ARCTIC OCEAN
Barents Sea
RUSSIAN FEDERATION
FINLAND
SWEDEN
ESTONIA
LATVIA
LITHUANIA
Baltic Sea
BELARUS
POLAND
CZECH REP.
SLOVAKIA
UKRAINE
HUNGARY
MOLDOVA
ROMANIA
BULGARIA
Black Sea
GEORGIA
ARMENIA
AZERBAIJAN
GREECE
TURKEY
MALTA
CYPRUS
LEBANON
ISRAEL
SYRIA
JORDAN
IRAQ
IRAN
KUWAIT
QATAR
BAHRAIN
U.A.E.
SAUDI ARABIA
OMAN
YEMEN
LIBYA
EGYPT
Red Sea
CHAD
SUDAN
ERITREA
DJIBOUTI
ETHIOPIA
SOMALIA
CENTRAL AFRICAN REPUBLIC
UGANDA
KENYA
Lake Victoria
CONGO
DEMOCRATIC REPUBLIC OF THE CONGO
RWANDA
BURUNDI
TANZANIA
ANGOLA
ZAMBIA
MALAWI
ZIMBABWE
MOZAMBIQUE
NAMIBIA
BOTSWANA
SWAZILAND
LESOTHO
SOUTH AFRICA
COMOROS
Mayotte (to France)
MADAGASCAR
MAURITIUS
Réunion (to France)
SEYCHELLES
Socotra (part of Yemen)
KAZAKHSTAN
Aral Sea
Caspian Sea
UZBEKISTAN
TURKMENISTAN
KYRGYZSTAN
TAJIKISTAN
Lake Balkhash
AFGHANISTAN
PAKISTAN
NEPAL
BHUTAN
BANGLADESH
INDIA
Arabian Sea
Bay of Bengal
Andaman Islands (part of India)
SRI LANKA
Nicobar Islands (part of India)
MALDIVES
MONGOLIA
Lake Baikal
CHINA
NORTH KOREA
SOUTH KOREA
Yellow Sea
Sea of Japan (East Sea)
JAPAN
East China Sea
TAIWAN
Hainan Dao
MYANMAR
LAOS
VIETNAM
THAILAND
CAMBODIA
South China Sea
PHILIPPINES
Philippine Sea
MALAYSIA
BRUNEI
SINGAPORE
Borneo
Sumatra
INDONESIA
Java Sea
Java
Moluccas
Flores Sea
EAST TIMOR
New Guinea
PAPUA NEW GUINEA
Sea of Okhotsk
Kurile Islands
Bering Sea
Arctic Circle
PACIFIC OCEAN
Tropic of Cancer
Northern Marianas Islands (to US)
Guam (to US)
FEDERATED STATES OF MICRONESIA
MARSHALL ISLANDS
PALAU
NAURU
Equator
KIRIBATI
TUVALU
SOLOMON ISLANDS
Wallis and Futuna (to France)
VANUATU
Coral Sea
Coral Sea Islands (to Australia)
New Caledonia (to France)
FIJI
Tropic of Capricorn
INDIAN OCEAN
AUSTRALIA
Tasman Sea
Tasmania
NEW ZEALAND
Antarctic Circle
ANTARCTICA

To Ethan, Madison, Marcus and Caleb. from Gammy Gail and Papa John July 8th 2005

DK

# Merriam-Webster Children's Dictionary

basketball

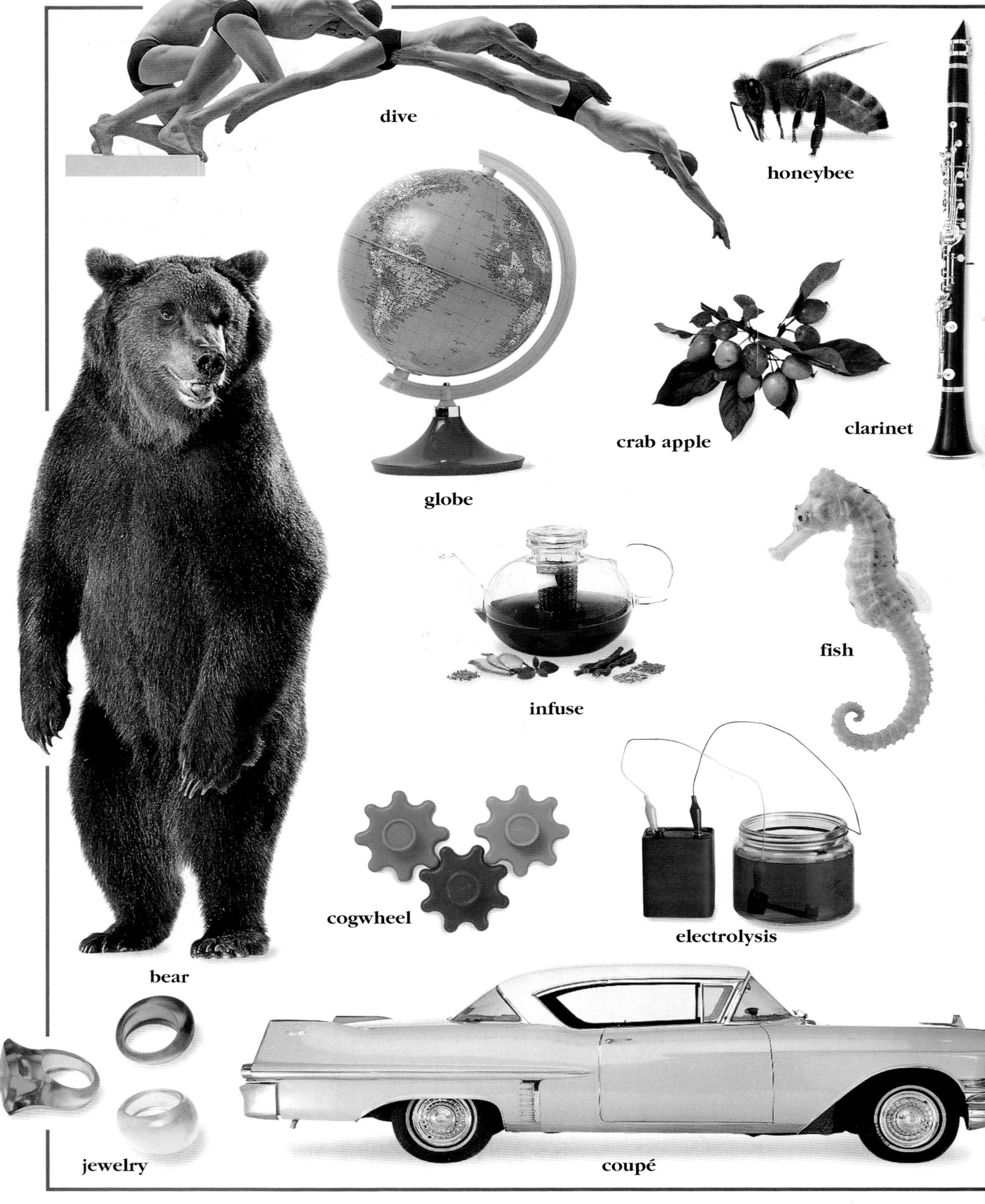
dive
honeybee
globe
crab apple
clarinet
bear
fish
infuse
cogwheel
electrolysis
jewelry
coupé

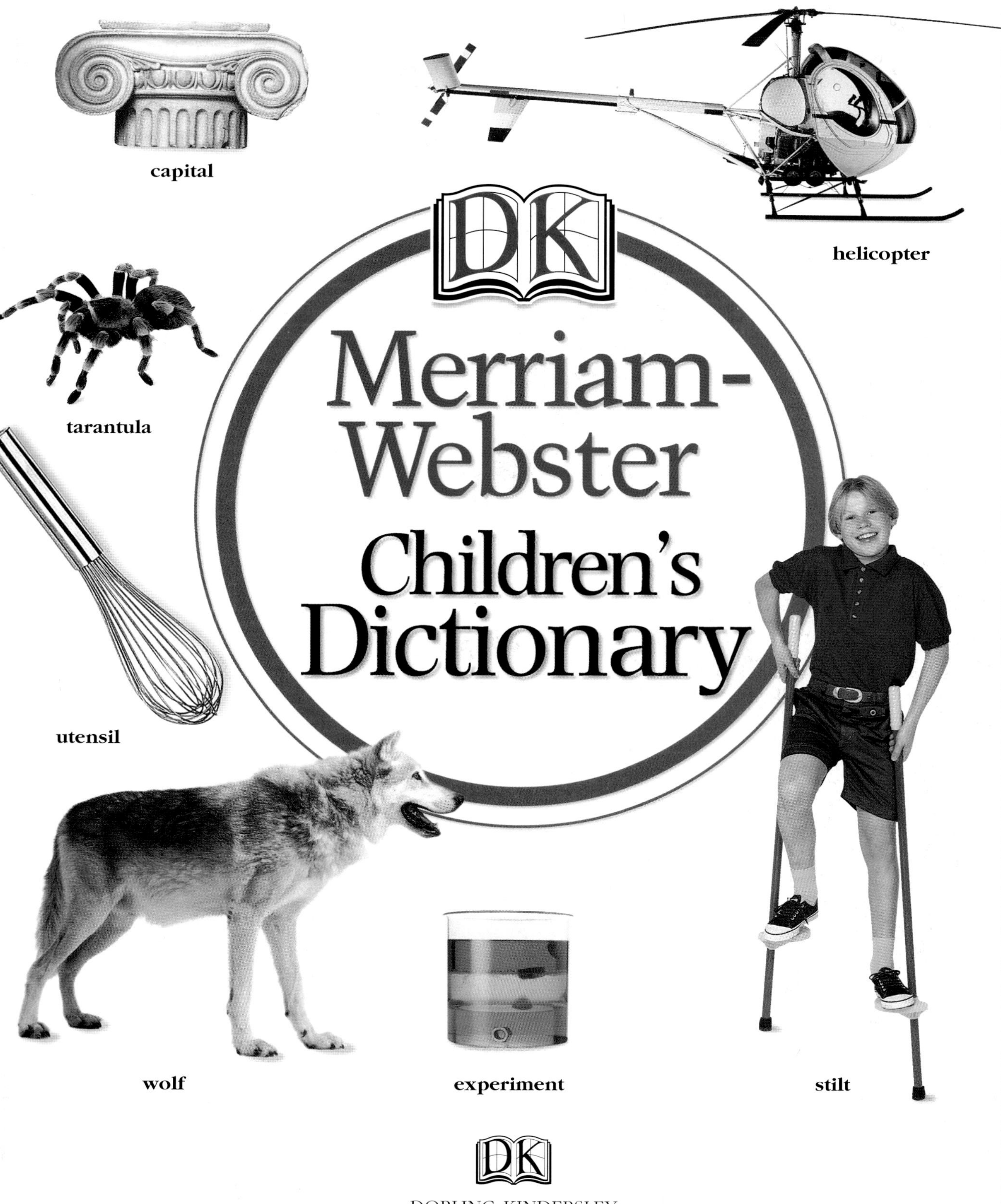


DK

DORLING KINDERSLEY

LONDON, NEW YORK, MUNICH, MELBOURNE, and DELHI

**For DK Publishing, Inc.**

**Senior Editor** Monica Byles
**Project Editor** Samantha Gray
**Editors** Azza Brown, Lucy Hurst, Dawn Rowley
**Managing Editor** Jayne Parsons
**Editorial Director** Sue Unstead
**Senior Production Controller** Kate Oliver
**Picture Research** Frances Vargo
**DTP Designer** Nomazwe Madonko
**Senior Art Editor** Esther van der Werf
**Project Art Editor** Tina Borg
**Designers** Ruth Jones, Clair Watson
**Managing Art Editor** Gillian Shaw
**Art Director** Linda Cole
**Production Assistant** Shivani Pandey
**DK Picture Library** Martin Copeland, Charlotte Oster, Romaine Werblow

**For DK India**

**Project Editor** Ranjana Saklani
**Editor** Atanu Raychaudhuri
**Editorial Director** Anita Roy
**Project Art Editor** Shuka Jain
**Designers** Prabal Mandal, Shefali Upadhyay
**Art Director** Alpana Khare
**DTP Designer** Sunil Sharma

**For Merriam-Webster, Incorporated**

**Senior Editor, Children's Dictionaries** Victoria Neufeldt
**Director of Editorial Operations** Madeline L. Novak
**Project Editors** Daniel J. Hopkins, Linda Picard Wood

**Revised Edition**

For DK Publishing, Inc.
**Editor** Rosie O'Neill
**Managing Art Editor** Diane Thistlethwaite
**Managing Editor** Linda Esposito

For DK India
**Manager** Aparna Sharma
**Designer** Romi Chakraborty
**DTP Designer** Balwant Singh
**Editor** Rohan Sinha

First American Edition, 2000

First published in the United States in 2000 by
DK Publishing, Inc., 375 Hudson Street, New York, NY, 10014
and Merriam-Webster, Incorporated, 47 Federal Street, Springfield, MA 01102

Revised editon published in 2005

05 06 07 08 09 10 9 8 7 6 5 4 3 2 1



Visit us on the World Wide Web at www.m-w.com



Library of Congress Cataloging-in-Publication Data

Dorling Kindersley Merriam-Webster children's dictionary --
1st American ed. p. cm.
Includes index.
Summary: Presents definitions for over 35,000 entries and includes
some 4,000 illustrations interspersed throughout the text.
ISBN 0-7566-1143-1
1. English language--Dictionaries, Juvenile.
2. Picture dictionaries, English--Juvenile literature.
[1. English language--Dictionaries.] I. DK Publishing, Inc. II.
Merriam-Webster, Inc.

PE1628.5. D67 2000
423--dc21

Color reproduction by Colourscan, Singapore
Printed in China by SNP Leefung

Discover more at
**www.dk.com**

# CONTENTS

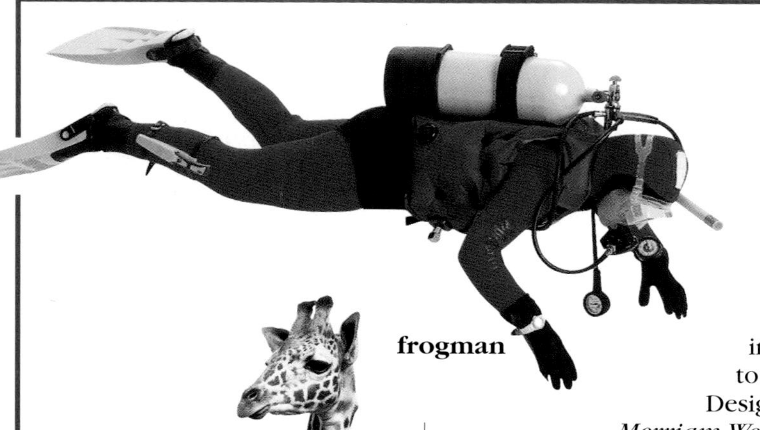

frogman

# Preface

THE VOLUME YOU ARE HOLDING IS THE FRUIT OF an extraordinary collaboration between two companies with formidable reputations — Merriam-Webster, certainly America's most eminent publisher of dictionaries, and Dorling Kindersley, whose books are renowned for their ability to make information visually exciting and accessible to readers of all ages.

giraffe

Designed for children ages 8 and up, *The DK Merriam-Webster Children's Dictionary* combines vibrant pictures from the Dorling Kindersley archive with authoritative text from Merriam-Webster. But this is no mere dictionary with illustrations. The thinking behind the selection of each individual picture has been as exacting as it has been for the choice of words. If we had added images only for their decorative value, this book would not serve as much more than a dictionary with pretty pictures. Instead, the choosing of images has been directed by their accuracy, usefulness, and potential for bringing unfamiliar subjects to life, and by their capacity to expand a word definition, illuminate the obscure, or cast light on those areas where the possibilities of verbal description are stretched to the limit. Special features have also been created to provide a wide range of themes with additional information: labels placed around images pinpoint individual features and expand the reader's vocabulary; diagrams, models, and cross sections enhance understanding and add detail to a host of topics; and collections of images establish the range of objects within a single theme.

These features combine to offer an exciting way to improve spelling, grammar, vocabulary, and understanding of our language — producing a handsome resource that children will look forward to using at home and at school.

Enjoy this dictionary, both as a remarkable work of the English language and as a colorful parade of words and illustrations. It has been a privilege to work with our colleagues at Merriam-Webster in creating it for your family's use.

NEAL PORTER
VICE PRESIDENT & PUBLISHER
DORLING KINDERSLEY PUBLISHING, INC.

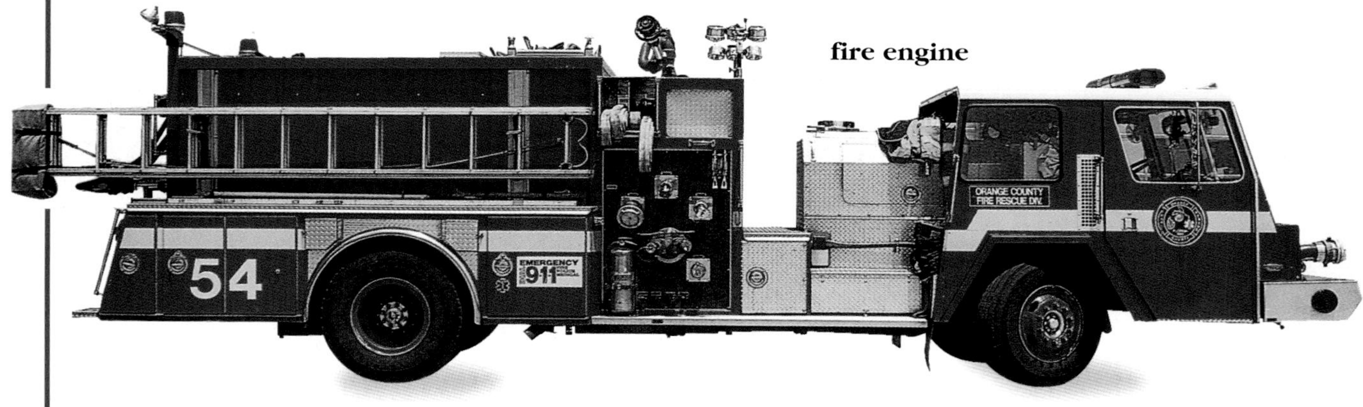


fire engine

The DK Merriam-Webster Children's Dictionary is written, designed, and illustrated for students in the elementary grades. It is meant to be a young student's first real dictionary. It has many of the features that appear in larger dictionaries that grown-ups use. Yet the definitions are in plain language that is easy to understand.

The text of the dictionary comes from Merriam-Webster and is based on the same information that goes into other Merriam-Webster dictionaries, including *Merriam-Webster's Collegiate Dictionary*. Dorling Kindersley created the design and illustrations that make this book a pleasure to browse and that help expand a student's understanding of words and their definitions.

Students using this dictionary will discover a world of information between its covers. They will learn about the meanings of words and how to spell and pronounce them. They will find out about synonyms, and they will discover the interesting histories of many words. There are examples to show how words are used, and thousands of illustrations and diagrams to provide additional information on many interesting topics. There are also special sections about nations and places around the world.

The dictionary includes entries for 32,000 words and phrases. They include all the words that students ordinarily use in talking and in writing and that they are likely to encounter in schoolwork and outside reading.

A dictionary is a very special book. In fact, it can become one of the most important books a student owns. It is not meant to be looked at once and then put away. Instead, it is a book that should be picked up often. The more a student uses this dictionary, the more it will become like a good friend — someone to go to whenever there is a question about words and someone who can always be relied upon for trustworthy answers.

John Morse
President & Publisher
Merriam-Webster, Inc.

**harness**

**quince**

**gaucho**

**germination**

**field glasses**

# How to Use Your Dictionary

THE FOLLOWING PAGES will help you understand all the features and conventions used in the *DK Merriam-Webster Children's Dictionary*, from the structure and content of individual word entries to a complete list of pronunciation symbols. The dictionary itself appears on pages 28-874, and is followed by an illustrated reference section, which includes maps of the world, listings of presidents and vice presidents of the USA, a guide to common abbreviations used in English, as well as a comprehensive picture index.

**Letter Information**
The start of each letter has an explanation describing the different sounds a letter can make

**Alphabet**
The alphabet helps users find their way through the dictionary

**Alphabet Locators**
Alphabetical sections are easily located using the color coding

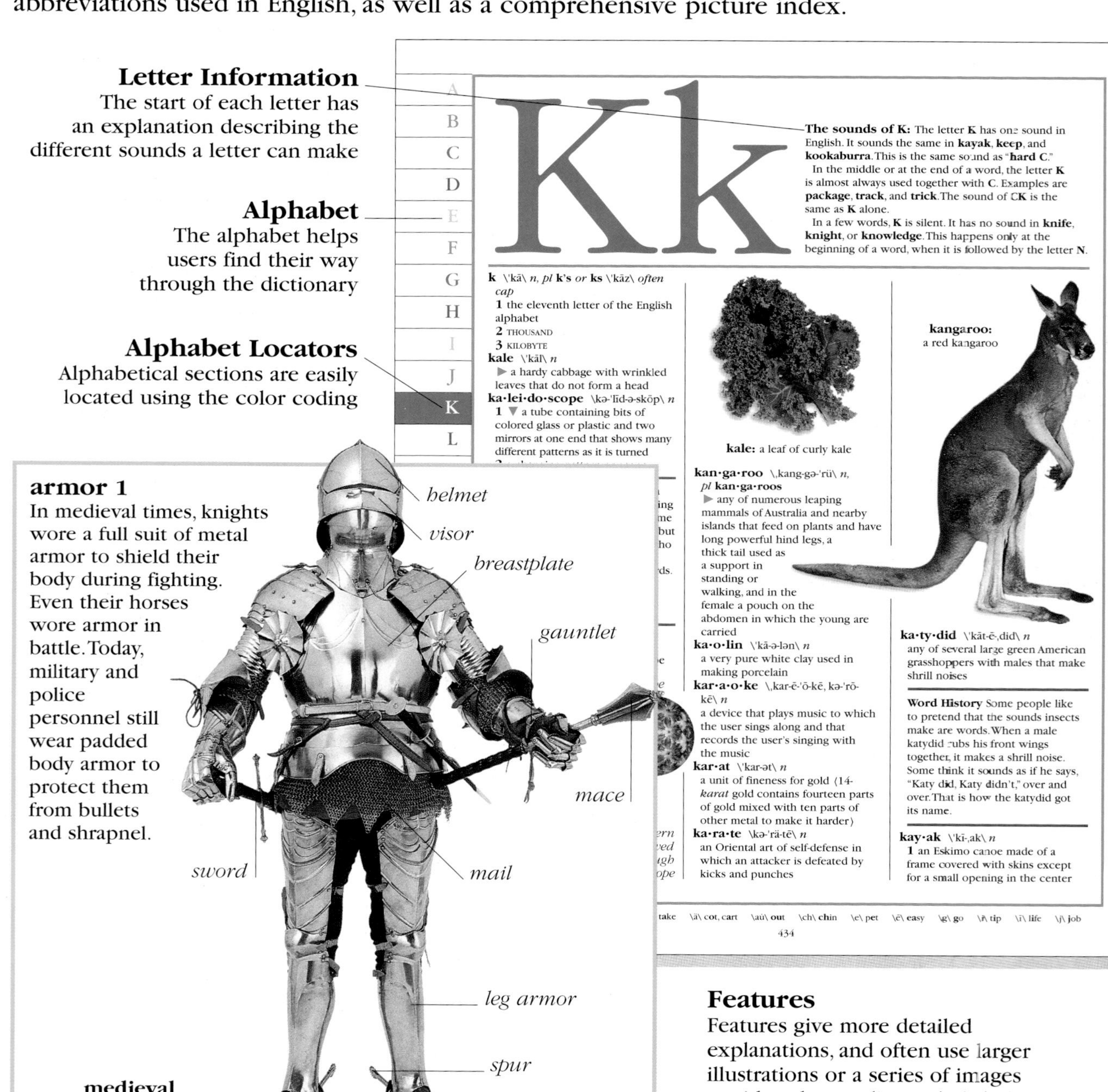

A
B
C
D
E
F
G
H
I
J
K
L
Kk
The sounds of K: The letter K has one sound in English. It sounds the same in kayak, keep, and kookaburra. This is the same sound as "hard C."
In the middle or at the end of a word, the letter K is almost always used together with C. Examples are package, track, and trick. The sound of CK is the same as K alone.
In a few words, K is silent. It has no sound in knife, knight, or knowledge. This happens only at the beginning of a word, when it is followed by the letter N.
k \'kā\ n, pl k's or ks \'kāz\ often cap
1 the eleventh letter of the English alphabet
2 THOUSAND
3 KILOBYTE
kale \'kāl\ n
a hardy cabbage with wrinkled leaves that do not form a head
ka·lei·do·scope \kə-'līd-ə-skōp\ n
1 a tube containing bits of colored glass or plastic and two mirrors at one end that shows many different patterns as it is turned
kale: a leaf of curly kale
kan·ga·roo \,kang-gə-'rü\ n, pl kan·ga·roos
any of numerous leaping mammals of Australia and nearby islands that feed on plants and have long powerful hind legs, a thick tail used as a support in standing or walking, and in the female a pouch on the abdomen in which the young are carried
ka·o·lin \'kā-ə-lən\ n
a very pure white clay used in making porcelain
kar·a·o·ke \,kar-ē-'ō-kē, kə-'rō-kē\ n
a device that plays music to which the user sings along and that records the user's singing with the music
kar·at \'kar-ət\ n
a unit of fineness for gold (14-karat gold contains fourteen parts of gold mixed with ten parts of other metal to make it harder)
ka·ra·te \kə-'rä-tē\ n
an Oriental art of self-defense in which an attacker is defeated by kicks and punches
kangaroo: a red kangaroo
ka·ty·did \'kāt-ē-,did\ n
any of several large green American grasshoppers with males that make shrill noises
Word History Some people like to pretend that the sounds insects make are words. When a male katydid rubs his front wings together, it makes a shrill noise. Some think it sounds as if he says, "Katy did, Katy didn't," over and over. That is how the katydid got its name.
kay·ak \'kī-,ak\ n
1 an Eskimo canoe made of a frame covered with skins except for a small opening in the center
take \ä\ cot, cart \aù\ out \ch\ chin \e\ pet \ē\ easy \g\ go \i\ tip \ī\ life \j\ job
434
armor 1
In medieval times, knights wore a full suit of metal armor to shield their body during fighting. Even their horses wore armor in battle. Today, military and police personnel still wear padded body armor to protect them from bullets and shrapnel.
helmet
visor
breastplate
gauntlet
mace
sword
mail
leg armor
spur
medieval suit of armor

**Features**
Features give more detailed explanations, and often use larger illustrations or a series of images to aid understanding. Labels help identify individual details or parts of the topic being illustrated.

## Picture Index

A picture index on pages 908–911 provides a quick reference to entries that are illustrated throughout the dictionary

## Guide Words

The right-hand page heading identifies the last word entry to appear in full on that page; the left-hand heading identifies the first entry to appear

**Word History** Look at the history of the word *kerchief* and you will see that it is a fine word for something that covers the head. The English word comes from an Old French word formed from two words. The first of these two French words was a verb that meant "to cover." The second was a noun that meant "head."

## Language Paragraphs

Some entries include short paragraphs providing word histories or synonyms. Word histories give fascinating information about the origin of words, and trace the development of meanings; synonyms provide cross-reference to similar words, and help to expand vocabulary.

**ketch**

a b c d e f g h i j k l m

**2** ▶ a boat styled like an Eskimo kayak
**ka·zoo** \kə-ˈzü\ *n, pl* **ka·zoos**
a toy musical instrument containing a membrane which produces a buzzing tone when one hums into the mouth hole
**KB** \ˈkā-ˈbē\ *n*
KILOBYTE
**[1]keel** \ˈkēl\ *n*
a timber or plate running lengthwise along the center of the bottom of a ship and usually sticking out from the bottom
**[2]keel** *vb*
to turn over
**keel over** *vb*
to fall suddenly (as in a faint)
**keen** \ˈkēn\ *adj*
**1** having a fine edge or point **:** SHARP ⟨a *keen* knife⟩
**2** seeming to cut or sting ⟨a *keen* wind⟩ ⟨a *keen* wit⟩
**3** full of enthusiasm **:** EAGER
**4** having or showing mental sharpness
**5** very sensitive (as in seeing or hearing) ⟨*keen* eyesight⟩
**synonyms** see EAGER
**keen·ly** *adv*
**keen·ness** *n*
**[1]keep** \ˈkēp\ *vb* **kept** \ˈkept\; **keep·ing**
**1** to be faithful to **:** FULFILL ⟨*keep* a promise⟩
**2** to act properly in relation to ⟨*keep* the Sabbath⟩
**3** PROTECT ⟨*keep* us from harm⟩
**4** to take care of **:** TEND
**5** to continue doing something
**6** to have in one's service or at one's disposal ⟨*keep* a car⟩
**7** to preserve a record in ⟨*keep* a diary⟩
**8** to have on hand regularly for sale ⟨*keep* neckties⟩
**9** to continue to have in one's possession or power
**10** to prevent from leaving **:** DETAIN ⟨*keep* a person in jail⟩
**11** to hold back ⟨*keep* a secret⟩
**12** to remain or cause to remain in a given place, situation, or condition ⟨*keep* off the grass⟩ ⟨*kept* us waiting⟩
**13** to continue in an unspoiled condition ⟨food that *keeps* well⟩
**14** [1]REFRAIN ⟨unable to *keep* from talking⟩

kayak — paddle

**kayak 2:** a girl paddling a kayak

**[2]keep** *n*
**1** the strongest part of a castle in the Middle Ages
**2** the necessities of life ⟨could not earn the family's *keep*⟩
**for keeps**
**1** with the understanding that one may keep what is won ⟨we'll play marbles *for keeps*⟩
**2** for a long time **:** PERMANENTLY
**keep·er** \ˈkē-pər\ *n*
a person who watches, guards, or takes care of something
**keep·ing** \ˈkē-piŋ\ *n*
**1** watchful attention **:** CARE
**2** a proper or fitting relationship **:** HARMONY ⟨a report in *keeping* with the facts⟩
**keep·sake** \ˈkēp-ˌsāk\ *n*
something kept or given to b… in memory of a person, place… happening
**keep up** *vb*
**1** MAINTAIN 1 ⟨*keep* standards…
**2** to stay well informed about… something ⟨*keep up* with the…
**3** to continue without interr… ⟨the rain *kept up* all night⟩
**4** to stay even with others (a… a race)
**keg** \ˈkeg\ *n*
**1** a small barrel holding abou… liters
**2** the contents of a keg
**kelp** \ˈkelp\ *n*
a large coarse brown seaweed
**ken** \ˈken\ *n*
**1** range of vision **:** SIGHT
**2** range of understanding
**ken·nel** \ˈken-ᵊl\ *n*
**1** a shelter for a dog
**2** a place where dogs are bred or housed

**kept**
*past of* KEEP
**ker·chief** \ˈkər-chəf\ *n, pl* **kerchiefs**
**1** a square of cloth worn as a head covering or as a scarf
**2** HANDKERCHIEF

**Word History** Look at the history of the word *kerchief* and you will see that it is a fine word for something that covers the head. The English word comes from an Old French word formed from two words. The first of these two French words was a verb that meant "to cover." The second was a noun that meant "head."

**ker·nel** \ˈkərn-ᵊl\ *n*

\ŋ\ sing \ō\ bone \ȯ\ saw \ȯi\ coin \th\ thin \t͟h\ this \ü\ food

435

## Quick-reference Guide to Word Entries

**[1]keel** \ˈkēl\ *n*
a timber or plate running lengthwise along the center of the bottom of a ship and usually sticking out from the bottom
**[2]keel** *vb*
to turn over
**keel over** *vb*
to fall suddenly (as in a faint)
**keen** \ˈkēn\ *adj*
**1** having a fine edge or point **:** SHARP ⟨a *keen* knife⟩
**2** seeming to cut or sting ⟨a *keen* wind⟩ ⟨a *keen* wit⟩
**3** full of enthusiasm **:** EAGER
**4** having or showing mental sharpness
**5** very sensitive (as in seeing or hearing) ⟨*keen* eyesight⟩
**synonyms** see EAGER
**keen·ly** *adv*
**keen·ness** *n*

*Numerals denote words that are spelled the same but have different functions or origins*

*Cross-reference to a word having the same meaning*

*Dark numbers introduce different senses of the same word*

*Dots in entry words show where words can be broken at the end of a line*

For a fuller explanation, and examples of all the elements found in a word entry, see pages 10–25.

*Functional label indicates the part of speech (such as noun, verb)*

*Pronunciation guide*

*Examples of usage show the word in action*

*Derived words help the reader increase word power*

## Pronunciation Symbols

An easy-reference guide to letter pronunciation runs across the bottom of each pair of facing pages

# Key to Using Your Dictionary

## 1. Main Entry Words

**saber–toothed tiger** \'sā-bər-ˌtütht-\ *n*
a very large prehistoric cat with long sharp curved eyeteeth
**²safe** *n*
a metal chest for keeping something (as money) safe

## 2. End-of-line Divisions

**sat·is·fac·tion** \ˌsat-əs-'fak-shən\ *n*
**1** the act of satisfying **:** the condition of being satisfied …

## 3. Pronunciation Symbols

**saun·ter** \'sȯnt-ər\ *vb*
to walk in a slow relaxed way **:** STROLL

## 4. Variant Spellings

**scep·ter** *or* **scep·tre** \'sep-tər\ *n*
a rod carried by a ruler as a sign of authority

## 5. Functional Labels

**sea·coast** \'sē-ˌkōst\ *n*
the shore of the sea

## 6. Homographs

**¹seal** \'sēl\ *n*
**1** a sea mammal that swims …
**²seal** *n*
**1** something (as a pledge) that …
**³seal** *vb*
**1** to mark with a seal …

## 7. Inflected Forms

**¹shade** \'shād\ *n*
**1** partial darkness ⟨the trees cast *shade*⟩…
**3 shades** *pl* **:** the shadows that gather as darkness falls …
**²shade** *vb* **shad·ed**; **shad·ing**

## 8. Usage Labels

**¹sire** \'sīr\ *n*
**1** *often cap* ¹FATHER 1 …

## 9. Definitions

**skim** \'skim\ *vb* **skimmed**; **skim·ming**
**1** to clean a liquid of scum or floating substance **:** remove (as cream or film) from the top part of a liquid
**2** to read or examine quickly and not thoroughly …

## 10. Synonyms and Cross-references

**slav·ery** \'slā-və-rē, 'slāv-rē\ *n*
**1** hard tiring labor **:** DRUDGERY
**2** the state of being a slave **:** BONDAGE …

## 11. Verbal Illustrations

[1]**snap** \'snap\ *vb* **snapped**; **snap·ping**
**1** to grasp or grasp at something suddenly with the mouth or teeth ⟨fish *snapping* at the bait⟩…
**4** to speak or utter sharply or irritably ⟨*snap* out a command⟩…

## 12. Visual Illustrations

**bird** \'bərd\ *n*
◀ an animal that lays eggs and has wings and a body covered with feathers

## 13. Run-in Entries

**sol·stice** \'säl-stəs, 'sōl-, 'sȯl-\ *n*
the time of the year when the sun is farthest north (**summer solstice**, about June 22) or south (**winter solstice**, about December 22) of the equator

## 14. Usage Notes

**son·ny** \'sən-ē\ *n, pl* **son·nies**
a young boy — used mostly to address a stranger

## 15. Undefined Run-on Entries

[1]**sour** \'sau̇r\ *adj* …
**sour·ish** \-ish\ *adj*
**sour·ly** *adv*
**sour·ness** *n*

## 16. Synonym Paragraphs

**splen·did** \'splen-dəd\ *adj*
**1** having or showing splendor **:** BRILLIANT …

**Synonyms** SPLENDID, GLORIOUS, and SUPERB mean very impressive. SPLENDID suggests that something is far above the ordinary in excellence or magnificence ⟨what a *splendid* idea⟩ ⟨a *splendid* jewel⟩. …

## 17. Defined Run-on Phrases

[1]**stand** \'stand\ *vb* **stood** \'stu̇d\; **stand·ing** …
**stand by** to be or remain loyal or true to ⟨*stand by* a promise⟩
**stand for**
**1** to be a symbol for **:** REPRESENT
**2** to put up with **:** PERMIT ⟨won't *stand for* any nonsense⟩

## 18. Word History Paragraphs

**sur·ly** \'sər-lē\ *adj* **sur·li·er**; **sur·li·est**
having a mean rude disposition **:** UNFRIENDLY

**Word History** The word *surly* comes from the word *sir*. Long ago, some Englishmen who had the title *Sir* became too proud of it. …

## 19. Guide Words

**arcade**

**ar·cade** \är-'kād\ *n*
**1** a row of arches with the columns that support them …

# Using Your Dictionary

## 1. Main Entry Words

When you open your dictionary to just about any page, you will find a list of words down the left-hand column printed in heavy black **boldface** type. Each of these is followed by information that explains or tells something about the word. The boldface word or phrase together with the explanation is a **dictionary entry**, and the boldface word itself is the **entry word** or **main entry**.

**s** \'es\ *n, pl* **s's** *or* **ss** \'es-əz\ *often cap*
**1** the nineteenth letter of the English alphabet
**2** a grade rating a student's work as satisfactory
[3]**-s** *vb suffix*
used to form the third person singular present of most verbs that do not end in *s, z, sh, ch*, or *y* following a consonant ⟨fall*s*⟩ ⟨take*s*⟩ ⟨play*s*⟩
**saber–toothed tiger** \'sā-bər-ˌtüht-\ *n*
a very large prehistoric cat with long sharp curved eyeteeth
[2]**safe** *n*
a metal chest for keeping something (as money) safe
[1]**safe·guard** \'sāf-ˌgärd\ *n*
something that protects and gives safety
**safety pin** *n*
a pin that is bent back on itself to form a spring and has a guard that covers the point

The main entry may take many forms. It may be a single letter like **s** or a single word like **safe**. It may also be a compound made up of two or more words written together (**safeguard**) or as separate words (**safety pin**) or with a hyphen (**saber–toothed tiger**). Sometimes an entry will be made up of all capital letters (**IOU** or **TV**) or of a letter and number (**A1**) or even of a letter and a word (**T–shirt**).

Finally some entries are only parts of words. The entry **-s** is one of these, and the entries **bi-** and **-graph**, shown below, are two more examples. Such entries all begin or end with a hyphen. They are the building blocks of our language, for they are used to create many new words.

**bi-** *prefix*
**1** two
**2** coming or occurring every two
**3** into two parts ⟨*bi*sect⟩
**4** twice : doubly : on both sides
**-graph** \ˌgraf\ *n suffix*
**1** something written
**2** instrument for making or sending records ⟨tele*graph*⟩

For example, **bi-** ("two") when combined with **cycle** gives us **bicycle** (literally "two wheels"). The word part **-graph** ("something written") combines with other word parts to give us such words as **autograph** and **paragraph**. The hyphen with the entry word is only there to show you where the word part is attached to other word parts. The entry **bi-** goes at the beginning of a word and is called a **prefix**. The entry **-graph** goes at the end of a word and is called a **suffix**.

Now that you know the kinds of entries you will find in your dictionary, you should know how the entries are arranged so you can find them easily and quickly.

All of the words in your dictionary are arranged in alphabetical order. To find a word, you simply look it up by the way it is spelled. Since **a** comes before **b** and **b** comes before **c** in the alphabet, you know that all of the words beginning with **a** will come before all of those beginning with **b**, the **b** words will all come before the **c** words, and so on all the way through the dictionary.

But merely grouping together all of the words that begin with the letter **a** would not help you find a particular word, like **alphabet**, very quickly. Well, alphabetical order also applies within each letter grouping. After all of the words are arranged by first letter, they are further grouped alphabetically by second letter. Then those words with the same first and second letters are arranged in alphabetical order by third letter and so on until every word has its own special place in the dictionary. So if you should want to look up the words **brat**, **bite**, and **bad**, you know that **bad** will come first, then **bite**, and finally **brat** because

**a** comes first in the alphabet and **i** comes ahead of **r**. The words **chop**, **chute**, **chili**, **chalk**, and **cheese** all begin with the letters **ch**, so their third letters must be used in ordering them: **chalk**, **cheese**, **chili**, **chop**, and **chute**.

Now when we arrange words in alphabetical order, we do not count spaces or hyphens between words. The words are arranged just as if the space or hyphen were not there. So you will find these words that begin **doub-** arranged in the dictionary in just the order you see them here.

> [4]**double** *n* ...
> **double bass** *n* ...
> **dou·ble–cross** \\ˌdəb-əl-ˈkrȯs\\ *vb* ...
> **dou·ble·head·er** \\ˌdəb-əl-ˈhed-ər\\ *n* ...

Some of the main entries in the *DK Merriam-Webster Children's Dictionary* are groups of letters that are not pronounced like ordinary words. But these entries, like **DDT** and **TV**, are still words, and they are arranged among the other words using the same rule of alphabetical order. Thus you will find **TV** between **tutor** and **twaddle**, because **v**, the second letter in **TV**, comes after **u** and before **w**.

Whenever the main entry has a number in it, like **A1**, it is arranged just as if the number were spelled out. You will find **A1** between the words **anywise** and **aorta** just as if it were spelled **A one**.

## 2. End-of-line Divisions

Most of the entry words in your dictionary are shown with dots at different places in the word. These dots are not a part of the spelling of the word but are there to show you end-of-line divisions — places where you can put a hyphen if you have to break up a word because there is room for only part of it at the end of a line.

> **sat·is·fac·tion** \\ˌsat-əs-ˈfak-shən\\ *n*
> **1** the act of satisfying **:** the condition of being satisfied
> **2** something that satisfies

In the example shown above, the word is normally written **satisfaction**, but if you have to divide it at the end of a line, the dots show you three places where you can put a hyphen.

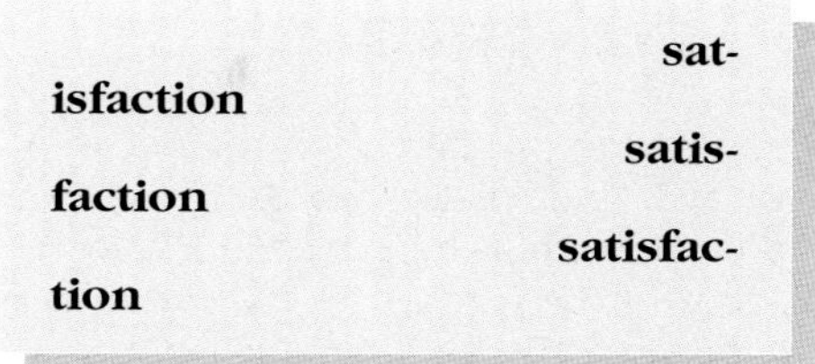


Words should not be divided so that only one letter comes at the end of a line or at the beginning of the next line.

> [1]**aban·don** \\ə-ˈban-dən\\ *vb* ...
> **ba·nana** \\bə-ˈnan-ə\\ *n* ...

For this reason no dot is shown after the first letter of the word **abandon** or before the last letter of the word **banana**. Thus, end-of-line divisions do not always separate the syllables of a word. Syllables are shown only in the pronunciation, explained in the next section.

When two or more main entries have the same spelling and the same end-of-line divisions, the dots are shown only in the first of these entries.

> [1]**mo·tion** \\ˈmō-shən\\ *n* ...
> [2]**motion** *vb* ...

## 3. Pronunciation Symbols

The English language is used in two different ways, in speaking and writing. Although the language is the same in both uses, writing and speaking are quite different from each other. Speech is made up of sounds and writing uses marks made on paper.

It is often hard to tell from the written spelling how to pronounce a word. Different letters may be used to spell the same sound, as in the words *right* and *write* or *sea* and *see*. One letter or a group of letters may be used to spell different sounds, like the letter **a** in the words *bat*, *car*, *late*, *any*, and *above*. There are also many words that have two or more pronunciations.

In order to show the sounds of words in this book, we use special **pronunciation symbols**. Each pronunciation symbol stands for one important sound in English. Most of the symbols look like letters of the regular alphabet. However, do not think of pronunciation symbols as letters. Learn the sound each symbol stands for. When you see a symbol, then think of its sound. Pronunciation symbols are always written between slant lines \ˌlīk-'this\ so you will know that they are not regular letters. To see how a pronunciation is given in an actual entry, look at the example **saunter** here.

> **saun·ter** \'sȯnt-ər\ *vb*
> to walk in a slow relaxed way
> **:** STROLL

A list of all the pronunciation symbols is printed on page 26. A shorter list is printed across the bottom of facing pages in the dictionary. In both lists the symbols are followed by words containing the sound of each symbol. The boldface letters in these words stand for the same sound as the symbol. If you say the sample word in your regular voice, you will hear the sound that the symbol stands for.

We use hyphens with the pronunciation symbols to show the syllables of a word, as in these examples.

> **beast** \'bēst\ *n* ...
> *(1 syllable)*
> **bed·side** \'bed-ˌsīd\ *n* ...
> *(2 syllables)*
> [1]**cast·away** \'kas-tə-ˌwā\ *adj* ...
> *(3 syllables)*
> **op·ti·mism** \'äp-tə-ˌmiz-əm\ *n*
> *(4 syllables)*

Of course, the syllables of words are not separated when we speak. One sound in a word follows right after another without pause.

Notice in the last two examples given above, **castaway** and **optimism**, that the number and position of the hyphens are not the same as the number and position of the dots in the entry words. The dots in the entry words are not meant to show the syllables in the word. Only the hyphens that you see in the pronunciation part of the entry will show you where the syllables are.

Some syllables of a word are spoken with greater force, or **stress**, than others. Three kinds of stress are shown in this dictionary. **Primary stress**, or **strong stress**, is shown by a high mark \'\ placed *before* a syllable. **Secondary stress**, or **medium stress**, is shown by a low mark \ˌ\ before a syllable. The third kind of stress is **weak stress**. There is no mark before syllables with weak stress. Each of these kinds of stress is shown in the pronunciation for **penmanship**.

> **pen·man·ship** \'pen-mən-ˌship\
> *n* ...

The first syllable has primary stress. The second syllable has weak stress. The third syllable has secondary stress. If you say the word to yourself, you will hear each kind of stress.

Many words are pronounced in two, three, or even more different ways. Two or more pronunciations for an entry are separated by commas. Look at the example **ration**.

> [1]**ra·tion** \'rash-ən, 'rā-shən\ *n* ...

The order in which different pronunciations are given does not mean that the pronunciation placed first is somehow better or more correct than the others. All the pronunciations that are shown in your dictionary are used by large numbers of educated people, and you will be correct whichever one you use. When you are learning a new word, you should choose the pronunciation that sounds most natural to you.

Sometimes when a second or third pronunciation is shown, only part of the pronunciation of a word changes. When this happens, we may show only the part that changes. To get the full second or third pronunciation of a word, just add the part that changes to the part that does not change.

> **greasy** \'grē-sē, -zē\ *adj* ...
> **pa·ja·mas** \pə-'jäm-əz, -'jam-əz\ *n*
> *pl* ...

The second pronunciation of **greasy** is \'grē-zē\ and the second pronunciation of **pajamas** is \pə-'jam-əz\.

If two or more entries are spelled the same and have the same pronunciation and end-of-line division, we show the pronunciation only for the first of these entries.

> [1]**se·cure** \si-'kyu̇r\ *adj* ...
> [2]**secure** *vb* ...

Many compound entries are made up of two or three separate words. If we do not show a pronunciation for all or part of such an entry, the missing pronunciation is the same as that for the individual word or words.

> **milk shake** *n*
> a drink made of milk, a flavoring syrup, and ice cream shaken or mixed thoroughly
> [1]**milk** \'milk\ *n* ...
> [1]**shake** \'shāk\ *vb* ...

No pronunciation is shown for the example **milk shake**. This means the two words are pronounced just like the separate entries **milk** and **shake**.

When a boldface word appears without a definition at the end of a main entry, sometimes we show only part of the pronunciation. This means the rest of the word is pronounced the same as part of the main entry.

> **post·pone** \pōst-'pōn\ *vb* ...
> **post·pone·ment** \-mənt\ *n*

In the example **postpone** the complete pronunciation of **postponement** is \pōst-'pōn-mənt\. Some of these entries will show no pronunciation at all. In these cases the pronunciation of the compound is the same as the pronunciation of the main entry plus the pronunciation of the word ending, which is found at its own alphabetical place in the dictionary.

> [1]**re·mote** \ri-'mōt\ *adj* ...
> **re·mote·ly** *adv*
> **re·mote·ness** *n*

In the example **remote**, the entry **remotely** is pronounced \ri-'mōt-lē\ and **remoteness** is pronounced \ri-'mōt-nəs\.

## 4. Variant Spellings

After the main entry word you may see a second or third spelling, also in boldface type. Additional spellings are called **variant spellings** or simply **variants**.

> **scep·ter** *or* **scep·tre** \'sep-tər\ *n*
> a rod carried by a ruler as a sign of authority

Variant spellings are usually separated by *or*. The *or* tells you that both spellings are common in good usage.

Usually we show variants in alphabetical order when one form is not used much more often than another. This is the case with the entry **scepter** *or* **sceptre**. If, however, one form does seem to be preferred, we show that one first. This sometimes means that variants will be out of alphabetical order.

> **Gyp·sy** *or* **Gip·sy** \'jip-sē\ *n, pl* ...

In the example **Gypsy** *or* **Gipsy** this is the case, since in strict alphabetical order the **Gipsy** spelling would come first. The order of the variants tells you that the spelling **Gypsy** is used a little more often than **Gipsy**.

Keep in mind that all of the variants shown in this dictionary are correct. However, you should pick one form and use it in all of your writing.

Occasionally you will see a variant spelling shown after the word *also*. Look at the example **pea**.

> **pea** \'pē\ *n, pl* **peas** *also* **pease**

The *also* tells you that the next spelling is much less common in ordinary usage than the first, although it is still a correct spelling.

When variant spellings are shown at the beginning of the entry, all of the variants are used in all meanings. If one variant form is shown at a particular definition, however, that spelling is more common for that meaning.

> **disk** *or* **disc** \'disk\ *n*
> **1** something that is or appears to be flat and round
> **2** *usually disc* a phonograph record ...
> **disk·like** \-ˌlīk\ *adj*

The information at the entry for **disk** *or* **disc** tells you that both spellings are used for both meanings. The form **disk** is more often used for meaning **1** (remember that when variants are not in alphabetical order you know the first one is used more often). The label *usually disc* at meaning **2** tells you that **disc** is more common than **disk** for meaning **2**.

## 5. Functional Labels

Words are used in many different ways in a sentence. You know, for example, that if a word is used as the name of something (**car**, **house**, **rainbow**), it is called a **noun**. If it describes some action or state of being (**run**, **stand**, **live**), the word is a **verb**. Words that show a quality of something (**tall**, **short**, **fast**) are **adjectives**, and words that tell how, when, or where something happens (**quickly**, **very**, **yesterday**, **here**) are **adverbs**. **Pronouns** (**them**, **you**, **that**) are words which substitute for nouns, and **conjunctions** (**and**, **but**, **yet**) join two words or groups of words. **Prepositions** (**to**, **for**, **by**) combine with nouns and pronouns to form phrases that answer such questions as where?, how?, and which?, and **interjections** (**hi**, **adios**, **ouch**) stand alone and often show a feeling or a reaction to something rather than a meaning.

To show you how the various entry words are used, or how they function in a sentence, we use **functional labels** before the definitions. These labels are usually abbreviations in slanting *italic* type, and they come right after the pronunciation — when one is shown — or immediately after the entry word.

> **sea·coast** \'sē-ˌkōst\ *n*
> the shore of the sea

The eight most common functions, known as **parts of speech**, are shown in the examples below.

> [2]**cereal** *n* ...
> [2]**fish** *vb* ...
> **hos·tile** \'häst-l\ *adj* ...
> [2]**just** *adv* ...
> [1]**none** \'nən\ *pron* ...
> [2]**since** *conj* ...
> [2]**under** *prep* ...
> [4]**why** \wī, hwī\ *interj* ...

In addition to these parts of speech, a few other special functional labels are used in this book. The words **the**, **a**, and **an** are used before nouns to show that a certain one or any one of a certain group is being talked about. Because the word **the** points out a certain one, it is called a **definite article**. The words **a** and **an**, which refer to any one of many, are called **indefinite articles**.

The prefixes and suffixes that we talked about in the section on main entries are also indicated by a functional label. Often it will be combined with a part-of-speech label when the suffix or prefix always makes one kind of word.

> **-g·ra·phy** \g-rə-fē\ *n suffix*

In the example, **-graphy** always combines with other words or word parts to form nouns (**photography**, **biography**), so its functional label is *noun suffix*.

There are a few special verbs that sometimes are used to help other verbs, such as **may** in a question like "May I go with you?" These special verbs are shown with the italic functional label *helping verb*.

> **may** \mā\ *helping verb, past* **might** \mīt\; *present sing & pl* **may** ...

## 6. Homographs

Often you will find two, three, or more main entries that come one after another and are spelled exactly alike.

**[1]seal** \'sēl\ *n*
**1** a sea mammal that swims with flippers, lives mostly in cold regions, mates and bears young on land, eats flesh, and is hunted for fur, hides, or oil
**2** the soft dense fur of a northern seal
**[2]seal** *n*
**1** something (as a pledge) that makes safe or secure
**2** a device with a cut or raised design or figure that can be stamped or pressed into wax or paper
**3** a piece of wax stamped with a design and used to seal a letter or package
**4** a stamp that may be used to close a letter or package ⟨Christmas *seals*⟩
**5** something that closes tightly
**6** a closing that is tight and perfect
**[3]seal** *vb*
**1** to mark with a seal
**2** to close or make fast with or as if with a seal
**seal·er** *n*

Although these words look alike, they are different words because they come from different sources and so have different meanings or because they are used in different ways in the sentence.

These similar entries are called **homographs** (from **homo-** "the same" and **-graph** "something written" — in this case "words written in the same way"). Each homograph has a small raised number before it. This number is used only in the dictionary entry to show you that these are different words. The number is not used when you write the word.

Let's look closely at the homographs for **seal** to see just why they are different. The first entry, a noun, is defined as "a sea mammal." The second **seal** entry is also a noun, but this meaning, "something (as a pledge) that makes safe or secure," is completely different from the meaning of the first entry. The third homograph of **seal** is certainly related to the second, but **[3]seal** is a verb, and since it has a different use in the sentence, we show it as a different entry word.

## 7. Inflected Forms

Whenever we talk about more than one of something, we have to use a special form of a noun. If we want to say that an action is taking place now or has happened already, we need a different form of the verb for each meaning. To say that this is bigger, smaller, or quicker than that, we have to use a special form of an adjective or adverb. These special forms usually involve a change in spelling. These forms are called **inflected forms** or **inflections** of the words.

**[1]shade** \'shād\ *n*
**1** partial darkness ⟨the trees cast *shade*⟩
**2** space sheltered from light or heat and especially from the sun ⟨sit in the *shade* of a tree⟩
**3 shades** *pl* **:** the shadows that gather as darkness falls ⟨the *shades* of night⟩
**4** GHOST, SPIRIT
**5** something that blocks off or cuts down light ⟨a lamp *shade*⟩ ⟨a window *shade*⟩
**6** the darkening of some objects in a painting or drawing to suggest that they are in shade
**7** the darkness or lightness of a color ⟨four *shades* of brown⟩
**8** a very small difference or amount ⟨just a *shade* taller⟩ ⟨*shades* of meaning⟩
**[2]shade** *vb* **shad·ed; shad·ing**
**1** to shelter from light or heat
**2** to mark with shades of light or color ⟨*shade* a drawing⟩
**3** to show or begin to have slight differences of color, value, or meaning
**shady** \'shād-ē\ *adj* **shad·i·er; shad·i·est**
**1** sheltered from the sun's rays
**2** not right or honest ⟨*shady* business deals⟩
**shad·i·ness** *n*

Nouns show more than one by means of **plural** forms — "the *shades* of night." Verbs can be made to show that something is happening now by the use of the **present participle** form — "that tree is *shading* our flowers" — or that something happened before but is not happening now by use of the **past tense** or the **past participle** forms — "I *shaded* my eyes; we have *shaded* parts of the drawing to show shadows." The **third person singular present tense** form of verbs shows what he, she, or it is doing now — "this umbrella *shades* us from the sun." Adjectives and adverbs show how one thing is compared with another or with all others of the same kind by **comparative** and **superlative** forms — "this spot is *shadier* than that, but over there is the *shadiest* spot in the garden."

For most words inflected forms are made in a regular way. That is, plurals usually are formed simply by adding **-s** or **-es** to the base word (*shade* ➛ *shades; box* ➛ *boxes*); verb inflections are formed by adding **-ed** for the past tense and past participle (*walk* ➛ *walked*), **-ing** for the present participle (*walk* ➛ *walking*), and **-s** or **-es** for the third person singular present tense form (*walk* ➛ *walks; wash* ➛ *washes*). Comparative and superlative forms of adjectives and adverbs are considered regular if they are formed by adding **-er** and **-est** to the base word or if the words *more* and *most* are used (*high* ➛ *higher, highest; natural* ➛ *more natural, most natural*).

We do not show most regular inflections in this dictionary since they should give you no problems in spelling.

> **bri·gade** \bri-'gād\ *n*
> **1** a body of soldiers consisting of two or more regiments ...
> **dif·fer** \'dif-ər\ *vb*
> **1** to be not the same : be unlike ...
> [1]**dull** \'dəl\ *adj*
> **1** mentally slow : STUPID ...

When you see entries like the examples **brigade**, **differ**, and **dull**, you will know that the inflected forms are regular. **Brigade** becomes **brigades** in the plural; the past and past participle of **differ** are both **differed**, the present participle is **differing**, and the third person singular is **differs**; and **dull** becomes **duller** in the comparative and **dullest** in the superlative.

We do show you inflections, however, when they are formed in any way other than by simply adding a suffix. If the base word is changed in any way when the suffix is added or if there are variant inflected forms, these forms are shown.

> **proph·e·cy** \'präf-ə-sē\ *n, pl* **proph·e·cies** ...
> [2]**model** *vb* **mod·eled** *or* **mod·elled**; **mod·el·ing** *or* **mod·el·ling** ...

We also show inflections for a word when no suffix is added

> **deer** \'dir\ *n, pl* **deer** ...

and for any words that have regular inflections when we think you might have questions about how they are formed.

> **chim·ney** \'chim-nē\ *n, pl* **chimneys** ...

For verb inflections only the past tense (the **-ed** form) and the present participle (the **-ing** form) are normally shown. The past participle is shown only when it is different from the past tense form. When it is shown, it comes between the past tense and present participle.

The third person singular present tense form (he *likes*, she *knows*, it *seems*) is the most regular of the verb inflections. For most verbs it is formed simply by adding **-s** or **-es** to the base word — even for verbs whose other inflections are not regular. We show this inflection only when we think its spelling or pronunciation might present a problem. When it is shown, this form comes after the present participle form.

> **go** \'gō\ *vb* **went** \'went\; **gone** \'gȯn\; **go·ing** \'gō-ing\; **goes** ...

Nouns are usually entered in the *DK Merriam-Webster Children's Dictionary* in the singular form, that is, in the form that means only one of something. And these words can either be used as a singular or be made into plural nouns. However, there are some entries that are used only in the plural. These are shown by the special label *n pl*.

> **aus·pic·es** \'ȯ-spə-səz\ *n pl* support and guidance of a sponsor ⟨a concert given under the *auspices* of the school⟩

Some words that end in an **-s**, like **gymnastics**, may be thought of as singular in some uses and as plural in others.

> **gym•nas•tics** \jim-'nas-tiks\ *n sing or pl*
> physical exercises for developing skill, strength, and control in the use of the body or a sport in which such exercises are performed

If you use this word for the sport, for example, you might think of it as singular, like this — "gymnastics is a sport in the Olympic Games." But if you think of the various exercises themselves, you might think of the word as a plural and use a plural verb, like this — "I think gymnastics are very hard to do." The *n sing or pl* label at such entries tells you that sometimes the word is used as a singular and sometimes as a plural.

There are a few entries in this dictionary that have unusual plural uses at individual meanings.

> [1]**dart** \'därt\ *n*
> **1** a small pointed object that is meant to be thrown
> **2 darts** *pl* a game in which darts are thrown at a target
> **3** a quick sudden movement
> **4** a stitched fold in a garment

These special uses we show by a *pl* label at the individual definitions. In the **dart** example, the *pl* label at meaning **2** tells you that the spelling is **darts** and it is plural in use. If the plural form has already been shown in boldface at the beginning of the entry, we show it in italic type before the individual definition.

Sometimes a noun entry will show variant plural forms, but only one of these variants is used in a particular meaning. To show this situation, we place the plural form after the *pl* label at the individual meaning.

> [1]**hose** \'hōz\ *n, pl* **hose** *or* **hos•es**
> **1** *pl hose* STOCKING, SOCK
> **2** a flexible tube for carrying fluid

This is shown in the example **hose**, where the *pl hose* label tells you that the plural form for this meaning is **hose** but the use is usually singular.

Occasionally you will see a noun entry where you think an inflected form should be shown but it is not. Words like **diplomacy** are not used as plurals, so no plural form is shown.

> **di•plo•ma•cy** \də-'plō-mə-sē\ *n*
> **1** the work of keeping up relations between the governments of different countries
> **2** skill in dealing with others

## 8. Usage Labels

In addition to functional labels at individual entries we use another kind of italic label to give you information about how a word is used. These **usage labels** come after the functional labels or, if they apply only to a particular meaning, just before the beginning of the definition.

> [1]**sire** \'sīr\ *n*
> **1** *often cap* [1]FATHER 1
> **2** ANCESTOR
> **3** the male parent of an animal

One of the things the usage label may tell you is whether or not a particular word is sometimes written with a capital letter. Whenever a word is always or usually written with a capital letter, it has a capital letter in the main entry.

> **Thurs•day** \'thərz-dē\ *n*
> the fifth day of the week

But some words are written with a small letter or a capital letter about equally often. These entries have an italic label *often cap*. Other words are written with a capital letter in some meanings and not in others. These words are usually shown in the dictionary with a small first letter. The italic label tells you when the word is always spelled with a capital letter (*cap*) or very frequently spelled with a capital letter (*often cap*).

> [4]**host** *n, often cap*
> the bread used in Christian Communion

In the example [4]**host**, the label tells you that sometimes the word is spelled with a capital letter and sometimes not.

**earth** \'ərth\ *n*
**1** [2]SOIL 1
**2** areas of land as distinguished from the sea and the air
**3** *often cap* the planet that we live on

In the example **earth**, the word is often written with a capital letter (notice the *often cap* label) when the meaning is **3** but with a small letter when the meaning is **1** or **2**.

**french fry** *n, often cap 1st F*
a strip of potato fried in deep fat ⟨steak and *french fries*⟩

See if you can tell what the label at the entry **french fry** means. Would you expect to see the word sometimes spelled **French fry**?

Another thing the usage labels can tell you is whether a word or a particular meaning is limited in use. One kind of word with limited use is one that is not used much anymore although it was quite common a long time ago.

**thou** \'thaü\ *pron, singular, archaic*

The *archaic* label at the sample entry **thou** tells you that **thou** is such a word. It is shown in this book because you may sometimes see it in very old writings, for example, in the Bible.

The last kind of usage label tells you a certain word or meaning is most commonly used in a limited area of the English-speaking world.

[2]**lift** *n* …
**4** *chiefly British* ELEVATOR 2 …

In the sample entry **lift** you will see that meaning **4** is labeled *chiefly British*. This means that the word in this meaning is used more often in Great Britain than in the United States.

## 9. Definitions

The definitions are what many people consider the most important part of the dictionary, because meanings are what people usually think of when they think of a dictionary.

**skim** \'skim\ *vb* **skimmed**; **skim·ming**
**1** to clean a liquid of scum or floating substance **:** remove (as cream or film) from the top part of a liquid
**2** to read or examine quickly and not thoroughly
**3** to throw so as to skip along the surface of water
**4** to pass swiftly or lightly over

All of the definitions in this dictionary start on a new line under the main entry words. Most of the words entered in this book have more than one meaning and therefore they have more than one definition. These separate meanings are shown by boldface numbers. **Skim** has four numbered meanings.

We have arranged the definitions in your dictionary in historical order. The oldest meaning is shown as meaning number **1** and the next oldest meaning is shown as meaning number **2**, and so on. The meanings that have most recently come into use are at the end. This allows you to see, just by reading the entry, how a word has grown in use from the first meaning to the last.

Let's look at meaning number **1** of **skim**. This meaning first came into use in English many centuries ago, and through the years it gained a more specific use, that of taking the cream off milk. This specific use is shown as the second definition at meaning **1**. The second definition does not change the original meaning. It only adds a little.

Meaning **2** of **skim** seems to have come into use as a figure of speech. If you think of a spoon barely touching the surface of water or milk or going just under the surface to scoop off something, you realize that the scoop is only taking off what can be seen on the surface. Most of the liquid remains behind. By first applying the word **skim** to reading or examining something and only getting what could be seen "on the surface" without going more deeply into the work, someone was using **skim** as a figure of speech. As more and more people used the word in this way, it came to have a set meaning.

Meaning **3**, which developed after meanings **1** and **2**, seems to have come from the first meaning in a similar way. This time, though, the idea of "just touching" a surface was the one that carried over to the act of causing rocks or other objects to bounce along the surface of a lake.

Can you guess at how meaning **4** came into use? Here it seems the meaning moved one more step away, from the idea of "just touching the surface" to that of "just missing the surface."

With the entry **skim**, you can see just how the word grew from one meaning to four. And the arrangement of the four meanings in historical order lets you follow that growth.

There may be times when you will look up a word and not be sure which of several meanings is the right one for the use you are checking. The way to tell which is the right definition is to substitute each definition in place of your word in the sentence until you find the one that is right.

Suppose you were reading the sentence "I just skimmed the book" and you were not certain what *skim* meant. By reading the definitions of **skim** in the sentence you would be able to find the right meaning by substitution. You know that "I just removed cream from the top of the book" certainly is not correct, and it is most unlikely that the writer was "throwing a book so that it skipped across the surface of water" or "passing swiftly over the book." But when you substitute meaning **2** in the sentence, you get a sentence that makes sense. "I was just reading or examining the book quickly and not thoroughly." This is using the method of substitution to find the right meaning.

## 10. Synonyms and Cross-references

**slav•ery** \'slā-və-rē, 'slāv-rē\ *n*
**1** hard tiring labor **:** DRUDGERY
**2** the state of being a slave **:** BONDAGE
**3** the custom or practice of owning slaves

In the entry **slavery** meanings **1** and **2** both have two definitions. The second definition in each case is a single word that means the same thing as the entry word **slavery** for that particular use. These words with the same meaning as the entry word are called **synonyms**. All synonyms in the *DK Merriam-Webster Children's Dictionary* are written in small capital letters. Any word in small capital letters is a **cross-reference**, referring you to another place in the book. In the case of these synonyms, the small capitals tell you to look at the entry for that word for a full explanation of the meaning or use.

You can see that **drudgery** is a synonym of the first meaning of **slavery** ("hard tiring labor") and **bondage** is a synonym of the second meaning ("the state of being a slave"). If you turn to the entry for **drudgery**, for example, you will find a definition that matches the definition for meaning **1** of **slavery**.

Sometimes an entry is defined only by a synonym.

**northern lights** *n pl*
AURORA BOREALIS

**au•ro•ra bo•re•al•is** \ə-ˌrōr-ə-ˌbōr-ē-'al-əs\ *n*
broad bands of light that have a magnetic and electrical source and that appear in the sky at night especially in the arctic regions

Look at the example **northern lights**. The cross-reference AURORA BOREALIS tells you to look at the entry **aurora borealis** for a definition. The definition at **aurora borealis** is the same as it would be for **northern lights**, since both words mean the same thing. When using synonymous cross-references, we have always put the full definition at the most common of the synonyms.

Sometimes you will see a number used as part of the cross-reference, as in the first meaning given for **host**.

**¹host** \'hōst\ *n*
**1** ARMY 1
**2** MULTITUDE

The cross-reference to ARMY **1** tells you to look at meaning number **1** of the entry **army** for a definition that fits this meaning of **host**.

Because the definition of the synonym must also be a good definition of the entry word, both the entry word and the synonym will always have the same part of speech. Thus, if the synonym of a verb is an entry with two or more homographs, you will always know that the right entry will be the homograph that is a verb. Nevertheless, your dictionary helps you by showing the proper homograph number at the cross-reference when necessary.

**¹dig** \'dig\ *vb* **dug** \'dəg\; **dig•ging**
. . .
**5** ¹PROD 1, POKE ⟨*dug* me in the ribs⟩

In the fifth meaning of the entry [1]**dig**, the cross-reference tells you that meaning **1** of the first homograph of **prod** is the synonym, because [1]**dig** is a noun and only the first homograph of **prod** is a noun.

The cross-reference printed in small capital letters is also used at certain entries that are variants or inflected forms of another entry.

**caught** *past of* CATCH

In the example **caught** the cross-reference tells you that you will find a definition or explanation at the entry shown in small capital letters.

## 11. Verbal Illustrations

[1]**snap** \'snap\ *vb* **snapped**; **snap·ping**
**1** to grasp or grasp at something suddenly with the mouth or teeth ⟨fish *snapping* at the bait⟩
**2** to grasp at something eagerly ⟨*snapped* at the chance to go⟩
**3** to get, take, or buy at once ⟨*snap* up a bargain⟩
**4** to speak or utter sharply or irritably ⟨*snap* out a command⟩ …

At times you may look up a word in your dictionary and understand the definition but still not be sure about the right way to use the word. Sometimes the several meanings are similar but the ways in which the word is actually used in a sentence are quite different. To help you better understand these more difficult words and usages, we have given along with some definitions a brief phrase or sentence called a **verbal illustration**. It shows you a typical use of the word. Most of the definitions at **snap** have verbal illustrations to show how the word is used in each of those meanings. A verbal illustration is always placed after the definition, it is enclosed in pointed brackets, and it has the entry word, or an inflection of it, printed in italic type.

## 12. Visual Illustrations

Sometimes a dictionary entry is illustrated with a picture. The colored triangle at the start of the definition points in the direction of the picture.

**bird** \'bərd\ *n*
◀ an animal that lays eggs and has wings and a body covered with feathers

Where there is more than one meaning, the colored triangle sits beside the entry number to show which meaning is illustrated. Often pictures are labeled with features that might interest you, and you can look these up in your dictionary too. Sometimes a word is illustrated by a group of pictures that show several examples of something or that illustrate several aspects of something.

## 13. Run-in Entries

Sometimes you will see boldface words in the middle of a definition. These are called **run-in entries**. Run-in entries are themselves defined by part of the main definition.

**sol·stice** \'säl-stəs, 'sōl-, 'sȯl-\ *n*
the time of the year when the sun is farthest north (**summer solstice**, about June 22) or south (**winter solstice**, about December 22) of the equator

Within the main entry **solstice** the run-in entry **summer solstice** is being defined as "the time of the year when the sun is farthest north of the equator," and **winter solstice** is being defined as "the time of the year when the sun is farthest south of the equator."

## 14. Usage Notes

The italic usage labels that come before definitions are one way we give you information on the usage of the entry word, and the verbal illustrations after the definitions are another way. In the *DK Merriam-Webster Children's Dictionary* we give information on usage in still another way — **usage notes** that follow definitions. Usage notes are short phrases that are separated from the definition by a dash. They tell you how or when the entry word is used.

**son·ny** \'sən-ē\ *n, pl* **son·nies**
a young boy — used mostly to address a stranger

The example **sonny** shows you one kind of usage note. The following examples show some other kinds of information found in these notes.

**cas·ta·net** \ˌkas-tə-ˈnet\ *n*
a rhythm instrument that consists of two small ivory, wooden, or plastic shells fastened to the thumb and clicked by the fingers in time to dancing and music — usually used in pl.
[2]**cheer** *vb* ...
**4** to grow or be cheerful — usually used with *up*

The note at **castanet** tells you that the word is usually used as a plural, **castanets**, although it is defined as a singular. This information is different from what would be given if the word had been entered as **castanets** or shown as **castanets** *pl* just before the definition. In both of those cases, you would be told that the word is defined as plural and is always plural in this use. Do you see how the note "usually used in pl." is different? It tells you that the word is singular — it is defined as a singular and may sometimes be used as singular — but is most often used in the plural form and with a plural verb.

Usage notes like the one at **cheer** tell you what words are usually used with the entry word in a sentence. In this case, the expression is usually *cheer up*.

In a few entries we use a usage note in place of a definition. This is done when the way the word is used is more important than what the word means.

[2]**both** *conj*
used before two words or phrases connected with *and* to stress that each is included ⟨*both* New York and London⟩

We also use a usage note in place of a definition for all interjections, which usually express a feeling or reaction to something rather than a meaning.

**amen** \ˈā-ˈmen, ˈä-\ *interj*
used to express agreement (as after a prayer or a statement of opinion)

## 15. Undefined Run-on Entries

[1]**sour** \ˈsau̇r\ *adj*
**1** having an acid taste
**2** having become acid through spoiling ⟨*sour* milk⟩
**3** suggesting decay ⟨a *sour* smell⟩
**4** not pleasant or friendly ⟨a *sour* look⟩
**5** acid in reaction ⟨*sour* soil⟩
**sour·ish** \-ish\ *adj*
**sour·ly** *adv*
**sour·ness** *n*

The boldface words at the end of the entry **sour** are **undefined run-on entries**. Each of these run-on entries is shown without a definition. You can easily discover the meaning of any of these words by simply combining the meaning of the base word (the main entry) and that of the suffix. For example, **sourish** is simply **sour** plus **-ish** ("somewhat") and so means "somewhat sour"; **sourly** is simply **sour** plus **-ly** ( "in a specified manner") and so means "in a sour manner"; and **sourness** is **sour** plus **-ness** ( "state : condition") and so means "the state or condition of being sour."

We have run on only words whose meanings you should have no trouble figuring out. Whenever a word derived from a main entry has a meaning that is not easily understandable from the meanings of the two parts, we have entered and defined it at its own alphabetical place.

## 16. Synonym Paragraphs

At the end of certain entries, you will see a special kind of cross-reference like the one at **sparkle**.

[1]**spar·kle** \ˈspär-kəl\ *vb* **spar·kled**; **spar·kling**
**1** to throw off sparks
**2** to give off small flashes of light ⟨the diamond *sparkled*⟩
**3** to be lively or active ⟨the conversation *sparkled*⟩ **synonyms** see GLEAM

The direction "**synonyms** see GLEAM" means "for a discussion of synonyms that includes **sparkle**, see the entry **gleam**."

At several entries in the *DK Merriam-Webster Children's Dictionary* like **gleam** and **splendid**, shown here, there are short discussions of the differences between certain synonyms.

**splen·did** \'splen-dəd\ *adj*
**1** having or showing splendor **:** BRILLIANT
**2** impressive in beauty, excellence, or magnificence ⟨did a *splendid* job⟩ ⟨a *splendid* palace⟩
**3** GRAND 4
**splen·did·ly** *adv*

**Synonyms** SPLENDID, GLORIOUS, and SUPERB mean very impressive. SPLENDID suggests that something is far above the ordinary in excellence or magnificence ⟨what a *splendid* idea⟩ ⟨a *splendid* jewel⟩. GLORIOUS suggests that something is radiant with light or beauty ⟨a *glorious* sunset⟩. SUPERB suggests the highest possible point of magnificence or excellence ⟨a *superb* museum⟩ ⟨the food was *superb*⟩.

These discussions are called **synonym paragraphs**. Synonyms can often be substituted freely for one another in a sentence because they mean basically the same thing. But some words that are synonyms because they mean nearly the same thing cannot always be substituted for one another. They may differ slightly in what they suggest to the reader — in the image they call to mind. These suggested meanings are what make one synonym a better choice than another in certain situations.

In the synonym paragraphs we indicate these little differences between synonyms. Any of the three words in the paragraph following the entry **splendid** might be satisfactory in the examples given to indicate something impressive. But through long usage people have come to think of the word **glorious** as more suited to describing something where light or beauty is involved, while **splendid** and **superb** are used of other things. And something described as **superb** is often thought of as more wonderful than something merely **splendid**.

## 17. Defined Run-on Phrases

The last kind of boldface entry you will find in your dictionary is the **defined run-on phrase**. These phrases are groups of words that, when used together, have a special meaning that is more than just the sum of the ordinary meanings of each word.

[1]**stand** \'stand\ *vb* **stood** \'stu̇d\; **stand·ing**
**1** to be in or take a vertical position on one's feet
**2** to take up or stay in a specified position or condition ⟨*stands* first in the class⟩ ⟨*stands* accused⟩ ⟨machines *standing* idle⟩
**3** to have an opinion ⟨how do you *stand* on taxes?⟩
**4** to rest, remain, or set in a usually vertical position ⟨*stand* the box in the corner⟩
**5** to be in a specified place ⟨the house *stands* on the hill⟩
**6** to stay in effect ⟨the order still *stands*⟩
**7** to put up with **:** ENDURE ⟨can't *stand* pain⟩
. . .
**stand by :** to be or remain loyal or true to ⟨*stand by* a promise⟩
**stand for**
**1** to be a symbol for **:** REPRESENT
**2** to put up with **:** PERMIT ⟨won't *stand for* any nonsense⟩

The **defined run-on phrases** are placed at the end of the entry that is the first major word of the phrase. Normally this will be the first noun or verb rather than an adjective or preposition. The phrases run on at **stand** all begin with the entry word **stand**. But some run-on phrases will not have the major word at the beginning. Keep in mind that the phrase will be entered at the first major word in the phrase. This word is usually a noun or a verb. Where do you think you would find the phrases **do away with**, **in the doghouse**, and **on fire**? If you said at the verb **do**, at the noun **doghouse**, and at the noun **fire**, then you understand how we enter phrases.

Where to find the phrase **read between the lines** may puzzle you at first, since it contains both a verb (**read**) and a noun (**lines**). But if you remember that the phrase will be entered at the *first* major word, in this case the verb **read**, you should have no trouble finding the phrases entered in this dictionary.

## 18. Word History Paragraphs

**sur·ly** \'sər-lē\ *adj* **sur·li·er**; **sur·li·est**
having a mean rude disposition
: UNFRIENDLY

**Word History** The word *surly* comes from the word *sir*. Long ago, some Englishmen who had the title *Sir* became too proud of it. Such men were called *sirly*, a word that meant "overbearing" and "arrogant." Over the years the spelling changed to *surly* and came to be used of anyone who is rude and unfriendly.

One of the important jobs of people who study words and write dictionaries is finding out where the words we use every day in English came from. Some of our words are made up by people using the language today. For example, scientists often make up names for the new elements they discover and the new drugs they create.

But most of the words in the English language have a long history. They usually can be traced back to other words in languages older than English. Many of these languages, like ancient Greek and Latin, are no longer spoken today. The study of the origins of words can be fascinating, for many of our words have very interesting stories behind them.

In this dictionary, we share with you some of the interesting stories of word origins and trace the development of meanings in special short **word history paragraphs**.

## 19. Guide Words

To save you from having to search up and down page after page looking for the word you want, we have printed a **guide word** at the top of each outside column of two facing pages. The guide word on the left-hand page is the first main entry word on the left page and the guide word on the right-hand page is the last main entry word on the right page. So the two guide words tell you the first and last entries on the two facing pages. By looking at the guide words and thinking about whether the word you are hunting will fit in alphabetically between them, you can quickly move from page to page until you find the right one.
Say, for example, you are looking up the word **array** and you have already turned to the section of words that begin with the letter **a**. You next would look at the guide words at the top of the pages. Let's take two pairs of pages, pages 62 and 63 and pages 64 and 65, as a sample to see how the system works.

**arcade** — *first main entry at top of left-hand page, page 62*

**ar·cade** \är-'kād\ *n*
**1** a row of arches with the columns that support them
**2** an arched or covered passageway often between two rows of shops

*last main entry at bottom of right-hand page, page 63* — **arid**

**ar·id** \'ar-əd\ *adj*
**1** not having enough rainfall to support agriculture
**2** UNINTERESTING, DULL ⟨an *arid* lecture⟩

On pages 62 and 63 in this sample are the guide words **arcade** and **arid**. You can see that **array** (arr-) comes after the last guide word, **arid** (ari-), so the page you want must be farther along.

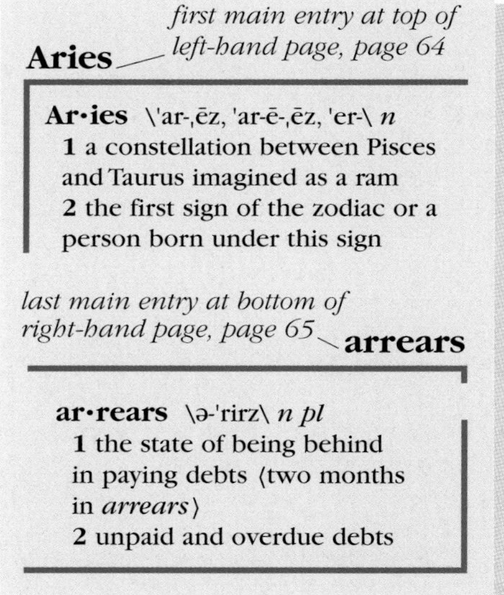

**Aries** — *first main entry at top of left-hand page, page 64*

**Ar·ies** \'ar-ˌēz, 'ar-ē-ˌēz, 'er-\ *n*
**1** a constellation between Pisces and Taurus imagined as a ram
**2** the first sign of the zodiac or a person born under this sign

*last main entry at bottom of right-hand page, page 65* — **arrears**

**ar·rears** \ə-'rirz\ *n pl*
**1** the state of being behind in paying debts ⟨two months in *arrears*⟩
**2** unpaid and overdue debts

The guide words on pages 64 and 65 are **Aries** and **arrears**. You can see that **array** (arra-) comes after **Aries** (ari-) and before **arrears** (arre-), so you know the word you are looking for will be found on one of these two pages.

# Pronunciation Symbols and Abbreviations

## Pronunciation Symbols

**ə** (called *schwa* \'shwä\) banana, collide, abut; in stressed syllables as in humdrum, mother, abut
**ər** further, learner
**a** mat, mad, gag
**ā** day, fade, mate, vacation
**ä** bother, cot, cart
**ȧ** father as pronounced by those who do not rhyme it with *bother.* (Not everyone uses this sound.)
**a** now, loud, out
**b** baby, rib
**ch** chin, match, nature \'nā-chər\
**d** did, ladder
**e** bed, pet
**ē** beat, easy, me, carefree
**f** fifty, cuff, phone
**g** go, dig, bigger
**h** hat, ahead
**hw** whale as pronounced by those who do not pronounce *whale* and *wail* the same
**i** bid, tip, banish, active
**ī** side, site, buy
**j** job, gem, judge
**k** kick, cook, ache
**l** lily, pool, cold, battle, metal
**m** murmur, dim, lamp
**n** no, own, cotton, maiden
**ng** sing \'sing\, singer \'sing-ər\, finger \'fing-gər\, ink \'ingk\
**ō** bone, know, soap
**ȯ** saw, all, moth, taut
**ȯi** coin, destroy
**p** pepper, lip
**r** red, rarity, rhyme, car
**s** source, less
**sh** shy, mission, machine, special
**t** tie, attack, hot, water
**th** thin, ether
**th** this, either
**ü** rule, youth, few \'fyü\, union \'yün-yən\
pull, wood, foot, cure \'kyu̇r\
**v** give, vivid
**w** we, away
**y** yet, you, cue \'kyü\, union \'yün-yən\
**yü** youth, union, cue, few, music
**y** cure, fury
**z** zone, raise
**zh** vision , azure \'azh-ər\

\ \ slant lines used to mark the beginning and end of a pronunciation: \'pen\
' mark at the beginning of a syllable with primary (strongest) stress: \'pen-mən\
ˌ mark at the beginning of a syllable with secondary (next-strongest) stress: \'pen-mən-ˌship\
- a hyphen separates syllables in pronunciations
, a comma separates pronunciation variants: \'rüm, 'ru̇m\

## Abbreviations

*adj* adjective
*adv* adverb
*cap* capitalized
*conj* conjunction
*interj* interjection
*n* noun
*n pl* noun plural
*pl* plural
*prep* preposition
*pron* pronoun
*sing* singular
*vb* verb

# THE ILLUSTRATED DICTIONARY

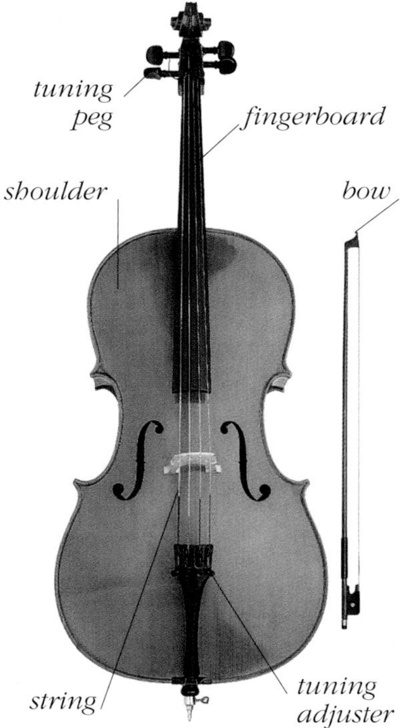


**cello** and bow

# Aa

**The sounds of A:** The letter **A** is used for several vowel sounds in English. These are the most common sounds of A:

In many words, **A** sounds like its own name. This sound is often called "**long A**." Some examples are **ache**, **cape**, **day**, **face**, **escape**, and **safety**.

But in most words, **A** has the sound called "**short A**." This sound is found in words such as **act**, **cap**, **dad**, **fact**, **establish**, **satisfy**, and many other words.

Another sound of **A** is the sound it has in **car**. **A** has this sound most often when it is followed by the letter R.

A fourth sound of **A** is its sound in words such as **all**, **awful**, and **chalk**.

---

[1]**a** \ā\ *n, pl* **a's** *or* **as** \āz\ *often cap*
**1** the first letter of the English alphabet
**2** a grade that shows a student's work is excellent

[2]**a** \ə, ā\ *indefinite article*
**1** some one not identified or known ⟨there's *a* dog in the yard⟩
**2** the same ⟨two of *a* kind⟩
**3** [1]ANY 1 ⟨it's hard for *a* person to bear⟩
**4** for or from each ⟨an apple *a* day⟩ ⟨charges ten dollars *a* person⟩

**a-** \ə\ *prefix*
**1** on **:** in **:** at ⟨*a*bed⟩
**2** in (such) a state, condition, or manner ⟨*a*fire⟩ ⟨*a*loud⟩
**3** in the act or process of ⟨gone *a*-hunting⟩

**aard·vark** \'ärd-,värk\ *n*
▼ an African animal with a long snout and a long sticky tongue that feeds mostly on ants and termites and is active at night

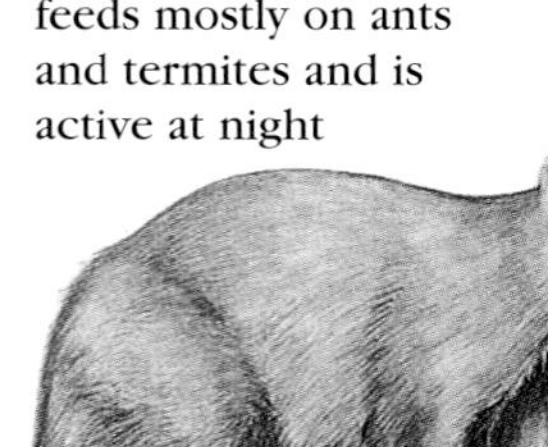

**aardvark**

**ab-** *prefix*
from **:** differing from ⟨*ab*normal⟩

**aback** \ə-'bak\ *adv*
by surprise ⟨taken *aback* by the change in plan⟩

**aba·cus** \'ab-ə-kəs\ *n, pl* **aba·ci** \'ab-ə-,sī\ *or* **aba·cus·es**

**abacus**

▲ an instrument for doing arithmetic by sliding counters along rods or in grooves

**abaft** \ə-'baft\ *adv*
toward or at the back part of a ship

**ab·a·lo·ne** \,ab-ə-'lō-nē\ *n*
▶ a large sea snail that has a flattened shell with a pearly lining

[1]**aban·don** \ə-'ban-dən\ *vb*
**1** to give up completely **:** FORSAKE ⟨*abandon* a sinking ship⟩
**2** to give (oneself) up to a feeling or emotion
**aban·don·ment** \-mənt\ *n*

---

**Synonyms** ABANDON, DESERT, and FORSAKE mean to give up completely. ABANDON suggests that one has no interest in what happens to the person or thing one has given up ⟨*abandoned* the wrecked car on the side of the road⟩. DESERT suggests leaving something to which one has a duty or responsibility ⟨*desert* one's family and job⟩. FORSAKE suggests that one is leaving someone or something for which one once had affection ⟨don't *forsake* old friends in times of trouble⟩.

---

[2]**abandon** *n*
a complete yielding to feelings or wishes ⟨drove with reckless *abandon*⟩

**aban·doned** \ə-'ban-dənd\ *adj*
given up **:** left empty or unused ⟨*abandoned* houses⟩

**abash** \ə-'bash\ *vb*
to destroy the self-confidence of

**abate** \ə-'bāt\ *vb* **abat·ed**; **abat·ing**
to make or become less ⟨the flood *abated* slowly⟩

**ab·bess** \'ab-əs\ *n*
the head of an abbey for women

**ab·bey** \'ab-ē\ *n, pl* **abbeys**
**1** MONASTERY, CONVENT
**2** a church that once belonged to an abbey ⟨Westminster *Abbey*⟩

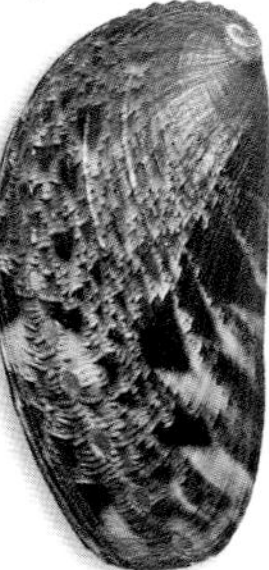

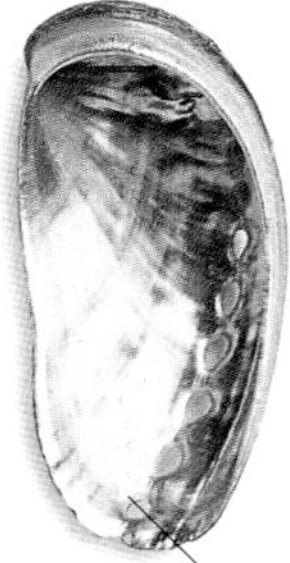

*mother-of-pearl lining*

**abalone**

**ab·bot** \'ab-ət\ *n*
the head of an abbey for men

**ab·bre·vi·ate** \ə-'brē-vē-,āt\ *vb* **ab·bre·vi·at·ed**; **ab·bre·vi·at·ing**
to make briefer **:** SHORTEN

**ab·bre·vi·a·tion** \ə-,brē-vē-'ā-shən\ *n*
**1** a making shorter
**2** a shortened form of a word or phrase

**ab·di·cate** \'ab-di-,kāt\ *vb* **ab·di·cat·ed**; **ab·di·cat·ing**
to give up a position of power or authority ⟨the ruler was forced to *abdicate*⟩

**ab·di·ca·tion** \ˌab-di-ˈkā-shən\ *n*
the giving up of a position of power or authority

**ab·do·men** \ˈab-də-mən, ab-ˈdō-\ *n*
1 the part of the body between the chest and the hips including the cavity in which the chief digestive organs lie
2 ▼ the hind part of the body of an arthropod (as an insect)

**abdomen 2:**
the abdomen of a tree wasp

**ab·dom·i·nal** \ab-ˈdäm-ən-l\ *adj*
of, relating to, or located in the abdomen

**ab·duct** \ab-ˈdəkt\ *vb*
to take a person away by force : KIDNAP

**ab·duc·tion** \ab-ˈdək-shən\ *n*
the act of abducting

**abeam** \ə-ˈbēm\ *adv or adj*
on a line at right angles to a ship's keel

**abed** \ə-ˈbed\ *adv or adj*
in bed

**ab·er·ra·tion** \ˌab-ə-ˈrā-shən\ *n*
a differing from what is normal or usual

**ab·hor** \ab-ˈhȯr\ *vb* **ab·horred**; **ab·hor·ring**
to shrink from in disgust : LOATHE

**ab·hor·rent** \ab-ˈhȯr-ənt\ *adj*
causing or deserving strong dislike

**abide** \ə-ˈbīd\ *vb* **abode** \-ˈbōd\ *or* **abid·ed**; **abid·ing**
1 to bear patiently : TOLERATE
2 ENDURE 1
3 to live in a place : DWELL
**abide by** to accept the terms of : OBEY

**abil·i·ty** \ə-ˈbil-ət-ē\ *n, pl* **abil·i·ties**
1 power to do something
2 natural talent or acquired skill

---

**Synonyms** ABILITY and TALENT mean bodily or mental power to do or accomplish something. ABILITY may suggest an inborn power to do something especially well ⟨the athlete's *ability* to run very fast⟩. TALENT suggests an unusual ability to create things ⟨you should develop your *talent* for writing short stories⟩.

---

**-abil·i·ty** *also* **-ibil·i·ty** \ə-ˈbil-ət-ē\ *n suffix, pl* **-abil·i·ties** *also* **-ibil·i·ties**
ability, fitness, or likeliness to act or be acted upon in (such) a way

**ab·ject** \ˈab-ˌjekt\ *adj*
being low in spirit or hope
**ab·ject·ly** *adv*
**ab·ject·ness** *n*

**ablaze** \ə-ˈblāz\ *adj*
1 being on fire
2 bright with light or color

**able** \ˈā-bəl\ *adj* **abler** \-blər\; **ablest** \-bləst\
1 having enough power or skill to do something ⟨*able* to swim⟩
2 having or showing much skill

---

**Synonyms** ABLE and CAPABLE mean having the power to do or accomplish. ABLE may suggest that one has exceptional skill and has done well in the past ⟨an *able* surgeon with years of experience⟩. CAPABLE stresses that one has the characteristics that make one suitable for a particular kind of work ⟨a very *capable* soldier⟩.

---

**-able** *also* **-ible** \ə-bəl\ *adj suffix*
1 capable of, fit for, or worthy of being ⟨lov*able*⟩
2 tending or likely to ⟨perish*able*⟩
**-ably** *also* **-ibly** \ə-blē\ *adv suffix*

**ably** \ˈā-blē\ *adv*
in an able way

**ab·nor·mal** \ab-ˈnȯr-məl\ *adj*
differing from the normal usually in a noticeable way
**ab·nor·mal·ly** *adv*

**¹aboard** \ə-ˈbōrd\ *adv*
on, onto, or within a ship, train, bus, or airplane

**²aboard** *prep*
on or into especially for passage ⟨go *aboard* ship⟩

**¹abode** \ə-ˈbōd\ *past of* ABIDE

**²abode** *n*
the place where one stays or lives

**abol·ish** \ə-ˈbäl-ish\ *vb*
to do away with : put an end to ⟨*abolish* discrimination⟩

**ab·o·li·tion** \ˌab-ə-ˈlish-ən\ *n*
a complete doing away with ⟨the *abolition* of war⟩

**A–bomb** \ˈā-ˌbäm\ *n*
ATOMIC BOMB

**abom·i·na·ble** \ə-ˈbäm-ə-nə-bəl\ *adj*
1 deserving or causing disgust
2 very disagreeable or unpleasant ⟨an *abominable* odor⟩
**abom·i·na·bly** \-blē\ *adv*

**abominable snow·man** \-ˈsnō-mən, -ˌman\ *n often cap A&S*
a mysterious creature with human or apelike characteristics reported to exist in the Himalayas

**abom·i·na·tion** \ə-ˌbäm-ə-ˈnā-shən\ *n*
something abominable

**ab·orig·i·nal** \ˌab-ə-ˈrij-ən-l\ *adj*
1 being the first of its kind in a region
2 of or relating to aborigines

**ab·orig·i·ne** \ˌab-ə-ˈrij-ə-nē\ *n, pl* **ab·orig·i·nes**
a member of the original race to live in a region : NATIVE

**abound** \ə-ˈbau̇nd\ *vb*
1 to be plentiful : TEEM
2 to be fully supplied ⟨the book *abounds* with pictures⟩

**¹about** \ə-ˈbau̇t\ *adv*
1 ALMOST, NEARLY ⟨*about* an hour ago⟩
2 on all sides : AROUND
3 in the opposite direction ⟨the ship came *about*⟩

**²about** *prep*
1 on every side of : AROUND ⟨trees *about* the house⟩
2 on the point of ⟨we're *about* to leave⟩
3 having to do with ⟨a story *about* dogs⟩

**¹above** \ə-ˈbəv\ *adv*
in or to a higher place

**²above** *prep*
1 higher than : OVER ⟨*above* the clouds⟩
2 too good for ⟨thought myself *above* that kind of work⟩
3 more than ⟨won't pay *above* ten dollars⟩

A B C D E F G H I J K L M N O P Q R S T U V W X Y Z

[3]**above** *adj*
said or written earlier

[1]**above·board** \ə-'bəv-,bōrd\ *adv*
in an honest open way

[2]**aboveboard** *adj*
free from tricks and secrecy

**ab·ra·ca·dab·ra** \,ab-rə-kə-'dab-rə\ *n*
a magical charm or word

**abrade** \ə-'brād\ *vb* **abrad·ed**; **abrad·ing**
to wear away by rubbing

[1]**abra·sive** \ə-'brā-siv\ *n*
a substance for grinding, smoothing, or polishing

[2]**abrasive** *adj*
having the effect of or like that of abrading ⟨an *abrasive* voice⟩

**abreast** \ə-'brest\ *adv or adj*
**1** side by side
**2** up to a certain level of knowledge ⟨keep *abreast* of the news⟩

**abridge** \ə-'brij\ *vb* **abridged**; **abridg·ing**
to shorten by leaving out some parts ⟨*abridge* a dictionary⟩

**abridg·ment** *or* **abridge·ment** \ə-'brij-mənt\ *n*
a shortened form of a written work

**abroad** \ə-'brȯd\ *adv or adj*
**1** over a wide area
**2** in the open **:** OUTDOORS
**3** in or to a foreign country
**4** known to many people ⟨the rumor soon got *abroad*⟩

**abrupt** \ə-'brəpt\ *adj*
**1** happening without warning **:** SUDDEN
**2** [1]STEEP 1 ⟨an *abrupt* drop⟩
**abrupt·ly** *adv*
**abrupt·ness** *n*

**ab·scess** \'ab-,ses\ *n*
a collection of pus with swollen and red tissue around it
**ab·scessed** \-,sest\ *adj*

**ab·sence** \'ab-səns\ *n*
**1** a being away
**2** [2]LACK 1, WANT

[1]**ab·sent** \'ab-sənt\ *adj*
**1** not present
**2** not existing
**3** showing that one is not paying attention ⟨an *absent* stare⟩

[2]**ab·sent** \ab-'sent\ *vb*
to keep (oneself) away

**ab·sen·tee** \,ab-sən-'tē\ *n*
a person who is absent

**ab·sent·mind·ed** \,ab-sənt-'mīn-dəd\ *adj*
not paying attention to what is going on or to what one is doing
**ab·sent·mind·ed·ly** *adv*
**ab·sent·mind·ed·ness** *n*

**ab·so·lute** \'ab-sə-,lüt\ *adj*
**1** free from imperfection **:** PERFECT, COMPLETE
**2** free from control or conditions ⟨*absolute* power⟩
**3** free from doubt **:** CERTAIN ⟨*absolute* proof⟩
**ab·so·lute·ly** *adv*
**ab·so·lute·ness** *n*

**ab·so·lu·tion** \,ab-sə-'lü-shən\ *n*
a forgiving of sins

**ab·solve** \əb-'zälv, -'sälv\ *vb* **ab·solved**; **ab·solv·ing**
to set free from a duty or from blame

**ab·sorb** \əb-'sȯrb, -'zȯrb\ *vb*
**1** ▼ to take in or swallow up ⟨a sponge *absorbs* water⟩
**2** to hold all of one's interest
**3** to receive without giving back ⟨a surface that *absorbs* sound⟩

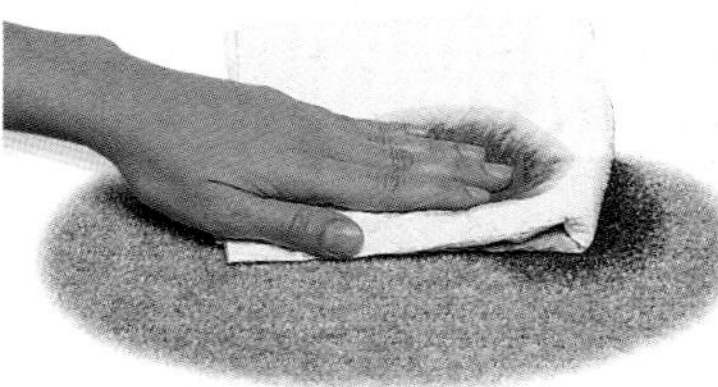

**absorb 1:**
a towel absorbs spilled liquid

**ab·sor·ben·cy** \əb-'sȯr-bən-sē, -'zȯr-\ *n*
the quality or state of being absorbent

**ab·sor·bent** \əb-'sȯr-bənt, -'zȯr-\ *adj*
able to absorb ⟨*absorbent* cotton⟩

**ab·sorp·tion** \əb-'sȯrp-shən, -'zȯrp-\ *n*
**1** the process of absorbing or being absorbed ⟨the *absorption* of water by soil⟩
**2** complete attention

**ab·stain** \əb-'stān\ *vb*
to keep oneself from doing something ⟨*abstain* from voting⟩
**ab·stain·er** *n*

**ab·sti·nence** \'ab-stə-nəns\ *n*
an avoiding by choice especially of certain foods or of liquor

[1]**ab·stract** \'ab-,strakt\ *adj*
**1** expressing a quality apart from an actual person or thing that possesses it ⟨"honesty" is an *abstract* word⟩
**2** hard to understand
**ab·stract·ly** *adv*
**ab·stract·ness** *n*

[2]**ab·stract** \'ab-,strakt\ *n*
[2]SUMMARY

[3]**ab·stract** \ab-'strakt\ *vb*
**1** to take away **:** SEPARATE
**2** SUMMARIZE

**ab·strac·tion** \ab-'strak-shən\ *n*
**1** the act of abstracting **:** the state of being abstracted
**2** an abstract idea

**ab·struse** \ab-'strüs\ *adj*
hard to understand
**ab·struse·ly** *adv*
**ab·struse·ness** *n*

**ab·surd** \əb-'sərd, -'zərd\ *adj*
completely unreasonable or untrue **:** RIDICULOUS
**ab·surd·ly** *adv*

---

**Synonyms** ABSURD, FOOLISH, and SILLY mean not showing good sense. ABSURD suggests that something is not in keeping with common sense, good reasoning, or accepted ideas ⟨the *absurd* notion that horses can talk⟩. FOOLISH suggests that something is not thought of by others as wise or sensible ⟨you made a *foolish* investment of your money⟩. SILLY suggests that something makes no sense and has no purpose ⟨a *silly* argument over who ate the most⟩.

---

**ab·sur·di·ty** \əb-'sərd-ət-ē, -'zərd-\ *n, pl* **ab·sur·di·ties**
**1** the fact of being absurd
**2** something that is absurd

**abun·dance** \ə-'bən-dəns\ *n*
a large quantity **:** PLENTY

**abun·dant** \ə-'bən-dənt\ *adj*
more than enough **:** PLENTIFUL
**abun·dant·ly** *adv*

[1]**abuse** \ə-'byüs\ *n*
**1** a dishonest practice ⟨election *abuses*⟩
**2** wrong or unfair treatment or use ⟨drug *abuse*⟩
**3** harsh insulting language

[2]**abuse** \ə-'byüz\ *vb* **abused**; **abus·ing**
**1** to blame or scold rudely
**2** to use wrongly **:** MISUSE ⟨*abuse* privileges⟩
**3** to treat cruelly **:** MISTREAT ⟨*abuse* a horse by overworking it⟩

**abu·sive** \ə-ˈbyü-siv, -ziv\ *adj*
using or characterized by abuse
**abu·sive·ly** *adv*
**abu·sive·ness** *n*

**abut** \ə-ˈbət\ *vb* **abut·ted**; **abut·ting**
to touch along a border or with a part that sticks out

**abut·ment** \ə-ˈbət-mənt\ *n*
something against which another thing rests its weight or pushes with force

**abyss** \ə-ˈbis\ *n*
a gulf so deep or space so great that it cannot be measured

**ac·a·dem·ic** \ˌak-ə-ˈdem-ik\ *adj*
**1** of or relating to schools or colleges
**2** having no practical importance ⟨an *academic* question⟩
**ac·a·dem·i·cal·ly** \-i-kə-lē\ *adv*

**acad·e·my** \ə-ˈkad-ə-mē\ *n, pl* **acad·e·mies**
**1** a private high school
**2** a high school or college where special subjects are taught ⟨a military *academy*⟩
**3** a society of learned persons

---

**Word History** In ancient Greece, a wise man named Plato started a school at a gymnasium. The gymnasium was named for a hero of Greek mythology. The English word *academy* came from the name of the hero for whom Plato's school was named.

---

**ac·cede** \ak-ˈsēd\ *vb* **ac·ced·ed**; **ac·ced·ing**
to agree to

**ac·cel·er·ate** \ak-ˈsel-ə-ˌrāt\ *vb* **ac·cel·er·at·ed**; **ac·cel·er·at·ing**
**1** to bring about earlier : HASTEN
**2** to move or cause to move faster

**ac·cel·er·a·tion** \ak-ˌsel-ə-ˈrā-shən\ *n*
a speeding up

**ac·cel·er·a·tor** \ak-ˈsel-ə-ˌrāt-ər\ *n*
a pedal in an automobile for controlling the speed of the motor

[1]**ac·cent** \ˈak-ˌsent, ak-ˈsent\ *vb*
**1** to give a greater force or stress
**2** to mark with a written or printed accent

[2]**ac·cent** \ˈak-ˌsent\ *n*
**1** a way of talking shared by a group (as the residents of a country)
**2** greater stress or force given to a syllable of a word in speaking or to a beat in music
**3** a mark (as ˈ or ˌ) used in writing or printing to show the place of greater stress on a syllable

**ac·cen·tu·ate** \ak-ˈsen-chə-ˌwāt\ *vb* **ac·cen·tu·at·ed**; **ac·cen·tu·at·ing**
**1** [1]ACCENT
**2** EMPHASIZE

**ac·cept** \ik-ˈsept, ak-\ *vb*
**1** to receive or take willingly ⟨*accept* a gift⟩
**2** to agree to

**ac·cept·able** \ik-ˈsep-tə-bəl, ak-\ *adj*
**1** worthy of being accepted ⟨an *acceptable* excuse⟩
**2** ADEQUATE ⟨plays an *acceptable* game of tennis⟩
**ac·cept·able·ness** *n*
**ac·cept·ably** \-blē\ *adv*

**ac·cep·tance** \ik-ˈsep-təns, ak-\ *n*
**1** the act of accepting
**2** the quality or state of being accepted or acceptable

**ac·cess** \ˈak-ˌses\ *n*
**1** the right or ability to approach, enter, or use ⟨*access* to secret information⟩
**2** a way or means of approach ⟨*access* to the sea⟩

**ac·ces·si·ble** \ak-ˈses-ə-bəl\ *adj*
**1** capable of being reached ⟨a resort *accessible* by train or bus⟩
**2** OBTAINABLE ⟨the book is *accessible* in your school library⟩
**ac·ces·si·bly** \-blē\ *adv*

**ac·ces·sion** \ak-ˈsesh-ən\ *n*
a coming to a position of power

[1]**ac·ces·so·ry** \ik-ˈses-ə-rē, ak-\ *n, pl* **ac·ces·so·ries**
**1** a person who helps another in doing wrong ⟨an *accessory* to murder⟩
**2** ▶ an object or device not necessary in itself but adding to the beauty or usefulness of something else ⟨clothing *accessories*⟩

[2]**accessory** *adj*
adding to or helping in a secondary way : SUPPLEMENTARY

**ac·ci·dent** \ˈak-səd-ənt, -sə-ˌdent\ *n*
**1** something that happens by chance or from unknown causes : MISHAP ⟨automobile *accident*⟩
**2** lack of intention or necessity : CHANCE

[1]**accessory 2**
Fashion accessories add color and style to an outfit.

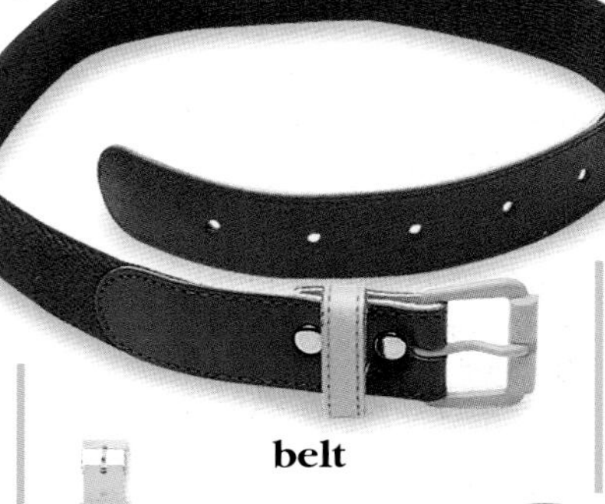
belt

watch

necklace

sunglasses

baseball cap

gloves

A B C D E F G H I J K L M N O P Q R S T U V W X Y Z

**ac·ci·den·tal** \ˌak-sə-ˈdent-l\ *adj*
1 happening by chance or unexpectedly ⟨an *accidental* discovery of oil⟩
2 not happening or done on purpose ⟨an *accidental* shooting⟩
**ac·ci·den·tal·ly** *adv*

[1]**ac·claim** \ə-ˈklām\ *vb*
[1]PRAISE 1 ⟨a book *acclaimed* by the critics⟩

[2]**acclaim** *n*
[2]PRAISE 1, APPLAUSE

**ac·cli·mate** \ə-ˈklī-mət, ˈak-lə-ˌmāt\ *vb* **ac·cli·mat·ed**; **ac·cli·mat·ing**
to change to fit a new climate or new surroundings

**ac·cli·ma·tize** \ə-ˈklī-mə-ˌtīz\ *vb* **ac·cli·ma·tized**; **ac·cli·ma·tiz·ing**
ACCLIMATE

**ac·com·mo·date** \ə-ˈkäm-ə-ˌdāt\ *vb* **ac·com·mo·dat·ed**; **ac·com·mo·dat·ing**
1 to provide with a place to stay or sleep
2 to provide with something needed : help out
3 to have room for ⟨the bus *accommodates* forty people⟩

**ac·com·mo·dat·ing** \ə-ˈkäm-ə-ˌdāt-ing\ *adj*
ready to help
**ac·com·mo·dat·ing·ly** *adv*

**ac·com·mo·da·tion** \ə-ˌkäm-ə-ˈdā-shən\ *n*
1 something supplied that is useful or handy
2 **accommodations** *pl* lodging and meals or traveling space and related services ⟨overnight *accommodations*⟩

**ac·com·pa·ni·ment** \ə-ˈkəm-pə-nē-mənt\ *n*
music played along with a solo part to enrich it

**ac·com·pa·nist** \ə-ˈkəm-pə-nist\ *n*
a musician who plays an accompaniment

**ac·com·pa·ny** \ə-ˈkəm-pə-nē\ *vb* **ac·com·pa·nied**; **ac·com·pa·ny·ing**
1 to go with as a companion
2 to play a musical accompaniment for
3 to happen at the same time as

**ac·com·plice** \ə-ˈkäm-pləs\ *n*
a partner in wrongdoing

**ac·com·plish** \ə-ˈkäm-plish\ *vb*
to succeed in doing : manage to do

**ac·com·plished** \ə-ˈkäm-plisht\ *adj*
skilled through practice or training : EXPERT ⟨an *accomplished* dancer⟩

**ac·com·plish·ment** \ə-ˈkäm-plish-mənt\ *n*
1 the act of accomplishing : COMPLETION
2 something accomplished
3 an acquired excellence or skill

[1]**ac·cord** \ə-ˈkȯrd\ *vb*
1 [1]GIVE 6 ⟨*accord* them special privileges⟩
2 to be in harmony : AGREE ⟨your story of the accident *accords* with theirs⟩

[2]**accord** *n*
1 AGREEMENT 1, HARMONY ⟨acted in *accord* with their parents' wishes⟩
2 willingness to act or to do something ⟨went of their own *accord*⟩

**ac·cor·dance** \ə-ˈkȯrd-ns\ *n*
AGREEMENT 1

**ac·cord·ing·ly** \ə-ˈkȯrd-ing-lē\ *adv*
1 in the necessary way : in the way called for
2 as a result : CONSEQUENTLY, SO

**ac·cord·ing to** *prep*
1 in agreement with ⟨everything was done *according to* the rules⟩
2 as stated by ⟨*according to* the experts⟩

[1]**ac·cor·di·on** \ə-ˈkȯrd-ē-ən\ *n*
▶ a portable keyboard musical instrument played by forcing air from a bellows past metal reeds

[2]**accordion** *adj*
folding or creased or hinged to fold like an accordion ⟨a skirt with *accordion* pleats⟩

**ac·cost** \ə-ˈkȯst\ *vb*
to approach and speak to often in a demanding or aggressive way

[1]**ac·count** \ə-ˈkau̇nt\ *n*
1 a record of money received and money paid out
2 a statement of explanation or of reasons or causes
3 a statement of facts or events : REPORT
4 [2]WORTH 1, IMPORTANCE
**on account of** for the sake of : BECAUSE OF
**on no account** not ever or for any reason

[2]**account** *vb*
1 to think of as : CONSIDER ⟨*account* them lucky⟩
2 to give an explanation ⟨try to *account* for what you did⟩
3 to be the only or chief reason ⟨heavy rains *accounted* for the flood⟩

**ac·coun·tant** \ə-ˈkau̇nt-nt\ *n*
a person whose job is accounting

**ac·count·ing** \ə-ˈkau̇nt-ing\ *n*
the work of keeping track of how much money is made and spent in a business

**ac·cu·mu·late** \ə-ˈkyü-myə-ˌlāt\ *vb* **ac·cu·mu·lat·ed**; **ac·cu·mu·lat·ing**
1 COLLECT 1, GATHER ⟨*accumulated* several swimming trophies⟩
2 to increase in quantity or number

**ac·cu·mu·la·tion** \ə-ˌkyü-myə-ˈlā-shən\ *n*
1 a collecting together ⟨a steady *accumulation* of snow⟩
2 something accumulated : COLLECTION ⟨an *accumulation* of junk⟩

**ac·cu·ra·cy** \ˈak-yə-rə-sē\ *n*
freedom from mistakes

**ac·cu·rate** \ˈak-yə-rət\ *adj*
free from mistakes : RIGHT ⟨an *accurate* answer⟩ **synonyms** see CORRECT
**ac·cu·rate·ly** *adv*
**ac·cu·rate·ness** *n*

[1]**accordion:**
a boy playing an accordion

**ac·cu·sa·tion** \ˌak-yə-ˈzā-shən\ *n*
a claim that someone has done something bad or illegal

**ac·cuse** \ə-ˈkyüz\ *vb* **ac·cused**; **ac·cus·ing**
to blame a fault, wrong, or crime on (a person)
**ac·cus·er** *n*

**ac•cus•tom** \ə-'kəs-təm\ *vb*
to cause (someone) to get used to something

**ac•cus•tomed** \ə-'kəs-təmd\ *adj*
**1** CUSTOMARY **2**, USUAL ⟨their *accustomed* lunch hour⟩
**2** familiar with **:** USED ⟨*accustomed* to hard luck⟩

[1]**ace** \'ās\ *n*
**1** ▼ a playing card with one figure in its center
**2** a person who is expert at something

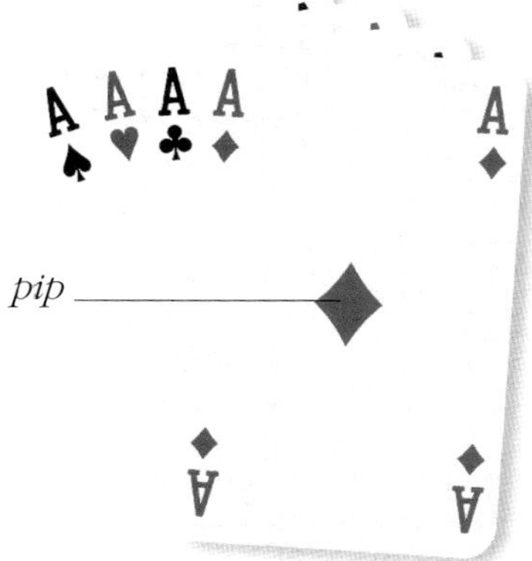


[1]**ace 1:**
aces on playing cards

**Word History** An Old French word referring to the side of a dice with a single spot came from a Latin word that meant "a unit" or "a single thing." The English word *ace* came from the Old French word. At first *ace* meant "the side of a dice that has a single spot." Later, however, the word *ace* came to be used for a playing card with a single mark in its center. Other meanings of *ace* have come from this meaning.

[2]**ace** *adj*
of the very best kind

[1]**ache** \'āk\ *vb* **ached**; **ach•ing**
**1** to suffer a dull continuous pain
**2** YEARN

[2]**ache** *n*
a dull continuous pain

**achieve** \ə-'chēv\ *vb* **achieved**; **achiev•ing**
**1** to bring about **:** ACCOMPLISH
**2** to get by means of one's own efforts **:** WIN **synonyms** see REACH

**achieve•ment** \ə-'chēv-mənt\ *n*
**1** the act of achieving
**2** something achieved especially by great effort

[1]**ac•id** \'as-əd\ *adj*
**1** having a taste that is sour, bitter, or stinging
**2** sour in temper **:** CROSS ⟨*acid* remarks⟩
**3** of, relating to, or like an acid

**ac•id•ly** *adv*

[2]**acid** *n*
▼ a chemical compound that tastes sour and forms a water solution which turns blue litmus paper red

**acid•i•ty** \ə-'sid-ət-ē\ *n, pl* **acid•i•ties**
the quality, state, or degree of being acid

[2]**acid**
Acids dissolve in water to form sharp-tasting solutions. Alkalis dissolve in water to form soapy solutions. The strength of a solution is measured by its value on a scale of acidity or alkalinity.

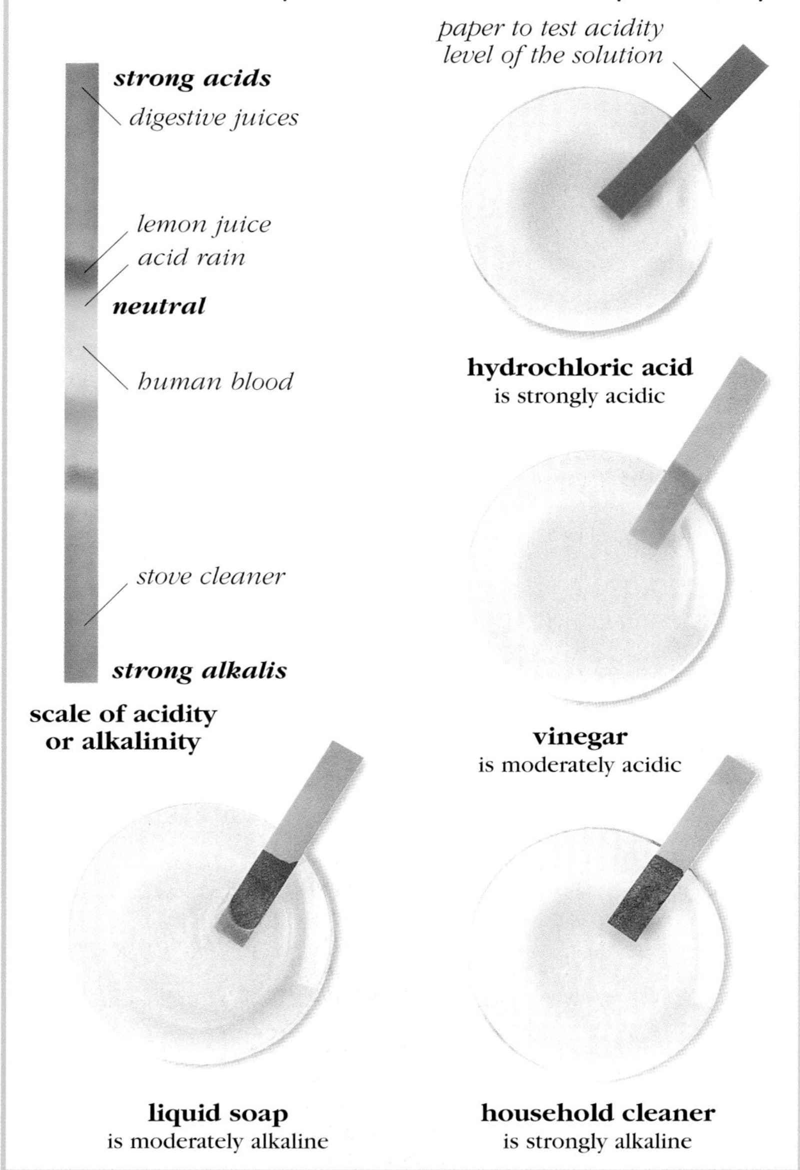


scale of acidity or alkalinity

**hydrochloric acid** is strongly acidic

**vinegar** is moderately acidic

**liquid soap** is moderately alkaline

**household cleaner** is strongly alkaline

**ac•knowl•edge** \ik-'näl-ij, ak-\ *vb* **ac•knowl•edged**; **ac•knowl•edg•ing**
**1** to admit the truth or existence of ⟨*acknowledged* their mistake⟩
**2** to recognize the rights or authority of
**3** to make known that something has been received or noticed

**ac•knowl•edged** \ik-'näl-ijd, ak-\ *adj* generally accepted ⟨the *acknowledged* leader⟩

**ac•knowl•edg•ment** *or* **ac•knowl•edge•ment** \ik-'näl-ij-mənt, ak-\ *n*
**1** an act of acknowledging some deed or achievement
**2** something done or given in return for something done or received

**ac•ne** \'ak-nē\ *n* a skin condition in which pimples and blackheads are present

**acorn** \'ā-,kȯrn, -kərn\ *n* ▶ the nut of the oak tree

acorn

**acous•tic** \ə-'kü-stik\ *or* **acous•ti•cal** \-sti-kəl\ *adj*
**1** of or relating to hearing or sound
**2** deadening sound ⟨*acoustical* tile⟩

**acous•tics** \ə-'kü-stiks\ *n sing or pl*
**1** a science dealing with sound
**2** the qualities in a room or hall that affect how well a person in it can hear

**ac•quaint** \ə-'kwānt\ *vb*
**1** to cause to know personally ⟨became *acquainted* at school⟩
**2** to make familiar : INFORM ⟨*acquaint* them with their duties⟩

**ac•quain•tance** \ə-'kwānt-ns\ *n*
**1** personal knowledge
**2** a person one knows slightly

**ac•qui•esce** \,ak-wē-'es\ *vb* **ac•qui•esced**; **ac•qui•esc•ing** to accept, agree, or give consent by keeping silent or by not making objections

**ac•qui•es•cence** \,ak-wē-'es-ns\ *n* the act of acquiescing

**ac•quire** \ə-'kwīr\ *vb* **ac•quired**; **ac•quir•ing** to get especially by one's own efforts : GAIN

## acropolis

The most famous acropolis of ancient Greece is found in Athens and was built almost 5,000 years ago. Many ruins still survive on this fortified citadel.

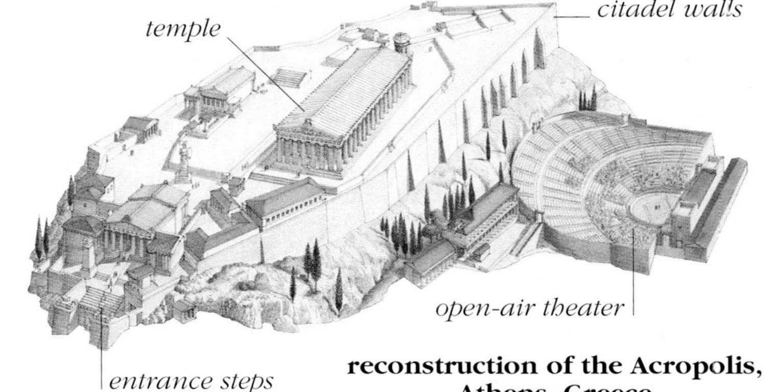


**reconstruction of the Acropolis, Athens, Greece**

**ac•qui•si•tion** \,ak-wə-'zish-ən\ *n*
**1** the act of acquiring
**2** something acquired

**ac•quis•i•tive** \ə-'kwiz-ət-iv\ *adj* GREEDY 2
**ac•quis•i•tive•ly** *adv*
**ac•quis•i•tive•ness** *n*

**ac•quit** \ə-'kwit\ *vb* **ac•quit•ted**; **ac•quit•ting**
**1** to declare innocent of a crime or of wrongdoing
**2** to conduct (oneself) in a certain way

**ac•quit•tal** \ə-'kwit-l\ *n* the act of acquitting someone

**acre** \'ā-kər\ *n* a measure of land area equal to 43,560 square feet (about 4047 square meters)

**acre•age** \'ā-kə-rij, 'ā-krij\ *n* area in acres

**ac•rid** \'ak-rəd\ *adj*
**1** sharp or bitter in taste or odor
**2** very harsh or unpleasant ⟨an *acrid* manner⟩

**ac•ro•bat** \'ak-rə-,bat\ *n* a person (as a circus performer) who is very good at stunts like jumping, balancing, tumbling, and swinging from things

**ac•ro•bat•ic** \,ak-rə-'bat-ik\ *adj* of or relating to acrobats or acrobatics

**ac•ro•bat•ics** \,ak-rə-'bat-iks\ *n sing or pl*
**1** the art or performance of an acrobat
**2** stunts of or like those of an acrobat

**ac•ro•nym** \'ak-rə-,nim\ *n* : a word (as *radar*) formed from the first letter or letters of the words of a compound term

**acrop•o•lis** \ə-'kräp-ə-ləs\ *n* ▲ the upper fortified part of an ancient Greek city

[1]**across** \ə-'krȯs\ *adv* from one side to the other

[2]**across** *prep*
**1** to or on the opposite side of ⟨ran *across* the street⟩
**2** so as to pass, go over, or intersect at an angle ⟨lay one stick *across* another⟩

[1]**act** \'akt\ *n*
**1** something that is done : DEED
**2** a law made by a governing body
**3** the doing of something ⟨caught in the *act* of stealing⟩
**4** a main division of a play

[2]**act** *vb*
**1** to perform (a part) on the stage ⟨*act* the hero in a play⟩
**2** to behave oneself in a certain way ⟨*acts* like a coward⟩
**3** to do something : MOVE ⟨*act* quickly in an emergency⟩
**4** to have a result : make something happen : WORK ⟨the medicine *acts* on the heart⟩ **synonyms** see IMPERSONATE

**act·ing** \'ak-ting\ *adj*
serving for a short time only or in place of another

**ac·tion** \'ak-shən\ *n*
**1** the working of one thing on another so as to produce a change
**2** the doing of something
**3** something done
**4** the way something runs or works
**5** combat in war

**action figure** *n*
a small figure often of a superhero used especially as a toy

**ac·ti·vate** \'ak-tə-,vāt\ *vb* **ac·ti·vat·ed**; **ac·ti·vat·ing**
to make active or more active

**ac·tive** \'ak-tiv\ *adj*
**1** producing or involving action or movement
**2** showing that the subject of a sentence is the doer of the action represented by the verb ⟨"hit" in "they hit the ball" is *active*⟩
**3** quick in physical movement : LIVELY ⟨an *active* child⟩
**4** taking part in an action or activity
**ac·tive·ly** *adv*

**ac·tiv·i·ty** \ak-'tiv-ət-ē\ *n*, *pl* **ac·tiv·i·ties**
**1** energetic action
**2** something done especially for relaxation or fun

**ac·tor** \'ak-tər\ *n*
a person who acts especially in a play or movie

**ac·tress** \'ak-trəs\ *n*
a woman or girl who acts especially in a play or movie

**ac·tu·al** \'ak-chə-wəl\ *adj*
really existing or happening : not false **synonyms** see REAL

**ac·tu·al·ly** \'ak-chə-wə-lē\ *adv*
in fact : REALLY

**acute** \ə-'kyüt\ *adj* **acut·er**; **acut·est**
**1** ▼ measuring less than a right angle ⟨*acute* angles⟩
**2** mentally sharp
**3** SEVERE ⟨*acute* distress⟩
**4** developing quickly and lasting only a short time ⟨*acute* illness⟩
**5** CRITICAL 4, URGENT ⟨an *acute* need for help⟩
**acute·ly** *adv*
**acute·ness** *n*



**acute 1:** an acute angle

**ad** \'ad\ *n*
ADVERTISEMENT

**ad·age** \'ad-ij\ *n*
an old familiar saying : PROVERB

**ad·a·mant** \'ad-ə-mənt\ *adj*
not giving in

**Ad·am's apple** \'ad-əmz-\ *n*
the lump formed in the front of a person's neck by cartilage in the throat

**adapt** \ə-'dapt\ *vb*
to make or become suitable or able to function
**adapt·er** *n*

**adapt·abil·i·ty** \ə-,dap-tə-'bil-ət-ē\ *n*
the quality or state of being adaptable

**adapt·able** \ə-'dap-tə-bəl\ *adj*
capable of adapting or being adapted

**ad·ap·ta·tion** \,ad-,ap-'tā-shən\ *n*
**1** the act or process of adapting
**2** something adapted or helping to adapt ⟨lungs are an *adaptation* to breathing air⟩

**add** \'ad\ *vb*
**1** to join or unite to something ⟨*add* a wing to the house⟩
**2** to say something more ⟨the teacher *added*, "It's not only wrong, it's foolish"⟩
**3** to combine numbers into a single sum

**ad·dend** \'ad-,end\ *n*
a number that is to be added to another number

**ad·den·dum** \ə-'den-dəm\ *n*, *pl* **ad·den·da** \ə-'den-də\
something added (as to a book)

**ad·der** \'ad-ər\ *n*
**1** any of several poisonous snakes of Europe or Africa
**2** ► any of several harmless North American snakes (as the **puff adder**)

[1]**ad·dict** \ə-'dikt\ *vb*
to cause to have a need for something ⟨*addicted* to drugs⟩

[2]**ad·dict** \'ad-,ikt\ *n*
a person who is addicted (as to a drug)

**ad·dic·tion** \ə-'dik-shən\ *n*
the state of being addicted (as to the use of harmful drugs)

**ad·di·tion** \ə-'dish-ən\ *n*
**1** the adding of numbers to obtain their sum
**2** something added ⟨an *addition* to a house⟩
**in addition** [2]BESIDES, ALSO
**in addition to** over and above : [1]BESIDES

**ad·di·tion·al** \ə-'dish-ən-l\ *adj*
[1]EXTRA ⟨we needed *additional* time to finish⟩
**ad·di·tion·al·ly** \-ē\ *adv*

[1]**ad·di·tive** \'ad-ət-iv\ *adj*
relating to or produced by addition

[2]**additive** *n*
a substance added to another in small amounts ⟨a gasoline *additive* to improve engine performance⟩

**ad·dle** \'ad-l\ *vb* **ad·dled**; **ad·dling**
to make confused

[1]**ad·dress** \ə-'dres\ *vb*
**1** to apply (oneself) to something ⟨*addressed* themselves to the problem⟩
**2** to speak or write to
**3** to put directions for delivery on ⟨*address* a letter⟩

[2]**ad·dress** \ə-'dres, 'ad-,res\ *n*
**1** a rehearsed speech : LECTURE
**2** the place where a person can usually be reached ⟨a business *address*⟩

**adder 2:** puff adder

a b c d e f g h i j k l m n o p q r s t u v w x y z

3 the directions for delivery placed on mail
4 the symbols (as numerals or letters) that identify the location where particular information (as a home page) is stored on a computer especially on the Internet

**ad·dress·ee** \ˌad-ˌres-ˈē\ *n*
the person to whom something is addressed

**ad·e·noids** \ˈad-n-ˌȯidz\ *n pl*
fleshy growths near the opening of the nose into the throat

**ad·ept** \ə-ˈdept\ *adj*
very good at something ⟨*adept* at swimming⟩
**adept·ly** *adv*
**adept·ness** *n*

---

**Word History** A long time ago people claimed to have found the trick of turning common metals to gold. No one could really do this. There was even a Latin word used to describe a person who could make gold from other metals. The English word *adept,* which means "highly skilled," came from this Latin word. Certainly, a person who could make gold in this way would have to be highly skilled.

---

**ad·e·quate** \ˈad-i-kwət\ *adj*
1 ¹ENOUGH ⟨the meal was not *adequate* to feed six people⟩
2 good enough ⟨your grades are barely *adequate*⟩
**ad·e·quate·ly** *adv*
**ad·e·quate·ness** *n*

**ad·here** \ad-ˈhir\ *vb* **ad·hered**; **ad·her·ing**
1 to stay loyal (as to a promise)
2 to stick tight : CLING

**ad·her·ence** \ad-ˈhir-əns\ *n*
steady or faithful attachment ⟨*adherence* to the truth⟩

**ad·her·ent** \ad-ˈhir-ənt\ *n*
a person who adheres to a belief, an organization, or a leader

**ad·he·sion** \ad-ˈhē-zhən\ *n*
the act or state of adhering

**¹ad·he·sive** \ad-ˈhē-siv, -ziv\ *adj*
tending to stick : STICKY
**ad·he·sive·ly** *adv*
**ad·he·sive·ness** *n*

**²adhesive** *n*
an adhesive substance

**adi·os** \ˌä-dē-ˈōs, ˌad-ē-\ *interj*
used instead of goodbye

**ad·ja·cent** \ə-ˈjās-nt\ *adj*
next to or near something
**ad·ja·cent·ly** *adv*

**ad·jec·ti·val** \ˌaj-ik-ˈtī-vəl\ *adj*
of, relating to, or functioning as an adjective ⟨an *adjectival* phrase⟩
**ad·jec·ti·val·ly** *adv*

**ad·jec·tive** \ˈaj-ik-tiv\ *n*
a word that says something about a noun or pronoun ⟨"good" in "good people," "someone good," "it's good to be here," and "they seem very good" is an *adjective*⟩

**ad·join** \ə-ˈjȯin\ *vb*
to be next to or in contact with

**ad·journ** \ə-ˈjərn\ *vb*
to bring or come to a close for a period of time ⟨*adjourn* a meeting⟩
**ad·journ·ment** \-mənt\ *n*

**ad·junct** \ˈaj-ˌəngkt\ *n*
something joined or added to something else but not a necessary part of it

**ad·just** \ə-ˈjəst\ *vb*
1 to settle or fix by agreement ⟨*adjust* conflicts⟩
2 to move the parts of an instrument or a machine to make them work better ⟨*adjust* the brakes on a car⟩
3 to become used to ⟨*adjust* to a new school⟩
**ad·just·er** *n*

**ad·just·able** \ə-ˈjəs-tə-bəl\ *adj*
▼ possible to adjust ⟨an *adjustable* wrench⟩

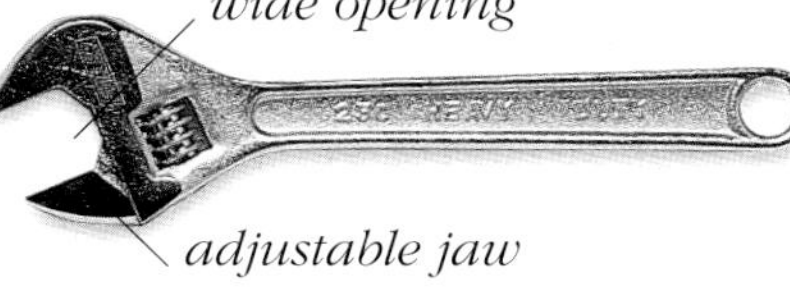


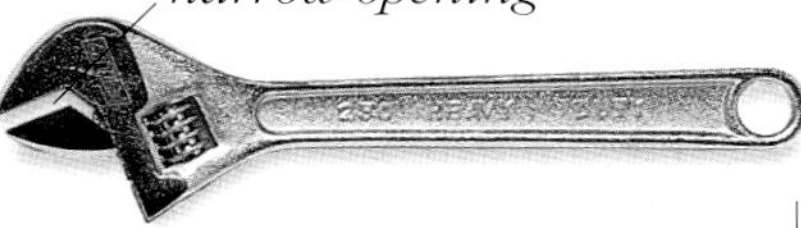


**adjustable** wrench

**ad·just·ment** \ə-ˈjəst-mənt\ *n*
1 the act or process of adjusting : the state of being adjusted
2 a deciding about and paying of a claim or debt
3 something that is used to adjust one part to another

**ad·ju·tant** \ˈaj-ət-ənt\ *n*
an officer who assists a commanding officer

**ad–lib** \ˈad-ˈlib\ *vb* **ad–libbed**; **ad–lib·bing**
to improvise something and especially music or spoken lines

**ad·min·is·ter** \əd-ˈmin-əs-tər\ *vb*
1 to be in charge of : MANAGE ⟨*administer* an athletic program⟩
2 to give out as deserved ⟨*administer* justice⟩
3 to give or supply as treatment ⟨*administer* a dose of medicine⟩

**ad·min·is·tra·tion** \əd-ˌmin-ə-ˈstrā-shən\ *n*
1 the act or process of administering
2 the work involved in managing something
3 the persons who direct the business of something (as a city or school)

**ad·min·is·tra·tive** \əd-ˈmin-ə-ˌstrāt-iv\ *adj*
of or relating to administration

**ad·mi·ra·ble** \ˈad-mə-rə-bəl, ˈad-mrə-bəl\ *adj*
deserving to be admired
**ad·mi·ra·bly** \-blē\ *adv*

**ad·mi·ral** \ˈad-mə-rəl, -mrəl\ *n*
a commissioned officer in the Navy or Coast Guard ranking above a vice admiral

---

**Word History** The word *admiral* looks a lot like the word *admire.* The two words, though, are not related. *Admire* came from a Latin verb that meant "to marvel at." *Admiral* came from an Arabic title that meant "commander of the." It was part of a phrase that meant "commander of the sea."

---

**ad·mi·ral·ty** \ˈad-mə-rəl-tē, -mrəl-\ *adj*
of or relating to conduct on the sea ⟨*admiralty* law⟩

**ad·mi·ra·tion** \ˌad-mə-ˈrā-shən\ *n*
great and delighted approval

**ad·mire** \əd-ˈmīr\ *vb* **ad·mired**; **ad·mir·ing**
to feel admiration for : think very highly of
**ad·mir·er** *n*

**ad·mis·si·ble** \əd-ˈmis-ə-bəl\ *adj*
deserving to be admitted or allowed : ALLOWABLE

**ad·mis·sion** \əd-'mish-ən\ *n*
1 an admitting of something that has not been proved ⟨an *admission* of guilt⟩
2 the act of admitting
3 the right or permission to enter ⟨*admission* to college⟩
4 the price of entrance

**ad·mit** \əd-'mit\ *vb* **ad·mit·ted**; **ad·mit·ting**
1 [1]PERMIT 2, ALLOW ⟨this law *admits* no exceptions⟩
2 to allow to enter : let in
3 to make known usually with some unwillingness ⟨*admitted* that they really didn't know⟩

**ad·mit·tance** \əd-'mit-ns\ *n*
permission to enter

**ad·mon·ish** \ad-'män-ish\ *vb*
1 to criticize or warn gently but seriously ⟨*admonish* a student for talking⟩
2 to give friendly advice or encouragement

**ad·mo·ni·tion** \ˌad-mə-'nish-ən\ *n*
a gentle or friendly criticism or warning

**ado** \ə-'dü\ *n*
fussy excitement or hurrying about

**ado·be** \ə-'dō-bē\ *n*
1 brick made of earth or clay dried in the sun
2 ▶ a building made of adobe

**ad·o·les·cence** \ˌad-l-'es-ns\ *n*
the period of life between childhood and adulthood

**ad·o·les·cent** \ˌad-l-'es-nt\ *n*
a person who is no longer a child but not yet adult

**adopt** \ə-'däpt\ *vb*
1 to take (a child of other parents) as one's own
2 to take up and practice as one's own
3 to accept and put into action
**adopt·er** *n*

**adop·tion** \ə-'däp-shən\ *n*
the act of adopting : the state of being adopted

**ador·able** \ə-'dōr-ə-bəl\ *adj*
CHARMING, LOVELY
**ador·able·ness** *n*
**ador·ably** \-blē\ *adv*

**ad·o·ra·tion** \ˌad-ə-'rā-shən\ *n*
deep love

**adore** \ə-'dōr\ *vb* **adored**; **ador·ing**
1 [2]WORSHIP 1
2 to be very fond of
**ador·er** *n*

**adorn** \ə-'dörn\ *vb*
to try to make prettier by adding decorations

**adorn·ment** \ə-'dörn-mənt\ *n*
1 DECORATION 1
2 [1]ORNAMENT 1

**adren·a·line** \ə-'dren-l-ən\ *n*
EPINEPHRINE

**adrift** \ə-'drift\ *adv or adj*
in a drifting state ⟨a ship *adrift* in the storm⟩

**adroit** \ə-'dröit\ *adj*
having or showing great skill or cleverness ⟨an *adroit* leader⟩
**adroit·ly** *adv*
**adroit·ness** *n*

**ad·u·la·tion** \ˌaj-ə-'lā-shən\ *n*
very great admiration

[1]**adult** \ə-'dəlt, 'ad-ˌəlt\ *adj*
fully developed and mature

[2]**adult** *n*
an adult person or thing

**adul·ter·ate** \ə-'dəl-tə-ˌrāt\ *vb* **adul·ter·at·ed**; **adul·ter·at·ing**
to make impure or weaker by adding something different or of poorer quality

**adult·hood** \ə-'dəlt-ˌhu̇d\ *n*
the period of being an adult

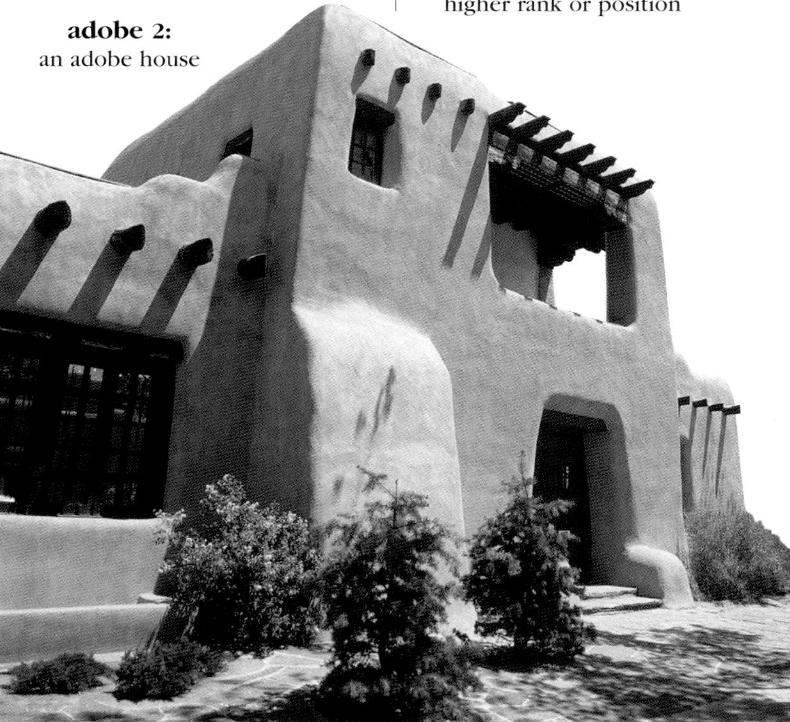

**adobe 2:** an adobe house

[1]**ad·vance** \əd-'vans\ *vb* **ad·vanced**; **ad·vanc·ing**
1 to help the progress of ⟨laws that *advance* freedom⟩
2 to move forward
3 to raise to a higher rank
4 to give ahead of time ⟨*advanced* me five dollars from my wages⟩
5 PROPOSE 1 ⟨*advance* a new plan⟩

[2]**advance** *n*
1 a forward movement
2 IMPROVEMENT 1
3 a rise in price, value, or amount
4 a first step or approach ⟨an unfriendly look discourages *advances*⟩
5 a giving (as of money) ahead of time ⟨asked for an *advance* on my salary⟩
**in advance** [1]BEFORE 1
**in advance of** ahead of

**ad·vanced** \əd-'vanst\ *adj*
1 being far along in years or progress ⟨an *advanced* civilization⟩
2 being beyond the elementary or introductory level ⟨*advanced* mathematics⟩

**ad·vance·ment** \əd-'van-smənt\ *n*
1 the action of advancing : the state of being advanced
2 a raising or being raised to a higher rank or position

**ad·van·tage** \əd-'vant-ij\ *n*
**1** the fact of being in a better position or condition
**2** personal benefit or gain ⟨it's to your own *advantage*⟩
**3** something that benefits the one it belongs to ⟨speed is an *advantage* in sports⟩

**ad·van·ta·geous** \,ad-vən-'tā-jəs, -,van-\ *adj*
giving an advantage **:** HELPFUL
**ad·van·ta·geous·ly** *adv*

**ad·vent** \'ad-,vent\ *n*
the arrival or coming of something ⟨the *advent* of spring⟩

**¹ad·ven·ture** \əd-'ven-chər\ *n*
**1** an action that involves unknown dangers and risks
**2** an unusual experience

**²adventure** *vb* **ad·ven·tured**; **ad·ven·tur·ing**
to expose to or go on in spite of danger or risk
**ad·ven·tur·er** \əd-'ven-chər-ər\ *n*

**ad·ven·ture·some** \əd-'ven-chər-səm\ *adj*
likely to take risks **:** DARING

**ad·ven·tur·ous** \əd-'ven-chə-rəs\ *adj*
**1** ready to take risks or to deal with new or unexpected problems ⟨*adventurous* explorers⟩
**2** DANGEROUS 1, RISKY ⟨an *adventurous* voyage⟩
**ad·ven·tur·ous·ly** *adv*
**ad·ven·tur·ous·ness** *n*

---

**Synonyms** ADVENTUROUS, VENTURESOME, and DARING mean taking risks that are not required by duty or courage. ADVENTUROUS suggests that one goes in search of adventure in spite of the possible dangers ⟨*adventurous* youngsters on a hike through the forest⟩. VENTURESOME suggests that one is willing to take many chances ⟨*venturesome* explorers searching for lost treasure⟩. DARING suggests that one is fearless and willing to take unnecessary risks ⟨the early airplane pilots were especially *daring*⟩.

---

**ad·verb** \'ad-,vərb\ *n*
a word used to modify a verb, an adjective, or another adverb and often used to show degree, manner, place, or time ⟨"almost" and "very" in "at almost three o'clock on a very hot day" are *adverbs*⟩

**ad·ver·bi·al** \ad-'vər-bē-əl\ *adj*
of, relating to, or used as an adverb
**ad·ver·bi·al·ly** *adv*

**ad·ver·sary** \'ad-vər-,ser-ē\ *n, pl* **ad·ver·sar·ies**
OPPONENT, ENEMY

**ad·verse** \ad-'vərs\ *adj*
**1** acting against or in an opposite direction ⟨*adverse* winds⟩
**2** not helping or favoring ⟨*adverse* circumstances⟩
**ad·verse·ly** *adv*
**ad·verse·ness** *n*

**ad·ver·si·ty** \ad-'vər-sət-ē\ *n, pl* **ad·ver·si·ties**
hard times **:** MISFORTUNE

**ad·ver·tise** \'ad-vər-,tīz\ *vb* **ad·ver·tised**; **ad·ver·tis·ing**
**1** to announce publicly ⟨*advertise* a coming event⟩
**2** to call to public attention to persuade to buy
**3** to put out a public notice or request ⟨*advertise* for a lost dog⟩
**synonyms** see DECLARE
**ad·ver·tis·er** *n*

**ad·ver·tise·ment** \,ad-vər-'tīz-mənt, ad-'vərt-əz-\ *n*
▶ a notice or short film advertising something

**ad·ver·tis·ing** \'ad-vər-,tī-zing\ *n*
**1** speech, writing, pictures, or films meant to persuade people to buy something
**2** the business of preparing advertisements

**ad·vice** \əd-'vīs\ *n*
suggestions about a decision or action ⟨took their *advice* on buying a new car⟩

**ad·vis·able** \əd-'vī-zə-bəl\ *adj*
reasonable or proper to do **:** DISCREET ⟨it is not *advisable* to swim after a meal⟩
**ad·vis·ably** \-blē\ *adv*

**ad·vise** \əd-'vīz\ *vb* **ad·vised**; **ad·vis·ing**
**1** to give advice to **:** COUNSEL
**2** to give information about something ⟨were *advised* of bad flying conditions⟩
**ad·vis·er** *or* **ad·vi·sor** \-'vī-zər\ *n*

**ad·vi·so·ry** \əd-'vī-zə-rē, -'vīz-rē\ *adj*
**1** having the power or right to advise
**2** containing advice

**¹ad·vo·cate** \'ad-və-kət, -,kāt\ *n*
**1** a person who argues for another in court
**2** a person who argues for or supports an idea or plan

**²ad·vo·cate** \'ad-və-,kāt\ *vb* **ad·vo·cat·ed**; **ad·vo·cat·ing**
to argue for

**adz** *or* **adze** \'adz\ *n*
▶ a cutting tool that has a thin curved blade at right angles to the handle and is used for shaping wood

blade

handle

**adz:**
an 18th-century adz

**aemia** see -EMIA

**ae·on** *or* **eon** \'ē-ən, 'ē-,än\ *n*
a very long period of time **:** AGE

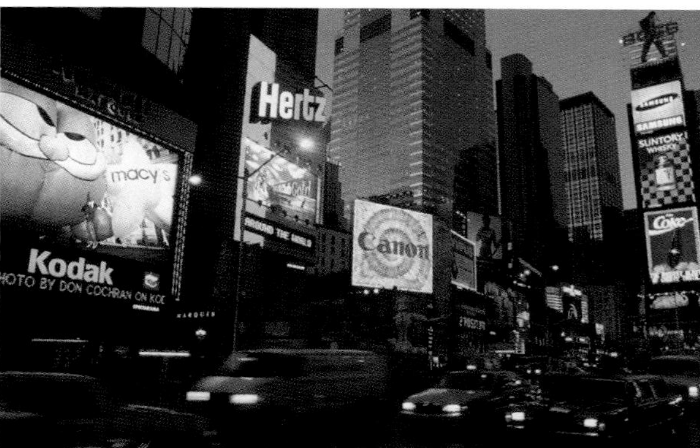


**advertisements** in Times Square, New York City

**aer-** *or* **aero-** *prefix*
air **:** atmosphere **:** gas ⟨*aer*ate⟩ ⟨*aero*sol⟩ ⟨*aero*space⟩

**aer·ate** \'aər-,āt, 'eər-\ *vb* **aer·at·ed**; **aer·at·ing**
**1** to supply (blood) with oxygen by breathing
**2** to supply or cause to be filled with air
**3** to combine or fill with gas
**aer·a·tor** \-ər\ *n*

**aer·a·tion** \aər-'ā-shən, eər-\ *n*
the process of aerating

**[1]ae·ri·al** \'ar-ē-əl, ā-'ir-ē-əl\ *adj*
1 of, relating to, or occurring in the air
2 running on cables or rails that are raised above the ground ⟨an *aerial* railway⟩
3 of or relating to aircraft ⟨*aerial* navigation⟩
4 taken from or used in or against aircraft ⟨*aerial* camera⟩ ⟨*aerial* warfare⟩
**ae·ri·al·ly** *adv*

**[2]aer·i·al** \'ar-ē-əl, 'er-\ *n*
ANTENNA 2

**ae·rie** \'ar-ē, 'er-, 'ir-, 'ā-ə-rē\ *n*
the nest of a bird (as an eagle) high on a cliff or a mountaintop

**aero·nau·ti·cal** \ˌar-ə-'nȯt-i-kəl\ *or* **aero·nau·tic** \-ik\ *adj*
of or relating to aeronautics ⟨*aeronautical* engineer⟩

**aero·nau·tics** \ˌar-ə-'nȯt-iks\ *n*
a science dealing with the building and flying of aircraft

**aero·sol** \'ar-ə-ˌsäl, 'er-, -ˌsȯl\ *n*
1 a substance (as an insecticide) that is dispensed from a container as a spray of tiny solid or liquid particles in gas
2 a container that dispenses an aerosol

**aero·space** \'ar-ō-ˌspās, 'er-\ *n*
1 the earth's atmosphere and the space beyond
2 a science dealing with aerospace

**aes·thet·ic** *or* **es·thet·ic** \es-'thet-ik\ *adj*
of or relating to beauty and what is beautiful
**aes·thet·i·cal·ly** \-i-kə-lē\ *adv*

**[1]afar** \ə-'fär\ *adv*
from, at, or to a great distance

**[2]afar** *n*
a long way off ⟨there came a voice from *afar*⟩

**af·fa·ble** \'af-ə-bəl\ *adj*
polite and friendly in talking to others
**af·fa·bly** \-blē\ *adv*

**af·fair** \ə-'faər, -'feər\ *n*
1 **affairs** *pl* BUSINESS 1 ⟨government *affairs*⟩
2 something that relates to or involves one ⟨that's no *affair* of mine⟩
3 an action or occasion only partly specified ⟨the *affair* of the year⟩

**[1]af·fect** \ə-'fekt\ *vb*
1 to be fond of using or wearing ⟨*affect* bright colors⟩
2 ASSUME 3

**[2]affect** *vb*
1 to attack or act on as a disease does
2 to have an effect on

**af·fect·ed** \ə-'fek-təd\ *adj*
not natural or genuine ⟨*affected* manners⟩
**af·fect·ed·ly** *adv*

**af·fect·ing** \ə-'fek-ting\ *adj*
causing pity or sadness ⟨an *affecting* story⟩

**af·fec·tion** \ə-'fek-shən\ *n*
a feeling of attachment **:** liking for someone

**af·fec·tion·ate** \ə-'fek-shə-nət\ *adj*
feeling or showing a great liking for a person or thing **:** LOVING
**af·fec·tion·ate·ly** *adv*

**af·fi·da·vit** \ˌaf-ə-'dā-vət\ *n*
a sworn statement in writing

**af·fil·i·ate** \ə-'fil-ē-ˌāt\ *vb*
**af·fil·i·at·ed**; **af·fil·i·at·ing**
to associate as a member or branch

**af·fin·i·ty** \ə-'fin-ət-ē\ *n,* *pl* **af·fin·i·ties**
a strong liking for or attraction to someone or something

**af·firm** \ə-'fərm\ *vb*
1 to declare to be true
2 to say with confidence **:** ASSERT

**af·fir·ma·tion** \ˌaf-ər-'mā-shən\ *n*
an act of affirming

**[1]af·fir·ma·tive** \ə-'fər-mət-iv\ *adj*
1 declaring that the fact is so
2 being positive or helpful

**[2]affirmative** *n*
1 an expression (as the word *yes*) of agreement
2 the affirmative side in a debate or vote

**[1]af·fix** \ə-'fiks\ *vb*
**:** FASTEN 1, 2, ATTACH

**[2]af·fix** \'af-ˌiks\ *n*
a letter or group of letters that comes at the beginning or end of a word and has a meaning of its own

**af·flict** \ə-'flikt\ *vb*
to cause pain or unhappiness to

**af·flic·tion** \ə-'flik-shən\ *n*
1 the state of being afflicted
2 something that causes pain or unhappiness

**af·flu·ence** \'af-ˌlü-əns\ *n*
the state of having much money or property

**af·flu·ent** \'af-ˌlü-ənt\ *adj*
having plenty of money and things that money can buy

**af·ford** \ə-'fōrd\ *vb*
1 to be able to do or bear without serious harm ⟨one cannot *afford* to waste one's strength⟩
2 to be able to pay for ⟨can't *afford* a new coat this winter⟩
3 to supply one with ⟨tennis *affords* good exercise⟩

**[1]af·front** \ə-'frənt\ *vb*
to insult openly

**[2]affront** *n*
[2]INSULT

**afield** \ə-'fēld\ *adv*
1 to, in, or into the countryside
2 away from home
3 outside of one's usual circle or way of doing
4 ASTRAY 2

**afire** \ə-'fīr\ *adj*
being on fire

**aflame** \ə-'flām\ *adj*
burning with flames

**afloat** \ə-'flōt\ *adv or adj*
▼ carried on or as if on water

**afloat:**
a toy boat afloat on water

**aflut·ter** \ə-'flət-ər\ *adj*
1 flapping quickly
2 very excited and nervous

**afoot** \ə-'fu̇t\ *adv or adj*
1 on foot ⟨traveled *afoot*⟩
2 happening now **:** going on

**afore·men·tioned** \ə-'fōr-ˌmen-chənd\ *adj*
mentioned before

**afore·said** \ə-'fōr-ˌsed\ *adj*
named before ⟨the *aforesaid* persons⟩

**afraid** \ə-'frād\ *adj*
filled with fear

**afresh** \ə-'fresh\ *adv*
again from the beginning **:** from a new beginning

A B C D E F G H I J K L M N O P Q R S T U V W X Y Z

**[1]Af·ri·can** \'af-ri-kən\ *n*
a person born or living in Africa

**[2]African** *adj*
of or relating to Africa or the Africans

**African–American** *n*
an American having African and especially black African ancestors
**African–American** *adj*

**African violet** *n*
▼ a tropical African plant grown often for its showy white, pink, or purple flowers and its velvety leaves

**African violet**

**Af·ro–Amer·i·can** \,af-rō-ə-'mer-ə-kən\ *n*
AFRICAN-AMERICAN
**Afro–American** *adj*

**aft** \'aft\ *adv*
toward or at the back part of a ship or the tail of an aircraft

**[1]af·ter** \'af-tər\ *adv*
following in time or place

**[2]after** *prep*
1 behind in time or place ⟨got there *after* me⟩
2 for the reason of catching, seizing, or getting ⟨run *after* the ball⟩ ⟨go *after* the championship⟩
3 with the name of ⟨named *after* his father⟩

**[3]after** *conj*
following the time when

**[4]after** *adj*
1 later in time ⟨in *after* years⟩
2 located toward the back part of a ship or aircraft

**af·ter·ef·fect** \'af-tər-ə-,fekt\ *n*
an effect that follows its cause after some time has passed

**af·ter·glow** \'af-tər-,glō\ *n*
a glow remaining (as in the sky after sunset) where a light has disappeared

**af·ter·life** \'af-tər-,līf\ *n*
an existence after death

**af·ter·math** \'af-tər-,math\ *n*
a usually bad result

**af·ter·noon** \,af-tər-'nün\ *n*
the part of the day between noon and evening

**af·ter·thought** \'af-tər-,thȯt\ *n*
a later thought about something one has done or said

**af·ter·ward** \'af-tər-wərd\ *or* **af·ter·wards** \-wərdz\ *adv*
at a later time

**again** \ə-'gen\ *adv*
1 once more : ANEW ⟨did it *again*⟩
2 on the other hand ⟨but then *again*, you might not⟩
3 in addition ⟨half as much *again*⟩

**against** \ə-'genst\ *prep*
1 opposed to ⟨war *against* disease⟩
2 as protection from ⟨a shield *against* aggression⟩
3 in or into contact with ⟨bounced *against* the wall⟩

**agape** \ə-'gāp\ *adj*
wide open ⟨with mouth *agape*⟩

**ag·ate** \'ag-ət\ *n*
1 ▼ a mineral that is a quartz with colors arranged in stripes, cloudy masses, or mossy forms
2 a child's marble of agate or of glass that looks like agate

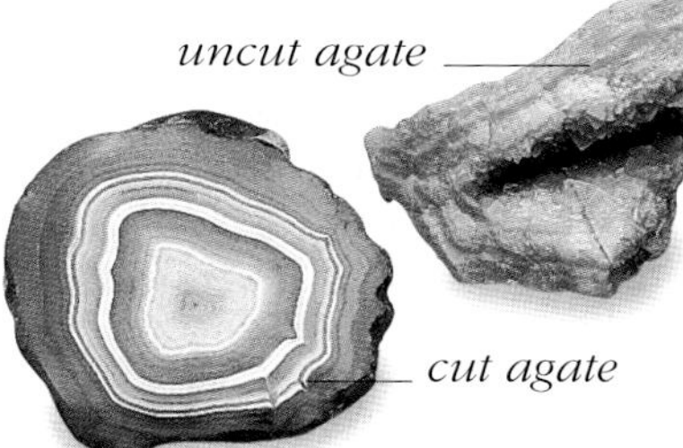


**agate 1**

**aga·ve** \ə-'gäv-ē\ *n*
a plant that has sword-shaped leaves with spiny edges and is sometimes grown for its large stalks of flowers

**[1]age** \'āj\ *n*
1 the time from birth to a specified date ⟨a child six years of *age*⟩
2 the time of life when a person receives full legal rights ⟨one comes of *age* at eighteen⟩
3 normal lifetime
4 the later part of life ⟨a mind as active in *age* as in youth⟩
5 a period of time associated with a special person or feature ⟨the machine *age*⟩
6 a long period of time **synonyms** see PERIOD

**[2]age** *vb* **aged** \'ājd\; **ag·ing** *or* **age·ing**
1 to grow old or cause to grow old
2 to remain or cause to remain undisturbed until fit for use : MATURE ⟨letting cheese *age*⟩

**-age** \ij\ *n suffix*
1 collection
2 action : process ⟨cover*age*⟩
3 result of
4 rate of ⟨shrink*age*⟩
5 house or place of ⟨orphan*age*⟩
6 state : rank
7 fee : charge ⟨post*age*⟩

**aged** \'ā-jəd *for 1*, 'ājd *for 2*\ *adj*
1 very old ⟨an *aged* oak⟩
2 of age ⟨a child *aged* ten⟩

**age·less** \'āj-ləs\ *adj*
not growing old or showing the effects of age
**age·less·ly** *adv*

**agen·cy** \'ā-jən-sē\ *n, pl* **agen·cies**
1 a person or thing through which power is used or something is achieved
2 the office or function of an agent
3 an establishment doing business for another ⟨automobile *agency*⟩
4 a part of a government that runs projects in a certain area ⟨a health *agency*⟩

**agen·da** \ə-'jen-də\ *n*
a list of things to be done or talked about

**agent** \'ā-jənt\ *n*
1 something that produces an effect ⟨cleansing *agents*⟩
2 a person who acts or does business for another

**ag·gra·vate** \'ag-rə-,vāt\ *vb* **ag·gra·vat·ed; ag·gra·vat·ing**
1 to make worse or more serious ⟨*aggravate* an injury⟩
2 to make angry by bothering again and again

**ag·gra·va·tion** \,ag-rə-'vā-shən\ *n*
1 an act or the result of aggravating
2 something that aggravates

**[1]ag·gre·gate** \'ag-ri-gət\ *adj*
formed by the collection of units or particles into one mass or sum

**[2]ag·gre·gate** \'ag-ri-,gāt\ *vb* **ag·gre·gat·ed; ag·gre·gat·ing**
to collect or gather into a mass or whole

[3]**ag·gre·gate** \'ag-ri-gət\ *n*
1 a mass or body of units or parts
2 the whole sum or amount

**ag·gre·ga·tion** \ˌag-ri-'gā-shən\ *n*
1 the collecting of units or parts into a mass or whole
2 a group, body, or mass composed of many distinct parts

**ag·gres·sion** \ə-'gresh-ən\ *n*
an attack made without reasonable cause

**ag·gres·sive** \ə-'gres-iv\ *adj*
1 showing a readiness to attack others ⟨an *aggressive* dog⟩
2 practicing aggression ⟨an *aggressive* nation⟩
3 being forceful and sometimes pushy
**ag·gres·sive·ly** *adv*
**ag·gres·sive·ness** *n*

**ag·gres·sor** \ə-'gres-ər\ *n*
a person or a country that attacks without reasonable cause

**ag·grieved** \ə-'grēvd\ *adj*
1 having a troubled or unhappy mind
2 having cause for complaint

**aghast** \ə-'gast\ *adj*
struck with terror or amazement

**ag·ile** \'aj-əl\ *adj*
1 able to move quickly and easily
2 having a quick mind
**ag·ile·ly** *adv*

**agil·i·ty** \ə-'jil-ət-ē\ *n*
the ability to move quickly and easily

**aging** *present participle of* AGE

**ag·i·tate** \'aj-ə-ˌtāt\ *vb* **ag·i·tat·ed**; **ag·i·tat·ing**
1 to move with an irregular rapid motion ⟨water *agitated* by wind⟩
2 to stir up : EXCITE ⟨*agitated* by bad news⟩
3 to try to stir up public feeling ⟨*agitate* for civil rights⟩
**ag·i·ta·tor** \-ər\ *n*

**ag·i·ta·tion** \ˌaj-ə-'tā-shən\ *n*
the act of agitating : the state of being agitated

**agleam** \ə-'glēm\ *adj*
giving off gleams of light

**aglow** \ə-'glō\ *adj*
glowing with light or color

**ago** \ə-'gō\ *adv*
before this time ⟨a week *ago*⟩

**agog** \ə-'gäg\ *adj*
full of excitement

**ag·o·nize** \'ag-ə-ˌnīz\ *vb* **ag·o·nized**; **ag·o·niz·ing**
to suffer greatly in body or mind

**ag·o·ny** \'ag-ə-nē\ *n, pl* **ag·o·nies**
great pain of body or mind

**agree** \ə-'grē\ *vb* **agreed**; **agree·ing**
1 to give one's approval or permission
2 to have the same opinion
3 ADMIT 3 ⟨*agreed* that I was right⟩
4 to be alike ⟨their stories don't *agree*⟩
5 to come to an understanding ⟨*agree* on a price⟩
6 to be fitting or healthful ⟨the climate *agrees* with you⟩

**agree·able** \ə-'grē-ə-bəl\ *adj*
1 pleasing to the mind or senses ⟨an *agreeable* taste⟩
2 willing to agree ⟨*agreeable* to my suggestion⟩
**agree·able·ness** *n*
**agree·ably** \-blē\ *adv*

**agree·ment** \ə-'grē-mənt\ *n*
1 the act or fact of agreeing
2 an arrangement made about action to be taken

**ag·ri·cul·tur·al** \ˌag-ri-'kəl-chə-rəl, -'kəlch-rəl\ *adj*
of, relating to, or used in agriculture

**ag·ri·cul·ture** \'ag-ri-ˌkəl-chər\ *n*
▼ the cultivating of the soil, producing of crops, and raising of livestock

## agriculture

People have grown crops and raised animals for thousands of years all over the world. Today, the main agricultural products of the US are cow's milk, corn, and soybeans.

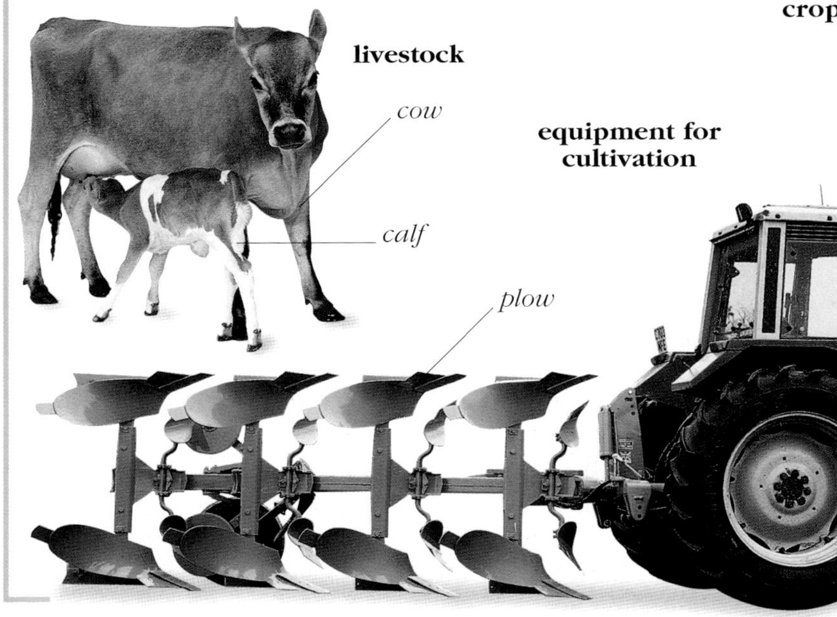

**aground** \ə-'graůnd\ *adv or adj*
on or onto the shore or the bottom of a body of water

**ah** \'ä\ *interj*
used to express delight, relief, disappointment, or scorn

**aha** \ä-'hä\ *interj*
used to express surprise, triumph, or scorn

**ahead** \ə-'hed\ *adv or adj*
**1** in or toward the front
**2** into or for the future

**ahead of** *prep*
**1** in front of ⟨stood *ahead of* me in line⟩
**2** earlier than

**ahoy** \ə-'hȯi\ *interj*
used in calling out to a passing ship or boat ⟨ship *ahoy*!⟩

[1]**aid** \'ād\ *vb*
[1]HELP 1, ASSIST

[2]**aid** *n*
**1** the act of helping
**2** help given
**3** someone or something that is of help or assistance

**aide** \'ād\ *n*
a person who acts as an assistant

**AIDS** \'ādz\ *n*
a serious disease of the human immune system in which large numbers of the cells that help the body fight infection are destroyed by the HIV virus carried in the blood and other fluids of the body

**ail** \'āl\ *vb*
**1** to be wrong with ⟨what *ails* you?⟩
**2** to suffer especially with ill health ⟨has been *ailing* for years⟩

**ai·le·ron** \'ā-lə-,rän\ *n*
a movable part of an airplane wing that is used to steer it to one side or the other

**ail·ment** \'āl-mənt\ *n*
SICKNESS 2

[1]**aim** \'ām\ *vb*
**1** to point a weapon toward an object
**2** INTEND ⟨we *aim* to please⟩
**3** to direct to or toward a specified object or goal

---

**Word History** Both *aim* and *estimate* come from a Latin word that meant "to estimate." An early French word, meaning "to guess" and "to aim" as well as "to estimate," came from this Latin word. The English word *aim* came from this French word. The English word *estimate* came directly from the Latin word that meant "to estimate."

---

[2]**aim** *n*
**1** the directing of a weapon or a missile at a mark
**2** [1]PURPOSE

**aim·less** \'ām-ləs\ *adj*
lacking purpose
**aim·less·ly** *adv*
**aim·less·ness** *n*

[1]**air** \'aər, 'eər\ *n*
**1** the invisible mixture of odorless tasteless gases that surrounds the earth
**2** air that is compressed ⟨a drill run by *air*⟩
**3** outward appearance ⟨an *air* of mystery⟩
**4** AIRCRAFT ⟨travel by *air*⟩
**5** AVIATION
**6** a radio or television system ⟨gave a speech on the *air*⟩
**7 airs** *pl* an artificial way of acting ⟨put on *airs*⟩

[2]**air** *vb*
**1** to place in the air for cooling, freshening, or cleaning ⟨*air* blankets⟩
**2** to make known in public ⟨*air* one's opinions⟩

**air bag** *n*
an automobile safety device consisting of a bag that will inflate automatically in front of a rider to act as a cushion in an accident

**air base** *n*
a base of operations for military aircraft

**air–con·di·tion** \,aər-kən-'dish-ən, ,eər-\ *vb*
to equip with a device for cleaning air and controlling its humidity and temperature
**air con·di·tion·er** *n*
**air–con·di·tion·ing** *n*

**air·craft** \'aər-,kraft, 'eər-\ *n, pl* **aircraft**
a vehicle (as a balloon, airplane, or helicopter) that can travel through the air and that is supported either

## airplane

Many airplanes share a design similar to the airliner below. The wings are attached to the middle of the fuselage, and the horizontal stabilizer and fin are attached to the rear.

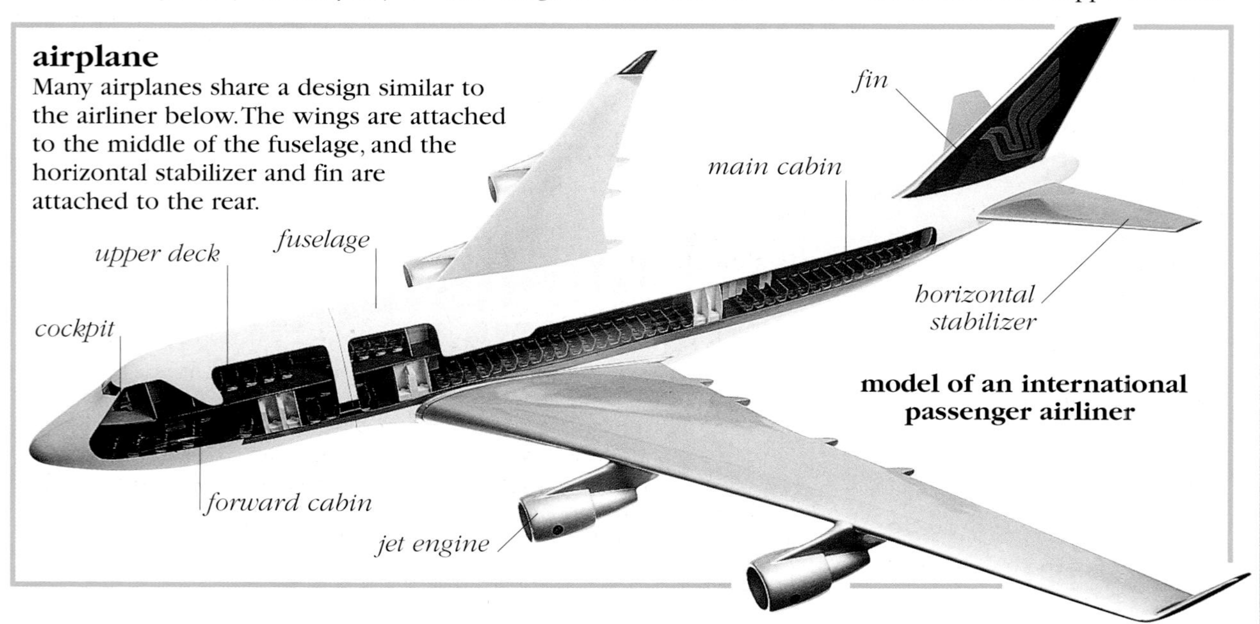


**model of an international passenger airliner**

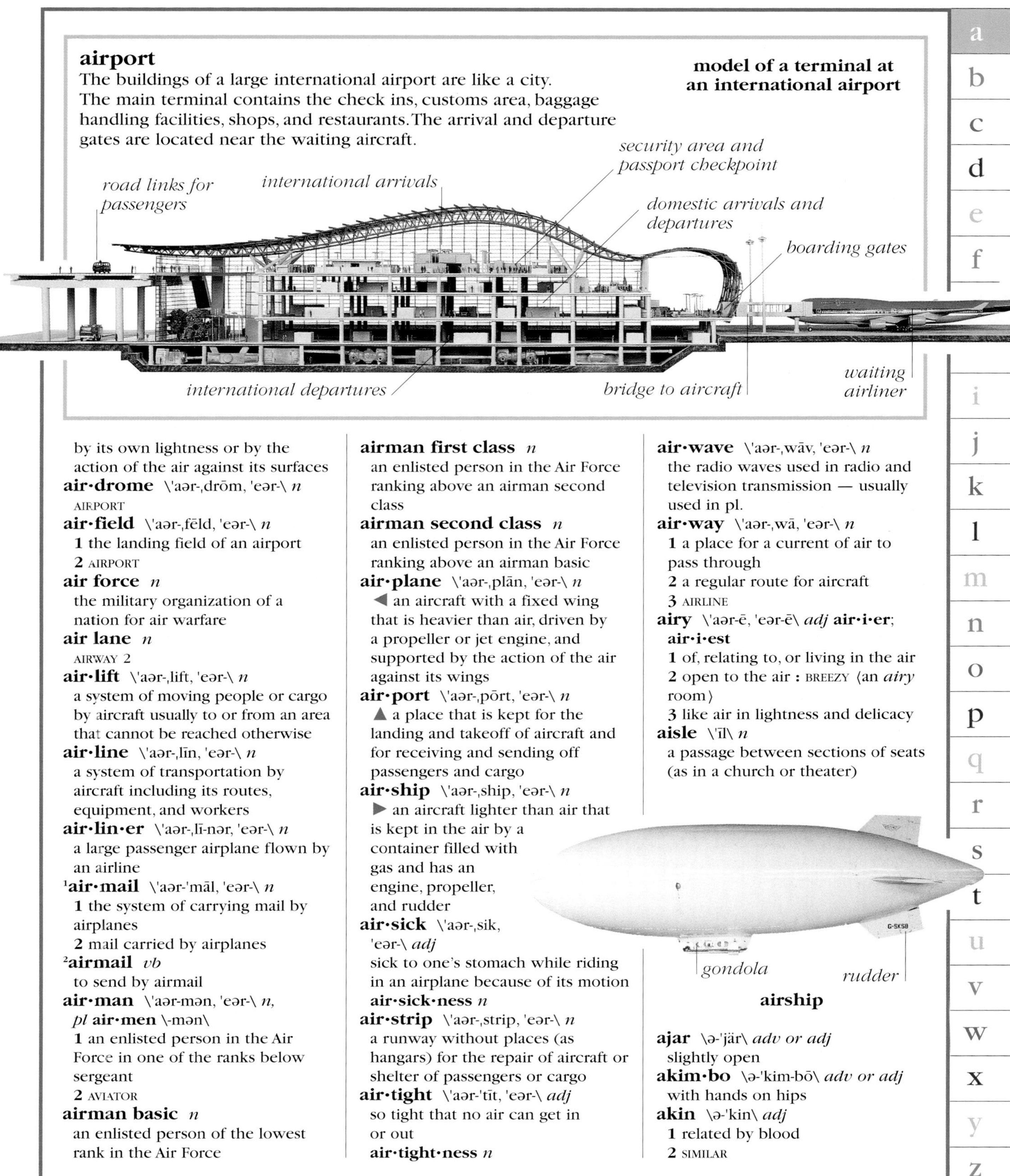


by its own lightness or by the action of the air against its surfaces

**air·drome** \'aər-ˌdrōm, 'eər-\ *n*
AIRPORT

**air·field** \'aər-ˌfēld, 'eər-\ *n*
**1** the landing field of an airport
**2** AIRPORT

**air force** *n*
the military organization of a nation for air warfare

**air lane** *n*
AIRWAY 2

**air·lift** \'aər-ˌlift, 'eər-\ *n*
a system of moving people or cargo by aircraft usually to or from an area that cannot be reached otherwise

**air·line** \'aər-ˌlīn, 'eər-\ *n*
a system of transportation by aircraft including its routes, equipment, and workers

**air·lin·er** \'aər-ˌlī-nər, 'eər-\ *n*
a large passenger airplane flown by an airline

**[1]air·mail** \'aər-'māl, 'eər-\ *n*
**1** the system of carrying mail by airplanes
**2** mail carried by airplanes

**[2]airmail** *vb*
to send by airmail

**air·man** \'aər-mən, 'eər-\ *n, pl* **air·men** \-mən\
**1** an enlisted person in the Air Force in one of the ranks below sergeant
**2** AVIATOR

**airman basic** *n*
an enlisted person of the lowest rank in the Air Force

**airman first class** *n*
an enlisted person in the Air Force ranking above an airman second class

**airman second class** *n*
an enlisted person in the Air Force ranking above an airman basic

**air·plane** \'aər-ˌplān, 'eər-\ *n*
◀ an aircraft with a fixed wing that is heavier than air, driven by a propeller or jet engine, and supported by the action of the air against its wings

**air·port** \'aər-ˌpōrt, 'eər-\ *n*
▲ a place that is kept for the landing and takeoff of aircraft and for receiving and sending off passengers and cargo

**air·ship** \'aər-ˌship, 'eər-\ *n*
▶ an aircraft lighter than air that is kept in the air by a container filled with gas and has an engine, propeller, and rudder

**air·sick** \'aər-ˌsik, 'eər-\ *adj*
sick to one's stomach while riding in an airplane because of its motion
**air·sick·ness** *n*

**air·strip** \'aər-ˌstrip, 'eər-\ *n*
a runway without places (as hangars) for the repair of aircraft or shelter of passengers or cargo

**air·tight** \'aər-'tīt, 'eər-\ *adj*
so tight that no air can get in or out
**air·tight·ness** *n*

**air·wave** \'aər-ˌwāv, 'eər-\ *n*
the radio waves used in radio and television transmission — usually used in pl.

**air·way** \'aər-ˌwā, 'eər-\ *n*
**1** a place for a current of air to pass through
**2** a regular route for aircraft
**3** AIRLINE

**airy** \'aər-ē, 'eər-ē\ *adj* **air·i·er**; **air·i·est**
**1** of, relating to, or living in the air
**2** open to the air **:** BREEZY ⟨an *airy* room⟩
**3** like air in lightness and delicacy

**aisle** \'īl\ *n*
a passage between sections of seats (as in a church or theater)

**ajar** \ə-'jär\ *adv or adj*
slightly open

**akim·bo** \ə-'kim-bō\ *adv or adj*
with hands on hips

**akin** \ə-'kin\ *adj*
**1** related by blood
**2** SIMILAR

[1]**-al** \əl, l\ *adj suffix*
of, relating to, or showing ⟨fiction*al*⟩

[2]**-al** *n suffix*
action : process ⟨rehears*al*⟩

**al·a·bas·ter** \'al-ə-ˌbas-tər\ *n*
a smooth usually white stone used for carving

**à la carte** \ˌal-ə-'kärt, ˌä-lə-\ *adv or adj*
with a separate price for each item on the menu

**alac·ri·ty** \ə-'lak-rət-ē\ *n*
a cheerful readiness to do something

[1]**alarm** \ə-'lärm\ *n*
**1** a warning of danger
**2** a device (as a bell) that warns or signals people
**3** the fear caused by sudden danger ⟨filled with *alarm* at the thought of flying⟩

[1]**alarm 2:** an alarm clock

[2]**alarm** *vb*
to cause a sense of danger in : FRIGHTEN

**alarm clock** *n*
▲ a clock that can be set to sound an alarm at any desired time

**alas** \ə-'las\ *interj*
used to express unhappiness, pity, or worry

**al·ba·tross** \'al-bə-ˌtrȯs\ *n*
a large seabird with webbed feet

**al·bi·no** \al-'bī-nō\ *n, pl* **al·bi·nos**
**1** ► a person or an animal that has little or no coloring matter in skin, hair, and eyes
**2** a plant with little or no coloring matter

**albino 1:** albino rabbits

**al·bum** \'al-bəm\ *n*
**1** a book with blank pages in which to put a collection (as of photographs, stamps, or autographs)
**2** one or more recordings (as on tape or disk) produced as one unit ⟨a two-CD *album*⟩

**al·bu·men** \al-'byü-mən\ *n*
**1** the white of an egg
**2** ALBUMIN

**al·bu·min** \al-'byü-mən\ *n*
any of various proteins that are soluble in water and occur in plant and animal tissues

**al·co·hol** \'al-kə-ˌhȯl\ *n*
**1** a colorless flammable liquid that in one form is the substance in fermented and distilled liquors (as beer, wine, or whiskey) that can make one drunk
**2** a drink containing alcohol

[1]**al·co·hol·ic** \ˌal-kə-'hȯl-ik, -'häl-\ *adj*
**1** of, relating to, or containing alcohol ⟨*alcoholic* drinks⟩
**2** affected with alcoholism

[2]**alcoholic** *n*
a person affected with alcoholism

**al·co·hol·ism** \'al-kə-ˌhȯl-ˌiz-əm\ *n*
a sickness of body and mind caused by too much use of alcoholic drinks

**al·cove** \'al-ˌkōv\ *n*
a small part of a room set back from the rest of it

**al·der** \'ȯl-dər\ *n*
a tree or shrub related to the birches that has toothed leaves and grows in moist soil

**al·der·man** \'ȯl-dər-mən\ *n*
a member of a lawmaking body in a city

**ale** \'āl\ *n*
an alcoholic drink made from malt and flavored with hops that is usually more bitter than beer

[1]**alert** \ə-'lərt\ *adj*
**1** watchful and ready to meet danger
**2** quick to understand and act
**3** ACTIVE 3, BRISK
**alert·ly** *adv*
**alert·ness** *n*

[2]**alert** *n*
**1** a signal (as an alarm) of danger
**2** the period during which an alert is in effect
**on the alert** watchful against danger

[3]**alert** *vb*
to call to a state of readiness : WARN

**al·fal·fa** \al-'fal-fə\ *n*
► a plant with purple flowers that is related to the clovers and is grown as a food for horses and cattle

**alfalfa** flowers

**al·ga** \'al-gə\ *n, pl* **al·gae** \'al-ˌjē\
► living things (as the seaweeds) that produce chlorophyll, that were once thought to be plants but that do not produce seeds and are not divisible into roots, stems, and leaves

chloroplast

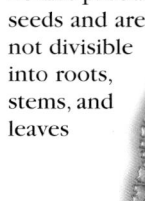

**alga:** microscopic photograph of a single-celled green alga

**al·ge·bra** \'al-jə-brə\ *n*
a branch of mathematics in which symbols (as letters and numbers) are combined according to the rules of arithmetic

**[1]alias** \'ā-lē-əs\ *adv*
otherwise known as

**[2]alias** *n*
a false name

**[1]al·i·bi** \'al-ə-,bī\ *n, pl* **al·i·bis**
**1** the explanation given by a person accused of a crime that he or she was somewhere else when the crime was committed
**2** [2]EXCUSE 2

**[2]alibi** *vb* **al·i·bied**; **al·i·bi·ing**
**1** to offer an excuse
**2** to make an excuse for

**[1]alien** \'ā-lē-ən, 'āl-yən\ *adj*
FOREIGN 2

**[2]alien** *n*
a resident who was born elsewhere and is not a citizen of the country in which he or she now lives

**alien·ate** \'ā-lē-ə-,nāt, 'āl-yə-\ *vb* **alien·at·ed**; **alien·at·ing**
to cause (one who used to be friendly or loyal) to become unfriendly or disloyal

**[1]alight** \ə-'līt\ *vb* **alight·ed** *also* **alit** \ə-'lit\; **alight·ing**
**1** to get down **:** DISMOUNT
**2** to come down from the air and settle ⟨ducks *alighting* on a pond⟩

**[2]alight** *adj*
full of light **:** lighted up

**align** \ə-'līn\ *vb*
to bring into line ⟨*align* the wheels of an automobile⟩
**align·er** *n*
**align·ment** \-mənt\ *n*

**[1]alike** \ə-'līk\ *adv*
in the same way

**[2]alike** *adj*
being like each other
**alike·ness** *n*

**al·i·men·ta·ry** \,al-ə-'ment-ə-rē, -'men-trē\ *adj*
of or relating to food and nourishment

**alimentary canal** *n*
a long tube made up of the esophagus, stomach, and intestine into which food is taken and digested and from which wastes are passed out

**al·i·mo·ny** \'al-ə-,mō-nē\ *n*
money for living expenses paid regularly by one spouse to another after their legal separation or divorce

**alit** *past of* ALIGHT

**alive** \ə-'līv\ *adj*
**1** having life **:** not dead
**2** being in force, existence, or operation ⟨it kept our hopes *alive*⟩
**3** aware of the existence of ⟨was *alive* to the danger⟩
**alive·ness** *n*

**al·ka·li** \'al-kə-,lī\ *n, pl* **al·ka·lies** *or* **al·ka·lis**
**1** any of numerous substances that have a bitter taste and react with an acid to form a salt
**2** a salt or a mixture of salts sometimes found in large amounts in the soil of dry regions

**al·ka·line** \'al-kə-,līn, -lən\ *adj*
of or relating to an alkali

**[1]all** \'ȯl\ *adj*
**1** the whole of ⟨sat up *all* night⟩
**2** the greatest possible ⟨told in *all* seriousness⟩
**3** every one of ⟨*all* students can go⟩

**[2]all** *adv*
**1** COMPLETELY ⟨sat *all* alone⟩ ⟨I'm *all* finished⟩
**2** so much ⟨is *all* the better for it⟩
**3** for each side ⟨the score is two *all*⟩

**[3]all** *pron*
**1** the whole number or amount ⟨*all* of us⟩ ⟨ate *all* of the candy⟩
**2** EVERYTHING ⟨*all* is lost⟩

**Al·lah** \'al-ə, ä-'lä\ *n*
the Supreme Being of Muslims

**all–around** \,ȯl-ə-'raùnd\ *adj*
**1** having ability in many areas
**2** useful in many ways

**al·lay** \ə-'lā\ *vb*
**1** to make less severe ⟨*allay* pain⟩
**2** to put to rest ⟨*allay* fears⟩

**al·lege** \ə-'lej\ *vb* **al·leged**; **al·leg·ing**
to state as fact but without proof ⟨*allege* a person's guilt⟩

**al·le·giance** \ə-'lē-jəns\ *n*
loyalty and service to a group, country, or idea **synonyms** see LOYALTY

**al·le·lu·ia** \,al-ə-'lü-yə\ *interj*
HALLELUJAH

**al·ler·gen** \'al-ər-jən\ *n*
▼ a substance that causes an allergic reaction

**al·ler·gic** \ə-'lər-jik\ *adj*
of, relating to, causing, or affected by allergy ⟨*allergic* to peanuts⟩ ⟨an *allergic* reaction⟩

### allergen
An allergen is a substance that may cause an allergic response in a person. Some allergens, such as flakes of a cat's skin, come into contact with the eyes or skin, while others, such as grass pollen and certain foods, are inhaled or swallowed. Allergic responses include hay fever, asthma, or hives.

**peanuts**

**strawberries**

**animal fur**

**grass pollen**

**al·ler·gist** \'al-ər-jəst\ *n*
a medical doctor who specializes in treating allergies

**al·ler·gy** \'al-ər-jē\ *n, pl* **al·ler·gies**
a condition in which a person is made sick by something that is harmless to most people

**al·le·vi·ate** \ə-'lē-vē-,āt\ *vb* **al·le·vi·at·ed**; **al·le·vi·at·ing**
to make easier to put up with

**al·ley** \'al-ē\ *n, pl* **al·leys**
**1** a narrow passageway between buildings
**2** a special narrow wooden floor on which balls are rolled in bowling

**al·li·ance** \ə-'lī-əns\ *n*
**1** connection between families, groups, or individuals
**2** an association formed by two or more nations for assistance and protection
**3** a treaty of alliance

**al·lied** \ə-'līd, 'al-,īd\ *adj*
**1** being connected or related in some way ⟨chemistry and *allied* subjects⟩
**2** joined in alliance ⟨*allied* nations⟩

**al·li·ga·tor** \'al-ə-,gāt-ər\ *n*
▼ a large four-footed water animal related to the snakes and lizards

**alligator**

**all·o·sau·rus** \,al-ə-'sȯr-əs\ *n*
any of several very large meat-eating dinosaurs that were related to the tyrannosaur

**al·lot** \ə-'lät\ *vb* **al·lot·ted**; **al·lot·ting**
to give out as a share or portion

**al·lot·ment** \ə-'lät-mənt\ *n*
**1** the act of allotting
**2** something that is allotted

**al·low** \ə-'lau̇\ *vb*
**1** to assign as a share or suitable amount (as of time or money)
**2** to take into account
**3** to accept as true : CONCEDE
**4** to give permission to
**5** to fail to prevent ⟨*allow* the dog to roam⟩
**6** to make allowance ⟨*allow* for growth⟩

**al·low·able** \ə-'lau̇-ə-bəl\ *adj*
not forbidden

**al·low·ance** \ə-'lau̇-əns\ *n*
**1** a share given out
**2** a sum given as repayment or for expenses ⟨a weekly *allowance*⟩
**3** the taking into account of things that could affect a result

**al·loy** \'al-,ȯi, ə-'lȯi\ *n*
a substance made of two or more metals melted together ⟨brass is an *alloy* of copper and zinc⟩

**all right** *adj or adv*
**1** satisfactory in quality or condition
**2** very well

**all–round** \'ȯl-'rau̇nd\ *adj*
ALL-AROUND

**all–star** \'ȯl-'stär\ *adj*
made up mainly or entirely of outstanding participants ⟨an *all-star* team⟩

**al·lude** \ə-'lüd\ *vb* **al·lud·ed**; **al·lud·ing**
to talk about or hint at without mentioning directly

**al·lure** \ə-'lu̇r\ *vb* **al·lured**; **al·lur·ing**
to try to influence by offering what seems to be a benefit or pleasure

**al·lu·sion** \ə-'lü-zhən\ *n*
an act of alluding or of hinting at something

[1]**al·ly** \ə-'lī, 'al-,ī\ *vb* **al·lied**; **al·ly·ing**
to form a connection between : join in an alliance

[2]**al·ly** \'al-,ī, ə-'lī\ *n, pl* **allies**
one (as a person or a nation) associated or united with another in a common purpose

**al·ma·nac** \'ȯl-mə-,nak, 'al-\ *n*
a book containing a calendar of days, weeks, and months and usually facts about weather and astronomy, and information of general interest

**al·mighty** \ȯl-'mīt-ē\ *adj, often cap*
having absolute power over all ⟨*Almighty* God⟩

**al·mond** \'ä-mənd, 'am-ənd\ *n*
► a nut that is the edible kernel of a small tree related to the peach

kernel

**almonds**

**al·most** \'ȯl-,mōst\ *adv*
only a little less than : very nearly

**alms** \'ämz, 'älmz\ *n, pl* **alms**
something and especially money given to help the poor : CHARITY

**aloft** \ə-'lȯft\ *adv or adj*
**1** at or to a great height
**2** in the air and especially in flight
**3** at, on, or to the top of the mast or the higher rigging of a ship

[1]**alone** \ə-'lōn\ *adj*
**1** separated from others
**2** not including anyone or anything else ⟨food *alone* is not enough for health⟩

**Synonyms** ALONE, SOLITARY, and LONELY mean separated from others. ALONE stresses that one is entirely by oneself ⟨I was left *alone* in the room⟩. SOLITARY may emphasize the fact of being alone ⟨an old tree with a *solitary* apple⟩ but often it stresses the pleasure this gives ⟨*solitary* people who choose peace and quiet⟩. LONELY suggests that one longs for company ⟨felt *lonely* after my friends left⟩.

[2]**alone** *adv*
**1** and nothing or no one else ⟨did it for money *alone*⟩

2 without company or help ⟨we thought we could do it *alone*⟩

[1]**along** \ə-'lȯng\ *prep*
1 on or near in a lengthwise direction ⟨walk *along* the trail⟩
2 at a point on ⟨stopped *along* the way⟩

[2]**along** *adv*
1 farther forward or on ⟨move *along*⟩
2 as a companion or associate ⟨brought a friend *along*⟩
3 throughout the time ⟨knew it all *along*⟩

**along·shore** \ə-'lȯng-,shōr\ *adv or adj*
along the shore or coast

[1]**along·side** \ə-'lȯng-,sīd\ *adv*
along or by the side

[2]**alongside** *prep*
parallel to ⟨boats *alongside* the dock⟩

[1]**aloof** \ə-'lüf\ *adv*
at a distance ⟨stood *aloof*⟩

[2]**aloof** *adj*
RESERVED 1 ⟨a shy *aloof* manner⟩
**aloof·ly** *adv*
**aloof·ness** *n*

**aloud** \ə-'lau̇d\ *adv*
using the voice so as to be clearly heard ⟨read *aloud*⟩

**al·paca** \al-'pak-ə\ *n*
▼ a South American animal related to the camel and llama that is raised for its long woolly hair which is woven into warm strong cloth

**al·pha·bet** \'al-fə-,bet\ *n*
the letters used in writing a language arranged in their regular order

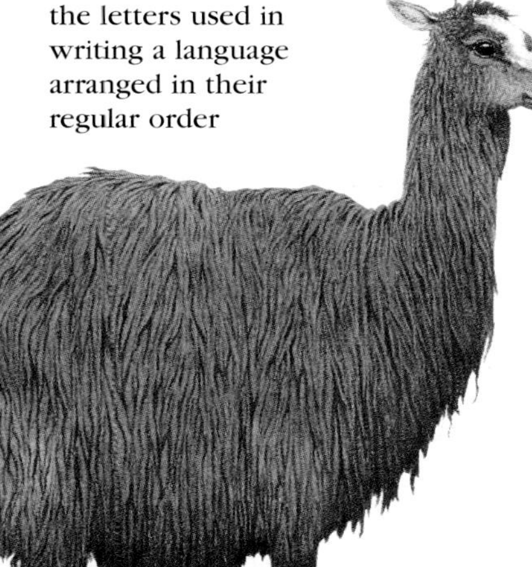

**alpaca**

**al·pha·bet·i·cal** \,al-fə-'bet-i-kəl\ *or* **al·pha·bet·ic** \-ik\ *adj*
arranged in the order of the letters of the alphabet
**al·pha·bet·i·cal·ly** *adv*

**al·pha·bet·ize** \'al-fə-bə-,tīz\ *vb*
**al·pha·bet·ized**; **al·pha·bet·iz·ing**
to arrange in alphabetical order

**al·ready** \ȯl-'red-ē\ *adv*
before a certain time **:** by this time ⟨I had *already* left when you called⟩

**al·so** \'ȯl-sō\ *adv*
in addition **:** TOO

**al·tar** \'ȯl-tər\ *n*
1 a usually raised place on which sacrifices are offered
2 a platform or table used as a center of worship

**al·ter** \'ȯl-tər\ *vb*
to change partly but not completely ⟨*alter* old clothes⟩
**synonyms** see CHANGE

**al·ter·ation** \,ȯl-tə-'rā-shən\ *n*
1 a making or becoming different in some respects
2 the result of altering **:** MODIFICATION

[1]**al·ter·nate** \'ȯl-tər-nət\ *adj*
1 occurring or following by turns ⟨*alternate* sunshine and rain⟩
2 arranged one above, beside, or next to another ⟨*alternate* layers of cake and filling⟩
3 every other **:** every second ⟨we have meat on *alternate* days⟩
**al·ter·nate·ly** *adv*

[2]**al·ter·nate** \'ȯl-tər-,nāt\ *vb*
**al·ter·nat·ed**; **al·ter·nat·ing**
to take place or cause to take place by turns

[3]**al·ter·nate** \'ȯl-tər-nət\ *n*
a person named to take the place of another whenever necessary ⟨*alternates* to a convention⟩

**alternating current** *n*
an electric current that reverses its direction of flow regularly many times per second

**al·ter·na·tion** \,ȯl-tər-'nā-shən\ *n*
the act, process, or result of alternating

[1]**al·ter·na·tive** \ȯl-'tər-nət-iv\ *adj*
offering or expressing a choice ⟨*alternative* plans⟩
**al·ter·na·tive·ly** *adv*

[2]**alternative** *n*
1 a chance to choose between two things
2 one of the things between which a choice is to be made

**al·though** \ȯl-'t͟hō\ *conj*
in spite of the fact that ⟨*although* you say it, you don't mean it⟩

**al·ti·tude** \'al-tə-,tüd, -,tyüd\ *n*
1 height above a certain level and especially above sea level
2 the perpendicular distance from the base of a geometric figure to the vertex or to the side parallel to the base **synonyms** see HEIGHT

**al·to** \'al-tō\ *n, pl* **altos**
1 the lowest female singing voice
2 the second highest part in four-part harmony
3 a singer or an instrument having an alto range or part

**al·to·geth·er** \,ȯl-tə-'get͟h-ər\ *adv*
1 COMPLETELY ⟨I'm not *altogether* sure⟩
2 on the whole ⟨*altogether* our school is one of the best⟩

**al·tru·ism** \'al-trü-,iz-əm\ *n*
unselfish interest in others

**al·um** \'al-əm\ *n*
either of two aluminum compounds that have a sweetish-sourish taste and puckering effect on the mouth and are used in medicine (as to stop bleeding)

**alu·mi·num** \ə-'lü-mə-nəm\ *n*
▼ a silver-white light metallic chemical element that is easily worked, conducts electricity well, resists weathering, and is the most plentiful metal in the earth's crust

**aluminum** foil

**alum·na** \ə-'ləm-nə\ *n, pl* **alum·nae** \-,nē\
a girl or woman who has attended or has graduated from a school, college, or university

A B C D E F G H I J K L M N O P Q R S T U V W X Y Z

**alum·nus** \ə-'ləm-nəs\ *n, pl* **alum·ni** \-,nī\
one who has attended or has graduated from a school, college, or university

**al·ways** \'ȯl-wēz, -wəz, -wāz\ *adv*
1 at all times ⟨*always* knows the answer⟩
2 throughout all time : FOREVER

**am** \əm, am\ *present 1st sing of* BE

**amal·gam·ation** \ə-,mal-gə-'mā-shən\ *n*
the combining of different elements into a single body

**amass** \ə-'mas\ *vb*
to collect or gather together ⟨*amass* a fortune⟩

**[1]am·a·teur** \'am-ə-,tər, -ət-ər\ *n*
1 a person who takes part in sports or occupations for pleasure and not for pay
2 a person who takes part in something without having experience or skill in it
**am·a·teur·ish** \,am-ə-'tər-ish\ *adj*

**Word History** The English word *amateur* came from a French word which in turn came from a Latin word that meant "lover." In English, amateurs are so called because they do something for the love of doing it and not for pay.

**[2]amateur** *adj*
of, relating to, or done by amateurs : not professional

**amaze** \ə-'māz\ *vb* **amazed**; **amaz·ing**
to surprise or puzzle very much
**synonyms** see SURPRISE

**amaze·ment** \ə-'māz-mənt\ *n*
great surprise

**am·bas·sa·dor** \am-'bas-ə-dər\ *n*
a person sent as the chief representative of his or her government in another country
**am·bas·sa·dor·ship** \-,ship\ *n*

**am·ber** \'am-bər\ *n*
1 ▶ a hard yellowish to brownish clear substance that is a fossil resin from trees long dead, takes a polish, and is used for ornamental objects (as beads)
2 a dark orange yellow

**ambi-** *prefix*
both

**am·bi·dex·trous** \,am-bi-'dek-strəs\ *adj*
using both hands with equal ease
**am·bi·dex·trous·ly** *adv*

**am·bi·gu·i·ty** \,am-bə-'gyü-ət-ē\ *n, pl* **am·bi·gu·ities**
the fact or state of being ambiguous

**am·big·u·ous** \am-'big-yə-wəs\ *adj*
able to be understood in more than one way ⟨an *ambiguous* answer⟩
**am·big·u·ous·ly** *adv*

**am·bi·tion** \am-'bish-ən\ *n*
1 a desire for success, honor, or power
2 the aim or object one tries for ⟨my *ambition* is to become a jet pilot⟩

**Word History** Like the candidates of today, some men ran for public office in ancient Rome by going around and asking people to vote for them. The Latin word for this practice meant "a going around." Since looking for votes showed "a desire for power or honor," the Latin word took on that meaning. The English word *ambition* came from the Latin word that once meant "a going around."

**am·bi·tious** \am-'bish-əs\ *adj*
1 possessing ambition ⟨*ambitious* to be president of the class⟩
2 showing ambition ⟨an *ambitious* plan⟩
**am·bi·tious·ly** *adv*

**[1]am·ble** \'am-bəl\ *vb* **am·bled**; **am·bling**
to go at an amble

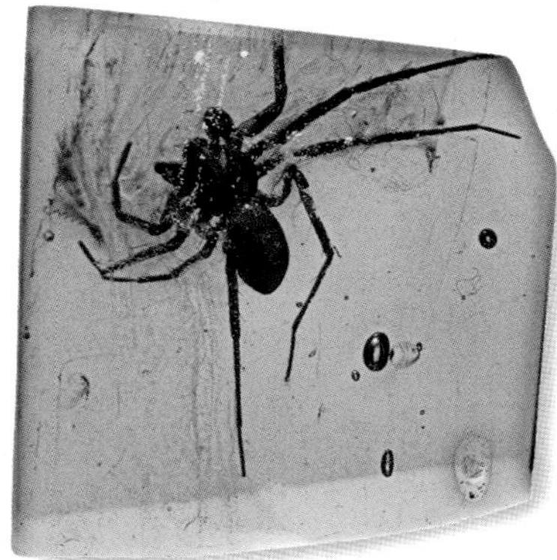

**amber 1:** amber containing a fossilized spider

**[2]amble** *n*
a slow easy way of walking

**am·bu·lance** \'am-byə-ləns\ *n*
▼ a vehicle meant to carry sick or injured persons

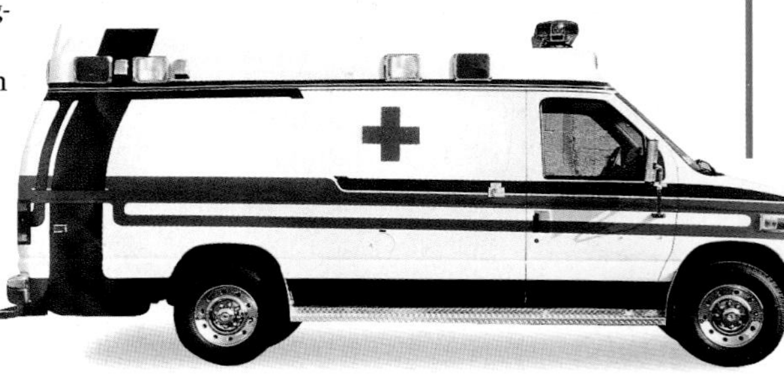

**ambulance**

**[1]am·bush** \'am-,bu̇sh\ *vb*
to attack from an ambush

**[2]ambush** *n*
a hidden place from which a surprise attack can be made

**amen** \'ā-'men, 'ä-\ *interj*
used to express agreement (as after a prayer or a statement of opinion)

**ame·na·ble** \ə-'mē-nə-bəl, -'men-ə-\ *adj*
readily giving in or agreeing ⟨*amenable* to our wishes⟩

**amend** \ə-'mend\ *vb*
1 to change for the better : IMPROVE
2 to change the wording or meaning of : ALTER ⟨*amend* a law in congress⟩

**amend·ment** \ə-'mend-mənt\ *n*
a change in wording or meaning especially in a law, bill, or motion

**amends** \ə-'mendz\ *n sing or pl*
something done or given by a person to make up for a loss or injury he or she has caused ⟨make *amends*⟩

**ame·ni·ty** \ə-'men-ət-ē, -'mē-nət-\ *n, pl* **ame·ni·ties**
1 the quality of being pleasant or agreeable
2 *amenities pl* something (as good manners or household appliances) that makes life easier or more pleasant

**[1]Amer·i·can** \ə-'mer-ə-kən\ *n*
1 a person born or living in North or South America
2 a citizen of the United States

**[2]American** *adj*
1 of or relating to North or South America or their residents

2 of or relating to the United States or its citizens

**American Indian** *n*
a member of any of the first peoples to live in North and South America except usually the Eskimos

**am·e·thyst** \'am-ə-thəst\ *n*
▼ a clear purple or bluish violet quartz used as a gem

**amethyst**

**Word History** People once believed that amethysts could cure drunkenness. The ancient Greeks gave the stone a name that reflected this belief. This name was formed from a prefix that meant "not" and a verb that meant "to be drunk." This verb came from a Greek word that meant "wine." The English word *amethyst* came from the Greek name for this stone.

**ami·a·ble** \'ā-mē-ə-bəl\ *adj*
having a friendly and pleasant manner
**ami·a·bly** \-blē\ *adv*

**am·i·ca·ble** \'am-i-kə-bəl\ *adj*
showing kindness or goodwill
**am·i·ca·bly** \-blē\ *adv*

**amid** \ə-'mid\ *or* **amidst** \-'midst\ *prep*
in or into the middle of ⟨advanced *amid* cheering crowds⟩

**amid·ships** \ə-'mid-ˌships\ *adv*
in or near the middle of a ship

**ami·no acid** \ə-'mē-nō-\ *n*
any of numerous acids that contain carbon and nitrogen, include some which are the building blocks of protein, and are made by living plant or animal cells or obtained from the diet

[1]**amiss** \ə-'mis\ *adv*
in the wrong way ⟨now, don't take this remark *amiss*⟩

[2]**amiss** *adj*
not right : WRONG

**am·i·ty** \'am-ət-ē\ *n, pl* **am·i·ties**
FRIENDSHIP

**am·me·ter** \'am-ˌēt-ər\ *n*
an instrument for measuring electric current in amperes

**am·mo·nia** \ə-'mō-nyə\ *n*
1 a colorless gas that is a compound of nitrogen and hydrogen, has a sharp smell and taste, can be easily made liquid by cold and pressure, and is used in making ice, fertilizers, and explosives
2 a solution of ammonia and water

**am·mu·ni·tion** \ˌam-yə-'nish-ən\ *n*
1 objects fired from guns
2 explosive objects used in war

**am·ne·sia** \am-'nē-zhə\ *n*
an abnormal and usually complete loss of one's memory

**amoe·ba** \ə-'mē-bə\ *n, pl* **amoe·bas** *or* **amoe·bae** \-bē\
a tiny water animal that is a single cell which flows about and takes in food

**among** \ə-'məng\ *also* **amongst** \-'məngst\ *prep*
1 in or through the middle of ⟨*among* the crowd⟩
2 in the presence of : WITH ⟨you're *among* friends⟩
3 through all or most of ⟨discontent *among* the poor⟩
4 in shares to each of ⟨candy divided *among* friends⟩
**synonyms** see BETWEEN

[1]**amount** \ə-'maůnt\ *vb*
1 to add up ⟨the bill *amounted* to ten dollars⟩
2 to be the same in meaning or effect ⟨acts that *amount* to treason⟩

[2]**amount** *n*
the total number or quantity

**am·pere** \'am-ˌpir\ *n*
a unit for measuring the strength of an electric current

**am·per·sand** \'am-pər-ˌsand\ *n*
a character & standing for the word *and*

**am·phet·amine** \am-'fet-ə-ˌmēn, -mən\ *n*
a drug that causes the nervous system to become more active

**am·phib·i·an** \am-'fib-ē-ən\ *n*
1 ▼ any of a group of cold-blooded animals (as frogs and toads) that have gills and live in water as larvae but breathe air as adults
2 an airplane designed to take off from and land on either land or water

**am·phib·i·ous** \am-'fib-ē-əs\ *adj*
1 able to live both on land and in water ⟨*amphibious* animals⟩

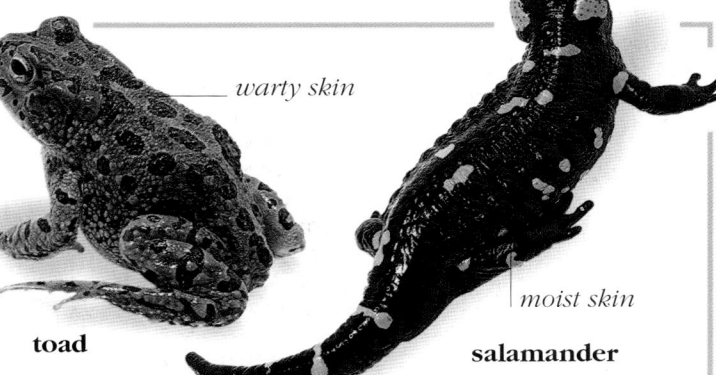

**amphibian 1**
Amphibians have skin that dries out quickly, so many species live in damp conditions. Some, however, have adapted to life in desert habitats.

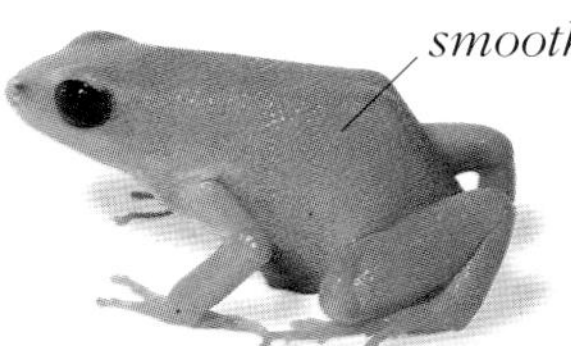

**frog**

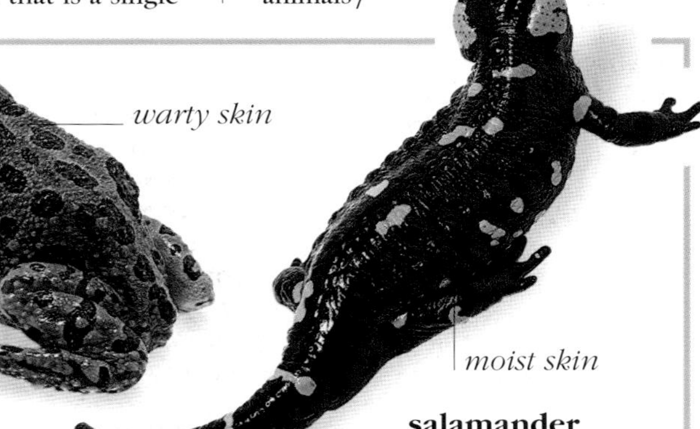

**toad**
**salamander**

A B C D E F G H I J K L M N O P Q R S T U V W X Y Z

## amphitheater

The ancient Greeks built elegant amphitheaters, where shows were staged for thousands of people. Amphitheaters are still used today for open-air performances in many parts of the world.

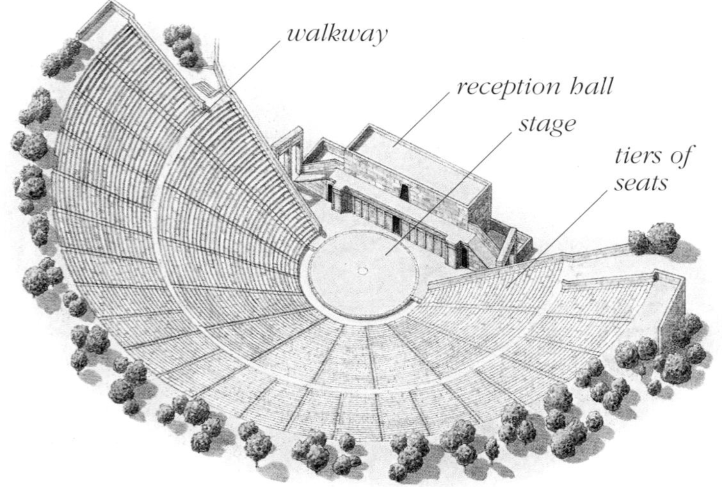


**reconstruction of an ancient Greek amphitheater**

**2** meant to be used on both land and water ⟨*amphibious* vehicles⟩
**3** made by land, sea, and air forces acting together ⟨*amphibious* attack⟩
**am·phib·i·ous·ly** *adv*
**am·phib·i·ous·ness** *n*

**am·phi·the·ater** \'am-fə-,thē-ət-ər\ *n*
▲ an arena with seats rising in curved rows around an open space

**am·ple** \'am-pəl\ *adj*
more than enough in amount or size ⟨an *ample* supply of food⟩
**am·ply** \-plē\ *adv*

**am·pli·fy** \'am-plə-,fī\ *vb*
**am·pli·fied**; **am·pli·fy·ing**
**1** to add to ⟨*amplify* a statement⟩
**2** to make louder or greater
**am·pli·fi·er** *n*

**am·pu·tate** \'am-pyə-,tāt\ *vb*
**am·pu·tat·ed**; **am·pu·tat·ing**
to cut off ⟨*amputate* a leg⟩

**am·u·let** \'am-yə-lət\ *n*
► a small object worn as a charm against evil

**amuse** \ə-'myüz\ *vb* **amused**; **amus·ing**
**1** to entertain with something pleasant ⟨*amuse* oneself with a book⟩
**2** to please the sense of humor of

**Synonyms** AMUSE and ENTERTAIN mean to cause the time to pass in an agreeable way. AMUSE suggests simply keeping one interested in anything that is pleasant or humorous ⟨the toy *amused* the child for hours⟩. ENTERTAIN suggests providing amusement for someone by doing something special ⟨the school put on a show to *entertain* the parents⟩.

**amuse·ment** \ə-'myüz-mənt\ *n*
**1** something that amuses or entertains
**2** the condition of being amused

**amusement park** *n*
a park with many rides (as roller coasters) and games for entertainment

**an** \ən, an\ *indefinite article*
[2]A — used before words beginning with a vowel sound ⟨*an* oak⟩ ⟨*an* hour⟩

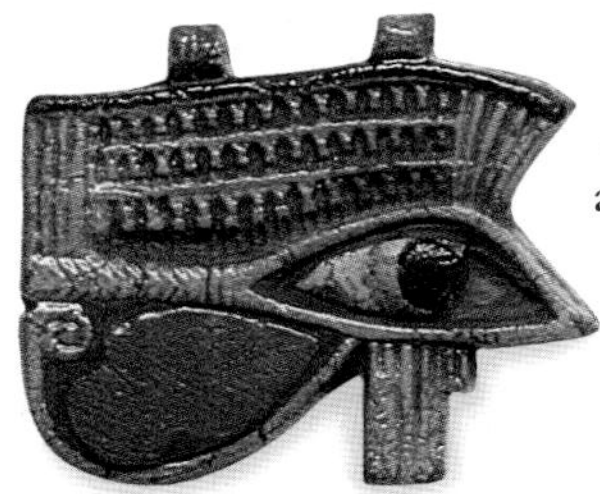

**amulet:** an ancient Egyptian amulet

**[1]-an** \ən\ *or* **-ian** *also* **-ean** \ē-ən, yən, ən\ *n suffix*
**1** one that belongs to ⟨Americ*an*⟩
**2** one skilled in or specializing in ⟨magic*ian*⟩

**[2]-an** *or* **-ian** *also* **-ean** *adj suffix*
**1** of or relating to ⟨Americ*an*⟩
**2** like : resembling

**an·a·bol·ic steroid** \,an-ə-'bäl-ik\ *n*
a hormone that is used in medicine to help tissue grow and is sometimes abused by athletes to increase muscle size and strength even though it may have unwanted or harmful effects (as stunted growth in teenagers)

**anaconda**

**an·a·con·da** \,an-ə-'kän-də\ *n*
▲ a large South American snake of the boa family

**anal·y·sis** \ə-'nal-ə-səs\ *n*, *pl* **anal·y·ses** \-ə-,sēz\
an examination of something to find out how it is made or works or what it is

**an·a·lyst** \'an-l-əst\ *n*
a person who analyzes or is skilled in analysis

**an·a·lyt·ic** \,an-l-'it-ik\ *or* **an·a·lyt·i·cal** \,an-l-'it-i-kəl\ *adj*
of, relating to, or skilled in analysis
**an·a·lyt·i·cal·ly** *adv*

**an·a·lyze** \'an-l-,īz\ *vb* **an·a·lyzed**; **an·a·lyz·ing**
to examine something to find out

what it is or what makes it work

**an·ar·chist** \'an-ər-kist\ *n*
a person who believes in or practices anarchy

**an·ar·chy** \'an-ər-kē\ *n*
**1** the condition of a country where there is no government or law and order
**2** a state of confused disorder or lawlessness

**an·a·tom·i·cal** \,an-ə-'täm-i-kəl\ *or* **an·a·tom·ic** \-'täm-ik\ *adj*
of or relating to anatomy

**anat·o·my** \ə-'nat-ə-mē\ *n, pl* **anat·o·mies**
**1** a science that has to do with the structure of the body
**2** the structural makeup especially of a person or animal ⟨the *anatomy* of the cat⟩

**-ance** \əns\ *n suffix*
**1** action or process ⟨perform*ance*⟩
**2** quality or state ⟨resembl*ance*⟩
**3** amount or degree

**an·ces·tor** \'an-,ses-tər\ *n*
one from whom an individual is descended

**an·ces·tral** \an-'ses-trəl\ *adj*
of, relating to, or coming from an ancestor ⟨their *ancestral* home⟩

**an·ces·try** \'an-,ses-trē\ *n, pl* **an·ces·tries**
one's ancestors

**[1]an·chor** \'ang-kər\ *n*
**1** ▼ a heavy iron or steel device attached to a ship by a cable or chain and so made that when thrown overboard it digs into the bottom and holds the ship in place
**2** something that keeps something else fastened or steady

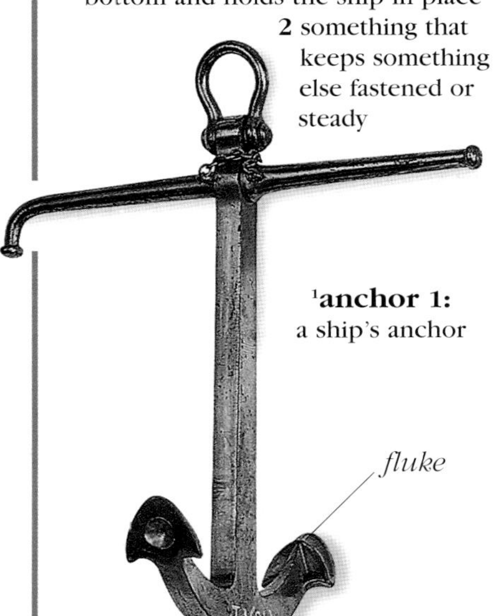


**[1]anchor 1:** a ship's anchor

**[2]anchor** *vb*
**1** to hold or become held in place with an anchor ⟨*anchor* a ship⟩
**2** to fasten tightly ⟨*anchor* the cables of a bridge⟩

**an·chor·age** \'ang-kə-rij\ *n*
a place where boats can be anchored

**[1]an·cient** \'ān-shənt, -chənt\ *adj*
**1** very old ⟨*ancient* customs⟩
**2** of or relating to a time long past or to those living in such a time

**[2]ancient** *n*
**1** a very old person
**2 ancients** *pl* the civilized peoples of ancient times and especially of Greece and Rome

**-an·cy** \ən-sē, -n-sē\ *n suffix, pl* **-an·cies**
quality or state ⟨buoy*ancy*⟩

**and** \ənd, and\ *conj*
**1** added to ⟨2 *and* 2 make 4⟩
**2** AS WELL AS, ALSO ⟨ice cream *and* cake⟩ ⟨strong *and* healthy⟩
**and so forth** and others or more of the same kind
**and so on** AND SO FORTH

**and·iron** \'an-,dī-ərn\ *n*
one of a pair of metal supports for firewood in a fireplace

**an·ec·dote** \'an-ik-,dōt\ *n*
a short story about something interesting or funny in a person's life

**ane·mia** \ə-'nē-mē-ə\ *n*
a sickness in which there is too little blood or too few red blood cells or too little hemoglobin in the blood

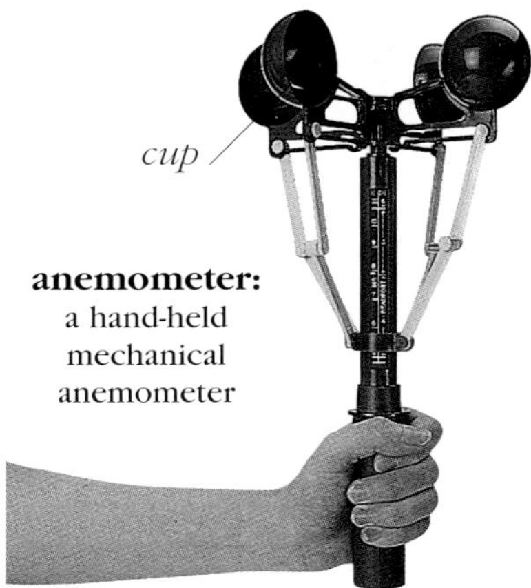


**anemometer:** a hand-held mechanical anemometer

**an·e·mom·e·ter** \,an-ə-'mäm-ət-ər\ *n*
▲ an instrument for measuring the speed of the wind

**anem·o·ne** \ə-'nem-ə-nē\ *n*
▼ a plant related to the buttercup that blooms in spring and is often grown for its large white or colored flowers

**anemone**

**an·es·the·sia** \,an-əs-'thē-zhə\ *n*
loss of feeling or consciousness

**[1]an·es·thet·ic** \,an-əs-'thet-ik\ *adj*
of, relating to, or capable of producing anesthesia

**[2]anesthetic** *n*
something that produces anesthesia

**anew** \ə-'nü, -'nyü\ *adv*
**1** over again ⟨begin *anew*⟩
**2** in a new or different form ⟨tear down and build *anew*⟩

**an·gel** \'ān-jəl\ *n*
**1** a spiritual being serving God especially as a messenger
**2** a person other people think to be like an angel (as in goodness or beauty)

**[1]an·ger** \'ang-gər\ *vb*
to make strongly displeased

**[2]anger** *n*
a strong feeling of displeasure and often of active opposition to an insult, injury, or injustice

**Synonyms** ANGER, RAGE, and FURY mean excitement of the feelings brought about by great displeasure. ANGER can be used of either a strong or a mild feeling ⟨I was able to hide my *anger*⟩. RAGE suggests such strong, violent feeling that one cannot control oneself ⟨screaming with *rage*⟩. FURY suggests an overwhelming rage that is almost like madness and may cause one to destroy things ⟨in their *fury* the people smashed windows and turned over cars⟩.

A B C D E F G H I J K L M N O P Q R S T U V W X Y Z

**¹an·gle** \'ang-gəl\ *n*
1 a sharp corner ⟨they stood in an *angle* of the building⟩
2 the figure formed by two lines meeting at a point
3 POINT OF VIEW ⟨consider a problem from a new *angle*⟩

**²angle** *vb* **an·gled**; **an·gling**
to turn, move, or direct at an angle

**³angle** *vb* **an·gled**; **an·gling**
1 to fish with hook and line
2 to try to get what one wants in a sly way ⟨*angle* for a compliment⟩

**an·gler** \'ang-glər\ *n*
▼ a person who fishes with hook and line especially for pleasure

angler

**an·gle·worm** \'ang-gəl-,wərm\ *n*
EARTHWORM

**an·gling** \'ang-gling\ *n*
fishing with a hook and line for pleasure

**An·glo-** \'ang-glō\ *prefix*
1 English
2 English and

**¹An·glo–Sax·on** \,ang-glō-'sak-sən\ *n*
1 a member of the German people who conquered England in the fifth century A.D.
2 a person whose ancestors were English

**²Anglo–Saxon** *adj*
► relating to the Anglo-Saxons

**an·go·ra** \ang-'gōr-ə\ *n*
► cloth or yarn made from the soft silky hair of a special usually white domestic rabbit (**Angora rabbit**) or from the long shiny wool of a goat (**Angora goat**)

**an·gry** \'ang-grē\ *adj*
**an·gri·er**; **an·gri·est**
feeling or showing anger

**an·gri·ly** \-grə-lē\ *adv*

**an·guish** \'ang-gwish\ *n*
great pain or trouble of body or mind

**an·guished** \'ang-gwisht\ *adj*
full of anguish ⟨an *anguished* cry⟩

**an·gu·lar** \'ang-gyə-lər\ *adj*
1 having angles or sharp corners
2 being lean and bony ⟨an *angular* face⟩

**an·i·mal** \'an-ə-məl\ *n*
1 any of the great group of living beings (as jellyfishes, crabs, birds, and people) that differ from plants typically in being able to move about, in not having cell walls made of cellulose, and in depending on plants and other animals as sources of food
2 any of the animals lower than humans in the natural order
3 MAMMAL

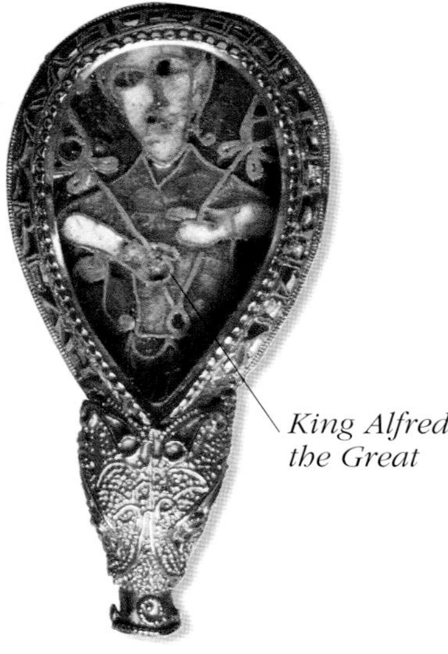

**²Anglo–Saxon:** a 9th-century jewel containing a portrait of an Anglo-Saxon king

**angora**
Fibers are collected from the coats of Angora rabbits or goats. The fibers are spun and dyed to make soft yarn.

**Angora rabbit**

**angora yarn**

**animal kingdom** *n*
a basic group of natural objects that includes all living and extinct animals

**¹an·i·mate** \'an-ə-mət\ *adj*
having life

**²an·i·mate** \'an-ə-,māt\ *vb*
**an·i·mat·ed**; **an·i·mat·ing**
1 to give life or energy to : make alive or lively
2 to make appear to move ⟨*animate* a cartoon⟩

**an·i·mat·ed** \'an-ə-,māt-əd\ *adj*
1 full of life and energy : LIVELY
2 appearing to be alive or moving

**an·i·mos·i·ty** \,an-ə-'mäs-ət-ē\ *n*, *pl* **an·i·mos·i·ties**
¹DISLIKE, HATRED

**an·kle** \'ang-kəl\ *n*
1 ▼ the joint between the foot and the leg
2 the area containing the ankle joint

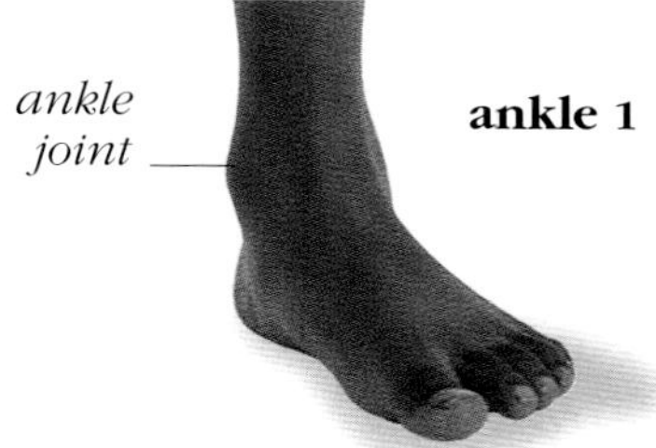

**ankle 1**

**an·klet** \'ang-klət\ *n*
a sock reaching slightly above the ankle

**ankylosaur:** a North American ankylosaur, *Euoplocephalus*

**an·ky·lo·saur** \'ang-kə-lō-,sȯr\ *n*
▲ any of several plant-eating dinosaurs with bony plates covering the back

**an·nals** \'an-lz\ *n pl*
**1** a record of events arranged in yearly sequence
**2** historical records **:** HISTORY

**an·neal** \ə-'nēl\ *vb*
to heat (as glass or steel) and then cool so as to toughen and make less brittle

[1]**an·nex** \ə-'neks, 'an-,eks\ *vb*
to add (something) to something else usually so as to become a part of it ⟨*annex* a postscript to a letter⟩ ⟨the United States *annexed* Texas and it became a state⟩

[2]**an·nex** \'an-,eks\ *n*
something (as a wing of a building) added on

**an·nex·ation** \,an-,ek-'sā-shən\ *n*
an annexing especially of new territory

**an·ni·hi·late** \ə-'nī-ə-,lāt\ *vb*
**an·ni·hi·lat·ed**; **an·ni·hi·lat·ing**
to destroy entirely **:** put completely out of existence

**an·ni·ver·sa·ry** \,an-ə-'vərs-ə-rē, -'vərs-rē\ *n, pl* **an·ni·ver·sa·ries**
the return every year of the date when something special (as a wedding) happened

**an·nounce** \ə-'nau̇ns\ *vb*
**an·nounced**; **an·nounc·ing**
**1** to make known publicly
**2** to give notice of the arrival, presence, or readiness of ⟨*announce* dinner⟩ **synonyms** see DECLARE

**an·nounce·ment** \ə-'nau̇n-smənt\ *n*
**1** the act of announcing
**2** a public notice announcing something

**an·nounc·er** \ə-'nau̇n-sər\ *n*
a person who introduces radio or television programs, makes announcements, and gives the news and station identification

**an·noy** \ə-'nȯi\ *vb*
to disturb or irritate especially by repeated disagreeable acts

**Synonyms** ANNOY, PESTER, and TEASE mean to disturb and upset a person. ANNOY suggests bothering someone to the point of anger ⟨I am *annoyed* by your bad behavior⟩. PESTER suggests bothering someone over and over ⟨stop *pestering* me for more money⟩. TEASE often suggests continually tormenting someone until that person is provoked or upset ⟨they *teased* the child to the point of tears⟩.

**an·noy·ance** \ə-'nȯi-əns\ *n*
**1** the act of annoying
**2** the feeling of being annoyed
**3** a source or cause of being annoyed ⟨the dog's barking was a constant *annoyance*⟩

**an·noy·ing** \ə-'nȯi-ing\ *adj*
causing annoyance ⟨an *annoying* habit⟩
**an·noy·ing·ly** *adv*

[1]**an·nu·al** \'an-yə-wəl\ *adj*
**1** coming, happening, done, made, or given once a year
**2** completing the life cycle in one growing season ⟨*annual* plants⟩
**an·nu·al·ly** *adv*

[2]**annual** *n*
◀ an annual plant

**annual ring** *n*
the layer of wood produced by one

[2]**annual**
Annuals complete their life cycle in a single season of growth. They flower soon after germination, then die after producing seeds.

poppy

sunflower

pot marigold

year's growth of a woody plant (as in the trunk of a tree)

**an·nu·ity** \ə-'nü-ət-ē, -'nyü-\ *n, pl* **an·nu·ities**
a sum of money paid at regular intervals

**an·nul** \ə-'nəl\ *vb* **an·nulled**; **an·nul·ling**
to cancel by law : take away the legal force of ⟨*annul* a marriage⟩
**an·nul·ment** \-mənt\ *n*

**an·ode** \'an-,ōd\ *n*
**1** the positive electrode of an electrolytic cell
**2** the negative end of a battery that is delivering electric current
**3** the electron-collecting electrode of an electron tube

**anoint** \ə-'nȯint\ *vb*
**1** to rub or cover with oil or grease
**2** to put oil on as part of a religious ceremony

**anon·y·mous** \ə-'nän-ə-məs\ *adj*
**1** not named or identified ⟨an *anonymous* caller⟩
**2** made or done by someone unknown ⟨an *anonymous* phone call⟩
**anon·y·mous·ly** *adv*

**¹an·oth·er** \ə-'nəth-ər\ *adj*
**1** some other ⟨choose *another* day⟩
**2** one more ⟨bring *another* cup⟩

**²another** *pron*
**1** one more ⟨hit one homer in the first game and *another* in the second⟩
**2** someone or something different ⟨horse-play is one thing, but vandalism is *another*⟩

**¹an·swer** \'an-sər\ *n*
**1** something said or written in reply (as to a question)
**2** a solution of a problem

**²answer** *vb*
**1** to speak or write in reply to
**2** to take responsibility ⟨*answered* for the children's safety⟩
**3** ¹SERVE 5, DO

**an·swer·able** \'an-sə-rə-bəl\ *adj*
**1** RESPONSIBLE 1 ⟨*answerable* for your actions⟩
**2** possible to answer ⟨an *answerable* argument⟩

**answering machine** *n*
a machine that receives telephone calls by playing a recorded message and usually also recording messages from callers

**ant** \'ant\ *n*
▼ a small insect related to the bees and wasps that lives in colonies and forms nests in the ground or in wood in which it stores food and raises its young

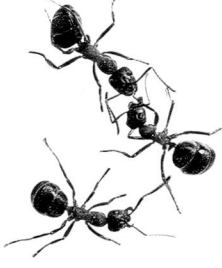

**ants**

**ant-** *see* ANTI-

**¹-ant** \ənt\ *n suffix*
**1** one that does or causes a certain thing ⟨deodor*ant*⟩
**2** thing that is acted upon in a certain way

**²-ant** *adj suffix*
**1** doing a certain thing or being a certain way
**2** causing a certain action

**an·tag·o·nism** \an-'tag-ə-,niz-əm\ *n*
a state of not liking and being against something

**an·tag·o·nist** \an-'tag-ə-nəst\ *n*
a person who is against something or someone else : OPPONENT

**an·tag·o·nis·tic** \an-,tag-ə-'nis-tik\ *adj*
being against something or someone : HOSTILE, UNFRIENDLY
**an·tag·o·nis·ti·cal·ly** \-ti-kə-lē\ *adv*

**antelope:** an Arabian oryx

**an·tag·o·nize** \an-'tag-ə-,nīz\ *vb* **an·tag·o·nized**; **an·tag·o·niz·ing**
to stir up dislike or anger in ⟨parents who *antagonize* their children⟩

**ant·arc·tic** \ant-'ärk-tik, -'ärt-ik\ *adj, often cap*
▼ of or relating to the south pole or to the region around it ⟨*antarctic* explorers⟩

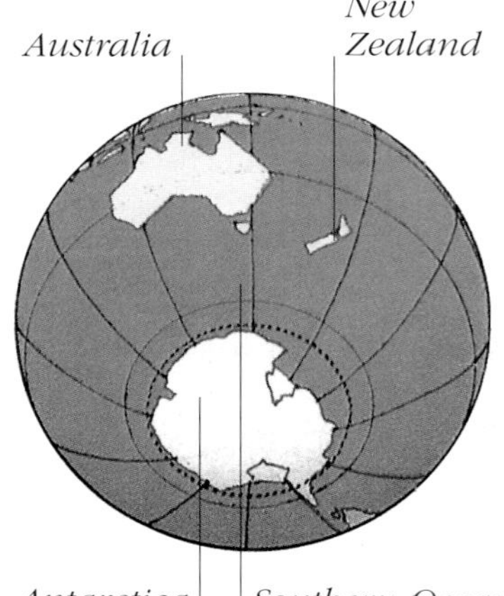


**antarctic:** map of the world showing the antarctic region

**ante-** \'ant-i\ *prefix*
**1** before in time : earlier ⟨*ante*date⟩
**2** in front of ⟨*ante*room⟩

**anteater:** a spiny anteater

**ant·eat·er** \'ant-,ēt-ər\ *n*
▲ any of several animals that have long noses and long sticky tongues and feed chiefly on ants

**an·te·cham·ber** \'ant-i-,chām-bər\ *n*
ANTEROOM

**an·te·lope** \'ant-l-,ōp\ *n*
◀ any of a group of cud-chewing animals that have horns that extend upward and backward

**an·ten·na** \an-'ten-ə\ *n*
**1** ▼ *pl* **an·ten·nae** \'ten-ē\ one of two or four threadlike movable feelers on the heads of insects or crustaceans (as lobsters)
**2** *pl* **an·ten·nas** a metallic device (as a rod or wire) for sending or receiving radio waves

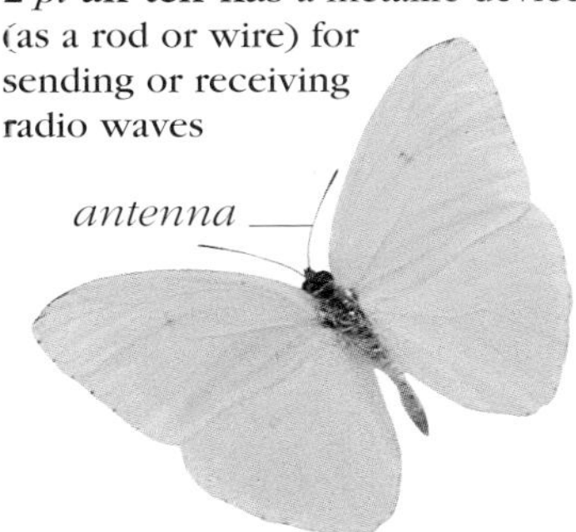


**antenna 1:** antennae of a butterfly

**Word History** Long ago, a wise man in Greece wrote about insects. His name was Aristotle. Aristotle used a Greek word that meant "horn" to refer to the insects' feelers. The Greek word for "horn" had another meaning—"sail yard." (A sail yard supports and spreads the sails on a sailing ship.) When Aristotle's book was translated into Latin, the Latin word for "sail yard" was used instead of the Latin word for "horn." That is how the Latin word that meant "sail yard" came to mean "feeler" as well. The English word *antenna* came from this Latin word.

**an·te·room** \'ant-i-,rüm, -,rům\ *n*
a room used as an entrance to another

**an·them** \'an-thəm\ *n*
**1** a sacred song usually sung by a church choir
**2** a patriotic song of praise and love for one's country

**an·ther** \'an-thər\ *n*
▶ the enlargement at the tip of a flower's stamen that contains pollen

**ant·hill** \'ant-,hil\ *n*
a mound of dirt thrown up by ants in digging their nest

**an·thol·o·gy** \an-'thäl-ə-jē\ *n, pl* **an·thol·o·gies**
a collection of writings (as stories and poems)

**an·thra·cite** \'an-thrə-,sīt\ *n*
a hard glossy coal that burns without much smoke

**an·thrax** \'an-,thraks\ *n*
a dangerous bacterial disease of warm-blooded animals that can affect humans

**an·thro·poid** \'an-thrə-,pȯid\ *adj*
looking somewhat like humans ⟨the *anthropoid* apes⟩

**an·thro·pol·o·gy** \,an-thrə-'päl-ə-jē\ *n*
a science that studies people and especially their history, development, distribution, and culture

**anti-** \'ant-i, 'an-,tī\ *or* **ant-** \ant\ *prefix*
**1** opposite in kind, position, or action ⟨*anti*cyclone⟩
**2** hostile toward ⟨*anti*social⟩

**an·ti·bi·ot·ic** \,ant-i-bī-'ät-ik\ *n*
a substance produced by living things and especially by bacteria and fungi that is used to kill or prevent the growth of harmful germs

**an·ti·body** \'ant-i-,bäd-ē\ *n, pl* **an·ti·bod·ies**
a substance produced by the body that counteracts the effects of a disease germ or its poisons

**an·tic** \'ant-ik\ *n*
a wildly playful or funny act or action

**an·tic·i·pate** \an-'tis-ə-,pāt\ *vb* **an·tic·i·pat·ed**; **an·tic·i·pat·ing**
**1** to foresee and deal with or provide for beforehand ⟨*anticipated* my objections⟩
**2** to look forward to ⟨*anticipating* their visit⟩

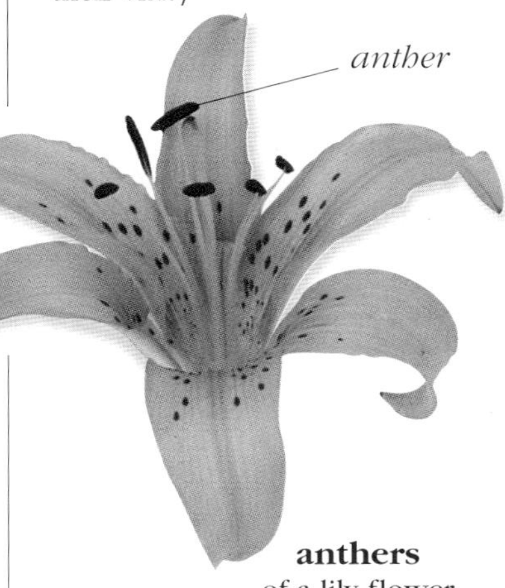


**anthers** of a lily flower

**an·tic·i·pa·tion** \an-,tis-ə-'pā-shən\ *n*
**1** an action that takes into account and deals with or prevents a later action
**2** pleasurable expectation
**3** a picturing beforehand of a future event or state

**an·ti·cy·clone** \,ant-i-'sī-,klōn\ *n*
a system of winds that is like a cyclone but that rotates about a center of high atmospheric pressure in a clockwise direction north of the equator and a counterclockwise direction south of the equator

**an·ti·dote** \'ant-i-,dōt\ *n*
something used to reverse or prevent the action of a poison

**an·ti·freeze** \'ant-i-,frēz\ *n*
a substance added to the liquid in an automobile radiator to prevent its freezing

**an·ti·mo·ny** \'ant-ə-,mō-nē\ *n*
a silvery white metallic chemical element

**an·tip·a·thy** \an-'tip-ə-thē\ *n, pl* **an·tip·a·thies**
a strong feeling of dislike

**an·ti·quat·ed** \'ant-ə-,kwāt-əd\ *adj*
OLD-FASHIONED 1, OBSOLETE

[1]**an·tique** \an-'tēk\ *n*
an object (as a piece of furniture) made at an earlier time

[2]**antique** *adj*
▼ belonging to or like a former style or fashion ⟨*antique* lamps⟩

[2]**antique:** an antique chair

a b c d e f g h i j k l m n o p q r s t u v w x y z

\ng\ sing \ō\ bone \ȯ\ saw \ȯi\ coin \th\ thin \t͟h\ this \ü\ food \u̇\ foot \y\ yet \yü\ few \yu̇\ cure \zh\ vision

**an·tiq·ui·ty** \an-'tik-wət-ē\ *n*
**1** ancient times
**2** very great age ⟨a castle of great *antiquity*⟩

[1]**an·ti·sep·tic** \ˌant-ə-'sep-tik\ *adj*
killing or making harmless the germs that cause decay or sickness ⟨iodine is *antiseptic*⟩

[2]**antiseptic** *n*
an antiseptic substance

**an·ti·so·cial** \ˌant-i-'sō-shəl, ˌan-ˌtī-\ *adj*
**1** being against or bad for society ⟨*antisocial* acts of the criminal⟩
**2** UNFRIENDLY

**an·tith·e·sis** \an-'tith-ə-səs\ *n, pl* **an·tith·e·ses** \-ə-ˌsēz\
the exact opposite

**an·ti·tox·in** \ˌant-i-'täk-sən\ *n*
a substance that is formed in the blood of one exposed to a disease and that prevents or acts against that disease

**ant·ler** \'ant-lər\ *n*
the entire horn or a branch of the horn of an animal of the deer family
**ant·lered** \-lərd\ *adj*

**ant lion** *n*
▼ an insect having a larva form with long jaws that digs a cone-shaped hole in which it waits for prey (as ants)

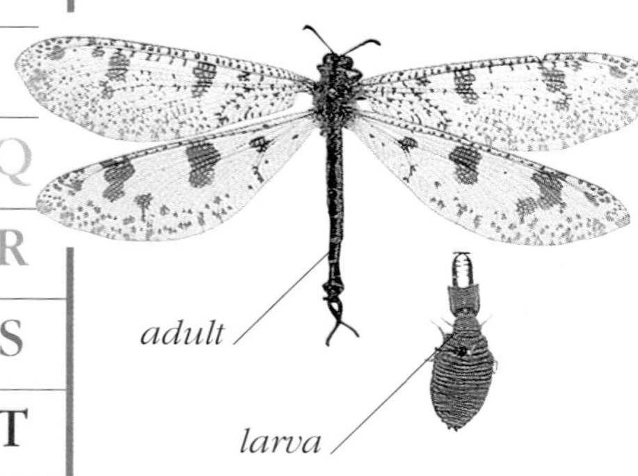


**ant lion**

**an·to·nym** \'an-tə-ˌnim\ *n*
a word of opposite meaning ⟨"hot" and "cold" are *antonyms*⟩

**an·vil** \'an-vəl\ *n*
an iron block on which pieces of metal are hammered into shape

**anx·i·ety** \ang-'zī-ət-ē\ *n, pl* **anx·i·eties**
fear or nervousness about what might happen

**anx·ious** \'angk-shəs\ *adj*
**1** afraid or nervous about what may happen ⟨*anxious* about the child's health⟩
**2** wanting very much **:** EAGER ⟨*anxious* to make good⟩
**synonyms** see EAGER
**anx·ious·ly** *adv*

[1]**any** \'en-ē\ *adj*
**1** whatever kind of ⟨*any* person you meet⟩
**2** of whatever number or amount ⟨need *any* help I can get⟩

[2]**any** *pron*
**1** any individuals ⟨are *any* of you ready⟩
**2** any amount ⟨is there *any* left⟩

[3]**any** *adv*
to the least amount or degree ⟨can't get it *any* cleaner⟩ ⟨was never *any* good⟩

**any·body** \'en-ē-ˌbäd-ē, -bəd-ē\ *pron*
ANYONE

**any·how** \'en-ē-ˌhau̇\ *adv*
**1** in any way, manner, or order
**2** at any rate **:** in any case

**any·more** \ˌen-ē-'mōr\ *adv*
NOWADAYS ⟨we never see them *anymore*⟩

**any·one** \'en-ē-ˌwən\ *pron*
any person ⟨*anyone* may come to the party⟩

**any·place** \'en-ē-ˌplās\ *adv*
in any place

**any·thing** \'en-ē-ˌthing\ *pron*
a thing of any kind ⟨didn't do *anything* all day⟩

**any·way** \'en-ē-ˌwā\ *adv*
ANYHOW

**any·where** \'en-ē-ˌhwear, -ˌwear, -ˌhwaər, -ˌwaər\ *adv*
in, at, or to any place

**any·wise** \'en-ē-ˌwīz\ *adv*
in any way whatever

**A1** \'ā-'wən\ *adj*
of the very best kind

**aor·ta** \ā-'ȯrt-ə\ *n*
the main artery that carries blood from the heart for distribution to all parts of the body

**apace** \ə-'pās\ *adv*
at a quick pace **:** FAST

**apart** \ə-'pärt\ *adv*
**1** away from each other ⟨towns many miles *apart*⟩
**2** as something separated **:** SEPARATELY ⟨considered *apart* from other points⟩
**3** into parts **:** to pieces ⟨took the clock *apart*⟩
**4** one from another ⟨could not tell the twins *apart*⟩

**apart·ment** \ə-'pärt-mənt\ *n*
**1** a room or set of rooms used as a home
**2** a building divided into individual apartments

**ap·a·thet·ic** \ˌap-ə-'thet-ik\ *adj*
having or showing little or no feeling or interest
**ap·a·thet·i·cal·ly** \-i-kə-lē\ *adv*

**ap·a·thy** \'ap-ə-thē\ *n*
lack of feeling or of interest **:** INDIFFERENCE

**apato·sau·rus** \ə-ˌpat-ə-'sȯr-əs\ *n*
BRONTOSAURUS

[1]**ape** \'āp\ *n*
▶ any of a group of tailless animals (as gorillas) that are most closely related to humans
**ape·like** \'āp-ˌlīk\ *adj*

[2]**ape** *vb* **aped**; **ap·ing**
to imitate (someone) awkwardly

**ap·er·ture** \'ap-ər-ˌchu̇r\ *n*
an opening or open space **:** HOLE

**apex** \'ā-ˌpeks\ *n, pl* **apex·es** *or* **api·ces** \'ā-pə-ˌsēz\
▼ the highest point **:** PEAK

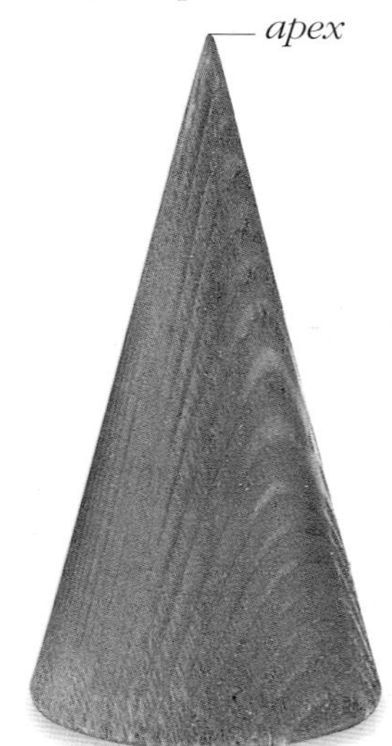


**apex** of a cone

**aphid** \'ā-fəd\ *n*
PLANT LOUSE

**apiece** \ə-'pēs\ *adv*
for each one

**aplomb** \ə-'pläm\ *n*
complete freedom from nervousness or uncertainty

**[1]ape**
Like their human relatives, apes have large brains and are among the most intelligent creatures on earth. Apes spend much of their time in trees, although most species can walk upright on two legs.

gibbon

chimpanzee

gorilla

orangutan

**apol•o•get•ic** \ə-ˌpäl-ə-'jet-ik\ *adj*
sorry for having done something wrong ⟨they were most *apologetic* about the mistake⟩
**apol•o•get•i•cal•ly** \-i-kə-lē\ *adv*

**apol•o•gize** \ə-'päl-ə-ˌjīz\ *vb*
**apol•o•gized**; **apol•o•giz•ing**
to make an apology

**apol•o•gy** \ə-'päl-ə-jē\ *n*, *pl* **apol•o•gies**
an expression of regret (as for a mistake or a rude remark)

**apos•tle** \ə-'päs-əl\ *n*
**1** ▶ one of the twelve close followers of Jesus sent out to teach the gospel
**2** the first Christian missionary to a region
**3** the person who first puts forward an important belief or starts a great reform
**apos•tle•ship** \-ˌship\ *n*

**apos•tro•phe** \ə-'päs-trə-fē\ *n*
a mark ' used to show that letters or figures are missing (as in "can't" for "cannot" or "'76" for "1776") or to show the possessive case (as in "James's") or the plural of letters or figures (as in "cross your t's")

**apoth•e•cary** \ə-'päth-ə-ˌker-ē\ *n*, *pl* **apoth•e•car•ies**
DRUGGIST

**ap•pall** \ə-'pȯl\ *vb*
to shock or overcome with horror

**ap•pall•ing** *adj*
being shocking and terrible

**apostle 1:** a 15th-century Italian painting by Fra Angelico showing Jesus and the apostles

**ap·pa·ra·tus** \,ap-ə-'rat-əs, -'rāt-\ *n, pl* **apparatus** *or* **ap·pa·ra·tus·es**
▼ the equipment or material for a particular use or job ⟨gymnasium *apparatus*⟩ ⟨laboratory *apparatus*⟩

[2]**appeal** *vb*
**1** to take action to have a case or decision reviewed by a higher court
**2** to ask for something badly needed or wanted
**3** to be pleasing or attractive

**ap·pear** \ə-'pir\ *vb*
**1** to come into sight
**2** to present oneself ⟨*appear* in court⟩
**3** SEEM 1 ⟨*appears* to be tired⟩
**4** to come before the public ⟨the book *appeared* last year⟩
**5** to come into existence

**ap·pear·ance** \ə-'pir-əns\ *n*
**1** the act or an instance of appearing ⟨a movie star's personal *appearance*⟩
**2** way of looking ⟨the room has a cool *appearance*⟩

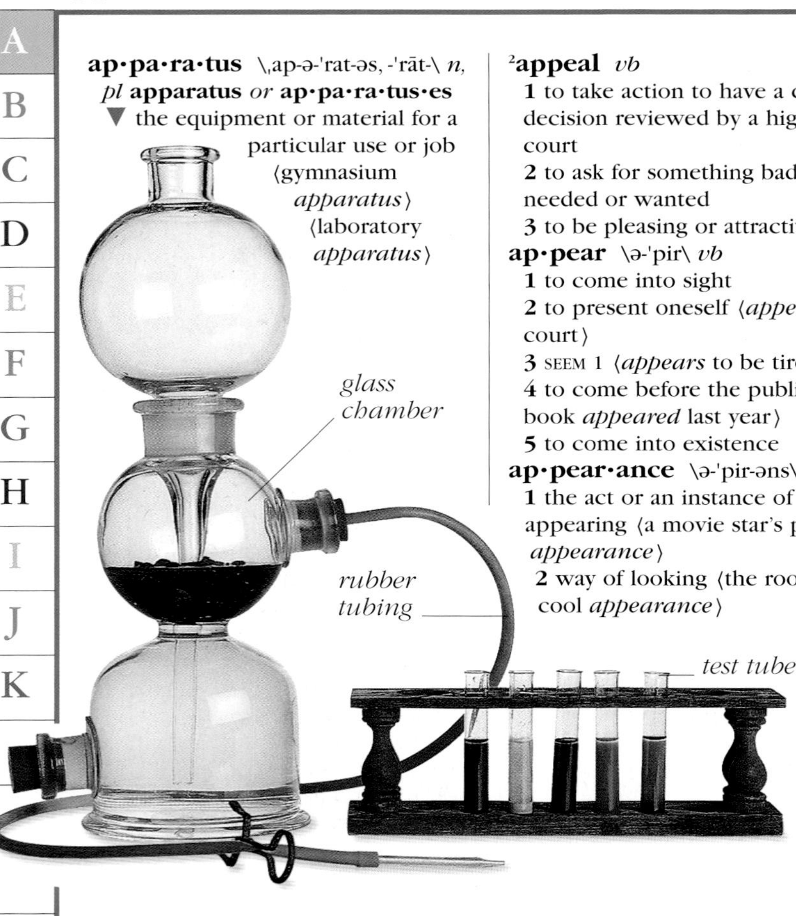


**apparatus** used in a science laboratory

**ap·pe·tite** \'ap-ə-,tīt\ *n*
**1** a natural desire especially for food
**2** [2]TASTE 4 ⟨an *appetite* for adventure⟩

**ap·pe·tiz·er** \'ap-ə-,tī-zər\ *n*
a food or drink usually served before a meal to make one hungrier

**ap·pe·tiz·ing** \'ap-ə-,tī-zing\ *adj*
pleasing to the appetite ⟨an *appetizing* smell⟩

**ap·plaud** \ə-'plȯd\ *vb*
**1** [1]PRAISE 1
**2** to show approval especially by clapping the hands

**ap·plause** \ə-'plȯz\ *n*
approval shown especially by clapping the hands

**ap·ple** \'ap-əl\ *n*
▼ the round or oval fruit with red, yellow, or green skin of a spreading tree (**apple tree**) that is related to the rose

core
pip
**apple**

**ap·par·el** \ə-'par-əl\ *n*
things that are worn : WEAR 2 ⟨summer *apparel*⟩

**ap·par·ent** \ə-'par-ənt, -'per-\ *adj*
**1** open to view : VISIBLE ⟨a night in which many stars are *apparent*⟩
**2** clear to the understanding : EVIDENT ⟨it was *apparent* that we could not win⟩
**3** appearing to be real or true ⟨the *apparent* meaning of the speech⟩
**ap·par·ent·ly** *adv*
**ap·par·ent·ness** *n*

**ap·pa·ri·tion** \,ap-ə-'rish-ən\ *n*
**1** an unusual or unexpected sight
**2** GHOST

[1]**ap·peal** \ə-'pēl\ *n*
**1** a legal action by which a case is brought to a higher court for review
**2** an asking for something badly needed or wanted : PLEA ⟨an *appeal* for funds⟩
**3** the power to cause enjoyment : ATTRACTION ⟨the *appeal* of music⟩

**ap·pease** \ə-'pēz\ *vb* **ap·peased**; **ap·peas·ing**
**1** to make calm or quiet ⟨*appease* their anger⟩
**2** to give in to
**ap·pease·ment** \-mənt\ *n*
**ap·peas·er** *n*

**ap·pend** \ə-'pend\ *vb*
to add as something extra ⟨*append* a postscript⟩

**ap·pend·age** \ə-'pen-dij\ *n*
something (as a leg) attached to a larger or more important thing

**ap·pen·di·ci·tis** \ə-,pen-də-'sīt-əs\ *n*
inflammation of the intestinal appendix

**ap·pen·dix** \ə-'pen-diks\ *n, pl* **ap·pen·dix·es** *or* **ap·pen·di·ces** \-də-,sēz\
**1** a part of a book giving added and helpful information (as notes or tables)
**2** a small tubelike part growing out from the intestine

**ap·pli·ance** \ə-'plī-əns\ *n*
**1** a device designed for a certain use
**2** ▶ a piece of household or office equipment that runs on gas or electricity

**ap·pli·ca·ble** \'ap-li-kə-bəl\ *adj*
capable of being put to use or put into practice

**ap·pli·cant** \'ap-li-kənt\ *n*
a person who applies for something (as a job)

**ap·pli·ca·tion** \,ap-lə-'kā-shən\ *n*
**1** the act or an instance of applying ⟨the *application* of paint to a house⟩
**2** something put or spread on a surface ⟨cold *applications* on a sprained ankle⟩
**3** [1]REQUEST 1 ⟨an *application* for a job⟩
**4** ability to be put to practical use

**ap·pli·ca·tor** \'ap-lə-ˌkāt-ər\ *n*
a device for applying a substance (as medicine or polish)

**ap·ply** \ə-'plī\ *vb* **ap·plied**; **ap·ply·ing**
1 to put to use ⟨*applied* my knowledge⟩
2 to lay or spread on ⟨*apply* a coat of paint⟩
3 to place in contact ⟨*apply* heat⟩
4 to give one's full attention ⟨*applied* myself to my work⟩
5 to have relation or a connection ⟨this law *applies* to everyone⟩
6 to request especially in writing ⟨*apply* for a job⟩

**ap·point** \ə-'pȯint\ *vb*
1 to decide on usually from a position of authority ⟨the teacher *appointed* a time for our meeting⟩
2 to choose for some duty, job, or office ⟨I was *appointed* to wash the dishes⟩ ⟨the school board *appointed* three new teachers⟩ ⟨the president *appoints* the cabinet⟩

**ap·poin·tee** \ə-ˌpȯin-'tē\ *n*
a person appointed to an office or position

**ap·point·ment** \ə-'pȯint-mənt\ *n*
1 the act or an instance of appointing ⟨holds office by *appointment*⟩
2 a position or office to which a person is named
3 an agreement to meet at a fixed time ⟨an eight-o'clock *appointment*⟩
4 **appointments** *pl* FURNISHINGS

**ap·po·si·tion** \ˌap-ə-'zish-ən\ *n*
a grammatical construction in which a noun is followed by another that explains it ⟨in "my friend the doctor," the word "doctor" is in *apposition* with "friend"⟩

**ap·pos·i·tive** \ə-'päz-ət-iv\ *n*
the second of a pair of nouns in apposition ⟨in "my friend the doctor," the word "doctor" is an *appositive*⟩

**ap·prais·al** \ə-'prā-zəl\ *n*
an act or instance of appraising

**ap·praise** \ə-'prāz\ *vb* **ap·praised**; **ap·prais·ing**
to set a value on

**ap·pre·cia·ble** \ə-'prē-shə-bəl\ *adj*
large enough to be noticed or measured

**ap·pre·cia·bly** \-blē\ *adv*

**ap·pre·ci·ate** \ə-'prē-shē-ˌāt\ *vb* **ap·pre·ci·at·ed**; **ap·pre·ci·at·ing**
1 to admire greatly and with understanding ⟨*appreciates* poetry⟩
2 to be fully aware of ⟨I *appreciate* how important this is⟩
3 to be grateful for ⟨we *appreciate* your help⟩
4 to increase in number or value

**Synonyms** APPRECIATE, TREASURE, and CHERISH mean to think very much of something. APPRECIATE suggests that one understands and enjoys the true worth of something ⟨I can *appreciate* good music⟩. TREASURE is often used of something of great sentimental value that one thinks of as precious and keeps in a safe place ⟨parents *treasure* gifts that their children make⟩. CHERISH suggests that one loves and cares for something very much and often for a long time ⟨*cherished* their friendship for many years⟩.

**appliance 2**
Household appliances save time in running a household. Many modern appliances, such as all of the examples shown here, run on electricity.

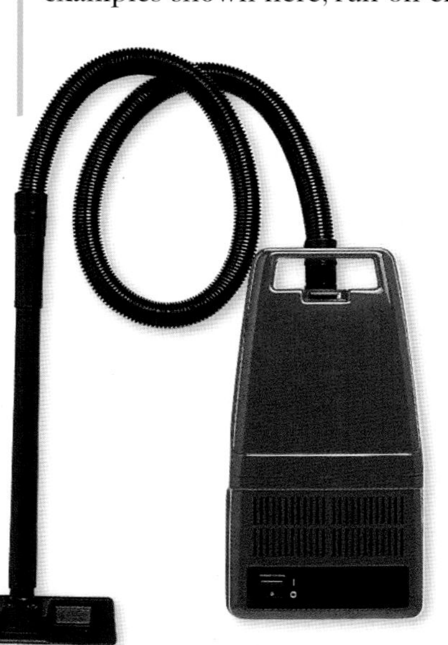
vacuum cleaner

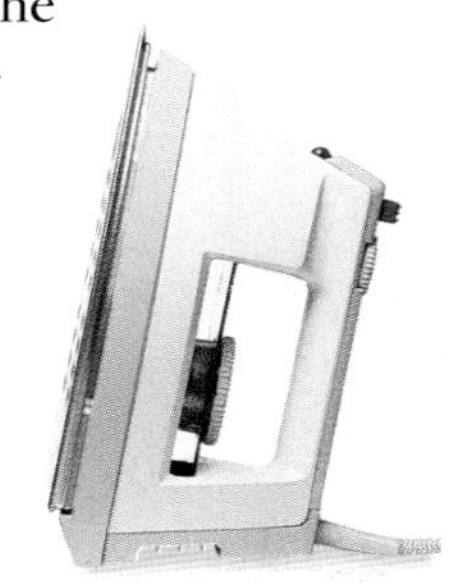
steam iron

toaster

refrigerator

a b c d e f g h i j k l m n o p q r s t u v w x y z

A
B
C
D
E
F
G
H
I
J
K
L
M
N
O
P
Q
R
S
T
U
V
W
X
Y
Z

**ap·pre·ci·a·tion** \ə-ˌprē-shē-ˈā-shən\ *n*
**1** the act of appreciating
**2** awareness or understanding of worth or value
**3** a rise in value

**ap·pre·cia·tive** \ə-ˈprē-shət-iv\ *adj*
having or showing appreciation ⟨an *appreciative* smile⟩
**ap·pre·cia·tive·ly** *adv*

**ap·pre·hend** \ˌap-ri-ˈhend\ *vb*
**1** [1]ARREST 2 ⟨*apprehend* a burglar⟩
**2** to look forward to with fear and uncertainty
**3** UNDERSTAND 1

**ap·pre·hen·sion** \ˌap-ri-ˈhen-chən\ *n*
**1** [2]ARREST
**2** an understanding of something
**3** fear of or uncertainty about what may be coming

**ap·pre·hen·sive** \ˌap-ri-ˈhen-siv\ *adj*
fearful of what may be coming
**ap·pre·hen·sive·ly** *adv*
**ap·pre·hen·sive·ness** *n*

[1]**ap·pren·tice** \ə-ˈprent-əs\ *n*
a person who is learning a trade or art by experience under a skilled worker

[2]**apprentice** *vb* **ap·pren·ticed**; **ap·pren·tic·ing**
to set at work as an apprentice

**ap·pren·tice·ship** \ə-ˈprent-əs-ˌship\ *n*
**1** service as an apprentice
**2** the period during which a person serves as an apprentice

[1]**ap·proach** \ə-ˈprōch\ *vb*
**1** to come near or nearer : draw close
**2** to begin to deal with ⟨*approach* a problem⟩

[2]**approach** *n*
**1** an act or instance of approaching
**2** a beginning step
**3** a way (as a path or road) to get to some place

**ap·proach·able** \ə-ˈprō-chə-bəl\ *adj*
easy to meet or deal with

[1]**ap·pro·pri·ate** \ə-ˈprō-prē-ˌāt\ *vb* **ap·pro·pri·at·ed**; **ap·pro·pri·at·ing**
**1** to take possession of
**2** to set apart for a certain purpose or use

[2]**ap·pro·pri·ate** \ə-ˈprō-prē-ət\ *adj*
especially suitable
**ap·pro·pri·ate·ly** *adv*
**ap·pro·pri·ate·ness** *n*

**ap·pro·pri·a·tion** \ə-ˌprō-prē-ˈā-shən\ *n*
**1** an act or instance of appropriating
**2** a sum of money appropriated for a specific use

**ap·prov·al** \ə-ˈprü-vəl\ *n*
an act or instance of approving

**ap·prove** \ə-ˈprüv\ *vb* **ap·proved**; **ap·prov·ing**
**1** to think well of
**2** to accept as satisfactory

[1]**ap·prox·i·mate** \ə-ˈpräk-sə-mət\ *adj*
nearly correct or exact ⟨the *approximate* cost⟩
**ap·prox·i·mate·ly** *adv*

[2]**ap·prox·i·mate** \ə-ˈpräk-sə-ˌmāt\ *vb* **ap·prox·i·mat·ed**; **ap·prox·i·mat·ing**
**1** to bring near or close
**2** to come near : APPROACH

**ap·prox·i·ma·tion** \ə-ˌpräk-sə-ˈmā-shən\ *n*
**1** a coming near or close (as in value)
**2** an estimate or figure that is almost exact

**apri·cot** \ˈap-rə-ˌkät, ˈā-prə-\ *n*
▼ a small oval orange-colored fruit that looks like the related peach and plum

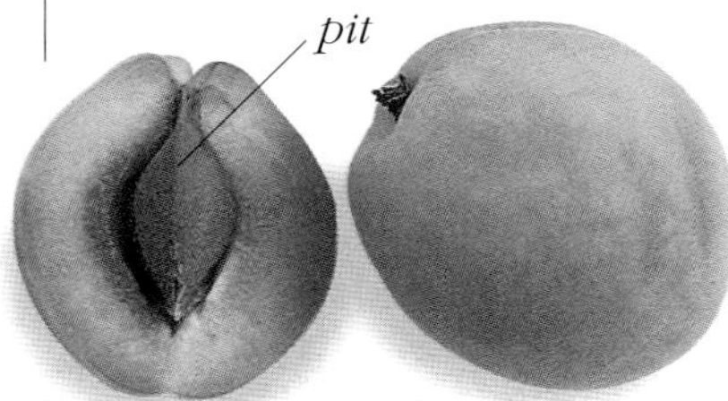

**apricot**

**April** \ˈā-prəl\ *n*
the fourth month of the year

**Word History** English *April* came from the Latin name of the month. We are not at all certain where the Latin name of the month came from. It may have been derived from the name of an ancient goddess.

**apron** \ˈā-prən\ *n*
**1** ▼ a piece of cloth worn on the front of the body to keep the clothing from getting dirty
**2** a paved area for parking or handling airplanes

**apron 1**

**apt** \ˈapt\ *adj*
**1** just right : SUITABLE ⟨an *apt* reply⟩
**2** having a tendency : LIKELY ⟨is *apt* to become angry over small things⟩
**3** quick to learn ⟨a pupil *apt* in arithmetic⟩
**apt·ly** *adv*
**apt·ness** *n*

**ap·ti·tude** \ˈap-tə-ˌtüd, -ˌtyüd\ *n*
**1** ability to learn
**2** natural ability : TALENT

**aqua** \ˈak-wə, ˈäk-\ *n*
a light greenish blue

**aqua·ma·rine** \ˌak-wə-mə-ˈrēn, ˌäk-\ *n*
▼ a transparent gem that is blue, blue-green, or green

**aquamarine**

**aqua·naut** \'ak-wə-ˌnòt, 'äk-\ *n*
a person who lives for a long while in an underwater shelter used as a base for research

**aquar·i·um** \ə-'kwer-ē-əm\ *n*
1 ▼ a container (as a tank or bowl) in which living water animals or water plants are kept

**aquarium 1**

2 a building in which water animals or water plants are exhibited

**Aquar·i·us** \ə-'kwar-ē-əs, -'kwer-\ *n*
1 a constellation between Capricorn and Pisces imagined as a man pouring water
2 the eleventh sign of the zodiac or a person born under this sign

**aquat·ic** \ə-'kwät-ik, -'kwat-\ *adj*
growing, living, or done in water ⟨*aquatic* animals⟩

**aq·ue·duct** \'ak-wə-ˌdəkt\ *n*
an artificial channel (as a structure that takes the water of a canal across a river or hollow) for carrying flowing water from one place to another

**aque·ous** \'ā-kwē-əs, 'ak-wē-\ *adj*
1 of, relating to, or like water
2 made of, by, or with water ⟨an *aqueous* solution⟩

**-ar** \ər\ *adj suffix*
of or relating to ⟨molecul*ar*⟩

[1]**Ar·ab** \'ar-əb\ *n*
1 a person born or living in the Arabian Peninsula
2 a member of a people that speaks Arabic

[2]**Arab** *adj*
of or relating to the Arabs : ARABIAN

[1]**Ara·bi·an** \ə-'rā-bē-ən\ *n*
[1]ARAB 1

[2]**Arabian** *adj*
of or relating to the Arabian Peninsula or Arabians

[1]**Ar·a·bic** \'ar-ə-bik\ *n*
a language spoken in the Arabian Peninsula, Iraq, Jordan, Lebanon, Syria, Egypt, and parts of northern Africa

[2]**Arabic** *adj*
1 of or relating to Arabia, the Arabs, or Arabic
2 expressed in or making use of Arabic numerals ⟨21 is an *Arabic* number⟩

**Arabic numeral** *n*
one of the number symbols 1, 2, 3, 4, 5, 6, 7, 8, 9, and 0

**ar·a·ble** \'ar-ə-bəl\ *adj*
fit for or cultivated by plowing : suitable for producing crops

**Arap·a·ho** *or* **Arap·a·hoe** \ə-'rap-ə-ˌhō\ *n, pl* **Arapaho** *or* **Arapahos** *or* **Arapahoe** *or* **Arapahoes**
▶ a member of an Indian people of the plains region of the United States and Canada

**Arapaho** ceremonial wand

**ar·bi·ter** \'är-bət-ər\ *n*
1 ARBITRATOR
2 a person having the power to decide what is right or proper

**ar·bi·trary** \'är-bə-ˌtrer-ē\ *adj*
1 coming from or given to free exercise of the will without thought of fairness or right ⟨*arbitrary* decisions⟩ ⟨an *arbitrary* ruler⟩
2 seeming to have been chosen by chance ⟨punctuation marks are *arbitrary* symbols⟩
**ar·bi·trari·ly** \ˌär-bə-'trer-ə-lē\ *adv*
**ar·bi·trar·i·ness** \'är-bə-ˌtrer-ē-nəs\ *n*

**ar·bi·trate** \'är-bə-ˌtrāt\ *vb*
**ar·bi·trat·ed**; **ar·bi·trat·ing**
1 to settle a disagreement after hearing the arguments of both sides
2 to refer a dispute to others for settlement

**ar·bi·tra·tion** \ˌär-bə-'trā-shən\ *n*
the settling of a disagreement in which both sides present their arguments to a third person or group for decision

**ar·bi·tra·tor** \'är-bə-ˌtrāt-ər\ *n*
a person chosen to settle differences in a disagreement

**ar·bor** \'är-bər\ *n*
a shelter of vines or branches or of a frame covered with growing vines

**ar·bo·re·al** \är-'bōr-ē-əl\ *adj*
1 of or relating to a tree
2 living in or often found in trees

**ar·bo·re·tum** \ˌär-bə-'rēt-əm\ *n, pl* **ar·bo·re·tums** *or* **ar·bo·re·ta** \-'rēt-ə\
a place where trees and plants are grown to be studied

**ar·bor·vi·tae** \ˌär-bər-'vīt-ē\ *n*
any of several evergreen trees with tiny scalelike leaves on flat branches shaped like fans

**ar·bu·tus** \är-'byüt-əs\ *n*
▶ a plant that spreads along the ground and in the spring has bunches of small fragrant flowers with five white or pink petals

**arbutus**

[1]**arc** \'ärk\ *n*
1 a glowing light across a gap in an electric circuit or between electrodes
2 a part of a curved line between any two points on it

[2]**arc** *vb* **arced** \'ärkt\; **arc·ing** \'är-king\
1 to form an electric arc
2 to follow an arc-shaped course ⟨the missile *arced* across the sky⟩

a b c d e f g h i j k l m n o p q r s t u v w x y z

A B C D E F G H I J K L M N O P Q R S T U V W X Y Z

**ar·cade** \är-ˈkād\ *n*
1 a row of arches with the columns that support them
2 an arched or covered passageway often between two rows of shops

**[1]arch** \ˈärch\ *n*
1 ▶ a usually curved part of a structure that is over an opening and serves as a support (as for the wall above the opening)
2 something suggesting an arch ⟨the *arch* of the foot⟩
**arched** \ˈärcht\ *adj*

**[2]arch** *vb*
1 to cover with an arch
2 to form or shape into an arch

**[3]arch** *adj*
1 [2]CHIEF 1, PRINCIPAL ⟨*arch*-villain⟩
2 being clever and mischievous ⟨an *arch* look⟩
**arch·ly** *adv*
**arch·ness** *n*

**ar·chae·ol·o·gy** *or* **ar·che·ol·o·gy** \ˌär-kē-ˈäl-ə-jē\ *n*
▼ a science that deals with past human life and activities as shown by fossils and the monuments and tools left by ancient peoples

**ar·cha·ic** \är-ˈkā-ik\ *adj*
1 of or relating to an earlier time
2 surviving from an earlier period

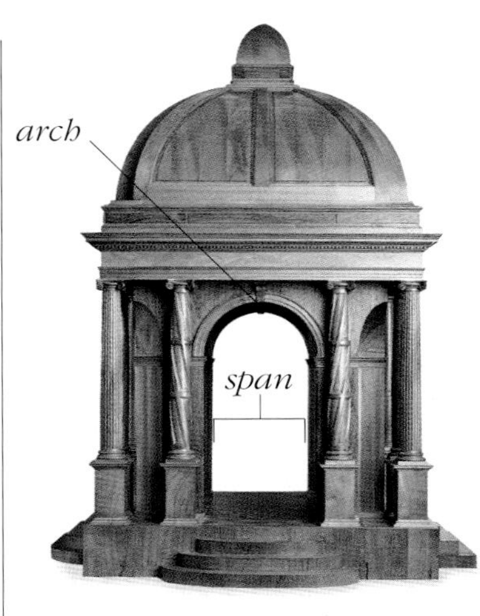


**[1]arch 1:** an arch in an architect's model

**arch·an·gel** \ˈär-ˌkān-jəl\ *n*
a chief angel

**arch·bish·op** \ˈärch-ˈbish-əp\ *n*
the bishop of highest rank in a group of dioceses

**ar·cher** \ˈär-chər\ *n*
▶ a person who shoots with a bow and arrow

**ar·chery** \ˈär-chə-rē, ˈärch-rē\ *n*
the sport or practice of shooting with bow and arrows

**ar·chi·pel·a·go** \ˌär-kə-ˈpel-ə-ˌgō, ˌär-chə-\ *n, pl* **ar·chi·pel·a·goes** *or* **ar·chi·pel·a·gos**
1 a body of water (as a sea) with many islands
2 a group of islands in an archipelago

**ar·chi·tect** \ˈär-kə-ˌtekt\ *n*
a person who designs buildings

**ar·chi·tec·tur·al** \ˌär-kə-ˈtek-chə-rəl\ *adj*
of or relating to architecture
**ar·chi·tec·tur·al·ly** *adv*

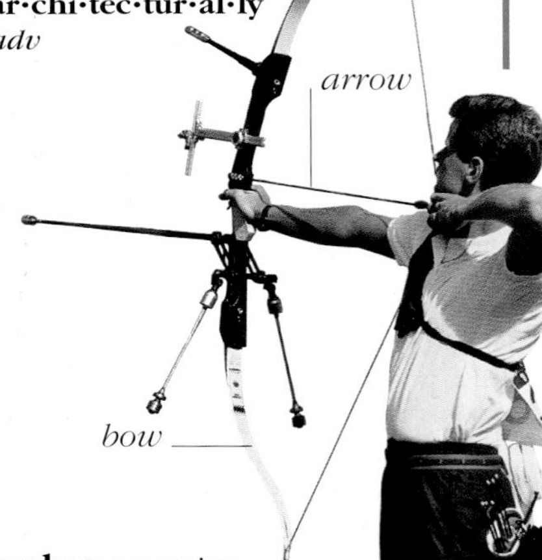


**archer** preparing to shoot an arrow

## archaeology

In archaeology, experts investigate remains such as tools, ornaments, and buildings to learn about the lives of ancient peoples.

**ancient burial doll from South America**

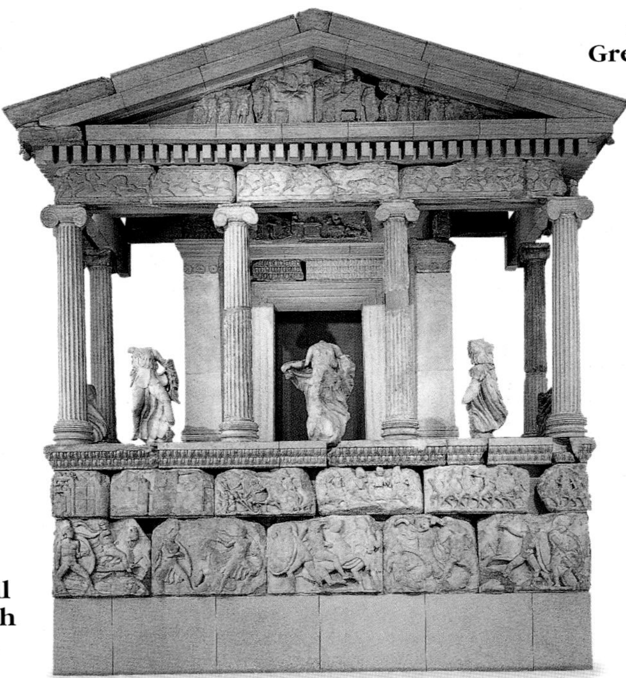

**ancient Greek temple**

**prehistoric spearhead**

## architecture 1

Architecture is the art of drawing plans for the construction of new buildings or for changes to existing ones. Many modern buildings, such as the one shown here, are built using concrete, glass, and steel.

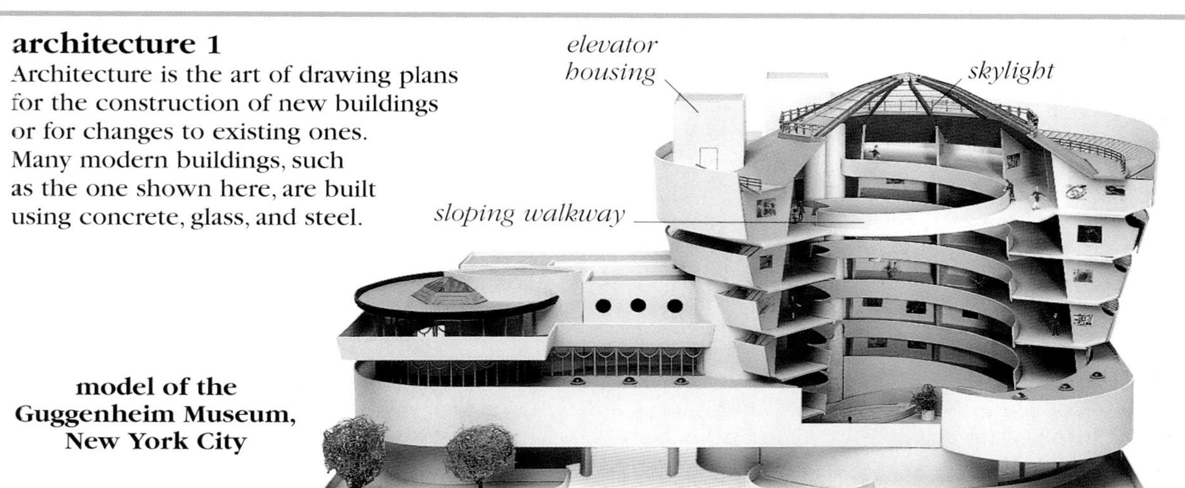


**model of the Guggenheim Museum, New York City**

**ar·chi·tec·ture** \'är-kə-ˌtek-chər\ *n*
1 ▲ the art of making plans for buildings
2 a style of building

**ar·chive** \'är-ˌkīv\ *n*
a place in which public records or historical papers are saved

**arch·way** \'ärch-ˌwā\ *n*
1 a passage under an arch
2 an arch over a passage

**-archy** \ˌär-kē, *in a few words also* ər-kē\ *n suffix , pl* **-archies**
rule : government ⟨mon*archy*⟩

**arc·tic** \'ärk-tik, 'ärt-ik\ *adj*
1 ▶ *often cap* of or relating to the north pole or to the region around it ⟨*arctic* explorers⟩
2 very cold

**Word History** The Big Dipper is a group of stars in the northern sky. It looks like a dipper to us, but ancient people thought it looked like a large bear. The ancient Greeks gave it a name that meant "bear." The English word *arctic* came from the Greek name for the Big Dipper. If we look at the Big Dipper we are looking toward the north pole. The word *arctic* refers to the region around the north pole.

**ar·dent** \'ärd-nt\ *adj*
showing or having warmth of feeling : PASSIONATE
**ar·dent·ly** *adv*

**ar·dor** \'ärd-ər\ *n*
1 warmth of feeling
2 great eagerness : ZEAL

**ar·du·ous** \'är-jə-wəs\ *adj*
DIFFICULT 1 ⟨an *arduous* climb⟩
**ar·du·ous·ly** *adv*
**ar·du·ous·ness** *n*

**are** \ər, är\ *present 2d sing or present pl of* BE

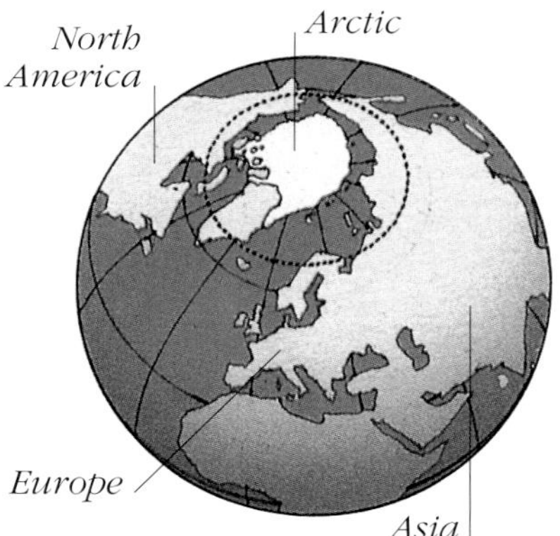


**arctic 1:** map of the world showing the arctic region

**ar·ea** \'ar-ē-ə, er-\ *n*
1 a flat surface or space
2 the amount of surface included within limits ⟨the *area* of a triangle⟩
3 REGION 1 ⟨a farming *area*⟩
4 a field of activity or study

**area code** *n*
a usually three-digit number that represents a telephone service area in a country

**are·na** \ə-'rē-nə\ *n*
1 an enclosed area used for public entertainment
2 a building containing an arena
3 a field of activity ⟨the political *arena*⟩

**Word History** In ancient Rome gladiators fought in big outdoor theaters. These theaters had a large open space in the middle covered with sand. The Latin word for this space meant "sand." The English word *arena* came from this Latin word.

**aren't** \ärnt, 'är-ənt\
are not

**ar·gue** \'är-gyü\ *vb* **ar·gued**; **ar·gu·ing**
1 to give reasons for or against something ⟨*argue* in favor of lower taxes⟩
2 to discuss some matter usually with different points of view ⟨*argue* about politics⟩
3 to persuade by giving reasons ⟨could not *argue* my parents into getting a new car⟩ **synonyms** see DISCUSS
**ar·gu·er** *n*

**ar·gu·ment** \'är-gyə-mənt\ *n*
1 a reason for or against something
2 a discussion in which reasons for and against something are given
3 an angry disagreement : QUARREL

**ar·id** \'ar-əd\ *adj*
1 not having enough rainfall to support agriculture
2 UNINTERESTING, DULL ⟨an *arid* lecture⟩

**Ar·ies** \'ar-,ēz, 'ar-ē-,ēz, 'er-\ *n*
**1** a constellation between Pisces and Taurus imagined as a ram
**2** the first sign of the zodiac or a person born under this sign

**aright** \ə-'rīt\ *adv*
in a correct way

**arise** \ə-'rīz\ *vb* **arose** \-'rōz\; **aris·en** \-'riz-n\; **aris·ing** \-'rī-zing\
**1** to move upward ⟨mist *arose* from the valley⟩
**2** to get up from sleep or after lying down
**3** to come into existence ⟨a dispute *arose*⟩

**ar·is·toc·ra·cy** \,ar-ə-'stäk-rə-sē\ *n, pl* **ar·is·toc·ra·cies**
**1** a government that is run by a small class of people
**2** an upper class that is usually based on birth and is richer and more powerful than the rest of a society
**3** persons thought of as being better than the rest of the community

**aris·to·crat** \ə-'ris-tə-,krat, 'ar-ə-stə-\ *n*
a member of an aristocracy

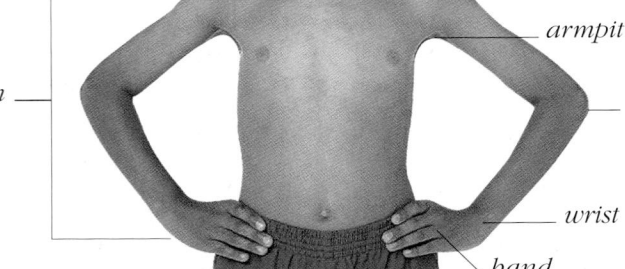

shoulder
armpit
arm
elbow
wrist
hand

[1]**arm 1**

**aris·to·crat·ic** \ə-,ris-tə-'krat-ik, ,ar-ə-stə-\ *adj*
of or relating to the aristocracy or aristocrats
**aris·to·crat·i·cal·ly** \-i-kə-lē\ *adv*

[1]**arith·me·tic** \ə-'rith-mə-,tik\ *n*
**1** a science that deals with the addition, subtraction, multiplication, and division of numbers
**2** an act or method of adding, subtracting, multiplying, or dividing

[2]**ar·ith·met·ic** \,ar-ith-'met-ik\ *or* **ar·ith·met·i·cal** \-i-kəl\ *adj*
of or relating to arithmetic

**ar·ith·met·ic mean** \,ar-ith-'met-ik-\ *n*
a quantity formed by adding quantities together and dividing by their number ⟨the *arithmetic mean* of 6, 4, and 5 is 5⟩

**ark** \'ärk\ *n*
**1** the ship in which an ancient Hebrew of the Bible named Noah and his family were saved from a great flood that God sent down on the world because of its wickedness
**2** a sacred chest in which the ancient Hebrews kept the two tablets of the Law
**3** a closet in a synagogue for the scrolls of the Law

[1]**arm** \'ärm\ *n*
**1** ▼ a human upper limb especially between the shoulder and wrist
**2** something like an arm in shape or position ⟨an *arm* of the sea⟩ ⟨the *arm* of a chair⟩
**3** [1]POWER 1 ⟨the long *arm* of the law⟩
**4** a foreleg of a four-footed animal
**armed** \'ärmd\ *adj*

[2]**arm** *vb*
**1** to provide with weapons
**2** to provide with a way of defense ⟨*armed* with facts⟩

[3]**arm** *n*
**1** WEAPON, FIREARM
**2** a branch of an army or of the military forces
**3** ▶ **arms** *pl* the designs on a shield or flag of a family or government
**4** **arms** *pl* actual fighting : WARFARE ⟨a call to *arms*⟩

**ar·ma·da** \är-'mäd-ə, -'mād-\ *n*
**1** a large fleet of warships
**2** a large number of moving things (as planes)

**ar·ma·dil·lo** \,är-mə-'dil-ō\ *n, pl* **ar·ma·dil·los**
▼ a small burrowing animal of Latin America and Texas whose head and body are protected by a hard bony armor

**armadillo**

**ar·ma·ment** \'är-mə-mənt\ *n*
**1** the military strength and equipment of a nation
**2** the supply of materials for war
**3** the process of preparing for war

**ar·ma·ture** \'är-mə-chər\ *n*
the part of an electric motor or generator that turns in a magnetic field

**arm·chair** \'ärm-,cheər, -,chaər\ *n*
a chair with arms

**arm·ful** \'ärm-,fu̇l\ *n, pl* **arm·fuls** \-,fu̇lz\ *or* **arms·ful** \'ärmz-,fu̇l\
as much as a person's arm can hold

**ar·mi·stice** \'är-mə-stəs\ *n*
a pause in fighting brought about by agreement between the two sides

[3]**arm 3:** coat of arms of Queen Elizabeth II of the United Kingdom

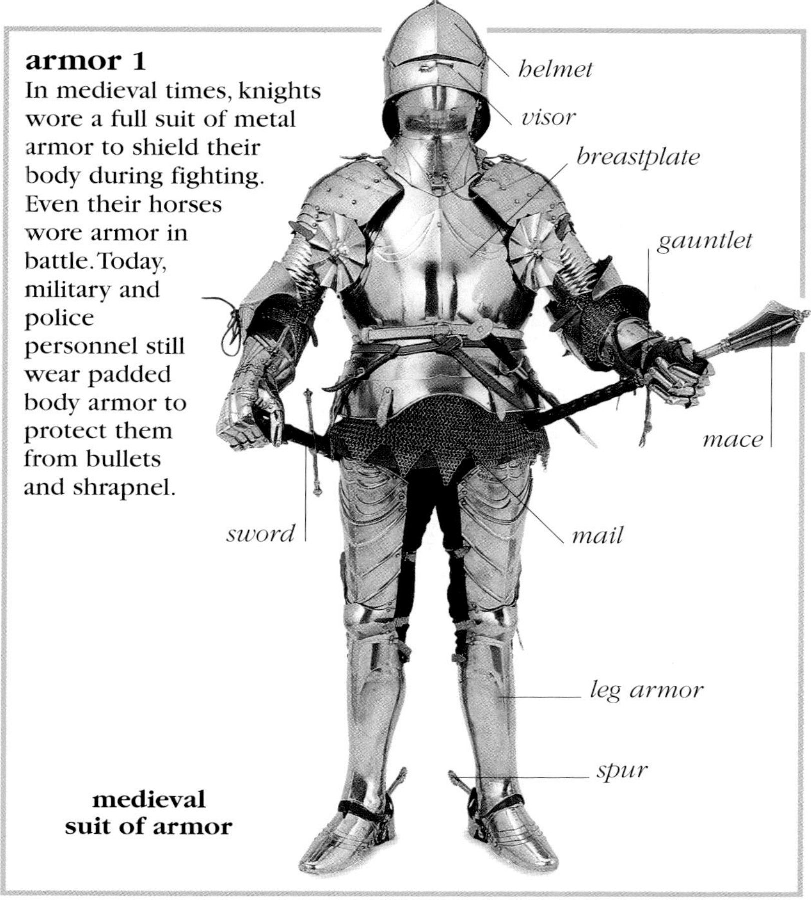


**armor 1**
In medieval times, knights wore a full suit of metal armor to shield their body during fighting. Even their horses wore armor in battle. Today, military and police personnel still wear padded body armor to protect them from bullets and shrapnel.

**medieval suit of armor**

**ar·mor** \'är-mər\ *n*
**1** ▲ a covering (as of metal) to protect the body in battle
**2** something that protects like metal armor ⟨safe in the *armor* of prosperity⟩
**3** armored forces and vehicles (as tanks)

**ar·mored** \'är-mərd\ *adj*
protected by or equipped with armor

**ar·mory** \'är-mə-rē\ *n, pl* **ar·mor·ies**
**1** a supply of arms
**2** a place where arms are kept and where soldiers are often trained
**3** a place where arms are made

**arm·pit** \'ärm-ˌpit\ *n*
the hollow under a person's arm where the arm joins the shoulder

**arm·rest** \'ärm-ˌrest\ *n*
a support for the arm

**ar·my** \'är-mē\ *n, pl* **armies**
**1** a large body of men and women trained for land warfare
**2** *often cap* the complete military organization of a nation for land warfare
**3** a great number of people or things
**4** a body of persons organized to advance an idea

**aro·ma** \ə-'rō-mə\ *n*
a noticeable and pleasant smell ⟨the *aroma* of coffee⟩

**ar·o·mat·ic** \ˌar-ə-'mat-ik\ *adj*
of, relating to, or having an aroma

**arose** *past of* ARISE

[1]**around** \ə-'rau̇nd\ *adv*
**1** in circumference ⟨a tree five feet *around*⟩
**2** in or along a curving course
**3** on all sides ⟨papers lying *around*⟩
**4** NEARBY ⟨stay *around* a while⟩
**5** here and there in various places ⟨travel *around* from state to state⟩
**6** to each in turn ⟨pass the candy *around*⟩
**7** in an opposite direction ⟨turn *around*⟩
**8** in the neighborhood of : APPROXIMATELY ⟨a price of *around* five dollars⟩

[2]**around** *prep*
**1** in a curving path along the outside boundary of ⟨walked *around* the house and peeked in the windows⟩
**2** on every side of
**3** here and there in ⟨travel *around* the country⟩
**4** near in number or amount ⟨they left *around* three o'clock⟩

**arouse** \ə-'rau̇z\ *vb* **aroused**; **arous·ing**
**1** to awaken from sleep
**2** to excite to action

**ar·range** \ə-'rānj\ *vb* **ar·ranged**; **ar·rang·ing**
**1** to put in order and especially a particular order
**2** to make plans for ⟨*arrange* a program⟩
**3** to come to an agreement about : SETTLE ⟨*arrange* a truce⟩
**4** to make a musical arrangement of
**ar·rang·er** *n*

**ar·range·ment** \ə-'rānj-mənt\ *n*
**1** a putting in order : the order in which things are put ⟨the *arrangement* of furniture in a room⟩
**2** preparation or planning done in advance ⟨make *arrangements* for a trip⟩
**3** something made by arranging ⟨a flower *arrangement*⟩
**4** a changing of a piece of music to suit voices or instruments for which it was not first written

[1]**ar·ray** \ə-'rā\ *vb*
**1** to set in order : DRAW UP ⟨soldiers *arrayed* for review⟩
**2** to dress especially in fine or beautiful clothing

[2]**array** *n*
**1** regular order or arrangement
**2** a group of persons (as soldiers) drawn up in regular order
**3** fine or beautiful clothing
**4** an impressive group
**5** a group of mathematical elements (as numbers or letters) arranged in rows and columns

**ar·rears** \ə-'rirz\ *n pl*
**1** the state of being behind in paying debts ⟨two months in *arrears*⟩
**2** unpaid and overdue debts

**art 4**
Paintings, films, music, and literature are all forms of art, created by artists to entertain or instruct their audience.

an oil painting

frames of movie film

a staff of music

printed books

**[1]ar·rest** \ə-ˈrest\ *vb*
**1** to stop the progress or movement of **:** CHECK ⟨*arrest* a disease⟩
**2** to take or keep in one's control by authority of law ⟨*arrest* someone on suspicion of robbery⟩
**3** to attract and hold the attention of

**[2]arrest** *n*
the act of taking or holding in one's control by authority of law

**ar·riv·al** \ə-ˈrī-vəl\ *n*
**1** the act of arriving
**2** a person or thing that has arrived

**ar·rive** \ə-ˈrīv\ *vb* **ar·rived**; **ar·riv·ing**
**1** to reach the place one started out for ⟨*arrive* home at six o'clock⟩
**2** to gain a goal or object ⟨*arrive* at a decision⟩
**3** COME 2 ⟨the time to leave finally *arrived*⟩
**4** to gain success

**ar·ro·gance** \ˈar-ə-gəns\ *n*
a sense of one's own importance that shows itself in a proud and insulting way

**ar·ro·gant** \ˈar-ə-gənt\ *adj*
overly proud of oneself or of one's own opinions
**ar·ro·gant·ly** *adv*

**ar·row** \ˈar-ō\ *n*
**1** ▶ a weapon that is made to be shot from a bow and is usually a stick with a point at one end and feathers at the other
**2** a mark to show direction

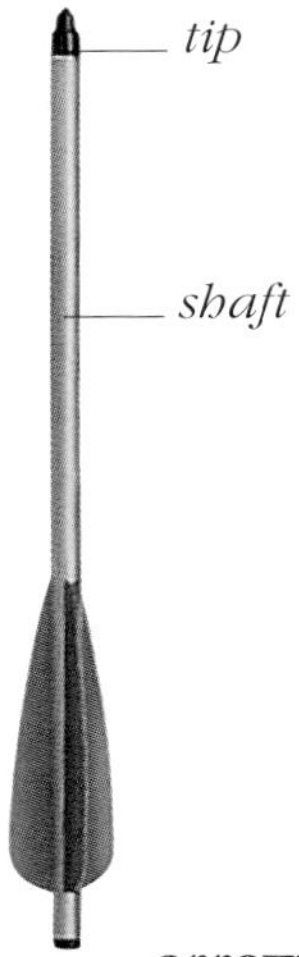

tip

shaft

**arrow 1**

**ar·row·head** \ˈar-ō-ˌhed\ *n*
the pointed end of an arrow

**ar·row·root** \ˈar-ō-ˌrüt, -ˌru̇t\ *n*
a starch obtained from the roots of a tropical plant

**ar·se·nal** \ˈärs-nəl, -n-əl\ *n*
a place where military equipment is made and stored

**ar·se·nic** \ˈärs-nik, -n-ik\ *n*
a solid poisonous chemical element that is usually steel gray and snaps easily

**ar·son** \ˈärs-n\ *n*
the illegal burning of a building or other property

**art** \ˈärt\ *n*
**1** skill that comes through experience or study ⟨the *art* of making friends⟩
**2** an activity that requires skill ⟨cooking is an *art*⟩
**3** an activity (as painting, music, or writing) whose purpose is making things that are beautiful to look at, listen to, or read
**4** ▲ works (as pictures, poems, or songs) made by artists

**ar·tery** \ˈärt-ə-rē\ *n, pl* **ar·ter·ies**
**1** one of the branching tubes that carry blood from the heart to all parts of the body
**2** a main road or waterway

**ar·te·sian well** \är-ˌtē-zhən-\ *n*
**1** a bored well from which water flows up like a fountain
**2** a deep bored well

**art·ful** \ˈärt-fəl\ *adj*
**1** done with or showing art or skill
**2** clever at taking advantage
**art·ful·ly** \-fə-lē\ *adv*
**art·ful·ness** *n*

**ar·thri·tis** \är-ˈthrīt-əs\ *n*
a condition in which the joints are painful and swollen

**ar·thro·pod** \ˈär-thrə-ˌpäd\ *n*
▶ any of a large group of animals (as crabs, insects, and spiders) with jointed limbs and a body made up of segments

**ar·ti·choke** \'ärt-ə-ˌchōk\ *n*
▶ a tall plant of the aster family with a flower head cooked and eaten as a vegetable

**artichoke:** flower head of an artichoke

**ar·ti·cle** \'ärt-i-kəl\ *n*
**1** a separate part of a document ⟨the third *article* of the constitution of the United States⟩
**2** a piece of writing other than fiction or poetry that forms a separate part of a publication (as a magazine)
**3** a word (as *a, an,* or *the*) used with a noun to limit it or make it clearer
**4** one of a class of things ⟨*articles* of clothing⟩

**[1]ar·tic·u·late** \är-'tik-yə-lət\ *adj*
**1** clearly understandable
**2** able to express oneself clearly and well
**ar·tic·u·late·ly** *adv*
**ar·tic·u·late·ness** *n*

**[2]ar·tic·u·late** \är-'tik-yə-ˌlāt\ *vb*
**ar·tic·u·lat·ed; ar·tic·u·lat·ing**
to speak clearly

**ar·tic·u·la·tion** \är-ˌtik-yə-'lā-shən\ *n*
the making of articulate sounds (as in speaking)

**ar·ti·fice** \'ärt-ə-fəs\ *n*
**1** a clever trick or device ⟨used every *artifice* to avoid work⟩
**2** clever skill ⟨a vase made with much *artifice*⟩

**artificial respiration** *n*
the forcing of air into and out of the lungs of a person whose breathing has stopped

**ar·til·lery** \är-'til-ə-rē\ *n*
**1** ▼ large firearms (as cannon or rockets)
**2** a branch of an army armed with artillery

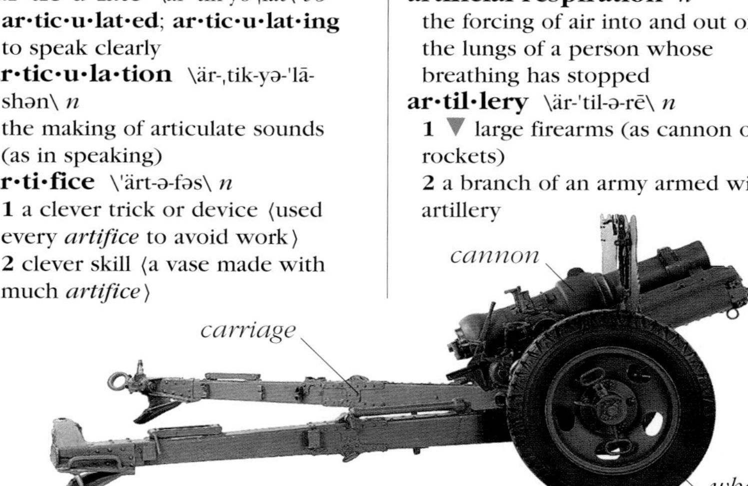


**artillery 1:** a mountain howitzer, capable of firing a shell in a high arc

**ar·ti·fi·cial** \ˌärt-ə-'fish-əl\ *adj*
**1** made by humans ⟨an *artificial* lake⟩
**2** not natural in quality ⟨an *artificial* smile⟩
**3** made to look like something natural ⟨*artificial* flowers⟩
**ar·ti·fi·cial·ly** *adv*

**ar·ti·san** \'ärt-ə-zən\ *n*
a person (as a carpenter) who works at a trade requiring skill with the hands

**art·ist** \'ärt-ist\ *n*
**1** ▼ a person skilled in one of the arts (as painting, sculpture, music, or writing)
**2** a person who has much ability in a job requiring skill

## arthropod

Arthropods have jointed outer skeletons — exoskeletons — which must be shed several times during their lives before they can grow to adult size.

**beetle**

**spider**

**lobster**

**artist 1**

**ar·tis·tic** \är-'tis-tik\ *adj*
**1** relating to art or artists
**2** showing skill and imagination
**ar·tis·ti·cal·ly** \-ti-kə-lē\ *adv*

**[1]-ary** \,er-ē, ə-rē\ *n suffix, pl* **-ar·ies**
thing or person belonging to or connected with ⟨bound*ary*⟩

**[2]-ary** *adj suffix*
of, relating to, or connected with ⟨legend*ary*⟩

**[1]as** \əz, az\ *adv*
**1** to the same degree or amount ⟨*as* good as gold⟩
**2** for example

**[2]as** *conj*
**1** in equal amount or degree with ⟨cold *as* ice⟩
**2** in the same way that ⟨do *as* I say⟩
**3** at the time that ⟨sang *as* they marched⟩
**4** BECAUSE, SINCE ⟨stayed home, *as* I had no car⟩

**[3]as** *pron*
**1** THAT, WHO, WHICH ⟨had the same name *as* my cousin⟩
**2** a fact that ⟨you are happy, *as* we all know⟩ ⟨*as* I said before, you must leave⟩

**[4]as** *prep*
**1** [4]LIKE 1 ⟨came dressed *as* a clown⟩
**2** in the position or role of ⟨works *as* an editor⟩

**as·bes·tos** \as-'bes-təs, az-\ *n*
a grayish mineral that separates easily into long flexible fibers and is used in making fireproof materials

**as·cend** \ə-'send\ *vb*
to go up : RISE

---

**Synonyms** ASCEND, MOUNT, and CLIMB mean to move upward or toward the top. ASCEND may suggest a gradual upward movement ⟨slowly *ascended* the staircase⟩. MOUNT suggests reaching the very top of something ⟨*mounted* the hill and placed a flag there⟩. CLIMB suggests effort and often the use of the hands and feet in moving up something ⟨*climbed* the rugged mountain⟩.

---

**as·cen·sion** \ə-'sen-chən\ *n*
the act or process of ascending

**as·cent** \ə-'sent\ *n*
**1** the act of rising or climbing upward
**2** an upward slope : RISE

**as·cer·tain** \,as-ər-'tān\ *vb*
to find out with certainty ⟨*ascertain* the date of the game⟩

**as·cribe** \ə-'skrīb\ *vb* **ascribed**; **as·crib·ing**
to think of as coming from a specified cause, source, or author

**asex·u·al** \'ā-'sek-shə-wəl\ *adj*
of, relating to, or being a process of reproduction (as the dividing of one cell into two cells) that does not involve the combining of male and female germ cells
**asex·u·al·ly** \-wə-lē\ *adv*

**[1]ash** \'ash\ *n*
▼ a common shade tree or timber tree that has winged seeds and bark with grooves

[1]ash

**[2]ash** *n*
**1** the solid matter left when something is completely burned
**2 ashes** *pl* the last remains of the dead human body

**ashamed** \ə-'shāmd\ *adj*
**1** feeling shame, guilt, or disgrace ⟨*ashamed* of my behavior⟩
**2** kept back by fear of shame ⟨*ashamed* to beg⟩

**ash·en** \'ash-ən\ *adj*
**1** of the color of ashes
**2** very pale

**ashore** \ə-'shōr\ *adv*
on or to the shore

**ash·tray** \'ash-,trā\ *n*
a container for tobacco ashes and cigarette and cigar butts

**ashy** \'ash-ē\ *adj* **ash·i·er**; **ash·i·est**
**1** of or relating to ashes
**2** very pale

**[1]Asian** \'ā-zhən\ *adj*
of or relating to Asia or the Asians

**[2]Asian** *n*
a person born or living in Asia

**Asian–Amer·i·can** \-ə-'mer-ə-kən\ *n*
an American who has Asian ancestors

**aside** \ə-'sīd\ *adv*
**1** to or toward the side ⟨stepped *aside*⟩
**2** out of the way : AWAY
**3** away from one's thought ⟨joking *aside*⟩

**aside from** *prep*
with the exception of ⟨*aside from* some bread, the food is gone⟩

**as if** *conj*
**1** the way it would be if ⟨it's *as if* we'd never left⟩
**2** the way one would if ⟨acted *as if* they'd never heard of me⟩
**3** [2]THAT 1 ⟨seems *as if* it never changes⟩

**ask** \'ask\ *vb*
**1** to seek information
**2** to make a request ⟨*ask* for help⟩
**3** to set as a price ⟨*ask* ten dollars⟩
**4** INVITE 2
**5** to behave as if looking ⟨you're *asking* for trouble⟩

**askance** \ə-'skans\ *adv*
**1** with a side glance
**2** with distrust or disapproval

**askew** \ə-'skyü\ *adv or adj*
out of line

*white asparagus*

*green asparagus*

**aslant** \ə-'slant\ *adv or adj*
in a slanting direction

**[1]asleep** \ə-'slēp\ *adj*
**1** being in a state of sleep
**2** having no feeling ⟨my foot was *asleep*⟩

**[2]asleep** *adv*
into a state of sleep

**as of** *prep*
[1]ON 5, AT ⟨we begin work *as of* Tuesday⟩ ⟨*as of* the moment, we are fine⟩

**as·par·a·gus** \ə-'spar-ə-gəs\ *n*
► a vegetable that is the thick young shoots of a garden plant that is related to the lilies and lives for many years

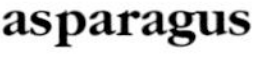

**asparagus**

**as·pect** \'as-ˌpekt\ *n*
**1** a position facing a certain direction
**2** a certain way in which something appears or may be thought of
**3** the appearance of an individual **:** LOOK

**as·pen** \'as-pən\ *n*
▼ a poplar tree whose leaves move easily in the breeze

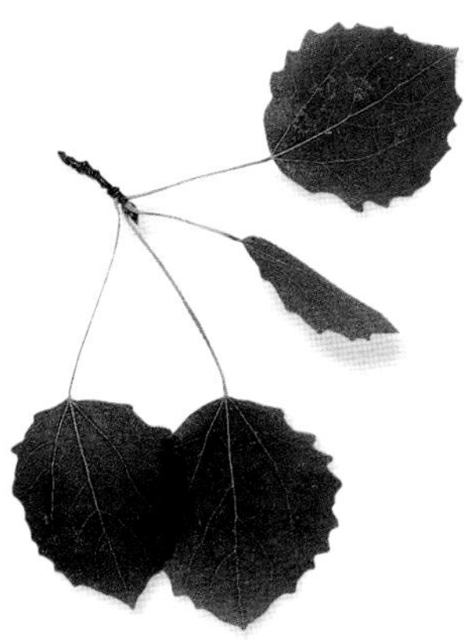

**aspen** leaves

**as·phalt** \'as-ˌfȯlt\ *n*
**1** a dark-colored substance obtained from natural beds or from petroleum
**2** any of various materials made of asphalt that are used for pavements and as a waterproof cement

**as·phyx·i·ate** \as-'fik-sē-ˌāt\ *vb* **as·phyx·i·at·ed**; **as·phyx·i·at·ing**
to cause (as a person) to become unconscious or die by cutting off the normal taking in of oxygen whether by blocking breathing or by replacing the oxygen of the air with another gas

**as·pi·rant** \'as-pə-rənt, ə-'spī-\ *n*
a person who aspires ⟨an *aspirant* to the presidency⟩

**as·pi·ra·tion** \ˌas-pə-'rā-shən\ *n*
a strong desire to achieve something high or great

**as·pire** \ə-'spīr\ *vb* **as·pired**; **as·pir·ing**
to very much want something and especially something high or fine ⟨*aspire* to greatness⟩

**as·pi·rin** \'as-prən, 'as-pə-rən\ *n*
a white drug used to relieve pain and fever

**ass** \'as\ *n*
**1** an animal that looks like but is smaller than the related horse and has shorter hair in mane and tail and longer ears **:** DONKEY
**2** a dull stupid person

**as·sail** \ə-'sāl\ *vb*
to attack violently with blows or words

**as·sail·ant** \ə-'sā-lənt\ *n*
a person who attacks

**as·sas·sin** \ə-'sas-n\ *n*
one who kills another person either for pay or from loyalty to a cause

**Word History** Long ago a secret Muslim group thought it was their religious duty to murder their enemies. Before they killed, the members of this group took a drug called "hashish." Because of this they became known in Arabic by a word that meant "a user of hashish." A Latin word was formed from this Arabic word. The English word *assassin* came from the Latin word.

**as·sas·si·nate** \ə-'sas-n-ˌāt\ *vb* **as·sas·si·nat·ed**; **as·sas·si·nat·ing**
to murder a usually important person by a surprise or secret attack **synonyms** see KILL

**as·sas·si·na·tion** \ə-ˌsas-n-'ā-shən\ *n*
the act of assassinating

[1]**as·sault** \ə-'sȯlt\ *n*
**1** a violent or sudden attack
**2** an unlawful attempt or threat to harm someone

[2]**assault** *vb*
to make an assault on

[1]**as·say** \'as-ˌā, a-'sā\ *n*
an analyzing (as of an ore or drug) to determine the presence, absence, or amount of one or more substances

[2]**as·say** \a-'sā, 'as-ˌā\ *vb*
to analyze (as an ore) for one or more valuable substances

**as·sem·blage** \ə-'sem-blij\ *n*
a collection of persons or things

**as·sem·ble** \ə-'sem-bəl\ *vb* **as·sem·bled**; **as·sem·bling**
**1** to collect in one place or group
**2** to fit (parts) together ⟨*assemble* a toy⟩
**3** to meet together ⟨the class *assembled*⟩ **synonyms** see GATHER
**as·sem·bler** *n*

**as·sem·bly** \ə-'sem-blē\ *n, pl* **as·sem·blies**
**1** a gathering of persons **:** MEETING ⟨a school *assembly*⟩
**2** *cap* a lawmaking body
**3** the act of assembling **:** the state of being assembled
**4** a collection of parts that make up a complete unit

[1]**as·sent** \ə-'sent\ *vb*
to agree to something

[2]**assent** *n*
an act of assenting **:** AGREEMENT

**as·sert** \ə-'sərt\ *vb*
**1** to state clearly and strongly ⟨*assert* an opinion loudly⟩
**2** to show the existence of ⟨*assert* your independence⟩
**assert oneself** to insist strongly that others respect one's rights

**as·ser·tion** \ə-'sər-shən\ *n*
**1** the act of asserting
**2** a positive statement

**as·sess** \ə-'ses\ *vb*
**1** to decide on the rate or amount of ⟨the jury *assessed* damages of $5000⟩
**2** to assign a value to for purposes of taxation
**3** to put a charge or tax on
**as·ses·sor** \-ər\ *n*

**as·set** \'as,et\ *n*
**1 assets** *pl* all the property belonging to a person or an organization
**2** ADVANTAGE 3 ⟨your sense of humor is an *asset*⟩

**as·sid·u·ous** \ə-'sij-ə-wəs\ *adj*
DILIGENT
**as·sid·u·ous·ly** *adv*
**as·sid·u·ous·ness** *n*

**as·sign** \ə-'sīn\ *vb*
**1** to appoint to a post or duty
**2** to give out with authority ⟨*assign* a lesson⟩
**3** to decide on definitely ⟨*assigned* a date for the trip⟩

**as·sign·ment** \ə-'sīn-mənt\ *n*
**1** the act of assigning ⟨the *assignment* of seats⟩
**2** something assigned ⟨an *assignment* in arithmetic⟩

**as·sim·i·late** \ə-'sim-ə-ˌlāt\ *vb* **as·sim·i·lat·ed**; **as·sim·i·lat·ing**
to take something in and make it part of the thing it has joined

A B C D E F G H I J K L M N O P Q R S T U V W X Y Z

**as·sim·i·la·tion** \ə-ˌsim-ə-ˈlā-shən\ *n*
the act or process of assimilating

[1]**as·sist** \ə-ˈsist\ *vb*
to give aid : HELP

[2]**assist** *n*
an act of assisting

**as·sis·tance** \ə-ˈsis-təns\ *n*
**1** the act of helping
**2** the help given

[1]**as·sis·tant** \ə-ˈsis-tənt\ *adj*
acting as a helper to another ⟨an *assistant* manager⟩

[2]**assistant** *n*
a person who assists another

[1]**as·so·ci·ate** \ə-ˈsō-shē-ˌāt\ *vb* **as·so·ci·at·ed**; **as·so·ci·at·ing**
**1** to join or come together as partners, friends, or companions
**2** to connect in thought ⟨*associate* soldiers with war⟩

[2]**as·so·ciate** \ə-ˈsō-shē-ət, -shət\ *adj*
**1** closely joined with another (as in duties or responsibility)
**2** having some but not all rights and privileges ⟨an *associate* member of the club⟩

[3]**as·so·ci·ate** \ə-ˈsō-shē-ət, -shət\ *n*
**1** a fellow worker : PARTNER
**2** a person who is one's friend or companion

**as·so·ci·a·tion** \ə-ˌsō-sē-ˈā-shən, -shē-\ *n*
**1** the act of associating : the state of being associated
**2** an organization of persons having a common interest ⟨an athletic *association*⟩
**3** a feeling, memory, or thought connected with a person, place, or thing

**as·so·cia·tive** \ə-ˈsō-shē-ˌāt-iv, -shət-iv\ *adj*
**1** serving to associate ⟨*associative* nerve cells⟩
**2** being a property of a mathematical operation (as addition or multiplication) in which the result is independent of the original grouping of the elements

**as·sort** \ə-ˈsȯrt\ *vb*
to sort into groups

**as·sort·ed** \ə-ˈsȯrt-əd\ *adj*
**1** made up of various kinds ⟨*assorted* chocolates⟩
**2** suited to one another ⟨a well *assorted* pair⟩

**as·sort·ment** \ə-ˈsȯrt-mənt\ *n*
**1** the act of assorting : the state of being assorted
**2** ▼ a collection of assorted things or persons

**as·sume** \ə-ˈsüm\ *vb* **as·sumed**; **as·sum·ing**
**1** to take upon oneself : UNDERTAKE ⟨*assume* new duties⟩
**2** to take over usually by force ⟨the dictator *assumed* power⟩
**3** to pretend to have or be ⟨*assumed* a look of happiness⟩
**4** to accept as true ⟨I *assume* you're right⟩

**assortment 2:** an assortment of vegetables

**as·sump·tion** \ə-ˈsəmp-shən\ *n*
**1** the act of assuming ⟨the *assumption* of power by a new ruler⟩
**2** something accepted as true ⟨the *assumption* that you will be here⟩

**as·sur·ance** \ə-ˈshu̇r-əns\ *n*
**1** the act of assuring
**2** the state of being certain
**3** a being sure and safe : SECURITY
**4** confidence in one's own self

**as·sure** \ə-ˈshu̇r\ *vb* **as·sured**; **as·sur·ing**
**1** to make safe : INSURE
**2** to give confidence to
**3** to make sure or certain ⟨*assure* the success of the plan⟩
**4** to inform positively

**as·sured** \ə-ˈshu̇rd\ *adj*
**1** made sure or certain
**2** very confident
**as·sured·ly** \-ˈshu̇r-əd-lē\ *adv*
**as·sured·ness** \-ˈshu̇r-əd-nəs\ *n*

**as·ter** \ˈas-tər\ *n*
▶ any of various herbs related to the daisies that have leafy stems and white, pink, purple, or yellow flower heads which bloom in the fall

**aster** flowers

**as·ter·isk** \ˈas-tə-ˌrisk\ *n*
a character * used in printing or in writing as a reference mark or to show that letters or words have been left out

**astern** \ə-ˈstərn\ *adv*
**1** behind a ship or airplane
**2** at or toward the stern
**3** [1]BACKWARD 1 ⟨full speed *astern*⟩

**as·ter·oid** \ˈas-tə-ˌrȯid\ *n*
▶ one of thousands of small planets that move in orbits mostly between those of Mars and Jupiter and have diameters from a fraction of a kilometer to nearly 800 kilometers

**asteroid**

**asth·ma** \ˈaz-mə\ *n*
an ailment of which difficult breathing, wheezing, and coughing are symptoms

**astir** \ə-ˈstər\ *adj*
**1** showing activity
**2** being out of bed : UP

**as to** *prep*
**1** with respect to : ABOUT ⟨confused *as to* what happened⟩
**2** ACCORDING TO 1 ⟨graded *as to* size and color⟩

**as·ton·ish** \ə-'stän-ish\ *vb*
to strike with sudden wonder or surprise **synonyms** see SURPRISE
**as·ton·ish·ment** \ə-'stän-ish-mənt\ *n*
great surprise : AMAZEMENT
**as·tound** \ə-'staund\ *vb*
to fill with puzzled wonder
**astray** \ə-'strā\ *adv or adj*
**1** off the right path or route
**2** in or into error
[1]**astride** \ə-'strīd\ *adv*
with one leg on each side
[2]**astride** *prep*
with one leg on each side of
**as·trin·gent** \ə-'strin-jənt\ *adj*
able or tending to shrink body tissues ⟨an *astringent* lotion⟩
**as·trin·gent·ly** *adv*
**astro-** \'as-trə, -trō\ *prefix*
star : heavens : astronomical
**as·trol·o·gy** \ə-'sträl-ə-jē\ *n*
the telling of fortunes by the stars
**as·tro·naut** \'as-trə-,nȯt\ *n*
▼ a traveler in a spacecraft

**astronaut**

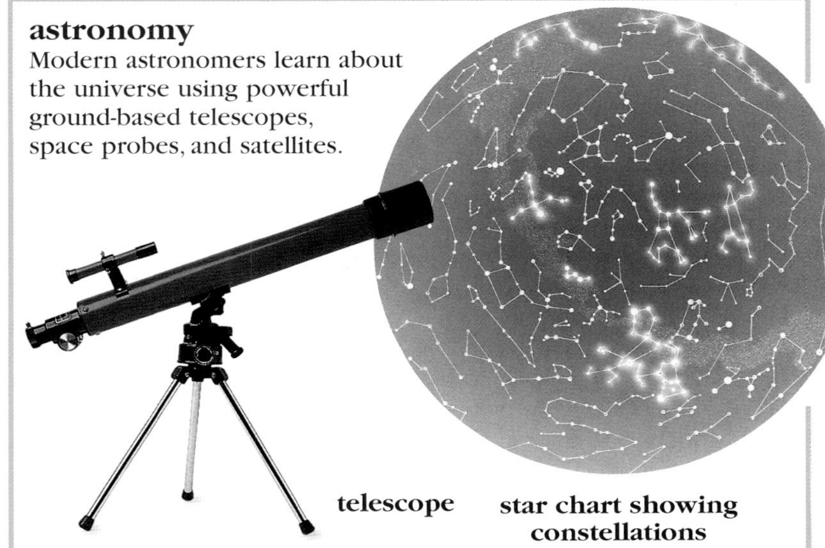


**as·tro·nau·tics** \,as-trə-'nȯt-iks\ *n*
the science of the construction and operation of spacecraft
**as·tron·o·mer** \ə-'strän-ə-mər\ *n*
a person who is skilled in astronomy
**as·tro·nom·i·cal** \,as-trə-'näm-i-kəl\ *or* **as·tro·nom·ic** \-ik\ *adj*
**1** of or relating to astronomy
**2** extremely or unbelievably large ⟨the cost was *astronomical*⟩
**as·tro·nom·i·cal·ly** *adv*
**as·tron·o·my** \ə-'strän-ə-mē\ *n*
▲ the science of celestial bodies and of their motions and makeup
**as·tute** \ə-'stüt, -'styüt\ *adj*
very alert and aware : CLEVER ⟨an *astute* observer⟩
**as·tute·ly** *adv*
**as·tute·ness** *n*
**asun·der** \ə-'sən-dər\ *adv or adj*
**1** into parts ⟨torn *asunder*⟩
**2** apart from each other in position ⟨their views of the problem were far *asunder*⟩
**as well as** *prep or conj*
in addition to : and also ⟨the cat is pretty *as well as* smart⟩
**asy·lum** \ə-'sī-ləm\ *n*
**1** a place of protection and shelter
**2** protection given especially to political refugees
**3** a place for the care of the poor or sick and especially of the insane
**at** \ət, at\ *prep*
**1** used to indicate a particular place or time ⟨they're *at* the door⟩ ⟨be here *at* six⟩
**2** used to indicate a goal ⟨swing *at* the ball⟩ ⟨laughed *at* me⟩
**3** used to indicate position or condition ⟨*at* rest⟩
**4** used to tell how or why something is done ⟨sold *at* auction⟩
**ate** *past of* EAT
[1]**-ate** \ət, ,āt\ *n suffix*
one acted upon in such a way
[2]**-ate** *n suffix*
office : rank : group of persons holding such an office or rank
[3]**-ate** *adj suffix*
marked by having
[4]**-ate** \,āt\ *vb suffix*
cause to be changed or influenced by : cause to become ⟨activ*ate*⟩ : furnish with ⟨aer*ate*⟩
**athe·ist** \'ā-thē-ist\ *n*
a person who believes there is no God
**ath·lete** \'ath-,lēt\ *n*
a person who is trained in or good at games and exercises that require physical skill, endurance, and strength
**athlete's foot** *n*
a fungus infection of the foot marked by blisters, itching, and cracks between and under the toes
**ath·let·ic** \ath-'let-ik\ *adj*
**1** of, relating to, or characteristic of athletes or athletics
**2** vigorously active
**3** STURDY 2

a b c d e f g h i j k l m n o p q r s t u v w x y z

A
B
C
D
E
F
G
H
I
J
K
L
M
N
O
P
Q
R
S
T
U
V
W
X
Y
Z

## athletics

Athletics events take place indoors or outdoors, on a track or in an arena. Some athletes compete for medals, while many people practice athletics for personal fitness.

**shot put** is a field event in which a heavy metallic ball — the shot — is "put" with a single pushing action.

**long jump** is a field event in which the athlete runs and then jumps from a mark on a board at the end of the run-up, landing into sand. The jump is measured from the mark to the nearest part of the sand touched by the athlete on landing.

**hurdling** is a track event in which the competitor runs and jumps over many hurdles to reach the end of the course.

**ath·let·ics** \ath-ˈlet-iks\ *n sing or pl*
◀ games, sports, and exercises requiring strength, endurance, and skill

**-ation** \ˈā-shən\ *n suffix*
action or process ⟨comput*ation*⟩ **:** something connected with an action or process ⟨discolor*ation*⟩

**-ative** \ət-iv, ˌāt-\ *adj suffix*
**1** of, relating to, or connected with ⟨authorit*ative*⟩
**2** tending to ⟨talk*ative*⟩

**at·las** \ˈat-ləs\ *n*
a book of maps

**ATM** \ˌā-ˌtē-ˈem\ *n*
a computerized machine that performs basic banking functions (as cash withdrawals)

**at·mo·sphere** \ˈat-mə-ˌsfir\ *n*
**1** ▼ the gas surrounding a celestial body **:** AIR
**2** the air in a particular place ⟨the stuffy *atmosphere* of this room⟩
**3** a surrounding influence or set of conditions ⟨the home *atmosphere*⟩

**at·mo·spher·ic** \ˌat-mə-ˈsfir-ik, -ˈsfer-\ *adj*
of or relating to the atmosphere

**atoll** \ˈa-ˌtȯl, -ˌtäl\ *n*
a ring-shaped coral island or string of islands consisting of a coral reef surrounding a lagoon

**at·om** \ˈat-əm\ *n*
**1** a tiny particle **:** BIT
**2** ▶ the smallest particle of an element that can exist alone or in combination

**Word History** The English word *atom* came from a Greek word that meant "not able to be divided." People believed that if something were divided into its smallest parts those parts would be atoms. The atoms themselves, however, could not be divided. This is how the atom got its name.

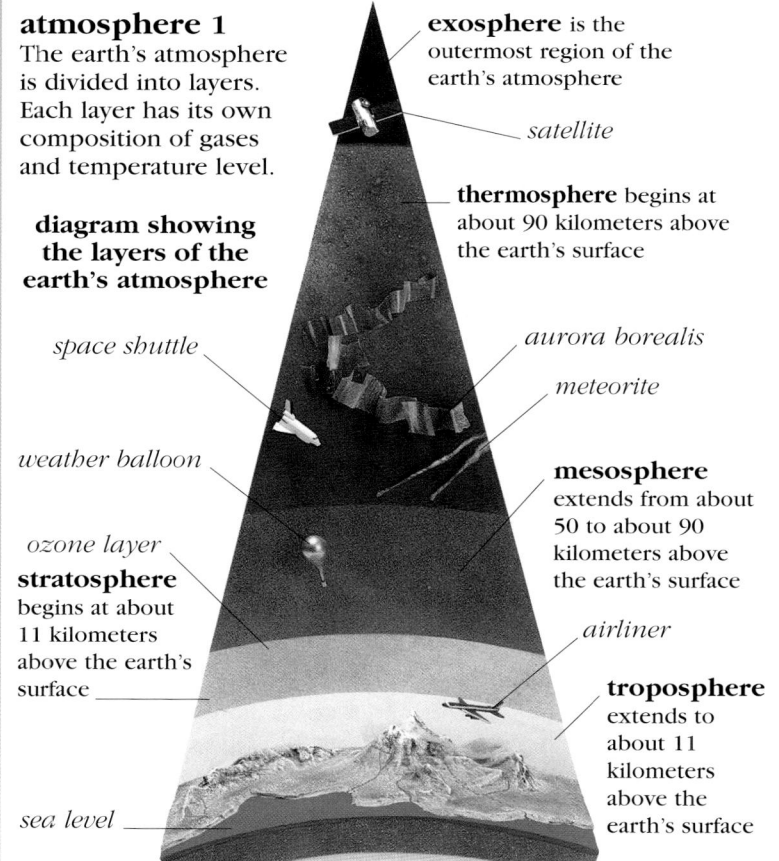

**atmosphere 1**
The earth's atmosphere is divided into layers. Each layer has its own composition of gases and temperature level.

**diagram showing the layers of the earth's atmosphere**

**exosphere** is the outermost region of the earth's atmosphere

*satellite*

**thermosphere** begins at about 90 kilometers above the earth's surface

*space shuttle*

*aurora borealis*

*meteorite*

*weather balloon*

**mesosphere** extends from about 50 to about 90 kilometers above the earth's surface

*ozone layer*

**stratosphere** begins at about 11 kilometers above the earth's surface

*airliner*

**troposphere** extends to about 11 kilometers above the earth's surface

*sea level*

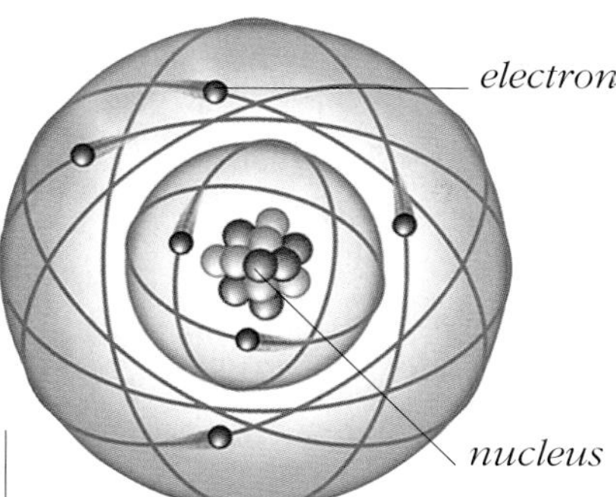

**atom 2:** diagram of the structure of an atom

**atom·ic** \ə-ˈtäm-ik\ *adj*
**1** of or relating to atoms ⟨*atomic* physics⟩
**2** NUCLEAR 3 ⟨*atomic* energy⟩

**atomic bomb** *n*
a bomb whose great power is due to the sudden release of the energy in the nuclei of atoms

**at·om·iz·er** \ˈat-ə-ˌmī-zər\ *n*
▼ a device for spraying a liquid (as a perfume or disinfectant)

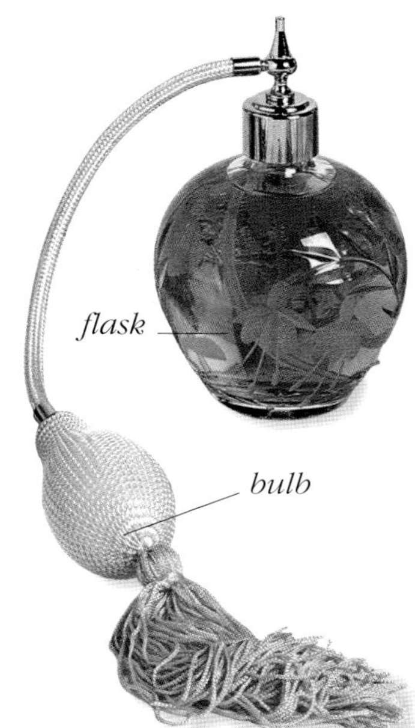

**atomizer:** perfume atomizer

**atone** \ə-ˈtōn\ *vb* **atoned; aton·ing**
to do something to make up for a wrong that has been done

**atone·ment** \ə-ˈtōn-mənt\ *n*
a making up for an offense or injury

**atop** \ə-ˈtäp\ *prep*
on top of

A B C D E F G H I J K L M N O P Q R S T U V W X Y Z

**atro·cious** \ə-'trō-shəs\ *adj*
**1** savagely brutal, cruel, or wicked
**2** very bad ⟨*atrocious* weather⟩
**atro·cious·ly** *adv*
**atro·cious·ness** *n*

**atroc·i·ty** \ə-'träs-ət-ē\ *n, pl* **atroc·i·ties**
an atrocious act, object, or situation

**at sign** *n*
the symbol @ used especially as part of an e-mail address

**at·tach** \ə-'tach\ *vb*
**1** to take (money or property) legally in order to obtain payment of a debt ⟨*attach* a person's salary⟩
**2** to fasten one thing to another
**3** to bind by feelings of affection ⟨a boy *attached* to his dog⟩
**4** to assign by authority ⟨*attach* an officer to headquarters⟩
**5** to think of as belonging to something ⟨*attach* no importance to it⟩

**at·tach·ment** \ə-'tach-mənt\ *n*
**1** connection by feelings of affection or regard
**2** a device that can be attached to a machine or tool
**3** a connection by which one thing is joined to another

**[1]at·tack** \ə-'tak\ *vb*
**1** to take strong action against : ASSAULT ⟨the dog *attacked* a skunk⟩
**2** to use unfriendly words against
**3** to begin to affect or to act upon harmfully ⟨the camp was *attacked* by fever⟩
**4** to start to work on ⟨*attacked* my homework⟩
**at·tack·er** *n*

**[2]attack** *n*
**1** the act of attacking
**2** beginning to work
**3** a spell of sickness

**at·tain** \ə-'tān\ *vb*
**1** to reach as a desired goal ⟨*attain* an ambition⟩
**2** to come into possession of
**3** to arrive at ⟨*attain* the hilltop ⟩
**at·tain·able** \ə-'tā-nə-bəl\ *adj*

**at·tain·ment** \ə-'tān-mənt\ *n*
**1** the act of attaining : the state of being attained
**2** ACCOMPLISHMENT 3

**at·tar** \'at-ər\ *n*
a sweet-smelling oil from flowers

**[1]at·tempt** \ə-'tempt\ *vb*
**1** to try to do or perform ⟨*attempt* an escape⟩
**2** to try to do something ⟨*attempt* to solve a problem⟩

**[2]attempt** *n*
the act or an instance of attempting

**at·tend** \ə-'tend\ *vb*
**1** to pay attention to ⟨*attend* to what I say⟩
**2** to go with especially as a servant or companion ⟨a ruler *attended* by the court⟩
**3** to care for ⟨nurses *attend* the sick⟩
**4** to go to or be present at ⟨*attend* a party⟩
**5** to take charge ⟨*attend* to taking out the rubbish⟩

**at·ten·dance** \ə-'ten-dəns\ *n*
**1** the act of attending
**2** the number of persons present

**[1]at·ten·dant** \ə-'ten-dənt\ *n*
a person who attends something or someone

**[2]attendant** *adj*
coming with or following closely as a result ⟨*attendant* circumstances⟩

**at·ten·tion** \ə-'ten-chən\ *n*
**1** the act or the power of fixing one's mind on something : careful listening or watching
**2** a state of being aware ⟨attract *attention*⟩
**3** careful thinking about something so as to be able to take action on it ⟨a matter requiring *attention*⟩
**4** an act of kindness or politeness
**5** a military posture with body stiff and straight, heels together, and arms at the sides

**attention deficit disorder** *n*
a condition in which a person has trouble paying attention or is so active and impulsive that it is difficult to function in school or at work

**at·ten·tive** \ə-'tent-iv\ *adj*
**1** paying attention ⟨an *attentive* listener⟩
**2** being thoughtful and polite ⟨*attentive* to their parents⟩
**at·ten·tive·ly** *adv*
**at·ten·tive·ness** *n*

**at·test** \ə-'test\ *vb*
to give proof of

**at·tic** \'at-ik\ *n*
a room or a space just under the roof of a building

**[1]at·tire** \ə-'tīr\ *vb* **at·tired**; **at·tir·ing**
to put clothes and especially fine clothes on

**[2]attire** *n*
▼ clothing meant for a particular occasion ⟨formal *attire*⟩

**[2]attire:** formal attire for performing in a concert

**at·ti·tude** \'at-ə-,tüd, -,tyüd\ *n*
**1** the position of the body, or of the parts of the body, or of an object
**2** a feeling or opinion about a certain fact or situation

**at·tor·ney** \ə-'tər-nē\ *n, pl* **at·tor·neys**
a person who acts as agent for another in dealing with business or legal matters

**at·tract** \ə-'trakt\ *vb*
**1** to draw to or toward oneself ⟨a magnet *attracts* iron⟩
**2** to draw by appealing to interest or feeling ⟨*attract* attention⟩

**at·trac·tion** \ə-'trak-shən\ *n*
**1** the act or power of attracting
**2** something that attracts or pleases

**at·trac·tive** \ə-'trak-tiv\ *adj*
having the power or quality of attracting : PLEASING
**at·trac·tive·ly** *adv*
**at·trac·tive·ness** *n*

[1]**at·tri·bute** \'at-rə-ˌbyüt\ *n*
**1** a quality belonging to a particular person or thing
**2** a word (as an adjective) indicating a quality

[2]**at·trib·ute** \ə-'trib-yət\ *vb*
**at·trib·ut·ed**; **at·trib·ut·ing**
**1** to explain as the cause of ⟨we *attribute* their success to hard work⟩
**2** to think of as likely to be a quality of a person or thing ⟨*attribute* stubbornness to mules⟩

**at·tri·bu·tion** \ˌat-rə-'byü-shən\ *n*
the act of attributing

**at·tune** \ə-'tün, -'tyün\ *vb*
**at·tuned**; **at·tun·ing**
to bring into harmony **:** TUNE

**atyp·i·cal** \'ā-'tip-i-kəl\ *adj*
not typical
**atyp·i·cal·ly** *adv*

**au·burn** \'ȯ-bərn\ *adj*
of a reddish brown color ⟨*auburn* hair⟩

[1]**auc·tion** \'ȯk-shən\ *n*
a public sale at which things are sold to those who offer to pay the most

[2]**auction** *vb*
to sell at auction

**auc·tion·eer** \ˌȯk-shə-'nir\ *n*
a person in charge of auctions

**au·da·cious** \ȯ-'dā-shəs\ *adj*
**1** very bold and daring **:** FEARLESS
**2** very rude **:** INSOLENT
**au·da·cious·ly** *adv*
**au·da·cious·ness** *n*

**au·dac·i·ty** \ȯ-'das-ət-ē\ *n, pl* **au·dac·i·ties**
the fact or an instance of being audacious

**au·di·ble** \'ȯd-ə-bəl\ *adj*
loud enough to be heard
**au·di·bly** \-blē\ *adv*

**au·di·ence** \'ȯd-ē-əns\ *n*
**1** a group that listens or watches (as at a play or concert)
**2** a chance to talk with a person of very high rank
**3** those of the general public who give attention to something said, done, or written

[1]**au·dio** \'ȯd-ē-ˌō\ *adj*
**1** of or relating to sound or its reproduction
**2** relating to or used in the transmitting or receiving of sound (as in radio or television)

[2]**audio** *n*
**1** the transmitting, receiving, or reproducing of sound
**2** the section of television equipment that deals with sound

**au·dio·tape** \'ȯd-ē-ō-ˌtāp\ *n*
a tape recording of sound

**au·dio·vi·su·al** \ˌȯd-ē-ō-'vizh-ə-wəl\ *adj*
of, relating to, or using both sound and sight ⟨*audiovisual* teaching aids⟩

[1]**au·dit** \'ȯd-ət\ *n*
a thorough check of business accounts

[2]**audit** *vb*
to make an audit of

[1]**au·di·tion** \ȯ-'dish-ən\ *n*
a short performance to test the talents of a singer, dancer, or actor

[2]**audition** *vb*
to test or try out in an audition

**au·di·tor** \'ȯd-ət-ər\ *n*
**1** a person who listens especially as a member of a radio or TV audience
**2** a person who audits business accounts

**au·di·to·ri·um** \ˌȯd-ə-'tōr-ē-əm\ *n*
**1** ▼ the part of a public building where an audience sits
**2** a hall used for public gatherings

**au·di·to·ry** \'ȯd-ə-ˌtōr-ē\ *adj*
of or relating to hearing

**au·ger** \'ȯ-gər\ *n*
a tool used for boring holes

**aught** \'ȯt\ *n*
ZERO 1

**aug·ment** \ȯg-'ment\ *vb*
to increase in size, amount, or degree

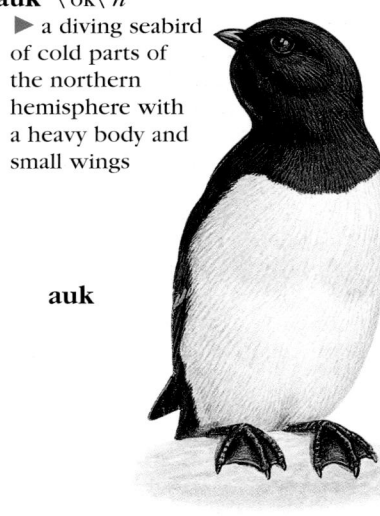

**auditorium 1:** model of an auditorium in a 19th-century theater

**au·gust** \ȯ-'gəst\ *adj*
being grand and noble **:** MAJESTIC
**au·gust·ly** *adv*
**au·gust·ness** *n*

**Au·gust** \'ȯ-gəst\ *n*
the eighth month of the year

**Word History** The first Roman calendar began the year with March. The sixth month was the one we now know as August. The first Latin name given to this month came from a Latin word that meant "sixth." Then the emperor Augustus decided that he wanted to have a month named after him. The sixth month was given his name. The English word *August* came from the emperor's Latin name.

**auk** \'ȯk\ *n*
► a diving seabird of cold parts of the northern hemisphere with a heavy body and small wings

**auk**

**aunt** \'ant, 'änt\ *n*
**1** a sister of one's parent
**2** the wife of one's uncle

**au·ra** \'ȯr-ə\ *n*
a feeling that seems to be given off by a person or thing ⟨an *aura* of mystery⟩

**au·ral** \'ȯr-əl\ *adj*
of or relating to the ear or sense of hearing
**au·ral·ly** *adv*

**au·ri·cle** \'ȯr-i-kəl\ *n*
the part of the heart that receives blood from the veins

**au·ro·ra bo·re·al·is** \ə-,rōr-ə-,bōr-ē-'al-əs\ *n*
▼ broad bands of light that have a magnetic and electrical source and that appear in the sky at night especially in the arctic regions

**aurora borealis**
in the night sky

**aus·pic·es** \'ȯ-spə-səz\ *n pl*
support and guidance of a sponsor ⟨a concert given under the *auspices* of the school⟩

**aus·pi·cious** \ȯ-'spish-əs\ *adj*
**1** promising success ⟨an *auspicious* beginning⟩
**2** PROSPEROUS 1 ⟨the team had a very *auspicious* season⟩
**aus·pi·cious·ly** *adv*

**aus·tere** \ȯ-'stir\ *adj*
**1** seeming or acting harsh and stern
**2** [1]PLAIN 1 ⟨an *austere* room⟩
**aus·tere·ly** *adv*

**aus·ter·i·ty** \ȯ-'ster-ət-ē\ *n, pl* **aus·ter·i·ties**
**1** an austere act or manner
**2** lack of all luxury

[1]**Aus·tra·lian** \ȯ-'strāl-yən\ *adj*
of or relating to Australia or the Australians

[2]**Australian** *n*
a person born or living in Australia

**aut-** \ȯt\ *or* **au·to-** \'ȯt-ə, 'ȯt-ō\ *prefix*
**1** self : same one ⟨*auto*biography⟩
**2** automatic

**au·then·tic** \ə-'thent-ik, ȯ-\ *adj*
being really what it seems to be : GENUINE ⟨an *authentic* signature⟩
**au·then·ti·cal·ly** \-i-kə-lē\ *adv*

**au·thor** \'ȯ-thər\ *n*
**1** a person who writes something (as a novel)
**2** one that starts or creates ⟨the *author* of a new tax system⟩

**au·thor·i·ta·tive** \ə-'thȯr-ə-,tāt-iv\ *adj*
having or coming from authority ⟨an *authoritative* order⟩
**au·thor·i·ta·tive·ly** *adv*
**au·thor·i·ta·tive·ness** *n*

**au·thor·i·ty** \ə-'thȯr-ət-ē\ *n, pl* **au·thor·i·ties**
**1** a fact or statement used to support a position
**2** a person looked to as an expert
**3** power to influence the behavior of others
**4** persons having powers of government ⟨state *authorities*⟩

**au·tho·rize** \'ȯ-thə-,rīz\ *vb* **au·tho·rized**; **au·tho·riz·ing**
**1** to give authority to : EMPOWER ⟨*authorized* to act for them⟩
**2** to give legal or official approval to

**au·thor·ship** \'ȯ-thər-,ship\ *n*
the profession of writing

**au·to** \'ȯt-ō\ *n, pl* **au·tos**
AUTOMOBILE

**auto-** see AUT-

**au·to·bi·og·ra·phy** \,ȯt-ə-bī-'äg-rə-fē\ *n, pl* **au·to·bi·og·ra·phies**
the biography of a person written by that person

[1]**au·to·graph** \'ȯt-ə-,graf\ *n*
a person's signature written by hand

[2]**autograph** *vb*
to write one's signature in or on (as a book)

**au·to·mate** \'ȯt-ə-,māt\ *vb* **au·to·mat·ed**; **au·to·mat·ing**
to make automatic ⟨*automate* a factory⟩

[1]**au·to·mat·ic** \,ȯt-ə-'mat-ik\ *adj*
**1** INVOLUNTARY ⟨*automatic* blinking of eyelids⟩
**2** being a machine or device that acts by or regulates itself ⟨an *automatic* washer⟩
**au·to·mat·i·cal·ly** \-i-kə-lē\ *adv*

[2]**automatic** *n*
**1** an automatic machine or device
**2** an automatic firearm

**au·to·ma·tion** \,ȯt-ə-'mā-shən\ *n*
**1** the method of making a machine, a process, or a system work automatically
**2** automatic working of a machine, process, or system by mechanical or electronic devices that take the place of humans

[1]**au·to·mo·bile** \,ȯt-ə-mō-'bēl, 'ȯt-ə-mō-,bēl\ *adj*
AUTOMOTIVE

[2]**automobile** *n*
▶ a usually four-wheeled vehicle that runs on its own power and is designed to carry passengers

## automobile

The first mass-produced automobiles were produced in the US about one hundred years ago. The US now manufactures almost 7 million automobiles each year.

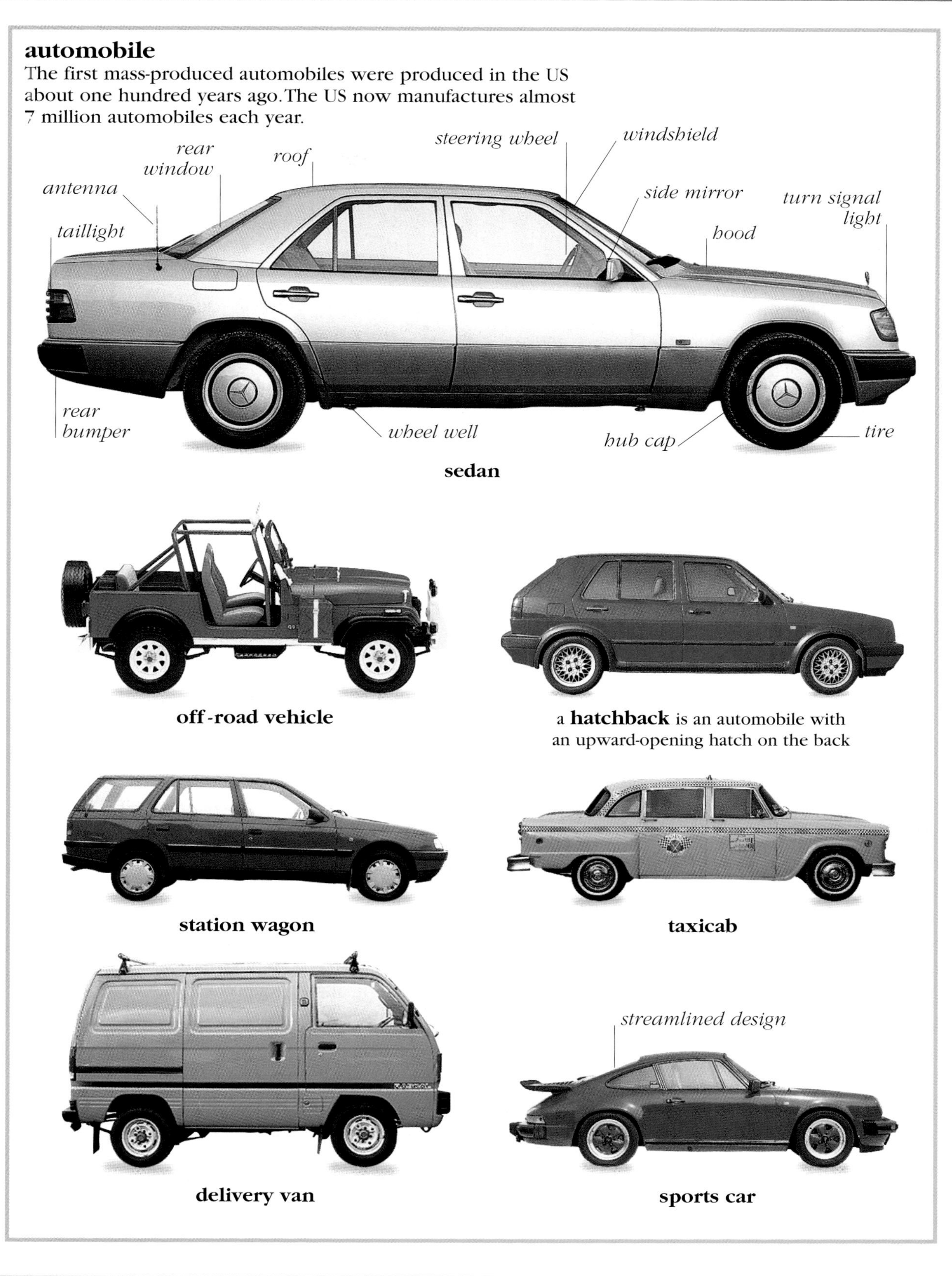


**sedan**

**off-road vehicle**

a **hatchback** is an automobile with an upward-opening hatch on the back

**station wagon**

**taxicab**



**delivery van**

**sports car**

**au·to·mo·tive** \ˌȯt-ə-ˈmōt-iv\ *adj*
SELF-PROPELLED

**au·tumn** \ˈȯt-əm\ *n*
the season between summer and winter that in the northern hemisphere is usually the months of September, October, and November

**au·tum·nal** \ȯ-ˈtəm-nəl\ *adj*
of or relating to autumn

**[1]aux·il·ia·ry** \ȯg-ˈzil-yə-rē, -ˈzil-ə-rē, -ˈzil-rē\ *adj*
available to provide something extra ⟨a sailboat with an *auxiliary* engine⟩

**[2]auxiliary** *n, pl* **aux·il·ia·ries**
**1** an auxiliary person, group, or device
**2** HELPING VERB

**[1]avail** \ə-ˈvāl\ *vb*
to be of use or help

**[2]avail** *n*
help toward reaching a goal **:** USE ⟨our work was of little *avail*⟩

**avail·able** \ə-ˈvā-lə-bəl\ *adj*
**1** SUITABLE, USABLE ⟨used every *available* excuse to get out of work⟩
**2** possible to get **:** OBTAINABLE ⟨*available* supplies⟩

**av·a·lanche** \ˈav-ə-ˌlanch\ *n*
a large mass of snow and ice or of earth or rock sliding down a mountainside or over a cliff

**av·a·rice** \ˈav-ə-rəs, ˈav-rəs\ *n*
strong desire for riches **:** GREED

**av·a·ri·cious** \ˌav-ə-ˈrish-əs\ *adj*
greedy for riches
**av·a·ri·cious·ly** *adv*
**av·a·ri·cious·ness** *n*

**avenge** \ə-ˈvenj\ *vb* **avenged**; **aveng·ing**
to take revenge for
**aveng·er** *n*

**av·e·nue** \ˈav-ə-ˌnü, -ˌnyü\ *n*
**1** a way of reaching a goal ⟨saw the job as an *avenue* to success⟩
**2** a usually wide street

**[1]av·er·age** \ˈav-ə-rij, ˈav-rij\ *n*
**1** ARITHMETIC MEAN
**2** something usual in a group, class, or series

**[2]average** *adj*
**1** equaling or coming close to an average ⟨the *average* age of the class is eleven⟩
**2** being ordinary or usual ⟨the *average* person⟩

**[3]average** *vb* **av·er·aged**; **av·er·ag·ing**
**1** to amount to usually
**2** to find the average of

**averse** \ə-ˈvərs\ *adj*
having a feeling of dislike ⟨*averse* to exercise⟩

**aver·sion** \ə-ˈvər-zhən\ *n*
**1** a strong dislike
**2** something strongly disliked

**avert** \ə-ˈvərt\ *vb*
**1** to turn away ⟨*avert* one's eyes⟩
**2** to keep from happening ⟨*avert* disaster⟩

**avi·ary** \ˈā-vē-ˌer-ē\ *n, pl* **avi·ar·ies**
a place (as a large cage) where birds are kept

**avi·a·tion** \ˌā-vē-ˈā-shən\ *n*
**1** the flying of aircraft
**2** the designing and making of aircraft

**avi·a·tor** \ˈā-vē-ˌāt-ər\ *n*
the pilot of an aircraft

**av·id** \ˈav-əd\ *adj*
very eager ⟨an *avid* football fan⟩
**av·id·ly** *adv*

**av·o·ca·do** \ˌav-ə-ˈkäd-ō, ˌäv-\ *n, pl* **av·o·ca·dos**
▼ a usually green fruit that is shaped like a pear or an egg, grows on a tropical American tree, and has a rich oily flesh

*pit*

**avocado**

**av·o·ca·tion** \ˌav-ə-ˈkā-shən\ *n*
an interest or activity that is not one's regular job **:** HOBBY

**avoid** \ə-ˈvȯid\ *vb*
to keep away from

**avoid·ance** \ə-ˈvȯid-ns\ *n*
a keeping away from something ⟨*avoidance* of trouble⟩

**avow** \ə-ˈvau̇\ *vb*
to declare openly and frankly

**avow·al** \ə-ˈvau̇-əl\ *n*
an open declaration

**await** \ə-ˈwāt\ *vb*
**1** to wait for ⟨*await* a train⟩
**2** to be ready or waiting for ⟨dinner was *awaiting* them on their arrival⟩

**[1]awake** \ə-ˈwāk\ *vb* **awoke** \-ˈwōk\; **awo·ken** \-ˈwō-kən\ *or* **awaked** \-ˈwākt\; **awak·ing**
**1** to arouse from sleep **:** wake up ⟨*awoke* at seven⟩
**2** to become conscious or aware of something ⟨*awoke* to their danger⟩

**[2]awake** *adj*
not asleep

**awak·en** \ə-ˈwā-kən\ *vb*
[1]AWAKE

**[1]award** \ə-ˈwȯrd\ *vb*
**1** to give by judicial decision ⟨*award* damages⟩
**2** to give or grant as deserved or needed ⟨*award* a medal⟩ ⟨*award* a pension⟩

**[2]award:** the Purple Heart, a military award

**[2]award** *n*
▲ something (as a prize) that is awarded

**aware** \ə-ˈwaər, -ˈweər\ *adj*
having or showing understanding or knowledge **:** CONSCIOUS ⟨*aware* of what's happening⟩
**aware·ness** *n*

**awash** \ə-ˈwȯsh, -ˈwäsh\ *adv or adj*
**1** washed by waves or tide
**2** floating about
**3** flooded or covered with water

**[1]away** \ə-ˈwā\ *adv*
1 from this or that place ⟨go *away*⟩
2 in another place or direction ⟨turn *away*⟩
3 out of existence ⟨the echo died *away*⟩
4 from one's possession ⟨gave *away* a fortune⟩
5 without stopping or slowing down ⟨talk *away*⟩
6 at or to a great distance in space or time **:** FAR ⟨*away* back in 1910⟩

**[2]away** *adj*
1 [1]ABSENT 1 ⟨be *away* from home⟩
2 DISTANT 1 ⟨a lake ten kilometers *away*⟩

**[1]awe** \ˈȯ\ *n*
a feeling of mixed fear, respect, and wonder

**[2]awe** *vb* **awed**; **aw·ing**
to fill with awe

**awe·some** \ˈȯ-səm\ *adj*
causing a feeling of awe

**aw·ful** \ˈȯ-fəl\ *adj*
1 causing fear or terror ⟨an *awful* disaster⟩
2 very disagreeable or unpleasant ⟨an *awful* cold⟩
3 very great ⟨an *awful* lot⟩

**aw·ful·ly** \ˈȯ-flē, *especially for 1* -fə-lē\ *adv*
1 in a disagreeable or unpleasant manner
2 to a very great degree ⟨was *awfully* tired⟩

**awhile** \ə-ˈhwīl, ə-ˈwīl\ *adv*
for a while **:** for a short time ⟨sit down and rest *awhile*⟩

**awk·ward** \ˈȯ-kwərd\ *adj*
1 not graceful **:** CLUMSY
2 likely to embarrass ⟨an *awkward* question⟩
3 difficult to use or handle ⟨*awkward* tools⟩
**awk·ward·ly** *adv*
**awk·ward·ness** *n*

**awl** \ˈȯl\ *n*
▼ a pointed tool for making small holes (as in leather or wood)

**awl**

**aw·ning** \ˈȯ-ning\ *n*
a cover (as of canvas) that shades or shelters like a roof

**awoke** *past of* AWAKE

**awoken** *past participle of* AWAKE

**awry** \ə-ˈrī\ *adv or adj*
1 turned or twisted to one side **:** ASKEW
2 out of the right course **:** AMISS ⟨the plans had gone *awry*⟩

**ax** *or* **axe** \ˈaks\ *n*
▼ a tool that has a heavy head with a sharp edge fixed to a handle and is used for chopping and splitting wood

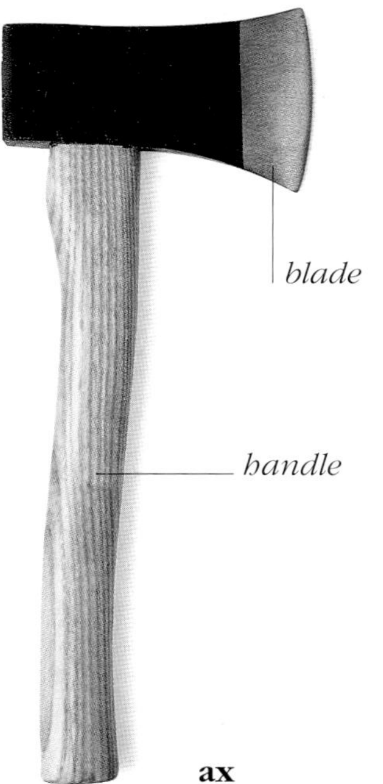


**ax**

**ax·i·om** \ˈak-sē-əm\ *n*
1 MAXIM
2 a statement thought to be clearly true

**ax·is** \ˈak-səs\ *n, pl* **ax·es** \ˈak-ˌsēz\
a straight line about which a body or a geometric figure rotates or may be supposed to rotate ⟨the earth's *axis*⟩

**ax·le** \ˈak-səl\ *n*
▼ a pin or shaft on or with which a wheel or pair of wheels turns

*direction of axle movement*
*wheel*
*axle*

**axle:** model of an axle

**ax·on** \ˈak-ˌsän\ *n*
a long fiber that carries impulses away from a nerve cell

**[1]aye** \ˈī\ *adv*
[1]YES 1 ⟨*aye, aye*, sir⟩

**[2]aye** \ˈī\ *n*
an affirmative vote or voter ⟨the *ayes* have it⟩

**aza·lea** \ə-ˈzāl-yə\ *n*
a usually small rhododendron that sheds its leaves in the fall and has flowers of many colors which are shaped like funnels

**azure** \ˈazh-ər\ *n*
the blue color of the clear daytime sky

# Bb

**The sounds of B:** The letter **B** is a consonant that has only one sound in English.

The sound of **B** is the same in words like **baby**, **blueprint**, **brown**, **rabbit**, **hubbub**, **tub**, **tube**, and most other words. A double **B** in a word sounds the same as a single **B**.

In a few words, the letter **B** is silent. It is not pronounced at all in words like **climb**, **crumb**, **comb**, and **doubt**. Silent **B** never occurs at the beginning of a word. It occurs most often following the letter **M**, at the end of a word or syllable.

**b** \'bē\ *n, pl* **b's** *or* **bs** \'bēz\ *often cap*
**1** the second letter of the English alphabet
**2** a grade that shows a student's work is good

[1]**baa** \'ba, 'bä\ *n*
the cry of a sheep

[2]**baa** *vb*
to make the cry of a sheep

[1]**bab·ble** \'bab-əl\ *vb* **bab·bled**; **bab·bling** \'bab-ə-ling, 'bab-ling\
**1** to make meaningless sounds
**2** to talk foolishly
**3** to make the sound of a brook
**bab·bler** \'bab-ə-lər, 'bab-lər\ *n*

[2]**babble** *n*
**1** talk that is not clear
**2** the sound of a brook

**babe** \'bāb\ *n*
[1]BABY 1 ⟨a *babe* in arms⟩

**baboons**

**ba·boon** \ba-'bün\ *n*
▲ a large monkey of Africa and Asia with a doglike face

[1]**ba·by** \'bā-bē\ *n, pl* **babies**
**1** a very young child
**2** the youngest of a group
**3** a childish person

[2]**baby** *adj*
[1]YOUNG 1 ⟨a *baby* deer⟩

[3]**baby** *vb* **ba·bied**; **ba·by·ing**
to treat as a baby

**ba·by·hood** \'bā-bē-,hu̇d\ *n*
**1** the time in a person's life when he or she is a baby
**2** the state of being a baby

**ba·by·ish** \'bā-bē-ish\ *adj*
like a baby

**ba·by–sit** \'bā-bē-,sit\ *vb* **ba·by–sat** \-,sat\; **ba·by–sit·ting**
to care for children usually during a short absence of the parents

**ba·by–sit·ter** \'bā-bē-,sit-ər\ *n*
a person who baby-sits

**baby tooth** *n*
: MILK TOOTH

**bach·e·lor** \'bach-ə-lər, 'bach-lər\
a man who has not married

**ba·cil·lus** \bə-'sil-əs\ *n, pl* **ba·cil·li** \-'sil-,ī\
**1** a rod-shaped bacterium that forms internal spores
**2** a bacterium that causes disease : GERM, MICROBE

[1]**back** \'bak\ *n*
**1** ▶ the rear part of the human body from the neck to the end of the spine : the upper part of the body of an animal
**2** the part of something that is opposite or away from the front part
**3** a player in a team game who plays behind the forward line of players
**backed** \'bakt\ *adj*

[2]**back** *adv*
**1** to, toward, or at the rear ⟨the crowd moved *back*⟩
**2** in or to a former time, state, or place ⟨some years *back*⟩ ⟨went *back* home⟩
**3** under control ⟨kept *back* my anger⟩
**4** in return or reply ⟨talk *back*⟩
**back and forth** backward and forward : from one place to another

[3]**back** *adj*
**1** located at the back ⟨the *back* door⟩
**2** not yet paid : OVERDUE ⟨*back* rent⟩
**3** no longer current ⟨*back* issues of a magazine⟩

[4]**back** *vb*
**1** to give support or help to
**2** to move back
**back·er** *n*

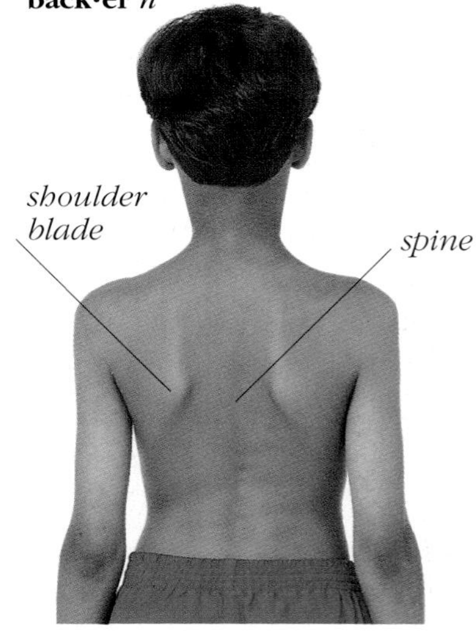


[1]**back 1:**
the back of a boy

**back·bone** \'bak-'bōn\ *n*
**1** the column of bones in the back : SPINAL COLUMN
**2** the strongest part of something
**3** firmness of character

[1]**back·fire** \'bak-,fīr\ *n*
**1** a fire that is set to stop the spread of a forest fire or a grass fire by burning off a strip of land ahead of it
**2** a loud engine noise that happens when fuel ignites with a valve open

[2]**backfire** *vb* **back·fired**; **back·fir·ing**
**1** to make a backfire
**2** to have a result opposite to what was planned ⟨the joke *backfired*⟩

**back·ground** \'bak-,grau̇nd\ *n*
**1** the scenery or ground that is behind a main figure or object
**2** a position that attracts little attention ⟨tried to keep in the *background*⟩
**3** the total of a person's experience, knowledge, and education

[1]**back·hand** \'bak-,hand\ *n*
**1** ▶ a stroke made with the back of the hand turned in the direction in which the hand is moving
**2** handwriting in which the letters slant to the left

[2]**backhand** *adv or adj*
with a backhand

**back·hand·ed** \'bak-,han-dəd\ *adj*
**1** [2]BACKHAND ⟨a *backhanded* blow⟩
**2** not sincere ⟨*backhanded* praise⟩

**back of** *prep*
[2]BEHIND 1

**back·pack** \'bak-,pak\ *n*
a carrying case strapped on the back : KNAPSACK

**back·stage** \'bak-'stāj\ *adv or adj*
in or to the area behind the stage

**back·track** \'bak-,trak\ *vb*
to go back over a course or a path

[1]**back·ward** \'bak-wərd\ *or* **back·wards** \-wərdz\ *adv*
**1** toward the back ⟨look *backward*⟩
**2** with the back first ⟨ride *backward*⟩
**3** opposite to the usual way ⟨count *backward*⟩

[2]**backward** *adj*
**1** turned toward the back
**2** BASHFUL
**3** slow in learning or development

**back·wa·ter** \'bak-,wȯt-ər, -,wät-\ *n*
**1** water held or turned back from its course
**2** a backward place or condition

**back·woods** \'bak-'wu̇dz\ *n pl*
**1** wooded or partly cleared areas away from cities
**2** a place that is backward in culture

**back·yard** \'bak-'yärd\ *n*
an area in the back of a house

**ba·con** \'bā-kən\ *n*
salted and smoked meat from the sides and the back of a pig

[1]**backhand 1:**
a backhand stroke in tennis

**bac·te·ri·al** \bak-'tir-ē-əl\ *adj*
relating to or caused by bacteria ⟨a *bacterial* infection⟩

**bac·te·ri·um** \bak-'tir-ē-əm\ *n, pl* **bac·te·ria** \-ē-ə\
any of numerous microscopic organisms that are single-celled and are important to humans because of their chemical activities and as causes of disease

**bad** \'bad\ *adj* **worse** \'wərs\; **worst** \'wərst\
**1** not good : POOR ⟨*bad* weather⟩
**2** not favorable ⟨a *bad* impression⟩
**3** not fresh or sound ⟨*bad* fish⟩
**4** not good or right : EVIL ⟨a *bad* person⟩ ⟨*bad* behavior⟩
**5** not enough ⟨*bad* lighting⟩
**6** UNPLEASANT ⟨*bad* news⟩
**7** HARMFUL ⟨*bad* for the health⟩
**8** SEVERE 4 ⟨a *bad* cold⟩
**9** not correct ⟨*bad* spelling⟩
**10** [1]ILL 4, SICK ⟨felt *bad* from a cold⟩
**11** SORRY 1 ⟨felt *bad* about my mistake⟩
**bad·ness** *n*

---

**Synonyms** BAD, EVIL, WICKED, and NAUGHTY mean not doing or being what is right. BAD is used of anyone or anything that is objectionable ⟨had to stay after school for *bad* behavior⟩. EVIL is a more powerful word than *bad* and often suggests something threatening ⟨criminals planning *evil* deeds⟩. WICKED is used of someone or something that is truly and deliberately bad ⟨a very *wicked* ruler who put many people to death⟩. NAUGHTY is usually used of children or of unimportant wrongdoing ⟨a *naughty* child knocked over the milk⟩.

---

**bade** *past of* BID

**badge** \'baj\ *n*
something worn to show that a person belongs to a certain group or rank

[1]**bad·ger** \'baj-ər\ *n*
▼ a furry burrowing animal with short thick legs and long claws on the front feet

[1]**badger**

[2]**badger** *vb*
to annoy again and again

**bad·ly** \'bad-lē\ *adv* **worse** \'wərs\; **worst** \'wərst\
**1** in a bad manner
**2** very much ⟨wanted the toy *badly*⟩

**bad·min·ton** \ˈbad-ˌmint-n\ *n*
▼ a game in which a shuttlecock is hit back and forth over a net by players using light rackets

*racket*
*shuttlecock*

**badminton**

**baf·fle** \ˈbaf-əl\ *vb* **baf·fled**; **baf·fling** \ˈbaf-ə-ling, ˈbaf-ling\
to defeat or check by confusing

**[1]bag** \ˈbag\ *n*
**1** a container made of flexible material (as paper or plastic)
**2** [1]PURSE 1, HANDBAG
**3** SUITCASE

**[2]bag** *vb* **bagged**; **bag·ging**
**1** to swell out
**2** to put into a bag
**3** to kill or capture in hunting

**ba·gel** \ˈbā-gəl\ *n*
a hard roll shaped like a doughnut

**bag·gage** \ˈbag-ij\ *n*
► the trunks, suitcases, and personal belongings of travelers

**baggage**

**bag·gy** \ˈbag-ē\ *adj* **bag·gi·er**; **bag·gi·est**
hanging loosely or puffed out like a bag ⟨*baggy* pants⟩

**bag·pipe** \ˈbag-ˌpīp\ *n*
a musical instrument played especially in Scotland that consists of a tube, a bag for air, and pipes from which the sound comes

**[1]bail** \ˈbāl\ *vb*
to dip and throw out water from a boat — usually used with *out* ⟨*bail* out a leaky boat⟩

**[2]bail** *n*
a promise or a deposit of money needed to free a prisoner until his or her trial

**[3]bail** *vb*
to get the release of (a prisoner) by giving bail

**bail out** *vb*
to jump out of an airplane with a parachute

**[1]bait** \ˈbāt\ *vb*
**1** to torment by mean or unjust attacks ⟨*baited* him by using a nickname he hated⟩
**2** to put bait on or in ⟨*bait* a trap⟩

**[2]bait** *n*
something used in luring especially to a hook or a trap ⟨used worms as *bait* for fish⟩

**bake** \ˈbāk\ *vb* **baked**; **bak·ing**
**1** to cook or become cooked in a dry heat especially in an oven
**2** to dry or harden by heat

**bak·er** \ˈbā-kər\ *n*
a person who bakes and sells bread, cakes, or pastry

**baker's dozen** *n*
THIRTEEN

**bak·ery** \ˈbā-kə-rē, ˈbā-krē\ *n, pl* **bak·er·ies**
a place where bread, cakes, and pastry are made or sold

**baking powder** *n*
a powder used to make the dough rise in making baked goods (as cakes or muffins)

**baking soda** *n*
SODIUM BICARBONATE

**[1]bal·ance** \ˈbal-əns\ *n*
**1** ▼ an instrument for weighing
**2** a steady position or condition ⟨kept my *balance*⟩
**3** equal total sums on the two sides of a bookkeeping account
**4** something left over : REMAINDER
**5** the amount by which one side of an account is greater than the other ⟨a *balance* of ten dollars on the credit side⟩

**[1]balance 1:** weighing scales

**Word History** The first meaning of the word *balance* was "an instrument used to weigh things." (Other meanings have come from this one.) Some weighing instruments have two scales. The English word *balance* came from a Latin word that meant "having two scales." This Latin word was a compound. It was formed from a Latin prefix that meant "two" and a Latin noun that meant "plate" or "scale."

**[2]balance** *vb* **bal·anced**; **bal·anc·ing**
**1** to make the two sides of (an account) add up to the same total
**2** to make equal in weight or number
**3** to weigh against one another : COMPARE
**4** to put in or as if in balance

**bal·co·ny** \ˈbal-kə-nē\ *n, pl* **bal·co·nies**
**1** a platform enclosed by a low wall or a railing built out from the side of a building
**2** a platform inside a building extending out over part of a main floor (as of a theater)

**bald** \'bȯld\ *adj*
**1** lacking a natural covering (as of hair)
**2** ¹PLAIN 3 ⟨the *bald* facts⟩
**bald·ness** *n*

**bald eagle** *n*
▼ the common North American eagle that when full-grown has white head and neck feathers

**¹bale** \'bāl\ *n*
a large bundle of goods tightly tied for storing or shipping ⟨a *bale* of cotton⟩

bald eagle

**²bale** *vb* **baled**; **bal·ing**
to make up into a bale
**bal·er** *n*

**ba·leen** \bə-'lēn\ *n*
a tough material that hangs down from the upper jaw of whales without teeth and is used by the whale to filter small ocean animals out of seawater

**¹balk** \'bȯk\ *n*
HINDRANCE

**²balk** *vb*
**1** to keep from happening or succeeding ⟨rain *balked* our plans for a hike⟩
**2** to stop short and refuse to go

**balky** \'bȯ-kē\ *adj* **balk·i·er**; **balk·i·est**
likely to balk ⟨a *balky* engine⟩

**¹ball** \'bȯl\ *n*
**1** something round or roundish ⟨a *ball* of twine⟩
**2** a usually round object used in a game or sport
**3** a game or sport (as baseball) played with a ball
**4** a solid usually round shot for a gun
**5** the rounded bulge at the base of the thumb or big toe ⟨the *ball* of the foot⟩
**6** a pitched baseball that is not hit and is not a strike

**²ball** *vb*
to make or come together into a ball

**³ball** *n*
a large formal party for dancing

**bal·lad** \'bal-əd\ *n*
**1** a simple song
**2** a short poem suitable for singing that tells a story in simple language

**ball–and–socket joint** *n*
a joint (as in the shoulder) in which a rounded part can move in many directions in a socket

**bal·last** \'bal-əst\ *n*
**1** heavy material used to make a ship steady or to control the rising of a balloon
**2** gravel, cinders, or crushed stone used in making a roadbed ⟨*ballast* for railroad tracks⟩

**ball bearing** *n*
**1** a bearing in which the revolving part turns on metal balls that roll easily in a groove
**2** one of the balls in a ball bearing

**bal·le·ri·na** \,bal-ə-'rē-nə\ *n*
► a female ballet dancer

**bal·let** \'ba-,lā, ba-'lā\ *n*
**1** a stage dance that tells a story in movement and pantomime
**2** a group that performs ballets

**¹bal·loon** \bə-'lün\ *n*
**1** a bag that rises and floats above the ground when filled with heated air or with a gas that is lighter than air
**2** a toy consisting of a rubber bag that can be blown up with air or gas
**3** an outline containing words spoken or thought by a character (as in a cartoon)

**²balloon** *vb*
to swell or puff out like a balloon

**¹bal·lot** \'bal-ət\ *n*
**1** an object and especially a printed sheet of paper used in voting
**2** the action or a system of voting
**3** the right to vote
**4** the number of votes cast

**Word History** The Italian city of Venice was a republic long ago. The people of Venice had secret voting. They used balls with different colors or marks to vote. The Italian word for a ball used to vote meant "little ball." The English word *ballot* came from this Italian word. Anything used to cast a secret vote can be called a *ballot*. It may be a ball. It may be a piece of paper.

**²ballot** *vb*
to vote or decide by ballot

**ball·point** \'bȯl-,pȯint\ *n*
a pen whose writing point is a small metal ball that inks itself from an inner supply

ballerina

**ball·room** \'bȯl-ˌrüm, -ˌru̇m\ *n*
a large room for dances

**balmy** \'bäm-ē, 'bäl-mē\ *adj* **balm·i·er**; **balm·i·est**
gently soothing ⟨a *balmy* breeze⟩

**bal·sa** \'bȯl-sə\ *n*
the very light but strong wood of a tropical American tree

**bal·sam** \'bȯl-səm\ *n*
**1** a material with a strong pleasant smell that oozes from some plants
**2** a plant (as the evergreen **balsam fir** often used as a Christmas tree) that yields balsam

**bal·us·ter** \'bal-əs-tər\ *n*
a short post that supports the upper part of a railing

**bal·us·trade** \'bal-əs-ˌtrād\ *n*
a row of balusters topped by a rail to serve as an open fence (as along the edge of a terrace or a balcony)

**bam·boo** \bam-'bü\ *n*
a tall treelike tropical grass with a hard jointed stem that is used in making furniture and in building

[1]**ban** \'ban\ *vb* **banned**; **ban·ning**
to forbid especially by law or social pressure

[2]**ban** *n*
an official order forbidding something ⟨a *ban* on the sale of a book⟩

**ba·nana** \bə-'nan-ə\ *n*
▶ a yellow or red fruit that is shaped somewhat like a finger and grows in bunches on a large treelike tropical plant (**banana plant** or **banana tree**) with very large leaves

banana

[1]**band** \'band\ *n*
**1** something that holds together or goes around something else
**2** a strip of material around or across something ⟨a hat *band*⟩
**3** a range of frequencies (as of radio waves)

[2]**band** *vb*
**1** to put a band on **:** tie together with a band
**2** to unite in a group ⟨*banded* together for protection⟩

[3]**band** *n*
**1** a group of persons or animals
**2** a group of musicians performing together

[1]**ban·dage** \'ban-dij\ *n*
a strip of material used especially to dress and bind up wounds

[2]**bandage** *vb* **ban·daged**; **ban·dag·ing**
to bind or cover with a bandage

**ban·dan·na** *or* **ban·dana** \ban-'dan-ə\ *n*
a large handkerchief usually with a colorful design printed on it

**ban·dit** \'ban-dət\ *n*
a lawless person **:** one who lives outside the law

**band·stand** \'band-ˌstand\ *n*
an outdoor platform used for band concerts

**band·wag·on** \'ban-ˌdwag-ən\ *n*
**1** a wagon carrying musicians in a parade
**2** a candidate, side, or movement that attracts growing support

[1]**bang** \'bang\ *vb*
to beat, strike, or shut with a loud noise

[2]**bang** *n*
**1** a violent blow
**2** a sudden loud noise
**3** [2]THRILL 1 ⟨I got a *bang* out of it⟩

[3]**bang** *n*
hair cut short across the forehead — usually used in pl.

[4]**bang** *vb*
to cut (hair) short and squarely across

**ban·ish** \'ban-ish\ *vb*
**1** to force to leave a country
**2** to drive away **:** DISMISS ⟨*banish* fears⟩

**ban·ish·ment** \'ban-ish-mənt\ *n*
a banishing from a country

**ban·is·ter** \'ban-ə-stər\ *n*
**1** one of the slender posts used to support the handrail of a staircase
**2** a handrail and its supporting posts
**3** the handrail of a staircase

**ban·jo** \'ban-jō\ *n, pl* **banjos**
▶ a musical instrument with four or five strings and a fretted neck

parchment-covered body

banjo

[1]**bank** \'bangk\ *n*
**1** a mound or ridge especially of earth
**2** something shaped like a mound ⟨a *bank* of clouds⟩
**3** an undersea elevation **:** SHOAL ⟨the *banks* of Newfoundland⟩
**4** the rising ground at the edge of a river, lake, or sea ⟨the *banks* of the Hudson⟩

[2]**bank** *vb*
**1** to raise a bank around
**2** to heap up in a bank ⟨*banked* the snow against the door⟩
**3** to build (a curve) with the road or track sloping upward from the inside edge
**4** to cover with fuel or ashes so as to reduce the speed of burning ⟨*bank* a fire⟩
**5** to tilt an airplane to one side when turning

[3]**bank** *n*
**1** a place of business that lends, exchanges, takes care of, or issues money
**2** a small closed container in which money may be saved
**3** a storage place for a reserve supply ⟨blood *bank*⟩

[4]**bank** *vb*
**1** to have an account in a bank ⟨we *bank* locally⟩
**2** to deposit in a bank ⟨*bank* ten dollars⟩

[5]**bank** *n*
a group or series of objects arranged together in a row ⟨a *bank* of seats⟩

**bank·er** \'bang-kər\ *n*
a person who is engaged in the business of a bank

**bank·ing** \'bang-king\ *n*
the business of a bank or banker

[1]**bank·rupt** \'bang-ˌkrəpt\ *n*
a person who becomes unable to pay his or her debts and whose property is by court order divided among the creditors

**[2]bankrupt** *adj*
unable to pay one's debts
**[3]bankrupt** *vb*
to make bankrupt
**bank·rupt·cy** \'bang-ˌkrəpt-sē\ *n*, *pl* **bank·rupt·cies**
the state of being bankrupt
**[1]ban·ner** \'ban-ər\ *n*
**1** [1]FLAG
**2** a piece of cloth with a design, a picture, or some writing on it
**[2]banner** *adj*
unusually good or satisfactory ⟨a *banner* year for apples⟩
**ban·quet** \'bang-kwət\ *n*
a formal dinner for many people often in honor of someone
**ban·tam** \'bant-əm\ *n*
▼ a miniature breed of domestic chicken often raised for a hobby

**bantam:** a bantam rooster

**[1]ban·ter** \'bant-ər\ *vb*
to speak to in a friendly but teasing way
**[2]banter** *n*
good-natured teasing and joking
**bap·tism** \'bap-ˌtiz-əm\ *n*
the act or ceremony of baptizing
**bap·tize** \bap-'tīz, 'bap-ˌtīz\ *vb* **bap·tized**; **bap·tiz·ing**
**1** to dip in water or sprinkle water on as a part of the ceremony of receiving into the Christian church
**2** to give a name to as in the ceremony of baptism **:** CHRISTEN
**[1]bar** \'bär\ *n*
**1** a usually slender rigid piece (as of wood or metal) that has many uses (as for a lever or barrier)

**[2]barbecue 1**

**2** a usually rectangular solid piece or block of something ⟨a *bar* of soap⟩
**3** something that blocks the way
**4** a submerged or partly submerged bank along a shore or in a river
**5** a court of law
**6** the profession of law
**7** a straight stripe, band, or line longer than it is wide
**8** a counter on which liquor is served
**9** a place of business for the sale of alcoholic drinks
**10** a vertical line across a musical staff marking equal measures of time
**11** [1]MEASURE 6
**[2]bar** *vb* **barred**; **bar·ring**
**1** to fasten with a bar ⟨*bar* the doors⟩
**2** to block off ⟨*barred* by a chain across the road⟩
**3** to shut out
**[3]bar** *prep*
with the exception of
**barb** \'bärb\ *n*
a sharp point that sticks out and backward (as from the tip of an arrow or fishhook)
**barbed** \'bärbd\ *adj*
**bar·bar·i·an** \bär-'ber-ē-ən, -'bar-\ *n*
an uncivilized person
**bar·bar·ic** \bär-'bar-ik\ *adj*
of, relating to, or characteristic of barbarians

**bar·ba·rous** \'bär-bə-rəs, -brəs\ *adj*
**1** not civilized ⟨a *barbarous* tribe⟩
**2** CRUEL 2, HARSH ⟨*barbarous* treatment of captives⟩
**bar·ba·rous·ly** *adv*
**[1]bar·be·cue** \'bär-bi-ˌkyü\ *vb* **bar·be·cued**; **bar·be·cu·ing**
**1** to cook over or before an open source of heat
**2** to cook in a highly seasoned sauce
**[2]barbecue** *n*
**1** ◀ a large animal roasted whole
**2** an outdoor social gathering at which food is barbecued and eaten
**bar·ber** \'bär-bər\ *n*
a person whose business is cutting and dressing hair and shaving beards
**bard** \'bärd\ *n*
**1** a person in ancient societies skilled at composing and singing songs about heroes
**2** POET
**[1]bare** \'baər, 'beər\ *adj* **bar·er**; **bar·est**
**1** ▼ having no covering **:** NAKED ⟨trees *bare* of leaves⟩
**2** [1]EMPTY 1 ⟨the cupboard was *bare*⟩
**3** having nothing left over or added **:** MERE
**4** [1]PLAIN 3 ⟨the *bare* facts⟩
**synonyms** see NAKED

*branches are bare in winter*

*branches have leaves in summer*

**[1]bare 1:**
a deciduous tree

[2]**bare** *vb* **bared**; **bar·ing**
UNCOVER 1, 2

**bare·back** \'baər-,bak, 'beər-\ *adv or adj*
on the bare back of a horse
**:** without a saddle

**bare·foot** \'baər-,fu̇t, 'beər-\ *adv or adj*
with the feet bare

**bare·head·ed** \'baər-'hed-əd, 'beər-\ *adv or adj*
with the head bare **:** without a hat

**bare·ly** \'baər-lē, 'beər-\ *adv*
with nothing to spare ⟨*barely* enough to eat⟩

[1]**bar·gain** \'bär-gən\ *n*
**1** an agreement between persons settling what each is to give and receive in a business deal ⟨make a *bargain* to mow a neighbor's lawn for five dollars⟩
**2** something bought or offered for sale at a desirable price

[2]**bargain** *vb*
to talk over the terms of a purchase or agreement

**barge** \'bärj\ *n*
a broad boat with a flat bottom used chiefly in harbors and on rivers and canals ⟨a coal *barge*⟩

**bar graph** *n*
a chart that uses parallel bars whose lengths are in proportion to the numbers represented

**bari·tone** \'bar-ə-,tōn\ *n*
**1** a male singing voice between bass and tenor in range
**2** a singer having a baritone voice
**3** a horn used in bands that is lower than the trumpet but higher than the tuba

[1]**bark** \'bärk\ *vb*
**1** to make the short loud cry of a dog
**2** to shout or speak sharply

[2]**bark** *n*
the sound made by a barking dog

[3]**bark** *n*
the outside covering of the trunk, branches, and roots of a tree

[4]**bark** *vb*
to rub or scrape the skin off

[5]**bark** *or* **barque** \'bärk\ *n*
**1** a small sailing boat
**2** a three-masted ship with foremast and mainmast square-rigged

**bark·er** \'bär-kər\ *n*
a person who stands at the entrance to a show or a store and tries to attract people to it

**bar·ley** \'bär-lē\ *n*
a cereal grass with flowers in dense heads that is grown for its grain which is used mostly to feed farm animals or make malt

**bar mitz·vah** \bär-'mits-və\ *n, often cap B&M*
**1** a Jewish boy who at 13 years of age takes on religious responsibilities
**2** the ceremony recognizing a boy as a bar mitzvah

**barnacle**

**barn** \'bärn\ *n*
a building used for storing grain and hay and for housing farm animals

**bar·na·cle** \'bär-ni-kəl\ *n*
▲ a small saltwater shellfish that fastens itself on rocks or on wharves and the bottoms of ships

**barn·yard** \'bärn-,yärd\ *n*
a usually fenced area next to a barn

*pressure scale*

**barometer**

**ba·rom·e·ter** \bə-'räm-ət-ər\ *n*
▲ an instrument that measures air pressure and is used to forecast changes in the weather

**bar·on** \'bar-ən\ *n*
a member of the lowest rank of the British nobility

**bar·on·ess** \'bar-ə-nəs\ *n*
**1** the wife or widow of a baron
**2** a woman who holds the rank of a baron in her own right

**bar·on·et** \'bar-ə-nət\ *n*
the holder of a rank of honor below a baron but above a knight

**ba·ro·ni·al** \bə-'rō-nē-əl\ *adj*
of, relating to, or suitable for a baron

**barque** *variant of* BARK

**bar·racks** \'bar-əks, -iks\ *n sing or pl*
a building or group of buildings in which soldiers live

**bar·rage** \bə-'räzh\ *n*
a barrier formed by continuous artillery or machine-gun fire directed upon a narrow strip of ground

[1]**bar·rel** \'bar-əl\ *n*
**1** a round bulging container that is longer than it is wide and has flat ends
**2** the amount contained in a full barrel
**3** something shaped like a cylinder

[2]**barrel** *vb* **bar·reled** *or* **bar·relled**; **bar·rel·ing** *or* **bar·rel·ling**
to move at a high speed

[1]**bar·ren** \'bar-ən\ *adj*
**1** unable to produce seed, fruit, or young ⟨*barren* plants⟩
**2** growing only poor or few plants ⟨*barren* soil⟩

[2]**barren** *n*
an area of barren land

**bar·rette** \bä-'ret, bə-\ *n*
a clasp or bar used to hold a girl's or woman's hair in place

[1]**bar·ri·cade** \'bar-ə-,kād\ *vb* **bar·ri·cad·ed**; **bar·ri·cad·ing**
to block off with a barricade

[2]**barricade** *n*
a barrier made in a hurry for protection against attack or for blocking the way

**bar·ri·er** \'bar-ē-ər\ *n*
**1** something (as a fence) that blocks the way
**2** something that keeps apart or makes progress difficult

**bar·ring** *prep*
aside from the possibility of

**barrow** *n*
**1** WHEELBARROW
**2** PUSHCART

**¹bar·ter** \'bärt-ər\ *vb*
to trade by exchanging one thing for another without the use of money

**²barter** *n*
the exchange of goods without the use of money

**¹base** \'bās\ *n*
**1** a thing or a part on which something rests : BOTTOM, FOUNDATION ⟨the *base* of a statue⟩
**2** a line or surface of a geometric figure upon which an altitude is or is thought to be constructed ⟨*base* of a triangle⟩
**3** the main substance in a mixture
**4** a supporting or carrying substance (as in a medicine or paint)
**5** a place where a military force keeps its supplies or from which it starts its operations ⟨an air force *base*⟩
**6** a number with reference to which a system of numbers is constructed
**7** a starting place or goal in various games
**8** any of the four stations a runner in baseball must touch in order to score
**9** a chemical substance (as lime or ammonia) that reacts with an acid to form a salt and turns red litmus paper blue

**²base** *vb* **based**; **bas·ing**
to provide with a base or basis

**³base** *adj* **bas·er**; **bas·est**
**1** of low value and not very good in some ways ⟨*base* metals⟩
**2** not honorable : MEAN ⟨*base* conduct⟩
**base·ness** *n*

**base·ball** \'bās-,bȯl\ *n*
**1** ▶ a game played with a bat and ball by two teams of nine players on a field with four bases that mark the course a runner must take to score
**2** the ball used in baseball

**base·board** \'bās-,bōrd\ *n*
a line of boards or molding extending around the walls of a room and touching the floor

**base·ment** \'bā-smənt\ *n*
the part of a building that is partly or entirely below ground level

**baseball 1**

This competitive sport is played by two teams who take turns at bat and in the field. The pitcher throws the ball and the batter attempts to hit it, then runs to each base in sequence to reach home base. When each team has had a turn at bat, this is known as an inning. A standard game lasts for nine innings.

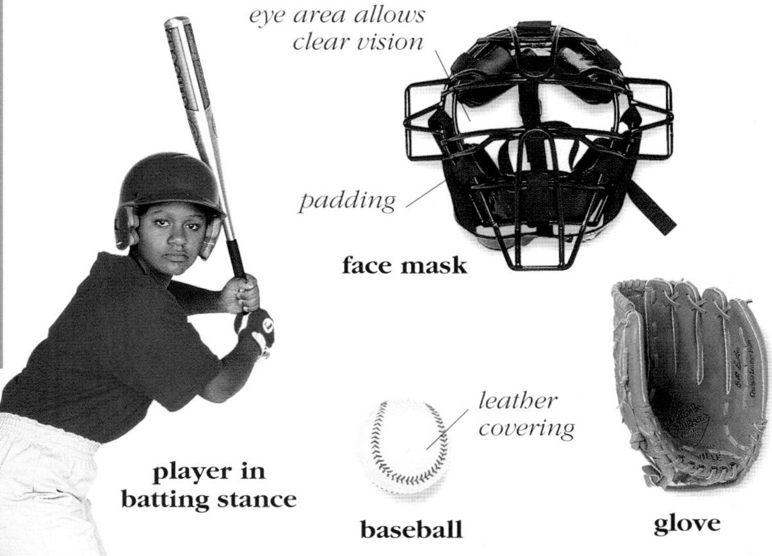


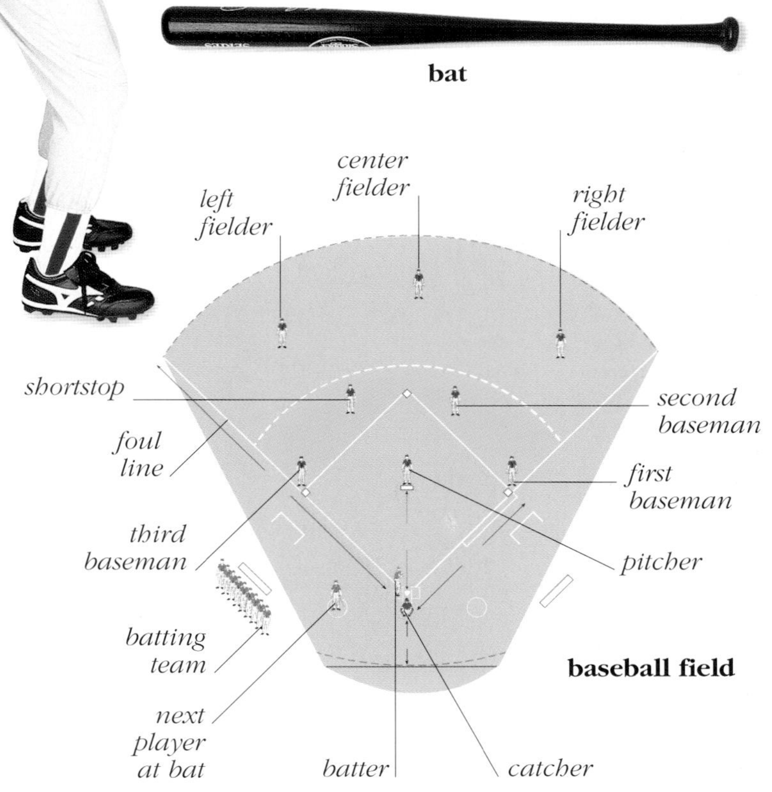

**bash** \'bash\ *vb*
to hit very hard

**bash·ful** \'bash-fəl\ *adj*
uneasy in the presence of others
**synonyms** see SHY

**ba·sic** \'bā-sik\ *adj*
**1** of, relating to, or forming the base of something ⟨the *basic* facts⟩
**2** relating to or characteristic of a chemical base
**ba·si·cal·ly** \-si-kə-lē\ *adv*

**ba·sil** \'baz-əl, 'bāz-\ *n*
▼ a fragrant mint used in cooking

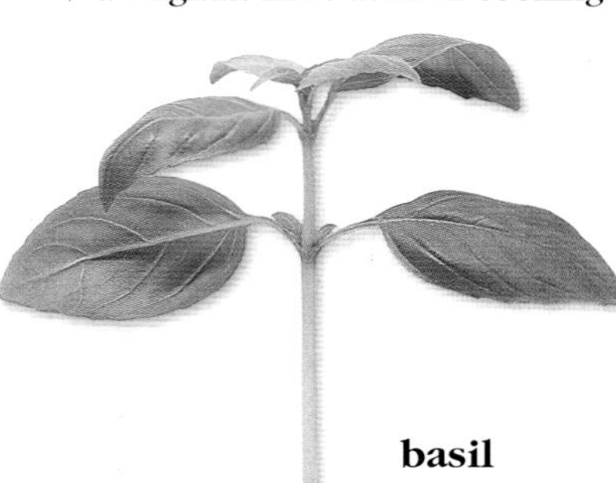

**basil**

**ba·sin** \'bās-n\ *n*
**1** a wide shallow usually round dish or bowl for holding liquids
**2** the amount that a basin holds
**3** a natural or artificial hollow or enclosure containing water ⟨a *basin* for anchoring ships⟩
**4** the land drained by a river and its branches

**ba·sis** \'bā-səs\ *n, pl* **ba·ses** \-,sēz\
FOUNDATION 2, BASE ⟨a story with a *basis* in fact⟩

**bask** \'bask\ *vb*
to lie or relax in pleasantly warm surroundings ⟨*bask* in the sun⟩

**bas·ket** \'bas-kət\ *n*
**1** a container made by weaving together materials (as reeds, straw, or strips of wood)
**2** the contents of a basket ⟨berries for sale at a dollar a *basket*⟩
**3** something that is like a basket in shape or use
**4** a goal in basketball
**bas·ket·like** \-,līk\ *adj*

**bas·ket·ball** \'bas-kət-,bȯl\ *n*
**1** ► a game in which each of two teams tries to throw a round inflated ball through a raised basketlike goal
**2** the ball used in basketball

**bas·ket·ry** \'bas-kə-trē\ *n*
**1** the making of objects (as baskets) by weaving or braiding long slender pieces (as of reed or wood)
**2** objects made of interwoven twigs or reeds

**bas–re·lief** \,bä-ri-'lēf\ *n*
a sculpture in which the design is raised very slightly from the background

**¹bass** \'bas\ *n, pl* **bass** *or* **bass·es**
any of numerous freshwater and sea fishes that are caught for sport and food

**²bass** \'bās\ *n*
**1** a tone of low pitch
**2** the lowest part in harmony that has four parts
**3** the lower half of the musical pitch range
**4** the lowest male singing voice
**5** a singer or an instrument having a bass range or part

**bass drum** \'bās-\ *n*
a large drum with two heads that produces a low booming sound when played

**bas·soon** \bə-'sün, ba-\ *n*
► a double-reed woodwind instrument with a usual range two octaves lower than an oboe

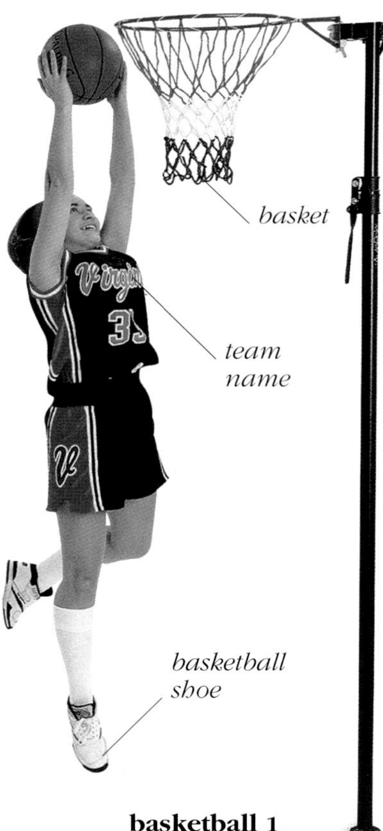


**basketball 1**

**Word History** The bassoon usually plays the lowest part among the woodwinds in an orchestra. The English name comes from the French name for the instrument which in turn comes from the Italian name. The Italian name was formed from a word that means "bass."

**bass viol** \'bās-\ *n*
DOUBLE BASS

**bass·wood** \'bas-,wu̇d\ *n*
a pale wood with straight grain from the linden or a related tree

**¹baste** \'bāst\ *vb* **bast·ed**; **bast·ing**
to sew with long loose stitches so as to hold the work temporarily in place

**²baste** *vb* **bast·ed**; **bast·ing**
to moisten (as with melted fat or juices) while roasting

**bassoon**

**¹bat** \'bat\ *n*
**1** a sharp blow or slap
**2** an implement used for hitting the ball in various games ⟨a baseball *bat*⟩
**3** a turn at batting

**²bat** *vb* **bat·ted**; **bat·ting**
**1** to strike with or as if with a bat
**2** to take one's turn at bat

**³bat** *n*
► any of a group of mammals that fly by means of long front limbs modified into wings

**batch** \'bach\ *n*
**1** a quantity of something baked at one time ⟨a *batch* of cookies⟩
**2** a quantity of material for use at one time or produced at one operation
**3** a group of persons or things

**bath** \'bath, 'bȧth\ *n, pl* **baths** \'baṯẖz, 'bȧṯẖz\
**1** a washing of the body
**2** water for bathing ⟨draw a *bath*⟩
**3** a place, room, or building where persons may bathe
**4** BATHTUB
**5** a liquid in which objects are placed so that it can act upon them

**bathe** \'bāṯẖ\ *vb* **bathed**; **bath·ing**
**1** to take a bath

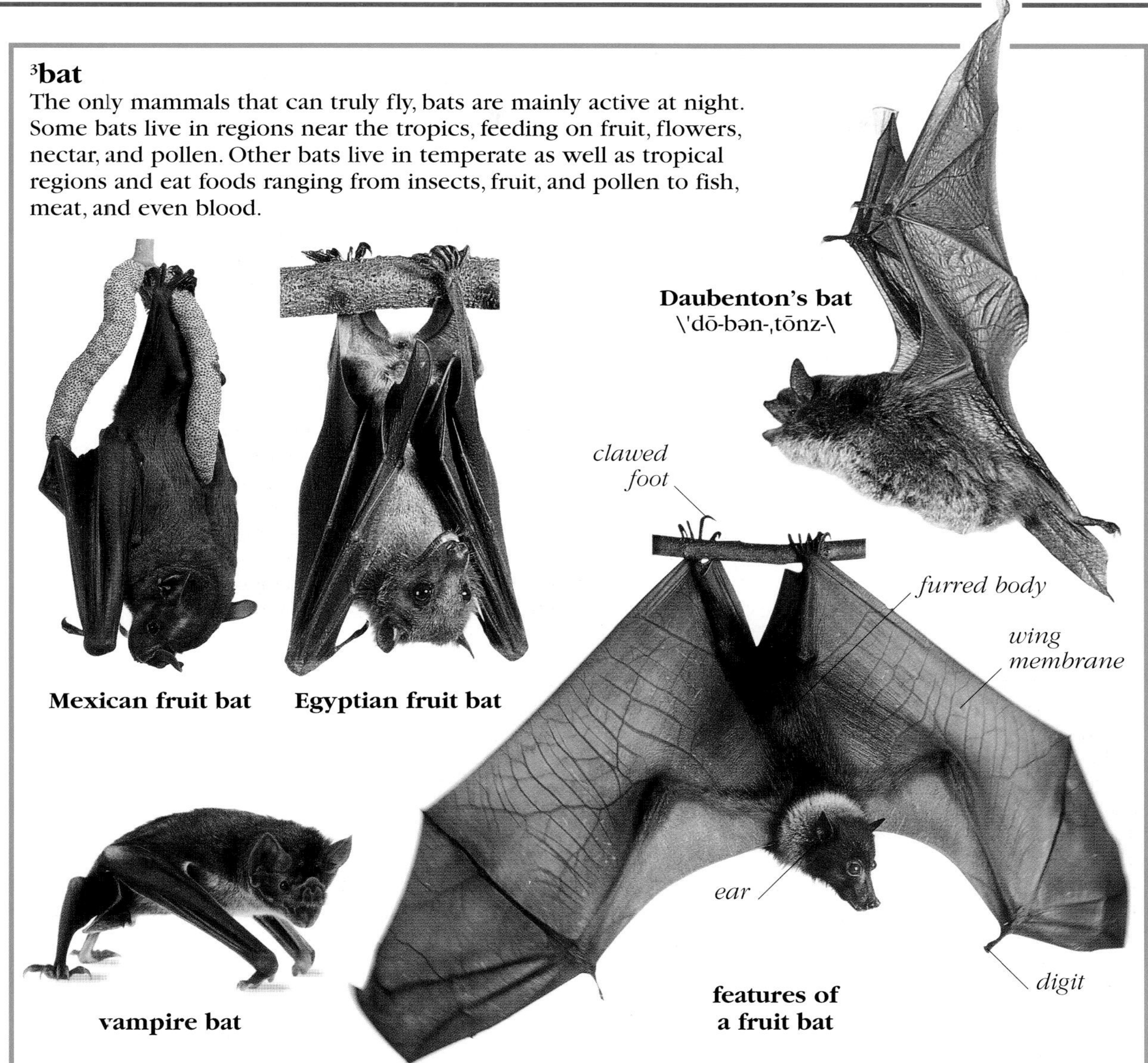

³bat
The only mammals that can truly fly, bats are mainly active at night. Some bats live in regions near the tropics, feeding on fruit, flowers, nectar, and pollen. Other bats live in temperate as well as tropical regions and eat foods ranging from insects, fruit, and pollen to fish, meat, and even blood.
Daubenton's bat \'dō-bən-ˌtōnz-\
clawed foot
furred body
wing membrane
ear
digit


Mexican fruit bat

Egyptian fruit bat

vampire bat

features of a fruit bat

2 to go swimming
3 to give a bath to ⟨*bathe* the baby⟩
4 to apply a liquid to ⟨*bathe* the eyes⟩
5 to cover with or as if with a liquid ⟨a scene *bathed* by moonlight⟩
**bath·er** *n*

**bathing suit** *n*
SWIMSUIT

**bath·room** \'bath-ˌrüm, 'bȧth-, -ˌru̇m\ *n*
a room containing a sink and toilet and often a bathtub or shower

**bath·tub** \'bath-ˌtəb, 'bȧth-\ *n*
a tub in which to take a bath

**bat mitz·vah** \bät-'mits-və\ *n, often cap B&M*
1 a Jewish girl who at 12 or 13 years of age takes on religious responsibilities
2 the ceremony recognizing a girl as a bat mitzvah

**ba·ton** \bə-'tän, ba-\ *n*
1 a stick with which a leader directs an orchestra or band
2 a rod with a ball on one end carried by a drum major or drum majorette

**bat·tal·ion** \bə-'tal-yən\ *n*
1 a part of an army consisting of two or more companies
2 a large body of persons organized to act together ⟨labor *battalions*⟩

**¹bat·ter** \'bat-ər\ *vb*
1 to beat with repeated violent blows ⟨a shore *battered* by waves⟩
2 to damage by blows or hard use ⟨the table was *battered* in the move⟩

**²batter** *n*
a thin mixture made chiefly of flour and a liquid beaten together and used in making cakes and biscuits

**³batter** *n*
the player whose turn it is to bat

**bat·tered** \'bat-ərd\ *adj*
worn down or injured by hard use ⟨wore a *battered* old hat⟩

**bat·ter·ing ram** \'bat-ə-ring-\ *n*
**1** an ancient military machine that consisted of a heavy beam with an iron tip mounted in a frame and swung back and forth in order to batter down walls
**2** a beam or bar with handles used to batter down doors or walls

**bat·tery** \'bat-ə-rē\ *n, pl* **bat·ter·ies**
**1** two or more big military guns that are controlled as a unit
**2** ▼ an electric cell for providing electric current or a group of such cells ⟨a flashlight *battery*⟩
**3** a number of machines or devices grouped together ⟨a *battery* of lights⟩

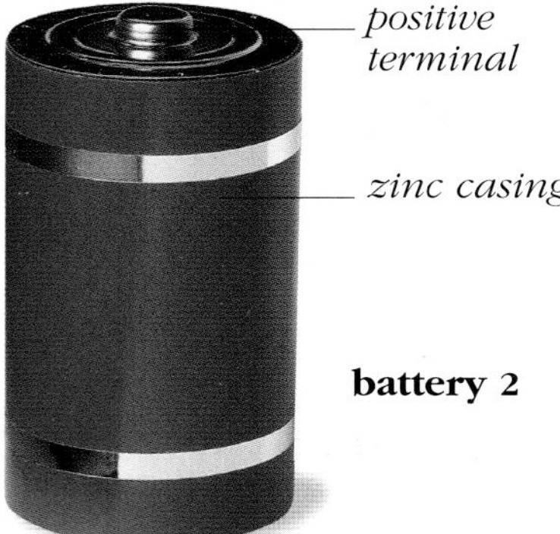


**battery 2**

**bat·ting** \'bat-ing\ *n*
cotton or wool in sheets used mostly for stuffing quilts or packaging goods

**¹bat·tle** \'bat-l\ *n*
**1** a fight between armies, warships, or airplanes
**2** a fight between two persons or animals
**3** a long or hard struggle or contest ⟨the *battle* against hunger⟩
**4** WARFARE

**²battle** *vb* **bat·tled**; **bat·tling**
to engage in battle

**bat·tle–ax** *or* **bat·tle–axe** \'bat-l-,aks\ *n*
▶ an ax with a broad blade formerly used as a weapon

**battle-ax**

**bat·tle·field** \'bat-l-,fēld\ *n*
a place where a battle is fought or was once fought

**bat·tle·ground** \'bat-l-,graůnd\ *n*
BATTLEFIELD

**bat·tle·ment** \'bat-l-mənt\ *n*
a low wall (as at the top of a castle or tower) with openings to shoot through

**bat·tle·ship** \'bat-l-,ship\ *n*
a large warship with heavy armor and large guns

**¹bawl** \'bȯl\ *vb*
**1** to shout or cry loudly ⟨*bawl* a command⟩
**2** to weep noisily

**²bawl** *n*
a loud cry

**bawl out** *vb*
to scold severely

**¹bay** \'bā\ *n*
**1** a reddish-brown horse
**2** a reddish brown

**²bay** *vb*
to bark with long deep tones

**³bay** *n*
**1** the baying of dogs
**2** the position of an animal or a person forced to face pursuers when it is impossible to escape ⟨brought to *bay*⟩
**3** the position of pursuers who are held off ⟨kept the hounds at *bay*⟩

**⁴bay** *n*
a part of a large body of water extending into the land

**⁵bay** *n*
▶ the laurel or a related tree or shrub

**⁵bay:** a bay tree

**bay·ber·ry** \'bā-,ber-ē\ *n, pl* **bay·ber·ries**
a shrub with leathery leaves and small bluish white waxy berries used in making candles

**¹bay·o·net** \'bā-ə-nət, ,bā-ə-'net\ *n*
a weapon like a dagger made to fit on the end of a rifle

**²bayonet** *vb* **bay·o·net·ted**; **bay·o·net·ting**
to stab with a bayonet

**bay·ou** \'bī-ō, -ü\ *n*
a creek that flows slowly through marshy land

**bay window** \'bā-\ *n*
a window or a set of windows that sticks out from the wall of a building

**ba·zaar** \bə-'zär\ *n*
**1** a marketplace (as in southwestern Asia and northern Africa) containing rows of small shops
**2** a large building where many kinds of goods are sold
**3** a fair for the sale of goods especially for charity

**ba·zoo·ka** \bə-'zü-kə\ *n*
a portable shoulder gun consisting of a tube open at both ends that shoots an explosive rocket able to pierce armor

**be** \bē\ *vb, past 1st & 3d sing* **was** \wəz, 'wəz, wäz\; *2d sing* **were** \wər, 'wər\; *pl* **were**; *past subjunctive* **were**; *past participle* **been** \bin\; *present participle* **be·ing** \'bē-ing\; *present 1st sing* **am** \əm, am\; *2d sing* **are** \ər, är\; *3d sing* **is** \iz, əz\; *pl* **are**; *present subjunctive* **be**
**1** to equal in meaning or identity ⟨that teacher *is* my neighbor⟩
**2** to have a specified character or quality ⟨the leaves *are* green⟩
**3** to belong to the class of ⟨apes *are* mammals⟩
**4** EXIST 1, LIVE ⟨once there *was* a knight⟩
**5** used as a helping verb with other verbs ⟨*was* walking along⟩ ⟨the ball *was* thrown⟩

**be-** *prefix*
**1** on : around : over
**2** provide with or cover with : dress up with ⟨*be*whiskered⟩
**3** about : to : upon ⟨*be*moan⟩
**4** make : cause to be ⟨*be*little⟩ ⟨*be*friend⟩

**¹beach** \'bēch\ *n*
a sandy or gravelly part of the shore of the sea or of a lake

**²beach** *vb*
to run or drive ashore ⟨*beach* a boat⟩

**beach·head** \'bēch-,hed\ *n*
an area on an enemy shore held by an advance force of an invading army to protect the later landing of troops or supplies

**bea·con** \'bē-kən\ *n*
**1** a guiding or warning light or fire on a high place
**2** a radio station that sends out signals to guide aircraft

**[1]bead** \'bēd\ *n*
**1** ▼ a small piece of solid material with a hole through it by which it can be strung on a thread
**2** a small round mass ⟨a *bead* of sweat⟩
**3** a small knob on a gun used in taking aim

**[1]bead 1**

**Word History** In early English the word *bead* meant "a prayer." Then, as now, people sometimes used strings of little round balls to keep track of their prayers. Each little ball stood for a prayer. In time the word that meant "prayer" came to be used for the little balls themselves. Now any small object that can be strung on a string is called a *bead*.

**[2]bead** *vb*
**1** to cover with beads
**2** to string together like beads

**beady** \'bēd-ē\ *adj* **bead·i·er**; **bead·i·est**
like a bead especially in being small, round, and shiny ⟨*beady* eyes⟩

**bea·gle** \'bē-gəl\ *n*
▼ a small hound with short legs and a smooth coat

**beagle**

**beak** \'bēk\ *n*
**1** the bill of a bird ⟨an eagle's *beak*⟩
**2** a part shaped like a beak
**beaked** \'bēkt\ *adj*

**bea·ker** \'bē-kər\ *n*
a deep cup or glass with a wide mouth and usually a lip for pouring

**[1]beam** \'bēm\ *n*
**1** a long heavy piece of timber or metal used as a main horizontal support of a building or a ship
**2** a ray of light
**3** a constant radio wave sent out from an airport to guide pilots along a course

**[2]beam** *vb*
**1** to send out beams of light
**2** to smile with joy
**3** to aim a radio broadcast by use of a special antenna

**bean** \'bēn\ *n*
**1** ▼ the edible seed or pod of a bushy or climbing garden plant related to the peas and clovers
**2** a seed or fruit like a bean ⟨coffee *beans*⟩

**bean 1**

Beans are a staple food around the world. They are high in protein and have many uses in cooking. There are many different types, varying in appearance and flavor.

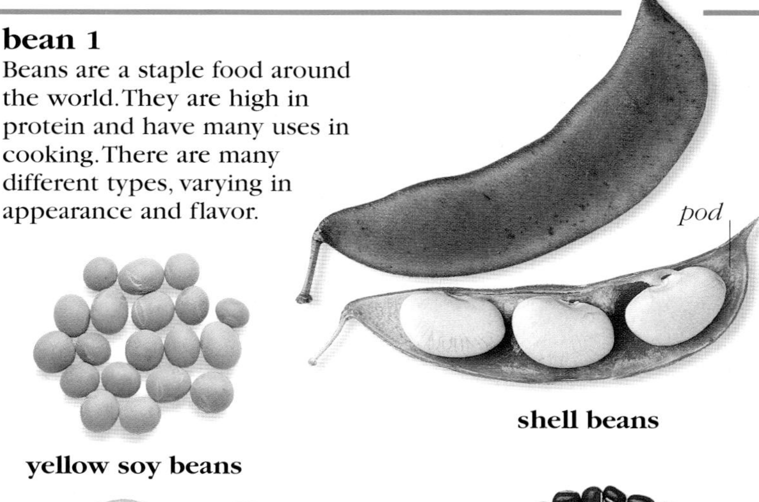


**shell beans**

**yellow soy beans**

**lima beans**

**adzuki beans**

**black kidney beans**

**red kidney beans**

**flageolet beans**

A B C D E F G H I J K L M N O P Q R S T U V W X Y Z

**[1]bear** \'baər, 'beər\ *n, pl* **bears**
**1** ▼ *or pl* **bear** a large heavy mammal with long shaggy hair and a very short tail
**2** a grumpy or glum person

**[1]bear 1**

**[2]bear** *vb* **bore** \'bōr\; **borne** \'bōrn\; **bear·ing**
**1** [1]SUPPORT 4 ⟨*bear* a burden⟩
**2** to have as a feature or characteristic ⟨*bear* marks of suffering⟩
**3** to bring forth **:** give birth to ⟨*bear* fruit⟩ ⟨*bear* children⟩
**4** to put up with ⟨could not *bear* pain⟩
**5** [2]PRESS 1 ⟨*bear* down hard on your crayon⟩
**6** to have a relation to the matter at hand ⟨facts *bearing* on the question⟩

**bear·able** \'bar-ə-bəl, 'ber-\ *adj* possible to bear

**beard** \'biərd\ *n*
**1** the hair on the face of a man
**2** a hairy growth or tuft

**bear·er** \'bar-ər, 'ber-\ *n*
**1** someone or something that bears, supports, or carries
**2** a person holding a check or an order for payment

**bear·ing** \'baər-ing, 'beər-\ *n*
**1** the manner in which one carries or conducts oneself ⟨has the *bearing* of a soldier⟩
**2** a part of a machine in which another part turns
**3** the position or direction of one point with respect to another or to the compass
**4** **bearings** *pl* understanding of one's position or situation ⟨lost my *bearings*⟩
**5** CONNECTION 2 ⟨personal feelings had no *bearing* on our decision⟩

**beast** \'bēst\ *n*
**1** a mammal with four feet (as a bear, deer, or rabbit) ⟨*beasts* of the field and fowls of the air⟩
**2** a farm animal especially when kept for work ⟨oxen and horses used as *beasts* of burden⟩
**3** a mean or horrid person

**[1]beat** \'bēt\ *vb* **beat**; **beat·en** \'bēt-n\ *or* **beat**; **beat·ing**
**1** to strike again and again ⟨*beat* a drum⟩
**2** [1]THROB 2, PULSATE ⟨heart still *beating*⟩
**3** to flap against ⟨wings *beating* the air⟩
**4** to mix by stirring rapidly ⟨*beat* two eggs⟩
**5** to win against ⟨*beat* the enemy⟩
**6** to measure or mark off by strokes ⟨*beat* time to the music⟩
**beat·er** *n*

**[2]beat** *n*
**1** a blow or a stroke made again and again ⟨the *beat* of drums⟩
**2** a single pulse (as of the heart)
**3** a measurement of time or accent in music
**4** an area or place regularly visited or traveled through ⟨a police officer's *beat*⟩

**[3]beat** *adj*
**1** being very tired
**2** having lost one's morale

**beat·en** \'bēt-n\ *adj* worn smooth by passing feet ⟨a *beaten* path⟩

**be·at·i·tude** \bē-'at-ə-,tüd, -,tyüd\ *n* one of the statements made in the Sermon on the Mount (Matthew 5: 3–12) beginning "Blessed are"

**beau** \'bō\ *n, pl* **beaux** \'bōz\ *or* **beaus** \'bōz\ BOYFRIEND

**beau·te·ous** \'byüt-ē-əs\ *adj* BEAUTIFUL

**beau·ti·cian** \byü-'tish-ən\ *n* a person who gives beauty treatments (as to skin and hair)

**beau·ti·ful** \'byüt-i-fəl\ *adj* having qualities of beauty **:** giving pleasure to the mind or senses
**beau·ti·ful·ly** *adv*

---

**Synonyms** BEAUTIFUL, PRETTY, and HANDSOME mean pleasing or delightful in some way. BEAUTIFUL is used of whatever is most pleasing to the senses or the mind ⟨a *beautiful* sunset⟩ ⟨a *beautiful* poem⟩. PRETTY is usually used of something that is small or dainty ⟨a *pretty* little doll⟩. HANDSOME is used of something that is well formed and therefore pleasing to look at ⟨a *handsome* desk⟩.

---

**beau·ti·fy** \'byüt-ə-,fī\ *vb* **beau·ti·fied**; **beau·ti·fy·ing** to make beautiful ⟨*beautified* the room with flowers⟩

**beau·ty** \'byüt-ē\ *n, pl* **beauties**
**1** the qualities of a person or a thing that give pleasure to the senses or to the mind ⟨the *beauty* of the landscape⟩ ⟨a poem of great *beauty*⟩
**2** a beautiful person or thing

**beauty shop** *n* a place of business for the care of customers' hair, skin, and nails

**bea·ver** \'bē-vər\ *n* ▼ an animal related to the rats and mice that has webbed hind feet and a broad flat tail, builds dams and houses of sticks and mud in water, and is prized for its soft but strong fur

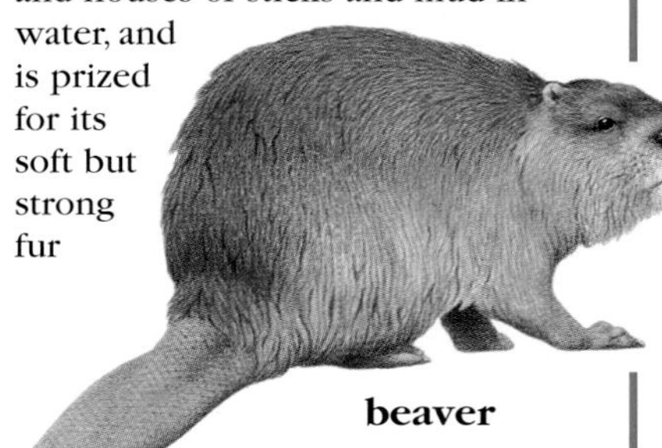

**beaver**

**be·calm** \bi-'käm, -'kälm\ *vb*
to bring to a stop because of lack of wind ⟨a ship *becalmed*⟩

**became** *past of* BECOME

**be·cause** \bi-'kȯz, bi-kəz\ *conj*
for the reason that ⟨I ran *because* I was scared⟩

**because of** *prep*
as a result of ⟨the game was canceled *because of* rain⟩

**beck** \'bek\ *n*
a beckoning motion

**beck·on** \'bek-ən\ *vb*
to call or signal by a motion (as a wave or nod) ⟨they *beckoned* to us to come over⟩

**be·come** \bi-'kəm\ *vb* **be·came** \-'kām\; **become**; **be·com·ing**
**1** to come or grow to be ⟨a tadpole *becomes* a frog⟩ ⟨days *become* shorter as summer ends⟩
**2** to be suitable to **:** SUIT ⟨look for clothes that *become* you⟩
**become of** to happen to ⟨what has *become of* my friend⟩

**be·com·ing** \bi-'kəm-ing\ *adj*
having a pleasing effect ⟨*becoming* clothes⟩
**be·com·ing·ly** *adv*

**¹bed** \'bed\ *n*
**1** ▶ a piece of furniture on which one may sleep or rest
**2** a place for sleeping or resting ⟨make a *bed* in the grass⟩
**3** a level piece of ground prepared for growing plants
**4** the bottom of something ⟨the *bed* of a river⟩
**5** LAYER 2 ⟨a thick *bed* of rock⟩

**²bed** *vb* **bed·ded**; **bed·ding**
**1** to put or go to bed
**2** to plant in beds

**bed·bug** \'bed-,bəg\ *n*
a small wingless insect that sucks blood and is sometimes found in houses and especially in beds

**bed·clothes** \'bed-,klōz, -klōthz\ *n pl*
coverings (as sheets and pillowcases) for a bed

**bed·ding** \'bed-ing\ *n*
**1** BEDCLOTHES
**2** material for a bed ⟨straw for the cows' *bedding*⟩

**be·dev·il** \bi-'dev-əl\ *vb*
to trouble or annoy again and again **:** PESTER, HARASS

**bed·lam** \'bed-ləm\ *n*
a place or scene of uproar and confusion

**Word History** *Bedlam*, an old form of *Bethlehem*, was the popular name for the *Hospital of Saint Mary of Bethlehem*. This hospital served as an insane asylum in London. The word *bedlam* came to be used for any place of uproar and confusion.

**be·drag·gled** \bi-'drag-əld\ *adj*
**1** limp and often wet as by exposure to rain ⟨*bedraggled* hair⟩
**2** soiled from or as if from being dragged in mud ⟨*bedraggled* clothes⟩

**bed·rid·den** \'bed-,rid-n\ *adj*
forced to stay in bed by sickness or weakness

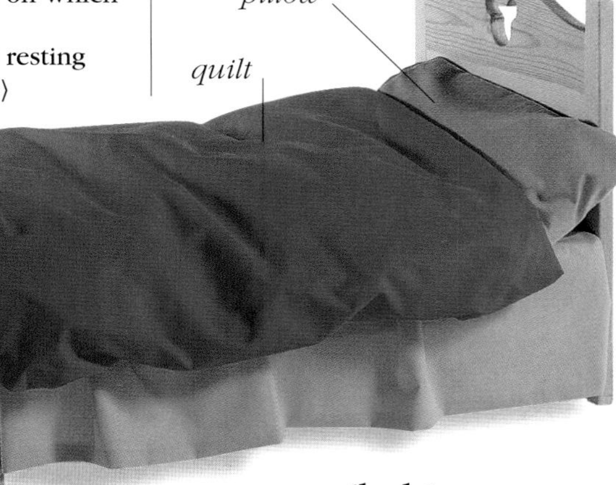

**¹bed 1**

**bed·rock** \'bed-,räk\ *n*
the solid rock found under surface materials (as soil)

**bed·room** \'bed-,rüm, -,rům\ *n*
a room to sleep in

**bed·side** \'bed-,sīd\ *n*
the place beside a bed

**bed·spread** \'bed-,spred\ *n*
a decorative top covering for a bed

**bed·stead** \'bed-,sted\ *n*
the framework of a bed

**bed·time** \'bed-,tīm\ *n*
time to go to bed

**bee** \'bē\ *n*
**1** ▼ an insect with four wings that is related to the wasps, gathers pollen and nectar from flowers from which it makes beebread and honey for food, and usually lives in large colonies
**2** a gathering of people to do something together ⟨a sewing *bee*⟩

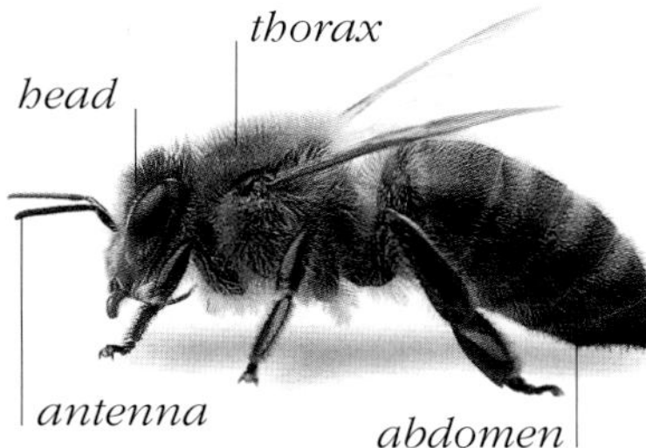

**bee 1:** a honeybee

**bee·bread** \'bē-,bred\ *n*
a bitter yellowish brown food material prepared by bees from pollen and stored in their honeycomb

**beech** \'bēch\ *n*
▼ a tree with smooth gray bark, deep green leaves, and small triangular nuts

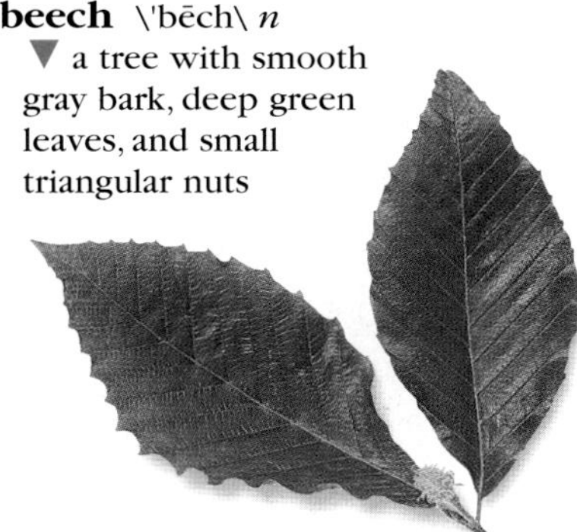
**beech: beech leaves**

**beef** \'bēf\ *n, pl* **beefs** \'bēfs\ *or* **beeves** \'bēvz\
**1** the flesh of a steer, cow, or bull
**2** a steer, cow, or bull especially when fattened for food
**beef·like** \'be-,flīk\ *adj*

**beef·steak** \'bēf-,stāk\ *n*
a slice of beef suitable for broiling or frying

**bee·hive** \'bē-,hīv\ *n*
HIVE 1

**bee·line** \'bē-,līn\ *n*
a straight direct course

**been** *past participle of* BE

**beer** \'biər\ *n*
an alcoholic drink made from malt and flavored with hops

**bees·wax** \'bēz-,waks\ *n*
wax made by bees and used by them in building honeycomb

**beet** \'bēt\ *n*
a leafy plant with a thick juicy root that is used as a vegetable or as a source of sugar

**bee·tle** \'bēt-l\ *n*
**1** ▼ any of a group of insects with four wings the outer pair of which are stiff cases that cover the others when folded
**2** an insect (as a bug) that looks like a beetle

**beeves** *pl of* BEEF

**be·fall** \bi-'fȯl\ *vb* **be·fell** \-'fel\; **be·fall·en** \-'fȯ-lən\; **be·fall·ing**
**1** to take place : HAPPEN
**2** to happen to

**be·fit** \bi-'fit\ *vb* **be·fit·ted**; **be·fit·ting**
to be suitable to or proper for

[1]**be·fore** \bi-'fōr\ *adv*
**1** in front : AHEAD ⟨go on *before*⟩
**2** in the past ⟨have been here *before*⟩
**3** at an earlier time ⟨come at six o'clock, not *before*⟩

[2]**before** *prep*
**1** in front of ⟨stand *before* a mirror⟩
**2** in the presence of ⟨spoke *before* the legislature⟩
**3** earlier than ⟨got there *before* me⟩

[3]**before** *conj*
**1** ahead of the time when ⟨wash *before* you eat⟩
**2** more willingly than ⟨I'd starve *before* I'd steal⟩

**be·fore·hand** \bi-'fōr-,hand\ *adv*
[1]BEFORE 1 : ahead of time

**be·friend** \bi-'frend\ *vb*
to act as a friend to : help in a friendly way

**beg** \'beg\ *vb* **begged**; **beg·ging**
**1** to ask for money, food, or help as a charity ⟨*beg* in the streets⟩
**2** to ask as a favor in an earnest or polite way ⟨*beg* to be taken to the circus⟩ ⟨*beg* pardon⟩

**beg·gar** \'beg-ər\ *n*
**1** one who lives by begging
**2** PAUPER

**be·gin** \bi-'gin\ *vb* **be·gan** \-'gan\; **be·gun** \-'gən\; **be·gin·ning**
**1** to do the first part of an action ⟨*begin* your homework⟩
**2** to come into existence

**be·gin·ner** \bi-'gin-ər\ *n*
a young or inexperienced person

**be·gin·ning** \bi-'gin-ing\ *n*
**1** the point at which something begins ⟨the *beginning* of the war⟩

**beetle 1**

The beetle is an insect that can be found in nearly all parts of the world. There are hundreds of thousands of different types, and they live in habitats that range from scorching deserts to muddy ponds and cold mountaintops. Some beetles eat plants, while others feed on dead animals. Many beetles are brilliantly colored or patterned.

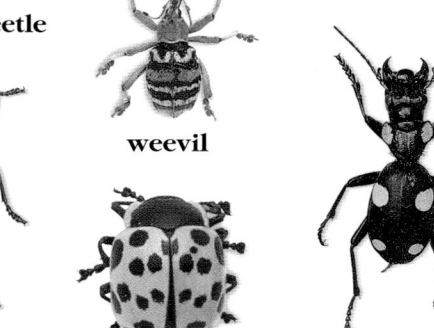

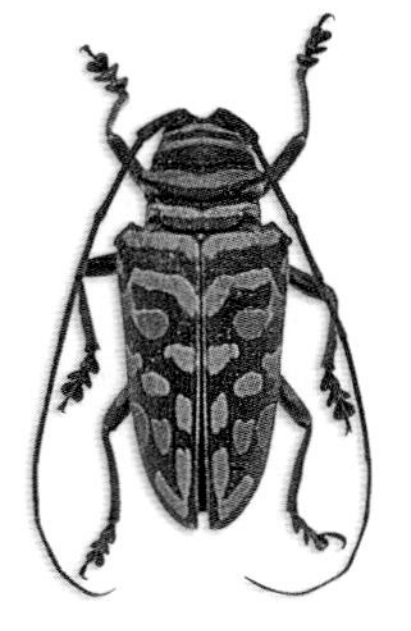

longhorn beetle

dung beetle

tortoise beetle

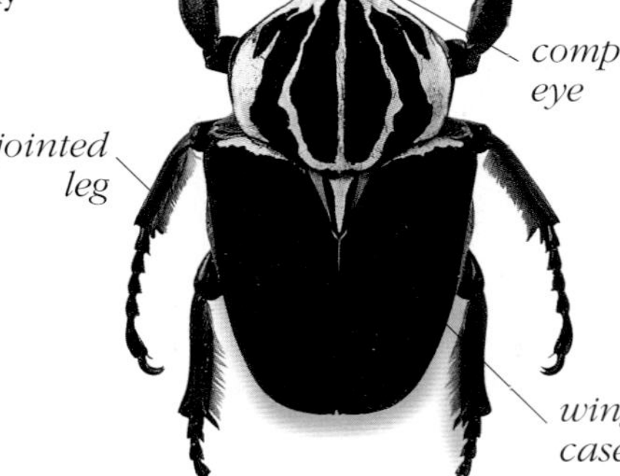


features of a Goliath beetle
\gə-'lī-əth\

weevil

jewel beetle

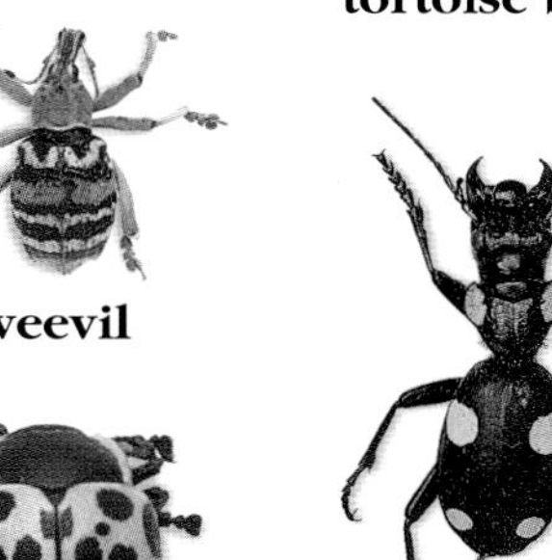

leaf beetle

tiger beetle

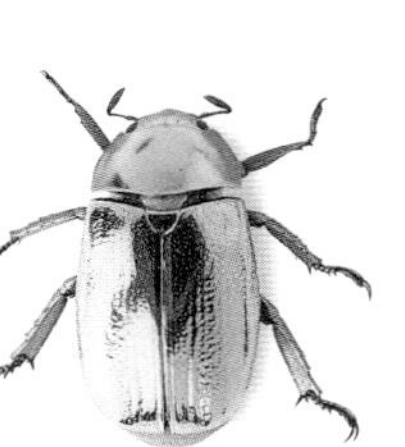

golden beetle

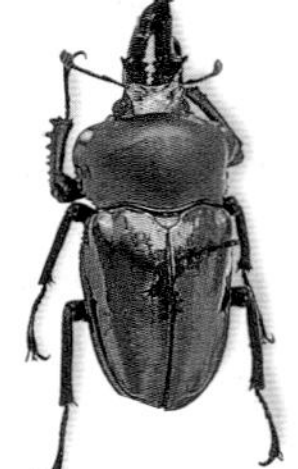

stag beetle

2 first part ⟨the *beginning* of the song⟩

**be·gone** \bi-'gȯn\ *vb* to go away **:** DEPART — used especially in the imperative mood ⟨*begone*, you rascal⟩

**be·go·nia** \bi-'gōn-yə\ *n* ▼ a plant with a juicy stem, ornamental leaves, and bright waxy flowers

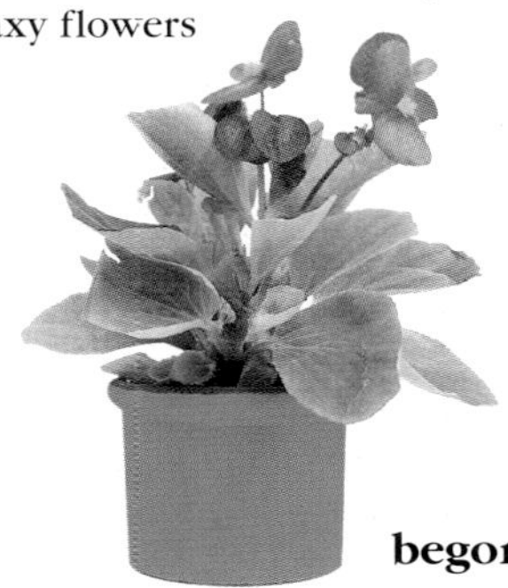
**begonia**

**be·grudge** \bi-'grəj\ *vb* **be·grudged; be·grudg·ing** to give or do reluctantly ⟨*begrudge* a person a favor⟩

**begun** *past of* BEGIN

**be·half** \bi-'haf, -'håf\ *n* one's interest or support ⟨argued in my *behalf*⟩

**be·have** \bi-'hāv\ *vb* **be·haved; be·hav·ing**
**1** to conduct oneself ⟨the children *behaved* well at the party⟩
**2** to conduct oneself properly ⟨tell them to *behave*⟩
**3** to act or function in a particular way ⟨the car *behaves* well on icy roads⟩

**be·hav·ior** \bi-'hāv-yər\ *n*
**1** the way in which one conducts oneself
**2** the whole activity of something and especially a living being

**be·head** \bi-'hed\ *vb* to cut off the head of

**¹be·hind** \bi-'hīnd\ *adv*
**1** in a place that is being or has been departed from ⟨leave your books *behind*⟩ ⟨stay *behind*⟩
**2** at, to, or toward the back ⟨look *behind*⟩ ⟨fall *behind*⟩
**3** not up to the general level ⟨*behind* in school⟩

**²behind** *prep*
**1** at or to the back of ⟨*behind* the door⟩
**2** not up to the level of ⟨*behind* the rest of the class⟩

**be·hold** \bi-'hōld\ *vb* **be·held** \-'held\; **be·hold·ing** to look upon **:** SEE
**be·hold·er** *n*

**beige** \'bāzh\ *n* a yellowish brown

**be·ing** \'bē-ing\ *n*
**1** the state of having life or existence
**2** one that exists in fact or thought
**3** a living thing

**be·la·bor** \bi-'lā-bər\ *vb* to keep working on to excess ⟨*belabor* the argument⟩

**be·lat·ed** \bi-'lāt-əd\ *adj* delayed beyond the usual or expected time

**¹belch** \'belch\ *vb*
**1** to force out gas suddenly from the stomach through the mouth
**2** to throw out or be thrown out violently ⟨smoke *belched* from the chimney⟩

**²belch** *n* a belching of gas

**bel·fry** \'bel-frē\ *n, pl* **belfries** ► a tower or room in a tower for a bell or set of bells

**Word History** The words *bell* and *belfry* sound similar. Belfries even have bells in them. These facts might make you think the two words must be related, but they are not. The word *bell* came from an Old English word meaning "bell." The word *belfry*, on the other hand, came from a Greek phrase meaning "a movable war tower."

**¹Bel·gian** \'bel-jən\ *adj* of or relating to Belgium or the Belgians

**²Belgian** *n* a person born or living in Belgium

**be·lief** \bə-'lēf\ *n*
**1** a feeling sure that a person or thing exists or is true or trustworthy ⟨*belief* in Santa Claus⟩ ⟨*belief* in democracy⟩
**2** religious faith **:** CREED
**3** something that one thinks is true ⟨it's my *belief* that our team really won⟩

**Synonyms** BELIEF and FAITH mean agreement with the truth of something. BELIEF suggests that there is some kind of evidence for believing even though the believer is not always sure of the truth ⟨my *belief* in ghosts⟩. FAITH suggests that the believer is certain even if there is no evidence or proof ⟨even after the robbery, I kept my *faith* in the goodness of people⟩. **Synonyms** see in addition OPINION.

**be·liev·able** \bə-'lē-və-bəl\ *adj* possible to believe ⟨a *believable* excuse⟩

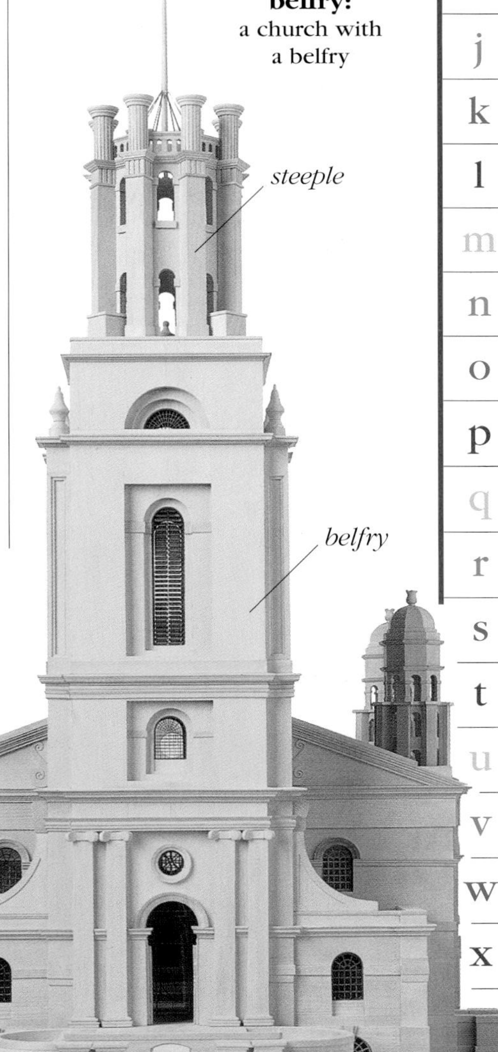

**belfry:** a church with a belfry

A B C D E F G H I J K L M N O P Q R S T U V W X Y Z

**be·lieve** \bə-ˈlēv\ *vb* **be·lieved**; **be·liev·ing**
**1** to have faith or confidence in the existence or worth of ⟨*believe* in ghosts⟩ ⟨*believes* in daily exercise⟩
**2** to accept as true ⟨*believe* the report⟩
**3** to accept the word of ⟨they didn't *believe* me⟩
**4** THINK 2

**be·liev·er** \bə-ˈlē-vər\ *n*
one who has faith (as in a religion)

**be·lit·tle** \bi-ˈlit-l\ *vb* **be·lit·tled**; **be·lit·tling**
to make (a person or a thing) seem small or unimportant

**bell** \ˈbel\ *n*
**1** ▼ a hollow metallic device that is shaped somewhat like a cup and makes a ringing sound when struck ⟨church *bells*⟩
**2** the stroke or sound of a bell that tells the hour
**3** the time indicated by the stroke of a bell
**4** a half-hour period of watch on shipboard
**5** something shaped like a bell ⟨the *bell* of a trumpet⟩

clapper
**bell 1**

**bell·boy** \ˈbel-ˌbȯi\ *n*
BELLHOP

**bell·hop** \ˈbel-ˌhäp\ *n*
a hotel or club employee who answers calls for service by bell or telephone and assists guests with luggage

**[1]bel·lig·er·ent** \bə-ˈlij-ə-rənt\ *adj*
**1** carrying on war
**2** eager to fight

**[2]belligerent** *n*
**1** a nation at war
**2** a person taking part in a fight

**bell jar** *n*
a usually glass vessel shaped like a bell and used to cover objects or to contain gases or a vacuum

**[1]bel·low** \ˈbel-ō\ *vb*
to give a loud deep roar like that of a bull

**[2]bellow** *n*
a loud deep roar

**bel·lows** \ˈbel-ōz, -əz\ *n sing or pl*
**1** a device that produces a strong current of air when its sides are pressed together
**2** the folding part of some cameras

**[1]bel·ly** \ˈbel-ē\ *n, pl* **bellies**
**1** ABDOMEN 1
**2** the under part of an animal's body
**3** STOMACH 1
**4** an internal cavity (as of the human body)
**5** the thick part of a muscle

**[2]belly** *vb* **bel·lied**; **bel·ly·ing**
to swell out

**belly button** *n*
NAVEL

**be·long** \bə-ˈlȯng\ *vb*
**1** to be in a proper place ⟨this book *belongs* on the top shelf⟩
**2** to be the property of a person or group of persons ⟨the watch *belongs* to me⟩
**3** to be a part of : be connected with : go with ⟨the tools that *belong* to the vacuum cleaner⟩

**be·long·ings** \bə-ˈlȯng-ingz\ *n pl*
the things that belong to a person

**be·lov·ed** \bə-ˈləv-əd, -ˈləvd\ *adj*
greatly loved : very dear

**[1]be·low** \bə-ˈlō\ *adv*
in or to a lower place

**[2]below** *prep*
lower than : BENEATH

**[1]belt** \ˈbelt\ *n*
**1** a strip of flexible material (as leather or cloth) worn around a person's body for holding in or supporting clothing or weapons or for ornament
**2** something like a belt : BAND, CIRCLE ⟨a *belt* of trees⟩
**3** a flexible endless band running around wheels or pulleys and used for moving or carrying something ⟨a fan *belt* on a car⟩
**4** a region suited to or producing something or having some special feature ⟨the cotton *belt*⟩
**belt·ed** \ˈbel-təd\ *adj*

**[2]belt** *vb*
**1** to put a belt on or around
**2** to strike hard

**be·moan** \bi-ˈmōn\ *vb*
to express grief over

**bench** \ˈbench\ *n*
**1** ▼ a long seat for two or more persons
**2** a long table for holding work and tools ⟨a carpenter's *bench*⟩
**3** the position or rank of a judge

**bench 1:** a park bench

**[1]bend** \ˈbend\ *vb* **bent** \ˈbent\; **bend·ing**
**1** to make, be, or become curved or angular rather than straight or flat
**2** to move out of a straight line or position : STOOP ⟨*bend* over and pick it up⟩
**3** to turn in a certain direction : DIRECT ⟨*bent* their steps toward home⟩

**[2]bend** *n*
something that is bent : CURVE

**[1]be·neath** \bi-ˈnēth\ *adv*
in a lower place

**[2]beneath** *prep*
**1** lower than : UNDER ⟨the sun sank *beneath* the horizon⟩
**2** not worthy of ⟨work *beneath* my dignity⟩

**bene·dic·tion** \ˌben-ə-ˈdik-shən\ *n*
**1** an expression of approval
**2** a short blessing by a minister or priest at the end of a religious service

**ben·e·fac·tor** \ˈben-ə-ˌfak-tər\ *n*
one who helps another especially by giving money

**ben·e·fi·cial** \ˌben-ə-ˈfish-əl\ *adj*
producing good results : HELPFUL
**ben·e·fi·cial·ly** *adv*

**ben·e·fi·cia·ry** \ˌben-ə-ˈfish-ē-ˌer-ē\ *n, pl* **ben·e·fi·cia·ries**
a person who benefits or is expected to benefit from something

**[1]ben·e·fit** \ˈben-ə-ˌfit\ *n*
**1** something that does good to a person or thing ⟨the *benefits* of sunshine⟩
**2** money paid in time of death, sickness, or unemployment or in old age (as by an insurance company)

**[2]benefit** *vb* **ben·e·fit·ed** *or* **ben·e·fit·ted**; **ben·e·fit·ing** *or* **ben·e·fit·ting**
**1** to be useful or profitable to
**2** to receive benefit

**be·nev·o·lence** \bə-ˈnev-ə-ləns\ *n*
KINDNESS, GENEROSITY

**be·nev·o·lent** \bə-ˈnev-ə-lənt\ *adj*
having a desire to do good : KINDLY, CHARITABLE

**be·nign** \bi-ˈnīn\ *adj*
**1** of a gentle disposition
**2** likely to bring about a good outcome
**be·nign·ly** *adv*

**[1]bent** \ˈbent\ *adj*
**1** changed by bending : CROOKED ⟨a *bent* pin⟩
**2** strongly favorable to : quite determined ⟨I am *bent* on going anyway⟩

**[2]bent** *n*
a strong or natural liking ⟨children with a *bent* for study⟩

**be·queath** \bi-ˈkwēth, -ˈkwēth\ *vb*
**1** to give or leave by means of a will ⟨my parents *bequeathed* me some money⟩
**2** to hand down ⟨knowledge *bequeathed* to later times⟩

**be·quest** \bi-ˈkwest\ *n*
**1** the act of bequeathing
**2** something given or left by a will

**[1]be·reaved** \bi-ˈrēvd\ *adj*
suffering the death of a loved one ⟨*bereaved* parents⟩

**[2]bereaved** *n, pl* **bereaved**
a bereaved person

**be·reft** \bi-ˈreft\ *adj*
**1** not having something needed, wanted, or expected
**2** [1]BEREAVED

**be·ret** \bə-ˈrā\ *n*
a soft round flat cap without a visor

**berg** \ˈbərg\ *n*
ICEBERG

**beri·beri** \ˌber-ē-ˈber-ē\ *n*
a disease caused by lack of a vitamin in which there is weakness, wasting, and damage to nerves

**[1]ber·ry** \ˈber-ē\ *n, pl* **berries**
**1** a small pulpy fruit (as a strawberry)
**2** ▼ a simple fruit (as a grape or tomato) in which the ripened ovary wall is fleshy
**3** a dry seed (as of the coffee tree)

**[2]berry** *vb* **ber·ried**; **ber·ry·ing**
to gather berries

**[1]berry 2**
A wide variety of flowering plants produce berries which have soft flesh and plentiful seeds. Many berries are cultivated for human consumption, but in the natural world their juicy flesh is eaten by animals and the seeds are dispersed to produce new plants.

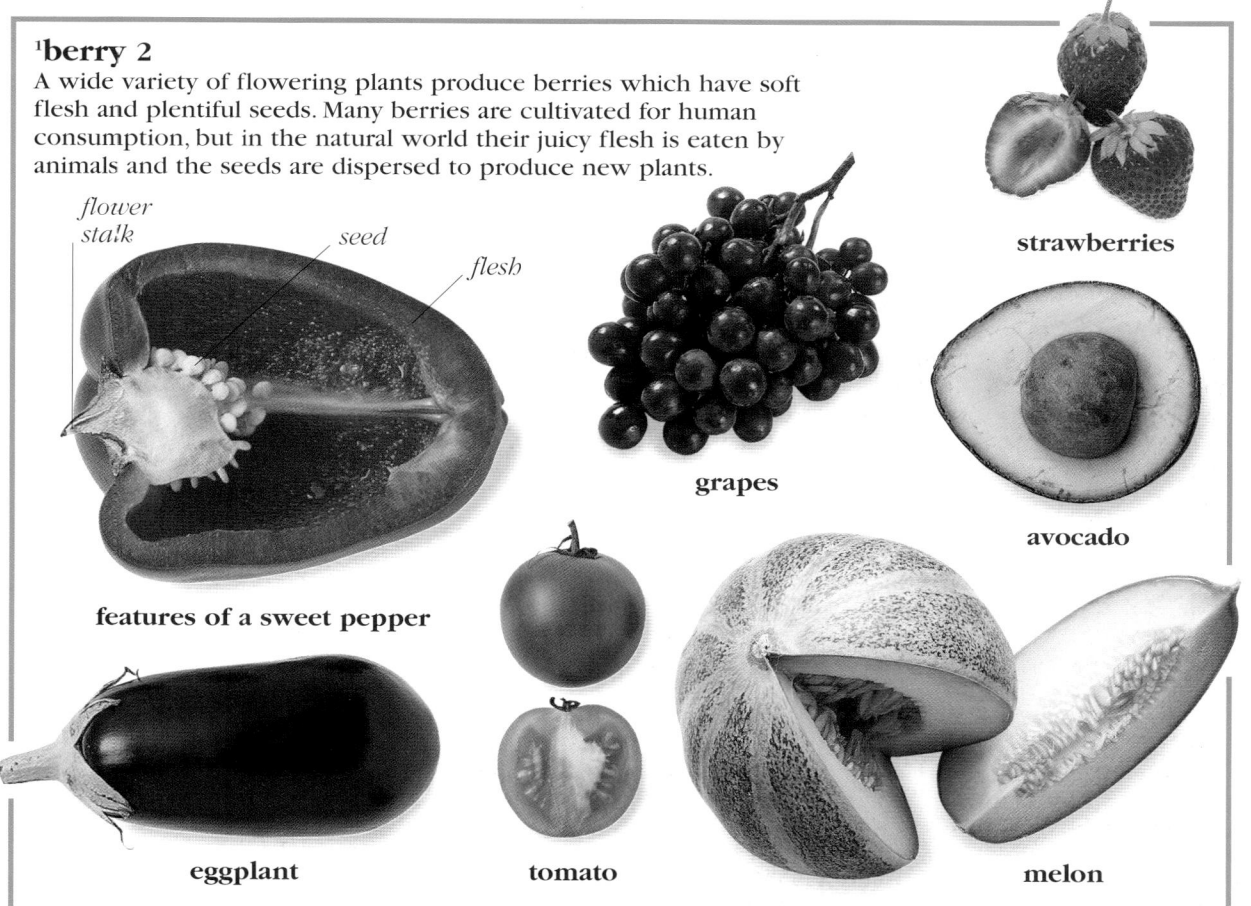

*flower stalk*
*seed*
*flesh*

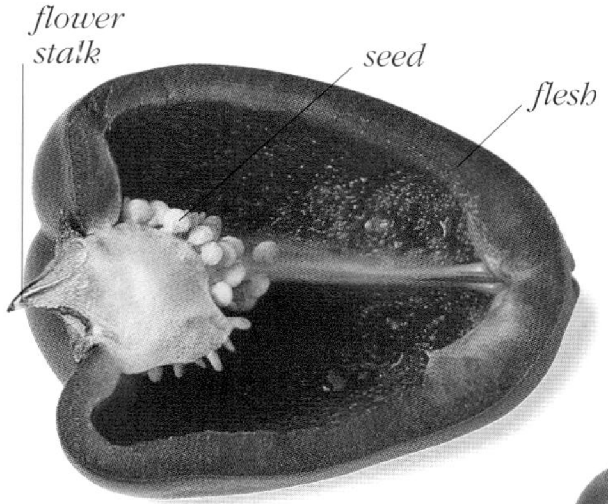

**features of a sweet pepper**

**grapes**

**strawberries**

**avocado**

**eggplant**

**tomato**

**melon**

A B C D E F G H I J K L M N O P Q R S T U V W X Y Z

**berth** \'bərth\ *n*
**1** a place where a ship lies at anchor or at a wharf
**2** a bed on a ship, train, or airplane

**be·seech** \bi-'sēch\ *vb* **be·sought** \-'sȯt\ *or* **be·seeched**; **be·seech·ing**
to ask earnestly

**be·set** \bi-'set\ *vb* **be·set**; **be·set·ting**
**1** to attack from all sides
**2** SURROUND

**be·side** \bi-'sīd\ *prep*
**1** by the side of : NEXT TO ⟨sit *beside* me⟩
**2** compared with ⟨looks small *beside* you⟩
**3** [1]BESIDES ⟨expect no one *beside* you⟩
**4** away from : wide of ⟨that remark is *beside* the point⟩
**beside oneself** very upset ⟨*beside myself* with worry⟩

[1]**be·sides** \bi-'sīdz\ *prep*
**1** in addition to ⟨*besides* cookies they also baked a cake⟩
**2** other than ⟨no one here *besides* me⟩

[2]**besides** *adv*
in addition : ALSO ⟨had ice cream and cake and candy *besides*⟩

**be·siege** \bi-'sēj\ *vb* **be·sieged**; **be·sieg·ing**
**1** to surround with armed forces for the purpose of capturing
**2** to crowd around
**be·sieg·er** *n*

**besought** *past of* BESEECH

[1]**best** \'best\ *adj, superlative of* GOOD
good or useful in the highest degree : most excellent
**best part** [3]MOST ⟨spent the *best part* of the day at school⟩

[2]**best** *adv, superlative of* WELL
**1** in the best way
**2** [2]MOST 1 ⟨*best* able to do the work⟩

[3]**best** *n*
**1** a person or thing or part of a thing that is best
**2** one's greatest effort

[4]**best** *vb*
to get the better of

**be·stir** \bi-'stər\ *vb* **be·stirred**; **be·stir·ring**
to stir up : rouse to action

**be·stow** \bi-'stō\ *vb*
to present as a gift

[1]**bet** \'bet\ *n*
**1** an agreement requiring the person who guesses wrong about the result of a contest or the outcome of an event to give something to the person who guesses right
**2** the money or thing risked in a bet

[2]**bet** *vb* **bet** *or* **bet·ted**; **bet·ting**
**1** to risk in a bet ⟨*bet* a dollar⟩
**2** to be sure enough to make a bet ⟨*bet* it will rain⟩

**be·tray** \bi-'trā\ *vb*
**1** to give over to an enemy by treason or fraud ⟨*betray* a fort⟩
**2** to be unfaithful to ⟨*betray* a friend⟩
**3** REVEAL 2, SHOW ⟨*betrayed* fear⟩

**be·troth** \bi-'träth, -'trȯth, -'trōth, *or with* th\ *vb*
to promise to marry or give in marriage

**be·troth·al** \bi-'trōth-əl, -'trȯth-, -'trōth-\ *n*
an engagement to be married

[1]**bet·ter** \'bet-ər\ *adj, comparative of* GOOD
**1** more satisfactory than another thing
**2** improved in health
**better part** more than half ⟨waited the *better part* of an hour⟩

[2]**better** *vb*
to make or become better
**bet·ter·ment** \-mənt\ *n*

[3]**better** *adv, comparative of* WELL
in a superior or more excellent way

[4]**better** *n*
**1** a better person or thing ⟨a change for the *better*⟩
**2** ADVANTAGE 1, VICTORY ⟨got the *better* of her opponent⟩

**bet·tor** *or* **bet·ter** \'bet-ər\ *n*
one that bets

[1]**be·tween** \bi-'twēn\ *prep*
**1** by the efforts of each of ⟨*between* us we can get the job done⟩
**2** in or into the interval separating ⟨*between* sundown and sunup⟩ ⟨*between* the two desks⟩
**3** functioning to separate or tell apart ⟨the differences *between* soccer and football⟩
**4** by comparing ⟨choose *between* two things⟩
**5** shared by ⟨a strong bond *between* parent and child⟩
**6** in shares to each of ⟨divided the money *between* the two children⟩

---

**Synonyms** BETWEEN and AMONG are both used to show the relationship of things in terms of their position or distribution. BETWEEN is always used of two objects ⟨divided the work *between* my brother and me⟩ ⟨competition *between* their school and ours⟩. AMONG is usually used of more than two objects ⟨divided the work *among* all of us⟩ ⟨competition *among* the three schools⟩.

---

[2]**between** *adv*
in a position between others

[1]**bev·el** \'bev-əl\ *n*
a slant or slope of one surface or line against another

---

**Word History** At first the word *bevel* was used for a certain kind of angle. This was the angle formed by two surfaces that are not at right angles. Look at the opening of such an angle. You may be able to imagine that it looks like an open mouth. The English word *bevel* came from an Old French word that meant "with open mouth." This word was formed from an Old French word that meant "to yawn."

---

[2]**bevel** *vb* **bev·eled** *or* **bev·elled**; **bev·el·ing** *or* **bev·el·ling**
to cut or shape (an edge or surface) so as to form a bevel

**bev·er·age** \'bev-ə-rij, 'bev-rij\ *n*
a liquid that is drunk for food or pleasure

**be·ware** \bi-'waər, -'weər\ *vb*
to be cautious or careful

**be·whis·kered** \bi-'hwis-kərd, -'wis-\ *adj*
having whiskers

**be·wil·der** \bi-'wil-dər\ *vb*
to fill with uncertainty : CONFUSE
**be·wil·der·ment** \-mənt\ *n*

**be·witch** \bi-'wich\ *vb*
**1** to gain an influence over by means of magic or witchcraft
**2** to attract or delight as if by magic
**be·witch·ment** \-mənt\ *n*

[1]**be·yond** \bē-'änd\ *adv*
on or to the farther side

**²beyond** *prep*
**1** on the other side of ⟨*beyond* the sea⟩
**2** out of the reach or sphere of ⟨*beyond* help⟩

**bi-** *prefix*
**1** two
**2** coming or occurring every two
**3** into two parts ⟨*bi*sect⟩
**4** twice : doubly : on both sides

**¹bi·as** \'bī-əs\ *n*
**1** a seam, cut, or stitching running in a slant across cloth
**2** a favoring of one way of feeling or acting over another : PREJUDICE

**²bias** *vb* **bi·ased** *or* **bi·assed**; **bi·as·ing** *or* **bi·as·sing**
to give a bias to

**bib** \'bib\ *n*
**1** a cloth or plastic shield tied under a child's chin to protect the clothes
**2** the upper part of an apron or of overalls

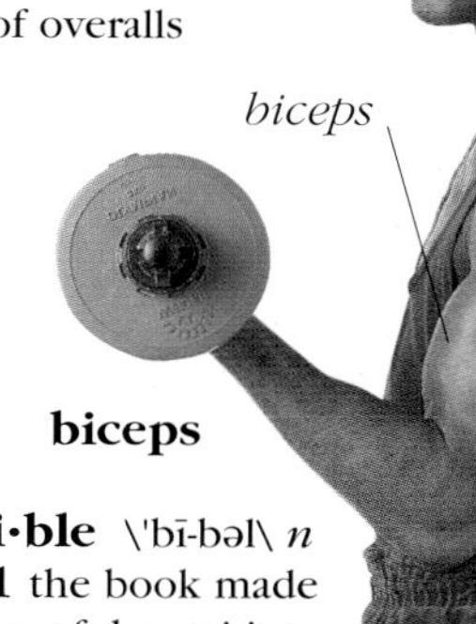


**biceps**

**Bi·ble** \'bī-bəl\ *n*
**1** the book made up of the writings accepted by Christians as coming from God
**2** a book containing the sacred writings of a religion

**bib·li·cal** \'bib-li-kəl\ *adj*
relating to, taken from, or found in the Bible

**bib·li·og·ra·phy** \,bib-lē-'äg-rə-fē\ *n, pl* **bib·li·og·ra·phies**
a list of writings about an author or a subject

**bi·car·bon·ate of soda** \bī-'kär-bə-nət-, -,nāt-\
SODIUM BICARBONATE

**bi·ceps** \'bī-,seps\ *n, pl* **biceps** *also* **bi·ceps·es**
◀ a large muscle of the upper arm

**bick·er** \'bik-ər\ *vb*
to quarrel in a cross or silly way ⟨*bickered* over who would pay⟩

**bi·cus·pid** \bī-'kəs-pəd\ *n*
either of the two teeth with double points on each side of each jaw of a person

**¹bi·cy·cle** \'bī-,sik-əl\ *n*
▼ a light vehicle having two wheels one behind the other, a saddle seat, and pedals by which it is made to move

## ¹bicycle

The bicycle is one of the most popular modes of transport in the world. The types available today are much more sophisticated than early examples such as the penny-farthing. They range from simple, gearless models for everyday use to specially equipped, multi-geared racing and mountain bicycles for competitive sports and cycling in rough terrain.

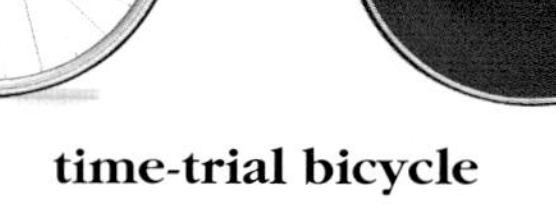


**time-trial bicycle**

**features of a mountain bicycle**

**child's bicycle**

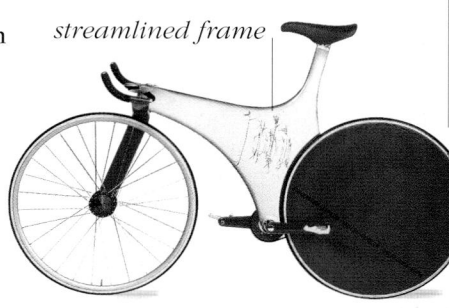

**penny-farthing** was a 19th-century bicycle

[2]**bicycle** *vb* **bi·cy·cled**; **bi·cy·cling** \'bī-,sik-ə-ling, -,sik-ling\
to ride a bicycle

**bi·cy·clist** \'bī-,sik-ləst\ *n*
a person who rides a bicycle

[1]**bid** \'bid\ *vb* **bade** \'bad\ *or* **bid**; **bid·den** \'bid-n\ *or* **bid**; **bid·ding**
**1** [1]ORDER 2, COMMAND ⟨do as I *bid* you⟩
**2** to express to ⟨*bade* our guests good-bye⟩
**3** to make an offer for something (as at an auction)
**bid·der** *n*

[2]**bid** *n*
**1** an offer to pay a certain sum for something or to do certain work at a stated fee
**2** INVITATION 2

**bide** \'bīd\ *vb* **bode** \'bōd\ *or* **bid·ed** \'bīd-əd\; **bid·ed**; **bid·ing**
to wait or wait for ⟨*bide* a while⟩ ⟨*bide* one's time⟩

[1]**bi·en·ni·al** \bī-'en-ē-əl\ *adj*
**1** occurring every two years
**2** growing stalks and leaves one year and flowers and fruit the next before dying
**bi·en·ni·al·ly** \-ē-ə-lē\ *adv*

[2]**biennial** *n*
a biennial plant

**bier** \'biər\ *n*
a stand on which a corpse or coffin is placed

**big** \'big\ *adj* **big·ger**; **big·gest**
**1** large in size
**2** IMPORTANT 1
**big·ness** *n*

**Big Dipper** *n*
a group of seven stars in the northern sky arranged in a form like a dipper with two stars that form the side opposite the handle pointing to the North Star

**big·horn** \'big-,hȯrn\ *n*
► a grayish brown wild sheep of mountainous western North America

**big tree** *n*
a very large California sequoia with light soft brittle wood

**bike** \'bīk\ *n*
**1** BICYCLE
**2** MOTORCYCLE

**bighorn** sheep

**bile** \'bīl\ *n*
a thick bitter yellow or greenish fluid supplied by the liver to aid in digestion

**bi·lin·gual** \,bī-'ling-gwəl, -gyə-wəl\ *adj*
of, expressed in, or using two languages ⟨a *bilingual* dictionary⟩ ⟨*bilingual* signs⟩

[1]**bill** \'bil\ *n*
**1** the jaws of a bird together with their horny covering
**2** a part of an animal (as a turtle) that suggests the bill of a bird
**billed** \'bild\ *adj*

[2]**bill** *n*
**1** a draft of a law presented to a legislature for consideration ⟨the representative introduced a *bill* in Congress⟩
**2** a record of goods sold, services performed, or work done with the cost involved ⟨a telephone *bill*⟩
**3** a sign or poster advertising something
**4** a piece of paper money ⟨a dollar *bill*⟩

[3]**bill** *vb*
to send a bill to

**bill·board** \'bil-,bōrd\ *n*
a flat surface on which outdoor advertisements are displayed

**bill·fold** \'bil-,fōld\ *n*
a folding pocketbook especially for paper money : WALLET

**bil·liards** \'bil-yərdz\ *n*
a game played by driving solid balls with a cue into each other or into pockets on a large rectangular table

**bil·lion** \'bil-yən\ *n*
**1** a thousand millions
**2** a very large number ⟨*billions* of dollars⟩

[1]**bil·lionth** \'bil-yənth\ *adj*
being last in a series of a billion

[2]**billionth** *n*
number 1,000,000,000 in a series

[1]**bil·low** \'bil-ō\ *n*
a great wave

[2]**billow** *vb*
**1** to roll in great waves ⟨the *billowing* ocean⟩
**2** to swell out ⟨sails *billowing* in the breeze⟩

**bil·ly club** \'bil-ē-\ *n*
a heavy club (as of wood) carried by a police officer

**billy goat** \'bil-ē-\ *n*
▼ a male goat

horn

**billy goat**

**bin** \'bin\ *n*
a box or enclosed place used for storage ⟨a coal *bin*⟩

**bi·na·ry** \'bī-nə-rē\ *adj*
of, relating to, or being a number system with a base of 2 ⟨the two *binary* digits are zero and 1⟩

**bind** \'bīnd\ *vb* **bound** \'baund\; **bind·ing**
**1** to fasten by tying
**2** to hold or restrict by force or obligation
**3** [2]BANDAGE
**4** to finish or decorate with a binding ⟨*bind* the hem of a skirt⟩
**5** to fasten together and enclose in a cover ⟨*bind* a book⟩

**bind·er** \'bīn-dər\ *n*
**1** a person who binds books
**2** a cover for holding together loose sheets of paper
**3** a machine that cuts grain and ties it into bundles

## biplane

Many early airplanes were constructed from wood and canvas, with two pairs of wings braced with wires, because these were stronger and more stable than a single pair. Although monoplanes were in use before 1910, biplanes continued to dominate airplane design until the 1930s.

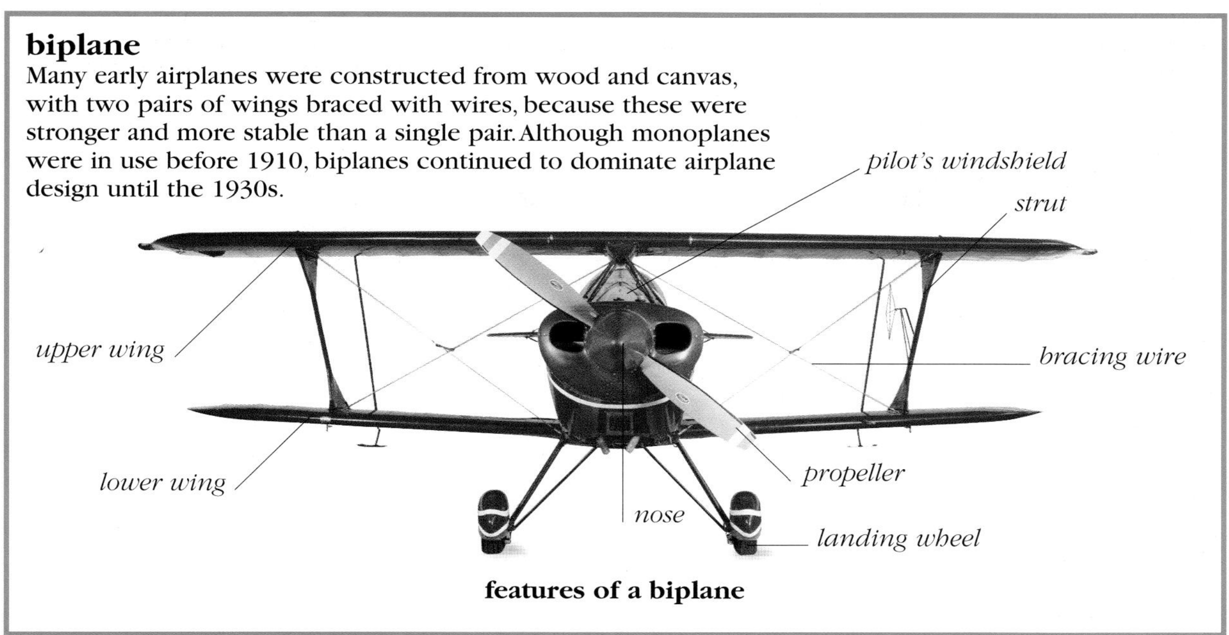


**features of a biplane**

**bind·ing** \'bīn-ding\ *n*
**1** the cover and the fastenings of a book
**2** a narrow strip of fabric used along the edge of an article of clothing

**bin·go** \'bing-gō\ *n*
a game of chance played by covering a numbered space on a card when the number is matched by one drawn at random and won by the first player to cover five spaces in a row

**bin·oc·u·lar** \bī-'näk-yə-lər, bə-\ *adj*
of, using, or suited for the use of both eyes

**bin·oc·u·lars** \bə-'näk-yə-lərz, bī-\ *n pl*
▼ a hand-held instrument for seeing at a distance that is made up of two telescopes usually having prisms

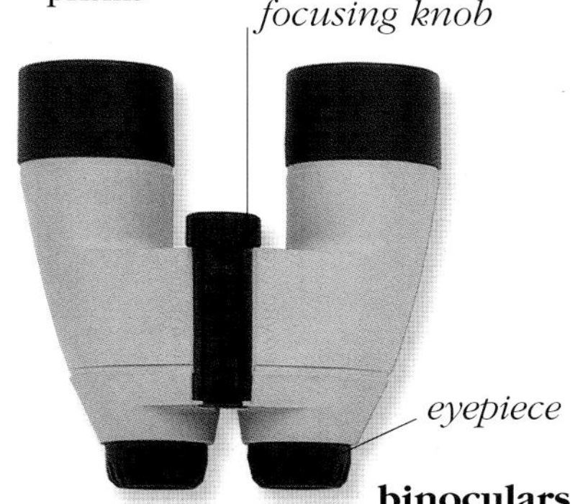


**binoculars**

**bio-** *prefix*
living matter

**bio·de·grad·able** \ˌbī-ō-di-'grād-ə-bəl\ *adj*
possible to break down and make harmless by the action of living things (as bacteria)

**bio·di·ver·si·ty** \ˌbī-ō-də-'vər-sə-tē, -dī-\ *n*
biological variety in an environment as shown by numbers of different kinds of plants and animals

**bio·graph·i·cal** \ˌbī-ə-'graf-i-kəl\ *adj*
of or relating to the history of people's lives

**bi·og·ra·phy** \bī-'äg-rə-fē\ *n, pl* **bi·og·ra·phies**
a written history of a person's life

**bi·o·log·i·cal** \ˌbī-ə-'läj-i-kəl\ *adj*
of or relating to biology

**bi·ol·o·gist** \bī-'äl-ə-jəst\ *n*
a specialist in biology

**bi·ol·o·gy** \bī-'äl-ə-jē\ *n*
a science that deals with living things and their relationships, distribution, and behavior

**bio·re·gion** \'bī-ō-ˌrē-jən\ *n*
a region whose limits are naturally defined by geographic and biological features (as mountains and ecosystems)
**bio·re·gion·al** \ˌbī-ō-'rē-jən-l\ *adj*

**bio·tech·nol·o·gy** \ˌbī-ō-tek-'näl-ə-jē\ *n*
the use of techniques from genetics to combine inherited characteristics selected from different kinds of organisms into one organism in order to produce useful products (as drugs)

**bi·ped** \'bī-ˌped\ *n*
an animal (as a person) that has only two feet

**bi·plane** \'bī-ˌplān\ *n*
▲ an airplane with two wings on each side of the body usually placed one above the other

**birch** \'bərch\ *n*
▼ a tree with hard wood and a smooth bark that can be peeled off in thin layers

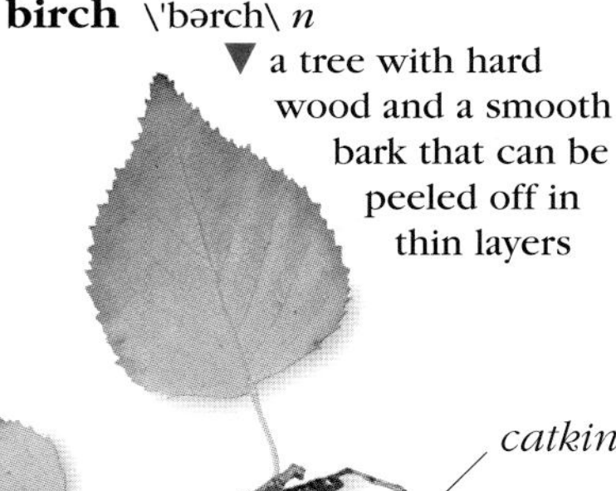

**birch**

## bird

All birds have a body covered with feathers, a pair of wings, a beak, and scaly legs and feet. They reproduce by laying eggs. Instead of teeth, birds have a special grinding organ called a gizzard. There are many bird species around the world, adapted to life in a wide range of habitats.

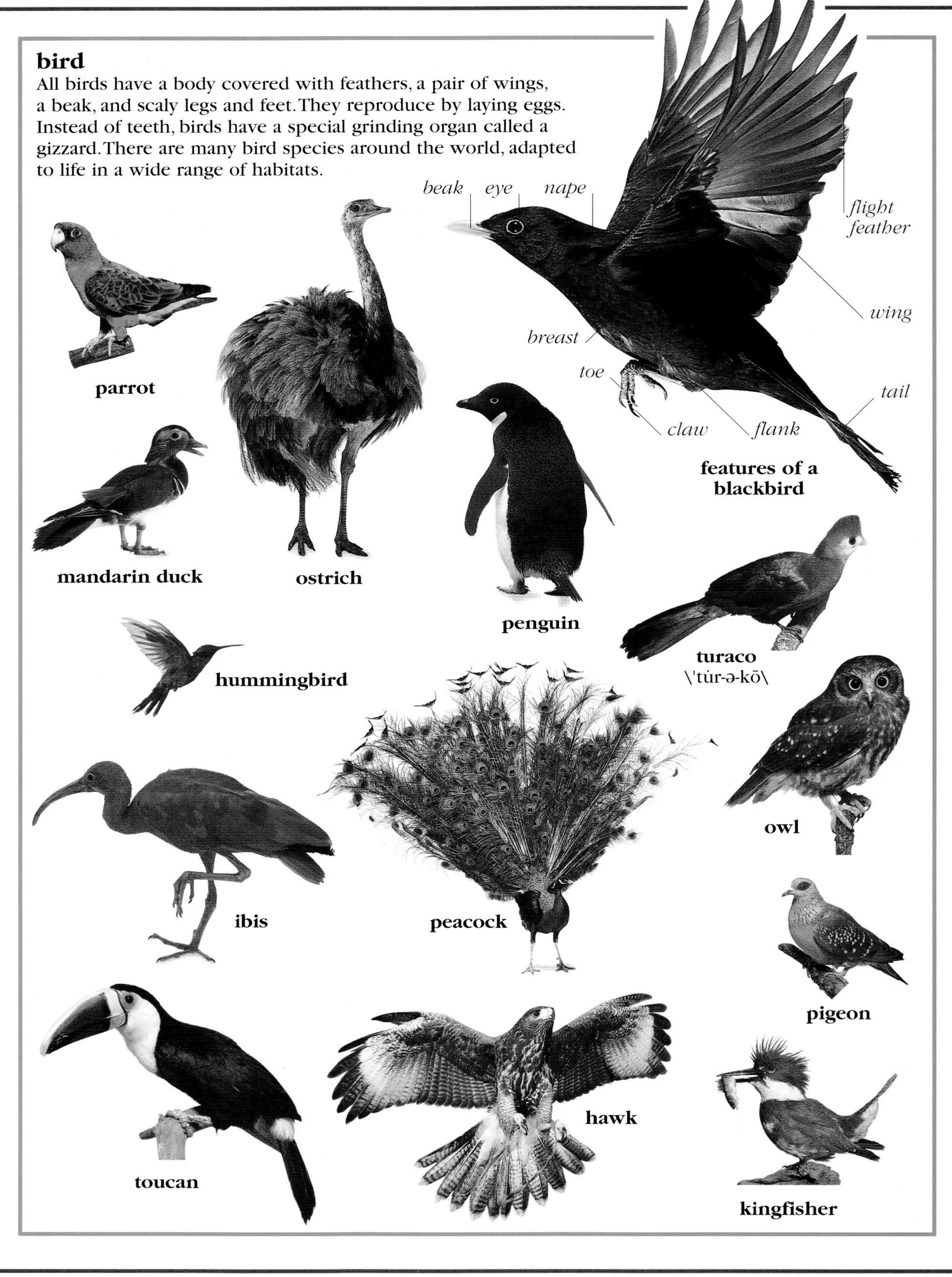

**bird** \'bərd\ *n*
◀ an animal that lays eggs and has wings and a body covered with feathers
**bird·bath** \'bərd-ˌbath, -ˌbȧth\ *n*
a basin for birds to bathe in
**bird dog** *n*
a dog trained to hunt or bring in game birds
**bird·house** \'bərd-ˌhau̇s\ *n*
**1** an artificial nesting place for birds
**2** AVIARY
**bird of prey**
a bird (as an eagle or owl) that feeds almost entirely on meat taken by hunting
**bird·seed** \'bərd-ˌsēd\ *n*
a mixture of small seeds used chiefly for feeding wild or caged birds
**bird's–eye** \'bərd-ˌzī\ *adj*
seen from above as if by a flying bird ⟨a *bird's-eye* view⟩
**birth** \'bərth\ *n*
**1** the coming of a new individual from the body of its parent
**2** the act of bringing into life
**3** LINEAGE 1 ⟨a person of noble *birth*⟩
**4** ORIGIN 2
**birth·day** \'bərth-ˌdā\ *n*
**1** the day on which a person is born
**2** a day of beginning ⟨July 4, 1776 is sometimes called the *birthday* of our country⟩
**3** the return each year of the date on which a person was born or something began
**birth·mark** \'bərth-ˌmärk\ *n*
an unusual mark or blemish on the skin at birth
**birth·place** \'bərth-ˌplās\ *n*
the place where a person was born or where something began ⟨the *birthplace* of freedom⟩
**birth·right** \'bərth-ˌrīt\ *n*
a right belonging to a person because of his or her birth
**bis·cuit** \'bis-kət\ *n*
**1** CRACKER
**2** a small cake of raised dough baked in an oven
**bi·sect** \'bī-ˌsekt\ *vb*
**1** to divide into two usually equal parts
**2** INTERSECT

**Word History** When you bisect something you are cutting it in two. The word *bisect* itself will tell you that if you know Latin. The word was formed in English, but it came from two Latin elements. The *bi-* came from a Latin prefix meaning "two." The *-sect* came from a Latin word meaning "to cut."

**bish·op** \'bish-əp\ *n*
**1** a member of the clergy of high rank
**2** ▶ a piece in the game of chess

**bishop 2**

**Word History** The main duty of a bishop is to watch over the members of a church as a shepherd watches over a flock. The English word *bishop* came from a Greek word. This Greek word meant "overseer" or "bishop." It was formed from two Greek words. The first meant "on" or "over," and the second meant "watcher."

**bis·muth** \'biz-məth\ *n*
a heavy grayish white metallic chemical element that is used in alloys and in medicine
**bi·son** \'bīs-n, 'bīz-\ *n, pl* **bison**
▼ a large animal with short horns and a shaggy mane that is related to the cows and oxen

**bison**

[1]**bit** \'bit\ *n*
**1** a part of a bridle that is put in the horse's mouth
**2** the cutting or boring edge or part of a tool
[2]**bit** *n*
**1** a small piece or quantity ⟨a *bit* of food⟩
**2** a short time ⟨rest a *bit*⟩
**3** [1]SOMEWHAT ⟨a *bit* of a fool⟩
[3]**bit** *n*
a unit of computer information that represents the selection of one of two possible choices (as *on* or *off*)
**bitch** \'bich\ *n*
a female dog
[1]**bite** \'bīt\ *vb* **bit** \'bit\; **bit·ten** \'bit-n\; **bit·ing** \'bīt-ing\
**1** to seize, grip, or cut into with or as if with teeth ⟨*bite* an apple⟩
**2** to wound or sting usually with a stinger or fang
**3** to cause to sting ⟨pepper *bites* the mouth⟩
**4** to take a bait ⟨the fish are *biting*⟩
[2]**bite** *n*
**1** a seizing of something with the teeth or the mouth
**2** a wound made by biting **:** STING ⟨a mosquito *bite*⟩
**3** the amount of food taken at a bite
**4** a sharp or biting sensation
**bit·ing** \'bīt-ing\ *adj*
producing bodily or mental distress **:** SHARP

\ng\ sing \ō\ bone \ȯ\ saw \ȯi\ coin \th\ thin \t͟h\ this \ü\ food \u̇\ foot \y\ yet \yü\ few \yu̇\ cure \zh\ vision

**bit·ter** \'bit-ər\ *adj*
**1** sharp, biting, and unpleasant to the taste
**2** hard to put up with ⟨a *bitter* disappointment⟩
**3** very harsh or sharp : BITING ⟨a *bitter* wind⟩
**4** caused by anger, distress, or sorrow ⟨*bitter* tears⟩
**bit·ter·ly** *adv*
**bit·ter·ness** *n*

**bit·tern** \'bit-ərn\ *n*
a brownish marsh bird which has a loud booming cry

**[1]bit·ter·sweet** \'bit-ər-,swēt\ *n*
**1** ▼ a poisonous vine with purple flowers and red berries
**2** a North American woody climbing plant with orange seedcases that open when ripe and show the red-coated seeds

berry

**[1]bittersweet 1**

**[2]bittersweet** *adj*
being partly bitter or sad and partly sweet or happy ⟨*bittersweet* memories of summer camp⟩

**bi·tu·mi·nous coal** \bə-'tü-mə-nəs-, -'tyü-\ *n*
a soft coal that gives much smoke when burned

**bi·zarre** \bə-'zär\ *adj*
very strange or odd

**blab** \'blab\ *vb* **blabbed**; **blab·bing**
to talk too much

**[1]black** \'blak\ *adj*
**1** of the color black
**2** very dark ⟨a *black* night⟩
**3** of or relating to any peoples having dark skin and especially any of the original peoples of Africa south of the Sahara
**4** *often cap* of or relating to Americans having ancestors from Africa south of the Sahara ⟨*black* studies⟩
**5** WICKED ⟨a *black* deed⟩
**6** very sad or gloomy ⟨in a *black* mood⟩
**7** UNFRIENDLY ⟨a *black* look⟩
**black·ness** *n*

**[2]black** *n*
**1** a black pigment or dye
**2** the color of coal : the opposite of white
**3** black clothing ⟨dressed in *black*⟩
**4** a person belonging to a people having dark skin and especially a black African
**5** *often cap* an American having black African ancestors

**[3]black** *vb*
BLACKEN 1

**black–and–blue** \,blak-ən-'blü\ *adj*
darkly discolored (as from a bruise)

**black·ber·ry** \'blak-,ber-ē\ *n*, *pl* **black·ber·ries**
the black or dark purple sweet juicy berry of a prickly plant related to the raspberry

**black·bird** \'blak-,bərd\ *n*
any of several birds of which the males are mostly black

**black·board** \'blak-,bōrd\ *n*
a hard smooth usually dark surface used especially in a classroom for writing or drawing on with chalk

**black·en** \'blak-ən\ *vb*
**1** to make or become black
**2** [2]SPOIL 2 ⟨*blacken* an enemy's reputation⟩

**black–eyed Su·san** \,blak-,īd-'süz-n\ *n*
▼ a daisy with yellow or orange petals and a dark center

**black-eyed Susan**

**black·head** \'blak-,hed\ *n*
a dark oily plug of hardened material blocking the opening of a skin gland

**black·ish** \'blak-ish\ *adj*
somewhat black

**[1]black·mail** \'blak-,māl\ *n*
**1** the forcing of someone to pay money by threatening to reveal a secret that might bring disgrace on him or her
**2** money paid under threat of blackmail

**[2]blackmail** *vb*
to threaten with the revealing of a secret unless money is paid
**black·mail·er** *n*

**black·out** \'blak-,au̇t\ *n*
**1** a period of darkness enforced as a protection against air raids
**2** a period of darkness caused by power failure
**3** a temporary loss of vision or consciousness

**black out** *vb*
to lose consciousness or the ability to see for a short time

**black·smith** \'blak-,smith\ *n*
a person who makes things out of iron by heating and hammering it

**black·snake** \'blak-,snāk\ *n*
either of two harmless snakes of the United States with blackish skins

**black·top** \'blak-,täp\ *n*
a black material used especially to pave roads

**black widow**

**black widow** *n*
▲ a poisonous spider the female of which is black with a red mark shaped like an hourglass on the underside of the abdomen

**blad·der** \'blad-ər\ *n*
**1** a pouch into which urine passes from the kidneys
**2** a container that can be filled with air or gas

**blade** \'blād\ *n*
**1** a leaf of a plant and especially of a grass
**2** the broad flat part of a leaf
**3** something that widens out like the blade of a leaf ⟨the *blade* of a propeller⟩ ⟨the *blade* of a fan⟩
**4** the cutting part of a tool or machine ⟨a knife *blade*⟩
**5** SWORD
**6** the runner of an ice skate
**blad·ed** \'blād-əd\ *adj*

[1]**blame** \'blām\ *vb* **blamed**; **blam·ing**
**1** to find fault with
**2** to hold responsible ⟨*blamed* me for everything⟩
**3** to place responsibility for ⟨don't *blame* it on us⟩

[2]**blame** *n*
**1** expression of disapproval ⟨receive both praise and *blame*⟩
**2** responsibility for something that fails ⟨took the *blame* for the defeat⟩
**blame·less** \'blām-ləs\ *adj*

**blame·wor·thy** \'blām-ˌwər-t͟hē\ *adj*
deserving blame

**blanch** \'blanch\ *vb*
**1** [1]BLEACH, WHITEN
**2** to scald so as to remove the skin from ⟨*blanch* almonds⟩
**3** to turn pale

[1]**blank** \'blangk\ *adj*
**1** seeming to be confused ⟨a *blank* look⟩
**2** not having any writing or marks ⟨a *blank* sheet of paper⟩
**3** having empty spaces to be filled in ⟨a *blank* form⟩

[2]**blank** *n*
**1** an empty space in a line of writing or printing
**2** a paper with empty spaces to be filled in ⟨an application *blank*⟩
**3** a cartridge loaded with powder but no bullet

[1]**blan·ket** \'blang-kət\ *n*
**1** ▶ a heavy woven covering used for beds
**2** a covering layer ⟨a *blanket* of snow⟩

[2]**blanket** *vb*
to cover with a blanket

[1]**blare** \'blaər, 'bleər\ *vb* **blared**; **blar·ing**
**1** to sound loud and harsh ⟨heard the trumpet *blare*⟩
**2** to present in a harsh noisy manner ⟨loudspeakers *blaring* advertisements⟩

[2]**blare** *n*
a harsh loud noise

[1]**blast** \'blast\ *n*
**1** a strong gust of wind ⟨the icy *blasts* of winter⟩
**2** a stream of air or gas forced through an opening
**3** the sound made by a wind instrument ⟨the *blast* of a whistle⟩
**4** EXPLOSION 1

[2]**blast** *vb*
**1** [2]BLIGHT
**2** to break to pieces by an explosion : SHATTER

**blast–off** \'blas-ˌtȯf\ *n*
an instance of blasting off (as of a rocket)

**blast off** \blas-'tȯf\ *vb*
to take off — used of vehicles using rockets for power

[1]**blaze** \'blāz\ *n*
**1** a bright hot flame
**2** great brightness and heat ⟨the *blaze* of the sun⟩
**3** OUTBURST 1 ⟨a *blaze* of anger⟩
**4** a bright display ⟨a *blaze* of color⟩

[2]**blaze** *vb* **blazed**; **blaz·ing**
**1** to burn brightly ⟨a fire *blazing* in the fireplace⟩
**2** to shine as if on fire ⟨eyes *blazing* with anger⟩

[3]**blaze** *n*
a mark made on a tree by chipping off a piece of the bark

[4]**blaze** *vb* **blazed**; **blaz·ing**
**1** to make a blaze on
**2** to mark by blazing trees ⟨*blaze* a trail⟩

[1]**bleach** \'blēch\ *vb*
to make white by removing the color or stains from

[2]**bleach** *n*
a preparation used for bleaching

[1]**blanket 1**

**bleach·er** \'blē-chər\ *n*
open seats for people to watch from (as at a game) usually arranged like steps — usually used in pl.

**bleak** \'blēk\ *adj*
**1** open to wind or weather ⟨a *bleak* coast⟩
**2** being cold and cutting ⟨a *bleak* wind⟩
**3** not hopeful or encouraging ⟨the future looks *bleak*⟩
**bleak·ly** *adv*
**bleak·ness** *n*

[1]**bleat** \'blēt\ *vb*
to make the cry of a sheep, goat, or calf

[2]**bleat** *n*
the sound of bleating

**bleed** \'blēd\ *vb* **bled** \'bled\; **bleed·ing**
**1** to lose or shed blood ⟨a cut finger *bleeds*⟩
**2** to feel pain or pity ⟨my heart *bleeds* for you⟩
**3** to draw fluid from ⟨*bleed* a tire⟩

[1]**blem·ish** \'blem-ish\ *vb*
to spoil by or as if by an ugly mark

[2]**blemish** *n*
a mark that makes something imperfect : FLAW

[1]**blend** \'blend\ *vb*
**1** to mix so completely that the separate things mixed cannot be told apart
**2** to shade into each other : HARMONIZE ⟨soft colors that *blend* well⟩ **synonyms** see MIX

[2]**blend** *n*
**1** a complete mixture : a product made by blending
**2** a word formed by combining parts of two or more other words so that they overlap ⟨"smog" is a *blend* of "smoke" and "fog"⟩
**3** a group of two or more consonants (as *gr-* in green) beginning a syllable without a vowel between

**bless** \'bles\ *vb* **blessed** \'blest\ *or* **blest**; **bless·ing**
**1** to make holy by a religious ceremony or words ⟨*bless* an altar⟩
**2** to ask the favor or protection of God for ⟨*bless* a congregation in church⟩
**3** to praise or honor as holy ⟨*bless* the Lord⟩
**4** to give happiness or good fortune to ⟨*blessed* with good health⟩

**bless·ed** \'bles-əd, 'blest\ *adj*
**1** HOLY 1
**2** enjoying happiness
**bless·ed·ness** \'bles-əd-nəs\ *n*

**bless·ing** \'bles-ing\ *n*
**1** the act of one who blesses
**2** APPROVAL ⟨gave their *blessing* to the plan⟩
**3** something that makes one happy or content ⟨the *blessings* of peace⟩

**blew** *past of* BLOW

[1]**blight** \'blīt\ *n*
**1** a plant disease marked by drying up without rotting
**2** an organism (as a germ or insect) that causes a plant blight

[2]**blight** *vb*
to injure or destroy by or as if by a blight

**blimp** \'blimp\ *n*
an airship filled with gas like a balloon

[1]**blind** \'blīnd\ *adj*
**1** unable or nearly unable to see
**2** lacking in judgment or understanding
**3** closed at one end ⟨a *blind* alley⟩
**4** using only the instruments within an airplane and not landmarks as a guide ⟨*blind* flying⟩
**blind·ly** *adv*
**blind·ness** *n*

[2]**blind** *vb*
**1** to make blind
**2** to make it impossible to see well **:** DAZZLE ⟨*blinded* by the lights of an approaching car⟩

[3]**blind** *n*
**1** a device to reduce sight or keep out light ⟨window *blinds*⟩
**2** a place of hiding ⟨shot the birds from a *blind*⟩

[4]**blind** *adv*
with only instruments as guidance ⟨fly *blind*⟩

[1]**blind·fold** \'blīnd-,fōld\ *vb*
to shut light out of the eyes of with or as if with a bandage

[2]**blindfold** *n*
a covering over the eyes

**blind·man's buff** \,blīnd-,manz-'bəf\ *n*
a game in which a blindfolded player tries to catch and identify one of the other players

**blink** \'blingk\ *vb*
**1** to look with partly shut eyes
**2** to shut and open the eyes quickly
**3** to shine with a light that goes or seems to go on and off ⟨lights *blinking*⟩

**blink·er** \'bling-kər\ *n*
a light that blinks

**bliss** \'blis\ *n*
great happiness **:** JOY
**bliss·ful** \-fəl\ *adj*
**bliss·ful·ly** \-fə-lē\ *adv*

[1]**blis·ter** \'blis-tər\ *n*
**1** a small raised area of the skin filled with a watery liquid
**2** a swelling (as in paint) that looks like a blister

[2]**blister** *vb*
**1** to develop a blister or blisters ⟨my heel *blistered* on the hike⟩ ⟨*blistering* paint⟩
**2** to cause blisters on ⟨tight shoes can *blister* your feet⟩

**blithe** \'blīth, 'blīth\ *adj* **blith·er**; **blith·est**
free from worry **:** MERRY, CHEERFUL
**blithe·ly** *adv*

**bliz·zard** \'bliz-ərd\ *n*
a long heavy snowstorm

**bloat** \'blōt\ *vb*
to make swollen with or as if with fluid

**blob** \'bläb\ *n*
a small lump or drop of something thick ⟨a *blob* of paint⟩

[1]**block** \'bläk\ *n*
**1** ▼ a solid piece of some material (as stone or wood) usually with one or more flat sides ⟨building *blocks*⟩
**2** something that stops or makes passage or progress difficult **:** OBSTRUCTION ⟨a traffic *block*⟩
**3** a case enclosing one or more pulleys
**4** a number of things thought of as forming a group or unit ⟨a *block* of seats⟩
**5** a large building divided into separate houses or shops ⟨an apartment *block*⟩
**6** a space enclosed by streets
**7** the length of one side of a block ⟨ran three *blocks*⟩

[1]**block 1:** toy building blocks

[2]**block** *vb*
**1** to stop or make passage through difficult **:** OBSTRUCT ⟨*block* the doorway with a bicycle⟩
**2** to stop or make the passage of difficult ⟨*block* a bill in Congress⟩
**3** to make an opponent's movement (as in football) difficult
**4** to mark the chief lines of ⟨*block* out a plan⟩

[1]**block·ade** \blä-'kād\ *vb*
**block·ad·ed**; **block·ad·ing**
to close off a place to prevent the coming in or going out of people or supplies ⟨warships *blockaded* the harbor⟩

[2]**blockade** *n*
the closing off of a place (as by warships) to prevent the coming in or going out of persons or supplies

**block·house** \'bläk-,haus\ *n*
a building (as of heavy timbers or of concrete) built with holes in its sides through which persons inside may fire out at an enemy

[1]**blond** \'bländ\ *adj*
**1** of a light color ⟨*blond* hair⟩
**2** having light hair and skin

[2]**blond** *or* **blonde** \'bländ\ *n*
someone who is blond

**blood** \'bləd\ *n*
**1** the red fluid that circulates in the heart, arteries, capillaries, and veins of persons and animals
**2** relationship through a common ancestor **:** KINSHIP ⟨ties of *blood*⟩
**blood·ed** \'bləd-əd\ *adj*

**blood bank** *n*
blood stored for emergency use in transfusion

**blood·hound** \'bləd-,haund\ *n*
▼ a large hound with long drooping ears, a wrinkled face, and a very good sense of smell

**bloodhound**

**blood pressure** *n*
pressure of the blood on the walls of blood vessels and especially arteries

**blood·shed** \'bləd-,shed\ *n*
[1]MURDER, SLAUGHTER

**blood·shot** \'bləd-,shät\ *adj*
being red and sore ⟨*bloodshot* eyes⟩

**blood·stream** \'bləd-,strēm\ *n*
the circulating blood in the living body

**blood·suck·er** \'bləd-,sək-ər\ *n*
an animal that sucks blood
**blood·suck·ing** \-,sək-ing\ *adj*

**blood·thirsty** \'bləd-,thərs-tē\ *adj*
eager to kill or hurt
**blood·thirst·i·ly** \-tə-lē\ *adv*
**blood·thirst·i·ness** \-tē-nəs\ *n*

**blood vessel** *n*
an artery, vein, or capillary of the body

**bloody** \'bləd-ē\ *adj* **blood·i·er**; **blood·i·est**
1 smeared or stained with blood
2 causing or accompanied by bloodshed

[1]**bloom** \'blüm\ *n*
1 [1]FLOWER 1
2 the period or state of blooming
3 a condition or time of beauty, freshness, and strength ⟨the *bloom* of youth⟩
4 the rosy color of the cheek
5 the delicate powdery coating on some fruits and leaves

[2]**bloom** *vb*
1 to produce blooms : FLOWER
2 to be in a state of youthful beauty and freshness

[1]**blos·som** \'bläs-əm\ *n*
1 [1]FLOWER 1
2 [1]BLOOM 2

[2]**blossom** *vb*
1 [2]BLOOM
2 to unfold like a blossom

[1]**blot** \'blät\ *n*
1 a spot or stain of dirt or ink
2 STIGMA 1, REPROACH ⟨the lie was a bad *blot* on my record⟩

[2]**blot** *vb* **blot·ted**; **blot·ting**
1 [2]SPOT 1
2 to hide completely ⟨the fog *blotted* out the lighthouse⟩
3 to dry with a blotter

**blotch** \'bläch\ *n*
1 a blemish on the skin
2 a large irregular spot of color or ink
**blotched** \'blächt\ *adj*

**blot·ter** \'blät-ər\ *n*
a piece of blotting paper

**blot·ting paper** \'blät-ing-\ *n*
a soft spongy paper used to absorb wet ink

**blouse** \'blau̇s\ *n*
1 a loose outer garment like a smock
2 the jacket of a uniform
3 a loose garment for women and children covering the body from the neck to the waist

[1]**blow** \'blō\ *vb* **blew** \'blü\; **blown** \'blōn\; **blow·ing**
1 to move or be moved usually with speed and force ⟨wind *blowing* from the north⟩
2 to move in or with the wind ⟨dust *blew* through the cracks⟩
3 to send forth a strong stream of air from the mouth or from a bellows ⟨*blow* on your hands⟩
4 to make a sound or cause to sound by blowing ⟨the whistle *blows*⟩ ⟨*blow* a horn⟩
5 to clear by forcing air through ⟨*blow* your nose⟩
6 to shape by forcing air into ⟨*blow* glass⟩
**blow·er** \'blō-ər\ *n*

[2]**blow** *n*
a blowing of wind : GALE

[3]**blow** *n*
1 an act of hitting (as with the fist or a weapon)
2 a sudden act
3 a sudden happening that causes suffering or loss ⟨the dog's death was a severe *blow*⟩

**blow·gun** \'blō-,gən\ *n*
a tube from which a dart may be shot by the force of the breath

**blow·out** \'blō-,au̇t\ *n*
a bursting of a container (as an automobile tire) by pressure of the contents on a weak spot

**bluebird**

**blow·pipe** \'blō-,pīp\ *n*
1 a small round tube for blowing air or gas into a flame so as to make it hotter
2 BLOWGUN

**blow·torch** \'blō-,tȯrch\ *n*
a small portable burner in which the flame is made hotter by a blast of air or oxygen

**blow up** *vb*
1 EXPLODE 1
2 to fill with a gas (as air) ⟨*blow* the balloon *up*⟩

[1]**blub·ber** \'bləb-ər\ *vb*
to weep noisily

[2]**blubber** *n*
the fat of various sea mammals (as whales) from which oil can be obtained

[1]**blue** \'blü\ *adj* **blu·er**; **blu·est**
1 of the color blue
2 low in spirits : MELANCHOLY

[2]**blue** *n*
1 the color in the rainbow between green and violet : the color of the clear daytime sky
2 something blue in color
**out of the blue** suddenly and unexpectedly

*bell-shaped flowers*

**bluebell**

**blue·bell** \'blü-,bel\ *n*
▲ a plant with blue flowers shaped like bells

**blue·ber·ry** \'blü-,ber-ē\ *n*, *pl* **blue·ber·ries**
a sweet blue berry that has small seeds and grows on a bush related to the huckleberry

**blue·bird** \'blü-,bərd\ *n*
◀ any of several small North American songbirds more or less blue above

a b c d e f g h i j k l m n o p q r s t u v w x y z

**blue·bot·tle** \'blü-,bät-l\ *n*
a large blue hairy fly

**blue cheese** *n*
▼ cheese ripened by and full of greenish blue mold

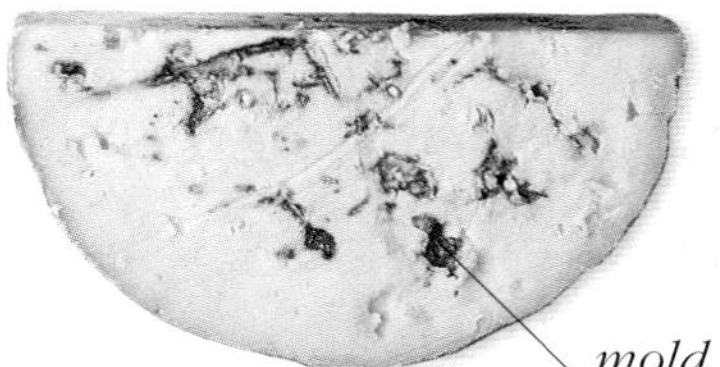


**blue cheese**

**blue·fish** \'blü-,fish\ *n*
a bluish saltwater food fish of the eastern coast of the United States

**blue·grass** \'blü-,gras\ *n*
a grass with bluish green stems

**blueing** *variant of* BLUING

**blue jay** \'blü-,jā\ *n*
any of several crested and mostly blue American birds related to the crows

**blue jeans** *n pl*
pants usually made of blue denim

[1]**blue·print** \'blü-,print\ *n*
**1** a photographic print made with white lines on a blue background and used for copying maps and building plans
**2** a detailed plan of something to be done

[2]**blueprint** *vb*
to make a blueprint of

**blues** \'blüz\ *n pl*
**1** low spirits ⟨overcome by the *blues*⟩
**2** a sad song in a style that was first used by American blacks

[2]**bluff** *n*
a high steep bank : CLIFF

[3]**bluff** *vb*
to deceive or frighten by pretending to have more strength or confidence than one really has
**bluff·er** *n*

[4]**bluff** *n*
**1** an act or instance of bluffing
**2** a person who bluffs

**blu·ing** *or* **blue·ing** \'blü-ing\ *n*
something made with blue or violet dyes that is added to the water when washing clothes to prevent yellowing of white fabrics

**blu·ish** \'blü-ish\ *adj*
somewhat blue

[1]**blun·der** \'blən-dər\ *vb*
**1** to move in a clumsy way
**2** to make a mistake
**blun·der·er** *n*

[2]**blunder** *n*
a bad or stupid mistake **synonyms** see ERROR

**blun·der·buss** \'blən-dər-,bəs\ *n*
a short gun that has a barrel which is larger at the end and that was used long ago for shooting at close range without taking exact aim

[1]**blunt** \'blənt\ *adj*
**1** having a thick edge or point : DULL ⟨a *blunt* knife⟩
**2** speaking or spoken in plain language without thought for other people's feelings
**blunt·ly** *adv*

[2]**blunt** *vb*
to make or become blunt

[1]**blur** \'blər\ *n*
something that cannot be seen clearly ⟨could see only a *blur*⟩

[1]**blush** ... shame, confusion, or embarrassment
**2** a rosy color

[2]**blush** *vb*
**1** to become red in the face from shame, confusion, or embarrassment
**2** to feel ashamed or embarrassed

[1]**blus·ter** \'bləs-tər\ *vb*
**1** to blow hard and noisily
**2** to talk or act in a noisy boastful way

[2]**bluster** *n*
noisy violent action or speech

**boa** \'bō-ə\ *n*
a large snake (as a python) that coils around and crushes its prey

**boar** \'bōr\ *n*
**1** a male pig
**2** a wild pig

[1]**board** \'bōrd\ *n*
**1** a sawed piece of lumber that is much broader and longer than it is thick
**2** a dining table
**3** meals given at set times for a price ⟨room and *board*⟩
**4** a number of persons having authority to manage or direct something ⟨the school *board*⟩
**5** a usually rectangular piece of rigid material used for some special purpose ⟨a diving *board*⟩ ⟨a game *board*⟩
**6** BLACKBOARD
**7 boards** *pl* the low wooden wall enclosing a hockey rink
**8** a sheet of insulating material carrying electronic parts (as for a computer)
**on board** ABOARD

**blue whale**

**blue whale** *n*
▲ a very large whale that is probably the largest living animal

[1]**bluff** \'bləf\ *adj*
**1** rising steeply with a broad front ⟨a *bluff* shoreline⟩
**2** frank and outspoken in a rough but good-natured way
**bluff·ly** *adv*
**bluff·ness** *n*

[2]**blur** *vb* **blurred**; **blur·ring**
**1** to make hard to see or read by smearing
**2** to make or become smeared or confused

**blurt** \'blərt\ *vb*
to say or tell suddenly and without thinking ⟨*blurt* out a secret⟩

[1]**blush** \'bləsh\ *n*
**1** a reddening of the face from shame, confusion, or embarrassment
**2** a rosy color

[2]**board** *vb*
**1** to go aboard ⟨*boarded* the plane in New York⟩
**2** to cover with boards ⟨the windows were *boarded* up⟩
**3** to give or get meals at set times for a price

**board·er** \'bōrd-ər\ *n*
a person who pays for meals or for meals and lodging at another's house

**board·ing·house** \ˈbōrd-ing-ˌhau̇s\ *n*
a house at which people are given meals and often lodging

**boarding school** *n*
a school at which most of the students live during the school year

**board·walk** \ˈbōrd-ˌwȯk\ *n*
a walk made of planks especially along a beach

[1]**boast** \ˈbōst\ *n*
**1** an act of boasting
**2** a cause for boasting or pride

[2]**boast** *vb*
**1** to praise what one has or has done ⟨*boasted* of their strength⟩
**2** to have and be proud of having

**boast·ful** \ˈbōst-fəl\ *adj*
**1** having the habit of boasting
**2** full of boasts

**boast·ful·ly** \-fə-lē\ *adv*
**boast·ful·ness** *n*

[1]**boat** \ˈbōt\ *n*
**1** ▼ a small vessel driven on the water by oars, paddles, sails, or a motor
**2** [1]SHIP 1

[2]**boat** *vb*
to use a boat
**boat·er** *n*

**boat·house** \ˈbōt-ˌhau̇s\ *n*
a house or shelter for boats

**boat·man** \ˈbōt-mən\ *n*, *pl* **boat·men** \-mən\
a person who works on or deals in boats

**boat·swain** \ˈbōs-ᵊn\ *n*
a warrant officer on a warship or a petty officer on a commercial ship who has charge of the hull, anchors, boats, and rigging

[1]**bob** \ˈbäb\ *vb* **bobbed**; **bob·bing**
**1** to move or cause to move with a short jerky motion
**2** to appear suddenly ⟨they may *bob* up anywhere⟩
**3** to try to seize something with the teeth ⟨*bob* for apples⟩

[2]**bob** *n*
a short jerky up-and-down motion

[3]**bob** *n*
**1** a float used to buoy up the baited end of a fishing line
**2** a woman's or child's short haircut

[4]**bob** *vb* **bobbed**; **bob·bing**
to cut in the style of a bob ⟨had my hair *bobbed*⟩

**bob·by pin** \ˈbäb-ē-\ *n*
a flat metal hairpin with the two ends pressed close together

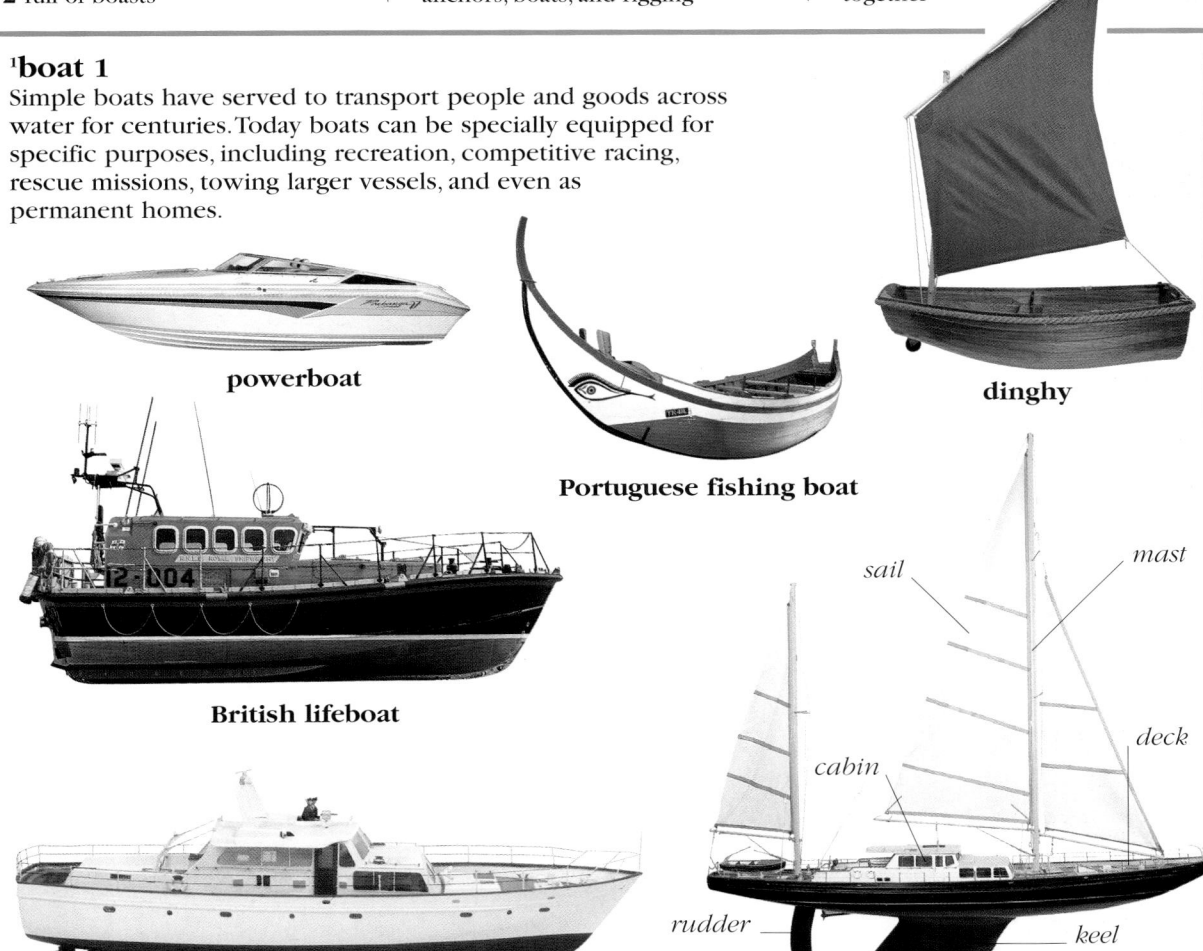

## [1]boat 1

Simple boats have served to transport people and goods across water for centuries. Today boats can be specially equipped for specific purposes, including recreation, competitive racing, rescue missions, towing larger vessels, and even as permanent homes.

**powerboat**

**Portuguese fishing boat**

**dinghy**

**British lifeboat**

**motor yacht**

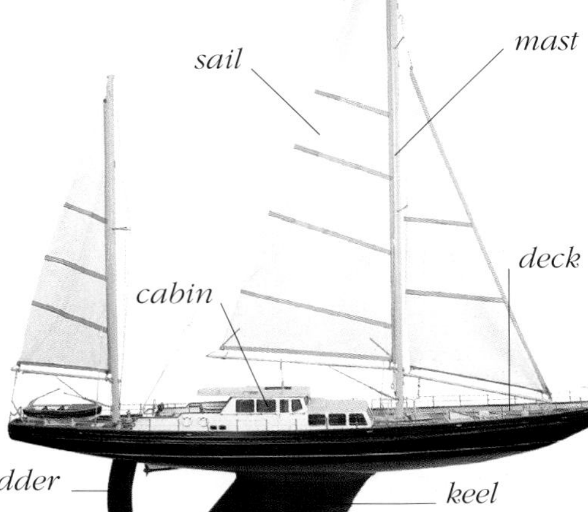


**features of a sailing yacht**

a b c d e f g h i j k l m n o p q r s t u v w x y z

A B C D E F G H I J K L M N O P Q R S T U V W X Y Z

**bob·cat** \'bäb-,kat\ *n*
▶ an American wildcat that is a small rusty brown variety of the lynx

**bobcat**

**bob·o·link** \'bäb-ə-,lingk\ *n*
an American songbird related to the blackbirds

**bob·sled** \'bäb-,sled\ *n*
a racing sled made with two sets of runners, a hand brake, and often a steering wheel

**bob·tail** \'bäb-,tāl\ *n*
**1** a short tail **:** a tail cut short
**2** an animal with a short tail

**bob·white** \bäb-'hwīt, -'wīt\ *n*
▼ an American quail with gray, white, and reddish coloring

**bobwhite**

**bode** *past of* BIDE

**bod·ice** \'bäd-əs\ *n*
the upper part of a dress

**bodi·ly** \'bäd-l-ē\ *adj*
of or relating to the body ⟨*bodily* comfort⟩

**body** \'bäd-ē\ *n, pl* **bod·ies**
**1** the material whole of a live or dead person or animal
**2** the main part of a person, animal, or plant
**3** the main or central part ⟨the *body* of a letter⟩
**4** a group of persons or things united for some purpose ⟨a *body* of troops⟩
**5** a mass or portion of something distinct from other masses ⟨a *body* of water⟩ ⟨a *body* of cold air⟩
**bod·ied** \'bäd-ēd\ *adj*

**body·guard** \'bäd-ē-,gärd\ *n*
a person or a group of persons whose duty it is to protect someone

**[1]bog** \'bäg, 'bȯg\ *n*
wet spongy ground that is usually acid and found next to a body of water (as a pond)

**[2]bog** *vb* **bogged**; **bog·ging**
to sink or stick fast in or as if in a bog ⟨the car *bogged* down⟩

**bo·gey** *or* **bo·gy** *or* **bo·gie** *n, pl* **bogeys** *or* **bogies**
**1** \'bu̇g-ē, 'bō-gē\ GHOST, GOBLIN
**2** \'bō-gē, 'bu̇g-ē\ something one is afraid of without reason

**[1]boil** \'bȯil\ *n*
a hot red painful lump in the skin that contains pus and is caused by infection

**[2]boil** *vb*
**1** to heat or become heated to the temperature (**boiling point**) at which bubbles rise and break at the surface ⟨*boil* water⟩
**2** to cook or become cooked in boiling water ⟨*boil* eggs⟩ ⟨let the stew *boil* slowly⟩
**3** to become angry or upset

**[3]boil** *n*
the state of something that is boiling

**boil·er** \'bȯi-lər\ *n*
**1** a container in which something is boiled
**2** a tank heating and holding water
**3** a strong metal container used in making steam (as to heat buildings)

**bois·ter·ous** \'bȯi-stə-rəs, -strəs\ *adj*
being rough and noisy
**bois·ter·ous·ly** *adv*
**bois·ter·ous·ness** *n*

**bold** \'bōld\ *adj*
**1** willing to meet danger or take risks **:** DARING
**2** not polite and modest **:** FRESH
**3** showing or calling for courage or daring ⟨a *bold* plan⟩ **synonyms** see BRAVE
**bold·ly** *adv*
**bold·ness** *n*

**bold·face** \'bōld-,fās\ *n*
a heavy black type
**bold–faced** \-,fāst\ *adj*

**bo·le·ro** \bə-'leər-ō\ *n, pl* **bo·le·ros**
**1** a Spanish dance or the music for it
**2** a loose short jacket open at the front

**boll** \'bōl\ *n*
the seedpod of a plant (as cotton)

**boll weevil** *n*
a grayish insect that lays its eggs in cotton bolls

**[1]bol·ster** \'bōl-stər\ *n*
a long pillow or cushion sometimes used to support bed pillows

**[2]bolster** *vb*
to support with or as if with a bolster ⟨help to *bolster* up their courage⟩

**[1]bolt** \'bōlt\ *n*
**1** a stroke of lightning **:** THUNDERBOLT
**2** ▼ a sliding bar used to fasten a door
**3** the part of a lock worked by a key
**4** a metal pin or rod usually with a head at one end and a screw thread at the other that is used to hold something in place
**5** a roll of cloth or wallpaper

**[1]bolt 2**

**[2]bolt** *vb*
**1** to move suddenly and rapidly ⟨*bolted* from the room⟩
**2** to run away ⟨the horse shied and *bolted*⟩
**3** to fasten with a bolt ⟨be sure to *bolt* the door⟩
**4** to swallow hastily or without chewing ⟨don't *bolt* your food⟩

**[1]bomb** \'bäm\ *n*
**1** a hollow case or shell filled with explosive material and made to be dropped from an airplane, thrown by hand, or set off by a fuse

2 a container in which something (as an insecticide) is stored under pressure and from which it is released in a fine spray

[2]**bomb** *vb*
to attack with bombs

**bom·bard** \bäm-'bärd\ *vb*
**1** to attack with heavy fire from big guns : SHELL ⟨*bombard* a fort⟩
**2** to attack again and again ⟨*bombard* a person with questions⟩

**bomb·er** \'bäm-ər\ *n*
an airplane specially made for dropping bombs

**bon·bon** \'bän-,bän\ *n*
a candy with a soft coating and a creamy center

[1]**bond** \'bänd\ *n*
**1** something that binds
**2** a force or influence that brings or holds together ⟨a *bond* of friendship⟩
**3** a legal agreement in which a person agrees to pay a sum of money if he or she fails to do a certain thing
**4** a government or business certificate promising to pay a certain sum by a certain day

[2]**bond** *vb*
to stick or cause to stick together

**bond·age** \'bän-dij\ *n*
SLAVERY

[1]**bone** \'bōn\ *n*
**1** the hard material of which the skeleton of most animals is formed
**2** ▼ any of the pieces into which the bone of the skeleton is naturally divided ⟨break a *bone* in one's arm⟩
**bone·less** \-ləs\ *adj*

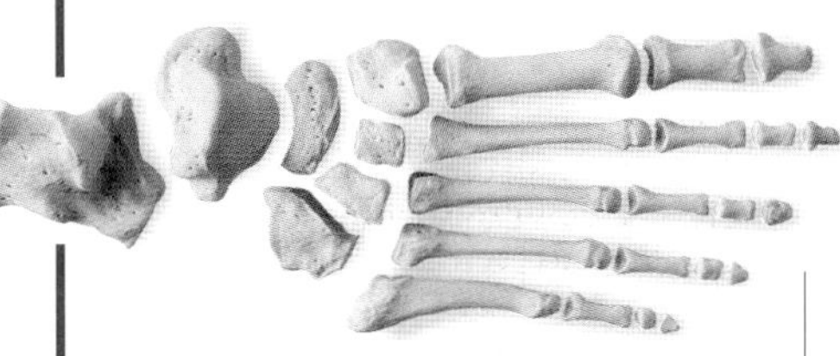

[1]**bone 2:** the bones of a human foot

[2]**bone** *vb* **boned**; **bon·ing**
to remove the bones from ⟨*bone* a fish⟩

**bon·fire** \'bän-,fīr\ *n*
a large fire built outdoors

**bong** \'bäng, 'bòng\ *n*
a deep sound like that of a large bell

**bon·go** \'bäng-gō, 'bòng-gō\ *n, pl* **bongos** *also* **bongoes**
either of a pair of small drums of different sizes fitted together and played with the fingers

**bon·net** \'bän-ət\ *n*
a child's or woman's hat usually tied under the chin by ribbons or strings

**bon·ny** *or* **bon·nie** \'bän-ē\ *adj* **bon·ni·er**; **bon·ni·est** *chiefly British*
HANDSOME 3, BEAUTIFUL

**bo·nus** \'bō-nəs\ *n*
something given to somebody (as a worker) in addition to what is usual or owed

**bony** \'bō-nē\ *adj* **bon·i·er**; **bon·i·est**
**1** of or relating to bone ⟨a *bony* skeleton⟩
**2** like bone especially in hardness ⟨*bony* material⟩
**3** having bones and especially large or noticeable bones ⟨a *bony* fish⟩

[1]**boo** \'bü\ *interj*
used to express disapproval or to startle or frighten

[2]**boo** *n, pl* **boos**
a cry expressing disapproval

[3]**boo** *vb*
to express disapproval of with boos

**boo·by** \'bü-bē\ *n, pl* **boobies**
an awkward foolish person

[1]**book** \'bùk\ *n*
**1** a set of sheets of paper bound together
**2** a long written work ⟨a *book* about birds⟩
**3** a large division of a written work ⟨the *books* of the Bible⟩
**4** a pack of small items bound together ⟨a *book* of matches⟩

**Word History** The word *book* is related to *beech*, the name of a tree. The ancestors of the early English people did not write on paper. They carved inscriptions on stone and wood. It is likely that the use of beech wood for this carved writing gave us the word *book*.

[2]**book** *vb*
to reserve for future use ⟨*book* rooms at the hotel⟩

**book·case** \'bùk-,kās\ *n*
a set of shelves to hold books

**book·end** \'bùk-,end\ *n*
a support at the end of a row of books to keep them standing up

**book·keep·er** \'bùk-,kē-pər\ *n*
a person who keeps accounts for a business

**book·keep·ing** \'bùk-,kē-ping\ *n*
the work of keeping business accounts

**book·let** \'bùk-lət\ *n*
a little book usually having paper covers and few pages

**book·mark** \'bùk-,märk\ *n*
something placed in a book to show the page one wants to return to later

**book·mo·bile** \'bùk-mō-,bēl\ *n*
a truck with shelves of books that is a traveling library

[1]**boom** \'büm\ *vb*
**1** to make a deep hollow rumbling sound ⟨the cannon *boomed*⟩
**2** to increase or develop rapidly ⟨business *boomed* during the war⟩

[2]**boom** *n*
**1** a booming sound
**2** a rapid increase in activity or popularity

[3]**boom** *n*
**1** ▼ a long pole used especially to stretch the bottom of a sail
**2** a long beam sticking out from the mast of a derrick to support or guide something that is being lifted

[3]**boom 1:** the boom on a sailboat

**boom box** *n*
a large portable radio and often tape player with two attached speakers

**boo·mer·ang** \'bü-mə-,rang\ *n*
▼ a curved club that can be thrown so as to return to the thrower

**boomerang**

**boon** \'bün\ *n*
**1** something asked or granted as a favor
**2** something pleasant or helpful that comes at just the right time ⟨the rain was a *boon* to the farmers⟩

[1]**boost** \'büst\ *vb*
**1** to raise or push up from below ⟨*boosted* me through the window⟩
**2** to make bigger or greater ⟨*boost* production⟩
**boost·er** *n*

[2]**boost** *n*
an act of boosting **:** a push up ⟨give me a *boost*⟩

[1]**boot** \'büt\ *n*
a covering usually of leather or rubber for the foot and part of the leg

[2]**boot** *vb*
[1]KICK 1

**boo·tee** *or* **boo·tie** \'büt-ē\ *n*
an infant's knitted sock

**booth** \'büth\ *n, pl* **booths** \'bü<u>th</u>z\
**1** a covered stall for selling or displaying goods (as at a fair or exhibition)
**2** a small enclosure giving privacy for one person ⟨a telephone *booth*⟩
**3** a section of a restaurant consisting of a table between two backed benches

**boo·ty** \'büt-ē\ *n*
goods seized from an enemy in war **:** PLUNDER

**bo·rax** \'bōr-,aks\ *n*
a compound of boron used as a cleansing agent and water softener

[1]**bor·der** \'bȯrd-ər\ *n*
**1** the outer edge of something ⟨the *border* of a lake⟩
**2** ► a boundary especially of a country or state
**3** an ornamental strip on or near the edge of a flat object

**Synonyms** BORDER, EDGE, and RIM mean a line or narrow space that marks the limit of something. BORDER is used of the area on or right next to the boundary line ⟨built several forts along the *border*⟩. EDGE is used of the line formed by two surfaces that meet ⟨a knife with a sharp *edge*⟩. RIM is used of the edge of something that is round or curving ⟨the *rim* of a bowl⟩.

[2]**border** *vb*
**1** to put a border on ⟨*border* the garden with flowers⟩
**2** to be close or next to ⟨the United States *borders* on Canada⟩

**bor·der·line** \'bȯrd-ər-,līn\ *adj*
not quite average, standard, or normal

[1]**bore** \'bōr\ *vb* **bored**; **bor·ing**
**1** to make a hole in especially with a drill ⟨*bore* a piece of wood⟩
**2** to make by piercing or drilling ⟨*bore* a hole⟩ ⟨*bore* a well⟩
**bor·er** *n*

[2]**bore** *n*
**1** a hole made by boring
**2** a cavity (as in a gun barrel) shaped like a cylinder
**3** the diameter of a hole or cylinder

[3]**bore** *past of* BEAR

[4]**bore** *n*
an uninteresting person or thing

[5]**bore** *vb* **bored**; **bor·ing**
to make weary and restless by being uninteresting ⟨this long-winded story *bores* me⟩

**bore·dom** \'bōrd-əm\ *n*
the state of being bored

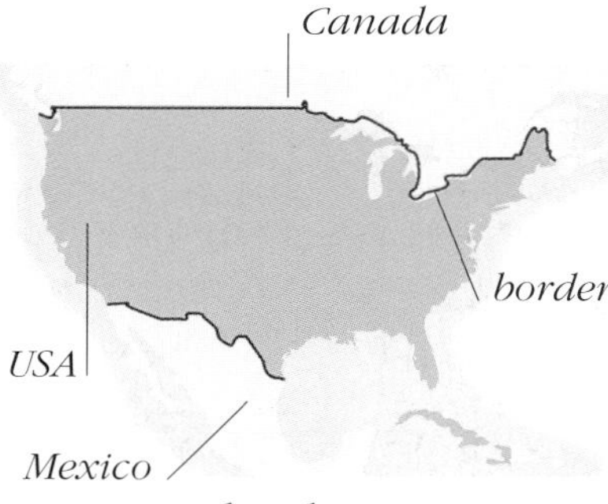


[1]**border 2:**
map showing international borders

**bo·ric acid** \,bōr-ik-\ *n*
a weak acid containing boron used to kill germs

**born** \'bȯrn\ *adj*
**1** brought into life by birth **:** brought forth
**2** having a certain characteristic from or as if from birth ⟨a *born* loser⟩ ⟨a *born* leader⟩

**borne** *past participle of* BEAR

**bo·ron** \'bōr-,än\ *n*
a powdery or hard solid chemical element that melts at a very high temperature and is found in nature only in combination

**bor·ough** \'bər-ō\ *n*
**1** a self-governing town or village in some states
**2** one of the five political divisions of New York City

**bor·row** \'bär-ō\ *vb*
**1** to take or receive something with the promise of returning it
**2** to take for one's own use something begun or thought up by another **:** ADOPT ⟨*borrow* an idea⟩
**bor·row·er** \'bär-ə-wər\ *n*

[1]**bos·om** \'bu̇z-əm\ *n*
**1** the front of the human chest
**2** the breasts of a woman

[2]**bosom** *adj*
[3]CLOSE 8, INTIMATE ⟨*bosom* friends⟩

[1]**boss** \'bȯs\ *n*
**1** the person (as an employer or foreman) who tells workers what to do
**2** the head of a group (as a political organization)

[2]**boss** *vb*
**1** to be in charge of ⟨*boss* a job⟩
**2** to give orders to ⟨don't *boss* me around⟩

**bossy** \'bȯ-sē\ *adj* **boss·i·er**; **boss·i·est**
liking to order people around

**bo·tan·i·cal** \bə-'tan-i-kəl\ *adj*
of or relating to botany

**bot·a·nist** \'bät-n-əst\ *n*
a specialist in botany

**bot·a·ny** \'bät-n-ē, 'bät-nē\ *n*
a branch of biology dealing with plants

**botch** \'bäch\ *vb*
to do clumsily and unskillfully **:** SPOIL, BUNGLE

[1]**both** \'bōth\ *pron*
the one and the other **:** the two ⟨*both* of us⟩

**²both** *conj*
used before two words or phrases connected with *and* to stress that each is included ⟨*both* New York and London⟩

**³both** *adj*
the two ⟨*both* books are mine⟩

**¹both·er** \'bäth-ər\ *vb*
**1** to trouble (someone) in body or mind : DISTRACT, ANNOY
**2** to cause to worry ⟨your illness *bothers* me⟩
**3** to take the time or trouble ⟨don't *bother* to dress up⟩

**²bother** *n*
**1** someone or something that bothers in a small way ⟨what a *bother* a cold can be⟩
**2** COMMOTION
**3** the condition of being bothered

**¹bot·tle** \'bät-l\ *n*
**1** ▶ a container (as of glass or plastic) usually having a narrow neck and mouth and no handle
**2** the quantity held by a bottle

**¹bottle 1**

**²bottle** *vb* **bot·tled**; **bot·tling**
**1** to put into a bottle
**2** to shut up as if in a bottle ⟨*bottle* up your feelings⟩

**bot·tle·neck** \'bät-l-,nek\ *n*
a place or condition where improvement or movement is held up

**bot·tom** \'bät-əm\ *n*
**1** the under surface of something ⟨the *bottom* of a shelf⟩
**2** a supporting surface or part : BASE ⟨chair *bottoms*⟩
**3** the bed of a body of water ⟨the lake *bottom*⟩
**4** the lowest part of something ⟨*bottom* of the heap⟩
**5** low land along a river ⟨Mississippi river *bottoms*⟩

**bot·tom·less** \'bät-əm-ləs\ *adj*
**1** having no bottom
**2** very deep ⟨a *bottomless* pit⟩

**bough** \'bau̇\ *n*
a usually large or main branch of a tree

**bought** *past of* BUY

**bouil·lon** \'bü-,yän, 'bu̇l-,yän, 'bu̇l-yən\ *n*
a clear soup made from meat (as beef or chicken)

**boul·der** \'bōl-dər\ *n*
a large detached and rounded or very worn mass of rock

**bou·le·vard** \'bu̇l-ə-,värd\ *n*
a wide avenue often having grass strips with trees along its center or sides

**Word History** The French made a word from a Dutch word that meant "bulwark." At first this French word meant "bulwark," but later it came to mean "boulevard" as well. The first boulevards were laid out where the city fortifications, or bulwarks, had been torn down. The English word *boulevard* came from the French word that meant "bulwark" or "boulevard."

**¹bounce** \'bau̇ns\ *vb* **bounced**; **bounc·ing**
**1** to spring back or up after hitting a surface ⟨the ball *bounced* into the street⟩
**2** to leap suddenly
**3** to cause to bounce ⟨*bounce* a ball⟩

**²bounce** *n*
**1** a sudden leap
**2** ²REBOUND 1

**¹bound** \'bau̇nd\ *adj*
going or intending to go ⟨homeward *bound*⟩

**²bound** *past of* BIND

**³bound** *vb*
to form the boundary of ⟨a farm *bounded* by a river on one side⟩

**⁴bound** *adj*
**1** tied or fastened with or as if with bands
**2** required by law or duty
**3** covered with binding ⟨a *bound* book⟩
**4** firmly determined ⟨we were *bound* we would succeed⟩
**5** very likely to do something : CERTAIN, SURE ⟨it is *bound* to rain⟩

**⁵bound** *n*
a fast easy leap

**⁶bound** *vb*
to make a bound or move in bounds

**bound·ary** \'bau̇n-də-rē, 'bau̇n-drē\ *n, pl* **bound·aries**
something that points out or shows a limit or end : a dividing line

**bound·less** \'bau̇nd-ləs\ *adj*
having no limits ⟨*boundless* energy⟩

**bounds** \'bau̇ndz\ *n pl*
a point or a line beyond which a person or thing cannot go ⟨out of *bounds*⟩

**boun·te·ous** \'bau̇nt-ē-əs\ *adj*
**1** LIBERAL 1
**2** ABUNDANT ⟨a *bounteous* harvest⟩

**boun·ti·ful** \'bau̇nt-i-fəl\ *adj*
**1** giving freely or generously ⟨a *bountiful* host⟩
**2** PLENTIFUL 2 ⟨a *bountiful* feast⟩
**boun·ti·ful·ly** \-fə-lē\ *adv*

**boun·ty** \'bau̇nt-ē\ *n, pl* **boun·ties**
**1** GENEROSITY 1
**2** generous gifts
**3** money given as a reward for killing certain harmful animals

**bou·quet** \bō-'kā, bü-\ *n*
▼ a bunch of flowers

**bouquet**

**bout** \'bau̇t\ *n*
**1** a contest of skill or strength between two persons ⟨a wrestling *bout*⟩
**2** ²ATTACK 3 ⟨a bad *bout* of flu⟩

**bou·tique** \bü-'tēk\ *n*
a small fashionable shop

**¹bow** \'bau̇\ *vb*
**1** ¹YIELD 8 ⟨*bow* to authority⟩
**2** to bend the head or body as an act of politeness or respect ⟨he *bowed* as he was introduced⟩

**²bow** *n*
the act of bending the head or body to express politeness or respect ⟨made a deep *bow* to the audience⟩

A B C D E F G H I J K L M N O P Q R S T U V W X Y Z

**[3]bow** \'bō\ *n*
**1** ▶ a weapon used for shooting arrows and usually made of a strip of wood bent by a cord connecting the two ends
**2** something shaped in a curve like a bow
**3** a rod with horsehairs stretched from end to end used for playing a stringed instrument (as a violin)
**4** a knot made with one or more loops ⟨tie the ribbon in a *bow*⟩

*grip*

*bowstring*

**[3]bow 1**

**[4]bow** \'bō\ *vb*
**1** to bend into a bow
**2** to play with a bow ⟨*bowed* two strings at once⟩

**[5]bow** \'bau̇\ *n*
the forward part of a ship

**bow·el** \'bau̇-əl\ *n*
**1** INTESTINE — usually used in pl.
**2** a part of the intestine ⟨the large *bowel*⟩

**bow·er** \'bau̇-ər\ *n*
a shelter in a garden made of boughs of trees or vines

**[1]bowl** \'bōl\ *n*
**1** a round hollow dish without handles
**2** the contents of a bowl ⟨eat a *bowl* of cereal⟩
**3** something in the shape of a bowl (as part of a spoon or pipe)

**[2]bowl** *n*
a rolling of a ball in bowling

**[3]bowl** *vb*
**1** to roll a ball in bowling
**2** to move rapidly and smoothly as if rolling
**3** [2]SURPRISE 3
**4** IMPRESS 2 ⟨was *bowled* over by her talent⟩

**bow·legged** \'bō-'leg-əd, -'legd\ *adj*
having the legs bowed outward

**bow·line** \'bō-lən\ *n*
▶ a knot used for making a loop that will not slip

**bowl·ing** \'bō-ling\ *n*
a game in which balls are rolled so as to knock down pins

**bow·man** \'bō-mən\ *n, pl* **bow·men** \-mən\
ARCHER

**bow·sprit** \'bau̇-ˌsprit, 'bō-\ *n*
a large spar sticking out forward from the bow of a ship

**bow·string** \'bō-ˌstring\ *n*
the cord connecting the two ends of a bow

**[1]box** \'bäks\ *n*
an evergreen shrub or small tree used for hedges

**[2]box** *n*
**1** a container usually having four sides, a bottom, and a cover
**2** the contents of a box ⟨eat a whole *box* of candy⟩
**3** an enclosed place for one or more persons ⟨a sentry *box*⟩ ⟨a *box* in a theater⟩

**[3]box** *vb*
to enclose in or as if in a box

**[4]box** *vb*
to engage in boxing

**box·car** \'bäk-ˌskär\ *n*
▼ a roofed freight car usually having sliding doors in the sides

**box elder** *n*
an American maple with leaves divided into several leaflets

**[1]box·er** \'bäk-sər\ *n*
a person who boxes

**[2]boxer** *n*
a compact dog of German origin that is of medium size with a square build and has a short and often tan coat with a black mask

**box·ing** \'bäk-sing\ *n*
the sport of fighting with the fists

**bowline**

**box office** *n*
a place where tickets to public entertainments (as sports or theatrical events) are sold

**boy** \'bȯi\ *n*
**1** a male child from birth to young manhood
**2** a male servant

**[1]boy·cott** \'bȯi-ˌkät\ *vb*
to join with others in refusing to deal with someone (as a person, organization, or country) usually to show disapproval or to force acceptance of terms

**[2]boycott** *n*
the process or an instance of boycotting

**boy·friend** \'bȯi-ˌfrend\ *n*
a regular male companion of a girl or woman

**boy·hood** \'bȯi-ˌhu̇d\ *n*
the time or condition of being a boy

**boy·ish** \'bȯi-ish\ *adj*
of, relating to, or having qualities often felt to be typical of boys
**boy·ish·ly** *adv*
**boy·ish·ness** *n*

**boxcar** on a model freight train

**Boy Scout** *n*
a member of a scouting program (as the Boy Scouts of America)

**bra** \'brä\ *n*
a woman's undergarment for breast support

[1]**brace** \'brās\ *vb* **braced**; **brac·ing**
to make strong, firm, or steady

[2]**brace** *n*
**1** two of a kind ⟨a *brace* of quail⟩
**2** a tool with a U-shaped bend that is used to turn wood-boring bits
**3** something that braces ⟨a *brace* for a fence post⟩ ⟨a *brace* for a crippled leg⟩
**4** a usually wire device worn on the teeth for changing faulty position
**5** a mark { or } used to connect words or items to be considered together

**brace·let** \'brā-slət\ *n*
a decorative band or chain usually worn on the wrist or arm

**brack·en** \'brak-ən\ *n*
a large coarse branching fern

[1]**brack·et** \'brak-ət\ *n*
**1** a support for a weight (as a shelf) that is usually attached to a wall
**2** one of a pair of marks [ ] (**square brackets**) used to enclose letters or numbers or in mathematics to enclose items to be treated together
**3** one of a pair of marks ⟨ ⟩ (**angle brackets**) used to enclose letters or numbers

[2]**bracket** *vb*
**1** to place within brackets
**2** to put into the same class : GROUP

**brack·ish** \'brak-ish\ *adj*
somewhat salty

**brad** \'brad\ *n*
a slender wire nail with a small longish but rounded head

**brag** \'brag\ *vb* **bragged**; **brag·ging**
[2]BOAST 1

**brag·gart** \'brag-ərt\ *n*
a person who brags a lot

[1]**braid** \'brād\ *vb*
to weave together into a braid ⟨*braided* rugs⟩

[2]**braid** *n*
a length of cord, ribbon, or hair formed of three or more strands woven together

**braille** \'brāl\ *n, often cap*
a system of printing for the blind in which the letters are represented by raised dots

---

**Word History** More than a hundred years ago, Louis Braille was a teacher in France. He taught blind people and was himself blind. He invented the system of printing for the blind called *braille*, which is named after him.

---

[1]**brain** \'brān\ *n*
**1** ▼ the part of the nervous system that is inside the skull, consists of grayish nerve cells and whitish nerve fibers, and is the organ of thought and the central control point for the nervous system
**2 brains** *pl* a good mind : INTELLIGENCE
**3** someone who is very smart

[2]**brain** *vb*
to hurt or kill by a blow on the head ⟨*brained* by a falling tree⟩

**brain·storm** \'brān-ˌstȯrm\ *n*
a sudden inspiration or idea

**brainy** \'brā-nē\ *adj* **brain·i·er**; **brain·i·est**
very smart

[1]**brake** \'brāk\ *n*
a thick growth of shrubs, small trees, or canes

[2]**brake** *n*
a device for slowing or stopping motion (as of a wheel) usually by friction

[3]**brake** *vb* **braked**; **brak·ing**
to slow or stop by using a brake

**brake·man** \'brāk-mən\ *n, pl* **brake·men** \-mən\
a crew member on a train whose duties include inspecting the train and helping the conductor

**bram·ble** \'bram-bəl\ *n*
► any of a group of woody plants with prickly stems that include the raspberries and blackberries and are related to the roses

*fruit*
*prickly stem*

**bramble**

**bran** \'bran\ *n*
the broken coat of the seed of cereal grain separated (as by sifting) from the flour or meal

### [1]brain 1

The brain monitors and regulates actions and reactions in the body. The brain stem controls breathing and heart rate. The cerebrum is the center of thinking, while the cerebellum coordinates movement and balance. The thalamus directs nerve impulses to specialized areas and the hypothalamus produces hormones for the nervous system.

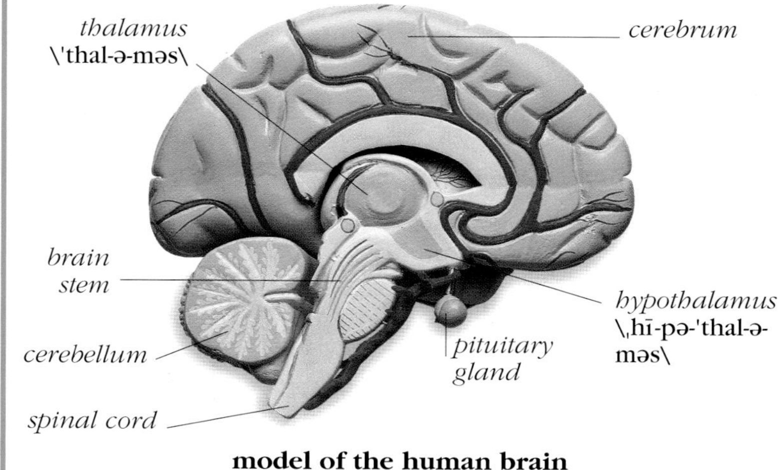


**model of the human brain**

A B C D E F G H I J K L M N O P Q R S T U V W X Y Z

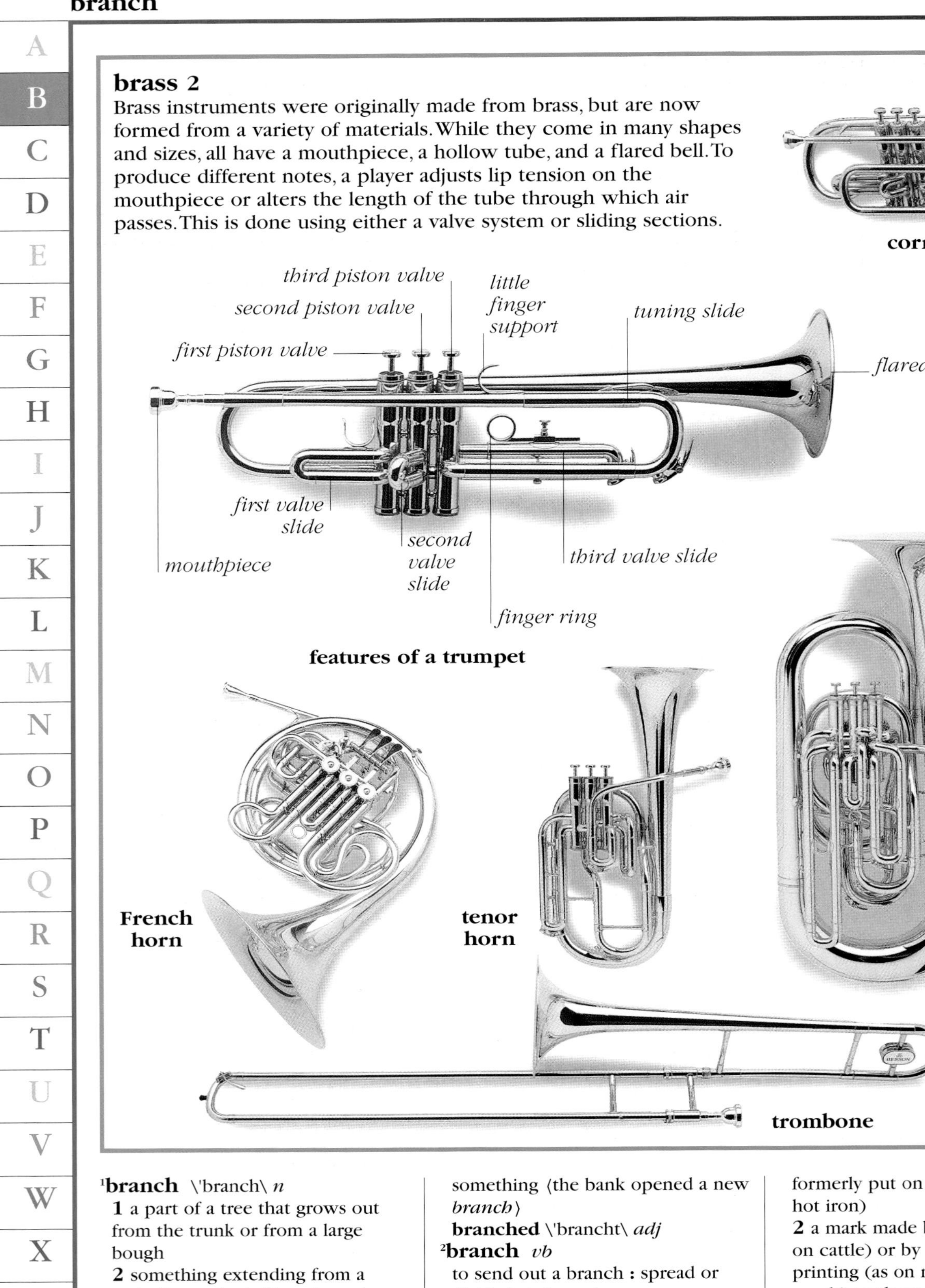


**¹branch** \'branch\ *n*
**1** a part of a tree that grows out from the trunk or from a large bough
**2** something extending from a main line or body like a branch ⟨a *branch* of a railroad⟩
**3** a division or subordinate part of something ⟨the bank opened a new *branch*⟩
**branched** \'brancht\ *adj*

**²branch** *vb*
to send out a branch **:** spread or divide into branches

**¹brand** \'brand\ *n*
**1** a mark of disgrace (as one formerly put on criminals with a hot iron)
**2** a mark made by burning (as on cattle) or by stamping or printing (as on manufactured goods) to show ownership, maker, or quality
**3** TRADEMARK

4 a class of goods identified by a name as the product of a certain maker

[2]**brand** *vb*
1 to mark with a brand
2 to show or claim (something) to be bad or wrong ⟨opponents *branded* the test a failure⟩

**bran·dish** \'bran-dish\ *vb*
to wave or shake in a threatening manner ⟨*brandishing* their swords⟩

**brand–new** \'bran-'nü, -'nyü\ *adj*
completely new and unused

**bran·dy** \'bran-dē\ *n, pl* **brandies**
an alcoholic liquor made from wine or fruit juice

**brass** \'bras\ *n*
1 an alloy made by combining copper and zinc
2 ◀ the musical instruments of an orchestra or band that are usually made of brass and include the cornets, trumpets, trombones, French horns, and tubas

**brat** \'brat\ *n*
a naughty annoying child

[1]**brave** \'brāv\ *adj* **brav·er**; **brav·est**
feeling or showing no fear
**brave·ly** *adv*

**Synonyms** BRAVE, COURAGEOUS, and BOLD mean showing no fear. BRAVE suggests that one has or shows no fear when faced with danger or difficulty ⟨the *brave* crew tried to save the ship⟩. COURAGEOUS suggests that one is always prepared to meet danger or difficulty ⟨the early pioneers were *courageous* people ready to put up with great hardships⟩. BOLD suggests that one welcomes dangerous situations ⟨*bold* explorers in search of adventure⟩.

[2]**brave** *vb* **braved**; **brav·ing**
to face or take bravely ⟨*braved* the raging storm⟩

[3]**brave** *n*
an American Indian warrior

**brav·ery** \'brā-və-rē, 'brāv-rē\ *n*
COURAGE

[1]**brawl** \'brȯl\ *vb*
to quarrel or fight noisily

[2]**brawl** *n*
a noisy quarrel or fight

**brawn** \'brȯn\ *n*
muscular strength

**brawny** \'brȯ-nē\ *adj* **brawn·i·er**; **brawn·i·est**
having large strong muscles

[1]**bray** \'brā\ *vb*
to make the loud harsh cry of a donkey

[2]**bray** *n*
a sound of braying

**bra·zen** \'brāz-n\ *adj*
1 made of brass
2 sounding harsh and loud ⟨*brazen* voices⟩
3 not ashamed of or embarrassed by one's bad behavior : IMPUDENT

**Bra·zil nut** \brə-,zil-\ *n*
a dark three-sided nut with a white kernel

[1]**breach** \'brēch\ *n*
1 a breaking of a law : a failure to do what one should
2 an opening made by breaking

[2]**breach** *vb*
to make a break in

[1]**bread** \'bred\ *n*
1 a baked food made from flour or meal
2 FOOD 1 ⟨our daily *bread*⟩

[2]**bread** *vb*
to cover with bread crumbs

**breadth** \'bredth\ *n*
1 distance measured from side to side
2 SCOPE 2

[1]**break** \'brāk\ *vb* **broke** \'brōk\; **bro·ken** \'brō-kən\; **break·ing**
1 to separate into parts suddenly or forcibly ⟨*break* a stick⟩ ⟨glass *breaks* easily⟩
2 to fail to keep ⟨*broke* the law⟩
3 to force a way ⟨*break* into a house⟩ ⟨*broke* out of jail⟩
4 [2]TAME 1 ⟨*break* a wild horse⟩
5 to reduce the force of ⟨*break* one's fall⟩
6 to do better than ⟨*broke* the school record⟩
7 to interrupt or put an end to : STOP ⟨a shout *broke* the silence⟩ ⟨let's *break* for lunch⟩
8 to develop or burst out suddenly ⟨day is *breaking*⟩ ⟨*broke* into laughter⟩
9 to make known ⟨*broke* the news⟩
10 SOLVE ⟨*break* a code⟩
11 [1]CHANGE 4 ⟨*break* a ten-dollar bill⟩

[2]**break** *n*
1 an act of breaking ⟨make a *break* for freedom⟩ ⟨at *break* of day⟩
2 something produced by breaking ⟨a bad *break* in the leg⟩
3 an accidental event ⟨a lucky *break*⟩

**break·down** \'brāk-,dau̇n\ *n*
bodily or mental collapse : FAILURE 6

**brea·ker** \'brā-kər\ *n*
1 a person or thing that breaks something ⟨a circuit *breaker*⟩
2 a wave that breaks on shore

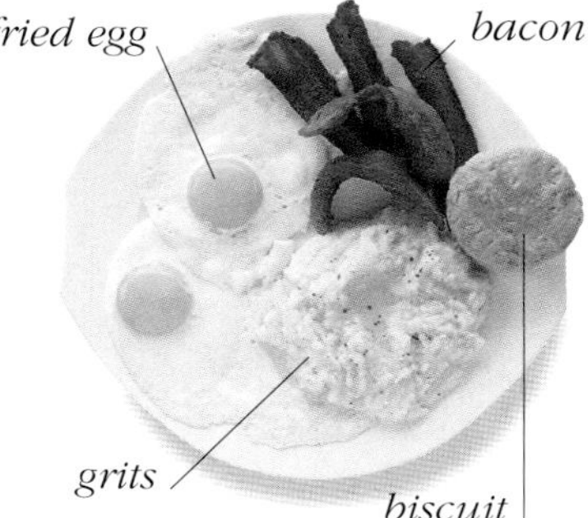


[1]**breakfast:**
a large traditional breakfast

[1]**break·fast** \'brek-fəst\ *n*
▲ the first meal of the day

[2]**breakfast** *vb*
to eat breakfast

**break·neck** \'brāk-,nek\ *adj*
very fast or dangerous ⟨*breakneck* speed⟩

**break out** *vb*
1 to develop a skin rash
2 to start up suddenly ⟨a fight *broke out*⟩

**break·through** \'brāk-,thrü\ *n*
a sudden advance or successful development ⟨a *breakthrough* in cancer research⟩

**break up** *vb*
1 to separate into parts
2 to bring or come to an end ⟨the fighting *broke up* the meeting⟩
3 to end a romance
4 to go into a fit of laughter

**break·wa·ter** \'brā-,kwȯt-ər, -,kwät-\ *n*
an offshore wall to protect a beach or a harbor from the sea

[1]**breast** \'brest\ *n*
1 a gland that produces milk
2 the front part of the body between the neck and the abdomen
**breast·ed** \'bres-təd\ *adj*

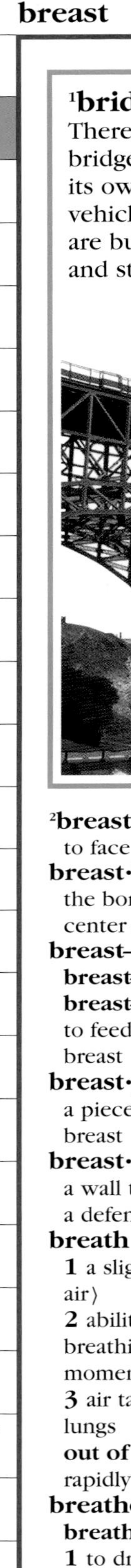


**[1]bridge 1**
There are a number of ways to construct a bridge to make it strong enough to support its own weight as well as that of the vehicles crossing it. Most modern bridges are built using a combination of concrete and steel for strength and flexibility.

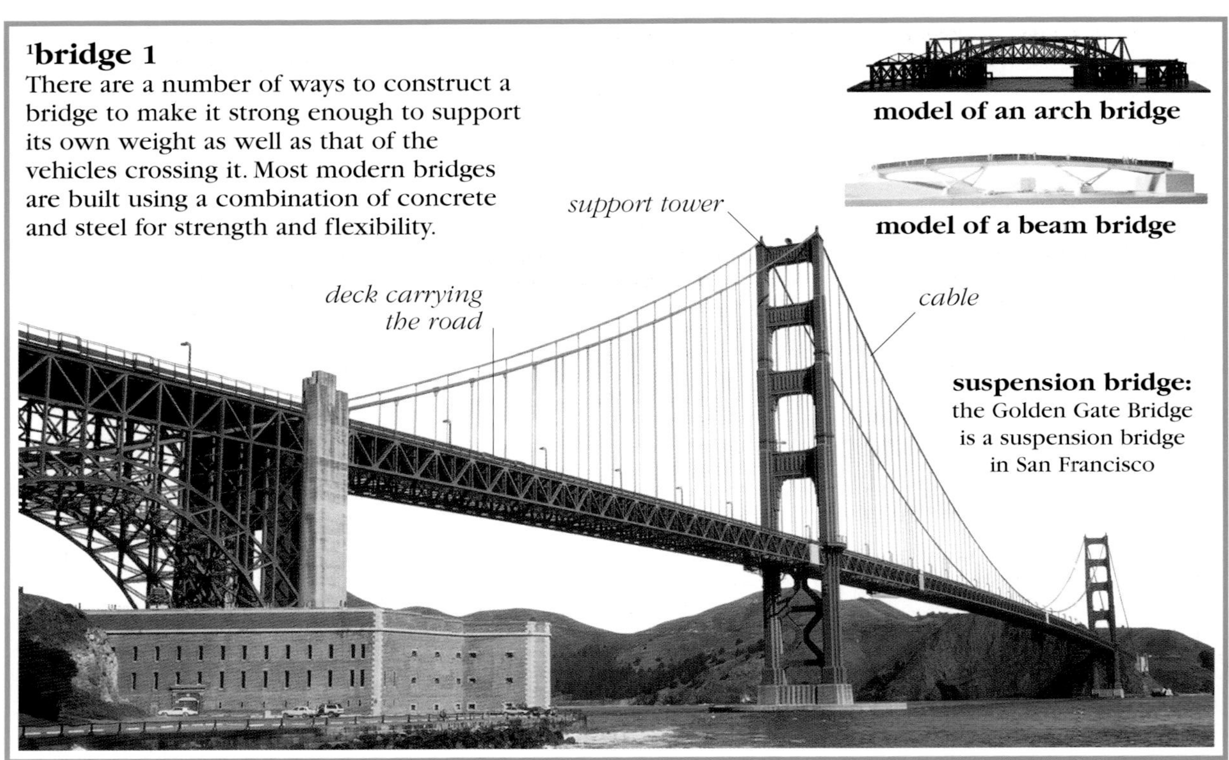


**model of an arch bridge**

**model of a beam bridge**

**suspension bridge:** the Golden Gate Bridge is a suspension bridge in San Francisco

**[2]breast** *vb*
to face or oppose bravely

**breast·bone** \'brest-'bōn\ *n*
the bony plate at the front and center of the breast

**breast–feed** \'brest-'fēd\ *vb* **breast–fed** \-'fed\; **breast–feed·ing**
to feed (a baby) from a mother's breast

**breast·plate** \'brest-ˌplāt\ *n*
a piece of armor for covering the breast

**breast·work** \'bres-ˌtwərk\ *n*
a wall thrown together to serve as a defense in battle

**breath** \'breth\ *n*
**1** a slight breeze ⟨not a *breath* of air⟩
**2** ability to breathe **:** ease of breathing ⟨lost my *breath* for a moment⟩
**3** air taken in or sent out by the lungs
**out of breath** breathing very rapidly as a result of hard exercise

**breathe** \'brēth\ *vb* **breathed**; **breath·ing**
**1** to draw air into and expel it from the lungs
**2** [1]LIVE 1
**3** [1]SAY 1, UTTER ⟨don't *breathe* a word of this⟩

**breath·er** \'brē-thər\ *n*
a pause for rest

**breath·less** \'breth-ləs\ *adj*
**1** panting from exertion
**2** holding one's breath from excitement or fear
**breath·less·ly** *adv*

**breath·tak·ing** \'breth-ˌtā-king\ *adj*
very exciting

**breech·es** \'brich-əz\ *n pl*
**1** ► short pants fastening below the knee
**2** PANTS

**[1]breed** \'brēd\ *vb* **bred** \'bred\; **breed·ing**
**1** to produce or increase (plants or animals) by sexual reproduction ⟨*breed* cattle for market⟩
**2** to produce offspring by sexual reproduction
**3** to bring up **:** TRAIN ⟨born and *bred* in this town⟩
**4** to bring about **:** CAUSE ⟨familiarity *breeds* contempt⟩
**breed·er** *n*

**[2]breed** *n*
**1** a kind of plant or animal that is found only under human care and is different from related kinds ⟨a beef *breed* of cattle⟩
**2** [1]CLASS 6, KIND

**breeches 1:** breeches as worn by a 16th-century gentleman

*breeches*

**breed·ing** \'brēd-ing\ *n*
training especially in manners **:** UPBRINGING ⟨your behavior shows good *breeding*⟩

**breeze** \'brēz\ *n*
a gentle wind

**breezy** \'brē-zē\ *adj* **breez·i·er**; **breez·i·est**
**1** somewhat windy

2 lively and somewhat carefree ⟨a *breezy* reply⟩
**breez·i·ly** \-zə-lē\ *adv*
**breez·i·ness** \-zē-nəs\ *n*

**breth·ren** \'bret͟h-rən\ *pl of* BROTHER
used chiefly in some formal or solemn situations

**breve** \'brēv, 'brev\ *n*
a mark ˘ placed over a vowel to show that the vowel is short

**brev·i·ty** \'brev-ət-ē\ *n*
the condition of being short or brief

[1]**brew** \'brü\ *vb*
**1** to make (beer) from water, malt, and hops
**2** to prepare by soaking in hot water ⟨*brew* the tea⟩
**3** [2]PLAN 2 ⟨*brewing* mischief⟩
**4** to start to form ⟨a storm is *brewing*⟩
**brew·er** *n*

[2]**brew** *n*
a brewed beverage

**brew·ery** \'brü-ə-rē\ *n, pl* **brew·er·ies**
a place where malt liquors are brewed

**bri·ar** *variant of* BRIER

[1]**bribe** \'brīb\ *n*
something given or promised to a person in order to influence a decision or action dishonestly

[2]**bribe** *vb* **bribed**; **brib·ing**
to influence or try to influence by a bribe

**brib·ery** \'brī-bə-rē\ *n, pl* **brib·er·ies**
the act of giving or taking a bribe

[1]**brick** \'brik\ *n*
**1** a building or paving material made from clay molded into blocks and baked
**2** a block made of brick

[2]**brick** *vb*
to close, face, or pave with bricks

**brick·lay·er** \'brik-ˌlā-ər\ *n*
a person who builds or paves with bricks

**brig**

A brig was a merchant ship of the 18th and 19th centuries. This model is shown fully rigged with extra "studding" sails to give more power with a light wind blowing from behind.

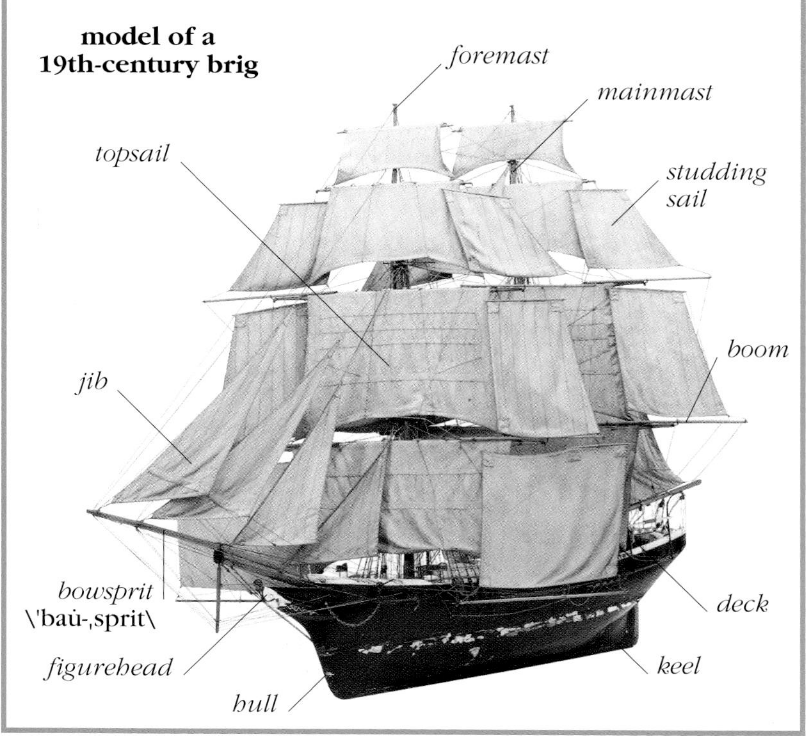


**brid·al** \'brīd-l\ *adj*
of or relating to a bride or a wedding

**bride** \'brīd\ *n*
a woman just married or about to be married

**bride·groom** \'brīd-ˌgrüm\ *n*
a man just married or about to be married

**brides·maid** \'brīdz-ˌmād\ *n*
a woman who attends a bride at her wedding

[1]**bridge** \'brij\ *n*
**1** ◀ a structure built over something (as water, a low place, or a railroad) so people can cross
**2** a platform above and across the deck of a ship for the captain or officer in charge
**3** something like a bridge ⟨the *bridge* of the nose⟩

[2]**bridge** *vb* **bridged**; **bridg·ing**
to make a bridge over or across ⟨*bridge* a gap⟩

[3]**bridge** *n*
a card game for four players in two teams

[1]**bri·dle** \'brīd-l\ *n*
a device for controlling a horse made up of a set of straps enclosing the head, a bit, and a pair of reins

[2]**bridle** *vb* **bri·dled**; **bri·dling** \'brīd-ling, -l-ing\
**1** to put a bridle on
**2** RESTRAIN 2 ⟨*bridle* one's anger⟩
**3** to hold the head high and draw in the chin as an expression of resentment ⟨*bridle* at criticism⟩

[1]**brief** \'brēf\ *adj*
not very long **:** SHORT
**brief·ly** *adv*

[2]**brief** *vb*
to give information or instructions to

**brief·case** \'brēf-ˌkās\ *n*
a flat case for carrying papers or books

**briefs** \'brēfs\ *n pl*
short snug underpants

**bri·er** *or* **bri·ar** \'brī-ər\ *n*
a plant (as the rose or blackberry) with a thorny or prickly woody stem

**brig** \'brig\ *n*
◀ a square-rigged sailing ship with two masts

**bri·gade** \bri-'gād\ *n*
**1** a body of soldiers consisting of two or more regiments
**2** a group of persons organizedfor acting together ⟨a fire *brigade*⟩

**brig·a·dier general** \ˌbrig-ə-ˌdiər-\ *n*
a commissioned officer in the Army, Air Force, or Marine Corps ranking above a colonel

**bright** \ˈbrīt\ *adj*
**1** giving off or filled with much light ⟨a *bright* fire⟩ ⟨a *bright* day⟩
**2** very clear or vivid in color ⟨a *bright* red⟩
**3** INTELLIGENT, CLEVER ⟨a *bright* child⟩
**4** CHEERFUL
**bright·ly** *adv*
**bright·ness** *n*

---

**Synonyms** BRIGHT, RADIANT, and BRILLIANT mean shining or glowing with light. BRIGHT can be used either of something that reflects a great amount of light ⟨a *bright* full moon⟩ or of something that produces much light ⟨*bright* stars⟩. RADIANT is more often used of something that sends forth its own light ⟨the sun is a *radiant* body⟩. BRILLIANT is used of something that shines with a sparkling or flashing light ⟨*brilliant* diamonds⟩.

---

**bright·en** \ˈbrīt-n\ *vb*
to make or become bright or brighter

**bril·liance** \ˈbril-yəns\ *n*
great brightness

**bril·liant** \ˈbril-yənt\ *adj*
**1** flashing with light : very bright ⟨*brilliant* jewels⟩
**2** very impressive ⟨a *brilliant* career⟩
**3** very smart or clever ⟨a *brilliant* student⟩ **synonyms** see BRIGHT, INTELLIGENT
**bril·liant·ly** *adv*

**¹brim** \ˈbrim\ *n*
**1** the edge or rim of something hollow ⟨a cup filled to the *brim*⟩
**2** the part of a hat that sticks out around the lower edge

**²brim** *vb* **brimmed**; **brim·ming**
to be or become full to overflowing ⟨*brimming* with happiness⟩

**brin·dled** \ˈbrin-dld\ *adj*
► having dark streaks or spots on a gray or brownish background

**brine** \ˈbrīn\ *n*
**1** water containing a great deal of salt
**2** OCEAN

**bring** \ˈbring\ *vb* **brought** \ˈbrȯt\; **bring·ing**
**1** to cause to come with oneself by carrying or leading : take along ⟨told to *bring* lunches⟩ ⟨*bring* your friend⟩
**2** to cause to reach a certain state or take a certain action ⟨*bring* water to a boil⟩ ⟨couldn't *bring* myself to say it⟩
**3** to cause to arrive or exist ⟨the storm *brought* snow and ice⟩
**4** to sell for ⟨the cow *brought* a high price⟩
**bring·er** *n*

**bring about** *vb*
to cause to happen : EFFECT

**bring forth** *vb*
to give birth to : PRODUCE

**bring out** *vb*
to produce and offer for sale ⟨*brought out* a new book⟩

**bring to** *vb*
to bring back from unconsciousness : REVIVE

**bring up** *vb*
to bring to maturity through care and education ⟨*bring up* a child⟩

**brink** \ˈbringk\ *n*
**1** the edge at the top of a steep place
**2** a point of beginning ⟨*brink* of crisis⟩

**briny** \ˈbrī-nē\ *adj* **brin·i·er**; **brin·i·est**
of or like salt water : SALTY

**brisk** \ˈbrisk\ *adj*
**1** very active : LIVELY
**2** very refreshing ⟨*brisk* fall weather⟩
**brisk·ly** *adv*
**brisk·ness** *n*

**¹bris·tle** \ˈbris-əl\ *n*
**1** a short stiff hair ⟨a hog's *bristle*⟩
**2** ▼ a stiff hair or something like a hair fastened in a brush

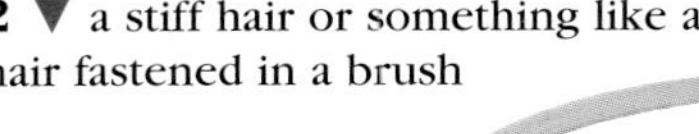

**¹bristle 2:** a bristle brush

**brindled** boxer

**²bristle** *vb* **bris·tled**; **bris·tling**
**1** to rise up and stiffen like bristles ⟨makes your hair *bristle*⟩
**2** to show signs of anger ⟨*bristled* at the insult⟩

**bris·tly** \ˈbris-lē\ *adj* **bris·tli·er**; **bris·tli·est**
of, like, or having many bristles

**britch·es** \ˈbrich-əz\ *n pl*
BREECHES

**¹Brit·ish** \ˈbrit-ish\ *adj*
of or relating to Great Britain or the British

**²British** *n pl*
the people of Great Britain

**brit·tle** \ˈbrit-l\ *adj* **brit·tler**; **brit·tlest**
hard but easily broken ⟨*brittle* glass⟩
**brit·tle·ness** *n*

---

**Synonyms** BRITTLE, CRISP, and FRAGILE mean easily broken. BRITTLE suggests that something is hard and dry ⟨*brittle* twigs snapping under our feet⟩. CRISP suggests that something is hard and dry but also fresh ⟨crackers no longer *crisp*⟩. FRAGILE is used of anything so delicate that it may be broken easily ⟨a piece of *fragile* china⟩.

---

**broach** \ˈbrōch\ *vb*
to bring up as a subject for discussion ⟨*broach* a question⟩

**broad** \ˈbrȯd\ *adj*
**1** not narrow : WIDE ⟨a *broad* stripe⟩
**2** extending far and wide : SPACIOUS ⟨*broad* prairies⟩
**3** ¹COMPLETE 1, FULL ⟨*broad* daylight⟩
**4** not limited ⟨a *broad* choice of subjects⟩
**5** not covering fine points : GENERAL ⟨gave a *broad* outline of the problem⟩
**broad·ly** *adv*

**brocade** dress

**¹broad·cast** \'bròd-,kast\ *adj*
**1** scattered in all directions
**2** made public by means of radio or television ⟨*broadcast* announcements⟩
**3** of or relating to radio or television broadcasting ⟨a *broadcast* network⟩

**²broadcast** *vb* **broadcast**; **broad·cast·ing**
**1** to scatter far and wide ⟨*broadcast* seed⟩
**2** to make widely known
**3** to send out by radio or television from a transmitting station ⟨the speech will be *broadcast*⟩
**broad·cast·er** *n*

**³broadcast** *n*
**1** an act of broadcasting
**2** the material broadcast by radio or television : a radio or television program

**broad·cloth** \'bròd-,klòth\ *n*
a fine cloth with a firm smooth surface

**broad·en** \'bròd-n\ *vb*
to make or become broad or broader : WIDEN

**broad–mind·ed** \'bròd-'mīn-dəd\ *adj*
willing to consider opinions, beliefs, and practices that are unusual or different from one's own
**broad–mind·ed·ly** *adv*
**broad–mind·ed·ness** *n*

**¹broad·side** \'bròd-,sīd\ *n*
**1** the part of a ship's side above the waterline
**2** a firing of all of the guns that are on the same side of a ship ⟨fire a *broadside*⟩

**²broadside** *adv*
**1** with one side forward ⟨turned *broadside*⟩
**2** from the side ⟨hit the other car *broadside*⟩

**broad·sword** \'bròd-,sōrd\ *n*
a sword having a broad blade

**bro·cade** \brō-'kād\ *n*
◀ a cloth with a raised design woven into it

**broc·co·li** \'bräk-ə-lē, 'bräk-lē\ *n*
▼ an open branching form of cauliflower whose green stalks and clustered flower buds are used as a vegetable

**broccoli**

**broil** \'bròil\ *vb*
**1** to cook or be cooked directly over or under a heat source (as a fire or flame)
**2** to make or be extremely hot ⟨a *broiling* sun⟩

**broil·er** \'bròi-lər\ *n*
a young chicken suitable for broiling

**¹broke** \'brōk\ *past of* BREAK

**²broke** *adj*
having no money

**bro·ken** \'brō-kən\ *adj*
**1** shattered into pieces ⟨*broken* glass⟩
**2** having gaps or breaks ⟨a *broken* line⟩
**3** not kept ⟨a *broken* promise⟩
**4** imperfectly spoken ⟨*broken* English⟩

**bro·ken·heart·ed** \,brō-kən-'härt-əd\ *adj*
overwhelmed by grief : very sad

**bro·ker** \'brō-kər\ *n*
a person who acts as an agent for others in the buying or selling of property

**bro·mine** \'brō-,mēn\ *n*
a chemical element that is a deep red liquid giving off an irritating vapor of disagreeable odor

**bron·chi·al** \'bräng-kē-əl\ *adj*
relating to the branches (**bronchial tubes**) of the windpipe

**bron·chi·tis** \brän-'kīt-əs\ *n*
a sore raw state of the bronchial tubes

**bron·co** \'bräng-kō\ *n, pl* **bron·cos**
MUSTANG

**bron·to·sau·rus** \,bränt-ə-'sòr-əs\ *n*
a huge plant-eating dinosaur with a long thin neck and tail and four thick legs

**¹bronze** \'bränz\ *vb* **bronzed**; **bronz·ing**
to give the appearance or color of bronze to ⟨a *bronzed* sculpture⟩

**²bronze** *n*
**1** an alloy of copper and tin and sometimes other elements
**2** a yellowish brown color

**brooch** \'brōch, 'brüch\ *n*
an ornamental pin or clasp for the clothing

**¹brood** \'brüd\ *n*
**1** ▼ the young of birds hatched at the same time ⟨a *brood* of chicks⟩
**2** a group of young children or animals having the same mother

**¹brood 1**

**²brood** *vb*
**1** to sit on eggs to hatch them
**2** to think long and anxiously about something ⟨*brooded* over the mistake⟩

a b c d e f g h i j k l m n o p q r s t u v w x y z

**brood·er** \'brüd-ər\ *n*
**1** one that broods
**2** a building or a compartment that can be heated and is used for raising young fowl

**brook** \'brůk\ *n*
a small stream
**brook·let** \-lət\ *n*

**broom** \'brüm, 'brům\ *n*
**1** a woody plant of the pea family with long slender branches along which grow many drooping yellow flowers
**2** a brush with a long handle used for sweeping

**broom·stick** \'brüm-,stik, 'brům-\ *n*
the handle of a broom

**broth** \'bròth\ *n*
the liquid in which a meat, fish, or vegetable has been boiled

**broth·er** \'brəth-ər\ *n, pl* **brothers** *also* **breth·ren** \'breth-rən\
**1** a boy or man related to another person by having the same parents
**2** a fellow member of an organization

**broth·er·hood** \'brəth-ər-,hůd\ *n*
**1** the state of being a brother
**2** an association of people for a particular purpose
**3** those who are engaged in the same business or profession

**broth·er–in–law** \'brəth-ər-ən-,lò\ *n, pl* **broth·ers–in–law**
**1** the brother of one's husband or wife
**2** the husband of one's sister

**broth·er·ly** \'brəth-ər-lē\ *adj*
**1** of or relating to brothers
**2** [1]KINDLY 2, AFFECTIONATE

**brought** *past of* BRING

**brow** \'braů\ *n*
**1** EYEBROW
**2** FOREHEAD
**3** the upper edge of a steep slope

[1]**brown** \'braůn\ *adj*
**1** of the color brown
**2** having a dark or tanned complexion

[2]**brown** *n*
a color like that of coffee or chocolate

[3]**brown** *vb*
to make or become brown

**brown·ie** \'braů-nē\ *n*
**1** a cheerful elf believed to perform helpful services at night
**2** *cap* a member of a program of the Girl Scouts for girls in the first through third grades in school
**3** a small rectangle of chewy chocolate cake

**brown·ish** \'braů-nish\ *adj*
somewhat brown

**browse** \'braůz\ *vb* **browsed**; **brows·ing**
**1** to nibble young shoots and foliage ⟨*browsing* cattle⟩
**2** to read or look over something (as in a book or a store) in a light or careless way

**brows·er** \'braů-zər\ *n*
**1** one that browses
**2** a computer program providing access to sites on the World Wide Web

**bru·in** \'brü-ən\ *n*
[1]BEAR 1

[1]**bruise** \'brüz\ *vb* **bruised**; **bruis·ing**
to injure the flesh (as by a blow) without breaking the skin

[2]**bruise** *n*
a black-and-blue spot on the body or a dark spot on fruit caused by bruising (as from a blow)

[1]**bru·net** *or* **brun·ette** \brü-'net\ *n*
▼ someone who is brunet

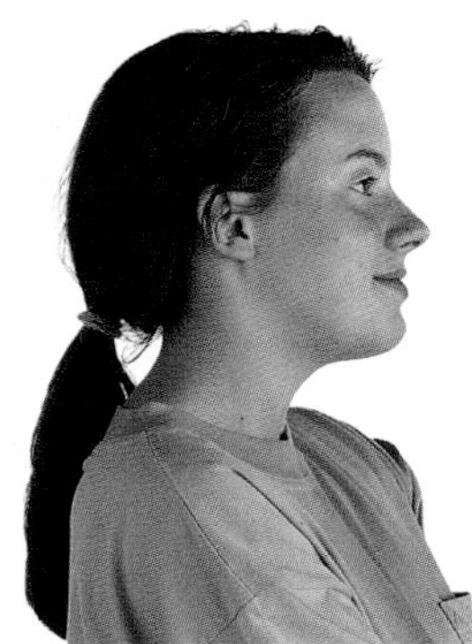

[1]**brunet**

[2]**brunet** *or* **brunette** *adj*
having dark brown or black hair and dark eyes

**brunt** \'brənt\ *n*
the main force or stress (as of an attack) ⟨the *brunt* of a storm⟩

[1]**brush** \'brəsh\ *n*
BRUSHWOOD

[2]**brush** *n*
**1** a tool made of bristles set in a handle and used for cleaning, smoothing, or painting
**2** a bushy tail ⟨a fox's *brush*⟩
**3** an act of brushing
**4** a light stroke ⟨a *brush* of the hand⟩

[3]**brush** *vb*
**1** to scrub or smooth with a brush ⟨*brush* your hair⟩
**2** to remove with or as if with a brush ⟨*brush* up the dirt⟩
**3** to pass lightly across ⟨a twig *brushed* my cheek⟩

[4]**brush** *n*
a brief fight or quarrel

**brush·wood** \'brəsh-,wůd\ *n*
**1** branches and twigs cut from trees
**2** a heavy growth of small trees and bushes

**brus·sels sprouts** \,brəs-əlz-\ *n pl, often cap B*
▼ green heads like tiny cabbages growing thickly on the stem of a plant of the cabbage family and used as a vegetable

**brussels sprouts**

**bru·tal** \'brüt-l\ *adj*
being cruel and inhuman
**bru·tal·ly** *adv*

**bru·tal·i·ty** \brü-'tal-ət-ē\ *n, pl* **bru·tal·i·ties**
**1** the quality of being brutal
**2** a brutal act or course of action

[1]**brute** \'brüt\ *adj*
**1** of or relating to beasts
**2** typical of beasts : like that of a beast ⟨*brute* force⟩

[2]**brute** *n*
**1** a four-footed animal especially when wild
**2** a brutal person

**brut·ish** \'brüt-ish\ *adj*
being unfeeling and stupid

[1]**bub·ble** \'bəb-əl\ *n*
**1** a tiny round body of air or gas in a liquid ⟨*bubbles* in boiling water⟩
**2** a round body of air within a solid ⟨a *bubble* in glass⟩
**3** a thin film of liquid filled with air or gas ⟨soap *bubbles*⟩

**[2]bubble** *vb* **bub·bled**; **bub·bling**
**1** to form or produce bubbles
**2** to flow with a gurgle ⟨a *bubbling* brook⟩

**bu·bon·ic plague** \bü-ˈbän-ik-, byü-\ *n*
a dangerous disease which is spread by rats and in which fever, weakness, and swollen lymph glands are present

**buc·ca·neer** \ˌbək-ə-ˈniər\ *n*
PIRATE

**[1]buck** \ˈbək\ *n*
a male deer or antelope or a male goat, hare, rabbit, or rat

**[2]buck** *vb*
**1** to spring or jump upward with head down and back arched ⟨a bronco *bucking*⟩
**2** to charge or push against ⟨*bucking* the waves⟩
**3** to act in opposition to **:** OPPOSE ⟨*bucking* the system⟩

**buck·board** \ˈbək-ˌbōrd\ *n*
a lightweight carriage with four wheels that has a seat supported by a springy platform

**buck·et** \ˈbək-ət\ *n*
**1** a usually round container with a handle for holding or carrying liquids or solids
**2** an object for collecting, scooping, or carrying something (as the scoop of an excavating machine)
**3** BUCKETFUL

**buck·et·ful** \ˈbək-ət-ˌfu̇l\ *n, pl* **buck·et·fuls** \-ˌfu̇lz\ *or* **buck·ets·ful** \ˈbək-əts-ˌfu̇l\
**1** as much as a bucket will hold
**2** a large quantity ⟨bought a *bucketful* of souvenirs⟩

**buck·eye** \ˈbək-ˌī\ *n*
a horse chestnut or a closely related tree or shrub

**[1]buck·le** \ˈbək-əl\ *n*
a fastening device which is attached to one end of a belt or strap and through which the other end is passed and held

**[2]buckle** *vb* **buck·led**; **buck·ling**
**1** to fasten with a buckle
**2** to apply oneself earnestly ⟨*buckle* down to business⟩
**3** to bend, crumple, or give way ⟨the pavement *buckled* in the heat⟩

**buck·shot** \ˈbək-ˌshät\ *n*
coarse lead shot

**buck·skin** \ˈbək-ˌskin\ *n*
▼ a soft flexible leather usually having a suede finish

**buckskin** jacket of the Algonquian people

**buck·wheat** \ˈbək-ˌhwēt, -ˌwēt\ *n*
a plant with pinkish white flowers that is grown for its dark triangular seeds which are used as a cereal grain

**[1]bud** \ˈbəd\ *n*
**1** a small growth at the tip or on the side of a stem that later develops into a flower or branch
**2** ► a flower that has not fully opened
**3** a part that grows out from the body of an organism and develops into a new organism ⟨a *bud* on a yeast plant⟩
**4** an early stage of development

**[1]bud 2:** a flower bud

**[2]bud** *vb* **bud·ded**; **bud·ding**
**1** to form or put forth buds
**2** to grow or reproduce by buds

**Bud·dhism** \ˈbü-ˌdiz-əm, ˈbu̇d-ˌiz-\ *n*
a religion of eastern and central Asia growing out of the teachings of Gautama Buddha

**Bud·dhist** \ˈbüd-əst, ˈbu̇d-\ *n*
a person whose religion is Buddhism

**bud·dy** \ˈbəd-ē\ *n, pl* **buddies**
[1]CHUM

**budge** \ˈbəj\ *vb* **budged**; **budg·ing**
to move or cause to move from one position to another

**[1]bud·get** \ˈbəj-ət\ *n*
**1** a statement of estimated income and expenses for a period of time ⟨the government *budget*⟩
**2** a plan for using money

**[2]budget** *vb*
**1** to include in a budget ⟨*budget* money for food⟩
**2** to plan as in a budget ⟨*budget* your time wisely⟩

**[1]buff** \ˈbəf\ *n*
**1** an orange yellow
**2** a stick or wheel with a soft surface for applying polish

**Word History** The French made a word from an Italian word that means "buffalo" or "wild ox." The English word *buff* came from this French word and at first meant "buffalo." Later *buff* came to mean "buffalo leather." It was also used to refer to the orange yellow color which is the color of buffalo leather. Still later a stick covered with buffalo leather and used for polishing was also called a *buff*.

**[2]buff** *vb*
to polish with or as if with a buff

**buf·fa·lo** \ˈbəf-ə-ˌlō\ *n, pl* **buffalo** *or* **buf·fa·loes**
any of several wild oxen and especially the American bison

**Word History** The ancient Greeks had a name for an African gazelle. This name came from the Greek word that meant "a bull or cow." The ancient Romans made a Latin word from the Greek name of the gazelle. This Latin word meant "wild ox." The Spanish made a word that meant "wild ox" from this Latin word, and the Italians did, too. The English word *buffalo* came from these Spanish and Italian words.

**buffalo wing** *n*
a deep-fried chicken wing coated with a spicy sauce and usually served with blue cheese dressing

**[1]buf·fet** \ˈbəf-ət\ *vb*
to pound repeatedly **:** BATTER

**[2]buf·fet** \ˌbə-ˈfā, bü-\ *n*
**1** a cabinet or set of shelves for the display of dishes and silver
**2** a meal set out on a buffet or table from which people serve themselves

**bug** \'bəg\ *n*
**1** an insect or other small creeping or crawling animal
**2** any of a large group of insects that have four wings, suck liquid food (as plant juices or blood), and have young which resemble the adults but lack wings
**3** FLAW ⟨a *bug* in a computer system⟩
**4** a person who is a fan of something ⟨I'm a camera *bug*⟩

**bug·a·boo** \'bəg-ə-ˌbü\ *n, pl* **bug·a·boos**
BUGBEAR

**bug·bear** \'bəg-ˌbaər, -ˌbeər\ *n*
**1** an imaginary creature used to frighten children
**2** something one is afraid of

**bug·gy** \'bəg-ē\ *n, pl* **buggies**
a light carriage with a single seat that is usually drawn by one horse

**bu·gle** \'byü-gəl\ *n*
an instrument like a simple trumpet used chiefly for giving military signals

**Word History** In early English *bugle* meant "a buffalo." It also meant "a musical instrument made from buffalo horn." The word *bugle* came from an Old French word that had these same meanings. This French word came from a Latin word that meant "a young steer."

**bu·gler** \'byü-glər\ *n*
a person who plays a bugle

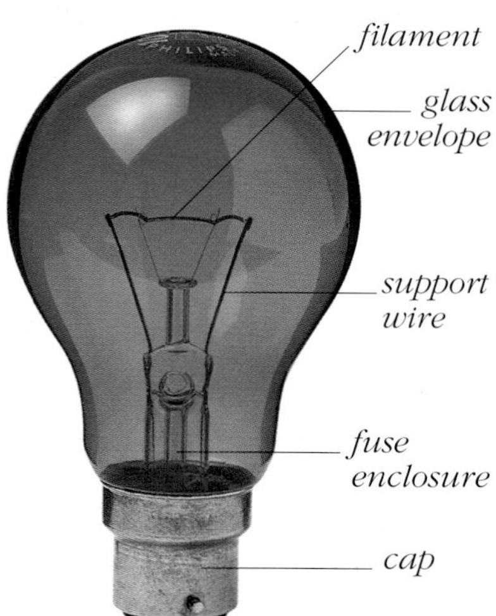


**bulb 3:** a lamp bulb

**¹build** \'bild\ *vb* **built** \'bilt\; **build·ing**
**1** to make by putting together parts or materials
**2** to produce or create gradually by effort ⟨*build* a winning team⟩
**3** to move toward a peak ⟨excitement was *building* up⟩

**Synonyms** BUILD, CONSTRUCT, and ERECT mean to make a structure. BUILD suggests putting together several parts or materials to form something ⟨*build* a house⟩. CONSTRUCT stresses the designing of something and the process of fitting its parts together ⟨*constructing* a system of dams across the river⟩. ERECT stresses the idea of building something that stands up ⟨*erected* a high tower⟩.

**²build** *n*
form or kind of structure
**:** PHYSIQUE

**build·er** \'bil-dər\ *n*
a person whose business is the construction of buildings

**build·ing** \'bil-ding\ *n*
**1** ▶ a permanent structure built as a dwelling, shelter, or place for human activities or for storage ⟨an office *building*⟩
**2** the art, work, or business of assembling materials into a structure

**built–in** \'bil-'tin\ *adj*
forming a permanent part of a structure ⟨*built-in* bookcases⟩

**bulb** \'bəlb\ *n*
**1** an underground resting form of a plant which consists of a short stem with one or more buds surrounded by thick leaves and from which a new plant can grow
**2** a plant structure (as a tuber) that is somewhat like a bulb
**3** ◀ a rounded object or part shaped more or less like a bulb ⟨a lamp *bulb*⟩

**bul·bous** \'bəl-bəs\ *adj*
**1** having a bulb
**2** like a bulb in being round and swollen

**¹bulge** \'bəlj\ *vb* **bulged**; **bulg·ing**
to swell or curve outward ⟨*bulging* muscles⟩

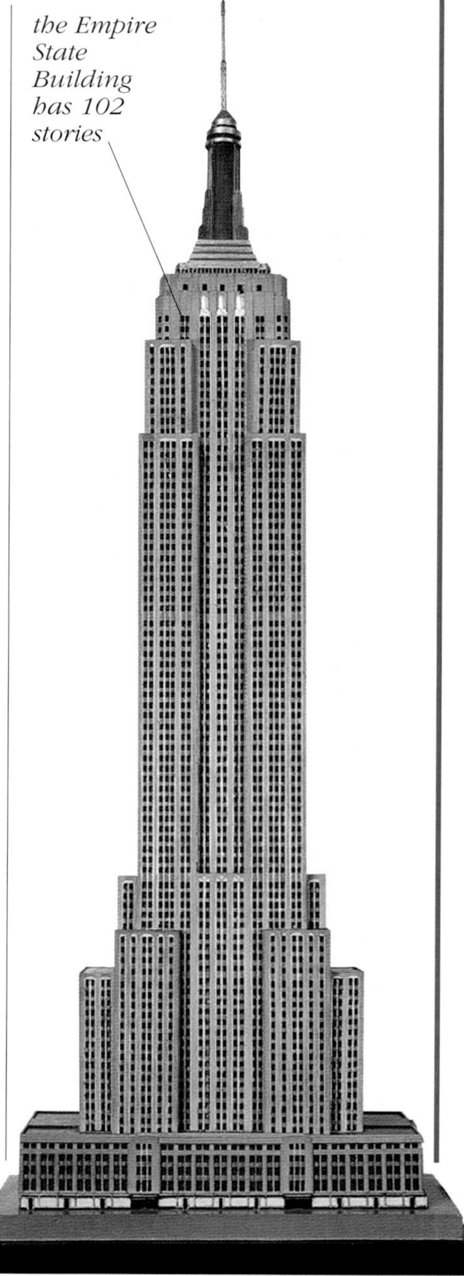


**building 1:** model of the Empire State Building, New York City

**²bulge** *n*
a swelling part **:** a part that sticks out

**bulk** \'bəlk\ *n*
**1** greatness of size or volume ⟨hard to handle because of its *bulk*⟩
**2** the largest or chief part

**bulk·head** \'bəlk-ˌhed\ *n*
a wall separating sections in a ship
**bulky** \'bəl-kē\ *adj* **bulk·i·er**; **bulk·i·est**
1 having bulk
2 being large and awkward to handle
**bull** \'bu̇l\ *n*
the male of an animal of the ox and cow family and of certain other large animals (as the elephant and the whale)
[1]**bull·dog** \'bu̇l-ˌdȯg\ *n*
a dog of English origin with short hair and a stocky powerful build
[2]**bulldog** *vb* **bull·dogged**; **bull·dog·ging**
to throw by seizing the horns and twisting the neck ⟨*bulldog* a steer⟩
**bull·doz·er** \'bu̇l-ˌdō-zər\ *n*
► a motor vehicle with beltlike tracks that has a broad blade for pushing (as in clearing land of trees)
**bul·let** \'bu̇l-ət\ *n*
a shaped piece of metal made to be shot from a firearm
**bul·let·proof** \ˌbu̇l-ət-'prüf\ *adj*
**bul·le·tin** \'bu̇l-ət-n\ *n*
a short public notice usually coming from an informed or official source
**bulletin board** *n*
a board for posting bulletins and announcements
**bull·fight** \'bu̇l-ˌfīt\ *n*
a public entertainment in which people excite bulls, display daring in escaping their charges, and finally kill them
**bull·fight·er** *n*
**bull·finch** \'bu̇l-ˌfinch\ *n*
▼ a European songbird that has a thick bill and a red breast and is often kept in a cage

bullfinch

**bull·frog** \'bu̇l-ˌfrȯg, -ˌfräg\ *n*
a large heavy frog that makes a booming or bellowing sound
**bull·head** \'bu̇l-ˌhed\ *n*
any of various fishes with large heads
**bul·lion** \'bu̇l-yən\ *n*
gold or silver metal in bars or blocks
**bul·lock** \'bu̇l-ək\ *n*
1 a young bull
2 [1]STEER, OX

bulldozer

**bull's–eye** \'bu̇l-ˌzī\ *n*
1 the center of a target
2 a shot that hits the center of a target
[1]**bul·ly** \'bu̇l-ē\ *n, pl* **bul·lies**
a person who teases, hurts, or threatens smaller or weaker persons
[2]**bully** *vb* **bul·lied**; **bul·ly·ing**
to act like a bully toward
**bul·rush** \'bu̇l-ˌrəsh\ *n*
any of several large rushes or sedges that grow in wet places
**bul·wark** \'bu̇l-wərk\ *n*
1 a solid structure like a wall built for defense against an enemy
2 something that defends or protects
**bum** \'bəm\ *n*
1 a person who avoids work and tries to live off others
2 [2]TRAMP 1, HOBO
**bum·ble·bee** \'bəm-bəl-ˌbē\ *n*
a large hairy bee that makes a loud humming sound
[1]**bump** \'bəmp\ *n*
1 a sudden heavy blow or shock
2 a rounded swelling of flesh as from a blow
3 an unevenness in a road surface
[2]**bump** *vb*
1 to strike or knock against something ⟨*bump* into a door⟩
2 to move along unevenly : JOLT
[1]**bum·per** \'bəm-pər\ *adj*
larger or finer than usual ⟨a *bumper* crop of corn⟩
[2]**bump·er** \'bəm-pər\ *n*
a bar across the front or back of a motor vehicle intended to lessen the shock or damage from collision
**bun** \'bən\ *n*
a sweet or plain round roll
[1]**bunch** \'bənch\ *n*
1 a number of things of the same kind growing together ⟨a *bunch* of grapes⟩
2 [1]GROUP ⟨a *bunch* of children⟩
[2]**bunch** *vb*
to gather in a bunch
[1]**bun·dle** \'bən-dl\ *n*
a number of things fastened or wrapped together : PACKAGE
[2]**bundle** *vb* **bun·dled**; **bun·dling**
to make into a bundle : WRAP
**bung** \'bəng\ *n*
1 the stopper in the bunghole of a barrel
2 BUNGHOLE
**bun·ga·low** \'bəng-gə-ˌlō\ *n*
a house with a single story
**bung·hole** \'bəng-ˌhōl\ *n*
a hole for emptying or filling a barrel

A B C D E F G H I J K L M N O P Q R S T U V W X Y Z

**bun·gle** \'bəng-gəl\ *vb* **bun·gled**; **bun·gling**
to act, do, make, or work badly ⟨*bungled* the job⟩
**bun·gler** *n*

**bun·ion** \'bən-yən\ *n*
a sore reddened swelling of the first joint of a big toe

[1]**bunk** \'bəngk\ *n*
**1** a built-in bed
**2** a sleeping place

[2]**bunk** *vb*
to share or sleep in a bunk

**bunk bed** *n*
one of two single beds usually placed one above the other

**bun·ny** \'bən-ē\ *n, pl* **bunnies**
RABBIT

[1]**bunt** \'bənt\ *vb*
to strike or push with the horns or head : BUTT

[2]**bunt** *n*
[2]BUTT, PUSH

[1]**bun·ting** \'bənt-ing\ *n*
▼ any of various birds that are similar to sparrows in size and habits but have stout bills

[1]**bunting:** an indigo bunting

[2]**bunting** *n*
**1** a thin cloth used chiefly for making flags and patriotic decorations
**2** flags or decorations made of bunting

[1]**buoy** \'bü-ē, 'bȯi\ *n*
**1** a floating object anchored in a body of water so as to mark a channel or to warn of danger
**2** LIFE BUOY

[2]**buoy** *vb*
**1** to keep from sinking : keep afloat
**2** to brighten the mood of ⟨*buoyed* by the hope of success⟩

**buoy·an·cy** \'bȯi-ən-sē, 'bü-yən-\ *n*
**1** the power of rising and floating (as on water or in air) ⟨the *buoyancy* of cork in water⟩
**2** the power of a liquid to hold up a floating body ⟨the *buoyancy* of seawater⟩

**buoy·ant** \'bȯi-ənt, 'bü-yənt\ *adj*
**1** able to rise and float in the air or on the top of a liquid ⟨*buoyant* cork⟩
**2** able to keep a body afloat
**3** LIGHT-HEARTED, CHEERFUL

**bur** *or* **burr** \'bər\ *n*
**1** a rough or prickly covering or shell of a seed or fruit
**2** something that is like a bur (as in sticking)

[1]**bur·den** \'bərd-n\ *n*
**1** something carried : LOAD
**2** something that is hard to take ⟨a heavy *burden* of sorrow⟩
**3** the carrying of loads ⟨beast of *burden*⟩
**4** the capacity of a ship for carrying cargo

[2]**burden** *vb*
to put a burden on

**bur·den·some** \'bərd-n-səm\ *adj*
so heavy or hard to take as to be a burden

**bur·dock** \'bər-ˌdäk\ *n*
a tall coarse weed related to the thistles that has prickly purplish heads of flowers

**bu·reau** \'byu̇r-ō\ *n*
**1** a low chest of drawers for use in a bedroom
**2** a division of a government department ⟨the Weather *Bureau*⟩
**3** a business office that provides services ⟨a travel *bureau*⟩

**bur·glar** \'bər-glər\ *n*
a person who is guilty of burglary

**bur·glary** \'bər-glə-rē\ *n, pl* **bur·glar·ies**
the act of breaking into a building to steal

**buri·al** \'ber-ē-əl\ *n*
the placing of a dead body in a grave or tomb

**bur·lap** \'bər-ˌlap\ *n*
a rough cloth made usually from jute or hemp and used mostly for bags and wrappings

**bur·ly** \'bər-lē\ *adj* **bur·li·er**; **bur·li·est**
strongly and heavily built
**bur·li·ness** *n*

[1]**burn** \'bərn\ *vb* **burned** \'bərnd\ *or* **burnt** \'bərnt\; **burn·ing**
**1** to be on fire or to set on fire
**2** to destroy or be destroyed by fire or heat ⟨*burn* the trash⟩ ⟨a house that *burned* to the ground⟩
**3** to make or produce by fire or heat ⟨*burn* a hole in a coat⟩
**4** to give light ⟨a light *burning*⟩
**5** to injure or affect by or as if by fire or heat ⟨*burned* my finger⟩
**6** to feel or cause to feel as if on fire ⟨*burn* with anger⟩

[2]**burn** *n*
an injury produced by burning

**burn·er** \'bər-nər\ *n*
the part of a stove or furnace where the flame or heat is produced

**bur·nish** \'bər-nish\ *vb*
to make shiny

**burr** *variant of* BUR

**bur·ro** \'bər-ō\ *n, pl* **burros**
a small donkey often used as a pack animal

[1]**bur·row** \'bər-ō\ *n*
► a hole in the ground made by an animal (as a rabbit or fox) for shelter or protection

[2]**burrow** *vb*
**1** to hide in or as if in a burrow
**2** to make a burrow
**3** to make one's way by or as if by digging

[1]**burst** \'bərst\ *vb* **burst**; **burst·ing**
**1** to break open or in pieces (as by an explosion from within) ⟨bombs *bursting* in air⟩ ⟨buds *bursting* open⟩
**2** to suddenly show one's feelings ⟨*burst* into tears⟩
**3** to come or go suddenly ⟨*burst* into the room⟩
**4** to be filled to the breaking point ⟨*bursting* with energy⟩

[2]**burst** *n*
a sudden release or effort ⟨a *burst* of laughter⟩ ⟨a *burst* of energy⟩

**bury** \'ber-ē\ *vb* **bur·ied**; **bury·ing**
**1** to put (a dead body) in a grave or tomb
**2** to place in the ground and cover over for concealment ⟨*buried* treasure⟩
**3** to cover up : HIDE ⟨*buried* my face in my hands⟩

**bus** \'bəs\ *n, pl* **bus·es** *or* **bus·ses**
a large motor vehicle for carrying passengers

## [1]burrow

A burrow protects animals against predators and against extremes of weather. In a burrow dug by moles, as shown here, different tunnels provide access to the surface or to the breeding nest beneath the molehill. They may also be used for food storage.

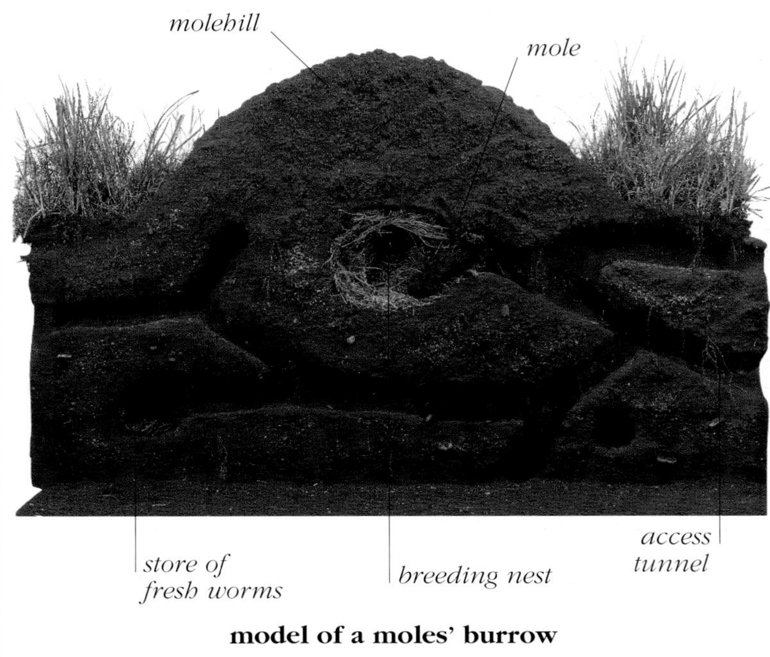


**model of a moles' burrow**

**bush** \'bu̇sh\ *n*
**1** a usually low shrub with many branches
**2** a stretch of uncleared or lightly settled country

**bush·el** \'bu̇sh-əl\ *n*
**1** a unit of dry capacity equal to four pecks or thirty-two quarts (about thirty-five liters)
**2** a container holding a bushel

**bushy** \'bu̇sh-ē\ *adj* **bush·i·er**; **bush·i·est**
**1** overgrown with bushes
**2** being thick and spreading ⟨a *bushy* beard⟩

**busi·ness** \'biz-nəs\ *n*
**1** the normal activity of a person or group ⟨learning is the *business* of a student⟩
**2** a commercial enterprise ⟨opened a new *business*⟩
**3** the making, buying, and selling of goods or services
**4** personal concerns ⟨none of your *business*⟩ **synonyms** see TRADE

**busi·ness·man** \'biz-nəs-ˌman\ *n*, *pl* **busi·ness·men** \-ˌmen\
a man in business especially as an owner or a manager

**busi·ness·wom·an** \'biz-nə-ˌswu̇m-ən\ *n*, *pl* **busi·ness·wom·en** \-ˌswim-ən\
a woman in business especially as an owner or a manager

**[1]bust** \'bəst\ *n*
**1** a piece of sculpture representing the upper part of the human figure including the head and neck
**2** a woman's bosom

**[2]bust** *vb*
**1** to hit with the fist
**2** [1]BREAK 1

**[1]bus·tle** \'bəs-əl\ *vb* **bus·tled**; **bus·tling**
to move about in a fussy or noisy way

**[2]bustle** *n*
fussy or noisy activity

**[1]busy** \'biz-ē\ *adj* **busi·er**; **busi·est**
**1** actively at work
**2** being used ⟨the line is *busy*⟩
**3** full of activity ⟨a *busy* day⟩
**busi·ly** \'biz-ə-lē\ *adv*

**[2]busy** *vb* **bus·ied**; **busy·ing**
to make busy ⟨*busy* oneself with chores⟩

**busy·body** \'biz-ē-ˌbäd-ē\ *n*, *pl* **busy·bod·ies**
a person who meddles in the affairs of others

**[1]but** \bət\ *conj*
**1** except that : UNLESS ⟨never rains *but* it pours⟩
**2** while just the opposite ⟨I ski *but* you don't⟩
**3** yet nevertheless ⟨fell *but* wasn't hurt⟩

**[2]but** *prep*
other than : EXCEPT ⟨everyone *but* you⟩

**[3]but** *adv*
[2]ONLY 1 ⟨we have *but* one choice⟩

**[1]butch·er** \'bu̇ch-ər\ *n*
**1** one whose business is killing animals for sale as food
**2** a dealer in meat
**3** a person who kills in large numbers or in a brutal manner

**[2]butcher** *vb*
**1** to kill and dress (an animal) for food
**2** [2]MASSACRE
**3** to make a mess of : BOTCH

**but·ler** \'bət-lər\ *n*
the chief male servant of a household

**[1]butt** \'bət\ *vb*
to strike or thrust with the head or horns

**[2]butt** *n*
a blow or thrust with the head or horns

**[3]butt** *n*
a target of ridicule or hurtful jokes ⟨he became the *butt* of their jokes⟩

**[4]butt** *n*
**1** the thicker or bottom end of something ⟨the *butt* of a rifle⟩
**2** an unused remainder ⟨a cigarette *butt*⟩

**butte** \'byüt\ *n*
an isolated hill with steep sides

**[1]but·ter** \'bət-ər\ *n*
**1** a solid yellowish fatty food obtained from cream or milk by churning
**2** a substance that is like butter in texture and use ⟨apple *butter*⟩ ⟨peanut *butter*⟩

a b c d e f g h i j k l m n o p q r s t u v w x y z

A B C D E F G H I J K L M N O P Q R S T U V W X Y Z

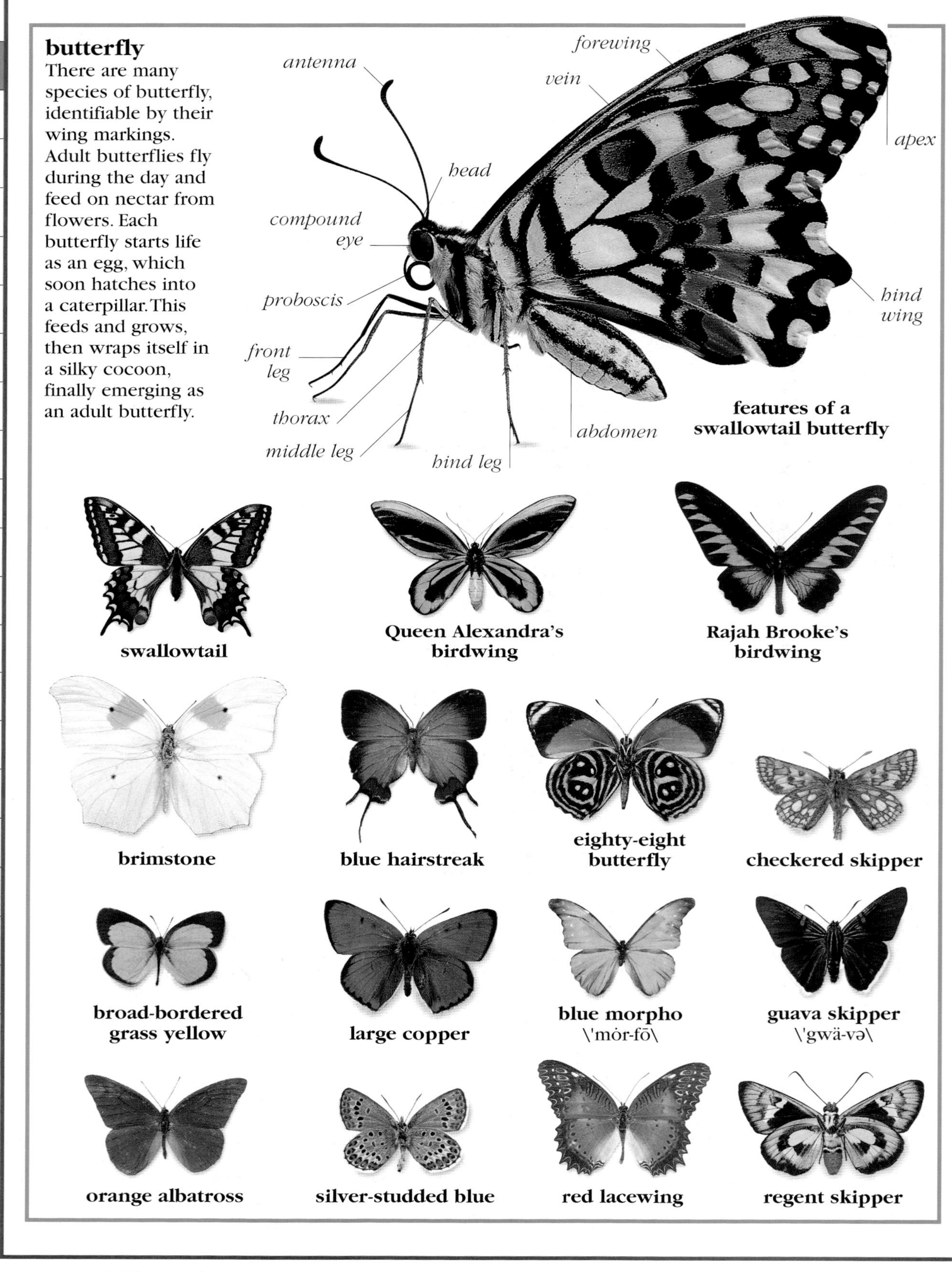


**butterfly**
There are many species of butterfly, identifiable by their wing markings. Adult butterflies fly during the day and feed on nectar from flowers. Each butterfly starts life as an egg, which soon hatches into a caterpillar. This feeds and grows, then wraps itself in a silky cocoon, finally emerging as an adult butterfly.

[2]**butter** *vb*
to spread with or as if with butter

**but·ter·cup** \'bət-ər-ˌkəp\ *n*
► a common wildflower with bright yellow blossoms

**but·ter·fat** \'bət-ər-ˌfat\ *n*
the natural fat of milk that is the chief ingredient of butter

**but·ter·fly** \'bət-ər-ˌflī\ *n, pl* **but·ter·flies**
◄ an insect that has a slender body and large colored wings covered with tiny overlapping scales and that flies mostly in the daytime

**buttercup**

**but·ter·milk** \'bət-ər-ˌmilk\ *n*
the liquid left after churning butter from milk or cream

**but·ter·nut** \'bət-ər-ˌnət\ *n*
an eastern North American tree that has sweet egg-shaped nuts and is related to the walnuts

**but·ter·scotch** \'bət-ər-ˌskäch\ *n*
a candy made from sugar, corn syrup, and water

**but·tock** \'bət-ək\ *n*
**1** the back of the hip which forms one of the rounded parts on which a person sits
**2 buttocks** *pl* RUMP 1

[1]**but·ton** \'bət-n\ *n*
**1** a small ball or disk used for holding parts of a garment together or as an ornament
**2** something that suggests a button ⟨push the light *button*⟩

[2]**button** *vb*
to close or fasten with buttons

**but·ton·hole** \'bət-n-ˌhōl\ *n*
a slit or loop for fastening a button

**but·ton·wood** \'bət-n-ˌwu̇d\ *n*
SYCAMORE 2

[1]**but·tress** \'bə-trəs\ *n*
**1** a structure built against a wall or building to give support and strength
**2** something that supports, props, or strengthens

[2]**buttress** *vb*
to support with or as if with a buttress

**bux·om** \'bək-səm\ *adj*
having a healthy plump form

[1]**buy** \'bī\ *vb* **bought** \'bȯt\; **buy·ing**
to get by paying for : PURCHASE
**buy·er** *n*

[2]**buy** *n*
[1]BARGAIN 2

[1]**buzz** \'bəz\ *vb*
**1** to make a low humming sound like that of bees
**2** to be filled with a low hum or murmur ⟨a room that *buzzed* with excitement⟩
**3** to fly an airplane low over

[2]**buzz** *n*
a sound of buzzing

**buz·zard** \'bəz-ərd\ *n*
▼ a usually large bird of prey that flies slowly

**buzzard**

**buzz·er** \'bəz-ər\ *n*
an electric signaling device that makes a buzzing sound

[1]**by** \bī\ *prep*
**1** close to : NEAR ⟨stood *by* the door⟩
**2** so as to go on ⟨went *by* the back road⟩ ⟨travel *by* bus⟩
**3** so as to go through ⟨left *by* the back window⟩
**4** so as to pass ⟨drove *by* the house⟩
**5** AT 1, DURING ⟨travel *by* night⟩
**6** no later than ⟨leave *by* noon⟩
**7** with the use or help of ⟨won *by* cheating⟩
**8** through the action of ⟨was seen *by* the others⟩
**9** ACCORDING TO ⟨play *by* the rules⟩
**10** with respect to ⟨a lawyer *by* profession⟩ ⟨a Canadian *by* birth⟩
**11** to the amount of ⟨won *by* a mile⟩
**12** used to join two or more measurements ⟨a room 4 meters wide *by* 6 meters long⟩ or to join the numbers in a statement of multiplication or division ⟨divide 8 *by* 4⟩

[2]**by** *adv*
**1** near at hand ⟨stand *by*⟩
**2** [4]PAST ⟨walk *by*⟩ ⟨in days gone *by*⟩

**by–and–by** \ˌbī-ən-'bī\ *n*
a future time

**by and by** \ˌbī-ən-'bī\ *adv*
after a while

**by·gone** \'bī-ˌgȯn\ *adj*
gone by : PAST

**by·gones** \'bī-ˌgȯnz\ *n pl*
events that are over and done with ⟨let *bygones* be *bygones*⟩

[1]**by·pass** \'bī-ˌpas\ *n*
**1** a way for passing to one side
**2** a road serving as a substitute route around a crowded area

[2]**bypass** *vb*
to make a detour around

**by–prod·uct** \'bī-ˌpräd-əkt\ *n*
something produced (as in manufacturing) in addition to the main product

**by·stand·er** \'bī-ˌstan-dər\ *n*
a person present or standing near but taking no part in what is going on

**byte** \'bīt\ *n*
a group of eight bits that a computer handles as a unit

**by·way** \'bī-ˌwā\ *n*
a less traveled road off a main highway

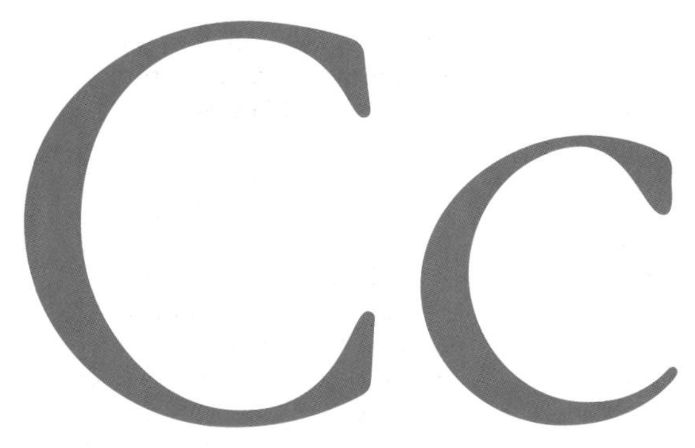

**The sounds of C**: The consonant **C** has two sounds. It usually sounds like the letter **K** when it occurs before the vowels **A**, **O**, or **U**. Examples are **cat**, **cot**, and **cut**.

When it occurs before the vowels **I** or **E** it usually sounds like the letter **S**. Examples are **cell** and **cider**.

**C** also occurs together with **H** to form a separate sound. Examples of this sound are **child** and **chili**.

When this combination occurs in the middle or at the end of a word, it is often preceded by the letter **T**, as in the word **match**. But the sound is the same as the **CH** alone.

In a few words, **CH** sounds like the **SH** in **ship**. An example is **chute**. In others, it sounds like **K**, as in **chaos** and **echo**.

**c** \'sē\ *n, pl* **c's** *or* **cs** \'sēz\ *often cap*
**1** the third letter of the English alphabet
**2** 100 in Roman numerals
**3** a grade that shows a student's work is fair

**cab** \'kab\ *n*
**1** a light closed carriage pulled by a horse
**2** TAXICAB
**3** the covered compartment for the engineer and the controls of a locomotive or for the operator of a truck, tractor, or crane

**ca·bana** \kə-'ban-ə, -yə\ *n*
a shelter usually with an open side facing the sea or a swimming pool

**cab·bage** \'kab-ij\ *n*
▼ a garden plant with a short stem and a firm head of leaves that is used as a vegetable

**cab·in** \'kab-ən\ *n*
**1** a private room on a ship
**2** a place below deck on a small boat for passengers or crew
**3** a part of an airplane for cargo, crew, or passengers
**4** a small simple dwelling usually having only one story

**cab·i·net** \'kab-ə-nət, 'kab-nət\ *n*
**1** a case or cupboard with shelves or drawers for keeping or displaying articles ⟨filing *cabinet*⟩
**2** a group of persons who act as advisers (as to the head of a country) ⟨a member of the president's *cabinet*⟩

[1]**ca·ble** \'kā-bəl\ *n*
**1** a very strong rope, wire, or chain
**2** ▼ a bundle of wires to carry electric current
**3** CABLEGRAM
**4** CABLE TELEVISION

plastic insulator

copper wires conduct electricity

**[1]cable 2:**
an electric cable

[2]**cable** *vb* **ca·bled**; **ca·bling**
to telegraph by underwater cable

**ca·ble·gram** \'kā-bəl-,gram\ *n*
a message sent by underwater cable

**cable television** \ *n*
a television system in which paying customers receive the television signals over electrical wires

**ca·boose** \kə-'büs\ *n*
a car usually at the rear of a freight train for the use of the train crew and railroad workers

**ca·cao** \kə-'kaù, kə-'kā-ō\ *n, pl* **cacaos**
a South American tree with fleshy yellow pods that contain fatty seeds from which chocolate is made

[1]**cache** \'kash\ *n*
**1** a place for hiding, storing, or preserving treasure or supplies
**2** something hidden or stored in a cache

[2]**cache** *vb* **cached**; **cach·ing**
to place, hide, or store in a cache

[1]**cack·le** \'kak-əl\ *vb* **cack·led**; **cack·ling**
**1** to make the noise or cry a hen makes especially after laying an egg
**2** to laugh or chatter noisily

[2]**cackle** *n*
a cackling sound

**cac·tus** \'kak-təs\ *n, pl* **cac·tus·es** *or* **cac·ti** \-,tī, -tē\
▼ any of a large group of flowering plants of dry regions that

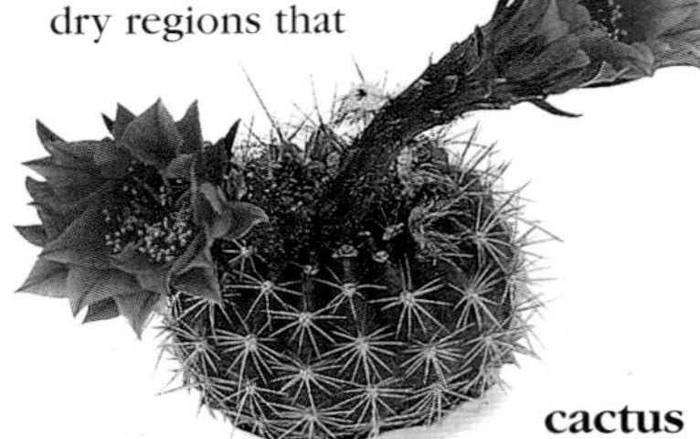

**cactus**

## cabbage

A leafy vegetable, cabbages are produced all year round. Most are round in shape, with leaves that are held loosely, or tightly curled around the heart — the central cluster of small leaves at the stalk. Cabbages may be white, red, or green. The leaves can be smooth or crinkled.

**roundhead cabbage**

**crinkled cabbage**

**Chinese cabbage**

have thick juicy stems and branches with scales or prickles

[1]**cad·die** *or* **cad·dy** \'kad-ē\ *n, pl* **cad·dies**
a person who carries a golfer's clubs

[2]**caddie** *or* **caddy** *vb* **cad·died**; **cad·dy·ing**
to work as a caddie

**cad·dis fly** \'kad-əs-\ *n*
an insect that has four wings and a larva which lives in water in a silk case covered with bits of wood or gravel and is often used for fish bait

**ca·dence** \'kād-ns\ *n*
the beat of rhythmic motion or sound (as of marching) : RHYTHM

**ca·det** \kə-'det\ *n*
a student in a military school or college

**ca·fé** *also* **ca·fe** \ka-'fā, kə-\ *n*
**1** [1]BAR 9
**2** RESTAURANT
**3** NIGHTCLUB

**caf·e·te·ria** \,kaf-ə-'tir-ē-ə\ *n*
a restaurant where the customers serve themselves or are served at a counter but carry their own food to their tables

**caf·feine** \ka-'fēn, 'ka-,fēn\ *n*
a stimulating substance in coffee and tea

[1]**cage** \'kāj\ *n*
**1** ▼ a box or enclosure that has large openings covered usually with wire net or bars and is used to confine or carry birds or animals
**2** an enclosure like a cage in shape or purpose

[2]**cage** *vb* **caged**; **cag·ing**
to put or keep in or as if in a cage

[1]**cage 1:** a bird cage

**ca·gey** \'kā-jē\ *adj* **ca·gi·er**; **ca·gi·est**
hard to trap or trick

**cais·son** \'kā-,sän\ *n*
**1** a chest for ammunition usually set on two wheels
**2** a watertight box or chamber used for doing construction work under water or used as a foundation

**ca·jole** \kə-'jōl\ *vb* **ca·joled**; **ca·jol·ing**
to coax or persuade especially by flattery or false promises : WHEEDLE

**Word History** The English word *cajole* came from a French word meaning "to chatter like a bird in a cage." This modern French word came in turn from an earlier French word that meant "bird cage." The French word that means "bird cage" came from a Latin word that meant "little cage." The English word *cave* is also related to this Latin word.

[1]**cake** \'kāk\ *n*
**1** a small piece of food (as dough or batter, meat, or fish) that is baked or fried
**2** ▼ a baked food made from a sweet batter or dough
**3** a substance hardened or molded into a solid piece ⟨a *cake* of soap⟩

[1]**cake 2:**
cherry and chocolate cake

[2]**cake** *vb* **caked**; **cak·ing**
**1** ENCRUST
**2** to form or harden into a cake

**ca·lam·i·ty** \kə-'lam-ət-ē\ *n, pl* **ca·lam·i·ties**
**1** great distress or misfortune
**2** an event that causes great harm

**cal·ci·um** \'kal-sē-əm\ *n*
a silvery soft metallic chemical element that is an essential for most plants and animals

**calcium carbonate** *n*
a solid substance that is found as limestone and marble and in plant ashes, bones, and shells

**cal·cu·late** \'kal-kyə-,lāt\ *vb* **cal·cu·lat·ed**; **cal·cu·lat·ing**
**1** to find by adding, subtracting, multiplying, or dividing : COMPUTE
**2** [1]ESTIMATE 1
**3** to plan by careful thought

**Word History** The English word *calculate* came from a Latin word that meant "to figure" or "to compute." Long ago pebbles were sometimes used in figuring. The Latin word that meant "to figure" came from another Latin word that meant "pebble."

**cal·cu·la·tion** \,kal-kyə-'lā-shən\ *n*
**1** the process or an act of calculating
**2** the result obtained by calculating

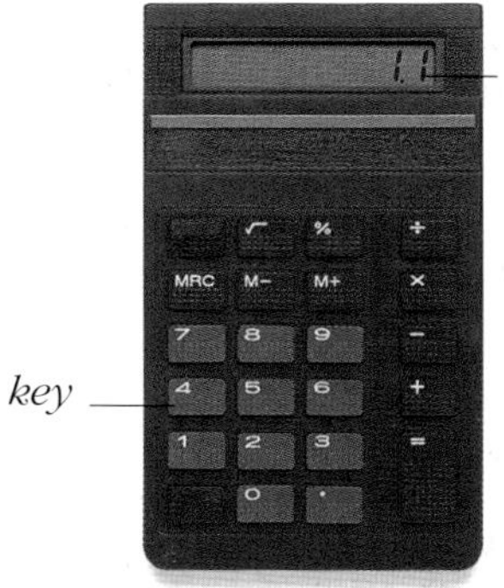

**calculator 2**

**cal·cu·la·tor** \'kal-kyə-,lāt-ər\ *n*
**1** a person who calculates
**2** ▲ a usually small electronic device for solving mathematical problems

**cal·cu·lus** \'kal-kyə-ləs\ *n*
TARTAR 2

**caldron** *variant of* CAULDRON

**cal·en·dar** \'kal-ən-dər\ *n*
**1** a chart showing the days, weeks, and months of the year
**2** a schedule of coming events ⟨a church *calendar*⟩

[1]**calf** \'kaf, 'kȧf\ *n, pl* **calves** \'kavz, 'kȧvz\
**1** the young of the cow
**2** the young of various large animals (as the elephant, moose, or whale)
**3** *pl* **calfs** CALFSKIN

[2]**calf** *n, pl* **calves**
the muscular back part of the leg below the knee

A B C D E F G H I J K L M N O P Q R S T U V W X Y Z

**calf·skin** \'kaf-,skin, 'kȧf-\ *n*
the skin of a calf or the leather made from it

**cal·i·ber** *or* **cal·i·bre** \'kal-ə-bər\ *n*
**1** the diameter of a bullet
**2** the diameter of the hole in the barrel of a gun

[1]**cal·i·co** \'kal-i-,kō\ *n, pl* **cal·i·coes** *or* **cal·i·cos**
cotton cloth especially with a colored pattern printed on one side

[2]**calico** *adj*
▼ marked with blotches of color ⟨a *calico* cat⟩

[2]**calico:** a calico cat

**cal·i·per** *or* **cal·li·per** \'kal-ə-pər\ *n*
an instrument with two adjustable legs used to measure the thickness of objects or the distance between surfaces — usually used in pl. ⟨a pair of *calipers*⟩

**ca·liph** *or* **ca·lif** \'kā-ləf\ *n*
an important official in some Arab countries

**cal·is·then·ics** \,kal-əs-'then-iks\ *n sing or pl*
exercise to develop strength and grace that is done without special equipment

[1]**call** \'kȯl\ *vb*
**1** to speak in a loud clear voice so as to be heard at a distance **:** SHOUT ⟨*call* for help⟩
**2** to say in a loud clear voice ⟨*call* an order to a worker⟩
**3** to announce with authority **:** PROCLAIM ⟨*call* a halt⟩
**4** SUMMON 1, 2 ⟨*call* children from play⟩
**5** to bring into action or discussion ⟨*call* up reserves⟩
**6** to make a request or demand ⟨*call* for an investigation⟩
**7** to get in touch with by telephone
**8** to make a visit ⟨*call* on a neighbor⟩
**9** [2]NAME 1 ⟨*called* the cat "Patches"⟩
**10** to estimate as ⟨*call* it an even dollar⟩
**call for** to require as necessary or suitable ⟨we'll do whatever is *called for*⟩

[2]**call** *n*
**1** a loud shout or cry
**2** a cry of an animal
**3** a request or command to come or assemble
**4** [1]DEMAND 1, CLAIM
**5** [1]REQUEST 1 ⟨*calls* for a recipe⟩
**6** a short visit ⟨a neighborly *call*⟩
**7** a name or thing called
**8** the act of calling on the telephone

**call down** *vb*
[2]REPRIMAND

**call·er** \'kȯ-lər\ *n*
one who calls **synonyms** see VISITOR

**call·ing** \'kȯ-ling\ *n*
OCCUPATION 1, PROFESSION

**cal·li·ope** \kə-'lī-ə-pē\ *n*
a keyboard musical instrument consisting of a set of steam whistles

**cal·lous** \'kal-əs\ *adj*
**1** having a callus
**2** feeling no sympathy for others

**cal·lus** \'kal-əs\ *n*
a hard thickened spot (as of skin)

[1]**calm** \'käm, 'kälm\ *n*
**1** a period or condition of freedom from storm, wind, or rough water
**2** a peaceful state **:** QUIET

**calm·ly** *adv*
**calm·ness** *n*

**Synonyms** CALM, PEACEFUL, and TRANQUIL mean quiet and free from disturbance. CALM suggests that one is free from disturbance even when there is cause for excitement ⟨stayed *calm* even during the fire⟩. PEACEFUL suggests that one has reached a quiet state after some period of disturbance ⟨the storm is over and the lake is *peaceful* again⟩. TRANQUIL suggests a total or lasting state of rest ⟨a *tranquil* village in the mountains⟩.

**cal·o·rie** \'kal-ə-rē, 'kal-rē\ *n*
**1** a unit for measuring heat equal to the heat required to raise the temperature of one gram of water one degree Celsius
**2** a unit equal to 1000 calories — used especially to indicate the value of foods for producing heat and energy in the human body

**camel**
There are two camel species: the dromedary and the Bactrian. The dromedary has one hump, while the Bactrian camel has two. The hump serves a useful purpose — storing fat for times when the camel's food of desert plants becomes scarce. As the fat is used up, the hump shrinks.

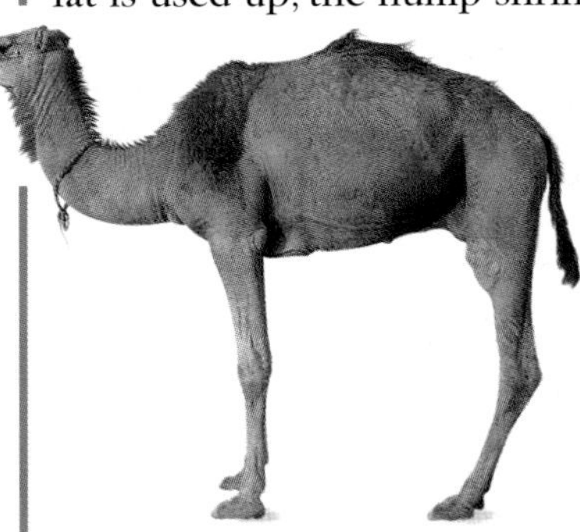

**dromedary**

**Bactrian camel**

[2]**calm** *vb*
to make or become calm

[3]**calm** *adj*
**1** not stormy or windy **:** STILL ⟨a *calm* night⟩
**2** not excited or angry ⟨a *calm* reply⟩

**calve** \'kav, 'kȧv\ *vb* **calved**; **calv·ing**
to give birth to a calf

**calves** *pl of* CALF

**ca·lyp·so** \kə-'lip-sō\ *n, pl* **calypsos**
a folk song or style of singing of the West Indies

**ca·lyx** \'kā-liks\ *n, pl* **ca·lyx·es** *or* **ca·ly·ces** \-lə-ˌsēz\
▼ the outer usually green or leafy part of a flower

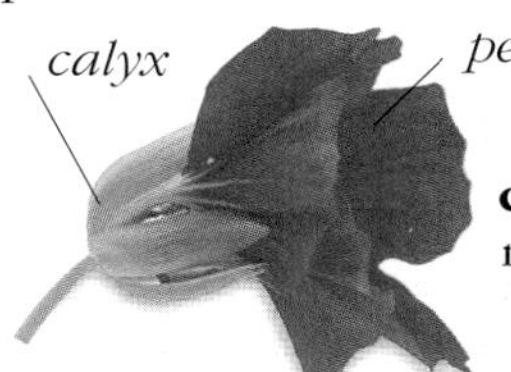


**calyx** of a nasturtium flower

**cam** \'kam\ *n*
a device (as a tooth on a wheel) by which circular motion is changed to back-and-forth motion

**cam·bi·um** \'kam-bē-əm\ *n, pl* **cam·bi·ums** *or* **cam·bia** \-bē-ə\
soft tissue in woody plants from which new wood and bark grow

**cam·cord·er** \'kam-ˌkȯrd-ər\ *n*
a small portable device that is a combination of a camera and a videotape recording device

**came** *past of* COME

**cam·el** \'kam-əl\ *n*
◀ a large hoofed animal that chews the cud and is used in the deserts of Asia and Africa for carrying burdens and for riding

**cam·era** \'kam-ə-rə, 'kam-rə\ *n*
**1** ▶ a box that has a lens on one side to let the light in and is used for taking pictures
**2** the part of a television sending device in which the image to be sent out is formed

**¹cam·ou·flage** \'kam-ə-ˌfläzh, -ˌfläj\ *n*
**1** the hiding or disguising of something by covering it up or changing the way it looks
**2** ◀ a disguise made for camouflage

brown and sand-colored uniform blends in with desert scene

**¹camouflage 2:** a soldier dressed in camouflage

**camera 1**

The most widely used cameras are those that hold films 35 mm in width. While many cameras adjust focus and lighting levels automatically, single-lens reflex — SLR — cameras must be set by hand, giving greater control to the photographer.

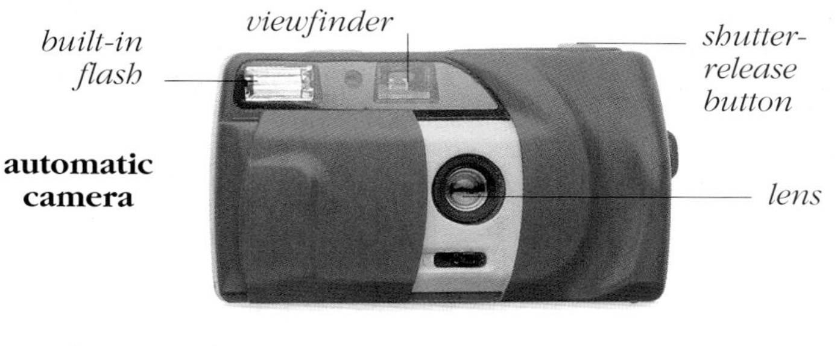


**automatic camera**

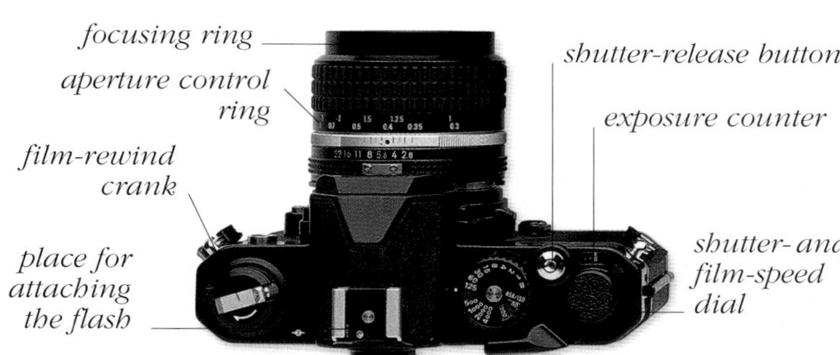


**SLR (single-lens reflex) camera**

**²camouflage** *vb* **cam·ou·flaged**; **cam·ou·flag·ing**
to hide or disguise by camouflage

**¹camp** \'kamp\ *n*
**1** a place where temporary shelters are erected
**2** a place usually in the country for recreation or instruction during the summer
**3** a group of people in a camp

**²camp** *vb*
**1** to make or occupy a camp
**2** to live in a camp or outdoors
**camp·er** *n*

**¹cam·paign** \kam-'pān\ *n*
**1** a series of military operations in a certain area or for a certain purpose ⟨the Italian *campaign*⟩
**2** a series of activities meant to get a certain thing done ⟨the election *campaign*⟩

**²campaign** *vb*
to take part in a campaign
**campaign·er** *n*

**Camp Fire Girl** *n*
a member of a national organization for girls from seven to eighteen

**cam·phor** \'kam-fər\ *n*
a white fragrant solid that comes from the wood and bark of a tall Asian tree (**camphor tree**) and is used mostly in medicine and in making plastics

**cam·pus** \'kam-pəs\ *n*
the grounds and buildings of a university, college, or school

**¹can** \kən, kan\ *helping verb, past* **could** \kəd, ku̇d\; *present sing & pl* **can**
**1** know how to ⟨we *can* read⟩
**2** be able to ⟨I *can* hear you⟩
**3** be permitted by conscience to ⟨they *can* hardly blame me⟩
**4** have permission to **:** MAY ⟨you *can* go now⟩

**²can** \'kan\ *n*
**1** a usually cylindrical metal container ⟨garbage *can*⟩
**2** the contents of a can ⟨a *can* of tomatoes⟩

**³can** \'kan\ *vb* **canned**; **can·ning**
to keep fit for later use by sealing (as in an airtight jar) ⟨*can* peaches for winter⟩

a b c d e f g h i j k l m n o p q r s t u v w x y z

**[1]Ca·na·di·an** \kə-ˈnād-ē-ən\ *adj*
of or relating to Canada or the Canadians

**[2]Canadian** *n*
a person born or living in Canada

**ca·nal** \kə-ˈnal\ *n*
**1** an artificial waterway for boats or for irrigation of land
**2** a tubelike passage in the body

**ca·nary** \kə-ˈneər-ē\ *n, pl* **ca·nar·ies**
▶ a small usually yellow songbird often kept in a cage

**canary**

**Word History** Long ago explorers from Africa went to a group of islands off the northern coast. On the islands they found great numbers of very large dogs. The Romans read about the dogs and gave the islands a Latin name that meant "dog islands." The English name *Canary Islands* came from the Latin name. In the sixteenth century small birds from the Canary Islands were sold in Europe. In England they were called *canary birds*. Later the name for these ancestors of our canaries was shortened to *canary*.

**can·cel** \ˈkan-səl\ *vb* **can·celed** *or* **can·celled**; **can·cel·ing** *or* **can·cel·ling**
**1** to cross out or strike out with a line : DELETE ⟨*cancel* what has been written⟩
**2** to take back : WITHDRAW ⟨*canceled* the invitation⟩
**3** to equal in force or effect : OFFSET
**4** to remove (a common divisor) from numerator and denominator : remove (equivalents) on opposite sides of an equation or account
**5** to mark (as a postage stamp) so as to make impossible to use again

**can·cel·la·tion** \ˌkan-sə-ˈlā-shən\ *n*
**1** an act of canceling ⟨*cancellation* of a game⟩
**2** a mark made to cancel something

**can·cer** \ˈkan-sər\ *n*
**1** a harmful growth on or in the body that may keep spreading and be fatal if not treated
**2** a condition of the body characterized by a cancer or cancers

**can·de·la·bra** \ˌkan-də-ˈlä-brə, -ˈlab-rə\ *n*
a candlestick or lamp that has several branches for lights

**can·de·la·brum** \ˌkan-də-ˈlä-brəm, -ˈlab-rəm\ *n, pl* **can·de·la·bra** \-ˈlä-brə, -ˈlab-rə\ *also* **can·de·la·brums**
CANDELABRA

**can·did** \ˈkan-dəd\ *adj*
**1** FRANK, STRAIGHTFORWARD
**2** relating to photography of people acting naturally without being posed
**can·did·ly** *adv*
**can·did·ness** *n*

**[1]candle**
In the days before electricity, candles provided the only means of lighting after dark. Today, they are still popular, especially for table settings. There are many styles to choose from, in different sizes, shapes, and colors.

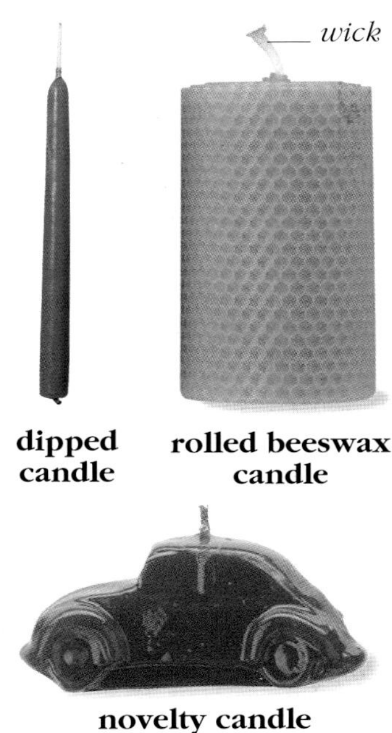


**dipped candle**

**rolled beeswax candle**

**novelty candle**

**can·di·da·cy** \ˈkan-də-də-sē\ *n, pl* **can·di·da·cies**
the state of being a candidate

**can·di·date** \ˈkan-də-ˌdāt\ *n*
a person who runs for or is nominated by others for an office or honor

**Word History** Men who ran for public office in ancient Rome wore white togas. The Latin word for such a man meant "one dressed in white" and came from another Latin word that meant "white." The English word *candidate* came from the Latin word meaning "one dressed in white."

**can·died** \ˈkan-dēd\ *adj*
preserved in or coated with sugar ⟨*candied* ginger⟩

**[1]can·dle** \ˈkan-dl\ *n*
◀ a stick of tallow or wax containing a wick and burned to give light

**[2]candle** *vb* **can·dled**; **can·dling**
to examine (as eggs) by holding between the eye and a light
**can·dler** *n*

**can·dle·light** \ˈkan-dl-ˌlīt\ *n*
**1** the light of a candle
**2** a soft artificial light

**can·dle·stick** \ˈkan-dl-ˌstik\ *n*
a holder for a candle

**can·dor** \ˈkan-dər\ *n*
sincere and honest expression

**[1]can·dy** \ˈkan-dē\ *n, pl* **can·dies**
a sweet made of sugar often with flavoring and filling

**[2]candy** *vb* **can·died**; **can·dy·ing**
**1** to coat or become coated with sugar often by cooking
**2** to crystallize into sugar

**[1]cane** \ˈkān\ *n*
**1** an often hollow, slender, and somewhat flexible plant stem
**2** a tall woody grass or reed (as sugarcane)
**3** WALKING STICK 1
**4** a rod for beating

**[2]cane** *vb* **caned**; **can·ing**
**1** to beat with a cane
**2** to make or repair with cane ⟨*cane* a chair seat⟩

**[1]ca·nine** \ˈkā-ˌnīn\ *n*
**1** a pointed tooth next to the incisors
**2** a canine animal

[2]**canine** *adj*
**1** of or relating to the dogs or to the group of animals (as wolves) to which the dog belongs
**2** like or typical of a dog

**can·is·ter** \'kan-əs-tər\ *n*
a small box or can for holding a dry product

**can·nery** \'kan-ə-rē\ *n, pl* **can·ner·ies**
a factory where foods are canned

**can·ni·bal** \'kan-ə-bəl\ *n*
**1** a human being who eats human flesh
**2** an animal that eats other animals of its own kind

**can·non** \'kan-ən\ *n, pl* **cannon** *also* **cannons**
**1** ▼ a heavy gun mounted on a carriage
**2** an automatic gun of heavy caliber on an airplane

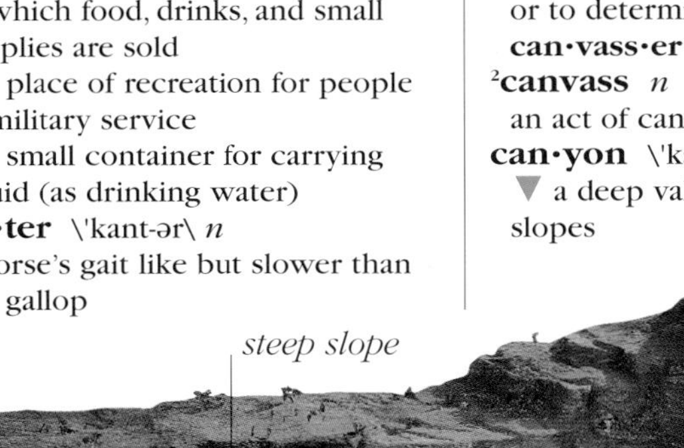


**cannon 1**

**can·non·ball** \'kan-ən-ˌbȯl\ *n*
a usually round solid missile for firing from a cannon

**can·not** \'kan-ˌät, kə-'nät\
can not

**can·ny** \'kan-ē\ *adj* **can·ni·er**; **can·ni·est**
watchful of one's own interest
**can·ni·ly** \'kan-l-ē\ *adv*

[1]**ca·noe** \kə-'nü\ *n*
a long light narrow boat with sharp ends and curved sides usually driven by paddles

[2]**canoe** *vb* **ca·noed**; **ca·noe·ing**
to travel or carry in a canoe
**ca·noe·ist** \-'nü-ist\ *n*

**can·on** \'kan-ən\ *n*
**1** a rule or law of a church
**2** an accepted rule ⟨the *canons* of good taste⟩

**can·o·py** \'kan-ə-pē\ *n, pl* **can·o·pies**
**1** a covering fixed over a bed or throne or carried on poles (as over a person of high rank)
**2** something that hangs over and shades or shelters something else

**can't** \kant, kȧnt, känt, kānt\
can not

**can·ta·loupe** \'kant-l-ˌōp\ *n*
▼ a muskmelon usually with a hard ridged or rough skin and reddish orange flesh

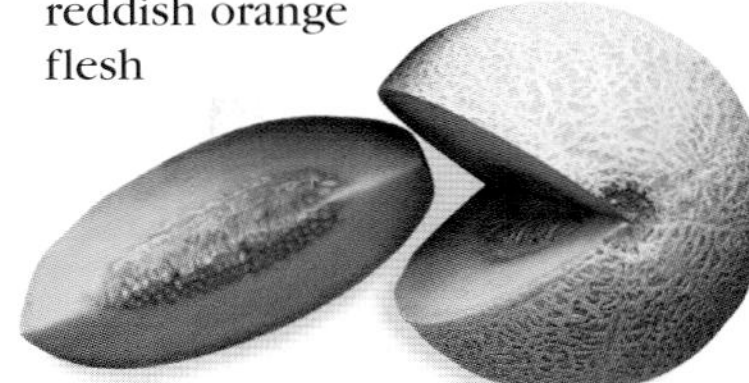

**cantaloupe**

**can·tan·ker·ous** \kan-'tang-kə-rəs\ *adj*
QUARRELSOME

**can·ta·ta** \kən-'tät-ə\ *n*
a poem or story set to music to be sung by a chorus and soloists

**can·teen** \kan-'tēn\ *n*
**1** a store (as in a camp or factory) in which food, drinks, and small supplies are sold
**2** a place of recreation for people in military service
**3** a small container for carrying liquid (as drinking water)

**can·ter** \'kant-ər\ *n*
a horse's gait like but slower than the gallop

**can·ti·le·ver** \'kant-l-ˌē-vər, -ˌev-ər\ *n*
**1** a beam or similar structure fastened (as by being built into a wall) only at one end
**2** either of two structures that extend from piers toward each other and when joined form a span in a bridge (**cantilever bridge**)

**can·to** \'kan-ˌtō\ *n, pl* **can·tos**
one of the major divisions of a long poem

**can·ton** \'kant-n, 'kan-ˌtän\ *n*
a division of a country (as Switzerland)

**can·tor** \'kant-ər\ *n*
a synagogue official who sings religious music and leads the congregation in prayer

**can·vas** \'kan-vəs\ *n*
**1** a strong cloth of hemp, flax, or cotton that is used sometimes for making tents and sails and as the material on which oil paintings are made
**2** something made of canvas or on canvas

**can·vas·back** \'kan-vəs-ˌbak\ *n*
a North American wild duck with reddish head and grayish back

[1]**can·vass** \'kan-vəs\ *vb*
to go through (a district) or go to (people) to ask for votes, contributions, or orders for goods or to determine public opinion
**can·vass·er** *n*

[2]**canvass** *n*
an act of canvassing

**can·yon** \'kan-yən\ *n*
▼ a deep valley with high steep slopes

**canyon:** cross section through a canyon

**[1]cap** \'kap\ *n*
**1** a head covering that has a visor and no brim
**2** something that serves as a cover or protection for something ⟨a bottle *cap*⟩
**3** a paper or metal container holding an explosive charge ⟨a toy pistol for shooting *caps*⟩

**[2]cap** *vb* **capped**; **cap·ping**
**1** to cover or provide with a cap ⟨*cap* a bottle⟩
**2** to match with something equal or better

**ca·pa·bil·i·ty** \,kā-pə-'bil-ət-ē\ *n, pl* **ca·pa·bil·i·ties**
the quality or state of being capable

**ca·pa·ble** \'kā-pə-bəl\ *adj*
**1** having the qualities (as ability, power, or strength) needed to do or accomplish something ⟨you are *capable* of better work⟩
**2** able to do one's job well **:** EFFICIENT ⟨a very *capable* teacher⟩ **synonyms** see ABLE
**ca·pa·bly** \-blē\ *adv*

**ca·pa·cious** \kə-'pā-shəs\ *adj*
able to hold a great deal ⟨a *capacious* pocket⟩

**ca·pac·i·ty** \kə-'pas-ət-ē\ *n, pl* **ca·pac·i·ties**
**1** ability to contain or deal with something ⟨the seating *capacity* of a room⟩ ⟨factories working to the limit of their *capacity*⟩
**2** mental or physical power ⟨you have the *capacity* to do better⟩
**3** VOLUME 3 ⟨a tank of twenty-gallon *capacity*⟩
**4** ROLE 1, STATUS ⟨in your *capacity* of student⟩

**[1]cape** \'kāp\ *n*
a point of land that juts out into the sea or into a lake

**[2]cape** *n*
a sleeveless garment worn so as to hang over the shoulders, arms, and back

**[1]ca·per** \'kā-pər\ *vb*
to leap about in a lively way

**[2]caper** *n*
**1** a gay bounding leap or spring
**2** a playful or mischievous trick
**3** an illegal or questionable act

**[1]cap·il·lary** \'kap-ə-,ler-ē\ *adj*
**1** having a long slender form and a small inner diameter ⟨a *capillary* tube⟩
**2** of or relating to capillary action or a capillary

**[2]capillary** *n, pl* **cap·il·lar·ies**
one of the slender hairlike tubes that are the smallest blood vessels and connect arteries with veins

**capillary action** *n*
the action by which the surface of a liquid where it is in contact with a solid (as in a capillary tube) is raised or lowered

**[1]cap·i·tal** \'kap-ət-l, 'kap-tl\ *n*
▼ the top part of an architectural column

capital
column

**[1]capital:** an ancient Greek capital

**[2]capital** *adj*
**1** punishable by or resulting in death ⟨a *capital* crime⟩ ⟨*capital* punishment⟩
**2** being like the letters A, B, C, etc. rather than a, b, c, etc. ⟨*capital* letters⟩
**3** being the location of a government ⟨the *capital* city of a state⟩
**4** of or relating to capital
**5** EXCELLENT ⟨a *capital* idea⟩

**[3]capital** *n*
**1** accumulated wealth especially as used to produce more wealth
**2** persons holding capital
**3** profitable use ⟨they made *capital* out of my weakness⟩
**4** a capital letter ⟨begin each sentence with a *capital*⟩
**5** a capital city ⟨name the *capital* of North Dakota⟩

**cap·i·tal·ism** \'kap-ət-l-,iz-əm\ *n*
a system under which the ownership of land and wealth is for the most part in the hands of private individuals

**[1]cap·i·tal·ist** \'kap-ət-l-ist\ *n*
**1** a person who has capital and especially business capital
**2** a person who favors capitalism

**[2]capitalist** *adj*
**1** owning capital
**2** CAPITALISTIC

**cap·i·tal·is·tic** \,kap-ət-l-'is-tik\ *adj*
**1** practicing or favoring capitalism
**2** of or relating to capitalism or capitalists
**cap·i·tal·is·ti·cal·ly** \-ti-kə-lē\ *adv*

**cap·i·tal·iza·tion** \,kap-ət-l-ə-'zā-shən\ *n*
**1** the act or process of capitalizing
**2** the amount of money used as capital in business

**cap·i·tal·ize** \'kap-ət-l-,īz\ *vb* **cap·i·tal·ized**; **cap·i·tal·iz·ing**
**1** to write with a beginning capital letter or in capital letters
**2** to use as capital (as in a business) **:** furnish capital for (a business)
**3** to gain by turning something to advantage ⟨*capitalize* on another's mistakes⟩

**cap·i·tol** \'kap-ət-l, 'kap-tl\ *n*
**1** the building in which a state legislature meets
**2** *cap* the building in Washington in which the United States Congress meets

**ca·po** \'kā-pō\ *n, pl* **capos**
a bar that can be fitted on the fingerboard especially of a guitar to raise the pitch of all the strings

**ca·pon** \'kā-,pän\ *n*
a castrated male chicken

**ca·price** \kə-'prēs\ *n*
a sudden change in feeling, opinion, or action **:** WHIM

**Word History** The English word *caprice* came from an Italian word which at first meant "a shiver of fear." It was formed from two Italian words. One meant "head," and the other meant "hedgehog." Try to picture very frightened people with their hair standing on end. They might look a bit like hedgehogs covered with spines. In time the meaning of the Italian word that meant "a shiver of fear" changed to "a sudden whim." This is the meaning of our English word *caprice*.

**ca·pri·cious** \kə-'prish-əs\ *adj*
moved or controlled by caprice **:** likely to change suddenly
**ca·pri·cious·ly** *adv*
**ca·pri·cious·ness** *n*

**cap·size** \'kap-ˌsīz\ *vb* **cap·sized**; **cap·siz·ing**
to turn over : UPSET ⟨*capsize* a canoe⟩

**cap·stan** \'kap-stən\ *n*
a device that consists of a drum to which a rope is fastened and that is used especially on ships for moving or raising weights

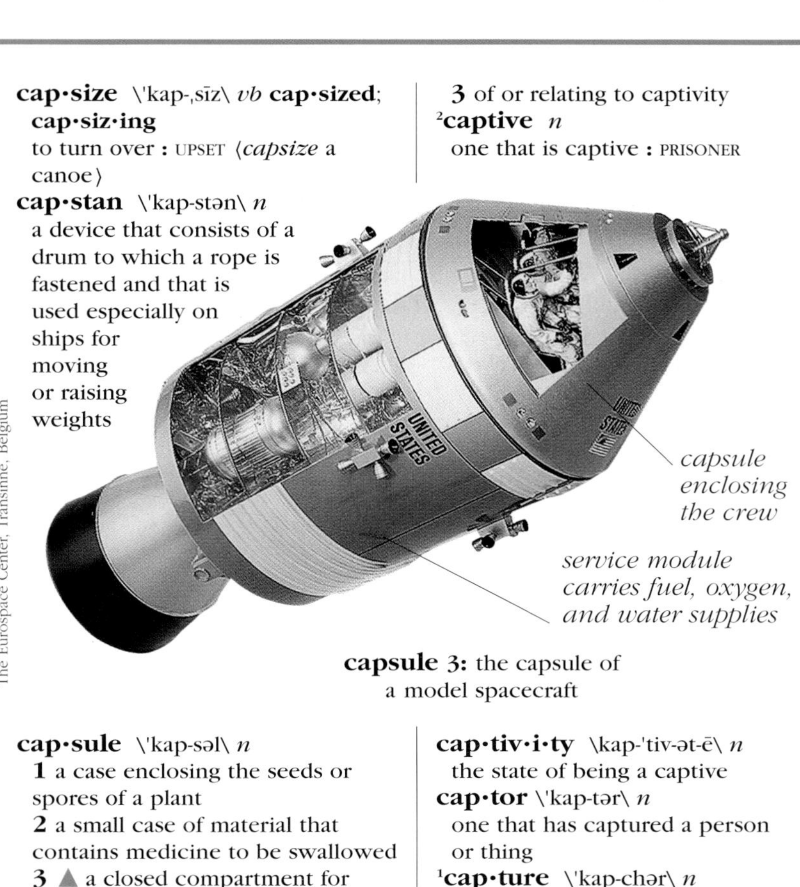

**capsule 3:** the capsule of a model spacecraft



**cap·sule** \'kap-səl\ *n*
**1** a case enclosing the seeds or spores of a plant
**2** a small case of material that contains medicine to be swallowed
**3** ▲ a closed compartment for travel in space

**¹cap·tain** \'kap-tən\ *n*
**1** a leader of a group : one in command ⟨the *captain* of a football team⟩
**2** a commissioned officer in the Navy or Coast Guard ranking above a commander
**3** a commissioned officer in the Army, Air Force, or Marine Corps ranking above a first lieutenant
**4** the commanding officer of a ship

**²captain** *vb*
to be captain of

**cap·tion** \'kap-shən\ *n*
**1** the heading especially of an article or document
**2** a comment or title that goes with a picture (as in a book)

**cap·ti·vate** \'kap-tə-ˌvāt\ *vb* **cap·ti·vat·ed**; **cap·ti·vat·ing**
to fascinate by some special charm

**¹cap·tive** \'kap-tiv\ *adj*
**1** taken and held prisoner especially in war
**2** kept within bounds or under control ⟨a *captive* balloon⟩
**3** of or relating to captivity

**²captive** *n*
one that is captive : PRISONER

**cap·tiv·i·ty** \kap-'tiv-ət-ē\ *n*
the state of being a captive

**cap·tor** \'kap-tər\ *n*
one that has captured a person or thing

**¹cap·ture** \'kap-chər\ *n*
the act of capturing

**²capture** *vb* **cap·tured**; **cap·tur·ing**
**1** to take and hold especially by force ⟨*capture* a city⟩
**2** to put into a lasting form ⟨*captured* the scene in a photo⟩
**synonyms** see CATCH

**car** \'kär\ *n*
**1** a vehicle (as an automobile) that moves on wheels
**2** the compartment of an elevator

**ca·rafe** \kə-'raf\ *n*
a bottle that has a lip and is used to hold water or beverages

**car·a·mel** \'kar-ə-məl, 'kär-məl\ *n*
**1** burnt sugar used for coloring and flavoring
**2** a firm chewy candy

**car·at** \'kar-ət\ *n*
a unit of weight for precious stones equal to 200 milligrams

**car·a·van** \'kar-ə-ˌvan\ *n*
**1** a group (as of merchants or pilgrims) traveling together on a long journey through desert or in dangerous places
**2** a group of vehicles traveling together one behind the other

**car·a·vel** \'kar-ə-ˌvel\ *n*
▼ a small sailing ship of the fifteenth and sixteenth centuries with a broad bow and high stern and three or four masts

**car·a·way** \'kar-ə-ˌwā\ *n*
an herb related to the carrots that is grown for its seeds used especially as a seasoning

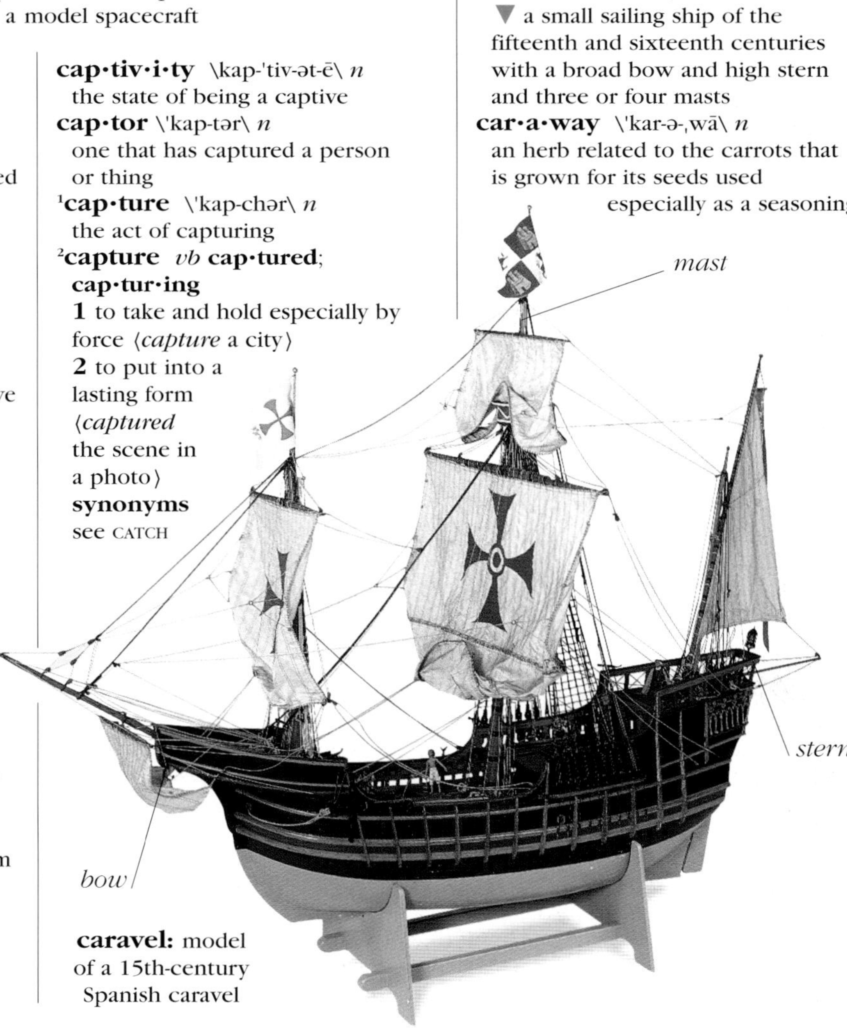

**caravel:** model of a 15th-century Spanish caravel

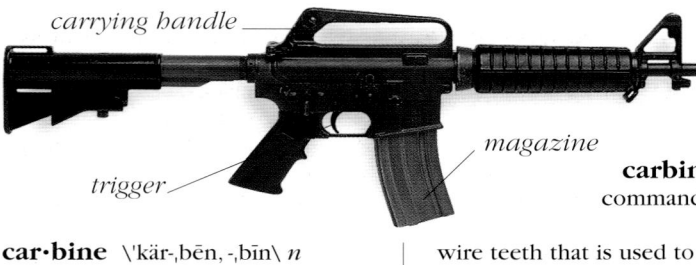

carrying handle
barrel
magazine
trigger

**carbine:** a US commando carbine

**car•bine** \'kär-ˌbēn, -ˌbīn\ *n*
▲ a short light rifle

**car•bo•hy•drate** \ˌkär-bō-'hī-ˌdrāt\ *n*
a nutrient that is rich in energy and is made up of carbon, hydrogen, and oxygen

**car•bol•ic acid** \ˌkär-ˌbäl-ik-\ *n*
a poison present in coal tar and wood tar that is diluted and used as an antiseptic

**car•bon** \'kär-bən\ *n*
a chemical element occurring as diamond and graphite, in coal and petroleum, and in plant and animal bodies

**car•bon•ate** \'kär-bə-ˌnāt\ *vb* **car•bon•ated**; **car•bon•at•ing**
to fill with carbon dioxide which escapes in the form of bubbles ⟨a *carbonated* soft drink⟩

**carbon di•ox•ide** \-dī-'äk-ˌsīd\ *n*
a heavy colorless gas that is formed by burning fuels and by decay and that is the simple raw material from which plants build up compounds for their nourishment

**carbon mon•ox•ide** \-mə-'näk-ˌsīd\ *n*
a colorless odorless very poisonous gas formed by incomplete burning of carbon

**carbon tet•ra•chlo•ride** \-ˌtet-rə-'klōr-ˌīd\ *n*
a colorless poisonous liquid that does not burn and is used for dissolving grease

**car•bu•re•tor** \'kär-bə-ˌrāt-ər\ *n*
the part of an engine in which liquid fuel (as gasoline) is mixed with air to make it burn easily

**car•cass** \'kär-kəs\ *n*
the body of an animal prepared for use as meat

[1]**card** \'kärd\ *vb*
to clean and untangle fibers and especially wool by combing with a card
**card•er** *n*

[2]**card** *n*
an instrument usually with bent wire teeth that is used to clean and untangle fibers (as wool)

[3]**card** *n*
**1** PLAYING CARD
**2 cards** *pl* a game played with playing cards
**3** a flat stiff piece of paper or thin pasteboard that can be written on or that contains printed information ⟨lost my library *card*⟩

**card•board** \'kärd-ˌbōrd\ *n*
a stiff material made of wood pulp that has been pressed and dried

**car•di•ac** \'kärd-ē-ˌak\ *adj*
of, relating to, or affecting the heart

[1]**car•di•nal** \'kärd-nəl, -n-əl\ *n*
**1** a high official of the Roman Catholic Church ranking next below the pope
**2** ▼ a bright red songbird with a crest and a whistling call

[1]**cardinal 2:** a common cardinal

[2]**cardinal** *adj*
of first importance **:** MAIN, PRINCIPAL ⟨a *cardinal* rule⟩

**cardinal flower** *n*
the bright red flower of a North American plant that blooms in late summer

**car•di•nal•i•ty** \ˌkärd-n-'al-ət-ē\ *n, pl* **car•di•nal•i•ties**
the number of elements in a given mathematical set

**cardinal number** *n*
a number (as 1, 5, 22) that is used in simple counting and answers the question "how many?"

**cardinal point** *n*
one of the four chief points of the compass which are north, south, east, west

[1]**care** \'keər, 'kaər\ *n*
**1** a heavy sense of responsibility
**2** serious attention ⟨take *care* in crossing streets⟩
**3** PROTECTION 1, SUPERVISION ⟨under a doctor's *care*⟩
**4** an object of one's care

[2]**care** *vb* **cared**; **car•ing**
**1** to feel interest or concern ⟨we *care* what happens⟩
**2** to give care ⟨*care* for the sick⟩
**3** to have a liking or desire ⟨do you *care* for more tea⟩

**ca•reer** \kə-'rir\ *n*
**1** the course followed or progress made in one's job or life's work
**2** a job followed as a life's work

**care•free** \'keər-ˌfrē, 'kaər-\ *adj*
free from care or worry

**care•ful** \'keər-fəl, 'kaər-\ *adj*
**1** using care ⟨a *careful* driver⟩
**2** made, done, or said with care ⟨gave a *careful* answer⟩
**care•ful•ly** \-fə-lē\ *adv*
**care•ful•ness** *n*

---

**Synonyms** CAREFUL and CAUTIOUS mean taking care to avoid trouble. CAREFUL suggests that one is alert and thus able to prevent mistakes or accidents ⟨be *careful* when you paint the fence⟩. CAUTIOUS suggests that one takes care to avoid further problems or difficulties ⟨a *cautious* driver will drive slowly in bad weather⟩.

---

**care•less** \'keər-ləs, 'kaər-\ *adj*
**1** CAREFREE
**2** not taking proper care
**3** said without being careful
**care•less•ly** *adv*
**care•less•ness** *n*

[1]**ca•ress** \kə-'res\ *n*
a tender or loving touch or hug

[2]**caress** *vb*
to touch in a tender or loving way

**care•tak•er** \'keər-ˌtā-kər, 'kaər-\ *n*
a person who takes care of property for another person

**car•fare** \'kär-ˌfaər, -ˌfeər\ *n*
the fare charged for carrying a passenger (as on a bus)

**car•go** \'kär-gō\ *n, pl* **cargoes** *or* **cargos**
the goods carried by a ship, airplane, or vehicle

**car•i•bou** \'kar-ə-ˌbü\ *n*
a large deer of northern and arctic North America that is closely related to the Old World reindeer

**car·ies** \'kaər-ēz, 'keər-\ *n, pl* **caries**
a decayed condition of a tooth or teeth

**car·il·lon** \'kar-ə-,län, -lən\ *n*
a set of bells sounded by hammers controlled by a keyboard

**car·nage** \'kär-nij\ *n*
[1]SLAUGHTER 3

**carnation**

**car·na·tion** \kär-'nā-shən\ *n*
▲ a fragrant usually white, pink, or red garden or greenhouse flower that is related to the pinks

**car·ne·lian** \kär-'nēl-yən\ *n*
► a hard reddish quartz used as a gem

**car·ni·val** \'kär-nə-vəl\ *n*
**1** a traveling group that puts on a variety of amusements
**2** an organized program of entertainment or exhibition **:** FESTIVAL ⟨a winter *carnival*⟩

**car·ni·vore** \'kär-nə-,vōr\ *n*
▼ an animal that feeds on meat

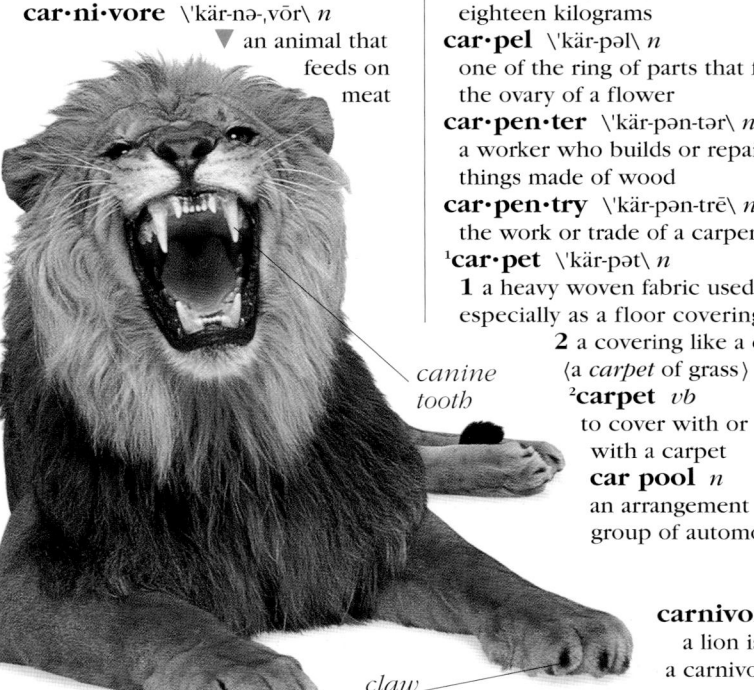

*canine tooth*

*claw*

**carnivore:** a lion is a carnivore

**car·niv·o·rous** \kär-'niv-ə-rəs\ *adj*
**1** feeding on animal flesh
**2** of or relating to carnivores

[1]**car·ol** \'kar-əl\ *n*
a usually religious song of joy

[2]**carol** *vb* **car·oled** *or* **car·olled**; **car·ol·ing** *or* **car·ol·ling**
**1** to sing in a joyful manner
**2** to sing carols and especially Christmas carols
**car·ol·er** *or* **car·ol·ler** *n*

[1]**car·om** \'kar-əm\ *n*
a bouncing back especially at an angle

[2]**carom** *vb*
to hit and bounce back at an angle

[1]**carp** \'kärp\ *vb*
to find fault

*uncut carnelian*

*cut carnelian*

**carnelian**

[2]**carp** *n*
► a freshwater fish that lives a long time and may weigh as much as eighteen kilograms

**car·pel** \'kär-pəl\ *n*
one of the ring of parts that form the ovary of a flower

**car·pen·ter** \'kär-pən-tər\ *n*
a worker who builds or repairs things made of wood

**car·pen·try** \'kär-pən-trē\ *n*
the work or trade of a carpenter

[1]**car·pet** \'kär-pət\ *n*
**1** a heavy woven fabric used especially as a floor covering
**2** a covering like a carpet ⟨a *carpet* of grass⟩

[2]**carpet** *vb*
to cover with or as if with a carpet

**car pool** *n*
an arrangement by a group of automobile owners in which each takes turns driving his or her car and giving the others a ride

**car·riage** \'kar-ij\ *n*
**1** the manner of holding the body **:** POSTURE
**2** a vehicle with wheels used for carrying persons
**3** a support with wheels used for carrying a load ⟨a gun *carriage*⟩
**4** a movable part of a machine that carries or supports some other moving part

**car·ri·er** \'kar-ē-ər\ *n*
**1** a person or thing that carries ⟨mail *carrier*⟩
**2** a person or business that transports passengers or goods
**3** one that carries disease germs and passes them on to others

**car·ri·on** \'kar-ē-ən\ *n*
dead and decaying flesh

**car·rot** \'kar-ət\ *n*
the long orange edible root of a garden plant **(carrot plant)**

**car·ry** \'kar-ē\ *vb* **car·ried**; **car·ry·ing**
**1** to take or transfer from one place to another ⟨*carry* a package⟩ ⟨*carry* a number in addition⟩
**2** [1]SUPPORT 4, BEAR ⟨pillars that *carry* an arch⟩
**3** WIN 4 ⟨*carry* an election⟩

[2]**carp**

**4** to contain and direct the course of ⟨a pipe *carrying* water⟩
**5** to wear or have on one's person or have within one ⟨*carry* a gun⟩ ⟨*carrying* an unborn child⟩
**6** to have as an element, quality, or part ⟨*carry* a guarantee⟩
**7** to hold or bear the body or some part of it ⟨*carry* your head high⟩
**8** to sing in correct pitch ⟨*carry* a tune⟩
**9** to have for sale ⟨the market *carries* fresh fish⟩
**10** PUBLISH 2 ⟨the paper *carries* weather reports⟩
**11** to go over or travel a distance ⟨your voice *carries* well⟩

A B C D E F G H I J K L M N O P Q R S T U V W X Y Z

**car·ry·all** \'kar-ē-ˌȯl\ *n*
a large bag or carrying case

**carry away** *vb*
to cause strong feeling in ⟨*carried away* by the music⟩

**carry on** *vb*
**1** MANAGE 1 ⟨*carry on* a business⟩
**2** to behave badly
**3** to continue in spite of difficulties

**carry out** *vb*
to put into action or effect

**car seat** *n*
a portable seat for a small child that attaches to an automobile seat and holds the child safely

[1]**cart** \'kärt\ *n*
**1** a heavy vehicle with two wheels usually drawn by horses and used for hauling
**2** a light vehicle pushed or pulled by hand

[2]**cart** *vb*
to carry in a cart
**cart·er** *n*

**car·ti·lage** \'kärt-l-ij\ *n*
an elastic tissue that makes up most of the skeleton of very young animals and is later mostly changed into bone

**car·ti·lag·i·nous** \ˌkärt-l-'aj-ə-nəs\ *adj*
of, relating to, or made of cartilage

**car·ton** \'kärt-n\ *n*
a cardboard container

**car·toon** \kär-'tün\ *n*
**1** a drawing (as in a newspaper) making people or objects look funny or foolish
**2** COMIC STRIP
**3** a movie composed of cartoons

**car·toon·ist** \kär-'tü-nist\ *n*
a person who draws cartoons

**car·tridge** \'kär-trij\ *n*
**1** a case or shell containing gunpowder and shot or a bullet for use in a firearm
**2** a case containing an explosive for blasting
**3** a container like a cartridge

**cart·wheel** \'kärt-ˌhwēl, -ˌwēl\ *n*
▶ a handspring made to the side with arms and legs sticking out

**carve** \'kärv\ *vb* **carved**; **carv·ing**
**1** to cut with care ⟨*carve* ivory⟩
**2** to make or get by cutting ⟨*carve* a figure⟩
**3** to slice and serve (meat) ⟨*carve* the turkey⟩
**carv·er** *n*

**cas·cade** \kas-'kād\ *n*
a steep usually small waterfall

**cas·cara** \ka-'skar-ə\ *n*
the dried bark of a western North American shrub used as a laxative

[1]**case** \'kās\ *n*
**1** a particular instance, situation, or example ⟨a *case* of injustice⟩
**2** a situation or an object that calls for investigation or action (as by the police)
**3** a question to be settled in a court of law
**4** a form of a noun, pronoun, or adjective showing its grammatical relation to other words
**5** the actual situation ⟨such is the *case*⟩
**6** a convincing argument
**7** an instance of disease or injury ⟨a *case* of measles⟩
**8** [2]PATIENT

[2]**case** *n*
**1** a container (as a box) for holding something
**2** a box and its contents ⟨a *case* of books⟩
**3** an outer covering
**4** the frame of a door or window

**ca·sein** \kā-'sēn\ *n*
a whitish to yellowish material made from milk especially by the action of acid and used in making paints and plastics

**case·ment** \'kā-smənt\ *n*
**1** a window sash opening on hinges
**2** a window with a casement

[1]**cash** \'kash\ *n*
**1** money in the form of coins or bills
**2** money or its equivalent (as a check) paid for goods at the time of purchase or delivery

[2]**cash** *vb*
to pay or obtain cash for

**cash·ew** \'kash-ü\ *n*
an edible nut that is shaped like a kidney and comes from a tropical American tree

[1]**ca·shier** \ka-'shir\ *vb*
to dismiss from service especially in disgrace

[2]**cash·ier** \ka-'shir\ *n*
a person who is responsible for money (as in a bank or business)

**cash·mere** \'kazh-ˌmir, 'kash-\ *n*
a soft yarn or fabric once made from the fine wool of an Indian goat but now often from sheep's wool

**cas·ing** \'kā-sing\ *n*
something that covers or encloses ⟨sausage *casings*⟩

**cask** \'kask\ *n*
**1** a container that is shaped like a barrel and is usually used for liquids
**2** the amount contained in a cask

**cas·ket** \'kas-kət\ *n*
**1** a small box for storage or safekeeping (as for jewels)
**2** COFFIN

**cas·se·role** \'kas-ə-ˌrōl\ *n*
**1** a deep dish in which food can be baked and served
**2** the food cooked and served in a casserole

**cartwheel**

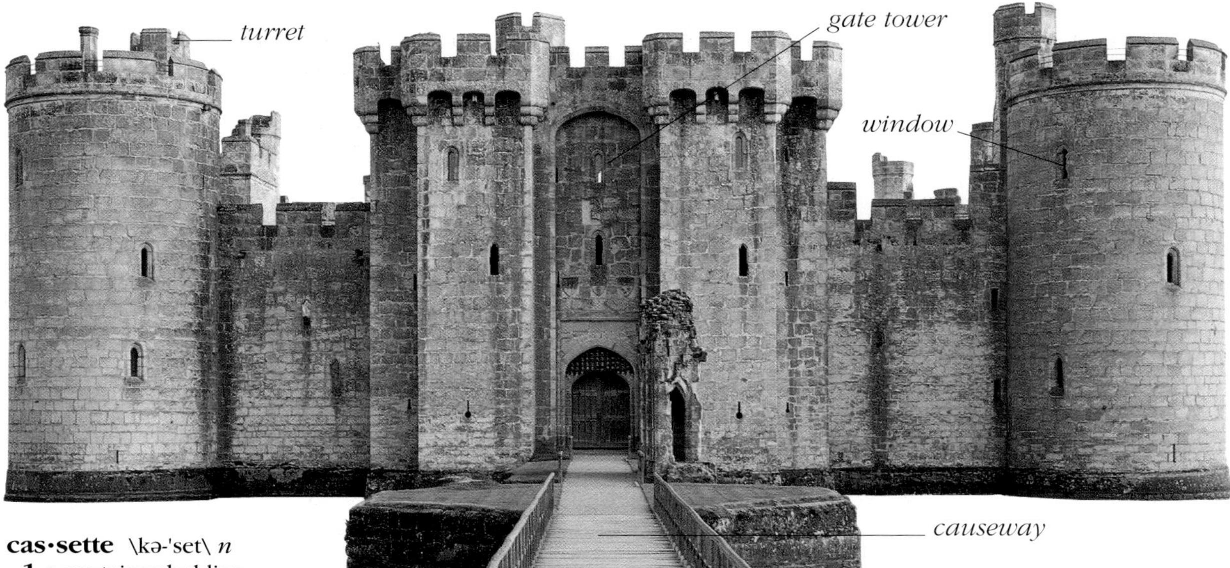


**castle 1**

**cas•sette** \kə-'set\ *n*
**1** a container holding photographic film or plates that can be easily loaded into a camera
**2** ▼ a container holding magnetic tape with the tape on one reel passing to the other

*magnetic tape* *reel*

**cassette 2**

**[1]cast** \'kast\ *vb* **cast**; **cast•ing**
**1** [1]THROW 1 ⟨*cast* a stone⟩ ⟨*cast* a fishing line⟩
**2** to throw out, off, or away **:** SHED ⟨snakes *cast* their skins⟩
**3** to direct to or toward something or someone ⟨*cast* a glance⟩
**4** to put on record ⟨*cast* a vote for class president⟩
**5** to assign a part or role to ⟨I was *cast* as the hero in the play⟩
**6** to give shape to liquid material by pouring it into a mold and letting it harden ⟨*cast* a statue in bronze⟩ ⟨*cast* steel⟩
**7** to make by looping or catching up ⟨*cast* on fifty stitches⟩
**cast lots** to take or receive an object at random in order to decide something by chance ⟨*cast lots* to see who goes first⟩

**[2]cast** *n*
**1** an act of casting **:** THROW, FLING
**2** the form in which a thing is made
**3** the characters or the people acting in a play or story
**4** the distance to which a thing can be thrown
**5** something formed by casting in a mold or form ⟨a bronze *cast* of a statue⟩
**6** a stiff surgical dressing of plaster hardened around a part of the body ⟨had a *cast* on my broken leg⟩
**7** a hint of color ⟨a bluish *cast*⟩
**8** [2]SHAPE 1 ⟨a face with a rugged *cast*⟩
**9** something (as the skin of an insect) thrown out or off

**cas•ta•net** \,kas-tə-'net\ *n*
► a rhythm instrument that consists of two small ivory, wooden, or plastic shells fastened to the thumb and clicked by the fingers in time to dancing and music — usually used in pl.

*wooden shell*

**castanet**

**[1]cast•away** \'kas-tə-,wā\ *adj*
**1** thrown away
**2** cast adrift or ashore

**[2]castaway** *n*
**1** something that has been thrown away
**2** a shipwrecked person

**caste** \'kast\ *n*
**1** one of the classes into which the people of India were formerly divided
**2** a division or class of society based on wealth, rank, or occupation
**3** social rank **:** PRESTIGE

**cast•er** \'kas-tər\ *n*
**1** one that casts
**2** a small container (as for salt or pepper) with holes in the top
**3** *or* **cas•tor** \'kas-tər\ a small wheel that turns freely and is used for supporting furniture

**cas•ti•gate** \'kas-tə-,gāt\ *vb* **cas•ti•gat•ed**; **cas•ti•gat•ing**
to punish or correct with words or blows

**cast•ing** \'kas-ting\ *n*
**1** the act or action of one that casts
**2** something that is cast in a mold ⟨a bronze *casting*⟩
**3** something (as skin or feathers) that is cast out or off

**cast iron** *n*
a hard and brittle alloy of iron, carbon, and silicon shaped by being poured into a mold while melted

**cas•tle** \'kas-əl\ *n*
**1** ▲ a large building or group of buildings usually having high walls with towers and a surrounding moat for protection
**2** a large or impressive house

A B C D E F G H I J K L M N O P Q R S T U V W X Y Z

## cat 1

Domesticated cats are descended from large wild cats such as lions. They are popular pets, being both affectionate toward people and skillful hunters, adept at controlling pests. Cats mostly search for their prey at night and can see well in low light levels, focusing on their prey from a distance. Excellent hearing and whiskers that are sensitive to touch also help them to find their way. There are more than 300 recognized breeds and varieties as well as non-pedigree types.

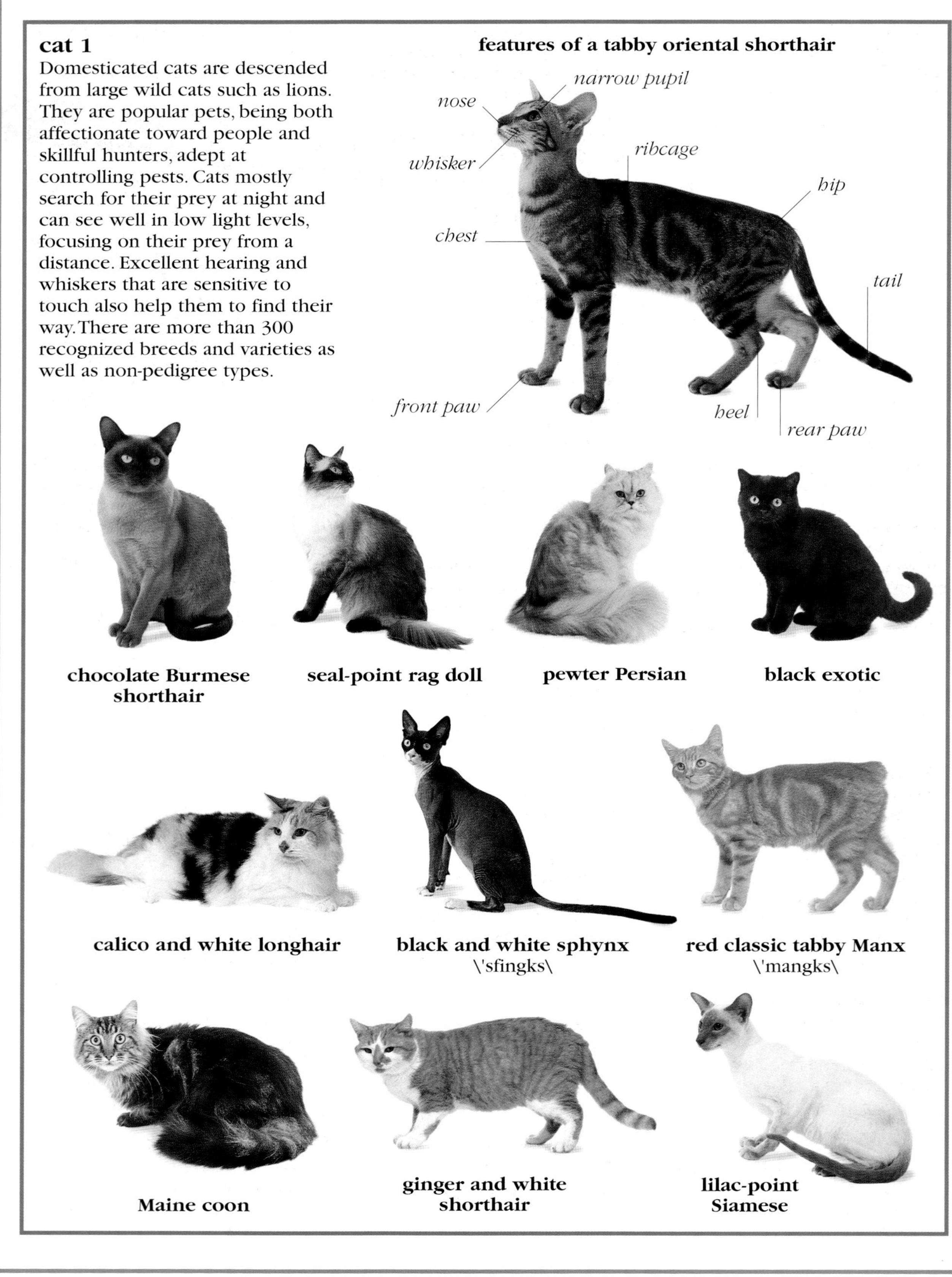


**chocolate Burmese shorthair**

**seal-point rag doll**

**pewter Persian**

**black exotic**

**calico and white longhair**

**black and white sphynx** \'sfingks\

**red classic tabby Manx** \'mangks\

**Maine coon**

**ginger and white shorthair**

**lilac-point Siamese**

**cast·off** *n*
a cast-off person or thing

**cast–off** \'kas-ˌtȯf\ *adj*
thrown away or aside

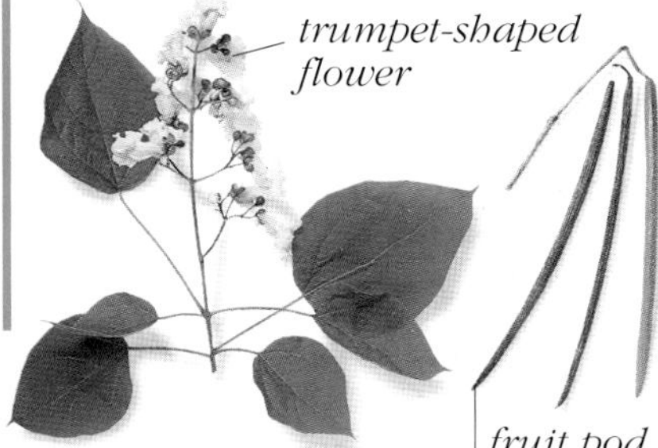


**catalpa**

**cas·tor oil** \'kas-tər-\ *n*
a thick yellowish liquid that comes from the seeds (**castor beans**) of a tropical herb and is used as a lubricant and as a strong laxative

**cas·trate** \'kas-ˌtrāt\ *vb* **cas·trat·ed**; **cas·trat·ing**
to remove the sex glands of

**ca·su·al** \'kazh-ə-wəl, 'kazh-wəl, 'kazh-əl\ *adj*
**1** happening unexpectedly or by chance **:** not planned or foreseen ⟨a *casual* meeting⟩
**2** occurring without regularity **:** OCCASIONAL
**3** showing or feeling little concern **:** NONCHALANT
**4** meant for informal use
**ca·su·al·ly** *adv*

**ca·su·al·ty** \'kazh-əl-tē\ *n, pl* **ca·su·al·ties**
**1** a serious or fatal accident **:** DISASTER
**2** a military person lost (as by death) during warfare
**3** a person or thing injured, lost, or destroyed

**cat** \'kat\ *n*
**1** ◀ a common furry flesh-eating animal kept as a pet or for catching mice and rats
**2** any of the group of mammals (as lions, tigers, and wildcats) to which the domestic cat belongs

**[1]cat·a·log** *or* **cat·a·logue** \'kat-l-ˌȯg\ *n*
**1** a list of names, titles, or articles arranged by some system
**2** a book or file containing a catalog

**[2]catalog** *or* **catalogue** *vb* **cat·a·loged** *or* **cat·a·logued**; **cat·a·log·ing** *or* **cat·a·logu·ing**
**1** to make a catalog of
**2** to enter in a catalog
**cat·a·log·er** *or* **cat·a·logu·er** *n*

**ca·tal·pa** \kə-'tal-pə\ *n*
◀ a tree of America and Asia with broad leaves, bright flowers, and long pods

**[1]cat·a·pult** \'kat-ə-ˌpəlt\ *n*
**1** ▶ an ancient military machine for hurling stones and arrows
**2** a device for launching an airplane from the deck of a ship

**[2]catapult** *vb*
**1** to throw or launch by or as if by a catapult
**2** to become catapulted

**ca·tarrh** \kə-'tär\ *n*
a red sore state of mucous membrane especially when chronic

**ca·tas·tro·phe** \kə-'tas-trə-fē\ *n*
**1** a sudden disaster
**2** complete failure **:** FIASCO

**cat·bird** \'kat-ˌbərd\ *n*
a dark gray songbird that has a call like a cat's mewing

**cat·boat** \'kat-ˌbōt\ *n*
a sailboat with a single mast set far forward and a single large sail with a long boom

**cat·call** \'kat-ˌkȯl\ *n*
a sound like the cry of a cat or a noise expressing disapproval (as at a sports event)

**[1]catch** \'kach, 'kech\ *vb* **caught** \'kȯt\; **catch·ing**
**1** to capture or seize something in flight or motion
**2** to discover unexpectedly ⟨*caught* them in the act⟩
**3** to check suddenly
**4** to take hold of
**5** to get tangled ⟨*catch* a sleeve on a nail⟩
**6** to hold firmly **:** FASTEN ⟨a lock that will not *catch*⟩
**7** to become affected by ⟨*catch* fire⟩ ⟨*catch* a cold⟩
**8** to take or get briefly or quickly ⟨*catch* a glimpse of a friend⟩
**9** to be in time for ⟨*catch* the next bus⟩
**10** to grasp by the senses or the mind
**11** to play catcher on a baseball team

**Synonyms** CATCH, CAPTURE, and TRAP mean to get into one's possession or under one's control by or as if by seizing. CATCH suggests that what one is trying to seize is moving or hiding ⟨*catch* that dog⟩. CAPTURE suggests a struggle or some other kind of difficulty ⟨*captured* the robbers as they tried to flee⟩. TRAP suggests the use of a device that catches and holds the prey ⟨made a living by *trapping* beavers⟩.

**[1]catapult 1:** model of a 14th-century catapult

**[2]catch** *n*
**1** something caught **:** the amount caught at one time ⟨a large *catch* of fish⟩
**2** the act of catching
**3** a pastime in which a ball is thrown and caught
**4** something that checks, fastens, or holds immovable ⟨a *catch* on a door⟩
**5** a hidden difficulty

**catch·er** \'kach-ər, 'kech-\ *n*
**1** one that catches
**2** a baseball player who plays behind home plate

**catch·ing** \'kach-iŋ, 'kech-\ *adj*
**1** INFECTIOUS 1, CONTAGIOUS
**2** likely to spread as if infectious ⟨the laughter was *catching*⟩

**catchy** \'kach-ē, 'kech-\ *adj* **catch·i·er**; **catch·i·est**
**1** likely to attract ⟨*catchy* music⟩
**2** TRICKY 2

**cat·e·chism** \'kat-ə-,kiz-əm\ *n*
**1** a series of questions and answers used in giving instruction and especially religious instruction
**2** a set of formal questions

**cat·e·go·ry** \'kat-ə-,gōr-ē\ *n, pl* **cat·e·go·ries**
a basic division or grouping of things ⟨many scientists now put birds in the same *category* as dinosaurs⟩

**ca·ter** \'kāt-ər\ *vb*
**1** to provide a supply of food ⟨*cater* for parties⟩
**2** to supply what is needed or wanted
**ca·ter·er** *n*

**cat·er·pil·lar** \'kat-ər-,pil-ər, 'kat-ə-,pil-\ *n*
▼ a wormlike often hairy larva of an insect (as a moth or butterfly)

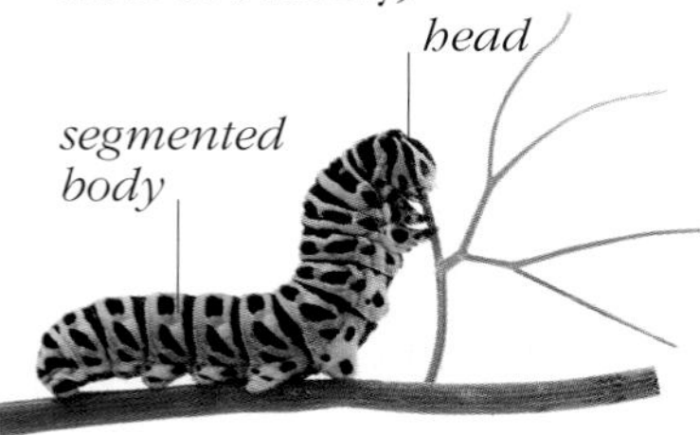


**caterpillar**

**Word History** The English word *caterpillar* came from an early French word that meant "caterpillar." The literal meaning of this French word was "hairy cat." It was formed from two French words. The first of these words meant "female cat." The second meant "hairy."

**cat·fish** \'kat-,fish\ *n*
any of a group of fishes with large heads and feelers about the mouth

**cat·gut** \'kat-,gət\ *n*
a tough cord made from intestines of animals (as sheep) and used for strings of musical instruments and rackets and for sewing in surgery

**ca·the·dral** \kə-'thē-drəl\ *n*
▼ the principal church of a district headed by a bishop

**cath·o·lic** \'kath-ə-lik, 'kath-lik\ *adj*
**1** broad in range ⟨a person of *catholic* interests⟩
**2** *cap* of or relating to the Roman Catholic Church

**Catholic** *n*
**1** a member of a Christian church tracing its history back to the apostles
**2** a member of the Roman Catholic Church

spire
steeple

**cathedral:** model of a 14th-century English cathedral

**cat·kin** \'kat-kən\ *n*
a flower cluster (as of the willow and birch) in which the flowers grow in close circular rows along a slender stalk

**cat·like** \'kat-,līk\ *adj*
like a cat (as in grace or slyness)

**cat·nap** \'kat-,nap\ *n*
a very short light nap

**cat·nip** \'kat-,nip\ *n*
a plant of the mint family enjoyed by cats

**cat–o'–nine–tails** \,kat-ə-'nīn-,tālz\ *n, pl* **cat–o'–nine–tails**
a whip made of nine knotted cords fastened to a handle

**cat·sup** \'kech-əp, 'kach-əp, 'kat-səp\ *variant of* KETCHUP

**cat·tail** \'kat-,tāl\ *n*
a tall plant with long flat leaves and tall furry stalks that grows in marshy areas

**cat·tle** \'kat-l\ *n, pl* **cattle**
domestic animals with four feet and especially cows, bulls, and calves

**cat·walk** \'kat-,wȯk\ *n*
a narrow walk or way (as along a bridge)

**caught** *past of* CATCH

**caul·dron** *or* **cal·dron** \'kȯl-drən\ *n*
a large kettle or boiler

**cau·li·flow·er** \'kȯ-li-,flaủ-ər, 'käl-i-\ *n*
a vegetable closely related to the cabbage that is grown for its white head of undeveloped flowers

[1]**caulk** \'kȯk\ *vb*
to fill up a crack, seam, or joint so as to make it watertight

[2]**caulk** *also* **caulk·ing** \'kȯk-iŋ\ *n*
material used to caulk

[1]**cause** \'kȯz\ *n*
**1** a person or thing that brings about a result ⟨carelessness is the *cause* of many accidents⟩
**2** a good or good enough reason for something ⟨a *cause* for rejoicing⟩
**3** something (as a question) to be decided
**4** something supported or deserving support ⟨a worthy *cause*⟩

[2]**cause** *vb* **caused**; **caus·ing**
to be the cause of

**cause·way** \'kȯz-,wā\ *n*
a raised road or way across wet ground or water

**caus·tic** \'kȯ-stik\ *adj*
**1** capable of eating away by chemical action **:** CORROSIVE
**2** [1]SHARP 8, BITING ⟨*caustic* remarks⟩

[1]**cau·tion** \'kȯ-shən\ *n*
**1** ADMONITION
**2** carefulness in regard to danger **:** PRECAUTION

[2]**caution** *vb*
to advise caution to **:** WARN

**cau·tious** \'kȯ-shəs\ *adj*
showing or using caution

**syn·onyms** see CAREFUL
**cau·tious·ly** *adv*
**cav·al·cade** \ˌkav-əl-ˈkād\ *n*
1 a procession especially of riders or carriages
2 a dramatic series (as of related events)
**¹cav·a·lier** \ˌkav-ə-ˈlir\ *n*
1 a mounted soldier
2 a brave and courteous gentleman
**²cavalier** *adj*
1 easy and lighthearted in manner
2 tending to disregard the rights or feelings of others : ARROGANT
**cav·al·ry** \ˈkav-əl-rē\ *n, pl* **cav·al·ries**
troops mounted on horseback or moving in motor vehicles
**cav·al·ry·man** \ˈkav-əl-rē-mən\ *n, pl* **cav·al·ry·men** \-mən\
a cavalry soldier
**¹cave** \ˈkāv\ *n*
▼ a hollow underground place with an opening on the surface
**²cave** *vb* **caved**; **cav·ing**
to fall or cause to fall in or down : COLLAPSE ⟨the mine *caved* in⟩
**cave·man** \ˈkāv-ˌman\ *n, pl* **cave·men** \-ˌmen\
a person living in a cave especially during the Stone Age
**cav·ern** \ˈkav-ərn\ *n*
a cave often of large or unknown size



**¹cave:** cross section of a limestone cave

**cav·ern·ous** \ˈkav-ər-nəs\ *adj*
1 having caverns or hollow places
2 like a cavern because large and hollow ⟨a *cavernous* cellar⟩
**cav·i·ty** \ˈkav-ət-ē\ *n, pl* **cav·i·ties**
a hollow place ⟨a *cavity* in a tooth⟩
**ca·vort** \kə-ˈvȯrt\ *vb*
to move or hop about in a lively way
**¹caw** \ˈkȯ\ *vb*
to make a caw
**²caw** *n*
the cry of a crow or a raven
**cay·enne pepper** \ˌkī-ˌen-, ˌkā-ˌen-\ *n*
dried ripe hot peppers ground and used to add flavor to food
**CD** \ˌsē-ˈdē\ *n*
COMPACT DISC
**CD–ROM** \ˌsē-ˌdē-ˈräm\ *n*
a compact disc that contains computer data that cannot be changed
**cease** \ˈsēs\ *vb* **ceased**; **ceas·ing**
to come or bring to an end : STOP
**cease·less** \ˈsēs-ləs\ *adj*
CONSTANT 3
**ce·cro·pia moth** \si-ˌkrō-pē-ə-\ *n*
a silkworm moth that is the largest moth of the eastern United States
**ce·dar** \ˈsēd-ər\ *n*
any of a number of trees having cones and a strong wood with a pleasant smell
**cede** \ˈsēd\ *vb* **ced·ed**; **ced·ing**
to give up especially by treaty ⟨territory *ceded* by one country to another⟩
**ceil·ing** \ˈsē-ling\ *n*
1 the overhead inside surface of a room
2 the greatest height at which an airplane can fly properly
3 the height above the ground of the bottom of the lowest layer of clouds
4 an upper limit
**cel·e·brate** \ˈsel-ə-ˌbrāt\ *vb* **cel·e·brat·ed**; **cel·e·brat·ing**
1 to perform publicly and according to certain rules ⟨*celebrate* Mass⟩
2 to observe in some special way (as by merrymaking or by staying away from business)
3 ¹PRAISE 1
**cel·e·brat·ed** \ˈsel-ə-ˌbrāt-əd\ *adj*
widely known and talked about
**cel·e·bra·tion** \ˌsel-ə-ˈbrā-shən\ *n*
1 the act of celebrating
2 the activities or ceremonies for celebrating a special occasion
**ce·leb·ri·ty** \sə-ˈleb-rət-ē\ *n, pl* **ce·leb·ri·ties**
1 FAME
2 a celebrated person
**cel·ery** \ˈsel-ə-rē, ˈsel-rē\ *n*
▶ a plant related to the carrots whose crisp leafstalks are used for food
**ce·les·ta** \sə-ˈles-tə\ *n*
a keyboard instrument with hammers that strike steel plates to make ringing sounds
**ce·les·tial** \sə-ˈles-chəl\ *adj*
1 of, relating to, or suggesting heaven
2 of or relating to the sky

**celery**

**cell** \ˈsel\ *n*
1 a very small room (as in a prison or a monastery)
2 a small enclosed part or division (as in a honeycomb)
3 a small mass of living matter that is made of protoplasm, includes a nucleus, is enclosed in a membrane, and is the basic unit of which all plants and animals are made up
4 a container with substances which can produce an electric current by chemical action
5 a device that converts light (as sunlight) that falls on it into electrical energy that is used as a power source
6 CELL PHONE
**celled** \ˈseld\ *adj*

**cel·lar** \'sel-ər\ *n*
a room or set of rooms below the surface of the ground
: BASEMENT

**cel·lo** \'chel-ō\ *n, pl* **cel·los**
▶ a large stringed instrument of the violin family that plays the bass part

**cel·lo·phane** \'sel-ə-,fān\ *n*
a thin clear material made from cellulose and used as a wrapping

**cell phone** *n*
a portable telephone that connects to other telephones by radio through a system of transmitters each of which covers a limited geographical area

**cel·lu·lar** \'sel-yə-lər\ *adj*
**1** of, relating to, or made up of cells ⟨*cellular* tissue⟩
**2** of, relating to, or being a telephone that connects to others by radio and is part of a system in which a geographical area is divided into small sections each served by a transmitter of limited range

**cel·lu·lose** \'sel-yə-,lōs\ *n*
a substance that is the chief part of the cell walls of plants and is used in making various products (as paper and rayon)

**cell wall** *n*
the firm outer nonliving boundary of a plant cell

**Cel·si·us** \'sel-sē-əs\ *adj*
relating to or having a thermometer scale on which the interval between the freezing point and the boiling point of water is divided into 100 degrees with 0° representing the freezing point and 100° the boiling point

**[1]ce·ment** \si-'ment\ *n*
**1** a powder that is made mainly from compounds of aluminum, calcium, silicon, and iron heated together and then ground, that combines with water and hardens into a mass, and that is used in mortar and concrete
**2** [2]CONCRETE, MORTAR
**3** a substance that by hardening sticks things together firmly

**[2]cement** *vb*
**1** to join together with or as if with cement
**2** to cover with concrete

**ce·men·tum** \si-'ment-əm\ *n*
a thin bony layer covering the part of a tooth inside the gum

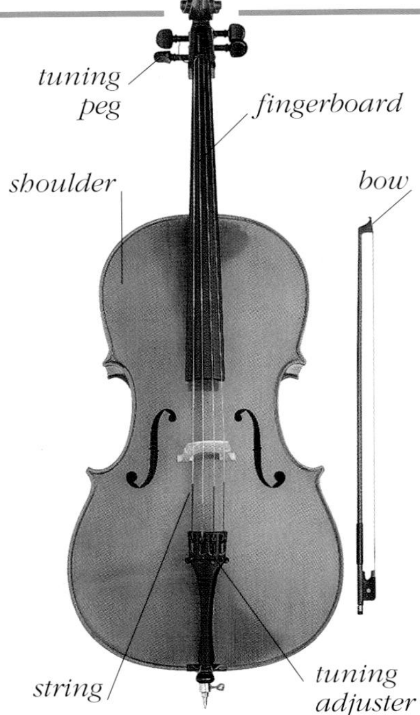


**cello** and bow

**cem·e·tery** \'sem-ə-,ter-ē\ *n, pl* **cem·e·ter·ies**
a place where dead people are buried : GRAVEYARD

**Ce·no·zo·ic** \,sē-nə-'zō-ik, ,sen-ə-\ *n*
an era of geological history lasting from seventy million years ago to the present time in which there has been a rapid evolution of mammals and birds and of flowering plants

**[1]cen·sor** \'sen-sər\ *n*
an official who checks writings or movies to take out things thought to be objectionable

**[2]censor** *vb*
to examine (as a book) to take out things thought to be objectionable

**[1]cen·sure** \'sen-chər\ *n*
**1** the act of finding fault with or blaming
**2** an official criticism

**[2]censure** *vb* **cen·sured**; **cen·sur·ing**
to find fault with especially publicly

**cen·sus** \'sen-səs\ *n*
a count of the number of people in a country, city, or town

**cent** \'sent\ *n*
**1** a hundredth part of the unit of the money system in a number of different countries ⟨in the United States 100 *cents* equal one dollar⟩
**2** a coin, token, or note representing one cent

**Word History** The English word for the hundredth part of a dollar came from a Latin word. This Latin word meant "hundred."

**cen·taur** \'sen-,tȯr\ *n*
a creature in Greek mythology that is part man and part horse

**cen·te·nar·i·an** \,sent-n-'er-ē-ən\ *n*
a person 100 or more years old

**[1]cen·ten·ni·al** \sen-'ten-ē-əl\ *n*
a 100th anniversary or a celebration of this event

**[2]centennial** *adj*
relating to a period of 100 years

**[1]cen·ter** \'sent-ər\ *n*
**1** the middle point of a circle or a sphere equally distant from every point on the circumference or surface
**2** one (as a person or area) that is very important to some activity or concern ⟨a shopping *center*⟩
**3** the middle part of something ⟨the *center* of the room⟩
**4** a player occupying a middle position on a team

**[2]center** *vb*
**1** to place or fix at or around a center or central area
**2** to collect at or around one point

**center of gravity**
▼ the point at which the entire weight of a body may be thought of as centered so that if supported at this point the body would balance perfectly

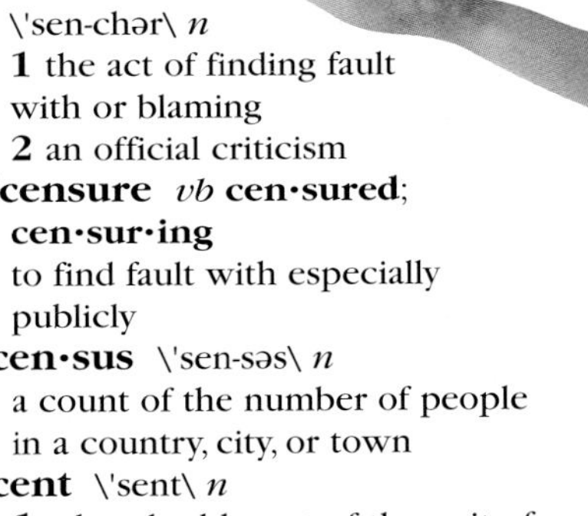


**center of gravity:** a balancing gymnast

a b c d e f g h i j k l m n o p q r s t u v w x y z

**[2]cereal 1**
Cereals are one of the world's most important food crops. Grain inside the ripe seed is harvested to make foods such as breakfast cereals, pasta, bread, and cakes. The stems can be used to weave baskets or, when dried, to provide straw for animal bedding and fodder.

millet corn rye

barley wheat oats

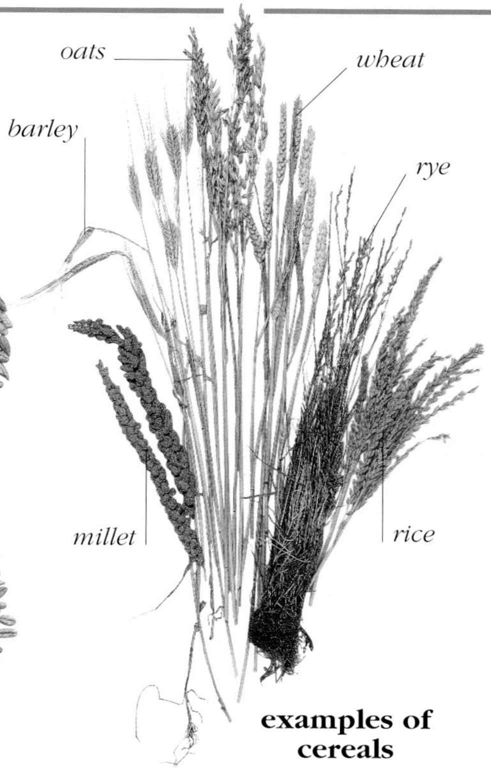

oats wheat barley rye millet rice

**examples of cereals**

**cen·ter·piece** \'sent-ər-ˌpēs\ *n*
a piece put in the center of something and especially a decoration (as flowers) for a table

**centi-** *prefix*
hundredth part ⟨*centi*meter⟩ — used in terms of the metric system

**cen·ti·grade** \'sent-ə-ˌgrād\ *adj*
CELSIUS

**cen·ti·gram** \'sent-ə-ˌgram\ *n*
a unit of weight equal to $^{1}/_{100}$ gram

**cen·ti·li·ter** \'sent-ə-ˌlēt-ər\ *n*
a unit of liquid capacity equal to $^{1}/_{100}$ liter

**cen·ti·me·ter** \'sent-ə-ˌmēt-ər\ *n*
a unit of length equal to $^{1}/_{100}$ meter

**cen·ti·pede** \'sent-ə-ˌpēd\ *n*
a small animal that has a long body and many legs and is related to the insects

**cen·tral** \'sen-trəl\ *adj*
**1** containing or being the center
**2** most important : CHIEF ⟨the *central* person in a story⟩
**3** placed at, in, or near the center
**cen·tral·ly** *adv*

**[1]Central American** *adj*
of or relating to Central America or the Central Americans

**[2]Central American** *n*
a person born or living in Central America

**central angle** *n*
an angle with its vertex at the center of a circle and with sides that are radii of the circle

**cen·tral·ize** \'sen-trə-ˌlīz\ *vb*
**cen·tral·ized**; **cen·tral·iz·ing**
to bring to a central point or under a single control

**central processing unit** *n*
PROCESSOR 3

**cen·trif·u·gal force** \sen-ˌtrif-yə-gəl-\ *n*
▶ the force that tends to cause a thing or parts of a thing to go outward from a center of rotation

*centrifugal force holds car on track*

**centrifugal force**

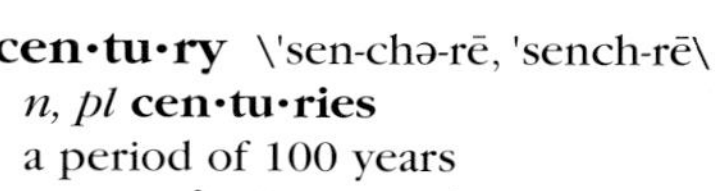

**cen·tu·ry** \'sen-chə-rē, 'sench-rē\ *n, pl* **cen·tu·ries**
a period of 100 years

**ce·ram·ic** \sə-'ram-ik\ *n*
**1** **ceramics** *pl* the art of making things (as pottery or tiles) of baked clay
**2** a product made by ceramics

**[1]ce·re·al** \'sir-ē-əl\ *adj*
**1** relating to grain or the plants that it comes from
**2** made of grain

**Word History** In Roman mythology Ceres was the goddess of agriculture. A Latin word meaning "of the goddess of agriculture" was formed from her name. Since Ceres was in charge of grain and grain plants, the word formed from her name came to mean "of grain" as well. The English word *cereal* came from this Latin word.

**[2]cereal** *n*
**1** ▲ a plant (as a grass) that yields grain for food
**2** a food prepared from grain

**cer•e•bel•lum** \ˌser-ə-ˈbel-əm\ *n, pl* **cer•e•bel•lums** *or* **cer•e•bel•la** \-ˈbel-ə\
a part of the brain concerned especially with the coordination of muscles and with keeping the body in proper balance

**ce•re•bral** \sə-ˈrē-brəl, ˈser-ə-brəl\ *adj*
**1** of or relating to the brain or mind
**2** of, relating to, or affecting the cerebrum

**ce•re•brum** \sə-ˈrē-brəm, ˈser-ə-brəm\ *n, pl* **ce•re•brums** *or* **ce•re•bra** \-brə\
the enlarged front and upper part of the brain that is the center of thinking

[1]**cer•e•mo•ni•al** \ˌser-ə-ˈmō-nē-əl\ *adj*
of, relating to, or being a ceremony

[2]**ceremonial** *n*
a ceremonial act, action, or system

**cer•e•mo•ni•ous** \ˌser-ə-ˈmō-nē-əs\ *adj*
**1** [1]CEREMONIAL
**2** given to ceremony : FORMAL
**cer•e•mo•ni•ous•ly** *adv*

**cer•e•mo•ny** \ˈser-ə-ˌmō-nē\ *n, pl* **cer•e•mo•nies**
**1** an act or series of acts performed in some regular way according to fixed rules
**2** very polite behavior : FORMALITY

[1]**cer•tain** \ˈsərt-n\ *adj*
**1** being fixed or settled ⟨a *certain* percentage of the profit⟩
**2** known but not named ⟨a *certain* person told me⟩
**3** sure to have an effect ⟨a *certain* cure⟩
**4** known to be true ⟨it's *certain* that they were here⟩
**5** bound by the way things are ⟨*certain* to succeed⟩
**6** assured in thought or action

[2]**certain** *pron*
certain ones ⟨*certain* of the students could work harder⟩

**cer•tain•ly** \ˈsərt-n-lē\ *adv*
**1** with certainty : without fail ⟨I will *certainly* see to it⟩
**2** without doubt ⟨it is *certainly* cool this evening⟩

**cer•tain•ty** \ˈsərt-n-tē\ *n, pl* **cer•tain•ties**
**1** something that is certain
**2** the quality or state of being certain ⟨answered with *certainty*⟩

**cer•tif•i•cate** \sər-ˈtif-i-kət\ *n*
**1** a written or printed statement that is proof of some fact ⟨a vaccination *certificate*⟩
**2** a paper showing that a person

**chair 1**
From earliest civilized times, chairs have been used for relaxation, and as seating around tables. Today, there are many different styles of chair to suit a range of functions within the office, home, and garden. Chairs may be simple, or padded and upholstered. Not always strictly practical, chairs reflect contemporary styles of fashion.

lawn chair

dining chair

office chair

armchair

baby's high chair

has met certain requirements
**3** a paper showing ownership

**cer·ti·fy** \'sərt-ə-ˌfī\ *vb* **cer·ti·fied**; **cer·ti·fy·ing**
**1** to show to be true or as claimed by a formal or official statement ⟨*certify* a student's record⟩
**2** to guarantee the quality, fitness, or value of officially ⟨*certify* a check⟩
**3** to show to have met certain requirements ⟨*certify* a student for graduation⟩

**ce·ru·le·an** \sə-'rü-lē-ən\ *adj* somewhat like the blue of the sky

**ces·sa·tion** \se-'sā-shən\ *n* a coming to a stop

**chafe** \'chāf\ *vb* **chafed**; **chaf·ing**
**1** IRRITATE 1, VEX
**2** to be bothered : FRET
**3** to warm by rubbing ⟨*chafed* my hands⟩
**4** to rub so as to wear away or make sore

**¹chaff** \'chaf\ *n*
**1** the husks of grains and grasses separated from the seed in threshing
**2** something worthless

**²chaff** *vb* to tease in a friendly way

**cha·grin** \shə-'grin\ *n* a feeling of being annoyed by failure or disappointment

**¹chain** \'chān\ *n*
**1** ▼ a series of links or rings usually of metal
**2** something that restricts or binds : BOND
**3** a series of things joined together as if by links ⟨a *chain* of mountains⟩ ⟨a *chain* of events⟩

**²chain** *vb* to fasten, bind, or connect with or as if with a chain

**¹chain 1:** an anchor chain

**chain saw** *n* a portable power saw that cuts using teeth that are linked together to form a continuous chain

**chair** \'cheər, 'chaər\ *n*
**1** ◀ a seat for one person usually having a back and either four legs or a swivel base
**2** an official seat or a seat of authority or honor ⟨take the *chair* at a meeting⟩
**3** an office or position of authority or honor
**4** an official who conducts a meeting

**chair·man** \'cheər-mən, 'chaər-\ *n, pl* **chair·men** \-mən\ CHAIR 4
**chair·man·ship** \-ˌship\ *n*

**chair·per·son** \'cheər-ˌpərs-n, 'chaər-\ *n* CHAIR 4

**chair·wom·an** \'cheər-ˌwu̇m-ən, 'chaər-\ *n, pl* **chair·wom·en** \-ˌwim-ən\ a woman who conducts a meeting

**chaise longue** \'shāz-'lȯŋ\ *n* a long chair somewhat like a couch

**chaise lounge** \'shāz-'lau̇nj, 'chās-\ *n* CHAISE LONGUE

**cha·let** \sha-'lā\ *n*
**1** a herdsman's hut in the Alps away from a town or village
**2** a Swiss dwelling with a roof that sticks far out past the walls
**3** a cottage built to look like a chalet

**chalice:** a 16th-century church chalice from Spain

**chal·ice** \'chal-əs\ *n* ▲ a drinking cup : GOBLET

**¹chalk** \'chȯk\ *n*
**1** a soft white, gray, or buff limestone made up mainly of very small seashells
**2** a material like chalk especially when used in the form of a crayon

**²chalk** *vb*
**1** to rub, mark, write, or draw with chalk
**2** to record or add up with or as if with chalk

**chalk·board** \'chȯk-ˌbōrd\ *n* BLACKBOARD

**chalky** \'chȯ-kē\ *adj* **chalk·i·er**; **chalk·i·est**
**1** made of or like chalk
**2** easily crumbled
**3** very pale ⟨*chalky* from fright⟩

**¹chal·lenge** \'chal-ənj\ *vb* **chal·lenged**; **chal·leng·ing**
**1** to halt and demand a password from
**2** to object to as bad or incorrect : DISPUTE
**3** to demand proof that something is right or legal ⟨*challenge* a vote⟩
**4** to invite or dare to take part in a contest ⟨*challenge* us to race⟩
**chal·leng·er** *n*

**²challenge** *n*
**1** an objection to something as not being true, genuine, correct, or proper or to a person (as a juror) as not being qualified or approved : PROTEST
**2** a demand that someone take part in a duel
**3** a call or dare for someone to compete in a contest or sport

**challenged** *adj* having a disability or deficiency

**cham·ber** \'chām-bər\ *n*
**1** a room in a house and especially a bedroom
**2** an enclosed space, cavity, or compartment (as in a gun)
**3** a meeting hall of a government body (as an assembly)
**4** a room where a judge conducts business out of court
**5** a group of people organized into a lawmaking body
**6** a board or council of volunteers (as businessmen)
**cham·bered** \-bərd\ *adj*

**cham·ber·lain** \'chām-bər-lən\ *n*
**1** a chief officer in the household of a ruler or noble
**2** TREASURER ⟨city *chamberlain*⟩

**cham·ber·maid** \'chām-bər-ˌmād\ *n* a maid who takes care of bedrooms (as in a hotel)

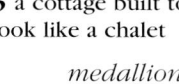

**chamber music** *n* instrumental music to be performed in a room or small hall

**cha·me·leon** \kə-ˈmēl-yən\ *n*
▼ a lizard that has the ability to change the color of its skin

**chameleon**

**Word History** Many of the lizards of the Old World must have looked quite startling. They may even have reminded the ancients of small lions. The Greeks gave these strange-looking lizards a name made up of two Greek words. The first meant "on the ground," and the second meant "lion." The English word *chameleon* came from the Greek name of the lizards.

**cham·ois** \ˈsham-ē\ *n*, *pl* **cham·ois** \-ē, -ēz\
**1** ► a small antelope living on the highest mountains of Europe and Asia
**2** a soft yellowish leather made from the skin of the chamois or from sheepskin

[1]**champ** \ˈchamp\ *vb*
to bite and chew noisily ⟨a horse *champing* its bit⟩

[2]**champ** *n*
[1]CHAMPION 2, 3

[1]**cham·pi·on** \ˈcham-pē-ən\ *n*
**1** a person who fights or speaks for another person or in favor of a cause
**2** a person accepted as better than all others in a sport or in a game of skill
**3** the winner of first place in a competition

[2]**champion** *vb*
to protect or fight for as a champion

**cham·pi·on·ship** \ˈcham-pē-ən-ˌship\ *n*
**1** the act of defending as a champion
**2** the position or title of champion
**3** a contest held to find a champion

[1]**chance** \ˈchans\ *n*
**1** the uncertain course of events ⟨they met by *chance*⟩
**2** OPPORTUNITY 1 ⟨had a *chance* to travel⟩
**3** [1]RISK, GAMBLE ⟨take *chances*⟩
**4** PROBABILITY 1 ⟨a slight *chance* of rain⟩
**5** a ticket in a raffle

[2]**chance** *vb* **chanced**; **chanc·ing**
**1** to take place by chance
**2** to come unexpectedly ⟨*chanced* on a bargain⟩
**3** to leave to chance : RISK

[3]**chance** *adj*
happening by chance ⟨a *chance* meeting⟩

**chan·cel·lor** \ˈchan-sə-lər, ˈchan-slər\ *n*
**1** a high state official (as in Germany)
**2** a high officer of some universities
**3** a chief judge in some courts
**chan·cel·lor·ship** \-ˌship\ *n*

**chamois 1**

**chan·de·lier** \ˌshan-də-ˈlir\ *n*
a lighting fixture with several branches that usually hangs from the ceiling

[1]**change** \ˈchānj\ *vb* **changed**; **chang·ing**
**1** to make or become different : ALTER ⟨*change* the looks of a room⟩ ⟨*changing* autumn leaves⟩
**2** to give a different position, course, or direction to ⟨*change* one's plans⟩
**3** to put one thing in the place of another : SWITCH, EXCHANGE ⟨*change* places⟩
**4** to give or receive an equal amount of money in usually smaller units of value or in the money of another country ⟨*change* a ten-dollar bill⟩
**5** to put fresh clothes or covering on ⟨*change* a bed⟩
**6** to put on different clothes ⟨we always *change* for dinner⟩

**Synonyms** CHANGE, ALTER, and VARY mean to make or become different. CHANGE may suggest making such a basic difference in a thing that it becomes something else ⟨they've *changed* the house into a restaurant⟩ or it may apply to substituting one thing for another ⟨*change* that shirt for a clean one⟩. ALTER suggests making a small difference in something ⟨*altered* the skirt by making it a bit shorter⟩. VARY suggests making a difference in order to break away from a routine ⟨*vary* the tasks given to each worker⟩.

[2]**change** *n*
**1** the act, process, or result of changing ⟨*change* of seasons⟩
**2** a fresh set of clothes ⟨take several *changes* on your vacation⟩
**3** money in small units of value received in exchange for an equal amount in larger units ⟨*change* for a ten-dollar bill⟩
**4** money returned when a payment is more than the amount due ⟨wait for your *change*⟩
**5** money in coins

**change·able** \ˈchān-jə-bəl\ *adj*
able or likely to change

[1]**chan·nel** \ˈchan-l\ *n*
**1** the bed of a stream
**2** the deeper part of a waterway (as a river or harbor)
**3** a strait or a narrow sea ⟨the English *Channel*⟩
**4** a closed course (as a tube) through which something flows
**5** a long groove
**6** a means by which something is passed or carried
**7** a range of frequencies used by a single radio or television station in broadcasting

[2]**channel** *vb* **chan·neled** *or* **chan·nelled**; **chan·nel·ing** *or* **chan·nel·ling**
**1** to form a channel in
**2** to direct into or through a channel

**[1]chant** \'chant\ *vb*
**1** to sing especially in the way a chant is sung
**2** to recite or speak with no change in tone

**[2]chant** *n*
**1** a melody in which several words or syllables are sung on one tone
**2** something spoken in the style of a chant

**cha·os** \'kā-,äs\ *n*
complete confusion and disorder

**cha·ot·ic** \kā-'ät-ik\ *adj*
being in a state of chaos

**[1]chap** \'chap\ *vb* **chapped**; **chap·ping**
to open in slits **:** CRACK ⟨lips *chapped* by wind and cold⟩

**[2]chap** *n*
[1]FELLOW 4

**chap·el** \'chap-əl\ *n*
**1** a building or a room or place for prayer or special religious services
**2** a religious service or assembly held in a school or college

**[1]chap·er·on** *or* **chap·er·one** \'shap-ə-,rōn\ *n*
an older person who goes with and is responsible for a young woman or a group of young people (as at a dance)

**[2]chaperon** *or* **chaperone** *vb* **chap·er·oned**; **chap·er·on·ing**
to act as a chaperon

**chap·lain** \'chap-lən\ *n*
**1** a member of the clergy officially attached to a special group (as the army)
**2** a person chosen to conduct religious services (as for a club)

**chaps** \'shaps, 'chaps\ *n pl*
▶ a set of leather coverings for the legs used especially by western ranch workers

**chap·ter** \'chap-tər\ *n*
**1** a main division of a book or story
**2** a local branch of a club or organization

**char** \'chär\ *vb* **charred**; **char·ring**
**1** to change to charcoal by burning
**2** to burn slightly **:** SCORCH

**char·ac·ter** \'kar-ək-tər\ *n*
**1** a mark, sign, or symbol (as a letter or figure) used in writing or printing
**2** [1]CHARACTERISTIC
**3** the group of qualities that make a person, group, or thing different from others
**4** a person who is unusual or peculiar
**5** a person in a story or play
**6** REPUTATION 1
**7** moral excellence ⟨a person of *character*⟩

**[1]char·ac·ter·is·tic** \,kar-ək-tə-'ris-tik\ *n*
a special quality or appearance that makes an individual or a group different from others

**[2]characteristic** *adj*
serving to stress some special quality of an individual or a group **:** TYPICAL ⟨replied with *characteristic* carelessness⟩

**char·ac·ter·is·ti·cal·ly** \,kar-ək-tə-'ris-ti-kə-lē\ *adv*
in a characteristic way

**char·ac·ter·ize** \'kar-ək-tə-,rīz\ *vb* **char·ac·ter·ized**; **char·ac·ter·iz·ing**
**1** to point out the character of an individual or a group **:** DESCRIBE
**2** to be characteristic of

**chaps:**
a cowboy wearing chaps

**char·coal** \'chär-,kōl\ *n*
▼ a black or dark absorbent carbon made by heating animal or vegetable material in the absence of air

**charcoal**

**[1]charge** \'chärj\ *n*
**1** the amount (as of ammunition or fuel) needed to load or fill something
**2** an amount of electricity available
**3** a task, duty, or order given to a person **:** OBLIGATION
**4** the work or duty of managing ⟨has *charge* of the building⟩
**5** a person or thing given to a person to look after
**6** [2]COMMAND 2 ⟨a judge's *charge* to a jury⟩
**7** the price demanded especially for a service ⟨storage *charges*⟩
**8** an amount listed as a debt on an account
**9** ACCUSATION
**10** a rushing attack **synonyms** see PRICE

**[2]charge** *vb* **charged**; **charg·ing**
**1** [1]FILL 1 ⟨*charge* a furnace with coal⟩
**2** to give an electric charge to
**3** to restore the active materials in a storage battery by passage of an electric current through it
**4** to give a task, duty, or responsibility to
**5** [1]COMMAND 1
**6** to accuse formally ⟨*charged* with speeding⟩
**7** to rush against **:** ASSAULT
**8** to take payment from or make responsible for payment ⟨you *charged* me too much⟩
**9** to enter as a debt or responsibility on a record ⟨*charge* a purchase to one's account⟩ ⟨*charge* books on a library card⟩
**10** to ask or set as a price ⟨they *charge* too much for everything⟩ ⟨*charged* $100 for repairs⟩

**charg·er** \'chär-jər\ *n*
a cavalry horse

A B C D E F G H I J K L M N O P Q R S T U V W X Y Z

**char·i·ot** \'char-ē-ət\ *n*
▶ a vehicle of ancient times that had two wheels, was pulled by horses, and was used in war and in races and parades

**char·i·ta·ble** \'char-ət-ə-bəl\ *adj*
**1** freely giving money or help to needy persons : GENEROUS
**2** given for the needy : of service to the needy
**3** kindly in judging other people

**char·i·ty** \'char-ət-ē\ *n, pl* **char·i·ties**
**1** love for others
**2** kindliness in judging others
**3** the giving of aid to the poor and suffering
**4** public aid for the poor
**5** an institution or fund for helping the needy

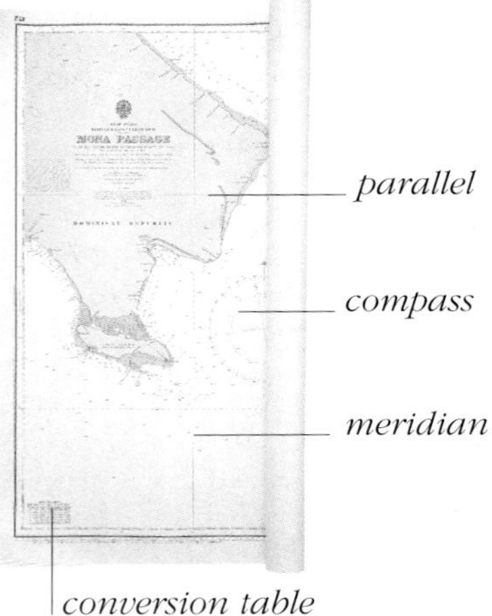


[1]**chart 2:** a nautical chart

**char·ley horse** \'chär-lē-,hȯrs\ *n*
pain and stiffness in a muscle (as in a leg)

[1]**charm** \'chärm\ *n*
**1** a word, action, or thing believed to have magic powers
**2** something worn or carried to keep away evil and bring good luck
**3** a small decorative object worn on a chain or bracelet
**4** a quality that attracts and pleases

[2]**charm** *vb*
**1** to affect or influence by or as if by a magic spell ⟨*charm* a snake⟩
**2** FASCINATE 2, DELIGHT ⟨sounds that *charm* the ear⟩
**3** to protect by or as if by a charm ⟨leads a *charmed* life⟩
**4** to attract by grace or beauty

**chariot:** an ancient Roman chariot

**charm·ing** \'chär-ming\ *adj*
very pleasing

[1]**chart** \'chärt\ *n*
**1** [1]MAP
**2** ◀ a map showing coasts, reefs, currents, and depths of water
**3** a sheet giving information in a table or lists or by means of diagrams

[2]**chart** *vb*
**1** to make a map or chart of ⟨*chart* the seas⟩
**2** to lay out a plan for

[1]**char·ter** \'chärt-ər\ *n*
**1** an official document granting, guaranteeing, or showing the limits of the rights and duties of the group to which it is given
**2** a contract by which the owners of a ship lease it to others

[2]**charter** *vb*
**1** to grant a charter to
**2** to hire (as a bus or an aircraft) for temporary use

**charter school** *n*
a school supported by taxes but run independently to achieve set goals under a charter between an official body (as a state government) and an outside group (as educators and businesses)

[1]**chase** \'chās\ *n*
**1** the act of chasing : PURSUIT
**2** the hunting of wild animals
**3** something pursued

[2]**chase** *vb* **chased**; **chas·ing**
**1** to follow in order to catch up with or capture ⟨*chase* a thief⟩ ⟨*chase* a bus⟩
**2** [1]HUNT 1 ⟨*chase* the fox⟩
**3** to drive away or out

**Synonyms** CHASE, PURSUE, and FOLLOW mean to go after someone or something. CHASE suggests that one moves swiftly in order to catch up with something ⟨*chased* the cat all over the yard⟩. PURSUE suggests a long, continual chase ⟨they *pursued* the bear for miles⟩. FOLLOW does not suggest speed or a desire to actually catch up with something ⟨*follow* the children and find out where their hideout is⟩.

**chasm** \'kaz-əm\ *n*
a deep split or gap in the earth

**chas·sis** \'shas-ē, 'chas-\ *n, pl* **chas·sis** \-ēz\
▼ a structure that supports the body (as of an automobile or airplane) or the parts (as of a television set)

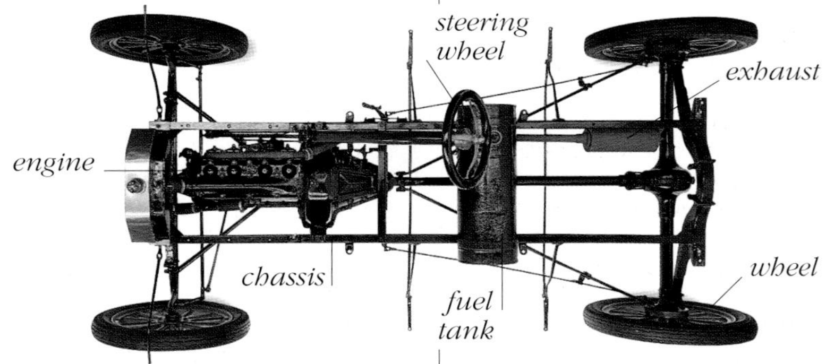


**chassis** of an automobile from 1912

**chaste** \'chāst\ *adj* **chast·er**; **chast·est**
**1** pure in thought and act : MODEST
**2** simple or plain in design

**chas·ten** \'chās-n\ *vb*
to correct by punishment or suffering : DISCIPLINE

**chas·tise** \chas-'tīz\ *vb* **chas·tised**; **chas·tis·ing**
to punish severely (as by whipping)

**chas·ti·ty** \'chas-tət-ē\ *n*
the quality or state of being chaste

[1]**chat** \'chat\ *vb* **chat·ted**; **chat·ting**
to talk in a friendly manner of things that are not serious

[2]**chat** *n*
a light friendly conversation

**chat room** *n*
an on-line computer site at which any visitor to the site can send messages that immediately appear on the screen for everyone to read

[1]**chat·ter** \'chat-ər\ *vb*
**1** to make quick sounds that suggest speech but lack meaning ⟨monkeys *chattering* in the trees⟩
**2** to talk without thinking, without stopping, or fast : JABBER
**3** to click again and again and without control ⟨teeth *chattering* from the cold⟩
**chat·ter·er** *n*

[2]**chatter** *n*
the act or sound of chattering

**chat·ter·box** \'chat-ər-ˌbäks\ *n*
a person who talks all the time

**chat·ty** \'chat-ē\ *adj* **chat·ti·er**; **chat·ti·est**
**1** TALKATIVE
**2** having the style and manner of friendly conversation ⟨a *chatty* letter⟩

**chauf·feur** \'shō-fər, shō-'fər\ *n*
a person hired to drive people around in a car

[1]**cheap** \'chēp\ *adj*
**1** not costing much ⟨a *cheap* watch⟩
**2** worth little : not very good
**3** gained without much effort ⟨a *cheap* victory⟩
**4** lowered in one's own opinion ⟨feel *cheap*⟩
**5** charging low prices ⟨a *cheap* hotel⟩
**cheap·ly** *adv*

[2]**cheap** *adv*
at low cost

**cheap·en** \'chē-pən\ *vb*
to make or become cheap or cheaper

[1]**cheat** \'chēt\ *vb*
**1** to take something away from or keep from having something by dishonest tricks : DEFRAUD
**2** to use unfair or dishonest methods to gain an advantage ⟨*cheat* on a test⟩ ⟨*cheat* at cards⟩

[2]**cheat** *n*
**1** an act of cheating : DECEPTION, FRAUD
**2** a dishonest person

[1]**check** \'chek\ *n*
**1** a sudden stopping of progress : PAUSE
**2** something that delays, stops, or holds back : RESTRAINT
**3** a standard or guide for testing and studying something
**4** EXAMINATION 1, INVESTIGATION
**5** a written order telling a bank to pay out money from a person's account to the one named on the order ⟨pay a bill by *check*⟩
**6** a ticket or token showing a person's ownership, identity, or claim to something ⟨a baggage *check*⟩
**7** a slip of paper showing the amount due : BILL ⟨who will pay the *check* at dinner⟩
**8** a pattern in squares
**9** ▼ material with a design in squares
**10** a mark typically ✓ placed beside a written or printed item to show that something has been specially noted

[1]**check 9:** a checked napkin

[2]**check** *vb*
**1** to bring to a sudden stop
**2** to keep from expressing ⟨*check* one's temper⟩
**3** to make sure that something is correct or satisfactory : VERIFY
**4** to mark with a check ⟨*check* the correct answer⟩
**5** to mark with squares ⟨a *checked* suit⟩
**6** to leave or accept for safekeeping or for shipment ⟨*check* baggage⟩
**7** to be the same on every point : TALLY

**check·er·board** \'chek-ər-ˌbōrd\ *n*
a board marked with sixty-four squares in two colors and used for games (as checkers)

**check·ers** \'chek-ərz\ *n*
▼ a game played on a checkerboard by two players each having twelve pieces

**checkers:** pieces laid out on a checkerboard

**check·up** \'chek-ˌəp\ *n*
**1** INSPECTION, EXAMINATION
**2** a physical examination

**cheek** \'chēk\ *n*
**1** the side of the face below the eye and above and beside the mouth
**2** IMPUDENCE

[1]**cheep** \'chēp\ *vb*
[1]PEEP, CHIRP

[2]**cheep** *n*
[1]CHIRP

[1]**cheer** \'chir\ *n*
**1** state of mind or heart : SPIRIT ⟨be of good *cheer*⟩
**2** good spirits ⟨full of *cheer*⟩
**3** something that gladdens ⟨words of *cheer*⟩
**4** a shout of praise or encouragement ⟨three *cheers* for the team⟩

[2]**cheer** *vb*
**1** to give hope to : make happier : COMFORT ⟨*cheer* the sick⟩
**2** to urge on especially with shouts or cheers ⟨*cheer* a team to victory⟩
**3** to shout with joy, approval, or enthusiasm
**4** to grow or be cheerful — usually used with *up*

a b c d e f g h i j k l m n o p q r s t u v w x y z

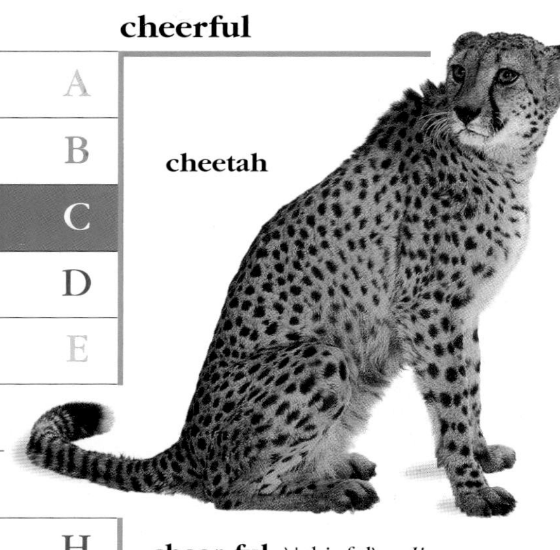
cheetah

**cheer·ful** \'chir-fəl\ *adj*
full of good spirits : PLEASANT
**cheer·ful·ly** \-fə-lē\ *adv*
**cheer·ful·ness** *n*

**cheer·less** \'chir-ləs\ *adj*
offering no cheer : GLOOMY ⟨a *cheerless* room⟩

**cheery** \'chir-ē\ *adj* **cheer·i·er**; **cheer·i·est**
merry and bright in manner or effect : CHEERFUL
**cheer·i·ly** \-ə-lē\ *adv*
**cheer·i·ness** \-ē-nəs\ *n*

**cheese** \'chēz\ *n*
▼ the curd of milk pressed for use as food

**cheese·cloth** \'chēz-ˌklȯth\ *n*
a thin loosely woven cotton cloth

**cheesy** \'chē-zē\ *adj* **chees·i·er**; **chees·i·est**
like or suggesting cheese

**chee·tah** \'chēt-ə\ *n*
◄ a long-legged spotted African and formerly Asian animal of the cat family that is the fastest animal on land

**chef** \'shef\ *n*
**1** a chief cook
**2** [1]COOK

[1]**chem·i·cal** \'kem-i-kəl\ *adj*
of or relating to chemistry or chemicals
**chem·i·cal·ly** *adv*

[2]**chemical** *n*
a substance (as an acid) that is formed when two or more other substances act upon one another or that is used to produce a change in another substance (as in making plastics)

**chem·ist** \'kem-ist\ *n*
a person trained or engaged in chemistry

**chem·is·try** \'kem-əs-trē\ *n*
**1** a science that deals with the composition and properties of substances and of the changes they undergo
**2** chemical composition and properties ⟨the *chemistry* of food⟩

**cher·ish** \'cher-ish\ *vb*
**1** to hold dear ⟨*cherish* a friend⟩

## cheese

Cheese is made from curdled milk or cream. The solid curds produced are put into molds to ripen. The time a cheese is left to mature and the type of milk used determine its texture and flavor. Hard cheese is matured for a long time, while soft cheese is ripened only briefly. Most cheese is produced from cow's milk, but milk from goats and sheep is also used.

**Parmesan** \'pär-mə-ˌzän\ is a very hard cheese

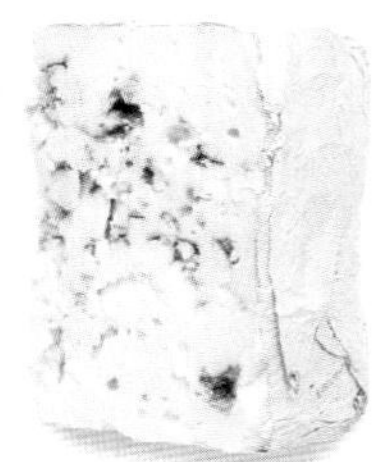
**blue cheese** has veins of greenish-blue mold

**mozzarella** \ˌmät-sə-'rel-ə\ is a soft cheese

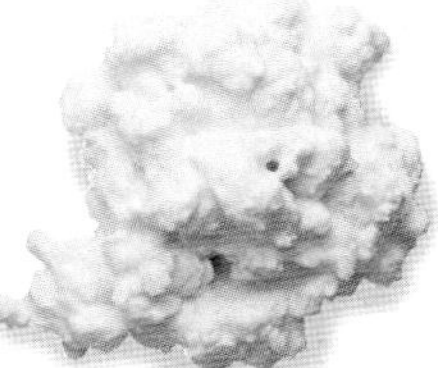
**cottage cheese** is a very soft cheese

**Edam** \'ē-dəm\ is a hard cheese

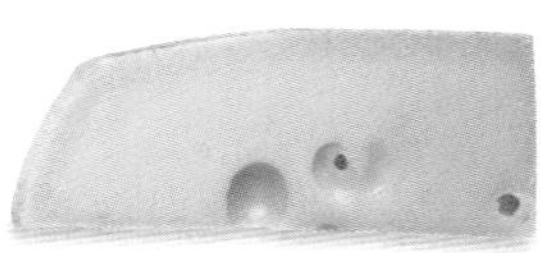
**Swiss cheese** is a hard cheese with large holes

**Brie** \'brē\ is a soft cheese

**Monterey Jack** \'män-tə-ˌrā-'jak\ is a semisoft cheese

**cheddar** \'ched-ər\ is a hard cheese

**feta** \'fe-tə\ is a crumbly goat cheese

**2** to keep deeply in mind **:** cling to ⟨*cherish* a belief⟩ **synonyms** see APPRECIATE

**Cher·o·kee** \'cher-ə-kē\ *n, pl* **Cherokee** *or* **Cherokees**
a member of an Indian people originally from the southern Appalachian mountains

**cher·ry** \'cher-ē\ *n, pl* **cherries**
**1** ▼ the round red or yellow fruit of a tree (**cherry tree**) that is related to the plum
**2** a medium red

**cherry 1**

**cher·ub** \'cher-əb\ *n*
**1** a painting or drawing of a beautiful child usually with wings
**2** a chubby rosy child

**chess** \'ches\ *n*
▼ a game of capture played on a board by two players each using sixteen pieces that have set moves

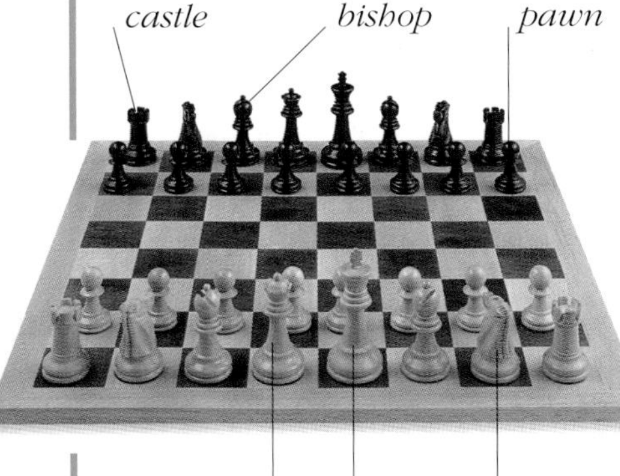


**chess:**
pieces laid out on a chessboard

**chest** \'chest\ *n*
**1** a container (as a box or case) for storing, safekeeping, or shipping ⟨tool *chest*⟩ ⟨linen *chest*⟩
**2** a public fund ⟨community *chest*⟩
**3** the part of the body enclosed by the ribs and breastbone
**chest·ed** \'ches-təd\ *adj*

**chest·nut** \'ches-nət\ *n*
**1** a sweet edible nut that grows in burs on a tree (**chestnut tree**) related to the beech
**2** a reddish brown

**chev·ron** \'shev-rən\ *n*
a sleeve badge of one or more bars or stripes usually in the shape of an upside down V indicating the wearer's rank (as in the armed forces)

**¹chew** \'chü\ *vb*
to crush or grind with the teeth

**²chew** *n*
**1** the act of chewing
**2** something for chewing ⟨a *chew* of tobacco⟩

**chew·ing gum** \'chü-ing-\ *n*
gum usually of sweetened and flavored chicle prepared for chewing

**chewy** \'chü-ē\ *adj* **chew·i·er**; **chew·i·est**
requiring chewing ⟨*chewy* candy⟩

**¹chic** \'shēk\ *n*
fashionable style

**²chic** *adj*
STYLISH, SMART ⟨*chic* clothes⟩

**Chi·ca·na** \chi-'kän-ə\ *n*
an American woman or girl of Mexican ancestry

**¹Chi·ca·no** \chi-'kän-ō\ *n, pl* **Chicanos**
an American of Mexican ancestry

**²Chicano** *adj*
of or relating to Chicanos

**chick** \'chik\ *n*
**1** ▶ a young chicken
**2** CHILD 2

**chick·a·dee** \'chik-ə-dē\ *n*
a small bird with fluffy grayish feathers and usually a black cap

**¹chick·en** \'chik-ən\ *n*
**1** the common domestic fowl especially when young **:** a young hen or rooster
**2** the flesh of a chicken for use as food

**²chicken** *adj*
CHICKENHEARTED

**chick·en·heart·ed** \ˌchik-ən-'härt-əd\ *adj*
COWARDLY, TIMID

**chicken pox** *n*
a contagious disease especially of children in which there is fever and the skin breaks out in watery blisters

**chick·weed** \'chik-ˌwēd\ *n*
a weedy plant related to the pinks that has small leaves and whitish flowers

**chi·cle** \'chik-əl, -lē\ *n*
a gum obtained from the sap of a tropical American tree and used in making chewing gum

**chide** \'chīd\ *vb* **chid** \'chid\ *or* **chid·ed** \'chīd-əd\; **chid** *or* **chid·den** \'chid-n\ *or* **chided**; **chid·ing**
to find fault with **:** SCOLD

**¹chief** \'chēf\ *n*
the head of a group **:** LEADER ⟨the *chief* of police⟩
**in chief** in the chief position or place ⟨editor *in chief*⟩

**²chief** *adj*
**1** highest in rank or authority
**2** most important **:** MAIN

**chief·ly** \'chē-flē\ *adv*
**1** above all
**2** for the most part

**chief master sergeant** *n*
a noncommissioned officer in the Air Force ranking above a senior master sergeant

**chief petty officer** *n*
a petty officer in the Navy or Coast Guard ranking above a petty officer first class

**chick 1**

**chief·tain** \'chēf-tən\ *n*
a chief especially of a band, tribe, or clan

**chief warrant officer** *n*
a warrant officer in any of the three top grades

**chig·ger** \'chig-ər\ *n*
the larva of some mites that has six legs, clings to the skin, and causes itching

**chil·blain** \'chil-ˌblān\ *n*
a red swollen itchy condition caused by cold that occurs especially on the hands or feet

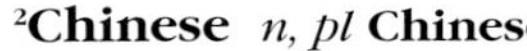

**child** \'chīld\ *n, pl* **chil·dren** \'chil-drən\
**1** an unborn or recently born person
**2** a young person of either sex between infancy and youth
**3** one's son or daughter of any age

**child·birth** \'chīld-,bərth\ *n*
the act or process of giving birth to a child

**child·hood** \'chīld-,hu̇d\ *n*
the period of life between infancy and youth

**child·ish** \'chīl-dish\ *adj*
**1** of, like, or thought to be suitable to children ⟨*childish* laughter⟩
**2** showing the less pleasing qualities (as silliness) often thought to be those of children

**child·like** \'chīld-,līk\ *adj*
**1** of or relating to a child or childhood
**2** showing the more pleasing qualities (as innocence and trustfulness) often thought to be those of children

**child·proof** \'chīld-,prüf\ *adj*
**1** made to prevent opening by children ⟨a *childproof* bottle⟩
**2** made safe for children ⟨a *childproof* house⟩

**chili** *or* **chile** \'chil-ē\ *n, pl* **chil·ies** *or* **chil·es**
**1** ▶ the small very sharply flavored fruit of a pepper plant
**2** a spicy stew of ground beef and chilies usually with beans

**chili 1**

**[1]chill** \'chil\ *n*
**1** a feeling of coldness accompanied by shivering
**2** unpleasant coldness

**[2]chill** *adj*
**1** unpleasantly cold : RAW ⟨a *chill* wind⟩
**2** not friendly ⟨a *chill* greeting⟩

**[3]chill** *vb*
**1** to make or become cold or chilly
**2** to make cool especially without freezing ⟨*chill* pudding for dessert⟩
**3** to harden the surface of (as metal) by sudden cooling

**chilly** \'chil-ē\ *adj* **chill·i·er**; **chill·i·est**
noticeably cold
**chill·i·ness** *n*

**[1]chime** \'chīm\ *vb* **chimed**; **chim·ing**
**1** to make sounds like a bell : ring chimes
**2** to call or indicate by chiming ⟨the clock *chimed* midnight⟩

**[2]chime** *n*
**1** a set of bells tuned to play music
**2** the music from a set of bells — usually used in pl.
**3** a musical sound suggesting bells

**chime in** *vb*
to break into or join in a discussion

**chim·ney** \'chim-nē\ *n, pl* **chimneys**
**1** a passage for smoke especially in the form of a vertical structure of brick or stone that reaches above the roof of a building
**2** a glass tube around a lamp flame

**chimney sweep** *n*
a person who cleans soot from chimneys

**chimney swift** *n*
a small dark gray bird with long narrow wings that often attaches its nest to chimneys

**chimp** \'chimp\ *n*
CHIMPANZEE

**chim·pan·zee** \,chim-,pan-'zē, chim-'pan-zē\ *n*
an African ape that lives mostly in trees and is smaller than the related gorilla

**[1]chin** \'chin\ *n*
the part of the face below the mouth and including the point of the lower jaw

**[2]chin** *vb* **chinned**; **chin·ning**
to raise oneself while hanging by the hands until the chin is level with the support

**chi·na** \'chī-nə\ *n*
**1** porcelain ware
**2** pottery (as dishes) for use in one's home

**chin·chil·la** \chin-'chil-ə\ *n*
a South American animal that is somewhat like a squirrel and is hunted or raised for its soft silvery gray fur

**[1]Chi·nese** \chī-'nēz\ *adj*
of or relating to China, the Chinese people, or Chinese

**[1]chisel**

**[2]Chinese** *n, pl* **Chinese**
**1** a person born or living in China
**2** a group of related languages used in China

**chink** \'chink\ *n*
a narrow slit or crack (as in a wall)

**[1]chip** \'chip\ *n*
**1** a small piece (as of wood, stone, or glass) cut or broken off
**2** a thin crisp piece of food ⟨tortilla *chip*⟩
**3** POTATO CHIP
**4** a flaw left after a small piece has been broken off ⟨a *chip* in the rim of a cup⟩
**5** INTEGRATED CIRCUIT
**6** a small slice of silicon containing electronic circuits (as for a computer)

**[2]chip** *vb* **chipped**; **chip·ping**
**1** to cut or break chips from
**2** to break off in small pieces

**chipmunk**

**chip·munk** \'chip-,məngk\ *n*
▲ a small striped animal related to the squirrels

**chip·ping sparrow** \'chip-ing-\ *n*
a small North American sparrow that often nests about houses and has a weak chirp as a call

**[1]chirp** \'chərp\ *n*
the short sharp sound made by crickets and some small birds

**[2]chirp** *vb*
to make a chirp

**[1]chis·el** \'chiz-əl\ *n*
◀ a metal tool with a sharp edge at the end of a usually flat piece used to chip away stone, wood, or metal

**[2]chisel** *vb* **chis·eled** *or* **chis·elled**; **chis·el·ing** *or* **chis·el·ling**
to cut or shape with a chisel

**chiv·al·rous** \'shiv-əl-rəs\ *adj*
**1** of or relating to chivalry
**2** having or showing honor, generosity, and courtesy
**3** showing special courtesy and regard to women

**chiv·al·ry** \'shiv-əl-rē\ *n*
**1** a body of knights
**2** the system, spirit, ways, or customs of knighthood
**3** chivalrous conduct

**chlo·rine** \'klōr-,ēn, -ən\ *n*
a chemical element that is a greenish yellow irritating gas of strong odor used as a bleach and as a disinfectant to purify water

[1]**chlo·ro·form** \'klōr-ə-,fórm\ *n*
a colorless heavy liquid used especially to dissolve fatty substances and in the past in medicine to deaden the pain of operations but now mostly replaced by less poisonous substances

[2]**chloroform** *vb*
to make unconscious or kill with chloroform

**chlo·ro·phyll** \'klōr-ə-,fil\ *n*
the green coloring matter by means of which green plants produce carbohydrates from carbon dioxide and water

**chlo·ro·plast** \'klōr-ə-,plast\ *n*
one of the tiny bodies in which chlorophyll is found

**chock–full** \'chäk-'fúl\ *or* **chuck–full** \'chək-\ *adj*
full to the limit

**choc·o·late** \'chäk-ə-lət, 'chäk-lət, 'chók-\ *n*
**1** a food prepared from ground roasted cacao beans
**2** a beverage of chocolate in water or milk
**3** ▼ a candy made or coated with chocolate

**chocolate 3**

[1]**choice** \'chóis\ *n*
**1** the act of choosing : SELECTION
**2** the power of choosing : OPTION
**3** a person or thing chosen
**4** the best part
**5** a large enough number and variety to choose among

[2]**choice** *adj* **choic·er**; **choic·est**
of very good quality

**choir** \'kwīr\ *n*
**1** an organized group of singers especially in a church
**2** the part of a church set aside for the singers

[1]**choke** \'chōk\ *vb* **choked**; **chok·ing**
**1** to keep from breathing in a normal way by cutting off the supply of air ⟨*choked* by thick smoke⟩
**2** to have the windpipe blocked entirely or partly ⟨*choke* on a bone⟩
**3** to slow or prevent the growth or action of ⟨flowers *choked* by weeds⟩
**4** to block by clogging ⟨leaves *choked* the sewer⟩

[2]**choke** *n*
**1** the act or sound of choking
**2** something that chokes

**choke·cher·ry** \'chōk-,cher-ē\ *n, pl* **choke·cher·ries**
a wild cherry tree with long clusters of reddish black fruits that pucker the mouth

**chol·era** \'käl-ə-rə\ *n*
a dangerous infectious disease of Asian origin in which violent vomiting and dysentery are present

**choose** \'chüz\ *vb* **chose** \'chōz\; **cho·sen** \'chōz-n\; **choos·ing**
**1** to select freely and after careful thought ⟨*choose* a leader⟩
**2** DECIDE 3 ⟨we *chose* to leave⟩
**3** to see fit ⟨do as you *choose*⟩

---

**Synonyms** CHOOSE, ELECT, and SELECT mean to decide upon one from among several. CHOOSE suggests that one does some thinking and makes a careful judgment before deciding ⟨*chose* to follow the right course⟩. ELECT may suggest that of two things one is deliberately picked and the other rejected ⟨*elect* one candidate for president⟩. SELECT suggests that there are many things from which to choose ⟨customers may *select* from a great variety of goods⟩.

---

**choosy** \'chü-zē\ *adj* **choos·i·er**; **choos·i·est**
careful in making choices

[1]**chop** \'chäp\ *vb* **chopped**; **chop·ping**
**1** to cut by striking especially over and over with something sharp ⟨*chop* down a tree⟩
**2** to cut into small pieces : MINCE ⟨*chop* meat⟩
**3** to strike quickly or again and again

[2]**chop** *n*
**1** a sharp downward blow or stroke (as with an ax)
**2** a small cut of meat often including a part of a rib ⟨a lamb *chop*⟩
**3** a short quick motion (as of a wave)

**chop·per** \'chäp-ər\ *n*
**1** someone or something that chops
**2** HELICOPTER

[1]**chop·py** \'chäp-ē\ *adj* **chop·pi·er**; **chop·pi·est**
frequently changing direction ⟨a *choppy* wind⟩

[2]**choppy** *adj* **chop·pi·er**; **chop·pi·est**
**1** rough with small waves
**2** JERKY

**chops** \'chäps\ *n pl*
the fleshy covering of the jaws

**chop·stick** \'chäp-,stik\ *n*
► one of two thin sticks used chiefly in Oriental countries to lift food to the mouth

**chopsticks**

**cho·ral** \'kōr-əl\ *adj*
of, relating to, or sung or recited by a chorus or choir or in chorus

**cho·rale** \kə-'ral\ *n*
**1** a hymn sung by the choir or congregation at a church service
**2** CHORUS 1

[1]**chord** \'kórd\ *n*
a group of tones sounded together to form harmony

[2]**chord** *n*
a straight line joining two points on a curve

**chore** \'chōr\ *n*
**1 chores** *pl* the regular light work about a home or farm
**2** an ordinary task
**3** a dull, unpleasant, or difficult task

**cho·re·og·ra·phy** \,kōr-ē-'äg-rə-fē\ *n*
the art of dancing or of arranging dances and especially ballets
**cho·re·og·ra·pher** \-fər\ *n*

**cho·ris·ter** \'kōr-ə-stər\ *n*
a singer in a choir

**chor·tle** \'chȯrt-l\ *vb* **chor·tled**; **chor·tling**
to chuckle especially in satisfaction

[1]**cho·rus** \'kōr-əs\ *n*
**1** a group of singers **:** CHOIR
**2** a group of dancers and singers (as in a musical comedy)
**3** a part of a song or hymn that is repeated every so often **:** REFRAIN
**4** a song meant to be sung by a group **:** group singing
**5** sounds uttered by a group of persons or animals together

[2]**chorus** *vb*
to speak, sing, or sound at the same time or together

**chose** *past of* CHOOSE

**cho·sen** \'chōz-n\ *adj*
**1** picked to be given favor or special privilege ⟨a *chosen* few⟩
**2** picked by God for special protection ⟨a *chosen* people⟩

**chow**

**chow** \'chau̇\ *n*
▲ a muscular dog with a blue-black tongue, a short tail curled close to the back, straight legs, and a thick coat

**chow·der** \'chau̇d-ər\ *n*
a soup or stew made of fish, clams, or a vegetable usually simmered in milk

**Christ** \'krīst\ *n*
JESUS

**Christmas tree**

**chris·ten** \'kris-n\ *vb*
**1** BAPTIZE 1
**2** to give a name to at baptism ⟨*christened* the baby Robin⟩
**3** to name or dedicate (as a ship) in a ceremony like that of baptism

**Chris·ten·dom** \'kris-n-dəm\ *n*
**1** the entire body of Christians
**2** the part of the world in which Christianity is most common

**chris·ten·ing** \'kris-ning, 'kris-n-ing\ *n*
BAPTISM

[1]**Chris·tian** \'kris-chən\ *n*
**1** a person who believes in Jesus and follows his teachings
**2** a member of a Christian church

[2]**Christian** *adj*
**1** of or relating to Jesus or the religion based on his teachings
**2** of or relating to Christians ⟨a *Christian* nation⟩
**3** being what a Christian should be or do ⟨*Christian* behavior toward others⟩

**Chris·tian·i·ty** \,kris-chē-'an-ət-ē\ *n*
**1** CHRISTENDOM 1
**2** the religion of Christians

**Christian name** *n*
the personal name given to a person at birth or christening

**Christ·mas** \'kris-məs\ *n*
December 25 celebrated in honor of the birth of Christ

**Christ·mas·tide** \'kris-mə-,stīd\ *n*
the season of Christmas

**Christmas tree** *n*
◀ a usually evergreen tree decorated at Christmas

**chro·mat·ic scale** \krō-,mat-ik-\ *n*
a musical scale that has all half steps

**chrome** \'krōm\ *n*
**1** CHROMIUM
**2** something plated with an alloy of chromium

**chro·mi·um** \'krō-mē-əm\ *n*
a bluish white metallic chemical element used especially in alloys

**chro·mo·some** \'krō-mə-,sōm\ *n*
one of the rodlike bodies of a cell nucleus that contain genes and divide when the cell divides

**chron·ic** \'krän-ik\ *adj*
**1** continuing for a long time or returning often ⟨a *chronic* disease⟩
**2** HABITUAL 2 ⟨a *chronic* complainer⟩
**chron·i·cal·ly** \-i-kə-lē\ *adv*

[1]**chron·i·cle** \'krän-i-kəl\ *n*
an account of events in the order of their happening **:** HISTORY

[2]**chronicle** *vb* **chron·i·cled**; **chron·i·cling**
to record in or as if in a chronicle

**chron·o·log·i·cal** \,krän-l-'äj-i-kəl\ *adj*
arranged in or according to the order of time ⟨*chronological* tables of American history⟩
**chron·o·log·i·cal·ly** *adv*

**chrys·a·lis** \'kris-ə-ləs\ *n*
a moth or butterfly pupa that is enclosed in a firm protective case

**chry·san·the·mum** \kri-'san-thə-məm\ *n*
▶ a plant related to the daisies that has deeply notched leaves and brightly colored often double flower heads

**chrysanthemum**

**chub·by** \'chəb-ē\ *adj* **chub·bi·er**; **chub·bi·est**
[4]PLUMP ⟨a *chubby* baby⟩

[1]**chuck** \'chək\ *vb*
**1** to give a pat or tap to ⟨*chucked* me under the chin⟩
**2** [1]TOSS 2 ⟨*chuck* a ball back and forth⟩

**²chuck** *n*
**1** a pat or nudge under the chin
**2** ²TOSS

**chuck–full** *variant of* CHOCK-FULL

**¹chuck·le** \'chək-əl\ *vb* **chuck·led; chuck·ling**
to laugh in a quiet way

**²chuckle** *n*
a low quiet laugh

**chuck wagon** \'chək-\ *n*
▶ a wagon carrying a stove and food for cooking

**¹chug** \'chəg\ *n*
a dull explosive sound

**²chug** *vb* **chugged; chug·ging**
to move with chugs ⟨an old car *chugging* along⟩

**¹chum** \'chəm\ *n*
a close friend : PAL

**²chum** *vb* **chummed; chum·ming**
to be chums

**chum·my** \'chəm-ē\ *adj* **chum·mi·er; chum·mi·est**
being on close friendly terms : SOCIABLE

**chunk** \'chəngk\ *n*
a short thick piece (as of ice)

**chunky** \'chəng-kē\ *adj* **chunk·i·er; chunk·i·est**
STOCKY

**church** \'chərch\ *n*
**1** a building for public worship and especially Christian worship
**2** an organized body of religious believers
**3** public worship

**church·yard** \'chərch-ˌyärd\ *n*
a yard that belongs to a church and is often used as a burial ground

**¹churn** \'chərn\ *n*
a container in which milk or cream is stirred or shaken in making butter

**churn** *vb*
**1** to stir or shake in a churn (as in making butter)
**2** to stir or shake violently

**chute** \'shüt\ *n*
**1** a sloping plane, trough, or passage down or through which things are slid or dropped
**2** ¹PARACHUTE

**ci·ca·da** \sə-'kād-ə\ *n*
an insect that has transparent wings and a stout body and is related to the true bugs

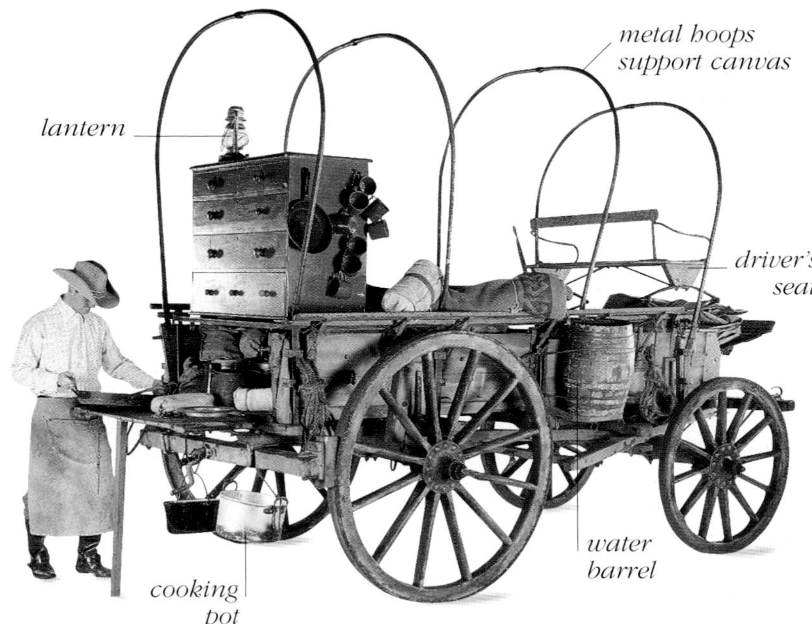

**chuck wagon**

**-cide** \ˌsīd\ *n suffix*
**1** killer ⟨insecti*cide*⟩
**2** killing

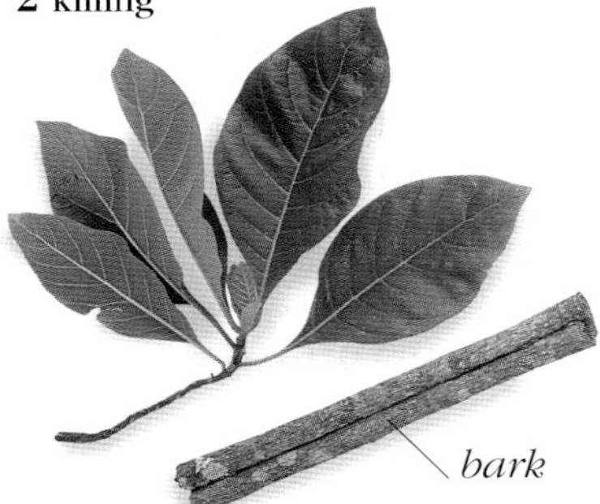

**cinchona**

**ci·der** \'sīd-ər\ *n*
the juice pressed out of fruit (as apples) and used especially as a drink and in making vinegar

**ci·gar** \si-'gär\ *n*
a small roll of tobacco leaf for smoking

**cig·a·rette** \ˌsig-ə-'ret\ *n*
a small roll of cut tobacco wrapped in paper for smoking

**cil·i·um** \'sil-ē-əm\ *n, pl* **cil·ia** \'sil-ē-ə\
any of the structures on the surface of some cells that look like tiny flexible eyelashes

**¹cinch** \'sinch\ *n*
**1** GIRTH 1
**2** a sure or an easy thing

**²cinch** *vb*
**1** to fasten or tighten a girth on ⟨*cinch* up a horse⟩
**2** to fasten with or as if with a girth ⟨*cinch* a saddle in place⟩

**cin·cho·na** \sing-'kō-nə\ *n*
◀ a South American tree whose bark yields quinine

**cin·der** \'sin-dər\ *n*
**1** SLAG
**2** a piece of partly burned coal or wood that is not burning
**3** EMBER
**4 cinders** *pl* ²ASH 1

**cin·e·ma** \'sin-ə-mə\ *n*
**1** a movie theater
**2** the movie industry

**cin·na·mon** \'sin-ə-mən\ *n*
▼ a spice made from the fragrant bark of tropical trees related to the Old World laurel

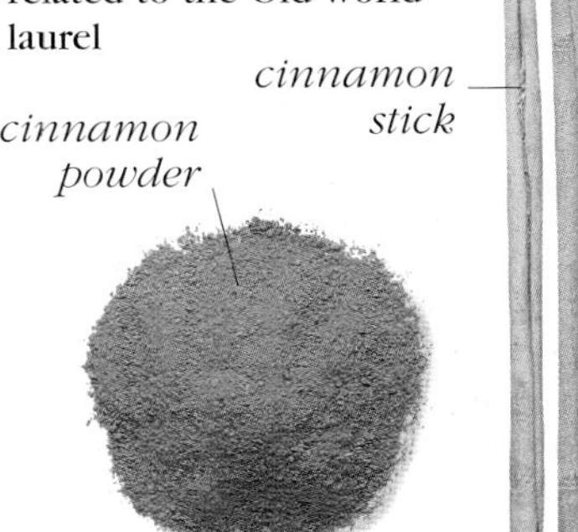

**cinnamon**

A B C D E F G H I J K L M N O P Q R S T U V W X Y Z

**¹ci·pher** \'sī-fər\ *n*
**1** ZERO 1
**2** an unimportant or worthless person : NONENTITY
**3** a method of secret writing or the alphabet or letters and symbols used in such writing
**4** a message in code

**²cipher** *vb*
to use figures in doing a problem in arithmetic : CALCULATE

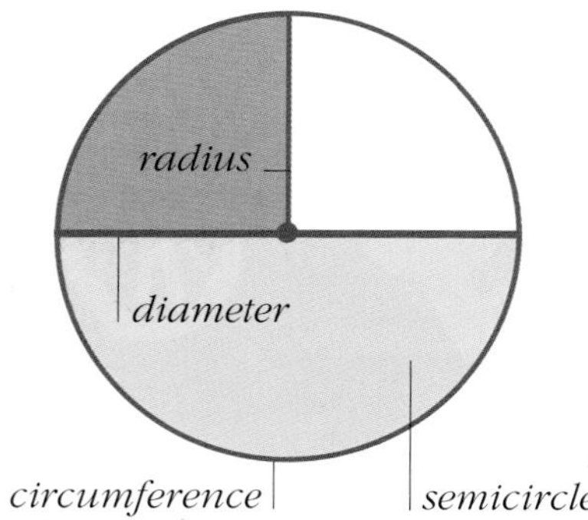


**¹circle 1**

**¹cir·cle** \'sər-kəl\ *n*
**1** ▲ a closed curve every point of which is equally distant from a central point within it : the space inside such a closed curve
**2** something in the form of a circle or part of a circle
**3** ¹CYCLE 2, ROUND ⟨the wheel has come full *circle*⟩
**4** a group of people sharing a common interest

**²circle** *vb* **cir·cled**; **cir·cling**
**1** to enclose in or as if in a circle
**2** to move or revolve around
**3** to move in or as if in a circle

**cir·cuit** \'sər-kət\ *n*
**1** a boundary line around an area
**2** an enclosed space
**3** a moving around (as in a circle) ⟨the *circuit* of the earth around the sun⟩
**4** a traveling from place to place in an area (as by a judge) so as to stop in each place at a certain time : a course so traveled
**5** the complete path of an electric current
**6** a group of electronic parts

**circuit breaker** *n*
a switch that automatically stops the flow of electric current if a circuit becomes overloaded

**cir·cu·i·tous** \,sər-'kyü-ət-əs\ *adj*
**1** having a circular or winding course
**2** not saying what one means in simple and sincere language

**¹cir·cu·lar** \'sər-kyə-lər\ *adj*
**1** having the form of a circle : ROUND ⟨a *circular* track⟩
**2** passing or going around in a circle ⟨*circular* motion⟩
**3** CIRCUITOUS 2
**4** sent around to a number of persons ⟨a *circular* letter⟩

**²circular** *n*
a printed notice or advertisement given or sent to many people

**cir·cu·late** \'sər-kyə-,lāt\ *vb*
**cir·cu·lat·ed**; **cir·cu·lat·ing**
**1** ▼ to move around in a course ⟨blood *circulates* in the body⟩
**2** to pass or be passed from place to place or from person to person

**cir·cu·la·tion** \,sər-kyə-'lā-shən\ *n*
**1** motion around in a course ⟨the *circulation* of air in a room⟩
**2** passage from place to place or person to person ⟨coins in *circulation*⟩
**3** the average number of copies (as of a newspaper) sold in a given period

**cir·cu·la·to·ry** \'sər-kyə-lə-,tōr-ē\ *adj*
of or relating to circulation (as of the blood)

**circulatory system** *n*
the system of the body that circulates blood and lymph and includes the heart and blood vessels

**circum-** *prefix*
around : about ⟨*circum*polar⟩

**cir·cum·fer·ence** \sər-'kəm-fə-rəns, -fərns\ *n*
**1** the line that goes around a circle
**2** a boundary line or circuit enclosing an area
**3** the distance around something

**cir·cum·nav·i·gate** \,sər-kəm-'nav-ə-,gāt\ *vb*

**circulate 1**
Blood flows around the body in a continuous circuit through a system of arteries, veins, and branching blood vessels. The heart acts as a pump to keep the blood circulating. Blood is carried from the heart by arteries to supply the cells of the body with vital oxygen and a range of nutrients. It is returned to the heart through the veins at the same rate at which it is pumped into the arteries.

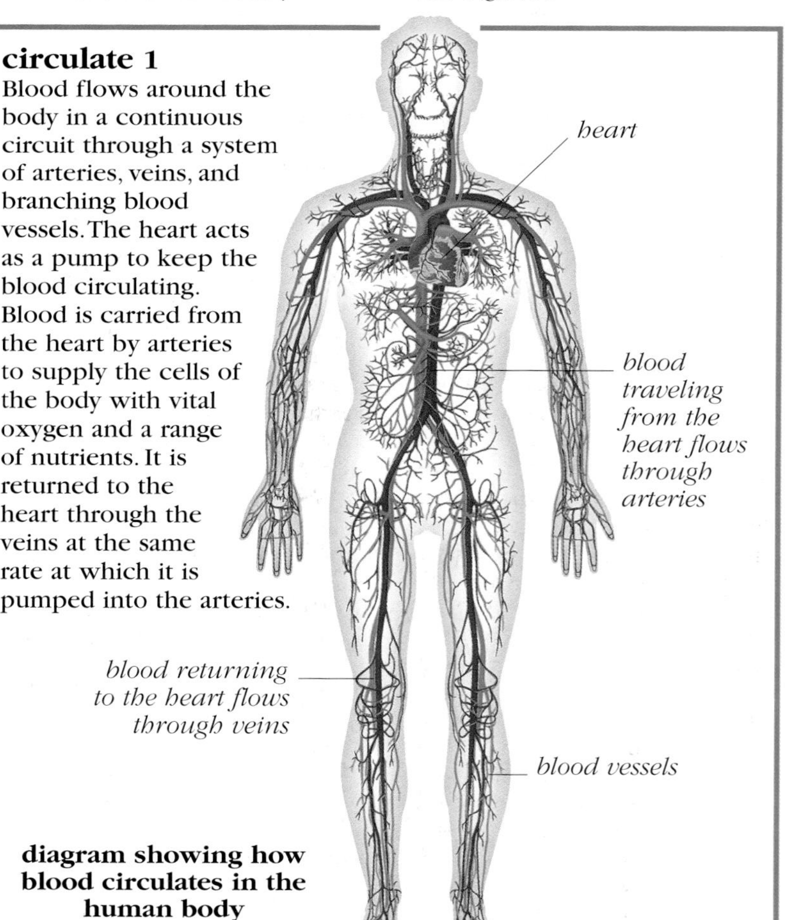


**diagram showing how blood circulates in the human body**

acrobat
clown
a firebrand is a piece of burning wood
clown
fire-eater
a unicycle is a one-wheeled vehicle moved by pedals

**circus 3**
The modern-style traveling circus dates from the mid-18th century and is still a popular form of family entertainment. Performances are traditionally held in a huge tent called the big top, with each act introduced by a ringmaster. Early circuses commonly featured performing wild animals, but today concern for animal welfare has led to the development of people-only circuses.

**cir·cum·nav·i·gat·ed; cir·cum·nav·i·gat·ing**
to go completely around (as the earth) especially by water

**cir·cum·po·lar** \ˌsər-kəm-ˈpō-lər\ *adj*
**1** continually visible above the horizon ⟨a *circumpolar* star⟩
**2** surrounding or found near the north pole or south pole

**cir·cum·stance** \ˈsər-kəm-ˌstans\ *n*
**1** a fact or event that must be considered along with another fact or event
**2 circumstances** *pl* conditions at a certain time or place ⟨under the *circumstances* I must leave home⟩
**3 circumstances** *pl* situation with regard to wealth ⟨in easy *circumstances*⟩
**4** [1]CHANCE 1, FATE ⟨an unfortunate victim of *circumstance*⟩

**cir·cum·vent** \ˌsər-kəm-ˈvent\ *vb*
**1** to go around : BYPASS
**2** to get the better of or avoid the force or effect of especially by trickery ⟨*circumvented* the tax laws⟩

**cir·cus** \ˈsər-kəs\ *n*
**1** a show that usually travels from place to place and that has a variety of exhibitions including riding, acrobatic feats, wild animal displays, and the performances of jugglers and clowns
**2** a circus performance
**3** ▲ the performers and equipment of a circus

**cir·rus** \ˈsir-əs\ *n, pl* **cir·ri** \ˈsir-ī\
a thin white cloud of tiny ice crystals that forms at a very high altitude

**cis·tern** \ˈsis-tərn\ *n*
an artificial reservoir or tank for storing water usually underground

**cit·a·del** \ˈsit-əd-l, -ə-ˌdel\ *n*
**1** a fortress that sits high above a city
**2** a strong fortress

**ci·ta·tion** \sī-ˈtā-shən\ *n*
**1** an act or instance of quoting
**2** QUOTATION 1
**3** a formal statement of what a person did to be chosen to receive an award

**cite** \ˈsīt\ *vb* **cit·ed**; **cit·ing**
**1** to quote as an example, authority, or proof
**2** to refer to especially in praise

**cit·i·zen** \ˈsit-ə-zən\ *n*
**1** a person who lives in a city or town
**2** a person who owes loyalty to a government and is protected by it

A B C D E F G H I J K L M N O P Q R S T U V W X Y Z

**cit·i·zen·ry** \'sit-ə-zən-rē\ *n*
the whole body of citizens

**cit·i·zen·ship** \'sit-ə-zən-,ship\ *n*
the state of being a citizen

**cit·ron** \'si-trən\ *n*
**1** a citrus fruit like the smaller lemon and having a thick rind that is preserved for use in cakes and puddings
**2** a small hard watermelon used especially in pickles and preserves

**cit·rus** \'si-trəs\ *adj*
▼ of or relating to a group of often thorny trees and shrubs of warm regions whose fruits include the lemon, lime, orange, and grapefruit

**city** \'sit-ē\ *n, pl* **cit·ies**
**1** a place in which people live that is larger than a town
**2** the people of a city

**city hall** *n*
the main administrative building of a city

**civ·ic** \'siv-ik\ *adj*
of or relating to a citizen, a city, or citizenship ⟨*civic* pride⟩ ⟨*civic* duty⟩

**civ·ics** \'siv-iks\ *n*
a study of the rights and duties of citizens

**civ·il** \'siv-əl\ *adj*
**1** of or relating to citizens ⟨*civil* liberties⟩
**2** of or relating to the state
**3** of or relating to ordinary or government affairs rather than to those of the military or the church
**4** polite without being friendly ⟨gave a *civil* answer⟩
**5** relating to court action between individuals having to do with private rights rather than criminal action

**Synonyms** CIVIL, POLITE, and COURTEOUS mean obeying the rules of good behavior. CIVIL suggests showing only enough proper behavior to avoid being actually rude ⟨that bank teller is barely *civil*⟩. POLITE suggests good manners and thoughtfulness ⟨the host was *polite* and made us feel at home⟩. COURTEOUS may suggest a politeness that is somewhat dignified ⟨the servants were taught to be *courteous* always⟩.

**[1]ci·vil·ian** \sə-'vil-yən\ *n*
a person not on active duty in a military, police, or fire-fighting force

**[2]civilian** *adj*
of or relating to a civilian

**ci·vil·i·ty** \sə-'vil-ət-ē\ *n, pl* **ci·vil·i·ties**
**1** civil behavior
**2** COURTESY 1

**civ·i·li·za·tion** \,siv-ə-lə-'zā-shən\ *n*
**1** an advanced stage (as in art, science, and government) of social development
**2** the way of life of a people ⟨Greek *civilization*⟩

**civ·i·lize** \'siv-ə-,līz\ *vb* **civ·i·lized**; **civ·i·liz·ing**
to cause to develop out of a primitive state

**civil service** *n*
the branch of a government that takes care of the business of running a state but that does not include the lawmaking branch, the military, or the court system

**civil war** *n*
a war between opposing groups of citizens of the same country

**[1]clack** \'klak\ *vb*
**1** PRATTLE
**2** to make or cause to make a clatter

**[2]clack** *n*
**1** rapid continous talk : CHATTER
**2** a sound of clacking ⟨the *clack* of a typewriter⟩

**clad** \'klad\ *adj*
being covered : wearing clothes

**[1]claim** \'klām\ *vb*
**1** to ask for as rightfully belonging to oneself
**2** to call for : REQUIRE ⟨business that *claims* attention⟩
**3** to state as a fact : MAINTAIN
**4** to make a claim ⟨*claims* to know nothing about it⟩

**[2]claim** *n*
**1** a demand for something due or believed to be due ⟨an insurance *claim*⟩
**2** a right to something

**citrus**
Citrus fruits are a major agricultural crop, produced in regions near the tropics for centuries. A good source of vitamin C, the flesh can be eaten, or squeezed to obtain the juice for drinking. In addition, the flesh, juice, and peel are used to flavor other foods in cooking. The peel also contains an aromatic oil that is used in soaps, perfumes, and lotions.

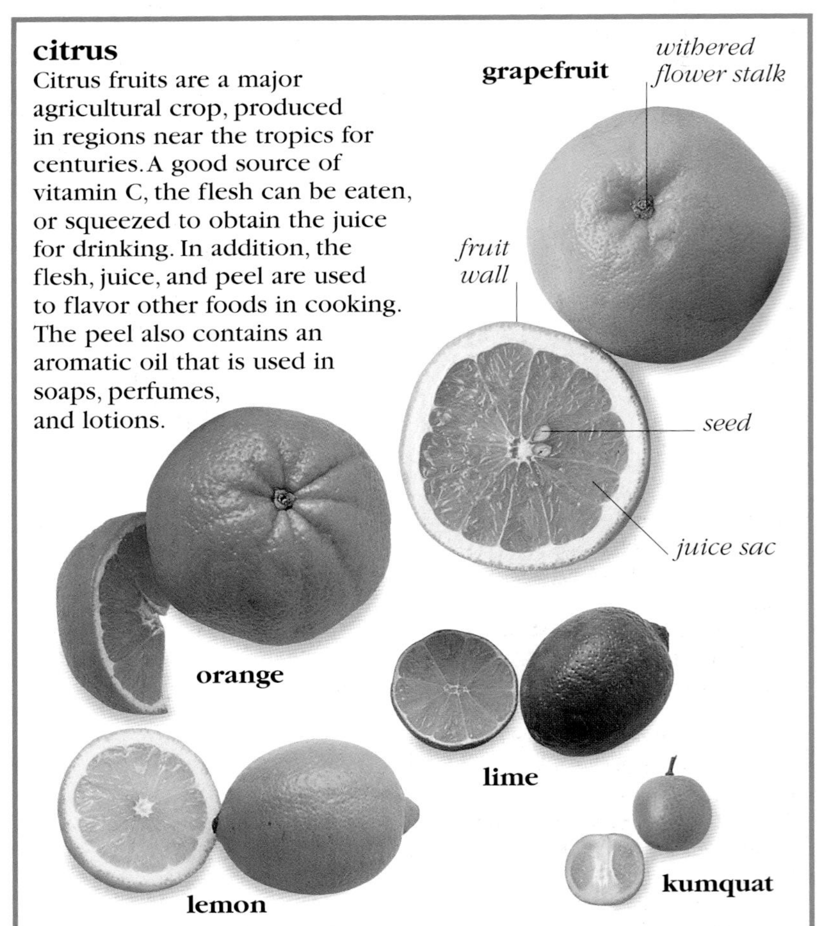

3 a statement that may be doubted
4 something (as an area of land) claimed as one's own ⟨a prospector's *claim*⟩

**[1]clam** \'klam\ *n*
▼ a shellfish with a soft body and a hinged double shell

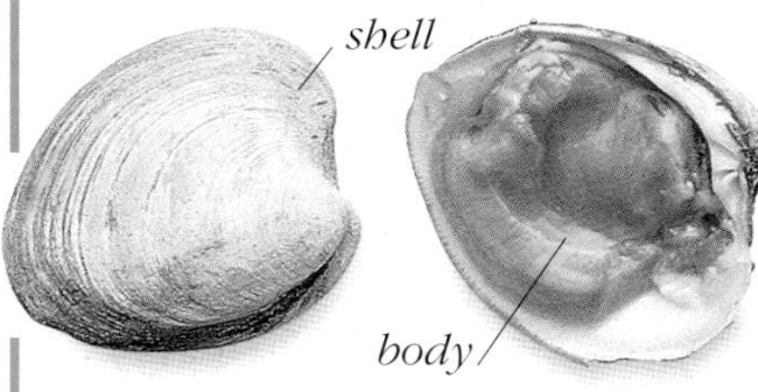

**[1]clam**

**[2]clam** *vb* **clammed**; **clam·ming**
to dig or gather clams

**clam·bake** \'klam-ˌbāk\ *n*
an outing where food is cooked usually on heated rocks covered by seaweed

**clam·ber** \'klam-bər\ *vb*
to climb in an awkward way (as by scrambling)

**clam·my** \'klam-ē\ *adj* **clam·mi·er**; **clam·mi·est**
unpleasantly damp, soft, sticky, and usually cool
**clam·mi·ly** \'klam-ə-lē\ *adv*
**clam·mi·ness** \'klam-ē-nəs\ *n*

**[1]clam·or** \'klam-ər\ *n*
1 a noisy shouting
2 a loud continous noise
3 strong and active protest or demand ⟨public *clamor* for a tax cut⟩

**[2]clamor** *vb*
to make a clamor

**clam·or·ous** \'klam-ə-rəs\ *adj*
full of clamor : very noisy

**[1]clamp** \'klamp\ *n*
► a device that holds or presses parts together firmly

**[2]clamp** *vb*
to fasten or to hold together with or as if with a clamp

**clan** \'klan\ *n*
1 a group (as in the Scottish Highlands) made up of households whose heads claim to have a common ancestor
2 a group of persons united by some common interest

**[1]clang** \'klang\ *vb*
to make or cause to make a loud ringing sound

**[2]clang** *n*
a loud ringing sound like that made by pieces of metal striking together

**[1]clank** \'klangk\ *vb*
1 to make or cause to make a clank or series of clanks ⟨the radiator hissed and *clanked*⟩
2 to move with a clank

**[2]clank** *n*
a sharp short ringing sound

**[1]clap** \'klap\ *vb* **clapped**; **clap·ping**
1 to strike noisily : SLAM, BANG ⟨*clap* two boards together⟩ ⟨the door *clapped* shut⟩
2 to strike (one's hands) together again and again in applause
3 to strike with the open hand ⟨*clap* a friend on the shoulder⟩
4 to put or place quickly or with force

**[2]clap** *n*
1 a loud noisy crash made by or as if by the striking together of two hard surfaces
2 a hard or a friendly slap

**clap·board** \'klab-ərd, -ˌōrd\ *n*
a narrow board thicker at one edge than at the other used as siding for a building

**clap·per** \'klap-ər\ *n*
one (as the tongue of a bell) that makes a clapping sound

**clar·i·fy** \'klar-ə-ˌfī\ *vb* **clar·i·fied**; **clar·i·fy·ing**
1 to make or to become pure or clear ⟨*clarify* a liquid⟩
2 to make or become more easily understood ⟨*clarify* a statement⟩

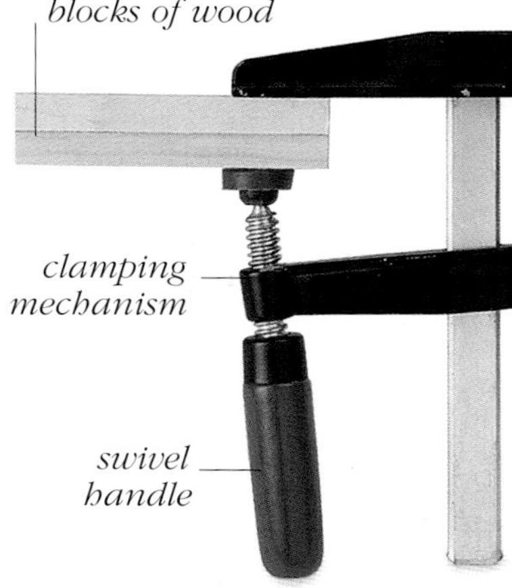

**[1]clamp:** a carpenter's clamp

**clar·i·net** \ˌklar-ə-'net\ *n*
▼ a woodwind instrument in the form of a tube with finger holes and keys

**clarinet**

**clar·i·on** \'klar-ē-ən\ *adj*
being loud and clear

**clar·i·ty** \'klar-ət-ē\ *n*
clear quality or state ⟨the *clarity* of the explanation⟩

**[1]clash** \'klash\ *vb*
1 to make or cause to make a clash ⟨*clashing* cymbals⟩
2 to come into conflict ⟨pickets *clashed* with the police⟩
3 to not match well ⟨our ideas *clashed*⟩ ⟨the colors *clashed*⟩

**[2]clash** *n*
1 a loud sharp sound usually of metal striking metal ⟨the *clash* of swords⟩
2 a struggle or strong disagreement

**[1]clasp** \'klasp\ *n*
1 a device for holding together objects or parts of something
2 [2]GRASP 1, GRIP
3 [2]EMBRACE

**[2]clasp** *vb*
1 to fasten with or as if with a clasp
2 [1]EMBRACE 1
3 [1]GRASP 1

A B C D E F G H I J K L M N O P Q R S T U V W X Y Z

**[1]class** \'klas\ *n*
**1** a group of pupils meeting at set times for study or instruction
**2** the period during which a study group meets
**3** a course of instruction ⟨a *class* in science⟩
**4** a body of students who are to graduate at the same time
**5** a group or rank of society ⟨the working *class*⟩
**6** a group of plants or animals that ranks above the order and below the phylum or division in scientific classification ⟨birds and mammals form two separate *classes* in the animal kingdom⟩
**7** a grouping or standing (as of goods or services) based on quality

**[2]class** *vb*
CLASSIFY

**[1]clas·sic** \'klas-ik\ *adj*
**1** serving as a standard of excellence
**2** fashionable year after year ⟨a *classic* style⟩
**3** of or relating to the ancient Greeks and Romans or their culture
**4** being very good or typical of its kind ⟨a *classic* example of good writing⟩

**[2]classic** *n*
**1** a written work or author of ancient Greece or Rome
**2** a great work of art
**3** something regarded as outstanding of its kind

**clas·si·cal** \'klas-i-kəl\ *adj*
**1** ▶ of or relating to the classics of literature or art and especially to the ancient Greek and Roman classics
**2** of or relating to serious music in the European tradition
**3** concerned with a general study of the arts and sciences

**clas·si·fi·ca·tion** \ˌklas-ə-fə-'kā-shən\ *n*
**1** the act of classifying or arranging in classes
**2** an arrangement in classes ⟨a *classification* of plants⟩

**clas·si·fy** \'klas-ə-ˌfī\ *vb*
**clas·si·fied**; **clas·si·fy·ing**
to group in classes

**class·mate** \'klas-ˌmāt\ *n*
a member of the same class in a school or college

**class·room** \'klas-ˌrüm, -ˌru̇m\ *n*
a room in a school or college in which classes meet

**[1]clat·ter** \'klat-ər\ *vb*
**1** to make or cause to make a rattling sound ⟨dishes *clattering* in the kitchen⟩
**2** to move or go with a clatter ⟨the cart *clattered* down the road⟩

**[2]clatter** *n*
**1** a rattling sound (as of hard objects striking together) ⟨the *clatter* of pots and pans⟩
**2** COMMOTION

**clause** \'klȯz\ *n*
**1** a separate part of a document (as a will)
**2** a group of words having its own subject and predicate but forming only part of a complete sentence ⟨"when it rained" in "when it rained they went inside" is a *clause*⟩

**clav·i·cle** \'klav-i-kəl\ *n*
COLLARBONE

**[1]claw** \'klȯ\ *n*
**1** a sharp usually thin and curved nail on the finger or toe of an animal (as a cat or bird)
**2** the end of a limb of a lower animal (as an insect, scorpion, or lobster) that is pointed or like pincers
**3** something like a claw in shape or use

**classical 1:** a classical statue of a nymph from ancient Greece

**[2]claw** *vb*
to scratch, seize, or dig with claws

**clay** \'klā\ *n*
**1** an earthy material that is sticky and easily molded when wet and hard when baked
**2** a plastic substance used like clay for modeling

**[1]clean** \'klēn\ *adj*
**1** free of dirt or evil ⟨put on a *clean* shirt⟩ ⟨the candidate has a *clean* record⟩
**2** free of objectionable behavior or language ⟨led a *clean* life⟩ ⟨a *clean* joke⟩
**3** THOROUGH 1, COMPLETE ⟨a *clean* sweep⟩
**4** having a simple graceful form : TRIM ⟨a ship with *clean* lines⟩
**5** [1]SMOOTH 1 ⟨the knife made a *clean* cut⟩

**[2]clean** *adv*
**1** so as to clean ⟨a new broom sweeps *clean*⟩
**2** in a clean way ⟨fight *clean*⟩
**3** all the way ⟨went *clean* through⟩

**[3]clean** *vb*
to make or become clean ⟨*clean* a room⟩ ⟨*clean* up for supper⟩
**clean·er** *n*

**clean·li·ness** \'klen-lē-nəs\ *n*
the condition of being clean : the habit of keeping clean

**[1]clean·ly** \'klēn-lē\ *adv*
in a clean way

**[2]clean·ly** \'klen-lē\ *adj*
**clean·li·er**; **clean·li·est**
**1** careful to keep clean ⟨a *cleanly* animal⟩
**2** kept clean ⟨*cleanly* surroundings⟩

**cleanse** \'klenz\ *vb* **cleansed**; **cleans·ing**
to make clean

**cleans·er** \'klen-zər\ *n*
a substance (as a scouring powder) used for cleaning

**[1]clear** \'klir\ *adj*
**1** BRIGHT 1, LUMINOUS ⟨*clear* sunlight⟩
**2** free of clouds, haze, or mist ⟨a *clear* day⟩
**3** UNTROUBLED ⟨a *clear* gaze⟩
**4** free of blemishes ⟨*clear* skin⟩
**5** easily seen through ⟨glass is *clear*⟩ ⟨*clear* water⟩
**6** easily heard, seen, or understood ⟨a *clear* voice⟩ ⟨the meaning is *clear*⟩
**7** free from doubt : SURE
**8** INNOCENT ⟨a *clear* conscience⟩

9 not blocked or limited ⟨a *clear* path⟩
**clear·ly** *adv*
**clear·ness** *n*

**[2]clear** *adv*
1 in a clear manner
2 all the way ⟨the hole goes *clear* through⟩

**[3]clear** *vb*
1 to make or become clear ⟨the sky *cleared*⟩
2 to go away **:** DISPERSE ⟨the clouds *cleared* away⟩
3 to free from blame ⟨*cleared* my name⟩
4 to approve or be approved by ⟨*cleared* for secret work⟩ ⟨the proposal *cleared* the committee⟩
5 EXPLAIN 1 ⟨*clear* the matter up⟩
6 to free of things blocking ⟨*clear* land of timber⟩
7 to get rid of **:** REMOVE ⟨*clear* the dishes from the table⟩
8 [4]NET
9 to go over or by without touching ⟨the hit ball *cleared* the fence⟩

**[4]clear** *n*
a clear space or part
**in the clear** free from guilt or suspicion

**clear·ance** \'klir-əns\ *n*
1 the act or process of clearing
2 the distance by which one object avoids hitting or touching another

**clear·ing** \'klir-ing\ *n*
an area of land from which trees and bushes have all been removed

**cleat** \'klēt\ *n*
1 a wooden or metal device used to fasten a line or a rope
2 ▶ a strip or projection fastened on or across something to give strength or a place to hold or to prevent slipping ⟨the *cleats* on football shoes⟩

**cleat 2:** cleats on the sole of a golf shoe

**cleav·age** \'klē-vij\ *n*
1 the tendency of a rock or mineral to split readily in one or more directions
2 the action of cleaving
3 the state of being cleft

**[1]cleave** \'klēv\ *vb* **cleaved** *or* **clove** \'klōv\; **cleav·ing**
to cling to a person or thing closely

**[2]cleave** *vb* **cleaved** *or* **cleft** \'kleft\ *or* **clove** \'klōv\; **cleaved** *or* **cleft** *or* **clo·ven** \'klō-vən\; **cleav·ing**
to divide by or as if by a cutting blow **:** SPLIT

**cleav·er** \'klē-vər\ *n*
▼ a heavy knife used for cutting up meat

**cleaver:**
a cleaver used in Chinese cooking

**clef** \'klef\ *n*
a sign placed on the staff in writing music to show what pitch is represented by each line and space

**[1]cleft** \'kleft\ *n*
1 a space or opening made by splitting or cracking **:** CREVICE
2 [1]NOTCH 1

**[2]cleft** *adj*
partly split or divided

**clem·en·cy** \'klem-ən-sē\ *n, pl* **clemencies**
1 MERCY 1
2 an act of mercy

**clench** \'klench\ *vb*
1 to hold tightly **:** CLUTCH
2 to set or close tightly ⟨*clench* your teeth⟩

**cler·gy** \'klər-jē\ *n, pl* **clergies**
the group of religious officials (as priests, ministers, and rabbis) specially prepared and authorized to lead religious services

**cler·gy·man** \'klər-ji-mən\ *n, pl* **cler·gy·men** \-mən\
a member of the clergy

**cler·i·cal** \'kler-i-kəl\ *adj*
1 of or relating to the clergy
2 of or relating to a clerk or office worker

**[1]clerk** \'klərk\ *n*
1 a person whose job is to keep records or accounts ⟨city *clerk*⟩
2 a salesperson in a store

**[2]clerk** *vb*
to act or work as a clerk

**clev·er** \'klev-ər\ *adj*
1 showing skill especially in using one's hands
2 having a quick inventive mind ⟨a *clever* designer⟩
3 showing wit or imagination ⟨a *clever* joke⟩ **synonyms** see INTELLIGENT
**clev·er·ly** *adv*
**clev·er·ness** *n*

**[1]click** \'klik\ *vb*
1 to make or cause to make a click ⟨*click* your tongue⟩
2 to fit in or work together smoothly ⟨by the middle of the season the team *clicked*⟩
3 to select or make a selection especially on a computer by pressing a button on a control device (as a mouse) ⟨*click* on the printer icon⟩

**[2]click** *n*
a slight sharp noise

**click·er** \'kli-kər\ *n*
REMOTE CONTROL 2

**cli·ent** \'klī-ənt\ *n*
a person who uses the professional advice or services of another ⟨a lawyer's *client*⟩

**cli·en·tele** \,klī-ən-'tel\ *n*
a group of clients

**cliff** \'klif\ *n*
▼ a high steep surface of rock

**cliff:** model of a cliff

A B C D E F G H I J K L M N O P Q R S T U V W X Y Z

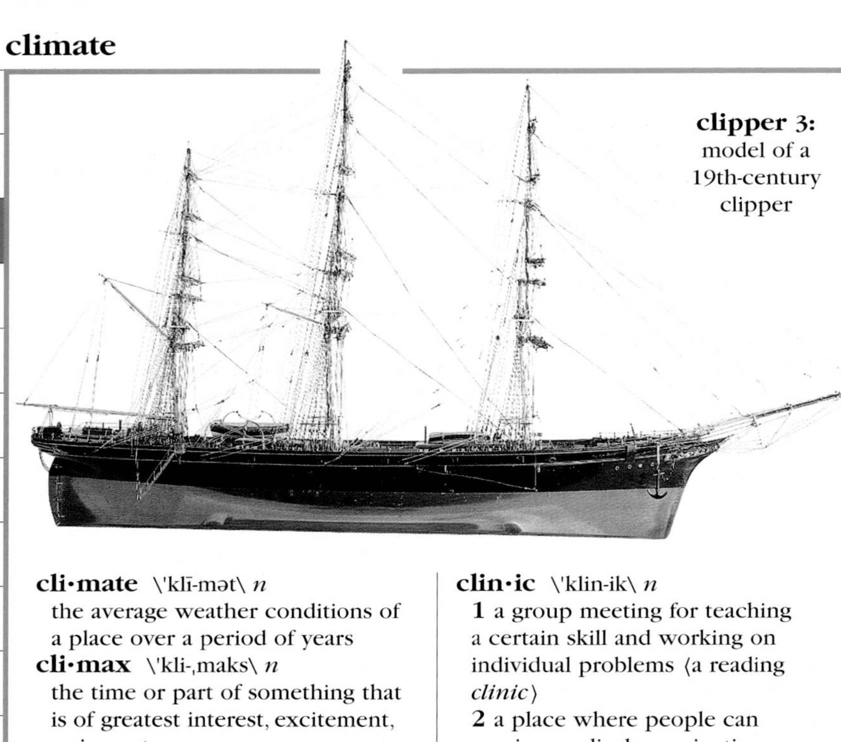

**clipper 3:** model of a 19th-century clipper

**cli·mate** \'klī-mət\ *n*
the average weather conditions of a place over a period of years

**cli·max** \'klī-ˌmaks\ *n*
the time or part of something that is of greatest interest, excitement, or importance

**¹climb** \'klīm\ *vb*
**1** to rise little by little to a higher point ⟨smoke *climbing* in the air⟩
**2** to go up or down often with the help of the hands in holding or pulling
**3** to go upward in growing (as by winding around something) ⟨a *climbing* vine⟩ **synonyms** see ASCEND
**climb·er** \'klī-mər\ *n*

**²climb** *n*
**1** a place where climbing is necessary
**2** the act of climbing

**clime** \'klīm\ *n*
CLIMATE

**¹clinch** \'klinch\ *vb*
**1** to turn over or flatten the end of (as a nail sticking out of a board)
**2** to fasten by clinching
**3** to show to be certain or true ⟨facts that *clinched* the argument⟩

**²clinch** *n*
a fastening with a clinched nail, bolt, or rivet **:** the clinched part of a nail, bolt, or rivet

**cling** \'kling\ *vb* **clung** \'kləng\; **cling·ing**
**1** to hold fast or stick closely to a surface
**2** to hold fast by grasping or winding around ⟨*cling* to a ladder⟩
**3** to remain close ⟨*clings* to the family⟩

**clin·ic** \'klin-ik\ *n*
**1** a group meeting for teaching a certain skill and working on individual problems ⟨a reading *clinic*⟩
**2** a place where people can receive medical examinations and usually treatment for minor ailments ⟨outpatient *clinic*⟩

**¹clink** \'klingk\ *vb*
to make or cause to make a slight short sound like that of metal being struck

**²clink** *n*
a clinking sound

**¹clip** \'klip\ *vb* **clipped**; **clip·ping**
to fasten with a clip ⟨*clip* the papers together⟩

**²clip** *n*
a device that holds or hooks

**³clip** *vb* **clipped**; **clip·ping**
**1** to shorten or remove by cutting (as with shears or scissors) ⟨*clip* a hedge⟩ ⟨*clip* out a news item⟩
**2** to cut off or trim the hair or wool of ⟨have a dog *clipped*⟩

**⁴clip** *n*
**1** an instrument with two blades for cutting the nails
**2** a sharp blow
**3** a rapid pace ⟨moved along at a good *clip*⟩

**clip art** *n*
ready-made illustrations sold in books or as software from which they may be taken for use in a printed work

**clip·board** \'klip-ˌbōrd\ *n*
**1** a small board with a clip at the top for holding papers
**2** a part of computer memory that is used to store data (as items to be copied to another file) temporarily

**clip·per** \'klip-ər\ *n*
**1** a person who clips
**2 clippers** *pl* a device used for clipping especially hair or nails
**3** ◀ a fast sailing ship with usually three tall masts and large square sails

**clip·ping** \'klip-ing\ *n*
something cut out or off ⟨grass *clippings*⟩ ⟨a newspaper *clipping*⟩

**clique** \'klēk, 'klik\ *n*
a small group of people that keep out outsiders

**¹cloak** \'klōk\ *n*
**1** a long loose outer garment
**2** something that hides or covers ⟨a *cloak* of secrecy surrounded the talks⟩

**²cloak** *vb*
to cover or hide with a cloak

**cloak·room** \'klō-ˌkrüm, -ˌkru̇m\ *n*
a room (as in a school) in which coats and hats may be kept

**¹clock** \'kläk\ *n*
▶ a device for measuring or telling the time and especially one not meant to be worn or carried by a person

**²clock** *vb*
**1** to time (as a person or a piece of work) by a timing device
**2** to show (as time or speed) on a recording device

**clock·wise** \'kläk-ˌwīz\ *adv or adj*
in the direction in which the hands of a clock turn

**clock·work** \'kläk-ˌwərk\ *n*
machinery (as in mechanical toys) like that which makes clocks go

**clod** \'kläd\ *n*
**1** a lump or mass especially of earth or clay
**2** a clumsy or stupid person

**¹clog** \'kläg\ *n*
**1** something that hinders or holds back
**2** a shoe having a thick usually wooden sole

**²clog** *vb* **clogged**; **clog·ging**
to make passage through difficult or impossible **:** PLUG ⟨snow *clogged* the roads⟩ ⟨a toy fell down the drain and *clogged* it up⟩

**¹clois·ter** \'klȯi-stər\ *n*
**1** MONASTERY, CONVENT
**2** a covered usually arched passage along or around the walls of a court

**²cloister** *vb*
**1** to shut away from the world
**2** to surround with a cloister

**clop** \'kläp\ *n*
a sound like that of a hoof against pavement

**[1]close** \'klōz\ *vb* **closed**; **clos•ing**
**1** to stop up : prevent passage through ⟨*close* a gap⟩ ⟨the street was *closed*⟩
**2** to fill or cause to fill an opening ⟨the door *closed* softly⟩
**3** to bring or come to an end ⟨*close* an account⟩ ⟨then the meeting *closed*⟩
**4** to end the operation of ⟨*closed* the school⟩
**5** to bring the parts or edges of together ⟨*closed* a book⟩
**6** [1]APPROACH 1 ⟨night *closed* in⟩

**[2]close** \'klōz\ *n*
the point at which something ends

**[3]close** \'klōs\ *adj* **clos•er**; **clos•est**
**1** having little space in which to move ⟨a *close* prisoner⟩ ⟨in *close* quarters⟩
**2** SECRETIVE
**3** lacking fresh or moving air ⟨a *close* room⟩
**4** not generous ⟨*close* with money⟩
**5** not far apart in space, time, degree, or effect ⟨*close* neighbors⟩ ⟨it's *close* to nine o'clock⟩
**6** [1]SHORT 1 ⟨a *close* haircut⟩
**7** very like ⟨the material is a *close* match with the curtains⟩
**8** having a strong liking each one for the other ⟨*close* friends⟩
**9** strict and careful in attention to details ⟨*close* examination⟩
**10** decided by a narrow margin ⟨a *close* election⟩
**close•ly** *adv*
**close•ness** *n*

**[4]close** \'klōs\ *adv*
[1]NEAR 1

**close call** \'klōs-\ *n*
a barely successful escape from a difficult or dangerous situation

**closed** \'klōzd\ *adj*
**1** not open ⟨a *closed* door⟩
**2** having mathematical elements that when subjected to an operation produce only elements of the same set ⟨whole numbers are *closed* under addition and multiplication⟩

**[1]clos•et** \'kläz-ət\ *n*
**1** a small room for privacy
**2** a small room for clothing or for supplies for the house ⟨clothes *closet*⟩

**[2]closet** *vb*
**1** to shut up in or as if in a closet
**2** to take into a private room for an interview

**close–up** \'klō-ˌsəp\ *n*
a photograph taken at close range

**clo•sure** \'klō-zhər\ *n*
**1** an act of closing
**2** the condition of being closed

**[1]clot** \'klät\ *n*
a lump made by some substance getting thicker and sticking together ⟨a blood *clot*⟩

**[2]clot** *vb* **clot•ted**; **clot•ting**
to thicken into a clot

**cloth** \'klȯth\ *n, pl* **cloths** \'klȯt͟hz, 'klȯths\
**1** a woven or knitted material (as of cotton or nylon)
**2** a piece of cloth for a certain use ⟨a polishing *cloth*⟩
**3** TABLECLOTH

**[1]clock**

There are 12 hours marked on a clock face, with time indicated by an hour hand and a minute hand. Some clocks also have a hand that measures the seconds, circling the face once every minute. There are different styles of clock, including traditional as well as modern digital types.

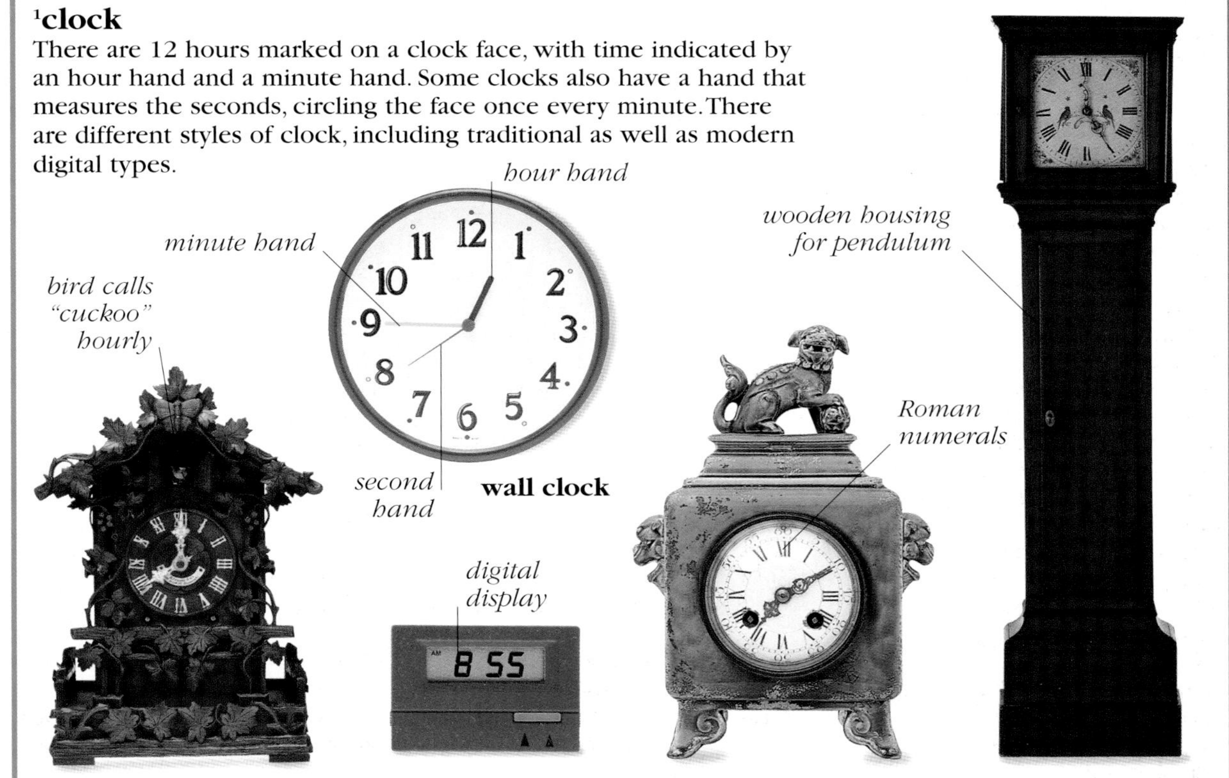


cuckoo clock · digital alarm clock · mantel clock · grandfather clock

**clothe** \'klōth\ *vb* **clothed** *or* **clad** \'klad\; **cloth·ing**
**1** to cover with or as if with clothing : DRESS
**2** to provide with clothes ⟨fed and *clothed* my family⟩
**3** to express in a certain way ⟨*clothed* their ideas in badly chosen words⟩

**clothes** \'klōz, 'klōthz\ *n pl*
CLOTHING 1

**clothes moth** *n*
a small yellowish moth whose larvae feed on wool, fur, and feathers

**clothes·pin** \'klōz-,pin, 'klōthz-\ *n*
a peg (as of wood) with the lower part slit or a clamp for holding clothes in place on a line

**cloth·ing** \'klō-thing\ *n*
**1** covering for the human body
**2** COVERING

**[1]cloud** \'klaůd\ *n*
**1** ▼ a visible mass of tiny bits of water or ice hanging in the air usually high above the earth
**2** a visible mass of small particles in the air ⟨a *cloud* of dust⟩
**3** something thought to be like a cloud ⟨a *cloud* of mosquitoes⟩
**cloud·less** \-ləs\ *adj*

**[2]cloud** *vb*
**1** to make or become cloudy
**2** to darken or hide as if by a cloud

**cloud·burst** \'klaůd-,bərst\ *n*
a sudden heavy rainfall

**cloudy** \'klaůd-ē\ *adj* **cloud·i·er**; **cloud·i·est**
**1** overspread with clouds ⟨a *cloudy* sky⟩
**2** showing confusion ⟨*cloudy* thinking⟩
**3** not clear ⟨a *cloudy* liquid⟩
**cloud·i·ness** *n*

**[1]clout** \'klaůt\ *n*
a blow especially with the hand

**[2]clout** *vb*
to hit hard

### [1]cloud 1

Clouds form when air containing water vapor rises and cools, changing into tiny water droplets or ice crystals. Clouds are grouped by their altitude and appearance, although this varies according to where they are in the world, the season, and the time of day. Low-lying clouds, such as cumulus, nimbostratus, and stratus, form at less than $1\frac{1}{2}$ miles (2 km) above sea level. Mid-level clouds, such as altocumulus and cumulonimbus, lie at $1\frac{1}{4}$–3 miles (2–5 km) in altitude. High-level clouds are wispy, and form at 3–$7\frac{1}{2}$ miles (5–12 km) above ground.

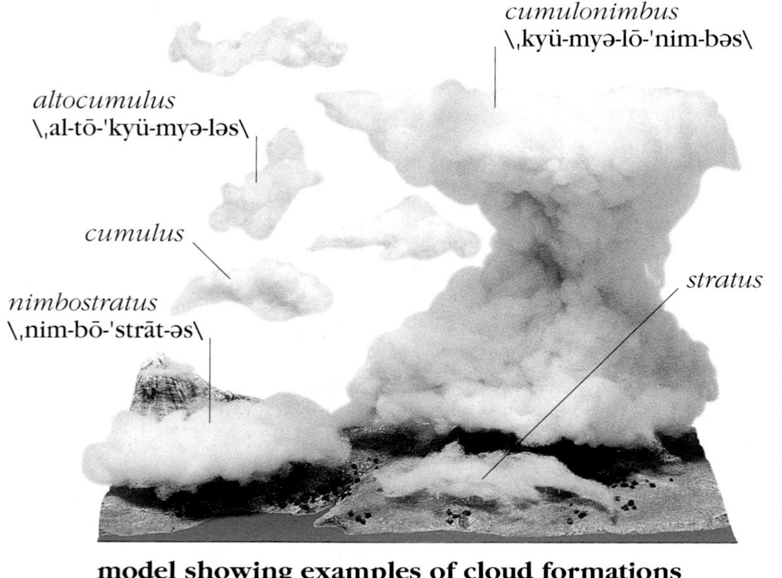


**model showing examples of cloud formations**

**[1]clove** \'klōv\ *n*
the dried flower bud of a tropical tree used as a spice

**[2]clove** *past of* CLEAVE

**clo·ven** \'klō-vən\ *past participle of* [2]CLEAVE

**cloven hoof** *n*
a hoof (as of a cow) with the front part divided into two sections

**clo·ver** \'klō-vər\ *n*
▶ any of various plants grown for hay and pasture that have leaves with three leaflets and usually roundish red, white, yellow, or purple flower heads

**clover:**
red clover

**[1]clown** \'klaůn\ *n*
**1** a rude and often stupid person
**2** a performer (as in a play or circus) who entertains by playing tricks and who usually wears comical clothes and makeup

**[2]clown** *vb*
to act like a clown : SHOW OFF

**[1]club** \'kləb\ *n*
**1** a heavy usually wooden stick used as a weapon
**2** a stick or bat used to hit a ball in various games ⟨golf *club*⟩
**3** a group of people associated because of a shared interest
**4** the meeting place of a club

**[2]club** *vb* **clubbed**; **club·bing**
to beat or strike with or as if with a club

**club·house** \'kləb-,haůs\ *n*
**1** a house used by a club
**2** locker rooms used by an athletic team

**club moss** *n*
a low often trailing evergreen plant that forms spores instead of seeds

**[1]cluck** \'klək\ *vb*
to make or call with a cluck

**[2]cluck** *n*
the call of a hen especially to her chicks

**clue** \'klü\ *n*
something that helps a person to find something or to solve a mystery

**¹clump** \'kləmp\ *n*
**1** a group of things clustered together ⟨a *clump* of bushes⟩
**2** a cluster or lump of something
**3** a heavy tramping sound
**²clump** *vb*
**1** to walk clumsily and noisily
**2** to form or cause to form clumps
**clum·sy** \'kləm-zē\ *adj*
**clum·si·er; clum·si·est**
**1** lacking skill or grace in movement ⟨*clumsy* fingers⟩
**2** not knowing how to get along with others
**3** badly or awkwardly made or done
**clum·si·ly** \-zə-lē\ *adv*
**clum·si·ness** \-zē-nəs\ *n*
**clung** *past of* CLING
**¹clus·ter** \'kləs-tər\ *n*
a number of similar things growing, collected, or grouped closely together : BUNCH ⟨a *cluster* of houses⟩
**²cluster** *vb*
to grow, collect, or assemble in a cluster
**¹clutch** \'kləch\ *vb*
**1** to grasp or hold tightly with or as if with the hands or claws
**2** to make a grab ⟨*clutching* at the falling child⟩
**²clutch** *n*
**1** the state of being clutched
**2** a device for gripping an object
**3** a coupling for connecting and disconnecting a driving and a driven part in machinery
**4** a lever or pedal operating a clutch
**¹clut·ter** \'klət-ər\ *vb*
to throw into disorder : fill or cover with scattered things
**²clutter** *n*
a crowded or confused collection : DISORDER
**co-** *prefix*
**1** with : together : joint : jointly
**2** in or to the same degree
**3** fellow : partner ⟨*co*author⟩

**¹coach** \'kōch\ *n*
**1** a large carriage that has four wheels and a raised seat outside in front for the driver and is drawn by horses
**2** a railroad passenger car without berths
**3** a class of passenger transportation in an airplane at a lower fare than first class
**4** a person who teaches students individually
**5** a person who instructs or trains a performer or team
**²coach** *vb*
to act as coach
**coach·man** \'kōch-mən\ *n, pl* **coach·men** \-mən\
a person whose business is driving a coach or carriage
**co·ag·u·late** \kō-'ag-yə-ˌlāt\ *vb*
**co·ag·u·lat·ed; co·ag·u·lat·ing**
to gather into a thick compact mass : CLOT

rotting vegetation
vegetation is pressed together to form peat
compressed peat forms brown coal
brown coal becomes bituminous coal
anthracite is the hardest coal
**coal 2:** layers showing how coal forms over millions of years

**¹coast:** a section of coast

**coal** \'kōl\ *n*
**1** a piece of glowing or charred wood : EMBER
**2** ▲ a black solid mineral substance that is formed by the partial decay of vegetable matter under the influence of moisture and often increased pressure and temperature within the earth and is mined for use as a fuel
**coarse** \'kōrs\ *adj*
**1** of poor or ordinary quality
**2** made up of large particles ⟨*coarse* sand⟩
**3** being harsh or rough ⟨*coarse* dry skin⟩ ⟨a *coarse* fabric⟩
**4** crude in taste, manners, or language
**coarse·ly** *adv*
**coarse·ness** *n*
**coars·en** \'kōrs-n\ *vb*
to make or become coarse ⟨hands *coarsened* by hard labor⟩
**¹coast** \'kōst\ *n*
◀ the land near a shore
**²coast** *vb*
**1** to slide downhill by the force of gravity over snow or ice
**2** to move along (as on a bicycle when not pedaling) without applying power
**coast·al** \'kōst-l\ *adj*
of, relating to, or located on, near, or along a coast ⟨*coastal* trade⟩

**coast·er** \'kō-stər\ *n*
**1** someone or something that coasts
**2** a sled or small wagon used in coasting

**coast guard** *n*
a military force that guards a coast

[1]**coat** \'kōt\ *n*
**1** an outer garment that differs in length and style according to fashion or use
**2** the outer covering (as fur or feathers) of an animal
**3** a layer of material covering a surface ⟨a *coat* of paint⟩
**coat·ed** \-əd\ *adj*

[2]**coat** *vb*
to cover with a coat or covering

**coat·ing** \'kōt-ing\ *n*
[1]COAT 3, COVERING ⟨a thin *coating* of ice⟩

**coat of arms**
the heraldic arms belonging to a person, family, or group or a representation of these (as on a shield)

**coat of mail**
a garment of metal scales or rings worn long ago as armor

**co·au·thor** \'kō-'ò-thər\ *n*
an author who works with another author

**coax** \'kōks\ *vb*
**1** to influence by gentle urging, special attention, or flattering
**2** to get or win by means of gentle urging or flattery ⟨*coaxed* a raise from the boss⟩

**cob** \'käb\ *n*
CORNCOB

**co·balt** \'kō-,bȯlt\ *n*
a tough shiny silvery white metallic chemical element found with iron and nickel

**cob·bled** \'käb-əld\ *adj*
paved or covered with cobblestones

**cob·bler** \'käb-lər\ *n*
**1** a person who mends or makes shoes
**2** a fruit pie with a thick upper crust and no bottom crust that is baked in a deep dish

**cob·ble·stone** \'käb-əl-,stōn\ *n*
a naturally rounded stone larger than a pebble and smaller than a boulder once used in paving streets

**co·bra** \'kō-brə\ *n*
◀ a very poisonous snake of Asia and Africa that puffs out the skin around its neck into a hood when excited

*extended hood*

**cobra**

**cob·web** \'käb-,web\ *n*
**1** the network spread by a spider : SPIDERWEB
**2** tangles of threads of a cobweb ⟨brushed the *cobwebs* off the old book⟩

**co·caine** \kō-'kān\ *n*
a habit-forming drug obtained from the leaves of a South American shrub and sometimes used as a medicine to deaden pain

**coc·cus** \'käk-əs\ *n*, *pl* **coc·ci** \'käk-,sī, -ī, -,sē, -,ē\
a bacterium shaped like a ball

[1]**cock** \'käk\ *n*
**1** a male bird : ROOSTER
**2** a faucet or valve for controlling the flow of a liquid or a gas
**3** a cocked position of the hammer of a gun ⟨a rifle at half *cock*⟩

[2]**cock** *vb*
**1** to draw back the hammer of (a gun) in readiness for firing ⟨*cock* a pistol⟩
**2** to set or draw back in readiness for some action ⟨*cock* your arm to throw⟩
**3** to turn or tip upward or to one side

[3]**cock** *n*
the act of tipping at an angle : TILT

**cock·a·too** \'käk-ə-,tü\ *n*, *pl* **cock·a·toos**
any of several large, noisy, and usually brightly colored crested parrots mostly of Australia

**cock·eyed** \'käk-'īd\ *adj*
**1** tilted to one side
**2** FOOLISH ⟨a *cockeyed* plan⟩

**cock·le** \'käk-əl\ *n*
an edible shellfish with a shell that has two parts and is shaped like a heart

**cock·le·bur** \'käk-əl-,bər, 'kək-\ *n*
a plant with prickly fruit that is related to the thistles

**cock·le·shell** \'käk-əl-,shel\ *n*
a shell of a cockle

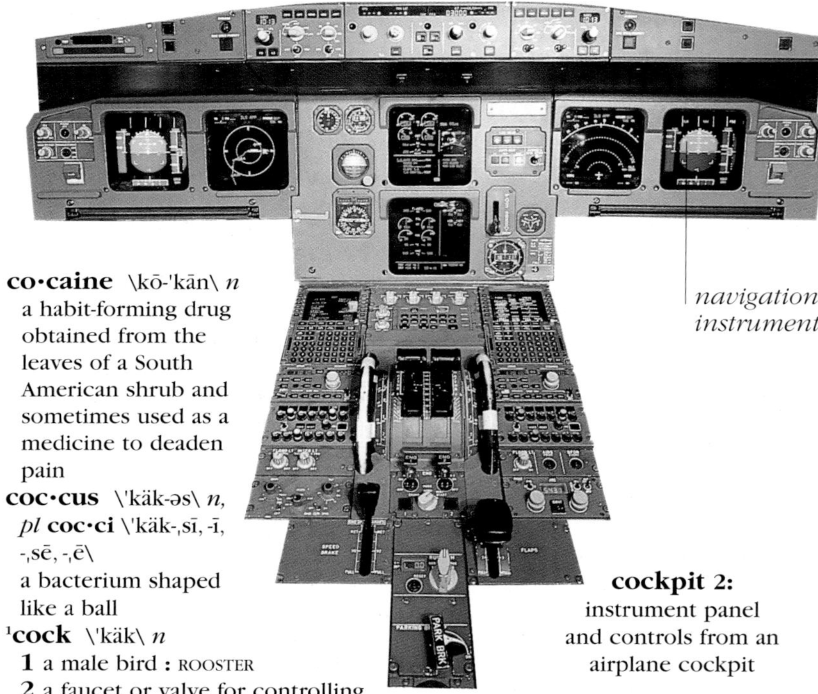


**cockpit 2:** instrument panel and controls from an airplane cockpit

**cock·pit** \'käk-,pit\ *n*
**1** an open space in the deck from which a small boat (as a yacht) is steered
**2** ▲ a space or compartment in an airplane from which it is piloted

**cock·roach** \'käk-,rōch\ *n*
a troublesome insect found in houses and ships and active chiefly at night

**cocky** \'käk-ē\ *adj* **cock·i·er**; **cock·i·est**
very sure of oneself : boldly self-confident

**co·coa** \'kō-kō\ *n*
**1** chocolate ground to a powder after some of its fat is removed
**2** a drink made from cocoa powder

**co·co·nut** \'kō-kə-nət, -ˌnət\ *n*
a large nutlike fruit that has a thick husk and grows on a tall tropical palm (**coconut palm**)

**co·coon** \kə-'kün\ *n*
the silky covering which caterpillars make around themselves and in which they are protected while changing into butterflies or moths

**cod** \'käd\ *n, pl* **cod**
▼ a large food fish found in the deep colder parts of the northern Atlantic Ocean

**cod**

**cod·dle** \'käd-l\ *vb* **cod·dled**; **cod·dling**
**1** to cook slowly in water below the boiling point ⟨*coddle* eggs⟩
**2** to treat with very much and usually too much care : PAMPER

**[1]code** \'kōd\ *n*
**1** a collection of laws arranged in some orderly way ⟨criminal *code*⟩
**2** a system of rules or principles ⟨moral *code*⟩
**3** a system of signals or letters and symbols with special meanings used for sending messages
**4** GENETIC CODE

**[2]code** *vb* **cod·ed**; **cod·ing**
to put in the form of a code

**cod·fish** \'käd-ˌfish\ *n, pl* **codfish** *or* **cod·fish·es**
COD

**cod·ger** \'käj-ər\ *n*
an odd or cranky man

**co·erce** \kō-'ərs\ *vb* **co·erced**; **co·erc·ing**
[2]FORCE 1, COMPEL

**cof·fee** \'kȯ-fē\ *n*
**1** a drink made from the roasted and ground seeds of a tropical plant
**2** the seeds of the coffee plant

**cof·fee·pot** \'kȯ-fē-ˌpät\ *n*
a covered utensil for preparing or serving coffee

**coffee table** *n*
a low table usually placed in front of a sofa

**cof·fer** \'kȯ-fər\ *n*
a box used especially for holding money and valuables

**cof·fin** \'kȯ-fən\ *n*
a box or case to hold a dead body

**cog** \'käg\ *n*
a tooth on the rim of a wheel or gear

**cog·i·tate** \'käj-ə-ˌtāt\ *vb* **cog·i·tat·ed**; **cog·i·tat·ing**
to think over : PONDER

**cog·i·ta·tion** \ˌkäj-ə-'tā-shən\ *n*
MEDITATION

**cog·wheel** \'käg-ˌhwēl, -ˌwēl\ *n*
▶ a wheel with cogs on the rim

**co·he·sion** \kō-'hē-zhən\ *n*
**1** the action of sticking together
**2** the force of attraction between the molecules in a mass

**[1]coil** \'kȯil\ *vb*
**1** to wind into rings or a spiral ⟨*coil* a rope⟩
**2** to form or lie in a coil

**[2]coil** *n*
**1** a circle, a series of circles, or a spiral made by coiling
**2** something coiled

*a quarter is a 25-cent coin*
*a penny is a 1-cent coin*
*a dime is a 10-cent coin*
*a nickel is a 5-cent coin*

**[1]coin 1:** a range of US coins

**[1]coin** \'kȯin\ *n*
**1** ▲ a piece of metal put out by government authority as money
**2** metal money ⟨change these bills for *coin*⟩

**[2]coin** *vb*
**1** to make coins especially by stamping pieces of metal : MINT
**2** to make metal (as gold or silver) into coins
**3** to make up (a new word or phrase)

**coin·age** \'kȯi-nij\ *n*
**1** the act or process of coining
**2** something coined

**co·in·cide** \ˌkō-ən-'sīd\ *vb* **co·in·cid·ed**; **co·in·cid·ing**
**1** to occupy the same space
**2** to happen at the same time
**3** to agree exactly

**co·in·ci·dence** \kō-'in-sə-dəns\ *n*
**1** a coinciding in space or time
**2** two things that happen at the same time by accident but seem to have some connection

**coke** \'kōk\ *n*
gray lumps of fuel made by heating soft coal in a closed chamber until some of its gases have passed off

**col-** see COM-

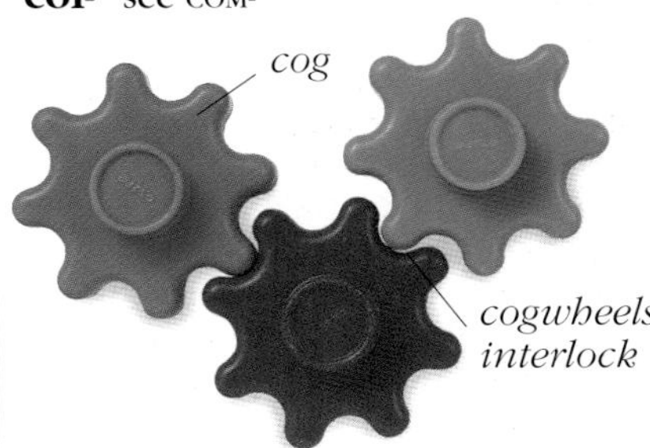


**cogwheel:** toy plastic cogwheels

**col·an·der** \'kəl-ən-dər, 'käl-\ *n*
a utensil with small holes for draining foods

**[1]cold** \'kōld\ *adj*
**1** having a low temperature or one much below normal ⟨a *cold* day⟩
**2** lacking warmth of feeling : UNFRIENDLY
**3** suffering from lack of warmth ⟨feel *cold*⟩
**cold·ly** *adv*
**cold·ness** *n*

**[2]cold** *n*
**1** a condition of low temperature : cold weather
**2** the bodily feeling produced by lack of warmth : CHILL
**3** COMMON COLD

**cold–blood·ed** \'kōld-'bləd-əd\ *adj*
**1** lacking or showing a lack of normal human feelings ⟨a *cold-blooded* criminal⟩
**2** having a body temperature that varies with the temperature of the environment ⟨frogs are *cold-blooded* animals⟩
**3** sensitive to cold

**co·le·us** \'kō-lē-əs\ *n*
a plant of the mint family grown for its many-colored leaves

**col·ic** \'käl-ik\ *n*
sharp pain in the bowels
**col·icky** \'käl-ə-kē\ *adj*

**col·i·se·um** \,käl-ə-'sē-əm\ *n*
▼ a large structure (as a stadium) for athletic contests or public entertainment

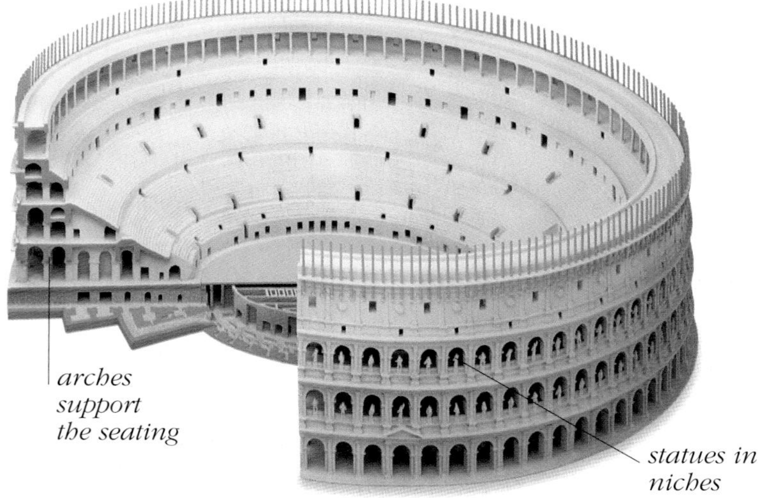


**coliseum:** reconstruction of the Coliseum, built in ancient Rome, Italy

**[1]col·lar** \'käl-ər\ *n*
**1** a band, strap, or chain worn around the neck or the neckline of a garment
**2** a part of the harness of draft animals fitted over the shoulders
**3** something (as a ring to hold a pipe in place) that is like a collar
**col·lar·less** \-ləs\ *adj*

**col·lab·o·rate** \kə-'lab-ə-,rāt\ *vb*
**col·lab·o·rat·ed**; **col·lab·o·rat·ing**
**1** to work with others (as in writing a book)
**2** to cooperate with an enemy force that has taken over one's country

**col·lage** \kə-'läzh\ *n*
a work of art made by gluing pieces of different materials to a flat surface

**[1]col·lapse** \kə-'laps\ *vb*
**col·lapsed**; **col·laps·ing**
**1** to break down completely : fall in
**2** to shrink together suddenly
**3** to suffer a physical or mental breakdown
**4** to fold together ⟨the umbrella *collapses* to pocket size⟩

**[2]collapse** *n*
the act or an instance of collapsing : BREAKDOWN

**col·laps·ible** \kə-'lap-sə-bəl\ *adj*
capable of collapsing or possible to collapse

**[2]collar** *vb*
**1** to seize by or as if by the collar : CAPTURE, GRAB
**2** to put a collar on

**col·lar·bone** \'käl-ər-,bōn\ *n*
a bone of the shoulder joined to the breastbone and the shoulder blade

**col·league** \'käl-,ēg\ *n*
an associate in a profession : a fellow worker

**col·lect** \kə-'lekt\ *vb*
**1** to bring or come together into one body or place
**2** to gather from a number of sources ⟨*collect* stamps⟩ ⟨*collect* taxes⟩
**3** to gain or regain control of ⟨*collected* my thoughts⟩
**4** to receive payment for ⟨*collect* a bill⟩ **synonyms** see GATHER

**col·lect·ed** \kə-'lek-təd\ *adj*
[3]CALM 2

**col·lec·tion** \kə-'lek-shən\ *n*
**1** the act or process of gathering together ⟨the *collection* of mail by the letter carrier⟩
**2** something collected and especially a group of objects gathered for study or exhibition
**3** a gathering of money (as for charitable purposes)

**col·lec·tive** \kə-'lek-tiv\ *adj*
**1** having to do with a number of persons or things thought of as a whole ⟨*collective* nouns⟩
**2** done or shared by a number of persons as a group ⟨made a *collective* effort⟩
**col·lec·tive·ly** *adv*

**col·lec·tor** \kə-'lek-tər\ *n*
**1** a person or thing that collects ⟨stamp *collector*⟩
**2** a person whose business it is to collect money ⟨a bill *collector*⟩

**col·lege** \'käl-ij\ *n*
a school higher than a high school

**col·le·giate** \kə-'lē-jət\ *adj*
**1** having to do with a college ⟨*collegiate* studies⟩
**2** of, relating to, or characteristic of college students ⟨*collegiate* clothes⟩ ⟨*collegiate* humor⟩

**col·lide** \kə-'līd\ *vb* **col·lid·ed**; **col·lid·ing**
**1** to strike against each other
**2** [1]CLASH 2

**col·lie** \'käl-ē\ *n*
▼ a large usually long-coated dog of a Scottish breed used to herd sheep

**collie**

**col·li·sion** \kə-'lizh-ən\ *n*
an act or instance of colliding

**col·lo·qui·al** \kə-'lō-kwē-əl\ *adj*
used in or suited to familiar and informal conversation

**col·lo·qui·al·ism** \kə-'lō-kwē-ə-,liz-əm\ *n*
a colloquial word or expression

**co·logne** \kə-'lōn\ *n*
a perfumed liquid made up of alcohol and fragrant oils

**[1]co·lon** \'kō-lən\ *n*
the main part of the large intestine

**[2]colon** *n*
a punctuation mark : used mostly to call attention to what follows (as a list, explanation, or quotation)

**col·o·nel** \'kərn-l\ *n*
a commissioned officer in the Army, Air Force, or Marine Corps ranking above a lieutenant colonel

**[1]co·lo·nial** \kə-'lō-nē-əl\ *adj*
**1** of, relating to, or characteristic of a colony
**2** *often cap* of or relating to the original thirteen colonies that formed the United States

**[2]colonial** *n*
a member of or a person living in a colony

**col·o·nist** \'käl-ə-nəst\ *n*
**1** a person living in a colony
**2** a person who helps to found a colony

**col·o·nize** \'käl-ə-ˌnīz\ *vb*
**col·o·nized**; **col·o·niz·ing**
**1** to establish a colony in or on
**2** to settle in a colony

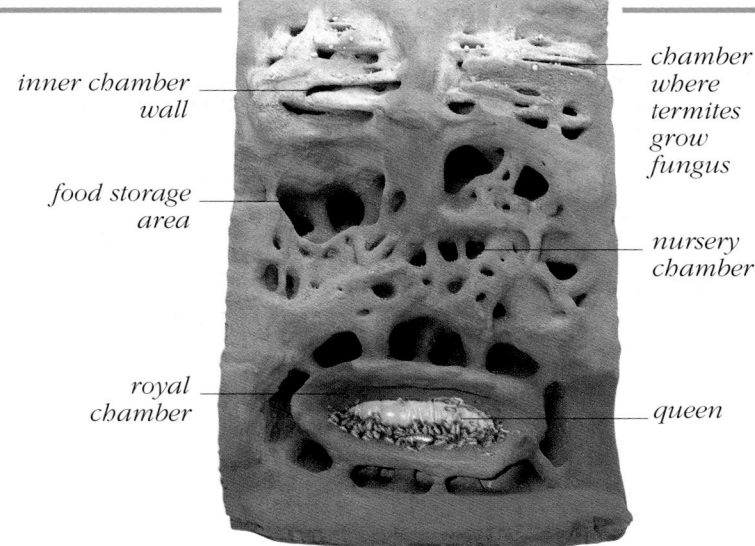

**colony 3:** cross section of a termite colony in the center of a mound

**col·on·nade** \ˌkäl-ə-'nād\ *n*
a row of columns usually supporting the base of a roof structure

**col·o·ny** \'käl-ə-nē\ *n*, *pl* **col·o·nies**
**1** a group of people sent out by a state to a new territory **:** the territory in which these people settle
**2** a distant territory belonging to or under the control of a nation
**3** ▲ a group of living things of one kind living together ⟨a *colony* of ants⟩
**4** a group of people with common qualities or interests located in close association ⟨an art *colony*⟩

**[1]color 1**

The color of an object is the way in which our eyes interpret light reflecting from it. In painting, the main, or primary, colors are red, blue, and yellow. If these three colors are combined, they create black. Mixing two primary colors makes the secondary colors orange, green, and violet. Further combinations make many more shades of color.

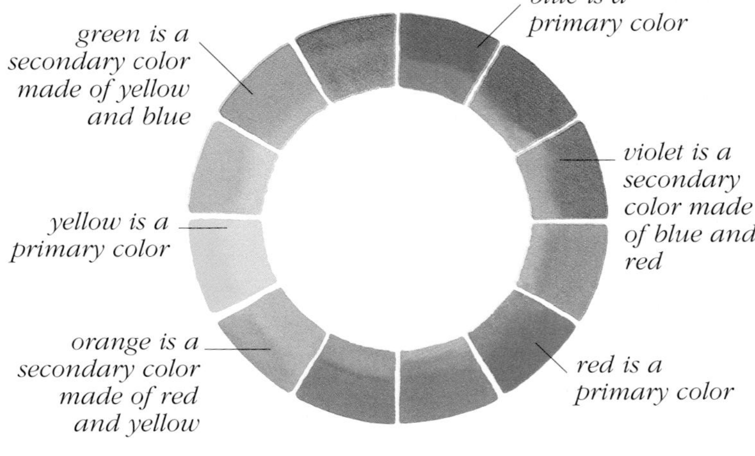

blue is a primary color
green is a secondary color made of yellow and blue
violet is a secondary color made of blue and red
yellow is a primary color
orange is a secondary color made of red and yellow
red is a primary color

**watercolor diagram of color relationships**

**[1]col·or** \'kəl-ər\ *n*
**1** ◄ the appearance of a thing apart from size and shape when light strikes it ⟨red is the *color* of blood⟩
**2** a hue other than black, white, or gray ⟨dressed in bright *colors*⟩
**3** outward show **:** APPEARANCE
**4** the normal rosy tint of skin
**5** [1]BLUSH
**6** **colors** *pl* an identifying flag
**7** **colors** *pl* military service
**8** [1]INTEREST 6

**[2]color** *vb*
**1** to give color to
**2** to change the color of
**3** MISREPRESENT ⟨*color* the truth⟩
**4** to take on or change color **:** BLUSH

**col·or·ation** \ˌkəl-ə-'rā-shən\ *n*
use or arrangement of colors or shades **:** COLORING

**color–blind** \'kəl-ər-ˌblīnd\ *adj*
unable to tell some colors apart

**col·ored** \'kəl-ərd\ *adj*
having color ⟨*colored* glass⟩

**col·or·ful** \'kəl-ər-fəl\ *adj*
**1** having bright colors
**2** full of variety or interest

**col·or·ing** \'kəl-ə-ring\ *n*
**1** the act of applying colors
**2** something that produces color ⟨vegetable *coloring*⟩
**3** the effect produced by the use of color
**4** natural color : COMPLEXION ⟨a person of delicate *coloring*⟩

**coloring book** *n*
a book of drawings made in solid lines for coloring

**col·or·less** \'kəl-ər-ləs\ *adj*
**1** having no color
**2** WAN, PALE
**3** [1]DULL 8

**co·los·sal** \kə-'läs-əl\ *adj*
very large : HUGE

**colt** \'kōlt\ *n*
**1** FOAL
**2** a young male horse

**col·um·bine** \'käl-əm-,bīn\ *n*
▶ a plant related to the buttercups that has leaves with three parts and showy flowers usually with five petals ending in spurs

**columbine**

**col·umn** \'käl-əm\ *n*
**1** one of two or more vertical sections of a printed page ⟨the left *column* of the page⟩
**2** a special regular feature in a newspaper or magazine ⟨a sports *column*⟩
**3** ▶ a pillar supporting a roof or gallery
**4** something like a column in shape, position, or use ⟨the spinal *column*⟩ ⟨a *column* of water⟩
**5** a long straight row (as of soldiers)

**col·um·nist** \'käl-əm-nəst, -ə-məst\ *n*
a writer of a column in a newspaper or magazine

**com-** *or* **col-** *or* **con-** *prefix*
with : together : jointly — usually *com-* before *b, p,* or *m, col-* before *l* and *con-* before other sounds

**co·ma** \'kō-mə\ *n*
a deep sleeplike state caused by sickness or injury

[1]**comb** \'kōm\ *n*
**1** a toothed implement used to smooth and arrange the hair or worn in the hair to hold it in place
**2** a toothed instrument used for separating fibers (as of wool or flax)
**3** ▶ a fleshy crest often with points suggesting teeth on the head of a fowl and some related birds
**4** [1]HONEYCOMB 1

[1]**comb 3:** a rooster's comb

[2]**comb** *vb*
**1** to smooth, arrange, or untangle with a comb
**2** to search over or through carefully ⟨police *combed* the building⟩

[1]**com·bat** \'käm-,bat\ *n*
**1** a fight or contest between individuals or groups
**2** [1]CONFLICT 2
**3** active military fighting ⟨soldiers lost in *combat*⟩

[2]**com·bat** \kəm-'bat, 'käm-,bat\ *vb* **com·bat·ed** *or* **com·bat·ted**; **com·bat·ing** *or* **com·bat·ting**
to fight with : fight against : OPPOSE ⟨*combat* disease⟩

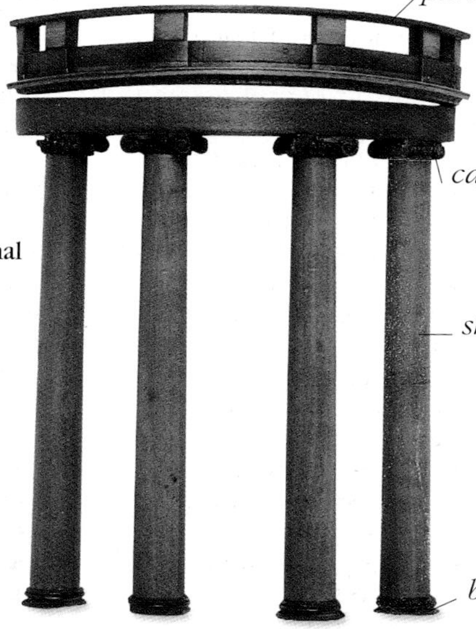

**column 3:** architect's model of columns supporting a parapet

[1]**com·bat·ant** \kəm-'bat-nt, 'käm-bət-ənt\ *n*
a person who takes part in a combat

[2]**combatant** *adj*
engaging in or ready to engage in combat

**com·bi·na·tion** \,käm-bə-'nā-shən\ *n*
**1** a result or product of combining or being combined
**2** a union of persons or groups for a purpose
**3** a series of letters or numbers which when dialed by a disk on a lock will operate or open the lock
**4** a union of different things

**combination lock** *n*
a lock with one or more dials or rings marked usually with numbers which are used to open the lock by moving them in a certain order to certain positions

[1]**com·bine** \kəm-'bīn\ *vb* **com·bined**; **com·bin·ing**
to join together so as to make or to seem one thing : UNITE, MIX

[2]**com·bine** \'käm-,bīn\ *n*
**1** a union of persons or groups of persons especially for business or political benefits
**2** a machine that harvests and threshes grain

**com·bus·ti·ble** \kəm-'bəs-tə-bəl\ *adj*
**1** possible to burn
**2** catching fire or burning easily

**com·bus·tion** \kəm-'bəs-chən\ *n*
the process of burning

**come** \'kəm, kəm\ *vb* **came** \'kām\; **come**; **com·ing** \'kəm-ing\
**1** to move toward : APPROACH ⟨*come* here⟩
**2** to reach the point of being or becoming ⟨the water *came* to a boil⟩ ⟨the rope *came* untied⟩
**3** to add up : AMOUNT ⟨the bill *comes* to ten dollars⟩
**4** to take place ⟨the holiday *comes* on Tuesday⟩
**5** ORIGINATE 2, ARISE ⟨they *come* from a good family⟩
**6** to be available ⟨these books *come* in four bindings⟩
**7** [1]REACH 3 ⟨the water *came* to our knees⟩

**co·me·di·an** \kə-'mēd-ē-ən\ *n*
**1** an actor who plays comic roles
**2** an amusing person

**com·e·dy** \'käm-ə-dē\ *n, pl* **com·e·dies**
**1** an amusing play that has a happy ending

2 an amusing and often ridiculous event

**come·ly** \'kəm-lē\ *adj* **come·li·er**; **come·li·est**
pleasing to the sight : good-looking

**com·et** \'käm-ət\ *n*
▶ a bright celestial body that develops a cloudy tail as it moves in an orbit around the sun

comet

**Word History** The tail of a comet looks rather like long hair streaming behind the head. The ancient Greeks gave comets a name that meant "long-haired." This Greek name was formed from a Greek word meaning "hair." The English word *comet* came from the Greek name for comets.

**come to** *vb*
to become conscious again

[1]**com·fort** \'kəm-fərt\ *vb*
1 to give hope and strength to : CHEER
2 to ease the grief or trouble of

[2]**comfort** *n*
1 acts or words that comfort
2 the feeling of the one that is comforted
3 something that makes a person comfortable ⟨the *comforts* of home⟩

**com·fort·able** \'kəm-fərt-ə-bəl, 'kəmf-tər-bəl\ *adj*
1 giving comfort and especially physical ease ⟨a *comfortable* chair⟩
2 more than what is needed ⟨a *comfortable* income⟩
3 physically at ease
**com·fort·ably** \-blē\ *adj*

**com·fort·er** \'kəm-fərt-ər\ *n*
1 one that gives comfort
2 [1]QUILT

**com·ic** \'käm-ik\ *adj*
1 of, relating to, or characteristic of comedy
2 FUNNY 1

**com·i·cal** \'käm-i-kəl\ *adj*
FUNNY 1, RIDICULOUS ⟨a *comical* sight⟩
**com·i·cal·ly** *adv*

**comic book** *n*
a magazine made up of a series of comic strips

**comic strip** *n*
▼ a series of cartoons that tell a story or part of a story

comic strip

**com·ma** \'käm-ə\ *n*
a punctuation mark , used chiefly to show separation of words or word groups within a sentence

[1]**com·mand** \kə-'mand\ *vb*
1 to order with authority
2 to have power or control over : be commander of
3 to have for one's use
4 to demand as right or due : EXACT ⟨*commands* a high fee⟩
5 to survey from a good position

[2]**command** *n*
1 the act of commanding
2 an order given ⟨obey a *command*⟩
3 the ability to control and use : MASTERY ⟨a good *command* of the language⟩
4 the authority, right, or power to command : CONTROL
5 the people, area, or unit (as of soldiers and weapons) under a commander
6 a position from which military operations are directed

**com·man·dant** \'käm-ən-,dant, -,dänt\ *n*
a commanding officer

**com·mand·er** \kə-'man-dər\ *n*
a commissioned officer in the Navy or Coast Guard ranking above a lieutenant commander

**commander in chief**
a person who holds supreme command of the armed forces of a nation

**com·mand·ment** \kə-'mand-mənt\ *n*
something given as a command and especially one of the Ten Commandments in the Bible

**com·man·do** \kə-'man-dō\ *n, pl* **com·man·dos** *or* **com·man·does**
1 a band or unit of troops trained for making surprise raids into enemy territory
2 a member of a commando unit

**command sergeant major** *n*
a noncommissioned officer in the Army ranking above a first sergeant

**com·mem·o·rate** \kə-'mem-ə-,rāt\ *vb* **com·mem·o·rat·ed**; **com·mem·o·rat·ing**
1 to call or recall to mind
2 to observe with a ceremony
3 to serve as a memorial of

**com·mem·o·ra·tion** \kə-,mem-ə-'rā-shən\ *n*
1 the act of commemorating
2 something (as a ceremony) that commemorates

**com·mence** \kə-'mens\ *vb* **com·menced**; **com·menc·ing**
BEGIN, START

**com·mence·ment** \kə-'mens-mənt\ *n*
1 the act or the time of commencing : BEGINNING
2 graduation exercises

**com·mend** \kə-'mend\ *vb*
1 to give into another's care : ENTRUST
2 to speak of with approval : PRAISE

**com·men·da·tion** \ˌkäm-ən-ˈdā-shən\ *n*
[2]PRAISE 1, APPROVAL

[1]**com·ment** \ˈkäm-ˌent\ *n*
**1** an expression of opinion either in speech or writing
**2** mention of something that deserves notice

[2]**comment** *vb*
to make a comment : REMARK

**com·men·ta·tor** \ˈkäm-ən-ˌtāt-ər\ *n*
**1** a person who makes comments
**2** a person who reports and discusses news events (as over radio)

**com·merce** \ˈkäm-ərs, -ˌərs\ *n*
the buying and selling of goods especially on a large scale and between different places : TRADE

[1]**com·mer·cial** \kə-ˈmər-shəl\ *adj*
**1** having to do with commerce
**2** having financial profit as the chief goal
**com·mer·cial·ly** *adv*

[2]**commercial** *n*
an advertisement broadcast on radio or television

**com·mer·cial·ize** \kə-ˈmər-shə-ˌlīz\ *vb* **com·mer·cial·ized**; **com·mer·cial·iz·ing**
to manage with the idea of making a profit

[1]**com·mis·sion** \kə-ˈmish-ən\ *n*
**1** an order or instruction granting the power to perform various acts or duties : the right or duty in question

**communication 3**
Modern technology allows information to be communicated and received faster than ever before. Traditional methods of communication include surface mail, but today there are many, swifter options. These include the telephone, fax, computer e-mail, and satellites. In addition, world news is conveyed via radio and television almost as soon as events occur.

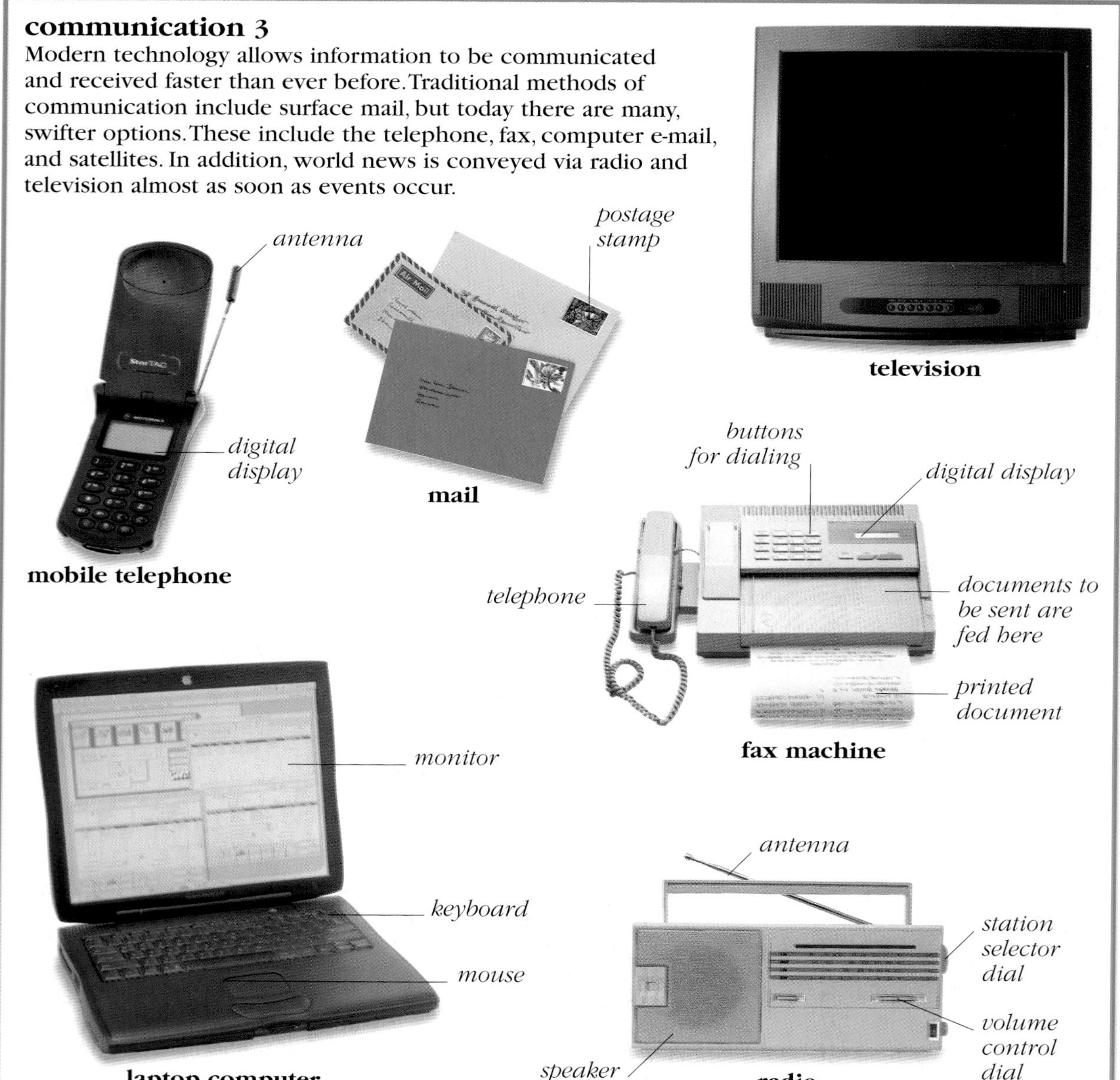

**2** a certificate that gives military or naval rank and authority **:** the rank and authority given
**3** authority to act as agent for another **:** a task or piece of business entrusted to an agent
**4** a group of persons given orders and authority to perform specified duties ⟨a housing *commission*⟩
**5** an act of doing something wrong ⟨the *commission* of a crime⟩
**6** a fee paid to an agent for taking care of a piece of business

**²commission** *vb*
**1** to give a commission to
**2** to put (a ship) into service

**commissioned officer** \kə-ˌmish-ənd-\ *n*
an officer in the armed forces who ranks above the enlisted persons or warrant officers and who is appointed by a commission from the president

**com·mis·sion·er** \kə-'mish-ə-nər, -'mish-nər\ *n*
**1** a member of a commission
**2** an official who is the head of a government department

**com·mit** \kə-'mit\ *vb*
**com·mit·ted**; **com·mit·ting**
**1** to make secure or put in safekeeping **:** ENTRUST
**2** to place in or send to a prison or mental institution
**3** to bring about **:** PERFORM ⟨*commit* a crime⟩
**4** to pledge or assign to a certain course or use
**com·mit·ment** \-mənt\ *n*

**com·mit·tee** \kə-'mit-ē\ *n*
a group of persons appointed or elected to consider some subject of interest or to perform some duty

**com·mod·i·ty** \kə-'mäd-ət-ē\ *n, pl* **com·mod·i·ties**
something produced by agriculture, mining, or manufacture

**com·mo·dore** \'käm-ə-ˌdōr\ *n*
**1** a former wartime commissioned officer rank in the Navy and Coast Guard between the ranks of captain and rear admiral
**2** the chief officer of a yacht club
**3** the senior captain of a line of merchant ships

**¹com·mon** \'käm-ən\ *adj*
**1** having to do with, belonging to, or used by everybody **:** PUBLIC
**2** belonging to or shared by two or more individuals or by the members of a family or group ⟨a *common* ancestor⟩
**3** ¹GENERAL 1 ⟨facts of *common* knowledge⟩
**4** occurring or appearing frequently
**5** not above the average in rank, excellence, or social position ⟨a *common* soldier⟩
**6** falling below ordinary standards (as in quality or manners) **:** INFERIOR
**7** COARSE 4, VULGAR

---

**Synonyms** COMMON, ORDINARY, and FAMILIAR mean occurring often. COMMON suggests that something is of the everyday sort and frequently occurs ⟨fishing boats are a *common* sight around here⟩. ORDINARY suggests that something is of the usual standard ⟨an *ordinary* TV show⟩. FAMILIAR suggests that something is well-known and easily recognized ⟨a *familiar* song⟩.

---

**²common** *n*
land (as a park) owned and used by a community
**in common** shared together

**common cold** *n*
a contagious disease which causes the lining of the nose and throat to be sore, swollen, and red and in which there is usually much mucus and coughing and sneezing

**common denominator** *n*
a common multiple of the denominators of a number of fractions

**com·mon·er** \'käm-ə-nər\ *n*
one of the common people

**common multiple** *n*
a multiple of each of two or more numbers

**common noun** *n*
a noun that names a class of persons or things or any individual of a class and that may occur with a limiting modifier (as *a*, *the*, *some*, or *every*) ⟨"child," "city," and "day" are *common nouns*⟩

**¹com·mon·place** \'käm-ən-ˌplās\ *n*
something that is often seen or met with

**²commonplace** *adj*
often seen or met with **:** ORDINARY

**common sense** *n*
ordinary good sense and judgment

**com·mon·wealth** \'käm-ən-ˌwelth\ *n*
**1** a political unit (as a nation or state)
**2** a state of the United States and especially Kentucky, Massachusetts, Pennsylvania, or Virginia

**com·mo·tion** \kə-'mō-shən\ *n*
noisy excitement and confusion **:** TURMOIL

**¹com·mune** \kə-'myün\ *vb*
**com·muned**; **com·mun·ing**
to be in close accord or communication with someone or something

**²com·mune** \'käm-ˌyün\ *n*
a community in which individuals have close personal ties to each other and share property and duties

**com·mu·ni·ca·ble** \kə-'myü-ni-kə-bəl\ *adj*
possible to communicate ⟨a *communicable* disease⟩

**com·mu·ni·cate** \kə-'myü-nə-ˌkāt\ *vb* **com·mu·ni·cat·ed**; **com·mu·ni·cat·ing**
**1** to make known
**2** to pass (as a disease) from one to another **:** SPREAD
**3** to get in touch (as by telephone)

**com·mu·ni·ca·tion** \kə-ˌmyü-nə-'kā-shən\ *n*
**1** the exchange (as by speech or letter) of information between persons
**2** information communicated
**3** ◀ **communications** *pl* a system of sending messages (as by telephone)
**4** **communications** *pl* a system of routes for moving troops, supplies, and vehicles

**com·mu·nion** \kə-'myü-nyən\ *n*
**1** an act or example of sharing
**2** a religious ceremony commemorating with bread and wine the last supper of Jesus
**3** the act of receiving the sacrament
**4** friendly communication
**5** a body of Christians having a common faith and discipline

**com·mu·nism** \'käm-yə-ˌniz-əm\ *n*
**1** a social system in which property and goods are held in common
**2** a theory that supports communism

**com·mu·nist** \'käm-yə-nəst\ *n*
**1** a person who believes in communism
**2** *cap* a member or follower of a Communist party or plan for change

**com·mu·ni·ty** \kə-'myü-nət-ē\ *n, pl* **com·mu·ni·ties**
**1** the people living in a certain place (as a village or city) **:** the area itself
**2** a natural group (as of kinds of plants and animals) living together and depending on one another for various necessities of life
**3** a group of people with common interests living together ⟨a *community* of artists⟩
**4** people in general **:** PUBLIC
**5** common ownership or participation

**com·mu·ta·tive** \'käm-yə-ˌtāt-iv\ *adj*
being a property of a mathematical operation (as addition or multiplication) in which the result of combining elements is independent of the order in which they are taken

**com·mute** \kə-'myüt\ *vb* **com·mut·ed**; **com·mut·ing**
**1** to change (as a penalty) to something less severe
**2** to travel back and forth regularly
**com·mut·er** *n*

[1]**com·pact** \kəm-'pakt, 'käm-ˌpakt\ *adj*
**1** closely united or packed
**2** arranged so as to save space ⟨a *compact* house⟩
**3** not wordy **:** BRIEF **synonyms** see DENSE
**com·pact·ly** *adv*
**com·pact·ness** *n*

[2]**com·pact** \'käm-ˌpakt\ *n*
**1** ▼ a small case for cosmetics
**2** a somewhat small automobile

[2]**compact 1:** a compact containing powder for the eyelids

[3]**com·pact** \'käm-ˌpakt\ *n* AGREEMENT 2

**compact disc** *n*
▼ a small plastic disc on which information (as music or computer data) is recorded

**compact disc**

**com·pan·ion** \kəm-'pan-yən\ *n*
**1** a person or thing that accompanies another
**2** one of a pair of matching things
**3** a person employed to live with and serve another

**Word History** The word *companion* came from a Latin word that meant "comrade." Comrades can be thought of as people who share bread or eat together. The Latin word meaning "comrade" was made up of two parts. The first was a Latin prefix that meant "together." The second was a Latin word that meant "bread."

**com·pan·ion·ship** \kəm-'pan-yən-ˌship\ *n* FELLOWSHIP 1, COMPANY

**com·pan·ion·way** \kəm-'pan-yən-ˌwā\ *n*
a ship's stairway from one deck to another

**com·pa·ny** \'kəm-pə-nē, 'kəmp-nē\ *n, pl* **com·pa·nies**
**1** FELLOWSHIP 1
**2** a person's companions or associates ⟨known by the *company* you keep⟩
**3** guests or visitors especially at one's home ⟨we have *company*⟩
**4** a group of persons or things
**5** a body of soldiers and especially an infantry unit normally led by a captain
**6** a band of musical or dramatic performers ⟨opera *company*⟩
**7** the officers and crew of a ship
**8** an association of persons carrying on a business

**com·pa·ra·ble** \'käm-pə-rə-bəl, -prə-bəl\ *adj*
being similar or about the same

[1]**com·par·a·tive** \kəm-'par-ət-iv\ *adj*
**1** of, relating to, or being the form of an adjective or adverb that shows a degree of comparison that is greater or less than its positive degree
**2** measured by comparisons **:** RELATIVE
**com·par·a·tive·ly** *adv*

[2]**comparative** *n*
the comparative degree or a comparative form in a language ⟨"taller" is the *comparative* of "tall"⟩

**com·pare** \kəm-'paər\ *vb* **com·pared**; **com·par·ing**
**1** to point out as similar **:** LIKEN ⟨*compare* an anthill to a town⟩
**2** to examine for likenesses or differences ⟨*compare* two bicycles⟩
**3** to appear in comparison to others ⟨*compares* well with the rest of the class⟩
**4** to state the positive, comparative, and superlative forms of an adjective or adverb

**Synonyms** COMPARE and CONTRAST mean to set side by side in order to show likenesses and differences. COMPARE stresses showing the likenesses between two or more things ⟨*compare* these sofas for size and comfort⟩. CONTRAST stresses showing the differences and especially the characteristics which are opposite ⟨*contrast* country and city life⟩.

**com·par·i·son** \kəm-'par-ə-sən\ *n*
**1** the act of comparing **:** the condition of being compared
**2** an examination of two or more objects to find the likenesses and differences between them
**3** change in the form and meaning of an adjective or an adverb (as by adding *-er* or *-est* to the word or by adding *more* or *most* before the word) to show different levels of quality, quantity, or relation

**com·part·ment** \kəm-'pärt-mənt\ *n*
**1** one of the parts into which a closed space is divided
**2** a separate division or section

**compass 4**

**com·pass** \'kəm-pəs\ *n*
**1** BOUNDARY, CIRCUMFERENCE
**2** a closed-in space
**3** [1]RANGE 6, SCOPE ⟨within the *compass* of my voice⟩
**4** ▲ a device having a magnetic needle that indicates direction on the earth's surface by pointing toward the north
**5** a device that indicates direction by means other than a magnetic needle
**6** an instrument for drawing circles or marking measurements consisting of two pointed legs joined at the top by a pivot — usually used in pl.

**com·pas·sion** \kəm-'pash-ən\ *n*
pity for and a desire to help another

**com·pas·sion·ate** \kəm-'pash-ə-nət\ *adj*
having or showing compassion

**com·pat·i·ble** \kəm-'pat-ə-bəl\ *adj*
capable of existing together in harmony

**com·pa·tri·ot** \kəm-'pā-trē-ət\ *n*
a person from one's own country

**com·pel** \kəm-'pel\ *vb*
**com·pelled**; **com·pel·ling**
to make (as a person) do something by the use of physical, moral, or mental pressure : FORCE ⟨lameness *compels* me to use a cane⟩ ⟨felt *compelled* to tell the truth⟩

**com·pen·sate** \'käm-pən-ˌsāt\ *vb*
**com·pen·sat·ed**; **com·pen·sat·ing**
**1** to make up for ⟨care can *compensate* for lack of experience⟩
**2** [1]RECOMPENSE, PAY ⟨*compensate* an injured worker⟩

**com·pen·sa·tion** \ˌkäm-pən-'sā-shən\ *n*
**1** something that makes up for or is given to make up for something else
**2** money paid regularly

**com·pete** \kəm-'pēt\ *vb*
**com·pet·ed**; **com·pet·ing**
to strive for something (as a prize or a reward) for which another is also striving

**com·pe·tence** \'käm-pət-əns\ *n*
the quality or state of being competent

**com·pe·tent** \'käm-pət-ənt\ *adj*
CAPABLE 1, EFFICIENT ⟨a *competent* teacher⟩

**com·pe·ti·tion** \ˌkäm-pə-'tish-ən\ *n*
**1** the act or process of competing
**2** a contest in which all who take part compete for the same thing

**com·pet·i·tive** \kəm-'pet-ət-iv\ *adj*
relating to, characterized by, or based on competition

**com·pet·i·tor** \kəm-'pet-ət-ər\ *n*
someone or something that competes especially in the selling of goods or services : RIVAL

**com·pile** \kəm-'pīl\ *vb*
**com·piled**; **com·pil·ing**
**1** to collect into a volume or list
**2** to collect information from books or documents and arrange it in a new form

**com·pla·cence** \kəm-'plās-ns\ *n*
calm or satisfied feeling about one's self or one's position

**com·pla·cen·cy** \kəm-'plās-n-sē\ *n*
COMPLACENCE

**com·pla·cent** \kəm-'plās-nt\ *adj*
feeling or showing complacence

**com·plain** \kəm-'plān\ *vb*
**1** to express grief, pain, or discontent : find fault
**2** to accuse someone of wrongdoing
**com·plain·er** *n*

**com·plaint** \kəm-'plānt\ *n*
**1** expression of grief, pain, or discontent
**2** a cause or reason for complaining ⟨the noise is my biggest *complaint*⟩
**3** a sickness or disease of the body
**4** a charge of wrongdoing against a person

[1]**com·ple·ment** \'käm-plə-mənt\ *n*
something that completes or fills : the number required to complete or make perfect

[2]**com·ple·ment** \'käm-plə-ˌment\ *vb*
to form or serve as a complement to ⟨a hat that *complements* the costume⟩

**com·ple·men·ta·ry** \ˌkäm-plə-'ment-ə-rē\ *adj*
serving as a complement

[1]**com·plete** \kəm-'plēt\ *adj*
**1** having no part lacking : ENTIRE ⟨a *complete* set of books⟩
**2** brought to an end
**3** THOROUGH 1
**com·plete·ness** *n*

[2]**complete** *vb* **com·plet·ed**; **com·plet·ing**
**1** to bring to an end : FINISH ⟨*complete* a job⟩
**2** to make whole or perfect

**com·plete·ly** \kəm-'plēt-lē\ *adv*
as much as possible : in every way or detail

**com·ple·tion** \kəm-'plē-shən\ *n*
the act or process of completing : the condition of being complete

**com·plex** \käm-'pleks, kəm-'pleks, 'käm-ˌpleks\ *adj*
**1** made up of two or more parts
**2** not simple

**complex fraction** *n*
a fraction with a fraction or mixed number in the numerator or denominator or both ⟨$5/1^3/_4$ is a *complex fraction*⟩

**com·plex·ion** \kəm-'plek-shən\ *n*
**1** the color or appearance of the skin and especially of the face
**2** general appearance or impression

**com·plex·i·ty** \kəm-'plek-sət-ē\ *n, pl* **com·plex·i·ties**
**1** the quality or condition of being complex ⟨the *complexity* of a problem⟩
**2** something complex ⟨the *complexities* of business⟩

**com·pli·cate** \'käm-plə-ˌkāt\ *vb*
**com·pli·cat·ed**; **com·pli·cat·ing**
to make or become complex or difficult

A B C D E F G H I J K L M N O P Q R S T U V W X Y Z

**com·pli·ca·tion** \,käm-plə-'kā-shən\ *n*
**1** a confused situation
**2** something that makes a situation more difficult

[1]**com·pli·ment** \'käm-plə-mənt\ *n*
**1** an act or expression of praise, approval, respect, or admiration
**2 compliments** *pl* best wishes

[2]**com·pli·ment** \'käm-plə-,ment\ *vb*
to pay a compliment to

**Synonyms** COMPLIMENT, PRAISE, and FLATTER mean to express approval or admiration to someone personally. COMPLIMENT suggests a courteous or pleasant statement of admiration ⟨*complimented* the students on their neat work⟩. PRAISE may suggest that the statement of approval comes from a person in authority ⟨the boss *praised* us for doing a good job⟩. FLATTER suggests complimenting a person too much and especially when one is not sincere ⟨we *flattered* the teacher in the hope of getting better grades⟩.

**com·pli·men·ta·ry** \,käm-plə-'ment-ə-rē, -'men-trē\ *adj*
**1** expressing or containing a compliment
**2** given free as a courtesy or favor ⟨*complimentary* tickets⟩

**com·ply** \kəm-'plī\ *vb*
**com·plied**; **com·ply·ing**
to act in agreement with another's wishes or in obedience to a rule

**com·po·nent** \kəm-'pō-nənt\ *n*
one of the parts or units of a combination, mixture, or system

**com·pose** \kəm-'pōz\ *vb*
**com·posed**; **com·pos·ing**
**1** to form by putting together ⟨*compose* a song⟩
**2** to be the parts or materials of ⟨cloth *composed* of silk and wool⟩
**3** to put in order : SETTLE ⟨*compose* one's mind⟩

**com·posed** \kəm-'pōzd\ *adj*
being calm and in control of oneself ⟨sat *composed* during the whole interview⟩

**com·pos·er** \kəm-'pō-zər\ *n*
**1** a person who composes
**2** a writer of music

**com·pos·ite** \kəm-'päz-ət\ *adj*
made up of different parts or elements

**composite number** *n*
an integer that is a product of two or more whole numbers each greater than 1

**com·po·si·tion** \,käm-pə-'zish-ən\ *n*
**1** the act of composing (as by writing)
**2** the manner in which the parts of a thing are put together
**3** MAKEUP 1, CONSTITUTION ⟨the *composition* of rubber⟩
**4** a literary, musical, or artistic production
**5** a short piece of writing done as a school exercise

**com·post** \'käm-,pōst\ *n*
decayed organic material used to improve soil for growing crops

**com·po·sure** \kəm-'pō-zhər\ *n*
calmness especially of mind, manner, or appearance

[1]**com·pound** \käm-'paund\ *vb*
**1** to mix or unite together into a whole
**2** to form by combining separate things ⟨*compound* a medicine⟩

[2]**com·pound** \'käm-,paund\ *adj*
made of or by the union of two or more parts

[3]**com·pound** \'käm-,paund\ *n*
**1** a word made up of parts that are themselves words ⟨"rowboat" and "hide-and-seek" are *compounds*⟩
**2** something (as a chemical) that is formed by combining two or more parts or elements

[4]**com·pound** \'käm-,paund\ *n*
an enclosed area containing a group of buildings

**compound fracture** *n*
a breaking of a bone in which bone fragments stick out through the flesh

**com·pre·hend** \,käm-pri-'hend\ *vb*
**1** to understand fully
**2** to take in : INCLUDE

**com·pre·hen·sion** \,käm-pri-'hen-chən\ *n*
ability to understand

**com·pre·hen·sive** \,käm-pri-'hen-siv\ *adj*
including much : INCLUSIVE ⟨a *comprehensive* course of study⟩ ⟨a *comprehensive* description⟩
**com·pre·hen·sive·ness** *n*

[1]**com·press** \kəm-'pres\ *vb*
**1** to press or squeeze together
**2** to reduce the volume of by pressure ⟨a pump for *compressing* air⟩

[2]**com·press** \'käm-,pres\ *n*
▼ a pad (as of folded cloth) applied firmly to a part of the body (as to check bleeding)



[2]**compress**

**com·pres·sion** \kəm-'presh-ən\ *n*
the process of compressing : the state of being compressed

**com·pres·sor** \kəm-'pres-ər\ *n*
**1** one that compresses
**2** a machine for compressing something (as air)

**com·prise** \kəm-'prīz\ *vb*
**com·prised**; **com·pris·ing**
**1** to be made up of : consist of
**2** [2]FORM 3

[1]**com·pro·mise** \'käm-prə-,mīz\ *n*
**1** an agreement over a dispute reached by each side changing or giving up some demands
**2** the thing agreed upon as a result of a compromise

[2]**compromise** *vb*
**com·pro·mised**; **com·pro·mis·ing**
**1** to settle by compromise
**2** to expose to risk, suspicion, or disgrace ⟨*compromise* national security⟩

**com·pul·sion** \kəm-'pəl-shən\ *n*
**1** an act of compelling : the state of being compelled
**2** a force that compels
**3** a very strong urge to do something

**com·pul·so·ry** \kəm-ˈpəls-ə-rē, -ˈpəls-rē\ *adj*
**1** required by or as if by law ⟨*compulsory* education⟩
**2** having the power of forcing someone to do something ⟨a *compulsory* law⟩

**com·pu·ta·tion** \ˌkäm-pyə-ˈtā-shən\ *n*
**1** the act or action of computing
**2** a result obtained by computing

**com·pute** \kəm-ˈpyüt\ *vb* **com·put·ed**; **com·put·ing**
to find out by using mathematics

**com·put·er** \kəm-ˈpyüt-ər\ *n*
▼ an automatic electronic machine that can store, recall, and process data

**com·put·er·ize** \kəm-ˈpyüt-ə-ˌrīz\ *vb* **com·put·er·ized**; **com·put·er·iz·ing**
**1** to carry out, control, or produce on a computer
**2** to equip with computers ⟨*computerize* a school⟩
**3** to put in a form that a computer can use

**com·rade** \ˈkäm-ˌrad, -rəd\ *n*
COMPANION 1

**[1]con** \ˈkän\ *adv*
on the negative side ⟨argue pro and *con*⟩

**[2]con** *n*
an opposing argument, person, or position ⟨the pros and *cons* of the question⟩

**con-** see COM-

**con·cave** \kän-ˈkāv\ *adj*
▼ hollow or rounded inward like the inside of a bowl

**concave:**
the inside of a bowl is concave

**con·ceal** \kən-ˈsēl\ *vb*
**1** to hide from sight ⟨a *concealed* weapon⟩
**2** to keep secret

**con·ceal·ment** \kən-ˈsēl-mənt\ *n*
**1** the act of hiding : the state of being hidden
**2** a hiding place

**con·cede** \kən-ˈsēd\ *vb* **con·ced·ed**; **con·ced·ing**
**1** to grant as a right or privilege
**2** to admit to be true ⟨*concede* defeat⟩

**con·ceit** \kən-ˈsēt\ *n*
too much pride in oneself or one's ability

**con·ceit·ed** \kən-ˈsēt-əd\ *adj*
VAIN 2

**con·ceiv·able** \kən-ˈsē-və-bəl\ *adj*
possible to conceive, imagine, or understand

**con·ceive** \kən-ˈsēv\ *vb* **con·ceived**; **con·ceiv·ing**
**1** to form an idea of : IMAGINE ⟨unable to *conceive* how it happened⟩
**2** THINK 2

**con·cen·trate** \ˈkän-sən-ˌtrāt\ *vb* **con·cen·trat·ed**; **con·cen·trat·ing**
**1** to bring or come to or direct toward a common center
**2** to make stronger or thicker by removing something (as water) ⟨*concentrated* orange juice⟩
**3** to fix one's powers, efforts, or attentions on one thing

**con·cen·tra·tion** \ˌkän-sən-ˈtrā-shən\ *n*
**1** the act or process of concentrating : the state of being concentrated
**2** close mental attention to a subject

## computer

Computers are a fast means of processing information. They perform a wide range of tasks, from air traffic control to weather forecasting. A computer is controlled by a central processing unit — CPU — within the computer's case. Programs, known as software, enable the computer to carry out instructions.

**computer and other items of hardware**

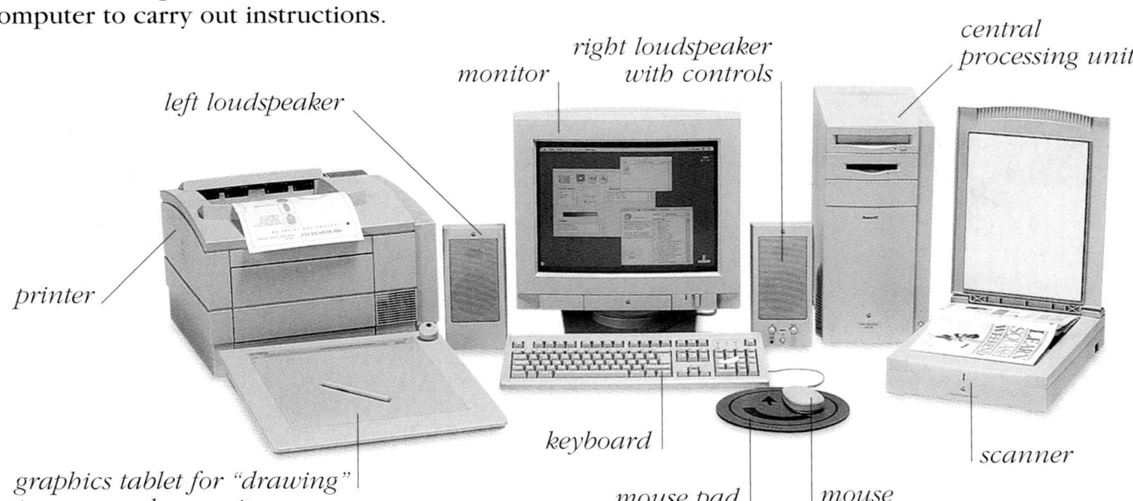

**con·cept** \'kän-,sept\ *n*
**1** ²THOUGHT 4
**2** a general idea

**¹con·cern** \kən-'sərn\ *vb*
**1** to relate to : be about
**2** to be of interest or importance to : AFFECT
**3** to be a care, trouble, or distress to ⟨an illness that *concerned* my parents⟩
**4** ENGAGE 3, OCCUPY

**²concern** *n*
**1** something that relates to or involves a person : AFFAIR
**2** a state of interest and uncertainty
**3** a business organization ⟨a banking *concern*⟩

**con·cerned** \kən-'sərnd\ *adj*
being worried and disturbed ⟨*concerned* parents⟩

**con·cern·ing** \kən-'sər-ning\ *prep*
relating to : ABOUT ⟨a notice *concerning* poor attendance⟩

**con·cert** \'kän-sərt, -,sərt\ *n*
**1** AGREEMENT 1 ⟨working in *concert* to finish the job⟩
**2** a musical performance by several voices or instruments or by both

**concertina**

**con·cer·ti·na** \,kän-sər-'tē-nə\ *n*
▲ a small musical instrument like an accordion

**con·cer·to** \kən-'chert-ō\ *n, pl* **con·cer·tos**
a musical composition usually in three parts for orchestra with one or more principal instruments

**con·ces·sion** \kən-'sesh-ən\ *n*
**1** the act or an instance of granting something
**2** something granted
**3** a special right or privilege given by an authority ⟨a *concession* to sell souvenirs on the beach⟩ ⟨a mining *concession*⟩

**conch** \'kängk, 'känch, 'kȯngk\ *n, pl* **conchs** \'kängks, 'kȯngks\ *or* **conch·es** \'kän-chəz\
▶ a very large sea snail with a tall thick spiral shell

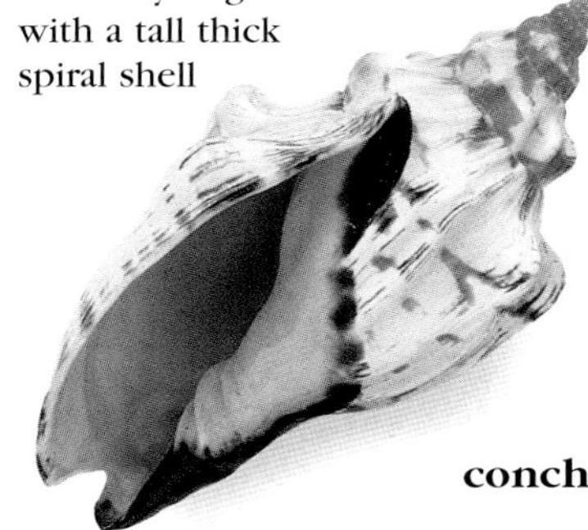

**conch**

**con·cil·i·ate** \kən-'sil-ē-,āt\ *vb* **con·cil·i·at·ed**; **con·cil·i·at·ing**
**1** to bring into agreement : RECONCILE ⟨it is hard to *conciliate* the true stories of what happened⟩
**2** to gain or regain the goodwill or favor of ⟨*conciliate* an angry friend by an apology⟩

**con·cise** \kən-'sīs\ *adj*
expressing much in few words

**con·clude** \kən-'klüd\ *vb* **con·clud·ed**; **con·clud·ing**
**1** to bring or come to an end : FINISH ⟨*conclude* a speech⟩
**2** to form an opinion ⟨I *conclude* that I was wrong⟩
**3** to bring about as a result ⟨*conclude* an agreement⟩

**con·clu·sion** \kən-'klü-zhən\ *n*
**1** final decision reached by reasoning
**2** the last part of something
**3** a final settlement

**con·clu·sive** \kən-'klü-siv\ *adj*
DECISIVE 1 ⟨*conclusive* evidence⟩
**con·clu·sive·ly** *adv*

**con·coct** \kən-'käkt, kän-\ *vb*
**1** to prepare (as food) by putting several different things together
**2** to make up : DEVISE ⟨*concoct* a plan⟩

**con·cord** \'kän-,kȯrd\ *n*
a state of agreement

**con·course** \'kän-,kōrs\ *n*
**1** a flocking, moving, or flowing together (as of persons or streams) : GATHERING
**2** a place where roads or paths meet
**3** an open space or hall (as in a mall or railroad terminal) where crowds gather

**¹con·crete** \kän-'krēt\ *adj*
**1** ¹MATERIAL 1, REAL
**2** made of or relating to concrete

**²con·crete** \'kän-,krēt\ *n*
a hardened mixture of cement, sand, and water with gravel or broken stone used in construction (as of pavements and buildings)

**con·cur** \kən-'kər\ *vb* **con·curred**; **con·cur·ring**
**1** to act or happen together
**2** to be in agreement (as in action or opinion) : ACCORD

**con·cus·sion** \kən-'kəsh-ən\ *n*
**1** a sharp hard blow or the effect of this
**2** injury to the brain by jarring (as from a blow)

**con·demn** \kən-'dem\ *vb*
**1** to declare to be wrong
**2** to declare guilty
**3** ²SENTENCE
**4** to declare to be unfit for use

**con·dem·na·tion** \,kän-,dem-'nā-shən, -dəm-\ *n*
**1** ¹CENSURE 1, BLAME
**2** the act of judicially condemning
**3** the state of being condemned

**con·den·sa·tion** \,kän-,den-'sā-shən, -dən-\ *n*
**1** the act or process of condensing
**2** something that has been condensed

**con·dense** \kən-'dens\ *vb* **con·densed**; **con·dens·ing**
to make or become more compact, more concise, closer, or denser : CONCENTRATE

**con·de·scend** \,kän-di-'send\ *vb*
**1** to stoop to a level considered lower than one's own
**2** to grant favors with a show of being better than others

**¹con·di·tion** \kən-'dish-ən\ *n*
**1** something agreed upon or necessary if some other thing is to take place
**2** **conditions** *pl* state of affairs
**3** state of being ⟨water in a frozen *condition*⟩
**4** situation in life ⟨people of humble *condition*⟩
**5** state of health or fitness

**²condition** *vb*
**1** to put into the proper or desired condition
**2** to change the habits of usually by training

**con·di·tion·al** \kən-ˈdish-ən-l\ *adj* depending on a condition ⟨a *conditional* promise⟩

ruff

**condor**

**con·dor** \ˈkän-dər, -ˌdȯr\ *n* ▶ a very large American vulture having a bare head and neck and a frill of white feathers on the neck

[1]**con·duct** \ˈkän-ˌdəkt\ *n*
**1** the act or way of carrying something on ⟨the *conduct* of foreign trade⟩
**2** personal behavior

[2]**con·duct** \kən-ˈdəkt\ *vb*
**1** [2]GUIDE 1
**2** to carry on or out from a position of command **:** LEAD ⟨*conduct* a business⟩
**3** BEHAVE 1 ⟨*conduct* oneself well at a party⟩
**4** to have the quality of transmitting light, heat, sound, or electricity

**conductor 2:**
the conductor of an orchestra

---

**Synonyms** CONDUCT, DIRECT, and MANAGE mean to provide the leadership or guidance for something. CONDUCT suggests leading something in person ⟨*conduct* an orchestra⟩. DIRECT suggests guiding something that needs constant attention ⟨*directed* the building of a new school⟩. MANAGE suggests the handling of the small items of something (as a business) or the careful guiding of something to a goal ⟨*manage* a political campaign⟩.

---

**con·duc·tion** \kən-ˈdək-shən\ *n*
**1** the act of transporting something ⟨pipes for the *conduction* of water⟩
**2** transmission through a conductor

**con·duc·tor** \kən-ˈdək-tər\ *n*
**1** a person in charge of a public means of transportation (as a train)
**2** ◀ a person or thing that directs or leads ⟨the *conductor* of our school orchestra⟩
**3** a substance or body capable of transmitting light, electricity, heat, or sound

**cone** \ˈkōn\ *n*
**1** ▶ the scaly fruit of certain trees (as the pine or fir)
**2** a solid body tapering evenly to a point from a circular base
**3** something resembling a cone in shape
**4** an ice-cream holder
**5** a cell of the retina of the eye that is sensitive to colored light

**con·fec·tion** \kən-ˈfek-shən\ *n* a fancy dish or sweet **:** DELICACY, CANDY

**con·fec·tion·er** \kən-ˈfek-shə-nər\ *n* a maker of or dealer in confections (as candies)

**con·fec·tion·ery** \kən-ˈfek-shə-ˌner-ē\ *n, pl* **con·fec·tion·er·ies**
**1** sweet things to eat (as candy)
**2** a confectioner's business or place of business

**con·fed·er·a·cy** \kən-ˈfed-ə-rə-sē\ *n, pl* **con·fed·er·a·cies**
**1** a league of persons, parties, or states
**2** *cap* the eleven southern states that seceded from the United States in 1860 and 1861

[1]**con·fed·er·ate** \kən-ˈfed-ə-rət\ *adj*
**1** united in a league
**2** *cap* of or relating to the Confederacy ⟨*Confederate* money⟩

[2]**confederate** *n*
**1** a member of a confederacy
**2** ACCOMPLICE
**3** *cap* a soldier of or a person who sided with the Confederacy

[3]**con·fed·er·ate** \kən-ˈfed-ə-ˌrāt\ *vb* **con·fed·er·at·ed**; **con·fed·er·at·ing** to unite in an alliance or confederacy

**con·fer** \kən-ˈfər\ *vb* **con·ferred**; **con·fer·ring**
**1** BESTOW, PRESENT
**2** to compare views especially in studying a problem

**con·fer·ence** \ˈkän-fə-rəns, -frəns\ *n* a meeting for discussion or exchange of opinions

**con·fess** \kən-ˈfes\ *vb*
**1** to tell of or make known (as something private or damaging to oneself)
**2** to make known one's sins to God or to a priest

**cone 1:**
a pine cone

**con·fes·sion** \kən-ˈfesh-ən\ *n*
**1** an act of confessing
**2** an admission of guilt
**3** a formal statement of religious beliefs

**con·fide** \kən-'fīd\ *vb* **con·fid·ed**; **con·fid·ing**
**1** to have or show faith
**2** to show confidence by telling secrets ⟨*confide* in a friend⟩
**3** to tell in confidence ⟨*confided* the secret to a pal⟩
**4** ENTRUST 2

**con·fi·dence** \'kän-fə-dəns\ *n*
**1** a feeling of trust or belief ⟨have *confidence* in a person⟩
**2** SELF-CONFIDENCE
**3** reliance on another's secrecy or loyalty
**4** [2]SECRET

**con·fi·dent** \'kän-fə-dənt\ *adj*
having or showing confidence
**con·fi·dent·ly** *adv*

**con·fi·den·tial** \ˌkän-fə-'den-chəl\ *adj*
**1** [1]SECRET 1 ⟨*confidential* information⟩
**2** [2]INTIMATE 2
**3** trusted with secret matters ⟨a *confidential* clerk⟩
**con·fi·den·tial·ly** *adv*

**con·fine** \kən-'fīn\ *vb* **con·fined**; **con·fin·ing**
**1** to keep within limits ⟨*confined* the message to twenty words⟩
**2** to shut up : IMPRISON
**3** to keep indoors ⟨*confined* by sickness⟩
**con·fine·ment** \-mənt\ *n*

**con·fines** \'kän-ˌfīnz\ *n pl*
the boundary or limits of something

**con·firm** \kən-'fərm\ *vb*
**1** to make firm or firmer (as in a habit, in faith, or in intention) : STRENGTHEN
**2** APPROVE 2, ACCEPT ⟨the senate *confirmed* the treaty⟩
**3** to administer the rite of confirmation to
**4** to make sure of the truth of ⟨*confirm* a suspicion⟩

**con·fir·ma·tion** \ˌkän-fər-'mā-shən\ *n*
**1** an act of confirming
**2** a religious ceremony admitting a person to full privileges in a church or synagogue
**3** something that confirms

**con·firmed** \kən-'fərmd\ *adj*
**1** being firmly established ⟨*confirmed* distrust of anything new⟩
**2** unlikely to change ⟨a *confirmed* drunkard⟩

**con·fis·cate** \'kän-fə-ˌskāt\ *vb* **con·fis·cat·ed**; **con·fis·cat·ing**
to seize by or as if by public authority

**con·fla·gra·tion** \ˌkän-flə-'grā-shən\ *n*
a large destructive fire

[1]**con·flict** \'kän-ˌflikt\ *n*
**1** an extended struggle : BATTLE
**2** a clashing disagreement (as between ideas or interests)

[2]**con·flict** \kən-'flikt\ *vb*
to be in opposition

**con·form** \kən-'fȯrm\ *vb*
**1** to make or be like : AGREE, ACCORD
**2** COMPLY ⟨*conform* to school customs⟩

**con·for·mi·ty** \kən-'fȯr-mət-ē\ *n, pl* **con·for·mi·ties**
**1** agreement in form, manner, or character
**2** action in accordance with some standard or authority

**con·found** \kən-'fau̇nd, kän-\ *vb*
to throw into disorder : mix up : CONFUSE

**con·front** \kən-'frənt\ *vb*
**1** to face especially in challenge : OPPOSE ⟨*confront* an enemy⟩
**2** to cause to face or meet ⟨*confronted* us with the evidence⟩

**con·fuse** \kən-'fyüz\ *vb* **con·fused**; **con·fus·ing**
**1** to make mentally foggy or uncertain : PERPLEX
**2** to make embarrassed
**3** to fail to tell apart ⟨teachers always *confused* the twins⟩

**con·fu·sion** \kən-'fyü-zhən\ *n*
**1** an act or instance of confusing
**2** the state of being confused

**con·geal** \kən-'jēl\ *vb*
**1** to change from a fluid to a solid state by or as if by cold : FREEZE
**2** to make or become hard, stiff, or thick

**con·ge·nial** \kən-'jē-nyəl\ *adj*
**1** alike or sympathetic in nature, disposition, or tastes
**2** existing together in harmony
**3** tending to please or satisfy ⟨*congenial* work⟩

**con·gest** \kən-'jest\ *vb*
to make too crowded or full : CLOG ⟨a *congested* neighborhood⟩

[1]**con·glom·er·ate** \kən-'gläm-ə-rət\ *adj*
made up of parts from various sources or of various kinds

[2]**conglomerate** *n*
▼ a mass (as a rock) formed of fragments from various sources

[2]**conglomerate**

**con·grat·u·late** \kən-'grach-ə-ˌlāt\ *vb* **con·grat·u·lat·ed**; **con·grat·u·lat·ing**
to express pleasure on account of success or good fortune ⟨*congratulate* the winner⟩

**con·grat·u·la·tion** \kən-ˌgrach-ə-'lā-shən\ *n*
**1** the act of congratulating
**2** an expression of joy or pleasure at another's success or good fortune — usually used in pl.

**con·gre·gate** \'käng-gri-ˌgāt\ *vb* **con·gre·gat·ed**; **con·gre·gat·ing**
to collect or gather into a crowd or group : ASSEMBLE

**con·gre·ga·tion** \ˌkäng-gri-'gā-shən\ *n*
**1** a gathering or collection of persons or things
**2** an assembly of persons gathered especially for religious worship
**3** the membership of a church or synagogue

**con·gress** \'käng-grəs\ *n*
**1** a formal meeting of delegates for discussion and action : CONFERENCE
**2** the chief lawmaking body of a nation and especially of a republic that in the United States is made up of separate houses of senators and representatives

**con·gress·man** \'käng-grə-smən\ *n, pl* **con·gress·men** \-smən\
a member of a congress and especially of the United States House of Representatives

**con·gress·wom·an** \'käng-grə-ˌswu̇m-ən\ *n,* *pl* **con·gress·wom·en** \-grə-ˌswim-ən\
a woman member of a congress and especially of the United States House of Representatives

**con·gru·ent** \kən-'grü-ənt, 'käng-grə-wənt\ *adj*
having the same size and shape ⟨*congruent* triangles⟩

**con·ic** \'kän-ik\ *adj*
**1** CONICAL
**2** of or relating to a cone

**con·i·cal** \'kän-i-kəl\ *adj*
shaped like a cone

**co·ni·fer** \'kän-ə-fər, 'kō-nə-\ *n*
▼ any of a group of mostly evergreen trees and shrubs (as pines) that produce cones
**co·nif·er·ous** \kō-'nif-ə-rəs,kə-\ *adj*

**conifer:** an Arizona cypress

[1]**con·jec·ture** \kən-'jek-chər\ *n*
[2]GUESS

[2]**conjecture** *vb* **con·jec·tured**; **con·jec·tur·ing**
[1]GUESS 1, SURMISE

**con·junc·tion** \kən-'jəngk-shən\ *n*
**1** a joining together : UNION
**2** a word or expression that joins together sentences, clauses, phrases, or words

**con·jure** \'kän-jər, 'kən-jər; *in sense 1* kən-'ju̇r\ *vb* **con·jured**; **con·jur·ing**
**1** to beg earnestly or solemnly : BESEECH
**2** to practice magical arts
**3** IMAGINE 1 ⟨*conjure* up an image⟩

**con·nect** \kə-'nekt\ *vb*
**1** to join or link together ⟨*connect* two wires⟩
**2** to attach by close personal relationship ⟨*connected* by marriage⟩
**3** to bring together in thought ⟨*connect* the smell of burning leaves with childhood⟩
**con·nec·tor** \-'nek-tər\ *n*

**con·nec·tion** \kə-'nek-shən\ *n*
**1** the act of connecting
**2** the fact or condition of being connected : RELATIONSHIP
**3** a thing that connects : BOND, LINK
**4** a person connected with others (as by kinship)
**5** a social, professional, or commercial relationship
**6** the act or the means of continuing a journey by transferring (as to another train)

**con·nois·seur** \ˌkän-ə-'sər\ *n*
a person qualified to act as a judge in matters involving taste and appreciation

**con·quer** \'käng-kər\ *vb*
**1** to get or gain by force : win by fighting
**2** OVERCOME 1

**con·quer·or** \'käng-kər-ər\ *n*
one that conquers : VICTOR

**con·quest** \'kän-ˌkwest\ *n*
**1** the act or process of conquering : VICTORY
**2** something that is conquered
**synonyms** see VICTORY

**con·quis·ta·dor** \kȯng-'kēs-tə-ˌdȯr\ *n, pl* **con·quis·ta·do·res** \-ˌkēs-tə-'dȯr-ēz\ *or* **con·quis·ta·dors**
▼ a leader in the Spanish conquest especially of Mexico and Peru in the sixteenth century

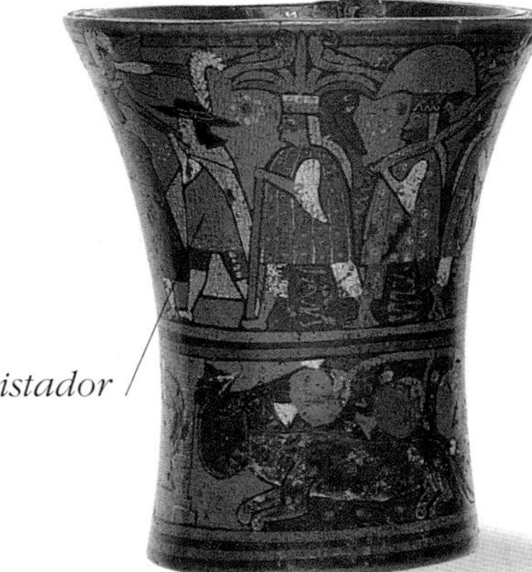


**conquistador:** a 16th-century beaker showing a Spanish conquistador

**con·science** \'kän-chəns\ *n*
knowledge of right and wrong and a feeling that one should do what is right

**con·sci·en·tious** \ˌkän-chē-'en-chəs\ *adj*
**1** guided by or agreeing with one's conscience
**2** using or done with careful attention

**con·scious** \'kän-chəs\ *adj*
**1** aware of facts or feelings ⟨*conscious* of the cold⟩
**2** known or felt by one's inner self ⟨*conscious* guilt⟩
**3** mentally awake or active
**4** INTENTIONAL
**con·scious·ly** *adv*

**con·scious·ness** \'kän-chəs-nəs\ *n*
**1** the condition of being conscious
**2** the upper level of mental life involving conscious thought and the will

**con·se·crate** \'kän-sə-ˌkrāt\ *vb* **con·se·crat·ed**; **con·se·crat·ing**
**1** to declare to be sacred or holy : set apart for the service of God ⟨*consecrate* a church⟩
**2** to dedicate to a particular purpose

**con·sec·u·tive** \kən-'sek-yət-iv\ *adj*
following one another in order without gaps

[1]**con·sent** \kən-'sent\ *vb*
to express willingness or approval : AGREE ⟨*consented* to speak at the banquet⟩

[2]**consent** *n*
approval of or agreement with what is done or suggested by another person

**con·se·quence** \'kän-sə-ˌkwens\ *n*
**1** something produced by a cause or following from a condition
**2** real importance ⟨a person of *consequence*⟩

**con·se·quent** \'kän-si-kwənt\ *adj*
following as a result or effect

**con·se·quent·ly** \'kän-sə-ˌkwent-lē\ *adv*
as a result

**con·ser·va·tion** \ˌkän-sər-'vā-shən\ *n*
**1** PROTECTION 1, PRESERVATION
**2** planned management of natural resources (as timber) to prevent waste, destruction, or neglect

[1]**con·ser·va·tive** \kən-ˈsər-vət-iv\ *adj*
**1** favoring a policy of keeping things as they are : opposed to change
**2** favoring established styles and standards ⟨*conservative* in dress⟩
**con·ser·va·tive·ly** *adv*

[2]**conservative** *n*
a person who holds conservative views : a cautious person

**con·ser·va·to·ry** \kən-ˈsər-və-ˌtōr-ē\ *n, pl* **con·ser·va·to·ries**
**1** GREENHOUSE
**2** a place of instruction in some special study (as music)

[1]**con·serve** \kən-ˈsərv\ *vb* **con·served**; **con·serv·ing**
to keep in a safe condition : SAVE

[2]**con·serve** \ˈkän-ˌsərv\ *n*
**1** a candied fruit
**2** ▼ a rich fruit preserve

jar
spoonful of conserve

[2]**conserve 2:**
raspberry conserve

**con·sid·er** \kən-ˈsid-ər\ *vb*
**1** to think over carefully : PONDER, REFLECT
**2** to treat in a kind or thoughtful way ⟨you never *consider* my feelings⟩
**3** to think of in a certain way : BELIEVE

**con·sid·er·able** \kən-ˈsid-ə-rə-bəl\ *adj*
rather large in extent, amount, or size ⟨a *considerable* estate⟩ ⟨was in *considerable* pain⟩
**con·sid·er·ably** \-blē\ *adv*

**con·sid·er·ate** \kən-ˈsid-ə-rət\ *adj*
thoughtful of the rights and feelings of others

**con·sid·er·ation** \kən-ˌsid-ə-ˈrā-shən\ *n*
**1** careful thought : DELIBERATION
**2** thoughtfulness for other people
**3** something that needs to be considered before deciding or acting
**4** a payment made in return for something

**con·sign** \kən-ˈsīn\ *vb*
**1** ENTRUST 2
**2** to give, transfer, or deliver to another
**3** to send (as goods) to an agent to be sold or cared for
**con·sign·ment** \-mənt\ *n*

**con·sist** \kən-ˈsist\ *vb*
to be made up or composed ⟨coal *consists* mostly of carbon⟩

**con·sis·ten·cy** \kən-ˈsis-tən-sē\ *n, pl* **con·sis·ten·cies**
**1** degree of compactness, firmness, or stickiness ⟨dough of the right *consistency*⟩
**2** agreement or harmony between parts or elements
**3** a sticking with one way of thinking or acting

**con·sis·tent** \kən-ˈsis-tənt\ *adj*
showing consistency ⟨*consistent* behavior⟩
**con·sis·tent·ly** *adv*

**con·so·la·tion** \ˌkän-sə-ˈlā-shən\ *n*
**1** the act of consoling : the state of being consoled
**2** something that lessens disappointment, misery, or grief

[1]**con·sole** \ˈkän-ˌsōl\ *n*
**1** the part of an organ at which the organist sits and which contains the keyboard and controls
**2** a panel or cabinet on which are dials and switches for controlling an electronic or mechanical device
**3** a radio, phonograph, or television cabinet that stands on the floor

[2]**con·sole** \kən-ˈsōl\ *vb* **con·soled**; **con·sol·ing**
to comfort in a time of grief or distress

**con·sol·i·date** \kən-ˈsäl-ə-ˌdāt\ *vb* **con·sol·i·dat·ed**; **con·sol·i·dat·ing**
**1** to join together into one whole : UNITE
**2** STRENGTHEN

**con·so·nant** \ˈkän-sə-nənt\ *n*
**1** a speech sound (as \p\, \n\, or \s\) produced by narrowing or closing the breath channel at one or more points
**2** a letter in the English alphabet other than *a, e, i, o*, or *u*

[1]**con·sort** \ˈkän-ˌsȯrt\ *n*
a wife or husband especially of a king or queen

[2]**con·sort** \kən-ˈsȯrt\ *vb*
to go together as companions : ASSOCIATE

**con·spic·u·ous** \kən-ˈspik-yə-wəs\ *adj*
**1** easily seen
**2** attracting attention : PROMINENT

**con·spir·a·cy** \kən-ˈspir-ə-sē\ *n, pl* **con·spir·a·cies**
**1** the act of conspiring or plotting
**2** an agreement among conspirators
**3** a group of conspirators

**con·spir·a·tor** \kən-ˈspir-ət-ər\ *n*
a person who conspires

**con·spire** \kən-ˈspīr\ *vb* **con·spired**; **con·spir·ing**
**1** to make an agreement especially in secret to do an unlawful act : PLOT
**2** to act together ⟨measles and the weather *conspired* to spoil our holiday⟩

**con·sta·ble** \ˈkän-stə-bəl, ˈkən-\ *n*
a police officer usually of a village or small town

**con·stan·cy** \ˈkän-stən-sē\ *n*
firmness and loyalty in one's beliefs or personal relationships

**con·stant** \ˈkän-stənt\ *adj*
**1** always faithful and true ⟨*constant* friends⟩
**2** remaining steady and unchanged ⟨a *constant* temperature⟩
**3** occurring over and over again ⟨*constant* headaches⟩
**con·stant·ly** *adv*

**con·stel·la·tion** \ˌkän-stə-ˈlā-shən\ *n*
▶ any of eighty-eight groups of stars forming patterns

**con·ster·na·tion** \ˌkän-stər-ˈnā-shən\ *n*
amazement, alarm, or disappointment that makes one feel helpless or confused

**con·sti·pate** \ˈkän-stə-ˌpāt\ *vb* **con·sti·pat·ed**; **con·sti·pat·ing**
to cause constipation in

**con·sti·pa·tion** \ˌkän-stə-ˈpā-shən\ *n*
difficult or infrequent passage of dry hard material from the bowels

[1]**con·stit·u·ent** \kən-ˈstich-ə-wənt\ *n*
**1** one of the parts or materials of which something is made : ELEMENT, INGREDIENT

2 any of the voters who elect a person to represent them

**²constituent** *adj*

1 serving to form or make up a unit or whole

2 having power to elect or appoint or to make or change a constitution ⟨a *constituent* assembly⟩

2 the basic structure of something

3 the basic beliefs and laws of a nation, state, or social group by which the powers and duties of the government are established and certain rights are guaranteed to the people

**constrictor:** a boa constrictor

**con·sti·tute** \'kän-stə-,tüt, -,tyüt\ *vb* **con·sti·tut·ed**; **con·sti·tut·ing**

1 to appoint to an office or duty ⟨the *constituted* authorities⟩

2 SET UP 2 ⟨a fund *constituted* to help needy students⟩

3 to make up **:** FORM ⟨twelve months *constitute* a year⟩

**con·sti·tu·tion** \,kän-stə-'tü-shən, -'tyü-\ *n*

1 the bodily makeup of an individual

**¹con·sti·tu·tion·al** \,kän-stə-'tü-shən-l, -'tyü-\ *adj*

1 having to do with a person's bodily or mental makeup

2 of, relating to, or in agreement with a constitution (as of a nation)

**²constitutional** *n*

an exercise (as a walk) taken for one's health

**con·strain** \kən-'strān\ *vb*

COMPEL, FORCE ⟨*constrained* to retire by ill health⟩

**constellation**

The sky around the earth is divided by astronomers into 88 interlocking constellations, all with clearly defined boundaries. Within each of these lies a pattern of stars. By drawing imaginary lines between these stars, it is possible to visualize the forms of objects, as well as human and animal figures.

**diagram showing the constellation of Andromeda** \an-'dräm-ə-də\

**con·straint** \kən-'strānt\ *n*

1 COMPULSION 1, 2 ⟨act under *constraint*⟩

2 a keeping back of one's natural feelings ⟨the *constraint* between former friends⟩

**con·strict** \kən-'strikt\ *vb*

to make narrower or smaller by drawing together **:** SQUEEZE

**con·stric·tion** \kən-'strik-shən\ *n*

an act or instance of constricting

**con·stric·tor** \kən-'strik-tər\ *n*

◀ a snake (as a boa) that kills prey by crushing in its coils

**con·struct** \kən-'strəkt\ *vb*

to make or form by combining parts **synonyms** see BUILD

**con·struc·tion** \kən-'strək-shən\ *n*

1 the arrangement of words and the relationship between words in a sentence

2 the process, art, or manner of constructing

3 something built or put together **:** STRUCTURE ⟨a flimsy *construction*⟩

4 INTERPRETATION ⟨believes in the strict *construction* of the constitution⟩

**construction paper** *n*

a thick paper available in many colors for school art work

**con·struc·tive** \kən-'strək-tiv\ *adj*

helping to develop or improve something ⟨*constructive* criticism⟩

**con·strue** \kən-'strü\ *vb* **con·strued**; **con·stru·ing**

to understand or explain the sense or intention of

**con·sul** \'kän-səl\ *n*

an official appointed by a government to live in a foreign country in order to look after the commercial interests of citizens of the appointing country

**con·sult** \kən-'səlt\ *vb*

1 to seek the opinion or advice of ⟨*consult* a doctor⟩

2 to seek information from ⟨*consult* a dictionary⟩

3 to talk something over ⟨will have to *consult* with my lawyer⟩

**con·sul·ta·tion** \,kän-səl-'tā-shən\ *n*

1 a discussion between doctors on a case or its treatment

2 the act of consulting

A B C D E F G H I J K L M N O P Q R S T U V W X Y Z

**con·sume** \kən-'süm\ *vb* **con·sumed**; **con·sum·ing**
1 to destroy by or as if by fire
2 to use up : SPEND
3 to eat or drink up
4 to take up the interest or attention of ⟨*consumed* with curiosity⟩

**con·sum·er** \kən-'sü-mər\ *n*
1 one that consumes
2 a person who buys and uses up goods

**con·sump·tion** \kən-'səmp-shən\ *n*
1 the act or process of consuming and especially of using up something (as food or coal)
2 a wasting away of the body especially from tuberculosis of the lungs

[1]**con·tact** \'kän-,takt\ *n*
1 a meeting or touching of persons or things
2 a person one knows who has influence especially in the business or political world

[2]**contact** *vb*
1 to come or bring into contact
2 to get in touch or communication with

[3]**contact** *adj*
involving or activated by contact ⟨*contact* sports⟩ ⟨*contact* poisons⟩

**contact lens** *n*
▼ a thin lens used to correct bad eyesight and worn right over the cornea of the eye

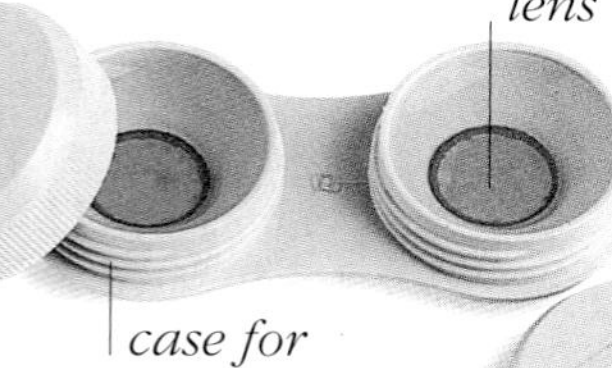


**contact lens:**
contact lenses in their case

**con·ta·gion** \kən-'tā-jən\ *n*
1 the passing of a disease from one individual to another as a result of some contact between them
2 a contagious disease

**con·ta·gious** \kən-'tā-jəs\ *adj*
spreading by contagion ⟨a *contagious* disease⟩

**con·tain** \kən-'tān\ *vb*
1 to keep within limits : RESTRAIN, CHECK ⟨tried to *contain* my anger⟩
2 to have within : HOLD ⟨the box *contained* some old books⟩
3 to consist of or include ⟨the building *contains* classrooms⟩

**con·tain·er** \kən-'tā-nər\ *n*
something into which other things can be put (as for storage)

**con·tam·i·nate** \kən-'tam-ə-,nāt\ *vb* **con·tam·i·nat·ed**; **con·tam·i·nat·ing**
1 to soil, stain, or infect by contact or association
2 to make unfit for use by adding something harmful or unpleasant

[4]**content 1:**
the content of a measuring cup

**con·tem·plate** \'känt-əm-,plāt\ *vb* **con·tem·plat·ed**; **con·tem·plat·ing**
1 to view with careful and thoughtful attention
2 to have in mind : plan on ⟨*contemplate* a trip to Europe⟩

**con·tem·pla·tion** \,känt-əm-'plā-shən\ *n*
1 the act of thinking about spiritual things : MEDITATION
2 the act of looking at or thinking about something for some time
3 a looking ahead to some future event

[1]**con·tem·po·rary** \kən-'tem-pə-,rer-ē\ *adj*
1 living or occurring at the same period of time
2 MODERN 1 ⟨our *contemporary* writers⟩

[2]**contemporary** *n, pl* **con·tem·po·rar·ies**
a person who lives at the same time or is of about the same age as another

**con·tempt** \kən-'tempt\ *n*
1 the act of despising : the state of mind of one who despises
2 the state of being despised

**con·tempt·ible** \kən-'temp-tə-bəl\ *adj*
deserving contempt ⟨a *contemptible* lie⟩

**con·temp·tu·ous** \kən-'temp-chə-wəs\ *adj*
feeling or showing contempt : SCORNFUL

**con·tend** \kən-'tend\ *vb*
1 COMPETE ⟨*contend* for a prize⟩
2 to try hard to deal with ⟨many problems to *contend* with⟩
3 to argue or state earnestly

[1]**con·tent** \kən-'tent\ *adj*
pleased and satisfied with what one has or is

[2]**content** *vb*
to make content : SATISFY

[3]**content** *n*
freedom from care or discomfort

[4]**con·tent** \'kän-,tent\ *n*
1 ◀ something contained — usually used in pl. ⟨the *contents* of a room⟩
2 the subject or topic treated (as in a book) — usually used in pl. ⟨a table of *contents*⟩
3 the important part or meaning (as of a book)
4 the amount contained or possible to contain ⟨oil with a high *content* of sulfur⟩ ⟨the jug has a *content* of one liter⟩

**con·tent·ed** \kən-'tent-əd\ *adj*
satisfied or showing satisfaction with one's possessions or one's situation in life ⟨a *contented* smile⟩

**con·ten·tion** \kən-'ten-chən\ *n*
1 an act or instance of contending
2 an idea or point for which a person argues (as in a debate or argument)
3 COMPETITION 2

**con·tent·ment** \kən-'tent-mənt\ *n*
freedom from worry or restlessness : peaceful satisfaction

[1]**con·test** \kən-'test\ *vb*
to make (something) a cause of dispute or fighting ⟨*contest* a claim⟩

[2]**con·test** \'kän-,test\ *n*
a struggle for victory : COMPETITION ⟨a *contest* for a prize⟩

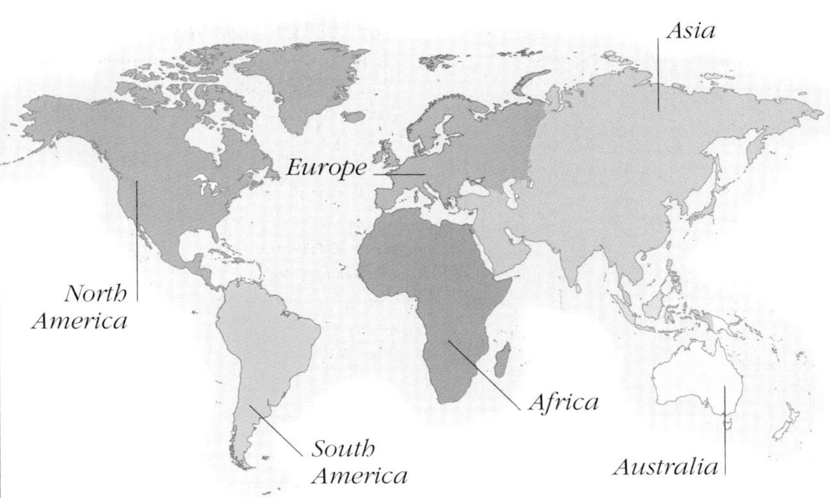


**continent 1:** the inhabited continents of the world

**con·tes·tant** \kən-'tes-tənt\ *n*
one who takes part in a contest ⟨a *contestant* on a quiz program⟩

**con·ti·nent** \'känt-n-ənt\ *n*
**1** ▲ one of the great divisions of land on the globe (as Africa, Antarctica, Asia, Australia, Europe, North America, or South America)
**2** *cap* the continent of Europe

**con·ti·nen·tal** \,känt-n-'ent-l\ *adj*
of or relating to a continent

**con·tin·gent** \kən-'tin-jənt\ *adj*
depending on something else that may or may not exist or occur ⟨our trip is *contingent* on our being able to get tickets⟩

**con·tin·u·al** \kən-'tin-yə-wəl\ *adj*
**1** going on without stopping
**2** occurring again and again at short intervals
**con·tin·u·al·ly** *adv*

**con·tin·u·ance** \kən-'tin-yə-wəns\ *n*
**1** the act of continuing
**2** the quality of being continual

**con·tin·u·a·tion** \kən-,tin-yə-'wā-shən\ *n*
**1** the making longer of a state or activity
**2** a going on after stopping
**3** a thing or part by which something is continued

**con·tin·ue** \kən-'tin-yü\ *vb*
**con·tin·ued**; **con·tinu·ing**
**1** to do or cause to do the same thing without changing or stopping ⟨I *continued* to work hard⟩ ⟨the weather *continued* hot and sunny⟩
**2** to begin again after stopping ⟨to be *continued* next week⟩

**con·ti·nu·ity** \,känt-n-'ü-ət-ē, -'yü-\ *n, pl* **con·ti·nu·ities**
the quality or state of being continuous

**con·tin·u·ous** \kən-'tin-yə-wəs\ *adj*
continuing without a stop
**con·tin·u·ous·ly** *adv*

**con·tort** \kən-'tȯrt\ *vb*
to give an unusual appearance or unnatural shape to by twisting

**con·tor·tion** \kən-'tȯr-shən\ *n*
**1** a twisting or a being twisted out of shape
**2** a contorted shape or thing

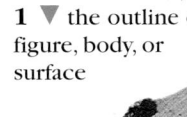

**con·tour** \'kän-,tu̇r\ *n*
**1** ▼ the outline of a figure, body, or surface
**2** a line or a drawing showing an outline

**contour 1:** a mountain with an irregular contour

**contra-** *prefix*
**1** against : contrary : contrasting
**2** pitched below normal bass

**con·tra·band** \'kän-trə-,band\ *n*
**1** goods forbidden by law to be owned or to be brought into or out of a country
**2** smuggled goods

[1]**con·tract** \'kän-,trakt\ *n*
**1** an agreement that the law can force one to keep
**2** a writing made to show the terms and conditions of a contract

[2]**con·tract** \kən-'trakt, *1 is also* 'kän-,trakt\ *vb*
**1** to agree by contract ⟨*contracted* to build a house⟩
**2** to become sick with : CATCH ⟨*contract* pneumonia⟩
**3** to draw together and make shorter and broader ⟨*contract* one's muscles⟩
**4** to make or become smaller : SHRINK ⟨cold metal *contracts*⟩
**5** to make (as a word) shorter by dropping sounds or letters

**con·trac·tion** \kən-'trak-shən\ *n*
**1** the act or process of contracting : the state of being contracted
**2** a shortening of a word or word group by leaving out a sound or letter
**3** a form (as *don't* or *they've*) produced by contraction

**con·tra·dict** \,kän-trə-'dikt\ *vb*
**1** to deny the truth of a statement : say the opposite of what someone else has said
**2** to be opposed to ⟨your actions *contradict* your words⟩

**con·tra·dic·tion** \,kän-trə-'dik-shən\ *n*
something (as a statement) that contradicts something else

**con·tra·dic·to·ry** \,kän-trə-'dik-tə-rē\ *adj*
involving, causing, or being a contradiction ⟨*contradictory* reports⟩

A B C D E F G H I J K L M N O P Q R S T U V W X Y Z

**con·tral·to** \kən-ˈtral-tō\ *n*, *pl* **con·tral·tos**
**1** the lowest female singing voice : ALTO
**2** a singer with a contralto voice

**con·trap·tion** \kən-ˈtrap-shən\ *n* GADGET

[1]**con·trary** \ˈkän-ˌtrer-ē\ *n*, *pl* **con·trar·ies**
something opposite or contrary
**on the contrary** just the opposite : NO

[2]**con·trary** \ˈkän-ˌtrer-ē, *4 is often* kən-ˈtreər-ē\ *adj*
**1** exactly opposite : altogether different ⟨we hold *contrary* opinions about that⟩
**2** being against or opposed to ⟨actions *contrary* to the law⟩
**3** not favorable ⟨*contrary* winds delayed the ship⟩
**4** unwilling to obey or behave well ⟨*contrary* children⟩

[1]**con·trast** \kən-ˈtrast\ *vb*
**1** to show noticeable differences
**2** to compare two persons or things so as to show the differences between them
**synonyms** see COMPARE

[2]**con·trast** \ˈkän-ˌtrast\ *n*
**1** a person or thing that shows differences when compared to another
**2** ▼ difference or unlikeness (as in color or brightness) between related things especially when very plain

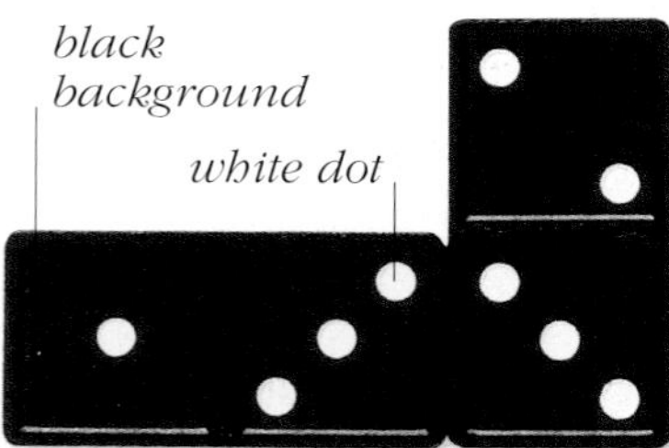


[2]**contrast 2:** the white dots on a domino are in sharp contrast with the black background

**con·trib·ute** \kən-ˈtrib-yət\ *vb*
**con·trib·ut·ed**; **con·trib·ut·ing**
**1** to give along with others
**2** to have a share in something ⟨you all *contributed* to the success of the plan⟩
**3** to supply (as an article) for publication especially in a magazine
**con·trib·u·tor** \kən-ˈtrib-yət-ər\ *n*

**con·tri·bu·tion** \ˌkän-trə-ˈbyü-shən\ *n*
**1** the act of contributing
**2** the sum or thing contributed

**con·trite** \ˈkän-ˌtrīt, kən-ˈtrīt\ *adj*
feeling or showing sorrow for some wrong that one has done : REPENTANT

**con·triv·ance** \kən-ˈtrī-vəns\ *n*
something (as a scheme or a mechanical device) produced with skill and cleverness

**con·trive** \kən-ˈtrīv\ *vb*
**con·trived**; **con·triv·ing**
**1** [2]PLAN 1, PLOT ⟨*contrive* a way to escape⟩
**2** to form or make in some skillful or clever way
**3** to manage to bring about or do

[1]**con·trol** \kən-ˈtrōl\ *vb*
**con·trolled**; **con·trol·ling**
**1** to keep within bounds : RESTRAIN ⟨learn to *control* your temper⟩ ⟨*control* a horse⟩
**2** to have power over

[2]**control** *n*
**1** the power or authority to control or command
**2** ability to control ⟨anger that is out of *control*⟩ ⟨lose *control* of an automobile⟩
**3** SELF-RESTRAINT
**4** REGULATION ⟨price *controls*⟩
**5** a device used to start, stop, or change the operation of a machine or system ⟨a radio *control*⟩
**6** something used in an experiment or study to provide a check on results

**con·tro·ver·sial** \ˌkän-trə-ˈvər-shəl\ *adj*
relating to or causing controversy ⟨a *controversial* law⟩

**con·tro·ver·sy** \ˈkän-trə-ˌvər-sē\ *n*, *pl* **con·tro·ver·sies**
**1** an often long or heated discussion of something about which there is great difference of opinion
**2** [1]QUARREL 2

**co·nun·drum** \kə-ˈnən-drəm\ *n* [1]RIDDLE

**con·va·lesce** \ˌkän-və-ˈles\ *vb*
**con·va·lesced**; **con·va·lesc·ing**
to regain health and strength gradually after sickness or injury

**con·va·les·cence** \ˌkän-və-ˈles-ns\ *n*
the period or process of convalescing

[1]**con·va·les·cent** \ˌkän-və-ˈles-nt\ *adj*
passing through convalescence

[2]**convalescent** *n*
a person who is convalescent

**con·vec·tion** \kən-ˈvek-shən\ *n*
motion in a gas (as air) or a liquid in which the warmer portions rise and the colder portions sink ⟨heat transferred by *convection*⟩

**con·vene** \kən-ˈvēn\ *vb*
**con·vened**; **con·ven·ing**
**1** ASSEMBLE 3 ⟨the legislature *convened* on Tuesday⟩
**2** to cause to assemble

**con·ve·nience** \kən-ˈvē-nyəns\ *n*
**1** the quality or state of being convenient
**2** personal comfort ⟨thought only of my own *convenience*⟩
**3** OPPORTUNITY 1 ⟨come at your earliest *convenience*⟩
**4** something that gives comfort or advantage ⟨a house with modern *conveniences*⟩

**con·ve·nient** \kən-ˈvē-nyənt\ *adj*
**1** suited to a person's comfort or ease ⟨a *convenient* time⟩ ⟨a *convenient* house⟩
**2** suited to a certain use ⟨*convenient* tools⟩
**3** easy to get to ⟨several *convenient* stores⟩
**con·ve·nient·ly** *adv*

**con·vent** \ˈkän-vənt, -ˌvent\ *n*
**1** a group of nuns living together
**2** a house or a set of buildings occupied by a community of nuns

**con·ven·tion** \kən-ˈven-chən\ *n*
**1** AGREEMENT 2 ⟨a *convention* among nations⟩
**2** a custom or a way of acting and doing things that is widely accepted and followed
**3** a meeting of persons gathered together for a common purpose ⟨a teachers' *convention*⟩

**con·ven·tion·al** \kən-ˈven-chən-l\ *adj*
**1** behaving according to convention ⟨very *conventional* people⟩
**2** used or accepted through convention ⟨*conventional* signs and symbols⟩

**con·ver·sa·tion** \ˌkän-vər-ˈsā-shən\ *n*
talking or a talk between two or more people

**con·verse** \kən-'vərs\ *vb* **con·versed**; **con·vers·ing** to have a conversation **synonyms** see SPEAK

**con·ver·sion** \kən-'vər-zhən\ *n* **1** the act of converting **:** the state of being converted **2** a change in the nature or form of a thing **3** a change of religion

[1]**con·vert** \kən-'vərt\ *vb* **1** to change from one belief, religion, view, or party to another **2** to change from one form to another **3** to exchange for an equivalent ⟨*convert* francs into dollars⟩

[2]**con·vert** \'kän-ˌvərt\ *n* a person who has been converted

[1]**con·vert·ible** \kən-'vərt-ə-bəl\ *adj* possible to change in form or use

**3** IMPART 2, COMMUNICATE ⟨we use words to *convey* our thoughts⟩

**con·vey·ance** \kən-'vā-əns\ *n* **1** the act of conveying **2** something used to carry goods or passengers

[1]**con·vict** \kən-'vikt\ *vb* to prove or find guilty

[2]**con·vict** \'kän-ˌvikt\ *n* a person serving a prison sentence usually for a long time

**con·vic·tion** \kən-'vik-shən\ *n* **1** the act of convicting **:** the state of being convicted **2** the state of mind of a person who is sure that what he or she believes or says is true **3** a strong belief or opinion

*folding top*

[2]**convertible 2:** a convertible car from the 1970s

[2]**convertible** *n* **1** something that is convertible **2** ▲ an automobile with a top that can be raised, lowered, or removed

**con·vex** \kän-'veks, 'kän-ˌveks\ *adj* ▶ rounded like the outside of a ball or circle

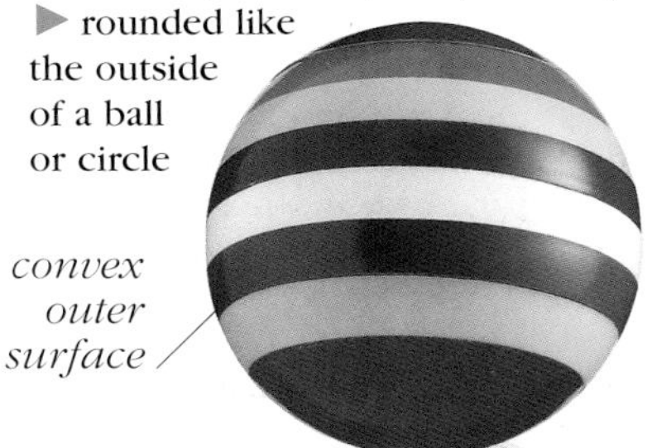


**convex:** the surface of a ball is convex

**con·vey** \kən-'vā\ *vb* **con·veyed**; **con·vey·ing** **1** to carry from one place to another **:** TRANSPORT **2** to serve as a way of carrying ⟨pipes *convey* water⟩

**con·vince** \kən-'vins\ *vb* **con·vinced**; **con·vinc·ing** to argue so as to make a person agree or believe ⟨*convinced* them to go along⟩ ⟨*convinced* me it was true⟩

**con·vinc·ing** \kən-'vin-sing\ *adj* causing one to believe or agree **:** PERSUASIVE
**con·vinc·ing·ly** *adv*

**con·vulse** \kən-'vəls\ *vb* **con·vulsed**; **con·vuls·ing** to shake violently or with jerky motions ⟨*convulsed* with laughter⟩

**con·vul·sion** \kən-'vəl-shən\ *n* **1** an attack of violent involuntary muscular contractions **:** FIT **2** a violent disturbance **:** UPHEAVAL

**con·vul·sive** \kən-'vəl-siv\ *adj* being or producing a convulsion
**con·vul·sive·ly** *adv*

[1]**coo** \'kü\ *vb* **cooed**; **coo·ing** **1** to make the soft sound made by doves and pigeons or one like it **2** to talk fondly or lovingly

[2]**coo** *n, pl* **coos** the sound made in cooing

[1]**cook** \'ku̇k\ *n* a person who prepares food for eating

[2]**cook** *vb* **1** to prepare food for eating by the use of heat **2** to go through the process of being cooked

**cook·book** \'ku̇k-ˌbu̇k\ *n* a book of cooking recipes and directions

**cook·ie** *or* **cooky** \'ku̇k-ē\ *n, pl* **cook·ies** ▶ a small sweet cake

**cookie:** a chocolate-chip cookie

**cook·out** \'ku̇k-ˌau̇t\ *n* an outing at which a meal is cooked and served outdoors

**cook up** *vb* to think up **:** DEVISE ⟨*cook up* a scheme⟩

[1]**cool** \'kül\ *adj* **1** somewhat cold **:** not warm ⟨a *cool* day⟩ ⟨a *cool* room⟩ **2** not letting or keeping in heat ⟨*cool* clothes⟩ **3** [3]CALM 2 **4** not friendly or interested **:** INDIFFERENT
**cool·ly** *adv*

[2]**cool** *vb* to make or become cool

[3]**cool** *n* a cool time or place

**cooler**

**cool·er** \'kü-lər\ *n* ▲ a container for keeping food or drink cool

**coon** \'kün\ *n*
RACCOON

**[1]coop** \'küp, 'ku̇p\ *n*
▶ a building for housing poultry

**[2]coop** *vb*
to restrict to a small space ⟨children *cooped* up by bad weather⟩

**coo·per** \'kü-pər, 'ku̇p-ər\ *n*
a worker who makes or repairs wooden casks, tubs, or barrels

**co·op·er·ate** \kō-'äp-ə-,rāt\ *vb* **co·op·er·at·ed**; **co–op·er·at·ing**
to act or work together so as to get something done

**co·op·er·a·tion** \kō-,äp-ə-'rā-shən\ *n*
the act or process of cooperating

**[1]co·op·er·a·tive** \kō-'äp-ə-rət-iv\ *adj*
**1** willing to cooperate or work with others
**2** of, relating to, or organized as a cooperative ⟨a *cooperative* store⟩

**copper 1:**
a copper pan

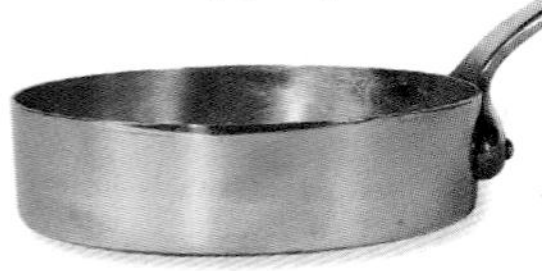

**[2]cooperative** *n*
an association formed to enable its members to buy or sell to better advantage

**[1]co·or·di·nate** \kō-'ȯrd-n-ət\ *adj*
equal in rank or importance

**[2]co·or·di·nate** \kō-'ȯrd-n-,āt\ *vb* **co·or·di·nat·ed**; **co·or·di·nat·ing**
to work or cause to work together smoothly

**co·or·di·na·tion** \kō-,ȯrd-n-'ā-shən\ *n*
smooth working together (as of parts) ⟨good muscular *coordination*⟩

**cop** \'käp\ *n*
POLICE OFFICER

**cope** \'kōp\ *vb* **coped**; **cop·ing**
to struggle or try to manage especially with some success ⟨*cope* with a tough problem⟩

**copi·er** \'käp-ē-ər\ *n*
**1** a person who copies
**2** a machine for making copies (as of letters or drawings)

**[1]coop:**
a hen coop

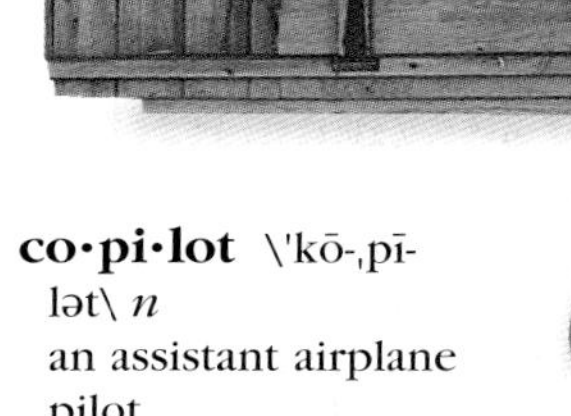

**co·pi·lot** \'kō-,pī-lət\ *n*
an assistant airplane pilot

**co·pi·ous** \'kō-pē-əs\ *adj*
very plentiful **:** ABUNDANT
**co·pi·ous·ly** *adv*

**cop·per** \'käp-ər\ *n*
**1** ◀ a tough reddish metallic chemical element that is one of the best conductors of heat and electricity
**2** a copper or bronze coin

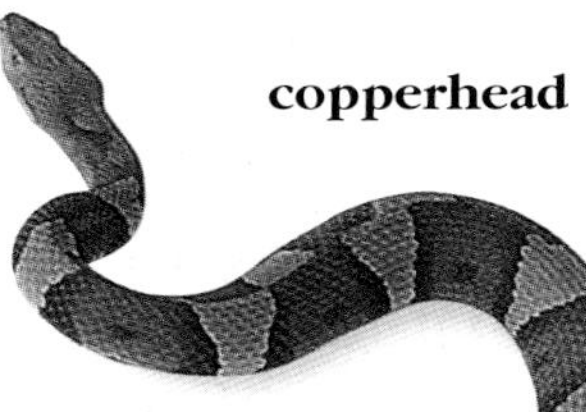

**copperhead**

**cop·per·head** \'käp-ər-,hed\ *n*
▲ a mottled reddish brown poisonous snake of the eastern United States

**cop·pice** \'käp-əs\ *n*
a thicket, grove, or growth of small trees

**co·pra** \'kō-prə\ *n*
dried coconut meat

**copse** \'käps\ *n*
COPPICE

**[1]copy** \'käp-ē\ *n, pl* **cop·ies**
**1** something that is made to look exactly like something else **:** DUPLICATE ⟨a *copy* of a letter⟩ ⟨a *copy* of a painting⟩
**2** one of the total number of books, magazines, or papers printed at one time
**3** written or printed material to be set in type

**[2]copy** *vb* **cop·ied**; **copy·ing**
**1** to make a copy of **:** DUPLICATE
**2** IMITATE 1, 3

---

**Synonyms** COPY, IMITATE, and MIMIC mean to make something so that it resembles something else. COPY suggests trying to duplicate a thing as much as possible ⟨*copy* this drawing exactly⟩. IMITATE suggests that one uses something as an example but does not try to make an exact copy ⟨*imitated* the actions of their parents⟩. MIMIC suggests carefully copying something (as a person's voice) often for the purpose of making fun of it ⟨the comedian *mimicked* a popular singer⟩.

---

**[1]copy·right** \'käp-ē-,rīt\ *n*
the legal right to be the only one to reproduce, publish, and sell the contents and form of a literary or artistic work

**[2]copyright** *vb*
to get a copyright on

**[1]coral 1:**
a colony of rose coral

**[1]cor·al** \'kȯr-əl\ *n*
**1** ▲ a stony or horny material consisting of the skeletons of tiny colonial sea animals related to the jellyfishes and including one kind that is red and used in jewelry
**2** one or a colony of the animals that form coral
**3** a dark pink

**[2]coral** *adj*
**1** made of coral ⟨a *coral* reef⟩
**2** of the color of coral

**coral snake** *n*
a small poisonous American snake brightly ringed with red, black, and yellow or white

**cord** \'kȯrd\ *n*
**1** material like a small thin rope that is used mostly for tying things
**2** something like a cord
**3** an amount of firewood equal to a pile of wood eight feet long, four feet high, and four feet wide or 128 cubic feet (about 3.6 cubic meters)
**4** a rib or ridge woven into cloth
**5** a ribbed fabric
**6** a small insulated cable used to connect an electrical appliance with an outlet

**cord·ed** \'kȯrd-əd\ *adj*
having or drawn into ridges or cords

**cor·dial** \'kȯr-jəl\ *adj*
being warm and friendly ⟨a *cordial* welcome⟩
**cor·dial·ly** *adv*

**cor·dial·i·ty** \,kȯr-jē-'al-ət-ē, kȯr-'jal-\ *n*
sincere affection and kindness

**cor·du·roy** \'kȯrd-ə-,rȯi\ *n*
**1** a heavy ribbed usually cotton cloth
**2 corduroys** *pl* trousers made of corduroy
**3** logs laid crosswise side by side to make a road surface

**[1]core** \'kōr\ *n*
**1** the central part of some fruits (as pineapples or pears)
**2** the central part of a heavenly body (as the earth or sun)
**3** a basic or central part of something ⟨the core of a problem⟩

**[2]core** *vb* **cored**; **cor·ing**
to remove the core from ⟨*core* an apple⟩

**[1]cork** \'kȯrk\ *n*
**1** the light but tough material that is the outer layer of bark of a tree (**cork oak**) and is used especially for stoppers and insulation
**2** a usually cork stopper for a bottle or jug

**[2]cork** *vb*
to stop with a cork ⟨*cork* a bottle⟩

**[1]cork·screw** \'kȯrk-,skrü\ *n*
► a pointed spiral piece of metal with a handle that is screwed into corks to draw them from bottles

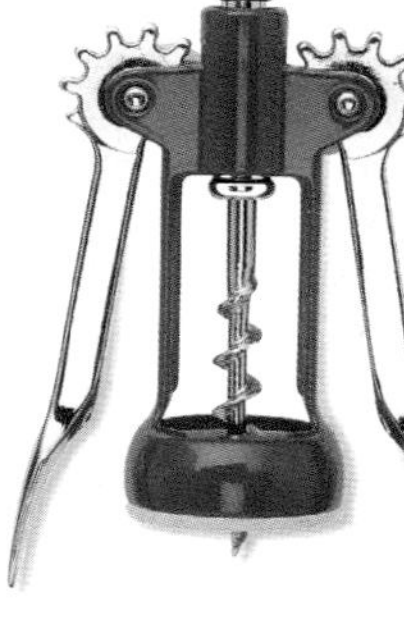

**[1]corkscrew**

**[2]corkscrew** *adj*
like a corkscrew

**cor·mo·rant** \'kȯr-mə-rənt\ *n*
▼ a large black seabird with a long neck and a slender hooked beak

**cormorant**

**[1]corn** \'kȯrn\ *n*
**1** the seeds or grain of a cereal plant (as wheat or oats)
**2** INDIAN CORN
**3** a plant whose seeds are corn

**[2]corn** *vb*
to preserve by packing with salt or by soaking in salty water ⟨*corned* beef⟩

**[3]corn** *n*
a hardening and thickening of the skin (as on a person's toe)

**corn·cob** \'kȯrn-,käb\ *n*
the woody core on which grains of Indian corn grow

**cor·nea** \'kȯr-nē-ə\ *n*
the transparent outer layer of the front of the eye covering the pupil and iris

**[1]cor·ner** \'kȯr-nər\ *n*
**1** the point or place where edges or sides meet
**2** the place where two streets or roads meet
**3** a piece used to mark, form, or protect a corner (as of a book)
**4** a place away from ordinary life or business ⟨a quiet *corner* of a big city⟩
**5** a position from which escape or retreat is difficult or impossible ⟨talked themselves into a *corner*⟩
**cor·nered** \-nərd\ *adj*

**[2]corner** *adj*
**1** located at a corner ⟨a *corner* store⟩
**2** used or usable in or on a corner

**[3]corner** *vb*
**1** to drive into a corner ⟨*corner* a rat⟩
**2** to put in a difficult position

**cor·net** \kȯr-'net\ *n*
a brass musical instrument similar to but shorter than a trumpet

**corn·flow·er** \'kȯrn-,flau̇-ər\ *n*
► a European plant related to the daisies that is often grown for its bright heads of blue, pink, or white flowers

**cor·nice** \'kȯr-nəs\ *n*
**1** an ornamental piece that forms the top edge of the front of a building or pillar
**2** an ornamental molding placed where the walls meet the ceiling of a room

**cornflower**

A B C D E F G H I J K L M N O P Q R S T U V W X Y Z

**corn·meal** \'kȯrn-'mēl\ *n*
meal ground from corn

**corn·stalk** \'kȯrn-,stȯk\ *n*
a stalk of Indian corn

**corn·starch** \'kȯrn-,stärch\ *n*
a fine starch made from Indian corn and used as a thickening agent in cooking

**corn syrup** *n*
a syrup made from cornstarch and used chiefly in baked goods and candy

**cor·nu·co·pia** \,kor-nə-'kō-pē-ə, -nyə-\ *n*
a container in the shape of a horn overflowing with fruits and flowers used as a symbol of plenty

**corny** \'kȯr-nē\ *adj* **corn·i·er**; **corn·i·est**
so simple, sentimental, or old-fashioned as to be annoying ⟨*corny* music⟩

**co·rol·la** \kə-'räl-ə\ *n*
the part of a flower that is formed by the petals

**cor·o·nary** \'kȯr-ə-,ner-ē\ *adj*
of or relating to the heart or its blood vessels

**cor·o·na·tion** \,kȯr-ə-'nā-shən\ *n*
the act or ceremony of crowning a king or queen

**cor·o·net** \,kȯr-ə-'net\ *n*
**1** a small crown worn by a person of noble but less than royal rank ⟨a duke's *coronet*⟩
**2** ▼ an ornamental wreath or band worn around the head

**coronet 2:**
a coronet of flowers and foliage

**¹cor·po·ral** \'kȯr-pə-rəl, 'kȯr-prəl\ *adj*
of or relating to the body : BODILY ⟨*corporal* punishment⟩

**²corporal** *n*
a noncommissioned officer ranking above a private in the Army or above a lance corporal in the Marine Corps

**cor·po·ra·tion** \,kȯr-pə-'rā-shən\ *n*
a group authorized by law to carry on an activity (as a business) with the rights and duties of a single person

**cor·po·re·al** \kȯr-'pōr-ē-əl\ *adj*
having, consisting of, or relating to a physical body

**corps** \'kōr\ *n, pl* **corps** \'kōrz\
**1** an organized branch of a country's military forces ⟨Marine *Corps*⟩
**2** a group of persons acting under one authority ⟨diplomatic *corps*⟩

**corpse** \'kȯrps\ *n*
a dead body

**cor·pu·lent** \'kȯr-pyə-lənt\ *adj*
very stout and heavy : extremely fat

**cor·pus·cle** \'kȯr-,pəs-əl\ *n*
one of the very small cells that float freely in the blood

**¹cor·ral** \kə-'ral\ *n*
an enclosure for keeping or capturing animals

**²corral** *vb* **cor·ralled**; **cor·ral·ling**
**1** to confine in or as if in a corral
**2** to get hold of or control over

**¹cor·rect** \kə-'rekt\ *vb*
**1** to make or set right ⟨*correct* a misspelled word⟩
**2** to change or adjust so as to bring to some standard or to a required condition
**3** to punish in order to improve ⟨*correct* a child for bad manners⟩
**4** to show how a thing can be improved or made right ⟨*correct* the students' papers⟩

**²correct** *adj*
**1** meeting or agreeing with some standard : APPROPRIATE ⟨*correct* behavior⟩ ⟨*correct* dress for a picnic⟩
**2** free from mistakes : ACCURATE
**cor·rect·ly** *adv*
**cor·rect·ness** *n*

**Synonyms** CORRECT, EXACT, and ACCURATE mean agreeing with a fact, truth, or standard. CORRECT stresses that something contains no error ⟨a *correct* answer⟩. EXACT stresses that something agrees very closely with fact or truth ⟨the *exact* measurements of the room⟩. ACCURATE stresses that great care has been taken to make sure that something agrees with the facts ⟨an *accurate* description of the battle⟩.

**cor·rec·tion** \kə-'rek-shən\ *n*
**1** the act of correcting
**2** a change that makes something right
**3** PUNISHMENT 1

**cor·re·spond** \,kȯr-ə-'spänd\ *vb*
**1** to be alike : AGREE ⟨what one gets seldom *corresponds* with what one hopes for⟩
**2** to be equivalent ⟨"give" and "donate" *correspond* closely in meaning⟩
**3** to communicate with a person by exchange of letters

**cor·re·spon·dence** \,kȯr-ə-'spän-dəns\ *n*
**1** agreement between certain things
**2** communication by means of letters : the letters exchanged

**cor·re·spon·dent** \,kȯr-ə-'spän-dənt\ *n*
**1** a person with whom another person communicates by letter
**2** a person who sends news stories or comment to a newspaper, magazine, or broadcasting company especially from a distant place

**cor·ri·dor** \'kȯr-ə-dər\ *n*
a passage into which rooms open

**cor·rode** \kə-'rōd\ *vb* **cor·rod·ed**; **cor·rod·ing**
to wear away little by little (as by rust or acid)

**cor·ro·sion** \kə-'rō-zhən\ *n*
the process or effect of corroding

**cor·ro·sive** \kə-'rō-siv, -ziv\ *adj*
tending or able to corrode

**cor·ru·gate** \'kȯr-ə-,gāt\ *vb* **cor·ru·gat·ed**; **cor·ru·gat·ing**
to make wrinkles in or shape into wavy folds ⟨*corrugated* paper⟩

**¹cor·rupt** \kə-'rəpt\ *vb*
**1** to change (as in morals, manners, or actions) from good to bad
**2** to influence a public official in an improper way (as by a bribe)

**²corrupt** *adj*
**1** morally bad : EVIL
**2** behaving in a bad or improper way : doing wrong ⟨*corrupt* judges who accept bribes⟩
**cor·rupt·ly** *adv*
**cor·rupt·ness** *n*

**cor·rup·tion** \kə-'rəp-shən\ *n*
**1** physical decay or rotting
**2** lack of honesty
**3** the causing of someone else to do something wrong
**4** a being changed for the worse ⟨*corruption* of art forms⟩

**cor·sage** \kȯr-'säzh\ *n*
▼ a bouquet of flowers usually worn on the shoulder

**corsage**

**corse·let** *or* **cors·let** \'kȯr-slət\ *n*
▼ the body armor worn by a knight especially on the upper part of the body

breastplate

backplate

**corselet:**
early 17th-century English corselet

## cosmetics

Throughout the centuries people have sought to improve their natural appearance. Today there is a vast cosmetics industry producing colored powders and creams to enhance the complexion and emphasize features such as eyes and lips.

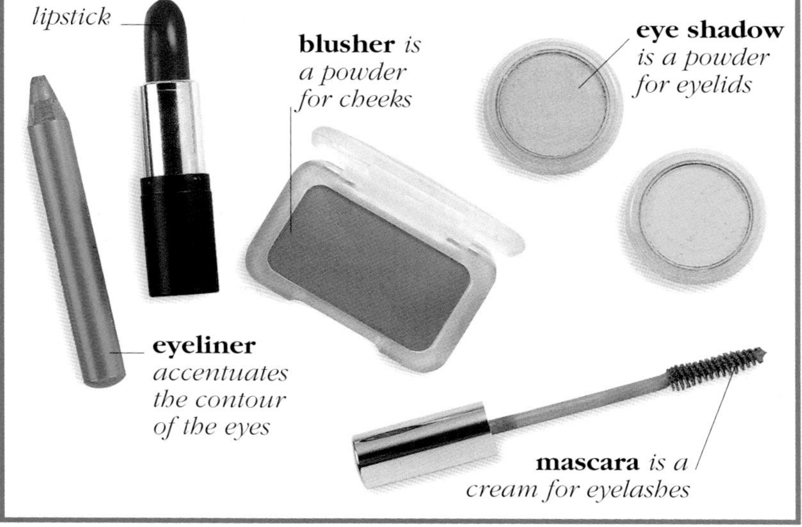
lipstick
**blusher** *is a powder for cheeks*
**eye shadow** *is a powder for eyelids*
**eyeliner** *accentuates the contour of the eyes*
**mascara** *is a cream for eyelashes*

**cor·set** \'kȯr-sət\ *n*
a tight undergarment worn to support or give shape to waist and hips

**cos·met·ic** \käz-'met-ik\ *n*
▲ material (as a cream, lotion, or powder) used to beautify especially the complexion

**cos·mic** \'käz-mik\ *adj*
of or relating to the whole universe

**cosmic ray** *n*
a stream of very penetrating particles that enter the earth's atmosphere from outer space at high speed

**cos·mo·naut** \'käz-mə-,nȯt\ *n*
a Soviet astronaut

**cos·mos** \'käz-məs, *1 is also* -,mōs, -,mäs\ *n*
**1** the orderly universe
**2** ► a tall garden plant related to the daisies that has showy white, pink, or rose-colored flower heads

[1]**cost** \'kȯst\ *n*
**1** the amount paid or charged for something : PRICE ⟨at a *cost* of eight dollars per book⟩
**2** loss or penalty involved in gaining something ⟨the greatest *cost* of war⟩ **synonyms** see PRICE

[2]**cost** *vb* **cost**; **cost·ing**
**1** to have a price of ⟨a ticket *costing* one dollar⟩
**2** to cause one to pay, spend, or lose ⟨it *cost* me my job⟩

**cost·ly** \'kȯst-lē\ *adj* **cost·li·er**; **cost·li·est**
**1** of great cost or value : EXPENSIVE, DEAR
**2** made at great expense or sacrifice

**cosmos 2**

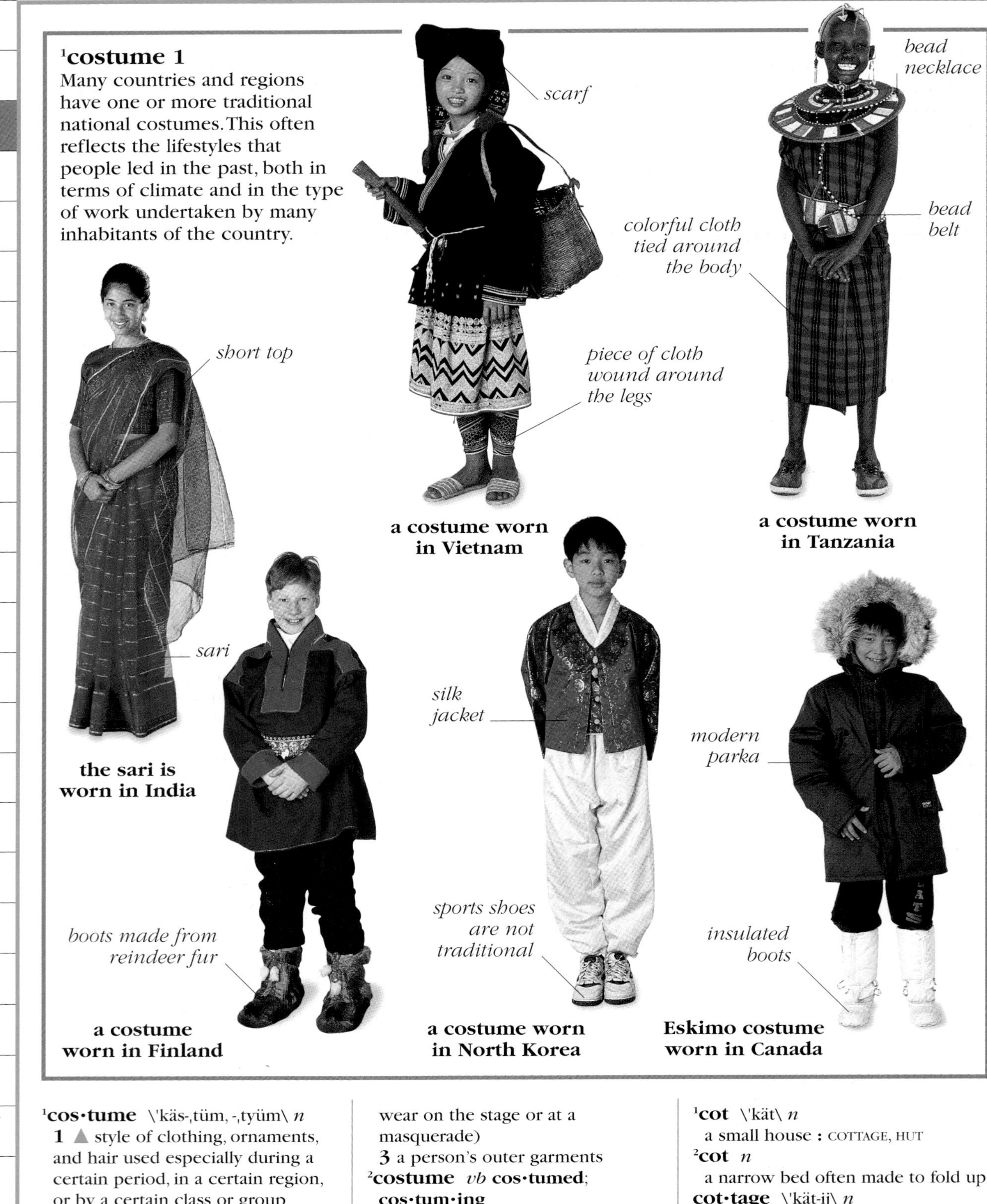


**a costume worn in Vietnam**

**a costume worn in Tanzania**

**the sari is worn in India**

**a costume worn in Finland**

**a costume worn in North Korea**

**Eskimo costume worn in Canada**

**[1]cos·tume** \ˈkäs-ˌtüm, -ˌtyüm\ *n*
**1** ▲ style of clothing, ornaments, and hair used especially during a certain period, in a certain region, or by a certain class or group ⟨ancient Roman *costume*⟩ ⟨peasant *costume*⟩
**2** special or fancy dress (as for wear on the stage or at a masquerade)
**3** a person's outer garments

**[2]costume** *vb* **cos·tumed**; **cos·tum·ing**
**1** to provide with a costume
**2** to design costumes for ⟨*costume* a play⟩

**[1]cot** \ˈkät\ *n*
a small house **:** COTTAGE, HUT

**[2]cot** *n*
a narrow bed often made to fold up

**cot·tage** \ˈkät-ij\ *n*
**1** a small usually frame house for one family
**2** a small house for vacation use

**cottage cheese** *n*
a very soft cheese made from soured skim milk

**[1]cot·ton** \'kät-n\ *n*
**1** a soft fluffy material made up of twisted hairs that surrounds the seeds of a tall plant (**cotton plant**) related to the mallows and that is spun into yarn
**2** thread, yarn, or cloth made from cotton

**[2]cotton** *adj*
made of cotton

**cotton gin** *n*
a machine for removing seeds from cotton

**cot·ton·mouth** \'kät-n-ˌmau̇th\ *n*
MOCCASIN 2

**cot·ton·seed** \'kät-n-ˌsēd\ *n*
the seed of the cotton plant from which comes a meal rich in protein and an oil used especially in cooking

**cot·ton·tail** \'kät-n-ˌtāl\ *n*
▼ a small rabbit with a white tail

**cottontail** rabbit

**cot·ton·wood** \'kät-n-ˌwu̇d\ *n*
any of several poplar trees that have seeds with bunches of hairs suggesting cotton and that include some which grow rapidly

**couch** \'kau̇ch\ *n*
a piece of furniture (as a bed or sofa) that one can sit or lie on

**cou·gar** \'kü-gər\ *n*
▶ a large yellowish brown North American wild animal related to the domestic cat

**Word History** The word *cougar* came from a word in the language of a group of Indians in Brazil. Their word for a cougar meant "false deer." A modern Latin word was formed from this Indian word. The French changed the Latin word and made a French word of it. The English word *cougar* came from this French word.

**[1]cough** \'kȯf\ *vb*
**1** to force air from the lungs with a sharp short noise or series of noises
**2** to get rid of by coughing ⟨*cough* up mucus⟩

**[2]cough** *n*
**1** a condition in which there is severe or frequent coughing
**2** an act or sound of coughing

**could** \kəd, ku̇d\ *past of* CAN
**1** used as a helping verb in the past ⟨*could* read at the age of five⟩
**2** used as a polite form instead of *can* ⟨*could* you help me⟩

**couldn't** \'ku̇d-nt\
could not

**coun·cil** \'kau̇n-səl\ *n*
a group of persons appointed or elected to make laws or give advice ⟨a city *council*⟩

**coun·cil·or** *or* **coun·cil·lor** \'kau̇n-sə-lər\ *n*
a member of a council ⟨a town *councilor*⟩

**[1]coun·sel** \'kau̇n-səl\ *n*
**1** advice given ⟨a parent's *counsel* to a child⟩
**2** the discussion of reasons for or against a thing **:** an exchange of opinions ⟨take *counsel* with friends⟩
**3** *pl* **counsel** a lawyer engaged in the trial and management of a case in court

**[2]counsel** *vb* **coun·seled** *or* **coun·selled**; **coun·sel·ing** *or* **coun·sel·ling**
**1** to give counsel **:** ADVISE ⟨*counsel* a student⟩
**2** to seek counsel ⟨*counsel* with a teacher⟩

**coun·sel·or** *or* **coun·sel·lor** \'kau̇n-sə-lər\ *n*
**1** a person who gives counsel
**2** LAWYER
**3** a supervisor of campers or activities at a summer camp

**[1]count** \'kau̇nt\ *vb*
**1** to add one by one in order to find the total number in a collection ⟨*count* the apples in a box⟩
**2** to name the numerals in order up to a particular point ⟨*count* ten⟩
**3** to name the numbers one by one or by groups ⟨*count* to 100 by fives⟩
**4** to include in counting or thinking about ⟨don't *count* Sunday as a work day⟩
**5** to consider or judge to be ⟨*count* myself lucky⟩
**6** to include or leave out by or as if by counting ⟨*counted* ourselves out⟩
**7** RELY, DEPEND ⟨you can *count* on them⟩
**8** [2]PLAN 1 ⟨*count* on our coming⟩
**9** to have value, force, or importance ⟨the people who really *count*⟩

**[2]count** *n*
**1** the act or process of counting
**2** a total arrived at by counting ⟨a *count* of ten⟩
**3** any one charge in a legal declaration or indictment ⟨guilty on all *counts*⟩

**[3]count** *n*
a European nobleman whose rank is like that of a British earl

**count·down** \'kau̇nt-ˌdau̇n\ *n*
a counting off of the time remaining before an event (as the launching of a rocket)

**[1]coun·te·nance** \'kau̇nt-n-əns\ *n*
the human face or its expression ⟨a kind *countenance*⟩

**[2]countenance** *vb* **coun·te·nanced**; **coun·te·nanc·ing**
to give approval or tolerance to

**[1]count·er** \'kau̇nt-ər\ *n*
**1** a piece (as of plastic or ivory) used in counting or in games
**2** a level surface usually higher than a table that is used for selling, serving food, displaying things, or working on

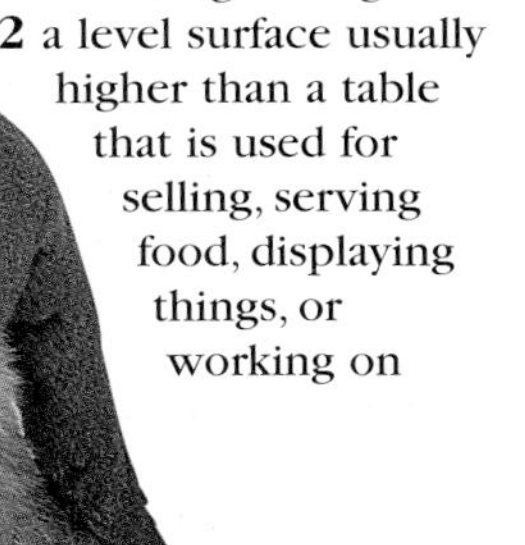

**cougar**

**²count·er** *n*
**1** one that counts
**2** a device for showing a number or amount

**³coun·ter** \'kau̇nt-ər\ *vb*
**1** to act in opposition to **:** OPPOSE
**2** RETALIATE

**⁴coun·ter** *adv*
in another or opposite direction ⟨go *counter* to advice⟩

**⁵coun·ter** *n*
an answering or opposing force or blow

**⁶coun·ter** *adj*
moving or acting in an opposite way **:** CONTRARY ⟨a *counter* tide⟩ ⟨made a *counter* offer⟩

**coun·ter-** *prefix*
**1** opposite ⟨*counter*clockwise⟩
**2** opposing
**3** like **:** matching ⟨*counter*part⟩
**4** duplicate **:** substitute

**coun·ter·act** \ˌkau̇nt-ər-'akt\ *vb*
to act against so as to prevent something from acting in its own way

**coun·ter·clock·wise** \ˌkau̇nt-ər-'kläk-ˌwīz\ *adv or adj*
in a direction opposite to that in which the hands of a clock move

**¹coun·ter·feit** \'kau̇nt-ər-ˌfit\ *adj*
**1** made in exact imitation of something genuine and meant to be taken as genuine ⟨*counterfeit* money⟩
**2** not sincere ⟨*counterfeit* sympathy⟩

**²counterfeit** *vb*
**1** PRETEND 2 ⟨*counterfeit* enthusiasm⟩
**2** to imitate or copy especially in order to deceive ⟨*counterfeiting* money⟩
**coun·ter·feit·er** *n*

**³counterfeit** *n*
something made to imitate another thing with the desire to deceive

**coun·ter·part** \'kau̇nt-ər-ˌpärt\ *n*
a person or thing that is very like or corresponds to another person or thing

**coun·ter·point** \'kau̇nt-ər-ˌpȯint\ *n*
one or more independent melodies added above or below and in harmony with a given melody

**coun·ter·sign** \'kau̇nt-ər-ˌsīn\ *n*
a secret signal that must be given by a person wishing to pass a guard **:** PASSWORD

**count·ess** \'kau̇nt-əs\ *n*
**1** the wife or widow of a count or an earl
**2** a woman who holds the rank of a count or an earl in her own right

**counting number** *n*
NATURAL NUMBER

**count·less** \'kau̇nt-ləs\ *adj*
too many to be counted ⟨*countless* grains of sand⟩

**coun·try** \'kən-trē\ *n, pl* **coun·tries**
**1** REGION 1, DISTRICT ⟨good farming *country*⟩
**2** ▼ a land lived in by a people with a common government
**3** the people of a nation ⟨a whole *country* in revolt⟩
**4** open rural land away from big towns and cities ⟨take a ride in the *country*⟩

**country 2:** map showing the country of Italy

**country and western** *n*
music coming from or imitating the folk music of the southern United States or the Western cowboy

**coun·try·man** \'kən-trē-mən\ *n, pl* **coun·try·men** \-mən\
**1** a person born in the same country as another **:** a fellow citizen
**2** a person living or raised in the country

**coun·try·side** \'kən-trē-ˌsīd\ *n*
a rural area or its people

**coun·ty** \'kau̇nt-ē\ *n, pl* **coun·ties**
a division of a state or country for local government

**coupe** *or* **cou·pé** \kü-'pā, *2 is usually* 'küp\ *n*
**1** a carriage with four wheels and an enclosed body seating two persons and with an outside seat for the driver in front
**2** ▲ an enclosed two-door automobile for usually two persons

**coupe 2:** a coupe from the 1950s

**¹cou·ple** \'kəp-əl\ *n*
**1** two persons who are paired together or closely associated
**2** two things of the same kind that are connected or that are thought of together

**²couple** *vb* **cou·pled**; **cou·pling**
**1** to join or link together **:** CONNECT ⟨*coupled* freight cars⟩
**2** to join in pairs

**cou·plet** \'kəp-lət\ *n*
two rhyming lines of verse one after another ⟨"The butcher, the baker,/ The candlestick maker" is an example of a *couplet*⟩

**cou·pling** \'kəp-ling\ *n*
**1** the act of bringing or coming together
**2** something that joins or connects two parts or things ⟨a pipe *coupling*⟩

**cou·pon** \'kü-ˌpän, 'kyü-\ *n*
**1** a ticket or form that allows the holder to receive some service, payment, or discount
**2** a part of an advertisement meant to be cut out for use as an order blank

**cour·age** \'kər-ij\ *n*
the strength of mind that makes one able to meet danger and difficulties with firmness

**cou·ra·geous** \kə-'rā-jəs\ *adj*
having or showing courage
**synonyms** see BRAVE
**cou·ra·geous·ly** *adv*

**[1]course** \'kōrs\ *n*
**1** motion from one point to another **:** progress in space or time ⟨the stars in their *course* through the sky⟩ ⟨during the *course* of a year⟩
**2** the path over which something moves
**3** direction of motion ⟨the *course* of a ship⟩
**4** a natural channel for water ⟨followed the river's *course*⟩
**5** way of doing something ⟨choose a *course* of action⟩
**6** a series of acts or proceedings arranged in regular order ⟨a *course* of lectures⟩
**7** a series of studies leading to a diploma or a degree ⟨a four-year *course* in law⟩
**8** a part of a meal served at one time ⟨finished the meat *course*⟩
**9** a continuous level range of brick or masonry throughout a wall
**of course** as might be expected

**[2]course** *vb* **coursed**; **cours·ing**
**1** to run through or over
**2** to move rapidly **:** RACE

**[1]court** \'kōrt\ *n*
**1** the home of a ruler
**2** a ruler's assembly of advisers and officers as a governing power
**3** the family and people who follow a ruler
**4** an open space completely or partly surrounded by buildings
**5** a short street
**6** a space arranged for playing a certain game ⟨tennis *court*⟩ ⟨basketball *court*⟩
**7** an official meeting led by a judge for settling legal questions or the place where it is held
**8** respect meant to win favor ⟨pay *court* to the king⟩

**[2]court** *vb*
**1** to try to gain or get the support of **:** SEEK ⟨*courting* favor with the authorities⟩ ⟨*court* the new voters⟩
**2** to seem to be asking for **:** TEMPT ⟨*court* disaster⟩
**3** to seek the liking of

**cour·te·ous** \'kərt-ē-əs\ *adj*
showing respect and consideration for others **:** POLITE
**synonyms** see CIVIL
**cour·te·ous·ly** *adv*
**cour·te·ous·ness** *n*

**cour·te·sy** \'kərt-ə-sē\ *n, pl* **cour·te·sies**
**1** the quality or state of being courteous
**2** a courteous act or expression
**3** something that is a favor and not a right

**court·house** \'kōrt-,haus\ *n*
**1** a building in which courts of law are held
**2** a building in which county offices are housed

**court·i·er** \'kōrt-ē-ər\ *n*
a member of a royal court

**court·ly** \'kōrt-lē\ *adj* **court·li·er**; **court·li·est**
suitable to a royal court **:** ELEGANT, POLITE ⟨*courtly* manners⟩

**court·ship** \'kōrt-,ship\ *n*
the act or process of courting or seeking the liking of someone

**court·yard** \'kōrt-,yärd\ *n*
[1]COURT 4

**cous·in** \'kəz-n\ *n*
a child of one's uncle or aunt

**cove** \'kōv\ *n*
a small sheltered inlet or bay

**cov·e·nant** \'kəv-ə-nənt\ *n*
a formal or solemn agreement ⟨a *covenant* between nations⟩

**[1]cov·er** \'kəv-ər\ *vb*
**1** to provide protection to or against ⟨*covered* the landing with artillery⟩
**2** to maintain a check on especially by patrolling ⟨police *cover* the highways⟩
**3** to hide from sight or knowledge ⟨*covered* my embarrassment⟩
**4** to place or spread something over ⟨*cover* the rolls with a cloth⟩
**5** to dot thickly ⟨*covered* with freckles⟩
**6** to form a cover or covering over ⟨snow *covered* the ground⟩
**7** to take into account ⟨a review *covering* the term's work⟩
**8** to have as one's field of activity or interest ⟨a reporter *covering* the courthouse⟩
**9** to pass over or through ⟨*cover* a country in one week⟩

**[2]cover** *n*
**1** something that protects, shelters, or hides
**2** something that is placed over or about another thing **:** LID, TOP
**3** a binding or a protecting case
**4** a covering (as a blanket) used on a bed
**5** an envelope or wrapper for mail

**cov·er·age** \'kəv-ə-rij, 'kəv-rij\ *n*
**1** insurance against something ⟨fire *coverage*⟩
**2** the value or amount of insurance ⟨a thousand dollars' *coverage*⟩

**cov·er·all** \'kəv-ə-,ròl\ *n*
an outer garment that combines shirt and pants and is worn to protect one's regular clothes — usually used in pl.

**covered wagon** *n*
▼ a large long wagon with a curving canvas top

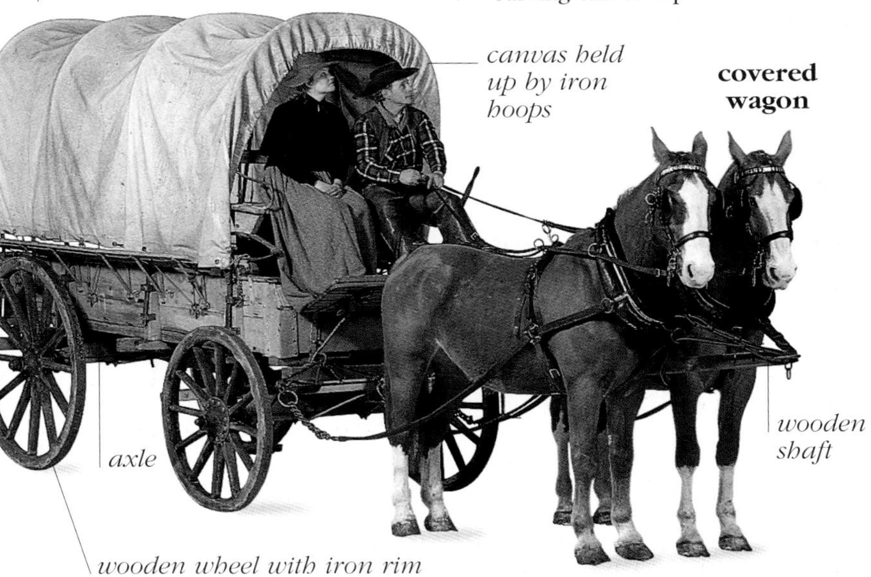

**covered wagon**

**cov·er·ing** \'kəv-ə-riŋ, 'kəv-riŋ\ *n*
something (as a roof or an envelope) that covers or conceals

**cov·er·let** \'kəv-ər-lət\ *n*
BEDSPREAD

[1]**co·vert** \'kəv-ərt, 'kō-vərt\ *adj*
made or done secretly ⟨a *covert* glance⟩ ⟨*covert* military operations⟩
**co·vert·ly** *adv*
**co·vert·ness** *n*

[2]**covert** *n*
**1** a hiding place (as a thicket that gives shelter to game animals)
**2** one of the small feathers around the bottom of the quills on the wings and tail of a bird

**cov·et** \'kəv-ət\ *vb*
to wish for greatly or with envy ⟨*covet* success⟩ ⟨*covet* a friend's happiness⟩

**cov·et·ous** \'kəv-ət-əs\ *adj*
having or showing too much desire for wealth or possessions or for something belonging to another person

**cov·ey** \'kəv-ē\ *n, pl* **coveys**
**1** a small flock (as of quail)
**2** [1]GROUP ⟨a *covey* of airplanes⟩

[1]**cow** \'kau̇\ *n*
▼ the adult female of cattle or of any of many large animals (as moose or seals)

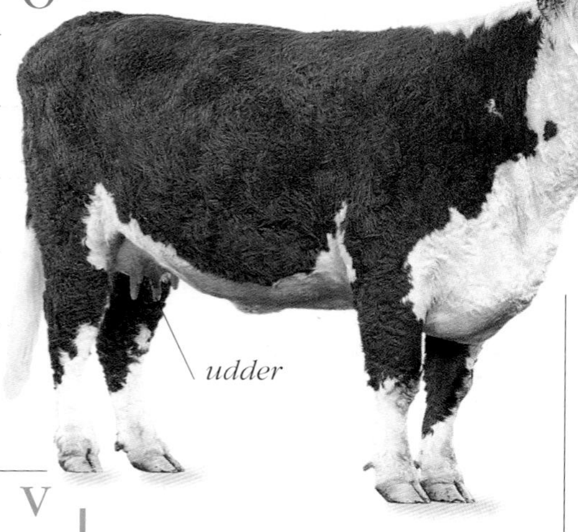


[1]**cow**

[2]**cow** *vb*
to lower the spirits or courage of **:** make afraid ⟨*cowed* by threats⟩

**cow·ard** \'kau̇-ərd\ *n*
a person who shows dishonorable fear

**cow·ard·ice** \'kau̇-ərd-əs\ *n*
dishonorable fear

**cow·ard·ly** \'kau̇-ərd-lē\ *adj*
being or behaving like a coward
**cow·ard·li·ness** *n*

**cow·bell** \'kau̇-ˌbel\ *n*
a bell hung around the neck of a cow to tell where it is

**cow·bird** \'kau̇-ˌbərd\ *n*
a small American blackbird that lays its eggs in the nests of other birds

**cow·boy** \'kau̇-ˌbȯi\ *n*
▶ a man or boy who works on a ranch or performs at a rodeo

**cow·catch·er** \'kau̇-ˌkach-ər\ *n*
a strong frame on the front of a railroad engine for moving things blocking the track

**cow·er** \'kau̇-ər\ *vb*
to shrink away or crouch down shivering (as from fear)

**cow·girl** \'kau̇-ˌgərl\ *n*
a girl or woman who works on a ranch or performs at a rodeo

**cow·hand** \'kau̇-ˌhand\ *n*
a person who works on a cattle ranch

**cow·herd** \'kau̇-ˌhərd\ *n*
a person who tends cows

**cow·hide** \'kau̇-ˌhīd\ *n*
**1** the hide of cattle or leather made from it
**2** a whip of rawhide or braided leather

**cowl** \'kau̇l\ *n*
a hood or long hooded cloak especially of a monk

**cow·lick** \'kau̇-ˌlik\ *n*
a small bunch of hair that sticks out and will not lie flat

**cow·pox** \'kau̇-ˌpäks\ *n*
a disease of cattle that when given to humans (as by vaccination) protects from smallpox

**cow·punch·er** \'kau̇-ˌpən-chər\ *n*
COWBOY

high-crowned hat
leather cuffs
riding whip
chaps
bridle
cowboy boot
spur

**cowboy**

**cow·slip** \'kau̇-ˌslip\ *n*
**1** a common Old World primrose with yellow or purple flowers
**2** MARSH MARIGOLD

**cox·swain** \'käk-sən, -ˌswān\ *n*
the person who steers a boat

**coy** \'kȯi\ *adj*
falsely shy or modest

**Word History** In earlier English *coy* meant "quiet" as well as "shy." The English word *coy* came from an early French word that meant "calm." This French word came from a Latin word that meant "quiet." The English word *quiet* also came from this Latin word.

**coy·ote** \'kī-ˌōt, kī-'ōt-ē\ *n*
a small wolf chiefly of western North America

[1]**co·zy** \'kō-zē\ *adj* **co·zi·er**; **co·zi·est**
enjoying or providing warmth and comfort
**co·zi·ly** \-zə-lē\ *adv*
**co·zi·ness** \-zē-nəs\ *n*

a b c d e f g h i j k l m n o p q r s t u v w x y z

[2]**co·zy** *n, pl* **co·zies**
a padded covering for a container (as a teapot) to keep the contents hot

**cpu** \ˌsē-ˌpē-ˈyü\ *n, often cap C&P&U*
the part of a computer that does most of the processing of data

[1]**crab** \ˈkrab\ *n*
a sea animal related to the lobsters but having a flat shell and a small abdomen pressed against the underside of the body

[2]**crab** *vb* **crabbed**; **crab·bing**
to find fault : COMPLAIN

[3]**crab** *n*
a person who is usually cross

**crab apple** *n*
**1** ▶ a small wild sour apple
**2** a cultivated apple with small usually brightly colored acid fruit

**crab·bed** \ˈkrab-əd\ *adj*
CRABBY

**crab·by** \ˈkrab-ē\ *adj* **crab·bi·er**; **crab·bi·est**
being cross and irritable

**crab·grass** \ˈkrab-ˌgras\ *n*
a weedy grass with coarse stems that root at the joints

[1]**crack** \ˈkrak\ *vb*
**1** to break or cause to break with a sudden sharp sound
**2** to make or cause to make a sound of cracking as if breaking ⟨*crack* a whip⟩
**3** to break often without completely separating into parts ⟨the ice *cracked* in several places⟩
**4** to tell (a joke) especially in a clever way
**5** to lose self-control : break down ⟨*cracked* under the strain of battle⟩
**6** to change in tone quality ⟨my voice *cracked* from emotion⟩
**7** to strike or receive a sharp blow

[2]**crack** *n*
**1** a sudden sharp noise
**2** a sharp clever remark
**3** a narrow break or opening ⟨a *crack* in the glass⟩
**4** a broken tone of the voice
**5** the beginning moment ⟨at the *crack* of dawn⟩
**6** a sharp blow
**7** [2]ATTEMPT ⟨my first *crack* at writing⟩

[3]**crack** *adj*
of high quality or ability ⟨*crack* troops⟩

**crack·er** \ˈkrak-ər\ *n*
a dry thin baked food made of flour and water

[1]**crack·le** \ˈkrak-əl\ *vb* **crack·led**; **crack·ling**
**1** to make many small sharp noises
**2** to form little cracks in a surface

[2]**crackle** *n*
the noise of repeated small cracks (as of burning wood)

**crack–up** \ˈkrak-ˌəp\ *n*
**1** BREAKDOWN
**2** [2]CRASH 3, WRECK ⟨*crack-up* of an airplane⟩

**crab apple 1**

**crack up** \ˈkrak-ˈəp\ *vb*
to cause or have a crack-up ⟨*crack up* a car⟩ ⟨you will *crack up* if you don't rest⟩

[1]**cra·dle** \ˈkrād-l\ *n*
**1** a baby's bed or cot usually on rockers
**2** place of beginning ⟨the *cradle* of civilization⟩
**3** a framework or support resembling a baby's cradle in appearance or use
**4** a rocking device used in panning gold
**5** a support for a telephone receiver

[2]**cradle** *vb* **cra·dled**; **cra·dling**
**1** to hold or support in or as if in a cradle ⟨*cradled* my head in my arms⟩
**2** to wash (as earth or sand) in a miner's cradle

**craft** \ˈkraft\ *n*
**1** skill in making things especially with the hands
**2** an occupation or trade requiring skill with the hands or as an artist ⟨carpentry is a *craft*⟩
**3** skill in deceiving for a bad purpose : CUNNING
**4** the members of a trade or a trade group
**5** *pl usually* **craft** a boat especially when of small size
**6** *pl usually* **craft** AIRCRAFT

**crafts·man** \ˈkraft-smən\ *n, pl* **crafts·men** \-smən\
**1** a person who works at a trade or handicraft
**2** a highly skilled worker in any field

**crafty** \ˈkraf-tē\ *adj* **craft·i·er**; **craft·i·est**
skillful at deceiving others : CUNNING
**craft·i·ly** \ˈkraf-tə-lē\ *adv*
**craft·i·ness** \-tē-nəs\ *n*

**crag** \ˈkrag\ *n*
a steep rock or cliff

**crag·gy** \ˈkrag-ē\ *adj* **crag·gi·er**; **crag·gi·est**
having many crags

**cram** \ˈkram\ *vb* **crammed**; **cram·ming**
**1** to stuff or pack tightly ⟨*cram* clothes into a bag⟩
**2** to fill full ⟨barns *crammed* with hay⟩
**3** to study hard just before a test
**synonyms** see PACK

[1]**cramp** \ˈkramp\ *n*
**1** a sudden painful involuntary tightening of a muscle
**2** sharp pain in the abdomen — usually used in pl.

[2]**cramp** *vb*
**1** to cause cramp in ⟨the cold water *cramped* the swimmer⟩
**2** to hold back from free action or expression : HAMPER

**cran·ber·ry** \ˈkran-ˌber-ē\ *n, pl* **cran·ber·ries**
a sour bright red berry that is eaten in sauces and jelly and is the fruit of an evergreen swamp plant related to the blueberries

[1]**crane** \ˈkrān\ *n*
**1** ▶ a tall wading bird that looks like a heron but is related to the rails
**2** a machine with a swinging arm for lifting and carrying heavy weights
**3** a mechanical arm that swings freely from a center and is used to support or carry a weight

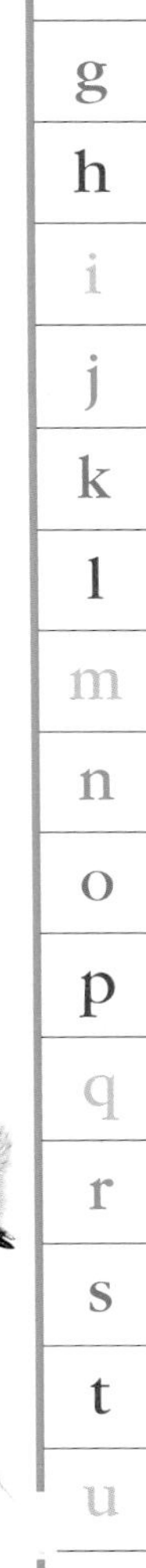

[1]**crane 1**

**[2]crane** *vb* **craned**; **cran·ing**
to stretch one's neck to see better ⟨*craned* out the window to see the parade⟩

**cra·ni·al** \'krā-nē-əl\ *adj*
of or relating to the cranium

**cra·ni·um** \'krā-nē-əm\ *n, pl* **cra·ni·ums** *or* **cra·nia** \-nē-ə\
**1** SKULL
**2** the part of the skull enclosing the brain

**[1]crank** \'krangk\ *n*
**1** a bent armlike part with a handle that is turned to start or run machinery
**2** a person with strange ideas
**3** a cross or irritable person

**[2]crank** *vb*
to start or run by turning a crank

**cranky** \'krang-kē\ *adj* **crank·i·er**; **crank·i·est**
easily angered or irritated
**crank·i·ness** *n*

**cran·ny** \'kran-ē\ *n, pl* **cran·nies**
a small break or slit (as in a cliff)

**crap·pie** \'kräp-ē\ *n*
either of two sunfishes native to the Great Lakes and Mississippi valley of which the larger and darker one (**black crappie**) is an important sport fish and the other (**white crappie**) is used as a table fish

**[1]crash** \'krash\ *vb*
**1** to break or go to pieces with or as if with violence and noise **:** SMASH
**2** to fall or strike something with noise and damage ⟨the plane *crashed* in the storm⟩ ⟨the lamp *crashed* to the floor⟩
**3** to hit or cause to hit something with force and noise ⟨the car *crashed* into a tree⟩
**4** to make or cause to make a loud noise ⟨thunder *crashed* overhead⟩
**5** to move or force a way roughly and noisily ⟨the door *crashed* shut⟩ ⟨we *crashed* the brush out of our path⟩

**[2]crash** *n*
**1** a loud sound (as of things smashing)
**2** a breaking to pieces by or as if by hitting something **:** SMASH, COLLISION
**3** the crashing of something ⟨was injured in the *crash*⟩
**4** a sudden weakening or failure (as of a business or prices)

**[1]crate** \'krāt\ *n*
a box or frame of wooden slats or boards for holding and protecting something in shipment

**[2]crate** *vb* **crat·ed**; **crat·ing**
to pack in a crate ⟨*crate* furniture for shipping⟩

**cra·ter** \'krāt-ər\ *n*
**1** a hollow in the shape of a bowl around the opening of a volcano or geyser
**2** ▶ a hole (as in the surface of the earth or moon) formed by an impact (as of a meteorite)

**cra·vat** \krə-'vat\ *n*
NECKTIE

**crave** \'krāv\ *vb* **craved**; **crav·ing**
**1** to ask for earnestly ⟨*crave* one's pardon⟩
**2** to want greatly **:** long for ⟨*craves* candy⟩ ⟨*craving* affection⟩
**synonyms** see DESIRE

**crater 2:** craters on the surface of the Moon

**cra·ven** \'krā-vən\ *adj*
COWARDLY

**crav·ing** \'krā-ving\ *n*
a great desire or longing

**craw** \'krȯ\ *n*
**1** [1]CROP 2
**2** the stomach of an animal

**[1]crayon:** wax crayons

**craw·fish** \'krȯ-ˌfish\ *n, pl* **crawfish**
CRAYFISH

**[1]crawl** \'krȯl\ *vb*
**1** to move slowly with the body close to the ground **:** move on hands and knees
**2** to go very slowly or carefully
**3** to be covered with or have the feeling of being covered with creeping things ⟨the food was *crawling* with flies⟩

**[2]crawl** *n*
**1** the act or motion of crawling
**2** a swimming stroke that looks a little like crawling

**cray·fish** \'krā-ˌfish\ *n, pl* **crayfish**
**1** a freshwater shellfish that looks like the related lobster but is much smaller
**2** a spiny saltwater shellfish that looks like the related lobster but lacks very large claws

**[1]cray·on** \'krā-ˌän, -ən\ *n*
◀ a stick of white or colored chalk or of colored wax used for writing or drawing

**[2]crayon** *vb*
to draw or color with a crayon

**craze** \'krāz\ *n*
something that is very popular for a short while

**cra·zy** \'krā-zē\ *adj* **cra·zi·er**; **cra·zi·est**
**1** having a diseased or abnormal mind **:** INSANE
**2** not sensible or logical ⟨a *crazy* idea⟩
**3** very excited or pleased ⟨*crazy* about their new house⟩
**cra·zi·ly** \'krā-zə-lē\ *adv*
**cra·zi·ness** \-zē-nəs\ *n*

**[1]creak** \'krēk\ *vb*
to make a long scraping or squeaking sound

[2]**creak** *n*
a long squeaking or scraping noise
**creaky** \'krē-kē\ *adj* **creak·i·er**; **creak·i·est**
making or likely to make a creaking sound
**creak·i·ly** \'krē-kə-lē\ *adv*
[1]**cream** \'krēm\ *n*
**1** the oily yellowish part of milk
**2** a food prepared with cream
**3** something having the smoothness and thickness of cream ⟨face *cream*⟩
**4** the best part ⟨the *cream* of the crop⟩
**5** a pale yellow
[2]**cream** *vb*
**1** to furnish, prepare, or treat with cream ⟨*cream* one's face⟩
**2** to rub or beat (as butter) until creamy
**cream·ery** \'krē-mə-rē, 'krēm-rē\ *n, pl* **cream·er·ies**
DAIRY 1, 3
**creamy** \'krē-mē\ *adj* **cream·i·er**; **cream·i·est**
**1** full of or containing cream
**2** like cream in appearance, color, or taste
**cream·i·ness** *n*
[1]**crease** \'krēs\ *n*
a line or mark usually made by folding or wrinkling
[2]**crease** *vb* **creased**; **creas·ing**
**1** to make a crease in or on
**2** to become creased
**cre·ate** \krē-'āt\ *vb* **cre·at·ed**; **cre·at·ing**
to cause to exist : bring into existence : PRODUCE **synonyms** see INVENT
**cre·a·tion** \krē-'ā-shən\ *n*
**1** the act of bringing the world into existence out of nothing
**2** the act of making, inventing, or producing something ⟨the *creation* of a poem⟩
**3** something created by human intelligence or imagination
**4** the created world ⟨throughout all *creation*⟩
**cre·a·tive** \krē-'āt-iv\ *adj*
able to create especially new and original things
**cre·a·tive·ly** *adv*
**cre·a·tive·ness** *n*
**cre·a·tor** \krē-'āt-ər\ *n*
**1** one that creates or produces
**2** *cap* GOD 1
**crea·ture** \'krē-chər\ *n*
**1** a living being
**2** a lower animal
**3** PERSON 1
**cred·i·ble** \'kred-ə-bəl\ *adj*
possible to believe : deserving belief
**cred·i·bly** \-blē\ *adv*
[1]**cred·it** \'kred-ət\ *n*
**1** the balance in an account in a person's favor
**2** trust given to a customer for future payment for goods purchased ⟨buy on *credit*⟩
**3** time given for payment ⟨extended them 30 days' *credit*⟩
**4** belief or trust in the truth of something ⟨rumors that deserve no *credit*⟩
**5** good reputation especially for honesty : high standing
**6** a source of honor or pride ⟨you are a *credit* to your school⟩
**7** recognition or honor received for some quality or work ⟨was given *credit* for the discovery⟩
**8** a unit of schoolwork ⟨took two *credits* in math⟩
[2]**credit** *vb*
**1** BELIEVE 2 ⟨*credit* a statement⟩
**2** to place something in a person's favor on (a business account) ⟨*credit* your account with ten dollars⟩
**3** to give credit or honor to for something ⟨*credited* them with discovering a new vaccine⟩
**cred·it·able** \'kred-ət-ə-bəl\ *adj*
good enough to deserve praise ⟨a *creditable* attempt⟩
**credit card** *n*
a card with which a person can buy things on credit
**cred·i·tor** \'kred-ət-ər\ *n*
a person to whom a debt is owed
**cred·u·lous** \'krej-ə-ləs\ *adj*
quick to believe especially without very good reasons
**creed** \'krēd\ *n*
**1** a statement of the basic beliefs of a religious faith
**2** a set of guiding rules or beliefs
**creek** \'krēk, 'krik\ *n*
a stream of water usually larger than a brook and smaller than a river
**creel** \'krēl\ *n*
► a basket for holding a catch of fish
[1]**creep** \'krēp\ *vb* **crept** \'krept\; **creep·ing**
**1** to move along with the body close to the ground or floor : move slowly on hands and knees : CRAWL
**2** to move or advance slowly, timidly, or quietly ⟨the tide *crept* up the beach⟩
**3** to grow or spread along the ground or along a surface ⟨ivy *creeping* up a wall⟩
[2]**creep** *n*
**1** a creeping movement
**2** a feeling as of insects crawling over one's skin : a feeling of horror — usually used in pl.
**creep·er** \'krē-pər\ *n*
**1** one that creeps
**2** a small bird that creeps about trees and bushes in search of insects
**3** a plant (as ivy) that grows by spreading over a surface
**creepy** \'krē-pē\ *adj* **creep·i·er**; **creep·i·est**
**1** having or causing a feeling as of insects creeping on the skin
**2** causing fear : SCARY ⟨a *creepy* story⟩
**creep·i·ness** *n*
**cre·mate** \'krē-,māt\ *vb* **cre·mat·ed**; **cre·mat·ing**
to burn (as a dead body) to ashes
**cre·ma·tion** \kri-'mā-shən\ *n*
the act or practice of cremating
**crepe** \'krāp\ *n*
a thin crinkled fabric (as of silk or wool)
**crepe paper** *n*
paper with a crinkled or puckered look and feel
**crept** *past of* CREEP
**cre·scen·do** \kri-'shen-dō\ *n, pl* **cre·scen·dos** *or* **cre·scen·does**
a gradual increase in the loudness of music

**creel**

A B C D E F G H I J K L M N O P Q R S T U V W X Y Z

**[1]cres·cent** \'kres-nt\ *n*
**1** the shape of the visible moon during about the first week after new moon or the last week before the next new moon
**2** something shaped like a crescent moon

**[2]crescent** *adj*
shaped like the new moon

**cress** \'kres\ *n*
▼ any of several salad plants of the mustard group

**cress**

**crest** \'krest\ *n*
**1** a showy growth (as of flesh or feathers) on the head of an animal
**2** an emblem or design on a helmet (as of a knight) or over a coat of arms
**3** something forming the top of something else ⟨the *crest* of the wave⟩ ⟨the *crest* of a hill⟩
**crest·ed** \'kres-təd\ *adj*

**crest·fall·en** \'krest-ˌfö-lən\ *adj*
feeling disappointment and loss of pride ⟨he was *crestfallen* when they said no⟩

**crev·ice** \'krev-əs\ *n*
a narrow opening (as in the earth) caused by cracking or splitting : FISSURE

**crew** \'krü\ *n*
**1** a gathering of people ⟨a happy *crew* on a picnic⟩
**2** a group of people working together ⟨the kitchen *crew*⟩
**3** the group of people who operate a ship, train, or airplane

**crib** \'krib\ *n*
**1** a manger for feeding animals
**2** ► a small bed frame with high sides for a child
**3** a building or bin for storing ⟨corn *crib*⟩

**[1]crick·et** \'krik-ət\ *n*
▼ a small leaping insect noted for the chirping notes of the males

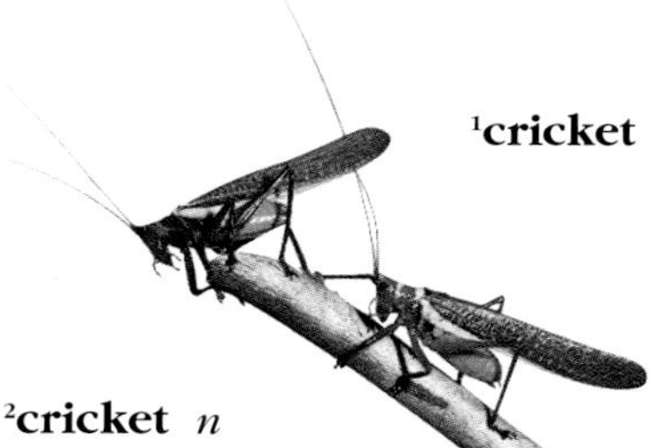

**[1]cricket**

**[2]cricket** *n*
a game played on a large field with bats, ball, and wickets by two teams of eleven players each

**cri·er** \'krī-ər\ *n*
one who calls out orders or announcements ⟨the town *crier*⟩

**crime** \'krīm\ *n*
**1** the doing of an act forbidden by law : the failure to do an act required by law
**2** an act that is sinful, foolish, or disgraceful ⟨it's a *crime* to waste food⟩

**[1]crim·i·nal** \'krim-ən-l\ *adj*
**1** being or guilty of crime ⟨a *criminal* act⟩
**2** relating to crime or its punishment ⟨*criminal* law⟩
**crim·i·nal·ly** \-ən-l-ē\ *adv*

**[2]criminal** *n*
a person who has committed a crime

**crim·son** \'krim-zən\ *n*
a deep purplish red

**cringe** \'krinj\ *vb* **cringed**; **cring·ing**
**1** to shrink in fear : COWER
**2** to behave in a very humble way : FAWN

**crin·kle** \'kring-kəl\ *vb* **crin·kled**; **crin·kling**
**1** to form or cause little waves or wrinkles on the surface : WRINKLE
**2** [1]RUSTLE 1

**crin·kly** \'kring-klē\ *adj* **crin·kli·er**; **crin·kli·est**
full of small wrinkles

**[1]crip·ple** \'krip-əl\ *n*
a lame or disabled person

**[2]cripple** *vb* **crip·pled**; **crip·pling**
**1** to cause to become a cripple ⟨*crippled* by rheumatism⟩
**2** to make useless or imperfect

**cri·sis** \'krī-səs\ *n, pl* **cri·ses** \'krī-ˌsēz\
**1** a turning point for better or worse in a disease
**2** an unstable or critical time or state of affairs

**[1]crisp** \'krisp\ *adj*
**1** being thin and hard and easily crumbled ⟨*crisp* potato chips⟩
**2** pleasantly firm and fresh ⟨*crisp* celery⟩
**3** having a sharp distinct outline ⟨*crisp* drawings⟩

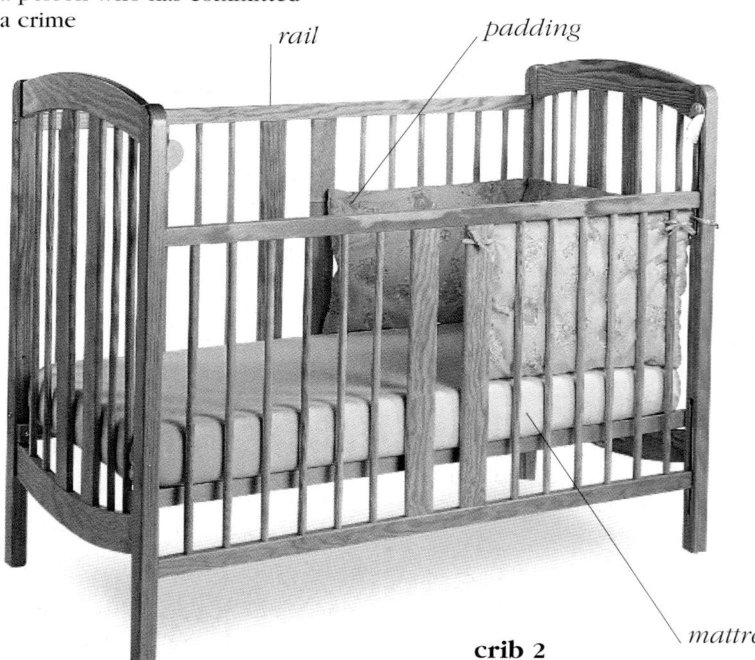


**crib 2**

**4** being clear and brief ⟨a *crisp* reply⟩
**5** pleasantly cool and invigorating : BRISK ⟨a *crisp* autumn day⟩
**synonyms** see BRITTLE

**²crisp** *vb*
to make or become crisp

**criss·cross** \'kris-ˌkȯs\ *vb*
**1** to mark with or make lines that cross one another
**2** to go or pass back and forth

**crit·ic** \'krit-ik\ *n*
**1** a person who makes or gives a judgment of the value, worth, beauty, or quality of something
**2** a person given to finding fault or complaining

**crit·i·cal** \'krit-i-kəl\ *adj*
**1** inclined to criticize especially in an unfavorable way
**2** consisting of or involving criticism or the judgment of critics ⟨*critical* writings⟩
**3** using or involving careful judgment ⟨a *critical* examination of a patient⟩
**4** of, relating to, or being a turning point or crisis ⟨the *critical* stage of a fever⟩
**crit·i·cal·ly** *adv*

**crit·i·cism** \'krit-ə-ˌsiz-əm\ *n*
**1** the act of criticizing and especially of finding fault
**2** a critical remark or comment
**3** a careful judgment or review especially by a critic

**crit·i·cize** \'krit-ə-ˌsīz\ *vb*
**crit·i·cized**; **crit·i·ciz·ing**
**1** to examine and judge as a critic
**2** to find fault with

**¹croak** \'krōk\ *vb*
**1** to make a deep harsh sound ⟨frogs *croaked*⟩
**2** to speak in a hoarse throaty voice

**²croak** *n*
a hoarse harsh sound or cry

**¹cro·chet** \krō-'shā\ *n*
work done or a fabric formed by crocheting

**²crochet** *vb*
to make (something) or create a fabric with a hooked needle by forming and interlacing loops in a thread

**crock** \'kräk\ *n*
a thick pot or jar of baked clay

**crock·ery** \'kräk-ə-rē\ *n*
EARTHENWARE

crocodile

**croc·o·dile** \'kräk-ə-ˌdīl\ *n*
▲ a very large animal related to the alligator that crawls on short legs about tropical marshes and rivers

**cro·cus** \'krō-kəs\ *n*
► a plant related to the irises that has grasslike leaves and is often planted for its white, yellow, or purple spring flowers

crocus

**cro·ny** \'krō-nē\ *n*, *pl* **cronies**
a close companion : CHUM

**¹crook** \'krůk\ *vb*
²BEND 2, CURVE ⟨*crook* your finger⟩

**²crook** *n*
**1** a shepherd's staff with one end curved into a hook
**2** a dishonest person (as a thief or swindler)
**3** a curved or hooked part of a thing : bend

**crook·ed** \'krůk-əd\ *adj*
**1** having bends and curves ⟨a *crooked* path⟩
**2** not set or placed straight ⟨the picture is *crooked*⟩
**3** DISHONEST ⟨a *crooked* card game⟩
**crook·ed·ly** *adv*
**crook·ed·ness** *n*

**croon** \'krün\ *vb*
to hum or sing in a low soft voice ⟨*croon* a lullaby⟩

**¹crop** \'kräp\ *n*
**1** a short riding whip
**2** an enlargement just above the stomach of a bird or insect in which food is stored for a while
**3** the amount gathered or harvested : HARVEST ⟨a *crop* of wheat⟩
**4** BATCH 3, LOT

**²crop** *vb* **cropped**; **crop·ping**
**1** to remove (as by cutting or biting) the upper or outer parts of : TRIM ⟨sheep *cropping* clover⟩
**2** to grow or yield a crop (as of grain) : cause (land) to bear a crop
**3** to come or appear when not expected ⟨problems *crop* up daily⟩

**cro·quet** \krō-'kā\ *n*
▼ a game in which players drive wooden balls with mallets through a series of wickets set out on a lawn

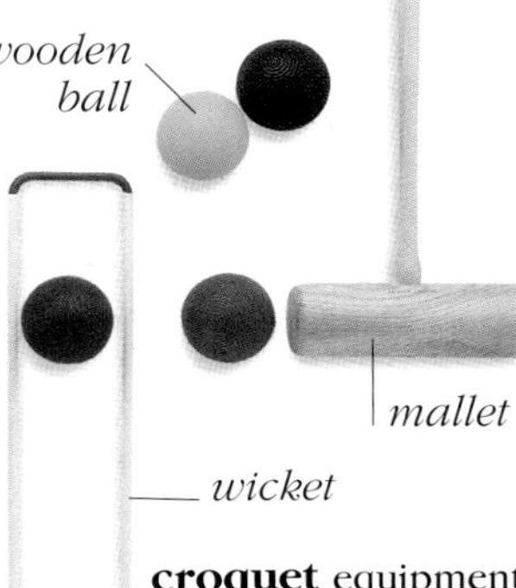


**croquet** equipment

**cro·quette** \krō-'ket\ *n*
a roll or ball of hashed meat, fish, or vegetables fried in deep fat

**¹cross** \'krȯs\ *n*
**1** a structure consisting of one bar crossing another at right angles
**2** *often cap* the structure on which Jesus was crucified used as a symbol of Christianity and of the Christian religion
**3** sorrow or suffering as test of patience or virtue ⟨had their *crosses* to bear⟩
**4** an object or mark shaped like a cross ⟨a stone *cross*⟩ ⟨put a *cross* next to the name⟩
**5** a mixing of breeds, races, or kinds : the product of such a mixing

[2]**cross** *vb*
**1** to lie or be situated across
**2** to divide by passing through or across (a line or area) : INTERSECT
**3** to move, pass, or extend across or past ⟨*cross* the street⟩
**4** to make the sign of the cross upon or over (as in prayer)
**5** to cancel by marking crosses on or by drawing a line through ⟨*cross* out a word⟩
**6** to place one over the other ⟨*cross* your legs⟩
**7** to act against : OPPOSE ⟨*crossed* my parent's wishes⟩
**8** to draw a line across ⟨*cross* your *t*'s⟩
**9** to cause (an animal or plant) to breed with one of another kind : produce hybrids
**10** to pass going in opposite directions ⟨their letters *crossed* in the mail⟩

[3]**cross** *adj*
**1** lying, falling, or passing across ⟨a *cross* street⟩
**2** [2]CONTRARY 1 ⟨at *cross* purposes⟩
**3** hard to get along with : IRRITABLE
**cross·ly** *adv*
**cross·ness** *n*

**cross·bar** \'krȯs-ˌbär\ *n*
a bar, piece, or stripe placed crosswise or across something

**cross·bones** \'krȯs-ˌbōnz\ *n pl*
► two leg or arm bones placed or pictured as lying across each other ⟨a skull and *crossbones*⟩

**cross·bow** \'krȯs-ˌbō\ *n*
▼ a short bow mounted crosswise near the end of a wooden stock that shoots short arrows

*wooden stock*
*bowstring*
**crossbow**

**cross–ex·am·ine** \ˌkrȯ-sig-'zam-ən\ *vb*
**cross–ex·am·ined**; **cross–ex·am·in·ing**
to question (a person) in an effort to show that statements or answers given earlier were false
**cross–ex·am·in·er** *n*

**cross–eyed** \'krȯ-'sīd\ *adj*
having one or both eyes turned toward the nose

**cross·ing** \'krȯ-sing\ *n*
**1** a point where two lines, tracks, or streets cross each other
**2** a place provided for going across a street, railroad tracks, or a stream
**3** a voyage across a body of water

**cross·piece** \'krȯ-ˌspēs\ *n*
something placed so as to cross something else

**cross–ref·er·ence** \'krȯs-'ref-ə-rəns, -'ref-rəns\ *n*
a reference made from one place to another (as in a dictionary)

**cross·roads** \'krȯs-ˌrōdz\ *n sing or pl*
a place where roads cross

**cross section** *n*
**1** a cutting made across something (as a log or an apple)
**2** a representation of a cross section ⟨a *cross section* of a wire⟩
**3** a number of persons or things selected from a group to stand for the whole

**crossbones**
on a 19th-century pirate's flag

**cross·walk** \'krȯ-ˌswȯk\ *n*
a specially paved or marked path for people walking across a street or road

**cross·wise** \'krȯ-ˌswīz\ *adv*
so as to cross something : ACROSS

**cross·word puzzle** \ˌkrȯ-ˌswərd-\ *n*
a puzzle in which words are filled into a pattern of numbered squares in answer to clues so that they read across and down

**crotch** \'kräch\ *n*
an angle formed by the spreading apart of two legs or branches or of a limb from its trunk ⟨the *crotch* of a tree⟩

[1]**crouch** \'krau̇ch\ *vb*
to stoop or bend low with the arms and legs close to the body

[2]**crouch** *n*
the position of crouching

**croup** \'krüp\ *n*
a children's disease in which a hoarse cough and hard breathing are present

[1]**crow** \'krō\ *n*
▼ a glossy black bird that has a harsh cry

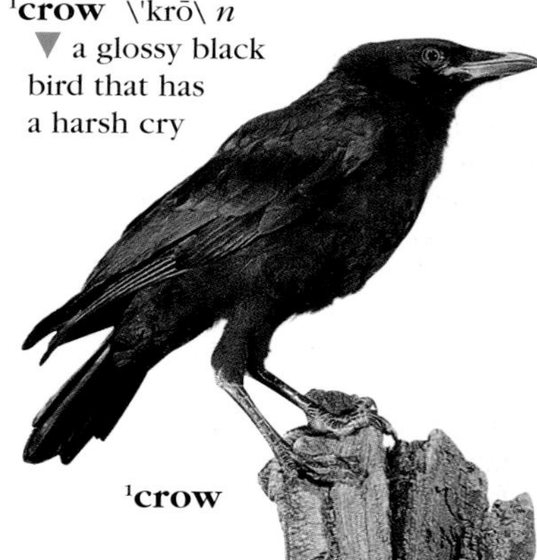

[1]**crow**

[2]**crow** *vb*
**1** to make the loud shrill sound that a rooster makes
**2** to make sounds of delight
**3** [2]BOAST 1 ⟨*crowed* over our victory⟩

[3]**crow** *n*
**1** the cry of a rooster
**2** a cry of triumph

**crow·bar** \'krō-ˌbär\ *n*
a metal bar used as a lever (as for prying things apart)

[1]**crowd** \'krau̇d\ *vb*
**1** to press or push forward ⟨*crowd* into an elevator⟩
**2** to press close ⟨the players *crowded* around the coach⟩
**3** to collect in numbers : THRONG
**4** to fill or pack by pressing together ⟨cars *crowded* the roads⟩

[2]**crowd** *n*
**1** a large number of persons collected together : THRONG
**2** the population as a whole : ordinary people ⟨books that appeal to the *crowd*⟩
**3** a group of people having a common interest ⟨running around with the wrong *crowd*⟩

**[1]crown** \'kraün\ *n*
**1** a wreath or band especially as a mark of victory or honor
**2** a royal headdress
**3** the highest part (as of a tree or mountain)
**4** the top of the head
**5** the top part of a hat
**6** the part of a tooth outside of the gum
**7** something suggesting a crown
**8** *cap* royal power or authority or one having such power
**9** any of various coins (as a British coin worth five shillings)
**crowned** \'kraünd\ *adj*

**[2]crown** *vb*
**1** to place a crown on : make sovereign
**2** to declare officially to be ⟨was *crowned* champion⟩
**3** to give something as a mark of honor or reward
**4** [2]TOP 2 ⟨snow *crowned* the mountain⟩
**5** to bring to a successful conclusion : COMPLETE, PERFECT
**6** to put an artificial crown on a damaged tooth
**7** to hit on the head

**crow's nest** *n*
▼ a partly enclosed place to stand high on the mast of a ship for use as a lookout

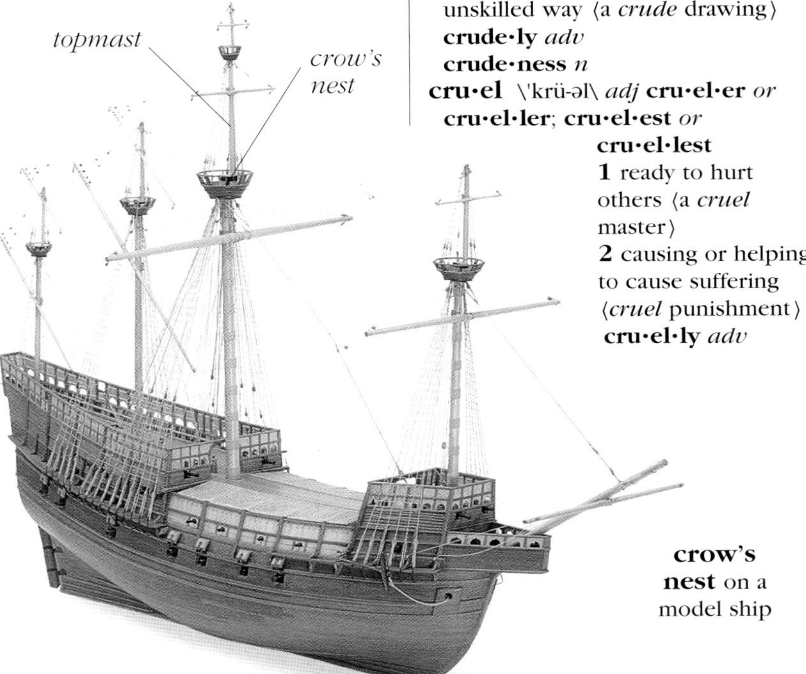


**crow's nest** on a model ship

**cru·cial** \'krü-shəl\ *adj*
**1** being a final or very important test or decision : DECISIVE ⟨a *crucial* battle⟩
**2** very important : SIGNIFICANT ⟨water is a *crucial* element in our weather⟩

**cru·ci·ble** \'krü-sə-bəl\ *n*
a pot made of a substance not easily damaged by fire that is used for holding something to be treated under great heat

**cru·ci·fix** \'krü-sə-,fiks\ *n*
a cross with a figure of Christ crucified on it

**cru·ci·fix·ion** \,krü-sə-'fik-shən\ *n*
**1** an act of crucifying
**2** *cap* the crucifying of Christ on the cross

**cru·ci·fy** \'krü-sə-,fī\ *vb*
**cru·ci·fied**; **cru·ci·fy·ing**
**1** to put to death by nailing or binding the hands and feet to a cross
**2** to treat cruelly : TORTURE, PERSECUTE ⟨were *crucified* in the newspapers⟩

**crude** \'krüd\ *adj* **crud·er**; **crud·est**
**1** in a natural state and not changed by special treatment : RAW ⟨*crude* oil⟩ ⟨*crude* sugar⟩
**2** not having or showing good manners : VULGAR
**3** planned or done in a rough or unskilled way ⟨a *crude* drawing⟩
**crude·ly** *adv*
**crude·ness** *n*

**cru·el** \'krü-əl\ *adj* **cru·el·er** *or* **cru·el·ler**; **cru·el·est** *or* **cru·el·lest**
**1** ready to hurt others ⟨a *cruel* master⟩
**2** causing or helping to cause suffering ⟨*cruel* punishment⟩
**cru·el·ly** *adv*

**cru·el·ty** \'krü-əl-tē\ *n, pl* **cru·el·ties**
**1** the quality or state of being cruel
**2** cruel treatment

**cru·et** \'krü-ət\ *n*
▼ a bottle for holding vinegar, oil, or sauce for table use

**cruet** for olive oil

**[1]cruise** \'krüz\ *vb* **cruised**; **cruis·ing**
**1** to travel by ship often stopping at a series of ports ⟨*cruise* along the coast⟩
**2** to travel for pleasure
**3** to travel at the best operating speed

**[2]cruise** *n*
an act or instance of cruising

**cruis·er** \'krü-zər\ *n*
**1** a warship that is smaller than a battleship
**2** a police car used for patrolling streets and equipped with radio for communicating with headquarters
**3** a motorboat equipped for living aboard

**crul·ler** \'krəl-ər\ *n*
a small sweet cake made of egg batter usually cut in strips or twists and fried in deep fat

**[1]crumb** \'krəm\ *n*
**1** a small piece especially of bread
**2** a little bit

**[2]crumb** *vb*
to break into crumbs : CRUMBLE

**crum·ble** \'krəm-bəl\ *vb*
**crum·bled**; **crum·bling**
**1** to break into small pieces ⟨*crumble* bread⟩
**2** to fall to pieces : fall into ruin

**²crush 1:**
a hand crushing an empty drink can

**crum·bly** \'krəm-blē\ *adj*
**crum·bli·er**; **crum·bli·est**
easily crumbled

**crum·ple** \'krəm-pəl\ *vb*
**crum·pled**; **crum·pling**
**1** to press or crush out of shape: RUMPLE ⟨*crumple* paper⟩
**2** to become crumpled
**3** ¹COLLAPSE 1

**¹crunch** \'krənch\ *vb*
**1** to chew or grind with a crushing noise ⟨*crunching* on hard candy⟩
**2** to make the sound of being crushed or squeezed ⟨the snow *crunching* underfoot⟩

**²crunch** *n*
an act or sound of crunching

**¹cru·sade** \krü-'sād\ *n*
**1** *cap* one of the military expeditions made by Christian countries in the eleventh, twelfth, and thirteenth centuries to recover the Holy Land from the Muslims
**2** a campaign to get things changed for the better

**²crusade** *vb* **cru·sad·ed**; **cru·sad·ing**
to take part in a crusade

**cru·sad·er** \krü-'sād-ər\ *n*
a person who takes part in a crusade

**¹crush** \'krəsh\ *vb*
**1** to squeeze together so as to change or destroy the natural shape or condition ⟨*crush* grapes⟩
**2** ¹HUG 1
**3** to break into fine pieces by pressure ⟨*crush* stone⟩
**4** OVERWHELM 2 ⟨*crush* an enemy⟩
**5** OPPRESS 1

**²crush** *n*
**1** ◄ an act of crushing
**2** a tightly packed crowd
**3** a foolish or very strong liking : INFATUATION ⟨have a *crush* on someone⟩

**crust** \'krəst\ *n*
**1** the hardened outside surface of bread
**2** a hard dry piece of bread
**3** the pastry cover of a pie
**4** a hard outer covering or surface layer ⟨a *crust* of snow⟩
**5** ► the outer part of the earth

**crus·ta·cean** \,krəs-'tā-shən\ *n*
▼ any of a large group of mostly water animals (as crabs, lobsters, and shrimps) with a body made of segments, a firm outer shell, two pairs of antennae, and limbs that are jointed



**crust 5:**
model showing the layers in the Earth's crust

## crustacean

Most crustaceans live in or near seawater. Crabs prefer sandy shores and rock pools, while lobsters search for food along the seabed. Shrimps dig into the sand to hide during the day, only coming out at night to hunt for food.

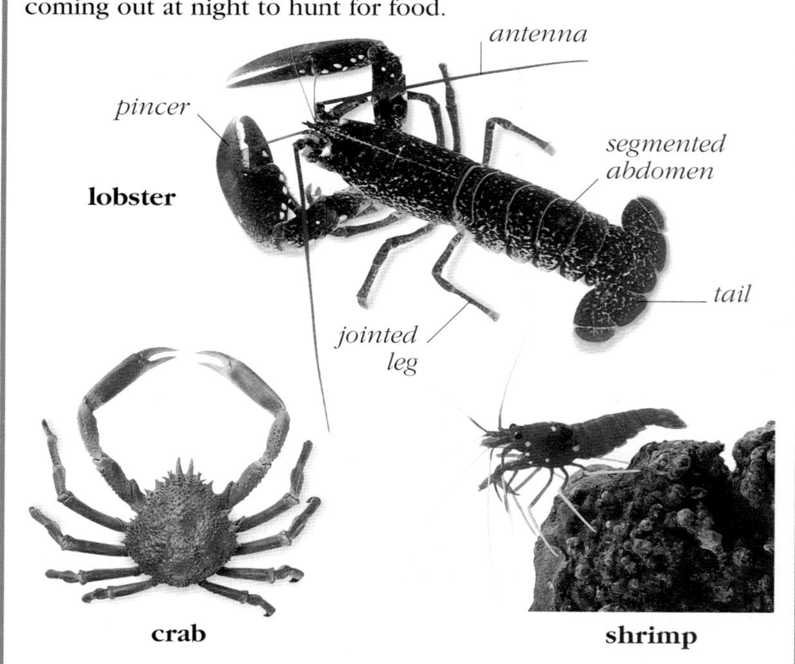

**crusty** \'krəs-tē\ *adj* **crust·i·er**; **crust·i·est**
1 having or being a crust
2 [3]CROSS 3 ⟨a *crusty* reply⟩

**crutch** \'krəch\ *n*
1 a support usually made with a piece at the top to fit under the armpit that is used by a lame person as an aid in walking
2 something (as a prop or support) like a crutch in shape or use

[1]**cry** \'krī\ *vb* **cried**; **cry·ing**
1 to make a loud call or cry : SHOUT, EXCLAIM
2 to shed tears : WEEP
3 to utter a special sound or call
4 to make known to the public : call out

**Word History** The English word *cry* came from an Old French word. This Old French word meant "to shout" or "to cry." It came from a Latin word meaning "to shout out" or "to scream." The literal meaning of the Latin word was "to cry out for help from a citizen." It was formed from a Latin word meaning "Roman citizen."

[1]**cube 1:** a solid cube

[2]**cry** *n, pl* **cries**
1 a loud call or shout (as of pain, fear, or joy)
2 [1]APPEAL 2 ⟨*cries* of the poor⟩
3 a fit of weeping ⟨had a good *cry*⟩
4 the special sound made by an animal

**cry·ba·by** \'krī-,bā-bē\ *n, pl* **cry·ba·bies**
a person who cries easily or who complains often

[1]**crys·tal** \'krist-l\ *n*
1 ▶ quartz that is colorless and transparent or nearly so
2 something transparent like crystal
3 a body formed by a substance hardening so that it has flat surfaces in an even arrangement ⟨an ice *crystal*⟩ ⟨a salt *crystal*⟩
4 a clear colorless glass of very good quality
5 the transparent cover over a clock or watch dial

[2]**crystal** *adj*
made of or being like crystal : CLEAR

**crys·tal·line** \'kris-tə-lən\ *adj*
1 made of crystal or composed of crystals
2 like crystal : TRANSPARENT

**crys·tal·lize** \'kris-tə-,līz\ *vb* **crys·tal·lized**; **crys·tal·liz·ing**
1 to form or cause to form crystals or grains
2 to take or cause to take definite form ⟨the plan *crystallized* slowly⟩

**cub** \'kəb\ *n*
1 ▶ the young of various animals (as the bear, fox, or lion)
2 CUB SCOUT

**cub·by·hole** \'kəb-ē-,hōl\ *n*
a snug place (as for storing things)

[1]**cube** \'kyüb\ *n*
1 ◀ a solid body having six equal square sides
2 the product obtained by multiplying the square of a number by the number itself ⟨27 is the *cube* of 3⟩

[2]**cube** *vb* **cubed**; **cub·ing**
1 to take (a number) as a factor three times ⟨3 *cubed* is 27⟩
2 to form into a cube or divide into cubes

**cu·bic** \'kyü-bik\ *adj*
being the volume of a cube whose edge is a specified unit ⟨a *cubic* centimeter⟩

**cu·bi·cal** \'kyü-bi-kəl\ *adj*
1 having the form of a cube
2 relating to volume

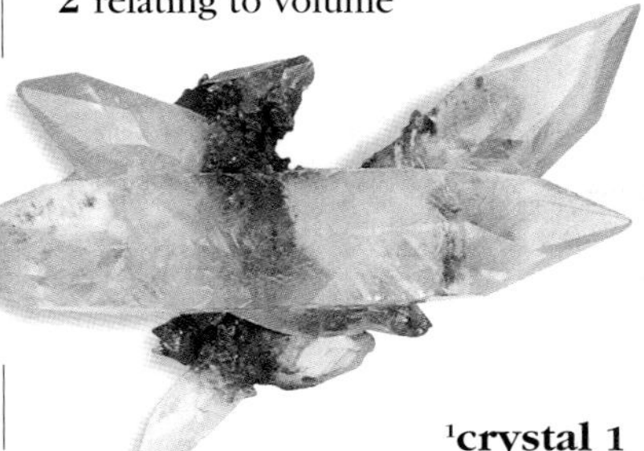

[1]**crystal 1**

**cub 1**

Newborn cubs are nourished by their mother's milk. At this early stage of life, they are helpless and dependent on parental care for survival. Within a few months they are running around and playing. As they continue to grow, they learn how to hunt for food so that they can survive on their own as adults.

**bear cub**

**lion cub**

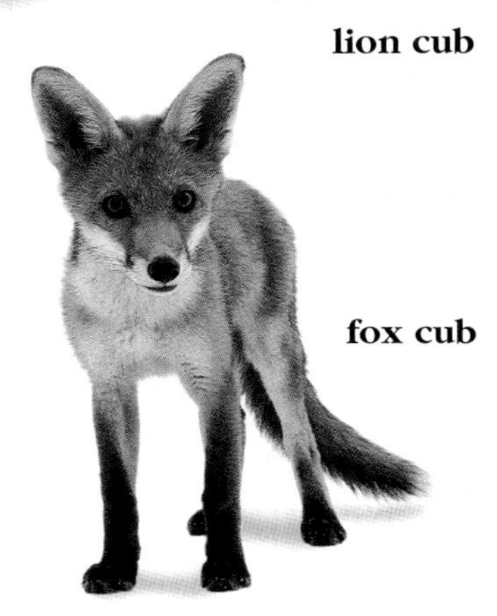

**fox cub**

**cu·bit** \'kyü-bət\ *n*
a unit of length usually equal to about forty-six centimeters

**Cub Scout** *n*
a member of a program of the Boy Scouts for boys in the first through fifth grades in school

a b c d e f g h i j k l m n o p q r s t u v w x y z

**cuck·oo** \'kük-ü, 'ku̇k-\ *n, pl* **cuckoos**
**1** ▼ any of several related birds (as a grayish brown European bird) that mostly lay their eggs in the nests of other birds for them to hatch
**2** the call of the European cuckoo

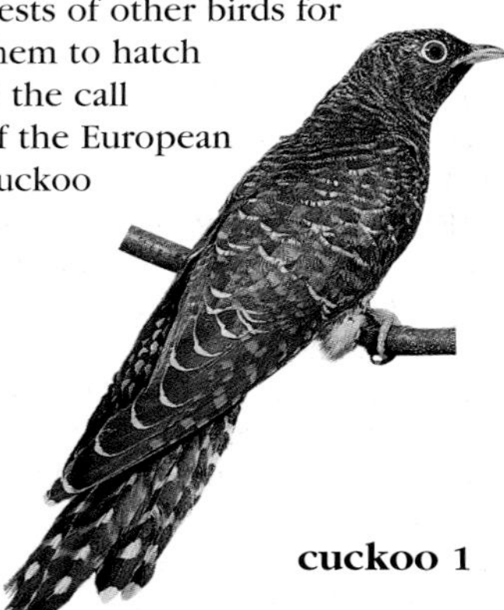

**cuckoo 1**

**cu·cum·ber** \'kyü-,kəm-bər\ *n*
▼ a long usually green-skinned vegetable that is used in salads and as pickles and is the fruit of a vine related to the melons and gourds

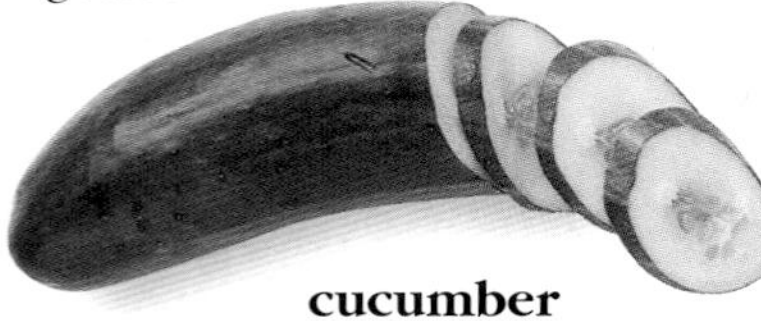

**cucumber**

**cud** \'kəd\ *n*
a portion of food brought up from the first stomach of some animals (as the cow and sheep) to be chewed again

**cud·dle** \'kəd-l\ *vb* **cud·dled**; **cud·dling**
**1** to hold close for warmth or comfort or in affection
**2** to lie close **:** NESTLE, SNUGGLE

[1]**cud·gel** \'kəj-əl\ *n*
a short heavy club

[2]**cudgel** *vb* **cud·geled** *or* **cud·gelled**; **cud·gel·ing** *or* **cud·gel·ling**
to beat with or as if with a cudgel

[1]**cue** \'kyü\ *n*
**1** a word, phrase, or action in a play serving as a signal for the next actor to speak or to do something
**2** something serving as a signal or suggestion **:** HINT

[2]**cue** *n*
a straight tapering stick used in playing billiards and pool

[1]**cuff** \'kəf\ *n*
**1** a band or turned-over piece at the end of a sleeve
**2** the turned-back hem of a trouser leg

[2]**cuff** *vb*
to strike especially with or as if with the palm of the hand **:** SLAP

[3]**cuff** *n*
[2]SLAP 1

[1]**cull** \'kəl\ *vb*
**1** to select from a group
**2** to identify and remove the culls from

[2]**cull** *n*
something rejected from a group or lot as not as good as the rest

**cul·mi·nate** \'kəl-mə-,nāt\ *vb* **cul·mi·nat·ed**; **cul·mi·nat·ing**
to reach the highest point

**cul·pa·ble** \'kəl-pə-bəl\ *adj*
deserving blame

**cul·prit** \'kəl-prət\ *n*
**1** one accused of or charged with a crime or fault
**2** one guilty of a crime or fault

**cul·ti·vate** \'kəl-tə-,vāt\ *vb* **cul·ti·vat·ed**; **cul·ti·vat·ing**
**1** to prepare land for the raising of crops
**2** to raise or assist the growth of crops by tilling or by labor and care
**3** to improve or develop by careful attention, training, or study **:** devote time and thought to
**4** to seek the company and friendship of

**cul·ti·vat·ed** \'kəl-tə-,vāt-əd\ *adj*
**1** raised or produced under cultivation ⟨*cultivated* fruits⟩
**2** having or showing good education and proper manners

**cul·ti·va·tion** \,kəl-tə-'vā-shən\ *n*
**1** the act or process of cultivating especially the soil
**2** REFINEMENT 2

**cul·ti·va·tor** \'kəl-tə-,vāt-ər\ *n*
**1** one (as a farmer) that cultivates something
**2** ▶ a tool or machine for loosening the soil between rows of a crop



**cultivator 2:** a hand cultivator

**cul·tur·al** \'kəl-chə-rəl\ *adj*
of or relating to culture
**cul·tur·al·ly** *adv*

**cul·ture** \'kəl-chər\ *n*
**1** CULTIVATION 1
**2** the raising or development (as of a crop or product) by careful attention ⟨grape *culture*⟩
**3** the improvement of the mind, tastes, and manners through careful training
**4** a certain stage, form, or kind of civilization ⟨Greek *culture*⟩

**cul·tured** \'kəl-chərd\ *adj*
**1** having or showing refinement in taste, speech, or manners
**2** produced under artificial conditions ⟨*cultured* pearls⟩

**cul·vert** \'kəl-vərt\ *n*
a drain or waterway crossing under a road or railroad

**cum·ber·some** \'kəm-bər-səm\ *adj*
hard to handle or manage because of size or weight

**cu·mu·la·tive** \'kyü-myə-lət-iv, -,lāt-\ *adj*
increasing (as in force, strength, or amount) by one addition after another ⟨a *cumulative* effect⟩

**cu·mu·lus** \'kyü-myə-ləs\ *n, pl* **cu·mu·li** \-,lī, -,lē\
a massive cloud form having a flat base and rounded outlines often piled up like a mountain

[1]**cu·ne·i·form** \kyu̇-'nē-ə-,fȯrm\ *adj*
**1** shaped like a wedge
**2** made up of or written with marks or letters shaped like wedges

[2]**cuneiform** *n*
▼ cuneiform writing

[2]**cuneiform:** cuneiform on a clay tablet from western Asia, about 2500 BC

**cupola 1**

**[1]cun·ning** \'kən-iŋ\ *adj*
**1** skillful and clever at using special knowledge or at getting something done ⟨a *cunning* plotter⟩
**2** showing craftiness and trickery ⟨a *cunning* scheme⟩
**3** CUTE, PRETTY ⟨a *cunning* baby⟩
**synonyms** see SLY

**[2]cunning** *n*
**1** SKILL 1, DEXTERITY
**2** cleverness in getting what one wants often by tricks or deceiving

**[1]cup** \'kəp\ *n*
**1** something to drink out of in the shape of a small bowl usually with a handle
**2** the contents of a cup : CUPFUL ⟨drink a *cup* of tea⟩
**3** a trophy in the shape of a cup with two handles
**4** something like a cup in shape or use

**[2]cup** *vb* **cupped**; **cup·ping**
to curve into the shape of a cup

**cup·board** \'kəb-ərd\ *n*
a closet usually with shelves for dishes or food

**cup·cake** \'kəp-,kāk\ *n*
a small cake baked in a mold shaped like a cup

**cup·ful** \'kəp-,fu̇l\ *n, pl* **cup·fuls** \-,fu̇lz\ *or* **cups·ful** \'kəps-,fu̇l\
**1** the amount held by a cup
**2** a half pint : eight ounces (about 236 milliliters)

**cu·pid** \'kyü-pəd\ *n*
a picture or statue of Cupid the Roman god of love often as a winged child with a bow and arrow

**cu·pid·i·ty** \kyu̇-'pid-ət-ē\ *n*
excessive desire for wealth : GREED

**cu·po·la** \'kyü-pə-lə\ *n*
**1** ◀ a rounded roof or ceiling : DOME
**2** a small structure built on top of a roof

**cur** \'kər\ *n*
a worthless or mongrel dog

**cur·able** \'kyu̇r-ə-bəl\ *adj*
possible to cure

**cu·rate** \'kyu̇r-ət\ *n*
a member of the clergy who assists the rector or vicar of a church

**[1]curb** \'kərb\ *n*
**1** ▶ a chain or strap on a horse's bit used to control the horse by pressing against the lower jaw
**2** [1]CHECK 2 ⟨a *curb* on rising prices⟩
**3** an enclosing border (as of stone or concrete) often along the edge of a street

**[2]curb** *vb*
to control by or furnish with a curb ⟨trying to *curb* their curiosity⟩

**curb·ing** \'kər-biŋ\ *n*
**1** material for making a curb
**2** [1]CURB 3

**curd** \'kərd\ *n*
the thickened or solid part of sour or partly digested milk

**cur·dle** \'kərd-l\ *vb* **cur·dled**; **cur·dling**
to change into curd : COAGULATE

**[1]cure** \'kyu̇r\ *n*
**1** a method or period of medical treatment
**2** recovery or relief from a disease
**3** [1]REMEDY 1 ⟨a *cure* for colds⟩

**[2]cure** *vb* **cured**; **cur·ing**
**1** to make or become healthy or sound again
**2** to prepare by a chemical or physical process for use or storage ⟨*cure* pork in brine⟩
**3** to undergo a curing process

**cur·few** \'kər-,fyü\ *n*
**1** a rule requiring certain or all people to be off the streets or at home at a stated time
**2** a signal (as the ringing of a bell) formerly given to announce the beginning of a curfew
**3** the time when a curfew is sounded

**cu·rio** \'kyu̇r-ē-,ō\ *n, pl* **cu·ri·os**
a rare or unusual article : CURIOSITY

**cu·ri·os·i·ty** \,kyu̇r-ē-'äs-ət-ē\ *n, pl* **cu·ri·os·i·ties**
**1** an eager desire to learn and often to learn what does not concern one
**2** something strange or unusual
**3** an object or article valued because it is strange or rare

**cu·ri·ous** \'kyu̇r-ē-əs\ *adj*
**1** eager to learn : INQUISITIVE
**2** attracting attention by being strange or unusual : ODD
**cu·ri·ous·ly** *adv*

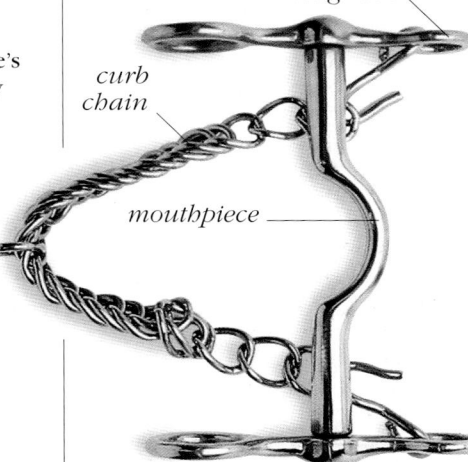

*ring rein*
*curb chain*
*mouthpiece*

**[1]curb 1:**
a curb bit from a horse's bridle

**[1]curl** \'kərl\ *vb*
**1** to twist or form into ringlets
**2** to take or move in a curved form ⟨*curl* up in a chair⟩ ⟨smoke *curling* from the chimney⟩

**[2]curl** *n*
**1** a lock of hair that coils : RINGLET
**2** something having a spiral or winding form : COIL ⟨a *curl* of smoke⟩
**3** the action of curling : the state of being curled

**curly** \'kər-lē\ *adj* **curl·i·er; curl·i·est**
**1** tending to curl
**2** having curls

**cur·rant** \'kər-ənt\ *n*
**1** a small seedless raisin used in baking and cooking
**2** a sour red or white edible berry produced by a low spreading shrub related to the gooseberry

**cur·ren·cy** \'kər-ən-sē\ *n, pl* **cur·ren·cies**
**1** common use or acceptance ⟨a rumor that had wide *currency*⟩
**2** money in circulation

[1]**cur·rent** \'kər-ənt\ *adj*
**1** now passing ⟨the *current* month⟩
**2** occurring in or belonging to the present time ⟨*current* events⟩
**3** generally and widely accepted, used, or practiced ⟨*current* customs⟩

[2]**current** *n*
**1** a body of fluid moving in a specified direction
**2** the swiftest part of a stream
**3** the general course : TREND ⟨the *current* of public opinion⟩
**4** a flow of charges of electricity

**cur·ric·u·lum** \kə-'rik-yə-ləm\ *n, pl* **cur·ric·u·la** \-lə\ *or* **cur·ric·u·lums**
all the courses of study offered by a school

**cur·ry** \'kər-ē\ *vb* **cur·ried; cur·ry·ing**
to rub and clean the coat of ⟨*curry* a horse⟩

[1]**curse** \'kərs\ *n*
**1** a calling for harm or injury to come to someone
**2** a word or an expression used in cursing or swearing
**3** evil or misfortune that comes as if in answer to a curse
**4** a cause of great harm or evil

[2]**curse** *vb* **cursed; curs·ing**
**1** to call upon divine power to send harm or evil upon
**2** SWEAR 5
**3** to bring unhappiness or evil upon : AFFLICT

**cur·sor** \'kər-sər, -ˌsȯr\ *n*
a symbol (as an arrow or blinking line) on a computer screen that shows where the user is working

**curt** \'kərt\ *adj*
rudely brief in language

**cur·tail** \ˌkər-'tāl\ *vb*
to shorten or reduce by cutting off the end or a part of ⟨had to *curtail* my speech⟩

[1]**cur·tain** \'kərt-n\ *n*
**1** a piece of material (as cloth) hung up to darken, hide, divide, or decorate
**2** something that covers, hides, or separates like a curtain ⟨a *curtain* of secrecy⟩

[2]**curtain** *vb*
**1** to furnish with curtains
**2** to hide or shut off with a curtain

[1]**curt·sy** *or* **curt·sey** \'kərt-sē\ *vb* **curt·sied** *or* **curt·seyed; curt·sy·ing** *or* **curt·sey·ing**
to lower the body slightly by bending the knees as an act of politeness or respect

[2]**curtsy:** a girl making a curtsy

[2]**curtsy** *or* **curtsey** *n, pl* **curtsies** *or* **curtseys**
▲ an act of politeness or respect made mainly by women and consisting of a slight lowering of the body by bending the knees

**cur·va·ture** \'kər-və-ˌchu̇r\ *n*
**1** a curving or bending
**2** the state of being curved

[1]**curve** \'kərv\ *vb* **curved; curv·ing**
**1** to turn or change from a straight line or course ⟨the road *curved* to the left⟩
**2** to cause to curve

[2]**curve** *n*
**1** a bending or turning without angles : BEND ⟨a *curve* in the road⟩
**2** something curved
**3** a ball thrown so that it moves away from a straight course

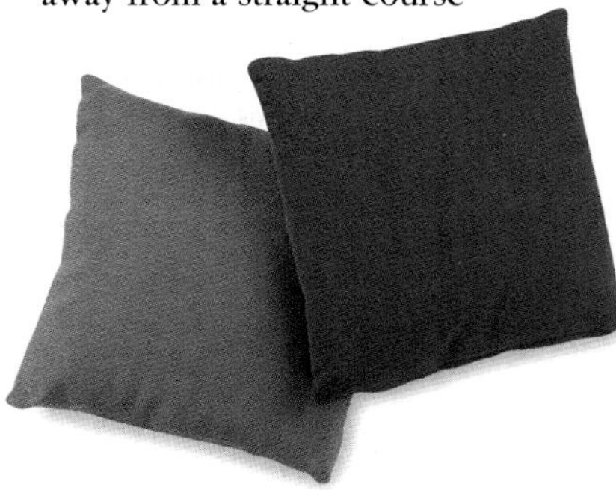

[1]**cushion 1:** a pair of cushions

[1]**cush·ion** \'ku̇sh-ən\ *n*
**1** ▲ a soft pillow or pad to rest on or against
**2** something like a cushion in use, shape, or softness
**3** something that serves to soften or lessen the effects of something bad or unpleasant

[2]**cushion** *vb*
**1** to place on or as if on a cushion
**2** to furnish with a cushion
**3** to soften or lessen the force or shock of

**cusp** \'kəsp\ *n*
a point or pointed end (as on the crown of a tooth)

**cus·pid** \'kəs-pəd\ *n*
[1]CANINE 1

**cuss** \'kəs\ *vb*
SWEAR 5

**cus·tard** \'kəs-tərd\ *n*
a sweetened mixture of milk and eggs baked, boiled, or frozen

**cus·to·di·an** \ˌkəs-'tōd-ē-ən\ *n*
one that guards and protects or takes care of ⟨the school *custodian*⟩

**cus·to·dy** \'kəs-tə-dē\ *n*
**1** direct responsibility for care and control
**2** the state of being arrested or held by police

[1]**cus·tom** \'kəs-təm\ *n*
**1** the usual way of doing things : the usual practice
**2 customs** *pl* duties or taxes paid on imports or exports

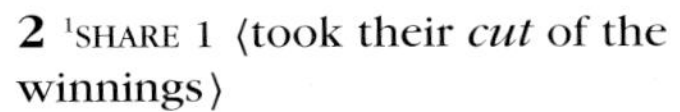

**3** support given to a business by its customers

**²custom** *adj*

**1** made or done to personal order

**2** specializing in custom work

**cus·tom·ary** \'kəs-tə-ˌmer-ē\ *adj*

**1** based on or existing by custom

**2** commonly done or observed

**cus·tom·er** \'kəs-tə-mər\ *n*

a person who buys from or uses the services of a company especially regularly

**¹cut** \'kət\ *vb* **cut**; **cut·ting**

**1** to penetrate or divide with or as if with an edged tool : CLEAVE ⟨*cut* a finger⟩ ⟨*cut* bread into slices⟩

**2** to undergo shaping or penetrating with an edged tool ⟨cheese *cuts* easily⟩

**3** to experience the growth of through the gum ⟨the baby is *cutting* teeth⟩

**4** to hurt someone's feelings ⟨that remark really *cut*⟩

**5** to strike sharply or at an angle ⟨the wind *cut* our faces⟩

**6** to make less ⟨*cut* costs⟩

**7** ²CROSS 2, INTERSECT ⟨the lines *cut* each other⟩

**8** to shape by carving or grinding ⟨*cut* a gem⟩

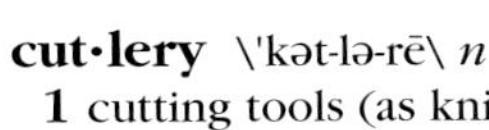

**cutlery 2**

**9** ¹SWERVE ⟨*cut* to avoid a hole in the road⟩

**10** to go by a short or direct path or course ⟨we *cut* across the lawn⟩

**11** to divide into two parts ⟨*cut* a deck of cards⟩

**12** to stop or cause to stop ⟨*cut* the motor⟩ ⟨*cut* that whispering⟩

**13** ¹SNUB ⟨*cut* a former friend⟩

**²cut** *n*

**1** something cut or cut off ⟨a *cut* of pie⟩ ⟨a *cut* of beef⟩

**2** ¹SHARE 1 ⟨took their *cut* of the winnings⟩

**3** something (as a gash or wound) produced by or as if by cutting

**4** a passage made by digging or cutting ⟨a railroad *cut*⟩

**5** a pictorial illustration (as in a book)

**6** something that is done or said that hurts the feelings ⟨an unkind *cut*⟩

**7** a straight path or course

**8** a cutting stroke or blow

**9** the way in which a thing is cut, formed, or made

**10** REDUCTION 1 ⟨a *cut* in pay⟩

**cute** \'kyüt\ *adj* **cut·er**; **cut·est**

**1** KEEN 4, SHREWD

**2** attractive especially in looks or actions

**cu·ti·cle** \'kyüt-i-kəl\ *n*

**1** an outer layer (as of skin or a leaf) often produced by the cells beneath

**2** a dead or horny layer of skin especially around a fingernail

**cut·lass** \'kət-ləs\ *n*

▼ a short heavy curved sword

**cutlass**

**cut·lery** \'kət-lə-rē\ *n*

**1** cutting tools (as knives and scissors)

**2** ◀ utensils used in cutting, serving, and eating food

**cut·let** \'kət-lət\ *n*

**1** a small slice of meat cut for broiling or frying

**2** a piece of food shaped like a cutlet

**cut·out** \'kət-ˌau̇t\ *n*

something cut out or intended to be cut out from something else ⟨a page of animal *cutouts*⟩

**cut out** \ˌkət-'au̇t\ *vb*

to form by cutting ⟨*cut out* a pattern⟩

**cut·ter** \'kət-ər\ *n*

**1** ▶ someone or something that cuts ⟨a diamond *cutter*⟩ ⟨a cookie *cutter*⟩

**2** a boat used by warships for carrying passengers and stores to and from the shore

**3** a small sailing boat with one mast

**4** a small armed boat used by the Coast Guard

**cut·ting** \'kət-ing\ *n*

a part (as a shoot) of a plant able to grow into a whole new plant

**cut·tle·fish** \'kət-l-ˌfish\ *n*

a sea animal with ten arms that is related to the squid and octopus

**cut·up** \'kət-ˌəp\ *n*

a person who clowns or acts in a noisy manner

**cut·worm** \'kət-ˌwərm\ *n*

a moth caterpillar that has a smooth body and feeds on the stems of plants at night

**-cy** \sē\ *n suffix, pl* **-cies**

**1** action : practice

**2** rank : office

**3** body : class

**4** state : quality ⟨accura*cy*⟩ ⟨bankrupt*cy*⟩

**cy·a·nide** \'sī-ə-ˌnīd\ *n*

any of several compounds containing carbon and nitrogen and including two very poisonous substances

**cyber-** *combining form*

relating to computers or computer networks

**cy·ber·space** \'sī-bər-ˌspās\ *n*

the on-line world of computer networks

**cy·cad** \'sī-kəd\ *n*

a tropical tree like a palm but related to the conifers

**¹cy·cle** \'sī-kəl\ *n*

**1** a period of time taken up by a series of events or actions that repeat themselves again and again in the same order ⟨the *cycle* of the seasons⟩

**2** a complete round or series

**3** a long period of time : AGE

**4** BICYCLE

**5** TRICYCLE

**6** MOTORCYCLE

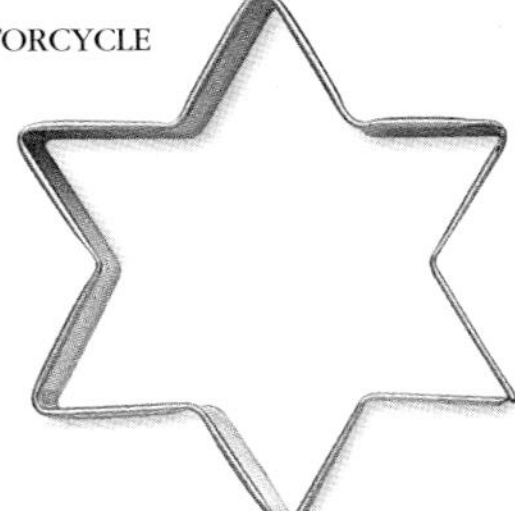

**cutter 1:** a cookie cutter

**[2]cycle** *vb* **cy·cled**; **cy·cling**
to ride a cycle

**cy·clist** \'sī-kləst\ *n*
a person who rides a cycle and especially a bicycle

**cy·clone** \'sī-ˌklōn\ *n*
**1** a storm or system of winds that rotates about a center of low atmospheric pressure in a counterclockwise direction north of the equator and that moves forward at a speed of thirty to fifty kilometers per hour and often brings heavy rain
**2** TORNADO

**cyl·in·der** \'sil-ən-dər\ *n*
▶ a long round body whether hollow or solid

**cy·lin·dri·cal** \sə-'lin-dri-kəl\ *adj*
having the shape of a cylinder

**cym·bal** \'sim-bəl\ *n*
a brass plate that is struck with a drumstick or is used in pairs struck together to make a clashing sound

**cylinder:** a solid cylinder

**cy·press** \'sī-prəs\ *n*
any of various evergreen trees and shrubs that are related to the pines and have overlapping leaves resembling scales

**cyst** \'sist\ *n*
**1** an abnormal sac in a living body
**2** a covering like a cyst or a body (as a spore) with such a covering

**cy·to·plasm** \'sīt-ə-ˌplaz-əm\ *n*
the protoplasm of a cell except for the nucleus

**czar** \'zär\ *n*
the ruler of Russia until the 1917 revolution

**cza·ri·na** \zä-'rē-nə\ *n*
**1** the wife of a czar
**2** a woman who has the rank of czar

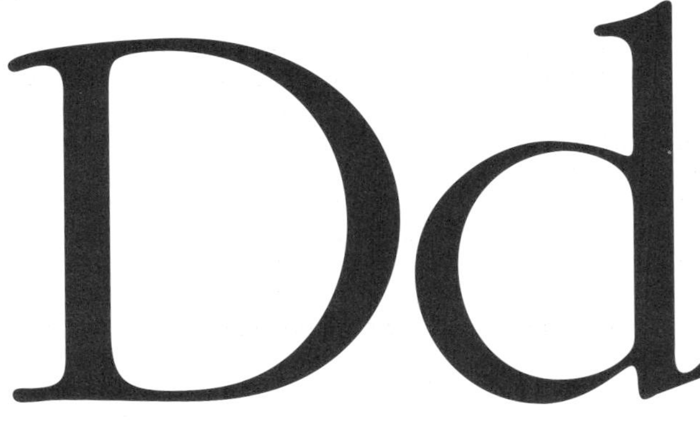

**The sounds of D:** The letter **D** has only one sound in English. It sounds the same in the words **daddy**, **dandelion**, **red**, and **heraldry**. A double **D** in a word sounds the same as a single **D**, as in **cuddle**.

In a few words, the letter **D** combines with a following vowel to make the sound of the letter **J**. But this is not really a different sound of **D**; it is just **D** plus another sound added to it. Examples of words in which **D** makes this sound are **soldier** and **educate**.

**d** \'dē\ *n, pl* **d's** *or* **ds** \'dēz\ *often cap*
**1** the fourth letter of the English alphabet
**2** 500 in Roman numerals
**3** a grade that shows a student's work is poor

[1]**dab** \'dab\ *n*
**1** a sudden poke
**2** a small amount ⟨a *dab* of butter⟩
**3** a light quick touch

[2]**dab** *vb* **dabbed**; **dab·bing**
**1** to strike or touch lightly
**2** to apply with light or uneven strokes ⟨*dab* on paint⟩
**dab·ber** *n*

**dab·ble** \'dab-əl\ *vb* **dab·bled**; **dab·bling**
**1** to wet by splashing **:** SPATTER
**2** to paddle in or as if in water
**3** to work without real interest or effort
**dab·bler** \'dab-lər\ *n*

**dace** \'dās\ *n, pl* **dace**
any of several small fishes related to the carps

**dachs·hund** \'däks-,hu̇nt, 'däk-sənt\ *n*
▶ a small hound with a long body, very short legs, and long drooping ears

**Word History** The Germans developed a dog with short legs and a long body. These dogs were used to hunt burrowing animals such as badgers. Such a dog could follow a badger right down its hole. The Germans gave these dogs a name that meant "badger dog." The English word *dachshund* came from this German name.

**dachshund:** a smooth-haired dachshund

**dad** \'dad\ *n*
[1]FATHER 1

**dad·dy** \'dad-ē\ *n, pl* **daddies**
[1]FATHER 1

**dad·dy long·legs** \,dad-ē-'lȯng-,legz\ *n, pl* **daddy longlegs**
**1** an insect like a spider but with a small rounded body and long slender legs
**2** a slender two-winged fly with long legs

**daf·fo·dil** \'daf-ə-,dil\ *n*
▼ a plant that grows from a bulb and has long slender leaves and yellow, white, or pinkish flowers suggesting trumpets and having a scalloped edge and leaflike parts at the base

**daffodil**

**daft** \'daft\ *adj*
FOOLISH, CRAZY
**daft·ly** *adv*
**daft·ness** *n*

**dag·ger** \'dag-ər\ *n*
▼ a short knife used for stabbing

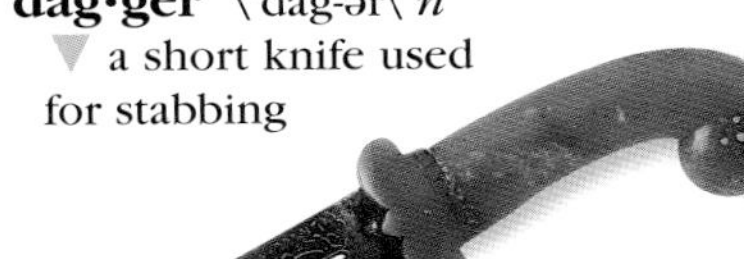

**dagger:** a 16th-century Turkish dagger

**dahl·ia** \'dal-yə, 'däl-\ *n*
▼ a tall plant related to the daisies and widely grown for its bright flowers

**dahlia**

[1]**dai·ly** \'dā-lē\ *adj*
**1** occurring, done, produced, or issued every day or every weekday
**2** given or paid for one day ⟨a *daily* wage⟩

[2]**daily** *adv*
every day ⟨jogs three miles *daily*⟩

[3]**daily** *n, pl* **dai·lies**
a newspaper published every weekday

[1]**dain·ty** \'dānt-ē\ *n, pl* **dain·ties**
DELICACY 1

[2]**dainty** *adj* **dain·ti·er**; **dain·ti·est**
**1** tasting good
**2** pretty in a delicate way
**3** having or showing delicate taste
**dain·ti·ly** \'dānt-l-ē\ *adv*
**dain·ti·ness** \'dānt-ē-nəs\ *n*

A B C D E F G H I J K L M N O P Q R S T U V W X Y Z

**dairy** \'deər-ē, 'daər-ē\ *n, pl* **dair·ies**
**1** a place where milk is stored or is made into butter and cheese
**2** a farm that produces milk
**3** a company or a store that sells milk products

**Word History** *Dairy* came from an Old English word that meant "kneader of dough." The modern English word *dough* is a relative of this word. In time the word that meant "kneader of dough" came to mean "maid." The word was also used for a special kind of maid, a dairymaid. A new word was formed later on by adding an ending meaning "place" to the word meaning "dairymaid." The new word then was used for the place where the dairymaid worked. The modern English word *dairy* came from this earlier English word. The ending can still be seen in the last two letters of the modern word.

**dairy·ing** \'der-ē-ing\ *n*
the business of producing milk or milk products

**dairy·maid** \'deər-ē-ˌmād\ *n*
a woman or girl who works in a dairy

**dairy·man** \'deər-ē-mən\ *n, pl* **dairy·men** \-mən\
a man who operates a dairy farm or works in a dairy

**da·is** \'dā-əs\ *n*
a raised platform (as in a hall or large room)

**dai·sy** \'dā-zē\ *n, pl* **daisies**
▼ any of a large group of plants with flower heads consisting of one or more rows of white or colored flowers like petals around a central disk of tiny often yellow flowers closely packed together

daisy

## ²dam

Most dams are built across river valleys to control flooding, create a reservoir for water storage, or provide hydroelectric power. Often constructed from reinforced concrete, dams are designed to suit the size and shape of a valley, and the types of rock and soil present.

model of an arch dam

**Word History** The modern English word *daisy* came from an Old English word that meant "daisy." The literal meaning of this Old English word was "day's eye." The yellow center of a daisy looks a bit like the sun. The sun may be thought of as the bright eye of the day.

**dale** \'dāl\ *n*
VALLEY

**dal·ly** \'dal-ē\ *vb* **dal·lied**; **dal·ly·ing**
**1** to act playfully
**2** to waste time
**3** LINGER, DAWDLE

**dal·ma·tian** \dal-'mā-shən\ *n, often cap*
► a large dog having a short white coat with black or brown spots

**¹dam** \'dam\ *n*
a female parent — used especially of a domestic animal

**²dam** *n*
▲ a barrier (as across a stream) to hold back a flow of water

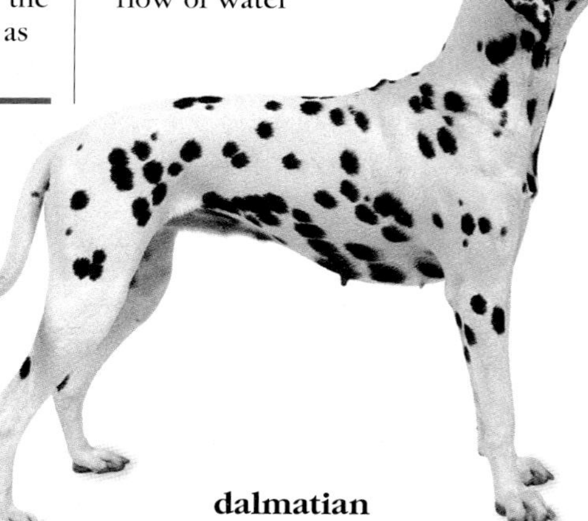

dalmatian

**³dam** *vb* **dammed**; **dam·ming**
to hold back or block with or as if with a dam

**¹dam·age** \'dam-ij\ *n*
**1** loss or harm due to injury
**2** **damages** *pl* money demanded or paid according to law for injury or damage **synonyms** see HARM

**²damage** *vb* **dam·aged**; **dam·ag·ing**
to cause damage to

**dam·ask** \'dam-əsk\ *n*
a fancy cloth used especially for household linen

**dame** \'dām\ *n*
a woman of high rank or social position

**¹damn** \'dam\ *vb*
**1** to condemn to everlasting punishment especially in hell
**2** to declare to be bad or a failure
**3** to swear at : CURSE

**²damn** *n*
the word *damn* used as a curse

**dam·na·ble** \'dam-nə-bəl\ *adj*
very bad : OUTRAGEOUS
**dam·na·bly** \-blē\ *adv*

**¹damned** \'damd\ *adj* **damned·er** \'dam-dər\; **damned·est** \-dəst\
**1** DAMNABLE ⟨a *damned* nuisance⟩
**2** REMARKABLE ⟨the *damnedest* sight⟩

**²damned** *adv*
to a high degree : VERY

**¹damp** \'damp\ *n*
**1** a harmful gas found especially in coal mines
**2** MOISTURE

**²damp** *vb*
DAMPEN

**³damp** *adj*
slightly wet : MOIST
**damp·ly** *adv*
**damp·ness** *n*

**damp·en** \'dam-pən\ *vb*
**1** to make dull or less active ⟨rain *dampened* our enthusiasm for a picnic⟩
**2** to make or become damp
**damp·en·er** *n*

**damp·er** \'dam-pər\ *n*
**1** something that checks, discourages, or deadens
**2** a valve or movable plate for controlling a flow of air

**dam·sel** \'dam-zəl\ *n*
GIRL 1, MAIDEN

**¹dance** \'dans\ *vb* **danced**; **danc·ing**
**1** to glide, step, or move through a series of movements usually in time to music
**2** to move about or up and down quickly and lightly
**3** to perform or take part in as a dancer
**danc·er** *n*

**²dance** *n*
**1** an act of dancing
**2** a social gathering for dancing
**3** a set of movements or steps for dancing usually in time to special music
**4** the art of dancing

**dan·de·li·on** \'dan-dl-,ī-ən\ *n*
▼ a weedy plant related to the daisies that has a ring of long deeply toothed leaves often eaten as cooked greens or in salad and bright yellow flowers with hollow stems

**dandelion**

**dan·druff** \'dan-drəf\ *n*
thin dry whitish flakes that form on the scalp and come off freely

**¹dan·dy** \'dan-dē\ *n, pl* **dandies**
**1** a man who pays a great deal of attention to his clothes
**2** an excellent or unusual example

**²dandy** *adj* **dan·di·er**; **dan·di·est**
very good

**Dane** \'dān\ *n*
a person born or living in Denmark

**dan·ger** \'dān-jər\ *n*
**1** the state of not being protected from harm or evil : PERIL
**2** something that may cause injury or harm

**Synonyms** DANGER, HAZARD, and RISK mean a threat of loss, injury, or death. DANGER suggests possible harm that may or may not be avoided ⟨the *danger* of a new war starting⟩. HAZARD suggests danger from something beyond one's control ⟨the *hazards* of mining for coal⟩. RISK suggests danger that may result from a chance voluntarily taken ⟨willing to take the *risks* that come with flying a plane⟩.

**dan·ger·ous** \'dān-jə-rəs, 'dānj-rəs\ *adj*
**1** full of danger ⟨*dangerous* work⟩
**2** able or likely to injure ⟨a *dangerous* tool⟩
**dan·ger·ous·ly** *adv*

**dan·gle** \'dang-gəl\ *vb* **dan·gled**; **dan·gling**
**1** to hang loosely especially with a swinging or jerking motion
**2** to depend on something else
**3** to cause to dangle

**¹Dan·ish** \'dā-nish\ *adj*
of or relating to Denmark, the Danes, or Danish

**²Danish** *n*
**1** the language of the Danes
**2** a piece of Danish pastry

**Danish pastry** *n*
a pastry made of rich raised dough

**dank** \'dangk\ *adj*
unpleasantly wet or moist
**dank·ly** *adv*
**dank·ness** *n*

**dap·per** \'dap-ər\ *adj*
neat and trim in dress or appearance

**dap·ple** \'dap-əl\ *vb* **dap·pled**; **dap·pling**
▼ to mark or become marked with rounded spots of color ⟨*dappled* horse⟩

**dapple:** a dappled horse

**[1]dare** \ˈdaər, ˈdeər\ *vb* **dared**; **dar·ing**
**1** to have courage enough for some purpose : be bold enough ⟨they *dared* to try something new⟩ — sometimes used as a helping verb ⟨we *dare* not say a word⟩
**2** to challenge to do something especially as a proof of courage ⟨I *dare* you to jump⟩

**[2]dare** *n*
a demand that one do something difficult or dangerous as proof of courage

**dare·dev·il** \ˈdaər-ˌdev-əl, ˈdeər-\ *n*
a person so bold as to be reckless

**[1]dar·ing** \ˈdaər-ing, ˈdeər-\ *adj*
ready to take risks : BOLD, VENTURESOME **synonyms** see ADVENTUROUS
**dar·ing·ly** *adv*

**[2]daring** *n*
bold fearlessness : readiness to take chances

**[1]dark** \ˈdärk\ *adj*
**1** being without light or without much light
**2** not light in color
**3** not bright and cheerful : GLOOMY
**4** being without knowledge and culture ⟨the *Dark* Ages⟩
**dark·ish** \ˈdär-kish\ *adj*
**dark·ly** *adv*
**dark·ness** *n*

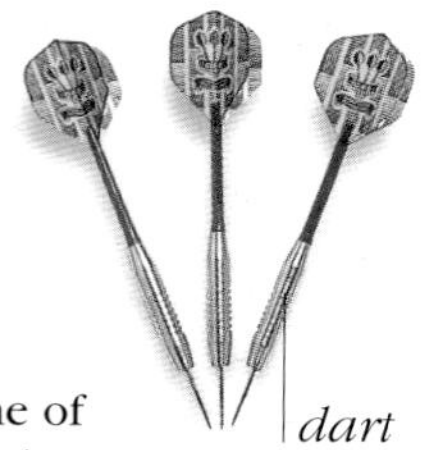

**[1]dart 1:** darts shown with the target

**[2]dark** *n*
**1** absence of light
**2** a place or time of little or no light ⟨got home before *dark*⟩

**dark·en** \ˈdär-kən\ *vb*
**1** to make or grow dark or darker
**2** to make or become gloomy
**dark·en·er** *n*

**dark·room** \ˈdär-ˌkrüm, -ˌkru̇m\ *n*
a usually small lightproof room used in developing photographic plates and film

**[1]dar·ling** \ˈdär-ling\ *n*
**1** a dearly loved person
**2** [1]FAVORITE ⟨the *darling* of the crowd⟩

**[2]darling** *adj*
**1** dearly loved
**2** very pleasing : CHARMING

**[1]darn** \ˈdärn\ *vb*
to mend by interlacing threads ⟨*darn* socks⟩

**[2]darn** *n*
a place that has been darned

**[3]darn** *n*
[2]DAMN

**darning needle** *n*
DRAGONFLY

**4** DESTROY 1 ⟨their hopes were *dashed*⟩
**5** to complete or do hastily ⟨*dash* off a note⟩
**6** to move with sudden speed

**[2]dash** *n*
**1** a sudden burst or splash ⟨a *dash* of cold water⟩
**2** a punctuation mark — that is used most often to show a break in the thought or structure of a sentence
**3** a small amount : TOUCH
**4** liveliness in style and action
**5** a sudden rush or attempt ⟨a *dash* for the goal⟩
**6** a short fast race ⟨100-yard *dash*⟩
**7** a long click or buzz forming a letter or part of a letter (as in telegraphy)
**8** DASHBOARD

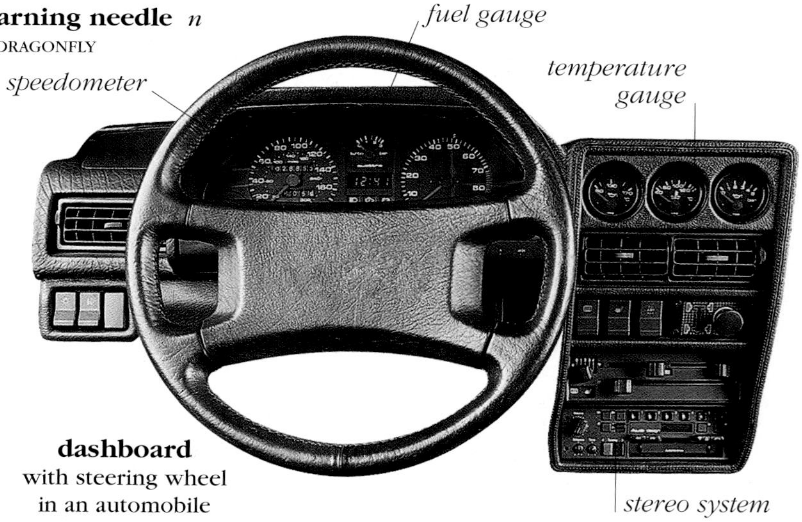

**dashboard**
with steering wheel in an automobile

**[1]dart** \ˈdärt\ *n*
**1** ◀ a small pointed object that is meant to be thrown
**2 darts** *pl* a game in which darts are thrown at a target
**3** a quick sudden movement
**4** a stitched fold in a garment

**[2]dart** *vb*
to move or shoot out suddenly and quickly ⟨a toad *darted* out its tongue⟩

**[1]dash** \ˈdash\ *vb*
**1** to knock, hurl, or shove violently
**2** [2]SMASH 1 ⟨*dash* the plate to pieces on the floor⟩
**3** [1]SPLASH 2 ⟨clothes *dashed* with mud⟩

**dash·board** \ˈdash-ˌbōrd\ *n*
▲ a panel across an automobile or aircraft below the windshield usually containing dials and controls

**dash·ing** \ˈdash-ing\ *adj*
having clothes or manners that are very fancy and stylish

**das·tard** \ˈdas-tərd\ *n*
a mean and sneaky coward

**das·tard·ly** \ˈdas-tərd-lē\ *adj*
of or like a dastard
**das·tard·li·ness** *n*

**da·ta** \ˈdāt-ə, ˈdat-ə\ *n sing or pl*
**1** facts about something that can be used in calculating, reasoning, or planning
**2** DATUM

**da·ta·base** \'dāt-ə-,bās, 'dat-\ *n*
a collection of data that is organized especially to be used by a computer

**¹date** \'dāt\ *n*
▶ the sweet brownish fruit of an Old World palm **(date palm)**

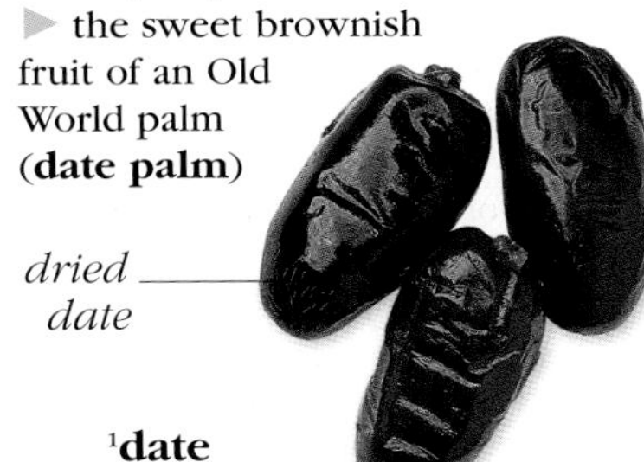


**¹date**

**Word History** The English word for the fruit of the date palm came from a Greek word. The first meaning of this Greek word was "finger," but it was also used for the fruit. A cluster of dates on a palm tree must have looked to someone rather like the cluster of fingers on a hand.

**²date** *n*
**1** the day, month, or year of a happening
**2** a statement of time on something (as a coin, letter, book, or building)
**3** APPOINTMENT 3
**4** a person with whom one has a social engagement

**Word History** Long ago the Romans wrote on their letters the place and date of sending. For example a Roman might use a Latin phrase that meant "given at Rome on the first of April." The first word of this phrase, which meant "given," came to be used to mean "date." The English word *date* came from this Latin word.

**³date** *vb* **dat·ed**; **dat·ing**
**1** to find or show the date of
**2** to write the date on ⟨*date* a letter⟩
**3** to make or have a date with
**4** to belong to or have survived from a time ⟨my house *dates* from the War of 1812⟩
**5** to show to be old-fashioned or belonging to a past time ⟨their slang *dates* them⟩

**da·tum** \'dāt-əm, 'dat-, 'dät-\ *n, pl* **da·ta** \-ə\ *or* **datums**
a single piece of information : FACT

**¹daub** \'dȯb\ *vb*
**1** to cover with something soft and sticky ⟨*daubed* with mud⟩
**2** to paint or color carelessly or badly
**daub·er** *n*

**²daub** *n*
something daubed on : SMEAR

**daugh·ter** \'dȯt-ər\ *n*
**1** a female child or offspring
**2** a woman or girl associated with or thought of as a child of something (as a country, race, or religion) ⟨the *daughters* of Africa⟩
**daugh·ter·ly** *adj*

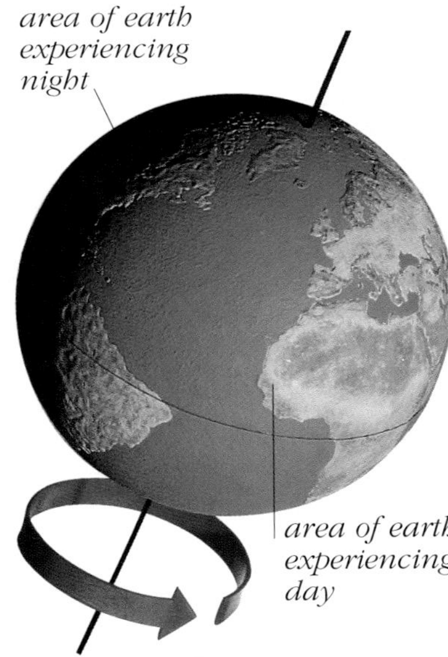


**day 1:**
model showing day on one-half of the earth

**daugh·ter–in–law** \'dȯt-ər-ən-,lȯ\ *n, pl* **daugh·ters–in–law**
the wife of one's son

**daunt** \'dȯnt\ *vb*
DISCOURAGE 1, INTIMIDATE ⟨dangers to *daunt* the bravest⟩

**daunt·less** \'dȯnt-ləs\ *adj*
bravely determined
**daunt·less·ly** *adv*
**daunt·less·ness** *n*

**dau·phin** \'dȯ-fən, 'dō-fən, ,dō-'fan\ *n*
the oldest son of a king of France

**dav·en·port** \'dav-ən-,pōrt\ *n*
a large sofa

**da·vit** \'dā-vət, 'dav-ət\ *n*
one of a pair of posts fitted with ropes and pulleys and used for supporting and lowering a ship's boat

**daw·dle** \'dȯd-l\ *vb* **daw·dled**; **daw·dling**
**1** to spend time wastefully : DALLY
**2** to move slowly and without purpose
**daw·dler** \'dȯd-lər\ *n*

**¹dawn** \'dȯn\ *vb*
**1** to begin to grow light as the sun rises
**2** to start becoming plain or clear ⟨it *dawned* on us that we were lost⟩

**²dawn** *n*
**1** the time when the sun comes up in the morning
**2** a first appearance : BEGINNING

**day** \'dā\ *n*
**1** ◀ the time between sunrise and sunset : DAYLIGHT
**2** the time the earth takes to make one turn on its axis
**3** a period of twenty-four hours beginning at midnight
**4** a specified day or date ⟨election *day*⟩
**5** a specified period : AGE ⟨in your grandparent's *day*⟩
**6** the time set apart by custom or law for work

**day·bed** \'dā-,bed\ *n*
a couch with low head and foot pieces

**day·break** \'dā-,brāk\ *n*
²DAWN 1

**day care** *n*
**1** care for children or disabled adults that is provided during the day by a person or organization
**2** a program or organization offering day care

**¹day·dream** \'dā-,drēm\ *n*
a happy or pleasant imagining about oneself or one's future

**²daydream** *vb*
to have a daydream
**day·dream·er** *n*

**day·light** \'dā-,līt\ *n*
**1** the light of day
**2** DAYTIME
**3** ²DAWN 1 ⟨from *daylight* to dark⟩
**4** *pl* mental state ⟨scared the *daylights* out of me⟩

**daylight saving time** *n*
time usually one hour ahead of standard time

**day·time** \'dā-,tīm\ *n*
the period of daylight

A B C D E F G H I J K L M N O P Q R S T U V W X Y Z

**[1]daze** \'dāz\ *vb* **dazed**; **daz·ing**
to stun especially by a blow
**[2]daze** *n*
a dazed state
**daz·zle** \'daz-əl\ *vb* **daz·zled**; **daz·zling**
**1** to confuse or be confused by too much light or by moving lights
**2** to confuse, surprise, or delight by being or doing something special and unusual
**daz·zler** \'daz-lər\ *n*
**daz·zling·ly** \'daz-ling-lē\ *adv*
**DDT** \,dē-,dē-'tē\ *n*
a chemical formerly used as an insecticide but found to damage the environment
**de-** *prefix*
**1** do the opposite of ⟨*de*code⟩
**2** reverse of
**3** remove or remove from a specified thing ⟨*de*forest⟩
**4** reduce
**5** get off of
**dea·con** \'dē-kən\ *n*
**1** an official in some Christian churches ranking just below a priest
**2** a church member who has special duties (as helping a minister)
**[1]dead** \'ded\ *adj*
**1** no longer living : LIFELESS
**2** having the look of death ⟨a *dead* faint⟩
**3** [1]NUMB 1
**4** very tired
**5** never having lived : INANIMATE ⟨*dead* matter⟩
**6** lacking motion, activity, energy, or power to function ⟨a *dead* battery⟩
**7** no longer in use : OBSOLETE ⟨*dead* languages⟩
**8** lacking warmth, vigor, or liveliness ⟨a *dead* fire⟩
**9** ACCURATE, PRECISE ⟨a *dead* shot⟩
**10** being sudden and complete ⟨a *dead* stop⟩
**11** [1]COMPLETE 1, TOTAL ⟨*dead* silence⟩
**[2]dead** *n, pl* **dead**
**1** *dead pl* those that are dead ⟨the living and the *dead*⟩
**2** the time of greatest quiet ⟨the *dead* of night⟩
**[3]dead** *adv*
**1** in a whole or complete manner ⟨*dead* right⟩
**2** suddenly and completely ⟨stopped *dead*⟩
**3** [2]STRAIGHT ⟨*dead* ahead⟩
**dead·en** \'ded-n\ *vb*
make less ⟨*deaden* pain⟩
**dead end** *n*
an end (as of a street) with no way out
**dead heat** *n*
a contest that ends in a tie
**dead letter** *n*
a letter that cannot be delivered by the post office or returned to the sender
**dead·line** \'ded-,līn\ *n*
a date or time by which something must be done
**[1]dead·lock** \'ded-,läk\ *n*
a stopping of action because both sides in a struggle are equally strong and neither will give in
**[2]deadlock** *vb*
to bring or come to a deadlock
**[1]dead·ly** \'ded-lē\ *adj* **dead·li·er**; **dead·li·est**
**1** causing or capable of causing death ⟨*deadly* weapons⟩
**2** meaning or hoping to kill or destroy ⟨*deadly* enemies⟩
**3** very accurate ⟨*deadly* aim⟩
**4** causing spiritual death
**5** suggestive of death
**6** [1]EXTREME 1 ⟨*deadly* seriousness⟩
**dead·li·ness** *n*

---

**Synonyms** DEADLY, MORTAL, and FATAL mean causing or capable of causing death. DEADLY is used of something that is certain or very likely to cause death ⟨a *deadly* poison⟩. MORTAL is used of something that already has caused death or is about to cause death ⟨received a *mortal* wound in battle⟩. FATAL stresses the certainty of death, even though there may be a period of time coming between the time death is caused (as by injury) and the time of death itself ⟨the wounds proved to be *fatal*, and death occurred three days later⟩.

---

**[2]deadly** *adv*
**1** in a way suggestive of death ⟨*deadly* pale⟩
**2** to an extreme degree ⟨*deadly* dull⟩
**deaf** \'def\ *adj*
**1** wholly or partly unable to hear
**2** unwilling to hear or listen
**deaf·ness** *n*
**deaf·en** \'def-ən\ *vb*
**1** to make deaf
**2** to stun with noise
**deaf–mute** \'def-,myüt\ *n*
a person who can neither hear nor speak
**[1]deal** \'dēl\ *n*
**1** an indefinite amount ⟨means a great *deal*⟩

**[1]deal 2:**
a player's deal in a card game

**2** ▲ one's turn to deal the cards in a card game
**[2]deal** *vb* **dealt** \'delt\; **deal·ing** \'dē-ling\
**1** to give out one or a few at a time
**2** [1]GIVE 5, ADMINISTER ⟨*dealt* the dog a blow⟩
**3** to have to do ⟨a book that *deals* with airplanes⟩
**4** to take action ⟨*deal* harshly with lawbreakers⟩
**5** to buy and sell regularly : TRADE
**deal·er** \'dē-lər\ *n*
**[3]deal** *n*
**1** an agreement to do business
**2** treatment received ⟨got a bad *deal*⟩
**3** a secret agreement
**4** [1]BARGAIN 2
**deal·ing** \'dē-ling\ *n*
**1** [3]DEAL 1
**2** a way of acting or doing business ⟨fair *dealing*⟩
**dean** \'dēn\ *n*
**1** a church official in charge of a cathedral
**2** the head of a section (as a college) of a university ⟨the *dean* of medicine⟩
**3** an official in charge of students or studies in a school or college ⟨the *dean* of women⟩
**dean·ship** \-,ship\ *n*

[1]**dear** \'dir\ *adj*
**1** greatly loved or cared about ⟨liberty is *dear* to our hearts⟩
**2** used as a form of address especially in letters ⟨*Dear* Sir⟩
**3** high-priced
**4** deeply felt : EARNEST ⟨my *dearest* wish⟩
**dear·ly** *adv*
**dear·ness** *n*

[2]**dear** *adv*
at a high price ⟨buy cheap and sell *dear*⟩

[3]**dear** *n*
a loved one : DARLING

**dearth** \'dərth\ *n*
SCARCITY, LACK

**death** \'deth\ *n*
**1** the end or ending of life ⟨sudden *death*⟩
**2** the cause of loss of life
**3** the state of being dead
**4** DESTRUCTION 2 ⟨the *death* of all hope⟩
**death·less** \-ləs\ *adj*
**death·like** \-ˌlīk\ *adj*

**death·bed** \'deth-ˌbed\ *n*
**1** the bed a person dies in
**2** the last hours of life

**death·blow** \'deth-ˌblō\ *n*
a fatal or crushing blow or event

[1]**death·ly** \'deth-lē\ *adj*
of, relating to, or suggesting death ⟨a *deathly* silence⟩

[2]**deathly** *adv*
in a way suggesting death ⟨*deathly* pale⟩

**de·bar** \di-'bär\ *vb* **de·barred**; **de·bar·ring**
to keep from having or doing something

**de·base** \di-'bās\ *vb* **de·based**; **de·bas·ing**
to make less good or valuable than before
**de·base·ment** \-mənt\ *n*

**de·bat·able** \di-'bāt-ə-bəl\ *adj*
possible to question or argue about

[1]**de·bate** \di-'bāt\ *n*
**1** a discussion or argument carried on between two teams
**2** DISCUSSION

[2]**debate** *vb* **de·bat·ed**; **de·bat·ing**
**1** to discuss a question by giving arguments on both sides : take part in a debate
**2** to consider reasons for and against **synonyms** see DISCUSS
**de·bat·er** *n*

**de·bil·i·tate** \di-'bil-ə-ˌtāt\ *vb* **de·bil·i·tat·ed**; **de·bil·i·tat·ing**
to make feeble : WEAKEN

**de·bil·i·ty** \di-'bil-ət-ē\ *n, pl* **de·bil·i·ties**
a weakened state especially of health

[1]**deb·it** \'deb-ət\ *vb*
to record as a debit

[2]**debit** *n*
a business record showing money paid out or owed

**deb·o·nair** \ˌdeb-ə-'naər, -'neər\ *adj*
gaily and gracefully charming ⟨a *debonair* manner⟩
**deb·o·nair·ly** *adv*
**deb·o·nair·ness** *n*

**de·bris** \də-'brē\ *n, pl* **de·bris** \-'brēz\
the junk or pieces left from something broken down or destroyed

**debt** \'det\ *n*
**1** [1]SIN
**2** something owed to another
**3** the condition of owing money

**debt·or** \'det-ər\ *n*
a person who owes a debt

**de·but** \'dā-ˌbyü, dā-'byü\ *n*
**1** a first public appearance ⟨a singer's *debut*⟩
**2** the formal entrance of a young woman into society

**deb·u·tante** \'deb-yu̇-ˌtänt\ *n*
a young woman making her debut

**deca-** *or* **dec-** *or* **deka-** *or* **dek-** *prefix*
ten ⟨*deca*gon⟩

**de·cade** \'dek-ˌād, de-'kād\ *n*
a period of ten years

**deca·gon** \'dek-ə-ˌgän\ *n*
▶ a closed figure having ten angles and ten sides

decagon

**de·cal** \'dē-ˌkal\ *n*
a design made to be transferred (as to glass) from specially prepared paper

**deca·logue** \'dek-ə-ˌlȯg\ *n, often cap*
the ten commandments of God given to Moses on Mount Sinai

**de·camp** \di-'kamp\ *vb*
to go away suddenly and usually secretly : run away

**de·cant·er** \di-'kant-ər\ *n*
an ornamental glass bottle used especially for serving wine

**de·cap·i·tate** \di-'kap-ə-ˌtāt\ *vb* **de·cap·i·tat·ed**; **de·cap·i·tat·ing**
to cut off the head of : BEHEAD

[1]**de·cay** \di-'kā\ *vb*
to weaken in health or soundness (as by aging or rotting)

[2]**decay** *n*
**1** the state of something that is decayed or decaying : a spoiled or rotting condition
**2** a gradual getting worse or failing ⟨the *decay* of civilization⟩
**3** a natural change of a radioactive element into another form of the same element or into a different element

[1]**de·cease** \di-'sēs\ *n*
DEATH 1

[2]**decease** *vb* **de·ceased**; **de·ceas·ing**
[1]DIE 1

**de·ce·dent** \di-'sēd-nt\ *n*
a dead person

**de·ceit** \di-'sēt\ *n*
**1** the act or practice of deceiving : DECEPTION
**2** a statement or act that misleads a person or causes him or her to believe what is false : TRICK

**de·ceit·ful** \di-'sēt-fəl\ *adj*
full of deceit : not honest
**de·ceit·ful·ly** \-fə-lē\ *adv*
**de·ceit·ful·ness** *n*

**de·ceive** \di-'sēv\ *vb* **de·ceived**; **de·ceiv·ing**
**1** to cause to believe what is not true : MISLEAD
**2** to be dishonest and misleading
**de·ceiv·er** *n*

**de·cel·er·ate** \dē-'sel-ə-ˌrāt\ *vb* **de·cel·er·at·ed**; **de·cel·er·at·ing**
to slow down

**De·cem·ber** \di-'sem-bər\ *n*
the twelfth month of the year

**Word History** The first Roman calendar started the year with the month of March. The tenth month was December. The Latin name for this month came from the Latin word that meant "ten." The English name *December* came from the Latin name for the tenth month in the Roman calendar.

**de·cen·cy** \ˈdē-sⁿn-sē\ *n, pl* **de·cen·cies**
**1** a way or habit of conducting oneself that is decent ⟨had the *decency* to say thank you⟩ **:** modest or proper behavior
**2** something that is right and proper

**de·cent** \ˈdē-sⁿnt\ *adj*
**1** meeting an accepted standard of good taste (as in speech, dress, or behavior)
**2** being moral and good **:** not dirty ⟨*decent* literature⟩
**3** fairly good ⟨a *decent* salary⟩
**de·cent·ly** *adv*

**de·cep·tion** \di-ˈsep-shən\ *n*
**1** the act of deceiving
**2** [1]TRICK 1

**de·cep·tive** \di-ˈsep-tiv\ *adj*
tending or able to deceive
**de·cep·tive·ly** *adv*

**deci-** *prefix*
tenth part ⟨*deci*meter⟩

**deci·bel** \ˈdes-ə-ˌbel, -bəl\ *n*
a unit for measuring the relative loudness of sounds

**de·cide** \di-ˈsīd\ *vb* **de·cid·ed; de·cid·ing**
**1** to make a judgment on ⟨the judge *decided* the case⟩
**2** to bring to an end ⟨one blow *decided* the fight⟩
**3** to make or cause to make a choice

**de·cid·ed** \di-ˈsīd-əd\ *adj*
**1** UNMISTAKABLE ⟨had a *decided* advantage⟩
**2** free from doubt ⟨a *decided* manner⟩
**de·cid·ed·ly** *adv*

**de·cid·u·ous** \di-ˈsij-ə-wəs\ *adj*
made up of or having a part that falls off at the end of a period of growth and use ⟨*deciduous* trees⟩

[1]**dec·i·mal** \ˈdes-ə-məl, ˈdes-məl\ *adj*
**1** based on the number 10 **:** numbered or counting by tens
**2** expressed in or including a decimal

[2]**decimal** *n*
a proper fraction in which the denominator is 10 or 10 multiplied one or more times by itself and is indicated by a point (**decimal point**) placed at the left of the numerator ⟨the *decimal* .2 = $^{2}/_{10}$, the *decimal* .25 = $^{25}/_{100}$, the *decimal* .025 = $^{25}/_{1000}$⟩

**deci·me·ter** \ˈdes-ə-ˌmēt-ər\ *n*
a unit of length equal to one tenth meter

**de·ci·pher** \dē-ˈsī-fər\ *vb*
**1** to translate from secret writing **:** DECODE
**2** to make out the meaning of something not clear ⟨*decipher* a blurred postmark⟩

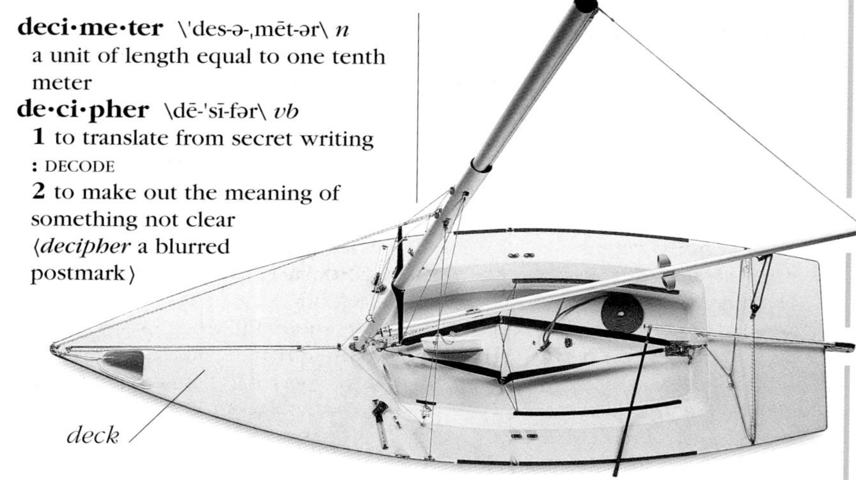

[1]**deck 1:** the deck of a sailboat

**de·ci·sion** \di-ˈsizh-ən\ *n*
**1** the act or result of deciding
**2** promptness and firmness in deciding

**de·ci·sive** \di-ˈsī-siv\ *adj*
**1** deciding or able to decide a question or dispute ⟨*decisive* proof⟩
**2** RESOLUTE ⟨*decisive* minds⟩
**3** [1]CLEAR 7, UNMISTAKABLE ⟨a *decisive* victory⟩
**de·ci·sive·ly** *adv*
**de·ci·sive·ness** *n*

[1]**deck** \ˈdek\ *n*
**1** a floor that goes from one side of a ship to the other
**2** something like the deck of a ship
**3** a pack of playing cards

[2]**deck** *vb*
to dress or decorate especially in a showy way

**dec·la·ra·tion** \ˌdek-lə-ˈrā-shən\ *n*
**1** an act of declaring
**2** something declared or a document containing such a declaration ⟨the *Declaration* of Independence⟩

*tree is covered with leaves in summer*

*tree is bare of leaves in winter*

**deciduous:** an oak tree in summer and winter

**de·clar·a·tive** \di-'klar-ət-iv, -'kler-\ *adj*
making a statement ⟨a *declarative* sentence⟩

**de·clare** \di-'klaər, -'kleər\ *vb* **de·clared**; **de·clar·ing**
**1** to make known in a clear or formal way ⟨*declare* war⟩
**2** to state as if certain

**Synonyms** DECLARE, ANNOUNCE, and ADVERTISE mean to make known to the public. DECLARE suggests that something is said very clearly and often in a formal manner ⟨the governor *declared* that all must pay the tax⟩. ANNOUNCE suggests that something of interest is declared for the first time ⟨*announced* the discovery of a new planet⟩. ADVERTISE suggests repeating a statement over and over and all around ⟨they *advertised* all over the neighborhood that they were getting a pony⟩.

**¹de·cline** \di-'klīn\ *vb* **de·clined**; **de·clin·ing**
**1** to bend or slope downward
**2** to pass toward a lower, worse, or weaker state ⟨prices *declined*⟩ ⟨*decline* in health⟩
**3** to refuse to accept, do, or agree ⟨*decline* an invitation⟩ ⟨*decline* to leave⟩

**²decline** *n*
**1** a gradual weakening in body or mind
**2** a change to a lower state or level ⟨a business *decline*⟩
**3** the time when something is nearing its end

**de·code** \dē-'kōd\ *vb* **de·cod·ed**; **de·cod·ing**
to change a message in code into ordinary language

**de·com·pose** \,dē-kəm-'pōz\ *vb* **de·com·posed**; **de·com·pos·ing**
**1** to separate a thing into its parts or into simpler compounds
**2** to break down in decaying
**de·com·pos·er** *n*

**de·com·po·si·tion** \,dē-,käm-pə-'zish-ən\ *n*
**1** the process of decomposing
**2** the state of being decomposed

**dec·o·rate** \'dek-ə-,rāt\ *vb* **dec·o·rat·ed**; **dec·o·rat·ing**
**1** to make more attractive by adding something nice looking ⟨*decorate* one's room⟩
**2** to award a decoration of honor to ⟨*decorate* a soldier for bravery⟩

**dec·o·ra·tion** \,dek-ə-'rā-shən\ *n*
**1** the act of decorating
**2** ¹ORNAMENT 1
**3** a badge of honor

**dec·o·ra·tive** \'dek-ə-rət-iv, 'dek-rət-\ *adj*
serving to decorate : ORNAMENTAL

**dec·o·ra·tor** \'dek-ə-,rāt-ər\ *n*
a person who decorates especially the rooms of houses

**de·co·rum** \di-'kōr-əm\ *n*
proper behavior

**¹de·coy** \di-'kȯi, 'dē-,kȯi\ *n*
▼ a person or thing (as an artificial bird) used to lead or lure into a trap or snare

**¹decoy:** artificial ducks used to attract live ducks toward hunters

**²decoy** *vb*
to lure by or as if by a decoy

**¹de·crease** \di-'krēs\ *vb* **de·creased**; **de·creas·ing**
to grow less or cause to grow less

**²de·crease** \'dē-,krēs\ *n*
**1** the process of decreasing
**2** REDUCTION 2

**¹de·cree** \di-'krē\ *n*
an order or decision given by a person or group in authority

**²decree** *vb* **de·creed**; **de·cree·ing**
to order by a decree

**de·crep·it** \di-'krep-ət\ *adj*
worn out or weakened by age or use

**de·cre·scen·do** \,dā-krə-'shen-dō\ *n*
a gradual decrease in the loudness of music

**ded·i·cate** \'ded-i-,kāt\ *vb* **ded·i·cat·ed**; **ded·i·cat·ing**
**1** to set apart for some purpose and especially for a sacred or serious purpose : DEVOTE
**2** to address or write something in (as a book) as a compliment to someone

**ded·i·ca·tion** \,ded-i-'kā-shən\ *n*
**1** an act of dedicating
**2** something written in dedicating a book
**3** devotion to the point of giving up what one needs or loves

**de·duct** \di-'dəkt\ *vb*
to take away an amount of something : SUBTRACT

**de·duc·tion** \di-'dək-shən\ *n*
**1** SUBTRACTION
**2** an amount deducted

**¹deed** \'dēd\ *n*
**1** a usually fine or brave act or action : FEAT
**2** a legal document containing the record of an agreement or especially of a transfer of real estate

**²deed** *vb*
to transfer by a deed

**deem** \'dēm\ *vb*
to hold as an opinion ⟨*deem* it wise to wait⟩

**¹deep** \'dēp\ *adj*
**1** reaching down far below the surface ⟨*deep* roots⟩ ⟨*deep* snow⟩
**2** reaching far back from the front or outer part ⟨a *deep* forest⟩
**3** hard to understand ⟨a *deep* book⟩
**4** located well below the surface or well within the boundaries of ⟨*deep* in the ground⟩
**5** fully developed : PROFOUND ⟨a *deep* sleep⟩ ⟨took *deep* pleasure in the gift⟩
**6** dark and rich in color ⟨a *deep* red⟩
**7** low in tone ⟨a *deep* voice⟩
**8** completely busy ⟨*deep* in study⟩
**deep·ly** *adv*

**²deep** *adv*
to a great depth : DEEPLY ⟨drink *deep*⟩

**³deep** *n*
**1** a very deep place or part ⟨the ocean *deeps*⟩
**2** OCEAN 1 ⟨the briny *deep*⟩

**deep·en** \'dē-pən\ *vb*
to make or become deep or deeper

**deep fat** *n*
hot fat or oil deep enough in a cooking utensil to cover the food to be fried

A B C D E F G H I J K L M N O P Q R S T U V W X Y Z

**deep–fry** \'dēp-'frī\ *vb*
to cook in deep fat

**deer** \'dir\ *n, pl* **deer**
▶ any of a group of mammals that chew the cud and have cloven hoofs and in the male antlers which are often branched

**deer·skin** \'dir-,skin\ *n*
leather made from the skin of a deer or a garment made of such leather

**de·face** \di-'fās\ *vb* **de·faced**; **de·fac·ing**
to destroy or mar the face or surface of
**de·face·ment** \-mənt\ *n*
**de·fac·er** *n*

[1]**de·fault** \di-'fȯlt\ *n*
failure to do something required by law or duty

[2]**default** *vb*
to fail to do one's duty
**de·fault·er** *n*

[1]**de·feat** \di-'fēt\ *vb*
**1** to bring to nothing ⟨*defeat* a hope⟩
**2** to win victory over

[2]**defeat** *n*
loss of a contest or battle

**de·fect** \'dē-,fekt, di-'fekt\ *n*
a lack of something necessary for completeness or perfection

**de·fec·tive** \di-'fek-tiv\ *adj*
lacking something necessary : FAULTY ⟨a *defective* plan⟩

**de·fend** \di-'fend\ *vb*
**1** to protect from danger or attack
**2** to act or speak in favor of when others are opposed
**de·fend·er** *n*

---

**Synonyms** DEFEND, PROTECT, and SAFEGUARD mean to keep secure. DEFEND suggests that danger or attack is actual or threatening ⟨*defended* the fort against enemy troops⟩. PROTECT stresses the use of some kind of shield to prevent possible attack or injury ⟨*protect* your eyes with dark glasses⟩. SAFEGUARD suggests the taking of a course of action to protect against merely possible danger ⟨public health rules that *safeguard* the city from epidemics⟩.

---

**de·fense** \di-'fens\ *n*
**1** the act of defending
**2** something that defends or protects

**deer:** a female red deer

**3** a defensive team
**de·fense·less** \-ləs\ *adj*

[1]**de·fen·sive** \di-'fen-siv\ *adj*
**1** serving or meant to defend or protect
**2** ▶ of or relating to the attempt to keep an opponent from scoring (as in a game)
**de·fen·sive·ly** *adv*

[2]**defensive** *n*
a defensive position or attitude

[1]**de·fer** \di-'fər\ *vb* **de·ferred**; **de·fer·ring**
to put off to a future time
**de·fer·ment** \mənt\ *n*

[2]**defer** *vb* **de·ferred**; **de·fer·ring**
to yield to the opinion or wishes of another

**def·er·ence** \'def-ə-rəns, 'def-rəns\ *n*
respect and consideration for the wishes of another

**de·fi·ance** \di-'fī-əns\ *n*
**1** an act of defying
**2** a willingness to resist

**de·fi·ant** \di-'fī-ənt\ *adj*
showing defiance
**de·fi·ant·ly** *adv*

**de·fi·cien·cy** \di-'fish-ən-sē\ *n, pl* **de·fi·cien·cies**
the state of being without something necessary and especially something required for health

**de·fi·cient** \di-'fish-ənt\ *adj*
lacking something necessary for completeness or health

**def·i·cit** \'def-ə-sət\ *n*
a shortage especially in money needed

**de·file** \di-'fīl\ *vb* **de·filed**; **de·fil·ing**
**1** to make filthy
**2** [1]CORRUPT 1
**3** [2]DISHONOR
**de·file·ment** \-mənt\ *n*

**de·fine** \di-'fīn\ *vb* **de·fined**; **de·fin·ing**
**1** to set or mark the limits of
**2** to make distinct in outline
**3** to find out and explain the meaning of ⟨*define* a word⟩
**de·fin·er** *n*

**def·i·nite** \'def-ə-nət\ *adj*
**1** having certain or distinct limits ⟨a *definite* period of time⟩
**2** clear in meaning ⟨a *definite* answer⟩
**3** UNQUESTIONABLE ⟨a *definite* improvement⟩
**def·i·nite·ly** *adv*
**def·i·nite·ness** *n*

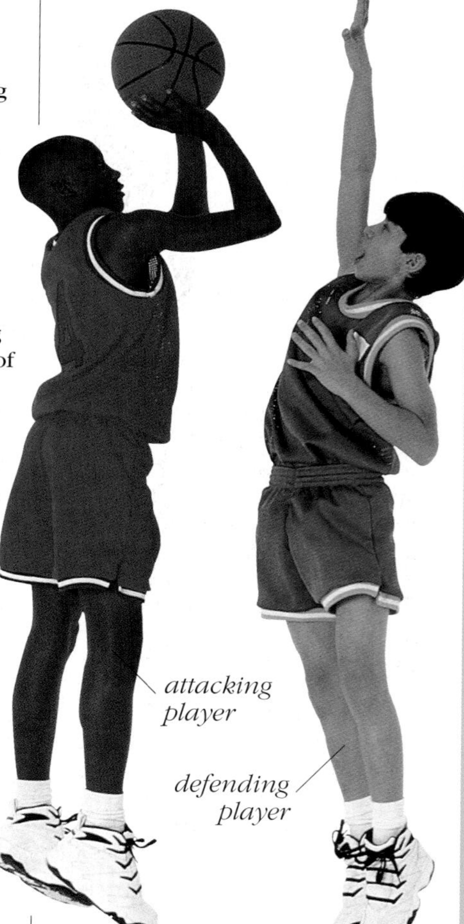


[1]**defensive 2:** a defensive action in basketball

**definite article** *n*
the article *the* used to show that the following noun refers to one or more specific persons or things

**def·i·ni·tion** \ˌdef-ə-ˈnish-ən\ *n*
**1** an act of defining
**2** a statement of the meaning of a word or a word group
**3** clearness of outline or detail

**de·flate** \di-ˈflāt\ *vb* **de·flat·ed**; **de·flat·ing**
**1** ▼ to let the air or gas out of something that has been blown up
**2** to reduce in size or importance

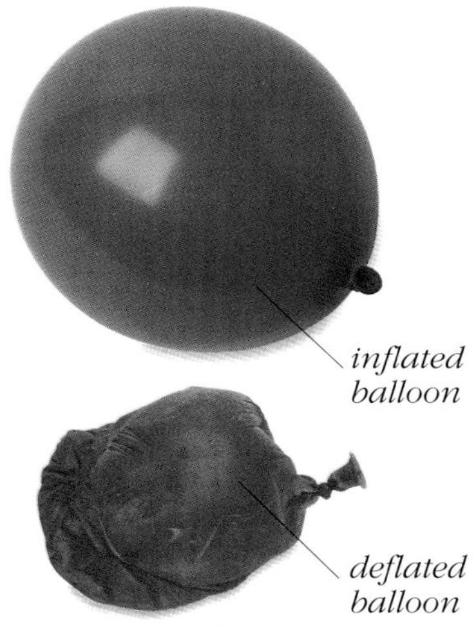

**deflate 1**

**de·flect** \di-ˈflekt\ *vb*
to turn aside

**de·for·est** \dē-ˈfȯr-əst\ *vb*
to clear of forests

**de·form** \di-ˈfȯrm\ *vb*
to spoil the form or the natural appearance of

**de·for·mi·ty** \di-ˈfȯr-mət-ē\ *n, pl* **de·for·mi·ties**
**1** the condition of being deformed
**2** a flaw or blemish in something and especially in the body of a person or animal

**de·frag·ment** \dē-ˈfrag-mənt\ *vb*
to reorganize fragments of computer data into a continuous series ⟨you need to *defragment* your hard drive⟩

**de·fraud** \di-ˈfrȯd\ *vb*
to take or keep something from by deceit : CHEAT

**de·frost** \di-ˈfrȯst\ *vb*
**1** to thaw out
**2** to remove ice from
**de·frost·er** *n*

**deft** \ˈdeft\ *adj*
quick and neat in action : SKILLFUL
**deft·ly** *adv*
**deft·ness** *n*

**de·fy** \di-ˈfī\ *vb* **de·fied**; **de·fy·ing**
**1** to challenge to do something thought to be impossible : DARE
**2** to refuse boldly to obey or yield to
**3** to resist the effects of or attempts at ⟨beauty that *defies* age⟩

**deg·ra·da·tion** \ˌdeg-rə-ˈdā-shən\ *n*
**1** an act of degrading
**2** the state of being degraded

**de·grade** \di-ˈgrād\ *vb* **de·grad·ed**; **de·grad·ing**
**1** to reduce from a higher to a lower rank or degree
**2** to bring to a low state : DEBASE, CORRUPT

**de·gree** \di-ˈgrē\ *n*
**1** a step in a series ⟨advanced by *degrees*⟩
**2** amount of something as measured by a series of steps ⟨a high *degree* of progress⟩
**3** one of the three forms an adjective or adverb may have when it is compared
**4** a title given (as to students) by a college or university ⟨a *degree* of doctor of medicine⟩
**5** one of the divisions marked on a measuring instrument (as a thermometer)
**6** a 360th part of the circumference of a circle
**7** a line or space of the staff in music or the difference in pitch between two notes

**de·hu·mid·i·fy** \ˌdē-hyü-ˈmid-ə-ˌfī\ *vb* **de·hu·mid·i·fied**; **de·hu·mid·i·fy·ing**
to take moisture from (as the air)
**de·hu·mid·i·fi·er** *n*

**de·hy·drate** \dē-ˈhī-ˌdrāt\ *vb* **de·hy·drat·ed**; **de·hy·drat·ing**
**1** to take water from (as foods)
**2** to lose water or body fluids

**de·ice** \dē-ˈīs\ *vb* **de·iced**; **de·ic·ing**
to free or keep free of ice ⟨*deice* an airplane⟩
**de·ic·er** *n*

**de·i·fy** \ˈdē-ə-ˌfī\ *vb* **de·i·fied**; **de·i·fy·ing**
to make a god of

**deign** \ˈdān\ *vb*
CONDESCEND 1

**de·i·ty** \ˈdē-ət-ē, ˈdā-\ *n, pl* **de·i·ties**
**1** *cap* GOD 1
**2** GOD 2, GODDESS ⟨Roman *deities*⟩

**de·ject·ed** \di-ˈjek-təd\ *adj*
low in spirits ⟨we were *dejected* at losing the game⟩
**de·ject·ed·ly** *adv*

**de·jec·tion** \di-ˈjek-shən\ *n*
a dejected state

**deka-** *or* **dek-** see DECA-

[1]**de·lay** \di-ˈlā\ *n*
**1** a putting off of something
**2** the time during which something is delayed

[2]**delay** *vb*
**1** to put off
**2** to stop or prevent for a time
**3** to move or act slowly

[1]**del·e·gate** \ˈdel-i-gət\ *n*
a person sent with power to act for another or others

[2]**del·e·gate** \ˈdel-ə-ˌgāt\ *vb* **del·e·gat·ed**; **del·e·gat·ing**
**1** to entrust to another ⟨the voters *delegate* power to their congressmen⟩
**2** to make responsible for getting something done ⟨we were *delegated* to clean up the yard⟩

**del·e·ga·tion** \ˌdel-ə-ˈgā-shən\ *n*
**1** the act of delegating
**2** one or more persons chosen to represent others

**de·lete** \di-ˈlēt\ *vb* **de·let·ed**; **de·let·ing**
to remove especially by erasing, crossing out, or cutting out

**de·le·tion** \di-ˈlē-shən\ *n*
**1** an act of deleting
**2** something deleted

[1]**de·lib·er·ate** \di-ˈlib-ə-ˌrāt\ *vb* **de·lib·er·at·ed**; **de·lib·er·at·ing**
to think about carefully

[2]**de·lib·er·ate** \di-ˈlib-ə-rət, -ˈlib-rət\ *adj*
**1** showing careful thought ⟨a *deliberate* decision⟩
**2** done or said on purpose ⟨a *deliberate* lie⟩
**3** slow in action : not hurried
**synonyms** see VOLUNTARY
**de·lib·er·ate·ly** *adv*
**de·lib·er·ate·ness** *n*

**de·lib·er·a·tion** \di-ˌlib-ə-ˈrā-shən\ *n*
**1** careful thought : CONSIDERATION
**2** the quality of being deliberate ⟨spoke with great *deliberation*⟩

A B C D E F G H I J K L M N O P Q R S T U V W X Y Z

**del·i·ca·cy** \'del-i-kə-sē\ *n,* *pl* **del·i·ca·cies**
**1** ▼ something pleasing to eat that is rare or a luxury
**2** fineness of structure ⟨lace of great *delicacy*⟩
**3** weakness of body **:** FRAILTY
**4** a situation needing careful handling
**5** consideration for the feelings of others

**delicacy 1:**
a cracker spread with smoked salmon and cream cheese

**del·i·cate** \'del-i-kət\ *adj*
**1** pleasing because of fineness or mildness ⟨a *delicate* flavor⟩ ⟨*delicate* blossoms⟩
**2** able to sense very small differences ⟨a *delicate* instrument⟩
**3** calling for skill and careful treatment ⟨a *delicate* operation⟩
**4** easily damaged
**5** SICKLY 1 ⟨a *delicate* child⟩
**6** requiring tact
**del·i·cate·ly** *adv*

**del·i·ca·tes·sen** \ˌdel-i-kə-'tes-n\ *n*
a store where prepared foods (as salads and meats) are sold

**de·li·cious** \di-'lish-əs\ *adj*
giving great pleasure especially to the taste or smell
**de·li·cious·ly** *adv*
**de·li·cious·ness** *n*

**[1]de·light** \di-'līt\ *n*
**1** great pleasure or satisfaction **:** JOY
**2** something that gives great pleasure

**[2]delight** *vb*
**1** to take great pleasure
**2** to give joy or satisfaction to

**de·light·ed** \di-'līt-əd\ *adj*
very pleased

**de·light·ful** \di-'līt-fəl\ *adj*
giving delight **:** very pleasing
**de·light·ful·ly** \-fə-lē\ *adv*

**de·lir·i·ous** \di-'lir-ē-əs\ *adj*
**1** suffering delirium
**2** wildly excited
**de·lir·i·ous·ly** *adv*

**de·lir·i·um** \di-'lir-ē-əm\ *n*
**1** a condition of mind in which thought and speech are confused and which often goes along with a high fever
**2** wild excitement

**de·liv·er** \di-'liv-ər\ *vb*
**1** to set free **:** RESCUE ⟨*deliver* us from evil⟩
**2** [1]TRANSFER 2 ⟨*deliver* a letter⟩ ⟨this store *delivers*⟩
**3** to help in childbirth
**4** [2]UTTER 2 ⟨*deliver* a speech⟩
**5** to send to an intended target
**de·liv·er·er** *n*

**de·liv·er·ance** \di-'liv-ə-rəns, -'liv-rəns\ *n*
an act of delivering or the state of being delivered **:** a setting free

**de·liv·ery** \di-'liv-ə-rē, -'liv-rē\ *n,* *pl* **de·liv·er·ies**
**1** a setting free (as from something that hampers or holds one back)
**2** the transfer of something from one place or person to another
**3** the act of giving birth
**4** speaking or manner of speaking (as of a formal speech)
**5** the act or way of throwing ⟨an underhand *delivery*⟩

**dell** \'del\ *n*
a small valley usually covered with trees

**del·phin·i·um** \del-'fin-ē-əm\ *n*
▶ a tall plant related to the buttercups and often grown for its large stalks of showy flowers

**delphinium**

**del·ta** \'del-tə\ *n*
a piece of land in the shape of a triangle or fan made by deposits of mud and sand at the mouth of a river

**de·lude** \di-'lüd\ *vb* **de·lud·ed**; **de·lud·ing**
DECEIVE, MISLEAD

**[1]del·uge** \'del-yüj\ *n*
**1** a flooding of land by water **:** FLOOD
**2** a drenching rain
**3** a sudden huge stream of something ⟨a *deluge* of mail⟩

**[2]deluge** *vb* **del·uged**; **del·ug·ing**
**1** [2]FLOOD 1
**2** to overwhelm as if with a deluge

**de·lu·sion** \di-'lü-zhən\ *n*
**1** an act of deluding or the state of being deluded
**2** a false belief that continues in spite of the facts

**de·luxe** \di-'lu̇ks, -'ləks\ *adj*
very fine or luxurious

**delve** \'delv\ *vb* **delved**; **delv·ing**
**1** DIG
**2** to work hard looking for information in written records
**delv·er** *n*

**[1]de·mand** \di-'mand\ *n*
**1** an act of demanding ⟨payable on *demand*⟩
**2** an expressed desire to own or use something ⟨the *demand* for new cars⟩
**3** a seeking or being sought after ⟨good teachers are in great *demand*⟩

**[2]demand** *vb*
**1** to claim as one's right ⟨*demand* an apology⟩
**2** to ask earnestly or in the manner of a command ⟨the sentry *demanded* the password⟩
**3** to call for **:** REQUIRE ⟨the situation *demands* attention⟩
**de·mand·er** *n*

**de·mean** \di-'mēn\ *vb* **de·meaned**; **de·mean·ing**
to behave or conduct (oneself) usually in a proper way

**de·mean·or** \di-'mē-nər\ *n*
outward manner or behavior

**de·ment·ed** \di-'ment-əd\ *adj*
INSANE 1, MAD
**de·ment·ed·ly** *adv*

**de·mer·it** \dē-'mer-ət\ *n*
a mark placed against a person's record for doing something wrong

**demi-** *prefix*
**1** half
**2** one that partly belongs to a specified type or class ⟨*demi*god⟩

**demi·god** \'dem-ē-ˌgäd\ *n*
one who is partly divine and partly human

**de·mo·bi·lize** \di-'mō-bə-ˌlīz\ *vb* **de·mo·bi·lized**; **de·mo·bi·liz·ing**
to let go from military service ⟨*demobilized* soldiers⟩

**de·moc·ra·cy** \di-ˈmäk-rə-sē\ *n, pl* **de·moc·ra·cies**
**1** government by the people **:** majority rule
**2** government in which the highest power is held by the people and is usually used through representatives
**3** a political unit (as a nation) governed by the people
**4** belief in or practice of the idea that all people are socially equal

**dem·o·crat** \ˈdem-ə-ˌkrat\ *n*
one who believes in or practices democracy

**dem·o·crat·ic** \ˌdem-ə-ˈkrat-ik\ *adj*
**1** of, relating to, or favoring political democracy
**2** believing in or practicing the idea that people are socially equal
**dem·o·crat·i·cal·ly** \-i-kə-lē\ *adv*

**de·mol·ish** \di-ˈmäl-ish\ *vb*
**1** to destroy by breaking apart ⟨*demolish* a building⟩
**2** to ruin completely **:** SHATTER

**de·mon** \ˈdē-mən\ *n*
**1** ▼ an evil spirit **:** DEVIL
**2** a person of great energy or skill

**demon 1:**
a demon mask from Korea

**dem·on·strate** \ˈdem-ən-ˌstrāt\ *vb* **dem·on·strat·ed**; **dem·on·strat·ing**
**1** to show clearly
**2** to prove or make clear by reasoning
**3** to explain (as in teaching) by use of examples or experiments
**4** to show to people the good qualities of an article or a product ⟨*demonstrate* a new car⟩
**5** to make a public display (as of feelings or military force)

**dem·on·stra·tion** \ˌdem-ən-ˈstrā-shən\ *n*
**1** an outward expression (as a show of feelings)
**2** an act or a means of demonstrating ⟨a cooking *demonstration*⟩
**3** a showing or using of an article for sale to display its good points
**4** a parade or a gathering to show public feeling

**de·mon·stra·tive** \di-ˈmän-strət-iv\ *adj*
**1** pointing out the one referred to and showing that it differs from others ⟨in "this is my dog" and "that is their dog," "this" and "that" are *demonstrative* pronouns⟩
**2** showing feeling freely ⟨a very *demonstrative* person⟩

**dem·on·stra·tor** \ˈdem-ən-ˌstrāt-ər\ *n*
**1** a person who makes or takes part in a demonstration
**2** a manufactured article used for demonstration

**de·mor·al·ize** \di-ˈmȯr-ə-ˌlīz\ *vb* **de·mor·al·ized**; **de·mor·al·iz·ing**
to weaken the discipline or spirit of

**de·mote** \di-ˈmōt\ *vb* **de·mot·ed**; **de·mot·ing**
to reduce to a lower grade or rank

**de·mure** \di-ˈmyu̇r\ *adj*
**1** MODEST 3
**2** pretending to be modest **:** COY
**de·mure·ly** *adv*
**de·mure·ness** *n*

**den** \ˈden\ *n*
**1** ▶ the shelter or resting place of a wild animal
**2** a quiet or private room in a home
**3** a hiding place (as for thieves)

**de·na·ture** \dē-ˈnā-chər\ *vb* **de·na·tured**; **de·na·tur·ing**
to make alcohol unfit for humans to drink

**den·drite** \ˈden-ˌdrīt\ *n*
any of the usually branched fibers that carry nerve impulses toward a nerve cell body

**de·ni·al** \di-ˈnī-əl\ *n*
**1** a refusal to give or agree to something asked for
**2** a refusal to admit the truth of a statement
**3** a refusal to accept or believe in someone or something
**4** a cutting down or limiting ⟨a *denial* of one's appetite⟩

**den·im** \ˈden-əm\ *n*
**1** ▼ a firm often coarse cotton cloth
**2 denims** *pl* overalls or pants of usually blue denim

**denim 1:** a shirt made of denim

**Word History** The word *denim* came from a French phrase that meant "serge of Nimes." Serge is a kind of sturdy cloth. Nimes is a city in the southern part of France. Making cloth is a big industry there even today. When the English borrowed the French phrase that meant "serge of Nimes" they made it *serge denim*. Later this phrase was shortened to *denim*.

**den 1:** red foxes emerging from the mouth of their den

**de·nom·i·na·tion** \di-ˌnäm-ə-'nā-shən\ *n*
**1** a name especially for a class of things
**2** a religious body made up of a number of congregations having the same beliefs
**3** a value in a series of values (as of money)

**de·nom·i·na·tor** \di-'näm-ə-ˌnāt-ər\ *n*
the part of a fraction that is below the line ⟨5 is the *denominator* of the fraction 3/5⟩

**de·note** \di-'nōt\ *vb* **de·not·ed**; **de·not·ing**
**1** to serve as a mark or indication of ⟨the hands of a clock *denote* the time⟩
**2** to have the meaning of **:** MEAN

**de·nounce** \di-'nau̇ns\ *vb* **de·nounced**; **de·nounc·ing**
**1** to point out as wrong or evil **:** CONDEMN
**2** to inform against **:** ACCUSE
**de·nounce·ment** \-mənt\ *n*
**de·nounc·er** *n*

**dense** \'dens\ *adj* **dens·er**; **dens·est**
**1** having its parts crowded together **:** THICK ⟨*dense* fog⟩
**2** STUPID 1
**dense·ly** *adv*
**dense·ness** *n*

---

**Synonyms** DENSE, THICK, and COMPACT mean having parts that are gathered tightly together. DENSE is used of something in which the parts are very close together ⟨a *dense* forest⟩. THICK is used of something that has many small parts that form a single mass ⟨a *thick* head of hair⟩. COMPACT is used of something that has a close and firm gathering of parts, especially within a small area ⟨a *compact* town where everything is within walking distance⟩.

---

**den·si·ty** \'den-sət-ē\ *n, pl* **den·si·ties**
**1** the state of being dense
**2** the amount of something in a specified volume or area

**¹dent** \'dent\ *vb*
**1** to make a dent in or on
**2** to become marked by a dent

**²dent** *n*
a notch or hollow made in a surface by a blow or by pressure

**den·tal** \'dent-l\ *adj*
of or relating to the teeth or dentistry
**den·tal·ly** *adv*

**dental floss** *n*
flat thread used for cleaning between teeth

*dental floss*

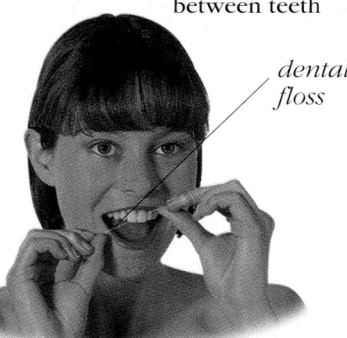

**dental floss:**
a woman using dental floss

**den·ti·frice** \'dent-ə-frəs\ *n*
a powder, paste, or liquid used in cleaning the teeth

**den·tin** \'dent-n\ *or* **den·tine** \'den-ˌtēn\ *n*
a hard bony material that makes up the main part of a tooth

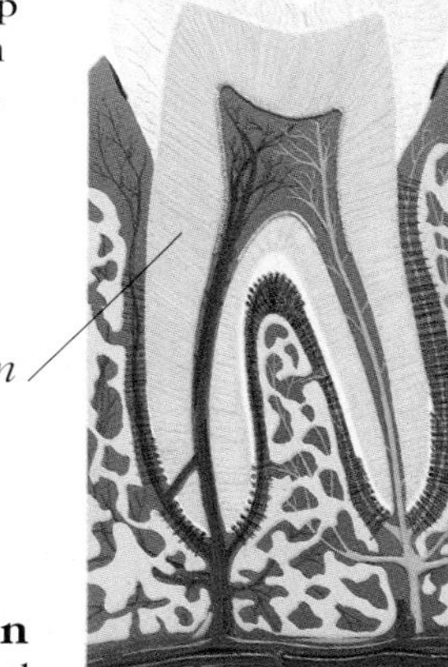


**dentin**
in a tooth

**den·tist** \'dent-əst\ *n*
a person whose profession is the care, treatment, and repair of the teeth

**den·tist·ry** \'dent-ə-strē\ *n*
the profession or practice of a dentist

**den·ture** \'den-chər\ *n*
a set of false teeth

**de·nude** \di-'nüd, -'nyüd\ *vb* **de·nud·ed**; **de·nud·ing**
to strip of covering **:** make bare

**de·ny** \di-'nī\ *vb* **de·nied**; **de·ny·ing**
**1** to declare not to be true ⟨*deny* a report⟩
**2** to refuse to grant ⟨*deny* a request⟩
**3** DISOWN, REPUDIATE ⟨*deny* one's religion⟩

**de·odor·ant** \dē-'ōd-ə-rənt\ *n*
something used to remove or hide unpleasant odors

**de·odor·ize** \dē-'ōd-ə-ˌrīz\ *vb* **de·odor·ized**; **de·odor·iz·ing**
to remove odor and especially a bad smell from

**de·part** \di-'pärt\ *vb*
**1** to go away or go away from **:** LEAVE
**2** ¹DIE 1
**3** to turn aside

**de·part·ment** \di-'pärt-mənt\ *n*
a special part or division of an organization (as a government or college)

**department store** *n*
a store having individual departments for different kinds of goods

**de·par·ture** \di-'pär-chər\ *n*
**1** a going away
**2** a setting out (as on a new course)
**3** a turning away or aside (as from a way of doing things)

**de·pend** \di-'pend\ *vb*
**1** to rely for support ⟨children *depend* on their parents⟩
**2** to be determined by or based on some action or condition ⟨success *depends* on hard work⟩
**3** ²TRUST 1, RELY

**de·pend·able** \di-'pen-də-bəl\ *adj*
TRUSTWORTHY, RELIABLE
**de·pend·ably** \-blē\ *adv*

**de·pen·dence** \di-'pen-dəns\ *n*
**1** a condition of being influenced and caused by something else
**2** a state of being dependent on someone or something
**3** ¹TRUST 1, RELIANCE

**¹de·pen·dent** \di-'pen-dənt\ *adj*
**1** CONTINGENT ⟨our plans are *dependent* on the weather⟩
**2** relying on someone else for support
**3** requiring something (as a drug) to feel or act normally

[2]**dependent** *n*
a person who depends upon another for support

**de·pict** \di-ˈpikt\ *vb*
**1** to represent by a picture
**2** to describe in words

**de·plete** \di-ˈplēt\ *vb* **de·plet·ed**; **de·plet·ing**
to reduce in amount by using up

**de·plor·able** \di-ˈplōr-ə-bəl\ *adj*
**1** deserving to be deplored **:** REGRETTABLE
**2** very bad **:** WRETCHED
**de·plor·ably** \-blē\ *adv*

**de·plore** \di-ˈplōr\ *vb* **de·plored**; **de·plor·ing**
**1** to regret strongly
**2** to consider deserving of disapproval

**de·port** \di-ˈpōrt\ *vb*
**1** BEHAVE 1, CONDUCT
**2** to force (a person who is not a citizen) to leave a country

**de·port·ment** \di-ˈpōrt-mənt\ *n*
BEHAVIOR 1

**de·pose** \di-ˈpōz\ *vb* **de·posed**; **de·pos·ing**
to remove from a high office ⟨*depose* a king⟩

[1]**de·pos·it** \di-ˈpäz-ət\ *vb*
**1** to place for or as if for safekeeping
**2** to put money in a bank
**3** to give as a pledge that a purchase will be made or a service used ⟨*deposit* ten dollars on a new bicycle⟩
**4** to lay down **:** PUT
**5** to let fall or sink

[2]**deposit** *n*
**1** the state of being deposited ⟨money on *deposit*⟩
**2** money that is deposited in a bank
**3** something given as a pledge or as part payment ⟨a *deposit* of ten dollars on a new bicycle⟩
**4** something laid or thrown down
**5** ▶ mineral matter built up in nature ⟨a coal *deposit*⟩

*crystal deposit*

[2]**deposit 5:** a crystal deposit on a rock

**de·pos·i·tor** \di-ˈpäz-ət-ər\ *n*
a person who makes a deposit especially of money in a bank

**de·pot** *usually* ˈdep-ˌō *for 1 & 2*, ˈdē-ˌpō *for 3*\ *n*
**1** a place where military supplies are kept
**2** STOREHOUSE 1
**3** a railroad or bus station

**de·pre·ci·ate** \di-ˈprē-shē-ˌāt\ *vb* **de·pre·ci·at·ed**; **de·pre·ci·at·ing**
**1** to lower the price or value of
**2** BELITTLE
**3** to lose value

**de·press** \di-ˈpres\ *vb*
**1** to press down ⟨*depress* a lever⟩
**2** to lessen the activity or strength of ⟨bad weather had *depressed* sales⟩
**3** to lower the spirits of **:** make sad and dull

**de·pres·sant** \di-ˈpres-nt\ *adj or n*
SEDATIVE

**de·pres·sion** \di-ˈpresh-ən\ *n*
**1** an act of depressing **:** a state of being depressed
**2** a hollow place or part ⟨a *depression* in a road⟩
**3** low spirits
**4** a period of low activity in business with much unemployment

**de·pri·va·tion** \ˌdep-rə-ˈvā-shən, ˌdē-ˌprī-\ *n*
**1** an act or instance of depriving
**2** the state of being deprived

**de·prive** \di-ˈprīv\ *vb* **de·prived**; **de·priv·ing**
to take something away from or keep from having or doing something ⟨*deprive* a ruler of power⟩ ⟨the noise *deprived* me of sleep⟩

**depth** \ˈdepth\ *n*
**1** a deep place in a body of water (as a sea or a lake)
**2** measurement from top to bottom or from front to back ⟨*depth* of a cupboard⟩
**3** the innermost part of something **:** MIDDLE, MIDST ⟨in the *depth* of winter⟩
**4** ABUNDANCE, COMPLETENESS ⟨*depth* of knowledge⟩
**5** the quality of being deep

**depth charge** *n*
an explosive for use underwater especially against submarines

**dep·u·tize** \ˈdep-yə-ˌtīz\ *vb* **dep·u·tized**; **dep·u·tiz·ing**
to appoint as deputy

**dep·u·ty** \ˈdep-yət-ē\ *n, pl* **dep·u·ties**
a person appointed to act for or in place of another

**de·rail** \di-ˈrāl\ *vb*
to cause to leave the rails ⟨*derail* a train⟩
**de·rail·ment** \-mənt\ *n*

**de·range** \di-ˈrānj\ *vb* **de·ranged**; **de·rang·ing**
**1** to put out of order **:** DISARRANGE
**2** to make insane
**de·range·ment** \-mənt\ *n*

**der·by** \ˈdər-bē\ *n, pl* **derbies**
**1** a horse race for three-year-olds usually held every year
**2** ◀ a stiff felt hat with a narrow brim and a rounded top

**derby 2**

**de·ride** \di-ˈrīd\ *vb* **de·rid·ed**; **de·rid·ing**
to laugh at in scorn **:** make fun of **:** RIDICULE

**der·i·va·tion** \ˌder-ə-ˈvā-shən\ *n*
**1** the formation of a word from an earlier word or root
**2** ETYMOLOGY
**3** ORIGIN 3, SOURCE
**4** an act or process of deriving

[1]**de·riv·a·tive** \di-ˈriv-ət-iv\ *n*
**1** a word formed by derivation
**2** something derived

[2]**derivative** *adj*
derived from something else
**de·riv·a·tive·ly** *adv*

**de·rive** \di-ˈrīv\ *vb* **de·rived**; **de·riv·ing**
**1** to receive or obtain from a source ⟨*derive* new ideas from reading⟩
**2** to trace the derivation of
**3** to come from a certain source

**der·mal** \ˈdər-məl\ *adj*
of or relating to skin

**der·mis** \ˈdər-məs\ *n*
the inner sensitive layer of the skin

**de·rog·a·to·ry** \di-ˈräg-ə-ˌtōr-ē\ *adj*
intended to hurt the reputation of a person or thing ⟨a *derogatory* remark⟩

a b c d e f g h i j k l m n o p q r s t u v w x y z

\ng\ sing \ō\ bone \ȯ\ saw \ȯi\ coin \th\ thin \t͟h\ this \ü\ food \u̇\ foot \y\ yet \yü\ few \yu̇\ cure \zh\ vision

A B C D E F G H I J K L M N O P Q R S T U V W X Y Z

**der·rick** \'der-ik\ *n*
**1** a machine for moving or lifting heavy weights by means of a long beam fitted with ropes and pulleys
**2** a framework or tower over an oil well for supporting machinery

**Word History** Once there was in London a hangman named *Derick*. The people of London called his gallows by his name. *Derick*, or *derrick*, was soon used as a term for any gallows. Later a machine for lifting came to be called *derrick* as well. This was because the machine looked a bit like a gallows.

**de·scribe** \di-'skrīb\ *vb*
**de·scribed**; **de·scrib·ing**
**1** to write or tell about ⟨*describe* a football game⟩
**2** to draw the outline of ⟨*describe* a circle⟩ **synonyms** see REPORT
**de·scrib·er** *n*

**de·scrip·tion** \di-'skrip-shən\ *n*
**1** an account of something especially of a kind that presents a picture to a person who reads or hears it
**2** [1]SORT 1, KIND ⟨people of every *description*⟩

**de·scrip·tive** \di-'skrip-tiv\ *adj*
serving to describe
**de·scrip·tive·ly** *adv*

[1]**desert:** a desert landscape

**de·scend** \di-'send\ *vb*
**1** to come or go down from a higher place or level to a lower one ⟨*descend* a hill⟩
**2** to come down in sudden attack ⟨locusts *descended* on the crops⟩
**3** to come down from an earlier time ⟨a custom *descended* from ancient times⟩
**4** to come down from a source : DERIVE ⟨*descended* from an ancient family⟩
**5** to be handed down to an heir ⟨the property will *descend* to the children⟩
**6** to sink in a social or moral scale : STOOP

**de·scen·dant** \di-'sen-dənt\ *n*
one that is descended from a particular ancestor or family

**de·scent** \di-'sent\ *n*
**1** a coming or going down
**2** one's line of ancestors
**3** a downward slope ⟨a steep *descent*⟩
**4** a sudden attack

**descendant:** the girl is the descendant of her parents and grandparents

**des·e·crate** \'des-i-,krāt\ *vb*
**des·e·crat·ed**; **des·e·crat·ing**
to treat a sacred place or sacred object shamefully or with great disrespect

**de·seg·re·gate** \dē-'seg-ri-,gāt\ *vb*
**de·seg·re·gat·ed**;
**de·seg·re·gat·ing**
to end segregation in : free of any law or practice setting apart members of a certain race

**de·seg·re·ga·tion** \dē-,seg-ri-'gā-shən\ *n*
the act or process or an instance of desegregating

[1]**des·ert** \'dez-ərt\ *n*
a dry land with few plants and little rainfall

[2]**desert** *adj*
of, relating to, or being a desert

[3]**de·sert** \di-'zərt\ *n*
**1** worthiness of reward or punishment ⟨rewarded according to their *deserts*⟩
**2** a just reward or punishment

[4]**de·sert** \di-'zərt\ *vb*
**1** to leave usually without intending to return
**2** to leave a person or a thing that one should stay with
**3** to fail in time of need ⟨my courage *deserted* me⟩ **synonyms** see ABANDON
**de·sert·er** *n*

**de·serve** \di-'zərv\ *vb* **de·served**; **de·serv·ing**
to be worthy of : MERIT

**Synonyms** DESERVE, MERIT, and EARN mean to be worthy of something. DESERVE suggests that one should rightly receive something good or bad because of what one has done or what one is ⟨a hard worker *deserves* to be rewarded⟩. MERIT stresses the fact that someone or something is especially worthy of reward, punishment, or consideration ⟨students who *merit* special praise⟩. EARN suggests that one has spent time and effort and that one actually gets what one deserves ⟨you've *earned* a long vacation⟩.

**de·served·ly** \di-'zər-vəd-lē, -'zərv-dlē\ *adv*
as one deserves ⟨*deservedly* punished⟩

**de·serv·ing** \di-'zər-ving\ *adj*
WORTHY

**[1]de·sign** \di-'zīn\ *vb*
1 to think up and plan out in the mind
2 to set apart for or have as a special purpose : INTEND ⟨*designed* for fun⟩
3 to make a pattern or sketch of
**de·sign·er** *n*

**[2]design** *n*
1 [1]PLAN 2, SCHEME
2 a planned intention ⟨had ambitious *designs* for their children⟩
3 a secret purpose : PLOT
4 ▶ a preliminary sketch, model, or plan
5 an arrangement of parts in a structure or a work of art
6 a decorative pattern

**des·ig·nate** \'dez-ig-,nāt\ *vb* **des·ig·nat·ed**; **des·ig·nat·ing**
1 to mark or point out : INDICATE
2 to appoint or choose for a special purpose : NAME ⟨*designate* a leader⟩
3 to call by a name or title

**des·ig·na·tion** \,dez-ig-'nā-shən\ *n*
1 an act of designating
2 a name, sign, or title that identifies something

**[2]design 4:** a designer planning the layout of a book

**de·sign·ing** \di-'zī-ning\ *adj*
CRAFTY

**de·sir·able** \di-'zī-rə-bəl\ *adj*
1 having pleasing qualities : ATTRACTIVE
2 worth having or seeking
**de·sir·ably** \-blē\ *adv*

**[1]de·sire** \di-'zīr\ *vb* **de·sired**; **de·sir·ing**
1 to long for : wish for in earnest ⟨*desire* peace⟩
2 to express a wish for : REQUEST

**Synonyms** DESIRE, WISH, and CRAVE mean to want something very much. DESIRE stresses great feeling and actual striving to get what one wants ⟨the immigrants *desired* a better life⟩. WISH may suggest wanting something that one has little or no chance of getting ⟨sat around and *wished* for wealth⟩. CRAVE suggests the force of bodily or mental needs (as hunger or love) ⟨*craving* for food⟩.

**[2]desire** *n*
1 a strong wish : LONGING
2 a wish made known : REQUEST
3 something desired

**de·sist** \di-'zist, -'sist\ *vb*
to stop doing something

**desk** \'desk\ *n*
▼ a piece of furniture with a flat or sloping surface for use in writing or reading

**desk·top** \'desk-,täp\ *n*
1 the top of a desk
2 an area on a computer screen in which items are arranged as if they are objects on top of a desk
3 a computer that is used on a desk or table and is too big to be moved easily

**desk**

**[1]des·o·late** \'des-ə-lət\ *adj*
1 ABANDONED ⟨a *desolate* ghost town⟩
2 having no comfort or companionship : LONELY
3 left neglected or in ruins
4 CHEERLESS, GLOOMY ⟨a *desolate* wasteland⟩

**[2]des·o·late** \'des-ə-,lāt\ *vb* **des·o·lat·ed**; **des·o·lat·ing**
to make or leave desolate

**des·o·la·tion** \,des-ə-'lā-shən\ *n*
1 the state of being desolated : RUIN
2 sadness resulting from grief or loneliness

**[1]de·spair** \di-'spaər, -'speər\ *vb*
to give up or lose all hope or confidence

**[2]despair** *n*
1 loss of hope : a feeling of complete hopelessness
2 a cause of hopelessness

**des·per·ate** \'des-pə-rət, -prət\ *adj*
1 being beyond or almost beyond hope : causing despair
2 reckless because of despair : RASH
**des·per·ate·ly** *adv*
**des·per·ate·ness** *n*

a b c d e f g h i j k l m n o p q r s t u v w x y z

A B C D E F G H I J K L M N O P Q R S T U V W X Y Z

**des·per·a·tion** \ˌdes-pə-ˈrā-shən\ *n*
a state of hopeless despair leading to recklessness

**de·spi·ca·ble** \di-ˈspik-ə-bəl, ˈdes-pik-\ *adj*
deserving to be despised
**de·spi·ca·bly** \-blē\ *adv*

**de·spise** \di-ˈspīz\ *vb* **de·spised**; **de·spis·ing**
to consider as beneath one's notice or respect : feel scorn and dislike for

**Synonyms** DESPISE and SCORN mean to consider a person or thing as not worthy of one's notice or interest. DESPISE may be used of feeling ranging from strong dislike to true hatred ⟨I *despise* liars⟩. SCORN is used of a deep and ready feeling of angry disgust for anything that one considers beneath oneself ⟨*scorned* the soldiers who were lazy or cowardly⟩.

**de·spite** \di-ˈspīt\ *prep*
in spite of

**de·spoil** \di-ˈspȯil\ *vb*
to rob of possessions or belongings : PLUNDER
**de·spoil·er** *n*

**des·ti·na·tion** \ˌdes-tə-ˈnā-shən\ *n*
a place that one starts out for or that something is sent to

**des·tine** \ˈdes-tən\ *vb* **des·tined**; **des·tin·ing**
**1** to decide in advance on the future condition, use, or action of ⟨soldiers *destined* to lead the attack received extra training⟩
**2** to set aside for a special purpose ⟨money *destined* for a new car⟩

**des·ti·ny** \ˈdes-tə-nē\ *n, pl* **des·ti·nies**
**1** the fate or lot to which a person or thing is destined
**2** the course of events held to be arranged by a superhuman power

**des·ti·tute** \ˈdes-tə-ˌtüt, -ˌtyüt\ *adj*
**1** lacking something needed or desirable ⟨a room *destitute* of comforts⟩
**2** very poor

**de·stroy** \di-ˈstrȯi\ *vb*
**1** to put an end to : do away with
**2** [1]KILL 1

**de·struc·ti·ble** \di-ˈstrək-tə-bəl\ *adj*
possible to destroy

**de·struc·tion** \di-ˈstrək-shən\ *n*
**1** the act or process of destroying something
**2** the state or fact of being destroyed : RUIN
**3** something that destroys

**de·struc·tive** \di-ˈstrək-tiv\ *adj*
**1** causing destruction ⟨a *destructive* storm⟩
**2** not positive or helpful ⟨*destructive* criticism⟩
**de·struc·tive·ly** *adv*
**de·struc·tive·ness** *n*

**de·tach** \di-ˈtach\ *vb*
to separate from something else or from others especially for a certain purpose
**de·tach·able** \-ə-bəl\ *adj*

**de·tached** \di-ˈtacht\ *adj*
**1** not joined or connected : SEPARATE
**2** not taking sides or being influenced by others ⟨a *detached* attitude⟩
**de·tached·ly** \-ˈtach-əd-lē, -ˈtach-tlē\ *adv*

**destroyer 2:** model of a destroyer

**de·spon·den·cy** \di-ˈspän-dən-sē\ *n*
MELANCHOLY, DEJECTION

**de·spon·dent** \di-ˈspän-dənt\ *adj*
feeling quite discouraged or depressed : being in very low spirits
**de·spon·dent·ly** *adv*

**des·pot** \ˈdes-pət\ *n*
a ruler having absolute power and authority and especially one who rules cruelly

**des·sert** \di-ˈzərt\ *n*
▶ a course of sweet food, fruit, or cheese served at the end of a meal

**de·stroy·er** \di-ˈstrȯi-ər\ *n*
**1** one that destroys
**2** ▲ a small fast warship armed with guns, depth charges, torpedoes, and sometimes missiles

**dessert:** apple pie and cream

**de·tach·ment** \di-ˈtach-mənt\ *n*
**1** SEPARATION 1
**2** a body of troops or ships sent on special duty
**3** a keeping apart : lack of interest in worldly concerns
**4** IMPARTIALITY

[1]**de·tail** \di-ˈtāl, ˈdē-ˌtāl\ *n*
**1** a dealing with something item by item ⟨go into *detail*⟩
**2** a small part : ITEM
**3** a soldier or group of soldiers picked for special duty

[2]**detail** *vb*
**1** to report in detail : give the details of

2 to select for some special duty
**de·tailed** \di-'tāld, 'dē-,tāld\ *adj* including many details ⟨a *detailed* report⟩
**de·tain** \di-'tān\ *vb*
1 to hold or keep in or as if in prison
2 to stop especially from going on : DELAY ⟨*detained* by an accident⟩
**de·tain·ment** \-mənt\ *n*
**de·tect** \di-'tekt\ *vb* to learn of the existence, presence, or fact of ⟨*detect* an odor of escaping gas⟩
**de·tec·tion** \di-'tek-shən\ *n* the act of detecting : the state or fact of being detected : DISCOVERY
[1]**de·tec·tive** \di-'tek-tiv\ *adj*
1 able to detect or used in detecting something ⟨a *detective* device⟩
2 of or relating to detectives or their work
[2]**detective** *n* a person (as a police officer) whose business is solving crimes and catching criminals or gathering information that is not easy to get
**de·ten·tion** \di-'ten-chən\ *n*
1 the act of detaining : the state of being detained : CONFINEMENT
2 a forced delay
**de·ter** \di-'tər\ *vb* **de·terred**; **de·ter·ring** to discourage or prevent from doing something
[1]**de·ter·gent** \di-'tər-jənt\ *adj* able to clean : used in cleaning
[2]**detergent** *n* a substance that is like soap in its ability to clean
**de·te·ri·o·rate** \di-'tir-ē-ə-,rāt\ *vb* **de·te·ri·o·rat·ed**; **de·te·ri·o·rat·ing** to make or become worse or of less value
**de·ter·mi·na·tion** \di-,tər-mə-'nā-shən\ *n*
1 a coming to a decision or the decision reached
2 a settling or making sure of the position, size, or nature of something
3 firm or fixed intention
**de·ter·mine** \di-'tər-mən\ *vb* **de·ter·mined**; **de·ter·min·ing**
1 to fix exactly and with certainty
2 to come to a decision
3 to learn or find out exactly
4 to be the cause of or reason for
**de·ter·mined** \di-'tər-mənd\ *adj*
1 free from doubt
2 not weak or uncertain : FIRM ⟨a very *determined* opponent⟩
**de·ter·mined·ly** *adv*
**de·ter·min·er** \di-'tər-mə-nər\ *n* a word belonging to a group of noun modifiers that can occur before descriptive adjectives modifying the same noun ⟨"the" in "the red house" is a *determiner*⟩
**de·test** \di-'test\ *vb* to dislike very much
**de·test·able** \di-'tes-tə-bəl\ *adj* causing or deserving strong dislike
**de·test·ably** \-blē\ *adv*
**de·throne** \di-'thrōn\ *vb* **de·throned**; **de·thron·ing** to drive from a throne : DEPOSE
**de·throne·ment** \-mənt\ *n*
[1]**de·tour** \'dē-,tu̇r\ *n* a roundabout way that temporarily replaces part of a regular route
[2]**detour** *vb* to use or follow a detour
**de·tract** \di-'trakt\ *vb* to take away (as from value or importance)
**det·ri·ment** \'de-trə-mənt\ *n* injury or damage or its cause : HARM
**dev·as·tate** \'dev-ə-,stāt\ *vb* **dev·as·tat·ed**; **dev·as·tat·ing** to reduce to ruin : lay waste
**dev·as·ta·tion** \,dev-ə-'stā-shən\ *n* the action of devastating : the state of being devastated
**de·vel·op** \di-'vel-əp\ *vb*
1 to make or become plain little by little : UNFOLD ⟨as the story *develops*⟩
2 ▼ to apply chemicals to exposed photographic material (as a film) in order to bring out the picture
3 to bring out the possibilities of : IMPROVE

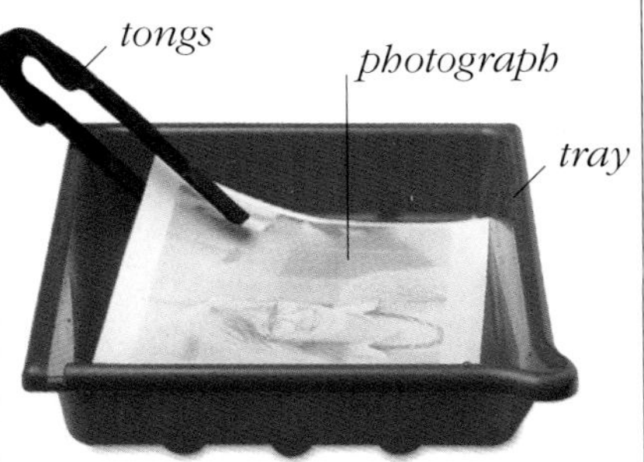


**develop 2:** a photograph emerging in a tray of developing solution

4 to make more available or usable ⟨*develop* land⟩
5 to gain gradually ⟨*develop* a taste for reading⟩
6 to grow toward maturity
**de·vel·op·er** *n*
**de·vel·oped** \di-'vel-əpt\ *adj* having many large industries and a complex economic system ⟨*developed* nations⟩
**de·vel·op·ment** \di-'vel-əp-mənt\ *n*
1 the act or process of developing : a result of developing
2 the state of being developed
**de·vi·ate** \'dē-vē-,āt\ *vb* **de·vi·at·ed**; **de·vi·at·ing** to turn aside from a course, principle, standard, or topic
**de·vice** \di-'vīs\ *n*
1 a scheme to deceive : TRICK
2 a piece of equipment or mechanism for a special purpose
3 [2]DESIRE 2, WILL ⟨left to our own *devices*⟩

[1]**devil 1:** a medieval sculpture of the devil

[1]**dev·il** \'dev-əl\ *n*
1 ▲ *often cap* the personal supreme spirit of evil
2 an evil spirit : DEMON, FIEND
3 a wicked or cruel person
4 a reckless or dashing person
5 a mischievous person
6 a person to be pitied ⟨poor *devils*⟩

[2]**devil** *vb* **dev·iled** *or* **dev·illed**; **dev·il·ing** *or* **dev·il·ling**
**1** to chop fine and season highly ⟨*deviled* eggs⟩
**2** [1]TEASE, ANNOY

**dev·il·ment** \'dev-əl-mənt\ *n*
reckless mischief

**de·vise** \di-'vīz\ *vb* **de·vised**; **de·vis·ing**
to think up : PLAN, INVENT
**de·vis·er** *n*

**de·void** \di-'vȯid\ *adj*
entirely lacking

**de·vote** \di-'vōt\ *vb* **de·vot·ed**; **de·vot·ing**
**1** to set apart for a special purpose
**2** to give up to entirely or in part ⟨*devote* oneself to reading⟩

**de·vot·ed** \di-'vōt-əd\ *adj*
**1** completely loyal ⟨*devoted* supporters and admirers⟩
**2** AFFECTIONATE, LOVING
**de·vot·ed·ly** *adv*

**de·vo·tion** \di-'vō-shən\ *n*
**1** a religious exercise or practice (as prayers) especially for use in private worship
**2** an act of devoting : the quality of being devoted ⟨felt a real *devotion* to music⟩
**3** deep love or affection

**de·vour** \di-'vau̇r\ *vb*
**1** to eat up greedily
**2** CONSUME 1 ⟨buildings *devoured* by flames⟩
**3** to take in eagerly by the senses or mind

**de·vout** \di-'vau̇t\ *adj*
**1** devoted to religion
**2** warmly sincere and earnest ⟨*devout* thanks⟩
**de·vout·ly** *adv*
**de·vout·ness** *n*

**dew** \'dü, 'dyü\ *n*
▼ moisture condensed on cool surfaces at night

**dew** on rose petals

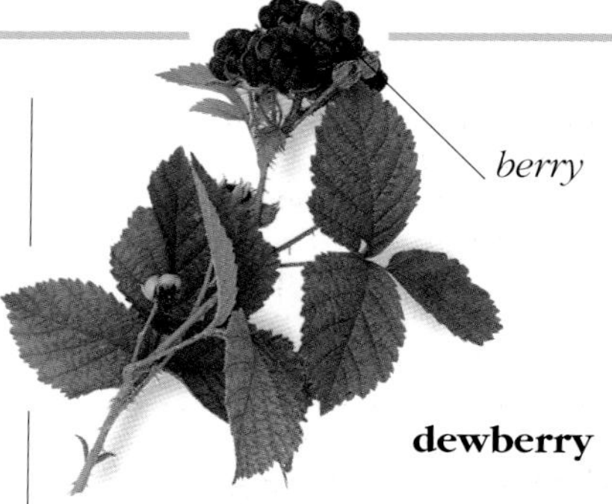

**dewberry**

**dew·ber·ry** \'dü-,ber-ē, 'dyü-\ *n, pl* **dew·ber·ries**
▲ a sweet edible berry that grows on a prickly vine and is related to the blackberries

**dewlap** on a mastiff

dewlap

**dew·lap** \'dü-,lap, 'dyü-\ *n*
▲ a hanging fold of skin under the neck of some animals

**dew point** *n*
the temperature at which the moisture in the air begins to turn to dew

**dewy** \'dü-ē, 'dyü-\ *adj* **dew·i·er**; **dew·i·est**
moist with or as if with dew
**dew·i·ly** \-ə-lē\ *adv*
**dew·i·ness** \-ē-nəs\ *n*

**dex·ter·i·ty** \dek-'ster-ət-ē\ *n, pl* **dex·ter·i·ties**
**1** skill and ease in bodily activity
**2** mental skill or quickness

**dex·ter·ous** *or* **dex·trous** \'dek-stə-rəs, -strəs\ *adj*
**1** skillful with the hands
**2** mentally skillful and clever
**3** done with skill
**dex·ter·ous·ly** *adv*
**dex·ter·ous·ness** *n*

**di·a·be·tes** \,dī-ə-'bēt-ēz, -'bēt-əs\ *n*
a disease in which too little insulin is produced and the body cannot use sugar and starch in the normal way

**di·a·bet·ic** \,dī-ə-'bet-ik\ *n*
a person with diabetes

**di·a·crit·i·cal mark** \,dī-ə-,krit-i-kəl-\ *n*
a mark used with a letter or group of letters to show a pronunciation different from that given a letter or group of letters not marked or marked in a different way

**di·a·dem** \'dī-ə-,dem\ *n*
a band for the head worn especially by monarchs

**di·ag·nose** \'dī-əg-,nōs\ *vb* **di·ag·nosed**; **di·ag·nos·ing**
to recognize (as a disease) by signs and symptoms

**di·ag·no·sis** \,dī-əg-'nō-səs\ *n, pl* **di·ag·no·ses** \-,sēz\
the art or act of recognizing a disease from its signs and symptoms

[1]**di·ag·o·nal** \dī-'ag-ən-l, -'ag-nəl\ *adj*
**1** ▼ running from one corner to the opposite corner of a figure with four sides
**2** running in a slanting direction ⟨*diagonal* stripes⟩
**di·ag·o·nal·ly** \-ē\ *adv*

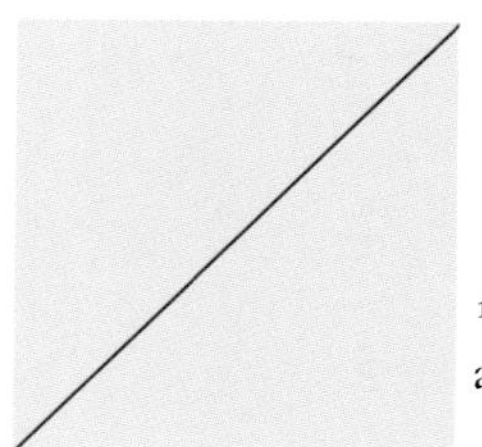
[1]**diagonal 1:** a diagonal line on a square

[2]**diagonal** *n*
a diagonal line, direction, or pattern

[1]**di·a·gram** \'dī-ə-,gram\ *n*
a drawing, sketch, plan, or chart that makes something clearer or easier to understand

[2]**diagram** *vb* **di·a·gramed** \'dī-ə-,gramd\ *or* **di·a·grammed**; **di·a·gram·ing** \-,gram-ing\ *or* **di·a·gram·ming**
to put in the form of a diagram

**¹di·al** \'dī-əl\ *n*
**1** the face of a watch or clock
**2** SUNDIAL
**3** a face or series of marks on which some measurement or other number is shown usually by means of a pointer ⟨the *dial* of a pressure gauge⟩
**4** a disk usually with a knob or holes that may be turned to operate something (as a telephone)

**²dial** *vb* **di·aled** *or* **di·alled**; **di·al·ing** *or* **di·al·ling**
to use a dial to operate or select ⟨*dialed* the wrong number⟩

**di·a·lect** \'dī-ə-ˌlekt\ *n*
**1** a form of a language belonging to a certain region
**2** a form of a language used by the members of a certain occupation or class

**di·a·logue** *or* **di·a·log** \'dī-ə-ˌlȯg\ *n*
**1** a conversation between two or more persons
**2** conversation given in a written story or a play

**di·am·e·ter** \dī-'am-ət-ər\ *n*
**1** a straight line that joins two points of a figure or body and passes through the center
**2** the distance through the center of an object from one side to the other **:** THICKNESS ⟨the *diameter* of a tree trunk⟩

**di·a·mond** \'dī-ə-mənd, 'dī-mənd\ *n*
**1** ▶ a very hard mineral that is a form of carbon, is usually nearly colorless, and is used especially in jewelry
**2** a flat figure ◊ like one of the surfaces of certain cut diamonds
**3** INFIELD 1

**di·a·per** \'dī-ə-pər, 'dī-pər\ *n*
a piece of absorbent material drawn up between the legs of a baby and fastened about the waist

**di·a·phragm** \'dī-ə-ˌfram\ *n*
**1** a muscular wall separating the chest from the abdomen
**2** a thin circular plate (as in a microphone) that vibrates when sound strikes it

**di·ar·rhea** \ˌdī-ə-'rē-ə\ *n*
abnormally frequent and watery bowel movements

**di·a·ry** \'dī-ə-rē, 'dī-rē\ *n, pl* **di·a·ries**
**1** a daily record especially of personal experiences and thoughts
**2** a book for keeping a diary

**¹dice** \'dīs\ *n, pl* **dice**
a small cube marked on each face with one to six spots and used usually in pairs in games

**²dice** *vb* **diced**; **dic·ing**
to cut into small cubes ⟨*dice* carrots⟩

**dick·er** \'dik-ər\ *vb*
²BARGAIN, HAGGLE

**¹dic·tate** \'dik-ˌtāt\ *vb* **dic·tat·ed**; **dic·tat·ing**
**1** to speak or read for someone else to write down or for a machine to record ⟨*dictate* a letter⟩
**2** to say or state with authority **:** ORDER

**²dictate** *n*
a statement made or direction given with authority **:** COMMAND

**dic·ta·tion** \dik-'tā-shən\ *n*
**1** the giving of orders often without thought of whether they are reasonable or fair
**2** the dictating of words
**3** something dictated or taken down from dictation

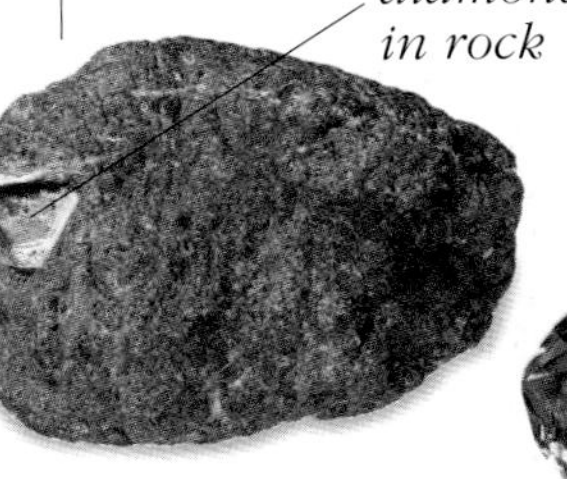


**diamond 1**

**dic·ta·tor** \'dik-ˌtāt-ər\ *n*
**1** a person who rules with total authority and often in a cruel or brutal manner
**2** a person who dictates
**dic·ta·tor·ship** \dik-'tāt-ər-ˌship\ *n*

**dic·ta·to·ri·al** \ˌdik-tə-'tōr-ē-əl\ *adj*
of, relating to, or like a dictator or a dictatorship

**dic·tion** \'dik-shən\ *n*
**1** choice of words especially with regard to correctness, clearness, and effectiveness
**2** ENUNCIATION

**dic·tio·nary** \'dik-shə-ˌner-ē\ *n, pl* **dic·tio·nar·ies**
**1** a book giving the meaning and usually the pronunciation of words listed in alphabetical order
**2** an alphabetical reference book explaining words and phrases of a field of knowledge ⟨a medical *dictionary*⟩ ⟨biographical *dictionary*⟩
**3** a book listing words of one language in alphabetical order with definitions in another language

**did** *past of* DO

**didn't** \'did-nt\
did not

**¹die** \'dī\ *vb* **died**; **dy·ing**
**1** to stop living
**2** to pass out of existence ⟨a *dying* race of people⟩
**3** to disappear little by little ⟨the wind *died* down⟩
**4** to wish eagerly ⟨*dying* to go⟩
**5** ¹STOP 4 ⟨the motor *died*⟩

**²die** *n*
**1** *pl* **dice** \'dīs\ ¹DICE
**2** *pl* **dies** \'dīz\ a device for forming or cutting material by pressure

**die·sel** \'dē-zəl, -səl\ *n*
**1** DIESEL ENGINE
**2** a vehicle driven by a diesel engine

**diesel engine** *n*
an engine in which the mixture of air and fuel is compressed until enough heat is created to ignite the mixture

**¹di·et** \'dī-ət\ *n*
**1** the food and drink that a person or animal usually takes
**2** the kind and amount of food selected or allowed in certain circumstances (as ill health)

**²diet** *vb*
to eat or cause to eat less or according to certain rules
**di·et·er** *n*

**³diet** *adj*
reduced in calories ⟨a *diet* soft drink⟩

**di·e·tary** \'dī-ə-ˌter-ē\ *adj*
of or relating to a diet or to rules of diet

**di·e·ti·tian** *or* **di·e·ti·cian** \ˌdī-ə-'tish-ən\ *n*
a person trained to apply the principles of nutrition to the planning of food and meals

**dif·fer** \'dif-ər\ *vb*
1 to be not the same : be unlike
2 DISAGREE 2

**dif·fer·ence** \'dif-ə-rens, 'dif-rəns\ *n*
1 what makes two or more persons or things different
2 a disagreement about something
3 REMAINDER 2

**dif·fer·ent** \'dif-ə-rənt, 'dif-rənt\ *adj*
1 not of the same kind
2 not the same ⟨went to *different* schools⟩
**dif·fer·ent·ly** *adv*

**dif·fer·en·ti·ate** \,dif-ə-'ren-chē-,āt\ *vb* **dif·fer·en·ti·at·ed**; **dif·fer·en·ti·at·ing**
1 to make or become different
2 to recognize or state the difference between ⟨*differentiate* two colors⟩

**dif·fer·en·ti·a·tion** \,dif-ə-,ren-chē-'ā-shən\ *n*
the process of change by which immature living structures develop to maturity

**dif·fi·cult** \'dif-i-,kəlt\ *adj*
1 hard to do or make ⟨a *difficult* climb⟩
2 hard to deal with ⟨a *difficult* child⟩
3 hard to understand

**dif·fi·cul·ty** \'dif-i-,kəl-tē\ *n, pl* **dif·fi·cul·ties**
1 the state of being difficult ⟨the *difficulty* of a task⟩
2 great effort
3 OBSTACLE
4 a difficult situation : TROUBLE ⟨in financial *difficulties*⟩

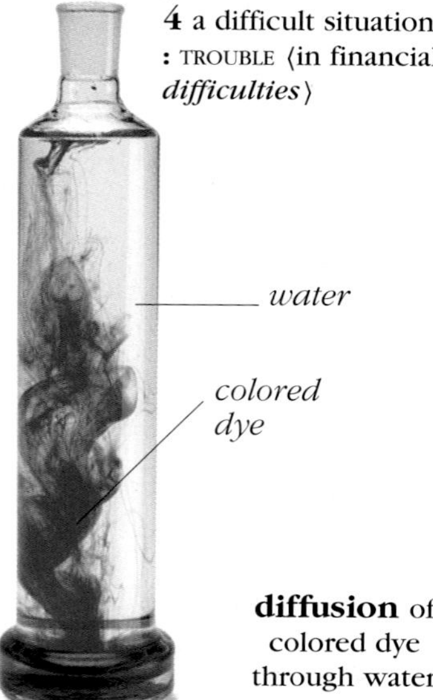


**diffusion** of colored dye through water

## digestion

Digestion begins in the mouth, where food is bitten into smaller chunks by the teeth. Saliva helps the tongue and teeth to form the food into a paste, which then travels into the pharynx, through the esophagus, and into the stomach, where it is further broken down by digestive juices. The food now passes into the small intestine, where secretions from the intestine, pancreas, gall bladder (not shown), and liver continue digestion, and nutrients are absorbed into the bloodstream. Any remaining waste is compressed in the large intestine, and expelled from the body via the rectum.

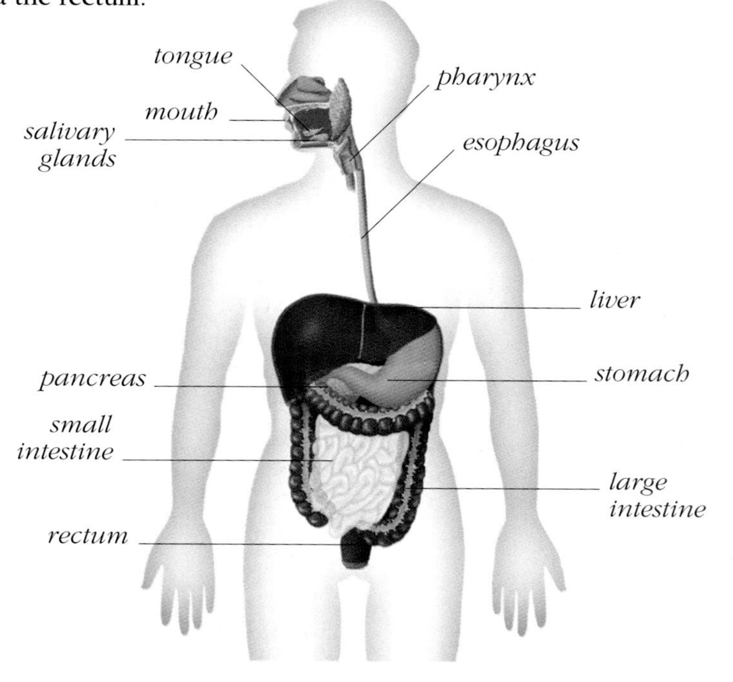


**parts of the human digestive system**

**dif·fi·dent** \'dif-əd-ənt\ *adj*
1 lacking confidence
2 RESERVED 1
**dif·fi·dent·ly** *adv*

**dif·fuse** \dif-'yüz\ *vb* **dif·fused**; **dif·fus·ing**
to undergo diffusion

**dif·fu·sion** \dif-'yü-zhən\ *n*
◄ the mixing of particles of liquids or gases so that they move from a region of high concentration to one of lower concentration

**[1]dig** \'dig\ *vb* **dug** \'dəg\; **dig·ging**
1 to turn up, loosen, or remove the soil
2 to form by removing earth ⟨*dig* a hole⟩ ⟨*dig* a cellar⟩
3 to uncover or search by or as if by turning up earth ⟨*dig* potatoes⟩ ⟨*dig* for gold⟩
4 DISCOVER, UNCOVER ⟨*dig* up information⟩
5 [1]PROD 1, POKE ⟨*dug* me in the ribs⟩
6 to work hard
**dig·ger** *n*

**[2]dig** *n*
1 [2]POKE, THRUST
2 a nasty remark

**[1]di·gest** \'dī-,jest\ *n*
information in shortened form

**[2]di·gest** \dī-'jest, də-\ *vb*
1 to think over and get straight in the mind ⟨*digest* a lesson⟩
2 to change (food) into simpler forms that can be taken in and used by the body
3 to become digested

**di·gest·ible** \dī-ˈjes-tə-bəl, də-\ *adj*
possible to digest

**di·ges·tion** \dī-ˈjes-chən, də-\ *n*
the process or power of digesting something (as food)

**di·ges·tive** \dī-ˈjes-tiv, də-\ *adj*
of, relating to, or functioning in digestion

**dig·it** \ˈdij-ət\ *n*
**1** any of the numerals 1 to 9 and the symbol 0
**2** [1]FINGER 1, [1]TOE 1

**dig·i·tal** \ˈdij-ət-l\ *adj*
**1** of, relating to, or done with a finger or toe
**2** of, relating to, or using calculation directly with digits rather than through measurable physical quantities
**3** of or relating to data in the form of numerical digits
**4** providing displayed or recorded information in numerical digits from an automatic device ⟨a *digital* watch⟩
**dig·i·tal·ly** \-l-ē\ *adv*

**digital camera** *n*
a camera that records images as electronic data instead of on film

**dig·ni·fied** \ˈdig-nə-ˌfīd\ *adj*
having or showing dignity

**dig·ni·fy** \ˈdig-nə-ˌfī\ *vb* **dig·ni·fied**; **dig·ni·fy·ing**
to give dignity or importance to

**dig·ni·tary** \ˈdig-nə-ˌter-ē\ *n, pl* **dig·ni·tar·ies**
a person of high position or honor

**dig·ni·ty** \ˈdig-nət-ē\ *n, pl* **dig·ni·ties**
**1** the quality or state of being worthy of honor and respect
**2** high rank or office
**3** a dignified look or manner

**dike** \ˈdīk\ *n*
**1** a channel dug in the earth to carry water
**2** a bank of earth built to control water

**di·lap·i·dat·ed** \də-ˈlap-ə-ˌdāt-əd\ *adj*
partly fallen apart or ruined from age or from lack of care

**di·late** \dī-ˈlāt\ *vb* **di·lat·ed**; **di·lat·ing**
to make or grow larger or wider

**di·lem·ma** \də-ˈlem-ə\ *n*
a situation in which a person has to choose between things that are all bad or unsatisfactory

**dil·i·gence** \ˈdil-ə-jəns\ *n*
careful and continued work

**dil·i·gent** \ˈdil-ə-jənt\ *adj*
showing steady and earnest care and effort ⟨a *diligent* search⟩
**dil·i·gent·ly** *adv*

**dill** \ˈdil\ *n*
an herb related to the carrot with fragrant leaves and seeds used mostly in flavoring pickles

dill

**dil·ly·dal·ly** \ˈdil-ē-ˌdal-ē\ *vb* **dil·ly·dal·lied**; **dil·ly·dal·ly·ing**
to waste time : DAWDLE

**di·lute** \dī-ˈlüt, də-\ *vb* **di·lut·ed**; **di·lut·ing**
to make thinner or more liquid

**di·lu·tion** \dī-ˈlü-shən, də-\ *n*
**1** the act of diluting : the state of being diluted
**2** something (as a solution) that is diluted

[1]**dim** \ˈdim\ *adj* **dim·mer**; **dim·mest**
**1** not bright or distinct : FAINT
**2** not seeing or understanding clearly
**dim·ly** *adv*
**dim·ness** *n*

[2]**dim** *vb* **dimmed**; **dim·ming**
**1** to make or become dim
**2** to reduce the light from

**dime** \ˈdīm\ *n*
a United States coin worth ten cents

dime

**Word History** Our name for the coin that is worth a tenth of a dollar came from an early French word. This early French word meant "tenth part." It came from a Latin word meaning "tenth," which in turn came from a Latin word meaning "ten."

**di·men·sion** \də-ˈmen-chən\ *n*
the length, width, or height of something

**di·men·sion·al** \də-ˈmen-chən-l\ *adj*
of or relating to dimensions ⟨a cube is three-*dimensional*⟩ ⟨a square is two-*dimensional*⟩

**di·min·ish** \də-ˈmin-ish\ *vb*
**1** to make less or cause to seem less
**2** BELITTLE
**3** DWINDLE
**di·min·ish·ment** \-mənt\ *n*

**di·min·u·en·do** \də-ˌmin-yə-ˈwen-dō\ *n, pl* **di·min·u·en·dos** *or* **di·min·u·en·does**
DECRESCENDO

**di·min·u·tive** \də-ˈmin-yət-iv\ *adj*
very small : TINY ⟨a *diminutive* tree⟩

**dim·mer** \ˈdim-ər\ *n*
a device for regulating the brightness of an electric lighting unit (as the lights of a room)

[1]**dim·ple** \ˈdim-pəl\ *n*
a slight hollow spot especially in the cheek or chin

[2]**dimple** *vb* **dim·pled**; **dim·pling**
to mark with or form dimples

[1]**din** \ˈdin\ *n*
loud confused noise

[2]**din** *vb* **dinned**; **din·ning**
**1** to make a din
**2** to repeat again and again in order to impress on someone's mind

**dine** \ˈdīn\ *vb* **dined**; **din·ing**
**1** to eat dinner ⟨*dine* out⟩
**2** to give a dinner to

**din·er** \ˈdī-nər\ *n*
**1** a person eating dinner
**2** a railroad dining car or a restaurant in the shape of one

**di·nette** \dī-ˈnet\ *n*
a separate area or small room used for dining

**ding·dong** \ˈding-ˌdȯng\ *n*
the sound of a bell ringing

**din·ghy** \ˈding-ē, ˈding-gē\ *n, pl* **dinghies**
**1** a small light rowboat
**2** a rubber life raft

**din·gle** \ˈding-gəl\ *n*
a small narrow wooded valley

**din·gy** \ˈdin-jē\ *adj* **din·gi·er**; **din·gi·est**
rather dark and dirty ⟨a *dingy* room⟩
**din·gi·ness** *n*

**din·ner** \'din-ər\ *n*
1 the main meal of the day
2 BANQUET
**di·no·saur** \'dī-nə-,sȯr\ *n*
▶ any of a group of extinct mostly land-dwelling reptiles that lived millions of years ago
**dint** \'dint\ *n*
1 the force or power of something ⟨succeeded by *dint* of hard work⟩
2 ²DENT
**di·o·cese** \'dī-ə-səs, -,sēz\ *n*
the district over which a bishop has authority
**¹dip** \'dip\ *vb* **dipped**; **dip·ping**
1 to sink or push briefly into a liquid ⟨*dip* a cloth into water⟩
2 to take out with or as if with a ladle
3 to lower and quickly raise again : drop or sink and quickly rise again
4 to sink out of sight ⟨the sun *dipped* below the horizon⟩
5 to slope downward
**²dip** *n*
1 a plunge into water for fun or exercise : a short swim
2 a downward slope
3 something obtained by or used in dipping ⟨a *dip* of ice cream⟩
4 a tasty sauce into which solid food may be dipped
**diph·the·ria** \dif-'thir-ē-ə, dip-\ *n*
a contagious disease in which the air passages become coated with a membrane that often makes breathing difficult
**diph·thong** \'dif-,thȯng, 'dip-\ *n*
two vowel sounds joined in one syllable to form one speech sound ⟨the sounds of "ou" in "out" and of "oy" in "boy" are *diphthongs*⟩
**di·plo·ma** \də-'plō-mə\ *n*
a certificate that shows a person has finished a course or graduated from a school
**di·plo·ma·cy** \də-'plō-mə-sē\ *n*
1 the work of keeping up relations between the governments of different countries
2 skill in dealing with others
**dip·lo·mat** \'dip-lə-,mat\ *n*
1 a person whose work is diplomacy
2 a person who is good at not saying or doing things that hurt or make people angry
**dip·lo·mat·ic** \,dip-lə-'mat-ik\ *adj*
1 of or relating to diplomats and their work
2 TACTFUL
**dip·lo·mat·i·cal·ly** \-i-kə-lē\ *adv*
**dip·per** \'dip-ər\ *n*
1 one that dips
2 a ladle or scoop for dipping
**dire** \'dīr\ *adj*
1 causing horror or terror : DREADFUL
2 very great ⟨in *dire* need⟩
**dire·ly** *adv*
**dire·ness** *n*
**¹di·rect** \də-'rekt, dī-\ *vb*
1 to put an address on (as a letter)
2 ¹AIM 3, TURN
3 to show or tell the way
4 to guide the production of ⟨*direct* a play⟩
5 ¹ORDER 2, COMMAND **synonyms** see CONDUCT
**²direct** *adj*
1 going from one point to another without turning or stopping : STRAIGHT
2 going straight to the point ⟨a *direct* answer⟩
3 being in an unbroken family line ⟨a *direct* ancestor⟩
**di·rect·ness** *n*
**³direct** *adv*
DIRECTLY 1
**direct current** *n*
an electric current flowing in one direction only
**di·rec·tion** \də-'rek-shən, dī-\ *n*
1 SUPERVISION, MANAGEMENT
2 an order or instruction to be followed
3 the path along which something moves, lies, or points
**di·rect·ly** \də-'rekt-lē, dī-\ *adv*
1 in a direct course or way ⟨the road runs *directly* north⟩
2 right away : IMMEDIATELY
**direct object** *n*
a word that represents the main goal or the result of the action of a verb ⟨"me" in "you hit me" is a *direct object*⟩
**di·rec·tor** \də-'rek-tər, dī-\ *n*
a person who directs something
**di·rec·to·ry** \də-'rek-tə-rē, dī-\ *n*, *pl* **di·rec·to·ries**
a book containing an alphabetical list of names and addresses
**dirge** \'dərj\ *n*
a song or hymn of grief
**di·ri·gi·ble** \'dir-ə-jə-bəl, də-'rij-ə-\ *n*
AIRSHIP
**dirk** \'dərk\ *n*
a long dagger with a straight blade
**dirt** \'dərt\ *n*
1 a filthy or soiling substance (as mud or dust)
2 ²SOIL ⟨packed *dirt* around the plant⟩
**¹dirty** \'dərt-ē\ *adj* **dirt·i·er**; **dirt·i·est**
1 soiled or polluted by dirt or impurities ⟨*dirty* clothes⟩
2 UNFAIR, MEAN ⟨a *dirty* trick⟩
3 INDECENT, VULGAR ⟨*dirty* talk⟩
4 not clear in color ⟨a *dirty* red⟩
5 showing dislike or anger ⟨gave me a *dirty* look⟩
**dirt·i·ness** *n*
**²dirty** *vb* **dirt·ied**; **dirty·ing**
to make or become dirty
**dis-** *prefix*
1 do the opposite of ⟨*dis*own⟩
2 deprive of ⟨*dis*able⟩
3 expel from ⟨*dis*bar⟩
4 opposite or absence of ⟨*dis*approval⟩
5 not ⟨*dis*agreeable⟩
**dis·abil·i·ty** \,dis-ə-'bil-ət-ē\ *n*, *pl* **dis·abil·i·ties**
1 the state of being disabled : lack of power to do something
2 something that disables
**dis·able** \dis-'ā-bəl\ *vb* **dis·abled**; **dis·abling**
to make unable or incapable
**dis·able·ment** \-bəl-mənt\ *n*
**disabled** *adj*
not having the ability to do certain mental or physical tasks ( as because of illness, injury, or a condition one is born with) that one would typically be expected to do
**dis·ad·van·tage** \,dis-əd-'vant-ij\ *n*
a state or condition that favors someone else
**dis·ad·van·ta·geous** \,dis-,ad-,van-'tā-jəs\ *adj*
making it harder for a person to succeed or do something
**dis·ad·van·ta·geous·ly** *adv*
**dis·ad·van·ta·geous·ness** *n*
**dis·agree** \,dis-ə-'grē\ *vb* **dis·agreed**; **dis·agree·ing**
1 to be unlike each other : be different
2 to have unlike ideas or opinions ⟨*disagreed* over the price⟩
3 QUARREL
4 to have an unpleasant effect ⟨fried foods *disagree* with me⟩

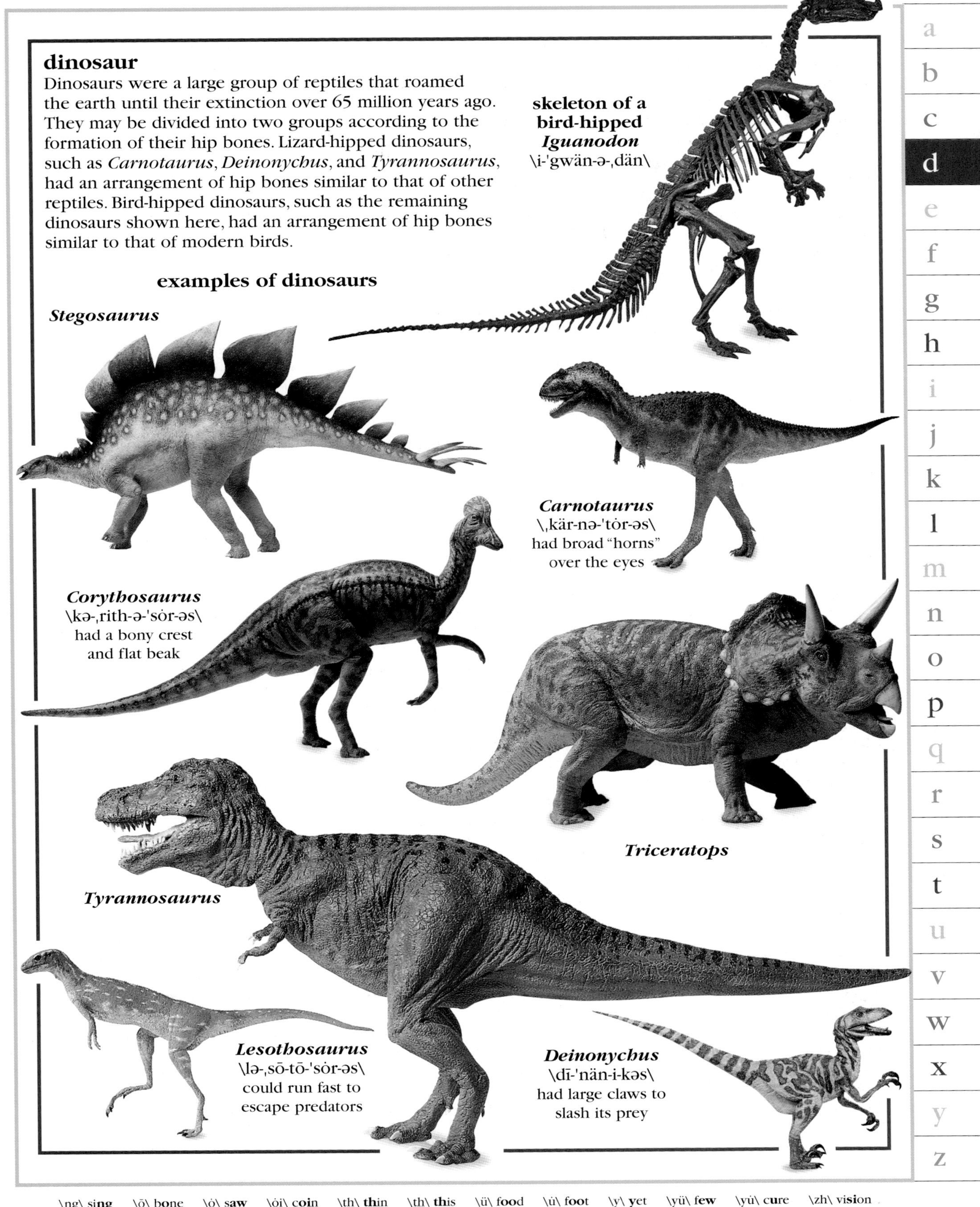
**dinosaur**
Dinosaurs were a large group of reptiles that roamed the earth until their extinction over 65 million years ago. They may be divided into two groups according to the formation of their hip bones. Lizard-hipped dinosaurs, such as *Carnotaurus*, *Deinonychus*, and *Tyrannosaurus*, had an arrangement of hip bones similar to that of other reptiles. Bird-hipped dinosaurs, such as the remaining dinosaurs shown here, had an arrangement of hip bones similar to that of modern birds.
skeleton of a bird-hipped *Iguanodon* \i-ˈgwän-ə-ˌdän\
examples of dinosaurs
*Stegosaurus*
*Carnotaurus* \ˌkär-nə-ˈtȯr-əs\ had broad "horns" over the eyes
*Corythosaurus* \kə-ˌrith-ə-ˈsȯr-əs\ had a bony crest and flat beak
*Triceratops*
*Tyrannosaurus*
*Lesothosaurus* \lə-ˌsō-tō-ˈsȯr-əs\ could run fast to escape predators
*Deinonychus* \dī-ˈnän-i-kəs\ had large claws to slash its prey
a
b
c
d
e
f
g
h
i
j
k
l
m
n
o
p
q
r
s
t
u
v
w
x
y
z

A B C D E F G H I J K L M N O P Q R S T U V W X Y Z

**dis·agree·able** \ˌdis-ə-ˈgrē-ə-bəl\ *adj*
**1** UNPLEASANT ⟨a *disagreeable* taste⟩
**2** having a bad disposition **:** PEEVISH ⟨a *disagreeable* child⟩
**dis·agree·ably** \-blē\ *adv*

**dis·agree·ment** \ˌdis-ə-ˈgrē-mənt\ *n*
**1** the act or fact of disagreeing
**2** the condition of being different
**3** a difference of opinion

**dis·ap·pear** \ˌdis-ə-ˈpir\ *vb*
**1** to stop being visible **:** pass out of sight
**2** to stop existing ⟨dinosaurs *disappeared* long ago⟩

**dis·ap·pear·ance** \ˌdis-ə-ˈpir-əns\ *n*
the act or fact of disappearing

**dis·ap·point** \ˌdis-ə-ˈpȯint\ *vb*
to fail to satisfy the hope or expectation of

**dis·ap·point·ment** \ˌdis-ə-ˈpȯint-mənt\ *n*
**1** the act of disappointing
**2** the condition or feeling of being disappointed
**3** one that disappoints

**dis·ap·prov·al** \ˌdis-ə-ˈprü-vəl\ *n*
the feeling of not liking or agreeing with something or someone

**dis·ap·prove** \ˌdis-ə-ˈprüv\ *vb* **dis·ap·proved**; **dis·ap·prov·ing**
to dislike or be against something

**dis·arm** \dis-ˈärm\ *vb*
**1** to take weapons from ⟨*disarm* a prisoner⟩
**2** to reduce the size and strength of the armed forces of a country
**3** to make harmless ⟨*disarm* a bomb⟩
**4** to remove any feelings of doubt, mistrust, or unfriendliness **:** win over ⟨a *disarming* smile⟩
**dis·ar·ma·ment** \-ˈär-mə-mənt\ *n*

**dis·ar·range** \ˌdis-ə-ˈrānj\ *vb* **dis·ar·ranged**; **dis·ar·rang·ing**
to make all mussed up or mixed up
**dis·ar·range·ment** \-mənt\ *n*

**disaster:**
a flood in Napa, California

**di·sas·ter** \diz-ˈas-tər, dis-\ *n*
▲ something (as a flood or a tornado) that happens suddenly and causes much suffering or loss **:** CALAMITY

**Word History** The word *disaster* came from an old Italian word. This Italian word was used in astrology. It was the term for a bad influence due to the positions of stars and planets. This Italian word was made up of two parts. The first was a negative prefix. The second was a word that meant "star."

**di·sas·trous** \diz-ˈas-trəs\ *adj*
being or resulting in a disaster
**di·sas·trous·ly** *adv*

**dis·band** \dis-ˈband\ *vb*
to break up and stop being a group
**dis·band·ment** \-mənt\ *n*

**dis·bar** \dis-ˈbär\ *vb* **dis·barred**; **dis·bar·ring**
to deprive (a lawyer) of the rights of membership in the legal profession
**dis·bar·ment** \-mənt\ *n*

**dis·be·lief** \ˌdis-bə-ˈlēf\ *n*
refusal or inability to believe

**dis·be·lieve** \ˌdis-bə-ˈlēv\ *vb* **dis·be·lieved**; **dis·be·liev·ing**
to think not to be true or real
**dis·be·liev·er** *n*

**dis·burse** \dis-ˈbərs\ *vb* **dis·bursed**; **dis·burs·ing**
to pay out
**dis·burse·ment** \-mənt\ *n*

**disc** *variant of* DISK

[1]**dis·card** \dis-ˈkärd\ *vb*
**1** to throw down an unwanted playing card from one's hand
**2** to get rid of as useless or unwanted

[2]**dis·card** \ˈdis-ˌkärd\ *n*
**1** the act of discarding
**2** something discarded

**dis·cern** \dis-ˈərn, diz-\ *vb*
to see, recognize, or understand something

[1]**dis·charge** \dis-ˈchärj\ *vb* **dis·charged**; **dis·charg·ing**
**1** to relieve of a load or burden **:** UNLOAD
**2** SHOOT 1, 2, FIRE ⟨*discharge* a gun⟩
**3** to set free ⟨*discharge* a prisoner⟩
**4** to dismiss from service ⟨*discharge* a worker⟩
**5** to let go or let off
**6** to give forth the contents (as a fluid)
**7** to get rid of by paying or doing ⟨*discharge* a debt⟩

[2]**dis·charge** \ˈdis-ˌchärj\ *n*
**1** the act of discharging, unloading, or releasing
**2** a certificate of release or payment
**3** a firing off
**4** a flowing out (as of blood or pus)
**5** a firing of a person from a job
**6** complete separation from military service

**dis·ci·ple** \di-ˈsī-pəl\ *n*
**1** a person who accepts and helps to spread the teachings of another
**2** APOSTLE 1

[1]**dis·ci·pline** \ˈdis-ə-plən\ *n*
**1** strict training that corrects or strengthens
**2** PUNISHMENT 1
**3** habits and ways of acting that are gotten through practice
**4** a system of rules

[2]**discipline** *vb* **dis·ci·plined**; **dis·ci·plin·ing**
**1** to punish for the sake of discipline
**2** to train in self-control or obedience
**3** to bring under control ⟨*discipline* troops⟩ **synonyms** see PUNISH

**disc jockey** *n*
a radio announcer who plays records

**dis·claim** \dis-ˈklām\ *vb*
to deny being part of or responsible for

**dis·close** \dis-ˈklōz\ *vb*
**dis·closed**; **dis·clos·ing**
to make known : REVEAL

**dis·clo·sure** \dis-ˈklō-zhər\ *n*
**1** an act of disclosing
**2** something disclosed

**dis·col·or** \dis-ˈkəl-ər\ *vb*
to change in color especially for the worse

**dis·col·or·a·tion** \dis-ˌkəl-ə-ˈrā-shən\ *n*
**1** change of color
**2** a discolored spot

**dis·com·fort** \dis-ˈkəm-fərt\ *n*
the condition of being uncomfortable

**dis·con·cert** \ˌdis-kən-ˈsərt\ *vb*
to make confused and a little upset

**dis·con·nect** \ˌdis-kə-ˈnekt\ *vb*
to undo the connection of ⟨*disconnect* a hose⟩

**dis·con·nect·ed** \ˌdis-kə-ˈnek-təd\ *adj*
INCOHERENT ⟨a *disconnected* speech⟩
**dis·con·nect·ed·ly** *adv*

**dis·con·so·late** \dis-ˈkän-sə-lət\ *adj*
too sad to be cheered up
**dis·con·so·late·ly** *adv*

**[1]dis·con·tent** \ˌdis-kən-ˈtent\ *vb*
to make dissatisfied

**[2]discontent** *n*
the condition of being dissatisfied

**dis·con·tent·ed** \ˌdis-kən-ˈtent-əd\ *adj*
not contented
**dis·con·tent·ed·ly** *adv*

**dis·con·tin·ue** \ˌdis-kən-ˈtin-yü\ *vb* **dis·con·tin·ued**; **dis·con·tinu·ing**
to bring to an end : STOP

**dis·cord** \ˈdis-ˌkȯrd\ *n*
lack of agreement or harmony

**dis·cor·dant** \dis-ˈkȯrd-nt\ *adj*
being in disagreement : not being in harmony

**[1]dis·count** \ˈdis-ˌkau̇nt\ *n*
an amount taken off a regular price

**[2]dis·count** \ˈdis-ˌkau̇nt, dis-ˈkau̇nt\ *vb*
**1** to lower the amount of a bill, debt, or charge usually in return for cash or quick payment
**2** to believe only partly ⟨*discount* a rumor⟩

**dis·cour·age** \dis-ˈkər-ij\ *vb*
**dis·cour·aged**; **dis·cour·ag·ing**
**1** to make less determined, hopeful, or sure of oneself ⟨*discouraged* by past failure⟩
**2** DETER ⟨tried to *discourage* the idea⟩
**3** to try to persuade not to do something
**dis·cour·age·ment** \-mənt\ *n*

**[1]dis·course** \ˈdis-ˌkōrs\ *n*
**1** CONVERSATION
**2** a long talk or composition about a subject

**[2]dis·course** \dis-ˈkōrs\ *vb*
**dis·coursed**; **dis·cours·ing**
to talk especially for a long time

**dis·cour·te·ous** \dis-ˈkərt-ē-əs\ *adj*
not polite : RUDE
**dis·cour·te·ous·ly** *adv*

**dis·cour·te·sy** \dis-ˈkərt-ə-sē\ *n, pl* **dis·cour·te·sies**
**1** rude behavior
**2** a rude act

**dis·cov·er** \dis-ˈkəv-ər\ *vb*
to find out, see, or learn of especially for the first time : FIND **synonyms** see INVENT
**dis·cov·er·er** *n*

**dis·cov·ery** \dis-ˈkəv-ə-rē, -ˈkəv-rē\ *n, pl* **dis·cov·er·ies**
**1** an act of discovering
**2** something discovered

**[1]dis·cred·it** \dis-ˈkred-ət\ *vb*
**1** to refuse to accept as true
**2** to cause to seem dishonest or untrue

**[2]discredit** *n*
loss of good name or respect ⟨brought *discredit* on the family⟩

**dis·creet** \dis-ˈkrēt\ *adj*
having or showing good judgment especially in conduct or speech
**dis·creet·ly** *adv*

**dis·cre·tion** \dis-ˈkresh-ən\ *n*
**1** good sense in making decisions
**2** the power of deciding for oneself ⟨I'll leave it to your *discretion*⟩

**dis·crim·i·nate** \dis-ˈkrim-ə-ˌnāt\ *vb* **dis·crim·i·nat·ed**; **dis·crim·i·nat·ing**
**1** to be able to tell the difference between things
**2** to treat some people better than others without any fair or proper reason

**dis·crim·i·na·tion** \dis-ˌkrim-ə-ˈnā-shən\ *n*
**1** the act of discriminating
**2** the ability to see differences
**3** the treating of some people better than others without any fair or proper reason

**dis·crim·i·na·to·ry** \dis-ˈkrim-ə-nə-ˌtōr-ē\ *adj*
showing discrimination : being unfair

**dis·cus** \ˈdis-kəs\ *n, pl* **dis·cus·es**
▼ an object that is shaped like a disk and hurled for distance in a track-and-field event

**dis·cuss** \dis-ˈkəs\ *vb*
**1** to argue or consider fully and openly
**2** to talk about

*discus*

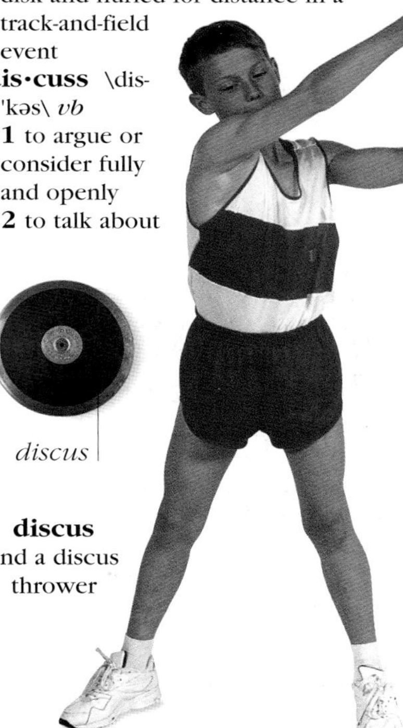
**discus** and a discus thrower

**Synonyms** DISCUSS, ARGUE, and DEBATE mean to talk about something in order to reach a decision or to convince someone of a point of view. DISCUSS suggests that there is an exchange of ideas and that statements both for and against something are made ⟨we will *discuss* plans for the school picnic⟩. ARGUE suggests the giving of evidence or reasons for something ⟨*argued* for the need for more hospitals⟩. DEBATE suggests an argument between opposing persons or groups according to rules and often before an audience ⟨the candidates will *debate* on TV⟩.

A B C D E F G H I J K L M N O P Q R S T U V W X Y Z

**dis·cus·sion** \dis-'kəsh-ən\ *n* conversation for the purpose of understanding a question or subject

[1]**dis·dain** \dis-'dān\ *n* a feeling of scorn for something considered beneath oneself
**dis·dain·ful** *adj*
**dis·dain·ful·ly** \-fə-lē\ *adv*

[2]**disdain** *vb*
**1** to think oneself far too good for something or someone ⟨*disdained* the younger children⟩
**2** to refuse because of scorn ⟨*disdained* to answer⟩

**dis·ease** \diz-'ēz\ *n*
**1** a change in a living body (as of a person or plant) that interferes with its normal functioning **:** ILLNESS
**2** an instance or a kind of disease
**dis·eased** \-'ēzd\ *adj*

**dis·em·bark** \,dis-əm-'bärk\ *vb* to go or put ashore from a ship

**dis·en·fran·chise** \,dis-n-'fran-,chīz\ *vb* **dis·en·fran·chised; dis·en·fran·chis·ing** to take away the right to vote

**dis·en·tan·gle** \,dis-n-'tang-gəl\ *vb* **dis·en·tan·gled**; **dis·en·tan·gling** to straighten out **:** UNTANGLE
**dis·en·tan·gle·ment** \-gəl -mənt\ *n*

**dis·fa·vor** \dis-'fā-vər\ *n*
**1** DISAPPROVAL
**2** the state of being disliked

**dis·fig·ure** \dis-'fig-yər\ *vb* **dis·fig·ured**; **dis·fig·ur·ing** to spoil the looks of
**dis·fig·ure·ment** \-mənt\ *n*

**dis·fran·chise** \dis-'fran-,chīz\ *vb* **dis·fran·chised**; **dis·fran·chis·ing** DISENFRANCHISE
**dis·fran·chise·ment** \-,chīz-mənt, -chəz-\ *n*

[1]**dis·grace** \dis-'grās\ *vb* **dis·graced**; **dis·grac·ing** to bring shame to
**dis·grac·er** *n*

[2]**disgrace** *n*
**1** the condition of being looked down on **:** loss of respect
**2** [1]DISHONOR 1
**3** a cause of shame ⟨you are a *disgrace* to your profession⟩

**dis·grace·ful** \dis-'grās-fəl\ *adj* bringing or deserving disgrace
**dis·grace·ful·ly** \-fə-lē\ *adv*
**dis·grace·ful·ness** *n*

**dis·grun·tle** \dis-'grənt-l\ *vb* **dis·grun·tled**; **dis·grun·tling** to make grouchy or cross

[1]**dis·guise** \dis-'gīz\ *vb* **dis·guised**; **dis·guis·ing**
**1** to change the looks of so as to conceal identity
**2** to keep from revealing ⟨*disguise* one's motive⟩

[2]**disguise** *n*
**1** clothing put on to hide one's true identity or to imitate another's
**2** an outward appearance that hides what something really is ⟨a blessing in *disguise*⟩

[1]**dis·gust** \dis-'gəst\ *n* the strong dislike one feels for something nasty and sickening

[2]**disgust** *vb* to cause to feel disgust
**dis·gust·ed·ly** *adv*

**dis·gust·ing** \dis-'gəs-ting\ *adj* causing disgust
**dis·gust·ing·ly** *adv*

[1]**dish** \'dish\ *n*
**1** ▼ a hollowed out vessel for serving food at table
**2** the contents of a dish ⟨a *dish* of strawberries⟩

[1]**dish 1:** a ceramic dish

[2]**dish** *vb* to put into a dish **:** SERVE

**dis·heart·en** \dis-'härt-n\ *vb* DISCOURAGE 1
**dis·heart·en·ing·ly** *adv*

**di·shev·eled** *or* **di·shev·elled** \di-'shev-əld\ *adj* mussed up **:** UNTIDY

**dis·hon·est** \dis-'än-əst\ *adj* not honest or trustworthy
**dis·hon·est·ly** *adv*

**dis·hon·es·ty** \dis-'än-ə-stē\ *n* lack of honesty **:** the quality of being dishonest

[1]**dis·hon·or** \dis-'än-ər\ *n*
**1** loss of honor or good name
**2** a cause of disgrace

[2]**dishonor** *vb* to bring shame on **:** DISGRACE

**dis·hon·or·able** \dis-'än-ə-rə-bəl\ *adj* not honorable **:** SHAMEFUL
**dis·hon·or·ably** \-blē\ *adv*

**dis·il·lu·sion** \,dis-ə-'lü-zhən\ *vb* to free from mistaken beliefs or foolish hopes
**dis·il·lu·sion·ment** \-mənt\ *n*

**dis·in·fect** \,dis-n-'fekt\ *vb* to free from germs that might cause disease

[1]**dis·in·fec·tant** \,dis-n-'fek-tənt\ *n* something that frees from germs

[2]**disinfectant** *adj* serving to disinfect

**dis·in·her·it** \,dis-n-'her-ət\ *vb* to deprive (an heir) of the right to inherit

**dis·in·te·grate** \dis-'int-ə-,grāt\ *vb* **dis·in·te·grat·ed**; **dis·in·te·grat·ing** to separate or break up into small parts or pieces

**dis·in·te·gra·tion** \dis-,int-ə-'grā-shən\ *n* the act or process of disintegrating **:** the state of being disintegrated

**dis·in·ter·est·ed** \dis-'in-trəs-təd, -'int-ə-rəs-\ *adj*
**1** not interested
**2** free of selfish interest
**dis·in·ter·est·ed·ly** *adv*
**dis·in·ter·est·ed·ness** *n*

**dis·joint·ed** \dis-'jȯint-əd\ *adj* not clear and orderly ⟨*disjointed* speech⟩
**dis·joint·ed·ly** *adv*

**disk** *or* **disc** \'disk\ *n*
**1** something that is or appears to be flat and round
**2** *usually disc* a phonograph record
**3** a round flat plate coated with a magnetic substance on which data for a computer is stored
**disk·like** \-,līk\ *adj*

**disk drive** *n* a device for transferring computer data to and from a magnetic disk

**disk·ette** \,dis-'ket\ *n* FLOPPY DISK

[1]**dis·like** \dis-'līk\ *n* a strong feeling of not liking or approving

[2]**dislike** *vb* **dis·liked**; **dis·lik·ing** to feel dislike for

**dis·lo·cate** \'dis-lō-,kāt, dis-'lō-\ *vb* **dis·lo·cat·ed**; **dis·lo·cat·ing** to displace a bone from its normal connections with another bone

**dis·lo·ca·tion** \,dis-lō-'kā-shən\ *n* the state of being dislocated

**dis·lodge** \dis-'läj\ *vb* **dis·lodged**; **dis·lodg·ing**

to force out of a place of resting, hiding, or defense

**dis·loy·al** \dis-ˈlȯi-əl\ *adj*
not loyal **synonyms** see FAITHLESS
**dis·loy·al·ly** *adv*

**dis·loy·al·ty** \dis-ˈlȯi-əl-tē\ *n, pl* **dis·loy·al·ties**
**1** lack of loyalty
**2** a disloyal act

**dis·mal** \ˈdiz-məl\ *adj*
very gloomy

**Word History** In the Middle Ages in Europe, people considered some days in each year to be unlucky. These days were given a Latin name that meant "evil days" and they were marked on calendars. The English name for the unlucky days was *dismal*. This noun came from the Latin name. Our adjective *dismal* came from the noun *dismal*. The noun is no longer used.

**dis·man·tle** \dis-ˈmant-l\ *vb* **dis·man·tled**; **dis·man·tling**
**1** to strip of furniture or equipment
**2** to take completely apart (as for storing or repair)
**dis·man·tle·ment** \-ˈmant-l-mənt\ *n*

**¹dis·may** \dis-ˈmā\ *vb*
to cause to be unable to act because of surprise, fear, or confusion

**²dismay** *n*
**1** sudden loss of courage or determination because of fear
**2** a feeling of fear or disappointment

**dis·miss** \dis-ˈmis\ *vb*
**1** to send away
**2** to discharge from an office or job
**3** to decide not to think about

**dis·miss·al** \dis-ˈmis-əl\ *n*
the act of dismissing : the state or fact of being dismissed

**dis·mount** \dis-ˈmau̇nt\ *vb*
**1** to get down from something (as a horse or bicycle)
**2** to cause to fall off or get off
**3** to take (as a cannon) off a support
**4** to take apart (as a machine)

**dis·obe·di·ence** \ˌdis-ə-ˈbēd-ē-əns\ *n*
an act or the fact of disobeying

**dis·obe·di·ent** \ˌdis-ə-ˈbēd-ē-ənt\ *adj*
not obeying
**dis·obe·di·ent·ly** *adv*

**dis·obey** \ˌdis-ə-ˈbā\ *vb* **dis·obeyed**; **dis·obey·ing**
to refuse, neglect, or fail to obey

**¹dis·or·der** \dis-ˈȯrd-ər\ *vb*
**1** to disturb the order of
**2** to disturb the regular or normal functioning of

**²disorder** *n*
**1** lack of order or of orderly arrangement : CONFUSION
**2** an abnormal state of body or mind : SICKNESS

**dis·or·der·ly** \dis-ˈȯrd-ər-lē\ *adj*
**1** not behaving quietly or well : UNRULY
**2** not neat or orderly
**dis·or·der·li·ness** *n*

**dis·or·ga·nize** \dis-ˈȯr-gə-ˌnīz\ *vb* **dis·or·ga·nized**; **dis·or·ga·niz·ing**
to break up the regular arrangement or system of

**dis·own** \dis-ˈōn\ *vb*
to refuse to accept any longer as one's own

**dis·par·age** \dis-ˈpar-ij\ *vb* **dis·par·aged**; **dis·par·ag·ing**
to speak of as unimportant or not much good : BELITTLE
**dis·par·age·ment** \-mənt\ *n*

**dis·pas·sion·ate** \dis-ˈpash-ə-nət\ *adj*
not influenced by strong feeling : CALM, IMPARTIAL
**dis·pas·sion·ate·ly** *adv*

**¹dis·patch** \dis-ˈpach\ *vb*
**1** to send away quickly to a certain place or for a certain reason
**2** ¹KILL 1 ⟨*dispatch* a sick animal⟩
**dis·patch·er** *n*

**²dispatch** *n*
**1** MESSAGE
**2** a news story sent in to a newspaper
**3** SPEED 1 ⟨act with *dispatch*⟩

**dis·pel** \dis-ˈpel\ *vb* **dis·pelled**; **dis·pel·ling**
to drive away

**dis·pense** \dis-ˈpens\ *vb* **dis·pensed**; **dis·pens·ing**
**1** to give out in shares : DISTRIBUTE ⟨*dispense* charity⟩
**2** ADMINISTER 2 ⟨*dispense* justice⟩
**3** to put up or prepare medicine in a form ready for use
**dispense with** to do or get along without

**dis·pens·er** \dis-ˈpen-sər\ *n*
a container that gives out something one at a time or a little at a time

**dis·perse** \dis-ˈpərs\ *vb* **dis·persed**; **dis·pers·ing**
to break up and scatter ⟨the clouds *dispersed*⟩ ⟨police *dispersed* the crowd⟩

**dispir·it** \dis-ˈpir-ət\ *vb*
to take away the cheerfulness or enthusiasm of

**dis·place** \dis-ˈplās\ *vb* **dis·placed**; **dis·plac·ing**
**1** to remove from the usual or proper place
**2** to remove from office : DISCHARGE
**3** to take the place of : REPLACE
**dis·place·ment** \-mənt\ *n*

**¹dis·play** \dis-ˈplā\ *vb*
**1** to put (something) in plain sight ⟨*display* toys in a store window⟩
**2** to make clear the existence or presence of : show plainly ⟨*display* anger⟩ ⟨*displayed* a gift for acting⟩

**²display** *n*
a showing of something ⟨a *display* of bad manners⟩

**dis·please** \dis-ˈplēz\ *vb* **dis·pleased**; **dis·pleas·ing**
to be or do something that makes (a person) cross or not pleased or satisfied

**dis·plea·sure** \dis-ˈplezh-ər\ *n*
a feeling of dislike and irritation : DISSATISFACTION

**dis·pos·able** \dis-ˈpō-zə-bəl\ *adj*
made to be thrown away after use ⟨*disposable* diapers⟩

**dis·pos·al** \dis-ˈpō-zəl\ *n*
**1** ARRANGEMENT 1
**2** ▼ a getting rid of ⟨trash *disposal*⟩
**3** right or power to use : CONTROL ⟨money at my *disposal*⟩

**disposal 2:** trash disposal

a b c d e f g h i j k l m n o p q r s t u v w x y z

A B C D E F G H I J K L M N O P Q R S T U V W X Y Z

**dis·pose** \dis-'pōz\ *vb* **dis·posed**; **dis·pos·ing**
1 to put in place : ARRANGE
2 to make ready and willing ⟨was *disposed* to help⟩
**dis·pos·er** *n*
**dispose of**
1 to finish with
2 to get rid of

**dis·po·si·tion** \ˌdis-pə-'zish-ən\ *n*
1 ARRANGEMENT 1
2 one's usual attitude or mood ⟨has a nasty *disposition*⟩
3 TENDENCY 2, LIKING

**dis·pro·por·tion** \ˌdis-prə-'pōr-shən\ *n*
lack of normal or usual proportions

**dis·prove** \dis-'prüv\ *vb* **dis·proved**; **dis·prov·ing**
to show to be false

**dis·put·able** \dis-'pyüt-ə-bəl, 'dis-pyət-\ *adj*
not yet proved : DEBATABLE
**dis·put·ably** \-blē\ *adv*

[1]**dis·pute** \dis-'pyüt\ *vb* **dis·put·ed**; **dis·put·ing**
1 ARGUE 2
2 to question or deny the truth or rightness of ⟨*dispute* a statement⟩
3 to fight over ⟨the two nations *disputed* the territory⟩
**dis·put·er** *n*

[2]**dispute** *n*
1 ARGUMENT 2, DEBATE
2 [1]QUARREL 2

**dis·qual·i·fy** \dis-'kwäl-ə-ˌfī\ *vb* **dis·qual·i·fied**; **dis·qual·i·fy·ing**
to make or declare unfit or not qualified

[1]**dis·qui·et** \dis-'kwī-ət\ *vb*
to make uneasy or worried : DISTURB

[2]**disquiet** *n*
an uneasy feeling

**dis·qui·et·ing** \dis-'kwī-ət-ing\ *adj*
causing worry or uneasiness
**dis·qui·et·ing·ly** *adv*

[1]**dis·re·gard** \ˌdis-ri-'gärd\ *vb*
to pay no attention to **synonyms** see NEGLECT

[2]**disregard** *n*
the act of disregarding : the state of being disregarded

**dis·re·pair** \ˌdis-ri-'paər, -'peər\ *n*
the condition of needing repair

**dis·rep·u·ta·ble** \dis-'rep-yət-ə-bəl\ *adj*
not respectable
**dis·rep·u·ta·bly** \-blē\ *adv*

**dis·re·spect** \ˌdis-ri-'spekt\ *n*
lack of respect : DISCOURTESY
**dis·re·spect·ful** *adj*
**dis·re·spect·ful·ly** \-fə-lē\ *adv*

**dis·robe** \dis-'rōb\ *vb* **dis·robed**; **dis·rob·ing**
UNDRESS

**dis·rupt** \dis-'rəpt\ *vb*
to throw into disorder : BREAK UP ⟨*disrupted* the class⟩ ⟨*disrupt* a friendship⟩

**dis·sat·is·fac·tion** \di-ˌsat-əs-'fak-shən\ *n*
a being dissatisfied

**dis·sat·is·fy** \di-'sat-əs-ˌfī\ *vb* **dis·sat·is·fied**; **dis·sat·is·fy·ing**
to fail to satisfy : DISPLEASE

**dis·sect** \di-'sekt\ *vb*
▼ to cut or take apart especially for examination

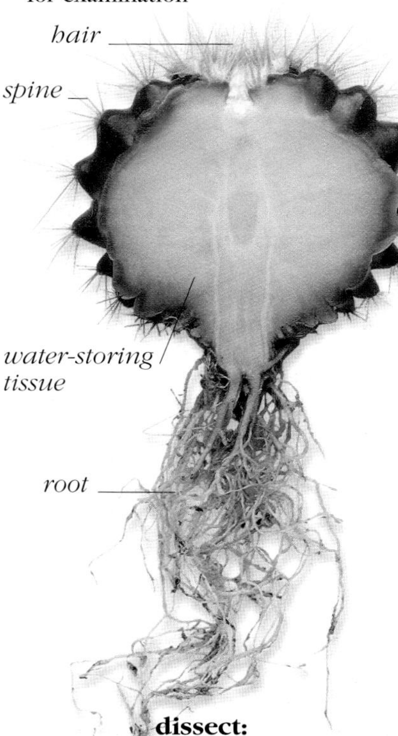


**dissect:**
a dissected cactus plant

**dis·sen·sion** \di-'sen-chən\ *n*
disagreement in opinion : DISCORD

[1]**dis·sent** \di-'sent\ *vb*
DISAGREE 2
**dis·sent·er** *n*

[2]**dissent** *n*
difference of opinion

**dis·ser·vice** \di-'sər-vəs\ *n*
a harmful, unfair, or unjust act

**dis·sim·i·lar** \di-'sim-ə-lər\ *adj*
not similar : DIFFERENT

**dis·si·pate** \'dis-ə-ˌpāt\ *vb* **dis·si·pat·ed**; **dis·si·pat·ing**
1 to break up and drive off : DISPERSE ⟨the sun *dissipated* the fog⟩
2 to scatter or waste foolishly : SQUANDER

**dis·si·pat·ed** \'dis-ə-ˌpāt-əd\ *adj*
enjoying bad, foolish, or harmful activities

**dis·si·pa·tion** \ˌdis-ə-'pā-shən\ *n*
1 the act of dissipating or the state of being dissipated
2 a dissipated way of life

**dis·so·lute** \'dis-ə-ˌlüt\ *adj*
having or showing bad morals or behavior
**dis·so·lute·ly** *adv*
**dis·so·lute·ness** *n*

**dis·solve** \di-'zälv\ *vb* **dis·solved**; **dis·solv·ing**
1 to mix or cause to mix with a liquid so that the result is a liquid that is the same throughout ⟨sugar *dissolves* in water⟩
2 to bring to an end : TERMINATE ⟨*dissolved* their partnership⟩
3 to fade away as if by melting or breaking up

**dis·so·nance** \'dis-ə-nəns\ *n*
an unpleasant combination of musical sounds

**dis·suade** \di-'swād\ *vb* **dis·suad·ed**; **dis·suad·ing**
to persuade or advise not to do something

**dis·tance** \'dis-təns\ *n*
1 how far from each other two points or places are
2 the quality or state of not being friendly : RESERVE
3 a distant point or region

**dis·tant** \'dis-tənt\ *adj*
1 separated in space or time ⟨two miles *distant* from the house⟩
2 REMOTE 1 ⟨a *distant* spot⟩
3 not closely related ⟨*distant* cousins⟩
4 [1]COLD 2, UNFRIENDLY
**dis·tant·ly** *adv*

**dis·taste** \dis-'tāst\ *n*
[1]DISLIKE

**dis·taste·ful** \dis-'tāst-fəl\ *adj*
UNPLEASANT

**dis·tend** \dis-'tend\ *vb*
EXPAND 2, SWELL

**dis·till** *also* **dis·til** \dis-'til\ *vb*
**dis·tilled**; **dis·till·ing**
to obtain or purify by distillation ⟨*distill* water⟩
**dis·till·er** *n*

**dis·til·la·tion** \ˌdis-tə-'lā-shən\ *n*
▼ the process of heating a liquid or solid until it sends off a gas or vapor and then cooling the gas or vapor until it becomes liquid

heated liquid produces water vapor
vapor begins to cool as it moves away from heat
cooling vapor turns into pure water
gas flame

**distillation:** experiment showing how pure water is distilled from a liquid mixture

**dis·tinct** \dis-'tingkt\ *adj*
**1** real and different from each other ⟨guilty of three *distinct* crimes⟩
**2** easy to see, hear, or understand ⟨a *distinct* sound⟩
**dis·tinct·ly** *adv*
**dis·tinct·ness** *n*

**dis·tinc·tion** \dis-'tingk-shən\ *n*
**1** the seeing or pointing out of a difference
**2** DIFFERENCE 1 ⟨the *distinction* between good and evil⟩
**3** great worth **:** EXCELLENCE ⟨a writer of *distinction*⟩
**4** something that makes a person or thing special or different ⟨has the *distinction* of being the oldest building in the state⟩

**dis·tinc·tive** \dis-'tingk-tiv\ *adj*
**1** clearly marking a person or a thing as different from others ⟨a *distinctive* walk⟩
**2** having or giving a special look or way ⟨*distinctive* clothes⟩
**dis·tinc·tive·ly** *adv*
**dis·tinc·tive·ness** *n*

**dis·tin·guish** \dis-'ting-gwish\ *vb*
**1** to recognize by some mark or quality ⟨*distinguish* the sound of the piano in the orchestra⟩
**2** to know the difference ⟨*distinguish* between right and wrong⟩
**3** to set apart as different or special ⟨*distinguished* themselves by heroic actions⟩

**dis·tin·guish·able** \dis-'ting-gwish-ə-bəl\ *adj*
possible to recognize or tell apart from others

**dis·tin·guished** \dis-'ting-gwisht\ *adj*
widely known and admired

**dis·tort** \dis-'tȯrt\ *vb*
**1** to tell in a way that is misleading **:** MISREPRESENT ⟨*distorted* the facts⟩
**2** to twist out of shape
**dis·tort·er** *n*

**dis·tor·tion** \dis-'tȯr-shən\ *n*
the act of distorting **:** the state or fact of being distorted

**dis·tract** \dis-'trakt\ *vb*
**1** to draw the mind or attention to something else
**2** to upset or trouble in mind to the point of confusion

**dis·trac·tion** \dis-'trak-shən\ *n*
**1** the act of distracting **:** the state of being distracted
**2** complete confusion of mind
**3** something that makes it hard to pay attention

**[1]dis·tress** \dis-'tres\ *n*
**1** suffering or pain of body or mind
**2** DANGER 1 ⟨a ship in *distress*⟩
**dis·tress·ful** *adj*

**[2]distress** *vb*
to cause distress to
**dis·tress·ing·ly** *adv*

**dis·trib·ute** \dis-'trib-yət\ *vb*
**dis·trib·ut·ed**; **dis·trib·ut·ing**
**1** to divide among several or many
**2** to spread out so as to cover something
**3** to divide or separate especially into classes **:** SORT

**dis·trib·u·tor** \dis-'trib-yət-ər\ *n*

**dis·tri·bu·tion** \ˌdis-trə-'byü-shən\ *n*
**1** the act of distributing
**2** the way things are distributed
**3** something distributed

**dis·trib·u·tive** \dis-'trib-yət-iv\ *adj*
**1** of or relating to distribution
**2** producing the same answer when operating on the sum of several numbers as when operating on each and collecting the results ⟨multiplication is *distributive*⟩
**dis·trib·u·tive·ly** *adv*

**dis·trict** \'dis-ˌtrikt\ *n*
**1** an area or section (as of a city or nation) set apart for some purpose ⟨our school *district*⟩
**2** an area or region with some special feature ⟨lived in a coal-mining *district*⟩

**[1]dis·trust** \dis-'trəst\ *n*
a lack of trust or confidence **:** SUSPICION
**dis·trust·ful** *adj*
**dis·trust·ful·ly** \-fə-lē\ *adv*

**[2]distrust** *vb*
to have no trust or confidence in

**dis·turb** \dis-'tərb\ *vb*
**1** to interfere with **:** INTERRUPT ⟨the bad weather *disturbed* our plans⟩
**2** to change the arrangements of **:** move from its place ⟨don't *disturb* the flowers⟩
**3** to trouble the mind of **:** UPSET ⟨I am very *disturbed* by your behavior⟩
**4** to make confused or disordered ⟨*disturb* the peace⟩

**dis·tur·bance** \dis-'tər-bəns\ *n*
**1** the act of disturbing **:** the state of being disturbed
**2** [2]DISORDER 1, COMMOTION

**dis·use** \dis-'yüs\ *n*
lack of use

**dis·used** \dis-'yüzd\ *adj*
not used any more

**[1]ditch** \'dich\ *n*
a long narrow channel or trench dug in the earth

**[2]ditch** *vb*
**1** to dig a ditch in or around (as for drainage)
**2** to get rid of **:** DISCARD
**3** to make a forced landing in an airplane on water

**dith·er** \'dith-ər\ *n*
a very nervous or excited state

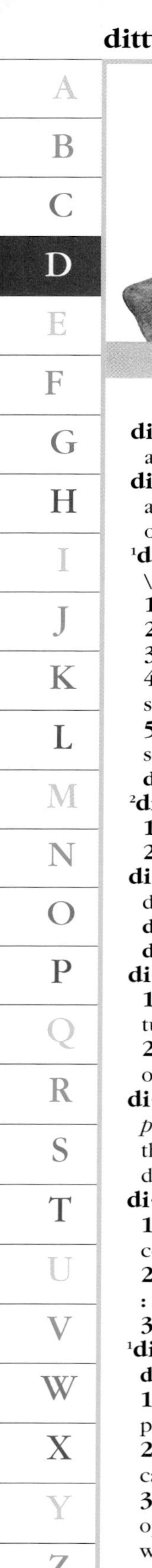

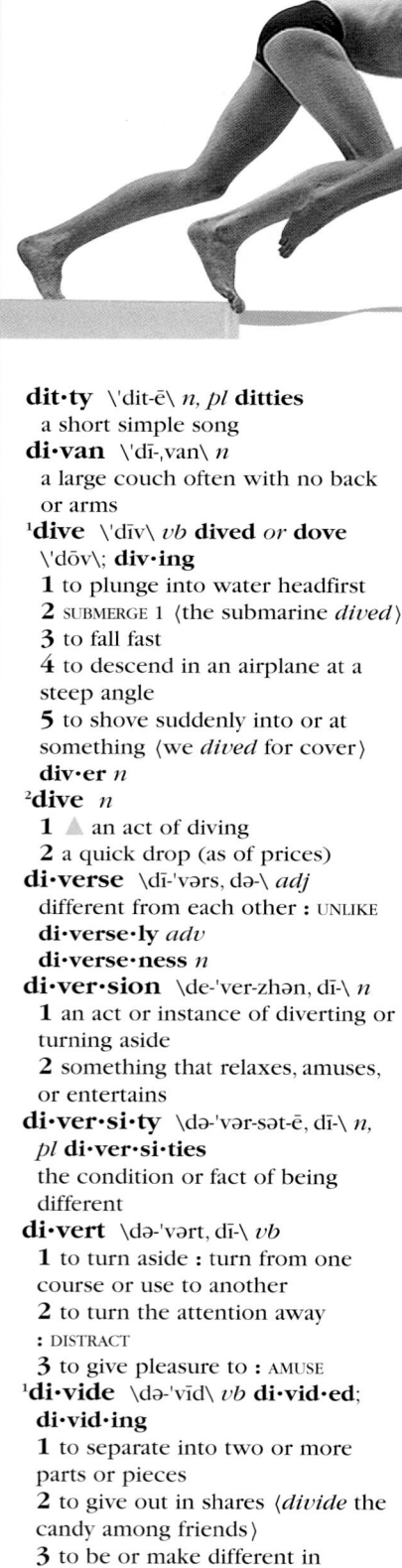

**[2]dive 1:** sequence showing a dive

**dit·ty** \'dit-ē\ *n, pl* **ditties**
a short simple song

**di·van** \'dī-,van\ *n*
a large couch often with no back or arms

**[1]dive** \'dīv\ *vb* **dived** *or* **dove** \'dōv\; **div·ing**
**1** to plunge into water headfirst
**2** SUBMERGE 1 ⟨the submarine *dived*⟩
**3** to fall fast
**4** to descend in an airplane at a steep angle
**5** to shove suddenly into or at something ⟨we *dived* for cover⟩
**div·er** *n*

**[2]dive** *n*
**1** ▲ an act of diving
**2** a quick drop (as of prices)

**di·verse** \dī-'vərs, də-\ *adj*
different from each other : UNLIKE
**di·verse·ly** *adv*
**di·verse·ness** *n*

**di·ver·sion** \de-'ver-zhən, dī-\ *n*
**1** an act or instance of diverting or turning aside
**2** something that relaxes, amuses, or entertains

**di·ver·si·ty** \də-'vər-sət-ē, dī-\ *n, pl* **di·ver·si·ties**
the condition or fact of being different

**di·vert** \də-'vərt, dī-\ *vb*
**1** to turn aside : turn from one course or use to another
**2** to turn the attention away : DISTRACT
**3** to give pleasure to : AMUSE

**[1]di·vide** \də-'vīd\ *vb* **di·vid·ed**; **di·vid·ing**
**1** to separate into two or more parts or pieces
**2** to give out in shares ⟨*divide* the candy among friends⟩
**3** to be or make different in opinion or interest ⟨the country was *divided* over the issue⟩
**4** to subject to mathematical division ⟨*divide* 10 by 2⟩
**5** to branch off : FORK ⟨the road *divides* here⟩ **synonyms** see SEPARATE
**di·vid·er** \də-'vīd-ər\ *n*

**[2]divide** *n*
WATERSHED 1

**div·i·dend** \'div-ə-,dend\ *n*
**1** a sum to be divided and given out
**2** a number to be divided by another number

**[1]di·vine** \də-'vīn\ *adj*
**1** of or relating to God or a god ⟨*divine* will⟩
**2** being in praise of God : RELIGIOUS, HOLY ⟨*divine* services⟩
**3** GODLIKE
**di·vine·ly** *adv*

**[2]divine** *n*
a member of the clergy

**di·vin·i·ty** \də-'vin-ət-ē\ *n, pl* **di·vin·i·ties**
**1** the quality or state of being divine
**2** DEITY
**3** the study of religion

**di·vis·i·ble** \də-'viz-ə-bəl\ *adj*
possible to divide or separate

**di·vi·sion** \də-'vizh-ən\ *n*
**1** ► the act or process of dividing : the state of being divided
**2** a part or portion of a whole
**3** a large military unit
**4** something that divides, separates, or marks off
**5** the finding out of how many times one number is contained in another
**6** a group of plants that ranks above the class in scientific classification and is the highest group of the plant kingdom

**di·vi·sor** \də-'vī-zər\ *n*
the number by which a dividend is divided

**[1]di·vorce** \də-'vōrs\ *n*
**1** a complete legal ending of a marriage
**2** complete separation

**[2]divorce** *vb* **di·vorced**; **di·vorc·ing**
**1** to make or keep separate ⟨our constitution *divorces* church and state⟩
**2** to end one's marriage legally : get a divorce

**di·vulge** \də-'vəlj, dī-\ *vb* **di·vulged**; **di·vulg·ing**
to make public : REVEAL, DISCLOSE

**whole apple**

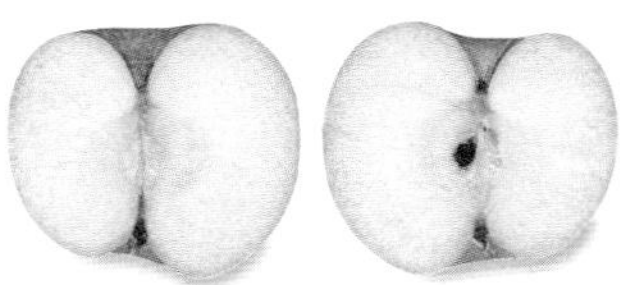

**two halves**

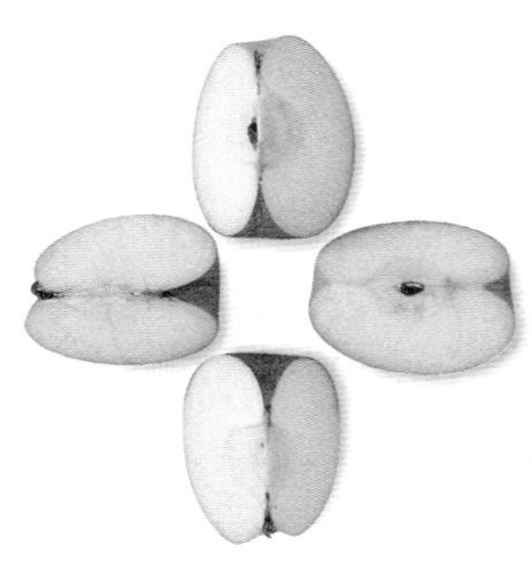

**four quarters**

**division 1:** the division of a whole apple into halves and quarters

**dix·ie·land** \'dik-sē-ˌland\ *n*
lively jazz music in a style developed in New Orleans

**diz·zy** \'diz-ē\ *adj* **diz·zi·er**; **diz·zi·est**
**1** having the feeling of whirling
**2** confused or unsteady in mind
**3** causing a dizzy feeling ⟨*dizzy* heights⟩
**diz·zi·ly** \'diz-ə-lē\ *adv*
**diz·zi·ness** \'diz-ē-nəs\ *n*

**DNA** \ˌdē-ˌen-'ā\ *n*
▶ a complicated organic acid that carries genetic information in the chromosomes

**[1]do** \'dü\ *vb* **did** \did\; **done** \'dən\; **do·ing** \'dü-ing\; **does** \'dəz, dəz\
**1** to cause (as an act or action) to happen : CARRY OUT, PERFORM ⟨tell me what to *do*⟩ ⟨*do* me a favor⟩
**2** [2]ACT 2, BEHAVE ⟨*do* as I say, not as I *do*⟩
**3** to meet one's needs : SUCCEED ⟨*doing* well in school⟩
**4** [1]FINISH 1 — used in the past participle ⟨the work is nearly *done*⟩
**5** to put forth : EXERT ⟨*do* your best⟩
**6** to work on, prepare, or put in order ⟨*do* your homework⟩ ⟨*do* the dishes⟩
**7** to work at as a paying job ⟨what does she *do*⟩
**8** to serve the purpose : SUIT ⟨this will *do* very well⟩
**9** used as a helping verb (1) before the subject in a question ⟨*do* you work⟩, (2) in a negative statement ⟨I *do* not know⟩, (3) for emphasis ⟨you *do* know⟩, and (4) as a substitute for a preceding predicate ⟨you work harder than I *do*⟩
**do away with**
**1** to get rid of
**2** [1]KILL 1

**[2]do** \'dō\ *n*
the first note of the musical scale

**doc·ile** \'däs-əl\ *adj*
easily taught, led, or managed
**doc·ile·ly** *adv*

**[1]dock** \'däk\ *vb*
**1** to cut off the end of
**2** to take away a part of ⟨*dock* your wages⟩

**[2]dock** *n*
**1** an artificial basin for ships that has gates to keep the water in or out
**2** a waterway usually between two piers to receive ships
**3** a wharf or platform for loading or unloading materials

**DNA**

Stored in the cells of all living things are chromosomes, made up of long spirals of DNA. Each molecule of DNA consists of millions of genes, responsible for characteristics such as hair and eye color.

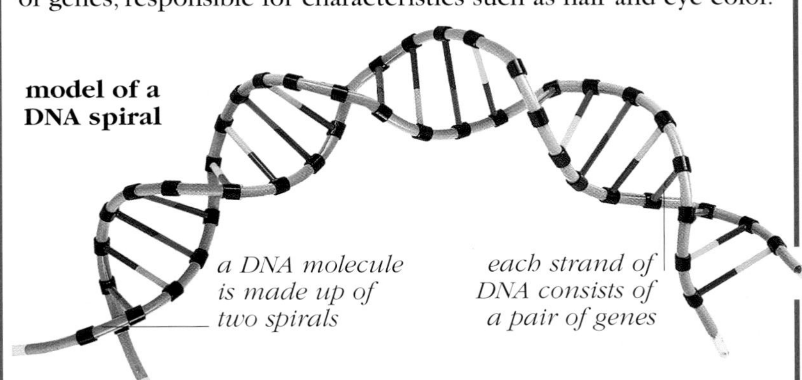
a DNA molecule is made up of two spirals
each strand of DNA consists of a pair of genes

**model of a DNA spiral**

**[3]dock** *vb*
**1** to haul or guide into a dock
**2** to come or go into a dock
**3** to join (as two spacecraft) mechanically while in space

**[4]dock** *n*
the place in a court where a prisoner stands or sits during trial

**[1]doc·tor** \'däk-tər\ *n*
a person (as a physician or veterinarian) skilled and specializing in the art of healing

**[2]doctor** *vb*
**1** to use remedies on or for ⟨*doctor* a boil⟩
**2** to practice medicine

**doc·trine** \'däk-trən\ *n*
something (as a rule or principle) that is taught, believed in, or considered to be true

**doc·u·ment** \'däk-yə-mənt\ *n*
**1** a written or printed paper that gives information about or proof of something
**2** a computer file (as a letter, essay, or chart) typed in by a user

**[1]dodge** \'däj\ *n*
a sudden movement to one side

**[2]dodge** *vb* **dodged**; **dodg·ing**
**1** to move suddenly aside or to and fro ⟨*dodged* through the crowd⟩
**2** to avoid by moving quickly ⟨*dodge* a blow⟩
**3** EVADE ⟨*dodged* the question⟩
**dodg·er** *n*

**dodge ball** *n*
a game in which players stand in a circle and try to hit a player inside the circle by throwing a large inflated ball

**do·do** \'dōd-ō\ *n*, *pl* **dodoes** *or* **dodos**
▼ a large heavy bird unable to fly that once lived on some of the islands of the Indian ocean

**dodo**

**doe** \'dō\ *n*
the female of an animal (as a deer) the male of which is called *buck*

**do·er** \'dü-ər\ *n*
one that does ⟨you are more a thinker than a *doer*⟩

**does** *present third sing of* DO

**doesn't** \'dəz-nt\
does not

**doff** \'däf, 'dȯf\ *vb*
to take off (as one's hat as an act of politeness)

a b c d e f g h i j k l m n o p q r s t u v w x y z

**[1]dog** \'dȯg\ *n*
**1** ▶ a domestic animal that eats meat and is related to the wolves and foxes
**2** a device (as a metal bar with a hook at the end) for holding, gripping, or fastening something
**dog·like** \'dȯ-ˌglīk\ *adj*

**[2]dog** *vb* **dogged**; **dog·ging**
to hunt, track, or follow like a hound

**dog·cart** \'dȯg-ˌkärt\ *n*
**1** a cart pulled by dogs
**2** a light one-horse carriage with two seats back to back

**dog·catch·er** \'dȯg-ˌkach-ər\ *n*
an official paid to catch and get rid of stray dogs

**dog days** *n pl*
the hot period between early July and early September

**Word History** The Latin name for a certain group of stars in the summer sky meant "the greater dog." The ancient Romans gave the brightest star in this group a name that meant "small dog." Some very hot days were associated with the rising of this star. The Latin name for these days meant "days of the small dog." In English *dog days* is a translation of this Latin name.

**dog–eared** \'dȯ-ˌgird\ *adj*
having a lot of pages with corners turned over ⟨a *dog-eared* book⟩

**dogfish**

**dog·fish** \'dȯg-ˌfish\ *n*
▲ any of several small sharks often seen near shore

**dog·ged** \'dȯ-gəd\ *adj*
stubbornly determined
**dog·ged·ly** *adv*
**dog·ged·ness** *n*

**dog·gy** *or* **dog·gie** \'dȯ-gē\ *n, pl* **doggies**
a usually small or young dog

**dog·house** \'dȯg-ˌhau̇s\ *n*
a shelter for a dog

**in the doghouse** in trouble over some wrongdoing

**dog·ma** \'dȯg-mə\ *n*
**1** something firmly believed
**2** a belief or set of beliefs taught by a church

**dog·mat·ic** \dȯg-'mat-ik\ *adj*
**1** of or relating to dogma
**2** seeming or sounding absolutely certain about something
**dog·mat·i·cal·ly** \-i-kə-lē\ *adv*

**[1]dog·trot** \'dȯg-ˌträt\ *n*
a slow trot

**[2]dogtrot** *vb* **dog·trot·ted**; **dog·trot·ting**
to move at a dogtrot

**dogwood**

**dog·wood** \'dȯg-ˌwu̇d\ *n*
▲ any of several shrubs and small trees with clusters of small flowers often surrounded by four showy leaves that look like petals

**doi·ly** \'dȯi-lē\ *n, pl* **doilies**
a small often ornamental mat used on a table

**do·ings** \'dü-ingz\ *n pl*
things that are done or that go on

**dol·drums** \'dōl-drəmz, 'däl-, 'dȯl-\ *n pl*
**1** a spell of low spirits
**2** a part of the ocean near the equator known for its calms

**[1]dole** \'dōl\ *n*
**1** a giving out especially of food, clothing, or money to the needy
**2** something given out as charity

**[2]dole** *vb* **doled**; **dol·ing**
**1** to give out as charity
**2** to give in small portions

**dole·ful** \'dōl-fəl\ *adj*
full of grief **:** SAD
**dole·ful·ly** \-fə-lē\ *adv*
**dole·ful·ness** *n*

**doll** \'däl\ *n*
a small figure of a human being used especially as a child's plaything

**dol·lar** \'däl-ər\ *n*
▼ any of various coins or pieces of paper money (as of the United States or Canada) equal to 100 cents

**dollar:** a dollar bill

**Word History** Many years ago there was a silver mine near a town in Bohemia. In German this town was called *Sankt Joachimsthal* and meant "Saint Joachim's valley." The German word for the silver coins made at Sankt Joachimsthal was formed from the name of the town. This word was *joachimstaler*, and in time it was shortened to *taler*. The English word *dollar* came from the German word *taler*.

**dolly** \'däl-ē\ *n, pl* **dollies**
**1** DOLL
**2** a platform on a roller or on wheels for moving heavy things

**dol·phin** \'däl-fən, 'dȯl-\ *n*
**1** ▼ a small whale with teeth and a long nose
**2** either of two large food fishes of the sea

**dolphin 1**

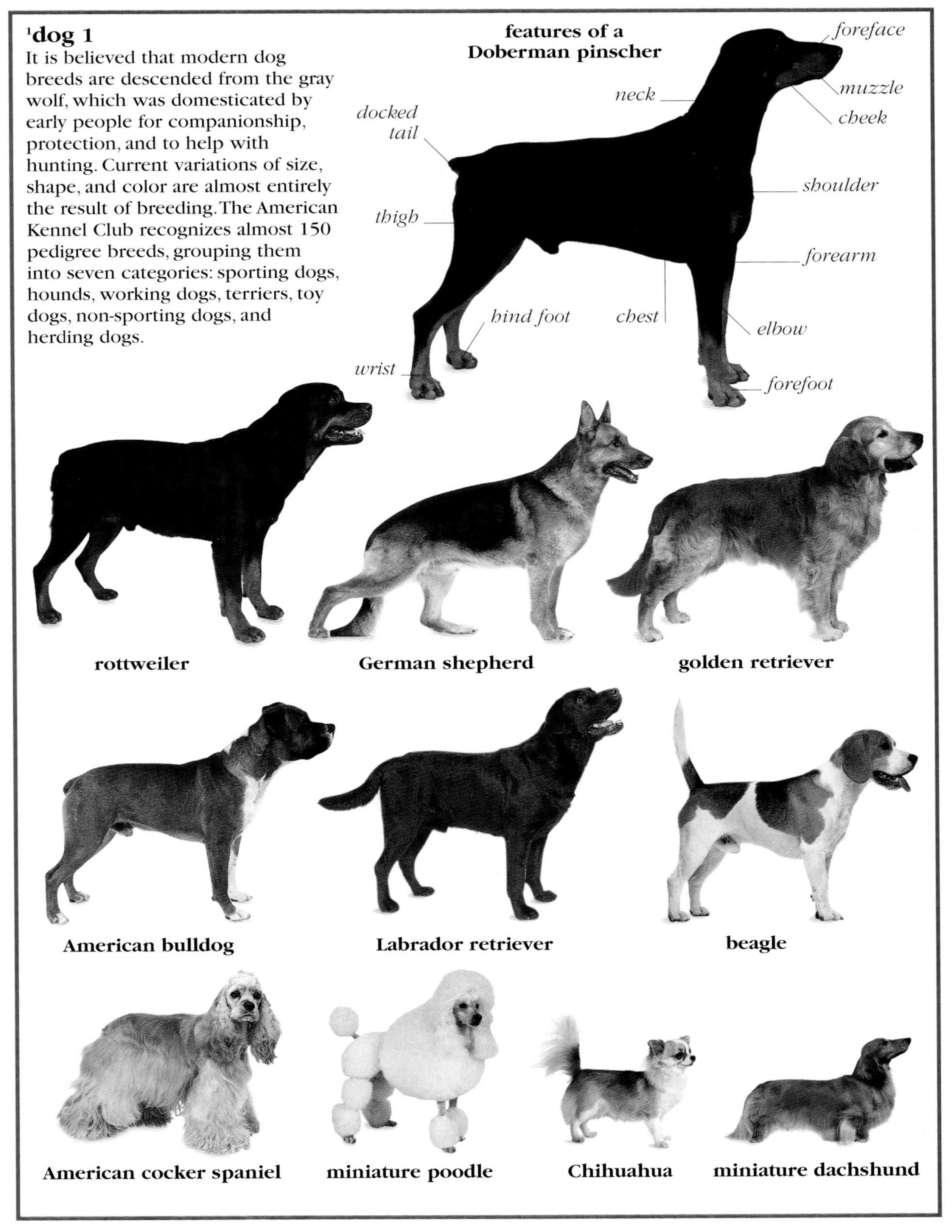
[1]dog 1
It is believed that modern dog breeds are descended from the gray wolf, which was domesticated by early people for companionship, protection, and to help with hunting. Current variations of size, shape, and color are almost entirely the result of breeding. The American Kennel Club recognizes almost 150 pedigree breeds, grouping them into seven categories: sporting dogs, hounds, working dogs, terriers, toy dogs, non-sporting dogs, and herding dogs.
features of a Doberman pinscher
foreface
muzzle
cheek
neck
docked tail
shoulder
thigh
forearm
hind foot
chest
elbow
wrist
forefoot
rottweiler
German shepherd
golden retriever
American bulldog
Labrador retriever
beagle
American cocker spaniel
miniature poodle
Chihuahua
miniature dachshund
a b c d e f g h i j k l m n o p q r s t u v w x y z

**dolt** \'dōlt\ *n*
a stupid person
**dolt·ish** \'dōl-tish\ *adj*
**dolt·ish·ly** *adv*
**dolt·ish·ness** *n*

**-dom** \dəm\ *n suffix*
**1** dignity **:** office
**2** realm **:** jurisdiction ⟨king*dom*⟩
**3** state or fact of being ⟨free*dom*⟩
**4** those having a certain office, occupation, interest, or character

**do·main** \dō-'mān\ *n*
**1** land under the control of a ruler or a government
**2** a field of knowledge or activity
**3** a main subdivision of the Internet

**dome** \'dōm\ *n*
▼ a bulge or a rounded top or roof that looks like half of a ball
**domed** \'dōmd\ *adj*

**dom·i·nance** \'däm-ə-nəns\ *n*
the state or fact of being dominant

**dom·i·nant** \'däm-ə-nənt\ *adj*
controlling or being over all others
**dom·i·nant·ly** *adv*

**dom·i·nate** \'däm-ə-,nāt\ *vb* **dom·i·nat·ed**; **dom·i·nat·ing**
to have a commanding position or controlling power over

**dom·i·neer** \,däm-ə-'nir\ *vb*
to rule or behave in a bossy way

**do·min·ion** \də-'min-yən\ *n*
**1** ruling or controlling power **:** SOVEREIGNTY
**2** a territory under the control of a ruler **:** DOMAIN

**dom·i·no** \'däm-ə-,nō\ *n, pl* **dom·i·noes** *or* **dom·i·nos**
one of a set of flat oblong dotted pieces used in playing a game (**dominoes**)

*dome*

**dome** of a planetarium

**[1]do·mes·tic** \də-'mes-tik\ *adj*
**1** of or relating to a household or a family ⟨*domestic* life⟩
**2** of, relating to, made in, or done in one's own country
**3** living with or under the care of human beings **:** TAME
**do·mes·ti·cal·ly** \-ti-kə-lē\ *adv*

**[2]domestic** *n*
a household servant

**do·mes·ti·cate** \də-'mes-ti-,kāt\ *vb* **do·mes·ti·cat·ed**; **do·mes·ti·cat·ing**
to bring under the control of and make usable by humans

**do·mi·cile** \'däm-ə-,sīl\ *n*
a dwelling place

**don** \'dän\ *vb* **donned**; **don·ning**
to put on

**do·nate** \'dō-,nāt\ *vb* **do·nat·ed**; **do·nat·ing**
to make a gift of **:** CONTRIBUTE
**synonyms** see GIVE
**do·na·tor** \'dō-,nāt-ər, dō-'nāt-\ *n*

**do·na·tion** \dō-'nā-shən\ *n*
a giving of something without charge **:** the thing given (as to charity)

**done** *past participle of* DO

**don·key** \'däng-kē, 'dəng-, 'dȯng-\ *n, pl* **donkeys**
**1** ► an animal related to but smaller than the horse that has short hair in mane and tail and very large ears
**2** a silly or stupid person

**do·nor** \'dō-nər\ *n*
one who gives, donates, or presents
**do·nor·ship** \-,ship\ *n*

**don't** \dōnt\
do not

**[1]doo·dle** \'düd-l\ *vb* **doo·dled**; **doo·dling**
to make a doodle
**doo·dler** \'düd-lər\ *n*

**[2]doodle** *n*
a scribble, design, or sketch done while thinking about something else

**doo·dle·bug** \'düd-l-,bəg\ *n*
ANT LION

**[1]doom** \'düm\ *n*
**1** a decision made by a court **:** SENTENCE
**2** a usually unhappy end **:** FATE

**[2]doom** *vb*
**1** to give judgment against **:** CONDEMN
**2** to make sure that something bad will happen ⟨the plan was *doomed* to failure⟩

**dooms·day** \'dümz-,dā\ *n*
the day of final judgment **:** the end of the world

**door** \'dōr\ *n*
**1** a usually swinging or sliding frame or barrier by which an entrance (as into a house) is closed and opened
**2** a part of a piece of furniture like a house's door
**3** DOORWAY

**door·man** \'dōr-,man, -mən\ *n, pl* **door·men** \-,men\
a person who tends a door of a building

**door·step** \'dōr-,step\ *n*
a step or a series of steps before an outer door

**door·way** \'dōr-,wā\ *n*
the opening or passage that a door closes

**donkey 1**

**door·yard** \'dōr-,yärd\ *n*
a yard outside the door of a house

**dope** \'dōp\ *n*
**1** a thick sticky material (as one used to make pipe joints tight)
**2** a narcotic substance
**3** a stupid person
**4** INFORMATION 2

**dop·ey** \'dō-pē\ *adj* **dop·i·er**; **dop·i·est**
**1** lacking alertness and activity **:** SLUGGISH
**2** STUPID 2 ⟨a *dopey* remark⟩

**dorm** \'dȯrm\ *n*
DORMITORY

**dor·mant** \'dȯr-mənt\ *adj*
being in an inactive state for the time being

**dor·mer** \'dȯr-mər\ *n*
**1** a window placed upright in a sloping roof
**2** the structure containing a dormer window

**dor·mi·to·ry** \'dȯr-mə-,tōr-ē\ *n, pl* **dor·mi·to·ries**
**1** a sleeping room especially for several people
**2** a residence hall having many sleeping rooms

**dor·mouse** \'dȯr-,maůs\ *n, pl* **dor·mice** \-,mīs\
▼ a small European animal that is like a squirrel, lives in trees, and feeds on nuts

**dormouse** hibernating in its nest

**dor·sal** \'dȯr-səl\ *adj*
▼ of, relating to, or being on or near the surface of the body that in humans is the back but in most animals is the upper surface ⟨a fish's *dorsal* fin⟩
**dor·sal·ly** *adv*

**dorsal** fin of a shark

**do·ry** \'dōr-ē\ *n, pl* **dories**
▼ a boat with a flat bottom, high sides that curve upward and outward, and a sharp bow

**dory:** a Portuguese dory

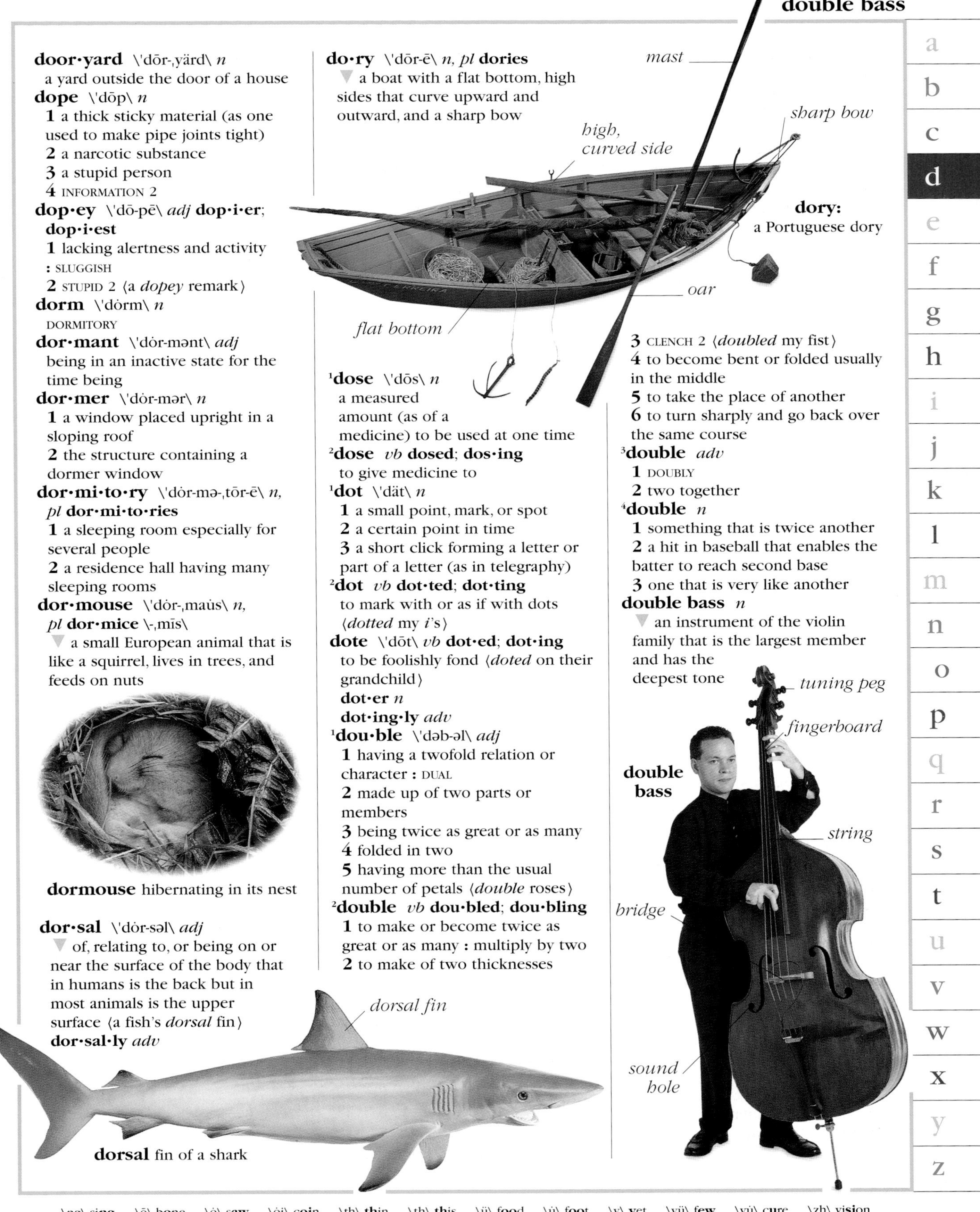


**¹dose** \'dōs\ *n*
a measured amount (as of a medicine) to be used at one time

**²dose** *vb* **dosed**; **dos·ing**
to give medicine to

**¹dot** \'dät\ *n*
**1** a small point, mark, or spot
**2** a certain point in time
**3** a short click forming a letter or part of a letter (as in telegraphy)

**²dot** *vb* **dot·ted**; **dot·ting**
to mark with or as if with dots ⟨*dotted* my *i*'s⟩

**dote** \'dōt\ *vb* **dot·ed**; **dot·ing**
to be foolishly fond ⟨*doted* on their grandchild⟩
**dot·er** *n*
**dot·ing·ly** *adv*

**¹dou·ble** \'dəb-əl\ *adj*
**1** having a twofold relation or character **:** DUAL
**2** made up of two parts or members
**3** being twice as great or as many
**4** folded in two
**5** having more than the usual number of petals ⟨*double* roses⟩

**²double** *vb* **dou·bled**; **dou·bling**
**1** to make or become twice as great or as many **:** multiply by two
**2** to make of two thicknesses
**3** CLENCH 2 ⟨*doubled* my fist⟩
**4** to become bent or folded usually in the middle
**5** to take the place of another
**6** to turn sharply and go back over the same course

**³double** *adv*
**1** DOUBLY
**2** two together

**⁴double** *n*
**1** something that is twice another
**2** a hit in baseball that enables the batter to reach second base
**3** one that is very like another

**double bass** *n*
▼ an instrument of the violin family that is the largest member and has the deepest tone

**double bass**

A B C D E F G H I J K L M N O P Q R S T U V W X Y Z

**dou·ble–cross** \ˌdəb-əl-ˈkrȯs\ *vb* BETRAY 2

**dou·ble·head·er** \ˌdəb-əl-ˈhed-ər\ *n* two games played one right after the other on the same day

**dou·ble–joint·ed** \ˌdəb-əl-ˈjȯint-əd\ *adj* having a joint that permits unusual freedom of movement of the parts that are joined

**double play** *n* a play in baseball by which two base runners are put out

*doublet*

**doublet:** a man dressed in a 16th-century doublet

**dou·blet** \ˈdəb-lət\ *n* ▶ a close-fitting jacket worn by men in Europe especially in the sixteenth century

**dou·ble–talk** \ˈdəb-əl-ˌtȯk\ *n* language that seems to make sense but is actually a mixture of sense and nonsense

**dou·bloon** \ˌdəb-ˈlün\ *n* an old gold coin of Spain and Spanish America

**dou·bly** \ˈdəb-lē\ *adv* to twice the amount or degree

**¹doubt** \ˈdau̇t\ *vb*
**1** to be uncertain about
**2** to lack confidence in : DISTRUST
**3** to consider unlikely
**doubt·er** *n*
**doubt·ing·ly** *adv*

**²doubt** *n*
**1** uncertainty of belief or opinion
**2** the condition of being undecided
**3** a lack of confidence : DISTRUST

**doubt·ful** \ˈdau̇t-fəl\ *adj*
**1** not clear or certain as to fact ⟨a *doubtful* claim⟩
**2** of a questionable kind ⟨*doubtful* intentions⟩
**3** undecided in opinion
**4** not certain in outcome
**doubt·ful·ly** \-fə-lē\ *adv*

**doubt·less** \ˈdau̇t-ləs\ *adv*
**1** without doubt
**2** in all probability

**dough** \ˈdō\ *n*
**1** a soft mass of moistened flour or meal thick enough to knead or roll
**2** MONEY 1, 2

**dough·nut** \ˈdō-ˌnət\ *n* a small ring of sweet dough fried in fat

**dough·ty** \ˈdau̇t-ē\ *adj* **dough·ti·er**; **dough·ti·est** very strong and brave
**dough·ti·ly** \ˈdau̇t-l-ē\ *adv*
**dough·ti·ness** \ˈdau̇t-ē-nəs\ *n*

**dour** \ˈdau̇r, ˈdu̇r\ *adj* looking or being stern or sullen
**dour·ly** *adv*
**dour·ness** *n*

**douse** \ˈdau̇s\ *vb* **doused**; **dous·ing**
**1** to stick into water
**2** to throw a liquid on
**3** to put out : EXTINGUISH ⟨*douse* a light⟩

**¹dove** \ˈdəv\ *n* ▶ any of various mostly small pigeons

**¹dove**

**²dove** \ˈdōv\ *past of* DIVE

**dowdy** \ˈdau̇d-ē\ *adj* **dowd·i·er**; **dowd·i·est**
**1** not neatly or well dressed or cared for
**2** not stylish
**dowd·i·ly** \ˈdau̇d-l-ē\ *adv*
**dowd·i·ness** \ˈdau̇d-ē-nəs\ *n*

**dow·el** \ˈdau̇-əl\ *n* a pin or peg used for fastening together two pieces of wood

**¹down** \ˈdau̇n\ *adv*
**1** toward or in a lower position
**2** to a lying or sitting position
**3** toward or to the ground, floor, or bottom
**4** in cash ⟨paid five dollars *down*⟩
**5** in a direction opposite to up
**6** to or in a lower or worse condition
**7** from a past time ⟨heirlooms handed *down*⟩
**8** to or in a state of less activity ⟨quiet *down*⟩

**²down** *prep* down in : down along : down on : down through ⟨fell *down* a hole⟩ ⟨walked *down* the road⟩

**³down** *vb* to go or cause to go or come down

**⁴down** *adj*
**1** being in a low position
**2** directed or going downward ⟨the *down* escalator⟩
**3** being at a lower level ⟨sales were *down*⟩
**4** low in spirits : DOWNCAST

**⁵down** *n* a low or falling period ⟨the ups and *downs* of life⟩

**⁶down** *n* a rolling grassy upland — usually used in pl.

*down*

**⁷down 1:** downy feathers on a duckling

**⁷down** *n*
**1** ▲ soft fluffy feathers (as of young birds)
**2** something soft and fluffy like down
**down·like** \-ˌlīk\ *adj*

**down·beat** \ˈdau̇n-ˌbēt\ *n* the first beat of a measure of music

**down·cast** \ˈdau̇n-ˌkast\ *adj*
**1** low in spirit : SAD
**2** directed down ⟨*downcast* eyes⟩

**down·fall** \ˈdau̇n-ˌfȯl\ *n* a sudden fall (as from power, happiness, or a high position) or the cause of such a fall
**down·fall·en** \-ˌfȯl-ən\ *adj*

**¹down·grade** \ˈdau̇n-ˌgrād\ *n* a downward slope (as of a road) ⟨lost my brakes on the *downgrade*⟩

**²downgrade** *vb* **down·grad·ed**; **down·grad·ing** to lower in grade, rank, position, or standing

**down·heart·ed** \'daůn-'härt-əd\ *adj*
DOWNCAST 1
**down·heart·ed·ly** *adv*
**down·heart·ed·ness** *n*

[1]**down·hill** \'daůn-'hil\ *adv*
[1]DOWNWARD 1

[2]**down·hill** \'daůn-,hil\ *adj*
sloping downhill

**down payment** *n*
a part of a price paid when something is bought or delivered leaving a balance to be paid later

**down·pour** \'daůn-,pōr\ *n*
a heavy rain

[1]**down·right** \'daůn-,rīt\ *adv*
REALLY, VERY ⟨that was *downright* stupid⟩

[2]**downright** *adj*
[2]OUTRIGHT 1, ABSOLUTE ⟨a *downright* lie⟩

**down·stage** \'daůn-'stāj\ *adv or adj*
toward or at the front of a theatrical stage

[1]**down·stairs** \'daůn-'staərz, -'steərz\ *adv*
down the stairs : on or to a lower floor

[2]**down·stairs** \'daůn-,staərz, -,steərz\ *adj*
situated on a lower floor or on the main or first floor

[3]**down·stairs** \'daůn-'staərz, -'steərz\ *n sing or pl*
the lower floor of a building

**down·stream** \'daůn-'strēm\ *adv*
in the direction a stream is flowing

**down·town** \'daůn-'taůn\ *adv or adj*
to, toward, or in the main business district ⟨walked *downtown*⟩ ⟨the *downtown* stores⟩

[1]**down·ward** \'daůn-wərd\ *or* **down·wards** \wərdz\ *adv*
**1** from a higher place or condition to a lower one
**2** from an earlier time

[2]**downward** *adj*
going or moving down

**down·wind** \'daůn-'wind\ *adv or adj*
in the direction the wind is blowing

**downy** \'daů-nē\ *adj* **down·i·er**; **down·i·est**
**1** like down
**2** covered with down

**dow·ry** \'daů-rē\ *n, pl* **dowries**
the property that a woman brings to her husband in marriage

[1]**doze** \'dōz\ *vb* **dozed**; **doz·ing**
to sleep lightly
**doz·er** *n*

[2]**doze** *n*
a light sleep

**doz·en** \'dəz-n\ *n, pl* **dozens** *or* **dozen**
a group of twelve

[1]**drab** \'drab\ *n*
a light olive brown

[2]**drab** *adj* **drab·ber**; **drab·best**
**1** of the color drab
**2** lacking change and interest : DULL ⟨a *drab* life⟩
**drab·ly** *adv*
**drab·ness** *n*

[1]**draft** \'draft, 'dråft\ *n*
**1** the act of pulling or hauling : the thing or amount pulled
**2** the act or an instance of drinking or inhaling : the portion drunk or inhaled at one time
**3** ▶ a medicine prepared for drinking
**4** something represented in words or lines : DESIGN, PLAN
**5** a quick sketch or outline from which a final work is produced
**6** the act of drawing out liquid (as from a cask) : a portion of liquid drawn out
**7** the depth of water a ship needs in order to float
**8** a picking of persons for required military service
**9** an order made by one party to another to pay money to a third party ⟨a bank *draft*⟩
**10** a current of air
**11** a device to regulate an air supply (as in a stove)

[2]**draft** *adj*
**1** used for pulling loads ⟨a *draft* animal⟩
**2** TENTATIVE ⟨a *draft* treaty⟩
**3** ready to be drawn from a container ⟨*draft* beer⟩

[3]**draft** *vb*
**1** to pick especially for required military service
**2** to make a draft of : OUTLINE ⟨*draft* a speech for the boss⟩
**3** COMPOSE 1, PREPARE ⟨quickly *drafted* an answer to the telegram⟩
**draft·er** *n*

**drafts·man** \'drafts-mən, 'dråfts-\ *n, pl* **drafts·men** \-mən\
a person who draws plans (as for machinery)
**drafts·man·ship** \-,ship\ *n*

**drafty** \'draf-tē, 'dråf-\ *adj* **draft·i·er**; **draft·i·est**
exposed to a draft or current of air ⟨a *drafty* hall⟩
**draft·i·ness** *n*

[1]**drag** \'drag\ *n*
**1** something without wheels (as a sledge for carrying heavy loads) that is dragged, pulled, or drawn along or over a surface
**2** something used for dragging (as a device used underwater to catch something)
**3** something that stops or holds back progress
**4** a dull event, person, or thing ⟨the party was a *drag*⟩

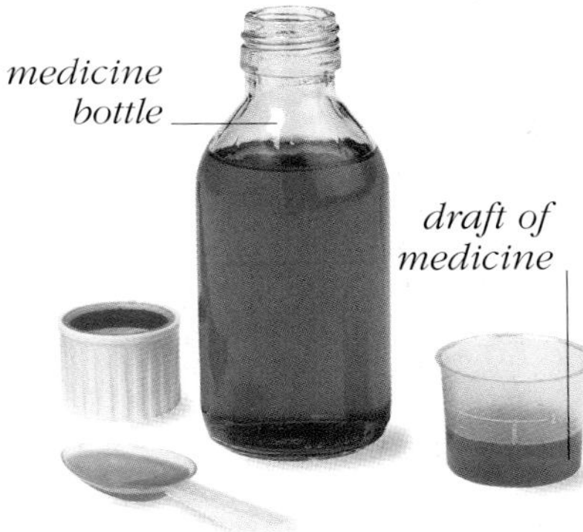

[1]**draft 3:** a draft of medicine

[2]**drag** *vb* **dragged**; **drag·ging**
**1** to haul slowly or heavily ⟨*drag* a trunk across a room⟩
**2** to move with distressing slowness or difficulty
**3** to pass or cause to pass slowly ⟨the hot day *dragged* on⟩
**4** to hang or lag behind
**5** to trail along on the ground
**6** to search or fish with a drag

**drag·gle** \'drag-əl\ *vb* **drag·gled**; **drag·gling**
**1** to make or become wet and dirty by dragging
**2** to follow slowly : STRAGGLE

**drag·net** \'drag-,net\ *n*
**1** a net to be drawn along in order to catch something
**2** a network of planned actions for going after and catching a criminal

A B C D E F G H I J K L M N O P Q R S T U V W X Y Z

**drag·on** \'drag-ən\ *n*
an imaginary animal usually pictured as a huge serpent or lizard with wings and large claws

**drag·on·fly** \'drag-ən-,flī\ *n*, *pl* **drag·on·flies**
a large insect with a long slender body and four wings

**dragonfly:** an adult dragonfly

**dra·goon** \drə-'gün\ *n*
a soldier on horseback

**drag race** *n*
a race for two vehicles at a time from a standstill to a point a quarter mile away

[1]**drain** \'drān\ *vb*
**1** to draw off or flow off gradually or completely ⟨*drain* water from a tank⟩
**2** to make or become dry or empty a little at a time ⟨*drain* a swamp⟩
**3** to let out surface or surplus water
**4** [1]EXHAUST 3

[2]**drain** *n*
**1** a means of draining (as a pipe, channel, or sewer)
**2** the act of draining
**3** a using up a little at a time

**drain·age** \'drā-nij\ *n*
**1** an act of draining
**2** something that is drained off
**3** a method of draining : system of drains

**drain·pipe** \'drān-,pīp\ *n*
a pipe for drainage

**drake** \'drāk\ *n*
a male duck

**dra·ma** \'dräm-ə, 'dram-ə\ *n*
**1** a written work that tells a story through action and speech and is meant to be acted out on a stage
**2** dramatic art, literature, or affairs

**dra·mat·ic** \drə-'mat-ik\ *adj*
**1** of or relating to the drama
**2** like that of the drama : VIVID
**dra·mat·i·cal·ly** \-i-kə-lē\ *adv*

**dra·ma·tist** \'dram-ət-əst, 'dräm-\ *n*
PLAYWRIGHT

**dra·ma·tize** \'dram-ə-,tīz, 'dräm-\ *vb* **dram·a·tized**; **dram·a·tiz·ing**
**1** to make into a drama
**2** to present or represent in a dramatic manner
**dra·ma·ti·za·tion** \,dram-ət-ə-'zā-shən, ,dräm-\ *n*

**drank** *past of* DRINK

[1]**drape** \'drāp\ *vb* **draped**; **drap·ing**
**1** to decorate or cover with or as if with folds of cloth
**2** to arrange or hang in flowing lines

[2]**drape** *n*
**1 drapes** *pl* DRAPERY 2
**2** arrangement in or of folds
**3** the cut or hang of clothing

[1]**draw 13:** a girl drawing with a pencil

**drap·ery** \'drā-pə-rē, 'drā-prē\ *n*, *pl* **drap·er·ies**
**1** a decorative fabric hung in loose folds
**2** curtains of heavy fabric often used over thinner curtains

**dras·tic** \'dras-tik\ *adj*
**1** acting rapidly and strongly
**2** severe in effect : HARSH
**dras·ti·cal·ly** \-ti-kə-lē\ *adv*

**draught** \'draft, 'dråft\ *chiefly British variant of* DRAFT

[1]**draw** \'dr̊o\ *vb* **drew** \'drü\; **drawn** \'drȯn\; **draw·ing**
**1** to cause to move by pulling : cause to follow
**2** to move or go usually steadily or a little at a time ⟨day was *drawing* to a close⟩
**3** ATTRACT 1 ⟨*draw* a crowd⟩
**4** to call forth : PROVOKE ⟨*draw* enemy fire⟩
**5** INHALE ⟨*draw* a deep breath⟩
**6** to bring or pull out ⟨the dentist *drew* the tooth⟩ ⟨*draw* a sword⟩
**7** to bring or get from a source ⟨*draw* a pail of water⟩
**8** to need (a certain depth) to float in ⟨the boat *draws* three feet of water⟩
**9** to take or receive at random ⟨*draw* lots⟩ ⟨*drew* the winning number⟩
**10** to bend (a bow) by pulling back the string
**11** to cause to shrink or pucker : WRINKLE
**12** to leave (a contest) undecided : TIE
**13** to produce a likeness of by making lines on a surface : SKETCH
**14** to write out in proper form ⟨*draw* a check⟩ — often used with *up* ⟨*draw* up a deed⟩
**15** FORMULATE ⟨*draw* a conclusion from facts⟩
**16** to produce or make use of a current of air ⟨the furnace *draws* well⟩

[2]**draw** *n*
**1** the act or the result of drawing
**2** a tie game or contest
**3** something that draws attention
**4** a gully shallower than a ravine

**draw·back** \'drȯ-,bak\ *n*
[1]HANDICAP 3

**draw·bridge** \'drȯ-,brij\ *n*
a bridge made to be drawn up, down, or aside to permit or prevent passage

**draw·er** \'drȯ-ər, 'drȯr\ *n*
**1** one that draws
**2** a sliding boxlike compartment (as in a desk)
**3 drawers** *pl* an undergarment for the lower part of the body

**draw·ing** \'drȯ-ing\ *n*
**1** an act or instance of drawing lots
**2** the act or art of making a figure, plan, or sketch by means of lines
**3** a picture made by drawing

**drawing room** *n*
a formal room for entertaining company

[1]**drawl** \'dról\ *vb*
to speak slowly with vowel sounds drawn out beyond their usual length

**drawl** *n*
a drawling way of speaking

**draw on** *vb*
to come closer : APPROACH ⟨as night *drew on*⟩

**draw out** *vb*
to cause or encourage to speak freely ⟨tried to *draw* the frightened child *out*⟩

**draw·string** \'dró-,string\ *n*
▶ a string, cord, or tape used to close a bag, control fullness in clothes, or open or close curtains

**draw up** *vb*
**1** to arrange (as a body of troops) in order
**2** to straighten (oneself) to an erect posture
**3** to bring or come to a stop

**dray** \'drā\ *n*
a strong low cart or wagon without sides for hauling heavy loads

[1]**dread** \'dred\ *vb*
**1** to fear greatly
**2** to be very unwilling to meet or face

[2]**dread** *n*
great fear especially of harm to come

[3]**dread** *adj*
causing great fear or anxiety ⟨a *dread* disease⟩

**dread·ful** \'dred-fəl\ *adj*
**1** causing a feeling of dread
**2** very disagreeable, unpleasant, or shocking ⟨had a *dreadful* cold⟩ ⟨such *dreadful* manners⟩
**dread·ful·ly** \-fə-lē\ *adv*
**dread·ful·ness** *n*

**dread·nought** \'dred-,nót\ *n*
a very large battleship

[1]**dream** \'drēm\ *n*
**1** a series of thoughts, pictures, or feelings occurring during sleep
**2** a dreamlike creation of the imagination : DAYDREAM
**3** something notable for its pleasing quality
**4** a goal that is longed for : IDEAL
**dream·like** \-,līk\ *adj*

[2]**dream** *vb* **dreamed** \'dremt, 'drēmd\ *or* **dreamt** \'dremt\; **dream·ing** \'drē-ming\
**1** to have a dream or dreams
**2** to spend time having daydreams
**3** to think of as happening or possible
**dream·er** \'drē-mər\ *n*

**drawstrings** on a military jacket

**dream·land** \'drēm-,land\ *n*
an unreal delightful country existing only in imagination or in dreams

**dream·less** \'drēm-ləs\ *adj*
having no dreams ⟨a *dreamless* sleep⟩
**dream·less·ly** *adv*
**dream·less·ness** *n*

**dreamy** \'drē-mē\ *adj* **dream·i·er**; **dream·i·est**
**1** tending to spend time dreaming
**2** having the quality of a dream
**3** being quiet and soothing ⟨*dreamy* music⟩
**4** SUPERB
**dream·i·ly** \-mə-lē\ *adv*
**dream·i·ness** \-mē-nəs\ *n*

**drea·ry** \'drir-ē\ *adj* **drea·ri·er**; **drea·ri·est**
DISMAL, GLOOMY
**drea·ri·ly** \'drir-ə-lē\ *adv*
**drea·ri·ness** \'drir-ē-nəs\ *n*

[1]**dredge** \'drej\ *vb* **dredged**; **dredg·ing**
to dig or gather with or as if with a dredge
**dredg·er** *n*

[2]**dredge** *n*
**1** a heavy iron frame with a net attached to be dragged (as for gathering oysters) over the sea bottom
**2** a machine for scooping up or removing earth usually by buckets on an endless chain or by a suction tube
**3** a barge used in dredging

**dregs** \'dregz\ *n pl*
**1** solids that settle out of a liquid
**2** the worst or most useless part

**drench** \'drench\ *vb*
to wet thoroughly

[1]**dress** \'dres\ *vb*
**1** to make or set straight (as soldiers on parade)
**2** to put clothes on : CLOTHE
**3** to wear formal or fancy clothes
**4** to trim or decorate for display ⟨*dress* a store window⟩
**5** to treat with remedies and bandage ⟨*dress* a wound⟩
**6** to arrange by combing, brushing, or curling ⟨*dress* hair⟩
**7** to prepare (a meat animal) for food
**8** to apply fertilizer to

[2]**dress** *n*
**1** CLOTHING 1, APPAREL
**2** an outer garment with a skirt for a woman or child

[1]**dress·er** \'dres-ər\ *n*
a piece of furniture (as a chest or a bureau) with a mirror

[2]**dresser** *n*
a person who dresses in a certain way ⟨a sloppy *dresser*⟩ ⟨a stylish *dresser*⟩

**dress·ing** \'dres-ing\ *n*
**1** the act or process of one who dresses
**2** a sauce added to a food (as a salad)
**3** a seasoned mixture used as a stuffing (as for a turkey)
**4** material used to cover an injury
**5** something used as a fertilizer

**dress·mak·er** \'dres-,mā-kər\ *n*
a person who makes dresses

**dress·mak·ing** \'dres-,mā-king\ *n*
the process or occupation of making dresses

**dress up** *vb*
**1** to put on one's best or formal clothes
**2** to put on strange or fancy clothes ⟨*dress up* for Halloween⟩

**dressy** \'dres-ē\ *adj* **dress·i·er**; **dress·i·est**
**1** showy in dress
**2** suitable for formal occasions

[2]**drill 1:** an electric drill

[1]**drib·ble** \'drib-əl\ *vb* **drib·bled**; **drib·bling**
**1** to fall or let fall in small drops **:** TRICKLE
**2** [1]SLOBBER, DROOL
**3** to move forward by bouncing, tapping, or kicking ⟨*dribble* a basketball⟩

[2]**dribble** *n*
**1** a trickling flow
**2** the act of dribbling a ball

**drib·let** \'drib-lət\ *n*
**1** a small amount
**2** a falling drop

**dri·er** *or* **dry·er** \'drī-ər\ *n*
**1** something that removes or absorbs moisture
**2** a substance that speeds up the drying of oils, paints, and inks
**3** *usually dryer* **:** a device for drying ⟨a clothes *dryer*⟩

[1]**drift** \'drift\ *n*
**1** the motion or course of something drifting
**2** a mass of matter (as snow or sand) piled in a heap by the wind
**3** a course something appears to be taking ⟨the *drift* of the conversation⟩
**4** the meaning of something said or implied ⟨I don't get your *drift*⟩

[2]**drift** *vb*
**1** to float or to be driven along by winds, waves, or currents
**2** to move along without effort or purpose ⟨*drift* through life⟩
**3** to pile up in drifts
**drift·er** *n*

**drift·wood** \'drift-,wu̇d\ *n*
wood drifted or floated by water

[1]**drill** \'dril\ *vb*
**1** to bore with a drill
**2** to teach by means of repeated practice
**drill·er** *n*

[2]**drill** *n*
**1** a tool for making holes in hard substances
**2** the training of soldiers (as in marching)
**3** regular strict training and instruction in a subject

[3]**drill** *n*
a farming implement for making holes or furrows and planting seeds in them

[4]**drill** *vb*
to sow seeds with or as if with a drill

**drily** *variant of* DRYLY

[1]**drink** \'dringk\ *vb* **drank** \'drangk\; **drunk** \'drəngk\; **drink·ing**
**1** to swallow liquid
**2** to absorb a liquid ⟨plants *drink* up water⟩
**3** to take in through the senses ⟨*drank* in the beautiful scenery⟩
**4** to drink alcoholic liquor
**drink·er** *n*

[2]**drink** *n*
**1** BEVERAGE
**2** alcoholic liquor

**drink·able** \'dring-kə-bəl\ *adj*
suitable or safe for drinking

[1]**drip** \'drip\ *vb* **dripped**; **drip·ping**
**1** to fall or let fall in or as if in drops
**2** to let fall drops of liquid ⟨a *dripping* faucet⟩

[2]**drip** *n*
**1** a falling in drops
**2** dripping liquid
**3** the sound made by falling drops

[1]**drive** \'drīv\ *vb* **drove** \'drōv\; **driv·en** \'driv-ən\; **driv·ing** \'drī-viŋ\
**1** to push or force onward
**2** to direct the movement or course of ⟨*drive* a car⟩
**3** to go or carry in a vehicle under one's own control ⟨*drive* into town⟩
**4** to set or keep in motion or operation ⟨machines *driven* by electricity⟩
**5** to carry through **:** CONCLUDE ⟨*drive* a bargain⟩
**6** to force to work or to act ⟨*driven* by hunger to steal⟩
**7** to bring into a specified condition ⟨the noise *drove* me crazy⟩
**driv·er** \'drī-vər\ *n*

[2]**drive** *n*
**1** a trip in a carriage or automobile
**2** a collecting and driving together of animals
**3** DRIVEWAY
**4** an often scenic public road
**5** an organized usually thorough effort to carry out a purpose
**6** the means for giving motion to a machine or machine part
**7** a device that transfers information to and from a storage material (as tape or disks) ⟨a disk *drive*⟩

**drive–in** \'drī-,vin\ *adj*
designed and equipped to serve customers while they remain in their automobiles ⟨a *drive-in* bank⟩

**drive·way** \'drīv-,wā\ *n*
a private road leading from the street to a house or garage

[1]**driz·zle** \'driz-əl\ *n*
a fine misty rain

[2]**drizzle** *vb* **driz·zled**; **driz·zling**
to rain in very small drops

**droll** \'drōl\ *adj*
having an odd or amusing quality ⟨a *droll* expression⟩
**droll·ness** *n*
**drol·ly** \'drōl-lē\ *adv*

**drom·e·dary** \'dräm-ə-,der-ē\ *n*, *pl* **drom·e·dar·ies**
**1** a speedy camel trained for riding
**2** the camel of western Asia and northern Africa that has only one hump

[1]**drone** \'drōn\ *n*
**1** a male bee
**2** a lazy person **:** one who lives on the labor of others

[2]**drone** *vb* **droned**; **dron·ing**
to make or to speak with a low dull monotonous hum

[3]**drone** *n*
a droning sound

**drool** \'drül\ *vb*
to let liquid flow from the mouth **:** SLOBBER

[1]**droop** \'drüp\ *vb*
**1** to sink, bend, or hang down ⟨flowers *drooping* in the hot sun⟩

2 to become sad or weak ⟨my spirits *drooped*⟩

[2]**droop** *n*
the condition or appearance of drooping

[1]**drop** \'dräp\ *n*
1 the amount of liquid that falls naturally in one rounded mass
2 **drops** *pl* a dose of medicine measured by drops
3 something (as a small round candy) that is shaped like a liquid drop
4 an instance of dropping
5 the distance of a fall

[2]**drop** *vb* **dropped**; **drop·ping**
1 to fall or let fall in drops
2 to let fall ⟨*drop* a book⟩
3 to lower in pitch and volume ⟨my voice *dropped*⟩
4 SEND 1 ⟨*drop* me a note about it⟩
5 to let go : DISMISS ⟨*drop* a subject⟩
6 to knock down : cause to fall
7 to go lower ⟨the temperature *dropped*⟩
8 to make a brief visit ⟨*drop* in on a friend⟩
9 to pass into a less active state ⟨*drop* off to sleep⟩
10 to withdraw from membership or from taking part ⟨*drop* out of school⟩
11 LOSE 4

**drop·let** \'dräp-lət\ *n*
a tiny drop

**drop·out** \'dräp-ˌau̇t\ *n*
one that drops out especially from school or a training program

**drop·per** \'dräp-ər\ *n*
1 one that drops
2 a short glass tube with a rubber bulb used to measure out liquids by drops

**drought** *or* **drouth** \'drau̇t, 'drau̇th\ *n*
1 lack of rain or water
2 a long period of dry weather

[1]**drove** \'drōv\ *n*
1 a group of animals being driven or moving in a body
2 a crowd of people moving or acting together

[2]**drove** *past of* DRIVE

**drov·er** \'drō-vər\ *n*
a worker who drives cattle or sheep

**drown** \'drau̇n\ *vb*
1 to suffocate in a liquid and especially in water
2 to cover with water : FLOOD
3 to overpower especially with noise ⟨*drowned* the speaker out with boos⟩

[1]**drowse** \'drau̇z\ *vb* **drowsed**; **drows·ing**
to be half asleep : sleep lightly

[2]**drowse** *n*
a light sleep : DOZE

**drowsy** \'drau̇-zē\ *adj* **drows·i·er**; **drows·i·est**
1 ready to fall asleep
2 making one sleepy ⟨the *drowsy* buzz of bees⟩
**drows·i·ly** \-zə-lē\ *adv*
**drows·i·ness** \-zē-nəs\ *n*

**drub** \'drəb\ *vb* **drubbed**; **drub·bing**
1 to beat severely
2 to defeat completely

**drudge** \'drəj\ *n*
a person who does hard or dull work

**drudg·ery** \'drəj-ə-rē\ *n, pl* **drudg·er·ies**
hard or dull work

[1]**drug** \'drəg\ *n*
1 a substance used as a medicine or in making medicines
2 medicine used to deaden pain or bring sleep
3 a substance that may harm or make an addict of a person who uses it

[2]**drug** *vb* **drugged**; **drug·ging**
1 to poison with or as if with a drug ⟨the wine was *drugged*⟩
2 to dull a person's senses with drugs

**drug·gist** \'drəg-əst\ *n*
a seller of drugs and medicines : PHARMACIST

**drug·store** \'drəg-ˌstōr\ *n*
a retail store where medicines and often other things are sold : PHARMACY

[1]**drum** \'drəm\ *n*
1 ▶ a percussion instrument usually consisting of a metal or wooden cylinder with flat ends covered by tightly stretched skin
2 a sound of or like a drum
3 an object shaped like a drum ⟨oil *drum*⟩

[2]**drum** *vb* **drummed**; **drum·ming**
1 to beat a drum
2 to beat or sound like a drum
3 to gather together by or as if by beating a drum ⟨*drum* up customers⟩
4 to drive or force by steady or repeated effort ⟨*drummed* the lesson into their heads⟩
5 to beat or tap in a rhythmic way

**drum major** *n*
the marching leader of a band or drum corps

**drum ma·jor·ette** \ˌdrəm-ˌmā-jə-'ret\ *n*
a girl who is a drum major

**drum·mer** \'drəm-ər\ *n*
1 a person who plays a drum
2 a traveling salesman

**drum·stick** \'drəm-ˌstik\ *n*
1 a stick for beating a drum
2 the lower section of the leg of a fowl

[1]**drunk** \'drəngk\ *past participle of* DRINK

[2]**drunk** *adj*
1 being so much under the influence of alcohol that normal thinking and acting become difficult or impossible
2 controlled by some feeling as if under the influence of alcohol ⟨*drunk* with power⟩

[1]**drum 1:** a girl playing a drum

[3]**drunk** *n*
1 a period of drinking too much alcoholic liquor
2 a drunken person

A B C D E F G H I J K L M N O P Q R S T U V W X Y Z

**drunk·ard** \'drəng-kərd\ *n*
a person who is often drunk

**drunk·en** \'drəng-kən\ *adj*
**1** [2]DRUNK 1
**2** resulting from being drunk ⟨a *drunken* sleep⟩
**drunk·en·ly** *adv*
**drunk·en·ness** *n*

[1]**dry** \'drī\ *adj* **dri·er**; **dri·est**
**1** free or freed from water or liquid **:** not wet or moist
**2** having little or no rain ⟨a *dry* climate⟩
**3** lacking freshness **:** STALE
**4** not being in or under water ⟨*dry* land⟩
**5** THIRSTY 1, 2
**6** no longer liquid or sticky ⟨the paint is *dry*⟩
**7** containing no liquid ⟨a *dry* creek⟩
**8** not giving milk ⟨a *dry* cow⟩
**9** not producing phlegm ⟨a *dry* cough⟩
**10** amusing in a sharp or acid way ⟨*dry* humor⟩
**11** UNINTERESTING ⟨a *dry* lecture⟩
**12** not sweet ⟨*dry* wines⟩
**dry·ly** *adv*
**dry·ness** *n*

[2]**dry** *vb* **dried**; **dry·ing**
to make or become dry

**dry cell** *n*
a small cell producing electricity by means of chemicals in a sealed container

**dry–clean** \'drī-,klēn\ *vb*
to clean (fabrics) with chemical solvents

**dry cleaner** *n*
one whose business is dry cleaning

**dry cleaning** *n*
**1** the cleaning of fabrics with a substance other than water
**2** something that is dry-cleaned ⟨picked up the *dry cleaning* on the way home⟩

**dryer** *variant of* DRIER

**dry goods** \'drī-,gu̇dz\ *n pl*
cloth goods (as fabrics, lace, and ribbon)

**dry ice** *n*
solidified carbon dioxide used chiefly to keep something very cold

**du·al** \'dü-əl, 'dyü-\ *adj*
consisting of two parts **:** having two like parts **:** DOUBLE ⟨a car with *dual* controls⟩
**du·al·ly** *adv*

[1]**dub** \'dəb\ *vb* **dubbed**; **dub·bing**
**1** to make a knight of by a light tapping on the shoulder with a sword
**2** [2]NAME 1, NICKNAME

[2]**dub** *vb* **dubbed**; **dub·bing**
to add (sound effects) to a film or broadcast

**du·bi·ous** \'dü-bē-əs, 'dyü-\ *adj*
**1** causing doubt **:** UNCERTAIN
**2** feeling doubt
**3** QUESTIONABLE 1
**du·bi·ous·ly** *adv*

**duch·ess** \'dəch-əs\ *n*
**1** the wife or widow of a duke
**2** a woman who holds the rank of a duke in her own right

[1]**duck** \'dək\ *n*
▼ any of a group of swimming birds that have broad flat bills and are smaller than the related geese and swans

broad flat bill
webbed feet

[1]**duck:** a male mallard

[2]**duck** *vb*
**1** to push or pull under water for a moment
**2** to lower the head or body suddenly
**3** [2]DODGE 1
**4** [2]DODGE 2 ⟨*duck* a blow⟩
**5** to avoid a duty, question, or responsibility

[3]**duck** *n*
**1** a coarse usually cotton fabric rather like canvas
**2 ducks** *pl* clothes (as trousers) made of duck

**duck·bill** \'dək-,bil\ *n*
PLATYPUS

**duck·ling** \'dək-ling\ *n*
a young duck

**duck·weed** \'dək-,wēd\ *n*
a very small stemless plant that floats in fresh water

**duct** \'dəkt\ *n*
a pipe, tube, or vessel that carries something (as a bodily secretion, water, or hot air)
**duct·less** \-ləs\ *adj*

**ductless gland** *n*
ENDOCRINE GLAND

**dud** \'dəd\ *n*
**1 duds** *pl* CLOTHING
**2** a complete failure
**3** a missile that fails to explode

**dude** \'düd, 'dyüd\ *n*
a man who pays too much attention to his clothes

[1]**due** \'dü, 'dyü\ *adj*
**1** owed or owing as a debt or a right
**2** SUITABLE ⟨treat one's teacher with *due* respect⟩
**3** being a result — used with *to* ⟨accidents *due* to carelessness⟩
**4** required or expected to happen ⟨*due* to arrive soon⟩

[2]**due** *n*
**1** something owed **:** DEBT ⟨give the devil his *due*⟩
**2 dues** *pl* a regular or legal charge or fee

[3]**due** *adv*
DIRECTLY 1 ⟨*due* north⟩

[1]**du·el** \'dü-əl, 'dyü-\ *n*
**1** a combat between two persons fought with deadly weapons by agreement and in the presence of witnesses
**2** a contest between two opponents

[2]**duel** *vb* **du·eled** *or* **du·elled**; **du·el·ing** *or* **du·el·ling**
to fight in a duel
**du·el·ist** \'dü-ə-list,'dyü-\ *n*

**du·et** \dü-'et, dyü-\ *n*
**1** a musical composition for two performers
**2** two performers playing or singing together

**due to** *prep*
because of

**dug** *past of* DIG

**dug·out** \'dəg-,au̇t\ *n*
**1** a boat made by hollowing out a log
**2** a shelter dug in a hillside or in the ground
**3** a low shelter facing a baseball diamond and containing the players' bench

**duke** \'dük, 'dyük\ *n*
a member of the highest rank of the British nobility

[1]**dull** \'dəl\ *adj*
**1** mentally slow **:** STUPID

2 LISTLESS ⟨was feeling *dull*⟩
3 slow in action : SLUGGISH ⟨business was *dull*⟩
4 not sharp in edge or point : BLUNT
5 lacking brightness or luster ⟨a *dull* finish⟩
6 not clear and ringing ⟨a *dull* sound⟩
7 CLOUDY 1, OVERCAST
8 not interesting : TEDIOUS
9 slightly grayish ⟨a *dull* red⟩
**dull·ness** *or* **dul·ness** *n*
**dul·ly** *adv*

[2]**dull** *vb*
to make or become dull

**du·ly** \'dü-lē, 'dyü-\ *adv*
in a due or suitable manner, time, or degree

**dumb** \'dəm\ *adj*
1 lacking the normal power of speech ⟨deaf and *dumb* persons⟩
2 normally unable to speak ⟨*dumb* animals⟩
3 not willing to speak : SILENT
4 STUPID 1, FOOLISH
**dumb·ly** *adv*
**dumb·ness** *n*

**dumb·bell** \'dəm-,bel\ *n*
1 ▶ a short bar with two weighted balls or disks at the ends usually used in pairs for strengthening the arms
2 a stupid person

**dumb·found** *or* **dum·found** \,dəm-'faůnd\ *vb*
to cause to become speechless with astonishment : AMAZE

**dumb·wait·er** \'dəm-'wāt-ər\ *n*
a small elevator for carrying food and dishes or other small items from one floor to another

**dum·my** \'dəm-ē\ *n, pl* **dummies**
1 a person who does not have or seems not to have the power of speech
2 a stupid person
3 an imitation used as a substitute for something ⟨*dummies* in a store window⟩

[1]**dump** \'dəmp\ *vb*
to let fall in a heap : get rid of

[2]**dump** *n*
1 a place for dumping something (as trash)
2 a place for storage of military materials or the materials stored
3 a messy or shabby place ⟨the *dump* we lived in then⟩

**dump·ling** \'dəmp-ling\ *n*
a small mass of dough cooked by boiling or steaming

**dumps** \'dəmps\ *n pl*
low spirits

**dumpy** \'dəm-pē\ *adj* **dump·i·er**; **dump·i·est**
short and thick in build
**dump·i·ness** *n*

[1]**dun** \'dən\ *n*
a slightly brownish dark gray

[2]**dun** *vb* **dunned**; **dun·ning**
to make repeated demands upon for payment

**dunce** \'dəns\ *n*
a stupid person

**dune** \'dün, 'dyün\ *n*
a hill or ridge of sand piled up by the wind

**dung** \'dəng\ *n*
FECES

**dun·ga·ree** \,dəng-gə-'rē\ *n*
1 a heavy cotton cloth
2 **dungarees** *pl* pants or work clothes made of dungaree

**dumbbell 1:**
a man exercising with dumbbells

**dun·geon** \'dən-jən\ *n*
a dark usually underground prison

**dung·hill** \'dəng-,hil\ *n*
a pile of manure

**dunk** \'dəngk\ *vb*
to dip (as a cookie) into liquid (as milk)

**duo** \'dü-ō, 'dyü-\ *n, pl* **du·os**
1 a duet especially for two performers at two pianos
2 [1]PAIR 1

[1]**dupe** \'düp, 'dyüp\ *n*
a person who has been or is easily deceived or cheated

[2]**dupe** *vb* **duped**; **dup·ing**
to make a dupe of : TRICK

**du·plex** \'dü-,pleks, 'dyü-\ *adj*
[1]DOUBLE 2

[1]**du·pli·cate** \'dü-pli-kət, 'dyü-\ *adj*
1 having two parts exactly the same or alike
2 being the same as another

[2]**du·pli·cate** \'dü-pli-,kāt, 'dyü-\ *vb* **du·pli·cat·ed**; **du·pli·cat·ing**
1 to make double
2 to make an exact copy of

[3]**du·pli·cate** \'dü-pli-kət, 'dyü-\ *n*
a thing that is exactly like another

**du·pli·ca·tion** \,dü-pli-'kā-shən, ,dyü-\ *n*
1 the act or process of duplicating
2 the state of being duplicated

**du·ra·bil·i·ty** \,důr-ə-'bil-ət-ē, ,dyůr-\ *n*
ability to last or to stand hard or continued use

**du·ra·ble** \'důr-ə-bəl, 'dyůr-\ *adj*
able to last a long time
**du·ra·ble·ness** *n*
**du·ra·bly** \-blē\ *adv*

**du·ra·tion** \dů-'rā-shən, dyů-\ *n*
the time during which something exists or lasts

**dur·ing** \,důr-ing, ,dyůr-\ *prep*
1 throughout the course of ⟨swims every day *during* the summer⟩
2 at some point in the course of ⟨you may phone me *during* the day⟩

**dusk** \'dəsk\ *n*
1 the darker part of twilight especially at night
2 partial darkness

**dusky** \'dəs-kē\ *adj* **dusk·i·er**; **dusk·i·est**
1 somewhat dark in color
2 somewhat dark : DIM ⟨a *dusky* room⟩
**dusk·i·ness** *n*

**[1]dust** \ˈdəst\ *n*
**1** fine dry powdery particles (as of earth) **:** a fine powder
**2** the powdery remains of bodies once alive
**3** something worthless
**4** the surface of the ground
**dust·less** \-ləs\ *adj*

**[2]dust** *vb*
**1** to make free of dust **:** brush or wipe away dust
**2** to sprinkle with or as if with fine particles
**dust·er** \ˈdəs-tər\ *n*

**[1]dwarf 1:** a dwarf tree, pruned to restrict its growth

**dust·pan** \ˈdəst-ˌpan\ *n*
a pan shaped like a shovel and used for sweepings

**dust storm** *n*
a violent wind carrying dust across a dry region

**dusty** \ˈdəs-tē\ *adj* **dust·i·er**; **dust·i·est**
**1** filled or covered with dust
**2** like dust

**[1]Dutch** \ˈdəch\ *adj*
of or relating to the Netherlands, its people, or the Dutch language

**[2]Dutch** *n*
**1 Dutch** *pl* the people of the Netherlands
**2** the language of the Dutch

**Dutch door** *n*
a door divided so that the lower part can be shut while the upper part remains open

**Dutch treat** *n*
a treat for which each person pays his or her own way

**du·ti·ful** \ˈdüt-i-fəl, ˈdyüt-\ *adj*
having or showing a sense of duty
**du·ti·ful·ly** \-fə-lē\ *adv*
**du·ti·ful·ness** *n*

**du·ty** \ˈdüt-ē, ˈdyüt-\ *n, pl* **duties**
**1** conduct owed to parents and those in authority
**2** the action required by one's position or occupation
**3** something a person feels he or she ought to do
**4** a tax especially on imports into a country **synonyms** see TASK

**DVD** \ˌdē-ˌvē-ˈdē\ *n*
a plastic disk the same size as a compact disc but with a much higher storage capacity that is used to store information (as computer data or a movie) and is read using a laser

**[1]dwarf** \ˈdwȯrf\ *n, pl* **dwarfs** \ˈdwȯrfs\ *also* **dwarves** \ˈdwȯrvz\
**1** ◀ a person, animal, or plant much below normal size
**2** a small legendary being usually pictured as a deformed and ugly person

**[2]dwarf** *vb*
**1** to prevent from growing to natural size **:** STUNT ⟨*dwarf* a tree⟩
**2** to cause to appear smaller

**[3]dwarf** *adj*
of less than the usual size

**dwell** \ˈdwel\ *vb* **dwelt** \ˈdwelt\ *or* **dwelled** \ˈdweld\; **dwell·ing**
**1** to stay for a while
**2** to live in a place **:** RESIDE
**3** to keep the attention directed ⟨*dwelt* on their mistakes⟩
**dwell·er** *n*

**dwell·ing** \ˈdwel-ing\ *n*
RESIDENCE 2, 3

**dwin·dle** \ˈdwin-dəl\ *vb* **dwin·dled**; **dwin·dling**
to make or become less ⟨*dwindling* fuel resources⟩

**[1]dye** \ˈdī\ *n*
a coloring matter ⟨most *dyes* give a permanent color⟩

**[2]dye :** experiment showing how dye colors paper

**[2]dye** *vb* **dyed**; **dye·ing**
▲ to give a new color to ⟨wool is often *dyed* before it is spun into yarn⟩

**dye·stuff** \ˈdī-ˌstəf\ *n*
material used for dyeing

**dying** *present participle of* DIE

**dy·nam·ic** \dī-ˈnam-ik\ *adj*
full of energy **:** ACTIVE, FORCEFUL

**[1]dy·na·mite** \ˈdī-nə-ˌmīt\ *n*
an explosive used in blasting

**[2]dynamite** *vb* **dy·na·mit·ed**; **dy·na·mit·ing**
to blow up with dynamite
**dy·na·mit·er** *n*

**dy·na·mo** \ˈdī-nə-ˌmō\ *n, pl* **dy·na·mos**
a machine for producing electric current

**dy·nas·ty** \ˈdī-nə-stē\ *n, pl* **dy·nas·ties**
a series of rulers of the same family

**dys·en·tery** \ˈdis-n-ˌter-ē\ *n*
a disease in which much watery material mixed with mucus and blood is passed from the bowels

**dys·lex·ia** \dis-ˈlek-sē-ə\ *n*
a learning disability in which one usually has a problem in reading, spelling, and writing

# Ee

**The sounds of E:** The letter **E** is used mainly for two vowel sounds in English.

In some words, **E** sounds like its own name. This sound is often called "**long E**." Examples are **evil**, **equal**, and **me**. **E** always makes this sound when it is doubled. Some examples with double **E** are **eel**, **tree**, **feet**, and **freedom**.

In most words, **E** has the sound called "**short E**." This sound is found in words such as **end**, **felt**, **fellow**, and **predator**.

These two sounds are also made by **E** and **A** together. Examples of the "**long E**" sound with **EA** are the words **east**, **feature**, and **steam**. Examples of the "**short E**" sound with **EA** are **thread** and **treasure**.

---

**e** \ˈē\ *n, pl* **e's** *or* **es** \ˈēz\ *often cap*
**1** the fifth letter of the English alphabet
**2** a grade that shows a student's work is failing

**[1]each** \ˈēch\ *adj*
being one of two or more individuals

**[2]each** *pron*
each one

**[3]each** *adv*
to or for each : APIECE

**each other** *pron*
each of two or more in a shared action or relationship ⟨greeted *each other*⟩

**ea·ger** \ˈē-gər\ *adj*
desiring very much : IMPATIENT
**ea·ger·ly** *adv*
**ea·ger·ness** *n*

---

**Synonyms** EAGER, ANXIOUS, and KEEN mean having or showing a strong desire or interest. EAGER suggests much enthusiasm and often impatience ⟨*eager* passengers waiting for the tour to start⟩. ANXIOUS suggests fear of failure or disappointment ⟨*anxious* to learn who won⟩. KEEN suggests great interest and readiness to act ⟨the new scouts are *keen* and willing to learn⟩.

---

**ea·gle** \ˈē-gəl\ *n*
▼ any of several large birds of prey noted for keen sight and powerful flight

**ea·glet** \ˈē-glət\ *n*
a young eagle

**-ean** see -AN

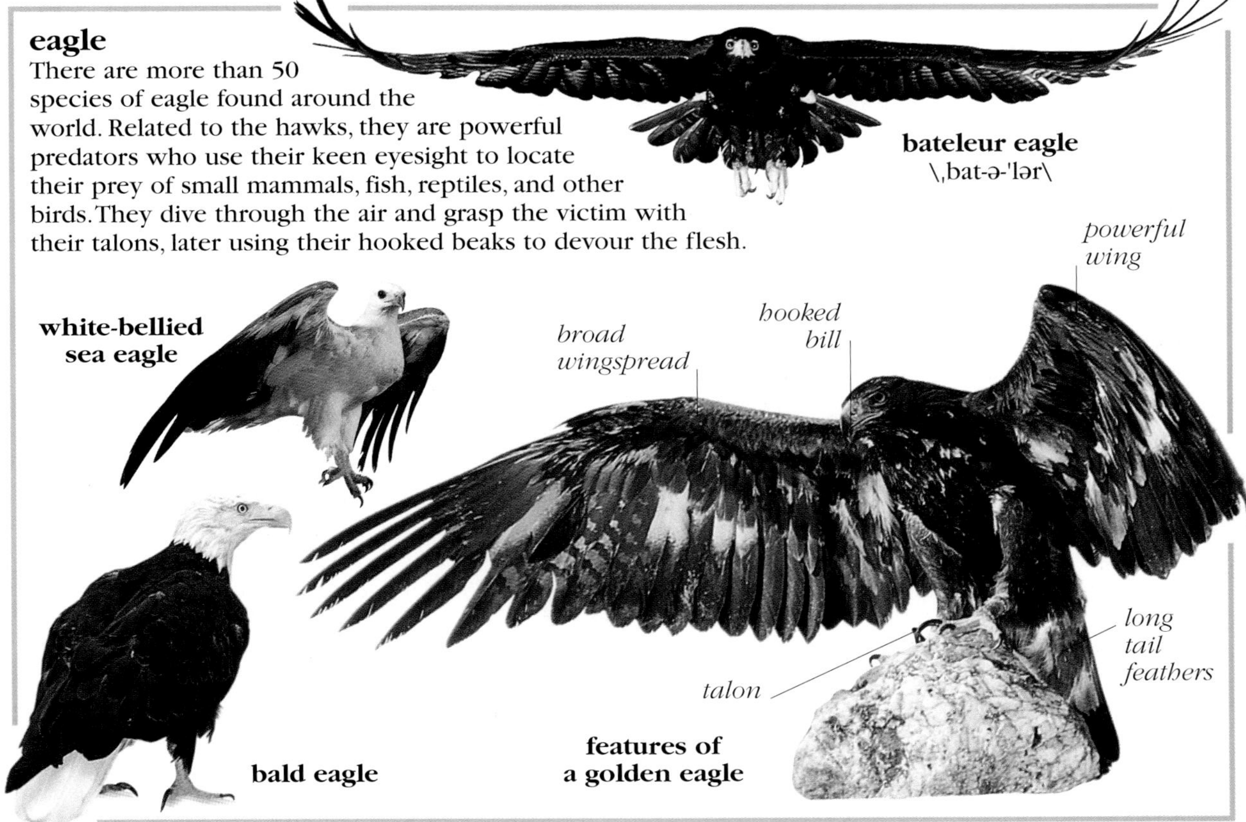

**eagle**
There are more than 50 species of eagle found around the world. Related to the hawks, they are powerful predators who use their keen eyesight to locate their prey of small mammals, fish, reptiles, and other birds. They dive through the air and grasp the victim with their talons, later using their hooked beaks to devour the flesh.

**[1]ear** \'ir\ *n*
**1** ▶ the organ of hearing
**2** the sense of hearing ⟨a good *ear* for music⟩
**3** willing or sympathetic attention ⟨give *ear* to a request⟩
**4** something like an ear in shape or position
**eared** \'iərd\ *adj*

**[2]ear** *n*
the seed-bearing head of a cereal grass

**ear·ache** \'ir-,āk\ *n*
an ache or pain in the ear

**ear·drum** \'ir-,drəm\ *n*
the membrane that separates the outer and middle parts of the ear and vibrates when sound waves strike it

**earl** \'ərl\ *n*
a member of the British nobility ranking below a marquess and above a viscount

**[1]ear·ly** \'ər-lē\ *adv* **ear·li·er**; **ear·li·est**
**1** at or near the beginning of a period of time or a series
**2** before the usual time

**[2]early** *adj* **ear·li·er**; **ear·li·est**
occurring near the beginning or before the usual time

**ear·muff** \'ir-,məf\ *n*
one of a pair of coverings joined by a flexible band and worn to protect the ears from cold or noise

**[1]ear 1**
The ear is used for hearing and balance. The outermost part of the ear receives sound waves which travel through the auditory canal and cause the eardrum and parts of the middle ear to vibrate. The vibrations reach the inner ear where they convert into nerve impulses to the brain.

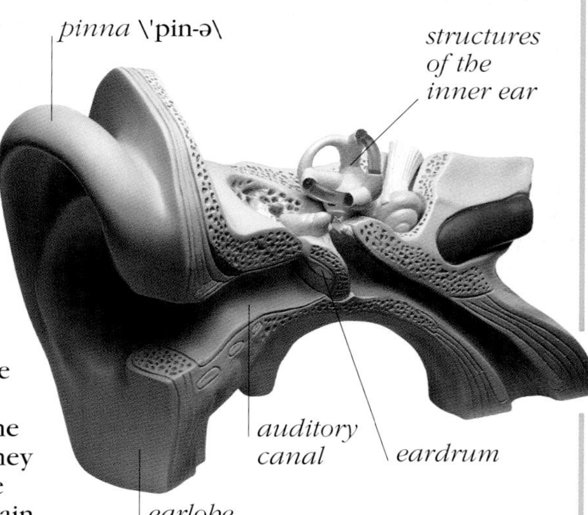


**model of the human ear in cross section**

**earn** \'ərn\ *vb*
**1** to get for services given ⟨*earn* a good wage⟩
**2** to deserve especially as a reward or punishment **synonyms** see DESERVE

**ear·nest** \'ər-nəst\ *adj*
not light or playful **synonyms** see SERIOUS
**ear·nest·ly** *adv*
**ear·nest·ness** *n*

**earn·ings** \'ər-ningz\ *n pl*
money received as wages or gained as profit

**ear·phone** \'ir-,fōn\ *n*
a device that converts electrical energy into sound and is worn over the opening of the ear or inserted into it

**ear·ring** \'ir-,ring\ *n*
an ornament worn on the ear lobe

**ear·shot** \'ir-,shät\ *n*
the range within which an unaided human voice can be heard

**earth** \'ərth\ *n*
**1** [2]SOIL 1
**2** areas of land as distinguished from the sea and the air
**3** ◀ *often cap* the planet that we live on

**earth·en** \'ər-thən\ *adj*
made of earth

**earth·en·ware** \'ər-thən-,waər, -,weər\ *n*
▶ things (as dishes) made of baked clay

**earthenware:** an earthenware crock

**earth 3**
The earth is the fifth largest planet in the solar system, and the only planet known to sustain life. It is made up of four main layers: the inner core, outer core, mantle, and crust, and is surrounded by the atmosphere.

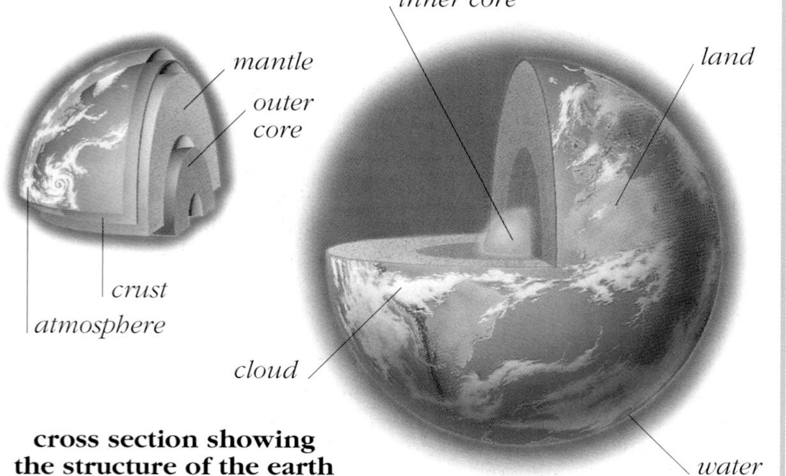


**cross section showing the structure of the earth**

**earth·ly** \'ərth-lē\ *adj*
**1** having to do with or belonging to the earth : not heavenly ⟨*earthly* joys⟩
**2** IMAGINABLE, POSSIBLE ⟨of no *earthly* use⟩

**earth·quake** \'ərth-ˌkwāk\ *n*
a shaking or trembling of a portion of the earth

**earth·worm** \'ərth-ˌwərm\ *n*
▼ a worm that has a long body made up of similar segments and lives in damp soil

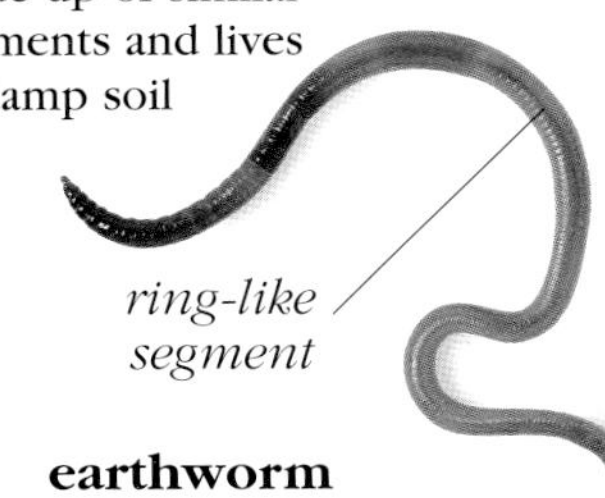


**earthworm**

**earthy** \'ər-thē\ *adj* **earth·i·er**; **earth·i·est**
**1** consisting of or like earth
**2** PRACTICAL 4
**3** not polite : CRUDE ⟨*earthy* humor⟩

**ear·wig** \'ir-ˌwig\ *n*
▼ an insect with long slender feelers and a large forcepslike organ at the end of its abdomen

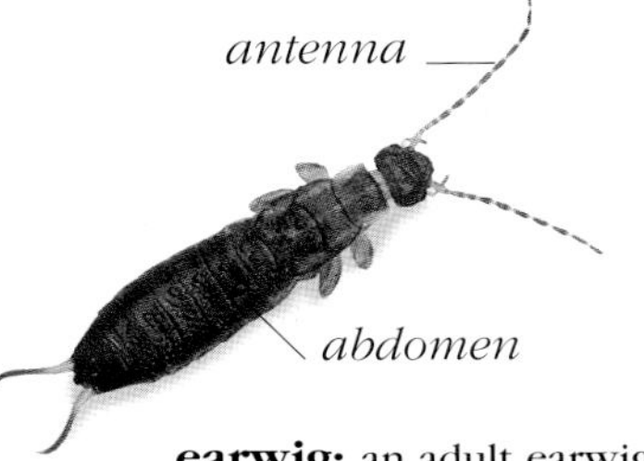


**earwig:** an adult earwig

**Word History** The modern English word *earwig* came from an Old English word that meant "earwig." This word was a compound of two Old English words. The first meant "ear." The second meant "insect." The earwig probably owes its name to an old belief that these insects crawl into human ears.

[1]**ease** \'ēz\ *n*
**1** freedom from pain or trouble : comfort of body or mind ⟨a life of *ease*⟩
**2** freedom from any feeling of difficulty or embarrassment

[2]**ease** *vb* **eased**; **eas·ing**
**1** to free from discomfort or worry : RELIEVE
**2** to make less tight : LOOSEN
**3** to move very carefully

**ea·sel** \'ē-zəl\ *n*
▶ a frame for holding a flat surface in an upright position

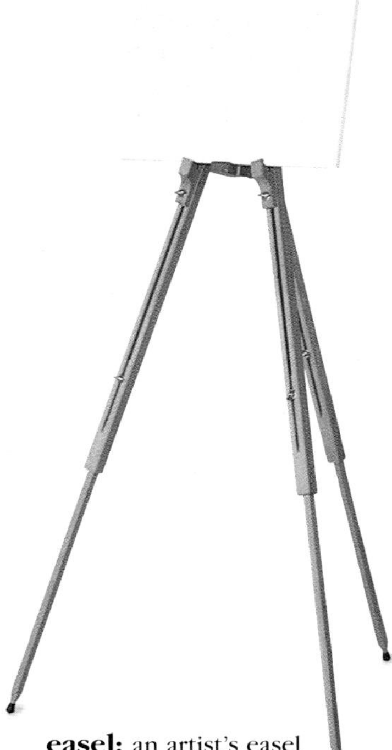

**easel:** an artist's easel

**Word History** The English word *easel* came from a Dutch word. The basic meaning of this Dutch word was "ass" or "donkey." Like a beast of burden, an easel is used to hold things. This must have been why the Dutch word that meant "ass" developed the meaning "easel."

**eas·i·ly** \'ē-zə-lē, 'ēz-lē\ *adv*
**1** in an easy manner : without difficulty ⟨won the race *easily*⟩
**2** without doubt or question ⟨*easily* the best person for the job⟩

[1]**east** \'ēst\ *adv*
to or toward the east

[2]**east** *adj*
placed toward, facing, or coming from the east

[3]**east** *n*
**1** the direction of sunrise : the compass point opposite to west
**2** *cap* regions or countries east of a certain point

**Eas·ter** \'ē-stər\ *n*
a Christian church festival observed in memory of the Resurrection

**Easter lily** *n*
▶ a white garden lily that blooms in spring

**Easter lily**

**east·er·ly** \'ē-stər-lē\ *adj or adv*
**1** toward the east
**2** from the east ⟨an *easterly* wind⟩

**east·ern** \'ē-stərn\ *adj*
**1** *often cap* of, relating to, or like that of the East
**2** lying toward or coming from the east

**east·ward** \'ēs-twərd\ *adv or adj*
toward the east

**easy** \'ē-zē\ *adj* **eas·i·er**; **eas·i·est**
**1** not hard to do or get : not difficult ⟨an *easy* lesson⟩
**2** not hard to please ⟨an *easy* teacher⟩
**3** free from pain, trouble, or worry ⟨an *easy* mind⟩
**4** COMFORTABLE ⟨an *easy* chair⟩
**5** showing ease : NATURAL ⟨an *easy* manner⟩

**eat** \'ēt\ *vb* **ate** \'āt\; **eat·en** \'ēt-n\; **eat·ing**
**1** to chew and swallow food
**2** to take a meal or meals ⟨*eat* at home⟩
**3** to destroy as if by eating : CORRODE
**eat·er** *n*

**eat·able** \'ēt-ə-bəl\ *adj*
fit to be eaten

**eaves** \'ēvz\ *n sing or pl*
the lower edge of a roof that sticks out past the wall

A B C D E F G H I J K L M N O P Q R S T U V W X Y Z

**eaves·drop** \'ēvz-,dräp\ *vb* **eaves·dropped**; **eaves·drop·ping** to listen secretly to private conversation

**Word History** An early English noun *eavesdrop* was used to refer to the water that falls in drops from the eaves of a house. The ground on which water fell from the eaves was called *eavesdrop*, too. A person might stand on this ground listening to what was going on inside a house. Such a person was called an *eavesdropper*. The verb *eavesdrop* probably came from this word.

**[1]ebb** \'eb\ *n*
**1** the flowing out of the tide
**2** a passing from a high to a low point or the time of this

**[2]ebb** *vb*
**1** to flow out or away : RECEDE
**2** [1]DECLINE 2, WEAKEN

**[1]eb·o·ny** \'eb-ə-nē\ *n, pl* **eb·o·nies** a hard heavy wood that wears well and comes from tropical trees related to the persimmon

**[2]ebony** *adj*
**1** made of or like ebony
**2** [1]BLACK 1

**[1]ec·cen·tric** \ik-'sen-trik, ek-\ *adj*
**1** acting or thinking in a strange way ⟨an *eccentric* person⟩
**2** not of the usual or normal kind ⟨*eccentric* behavior⟩

**[2]eccentric** *n* an eccentric person

**ec·cle·si·as·ti·cal** \i-,klē-zē-'as-ti-kəl\ *adj* of or relating to the church or its affairs

**[1]echo** \'ek-ō\ *n, pl* **ech·oes** the repeating of a sound caused by the reflection of sound waves

**[2]echo** *vb* **ech·oed**; **echo·ing**
**1** to send back or repeat a sound
**2** to say what someone else has already said

**éclair** \ā-'klaər, ā-'kleər\ *n* ► an oblong pastry with whipped cream or custard filling

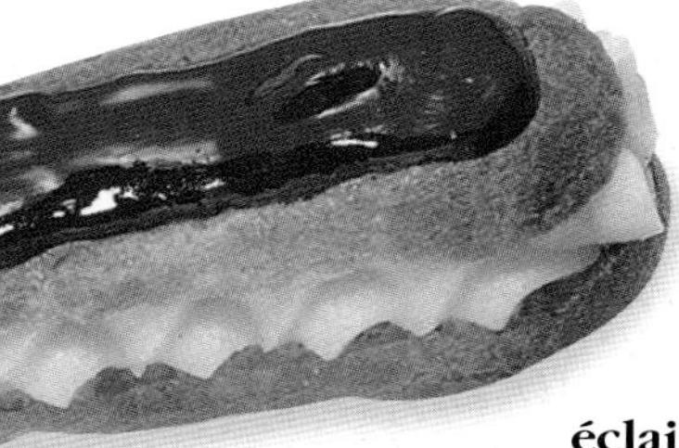

**éclair:** a chocolate éclair

**Word History** The English word *éclair* came from a French word, whose first meaning was "lightning" or "a flash of lightning." We are not sure why the éclair was named after lightning. Some say it was because it is so light a pastry. Others say that the éclair got its name because it is likely to be eaten in a flash.

**[1]eclipse** \i-'klips\ *n*
**1** ▼ a complete or partial hiding of the sun (**solar eclipse**) caused by the moon's passing between the sun and the earth
**2** a darkening of the moon (**lunar eclipse**) caused by the moon's entering the shadow of the earth
**3** the hiding of any celestial body by another
**4** a falling into disgrace or out of use or public favor

**[1]eclipse 1:** a total eclipse of the sun

**[2]eclipse** *vb* **eclipsed**; **eclips·ing**
**1** to cause an eclipse of
**2** to be or do much better than : OUTSHINE

**eco·log·i·cal** \,ē-kə-'läj-i-kəl, ,ek-ə-\ *adj* of or relating to the science of ecology or the ecology of a particular environment and the living things in it ⟨doing *ecological* damage⟩

**ecol·o·gist** \i-'käl-ə-jəst\ *n* a specialist in ecology

**ecol·o·gy** \i-'käl-ə-jē\ *n*
**1** a branch of science dealing with the relation of living things to their environment
**2** the pattern of relations between living things and their environment ⟨the *ecology* of a rain forest⟩

**eco·nom·ic** \,ek-ə-'näm-ik, ,ē-kə-\ *adj*
**1** of or relating to economics
**2** of, relating to, or based on the making, selling, and using of goods and services

**eco·nom·i·cal** \,ek-ə-'näm-i-kəl, ,ē-kə-\ *adj*
**1** using what one has carefully and without waste : FRUGAL
**2** operating with little waste or at a saving ⟨an *economical* car⟩

**eco·nom·i·cal·ly** *adv*

**Synonyms** ECONOMICAL, THRIFTY, and SPARING mean careful in the use of money or goods. ECONOMICAL suggests that one makes the most of what one has, using things in the best possible way and not wasting anything ⟨an *economical* cook who feeds us well⟩. THRIFTY suggests that one manages things well and is industrious ⟨the *thrifty* shopkeeper was able to save much money⟩. SPARING suggests that one spends or uses as little as possible ⟨very *sparing* in giving money to charity⟩.

**eco·nom·ics** \,ek-ə-'näm-iks, ,ē-kə-\ *n* the science that studies and explains facts about the making, selling, and using of goods and services

**econ·o·mize** \i-'kän-ə-,mīz\ *vb* **econ·o·mized**; **econ·o·miz·ing**
**1** to practice economy : be thrifty
**2** to reduce expenses : SAVE

**econ·o·my** \i-'kän-ə-mē\ *n, pl* **econ·o·mies**
**1** the careful use of money and goods : THRIFT

2 the way an economic system (as of a country or a period in history) is organized

**eco·sys·tem** \'ē-kō-ˌsis-təm, 'ek-ō-\ *n*
▶ the whole group of living and nonliving things that make up an environment and affect each other

**ec·sta·sy** \'ek-stə-sē\ *n, pl* **ec·sta·sies**
very great happiness : extreme delight

**ec·stat·ic** \ek-'stat-ik\ *adj*
of, relating to, or showing ecstasy

**ec·ze·ma** \ig-'zē-mə, 'eg-zə-mə, 'ek-sə-mə\ *n*
a disease in which the skin is red, itchy, and marred by scaly or crusted spots

**[1]-ed** \d *after a vowel or* b, g, j, l, m, n, ng, r, th, v, z, zh; əd, id *after* d, t; t *after other sounds*\ *vb suffix or adj suffix*
**1** used to form the past participle of verbs ⟨end*ed*⟩ ⟨fad*ed*⟩ ⟨tri*ed*⟩ ⟨patt*ed*⟩
**2** having : showing ⟨cultur*ed*⟩
**3** having the characteristics of ⟨dogg*ed*⟩

**[2]-ed** *vb suffix*
used to form the past tense of verbs ⟨judg*ed*⟩ ⟨deni*ed*⟩ ⟨dropp*ed*⟩

**[1]ed·dy** \'ed-ē\ *n, pl* **eddies**
a current of air or water running against the main current or in a circle

**[2]eddy** *vb* **ed·died**; **ed·dy·ing**
to move in an eddy

**[1]edge** \'ej\ *n*
**1** the cutting side of a blade
**2** the line where a surface ends : MARGIN, BORDER **synonyms** see BORDER
**edged** \'ejd\ *adj*
**on edge** NERVOUS 3, TENSE

**[2]edge** *vb* **edged**; **edg·ing**
**1** to give an edge to
**2** to move slowly and little by little

**edge·ways** \'ej-ˌwāz\ *or* **edge·wise** \-ˌwīz\ *adv*
with the edge in front : SIDEWAYS

**ed·i·ble** \'ed-ə-bəl\ *adj*
fit or safe to eat

**edict** \'ē-ˌdikt\ *n*
a command or law given or made by an authority (as a ruler)

**ed·i·fice** \'ed-ə-fəs\ *n*
a large or impressive building (as a church)

## ecosystem

A typical ecosystem includes sunlight, water, plants, animals, and microorganisms. Sunlight and water help plants to grow, which offer food and protection to the animals. These feed on the plants and hunt other creatures, while the microorganisms help to break down decaying material.

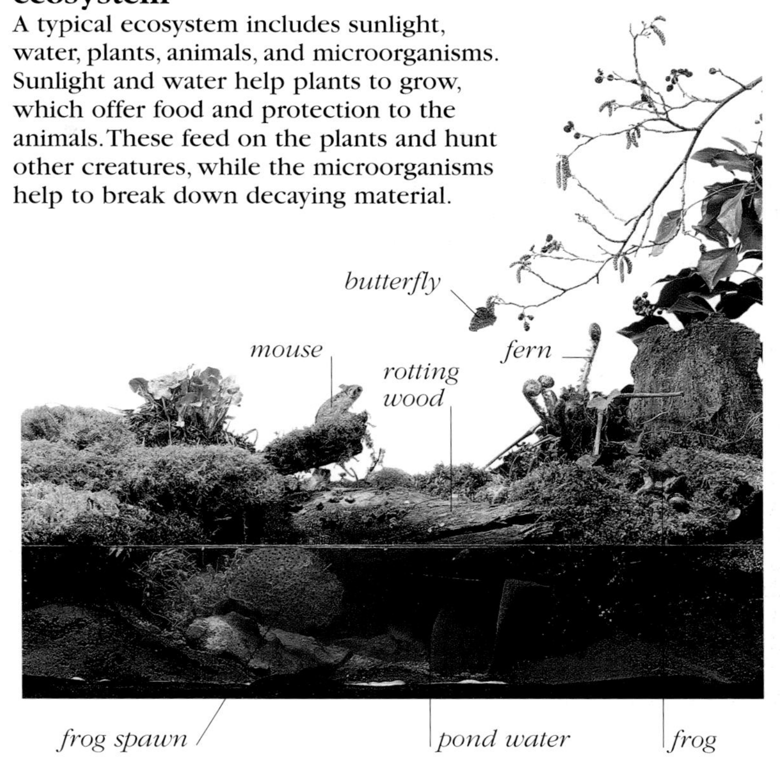


**a pond ecosystem**

**ed·it** \'ed-ət\ *vb*
**1** to correct, revise, and get ready for publication : collect and arrange material to be printed ⟨*edit* a book of poems⟩
**2** to be in charge of the publication of something (as an encyclopedia or a newspaper) that is the work of many writers

**edi·tion** \i-'dish-ən\ *n*
**1** the form in which a book is published ⟨an illustrated *edition*⟩
**2** the whole number of copies of a book, magazine, or newspaper published at one time
**3** one of several issues of a newspaper for a single day ⟨the evening *edition*⟩

**ed·i·tor** \'ed-ət-ər\ *n*
**1** a person who edits
**2** a person who writes editorials

**[1]ed·i·to·ri·al** \ˌed-ə-'tōr-ē-əl\ *adj*
**1** of or relating to an editor ⟨an *editorial* office⟩
**2** being or like an editorial ⟨an *editorial* statement⟩

**[2]editorial** *n*
a newspaper or magazine article that gives the opinions of its editors or publishers

**ed·u·cate** \'ej-ə-ˌkāt\ *vb* **ed·u·cat·ed**; **ed·u·cat·ing**
**1** to provide schooling for
**2** to develop the mind and morals of especially by formal instruction : TRAIN
**ed·u·ca·tor** \'ej-ə-ˌkāt-ər\ *n*

**ed·u·ca·tion** \ˌej-ə-'kā-shən\ *n*
**1** the act or process of educating or of being educated
**2** knowledge, skill, and development gained from study or training
**3** the study or science of the methods and problems of teaching

**ed·u·ca·tion·al** \ˌej-ə-'kā-shən-l\ *adj*
**1** having to do with education
**2** offering information or something of value in learning ⟨an *educational* film⟩
**ed·u·ca·tion·al·ly** *adv*

a b c d e f g h i j k l m n o p q r s t u v w x y z

**[1]-ee** \'ē, ˌē\ *n suffix*
**1** person who receives or benefits from a specified thing or action ⟨appoint*ee*⟩
**2** person who does a specified thing

**[2]-ee** *n suffix*
**1** a certain and especially a small kind of ⟨boot*ee*⟩
**2** one like or suggesting ⟨goat*ee*⟩

**eel** \'ēl\ *n*
▶ a long snakelike fish with a smooth slimy skin

**e'en** \ēn\ *adv*
EVEN

eel

**-eer** \'ir\ *n suffix*
person who is concerned with or conducts or produces as a profession ⟨auction*eer*⟩

**e'er** \eər, aər\ *adv*
EVER

**ee·rie** *also* **ee·ry** \'ir-ē\ *adj*
**ee·ri·er**; **ee·ri·est**
causing fear and uneasiness : STRANGE

**ef·face** \i-'fās\ *vb* **ef·faced**; **ef·fac·ing**
to erase or blot out completely

**[1]ef·fect** \i-'fekt\ *n*
**1** an event, condition, or state of affairs that is produced by a cause
**2** EXECUTION 1, OPERATION ⟨the law went into *effect* today⟩
**3** REALITY 1, FACT ⟨the hint was in *effect* an order⟩
**4** the act of making a certain impression ⟨tears that were only for *effect*⟩
**5** [1]INFLUENCE 1 ⟨the *effect* of climate on growth⟩
**6 effects** *pl* personal property or possessions ⟨household *effects*⟩

**[2]effect** *vb*
BRING ABOUT

**ef·fec·tive** \i-'fek-tiv\ *adj*
**1** producing or able to produce a desired effect ⟨*effective* measures to reduce traffic accidents⟩
**2** IMPRESSIVE ⟨an *effective* speech⟩
**3** being in actual operation ⟨the law will become *effective* next year⟩
**ef·fec·tive·ly** *adv*
**ef·fec·tive·ness** *n*

**ef·fec·tu·al** \i-'fek-chə-wəl\ *adj*
producing or able to produce a desired effect

**ef·fi·ca·cy** \'ef-i-kə-sē\ *n*, *pl* **ef·fi·ca·cies**
power to produce effects : efficient action

**ef·fi·cien·cy** \i-'fish-ən-sē\ *n*, *pl* **ef·fi·cien·cies**
the quality or degree of being efficient

**ef·fi·cient** \i-'fish-ənt\ *adj*
capable of bringing about a desired result with little waste (as of time or energy)
**ef·fi·cient·ly** *adv*

**ef·fort** \'ef-ərt\ *n*
**1** hard work of mind or body : EXERTION
**2** a serious attempt : TRY

**ef·fort·less** \'ef-ərt-ləs\ *adj*
showing or needing little or no effort
**ef·fort·less·ly** *adv*

**[1]egg** \'eg, 'āg\ *vb*
INCITE, URGE ⟨we *egged* them on to fight it out⟩

**[2]egg** *n*
**1** ▶ a shelled oval or rounded body by which some animals (as birds or snakes) reproduce and from which the young hatches out
**2** an egg cell usually together with its protective coverings

**egg cell** *n*
a cell produced by an ovary that when fertilized by a sperm cell can develop into an embryo and finally a new mature being

**egg·nog** \'eg-ˌnäg, 'āg-\ *n*
a drink made of eggs beaten with sugar, milk or cream, and often alcoholic liquor

**egg·plant** \'eg-ˌplant, 'āg-\ *n*
▼ an oval vegetable with a usually glossy purplish skin and white flesh that is the fruit of a plant related to the tomato

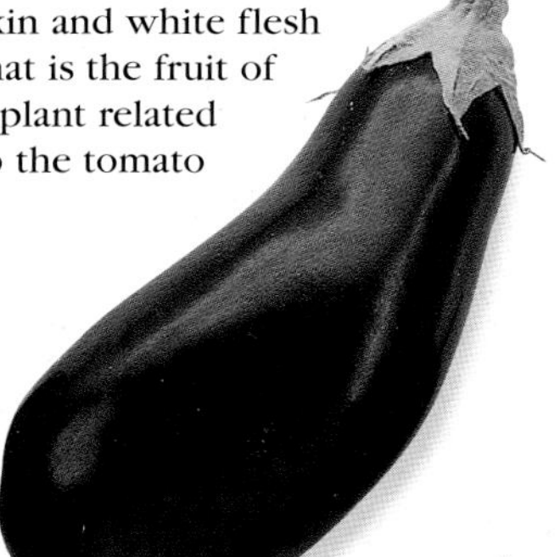

eggplant

**egg·shell** \'eg-ˌshel, 'āg-\ *n*
the shell of an egg

**egret** \'ē-grət, i-'gret\ *n*
any of various herons that have long plumes during the breeding season

**[1]Egyp·tian** \i-'jip-shən\ *adj*
of or relating to Egypt or the Egyptians

**[2]Egyptian** *n*
**1** a person who is born or lives in Egypt
**2** the language of the ancient Egyptians

**ei·der** \'ī-dər\ *n*
▼ a large northern sea duck that is mostly white above and black below and has very soft down

eider

**ei·der·down** \'ī-dər-ˌdau̇n\ *n*
**1** the down of the eider used for filling quilts and pillows
**2** a quilt filled with down

**[1]eight** \'āt\ *adj*
being one more than seven

**[2]eight** *n*
one more than seven : two times four : 8

**[1]eigh·teen** \ā-'tēn, āt-\ *adj*
being one more than seventeen

**[2]eighteen** *n*
one more than seventeen : three times six : 18

**[1]eigh·teenth** \ā-'tēnth, āt-\ *adj*
coming right after seventeenth

**[2]eighteenth** *n*
number eighteen in a series

**[1]eighth** \'ātth\ *adj*
coming right after seventh

**[2]eighth** *n*
**1** number eight in a series
**2** one of eight equal parts

**[1]eight·i·eth** \'āt-ē-əth\ *adj*
coming right after seventy-ninth

**[2]eightieth** *n*
number eighty in a series

### [2]egg 1

While the eggs of most mammals, including humans, develop within the mother's body, the eggs of other animal groups — such as reptiles, birds, and insects — develop externally, protected by a hard or soft covering. The embryo inside a bird's egg is surrounded by fluid enclosed in a membrane, and is nourished from a supply of yolk. Small pores in the egg's shell allow oxygen to reach the embryo.

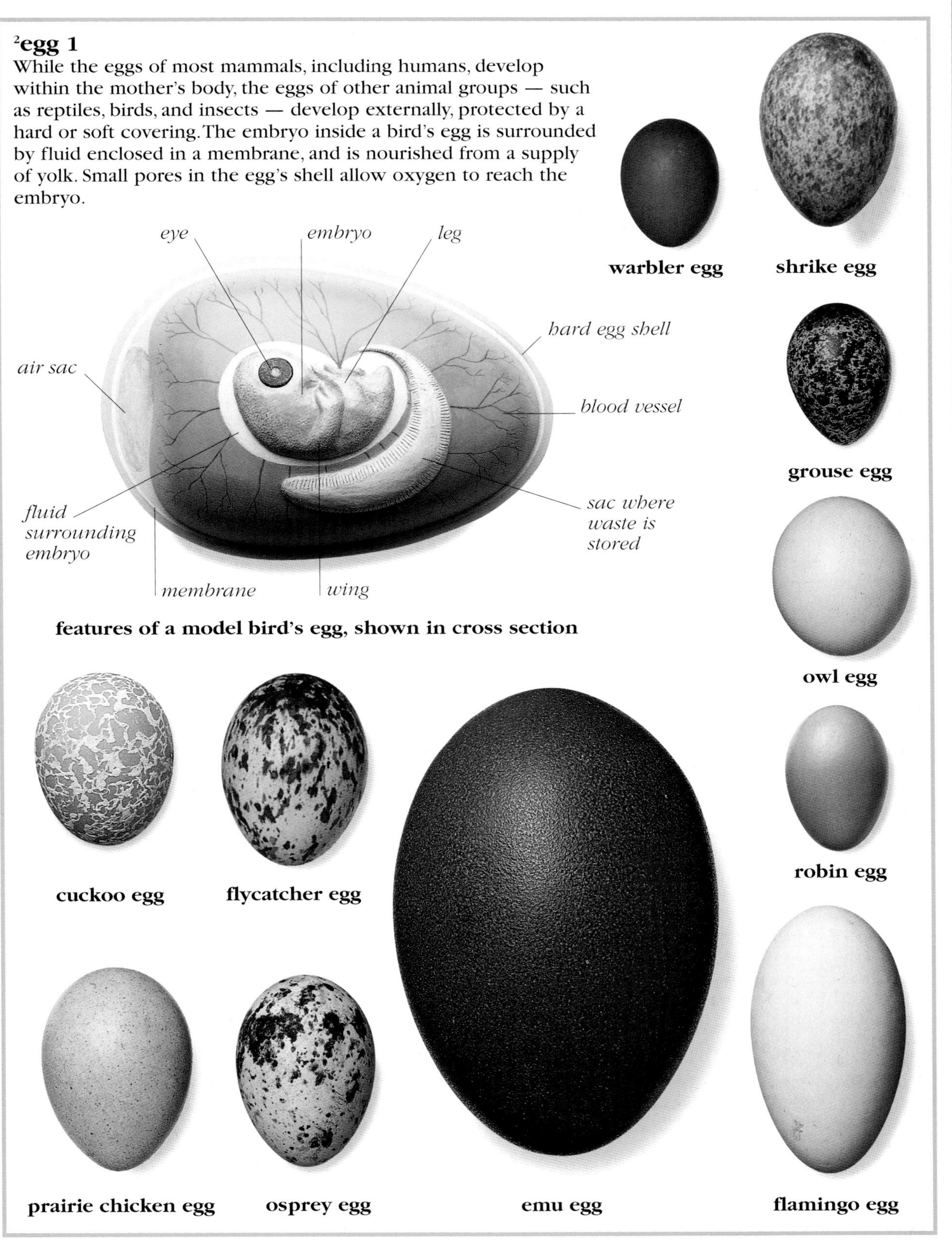


**features of a model bird's egg, shown in cross section**

**warbler egg** **shrike egg** **grouse egg** **owl egg** **robin egg** **cuckoo egg** **flycatcher egg** **prairie chicken egg** **osprey egg** **emu egg** **flamingo egg**

## eighty

A B C D E F G H I J K L M N O P Q R S T U V W X Y Z

**[1]eighty** \'āt-ē\ *adj*
being eight times ten

**[2]eighty** *n*
eight times ten : 80

**[1]ei·ther** \'ē-t͟hər, 'ī-\ *adj*
**1** [1]EACH ⟨flowers on *either* side of the road⟩
**2** being one or the other ⟨take *either* road⟩

**[2]either** *pron*
the one or the other

**[3]either** *conj*
used before words or phrases the last of which follows "or" to show that they are choices or possibilities ⟨you can *either* go or stay⟩

**ejac·u·late** \i-'jak-yə-,lāt\ *vb* **ejac·u·lat·ed**; **ejac·u·lat·ing**
EXCLAIM

**eject** \i-'jekt\ *vb*
to drive out or throw off or out ⟨was *ejected* from the meeting⟩

**eke out** \'ēk-'au̇t\ *vb* **eked out**; **ek·ing out**
**1** to add to bit by bit ⟨*eked out* a pension with odd jobs⟩
**2** to get with great effort ⟨*eke out* a living⟩

**[1]elab·o·rate** \i-'lab-ə-rət, -'lab-rət\ *adj*
worked out with great care or with much detail ⟨an *elaborate* plot⟩
**elab·o·rate·ly** *adv*

**[2]elab·o·rate** \i-'lab-ə-,rāt\ *vb* **elab·o·rat·ed**; **elab·o·rat·ing**
to work out in detail

**elapse** \i-'laps\ *vb* **elapsed**; **elaps·ing**
to slip past : go by ⟨nearly a year *elapsed*⟩

**[1]elas·tic** \i-'las-tik\ *adj*
capable of returning to original shape or size after being stretched, pressed, or squeezed together

**[2]elastic** *n*
**1** an elastic fabric made of yarns containing rubber
**2** a rubber band

**elas·tic·i·ty** \i-,las-'tis-ət-ē\ *n*
the quality or state of being elastic

**elate** \i-'lāt\ *vb* **elat·ed**; **elat·ing**
to fill with joy or pride

**ela·tion** \i-'lā-shən\ *n*
the quality or state of being elated

**[1]el·bow** \'el-,bō\ *n*
**1** ▶ the joint of the arm or of the same part of an animal's forelimb
**2** a part (as of a pipe) bent like an elbow

**[2]elbow** *vb*
to push or force a way through with the elbows

**[1]el·der** \'el-dər\ *n*
a shrub or small tree related to the honeysuckles that has flat clusters of white flowers followed by fruits like berries

**[2]elder** *adj*
being older than another person ⟨an *elder* cousin⟩

**[3]elder** *n*
**1** one who is older
**2** a person having authority because of age and experience ⟨*elders* of the village⟩
**3** an official in some churches

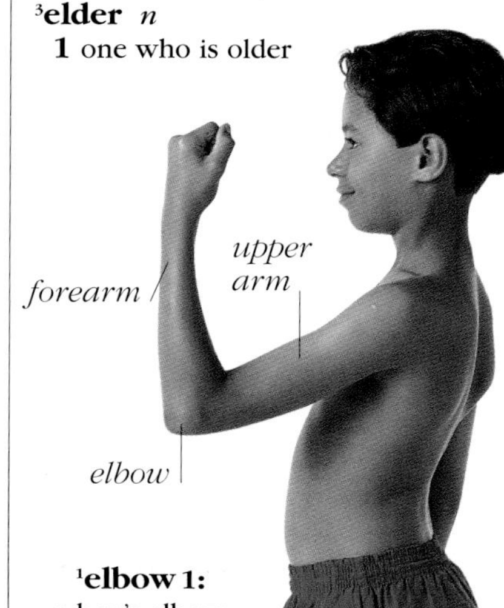


**[1]elbow 1:** a boy's elbow

**el·der·ber·ry** \'el-dər-,ber-ē\ *n*, *pl* **el·der·ber·ries**
the juicy black or red fruit of the elder

**el·der·ly** \'el-dər-lē\ *adj*
somewhat old : past middle age

**el·dest** \'el-dəst\ *adj*
being oldest of a group of people (as siblings) ⟨the *eldest* child⟩

**[1]elect** \i-'lekt\ *adj*
chosen for office but not yet holding office ⟨the president-*elect*⟩

**[2]elect** *vb*
**1** to select by vote ⟨*elect* a senator⟩
**2** to make a choice ⟨the home team *elected* to kick off⟩
**synonyms** see CHOOSE

**elec·tion** \i-'lek-shən\ *n*
an electing or being elected especially by vote

**elec·tive** \i-'lek-tiv\ *adj*
chosen or filled by election

**elec·tor** \i-'lek-tər\ *n*
a person qualified or having the right to vote in an election

**electr-** *or* **electro-** *prefix*
**1** electricity
**2** electric

## electrolysis

In electrolysis, an electric current passed through a liquid solution causes chemical changes to substances in the solution. In the experiment shown here, copper is drawn from a copper sulfate solution to coat the surface of a key.

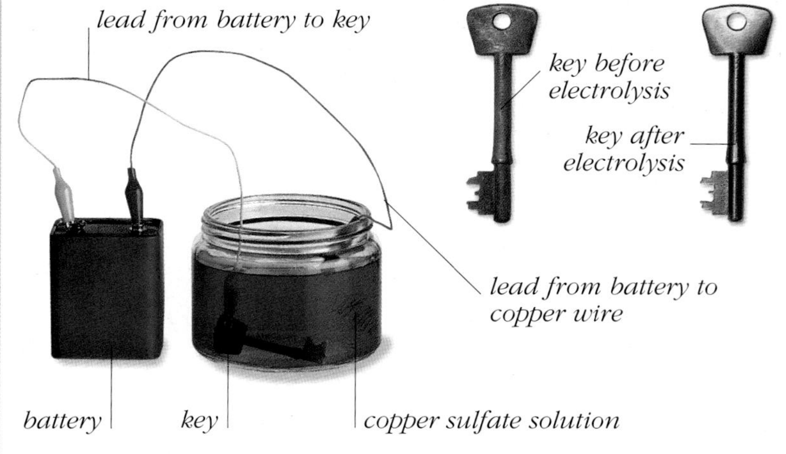


**experiment showing the effect of electrolysis**

3 electric and
4 electrically

**elec·tric** \i-'lek-trik\ *or* **elec·tri·cal** \-tri-kəl\ *adj*
1 of or relating to electricity or its use ⟨an *electric* current⟩ ⟨*electrical* engineering⟩
2 heated, moved, made, or run by electricity ⟨an *electric* iron⟩ ⟨an *electric* locomotive⟩
3 having a thrilling effect
4 giving off sounds through an electronic amplifier ⟨an *electric* guitar⟩
**elec·tri·cal·ly** *adv*

**Word History** A man in ancient Greece found that if he rubbed a piece of amber it would attract light things like straws and small feathers. In other words, the rubbing gave the amber an electric charge. We owe the English word *electric* to this property of amber. Our word came from a Greek word that meant "amber."

**elec·tri·cian** \i-,lek-'trish-ən\ *n*
a person who installs, operates, or repairs electrical equipment

**elec·tric·i·ty** \i-,lek-'tris-ət-ē\ *n*
1 ▼ an important form of energy that is found in nature but that can be artificially produced by rubbing together two unlike things (as glass and silk), by the action of chemicals, or by means of a generator
2 electric current

**electricity 1:** rubbing a balloon on hair creates static electricity

**elec·tri·fy** \i-'lek-trə-,fī\ *vb*
**elec·tri·fied**; **elec·tri·fy·ing**
1 to charge with electricity
2 to equip for use of electric power
3 to supply with electric power
4 to excite suddenly and sharply : THRILL

**elec·tro·cute** \i-'lek-trə-,kyüt\ *vb*
**elec·tro·cut·ed**; **elec·tro·cut·ing**
to kill by an electric shock

**elec·trode** \i-'lek-,trōd\ *n*
a conductor (as a metal or carbon) used to make electrical contact with a part of an electrical circuit that is not metallic

**elec·trol·y·sis** \i-,lek-'träl-ə-səs\ *n*
◀ the producing of chemical changes by passage of an electric current through a liquid

**elec·tro·lyte** \i-'lek-trə-,līt\ *n*
a substance (as an acid or salt) that when dissolved (as in water) conducts an electric current

**elec·tro·lyt·ic** \i-,lek-trə-'lit-ik\ *adj*
of or relating to electrolysis or an electrolyte

**elec·tro·mag·net** \i-,lek-trō-'mag-nət\ *n*
▼ a piece of iron encircled by a coil of wire through which an electric current is passed to magnetize the iron

**elec·tro·mag·net·ic** \i-,lek-trō-mag-,net-ik\ *adj*
of or relating to a magnetic field produced by an electric current

**electromagnetic wave** *n*
a wave (as a radio wave or wave of light) that travels at the speed of light and consists of a combined electric and magnetic effect

### electromagnet

A simple electromagnet is made by passing an electric current from a battery through a copper wire wrapped around an iron bar. An electromagnetic field forms around the iron bar, which then attracts metal objects, such as paper clips. If the battery is disconnected, the electromagnetic field is switched off, and the paper clips drop.

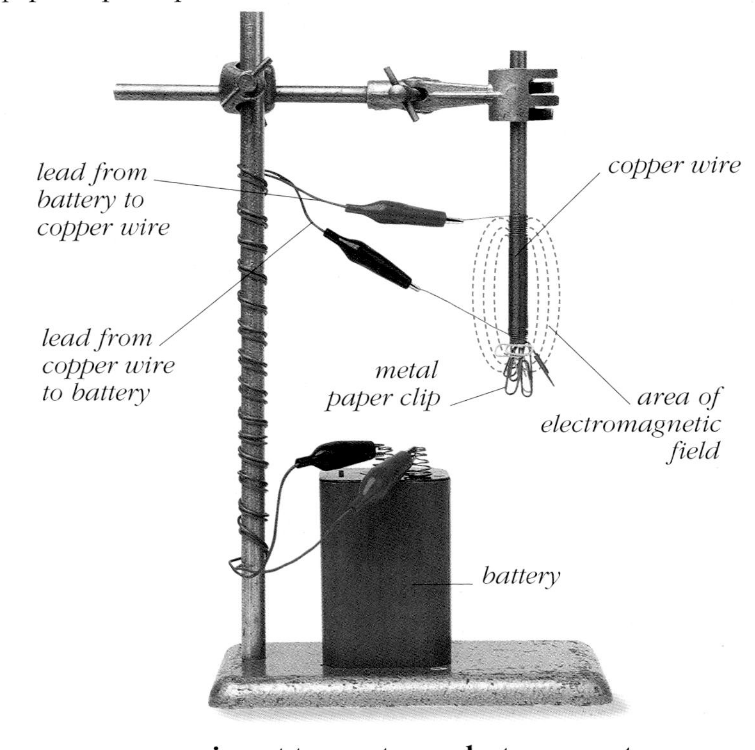


**experiment to create an electromagnet**

A B C D E F G H I J K L M N O P Q R S T U V W X Y Z

**elec·tron** \i-'lek-,trän\ *n*
a very small particle that has a negative charge of electricity and travels around the nucleus of an atom

**elec·tron·ic** \i-,lek-'trän-ik\ *adj*
**1** of, relating to, or using the principles of electronics ⟨an *electronic* device⟩
**2** operating by means of or using an electronic device (as a computer) ⟨an *electronic* typewriter⟩ ⟨*electronic* banking⟩
**elec·tron·i·cal·ly** *adv*

**electronic mail** *n*
E-MAIL

**elec·tron·ics** \i-,lek-'trän-iks\ *n*
a science that deals with the giving off, action, and effects of electrons in vacuums, gases, and semiconductors and with devices using such electrons

**electron tube** *n*
a device in which conduction of electricity by electrons takes place through a vacuum or a gas within a sealed container and which has various uses (as in radio and television)

**elec·tro·scope** \i-'lek-trə-,skōp\ *n*
an instrument for discovering the presence of an electric charge on a body and for finding out whether the charge is positive or negative

**el·e·gance** \'el-i-gəns\ *n*
**1** refined gracefulness
**2** decoration that is rich but in good taste

**el·e·gant** \'el-i-gənt\ *adj*
showing good taste (as in dress or manners) **:** having or showing beauty and refinement
**el·e·gant·ly** *adv*

**el·e·gy** \'el-ə-jē\ *n, pl* **el·e·gies**
a sad or mournful poem usually expressing sorrow for one who is dead

**el·e·ment** \'el-ə-mənt\ *n*
**1** one of the parts of which something is made up
**2** something that must be learned before one can advance ⟨the *elements* of arithmetic⟩
**3** a member of a mathematical set
**4** any of more than 100 substances that cannot by ordinary chemical means be separated into different substances ⟨gold and carbon are *elements*⟩

## elephant

The African and the Indian elephant are the largest land animals on earth, and the last two living species of a group of animals with a long, flexible snout. Elephants are intelligent and sociable creatures. Females and calves live in family herds, led by an older female, while males past puberty form their own herds or travel alone. Elephants feed on vegetation such as grass and leaves.

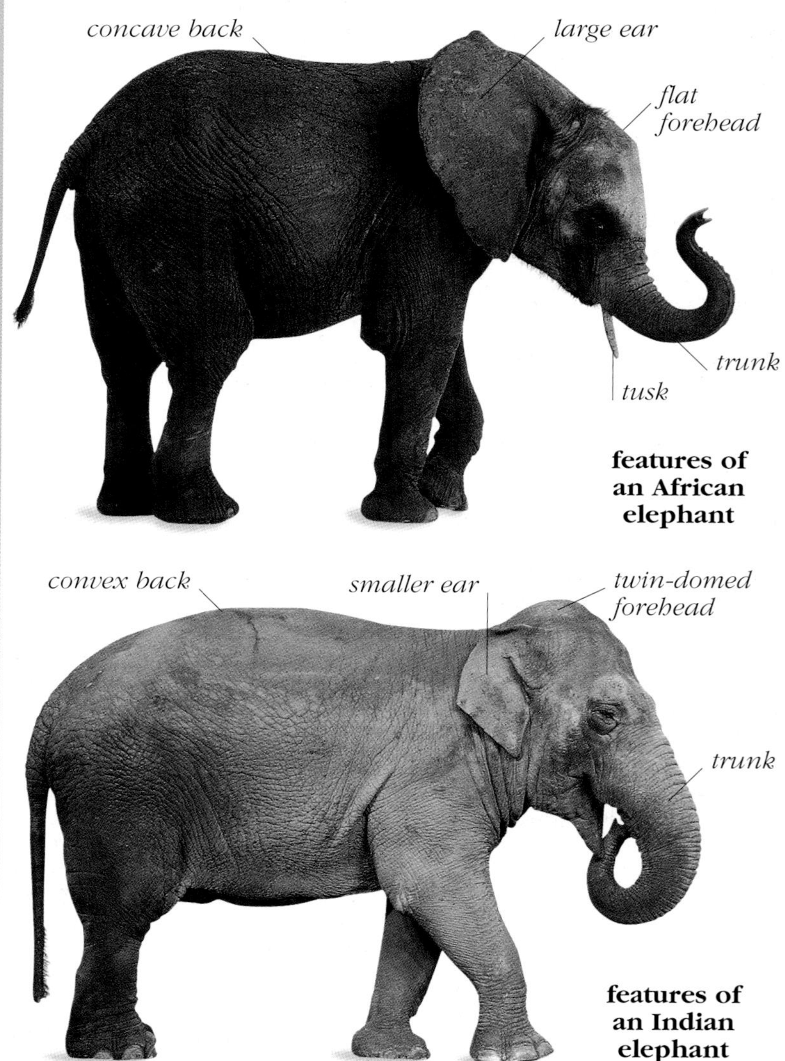


**features of an African elephant**

**features of an Indian elephant**

**el·e·men·ta·ry** \,el-ə-'ment-ə-rē, -'men-trē\ *adj*
of or relating to the beginnings or first principles of a subject ⟨*elementary* arithmetic⟩

**el·e·phant** \'el-ə-fənt\ *n*
▲ a huge thickset mammal with the nose drawn out into a long trunk and two large curved tusks

**el·e·vate** \'el-ə-,vāt\ *vb*
**el·e·vat·ed; el·e·vat·ing**
to lift up **:** RAISE

**el·e·va·tion** \,el-ə-'vā-shən\ *n*
**1** height especially above sea level **:** ALTITUDE ⟨a hill with an *elevation* of 1500 feet⟩
**2** a raised place (as a hill)
**3** the act of elevating **:** the

condition of being elevated
**synonyms** see HEIGHT

**el·e·va·tor** \'el-ə-,vāt-ər\ *n*
**1** a device (as an endless belt) for raising material
**2** a floor or little room that can be raised or lowered for carrying persons or goods from one level to another
**3** a building for storing grain
**4** a winglike device on an airplane to produce motion up or down

[1]**elev·en** \i-'lev-ən\ *adj*
being one more than ten

[2]**eleven** *n*
one more than ten **:** 11

[1]**elev·enth** \i-'lev-ənth\ *adj*
coming right after tenth

[2]**eleventh** *n*
number eleven in a series

**elf** \'elf\ *n, pl* **elves** \'elvz\
an often mischievous fairy

**elf·in** \'el-fən\ *adj*
**1** of or relating to elves
**2** having a strange beauty or charm

**el·i·gi·ble** \'el-i-jə-bəl\ *adj*
worthy or qualified to be chosen

**elim·i·nate** \i-'lim-ə-,nāt\ *vb* **elim·i·nat·ed**; **elim·i·nat·ing**
to get rid of **:** do away with

**elim·i·na·tion** \i-,lim-ə-'nā-shən\ *n*
a getting rid especially of waste from the body

**elk** \'elk\ *n*
**1** the moose of Europe and Asia
**2** ▼ a large North American deer with curved antlers having many branches

**elk 2**

**el·lipse** \i-'lips\ *n*
a closed curve that looks like a circle pulled out on opposite sides

**el·lip·ti·cal** \i-'lip-ti-kəl\ *or* **el·lip·tic** \-tik\ *adj*
of or like an ellipse

**elm** \'elm\ *n*
a tall shade tree with a broad rather flat top and spreading branches

**el·o·cu·tion** \,el-ə-'kyü-shən\ *n*
the art of reading or speaking well in public

**elo·dea** \i-'lōd-ē-ə\ *n*
a common floating water plant with small green leaves

**elon·gate** \i-'lȯng-,gāt\ *vb* **elon·gat·ed**; **elon·gat·ing**
to make or grow longer

**elope** \i-'lōp\ *vb* **eloped**; **elop·ing**
to run away to be married
**elope·ment** \-mənt\ *n*

**el·o·quence** \'el-ə-kwəns\ *n*
**1** speaking or writing that is forceful and able to persuade
**2** the art or power of speaking or writing with force and in a way to persuade

**el·o·quent** \'el-ə-kwənt\ *adj*
**1** expressing oneself or expressed clearly and with force ⟨an *eloquent* speaker⟩
**2** clearly showing some feeling or meaning ⟨an *eloquent* look⟩
**el·o·quent·ly** *adv*

[1]**else** \'els\ *adv*
**1** in a different way or place or at a different time ⟨nowhere *else* to go⟩
**2** if the facts are or were different **:** if not

[2]**else** *adj*
**1** being other and different ⟨ask someone *else*⟩
**2** being in addition ⟨what *else* can you bring⟩

**else·where** \'els-,hweər, -,hwaər, -,weər, -,waər\ *adv*
in or to another place

**elude** \i-'lüd\ *vb* **elud·ed**; **elud·ing**
to avoid or escape by being quick, skillful, or tricky

**elu·sive** \i-'lü-siv\ *adj*
**1** clever in eluding
**2** hard to understand or define

**elves** *pl of* ELF

**em-** see EN-

**e–mail** \'ē-,māl\ *n*
▼ messages sent and received electronically (as between computer terminals linked by telephone lines)

Eudora Light - [joe@abc.superserve., I'm back]
File Edit Mailbox Message Transfer Special Window Help
Send
To: joe@abc.superserve.co.uk
From: Susan Jacobs <sue@xyz.superserve.co.uk>
Subject: I'm back
Cc:
Bcc:
Attachments:

Dear Joe,

I'm back from New York. I've brought you a surprise.

Sue

**e-mail:** an e-mail message

**e–mail** \'ē-,māl\ *vb*
to send e-mail ⟨*e-mailed* all her friends⟩ ⟨*e-mail* a birthday greeting⟩
**e–mailer** \-,māl-ər\ *n*

**eman·ci·pate** \i-'man-sə-,pāt\ *vb* **eman·ci·pat·ed**; **eman·ci·pat·ing**
to set free from control or slavery **:** LIBERATE

**eman·ci·pa·tion** \i-,man-sə-'pā-shən\ *n*
a setting free ⟨the *emancipation* of slaves⟩

**em·balm** \im-'bäm, -'bälm\ *vb*
to treat a dead body so as to preserve it from decay
**em·balm·er** *n*

**em·bank·ment** \im-'bangk-mənt\ *n*
a raised bank or wall to carry a roadway, prevent floods, or hold back water

**em·bar·go** \im-'bär-gō\ *n, pl* **em·bar·goes**
an order of a government prohibiting commercial shipping from leaving its ports

**em·bark** \im-'bärk\ *vb*
**1** to go on or put on board a ship or an airplane
**2** to begin some project or task

**em·bar·rass** \im-'bar-əs\ *vb*
**1** to involve in financial difficulties
**2** to cause to feel confused and distressed **:** FLUSTER

**em·bas·sy** \'em-bə-sē\ *n,* *pl* **em·bas·sies**
**1** an ambassador and his assistants
**2** the residence or office of an ambassador

**em·bed** *or* **im·bed** \im-'bed\ *vb* **em·bed·ded** *or* **im·bed·ded**; **em·bed·ding** *or* **im·bed·ding**
to set solidly in or as if in a bed ⟨*embed* a post in concrete⟩

**em·bel·lish** \im-'bel-ish\ *vb*
to add ornamental details to
**em·bel·lish·ment** \-mənt\ *n*

**em·ber** \'em-bər\ *n*
a glowing piece of coal or wood in the ashes from a fire

**em·bez·zle** \im-'bez-əl\ *vb* **em·bez·zled**; **em·bez·zling**
to take (property entrusted to one's care) dishonestly for one's own use

**em·bit·ter** \im-'bit-ər\ *vb*
to make bitter **:** stir bitter feeling in

**em·blem** \'em-bləm\ *n*
▼ an object or a likeness of an object used to suggest a thing that cannot be pictured **:** SYMBOL

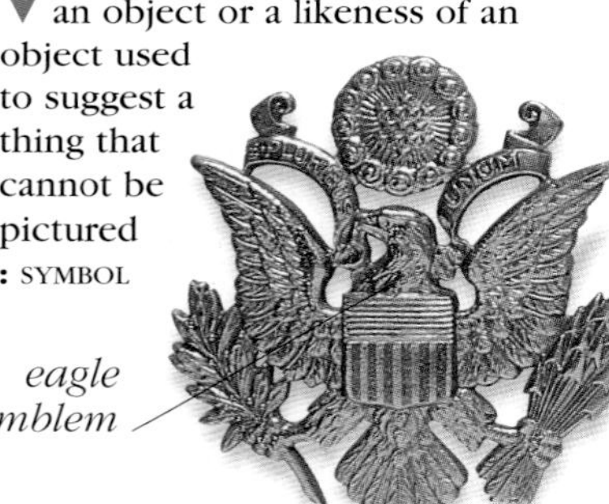
eagle emblem

**emblem** from a US Army officer's cap in World War II (1941–45)

**Synonyms** EMBLEM, SYMBOL, and TOKEN mean a visible thing that stands for something that cannot be pictured. EMBLEM is usually used of an object or a picture that represents a group such as a family, an organization, or a nation ⟨the eagle is one of our national *emblems*⟩. SYMBOL may be used of anything that serves as an outward sign for something else and especially for something ideal or spiritual ⟨the lion is the *symbol* of courage⟩. TOKEN is used of an object or act that gives evidence of the existence of something else ⟨this gift is a *token* of our love⟩.

**em·body** \im-'bäd-ē\ *vb* **em·bod·ied**; **em·body·ing**
**1** to give form to ⟨*embodied* her ideas in words⟩
**2** to cause to become a body or system or part of a body or system ⟨the basic law of the United States is *embodied* in its constitution⟩
**3** to represent in visible form

**em·boss** \im-'bäs, -'bȯs\ *vb*
to ornament with a raised pattern or design

**[1]em·brace** \im-'brās\ *vb* **em·braced**; **em·brac·ing**
**1** to clasp in the arms
**2** to enclose on all sides ⟨low hills *embraced* the valley⟩
**3** to take up readily or gladly ⟨*embrace* an opportunity⟩
**4** TAKE IN 5, INCLUDE ⟨mathematics *embraces* arithmetic, algebra, and geometry⟩

**[2]embrace** *n*
an encircling with the arms **:** HUG

**em·broi·der** \im-'brȯid-ər\ *vb*
**1** to make or fill in a design with needlework ⟨*embroider* a flower on a towel⟩
**2** to decorate with needlework
**3** to add to the interest of (as a story) with details far beyond the truth

**em·broi·dery** \im-'brȯid-ə-rē\ *n,* *pl* **em·broi·der·ies**
**1** needlework done to decorate cloth
**2** the act or art of embroidering

**em·bryo** \'em-brē-ˌō\ *n,* *pl* **em·bry·os**
**1** ▼ an animal in the earliest stages of growth when its basic structures are being formed
**2** a tiny young plant inside a seed

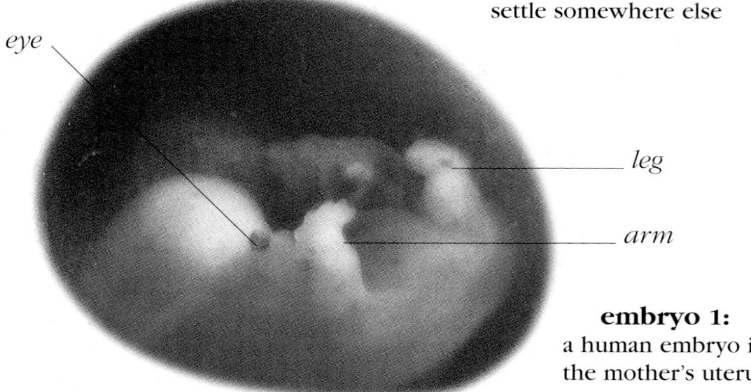


**embryo 1:** a human embryo in the mother's uterus

**[1]em·er·ald** \'em-ə-rəld, 'em-rəld\ *n*
▼ a precious stone of a rich green color

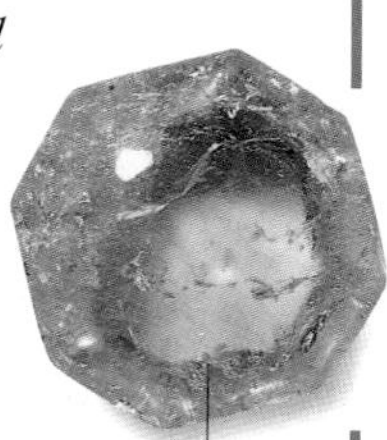


**[1]emerald**

**[2]emerald** *adj*
brightly or richly green

**emerge** \i-'mərj\ *vb* **emerged**; **emerg·ing**
**1** to come out or into view (as from water or a hole)
**2** to become known especially as a result of study or questioning

**emer·gen·cy** \i-'mər-jən-sē\ *n,* *pl* **emer·gen·cies**
an unexpected situation calling for prompt action

**emergency room** *n*
a room or place in a hospital with doctors, nurses, and medical equipment for treating people who need medical care immediately

**em·ery** \'em-ə-rē, 'em-rē\ *n,* *pl* **em·er·ies**
a mineral used in the form of powder or grains for polishing and grinding

**-emia** *or* **-ae·mia** \'ē-mē-ə\ *n suffix*
condition of having a specified disorder of the blood

**em·i·grant** \'em-i-grənt\ *n*
a person who emigrates

**em·i·grate** \'em-ə-ˌgrāt\ *vb* **em·i·grat·ed**; **em·i·grat·ing**
to leave a country or region to settle somewhere else

**em·i·gra·tion** \ˌem-ə-ˈgrā-shən\ *n*
a going away from one region or country to live in another

**em·i·nence** \ˈem-ə-nəns\ *n*
**1** the condition of being eminent
**2** a piece of high ground **:** HILL

**em·i·nent** \ˈem-ə-nənt\ *adj*
standing above others in rank, merit, or worth

**em·is·sary** \ˈem-ə-ˌser-ē\ *n, pl* **em·is·sar·ies**
a person sent on a mission to represent another

**emit** \ē-ˈmit\ *vb* **emit·ted**; **emit·ting**
to give out **:** send forth ⟨*emit* light⟩ ⟨*emit* a shriek⟩

**emo·tion** \i-ˈmō-shən\ *n*
**1** strong feeling ⟨speak with *emotion*⟩
**2** a mental and bodily reaction (as anger or fear) accompanied by strong feeling

**emo·tion·al** \i-ˈmō-shən-l\ *adj*
**1** of or relating to the emotions ⟨an *emotional* upset⟩
**2** likely to show or express emotion
**3** expressing emotion ⟨an *emotional* speech⟩
**emo·tion·al·ly** *adv*

**em·per·or** \ˈem-pər-ər\ *n*
the supreme ruler of an empire

**em·pha·sis** \ˈem-fə-səs\ *n, pl* **em·pha·ses** \-ˌsēz\
**1** a forcefulness of expression that gives special importance to something
**2** special force given to one or more words or syllables in speaking or reading
**3** special importance given to something

**em·pha·size** \ˈem-fə-ˌsīz\ *vb* **em·pha·sized**; **em·pha·siz·ing**
to give emphasis to

**em·phat·ic** \im-ˈfat-ik\ *adj*
showing or spoken with emphasis ⟨an *emphatic* refusal⟩

**em·phy·se·ma** \ˌem-fə-ˈzē-mə, -ˈsē-mə\ *n*
a disease in which the lungs become stretched and inefficient

**em·pire** \ˈem-ˌpīr\ *n*
**1** a group of territories or peoples under one ruler ⟨the Roman *empire*⟩
**2** a country whose ruler is called an emperor
**3** the power or rule of an emperor

**[1]em·ploy** \im-ˈplȯi\ *vb*
**1** to make use of ⟨*employ* bricks in building⟩
**2** to use the services of **:** hire for wages or salary

**[2]employ** *n*
the state of being employed

**em·ploy·ee** *or* **em·ploye** \im-ˌplȯi-ˈē\ *n*
a person who works for pay in the service of an employer

**em·ploy·er** \im-ˈplȯi-ər\ *n*
one that employs others

**em·ploy·ment** \im-ˈplȯi-mənt\ *n*
**1** OCCUPATION 1, ACTIVITY
**2** the act of employing **:** the state of being employed

**em·pow·er** \im-ˈpau̇-ər\ *vb*
to give authority or legal power to

**em·press** \ˈem-prəs\ *n*
**1** the wife of an emperor
**2** a woman who is the ruler of an empire in her own right

**[1]emp·ty** \ˈemp-tē\ *adj* **emp·ti·er**; **emp·ti·est**
**1** containing nothing
**2** not occupied or lived in **:** VACANT
**emp·ti·ness** *n*

---

**Synonyms** EMPTY and VACANT mean lacking contents which could or should be present. EMPTY may suggest that a thing has nothing in it at all ⟨an *empty* milk bottle⟩ or it may replace *vacant* ⟨the company left and the room is *empty*⟩. VACANT is the opposite of *occupied* and is used of something that is not occupied usually only for a while ⟨the hotel room is *vacant* now⟩.

---

**[2]empty** *vb* **emp·tied**; **emp·ty·ing**
**1** to make empty **:** remove the contents of ⟨*empty* a barrel⟩
**2** to transfer by emptying a container ⟨*empty* corn into a bin⟩
**3** to become empty
**4** [1]DISCHARGE 6 ⟨the river *empties* into the gulf⟩

**emp·ty–hand·ed** \ˌemp-tē-ˈhan-dəd\ *adj*
**1** having nothing in the hands
**2** having gotten or gained nothing ⟨walked away from the contest *empty-handed*⟩

**emp·ty–head·ed** \ˌemp-tē-ˈhed-əd\ *adj*
having a merry silly nature

**EMT** \ˌē-ˌem-ˈtē\ *n*
a person that is trained to give medical care in an emergency to a patient before or during the trip to a hospital

**emu** \ˈē-ˌmyü\ *n*
▼ a fast-running Australian bird that is like but smaller than the related ostrich

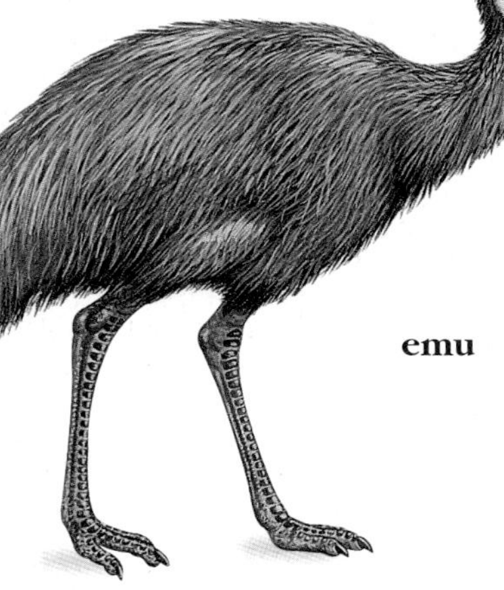
**emu**

**em·u·late** \ˈem-yə-ˌlāt\ *vb* **em·u·lat·ed**; **em·u·lat·ing**
to try hard to equal or do better than ⟨*emulate* great people⟩

**em·u·la·tion** \ˌem-yə-ˈlā-shən\ *n*
ambition or effort to equal or do better than others

**emul·si·fy** \i-ˈməl-sə-ˌfī\ *vb* **emul·si·fied**; **emul·si·fy·ing**
to make an emulsion of

**emul·sion** \i-ˈməl-shən\ *n*
a material consisting of a mixture of liquids so that fine drops of one liquid are scattered throughout the other ⟨an *emulsion* of oil in water⟩

**en-** *also* **em-** *prefix*
**1** put into or onto ⟨*en*case⟩ ⟨*en*throne⟩ **:** go into or onto
**2** cause to be ⟨*en*slave⟩
**3** provide with ⟨*em*power⟩ — in all senses usually *em-* before *b*, *m*, or *p*

**[1]-en** \ən, -n\ *also* **-n** \n\ *adj suffix*
made of **:** consisting of ⟨earth*en*⟩ ⟨wool*en*⟩

**[2]-en** *vb suffix*
**1** become or cause to be ⟨sharp*en*⟩
**2** cause or come to have ⟨length*en*⟩

**en·able** \in-ˈā-bəl\ *vb* **en·abled**; **en·abling**
to give strength, power, or ability to **:** make able

a b c d e f g h i j k l m n o p q r s t u v w x y z

**en·act** \in-'akt\ *vb*
**1** to make into law
**2** to act the part of (as in a play)
**en·act·ment** \-mənt\ *n*

[1]**enam·el** \i-'nam-əl\ *vb*
**enam·eled** *or* **enam·elled**; **enam·el·ing** *or* **enam·el·ling**
to cover with or as if with enamel

[2]**enamel** *n*
**1** ▼ a glassy substance used for coating the surface of metal, glass, and pottery

[2]**enamel 1:**
a bird-shaped enamel brooch

**2** the hard outer surface of the teeth
**3** a paint that forms a hard glossy coat

**en·camp** \in-'kamp\ *vb*
to set up and occupy a camp

**en·camp·ment** \in-'kamp-mənt\ *n*
**1** the act of making a camp
**2** CAMP

**en·case** \in-'kās\ *vb* **en·cased**; **en·cas·ing**
to enclose in or as if in a case

**-ence** \əns, -ns\ *n suffix*
action or process ⟨refer*ence*⟩

**en·chant** \in-'chant\ *vb*
**1** to put under a spell by or as if by charms or magic
**2** to please greatly
**en·chant·er** *n*
**en·chant·ment** \-mənt\ *n*

**en·chant·ing** \in-'chant-ing\ *adj*
very attractive : CHARMING

**en·chant·ress** \in-'chan-trəs\ *n*
a woman who enchants : WITCH, SORCERESS

**en·cir·cle** \in-'sər-kəl\ *vb*
**en·cir·cled**; **en·cir·cling**
**1** to form a circle around : SURROUND
**2** to pass completely around

**en·close** *or* **in·close** \in-'klōz\ *vb*
**en·closed** *or* **in·closed**; **en·clos·ing** *or* **in·clos·ing**
**1** to close in all around : SURROUND ⟨a porch *enclosed* with glass⟩
**2** to put in the same parcel or envelope with something else ⟨*enclose* a snapshot with a letter⟩

**Synonyms** ENCLOSE, ENVELOP, and FENCE mean to surround something and in this way close it off. ENCLOSE suggests putting up barriers (as walls) or a cover around something so as to give it protection or privacy ⟨a high hedge *encloses* the garden⟩. ENVELOP suggests something is completely surrounded by some kind of soft layer or covering that serves to screen or protect ⟨clouds *enveloped* the peaks of the mountains⟩. FENCE suggests that something is enclosed with or as if with a fence so that nothing may freely enter or leave ⟨a stone wall *fences* in the yard⟩.

**en·clo·sure** *or* **in·clo·sure** \in-'klō-zhər\ *n*
**1** the act of enclosing
**2** an enclosed space
**3** something (as a fence) that encloses
**4** something enclosed (as in a letter)

**en·com·pass** \in-'kəm-pəs\ *vb*
**1** ENCIRCLE 1
**2** INCLUDE

[1]**en·core** \'än-,kōr\ *n*
**1** a demand for the repeating of something on a program made by applause from an audience
**2** a further appearance or performance given in response to applause

[2]**encore** *vb* **en·cored**; **en·cor·ing**
to call for an encore

[1]**en·coun·ter** \in-'kau̇nt-ər\ *vb*
**1** to meet as an enemy : FIGHT
**2** to meet face-to-face or unexpectedly ⟨*encounter* a friend⟩

[2]**encounter** *n*
**1** a meeting with an enemy : COMBAT
**2** a meeting face-to-face and often by chance

## endocrine gland

The endocrine glands are situated in different parts of the body. Together with related organs they form the endocrine system. The endocrine glands secrete hormones into the bloodstream. Hormones are needed for healthy growth and for the body to work properly.

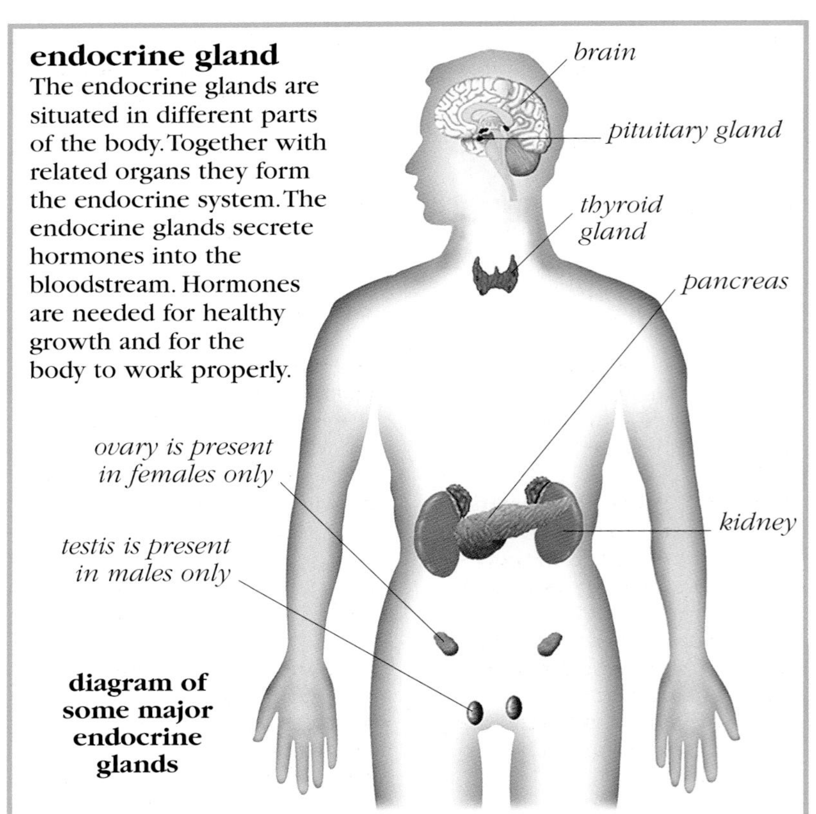


**diagram of some major endocrine glands**

**en·cour·age** \in-'kər-ij\ *vb* **en·cour·aged; en·cour·ag·ing**
**1** to give courage, spirit, or hope to **:** HEARTEN
**2** to give help to **:** AID

**en·cour·age·ment** \in-'kər-ij-mənt\ *n*
**1** the act of encouraging **:** the state of being encouraged
**2** something that encourages

**endive**

**en·croach** \in-'krōch\ *vb*
**1** to take over the rights or possessions of another little by little or in secret
**2** to go beyond the usual or proper limits

**en·crust** *also* **in·crust** \in-'krəst\ *vb*
to cover with or as if with a crust

**en·cum·ber** \in-'kəm-bər\ *vb*
**1** to weigh down **:** BURDEN
**2** HINDER, HAMPER

**-en·cy** \ən-sē, -n-sē\ *n suffix, pl* **-en·cies**
quality or state ⟨despondency⟩

**en·cy·clo·pe·dia** \in-,sī-klə-'pēd-ē-ə\ *n*
a book or a set of books containing information on all branches of learning in articles arranged alphabetically by subject

[1]**end** \'end\ *n*
**1** the part near the boundary of an area ⟨the south *end* of a town⟩
**2** the point (as of time or space) where something ceases to exist ⟨the *end* of vacation⟩
**3** the first or last part of a thing ⟨the front *end* of the car⟩ ⟨knotted the *end* of the rope⟩
**4** DEATH 1, DESTRUCTION ⟨a ship met its *end* in the storm⟩
**5** [1]PURPOSE, GOAL

[2]**end** *vb*
to bring or come to an end **:** STOP

**en·dan·ger** \in-'dān-jər\ *vb*
[2]RISK 1

**en·dear** \in-'dir\ *vb*
to make dear or beloved

**en·dear·ment** \in-'dir-mənt\ *n*
a word or an act that shows love or affection

[1]**en·deav·or** \in-'dev-ər\ *vb*
to make an effort **:** TRY

[2]**endeavor** *n*
a serious determined effort

**end·ing** \'en-ding\ *n*
the final part **:** END

**en·dive** \'en-,dīv\ *n*
◀ either of two plants related to the daisies and often used in salads

**end·less** \'end-ləs\ *adj*
**1** having or seeming to have no end
**2** joined at the ends ⟨an *endless* belt⟩
**end·less·ly** *adv*
**end·less·ness** *n*

**en·do·crine gland** \,en-də-krən-, -,krīn-\ *n*
◀ any of several glands (as the thyroid or pituitary) that secrete hormones directly into the blood

**en·dorse** *also* **in·dorse** \in-'dȯrs\ *vb* **en·dorsed** *also* **in·dorsed; en·dors·ing** *or* **in·dors·ing**
**1** to sign one's name on the back of (a check) to obtain payment
**2** to give one's support to openly ⟨*endorse* a candidate⟩
**en·dorse·ment** \-mənt\ *n*

**en·dow** \in-'daů\ *vb*
**1** to provide with money for support ⟨*endow* a hospital⟩
**2** to provide with something freely or naturally ⟨humans are *endowed* with reason⟩

**en·dow·ment** \in-'daů-mənt\ *n*
the providing of a permanent fund for support or the fund provided

**end·point** \'end-,pȯint\ *n*
either of two points that mark the ends of a line segment or a point that marks the end of a ray

**en·dur·ance** \in-'důr-əns, -'dyůr-\ *n*
the ability to put up with strain, suffering, or hardship

**en·dure** \in-'důr, -'dyůr\ *vb* **en·dured; en·dur·ing**
**1** to continue in existence **:** LAST
**2** to put up with (as pain) patiently or firmly

**end·ways** \'en-,dwāz\ *adv or adj*
**1** on end
**2** with the end forward
**3** [1]LENGTHWISE

**en·e·ma** \'en-ə-mə\ *n*
the injection of liquid into the bowel or the liquid injected

**en·e·my** \'en-ə-mē\ *n, pl* **en·e·mies**
**1** one that hates another **:** one that attacks or tries to harm another
**2** something that harms or threatens
**3** a nation with which one's own country is at war or a person belonging to such a nation

**en·er·get·ic** \,en-ər-'jet-ik\ *adj*
having or showing energy **:** ACTIVE, VIGOROUS
**en·er·get·i·cal·ly** \-i-kə-lē\ *adv*

**en·er·gize** \'en-ər-,jīz\ *vb* **en·er·gized; en·er·giz·ing**
to give energy to

**en·er·gy** \'en-ər-jē\ *n, pl* **en·er·gies**
**1** ability to be active **:** strength of body or mind to do things or to work
**2** usable power or the resources (as oil) for producing such power
**synonyms** see POWER

**en·fold** \in-'fōld\ *vb*
**1** to wrap up **:** cover with or as if with folds
**2** [1]EMBRACE 1

**en·force** \in-'fōrs\ *vb* **en·forced; en·forc·ing**
**1** to demand and see that one gets ⟨*enforce* obedience to school rules⟩
**2** to put into force ⟨*enforce* a law⟩
**en·force·ment** \mənt\ *n*

**en·gage** \in-'gāj\ *vb* **en·gaged; en·gag·ing**
**1** to pledge (as oneself) to do something **:** PROMISE
**2** to catch and hold fast (as the attention) ⟨*engaged* my interest⟩
**3** to take part in something ⟨*engage* in a sport⟩
**4** to enter into contest or battle with ⟨*engage* the enemy⟩
**5** to arrange for the services or use of **:** HIRE ⟨*engage* a plumber⟩ ⟨*engage* a room at the hotel⟩
**6** to put or become in gear **:** MESH

a b c d e f g h i j k l m n o p q r s t u v w x y z

**en·gaged** \in-'gājd\ *adj*
1 busy with some activity ⟨I am *engaged* just now⟩
2 pledged to be married ⟨an *engaged* couple⟩

**en·gage·ment** \in-'gāj-mənt\ *n*
1 the act of engaging **:** the state of being engaged
2 EMPLOYMENT 2 ⟨a week's *engagement* at the theater⟩
3 an appointment at a certain time and place
4 a fight between armed forces

**en·gag·ing** \in-'gā-jing\ *adj*
ATTRACTIVE ⟨an *engaging* smile⟩

**en·gen·der** \in-'jen-dər\ *vb*
to cause to be or develop **:** PRODUCE

**en·gine** \'en-jən\ *n*
1 a mechanical tool or device ⟨tanks, planes, and other *engines* of war⟩
2 a machine for driving or operating something especially by using the energy of steam, gasoline, or oil
3 [1]LOCOMOTIVE

**Word History** The English word *engine* came from a Latin word that meant "natural talent." At first the word *engine* meant "skill" or "cleverness." In time the word came to be used for things that are products of human skills — tools and machines, for example.

[1]**en·gi·neer** \,en-jə-'nir\ *n*
1 a member of a military group devoted to engineering work
2 a person who specializes in engineering ⟨an electrical *engineer*⟩ ⟨a mining *engineer*⟩
3 a person who runs or has charge of an engine or of machinery or technical equipment

[2]**engineer** *vb*
1 to plan, build, or manage as an engineer
2 to plan out **:** CONTRIVE

**en·gi·neer·ing** \,en-jə-'nir-ing\ *n*
a science by which the properties of matter and the sources of energy in nature are made useful to man in structures (as roads and dams), machines (as automobiles and computers), and products (as plastics and radios)

[1]**En·glish** \'ing-glish\ *adj*
of or relating to England, its people, or the English language

[2]**English** *n*
1 the language of England, the United States, and some other countries now or at one time under British rule
2 **English** *pl* the people of England

**English horn** *n*
a woodwind instrument that is similar to an oboe but is longer and has a deeper tone

**en·grave** \in-'grāv\ *vb* **en·graved**; **en·grav·ing**
1 to cut or carve (as letters or designs) on a hard surface
2 to cut lines, letters, figures, or designs on or into (a hard surface) often for use in printing
3 to print from a cut surface ⟨an *engraved* invitation⟩
**en·grav·er** *n*

**en·grav·ing** \in-'grā-ving\ *n*
1 the art of cutting something especially into the surface of wood, stone, or metal
2 ▼ a print made from an engraved surface

**engraving 2:** an engraving printed from a block

**en·gross** \in-'grōs\ *vb*
to take up the whole interest of ⟨be *engrossed* in a puzzle⟩

**en·gulf** \in-'gəlf\ *vb*
to flow over and swallow up ⟨the town was *engulfed* by the flood⟩ ⟨a person *engulfed* by fear⟩

**en·hance** \in-'hans\ *vb* **en·hanced**; **en·hanc·ing**
to make greater or better

**enig·ma** \i-'nig-mə\ *n*
something hard to understand

**en·joy** \in-'jȯi\ *vb*
1 to take pleasure or satisfaction in ⟨*enjoy* camping⟩
2 to have for one's use or benefit ⟨*enjoy* good health⟩

**en·joy·able** \in-'jȯi-ə-bəl\ *adj*
being a source of pleasure

**en·joy·ment** \in-'jȯi-mənt\ *n*
1 the action or condition of enjoying something
2 something that gives pleasure
**synonyms** see PLEASURE

**en·large** \in-'lärj\ *vb* **en·larged**; **en·larg·ing**
to make or grow larger **:** EXPAND

**en·large·ment** \in-'lärj-mənt\ *n*
1 an act of enlarging
2 the state of being enlarged
3 a photographic print made larger than the negative

**en·light·en** \in-'līt-n\ *vb*
to give knowledge to

**en·list** \in-'list\ *vb*
1 to join the armed forces as a volunteer
2 to obtain the help of ⟨*enlist* friends in painting the house⟩
**en·list·ment** \-mənt\ *n*

**en·list·ed man** \in-'lis-təd-\ *n*
a man or woman serving in the armed forces who ranks below a commissioned officer or warrant officer

**en·liv·en** \in-'lī-vən\ *vb*
to put life or spirit into **:** make active or cheerful

**en·mi·ty** \'en-mət-ē\ *n*, *pl* **en·mi·ties**
hatred especially when shared **:** ILL WILL

**enor·mous** \i-'nȯr-məs\ *adj*
unusually large **:** HUGE
**enor·mous·ly** *adv*

[1]**enough** \i-'nəf\ *adj*
equal to the needs or demands ⟨there was just *enough* food⟩

[2]**enough** *adv*
in sufficient amount or degree ⟨are you warm *enough*⟩

[3]**enough** *pron*
a sufficient number or amount ⟨we have *enough* to meet our needs⟩

**en·rage** \in-'rāj\ *vb* **en·raged**; **en·rag·ing**
to fill with rage **:** ANGER

**en·rich** \in-'rich\ *vb*
1 to make rich or richer

2 to improve the quality of food by adding vitamins and minerals
3 to make more fertile ⟨*enrich* soil with fertilizer⟩

**en·roll** *or* **en·rol** \in-ˈrōl\ *vb* **en·rolled**; **en·roll·ing**
to include (as a name) on a roll or list

**en·roll·ment** *or* **en·rol·ment** \in-ˈrōl-mənt\ *n*
1 the act of enrolling or being enrolled
2 the number of persons enrolled

**en route** \än-ˈrüt\ *adv*
on or along the way

**en·sem·ble** \än-ˈsäm-bəl\ *n*
a group of musicians or dancers performing together

**en·shrine** \in-ˈshrīn\ *vb* **en·shrined**; **en·shrin·ing**
to cherish as if sacred

**en·sign** \ˈen-sən, *1 is also* -ˌsīn\ *n*
1 a flag flown as the symbol of nationality
2 a commissioned officer of the lowest rank in the Navy or Coast Guard

**en·slave** \in-ˈslāv\ *vb* **en·slaved**; **en·slav·ing**
to make a slave of

**en·sue** \in-ˈsü\ *vb* **en·sued**; **en·su·ing**
to come after in time or as a result : FOLLOW

**en·sure** \in-ˈshu̇r\ *vb* **en·sured**; **en·sur·ing**
to make sure, certain, or safe : GUARANTEE

**en·tan·gle** \in-ˈtang-gəl\ *vb* **en·tan·gled**; **en·tan·gling**
1 to make tangled or confused
2 to catch in a tangle
— **en·tan·gle·ment** \-gəl-mənt\ *n*

**en·ter** \ˈent-ər\ *vb*
1 to come or go in or into ⟨you may *enter* now⟩ ⟨*enter* a room⟩
2 to put into a list : write down
3 to become a member or a member of : JOIN
4 to become a party to or take an interest in something ⟨*enter* into a treaty⟩
5 PENETRATE 1, PIERCE ⟨the thorn *entered* my thumb⟩
6 to cause to be admitted (as to a school) ⟨*enter* students in college⟩

**en·ter·prise** \ˈent-ər-ˌprīz\ *n*
1 an undertaking requiring courage and energy
2 willingness to engage in daring or difficult action
3 a business organization or activity

**en·ter·pris·ing** \ˈent-ər-ˌprī-zing\ *adj*
bold and energetic in trying or experimenting

**en·ter·tain** \ˌent-ər-ˈtān\ *vb*
1 to greet in a friendly way and provide for especially in one's home : have as a guest ⟨*entertain* friends over the weekend⟩
2 to have in mind ⟨*entertain* kind thoughts⟩
3 to provide amusement for
**synonyms** see AMUSE

**en·ter·tain·er** \ˌent-ər-ˈtā-nər\ *n*
a person who performs for public entertainment

**en·ter·tain·ment** \ˌent-ər-ˈtān-mənt\ *n*
1 the act of entertaining or amusing
2 something (as a show) that is a form of amusement or recreation

**en·thrall** *or* **en·thral** \in-ˈthrȯl\ *vb* **en·thralled**; **en·thrall·ing**
to hold the attention of completely : CHARM

**en·throne** \in-ˈthrōn\ *vb* **en·throned**; **en·thron·ing**
1 to seat on a throne
2 to place in a high position

**en·thu·si·asm** \in-ˈthü-zē-ˌaz-əm, -ˈthyü-\ *n*
strong feeling in favor of something ⟨their *enthusiasm* for sports⟩

**en·thu·si·ast** \in-ˈthü-zē-ˌast, -ˈthyü-\ *n*
a person filled with enthusiasm

**en·thu·si·as·tic** \in-ˌthü-zē-ˈas-tik, -ˌthyü-\ *adj*
full of enthusiasm : EAGER

**en·thu·si·as·ti·cal·ly** \in-ˌthü-zē-ˈas-ti-kə-lē, -ˌthyü-\ *adv*
with enthusiasm

**en·tice** \in-ˈtīs\ *vb* **en·ticed**; **en·tic·ing**
to attract by raising hope or desire : TEMPT

**en·tire** \in-ˈtīr\ *adj*
complete in all parts or respects ⟨the *entire* day⟩ ⟨was in *entire* control⟩
— **en·tire·ly** *adv*

**en·tire·ty** \in-ˈtī-rət-ē, -ˈtīr-tē\ *n, pl* **en·tire·ties**
1 a state of completeness
2 [2]WHOLE 2

**en·ti·tle** \in-ˈtīt-l\ *vb* **en·ti·tled**; **en·ti·tling**
1 to give a title to
2 to give a right or claim to ⟨buying a ticket *entitles* you to a seat⟩

**en·trails** \ˈen-trəlz, -ˌtrālz\ *n pl*
the internal parts of an animal

[1]**en·trance** \ˈen-trəns\ *n*
1 the act of entering
2 a door, gate, or way for entering
3 permission to enter : ADMISSION ⟨apply for *entrance* to college⟩

[2]**en·trance** \in-ˈtrans\ *vb* **en·tranced**; **en·tranc·ing**
1 to put into a trance
2 to fill with delight and wonder

**en·trap** \in-ˈtrap\ *vb* **en·trapped**; **en·trap·ping**
to catch in or as if in a trap

**en·treat** \in-ˈtrēt\ *vb*
to ask in an earnest way

**en·treaty** \in-ˈtrēt-ē\ *n, pl* **en·treat·ies**
an act of entreating : PLEA

**en·trust** *or* **in·trust** \in-ˈtrəst\ *vb*
1 to give care of something to as a trust ⟨*entrusted* me with their money⟩
2 to give to another with confidence ⟨I'll *entrust* the job to you⟩

**en·try** \ˈen-trē\ *n, pl* **en·tries**
1 the act of entering : ENTRANCE
2 a place (as a hall or door) through which entrance is made
3 the act of making (as in a book or a list) a written record of something
4 something entered in a list or a record ⟨dictionary *entries*⟩
5 a person or thing entered in a contest

**en·twine** \in-ˈtwīn\ *vb* **en·twined**; **en·twin·ing**
to twist or twine together or around

**enu·mer·ate** \i-ˈnü-mə-ˌrāt, -ˈnyü-\ *vb* **enu·mer·at·ed**; **enu·mer·at·ing**
1 [1]COUNT 1
2 to name one after another : LIST

**enun·ci·ate** \ē-ˈnən-sē-ˌāt\ *vb* **enun·ci·at·ed**; **enun·ci·at·ing**
1 ANNOUNCE 1
2 to pronounce words or parts of words

**enun·ci·a·tion** \ē-ˌnən-sē-ˈā-shən\ *n*
clearness of pronunciation

a b c d e f g h i j k l m n o p q r s t u v w x y z

A B C D E F G H I J K L M N O P Q R S T U V W X Y Z

**en·vel·op** \in-'vel-əp\ *vb* to put a covering completely around **:** wrap up or in **synonyms** see ENCLOSE

**en·ve·lope** \'en-və-,lōp, 'än-\ *n* ▼ an enclosing cover or wrapper (as for a letter)

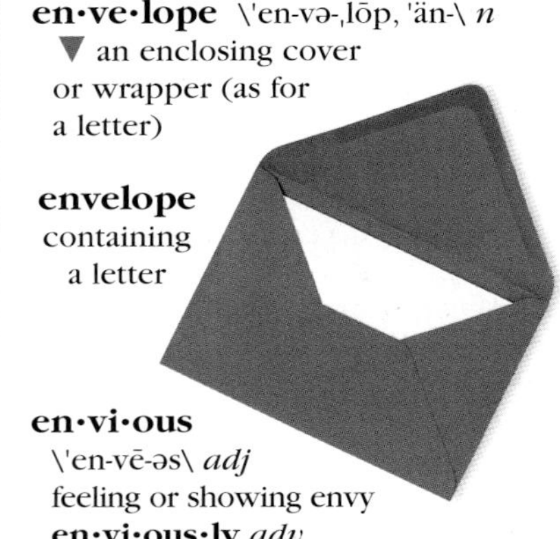

**envelope** containing a letter

**en·vi·ous** \'en-vē-əs\ *adj* feeling or showing envy **en·vi·ous·ly** *adv* **en·vi·ous·ness** *n*

**en·vi·ron·ment** \in-'vī-rən-mənt, -'vī-ərn-mənt\ *n* **1** SURROUNDINGS ⟨their home was in a comfortable rural *environment*⟩ **2** the surrounding conditions or forces (as soil, climate, and living things) that influence the form and ability to survive of a plant or animal or ecological community **3** the social and cultural conditions that influence the life of a person or human community ⟨a happy home *environment*⟩

**en·voy** \'en-,vȯi, 'än-\ *n* **1** a representative sent by one government to another **2** MESSENGER

**¹en·vy** \'en-vē\ *n, pl* **envies** **1** a feeling of discontent at another's good fortune together with a desire to have the same good fortune oneself ⟨filled with *envy* on seeing her success⟩ **2** a person or a thing that is envied ⟨the *envy* of all my friends⟩

**²envy** *vb* **en·vied**; **en·vy·ing** to feel envy toward or because of

**en·zyme** \'en-,zīm\ *n* one of the substances produced by body cells that help bodily chemical activities (as digestion) to take place but are not destroyed in so doing

**eon** *variant of* AEON

**¹ep·ic** \'ep-ik\ *adj* of, relating to, or characteristic of an epic

**²epic** *n* a long poem that tells the story of a hero's deeds

**¹ep·i·dem·ic** \,ep-ə-'dem-ik\ *adj* spreading widely and affecting large numbers of people at the same time ⟨an *epidemic* disease⟩

**²epidemic** *n* **1** a rapidly spreading outbreak of disease **2** something that spreads or develops rapidly like an epidemic disease

**epi·der·mis** \,ep-ə-'dər-məs\ *n* **1** a thin outer layer of skin covering the dermis **2** any of various thin outer layers of plants or animals

$$d + h = 35$$

$$\text{So } h = 35 - d$$

**equation 1:** two related mathematical equations

**ep·i·neph·rine** \,ep-ə-'nef-rən\ *n* a hormone that causes blood vessels to narrow and the blood pressure to increase

**ep·i·sode** \'ep-ə-,sōd\ *n* an event or one of a series of events that stands out clearly in one's life, in history, or in a story

**epis·tle** \i-'pis-əl\ *n* ¹LETTER 2

**ep·i·taph** \'ep-ə-,taf\ *n* a brief statement on a tombstone in memory of a dead person

**ep·och** \'ep-ək\ *n* a period marked by unusual or important events

**¹equal** \'ē-kwəl\ *adj* **1** exactly the same in number, amount, degree, rank, or quality **2** evenly balanced ⟨an *equal* contest⟩ **3** having enough strength, ability, or means **:** ADEQUATE ⟨*equal* to the task⟩ **synonyms** see SAME **equal·ly** \'ē-kwə-lē\ *adv*

**²equal** *vb* **equaled** *or* **equalled**; **equal·ing** *or* **equal·ling** to be equal to

**³equal** *n* one that is equal to another

**equal·i·ty** \i-'kwäl-ət-ē\ *n, pl* **equal·i·ties** the condition or state of being equal

**equal·ize** \'ē-kwə-,līz\ *vb* **equal·ized**; **equal·iz·ing** to make equal or even

**equa·tion** \i-'kwā-zhən\ *n* **1** ◀ a statement of the equality of two mathematical expressions **2** an expression representing a chemical reaction by means of chemical symbols

**equa·tor** \i-'kwāt-ər\ *n* ▼ an imaginary circle around the earth everywhere equally distant from the north pole and the south pole

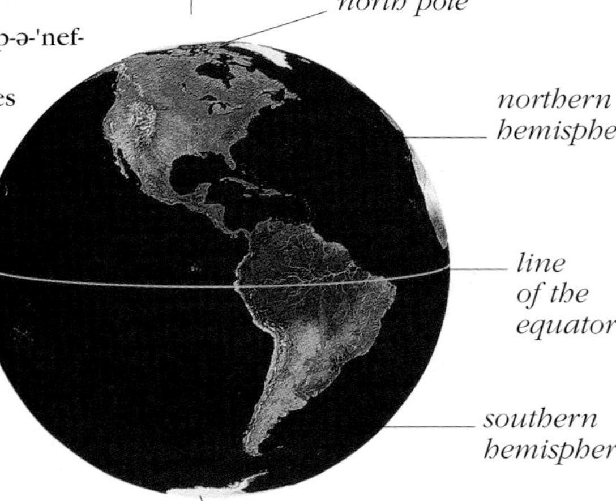


**equator** encircling the earth

**equa·to·ri·al** \,ē-kwə-'tōr-ē-əl, ,ek-wə-\ *adj* **1** of, relating to, or lying near the equator **2** of, coming from, or suggesting the region at or near the equator

**eques·tri·an** \i-'kwes-trē-ən\ *adj* of or relating to horses or to the riding or riders of horses

**equi·lat·er·al** \,ē-kwə-'lat-ə-rəl, ,ek-wə-\ *adj* having all sides of equal length ⟨an *equilateral* triangle⟩

**equi·lib·ri·um** \ˌē-kwə-ˈlib-rē-əm, ˌek-wə-\ *n*
**1** a state of balance between opposing weights, forces, or influences
**2** the normal bodily adjustment of a person or animal in relation to its environment

**equi·nox** \ˈē-kwə-ˌnäks, ˈek-wə-\ *n*
▼ either of the two times each year when the sun's center crosses the equator and day and night (as on March 21 and September 23) are everywhere of equal length

**equip** \i-ˈkwip\ *vb* **equipped**; **equip·ping**
to make ready for a purpose by supplying what is necessary

**equip·ment** \i-ˈkwip-mənt\ *n*
**1** an act of equipping
**2** supplies and tools needed for a special purpose

[1]**equiv·a·lent** \i-ˈkwiv-ə-lənt\ *adj*
alike or equal in number, value, or meaning

[2]**equivalent** *n*
something equivalent

[1]**-er** \ər\ *adj suffix or adv suffix*
used to form the comparative degree of adjectives and adverbs of one syllable ⟨hott*er*⟩ ⟨dri*er*⟩ and of some adjectives and adverbs of two or more syllables ⟨complet*er*⟩ ⟨earli*er*⟩

[2]**-er** \ər\ *also* **-ier** \ē-ər, yər\ *or* **-yer** \yər\ *n suffix*
**1** a person whose work or business is connected with ⟨hatt*er*⟩ ⟨furr*ier*⟩ ⟨law*yer*⟩
**2** a person or thing belonging to or associated with ⟨old-tim*er*⟩
**3** a native of : resident of ⟨New York*er*⟩
**4** one that has
**5** one that produces
**6** one that does or performs a specified action ⟨report*er*⟩
**7** one that is a suitable object of a specified action
**8** one that is ⟨foreign*er*⟩

**era** \ˈir-ə, ˈer-ə\ *n*
**1** a period of time starting from some special date or event ⟨the Christian *era*⟩
**2** an important period of history ⟨the colonial *era*⟩

### equinox

Twice a year, in March and September, an equinox occurs when the center of the sun crosses directly over the equator, and day and night are of equal length. From the March equinox, the northern hemisphere experiences spring, while the southern hemisphere experiences fall. From the September equinox, the seasons in the hemispheres are reversed.

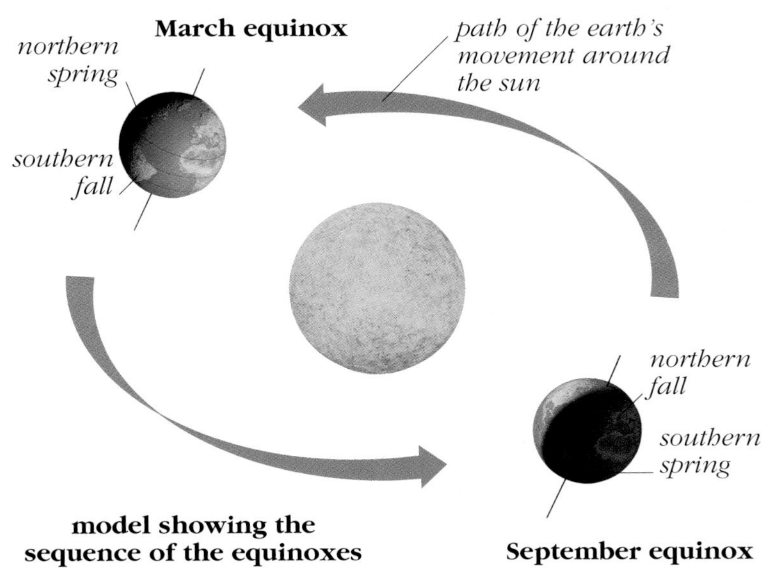


model showing the sequence of the equinoxes

**erad·i·cate** \i-ˈrad-ə-ˌkāt\ *vb* **erad·i·cat·ed**; **erad·i·cat·ing**
to remove by or as if by tearing up by the roots : destroy completely

**erase** \i-ˈrās\ *vb* **erased**; **eras·ing**
**1** to cause to disappear by rubbing or scraping ⟨*erase* a chalk mark⟩
**2** to remove recorded matter from ⟨*erase* a videotape⟩

**eras·er** \i-ˈrā-sər\ *n*
something for erasing marks

**era·sure** \i-ˈrā-shər\ *n*
**1** an act of erasing
**2** something erased

[1]**ere** \eər, aər\ *prep*
[2]BEFORE 3

[2]**ere** *conj*
[3]BEFORE 2

[1]**erect** \i-ˈrekt\ *adj*
being straight up and down
**erect·ly** *adv*
**erect·ness** *n*

[2]**erect** *vb*
**1** to put up by fitting together materials or parts
**2** to set straight up **synonyms** see BUILD
**erec·tor** \i-ˈrek-tər\ *n*

**er·mine** \ˈər-mən\ *n*
a weasel of northern regions that is valued for its winter coat of white fur with a tail tipped in black

**erode** \i-ˈrōd\ *vb* **erod·ed**; **erod·ing**
to eat into : wear away : destroy by wearing away ⟨a shore *eroded* by the sea⟩

**ero·sion** \i-ˈrō-zhən\ *n*
the act of eroding : the state of being eroded

**err** \ˈeər, ˈər\ *vb*
**1** to make a mistake
**2** to do wrong : SIN

**er·rand** \ˈer-ənd\ *n*
**1** a short trip made to take care of some business
**2** the business done on an errand

**er·rant** \ˈer-ənt\ *adj*
**1** wandering in search of adventure ⟨an *errant* knight⟩
**2** straying from a proper course

**er·rat·ic** \i-ˈrat-ik\ *adj*
not following the usual or expected course

**er·ro·ne·ous** \i-ˈrō-nē-əs\ *adj*
INCORRECT 1

**er·ror** \ˈer-ər\ *n*
a failure to be correct or accurate : MISTAKE ⟨an *error* in adding figures⟩

A B C D E F G H I J K L M N O P Q R S T U V W X Y Z

**Synonyms** ERROR, MISTAKE, and BLUNDER mean an act or statement that is not right or true or proper. ERROR suggests that one fails to follow a model correctly ⟨an *error* in addition⟩. MISTAKE suggests that one misunderstands something or does not intend to do wrong ⟨took someone else's coat by *mistake*⟩. BLUNDER suggests a really bad mistake made because of a lack of knowledge, intelligence, caution, or care ⟨the actors made several *blunders* during the play⟩.

**erupt** \i-'rəpt\ *vb*
**1** to burst forth or cause to burst forth ⟨lava *erupting* from a volcano⟩
**2** to break through a surface
**3** to break out (as with a skin rash)

**erup·tion** \i-'rəp-shən\ *n*
**1** ▶ a bursting forth ⟨*eruption* of lava from a volcano⟩
**2** a breaking out (as of a skin rash) or the resulting rash

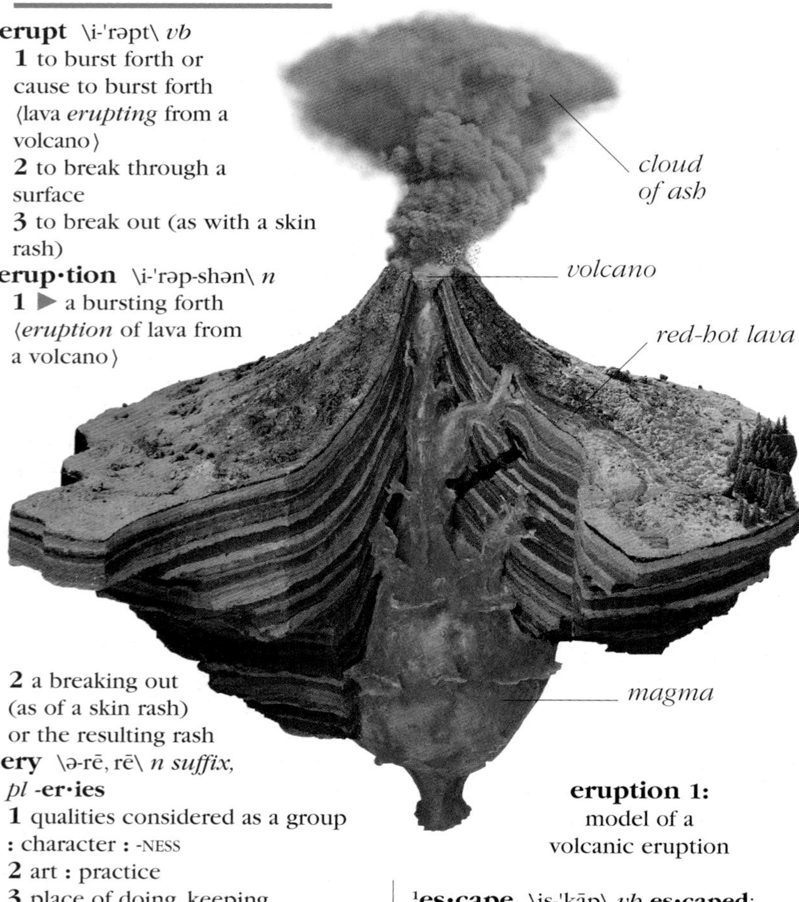


**eruption 1:** model of a volcanic eruption

**-ery** \ə-rē, rē\ *n suffix, pl* **-er·ies**
**1** qualities considered as a group : character : -NESS
**2** art : practice
**3** place of doing, keeping, producing, or selling ⟨fish*ery*⟩ ⟨bak*ery*⟩
**4** collection : aggregate ⟨fin*ery*⟩
**5** state or condition ⟨slav*ery*⟩

**¹-es** \əz, iz *after* s, z, sh, ch; z *after* v *or a vowel*\ *n pl suffix*
**1** used to form the plural of most nouns that end in *s* ⟨glass*es*⟩, *z* ⟨buzz*es*⟩, *sh* ⟨bush*es*⟩, *ch* ⟨peach*es*⟩, or a final *y* that changes to *i* ⟨lad*ies*⟩ and of some nouns ending in *f* that changes to *v* ⟨loav*es*⟩
**2** ¹-S 2

**²-es** *vb suffix*
used to form the third person singular present of most verbs that end in *s* ⟨bless*es*⟩, *z* ⟨fizz*es*⟩, *sh* ⟨hush*es*⟩, *ch* ⟨catch*es*⟩, or a final *y* that changes to *i* ⟨def*ies*⟩

**es·ca·la·tor** \'es-kə-,lāt-ər\ *n*
a moving stairway arranged like an endless belt

**es·ca·pade** \'es-kə-,pād\ *n*
a daring or reckless adventure

**¹es·cape** \is-'kāp\ *vb* **es·caped**; **es·cap·ing**
**1** to get away : get free or clear ⟨*escape* from a burning building⟩
**2** to keep free of : AVOID ⟨managed to *escape* injury⟩
**3** to fail to be noticed or remembered by ⟨the name *escapes* me⟩
**4** to leak out from some enclosed place

**Word History** Picture a person who is held fast by a cape or cloak. The person being held may be able to slip out of the garment and so escape from the captor. The word *escape* is based on such a picture. The English word *escape* came from an Old French word that came from two Latin words. The first of these Latin words meant "out of" and the second meant "cloak."

**²escape** *n*
**1** the act of escaping
**2** a way of escaping

**¹es·cort** \'es-,kȯrt\ *n*
**1** one (as a person or group) that accompanies another to give protection or show courtesy
**2** the man who goes on a date with a woman

**²es·cort** \is-'kȯrt\ *vb*
to accompany as an escort

**¹-ese** \'ēz\ *adj suffix*
of, relating to, or coming from a certain place or country ⟨Japan*ese*⟩

**²-ese** *n suffix, pl* **-ese**
**1** native or resident of a specified place or country ⟨Chin*ese*⟩
**2** language of a particular place, country, or nationality
**3** speech or literary style of a specified place, person, or group

**Es·ki·mo** \'es-kə-,mō\ *n, pl* **Es·ki·mos**
a member of a group of peoples of Alaska, northern Canada, Greenland, and northeastern Siberia

**Eskimo dog**

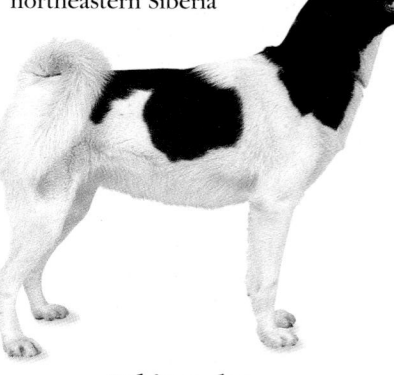

**Eskimo dog** *n*
▲ a sled dog of northern North America

**esoph·a·gus** \i-'säf-ə-gəs\ *n, pl* **esoph·a·gi** \-ˌgī, -ˌjī\
the tube that leads from the mouth through the throat to the stomach

**es·pe·cial** \is-'pesh-əl\ *adj*
SPECIAL
**es·pe·cial·ly** *adv*

**es·pi·o·nage** \'es-pē-ə-ˌnäzh\ *n*
the practice of spying : the use of spies

**es·py** \is-'pī\ *vb* **es·pied**; **es·py·ing**
to catch sight of

**-ess** \əs\ *n suffix*
female ⟨godd*ess*⟩

[1]**es·say** \e-'sā, 'es-ˌā\ *vb*
[1]TRY 6

[2]**es·say** \'es-ˌā, *1 also* e-'sā\ *n*
**1** [2]ATTEMPT
**2** a usually short piece of writing dealing with a subject from a personal point of view

**es·say·ist** \'es-ˌā-ist\ *n*
a writer of essays

**es·sence** \'es-ns\ *n*
**1** the basic part of something ⟨freedom is the *essence* of democracy⟩
**2** a substance made from a plant or drug and having its special qualities
**3** [1]PERFUME 2

[1]**es·sen·tial** \i-'sen-chəl\ *adj*
**1** forming or belonging to the basic part of something ⟨free speech is an *essential* right of citizenship⟩
**2** important in the highest degree
**es·sen·tial·ly** *adv*

[2]**essential** *n*
something that is essential

**-est** \əst\ *adj suffix or adv suffix*
used to form the superlative degree of adjectives and adverbs of one syllable ⟨fatt*est*⟩ ⟨lat*est*⟩ and of some adjectives and adverbs of two or more syllables ⟨luck*iest*⟩ ⟨often*est*⟩

**es·tab·lish** \is-'tab-lish\ *vb*
**1** to bring into being : FOUND ⟨*establish* a colony⟩
**2** to put beyond doubt : PROVE

**es·tab·lish·ment** \is-'tab-lish-mənt\ *n*
**1** the act of establishing
**2** a place for residence or for business

**es·tate** \is-'tāt\ *n*
**1** [1]STATE 1 ⟨the low *estate* of the poor⟩
**2** the property of all kinds that a person leaves at death
**3** a fine country house on a large piece of land

[1]**es·teem** \is-'tēm\ *n*
high regard

[2]**esteem** *vb*
to think well or highly of

**esthetic** *variant of* AESTHETIC

[1]**es·ti·mate** \'es-tə-ˌmāt\ *vb* **es·ti·mat·ed**; **es·ti·mat·ing**
**1** to give or form a general idea of (as the value, size, or cost of something)
**2** to form an opinion ⟨I *estimate* our team will win⟩

[2]**es·ti·mate** \'es-tə-mət\ *n*
**1** an opinion or judgment especially of the value or quality of something
**2** an approximation of the size or cost of something

**es·ti·ma·tion** \ˌes-tə-'mā-shən\ *n*
**1** the making of an estimate : JUDGMENT
**2** an estimate formed : OPINION

**es·tu·ary** \'es-chə-ˌwer-ē\ *n, pl* **es·tu·ar·ies**
an arm of the sea at the lower end of a river

**et cet·era** \et-'set-ə-rə, -'se-trə\
and others of the same kind : and so forth : and so on

**etch** \'ech\ *vb*
to produce designs or figures on metal or glass by lines eaten into the substance by acid

**etch·ing** \'ech-ing\ *n*
**1** the art or process of producing drawings or pictures by printing from etched plates
**2** a picture made from an etched plate

**eter·nal** \i-'tərn-l\ *adj*
**1** lasting forever : having no beginning and no end
**2** continuing without interruption

**eter·ni·ty** \i-'tər-nət-ē\ *n, pl* **eter·ni·ties**
**1** time without end
**2** the state after death
**3** a period of time that seems to be endless

**-eth** see -TH

**ether** \'ē-thər\ *n*
**1** the clear upper part of the sky
**2** a light flammable liquid used to dissolve fats and as an anesthetic

**ethe·re·al** \i-'thir-ē-əl\ *adj*
**1** HEAVENLY 1
**2** very delicate : AIRY

**eth·i·cal** \'eth-i-kəl\ *adj*
**1** of or relating to ethics
**2** following accepted rules of behavior ⟨an *ethical* doctor⟩

**eth·ics** \'eth-iks\ *n sing or pl*
**1** a branch of philosophy dealing with moral duty and with questions of what is good and bad
**2** the rules of moral behavior governing an individual or a group

**eth·nic** \'eth-nik\ *adj*
of or relating to groups of people with common characteristics and customs
**eth·ni·cal·ly** \-ni-kə-lē\ *adv*

**et·i·quette** \'et-i-kət, -ˌket\ *n*
the rules governing the proper way to behave or to do something

**-ette** \'et\ *n suffix*
**1** little one ⟨kitchen*ette*⟩
**2** female
**3** imitation

**et·y·mol·o·gy** \ˌet-ə-'mäl-ə-jē\ *n, pl* **et·y·mol·o·gies**
the history of a word shown by tracing it or its parts back to the earliest known forms and meanings both in its own language and any other language from which it may have been taken

**Word History** We can trace the English word *etymology* back to a Greek word. This Greek word meant "the true meaning of a word based on its origin." This word came in turn from a Greek word which meant "true."

**eu·ca·lyp·tus** \ˌyü-kə-'lip-təs\ *n, pl* **eu·ca·lyp·ti** \-ˌtī\ *or* **eu·ca·lyp·tus·es**
▶ a tree of a kind native mainly to western Australia and widely grown for shade, timber, gum, and oil

**eucalyptus**

a b c d e f g h i j k l m n o p q r s t u v w y z

**Eu·cha·rist** \'yü-kə-rəst\ *n*
COMMUNION 2

**eu·gle·na** \yu̇-'glē-nə\ *n*
▶ any of numerous tiny single-celled organisms that contain chlorophyll, swim about by means of a flagellum, and are often classified in science as algae

nucleus

flagellum

**euglena**

**eu·ro** \'yu̇r-ō\ *n, pl* **euros**
a coin or bill used by countries of the European Union

**[1]Eu·ro·pe·an** \ˌyu̇r-ə-'pē-ən\ *adj*
of or relating to Europe or the Europeans

**[2]European** *n*
a native or resident of Europe

**evac·u·ate** \i-'vak-yə-ˌwāt\ *vb*
**evac·u·at·ed**; **evac·u·at·ing**
**1** to make empty **:** empty out
**2** to discharge waste matter from the body
**3** to remove troops or people from a place of danger ⟨*evacuate* a city⟩

**evade** \i-'vād\ *vb* **evad·ed**; **evad·ing**
to get away from or avoid meeting directly ⟨*evade* a question⟩

**eval·u·ate** \i-'val-yə-ˌwāt\ *vb*
**eval·u·at·ed**; **eval·u·at·ing**
to find or estimate the value of

**eval·u·a·tion** \i-ˌval-yə-'wā-shən\ *n*
the act or result of evaluating

**evan·ge·list** \i-'van-jə-ləst\ *n*
a Christian preacher who goes about from place to place trying to change or increase people's religious feelings

**evap·o·rate** \i-'vap-ə-ˌrāt\ *vb*
**evap·o·rat·ed**; **evap·o·rat·ing**
**1** to change into vapor ⟨a liquid that *evaporates* quickly⟩
**2** to disappear without being seen to go
**3** to remove some of the water from something (as by heating)

**evap·o·ra·tion** \i-ˌvap-ə-'rā-shən\ *n*
the process of evaporating

**eve** \'ēv\ *n*
**1** EVENING
**2** the evening or day before a special day ⟨Christmas *eve*⟩
**3** the period just before an important event

**[1]even** \'ē-vən\ *adj*
**1** being without breaks or bumps ⟨*even* ground⟩
**2** staying the same over a period of time ⟨*even* breathing⟩
**3** being on the same line or level ⟨water *even* with the rim of a glass⟩
**4** equal in size, number, or amount ⟨bread cut in *even* slices⟩
**5** [1]EQUAL 2, FAIR ⟨an *even* trade⟩
**6** possible to divide by two ⟨*even* numbers⟩ **synonyms** see LEVEL
**even·ly** *adv*
**even·ness** *n*

**[2]even** *adv*
**1** at the very time **:** JUST ⟨*even* as the clock struck⟩
**2** INDEED ⟨we were willing, *even* eager, to help⟩
**3** used to stress an extreme or highly unlikely condition or instance ⟨so simple *even* a child can do it⟩
**4** to a greater extent or degree **:** STILL ⟨*even* better⟩
**5** so much as ⟨didn't *even* offer to help⟩

**[3]even** *vb*
to make or become even

**evolution 2**

Evolution is a theory that explains the process by which all living things slowly develop new features over time. From studying fossil remains, for example, scientists believe that the modern elephant may have evolved from a much smaller ancestor, belonging to or resembling the genus *Moeritherium*, which has long been extinct.

**the modern elephant with some extinct relatives**

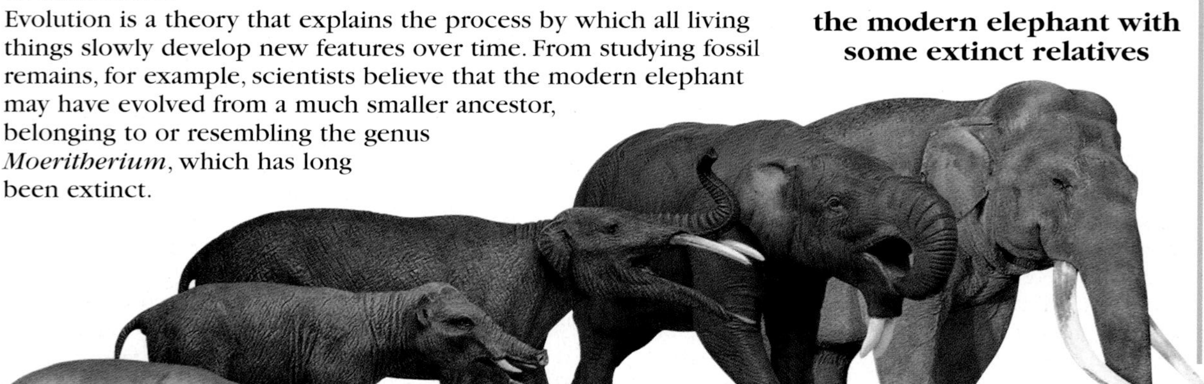

***Moeritherium*** \ˌmir-ə-'thir-ē-əm\ died out about 35 million years ago

***Phiomia*** \fī-'ō-mē-ə\ died out more than 24 million years ago

***Gomphotherium*** \ˌgäm-fō-'thir-ē-əm\ died out about 20 million years ago

***Deinotherium*** \ˌdī-nə-'thir-ē-əm\ died out about 2 million years ago

**elephant** is a modern-day species

**eve·ning** \'ēv-ning\ *n*
the final part of the day and early part of the night

**evening star** *n*
a bright planet (as Venus) seen in the western sky after sunset

**event** \i-'vent\ *n*
**1** something usually of importance that happens
**2** a social occasion (as a party)
**3** the fact of happening ⟨in the *event* of rain⟩
**4** a contest in a program of sports
**synonyms** see INCIDENT

**event·ful** \i-'vent-fəl\ *adj*
**1** filled with events
**2** very important

**even·tide** \'ē-vən-ˌtīd\ *n*
EVENING

**even·tu·al** \i-'ven-chə-wəl\ *adj*
coming at some later time ⟨*eventual* success⟩
**even·tu·al·ly** *adv*

**ev·er** \'ev-ər\ *adv*
**1** at all times **:** ALWAYS ⟨*ever* faithful⟩
**2** at any time ⟨has this *ever* been done before⟩
**3** in any way ⟨how can I *ever* thank you⟩

**ev·er·glade** \'ev-ər-ˌglād\ *n*
a swampy grassland

[1]**ev·er·green** \'ev-ər-ˌgrēn\ *n*
**1** an evergreen plant (as a pine or a laurel)
**2 evergreens** *pl* branches and leaves of evergreens used for decorations

[2]**evergreen** *adj*
having leaves that stay green through more than one growing season

**ev·er·last·ing** \ˌev-ər-'las-ting\ *adj*
**1** lasting forever **:** ETERNAL ⟨*everlasting* fame⟩
**2** going on for a long time or for too long a time ⟨stop that *everlasting* noise⟩
**ev·er·last·ing·ly** *adv*

**ev·er·more** \ˌev-ər-'mōr\ *adj*
FOREVER 1

**ev·ery** \'ev-rē\ *adj*
being each of a group or series without leaving out any ⟨heard *every* word you said⟩

**ev·ery·body** \'ev-ri-ˌbäd-ē, -bəd-ē\ *pron*
every person

**ewe** and her lamb

**ev·ery·day** \ˌev-rē-ˌdā\ *adj*
used or suitable for every day **:** ORDINARY

**ev·ery·one** \'ev-rē-wən, -ˌwən\ *pron*
every person

**ev·ery·thing** \'ev-rē-ˌthing\ *pron*
every thing **:** ALL

**ev·ery·where** \'ev-rē-ˌhweər, -ˌhwaər, -ˌweər, -ˌwaər\ *adv*
in or to every place or part

**evict** \i-'vikt\ *vb*
to put out from property by legal action

**ev·i·dence** \'ev-ə-dəns\ *n*
**1** an outward sign **:** INDICATION ⟨find *evidence* of a robbery⟩
**2** material presented to a court to help find the truth in a matter

**ev·i·dent** \'ev-ə-dənt\ *adj*
clear to the sight or to the mind **:** PLAIN
**ev·i·dent·ly** \-dənt-lē, -ˌdent-\ *adv*

[1]**evil** \'ē-vəl\ *adj*
**1** morally bad **:** WICKED ⟨*evil* deeds⟩
**2** causing harm **:** tending to injure
**synonyms** see BAD

[2]**evil** *n*
**1** something that brings sorrow, trouble, or destruction ⟨the *evils* of poverty⟩
**2** the fact of suffering or wrongdoing

**evoke** \i-'vōk\ *vb* **evoked**; **evok·ing**
to call forth or up **:** SUMMON

**evo·lu·tion** \ˌev-ə-'lü-shən, ˌē-və-\ *n*
**1** the process of development of an animal or a plant
**2** ◀ the theory that the various kinds of existing animals and plants have come from kinds that existed in the past

**evolve** \i-'välv\ *vb* **evolved**; **evolv·ing**
to grow or develop out of something

**ewe** \'yü\ *n*
◀ a female sheep

**ex-** \'eks\ *prefix*
**1** out of **:** outside
**2** former

[1]**ex·act** \ig-'zakt\ *vb*
to demand and get by force or threat

[2]**exact** *adj*
showing close agreement with fact **:** ACCURATE **synonyms** see CORRECT
**ex·act·ly** *adv*
**ex·act·ness** *n*

**ex·act·ing** \ig-'zak-ting\ *adj*
making many or difficult demands upon a person **:** TRYING

**ex·ag·ger·ate** \ig-'zaj-ə-ˌrāt\ *vb* **ex·ag·ger·at·ed**; **ex·ag·ger·at·ing**
to enlarge a fact or statement beyond what is true

**ex·ag·ger·a·tion** \ig-ˌzaj-ə-'rā-shən\ *n*
**1** the act of exaggerating
**2** an exaggerated statement

**ex·alt** \ig-'zȯlt\ *vb*
**1** to raise in rank or power
**2** to praise highly

**ex·am** \ig-'zam\ *n*
EXAMINATION

**ex·am·i·na·tion** \ig-ˌzam-ə-'nā-shən\ *n*
**1** the act of examining or state of being examined ⟨go to the doctor for a physical *examination*⟩
**2** a test given to determine progress, fitness, or knowledge ⟨a college entrance *examination*⟩

**ex·am·ine** \ig-'zam-ən\ *vb* **ex·am·ined**; **ex·am·in·ing**
**1** to look at or check carefully
**2** to question closely

**ex·am·ple** \ig-'zam-pəl\ *n*
**1** a sample of something taken to show what the whole is like **:** INSTANCE
**2** something to be imitated **:** MODEL ⟨set a good *example*⟩
**3** something that is a warning to others
**4** a problem to be solved to show how a rule works ⟨an *example* in arithmetic⟩ **synonyms** see MODEL

A B C D E F G H I J K L M N O P Q R S T U V W X Y Z

**ex·as·per·ate** \ig-ˈzas-pə-ˌrāt\ *vb*
**ex·as·per·at·ed**; **ex·as·per·at·ing**
to make angry

**ex·as·per·a·tion** \ig-ˌzas-pə-ˈrā-shən\ *n*
extreme annoyance : ANGER

**ex·ca·vate** \ˈeks-kə-ˌvāt\ *vb*
**ex·ca·vat·ed**; **ex·ca·vat·ing**
**1** to hollow out : form a hole in ⟨*excavate* the side of a hill⟩
**2** to make by hollowing out
**3** to dig out and remove ⟨*excavate* iron ore⟩
**4** to expose to view by digging away a covering (as of earth) ⟨*excavate* the remains of an ancient city⟩

**ex·ca·va·tion** \ˌeks-kə-ˈvā-shən\ *n*
**1** the act of excavating
**2** a hollow place formed by excavating

**ex·ceed** \ik-ˈsēd\ *vb*
**1** to go or be beyond the limit of ⟨*exceed* the speed limit⟩
**2** to be greater than ⟨the cost must not *exceed* your allowance⟩

**ex·ceed·ing·ly** \ik-ˈsēd-ing-lē\ *adv*
to a very great degree

**ex·cel** \ik-ˈsel\ *vb* **ex·celled**; **ex·cel·ling**
to do better than others : SURPASS

**ex·cel·lence** \ˈek-sə-ləns\ *n*
**1** high quality
**2** an excellent quality : VIRTUE

**ex·cel·lent** \ˈek-sə-lənt\ *adj*
very good of its kind
**ex·cel·lent·ly** *adv*

[1]**ex·cept** \ik-ˈsept\ *prep*
**1** not including ⟨daily *except* Sundays⟩
**2** other than : BUT ⟨take no orders *except* from me⟩

[2]**except** *vb*
to leave out from a number or a whole : EXCLUDE

[3]**except** *conj*
if it were not for the fact that : ONLY ⟨I'd go, *except* it's too far⟩

**ex·cep·tion** \ik-ˈsep-shən\ *n*
**1** the act of leaving out
**2** a case to which a rule does not apply
**3** an objection or a reason for objecting

**ex·cep·tion·al** \ik-ˈsep-shən-l\ *adj*
**1** forming an exception ⟨an *exceptional* amount of rain⟩
**2** better than average : SUPERIOR
**ex·cep·tion·al·ly** *adv*

[1]**ex·cess** \ik-ˈses, ˈek-ˌses\ *n*
**1** a state of being more than enough ⟨eat to *excess*⟩
**2** the amount by which something is more than what is needed or allowed

[2]**excess** *adj*
more than is usual or acceptable

**ex·ces·sive** \ik-ˈses-iv\ *adj*
showing excess
**ex·ces·sive·ly** *adv*

[1]**ex·change** \iks-ˈchānj\ *n*
**1** a giving or taking of one thing in return for another : TRADE ⟨a fair *exchange*⟩
**2** the act of substituting one thing for another
**3** the act of giving and receiving between two groups ⟨an *exchange* of students between two countries⟩
**4** a place where goods or services are exchanged

[2]**exchange** *vb* **ex·changed**; **ex·chang·ing**
to give in exchange : TRADE, SWAP

**ex·cit·able** \ik-ˈsīt-ə-bəl\ *adj*
easily excited

**ex·cite** \ik-ˈsīt\ *vb* **ex·cit·ed**; **ex·cit·ing**
**1** to increase the activity of
**2** to stir up feeling in : ROUSE

**ex·cite·ment** \ik-ˈsīt-mənt\ *n*
**1** the state of being excited : AGITATION
**2** something that excites or stirs up

**ex·cit·ing** \ik-ˈsīt-ing\ *adj*
producing excitement ⟨an *exciting* adventure⟩

**ex·claim** \iks-ˈklām\ *vb*
to cry out or speak out suddenly or with strong feeling

**ex·cla·ma·tion** \ˌeks-klə-ˈmā-shən\ *n*
**1** a sharp or sudden cry of strong feeling
**2** strong expression of anger or complaint

**exclamation point** *n*
a punctuation mark ! used mostly to show a forceful way of speaking or strong feeling

**ex·clam·a·to·ry** \iks-ˈklam-ə-ˌtōr-ē\ *adj*
containing or using exclamation

**ex·clude** \iks-ˈklüd\ *vb*
**ex·clud·ed**; **ex·clud·ing**
to shut out : keep out

**ex·clu·sion** \iks-ˈklü-zhən\ *n*
the act of excluding : the state of being excluded

**ex·clu·sive** \iks-ˈklü-siv, -ziv\ *adj*
**1** excluding or trying to exclude others ⟨an *exclusive* neighborhood⟩
**2** [4]SOLE 2 ⟨that family has *exclusive* use of a bathing beach⟩
**3** ENTIRE, COMPLETE ⟨give me your *exclusive* attention⟩
**4** not including ⟨on weekdays, *exclusive* of Saturdays⟩
**ex·clu·sive·ly** *adv*

**ex·crete** \ik-ˈskrēt\ *vb* **ex·cret·ed**; **ex·cret·ing**
to separate and give off waste matter from the body usually as urine or sweat

**ex·cre·tion** \ik-ˈskrē-shən\ *n*
**1** the process of excreting
**2** waste material excreted

**ex·cre·to·ry** \ˈek-skrə-ˌtōr-ē\ *adj*
of or relating to excretion : used in excreting

**ex·cur·sion** \ik-ˈskər-zhən\ *n*
**1** a brief pleasure trip
**2** a trip at special reduced rates

**ex·cus·able** \ik-ˈskyü-zə-bəl\ *adj*
possible to excuse

[1]**ex·cuse** \ik-ˈskyüz\ *vb* **ex·cused**; **ex·cus·ing**
**1** to make apology for ⟨*excuse* yourself for being late⟩
**2** to overlook or pardon as of little importance ⟨please *excuse* my clumsiness⟩
**3** to let off from doing something ⟨*excused* from chores for a week⟩
**4** to be an acceptable reason for ⟨nothing *excuses* bad manners⟩

[2]**ex·cuse** \ik-ˈskyüs\ *n*
**1** the act of excusing
**2** something offered as a reason for being excused
**3** something that excuses or is a reason for excusing

**ex·e·cute** \ˈek-sə-ˌkyüt\ *vb*
**ex·e·cut·ed**; **ex·e·cut·ing**
**1** to put into effect : CARRY OUT, PERFORM ⟨*execute* a plan⟩
**2** to put to death according to a legal order
**3** to make according to a design

**ex·e·cu·tion** \ˌek-sə-ˈkyü-shən\ *n*
**1** a carrying through of something to its finish
**2** a putting to death as a legal penalty

[1]**ex·ec·u·tive** \ig-'zek-yət-iv\ *adj*
**1** fitted for or relating to the carrying of things to completion ⟨*executive* skills⟩
**2** concerned with or relating to the carrying out of the law and the conduct of public affairs ⟨the *executive* branch of our government⟩

[2]**executive** *n*
**1** the executive branch of a government
**2** a person who manages or directs ⟨a sales *executive*⟩

**ex·em·pli·fy** \ig-'zem-plə-ˌfī\ *vb* **ex·em·pli·fied**; **ex·em·pli·fy·ing**
to show by example

[1]**ex·empt** \ig-'zempt\ *adj*
free or released from some condition or requirement that other persons must meet or deal with

[2]**exempt** *vb*
to make exempt

**ex·emp·tion** \ig-'zemp-shən\ *n*
**1** the act of exempting : the state of being exempt
**2** something that is exempted

[1]**ex·er·cise** \'ek-sər-ˌsīz\ *n*
**1** the act of putting into use, action, or practice ⟨the *exercise* of patience⟩
**2** ► bodily activity for the sake of health ⟨go walking for *exercise*⟩
**3** a school lesson or other task performed to develop skill : practice work : DRILL ⟨finger *exercises*⟩
**4** **exercises** *pl* a program of songs, speeches, and announcing of awards and honors ⟨graduation *exercises*⟩

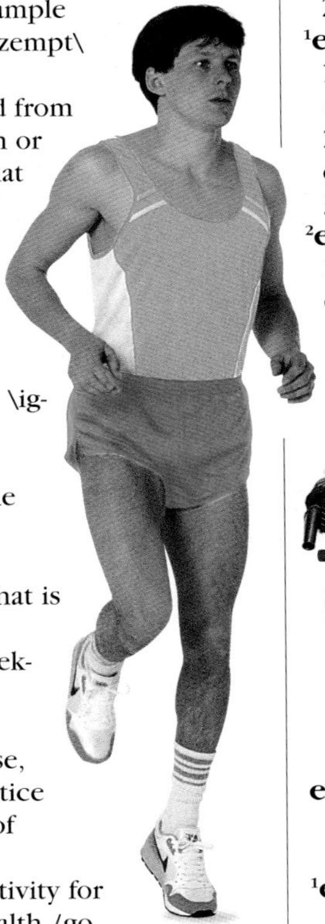

[1]**exercise 2:** a man jogging for exercise

[2]**exercise** *vb* **ex·er·cised**; **ex·er·cis·ing**
**1** to put into use : EXERT ⟨*exercise* authority⟩
**2** to use again and again to train or develop ⟨*exercise* a muscle⟩
**3** to take part in bodily activity for the sake of health or training

**ex·ert** \ig-'zərt\ *vb*
**1** to put forth (as strength) : bring into play
**2** to put (oneself) into action or to tiring effort

**ex·er·tion** \ig-'zər-shən\ *n*
**1** the act of exerting ⟨they won by the *exertion* of great effort⟩
**2** use of strength or ability

**ex·hale** \eks-'hāl\ *vb* **ex·haled**; **ex·hal·ing**
**1** to breathe out
**2** to send forth : give off

[1]**ex·haust** \ig-'zȯst\ *vb*
**1** to draw out or let out completely ⟨*exhaust* the water from a tank⟩
**2** to use up completely ⟨*exhausted* our supplies on the camping trip⟩
**3** to tire out : FATIGUE

[2]**exhaust** *n*
**1** the gas that escapes from an engine
**2** ▼ a system of pipes through which exhaust escapes

engine
central exhaust pipe
exhaust tail pipe
muffler

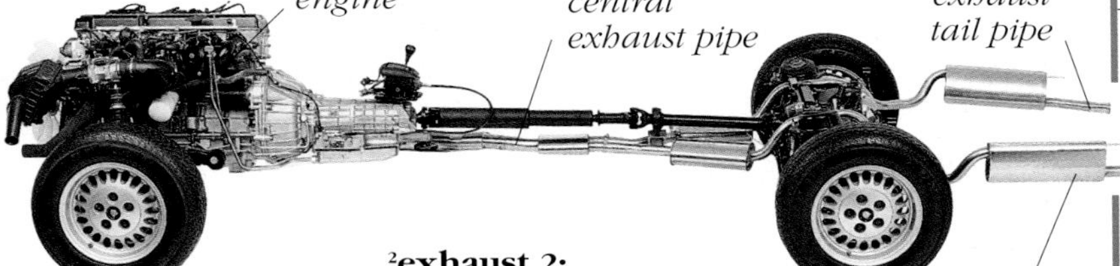

[2]**exhaust 2:** features of an automobile dual exhaust system

**ex·haus·tion** \ig-'zȯs-chən\ *n*
**1** the act of exhausting
**2** the condition of being exhausted

[1]**ex·hib·it** \ig-'zib-ət\ *vb*
**1** to show by outward signs : REVEAL ⟨*exhibit* interest in something⟩
**2** to put on display ⟨*exhibit* a collection of paintings⟩ **synonyms** see SHOW

[2]**exhibit** *n*
**1** an article or collection shown in an exhibition
**2** an article presented as evidence in a law court

**ex·hi·bi·tion** \ˌek-sə-'bish-ən\ *n*
**1** the act of exhibiting
**2** a public showing (as of athletic skill or works of art)

**ex·hil·a·rate** \ig-'zil-ə-ˌrāt\ *vb* **ex·hil·a·rat·ed**; **ex·hil·a·rat·ing**
to make cheerful or lively

**ex·hort** \ig-'zȯrt\ *vb*
to try to influence by words or advice : urge strongly

[1]**ex·ile** \'eg-ˌzīl, 'ek-ˌsīl\ *n*
**1** the sending or forcing of a person away from his or her own country or the situation of a person who is sent away
**2** a person who is expelled from his or her own country

[2]**exile** *vb* **ex·iled**; **ex·il·ing**
to force to leave one's own country

**ex·ist** \ig-'zist\ *vb*
**1** to have actual being : be real ⟨wonder if other worlds than ours *exist*⟩
**2** to continue to live
**3** to be found : OCCUR

**ex·is·tence** \ig-'zis-təns\ *n*
**1** the fact or the condition of being or of being real ⟨the largest animal in *existence*⟩
**2** the state of being alive : LIFE ⟨owe one's *existence* to medical skill⟩

[1]**ex·it** \'eg-zət, 'ek-sət\ *n*
**1** the act of going out of or away from a place : DEPARTURE
**2** a way of getting out of a place

[2]**exit** *vb*
to go out : LEAVE, DEPART

**ex·o·dus** \'ek-sə-dəs\ *n*
the going out or away of a large number of people

**ex·or·bi·tant** \ig-'zȯr-bət-ənt\ *adj*
going beyond the limits of what is fair, reasonable, or expected ⟨*exorbitant* prices⟩

**exo·sphere** \'ek-sō-ˌsfir\ *n*
the outer fringe region of the atmosphere

**ex·ot·ic** \ig-'zät-ik\ *adj*
introduced from a foreign country ⟨an *exotic* flower⟩

a b c d e f g h i j k l m n o p q r s t u v w x y z

**ex·pand** \ik-'spand\ *vb*
**1** to open wide : UNFOLD
**2** to take up or cause to take up more space ⟨metals *expand* under heat⟩
**3** to work out in greater detail ⟨*expand* a plan⟩

**ex·panse** \ik-'spans\ *n*
a wide area or stretch ⟨a vast *expanse* of desert⟩

**ex·pan·sion** \ik-'span-chən\ *n*
the act of expanding or the state of being expanded : ENLARGEMENT

**ex·pect** \ik-'spekt\ *vb*
**1** to look for or look forward to something that ought to or probably will happen ⟨*expect* rain⟩ ⟨*expects* to go to town tomorrow⟩
**2** to consider to be obliged ⟨*expected* you to pay your debts⟩

**ex·pec·tant** \ik-'spek-tənt\ *adj*
looking forward to or waiting for something

**ex·pec·ta·tion** \,ek-,spek-'tā-shən\ *n*
a looking forward to or waiting for something

**ex·pe·di·ent** \ik-'spēd-ē-ənt\ *adj*
suitable for bringing about a desired result often without regard to what is fair or right
**ex·pe·di·ent·ly** *adv*

**ex·pe·di·tion** \,ek-spə-'dish-ən\ *n*
**1** a journey for a particular purpose (as for exploring)
**2** the people making an expedition

**ex·pel** \ik-'spel\ *vb* **ex·pelled**; **ex·pel·ling**
**1** to force out
**2** to drive away

**ex·pend** \ik-'spend\ *vb*
**1** to pay out : SPEND
**2** to use up

**ex·pen·di·ture** \ik-'spen-di-chər\ *n*
**1** the act of spending (as money, time, or energy)
**2** something that is spent

**ex·pense** \ik-'spens\ *n*
**1** something spent or required to be spent : COST ⟨*expenses* of a trip⟩
**2** a cause for spending ⟨a car can be a great *expense*⟩

**ex·pen·sive** \ik-'spen-siv\ *adj*
COSTLY 1
**ex·pen·sive·ly** *adv*

[1]**ex·pe·ri·ence** \ik-'spir-ē-əns\ *n*
**1** the actual living through an event or events ⟨learn by *experience*⟩
**2** the skill or knowledge gained by actually doing a thing ⟨a job that requires someone with *experience*⟩
**3** something that one has actually done or lived through ⟨a soldier's *experiences* in war⟩

[2]**experience** *vb* **ex·pe·ri·enced**; **ex·pe·ri·enc·ing**
to have experience of : UNDERGO

**ex·pe·ri·enced** \ik-'spir-ē-ənst\ *adj*
made skillful or wise through experience

[1]**ex·per·i·ment** \ik-'sper-ə-mənt\ *n*
▼ a trial or test made to find out about something

plastic block
hazelnut
vegetable oil
colored water
syrup
bolt
grape

[1]**experiment:** an experiment to measure the density of different liquids and the weight of different objects

[2]**ex·per·i·ment** \ik-'sper-ə-,ment\ *vb*
to make experiments ⟨*experiment* with a new hairstyle⟩

**ex·per·i·men·tal** \ik-,sper-ə-'ment-l\ *adj*
of, relating to, or based on experiment ⟨an *experimental* science⟩

[1]**ex·pert** \'ek-,spərt, ik-'spərt\ *adj*
showing special skill or knowledge gained from experience or training
**synonyms** see SKILLFUL
**ex·pert·ly** *adv*
**ex·pert·ness** *n*

[2]**ex·pert** \'ek-,spərt\ *n*
a person with special skill or knowledge of a subject

**ex·pi·ra·tion** \,ek-spə-'rā-shən\ *n*
an act or instance of expiring

**ex·pire** \ik-'spīr\ *vb* **ex·pired**; **ex·pir·ing**
**1** [1]DIE 1
**2** to come to an end ⟨when your insurance *expires*⟩
**3** to breathe out : EXHALE

**ex·plain** \ik-'splān\ *vb*
**1** to make clear : CLARIFY 2
**2** to give the reasons for or cause of
**ex·plain·able** \-'splā-nə-bəl\ *adj*

**ex·pla·na·tion** \,ek-splə-'nā-shən\ *n*
**1** the act or process of explaining
**2** a statement that makes something clear

**ex·plan·a·to·ry** \ik-'splan-ə-,tōr-ē\ *adj*
giving explanation : helping to explain

**ex·plic·it** \ik-'splis-ət\ *adj*
so clear in statement that there is no doubt about the meaning

**ex·plode** \ik-'splōd\ *vb* **ex·plod·ed**; **ex·plod·ing**
**1** to burst or cause to burst with violence and noise ⟨*explode* a bomb⟩
**2** to burst forth ⟨*exploded* with anger⟩

[1]**ex·ploit** \'ek-,splȯit\ *n*
a brave or daring act

[2]**ex·ploit** \ik-'splȯit\ *vb*
**1** to get the value or use out of ⟨*exploit* a coal mine⟩
**2** to make use of unfairly for one's own benefit

**ex·plo·ra·tion** \,ek-splə-'rā-shən\ *n*
the act or an instance of exploring

**ex·plore** \ik-'splōr\ *vb* **ex·plored**; **ex·plor·ing**
**1** to search through or into : examine closely ⟨*explore* old writings⟩
**2** to go into or through for purposes of discovery ⟨*explore* a cave⟩

**ex·plor·er** \ik-'splōr-ər\ *n*
a person (as a traveler seeking new geographical or scientific information) who explores something

**ex·plo·sion** \ik-'splō-zhən\ *n*
**1** the act of exploding : a sudden and noisy bursting (as of a bomb)
**2** a sudden outburst of feeling

**[1]ex·plo·sive** \ik-'splō-siv, -ziv\ *adj*
**1** able to cause explosion ⟨the *explosive* power of gunpowder⟩
**2** likely to explode ⟨an *explosive* temper⟩
**ex·plo·sive·ly** *adv*

**[2]explosive** *n*
an explosive substance

**ex·po·nent** \ik-'spō-nənt\ *n*
a numeral written above and to the right of a number to show how many times the number is to be used as a factor ⟨the *exponent* 3 in $10^3$ indicates 10 × 10 × 10⟩

**[1]ex·port** \ek-'spōrt\ *vb*
to send or carry abroad especially for sale in foreign countries

**[2]ex·port** \'ek-,spōrt\ *n*
**1** something that is exported
**2** the act of exporting

**ex·pose** \ik-'spōz\ *vb* **ex·posed**; **ex·pos·ing**
**1** to leave without protection, shelter, or care
**2** to let light strike the photographic film or plate in taking a picture
**3** to put on exhibition : display for sale
**4** to make known ⟨*expose* a dishonest scheme⟩

**ex·po·si·tion** \,ek-spə-'zish-ən\ *n*
**1** an explaining of something
**2** a public exhibition

**ex·po·sure** \ik-'spō-zhər\ *n*
**1** an act of making something public ⟨the *exposure* of a plot⟩
**2** the condition of being exposed ⟨suffer from *exposure* to the cold⟩
**3** the act of letting light strike a photographic film or the time during which a film is exposed
**4** a section of a roll of film for one picture
**5** position with respect to direction ⟨a room with a southern *exposure*⟩

**ex·pound** \ik-'spau̇nd\ *vb*
**1** EXPLAIN 1, INTERPRET
**2** to talk especially for a long time

**[1]ex·press** \ik-'spres\ *adj*
**1** clearly stated ⟨an *express* order⟩
**2** of a certain sort ⟨came for an *express* purpose⟩
**3** sent or traveling at high speed ⟨*express* mail⟩

**[2]express** *n*
**1** a system for the special transportation of goods ⟨send a package by *express*⟩
**2** a vehicle (as a train or elevator) run at special speed with few or no stops

**[3]express** *vb*
**1** to make known especially in words ⟨*express* disapproval⟩
**2** to represent by a sign or symbol
**3** to send by express

**ex·pres·sion** \ik-'spresh-ən\ *n*
**1** the act or process of expressing especially in words

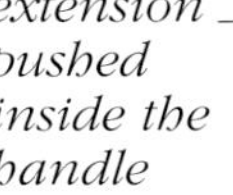
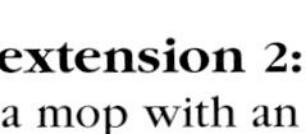


**extension 2:** a mop with an extension

**2** a meaningful word or saying ⟨an odd *expression*⟩
**3** a way of speaking, singing, or playing that shows mood or feeling ⟨read with *expression*⟩
**4** the look on one's face ⟨a pleased *expression*⟩
**ex·pres·sion·less** \-ləs\ *adj*

**ex·pres·sive** \ik-'spres-iv\ *adj*
expressing something : full of expression
**ex·pres·sive·ly** *adv*
**ex·pres·sive·ness** *n*

**ex·press·way** \ik-'spres-,wā\ *n*
a divided highway for rapid traffic

**ex·pul·sion** \ik-'spəl-shən\ *n*
the act of expelling : the state of being expelled

**ex·qui·site** \ek-'skwiz-ət, 'ek-skwiz-\ *adj*
**1** finely made or done ⟨*exquisite* workmanship⟩
**2** very pleasing (as through beauty or fitness) ⟨*exquisite* flowers⟩
**3** very severe : INTENSE ⟨*exquisite* pain⟩

**ex·tend** \ik-'stend\ *vb*
**1** [1]STRETCH 2 ⟨*extend* a sail⟩
**2** to hold out ⟨*extend* a hand⟩
**3** to make longer ⟨*extend* a visit⟩
**4** ENLARGE ⟨*extend* the meaning of a word⟩
**5** to stretch out or across something ⟨flood water *extended* to the door⟩ ⟨a bridge *extends* across the stream⟩

**ex·ten·sion** \ik-'sten-chən\ *n*
**1** a stretching out : an increase in length or time
**2** ◀ a part forming an addition or enlargement

**ex·ten·sive** \ik-'sten-siv\ *adj*
having wide extent : BROAD

**ex·tent** \ik-'stent\ *n*
**1** the distance or range over which something extends
**2** the point, degree, or limit to which something extends

**[1]ex·te·ri·or** \ek-'stir-ē-ər\ *adj*
EXTERNAL

**[2]exterior** *n*
an exterior part or surface

**ex·ter·mi·nate** \ik-'stər-mə-,nāt\ *vb* **ex·ter·mi·nat·ed**; **ex·ter·mi·nat·ing**
to get rid of completely : wipe out ⟨*exterminate* rats⟩

**[1]ex·ter·nal** \ek-'stərn-l\ *adj*
situated on or relating to the outside : OUTSIDE

**[2]external** *n*
something that is external

**ex·tinct** \ik-'stingkt\ *adj*
**1** no longer active ⟨an *extinct* volcano⟩
**2** no longer existing

**ex·tinc·tion** \ik-'stingk-shən\ *n*
**1** an act of extinguishing or an instance of being extinguished
**2** the state of being extinct

**ex·tin·guish** \ik-'sting-gwish\ *vb*
**1** to cause to stop burning
**2** to cause to die out : DESTROY
**ex·tin·guish·er** *n*

**ex·tol** \ik-ˈstōl\ *vb* **ex·tolled**; **ex·tol·ling**
to praise highly : GLORIFY

**[1]ex·tra** \ˈek-strə\ *adj*
being more than what is usual, expected, or due

**[2]extra** *n*
**1** something extra
**2** an added charge
**3** a special edition of a newspaper
**4** a person hired for a group scene (as in a movie)

**[3]extra** *adv*
beyond the usual size, amount, or degree ⟨*extra* large eggs⟩

**extra-** *prefix*
outside : beyond

**[1]ex·tract** \ik-ˈstrakt\ *vb*
**1** to remove by pulling ⟨*extract* a tooth⟩
**2** to get out by pressing, distilling, or by a chemical process ⟨*extract* juice from apples⟩
**3** to choose and take out for separate use ⟨*extract* a few lines from a poem⟩

**[2]ex·tract** \ˈek-ˌstrakt\ *n*
**1** a selection from a writing
**2** a product obtained by extraction

**ex·trac·tion** \ik-ˈstrak-shən\ *n*
**1** an act of extracting ⟨the *extraction* of a tooth⟩
**2** ORIGIN 1, DESCENT ⟨of French *extraction*⟩

**ex·tra·cur·ric·u·lar** \ˌek-strə-kə-ˈrik-yə-lər\ *adj*
of or relating to those activities (as athletics) that are offered by a school but are not part of the course of study

**ex·traor·di·nary** \ik-ˈstrȯrd-n-ˌer-ē, ˌek-strə-ˈȯrd-\ *adj*
so unusual as to be remarkable
**ex·traor·di·nari·ly** \ik-ˌstrȯrd-n-ˈer-ə-lē, ˌek-strə-ˌȯrd-n-ˈer-\ *adv*

**[1]eye 1**
The human eye lies in a bony socket in the skull. Light rays enter the pupil, and are focused by the cornea and lens to form upside-down images on the retina. The images are then transmitted as impulses along the optic nerve to the brain, which interprets them so that they appear right way up.

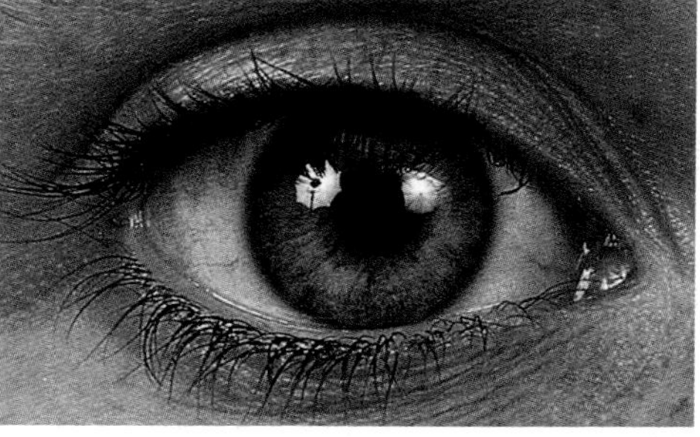

**front view of the human eye**

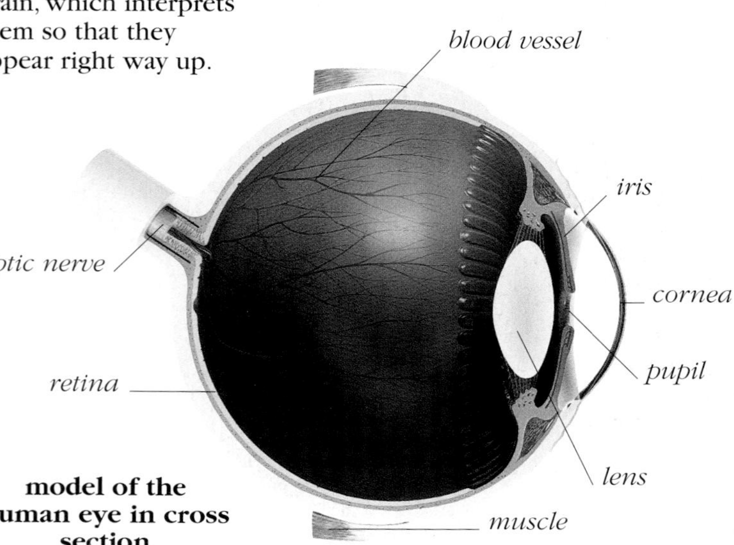


**model of the human eye in cross section**

**ex·trav·a·gance** \ik-ˈstrav-ə-gəns\ *n*
**1** the wasteful or careless spending of money
**2** something that is extravagant
**3** the quality or fact of being extravagant

**ex·trav·a·gant** \ik-ˈstrav-ə-gənt\ *adj*
**1** going beyond what is reasonable or suitable ⟨*extravagant* praise⟩
**2** wasteful especially of money
**ex·trav·a·gant·ly** *adv*

**[1]ex·treme** \ik-ˈstrēm\ *adj*
**1** existing to a very great degree ⟨*extreme* heat⟩ ⟨*extreme* poverty⟩
**2** farthest from a center ⟨the *extreme* edge⟩
**ex·treme·ly** *adv*

**[2]extreme** *n*
**1** something as far as possible from a center or from its opposite ⟨*extremes* of heat and cold⟩
**2** the greatest possible degree : MAXIMUM

**ex·trem·i·ty** \ik-ˈstrem-ət-ē\ *n, pl* **ex·trem·i·ties**
**1** the farthest limit, point, or part ⟨the *extremity* of the island⟩
**2** an end part of a limb of the body (as a foot)
**3** an extreme degree (as of emotion or distress)

**ex·tri·cate** \ˈek-strə-ˌkāt\ *vb* **ex·tri·cat·ed**; **ex·tri·cat·ing**
to free from entanglement or difficulty

**ex·ult** \ig-ˈzəlt\ *vb*
to be in high spirits : REJOICE

**Word History** When we exult we feel like jumping for joy though we may not really move at all. At first the English word *exult* meant "to jump for joy." *Exult* came from a Latin word meaning "to jump up." This Latin word was formed from a prefix meaning "out" and a verb meaning "to jump."

**ex·ul·tant** \ig-ˈzəlt-nt\ *adj*
full of or expressing joy or triumph
**ex·ul·tant·ly** *adv*

**-ey** see -Y

**[1]eye** \ˈī\ *n*
**1** ◀ the organ of seeing
**2** the ability to see
**3** the ability to recognize ⟨a keen *eye* for a bargain⟩

**4** GLANCE ⟨caught my *eye*⟩
**5** close attention **:** WATCH ⟨keep an *eye* on the dinner⟩
**6** JUDGMENT 1 ⟨guilty in the *eyes* of the law⟩
**7** something like or suggesting an eye ⟨the *eye* of a needle⟩
**8** the center of something ⟨the *eye* of a hurricane⟩
**eyed** \ˈīd\ *adj*
**eye·less** \ˈī-ləs\ *adj*

[2]**eye** *vb* **eyed**; **eye·ing** *or* **ey·ing**
to look at **:** watch closely

**eye·ball** \ˈī-ˌbȯl\ *n*
the whole eye

**eye·brow** \ˈī-ˌbrau̇\ *n*
the arch or ridge over the eye **:** the hair on the ridge over the eye

**eye·drop·per** \ˈī-ˌdräp-ər\ *n*
DROPPER 2

**eye·glass** \ˈī-ˌglas\ *n*
**1** a glass lens used to help one to see clearly
**2** ► **eyeglasses** *pl* a pair of glass lenses set in a frame and used to help one to see clearly

**eye·lash** \ˈī-ˌlash\ *n*
a single hair of the fringe on the eyelid

**eye·let** \ˈī-lət\ *n*
**1** ► a small hole (as in cloth or leather) for a lace or rope
**2** GROMMET

**eye·lid** \ˈī-ˌlid\ *n*
the thin movable cover of an eye

**eye·piece** \ˈī-ˌpēs\ *n*
the lens or combination of lenses at the eye end of an optical instrument (as a microscope or telescope)

**eyeglass 2:**
eyeglasses

**eyelet 1:**
eyelets on a tennis shoe

**eye·sight** \ˈī-ˌsīt\ *n*
[1]SIGHT 4, VISION

**eye·sore** \ˈī-ˌsōr\ *n*
something displeasing to the sight ⟨that old building is an *eyesore*⟩

**eye·strain** \ˈī-ˌstrān\ *n*
a tired or irritated state of the eyes (as from too much use)

**eye·tooth** \ˈī-ˈtüth\ *n, pl* **eye·teeth** \-ˈtēth\
a canine tooth of the upper jaw

**ey·rie** \ˈīr-ē, *or same as* AERIE\ *n*
AERIE

a b c d e f g h i j k l m n o p q r s t u v w x y z

**The sounds of F:** The letter **F** has one main sound in English. It sounds the same in the words **father**, **after**, and **roof**. A double **F** in a word sounds the same as a single **F**, as in the word **coffee**.

There is one very common word in which the letter **F** has the sound of **V**. That is the word **of**.

The **F** sound is sometimes spelled **PH**. Examples of words with this spelling are **phone**, **photo**, **pharaoh**, and **aphid**.

In a few other words, the sound of **F** is spelled **GH**; but this never happens at the beginning of a word. Examples of words in which **GH** sounds like **F** are **laugh** and **cough**.

**f** \'ef\ *n, pl* **f's** *or* **fs** \'efs\ *often cap*
**1** the sixth letter of the English alphabet
**2** a grade that shows a student's work is failing

**fa** \'fä\ *n*
the fourth note of the musical scale

**fa·ble** \'fā-bəl\ *n*
**1** a story that is not true
**2** a story in which animals speak and act like people and which is usually meant to teach a lesson

**fab·ric** \'fab-rik\ *n*
**1** the basic structure ⟨the *fabric* of society⟩
**2** CLOTH 1
**3** a structural plan or material

**fab·u·lous** \'fab-yə-ləs\ *adj*
**1** like a fable especially in being marvelous or beyond belief ⟨*fabulous* wealth⟩
**2** told in or based on fable

**fa·cade** \fə-'säd\ *n*
▶ the face or front of a building

[1]**face** \'fās\ *n*
**1** the front part of the head
**2** an expression of the face ⟨put on a sad *face*⟩
**3** outward appearance ⟨looks easy on the *face* of it⟩
**4** GRIMACE ⟨made a *face*⟩
**5** DIGNITY 1, PRESTIGE ⟨afraid of losing *face*⟩
**6** a front, upper, or outer surface
**7** one of the flat surfaces that bound a solid ⟨a *face* of a prism⟩

[2]**face** *vb* **faced**; **fac·ing**
**1** to cover the front or surface of ⟨a building *faced* with marble⟩
**2** to have the front or face toward ⟨the house *faces* east⟩ ⟨*face* the class⟩
**3** to oppose firmly ⟨*face* danger⟩

**fac·et** \'fas-ət\ *n*
▶ one of the small flat surfaces on a cut gem

**fa·ce·tious** \fə-'sē-shəs\ *adj*
intended or trying to be funny

**face–to–face** \ˌfās-tə-ˌfās\ *adv or adj*
in person ⟨met *face-to-face*⟩

**fa·cial** \'fā-shəl\ *adj*
of or relating to the face
**fa·cial·ly** *adv*

**fa·cil·i·tate** \fə-'sil-ə-ˌtāt\ *vb*
**fa·cil·i·tat·ed**; **fa·cil·i·tat·ing**
to make easier

**fa·cil·i·ty** \fə-'sil-ət-ē\ *n, pl* **fa·cil·i·ties**
**1** freedom from difficulty
**2** ease in doing something : APTITUDE ⟨shows *facility* in reading⟩
**3** something that makes an action, operation, or activity easier ⟨cooking *facilities*⟩

**facets** of a diamond

**fac·sim·i·le** \fak-'sim-ə-lē\ *n*
**1** an exact copy
**2** a system of transmitting and reproducing printed matter or pictures by means of signals sent over telephone lines

**fact** \'fakt\ *n*
**1** something (as an event or an act) that really exists or has occurred ⟨life and death are *facts*⟩

**facade** of a 19th-century building in New York City

2 physical reality or actual experience ⟨this is a matter of *fact*, not fiction⟩

[1]**fac·tor** \'fak-tər\ *n*
1 something that helps produce a result
2 any of the numbers that when multiplied together form a product

[2]**factor** *vb*
to find the factors of a number

**fac·to·ry** \'fak-tə-rē, 'fak-trē\ *n, pl* **fac·to·ries**
▶ a place where goods are manufactured

**fac·tu·al** \'fak-chə-wəl\ *adj*
of, relating to, or based on facts
**fac·tu·al·ly** *adv*

**fac·ul·ty** \'fak-əl-tē\ *n, pl* **fac·ul·ties**
1 ability to do something : TALENT ⟨a *faculty* for making friends⟩
2 one of the powers of the mind or body ⟨the *faculty* of hearing⟩
3 the teachers in a school or college

**fad** \'fad\ *n*
a way of doing or an interest widely followed for a time
**synonyms** see FASHION

**fade** \'fād\ *vb* **fad·ed**; **fad·ing**
1 to dry up : WITHER ⟨a *faded* flower⟩
2 to lose or cause to lose brightness of color
3 to grow dim or faint ⟨the path *faded* out⟩

**Fahr·en·heit** \'far-ən-,hīt\ *adj*
relating to or having a temperature scale on which the boiling point of water is at 212 degrees above the zero of the scale and the freezing point is at 32 degrees above zero

[1]**fail** \'fāl\ *vb*
1 to lose strength : WEAKEN ⟨*failing* in health⟩
2 to die away
3 to stop functioning ⟨the engine *failed*⟩
4 to fall short ⟨their try *failed* of success⟩
5 to be or become absent or not enough ⟨the water supply *failed*⟩
6 to be unsuccessful ⟨*failed* the test⟩ ⟨*failed* in the new job⟩
7 to become bankrupt ⟨the business *failed*⟩
8 DISAPPOINT, DESERT ⟨*fail* a friend in need⟩
9 [1]NEGLECT 2 ⟨*fail* to answer the phone⟩

[2]**fail** *n*
FAILURE 1 ⟨promised to go without *fail*⟩

**factory:** engines being assembled in an automobile factory

**fail·ing** \'fā-ling\ *n*
a slight moral weakness or flaw

**fail·ure** \'fāl-yər\ *n*
1 a failing to do or perform ⟨*failure* to keep a promise⟩
2 a state of being unable to work in a normal way ⟨heart *failure*⟩
3 a lack of success ⟨*failure* in a test⟩
4 BANKRUPTCY
5 a falling short ⟨crop *failure*⟩
6 a breaking down ⟨a *failure* of memory⟩
7 a person or thing that has failed

[1]**faint** \'fānt\ *adj*
1 lacking courage : COWARDLY
2 being weak or dizzy and likely to collapse ⟨feel *faint*⟩
3 lacking strength : FEEBLE ⟨a *faint* attempt⟩
4 not clear or plain : DIM
**faint·ly** *adv*
**faint·ness** *n*

[2]**faint** *vb*
to lose consciousness

[3]**faint** *n*
an act or condition of fainting

**faint·heart·ed** \'fānt-'härt-əd\ *adj*
TIMID

[1]**fair** \'faər, 'feər\ *adj*
1 attractive in appearance : BEAUTIFUL ⟨our *fair* city⟩
2 not stormy or cloudy ⟨*fair* weather⟩
3 not favoring one over another ⟨received *fair* treatment⟩
4 observing the rules ⟨*fair* play⟩
5 being within the foul lines ⟨*fair* ball⟩
6 not dark : BLOND ⟨*fair* hair⟩
7 neither good nor bad ⟨a *fair* grade in spelling⟩
**fair·ness** *n*

[2]**fair** *adv*
in a fair manner ⟨play *fair*⟩

[3]**fair** *n*
1 a gathering of buyers and sellers at a certain time and place for trade
2 an exhibition (as of livestock or farm products) usually along with entertainment and amusements ⟨county *fair*⟩
3 a sale of articles for a charitable purpose ⟨a church *fair*⟩

**fair·ground** \'faər-,graund, 'feər-\ *n*
▼ an area set aside for fairs, circuses, or exhibitions

**fairground:** the Maryland State Fair

**fair·ly** \'faər-lē, 'feər-\ *adv*
1 in a manner of speaking : QUITE ⟨*fairly* bursting with pride⟩
2 in a fair manner : JUSTLY ⟨treated *fairly*⟩
3 for the most part : RATHER ⟨a *fairly* easy job⟩

**[1]fairy** \'faər-ē, 'feər-ē\ *n, pl* **fair·ies**
an imaginary being who has the form of a very tiny human being and has magic powers

**Word History** The English word *fairy* was derived from an Old French word that meant "fairy." This Old French word came from the Latin name of the Roman goddess of fate, who got her name from a Latin word that meant "fate." The English word *fate* came from this same Latin word.

**[2]fairy** *adj*
of, relating to, or like a fairy

**fairy·land** \'faər-ē-,land, 'feər-\ *n*
**1** the land of fairies
**2** a place of delicate beauty or magical charm

**fairy tale** *n*
**1** a story about fairies
**2** a small lie **:** FIB

**faith** \'fāth\ *n*
**1** loyalty to duty or to a person
**2** belief in God
**3** firm belief even in the absence of proof
**4** a system of religious beliefs **:** RELIGION **synonyms** see BELIEF

**faith·ful** \'fāth-fəl\ *adj*
**1** RELIABLE ⟨a *faithful* worker⟩
**2** firm in devotion or support ⟨a *faithful* friend⟩
**3** true to the facts **:** ACCURATE
**faith·ful·ly** \-fə-lē\ *adv*
**faith·ful·ness** *n*

**Synonyms** FAITHFUL, LOYAL, and TRUE mean firm in one's allegiance to something. FAITHFUL suggests that one has a firm and constant allegiance to something to which one is united by or as if by a promise or pledge ⟨always be *faithful* to your duty⟩. LOYAL suggests that one firmly refuses to desert or betray ⟨citizens who are *loyal* to their country⟩. TRUE stresses that one is personally devoted to someone or something ⟨a *true* friend who was ready to help in time of need⟩.

**faith·less** \'fāth-ləs\ *adj*
not true to allegiance or duty
**faith·less·ly** *adv*
**faith·less·ness** *n*

**Synonyms** FAITHLESS, DISLOYAL, and TRAITOROUS mean not being true to something that has a right to one's allegiance. FAITHLESS suggests breaking a promise or pledge to remain loyal to someone or something ⟨our *faithless* friends left us at the first sign of trouble⟩. DISLOYAL suggests that one is unfaithful to someone or something that has the right to expect loyalty ⟨*disloyal* citizens will be punished⟩. TRAITOROUS suggests either actual treason or a betrayal of trust ⟨the *traitorous* soldier was giving secrets to the enemy⟩.

**[1]fake** \'fāk\ *adj*
[1]COUNTERFEIT

**[2]fake** *n*
a person or thing that is not really what is pretended

**[3]fake** *vb* **faked**; **fak·ing**
**1** to change or treat in a way that gives a false effect
**2** [2]COUNTERFEIT 2 ⟨*fake* a signature⟩
**3** PRETEND 1 ⟨*fake* surprise⟩

**fal·con** \'fal-kən, 'fȯl-\ *n*
**1** a hawk trained for use in hunting small game
**2** ► any of several small hawks with long wings and swift flight

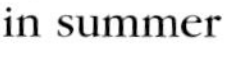
**falcon 2**

**fal·con·ry** \'fal-kən-rē, 'fȯl-\ *n*
the art or sport of hunting with a falcon

**[1]fall** \'fȯl\ *vb* **fell** \'fel\; **fall·en** \'fȯl-ən\; **fall·ing**
**1** to come or go down freely by the force of gravity ⟨an apple *fell* from the tree⟩
**2** to come as if by falling ⟨night *fell*⟩
**3** to become lower (as in degree or value) ⟨the temperature *fell* ten degrees⟩
**4** to topple from an upright position ⟨the tree *fell*⟩
**5** to collapse wounded or dead ⟨*fall* in battle⟩
**6** to become captured ⟨the city *fell* to the enemy⟩
**7** to occur at a certain time ⟨*falls* on the first Monday in September⟩
**8** to pass from one condition of body or mind to another ⟨*fall* asleep⟩ ⟨*fall* ill⟩
**fall short** be lacking in something

**[2]fall** *n*
**1** the act or an instance of falling ⟨a *fall* from a horse⟩
**2** AUTUMN
**3** a thing or quantity that falls ⟨a heavy *fall* of snow⟩
**4** a loss of greatness **:** DOWNFALL ⟨the *fall* of Rome⟩
**5** WATERFALL — usually used in pl. ⟨Niagara *Falls*⟩
**6** a decrease in size, amount, or value ⟨a *fall* in prices⟩
**7** the distance something falls

**fal·la·cy** \'fal-ə-sē\ *n, pl* **fal·la·cies**
**1** a false or mistaken idea
**2** false reasoning

**fall back** *vb*
[2]RETREAT

**fall·out** \'fȯ-,lau̇t\ *n*
the usually radioactive particles falling through the atmosphere as a result of the explosion of an atomic bomb

**fall out** \fȯ-'lau̇t\ *vb*
[2]QUARREL 2

**[1]fal·low** \'fal-ō\ *n*
land for crops that lies idle

**[2]fallow** *vb*
to till without planting a crop

**[3]fallow** *adj*
not tilled or planted

**fallow deer** *n*
▼ a small European deer with broad antlers and a pale yellowish coat spotted with white in summer

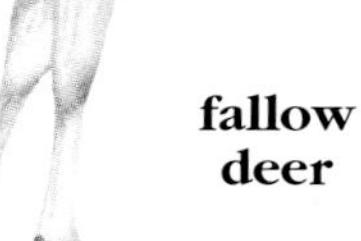
**fallow deer**

**[1]false** \'fȯls\ *adj* **fals·er**; **fals·est**
**1** not true, genuine, or honest ⟨*false* testimony⟩ ⟨*false* documents⟩ ⟨*false* teeth⟩
**2** not faithful or loyal ⟨*false* friends⟩
**3** not based on facts or sound judgment ⟨a *false* feeling of security⟩
**false·ly** *adv*
**false·ness** *n*

**[2]false** *adv*
in a false or misleading manner

**false·hood** \'fȯls-,hu̇d\ *n*
**1** [3]LIE
**2** the habit of lying ⟨given to *falsehood*⟩

**fal·si·fy** \'fȯl-sə-,fī\ *vb* **fal·si·fied**; **fal·si·fy·ing**
to make false ⟨*falsified* the accounts to cover up a theft⟩

**fal·si·ty** \'fȯl-sət-ē\ *n, pl* **fal·si·ties**
**1** something false
**2** the quality or state of being false

**fal·ter** \'fȯl-tər\ *vb*
**1** to move unsteadily : WAVER
**2** to hesitate in speech
**3** to hesitate in purpose or action

**fame** \'fām\ *n*
the fact or condition of being known to and usually thought well of by the public : RENOWN

**famed** \'fāmd\ *adj*
known widely and well : FAMOUS

**fa·mil·ial** \fə-'mil-yəl\ *adj*
of, relating to, or typical of a family

**fa·mil·iar** \fə-'mil-yər\ *adj*
**1** closely acquainted : INTIMATE ⟨*familiar* friends⟩
**2** INFORMAL 1 ⟨spoke in a *familiar* way⟩
**3** too friendly or bold
**4** often seen or experienced
**5** having a good knowledge of ⟨parents should be *familiar* with their children's schools⟩
**synonyms** see COMMON

safety cage
rotating blade

**[1]fan 1:** an electric fan

**fa·mil·iar·i·ty** \fə-,mil-'yar-ət-ē, -,mil-ē-'ar-\ *n, pl* **fa·mil·iar·i·ties**
**1** close friendship : INTIMACY
**2** good knowledge of something
**3** INFORMALITY 1

**fa·mil·iar·ize** \fə-'mil-yə-,rīz\ *vb* **fa·mil·iar·ized**; **fa·mil·iar·iz·ing**
to make familiar ⟨*familiarized* students with the library⟩

**[2]fan** *vb* **fanned**; **fan·ning**
**1** to move air with a fan
**2** to direct a current of air upon with a fan

**[3]fan** *n*
an enthusiastic follower or admirer

**[1]fa·nat·ic** \fə-'nat-ik\ *adj*
too enthusiastic or devoted

**family 5:** three members of the rose family

**fam·i·ly** \'fam-ə-lē, 'fam-lē\ *n, pl* **fam·i·lies**
**1** a group of persons who come from the same ancestor
**2** a group of persons living under one roof or one head
**3** a group of things sharing certain characteristics ⟨a *family* of languages⟩
**4** a social group made up of parents and their children
**5** ▲ a group of related plants or animals that ranks above the genus and below the order in scientific classification ⟨domestic cats, lions, and tigers are some of the members of the cat *family*⟩

**fam·ine** \'fam-ən\ *n*
**1** a very great and general lack of food
**2** a great shortage

**fam·ish** \'fam-ish\ *vb*
to suffer from hunger : STARVE

**fam·ished** \'fam-isht\ *adj*
very hungry

**fa·mous** \'fā-məs\ *adj*
very well-known

**fa·mous·ly** \'fā-məs-lē\ *adv*
very well

**[1]fan** \'fan\ *n*
**1** ◀ something (as a hand-waved semicircular device or a mechanism with rotating blades) for producing a current of air
**2** something like a fan
**fan·like** \-,līk\ *adj*

**Word History** The word *fanatic* can be traced back to a Latin noun that meant "temple." A Latin adjective was formed from this noun. At first the adjective meant "of a temple," but later it was used to refer to people who were thought to be inspired by the gods. Since insane people were believed to be possessed by gods, the adjective later came to mean "frantic" or "insane." Our English word *fanatic* came from this Latin adjective, and at first it too meant "insane" or "frantic."

**[2]fanatic** *n*
a fanatic person

**fan·ci·ful** \'fan-si-fəl\ *adj*
**1** showing free use of the imagination ⟨a *fanciful* tale⟩
**2** coming from fancy rather than reason ⟨a *fanciful* scheme for getting rich⟩
**fan·ci·ful·ly** \-fə-lē\ *adv*
**fan·ci·ful·ness** *n*

**[1]fan·cy** \'fan-sē\ *vb* **fan·cied**; **fan·cy·ing**
**1** [1]LIKE 1, ENJOY ⟨*fancies* candied apples⟩
**2** IMAGINE 1 ⟨well, *fancy* that⟩

**[2]fancy** *n, pl* **fancies**
**1** the power of the mind to think of things that are not present or real : IMAGINATION
**2** LIKING ⟨took a *fancy* to them⟩
**3** IDEA 2, NOTION

[3]**fancy** *adj* **fan·ci·er**; **fan·ci·est**
**1** not plain or ordinary ⟨a *fancy* dress⟩
**2** being above the average (as in quality or price) ⟨*fancy* fruits⟩
**3** done with great skill and grace ⟨*fancy* diving⟩
**fan·ci·ly** \'fan-sə-lē\ *adv*
**fan·ci·ness** \-sē-nəs\ *n*

**fang** \'fang\ *n*
**1** a long sharp tooth by which animals seize and hold their prey
**2** ▶ one of the usually two long hollow or grooved teeth by which a poisonous snake injects its poison
**fanged** \'fangd\ *adj*

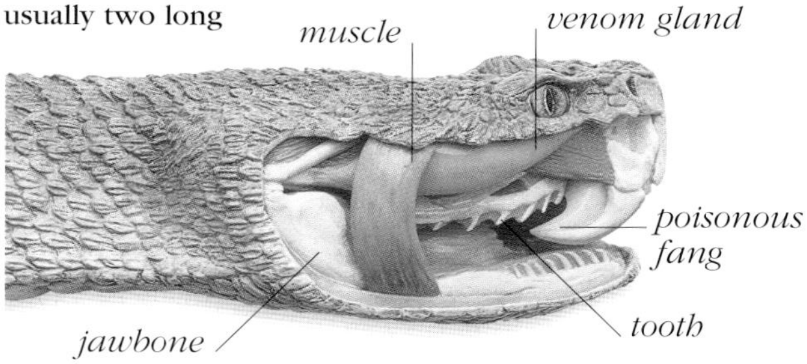

**fang 2:** fang on model head of a rattlesnake

**fan·tas·tic** \fan-'tas-tik\ *adj*
**1** produced by or like something produced by the fancy ⟨a *fantastic* scheme⟩
**2** barely believable
**fan·tas·ti·cal·ly** \-ti-kə-lē\ *adv*

**fan·ta·sy** *or* **phan·ta·sy** \'fant-ə-sē, -zē\ *n, pl* **fan·ta·sies** *or* **phan·ta·sies**
**1** IMAGINATION 1
**2** something produced by the imagination

[1]**far** \'fär\ *adv* **far·ther** \'fär-t͟hər\ *or* **fur·ther** \'fər-\; **far·thest** \'fär-t͟həst\ *or* **fur·thest** \'fər-\
**1** at or to a great distance in space or time ⟨*far* from home⟩ ⟨read *far* into the night⟩
**2** to a great extent : MUCH ⟨*far* better⟩
**3** to or at a definite distance or point ⟨as *far* as I know⟩
**4** to an advanced point ⟨a smart student can go *far*⟩

[2]**far** *adj* **far·ther** *or* **fur·ther**; **far·thest** *or* **fur·thest**
**1** very distant in space or time ⟨a *far* country⟩
**2** LONG 3 ⟨a *far* journey⟩
**3** the more distant of two ⟨on the *far* side of the stream⟩

**far·away** \,fär-ə-,wā\ *adj*
**1** REMOTE 1, DISTANT ⟨*faraway* lands⟩
**2** PREOCCUPIED ⟨a *faraway* look⟩

[1]**fare** \'faər, 'feər\ *vb* **fared**; **far·ing**
to get along : SUCCEED

[2]**fare** *n*
**1** the money a person pays to travel (as on a bus)
**2** a person paying a fare
**3** FOOD 1

[1]**fare·well** \faər-'wel, feər-\ *n*
an expression of good wishes at parting — often used as an interjection

[2]**fare·well** \,faər-,wel, ,feər-\ *adj*
of or relating to a time or act of leaving : FINAL ⟨a *farewell* speech⟩

**far-fetched** \'fär-'fecht\ *adj*
not likely to be true

[1]**farm** \'färm\ *n*
**1** a piece of land used for raising crops or animals
**2** an area of water where fish or shellfish are grown

[2]**farm** *vb*
to work on or run a farm
**farm·er** *n*

**farm·hand** \'färm-,hand\ *n*
a farm laborer

**farm·house** \'färm-,hau̇s\ *n*
the dwelling house of a farm

**farm·yard** \'färm-,yärd\ *n*
▼ the yard around or enclosed by farm buildings

**far–off** \'fär-'ȯf\ *adj*
distant in time or space

**far–reach·ing** \'fär-'rē-ching\ *adj*
EXTENSIVE

**far·sight·ed** \'fär-'sīt-əd\ *adj*
**1** able to see distant things more clearly than near ones
**2** able to judge how something will work out in the future
**far·sight·ed·ness** *n*

[1]**far·ther** \'fär-t͟hər\ *adv*
**1** at or to a greater distance or more advanced point
**2** [2]BESIDES

[2]**farther** *adj*
more distant

[1]**far·thest** \'fär-t͟həst\ *adj*
most distant

[2]**farthest** *adv*
**1** to or at the greatest distance in space or time
**2** to the most advanced point

**fas·ci·nate** \'fas-n-,āt\ *vb* **fas·ci·nat·ed**; **fas·ci·nat·ing**
**1** to seize and hold the attention of
**2** to attract greatly

**fas·ci·na·tion** \,fas-n-'ā-shən\ *n*
the state of being fascinated

**fas·cism** \'fash-,iz-əm\ *n*
a political system headed by a dictator in which the government controls business and labor and opposition is not permitted

**fas·cist** \'fash-əst\ *n, often cap*
one who approves of or practices fascism

**farmyard:** model of a 19th-century farmyard

**[1]fash·ion** \'fash-ən\ *n*
**1** the make or form of something
**2** MANNER 2, WAY
**3** ▶ the popular style of a thing at a certain time

**Synonyms** FASHION, STYLE, and FAD mean the way that up-to-date people do things. FASHION is used of any custom (as a way of dressing or behaving) that is widely accepted at any one time or place ⟨it was once the *fashion* for everyone to wear hats⟩. STYLE may suggest a fashion that is approved of by people with money and taste ⟨the house was decorated in the latest *style*⟩. FAD suggests something (as a way of dressing) that is very popular and often only for a short time ⟨running as a popular sport may be just a *fad*⟩.

**[2]fashion** *vb*
to give shape or form to : MOLD

**fash·ion·able** \'fash-ə-nə-bəl, 'fash-nə-\ *adj*
following the fashion or established style
**fash·ion·ably** \-blē\ *adv*

**[1]fast** \'fast\ *adj*
**1** firmly placed ⟨tent pegs *fast* in the ground⟩
**2** totally loyal ⟨*fast* friends⟩
**3** moving, operating, or acting quickly ⟨a *fast* train⟩ ⟨a *fast* thinker⟩
**4** taking a short time ⟨a *fast* trip⟩
**5** indicating ahead of the correct time ⟨the clock is *fast*⟩
**6** not likely to fade ⟨*fast* colors⟩

**Synonyms** FAST, RAPID, and SWIFT mean moving, proceeding, or acting with great speed. FAST is used of the thing that moves ⟨a *fast* horse⟩. RAPID is used of the movement itself ⟨the horse moved at a *rapid* pace⟩. SWIFT suggests ease of movement along with great speed ⟨the *swift* horse easily jumped the high fence⟩.

**[2]fast** *adv*
**1** in a fast or fixed way ⟨stuck *fast* in the mud⟩
**2** to the full extent : SOUND ⟨*fast* asleep⟩
**3** with great speed ⟨run *faster* than a rabbit⟩

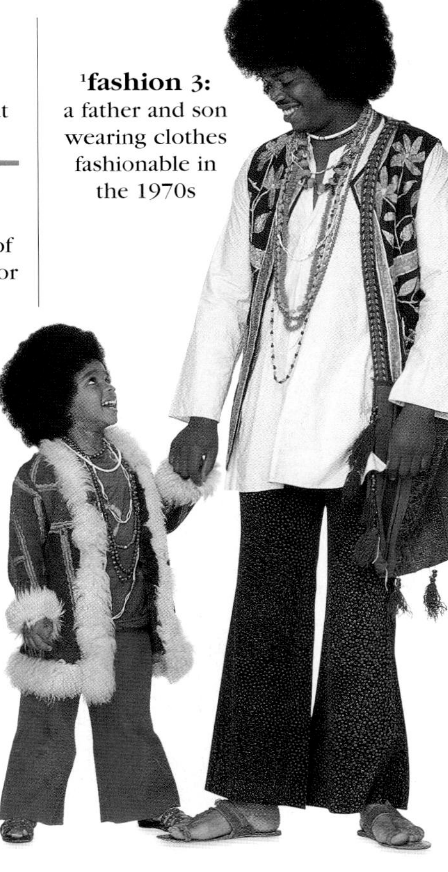

**[1]fashion 3:** a father and son wearing clothes fashionable in the 1970s

**[3]fast** *vb*
**1** to go without eating
**2** to eat in small amounts or only certain foods

**[4]fast** *n*
**1** the act of fasting
**2** a period of fasting

**fas·ten** \'fas-n\ *vb*
**1** to attach or join by or as if by pinning, tying, or nailing ⟨*fasten* clothes on a line⟩
**2** to fix firmly
**3** to become fixed or joined
**fas·ten·er** *n*

**fas·ten·ing** \'fas-n-ing\ *n*
something that holds another thing shut or in the right position

**fast–food** \'fast-ˌfüd\ *adj*
of, relating to, or specializing in food that can be prepared and served quickly ⟨a *fast-food* restaurant⟩
**fast–food** *n*

**fas·tid·i·ous** \fas-'tid-ē-əs\ *adj*
hard to please : very particular

**[1]fat** \'fat\ *adj* **fat·ter**; **fat·test**
**1** having much body fat ⟨a *fat* puppy⟩
**2** [1]THICK 1 ⟨a *fat* book of poems⟩
**3** richly rewarding or profitable ⟨signed a *fat* contract⟩
**4** swollen up ⟨got a *fat* lip in the fight⟩
**fat·ness** *n*

**Synonyms** FAT, STOUT, and PLUMP mean having much flesh. FAT suggests that there is too much soft fatty tissue ⟨their dog is *fat* because they feed it too much⟩. STOUT suggests a thick figure with a large amount of flesh that is usually more muscular ⟨many wrestlers are *stout*⟩. PLUMP suggests a soft, pleasing, full figure ⟨people just love *plump* little babies⟩.

**[2]fat** *n*
**1** animal or plant tissue containing much greasy or oily material
**2** any of numerous compounds of carbon, hydrogen, and oxygen that make up most of animal or plant fat and that are important to nutrition as sources of energy
**3** a solid fat as distinguished from an oil
**4** the best or richest part ⟨the *fat* of the land⟩

**fa·tal** \'fāt-l\ *adj*
**1** FATEFUL ⟨on that *fatal* day⟩
**2** causing death : MORTAL ⟨received a *fatal* blow from a falling tree⟩
**synonyms** see DEADLY
**fa·tal·ly** *adv*

**fa·tal·i·ty** \fā-'tal-ət-ē\ *n*, *pl* **fa·tal·i·ties**
a death resulting from a disaster or accident

**fate** \'fāt\ *n*
**1** a power beyond human control that is held to determine what happens : DESTINY ⟨blamed their failure on *fate*⟩
**2** something that happens as though determined by fate : FORTUNE
**3** final outcome

**fate·ful** \'fāt-fəl\ *adj*
having serious results ⟨a *fateful* decision⟩ ⟨that *fateful* day⟩
**fate·ful·ly** \-fə-lē\ *adv*
**fate·ful·ness** *n*

**[1]fa·ther** \'fäth-ər, 'fàth-\ *n*
**1** a male parent
**2** *cap* GOD 1
**3** ANCESTOR
**4** one who cares for another as a father might
**5** one deserving the respect and love given to a father
**6** a person who invents or begins something ⟨the *father* of science⟩
**7** PRIEST — used especially as a title
**fa·ther·hood** \-,hu̇d\ *n*
**fa·ther·less** \-ləs\ *adj*

**[2]father** *vb*
**1** to become the father of
**2** to care for as a father

**fa·ther–in–law** \'fäth-ər-ən-,lȯ, 'fàth-\ *n, pl* **fa·thers–in–law**
the father of one's husband or wife

**fa·ther·land** \'fäth-ər-,land, 'fàth-\ *n*
one's native land

**fa·ther·ly** \'fäth-ər-lē, 'fàth-\ *adj*
**1** of or like a father
**2** showing the affection or concern of a father

**[1]fath·om** \'fath-əm\ *n*
a unit of length equal to six feet (about 1.8 meters) used chiefly in measuring the depth of water

**[2]fathom** *vb*
**1** to measure the depth of water by means of a special line
**2** to see into and come to understand ⟨can't *fathom* their reasons⟩

**[1]fa·tigue** \fə-'tēg\ *n*
a state of being very tired

**[2]fatigue** *vb* **fa·tigued**; **fa·tigu·ing**
to tire by work or exertion

**fat·ten** \'fat-n\ *vb*
to make or become fat

**fat·ty** \'fat-ē\ *adj* **fat·ti·er**; **fat·ti·est**
containing or like fat

**fault 5:** aerial view of the San Andreas Fault in California

**fau·cet** \'fȯ-sət\ *n*
a fixture for controlling the flow of a liquid (as from a pipe or cask)

**Word History** The English word *faucet* can be traced back to a Latin adjective that meant "false." A Latin verb meaning "to falsify" was formed from this adjective. A French verb came from this Latin verb. But in French the verb meant "to hurt or break" as well as "to falsify." A French noun for the stopper that is used to plug a cask was formed from the French verb. If you think about it, a stopper does look as though it might be breaking into the cask. Our English word *faucet* came from the French word for stopper. *Faucet* is now used not only for a stopper but for any fixture used to get liquid from a cask or pipe.

**fault** \'fȯlt\ *n*
**1** a weakness in character : FAILING
**2** FLAW, IMPERFECTION ⟨a *fault* in the weaving of the cloth⟩
**3** ERROR ⟨found a *fault* in the text⟩
**4** responsibility for something wrong ⟨your own *fault*⟩
**5** ◀ a crack in the earth's crust along which movement occurs
**at fault** BLAMEWORTHY

**fault·less** \'fȯlt-ləs\ *adj*
free from fault : PERFECT
**fault·less·ly** *adv*
**fault·less·ness** *n*

**faulty** \'fȯl-tē\ *adj* **fault·i·er**; **fault·i·est**
having a fault or blemish : IMPERFECT
**fault·i·ly** \-tə-lē\ *adv*
**fault·i·ness** \-tē-nəs\ *n*

**faun** \'fȯn\ *n*
▶ a Roman god of country life represented as part goat and part man

**faun:** an ancient Roman statue of a faun

**fau·na** \'fȯ-nə\ *n*
the animal life typical of a region, period, or special environment

**[1]fa·vor** \'fā-vər\ *n*
**1** APPROVAL, LIKING ⟨look with *favor* on a plan⟩
**2** a preferring of one side over another : PARTIALITY
**3** an act of kindness ⟨do me a *favor*⟩
**4** a small gift or decorative item ⟨party *favors*⟩

**[2]favor** *vb*
**1** to regard with favor ⟨*favors* a bill to cut taxes⟩
**2** OBLIGE 3
**3** to prefer especially unfairly
**4** to make possible or easier ⟨the weather *favored* our plan for a picnic⟩
**5** to look like

**fa·vor·able** \'fā-və-rə-bəl, 'fāv-rə-\ *adj*
**1** showing favor ⟨a *favorable* opinion⟩

**2** PROMISING ⟨*favorable* weather⟩
**fa·vor·able·ness** *n*
**fa·vor·ably** \-blē\ *adv*

**[1]fa·vor·ite** \'fā-və-rət, 'fāv-rət\ *n*
a person or a thing that is favored above others

**[2]favorite** *adj*
being a favorite ⟨our *favorite* food⟩

**[1]fawn** \'fȯn\ *vb*
**1** to show affection — used especially of a dog
**2** to try to win favor by behavior that shows lack of self-respect

**[2]fawn** *n*
**1** a young deer
**2** a light grayish brown

**[1]fax** \'faks\ *n*
**1** FACSIMILE 2
**2** a machine used to send or receive material by facsimile
**3** something sent or received by facsimile

**[2]fax** *vb*
to send material by facsimile

**faze** \'fāz\ *vb* **fazed**; **faz·ing**
DAUNT

**[1]fear** \'fir\ *vb*
to be afraid of : feel fear

**[2]fear** *n*
a strong unpleasant feeling caused by being aware of danger or expecting something bad to happen

**fear·ful** \'fir-fəl\ *adj*
**1** causing fear ⟨the *fearful* roar of a lion⟩
**2** filled with fear ⟨*fearful* of danger⟩
**3** showing or caused by fear
**fear·ful·ly** \-fə-lē\ *adv*
**fear·ful·ness** *n*

**fear·less** \'fir-ləs\ *adj*
free from fear : BRAVE
**fear·less·ly** *adv*
**fear·less·ness** *n*

**fear·some** \'fir-səm\ *adj*
causing fear

**fea·si·ble** \'fē-zə-bəl\ *adj*
possible to do or carry out ⟨a *feasible* plan⟩

**[1]feast** \'fēst\ *n*
**1** a fancy meal
**2** a religious festival

**[2]feast** *vb*
**1** to eat well
**2** [2]DELIGHT 1

**feat** \'fēt\ *n*
an act showing courage, strength, or skill

**[1]feath·er** \'fe<u>th</u>-ər\ *n*
**1** ▼ one of the light horny growths that make up the outer covering of a bird
**2** VARIETY 3, SORT ⟨people of that *feather*⟩
**feath·ered** \-ərd\ *adj*
**feath·er·less** \-ər-ləs\ *adj*

**[2]feather** *vb*
to grow or form feathers

**feather bed** *n*
**1** a mattress filled with feathers
**2** a bed with a feather mattress

**feath·ery** \'fe<u>th</u>-ə-rē\ *adj*
**1** like a feather or tuft of feathers
**2** covered with feathers

**[1]fea·ture** \'fē-chər\ *n*
**1** a single part (as the nose or the mouth) of the face
**2** something especially noticeable
**3** a main attraction
**4** a special story in a newspaper or magazine

**[2]feature** *vb* **fea·tured**; **fea·tur·ing**
to stand out or cause to stand out ⟨health care *features* in the new law⟩ ⟨*featured* a new singer⟩

**Feb·ru·ary** \'feb-yə-ˌwer-ē, 'feb-rə-, 'feb-ə-\ *n*
the second month of the year

---

**Word History** In ancient Rome a feast of purification, or cleansing, was held each year. It took place in the middle of the second month. The Latin name for this month was formed from the name of the feast. English *February* came from the Latin name of the month.

---

**fe·ces** \'fē-ˌsēz\ *n pl*
body waste that passes out from the intestine

**fed·er·al** \'fed-ə-rəl, 'fed-rəl\ *adj*
of or relating to a nation formed by the union of several states or nations

**fee** \'fē\ *n*
**1** a fixed charge ⟨admission *fees*⟩
**2** a charge for services ⟨a doctor's *fee*⟩

**fee·ble** \'fē-bəl\ *adj* **fee·bler** \-blər\; **fee·blest** \-bləst\
**1** lacking in strength or endurance
**2** not loud ⟨a *feeble* cry⟩
**synonyms** see WEAK
**fee·ble·ness** \-bəl-nəs\ *n*
**fee·bly** \-blē\ *adv*

### [1]feather 1

Unique to adult birds, feathers are lightweight and waterproof, kept in condition by regular preening. In flight, wing feathers increase lift, while tail feathers help with balance and maneuvering. Fluffy body feathers insulate the bird against extremes of weather. Many birds have colorful feathers to attract a mate, while others have feathers that provide protective camouflage.

**features of a macaw's wing feather**

**inner wing feather** of an owl

**tail feather** of a parrot

**body feathers** of a parrot

**outer wing feather** of a parakeet

[1]**feed** \'fēd\ *vb* **fed** \'fed\; **feed·ing**
**1** to give food to or give as food ⟨*fed* the baby⟩ ⟨*fed* cereal to the baby⟩
**2** to take food into the body : EAT ⟨cattle *feeding* on hay⟩
**3** to supply with something necessary (as to growth or operation) ⟨*feed* plants with fertilizer⟩
**feed·er** *n*

[2]**feed** *n*
food especially for livestock

[1]**feel** \'fēl\ *vb* **felt** \'felt\; **feel·ing**
**1** to be aware of through physical contact ⟨*feel* cold⟩
**2** to examine or test by touching
**3** to be conscious of ⟨*felt* a fear of the dark⟩
**4** to seem especially to the touch ⟨*feels* like silk⟩
**5** to sense oneself to be ⟨*felt* sick⟩

[2]**feel** *n*
**1** SENSATION 2, FEELING
**2** the quality of something as learned through or as if through touch

**feel·er** \'fē-lər\ *n*
**1** a long flexible structure (as an insect's antenna) that is an organ of touch
**2** a suggestion or remark made to find out the views of other people

**feel·ing** \'fē-ling\ *n*
**1** the sense by which a person knows whether things are hard or soft, hot or cold, heavy or light
**2** a sensation of temperature or pressure ⟨a *feeling* of cold⟩ ⟨a *feeling* of pain⟩
**3** a state of mind ⟨a *feeling* of joy⟩
**4** **feelings** *pl* the state of a person's emotions ⟨hurt my *feelings*⟩
**5** the condition of being aware
**6** IMPRESSION 4

**feet** *pl of* FOOT

**feign** \'fān\ *vb*
PRETEND 2

[1]**feint** \'fānt\ *n*
a pretended blow or attack at one point or in one direction to take attention away from the point or direction one really intends to attack

[2]**feint** *vb*
to make a feint

[1]**fe·line** \'fē-,līn\ *adj*
**1** of or relating to cats or the cat family
**2** like or like that of a cat

[2]**feline** *n*
a feline animal : CAT

[1]**fell** \'fel\ *vb*
to cut or knock down

[2]**fell** *past of* FALL

[1]**fel·low** \'fel-ō\ *n*
**1** COMPANION 1, COMRADE
**2** an equal in rank, power, or character
**3** one of a pair : MATE
**4** a male person

[2]**fellow** *adj*
being a companion, mate, or equal

**fel·low·man** \,fel-ō-'man\ *n*, *pl* **fel·low·men** \-'men\
a fellow human being

**fel·low·ship** \'fel-ō-,ship\ *n*
**1** friendly relationship existing among persons
**2** a group with similar interests

**fel·on** \'fel-ən\ *n*
[2]CRIMINAL

**fel·o·ny** \'fel-ə-nē\ *n*, *pl* **fel·o·nies**
a very serious crime

[1]**felt** \'felt\ *n*
a heavy material made by rolling and pressing fibers together

[2]**felt** *past of* FEEL

[1]**fe·male** \'fē-,māl\ *adj*
**1** of, relating to, or being the sex that bears young or lays eggs
**2** having a pistil but no stamens
**3** of, relating to, or characteristic of females
**fe·male·ness** *n*

[2]**female** *n*
a female being

**fem·i·nine** \'fem-ə-nən\ *adj*
**1** [1]FEMALE 1
**2** [1]FEMALE 3

**fem·i·nism** \'fem-ə-,niz-əm\ *n*
**1** the theory that women and men should have equal rights and opportunities
**2** organized activity on behalf of women's rights and interests
**fem·i·nist** \-nist\ *n or adj*

**fen** \'fen\ *n*
low land covered by water

[1]**fence** \'fens\ *n*
a barrier (as of wood or wire) to prevent escape or entry or to mark a boundary

[2]**fence** *vb* **fenced**; **fenc·ing**
**1** to enclose with a fence
**2** to practice fencing **synonyms** see ENCLOSE
**fenc·er** *n*

**fenc·ing** \'fen-sing\ *n*
▼ the sport of having a pretended fight with blunted swords

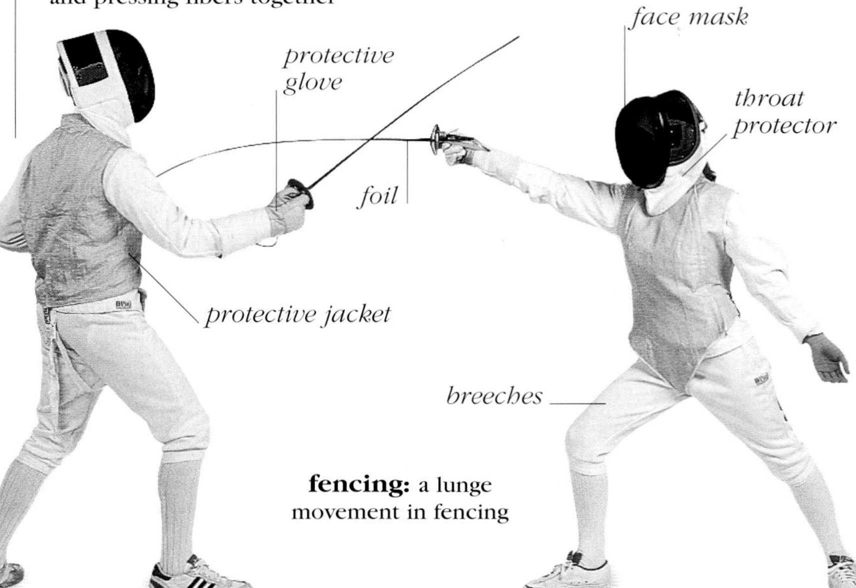


**fencing:** a lunge movement in fencing

**fend** \'fend\ *vb*
**1** REPEL 1 ⟨*fend* off an attack⟩
**2** to try to get along without help ⟨*fend* for oneself⟩

**fend·er** \'fen-dər\ *n*
**1** a frame on the lower front of a locomotive or streetcar to catch or throw off anything that is hit

2 a guard over an automobile or cycle wheel

**[1]fer·ment** \fər-'ment\ *vb*
to undergo or cause to undergo fermentation

**[2]fer·ment** \'fər-,ment\ *n*
**1** something (as yeast) that causes fermentation
**2** a state of excitement

**fer·men·ta·tion** \,fər-mən-'tā-shən\ *n*
a chemical breaking down of an organic material that is controlled by an enzyme and usually does not require oxygen

**fern** \'fərn\ *n*
▼ a plant that produces spores instead of seeds and no flowers and whose leaves are usually divided into many parts
**fern·like** \-,līk\ *adj*

**fern**

**fe·ro·cious** \fə-'rō-shəs\ *adj*
FIERCE 1, SAVAGE
**fe·ro·cious·ly** *adv*
**fe·ro·cious·ness** *n*

**fe·roc·i·ty** \fə-'räs-ət-ē\ *n, pl* **fe·roc·i·ties**
the quality or state of being ferocious

**[1]fer·ret** \'fer-ət\ *n*
a partly domesticated European polecat of a pale color sometimes kept for hunting vermin (as rats)

**[2]ferret** *vb*
**1** to hunt with a ferret
**2** to find by eager searching ⟨*ferret* out the answer⟩

**Fer·ris wheel** \'fer-əs-\ *n*
an amusement device consisting of a large vertical wheel that is driven by a motor and has seats around its rim

**fertilization 2**
In mammals, fertilization takes place when a male sex cell, or sperm, penetrates the female sex cell, or egg. The genes from each one combine, so that the fertilized egg develops into a new individual with characteristics inherited from both parents.

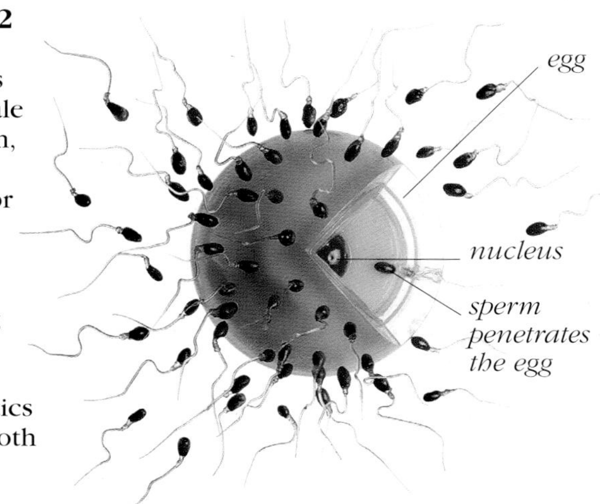


**model in cross section showing how an egg is fertilized**

**[1]fer·ry** \'fer-ē\ *vb* **fer·ried**; **fer·ry·ing**
**1** to carry by boat over a body of water
**2** to cross by a ferry
**3** to deliver an airplane under its own power
**4** to transport in an airplane

**[2]ferry** *n, pl* **fer·ries**
**1** a place where persons or things are ferried
**2** FERRYBOAT

**fer·ry·boat** \'fer-ē-,bōt\ *n*
▼ a boat used to ferry passengers, vehicles, or goods

**ferryboat**

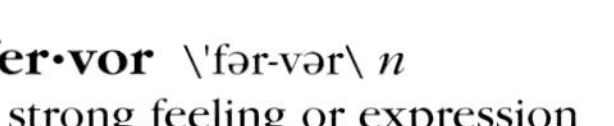

**fer·tile** \'fərt-l\ *adj*
**1** producing much vegetation or large crops
**2** capable of developing and growing ⟨a *fertile* egg⟩

**fer·til·i·ty** \,fər-'til-ət-ē\ *n*
the condition of being fertile

**fer·til·iza·tion** \,fərt-l-ə-'zā-shən\ *n*
**1** an act or process of making fertile
**2** ▲ the joining of an egg cell and a sperm cell to form the first stage of an embryo

**fer·til·ize** \'fərt-l-,īz\ *vb* **fer·til·ized**; **fer·til·iz·ing**
to make fertile or more fertile

**fer·til·iz·er** \'fərt-l-,ī-zər\ *n*
material added to soil to make it more fertile

**fer·vent** \'fər-vənt\ *adj*
very warm in feeling : ARDENT
**fer·vent·ly** *adv*

**fer·vor** \'fər-vər\ *n*
strong feeling or expression

**fes·ter** \'fes-tər\ *vb*
to become painfully red and sore and usually full of pus

**fes·ti·val** \'fes-tə-vəl\ *n*
**1** a time of celebration ⟨a harvest *festival*⟩
**2** a program of cultural events or entertainment

**fes·tive** \'fes-tiv\ *adj*
**1** having to do with a feast or festival
**2** very merry and joyful ⟨a *festive* party⟩

**fes·tiv·i·ty** \fes-'tiv-ət-ē\ *n, pl* **fes·tiv·i·ties**
**1** a festive state
**2** festive activity **:** MERRYMAKING

**¹fes·toon** \fes-'tün\ *n*
an ornament (as a chain) hanging between two points

**²festoon** *vb*
to hang or form festoons on

**fetch** \'fech\ *vb*
**1** to go after and bring back
**2** to bring as a price **:** sell for

**fetch·ing** \'fech-ing\ *adj*
very attractive
**fetch·ing·ly** *adv*

**¹fet·ter** \'fet-ər\ *n*
**1** a shackle for the feet
**2** something that holds back **:** RESTRAINT

**²fetter** *vb*
**1** to put fetters on
**2** to keep from moving or acting freely

**fe·tus** \'fēt-əs\ *n*
an animal not yet born or hatched but more developed than an embryo

**¹feud** \'fyüd\ *n*
a long bitter quarrel carried on especially between families or clans and usually having acts of violence and revenge

**²feud** *vb*
to carry on a feud

**feu·dal** \'fyüd-l\ *adj*
of or relating to feudalism

**feu·dal·ism** \'fyüd-l-ˌiz-əm\ *n*
a system of social organization existing in medieval Europe in which a vassal served a lord and received protection and land in return

**fe·ver** \'fē-vər\ *n*
**1** a rise of body temperature above normal
**2** a disease in which fever is present

**fe·ver·ish** \'fē-və-rish\ *adj*
**1** having a fever
**2** of, relating to, or being fever
**3** showing great emotion or activity **:** HECTIC
**fe·ver·ish·ly** *adv*
**fe·ver·ish·ness** *n*

**¹few** \'fyü\ *pron*
not many **:** a small number

**²few** *adj*
not many but some ⟨caught a *few* fish⟩ ⟨they had *few* pleasures⟩

**³few** *n*
a small number of individuals ⟨a *few* of the students⟩

**fez** \'fez\ *n, pl* **fez·zes**
▼ a round red felt hat that usually has a tassel but no brim



**fez**

**fi·as·co** \fē-'as-kō\ *n, pl* **fi·as·coes**
a complete failure

**¹fib** \'fib\ *n*
an unimportant lie

**²fib** *vb* **fibbed**; **fib·bing**
to tell a fib
**fib·ber** *n*

**fi·ber** *or* **fi·bre** \'fī-bər\ *n*
a long slender threadlike structure

**fi·ber·glass** *also* **fi·bre·glass** \'fī-bər-ˌglas\ *n*
**1** glass in the form of fibers used in various products (as filters and insulation)
**2** a material of plastic and fiberglass

**fiber op·tics** \-'äp-tiks\ *n pl*
▶ thin transparent fibers of glass or plastic that transmit light throughout their length



**fiber optics:** a fiber-optic cable

**fi·brous** \'fī-brəs\ *adj*
containing, consisting of, or like fibers ⟨*fibrous* roots⟩

**-fi·ca·tion** \fə-'kā-shən\ *n suffix*
the act or process of or the result of ⟨ampli*fication*⟩

**fick·le** \'fik-əl\ *adj*
INCONSTANT ⟨*fickle* friends⟩ ⟨*fickle* weather⟩
**fick·le·ness** *n*

**fic·tion** \'fik-shən\ *n*
**1** something told or written that is not fact
**2** a made-up story

**fic·tion·al** \'fik-shən-l\ *adj*
of, relating to, or suggesting fiction
**fic·tion·al·ly** \-l-ē\ *adv*

**fic·ti·tious** \fik-'tish-əs\ *adj*
not real

**¹fid·dle** \'fid-l\ *n*
VIOLIN

**²fiddle** *vb* **fid·dled**; **fid·dling**
**1** to play on a fiddle
**2** to move the hands or fingers restlessly ⟨kept *fiddling* with a ring⟩
**3** to spend time in aimless activity ⟨*fiddled* around and did nothing⟩
**4** TAMPER ⟨*fiddled* with the lock⟩
**fid·dler** \'fid-lər\ *n*

**fid·dle·sticks** \'fid-l-ˌstiks\ *n*
NONSENSE 1 — used as an interjection

**fi·del·i·ty** \fə-'del-ət-ē, fī-\ *n*
**1** LOYALTY
**2** ACCURACY

**fidg·et** \'fij-ət\ *vb*
to move in a restless or nervous way

**fidg·ets** \'fij-əts\ *n pl*
uneasy restlessness shown by nervous movements

**fidg·ety** \'fij-ət-ē\ *adj*
tending to fidget

**fief** \'fēf\ *n*
an estate given to a vassal by a feudal lord

**¹field** \'fēld\ *n*
**1** a piece of open, cleared, or cultivated land
**2** a piece of land put to a special use or giving a special product ⟨a ball *field*⟩ ⟨an oil *field*⟩
**3** an open space
**4** an area of activity or influence ⟨the *field* of science⟩
**5** a background on which something is drawn, painted, or mounted

**²field** *adj*
of or relating to a field

**³field** *vb*
to catch or stop and throw a ball

**field·er** \'fēl-dər\ *n*
a baseball player other than the pitcher or catcher on the team that is not at bat

**field glasses** *n pl*
▼ a hand-held instrument for seeing at a distance that is made up of two telescopes usually without prisms

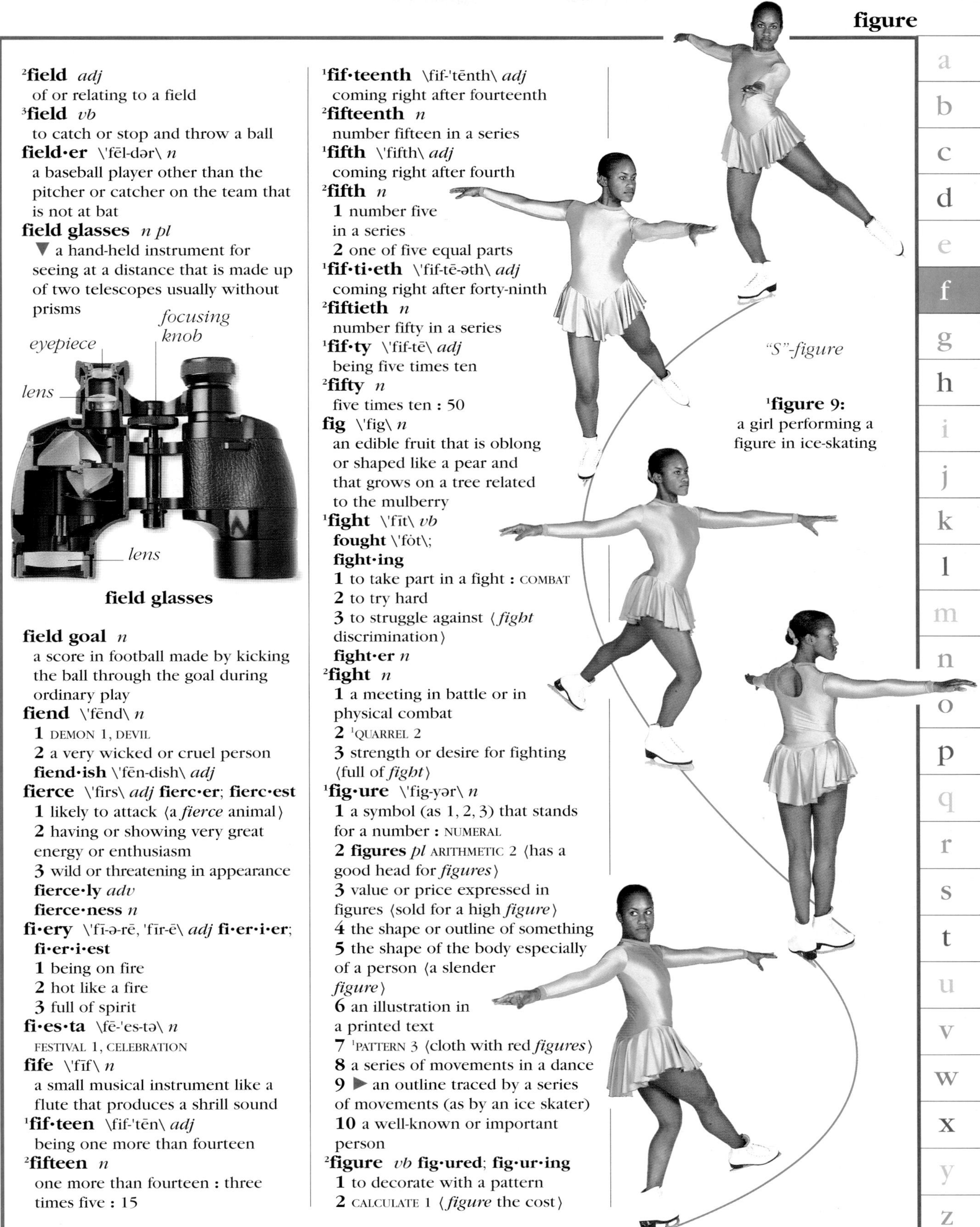


**field glasses**

**field goal** *n*
a score in football made by kicking the ball through the goal during ordinary play

**fiend** \'fēnd\ *n*
**1** DEMON 1, DEVIL
**2** a very wicked or cruel person
**fiend·ish** \'fēn-dish\ *adj*

**fierce** \'firs\ *adj* **fierc·er**; **fierc·est**
**1** likely to attack ⟨a *fierce* animal⟩
**2** having or showing very great energy or enthusiasm
**3** wild or threatening in appearance
**fierce·ly** *adv*
**fierce·ness** *n*

**fi·ery** \'fī-ə-rē, 'fīr-ē\ *adj* **fi·er·i·er**; **fi·er·i·est**
**1** being on fire
**2** hot like a fire
**3** full of spirit

**fi·es·ta** \fē-'es-tə\ *n*
FESTIVAL 1, CELEBRATION

**fife** \'fīf\ *n*
a small musical instrument like a flute that produces a shrill sound

**¹fif·teen** \fif-'tēn\ *adj*
being one more than fourteen

**²fifteen** *n*
one more than fourteen : three times five : 15

**¹fif·teenth** \fif-'tēnth\ *adj*
coming right after fourteenth

**²fifteenth** *n*
number fifteen in a series

**¹fifth** \'fifth\ *adj*
coming right after fourth

**²fifth** *n*
**1** number five in a series
**2** one of five equal parts

**¹fif·ti·eth** \'fif-tē-əth\ *adj*
coming right after forty-ninth

**²fiftieth** *n*
number fifty in a series

**¹fif·ty** \'fif-tē\ *adj*
being five times ten

**²fifty** *n*
five times ten : 50

**fig** \'fig\ *n*
an edible fruit that is oblong or shaped like a pear and that grows on a tree related to the mulberry

**¹fight** \'fīt\ *vb*
**fought** \'fȯt\;
**fight·ing**
**1** to take part in a fight : COMBAT
**2** to try hard
**3** to struggle against ⟨*fight* discrimination⟩
**fight·er** *n*

**²fight** *n*
**1** a meeting in battle or in physical combat
**2** ¹QUARREL 2
**3** strength or desire for fighting ⟨full of *fight*⟩

**¹fig·ure** \'fig-yər\ *n*
**1** a symbol (as 1, 2, 3) that stands for a number : NUMERAL
**2 figures** *pl* ARITHMETIC 2 ⟨has a good head for *figures*⟩
**3** value or price expressed in figures ⟨sold for a high *figure*⟩
**4** the shape or outline of something
**5** the shape of the body especially of a person ⟨a slender *figure*⟩
**6** an illustration in a printed text
**7** ¹PATTERN 3 ⟨cloth with red *figures*⟩
**8** a series of movements in a dance
**9** ▶ an outline traced by a series of movements (as by an ice skater)
**10** a well-known or important person

**²figure** *vb* **fig·ured**; **fig·ur·ing**
**1** to decorate with a pattern
**2** CALCULATE 1 ⟨*figure* the cost⟩

**¹figure 9:**
a girl performing a figure in ice-skating

A B C D E F G H I J K L M N O P Q R S T U V W X Y Z

**fig·ure·head** \'fig-yər-,hed\ *n*
▶ a figure, statue, or bust on the bow of a ship

**figure of speech**
an expression (as a simile or a metaphor) that uses words in other than a plain or literal way

**figurehead:** a 19th-century ship's figurehead

**figure out** *vb*
to work out in the mind ⟨*figure out* the answer⟩

**fil·a·ment** \'fil-ə-mənt\ *n*
1 a fine thread ⟨a *filament* of silk⟩
2 a fine wire (as in a light bulb) that is made to glow by the passage of an electric current
3 the stalk of a plant stamen that bears the anther
**fil·a·men·tous** \,fil-ə-'ment-əs\ *adj*

**fil·bert** \'fil-bərt\ *n*
the hazel or its nut

**Word History** Hazels are common in England. Their nuts are picked in late summer. The feast day of a certain saint (Saint Philbert) falls about the time that people pick hazelnuts. *Filbert*, a word for hazelnuts, came from the name of this saint.

**filch** \'filch\ *vb*
PILFER

**¹file** \'fīl\ *n*
a steel tool with sharp ridges or teeth for smoothing or rubbing down hard substances

**²file** *vb* **filed**; **fil·ing**
to rub, smooth, or cut away with a file

**³file** *vb* **filed**; **fil·ing**
1 to arrange in order ⟨*filed* the cards in alphabetical order⟩
2 to enter or record officially ⟨*file* a claim⟩

**⁴file** *n*
1 a device for keeping papers or records
2 a collection of papers or records kept in a file
3 a collection of data treated as a unit by a computer

**⁵file** *n*
a row of persons or things arranged one behind the other ⟨walk in single *file*⟩

**⁶file** *vb* **filed**; **fil·ing**
to move in a file ⟨*file* out of the building⟩

**fil·ial** \'fil-ē-əl, 'fil-yəl\ *adj*
1 of, relating to, or suitable for a son or daughter ⟨*filial* obedience⟩
2 being or having the relation of offspring

**¹fill** \'fil\ *vb*
1 to make or become full ⟨*fill* a pail⟩ ⟨the pail *filled* slowly⟩
2 to occupy fully ⟨cars *filled* the street⟩
3 to spread through ⟨laughter *filled* the room⟩
4 to stop up : PLUG ⟨*fill* a tooth⟩
5 to write information on or in : COMPLETE ⟨*fill* in the blanks⟩ ⟨*fill* out a form⟩
6 to do the duties of ⟨*fill* the office of president⟩
7 to supply according to directions ⟨*fill* a prescription⟩

**²fill** *n*
1 an amount that satisfies ⟨ate my *fill*⟩
2 material for filling something

**fill·er** \'fil-ər\ *n*
1 one that fills
2 a material used for filling

**fil·let** \'fil-ət, fi-'lā\ *n*
a piece of lean boneless meat or fish

**fill·ing** \'fil-ing\ *n*
a substance used to fill something else ⟨a *filling* for a tooth⟩

**filling station** *n*
SERVICE STATION

**fil·ly** \'fil-ē\ *n, pl* **fillies**
a female foal : a young female horse

**¹film** \'film\ *n*
1 a thin coating or layer ⟨a *film* of ice⟩
2 a roll of material prepared for taking pictures
3 MOVIE

**²film** *vb*
1 to cover or become covered with film
2 to photograph on a film
3 to make a movie

**film·strip** \'film-,strip\ *n*
a strip of film for projecting still pictures on a screen

**filmy** \'fil-mē\ *adj* **film·i·er**; **film·i·est**
of, like, or made of film

**¹fil·ter** \'fil-tər\ *n*
1 a device or a mass of material (as sand) with tiny openings through which a gas or liquid is passed to separate out something which it contains ⟨a *filter* for removing dust from the air⟩
2 ◀ a transparent material that absorbs light of some colors and is used for changing light (as in photography)

**²filter** *vb*
1 to pass through a filter ⟨*filter* water⟩
2 to remove by means of a filter

**filth** \'filth\ *n*
disgusting dirt

**¹filter 2**
When a photographer places a filter over a camera lens, only light of similar color can pass through to the film. This can dramatically alter the look of a picture, as shown below.

photo taken without filter

yellow filter

orange filter

blue filter

**a vase photographed using three different color filters**

**filthy** \'fil-thē\ *adj* **filth·i·er**; **filth·i·est**
disgustingly dirty
**filth·i·ness** *n*

**fil·tra·tion** \fil-'trā-shən\ *n*
the process of filtering

**fin** \'fin\ *n*
**1** any of the thin parts that stick out from the body of a water animal and especially a fish and are used in moving or guiding the body through the water
**2** something shaped like a fin

[1]**fi·nal** \'fīn-l\ *adj*
**1** not to be changed : CONCLUSIVE ⟨the decision of the judges is *final*⟩
**2** coming or happening at the end ⟨*final* examinations⟩ **synonyms** see LAST
**fi·nal·ly** *adv*

[2]**final** *n*
**1** the last match or game of a tournament
**2** a final examination in a course

**fi·na·le** \fə-'nal-ē\ *n*
the close or end of something (as a musical work)

**fi·nal·i·ty** \fī-'nal-ət-ē\ *n*
the condition of being final

[1]**fi·nance** \fə-'nans, 'fī-,nans\ *n*
**1 finances** *pl* money available to a government, business, or individual
**2** the system that includes the circulation of money, the providing of banks and credit, and the making of investments

[2]**finance** *vb* **fi·nanced**; **fi·nanc·ing**
to provide money for ⟨*finance* a trip⟩

**fi·nan·cial** \fə-'nan-chəl, fī-\ *adj*
having to do with finance or with finances ⟨a *financial* expert⟩ ⟨*financial* worries⟩
**fi·nan·cial·ly** *adv*

**fin·an·cier** \,fin-ən-'sir\ *n*
a specialist in finance and especially in the financing of businesses

**finch** \'finch\ *n*
a small songbird (as a sparrow, bunting, or canary) that eats seeds

[1]**find** \'fīnd\ *vb* **found** \'faủnd\; **find·ing**
**1** to come upon by chance ⟨*found* a dime⟩
**2** to come upon by searching, study, or effort ⟨finally *found* the answer⟩
**3** to decide on ⟨*find* a verdict⟩
**4** to know by experience ⟨people *found* the child honest⟩
**5** to gain or regain the use of ⟨*found* my voice again⟩
**find fault** to criticize in an unfavorable way

[2]**find** *n*
something found

**find·er** \'fīn-dər\ *n*
**1** one that finds
**2** a device on a camera that shows the view being photographed

**find out** *vb*
to learn by studying or watching : DISCOVER

[1]**fine** \'fīn\ *n*
a sum of money to be paid as a punishment

[2]**fine** *vb* **fined**; **fin·ing**
to punish by a fine

[3]**fine** *adj* **fin·er**; **fin·est**
**1** very small or thin ⟨*fine* print⟩
**2** not coarse ⟨*fine* sand⟩
**3** very good in quality or appearance ⟨a *fine* person⟩
**fine·ly** *adv*
**fine·ness** *n*

[4]**fine** *adv*
very well ⟨doing *fine*⟩

**fin·ery** \'fī-nə-rē\ *n, pl* **fin·er·ies**
stylish or showy clothes and jewelry

[1]**fin·ger** \'fing-gər\ *n*
**1** one of the five divisions of the end of the hand including the thumb
**2** something that is like or does the work of a finger
**3** the part of a glove into which a finger goes
**fin·ger·like** \-,līk\ *adj*

[2]**finger** *vb*
to touch with the fingers : HANDLE

**fin·ger·board** \'fing-gər-,bōrd\ *n*
a strip on the neck of a stringed instrument (as a guitar) against which the fingers press the strings to change the pitch

**finger hole** *n*
any of a group of holes in a wind instrument that may be covered with a finger to change the pitch

**fin·ger·ling** \'fing-gər-ling\ *n*
a young fish

**fin·ger·nail** \'fing-gər-,nāl\ *n*
the hard covering at the end of a finger

[1]**fin·ger·print** \'fing-gər-,print\ *n*
► the pattern of marks made by pressing a finger on a surface especially when the pattern is made in ink in order to identify a person

[1]**fingerprint**

[2]**fingerprint** *vb*
to take the fingerprints of

**fin·icky** \'fin-i-kē\ *adj*
very hard to please : FUSSY
**fin·ick·i·ness** *n*

[1]**fin·ish** \'fin-ish\ *vb*
**1** to bring or come to an end : COMPLETE, TERMINATE
**2** to put a final coat or surface on

[2]**finish** *n*
**1** [1]END 2, CONCLUSION ⟨a close *finish* in a race⟩
**2** the final treatment or coating of a surface or the appearance given by finishing

**fi·nite** \'fī-,nīt\ *adj*
having certain limits

**Finn** \'fin\ *n*
a person born or living in Finland

**finned** \'find\ *adj*
having fins

[1]**Finn·ish** \'fin-ish\ *adj*
of or relating to Finland, its people, or the Finnish language

[2]**Finnish** *n*
the language of the Finns

**fiord** *variant of* FJORD

**fir** \'fər\ *n*
a tall evergreen tree related to the pine that yields useful lumber

[1]**fire** \'fīr\ *n*
**1** the light and heat and especially the flame produced by burning
**2** fuel that is burning (as in a fireplace or stove)
**3** the destructive burning of something (as a building or a forest)
**4** a being lively : ENTHUSIASM
**5** the shooting of firearms ⟨rifle *fire*⟩
**on fire** actively burning
**under fire**
**1** exposed to the firing of enemy guns
**2** under attack

a b c d e f g h i j k l m n o p q r s t u v w x y z

A B C D E F G H I J K L M N O P Q R S T U V W X Y Z

**²fire** *vb* **fired**; **fir·ing**
**1** to set on fire ⟨vandals *fired* the barn⟩
**2** EXCITE 2, STIR ⟨a story to *fire* the imagination⟩
**3** to dismiss from employment
**4** to set off **:** EXPLODE ⟨*fire* a firecracker⟩
**5** ¹SHOOT 2 ⟨*fire* a gun⟩
**6** to subject to great heat ⟨*fire* pottery⟩

**fire·alarm** *n*
an alarm sounded to signal that a fire has broken out

**fire·arm** \'fīr-,ärm\ *n*
a small weapon from which shot or a bullet is driven by the explosion of gunpowder

**fire·bug** \'fīr-,bəg\ *n*
a person who sets destructive fires on purpose

**fire·crack·er** \'fīr-,krak-ər\ *n*
a paper tube containing an explosive to be set off for amusement

**2** a person who tends a fire (as in a large furnace)

**fire·place** \'fīr-,plās\ *n*
a structure with a hearth on which an open fire can be built for heating or especially outdoors for cooking

**fire·plug** \'fīr-,pləg\ *n*
HYDRANT

**fire·proof** \'fīr-'prüf\ *adj*
not easily burned **:** made safe against fire

**fire·side** \'fīr-,sīd\ *n*
**1** a place near the hearth
**2** ¹HOME 1

**fire station** *n*
a building housing fire engines and usually firefighters

**fire·wood** \'fīr-,wu̇d\ *n*
wood cut for fuel

**fire·work** \'fīr-,wərk\ *n*
**1** a device that makes a display of light or noise by the burning of explosive or flammable materials
**2 fireworks** *pl* a display of fireworks

**2** coming before all others

**²first** *adv*
**1** before any other ⟨reached the goal *first*⟩
**2** for the first time ⟨we *first* met at a party⟩

**³first** *n*
**1** number one in a series
**2** something or someone that is first

**first aid** *n*
care or treatment given to an ill or injured person before regular medical help can be gotten

**first·hand** \'fərst-'hand\ *adj or adv*
coming right from the original source

**first lieutenant** *n*
a commissioned officer in the Army, Air Force, or Marine Corps ranking above a second lieutenant

**first–rate** \'fərst-'rāt\ *adj*
EXCELLENT

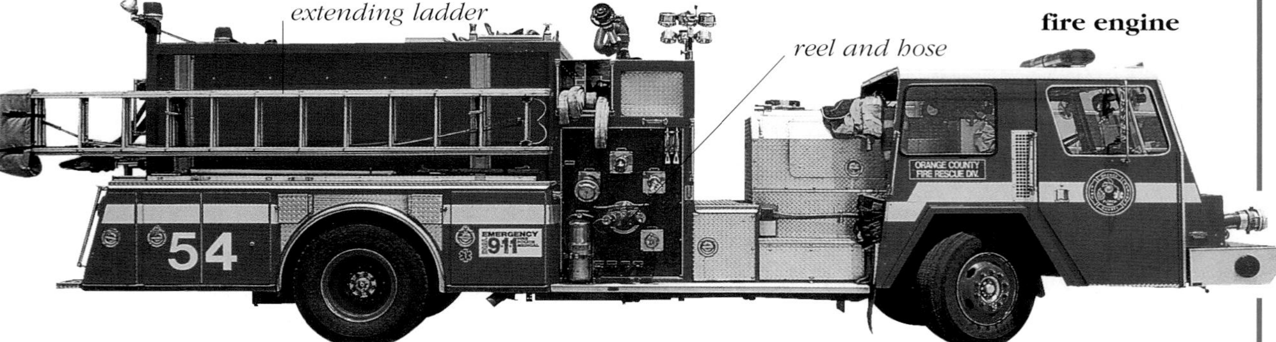


**fire engine** *n*
▲ a truck equipped to fight fires

**fire escape** *n*
a stairway that provides a way of escape from a building in case of fire

**fire extinguisher** *n*
something (as a metal container filled with chemicals) that is used to put out a fire

**fire·fight·er** \'fīr-,fīt-ər\ *n*
a person whose job is to put out fires

**fire·fly** \'fīr-,flī\ *n, pl* **fire·flies**
a small beetle producing a soft light

**fire·house** \'fīr-,hau̇s\ *n*
FIRE STATION

**fire·man** \'fīr-mən\ *n, pl* **fire·men** \-mən\
**1** FIREFIGHTER

**¹firm** \'fərm\ *adj*
**1** STRONG 1, VIGOROUS ⟨had a *firm* grip on the wheel⟩
**2** having a solid compact texture ⟨*firm* ground⟩
**3** not likely to be changed ⟨a *firm* price⟩
**4** not easily moved or shaken **:** FAITHFUL ⟨a *firm* believer⟩ ⟨*firm* friends⟩
**5** showing no weakness
**synonyms** see HARD
**firm·ly** *adv*
**firm·ness** *n*

**²firm** *n*
BUSINESS 2

**fir·ma·ment** \'fər-mə-mənt\ *n*
the arch of the sky

**¹first** \'fərst\ *adj*
**1** being number one ⟨the *first* day of the week⟩

**first sergeant** *n*
**1** a noncommissioned officer serving as the chief assistant to a military commander
**2** a noncommissioned officer ranking above a sergeant first class in the Army or above a gunnery sergeant in the Marine Corps

**firth** \'fərth\ *n*
a narrow arm of the sea

**¹fish** \'fish\ *n, pl* **fish** *or* **fish·es**
**1** an animal that lives in water — usually used in combination ⟨star*fish*⟩ ⟨shell*fish*⟩
**2** ► any of a large group of vertebrate animals that live in water, breathe with gills, and usually have fins and scales
**fish·like** \-,līk\ *adj*

## [1]fish 2

Fish are cold-blooded animals that live in water. They use their fins and tail to move around, and breathe through their gills. Fish can be divided into three main groups: bony, cartilaginous, and jawless fish. Bony fish have a bony skeleton, while cartilaginous fish have a skeleton made of cartilage. Jawless fish have a sucker-like mouth.

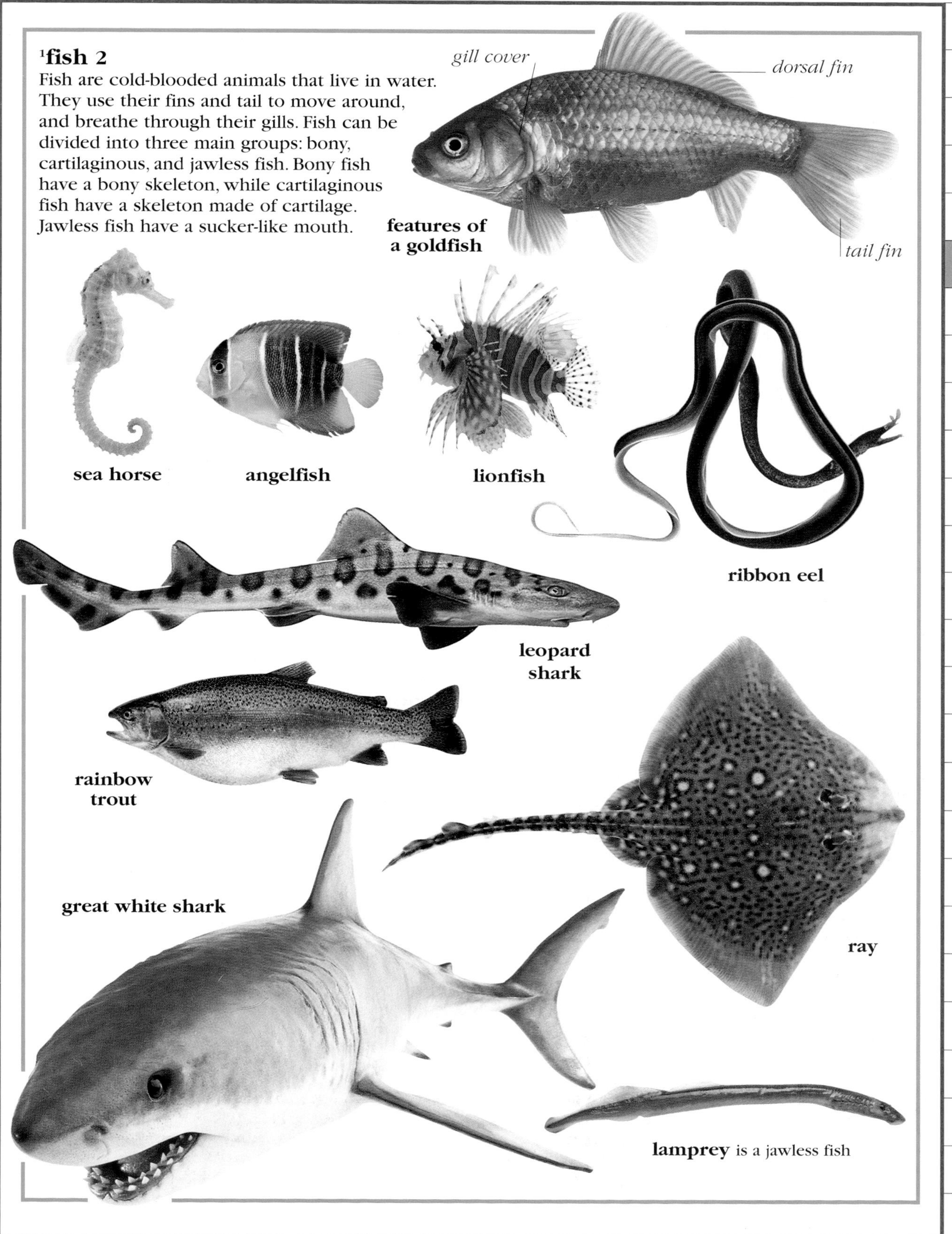


**features of a goldfish**

**sea horse**

**angelfish**

**lionfish**

**ribbon eel**

**leopard shark**

**rainbow trout**

**great white shark**

**ray**

**lamprey** is a jawless fish

a b c d e f g h i j k l m n o p q r s t u v w x y z

**[2]fish** *vb*
**1** to attempt to catch fish
**2** to try to find or to find out something by groping

**fish·er·man** \'fish-ər-mən\ *n, pl* **fish·er·men** \-mən\
a person who fishes

**fish·ery** \'fish-ə-rē\ *n, pl* **fish·er·ies**
**1** the business of catching fish
**2** a place for catching fish

**fish·hook** \'fish-,hu̇k\ *n*
▼ a hook used for catching fish

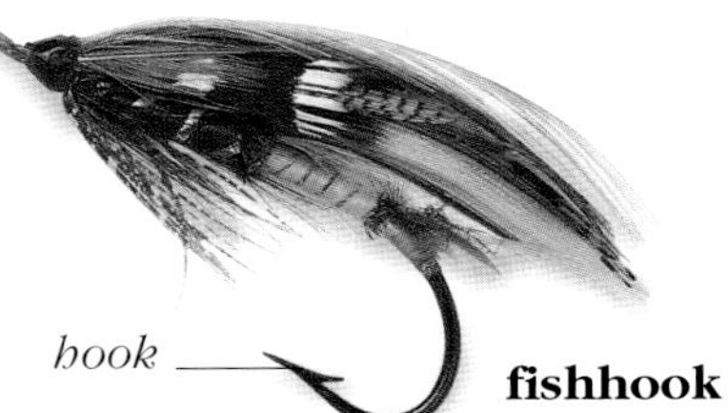

**fishhook**

**fishy** \'fish-ē\ *adj* **fish·i·er**; **fish·i·est**
**1** of or like fish ⟨a *fishy* odor⟩
**2** QUESTIONABLE ⟨the story sounds *fishy* to me⟩

**fis·sion** \'fish-ən\ *n*
**1** a splitting or breaking into parts
**2** a method of reproduction in which a living cell or body divides into two or more parts each of which grows into a whole new individual
**3** the splitting of an atomic nucleus with the release of large amounts of energy

**fis·sure** \'fish-ər\ *n*
a narrow opening or crack ⟨a *fissure* in rock⟩

**fist** \'fist\ *n*
the hand with the fingers doubled tight into the palm

**[1]fit** \'fit\ *adj* **fit·ter**; **fit·test**
**1** good enough ⟨*fit* to eat⟩
**2** healthy in mind and body ⟨feel *fit*⟩
**fit·ness** *n*

**[2]fit** *n*
a sudden attack or outburst

**[3]fit** *vb* **fit·ted**; **fit·ting**
**1** to be suitable for or to ⟨dressed to *fit* the occasion⟩
**2** to be the right shape or size ⟨this shirt doesn't *fit*⟩
**3** to bring to the right shape or size ⟨have a suit *fitted*⟩
**4** EQUIP ⟨*fitted* the ship with new engines⟩

**[4]fit** *n*
**1** the way something fits
**2** a piece of clothing that fits

**fit·ful** \'fit-fəl\ *adj*
IRREGULAR 4 ⟨*fitful* sleep⟩

**[1]fit·ting** \'fit-ing\ *adj*
[2]APPROPRIATE, SUITABLE
**fit·ting·ly** *adv*

**[2]fitting** *n*
a small accessory part ⟨a pipe *fitting*⟩

**[1]five** \'fīv\ *adj*
being one more than four

**[2]five** *n*
**1** one more than four : 5
**2** the fifth in a set or series

**[1]fix** \'fiks\ *vb*
**1** to make firm or secure ⟨*fix* a machine in place⟩
**2** to cause to combine chemically ⟨bacteria that *fix* nitrogen⟩
**3** to set definitely : ESTABLISH ⟨*fix* the date of a meeting⟩
**4** to get ready : PREPARE ⟨*fix* dinner⟩
**5** [1]REPAIR 1, MEND
**fix·er** \'fik-sər\ *n*

**[2]fix** *n*
an unpleasant or difficult position

**fixed** \'fikst\ *adj*
**1** not changing : SET ⟨living on a *fixed* income⟩
**2** not moving : INTENT ⟨a *fixed* stare⟩
**fix·ed·ly** \'fik-səd-lē\ *adv*

**fixed star** *n*
a star so distant that its motion can be measured only by very careful observations over long periods

**fix·ture** \'fiks-chər\ *n*
something attached as a permanent part ⟨bathroom *fixtures*⟩

**[1]fizz** \'fiz\ *vb*
to make a hissing or sputtering sound

**[2]fizz** *n*
**1** a hissing or sputtering sound
**2** a bubbling drink

**[1]fiz·zle** \'fiz-əl\ *vb* **fiz·zled**; **fiz·zling**
to fail after a good start

**[2]fizzle** *n*
FAILURE 3

**fjord** *or* **fiord** \fē-'ȯrd\ *n*
a narrow inlet of the sea between cliffs or steep slopes

**flab·by** \'flab-ē\ *adj* **flab·bi·er**; **flab·bi·est**
not hard and firm : SOFT
**flab·bi·ness** *n*

**[1]flag** \'flag\ *n*
▼ a piece of cloth with a special design or color that is used as a symbol (as of a nation) or as a signal

**[1]flag:**
the Stars and Stripes of the USA

**[2]flag** *vb* **flagged**; **flag·ging**
to signal with or as if with a flag

**[3]flag** *vb* **flagged**; **flag·ging**
to become weak

**fla·gel·lum** \flə-'jel-əm\ *n, pl* **fla·gel·la** \-'jel-ə\
a long whiplike structure by which some tiny plants and animals move

**flag·man** \'flag-mən\ *n, pl* **flag·men** \-mən\
a person who signals with a flag

**flag·on** \'flag-ən\ *n*
a container for liquids usually having a handle, spout, and lid

**flag·pole** \'flag-,pōl\ *n*
a pole from which a flag flies

**fla·grant** \'flā-grənt\ *adj*
so bad as to be impossible to overlook ⟨a *flagrant* violation of the rules⟩
**fla·grant·ly** *adv*

**flag·ship** \'flag-,ship\ *n*
the ship carrying the commander of a group of ships and flying a flag that tells the commander's rank

**flag·staff** \'flag-,staf\ *n, pl* **flag·staffs**
FLAGPOLE

**flag·stone** \'flag-,stōn\ *n*
a piece of hard flat rock used for paving

**[1]flail** \'flāl\ *n*
▶ a tool for threshing grain by hand

**[1]flail:**
a 19th-century wooden flail from Russia

**[2]flail** *vb*
to hit with or as if with a flail

**flair** \'flaər, 'fleər\ *n*
natural ability

**¹flake** \'flāk\ *n*
a small thin flat piece

**²flake** *vb* **flaked**; **flak·ing**
to form or separate into flakes

**flaky** \'flā-kē\ *adj* **flak·i·er**; **flak·i·est**
tending to flake ⟨a *flaky* pie crust⟩
**flak·i·ness** *n*

**flam·boy·ant** \flam-'bȯi-ənt\ *adj*
liking or making a dashing show
**flam·boy·ant·ly** *adv*

**¹flame** \'flām\ *n*
**1** the glowing gas that makes up part of a fire ⟨the *flame* of a candle⟩
**2** a condition or appearance suggesting a flame

**²flame** *vb* **flamed**; **flam·ing**
to burn with or as if with a flame

**flame·throw·er** \'flām-,thrō-ər\ *n*
a device that shoots a burning stream of fuel

**fla·min·go** \flə-'ming-gō\ *n, pl* **fla·min·gos** *or* **fla·min·goes**
► a waterbird with very long neck and legs, scarlet wings, and a broad bill bent downward at the end

**Word History** The English word *flamingo* came from the bird's Spanish name. It is likely that this Spanish word was taken from a language of southern France. The word for a flamingo in this language came from a Latin word. This Latin word meant "flame." When a flamingo takes flight there is a sudden bright flash of its scarlet wing feathers. This looks a bit like a burst of flame.

**flam·ma·ble** \'flam-ə-bəl\ *adj*
capable of being easily set on fire and of burning quickly ⟨a *flammable* liquid⟩

**¹flank** \'flangk\ *n*
**1** the fleshy part of the side between the ribs and the hip
**2** ¹SIDE 3
**3** the right or left side of a formation (as of soldiers)

**²flank** *vb*
**1** to pass around the flank of
**2** to be located at the side of **:** BORDER

**flank·er** \'flang-kər\ *n*
a football player stationed wide of the formation

**flan·nel** \'flan-l\ *n*
a soft cloth made of wool or cotton

**¹flap** \'flap\ *n*
**1** something broad and flat or limber that hangs loose
**2** the motion made by something broad and limber (as a sail or wing) moving back and forth or the sound produced

**²flap** *vb* **flapped**; **flap·ping**
**1** to give a quick light blow
**2** to move with a beating or fluttering motion ⟨birds *flapping* their wings⟩

**flap·jack** \'flap-,jak\ *n*
PANCAKE

**¹flare** \'flaər, 'fleər\ *vb* **flared**; **flar·ing**
**1** to burn with an unsteady flame
**2** to shine with great or sudden light
**3** to become angry ⟨*flared* up at the remarks⟩
**4** to spread outward

flamingo

**²flare** *n*
**1** a sudden blaze of light
**2** a blaze of light used to signal, light up something, or attract attention
**3** a device or material used to produce a flare
**4** a sudden outburst (as of sound or anger)
**5** a spreading outward **:** a part that spreads outward

**¹flash** \'flash\ *vb*
**1** to shine in or like a sudden flame ⟨lightning *flashed*⟩
**2** to send out in or as if in flashes ⟨*flash* a message⟩
**3** to come or pass very suddenly ⟨a car *flashed* by⟩
**4** to make a sudden display (as of feeling)

**²flash** *n*
**1** a sudden burst of or as if of light ⟨a *flash* of wit⟩
**2** a very short time

**³flash** *adj*
beginning suddenly and lasting only a short time ⟨*flash* floods⟩

**flash·light** \'flash-,līt\ *n*
▼ a small portable electric light that runs on batteries

flashlight

**flashy** \'flash-ē\ *adj* **flash·i·er**; **flash·i·est**
GAUDY, SHOWY 2 ⟨*flashy* clothes⟩

**flask** \'flask\ *n*
a container like a bottle with a flat or rounded body

**¹flat** \'flat\ *adj* **flat·ter**; **flat·test**
**1** having a smooth level surface ⟨a *flat* rock⟩
**2** spread out on or along a surface ⟨*flat* on the ground⟩
**3** having a broad smooth surface and little thickness ⟨a compact disc is *flat*⟩
**4** ²OUTRIGHT 1, POSITIVE ⟨a *flat* refusal⟩
**5** FIXED 1 ⟨charge a *flat* rate⟩
**6** having nothing lacking or left over **:** EXACT ⟨got there in two minutes *flat*⟩
**7** INSIPID ⟨a *flat* story⟩ ⟨the stew is too *flat*⟩
**8** having lost air pressure ⟨a *flat* tire⟩
**9** lower than the true musical pitch
**10** lower by a half step in music
**11** free from gloss ⟨*flat* paint⟩
**synonyms** see LEVEL
**flat·ly** *adv*
**flat·ness** *n*

a b c d e f g h i j k l m n o p q r s t u v w x y z

A B C D E F G H I J K L M N O P Q R S T U V W X Y Z

**[2]flat** *n*
**1** a level place : PLAIN
**2** a flat part or surface
**3** a note or tone that is a half step lower than the note named
**4** a sign ♭ meaning that the pitch of a musical note is to be lower by a half step
**5** a deflated tire

**[3]flat** *adv*
**1** on or against a flat surface ⟨lie *flat*⟩
**2** below the true musical pitch ⟨sang *flat*⟩

**[4]flat** *n*
an apartment on one floor

**flat·boat** \'flat-ˌbōt\ *n*
a large boat with a flat bottom and square ends

**flat·car** \-ˌkär\ *n*
a railroad car without sides or a roof that is used to carry freight

**flat·fish** \'flat-ˌfish\ *n*
a fish (as the flounder) that swims on its side and has both eyes on the upper side

**flea**

**flat·iron** \'flat-ˌī-ərn\ *n*
[1]IRON

**flat·ten** \'flat-n\ *vb*
to make or become flat

**flat·ter** \'flat-ər\ *vb*
**1** to praise but not sincerely
**2** to show too favorably ⟨a picture that *flatters* me⟩ **synonyms** see COMPLIMENT
**flat·ter·er** *n*
**flat·ter·ing·ly** *adv*

**flat·tery** \'flat-ə-rē\ *n, pl* **flat·ter·ies**
praise that is not deserved or meant

**flaunt** \'flȯnt\ *vb*
**1** to wave or flutter in a showy way
**2** to make too much show of

**[1]fla·vor** \'flā-vər\ *n*
**1** the quality of something that affects the sense of taste
**2** a substance added to food to give it a desired taste
**fla·vored** \-vərd\ *adj*

**[2]flavor** *vb*
to give or add a flavor to

**fla·vor·ing** \'flā-və-riŋ, 'flāv-riŋ\ *n*
[1]FLAVOR 2

**flaw** \'flȯ\ *n*
a small often hidden fault

**flax** \'flaks\ *n*
▶ a plant with blue flowers that is grown for its fiber from which linen is made and for its seed from which oil and livestock feed are obtained

**flax**

**flax·en** \'flak-sən\ *adj*
**1** made of flax
**2** having a light straw color ⟨*flaxen* hair⟩

**flax·seed** \'flak-ˌsēd\ *n*
the seed of flax from which linseed oil comes and which is used in medicine

**flay** \'flā\ *vb*
**1** [2]SKIN
**2** to scold severely

**flea** \'flē\ *n*
◀ a small bloodsucking insect that has no wings and a hard body

**[1]fleck** \'flek\ *vb*
to mark with small streaks or spots ⟨bananas *flecked* with brown⟩

**[2]fleck** *n*
**1** [1]SPOT 2, MARK
**2** [1]FLAKE, PARTICLE

**fledg·ling** \'flej-liŋ\ *n*
a young bird that has just grown the feathers needed to fly

**flee** \'flē\ *vb* **fled** \'fled\; **flee·ing**
to run away or away from : FLY

**[1]fleece** \'flēs\ *n*
▶ the woolly coat of an animal and especially a sheep

**[1]fleece:** a farmer shearing fleece from a sheep

**[2]fleece** *vb* **fleeced**; **fleec·ing**
to take money or property from by trickery

**fleecy** \'flē-sē\ *adj* **fleec·i·er**; **fleec·i·est**
covered with, made of, or like fleece

**[1]fleet** \'flēt\ *n*
**1** a group of warships under one command
**2** a country's navy
**3** a group of ships or vehicles that move together or are under one management ⟨a fishing *fleet*⟩ ⟨a *fleet* of taxis⟩

**[2]fleet** *adj*
very swift ⟨*fleet* of foot⟩
**fleet·ly** *adv*
**fleet·ness** *n*

**Fleet Admiral** *n*
the highest ranking commissioned officer in the Navy ranking above an admiral

**flesh** \'flesh\ *n*
**1** the soft and especially the edible muscular parts of an animal's body
**2** a fleshy edible plant part (as the pulp of a fruit)
**fleshed** \'flesht\ *adj*

**fleshy** \'flesh-ē\ *adj* **flesh·i·er**; **flesh·i·est**
**1** like or consisting of flesh
**2** rather stout

**flew** *past of* FLY

**flex** \'fleks\ *vb*
to bend often again and again

**flex·i·bil·i·ty** \ˌflek-sə-'bil-ət-ē\ *n*
the quality or state of being flexible

**flex·i·ble** \'flek-sə-bəl\ *adj*
**1** possible to bend or flex
**2** able or suitable to meet new situations ⟨a *flexible* mind⟩
**flex·i·bly** \'flek-sə-blē\ *adv*

**[1]flick** \'flik\ *n*
a light snapping stroke

**[2]flick** *vb*
to strike or move with a quick motion

**[1]flick·er** \'flik-ər\ *vb*
to burn unsteadily ⟨a *flickering* candle⟩

**[2]flicker** *n*
1 a quick small movement ⟨a *flicker* of the eyelids⟩
2 a flickering light

**[3]flicker** *n*
a large North American woodpecker

**fli·er** *or* **fly·er** \'flī-ər\ *n*
1 one that flies
2 AVIATOR

**[1]flight** \'flīt\ *n*
1 an act or instance of passing through the air by the use of wings
2 a passing through the air or space ⟨a balloon *flight*⟩ ⟨the *flight* of a rocket to the moon⟩
3 the distance covered in a flight
4 a scheduled trip by an airplane ⟨a four o'clock *flight*⟩
5 a group of similar things flying through the air together ⟨a *flight* of ducks⟩ ⟨a *flight* of bombers⟩
6 a passing above or beyond ordinary limits ⟨*flights* of imagination⟩
7 a continuous series of stairs

**[2]flight** *n*
the act of running away

**flight·less** \'flīt-ləs\ *adj*
▶ unable to fly

**flightless:** the penguin is a flightless bird

**flighty** \'flīt-ē\ *adj* **flight·i·er**; **flight·i·est**
1 easily excited : SKITTISH ⟨a *flighty* horse⟩
2 not wise or sober : FRIVOLOUS

**flim·sy** \'flim-zē\ *adj* **flim·si·er**; **flim·si·est**
not strong or solid ⟨a *flimsy* cardboard suitcase⟩ ⟨a *flimsy* excuse⟩
**flim·si·ly** \-zə-lē\ *adv*
**flim·si·ness** \-zē-nəs\ *n*

**flinch** \'flinch\ *vb*
to draw back from or as if from pain ⟨*flinch* at a loud noise⟩

**[1]fling** \'fling\ *vb* **flung** \'fləng\; **fling·ing**
1 to move suddenly
2 to throw hard or without care ⟨*flung* the junk out the window⟩

**[2]fling** *n*
1 an act of flinging
2 a time of freedom for pleasure

**flint** \'flint\ *n*
a very hard stone that produces a spark when struck by steel

**flint·lock** \'flint-,läk\ *n*
▼ an old-fashioned firearm using a flint for striking a spark to fire the charge

**flintlock:** a 19th-century flintlock pistol from England

**[1]flip** \'flip\ *vb* **flipped**; **flip·ping**
to move or turn by or as if by tossing ⟨*flip* a coin⟩ ⟨*flip* a switch⟩

**[2]flip** *n*
an act of flipping : TOSS

**flip·pant** \'flip-ənt\ *adj*
not respectful : SAUCY
**flip·pant·ly** *adv*

**flip·per** \'flip-ər\ *n*
1 a broad flat limb (as of a seal) specialized for swimming
2 a flat rubber shoe with the front expanded into a paddle used in swimming

**[1]flirt** \'flərt\ *vb*
to show a liking for someone of the opposite sex just for the fun of it

**[2]flirt** *n*
a person who flirts a lot

**flit** \'flit\ *vb* **flit·ted**; **flit·ting**
to move by darting about

**[1]float** \'flōt\ *n*
1 something that floats in or on the surface of a liquid
2 a cork or bob that holds up the baited end of a fishing line
3 a floating platform anchored near a shore for the use of swimmers or boats
4 a hollow ball that controls the flow or level of the liquid it floats on (as in a tank)
5 a vehicle with a platform used to carry an exhibit in a parade

**[2]float** *vb*
1 to rest on the surface of a liquid ⟨cork will *float*⟩
2 to drift on or through or as if on or through a fluid ⟨dust *floating* through the air⟩
3 to cause to float
**float·er** *n*

**[1]flock** \'fläk\ *n*
1 a group of animals (as geese or sheep) living or kept together
2 a group someone (as a minister) watches over

**[2]flock** *vb*
to gather or move in a crowd

**floe** \'flō\ *n*
▼ a sheet or mass of floating ice

**floe:** model showing floes broken away from a shelf of ice

**flog** \'fläg\ *vb* **flogged**; **flog·ging**
to beat severely with a rod or whip

[1]**flood** \'fləd\ *n*
**1** a huge flow of water that rises and spreads over the land
**2** the flowing in of the tide
**3** a very large number or amount ⟨a *flood* of requests⟩

[2]**flood** *vb*
**1** to cover or become filled with water
**2** to fill as if with a flood

**flood·light** \'fləd-,līt\ *n*
a lamp that gives a bright broad beam of light

**flood·plain** \'fləd-,plān\ *n*
low flat land along a stream that is flooded when the stream overflows

**flood·wa·ter** \'fləd-,wȯt-ər, -,wät-\ *n*
the water of a flood

[1]**floor** \'flōr\ *n*
**1** the part of a room on which one stands
**2** the lower inside surface of a hollow structure ⟨the *floor* of a car⟩
**3** a ground surface ⟨the ocean *floor*⟩
**4** a story of a building

[2]**floor** *vb*
**1** to cover or provide with a floor ⟨*floor* a garage with concrete⟩
**2** to knock down

**floor·ing** \'flōr-ing\ *n*
**1** [1]FLOOR 1
**2** material for floors

[1]**flop** \'fläp\ *vb* **flopped**; **flop·ping**
**1** to flap about ⟨a fish *flopping* on the deck⟩
**2** to drop or fall limply ⟨*flopped* into the chair⟩
**3** [1]FAIL 6

[2]**flop** *n*
**1** the act or sound of flopping
**2** FAILURE 3

[1]**flop·py** \'fläp-ē\ *adj* **flop·pi·er**; **flop·pi·est**
being soft and flexible

[2]**floppy** *n, pl* **floppies**
FLOPPY DISK

**floppy disk** *n*
a small flexible plastic disk with a magnetic coating on which computer data can be stored

**flo·ra** \'flōr-ə\ *n*
the plant life typical of a region, period, or special environment

**flo·ral** \'flōr-əl\ *adj*
of or relating to flowers

**flo·ret** \'flōr-ət\ *n*
a small flower

**flo·rist** \'flōr-əst\ *n*
a person who sells flowers and ornamental plants

[1]**floss** \'fläs, 'flȯs\ *n*
**1** soft thread used in embroidery
**2** fluffy material full of fibers

[2]**floss** *vb*
to use dental floss on (one's teeth)

**flo·til·la** \flō-'til-ə\ *n*
a fleet of usually small ships

[1]**flounce** \'flau̇ns\ *vb* **flounced**; **flounc·ing**
to move with exaggerated jerky motions

[2]**flounce** *n*
a strip of fabric attached by its upper edge ⟨a *flounce* on a skirt⟩

[1]**floun·der** \'flau̇n-dər\ *n*
a flatfish used for food

[2]**flounder** *vb*
**1** to struggle to move or get footing ⟨*floundering* in the mud⟩
**2** to behave or do something in a clumsy way ⟨*floundered* through the speech⟩

**flour** \'flau̇r\ *n*
▼ the finely ground meal of a cereal grain and especially of wheat

[1]**flour·ish** \'flər-ish\ *vb*
**1** to grow well : THRIVE ⟨plants *flourish* in this rich soil⟩
**2** to do well : PROSPER
**3** to make sweeping movements with ⟨*flourish* a sword⟩

[2]**flourish** *n*
**1** a fancy bit of decoration added to something (as handwriting)
**2** a sweeping motion

**flout** \'flau̇t\ *vb*
to show lack of respect for : DISREGARD ⟨*flouted* their parents' advice⟩

[1]**flow** \'flō\ *vb*
**1** to move in a stream
**2** to glide along smoothly
**3** to hang loose and waving

[2]**flow** *n*
**1** an act of flowing ⟨a dam to stop the *flow* of water⟩
**2** the rise of the tide ⟨the ebb and *flow* of the tide⟩
**3** a smooth even movement : STREAM ⟨*flow* of conversation⟩ ⟨a *flow* of information⟩

[1]**flow·er** \'flau̇-ər\ *n*
**1** ▶ a plant part that produces seed
**2** a plant grown chiefly for its showy flowers
**3** the state of bearing flowers ⟨in full *flower*⟩
**4** the best part or example
**flow·ered** \-ərd\ *adj*
**flow·er·less** \-ər-ləs\ *adj*

[2]**flower** *vb*
to produce flowers

**flower head** *n*
a tight cluster of small flowers that are arranged so that the whole looks like a single flower

**flowering plant** *n*
a seed plant whose seeds are produced in the ovary of a flower

**flow·er·pot** \'flau̇-ər-,pät\ *n*
a pot in which to grow plants

**flow·ery** \'flau̇-ə-rē\ *adj*
**1** having many flowers
**2** full of fine words ⟨*flowery* language⟩
**flow·er·i·ness** *n*

**flown** *past participle of* FLY

**flu** \'flü\ *n*
**1** INFLUENZA
**2** any of several virus diseases something like a cold

**fluc·tu·ate** \'flək-chə-,wāt\ *vb* **fluc·tu·at·ed**; **fluc·tu·at·ing**
to change continually and especially up and down ⟨the temperature *fluctuated*⟩

**flour**

Wheat flour is a staple food of western culture. It contains a protein (called gluten) that, when mixed with water, becomes elastic and gives dough its structure. The dough can then be baked into bread, crackers, and other products.

## [1]flower 1

A flower is the reproductive part of a flowering plant. It may contain the male reproductive organs (filaments and pollen-bearing anthers), or the female organs (stigma, style, and ovule-bearing ovaries), or both. Pollination takes place when pollen is transferred from the anthers to the stigma within the same flower, or to another flower by the action of wind, insects, or birds.

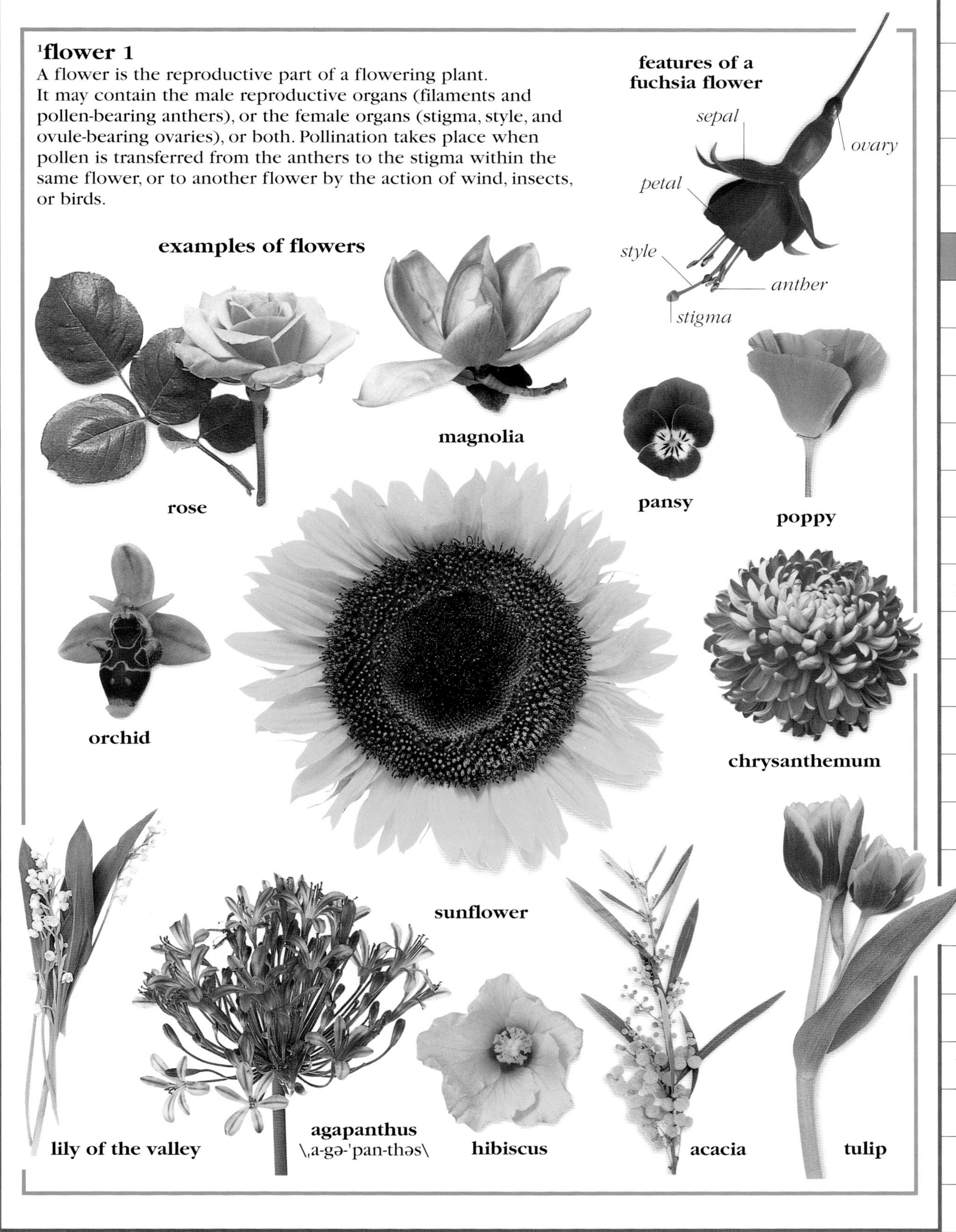


a b c d e f g h i j k l m n o p q r s t u v w x y z

A B C D E F G H I J K L M N O P Q R S T U V W X Y Z

**fluorescent 2:** a fluorescent bulb

**flue** \'flü\ *n*
an enclosed passage (as in a chimney) for smoke or air

**flu·en·cy** \'flü-ən-sē\ *n*
the ability to speak easily and well

**flu·ent** \'flü-ənt\ *adj*
**1** able to speak easily and well ⟨was *fluent* in Spanish⟩
**2** that is smooth and correct : GOOD ⟨speaks *fluent* German⟩
**flu·ent·ly** \-ənt-lē\ *adv*

**¹fluff** \'fləf\ *n*
¹DOWN, NAP

**²fluff** *vb*
to make or become fluffy

**fluffy** \'fləf-ē\ *adj* **fluff·i·er**; **fluff·i·est**
having, covered with, or like down ⟨a *fluffy* little chick⟩

**¹flu·id** \'flü-əd\ *adj*
**1** capable of flowing like a liquid or gas
**2** being smooth and easy
**flu·id·ly** *adv*

**²fluid** *n*
something that tends to flow and take the shape of its container

**flung** *past of* FLING

**flunk** \'fləngk\ *vb*
¹FAIL 6 ⟨*flunk* a test⟩

**fluo·res·cent** \flu̇-'res-nt, flō-\ *adj*
**1** giving out visible light when exposed to external radiation ⟨a *fluorescent* coating⟩
**2** ◀ producing visible light by means of a fluorescent coating ⟨a *fluorescent* bulb⟩
**3** extremely bright or glowing ⟨*fluorescent* colors⟩

**fluo·ri·date** \'flu̇r-ə-ˌdāt, 'flōr-\ *vb* **fluo·ri·dat·ed**; **fluo·ri·dat·ing**
to add a fluoride to (as drinking water) to reduce tooth decay

**fluo·ri·da·tion** \ˌflu̇r-ə-'dā-shən, ˌflōr-\ *n*
the act of fluoridating

**fluo·ride** \'flȯr-ˌīd, 'flu̇r-\ *n*
a compound of fluorine ⟨toothpaste with *fluoride*⟩

**fluo·rine** \'flu̇r-ˌēn, 'flȯr-\ *n*
a yellowish flammable irritating gaseous chemical element

**¹flur·ry** \'flər-ē\ *n, pl* **flurries**
**1** a gust of wind
**2** a brief light snowfall
**3** a brief outburst (as of activity)

**²flurry** *vb* **flur·ried**; **flur·ry·ing**
¹FLUSTER, EXCITE

**¹flush** \'fləsh\ *vb*
to begin or cause to begin flight suddenly ⟨a hunting dog *flushing* quail⟩

**²flush** *n*
**1** an act of flushing
**2** ¹BLUSH 1

**³flush** *vb*
**1** ²BLUSH ⟨*flushed* with pleasure⟩
**2** to pour water over or through

**⁴flush** *adj*
having one edge or surface even with the next ⟨*flush* paneling⟩ ⟨a *flush* joint⟩

**⁵flush** *adv*
so as to be flush

**¹flus·ter** \'fləs-tər\ *vb*
to make nervous and confused : UPSET

**²fluster** *n*
a state of nervous confusion

**¹flute** \'flüt\ *n*
▶ a woodwind instrument in the form of a hollow slender tube open at only one end that is played by blowing across a hole near the closed end

**¹flute**

**³fly 2**
Flies are a huge group of insects with large compound eyes, and feet with sticky pads and claws that allow them to walk on any surface. The larvae of flies are called maggots.

thorax
abdomen
compound eye
mouthpart

**crane fly**

**robber fly**

**housefly**

**syrphid fly** \'sər-fəd-\

**features of a greenbottle fly** \'grēn-ˌbät-l-\

**[2]flute** *vb* **flut·ed**; **flut·ing**
to make a sound like that of a flute

**[1]flut·ter** \'flət-ər\ *vb*
**1** to move the wings rapidly without flying or in making short flights ⟨butterflies *flutter*⟩
**2** to move with a quick flapping motion ⟨flags *fluttered* in the wind⟩
**3** to move about busily without getting much done

**[2]flutter** *n*
an act of fluttering

**[1]fly** \'flī\ *vb* **flew** \'flü\; **flown** \'flōn\; **fly·ing**
**1** to move in or pass through the air with wings ⟨birds *fly*⟩
**2** to move through the air or before the wind ⟨paper *flying* in all directions⟩
**3** to float or cause to float, wave, or soar in the wind ⟨*fly* a kite⟩ ⟨*fly* a flag⟩
**4** to run away : FLEE
**5** to move or pass swiftly ⟨how time does *fly*⟩
**6** to operate or travel in an aircraft

**[2]fly** *n, pl* **flies**
**1** a flap of material to cover a fastening in a garment
**2** the outer canvas of a tent that has a double top
**3** a baseball hit high in the air

**[3]fly** *n, pl* **flies**
**1** a winged insect
**2** ◀ any of a large group of mostly stout-bodied two-winged insects (as the common housefly)
**3** a fishhook made to look like an insect

**fly·catch·er** \'flī-,kach-ər\ *n*
a small bird that eats flying insects

**flyer** *variant of* FLIER

**fly·ing boat** \'flī-ing-\ *n*
a seaplane with a hull designed to support it on the water

**flying fish** *n*
a fish with large fins that let it jump from the water and move for a distance through the air

**fly·pa·per** \'flī-,pā-pər\ *n*
sticky paper to catch and kill flies

**fly·speck** \'flī-,spek\ *n*
a spot of feces left by a fly on a surface

**fly·way** \'flī-,wā\ *n*
a route regularly followed by migratory birds

**[1]foal** \'fōl\ *n*
▼ a young animal of the horse family especially while less than one year old

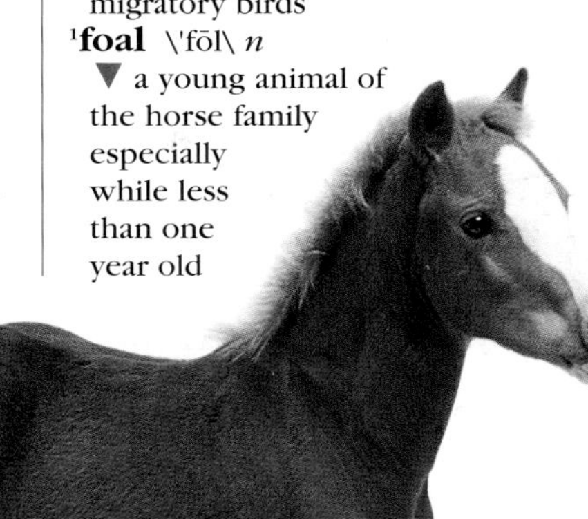

**[1]foal**

**[2]foal** *vb*
to give birth to a foal

**[1]foam** \'fōm\ *n*
a mass of tiny bubbles that forms in or on the surface of liquids or in the mouths or on the skins of animals

**[2]foam** *vb*
to produce or form foam

**foamy** \'fō-mē\ *adj* **foam·i·er**; **foam·i·est**
covered with or looking like foam ⟨the *foamy* tops of the waves⟩
**foam·i·ness** *n*

**fo·cal** \'fō-kəl\ *adj*
of, relating to, or having a focus

**[1]fo·cus** \'fō-kəs\ *n, pl* **fo·cus·es** *or* **fo·ci** \'fō-,sī\
**1** a point at which rays (as of light, heat, or sound) meet after being reflected or bent : the point at which an image is formed
**2** the distance from a lens or mirror to a focus
**3** an adjustment (as of a person's eyes or glasses) that gives clear vision ⟨bring into *focus*⟩
**4** a center of activity or interest

**[2]focus** *vb* **fo·cused** *or* **fo·cussed**; **fo·cus·ing** *or* **fo·cus·sing**
**1** to bring or come to a focus ⟨*focus* rays of light⟩
**2** to adjust the focus of ⟨*focus* the eyes⟩

**fod·der** \'fäd-ər\ *n*
coarse dry food (as stalks of corn) for livestock

**foe** \'fō\ *n*
an enemy especially in war

**[1]fog** \'fög, 'fäg\ *n*
**1** fine particles of water floating in the air at or near the ground
**2** a confused state of mind ⟨this problem has me in a *fog*⟩

**[2]fog** *vb* **fogged**; **fog·ging**
to cover or become covered with fog

**fog·gy** \'fög-ē, 'fäg-\ *adj* **fog·gi·er**; **fog·gi·est**
**1** filled with fog
**2** confused as if by fog
**fog·gi·ness** *n*

**fog·horn** \'fög-,hörn, 'fäg-\ *n*
a loud horn sounded in a fog to give warning

**fo·gy** \'fō-gē\ *n, pl* **fogies**
a person with old-fashioned ideas

**foi·ble** \'föi-bəl\ *n*
an unimportant weakness or failing

**[1]foil** \'föil\ *vb*
to keep from succeeding or from reaching a goal

**[2]foil** *n*
**1** a very thin sheet of metal ⟨aluminum *foil*⟩
**2** something that makes another thing more noticeable by being very different from it

**[3]foil** *n*
▶ a fencing weapon having a light flexible blade with a blunt point

**[1]fold** \'fōld\ *n*
an enclosure or shelter for sheep

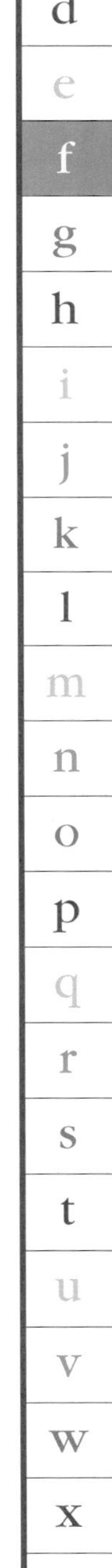

**[3]foil:**
a fencing foil

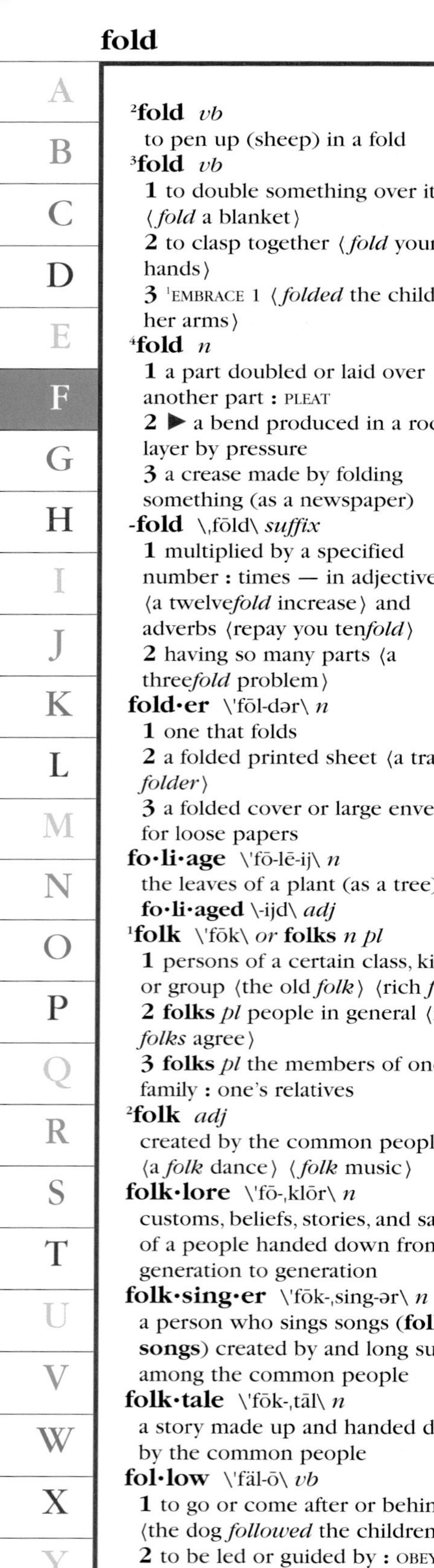

[2]**fold** *vb*
to pen up (sheep) in a fold

[3]**fold** *vb*
**1** to double something over itself ⟨*fold* a blanket⟩
**2** to clasp together ⟨*fold* your hands⟩
**3** [1]EMBRACE 1 ⟨*folded* the child in her arms⟩

[4]**fold** *n*
**1** a part doubled or laid over another part **:** PLEAT
**2** ► a bend produced in a rock layer by pressure
**3** a crease made by folding something (as a newspaper)

**-fold** \ˌfōld\ *suffix*
**1** multiplied by a specified number **:** times — in adjectives ⟨a twelve*fold* increase⟩ and adverbs ⟨repay you ten*fold*⟩
**2** having so many parts ⟨a three*fold* problem⟩

**fold·er** \ˈfōl-dər\ *n*
**1** one that folds
**2** a folded printed sheet ⟨a travel *folder*⟩
**3** a folded cover or large envelope for loose papers

**fo·li·age** \ˈfō-lē-ij\ *n*
the leaves of a plant (as a tree)
**fo·li·aged** \-ijd\ *adj*

[1]**folk** \ˈfōk\ *or* **folks** *n pl*
**1** persons of a certain class, kind, or group ⟨the old *folk*⟩ ⟨rich *folks*⟩
**2 folks** *pl* people in general ⟨most *folks* agree⟩
**3 folks** *pl* the members of one's family **:** one's relatives

[2]**folk** *adj*
created by the common people ⟨a *folk* dance⟩ ⟨*folk* music⟩

**folk·lore** \ˈfō-ˌklōr\ *n*
customs, beliefs, stories, and sayings of a people handed down from generation to generation

**folk·sing·er** \ˈfōk-ˌsing-ər\ *n*
a person who sings songs (**folk songs**) created by and long sung among the common people

**folk·tale** \ˈfōk-ˌtāl\ *n*
a story made up and handed down by the common people

**fol·low** \ˈfäl-ō\ *vb*
**1** to go or come after or behind ⟨the dog *followed* the children⟩
**2** to be led or guided by **:** OBEY ⟨*follow* instructions⟩
**3** to proceed along ⟨*follow* a path⟩
**4** to work in or at something as a way of life ⟨*follow* the sea⟩
**5** to come after in time or place ⟨spring *follows* winter⟩
**6** to result from ⟨panic *followed* the fire⟩
**7** to keep one's eyes or attention on ⟨*follow* the bouncing ball⟩
**synonyms** see CHASE

**fol·low·er** \ˈfäl-ə-wər\ *n*

**follow suit**
**1** to play a card that belongs to the same group (as hearts or spades) as the one led
**2** to do the same thing someone else has just done

[1]**fol·low·ing** \ˈfäl-ə-wing\ *adj*
coming just after

[2]**following** *n*
a group of followers

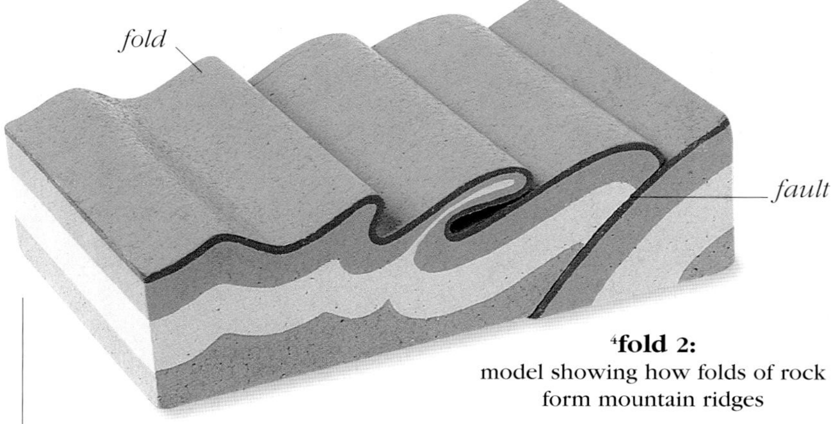


[4]**fold 2:**
model showing how folds of rock form mountain ridges

**food 1**

Foods contain many chemicals that allow the body to function. Some foods are most important as sources of energy, while others help the body fight infection or keep fluid levels in balance. A healthy diet includes food from all six main food groups: the bread, cereal, rice and pasta group, which forms the base of the diet; the vegetable group; the fruit group; the meat, poultry, fish, beans, eggs, and nuts group; the milk, yogurt, and cheese group; and lastly, the group of fats, oils, and sugars, which should be eaten sparingly.

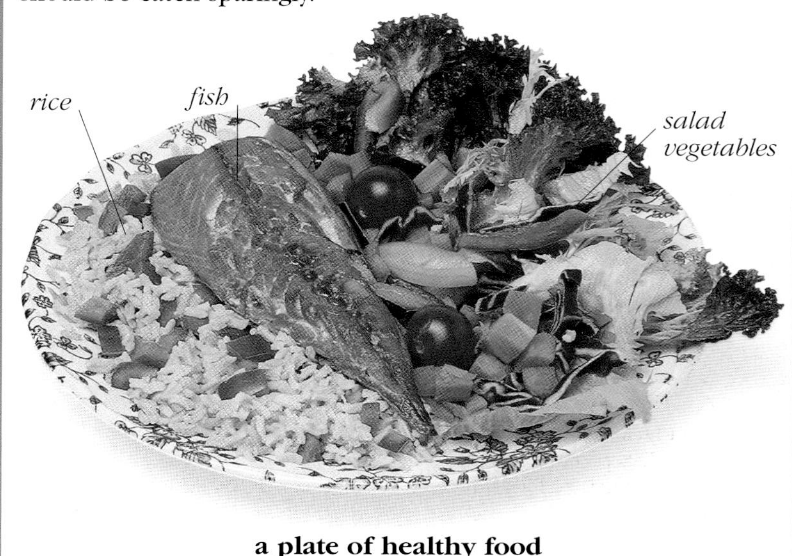


**a plate of healthy food**

**follow through** *vb*
to complete an action

**follow up** *vb*
to show continued interest in or take further action regarding

**fol·ly** \'fäl-ē\ *n, pl* **follies**
**1** lack of good sense
**2** a foolish act or idea

**fond** \'fänd\ *adj*
**1** having a liking or love ⟨*fond* of candy⟩
**2** AFFECTIONATE, LOVING ⟨a *fond* farewell⟩
**fond·ly** *adv*
**fond·ness** *n*

**fon·dle** \'fän-dl\ *vb* **fon·dled**; **fon·dling**
to touch or handle in a tender or loving manner

**font** \'fänt\ *n*
a basin to hold water for baptism

**food** \'füd\ *n*
**1** ◀ material containing carbohydrates, fats, proteins, and supplements (as minerals and vitamins) that is taken in by and used in the living body for growth and repair and as a source of energy for activities
**2** inorganic substances taken in by green plants and used to build organic nutrients
**3** organic materials formed by plants and used in their growth and activities
**4** solid food as distinguished from drink

**food chain** *n*
▶ a sequence of organisms in which each depends on the next and usually lower member as a source of food

**food·stuff** \'füd-ˌstəf\ *n*
a substance with food value

**[1]fool** \'fül\ *n*
**1** a person without good sense or judgment
**2** JESTER 1

---

**Word History** In Latin there was a word that meant "bellows" or "bag." This word came to be used to refer to fools, whose heads seem, like bellows or bags, to be empty of all but air. The English word *fool* came from this Latin word.

---

## food chain

This simplified food chain is shown in the form of a pyramid with the owl, the highest member of the food chain, at the top. The owl would eat the weasels, voles, and mice in the levels below it. The weasels, in turn, would eat the mice and voles, while the mice and voles, at the bottom of the chain, would eat plants and insects. The chart shows that it takes several weasels to feed a single owl, and many more mice and voles to feed the weasels, as well as the owl.

**[2]fool** *vb*
**1** to spend time idly ⟨just *fooling* around⟩
**2** to meddle or tamper with something ⟨don't *fool* with that gun⟩
**3** to speak or act in a playful way or in fun : JOKE ⟨we were only *fooling*⟩
**4** [2]TRICK ⟨I *fooled* you⟩

**fool·har·dy** \'fül-ˌhärd-ē\ *adj* **fool·har·di·er**; **fool·har·di·est**
foolishly adventurous or bold

**fool·ish** \'fü-lish\ *adj*
showing or resulting from lack of good sense : SENSELESS **synonyms** see ABSURD
**fool·ish·ly** *adv*
**fool·ish·ness** *n*

**fool·proof** \'fül-'prüf\ *adj*
done, made, or planned so well that nothing can go wrong

**[1]foot** \'fu̇t\ *n, pl* **feet** \'fēt\
**1** the end part of the leg of an animal or person : the part of an animal on which it stands or moves
**2** a unit of length equal to twelve inches (about .3 meter)
**3** something like a foot in position or use ⟨*foot* of a hill⟩ ⟨*foot* of the bed⟩
**on foot** by walking

**[2]foot** *vb*
**1** to go on foot
**2** [1]PAY 2 ⟨*foot* the bill⟩

**foot·ball** \'fu̇t-ˌbȯl\ *n*
**1** ▶ a game played with a blown up oval ball on a large field by two teams of eleven players that move the ball by kicking, passing, or running with it
**2** the ball used in football

**foot·ed** \'fu̇t-əd\ *adj*
**1** having a foot or feet ⟨a *footed* goblet⟩
**2** having such or so many feet ⟨four-*footed* animals⟩

**foot·fall** \'fu̇t-ˌfȯl\ *n*
the sound of a footstep

**foot·hill** \'fu̇t-ˌhil\ *n*
a hill at the foot of higher hills

**foot·hold** \'fu̇t-ˌhōld\ *n*
a place where the foot may be put (as for climbing)

**foot·ing** \'fu̇t-ing\ *n*
**1** a firm position or placing of the feet ⟨lost my *footing*⟩
**2** FOOTHOLD
**3** position in relation to others ⟨we all started on the same *footing*⟩
**4** social relationship ⟨on good *footing* with the neighbors⟩

**foot·lights** \'fu̇t-ˌlīts\ *n pl*
a row of lights set across the front of a stage floor

**foot·man** \'fu̇t-mən\ *n*, *pl* **foot·men** \-mən\
a male servant who lets visitors in and waits on table

**foot·note** \'fu̇t-ˌnōt\ *n*
a note at the bottom of a page

**foot·path** \'fu̇t-ˌpath, -ˌpȧth\ *n*
a path for walkers

**foot·print** \'fu̇t-ˌprint\ *n*
a track left by a foot

**foot·sore** \'fu̇t-ˌsōr\ *adj*
having sore feet from walking a lot

**foot·step** \'fu̇t-ˌstep\ *n*
**1** a step of the foot
**2** the distance covered by a step
**3** FOOTPRINT

**foot·stool** \'fu̇t-ˌstül\ *n*
a low stool to support the feet

**foot·work** \'fu̇t-ˌwərk\ *n*
the skill with which the feet are moved (as in boxing)

[1]**for** \fər, fȯr\ *prep*
**1** by way of getting ready ⟨wash up *for* supper⟩
**2** toward the goal of ⟨saved *for* a new bike⟩
**3** in order to reach ⟨left *for* home⟩
**4** as being ⟨took me *for* a fool⟩
**5** because of ⟨cried *for* joy⟩

## football 1

Football is a highly physical game played by two teams, each of 11 players. All players wear protective equipment and are allowed to throw, kick, or run with the ball. Points are scored for touchdowns and for kicking the ball through the goalposts.

**features of a football field**

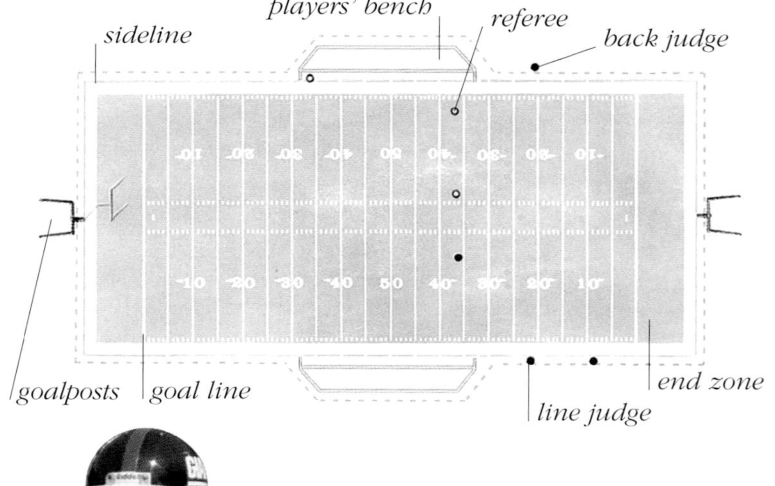

**shoulder pads**

**player**

**helmet**

**football**

cleat

**football shoes**

**6** used to show who or what is to receive something ⟨a letter *for* you⟩
**7** in order to help or defend ⟨fought *for* their country⟩
**8** directed at : AGAINST ⟨a cure *for* cancer⟩
**9** in exchange as equal to ⟨pay ten dollars *for* a hat⟩
**10** with regard to : CONCERNING ⟨a talent *for* music⟩
**11** taking into account ⟨tall *for* your age⟩
**12** through the period of ⟨slept *for* ten hours⟩

**[2]for** *conj*
BECAUSE ⟨I know we won, *for* I heard the cheers⟩

**[1]for·age** \'fȯr-ij\ *n*
food (as pasture) for browsing or grazing animals

**[2]forage** *vb* **for·aged**; **for·ag·ing**
[1]SEARCH 1

**for·ay** \'fȯr-,ā\ *n*
[1]RAID

**for·bear** \fȯr-'baər, -'beər\ *vb* **for·bore** \-'bōr\; **for·borne** \-'bōrn\; **for·bear·ing**
**1** to hold back ⟨*forbore* from striking the bully⟩
**2** to control oneself when provoked

**for·bid** \fər-'bid\ *vb* **for·bade** \-'bad\ *or* **for·bad**; **for·bid·den** \-'bid-n\; **for·bid·ding**
to order not to do something

**for·bid·ding** \fər-'bid-ing\ *adj*
tending to frighten or discourage

**[1]force** \'fōrs\ *n*
**1** POWER 4 ⟨the *force* of the wind⟩
**2** the state of existing and being enforced : EFFECT ⟨that law is still in *force*⟩
**3** a group of persons gathered together and trained for action ⟨a police *force*⟩
**4** power or violence used on a person or thing ⟨opened the door by *force*⟩
**5** ► an influence (as a push or pull) that tends to produce a change in the speed or direction of motion of something ⟨the *force* of gravity⟩

**[2]force** *vb* **forced**; **forc·ing**
**1** to make (as a person) do something ⟨*forced* them to work⟩
**2** to get or make by using force ⟨*forced* their way into the room⟩
**3** to break open by force ⟨*forced* the door⟩
**4** to speed up the development of

**force·ful** \'fōrs-fəl\ *adj*
having much force : VIGOROUS ⟨*forceful* action⟩ ⟨a *forceful* speech⟩
**force·ful·ly** \-fə-lē\ *adv*
**force·ful·ness** *n*

**for·ceps** \'fȯr-səps\ *n, pl* **forceps**
▼ an instrument for grasping, holding, or pulling on things especially in delicate operations (as by a jeweler or surgeon)

**forceps:**
a pair of surgical forceps

**forc·ible** \'fōr-sə-bəl\ *adj*
**1** got, made, or done by force or violence ⟨a *forcible* entrance⟩
**2** showing a lot of force or energy
**forc·ibly** \-blē\ *adv*

**[1]ford** \'fōrd\ *n*
a shallow place in a body of water where one can wade across

**[2]ford** *vb*
to cross by wading

**[1]fore** \'fōr\ *adv*
in or toward the front

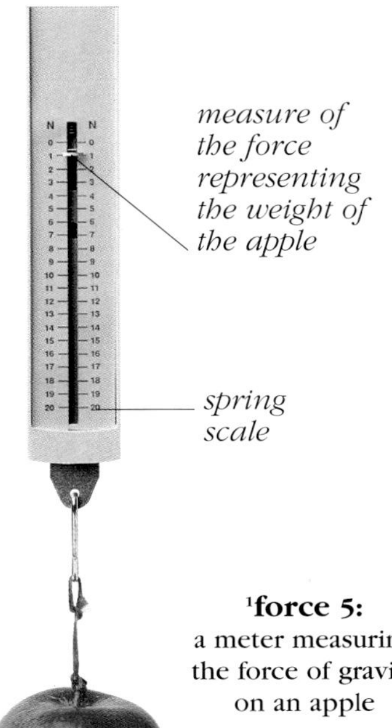


**[1]force 5:**
a meter measuring the force of gravity on an apple

**[2]fore** *adj*
being or coming before in time, place, or order

**[3]fore** *n*
[1]FRONT 2 ⟨came to the *fore*⟩

**[4]fore** *interj*
used by a golfer to warn someone within range of a hit ball

**fore-** *prefix*
**1** earlier : beforehand ⟨*fore*see⟩
**2** at the front : in front ⟨*fore*leg⟩
**3** front part of something specified ⟨*fore*arm⟩

**fore–and–aft** \,fōr-ə-'naft\ *adj*
being in line with the length of a ship ⟨*fore-and-aft* sails⟩

**fore·arm** \'fōr-,ärm\ *n*
the part of the arm between the elbow and the wrist

**fore·bear** \'fōr-,baər, -,beər\ *n*
ANCESTOR

**fore·bod·ing** \fōr-'bōd-ing\ *n*
a feeling that something bad is going to happen

**[1]fore·cast** \'fōr-,kast\ *vb* **forecast** *or* **fore·cast·ed**; **fore·cast·ing**
to predict often after thought and study of available evidence
**synonyms** see FORETELL
**fore·cast·er** *n*

**[2]forecast** *n*
a prediction of something in the future ⟨a weather *forecast*⟩

**fore·cas·tle** \'fōk-səl\ *n*
**1** the forward part of the upper deck of a ship
**2** quarters for the crew in the forward part of a ship

**fore·fa·ther** \'fōr-,fäth-ər, -,fath-\ *n*
ANCESTOR

**fore·fin·ger** \'fōr-,fing-gər\ *n*
INDEX FINGER

**fore·foot** \'fōr-,fu̇t\ *n, pl* **fore·feet** \-,fēt\
one of the front feet of an animal with four feet

**fore·front** \'fōr-,frənt\ *n*
the very front : VANGUARD

**forego** *variant of* FORGO

**fore·go·ing** \fōr-'gō-ing\ *adj*
being before in time or place

**fore·gone conclusion** \'fōr-,gȯn-\ *n*
something felt to be sure to happen

**fore·ground** \'fōr-,grau̇nd\ *n*
the part of a picture or scene that seems to be nearest to and in front of the person looking at it

**fore·hand** \'fōr-ˌhand\ *n*
▶ a stroke (as in tennis) made with the palm of the hand turned in the direction in which the hand is moving

**forehand**

**fore·head** \'fȯr-əd, 'fōr-ˌhed\ *n*
the part of the face above the eyes

**for·eign** \'fȯr-ən\ *adj*
**1** located outside of a place or country and especially outside of one's country ⟨a *foreign* nation⟩
**2** belonging to a place or country other than the one under consideration ⟨many Danes speak *foreign* languages⟩
**3** relating to or having to do with other nations ⟨*foreign* trade⟩ ⟨*foreign* affairs⟩
**4** not normal or wanted ⟨*foreign* material in food⟩

**for·eign·er** \'fȯr-ə-nər\ *n*
a person who is from a foreign country

**fore·leg** \'fōr-ˌleg\ *n*
a front leg

**fore·limb** \'fōr-ˌlim\ *n*
an arm, fin, wing, or leg that is or occupies the position of a foreleg

**fore·man** \'fōr-mən\ *n, pl* **fore·men** \-mən\
the leader of a group of workers

**fore·mast** \'fōr-ˌmast, -məst\ *n*
the mast nearest the bow of the ship

[1]**fore·most** \'fōr-ˌmōst\ *adj*
first in time, place, or order : most important

[2]**foremost** *adv*
in the first place

**fore·noon** \'fōr-ˌnün\ *n*
MORNING

**fore·quar·ter** \'fōr-ˌkwȯrt-ər\ *n*
the front half of a side of the body or carcass of an animal with four feet ⟨a *forequarter* of beef⟩

**fore·run·ner** \'fōr-ˌrən-ər\ *n*
one that comes before especially as a sign of the coming of another

**fore·see** \fōr-'sē\ *vb* **fore·saw** \-'sȯ\; **fore·seen** \-'sēn\; **fore·see·ing**
to see or know about beforehand

**fore·sight** \'fōr-ˌsīt\ *n*
**1** the act or power of foreseeing
**2** care for the future : PRUDENCE

*anvil*

[1]**forge:** a blacksmith at work in a traditional forge

**for·est** \'fȯr-əst\ *n*
a growth of trees and underbrush covering a large area
**for·est·ed** \-əs-təd\ *adj*

**fore·stall** \fōr-'stȯl\ *vb*
to keep out, interfere with, or prevent by steps taken in advance

**forest ranger** *n*
a person in charge of the management and protection of a part of a public forest

**for·est·ry** \'fȯr-ə-strē\ *n*
the science and practice of caring for forests
**for·est·er** \-stər\ *n*

**fore·tell** \fōr-'tel\ *vb* **fore·told** \-'tōld\; **fore·tell·ing**
to tell of a thing before it happens

**Synonyms** FORETELL, PREDICT, and FORECAST mean to tell about or announce something before it happens. FORETELL may suggest the use of extraordinary powers to reveal the future ⟨the wizards *foretold* a great war⟩. PREDICT may suggest a fairly exact statement that is the result of the gathering of information and the use of scientific methods ⟨scientists can sometimes *predict* earthquakes⟩. FORECAST often suggests that one has weighed evidence and is telling what is most likely to happen ⟨*forecasted* that it would snow⟩.

**fore·thought** \'fōr-ˌthȯt\ *n*
a thinking or planning for the future

**for·ev·er** \fə-'rev-ər\ *adv*
**1** for a limitless time ⟨will last *forever*⟩
**2** at all times ⟨is *forever* bothering the teacher⟩

**for·ev·er·more** \fə-ˌrev-ər-'mōr\ *adv*
FOREVER 1

**fore·word** \'fōr-ˌwərd\ *n*
PREFACE

[1]**for·feit** \'fȯr-fət\ *n*
something forfeited

[2]**forfeit** *vb*
to lose or lose the right to something through a fault, error, or crime

[1]**forge** \'fōrj\ *n*
◀ a furnace or a place with a furnace where metal is shaped and worked by heating and hammering

[2]**forge** *vb* **forged**; **forg·ing**
1 to shape and work metal by heating and hammering
2 to produce something that is not genuine : COUNTERFEIT ⟨*forge* a check⟩
**forg·er** *n*

[3]**forge** *vb* **forged**; **forg·ing**
to move forward slowly but steadily ⟨*forged* ahead through the blizzard⟩

**forg·ery** \'fōr-jə-rē\ *n, pl* **forg·er·ies**
1 the crime of falsely making or changing a written paper or signing someone else's name
2 something that has been forged

**for·get** \fər-'get\ *vb* **for·got** \-'gät\; **for·got·ten** \-'gät-n\ *or* **for·got**; **for·get·ting**
1 to be unable to think of or recall ⟨*forget* a name⟩
2 to fail by accident to do (something) : OVERLOOK ⟨*forgot* to pay the bill⟩

**for·get·ful** \fər-'get-fəl\ *adj*
forgetting easily
**for·get·ful·ly** \-fə-lē\ *adv*
**for·get·ful·ness** *n*

**for·get–me–not** \fər-'get-mē-ˌnät\ *n*
► a small low plant with bright blue flowers

**forget-me-not**

**for·give** \fər-'giv\ *vb* **for·gave** \-'gāv\; **for·giv·en** \-'giv-ən\; **for·giv·ing**
to stop feeling angry at or hurt by

**for·give·ness** \fər-'giv-nəs\ *n*
the act of forgiving or the state of being forgiven

**for·go** *or* **fore·go** \fȯr-'gō, fōr-\ *vb* **for·went** *or* **fore·went** \-'went\; **for·gone** *or* **fore·gone** \-'gȯn\; **for·go·ing** *or* **fore·go·ing**
to hold oneself back from : GIVE UP ⟨*forgo* an opportunity⟩

[1]**fork** \'fȯrk\ *n*
1 ► an implement having a handle and two or more prongs for taking up (as in eating), pitching, or digging
2 something like a fork in shape
3 the place where something divides or branches ⟨a *fork* in the road⟩
4 one of the parts into which something divides or branches ⟨the left *fork*⟩
**forked** \'fȯrkt, 'fȯr-kəd\ *adj*

[1]**fork 1:** a fork for eating

[2]**fork** *vb*
1 to divide into branches
2 to pitch or lift with a fork

**for·lorn** \fər-'lȯrn\ *adj*
sad from being left alone
**for·lorn·ly** *adv*

[1]**form** \'fȯrm\ *n*
1 the shape and structure of something
2 an established way of doing something ⟨different *forms* of worship⟩
3 a printed sheet with blank spaces for information ⟨fill out a *form*⟩
4 a mold in which concrete is placed to set
5 [1]SORT 1, KIND ⟨early *forms* of plant life⟩ ⟨coal is one *form* of carbon⟩
6 a plan of arrangement or design (as for a work of art)
7 one of the different pronunciations, spellings, or inflections a word may have

[2]**form** *vb*
1 to give form or shape to
2 DEVELOP 5
3 to come or bring together in making
4 to take form : come into being ⟨clouds will *form*⟩ **synonyms** see MAKE

[1]**for·mal** \'fȯr-məl\ *adj*
following established form, custom, or rule
**for·mal·ly** *adv*

[2]**formal** *n*
something (as a dress) formal in character

**for·mal·i·ty** \fȯr-'mal-ət-ē\ *n, pl* **for·mal·i·ties**
1 the quality or state of being formal
2 an established way of doing something

**for·ma·tion** \fȯr-'mā-shən\ *n*
1 a forming of something ⟨the *formation* of good habits⟩
2 something that is formed ⟨a cloud *formation*⟩
3 an arrangement of something (as persons or ships) ⟨battle *formation*⟩ ⟨punt *formation*⟩

**for·mer** \'fȯr-mər\ *adj*
coming before in time ⟨a *former* president⟩

**for·mer·ly** \'fȯr-mər-lē\ *adv*
at an earlier time

**for·mi·da·ble** \'fȯr-mə-də-bəl\ *adj*
1 exciting fear or awe ⟨a *formidable* problem⟩
2 offering serious difficulties

**form·less** \'fȯrm-ləs\ *adj*
having no regular form or shape
**form·less·ly** *adv*
**form·less·ness** *n*

**for·mu·la** \'fȯr-myə-lə\ *n*
1 a direction giving amounts of the substances for the preparation of something (as a medicine)
2 a milk mixture or substitute for feeding a baby
3 a general fact or rule expressed in symbols ⟨a *formula* for finding the size of an angle⟩
4 an expression in symbols giving the makeup of a substance ⟨the *formula* for water is $H_2O$⟩
5 an established form or method

**for·mu·late** \'fȯr-myə-ˌlāt\ *vb* **for·mu·lat·ed**; **for·mu·lat·ing**
to state definitely and clearly

**for·sake** \fər-'sāk\ *vb* **for·sook** \-'su̇k\; **for·sak·en** \-'sā-kən\; **for·sak·ing**
to give up or leave entirely
**synonyms** see ABANDON

**for·syth·ia** \fər-'sith-ē-ə\ *n*
▼ a bush often grown for its bright yellow flowers that appear in early spring

**forsythia**

**fort** \'fōrt\ *n*
▶ a strong or fortified place

**forth** \'fōrth\ *adv*
**1** onward in time, place, or order ⟨from that time *forth*⟩
**2** out into view

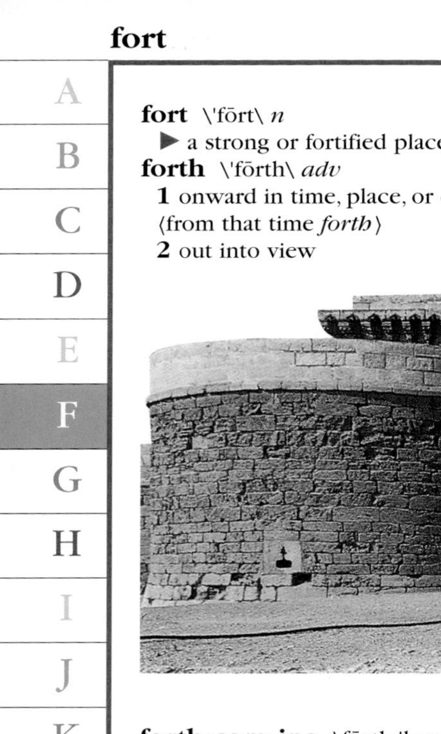

**fort:**
a 14th-century fort in Spain

**forth·com·ing** \fōrth-'kəm-ing\ *adj*
**1** being about to appear
**2** ready or available when needed

**forth·right** \'fōr-,thrīt\ *adj*
going straight to the point clearly and firmly ⟨a *forthright* answer⟩
**forth·right·ly** *adv*

**forth·with** \fōrth-'with, -'with\ *adv*
without delay : IMMEDIATELY

[1]**for·ti·eth** \'fórt-ē-əth\ *adj*
coming right after thirty-ninth

[2]**fortieth** *n*
number forty in a series

**for·ti·fi·ca·tion** \,fórt-ə-fə-'kā-shən\ *n*
**1** the act of fortifying
**2** something that strengthens or protects

**for·ti·fy** \'fórt-ə-,fī\ *vb* **for·ti·fied**; **for·ti·fy·ing**
**1** to make strong (as by building defenses)
**2** ENRICH 2, 3 ⟨*fortify* food with vitamins⟩

**for·ti·tude** \'fórt-ə-,tüd, -,tyüd\ *n*
strength of mind that lets a person meet and put up with trouble

**fort·night** \'fōrt-,nīt\ *n*
two weeks

**for·tress** \'fór-trəs\ *n*
a fortified place

**for·tu·nate** \'fór-chə-nət\ *adj*
**1** bringing some unexpected good
**2** receiving some unexpected good : LUCKY
**for·tu·nate·ly** *adv*

**for·tune** \'fór-chən\ *n*
**1** favorable results that come partly by chance
**2** what happens to a person : good or bad luck
**3** what is to happen to one in the future ⟨had my *fortune* told⟩
**4** WEALTH

**for·tune–tell·er** \'fór-chən-,tel-ər\ *n*
a person who claims to foretell future events

[1]**for·ty** \'fórt-ē\ *adj*
being four times ten

[2]**forty** *n*
four times ten : 40

**for·ty–nin·er** \'fórt-ē-'nī-nər\ *n*
a person in the California gold rush of 1849

**fo·rum** \'fōr-əm\ *n*
**1** the marketplace or public place of an ancient Roman city serving as the center for public business
**2** a program of open discussion

[1]**for·ward** \'fór-wərd\ *adj*
**1** near, at, or belonging to the front part ⟨a ship's *forward* gun⟩
**2** lacking proper modesty or reserve
**3** moving, tending, or leading to a position in front

[2]**forward** *adv*
to or toward what is in front

[3]**forward** *vb*
**1** to help onward : ADVANCE
**2** to send on or ahead ⟨*forward* a letter⟩

[4]**forward** *n*
a player at or near the front of his or her team or near the opponent's goal

**for·wards** \'fór-wərdz\ *adv*
[2]FORWARD

**fos·sil** \'fäs-əl\ *n*
▶ a trace or print or the remains of a plant or animal of a past age preserved in earth or rock

[1]**fos·ter** \'fós-tər\ *adj*
giving, receiving, or sharing parental care even though not related by blood or legal ties ⟨a *foster* parent⟩

[2]**foster** *vb*
**1** to give parental care to
**2** to help the growth and development of

**fought** *past of* FIGHT

[1]**foul** \'faùl\ *adj*
**1** disgusting in looks, taste, or smell ⟨a *foul* sewer⟩
**2** full of or covered with dirt
**3** being vulgar or insulting ⟨*foul* language⟩
**4** being wet and stormy ⟨*foul* weather⟩
**5** very unfair ⟨would use fair means or *foul*⟩
**6** breaking a rule in a game or sport ⟨a *foul* blow in boxing⟩
**7** being outside the foul lines ⟨hit a *foul* ball⟩
**foul·ly** \'faùl-lē\ *adv*
**foul·ness** *n*

## fossil

Fossils are the remains of plants and animals that were quickly sealed off from air and moisture after death. Some fossils are formed as minerals that are harder than the surrounding sediments. Other fossils are formed in coal deposits over millions of years. Fossilized leaf prints are like casts left in stone that once was mud. Sometimes whole creatures are frozen in ice or preserved in amber.

**fossil of a beetle in sand and tar**

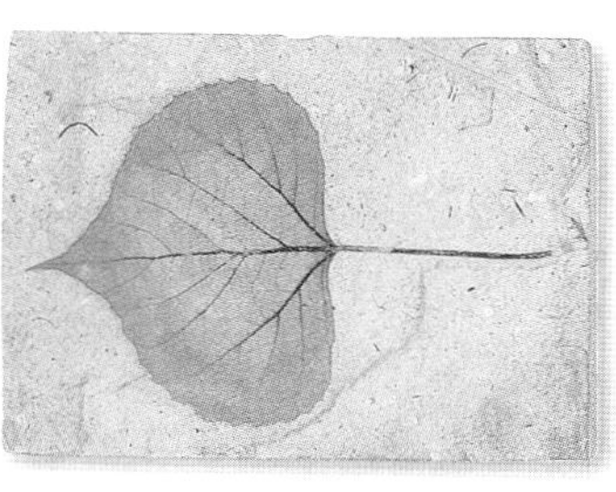

**impression of a leaf in stone formed from mud**

**mineral fossil of an ammonite**

**impression of a sea urchin in sandstone**

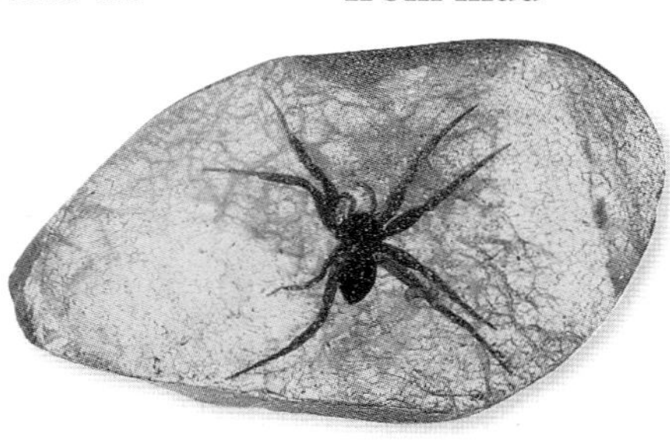

**a spider in amber**

**[2]foul** *n*
**1** a breaking of the rules in a game or sport
**2** a foul ball in baseball

**[3]foul** *vb*
**1** to make or become foul or filthy ⟨*foul* the air⟩ ⟨*foul* a stream⟩
**2** to make a foul
**3** to become or cause to become entangled

**foul line** *n*
either of two straight lines running from the rear corner of home plate through first and third base to the boundary of a baseball field

**foul play** *n*
VIOLENCE 1

**[1]found** \'faund\ *past of* FIND

**[2]found** *vb*
ESTABLISH 1 ⟨*found* a college⟩

**foun·da·tion** \faun-'dā-shən\ *n*
**1** the act of founding
**2** the support upon which something rests ⟨the *foundation* of a building⟩

**[1]found·er** \'faun-dər\ *n*
a person who founds something

**[2]foun·der** \'faun-dər\ *vb*
[1]SINK 1

**found·ling** \'faund-ling\ *n*
an infant found after being abandoned by unknown parents

**found·ry** \'faun-drē\ *n, pl* **foundries**
a building or factory where metals are cast

**foun·tain** \'faunt-n\ *n*
**1** a spring of water
**2** SOURCE 1
**3** an artificial stream or spray of water (as for drinking or ornament) or the device from which it comes

**fountain pen** *n*
▼ a pen with ink inside that is fed as needed to the writing point

**fountain pen**

**[1]four** \'fōr\ *adj*
being one more than three

**[2]four** *n*
**1** one more than three : two times two : 4
**2** the fourth in a set or series

**four·fold** \'fōr-,fōld\ *adj*
being four times as great or as many

**four·score** \'fōr-,skōr\ *adj*
[1]EIGHTY

**four·some** \'fōr-səm\ *adj*
a group of four persons or things

**[1]four·teen** \fōr-'tēn, fōrt-\ *adj*
being one more than thirteen

**[2]fourteen** *n*
one more than thirteen : two times seven : 14

**[1]four·teenth** \fōr-'tēnth, fōrt-\ *adj*
coming right after thirteenth

**[2]fourteenth** *n*
number fourteen in a series

**[1]fourth** \'fōrth\ *adj*
coming right after third

**[2]fourth** *n*
**1** number four in a series
**2** one of four equal parts

**Fourth of July** *n*
INDEPENDENCE DAY

**fowl** \'faůl\ *n, pl* **fowl** *or* **fowls**
**1** BIRD ⟨wild *fowls*⟩
**2** a common domestic rooster or hen
**3** the flesh of a mature domestic fowl for use as food

**fox** \'fäks\ *n*
▼ a wild animal closely related to the dog that has a sharp snout, pointed ears and a long bushy tail

**fox**

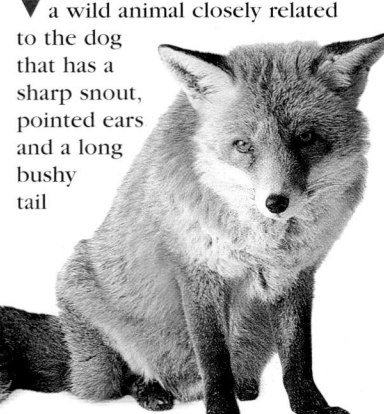

**foxy** \'fäk-sē\ *adj* **fox·i·er**; **fox·i·est**
cunning and careful in planning and action
**fox·i·ly** \-sə-lē\ *adv*
**fox·i·ness** \-sē-nəs\ *n*

**foy·er** \'fȯi-ər, 'fȯi-,ā\ *n*
**1** a lobby especially in a theater
**2** an entrance hall

**fra·cas** \'frāk-əs, 'frak-\ *n*
a noisy quarrel **:** BRAWL

**frac·tion** \'frak-shən\ *n*
**1** a part of a whole **:** FRAGMENT
**2** a number (as $^{1}/_{2}$, $^{2}/_{3}$, $^{17}/_{100}$) that indicates one or more equal parts of a whole or group and that may be considered as indicating also division of the number above the line by the number below the line

**frac·tion·al** \'frak-shən-l\ *adj*
**1** of, relating to, or being a fraction
**2** fairly small

**[1]frac·ture** \'frak-chər\ *n*
**1** a breaking or being broken (as of a bone)
**2** damage or an injury caused by breaking

**[2]fracture** *vb* **frac·tured**; **frac·tur·ing**
to cause a fracture in **:** BREAK

**frag·ile** \'fraj-əl\ *adj*
easily broken **:** DELICATE **synonyms** see BRITTLE

**frag·ment** \'frag-mənt\ *n*
a part broken off or incomplete

**frag·men·tary** \'frag-mən-,ter-ē\ *adj*
made up of fragments **:** INCOMPLETE

**fra·grance** \'frā-grəns\ *n*
a sweet or pleasant smell

**fra·grant** \'frā-grənt\ *adj*
sweet or pleasant in smell
**fra·grant·ly** *adv*

**frail** \'frāl\ *adj*
very delicate or weak in structure or being **synonyms** see WEAK

**frail·ty** \'frāl-tē\ *n, pl* **frailties**
**1** the quality or state of being weak
**2** a weakness of character

**[1]frame** \'frām\ *vb* **framed**; **fram·ing**
**1** [2]FORM 1, CONSTRUCT
**2** to enclose in a frame

**[2]frame** *n*
**1** the structure of an animal and especially a human body **:** PHYSIQUE
**2** ▼ an arrangement of parts that give form or support to something ⟨the *frame* of a house⟩
**3** an open case or structure for holding or enclosing something ⟨window *frame*⟩ ⟨picture *frame*⟩
**4** a particular state or mood ⟨in a pleasant *frame* of mind⟩

**[3]frame** *adj*
having a wooden frame ⟨a two-story *frame* house⟩

**frame·work** \'frām-,wərk\ *n*
a basic supporting part or structure ⟨the *framework* of an argument⟩

**franc** \'frangk\ *n*
**1** a French coin or bill
**2** any of various coins or bills used in countries where French is widely spoken

**Fran·co-** \'frang-kō\ *prefix*
**1** French and
**2** French

**frank** \'frangk\ *adj*
free in speaking one's feelings and opinions
**frank·ly** *adv*
**frank·ness** *n*

**Word History** The word *frank* came from the name of a group of people, the Franks, who controlled France a long time ago. When the Franks were in power, they were the only people in the country who had complete freedom. A Latin word that meant "free" was formed from the Latin word that meant "a Frank." The English word *frank* came from the Latin word that meant "free." At first English *frank* meant "free," but now it has a more specific meaning.

**[2]frame 2:**
the wooden frame of a house under construction

**frank·furt·er** \'frangk-fərt-ər\ *n*
▼ a cooked sausage (as of beef or beef and pork)

frankfurter

**frank·in·cense** \'frang-kən-,sens\ *n*
a fragrant gum that is burned for its sweet smell

**fran·tic** \'frant-ik\ *adj*
wildly excited

**fran·ti·cal·ly** \'frant-i-kə-lē\ *adv*
in a frantic way

**fra·ter·nal** \frə-'tərn-l\ *adj*
**1** having to do with brothers
**2** made up of members banded together like brothers

**fra·ter·ni·ty** \frə-'tər-nət-ē\ *n, pl* **fra·ter·ni·ties**
a society of boys or men (as in a college)

**fraud** \'frȯd\ *n*
**1** TRICKERY, DECEIT
**2** an act of deceiving **:** TRICK
**3** a person who pretends to be what he or she is not

**fraud·u·lent** \'frȯ-jə-lənt\ *adj*
based on or done by fraud
**fraud·u·lent·ly** *adv*

**fraught** \'frȯt\ *adj*
full of some quality ⟨a situation *fraught* with danger⟩

**[1]fray** \'frā\ *n*
[2]FIGHT 1, BRAWL

**[2]fray** *vb*
to wear into shreds

**fraz·zle** \'fraz-əl\ *n*
a tired or nervous condition ⟨worn to a *frazzle*⟩

**[1]freak** \'frēk\ *n*
a strange, abnormal, or unusual person, thing, or event ⟨circus *freaks*⟩

**[2]freak** *adj*
being or suggesting a freak **:** IMPROBABLE ⟨a *freak* accident⟩

**[1]freck·le** \'frek-əl\ *n*
► a small brownish spot on the skin

**[2]freckle** *vb* **freck·led**; **freck·ling**
to mark or become marked with freckles ⟨a *freckled* face⟩

**[1]free** \'frē\ *adj* **fre·er** \'frē-ər\; **fre·est** \'frē-əst\
**1** having liberty **:** not being a slave ⟨*free* citizens⟩
**2** not controlled by others ⟨a *free* country⟩
**3** released or not suffering from something unpleasant or painful ⟨*free* from worry⟩
**4** given without charge ⟨a *free* ticket⟩
**5** not held back by fear or distrust **:** OPEN ⟨a *free* expression of opinion⟩
**6** not blocked **:** CLEAR
**7** not combined ⟨*free* oxygen⟩
**free·ly** *adv*

**[2]free** *vb* **freed**; **free·ing**
to make or set free

**[3]free** *adv*
**1** in a free manner **:** FREELY
**2** without charge

**freed·man** \'frēd-mən\ *n, pl* **freed·men** \-mən\
a person freed from slavery

**free·dom** \'frēd-əm\ *n*
**1** the condition of being free **:** LIBERTY, INDEPENDENCE
**2** ability to move or act freely
**3** the quality of being very frank **:** CANDOR
**4** free and unlimited use

**free·hand** \'frē-,hand\ *adj or adv*
done without mechanical aids ⟨a *freehand* drawing⟩

**free·man** \'frē-mən\ *n, pl* **free·men** \-mən\
a free person **:** one who is not a slave

**free·stand·ing** \'frē-'stan-ding\ *adj*
standing alone or on its own foundation free of attachment or support

**free·way** \'frē-,wā\ *n*
an expressway that can be used without paying tolls

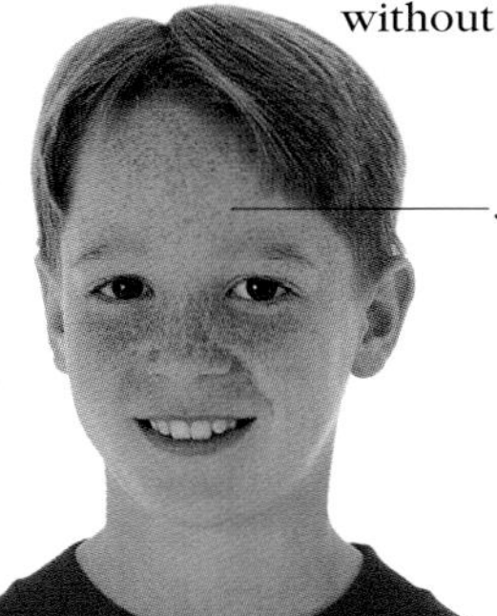

*freckled skin*

**[1]freckle:** a boy with freckles on his face

**[1]freeze** \'frēz\ *vb* **froze** \'frōz\; **fro·zen** \'frōz-n\; **freez·ing**
**1** to harden into or be hardened into a solid (as ice) by loss of heat ⟨the river *froze* over⟩ ⟨*freeze* cream⟩
**2** to be or become uncomfortably cold
**3** to damage by cold ⟨plants *frozen* by heavy frost⟩
**4** to clog or become clogged by ice ⟨water pipes *frozen* overnight⟩
**5** to become fixed or motionless ⟨*freeze* in your tracks⟩

**[2]freeze** *n*
**1** a period of freezing weather **:** cold weather
**2** an act or instance of freezing
**3** the state of being frozen

**freez·er** \'frē-zər\ *n*
a compartment or room used to freeze food or keep it frozen

**freezing point** *n*
the temperature at which a liquid becomes solid

**[1]freight** \'frāt\ *n*
**1** the amount paid (as to a shipping company) for carrying goods
**2** goods or cargo carried by a ship, train, truck, or airplane
**3** the carrying (as by truck) of goods from one place to another
**4** a train that carries freight

**[2]freight** *vb*
to send by freight

**freight·er** \'frāt-ər\ *n*
a ship or airplane used to carry freight

**[1]French** \'french\ *adj*
of or relating to France, its people, or the French language

**[2]French** *n*
**1 French** *pl* the people of France
**2** the language of the French

**french fry** *n, often cap 1st F*
a strip of potato fried in deep fat ⟨steak and *french fries*⟩

**French horn** *n*
a circular brass musical instrument with a large opening at one end and a mouthpiece shaped like a small funnel

**fren·zied** \'fren-zēd\ *adj*
very excited and upset

**fren·zy** \'fren-zē\ *n, pl* **frenzies**
great and often wild or disorderly activity

a b c d e f g h i j k l m n o p q r s t u v w x y z

\ng\ sing \ō\ bone \ȯ\ saw \ȯi\ coin \th\ thin \t͟h\ this \ü\ food \u̇\ foot \y\ yet \yü\ few \yu̇\ cure \zh\ vision

A
B
C
D
E
F
G
H
I
J
K
L
M
N
O
P
Q
R
S
T
U
V
W
X
Y
Z

**frog 1**
Frogs generally have squat bodies, smooth skin, strongly muscled hind legs for leaping, and webbed feet. Most frogs reproduce in water, and lay eggs that develop into larvae known as tadpoles. Frogs are the most commonly found amphibians in the world, living in habitats ranging from moist areas such as lakes, marshes, and rain forests to dry regions such as mountains and deserts.
South American frog
poison-dart frog
European common frog
tomato frog

**fre·quen·cy** \'frē-kwən-sē\ *n, pl* **fre·quen·cies**
**1** frequent repetition
**2** rate of repetition

[1]**fre·quent** \frē-'kwent\ *vb*
to visit often ⟨we *frequented* the beach during the summer⟩

[2]**fre·quent** \'frē-kwənt\ *adj*
happening often ⟨*frequent* trips to town⟩
**fre·quent·ly** *adv*

**fresh** \'fresh\ *adj*
**1** not salt ⟨*fresh* water⟩
**2** PURE 1, BRISK ⟨*fresh* air⟩ ⟨a *fresh* breeze⟩
**3** not frozen, canned, or pickled ⟨*fresh* vegetables⟩
**4** not stale, sour, or spoiled ⟨*fresh* bread⟩ ⟨meat kept *fresh* in the refrigerator⟩
**5** not dirty or rumpled ⟨a *fresh* shirt⟩
**6** NEW 6 ⟨make a *fresh* start⟩
**7** newly made or received ⟨a *fresh* wound⟩ ⟨*fresh* news⟩
**8** IMPUDENT ⟨*fresh* talk⟩
**fresh·ly** *adv*
**fresh·ness** *n*

**fresh·en** \'fresh-ən\ *vb*
to make or become fresh ⟨took a shower to *freshen* up⟩ ⟨the wind *freshened*⟩

**fresh·et** \'fresh-ət\ *n*
a sudden overflowing of a stream

**fresh·man** \'fresh-mən\ *n, pl* **fresh·men** \-mən\
a first year student (as in college)

**fresh·wa·ter** \,fresh-,wȯt-ər, -,wät-\ *adj*
of, relating to, or living in fresh water

[1]**fret** \'fret\ *vb* **fret·ted**; **fret·ting**
to make or become worried ⟨*fret* over a problem⟩

[2]**fret** *n*
an irritated or worried state

[3]**fret** *n*
a design of short lines or bars

[4]**fret** *n*
▶ one of a series of ridges fixed across the fingerboard of a stringed musical instrument
**fret·ted** *adj*

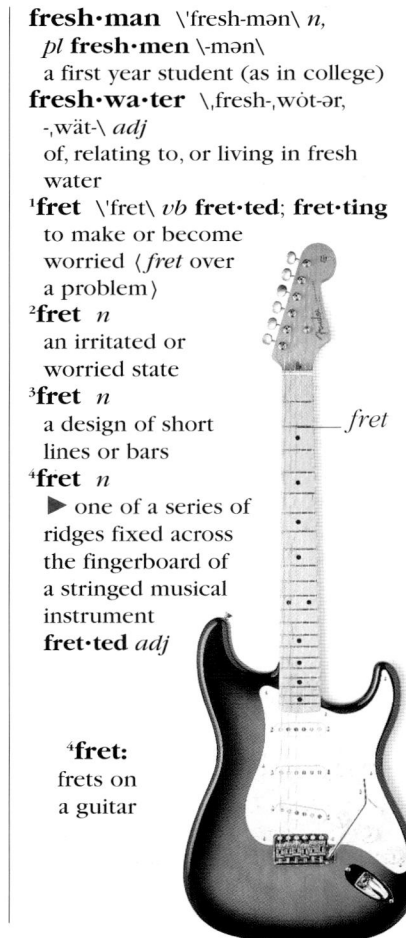

*fret*

[4]**fret:** frets on a guitar

**fret·ful** \'fret-fəl\ *adj*
likely to fret : IRRITABLE ⟨a *fretful* baby⟩
**fret·ful·ly** \-fə-lē\ *adv*
**fret·ful·ness** *n*

**fri·ar** \'frī-ər\ *n*
a member of a Roman Catholic religious order for men

**fric·tion** \'frik-shən\ *n*
**1** the rubbing of one thing against another
**2** resistance to motion between bodies in contact ⟨the *friction* of a box sliding along the floor⟩
**3** disagreement among persons or groups

**Fri·day** \'frīd-ē\ *n*
the sixth day of the week

**friend** \'frend\ *n*
**1** a person who has a strong liking for and trust in another person
**2** a person who is not an enemy ⟨*friend* or foe⟩
**3** a person who aids or favors something ⟨was a *friend* to good causes⟩
**friend·less** \-ləs\ *adj*

**friend·ly** \'frend-lē\ *adj* **friend·li·er**; **friend·li·est**
**1** showing friendship
**2** being other than an enemy
**friend·li·ness** *n*

**friend·ship** \'frend-,ship\ *n*
the state of being friends

**frieze** \'frēz\ *n*
a band or stripe (as around a building) used as a decoration

**frig·ate** \'frig-ət\ *n*
**1** a square-rigged warship

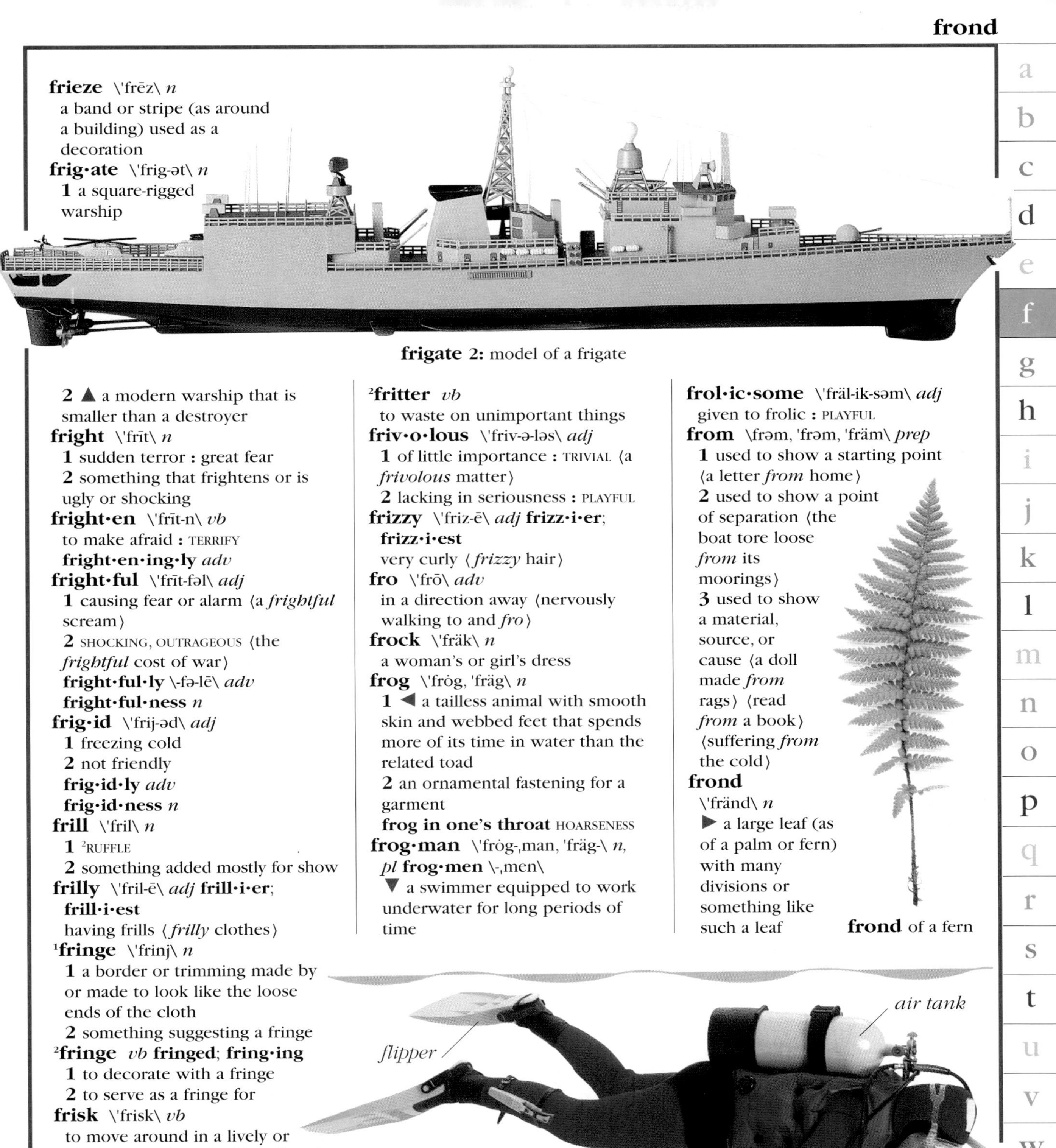


**frigate 2:** model of a frigate

**2** ▲ a modern warship that is smaller than a destroyer

**fright** \'frīt\ *n*
**1** sudden terror : great fear
**2** something that frightens or is ugly or shocking

**fright·en** \'frīt-n\ *vb*
to make afraid : TERRIFY
**fright·en·ing·ly** *adv*

**fright·ful** \'frīt-fəl\ *adj*
**1** causing fear or alarm ⟨a *frightful* scream⟩
**2** SHOCKING, OUTRAGEOUS ⟨the *frightful* cost of war⟩
**fright·ful·ly** \-fə-lē\ *adv*
**fright·ful·ness** *n*

**frig·id** \'frij-əd\ *adj*
**1** freezing cold
**2** not friendly
**frig·id·ly** *adv*
**frig·id·ness** *n*

**frill** \'fril\ *n*
**1** [2]RUFFLE
**2** something added mostly for show

**frilly** \'fril-ē\ *adj* **frill·i·er**; **frill·i·est**
having frills ⟨*frilly* clothes⟩

[1]**fringe** \'frinj\ *n*
**1** a border or trimming made by or made to look like the loose ends of the cloth
**2** something suggesting a fringe

[2]**fringe** *vb* **fringed**; **fring·ing**
**1** to decorate with a fringe
**2** to serve as a fringe for

**frisk** \'frisk\ *vb*
to move around in a lively or playful way ⟨dogs *frisking* about⟩

**frisky** \'fris-kē\ *adj* **frisk·i·er**; **frisk·i·est**
tending to frisk : PLAYFUL, LIVELY

[1]**frit·ter** \'frit-ər\ *n*
a small amount of fried batter often containing fruit or meat

[2]**fritter** *vb*
to waste on unimportant things

**friv·o·lous** \'friv-ə-ləs\ *adj*
**1** of little importance : TRIVIAL ⟨a *frivolous* matter⟩
**2** lacking in seriousness : PLAYFUL

**frizzy** \'friz-ē\ *adj* **frizz·i·er**; **frizz·i·est**
very curly ⟨*frizzy* hair⟩

**fro** \'frō\ *adv*
in a direction away ⟨nervously walking to and *fro*⟩

**frock** \'fräk\ *n*
a woman's or girl's dress

**frog** \'frȯg, 'fräg\ *n*
**1** ◀ a tailless animal with smooth skin and webbed feet that spends more of its time in water than the related toad
**2** an ornamental fastening for a garment
**frog in one's throat** HOARSENESS

**frog·man** \'frȯg-,man, 'fräg-\ *n*, *pl* **frog·men** \-,men\
▼ a swimmer equipped to work underwater for long periods of time

**frogman**

[1]**frol·ic** \'fräl-ik\ *vb* **frol·icked**; **frol·ick·ing**
to play about happily : ROMP ⟨the dog *frolicked* in the snow⟩

[2]**frolic** *n*
FUN 1, GAIETY

**frol·ic·some** \'fräl-ik-səm\ *adj*
given to frolic : PLAYFUL

**from** \frəm, 'frəm, 'främ\ *prep*
**1** used to show a starting point ⟨a letter *from* home⟩
**2** used to show a point of separation ⟨the boat tore loose *from* its moorings⟩
**3** used to show a material, source, or cause ⟨a doll made *from* rags⟩ ⟨read *from* a book⟩ ⟨suffering *from* the cold⟩

**frond** \'fränd\ *n*
► a large leaf (as of a palm or fern) with many divisions or something like such a leaf

**frond** of a fern

**[1]front** \'frənt\ *n*
**1** a region in which active warfare is taking place
**2** the forward part or surface
**3** ▶ the boundary between bodies of air at different temperatures ⟨a cold *front*⟩

**[2]front** *vb*
[2]FACE 2 ⟨the cottage *fronts* on the lake⟩

**[3]front** *adj*
of, relating to, or situated at the front

**fron·tal** \'frənt-l\ *adj*
of, relating to, or directed at the front ⟨a *frontal* attack⟩

**fron·tier** \,frən-'tir\ *n*
**1** a border between two countries
**2** the edge of the settled part of a country

**fron·tiers·man** \,frən-'tirz-mən\ *n, pl* **fron·tiers·men** \-mən\
a person living on the frontier

**[1]frost** \'frȯst\ *n*
**1** temperature cold enough to cause freezing
**2** a covering of tiny ice crystals on a cold surface formed from the water vapor in the air

**[2]frost** *vb*
to cover with frost or with something suggesting frost ⟨*frost* a cake⟩

**frost·bite** \'frȯst-,bīt\ *n*
slight freezing of a part of the body or the effect of this

**frost·ing** \'frȯs-ting\ *n*
**1** ICING
**2** a dull finish on glass

**frosty** \'frȯ-stē\ *adj* **frost·i·er**; **frost·i·est**
**1** cold enough to produce frost ⟨a *frosty* evening⟩
**2** covered with or appearing to be covered with frost ⟨a *frosty* glass⟩
**frost·i·ly** \-stə-lē\ *adv*
**frost·i·ness** \-stē-nəs\ *n*

**[1]froth** \'frȯth\ *n*
bubbles formed in or on liquids

**[2]froth** *vb*
to produce or form froth

**frothy** \'frȯ-thē, -t͟hē\ *adj* **froth·i·er**; **froth·i·est**
full of or made up of froth
**froth·i·ness** *n*

**[1]frown** \'frau̇n\ *vb*
**1** to wrinkle the forehead (as in anger or thought)
**2** to look with disapproval

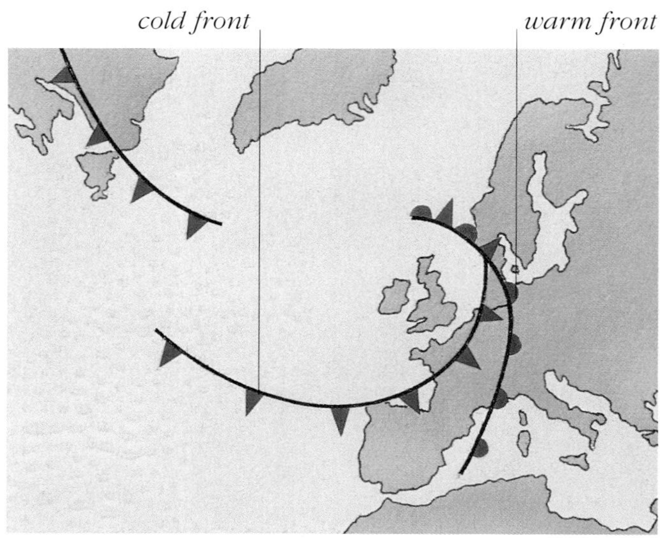


**[1]front 3:** a cold front advancing over Europe

**[2]frown** *n*
a wrinkling of the brow

**froze** *past of* FREEZE

**frozen** *past participle of* FREEZE

**fru·gal** \'frü-gəl\ *adj*
careful in spending or using resources
**fru·gal·ly** *adv*

**[1]fruit** \'früt\ *n*
**1** a pulpy or juicy plant part (as rhubarb or a strawberry) that is often eaten as a dessert and is distinguished from a vegetable
**2** ▶ a reproductive body of a seed plant that consists of the ripened ovary of a flower with its included seeds
**3** [2]RESULT 1, PRODUCT ⟨the *fruits* of your labors⟩
**fruit·ed** \-əd\ *adj*

**[2]fruit** *vb*
to bear or cause to bear fruit

**fruit·cake** \'früt-,kāk\ *n*
▶ a rich cake containing nuts, dried or candied fruits, and spices

**fruit·ful** \'früt-fəl\ *adj*
**1** very productive ⟨a *fruitful* soil⟩
**2** bringing results ⟨a *fruitful* idea⟩
**fruit·ful·ly** \-fə-lē\ *adv*
**fruit·ful·ness** *n*

**fruit·less** \'früt-ləs\ *adj*
**1** not bearing fruit
**2** UNSUCCESSFUL
**fruit·less·ly** *adv*
**fruit·less·ness** *n*

**fruity** \'früt-ē\ *adj* **fruit·i·er**; **fruit·i·est**
relating to or suggesting fruit ⟨a *fruity* smell⟩

**frus·trate** \'frəs-,trāt\ *vb* **frus·trat·ed**; **frus·trat·ing**
**1** to prevent from carrying out a purpose
**2** [1]DEFEAT 1
**3** DISCOURAGE 1

**frus·tra·tion** \,frəs-'trā-shən\ *n*
DISAPPOINTMENT 2, DEFEAT

**[1]fry** \'frī\ *vb* **fried**; **fry·ing**
to cook in fat

**[2]fry** *n, pl* **fry**
**1** recently hatched or very young fishes
**2** persons of a particular group ⟨small *fry*⟩

**fudge** \'fəj\ *n*
a soft creamy candy often containing nuts

**fruitcake**

**[1]fu·el** \'fyü-əl\ *n*
a substance (as oil) that can be burned to produce heat or power

**[1]fruit 2**

A fruit develops from the ovary of a flower that has been pollinated, and is the part of a plant that contains the seeds. There are two main types of fruit: dry fruits, and succulent fruits, which are juicy and colorful. Of the succulent fruits, some have a single, large seed in a hard case — the stone — while others have many tiny seeds.

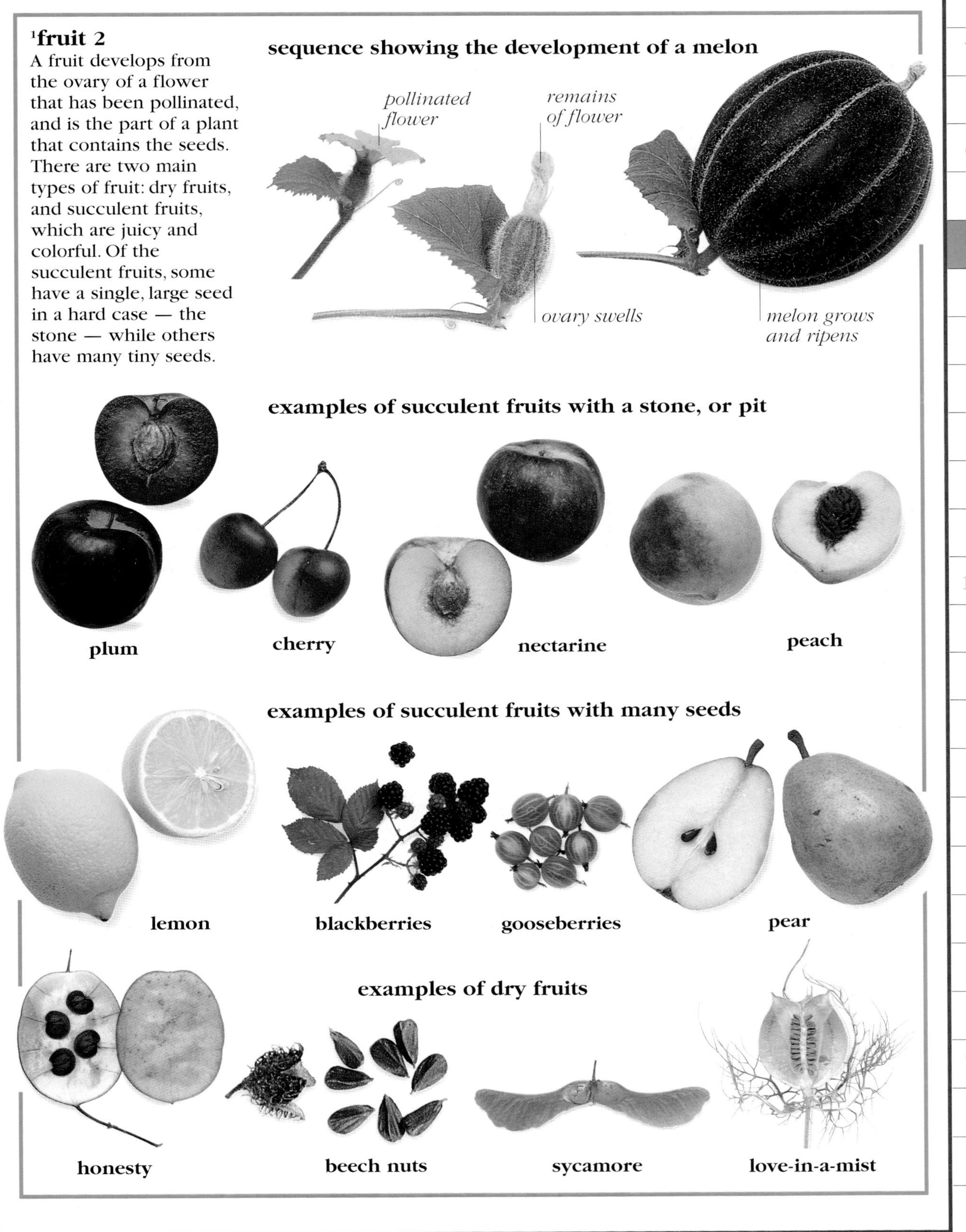

[2]**fuel** *vb* **fu·eled** *or* **fu·elled**; **fu·el·ing** *or* **fu·el·ling**
to supply with or take on fuel

[1]**fu·gi·tive** \'fyü-jət-iv\ *adj*
running away or trying to escape ⟨a *fugitive* slave⟩

[2]**fugitive** *n*
a person who is running away

[1]**-ful** \fəl\ *adj suffix*
**1** full of ⟨event*ful*⟩
**2** characterized by ⟨peace*ful*⟩
**3** having the qualities of ⟨master*ful*⟩
**4** -ABLE ⟨mourn*ful*⟩

[2]**-ful** \,fu̇l\ *n suffix*
number or quantity that fills or would fill ⟨spoon*ful*⟩

**ful·crum** \'fu̇l-krəm, 'fəl-\ *n, pl* **fulcrums** *or* **ful·cra** \-krə\
the support on which a lever turns in lifting something

**ful·fill** *or* **ful·fil** \fu̇l-'fil\ *vb* **ful·filled**; **ful·fill·ing**
**1** ACCOMPLISH ⟨*fulfill* a plan⟩
**2** SATISFY 1 ⟨*fulfill* a requirement⟩
**ful·fill·ment** \-mənt\ *n*

[1]**full** \'fu̇l\ *adj*
**1** containing as much as possible or normal ⟨a *full* glass⟩
**2** [1]COMPLETE 1 ⟨waited a *full* year⟩
**3** plump and rounded in outline ⟨a *full* face⟩
**4** having much material ⟨a *full* skirt⟩
**full·ness** *n*

[2]**full** *adv*
**1** [2]VERY 1
**2** COMPLETELY ⟨fill the glass *full*⟩

[3]**full** *n*
**1** the highest state, extent, or degree
**2** the complete amount ⟨paid in *full*⟩

**full moon** *n*
the moon with its whole disk lighted

**ful·ly** \'fu̇l-ē\ *adv*
**1** COMPLETELY
**2** at least ⟨*fully* half of them⟩

[1]**fum·ble** \'fəm-bəl\ *vb* **fum·bled**; **fum·bling**
to feel about for or handle something clumsily

[2]**fumble** *n*
an act of fumbling

[1]**fume** \'fyüm\ *n*
a disagreeable smoke, vapor, or gas — usually used in pl.

[2]**fume** *vb* **fumed**; **fum·ing**
**1** to give off fumes
**2** to show bad temper : be angry

**fungus**

Fungi absorb nutrients from dead or living organic matter, and most reproduce by spores. Fungi vary in size from microscopic, single-celled organisms such as yeast, to large, globe-shaped puffballs. Some fungi, such as truffles and mushrooms, are an important source of food, but many others are highly poisonous.

**poisonous fly mushroom**

**edible oyster mushrooms**

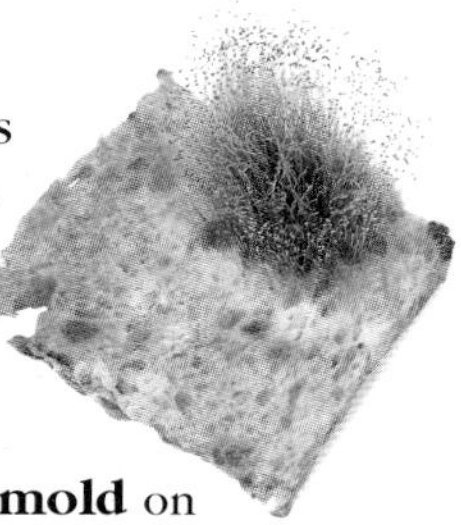

**mold** on stale bread

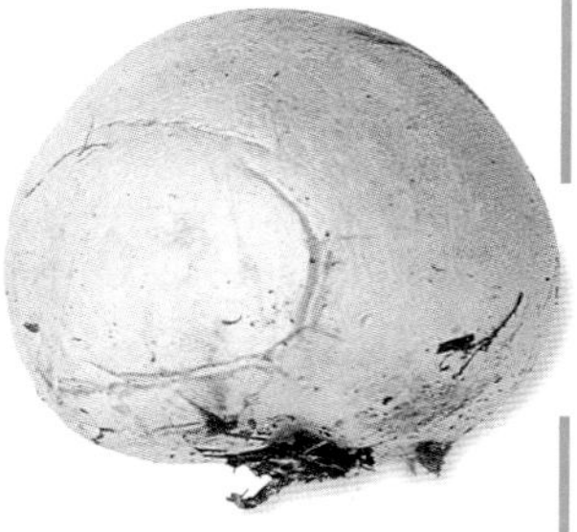

**puffball** is a globe-shaped fungus

**truffle** is an edible fungus

**bracket fungus** has a shape like a shelf

**fu·mi·gate** \'fyü-mə-,gāt\ *vb* **fu·mi·gat·ed**; **fu·mi·gat·ing**
to disinfect by exposing to smoke, vapor, or gas

**fun** \'fən\ *n*
**1** someone or something that provides amusement or enjoyment ⟨they were *fun* to play with⟩
**2** a good time : AMUSEMENT ⟨we had a lot of *fun*⟩ ⟨made up stories for *fun*⟩
**3** words or actions to make someone or something an object of unkind laughter ⟨made *fun* of their singing⟩

[1]**func·tion** \'fəngk-shən\ *n*
**1** the action for which a person or thing is specially fitted or used : PURPOSE
**2** a large important ceremony or social affair

[2]**function** *vb*
to serve a certain purpose : WORK ⟨the new machine *functions* well⟩

**function key** *n*
any of a set of keys on a computer keyboard that have or can be programmed to have special functions

**fund** \'fənd\ *n*
**1** [1]STOCK 4, SUPPLY ⟨a *fund* of jokes⟩
**2** a sum of money for a special purpose ⟨a book *fund*⟩
**3 funds** *pl* available money ⟨out of *funds*⟩

[1]**fun·da·men·tal** \,fən-də-'ment-l\ *adj*
being or forming a foundation : BASIC, ESSENTIAL ⟨a discovery *fundamental* to modern science⟩ ⟨our *fundamental* rights⟩
**fun·da·men·tal·ly** *adv*

[2]**fundamental** *n*
a basic part ⟨the *fundamentals* of arithmetic⟩

**fu·ner·al** \'fyü-nə-rəl, 'fyün-rəl\ *n*
the ceremonies held for a dead person (as before burial)

**fun·gi·cide** \'fən-jə-,sīd\ *n*
a substance used to kill fungi
**fun·gi·cid·al** \,fən-jə-'sīd-l\ *adj*

**fun·gous** \'fəng-gəs\ *or* **fun·gal** \-gəl\ *adj*
of, relating to, or caused by fungi

**fun·gus** \'fəng-gəs\ *n, pl* **fun·gi** \'fən-ˌjī, -ˌgī\ *also* **fun·gus·es**
◀ any of a large group of plantlike organisms (as mushrooms, molds, and rusts) that have no chlorophyll and must live on other plants or animals or on decaying material

**fun·nel** \'fən-l\ *n*
**1** ▶ a utensil usually shaped like a hollow cone with a tube extending from the point and used to catch and direct a downward flow (as of liquid)
**2** a large pipe for the escape of smoke or for ventilation (as on a ship)

**funnel 1:** a funnel in the neck of a bottle

**fun·nies** \'fən-ēz\ *n pl*
comic strips or a section containing comic strips (as in a newspaper)

**fun·ny** \'fən-ē\ *adj* **fun·ni·er**; **fun·ni·est**
**1** causing laughter
**2** STRANGE 3 ⟨a *funny* noise⟩

**fur** \'fər\ *n*
**1** a piece of the pelt of an animal
**2** an article of clothing made with fur
**3** the hairy coat of a mammal especially when fine, soft, and thick
**furred** \'fərd\ *adj*

**Word History** At first the pelt of an animal was called *fur* only when it was part of a person's garment. The English noun *fur* came from an earlier verb *fur*. This verb meant "to line or trim with fur." The English verb *fur* came from an early French verb. This early French verb came from an early French noun that meant "sheath." Lining or trimming a garment with fur was likened to putting a knife in a sheath.

**fu·ri·ous** \'fyu̇r-ē-əs\ *adj*
**1** very angry
**2** very active : VIOLENT ⟨a *furious* storm⟩
**fu·ri·ous·ly** *adv*

**furl** \'fərl\ *vb*
to wrap or roll close to or around something ⟨*furl* a flag⟩

**fur·long** \'fər-ˌlȯng\ *n*
a unit of length equal to 220 yards (about 201 meters)

**fur·lough** \'fər-lō\ *n*
a leave of absence from duty ⟨a soldier's *furlough*⟩

**fur·nace** \'fər-nəs\ *n*
▶ an enclosed structure in which heat is produced (as for heating a house or for melting metals)

**fur·nish** \'fər-nish\ *vb*
**1** to provide with what is needed ⟨the cave *furnished* us with shelter⟩
**2** to supply to someone or something ⟨*furnish* food to the guests⟩

**fur·nish·ings** \'fər-nish-ingz\ *n pl*
articles of furniture for a room or building

**fur·ni·ture** \'fər-ni-chər\ *n*
movable articles used to furnish a room

**fur·ri·er** \'fər-ē-ər\ *n*
a dealer in furs

[1]**fur·row** \'fər-ō\ *n*
**1** a trench made by or as if by a plow
**2** a narrow groove : WRINKLE

[2]**furrow** *vb*
to make furrows in

**fur·ry** \'fər-ē\ *adj* **fur·ri·er**; **fur·ri·est**
**1** like fur
**2** covered with fur

[1]**fur·ther** \'fər-t͟hər\ *adv*
**1** [1]FARTHER 1
**2** [2]BESIDES, ALSO
**3** to a greater degree or extent

[2]**further** *vb*
to help forward : PROMOTE

[3]**further** *adj*
**1** [2]FARTHER
**2** going or extending beyond : ADDITIONAL ⟨*further* study⟩

**furnace:** molten iron being poured from a furnace

**fur·ther·more** \'fər-t͟hər-ˌmōr\ *adv*
MOREOVER ⟨they came, *furthermore* they came on time⟩

**fur·ther·most** \'fər-t͟hər-ˌmōst\ *adj*
most distant : FARTHEST

**fur·thest** \'fər-t͟həst\ *adv or adj*
FARTHEST

**fur·tive** \'fərt-iv\ *adj*
done in a sneaky or sly manner
**fur·tive·ly** *adv*
**fur·tive·ness** *n*

**fu·ry** \'fyu̇r-ē\ *n, pl* **furies**
**1** violent anger : RAGE
**2** wild and dangerous force ⟨the *fury* of the storm⟩ **synonyms** see ANGER

[1]**fuse** \'fyüz\ *vb* **fused**; **fus·ing**
**1** to change into a liquid or to a plastic state by heat
**2** to unite by or as if by melting together

**²fuse** *n*
▶ a device having a metal wire or strip that melts and interrupts an electrical circuit when the current becomes too strong

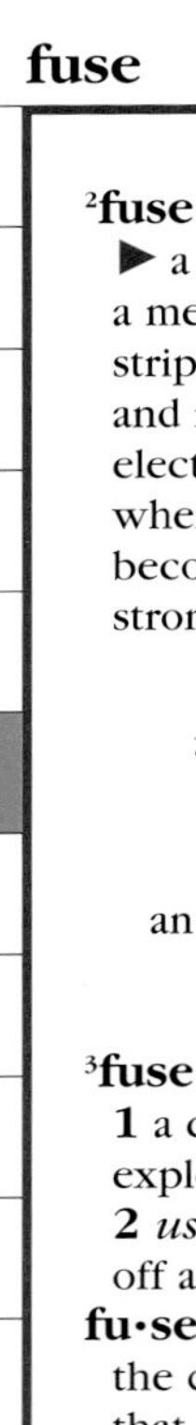

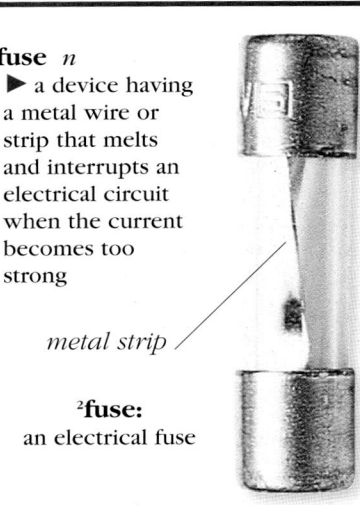

**²fuse:** an electrical fuse

**³fuse** *n*
**1** a cord that is set afire to ignite an explosive by carrying fire to it
**2** *usually* **fuze** a device for setting off a bomb or torpedo

**fu·se·lage** \ˈfyü-sə-ˌläzh, -zə-\ *n*
the central body part of an airplane that holds the crew, passengers, and cargo

**fu·sion** \ˈfyü-zhən\ *n*
**1** a fusing or melting together
**2** union by or as if by melting
**3** union of atomic nuclei to form heavier nuclei resulting in the release of enormous quantities of energy

**¹fuss** \ˈfəs\ *n*
**1** unnecessary activity or excitement often over something unimportant
**2** ¹PROTEST 2
**3** a great show of interest ⟨made a *fuss* over the baby⟩

**²fuss** *vb*
to make a fuss

**fussy** \ˈfəs-ē\ *adj* **fuss·i·er**; **fuss·i·est**
**1** inclined to complain or whine ⟨a *fussy* child⟩
**2** needing much attention to details ⟨a *fussy* job⟩
**3** hard to please ⟨*fussy* about food⟩

**fu·tile** \ˈfyüt-l\ *adj*
having no result or effect : USELESS ⟨their efforts to win were *futile*⟩
**fu·tile·ly** *adv*
**fu·tile·ness** *n*

**fu·til·i·ty** \fyu̇-ˈtil-ət-ē\ *n*
the quality or state of being futile

**¹fu·ture** \ˈfyü-chər\ *adj*
coming after the present ⟨*future* events⟩

**²future** *n*
**1** future time
**2** the chance of future success ⟨you've a bright *future*⟩

**fuze** *variant of* FUSE

**fuzz** \ˈfəz\ *n*
fine light particles or fibers

**fuzzy** \ˈfəz-ē\ *adj* **fuzz·i·er**; **fuzz·i·est**
**1** covered with or looking like fuzz
**2** not clear
**fuzz·i·ly** \ˈfəz-ə-lē\ *adv*
**fuzz·i·ness** \ˈfəz-ē-nəs\ *n*

**-fy** \ˌfī\ *vb suffix* **-fied**; **-fy·ing**
**1** make : form into ⟨solidi*fy*⟩
**2** make similar to ⟨beauti*fy*⟩

**The sounds of G:** The letter **G** has two sounds in English.

Its most common sound is the sound it has in the words **get**, **give**, **goofy**, **dog**, and **gurgle**. This is often called the "**hard G**" sound. **G** always has this sound when it occurs before another consonant, as in **ghost**, **glad**, or **grandfather**, or when it is doubled, as in **wiggle**.

Its second sound is like the sound of the letter **J**, called a "**soft G**." It sometimes has this sound before an **I** or an **E**. Examples of words with a soft **G** are **geranium**, **gene**, **giant**, **gingersnap**, **legible**, and **plumage**.

**G** is silent in a few words such as **gnaw** and **gnu**.

**g** \'jē\ *n, pl* **g's** *or* **gs** \'jēz\ *often cap*
**1** the seventh letter of the English alphabet
**2** a unit of force equal to the weight of a body on which the force acts ⟨an astronaut during takeoff of the rocket vehicle may experience ten *G's*⟩

hook

gaff 1

**[1]gab** \'gab\ *vb* **gabbed**; **gab·bing**
to talk in an idle way

**[2]gab** *n*
idle talk **:** CHATTER

**gab·ar·dine** \'gab-ər-ˌdēn\ *n*
a firm cloth with diagonal ribs and a hard smooth finish

**[1]gab·ble** \'gab-əl\ *vb* **gab·bled**; **gab·bling**
[1]CHATTER 2

**[2]gabble** *n*
loud or fast talk that has no meaning

**gab·by** \'gab-ē\ *adj* **gab·bi·er**; **gab·bi·est**
given to talking a lot **:** TALKATIVE

**ga·ble** \'gā-bəl\ *n*
the triangular part of an outside wall of a building formed by the sides of the roof sloping down from the ridgepole to the eaves

**gad** \'gad\ *vb* **gad·ded**; **gad·ding**
to roam about **:** WANDER

**gad·about** \'gad-ə-ˌbau̇t\ *n*
a person who goes from place to place without much reason

**gad·fly** \'gad-ˌflī\ *n, pl* **gad·flies**
**1** a large biting fly
**2** a person who is an annoying pest

**gad·get** \'gaj-ət\ *n*
an interesting, unfamiliar, or unusual device

**gaff** \'gaf\ *n*
**1** ◀ an iron hook with a handle
**2** something hard to take ⟨couldn't stand the *gaff*⟩

**[1]gag** \'gag\ *vb* **gagged**; **gag·ging**
**1** to keep from speaking or crying out by or as if by stopping up the mouth
**2** to cause to feel like vomiting **:** RETCH

**[2]gag** *n*
**1** something that gags
**2** [1]JOKE 1, 2

**gage** *variant of* GAUGE

**gai·ety** \'gā-ət-ē\ *n, pl* **gai·eties**
**1** MERRYMAKING 1
**2** bright spirits or manner

**gai·ly** \'gā-lē\ *adv*
**1** in a merry or lively way
**2** in a bright or showy way ⟨*gaily* dressed crowds⟩

**[1]gain** \'gān\ *n*
**1** advantage gained or increased **:** PROFIT ⟨financial *gains*⟩
**2** an increase in amount, size, or degree ⟨a *gain* in weight⟩

**[2]gain** *vb*
**1** to get hold of often by effort or with difficulty **:** WIN ⟨*gain* knowledge by study⟩ ⟨*gain* strength by exercise⟩ ⟨*gained* a great victory⟩
**2** to get to **:** REACH ⟨the swimmer *gained* the shore⟩
**3** to get advantage **:** PROFIT ⟨we all *gained* from the lesson⟩

**synonyms** see REACH

**gain·er** *n*

**gain·ful** \'gān-fəl\ *adj*
producing gain

**gait** \'gāt\ *n*
way of walking or running

**[1]ga·la** \'gā-lə, 'gal-ə, 'gäl-ə\ *n*
a large showy entertainment celebrating a special occasion ⟨the mayor's annual *gala*⟩

**[2]gala** *adj*
of or being a gala ⟨a *gala* charity ball⟩

**ga·lac·tic** \gə-'lak-tik\ *adj*
of or relating to a galaxy ⟨*galactic* light⟩

**galaxy 2:** a spiral galaxy

**gal·axy** \'gal-ək-sē\ *n, pl* **gal·ax·ies**
**1** MILKY WAY GALAXY
**2** ▲ one of billions of collections of stars, gas, and dust that make up the universe

**Word History** A band of light in the night sky is caused by many faint stars. We call this band the *Milky Way* because it looks a bit like a stream of milk. The stars of the Milky Way belong to our galaxy, the Milky Way galaxy. The idea that the Milky Way looks like milk is much older than the English language. The ancient Greek name for this star system was formed from the Greek word for milk. The English word *galaxy* came from the Greek name for the Milky Way.

**gale** \'gāl\ *n*
1 a strong wind
2 a wind of from about fourteen to twenty-four meters per second
3 OUTBURST 1 ⟨*gales* of laughter⟩

**ga·le·na** \gə-'lē-nə\ *n*
▶ a bluish gray mineral that is the main ore of lead

galena

**¹gall** \'gȯl\ *n*
1 bile especially when obtained from an animal and used in the arts or medicine
2 rude boldness ⟨had the *gall* to return my gift⟩

**²gall** *n*
a sore spot (as on a horse's back) caused by rubbing

**³gall** *vb*
1 to make sore by rubbing
2 IRRITATE 1

**⁴gall** *n*
a swelling or growth on a twig or leaf

**gal·lant** \'gal-ənt\ *adj*
1 showing no fear : BRAVE
2 CHIVALROUS 2, NOBLE
3 \gə-'lant, -'länt\ very polite to women

**gal·lant·ry** \'gal-ən-trē\ *n*
1 polite attention shown to women
2 COURAGE, BRAVERY

**gall·blad·der** \'gȯl-ˌblad-ər\ *n*
a small sac in which bile from the liver is stored

**gal·le·on** \'gal-ē-ən\ *n*
a large sailing ship of the time of Columbus and later

**gal·lery** \'gal-ə-rē, 'gal-rē\ *n, pl* **gal·ler·ies**
1 a long narrow room or hall
2 an indoor structure (as in a theater or church) built out from one or more walls
3 a room or hall used for a special purpose (as showing pictures)

**gal·ley** \'gal-ē\ *n, pl* **galleys**
1 a large low ship of olden times moved by oars and sails
2 the kitchen of a ship

**galley slave** *n*
a person forced to row on a galley

**gal·li·vant** \'gal-ə-ˌvant\ *vb*
GAD

**gal·lon** \'gal-ən\ *n*
a unit of liquid capacity equal to four quarts (about 3.8 liters)

**¹gal·lop** \'gal-əp\ *vb*
to go or cause to go at a gallop

**²gallop** *n*
1 a fast springing way of running of an animal with four feet and especially a horse
2 a ride or run at a gallop

**gal·lows** \'gal-ōz\ *n, pl* **gallows** *or* **gal·lows·es**
a structure from which criminals are hanged

**ga·lore** \gə-'lōr\ *adj*
marked by large amounts — used after the word it modifies ⟨a ride with thrills *galore*⟩

**ga·losh** \gə-'läsh\ *n*
an overshoe worn in snow or wet weather

**gal·va·nize** \'gal-və-ˌnīz\ *vb* **gal·va·nized**; **gal·va·niz·ing**
1 to excite or stir by or as if by an electric shock
2 ▶ to coat with zinc for protection

**galvanize 2:** a galvanized bucket

**¹gam·ble** \'gam-bəl\ *vb* **gam·bled**; **gam·bling**
1 to play a game in which something (as money) is risked : BET
2 to take risks on the chance of gain : take a chance ⟨we *gambled* on not being seen⟩

**²gamble** *n*
something that is risky to do

**gam·bler** \'gam-blər\ *n*
a person who gambles

**gam·bol** \'gam-bəl\ *vb* **gam·boled** *or* **gam·bolled**; **gam·bol·ing** *or* **gam·bol·ling**
to run or skip about playfully : FROLIC

**¹game** \'gām\ *n*
1 AMUSEMENT, PLAY ⟨children happy at their *games*⟩
2 a contest carried on according to rules with the players in direct opposition to each other
3 animals hunted for sport or for food
4 the meat from game animals

**²game** *adj* **gam·er**; **gam·est**
1 full of spirit or eagerness
2 of or relating to animals that are hunted ⟨the *game* laws⟩

**game·cock** \'gām-ˌkäk\ *n*
a rooster trained for fighting

**game·keep·er** \'gām-ˌkē-pər\ *n*
a person in charge of the breeding and protection of game animals or birds on private land

**game·ly** \'gām-lē\ *adv*
with spirit and courage

**game·ness** \'gām-nəs\ *n*
the quality or state of being spirited and courageous

**game show** *n*
a television program on which contestants compete for prizes in a game (as a quiz)

**game warden** *n*
a person who sees that fishing and hunting laws are obeyed

**gam·ing** \'gā-ming\ *n*
the practice of gambling

**gam·ma rays** \'gam-ə-\ *n pl*
very penetrating rays like X rays but of shorter wavelength

**gamy** \'gā-mē\ *adj* **gam·i·er**; **gam·i·est**
having the flavor of wild game especially when slightly spoiled

**gan·der** \'gan-dər\ *n*
a male goose

**gang** \'gang\ *n*
1 a group of persons working or going about together
2 a group of persons acting together to do something illegal

**gan·gli·on** \'gang-glē-ən\ *n, pl* **gan·glia** \-glē-ə\
a mass of nerve cells especially outside the brain or spinal cord

**gang·plank** \'gang-ˌplangk\ *n*
a movable bridge from a ship to the shore

**gan·grene** \'gang-ˌgrēn\ *n*
death of body tissue when the blood supply is cut off

**gang·ster** \'gang-stər\ *n*
a member of a gang of criminals

**gang·way** \'gang-ˌwā\ *n*
**1** a way into, through, or out of an enclosed space
**2** GANGPLANK

**gan·net** \'gan-ət\ *n*
► a large bird that eats fish and spends much time far from land

**gannet**

**gan·try** \'gan-trē\ *n, pl* **gantries**
**1** a structure over railroad tracks for holding signals
**2** a movable structure for preparing a rocket for launching

**gap** \'gap\ *n*
**1** an opening made by a break or a coming apart
**2** an opening between mountains
**3** a hole or space where something is missing

[1]**gape** \'gāp\ *vb* **gaped**; **gap·ing**
**1** to open the mouth wide
**2** to stare with open mouth
**3** to open or part widely

[2]**gape** *n*
an act or instance of gaping

[1]**ga·rage** \gə-'räzh, -'räj\ *n*
a building where automobiles or trucks are repaired or kept when not in use

[2]**garage** *vb* **ga·raged**; **ga·rag·ing**
to keep or put in a garage

[1]**garb** \'gärb\ *n*
style or kind of clothing

[2]**garb** *vb*
CLOTHE 1

**gar·bage** \'gär-bij\ *n*
waste food especially from a kitchen

**gar·ble** \'gär-bəl\ *vb* **gar·bled**; **gar·bling**
to change or twist the meaning or sound of

---

**Word History** At first the word *garble* meant "to sift" or "to sort or pick out." If you pick out a few misleading parts of a message and report only those parts, you distort the message. *Garble* came to mean "to distort." It is the meaning "sift," however, that reflects the origin of *garble*. The English word *garble* came from an old Italian word that meant "to sift." This word came in turn from an Arabic word that meant "sieve." The Arabs took this word from a Latin word that meant "sieve."

---

[1]**gar·den** \'gärd-n\ *n*
**1** a piece of ground in which fruits, flowers, or vegetables are grown
**2** an enclosure for the public showing of plants or animals ⟨a botanical *garden*⟩

[2]**garden** *vb*
to make or work in a garden

**gar·den·er** \'gärd-nər, -n-ər\ *n*
a person who gardens especially for pay

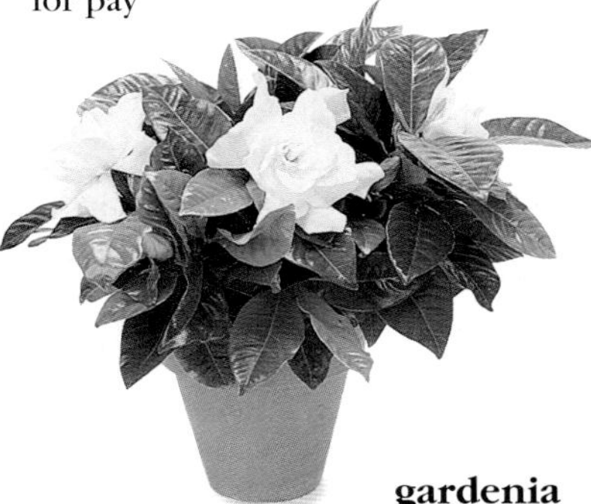
**gardenia**

**gar·de·nia** \gär-'dē-nyə\ *n*
▲ a large white or yellowish flower with a fragrant smell

[1]**gar·gle** \'gär-gəl\ *vb* **gar·gled**; **gar·gling**
to rinse the throat with a liquid kept in motion by air forced through it from the lungs

[2]**gargle** *n*
**1** a liquid used in gargling
**2** a gargling sound

**gar·goyle** \'gär-ˌgȯil\ *n*
▼ a waterspout in the form of a strange or frightening human or animal figure sticking out at the roof or eaves of a building

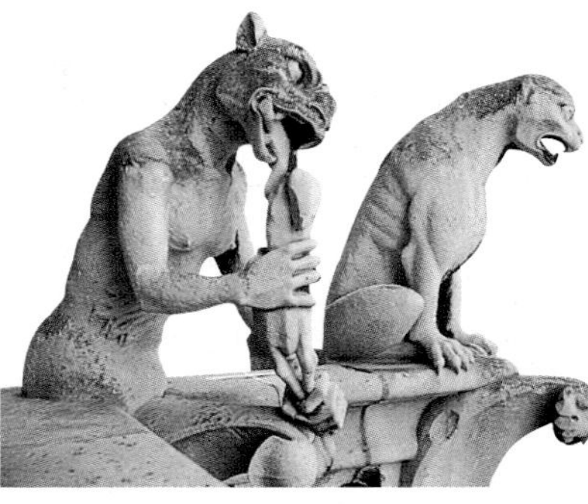
**gargoyles** on a cathedral in Paris, France

**gar·ish** \'gaər-ish, 'geər-\ *adj*
too bright or showy : GAUDY ⟨dressed in *garish* colors⟩

[1]**gar·land** \'gär-lənd\ *n*
a wreath or rope of leaves or flowers

[2]**garland** *vb*
to form into or decorate with a garland

**gar·lic** \'gär-lik\ *n*
a plant related to the onion and grown for its bulbs that have a strong smell and taste and are used to flavor foods

**gar·ment** \'gär-mənt\ *n*
an article of clothing

**gar·ner** \'gär-nər\ *vb*
to gather in and store

**gar·net** \'gär-nət\ *n*
▼ a deep red mineral used as a gem

**garnet**

[1]**gar·nish** \'gär-nish\ *vb*
to add decorations or seasoning (as to food)

[2]**garnish** *n*
something used in garnishing

**gar·ret** \'gar-ət\ *n*
a room or unfinished part of a house just under the roof

**[1]gar·ri·son** \'gar-ə-sən\ *n*
a place in which troops are regularly stationed

**[2]garrison** *vb*
**1** to station troops in
**2** to send (troops) to a garrison

**gar·ter** \'gärt-ər\ *n*
a band worn to hold up a stocking or sock

**garter snake** *n*
▶ any of numerous harmless American snakes with stripes along the back

**[1]gas** \'gas\ *n, pl* **gas·es**
**1** a substance (as oxygen or hydrogen) having no fixed shape and tending to expand without limit
**2** a gas or a mixture of gases used as a fuel or to make one unconscious (as for an operation)
**3** a fluid that poisons the air or makes breathing difficult
**4** GASOLINE

**[2]gas** *vb* **gassed**; **gas·sing**; **gas·ses**
**1** to treat with gas
**2** to poison with gas
**3** to supply with gas

**gas·eous** \'gas-ē-əs, 'gash-əs\ *adj*
of or relating to gas

**[1]gash** \'gash\ *n*
a long deep cut

**[2]gash** *vb*
to make a long deep cut in

**gas mask** *n*
▼ a mask connected to a chemical air filter and used to protect the face and lungs from poisonous gases

**gas mask:**
a gas mask used for protection from volcanic gas and dust

**gas·o·line** \'gas-ə-ˌlēn, ˌgas-ə-'lēn\ *n*
a flammable liquid made especially from gas found in the earth and from petroleum and used mostly as an automobile fuel

**[1]gasp** \'gasp\ *vb*
**1** to breathe with difficulty : PANT ⟨*gasping* after a race⟩
**2** to utter with quick difficult breaths

**garter snake**

**[2]gasp** *n*
**1** the act of gasping
**2** something gasped ⟨a *gasp* of surprise⟩

**gas station** *n*
SERVICE STATION

**gas·tric juice** \'gas-trik-\ *n*
an acid liquid made by the stomach that helps to digest food

**gate** \'gāt\ *n*
**1** an opening in a wall or fence often with a movable frame or door for closing it
**2** a part of a barrier (as a fence) that opens and closes like a door

**[1]gath·er** \'gath-ər\ *vb*
**1** to bring or come together
**2** to pick out and collect ⟨*gather* fruit⟩
**3** to gain little by little ⟨*gather* speed⟩
**4** to get an idea : CONCLUDE
**5** to draw together in folds

**Synonyms** GATHER, COLLECT, and ASSEMBLE mean to come or bring together. GATHER may suggest the coming or bringing together of different kinds of things ⟨*gathered* all the goods in the house and sold them⟩. COLLECT may suggest a careful or orderly gathering of things that are often of one kind ⟨it's fun to *collect* coins⟩. ASSEMBLE suggests a gathering of units into an orderly whole ⟨the choir *assembled* and started to sing⟩

**[2]gather** *n*
the result of gathering cloth : PUCKER

**gath·er·ing** \'gath-ə-riŋ\ *n*
a coming together of people : MEETING

**gau·cho** \'gau̇-chō\ *n, pl* **gauchos**
▼ a South American cowboy

**gaucho** in traditional clothes

**gaudy** \'gȯd-ē\ *adj* **gaud·i·er**; **gaud·i·est**
too showy

**[1]gauge** *or* **gage** \'gāj\ *n*
**1** measurement according to a standard
**2** SIZE 2
**3** an instrument for measuring, testing, or registering ⟨a rain *gauge*⟩ ⟨a steam *gauge*⟩

[2]**gauge** *or* **gage** *vb* **gauged** *or* **gaged**; **gaug·ing** *or* **gag·ing**
**1** to measure exactly ⟨*gauge* rainfall⟩
**2** to find out the capacity or contents of
**3** [1]ESTIMATE 1, JUDGE

**gaunt** \'gȯnt\ *adj*
very thin and bony (as from illness or starvation)

[1]**gaunt·let** \'gȯnt-lət\ *n*
**1** ▼ a glove made of small metal plates and worn with a suit of armor
**2** a glove with a wide cuff that covers and protects the wrist and part of the arm

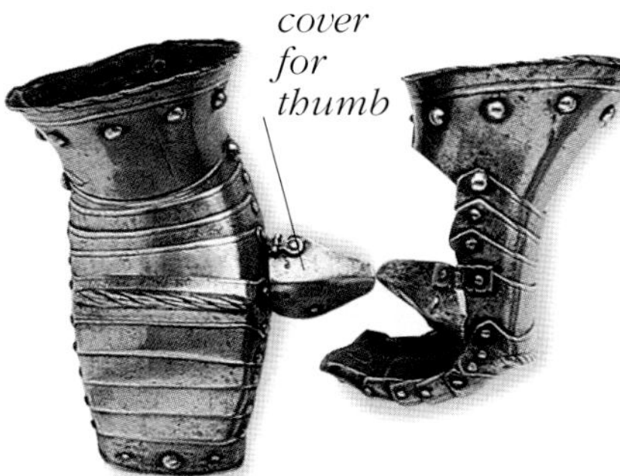


[1]**gauntlet 1:** gauntlets from a 16th-century Italian suit of armor

[2]**gauntlet** *n*
a double file of persons who beat someone forced to run between them

**gauze** \'gȯz\ *n*
▼ a thin transparent fabric

**gauze** bandage

**gauzy** \'gȯ-zē\ *adj* **gauz·i·er**; **gauz·i·est**
thin and transparent like gauze

**gave** *past of* GIVE

**gav·el** \'gav-əl\ *n*
a mallet with which the person in charge raps to call a meeting or court to order

**gawk** \'gȯk\ *vb*
to stare stupidly

**gawky** \'gȯ-kē\ *adj* **gawk·i·er**; **gawk·i·est**
AWKWARD 1, CLUMSY
**gawk·i·ly** \-kə-lē\ *adv*
**gawk·i·ness** \-kē-nəs\ *n*

**gay** \'gā\ *adj* **gay·er**; **gay·est**
**1** MERRY
**2** brightly colored

[1]**gaze** \'gāz\ *vb* **gazed**; **gaz·ing**
to fix the eyes in a long steady look

---

**Synonyms** GAZE, STARE, and GLARE mean to look at with concentration. GAZE suggests a long and fixed look ⟨stood *gazing* at the sunset⟩. STARE suggests a wide-eyed often curious, rude, or absentminded gaze ⟨*stared* in surprise at the strange creature⟩. GLARE suggests an angry stare ⟨*glared* at the naughty children until they behaved themselves⟩.

---

[2]**gaze** *n*
a long steady look

**ga·zelle** \gə-'zel\ *n*
► a swift graceful antelope with large bright eyes

**ga·zette** \gə-'zet\ *n*
**1** NEWSPAPER
**2** a journal giving official information

**gaz·et·teer** \ˌgaz-ə-'tir\ *n*
a geographical dictionary

**ga·zil·lion** \gə-'zil-yən\ *n*
a large number ⟨a *gazillion* fallen leaves⟩
**gazillion** *adj*

[1]**gear** \'gir\ *n*
**1** EQUIPMENT 2
**2** a group of parts that has a specific function in a machine ⟨steering *gear*⟩
**3** a toothed wheel **:** COGWHEEL
**4** the position the gears of a machine are in when they are ready to work ⟨in *gear*⟩
**5** one of the adjustments in a motor vehicle that determine the direction of travel and the relative speed between the engine and the motion of the vehicle ⟨second *gear*⟩ ⟨reverse *gear*⟩

[2]**gear** *vb*
**1** to make ready for operation ⟨*gear* up for production⟩
**2** to make suitable ⟨a book *geared* to children⟩

**gear·shift** \'gir-ˌshift\ *n*
a mechanism by which gears are connected and disconnected

**gee** \'jē\ *interj*
used to show surprise or enthusiasm

**geese** *pl of* GOOSE

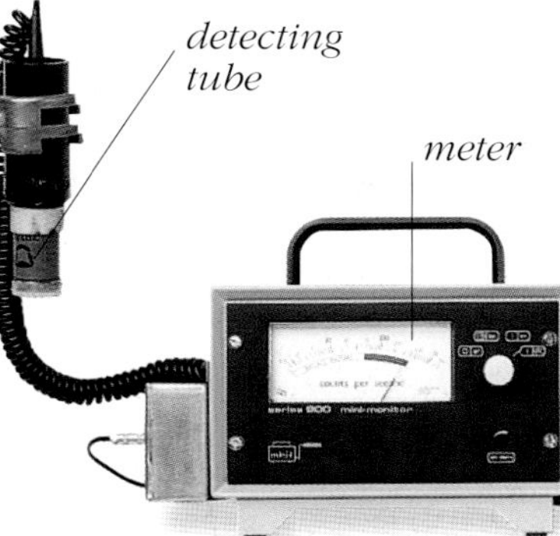


**Geiger counter**

**Gei·ger counter** \ˈgī-gər-\ *n*
▲ an instrument for detecting the presence of cosmic rays or radioactive substances

**gel·a·tin** \'jel-ət-n\ *n*
**1** a protein obtained by boiling animal tissues and used especially as food
**2** an edible jelly formed with gelatin

**gazelle**

a b c d e f g h i j k l m n o p q r s t u v w x y z

## gem

The characteristics that define a gem are a beautiful color, ability to reflect light, rarity, and durability. Most gems, including rubies and emeralds, are minerals that have formed crystals within the earth's crust. Organic gems, such as jet, amber, and pearls, are produced by plants and animals. Mineral gems are usually cut into facets, while organic gems are mostly carved and polished.

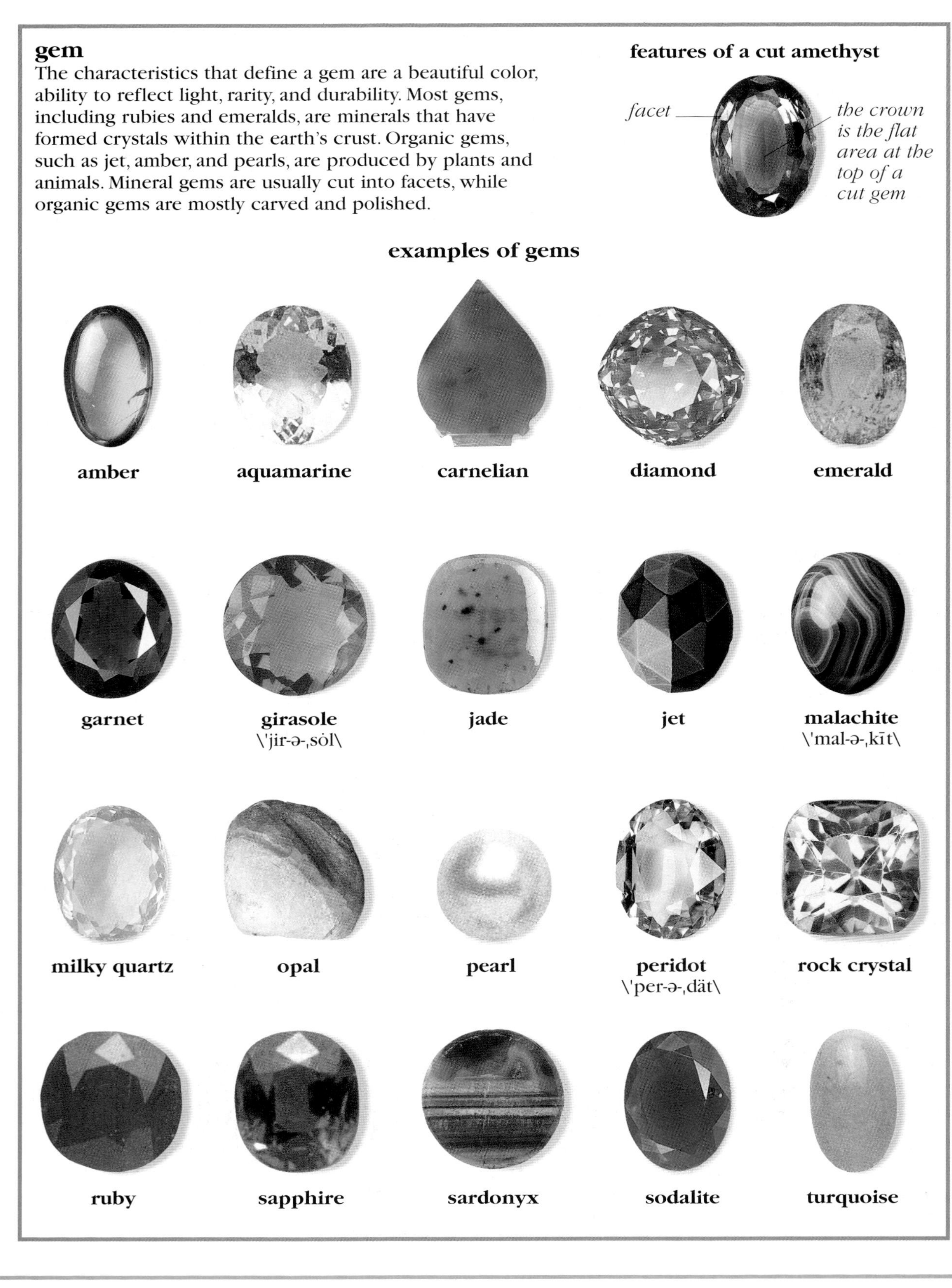

**gem** \'jem\ *n*
◀ a usually valuable stone cut and polished for jewelry

**Gem·i·ni** \'jem-ə-nē, -,nī\ *n*
1 ▼ a constellation between Taurus and Cancer imagined as twins
2 the third sign of the zodiac or a person born under this sign

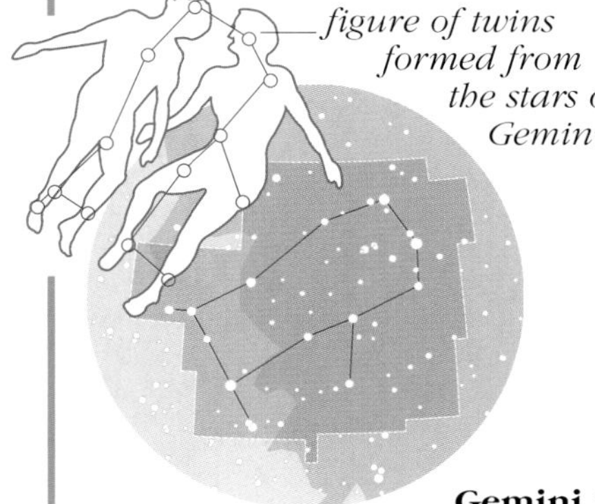


**Gemini 1**

**gen·der** \'jen-dər\ *n*
SEX 1

**gene** \'jēn\ *n*
a unit of DNA that controls the development of a single characteristic in an individual

**ge·ne·al·o·gy** \,jē-nē-'äl-ə-jē\ *n*
*pl* **ge·ne·al·o·gies**
1 a line or a history of a line of ancestors of a person or family
2 the study of family lines of ancestors

**genera** *pl of* GENUS

**¹gen·er·al** \'jen-ə-rəl, 'jen-rəl\ *adj*
1 having to do with the whole ⟨a matter of *general* interest⟩
2 not specific or detailed
3 not specialized ⟨a *general* store⟩

**²general** *n*
a military officer ranking above a lieutenant general

**gen·er·al·iza·tion** \,jen-ə-rə-lə-'zā-shən\ *n*
1 the act of generalizing
2 a general statement

**gen·er·al·ize** \'jen-ə-rə-,līz, 'jen-rə-\ *vb* **gen·er·al·ized**; **gen·er·al·iz·ing**
to put in the form of a general rule : draw or state a general conclusion from different items or instances

**gen·er·al·ly** \'jen-ə-rə-lē, 'jen-rə-\ *adv*
as a rule : USUALLY

**General of the Air Force**
a general of the highest rank in the Air Force

**General of the Army**
a general of the highest rank in the Army

**gen·er·ate** \'jen-ə-,rāt\ *vb* **gen·er·at·ed**; **gen·er·at·ing**
to cause to come into being

**gen·er·a·tion** \,jen-ə-'rā-shən\ *n*
1 those being a step in a line from one ancestor ⟨a family living in town for four *generations*⟩
2 a group of individuals born about the same time ⟨the younger *generation*⟩
3 the act of generating something

**gen·er·a·tor** \'jen-ə-,rāt-ər\ *n*
DYNAMO

**gen·er·os·i·ty** \,jen-ə-'räs-ət-ē\ *n*, *pl* **gen·er·os·i·ties**
1 willingness to give or to share
2 a generous act

**gen·er·ous** \'jen-ə-rəs, 'jen-rəs\ *adj*
1 free in giving or sharing
2 ABUNDANT ⟨a *generous* supply⟩
**gen·er·ous·ly** *adv*

**gen·e·sis** \'jen-ə-səs\ *n*, *pl* **gen·e·ses** \-,sēz\
a coming into being

**ge·net·ic** \jə-'net-ik\ *adj*
of or relating to genetics

**genetic code** *n*
the arrangement of chemical groups within the genes by which genetic information is passed on

**ge·net·i·cist** \jə-'net-ə-səst\ *n*
a specialist in genetics

**ge·net·ics** \jə-'net-iks\ *n*
a branch of biology that deals with the heredity and variation of living things

**ge·nial** \'jēn-yəl\ *adj*
pleasantly cheerful
**ge·nial·ly** \'jēn-yə-lē\ *adv*

**ge·nie** \'jē-nē\ *n*
a magic spirit believed to take human form and serve the person who calls it

**gen·i·tal** \'jen-ə-tl\ *adj*
of or relating to reproduction or sex

**ge·nius** \'jēn-yəs\ *n*
1 great natural ability ⟨a person of *genius*⟩
2 a very gifted person

**gen·teel** \jen-'tēl\ *adj*
1 relating to the upper classes
2 ELEGANT, GRACEFUL
3 showing good manners or taste

**gen·tian** \'jen-chən\ *n*
▼ an herb with smooth opposite leaves and usually blue flowers

**¹gen·tile** \'jen-,tīl\ *n, often cap*
a person who is not Jewish

**²gentile** *adj, often cap*
of or relating to people not Jewish

**gen·til·i·ty** \jen-'til-ət-ē\ *n*
1 good birth and family
2 the qualities of a well-bred person
3 good manners

**gen·tle** \'jent-l\ *adj* **gen·tler**; **gen·tlest**
1 easily handled : not wild
2 not harsh or stern : MILD
3 ¹MODERATE 1
**gen·tle·ness** \'jent-l-nəs\ *n*

**gen·tle·folk** \'jent-l-,fōk\ *n pl*
GENTRY 1

**gen·tle·man** \'jent-l-mən\ *n*, *pl* **gen·tle·men** \-mən\
1 a man of good birth and position
2 a man of good education and social position
3 a man with very good manners
4 MAN — used in the plural when speaking to a group of men
**gen·tle·man·ly** *adj*

**gen·tle·wom·an** \'jent-l-,wu̇m-ən\ *n*, *pl* **gen·tle·wom·en** \-,wim-ən\
1 a woman of good birth and position
2 a woman with very good manners : LADY 2

**gen·tly** \'jent-lē\ *adv*
in a gentle manner

**gen·try** \'jen-trē\ *n*
1 people of good birth, breeding, and education
2 people of a certain class

**gen·u·flect** \'jen-yə-,flekt\ *vb*
to kneel on one knee and rise again as an act of deep respect

**gentian**

A B C D E F G H I J K L M N O P Q R S T U V W X Y Z

**gen•u•ine** \'jen-yə-wən\ *adj*
**1** being just what it seems to be : REAL ⟨*genuine* gold⟩
**2** HONEST 1, SINCERE ⟨*genuine* interest⟩
**gen•u•ine•ly** *adv*
**gen•u•ine•ness** *n*

**geranium:** a type of geranium sometimes grown in gardens

**ge•nus** \'jē-nəs\ *n, pl* **gen•era** \'jen-ə-rə\
a group of related plants or animals that ranks below the family in scientific classification and is made up of one or more species ⟨the camel *genus* is made up of only two species: the one-humped camel and the two-humped camel⟩

**geo-** *prefix*
**1** earth ⟨*geo*chemistry⟩
**2** geographical

**geo•chem•is•try** \,jē-ō-'kem-ə-strē\ *n*
chemistry that deals with the earth's crust

**geo•graph•ic** \,jē-ə-'graf-ik\ *or* **geo•graph•i•cal** \-i-kəl\ *adj*
of or relating to geography

**ge•og•ra•phy** \jē-'äg-rə-fē\ *n*
**1** a science that deals with the location of living and nonliving things on earth and the way they affect one another
**2** the natural features of an area

**geo•log•ic** \,jē-ə-'läj-ik\ *or* **geo•log•i•cal** \-i-kəl\ *adj*
of or relating to geology

**ge•ol•o•gist** \jē-'äl-ə-jəst\ *n*
a specialist in geology

**ge•ol•o•gy** \jē-'äl-ə-jē\ *n*
**1** a science that deals with the history of the earth and its life especially as recorded in rocks
**2** the geologic features (as mountains or plains) of an area

**geo•mag•net•ic** \,jē-ō-mag-'net-ik\ *adj*
of or relating to the magnetism of the earth

**geo•met•ric** \,jē-ə-'met-rik\ *adj*
of or relating to geometry

**ge•om•e•try** \jē-'äm-ə-trē\ *n*
a branch of mathematics that deals with points, lines, angles, surfaces, and solids

**ge•ra•ni•um** \jə-'rā-nē-əm\ *n*
◀ an herb often grown for its bright flowers

**Word History** Many of the plants of the geranium family have long, thin, pointed fruits. These fruits look a bit like the bill of a bird. The ancient Greeks thought that the fruit of the wild geranium looked like the bill of a crane. They gave the plant a name that meant "little crane." The English word *geranium* came from this Greek name.

**ger•bil** \'jər-bəl\ *n*
▼ a small Old World leaping desert rodent

**gerbil**

**germ** \'jərm\ *n*
**1** a bit of living matter capable of forming a new individual
**2** a source from which something develops ⟨the *germ* of an idea⟩
**3** a microbe that causes disease

[1]**Ger•man** \'jər-mən\ *n*
**1** a person born or living in Germany
**2** the language spoken mainly in Germany, Austria, and parts of Switzerland

[2]**German** *adj*
of or relating to Germany, the Germans, or the German language

**ger•ma•ni•um** \jər-'mā-nē-əm\ *n*
a white hard brittle element used as a semiconductor

**germ cell** *n*
a reproductive cell (as an egg or sperm cell)

**ger•mi•cide** \'jər-mə-,sīd\ *n*
a substance that destroys germs

**ger•mi•nate** \'jər-mə-,nāt\ *vb* **ger•mi•nat•ed; ger•mi•nat•ing**
[1]SPROUT

**ger•mi•na•tion** \,jər-mə-'nā-shən\ *n*
▼ a beginning of development (as of a seed)

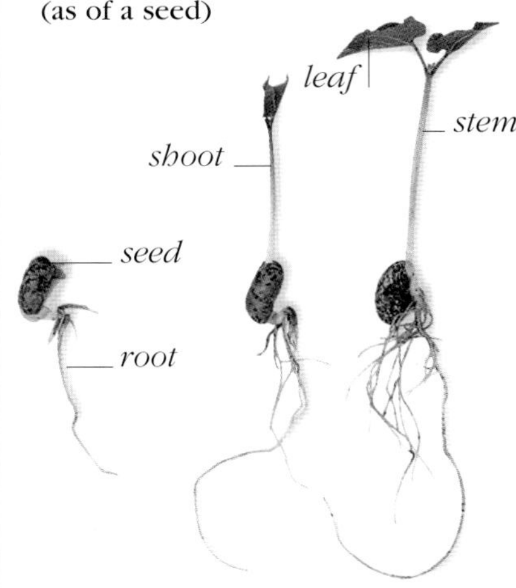


**germination** of a seed shown in stages

**ges•tic•u•late** \jes-'tik-yə-,lāt\ *vb* **ges•tic•u•lat•ed; ges•tic•u•lat•ing**
to make gestures especially when speaking

[1]**ges•ture** \'jes-chər\ *n*
**1** a motion of the limbs or body that expresses an idea or a feeling
**2** something said or done that shows one's feelings ⟨a *gesture* of friendship⟩

[2]**gesture** *vb* **ges•tured; ges•tur•ing**
to make or direct with a gesture

**get** \'get\ *vb* **got** \'gät\; **got** *or* **got•ten** \'gät-n\; **get•ting** \'get-ing\
**1** to gain possession of (as by receiving, earning, buying, or winning) ⟨*get* a present⟩ ⟨*got* new clothes⟩
**2** ARRIVE 1 ⟨*get* home early⟩
**3** GO 1, MOVE ⟨*get* out⟩ ⟨*get* about on crutches⟩
**4** BECOME 1 ⟨*get* angry⟩
**5** [1]CATCH 7 ⟨*get* pneumonia⟩
**6** to cause to be ⟨*get* your hair cut⟩
**7** UNDERSTAND 1 ⟨now I've *got* it⟩
**8** PERSUADE ⟨*get* them to lower the price⟩
**get ahead** to achieve success (as in business)

**get around**
1 to get the better of
2 EVADE ⟨*get around* a tax law⟩
**get at**
1 to reach with or as if with the hand ⟨can't *get at* the switch⟩
2 to turn one's attention to
3 to try to prove or make clear ⟨what are you *getting at*?⟩
**get away with** to do (as something wrong) without being caught

**geyser** in California

**get back at** to get even with
**get even** to get revenge
**get even with** to pay back for a real or imagined injury
**get one's goat** to make one angry or annoyed
**get over** to recover from
**get together**
1 to bring or come together
2 to reach agreement
**get wind of** to become aware of : hear about

**get along** *vb*
1 to approach old age
2 to meet one's needs ⟨*getting along* on a small income⟩
3 to stay friendly ⟨we *get along* well⟩

**get by** *vb*
1 GET ALONG 2
2 to succeed with the least possible effort or accomplishment ⟨barely *got by* on the test⟩

**get off** *vb*
1 START ⟨*got off* on their trip to Europe⟩
2 to escape punishment or harm ⟨*got off* with just a warning⟩

**get out** *vb*
1 ESCAPE ⟨might not *get out* alive⟩
2 to become known ⟨their secret *got out*⟩

**get–to·geth·er** \'get-tə-ˌgeth-ər\ *n*
an informal social gathering

**get up** *vb*
1 to arise from bed
2 to rise to one's feet
3 PREPARE, ORGANIZE ⟨*get up* a new club⟩
4 DRESS ⟨was *got up* as a pirate⟩

**gey·ser** \'gī-zər\ *n*
◀ a spring that now and then shoots up hot water and steam

**ghast·ly** \'gast-lē\ *adj* **ghast·li·er**; **ghast·li·est**
1 HORRIBLE, SHOCKING ⟨a *ghastly* crime⟩
2 like a ghost : PALE ⟨a *ghastly* face⟩

**ghet·to** \'get-ō\ *n, pl* **ghettos** *or* **ghettoes**
a part of a city in which members of a minority group live because of social, legal, or economic pressure

**ghost** \'gōst\ *n*
the spirit of a dead person thought of as living in an unseen world or as appearing to living people

**ghost·ly** \'gōst-lē\ *adj* **ghost·li·er**; **ghost·li·est**
of, relating to, or like a ghost

**ghost town** *n*
a town deserted because some nearby natural resource has been used up

**ghoul** \'gül\ *n*
1 an evil being of legend that robs graves and feeds on corpses
2 someone whose activities suggest those of a ghoul

**[1]gi·ant** \'jī-ənt\ *n*
1 an imaginary person of great size and strength
2 a person or thing that is very large or powerful

**[2]giant** *adj*
much larger than ordinary : HUGE

**giant panda** *n*
▼ a large black-and-white mammal of the bear family found mainly in central China

**giant panda**

**gib·ber·ish** \'jib-ə-rish\ *n*
confused meaningless talk

**gib·bon** \'gib-ən\ *n*
▼ a small ape of southwestern Asia that has long arms and legs and lives mostly in trees

**gibbon:**
a mother gibbon with her baby

**[1]gibe** *or* **jibe** \'jīb\ *vb* **gibed**; **gib·ing**
[1]JEER

**[2]gibe** *or* **jibe** *n*
[2]JEER

**gib·let** \'jib-lət\ *n*
an edible inner organ (as the heart or liver) of a fowl ⟨*giblet* gravy⟩

a b c d e f g h i j k l m n o p q r s t u v w x y z

**gid·dy** \'gid-ē\ *adj* **gid·di·er**; **gid·di·est**
1 having a feeling of whirling or spinning about : DIZZY
2 causing dizziness ⟨a *giddy* height⟩
3 SILLY 3
**gid·di·ness** *n*

**gift** \'gift\ *n*
1 a special ability : TALENT ⟨a *gift* for music⟩
2 something given : PRESENT

**gift·ed** \'gif-təd\ *adj*
having great ability ⟨a *gifted* child⟩

**gig** \'gig\ *n*
1 a long light boat for a ship's captain
2 ▼ a light carriage having two wheels and pulled by a horse

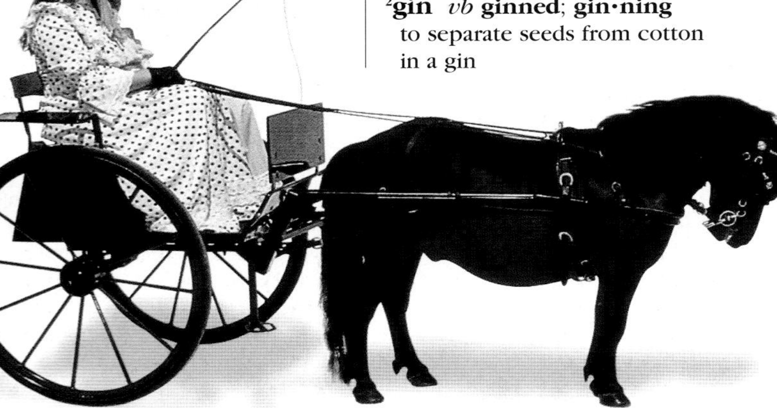

**gig 2:** a girl driving a gig

**giga·byte** \'jig-ə-,bīt, 'gig-ə-\ *n*
a unit of computer information storage capacity equal to 1,073,741,824 bytes

**gi·gan·tic** \jī-'gant-ik\ *adj*
like a giant (as in size, weight, or strength)

**gig·gle** \'gig-əl\ *vb* **gig·gled**; **gig·gling**
to laugh with repeated short high sounds

**Gila monster**

**Gi·la monster** \,hē-lə-\ *n*
► a large black and orange poisonous lizard of the southwestern United States

**gild** \'gild\ *vb* **gild·ed** *or* **gilt** \'gilt\; **gild·ing**
to cover with a thin coating of gold

**[1]gill** \'jil\ *n*
a unit of liquid capacity equal to a quarter of a pint (about 120 milliliters)

**[2]gill** \'gil\ *n*
an organ (as of a fish) for taking oxygen from water

**[1]gilt** \'gilt\ *n*
gold or something like gold applied to a surface

**[2]gilt** *n*
a young female hog

**gim·let** \'gim-lət\ *n*
a small tool for boring

**[1]gin** \'jin\ *n*
a machine to separate seeds from cotton

**[2]gin** *vb* **ginned**; **gin·ning**
to separate seeds from cotton in a gin

**[3]gin** *n*
a strong alcoholic liquor flavored with juniper berries

**gin·ger** \'jin-jər\ *n*
a hot spice obtained from the root of a tropical plant and used to season foods (as cookies) or in medicine

**ginger ale** *n*
a soft drink flavored with ginger

**gin·ger·bread** \'jin-jər-,bred\ *n*
a dark cake flavored with ginger and molasses

**gin·ger·ly** \'jin-jər-lē\ *adv*
with great caution or care

**gin·ger·snap** \'jin-jər-,snap\ *n*
a thin brittle cookie flavored with ginger

**ging·ham** \'ging-əm\ *n*
a cotton cloth in plain weave

**gipsy** *variant of* GYPSY

**gi·raffe** \jə-'raf\ *n*
► a spotted mammal of Africa that has a long neck and chews the cud

**giraffe**

**gird** \'gərd\ *vb* **gird·ed** *or* **girt** \'gərt\; **gird·ing**
to encircle or fasten with or as if with a belt or cord

**gird·er** \'gərd-ər\ *n*
a horizontal main supporting beam ⟨a *girder* of a bridge⟩

**[1]gir·dle** \'gərd-l\ *n*
1 something (as a belt or sash) that encircles or binds
2 a light corset worn below the waist

**[2]girdle** *vb* **gir·dled**; **gir·dling**
1 to bind with or as if with a girdle, belt, or sash : ENCIRCLE
2 to strip a ring of bark from a tree trunk

**girl** \'gərl\ *n*
1 a female child or young woman
2 a female servant
3 GIRLFRIEND

**girl·friend** *n* \'gərl-,frend\
1 a female friend
2 a regular female companion of a boy or man

**girl·hood** \'gərl-,hu̇d\ *n*
the state or time of being a girl

**girl·ish** \'gər-lish\ *adj*
of, relating to, or having qualities often felt to be typical of a girl
**girl·ish·ly** *adv*
**girl·ish·ness** *n*

**Girl Scout** *n*
a member of the Girl Scouts of the United States of America

**girth** \'gərth\ *n*
**1** a band put around the body of an animal to hold something (as a saddle) on its back
**2** the measure or distance around something ⟨a person of huge *girth*⟩ ⟨the *girth* of a tree⟩

**gist** \'jist\ *n*
the main point of a matter

**[1]give** \'giv\ *vb* **gave** \'gāv\; **giv·en** \'giv-ən\; **giv·ing**
**1** to hand over to be kept : PRESENT ⟨*give* a friend a present⟩
**2** [1]PAY 1
**3** [2]UTTER ⟨*give* a yell⟩ ⟨*give* a speech⟩
**4** FURNISH, PROVIDE ⟨a candle that *gives* light⟩ ⟨*give* a party⟩
**5** to cause to have ⟨*give* someone a lot of trouble⟩
**6** to let someone or something have ⟨*give* permission⟩
**7** to yield slightly ⟨the mattress *gave* under our weight⟩
**8** to yield as a product : PRODUCE ⟨2 plus 2 *gives* 4⟩

**Synonyms** GIVE, PRESENT, and DONATE mean to hand over to someone without looking for a return. GIVE can be used of anything that is delivered in any way ⟨*give* me your coat⟩ ⟨*give* a friend a gift⟩. PRESENT suggests that something is given with some ceremony ⟨*presented* a trophy to the winner⟩. DONATE suggests giving to a charity ⟨some kind person *donated* the toys⟩.

**give way**
**1** to yield oneself without control ⟨*give way* to tears⟩
**2** to break down : COLLAPSE ⟨the bridge *gave way*⟩

**[2]give** *n*
the quality of being able to bend under pressure

**give in** *vb*
**1** [1]OFFER 2 ⟨*give in* one's resignation⟩
**2** [1]SURRENDER 1, YIELD

**giv·en** \'giv-ən\ *adj*
**1** being likely to have or do something ⟨*given* to quarreling⟩
**2** decided on beforehand ⟨at a *given* time⟩

**given name** *n*
a first name (as *John* or *Susan*)

**give up** *vb*
**1** to let go : ABANDON ⟨*give up* a plan⟩
**2** to stop trying : QUIT ⟨refused to *give up*⟩

**giz·zard** \'giz-ərd\ *n*
a large muscular part of the digestive tube (as of a bird) in which food is churned and ground small

**gla·cial** \'glā-shəl\ *adj*
**1** very cold
**2** of or relating to glaciers

**gla·cier** \'glā-shər\ *n*
▼ a large body of ice moving slowly down a slope or over a wide area of land

**glad** \'glad\ *adj* **glad·der**; **glad·dest**
**1** being happy and joyful
**2** bringing or causing joy ⟨*glad* news⟩
**3** very willing ⟨I'd be *glad* to help⟩
**glad·ly** *adv*
**glad·ness** *n*

**glacier** in Glacier Bay National Park, Alaska

**glad·den** \'glad-n\ *vb*
to make glad

**glade** \'glād\ *n*
a grassy open space in a forest

**glad·i·a·tor** \'glad-ē-,āt-ər\ *n*
a person taking part in a fight to the death as public entertainment for the ancient Romans

**glad·i·o·lus** \,glad-ē-'ō-ləs\ *n*, *pl* **glad·i·o·li** \-lē, -,lī\ *or* **gladiolus** *or* **glad·i·o·lus·es**
a plant with long stiff pointed leaves and stalks of brightly colored flowers

**glad·some** \'glad-səm\ *adj*
giving or showing joy

**glam·or·ous** \'glam-ə-rəs\ *adj*
full of glamour

**glam·our** *or* **glam·or** \'glam-ər\ *n*
**1** appeal or attractiveness especially when it is misleading
**2** tempting or fascinating personal attraction

**Word History** A long time ago, back when the spelling of English was not fixed as it is for most words now, *glamour* was just another way to spell *grammar*. In those days *grammar* could mean not only the study of how language is used but also any kind of learning or study. Latin was the language used by learned people then, and the common people who did not understand Latin were often afraid of those who spoke it. For all they knew students of grammar might be wicked magicians or enchanters. In time *grammar* and *glamour* came to mean "a magic spell." After a while, as people learned to feel less fear of scholars, *grammar* lost this sense completely and *glamour* just meant "a mysterious attraction" without any real suggestion of magic. Even today, though, someone who has *glamour* may seem to cast a spell over us.

**[1]glance** \'glans\ *vb* **glanced**; **glanc·ing**
**1** to strike at an angle and fly off to one side
**2** to give a quick look

[2]**glance** *n*
a quick look

**gland** \'gland\ *n*
an organ in the body that prepares a substance to be used by the body or given off from it ⟨a saliva *gland*⟩

**glan·du·lar** \'glan-jə-lər\ *adj*
of or relating to glands

[1]**glare** \'glaər, 'gleər\ *vb* **glared**; **glar·ing**
**1** to shine with a harsh bright light
**2** to look fiercely or angrily
**synonyms** see GAZE

[2]**glare** *n*
**1** a harsh bright light
**2** a fierce or angry look

**glar·ing** \'glaər-ing, 'gleər-\ *adj*
**1** so bright as to be harsh ⟨*glaring* sunlight⟩
**2** ANGRY, FIERCE ⟨a *glaring* look⟩
**3** very noticeable **:** OBVIOUS ⟨a *glaring* error⟩

[1]**glass** \'glas\ *n*
**1** ▼ a hard brittle usually transparent substance commonly made from sand heated with chemicals
**2** something made of glass
**3 glasses** *pl* EYEGLASS 2
**4** the contents of a glass

[1]**glass 1:** a bottle made of glass

[2]**glass** *vb*
to fit or protect with glass ⟨*glass* in a porch⟩

**glass·blow·ing** \'glas-,blō-ing\ *n*
the art of shaping a mass of melted glass by blowing air into it through a tube

**glass·ful** \'glas-,fu̇l\ *n*
the amount a glass will hold

**glass·ware** \'glas-,waər, -,weər\ *n*
articles of glass

**glassy** \'glas-ē\ *adj* **glass·i·er**; **glass·i·est**
**1** like glass (as in smoothness)
**2** not shiny or bright **:** DULL ⟨*glassy* eyes⟩

[1]**glaze** \'glāz\ *vb* **glazed**; **glaz·ing**
**1** to set glass in ⟨*glaze* a window⟩
**2** to cover with a glassy surface ⟨*glaze* pottery⟩
**3** to become shiny or glassy in appearance

[2]**glaze** *n*
a glassy surface or coating

**gla·zier** \'glā-zhər\ *n*
a person who sets glass in window frames

[1]**gleam** \'glēm\ *n*
**1** a faint, soft, or reflected light ⟨the first *gleam* of dawn⟩
**2** a small bright light
**3** a short or slight appearance ⟨a *gleam* of hope⟩



**glider 1**

[2]**gleam** *vb*
**1** to shine with a soft light
**2** to give out gleams of light

**Synonyms** GLEAM, SPARKLE, and GLITTER mean to send forth light. GLEAM is likely to suggest that the light shines through something else or is reflected or shines against a dark background ⟨the lighthouse *gleamed* through the fog⟩. SPARKLE suggests that something has several changing points of light ⟨the water *sparkled* in the sunlight⟩. GLITTER suggests a very cold sort of sparkling ⟨the jewels *glittered* brightly⟩.

**glean** \'glēn\ *vb*
**1** to gather from a field what is left by the harvesters
**2** to gather (as information) little by little with patient effort

**glee** \'glē\ *n*
great joy **:** DELIGHT

**glee club** *n*
a singing group organized especially as a social activity in a school or college

**glee·ful** \'glē-fəl\ *adj*
full of glee

**glen** \'glen\ *n*
a narrow hidden valley

**glib** \'glib\ *adj* **glib·ber**; **glib·best**
speaking or spoken with careless ease and often with little regard for the truth
**glib·ly** *adv*
**glib·ness** *n*

[1]**glide** \'glīd\ *vb* **glid·ed**; **glid·ing**
to move with a smooth silent motion

[2]**glide** *n*
the act or action of gliding

**glid·er** \'glīd-ər\ *n*
**1** ▼ an aircraft without an engine that glides on air currents
**2** a porch seat hung from a frame (as by chains)

[1]**glim·mer** \'glim-ər\ *vb*
to shine faintly and unsteadily

[2]**glimmer** *n*
a faint unsteady light

[1]**glimpse** \'glimps\ *vb* **glimpsed**; **glimps·ing**
to catch a quick view of

[2]**glimpse** *n*
a short hurried look

[1]**glint** \'glint\ *vb*
to shine with tiny bright flashes

[2]**glint** *n*
a brief flash

**glis·ten** \'glis-n\ *vb*
to shine with a soft reflected light

**glitch** \'glich\ *n*
a usually minor problem ⟨a *glitch* in a computer program⟩

[1]**glit·ter** \'glit-ər\ *vb*
**1** to sparkle brightly
**2** to sparkle with a harsh, cold light
**3** to be very bright and showy
**synonyms** see GLEAM

[2]**glitter** *n*
sparkling brightness

**gloat** \'glōt\ *vb*
to gaze at or think about something with great and often mean satisfaction

**glob·al** \'glō-bəl\ *adj*
**1** shaped like a globe
**2** having to do with the whole earth

**global warming** *n*
a warming of the earth's atmosphere and oceans as a result of air pollution

**globe** \'glōb\ *n*
**1** a round object : BALL, SPHERE
**2** EARTH 3
**3** ▼ a round model of the earth or heavens

**globe 3:**
a globe of the earth

**globe–trot·ter** \'glōb-,trät-ər\ *n*
a person who travels widely

**glob·u·lar** \'gläb-yə-lər\ *adj*
shaped like a globe : SPHERICAL

**glob·ule** \'gläb-yül\ *n*
a small round mass ⟨fat *globules*⟩

**glock·en·spiel** \'gläk-ən-,spēl\ *n*
a portable musical instrument consisting of a series of metal bars played with hammers

**gloom** \'glüm\ *n*
**1** partial or complete darkness
**2** a sad mood

**gloomy** \'glü-mē\ *adj* **gloom·i·er**; **gloom·i·est**
**1** partly or completely dark
**2** SAD 1, BLUE
**3** causing lowness of spirits ⟨a *gloomy* story⟩
**4** not hopeful : PESSIMISTIC ⟨the future looks *gloomy*⟩

**glo·ri·fi·ca·tion** \,glōr-ə-fə-'kā-shən\ *n*
the act of glorifying : the state of being glorified

**glo·ri·fy** \'glōr-ə-,fī\ *vb* **glo·ri·fied**; **glo·ri·fy·ing**
**1** to honor or praise as divine : WORSHIP ⟨*glorify* God⟩
**2** to give honor and praise to
**3** to show in a way that looks good ⟨*glorify* war⟩

**glo·ri·ous** \'glōr-ē-əs\ *adj*
**1** having or deserving glory ⟨*glorious* deeds⟩
**2** having great beauty or splendor
**3** DELIGHTFUL **synonyms** see SPLENDID

[1]**glo·ry** \'glōr-ē\ *n, pl* **glories**
**1** praise, honor, and admiration given to a person by others
**2** something that brings honor, praise, or fame ⟨the *glories* of ancient Greece⟩
**3** BRILLIANCE, SPLENDOR
**4** HEAVEN 2

[2]**glory** *vb* **glo·ried**; **glo·ry·ing**
to rejoice proudly : be proud or boastful

[1]**gloss** \'gläs, 'glȯs\ *n*
**1** brightness from a smooth surface : LUSTER, SHEEN
**2** a falsely attractive surface appearance

[2]**gloss** *vb*
**1** to give a gloss to
**2** to smooth over : explain away ⟨*gloss* over a mistake⟩

**glos·sa·ry** \'gläs-ə-rē, 'glȯs-\ *n, pl* **glos·sa·ries**
a list of the hard or unusual words used in a book given with their meanings

**glossy** \'gläs-ē, 'glȯs-ē\ *adj* **gloss·i·er**; **gloss·i·est**
smooth and shining on the surface

**glove** \'gləv\ *n*
▶ a covering for the hand having a separate section for each finger

**glove:**
a pair of rubber gloves

[1]**glow** \'glō\ *vb*
**1** to shine with or as if with great heat
**2** to show strong bright color
**3** to be or to look warm and flushed (as with exercise)

[2]**glow** *n*
**1** light such as comes from something that is very hot but not flaming
**2** brightness or warmth of color
**3** a feeling of physical warmth (as from exercise)
**4** warmth of feeling

**glow·er** \'glau̇-ər\ *vb*
to stare angrily : SCOWL

**glow·worm** \'glō-,wərm\ *n*
▶ an insect or insect larva that gives off light

**glowworm:**
a larva of a firefly

**glu·cose** \'glü-,kōs\ *n*
a sugar in plant saps and fruits that is the usual form in which carbohydrate is taken in by the animal body

[1]**glue** \'glü\ *n*
a substance used to stick things tightly together

[2]**glue** *vb* **glued**; **glu·ing**
to stick with or as if with glue

**glu·ey** \'glü-ē\ *adj* **glu·i·er**; **glu·i·est**
**1** sticky like glue
**2** covered with glue

**glum** \'gləm\ *adj* **glum·mer**; **glum·mest**
**1** [1]SULKY
**2** seeming gloomy and sad
**glum·ly** *adv*
**glum·ness** *n*

[1]**glut** \'glət\ *vb* **glut·ted**; **glut·ting**
**1** to make quite full : fill completely
**2** to flood with goods so that supply is greater than demand

[2]**glut** *n*
too much of something

**glu·ti·nous** \'glüt-n-əs\ *adj*
like glue : STICKY
**glu·ti·nous·ly** *adv*

**glut·ton** \'glət-n\ *n*
a person or animal that overeats
**glut·ton·ous** \'glət-n-əs\ *adj*
**glut·ton·ous·ly** *adv*

**glut·tony** \'glət-n-ē\ *n, pl* **glut·ton·ies**
the act or habit of eating or drinking too much

**glyc·er·in** *or* **glyc·er·ine** \'glis-ə-rən\ *n*
a sweet thick liquid that is found in various oils and fats and is used to moisten or dissolve things

**gly·co·gen** \'glī-kə-jən\ *n*
a white tasteless starchy substance that is the chief stored carbohydrate of animals

**G–man** \'jē-,man\ *n, pl* **G–men** \-,men\
a special agent of the Federal Bureau of Investigation

**gnarled** \'närld\ *adj*
being full of knots, twisted, and rugged ⟨a *gnarled* old oak⟩

**gnash** \'nash\ *vb*
to strike or grind (the teeth) together (as in anger)

**gnat** \'nat\ *n*
a very small two-winged fly

**gnaw** \'nȯ\ *vb* **gnawed**; **gnaw·ing**
to bite so as to wear away little by little **:** bite or chew upon ⟨the dog *gnawed* the bone⟩

**gnome** \'nōm\ *n*
one of an imaginary race of dwarfs believed to live inside the earth and guard treasure

**gnu** \'nü, 'nyü\ *n, pl* **gnu** *or* **gnus**
▶ a large African antelope with a head like that of an ox, curving horns, a short mane, and a tail somewhat like that of a horse

gnu

**go** \'gō\ *vb* **went** \'went\; **gone** \'gȯn\; **go·ing** \'gō-iŋ\; **goes**
**1** to pass from one place to or toward another ⟨we *went* home⟩
**2** to move away **:** LEAVE ⟨the crowd has *gone*⟩
**3** to become lost, used, or spent ⟨our money was all *gone*⟩
**4** to continue its course or action **:** RUN ⟨some machines *go* by electricity⟩
**5** to make its own special sound ⟨a kitten *goes* like this⟩
**6** to be suitable **:** MATCH ⟨the scarf *goes* with the coat⟩
**7** to reach some state ⟨*go* to sleep⟩ ⟨the tire *went* flat⟩

**[1]goad** \'gōd\ *n*
**1** a pointed rod used to keep an animal moving
**2** something that stirs one to action

**[2]goad** *vb*
to drive or stir with a goad

**goal** \'gōl\ *n*
**1** the point at which a race or journey is to end
**2** an area to be reached safely in certain games
**3** [1]PURPOSE ⟨one's *goal* in life⟩
**4** an object into which a ball or puck must be driven in various games in order to score
**5** a scoring of one or more points by driving a ball or puck into a goal

**goal·ie** \'gō-lē\ *n*
GOALKEEPER

**goal·keep·er** \'gōl-,kē-pər\ *n*
a player who defends a goal

**goal·post** \'gōl-,pōst\ *n*
one of two usually upright posts often with a crossbar that serve as the goal in various games

**goal·tend·er** \'gōl-,ten-dər\ *n*
GOALKEEPER

**goat** \'gōt\ *n*
a horned animal that chews the cud and is related to but more lively than the sheep
**goat·like** \-,līk\ *adj*

**goa·tee** \gō-'tē\ *n*
a small beard trimmed to a point

**goat·herd** \'gōt-,hərd\ *n*
a person who tends goats

**goat·skin** \'gōt-,skin\ *n*
the skin of a goat or leather made from it

**gob** \'gäb\ *n*
[1]LUMP ⟨a *gob* of mud⟩

**[1]gob·ble** \'gäb-əl\ *vb* **gob·bled**; **gob·bling**
to eat fast or greedily

**[2]gobble** *vb* **gob·bled**; **gob·bling**
to make the call of a turkey or a similar sound

**[3]gobble** *n*
the loud harsh call of a turkey

**go–be·tween** \'gō-bə-,twēn\ *n*
a person who acts as a messenger or peacemaker

**gob·let** \'gäb-lət\ *n*
a drinking glass with a foot and stem

**gob·lin** \'gäb-lən\ *n*
an ugly imaginary creature with evil or sly ways

**god** \'gäd\ *n*
**1** *cap* the Being considered the holy and ruling power who made and sustains all things of the universe
**2** a being believed to have more than human powers ⟨ancient peoples worshiped many *gods*⟩
**3** a natural or artificial object worshiped as divine
**4** something believed to be the most important thing in existence ⟨money is their *god*⟩

**god·child** \'gäd-,chīld\ *n, pl* **god·chil·dren** \-,chil-drən\
a person for whom another person is sponsor at baptism

**god·dess** \'gäd-əs\ *n*
a female god

**god·fa·ther** \'gäd-,fäth-ər, -,fäth-\ *n*
a boy or man who is sponsor for a child at its baptism

**god·less** \'gäd-ləs\ *adj*
**1** not believing in God or a god
**2** WICKED 1, EVIL
**god·less·ness** *n*

**god·like** \'gäd-,līk\ *adj*
like or suitable for God or a god

**god·ly** \'gäd-lē\ *adj* **god·li·er**; **god·li·est**
DEVOUT 1, PIOUS
**god·li·ness** *n*

**god·moth·er** \'gäd-,məth-ər\ *n*
a girl or woman who is sponsor for a child at its baptism

**god·par·ent** \'gäd-,par-ənt, -,per-\ *n*
a sponsor at baptism

**god·send** \'gäd-,send\ *n*
some badly needed thing that comes unexpectedly

**goes** *present 3d sing of* GO

**go–get·ter** \'gō-,get-ər\ *n*
a very active and aggressive person

**gog·gle** \'gäg-əl\ *vb* **gog·gled**; **gog·gling**
**1** to roll the eyes
**2** to stare with bulging or rolling eyes

**gog·gle–eyed** \,gäg-ə-'līd\ *adj*
having bulging or rolling eyes

**gog·gles** \'gäg-əlz\ *n pl*
eyeglasses worn to protect the eyes (as from dust, sun, or wind)

**go·ings–on** \ˌgō-ing-ˈzȯn, -ˈzän\ *n pl*
things that happen

**goi·ter** \ˈgȯit-ər\ *n*
a swelling on the front of the neck caused by enlargement of the thyroid gland

**gold** \ˈgōld\ *n*
**1** a soft yellow metallic chemical element used especially in coins and jewelry
**2** gold coins
**3** MONEY 3
**4** a deep yellow

**gold·en** \ˈgōl-dən\ *adj*
**1** like, made of, or containing gold
**2** of the color of gold
**3** very good or desirable ⟨a *golden* opportunity⟩
**4** being prosperous and happy ⟨a *golden* age⟩

**gold·en·rod** \ˈgōl-dən-ˌräd\ *n*
a plant with tall stiff stems topped with rows of tiny yellow flower heads on slender branches

**golden rule** *n*
a rule that one should treat others as one would want others to treat oneself

**gold·finch** \ˈgōld-ˌfinch\ *n*
**1** a European finch with a yellow patch on each wing
**2** ► an American finch that looks like the canary

**goldfinch 2**

**gold·fish** \ˈgōld-ˌfish\ *n*
a small usually golden yellow or orange carp often kept in aquariums

**gold·smith** \ˈgōld-ˌsmith\ *n*
a person who makes or deals in articles of gold

**golf** \ˈgälf, ˈgȯlf\ *n*
► a game played by driving a small ball (**golf ball**) with one of a set of clubs (**golf clubs**) around an outdoor course (**golf course**) and into various holes in as few strokes as possible

## golf

Starting from a tee, golfers aim to hit a ball into a series of 18 holes positioned some distance apart. The object is to hit the ball along a flat strip of grass, avoiding areas of rough and bunkers, to reach a putting green and sink the ball into a hole, all using as few strokes as possible. Golfers use a range of clubs for different purposes.

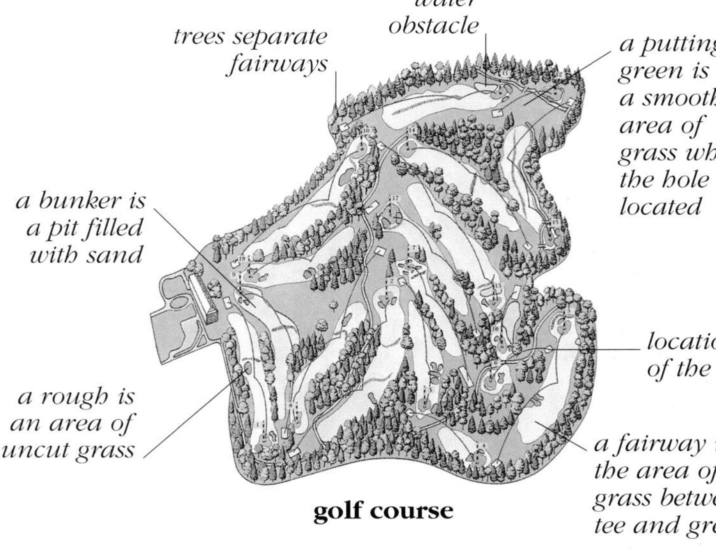

water obstacle
trees separate fairways
a putting green is a smooth area of grass where the hole is located
a bunker is a pit filled with sand
location of the tee
a rough is an area of uncut grass
a fairway is the area of grass between tee and green

**golf course**

golf club

**golf ball**

**golf shoe**

**tees**

**golfer preparing to roll the ball toward the hole**

**golf bag**

A B C D E F G H I J K L M N O P Q R S V W X Y Z

**golf·er** \'gäl-fər, 'gȯl-\ *n*
a person who plays golf

**gol·ly** \'gäl-ē\ *interj*
used to express surprise or annoyance

**gon·do·la** \'gän-də-lə, *2 and 3 also* gän-'dō-lə\ *n*
**1** ▼ a long narrow boat used in the canals of Venice, Italy
**2** a freight car with no top
**3** an enclosure that hangs from a balloon and carries passengers or instruments

*oar*

**gondola 1**

**gone** \'gȯn\ *adj*
**1** ADVANCED 1 ⟨far *gone* in crime⟩
**2** INFATUATED ⟨*gone* on each other⟩
**3** [1]DEAD 1
**4** WEAK 1, LIMP ⟨had a *gone* feeling⟩

**gon·er** \'gȯ-nər\ *n*
one whose case is hopeless

**gong** \'gäng, 'gȯng\ *n*
▼ a metallic disk that produces a harsh ringing tone when struck

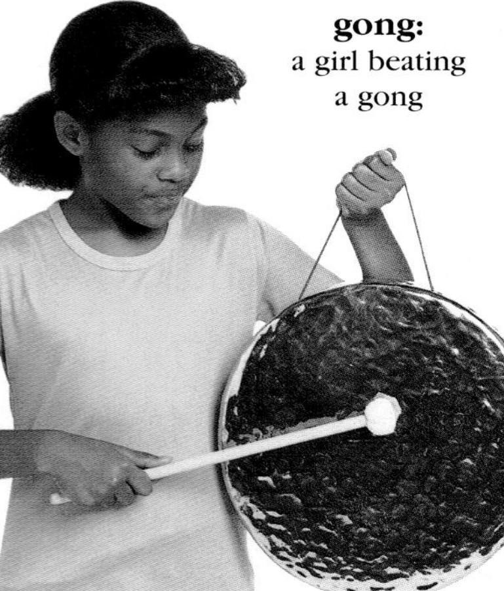

**gong:** a girl beating a gong

**[1]good** \'gu̇d\ *adj* **bet·ter** \'bet-ər\; **best** \'best\
**1** suitable for a use **:** SATISFACTORY ⟨a *good* light for reading⟩
**2** being at least the amount mentioned ⟨it takes a *good* hour to get there⟩
**3** CONSIDERABLE ⟨a *good* bit of trouble⟩
**4** DESIRABLE, ATTRACTIVE ⟨looking for a *good* job⟩
**5** HELPFUL, KIND ⟨how *good* of you to wait⟩
**6** behaving well ⟨a *good* child⟩
**7** being honest and upright
**8** showing good sense or judgment ⟨*good* advice⟩
**9** better than average ⟨*good* work⟩

**[2]good** *n*
**1** something good
**2** WELFARE 1, BENEFIT ⟨for your own *good*⟩
**3 goods** *pl* WARE 2 ⟨canned *goods*⟩
**4 goods** *pl* personal property
**5 goods** *pl* a length of cloth

**[1]good–bye** *or* **good–by** \gu̇d-'bī\ *interj*
used as a farewell remark

**[2]good–bye** *or* **good–by** *n*
a farewell remark ⟨said our *good-byes*⟩

**good–heart·ed** \'gu̇d-'härt-əd\ *adj*
having a kindly generous disposition
**good–heart·ed·ly** *adv*
**good–heart·ed·ness** *n*

**good–hu·mored** \'gu̇d-'hyü-mərd, -'yü-\ *adj*
GOOD-NATURED
**good–hu·mored·ly** *adv*
**good–hu·mored·ness** *n*

**good·ly** \'gu̇d-lē\ *adj* **good·li·er**; **good·li·est**
**1** of pleasing appearance ⟨a *goodly* person⟩
**2** LARGE, CONSIDERABLE ⟨a *goodly* number⟩

**good–na·tured** \'gu̇d-'nā-chərd\ *adj*
having or showing a pleasant disposition
**good–na·tured·ly** *adv*

**good·ness** \'gu̇d-nəs\ *n*
**1** the quality or state of being good
**2** excellence of morals and behavior

**good–tem·pered** \'gu̇d-'tem-pərd\ *adj*
not easily angered or upset

**good·will** \'gu̇d-'wil\ *n*
**1** kindly feelings
**2** the value of the trade a business has built up

**goody** \'gu̇d-ē\ *n, pl* **good·ies**
something especially good to eat

**[1]goof** \'güf\ *n*
**1** a stupid or silly person
**2** [2]BLUNDER

**[2]goof** *vb*
to make a blunder

**goofy** \'gü-fē\ *adj* **goof·i·er**; **goof·i·est**
SILLY 1

**goose** \'güs\ *n, pl* **geese** \'gēs\
**1** a waterbird with webbed feet that is related to the smaller duck and the larger swan
**2** a female goose
**3** the flesh of a goose used as food
**4** a silly person

**goose·ber·ry** \'güs-ˌber-ē, 'güz-\ *n, pl* **goose·ber·ries**
the sour berry of a thorny bush related to the currant

**goose bumps** *n pl*
a roughness of the skin caused by cold, fear, or a sudden feeling of excitement

**goose·flesh** \'güs-ˌflesh\ *n*
GOOSE BUMPS

**goose pimples** *n pl*
GOOSE BUMPS

**go·pher** \'gō-fər\ *n*
**1** a burrowing animal that is about the size of a rat and has strong claws on the forefeet and very large outside cheek pouches
**2** a striped ground squirrel of the prairies
**3** a burrowing American land tortoise

**[1]gore** \'gōr\ *n*
shed or clotted blood

**[2]gore** *vb* **gored**; **gor·ing**
to pierce or wound with a horn or tusk

**[1]gorge** \'gȯrj\ *n*
a narrow steep-walled canyon or part of a canyon

**[2]gorge** *vb* **gorged**; **gorg·ing**
to eat greedily

**gor·geous** \'gȯr-jəs\ *adj*
very beautiful
**gor·geous·ly** *adv*
**gor·geous·ness** *n*

---

**Word History** We can trace the word *gorgeous* back to an early French word that meant "throat." A long time ago women wore a kind of headdress that surrounded the neck and head. Only the face was not covered. The French word for such a headdress was formed from the French word that meant "throat." An elegant headdress was the mark of a lady of fashion. The French word for the headdress came to mean "elegant." The English word *gorgeous* came from this French word.

---

**go·ril·la** \gə-'ril-ə\ *n*
► a very large ape of the forests of central Africa that lives mostly on the ground

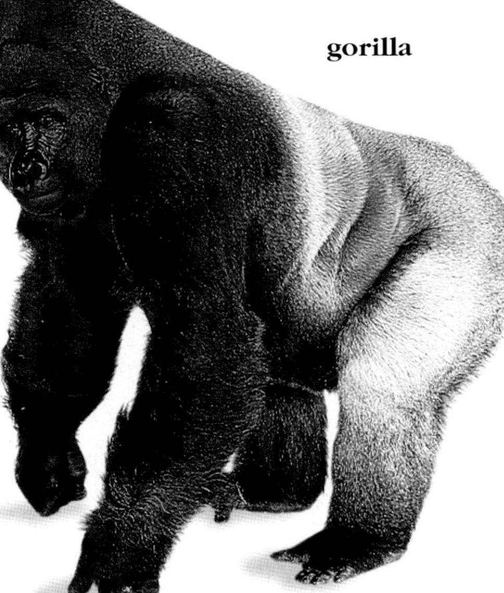

**gorilla**

**gory** \'gōr-ē\ *adj* **gor·i·er**; **gor·i·est**
covered with gore

**gos·ling** \'gäz-liŋ\ *n*
a young goose

**gos·pel** \'gäs-pəl\ *n*
**1** *often cap* the teachings of Christ and the apostles
**2** something told or accepted as being absolutely true

**gos·sa·mer** \'gäs-ə-mər, 'gäz-\ *adj*
very light and flimsy

**[1]gos·sip** \'gäs-əp\ *n*
**1** a person who repeats stories about other people
**2** talk or rumors having no worth

---

**Word History** At first the word *gossip* meant "godparent." Later it came to mean "close friend" as well. Close friends, of course, share secrets. *Gossip* has come to refer to anyone, close friend or not, who is eager to share the secrets of others.

---

**[2]gossip** *vb*
to spread gossip

**got** *past of* GET

**gotten** *past participle of* GET

**[1]gouge** \'gau̇j\ *n*
**1** a chisel with a curved blade for scooping or cutting holes
**2** a hole or groove made with or as if with a gouge

**[2]gouge** *vb* **gouged**; **goug·ing**
to dig out with or as if with a gouge

**gou·lash** \'gü-ˌläsh\ *n*
a beef stew made with vegetables and paprika

**gourd** \'gōrd\ *n*
the fruit of a vine (**gourd vine**) related to the pumpkin and melon

**gour·met** \'gu̇r-ˌmā\ *n*
a person who appreciates fine food and drink

**gov·ern** \'gəv-ərn\ *vb*
**1** [2]RULE 2
**2** to influence the actions and conduct of **:** CONTROL

**gov·ern·able** \'gəv-ər-nə-bəl\ *adj*
possible to govern

**gov·ern·ess** \'gəv-ər-nəs\ *n*
a woman who teaches and trains a child especially in a private home

**gov·ern·ment** \'gəv-ərn-mənt, -ər-mənt\ *n*
**1** control and direction of public business (as of a city or a nation)
**2** a system of control **:** an established form of political rule ⟨a democratic *government*⟩
**3** the persons making up a governing body

**gov·ern·men·tal** \ˌgəv-ərn-'ment-l, -ər-'ment-l\ *adj*
of or relating to government or the government

**gov·er·nor** \'gəv-ər-nər, 'gəv-ə-nər\ *n*
**1** a person who governs and especially the elected head of a state of the United States
**2** a device attached to an engine for controlling its speed

**gov·er·nor·ship** \'gəv-ər-nər-ˌship, 'gəv-ə-nər-\ *n*
**1** the office or position of governor
**2** the term of office of a governor

**gown** \'gau̇n\ *n*
**1** ► a woman's dress ⟨an evening *gown*⟩
**2** a loose robe

**gown 1:** a woman wearing an evening gown

**[1]grab** \'grab\ *vb* **grabbed**; **grab·bing**
[1]SNATCH

**[2]grab** *n*
the act or an instance of grabbing

**[1]grace** \'grās\ *n*
**1** GOODWILL 1, FAVOR ⟨saved by the *grace* of God⟩
**2** a short prayer at a meal
**3** pleasing and attractive behavior or quality ⟨social *graces*⟩
**4** the condition of being in favor ⟨in their good *graces*⟩
**5** a sense of what is proper ⟨accept criticism with good *grace*⟩
**6** beauty and ease of movement

**[2]grace** *vb* **graced**; **grac·ing**
**1** to do credit to **:** HONOR
**2** to make more attractive **:** ADORN

**grace·ful** \'grās-fəl\ *adj*
showing grace or beauty in form or action
**grace·ful·ly** \-fə-lē\ *adv*
**grace·ful·ness** *n*

**grace·less** \'grās-ləs\ *adj*
lacking grace
**grace·less·ly** *adv*
**grace·less·ness** *n*

**gra·cious** \'grā-shəs\ *adj*
**1** being kind and courteous
**2** GRACEFUL
**gra·cious·ly** *adv*
**gra·cious·ness** *n*

**grack·le** \'grak-əl\ *n*
▼ a large blackbird with shiny feathers that show changeable green, purple, and bronze colors

grackle

**¹grade** \'grād\ *n*
**1** a position in a scale of rank, quality, or order ⟨a high *grade* in the army⟩ ⟨leather of the poorer *grades*⟩
**2** a class of things that are of the same rank, quality, or order
**3** a division of a school course representing a year's work ⟨start the fourth *grade*⟩
**4** the group of pupils in a school grade
**5 grades** *pl* the elementary school system ⟨teach in the *grades*⟩
**6** a mark or rating especially in school
**7** the degree of slope (as of a road or railroad track) **:** SLOPE

**²grade** *vb* **grad·ed**; **grad·ing**
**1** to arrange in grades **:** SORT ⟨*grade* apples⟩
**2** to make level or evenly sloping ⟨*grade* a highway⟩
**3** to give a grade to
**4** to assign to a grade

**grade school** *n*
a school including the first six or the first eight grades

**grad·u·al** \'graj-ə-wəl\ *adj*
moving or happening by steps or degrees
**grad·u·al·ly** *adv*

**¹grad·u·ate** \'graj-ə-wət\ *n*
a person who has completed the required course of study in a college or school

**²grad·u·ate** \'graj-ə-,wāt\ *vb*
**grad·u·at·ed**; **grad·u·at·ing**
to become a graduate **:** finish a course of study

**grad·u·a·tion** \,graj-ə-'wā-shən\ *n*
**1** the act or process of graduating
**2** COMMENCEMENT 2

**Graeco-** see GRECO-

**graf·fi·ti** \grə-'fēt-ē\ *n*
writing or drawing made on a public structure without permission

**¹graft** \'graft\ *n*
**1** a grafted plant
**2** the act of grafting
**3** something (as skin or a bud) used in grafting
**4** something (as money or advantage) gotten in a dishonest way and especially by betraying a public trust

**²graft** *vb*
**1** ► to insert a twig or bud from one plant into another plant so they are joined and grow together
**2** to join one thing to another as if by grafting ⟨*graft* skin or bone⟩
**3** to gain money or advantage in a dishonest way
**graft·er** *n*

**grain** \'grān\ *n*
**1** the edible seed or seedlike fruit of some grasses (as wheat or oats) or a few other plants (as buckwheat)
**2** plants that produce grain
**3** a small hard particle
**4** a tiny amount **:** BIT ⟨a *grain* of sense in what they were saying⟩
**5** a unit of weight equal to 0.0648 gram
**6** the arrangement of fibers in wood
**grained** \'grānd\ *adj*

**gram** \'gram\ *n*
a unit of mass in the metric system equal to 1/1000 kilogram

**-gram** \,gram\ *n suffix*
drawing **:** writing **:** record ⟨tele*gram*⟩

**gram·mar** \'gram-ər\ *n*
**1** the study of the classes of words and their uses and relations in sentences
**2** the study of what is good and bad to use in speaking and writing
**3** speech or writing judged according to the rules of grammar

**gram·mat·i·cal** \grə-'mat-i-kəl\ *adj*
of, relating to, or following the rules of grammar
**gram·mat·i·cal·ly** *adv*

**gra·na·ry** \'grā-nə-rē, 'gran-ə-\ *n, pl* **gra·na·ries**
a storehouse for grain

**grand** \'grand\ *adj*
**1** higher in rank than others **:** FOREMOST ⟨the *grand* prize⟩
**2** great in size
**3** COMPREHENSIVE, INCLUSIVE ⟨a *grand* total⟩
**4** showing wealth or high social standing
**5** IMPRESSIVE ⟨a *grand* view⟩
**6** very good ⟨*grand* weather⟩
**grand·ly** *adv*
**grand·ness** *n*

stock

**²graft 1:** grafted apple tree twigs

**grand·aunt** \'grand-'ant, -'ánt\ *n*
GREAT-AUNT

**grand·child** \'grand-,chīld, 'gran-\ *n, pl* **grand·chil·dren** \-,chil-drən\
a child of one's son or daughter

**grand·daugh·ter** \'gran-,dȯt-ər\ *n*
a daughter of one's son or daughter

**gran·deur** \'gran-jər\ *n*
impressive greatness (as of power or nature)

**grand·fa·ther** \'grand-,fäth-ər, 'gran-, -,fäth-\ *n*
**1** the father of one's father or mother

2 ANCESTOR
**grand·fa·ther·ly** *adj*

**grandfather clock** *n*
a tall clock standing directly on the floor

**grand·ma** \'gram-,ȯ, 'gram-,ä, 'gran-,mȯ, 'gran-,mä\ *n*
GRANDMOTHER 1

**grand·moth·er** \'grand-,məth-ər, 'gran-\ *n*
**1** the mother of one's father or mother
**2** a female ancestor
**grand·moth·er·ly** *adj*

**grand·neph·ew** \'grand-'nef-yü, 'gran-\ *n*
a grandson of one's brother or sister

**grand·niece** \'grand-'nēs, 'gran-\ *n*
a granddaughter of one's brother or sister

**grand·pa** \'gram-,pȯ, 'gram-,pä, 'gran-\ *n*
GRANDFATHER 1

**grand·par·ent** \'grand-,par-ənt, 'gran-, -,per-\ *n*
a parent of one's father or mother

**grand·son** \'grand-,sən, 'gran-\ *n*
a son of one's son or daughter

**grand·stand** \'grand-,stand, 'gran-\ *n*
the main stand (as on an athletic field) for spectators

**grand·un·cle** \'gran-'dəng-kəl\ *n*
GREAT-UNCLE

**gran·ite** \'gran-ət\ *n*
▼ a very hard rock that is used for building and for monuments

**granite:** a rough piece of granite

**gran·ny** \'gran-ē\ *n, pl* **gran·nies**
GRANDMOTHER 1

**granny knot** *n*
▼ a knot that is not very firm and is often made accidentally instead of a square knot

**gra·no·la** \grə-'nō-lə\ *n*
a mixture of oats and other ingredients (as raisins, coconut, or nuts) that is eaten especially for breakfast or as a snack

**granny knot**

**¹grant** \'grant\ *vb*
**1** to agree to ⟨*grant* a request⟩
**2** to give as a favor or right
**3** to admit (something not yet proved) to be true

**²grant** *n*
**1** the act of granting
**2** GIFT 2

**grape** \'grāp\ *n*
a juicy berry that has a smooth green or whitish to deep red, purple, or black skin and grows in clusters on a woody vine **(grapevine)**

**grape·fruit** \'grāp-,früt\ *n*
▶ a large fruit with a yellow skin that is related to the orange and lemon

**grapefruit:** a pink grapefruit

**graph** \'graf\ *n*
a diagram that by means of dots and lines shows a system of relationships between things ⟨a *graph* showing the rise and fall in temperature during a period of time⟩

**-graph** \,graf\ *n suffix*
**1** something written
**2** instrument for making or sending records ⟨tele*graph*⟩

**¹graph·ic** \'graf-ik\ *adj*
**1** being written, drawn, printed, or engraved
**2** told or described in a clear vivid way ⟨a *graphic* account of an accident⟩
**3** of or relating to the pictorial arts or to printing
**graph·i·cal·ly** \-i-kə-lē\ *adv*

**²graphic** *n*
**1** a picture, map, or graph used for illustration
**2 graphics** *pl* a display (as of pictures or graphs) generated by a computer on a screen or printer

**graph·ite** \'graf-,īt\ *n*
a soft black carbon used in making lead pencils and as a lubricant

**-g·ra·phy** \g-rə-fē\ *n suffix, pl* **-g·ra·phies**
writing or picturing in a special way, by a special means, or of a special thing

**grap·nel** \'grap-nl\ *n*
a small anchor with several claws that can be used to anchor a boat or to take and keep a hold on an object (as another boat or something under water)

**¹grap·ple** \'grap-əl\ *n*
**1** the act of grappling or seizing
**2** a device for grappling

**²grapple** *vb* **grap·pled; grap·pling**
**1** to seize or hold with an instrument (as a hook)
**2** to seize and struggle with another

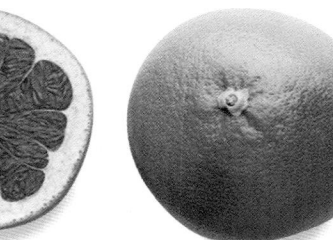

**¹grasp** \'grasp\ *vb*
**1** to seize and hold with or as if with the hand **:** GRIP
**2** to make the motion of seizing
**3** UNDERSTAND 1, COMPREHEND
**synonyms** see TAKE

**²grasp** *n*
**1** the act of grasping **:** a grip of the hand
**2** ²CONTROL 1, HOLD ⟨a land in the *grasp* of a tyrant⟩
**3** the power of seizing and holding **:** REACH
**4** ¹UNDERSTANDING 1, COMPREHENSION ⟨have a *grasp* of a subject⟩

**grasp·ing** \'gras-ping\ *adj*
GREEDY 2

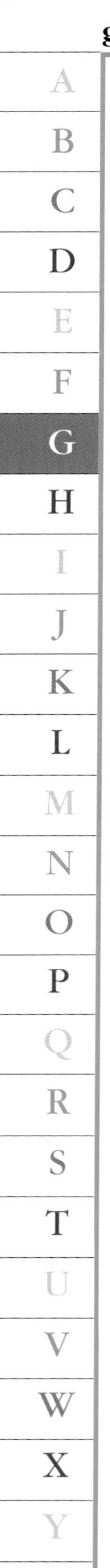


**grass** \'gras\ *n*
**1** plants suitable for or eaten by grazing animals
**2** ▼ any of a large natural group of green plants with jointed stems, long slender leaves, and stalks of clustered flowers
**3** GRASSLAND
**grass·like** \-,līk\ *adj*

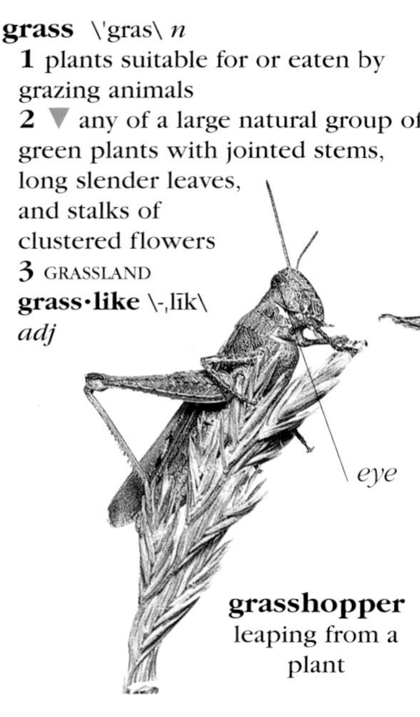


wing

hind leg

**grasshopper**
leaping from a plant

**grass·hop·per** \'gras-,häp-ər\ *n*
▲ a common leaping insect that feeds on plants

**grass·land** \'gras-,land\ *n*
land covered with herbs (as grass and clover) rather than shrubs and trees

**grassy** \'gras-ē\ *adj* **grass·i·er**; **grass·i·est**
of, like, or covered with grass

**¹grate** \'grāt\ *vb* **grat·ed**; **grat·ing**
**1** to break into small pieces by rubbing against something rough
**2** to grind or rub against something with a scratching noise
**3** to have a harsh effect ⟨a *grating* sound⟩

**²grate** *n*
**1** a frame containing parallel or crossed bars (as in a window)
**2** a frame of iron bars for holding burning fuel

**grate·ful** \'grāt-fəl\ *adj*
**1** feeling or showing thanks
**2** providing pleasure or comfort
**grate·ful·ly** \-fə-lē\ *adv*
**grate·ful·ness** *n*

**grat·er** \'grāt-ər\ *n*
► a device with a rough surface for grating

**grater:**
a cheese grater

**grat·i·fi·ca·tion** \,grat-ə-fə-'kā-shən\ *n*
**1** the act of gratifying **:** the state of being gratified
**2** something that gratifies

**grat·i·fy** \'grat-ə-,fī\ *vb* **grat·i·fied**; **grat·i·fy·ing**
to give pleasure or satisfaction to

**grat·ing** \'grāt-ing\ *n*
²GRATE 1

**grat·i·tude** \'grat-ə-,tüd, -,tyüd\ *n*
the state of being grateful

**¹grave** \'grāv\ *n*
a hole in the ground for burying a dead body

**²grave** *adj* **grav·er**; **grav·est**
**1** deserving serious thought **:** IMPORTANT
**2** having a serious look or way of acting
**grave·ly** *adv*
**grave·ness** *n*

**grav·el** \'grav-əl\ *n*
small pieces of rock and pebbles larger than grains of sand

**grass 2**

There are about 9,000 species of grass, growing in a wide range of habitats throughout the world. Grasses are pollinated by the wind, and so have no need of showy flowers to attract insects. Instead, their small flowers produce many grains of pollen that are easily blown by the wind.

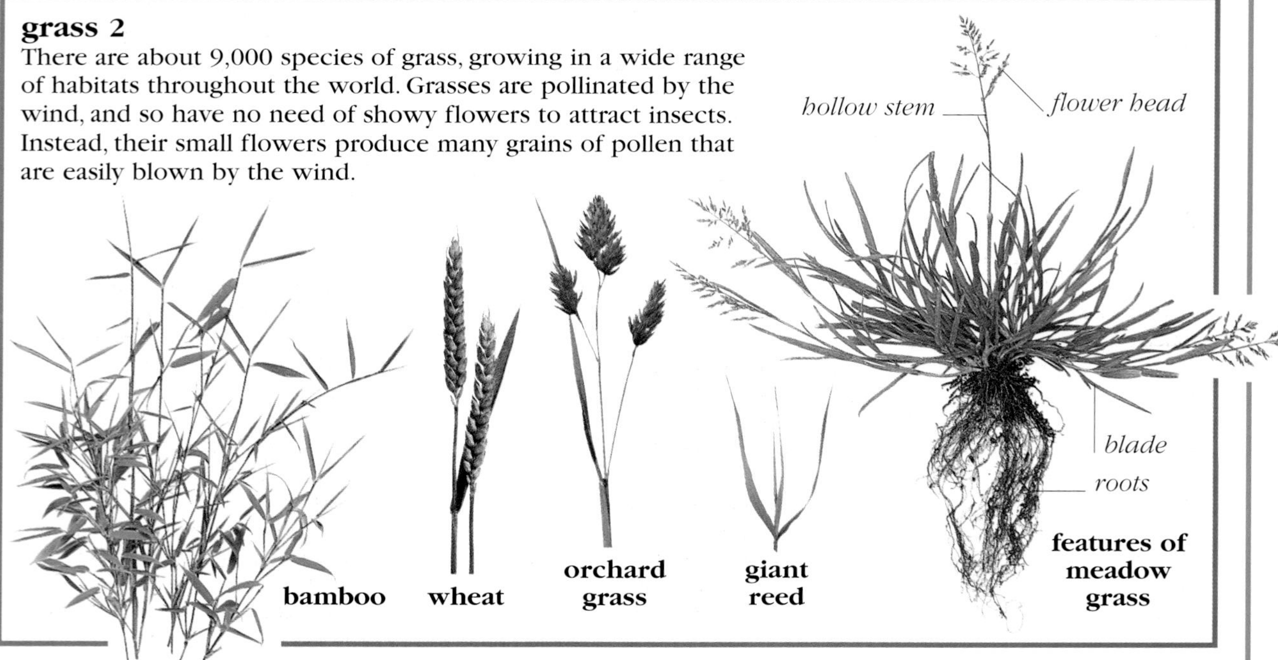


**bamboo** **wheat** **orchard grass** **giant reed** **features of meadow grass**

**grav·el·ly** \'grav-ə-lē\ *adj*
**1** containing or made up of gravel
**2** sounding harsh or scratchy ⟨a *gravelly* voice⟩

**grave·stone** \'grāv-,stōn\ *n*
a monument on a grave

**grave·yard** \'grāv-,yärd\ *n*
CEMETERY

**grav·i·tate** \'grav-ə-,tāt\ *vb* **grav·i·tat·ed**; **grav·i·tat·ing**
to move or be drawn toward something

**grav·i·ta·tion** \,grav-ə-'tā-shən\ *n*
**1** a force of attraction that tends to draw particles or bodies together
**2** the act or process of gravitating

**grav·i·ty** \'grav-ət-ē\ *n, pl* **grav·i·ties**
**1** the condition of being grave
**2** ▶ the attraction of bodies by gravitation toward the center of the earth
**3** GRAVITATION 1

**gravity 2**
A juggling ball thrown into the air is pulled down toward the earth by gravity. This slows the ball as it rises, and speeds it up as it falls.

gravity slows the ball as it rises
ball pulled down to the earth by gravity
ball is thrown up in the air

**motion of a ball showing the effect of gravity**

**gra·vy** \'grā-vē\ *n, pl* **gravies**
a sauce made from the juice of cooked meat

[1]**gray** *or* **grey** \'grā\ *adj*
**1** of the color gray
**2** having gray hair
**3** lacking cheer or brightness ⟨a *gray* day⟩
**gray·ness** *n*

[2]**gray** *or* **grey** *n*
**1** something gray in color
**2** a color that is a blend of black and white

[3]**gray** *or* **grey** *vb*
to make or become gray

**gray·ish** \'grā-ish\ *adj*
somewhat gray

[1]**graze** \'grāz\ *vb* **grazed**; **graz·ing**
**1** to eat grass
**2** to supply with grass or pasture

[2]**graze** *vb* **grazed**; **graz·ing**
**1** to rub lightly in passing : barely touch
**2** to scrape by rubbing against something

[3]**graze** *n*
a scrape or mark caused by grazing

[1]**grease** \'grēs\ *n*
**1** a more or less solid substance obtained from animal fat by melting
**2** oily material
**3** a thick lubricant

[2]**grease** \'grēs, 'grēz\ *vb* **greased**; **greas·ing**
**1** to smear with grease
**2** to lubricate with grease

**grease·paint** \'grēs-,pānt\ *n*
actors' makeup

**greasy** \'grē-sē, -zē\ *adj* **greas·i·er**; **greas·i·est**
**1** smeared with grease
**2** like or full of grease

**great** \'grāt\ *adj*
**1** very large in size : HUGE
**2** large in number : NUMEROUS ⟨a *great* crowd⟩
**3** long continued ⟨a *great* while⟩
**4** much beyond the average or ordinary ⟨a *great* weight⟩
**5** IMPORTANT 1, DISTINGUISHED ⟨a *great* artist⟩
**6** remarkable in knowledge or skill ⟨*great* at diving⟩
**7** GRAND 6
**great·ly** *adv*

**great–aunt** \'grāt-'ant, -'ånt\ *n*
an aunt of one's father or mother

**great–grand·child** \'grāt-'grand-,chīld, -'gran-\ *n, pl* **great–grand·chil·dren** \-,chil-drən\
a grandson (**great–grandson**) or granddaughter (**great–granddaughter**) of one's son or daughter

**great–grand·par·ent** \'grāt-'grand-,par-ənt, -'gran-, -,per-\ *n*
a grandfather (**great–grandfather**) or grandmother (**great–grandmother**) of one's father or mother

**great–un·cle** \'grāt-'əng-kəl\ *n*
an uncle of one's father or mother

**grebe** \'grēb\ *n*
any of a group of swimming and diving birds related to the loons

**Gre·cian** \'grē-shən\ *adj*
[2]GREEK

**Gre·co-** *or* **Grae·co-** \'grē-kō\ *prefix*
**1** Greece : Greeks
**2** Greek and

**greed** \'grēd\ *n*
greedy desire (as for money or food)

**greedy** \'grēd-ē\ *adj* **greed·i·er**; **greed·i·est**
**1** having a strong appetite for food or drink : very hungry
**2** trying to grab more than one needs or more than one's share
**greed·i·ly** \'grēd-l-ē\ *adv*
**greed·i·ness** \'grēd-ē-nəs\ *n*

[1]**Greek** \'grēk\ *n*
**1** a person born or living in Greece
**2** the language of the Greeks

[2]**Greek** *adj*
of or relating to Greece, its people, or the Greek language

a b c d e f g h i j k l m n o p q r s t u v w x y z

**[1]green** \'grēn\ *adj*
**1** of the color green
**2** covered with green vegetation ⟨*green* fields⟩
**3** made of green plants or of the leafy parts of plants ⟨a *green* salad⟩
**4** not ripe ⟨*green* bananas⟩
**5** not fully processed, treated, or seasoned ⟨*green* lumber⟩
**6** lacking training or experience ⟨*green* troops⟩
**7** supporting the preservation or improvement of the natural environment (as by controlling pollution)
**8** helping to preserve the environment (as by being recyclable or not polluting) ⟨*green* household products⟩
**green·ly** *adv*
**green·ness** *n*

**[2]green** *n*
**1** a color that ranges between blue and yellow
**2 greens** *pl* leafy parts of plants used for decoration or food
**3** a grassy plain or plot

**green·ery** \'grē-nə-rē\ *n, pl* **green·er·ies**
green plants or foliage

**green·horn** \'grēn-ˌhȯrn\ *n*
a person who is new at something

**green·house** \'grēn-ˌhau̇s\ *n*
a building with glass walls and roof for growing plants

**greenhouse effect** *n*
► warming of the lower atmosphere of the earth that occurs when radiation from the sun is absorbed by the earth and then given off again and absorbed by carbon dioxide and water vapor in the atmosphere

**green·ish** \'grē-nish\ *adj*
somewhat green

**green·ling** \'grēn-ling\ *n*
any of a group of food and sport fishes of the Pacific coast

**green manure** *n*
a leafy crop (as of clover) plowed under to improve the soil

**green thumb** *n*
an unusual ability to make plants grow

**green·wood** \'grēn-ˌwu̇d\ *n*
a forest green with leaves

**greet** \'grēt\ *vb*
**1** to speak to in a friendly polite way upon arrival or meeting

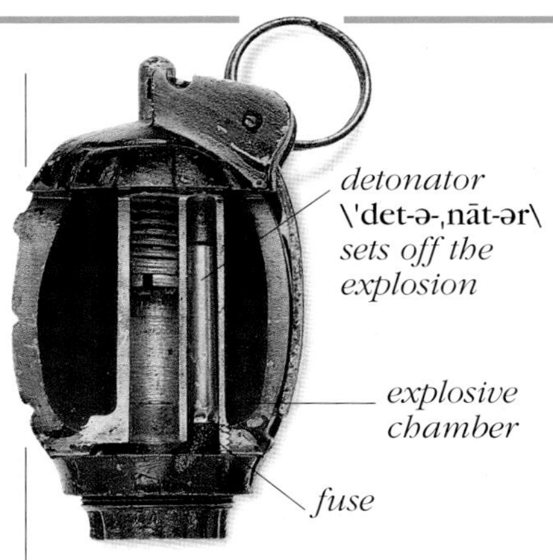


**grenade**

**2** to receive or react to in a certain way ⟨*greeted* the speech with boos⟩
**3** to present itself to ⟨a pretty scene *greeted* them⟩
**greet·er** *n*

**greet·ing** \'grēt-ing\ *n*
**1** an expression of pleasure on meeting someone
**2** SALUTATION 2
**3** an expression of good wishes ⟨holiday *greetings*⟩

**gre·gar·i·ous** \gri-'gar-ē-əs\ *adj*
tending to live together with or associate with others of one's own kind ⟨*gregarious* insects⟩
**gre·gar·i·ous·ly** *adv*
**gre·gar·i·ous·ness** *n*

**gre·nade** \grə-'nād\ *n*
◄ a small bomb designed to be thrown by hand or fired (as by a rifle)

**gren·a·dier** \ˌgren-ə-'dir\ *n*
a member of a European regiment formerly armed with grenades

**grew** *past of* GROW

**greyhound**

**grey** *variant of* GRAY

**grey·hound** \'grā-ˌhau̇nd\ *n*
▲ a tall swift dog with a smooth coat and good eyesight

## greenhouse effect

The sun's heat is directed toward the earth, but not all of the reflected heat escapes from the atmosphere, so that the earth becomes warmer. Many scientists studying the effect think it is worsened by the buildup of pollution, which traps even more of the sun's heat. These scientists think that as the climate grows warmer, weather patterns will change, and different parts of the world will experience droughts, storms, and floods.

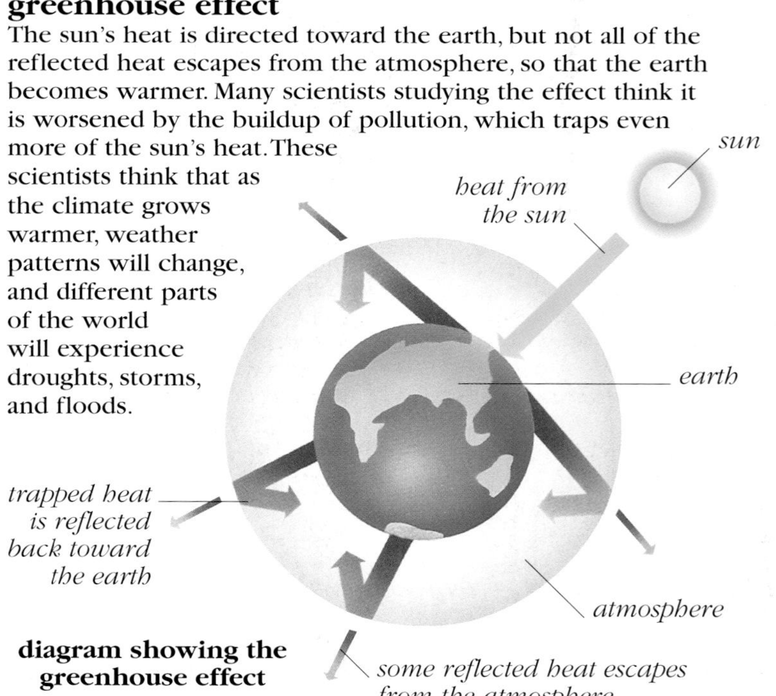


**diagram showing the greenhouse effect**

**grid** \'grid\ *n*
**1** a group of electrical conductors that form a network
**2** a network of horizontal and perpendicular lines (as for locating places on a map)

**grid·dle** \'grid-l\ *n*
a flat surface or pan on which food is cooked

**griddle cake** *n*
PANCAKE

**grid·iron** \'grid-,ī-ərn\ *n*
**1** a grate with parallel bars for broiling food
**2** a football field

**grief** \'grēf\ *n*
**1** very deep sorrow
**2** a cause of sorrow
**3** MISHAP **synonyms** see SORROW

**griev·ance** \'grē-vəns\ *n*
**1** a cause of uneasiness or annoyance
**2** a formal complaint

**grieve** \'grēv\ *vb* **grieved**; **griev·ing**
**1** to cause grief to
**2** to feel or show grief

**griev·ous** \'grē-vəs\ *adj*
**1** causing suffering
**2** SERIOUS 5, GRAVE ⟨a *grievous* error⟩

**¹grill** \'gril\ *vb*
**1** to broil on a grill
**2** to distress with continued questioning

**²grill** *n*
**1** a grate on which food is broiled
**2** a dish of broiled food
**3** a simple restaurant

**grille** *or* **grill** \'gril\ *n*
an often ornamental arrangement of bars (as of metal) forming a barrier or screen

**grim** \'grim\ *adj* **grim·mer**; **grim·mest**
**1** ¹SAVAGE 2, CRUEL
**2** harsh in appearance : STERN ⟨a *grim* look⟩
**3** UNYIELDING 2 ⟨*grim* determination⟩
**4** FRIGHTFUL 1 ⟨a *grim* tale⟩
**grim·ly** *adv*
**grim·ness** *n*

**¹gri·mace** \'grim-əs, gri-'mās\ *n*
a twisting of the face (as in disgust)

**²grim·ace** *vb* **grim·aced**; **grim·ac·ing**
to make a grimace

**grime** \'grīm\ *n*
dirt rubbed into a surface

**grimy** \'grī-mē\ *adj* **grim·i·er**; **grim·i·est**
full of grime : DIRTY

**¹grin** \'grin\ *vb* **grinned**; **grin·ning**
to draw back the lips and show the teeth

**²grin** *n*
an act of grinning

**¹grind** \'grīnd\ *vb* **ground** \'grau̇nd\; **grind·ing**
**1** to make or be made into meal or powder by rubbing
**2** to wear down, polish, or sharpen by friction ⟨*grind* an ax⟩
**3** to rub together with a scraping noise ⟨*grind* the teeth⟩
**4** to operate or produce by or as if by turning a crank

**²grind** *n*
**1** an act of grinding
**2** steady hard work

**grind·stone** \'grīnd-,stōn\ *n*
a flat round stone that turns on an axle and is used for sharpening tools and for shaping and smoothing

**¹grip** \'grip\ *vb* **gripped**; **grip·ping**
**1** to grasp firmly
**2** to hold the interest of

**²grip** *n*
**1** a strong grasp
**2** strength in holding : POWER ⟨the *grip* of a disease⟩
**3** ¹HANDLE
**4** a small suitcase

**grippe** \'grip\ *n*
a disease like or the same as influenza

**gris·ly** \'griz-lē\ *adj* **gris·li·er**; **gris·li·est**
HORRIBLE, GHASTLY ⟨a *grisly* murder⟩

**grist** \'grist\ *n*
grain to be ground or that is already ground

**gris·tle** \'gris-əl\ *n*
CARTILAGE
**gris·tli·ness** \'gris-lē-nəs\ *n*
**gris·tly** \'gris-lē\ *adj*

**grist·mill** \'grist-,mil\ *n*
a mill for grinding grain

**¹grit** \'grit\ *n*
**1** rough hard bits especially of sand
**2** strength of mind or spirit

**²grit** *vb* **grit·ted**; **grit·ting**
¹GRIND 3, GRATE

**grits** \'grits\ *n pl*
coarsely ground hulled grain

**grit·ty** \'grit-ē\ *adj* **grit·ti·er**; **grit·ti·est**
**1** containing or like grit
**2** bravely refusing to yield : PLUCKY
**grit·ti·ness** *n*

**griz·zled** \'griz-əld\ *adj*
streaked or mixed with gray

**griz·zly** \'griz-lē\ *adj* **griz·zli·er**; **griz·zli·est**
GRIZZLED, GRAYISH

**grizzly bear** *n*
▼ a large powerful usually brownish yellow bear of western North America

grizzly bear

**¹groan** \'grōn\ *vb*
**1** to make or express with a deep moaning sound
**2** to creak under a strain

**²groan** *n*
a low moaning sound

**gro·cer** \'grō-sər\ *n*
a dealer in food

**gro·cery** \'grōs-ə-rē, 'grōs-rē\ *n, pl* **gro·cer·ies**
**1** *groceries pl* the goods sold by a grocer
**2** a grocer's store

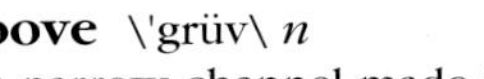

**grog·gy** \'gräg-ē\ *adj* **grog·gi·er**; **grog·gi·est**
weak and confused and unsteady on one's feet
**grog·gi·ly** \'gräg-ə-lē\ *adv*
**grog·gi·ness** \'gräg-ē-nəs\ *n*

---

**Word History** Once there was an English admiral who was nicknamed "Old Grog." He gave his sailors a daily ration of rum mixed with water. The sailors called this rum *grog*, after Old Grog. In time the word *grog* came to be used for any liquor. Now a person who acts weak and confused as if drunk is called *groggy*.

---

**groin** \'gròin\ *n*
the fold or area where the abdomen joins the thigh

**grom·met** \'gräm-ət\ *n*
an eyelet of firm material to strengthen or protect an opening

**[1]groom** \'grüm\ *n*
**1** a servant especially in charge of horses
**2** BRIDEGROOM

**[2]groom** *vb*
**1** ▼ to make neat and attractive (as by cleaning and brushing) ⟨*groom* a dog⟩
**2** to make fit or ready ⟨*groom* a candidate for office⟩

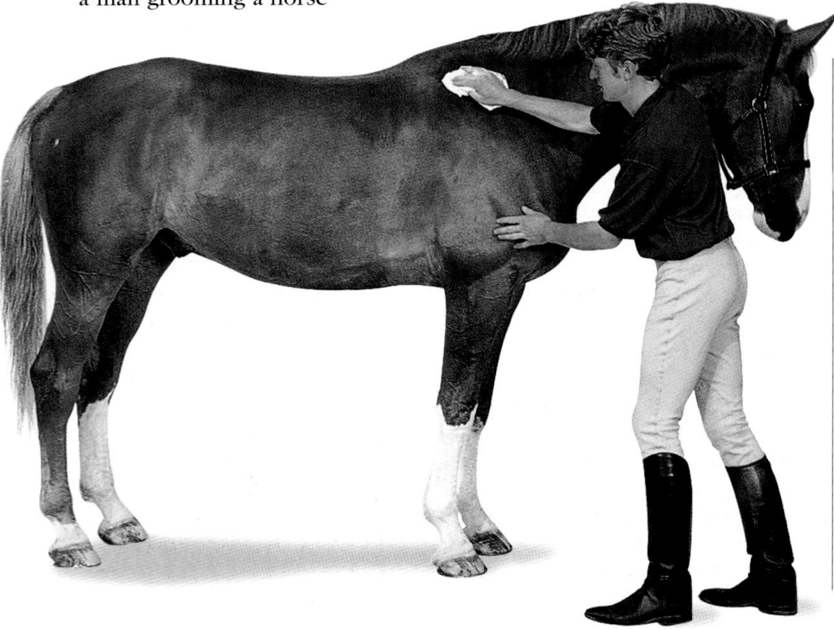

**[2]groom 1:**
a man grooming a horse

**[1]groove** \'grüv\ *n*
**1** a narrow channel made in a surface (as by cutting)
**2** [1]ROUTINE

**[2]groove** *vb* **grooved**; **groov·ing**
to form a groove in

**groovy** \'grü-vē\ *adj* **groov·i·er**; **groov·i·est**
very good **:** EXCELLENT

**grope** \'grōp\ *vb* **groped**; **grop·ing**
**1** to feel one's way ⟨*groping* along the dark hallway⟩
**2** to seek by or as if by feeling around ⟨*groping* for the light switch⟩ ⟨*grope* for an answer⟩

**gros·beak** \'grōs-ˌbēk\ *n*
▶ a finch with a strong conical bill

**grosbeak**

**[1]gross** \'grōs\ *adj*
**1** GLARING 3 ⟨a *gross* error⟩
**2** BIG 1
**3** [1]THICK 3
**4** consisting of a whole before anything is deducted ⟨*gross* earnings⟩
**5** COARSE 4, VULGAR ⟨*gross* words⟩

**[2]gross** *n*
the whole before anything is deducted

**[3]gross** *n, pl* **gross**
twelve dozen

**gro·tesque** \grō-'tesk\ *adj*
very strange and unexpected **:** FANTASTIC

**grot·to** \'grät-ō\ *n, pl* **grottoes**
**1** [1]CAVE, CAVERN
**2** an artificial structure like a cave

**[1]grouch** \'grau̇ch\ *n*
**1** a fit of bad temper
**2** a person with a bad disposition

**[2]grouch** *vb*
[1]GRUMBLE 1, COMPLAIN

**grouchy** \'grau̇-chē\ *adj* **grouch·i·er**; **grouch·i·est**
having a bad disposition **:** CANTANKEROUS
**grouch·i·ly** \-chə-lē\ *adv*
**grouch·i·ness** \-chē-nəs\ *n*

**[1]ground** \'grau̇nd\ *n*
**1** the bottom of a body of water ⟨the boat struck *ground*⟩
**2 grounds** *pl* SEDIMENT 1 ⟨coffee *grounds*⟩
**3** a reason for a belief, action, or argument ⟨*ground* for complaint⟩
**4** the surface or material upon which something is made or displayed or against which it appears
**5** the surface of the earth **:** SOIL
**6** an area used for some purpose ⟨a hunting *ground*⟩
**7 grounds** *pl* the land around and belonging to a building ⟨the capitol *grounds*⟩
**8** an area to be won or defended as if in a battle ⟨gain *ground*⟩

**[2]ground** *vb*
**1** to instruct in basic knowledge or understanding
**2** to run or cause to run aground
**3** to connect electrically with the ground
**4** to prevent (a plane or pilot) from flying

**[3]ground** *past of* GRIND

**ground crew** *n*
the mechanics and technicians who take care of an airplane

**ground·hog** \'grau̇nd-ˌhòg, -ˌhäg\ *n*
WOODCHUCK

**ground·less** \'grau̇n-dləs\ *adj*
being without foundation or reason ⟨*groundless* fears⟩

**ground swell** *n*
a broad deep ocean swell caused by a distant storm or earthquake

**ground·work** \'grau̇n-ˌdwərk\ *n*
FOUNDATION 2

**[1]group** \'grüp\ *n*
a number of persons or things that form one whole

**[2]group** *vb*
to arrange in or put into a group

**[1]grouse** \'grau̇s\ *n, pl* **grouse**
▼ a game bird that is much like the domestic fowl

**[1]grouse**

**[2]grouse** *vb* **groused**; **grous·ing**
[1]GRUMBLE 1, GROUCH

**grove** \'grōv\ *n*
a small wood or a planting of trees

**grov·el** \'gräv-əl, 'grəv-\ *vb* **grov·eled** *or* **grov·elled**; **grov·el·ing** *or* **grov·el·ling**
**1** to creep or lie face down on the ground (as in fear)
**2** CRINGE
**grov·el·er** *or* **grov·el·ler** *n*

**grow** \'grō\ *vb* **grew** \'grü\; **grown** \'grōn\; **grow·ing**
**1** to spring up and develop to maturity ⟨the crop is *growing* well⟩
**2** to be able to live and develop ⟨most algae *grow* in water⟩
**3** to be related in some way by reason of growing ⟨tree branches *grown* together⟩
**4** [1]INCREASE, EXPAND ⟨the city *grew*⟩
**5** BECOME 1 ⟨*grow* old⟩
**6** to cause to grow : RAISE
**grow·er** *n*

**growing pains** *n pl*
pains that occur in the legs of growing children but have not been proven to be caused by growth

**[1]growl** \'grau̇l\ *vb*
**1** to make a rumbling noise
**2** to make a growl
**3** [1]GRUMBLE 1

**[2]growl** *n*
**1** a deep threatening sound (as of an animal)
**2** a grumbling or muttered complaint

**grown** \'grōn\ *adj*
having reached full growth : MATURE ⟨a *grown* person⟩

**[1]grown–up** \'grō-ˌnəp\ *adj*
[1]ADULT

**[2]grown–up** *n*
an adult person

**growth** \'grōth\ *n*
**1** a stage or condition in growing ⟨reach one's full *growth*⟩
**2** a process of growing ⟨*growth* of a crystal⟩
**3** a gradual increase ⟨the *growth* of wealth⟩
**4** something (as a covering of plants) produced by growing

**grow up** *vb*
to become adult

**[1]grub** \'grəb\ *vb* **grubbed**; **grub·bing**
**1** to root out by digging : DIG ⟨*grub* out potatoes⟩
**2** to work hard

**[2]grub 1:** a flour beetle grub

**[2]grub** *n*
**1** ▲ a soft thick wormlike larva (as of a beetle)
**2** FOOD 1

**grub·by** \'grəb-ē\ *adj* **grub·bi·er**; **grub·bi·est**
[1]DIRTY 1
**grub·bi·ly** \'grəb-ə-lē\ *adv*
**grub·bi·ness** \'grəb-ē-nəs\ *n*

**[1]grub·stake** \'grəb-ˌstāk\ *n*
supplies or funds given to a prospector in return for a promise of a share in the finds

**[2]grubstake** *vb* **grub·staked**; **grub·stak·ing**
to provide with a grubstake

**[1]grudge** \'grəj\ *vb* **grudged**; **grudg·ing**
BEGRUDGE

**[2]grudge** *n*
a feeling of sullen dislike that lasts a long time

**gru·el** \'grü-əl\ *n*
a thin porridge

**gru·el·ing** *or* **gru·el·ling** \'grü-ə-liŋ\ *adj*
calling for much effort ⟨a *grueling* run⟩

**grue·some** \'grü-səm\ *adj*
HORRIBLE, GHASTLY
**grue·some·ly** *adv*
**grue·some·ness** *n*

**gruff** \'grəf\ *adj*
rough in speech or manner : HARSH
**gruff·ly** *adv*
**gruff·ness** *n*

**[1]grum·ble** \'grəm-bəl\ *vb* **grum·bled**; **grum·bling**
**1** to complain or mutter in discontent
**2** [1]RUMBLE

**[2]grumble** *n*
**1** the act of grumbling
**2** [2]RUMBLE

**grumpy** \'grəm-pē\ *adj* **grump·i·er**; **grump·i·est**
GROUCHY, CROSS
**grump·i·ly** \-pə-lē\ *adv*
**grump·i·ness** \-pē-nəs\ *n*

**[1]grunt** \'grənt\ *vb*
to make a grunt
**grunt·er** *n*

**[2]grunt** *n*
a deep short sound (as of a hog)

**[1]guar·an·tee** \ˌgar-ən-'tē, ˌgär-\ *n*
**1** GUARANTOR
**2** the act of guaranteeing
**3** a promise that something will work the way it should
**4** SECURITY 2

**[2]guarantee** *vb* **guar·an·teed**; **guar·an·tee·ing**
**1** to promise to answer for the debt or duty of another person ⟨*guarantee* that a loan will be repaid⟩
**2** to give a guarantee on or about ⟨*guarantee* a car for one year⟩

**guar·an·tor** \ˌgar-ən-'tȯr, ˌgär-\ *n*
a person who gives a guarantee

**[1]guard** \'gärd\ *n*
**1** the act or duty of keeping watch
**2** a person or a body of persons that guards against injury or danger
**3** a device giving protection

**[2]guard** *vb*
**1** to protect from danger : DEFEND
**2** to watch over so as to prevent escape
**3** to keep careful watch ⟨*guard* against mistakes⟩

**guard·ed** \'gärd-əd\ *adj*
CAUTIOUS ⟨a *guarded* answer⟩

**guard·house** \'gärd-ˌhau̇s\ *n*
**1** a building used as a headquarters by soldiers on guard duty
**2** a military jail

a b c d e f g h i j k l m n o p q r s t u v w x y z

**guard·ian** \'gärd-ē-ən\ *n*
**1** a person who guards or looks after something : CUSTODIAN
**2** a person who legally has the care of another person or of that person's property
**guard·ian·ship** \-,ship\ *n*

**guard·room** \'gärd-,rüm, -,rům\ *n*
a room used by a military guard while on duty

**guards·man** \'gärdz-mən\ *n, pl* **guards·men** \-mən\
a member of a military guard

**gu·ber·na·to·ri·al** \,gü-bər-nə-'tōr-ē-əl, ,gyü-\ *adj*
of or relating to a governor

**guer·ril·la** *or* **gue·ril·la** \gə-'ril-ə\ *n*
a member of a band of persons carrying on warfare but not part of a regular army

[1]**guess** \'ges\ *vb*
**1** to judge without sure knowledge ⟨*guess* at a person's weight⟩
**2** to solve correctly ⟨*guess* a riddle⟩
**3** THINK 2, BELIEVE
**guess·er** *n*

[2]**guess** *n*
an opinion formed by guessing

**guess·work** \'ges-,wərk\ *n*
work done or results gotten by guessing

**guest** \'gest\ *n*
**1** a person entertained in one's house or at one's table
**2** a person using a hotel, motel, inn, or restaurant **synonyms** see VISITOR

[1]**guf·faw** \,gə-'fò\ *n*
a burst of loud laughter

[2]**guffaw** *vb*
to laugh noisily

**guid·ance** \'gīd-ns\ *n*
the act or process of guiding or being guided : DIRECTION

[1]**guide** \'gīd\ *n*
someone or something (as a book) that leads, directs, or shows the right way

[2]**guide** *vb* **guid·ed**; **guid·ing**
**1** to show the way to ⟨*guide* a group on a tour⟩
**2** DIRECT, INSTRUCT

**guide·book** \'gīd-,bůk\ *n*
a book of information for travelers

**guide dog** *n*
a dog trained to lead a person who is blind

**guide·post** \'gīd-,pōst\ *n*
a post with signs giving directions for travelers

**guinea fowl**

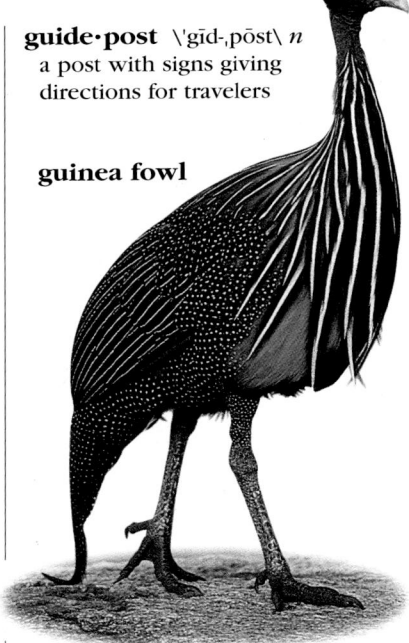

**guide word** *n*
either of the terms at the head of a page of an alphabetical reference work (as a dictionary) usually showing the first and last entries on the page

**guild** \'gild\ *n*
an association of persons with similar aims or common interests

**guile** \'gīl\ *n*
sly trickery
**guile·ful** \'gīl-fəl\ *adj*
**guile·ful·ly** \-fə-lē\ *adv*

[1]**guil·lo·tine** \'gil-ə-,tēn\ *n*
a machine for cutting off a person's head with a heavy blade that slides down two grooved posts

[2]**guillotine** *vb* **guil·lo·tined**; **guil·lo·tin·ing**
to cut off a person's head with a guillotine

**guilt** \'gilt\ *n*
**1** the fact of having done something wrong and especially something punishable by law
**2** conduct that causes one to feel shame or regret or the feeling experienced
**guilt·less** \-ləs\ *adj*

**guilty** \'gil-tē\ *adj* **guilt·i·er**; **guilt·i·est**
**1** having done wrong
**2** aware of, suffering from, or showing guilt ⟨feel *guilty*⟩ ⟨had a *guilty* look⟩
**guilt·i·ly** \-tə-lē\ *adv*
**guilt·i·ness** \-tē-nəs\ *n*

**guin·ea** \'gin-ē\ *n*
an old British gold coin

**guinea fowl** *n*
◀ an African bird related to the pheasants that has a bare head and neck and usually dark gray feathers with white speckles and is sometimes raised for food

**guinea pig** *n*
▼ a stocky rodent with short ears and a very short tail

**guinea pig**

**guise** \'gīz\ *n*
**1** a style of dress
**2** outward appearance

**gui·tar** \gə-'tär\ *n*
▼ a musical instrument with six strings played by plucking or strumming

**gulch** \'gəlch\ *n*
RAVINE

electric guitar
an acoustic guitar is not electronically amplified

**guitars**

**gulf** \'gəlf\ *n*
**1** a part of an ocean or sea extending into the land ⟨the *Gulf* of Mexico⟩
**2** CHASM, ABYSS
**3** a wide separation (as in age)

**gull** \'gəl\ *n*
a waterbird with webbed feet that is usually blue-gray or whitish in color and has a thick strong bill

**gul·let** \'gəl-ət\ *n*
THROAT 2, ESOPHAGUS

**gull·ible** \'gəl-ə-bəl\ *adj*
easily tricked or misled

**gul·ly** \'gəl-ē\ *n, pl* **gullies**
a trench worn in the earth by running water

[1]**gulp** \'gəlp\ *vb*
**1** to swallow eagerly or in large amounts at a time
**2** to keep back as if by swallowing ⟨*gulp* down a sob⟩
**3** to catch the breath as if after a long drink

[2]**gulp** *n*
**1** the act of gulping
**2** a large swallow

[1]**gum** \'gəm\ *n*
the flesh along the jaws at the roots of the teeth

**gump·tion** \'gəmp-shən\ *n*
[1]SPIRIT 5, COURAGE

[1]**gun** \'gən\ *n*
**1** CANNON 1
**2** a portable firearm (as a rifle, shotgun, or pistol)
**3** something like a gun in shape or function
**4** a discharge of a gun (as in a salute)

[2]**gun** *vb* **gunned**; **gun·ning**
**1** to hunt with a gun
**2** to open the throttle of quickly so as to increase speed ⟨*gun* the engine⟩

**gun·boat** \'gən-ˌbōt\ *n*
▼ a small armed ship for use in coastal waters

**gunboat:** a torpedo gunboat

**gun·shot** \'gən-ˌshät\ *n*
**1** a shot from a gun
**2** the effective range of a gun

**gun·wale** \'gən-l\ *n*
the upper edge of a ship's side

**gup·py** \'gəp-ē\ *n, pl* **guppies**
▼ a small tropical minnow often kept as an aquarium fish

**guppy**

[1]**gur·gle** \'gər-gəl\ *vb* **gur·gled**; **gur·gling**
**1** to flow in a broken uneven noisy current
**2** to sound like a liquid flowing with a gurgle

[2]**gurgle** *n*
a sound of or like gurgling liquid

[1]**gush** \'gəsh\ *vb*
**1** [1]SPOUT 1, 3
**2** to be too affectionate or enthusiastic



[2]**gum** *n*
**1** a sticky substance obtained from plants that hardens on drying
**2** a substance like a plant gum (as in stickiness)
**3** CHEWING GUM

[3]**gum** *vb* **gummed**; **gum·ming**
to smear, stick together, or clog with or as if with gum

**gum·bo** \'gəm-ˌbō\ *n, pl* **gumbos**
a rich soup thickened with okra pods

**gum·drop** \'gəm-ˌdräp\ *n*
a candy usually made from corn syrup and gelatin

**gum·my** \'gəm-ē\ *adj* **gum·mi·er**; **gum·mi·est**
**1** consisting of, containing, or covered with gum
**2** GLUEY, STICKY

**gun·fire** \'gən-ˌfīr\ *n*
the firing of guns

**gun·man** \'gən-mən\ *n, pl* **gun·men** \-mən\
a criminal armed with a gun

**gun·ner** \'gən-ər\ *n*
a person who operates a gun

**gun·nery** \'gən-ə-rē\ *n*
the use of guns

**gunnery sergeant** *n*
a noncommissioned officer in the Marine Corps ranking above a staff sergeant

**gun·ny** \'gən-ē\ *n, pl* **gun·nies**
**1** coarse jute sacking
**2** BURLAP

**gun·pow·der** \'gən-ˌpau̇d-ər\ *n*
an explosive powder used in guns and blasting

[2]**gush** *n*
a sudden free pouring out

**gush·er** \'gəsh-ər\ *n*
an oil well with a large natural flow

**gust** \'gəst\ *n*
**1** a sudden brief rush of wind
**2** a sudden outburst (as of emotion)

**gusty** \'gəs-tē\ *adj* **gust·i·er**; **gust·i·est**
WINDY

[1]**gut** \'gət\ *n*
**1** ENTRAILS — usually used in pl.
**2** the digestive tube or a part of this ⟨the small *gut*⟩
**3** CATGUT
**4** **guts** *pl* COURAGE

[2]**gut** *vb* **gut·ted**; **gut·ting**
**1** to remove the entrails from
**2** to destroy the inside of ⟨fire *gutted* the building⟩

## gymnastics

Three main types of gymnastics are popular: rhythmic gymnastics, artistic gymnastics, and sports acrobatics. In rhythmic gymnastics, girls and women work with a small hand apparatus, such as a ball, hoop, or ribbon. Artistic gymnastics, for both sexes, involves work on an apparatus such as a vaulting horse or a bar, as well as on the floor. Balance positions are a major part of sports acrobatics, in which both sexes take part.

[1]**gut·ter** \'gət-ər\ *n*
**1** a trough along the eaves of a house to catch and carry off water
**2** a low area (as at the side of a road) to carry off surface water

[2]**gutter** *vb*
**1** to flow in small streams
**2** to have wax flowing down the sides after melting through the rim ⟨a *guttering* candle⟩

[1]**guy** \'gī\ *n*
a rope, chain, rod, or wire (**guy wire**) attached to something to steady it

[2]**guy** *n*
PERSON 1, FELLOW

**Word History** Once a group of men made a plot to blow up the Houses of Parliament in London on November 5. The plot was foiled. One of the plotters, a man named Guy Fawkes, was put to death. November 5 is now celebrated in England as Guy Fawkes Day. Figures made of old clothes stuffed with straw or rags are burned. These figures are called *guys*, for Guy Fawkes. In the United States *guy* came to be used as a general term for a person.

**gym** \'jim\ *n*
GYMNASIUM

**gym·na·si·um** \jim-'nā-zē-əm\ *n*
a room or building for sports events or gymnastics

**gym·nast** \'jim-,nast, -nəst\ *n*
a person who is skilled in gymnastics

**gym·nas·tic** \jim-'nas-tik\ *adj*
of or relating to gymnastics

**gym·nas·tics** \jim-'nas-tiks\ *n sing or pl*
◀ physical exercises for developing skill, strength, and control in the use of the body or a sport in which such exercises are performed

**Gyp·sy** *or* **Gip·sy** \'jip-sē\ *n*, *pl* **Gyp·sies** *or* **Gip·sies**
a member of a group of people coming from India to Europe long ago and living a wandering way of life

**Word History** Gypsies first came to England about four hundred years ago. The English thought that these strangers had come from Egypt. They gave them the name *Egyptian*. In time this name was shortened and altered to *Gypsy*.

**gypsy moth** *n*
a moth whose caterpillar has a spotty grayish look and does great damage to trees by eating the leaves

**gy·rate** \'jī-,rāt\ *vb* **gy·rat·ed**; **gy·rat·ing**
to move in a circle around a center : SPIN ⟨the child set the top *gyrating*⟩

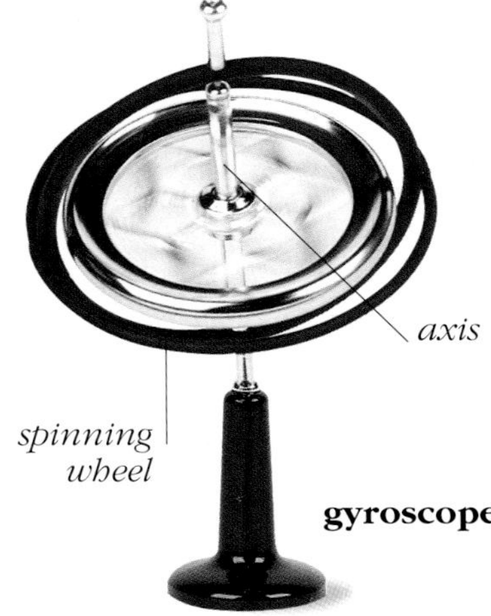


**gyroscope**

**gy·ro·scope** \'jī-rə-,skōp\ *n*
▲ a wheel mounted to spin rapidly so that its axis is free to turn in various directions

**gy·ro·scop·ic** \,jī-rə-'skäp-ik\ *adj*
of or relating to a gyroscope

**The sounds of H:** The letter **H** has only one sound in English. It sounds the same in **happy**, **help**, **home**, **hurry**, and **inhale**.

The letter **H** is sometimes silent. It has no sound in the words **heirloom**, **hour**, **honest**, **ghost**, and **mynah**.

**H** also combines with a few other consonants to form completely different sounds. For example: **S + H** produces the "**SH**" sound, as in **ship**; **C + H** produces the "**CH**" sound, as in **chip**; **T + H** produces the two "**TH**" sounds, as in **this** and **thin**; and **P + H** produces the sound of **F**, as in **phone**.

**h** \'āch\ *n, pl* **h's** *or* **hs** \'ā-chəz\ *often cap*
the eighth letter of the English alphabet

**ha** \'hä\ *interj*
used to show surprise or joy

**hab·it** \'hab-ət\ *n*
1 ▼ clothing worn for a special purpose ⟨a riding *habit*⟩

**habit 1:** a riding habit

2 usual way of behaving ⟨the *habits* of a wild animal⟩
3 a way of acting or doing that has become fixed by being repeated often
4 characteristic way of growing ⟨trees of spreading *habit*⟩

**hab·it·able** \'hab-ət-ə-bəl\ *adj*
suitable or fit to live in ⟨a *habitable* house⟩

**hab·i·tat** \'hab-ə-ˌtat\ *n*
the place where a plant or animal grows or lives in nature

**hab·i·ta·tion** \ˌhab-ə-'tā-shən\ *n*
1 the act of living in a place
2 a place to live

**ha·bit·u·al** \hə-'bich-ə-wəl\ *adj*
1 being or done by habit ⟨*habitual* kindness⟩
2 doing or acting by force of habit ⟨*habitual* criminals⟩
3 [1]REGULAR
**ha·bit·u·al·ly** \-wə-lē\ *adv*
**ha·bit·u·al·ness** *n*

**ha·ci·en·da** \ˌhä-sē-'en-də\ *n*
1 a large estate especially in a Spanish-speaking country
2 the main house of a hacienda

[1]**hack** \'hak\ *vb*
1 to cut with repeated chopping blows
2 to cough in a short broken way
3 to write computer programs for enjoyment
4 to gain access to a computer illegally

[2]**hack** *n*
a short broken cough

[3]**hack** *n*
1 a horse let out for hire or used for varied work
2 a person who works for pay at a routine writing job
3 a writer who is not very good

**hack·er** \'hak-ər\ *n*
1 one that hacks
2 a person who is unskilled at a particular activity
3 an expert at programming and solving problems with a computer
4 a person who illegally gains access to a computer system

**hack·les** \'hak-əlz\ *n pl*
hairs (as on the neck of a dog) that can be made to stand up

**hack·ney** \'hak-nē\ *n, pl* **hack·neys**
a horse for ordinary riding or driving

**hacksaw**

**hack·saw** \'hak-ˌsȯ\ *n*
▲ a saw used for cutting hard materials (as metal) that consists of a frame and a blade with small teeth

**had** *past of* HAVE

**haddock**

**had·dock** \'had-ək\ *n, pl* **haddock** *or* **haddocks**
▲ a food fish related to but smaller than the cod

**hadn't** \'had-nt\
had not

**haf·ni·um** \'haf-nē-əm\ *n*
a gray metallic chemical element

**hag** \'hag\ *n*
**1** WITCH 1
**2** an ugly old woman

**hag·gard** \'hag-ərd\ *adj*
having a hungry, tired, or worried look

**hag·gle** \'hag-əl\ *vb*
**hag·gled**; **hag·gling**
to argue especially over a price
**hag·gler** \'hag-lər\ *n*

**ha–ha** \hä-'hä\ *interj*
used to show amusement or scorn

**hai·ku** \'hī-,kü\ *n, pl* **haiku**
**1** a Japanese verse form without rhyme having three lines with the first and last lines having five syllables and the middle having seven
**2** a poem written in this form

**¹hail** \'hāl\ *n*
**1** small lumps of ice and snow that fall from the clouds sometimes during thunderstorms
**2** ¹VOLLEY 1 ⟨a *hail* of bullets⟩

**²hail** *vb*
**1** to fall as hail
**2** to pour down like hail

**³hail** *interj*
used to show enthusiastic approval

**⁴hail** *vb*
**1** GREET 1, WELCOME
**2** to call out to ⟨*hail* a taxi⟩
**hail from** to come from ⟨*hails from* Oklahoma⟩

**⁵hail** *n*
an exclamation of greeting, approval, or praise

**hail·stone** \'hāl-,stōn\ *n*
a lump of hail

**hail·storm** \'hāl-,stȯrm\ *n*
a storm that brings hail

**hair** \'haər, 'heər\ *n*
**1** a threadlike growth from the skin of a person or lower animal
**2** a covering or growth of hairs (as on one's head)
**3** something (as a growth on a leaf) like an animal hair
**haired** \'haərd, 'heərd\ *adj*
**hair·less** \'haər-ləs, 'heər-\ *adj*
**hair·like** \-,līk\ *adj*

**hair·brush** \'haər-,brəsh, 'heər-\ *n*
a brush for the hair

**hair·cut** \'haər-,kət, 'heər-\ *n*
the act, process, or result of cutting the hair

*braided hair*

**hairdo**

**hair·do** \'haər-,dü, 'heər-\ *n, pl* **hairdos**
▲ a way of arranging a person's hair

**hair·dress·er** \'haər-,dres-ər, 'heər-\ *n*
one who dresses or cuts hair
**hair·dress·ing** *n*

**hair·pin** \'haər-,pin, 'heər-\ *n*
a pin in the shape of a U for holding the hair in place

**hair–rais·ing** \'haər-,rā-zing, 'heər-\ *adj*
causing terror, excitement, or great surprise

**hair·style** \'haər-,stīl, 'heər-\ *n*
HAIRDO

**hairy** \'haər-ē, 'heər-ē\ *adj*
**hair·i·er**; **hair·i·est**
covered with hair
**hair·i·ness** *n*

**¹hale** \'hāl\ *adj*
being strong and healthy

**²hale** *vb* **haled**; **hal·ing**
to force to go ⟨*haled* them into court⟩

**¹half** \'haf, 'hȧf\ *n, pl* **halves** \'havz, 'hȧvz\
**1** one of two equal parts into which something can be divided
**2** a part of something that is about equal to the remainder ⟨*half* the distance⟩
**3** one of a pair

**²half** *adj*
**1** being one of two equal parts ⟨a *half* liter of oil⟩
**2** amounting to about a half : PARTIAL ⟨a *half* success⟩

**³half** *adv*
**1** to the extent of half ⟨*half* full⟩
**2** not completely ⟨*half* persuaded⟩

**half brother** *n*
a brother by one parent only

**half·heart·ed** \'haf-'härt-əd, 'hȧf-\ *adj*
lacking spirit or interest
**half·heart·ed·ly** *adv*
**half·heart·ed·ness** *n*

**half–knot** \'haf-,nät, 'hȧf-\ *n*
a knot in which two rope ends are wrapped once around each other and which is used to start other knots

**half–life** \'haf-,līf, 'hȧf-\ *n, pl* **half–lives** \-,līvz\
the time required for half of the atoms of a radioactive substance to change composition

**half sister** *n*
a sister by one parent only

**¹half·way** \'haf-'wā, 'hȧf-\ *adv*
at or to half the distance ⟨open the door *halfway*⟩

**²halfway** *adj*
**1** midway between two points
**2** PARTIAL 3 ⟨*halfway* measures⟩

**half–wit** \'haf-,wit, 'hȧf-\ *n*
a very stupid person
**half–wit·ted** \-'wit-əd\ *adj*

**hal·i·but** \'hal-ə-bət\ *n, pl* **halibut** *or* **halibuts**
a very large flatfish much used for food

**hall** \'hȯl\ *n*
**1** a large building used for public purposes ⟨city *hall*⟩
**2** a building (as of a college) set apart for a special purpose ⟨Science *Hall*⟩
**3** an entrance room
**4** CORRIDOR
**5** AUDITORIUM

**hal·le·lu·jah** \,hal-ə-'lü-yə\ *interj*
used to express praise, joy, or thanks

**hal·low** \'hal-ō\ *vb*
to set apart for holy purposes : treat as sacred

a b c d e f g **h** i j k l m n o p q r s t u v w x y z

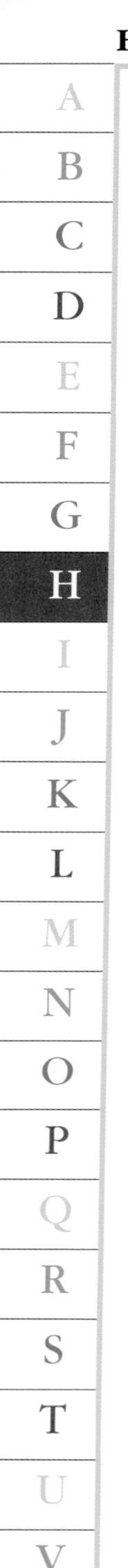


## Halloween

The festival of Halloween is based on the old belief that ghosts and witches haunt the earth on the last night of October. Today, Halloween is often celebrated by dressing up in scary or fantastic costumes and masks. Children visit their neighbors' homes to play trick or treat, and jack-o'-lanterns are placed in windows, traditionally to keep away evil spirits.

*monster*

*fairy princess*

*witch*

*cowboy*

*jack-o'-lantern*

**children wearing Halloween costumes**

**Hal·low·een** \\,hal-ə-'wēn, ,häl-\\ *n*
▲ October 31 observed with parties and with the playing of tricks by children during the evening

**Word History** The first of November is All Saints' Day in the Christian calendar. It is celebrated in honor of all the saints in heaven. An old name for this day was *All Hallow Day*. (*Hallow* was an old word that meant "saint.") The day before *All Hallow Day* was called *All Hallow Eve* or *All Hallow Even*. (*Even* was an old word for "evening.") This name has been contracted to *Halloween*.

**hal·lu·ci·na·tion** \\hə-,lüs-n-'ā-shən\\ *n*
the seeing of objects or the experiencing of feelings that are not real but are usually the result of mental disorder or the effect of a drug

**hal·lu·ci·no·gen** \\hə-'lüs-n-ə-jən\\ *n*
a drug that causes hallucinations
**hal·lu·ci·no·gen·ic** \\hə-,lüs-n-ə-'jen-ik\\ *adj*

**hall·way** \\'hȯl-,wā\\ *n*
CORRIDOR

**ha·lo** \\'hā-lō\\ *n, pl* **halos** *or* **haloes**
**1** a circle of light around the sun or moon caused by tiny ice crystals in the air
**2** ► a circle drawn or painted around the head of a person in a picture as a symbol of holiness

**[1]halt** \\'hȯlt\\ *vb*
HESITATE 1

**[2]halt** *n*
[1]END 2 ⟨call a *halt*⟩

**[3]halt** *vb*
**1** to stop or cause to stop marching or traveling
**2** [2]END ⟨*halt* work⟩

**halo 2:** a 14th-century painting from Florence, Italy

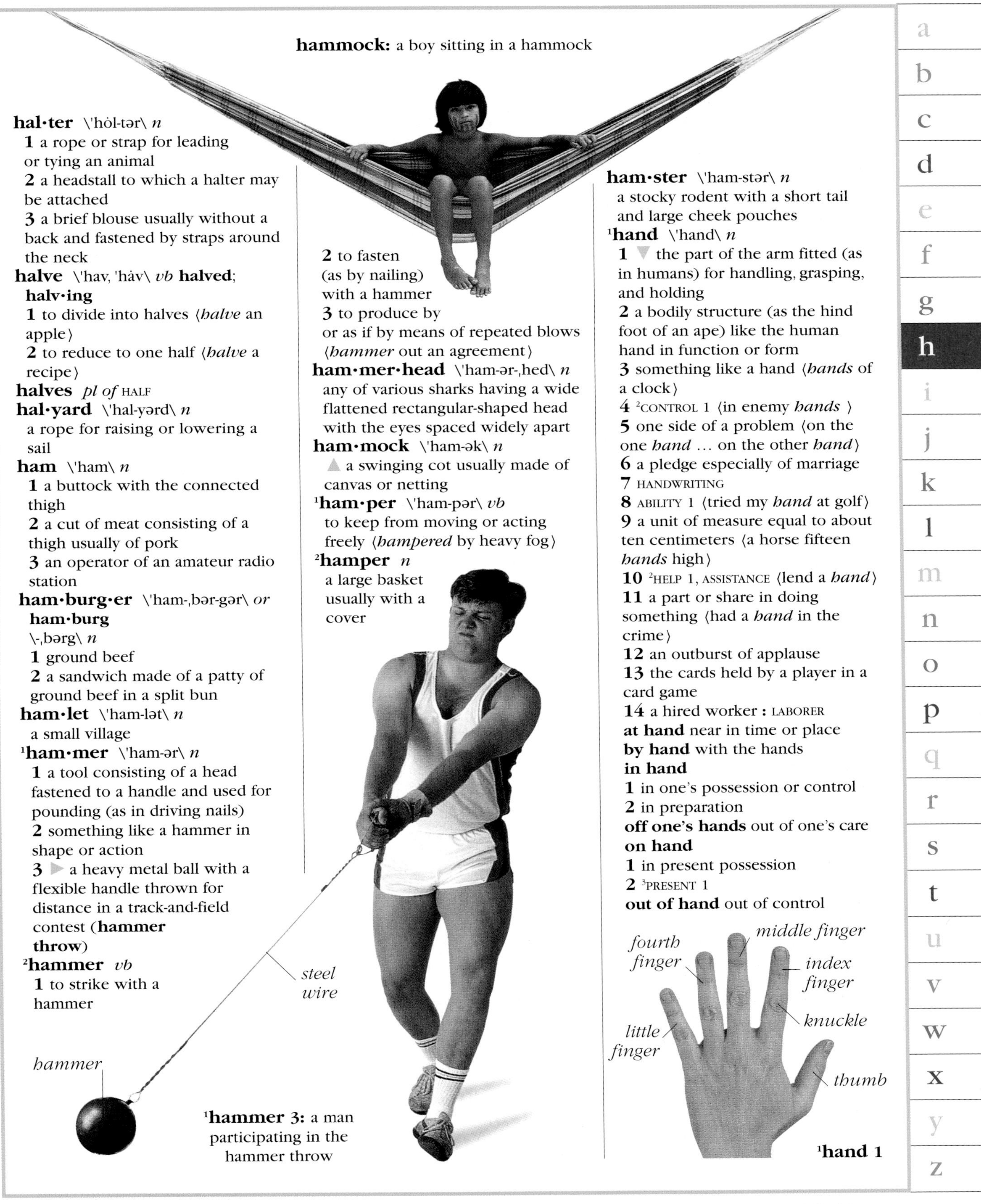


hammock: a boy sitting in a hammock

**hal·ter** \'hȯl-tər\ *n*
**1** a rope or strap for leading or tying an animal
**2** a headstall to which a halter may be attached
**3** a brief blouse usually without a back and fastened by straps around the neck

**halve** \'hav, 'hȧv\ *vb* **halved**; **halv·ing**
**1** to divide into halves ⟨*halve* an apple⟩
**2** to reduce to one half ⟨*halve* a recipe⟩

**halves** *pl of* HALF

**hal·yard** \'hal-yərd\ *n*
a rope for raising or lowering a sail

**ham** \'ham\ *n*
**1** a buttock with the connected thigh
**2** a cut of meat consisting of a thigh usually of pork
**3** an operator of an amateur radio station

**ham·burg·er** \'ham-,bər-gər\ *or* **ham·burg** \-,bərg\ *n*
**1** ground beef
**2** a sandwich made of a patty of ground beef in a split bun

**ham·let** \'ham-lət\ *n*
a small village

**¹ham·mer** \'ham-ər\ *n*
**1** a tool consisting of a head fastened to a handle and used for pounding (as in driving nails)
**2** something like a hammer in shape or action
**3** ▶ a heavy metal ball with a flexible handle thrown for distance in a track-and-field contest (**hammer throw**)

**²hammer** *vb*
**1** to strike with a hammer
**2** to fasten (as by nailing) with a hammer
**3** to produce by or as if by means of repeated blows ⟨*hammer* out an agreement⟩

**ham·mer·head** \'ham-ər-,hed\ *n*
any of various sharks having a wide flattened rectangular-shaped head with the eyes spaced widely apart

**ham·mock** \'ham-ək\ *n*
▲ a swinging cot usually made of canvas or netting

**¹ham·per** \'ham-pər\ *vb*
to keep from moving or acting freely ⟨*hampered* by heavy fog⟩

**²hamper** *n*
a large basket usually with a cover

**¹hammer 3:** a man participating in the hammer throw

**ham·ster** \'ham-stər\ *n*
a stocky rodent with a short tail and large cheek pouches

**¹hand** \'hand\ *n*
**1** ▼ the part of the arm fitted (as in humans) for handling, grasping, and holding
**2** a bodily structure (as the hind foot of an ape) like the human hand in function or form
**3** something like a hand ⟨*hands* of a clock⟩
**4** ²CONTROL 1 ⟨in enemy *hands* ⟩
**5** one side of a problem ⟨on the one *hand* … on the other *hand*⟩
**6** a pledge especially of marriage
**7** HANDWRITING
**8** ABILITY 1 ⟨tried my *hand* at golf⟩
**9** a unit of measure equal to about ten centimeters ⟨a horse fifteen *hands* high⟩
**10** ²HELP 1, ASSISTANCE ⟨lend a *hand*⟩
**11** a part or share in doing something ⟨had a *hand* in the crime⟩
**12** an outburst of applause
**13** the cards held by a player in a card game
**14** a hired worker **:** LABORER

**at hand** near in time or place
**by hand** with the hands
**in hand**
**1** in one's possession or control
**2** in preparation
**off one's hands** out of one's care
**on hand**
**1** in present possession
**2** ³PRESENT 1
**out of hand** out of control

**¹hand 1**

A B C D E F G H I J K L M N O P Q R S T U V W X Y Z

²**hand** *vb*
to give or pass with the hand

**hand·bag** \'hand-,bag\ *n*
a bag used for carrying money and small personal articles

**hand·ball** \'hand-,bȯl\ *n*
a game played by hitting a small rubber ball against a wall or board with the hand

**hand·bill** \'hand-,bil\ *n*
a printed sheet (as of advertising) distributed by hand

**hand·book** \'hand-,bu̇k\ *n*
a book of facts usually about one subject

**hand·car** \'hand-,kär\ *n*
a small railroad car that is made to move by hand or by a small motor

**hand·cart** \'hand-,kärt\ *n*
a cart drawn or pushed by hand

¹**hand·cuff** \'hand-,kəf\ *n*
a metal fastening that can be locked around a person's wrist

²**handcuff** *vb*
to put handcuffs on

**hand·ed** \'han-dəd\ *adj*
having or using such or so many hands ⟨a right-*handed* child⟩

**hand·ful** \'hand-,fu̇l\ *n, pl* **handfuls** \-,fu̇lz\ *or* **hands·ful** \'handz-,fu̇l\
1 as much or as many as the hand will grasp
2 a small amount or number

¹**hand·i·cap** \'han-di-,kap\ *n*
1 a contest in which one more skilled is given a disadvantage and one less skilled is given an advantage
2 the disadvantage or advantage given in a contest
3 a disadvantage that makes progress or success difficult

²**handicap** *vb* **hand·i·capped**; **hand·i·cap·ping**
1 to give a handicap to
2 to put at a disadvantage

**hand·i·craft** \'han-di-,kraft\ *n*
1 an occupation (as weaving or pottery making) that requires skill with the hands
2 articles made by one working at handicraft

**hand·i·ly** \'han-də-lē\ *adv*
in a handy manner : EASILY ⟨won *handily*⟩

**hand·i·work** \'han-di-,wərk\ *n*
work done by the hands

**hand·ker·chief** \'hang-kər-chif\ *n, pl* **hand·ker·chiefs** \-chifs, -,chēvz\
a small usually square piece of cloth used for wiping the face, nose, or eyes

¹**han·dle** \'han-dəl\ *n*
the part by which something (as a dish or tool) is picked up or held
**han·dled** \-dəld\ *adj*

²**handle** *vb* **han·dled**; **han·dling**
1 to touch, feel, hold, or move with the hand
2 to manage with the hands
3 to deal with (as in writing or speaking)
4 MANAGE 1, DIRECT
5 to deal with or act on
6 to deal or trade in
**han·dler** \-dlər\ *n*

**han·dle·bars** \'han-dəl-,bärz\ *n pl*
◀ a bar (as on a bicycle) that has a handle at each end and is used for steering

**hand·made** \'hand-'mād\ *adj*
made by hand rather than by machine

**hand–me–downs** \'hand-mē-,dau̇nz\ *n pl*
used clothes

**hand organ** *n*
a small musical instrument cranked by hand

**hand·out** \'han-,dau̇t\ *n*
something (as food) given to a beggar

**hand·rail** \'han-,drāl\ *n*
a rail to be grasped by the hand for support

**hands down** \'handz-'dau̇n\ *adv*
without question : EASILY ⟨won the race *hands down*⟩

**hand·shake** \'hand-,shāk\ *n*
a clasping of hands by two people (as in greeting)

**hand·some** \'han-səm\ *adj* **hand·som·er**; **hand·som·est**
1 CONSIDERABLE ⟨a *handsome* sum⟩
2 more than enough ⟨a *handsome* tip⟩
3 having a pleasing and impressive appearance **synonyms** see BEAUTIFUL

**hand·spring** \'hand-,spring\ *n*
▼ a feat of tumbling in which the body turns forward or backward in a full circle from a standing position and lands first on the hands and then on the feet

**hand·stand** \'hand-,stand\ *n*
a stunt in which a person balances the body in the air upside down supported on the hands

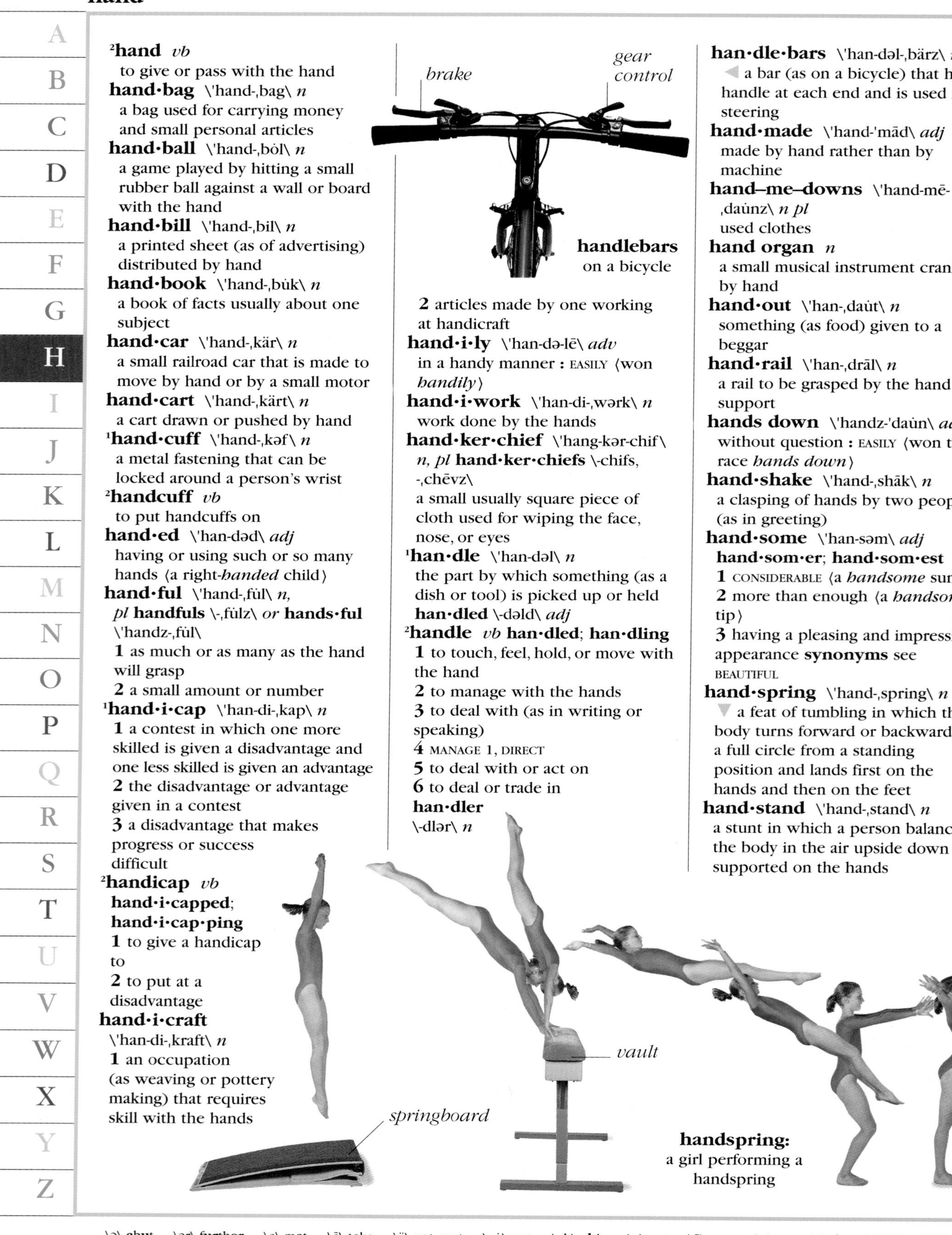


**handlebars** on a bicycle

**handspring:** a girl performing a handspring

**hand–to–hand** \ˌhan-tə-ˈhand\ *adj*
involving bodily contact ⟨*hand-to-hand* combat⟩
**hand•work** \ˈhan-ˌdwərk\ *n*
work done by hand and not by machine
**hand•writ•ing** \ˈhan-ˌdrīt-ing\ *n*
writing done by hand
**handy** \ˈhan-dē\ *adj* **hand•i•er**; **hand•i•est**
**1** within easy reach
**2** easy to use or manage
**3** VERSATILE 2
**4** DEXTEROUS 1 ⟨*handy* at small jobs⟩
[1]**hang** \ˈhang\ *vb* **hung** \ˈhəng\ *also* **hanged**; **hang•ing**
**1** to fasten or be fastened to something without support from below **:** SUSPEND ⟨*hang* curtains⟩
**2** to kill or be killed by suspending (as from a gallows) by a rope tied around the neck
**3** to fasten so as to allow free motion forward and backward ⟨*hang* a door⟩
**4** to cause to droop ⟨*hang* one's head⟩
**hang on to** to hold or keep with determination
[2]**hang** *n*
**1** the way in which a thing hangs
**2** MEANING 1
**3** KNACK 1 ⟨soon got the *hang* of it⟩
**han•gar** \ˈhang-ər\ *n*
a shelter for housing and repairing aircraft
**hang•er** \ˈhang-ər\ *n*
▼ a device on which something hangs

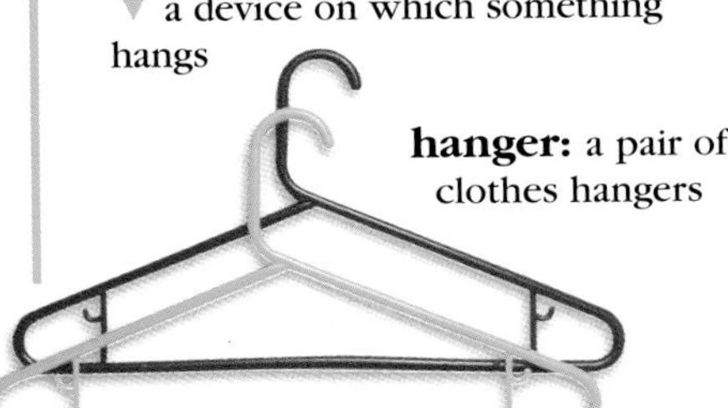

**hanger:** a pair of clothes hangers

**hang•man** \ˈhang-mən\ *n, pl* **hang•men** \-mən\
one who hangs criminals
**hang•nail** \ˈhang-ˌnāl\ *n*
a bit of skin hanging loose about a fingernail
**hang•out** \ˈhang-ˌaùt\ *n*
a place where a person spends much idle time or goes often
**hang•over** \ˈhang-ˌō-vər\ *n*
**1** something (as a surviving custom) that remains from what is past
**2** a sick uncomfortable state that comes from drinking too much liquor
**han•ker** \ˈhang-kər\ *vb*
to have a great desire ⟨*hankering* for candy⟩
**han•som** \ˈhan-səm\ *n*
a light covered carriage that has two wheels and a driver's seat elevated at the rear
**Ha•nuk•kah** \ˈhän-ə-kə\ *n*
a Jewish holiday lasting eight days and celebrating the cleansing and second dedication of the Temple after the Syrians were driven out of Jerusalem in 165 B.C.
**hap•haz•ard** \hap-ˈhaz-ərd\ *adj*
marked by lack of plan, order, or direction
**hap•haz•ard•ly** *adv*
**hap•haz•ard•ness** *n*
**hap•less** \ˈhap-ləs\ *adj*
[1]UNFORTUNATE 1
**hap•pen** \ˈhap-ən\ *vb*
**1** to occur or come about by chance
**2** to take place
**3** to have opportunity **:** CHANCE ⟨I *happened* to overhear this⟩
**4** to come especially by way of injury or harm ⟨nothing will *happen* to you⟩
**hap•pen•ing** \ˈhap-ə-ning, ˈhap-ning\ *n*
something that happens
**hap•py** \ˈhap-ē\ *adj* **hap•pi•er**; **hap•pi•est**
**1** FORTUNATE 1, LUCKY
**2** being suitable for something ⟨a *happy* choice⟩
**3** enjoying one's condition **:** CONTENT
**4** JOYFUL
**5** feeling or showing pleasure **:** GLAD
**hap•pi•ly** \ˈhap-ə-lē\ *adv*
**hap•pi•ness** \ˈhap-ē-nəs\ *n*
**hap•py–go–lucky** \ˌhap-ē-gō-ˈlək-ē\ *adj*
free from care
**ha•rangue** \hə-ˈrang\ *n*
a scolding speech or writing
**ha•rass** \hə-ˈras, ˈhar-əs\ *vb*
**1** to worry and hinder by repeated attacks
**2** to annoy again and again
**ha•rass•ment** \-mənt\ *n*

**Word History** The English word *harass* came from a French word. This French word came from an earlier French word that meant "to set a dog on." The earlier word was formed from a cry used long ago by French hunters to urge their dogs to chase game.

[1]**har•bor** \ˈhär-bər\ *n*
**1** a place of safety and comfort **:** REFUGE
**2** ▼ a part of a body of water (as a sea or lake) so protected as to be a place of safety for ships **:** PORT

[1]**harbor 2:** a harbor in New York City

A B C D E F G H I J K L M N O P Q R S T U V W X Y Z

[2]**harbor** *vb*
**1** to give shelter to
**2** to have or hold in the mind ⟨*harbor* a belief⟩

[1]**hard** \'härd\ *adj*
**1** not easily cut, pierced, or divided : not soft
**2** high in alcoholic content
**3** containing substances that prevent lathering with soap
**4** difficult to put up with : SEVERE ⟨*hard* words⟩ ⟨a *hard* winter⟩
**5** UNFEELING 2
**6** carried on with steady and earnest effort ⟨hours of *hard* study⟩
**7** DILIGENT, ENERGETIC ⟨a *hard* worker⟩
**8** sounding as in *cold* and *geese* — used of *c* and *g*
**9** difficult to do or to understand ⟨a *hard* job⟩ ⟨a *hard* book⟩

**Synonyms** HARD, FIRM, and SOLID mean having a structure that can stand up against pressure. HARD is used of something that does not easily bend, stretch, or dent ⟨steel is *hard*⟩. FIRM is used of something that is flexible but also tough or compact ⟨*firm* muscles⟩. SOLID is used of something that has a fixed structure and is heavy and compact all the way through ⟨a *solid* wall of bricks⟩.

[2]**hard** *adv*
**1** with great effort or energy
**2** in a violent way ⟨the wind blew *hard*⟩
**3** with pain, bitterness, or resentment ⟨took the defeat *hard*⟩

**hard copy** *n*
a copy of information (as from computer storage) produced on paper in normal size ⟨a *hard copy* of an e-mail message⟩

**hard disk** *n*
**1** a rigid metal disk used to store computer data
**2** HARD DRIVE

**hard drive** *n*
a computer-data storage device containing one or more hard disks

**hard·en** \'härd-n\ *vb*
**1** to make or become hard or harder
**2** to make or become hardy or strong
**3** to make or become stubborn or unfeeling ⟨*harden* your heart⟩
**hard·en·er** *n*

**hard·head·ed** \'härd-'hed-əd\ *adj*
**1** STUBBORN 1
**2** using or showing good judgment
**hard·head·ed·ly** *adv*
**hard·head·ed·ness** *n*

**hard·heart·ed** \'härd-'härt-əd\ *adj*
showing or feeling no pity : UNFEELING
**hard·heart·ed·ly** *adv*
**hard·heart·ed·ness** *n*

**hard·ly** \'härd-lē\ *adv*
only just : BARELY

**hard·ness** \'härd-nəs\ *n*
the quality or state of being hard

**hard palate** *n*
the bony front part of the roof of the mouth

**hard·ship** \'härd-,ship\ *n*
something (as a loss or injury) that is hard to put up with

**hard·tack** \'härd-,tak\ *n*
a hard biscuit made of flour and water without salt

**hard·ware** \'här-,dwaər, -,dweər\ *n*
**1** things (as tools, cutlery, or parts of machines) made of metal
**2** items of equipment or their parts used for a particular purpose ⟨computer *hardware* such as monitors and keyboards⟩

[1]**hard·wood** \'här-,dwu̇d\ *n*
the usually hard wood of a tree belonging to the group bearing broad leaves as distinguished from the wood of a tree (as a pine) with leaves that are needles

[2]**hardwood** *adj*
having or made of hardwood ⟨*hardwood* trees⟩ ⟨*hardwood* floors⟩

**har·dy** \'härd-ē\ *adj* **har·di·er**; **har·di·est**
**1** BOLD 1, BRAVE
**2** able to stand weariness, hardship, or severe weather
**har·di·ness** \'härd-ē-nəs\ *n*

**hare** \'haər, 'heər\ *n*
▶ a timid animal like the related rabbit but having young that are born with the eyes open and a furry coat

**hare:** a European brown hare

**hare·brained** \'haər-'brānd, 'heər-\ *adj*
FOOLISH

**hark** \'härk\ *vb*
LISTEN

[1]**harm** \'härm\ *n*
**1** physical or mental damage : INJURY ⟨the storm did little *harm* to the sheltered beach⟩
**2** MISCHIEF 1 ⟨meant no *harm*⟩

**Synonyms** HARM, INJURY, and DAMAGE mean an act that causes loss or pain. HARM can be used of anything that causes suffering or loss⟨the frost did great *harm* to the crops⟩ ⟨received no *harm* in the fight⟩. INJURY is likely to be used of something that has as a result the loss of health or success ⟨an *injury* to the eyes⟩. DAMAGE stresses the idea of loss (as of value or fitness) ⟨the fire caused much *damage* to the furniture⟩.

[2]**harm** *vb*
to cause harm to : HURT

**harm·ful** \'härm-fəl\ *adj*
causing harm : INJURIOUS
**harm·ful·ly** \-fə-lē\ *adv*
**harm·ful·ness** *n*

**harm·less** \'härm-ləs\ *adj*
not harmful
**harm·less·ly** *adv*
**harm·less·ness** *n*

**har·mon·ic** \här-'män-ik\ *adj*
of or relating to musical harmony rather than melody or rhythm
**har·mon·i·cal·ly** \-i-kə-lē\ *adv*

**har·mon·i·ca** \här-'män-i-kə\ *n*
a small musical instrument held in the hand and played by the mouth : MOUTH ORGAN

**har·mo·ni·ous** \här-'mō-nē-əs\ *adj*
**1** having a pleasant sound : MELODIOUS
**2** combining so as to produce a pleasing result ⟨*harmonious* colors⟩
**3** showing harmony in action or feeling
**har·mo·ni·ous·ly** *adv*
**har·mo·ni·ous·ness** *n*

**1harness:** a horse in harness pulling a sulky in a trotting race

**har·mo·nize** \'här-mə-ˌnīz\ *vb* **har·mo·nized; har·mo·niz·ing**
1 to play or sing in harmony
2 to be in harmony
**har·mo·niz·er** *n*

**har·mo·ny** \'här-mə-nē\ *n, pl* **har·mo·nies**
1 the playing of musical tones together in chords
2 a pleasing arrangement of parts
3 AGREEMENT 1, ACCORD

**1har·ness** \'här-nəs\ *n*
▶ an arrangement of straps and fastenings placed on an animal so as to control it or prepare it to pull a load

**2harness** *vb*
1 to put a harness on
2 to put to work : UTILIZE ⟨*harness* a waterfall⟩

**1harp** \'härp\ *n*
▼ a musical instrument consisting of a triangular frame set with strings that are plucked by the fingers

**1harp:** a 19th-century Irish harp

**2harp** *vb*
to call attention to something over and over again

**1har·poon** \här-'pün\ *n*
▼ a barbed spear used especially for hunting whales and large fish

**2harpoon** *vb*
to strike with a harpoon

**harp·si·chord** \'härp-si-ˌkȯrd\ *n*
a keyboard instrument similar to a piano with strings that are plucked

**1har·row** \'har-ō\ *n*
a heavy frame set with metal teeth or disks used in farming for breaking up and smoothing soil

**2harrow** *vb*
1 to drag a harrow over (plowed ground)
2 2DISTRESS

**har·ry** \'har-ē\ *vb* **har·ried; har·ry·ing**
HARASS

**harsh** \'härsh\ *adj*
1 having a coarse surface : rough to the touch
2 disagreeable to any of the senses ⟨a *harsh* taste⟩
3 causing physical discomfort ⟨a *harsh* wind⟩
4 SEVERE 1 ⟨*harsh* punishment⟩
**harsh·ly** *adv*
**harsh·ness** *n*

---

**Synonyms** HARSH, ROUGH, and RUGGED mean not smooth or even. HARSH suggests that something has a surface or texture that is unpleasant to the touch ⟨used a *harsh* sandpaper on the floor⟩. ROUGH suggests a surface with points or ridges ⟨a *rough* piece of wood⟩. RUGGED is used of a surface on land that is very uneven ⟨a *rugged* road up the mountain⟩.

---

**1harpoon:** a harpoon from a modern whaling ship

**1har·vest** \'här-vəst\ *n*
1 the season when crops are gathered
2 the gathering of a crop
3 a ripe crop (as of grain)

**2harvest** *vb*
to gather in a crop

**har·vest·er** \'här-və-stər\ *n*
1 one that gathers by or as if by harvesting
2 a machine for harvesting field crops

**has** *present 3d sing of* HAVE

**1hash** \'hash\ *vb*
to chop into small pieces

**2hash** *n*
1 cooked meat and vegetables chopped together and browned
2 2JUMBLE

**hash·ish** \'hash-ˌēsh\ *n*
a drug from the hemp plant that causes hallucinations

**hash over** *vb*
to talk about : DISCUSS

**hasn't** \'haz-nt\
has not

**hasp** \'hasp\ *n*
a fastener (as for a door) consisting of a hinged metal strap that fits over a staple and is held by a pin or padlock

**has·sle** \'has-əl\ *n*
1 a loud angry argument
2 a brief fight
3 something that annoys or bothers

**has·sock** \'has-ək\ *n*
a firm stuffed cushion used as a seat or leg rest

a b c d e f g h i j k l m n o p q r s t u v w x y z

A B C D E F G H I J K L M N O P Q R S T U V W X Y Z

**haste** \'hāst\ *n*
**1** quickness of motion or action : SPEED
**2** hasty action ⟨*haste* makes waste⟩

**has·ten** \'hās-n\ *vb*
to move or act fast : HURRY

**hasty** \'hā-stē\ *adj* **hast·i·er**; **hast·i·est**
**1** done or made in a hurry ⟨a *hasty* trip⟩
**2** made, done, or decided without proper care and thought ⟨a *hasty* decision⟩
**hast·i·ly** \-stə-lē\ *adv*

**hat** \'hat\ *n*
▼ a covering for the head having a crown and usually a brim

**hat:** a woman wearing a hat

**¹hatch** \'hach\ *n*
**1** an opening in the deck of a ship or in the floor or roof of a building
**2** a small door or opening (as in an airplane) ⟨escape *hatch*⟩
**3** the cover for a hatch

**²hatch** *vb*
**1** to produce from eggs
**2** to come forth from an egg
**3** to develop usually in secret ⟨*hatch* a plan⟩

**hatch·ery** \'hach-ə-rē\ *n, pl* **hatch·er·ies**
a place for hatching eggs ⟨a chick *hatchery*⟩

**hatch·et** \'hach-ət\ *n*
a small ax with a short handle

**hatch·way** \'hach-ˌwā\ *n*
a hatch usually having a ladder or stairs

**¹hate** \'hāt\ *n*
deep and bitter dislike

**²hate** *vb* **hat·ed**; **hat·ing**
to feel great dislike toward

**hate·ful** \'hāt-fəl\ *adj*
**1** full of hate
**2** causing or deserving hate ⟨a *hateful* crime⟩
**hate·ful·ly** \-fə-lē\ *adv*
**hate·ful·ness** *n*

**ha·tred** \'hā-trəd\ *n*
¹HATE

**hat·ter** \'hat-ər\ *n*
a person who makes, sells, or cleans and repairs hats

**haugh·ty** \'hȯt-ē\ *adj* **haugh·ti·er**; **haugh·ti·est**
acting as if other people are not as good as oneself
**haugh·ti·ly** \'hȯt-l-ē\ *adv*
**haugh·ti·ness** \'hȯt-ē-nəs\ *n*

**¹haul** \'hȯl\ *vb*
**1** to pull or drag with effort
**2** to transport in a vehicle

**²haul** *n*
**1** the act of hauling
**2** an amount collected ⟨a burglar's *haul*⟩
**3** the distance or route over which a load is moved ⟨a long *haul*⟩

**haunch** \'hȯnch\ *n*
**1** HIP
**2** HINDQUARTER

**¹haunt** \'hȯnt\ *vb*
**1** to visit often
**2** to come to mind frequently ⟨the song *haunts* me⟩
**3** to visit or live in as a ghost

**²haunt** *n*
a place often visited

**have** \hav, həv, əv, *in sense 3 before "to" usually* 'haf\ *vb, past & past participle* **had** \had, həd, əd\; *present participle* **hav·ing** \'hav-ing\; *present 3d sing* **has** \has, həz, əz\
**1** to hold for one's use or as property ⟨*have* the tickets⟩
**2** to consist of ⟨April *has* 30 days⟩
**3** to be forced or feel obliged ⟨*have* to stay⟩
**4** to stand in some relationship to ⟨a bad person to *have* as an enemy⟩
**5** OBTAIN, GAIN, GET ⟨the best car to be *had*⟩
**6** to possess as a characteristic ⟨*has* red hair⟩
**7** ²EXERCISE 1 ⟨*have* mercy⟩
**8** to be affected by ⟨*have* a cold⟩
**9** to be in : CARRY ON ⟨*had* a fight⟩
**10** to hold in the mind ⟨*have* doubts⟩
**11** to cause to be ⟨*have* your hair cut⟩
**12** to cause to ⟨I'll *have* them call you⟩
**13** ¹PERMIT 1 ⟨we'll *have* none of that⟩
**14** ²TRICK ⟨we've been *had*⟩
**15** to give birth to ⟨*had* twins⟩
**16** to partake of ⟨*have* dinner⟩
**17** used as a helping verb with the past participle of another verb ⟨*has* gone home⟩

**ha·ven** \'hā-vən\ *n*
a safe place

**haven't** \'hav-ənt\
have not

**hav·er·sack** \'hav-ər-ˌsak\ *n*
▼ a bag worn over one shoulder for carrying supplies

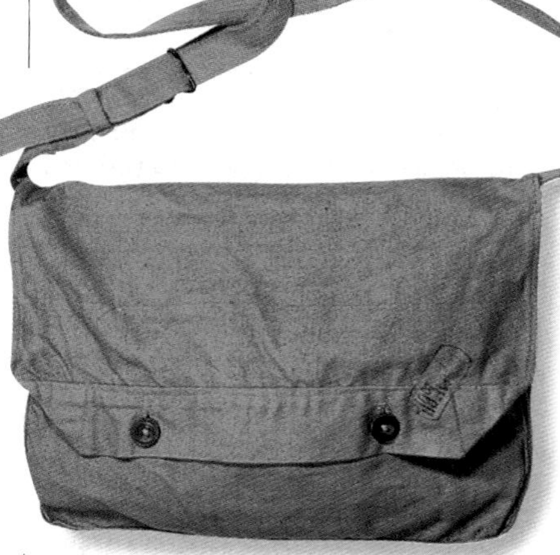

**haversack**

**Word History** The English word *haversack* came from a French word. This French word came in turn from a German word that meant "a bag for oats." This German word was a compound of a word that meant "oats" and another that meant "bag, sack."

**hav·oc** \'hav-ək\ *n*
**1** wide destruction
**2** great confusion and lack of order

**Ha·wai·ian** \hə-'wä-yən\ *n*
**1** a person born or living in Hawaii
**2** the language of the Hawaiians

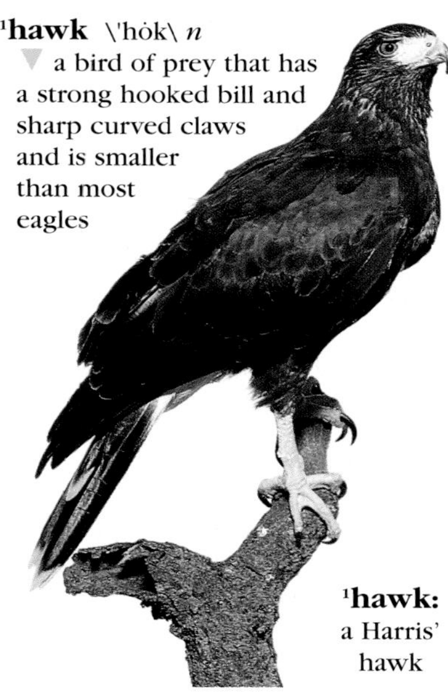

**[1]hawk** \'hȯk\ *n*
▼ a bird of prey that has a strong hooked bill and sharp curved claws and is smaller than most eagles

**[1]hawk:** a Harris' hawk

**[2]hawk** *vb*
to make a harsh coughing sound in clearing the throat

**[3]hawk** *vb*
to offer for sale by calling out in the street ⟨*hawk* fruit⟩
**hawk·er** *n*

**haw·ser** \'hȯ-zər\ *n*
a large rope for towing or tying up a ship

**haw·thorn** \'hȯ-ˌthȯrn\ *n*
▼ any of several thorny shrubs or small trees with shiny leaves, white, pink, or red flowers, and small red fruits

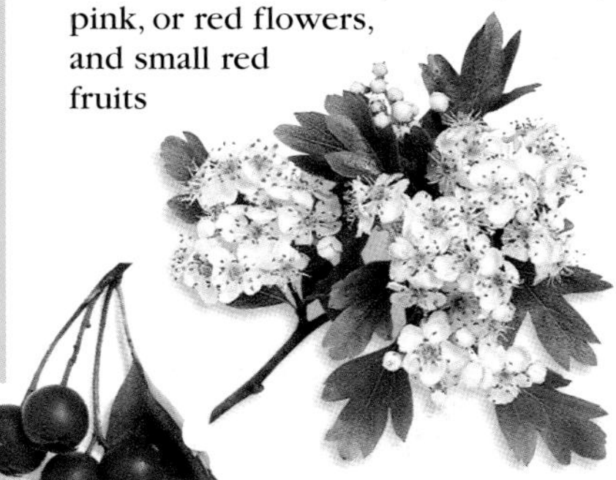

**hawthorn**

**[1]hay** \'hā\ *n*
any of various herbs (as grasses) cut and dried for use as fodder

**[2]hay** *vb*
to cut plants for hay

**hay fever** *n*
a sickness like a cold usually affecting people sensitive to plant pollen

**hay·loft** \'hā-ˌlȯft\ *n*
a loft in a barn or stable for storing hay

**hay·mow** \'hā-ˌmau̇\ *n*
HAYLOFT

**hay·stack** \'hā-ˌstak\ *n*
a large pile of hay stored outdoors

**hay·wire** \'hā-ˌwīr\ *adj*
**1** working badly or in an odd way ⟨the TV went *haywire*⟩
**2** CRAZY 1, WILD

**[1]haz·ard** \'haz-ərd\ *n*
a source of danger ⟨a fire *hazard*⟩
**synonyms** see DANGER

---

**Word History** English *hazard* was originally the name of a game of chance played with dice. The English word was taken from an early French word for this game. This French word came in turn from an Arabic word that meant "the die" (that is, "one of the dice").

---

**[2]hazard** *vb*
to risk something **:** take a chance

**haz·ard·ous** \'haz-ərd-əs\ *adj*
DANGEROUS
**haz·ard·ous·ly** *adv*
**haz·ard·ous·ness** *n*

**[1]haze** \'hāz\ *n*
fine dust, smoke, or fine particles of water in the air

**[2]haze** *vb* **hazed**; **haz·ing**
to make or become hazy or cloudy

**ha·zel** \'hā-zəl\ *n*
**1** ▶ a shrub or small tree that bears an edible nut
**2** a light brown

**ha·zel·nut** \'hā-zəl-ˌnət\ *n*
the nut of a hazel

**hazy** \'hā-zē\ *adj* **haz·i·er**; **haz·i·est**
**1** partly hidden by haze
**2** not clear in thought or meaning **:** VAGUE
**haz·i·ly** \-zə-lē\ *adv*
**haz·i·ness** \-zē-nəs\ *n*

**H–bomb** \'āch-ˌbäm\ *n*
HYDROGEN BOMB

**he** \hē, ē\ *pron*
**1** that male one
**2** a or the person **:** [3]ONE 2 ⟨*he* who hesitates is lost⟩

**[1]head** \'hed\ *n*
**1** the part of the body containing the brain, eyes, ears, nose, and mouth
**2** [1]MIND 2 ⟨a good *head* for figures⟩
**3** control of the mind or feelings ⟨kept a level *head* in time of danger⟩
**4** the side of a coin or medal usually thought of as the front
**5** each person among a number ⟨count *heads*⟩
**6** *pl* **head** a unit of number ⟨thirty *head* of cattle⟩
**7** something like a head in position or use ⟨the *head* of a bed⟩
**8** the place a stream begins
**9** a skin stretched across one or both ends of a drum
**10** DIRECTOR, LEADER
**11** a compact mass of plant parts (as leaves or flowers) ⟨a *head* of cabbage⟩
**12** a part of a machine, tool, or weapon that performs the main work ⟨*head* of a spear⟩ ⟨shower *head*⟩
**13** a place of leadership or honor ⟨*head* of one's class⟩
**14** CLIMAX, CRISIS ⟨events came to a *head*⟩
**out of one's head** DELIRIOUS 1
**over one's head** beyond one's understanding

**[2]head** *adj*
**1** [2]CHIEF 1
**2** located at the head
**3** coming from in front ⟨*head* wind⟩

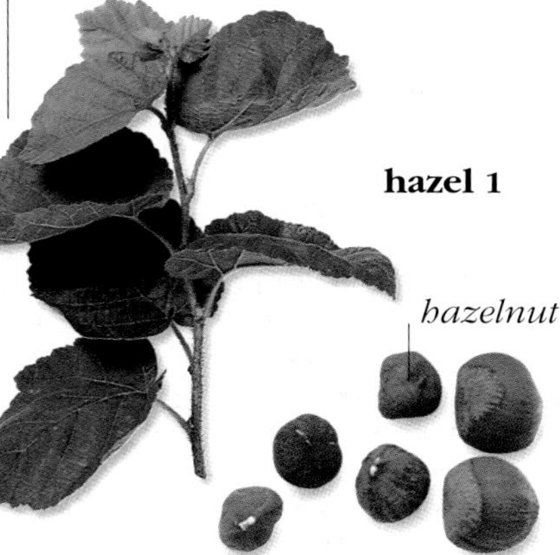


**hazel 1**

**[3]head** *vb*
**1** to provide with or form a head ⟨this cabbage *heads* early⟩
**2** to be or put oneself at the head of ⟨*head* a revolt⟩
**3** to be or get in front of ⟨*head* off the runaway⟩ ⟨*head* the list⟩
**4** to go or cause to go in a certain direction ⟨let's *head* for home⟩

**head·ache** \'hed-,āk\ *n*
**1** pain in the head
**2** something that annoys or confuses

**head·band** \'hed-,band\ *n*
a band worn on or around the head

**head·board** \'hed-,bō(ə)rd, -,bȯ(ə)rd\ *n*
a board forming the head (as of a bed)

**head·dress** \'hed-,dres\ *n*
a covering or ornament for the head

**head·ed** \'hed-əd\ *adj*
having such a head or so many heads ⟨curly-*headed*⟩ ⟨a gold-*headed* cane⟩

**head·first** \'hed-'fərst\ *adv*
with the head in front ⟨fell *headfirst* down the stairs⟩

**head·gear** \'hed-,gir\ *n*
something worn on the head

**head·ing** \'hed-ing\ *n*
something (as a title or an address) at the top or beginning (as of a letter)

**head·land** \'hed-lənd\ *n*
▶ a point of high land sticking out into the sea

**head·light** \'hed-,līt\ *n*
a light at the front of a vehicle

[1]**head·line** \'hed-,līn\ *n*
▼ a title of an article in a newspaper

CHICAGO DAILY NEWS
RED STREAK

PRESIDENT IS KILLED

Texas Sniper Escapes; Johnson Sworn In

Story Begins on Next Page

[1]**headline:** a front page headline

[2]**headline** *vb* **head·lined**; **head·lin·ing**
to provide with a headline

[1]**head·long** \'hed-'lȯng\ *adv*
**1** HEADFIRST
**2** without waiting to think things through

[2]**headlong** \'hed-,lȯng\ *adj*
**1** [1]RASH, IMPULSIVE
**2** plunging headfirst ⟨a *headlong* dive⟩

**head·mas·ter** \'hed-,mas-tər\ *n*
a man who heads the staff of a private school

**head·mis·tress** \'hed-,mis-trəs\ *n*
a woman who heads the staff of a private school

**headland**

**head–on** \'hed-'ȯn, -'än\ *adv or adj*
with the front hitting or facing an object ⟨struck the tree *head-on*⟩

**head·phone** \'hed-,fōn\ *n*
▶ an earphone held over the ear by a band worn on the head

**headphones**

**head·quar·ters** \'hed-,kwȯrt-ərz\ *n sing or pl*
a place where a leader gives out orders

**head·stall** \'hed-,stȯl\ *n*
an arrangement of straps or rope that fits around the head of an animal and forms part of a bridle or halter

**head start** *n*
an advantage given at the beginning (as to a school child or a runner)

**head·stone** \'hed-,stōn\ *n*
a stone at the head of a grave

**head·strong** \'hed-,strȯng\ *adj*
always wanting one's own way

**head·wait·er** \'hed-'wāt-ər\ *n*
the head of the staff of a restaurant or of the dining room of a hotel

**head·wa·ters** \'hed-,wȯt-ərz, -,wät-\ *n pl*
the beginning and upper part of a stream

**head·way** \'hed-,wā\ *n*
**1** movement in a forward direction (as of a ship)
**2** [1]PROGRESS 2

**heal** \'hēl\ *vb*
**1** [2]CURE 1
**2** to return to a sound or healthy condition
**heal·er** *n*

**health** \'helth\ *n*
**1** the condition of being free from illness or disease
**2** the overall condition of the body ⟨in poor *health*⟩

**health·ful** \'helth-fəl\ *adj*
good for the health
**health·ful·ly** *adv*
**health·ful·ness** *n*

**healthy** \'hel-thē\ *adj* **health·i·er**; **health·i·est**
**1** being sound and well **:** not sick
**2** showing good health
**3** aiding or building up health ⟨*healthy* exercise⟩
**health·i·ly** \-thə-lē\ *adv*
**health·i·ness** \-thē-nəs\ *n*

[1]**heap** \'hēp\ *n*
**1** things or material piled together ⟨a rubbish *heap*⟩ ⟨a *heap* of earth⟩
**2** a large number or amount ⟨*heaps* of fun⟩

[2]**heap** *vb*
**1** to throw or lay in a heap **:** make into a pile
**2** to provide in large amounts ⟨*heaped* scorn on our efforts⟩
**3** to fill to capacity ⟨*heap* a plate with food⟩

**hear** \'hir\ *vb* **heard** \'hərd\; **hear·ing** \'hir-ing\
**1** to take in through the ear **:** have the power of hearing

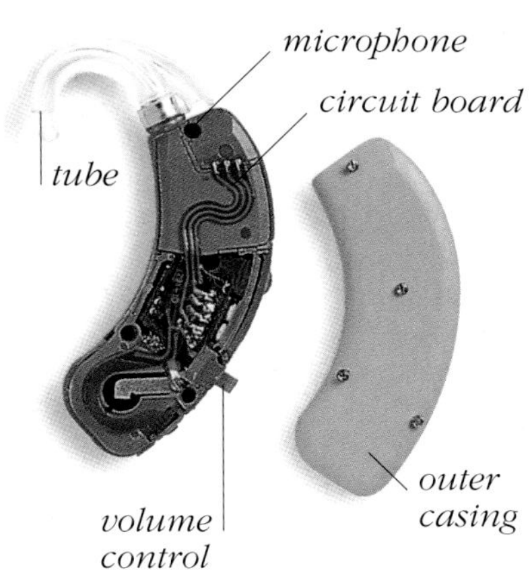


**hearing aid:** a hearing aid worn behind the ear

**2** to gain knowledge of by hearing
**3** to listen to with care and attention ⟨*hear* both sides of a story⟩
**hear·er** \'hir-ər\ *n*

**hear·ing** \'hir-ing\ *n*
**1** the act or power of taking in sound through the ear : the sense by which a person hears
**2** EARSHOT
**3** a chance to be heard or known ⟨give both sides a fair *hearing*⟩

**hearing aid** *n*
◀ an electronic device used by a partly deaf person to make sounds louder

**hear·ken** \'här-kən\ *vb*
LISTEN

**hear·say** \'hir-,sā\ *n*
something heard from another : RUMOR

**hearse** \'hərs\ *n*
a vehicle for carrying the dead to the grave

**heart** \'härt\ *n*
**1** ▼ a hollow organ of the body that expands and contracts to move blood through the arteries and veins
**2** something shaped like a heart
**3** the part nearest the center
**4** the most essential part
**5** human feelings ⟨speak from the *heart*⟩
**6** COURAGE
**by heart** so as to be able to repeat from memory ⟨learn a song *by heart*⟩

**heart·ache** \'härt-,āk\ *n*
[1]SORROW 1, 2

**heart 1**

A hollow muscle in the middle of the chest, the heart acts as a pump that beats rhythmically to send blood around the body. It is divided lengthways by a muscular wall, and each side is separated by a valve into an upper chamber and lower ventricle. Blood is squeezed through the upper chambers and ventricles when the heart muscle contracts.

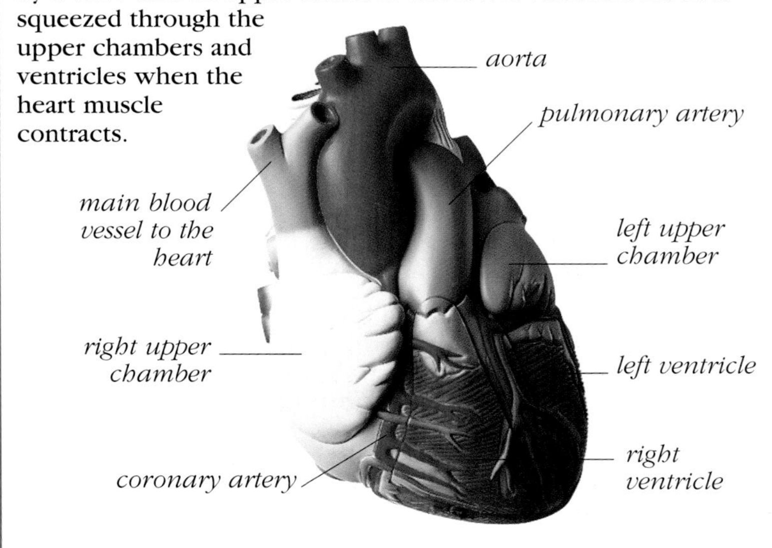


**model of the human heart**

**heart·beat** \'härt-,bēt\ *n*
a single contracting and expanding of the heart

**heart·break** \'härt-,brāk\ *n*
very great or deep grief

**heart·break·ing** \'härt-,brā-king\ *adj*
causing great sorrow

**heart·bro·ken** \'härt-,brō-kən\ *adj*
overcome by sorrow

**heart·en** \'härt-n\ *vb*
to give new hope or courage to

**heart·felt** \'härt-,felt\ *adj*
deeply felt : SINCERE

**hearth** \'härth\ *n*
**1** an area (as of brick) in front of a fireplace
**2** the floor of a fireplace
**3** [1]HOME 1

**hearth·stone** \'härth-,stōn\ *n*
a stone forming a hearth

**heart·i·ly** \'härt-l-ē\ *adv*
**1** with sincerity or enthusiasm ⟨I agree *heartily*⟩
**2** COMPLETELY ⟨I am *heartily* sick of this arguing⟩

**heart·less** \'härt-ləs\ *adj*
UNFEELING 2, CRUEL
**heart·less·ly** *adv*
**heart·less·ness** *n*

**heart·sick** \'härt-,sik\ *adj*
DESPONDENT

**heart·wood** \'härt-,wu̇d\ *n*
▼ the usually dark wood in the center of a tree

**heartwood** seen in a cross section of a tree trunk

**hearty** \'härt-ē\ *adj* **heart·i·er**; **heart·i·est**
**1** friendly and enthusiastic ⟨a *hearty* welcome⟩
**2** strong, healthy, and active
**3** having a good appetite
**4** AMPLE ⟨a *hearty* meal⟩
**heart·i·ness** *n*

[1]**heat** \'hēt\ *vb*
to make or become warm or hot

[2]**heat** *n*
**1** a condition of being hot **:** WARMTH
**2** high temperature
**3** a form of energy that causes a body to rise in temperature
**4** strength of feeling or force of action
**5** a single race in a contest that includes two or more races

**heat·ed** \'hēt-əd\ *adj*
**1** HOT 1
**2** ANGRY ⟨*heated* words⟩
**heat·ed·ly** *adv*

**heat·er** \'hēt-ər\ *n*
a device for heating

**heath** \'hēth\ *n*
**1** any of a group of low, woody, and often evergreen plants that grow on poor sour wet soil
**2** a usually open level area of land on which heaths can grow

[1]**hea·then** \'hē-th̲ən\ *adj*
**1** of or relating to the heathen
**2** UNCIVILIZED 1

[2]**heathen** *n, pl* **heathens** *or* **heathen**
**1** a person who does not know about and worship the God of the Bible **:** PAGAN
**2** an uncivilized person

**heath·er** \'heth̲-ər\ *n*
an evergreen heath of northern and mountainous areas with pink flowers and needlelike leaves

[1]**heave** \'hēv\ *vb* **heaved** *or* **hove** \'hōv\; **heav·ing**
**1** to raise with an effort ⟨*heave* a trunk onto a truck⟩
**2** HURL, THROW ⟨*heave* a rock⟩
**3** to utter with an effort ⟨*heave* a sigh⟩
**4** to rise and fall again and again ⟨the runner's chest was *heaving*⟩
**5** to be thrown or raised up

[2]**heave** *n*
**1** an effort to lift or raise
**2** a forceful throw
**3** an upward motion (as of the chest in breathing)

**heav·en** \'hev-ən\ *n*
**1** SKY 1 — usually used in pl.
**2** *often cap* the dwelling place of God and of the blessed dead
**3** *cap* GOD 1
**4** a place or condition of complete happiness

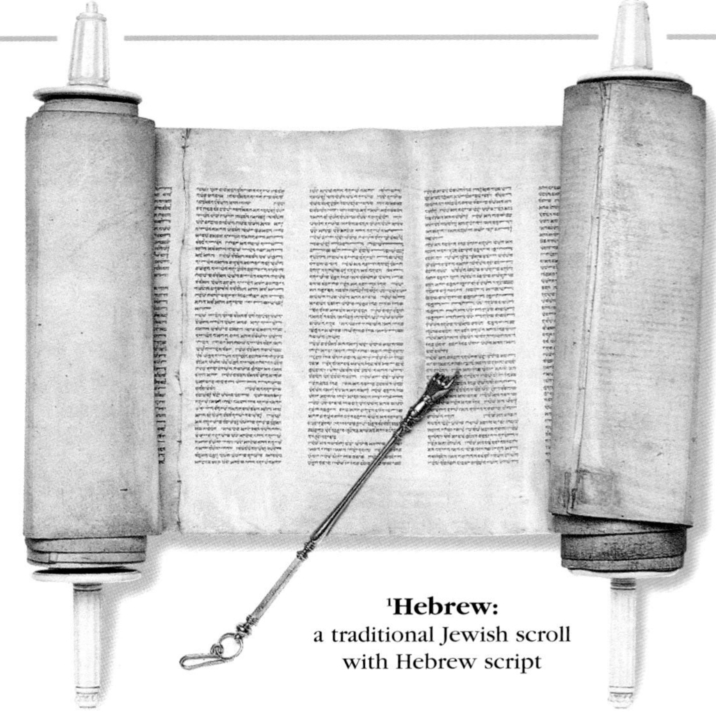

[1]**Hebrew:** a traditional Jewish scroll with Hebrew script

**heav·en·ly** \'hev-ən-lē\ *adj*
**1** of or relating to heaven or the heavens ⟨*heavenly* bodies such as the sun, moon, and stars⟩
**2** of or relating to the Heaven of God and the blessed dead ⟨*heavenly* angels⟩
**3** entirely delightful ⟨a *heavenly* day⟩

**heav·i·ly** \'hev-ə-lē\ *adv*
**1** with or as if with weight ⟨bear down *heavily*⟩
**2** in a slow and difficult way ⟨breathing *heavily*⟩
**3** very much ⟨*heavily* damaged⟩

**heavy** \'hev-ē\ *adj* **heavi·er**; **heavi·est**
**1** having great weight
**2** hard to put up with ⟨a *heavy* sorrow⟩
**3** burdened by something important or troubling ⟨a *heavy* heart⟩
**4** having little strength or energy
**5** unusually great in amount, force, or effect ⟨*heavy* rain⟩ ⟨*heavy* sleep⟩
**heav·i·ness** *n*

[1]**He·brew** \'hē-brü\ *adj*
▲ of or relating to the Hebrew peoples or Hebrew

[2]**Hebrew** *n*
**1** a member of any of a group of peoples including the ancient Jews
**2** JEW
**3** the language of the Hebrews

**hec·tic** \'hek-tik\ *adj*
filled with excitement, activity, or confusion ⟨a *hectic* day of shopping⟩

**hecto-** *prefix*
hundred ⟨*hecto*meter⟩

**hec·to·me·ter** \'hek-tə-ˌmēt-ər\ *n*
a unit of length in the metric system equal to 100 meters

**he'd** \hēd, ēd\
he had **:** he would

[1]**hedge** \'hej\ *n*
a fence or boundary made up of a thick growth of shrubs or low trees

[2]**hedge** *vb* **hedged**; **hedg·ing**
**1** to surround or protect with a hedge
**2** to avoid giving a direct or exact answer or promise

**hedge·hog** \'hej-ˌhȯg, -ˌhäg\ *n*
**1** ▼ a European mammal that eats insects, has sharp spines mixed with the hair on its back, and is able to roll itself up into a ball
**2** PORCUPINE

**hedgehog 1:** a hedgehog rolled up into a ball

## helicopter

The most versatile of all flying machines, helicopters have spinning rotor blades powered by an engine. Unlike airplanes, they can fly backward and sideways as well as forward, hover in the air, rise directly upward on takeoff, and land without a runway. They have many uses, including airlift rescue, and monitoring ground situations such as highway traffic.

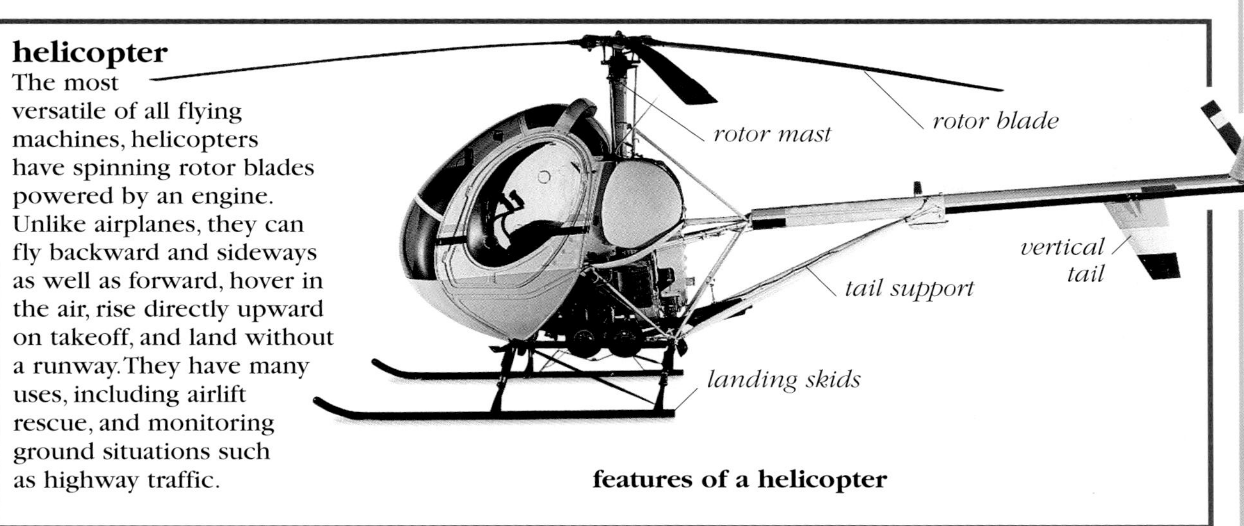


**features of a helicopter**

**hedge·row** \'hej-ˌrō\ *n*
a hedge of shrubs or trees around a field

**[1]heed** \'hēd\ *vb*
to pay attention to : MIND

**[2]heed** *n*
ATTENTION 1 ⟨pay *heed* to a sign⟩
**heed·ful** *adj*
**heed·ful·ly** \-fə-lē\ *adv*

**heed·less** \'hēd-ləs\ *adj*
not taking heed : CARELESS
**heed·less·ly** *adv*
**heed·less·ness** *n*

**[1]heel** \'hēl\ *n*
**1** the back part of the human foot behind the arch and below the ankle
**2** the part of an animal's limb corresponding to a person's heel
**3** one of the crusty ends of a loaf of bread
**4** a part (as of a stocking) that covers the human heel
**5** ▼ the solid part of a shoe that supports the heel
**6** a rear, low, or bottom part
**7** a mean selfish person
**heel·less** \'hēl-ləs\ *adj*

**[2]heel** *vb*
to lean to one side ⟨a boat *heeling* in the wind⟩

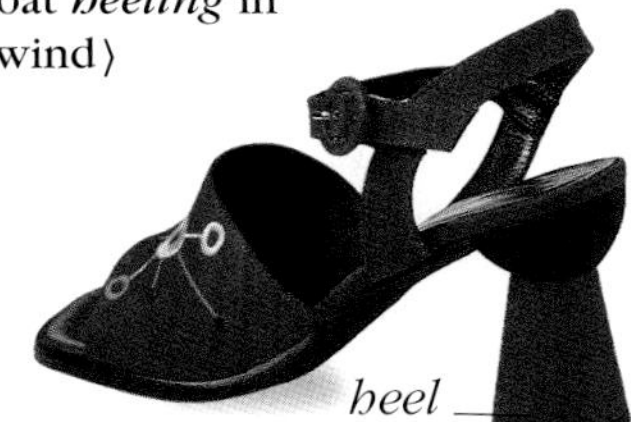


**[1]heel 5:** heel of a shoe

**heft** \'heft\ *vb*
to test the weight of by lifting

**hefty** \'hef-tē\ *adj* **heft·i·er**; **heft·i·est**
HEAVY 1

**heif·er** \'hef-ər\ *n*
a young cow

**height** \'hīt\ *n*
**1** the highest point or greatest degree ⟨the *height* of stupidity⟩
**2** the distance from the bottom to the top of something standing upright
**3** distance upward

---

**Synonyms** HEIGHT, ALTITUDE, and ELEVATION mean distance upward. HEIGHT may be used in measuring something from bottom to top ⟨a wall that is ten feet in *height*⟩. ALTITUDE is used in measuring the distance above a fixed level ⟨a plane flying at a low *altitude*⟩. ELEVATION is used in measuring the height to which something is raised ⟨the *elevation* of the tower is 300 feet⟩.

---

**height·en** \'hīt-n\ *vb*
**1** to make greater : INCREASE ⟨*heightened* their interest⟩
**2** to make or become high or higher

**Heim·lich maneuver** \'hīm -lik-\ *n*
the use of upward pressure upon the upper abdomen of a choking person to force out an object blocking the airway

**heir** \'aər, 'eər\ *n*
**1** a person who inherits or has the right to inherit property after the death of its owner
**2** a person who has legal claim to a title or a throne when the person holding it dies

**heir·ess** \'ar-əs, 'er-\ *n*
a female heir

**heir·loom** \'aər-ˌlüm, 'eər-\ *n*
a piece of personal property handed down in a family from one generation to another

**held** *past of* HOLD

**he·li·cop·ter** \'hel-ə-ˌkäp-tər, 'hē-lə-\ *n*
▲ an aircraft supported in the air by horizontal propellers

**he·li·port** \'hel-ə-ˌpōrt, 'hē-lə-\ *n*
a place for a helicopter to land and take off

**he·li·um** \'hē-lē-əm\ *n*
a very light, nonflammable gaseous chemical element found in various natural gases that is used in balloons

**hell** \'hel\ *n*
**1** a place where souls of the dead are believed to exist
**2** a place or state of punishment for the wicked after death
**3** a place or state of misery or wickedness
**hell·ish** \-ish\ *adj*

**he'll** \hēl, ēl\
he shall : he will

**hell·ben·der** \'hel-ˌben-dər\ *n*
a large American salamander that lives in water

**hel·lo** \hə-'lō, he-\ *interj*
used as a greeting or to express surprise

A B C D E F G **H** I J K L M N O P Q R S T U V W X Y Z

**helm** \'helm\ *n*
**1** a lever or wheel for steering a ship
**2** a position of control

**hel·met** \'hel-mət\ *n*
a protective covering for the head

**helmet:**
a helmet worn by a goalkeeper in the game of field hockey

**[1]help** \'help\ *vb*
**1** to provide with what is useful in achieving an end : AID, ASSIST
**2** to give relief from pain or disease
**3** PREVENT 1 ⟨couldn't *help* laughing⟩
**4** [1]SERVE 9 ⟨*help* yourself to candy⟩

**[2]help** *n*
**1** an act or instance of helping : AID
**2** the state of being helped ⟨we are beyond *help*⟩
**3** a person or a thing that helps ⟨you've been a real *help*⟩
**4** a body of hired helpers

**help·er** \'hel-pər\ *n*
**1** one that helps
**2** a less skilled person who helps a skilled worker

**help·ful** \'help-fəl\ *adj*
providing help ⟨a *helpful* idea⟩
**help·ful·ly** \-fə-lē\ *adv*
**help·ful·ness** *n*

**help·ing** \'hel-ping\ *n*
a serving of food

**helping verb** *n*
a verb (as *am, may*, or *will*) that is used with another verb to express person, number, mood, or tense

**help·less** \'help-ləs\ *adj*
not able to help or protect oneself
**help·less·ly** *adv*
**help·less·ness** *n*

**hel·ter–skel·ter** \,hel-tər-'skel-tər\ *adv*
in great disorder

**[1]hem** \'hem\ *n*
a border of a cloth article made by folding back an edge and sewing it down

**[2]hem** *vb* **hemmed**; **hem·ming**
**1** to finish with or make a hem
**2** SURROUND ⟨a village *hemmed* in by mountains⟩

**hemi-** *prefix*
half ⟨*hemi*sphere⟩

**hemi·sphere** \'hem-ə-,sfir\ *n*
**1** one of the halves of the earth as divided by the equator into northern and southern parts (**northern hemisphere, southern hemisphere**) or by a meridian into two parts so that one half (**eastern hemisphere**) to the east of the Atlantic ocean includes Europe, Asia, and Africa and the half (**western hemisphere**) to the west includes North and South America and surrounding waters
**2** a half of a sphere
**3** either the left or the right half of the cerebrum

**hemi·spher·ic** \,hem-ə-'sfir-ik, -'sfer-\ *or* **hemi·spher·i·cal** \-'sfir-i-kəl, -'sfer-\ *adj*
of or relating to a hemisphere

**hem·lock** \'hem-,läk\ *n*
**1** a poisonous plant of the carrot family
**2** an evergreen tree of the pine family

**he·mo·glo·bin** \'hē-mə-,glō-bən\ *n*
the coloring material of the red blood cells that carry oxygen from the lungs to the tissues

**hem·or·rhage** \'hem-ə-rij\ *n*
great loss of blood by bleeding

**hemp** \'hemp\ *n*
a tall plant grown for its tough woody fiber that is used in making rope and for its flowers and leaves that yield drugs (as marijuana)

**hen** \'hen\ *n*
**1** a female domestic fowl
**2** a female bird

**hence** \'hens\ *adv*
**1** from this place
**2** from this time
**3** as a result : THEREFORE

**hence·forth** \'hens-,fōrth\ *adv*
from this time on

**hench·man** \'hench-mən\ *n, pl* **hench·men** \-mən\
a trusted follower or supporter

**hep·a·ti·tis** \,hep-ə-'tīt-əs\ *n*
a disease which is caused by a virus and in which the liver is damaged and there is yellowing of the skin and fever

**hepta-** *or* **hept-** *prefix*
seven

**hep·ta·gon** \'hep-tə-,gän\ *n*
a closed figure having seven angles and seven sides

**[1]her** \hər, ər\ *adj*
of, relating, or belonging to her or herself ⟨*her* book⟩ ⟨*her* illness⟩

**[2]her** \ər, hər, 'hər\ *pron, objective case of* SHE

**[1]her·ald** \'her-əld\ *n*
**1** an official messenger
**2** a person who brings news or announces something

**[2]herald** *vb*
to give notice of : ANNOUNCE

**he·ral·dic** \he-'ral-dik\ *adj*
of or relating to heralds or heraldry

**her·ald·ry** \'her-əl-drē\ *n*
the art or science of tracing a person's ancestors and determining what coat of arms his or her family has the right to

**herb** \'ərb, 'hərb\ *n*
**1** a plant with soft stems that die down at the end of the growing season
**2** a plant or plant part used in medicine or in seasoning foods

**her·biv·o·rous** \,hər-'biv-ə-rəs, ,ər-'biv-\ *adj*
eating or living on plants

**[1]herd** \'hərd\ *n*
a number of animals of one kind kept or living together ⟨a *herd* of cows⟩

**[2]herd** *vb*
**1** to gather or join in a herd
**2** to form into or move as a herd
**herd·er** \'hərd-ər\ *n*

**herds·man** \'hərdz-mən\ *n, pl* **herds·men** \-mən\
one who owns or tends livestock

**[1]here** \'hir\ *adv*
**1** in or at this place ⟨stand *here*⟩
**2** [1]NOW 1 ⟨*here* it is Monday again⟩
**3** to or into this place : HITHER ⟨come *here*⟩

**[2]here** *n*
this place ⟨get away from *here*⟩

**here·abouts** \'hir-ə-,bau̇ts\ *or* **here·about** \-,bau̇t\ *adv*
near or around this place

**[1]here·af·ter** \hir-'af-tər\ *adv*
**1** after this
**2** in some future time or state

## herb 2

Many of the most popular herbs are used for seasoning food. These are known as culinary — or cooking — herbs, and they are generally available fresh or dried. All herbs have their own distinctive taste and aroma, so that different types are preferred for flavoring particular foods. Some culinary herbs are added during cooking, while others are eaten fresh in salads or used to decorate meals or drinks.

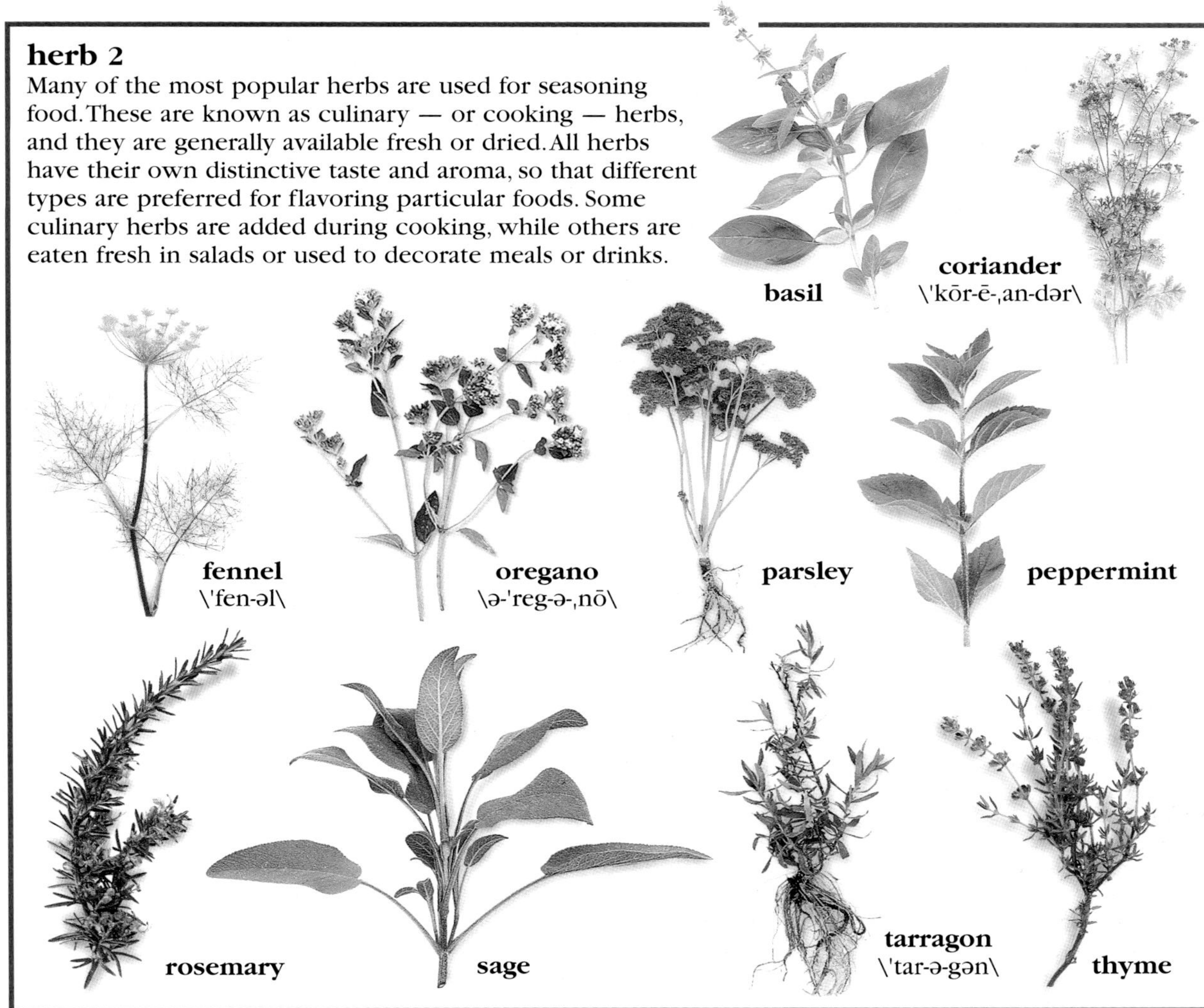


**²hereafter** *n*
 **1** ²FUTURE 1
 **2** life after death

**here·by** \hir-'bī\ *adv*
 by means of this

**he·red·i·tary** \hə-'red-ə-ˌter-ē\ *adj*
 **1** capable of being passed from parent to offspring ⟨*hereditary* disease⟩
 **2** received or passing from an ancestor to an heir

**he·red·i·ty** \hə-'red-ət-ē\ *n, pl* **he·red·i·ties**
 the passing on of characteristics (as looks or ability) from parents to offspring

**here·in** \hir-'in\ *adv*
 in this

**here·of** \hir-'əv, -'äv\ *adv*
 of this

**here·on** \hir-'ȯn, -'än\ *adv*
 on this

**her·e·sy** \'her-ə-sē\ *n, pl* **her·e·sies**
 **1** the holding of religious beliefs opposed to church doctrine **:** such a belief
 **2** an opinion opposed to a generally accepted belief

**her·e·tic** \'her-ə-ˌtik\ *n*
 a person who believes or teaches something opposed to accepted beliefs (as of a church)

**he·ret·i·cal** \hə-'ret-i-kəl\ *adj*
 of, relating to, or being heresy

**here·to·fore** \'hir-tə-ˌfōr\ *adv*
 HITHERTO

**here·up·on** \'hir-ə-ˌpȯn, -ˌpän\ *adv*
 right after this

**here·with** \hir-'wi<u>th</u>, -'with\ *adv*
 with this

**her·i·tage** \'her-ət-ij\ *n*
 something that comes to one from one's ancestors

**her·mit** \'hər-mət\ *n*
 one who lives apart from others especially for religious reasons

**hermit crab** *n*
 any of various small crabs that live in the empty shells of mollusks (as snails)

**he·ro** \'hir-ō, 'hē-rō\ *n, pl* **heroes**
 **1** a person admired for great deeds or fine qualities ⟨*heroes* of a nation's history⟩
 **2** one who shows great courage
 **3** the chief male character in a story, play, or poem

**he·ro·ic** \hi-'rō-ik\ *adj*
 **1** of, relating to, or like heroes
 **2** COURAGEOUS, DARING ⟨a *heroic* feat⟩
 **he·ro·ical·ly** \-i-kə-lē\ *adv*

**her·o·in** \'her-ə-wən\ *n*
a very harmful drug that comes from morphine

**her·o·ine** \'her-ə-wən\ *n*
**1** a woman admired for great deeds or fine qualities
**2** the chief female character in a story, poem, or play

**her·o·ism** \'her-ə-,wiz-əm\ *n*
**1** great courage especially for a noble purpose
**2** the qualities of a hero

**her·on** \'her-ən\ *n*
▼ a wading bird that has long legs, a long neck, a long thin bill, and large wings

**her·ring** \'her-ing\ *n*
a widely used food fish of the north Atlantic ocean

**hers** \'hərz\ *pron*
that which belongs to her ⟨this book is *hers*⟩ ⟨these books are *hers*⟩

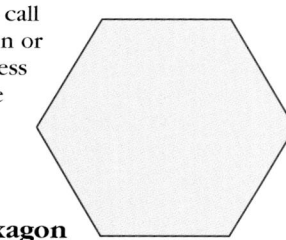

**heron:** a great blue heron

**her·self** \hər-'self, ər-\ *pron*
her own self ⟨she hurt *herself*⟩ ⟨she *herself* did it⟩

**he's** \hēz, ēz\
he is : he has

**hes·i·tan·cy** \'hez-ə-tən-sē\ *n*
the quality or state of being hesitant

**hes·i·tant** \'hez-ə-tənt\ *adj*
feeling or showing hesitation
**hes·i·tant·ly** *adv*

**hes·i·tate** \'hez-ə-,tāt\ *vb*
**hes·i·tat·ed**; **hes·i·tat·ing**
**1** to pause because of forgetfulness or uncertainty
**2** to speak or say in a weak or broken way

**hes·i·ta·tion** \,hez-ə-'tā-shən\ *n*
an act or instance of hesitating

**hew** \'hyü\ *vb* **hewed** *or* **hewn** \'hyün\; **hew·ing**
**1** to chop down
**2** to shape by cutting with an ax

**hex** \'heks\ *n*
a harmful spell : JINX

**hexa-** *or* **hex-** *prefix*
six

**hexa·gon** \'hek-sə-,gän\ *n*
▼ a closed figure having six angles and six sides

**hex·ag·o·nal** \hek-'sag-ən-l\ *adj*
having six sides
**hex·ag·o·nal·ly** *adv*

**hey** \'hā\ *interj*
used to call attention or to express surprise or joy

**hexagon**

**hey·day** \'hā-,dā\ *n*
the time of greatest strength, energy, or success

**hi** \'hī\ *interj*
used especially as a greeting

**hi·ber·nate** \'hī-bər-,nāt\ *vb*
**hi·ber·nat·ed**; **hi·ber·nat·ing**
to pass the winter in a resting state
**hi·ber·na·tor** \-,nāt-ər\ *n*

**hi·ber·na·tion** \,hī-bər-'nā-shən\ *n*
▼ the state of one that hibernates

[1]**hic·cup** \'hik-,əp\ *n*
a gulping sound caused by sudden movements of muscles active in breathing

[2]**hiccup** *vb* **hic·cuped** *also* **hic·cupped**; **hic·cup·ing** *also* **hic·cup·ping**
to make a hiccup

**hibernation:** a squirrel in hibernation

**hick·o·ry** \'hik-ə-rē, 'hik-rē\ *n*, *pl* **hick·o·ries**
a tall tree related to the walnuts that has strong tough elastic wood and bears an edible nut (**hickory nut**) in a hard shell

[1]**hide** \'hīd\ *vb* **hid** \'hid\; **hid·den** \'hid-n\ *or* **hid**; **hid·ing** \'hīd-ing\
**1** to put or stay out of sight
**2** to keep secret
**3** to screen from view ⟨clouds *hiding* the sun⟩

[2]**hide** *n*
the skin of an animal whether fresh or prepared for use

**hide–and–go–seek** \,hīd-n-gō-'sēk\ *n*
HIDE-AND-SEEK

**hide–and–seek** \,hīd-n-'sēk\ *n*
a game in which one player covers his or her eyes and after giving the others time to hide goes looking for them

**hide·away** \'hīd-ə-,wā\ *n*
[1]RETREAT 3, HIDEOUT

**hid·eous** \'hid-ē-əs\ *adj*
very ugly or disgusting : FRIGHTFUL
**hid·eous·ly** *adv*
**hid·eous·ness** *n*

**hide·out** \'hī-,dau̇t\ *n*
a secret place for hiding (as from the police)

**hi·ero·glyph·ic** \,hī-ə-rə-'glif-ik\ *n*
▶ any of the symbols in the picture writing of ancient Egypt

**hi–fi** \'hī-'fī\ *n*
**1** HIGH FIDELITY
**2** equipment for reproduction of sound with high fidelity

**hig·gle·dy–pig·gle·dy** \,hig-əl-dē-'pig-əl-dē\ *adv or adj*
in confusion : TOPSY-TURVY

[1]**high** \'hī\ *adj*
**1** extending to a great distance above the ground
**2** having a specified elevation : TALL
**3** of greater degree, size, amount, or cost than average

**hieroglyphic:** an ancient Egyptian door plate inscribed with hieroglyphics

4 of more than usual importance ⟨*high* crimes⟩
5 having great force ⟨*high* winds⟩
6 pitched or sounding above some other sound

**Synonyms** HIGH, TALL, and LOFTY mean above the usual level in height. HIGH is used of height that is measured from the ground or some other standard ⟨a *high* hill⟩. TALL is used of something that is considered high when compared to others of the same kind ⟨a *tall* youngster for that age⟩. LOFTY is used of something that rises to a grand or impressive height ⟨*lofty* mountains⟩.

**[2]high** *adv*
at or to a high place or degree

**[3]high** *n*
1 the space overhead **:** SKY ⟨watched the birds on *high*⟩
2 a region of high barometric pressure
3 a high point or level ⟨prices reached a new *high*⟩
4 the arrangement of gears in an automobile giving the highest speed of travel

**high·brow** \'hī-ˌbrau̇\ *n*
a person of great learning or culture

**high fidelity** *n*
the reproduction of sound with a high degree of accuracy

**high·land** \'hī-lənd\ *n*
high or hilly country

**[1]high·light** \'hī-ˌlīt\ *n*
a very interesting event or detail ⟨*highlights* of the trip⟩

**[2]highlight** *vb* **high·light·ed**; **high·light·ing**
1 EMPHASIZE ⟨the speech *highlighted* the problems⟩
2 to be a highlight of
3 to mark with a highlighter ⟨*highlight* your spelling words on the page⟩
4 to cause (something on a computer screen) to be displayed in such a way that stands out

**high·light·er** \'hī-ˌlīt-ər\ *n*
a pen with a wide felt tip and brightly colored ink for marking text on a page

**high·ly** \'hī-lē\ *adv*
1 to a high degree **:** very much
2 with much approval

**high·ness** \'hī-nəs\ *n*
1 the quality or state or being high
2 used as a title for a person of very high rank ⟨Your Royal *Highness*⟩

**high school** *n*
a school usually including the ninth to twelfth or tenth to twelfth grades

**high seas** *n pl*
the open part of a sea or ocean

**high–spir·it·ed** \'hī-'spir-ət-əd\ *adj*
LIVELY 1

**high–strung** \'hī-'strəng\ *adj*
very sensitive or nervous ⟨a *high-strung* horse⟩

**high tide** *n*
the tide when the water is at its greatest height

**high·way** \'hī-ˌwā\ *n*
a main road

**high·way·man** \'hī-ˌwā-mən\ *n*, *pl* **high·way·men** \-mən\
a person who robs travelers on a road

**hi·jack** *also* **high·jack** \'hī-ˌjak\ *vb*
1 to stop and steal from a moving vehicle
2 to force a pilot to fly a plane where one wants—**high·jack·er** *n*

**[1]hike** \'hīk\ *vb* **hiked**; **hik·ing**
to take a long walk
**hik·er** *n*

**[2]hike** *n*
a long walk especially for pleasure or exercise

**hi·lar·i·ous** \hil-'ar-ē-əs, -'er-\ *adj*
enjoying or causing hilarity **:** MERRY
**hi·lar·i·ous·ly** *adv*
**hi·lar·i·ous·ness** *n*

**hi·lar·i·ty** \hil-'ar-ət-ē, -'er-\ *n*
noisy fun

**[1]hill** \'hil\ *n*
1 a usually rounded elevation of land lower than a mountain
2 a little heap or mound of earth
3 several seeds or plants planted in a group rather than a row

**[2]hill** *vb*
1 to form into a heap
2 to draw earth around the roots or base of ⟨*hill* corn⟩

**hill·bil·ly** \'hil-ˌbil-ē\ *n*, *pl* **hill·bil·lies**
a person from a backwoods area

**hill·ock** \'hil-ək\ *n*
a small hill

**hill·side** \'hil-ˌsīd\ *n*
the part of a hill between the top and the foot

**hill·top** \'hil-ˌtäp\ *n*
the highest part of a hill

**hilly** \'hil-ē\ *adj* **hill·i·er**; **hill·i·est**
having many hills ⟨a *hilly* city⟩

**hilt** \'hilt\ *n*
▶ a handle especially of a sword or dagger

**hilt** on a traditional Indian dagger

**him** \him, im\ *pron*, *objective case of* HE

**him·self** \him-'self, im-\ *pron*
his own self ⟨he hurt *himself*⟩ ⟨he *himself* did it⟩

**hind** \'hīnd\ *adj*
being at the end or back **:** REAR

**hin·der** \'hin-dər\ *vb*
to make slow or difficult ⟨snow and high winds *hindered* our trip⟩

**hind·quar·ter** \'hīnd-ˌkwȯrt-ər\ *n*
the back half of a complete side of a four-footed animal or carcass

**hin·drance** \'hin-drəns\ *n*
something that hinders **:** OBSTACLE

**hind·sight** \'hīnd-ˌsīt\ *n*
understanding of something only after it has happened

**Hin·du·ism** \'hin-ˌdü-ˌiz-əm\ *n*
a set of cultural and religious beliefs and practices that originated in India

**[1]hinge** \'hinj\ *n*
a jointed piece on which a door, gate, or lid turns or swings

**[2]hinge** *vb* **hinged**; **hing·ing**
1 to attach by or provide with hinges
2 DEPEND 2

**[1]hint** \'hint\ *n*
1 information that helps one guess an answer or do something more easily
2 a small amount **:** TRACE

**[2]hint** *vb*
to suggest something without plainly asking or saying it ⟨*hint* for some help⟩

**hin·ter·land** \'hint-ər-ˌland\ *n*
a region far from cities

**hip** \'hip\ *n*
the part of the body that curves out below the waist on each side

**hip·pie** *or* **hip·py** \'hip-ē\ *n*, *pl* **hippies**
a usually young person who typically has long hair, is against the values and practices of society, and often lives together with others

a b c d e f g h i j k l m n o p q r s t u v w x y z

**hip·po** \'hip-ō\ *n, pl* **hip·pos**
HIPPOPOTAMUS

**hip·po·pot·a·mus** \,hip-ə-'pät-ə-məs\ *n, pl* **hip·po·pot·a·mus·es** *or* **hip·po·pot·a·mi** \-,mī\
a large hoglike animal with thick hairless skin that eats plants and lives in African rivers

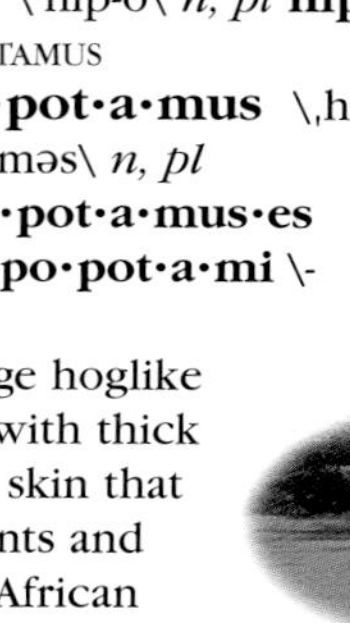

**hippopotamus**

**Word History** The English word *hippopotamus* came from the Greek name for the animal. The ancient Greeks made up a good name for a beast that spends most of its time in rivers. This Greek name was a compound of two Greek words. The first meant "horse," and the second meant "river."

**hire** \'hīr\ *vb* **hired**; **hir·ing**
**1** [1]EMPLOY 2
**2** to get the temporary use of in return for pay ⟨*hire* a hall⟩
**3** to take a job ⟨*hired* out as a cook⟩

**Synonyms** HIRE, LET, and RENT mean to use or to let another use something for a price. HIRE more often suggests that one pays to use something ⟨*hire* a machine to clean the carpet⟩. LET usually suggests that one receives money for the use of something ⟨the family has a spare room to *let*⟩. RENT stresses the payment of money in exchange for the use of property ⟨*rented* a car for fifty dollars⟩.

[1]**his** \hiz, iz\ *adj*
of or relating to him or himself ⟨*his* desk⟩ ⟨*his* turn⟩

[2]**his** \'hiz\ *pron*
that which belongs to him ⟨the book is *his*⟩ ⟨the books are *his*⟩

[1]**His·pan·ic** \his-'pan-ik\ *adj*
of or relating to people of Latin American origin

[2]**Hispanic** *n*
a person of Latin American origin

[1]**hiss** \'his\ *vb*
**1** to make a hiss
**2** to show dislike by hissing

[2]**hiss** *n*
a sound like a long \s\ sometimes used as a sign of dislike ⟨the *hiss* of steam⟩

**his·to·ri·an** \his-'tōr-ē-ən\ *n*
a person who studies or writes about history

**his·tor·ic** \his-'tȯr-ik\ *adj*
famous in history

**his·tor·i·cal** \his-'tȯr-i-kəl\ *adj*
**1** of, relating to, or based on history ⟨*historical* writings⟩
**2** known to be true ⟨*historical* fact⟩
**his·tor·i·cal·ly** *adv*

**his·to·ry** \'his-tə-rē\ *n, pl* **his·to·ries**
**1** a telling of events **:** STORY
**2** a written report of past events
**3** a branch of knowledge that records and explains past events

[1]**hit** \'hit\ *vb* **hit**; **hit·ting**
**1** to touch or cause to touch with force
**2** to strike or cause to strike something aimed at ⟨the arrow *hit* the target⟩
**3** to affect as if by a blow ⟨*hit* hard by the loss⟩
**4** OCCUR 2 ⟨the storm *hit* without warning⟩
**5** to happen to get **:** come upon ⟨*hit* upon the right answer⟩
**6** to arrive at ⟨prices *hit* a new high⟩
**hit·ter** *n*

[2]**hit** *n*
**1** a blow striking an object aimed at ⟨score a *hit*⟩
**2** COLLISION
**3** something very successful
**4** a batted baseball that enables the batter to reach base safely
**5** a match in a computer search ⟨the search produced over a thousand *hits*⟩

**hit–and–run** \,hit-n-'rən\ *adj*
being or involving a driver who does not stop after being in an automobile accident

[1]**hitch** \'hich\ *vb*
**1** to move by jerks
**2** to fasten by or as if by a hook or knot
**3** HITCHHIKE

[2]**hitch** *n*
**1** a jerky movement or pull ⟨give one's pants a *hitch*⟩
**2** an unexpected stop or obstacle
**3** a knot used for a temporary fastening

**hitch·hike** \'hich-,hīk\ *vb* **hitch·hiked**; **hitch·hik·ing**
to travel by getting free rides in passing vehicles
**hitch·hik·er** *n*

**hith·er** \'hith-ər\ *adv*
to this place

**hith·er·to** \'hith-ər-,tü\ *adv*
up to this time

**HIV** \,āch-,ī-'vē\ *n*
a virus that causes AIDS by destroying the cells that help the human body fight infection

**hive** \'hīv\ *n*
**1** a container for housing honeybees
**2** the nest of bees
**3** a colony of bees
**4** a place swarming with busy people

**hive 1:** a beekeeper collecting honey from a hive

**hives** \'hīvz\ *n pl*
an allergic condition in which the skin breaks out in large red itching patches

**ho** \'hō\ *interj*
used especially to attract attention

**[1]hoard** \'hōrd\ *n*
a supply usually of something of value stored away or hidden

**[2]hoard** *vb*
to gather and store away
**hoard•er** *n*

**hoar•frost** \'hōr-,frȯst\ *n*
[1]FROST 2

**hoarse** \'hōrs\ *adj* **hoars•er**; **hoars•est**
1 harsh in sound
2 having a rough voice
**hoarse•ly** *adv*
**hoarse•ness** *n*

**hoary** \'hōr-ē\ *adj* **hoar•i•er**; **hoar•i•est**
gray or white with age

**[1]hoax** \'hōks\ *vb*
to trick into thinking something is true or real when it isn't

**[2]hoax** *n*
1 an act meant to fool or deceive
2 something false passed off as real

**[1]hob•ble** \'häb-əl\ *vb* **hob•bled**; **hob•bling**
1 to walk with difficulty : LIMP
2 to tie the legs of to make movement difficult

**[2]hobble** *n*
1 a limping walk
2 something used to hobble an animal

**hob•by** \'häb-ē\ *n, pl* **hobbies**
an interest or activity engaged in for pleasure

**hob•by•horse** \'häb-ē-,hȯrs\ *n*
1 a stick with a horse's head on which children pretend to ride
2 ROCKING HORSE

**hob•gob•lin** \'häb-,gäb-lən\ *n*
1 a mischievous elf
2 BOGEY 2

**hob•nail** \'häb-,nāl\ *n*
a short nail with a large head driven into soles of heavy shoes to protect against wear
**hob•nailed** \-,nāld\ *adj*

**ho•bo** \'hō-bō\ *n, pl* **hoboes**
[1]VAGRANT

**hock•ey** \'häk-ē\ *n*
▼ a game played on ice or in a field by two teams who try to drive a puck or ball through a goal by hitting it with a stick

## hockey

Ice hockey originated as a winter version of hockey, played on frozen ponds and lakes. Today, indoor play on an ice rink is more common. A much faster game than field hockey, ice hockey is played by two teams of six players who use sticks to try to hit a hard rubber puck into the opponent's goal.

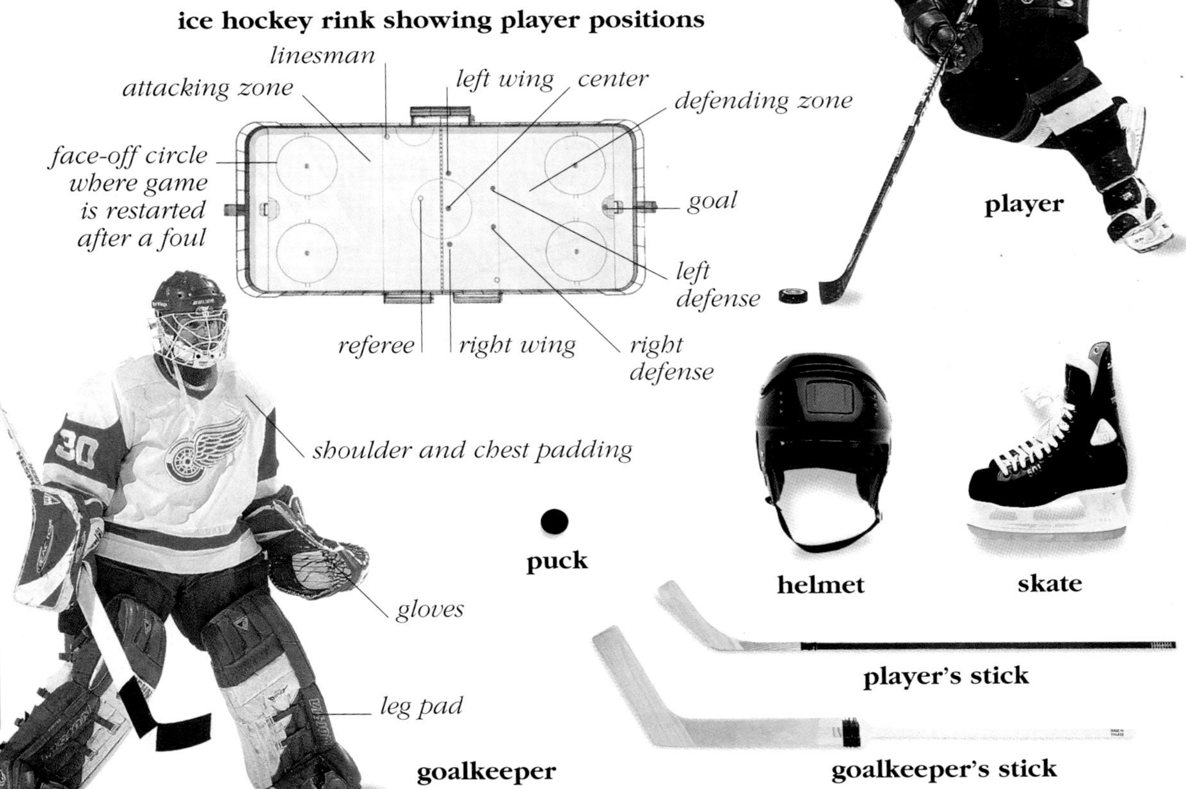

chimney hole

entrance

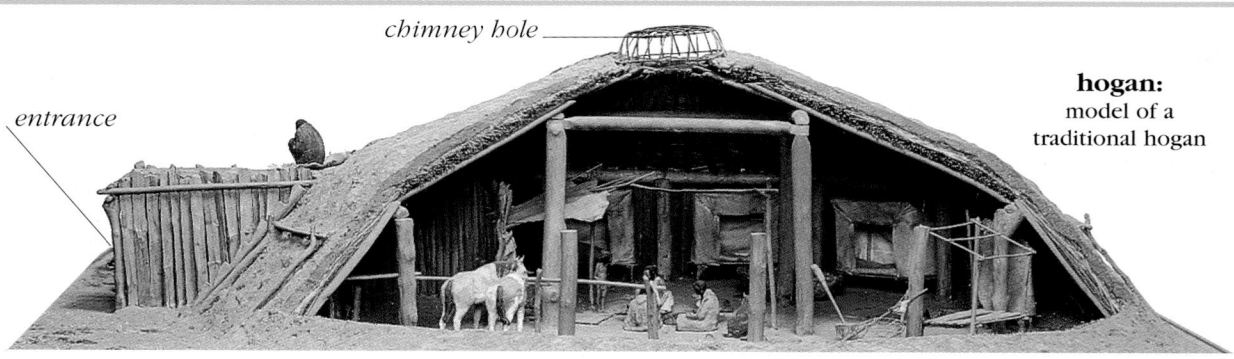

**hogan:** model of a traditional hogan

**hod** \'häd\ *n*
**1** a wooden tray or trough that has a long handle and is used to carry mortar or bricks
**2** a bucket for holding or carrying coal

**hodge·podge** \'häj-,päj\ *n*
a disorderly mixture

**[1]hoe** \'hō\ *n*
a tool with a long handle and a thin flat blade used for weeding and cultivating

**[2]hoe** *vb* **hoed**; **hoe·ing**
to weed or loosen the soil around plants with a hoe

**[1]hog** \'hȯg, 'häg\ *n*
**1** an adult domestic swine
**2** a greedy or dirty person

**[2]hog** *vb* **hogged**; **hog·ging**
to take more than one's share

**ho·gan** \'hō-,gän\ *n*
▲ a Native American dwelling made of logs and mud with a door traditionally facing east

**hog·gish** \'hȯg-ish, 'häg-\ *adj*
very selfish or greedy
**hog·gish·ly** *adv*
**hog·gish·ness** *n*

**hogs·head** \'hȯgz-,hed, 'hägz-\ *n*
**1** a very large cask
**2** a unit of liquid measure equal to sixty-three gallons (about 238 liters)

**[1]hoist** \'hȯist\ *vb*
to lift up especially with a pulley
**synonyms** see LIFT

**[2]hoist** *n*
**1** an act of hoisting
**2** a device used for lifting heavy loads

**[1]hold** \'hōld\ *vb* **held** \'held\; **hold·ing**
**1** to have or keep in one's possession or under one's control ⟨*hold* a fort⟩ ⟨*hold* territory⟩
**2** to limit the movement or activity of **:** RESTRAIN ⟨the nut *held* the bolt⟩ ⟨*hold* the dogs⟩
**3** to make accept a legal or moral duty ⟨they *held* me to my promise⟩
**4** to have or keep in one's grasp ⟨*hold* a book⟩
**5** [1]SUPPORT 4 ⟨a floor that will *hold* ten tons⟩
**6** to take in and have within **:** CONTAIN ⟨a jar that *holds* a quart⟩
**7** to have in mind ⟨*hold* opposing opinions⟩
**8** CONSIDER 3, REGARD
**9** to carry on by group action ⟨*hold* a meeting⟩
**10** to continue in the same way or state **:** LAST ⟨believes the good weather will *hold*⟩
**11** to remain fast or fastened ⟨the lock *held*⟩
**12** to bear or carry oneself

**[2]hold** *n*
**1** the act or way of holding **:** GRIP
**2** [1]INFLUENCE 1 ⟨the *hold* of the school on our minds⟩
**3** a note or rest in music kept up longer than usual

**[3]hold** *n*
**1** the part of a ship below the decks in which cargo is stored
**2** the cargo compartment of an airplane

**hold·er** \'hōl-dər\ *n*
one that holds

**hold out** *vb*
to refuse to yield or agree ⟨*held out* until help arrived⟩

**hold·up** \'hōl-,dəp\ *n*
**1** robbery by an armed robber
**2** [1]DELAY

**hold up** \hōl-'dəp\ *vb*
**1** [2]DELAY 2
**2** to rob while threatening with a weapon

**hole** \'hōl\ *n*
**1** an opening into or through something
**2** CAVITY
**3** DEN 1, BURROW

**hol·i·day** \'häl-ə-,dā\ *n*
**1** a day of freedom from work especially when celebrating some event
**2** VACATION

**ho·li·ness** \'hō-lē-nəs\ *n*
**1** the quality or state of being holy
**2** used as a title for persons of high religious position ⟨His *Holiness* the Pope⟩

**[1]hol·ler** \'häl-ər\ *vb*
to cry out **:** SHOUT

**[2]holler** *n*
[2]SHOUT, CRY

**[1]hol·low** \'häl-ō\ *n*
**1** a low spot in a surface ⟨the *hollow* of the land⟩
**2** VALLEY
**3** CAVITY

**[2]hollow** *adj*
**1** curved inward **:** SUNKEN
**2** having a space inside **:** not solid
**3** suggesting a sound made in an empty place ⟨a *hollow* roar⟩
**4** not sincere
**hol·low·ly** *adv*
**hol·low·ness** *n*

**[3]hollow** *vb*
to make or become hollow

**hol·ly** \'häl-ē\ *n, pl* **hollies**
▼ an evergreen tree or shrub that has shiny leaves with prickly edges and red berries much used for Christmas decorations

**holly**

**hol·ly·hock** \'häl-ē-,häk\ *n*
a plant with large rounded leaves and tall stalks of bright showy flowers

**ho·lo·caust** \'häl-ə-,kȯst, 'hō-lə-\ *n*
a complete destruction especially by fire

**Word History** At first the English word *holocaust* meant "a burnt sacrifice." This English word came from a Greek word that meant "burnt whole." This Greek word was a compound of a word that meant "whole" and another that meant "burnt."

**ho·lo·gram** \'hō-lə-,gram, 'hä-\ *n*
a three-dimensional picture made by laser light reflected onto a photographic substance without the use of a camera

**hol·ster** \'hōl-stər\ *n*
a usually leather case in which a pistol is carried or worn

**ho·ly** \'hō-lē\ *adj* **ho·li·er**; **ho·li·est**
**1** set apart for the service of God or of a divine being **:** SACRED ⟨a *holy* temple⟩
**2** having a right to expect complete devotion ⟨the *holy* Lord God⟩
**3** pure in spirit

**hom-** *or* **homo-** *prefix*
one and the same **:** similar **:** alike ⟨*homo*graph⟩

**hom·age** \'häm-ij, 'äm-\ *n*
**1** a feudal ceremony in which a person pledges loyalty to a lord and becomes a vassal
**2** [1]RESPECT 2

**[1]home** \'hōm\ *n*
**1** the house in which one or one's family lives
**2** the place where one was born or grew up
**3** HABITAT
**4** a place for the care of persons unable to care for themselves
**5** the social unit formed by a family living together
**6** [1]HOUSE 1 ⟨new *homes* for sale⟩
**7** the goal or point to be reached in some games
**home·less** \-ləs\ *adj*

**[2]home** *adv*
**1** to or at home
**2** to the final place or limit ⟨drive a nail *home*⟩

**home·land** \'hōm-,land\ *n*
native land

**home·like** \'hōm-,līk\ *adj*
like a home (as in comfort and kindly warmth) ⟨a *homelike* atmosphere⟩

**home·ly** \'hōm-lē\ *adj* **home·li·er**; **home·li·est**
**1** suggesting home life ⟨*homely* comfort⟩
**2** not handsome

**home·made** \'hōm-'mād\ *adj*
made in the home ⟨*homemade* bread⟩

**home·mak·er** \'hōm-,mā-kər\ *n*
a person who manages a household especially as a wife and mother
**home·mak·ing** \-,mā-king\ *n or adj*

**home page** *n*
▶ the page of a World Wide Web site that is usually seen first and that usually contains links to the other pages of the site or to other sites

**home plate** *n*
the base that a baseball runner must touch to score

**hom·er** \'hō-mər\ *n*
HOME RUN

**home·room** \'hōm-,rüm, -,ru̇m\ *n*
a schoolroom where pupils of the same class report at the start of each day

**home run** *n*
a hit in baseball that enables the batter to go around all the bases and score

**home·school** \'hōm-,skül\ *vb*
to teach school subjects to one's children at home ⟨she *homeschools* her third-grade son⟩

**home·school·er** \'hōm-,skü-lər\ *n*
**1** one that homeschools
**2** a child who is homeschooled

**home·sick** \'hōm-,sik\ *adj*
longing for home and family
**home·sick·ness** *n*

**[1]home·spun** \'hōm-,spən\ *adj*
**1** spun or made at home
**2** made of homespun
**3** not fancy **:** SIMPLE ⟨*homespun* humor⟩

**[2]homespun** *n*
a loosely woven usually woolen or linen fabric originally made from homespun yarn

**[1]home·stead** \'hōm-,sted\ *n*
**1** a home and the land around it
**2** a piece of land gained from United States public lands by living on and farming it

**[2]homestead** *vb*
to acquire or settle on public land for use as a homestead
**home·stead·er** \'hōm-,sted-ər\ *n*

**home·ward** \'hōm-wərd\ *or* **home·wards** \-wərdz\ *adv or adj*
toward home

**home·work** \'hōm-,wərk\ *n*
work (as school lessons) to be done at home

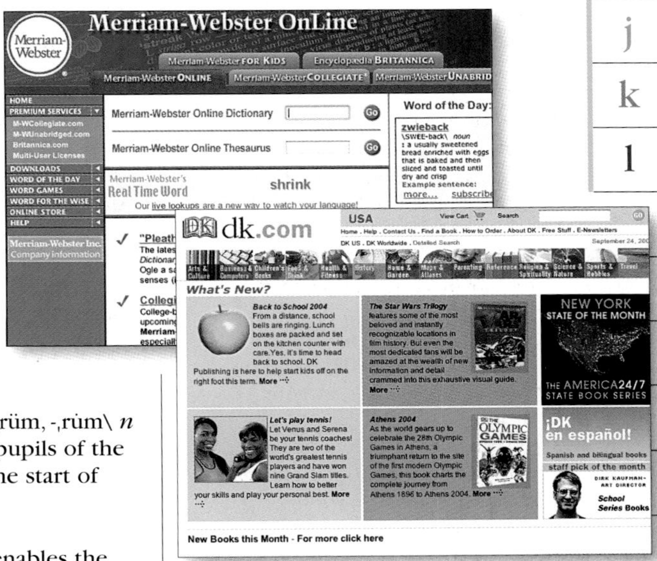

**home page:**
the Merriam-Webster and DK home pages

**hom·ey** \'hō-mē\ *adj* **hom·i·er**; **hom·i·est**
HOMELIKE
**hom·ey·ness** *or* **hom·i·ness** *n*

**ho·mi·cide** \'häm-ə-,sīd, 'hō-mə-\ *n*
a killing of one human being by another

**hom·ing pigeon** \,hō-ming-\ *n*
a racing pigeon trained to return home

**hom·i·ny** \'häm-ə-nē\ *n*
hulled corn with the germ removed

## honeybee

For centuries, people have built hives for honeybees. Modern hives have removable frames to make the collection of honey easier. A modern hive contains only three types of honeybee — the queen, male drones, and female workers. The queen lays all the eggs from which new larvae hatch, while the drones exist only to mate with the queen. The workers build the honeycomb and take care of the queen and larvae.

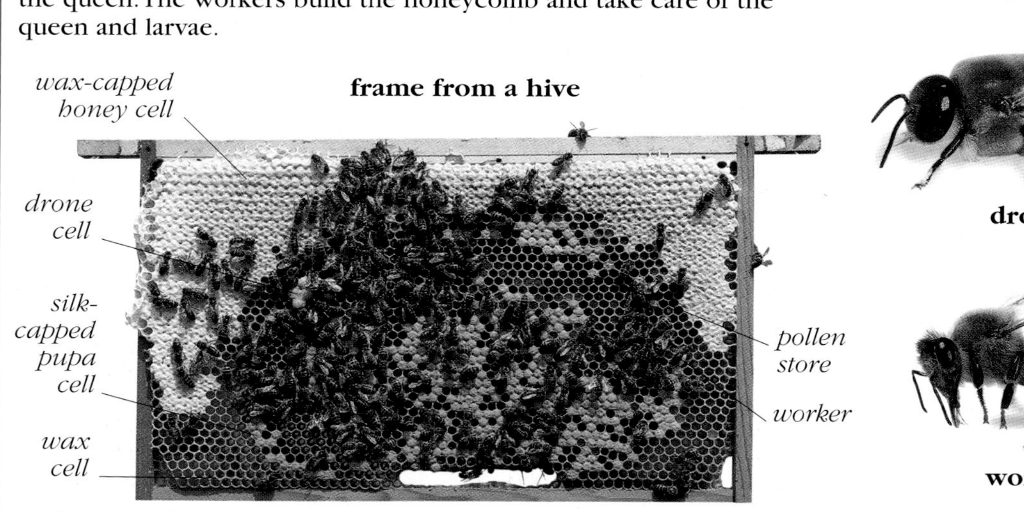


**frame from a hive**

**queen**

**drone**

**worker**

**homo-** see HOM-

**ho·mog·e·nize** \hō-ˈmäj-ə-ˌnīz, hə-\ *vb* **ho·mog·e·nized**; **ho·mog·e·niz·ing**
to reduce the particles in (as milk or paint) to the same size and spread them evenly in the liquid

**ho·mo·graph** \ˈhäm-ə-ˌgraf, ˈhō-mə-\ *n*
one of two or more words spelled alike but different in meaning or origin or pronunciation ⟨the noun "conduct" and the verb "conduct" are *homographs*⟩

**hom·onym** \ˈhäm-ə-ˌnim, ˈhō-mə-\ *n*
**1** HOMOPHONE
**2** HOMOGRAPH
**3** one of two or more words spelled and pronounced alike but different in meaning ⟨the noun "bear" and the verb "bear" are *homonyms*⟩

**ho·mo·phone** \ˈhäm-ə-ˌfōn, ˈhō-mə-\ *n*
one of two or more words pronounced alike but different in meaning or origin or spelling ⟨"to," "too," and "two" are *homophones*⟩

**hone** \ˈhōn\ *vb* **honed**; **hon·ing**
to sharpen with or as if with a fine abrasive stone

**hon·est** \ˈän-əst\ *adj*
**1** free from fraud or trickery : STRAIGHTFORWARD ⟨an *honest* answer⟩
**2** not given to cheating, stealing, or lying : UPRIGHT, TRUSTWORTHY
**3** being just what is indicated : REAL, GENUINE ⟨put in a day's *honest* work⟩ **synonyms** see UPRIGHT

**hon·es·ty** \ˈän-ə-stē\ *n*
the quality or state of being honest

**hon·ey** \ˈhən-ē\ *n*
**1** a sweet sticky fluid made by bees from the liquid drawn from flowers
**2** an outstanding example ⟨a *honey* of a fight⟩

**hon·ey·bee** \ˈhən-ē-ˌbē\ *n*
a bee whose honey is used by people as food

[1]**hon·ey·comb** \ˈhən-ē-ˌkōm\ *n*
**1** a mass of wax cells built by honeybees in their nest to contain young bees and stores of honey
**2** something like a honeycomb in structure or appearance

[2]**honeycomb** *vb*
to make or become full of holes like a honeycomb

**hon·ey·dew melon** \ˌhən-ē-ˌdü-, -ˌdyü-\ *n*
a pale muskmelon with greenish sweet flesh and smooth skin

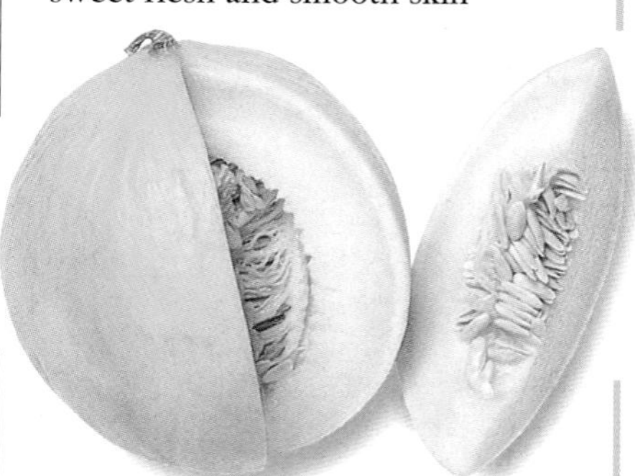

**honeydew melon**

[1]**hon·ey·moon** \ˈhən-ē-ˌmün\ *n*
**1** a holiday taken by a recently married couple
**2** a period of harmony especially just after marriage

[2]**honeymoon** *vb*
to have a honeymoon
**hon·ey·moon·er** *n*

**hon·ey·suck·le** \ˈhən-ē-ˌsək-əl\ *n*
a climbing vine or a bush with fragrant white, yellow, or red flowers

**¹honk** \'häŋk, 'hȯŋk\ *vb*
to make a honk

**²honk** *n*
**1** the cry of a goose
**2** a sound like the cry of a goose ⟨the *honk* of a horn⟩

**¹hon·or** \'än-ər\ *n*
**1** public admiration : REPUTATION
**2** outward respect : RECOGNITION ⟨a dinner in *honor* of a new coach⟩
**3** PRIVILEGE ⟨you will have the *honor* of leading the parade⟩
**4** used especially as a title for an official of high rank (as a judge) ⟨if Your *Honor* please⟩
**5** a person whose worth brings respect or fame ⟨an *honor* to your profession⟩
**6** evidence or a symbol of great respect ⟨a writer who has won many national *honors*⟩
**7** high moral standards of behavior

**²honor** *vb*
**1** ²RESPECT ⟨*honor* your parents⟩
**2** to give an honor to

**hon·or·able** \'än-ə-rə-bəl, 'än-rə-bəl\ *adj*
**1** bringing about or deserving honor ⟨an *honorable* achievement⟩
**2** observing ideas of honor or reputation ⟨seeking an *honorable* peace⟩
**3** having high moral standards of behavior : ETHICAL, UPRIGHT ⟨too *honorable* to stoop to scheming⟩

**hon·or·ary** \'än-ə-ˌrer-ē\ *adj*
given or done as an honor ⟨an *honorary* degree⟩

**¹hood** \'hu̇d\ *n*
**1** a covering for the head and neck and sometimes the face
**2** something like a hood
**3** the movable covering for an automobile engine
**hood·ed** \'hu̇d-əd\ *adj*

**²hood** *vb*
to cover with or as if with a hood

**-hood** \ˌhu̇d\ *n suffix*
**1** state : condition : quality : nature ⟨child*hood*⟩ ⟨hardi*hood*⟩
**2** instance of a specified state or quality ⟨false*hood*⟩
**3** individuals sharing a specified state or character

**hood·lum** \'hüd-ləm, 'hu̇d-\ *n*
a brutal ruffian : THUG

**hood·wink** \'hu̇d-ˌwiŋk\ *vb*
to mislead by trickery

**hoof** \'hu̇f, 'hüf\ *n, pl* **hooves** \'hu̇vz, 'hüvz\ *or* **hoofs**
**1** ▼ a covering of horn that protects the ends of the toes of some animals (as horses, oxen, or swine)
**2** a hoofed foot (as of a horse)
**hoofed** \'hu̇ft, 'hüft\ *adj*

**¹hook** \'hu̇k\ *n*
**1** ► a curved device (as a piece of bent metal) for catching, holding, or pulling something
**2** something curved or bent like a hook
**by hook or by crook** in any way : fairly or unfairly

**¹hook 1**

**²hook** *vb*
**1** to bend in the shape of a hook
**2** to catch or fasten with a hook ⟨*hook* a fish⟩

**hook·worm** \'hu̇k-ˌwərm\ *n*
a small worm that lives in the intestines and makes people sick by sucking their blood

**hoop** \'hu̇p, 'hüp\ *n*
**1** a circular band used for holding together the strips that make up the sides of a barrel or tub
**2** a circular figure or object ⟨embroidery *hoops*⟩
**3** a circle or series of circles of flexible material (as wire) used for holding a woman's skirt out from the body

**hooray** *variant of* HURRAH

**¹hoot** \'hüt\ *vb*
**1** to utter a loud shout usually to show disapproval
**2** to make the noise of an owl or a similar cry
**3** to express by hoots ⟨*hooted* disapproval⟩

**hoof 1**
There are two types of hoofed mammals: those with an uneven number of one or three toes, and those with an even number of two or four. Uneven-toed mammals include zebras, horses, and rhinoceroses, and even-toed mammals include cattle, pigs, sheep, giraffes, hippopotamuses, and camels. Hooves, such as those of cattle, that have two toes with a small gap in between, are known as cloven hooves.

**cow** is an even-toed mammal

*cloven hoof*

*hoof with an uneven number of toes*

**rhinoceros** is an uneven-toed mammal

**[2]hoot** *n*
**1** a sound of hooting
**2** the least bit ⟨doesn't care a *hoot*⟩

**[1]hop** \'häp\ *vb* **hopped**; **hop·ping**
**1** to move by short quick jumps
**2** to jump on one foot
**3** to jump over ⟨*hop* a puddle⟩
**4** to get aboard by or as if by hopping ⟨*hop* a bus⟩
**5** to make a quick trip especially by air

**[2]hop** *n*
**1** a short quick jump especially on one leg
**2** [2]DANCE 2
**3** a short trip especially by air

**[3]hop** *n*
**1** a twining vine whose greenish flowers look like cones
**2 hops** *pl* the dried flowers of the hop plant used chiefly in making beer and ale and in medicine

**[1]hope** \'hōp\ *vb* **hoped**; **hop·ing**
to desire especially with expectation that the wish will be granted

**[2]hope** *n*
**1** [1]TRUST 1
**2** desire together with the expectation of getting what is wanted
**3** a cause for hope
**4** something hoped for

**hope·ful** \'hōp-fəl\ *adj*
**1** full of hope
**2** giving hope : PROMISING ⟨a *hopeful* sign⟩
**hope·ful·ly** \-fə-lē\ *adv*
**hope·ful·ness** *n*

**hope·less** \'hō-pləs\ *adj*
**1** having no hope ⟨*hopeless* about the future⟩
**2** offering no hope ⟨the situation looks *hopeless*⟩
**hope·less·ly** *adv*
**hope·less·ness** *n*

**hop·per** \'häp-ər\ *n*
**1** one that hops
**2** an insect that moves by leaping
**3** a container usually shaped like a funnel for delivering material (as grain or coal) into a machine or a bin
**4** a tank holding liquid and having a device for releasing its contents through a pipe

**hop·scotch** \'häp-ˌskäch\ *n*
► a game in which a player tosses a stone into sections of a figure drawn on the ground and hops through the figure and back to pick up the stone

**horde** \'hōrd\ *n*
MULTITUDE, SWARM ⟨a *horde* of ants⟩

**ho·ri·zon** \hə-'rī-zᵊn\ *n*
**1** the line where the earth or sea seems to meet the sky
**2** the limit of a person's outlook or experience

**[1]hor·i·zon·tal** \ˌhȯr-ə-'zänt-l\ *adj*
level with the horizon
**hor·i·zon·tal·ly** *adv*

**[2]horizontal** *n*
something (as a line or plane) that is horizontal

**hor·mone** \'hȯr-ˌmōn\ *n*
a secretion of an endocrine gland

**horn 1:** a goat with large horns

**horn** \'hȯrn\ *n*
**1** ▲ one of the hard bony growths on the head of many hoofed animals (as cattle, goats, or sheep)
**2** the material of which horns are composed or a similar material ⟨a knife with a *horn* handle⟩
**3** something made from a horn ⟨each soldier carried a *horn* of powder⟩
**4** something shaped like a horn
**5** a musical or signaling instrument made from an animal's horn
**6** a brass musical instrument (as a trumpet or French horn)
**7** a usually electrical device that makes a noise like that of a horn ⟨motorists blowing their *horns*⟩

**hopscotch**

**horned** \'hȯrnd\ *adj*
**horn·less** \'hȯrn-ləs\ *adj*
**horn·like** \-ˌlīk\ *adj*

**horned toad** *n*
▼ a small harmless lizard with scales and hard pointed growths on the skin

**horned toad**

**hor·net** \'hȯr-nət\ *n*
a large wasp that can give a severe sting

**horn of plenty**
CORNUCOPIA

**horny** \'hȯr-nē\ *adj* **horn·i·er**; **horn·i·est**
like or made of horn

**hor·ri·ble** \'hȯr-ə-bəl\ *adj*
causing horror : TERRIBLE
**hor·ri·bly** \-blē\ *adv*

**hor·rid** \'hȯr-əd\ *adj*
**1** HORRIBLE
**2** very unpleasant : DISGUSTING
**hor·rid·ly** *adv*

**hor·ri·fy** \'hȯr-ə-ˌfī\ *vb* **hor·ri·fied**; **hor·ri·fy·ing**
to cause to feel horror

**hor·ror** \'hȯr-ər\ *n*
**1** great and painful fear, dread, or shock
**2** great dislike
**3** a quality or thing that causes horror

**horse** \'hȯrs\ *n*
**1** ► a large hoofed animal that feeds on grasses and is used as a work animal and for riding
**2** a frame that supports something (as wood while being cut)
**3** a piece of gymnasium equipment used for vaulting exercises
**horse·less** \'hȯr-sləs\ *adj*
**from the horse's mouth**
from the original source

## horse 1

The first horses evolved millions of years ago, with separate breeds developing in different habitats. Once horses were tamed, certain characteristics were encouraged by breeding from the best animals. Today there are more than 300 breeds of domestic horse. They can broadly be divided into three main types — light horses, heavy horses, and ponies, which are the smallest variety. Various breeds are suited to specific purposes, such as riding, racing, and harness work.

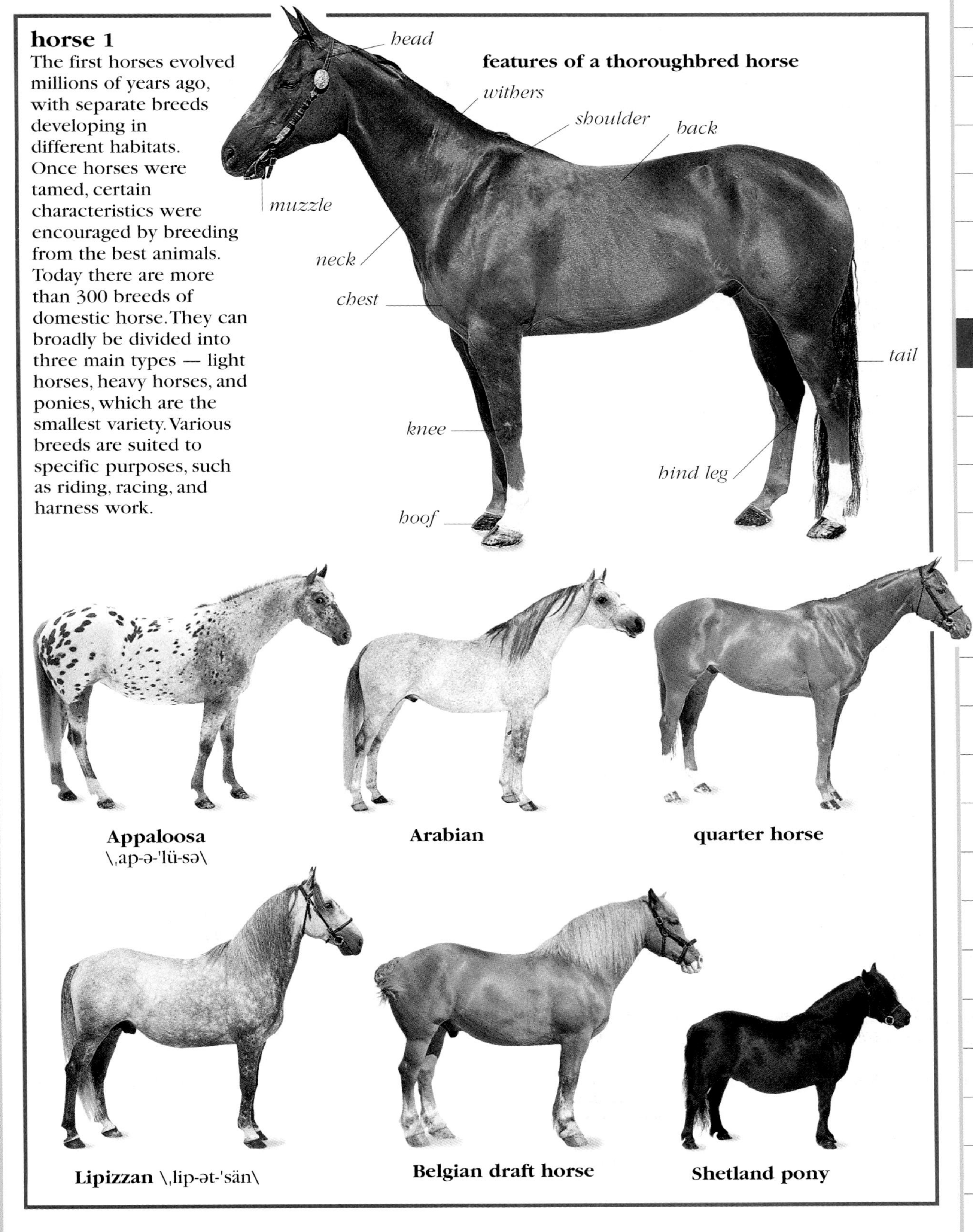


**Appaloosa** \ˌap-ə-ˈlü-sə\

**Arabian**

**quarter horse**

**Lipizzan** \ˌlip-ət-ˈsän\

**Belgian draft horse**

**Shetland pony**

A B C D E F G H I J K L M N O P Q R S T U V W X Y Z

**¹horse·back** \'hȯrs-,bak\ *n*
the back of a horse

**²horseback** *adv*
on horseback

**horse·car** \'hȯr-,skär\ *n*
**1** a streetcar drawn by horses
**2** a car for transporting horses

**horse chestnut** *n*
▶ a shiny brown nut that is unfit to eat and is the fruit of a tall tree with leaves divided into fingerlike parts and large flower clusters shaped like cones

**horse chestnut**

**horse·fly** \'hȯrs-,flī\ *n, pl* **horse·flies**
a large swift two-winged fly the females of which suck blood from animals

**horse·hair** \'hȯrs-,haər, -,heər\ *n*
**1** the hair of a horse especially from the mane or tail
**2** cloth made from horsehair

**horse latitudes** *n pl*
either of two regions in the neighborhoods of 30° north and 30° south of the equator marked by calms and light changeable winds

**horse·man** \'hȯr-smən\ *n, pl* **horse·men** \-smən\
**1** a horseback rider
**2** a person skilled in handling horses
**horse·man·ship** \-,ship\ *n*

**horse opera** *n*
a movie or a radio or television play about cowboys

**horse·play** \'hȯr-,splā\ *n*
rough play

**horse·pow·er** \'hȯr-,spau̇-ər\ *n*
a unit of power that equals the work done in raising 550 pounds one foot in one second

**horse·rad·ish** \'hȯrs-,rad-ish\ *n*
a hot relish made from the root of an herb of the mustard family

**horse·shoe** \'hȯrs-,shü\ *n*
**1** ▶ a protective iron plate that is nailed to the rim of a horse's hoof
**2** something shaped like a horseshoe
**3 horseshoes** *pl* a game in which horseshoes are tossed at a stake in the ground

**horseshoe 1**

**horse·tail** \'hȯr-,stāl\ *n*
any of a group of primitive plants that produce spores and have hollow stems with joints and leaves reduced to sheaths about the joints

**horse·whip** \'hȯr-,swip, 'hȯrs-,hwip\ *vb* **horse·whipped**; **horse·whip·ping**
to beat severely with a whip made to be used on a horse

**horse·wom·an** \'hȯr-,swu̇m-ən\ *n, pl* **horse·wom·en** \-,swim-ən\
a woman skilled in riding on horseback or in handling horses

**hors·ey** *or* **horsy** \'hȯr-sē\ *adj* **hors·i·er**; **hors·i·est**
of or relating to horses or horsemen and horsewomen

**ho·san·na** \hō-'zan-ə\ *interj*
used as a cry of approval, praise, or love

**¹hose 2:**
a fire fighter with a hose

**¹hose** \'hōz\ *n, pl* **hose** *or* **hos·es**
**1** *pl hose* STOCKING, SOCK
**2** ▲ a flexible tube for carrying fluid

**²hose** *vb* **hosed**; **hos·ing**
to spray, water, or wash with a hose

**ho·siery** \'hō-zhə-rē\ *n*
stockings or socks in general

**hos·pi·ta·ble** \hä-'spit-ə-bəl, 'häs-pit-\ *adj*
**1** friendly and generous in entertaining guests
**2** willing to deal with something new
**hos·pi·ta·bly** \-blē\ *adv*

**hos·pi·tal** \'häs-,pit-l\ *n*
a place where the sick and injured are cared for

**hos·pi·tal·i·ty** \,häs-pə-'tal-ət-ē\ *n*
friendly and generous treatment of guests

**hos·pi·tal·ize** \'häs-,pit-l-,īz\ *vb* **hos·pi·tal·ized**; **hos·pi·tal·iz·ing**
to place in a hospital for care and treatment
**hos·pi·tal·iza·tion** \,häs-,pit-l-ə-'zā-shən\ *n*

**¹host** \'hōst\ *n*
**1** ARMY 1
**2** MULTITUDE

**²host** *n*
one who receives or entertains guests

**³host** *vb*
to serve as host to or at ⟨*host* friends⟩ ⟨*hosting* a party⟩

**⁴host** *n, often cap*
the bread used in Christian Communion

**hos·tage** \'häs-tij\ *n*
a person given or held to make certain that promises will be kept

**hos·tel** \'häst-l\ *n*
a place providing inexpensive lodging for use by young travelers

**host·ess** \'hō-stəs\ *n*
a woman who receives or entertains guests

**hos·tile** \'häst-l\ *adj*
**1** of or relating to an enemy ⟨in *hostile* territory⟩
**2** UNFRIENDLY

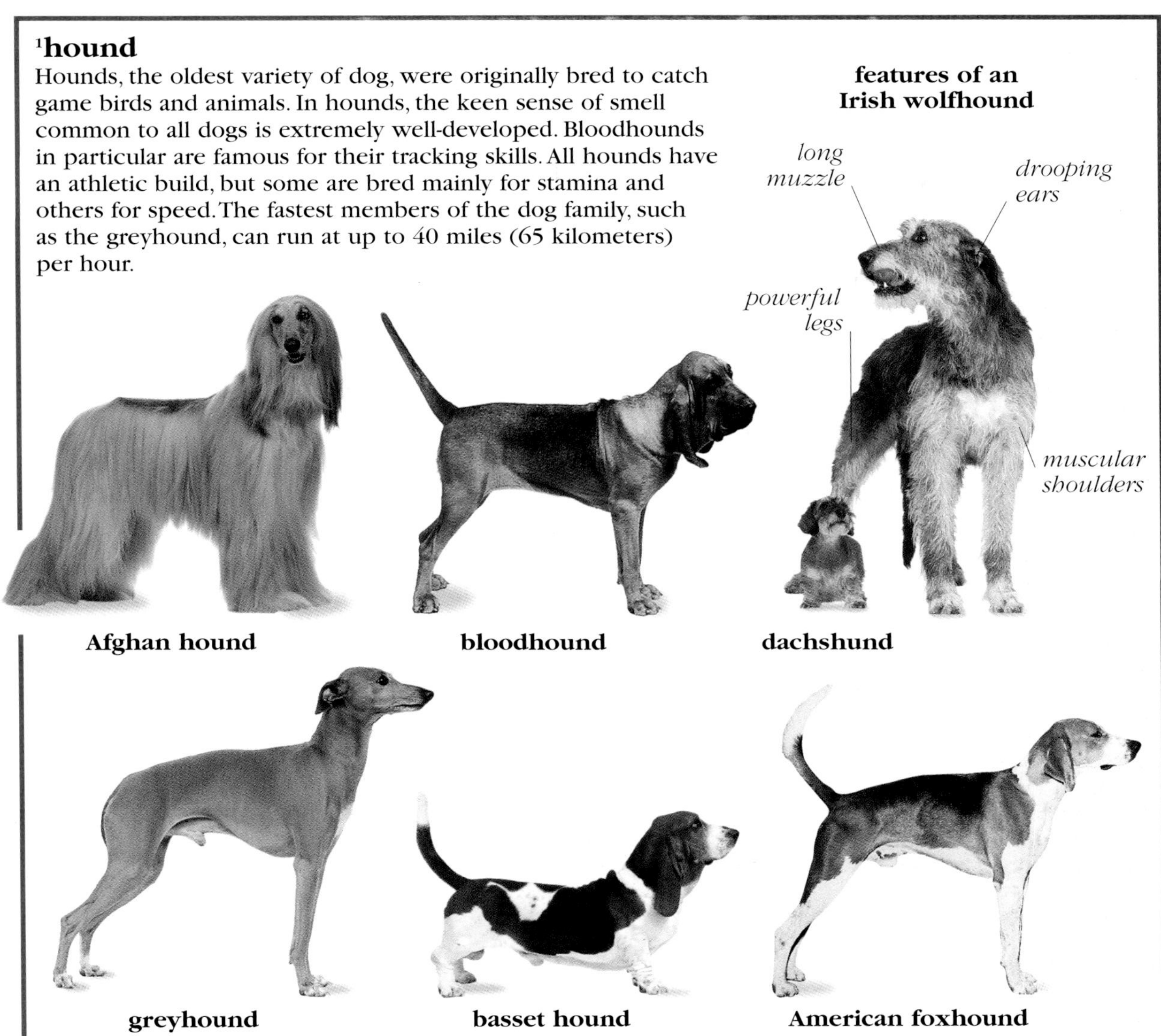


**[1]hound**
Hounds, the oldest variety of dog, were originally bred to catch game birds and animals. In hounds, the keen sense of smell common to all dogs is extremely well-developed. Bloodhounds in particular are famous for their tracking skills. All hounds have an athletic build, but some are bred mainly for stamina and others for speed. The fastest members of the dog family, such as the greyhound, can run at up to 40 miles (65 kilometers) per hour.

Afghan hound · bloodhound · dachshund · greyhound · basset hound · American foxhound

**hos·til·i·ty** \hä-'stil-ət-ē\ *n*, *pl* **hos·til·i·ties**
**1** a hostile state, attitude, or action
**2** *hostilities pl* acts of warfare

**hot** \'hät\ *adj* **hot·ter**; **hot·test**
**1** having a high temperature ⟨a *hot* stove⟩ ⟨a *hot* day⟩
**2** easily excited ⟨a *hot* temper⟩
**3** having or causing the sensation of an uncomfortable degree of body heat
**4** recently made or received ⟨*hot* news⟩
**5** close to something sought ⟨keep looking, you're getting *hot*⟩
**6** PUNGENT ⟨*hot* mustard⟩
**7** RADIOACTIVE
**8** recently stolen ⟨*hot* jewels⟩
**hot·ly** *adv*
**hot·ness** *n*

**hot·bed** \'hät-ˌbed\ *n*
a bed of heated earth covered by glass for growing tender plants early in the season

**hot dog** \'hät-ˌdȯg\ *n*
a frankfurter and especially a cooked one served in a long split roll

**ho·tel** \hō-'tel\ *n*
a place that provides lodging and meals for the public : INN

**hot·head** \'hät-ˌhed\ *n*
a person who is easily excited or angered
**hot·head·ed** \-'hed-əd\ *adj*

**hot·house** \'hät-ˌhau̇s\ *n*
a heated building enclosed by glass for growing plants

**hot plate** \'hät-ˌplāt\ *n*
a small portable appliance for heating or cooking

**hot rod** *n*
an automobile rebuilt for high speed and fast acceleration

**hot water** *n*
a difficult or distressing situation : TROUBLE

**[1]hound** \'hau̇nd\ *n*
▲ a dog with drooping ears and deep bark that is used in hunting and follows game by the sense of smell

**[2]hound** *vb*
to hunt, chase, or annoy without ceasing

**hour** \'au̇r\ *n*
**1** one of the twenty-four divisions of a day **:** sixty minutes
**2** the time of day
**3** a fixed or particular time
**4** a measure of distance figured by the amount of time it takes to cover it ⟨it's two *hours* by car⟩

**hour·glass** \'au̇r-ˌglas\ *n*
a device for measuring time in which sand runs from the upper into the lower part of a glass in an hour

**[1]hour·ly** \'au̇r-lē\ *adv*
at or during every hour ⟨planes leaving *hourly*⟩

**[2]hourly** *adj*
**1** occurring every hour
**2** figured by the hour ⟨an *hourly* wage⟩

**[1]house** \'hau̇s\ *n, pl* **hous·es** \'hau̇-zəz\
**1** a place built for people to live in
**2** something (as a nest or den) used by an animal for shelter
**3** a building in which something is kept ⟨a carriage *house*⟩
**4** [1]HOUSEHOLD
**5** FAMILY 1 ⟨the *house* of Windsor⟩
**6** a body of persons assembled to make the laws for a country ⟨the two *houses* of the United States Congress⟩
**7** a business firm ⟨a fashion *house*⟩
**8** the audience in a theater or concert hall
**on the house** free of charge

**[2]house** \'hau̇z\ *vb*
**1** to provide with living quarters or shelter
**2** CONTAIN 3

**house·boat** \'hau̇s-ˌbōt\ *n*
a roomy pleasure boat fitted for use as a place to live

**house·boy** \'hau̇s-ˌbȯi\ *n*
a boy or man hired to do housework

**house·fly** \'hau̇s-ˌflī\ *n, pl* **house·flies**
a two-winged fly that is common about houses and often carries disease germs

**[1]house·hold** \'hau̇s-ˌhōld\ *n*
all the persons who live as a family in one house

**[2]household** *adj*
**1** of or relating to a household
**2** FAMILIAR

**house·hold·er** \'hau̇s-ˌhōl-dər\ *n*
one who lives in a dwelling alone or as the head of a household

**house·keep·er** \'hau̇-ˌskē-pər\ *n*
a person employed to take care of a house

**house·keep·ing** \'hau̇-ˌskē-piŋ\ *n*
the care and management of a house

**house·maid** \'hau̇-ˌsmād\ *n*
a woman or girl hired to do housework

**house·moth·er** \'hau̇-ˌsmət͟h-ər\ *n*
a woman who acts as hostess, supervisor, and often housekeeper in a residence for young people

**house·plant** \'hau̇-ˌsplant\ *n*
▶ a plant grown or kept indoors

**houseplant:** a rubber plant

**house·top** \'hau̇-ˌstäp\ *n*
[1]ROOF 1

**house·warm·ing** \'hau̇-ˌswȯr-miŋ\ *n*
a party to celebrate moving into a new home

**house·wife** \'hau̇-ˌswīf\ *n, pl* **house·wives** \-ˌswīvz\
a married woman in charge of a household

**house·work** \'hau̇-ˌswərk\ *n*
the actual labor involved in housekeeping

**hous·ing** \'hau̇-ziŋ\ *n*
**1** dwellings provided for a number of people ⟨*housing* for the aged⟩
**2** something that covers or protects

**hove** *past of* HEAVE

**hov·el** \'həv-əl, 'häv-\ *n*
a small poorly built usually dirty house

**hov·er** \'həv-ər, 'häv-\ *vb*
**1** to hang fluttering in the air or on the wing
**2** to move to and fro near a place ⟨waiters *hovered* about⟩

**[1]how** \'hau̇\ *adv*
**1** in what way **:** by what means ⟨*how* do you work this thing⟩ ⟨*how* did they get here⟩
**2** for what reason ⟨*how* can you treat me so⟩
**3** to what degree, number, or amount ⟨*how* cold is it⟩
**4** in what state or condition ⟨*how* are you⟩
**how about** what do you say to or think of ⟨*how about* a soda⟩
**how come** [1]WHY
**how do you do** HELLO

**[2]how** *conj*
in what manner or condition ⟨study *how* plants grow⟩ ⟨asked them *how* they were⟩

**how·ev·er** \hau̇-'ev-ər\ *adv*
**1** to whatever degree or extent ⟨*however* long it takes⟩
**2** in whatever way ⟨*however* you want to do it⟩
**3** in spite of that ⟨*however*, we did try to help⟩

**[1]howl** \'hau̇l\ *vb*
**1** to make a loud long mournful sound like that of a dog ⟨wind *howling* through the trees⟩
**2** to cry out loudly (as with pain)

**[2]howl** *n*
**1** a loud long mournful sound made by dogs
**2** a long loud cry (as of distress, disappointment, or rage)
**3** COMPLAINT 1 ⟨set up a *howl* over taxes⟩
**4** something that causes laughter

**HTML** \ˌāch-(ˌ)tē-(ˌ)em-'el\ *n*
a computer language that is used to create pages on the World Wide Web that can include text, pictures, sound, video, and links to other Web pages

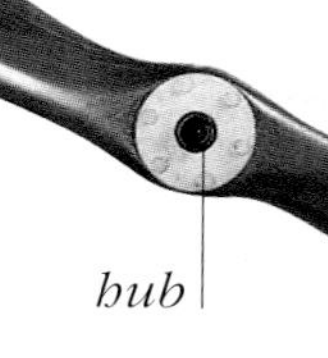


**hub 1:** the hub on an airplane's propeller

**hub** \'həb\ *n*
**1** ▲ the center of a wheel, propeller, or fan
**2** a center of activity

**hub·bub** \'həb-ˌəb\ *n*
UPROAR

**huck·le·ber·ry** \'hək-əl-ˌber-ē\ *n, pl* **huck·le·ber·ries**
a dark edible berry with many hard seeds that grows on a bush

**huck·ster** \'hək-stər\ *n*
**1** PEDDLER, HAWKER
**2** a writer of advertising

[1]**hud·dle** \'həd-l\ *vb* **hud·dled; hud·dling**
**1** to crowd, push, or pile together ⟨people *huddled* in a doorway⟩
**2** to get together to talk something over
**3** to curl up ⟨*huddled* under a blanket⟩

[2]**huddle** *n*
**1** a closely packed group
**2** a private meeting or conference

**hue** \'hyü\ *n*
**1** [1]COLOR 1 ⟨flowers of every *hue*⟩
**2** a shade of a color

[1]**huff** \'həf\ *vb*
to give off puffs (as of air or steam)

[2]**huff** *n*
a fit of anger or temper

**huffy** \'həf-ē\ *adj* **huff·i·er; huff·i·est**
**1** easily offended : PETULANT
**2** [1]SULKY
**huff·i·ly** \'həf-ə-lē\ *adv*
**huff·i·ness** \'həf-ē-nəs\ *n*

[1]**hug** \'həg\ *vb* **hugged; hug·ging**
**1** to clasp in the arms : EMBRACE
**2** to keep close to

[2]**hug** *n*
[2]EMBRACE

**huge** \'hyüj, 'yüj\ *adj* **hug·er; hug·est**
very large : VAST

**hulk** \'həlk\ *n*
**1** a person or thing that is bulky or clumsy
**2** the remains of an old or wrecked ship

**hulk·ing** \'həl-king\ *adj*
very large and strong : MASSIVE

[1]**hull** \'həl\ *n*
**1** the outside covering of a fruit or seed
**2** the frame or body of a ship, flying boat, or airship

[2]**hull** *vb*
to remove the hulls of
**hull·er** *n*

**hul·la·ba·loo** \'həl-ə-bə-ˌlü\ *n, pl* **hul·la·ba·loos**
a confused noise : HUBBUB, COMMOTION

[1]**hum** \'həm\ *vb* **hummed; hum·ming**
**1** to utter a sound like a long \m\
**2** to make the buzzing noise of a flying insect
**3** to sing with closed lips
**4** to give forth a low murmur of sounds ⟨a street *humming* with activity⟩
**5** to be very busy or active

[2]**hum** *n*
the act or an instance of humming : the sound produced by humming

[1]**hu·man** \'hyü-mən, 'yü-\ *adj*
**1** of, relating to, being, or characteristic of people as distinct from lower animals
**2** having human form or characteristics

[2]**human** *n*
a human being
**hu·man·like** \'hyü-mən-ˌlīk, 'yü-\ *adj*

**hu·mane** \hyü-'mān, yü-\ *adj*
having sympathy and consideration for others
**hu·mane·ly** *adv*
**hu·mane·ness** *n*

[1]**hu·man·i·tar·i·an** \hyü-ˌman-ə-'ter-ē-ən, yü-\ *n*
a person devoted to and working for the health and happiness of other people

[2]**humanitarian** *adj*
of, relating to, or characteristic of humanitarians

**hu·man·i·ty** \hyü-'man-ət-ē, yü-\ *n, pl* **hu·man·i·ties**
**1** KINDNESS 2, SYMPATHY
**2** the quality or state of being human
**3** *humanities pl* studies (as literature, history, and art) concerned primarily with human culture
**4** the human race

**hu·man·ly** \'hyü-mən-lē, 'yü-\ *adv*
within the range of human ability ⟨a task not *humanly* possible⟩

[1]**hum·ble** \'həm-bəl\ *adj* **hum·bler; hum·blest**
**1** not bold or proud : MODEST
**2** expressing a spirit of respect for the wishes of another ⟨*humble* apologies⟩
**3** low in rank or condition ⟨people of *humble* origin⟩
**hum·bly** \-blē\ *adv*

[2]**humble** *vb* **hum·bled; hum·bling**
**1** to make humble
**2** to destroy the power of

[1]**hum·bug** \'həm-ˌbəg\ *n*
**1** FRAUD 3
**2** NONSENSE 1

[2]**humbug** *vb* **hum·bugged; hum·bug·ging**
DECEIVE 1

**hum·ding·er** \'həm-'ding-ər\ *n*
something striking or extraordinary

**hum·drum** \'həm-ˌdrəm\ *adj*
MONOTONOUS

**hu·mid** \'hyü-məd, 'yü-\ *adj*
MOIST ⟨*humid* day⟩

**hu·mid·i·fy** \hyü-'mid-ə-ˌfī, yü-\ *vb* **hu·mid·i·fied; hu·mid·i·fy·ing**
to make (as the air of a room) more moist
**hu·mid·i·fi·er** *n*

**hu·mid·i·ty** \hyü-'mid-ət-ē, yü-\ *n, pl* **hu·mid·i·ties**
the degree of wetness especially of the atmosphere : MOISTURE

**hu·mil·i·ate** \hyü-'mil-ē-ˌāt, yü-\ *vb* **hu·mil·i·at·ed; hu·mil·i·at·ing**
to lower the pride or self-respect of

**hu·mil·i·a·tion** \hyü-ˌmil-ē-'ā-shən, yü-\ *n*
**1** the state of being humiliated
**2** an instance of being humiliated

**hu·mil·i·ty** \hyü-'mil-ət-ē, yü-\ *n*
the quality of being humble

**hum·ming·bird** \'həm-ing-ˌbərd\ *n*
▼ a tiny brightly colored American bird whose wings make a humming sound in flight

**hummingbird**

A B C D E F G H I J K L M N O P Q R S T U V W X Y Z

**hum·mock** \'həm-ək\ *n*
**1** a rounded mound of earth **:** KNOLL
**2** a ridge or pile of ice

[1]**hu·mor** \'hyü-mər, 'yü-\ *n*
**1** state of mind **:** MOOD ⟨in a bad *humor*⟩
**2** the amusing quality of something ⟨the *humor* of a situation⟩
**3** the ability to see or report the amusing quality of things

[2]**humor** *vb*
to give in to the wishes of

**hu·mor·ist** \'hyü-mə-rist, 'yü-\ *n*
a person who writes or talks in a humorous way

**hu·mor·ous** \'hyü-mə-rəs, 'yü-\ *adj*
full of humor **:** FUNNY
**hu·mor·ous·ly** *adv*

**hump** \'həmp\ *n*
**1** ▶ a rounded bulge or lump (as on the back of a camel)
**2** a difficult part (as of a task)
**humped** \'həmpt\ *adj*

**hump·back** \'həmp-,bak\ *n*
**1** a humped back
**2** HUNCHBACK 2
**hump·backed** \-'bakt\ *adj*

**hu·mus** \'hyü-məs, 'yü-\ *n*
the dark rich part of earth formed from decaying material

[1]**hunch** \'hənch\ *vb*
**1** to bend one's body into an arch or hump ⟨don't *hunch* over when you walk⟩
**2** to draw up close together or into an arch ⟨*hunch* one's shoulders⟩ ⟨the cat *hunched* its back⟩

[2]**hunch** *n*
**1** HUMP 1
**2** a strong feeling about what will happen

**hunch·back** \'hənch-,bak\ *n*
**1** HUMPBACK 1
**2** a person with a humped or crooked back

[1]**hun·dred** \'hən-drəd\ *n*
**1** ten times ten **:** 100
**2** a very large number ⟨*hundreds* of times⟩

[2]**hundred** *adj*
being 100

[1]**hun·dredth** \'hən-drədth\ *adj*
coming right after ninety-ninth

[2]**hundredth** *n*
number 100 in a series

**hung** *past of* HANG

[1]**hun·ger** \'həng-gər\ *n*
**1** a desire or a need for food
**2** a strong desire

[2]**hunger** *vb*
**1** to feel hunger
**2** to have a strong desire

**hun·gry** \'həng-grē\ *adj* **hun·gri·er**; **hun·gri·est**
**1** feeling or showing hunger
**2** having a strong desire
**hun·gri·ly** \-grə-lē\ *adv*

**hunk** \'həngk\ *n*
a large lump or piece

[1]**hunt** \'hənt\ *vb*
**1** to follow after in order to capture or kill ⟨*hunt* deer⟩
**2** to try to find **synonyms** see SEEK

**hump 1:** a camel with one hump

[2]**hunt** *n*
an instance or the practice of hunting

**hunt·er** \'hənt-ər\ *n*
**1** a person who hunts game
**2** a dog or horse used or trained for hunting
**3** a person who searches for something ⟨a bargain *hunter*⟩

**hunts·man** \'hənt-smən\ *n, pl* **hunts·men** \-smən\
HUNTER 1

[1]**hur·dle** \'hərd-l\ *n*
**1** ▶ a barrier to be jumped in a race (**hurdles**)
**2** OBSTACLE

[2]**hurdle** *vb* **hur·dled**; **hur·dling**
**1** to leap over while running
**2** OVERCOME ⟨difficulties to be *hurdled*⟩

**hur·dy–gur·dy** \,hərd-ē-'gərd-ē\ *n, pl* **hur·dy–gur·dies**
HAND ORGAN

**hurl** \'hərl\ *vb*
to throw with force **synonyms** see THROW

**hur·rah** \hu̇-'rȯ, -'rä\ *or* **hoo·ray** *also* **hur·ray** \hu̇-'rā\ *interj*
used to express joy, approval, or encouragement

**hur·ri·cane** \'hər-ə-,kān, 'hər-i-kən\ *n*
a tropical cyclone with winds of thirty-three meters per second or greater usually accompanied by rain, thunder, and lightning

**hur·ried** \'hər-ēd\ *adj*
**1** going or working with speed **:** FAST ⟨the *hurried* life of the city⟩
**2** done in a hurry
**hur·ried·ly** *adv*

[1]**hur·ry** \'hər-ē\ *vb* **hur·ried**; **hur·ry·ing**
**1** to carry or cause to go with haste
**2** to move or act with haste
**3** to speed up ⟨*hurried* the repair job⟩

[2]**hurry** *n*
a state of eagerness or urgent need **:** extreme haste

[1]**hurt** \'hərt\ *vb* **hurt**; **hurt·ing**
**1** to feel or cause pain
**2** to do harm to **:** DAMAGE
**3** [2]DISTRESS, OFFEND
**4** to make poorer or more difficult ⟨the fumble *hurt* our team's chance of winning⟩



[1]**hurdle 1:** an athlete leaping over a hurdle

**[2]hurt** *n*
**1** an injury or wound to the body
**2** SUFFERING 1, ANGUISH ⟨sympathy eases the *hurt*⟩
**3** [1]WRONG ⟨you cannot undo the *hurt*⟩

**hurt•ful** \'hərt-fəl\ *adj*
causing injury or suffering

**hur•tle** \'hərt-l\ *vb* **hur•tled**; **hur•tling**
**1** to rush suddenly or violently ⟨rocks *hurtled* down the hill⟩
**2** to drive or throw violently

**[1]hus•band** \'həz-bənd\ *n*
a married man

**[2]husband** *vb*
to manage with thrift : use carefully ⟨*husbanding* my money⟩

**hus•band•ry** \'həz-bən-drē\ *n*
**1** the management or wise use of resources : THRIFT
**2** the business and activities of a farmer

**[1]hush** \'həsh\ *vb*
to make or become quiet, calm, or still : SOOTHE ⟨*hush* a baby⟩

**[2]hush** *n*
[1]QUIET

**hush–hush** \'həsh-,həsh\ *adj*
[1]SECRET 1, CONFIDENTIAL

**[1]husk** \'həsk\ *n*
the outer covering of a fruit or seed

**[2]husk** *vb*
to strip the husk from
**husk•er** *n*

**[1]hus•ky** \'həs-kē\ *adj* **hus•ki•er**; **hus•ki•est**
HOARSE
**husk•i•ly** \-kə-lē\ *adv*
**husk•i•ness** \-kē-nəs\ *n*

**[2]husky** *n, pl* **huskies**
▼ a strong dog with a thick coat used to pull sleds in the Arctic

**[3]husky** *n, pl* **huskies**
a husky person or thing

**[2]husky:** huskies pulling a sled

*sled*

*husky*

**[4]husky** *adj* **hus•ki•er**; **hus•ki•est**
STRONG 1, BURLY
**husk•i•ness** *n*

**[1]hus•tle** \'həs-əl\ *vb* **hus•tled**; **hus•tling**
**1** to push, crowd, or force forward roughly ⟨*hustled* the prisoner to jail⟩
**2** HURRY

**[2]hustle** *n*
energetic activity

**hus•tler** \'həs-lər\ *n*
an energetic person who works fast

**hut** \'hət\ *n*
a small roughly made and often temporary dwelling

**hutch** \'həch\ *n*
**1** a low cupboard usually having open shelves on top
**2** a pen or coop for an animal

**hyacinth**

**hy•a•cinth** \'hī-ə-sinth\ *n*
▲ a plant of the lily family with stalks of fragrant flowers shaped like bells

**[1]hy•brid** \'hī-brəd\ *n*
**1** an animal or plant whose parents differ in some hereditary characteristic or belong to different groups (as breeds, races, or species)
**2** something that is of mixed origin or composition

**[2]hybrid** *adj*
of or relating to a hybrid : of mixed origin

**hydr-** *or* **hydro-** *prefix*
**1** water ⟨*hydro*electric⟩
**2** hydrogen ⟨*hydro*carbon⟩

**hy•drant** \'hī-drənt\ *n*
a pipe with a spout through which water may be drawn from the main pipes ⟨a fire *hydrant*⟩

**hy•drau•lic** \hī-'dró-lik\ *adj*
**1** operated, moved, or brought about by means of water
**2** operated by liquid forced through a small hole or through a tube ⟨*hydraulic* brakes⟩
**hy•drau•li•cal•ly** \-li-kə-lē\ *adv*

**hy•dro•car•bon** \,hī-drə-'kär-bən\ *n*
a substance containing only carbon and hydrogen

**hy•dro•chlo•ric acid** \,hī-drə-,klōr-ik-\ *n*
a strong acid formed by dissolving in water a gas made up of hydrogen and chlorine

**hy•dro•elec•tric** \,hī-drō-i-'lek-trik\ *adj*
relating to or used in the making of electricity by waterpower

**hy•dro•gen** \'hī-drə-jən\ *n*
a colorless, odorless, and tasteless flammable gas that is the lightest of the chemical elements

**Word History** When hydrogen is burned it combines with oxygen to make water. That fact accounts for the name of this gas. The word *hydrogen* was formed from two Greek elements. The first meant "water," and the second meant "born."

**hydrogen bomb** *n*
a bomb whose great power is due to the sudden release of energy when the central portions of hydrogen atoms unite

**hydrogen peroxide** *n*
a liquid chemical containing hydrogen and oxygen and used for bleaching and as an antiseptic

**hy•dro•pho•bia** \,hī-drə-'fō-bē-ə\ *n*
RABIES

**hy·dro·plane** \'hī-drə-,plān\ *n*
**1** a speedboat whose hull is completely or partly raised as it glides over the water
**2** SEAPLANE

hydroplane 1

**hy·e·na** \hī-'ē-nə\ *n*
a large mammal of Asia and Africa that lives on flesh

**Word History** Some hogs have bristly manes. When the ancient Greeks first saw hyenas they thought that the animals' short, bristly manes looked like the manes of hogs. They gave the strange animals a name that was formed from a Greek word that meant "hog." The English word *hyena* came from this Greek name.

**hy·giene** \'hī-,jēn\ *n*
**1** a science that deals with the bringing about and keeping up of good health in the individual and the group
**2** conditions or practices necessary for health

**hy·gien·ic** \,hī-jē-'en-ik, hī-'jen-ik\ *adj*
of, relating to, or leading toward health or hygiene
**hy·gien·i·cal·ly** \-i-kə-lē\ *adv*

**hy·gien·ist** \hī-'jē-nist\ *n*
a person skilled in hygiene and especially in a specified branch of hygiene ⟨a dental *hygienist*⟩

**hy·grom·e·ter** \hī-'gräm-ət-ər\ *n*
an instrument for measuring the humidity of the air

**hymn** \'him\ *n*
a song of praise especially to God

**hym·nal** \'him-nəl\ *n*
a book of hymns

hygrometer

**hyper-** *prefix*
excessively ⟨*hyper*sensitive⟩

**hy·per·link** \'hī-pər-,lingk\ *n*
an electronic link that allows a computer user to move directly from a marked place in a hypertext document to another in the same or a different document
**hyperlink** *vb*

**hy·per·sen·si·tive** \,hī-pər-'sen-sət-iv\ *adj*
very sensitive

**hy·per·text** \'hī-pər-,tekst\ *n*
an arrangement of the information in a computer database that allows the user to get other information by clicking on text displayed on the screen

**hyena:** a spotted hyena and a striped hyena

**hy·pha** \'hī-fə\ *n, pl* **hy·phae** \-,fē\
one of the fine threads that make up the body of a fungus

[1]**hy·phen** \'hī-fən\ *n*
a mark - used to divide or to compound words or word elements

[2]**hyphen** *vb*
HYPHENATE

**hy·phen·ate** \'hī-fə-,nāt\ *vb*
**hy·phen·at·ed**; **hy·phen·at·ing**
to connect or mark with a hyphen

**hyp·no·sis** \hip-'nō-səs\ *n*
a state which resembles sleep but is produced by a person who can then make suggestions to which the hypnotized person will respond

**hyp·no·tism** \'hip-nə-,tiz-əm\ *n*
the study or act of producing a state like sleep in which the person in this state will respond to suggestions made by the hypnotist

**hyp·no·tist** \'hip-nə-təst\ *n*
a person who practices hypnotism

**hyp·no·tize** \'hip-nə-,tīz\ *vb*
**hyp·no·tized**; **hyp·no·tiz·ing**
to affect by or as if by hypnotism

**hy·poc·ri·sy** \hi-'päk-rə-sē\ *n, pl* **hy·poc·ri·sies**
a pretending to be what one is not or to believe what one does not

**hyp·o·crite** \'hip-ə-,krit\ *n*
a person who practices hypocrisy

**hy·po·der·mic needle** \,hī-pə-'dər-mik-\ *n*
**1** [1]NEEDLE 5
**2** a hypodermic syringe complete with needle

**hypodermic syringe** *n*
a small syringe used with a hollow needle to inject material (as a vaccine) into or beneath the skin

**hy·pot·e·nuse** \hī-'pät-n-,üs, -,yüs\ *n*
the side of a right triangle that is opposite the right angle

**hy·poth·e·sis** \hī-'päth-ə-səs\ *n, pl* **hy·poth·e·ses** \-ə-,sēz\
something not proved but assumed to be true for purposes of argument or further study or investigation

**hy·po·thet·i·cal** \,hī-pə-'thet-i-kəl\ *adj*
**1** involving or based on a hypothesis
**2** being merely supposed ⟨a *hypothetical* situation⟩
**hy·po·thet·i·cal·ly** *adv*

**hys·te·ria** \his-'ter-ē-ə\ *n*
**1** a nervous disorder in which one loses control over the emotions
**2** a wild uncontrolled outburst of emotion
**hys·ter·i·cal** \-'ter-i-kəl\ *adj*
**hys·ter·i·cal·ly** *adv*

**hys·ter·ics** \his-'ter-iks\ *n sing or pl*
a fit of uncontrollable laughing or crying : HYSTERIA

# Ii

**The sounds of I:** The letter **I** is used mainly for two vowel sounds in English.
In many words, **I** sounds like its own name. This sound is often called "**long I**." Examples of words with this sound are **ice**, **ivory**, **idolize**, **dime**, **file**, **might**, **describe**, and **diagonal**.
The other main sound of **I** is the "**short I**." This is the sound of **I** in the words **itch**, **image**, **insist**, **dim**, **fill**, **bridge**, **dingy**, and **deliberate**.
There is a third, less common, sound of **I**. This is the same as the "**long E**" sound. This sound is heard especially in suffixes such as **-ia**, **-ial**, **-ian**, or **-iate**. Examples are **hysteria**, **aerial**, **Arabian**, and **appreciate**.

**i** \'ī\ *n, pl* **i's** *or* **is** \'īz\ *often cap*
**1** the ninth letter of the English alphabet
**2** one in Roman numerals

**I** \ī, 'ī\ *pron*
the person speaking or writing

**-ial** \ē-əl, yəl, əl\ *adj suffix*
[1]-AL ⟨aer*ial*⟩

**-ian** see -AN

**ibex** \'ī-ˌbeks\ *n, pl* **ibex** *or* **ibex·es**
▼ a wild goat of the Old World with horns that curve backward

**ibex:** a Siberian ibex

**-ibility** see -ABILITY

**ibis** \'ī-bəs\ *n, pl* **ibis** *or* **ibis·es**
a bird related to the herons but having a slender bill that curves down

**-ible** see -ABLE

**-ic** \ik\ *adj suffix*
**1** of, relating to, or having the form of : being
**2** coming from, consisting of, or containing ⟨alcohol*ic*⟩
**3** in the manner of
**4** associated or dealing with : using ⟨electron*ic*⟩
**5** characterized by : exhibiting : affected with ⟨allerg*ic*⟩

**-ical** \i-kəl\ *adj suffix*
-IC ⟨symmetr*ical*⟩

[1]**ice** \'īs\ *n*
**1** frozen water
**2** a substance like ice
**3** a frozen dessert usually made with sweetened fruit juice

[2]**ice** *vb* **iced**; **ic·ing**
**1** to coat or become coated with ice
**2** to chill with ice : supply with ice
**3** to cover with icing

**ice age** *n*
a period of time during which much of the earth is covered with glaciers

**ice·berg** \'īs-ˌbərg\ *n*
a large floating mass of ice that has broken away from a glacier

**ice·boat** \'īs-ˌbōt\ *n*
a boatlike frame driven by sails and gliding over ice on runners

**ice·bound** \'īs-ˌbau̇nd\ *adj*
surrounded or blocked by ice

**ice·box** \'īs-ˌbäks\ *n*
REFRIGERATOR

**ice·break·er** \'īs-ˌbrā-kər\ *n*
▼ a ship equipped to make and keep open a channel through ice

**ice cap** *n*
a large more or less level glacier flowing outward in all directions from its center

**ice–cold** \'ī-'skōld\ *adj*
very cold

**ice cream** *n*
a frozen food containing sweetened and flavored cream or butterfat

**ice-skate:** a girl ice-skating

**ice–skate** \'īs-ˌskāt\ *vb*
▲ to skate on ice
**ice skat·er** *n*

**ici·cle** \'ī-ˌsik-əl\ *n*
a hanging mass of ice formed from dripping water

**ic·ing** \'ī-sing\ *n*
a sweet coating for baked goods

**icebreaker:** model of a Finnish icebreaker

A B C D E F G H I J K L M N O P Q R S T U V W X Y Z

**icon** \ˈī-ˌkän\ *n*
**1** a picture that represents something
**2** a religious image usually painted on a small wooden panel
**3** a small picture or symbol on a computer screen that suggests a function that the computer can perform ⟨click on the printer *icon* to print out the document⟩

**-ics** \iks\ *n sing or pl suffix*
**1** study : knowledge : skill : practice ⟨electron*ics*⟩
**2** characteristic actions or qualities ⟨acrobat*ics*⟩

**icy** \ˈī-sē\ *adj* **ic·i·er**; **ic·i·est**
**1** covered with, full of, or being ice ⟨*icy* roads⟩
**2** very cold
**3** UNFRIENDLY ⟨an *icy* look⟩
**ic·i·ly** \ˈī-sə-lē\ *adv*
**ic·i·ness** \ˈī-sē-nəs\ *n*

**I'd** \īd\
I had : I should : I would

**idea** \ī-ˈdē-ə\ *n*
**1** a plan of action : INTENTION ⟨my *idea* is to study law⟩
**2** something imagined or pictured in the mind : NOTION
**3** a central meaning or purpose ⟨do you get the *idea*⟩

**¹ide·al** \ī-ˈdē-əl\ *adj*
**1** existing only in the mind
**2** having no flaw : PERFECT ⟨*ideal* weather⟩
**ide·al·ly** *adv*

**²ideal** *n*
**1** a standard of perfection, beauty, or excellence
**2** a perfect type **synonyms** see MODEL

**iden·ti·cal** \ī-ˈdent-i-kəl\ *adj*
**1** being one and the same
**2** being exactly alike or equal
**synonyms** see SAME

**iden·ti·fi·ca·tion** \ī-ˌdent-ə-fə-ˈkā-shən\ *n*
**1** an act of identifying : the state of being identified
**2** something that shows or proves identity

**iden·ti·fy** \ī-ˈdent-ə-ˌfī\ *vb* **iden·ti·fied**; **iden·ti·fy·ing**
**1** to think of as identical
**2** ¹ASSOCIATE 2
**3** to find out or show the identity of

**iden·ti·ty** \ī-ˈdent-ət-ē\ *n, pl* **iden·ti·ties**
**1** the fact or condition of being exactly alike : SAMENESS
**2** INDIVIDUALITY 1
**3** the fact of being the same person or thing as claimed ⟨prove one's *identity*⟩

**id·i·o·cy** \ˈid-ē-ə-sē\ *n, pl* **id·i·o·cies**
**1** great lack of intelligence
**2** something very stupid or foolish

**id·i·om** \ˈid-ē-əm\ *n*
an expression that cannot be understood from the meanings of its separate words but must be learned as a whole ⟨the expression "give way," meaning "retreat," is an *idiom*⟩

**id·i·ot** \ˈid-ē-ət\ *n*
**1** a person of very low intelligence
**2** a silly or foolish person

**Word History** The word *idiot* came from a Greek word that meant "a private person." This word was used for those who held no public office. In time this Greek word came to mean "a common person." Later it meant "an ignorant person." Most of the common people of ancient Greece were not learned. At first the English word *idiot* meant "an ignorant person." Now the meaning of the word is much stronger.

**id·i·ot·ic** \ˌid-ē-ˈät-ik\ *adj*
showing idiocy : FOOLISH, STUPID ⟨*idiotic* behavior⟩
**id·i·ot·i·cal·ly** \-i-kə-lē\ *adv*

**¹idle** \ˈīd-l\ *adj* **idler** \ˈīd-lər\; **idlest** \ˈīd-ləst\
**1** not based on facts ⟨*idle* gossip⟩
**2** not working or in use ⟨*idle* workers⟩ ⟨an *idle* factory⟩
**3** LAZY 1
**idle·ness** \ˈīd-l-nəs\ *n*
**idly** \ˈīd-lē\ *adv*

**²idle** *vb* **idled** \ˈīd-ld\; **idling** \ˈīd-ling\
**1** to spend time doing nothing
**2** to run without being connected for doing useful work ⟨the engine is *idling*⟩
**idler** \ˈīd-lər\ *n*

**idol** \ˈīd-l\ *n*
**1** an image worshiped as a god
**2** a much loved person or thing

**idol·ize** \ˈīd-l-ˌīz\ *vb* **idol·ized**; **idol·iz·ing**
to make an idol of : love or admire too much

**-ie** *also* **-y** \ē\ *n suffix, pl* **-ies**
little one ⟨lass*ie*⟩

**-ier** see ²-ER

**if** \if\ *conj*
**1** in the event that ⟨*if* it rains we'll stay home⟩
**2** WHETHER 1 ⟨see *if* they have left⟩

**-ify** \ə-ˌfī\ *vb suffix* **-ified**; **-ify·ing**
-FY

**ig·loo** \ˈig-lü\ *n, pl* **igloos**
an Eskimo house often made of blocks of snow and shaped like a dome

**ig·ne·ous** \ˈig-nē-əs\ *adj*
▼ formed by hardening of melted mineral material ⟨*igneous* rock⟩

**igneous:**
pink granite is an igneous rock

**ig·nite** \ig-ˈnīt\ *vb* **ig·nit·ed**; **ig·nit·ing**
**1** to set on fire : LIGHT
**2** to catch fire

**ig·ni·tion** \ig-ˈnish-ən\ *n*
**1** the act or action of igniting
**2** the process or means (as an electric spark) of igniting a fuel mixture

**ig·no·ble** \ig-ˈnō-bəl\ *adj*
DISHONORABLE ⟨an *ignoble* act⟩
**ig·no·bly** \-blē\ *adv*

**ig·no·rance** \ˈig-nə-rəns\ *n*
the state of being ignorant

**ig·no·rant** \ˈig-nə-rənt\ *adj*
**1** having little or no knowledge : not educated
**2** not knowing : UNAWARE ⟨*ignorant* of the plot⟩
**3** resulting from or showing lack of knowledge
**ig·no·rant·ly** *adv*

**iguana:** a common iguana

**ig•nore** \ig-'nōr\ *vb* **ig•nored; ig•nor•ing** to pay no attention to ⟨*ignore* a rude remark⟩

**igua•na** \i-'gwän-ə\ *n* ▲ a very large tropical American lizard with a ridge of tall scales along its back

**il-** see IN-

**[1]ill** \'il\ *adj* **worse** \'wərs\; **worst** \'wərst\
1 [1]EVIL 2 ⟨*ill* deeds⟩
2 causing suffering or distress ⟨*ill* weather⟩
3 not normal or sound ⟨*ill* health⟩
4 not in good health ⟨an *ill* person⟩
5 [1]UNFORTUNATE 1, UNLUCKY ⟨an *ill* omen⟩
6 UNKIND, UNFRIENDLY ⟨*ill* feeling⟩
7 not right or proper

**[2]ill** *adv* **worse; worst**
1 with displeasure ⟨the remark was *ill* received⟩
2 in a harsh way ⟨*ill* treated⟩
3 SCARCELY 1, HARDLY ⟨can *ill* afford it⟩
4 in a faulty way ⟨*ill*-prepared to face the winter⟩

**[3]ill** *n*
1 the opposite of good ⟨for good or *ill*⟩
2 SICKNESS 2 ⟨childhood *ills*⟩
3 [2]TROUBLE 2 ⟨society's *ills*⟩

**I'll** \īl\ I shall : I will

**il•le•gal** \il-'ē-gəl\ *adj* contrary to law : UNLAWFUL
**il•le•gal•ly** \il-'ē-gə-lē\ *adv*

**il•leg•i•ble** \il-'ej-ə-bəl\ *adj* impossible to read
**il•leg•i•bly** \-blē\ *adv*

**il•le•git•i•mate** \,il-i-'jit-ə-mət\ *adj* not legitimate
**il•le•git•i•mate•ly** *adv*

**illusion 1:** an optical illusion that plays tricks with perspective

**il•lic•it** \il-'is-ət\ *adj* not permitted : UNLAWFUL
**il•lic•it•ly** *adv*

**il•lit•er•a•cy** \il-'it-ə-rə-sē\ *n* the quality or state of being illiterate

**[1]il•lit•er•ate** \il-'it-ə-rət\ *adj*
1 unable to read or write
2 showing lack of education
**il•lit•er•ate•ly** *adv*

**[2]illiterate** *n* an illiterate person

**ill–man•nered** \'il-'man-ərd\ *adj* not polite

**ill–na•tured** \'il-'nā-chərd\ *adj* having a bad disposition
**ill–na•tured•ly** *adv*

**ill•ness** \'il-nəs\ *n* SICKNESS 1, 2

**il•log•i•cal** \il-'äj-i-kəl\ *adj* not using or following good reasoning
**il•log•i•cal•ly** *adv*

**ill–tem•pered** \'il-'tem-pərd\ *adj* ILL-NATURED

**ill–treat** \'il-'trēt\ *vb* to treat in a cruel or improper way
**ill–treat•ment** \-'trēt-mənt\ *n*

**il•lu•mi•nate** \il-'ü-mə-,nāt\ *vb* **il•lu•mi•nat•ed; il•lu•mi•nat•ing**
1 to supply with light : light up
2 to make clear : EXPLAIN

**il•lu•mi•na•tion** \il-,ü-mə-'nā-shən\ *n*
1 the action of illuminating : the state of being illuminated
2 the amount of light

**ill–use** \'il-'yüz\ *vb* ILL-TREAT

**il•lu•sion** \il-'ü-zhən\ *n*
1 ◄ a misleading image presented to the eye
2 the state or fact of being led to accept as true something unreal or imagined
3 a mistaken idea

**il•lu•sive** \il-'ü-siv\ *adj* ILLUSORY

**il•lu•so•ry** \il-'ü-sə-rē\ *adj* based on or producing illusion : DECEPTIVE

**il•lus•trate** \'il-əs-,trāt\ *vb* **il•lus•trat•ed; il•lus•trat•ing**
1 to make clear by using examples
2 to supply with pictures or diagrams meant to explain or decorate
3 to serve as an example

**il•lus•tra•tion** \,il-əs-'trā-shən\ *n*
1 the action of illustrating : the condition of being illustrated
2 an example or instance used to make something clear
3 a picture or diagram that explains or decorates ⟨a dictionary with color *illustrations*⟩

**il•lus•tra•tive** \il-'əs-trət-iv\ *adj* serving or meant to illustrate ⟨*illustrative* examples⟩

**il•lus•tra•tor** \'il-əs-,trāt-ər\ *n* an artist who makes illustrations (as for books)

**il•lus•tri•ous** \il-'əs-trē-əs\ *adj* EMINENT

**ill will** *n* unfriendly feeling

**im-** see IN-

**I'm** \īm\ I am

**[1]im•age** \'im-ij\ *n*
1 something (as a statue) made to look like a person or thing
2 ▼ a picture of a person or thing formed by a device (as a mirror or lens)

**[1]image 2:** the mirror shows an image of the flowers in the vase

3 a person very much like another
4 a mental picture of something not present : IMPRESSION
5 a graphic representation

A B C D E F G H I J K L M N O P Q R S T U V W X Y Z

**²image** *vb* **im·aged**; **im·ag·ing**
**1** to describe in words or pictures
**2** REFLECT 2

**imag·in·able** \im-ˈaj-ə-nə-bəl\ *adj*
possible to imagine

**imag·i·nary** \im-ˈaj-ə-ˌner-ē\ *adj*
existing only in the imagination : not real

**imag·i·na·tion** \im-ˌaj-ə-ˈnā-shən\ *n*
**1** the act, process, or power of forming a mental picture of something not present and especially of something one has not known or experienced
**2** creative ability
**3** a creation of the mind

**imag·i·na·tive** \im-ˈaj-ə-nət-iv\ *adj*
**1** of, relating to, or showing imagination
**2** having a lively imagination
**imag·i·na·tive·ly** *adv*

**imag·ine** \im-ˈaj-ən\ *vb*
**imag·ined**; **imag·in·ing**
**1** to form a mental picture of
**2** THINK 2

**¹im·be·cile** \ˈim-bə-səl\ *n*
a person of such low intelligence as to need help in simple personal care

**²imbecile** *or* **im·be·cil·ic** \ˌim-bə-ˈsil-ik\ *adj*
of very low intelligence : very stupid

**im·be·cil·i·ty** \ˌim-bə-ˈsil-ət-ē\ *n*, *pl* **im·be·cil·i·ties**
**1** the quality or state of being imbecile
**2** something very foolish

**imbed** *variant of* EMBED

**im·i·tate** \ˈim-ə-ˌtāt\ *vb*
**im·i·tat·ed**; **im·i·tat·ing**
**1** to follow as a pattern, model, or example
**2** to be or appear like : RESEMBLE
**3** to copy exactly : MIMIC
**synonyms** see COPY

**¹im·i·ta·tion** \ˌim-ə-ˈtā-shən\ *n*
**1** an act of imitating
**2** ¹COPY 1

**²imitation** *adj*
like something else and especially something better ⟨*imitation* leather⟩

**im·i·ta·tive** \ˈim-ə-ˌtāt-iv\ *adj*
**1** involving imitation
**2** given to imitating

**im·mac·u·late** \im-ˈak-yə-lət\ *adj*
**1** having no stain or blemish : PURE
**2** perfectly clean
**im·mac·u·late·ly** *adv*

**im·ma·te·ri·al** \ˌim-ə-ˈtir-ē-əl\ *adj*
not important : INSIGNIFICANT

**im·ma·ture** \ˌim-ə-ˈtu̇r, -ˈtyu̇r\ *adj*
not yet fully grown or ripe
**im·ma·ture·ly** *adv*

**im·mea·sur·able** \im-ˈezh-ə-rə-bəl\ *adj*
impossible to measure
**im·mea·sur·ably** \-blē\ *adv*

**im·me·di·ate** \im-ˈēd-ē-ət\ *adj*
**1** acting or being without anything else between ⟨the *immediate* cause of death⟩
**2** being next in line or nearest in relationship ⟨my *immediate* family⟩
**3** closest in importance ⟨our *immediate* needs⟩
**4** acting or being without any delay
**5** not far away in time or space ⟨in the *immediate* future⟩

**im·me·di·ate·ly** \im-ˈēd-ē-ət-lē\ *adv*
**1** with nothing between
**2** right away

**im·mense** \im-ˈens\ *adj*
very great in size or amount : HUGE
**im·mense·ly** *adv*

**im·men·si·ty** \im-ˈen-sət-ē\ *n*, *pl* **im·men·si·ties**
the quality or state of being immense

**im·merse** \im-ˈərs\ *vb*
**im·mersed**; **im·mers·ing**
**1** ▼ to plunge into something (as a fluid) that surrounds or covers
**2** to become completely involved with

**immerse 1:**
a swimmer immersed in water

**im·mi·grant** \ˈim-i-grənt\ *n*
a person who comes to a country to live there

**im·mi·grate** \ˈim-ə-ˌgrāt\ *vb*
**im·mi·grat·ed**; **im·mi·grat·ing**
to come into a foreign country to live

**im·mi·gra·tion** \ˌim-ə-ˈgrā-shən\ *n*
an act or instance of immigrating

**im·mi·nent** \ˈim-ə-nənt\ *adj*
being about to happen
**im·mi·nent·ly** *adv*

**im·mo·bile** \im-ˈō-bəl\ *adj*
unable to move or be moved

**im·mo·bi·lize** \im-ˈō-bə-ˌlīz\ *vb*
**im·mo·bi·lized**; **im·mo·bi·liz·ing**
to fix in place : make immovable

**im·mod·est** \im-ˈäd-əst\ *adj*
not modest ⟨*immodest* conduct⟩
**im·mod·est·ly** *adv*

**im·mod·es·ty** \im-ˈäd-ə-stē\ *n*
lack of modesty

**im·mor·al** \im-ˈȯr-əl\ *adj*
not moral : BAD 4
**im·mor·al·ly** *adv*

**im·mo·ral·i·ty** \ˌim-ȯ-ˈral-ət-ē\ *n*, *pl* **im·mo·ral·i·ties**
**1** the quality or state of being immoral
**2** an immoral act or custom

**¹im·mor·tal** \im-ˈȯrt-l\ *adj*
living or lasting forever
**im·mor·tal·ly** *adv*

**²immortal** *n*
**1** an immortal being
**2** a person of lasting fame

**im·mor·tal·i·ty** \ˌim-ȯr-ˈtal-ət-ē\ *n*
**1** the quality or state of being immortal : endless life
**2** lasting fame or glory

**im·mov·able** \im-ˈü-və-bəl\ *adj*
impossible to move : firmly fixed
**im·mov·ably** \-blē\ *adv*

**im·mune** \im-ˈyün\ *adj*
**1** ¹EXEMPT ⟨*immune* from punishment⟩
**2** having a strong or special power to resist

**immune system** *n*
▶ the system of the body that fights infection and disease and that includes especially the white blood cells and antibodies and the organs that produce them

## immune system

The human immune system responds to any threat to the body's health. The system consists of a clear fluid, lymph, which circulates constantly around the body through a network of lymphatic vessels. Organs such as the spleen produce white blood cells and antibodies, which travel through the body in the lymph and attack any sign of illness or contagion.

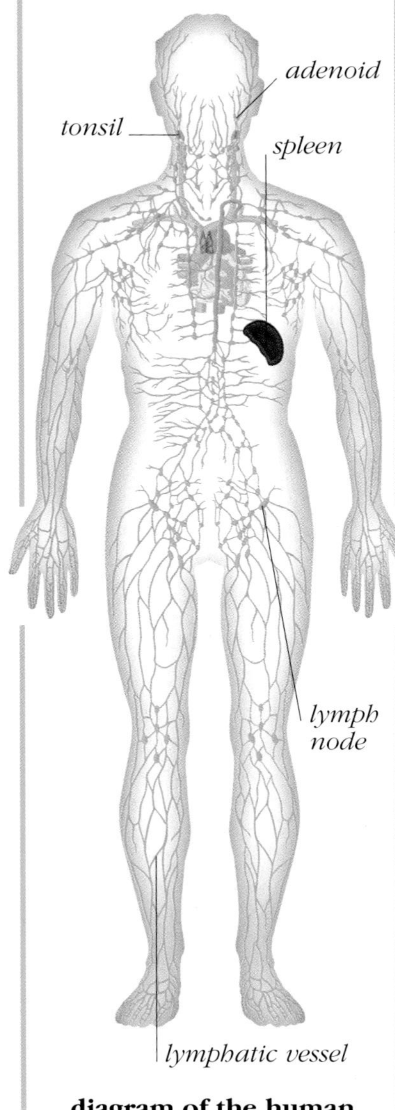


**diagram of the human immune system**

**im·mu·ni·ty** \im-'yü-nət-ē\ *n, pl* **im·mu·ni·ties**
**1** EXEMPTION 1 ⟨*immunity* from a tax⟩
**2** power to resist infection whether natural or acquired (as by vaccination)

**im·mu·ni·za·tion** \ˌim-yə-nə-'zā-shən\ *n*
treatment (as with a vaccine) to produce immunity to a disease

**im·mu·nize** \'im-yə-ˌnīz\ *vb* **im·mu·nized**; **im·mu·niz·ing**
to make immune

**imp** \'imp\ *n*
**1** a small demon
**2** a mischievous child

**im·pact** \'im-ˌpakt\ *n*
**1** ▶ a striking together of two bodies
**2** a strong effect

**im·pair** \im-'paər, -'peər\ *vb*
to make less (as in quantity, value, or strength) or worse : DAMAGE

**im·pale** \im-'pāl\ *vb* **im·paled**; **im·pal·ing**
to pierce with something pointed

**im·part** \im-'pärt\ *vb*
**1** to give or grant from a supply ⟨the sun *imparts* warmth⟩
**2** to make known

**im·par·tial** \im-'pär-shəl\ *adj*
not partial or biased : FAIR, JUST
**im·par·tial·ly** *adv*

**im·par·tial·i·ty** \im-ˌpär-shē-'al-ət-ē\ *n*
the quality or state of being impartial

**im·pass·able** \im-'pas-ə-bəl\ *adj*
impossible to pass, cross, or travel

**im·pas·sioned** \im-'pash-ənd\ *adj*
showing very strong feeling

**im·pas·sive** \im-'pas-iv\ *adj*
not feeling or showing emotion
**im·pas·sive·ly** *adv*

**im·pa·tience** \im-'pā-shəns\ *n*
**1** lack of patience
**2** restless or eager desire

**im·pa·tient** \im-'pā-shənt\ *adj*
**1** not patient
**2** showing or coming from impatience ⟨an *impatient* reply⟩
**3** restless and eager ⟨*impatient* to leave⟩
**im·pa·tient·ly** *adv*

**im·peach** \im-'pēch\ *vb*
to charge a public official formally with misconduct in office

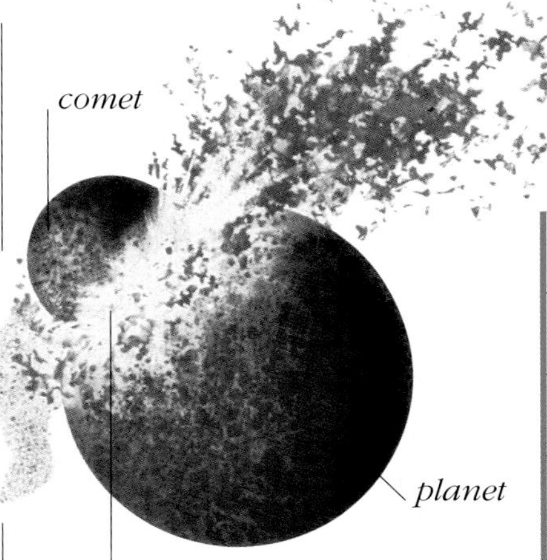


**impact 1:**
diagram showing the impact between a comet and a planet

**Word History** The English word *impeach* originally meant "to hinder." It came from an early French word that had the same meaning. This early French word came from a Latin word that meant "to put shackles on the feet." This word was derived from two Latin words. The first meant "in" or "on" and the second meant "foot."

**im·pede** \im-'pēd\ *vb* **im·ped·ed**; **im·ped·ing**
to disturb the movement or progress of

**im·ped·i·ment** \im-'ped-ə-mənt\ *n*
**1** something that impedes
**2** a defect in speech

**im·pel** \im-'pel\ *vb* **im·pelled**; **im·pel·ling**
to urge or drive forward or into action : FORCE

**im·pend** \im-'pend\ *vb*
to threaten to occur very soon ⟨an *impending* storm⟩

**im·pen·e·tra·ble** \im-'pen-ə-trə-bəl\ *adj*
**1** impossible to penetrate ⟨*impenetrable* walls⟩
**2** impossible to understand ⟨an *impenetrable* mystery⟩
**im·pen·e·tra·bly** \-blē\ *adv*

**im·pen·i·tent** \im-'pen-ə-tənt\ *adj*
not penitent

**im·per·a·tive** \im-'per-ət-iv\ *adj*
**1** expressing a command, request, or strong encouragement ⟨"Come here" is an *imperative* sentence⟩
**2** impossible to avoid or ignore **:** URGENT

**im·per·cep·ti·ble** \ˌim-pər-'sep-tə-bəl\ *adj*
**1** not perceptible by the senses or by the mind
**2** very small or gradual
**im·per·cep·ti·bly** \-blē\ *adv*

**im·per·fect** \im-'pər-fikt\ *adj*
not perfect **:** FAULTY
**im·per·fect·ly** *adv*

**im·per·fec·tion** \ˌim-pər-'fek-shən\ *n*
**1** the quality or state of being imperfect
**2** FLAW, FAULT

**im·pe·ri·al** \im-'pir-ē-əl\ *adj*
of or relating to an empire or its ruler ⟨an *imperial* decree⟩
**im·pe·ri·al·ly** *adv*

**im·per·il** \im-'per-əl\ *vb*
**im·per·iled** *or* **im·per·illed**; **im·per·il·ing** *or* **im·per·il·ling**
to place in great danger **:** ENDANGER

**im·per·ish·able** \im-'per-ish-ə-bəl\ *adj*
INDESTRUCTIBLE
**im·per·ish·ably** \-blē\ *adv*

**im·per·son·al** \im-'pərs-n-əl\ *adj*
not referring or belonging to a specific person
**im·per·son·al·ly** *adv*

**im·per·son·ate** \im-'pərs-n-ˌāt\ *vb* **im·per·son·at·ed**; **im·per·son·at·ing**
to pretend to be another person ⟨*impersonate* a police officer⟩

**Synonyms** IMPERSONATE, PLAY, and ACT mean to pretend to be somebody else. IMPERSONATE suggests that one tries to make oneself look and sound like some other person as much as possible ⟨you are very good at *impersonating* famous people⟩. PLAY suggests that one takes a part in a play, movie, or TV show ⟨you can *play* the part of the spy⟩. ACT may be used in situations other than performing in a drama or pretending to be a person ⟨*act* like you're a dog begging for a bone⟩.

**im·per·son·a·tion** \im-ˌpərs-n-'ā-shən\ *n*
the act of impersonating

**im·per·ti·nence** \im-'pərt-n-əns\ *n*
**1** the quality or state of being impertinent
**2** a rude act or remark

**im·per·ti·nent** \im-'pərt-n-ənt\ *adj*
INSOLENT, RUDE
**im·per·ti·nent·ly** *adv*

**im·per·turb·able** \ˌim-pər-'tər-bə-bəl\ *adj*
hard to disturb or upset
**im·per·turb·ably** \-blē\ *adv*

**im·per·vi·ous** \im-'pər-vē-əs\ *adj*
not letting something enter or pass through ⟨a coat *impervious* to rain⟩

**im·pet·u·ous** \im-'pech-ə-wəs\ *adj*
IMPULSIVE, RASH
**im·pet·u·ous·ly** *adv*

**im·pi·ous** \'im-pē-əs\ *adj*
not pious **:** IRREVERENT
**im·pi·ous·ly** *adv*

**imp·ish** \'im-pish\ *adj*
MISCHIEVOUS 3 ⟨an *impish* glance⟩
**imp·ish·ly** *adv*

**im·pla·ca·ble** \im-'plak-ə-bəl, -'plā-kə-\ *adj*
impossible to please, satisfy, or change ⟨*implacable* enemies⟩
**im·pla·ca·bly** \-blē\ *adv*

**im·plant** \im-'plant\ *vb*
to fix or set securely or deeply

**im·ple·ment** \'im-plə-mənt\ *n*
▼ an article (as a tool) intended for a certain use ⟨farm *implements*⟩

**im·pli·cate** \'im-plə-ˌkāt\ *vb*
**im·pli·cat·ed**; **im·pli·cat·ing**
to show to be connected or involved

**im·pli·ca·tion** \ˌim-plə-'kā-shən\ *n*
**1** the act of implicating **:** the state of being implicated
**2** the act of implying
**3** something implied

**im·plic·it** \im-'plis-ət\ *adj*
**1** understood though not put clearly into words
**2** ABSOLUTE 2 ⟨*implicit* trust⟩
**im·plic·it·ly** *adv*

**im·plore** \im-'plōr\ *vb*
**im·plored**; **im·plor·ing**
to call upon with a humble request **:** BESEECH

**implement**
Many hand implements once used by farmers, such as the plow, have generally been replaced by machines powered by gas, diesel, or electricity. For smaller tasks, however, hand implements such as pitchforks and sickles are still used and remain similar to those used for hundreds of years.

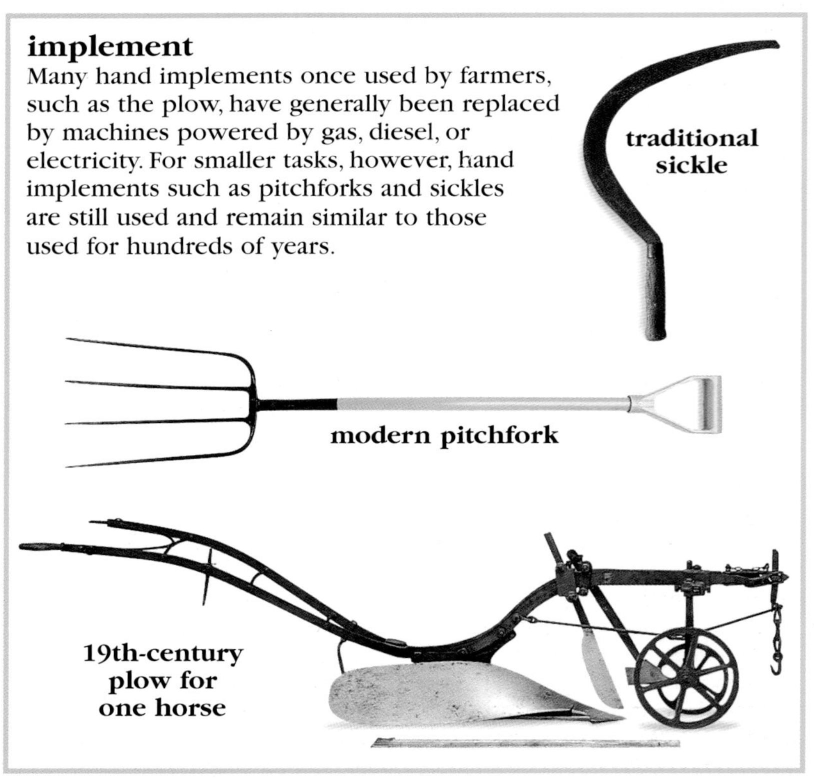

**im·ply** \im-'plī\ *vb* **im·plied**; **im·ply·ing**
to express indirectly : suggest rather than say plainly

**im·po·lite** \,im-pə-'līt\ *adj*
not polite
**im·po·lite·ly** *adv*
**im·po·lite·ness** *n*

**[1]im·port** \im-'pōrt\ *vb*
**1** [2]MEAN 3
**2** to bring (as goods) into a country usually for selling

**[2]im·port** \'im-,pōrt\ *n*
**1** MEANING 1
**2** IMPORTANCE
**3** something brought into a country

**im·por·tance** \im-'pȯrt-ns\ *n*
the quality or state of being important : SIGNIFICANCE

**im·por·tant** \im-'pȯrt-nt\ *adj*
**1** SIGNIFICANT ⟨graduation is an *important* day in your lives⟩
**2** having power or authority ⟨an *important* leader⟩
**im·por·tant·ly** *adv*

**im·por·ta·tion** \,im-,pōr-'tā-shən\ *n*
**1** the act or practice of importing
**2** something imported

**im·por·tu·nate** \im-'pȯr-chə-nət\ *adj*
making a nuisance of oneself with requests and demands
**im·por·tu·nate·ly** *adv*

**im·por·tune** \,im-pər-'tün, -'tyün\ *vb* **im·por·tuned**; **im·por·tun·ing**
to beg or urge so much as to be a nuisance

**im·pose** \im-'pōz\ *vb* **im·posed**; **im·pos·ing**
**1** to establish or apply as a charge or penalty ⟨*impose* a tax⟩
**2** to force someone to accept or put up with ⟨*impose* one's will on another⟩
**3** to take unfair advantage ⟨*impose* on a friend⟩

**im·pos·ing** \im-'pō-zing\ *adj*
impressive because of size, dignity, or magnificence

**im·pos·si·bil·i·ty** \im-,päs-ə-'bil-ət-ē\ *n, pl* **im·pos·si·bil·i·ties**
**1** the quality or state of being impossible
**2** something impossible

**im·pos·si·ble** \im-'päs-ə-bəl\ *adj*
**1** incapable of being or of occurring

**impression 2:** an impression made with ink on paper

**2** HOPELESS 2 ⟨an *impossible* situation⟩
**3** very bad or unpleasant
**im·pos·si·bly** \-blē\ *adv*

**im·pos·tor** \im-'päs-tər\ *n*
a person who pretends to be someone else in order to deceive

**im·pos·ture** \im-'päs-chər\ *n*
the act or conduct of an impostor

**im·po·tence** \'im-pə-təns\ *n*
the quality or state of being impotent

**im·po·tent** \'im-pə-tənt\ *adj*
lacking in power or strength
**im·po·tent·ly** *adv*

**im·pound** \im-'pau̇nd\ *vb*
to shut up in or as if in an enclosed place ⟨*impound* cattle⟩

**im·pov·er·ish** \im-'päv-ə-rish\ *vb*
**1** to make poor
**2** to use up the strength or richness of ⟨*impoverished* soil⟩

**im·prac·ti·ca·ble** \im-'prak-ti-kə-bəl\ *adj*
difficult to put into practice or use ⟨an *impracticable* plan⟩

**im·prac·ti·cal** \im-'prak-ti-kəl\ *adj*
not practical ⟨an *impractical* idea⟩
**im·prac·ti·cal·ly** *adv*

**im·pre·cise** \,im-pri-'sīs\ *adj*
not clear or exact
**im·pre·cise·ly** *adv*

**im·preg·nate** \im-'preg-,nāt\ *vb* **im·preg·nat·ed**; **im·preg·nat·ing**
**1** to make pregnant
**2** to cause (a material) to be filled with something

**im·press** \im-'pres\ *vb*
**1** to fix in or on one's mind ⟨*impress* these rules in your minds⟩
**2** to move or affect strongly ⟨*impressed* by the size of the city⟩

**im·pres·sion** \im-'presh-ən\ *n*
**1** the act or process of impressing
**2** ◀ something (as a design) made by pressing or stamping
**3** something that impresses or is impressed on one's mind ⟨these words made a strong *impression*⟩
**4** a memory or belief that is vague or uncertain

**im·pres·sion·able** \im-'presh-ə-nə-bəl\ *adj*
easy to impress or influence

**im·pres·sive** \im-'pres-iv\ *adj*
having the power to impress the mind or feelings ⟨an *impressive* speech⟩
**im·pres·sive·ly** *adv*

**[1]im·print** \im-'print\ *vb*
**1** to mark by pressure : STAMP
**2** to fix firmly

**[2]im·print** \'im-,print\ *n*
something imprinted or printed : IMPRESSION

**im·pris·on** \im-'priz-n\ *vb*
to put in prison

**im·pris·on·ment** \im-'priz-n-mənt\ *n*
the act of imprisoning : the state of being imprisoned

**im·prob·a·bil·i·ty** \im-,präb-ə-'bil-ət-ē\ *n*
the quality or state of being improbable

**im·prob·a·ble** \im-'präb-ə-bəl\ *adj*
not probable
**im·prob·a·bly** \-blē\ *adv*

**im·prop·er** \im-'präp-ər\ *adj*
not proper, right, or suitable
**im·prop·er·ly** *adv*

**improper fraction** *n*
a fraction whose numerator is equal to or larger than the denominator ⟨$^{13}/_{4}$ is an *improper fraction*⟩

**im·prove** \im-'prüv\ *vb* **im·proved**; **im·prov·ing**
to make or become better
**im·prov·er** *n*

**im·prove·ment** \im-'prüv-mənt\ *n*
**1** the act or process of improving
**2** increased value or excellence
**3** something that adds to the value or appearance (as of a house)

**im·prov·i·sa·tion** \im-ˌpräv-ə-ˈzā-shən\ *n*
**1** the act or art of improvising
**2** something that is improvised

**im·pro·vise** \ˈim-prə-ˌvīz\ *vb*
**im·pro·vised**; **im·pro·vis·ing**
**1** to compose, recite, or sing without studying or practicing ahead of time
**2** to make, invent, or arrange with whatever is at hand

**im·pu·dence** \ˈim-pyəd-əns\ *n*
impudent behavior or speech **:** INSOLENCE, DISRESPECT

**im·pu·dent** \ˈim-pyə-dənt\ *adj*
being bold and disrespectful **:** INSOLENT
**im·pu·dent·ly** *adv*

**4** WITH 7 ⟨wrote *in* pencil⟩
**5** used to show a state or condition ⟨you're *in* luck⟩ ⟨we're *in* trouble⟩
**6** used to show manner or purpose ⟨*in* a hurry⟩ ⟨said *in* reply⟩
**7** INTO 2 ⟨broke *in* pieces⟩

[2]**in** \ˈin\ *adv*
**1** to or toward the inside ⟨went *in* and closed the door⟩
**2** to or toward some particular place ⟨flew *in* yesterday⟩
**3** [1]NEAR 1 ⟨play close *in*⟩
**4** into the midst of something ⟨mix *in* the flour⟩
**5** to or at its proper place ⟨fit a piece *in*⟩

**in·ac·cu·ra·cy** \in-ˈak-yə-rə-sē\ *n, pl* **in·ac·cu·ra·cies**
**1** lack of accuracy
**2** ERROR, MISTAKE

**in·ac·cu·rate** \in-ˈak-yə-rət\ *adj*
not right or correct **:** not exact
**in·ac·cu·rate·ly** *adv*

**in·ac·tive** \in-ˈak-tiv\ *adj*
not active **:** IDLE

**in·ac·tiv·i·ty** \ˌin-ak-ˈtiv-ət-ē\ *n*
the state of being inactive

**in·ad·e·qua·cy** \in-ˈad-i-kwə-sē\ *n, pl* **in·ad·e·qua·cies**
the condition of being not enough or not good enough

**in·ad·e·quate** \in-ˈad-i-kwət\ *adj*
not enough or not good enough

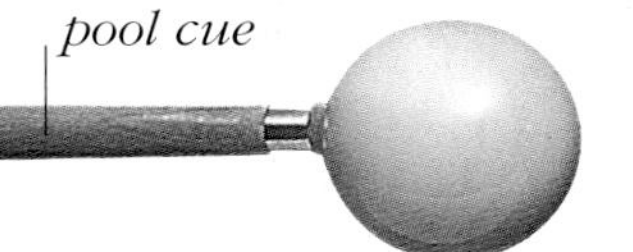

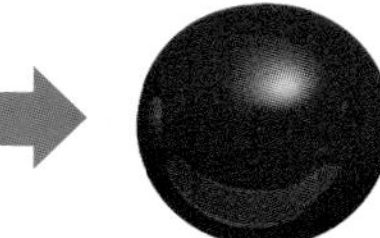

**impulse 1:** the pool cue taps the white ball toward the red ball, providing the impulse for both balls to move

**im·pulse** \ˈim-ˌpəls\ *n*
**1** ▲ a force that starts a body into motion
**2** the motion produced by a starting force
**3** a sudden stirring up of the mind and spirit to do something
**4** the wave of change that passes along a stimulated nerve and carries information to the brain

**im·pul·sive** \im-ˈpəl-siv\ *adj*
**1** acting or tending to act on impulse
**2** resulting from a sudden impulse
**im·pul·sive·ly** *adv*

**im·pure** \im-ˈpyu̇r\ *adj*
**1** not pure **:** UNCLEAN, DIRTY
**2** mixed with something else that is usually not as good
**im·pure·ly** *adv*

**im·pu·ri·ty** \im-ˈpyu̇r-ət-ē\ *n, pl* **im·pu·ri·ties**
**1** the quality or state of being impure
**2** something that is or makes impure

[1]**in** \in\ *prep*
**1** enclosed or surrounded by **:** WITHIN ⟨swim *in* the lake⟩
**2** INTO 1 ⟨ran *in* the house⟩
**3** DURING ⟨*in* the summer⟩

**6** on the inner side **:** WITHIN ⟨everyone is *in*⟩
**7** at hand or on hand ⟨the evidence is *in*⟩

[3]**in** \ˈin\ *adj*
**1** being inside or within ⟨the *in* part⟩
**2** headed or bound inward ⟨the *in* train⟩

[1]**in-** *or* **il-** *or* **im-** *or* **ir-** *prefix*
not **:** NON-, UN- — usually *il-* before *l* ⟨*il*logical⟩ and *im-* before *b, m,* or *p* ⟨*im*moral⟩ ⟨*im*practical⟩ and *ir-* before *r* ⟨*ir*reducible⟩ and *in-* before other sounds ⟨*in*complete⟩

[2]**in-** *or* **il-** *or* **im-** *or* **ir-** *prefix*
**1** in **:** within **:** into **:** toward **:** on ⟨*in*set⟩ — usually *il-* before *l*, *im-* before *b, m,* or *p*, *ir-* before *r*, and *in-* before other sounds
**2** EN- ⟨*im*peril⟩

**in·abil·i·ty** \ˌin-ə-ˈbil-ət-ē\ *n*
the condition of being unable to do something **:** lack of ability

**in·ac·ces·si·bil·i·ty** \ˌin-ak-ˌses-ə-ˈbil-ət-ē\ *n*
the quality or state of being inaccessible

**in·ac·ces·si·ble** \ˌin-ak-ˈses-ə-bəl\ *adj*
hard or impossible to get to or at

**in·ad·vis·able** \ˌin-əd-ˈvī-zə-bəl\ *adj*
not wise to do **:** UNWISE

**in·alien·able** \in-ˈāl-yə-nə-bəl\ *adj*
impossible to take away or give up ⟨*inalienable* rights⟩

**inane** \i-ˈnān\ *adj*
silly and pointless ⟨*inane* remarks⟩
**inane·ly** *adv*

**in·an·i·mate** \in-ˈan-ə-mət\ *adj*
not living **:** LIFELESS

**in·ap·pro·pri·ate** \ˌin-ə-ˈprō-prē-ət\ *adj*
not appropriate
**in·ap·pro·pri·ate·ly** *adv*

**in·as·much as** \ˌin-əz-ˌməch-əz\ *conj*
considering that **:** [2]SINCE 2

**in·at·ten·tion** \ˌin-ə-ˈten-chən\ *n*
failure to pay attention

**in·at·ten·tive** \ˌin-ə-ˈtent-iv\ *adj*
not paying attention
**in·at·ten·tive·ly** *adv*

**in·au·di·ble** \in-ˈȯd-ə-bəl\ *adj*
impossible to hear
**in·au·di·bly** \-blē\ *adv*

**in·au·gu·ral** \in-ˈȯ-gyə-rəl\ *adj*
of or relating to an inauguration ⟨an *inaugural* ball⟩

**in·au·gu·rate** \in-'ȯ-gyə-,rāt\ *vb* **in·au·gu·rat·ed**; **in·au·gu·rat·ing**
1 to introduce into office with suitable ceremonies : INSTALL
2 to celebrate the opening of
3 to bring into being or action

**in·au·gu·ra·tion** \in-,ȯ-gyə-'rā-shən\ *n*
an act or ceremony of inaugurating

**in·born** \'in-'bȯrn\ *adj*
INSTINCTIVE

**in·breed** \'in-'brēd\ *vb* **in·bred** \-'bred\; **in·breed·ing**
to breed with closely related individuals

**in·can·des·cent** \,in-kən-'des-nt\ *adj*
white or glowing with great heat

**incandescent lamp** *n*
▶ a lamp whose light is produced by the glow of a wire heated by an electric current

**in·ca·pa·ble** \in-'kā-pə-bəl\ *adj*
not able to do something

[1]**in·cense** \'in-,sens\ *n*
1 material used to produce a perfume when burned
2 the perfume given off by burning incense

[2]**in·cense** \in-'sens\ *vb* **in·censed**; **in·cens·ing**
to make very angry

**in·cen·tive** \in-'sent-iv\ *n*
something that makes a person try or work hard or harder

**in·ces·sant** \in-'ses-nt\ *adj*
going on and on : not stopping or letting up
**in·ces·sant·ly** *adv*

[1]**inch** \'inch\ *n*
a unit of length equal to $^1/_{36}$ yard or 2.54 centimeters

[2]**inch** *vb*
to move a little bit at a time

**inch·worm** \'inch-,wərm\ *n*
any of numerous small caterpillars that are larvae of moths and move by bringing forward the hind part of the body and then extending forward the front part of the body

**in·ci·dent** \'in-sə-dənt\ *n*
an often unimportant happening that may form a part of a larger event

**Synonyms** INCIDENT, OCCURRENCE, and EVENT mean something that happens. INCIDENT suggests something that is brief and not very important ⟨although there were a few unpleasant *incidents*, the trip was a success⟩. OCCURRENCE may suggest something that is not planned or expected ⟨those *occurrences* could not have been predicted⟩. EVENT is often used of something that is important ⟨the big *events* of last year⟩.

**incandescent lamp**

[1]**in·ci·den·tal** \,in-sə-'dent-l\ *adj*
1 happening by chance
2 of minor importance ⟨*incidental* expenses⟩

[2]**incidental** *n*
something incidental

**in·ci·den·tal·ly** \,in-sə-'dent-l-ē\ *adv*
as a matter of less interest or importance

**in·cin·er·ate** \in-'sin-ə-,rāt\ *vb* **in·cin·er·at·ed**; **in·cin·er·at·ing**
to burn to ashes

**in·cin·er·a·tor** \in-'sin-ə-,rāt-ər\ *n*
a furnace or a container for burning waste materials

**in·cise** \in-'sīz\ *vb* **in·cised**; **in·cis·ing**
to cut into : CARVE, ENGRAVE

**in·ci·sion** \in-'sizh-ən\ *n*
a cutting into something or the cut or wound that results

**in·ci·sor** \in-'sī-zər\ *n*
a tooth (as any of the four front teeth of the human upper or lower jaw) for cutting

**in·cite** \in-'sīt\ *vb* **in·cit·ed**; **in·cit·ing**
to move to action : stir up : ROUSE

**in·clem·ent** \in-'klem-ənt\ *adj*
STORMY 1 ⟨*inclement* weather⟩

**in·cli·na·tion** \,in-klə-'nā-shən\ *n*
1 an act or the action of bending or leaning
2 a usually favorable feeling toward something
3 [1]SLANT, TILT

[1]**in·cline** \in-'klīn\ *vb* **in·clined**; **in·clin·ing**
1 to cause to bend or lean
2 to be drawn to an opinion or course of action
3 [1]SLOPE, LEAN

[2]**in·cline** \'in-,klīn\ *n*
[2]SLOPE 2

**in·clined** \in-'klīnd\ *adj*
1 having an inclination ⟨not *inclined* to answer⟩
2 having a slope

**inclose, inclosure** *variant of* ENCLOSE, ENCLOSURE

**in·clude** \in-'klüd\ *vb* **in·clud·ed**; **in·clud·ing**
to take in or have as part of a whole

**in·clu·sion** \in-'klü-zhən\ *n*
1 an act of including : the state of being included
2 something included

**in·clu·sive** \in-'klü-siv, -ziv\ *adj*
1 covering everything or all important points ⟨an *inclusive* fee⟩
2 including the stated limits and all in between ⟨from ages three to ten *inclusive*⟩

**in·cog·ni·to** \,in-,käg-'nēt-ō, in-'käg-nə-,tō\ *adv or adj*
with one's identity kept secret

**in·co·her·ence** \,in-kō-'hir-əns\ *n*
the quality or state of being incoherent

**in·co·her·ent** \,in-kō-'hir-ənt\ *adj*
not connected in a clear or logical way
**in·co·her·ent·ly** *adv*

**in·come** \'in-,kəm\ *n*
a gain usually measured in money that comes in from labor, business, or property

**income tax** *n*
a tax on the income of a person or business

**in·com·pa·ra·ble** \in-'käm-pə-rə-bəl\ *adj*
MATCHLESS
**in·com·pa·ra·bly** \-blē\ *adv*

**in·com·pat·i·ble** \,in-kəm-'pat-ə-bəl\ *adj*
not able to live or work together in harmony
**in·com·pat·i·bly** \-blē\ *adv*

A B C D E F G H I J K L M N O P Q R S T U V W X Y Z

**in·com·pe·tence** \in-'käm-pət-əns\ *n*
the state or fact of being incompetent
**in·com·pe·tent** \in-'käm-pət-ənt\ *adj*
not able to do a good job
**in·com·pe·tent·ly** *adv*
**in·com·plete** \,in-kəm-'plēt\ *adj*
▶ not complete : not finished
**in·com·plete·ly** *adv*
**in·com·pre·hen·si·ble** \,in-,käm-pri-'hen-sə-bəl\ *adj*
impossible to understand
**in·com·pre·hen·si·bly** \-blē\ *adv*
**in·con·ceiv·able** \,in-kən-'sē-və-bəl\ *adj*
**1** impossible to imagine or put up with
**2** hard to believe
**in·con·ceiv·ably** \-blē\ *adv*
**in·con·gru·ous** \in-'käng-grə-wəs\ *adj*
not harmonious, suitable, or proper ⟨*incongruous* colors⟩
**in·con·gru·ous·ly** *adv*
**in·con·sid·er·ate** \,in-kən-'sid-ə-rət\ *adj*
careless of the rights or feelings of others
**in·con·sis·tent** \,in-kən-'sis-tənt\ *adj*
**1** not being in agreement
**2** not keeping to the same thoughts or practices : CHANGEABLE
**in·con·spic·u·ous** \,in-kən-'spik-yə-wəs\ *adj*
not easily seen or noticed
**in·con·spic·u·ous·ly** *adv*
**¹in·con·ve·nience** \,in-kən-'vē-nyəns\ *n*
**1** the quality or state of being inconvenient
**2** something inconvenient
**²inconvenience** *vb*
**in·con·ve·nienced**;
**in·con·ve·nienc·ing**
to cause inconvenience to
**in·con·ve·nient** \,in-kən-'vē-nyənt\ *adj*
not convenient
**in·con·ve·nient·ly** *adv*
**in·cor·po·rate** \in-'kȯr-pə-,rāt\ *vb*
**in·cor·po·rat·ed**;
**in·cor·po·rat·ing**
**1** to join or unite closely into a single mass or body

**incomplete:** the jigsaw puzzle is incomplete

**2** to make a corporation of ⟨decided to *incorporate* the family business⟩
**in·cor·po·ra·tion** \in-,kȯr-pə-'rā-shən\ *n*
an act of incorporating : the state of being incorporated
**in·cor·rect** \,in-kə-'rekt\ *adj*
**1** not correct : not accurate or true : WRONG
**2** showing no care for duty or for moral or social standards
**in·cor·rect·ly** *adv*
**in·cor·rect·ness** *n*
**¹in·crease** \in-'krēs\ *vb*
**in·creased**; **in·creas·ing**
to make or become greater (as in size)
**²in·crease** \'in-,krēs\ *n*
**1** the act of increasing
**2** something added (as by growth)
**in·creas·ing·ly** \in-'krē-sing-lē\ *adv*
more and more ⟨the path was *increasingly* rough⟩
**in·cred·i·ble** \in-'kred-ə-bəl\ *adj*
too strange or unlikely to be believed ⟨an *incredible* tale of adventure⟩
**in·cred·i·bly** \-blē\ *adv*
**in·cre·du·li·ty** \,in-kri-'dü-lət-ē, -'dyü-\ *n*
the quality or state of being incredulous
**in·cred·u·lous** \in-'krej-ə-ləs\ *adj*
feeling or showing disbelief : SKEPTICAL
**in·cred·u·lous·ly** *adv*
**in·crim·i·nate** \in-'krim-ə-,nāt\ *vb*
**in·crim·i·nat·ed**;
**in·crim·i·nat·ing**
to charge with or involve in a crime or fault : ACCUSE

**incrust** *variant of* ENCRUST
**in·cu·bate** \'ing-kyə-,bāt\ *vb*
**in·cu·bat·ed**; **in·cu·bat·ing**
**1** to sit upon eggs to hatch them by warmth
**2** to keep under conditions good for hatching or development
**in·cu·ba·tion** \,ing-kyə-'bā-shən\ *n*
**1** an act of incubating : the state of being incubated
**2** the time between infection with germs and the appearance of disease symptoms
**in·cu·ba·tor** \'ing-kyə-,bāt-ər\ *n*
**1** an apparatus that provides enough heat to hatch eggs artificially
**2** ▼ an apparatus to help the growth of tiny newborn babies

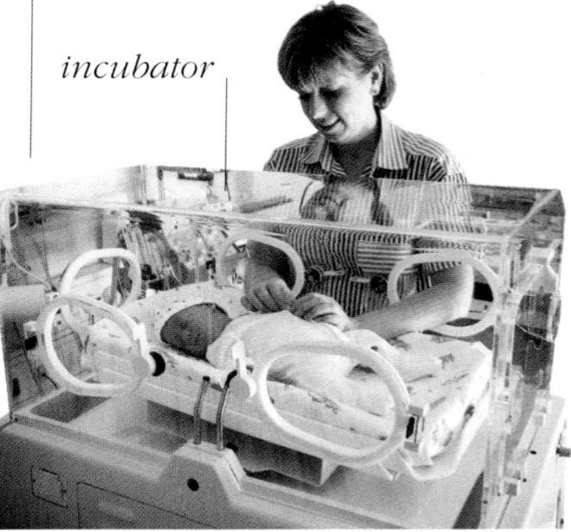


**incubator 2:** a hospital incubator for a premature baby

**in·cum·bent** \in-'kəm-bənt\ *n*
the holder of an office or position
**in·cur** \in-'kər\ *vb* **in·curred**; **in·cur·ring**
to bring upon oneself ⟨*incur* suspicion⟩
**in·cur·able** \in-'kyu̇r-ə-bəl\ *adj*
impossible to cure
**in·cur·ably** \-blē\ *adv*
**in·debt·ed** \in-'det-əd\ *adj*
being in debt : owing something
**in·debt·ed·ness** *n*
**in·de·cen·cy** \in-'dēs-n-sē\ *n, pl* **in·de·cen·cies**
**1** lack of decency
**2** an indecent act or word
**in·de·cent** \in-'dēs-nt\ *adj*
not decent : COARSE, VULGAR
**in·de·ci·sion** \,in-di-'sizh-ən\ *n*
a swaying between two or more courses of action

**in·de·ci·sive** \ˌin-di-ˈsī-siv\ *adj*
**1** not decisive or final ⟨an *indecisive* battle⟩
**2** finding it hard to make decisions ⟨an *indecisive* person⟩
**in·de·ci·sive·ly** *adv*
**in·de·ci·sive·ness** *n*

**in·deed** \in-ˈdēd\ *adv*
in fact : TRULY

**in·de·fen·si·ble** \ˌin-di-ˈfen-sə-bəl\ *adj*
impossible to defend

**in·def·i·nite** \in-ˈdef-ə-nət\ *adj*
**1** not clear or fixed in meaning or details
**2** not limited (as in amount or length)
**in·def·i·nite·ly** *adv*

**indefinite article** *n*
either of the articles *a* or *an* used to show that the following noun refers to any person or thing of the kind named

**in·del·i·ble** \in-ˈdel-ə-bəl\ *adj*
**1** impossible to erase, remove, or blot out ⟨an *indelible* impression⟩
**2** making marks not easily removed
**in·del·i·bly** \-blē\ *adv*

**in·del·i·cate** \in-ˈdel-i-kət\ *adj*
not polite or proper : COARSE
**in·del·i·cate·ly** *adv*

**in·dent** \in-ˈdent\ *vb*
to set (as the first line of a paragraph) in from the margin

**in·den·ta·tion** \ˌin-ˌden-ˈtā-shən\ *n*
**1** a cut or dent in something
**2** the action of indenting or the state of being indented

**in·de·pen·dence** \ˌin-də-ˈpen-dəns\ *n*
the quality or state of being independent

**Independence Day** *n*
July 4 observed as a legal holiday in honor of the adoption of the Declaration of Independence in 1776

**¹in·de·pen·dent** \ˌin-də-ˈpen-dənt\ *adj*
**1** not under the control or rule of another
**2** not connected with something else : SEPARATE
**3** not depending on anyone else for money to live on
**4** able to make up one's own mind
**in·de·pen·dent·ly** *adv*

**²independent** *n*
an independent person (as a voter who belongs to no political party)

**in·de·scrib·able** \ˌin-di-ˈskrī-bə-bəl\ *adj*
impossible to describe
**in·de·scrib·ably** \-blē\ *adv*

**in·de·struc·ti·ble** \ˌin-di-ˈstrək-tə-bəl\ *adj*
impossible to destroy
**in·de·struc·ti·bly** \-blē\ *adv*

**¹in·dex** \ˈin-ˌdeks\ *n, pl* **in·dex·es** *or* **in·di·ces** \ˈin-də-ˌsēz\
**1** a list of names or topics (as in a book) given in alphabetical order and showing where each is to be found
**2** POINTER 1 ⟨the *index* on a scale⟩
**3** ¹SIGN 5, INDICATION ⟨the price of goods is an *index* of business conditions⟩

**²index** *vb*
**1** to provide with an index
**2** to list in an index

**index finger** *n*
the finger next to the thumb

**¹In·di·an** \ˈin-dē-ən\ *n*
**1** a person born or living in India
**2** AMERICAN INDIAN

---

**Word History** Once the name *India* was not used just for the land that we now call *India*. The whole of the distant East was often called *India*. Columbus went west hoping to sail to the far East. When he reached the West Indies, he thought that he had come to the outer islands of "India," the far East. That is why the people that he found there were given the name *Indian*.

---

**²Indian** *adj*
**1** of or relating to India or its peoples
**2** of or relating to the American Indians or their languages

**Indian club** *n*
▼ a wooden club swung for exercise

**Indian clubs**

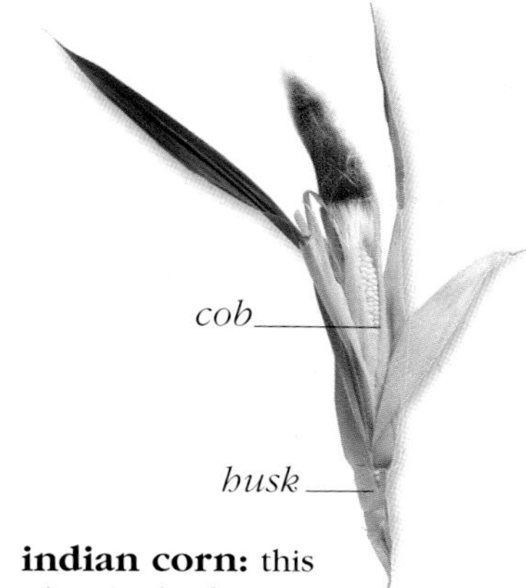


**indian corn:** this plant is also known as maize

**Indian corn** *n*
▲ a tall American cereal grass widely grown for its large ears of grain which are used as food or for feeding livestock

**Indian pipe** *n*
a waxy white leafless woodland herb with nodding flowers

**Indian summer** *n*
a period of mild weather in late autumn or early winter

**in·di·cate** \ˈin-də-ˌkāt\ *vb*
**in·di·cat·ed**; **in·di·cat·ing**
**1** to point out or point to
**2** to state or express briefly

**in·di·ca·tion** \ˌin-də-ˈkā-shən\ *n*
**1** the act of indicating
**2** something that indicates

**in·dic·a·tive** \in-ˈdik-ət-iv\ *adj*
**1** representing an act or state as a fact that can be known or proved ⟨in "I am here," the verb "am" is in the *indicative* mood⟩
**2** pointing out

**in·di·ca·tor** \ˈin-də-ˌkāt-ər\ *n*
**1** one that indicates
**2** a pointer on a dial or scale
**3** ¹DIAL 3, GAUGE 3

**indices** *pl of* INDEX

**in·dict** \in-ˈdīt\ *vb*
to charge with an offense or crime : ACCUSE
**in·dict·ment** \-ˈdīt-mənt\ *n*

**in·dif·fer·ence** \in-ˈdif-ə-rəns, -ˈdif-rəns\ *n*
**1** the condition or fact of being indifferent
**2** lack of interest

A B C D E F G H I J K L M N O P Q R S T U V W X Y Z

**in·dif·fer·ent** \in-'dif-ə-rənt, -'dif-rənt\ *adj*
**1** having no choice **:** showing neither interest nor dislike
**2** neither good nor bad
**in·dif·fer·ent·ly** *adv*

**in·di·gest·ible** \,in-dī-'jes-tə-bəl, -də-\ *adj*
not digestible **:** not easy to digest

**in·di·ges·tion** \,in-dī-'jes-chən, -də-\ *n*
discomfort caused by slow or painful digestion

**in·dig·nant** \in-'dig-nənt\ *adj*
filled with or expressing indignation
**in·dig·nant·ly** *adv*

**in·dig·na·tion** \,in-dig-'nā-shən\ *n*
anger caused by something unjust or unworthy

**in·dig·ni·ty** \in-'dig-nət-ē\ *n, pl* **in·dig·ni·ties**
**1** an act that injures one's dignity or self-respect
**2** treatment that shows a lack of respect

**in·di·go** \'in-di-,gō\ *n, pl* **in·di·gos** *or* **in·di·goes**
**1** ▼ a blue dye made artificially and formerly obtained from plants (**indigo plants**)
**2** a dark grayish blue

*indigo dye*

**indigo 1:**
a bottle of indigo dye

**in·di·rect** \,in-də-'rekt, -dī-\ *adj*
**1** not straight or direct ⟨an *indirect* route⟩
**2** not straightforward ⟨*indirect* methods⟩
**3** not having a plainly seen connection ⟨an *indirect* cause⟩
**in·di·rect·ly** *adv*
**in·di·rect·ness** *n*

**indirect object** *n*
an object that represents the secondary goal of the action of its verb ⟨"me" in "you gave me the book" is an *indirect object*⟩

**in·dis·creet** \,in-dis-'krēt\ *adj*
not discreet
**in·dis·creet·ly** *adv*

**in·dis·cre·tion** \,in-dis-'kresh-ən\ *n*
**1** lack of discretion
**2** an indiscreet act or remark

**in·dis·crim·i·nate** \,in-dis-'krim-ə-nət\ *adj*
showing lack of discrimination

**in·dis·pens·able** \,in-dis-'pen-sə-bəl\ *adj*
[1]ESSENTIAL 2 ⟨an *indispensable* employee⟩
**in·dis·pens·ably** \-blē\ *adv*

**in·dis·posed** \,in-dis-'pōzd\ *adj*
**1** somewhat unwell
**2** not willing

**in·dis·po·si·tion** \,in-,dis-pə-'zish-ən\ *n*
the condition of being indisposed **:** a slight illness

**in·dis·put·able** \,in-dis-'pyüt-ə-bəl, in-'dis-pyət-\ *adj*
not disputable **:** UNQUESTIONABLE
**in·dis·put·ably** \-blē\ *adv*

**in·dis·tinct** \,in-dis-'tingkt\ *adj*
not distinct
**in·dis·tinct·ly** *adv*
**in·dis·tinct·ness** *n*

**in·dis·tin·guish·able** \,in-dis-'ting-gwish-ə-bəl\ *adj*
impossible to distinguish clearly
**in·dis·tin·guish·ably** \-blē\ *adv*

[1]**in·di·vid·u·al** \,in-də-'vij-ə-wəl\ *adj*
**1** of or relating to an individual
**2** intended for one person
**3** [1]PARTICULAR 1, SEPARATE
**4** having a special quality **:** DISTINCTIVE 1 ⟨an *individual* style⟩
**in·di·vid·u·al·ly** *adv*

[2]**individual** *n*
**1** a single member of a class
**2** a single human being

**in·di·vid·u·al·i·ty** \,in-də-,vij-ə-'wal-ət-ē\ *n, pl* **in·di·vid·u·al·i·ties**
**1** the qualities that set one person or thing off from all others
**2** the quality or state of being an individual

**in·di·vis·i·ble** \,in-də-'viz-ə-bəl\ *adj*
impossible to divide or separate
**in·di·vis·i·bly** \-blē\ *adv*

**in·doc·tri·nate** \in-'däk-trə-,nāt\ *vb* **in·doc·tri·nat·ed**; **in·doc·tri·nat·ing**
**1** INSTRUCT 1, TEACH
**2** to teach the ideas, opinions, or beliefs of a certain group

**in·doc·tri·na·tion** \in-,däk-trə-'nā-shən\ *n*
the act or process of indoctrinating

**in·do·lence** \'in-də-ləns\ *n*
LAZINESS

**in·do·lent** \'in-də-lənt\ *adj*
LAZY, IDLE

**in·dom·i·ta·ble** \in-'däm-ət-ə-bəl\ *adj*
UNCONQUERABLE
**in·dom·i·ta·bly** \-blē\ *adv*

**in·door** \,in-,dōr\ *adj*
**1** of or relating to the inside of a building
**2** done, used, or belonging within a building ⟨an *indoor* job⟩ ⟨*indoor* clothes⟩

**in·doors** \'in-'dōrz\ *adv*
in or into a building ⟨games to be played *indoors*⟩

**indorse** *variant of* ENDORSE

**in·du·bi·ta·ble** \in-'dü-bət-ə-bəl, -'dyü-\ *adj*
being beyond question or doubt
**in·du·bi·ta·bly** \-blē\ *adv*

**in·duce** \in-'düs, -'dyüs\ *vb* **in·duced**; **in·duc·ing**
**1** to lead on to do something
**2** to bring about **:** CAUSE
**3** to produce (as an electric current) by induction

**in·duce·ment** \in-'düs-mənt, -'dyüs-\ *n*
**1** the act of inducing
**2** something that induces

**in·duct** \in-'dəkt\ *vb*
**1** to place in office **:** INSTALL
**2** to take in as a member of a military service

**in·duc·tion** \in-'dək-shən\ *n*
**1** the act or process of inducting
**2** the production of an electrical or magnetic effect through the influence of a nearby magnet, electrical current, or electrically charged body

**in·dulge** \in-'dəlj\ *vb* **in·dulged**; **in·dulg·ing**
**1** to give in to one's own or another's desires **:** HUMOR
**2** to allow oneself the pleasure of having or doing something

**in·dul·gence** \in-'dəl-jəns\ *n*
1 the act of indulging : the state of being indulgent
2 an indulgent act
3 something indulged in

**in·dul·gent** \in-'dəl-jənt\ *adj*
characterized by indulgence : LENIENT
**in·dul·gent·ly** *adv*

**in·dus·tri·al** \in-'dəs-trē-əl\ *adj*
1 of, relating to, or engaged in industry ⟨*industrial* work⟩
2 having highly developed industries ⟨*industrial* nations⟩
**in·dus·tri·al·ly** *adv*

**in·dus·tri·al·ist** \in-'dəs-trē-ə-list\ *n*
a person owning or engaged in the management of an industry

**in·dus·tri·al·i·za·tion** \in-ˌdəs-trē-ə-lə-'zā-shən\ *n*
the process of industrializing : the state of being industrialized

**in·dus·tri·al·ize** \in-'dəs-trē-ə-ˌlīz\ *vb* **in·dus·tri·al·ized**; **in·dus·tri·al·iz·ing**
to make or become industrial

**in·dus·tri·ous** \in-'dəs-trē-əs\ *adj*
working hard and steadily : DILIGENT
**in·dus·tri·ous·ly** *adv*

**in·dus·try** \'in-dəs-trē\ *n*, *pl* **in·dus·tries**
1 the habit of working hard and steadily
2 ▼ businesses that provide a certain product or service ⟨the oil *industry*⟩ ⟨the shipping *industry*⟩
3 manufacturing activity ⟨*industry* was slowing down⟩

**-ine** \ˌīn, ən, ˌēn\ *adj suffix*
of, relating to, or like ⟨alkal*ine*⟩

**in·ed·i·ble** \in-'ed-ə-bəl\ *adj*
not fit for food

**in·ef·fec·tive** \ˌin-ə-'fek-tiv\ *adj*
not producing the desired effect
**in·ef·fec·tive·ly** *adv*

**in·ef·fec·tu·al** \ˌin-ə-'fek-chə-wəl\ *adj*
not producing the proper or usual effect
**in·ef·fec·tu·al·ly** *adv*

**in·ef·fi·cien·cy** \ˌin-ə-'fish-ən-sē\ *n*, *pl* **in·ef·fi·cien·cies**
the state or an instance of being inefficient

**in·ef·fi·cient** \ˌin-ə-'fish-ənt\ *adj*
1 not effective : INEFFECTUAL
2 not able or willing to do something well ⟨*inefficient* workers⟩
**in·ef·fi·cient·ly** *adv*

**in·elas·tic** \ˌin-ə-'las-tik\ *adj*
not elastic

**in·el·i·gi·bil·i·ty** \in-ˌel-ə-jə-'bil-ət-ē\ *n*
the condition or fact of being ineligible

**in·el·i·gi·ble** \in-'el-ə-jə-bəl\ *adj*
not eligible

**in·ept** \in-'ept\ *adj*
1 not suited to the occasion ⟨an *inept* remark⟩
2 lacking in skill or ability
**in·ept·ly** *adv*
**in·ept·ness** *n*

**in·equal·i·ty** \ˌin-i-'kwäl-ət-ē\ *n*, *pl* **in·equal·i·ties**
1 the quality of being unequal or uneven
2 an instance of being uneven

**in·ert** \in-'ərt\ *adj*
unable or slow to move or react ⟨*inert* gas⟩
**in·ert·ly** *adv*
**in·ert·ness** *n*

**in·er·tia** \in-'ər-shə\ *n*
1 ▶ a property of matter by which it remains at rest or in motion in the same straight line unless acted upon by some external force
2 a tendency not to move or change

**in·er·tial** \in-'ər-shəl\ *adj*
of or relating to inertia

**industry 2:** an oil refinery processes products for the oil industry

**in·es·cap·able** \ˌin-ə-'skā-pə-bəl\ *adj*
INEVITABLE
**in·es·cap·ably** \-blē\ *adv*

**in·ev·i·ta·bil·i·ty** \in-ˌev-ət-ə-'bil-ət-ē\ *n*
the quality or state of being inevitable

**in·ev·i·ta·ble** \in-'ev-ət-ə-bəl\ *adj*
sure to happen : CERTAIN
**in·ev·i·ta·bly** \-blē\ *adv*

**in·ex·act** \ˌin-ig-'zakt\ *adj*
INACCURATE
**in·ex·act·ly** *adv*
**in·ex·act·ness** *n*

**inertia 1:** the bicycle would be stationary if the cyclist did not press on the pedals

**in·ex·cus·able** \ˌin-ik-'skyü-zə-bəl\ *adj*
not to be excused
**in·ex·cus·ably** \-blē\ *adv*

**in·ex·haust·ible** \ˌin-ig-'zȯs-tə-bəl\ *adj*
plentiful enough not to give out or be used up
**in·ex·haust·ibly** \-blē\ *adv*

**in·ex·o·ra·ble** \in-'ek-sə-rə-bəl\ *adj*
RELENTLESS
**in·ex·o·ra·bly** \-blē\ *adv*

**in·ex·pe·di·ent** \ˌin-ik-'spēd-ē-ənt\ *adj*
not suitable or advisable

**in·ex·pen·sive** \ˌin-ik-'spen-siv\ *adj*
[1]CHEAP 1
**in·ex·pen·sive·ly** *adv*
**in·ex·pen·sive·ness** *n*

a b c d e f g h i j k l m n o p q r s t u v w x y z

A B C D E F G H I J K L M N O P Q R S T U V W X Y Z

**in·ex·pe·ri·ence** \ˌin-ik-ˈspir-ē-əns\ *n*
lack of experience

**in·ex·pe·ri·enced** \ˌin-ik-ˈspir-ē-ənst\ *adj*
having little or no experience

**in·ex·pli·ca·ble** \ˌin-ik-ˈsplik-ə-bəl, in-ˈek-splik-\ *adj*
impossible to explain or account for ⟨an *inexplicable* mystery⟩
**in·ex·pli·ca·bly** \-blē\ *adv*

**in·ex·press·ible** \ˌin-ik-ˈspres-ə-bəl\ *adj*
being beyond one's power to express : INDESCRIBABLE
**in·ex·press·ibly** \-blē\ *adv*

**in·fal·li·ble** \in-ˈfal-ə-bəl\ *adj*
**1** not capable of being wrong
**2** not likely to fail : SURE ⟨an *infallible* remedy⟩
**in·fal·li·bly** \-blē\ *adv*

**in·fa·mous** \ˈin-fə-məs\ *adj*
**1** having an evil reputation ⟨an *infamous* person⟩
**2** DETESTABLE ⟨an *infamous* crime⟩
**in·fa·mous·ly** *adv*

**in·fa·my** \ˈin-fə-mē\ *n, pl* **in·fa·mies**
**1** an evil reputation
**2** an infamous act

**in·fan·cy** \ˈin-fən-sē\ *n, pl* **in·fan·cies**
**1** early childhood
**2** a beginning or early period of existence ⟨the *infancy* of our country⟩

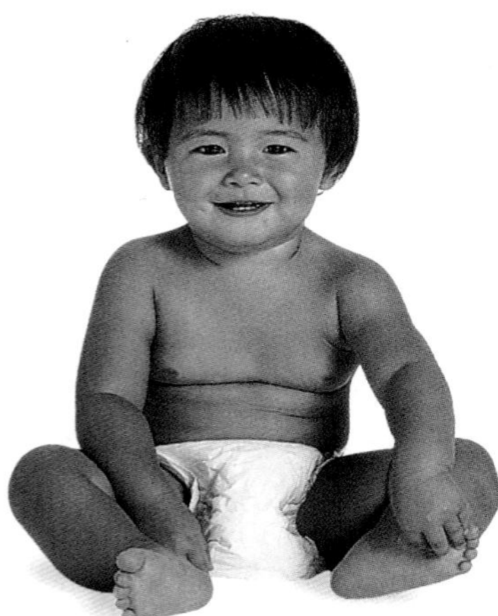
**[1]infant 1**

**[1]in·fant** \ˈin-fənt\ *n*
**1** ▲ a child in the first period of life
**2** [2]MINOR

**Word History** The word *infant* came from a Latin word. The basic meaning of this Latin word was "not talking." This Latin word was used to refer to children who were too young to talk. In time the Latin word came to be used for older children as well. The English word *infant* is most often used for a very young child.

**[2]infant** *adj*
**1** of or relating to infancy
**2** intended for young children ⟨*infant* food⟩

**in·fan·tile** \ˈin-fən-ˌtīl\ *adj*
CHILDISH

**infantile paralysis** *n*
POLIO

**in·fan·try** \ˈin-fən-trē\ *n, pl* **in·fan·tries**
a branch of an army composed of soldiers trained to fight on foot

**in·fat·u·at·ed** \in-ˈfach-ə-ˌwāt-əd\ *adj*
having a foolish or very strong love or admiration

**in·fat·u·a·tion** \in-ˌfach-ə-ˈwā-shən\ *n*
the state of being infatuated

**in·fect** \in-ˈfekt\ *vb*
**1** to cause disease germs to be present in or on ⟨*infected* bedding⟩
**2** to pass on a germ or disease to
**3** to enter and cause disease in ⟨bacteria that *infect* wounds⟩
**4** to cause to share one's feelings

**in·fec·tion** \in-ˈfek-shən\ *n*
**1** the act or process of infecting : the state of being infected
**2** any disease caused by germs

**in·fec·tious** \in-ˈfek-shəs\ *adj*
**1** passing from one to another in the form of a germ
**2** capable of being easily spread ⟨an *infectious* laugh⟩

**in·fer** \in-ˈfər\ *vb* **in·ferred**; **in·fer·ring**
**1** to arrive at as a conclusion
**2** [2]SURMISE
**3** to point out
**4** HINT, SUGGEST

**in·fer·ence** \ˈin-fə-rəns\ *n*
**1** the act or process of inferring
**2** something inferred

**[1]in·fe·ri·or** \in-ˈfir-ē-ər\ *adj*
**1** situated lower down (as in place or importance)
**2** of little or less importance, value, or merit

**[2]inferior** *n*
an inferior person or thing

**in·fe·ri·or·i·ty** \in-ˌfir-ē-ˈȯr-ət-ē\ *n*
**1** the state of being inferior
**2** a sense of being inferior

**in·fer·nal** \in-ˈfərn-l\ *adj*
**1** of or relating to hell ⟨the *infernal* regions⟩
**2** very bad or unpleasant : DAMNABLE ⟨stop that *infernal* noise⟩
**in·fer·nal·ly** *adv*

**in·fer·tile** \in-ˈfərt-l\ *adj*
not fertile

**in·fest** \in-ˈfest\ *vb*
to spread or swarm in or over in a troublesome manner

**in·fi·del** \ˈin-fəd-l, -fə-ˌdel\ *n*
a person who does not believe in a certain religion

**in·fi·del·i·ty** \ˌin-fə-ˈdel-ət-ē\ *n, pl* **in·fi·del·i·ties**
**1** lack of belief in a certain religion
**2** DISLOYALTY

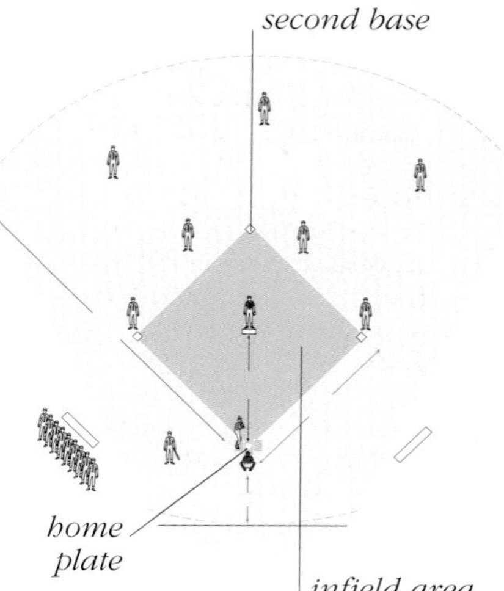


**infield 1:** diagram showing the infield area on a baseball field

**in·field** \ˈin-ˌfēld\ *n*
**1** ▲ the diamond-shaped part of a baseball field inside the bases and home plate
**2** the players in the infield

**in·field·er** \ˈin-ˌfēl-dər\ *n*
a baseball player who plays in the infield

**in·fi·nite** \ˈin-fə-nət\ *adj*
**1** having no limits of any kind

**2** seeming to be without limits ⟨took *infinite* care⟩
**in·fi·nite·ly** *adv*

**in·fin·i·tive** \in-'fin-ət-iv\ *n*
a verb form serving as a noun or as a modifier and at the same time taking objects and adverbial modifiers ⟨"to do" in "I have nothing to do" is an *infinitive*⟩

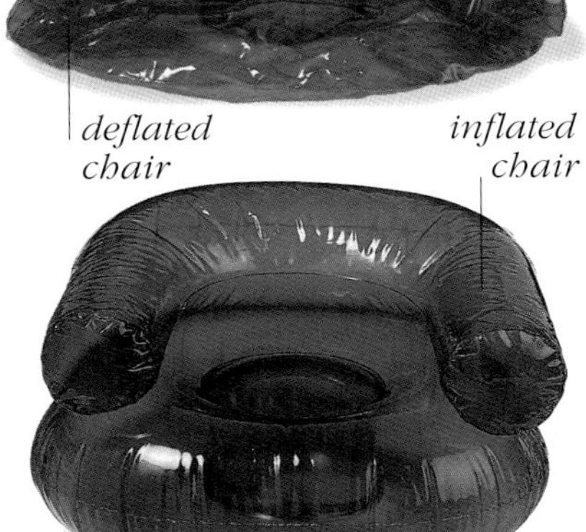


**inflatable:**
an inflatable plastic chair

**in·fin·i·ty** \in-'fin-ət-ē\ *n, pl* **in·fin·i·ties**
**1** the quality of being infinite
**2** a space, quantity, or period of time that is without limit

**in·firm** \in-'fərm\ *adj*
weak or frail in body (as from age or disease)

**in·fir·ma·ry** \in-'fər-mə-rē\ *n, pl* **in·fir·ma·ries**
a place for the care and housing of infirm or sick people

**in·fir·mi·ty** \in-'fər-mət-ē\ *n, pl* **in·fir·mi·ties**
the condition of being infirm

**in·flame** \in-'flām\ *vb* **in·flamed**; **in·flam·ing**
**1** to excite to too much action or feeling
**2** to cause to redden or grow hot (as from anger)
**3** to make or become sore, red, and swollen

**in·flam·ma·ble** \in-'flam-ə-bəl\ *adj*
**1** FLAMMABLE
**2** easily inflamed : EXCITABLE

**in·flam·ma·tion** \,in-flə-'mā-shən\ *n*
**1** the act of inflaming : the state of being inflamed
**2** a bodily response to injury in which heat, redness, and swelling are present

**in·flam·ma·to·ry** \in-'flam-ə-,tōr-ē\ *adj*
**1** tending to excite anger or disorder ⟨an *inflammatory* speech⟩
**2** causing or having inflammation ⟨an *inflammatory* disease⟩

**in·flat·able** \in-'flāt-ə-bəl\ *adj*
◀ possible to inflate ⟨an *inflatable* toy⟩

**in·flate** \in-'flāt\ *vb* **in·flat·ed**; **in·flat·ing**
**1** to swell or fill with air or gas ⟨*inflate* a balloon⟩
**2** to cause to increase beyond proper limits ⟨*inflated* prices⟩

**in·fla·tion** \in-'flā-shən\ *n*
**1** an act of inflating : the state of being inflated
**2** a continual rise in the price of goods and services

**in·flect** \in-'flekt\ *vb*
**1** to change a word by inflection
**2** to change the pitch of a person's voice

**in·flec·tion** \in-'flek-shən\ *n*
**1** a change in the pitch of a person's voice
**2** a change in a word that shows a grammatical difference (as of number, person, or tense)

**in·flec·tion·al** \in-'flek-shən-l\ *adj*
of or relating to inflection ⟨"darkened" and "darkening" are *inflectional* forms of the verb "darken"⟩

**in·flex·i·ble** \in-'flek-sə-bəl\ *adj*
**1** not easily bent or twisted : RIGID
**2** not easily influenced or persuaded : FIRM

**in·flict** \in-'flikt\ *vb*
**1** to give by or as if by striking ⟨*inflict* a wound⟩
**2** to cause to be put up with ⟨*inflict* punishment⟩

**in·flo·res·cence** \,in-flə-'res-ns\ *n*
▼ the arrangement of flowers on a stalk

**[1]in·flu·ence** \'in-,flü-əns\ *n*
**1** the act or power of producing an effect without apparent force or direct authority
**2** a person or thing that influences

## inflorescence

Flowers often grow in clusters known as inflorescences. The examples shown here demonstrate some of the different types of inflorescence.

**panicle** \'pan-i-kəl\ is a branched cluster of flowers

**raceme** \rā-'sēm\ has flowers on short stalks set towards the top of a stem

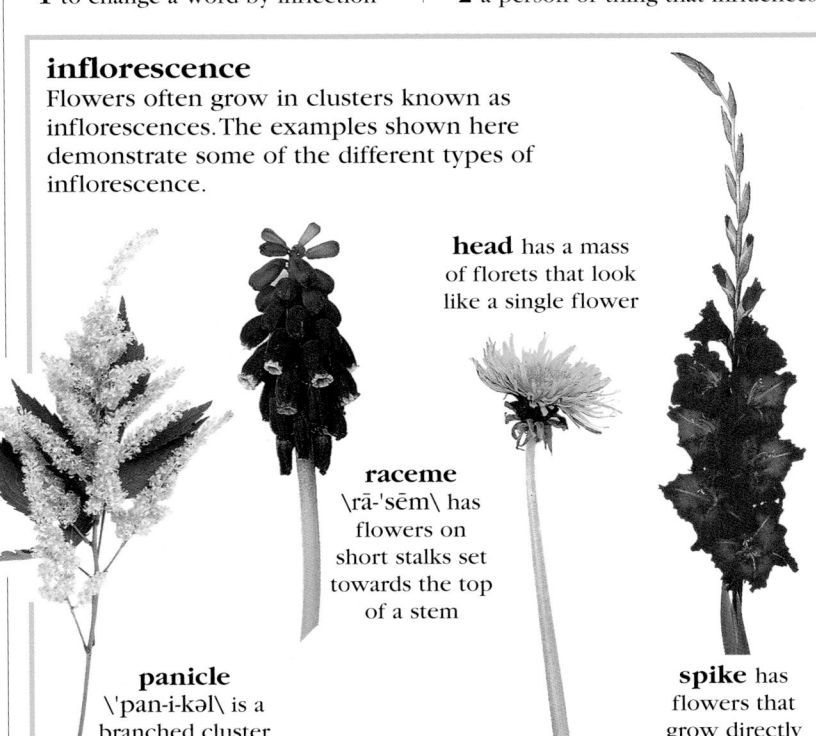

**head** has a mass of florets that look like a single flower

**spike** has flowers that grow directly from the stem

A B C D E F G H I J K L M N O P Q R S T U V W X Y Z

**²influence** *vb* **in·flu·enced**; **in·flu·enc·ing**
to have an influence on

**in·flu·en·tial** \ˌin-flü-ˈen-chəl\ *adj*
having influence

**in·flu·en·za** \ˌin-flü-ˈen-zə\ *n*
a very contagious virus disease like a severe cold with fever

**Word History** Once people blamed the stars for things that happened on earth. They even thought that some diseases were caused by the influence of the stars. An Italian word that meant "influence" came to be used for a disease as well. This disease broke out in Rome and spread through much of Europe. It was then that the word *influenza* came into the English language. It came from the Italian word that meant "influence."

**in·fo·mer·cial** \ˈin-(ˌ)fō-ˌmər-shəl, -fə-\ *n*
a television program that is a long commercial often including a discussion or demonstration

**in·form** \in-ˈfȯrm\ *vb*
**1** to let a person know something
**2** to give information so as to accuse or cause suspicion
**in·form·er** *n*

**in·for·mal** \in-ˈfȯr-məl\ *adj*
**1** not formal ⟨an *informal* party⟩
**2** suitable for ordinary or everyday use ⟨*informal* clothes⟩
**in·for·mal·ly** *adv*

**in·for·mal·i·ty** \ˌin-fȯr-ˈmal-ət-ē\ *n, pl* **in·for·mal·i·ties**
**1** the quality or state of being informal
**2** an informal act

**in·form·ant** \in-ˈfȯr-mənt\ *n*
a person who informs

**infuse 2:**
infusing tea leaves in a teapot

**in·for·ma·tion** \ˌin-fər-ˈmā-shən\ *n*
**1** the giving or getting of knowledge
**2** knowledge obtained from investigation, study, or instruction
**3** NEWS 3

**Synonyms** INFORMATION, KNOWLEDGE, and LEARNING mean what is or can be known. INFORMATION may suggest a collection of facts gathered from many places ⟨a book with much *information* about baseball⟩. KNOWLEDGE suggests a body of known facts and a set of ideas that are the product of study, observation, or experience ⟨a *knowledge* of birds⟩. LEARNING suggests knowledge acquired by long and careful study ⟨the *learning* of a lifetime went into that book⟩.

**information superhighway** *n*
INTERNET

**in·for·ma·tive** \in-ˈfȯr-mət-iv\ *adj*
giving information **:** INSTRUCTIVE

**in·frac·tion** \in-ˈfrak-shən\ *n*
VIOLATION

**in·fra·red** \ˌin-frə-ˈred\ *adj*
being, relating to, or producing rays like light but lying outside the visible spectrum at its red end

**in·fre·quent** \in-ˈfrē-kwənt\ *adj*
**1** seldom happening **:** RARE
**2** not placed, made, or done at frequent intervals ⟨made *infrequent* stops⟩
**in·fre·quent·ly** *adv*

**in·fringe** \in-ˈfrinj\ *vb* **in·fringed**; **in·fring·ing**
**1** to fail to obey or act in agreement with **:** VIOLATE ⟨*infringe* a law⟩
**2** to go further than is right or fair to another **:** ENCROACH
**in·fringe·ment** \-mənt\ *n*

**in·fu·ri·ate** \in-ˈfyu̇r-ē-ˌāt\ *vb* **in·fu·ri·at·ed**; **in·fu·ri·at·ing**
to make furious **:** ENRAGE

**in·fuse** \in-ˈfyüz\ *vb* **in·fused**; **in·fus·ing**
**1** to put in as if by pouring ⟨*infused* a spirit of cooperation into the group⟩
**2** ◀ to steep without boiling ⟨*infuse* tea leaves to make tea⟩

**in·fu·sion** \in-ˈfyü-zhən\ *n*

**¹-ing** \iŋ\ *n suffix*
**1** action or process ⟨meet*ing*⟩
**2** product or result of an action or process ⟨engrav*ing*⟩ ⟨earn*ings*⟩
**3** something used in or connected with making or doing ⟨bedd*ing*⟩ ⟨roof*ing*⟩

**²-ing** *vb suffix or adj suffix*
used to form the present participle ⟨sail*ing*⟩ and sometimes to form adjectives that do not come from a verb ⟨hulk*ing*⟩

**in·ge·nious** \in-ˈjēn-yəs\ *adj*
showing ingenuity **:** CLEVER ⟨an *ingenious* idea⟩
**in·ge·nious·ly** *adv*

**in·ge·nu·i·ty** \ˌin-jə-ˈnü-ət-ē, -ˈnyü-\ *n, pl* **in·ge·nu·i·ties**
skill or cleverness in discovering, inventing, or planning

**in·gen·u·ous** \in-ˈjen-yə-wəs\ *adj*
**1** FRANK, STRAIGHTFORWARD
**2** NAIVE 1
**in·gen·u·ous·ly** *adv*
**in·gen·u·ous·ness** *n*

**in·got** \ˈiŋ-gət\ *n*
▶ a mass of metal cast into a shape that is easy to handle or store

**ingot:**
a gold ingot from Mozambique

**in·gra·ti·ate** \in-ˈgrā-shē-ˌāt\ *vb* **in·gra·ti·at·ed**; **in·gra·ti·at·ing**
to gain favor for by effort

**in·gra·ti·at·ing** \in-ˈgrā-shē-ˌāt-iŋ\ *adj*
**1** PLEASING ⟨an *ingratiating* smile⟩
**2** intended to gain someone's favor ⟨*ingratiating* behavior⟩
**in·gra·ti·at·ing·ly** *adv*

**in·grat·i·tude** \in-ˈgrat-ə-ˌtüd, -ˌtyüd\ *n*
lack of gratitude

**in·gre·di·ent** \in-ˈgrēd-ē-ənt\ *n*
one of the substances that make up a mixture

**in·hab·it** \in-ˈhab-ət\ *vb*
to live or dwell in

**in·hab·i·tant** \in-ˈhab-ət-ənt\ *n*
one who lives in a place permanently

**in·ha·la·tion** \ˌin-ə-ˈlā-shən, -hə-\ *n*
the act or an instance of inhaling

**in·hale** \in-ˈhāl\ *vb* **in·haled**; **in·hal·ing**
**1** to draw in by breathing
**2** to breathe in

**in·hal·er** \in-ˈhā-lər\ *n*
a device used for inhaling medicine

**in·her·ent** \in-ˈhir-ənt\ *adj*
belonging to or being a part of the nature of a person or thing
**in·her·ent·ly** *adv*

**in·her·it** \in-ˈher-ət\ *vb*
**1** to get by legal right from a person at his or her death
**2** to get by heredity ⟨*inherit* red hair⟩

**in·her·i·tance** \in-ˈher-ət-əns\ *n*
**1** the act of inheriting
**2** something inherited

**in·hib·it** \in-ˈhib-ət\ *vb*
to prevent or hold back from doing something

**in·hos·pi·ta·ble** \ˌin-ˌhäs-ˈpit-ə-bəl, in-ˈhäs-pit-\ *adj*
not friendly or generous : not showing hospitality
**in·hos·pi·ta·bly** \-blē\ *adv*

**in·hu·man** \in-ˈhyü-mən, -ˈyü-\ *adj*
**1** lacking pity or kindness
**2** unlike what might be expected by a human ⟨*inhuman* screams⟩
**in·hu·man·ly** *adv*

**in·hu·mane** \ˌin-hyü-ˈmān, -yü-\ *adj*
not humane ⟨*inhumane* treatment⟩

**in·hu·man·i·ty** \ˌin-hyü-ˈman-ət-ē\ *n, pl* **in·hu·man·i·ties**
a cruel act or attitude

**in·iq·ui·tous** \in-ˈik-wət-əs\ *adj*
WICKED 1

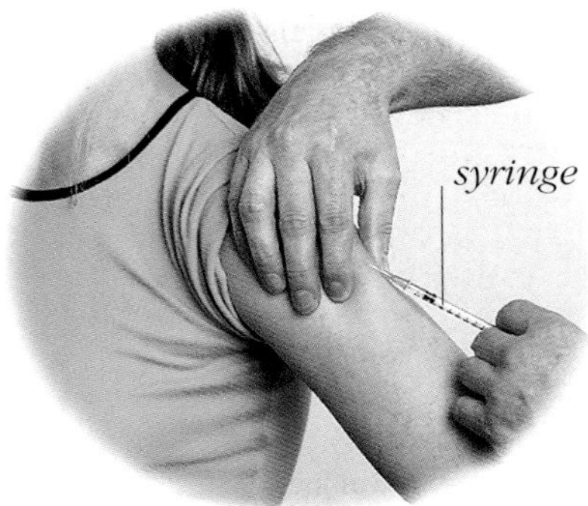


**injection 2:** a girl receiving an injection in her arm

**in·iq·ui·ty** \in-ˈik-wət-ē\ *n, pl* **in·iq·ui·ties**
[1]SIN 1

**[1]ini·tial** \in-ˈish-əl\ *adj*
**1** of, relating to, or being a beginning ⟨an *initial* effort⟩
**2** placed or standing at the beginning : FIRST

**[2]initial** *n*
**1** the first letter of a name
**2** ▶ a large letter beginning a text or a paragraph

**[2]initial 2:** the initial P from a 12th-century Latin Bible

**[3]initial** *vb* **ini·tialed** *or* **ini·tialled**; **ini·tial·ing** *or* **ini·tial·ling**
to mark with an initial or with one's initials

**ini·ti·ate** \in-ˈish-ē-ˌāt\ *vb* **ini·ti·at·ed**; **ini·ti·at·ing**
**1** to set going
**2** to admit into a club by special ceremonies

**ini·ti·a·tion** \in-ˌish-ē-ˈā-shən\ *n*
**1** the act or an instance of initiating : the process of being initiated
**2** the ceremonies with which a person is made a member of a club

**ini·tia·tive** \in-ˈish-ət-iv\ *n*
**1** a first step or movement ⟨take the *initiative*⟩
**2** energy shown in initiating action ⟨a person of great *initiative*⟩

**in·ject** \in-ˈjekt\ *vb*
**1** to throw or drive into something
**2** to force a fluid into (as a part of the body) for medical reasons

**in·jec·tion** \in-ˈjek-shən\ *n*
**1** an act or instance of injecting
**2** ◀ something injected

**in·junc·tion** \in-ˈjəngk-shən\ *n*
a court order commanding or forbidding the doing of some act

**in·jure** \ˈin-jər\ *vb* **in·jured**; **in·jur·ing**
**1** to do an injustice to : WRONG
**2** to cause pain or harm to

**in·ju·ri·ous** \in-ˈju̇r-ē-əs\ *adj*
causing injury

**in·ju·ry** \ˈin-jə-rē\ *n, pl* **in·ju·ries**
**1** an act that damages or hurts
**2** hurt, damage, or loss suffered
**synonyms** see HARM

**in·jus·tice** \in-ˈjəs-təs\ *n*
**1** violation of a person's rights
**2** an unjust act

**[1]ink** \ˈiŋk\ *n*
a usually liquid material for writing or printing

**[2]ink** *vb*
to put ink on

**ink–jet** \ˈīngk-ˈjet\ *adj*
relating to or being a printer in which droplets of ink are sprayed onto the paper

**in·kling** \ˈing-kling\ *n*
a vague notion : HINT

**ink·stand** \ˈingk-ˌstand\ *n*
a small stand for holding ink and pens

**ink·well** \ˈing-ˌkwel\ *n*
a container for ink

**inky** \ˈing-kē\ *adj* **ink·i·er**; **ink·i·est**
**1** consisting of or like ink ⟨*inky* darkness⟩
**2** soiled with or as if with ink

**in·laid** \ˈin-ˈlād\ *adj*
**1** set into a surface in a decorative design
**2** ▼ decorated with a design or material set into a surface

**inlaid 2:** an inlaid box

**[1]in·land** \ˈin-ˌland, -lənd\ *adj*
of or relating to the part of a country away from the coast

**[2]inland** *n*
the part of a country away from the coast or boundaries

**[3]inland** *adv*
into or toward the area away from a coast

**in–law** \'in-,lȯ\ *n*
a relative by marriage

**[1]in·lay** \'in-'lā\ *vb* **in·laid** \-'lād\; **in·lay·ing**
to set into a surface for decoration or strengthening

**[2]in·lay** \'in-,lā\ *n*
inlaid work **:** material used in inlaying

**in·let** \'in-,let\ *n*
**1** a small or narrow bay
**2** an opening for intake

**in–line skate** \'in-'līn-\ *n*
a roller skate whose wheels are set in a line one behind the other

**in·mate** \'in-,māt\ *n*
**1** one of a group living in a single residence
**2** a person confined in an institution (as a hospital or prison)

**in·most** \'in-,mōst\ *adj*
INNERMOST

**inn** \'in\ *n*
a place that provides a place to sleep and food for travelers

**in·ner** \'in-ər\ *adj*
**1** located farther in
**2** of or relating to the mind or spirit

**inner ear** *n*
the inner hollow part of the ear that contains sense organs which perceive sound and help keep the body properly balanced

**in·ner·most** \'in-ər-,mōst\ *adj*
farthest inward

**in·ning** \'in-ing\ *n*
a division of a baseball game that consists of a turn at bat for each team

**inn·keep·er** \'in-,kē-pər\ *n*
the person who runs an inn

**in·no·cence** \'in-ə-səns\ *n*
the quality or state of being innocent

**in·no·cent** \'in-ə-sənt\ *adj*
**1** free from sin **:** PURE
**2** free from guilt or blame
**3** free from evil influence or effect **:** HARMLESS ⟨*innocent* fun⟩
**in·no·cent·ly** *adv*

**in·noc·u·ous** \in-'äk-yə-wəs\ *adj*
not harmful

**in·no·va·tion** \,in-ə-'vā-shən\ *n*
**1** the introduction of something new
**2** a new idea, method, or device **:** NOVELTY

**in·nu·mer·a·ble** \in-'ü-mə-rə-bəl, -'yü-\ *adj*
too many to be counted

**in·oc·u·late** \in-'äk-yə-,lāt\ *vb* **in·oc·u·lat·ed**; **in·oc·u·lat·ing**
to inject a serum, vaccine, or weakened germ into to protect against or treat a disease

---

**Word History** You can insert a bud from one plant in another plant. If you are skillful and lucky, the bud will grow. The English word *inoculate* at first meant "to insert a bud in a plant." It came from a Latin word. This Latin word was formed from two Latin words. One meant "in." The other meant "eye" or "bud."

---

**in·oc·u·la·tion** \in-,äk-yə-'lā-shən\ *n*
**1** the act or an instance of inoculating
**2** material used in inoculating

**in·of·fen·sive** \,in-ə-'fen-siv\ *adj*
**1** not harmful
**2** PEACEFUL 1
**3** not offensive

**in·op·por·tune** \in-,äp-ər-'tün, -'tyün\ *adj*
INCONVENIENT ⟨an *inopportune* time⟩

**[1]in·put** \'in-,pu̇t\ *n*
**1** something (as power, a signal, or data) that is put into a machine or system
**2** the point at which an input is made
**3** the act of or process of putting in

**[2]input** *vb* **in·put·ted** *or* **input**; **in·put·ting**
to enter (as data) into a computer

**in·quest** \'in-,kwest\ *n*
an official investigation especially into the cause of a death

**in·quire** \in-'kwīr\ *vb* **in·quired**; **in·quir·ing**
**1** to ask about ⟨*inquired* the way to the station⟩
**2** to make an investigation
**3** to ask a question ⟨*inquired* about the weather⟩
**in·quir·er** *n*
**in·quir·ing·ly** *adv*

**in·qui·ry** \'in-,kwī-rē, -kwə-\ *n*, *pl* **in·qui·ries**
**1** the act of inquiring
**2** a request for information
**3** a thorough examination

**in·quis·i·tive** \in-'kwiz-ət-iv\ *adj*
**1** given to seeking information
**2** tending to ask questions
**in·quis·i·tive·ly** *adv*
**in·quis·i·tive·ness** *n*

**in·sane** \in-'sān\ *adj*
**1** not normal or healthy in mind
**2** used by or for people who are insane
**in·sane·ly** *adv*

**in·san·i·ty** \in-'san-ət-ē\ *n*
the condition of being insane **:** mental illness

**in·sa·tia·ble** \in-'sā-shə-bəl\ *adj*
impossible to satisfy ⟨*insatiable* thirst⟩

**in·scribe** \in-'skrīb\ *vb* **in·scribed**; **in·scrib·ing**
**1** to write, engrave, or print as a lasting record
**2** to write, engrave, or print something on or in ⟨*inscribe* a book⟩

**in·scrip·tion** \in-'skrip-shən\ *n*
something that is inscribed

**in·sect** \'in-,sekt\ *n*
**1** ► a small and often winged animal that has six jointed legs and a body formed of three parts ⟨flies, bees, and lice are true *insects*⟩
**2** an animal (as a spider or a centipede) similar to the true insects

---

**Word History** The bodies of most insects are divided into parts. They look as if someone might have cut into them. The ancient Greeks gave insects a name that meant "cut up." The Latin word for an insect was a translation of the Greek name. This Latin word was formed from two Latin words. One meant "in" and the other meant "to cut." The English word *insect* came from the Latin word for an insect.

---

**in·sec·ti·cide** \in-'sek-tə-,sīd\ *n*
a chemical used to kill insects

**in·se·cure** \,in-si-'kyu̇r\ *adj*
not safe or secure
**in·se·cure·ly** *adv*

**in·se·cu·ri·ty** \,in-si-'kyu̇r-ət-ē\ *n*
the quality or state of being insecure

**in·sen·si·ble** \in-'sen-sə-bəl\ *adj*
**1** UNCONSCIOUS 2
**2** not able to feel ⟨*insensible* to pain⟩
**3** not aware of or caring about something ⟨*insensible* to fear⟩

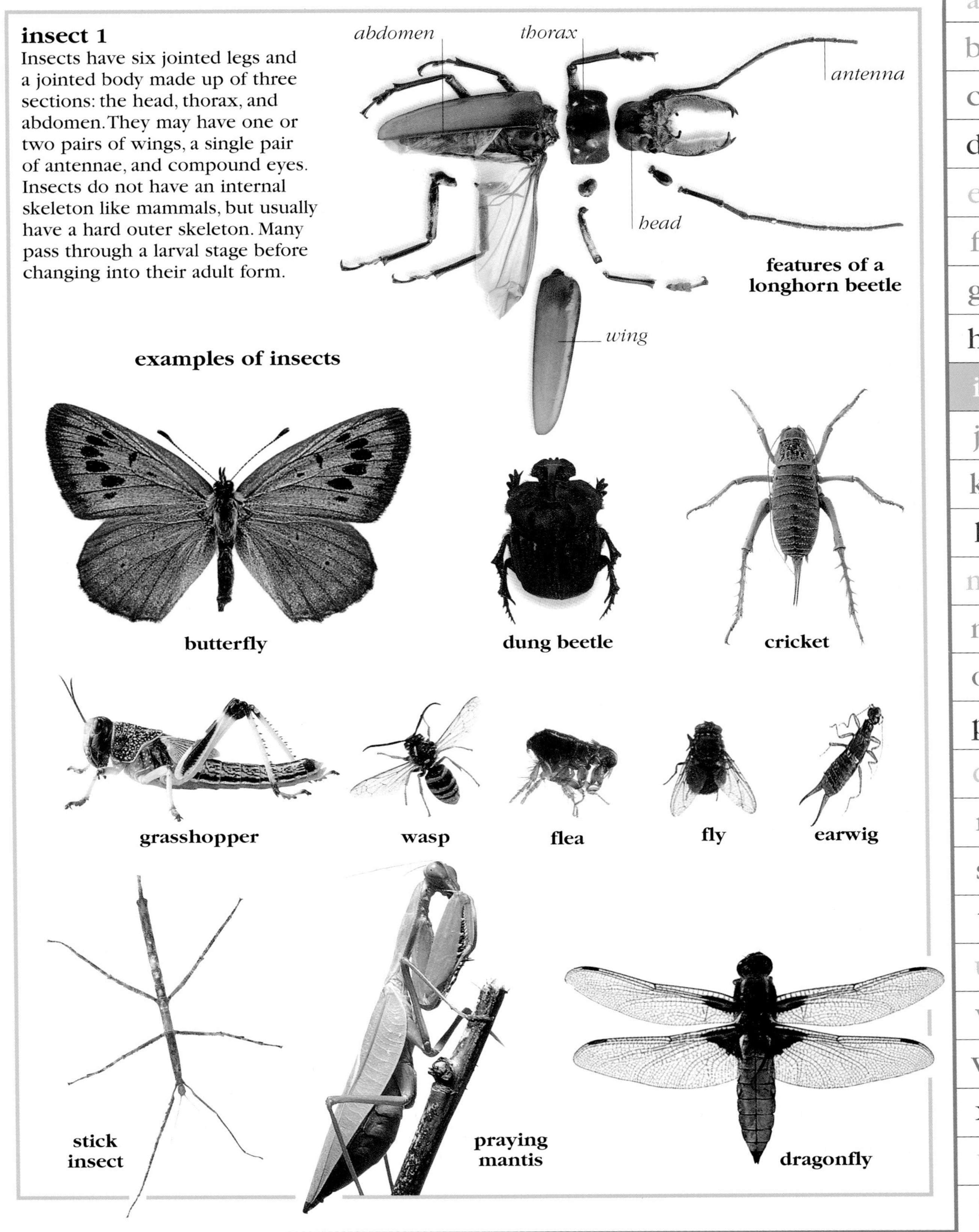


**insect 1**
Insects have six jointed legs and a jointed body made up of three sections: the head, thorax, and abdomen. They may have one or two pairs of wings, a single pair of antennae, and compound eyes. Insects do not have an internal skeleton like mammals, but usually have a hard outer skeleton. Many pass through a larval stage before changing into their adult form.

**in·sen·si·tive** \in-'sen-sət-iv\ *adj*
not sensitive : lacking feeling
**in·sen·si·tive·ly** *adv*

**in·sen·si·tiv·i·ty** \in-,sen-sə-'tiv-ət-ē\ *n*
lack of sensitivity

**in·sep·a·ra·bil·i·ty** \in-,sep-ə-rə-'bil-ət-ē\ *n*
the quality or state of being inseparable

**in·sep·a·ra·ble** \in-'sep-ə-rə-bəl\ *adj*
impossible to separate
**in·sep·a·ra·bly** \-blē\ *adv*

[1]**in·sert** \in-'sərt\ *vb*
**1** to put in ⟨*insert* one's hands in one's pockets⟩
**2** to set in and make fast ⟨*insert* a patch in the sleeve⟩

[2]**in·sert** \'in-,sərt\ *n*
something that is or is meant to be inserted

**in·ser·tion** \in-'sər-shən\ *n*
**1** the act or process of inserting
**2** [2]INSERT

[1]**in·set** \'in-,set\ *n*
[2]INSERT

[2]**inset** *vb* **in·set** *or* **in·set·ted**; **in·set·ting**
[1]INSERT 2

[1]**in·side** \in-'sīd, 'in-,sīd\ *n*
**1** an inner side, surface, or space : INTERIOR ⟨the *inside* of a box⟩
**2** ENTRAILS — usually used in pl.

[2]**inside** *adv*
**1** on the inner side ⟨cleaned my car *inside* and out⟩
**2** in or into the interior ⟨go *inside*⟩

[3]**inside** *adj*
**1** of, relating to, or being on or near the inside ⟨an *inside* wall⟩
**2** relating or known to a certain few people ⟨*inside* information⟩

[4]**inside** *prep*
**1** to or on the inside of ⟨they are *inside* the house⟩
**2** before the end of : WITHIN ⟨I'll finish *inside* an hour⟩

**in·sid·er** \in-'sīd-ər\ *n*
a person having information not generally available

**in·sight** \'in-,sīt\ *n*
the power or act of seeing what's really important about a situation

**in·sig·nia** \in-'sig-nē-ə\ *or* **in·sig·ne** \-nē\ *n, pl* **insignia** *or* **in·sig·ni·as**
▶ an emblem of a certain office, authority, or honor

**in·sig·nif·i·cance** \,in-sig-'nif-i-kəns\ *n*
the quality or state of being insignificant

**in·sig·nif·i·cant** \,in-sig-'nif-i-kənt\ *adj*
not significant : UNIMPORTANT
**in·sig·nif·i·cant·ly** *adv*

**in·sin·cere** \,in-sin-'sir\ *adj*
not sincere
**in·sin·cere·ly** *adv*

**in·sin·cer·i·ty** \,in-sin-'ser-ət-ē\ *n*
lack of sincerity

**in·sin·u·ate** \in-'sin-yə-,wāt\ *vb* **in·sin·u·at·ed**; **in·sin·u·at·ing**
**1** to bring or get in little by little or in a secret way
**2** [2]HINT, IMPLY ⟨*insinuated* that I had cheated⟩

**in·sip·id** \in-'sip-əd\ *adj*
**1** having little taste or flavor : TASTELESS
**2** not interesting or challenging : DULL

**in·sist** \in-'sist\ *vb*
**1** to place special stress or great importance ⟨*insists* on accuracy⟩
**2** to make a demand

**in·sis·tence** \in-'sis-təns\ *n*
the quality or state of being insistent

**in·sis·tent** \in-'sis-tənt\ *adj*
demanding attention : PERSISTENT
**in·sis·tent·ly** *adv*

**in·so·lence** \'in-sə-ləns\ *n*
lack of respect for rank or authority

**in·so·lent** \'in-sə-lənt\ *adj*
showing insolence
**in·so·lent·ly** *adv*

**in·sol·u·bil·i·ty** \in-,säl-yə-'bil-ət-ē\ *n*
the quality or state of being insoluble

**in·sol·u·ble** \in-'säl-yə-bəl\ *adj*
**1** having no solution or explanation ⟨an *insoluble* problem⟩
**2** difficult or impossible to dissolve ⟨*insoluble* in water⟩
**in·sol·u·bly** \-blē\ *adv*

*insignia*

**insignia** on the cap of an officer in the US Navy

**in·spect** \in-'spekt\ *vb*
**1** to examine closely
**2** to view and examine in an official way ⟨*inspected* the troops⟩

**in·spec·tion** \in-'spek-shən\ *n*
the act of inspecting

**in·spec·tor** \in-'spek-tər\ *n*
a person who makes inspections

**in·spi·ra·tion** \,in-spə-'rā-shən\ *n*
**1** the act of breathing in
**2** the act or power of arousing the mind or the emotions ⟨the *inspiration* of music⟩
**3** the state of being inspired
**4** something that is or seems inspired
**5** an inspiring agent or influence

**in·spire** \in-'spīr\ *vb* **in·spired**; **in·spir·ing**
**1** to move or guide by divine influence
**2** to give inspiration to : ENCOURAGE
**3** AROUSE 2
**4** to bring about : CAUSE
**5** INHALE

**in·sta·bil·i·ty** \,in-stə-'bil-ət-ē\ *n*
the quality or state of being unstable

**in·stall** \in-'stȯl\ *vb*
**1** to put in office with ceremony
**2** to set up for use or service ⟨*install* the plumbing⟩

**in·stal·la·tion** \,in-stə-'lā-shən\ *n*
**1** the act of installing : the state of being installed
**2** something installed for use

[1]**in·stall·ment** *or* **in·stal·ment** \in-'stȯl-mənt\ *n*
INSTALLATION 1

[2]**installment** *n*
one of the parts of a series

**in·stance** \'in-stəns\ *n*
**1** EXAMPLE 1
**2** a certain point in an action or process

[1]**in·stant** \'in-stənt\ *n*
MOMENT 1

[2]**instant** *adj*
**1** happening or done at once ⟨an *instant* success⟩
**2** partially prepared by the manufacturer so that only final mixing is needed ⟨*instant* cake mix⟩
**3** made to dissolve quickly in a liquid ⟨*instant* coffee⟩

**in·stan·ta·neous** \,in-stən-'tā-nē-əs\ *adj*
**1** happening in an instant
**2** done without delay
**in·stan·ta·neous·ly** *adv*

**in·stant·ly** \'in-stənt-lē\ *adv*
IMMEDIATELY 2

**in·stead** \in-'sted\ *adv*
as a substitute

**in·stead of** \in-ˌsted-əv\ *prep*
as a substitute for : rather than ⟨had milk *instead of* juice⟩

**in·step** \'in-ˌstep\ *n*
▼ the arched middle part of the human foot in front of the ankle joint

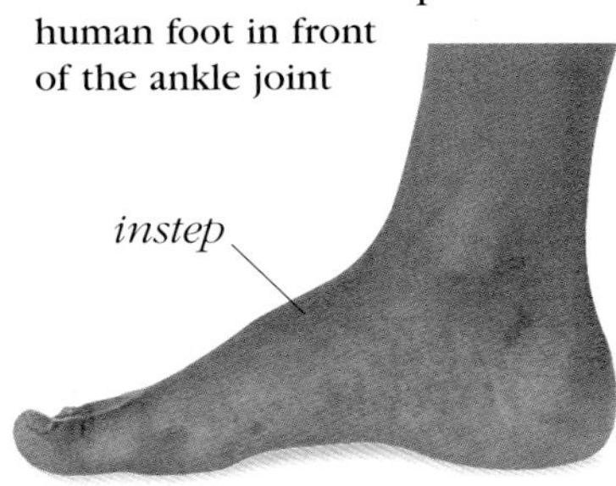


**instep**

**in·sti·gate** \'in-stə-ˌgāt\ *vb*
**in·sti·gat·ed**; **in·sti·gat·ing**
PROVOKE 2, INCITE

**in·still** \in-'stil\ *vb*
to put into the mind little by little

**in·stinct** \'in-ˌstingkt\ *n*
1 a natural ability
2 an act or course of action in response to a stimulus that is automatic rather than learned
3 behavior based on automatic reactions

**in·stinc·tive** \in-'stingk-tiv\ *adj*
of or relating to instinct : resulting from instinct
**in·stinc·tive·ly** *adv*

**¹in·sti·tute** \'in-stə-ˌtüt, -ˌtyüt\ *vb*
**in·sti·tut·ed**; **in·sti·tut·ing**
1 ESTABLISH 1
2 to set going : INAUGURATE

**²institute** *n*
1 an organization for the promotion of a cause ⟨an *institute* for mental health⟩
2 a place for study usually in a special field ⟨the new art *institute*⟩

**in·sti·tu·tion** \ˌin-stə-'tü-shən, -'tyü-\ *n*
1 the act of instituting : ESTABLISHMENT
2 an established custom, practice, or law
3 an established organization ⟨business *institutions*⟩

**in·sti·tu·tion·al** \ˌin-stə-'tü-shən-l, -'tyü-\ *adj*
of or relating to an institution

**in·struct** \in-'strəkt\ *vb*
1 to help to get knowledge to : TEACH
2 to give information to
3 to give commands to : DIRECT
**synonyms** see TEACH

**in·struc·tion** \in-'strək-shən\ *n*
1 LESSON 3
2 **instructions** *pl* DIRECTION 2, ORDER ⟨I left *instructions* that I was not to be disturbed⟩
3 **instructions** *pl* an outline of how something is to be done ⟨follow the *instructions* on the blackboard⟩
4 the practice or method used by a teacher

**in·struc·tive** \in-'strək-tiv\ *adj*
helping to give knowledge
**in·struc·tive·ly** *adv*

**in·struc·tor** \in-'strək-tər\ *n*
TEACHER

**in·stru·ment** \'in-strə-mənt\ *n*
1 a way of getting something done
2 ▼ a device for doing a particular kind of work
3 a device used to produce music
4 a legal document (as a deed)
5 a measuring device

**Synonyms** INSTRUMENT, TOOL, and UTENSIL mean a device for doing work. INSTRUMENT suggests a device that can be used to do complicated work ⟨the heart surgeon's *instruments*⟩. TOOL suggests a device used for a particular job and often suggests that a special skill is needed to use it ⟨a carpenter's *tools* such as hammers and saws⟩. UTENSIL may suggest a simple device used in jobs around the house ⟨kitchen *utensils* such as spoons and knives⟩.

**in·stru·men·tal** \ˌin-strə-'ment-l\ *adj*
1 acting to get something done ⟨was *instrumental* in organizing the club⟩
2 of or relating to an instrument
3 being music played on an instrument rather than sung
**in·stru·men·tal·ly** \-l-ē\ *adv*

**instrument 2**
Instruments are devices which enable a person to perform a particular task. A pair of compasses ensure that a perfect circle can be drawn. A microscope allows doctors and other scientists to view tiny things. Doctors also use a stethoscope to hear sounds inside the body, such as the beating of the heart.

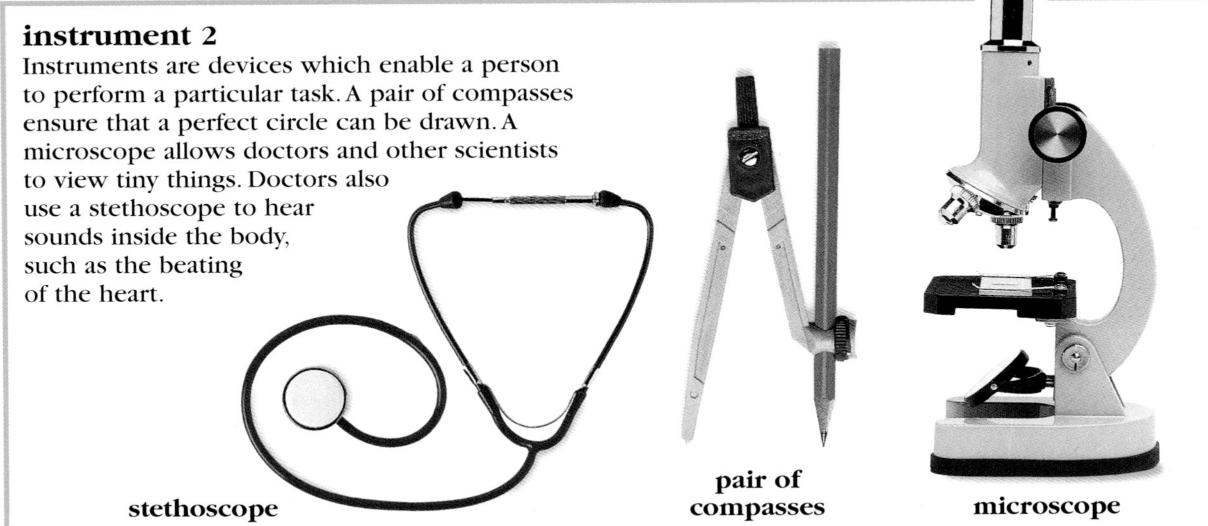

stethoscope

pair of compasses

microscope

**in·sub·or·di·nate** \ˌin-sə-ˈbȯrd-n-ət\ *adj*
unwilling to obey authority
: DISOBEDIENT

**in·sub·or·di·na·tion** \ˌin-sə-ˌbȯrd-n-ˈā-shən\ *n*
failure to obey authority

**in·sub·stan·tial** \ˌin-səb-ˈstan-chəl\ *adj*
**1** not real : IMAGINARY
**2** not firm or solid
**in·sub·stan·tial·ly** *adv*

**in·suf·fer·able** \in-ˈsəf-ə-rə-bəl\ *adj*
impossible to endure : INTOLERABLE ⟨*insufferable* behavior⟩
**in·suf·fer·ably** \-blē\ *adv*

**in·suf·fi·cien·cy** \ˌin-sə-ˈfish-ən-sē\ *n, pl* **in·suf·fi·cien·cies**
**1** the quality or state of being insufficient
**2** a shortage of something

**in·suf·fi·cient** \ˌin-sə-ˈfish-ənt\ *adj*
not sufficient : INADEQUATE
**in·suf·fi·cient·ly** *adv*

**in·su·late** \ˈin-sə-ˌlāt\ *vb* **in·su·lat·ed**; **in·su·lat·ing**
**1** to separate from others : ISOLATE
**2** to separate a conductor of electricity, heat, or sound from other conducting bodies by means of something that will not conduct electricity, heat, or sound

**in·su·la·tion** \ˌin-sə-ˈlā-shən\ *n*
**1** the act of insulating : the state of being insulated
**2** material used in insulating

**in·su·la·tor** \ˈin-sə-ˌlāt-ər\ *n*
**1** a material (as rubber or glass) that is a poor conductor of electricity or heat
**2** ▼ a device made of an electrical insulating material and used for separating or supporting electrical conductors

**in·su·lin** \ˈin-sə-lən\ *n*
a hormone from the pancreas that prevents or controls diabetes

*electrical cable*
*insulator*

**insulator 2:** a plastic insulator surrounding an electrical cable

[1]**in·sult** \in-ˈsəlt\ *vb*
to treat with disrespect or scorn

[2]**in·sult** \ˈin-ˌsəlt\ *n*
an act or expression showing disrespect or scorn

**in·sur·ance** \in-ˈshu̇r-əns\ *n*
**1** the act of insuring : the state of being insured
**2** the business of insuring persons or property
**3** a contract by which someone guarantees for a fee to pay someone else for the value of property lost or damaged (as through theft or fire) or usually a specified amount for injury or death
**4** the amount for which something is insured

**in·sure** \in-ˈshu̇r\ *vb* **in·sured**; **in·sur·ing**
**1** to give or get insurance on or for
**2** ENSURE ⟨*insure* the comfort of a guest⟩
**in·sur·er** *n*

**in·sured** \in-ˈshu̇rd\ *n*
a person whose life or property is insured

[1]**in·sur·gent** \in-ˈsər-jənt\ *n*
[2]REBEL

[2]**insurgent** *adj*
REBELLIOUS 1

**in·sur·rec·tion** \ˌin-sə-ˈrek-shən\ *n*
an act or instance of rebelling against a government

**in·tact** \in-ˈtakt\ *adj*
not touched especially by anything that harms

**in·take** \ˈin-ˌtāk\ *n*
**1** a place where liquid or air is taken into something (as a pump)
**2** the act of taking in
**3** something taken in

[1]**in·tan·gi·ble** \in-ˈtan-jə-bəl\ *adj*
**1** not possible to touch ⟨light is *intangible*⟩
**2** not possible to think of as matter or substance ⟨goodwill is an *intangible* asset⟩

[2]**intangible** *n*
something intangible

**in·te·ger** \ˈint-i-jər\ *n*
a number that is a natural number (as 1, 2, or 3), the negative of a natural number (as −1, −2, −3), or 0

**in·te·gral** \ˈint-i-grəl\ *adj*
needed to make something complete ⟨an *integral* part⟩

**in·te·grate** \ˈint-ə-ˌgrāt\ *vb* **in·te·grat·ed**; **in·te·grat·ing**
**1** to form into a whole : UNITE
**2** to make a part of a larger unit
**3** to make open to all races ⟨*integrate* the schools⟩

**integrated circuit** *n*
▼ a tiny group of electronic devices and their connections that is produced in or on a small slice of material (as silicon)

**integrated circuit:** a silicon board with an integrated circuit

**in·te·gra·tion** \ˌint-ə-ˈgrā-shən\ *n*
an act, process, or instance of integrating

**in·teg·ri·ty** \in-ˈteg-rət-ē\ *n*
**1** the condition of being free from damage or defect
**2** total honesty and sincerity

**in·tel·lect** \ˈint-l-ˌekt\ *n*
**1** the power of knowing
**2** the capacity for thought especially when highly developed
**3** a person with great powers of thinking and reasoning

[1]**in·tel·lec·tu·al** \ˌint-l-ˈek-chə-wəl\ *adj*
**1** of or relating to the intellect or understanding ⟨*intellectual* processes⟩
**2** having or showing greater than usual intellect
**3** requiring study and thought ⟨*intellectual* work⟩
**in·tel·lec·tu·al·ly** \-wə-lē\ *adv*

[2]**intellectual** *n*
an intellectual person

**in·tel·li·gence** \in-ˈtel-ə-jəns\ *n*
**1** the ability to learn and understand
**2** NEWS 3, INFORMATION
**3** an agency that obtains information about an enemy or a possible enemy

**in·tel·li·gent** \in-'tel-ə-jənt\ *adj*
having or showing intelligence or intellect
**in·tel·li·gent·ly** *adv*

---

**Synonyms** INTELLIGENT, CLEVER, and BRILLIANT mean having a good amount of mental ability. INTELLIGENT suggests that one can handle new situations and solve problems ⟨an *intelligent* person who knew what to do in an emergency⟩. CLEVER suggests that one learns very quickly ⟨the *clever* youngster learned how to do the trick in a few minutes⟩. BRILLIANT suggests that one's mental ability is much higher than normal ⟨a *brilliant* doctor discovered the cure for that disease⟩.

---

**in·tel·li·gi·ble** \in-'tel-ə-jə-bəl\ *adj*
possible to understand
**in·tel·li·gi·bly** \-blē\ *adv*

**in·tem·per·ance** \in-'tem-pə-rəns\ *n*
lack of self-control (as in satisfying an appetite)

**in·tem·per·ate** \in-'tem-pə-rət\ *adj*
**1** not moderate or mild ⟨*intemperate* weather⟩
**2** lacking or showing a lack of self-control (as in the use of alcoholic drinks)
**in·tem·per·ate·ly** *adv*

**in·tend** \in-'tend\ *vb*
to have in mind as a purpose or aim : PLAN ⟨*intend* to do better⟩

**in·tense** \in-'tens\ *adj*
**1** [1]EXTREME 1 ⟨*intense* heat⟩
**2** done with great energy, enthusiasm, or effort ⟨*intense* concentration⟩
**3** having very strong feelings ⟨an *intense* person⟩
**in·tense·ly** *adv*

**in·ten·si·fi·ca·tion** \in-,ten-sə-fə-'kā-shən\ *n*
the act or process of intensifying

**in·ten·si·fy** \in-'ten-sə-,fī\ *vb*
**in·ten·si·fied**; **in·ten·si·fy·ing**
to make or become intense or more intensive : HEIGHTEN

**in·ten·si·ty** \in-'ten-sət-ē\ *n, pl* **in·ten·si·ties**
**1** extreme strength or force
**2** the degree or amount of a quality or condition

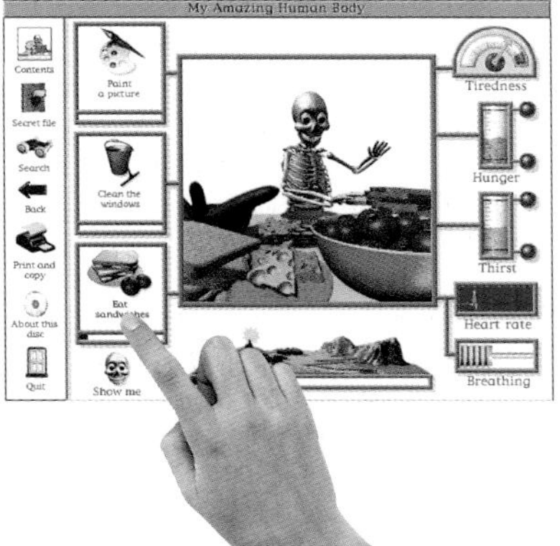


**interactive 2:** an interactive computer screen where touch leads the user to the next window

[1]**in·ten·sive** \in-'ten-siv\ *adj*
**1** involving special effort or concentration : THOROUGH
**2** used to stress something ⟨the *intensive* pronoun "myself" in "I myself did it"⟩

[2]**intensive** *n*
an intensive word

[1]**in·tent** \in-'tent\ *n*
**1** [1]PURPOSE, INTENTION ⟨with *intent* to kill⟩
**2** MEANING 1 ⟨the *intent* of a letter⟩

[2]**intent** *adj*
**1** showing concentration or great attention ⟨an *intent* gaze⟩
**2** showing great determination ⟨were *intent* on going⟩
**in·tent·ly** *adv*
**in·tent·ness** *n*

**in·ten·tion** \in-'ten-chən\ *n*
**1** a determination to act in a particular way
**2** [1]PURPOSE, AIM
**3** MEANING 1, INTENT

**in·ten·tion·al** \in-'ten-chən-l\ *adj*
done by intention : not accidental **synonyms** see VOLUNTARY
**in·ten·tion·al·ly** *adv*

**in·ter** \in-'tər\ *vb* **in·terred**; **in·ter·ring**
BURY 1

**inter-** *prefix*
**1** between : among : together ⟨*inter*mingle⟩ ⟨*inter*twine⟩
**2** mutual : mutually : reciprocal : reciprocally ⟨*inter*relation⟩
**3** located, occurring, or carried on between ⟨*inter*national⟩

**in·ter·act** \,int-ə-'rakt\ *vb*
to act upon one another

**in·ter·ac·tion** \,int-ə-'rak-shən\ *n*
the action or influence of people, groups, or things on one another

**in·ter·ac·tive** \,int-ə-'rak-tiv\ *adj*
**1** active between people, groups, or things
**2** ◀ of, relating to, or allowing two-way electronic communications (as between a person and a computer)
**in·ter·ac·tive·ly** *adv*

**in·ter·cede** \,int-ər-'sēd\ *vb*
**in·ter·ced·ed**; **in·ter·ced·ing**
**1** to try to help settle differences between unfriendly individuals or groups
**2** to plead for the needs of someone else

**in·ter·cept** \,int-ər-'sept\ *vb*
to take, seize, or stop before reaching an intended destination ⟨*intercept* a letter⟩
**in·ter·cep·tor** \-'sep-tər\ *n*

**in·ter·ces·sion** \,int-ər-'sesh-ən\ *n*
the act of interceding

**in·ter·ces·sor** \,int-ər-'ses-ər\ *n*
a person who intercedes

[1]**in·ter·change** \,int-ər-'chānj\ *vb*
**in·ter·changed**; **in·ter·chang·ing**
to put each in the place of the other : EXCHANGE

[2]**in·ter·change** \'int-ər-,chānj\ *n*
**1** an act or instance of interchanging
**2** ▼ a joining of highways that permits moving from one to the other without crossing traffic lanes

[2]**interchange 2:** an aerial view of an interchange

## intercom

With an intercom, the person who receives a call hears the caller's voice through a loudspeaker or telephone, and may see his or her face on a video screen. The receiver then presses a button to open the door, allowing the caller into the building.

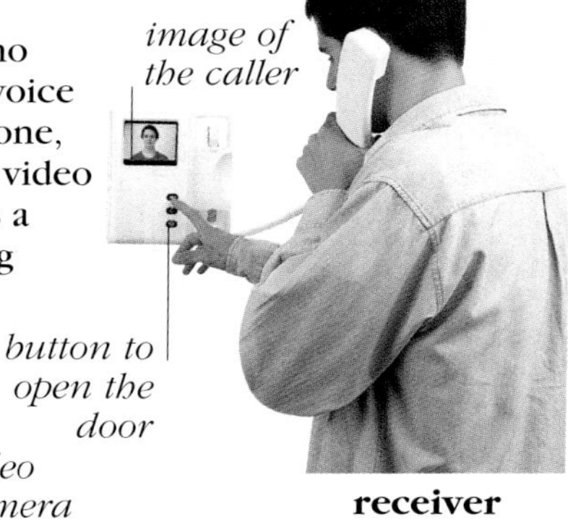

**a video intercom system**

**in·ter·change·able** \ˌint-ər-ˈchān-jə-bəl\ *adj*
possible to interchange
**in·ter·change·ably** \-blē\ *adv*

**in·ter·com** \ˈint-ər-ˌkäm\ *n*
▲ a communication system with a microphone and loudspeaker at each end

**in·ter·course** \ˈint-ər-ˌkōrs\ *n*
dealings between persons or groups

**in·ter·de·pen·dence** \ˌint-ər-di-ˈpen-dəns\ *n*
the quality or state of being interdependent

**in·ter·de·pen·dent** \ˌint-ər-di-ˈpen-dənt\ *adj*
depending on one another
**in·ter·de·pen·dent·ly** *adv*

**¹in·ter·est** \ˈin-trəst, ˈint-ə-rəst\ *n*
**1** a right, title, or legal share in something ⟨have an *interest* in the business⟩
**2** WELFARE 1, BENEFIT ⟨have only your *interest* in mind⟩
**3** the money paid by a borrower for the use of borrowed money
**4 interests** *pl* **:** a group financially interested in an industry or business ⟨mining *interests*⟩
**5** a feeling of concern, curiosity, or desire to be involved with something ⟨an *interest* in music⟩
**6** the quality of attracting special attention or arousing curiosity
**7** something in which one is interested

**²interest** *vb*
**1** to persuade to become involved in
**2** to arouse and hold the interest of

**in·ter·est·ed** \ˈin-trəs-təd, ˈint-ə-rəs-\ *adj*
having or showing interest

**in·ter·est·ing** \ˈin-trəs-ting, ˈint-ə-rəs-\ *adj*
holding the attention **:** arousing interest
**in·ter·est·ing·ly** *adv*

**in·ter·fere** \ˌint-ər-ˈfir\ *vb*
**in·ter·fered**; **in·ter·fer·ing**
**1** to be in opposition **:** CLASH
**2** to take a part in the concerns of others **synonyms** see MEDDLE

**in·ter·fer·ence** \ˌint-ər-ˈfir-əns\ *n*
**1** the act or process of interfering
**2** something that interferes

**in·ter·im** \ˈin-tə-rəm\ *n*
INTERVAL 1

**¹in·te·ri·or** \in-ˈtir-ē-ər\ *adj*
**1** being or occurring within the limits **:** INNER
**2** far from the border or shore **:** INLAND

**²interior** *n*
the inner part of something

**in·ter·ject** \ˌint-ər-ˈjekt\ *vb*
to put between or among other things ⟨*interject* a remark⟩

**in·ter·jec·tion** \ˌint-ər-ˈjek-shən\ *n*
**1** an interjecting of something
**2** something interjected
**3** a word or cry (as "ouch") expressing sudden or strong feeling

**in·ter·lace** \ˌint-ər-ˈlās\ *vb*
**in·ter·laced**; **in·ter·lac·ing**
to unite by or as if by lacing together

**in·ter·lock** \ˌint-ər-ˈläk\ *vb*
to lock together

**in·ter·lop·er** \ˌint-ər-ˈlō-pər\ *n*
INTRUDER

**in·ter·lude** \ˈint-ər-ˌlüd\ *n*
**1** an entertainment between the acts of a play
**2** a period or event that comes between others
**3** a musical composition between parts of a longer composition or of a drama

**in·ter·mar·riage** \ˌint-ər-ˈmar-ij\ *n*
marriage between members of different groups

**in·ter·mar·ry** \ˌint-ər-ˈmar-ē\ *vb*
**in·ter·mar·ried**; **in·ter·mar·ry·ing**
to become connected by intermarriage

**in·ter·me·di·ary** \ˌint-ər-ˈmēd-ē-ˌer-ē\ *n, pl* **in·ter·me·di·ar·ies**
GO-BETWEEN

**¹in·ter·me·di·ate** \ˌint-ər-ˈmēd-ē-ət\ *adj*
being or occurring in the middle or between
**in·ter·me·di·ate·ly** *adv*

**²intermediate** *n*
someone or something that is intermediate

**in·ter·ment** \in-ˈtər-mənt\ *n*
BURIAL

**in·ter·mi·na·ble** \in-ˈtər-mə-nə-bəl\ *adj*
ENDLESS 1
**in·ter·mi·na·bly** \-blē\ *adv*

**in·ter·min·gle** \ˌint-ər-ˈming-gəl\ *vb* **in·ter·min·gled**; **in·ter·min·gling**
to mix together

**in·ter·mis·sion** \ˌint-ər-ˈmish-ən\ *n*
**1** ¹PAUSE 1, INTERRUPTION ⟨continuing without *intermission*⟩
**2** a temporary halt (as between acts of a play)

**in·ter·mit·tent** \ˌint-ər-ˈmit-nt\ *adj*
starting, stopping, and starting again ⟨*intermittent* showers⟩
**in·ter·mit·tent·ly** *adv*

[1]**in·tern** \'in-,tərn\ *vb*
to force to stay within certain limits especially during a war
**in·tern·ment** \in-'tərn-mənt\ *n*

[2]**in·tern** *or* **in·terne** \'in-,tərn\ *n*
a medical school graduate getting practical experience in a hospital
**in·tern·ship** \-,ship\ *n*

[3]**in·tern** \'in-,tərn\ *vb*
to work as an intern

**in·ter·nal** \in-'tərn-l\ *adj*
**1** being within something : INTERIOR, INNER
**2** having to do with the inside of the body
**3** of or relating to the domestic affairs of a country
**in·ter·nal·ly** *adv*

**in·ter·na·tion·al** \,int-ər-'nash-ən-l\ *adj*
of, relating to, or affecting two or more nations
**in·ter·na·tion·al·ly** *adv*

**In·ter·net** \'in-tər-,net\ *n*
a communications system that connects groups of computers and databases all over the world

**in·ter·plan·e·tary** \,int-ər-'plan-ə-,ter-ē\ *adj*
existing, carried on, or operating between planets ⟨*interplanetary* travel⟩

**in·ter·play** \'int-ər-,plā\ *n*
INTERACTION

**in·ter·pose** \,int-ər-'pōz\ *vb*
**in·ter·posed**; **in·ter·pos·ing**
**1** to put between
**2** to introduce between parts of a conversation ⟨*interpose* a question⟩
**3** to be or come between

**in·ter·po·si·tion** \,int-ər-pə-'zish-ən\ *n*
**1** the act of interposing : the state of being interposed
**2** something that interposes or is interposed

**in·ter·pret** \in-'tər-prət\ *vb*
**1** to tell the meaning of : EXPLAIN, TRANSLATE
**2** to understand according to one's own belief, judgment, or interest
**3** to bring out the meaning of ⟨an actor *interprets* a role⟩
**in·ter·pret·er** *n*

**in·ter·pre·ta·tion** \in-,tər-prə-'tā-shən\ *n*
the act or the result of interpreting

**in·ter·pre·ta·tive** \in-'tər-prə-,tāt-iv\ *adj*
designed or serving to interpret

**in·ter·pre·tive** \in-'tər-prət-iv\ *adj*
INTERPRETATIVE

**in·ter·ra·cial** \,int-ər-'rā-shəl\ *adj*
of or involving members of different races

**in·ter·re·late** \,int-ər-ri-'lāt\ *vb*
**in·ter·re·lat·ed**; **in·ter·re·lat·ing**
to bring into or have a relationship with each other

**in·ter·re·la·tion** \,int-ər-ri-'lā-shən\ *n*
relation with each other
**in·ter·re·la·tion·ship** \-,ship\ *n*

**in·ter·ro·gate** \in-'ter-ə-,gāt\ *vb*
**in·ter·ro·gat·ed**; **in·ter·ro·gat·ing**
to question thoroughly ⟨*interrogate* a prisoner⟩

**in·ter·ro·ga·tion** \in-,ter-ə-'gā-shən\ *n*
the act of interrogating

**interrogation point** *n*
QUESTION MARK

**in·ter·rog·a·tive** \,int-ə-'räg-ət-iv\ *adj*
asking a question ⟨an *interrogative* sentence⟩

**in·ter·rog·a·to·ry** \,int-ə-'räg-ə-,tōr-ē\ *adj*
containing or expressing a question

**in·ter·rupt** \,int-ə-'rəpt\ *vb*
**1** to stop or hinder by breaking in
**2** to put or bring a difference into

**in·ter·rup·tion** \,int-ə-'rəp-shən\ *n*
an act of interrupting : a state of being interrupted

**in·ter·scho·las·tic** \,int-ər-skə-'las-tik\ *adj*
existing or carried on between schools

**in·ter·sect** \,int-ər-'sekt\ *vb*
to cut or divide by passing through or across : CROSS

**in·ter·sec·tion** \,int-ər-'sek-shən\ *n*
**1** the act or process of intersecting
**2** the place or point where two or more things (as streets) intersect : CROSSING
**3** the set of mathematical elements common to two or more sets

**in·ter·sperse** \,int-ər-'spərs\ *vb*
**in·ter·spersed**; **in·ter·spers·ing**
**1** to insert here and there
**2** to insert something at various places in or among

**in·ter·state** \,int-ər-'stāt\ *adj*
existing between or including two or more states

**in·ter·stel·lar** \,int-ər-'stel-ər\ *adj*
existing or taking place among the stars

**in·ter·twine** \,int-ər-'twīn\ *vb*
**in·ter·twined**; **in·ter·twin·ing**
to twine or cause to twine about one another

**in·ter·val** \'int-ər-vəl\ *n*
**1** a space of time between events or states
**2** a space between things
**3** the difference in pitch between two tones

**in·ter·vene** \,int-ər-'vēn\ *vb*
**in·ter·vened**; **in·ter·ven·ing**
**1** to come between events, places, or points of time
**2** to interfere with something so as to stop, settle, or change ⟨*intervene* in a quarrel⟩

**in·ter·ven·tion** \,int-ər-'ven-chən\ *n*
the act or fact of intervening

[1]**in·ter·view** \'int-ər-,vyü\ *n*
**1** a meeting face to face to give or get information or advice
**2** a written report of an interview for publication

[2]**interview** *vb*
▼ to meet and question in an interview ⟨*interview* people for a job⟩
**in·ter·view·er** *n*

[2]**interview:** an employer interviews a candidate for a job

**in·ter·weave** \ˌint-ər-ˈwēv\ *vb*
**in·ter·wove** \-ˈwōv\;
**in·ter·wo·ven** \-ˈwō-vən\;
**in·ter·weav·ing**
**1** to weave together
**2** INTERMINGLE

**in·tes·ti·nal** \in-ˈtes-tən-l\ *adj*
of or relating to the intestine

**in·tes·tine** \in-ˈtes-tən\ *n*
▼ the lower narrower part of the digestive canal in which most of the digestion and absorption of food occurs and through which waste material passes to be discharged

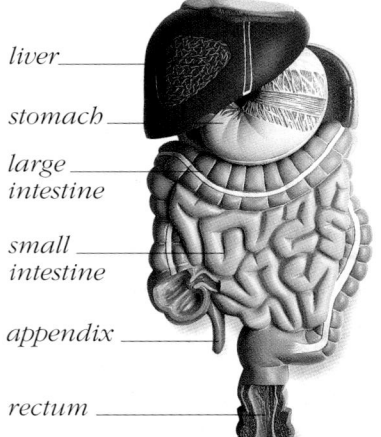

liver
stomach
large intestine
small intestine
appendix
rectum

**intestine:**
model of the human intestine

**in·ti·ma·cy** \ˈint-ə-mə-sē\ *n, pl* **in·ti·ma·cies**
the state or an instance of being intimate

**¹in·ti·mate** \ˈint-ə-ˌmāt\ *vb*
**in·ti·mat·ed**; **in·ti·mat·ing**
to express (as an idea) indirectly : HINT

**²in·ti·mate** \ˈint-ə-mət\ *adj*
**1** most private : PERSONAL ⟨one's *intimate* thoughts⟩
**2** marked by very close association ⟨*intimate* friends⟩
**3** suggesting comfortable warmth or privacy : COZY ⟨*intimate* clubs⟩
**in·ti·mate·ly** *adv*

**³in·ti·mate** \ˈint-ə-mət\ *n*
a very close friend

**in·ti·ma·tion** \ˌint-ə-ˈmā-shən\ *n*
**1** the act of intimating
**2** ¹HINT 1

**in·tim·i·date** \in-ˈtim-ə-ˌdāt\ *vb*
**in·tim·i·dat·ed**; **in·tim·i·dat·ing**
to frighten especially by threats

**in·tim·i·da·tion** \in-ˌtim-ə-ˈdā-shən\ *n*
the act of intimidating : the state of being intimidated

**in·to** \ˈin-tə, -tü\ *prep*
**1** to the inside of ⟨ran *into* the house⟩
**2** to the state, condition, or form of ⟨got *into* mischief⟩ ⟨cut the cake *into* eight pieces⟩
**3** so as to hit : AGAINST ⟨ran *into* the wall⟩

**in·tol·er·a·ble** \in-ˈtäl-ə-rə-bəl\ *adj*
UNBEARABLE
**in·tol·er·a·bly** \-blē\ *adv*

**in·tol·er·ance** \in-ˈtäl-ə-rəns\ *n*
the quality or state of being intolerant

**in·tol·er·ant** \in-ˈtäl-ə-rənt\ *adj*
not tolerant
**in·tol·er·ant·ly** \-rənt-lē\ *adv*

**in·to·na·tion** \ˌin-tə-ˈnā-shən\ *n*
the rise and fall in pitch of the voice in speech

**in·tox·i·cate** \in-ˈtäk-sə-ˌkāt\ *vb*
**in·tox·i·cat·ed**; **in·tox·i·cat·ing**
**1** to make drunk
**2** to make wildly excited or enthusiastic

**in·tox·i·ca·tion** \in-ˌtäk-sə-ˈkā-shən\ *n*
**1** an unhealthy state that is or is like a poisoning ⟨intestinal *intoxication*⟩
**2** the state of one who has drunk too much liquor : DRUNKENNESS

**in·tra·mu·ral** \ˌin-trə-ˈmyu̇r-əl\ *adj*
being or occurring within the limits usually of a school ⟨*intramural* sports⟩

**in·tran·si·tive** \in-ˈtrans-ət-iv, -ˈtranz-\ *adj*
not having or containing a direct object ⟨an *intransitive* verb⟩

**in·trep·id** \in-ˈtrep-əd\ *adj*
feeling no fear : BOLD
**in·trep·id·ly** *adv*

**in·tri·ca·cy** \ˈin-tri-kə-sē\ *n, pl* **in·tri·ca·cies**
**1** the quality or state of being intricate
**2** something intricate

**in·tri·cate** \ˈin-tri-kət\ *adj*
**1** ▶ having many closely combined parts or elements ⟨an *intricate* design⟩
**2** very difficult to follow or understand
**in·tri·cate·ly** *adv*

**¹in·trigue** \in-ˈtrēg\ *vb* **in·trigued**; **in·trigu·ing**
**1** ²PLOT 2, SCHEME
**2** to arouse the interest or curiosity of

**²in·trigue** \ˈin-ˌtrēg, in-ˈtrēg\ *n*
a secret or sly scheme often for selfish purposes

**in·tro·duce** \ˌin-trə-ˈdüs, -ˈdyüs\ *vb*
**in·tro·duced**; **in·tro·duc·ing**
**1** to bring into practice or use
**2** to lead or bring in especially for the first time
**3** to cause to be acquainted : make known
**4** to bring forward for discussion
**5** to put in : INSERT
**in·tro·duc·er** *n*

**in·tro·duc·tion** \ˌin-trə-ˈdək-shən\ *n*
**1** the action of introducing
**2** something introduced
**3** the part of a book that leads up to and explains what will be found in the main part
**4** the act of making persons known to each other

**in·tro·duc·to·ry** \ˌin-trə-ˈdək-tə-rē\ *adj*
serving to introduce : PRELIMINARY

**in·trude** \in-ˈtrüd\ *vb* **in·trud·ed**; **in·trud·ing**
**1** to force in, into, or on especially where not right or proper ⟨*intruded* an unwanted opinion⟩
**2** to come or go in without an invitation or right
**in·trud·er** *n*

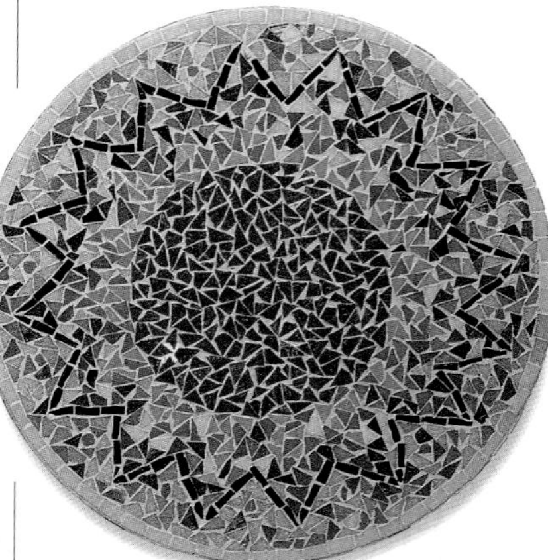

**intricate 1:** an intricate mosaic design on a table top

**in·tru·sion** \in-'trü-zhən\ *n*
the act of intruding

**intrust** *variant of* ENTRUST

**in·tu·i·tion** \,in-tü-'ish-ən, -tyü-\ *n*
a knowing or something known without mental effort

**in·un·date** \'in-ən-,dāt\ *vb* **in·un·dat·ed**; **in·un·dat·ing**
to cover with a flood : OVERFLOW

**in·un·da·tion** \,in-ən-'dā-shən\ *n*
[1]FLOOD 1

**in·vade** \in-'vād\ *vb* **in·vad·ed**; **in·vad·ing**
**1** to enter by force to conquer or plunder
**2** to show lack of respect for ⟨*invaded* their privacy⟩
**in·vad·er** *n*

### invention 1

An invention is something that has been thought of and created for the first time by a human being. It can be a simple idea like the wheel, or a complex one such as television. Some inventions dramatically change the way in which people live.

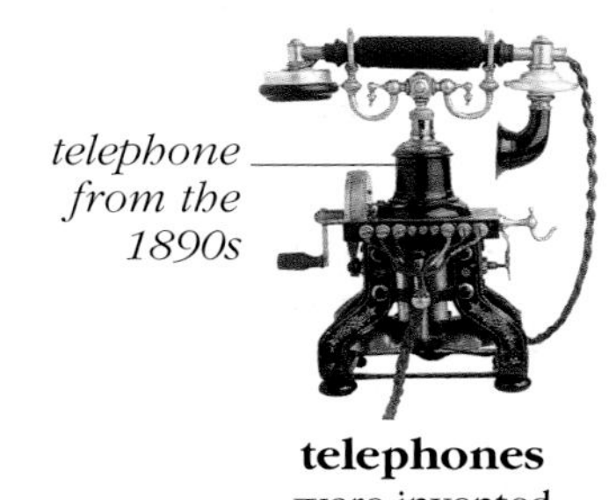

*telephone from the 1890s*

**telephones** were invented in the 1870s

**motor cars** were invented in the 1880s

*automobile from the 1910s*

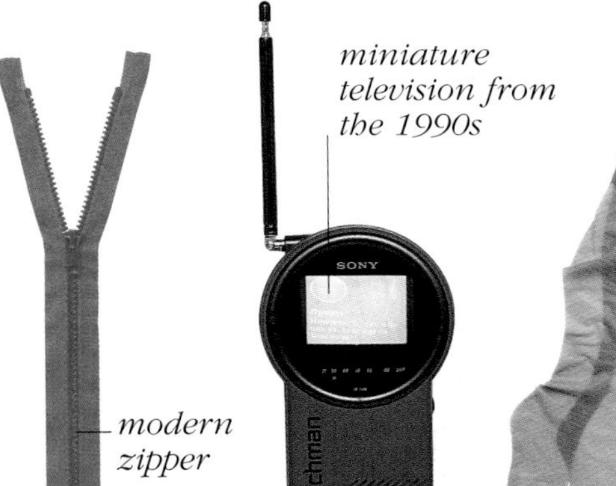

*modern zipper*

**zippers** were invented in the 1890s

*miniature television from the 1990s*

**television** was first broadcast in the 1920s

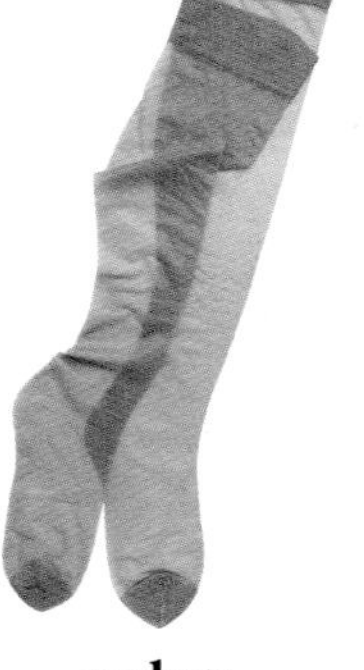

**nylon stockings** were first sold in the 1940s

**integrated circuits** were invented in the 1950s

[1]**in·val·id** \in-'val-əd\ *adj*
not valid

[2]**in·va·lid** \'in-və-ləd\ *adj*
**1** SICKLY 1
**2** of or relating to a sick person ⟨*invalid* diet⟩

[3]**in·va·lid** \'in-və-ləd\ *n*
a sick or disabled person
**in·va·lid·ism** \-,iz-əm\ *n*

**in·val·i·date** \in-'val-ə-,dāt\ *vb* **in·val·i·dat·ed**; **in·val·i·dat·ing**
to weaken or destroy the effect of

**in·valu·able** \in-'val-yə-wə-bəl\ *adj*
having value too great to be estimated : PRICELESS

**in·var·i·a·bil·i·ty** \in-,ver-ē-ə-'bil-ət-ē\ *n*
the quality or state of being invariable

**in·vari·able** \in-'ver-ē-ə-bəl\ *adj*
not changing or capable of change
**in·vari·ably** \-'ver-ē-ə-blē\ *adv*

**in·va·sion** \in-'vā-zhən\ *n*
an act of invading

**in·vei·gle** \in-'vā-gəl, -'vē-\ *vb* **in·vei·gled**; **in·vei·gling**
to win over or obtain by flattery ⟨I *inveigled* an invitation to the party⟩

**in·vent** \in-'vent\ *vb*
**1** to think up : make up
**2** to create or produce for the first time
**in·ven·tor** \-'vent-ər\ *n*

**Synonyms** INVENT, CREATE, and DISCOVER mean to bring something new into existence. INVENT suggests making something new for the first time and usually after some thinking and experimenting ⟨*invented* the first camera⟩. CREATE suggests making something out of nothing ⟨God *created* the world⟩ or producing something for its own sake ⟨*creates* unusual toys out of odds and ends⟩. DISCOVER is used when one finds and makes known something that already exists but is not known to others ⟨*discovered* an unknown planet⟩.

**in·ven·tion** \in-'ven-chən\ *n*
**1** ◀ an original device or process
**2** [3]LIE
**3** the act or process of inventing

A B C D E F G H I J K L M N O P Q R S T U V W X Y Z

**in·ven·tive** \in-'vent-iv\ *adj*
CREATIVE

[1]**in·ven·to·ry** \'in-vən-,tōr-ē\ *n, pl* **in·ven·to·ries**
**1** a list of items (as goods on hand)
**2** the act or process of making an inventory

[2]**inventory** *vb* **in·ven·to·ried**; **in·ven·to·ry·ing**
to make an inventory of

[1]**in·verse** \in-'vərs\ *adj*
**1** opposite in order, nature, or effect
**2** being a mathematical operation that is opposite in effect to another operation
**in·verse·ly** *adv*

[2]**inverse** *n*
something inverse

**in·vert** \in-'vərt\ *vb*
**1** to turn inside out or upside down
**2** to reverse the order or position of

[1]**in·ver·te·brate** \in-'vərt-ə-brət\ *adj*
having no backbone

[2]**invertebrate** *n*
▶ an invertebrate animal

[1]**in·vest** \in-'vest\ *vb*
**1** to give power or authority to
**2** BESIEGE 1

[2]**invest** *vb*
**1** to put out money in order to gain a financial return ⟨*invest* in a business⟩
**2** to put out (as effort) in support of a usually worthy cause
**in·ves·tor** \-'ves-tər\ *n*

**in·ves·ti·gate** \in-'ves-tə-,gāt\ *vb* **in·ves·ti·gat·ed**; **in·ves·ti·gat·ing**
to study by close and careful observation
**in·ves·ti·ga·tor** \-ər\ *n*

**in·ves·ti·ga·tion** \in-,ves-tə-'gā-shən\ *n*
the act or process of investigating

**in·ves·ti·ture** \in-'ves-tə-,chu̇r\ *n*
the act of placing in office

**in·vest·ment** \in-'vest-mənt\ *n*
**1** the investing of money
**2** a sum of money invested
**3** a property in which money is invested

**in·vig·o·rate** \in-'vig-ə-,rāt\ *vb* **in·vig·o·rat·ed**; **in·vig·o·rat·ing**
to give life and energy to

### [2]invertebrate

There are two main groups of animals: vertebrates, which have backbones, and the larger group, invertebrates, which do not. Animals without backbones include mollusks, worms, insects, spiders, and crustaceans. Insects, such as beetles, form the largest group of invertebrates.

**examples of invertebrates**

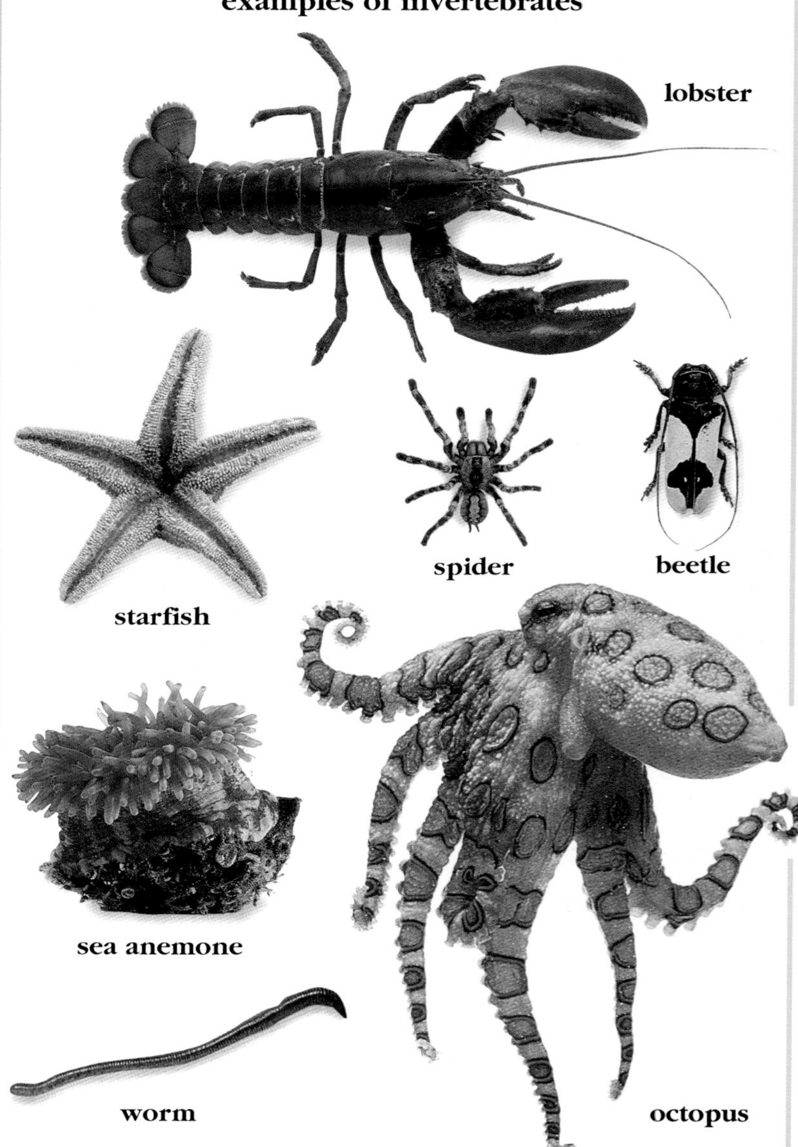


**in·vin·ci·bil·i·ty** \in-,vin-sə-'bil-ət-ē\ *n*
the quality or state of being invincible

**in·vin·ci·ble** \in-'vin-sə-bəl\ *adj*
impossible to defeat
**in·vin·ci·bly** \-'vin-sə-blē\ *adv*

**in·vi·o·la·ble** \in-'vī-ə-lə-bəl\ *adj*
**1** too sacred to be treated with disrespect
**2** impossible to harm or destroy by violence

**in·vi·o·late** \in-'vī-ə-lət\ *adj*
not violated

**in·vis·i·bil·i·ty** \in-ˌviz-ə-ˈbil-ət-ē\ *n*
the quality or state of being invisible

**in·vis·i·ble** \in-ˈviz-ə-bəl\ *adj*
**1** impossible to see
**2** being out of sight
**3** IMPERCEPTIBLE 1
**in·vis·i·ble·ness** \-ˈviz-ə-bəl-nəs\ *n*
**in·vis·i·bly** \-blē\ *adv*

**in·vi·ta·tion** \ˌin-və-ˈtā-shən\ *n*
**1** the act of inviting
**2** the written or spoken expression by which a person is invited

**in·vite** \in-ˈvīt\ *vb* **in·vit·ed**; **in·vit·ing**
**1** to tend to bring on ⟨behavior that *invites* criticism⟩
**2** to request the presence or company of
**3** [1]WELCOME 2 ⟨*invite* suggestions⟩

**in·vit·ing** \in-ˈvīt-ing\ *adj*
ATTRACTIVE
**in·vit·ing·ly** *adv*

**in·vo·ca·tion** \ˌin-və-ˈkā-shən\ *n*
a prayer for blessing or guidance (as at the beginning of a service)

[1]**in·voice** \ˈin-ˌvȯis\ *n*
a list of goods shipped usually showing the price and the terms of sale

[2]**invoice** *vb* **in·voiced**; **in·voic·ing**
to make an invoice of

**in·voke** \in-ˈvōk\ *vb* **in·voked**; **in·vok·ing**
**1** to call on for aid or protection (as in prayer)
**2** to call forth by magic ⟨*invoke* spirits⟩
**3** to appeal to as an authority or for support

**in·vol·un·tary** \in-ˈväl-ən-ˌter-ē\ *adj*
**1** not made or done willingly or from choice
**2** not under the control of the will
**in·vol·un·tari·ly** \ˌin-ˌväl-ən-ˈter-ə-lē\ *adv*

**in·volve** \in-ˈvälv, -ˈvȯlv\ *vb* **in·volved**; **in·volv·ing**
**1** to draw into a situation : ENGAGE
**2** INCLUDE ⟨one problem *involves* others⟩
**3** to be sure to or need to be accompanied by ⟨the plan *involves* some risk⟩
**in·volve·ment** \-mənt\ *n*

**in·volved** \in-ˈvälvd, -ˈvȯlvd\ *adj*
COMPLEX 2

**in·vul·ner·a·bil·i·ty** \in-ˌvəl-nə-rə-ˈbil-ət-ē\ *n*
the quality or state of being invulnerable

**in·vul·ner·a·ble** \in-ˈvəl-nə-rə-bəl\ *adj*
**1** impossible to injure or damage
**2** safe from attack
**in·vul·ner·a·bly** \-ˈvəl-nə-rə-blē\ *adv*

[1]**in·ward** \ˈin-wərd\ *adj*
**1** situated on the inside : INNER
**2** of or relating to the mind or spirit
**3** directed toward the interior ⟨an *inward* flow⟩

[2]**inward** *or* **in·wards** \-wərdz\ *adv*
**1** toward the inside or center ⟨slope *inward*⟩
**2** toward the mind or spirit ⟨turned my thoughts *inward*⟩

**in·ward·ly** \ˈin-wərd-lē\ *adv*
**1** in the mind or spirit
**2** beneath the surface
**3** to oneself : PRIVATELY
**4** toward the inside

**io·dine** \ˈī-ə-ˌdīn, -əd-n\ *n*
**1** a chemical element found in seawater and seaweeds and used especially in medicine and photography
**2** ▼ a solution of iodine in alcohol used to kill germs

**io·dize** \ˈī-ə-ˌdīz\ *vb* **io·dized**; **io·diz·ing**
to add iodine to ⟨*iodized* salt⟩

**iodine 2**

**ion** \ˈī-ən, ˈī-ˌän\ *n*
an atom or group of atoms that carries an electric charge

**-ion** *n suffix*
**1** act or process ⟨construct*ion*⟩
**2** result of an act or process ⟨regulat*ion*⟩ ⟨erupt*ion*⟩
**3** state or condition ⟨perfect*ion*⟩

**ion·ize** \ˈī-ə-ˌnīz\ *vb* **ion·ized**; **ion·iz·ing**
to change into ions

**ion·o·sphere** \ī-ˈän-ə-ˌsfir\ *n*
the part of the earth's atmosphere beginning at an altitude of about 30 miles (50 kilometers) and extending outward that contains electrically charged particles

**io·ta** \ī-ˈōt-ə\ *n*
a tiny amount : JOT

**IOU** \ˌī-ō-ˈyü\ *n*
a written promise to pay a debt

**-ious** *adj suffix*
-OUS ⟨capac*ious*⟩

**ir-** see IN-

[1]**Iraqi** \i-ˈräk-ē\ *n, pl* **Iraqis**
a person born or living in Iraq

[2]**Iraqi** *adj*
of or relating to Iraq or its people

**iras·ci·ble** \ir-ˈas-ə-bəl\ *adj*
easily angered

**irate** \ī-ˈrāt\ *adj*
ANGRY
**irate·ly** *adv*
**irate·ness** *n*

**ire** \ˈīr\ *n*
[2]ANGER, WRATH

**ir·i·des·cence** \ˌir-ə-ˈdes-ns\ *n*
a shifting and constant change of colors producing rainbow effects

**ir·i·des·cent** \ˌir-ə-ˈdes-nt\ *adj*
having iridescence
**ir·i·des·cent·ly** *adv*

**irid·i·um** \i-ˈrid-ē-əm\ *n*
a hard brittle heavy metallic chemical element

**iris** \ˈī-rəs\ *n*
**1** the colored part around the pupil of an eye
**2** ▼ a plant with long pointed leaves and large usually brightly colored flowers

**iris 2**

[1]**Irish** \ˈīr-ish\ *adj*
of or relating to Ireland, its people, or the Irish language

[2]**Irish** *n*
**1** **Irish** *pl* the people of Ireland
**2** a language of Ireland

**irk** \ˈərk\ *vb*
to make weary, irritated, or bored

A B C D E F G H I J K L M N O P Q R S T U V W X Y Z

**irk•some** \'ərk-səm\ *adj*
causing boredom : TIRESOME
**irk•some•ness** *n*

**[1]iron** \'ī-ərn\ *n*
**1** a heavy silvery white metallic chemical element that rusts easily, is strongly attracted by magnets, occurs in meteorites and combined in minerals, and is necessary in biological processes
**2** something made of iron
**3 irons** *pl* handcuffs or chains used to bind or to hinder movement
**4** ▶ a device that is heated and used for pressing cloth

**[2]iron** *adj*
**1** made of or relating to iron
**2** like iron

**[3]iron** *vb*
to press with a heated iron
**iron•er** *n*

**iron•ic** \ī-'rän-ik\ *or* **iron•i•cal** \-i-kəl\ *adj*
relating to, containing, or showing irony
**iron•i•cal•ly** \-i-kə-lē\ *adv*

**iron lung** *n*
an apparatus in which a person whose breathing is damaged (as by polio) can be placed to help the breathing

**iron•work** \'ī-ərn-,wərk\ *n*
**1** work in iron
**2 ironworks** *pl* a mill where iron or steel is smelted or heavy iron or steel products are made

**iro•ny** \'ī-rə-nē\ *n, pl* **iro•nies**
**1** the use of words that mean the opposite of what one really intends
**2** a result opposite to what was expected

**ir•ra•di•ate** \ir-'ād-ē-,āt\ *vb*
**ir•ra•di•at•ed**; **ir•ra•di•at•ing**
**1** to cast rays of light on
**2** to affect or treat with radiations (as X rays)

**ir•ra•di•a•tion** \ir-,ād-ē-'ā-shən\ *n*
**1** the giving off of radiant energy (as heat)
**2** exposure to irradiation (as of X rays)

**ir•ra•tio•nal** \ir-'ash-ən-l\ *adj*
**1** not able to reason
**2** not based on reason ⟨*irrational* fears⟩
**ir•ra•tio•nal•ly** *adv*

**ir•rec•on•cil•able** \ir-,ek-ən-'sī-lə-bəl\ *adj*
impossible to bring into harmony

**ir•re•cov•er•able** \,ir-i-'kəv-ə-rə-bəl\ *adj*
impossible to recover or set right

**ir•re•deem•able** \,ir-i-'dē-mə-bəl\ *adj*
impossible to redeem

**[1]iron 4:**
an electric iron

**ir•re•duc•ible** \,ir-i-'düs-ə-bəl, -'dyüs-\ *adj*
not possible to reduce

**ir•re•fut•able** \,ir-i-'fyüt-ə-bəl, ir-'ef-yət-\ *adj*
impossible to refute : INDISPUTABLE

**ir•reg•u•lar** \ir-'eg-yə-lər\ *adj*
**1** not following custom or rule
**2** not following the usual manner of inflection ⟨the *irregular* verb "sell"⟩
**3** not even or having the same shape on both sides ⟨*irregular* flowers⟩
**4** not continuous or coming at set times
**ir•reg•u•lar•ly** *adv*

**ir•reg•u•lar•i•ty** \ir-,eg-yə-'lar-ət-ē\ *n, pl* **ir•reg•u•lar•i•ties**
**1** the quality or state of being irregular
**2** something irregular

**ir•rel•e•vance** \ir-'el-ə-vəns\ *n*
**1** the quality or state of being irrelevant
**2** something irrelevant

**ir•rel•e•vant** \ir-'el-ə-vənt\ *adj*
not relevant
**ir•rel•e•vant•ly** \-vənt-lē\ *adv*

**ir•re•li•gious** \,ir-i-'lij-əs\ *adj*
not having or acting as if one has religious emotions or beliefs

**ir•rep•a•ra•ble** \ir-'ep-ə-rə-bəl\ *adj*
impossible to get back or to make right
**ir•rep•a•ra•bly** \-blē\ *adv*

**ir•re•place•able** \,ir-i-'plā-sə-bəl\ *adj*
impossible to replace

**ir•re•press•ible** \,ir-i-'pres-ə-bəl\ *adj*
impossible to repress or control

**ir•re•proach•able** \,ir-i-'prō-chə-bəl\ *adj*
being beyond reproach

**ir•re•sist•ible** \,ir-i-'zis-tə-bəl\ *adj*
impossible to resist
**ir•re•sist•ibly** \-blē\ *adv*

**ir•res•o•lute** \ir-'ez-ə-,lüt\ *adj*
uncertain how to act or proceed
**ir•res•o•lute•ly** *adv*

**ir•re•spec•tive of** \,ir-i-'spek-tiv-əv\ *prep*
without regard to ⟨open to anyone *irrespective of* age⟩

**ir•re•spon•si•bil•i•ty** \,ir-i-,spän-sə-'bil-ət-ē\ *n*
the quality or state of being irresponsible

**ir•re•spon•si•ble** \,ir-i-'spän-sə-bəl\ *adj*
having or showing little or no sense of responsibility
**ir•re•spon•si•bly** \-'spän-sə-blē\ *adv*

**ir•re•triev•able** \,ir-i-'trē-və-bəl\ *adj*
impossible to get back
**ir•re•triev•ably** \-blē\ *adv*

**ir•rev•er•ence** \ir-'ev-ə-rəns\ *n*
**1** lack of reverence
**2** something said or done that is irreverent

**ir•rev•er•ent** \ir-'ev-ə-rənt\ *adj*
not reverent : DISRESPECTFUL
**ir•rev•er•ent•ly** *adv*

**ir•re•vers•i•ble** \,ir-i-'vər-sə-bəl\ *adj*
impossible to reverse

**ir•rev•o•ca•ble** \ir-'ev-ə-kə-bəl\ *adj*
impossible to take away or undo
**ir•rev•o•ca•bly** \-blē\ *adv*

**ir•ri•gate** \'ir-ə-,gāt\ *vb*
**ir•ri•gat•ed**; **ir•ri•gat•ing**
**1** to supply (as land) with water by artificial means
**2** to flush with a liquid

**ir•ri•ga•tion** \,ir-ə-'gā-shən\ *n*
an act or process of irrigating

**ir·ri·ta·bil·i·ty** \ˌir-ət-ə-'bil-ət-ē\ *n*
the quality or state of being irritable

**ir·ri·ta·ble** \'ir-ət-ə-bəl\ *adj*
easily irritated
**ir·ri·ta·bly** \-blē\ *adv*

[1]**ir·ri·tant** \'ir-ə-tənt\ *adj*
tending to cause irritation

[2]**irritant** *n*
something that irritates

**ir·ri·tate** \'ir-ə-ˌtāt\ *vb* **ir·ri·tat·ed**; **ir·ri·tat·ing**
**1** to cause anger or impatience in : ANNOY
**2** to make sensitive or sore

**ir·ri·ta·tion** \ˌir-ə-'tā-shən\ *n*
**1** the act of irritating : the state of being irritated
**2** [2]IRRITANT

**is** \iz\ *present 3d sing of* BE

**-ish** \ish\ *adj suffix*
**1** of, relating to, or being ⟨Finn*ish*⟩
**2** characteristic of ⟨boy*ish*⟩ ⟨mul*ish*⟩
**3** somewhat ⟨purpl*ish*⟩
**4** about ⟨forty*ish*⟩

**isin·glass** \'īz-n-ˌglas, 'ī-zing-ˌglas\ *n*
mica in thin sheets

**Is·lam** \is-'läm, iz-\ *n*
a religion based on belief in Allah as the only God, in Muhammad as his prophet, and in the Koran
**Is·lam·ic** \is-'läm-ik, iz-\ *adj*

**is·land** \'ī-lənd\ *n*
**1** ▶ an area of land surrounded by water and smaller than a continent
**2** something suggesting an island in its isolation

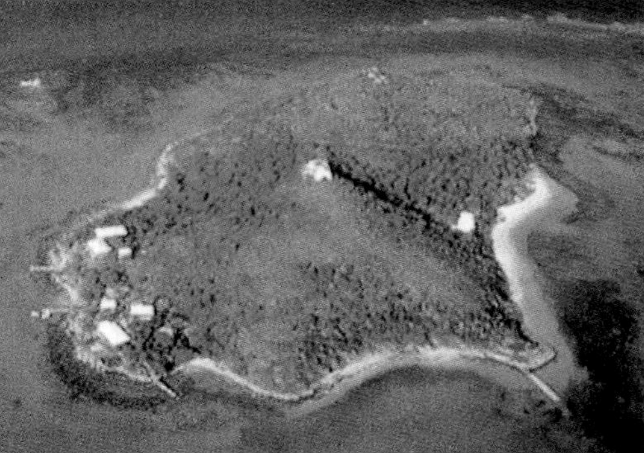

**island 1:** an island in the Caribbean Sea

**is·land·er** \'ī-lən-dər\ *n*
a person who lives on an island

**isle** \'īl\ *n*
a usually small island

**is·let** \'ī-lət\ *n*
a small island

**-ism** \ˌiz-əm\ *n suffix*
**1** act : practice : process ⟨bapt*ism*⟩ ⟨critic*ism*⟩
**2** manner of action or behavior like that of a specified person or thing ⟨hero*ism*⟩
**3** state : condition ⟨alcohol*ism*⟩
**4** teachings : theory : cult : system

**isn't** \'iz-nt\
is not

**iso·bar** \'ī-sə-ˌbär\ *n*
a line on a map to indicate areas having the same atmospheric pressure

**iso·late** \'ī-sə-ˌlāt\ *vb* **iso·lat·ed**; **iso·lat·ing**
to place or keep apart from others

**iso·la·tion** \ˌī-sə-'lā-shən\ *n*
the act of isolating : the condition of being isolated

**isos·ce·les triangle** \ī-ˌsäs-ə-ˌlēz-\ *n*
▶ a triangle having two sides of equal length

**isosceles triangle**

**ISP** \ˌī-ˌes-'pē\ *n*
a company that provides access to the Internet for a fee : Internet service provider

[1]**Is·rae·li** \iz-'rā-lē\ *adj*
of or relating to the Republic of Israel or the Israelis

[2]**Israeli** *n*
a person born or living in the Republic of Israel

**Is·ra·el·ite** \'iz-rē-ə-ˌlīt\ *n*
a member of the Hebrew people having Jacob as an ancestor

**is·su·ance** \'ish-ù-əns\ *n*
the act of issuing

[1]**is·sue** \'ish-ü\ *n*
**1** the action of going, coming, or flowing out
**2** OFFSPRING, PROGENY
**3** what finally happens : RESULT
**4** something that is disputed
**5** a giving off (as of blood) from the body
**6** the act of bringing out, offering, or making available
**7** the thing or the whole quantity of things given out ⟨the latest *issue* of a magazine⟩

[2]**issue** *vb* **is·sued**; **is·su·ing**
**1** to go, come, or flow out
**2** [1]RESULT 1
**3** to distribute officially
**4** to send out for sale or circulation

**-ist** \əst\ *n suffix*
**1** performer of a specified action ⟨cycl*ist*⟩ : maker : producer ⟨novel*ist*⟩
**2** one who plays a specified musical instrument or operates a specified mechanical device ⟨pian*ist*⟩
**3** one who specializes in a specified art or science or skill ⟨geolog*ist*⟩
**4** one who follows or favors a specified teaching, practice, system, or code of behavior

**isth·mus** \'is-məs\ *n*
▼ a neck of land separating two bodies of water and connecting two larger areas of land

[1]**it** \it, ət\ *pron*
**1** the thing, act, or matter about which these words are spoken or written
**2** the whole situation ⟨how's *it* going⟩
**3** used with little meaning of its own in certain kinds of sentences ⟨*it*'s cold⟩

**isthmus:** map showing the isthmus between North and South America

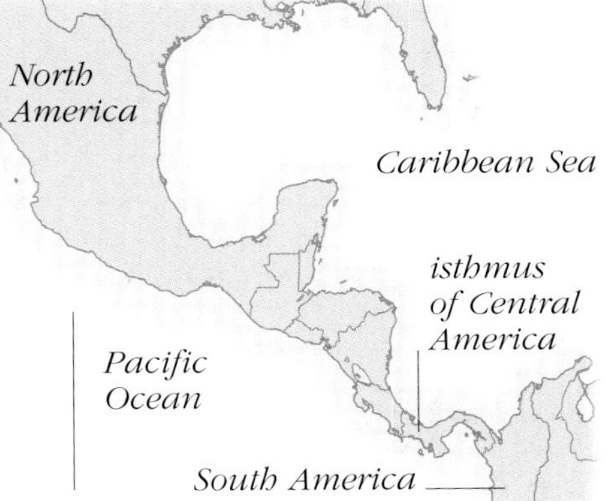

**[2]it** \'it\ *n*
the player who has to do something special in a children's game

**[1]Ital·ian** \i-'tal-yən\ *n*
**1** a person born or living in Italy
**2** the language of the Italians

**[2]Italian** *adj*
of or relating to Italy, its people, or the Italian language

**[1]ital·ic** \i-'tal-ik\ *adj*
of or relating to a type style with letters that slant to the right (as in *"these characters are italic"*)

**[2]italic** *n*
an italic letter or italic type

**ital·i·cize** \i-'tal-ə-,sīz\ *vb* **ital·i·cized**; **ital·i·ciz·ing**
**1** to print in italics
**2** UNDERLINE 1

**[1]itch** \'ich\ *vb*
to have or cause an itch

**[2]itch** *n*
**1** an uneasy irritating sensation in the skin
**2** a skin disorder in which an itch is present
**3** a restless usually constant desire

**itchy** \'ich-ē\ *adj* **itch·i·er**; **itch·i·est**
that itches

**it'd** \,it-əd\
it had : it would

**-ite** \,īt\ *n suffix*
**1** native : resident
**2** descendant ⟨Adam*ite*⟩
**3** adherent : follower

**item** \'īt-əm\ *n*
**1** a single thing in a list, account, or series
**2** a brief piece of news

**item·ize** \'īt-ə-,mīz\ *vb* **item·ized**; **item·iz·ing**
to set down one by one : LIST

**[1]itin·er·ant** \ī-'tin-ə-rənt\ *adj*
traveling from place to place

**[2]itinerant** *n*
a person who travels about

**-itis** \'īt-əs\ *n suffix*
inflammation of ⟨tonsil*litis*⟩ ⟨appendic*itis*⟩

**it'll** \,it-l\
it shall : it will

**its** \its\ *adj*
of or relating to it or itself

**it's** \its\
**1** it is
**2** it has

**it·self** \it-'self\ *pron*
its own self ⟨the cat gave *itself* a bath⟩ ⟨this *itself* is a good enough reason⟩

**-ity** \ət-ē\ *n suffix, pl* **-ities**
quality : state : degree ⟨similar*ity*⟩

**I've** \īv\
I have

**-ive** \iv\ *adj suffix*
that does or tends to do a specified action

**ivo·ry** \'ī-və-rē, 'īv-rē\ *n, pl* **ivo·ries**
**1** ► the hard creamy-white material of which the tusks of a tusked mammal (as an elephant) are made
**2** a very pale yellow

**ivory 1:** a 6th-century Italian horn made of ivory

**ivy** \'ī-vē\ *n, pl* **ivies**
**1** ▼ a woody vine with evergreen leaves, small yellowish flowers, and black berries often found growing on buildings
**2** a plant like ivy

**ivy 1:** English ivy

**-i·za·tion** \ə-'zā-shən, ī-; *the second is to be understood at entries*\ *n suffix*
action : process : state

**-ize** \,īz\ *vb suffix* **-ized**; **-iz·ing**
**1** cause to be or be like : form or cause to be formed into ⟨crystal*lize*⟩
**2** cause to experience a specified action
**3** saturate, treat, or combine with
**4** treat like ⟨idol*ize*⟩
**5** engage in a specified activity

# Jj

**The sounds of J:** The letter **J** has one main sound in English. It sounds the same in the words **joke**, **jump**, **jaguar**, **object**, **major**, and **enjoy**.

This letter is not used in very many words. The sound of **J** is quite common in English, but it is often spelled with a different letter. That is the letter **G**. The "**soft G**" sound, as in the words **gem** and **plumage**, is the same as the sound of **J**.

**j** \'jā\ *n, pl* **j's** *or* **js** \'jāz\ *often cap*
the tenth letter of the English alphabet

[1]**jab** \'jab\ *vb* **jabbed**; **jab·bing**
to poke quickly or suddenly with or as if with something sharp

[2]**jab** *n*
a quick or sudden poke

[1]**jab·ber** \'jab-ər\ *vb*
to talk too fast or not clearly enough to be understood

[2]**jabber** *n*
confused talk : GIBBERISH

[1]**jack** \'jak\ *n*
**1** a playing card marked with the figure of a man
**2** a device for lifting something heavy a short distance
**3** JACKASS 1
**4** ► a small six-pointed object used in a children's game (**jacks**)
**5** a small national flag flown by a ship
**6** a socket used with a plug to connect one electric circuit with another

[1]**jack 4:** a set of jacks

[2]**jack** *vb*
to move or lift by or as if by a jack

**jack·al** \'jak-əl\ *n*
any of several Old World wild dogs like but smaller than wolves

**jack·ass** \'jak-ˌas\ *n*
**1** a male donkey
**2** DONKEY 1
**3** a stupid person

**jack·daw** \'jak-ˌdȯ\ *n*
a European bird somewhat like a crow

**jack·et** \'jak-ət\ *n*
**1** a short coat or coatlike garment
**2** an outer cover or casing ⟨a book *jacket*⟩

**Jack Frost** \'jak-'frȯst\ *n*
frost or frosty weather thought of as a person

**jack–in–the–box** \'jak-ən-t͟hə-ˌbäks\ *n, pl* **jack–in–the–box·es** *or* **jacks–in–the–box** \'jak-sən-\
a small box out of which a comical toy figure springs when the lid is raised

**jack–in–the–pul·pit** \ˌjak-ən-t͟hə-'pu̇l-ˌpit\ *n, pl* **jack–in–the–pul·pits** *or* **jacks–in–the–pul·pit** \ˌjak-sən-\
a plant that grows in moist shady woods and has a stalk of tiny yellowish flowers protected by a leaf bent over like a hood

[1]**jack·knife** \'jak-ˌnīf\ *n, pl* **jack·knives** \-ˌnīvz\
a knife with folding blade or blades that can be carried in one's pocket

[2]**jackknife** *vb* **jack·knifed**; **jack·knif·ing**
to double up like a jackknife

**jack–of–all–trades** \ˌjak-ə-'vȯl-ˌtrādz\ *n, pl* **jacks–of–all–trades** \ˌjak-səv-\
a person who can do several kinds of work fairly well

**jack–o'–lan·tern** \'jak-ə-ˌlant-ərn\ *n*
a lantern made of a pumpkin cut to look like a human face

**jack·pot** \'jak-ˌpät\ *n*
a large and often unexpected success or reward

**jack·rab·bit** \'jak-ˌrab-ət\ *n*
a large North American hare with very long ears and long hind legs

**jade** \'jād\ *n*
► a usually green mineral used for jewelry and carvings

**jade:** an 18th-century jade mask from Mexico

**jag·ged** \'jag-əd\ *adj*
having a sharply uneven edge or surface ⟨a *jagged* tear in the sleeve⟩
**jag·ged·ly** *adv*

**jag·uar** \'jag-ˌwär\ *n*
▼ a large yellowish brown black-spotted animal of the cat family found from Texas to Paraguay

**jaguar**

A B C D E F G H I J K L M N O P Q R S T U V W X Y Z

**[1]jail** \'jāl\ *n*
PRISON

**[2]jail** *vb*
to shut up in or as if in a prison

**jail·bird** \'jāl-,bərd\ *n*
a person who is or has been locked up in prison

**jail·break** \'jāl-,brāk\ *n*
escape from prison by the use of force

**jail·er** *or* **jail·or** \'jā-lər\ *n*
a keeper of a prison

**ja·lopy** \jə-'läp-ē\ *n, pl* **ja·lop·ies**
a worn shabby old automobile or airplane

**[1]jam** \'jam\ *vb* **jammed**; **jam·ming**
**1** to crowd, squeeze, or wedge into a tight position
**2** to put into action hard or suddenly ⟨*jammed* the brake on⟩ ⟨*jammed* my foot on the brake⟩
**3** to hurt by pressure ⟨*jammed* a finger in the car door⟩
**4** to be or cause to be stuck or unable to work because a part is wedged tight ⟨paper *jammed* the copier⟩
**5** to cause interference in (radio or television signals)

**[2]jam** *n*
**1** a crowded mass of people or things that blocks something ⟨a traffic *jam*⟩
**2** a difficult state of affairs

**[3]jam** *n*
a food made by boiling fruit with sugar until it is thick

**jamb** \'jam\ *n*
a vertical piece forming the side of an opening (as for a doorway)

**jam·bo·ree** \,jam-bə-'rē\ *n*
**1** a large jolly get-together
**2** a national or international camping assembly of Boy Scouts

**[1]jan·gle** \'jang-gəl\ *vb* **jan·gled**; **jan·gling**
to make or cause to make a harsh sound

**[2]jangle** *n*
a harsh often ringing sound

**jan·i·tor** \'jan-ət-ər\ *n*
a person who takes care of a building (as a school)

**Jan·u·ary** \'jan-yə-,wer-ē\ *n*
the first month of the year

**Word History** The ancient Romans believed in many gods. One of these named Janus was the god of doors and gates and of beginnings. He had two faces, one that looked forward and one that looked back. The Latin name of the first month of the year came from the name of this god. The English word *January* came from the Latin name of the month.

**[1]Jap·a·nese** \,jap-ə-'nēz\ *adj*
of or relating to Japan, its people, or the Japanese language

**[2]Japanese** *n, pl* **Japanese**
**1** a person born or living in Japan
**2** the language of the Japanese

**Japanese beetle** *n*
a small glossy green or brown Asian beetle now found in the United States that as a grub feeds on roots and as an adult eats leaves and fruits

**[1]jar** \'jär\ *vb* **jarred**; **jar·ring**
**1** to make a harsh unpleasant sound
**2** to have a disagreeable effect
**3** to shake or cause to shake hard ⟨the bolt *jarred* loose⟩

**[2]jar** *n*
**1** a harsh sound
**2** [2]JOLT 1
**3** [2]SHOCK 3

**[3]jar** *n*
a usually glass or pottery container with a wide mouth

**jar·gon** \'jär-gən, -,gän\ *n*
**1** the special vocabulary of an activity or group ⟨sports *jargon*⟩
**2** language that is not clear and is full of long words

**jas·mine** \'jaz-mən\ *n*
any of various mostly climbing plants of warm regions with fragrant flowers

**jas·per** \'jas-pər\ *n*
an opaque usually red, green, brown, or yellow stone used for making ornamental objects (as vases)

**[1]jaunt** \'jȯnt\ *vb*
to make a short trip for pleasure

**[2]jaunt** *n*
a short pleasure trip

**jaun·ty** \'jȯnt-ē\ *adj* **jaun·ti·er**; **jaun·ti·est**
lively in manner or appearance ⟨wearing my hat at a *jaunty* angle⟩
**jaun·ti·ly** \'jȯnt-l-ē\ *adv*
**jaun·ti·ness** \'jȯnt-ē-nəs\ *n*

**Ja·va man** \,jä-və-\ *n*
a small-brained prehistoric human known from skulls found in Java

**jav·e·lin** \'jav-lən, 'jav-ə-lən\ *n*
**1** a light spear
**2** ◀ a slender rod thrown for distance in a track-and-field contest (**javelin throw**)

*javelin*

**javelin 2:** an athlete throwing a javelin

**jaw** \'jȯ\ *n*
**1** either of the bony structures that support the soft parts of the mouth and usually bear teeth on their edge
**2** a part of an invertebrate animal (as an insect) that resembles or does the work of a jaw
**3** one of a pair of moving parts that open and close for holding or crushing something ⟨*jaws* of a vise⟩

**jaw·bone** \'jȯ-ˌbōn\ *n*
JAW 1

**jay** \'jā\ *n*
▼ a noisy bird related to the crow but with brighter colors

**jay:**
a blue jay

**jay·walk** \'jā-ˌwȯk\ *vb*
to cross a street in a place or in a way that is against traffic regulations
**jay·walk·er** *n*

**jazz** \'jaz\ *n*
lively American music that developed from ragtime

**jeal·ous** \'jel-əs\ *adj*
**1** demanding complete faithfulness
**2** feeling a mean resentment toward someone more successful than oneself
**3** CAREFUL 1, WATCHFUL ⟨*jealous* of our rights⟩
**jeal·ous·ly** *adv*

**jeal·ou·sy** \'jel-ə-sē\ *n, pl* **jeal·ou·sies**
a jealous attitude or feeling

**jeans** \'jēnz\ *n pl*
pants made of a heavy cotton cloth

**Word History** *Jeans*, a word for a kind of pants, came from *jean*, a word for a kind of cloth. At first the word *jean* was an adjective. It was used to describe a kind of sturdy cotton cloth. This word *jean* came from *Gene*, an early English name for the city of Genoa, Italy, where the cloth was made.

**jeep** \'jēp\ *n*
a small motor vehicle used by the United States Army during World War II

**[1]jeer** \'jir\ *vb*
**1** to speak or cry out in scorn
**2** to scorn or mock with jeers

**[2]jeer** *n*
a scornful remark or sound : TAUNT

**Je·ho·vah** \ji-'hō-və\ *n*
GOD 1

**jell** \'jel\ *vb*
**1** to become as firm as jelly : SET
**2** to take shape ⟨an idea *jelled*⟩

**[1]jel·ly** \'jel-ē\ *n, pl* **jellies**
a soft springy food made from fruit juice boiled with sugar, from meat juices, or from gelatin
**jel·ly·like** \-ˌlīk\ *adj*

**[2]jelly** *vb* **jel·lied**; **jel·ly·ing**
**1** JELL 1
**2** to make jelly

**jelly bean** *n*
a chewy bean-shaped candy

**jel·ly·fish** \'jel-ē-ˌfish\ *n*
a free-swimming sea animal related to the corals that has a jellylike body shaped like a saucer

**jeop·ar·dize** \'jep-ər-ˌdīz\ *vb* **jeop·ar·dized**; **jeop·ar·diz·ing**
to expose to danger

**jeop·ar·dy** \'jep-ər-dē\ *n*
DANGER 1

**Word History** In French there is a phrase that means "divided game." This phrase was used for a situation in a game of chess where one could not be sure which of two plays would be better. With either play one would risk losing the game. The English word *jeopardy* came from the French phrase. At first the word was used for the risky situation in chess. Later it came to mean "risk" or "danger."

**[1]jerk** \'jərk\ *n*
**1** a short quick pull or jolt
**2** a foolish person

**[2]jerk** *vb*
**1** to give a quick sharp pull or twist to
**2** to move with jerks

**jer·kin** \'jər-kən\ *n*
a close-fitting sleeveless jacket that extends to or just over the hips

**jerky** \'jər-kē\ *adj* **jerk·i·er**; **jerk·i·est**
moving with sudden starts and stops
**jerk·i·ly** \-kə-lē\ *adv*
**jerk·i·ness** \-kē-nəs\ *n*

**jer·sey** \'jər-zē\ *n, pl* **jerseys**
**1** a knitted cloth (as of wool or cotton) used mostly for clothing
**2** a close-fitting knitted garment (as a shirt)

**[1]jest** \'jest\ *n*
**1** a comic act or remark : JOKE
**2** a playful mood or manner ⟨many a true word is spoken in *jest*⟩

**[2]jest** *vb*
to make jests : JOKE

**jest·er** \'jes-tər\ *n*
**1** a person formerly kept in royal courts to amuse people
**2** a person who often jests

**Je·sus** \'jē-zəs\ *n*
the founder of the Christian religion

**[1]jet** \'jet\ *n*
**1** a black mineral that is often used for jewelry
**2** a very dark black

**[2]jet** *vb* **jet·ted**; **jet·ting**
[1]SPURT 1

**[3]jet** *n*
**1** a rush of liquid, gas, or vapor through a narrow opening or a nozzle
**2** a nozzle for a jet of gas or liquid
**3** JET ENGINE
**4** JET AIRPLANE

**jet airplane** *n*
▼ an airplane powered by a jet engine

*jet engine*

**jet airplane:**
a military fighter plane

**jet engine** *n*
an engine in which fuel burns to produce a jet of heated air and gases that shoot out from the rear and drive the engine forward

**jet plane** *n*
JET AIRPLANE

**jet–pro·pelled** \ˌjet-prə-ˈpeld\ *adj*
driven forward or onward by a jet engine

**jet·sam** \ˈjet-səm\ *n*
goods thrown overboard to lighten a ship in danger of sinking

**jet stream** *n*
high-speed winds blowing from a westerly direction several kilometers above the earth's surface

**jet·ti·son** \ˈjet-ə-sən\ *vb*
to throw out especially from a ship or an airplane

**jet·ty** \ˈjet-ē\ *n, pl* **jetties**
**1** a pier built to change the path of the current or tide or to protect a harbor
**2** a landing wharf

**Jew** \ˈjü\ *n*
a person who is a descendant of the ancient Hebrews or whose religion is Judaism

**jew·el** \ˈjü-əl\ *n*
**1** an ornament of precious metal often set with precious stones and worn on the person
**2** a person who is greatly admired
**3** GEM
**4** a bearing in a watch made of crystal or a precious stone

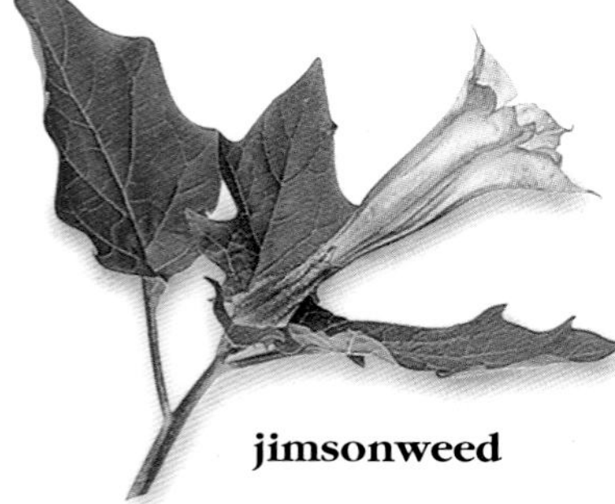

**jimsonweed**

**jew·el·er** *or* **jew·el·ler** \ˈjü-ə-lər\ *n*
a person who makes or deals in jewelry and related articles (as silverware)

**jew·el·ry** \ˈjü-əl-rē\ *n*
► ornamental pieces (as rings or necklaces) worn on the person

**Jew·ish** \ˈjü-ish\ *adj*
of or relating to Jews or Judaism

**Jew's harp** *or* **Jews' harp** \ˈjüz-ˌhärp\ *n*
a small musical instrument that is held in the mouth and struck with the finger to give off a tone

**jib** \ˈjib\ *n*
a three-cornered sail extending forward from the foremast

[1]**jibe** \ˈjīb\ *variant of* GIBE

[2]**jibe** *vb* **jibed**; **jib·ing**
**1** to shift suddenly from side to side
**2** to change the course of a boat so that the sail jibes

[3]**jibe** *vb* **jibed**; **jib·ing**
to be in agreement

**jif·fy** \ˈjif-ē\ *n, pl* **jiffies**
MOMENT 1

[1]**jig** \ˈjig\ *n*
a lively dance

[2]**jig** *vb* **jigged**; **jig·ging**
to dance a jig

[1]**jig·gle** \ˈjig-əl\ *vb* **jig·gled**; **jig·gling**
to move or cause to move with quick little jerks

[2]**jiggle** *n*
a quick little jerk

**jig·saw** \ˈjig-ˌsȯ\ *n*
a machine saw used to cut curved and irregular lines or openwork patterns

**jigsaw puzzle** *n*
a puzzle made by cutting a picture into small pieces that must be fitted together again

**jim·son·weed** \ˈjim-sən-ˌwēd\ *n*
◄ a coarse poisonous weedy plant related to the potato that is sometimes grown for its showy white or purple flowers

[1]**jin·gle** \ˈjing-gəl\ *vb* **jin·gled**; **jin·gling**
to make or cause to make a light clinking sound

[2]**jingle** *n*
**1** a light clinking sound
**2** a short verse or song that repeats bits in a catchy way
**jin·gly** \ˈjing-glē\ *adj*

**jinx** \ˈjingks\ *n*
a bringer of bad luck

**jit·ters** \ˈjit-ərz\ *n pl*
extreme nervousness

**jit·tery** \ˈjit-ə-rē\ *adj*
very nervous

**job** \ˈjäb\ *n*
**1** a piece of work usually done on order at an agreed rate
**2** something produced by or as if by work ⟨can do a better *job*⟩
**3** a regular paying employment ⟨has a good *job*⟩
**4** a special duty or function
**synonyms** see TASK
**job·less** \-ləs\ *adj*

jockey

**jockey 1:**
a jockey mounted on a horse

**jock·ey** \ˈjäk-ē\ *n, pl* **jockeys**
**1** ▲ a professional rider in a horse race
**2** OPERATOR 1

[1]**jog** \ˈjäg\ *vb* **jogged**; **jog·ging**
**1** to give a slight shake or push to : NUDGE
**2** to rouse to alertness ⟨*jog* one's memory⟩
**3** to move or cause to move at a jog
**4** to run slowly (as for exercise) ⟨*jogs* two miles every day⟩
**jog·ger** *n*

[2]**jog** *n*
**1** a slight shake or push
**2** a slow jolting gait (as of a horse)
**3** a slow run

[3]**jog** *n*
a short change in direction ⟨a *jog* in a road⟩

**jog·gle** \ˈjäg-əl\ *vb* **jog·gled**; **jog·gling**
to shake or cause to shake slightly

**john·ny·cake** \ˈjän-ē-ˌkāk\ *n*
a bread made of cornmeal, water or milk, and leavening with or without flour, shortening, and eggs

## jewelry

Decorative objects such as rings, brooches, necklaces, and earrings have been treasured since earliest times. The first jewelry was created using readily available elements such as carved bone or wood. Later pieces were made from gold and other metals, sometimes set with precious stones. Modern jewelry is made from a broad variety of materials, including plated metals, plastic, and enamel.

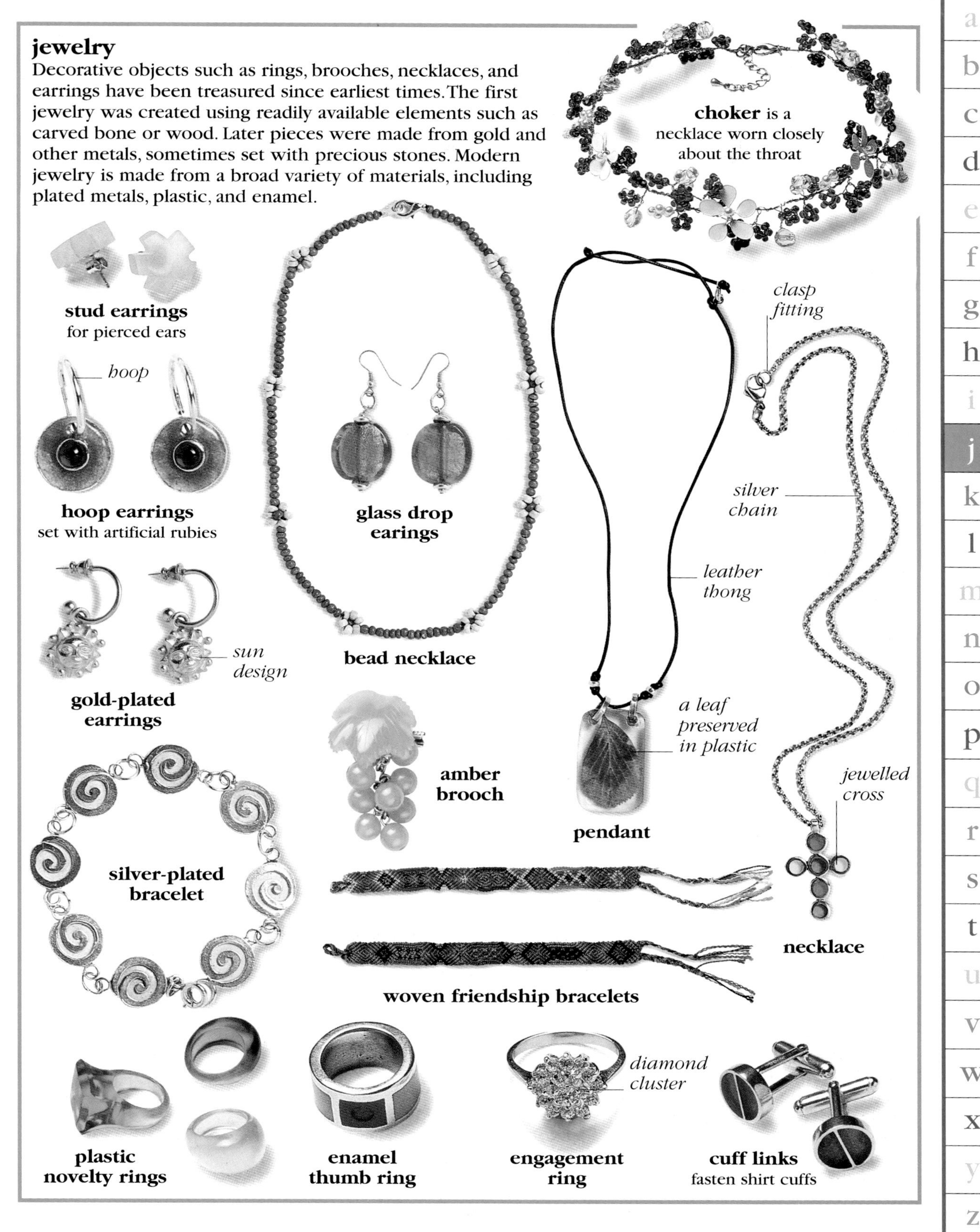


a b c d e f g h i j k l m n o p q r s t u v w x y z

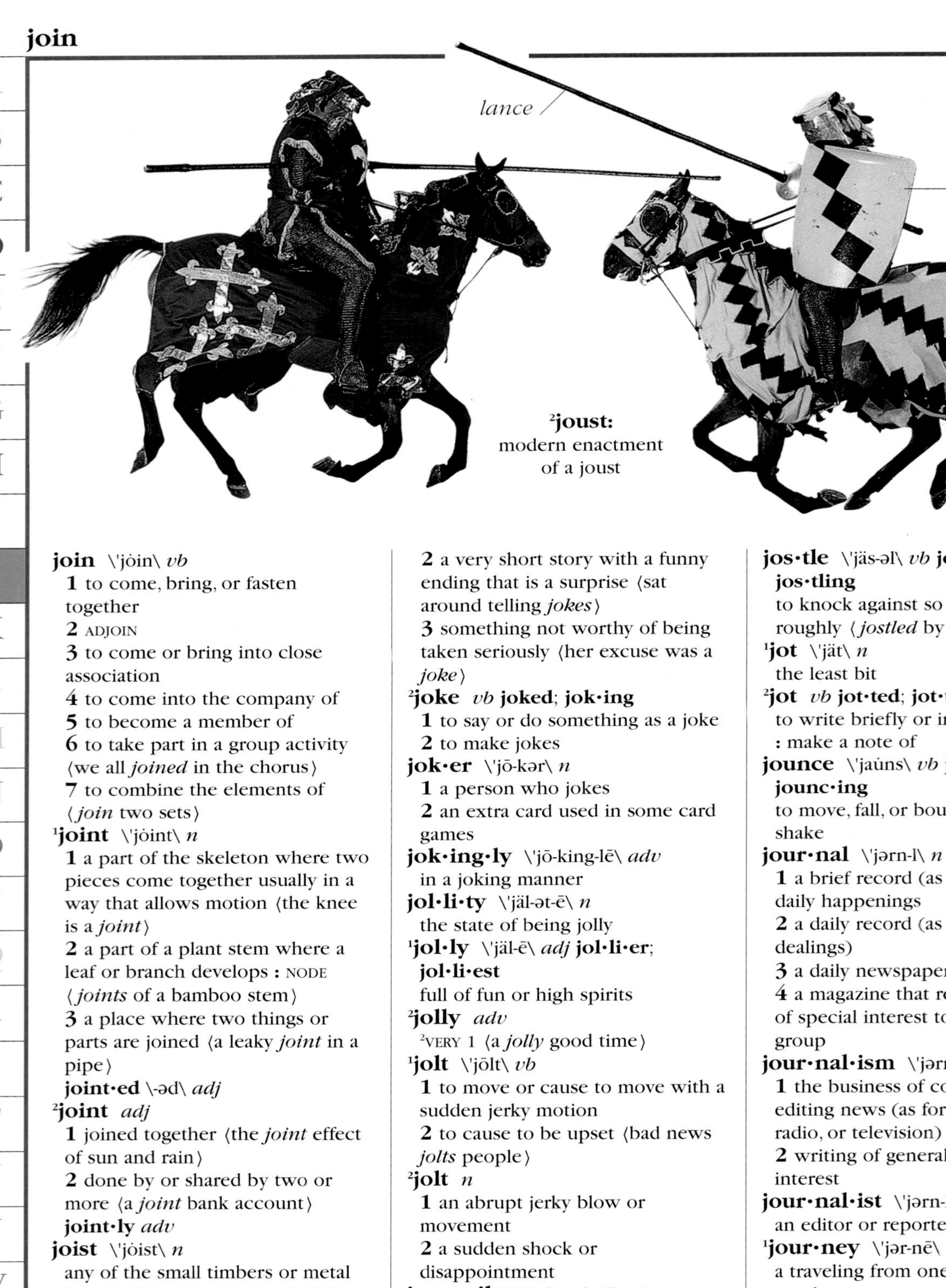


**²joust:** modern enactment of a joust

**join** \'jȯin\ *vb*
**1** to come, bring, or fasten together
**2** ADJOIN
**3** to come or bring into close association
**4** to come into the company of
**5** to become a member of
**6** to take part in a group activity ⟨we all *joined* in the chorus⟩
**7** to combine the elements of ⟨*join* two sets⟩

**¹joint** \'jȯint\ *n*
**1** a part of the skeleton where two pieces come together usually in a way that allows motion ⟨the knee is a *joint*⟩
**2** a part of a plant stem where a leaf or branch develops **:** NODE ⟨*joints* of a bamboo stem⟩
**3** a place where two things or parts are joined ⟨a leaky *joint* in a pipe⟩
**joint·ed** \-əd\ *adj*

**²joint** *adj*
**1** joined together ⟨the *joint* effect of sun and rain⟩
**2** done by or shared by two or more ⟨a *joint* bank account⟩
**joint·ly** *adv*

**joist** \'jȯist\ *n*
any of the small timbers or metal beams laid crosswise in a building to support a floor or ceiling

**¹joke** \'jōk\ *n*
**1** something said or done to cause laughter or amusement ⟨hid his shoes as a *joke*⟩ ⟨play a *joke* on someone⟩
**2** a very short story with a funny ending that is a surprise ⟨sat around telling *jokes*⟩
**3** something not worthy of being taken seriously ⟨her excuse was a *joke*⟩

**²joke** *vb* **joked**; **jok·ing**
**1** to say or do something as a joke
**2** to make jokes

**jok·er** \'jō-kər\ *n*
**1** a person who jokes
**2** an extra card used in some card games

**jok·ing·ly** \'jō-king-lē\ *adv*
in a joking manner

**jol·li·ty** \'jäl-ət-ē\ *n*
the state of being jolly

**¹jol·ly** \'jäl-ē\ *adj* **jol·li·er**; **jol·li·est**
full of fun or high spirits

**²jolly** *adv*
²VERY 1 ⟨a *jolly* good time⟩

**¹jolt** \'jōlt\ *vb*
**1** to move or cause to move with a sudden jerky motion
**2** to cause to be upset ⟨bad news *jolts* people⟩

**²jolt** *n*
**1** an abrupt jerky blow or movement
**2** a sudden shock or disappointment

**jon·quil** \'jän-kwəl, 'jäng-\ *n*
a plant related to the daffodil but with fragrant yellow or white flowers with a short central tube

**josh** \'jäsh\ *vb*
**1** ²KID 1
**2** ²JOKE

**jos·tle** \'jäs-əl\ *vb* **jos·tled**; **jos·tling**
to knock against so as to jar **:** push roughly ⟨*jostled* by a crowd⟩

**¹jot** \'jät\ *n*
the least bit

**²jot** *vb* **jot·ted**; **jot·ting**
to write briefly or in a hurry **:** make a note of

**jounce** \'jau̇ns\ *vb* **jounced**; **jounc·ing**
to move, fall, or bounce so as to shake

**jour·nal** \'jərn-l\ *n*
**1** a brief record (as in a diary) of daily happenings
**2** a daily record (as of business dealings)
**3** a daily newspaper
**4** a magazine that reports on things of special interest to a particular group

**jour·nal·ism** \'jərn-l-,iz-əm\ *n*
**1** the business of collecting and editing news (as for newspapers, radio, or television)
**2** writing of general or popular interest

**jour·nal·ist** \'jərn-l-ist\ *n*
an editor or reporter of the news

**¹jour·ney** \'jər-nē\ *n, pl* **jour·neys**
a traveling from one place to another

**Synonyms** JOURNEY, TRIP, and TOUR mean travel from one place to another. JOURNEY usually suggests traveling a long distance and often that the traveling may be dangerous or difficult ⟨the long *journey* across the desert⟩. TRIP suggests that the traveling is brief, swift, or ordinary ⟨our weekly *trip* to the supermarket⟩. TOUR suggests a circular journey with several stopping places and an end at the place where one began ⟨the sightseers took a *tour* of the city⟩.

**²journey** *vb* **jour·neyed**; **jour·ney·ing**
to go on a journey : TRAVEL
**jour·ney·er** *n*

**jour·ney·man** \'jər-nē-mən\ *n, pl* **jour·ney·men** \-mən\
a worker who has learned a trade and usually works for another person by the day

**¹joust** \'jau̇st\ *vb*
to take part in a joust : TILT

**²joust** *n*
◀ a combat on horseback between two knights with lances

**jo·vial** \'jō-vē-əl\ *adj*
¹JOLLY
**jo·vial·ly** *adv*

**¹jowl** \'jau̇l\ *n*
loose flesh (as a double chin) hanging from the lower jaw and throat

**²jowl** *n*
1 an animal's jaw and especially the lower jaw
2 CHEEK 1

**joy** \'jȯi\ *n*
1 a feeling of pleasure or happiness that comes from success, good fortune, or a sense of well-being
2 something that gives pleasure or happiness **synonyms** see PLEASURE

**joy·ful** \'jȯi-fəl\ *adj*
feeling, causing, or showing joy
**joy·ful·ly** \-fə-lē\ *adv*
**joy·ful·ness** *n*

**joy·ous** \'jȯi-əs\ *adj*
JOYFUL ⟨a *joyous* occasion⟩
**joy·ous·ly** *adv*
**joy·ous·ness** *n*

**joy·stick** \'jȯi-ˌstik\ *n*
a control lever (as for a computer display or an airplane) capable of motion in two or more directions

**ju·bi·lant** \'jü-bə-lənt\ *adj*
expressing great joy especially with shouting : noisily happy

**judo:** children performing an exercise in judo

**ju·bi·lee** \'jü-bə-ˌlē, ˌjü-bə-'lē\ *n*
1 a fiftieth anniversary
2 time of celebration

**Word History** In ancient Hebrew law every fiftieth year was a special year. At the beginning of the special year trumpets made of rams' horns were blown. The Hebrew name for the year came from a Hebrew word that meant "ram's horn." The English word *jubilee* came from this Hebrew name.

**Ju·da·ism** \'jüd-ə-ˌiz-əm, 'jüd-ē-\ *n*
a religion developed among the ancient Hebrews that stresses belief in one God and faithfulness to the moral laws of the Old Testament

**¹judge** \'jəj\ *vb* **judged**; **judg·ing**
1 to form an opinion after careful consideration
2 to act as a judge (as in a trial)
3 THINK 2

**²judge** *n*
1 a public official whose duty is to decide questions brought before a court
2 a person appointed to decide in a contest or competition
3 a person with the experience to give a meaningful opinion : CRITIC

**judg·ment** *or* **judge·ment** \'jəj-mənt\ *n*
1 a decision or opinion (as of a court) given after judging
2 an opinion or estimate formed by examining and comparing
3 the ability for judging

**ju·di·cial** \jü-'dish-əl\ *adj*
of or relating to the providing of justice
**ju·di·cial·ly** *adv*

**ju·di·cious** \jü-'dish-əs\ *adj*
having, using, or showing good judgment : WISE
**ju·di·cious·ly** *adv*
**ju·di·cious·ness** *n*

**ju·do** \'jü-dō\ *n*
◀ a Japanese form of wrestling in which each person tries to throw or pin the opponent

**jug** \'jəg\ *n*
a large deep usually earthenware or glass container with a narrow mouth and a handle

**jug·gle** \'jəg-əl\ *vb* **jug·gled**; **jug·gling**
1 ▼ to keep several things moving in the air at the same time
2 to mix things up in order to deceive
3 to hold or balance insecurely
**jug·gler** \'jəg-lər\ *n*

**juggle 1:**
an entertainer juggling Indian clubs

a b c d e f g h i j k l m n o p q r s t u v w x y z

**juice** \'jüs\ *n*
**1** the liquid part that can be squeezed out of vegetables and fruit
**2** the fluid part of meat

**juicy** \'jü-sē\ *adj* **juic·i·er**; **juic·i·est**
having much juice
**juic·i·ness** *n*

**Ju·ly** \jü-'lī\ *n*
the seventh month of the year

**Word History** The first Roman calendar began the year with March. The fifth month was the one we now know as *July*. The first Latin name given to this month came from the Latin word that meant "fifth." The Roman senate wanted to honor a Roman statesman named Julius Caesar so it decided to name this month after him. The English name *July* came from the Latin name *Julius*.

[1]**jum·ble** \'jəm-bəl\ *vb* **jum·bled**; **jum·bling**
to mix in a confused mass

[2]**jumble** *n*
a disorderly mass or pile

**jum·bo** \'jəm-bō\ *n, pl* **jumbos**
something very large of its kind

**Word History** *Jumbo* was a famous circus elephant. The name *Jumbo* probably came from a word that meant "elephant" in a language of Africa. Our word *jumbo* came from the name of the famous elephant.

[1]**jump** \'jəmp\ *vb*
**1** to spring into the air : LEAP
**2** to make a sudden movement : START
**3** to have or cause a sudden sharp increase ⟨prices *jumped*⟩
**4** to make a hasty judgement
**5** to make a sudden attack ⟨*jumped* on me for being late⟩
**6** to pass over or cause to pass over with or as if with a leap ⟨*jump* the fence⟩
**jump the gun**
**1** to start in a race before the starting signal
**2** to do something before the proper time

[2]**jump** *n*
**1** an act or instance of jumping : LEAP
**2** a sudden involuntary movement : START
**3** a sharp sudden increase
**4** an initial advantage ⟨we got the *jump* on the other team⟩

**jum·per** \'jəm-pər\ *n*
**1** a loose blouse or jacket often worn by workmen
**2** a sleeveless dress worn usually with a blouse

**jumpy** \'jəm-pē\ *adj* **jump·i·er**; **jump·i·est**
NERVOUS 3

**jun·co** \'jəng-kō\ *n, pl* **juncos** *or* **juncoes**
a small mostly gray American finch usually having a pink bill

**junc·tion** \'jəngk-shən\ *n*
**1** an act of joining
**2** a place or point of meeting

**June** \'jün\ *n*
the sixth month of the year

**Word History** The word *June* came from the Latin name of the month. It is most likely that this name came from an ancient Roman family name.

**jun·gle** \'jəng-gəl\ *n*
**1** a thick or tangled growth of plants
**2** a large area of land usually in a tropical region covered with a thick tangled growth of plants

[1]**ju·nior** \'jün-yər\ *adj*
**1** being younger — used to distinguish a son from a father with the same name ⟨John Doe, *Junior*⟩
**2** lower in rank
**3** of or relating to juniors ⟨*junior* class⟩

[2]**junior** *n*
**1** a person who is younger or lower in rank than another
**2** a student in the next-to-last year (as at high school)

**ju·ni·per** \'jü-nə-pər\ *n*
▼ any of various evergreen trees and shrubs related to the pines but having tiny berrylike cones

**juniper**

[1]**junk** \'jəngk\ *n*
**1** old iron, glass, paper, or waste : RUBBISH
**2** a poorly made product

[2]**junk** *vb*
to get rid of as worthless : SCRAP

[3]**junk** *n*
▼ a sailing ship of Chinese waters

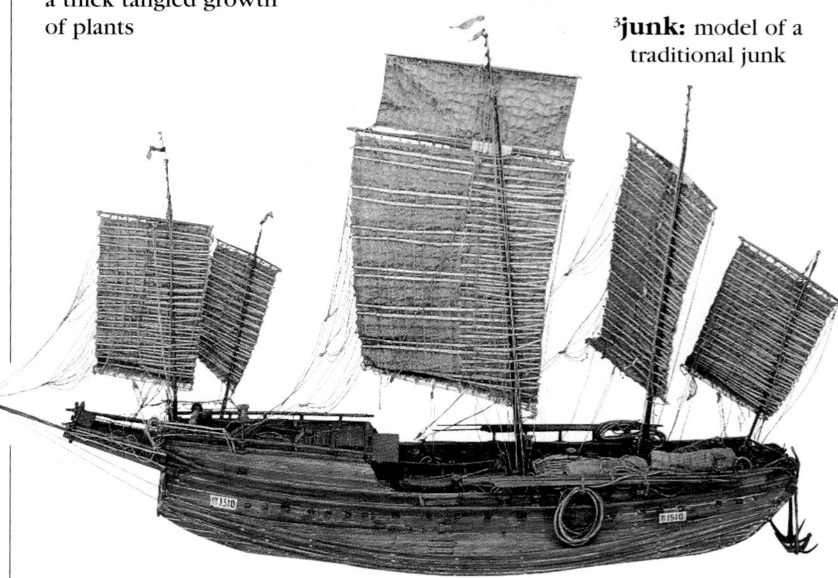
[3]**junk:** model of a traditional junk

**junk food** *n*
food that is high in calories but low in nutritional content

**Ju·pi·ter** \'jü-pət-ər\ *n*
▼ the planet that is fifth in order of distance from the sun and is the largest of the planets with a diameter of about 140,000 kilometers

**ju·ror** \'jůr-ər\ *n*
a member of a jury

*Great Red Spot is thought to consist of swirling gases*

**Jupiter**

**ju·ry** \'jůr-ē\ *n, pl* **juries**
**1** a body of persons sworn to seek for and try to learn the truth about a matter put before them for decision
**2** a committee that judges and awards prizes (as at an exhibition)

**[1]just** \'jəst\ *adj*
**1** having a foundation in fact or reason **:** REASONABLE
**2** agreeing with a standard of correctness
**3** morally right or good
**4** legally right **synonyms** see UPRIGHT
**just·ly** *adv*

**[2]just** *adv*
**1** exactly as wanted ⟨*just* right⟩
**2** very recently ⟨*just* got here⟩
**3** by a very small amount ⟨*just* enough⟩
**4** by a very short distance ⟨*just* east of here⟩
**5** nothing more than ⟨*just* a child⟩
**6** [2]VERY 2 ⟨*just* wonderful⟩

**jus·tice** \'jəs-təs\ *n*
**1** just or right action or treatment
**2** [2]JUDGE 1
**3** the carrying out of law ⟨a court of *justice*⟩
**4** the quality of being fair or just

**jus·ti·fi·able** \'jəs-tə-ˌfī-ə-bəl\ *adj*
possible to justify
**jus·ti·fi·ably** \-blē\ *adv*

**jus·ti·fi·ca·tion** \ˌjəs-tə-fə-'kā-shən\ *n*
**1** the act or an instance of justifying
**2** something that justifies

**jus·ti·fy** \'jəs-tə-ˌfī\ *vb* **jus·ti·fied**; **jus·ti·fy·ing**
to prove or show to be just, right, or reasonable

**jut** \'jət\ *vb* **jut·ted**; **jut·ting**
to extend or cause to extend above or beyond a surrounding area

**jute** \'jüt\ *n*
► a strong glossy fiber from a tropical plant used chiefly for making sacks and twine

**jute:** a bunch of jute fibers

**[1]ju·ve·nile** \'jü-və-ˌnīl, -vən-l\ *adj*
**1** incompletely developed **:** IMMATURE
**2** of, relating to, or characteristic of children or young people

**[2]juvenile** *n*
a young person **:** YOUTH

A
B
C
D
E
F
G
H
I
J
K
L
M
N
O
P
Q
R
S
T
U
V
W
X
Y
Z

**The sounds of K:** The letter **K** has one sound in English. It sounds the same in **kayak**, **keep**, and **kookaburra**. This is the same sound as "**hard C**."

In the middle or at the end of a word, the letter **K** is almost always used together with **C**. Examples are **package**, **track**, and **trick**. The sound of **CK** is the same as **K** alone.

In a few words, **K** is silent. It has no sound in **knife**, **knight**, or **knowledge**. This happens only at the beginning of a word, when it is followed by the letter **N**.

**k** \\'kā\\ *n, pl* **k's** *or* **ks** \\'kāz\\ *often cap*
**1** the eleventh letter of the English alphabet
**2** THOUSAND
**3** KILOBYTE

**kale** \\'kāl\\ *n*
▶ a hardy cabbage with wrinkled leaves that do not form a head

**ka·lei·do·scope** \\kə-'līd-ə-skōp\\ *n*
**1** ▼ a tube containing bits of colored glass or plastic and two mirrors at one end that shows many different patterns as it is turned
**2** a changing pattern or scene

**Word History** If you look into a kaleidoscope you will see changing shapes and pretty colors. The name of the device may seem strange, but it will make sense to a person who knows Greek. *Kaleidoscope* was made up out of three Greek words. The first means "beautiful," the second "shape," and the third "to look at."

**kaleidoscope 1:**
a girl looking into a kaleidoscope

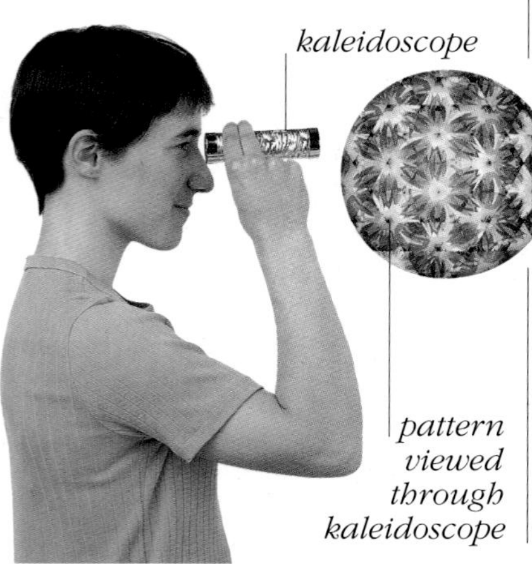

**kale:** a leaf of curly kale

**kan·ga·roo** \\,kang-gə-'rü\\ *n, pl* **kan·ga·roos**
▶ any of numerous leaping mammals of Australia and nearby islands that feed on plants and have long powerful hind legs, a thick tail used as a support in standing or walking, and in the female a pouch on the abdomen in which the young are carried

**ka·o·lin** \\'kā-ə-lən\\ *n*
a very pure white clay used in making porcelain

**kar·a·o·ke** \\,kar-ē-'ō-kē, kə-'rō-kē\\ *n*
a device that plays music to which the user sings along and that records the user's singing with the music

**kar·at** \\'kar-ət\\ *n*
a unit of fineness for gold ⟨14-*karat* gold contains fourteen parts of gold mixed with ten parts of other metal to make it harder⟩

**ka·ra·te** \\kə-'rä-tē\\ *n*
an Oriental art of self-defense in which an attacker is defeated by kicks and punches

**kangaroo:**
a red kangaroo

**ka·ty·did** \\'kāt-ē-,did\\ *n*
any of several large green American grasshoppers with males that make shrill noises

**Word History** Some people like to pretend that the sounds insects make are words. When a male katydid rubs his front wings together, it makes a shrill noise. Some think it sounds as if he says, "Katy did, Katy didn't," over and over. That is how the katydid got its name.

**kay·ak** \\'kī-,ak\\ *n*
**1** an Eskimo canoe made of a frame covered with skins except for a small opening in the center

2 ▶ a boat styled like an Eskimo kayak

**ka•zoo** \kə-'zü\ *n, pl* **ka•zoos**
a toy musical instrument containing a membrane which produces a buzzing tone when one hums into the mouth hole

**KB** \'kā-'bē\ *n*
KILOBYTE

**¹keel** \'kēl\ *n*
a timber or plate running lengthwise along the center of the bottom of a ship and usually sticking out from the bottom

**²keel** *vb*
to turn over

**keel over** *vb*
to fall suddenly (as in a faint)

**keen** \'kēn\ *adj*
1 having a fine edge or point : SHARP ⟨a *keen* knife⟩
2 seeming to cut or sting ⟨a *keen* wind⟩ ⟨a *keen* wit⟩
3 full of enthusiasm : EAGER
4 having or showing mental sharpness
5 very sensitive (as in seeing or hearing) ⟨*keen* eyesight⟩
**synonyms** see EAGER
**keen•ly** *adv*
**keen•ness** *n*

**¹keep** \'kēp\ *vb* **kept** \'kept\; **keep•ing**
1 to be faithful to : FULFILL ⟨*keep* a promise⟩
2 to act properly in relation to ⟨*keep* the Sabbath⟩
3 PROTECT ⟨*keep* us from harm⟩
4 to take care of : TEND
5 to continue doing something
6 to have in one's service or at one's disposal ⟨*keep* a car⟩
7 to preserve a record in ⟨*keep* a diary⟩
8 to have on hand regularly for sale ⟨*keep* neckties⟩
9 to continue to have in one's possession or power
10 to prevent from leaving : DETAIN ⟨*keep* a person in jail⟩
11 to hold back ⟨*keep* a secret⟩
12 to remain or cause to remain in a given place, situation, or condition ⟨*keep* off the grass⟩ ⟨*kept* us waiting⟩
13 to continue in an unspoiled condition ⟨food that *keeps* well⟩
14 ¹REFRAIN ⟨unable to *keep* from talking⟩

**kayak 2:** a girl paddling a kayak

**²keep** *n*
1 the strongest part of a castle in the Middle Ages
2 the necessities of life ⟨could not earn the family's *keep*⟩
**for keeps**
1 with the understanding that one may keep what is won ⟨we'll play marbles *for keeps*⟩
2 for a long time : PERMANENTLY

**keep•er** \'kē-pər\ *n*
a person who watches, guards, or takes care of something

**keep•ing** \'kē-ping\ *n*
1 watchful attention : CARE
2 a proper or fitting relationship : HARMONY ⟨a report in *keeping* with the facts⟩

**keep•sake** \'kēp-ˌsāk\ *n*
something kept or given to be kept in memory of a person, place, or happening

**keep up** *vb*
1 MAINTAIN 1 ⟨*keep* standards *up*⟩
2 to stay well informed about something ⟨*keep up* with the news⟩
3 to continue without interruption ⟨the rain *kept up* all night⟩
4 to stay even with others (as in a race)

**keg** \'keg\ *n*
1 a small barrel holding about 114 liters
2 the contents of a keg

**kelp** \'kelp\ *n*
a large coarse brown seaweed

**ken** \'ken\ *n*
1 range of vision : SIGHT
2 range of understanding

**ken•nel** \'ken-l\ *n*
1 a shelter for a dog
2 a place where dogs are bred or housed

**kept** *past of* KEEP

**ker•chief** \'kər-chəf\ *n, pl* **kerchiefs**
1 a square of cloth worn as a head covering or as a scarf
2 HANDKERCHIEF

**Word History** Look at the history of the word *kerchief* and you will see that it is a fine word for something that covers the head. The English word comes from an Old French word formed from two words. The first of these two French words was a verb that meant "to cover." The second was a noun that meant "head."

**ker•nel** \'kərn-l\ *n*
1 the inner softer part of a seed, fruit stone, or nut
2 the whole grain or seed of a cereal

**ker•o•sene** *or* **ker•o•sine** \'ker-ə-ˌsēn\ *n*
a thin oil obtained from petroleum and used as a fuel and solvent

**ketch** \'kech\ *n*
▼ a fore-and-aft rigged ship with two masts

**ketch:** model of a ketch

**ket·chup** \'kech-əp, 'kach-\ *n*
a thick seasoned sauce usually made from tomatoes

**ket·tle** \'ket-l\ *n*
**1** a pot for boiling liquids
**2** TEAKETTLE

**ket·tle·drum** \'ket-l-,drəm\ *n*
▼ a large brass or copper drum that has a rounded bottom and can be varied in pitch

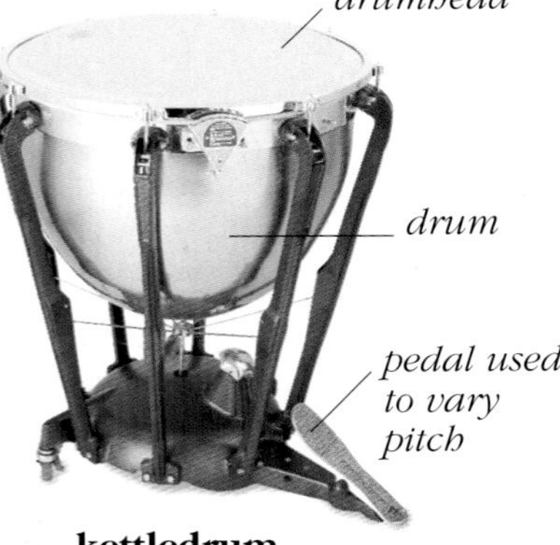


**kettledrum**

**[1]key** \'kē\ *n*
**1** an instrument by which the bolt of a lock (as on a door) is turned
**2** a device having the form or function of a key ⟨a *key* for opening a can of meat⟩
**3** a means of gaining or preventing entrance, possession, or control
**4** something (as a map legend) that gives an explanation : SOLUTION
**5** one of the levers with a flat surface that is pressed with a finger to activate a mechanism of a machine or instrument
**6** a system of seven musical tones arranged in relation to a keynote from which the system is named ⟨the *key* of C⟩
**7** a characteristic way (as of thought)
**8** a small switch for opening or closing an electric circuit

**[2]key** *vb* **keyed**; **key·ing**
**1** to regulate the musical pitch of
**2** to bring into harmony

**[3]key** *adj*
of great importance : most important ⟨the *key* question is "Can we afford it?"⟩ ⟨the *key* people in the organization⟩

**[4]key** *n*
a low island or reef ⟨the Florida *Keys*⟩

**key·board** \'kē-,bōrd\ *n*
**1** a row of keys by which a musical instrument (as a piano) is played
**2** ▶ a portable electronic musical instrument with a keyboard like that of a piano
**3** the whole arrangement of keys (as on a typewriter or computer)

key

**keyboard 2**

**key·hole** \'kē-,hōl\ *n*
a hole for receiving a key

**key·note** \'kē-,nōt\ *n*
**1** the first and harmonically fundamental tone of a scale
**2** the fundamental fact, idea, or mood

**key·stone** \'kē-,stōn\ *n*
**1** ▼ the wedge-shaped piece at the top of an arch that locks the other pieces in place
**2** something on which other things depend for support

**keystone 1:** a keystone on a building in New York City

**key up** *vb*
to make nervous or tense

**kha·ki** \'kak-ē, 'kä-kē\ *n*
**1** a light yellowish brown
**2** a light yellowish brown cloth used especially for military uniforms

**khan** \'kän, 'kan\ *n*
**1** a Mongolian leader
**2** a local chieftain or man of rank in some countries of central Asia

**ki·bitz·er** \'kib-ət-sər\ *n*
a person who looks on and often offers unwanted advice

**[1]kick** \'kik\ *vb*
**1** to strike out or hit with the foot
**2** to object strongly : PROTEST
**3** to spring back when fired

**[2]kick** *n*
**1** a blow with the foot
**2** a sudden moving (as of a ball) with the foot
**3** the sudden move backward of a gun when fired
**4** a feeling of or cause for objection
**5** a feeling or source of pleasure

**kick·ball** \'kik-,bȯl\ *n*
a form of baseball played with a large rubber ball that is kicked instead of hit with a bat

**kick·off** \'kik-,ȯf\ *n*
a kick that puts the ball into play (as in football or soccer)

**kick off** \kik-'ȯf, 'kik-\ *vb*
**1** to make a kickoff
**2** BEGIN 1

**kick·stand** \'kik-,stand\ *n*
a metal bar or rod attached to a two-wheeled vehicle (as a bicycle) and used to prop the vehicle up when it is not in use

**[1]kid** \'kid\ *n*
**1** the young of a goat or a related animal
**2** the flesh, fur, or skin of a kid or something (as leather) made from one of these
**3** CHILD
**kid·dish** \'kid-ish\ *adj*

**[2]kid** *vb* **kid·ded**; **kid·ding**
**1** to deceive or trick as a joke
**2** [1]TEASE
**kid·der** *n*

**kid·nap** \'kid-,nap\ *vb*
**kid·napped** *or* **kid·naped** \-,napt\; **kid·nap·ping** *or* **kid·nap·ing**
to carry away a person by force or

by fraud and against his or her will
**kid·nap·per** *or* **kid·nap·er** *n*

**kid·ney** \'kid-nē\ *n, pl* **kid·neys**
▶ either of a pair of organs near the backbone that give off waste from the body in the form of urine

**kidney bean** *n*
a common garden bean and especially one having large dark red seeds

**[1]kill** \'kil\ *vb*
1 to end the life of : SLAY
2 to put an end to ⟨*kill* all chance of success⟩
3 to use up ⟨*kill* time⟩
4 [1]DEFEAT 1 ⟨*kill* a proposed law⟩

**Synonyms** KILL, MURDER, and ASSASSINATE mean to take the life of. KILL suggests nothing about the manner of death and can apply to the death of anything ⟨the early frost *killed* the crops⟩ ⟨a person *killed* in an accident⟩. MURDER applies to the deliberate and unlawful killing of a person ⟨planned to *murder* the old merchant⟩. ASSASSINATE usually suggests the murder of an important person often for political reasons ⟨a plan to *assassinate* the President⟩.

**[2]kill** *n*
1 an act of killing
2 an animal killed ⟨a lion devouring its *kill*⟩

**kill·deer** \'kil-ˌdir\ *n*
a grayish brown North American plover that has a shrill mournful call

**Word History** Killdeers are not vicious birds. They have no particular hatred for deer, but to some people the cry of these birds sounds like "Kill deer! Kill deer! Kill deer!" That is why the killdeers got their unusual name.

**[1]kill·er** \'kil-ər\ *n*
one that kills

**[2]killer** *adj*
1 very impressive or effective ⟨a *killer* smile⟩
2 very difficult ⟨a *killer* exam⟩
3 causing death or ruin ⟨a *killer* tornado⟩

**kill·joy** \'kil-ˌjȯi\ *n*
a person who spoils the pleasure of others

## kidney

Humans have a pair of kidneys at the back of the abdomen. The kidneys maintain correct levels of water and salt in the body, filter toxic substances from the blood, and excrete excess water and waste in the form of urine, which drains to the bladder.

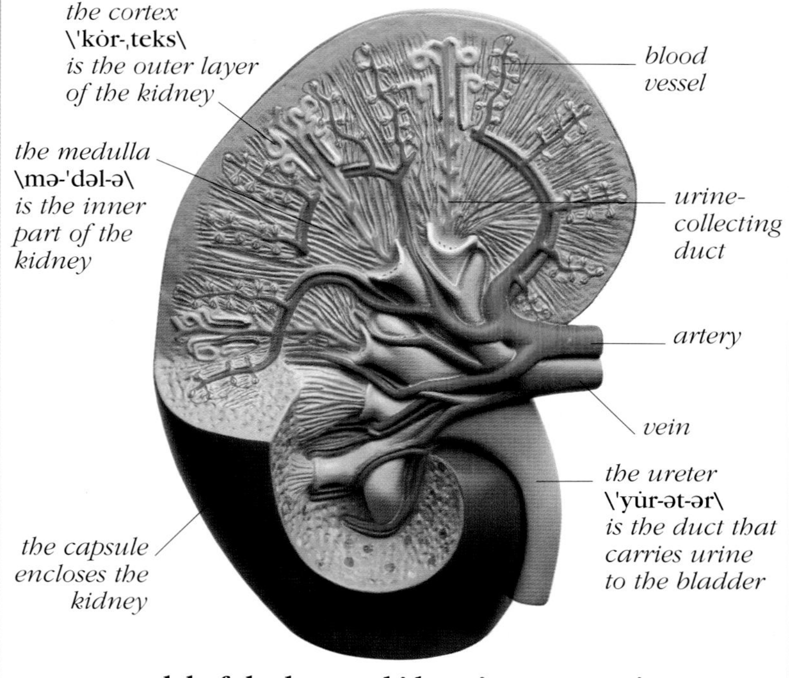
the cortex \'kȯr-ˌteks\ is the outer layer of the kidney
blood vessel
the medulla \mə-'dəl-ə\ is the inner part of the kidney
urine-collecting duct
artery
vein
the ureter \'yu̇r-ət-ər\ is the duct that carries urine to the bladder
the capsule encloses the kidney

**model of the human kidney in cross section**

**kiln** \'kiln, 'kil\ *n*
▶ a furnace or oven in which something (as pottery) is hardened, burned, or dried

**ki·lo** \'kē-lō\ *n, pl* **kilos**
KILOGRAM

**kilo-** *prefix*
thousand ⟨*kilo*meter⟩

**ki·lo·byte** \'kil-ə-ˌbīt\ *n*
a unit of computer information storage capacity equal to 1024 bytes

**ki·lo·gram** \'kil-ə-ˌgram\ *n*
a metric unit of weight equal to 1000 grams

**ki·lo·me·ter** \kil-'äm-ət-ər, 'kil-ə-ˌmēt-ər\ *n*
a metric unit of length equal to 1000 meters

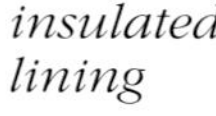
insulated lining

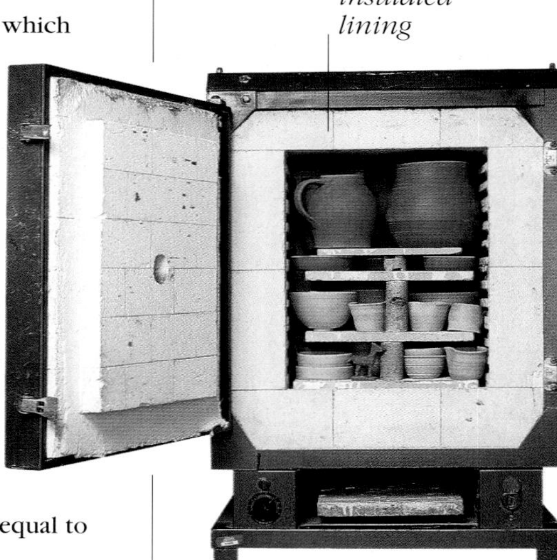

**kiln:** a kiln stacked with pottery, ready for firing

**kilo·watt** \'kil-ə-ˌwät\ *n*
a unit of electrical power equal to 1000 watts

**kilt** \'kilt\ *n*
a knee-length pleated skirt usually of tartan worn by men in Scotland

**kil·ter** \'kil-tər\ *n*
proper condition ⟨the TV is out of *kilter*⟩

**ki·mo·no** \kə-'mō-nō\ *n, pl* **ki·mo·nos**
**1** ▶ a loose robe with wide sleeves that is traditionally worn with a broad sash as an outer garment by the Japanese
**2** a loose dressing gown worn chiefly by women

*sash*
*sleeve*

**kimono 1:** a kimono worn by a Japanese girl

**kin** \'kin\ *n*
**1** a person's relatives
**2** KINSMAN

**-kin** \kən\ *also* **-kins** \kənz\ *n suffix*
little ⟨lamb*kin*⟩

**[1]kind** \'kīnd\ *n*
a group of persons or things that can be recognized as belonging together or having something in common ⟨all *kinds* of people⟩

**[2]kind** *adj*
**1** wanting or liking to do good and to bring happiness to others **:** CONSIDERATE
**2** showing or growing out of gentleness or goodness of heart ⟨a *kind* act⟩

**kin·der·gar·ten** \'kin-dər-ˌgärt-n\ *n*
a school or a class for very young children

**kind·heart·ed** \'kīnd-'härt-əd\ *adj*
having or showing a kind and sympathetic nature
**kind·heart·ed·ly** *adv*
**kind·heart·ed·ness** *n*

**kin·dle** \'kin-dəl\ *vb* **kin·dled**; **kin·dling**
**1** to set on fire **:** LIGHT
**2** to stir up **:** EXCITE ⟨the unfairness of the answer *kindled* our anger⟩

**kin·dling** \'kin-dling\ *n*
material that burns easily and is used for starting a fire

**[1]kind·ly** \'kīn-dlē\ *adj* **kind·li·er**; **kind·li·est**
**1** pleasant or wholesome in nature ⟨a *kindly* climate⟩
**2** sympathetic or generous in nature
**kind·li·ness** *n*

**[2]kindly** *adv*
**1** in a willing manner ⟨take *kindly* to a change⟩
**2** in a kind manner
**3** in an appreciative manner
**4** in an obliging manner

**kind·ness** \'kīnd-nəs\ *n*
**1** a kind deed **:** FAVOR
**2** the quality or state of being kind

**kind of** \ˌkīn-dəv, -də\ *adv*
to a moderate degree **:** SOMEWHAT ⟨it's *kind of* dark in here⟩

**[1]kin·dred** \'kin-drəd\ *n*
**1** a group of related individuals
**2** a person's relatives

**[2]kindred** *adj*
alike in nature or character

**kin·folk** \'kin-ˌfōk\ *n*
[1]KINDRED 2

**king** \'king\ *n*
**1** a male ruler of a country who usually inherits his position and rules for life
**2** a chief among competitors ⟨an oil *king*⟩
**3** the chief piece in the game of chess
**4** a playing card bearing the figure of a king
**5** a piece in checkers that has reached the opponent's back row
**king·ly** *adj*

**king·dom** \'king-dəm\ *n*
**1** a country whose ruler is a king or queen
**2** one of the three basic divisions (**animal kingdom**, **plant kingdom**, **mineral kingdom**) into which natural objects are commonly grouped
**3** a major category in scientific biological classification that ranks above the phylum and division and is the highest and broadest group

**king·fish·er** \'king-ˌfish-ər\ *n*
▼ any of a group of usually crested birds with a short tail, long sharp bill, and bright feathers

**king·let** \'king-lət\ *n*
a small bird resembling a warbler

**king–size** \'king-ˌsīz\ *or* **king–sized** \-ˌsīzd\ *adj*
unusually large ⟨a *king-size* bed⟩

**kingfisher:** a belted kingfisher eating a fish

**[1]kink** \'kingk\ *n*
**1** a short tight twist or curl (as in a thread or rope)
**2** [1]CRAMP 1 ⟨a *kink* in my back⟩
**3** an imperfection that makes something hard to use or work
**kinky** \'kingk-ē\ *adj*

**[2]kink** *vb*
to form or cause to form a kink in

**-kins** see -KIN

**kin·ship** \'kin-ˌship\ *n*
the quality or state of being kin

**kins·man** \'kinz-mən\ *n, pl* **kins·men** \-mən\
a relative usually by birth

**kins·wom·an** \'kinz-ˌwu̇m-ən\ *n, pl* **kins·wom·en** \-ˌwim-ən\
a woman who is a relative usually by birth

**[1]kiss** \'kis\ *vb*
**1** to touch with the lips as a mark of love or greeting
**2** to touch gently or lightly ⟨wind *kissing* the trees⟩

**[2]kiss** *n*
**1** a loving touch with the lips
**2** a gentle touch or contact
**3** a bite-size candy often wrapped in paper or foil

**kit** \'kit\ *n*
**1** a set of articles for personal use ⟨a travel *kit*⟩
**2** a set of tools or supplies
**3** a set of parts to be put together ⟨a model-airplane *kit*⟩
**4** a container (as a bag or case) for a kit

**kitch•en** \'kich-ən\ *n*
a room in which cooking is done

**kitch•en•ette** \ˌkich-ə-'net\ *n*
a small kitchen

**kitchen garden** *n*
a piece of land where vegetables are grown for household use

**kite** \'kīt\ *n*
**1** a hawk with long narrow wings and deeply forked tail that feeds mostly on insects and small reptiles
**2** ▼ a light covered frame for flying in the air at the end of a long string

**kith** \'kith\ *n*
familiar friends and neighbors or relatives ⟨our *kith* and kin⟩

**kit•ten** \'kit-n\ *n*
a young cat
**kit•ten•ish** \'kit-n-ish\ *adj*

**kit•ty** \'kit-ē\ *n, pl* **kitties**
CAT, KITTEN

**ki•wi** \'kē-wē\ *n*
**1** ▼ a grayish-brown bird of New Zealand that is unable to fly
**2** KIWIFRUIT

**kiwi**

**ki•wi•fruit** \-ˌfrüt\ *n*
the fruit of a Chinese vine having a fuzzy brown skin and slightly tart green flesh

**klutz** \'kləts\ *n*
a clumsy person

**knack** \'nak\ *n*
**1** a clever or skillful way of doing something : TRICK
**2** a natural ability : TALENT ⟨a *knack* for making friends⟩

**knap•sack** \'nap-ˌsak\ *n*
a carrying case or pouch slung from the shoulders over the back

**knave** \'nāv\ *n*
**1** RASCAL 1
**2** [1]JACK 1

**knead** \'nēd\ *vb*
**1** to work and press into a mass with or as if with the hands ⟨*knead* dough⟩
**2** [2]MASSAGE
**knead•er** *n*

**knee** \'nē\ *n*
**1** the joint or region in which the thigh and lower leg come together
**2** something resembling a knee
**3** the part of a garment covering the knee

**knee•cap** \'nē-ˌkap\ *n*
a thick flat movable bone forming the front part of the knee

**kneel** \'nēl\ *vb* **knelt** \'nelt\ *or* **kneeled** \'nēld\; **kneel•ing**
to bend the knee : support oneself on one's knees

**kite 2**
Kites were probably invented by the Chinese over 2,500 years ago to spy on the enemy and carry archers over their opponents in battle. Modern kites are flown for pleasure or sport, and may have a light wooden frame, covered with nylon fabric or paper. Once launched, a kite is lifted by the wind and controlled by a person holding the end of a long line.

**novelty kite**

**triangular kite**

**box kite**

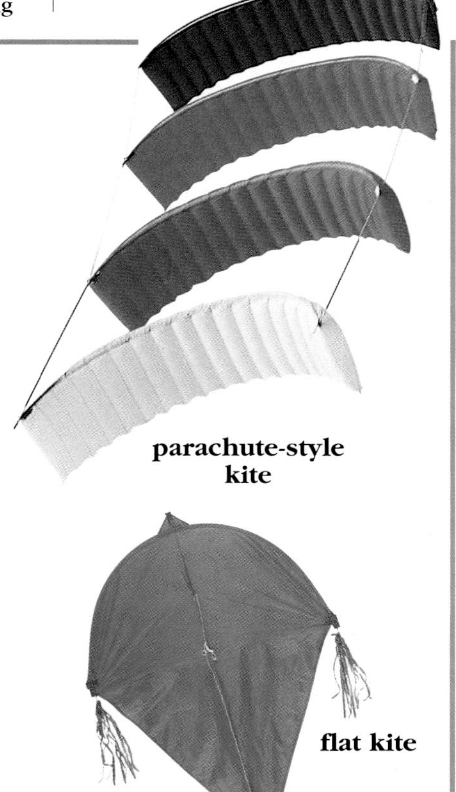
**parachute-style kite**

**flat kite**

**[1]knell** \'nel\ *vb*
**1** to ring slowly and solemnly : TOLL
**2** to summon or warn by a knell

**[2]knell** *n*
**1** a stroke or sound of a bell especially when rung slowly for a death, funeral, or disaster
**2** an indication (as a sound) of the end or failure of something

**knew** *past of* KNOW

**knick·ers** \'nik-ərz\ *n pl*
loose-fitting short pants gathered at the knee

**knick·knack** \'nik-,nak\ *n*
a small ornamental object

**[1]knife** \'nīf\ *n, pl* **knives** \'nīvz\
**1** a cutting instrument consisting of a sharp blade fastened to a handle
**2** a cutting blade in a machine

**[2]knife** *vb* **knifed**; **knif·ing**
to stab, slash, or wound with a knife

**[1]knight** \'nīt\ *n*
**1** ▶ a warrior of olden times who fought on horseback, served a king, held a special military rank, and swore to behave in a noble way
**2** a man honored by a sovereign for merit and in Great Britain ranking below a baronet
**3** one of the pieces in the game of chess
**knight·ly** *adj*

**[2]knight** *vb*
to make a knight of

**knight·hood** \'nīt-,hu̇d\ *n*
**1** the rank, dignity, or profession of a knight
**2** the qualities that a knight should have
**3** knights as a class or body

**knit** \'nit\ *vb* **knit** *or* **knit·ted**; **knit·ting**
**1** to form a fabric or garment by interlacing yarn or thread in connected loops with needles (**knitting needles**) ⟨*knit* a sweater⟩
**2** to draw or come together closely as if knitted : unite firmly
**3** [2]WRINKLE ⟨*knit* one's brow⟩
**knit·ter** *n*

**knob** \'näb\ *n*
**1** a rounded lump
**2** a small rounded handle
**3** a rounded hill

**[1]knock** \'näk\ *vb*
**1** to strike with a sharp blow
**2** to bump against something
**3** to make a pounding noise
**4** to find fault with

**[1]knight 1:**
a man dressed as a 14th-century knight preparing for battle

**[2]knock** *n*
**1** a sharp blow
**2** a severe misfortune or hardship
**3** a pounding noise

**knock·er** \'näk-ər\ *n*
a device made like a hinge and fastened to a door for use in knocking

**knock–kneed** \'näk-'nēd\ *adj*
having the legs bowed inward

**knoll** \'nōl\ *n*
a small round hill

**[1]knot** \'nät\ *n*
**1** ▶ an interlacing (as of string or ribbon) that forms a lump or knob
**2** PROBLEM 2
**3** a bond of union ⟨the marriage *knot*⟩
**4** the inner end of a branch enclosed in a plant stem or a section of this in sawed lumber
**5** a cluster of persons or things
**6** an ornamental bow of ribbon
**7** one nautical mile per hour (about two kilometers per hour)

**[2]knot** *vb* **knot·ted**; **knot·ting**
**1** to tie in or with a knot
**2** to unite closely

## [1]knot 1

There are many types of knot, tied either from single or double lengths of thread, twine, or rope. Each knot has a different purpose — some are used to prevent lines from sliding, or to add weight to a line, while others are used to tie sails, to join two ropes together, or to tether animals.

**hitch knot**

**overhand knot** is used to prevent the end of a rope from fraying

**bend knot** is used to fasten one rope to another

**reef knot** is used to tie in or let out a sail

**butterfly knot** is used to secure ropes linking rock climbers

**knot·hole** \'nät-,hōl\ *n*
a hole in wood where a knot has come out

**knot·ty** \'nät-ē\ *adj* **knot·ti·er**; **knot·ti·est**
**1** full of knots
**2** DIFFICULT 3 ⟨a *knotty* problem⟩

**koala:** a koala mother and baby

**know** \'nō\ *vb* **knew** \'nü, 'nyü\; **known** \'nōn\; **know·ing**
**1** to have understanding of ⟨*know* yourself⟩
**2** to recognize the nature of ⟨*knew* them to be honest⟩
**3** to recognize the identity of ⟨*knew* me by my walk⟩
**4** to be acquainted or familiar with ⟨*knows* the city well⟩
**5** to be aware of the truth of ⟨*know* that the earth is round⟩
**6** to have a practical understanding of ⟨*knows* how to speak Spanish fluently⟩
**7** to have information or knowledge ⟨ask someone who *knows*⟩
**8** to be or become aware ⟨*knew* about the problem⟩

**know·ing** \'nō-ing\ *adj*
**1** having or showing special knowledge, information, or intelligence
**2** shrewdly and keenly alert
**3** INTENTIONAL
**know·ing·ly** *adv*

**know–it–all** \'nō-ət-,ȯl\ *n*
a person who always claims to know everything

**knowl·edge** \'näl-ij\ *n*
**1** understanding and skill gained by experience ⟨a *knowledge* of carpentry⟩
**2** the state of being aware of something or of having information
**3** range of information or awareness
**4** something learned and kept in the mind **:** LEARNING **synonyms** see INFORMATION

**knuck·le** \'nək-əl\ *n*
the rounded lump formed by the ends of two bones (as of a finger) where they come together in a joint

**ko·ala** \kō-'ä-lə\ *n*
◀ a tailless Australian animal with thick fur and big hairy ears, sharp claws for climbing, and a pouch like the kangaroo's for carrying its young

**kohl·ra·bi** \kōl-'rä-bē\ *n*
▼ a cabbage that forms no head but has a fleshy edible stem

**Word History** Kohlrabi is a kind of cabbage. Its large stem looks a bit like the root of a turnip. The Italians gave this plant a name made up of two Italian words. The first means "cabbage" and the second means "turnip." The Germans took the Italian name but changed it to fit their own way of speaking. The English word *kohlrabi* comes from the plant's German name.

**Ko·mo·do dragon** \kə-'mōd-ō-\ *n*
a lizard of Indonesia that is the largest of all known lizards

**kook·a·bur·ra** \'ku̇k-ə-,bər-ə\ *n*
an Australian kingfisher that has a call resembling loud laughter

**Ko·ran** \kə-'ran, -'rän\ *n*
a book of sacred writings accepted by Muslims as revealed to Muhammad by Allah

**kohlrabi**
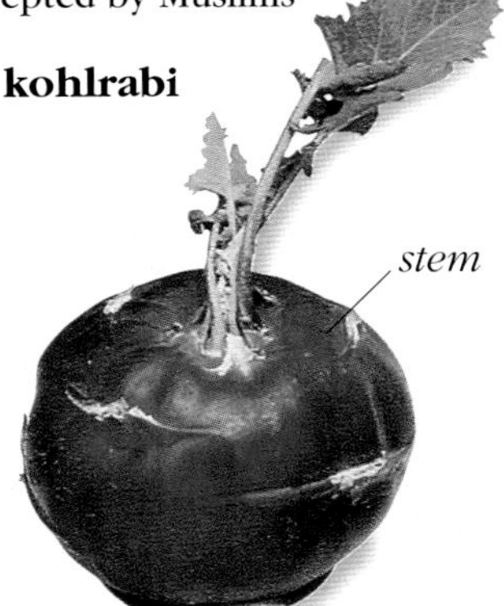


[1]**Ko·re·an** \kə-'rē-ən\ *n*
**1** a person born or living in North Korea or South Korea
**2** the language of the Koreans

[2]**Korean** *adj*
of or relating to North Korea or South Korea, the Korean people, or their language

**ko·sher** \'kō-shər\ *adj*
**1** accepted by Jewish law
**2** prepared as required by Jewish law

**krill** \'kril\ *n*
▼ tiny floating sea creatures that are a chief food of whales

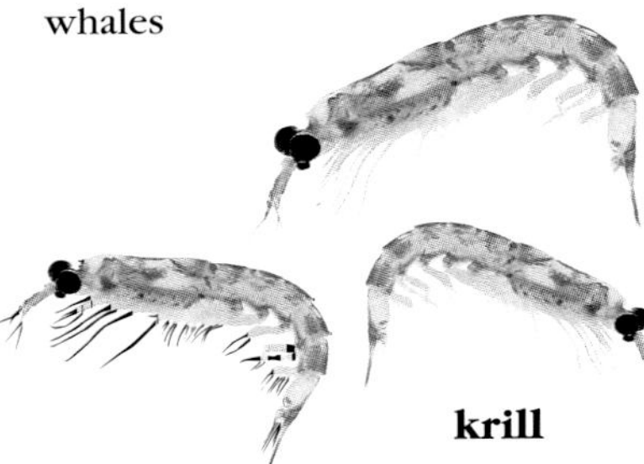
**krill**

**kud·zu** \'ku̇d-zü\ *n*
an Asian vine of the pea family that is widely grown for hay and for use in erosion control and is often a serious weed in the southeastern United States

**kum·quat** \'kəm-,kwät\ *n*
▶ a small citrus fruit with sweet rind and sour pulp that is used mostly in preserves

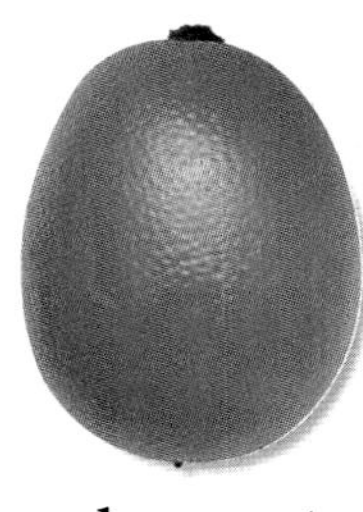
**kumquat**

**Word History** Kumquats first grew in China and Japan. The English got the fruit and its name from China. The word *kumquat* comes from a word in a variety of Chinese spoken in and near the city of Canton. The Chinese name for the kumquat is made up of two Chinese words. The first means "gold". The second is the word for the fruit we call *orange*.

**Kwan·zaa** \'kwän-zə\ *n*
an African-American cultural festival held from December 26 to January 1

A
B
C
D
E
F
G
H
I
J
K
L
M
N
O
P
Q
R
S
T
U
V
W
X
Y
Z

# Ll

**The sounds of L:** The letter **L** has only one sound in English. It sounds the same in **letter**, **alike**, **silly**, **illustrate**, and **wall**. Double **L** sounds the same as single **L**.

The letter **L** is usually silent before **F, K,** or **M** at the end of a word, and in **calf**, **half**, **walk**, **chalk**, **yolk**, **calm**, and **palm.** However, some people pronounce the **L** in **calm** and **palm**.

**l** \'el\ *n, pl* **l's** *or* **ls** \'elz\ *often cap*
**1** the twelfth letter of the English alphabet
**2** fifty in Roman numerals

**la** \'lä\ *n*
the sixth note of the musical scale

**lab** \'lab\ *n*
LABORATORY

[1]**la·bel** \'lā-bəl\ *n*
**1** a slip (as of paper or cloth) attached to something to identify or describe it
**2** a word or phrase that describes or names something ⟨a part-of-speech *label*⟩

[2]**label** *vb* **la·beled** *or* **la·belled**; **la·bel·ing** *or* **la·bel·ling**
**1** to attach a label to
**2** to name or describe with or as if with a label

**la·bi·al** \'lā-bē-əl\ *adj*
of or relating to the lips

[1]**la·bor** \'lā-bər\ *n*
**1** effort that is hard and usually physical ⟨rest from *labor*⟩
**2** the effort involved in giving birth
**3** something that has to be done **:** TASK
**4** workers as a body or class

**Synonyms** LABOR and WORK mean action involving effort or exertion. WORK can apply to either mental or bodily effort and may involve something that is enjoyable but tiring ⟨decorating the gym was hard *work*⟩. LABOR suggests great or unpleasant exertion, especially of the body, and indicates that the work is done of necessity ⟨the dull *labor* of cleaning the stove⟩.

[2]**labor** *vb*
**1** to work hard **:** TOIL
**2** to move slowly or heavily ⟨a truck *laboring* up the hill⟩

**lab·o·ra·to·ry** \'lab-rə-ˌtōr-ē, 'lab-ə-rə-\ *n, pl* **lab·o·ra·to·ries**
a room or building in which experiments and tests are done

**Labor Day** *n*
the first Monday in September observed as a legal holiday to honor the worker

**la·bored** \'lā-bərd\ *adj*
produced or done with effort or difficulty ⟨*labored* breathing⟩

**la·bor·er** \'lā-bər-ər\ *n*
a person who works on jobs that require strength rather than skill

**la·bo·ri·ous** \lə-'bōr-ē-əs\ *adj*
requiring much effort ⟨a *laborious* climb⟩
**la·bo·ri·ous·ly** *adv*

**labor union** *n*
an organization of workers designed to help them get better pay and working conditions

[1]**lace** \'lās\ *vb* **laced**; **lac·ing**
to fasten with a lace

[2]**lace** *n*
**1** a cord or string for pulling and holding together opposite edges (as of a shoe)
**2** ▶ an ornamental net of thread or cord usually with a design

**Word History** We usually try to avoid knotting our shoelaces. It might seem strange, then, that the English word *lace* comes from an Old French word that meant "a knotted cord," but that is true. This Old French word came, in turn, from a Latin word that meant "snare" or "noose."

**lac·er·ate** \'las-ə-ˌrāt\ *vb* **lac·er·at·ed**; **lac·er·at·ing**
to injure by tearing ⟨a *lacerated* knee⟩

**lac·er·a·tion** \ˌlas-ə-'rā-shən\ *n*
a lacerated place or wound

[1]**lack** \'lak\ *vb*
**1** to be missing ⟨something is *lacking*⟩
**2** to need or be without something ⟨you will never *lack* for friends⟩

[2]**lack** *n*
**1** the fact or state of being absent or needed ⟨a *lack* of time⟩
**2** something that is absent or needed

[2]**lace 2:** a scarf of lace from Spain

[1]**lac·quer** \'lak-ər\ *n*
a material like varnish that dries quickly into a shiny layer (as on wood or metal)

[2]**lacquer** *vb*
to coat with lacquer

**la·crosse** \lə-'kròs\ *n*
▶ a ball game played outdoors using a long-handled stick with a shallow net for catching, throwing, and carrying the ball

**lac·tose** \'lak-ˌtōs\ *n*
a sugar that is found in milk

**lacy** \'lā-sē\ *adj* **lac·i·er**; **lac·i·est**
like or made of lace

**lad** \'lad\ *n*
BOY 1, YOUTH

**lad·der** \'lad-ər\ *n*
a device used for climbing usually consisting of two long pieces of wood, rope, or metal joined at short distances by horizontal pieces

**lad·die** \'lad-ē\ *n*
BOY 1, LAD

**lad·en** \'lād-n\ *adj*
heavily loaded ⟨a truck *laden* with gravel⟩

[1]**la·dle** \'lād-l\ *n*
a spoon with a long handle and a deep bowl that is used for dipping

[2]**ladle** *vb* **la·dled**; **la·dling**
to take up and carry in a ladle

**la·dy** \'lād-ē\ *n, pl* **la·dies**
**1** a woman of high social position
**2** a pleasant well-bred woman or girl
**3** a woman of any kind or class — often used in speaking to a stranger ⟨*lady*, you dropped something⟩
**4** WIFE
**5** a British noblewoman — used as a title ⟨*Lady* Jane Grey⟩

**Word History** There was in Old English a word *hlāf* that meant "bread" or "loaf." The modern English word *loaf* comes from this Old English word. A suffix *-dige* meaning "kneader" was long ago added to the old word for bread. The modern word *dough* is related to that Old English suffix. Together *hlāf* and *-dige* made a word *hlǣfdige* that meant "one who kneads bread." This word was used for a woman who was the head of a household. The modern English word *lady* comes from this old word.

**la·dy·bird** \'lād-ē-ˌbərd\ *n*
LADYBUG

**la·dy·bug** \'lād-ē-ˌbəg\ *n*
a small rounded beetle that feeds mostly on plant lice

**la·dy·like** \'lād-ē-ˌlīk\ *adj*
WELL-BRED

**la·dy·ship** \'lād-ē-ˌship\ *n*
the rank of a lady — used as a title ⟨her *Ladyship* is not at home⟩

**lady's slipper** *or* **lady slipper** *n*
any of several North American wild orchids whose flowers suggest a slipper in shape

[1]**lag** \'lag\ *n*
the act or the amount of lagging

[2]**lag** *vb* **lagged**; **lag·ging**
to move or advance slowly ⟨work *lagging* behind schedule⟩

[1]**lag·gard** \'lag-ərd\ *adj*
lagging behind : SLOW

[2]**laggard** *n*
a person who lags

**la·goon** \lə-'gün\ *n*
a shallow channel or pond near or connected to a larger body of water

**laid** *past of* LAY

**lain** *past participle of* LIE

**lair** \'laər, 'leər\ *n*
the den or resting place of a wild animal

## lacrosse

In the sport of lacrosse, players use a stick with a net to throw, catch, and carry the ball. They can also roll or kick the ball in any direction. The players try to score a goal by aiming the ball into the other team's net. Women's lacrosse teams are made up of 12 players, whereas men's teams have 10 players.

**women's lacrosse field**

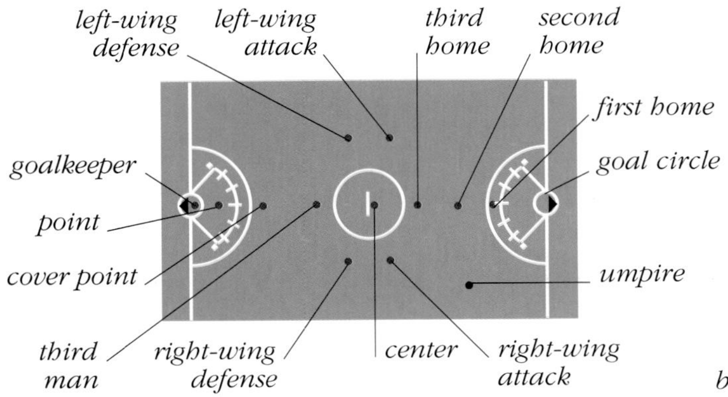

*left-wing defense*, *left-wing attack*, *third home*, *second home*, *first home*, *goalkeeper*, *goal circle*, *point*, *cover point*, *umpire*, *third man*, *right-wing defense*, *center*, *right-wing attack*

**player**

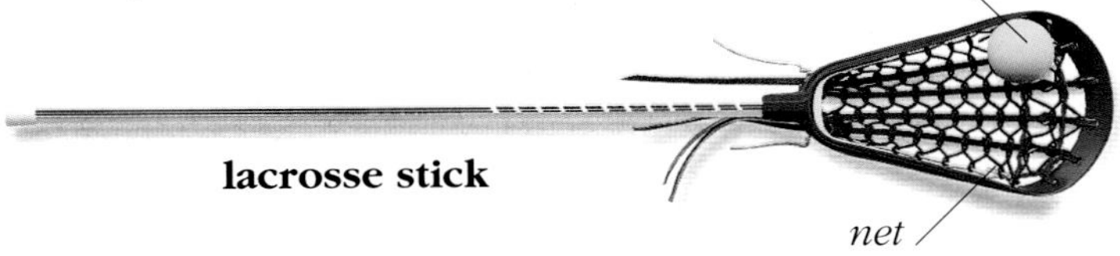

*ball*

**lacrosse stick**

*net*

**lake** in Misty Fjords National Monument, Alaska

**lake** \'lāk\ *n*
▲ a large inland body of still water

**[1]lamb** \'lam\ *n*
▼ a young sheep usually less than one year old

**[1]lamb**

**[2]lamb** *vb*
to give birth to a lamb

**lamb·kin** \'lam-kən\ *n*
a young lamb

**[1]lame** \'lām\ *adj* **lam·er**; **lam·est**
**1** not able to get around without pain or difficulty
**2** being stiff and sore ⟨a *lame* shoulder⟩
**3** not very convincing **:** WEAK ⟨a *lame* excuse⟩
**lame·ly** *adv*
**lame·ness** *n*

**[2]lame** *vb* **lamed**; **lam·ing**
to make or become lame ⟨*lamed* in a fall⟩

**[1]la·ment** \lə-'ment\ *vb*
**1** to mourn aloud **:** WAIL
**2** to show sorrow for

**[2]lament** *n*
**1** a crying out in sorrow
**2** a sad song or poem

**la·men·ta·ble** \'lam-ən-tə-bəl\ *adj*
REGRETTABLE ⟨a *lamentable* accident⟩

**lam·en·ta·tion** \,lam-ən-'tā-shən\ *n*
the act of lamenting

**lam·i·nat·ed** \'lam-ə-,nāt-əd\ *adj*
made of layers of material firmly joined together

**lamp** \'lamp\ *n*
a device for producing light ⟨a kerosene *lamp*⟩ ⟨an electric *lamp*⟩

**lam·prey** \'lam-prē\ *n*, *pl* **lampreys**
a water animal that looks like an eel but has a sucking mouth with no jaws

**[1]lance** \'lans\ *n*
▶ a weapon with a long handle and a sharp steel head used by knights on horseback

**[2]lance** *vb*
to cut open with a small sharp instrument ⟨the doctor *lanced* the boil⟩

**lance corporal** *n*
an enlisted person in the Marine Corps ranking above a private first class

**[1]land** \'land\ *n*
**1** the solid part of the surface of the earth
**2** a part of the earth's surface (as a country or a farm) marked off by boundaries
**3** the people of a country
**land·less** \-ləs\ *adj*

**[2]land** *vb*
**1** to go ashore or cause to go ashore from a ship
**2** to cause to reach or come to rest where planned ⟨*land* an arrow in the target⟩
**3** to catch and bring in ⟨*land* a fish⟩
**4** to get for oneself by trying ⟨*land* a job⟩
**5** to come down or bring down and settle on a surface ⟨*landed* on the moon⟩ ⟨*land* an airplane⟩

**land breeze** *n*
a breeze blowing toward the sea

**land·fill** \'land-,fil\ *n*
**1** a system of garbage and trash disposal in which trash and garbage are buried between layers of earth
**2** an area built up by such a landfill

**land·hold·er** \'land-,hōl-dər\ *n*
an owner of land

**land·ing** \'lan-ding\ *n*
**1** the act of one that lands

*lance*

**[1]lance:** a 15th-century painting of a knight on horseback holding a lance

a b c d e f g h i j k l m n o p q r s t u v w x y z

**2** a place for unloading or taking on passengers and cargo
**3** the level part of a staircase (as between flights of stairs)

**landing field** *n*
a field where aircraft land and take off

**landing strip** *n*
AIRSTRIP

**land·la·dy** \'land-ˌlād-ē\ *n, pl* **land·la·dies**
**1** a woman who owns land or houses that she rents
**2** a woman who runs an inn or rooming house

**land·locked** \'land-ˌläkt\ *adj*
**1** shut in or nearly shut in by land ⟨a *landlocked* harbor⟩
**2** kept from leaving fresh water by some barrier ⟨*landlocked* salmon⟩

**land·lord** \'land-ˌlȯrd\ *n*
**1** a man who owns land or houses that he rents
**2** a man who runs an inn or rooming house

**land·lub·ber** \'land-ˌləb-ər\ *n*
a person who lives on land and knows little or nothing about the sea

**land·mark** \'land-ˌmärk\ *n*
**1** ▶ something (as a building, a large tree, or a statue) that is easy to see and can help a person find the way to a place near it
**2** a very important event
**3** a building of historical importance

**land mine** *n*
a mine placed just below the surface of the ground and designed to be exploded by the weight of vehicles or troops passing over it

**land·own·er** \'lan-ˌdō-nər\ *n*
a person who owns land

**[1]land·scape** \'land-ˌskāp\ *n*
**1** a picture of natural scenery
**2** the land that can be seen in one glance

**[2]landscape** *vb* **land·scaped**; **land·scap·ing**
to improve the natural beauty of a piece of land

**land·slide** \'land-ˌslīd\ *n*
**1** the slipping down of a mass of rocks or earth on a steep slope
**2** the material that moves in a landslide
**3** the winning of an election by a very large number of votes

**lane** \'lān\ *n*
**1** a narrow path or road (as between fences or hedges) that is not used as a highway
**2** a special route (as for ships)
**3** a strip of road used for a single line of traffic

**lan·guage** \'lang-gwij\ *n*
**1** the words and expressions used and understood by a large group of people ⟨the English *language*⟩
**2** the speech of human beings
**3** a means of expressing ideas or feelings ⟨sign *language*⟩
**4** a formal system of signs and symbols that is used to carry information ⟨a computer *language*⟩
**5** the way in which words are used ⟨forceful *language*⟩
**6** the special words used by a certain group or in a certain field ⟨the *language* of science⟩
**7** the study of languages

**lan·guid** \'lang-gwəd\ *adj*
having very little strength or energy

**landmark 1:**
the Statue of Liberty, a famous US landmark, in New York City

**lan·guid·ly** *adv*
**lan·guid·ness** *n*

**lan·guish** \'lang-gwish\ *vb*
to become weak especially from a lack of something needed or wanted
**lan·guish·er** *n*
**lan·guish·ing** *adj*
**lan·guish·ing·ly** *adv*

**lan·guor** \'lang-gər\ *n*
**1** weakness or weariness of body or mind
**2** a state of dreamy idleness
**lan·guor·ous** *adj*
**lan·guor·ous·ly** *adv*

**lank** \'langk\ *adj*
**1** not well filled out **:** THIN ⟨*lank* cattle⟩
**2** hanging straight and limp without spring or curl ⟨*lank* hair⟩
**lank·ly** *adv*
**lank·ness** *n*

**lanky** \'lang-kē\ *adj* **lank·i·er**; **lank·i·est**
being very tall and thin
**lank·i·ly** \-kə-lē\ *adv*
**lank·i·ness** \-kē-nəs\ *n*

**lan·tern** \'lant-ərn\ *n*
▶ a usually portable lamp with a protective covering

**lantern:**
a barn lantern

**lan·yard** \'lan-yərd\ *n*
**1** a short rope or cord used as a fastening on ships
**2** a cord worn around the neck to hold a knife or whistle
**3** a strong cord with a hook at one end used in firing cannon

**[1]lap** \'lap\ *n*
the front part of a person between the waist and the knees when seated

**[2]lap** *vb* **lapped**; **lap·ping**
OVERLAP

**[3]lap** *n*
**1** a part of something that overlaps another part
**2** one time around a racetrack
**3** a stage in a trip

**[4]lap** *vb* **lapped**; **lap·ping**
**1** to scoop up food or drink with the tip of the tongue
**2** to splash gently

**[5]lap** *n*
the act or sound of lapping

**lap·dog** \'lap-,dȯg\ *n*
a dog small enough to be held in the lap

**la·pel** \lə-'pel\ *n*
the part of the front of a collar that is turned back ⟨coat *lapels*⟩

**lap·ful** \'lap-,fu̇l\ *n, pl* **lap·fuls** \-fu̇lz\ *or* **laps·ful** \'laps-,fu̇l\
as much as the lap can hold

**[1]lapse** \'laps\ *n*
**1** a slight error or slip ⟨a *lapse* of memory⟩
**2** a gradual falling away from a higher to a lower condition
**3** a gradual passing of time

**[2]lapse** *vb* **lapsed**; **laps·ing**
**1** to slip, pass, or fall gradually ⟨*lapse* into silence⟩
**2** to become little used ⟨a custom that had *lapsed*⟩
**3** to come to an end ⟨the car insurance *lapsed*⟩
**laps·er** *n*

**[1]lap·top** \'lap-,täp\ *adj*
small enough to fit on one's lap

**[2]laptop** *n*
a portable computer that is small enough to be used on one's lap, can run on battery power, and has the main parts (as keyboard and display screen) combined into a single unit

**lar·board** \'lär-bərd\ *n*
[3]PORT

**lar·ce·ny** \'lärs-n-ē\ *n, pl* **lar·ce·nies**
the unlawful taking of personal property without the owner's consent : THEFT

**Word History** The ancient Romans had a word for a soldier who served merely for pay and not for a cause. Many people did not think highly of such soldiers. They thought that a soldier like that was not much better than a thief. So the Romans made a new word that meant "theft." This word was based on the word for a hired soldier. The English word *larceny* comes from that old word in Latin.

**larch** \'lärch\ *n*
a tree related to the pine that sheds its needles each fall

**[1]lard** \'lärd\ *vb*
to smear or soil with grease

**[2]lard** *n*
a white soft fat from fatty tissue of the hog

**lar·der** \'lärd-ər\ *n*
a place where food is kept

**large** \'lärj\ *adj* **larg·er**; **larg·est**
more than most others of a similar kind in amount or size : BIG
**large·ness** *n*
**at large**
**1** not locked up : FREE ⟨the bank robbers are still *at large*⟩
**2** as a whole ⟨the public *at large*⟩
**3** representing a whole state or district ⟨a delegate-*at-large*⟩

**large–heart·ed** \'lärj-'härt-əd\ *adj*
GENEROUS 1

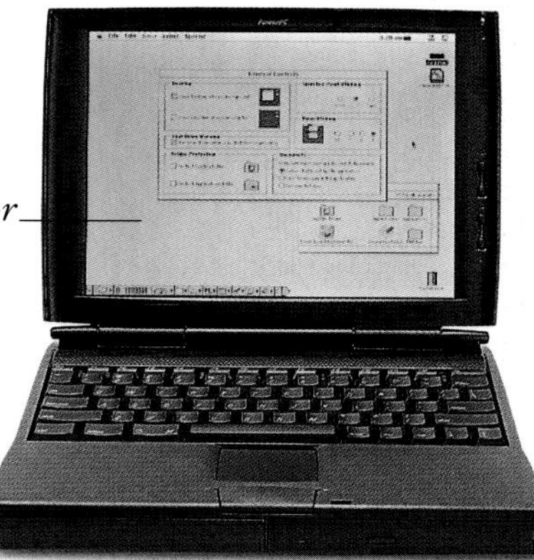


laptop

**large intestine** *n*
the wide lower part of the intestine from which water is absorbed and in which feces are made ready for passage

**large·ly** \'lärj-lē\ *adv*
MOSTLY, CHIEFLY

**lar·i·at** \'lar-ē-ət, 'ler-\ *n*
a long light rope used to catch livestock or tie up grazing animals

**[1]lark** \'lärk\ *n*
any of a group of mostly brownish songbirds of Europe and Asia

**[2]lark** *n*
something done for fun : PRANK

**lark·spur** \'lärk-,spər\ *n*
a tall branching plant related to the buttercups that is often grown for its stalks of showy blue, purple, pink, or white flowers

**lar·va** \'lär-və\ *n, pl* **lar·vae** \-vē\
**1** a wingless form (as a grub or caterpillar) in which many insects hatch from the egg
**2** an early form of any animal that at birth or hatching is very different from its parents

**Word History** Many insects have different forms at different times in their lives. A young moth, for instance, looks a bit like a worm. We may think of the different forms as masks of the insect. Scientists who thought this way gave the young form the name *larva*. This word comes from a Latin word which looked like English *larva*. This Latin word meant "mask" or "ghost."

**lar·yn·gi·tis** \,lar-ən-'jīt-əs\ *n*
inflammation of the larynx : a sore throat

**lar·ynx** \'lar-ingks\ *n, pl* **la·ryn·ges** \lə-'rin-,jēz\ *or* **lar·ynx·es**
the upper part of the windpipe that contains the vocal cords

**la·ser** \'lā-zər\ *n*
a device that produces a very powerful beam of light

**laser printer** *n*
a printer for computer output that produces high-quality images formed by a laser

**[1]lash** \'lash\ *vb*
**1** to move violently or suddenly
**2** to hit with a whip

**[2]lash** *n*
**1** a blow with a whip or switch
**2** the flexible part of a whip
**3** a sudden swinging blow
**4** EYELASH

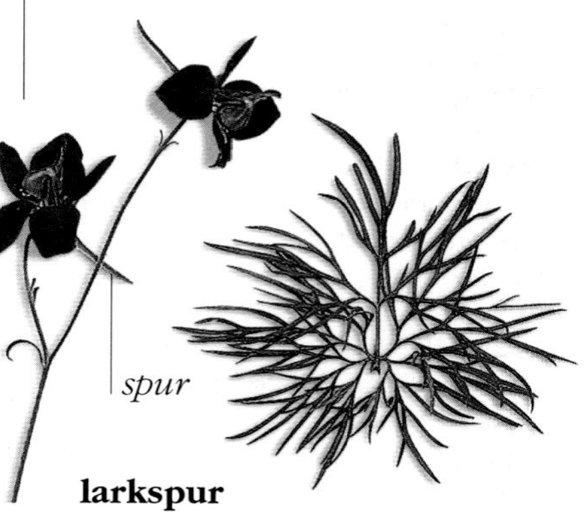


larkspur

**³lash** *vb*
to tie down with a rope or chain
**lash·ing** \'lash-ing\ *n*
something used for tying, wrapping, or fastening
**lass** \'las\ *n*
GIRL 1
**lass·ie** \'las-ē\ *n*
GIRL 1, LASS
**¹las·so** \'las-ō, la-'sü\ *vb*
to catch with a lasso
**²lasso** *n, pl* **lassos** *or* **lassoes**
a rope or long leather thong with a slipknot for catching animals
**¹last** \'last\ *vb*
**1** to go on ⟨the game *lasted* till dark⟩
**2** to stay in good condition ⟨the flowers *lasted* well⟩
**last·er** *n*
**²last** *adv*
**1** at the end
**2** most recently
**³last** *adj*
**1** following all the rest : FINAL
**2** most recent ⟨*last* week⟩
**3** lowest in rank or position
**4** most unlikely

**Synonyms** LAST and FINAL mean following all the others. LAST suggests being at the end of a series but it does not always suggest that the series is complete or permanently ended ⟨spent my *last* dollar on a ticket⟩. FINAL applies to something that positively closes a series and forever settles the matter ⟨the *final* game of the tennis championship⟩.

**⁵last** *n*
a person or thing that is last
**last·ing** \'las-ting\ *adj*
continuing for a long while
**last·ing·ly** *adv*
**last·ing·ness** *n*
**last·ly** \'last-lē\ *adv*
at or as the end
**¹latch** \'lach\ *n*
a movable piece that holds a door or gate closed
**²latch** *vb*
to fasten with a latch
**¹late** \'lāt\ *adj* **lat·er**; **lat·est**
**1** coming or remaining after the usual or proper time
**2** coming toward the end (as of the day or night) ⟨a *late* hour⟩

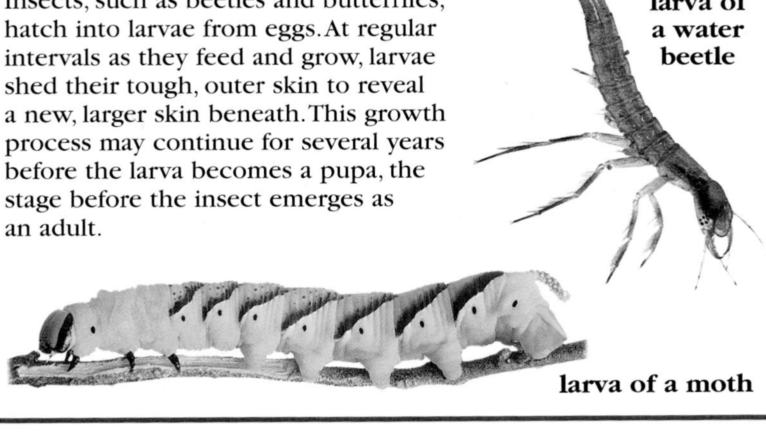


**larva 1**
Insects, such as beetles and butterflies, hatch into larvae from eggs. At regular intervals as they feed and grow, larvae shed their tough, outer skin to reveal a new, larger skin beneath. This growth process may continue for several years before the larva becomes a pupa, the stage before the insect emerges as an adult.

**3** having died or recently left a certain position ⟨the *late* king⟩
**4** RECENT 2
**late·ness** *n*
**²late** *adv* **lat·er**; **lat·est**
**1** after the usual or proper time
**2** LATELY
**late·com·er** \'lāt-ˌkəm-ər\ *n*
a person who arrives late
**late·ly** \'lāt-lē\ *adv*
not long ago : RECENTLY
**la·tent** \'lāt-nt\ *adj*
present but not visible or active ⟨*latent* infection⟩
**la·tent·ly** *adv*
**lat·er·al** \'lat-ə-rəl\ *adj*
being on or directed toward the side
**lat·er·al·ly** *adv*
**la·tex** \'lā-ˌteks\ *n*
**1** a milky plant juice that is the source of rubber
**2** a mixture of water and tiny particles of rubber or plastic used especially in paints
**lath** \'lath\ *n, pl* **laths** \'lathz, 'laths\
a thin strip of wood used (as in a wall or ceiling) as a base for plaster
**lathe** \'lāth\ *n*
a machine in which a piece of material is held and turned while being shaped by a tool
**¹lath·er** \'lath-ər\ *n*
**1** the foam made by stirring soap and water together
**2** foam from sweating
**²lather** *vb*
**1** to spread lather over
**2** to form a lather ⟨this soap *lathers* well⟩

**¹Lat·in** \'lat-n\ *adj*
**1** of or relating to the language of the ancient Romans ⟨*Latin* courses⟩
**2** of or relating to Latin America or the Latin Americans
**²Latin** *n*
**1** the language of the ancient Romans
**2** a member of a people whose language and customs have descended from the ancient Romans
**3** a person born or living in Latin America
**La·ti·na** \lə-'tē-nə\ *n*
a woman or girl born or living in Latin America or of Latin-American origin living in the United States
**Lat·in–Amer·i·can** \ˌlat-n-ə-'mer-ə-kən\ *adj*
of or relating to Latin America or its people
**Latin American** *n*
a person born or living in Latin America
**La·ti·no** \lə-'tē-nō\ *n, pl* **Latinos**
a person born or living in Latin America or of Latin-American origin living in the United States
**lat·i·tude** \'lat-ə-ˌtüd, -ˌtyüd\ *n*
**1** the distance north or south of the equator measured in degrees
**2** REGION 3 ⟨cold *latitudes*⟩
**3** freedom to act or speak as one wishes
**lat·ter** \'lat-ər\ *adj*
**1** relating to or coming near the end ⟨the *latter* stage of the job⟩
**2** of, relating to, or being the second of two things referred to

A B C D E F G H I J K L M N O P Q R S T U V W X Y Z

**lat·tice** \'lat-əs\ *n*
**1** a structure made of thin strips of wood or metal that cross each other to form a network
**2** ▼ a window or gate having a lattice

**lattice 2:** a 16th-century window from England

**[1]laud** \'lȯd\ *n*
[2]PRAISE 1, ACCLAIM

**[2]laud** *vb*
[1]PRAISE 1, ACCLAIM

**[1]laugh** \'laf, 'ȧf\ *vb*
to show amusement, joy, or scorn by smiling and making sounds (as chuckling) in the throat

**[2]laugh** *n*
the act or sound of laughing

**laugh·able** \'laf-ə-bəl, 'ȧf-\ *adj*
causing or likely to cause laughter
**laugh·able·ness** *n*
**laugh·ably** \-blē\ *adv*

**laugh·ing·stock** \'laf-ing-,stäk, 'ȧf-\ *n*
a person or thing that is made fun of

**laugh·ter** \'laf-tər, 'ȧf-\ *n*
the action or sound of laughing

**[1]launch** \'lȯnch\ *vb*
**1** [1]THROW 1, 2, HURL ⟨*launch* a spear⟩
**2** to set afloat ⟨*launch* a ship⟩
**3** to send off especially with force ⟨*launch* an aircraft⟩ ⟨*launch* a spacecraft⟩
**4** to give a start to ⟨*launch* a plan⟩

**[2]launch** *n*
an act of launching

**[3]launch** *n*
MOTORBOAT

**launch·pad** \'lȯnch-,pad\ *n*
▼ a nonflammable platform from which a rocket can be launched

**laun·der** \'lȯn-dər\ *vb*
to wash or wash and iron clothes
**laun·der·er** *n*

**laun·dress** \'lȯn-drəs\ *n*
a woman whose work is washing clothes

**laun·dry** \'lȯn-drē\ *n*, *pl* **laundries**
**1** clothes or linens that have been laundered or are to be laundered
**2** a place where laundering is done

**launchpad:** a French rocket on a launchpad

rocket
launchpad

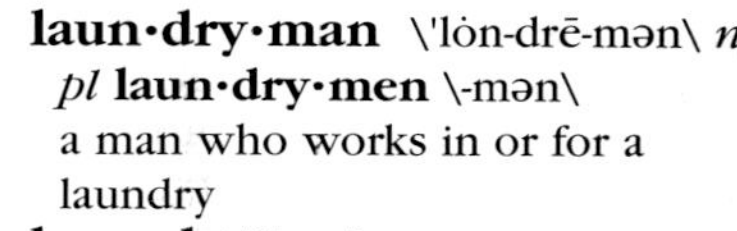

**laun·dry·man** \'lȯn-drē-mən\ *n*, *pl* **laun·dry·men** \-mən\
a man who works in or for a laundry

**lau·rel** \'lȯr-əl\ *n*
**1** a small evergreen European tree with shiny pointed leaves used in ancient times to crown victors (as in sports)
**2** any of various plants (as the American **mountain laurel**) that resemble the European laurel
**3** a crown of laurel used as a mark of honor

**lava 2:** a block of hardened lava

**la·va** \'läv-ə, 'lav-ə\ *n*
**1** melted rock coming from a volcano
**2** ▲ lava that has cooled and hardened

**lav·a·to·ry** \'lav-ə-,tōr-ē\ *n*, *pl* **lav·a·to·ries**
**1** a small sink (as in a bathroom)
**2** a room for washing that usually has a toilet
**3** TOILET 3

**lav·en·der** \'lav-ən-dər\ *n*
**1** ► a European mint with narrow somewhat woolly leaves and stalks of small sweet-smelling pale violet flowers
**2** a pale purple

**lavender 1**

**[1]lav·ish** \'lav-ish\ *adj*
**1** spending or giving more than is necessary **:** EXTRAVAGANT ⟨*lavish* with money⟩
**2** spent, produced, or given freely ⟨*lavish* gifts⟩
**lav·ish·ly** *adv*
**lav·ish·ness** *n*

**Word History** *Lavish* comes from an early English noun *lavish* that meant "plenty." This noun came from a French word that meant "a heavy rain." This French word can be traced back to a Latin verb that meant "to wash." Other English words that come from this Latin verb are *deluge, launder, laundry*, and *lavatory*.

[2]**lavish** *vb*
to spend, use, or give freely

**law** \'lȯ\ *n*
**1** a rule of conduct or action that a nation or a group of people agrees to follow
**2** a whole collection of established rules ⟨the *law* of the land⟩
**3** a rule or principle that always works the same way under the same conditions ⟨the *law* of gravity⟩
**4** a bill passed by a legislative group
**5** [2]POLICE
**6** *cap* the first part of the Jewish scriptures
**7** trial in court ⟨go to *law*⟩
**8** the profession of a lawyer

**law–abid·ing** \'lȯ-ə-,bīd-iŋ\ *adj*
obeying the law

**law·break·er** \'lȯ-,brā-kər\ *n*
a person who breaks the law

**law·ful** \'lȯ-fəl\ *adj*
**1** permitted by law
**2** approved by law
**law·ful·ly** \-fə-lē\ *adv*
**law·ful·ness** *n*

**law·less** \'lȯ-ləs\ *adj*
**1** having no laws : not based on or controlled by law ⟨a *lawless* frontier society⟩
**2** uncontrolled by law : UNRULY ⟨a *lawless* mob⟩
**law·less·ly** *adv*
**law·less·ness** *n*

**law·mak·er** \'lȯ-,mā-kər\ *n*
one who takes part in writing and passing laws : LEGISLATOR
**law·mak·ing** \-,mā-kiŋ\ *adj or n*

**lawn** \'lȯn, 'län\ *n*
ground (as around a house) covered with grass that is kept mowed

**lawn mower** *n*
▶ a machine used to mow the grass on lawns

**lawn tennis** *n*
TENNIS

**law·suit** \'lȯ-,süt\ *n*
a complaint brought before a court of law for decision

**law·yer** \'lȯ-yər, 'lȯi-ər\ *n*
a person whose profession is to handle lawsuits for people or to give advice about legal rights and duties

**lax** \'laks\ *adj*
**1** not firm or tight : LOOSE
**2** not stern or strict ⟨*lax* discipline⟩
**lax·ly** *adv*
**lax·ness** *n*

[1]**lax·a·tive** \'lak-sət-iv\ *adj*
helpful against constipation

[2]**laxative** *n*
a laxative medicine that is nearly always mild

[1]**lay** \'lā\ *vb* **laid** \'lād\; **lay·ing**
**1** to bring down (as with force) ⟨crops *laid* flat by the gale⟩
**2** to put down ⟨*laid* my hat on the table⟩
**3** to produce an egg
**4** to cause to disappear ⟨*laid* my fears⟩
**5** to spread over a surface ⟨*lay* a pavement⟩
**6** PREPARE 1, ARRANGE ⟨*lay* plans⟩
**7** to put to : APPLY ⟨*laid* the watch to my ear⟩

[2]**lay** *n*
the way a thing lies in relation to something else ⟨the *lay* of the land⟩

[3]**lay** *past of* LIE

**lay·away** \'lā-ə-,wā\ *n*
something held for a customer until the price is paid

**lay away** *vb*
to put aside for later use or delivery

**lay·er** \'lā-ər\ *n*
**1** one that lays something
**2** one thickness of something laid over another

**lay in** *vb*
to store for later use

**lay·man** \'lā-mən\ *n, pl* **lay·men** \-mən\
**1** a person who is not a member of the clergy
**2** a person who is not a member of a certain profession

**lay off** *vb*
**1** to stop employing (a person) usually temporarily
**2** to let alone

**lay·out** \'lā-,au̇t\ *n*
[1]PLAN 1, ARRANGEMENT

**lay out** \lā-'au̇t\ *vb*
**1** to plan in detail
**2** ARRANGE 1, DESIGN

**lay up** *vb*
**1** to store up
**2** to be confined by illness or injury

**la·zy** \'lā-zē\ *adj* **la·zi·er**; **la·zi·est**
**1** not willing to act or work
**2** [1]SLOW 3, SLUGGISH ⟨a *lazy* stream⟩
**la·zi·ly** \-zə-lē\ *adv*
**la·zi·ness** \-zē-nəs\ *n*

**leach** \'lēch\ *vb*
**1** to treat (as earth) with a liquid (as water) to remove something soluble
**2** to remove (as a soluble salt) by leaching

[1]**lead** \'lēd\ *vb* **led** \'led\; **lead·ing**
**1** to guide on a way often by going ahead
**2** to be at the head of ⟨*lead* the class⟩
**3** to go through : LIVE ⟨*lead* a happy life⟩
**4** to reach or go in a certain direction ⟨this road *leads* to town⟩

**lawn mower:**
a gasoline-powered lawn mower

**²lead** *n*
**1** position at the front ⟨take the *lead*⟩
**2** the distance that a person or thing is ahead
**3** the first part of a news story

**³lead** \'led\ *n*
**1** a heavy soft gray metallic element that is easily bent and shaped
**2** AMMUNITION 1 ⟨a shower of *lead*⟩
**3** a long thin piece of graphite used in pencils

**lead·en** \'led-n\ *adj*
**1** made of lead
**2** heavy as lead
**3** dull gray
**lead·en·ly** *adv*
**lead·en·ness** *n*

**lead·er** \'lēd-ər\ *n*
one that leads or is able to lead
**lead·er·ship** \-,ship\ *n*

**¹leaf** \'lēf\ *n,*
*pl* **leaves** \'lēvz\
**1** ▼ one of the usually flat green parts that grow from a plant stem and that together make up the foliage
**2** FOLIAGE ⟨trees in full *leaf*⟩

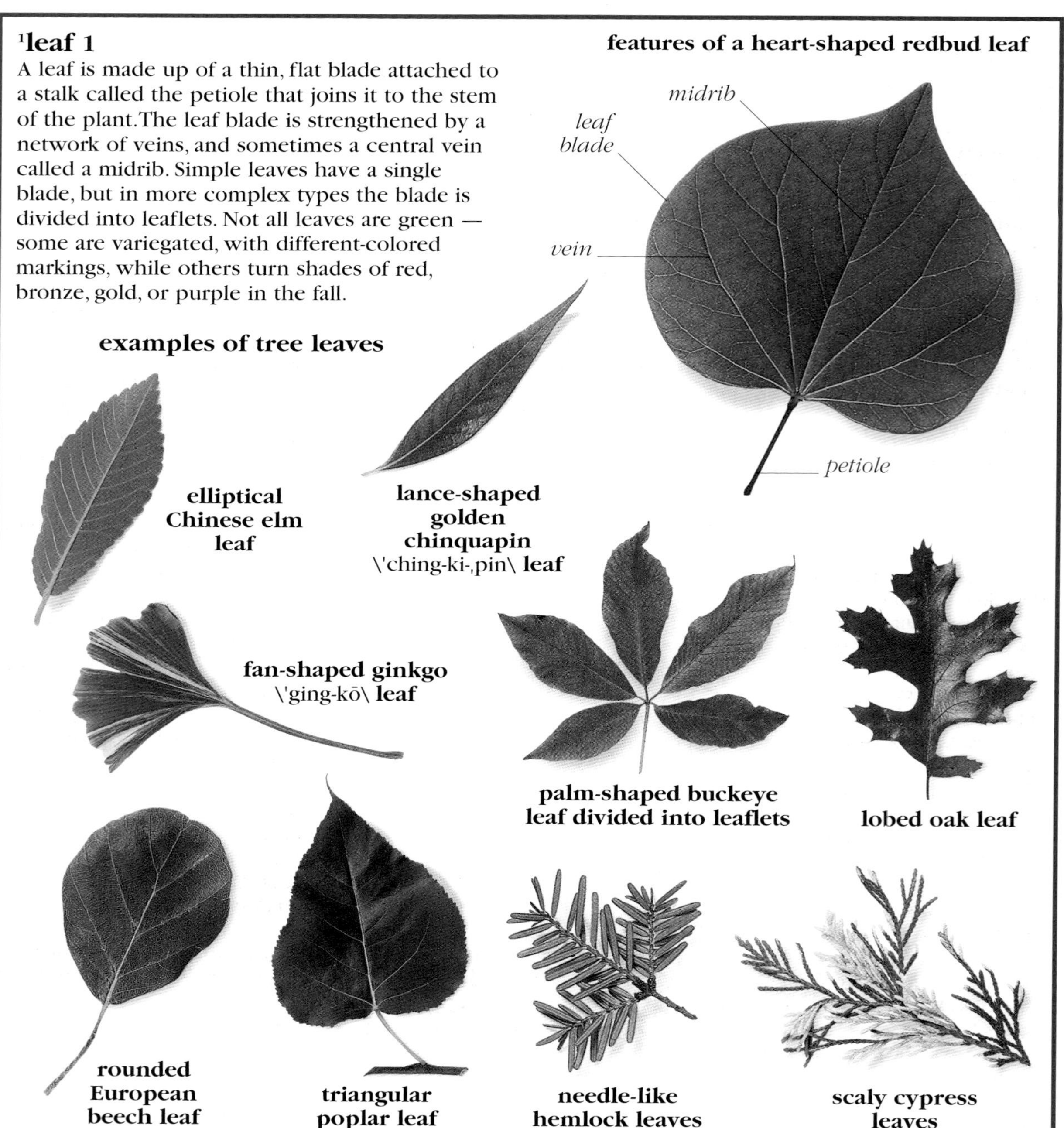

**¹leaf 1**
A leaf is made up of a thin, flat blade attached to a stalk called the petiole that joins it to the stem of the plant. The leaf blade is strengthened by a network of veins, and sometimes a central vein called a midrib. Simple leaves have a single blade, but in more complex types the blade is divided into leaflets. Not all leaves are green — some are variegated, with different-colored markings, while others turn shades of red, bronze, gold, or purple in the fall.
**features of a heart-shaped redbud leaf**
midrib
leaf blade
vein
petiole
**examples of tree leaves**
**elliptical Chinese elm leaf**
**lance-shaped golden chinquapin** \'ching-ki-,pin\ **leaf**
**fan-shaped ginkgo** \'ging-kō\ **leaf**
**palm-shaped buckeye leaf divided into leaflets**
**lobed oak leaf**
**rounded European beech leaf**
**triangular poplar leaf**
**needle-like hemlock leaves**
**scaly cypress leaves**

3 a single sheet of a book making two pages
4 a movable part of a table top
**leaf·less** \'lē-fləs\ *adj*
**leaf·like** \'lē-,flīk\ *adj*

[2]**leaf** *vb*
1 to grow leaves ⟨trees *leafing* out in spring⟩
2 to turn the leaves of a book

**leaf·let** \'lē-flət\ *n*
1 a young or small leaf
2 a division of a compound leaf
3 PAMPHLET

**leaf·stalk** \'lēf-,stȯk\ *n*
PETIOLE

**leafy** \'lē-fē\ *adj* **leaf·i·er**; **leaf·i·est**
having, covered with, or like leaves

[1]**league** \'lēg\ *n*
1 a group of nations working together for a common purpose
2 an association of persons or groups with common interests or goals
3 [1]CLASS 7 ⟨out of one's *league*⟩

[2]**league** *vb* **leagued**; **leagu·ing**
to form a league

[1]**leak** \'lēk\ *vb*
1 to enter or escape or let enter or escape usually by accident ⟨fumes *leaking* in⟩
2 to make or become known

[2]**leak** *n*
1 a crack or hole that accidentally lets fluid in or out
2 something that accidentally or secretly causes or permits loss
3 the act of leaking : LEAKAGE

**leak·age** \'lē-kij\ *n*
1 the act or process of leaking
2 the thing or amount that leaks

**leaky** \'lē-kē\ *adj* **leak·i·er**; **leak·i·est**
letting fluid leak in or out
**leak·i·ness** *n*

[1]**lean** \'lēn\ *vb*
1 to bend or tilt from a straight position ⟨a tree that *leans* badly⟩ ⟨*lean* the ladder against the wall⟩
2 to bend and rest one's weight on ⟨*lean* on me⟩
3 DEPEND 1, RELY
4 to tend or move toward in opinion, taste, or desire

[2]**lean** *adj*
1 having too little flesh : SKINNY ⟨*lean* cattle⟩
2 containing little fat ⟨*lean* meat⟩
3 not large or plentiful ⟨a *lean* harvest⟩
**lean·ness** *n*

---

**Synonyms** LEAN, THIN, SKINNY mean not having a great amount of flesh. LEAN suggests a lack of unnecessary flesh and may also suggest the tough, muscular frame of an athlete ⟨the hard, *lean* body of a runner⟩. THIN applies to a person having not much flesh or fat and often having an amount less than is desirable for good health ⟨a *thin* and sickly child⟩. SKINNY suggests a bony, noticeably thin appearance that may indicate poor nourishment ⟨*skinny* stray cats⟩.

---

**lean–to** \'lēn-,tü\ *n, pl* **lean–tos**
1 a building that has a roof with only one slope and is usually joined to another building
2 a rough shelter held up by posts, rocks, or trees

[1]**leap** \'lēp\ *vb* **leaped** *or* **leapt** \'lēpt, 'lept\; **leap·ing** \'lē-ping\
1 to jump or cause to jump from a surface ⟨*leaped* from the chair⟩
2 to move, act, or pass quickly
**leap·er** \'lē-pər\ *n*

[2]**leap** *n*
1 an act of leaping : JUMP
2 a place leaped over
3 a distance leaped

[1]**leash:** a woman holding a dog on a leash

leash

**leap·frog** \'lēp-,frȯg, -,fräg\ *n*
a game in which one player bends down and another leaps over

**leap year** *n*
a year of 366 days with February 29 as the extra day

**learn** \'lərn\ *vb* **learned** \'lərnd\ *also* **learnt** \'lərnt\; **learn·ing**
1 to get knowledge of or skill in (by studying or practicing) ⟨*learn* algebra⟩
2 MEMORIZE
3 to become able through practice ⟨a baby *learning* to walk⟩
4 to find out ⟨*learned* the news⟩
5 to gain knowledge ⟨children eager to *learn*⟩

**learned** \'lər-nəd\ *adj*
having or showing knowledge or learning

**learn·ing** \'lər-ning\ *n*
1 the act of a person who learns
2 knowledge or skill gained from teaching or study **synonyms** see INFORMATION

**learning disability** *n*
any of various conditions (as attention deficit disorder and dyslexia) that make learning difficult
**learning disabled** *adj*

[1]**lease** \'lēs\ *n*
1 an agreement by which a person exchanges property (as real estate) for a period of time for rent or services
2 the period of time for which property is leased
3 a piece of property that is leased

[2]**lease** *vb* **leased**; **leas·ing**
to give or get the use of (property) in return for services or rent

[1]**leash** \'lēsh\ *n*
◀ a line for leading or holding an animal

[2]**leash** *vb*
to put on a leash

[1]**least** \'lēst\ *adj*
smallest in size or degree

[2]**least** *n*
the smallest or lowest amount or degree ⟨doesn't mind in the *least*⟩

[3]**least** *adv*
in or to the smallest degree

**leath·er** \'leth-ər\ *n*
1 the tanned skin of an animal
2 something made of leather

**leath·ery** \'leth-ə-rē\ *adj*
like leather

**[1]leave** \'lēv\ *vb* **left** \'left\; **leav·ing**
**1** to fail to include or take along ⟨*left* my books at home⟩
**2** to have remaining ⟨a wound that *left* a scar⟩ ⟨taking 7 from 10 *leaves* 3⟩
**3** to give by will ⟨*left* property to the children⟩
**4** to let stay without interference ⟨*leave* them alone⟩
**5** to go away from ⟨*leave* the house⟩
**6** to give up
**7** DELIVER 2 ⟨agreed to *leave* the package on the way home⟩

**[2]leave** *n*
**1** PERMISSION ⟨ask *leave* to be absent⟩
**2** permitted absence from one's duty or work
**3** the act of leaving and saying good-bye ⟨take *leave* of a friend⟩
**4** a period of time during which a person is allowed to be absent from duties

**leaved** \'lēvd\ *adj* having leaves

**leaves** *pl of* LEAF

**leav·ings** \'lē-vingz\ *n pl* things remaining

**[1]lec·ture** \'lek-chər\ *n*
**1** a talk that teaches something
**2** a severe scolding

**[2]lecture** *vb* **lec·tured**; **lec·tur·ing**
**1** to give a lecture
**2** [2]SCOLD
**lec·tur·er** *n*

**led** *past of* LEAD

**LED** \,el-,ē-'dē\ *n* an electronic device that emits light when power is supplied to it

**ledge** \'lej\ *n*
**1** a piece projecting from a top or an edge like a shelf ⟨the outer *ledge* of a window⟩
**2** SHELF 2

**[1]lee** \'lē\ *n*
**1** a protecting shelter
**2** the side (as of a ship) sheltered from the wind

**[2]lee** *adj* of or relating to the lee

**leech** \'lēch\ *n*
**1** a bloodsucking worm related to the earthworm
**2** a person who clings like a leech to another person for what can be gained

---

**Word History** At first the English word *leech* meant "doctor." Many years ago doctors thought that a good way to cure sick people was to make them bleed. They thought that the blood of a sick person had harmful things in it that would flow away with the blood. To take bad blood out of sick people, early doctors often used little worms that suck blood. Soon *leech*, the word for a doctor, was used for these worms as well.

---

**leek** \'lēk\ *n* ▶ a garden plant grown for its thick stems which taste like a mild onion

**leek** with trimmed leaves

**[1]leer** \'lir\ *vb* to look with a leer

**[2]leer** *n* a mean or nasty glance

**leery** \'lir-ē\ *adj* SUSPICIOUS 2, WARY

**[1]lee·ward** \'lē-wərd\ *n* the lee side ⟨sail to the *leeward* of the buoy⟩

**[2]leeward** *adj* located away from the wind ⟨the *leeward* side of the house⟩

**[1]left** \'left\ *adj*
**1** on the same side of the body as the heart ⟨the *left* leg⟩
**2** located nearer to the left side of the body than to the right ⟨the *left* side of the road⟩

**[2]left** *n* the left side or the part on the left side

**[3]left** *past of* LEAVE

**left–hand** \'left-'hand\ *adj*
**1** located on the left
**2** LEFT-HANDED

**left–hand·ed** \'left-'han-dəd\ *adj*
**1** using the left hand better or more easily than the right
**2** done or made with or for the left hand

**left·over** \'lef-,tō-vər\ *n* something left over ⟨we had *leftovers* for supper⟩

**lefty** \'lef-tē\ *n, pl* **left·ies** a left-handed person

**leg** \'leg\ *n*
**1** ▶ one of the limbs of an animal or person that support the body and are used in walking and running
**2** the part of the leg between the knee and the foot

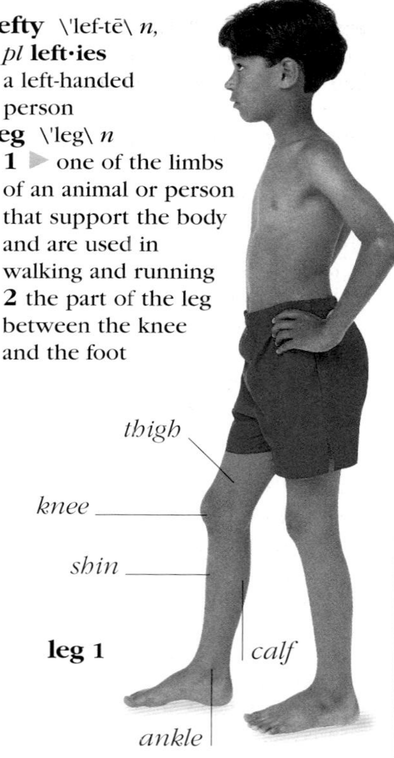


**leg 1**

**3** something like a leg in shape or use ⟨the *legs* of a table⟩
**4** the part of a garment that covers the leg
**5** a stage or part of a journey ⟨the first *leg* of a trip⟩

**leg·a·cy** \'leg-ə-sē\ *n, pl* **leg·a·cies** something left to a person by or as if by a will

**le·gal** \'lē-gəl\ *adj*
**1** of or relating to law or lawyers ⟨*legal* books⟩
**2** based on law ⟨a *legal* right⟩
**3** allowed by law or rules ⟨*legal* conduct⟩ ⟨a *legal* play in a game⟩
**le·gal·ly** *adv*

**le·gal·i·ty** \li-'gal-ət-ē\ *n, pl* **le·gal·i·ties** the quality or state of being legal

**le·gal·ize** \'lē-gə-,līz\ *vb* **le·gal·ized**; **le·gal·iz·ing** to make legal ⟨*legalized* gambling⟩
**le·gal·iza·tion** \,lē-gə-lə-'zā-shən\ *n*

**leg·end** \'lej-ənd\ *n*
**1** an old story that is widely believed but cannot be proved to be true
**2** writing or a title on an object
**3** a list of symbols used (as on a map)

**leg·end·ary** \'lej-ən-ˌder-ē\ *adj* of, relating to, or like a legend

**leg·ged** \'leg-əd, 'legd\ *adj* having legs

**leg·ging** \'leg-ən, 'leg-ing\ *n* an outer covering for the leg usually of cloth or leather ⟨a pair of *leggings*⟩

**leg·i·ble** \'lej-ə-bəl\ *adj* clear enough to be read
**leg·i·bly** \-blē\ *adv*

**le·gion** \'lē-jən\ *n*
**1** a group of from 3000 to 6000 soldiers that made up the chief army unit in ancient Rome
**2** ARMY 1
**3** a very great number ⟨has a *legion* of admirers⟩

**leg·is·late** \'lej-ə-ˌslāt\ *vb*
**leg·is·lat·ed**; **leg·is·lat·ing** to make laws
**leg·is·la·tor** \-ər\ *n*

**leg·is·la·tion** \ˌlej-ə-'slā-shən\ *n*
**1** the action of making laws
**2** the laws that are made

**leg·is·la·tive** \'lej-ə-ˌslāt-iv\ *adj*
**1** having the power or authority to make laws
**2** of or relating to legislation
**leg·is·la·tive·ly** *adv*

**leg·is·la·ture** \'lej-ə-ˌslā-chər\ *n* a body of persons having the power to make, change, or cancel laws

**le·git·i·ma·cy** \li-'jit-ə-mə-sē\ *n* the quality or state of being legitimate

**le·git·i·mate** \li-'jit-ə-mət\ *adj*
**1** accepted by the law as rightful : LAWFUL ⟨a *legitimate* heir⟩
**2** being right or acceptable ⟨a *legitimate* excuse⟩
**le·git·i·mate·ly** *adv*

**leg·less** \'leg-ləs\ *adj* having no legs

**le·gume** \'leg-ˌyüm\ *n* any of a large group of plants (as peas, beans, and clover) with fruits that are pods and root nodules containing bacteria that fix nitrogen

**lei·sure** \'lē-zhər\ *n*
**1** freedom from work ⟨a time of *leisure*⟩
**2** time that is free for use as one wishes

**lei·sure·ly** \'lē-zhər-lē\ *adj* UNHURRIED ⟨a *leisurely* walk⟩

**lem·on** \'lem-ən\ *n*
**1** ▼ an oval yellow fruit with a sour juice that is related to the orange and grows on a small spiny tree
**2** something unsatisfactory : DUD

**lemon 1**

**lem·on·ade** \ˌlem-ə-'nād\ *n* a drink made of lemon juice, sugar, and water

**lend** \'lend\ *vb* **lent** \'lent\; **lend·ing**
**1** ²LOAN 1
**2** to give usually for a time ⟨*lend* help to flood victims⟩
**3** to make a loan or loans
**lend·er** *n*

**length** \'length\ *n*
**1** the measured distance from one end to the other of the longer or longest side of an object
**2** a measured distance ⟨three meters in *length*⟩
**3** amount of time something takes ⟨the *length* of a visit⟩
**4** the sound of a vowel or syllable as it is affected by the time needed to pronounce it
**5** a piece of something that is long ⟨a *length* of pipe⟩
**at length**
**1** very fully ⟨tell a story *at length*⟩
**2** at the end

**length·en** \'leng-thən\ *vb* to make or become longer ⟨*lengthen* a dress⟩

**length·ways** \'length-ˌwāz\ *adv* LENGTHWISE

**length·wise** \'length-ˌwīz\ *adv or adj* in the direction of the length ⟨fold the paper *lengthwise*⟩ ⟨a *lengthwise* fold⟩

**lengthy** \'leng-thē\ *adj*
**length·i·er**; **length·i·est** very long ⟨a *lengthy* argument⟩
**length·i·ly** \-thə-lē\ *adv*
**length·i·ness** \-thē-nəs\ *n*

**le·nient** \'lē-nē-ənt, 'lēn-yənt\ *adj* being kind and patient ⟨a *lenient* teacher⟩
**le·nient·ly** *adv*

**lens** \'lenz\ *n*
**1** a clear curved piece of material (as glass) used to bend the rays of light to form an image
**2** a part of the eye that focuses rays of light so as to form clear images

**lent** *past of* LEND

**len·til** \'lent-l\ *n* the flattened round edible seed of a plant related to the pea

**Leo** \'lē-ō\ *n*
**1** a constellation between Cancer and Virgo imagined as a lion
**2** the fifth sign of the zodiac or a person born under this sign

**leop·ard** \'lep-ərd\ *n* ▼ a large cat of Asia and Africa that has a brownish buff coat with black spots

**leopard**

**leop·ard·ess** \'lep-ərd-əs\ *n* a female leopard

**le·o·tard** \'lē-ə-ˌtärd\ *n* a tight one-piece garment worn by dancers or acrobats

**le·sion** \'lē-zhən\ *n* an abnormal spot or area of the body caused by sickness or injury

**[1]less** \'les\ *adj*
**1** being fewer ⟨*less* than ten people showed up⟩
**2** of lower rank, degree, or importance
**3** not so much **:** a smaller amount of ⟨we need *less* talk and more work⟩

**[2]less** *adv*
not so much or so well ⟨*less* difficult⟩

**[3]less** *n*
**1** a smaller number or amount
**2** a thing that is poorer than another ⟨of two evils choose the *less*⟩

**[4]less** *prep*
[1]MINUS 1 ⟨the regular price *less* a discount⟩

**-less** \ləs\ *adj suffix*
**1** not having ⟨friend*less*⟩
**2** not able to be acted on or to act in a specified way ⟨cease*less*⟩

**less·en** \'les-n\ *vb*
to make or become less

**[1]less·er** \'les-ər\ *adj*
of smaller size or importance

**[2]lesser** *adv*
[2]LESS ⟨*lesser*-known writers⟩

**les·son** \'les-n\ *n*
**1** a part of the Scripture read in a church service
**2** a reading or exercise assigned for study
**3** something learned or taught

**lest** \,lest\ *conj*
for fear that ⟨tied the dog *lest* it should escape⟩

**let** \'let\ *vb* **let**; **let·ting**
**1** to cause to **:** MAKE ⟨*let* it be known⟩
**2** to give use of in return for payment ⟨rooms to *let*⟩
**3** to allow or permit to ⟨*let* them go⟩
**4** to allow to go or pass ⟨*let* me through⟩ **synonyms** see HIRE

**-let** \lət\ *n suffix*
**1** small one ⟨book*let*⟩
**2** something worn on ⟨ank*let*⟩

**let·down** \'let-,daůn\ *n*
DISAPPOINTMENT 2

**let down** \let-'daůn\ *vb*
**1** DISAPPOINT ⟨don't *let* me *down*⟩
**2** RELAX 3

**let on** *vb*
**1** ADMIT 3
**2** PRETEND 1

**let's** \lets\
let us

**[1]let·ter** \'let-ər\ *n*
**1** one of the marks that are symbols for speech sounds in writing or print and that make up the alphabet
**2** ▶ a written or printed communication (as one sent through the mail)
**3 letters** *pl* LITERATURE 2
**4** the strict or outward meaning ⟨the *letter* of the law⟩
**5** the initial of a school awarded to a student usually for athletic achievement

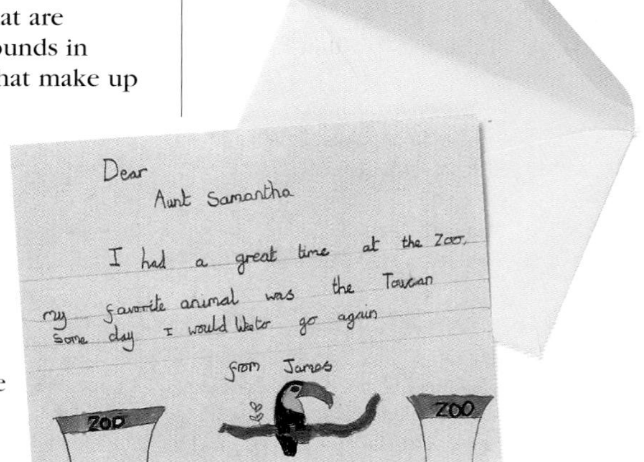


**[1]letter 2:** a thank-you letter from a young child

**[2]letter** *vb*
to mark with letters

**letter carrier** *n*
a person who delivers mail

**let·ter·head** \'let-ər-,hed\ *n*
**1** stationery having a printed or engraved heading
**2** the heading of a letterhead

**let·ter·ing** \'let-ə-ring\ *n*
letters used in an inscription

**let·tuce** \'let-əs\ *n*
▼ a garden plant related to the daisies that has large crisp leaves eaten in salad

**lettuce:** a head of iceberg lettuce

**Word History** Many kinds of lettuce have a milky white juice. Lettuce owes its name to this fact. The Latin name for lettuce, from which we get English *lettuce*, came from the Latin word for milk.

**let up** \let-'əp\ *vb*
**1** to slow down
**2** [1]STOP 4, CEASE ⟨the rain *let up*⟩

**leu·ke·mia** \lü-'kē-mē-ə\ *n*
a dangerous disease in which too many white blood cells are formed

**le·vee** \'lev-ē\ *n*
**1** a bank built along a river to prevent flooding
**2** a landing place along a river

**[1]lev·el** \'lev-əl\ *n*
**1** a device used (as by a carpenter) to find a horizontal line or surface
**2** a horizontal line or surface usually at a named height ⟨hold it at eye *level*⟩
**3** a step or stage in height, position, or rank ⟨rose to the *level* of manager⟩

**[2]level** *vb* **lev·eled** *or* **lev·elled**; **lev·el·ing** *or* **lev·el·ling**
to make or become level, flat, or even
**lev·el·er** *or* **lev·el·ler** *n*

**[3]level** *adj*
**1** having a flat even surface ⟨a *level* lawn⟩
**2** HORIZONTAL ⟨in a *level* position⟩
**3** of the same height or rank **:** EVEN
**4** steady and cool in judgment ⟨people with *level* heads⟩
**lev·el·ly** *adv*
**lev·el·ness** *n*

**Synonyms** LEVEL, FLAT, EVEN mean having a surface without bends, curves, or interruptions. LEVEL applies especially to a surface or a line that does not slant up or down ⟨a *level* road between two hills⟩.

FLAT applies to a surface that is free from curves or bumps or hollows whether or not it is parallel to the ground ⟨a *flat* work surface⟩. EVEN stresses the lack of breaks or bumps in a line or surface but need not suggest that the object is level or straight ⟨trimmed the top of the hedge to make it *even*⟩.

**¹le·ver** \'lev-ər, 'lē-vər\ *n*
**1** a bar used to pry or move something
**2** a stiff bar for lifting a weight at one point of its length by pressing or pulling at a second point while the bar turns on a support
**3** a bar or rod used to run or adjust something ⟨a gearshift *lever*⟩

**²lever** *vb*
to raise or move with a lever

**lev·i·tate** \'lev-ə-,tāt\ *vb* **lev·i·tat·ed**; **lev·i·tat·ing**
to rise or make rise up in the air

**¹levy** \'lev-ē\ *n, pl* **lev·ies**
**1** a collection (as of taxes) by authority of the law
**2** the calling of troops into service
**3** something (as taxes) collected by authority of the law

**²levy** *vb* **lev·ied**; **levy·ing**
**1** to collect legally ⟨*levy* taxes⟩
**2** to raise or collect troops for service

**li·a·ble** \'lī-ə-bəl\ *adj*
**1** forced by law or by what is right to make good ⟨we are *liable* for damage that we do⟩
**2** not sheltered or protected (as from danger or accident)
**3** LIKELY 1 ⟨it's *liable* to rain soon⟩

**li·ar** \'lī-ər\ *n*
a person who tells lies

**¹li·bel** \'lī-bəl\ *n*
something spoken or written that hurts a person's good name

**²libel** *vb* **li·beled** *or* **li·belled**; **li·bel·ing** *or* **li·bel·ling**
to hurt by a libel
**li·bel·er** *or* **li·bel·ler** *n*

**lib·er·al** \'lib-ə-rəl, 'lib-rəl\ *adj*
**1** not stingy : GENEROUS ⟨a *liberal* giver⟩
**2** being more than enough ⟨a *liberal* spending allowance⟩
**3** not strict
**4** BROAD 4 ⟨a *liberal* education⟩
**lib·er·al·ly** *adv*

**lib·er·ate** \'lib-ə-,rāt\ *vb* **lib·er·at·ed**; **lib·er·at·ing**
to set free

**lib·er·ty** \'lib-ərt-ē\ *n, pl* **lib·er·ties**
**1** the state of those who are free and independent : FREEDOM
**2** freedom to do what one pleases ⟨give a child some *liberty*⟩
**3** the state of not being busy : LEISURE
**4** behavior or an act that is too free ⟨take *liberties* with the truth⟩

**Li·bra** \'lē-brə, 'lī-\ *n*
**1** a constellation between Virgo and Scorpio imagined as a pair of scales
**2** the seventh sign of the zodiac or a person born under this sign

**li·brar·i·an** \lī-'brer-ē-ən\ *n*
a person in charge of a library

**li·brary** \'lī-,brer-ē\ *n, pl* **li·brar·ies**
**1** a place where especially literary or reference materials (as books, manuscripts, recordings, or films) are kept for use but not for sale
**2** a collection of such materials

**lice** *pl of* LOUSE

**¹li·cense** *or* **li·cence** \'līs-ns\ *n*
**1** permission granted by qualified authority to do something
**2** a paper showing legal permission ⟨a driver's *license*⟩
**3** liberty of action that is carried too far

**²license** *or* **licence** *vb* **li·censed** *or* **li·cenced**; **li·cens·ing** *or* **li·cenc·ing**
to permit or authorize by license

**li·chen** \'lī-kən\ *n*
▼ a plant made up of an alga and a fungus growing together

**lichen** growing on a rock

**¹lick** \'lik\ *vb*
**1** to pass the tongue over ⟨*lick* a spoon⟩
**2** to touch or pass over like a tongue ⟨flames *licking* a wall⟩
**3** to hit again and again : BEAT
**4** to get the better of
**lick·ing** *n*

**²lick** *n*
**1** the act of licking
**2** a small amount ⟨never did a *lick* of work⟩
**3** a place (**salt lick**) where salt is found on the top of the ground and animals come to lick it up

**lick·e·ty–split** \,lik-ət-ē-'split\ *adv*
at top speed

**lic·o·rice** \'lik-ə-rish, -rəs\ *n*
**1** the dried root of a European plant related to the peas or a juice from it used in medicine and in candy
**2** ▼ candy flavored with licorice

**licorice 2**

**lid** \'lid\ *n*
**1** a movable cover ⟨the *lid* of a box⟩
**2** EYELID
**lid·ded** \'lid-əd\ *adj*
**lid·less** \'lid-ləs\ *adj*

**¹lie** \'lī\ *vb* **lay** \'lā\; **lain** \'lān\; **ly·ing** \'lī-ing\
**1** to stretch out or be stretched out (as on a bed or on the ground)
**2** to be spread flat so as to cover ⟨snow *lying* on the fields⟩
**3** to be located or placed ⟨Ohio *lies* east of Indiana⟩
**4** to be or stay ⟨the book *lies* on the table⟩

**²lie** *vb* **lied**; **ly·ing**
to make a statement that one knows to be untrue

**³lie** *n*
something said or done in the hope of deceiving : an untrue statement

**¹liege** \'lēj\ *adj*
**1** having the right to receive service and loyalty ⟨*liege* lord⟩
**2** owing or giving service to a lord

A B C D E F G H I J K L M N O P Q R S T U V W X Y Z

**²liege** *n*
**1** VASSAL 1
**2** a feudal lord

**lieu·ten·ant** \lü-'ten-ənt\ *n*
**1** an official who acts for a higher official
**2** a first lieutenant or second lieutenant (as in the Army)
**3** a commissioned officer in the Navy or Coast Guard ranking above a lieutenant junior grade

**lieutenant colonel** *n*
a commissioned officer in the Army, Air Force, or Marine Corps ranking above a major

**lieutenant commander** *n*
a commissioned officer in the Navy or Coast Guard ranking above a lieutenant

**lieutenant general** *n*
a commissioned officer in the Army, Air Force, or Marine Corps ranking above a major general

**lieutenant junior grade** *n*
a commissioned officer in the Navy or Coast Guard ranking above an ensign

**life** \'līf\ *n, pl* **lives** \līvz\
**1** the quality that separates plants and animals from such things as water or rock **:** the quality that plants and animals lose when they die
**2** all the experiences that make up the existence of a person **:** the course of existence ⟨I never heard of such a thing in my *life*⟩
**3** BIOGRAPHY
**4** the period during which a person or thing is alive or exists
**5** a way of living ⟨the *life* of the ant⟩
**6** a living being ⟨many *lives* being saved by quick action⟩
**7** ¹SPIRIT 5 ⟨put a lot of *life* into the dance⟩

**life belt** *n*
a life preserver worn like a belt

**life·boat** \'līf-,bōt\ *n*
a sturdy boat (as one carried by a ship) for use in an emergency and especially for saving lives at sea

**life buoy** *n*
▶ life preserver in the shape of a ring

**life·guard** \'līf-,gärd\ *n*
a guard employed at a beach or swimming pool to protect swimmers from drowning

**life jacket** *n*
a life preserver in the form of a vest

**life·less** \'lī-fləs\ *adj*
having no life

**life·like** \'lī-,flīk\ *adj*
very like something that is alive

**life·long** \'lī-,flȯng\ *adj*
continuing through life ⟨a *lifelong* friendship⟩

**life preserver** *n*
a device (as a life jacket or life buoy) designed to save a person from drowning by keeping the person afloat

**life raft** *n*
a raft usually made of wood or an inflatable material for use by people forced into the water

**life·sav·er** \'līf-,sā-vər\ *n*
a person trained in lifesaving

**life·sav·ing** \'līf-,sā-ving\ *n*
the methods that can be used to save lives especially of drowning persons ⟨took a course in *lifesaving*⟩

**life–size** \'līf-'sīz\ *or* **life–sized** \-'sīzd\ *adj*
of natural size **:** having the same size as the original ⟨a *life-size* portrait⟩

**life·style** \'līf-'stī(ə)l\ *n*
the usual way of life of a person, group, or society **:** the way we live ⟨an active *lifestyle*⟩

**life·time** \'līf-,tīm\ *n*
LIFE 4

**life vest** *n*
LIFE JACKET

**¹lift** \'lift\ *vb*
**1** to raise from a lower to a higher position, rate, or amount
**2** to rise from the ground ⟨planes *lifting* from the runway⟩
**3** to move upward and disappear or become scattered ⟨the haze *lifted* when the sun rose⟩
**lift·er** *n*

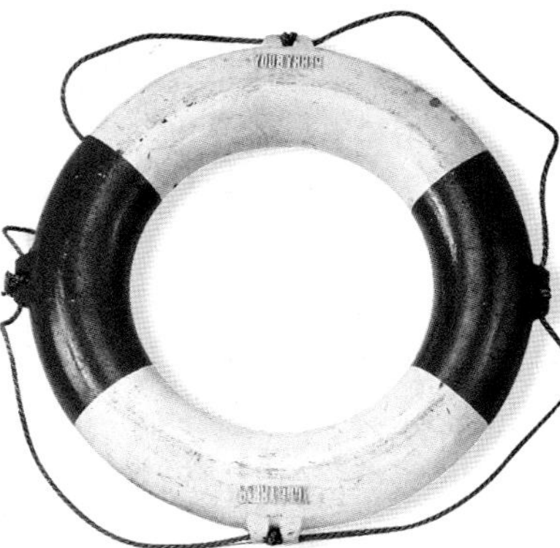

**life buoy**

**Synonyms** LIFT, RAISE, HOIST mean to move from a lower to a higher place or position. LIFT suggests a bringing up especially from the ground and also the need for exertion in order to pick up something heavy ⟨*lift* those boxes onto the table⟩. RAISE often suggests a suitable or intended higher position to which something is brought ⟨*raise* the flag a little higher⟩. HOIST often suggests the use of pulleys to increase the force applied in raising something very heavy ⟨*hoist* the crates onto the ship⟩.

**²lift** *n*
**1** the amount that may be lifted at one time **:** LOAD
**2** the action or an instance of lifting
**3** help especially in the form of a ride ⟨give a person a *lift*⟩
**4** *chiefly British* ELEVATOR 2
**5** an upward force (as on an airplane wing) that opposes the pull of gravity

**liftoff** \'lif-,tȯf\ *n*
a vertical takeoff (as by a rocket)

**lig·a·ment** \'lig-ə-mənt\ *n*
a tough band of tissue or fibers that holds bones together or keeps an organ in place in the body

**¹light** \'līt\ *n*
**1** the bright form of energy given off by something (as the sun) that lets one see objects
**2** a source (as a lamp) of light
**3** DAYLIGHT 1
**4** public knowledge ⟨facts brought to *light*⟩
**5** something that helps one to know or understand ⟨the teacher's explanation threw *light* on the problem⟩

**²light** *adj*
**1** having light **:** BRIGHT ⟨a *light* room⟩
**2** not dark or deep in color

**³light** *vb* **light·ed** *or* **lit** \'lit\; **light·ing**
**1** to make or become bright

**lighthouse**
under George Washington Bridge, New York City

2 to burn or cause to burn ⟨*light* the gas⟩
3 to lead with a light ⟨*light* a guest up the stairs⟩

**[4]light** *adj*
1 having little weight : not heavy
2 not strong or violent ⟨a *light* breeze⟩
3 not hard to bear, do, pay, or digest ⟨*light* punishment⟩
4 active in motion ⟨*light* on my feet⟩
5 not severe ⟨a *light* case of measles⟩
6 free from care : HAPPY ⟨a *light* heart⟩
7 intended mainly to entertain ⟨*light* verse⟩
**light·ly** *adv*
**light·ness** *n*

**[5]light** *adv*
with little baggage ⟨travel *light*⟩

**[6]light** *vb* **light·ed** *or* **lit** \'lit\; **light·ing**
1 [2]PERCH, SETTLE ⟨a bird *lighting* on a twig⟩
2 to come by chance ⟨*light* on a solution⟩

**light bulb** *n*
INCANDESCENT LAMP

**[1]light·en** \'līt-n\ *vb*
1 to make or become light or lighter : BRIGHTEN
2 to grow bright with lightning
**light·en·er** *n*

**[2]lighten** *vb*
to make or become less heavy
**light·en·er** *n*

**light·face** \'līt-ˌfās\ *n*
a type having light thin lines
**light·faced** \-ˌfāst\ *adj*

**light·heart·ed** \'līt-'härt-əd\ *adj*
free from worry
**light·heart·ed·ly** *adv*
**light·heart·ed·ness** *n*

**light·house** \'līt-ˌhau̇s\ *n*
◀ a tower with a powerful light at the top that is built on the shore to guide sailors at night

**light·ing** \'līt-ing\ *n*
supply of light or of lights ⟨the only *lighting* came through a small window⟩

**light·ning** \'līt-ning\ *n*
▶ the flashing of light caused by the passing of electricity from one cloud to another or between a cloud and the earth

**lightning:**
forked lightning over San Francisco, California

**lightning bug** *n*
FIREFLY

**light·proof** \'līt-'prüf\ *adj*
not letting in light ⟨*lightproof* box⟩

**light·weight** \'līt-ˌwāt\ *adj*
having less than the usual or expected weight

**light–year** \'līt-ˌyir\ *n*
a unit of length in astronomy equal to the distance that light travels in one year or 9,458,000,000,000 kilometers

**lik·able** *or* **like·able** \'lī-kə-bəl\ *adj*
easily liked
**lik·able·ness** *n*

**[1]like** \'līk\ *vb* **liked**; **lik·ing**
1 to have a liking for : ENJOY ⟨*likes* games⟩
2 to feel toward : REGARD ⟨how do you *like* snow⟩
3 CHOOSE 3, PREFER ⟨did as they *liked*⟩

**[2]like** *n*
LIKING, PREFERENCE ⟨*likes* and dislikes are very personal things⟩

**[3]like** *adj*
1 SIMILAR, ALIKE ⟨the twins are very *like*⟩
2 similar to or to that of — used after the word modified ⟨wolves are dog*like* animals⟩ ⟨a life*like* statue⟩

**[4]like** *prep*
1 similar or similarly to ⟨you're not *like* the rest of them⟩ ⟨they act *like* fools⟩
2 typical of ⟨it is just *like* them to leave without paying⟩
3 likely to ⟨looks *like* rain⟩
4 such as ⟨a subject *like* arithmetic⟩

**[5]like** *n*
[3]EQUAL, COUNTERPART ⟨never saw their *like* before⟩

**[6]like** *conj*
1 AS IF ⟨it looks *like* it might rain⟩
2 in the same way that : [2]AS 2 ⟨sounds just *like* I do⟩

**like·li·hood** \'līk-lē-ˌhu̇d\ *n*
PROBABILITY 1 ⟨in all *likelihood* we will go⟩

a b c d e f g h i j k l m n o p q r s t u v w x y z

**[1]like·ly** \'lī-klē\ *adj*
**1** very possibly going to happen ⟨that bomb is *likely* to explode⟩
**2** seeming to be the truth **:** BELIEVABLE ⟨a *likely* story⟩
**3** giving hope of turning out well **:** PROMISING ⟨a *likely* spot for a picnic⟩ **synonyms** see POSSIBLE
**like·li·ness** *n*

**[2]likely** *adv*
without great doubt

**lik·en** \'lī-kən\ *vb*
COMPARE 1

**like·ness** \'līk-nəs\ *n*
**1** the state of being like **:** RESEMBLANCE
**2** a picture of a person **:** PORTRAIT

**like·wise** \'lī-,kwīz\ *adv*
**1** in like manner ⟨do *likewise*⟩
**2** ALSO ⟨you *likewise*⟩

**lik·ing** \'lī-king\ *n*
a being pleased with someone or something

**li·lac** \'lī-lək, -,lak, -,läk\ *n*
**1** a bush having clusters of fragrant grayish pink, purple, or white flowers
**2** a medium purple

**lilt** \'lilt\ *vb*
to sing or play in a lively cheerful manner
**lilt·ing·ly** *adv*

**lily** \'lil-ē\ *n, pl* **lil·ies**
▼ a plant (as the **Easter lily** or the **tiger lily**) with a leafy stem that grows from a bulb and has funnel-shaped flowers

**lily:**
a tiger lily

**lily of the valley**
a low plant related to the lilies that has usually two leaves and a stalk of fragrant flowers shaped like bells

**li·ma bean** \,lī-mə-\ *n*
a bean with flat pale green or white seeds

**limb** \'lim\ *n*
**1** any of the paired parts (as an arm, wing, or leg) of an animal that stick out from the body and are used mostly in moving or grasping
**2** a large branch of a tree
**limbed** \'limd\ *adj*
**limb·less** \'lim-ləs\ *adj*

**[1]lim·ber** \'lim-bər\ *adj*
bending easily
**lim·ber·ly** *adv*
**lim·ber·ness** *n*

**[2]limber** *vb*
to make or become limber ⟨*limber* up with exercises⟩

**[1]lime** \'līm\ *n*
a white substance made by heating limestone or shells that is used in making plaster and cement and in farming

**[2]lime** *vb* **limed**; **lim·ing**
to treat or cover with lime ⟨*lime* a garden⟩

**[3]lime** *n*
a small greenish yellow fruit that is related to the lemon and orange

**lim·er·ick** \'lim-ə-rik\ *n*
a humorous poem five lines long

**lime·stone** \'līm-,stōn\ *n*
▶ a rock formed chiefly from animal remains (as shells or coral) that is used in building and gives lime when burned

**lime·wa·ter** \'līm-,wȯt-ər, -,wät-\ *n*
a colorless water solution that contains calcium and turns white when carbon dioxide is blown through it

**[1]lim·it** \'lim-ət\ *n*
**1** a boundary line ⟨the city *limits*⟩
**2** a point beyond which a person or thing cannot go

**[2]limit** *vb*
to set limits to ⟨*limit* expenses⟩

**lim·i·ta·tion** \,lim-ə-'tā-shən\ *n*
**1** an act or instance of limiting
**2** the quality or state of being limited

**lim·it·less** \'lim-ət-ləs\ *adj*
having no limits

**[1]limp** \'limp\ *vb*
to walk lamely

**[2]limp** *n*
a limping movement or gait

**[3]limp** *adj*
not firm or stiff
**limp·ly** *adv*
**limp·ness** *n*

**limy** \'lī-mē\ *adj* **lim·i·er**; **lim·i·est**
containing lime or limestone

**lin·den** \'lin-dən\ *n*
a shade tree with heart-shaped toothed leaves, drooping clusters of yellowish white flowers, and hard fruits like peas

**[1]line** \'līn\ *n*
**1** a long thin cord ⟨fishing *lines*⟩
**2** a pipe carrying a fluid (as steam, water, or oil)
**3** an outdoor wire carrying electricity for a telephone or power company
**4** a row of letters or words across a page or column
**5 lines** *pl* the words of a part in a play
**6** the direction followed by something in motion ⟨the *line* of flight of an arrow⟩

**limestone**

**7** the boundary or limit of a place or lot ⟨the town *line*⟩
**8** the track of a railway
**9** AGREEMENT 1, HARMONY ⟨bring their ideas into *line*⟩
**10** a course of behavior or thought ⟨a liberal political *line*⟩
**11** FAMILY 1 ⟨born of a royal *line*⟩
**12** a system of transportation ⟨a bus *line*⟩
**13** a long narrow mark (as one drawn by a pencil)
**14** the football players whose positions are along the line of scrimmage
**15** a geometric element produced by moving a point **:** a set of points
**16** [1]OUTLINE 1, CONTOUR ⟨a ship's *lines*⟩

**17** a plan for making or doing something ⟨a story along these *lines*⟩

**[2]line** *vb* **lined**; **lin·ing**
**1** to mark with a line or lines
**2** to place or be placed in a line along
**3** to form a line **:** form into lines

**[3]line** *vb* **lined**; **lin·ing**
to cover the inner surface of ⟨*line* a coat⟩

**lin·eage** \'lin-ē-ij\ *n*
**1** the ancestors from whom a person is descended
**2** people descended from the same ancestor

**lin·ear** \'lin-ē-ər\ *adj*
**1** of, relating to, or like a line **:** STRAIGHT
**2** involving a single dimension

**lin·en** \'lin-ən\ *n*
**1** smooth strong cloth or yarn made from flax
**2** household articles (as tablecloths or sheets) or clothing (as shirts or underwear) once often made of linen

**line of scrimmage**
an imaginary line in football parallel to the goal lines and running through the place where the ball is laid before each play begins

**[1]lin·er** \'lī-nər\ *n*
▼ a ship or airplane of a regular transportation line ⟨an ocean *liner*⟩

**[2]liner** *n*
one that lines or is used to line something

**line segment** *n*
SEGMENT 3

**line·up** \'lī-,nəp\ *n*
**1** a line of persons arranged especially for police identification
**2** a list of players taking part in a game (as baseball)

**-ling** \ling\ *n suffix*
**1** one associated with ⟨nest*ling*⟩
**2** young, small, or minor one ⟨duck*ling*⟩

**lin·ger** \'ling-gər\ *vb*
to be slow in leaving **:** DELAY

**linnet**

**lin·guist** \'ling-gwəst\ *n*
**1** a person skilled in languages
**2** a person who specializes in linguistics

**lin·guis·tics** \ling-'gwis-tiks\ *n*
the study of human speech including the units, nature, structure, and development of language, languages, or a language

**lin·i·ment** \'lin-ə-mənt\ *n*
a liquid medicine rubbed on the skin (as to ease pain)

**lin·ing** \'lī-ning\ *n*
material that lines an inner surface ⟨a coat *lining*⟩

**[1]link** \'lingk\ *n*
**1** a single ring of a chain
**2** something that connects ⟨evidence for a *link* between dinosaurs and birds⟩
**3** HYPERLINK ⟨*links* to other Web sites⟩

**[2]link** *vb*
to join with or as if with links ⟨towns *linked* by a road⟩ ⟨*linked* to the crime⟩

**linking verb** *n*
an intransitive verb that links a subject with a word or words in the predicate ⟨"look" in "you look tired" and "are" in "my favorite fruits are apples and oranges" are *linking verbs*⟩

**lin·net** \'lin-ət\ *n*
◄ a common small European finch often kept as a cage bird

**Word History** Linnets eat seeds, and they are especially fond of the seeds of flax plants. This liking for flax seeds has given the birds their name. The word *linnet* comes from the Latin word for flax. *Linen*, the English name for a cloth made from flax, comes from the same Latin word.

**li·no·leum** \lə-'nō-lē-əm, -'nōl-yəm\ *n*
a floor covering with a canvas back and a surface of hardened linseed oil and usually cork dust

**lin·seed** \'lin-,sēd\ *n*
FLAXSEED

**linseed oil** *n*
a yellowish oil obtained from flaxseed

**lint** \'lint\ *n*
**1** loose bits of thread
**2** [1]COTTON 1

**lin·tel** \'lint-l\ *n*
a horizontal piece or part across the top of an opening (as of a door) to carry the weight of the structure above it

**[1]liner:**
model of an ocean liner

*portbole*
*lifeboat*

A B C D E F G H I J K L M N O P Q R S T U V W X Y Z

lion

cub

lioness

**lions:** a family of lions

**li·on** \'lī-ən\ *n*
▲ a large flesh-eating animal of the cat family that has a brownish buff coat, a tufted tail, and in the male a shaggy mane and that lives in Africa and southern Asia

**li·on·ess** \'lī-ə-nəs\ *n*
a female lion

**lip** \'lip\ *n*
**1** either of the two folds of flesh that surround the mouth
**2** an edge (as of a flower or a wound) like or of flesh
**3** the edge of a hollow container especially where it is slightly spread out
**lip·less** \-ləs\ *adj*
**lip·like** \-,līk\ *adj*
**lipped** \'lipt\ *adj*

**lip·stick** \'lip-,stik\ *n*
a waxy solid colored cosmetic for the lips usually in stick form

**liq·ue·fy** \'lik-wə-,fī\ *vb*
**liq·ue·fied**; **liq·ue·fy·ing**
to make or become liquid

**[1]liq·uid** \'lik-wəd\ *adj*
**1** flowing freely like water
**2** neither solid nor gaseous
**3** like liquid in clearness or smoothness ⟨large *liquid* eyes⟩
**4** made up of or easily changed into cash
**liq·uid·ly** *adv*
**liq·uid·ness** *n*

**[2]liquid** *n*
a liquid substance

**liq·uor** \'lik-ər\ *n*
**1** a liquid substance or solution ⟨*liquor* from boiled meat⟩
**2** a strong alcoholic beverage (as whiskey)

**[1]lisp** \'lisp\ *vb*
to pronounce the sounds \s\ and \z\ as \th\ and \th\

**[2]lisp** *n*
the act or habit of lisping

**[1]list** \'list\ *n*
a leaning over to one side

**[2]list** *vb*
to lean to one side ⟨a *listing* ship⟩

**[3]list** *n*
a record or catalog of names or items

**[4]list** *vb*
to put into a list

**lis·ten** \'lis-n\ *vb*
**1** to pay attention in order to hear
**2** to give heed : follow advice
**lis·ten·er** \'lis-nər, -n-ər\ *n*

**list·less** \'list-ləs\ *adj*
too tired or too little interested to want to do things
**list·less·ly** *adv*
**list·less·ness** *n*

**lit** *past of* LIGHT

**li·ter** \'lēt-ər\ *n*
a metric unit of liquid capacity equal to 1.057 quarts

**lit·er·al** \'lit-ə-rəl\ *adj*
**1** following the ordinary or usual meaning of the words ⟨the *literal* meaning of a passage⟩
**2** true to fact ⟨a *literal* account⟩
**lit·er·al·ly** *adv*
**lit·er·al·ness** *n*

**lit·er·ary** \'lit-ə-,rer-ē\ *adj*
of or relating to literature

**lit·er·ate** \'lit-ə-rət\ *adj*
**1** well educated : WELL-BRED
**2** able to read and write

**lit·er·a·ture** \'lit-ə-rə-,chu̇r\ *n*
**1** written works having excellence of form or expression and ideas of lasting and widespread interest
**2** written material (as of a period or on a subject)

**lithe** \'līth, 'līth\ *adj*
[1]LIMBER, SUPPLE
**lithe·ly** *adv*
**lithe·ness** *n*

**lith·o·sphere** \'lith-ə-,sfir\ *n*
the outer part of the solid earth

**lit·mus paper** \'lit-məs-\ *n*
paper treated with coloring matter that turns red in acid solutions and blue in alkaline solutions

**[1]lit·ter** \'lit-ər\ *n*
**1** a covered and curtained couch having poles and used for carrying a single passenger
**2** a stretcher for carrying a sick or wounded person
**3** material spread out like a bed in places where farm animals (as cows or chickens) are kept to soak up their urine and feces
**4** ▼ the young born to an animal at a single time ⟨a *litter* of pigs⟩
**5** a messy collection of things scattered about : RUBBISH

**[1]litter 4:** a pig with her litter of piglets

**Word History** At first the English word *litter* meant "bed." It came from a Latin word that meant "bed." English *litter* does not mean "bed" any longer, but the different meanings of *litter* all come from the meaning "bed." A covered couch that a person is carried on is rather like a bed. So is a stretcher. Straw spread out as a bed for an animal is called *litter*. So are the young animals born at one time on such a bed. And trash scattered about might remind someone of the scattered straw of an animal's bed. This is called *litter* too.

**²litter** *vb*
**1** to cover with litter ⟨*litter* a road⟩
**2** to scatter about in disorder

**lit·ter·bug** \'lit-ər-,bəg\ *n*
one that litters a public area

**¹lit·tle** \'lit-l\ *adj* **lit·tler** \'lit-lər\ *or* **less** \'ləs\; **lit·tlest** \'lit-ləst\ *or* **least** \'lēst\
**1** small in size ⟨*little* feet⟩
**2** small in quantity ⟨*little* food to eat⟩
**3** small in importance ⟨concerned with *little* matters⟩
**4** NARROW-MINDED, MEAN ⟨people with *little* minds⟩
**5** short in duration or extent ⟨had *little* time left⟩
**lit·tle·ness** *n*

**²little** *adv* **less** \'les\; **least** \'lēst\
in a very small quantity or degree

**³little** *n*
a small amount or quantity

**Little Dipper** *n*
▶ a group of seven stars in the northern sky arranged in a form like a dipper with the North Star forming the tip of the handle

**li·tur·gi·cal** \lə-'tər-ji-kəl\ *adj*
of, relating to, or like liturgy

**lit·ur·gy** *n, pl* **lit·ur·gies**
a religious rite or body of rites

**¹live** \'liv\ *vb* **lived**; **liv·ing**
**1** to be alive
**2** to continue in life ⟨*live* to a great age⟩
**3** DWELL 2
**4** to pass one's life ⟨*live* peacefully⟩
**live it up** to live with great enthusiasm and excitement

**²live** \'līv\ *adj*
**1** not dead : ALIVE
**2** burning usually without flame ⟨*live* coals⟩
**3** not exploded ⟨a *live* cartridge⟩
**4** of present and continuing interest
**5** charged with an electric current
**6** broadcast at the time of production ⟨a *live* television program⟩

**live·li·hood** \'līv-lē-,hu̇d\ *n*
²LIVING 3 ⟨an honest *livelihood*⟩

**live·long** \,liv-,lȯng\ *adj*
during all of ⟨we worked the *livelong* day⟩

**live·ly** \'līv-lē\ *adj* **live·li·er**; **live·li·est**
**1** full of life : ACTIVE ⟨a *lively* puppy⟩
**2** KEEN 4 ⟨a *lively* interest⟩
**3** full of spirit or feeling : ANIMATED ⟨*lively* music⟩
**live·li·ness** *n*

**liv·en** \'lī-vən\ *vb*
to make or become lively

**live oak** \'lī-,vōk\ *n*
any of several American oaks that have evergreen leaves

**liv·er** \'liv-ər\ *n*
a large gland of vertebrates (as fishes and humans) that has a rich blood supply, secretes bile, and helps in storing some nutrients and in forming some body wastes

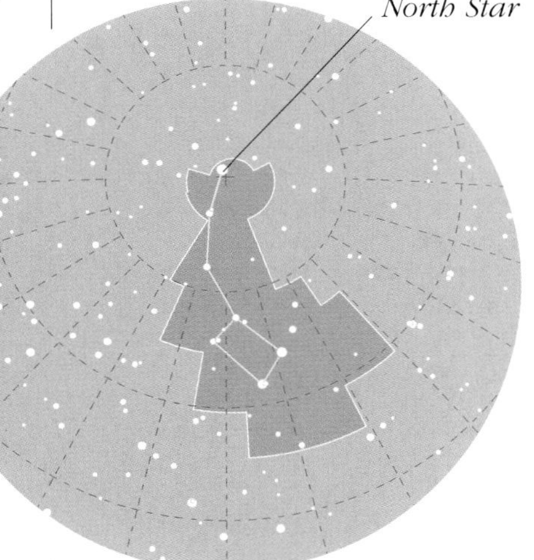


**Little Dipper:**
diagram showing the Little Dipper

**liv·er·ied** \'liv-ə-rēd\ *adj*
wearing a livery

**liv·er·wort** \'liv-ər-,wərt, -,wȯrt\ *n*
▼ any of a group of flowerless plants that are somewhat like mosses

**liverwort**

**liv·ery** \'liv-ə-rē, 'liv-rē\ *n, pl* **liv·er·ies**
**1** a special uniform worn by the servants of a wealthy household ⟨a footman in *livery*⟩
**2** the clothing worn to distinguish an association of persons ⟨the *livery* of a school⟩
**3** the care and stabling of horses for pay
**4** the keeping of horses and vehicles for hire or a place (**livery stable**) engaged in this

**lives** *pl of* LIFE

**live·stock** \'līv-,stäk\ *n*
animals kept or raised especially on a farm and for profit

**live wire** *n*
an alert active forceful person

**liv·id** \'liv-əd\ *adj*
**1** discolored by bruising
**2** pale as ashes ⟨*livid* with rage⟩
**liv·id·ly** *adv*
**liv·id·ness** *n*

**¹liv·ing** \'liv-ing\ *adj*
**1** not dead : ALIVE ⟨*living* authors⟩
**2** ACTIVE 4 ⟨*living* faith⟩
**3** true to life ⟨the *living* image of your parents⟩

**²living** *n*
**1** the condition of being alive
**2** conduct or manner of life
**3** what one has to have to meet one's needs ⟨made a *living* as a cook⟩

**living room** *n*
a room in a house for general family use

**liz·ard** \'liz-ərd\ *n*
▶ any of a group of reptiles having movable eyelids, ears that are outside the body, and usually four legs

**lla·ma** \'lä-mə\ *n*
▶ a South American hoofed animal that chews the cud

**lo** \'lō\ *interj*
used to call attention or to show wonder or surprise

**¹load** \'lōd\ *n*
**1** something taken up and carried : BURDEN
**2** a mass or weight supported by something
**3** something that depresses the mind or spirits
**4** a charge for a firearm
**5** the quantity of material loaded into a device at one time

**²load** *vb*
**1** to put a load in or on ⟨*load* a truck⟩
**2** to supply abundantly ⟨*load* a person with honors⟩
**3** to put a load into ⟨*load* film into a camera⟩
**load·er** *n*

**¹loaf** \'lōf\ *n, pl* **loaves** \'lōvz\
**1** a usually oblong mass of bread
**2** a dish (as of meat) baked in the form of a loaf

**²loaf** *vb*
to spend time idly or lazily
**loaf·er** *n*

**loam** \'lōm\ *n*
a soil having the right amount of silt, clay, and sand for good plant growth

**loamy** \'lō-mē\ *adj*
made up of or like loam

**¹loan** \'lōn\ *n*
**1** money loaned at interest
**2** something loaned for a time to a borrower
**3** permission to use something for a time

**²loan** *vb*
**1** to give to another for temporary use with the understanding that the same or a like thing will be returned ⟨*loan* a book⟩
**2** LEND 3

**loath** *or* **loth** \'lōth, 'lō<u>th</u>\ *adj*
not willing

**llama:** a man from Peru with a llama

**loathe** \'lō<u>th</u>\ *vb* **loathed**; **loath·ing**
to dislike greatly

**loathing** *n*
very great dislike

**loath·some** \'lōth-səm, 'lō<u>th</u>-\ *adj*
very unpleasant : OFFENSIVE
**loath·some·ly** *adv*
**loath·some·ness** *n*

**loaves** *pl of* LOAF

**¹lob** \'läb\ *vb* **lobbed**; **lob·bing**
to send (as a ball) in a high arc by hitting or throwing easily

**²lob** *n*
a lobbed throw or shot (as in tennis)

**lob·by** \'läb-ē\ *n, pl* **lobbies**
a hall or entry especially when large enough to serve as a waiting room ⟨a hotel *lobby*⟩

**lobe** \'lōb\ *n*
a rounded part ⟨the *lobe* of the ear⟩
**lobed** \'lōbd\ *adj*

**lob·ster** \'läb-stər\ *n*
a large edible sea crustacean with five pairs of legs of which the first pair usually has large claws

**¹lo·cal** \'lō-kəl\ *adj*
**1** of or relating to position in space
**2** relating to a particular place ⟨*local* news⟩
**lo·cal·ly** *adv*

**²local** *n*
**1** a public vehicle (as a bus or train) that makes all or most stops on its run
**2** a local branch (as of a lodge or labor union)

**local area network** *n*
a computer network that covers a small area (as an office building or a home)

**lo·cal·i·ty** \lō-'kal-ət-ē\ *n, pl* **lo·cal·i·ties**
a place and its surroundings

**lo·cal·ize** \'lō-kə-,līz\ *vb* **lo·cal·ized**; **lo·cal·iz·ing**
to make or become local

**lo·cate** \'lō-,kāt\ *vb* **lo·cat·ed**; **lo·cat·ing**
**1** to state and fix exactly the place or limits of ⟨*locate* a mining claim⟩
**2** to settle or establish in a locality
**3** to look and find the position of ⟨*locate* a city on the map⟩

**lo·ca·tion** \lō-'kā-shən\ *n*
**1** the act or process of locating
**2** a place fit for some use (as a building)

**¹lock** \'läk\ *n*
a small bunch of hair or of fiber (as cotton or wool)

**²lock** *n*
**1** a fastening (as for a door) in which a bolt is operated (as by a key)
**2** the device for exploding the charge or cartridge of a firearm
**3** an enclosure (as in a canal) with gates at each end used in raising or lowering boats as they pass from level to level

**³lock** *vb*
**1** to fasten with or as if with a lock
**2** to shut in or out by or as if by means of a lock
**3** to make fast by the linking of parts together

**lock·er** \'läk-ər\ *n*
a cabinet, compartment, or chest for personal use or for storing frozen food at a low temperature

**lock·et** \'läk-ət\ *n*
a small ornamental case usually worn on a chain

**lock·jaw** \'läk-,jȯ\ *n*
TETANUS

## lizard

More than half of the world's reptiles are lizards, and they live in habitats as varied as mountains, seashores, deserts, and rain forests. Cold-blooded reptiles, many lizards enjoy basking in the sun — although there are also lizards that live underground or prefer to be active at night. Some lizards eat plants, but most feed on small animals such as insects. Lizards vary greatly in size, and there are even species, such as glass snakes, that have no legs and resemble snakes.

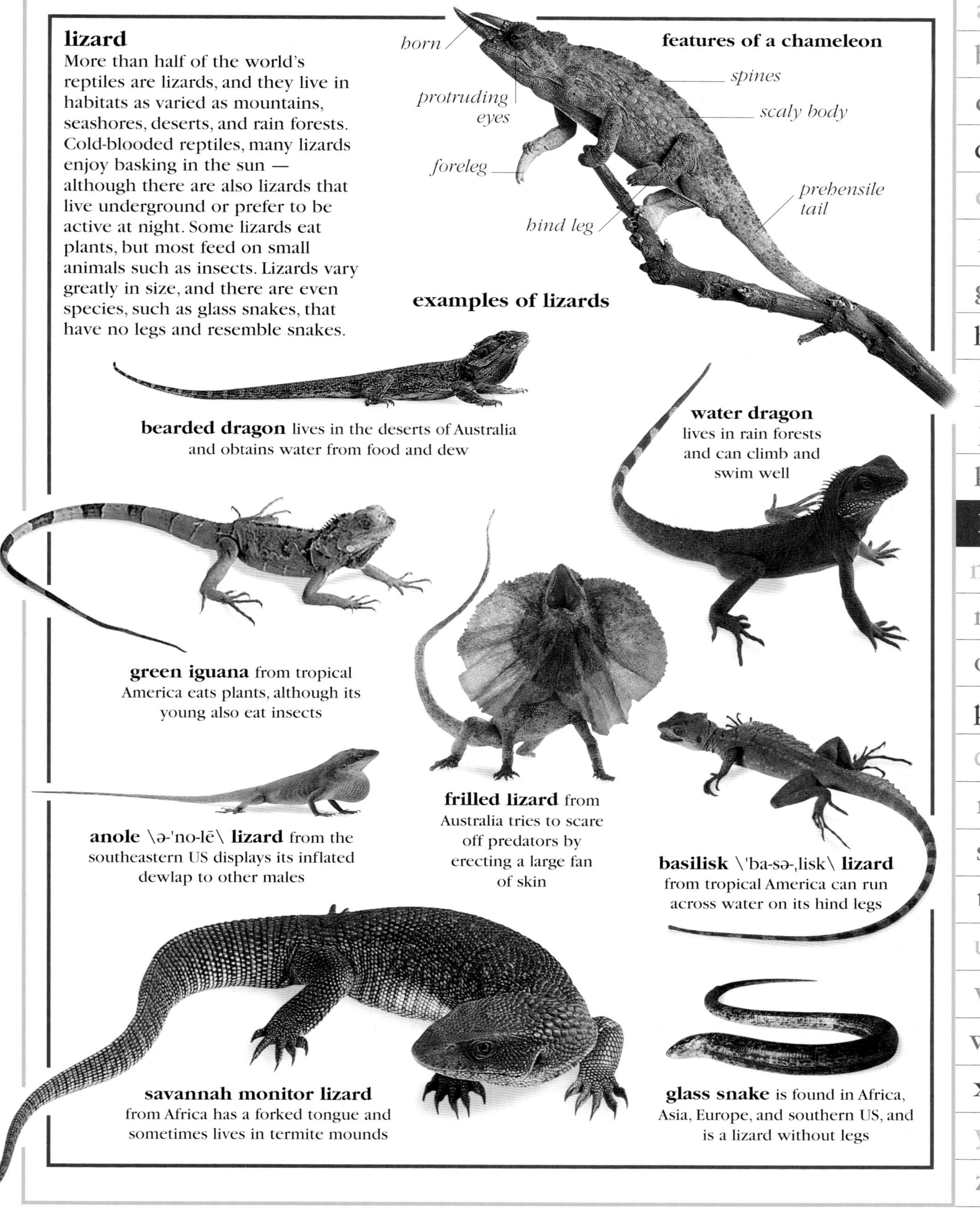


**bearded dragon** lives in the deserts of Australia and obtains water from food and dew

**water dragon** lives in rain forests and can climb and swim well

**green iguana** from tropical America eats plants, although its young also eat insects

**anole** \ə-'nō-lē\ **lizard** from the southeastern US displays its inflated dewlap to other males

**frilled lizard** from Australia tries to scare off predators by erecting a large fan of skin

**basilisk** \'ba-sə-ˌlisk\ **lizard** from tropical America can run across water on its hind legs

**savannah monitor lizard** from Africa has a forked tongue and sometimes lives in termite mounds

**glass snake** is found in Africa, Asia, Europe, and southern US, and is a lizard without legs

**lock·smith** \'läk-,smith\ *n*
a worker who makes or repairs locks

**lock·up** \'läk-,əp\ *n*
PRISON

**lo·co** \'lō-kō\ *adj*
not sane : CRAZY

**lo·co·mo·tion** \,lō-kə-'mō-shən\ *n*
the act or power of moving from place to place

**lo·co·mo·tive** \,lō-kə-'mōt-iv\ *n*
▼ a vehicle that moves under its own power and is used to haul cars on a railroad

**lodging** \'läj-ing\ *n*
**1** a temporary living or sleeping place
**2 lodgings** *pl* a room or rooms in the house of another person rented as a place to live

**loft** \'lȯft\ *n*
**1** an upper room or upper story of a building
**2** a balcony in a church
**3** an upper part of a barn

**lofty** \'lȯf-tē\ *adj* **loft·i·er**; **loft·i·est**
**1** PROUD 1 ⟨a *lofty* air⟩
**2** of high rank or fine quality
**3** rising to a great height ⟨*lofty* trees⟩ **synonyms** see HIGH

⟨a *logical* argument⟩
**3** according to what is reasonably expected ⟨the *logical* result⟩
**log·i·cal·ly** *adv*
**log·i·cal·ness** *n*

**log in** *vb*
LOG ON

**log–in** \'lȯg-,in, 'läg-\ *n*

**log on** *vb*
to establish a connection to and begin using a computer or network ⟨*log on* to the World Wide Web⟩

**log–on** \'lȯg-,ȯn, 'läg-\ *n*

**-logy** \l-ə-jē\ *n suffix*
area of knowledge : science

**loin** \'lȯin\ *n*
**1** the part of the body between the hip and the lower ribs
**2** a piece of meat (as beef) from the loin of an animal

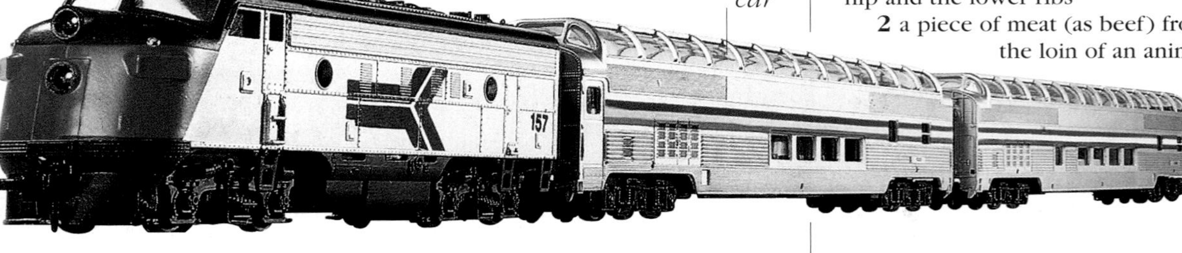


**locomotive:** model of a 1950s American locomotive

**lo·cust** \'lō-kəst\ *n*
**1** a grasshopper that moves in huge swarms and eats up the plants in its course
**2** CICADA
**3** a hardwood tree with feathery leaves and drooping flower clusters

**lode·stone** \'lōd-,stōn\ *n*
**1** a rocky substance having magnetic properties
**2** something that attracts strongly

**¹lodge** \'läj\ *vb* **lodged**; **lodg·ing**
**1** to provide temporary quarters for ⟨*lodge* guests for the night⟩
**2** to use a place for living or sleeping ⟨we *lodged* in motels⟩
**3** to come to rest ⟨the bullet *lodged* in a tree⟩
**4** ³FILE 2 ⟨*lodge* a complaint⟩

**²lodge** *n*
**1** a house set apart for residence in a special season or by an employee on an estate ⟨a hunting *lodge*⟩ ⟨the caretaker's *lodge*⟩
**2** the meeting place of a branch of a secret society

**lodg·er** \'läj-ər\ *n*
a person who lives in a rented room in another's house

**loft·i·ly** \-tə-lē\ *adv*
**loft·i·ness** \-tē-nəs\ *n*

**¹log** \'lȯg, 'läg\ *n*
**1** a large piece of rough timber : a long piece of a tree trunk trimmed and ready for sawing
**2** a device for measuring the speed of a ship
**3** the daily record of a ship's speed and progress
**4** the record of a ship's voyage or of an aircraft's flight
**5** a record of how something (as a piece of equipment) works in actual use

**²log** *vb* **logged**; **log·ging**
**1** to engage in cutting and hauling logs for timber
**2** to put details of or about in a log

**log·ger·head** \'lȯg-ər-,hed, 'läg-\ *n*
▶ a very large sea turtle found in the warmer parts of the Atlantic ocean

**log·ic** \'läj-ik\ *n*
**1** a science that deals with the rules and tests of sound thinking and reasoning
**2** sound reasoning

**log·i·cal** \'läj-i-kəl\ *adj*
**1** having to do with logic
**2** according to the rules of logic

**loi·ter** \'lȯit-ər\ *vb*
**1** to linger on one's way
**2** to hang around idly
**loi·ter·er** *n*

**loll** \'läl\ *vb*
**1** to hang loosely : DANGLE
**2** to lie around lazily

**lol·li·pop** *or* **lol·ly·pop** \'läl-ē-,päp\ *n*
▶ a lump of hard candy on the end of a stick

**lollipop**

**lone** \'lōn\ *adj*
**1** having no companion ⟨a *lone* sentinel⟩
**2** being by itself ⟨a *lone* outpost⟩

**lone·ly** \'lōn-lē\ *adj* **lone·li·er**; **lone·li·est**
**1** LONE 1
**2** not often visited
**3** longing for companions
**synonyms** see ALONE
**lone·li·ness** *n*

**loggerhead** turtle

**lone·some** \'lōn-səm\ *adj*
**1** saddened by a lack of companions
**2** not often visited or traveled over
**lone·some·ly** *adv*
**lone·some·ness** *n*

[1]**long** \'lȯng\ *adj* **lon·ger** \'lȯng-gər\; **lon·gest** \'lȯng-gəst\
**1** of great length from end to end **:** not short
**2** having a greater length than breadth
**3** lasting for some time **:** not brief ⟨a *long* program at assembly⟩
**4** having a stated length (as in distance or time) ⟨a meter *long*⟩ ⟨an hour *long*⟩
**5** of, relating to, or being one of the vowel sounds \ā, ȧ, ē, ī, ō, ü\ and sometimes \ä\ and \ȯ\

[2]**long** *adv*
**1** for or during a long time ⟨were you away *long*⟩
**2** for the whole length of ⟨slept all night *long*⟩
**3** at a distant point of time ⟨*long* ago⟩

[3]**long** *n*
a long time ⟨they'll be here before *long*⟩

[4]**long** *vb*
to wish for something very much
**synonyms** see YEARN
**long·ing·ly** *adv*

**long·hand** \'lȯng-ˌhand\ *n*
HANDWRITING

**long·horn** \'lȯng-ˌhȯrn\ *n*
▼ any of the half-wild cattle with very long horns that were once common in the southwestern United States

**long–horned** \'lȯng-'hȯrnd\ *adj*
having long horns or antennae ⟨a *long-horned* grasshopper⟩

**long·ing** \'lȯng-ing\ *n*
an eager desire

**long·ish** \'lȯng-ish\ *adj*
somewhat long

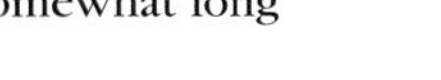


**longhorn**

**lon·gi·tude** \'län-jə-ˌtüd, -ˌtyüd\ *n*
distance measured in degrees east or west of a line drawn (as through Greenwich, England) between the north and south poles ⟨the *longitude* of New York is 74 degrees west of Greenwich⟩

**lon·gi·tu·di·nal** \ˌlän-jə-'tüd-n-əl, -'tyüd-\ *adj*
placed or running lengthwise
**lon·gi·tu·di·nal·ly** *adv*

**long–lived** \'lȯng-'līvd, -'livd\ *adj*
living or lasting for a long time

**long–range** \'lȯng-'rānj\ *adj*
**1** capable of traveling or shooting great distances
**2** lasting over or providing for a long period

**long·sight·ed** \'lȯng-'sīt-əd\ *adj*
FARSIGHTED
**long·sight·ed·ness** *n*

**long–suf·fer·ing** \'lȯng-'səf-ə-ring, -'səf-ring\ *adj*
very patient and forgiving

**long–wind·ed** \'lȯng-'win-dəd\ *adj*
**1** too long ⟨a *long-winded* speech⟩
**2** given to talking too long ⟨a *long-winded* speaker⟩

[1]**look** \'lu̇k\ *vb*
**1** to use the power of vision **:** SEE
**2** to appear suitable to ⟨*looks* the part⟩
**3** SEEM 1 ⟨*looks* thin⟩
**4** to turn one's attention or eyes ⟨*look* in the mirror⟩
**5** [2]FACE 2 ⟨the house *looks* east⟩
**look after** to take care of
**look down on** to regard with contempt
**look up to** RESPECT 1

[2]**look** *n*
**1** an act of looking ⟨we took a *look* around⟩
**2** the way one appears to others ⟨I liked their *looks*⟩ ⟨the child had an innocent *look*⟩
**3** appearance that suggests what something is or means ⟨the cloth has a *look* of linen⟩ ⟨black clouds with a *look* of rain⟩

**looking glass** *n*
[1]MIRROR 1

**look·out** \'lu̇k-ˌau̇t\ *n*
**1** a careful watch for something expected or feared ⟨on the *lookout* for trouble⟩
**2** a high place from which a wide view is possible
**3** a person who keeps watch

[1]**loom** \'lüm\ *n*
▼ a device for weaving cloth

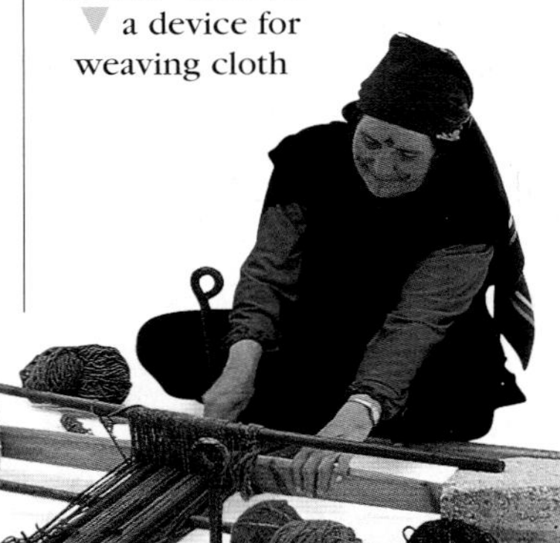

[1]**loom:**
a North African woman weaving cloth on a traditional loom

[2]**loom** *vb*
to come into sight suddenly and often with a dim or strange appearance

**loon** \'lün\ *n*
a large diving bird that lives on fish and has webbed feet, a black head, and a black back spotted with white

[1]**loop** \'lüp\ *n*
**1** an almost oval form produced when something flexible and thin (as a wire or a rope) crosses itself
**2** something (as a figure or bend) suggesting a flexible loop ⟨make letters with large *loops*⟩

[2]**loop** *vb*
to make a loop or loops in

A B C D E F G H I J K L M N O P Q R S T U V W X Y Z

**loop·hole** \ˈlüp-ˌhōl\ *n*
a way of escaping something ⟨a *loophole* in the law⟩

**[1]loose** \ˈlüs\ *adj* **loos·er**; **loos·est**
**1** not tightly fixed or fastened ⟨a *loose* board⟩
**2** not pulled tight ⟨a *loose* belt⟩
**3** not tied up or shut in ⟨a *loose* horse⟩
**4** not brought together in a package or binding ⟨*loose* sheets of paper⟩
**5** not respectable ⟨*loose* conduct⟩
**6** having parts that are not squeezed tightly together ⟨*loose* gravel⟩ ⟨cloth of *loose* weave⟩
**7** not exact or careful ⟨*loose* thinking⟩
**loose·ly** *adv*
**loose·ness** *n*

**[2]loose** *vb* **loosed**; **loos·ing**
**1** to make loose : UNTIE
**2** to set free

**loose–leaf** \ˈlü-ˈslēf\ *adj*
arranged so that pages can be put in or taken out ⟨a *loose-leaf* notebook⟩

**loos·en** \ˈlüs-ⁿn\ *vb*
to make or become loose

**[1]loot** \ˈlüt\ *n*
something stolen or taken by force

**[2]loot** *vb*
[1]PLUNDER
**loot·er** *n*

**[1]lope** \ˈlōp\ *n*
a gait with long smooth steps

**[2]lope** *vb* **loped**; **lop·ing**
to go or ride at a lope

**lop–eared** \ˈläp-ˈird\ *adj*
having ears that droop

**lop·sid·ed** \ˈläp-ˈsīd-əd\ *adj*
UNBALANCED 1
**lop·sid·ed·ly** *adv*
**lop·sid·ed·ness** *n*

**[1]lord** \ˈlȯrd\ *n*
**1** a person having power and authority over others
**2** *cap* GOD 1
**3** *cap* JESUS
**4** a British nobleman or a bishop of the Church of England entitled to sit in the House of Lords — used as a title ⟨*Lord* Cornwallis⟩ ⟨my *Lord* Archbishop⟩

**lop-eared** rabbit

---

**Word History** There was in Old English a word *hlāf* that meant "bread" or "loaf." The modern English word *loaf* comes from this Old English word. Another Old English word *weard* meant "keeper" or "guard." The modern English word *ward* is related to that Old English word. *Hlāf* and *weard* were put together to make a word *hlāford* that meant "one who guards or keeps bread." This word was used for a man who was the head of a household. The modern English word *lord* comes from this old word.

---

**[2]lord** *vb*
to act in a proud or bossy way toward others ⟨always tried to *lord* it over us⟩

**lord·ship** \ˈlȯrd-ˌship\ *n*
the rank or dignity of a lord — used as a title ⟨his *Lordship* is not at home⟩

**lore** \ˈlōr\ *n*
common knowledge or belief

**lose** \ˈlüz\ *vb* **lost** \ˈlȯst\; **los·ing** \ˈlü-ziŋ\
**1** to be unable to find or have at hand : MISLAY ⟨I *lost* my keys⟩
**2** to be deprived of ⟨*lose* money on a deal⟩
**3** [2]WASTE 2 ⟨*lost* a morning daydreaming⟩
**4** to be defeated in ⟨*lost* the game⟩
**5** to fail to keep ⟨*lost* my temper⟩
**los·er** *n*
**lose one's way** to stray from the right path

**loss** \ˈlȯs\ *n*
**1** the act or fact of losing something ⟨the *loss* of a ship⟩ ⟨anger may cause a *loss* of self-control⟩
**2** harm or distress that comes from losing something ⟨it was a real *loss* when our teacher retired⟩
**3** something that is lost ⟨heat *loss* from bad insulation⟩
**4** failure to win ⟨the team's first *loss* after two wins⟩

**[1]lost** \ˈlȯst\ *past of* LOSE

**[2]lost** *adj*
**1** not used, won, or claimed ⟨a *lost* opportunity⟩
**2** unable to find the way ⟨a *lost* puppy⟩
**3** come or brought to a bad end ⟨a *lost* sinner⟩
**4** no longer possessed or known ⟨a *lost* art⟩ ⟨long *lost* cousins⟩
**5** fully occupied ⟨*lost* in thought⟩

**lot** \ˈlät\ *n*
**1** an object used in deciding something by chance or the use of such an object to decide something ⟨draw *lots*⟩ ⟨choose by *lot*⟩
**2** FATE 2 ⟨it was their *lot* to do the hard work⟩
**3** a piece or plot of land
**4** a large number or amount ⟨*lots* of books⟩ ⟨a *lot* of help⟩

**loth** \ˈlōth, ˈlōth\ *variant of* LOATH

**lo·tion** \ˈlō-shən\ *n*
a liquid preparation used on the skin for healing or as a cosmetic

**lot·tery** \ˈlät-ə-rē\ *n, pl* **lot·ter·ies**
a way of raising money in which many tickets are sold and a few of these are drawn to win prizes

**lo·tus** \ˈlōt-əs\ *n*
any of various water lilies

**lotus**

**[1]loud** \ˈlau̇d\ *adj*
**1** not low, soft, or quiet in sound : NOISY ⟨a *loud* cry⟩
**2** not quiet or calm in expression ⟨a *loud* complaint⟩
**3** too bright or showy to be pleasing ⟨*loud* clothes⟩
**loud·ly** *adv*
**loud·ness** *n*

**loudspeakers**
on either side of a stereo unit

**²loud** *adv*
in a loud manner

**loud·speak·er** \'lau̇d-'spē-kər\ *n*
▶ an electronic device that makes sound louder

**¹lounge** \'lau̇nj\ *vb* **lounged**; **loung·ing**
**1** to move or act in a slow, tired, or lazy way
**2** to stand, sit, or lie in a relaxed manner

**²lounge** *n*
**1** a comfortable room where one can relax or lounge
**2** SOFA

**louse** \'lau̇s\ *n, pl* **lice** \'līs\
**1** a small, wingless, and usually flat insect that lives on the bodies of warm-blooded animals
**2** PLANT LOUSE

**lov·able** \'ləv-ə-bəl\ *adj*
deserving to be loved or admired ⟨a *lovable* child⟩
**lov·able·ness** *n*
**lov·ably** \-blē\ *adv*

**¹love** \'ləv\ *n*
**1** great and warm affection (as of a child for a parent)
**2** a great liking ⟨children with a *love* for reading⟩
**3** a beloved person

**²love** *vb* **loved**; **lov·ing**
**1** to feel warm affection for
**2** to like very much ⟨*loves* to ski⟩
**lov·er** *n*

**love·ly** \'ləv-lē\ *adj* **love·li·er**; **love·li·est**
**1** very beautiful
**2** very pleasing ⟨had a *lovely* time⟩
**love·li·ness** *n*

**lov·ing** \'ləv-iŋ\ *adj*
feeling or showing love : AFFECTIONATE
**lov·ing·ly** *adv*

**¹low** \'lō\ *vb*
to make the calling sound of a cow : MOO

**²low** *n*
the mooing of a cow : MOO

**³low** *adj*
**1** not high : not tall ⟨a *low* building⟩
**2** lying or going below the usual level ⟨*low* ground⟩ ⟨a *low* bow⟩
**3** not loud : SOFT ⟨a *low* whisper⟩
**4** deep in pitch ⟨a *low* note⟩
**5** ¹PROSTRATE 3
**6** SAD 1 ⟨in *low* spirits⟩
**7** less than usual (as in quantity or value) ⟨*low* prices⟩ ⟨*low* pressure⟩
**8** COARSE 4, VULGAR ⟨*low* talk⟩
**9** not favorable : POOR ⟨a *low* opinion of someone⟩
**low·ness** *n*

**⁴low** *n*
**1** something that is low
**2** a region of low barometric pressure
**3** the arrangement of gears in an automobile that gives the lowest speed of travel

**⁵low** *adv*
so as to be low ⟨fly *low*⟩ ⟨sing *low*⟩

**¹low·er** \'lō-ər\ *adj*
**1** being below the other of two similar persons or things ⟨the *lower* floor⟩
**2** less advanced ⟨pupils in the *lower* grades⟩

**²lower** *vb*
**1** to move to a lower level : SINK ⟨the sun *lowered* in the west⟩ ⟨water *lowered* in the well⟩
**2** to let or pull down ⟨*lower* a flag⟩ ⟨*lowered* the window shade⟩
**3** to make or become less (as in value or amount) ⟨*lower* the price of food⟩
**4** to make or become lower ⟨*lower* a fence⟩ ⟨their voices *lowered*⟩

**low·land** \'lō-lənd\ *n*
low flat country

**¹low·ly** \'lō-lē\ *adv*
in a humble way

**²lowly** *adj* **low·li·er**; **low·li·est**
of low rank or condition : HUMBLE
**low·li·ness** *n*

**loy·al** \'lȯi-əl\ *adj*
**1** faithful to one's country
**2** faithful to a person or thing one likes or believes in ⟨*loyal* to the home team⟩ **synonyms** see FAITHFUL
**loy·al·ly** *adv*

**loy·al·ty** \'lȯi-əl-tē\ *n, pl* **loy·al·ties**
the quality or state of being loyal

---

**Synonyms** LOYALTY and ALLEGIANCE mean faithfulness to whatever one is tied to by duty or by a pledge or promise. LOYALTY suggests a very personal or powerful kind of faithfulness and also often suggests a fighting of an urge to desert or betray ⟨I felt great *loyalty* to my teammates⟩. ALLEGIANCE stresses a duty to something other than a person, especially to a government or idea ⟨pledge *allegiance* to the flag⟩.

---

**loz·enge** \'läz-nj\ *n*
a small candy often containing medicine

**LSD** \,el-,es-'dē\ *n*
a dangerous drug that causes hallucinations

**lu·bri·cant** \'lü-bri-kənt\ *n*
something (as oil or grease) that makes a surface smooth or slippery

**lu·bri·cate** \'lü-brə-,kāt\ *vb* **lu·bri·cat·ed**; **lu·bri·cat·ing**
**1** to make smooth or slippery
**2** to apply oil or grease to ⟨*lubricate* a car⟩

**lu·bri·ca·tion** \,lü-brə-'kā-shən\ *n*
the act or process of lubricating or the state of being lubricated

**lu·cid** \'lü-səd\ *adj*
**1** showing a normal state of mind ⟨*lucid* behavior⟩
**2** easily understood ⟨*lucid* writing⟩
**lu·cid·ly** *adv*
**lu·cid·ness** *n*

**luck** \'lək\ *n*
**1** something that happens to a person by or as if by chance
**2** the accidental way events occur
**3** good fortune

**lucky** \'lək-ē\ *adj* **luck·i·er**; **luck·i·est**
**1** helped by luck : FORTUNATE ⟨a *lucky* person⟩
**2** happening because of good luck ⟨a *lucky* hit⟩
**3** thought of as bringing good luck ⟨a *lucky* charm⟩
**luck·i·ly** \'lək-ə-lē\ *adv*

**lu·di·crous** \'lü-də-krəs\ *adj*
funny because of being ridiculous **:** ABSURD
**lu·di·crous·ly** *adv*
**lu·di·crous·ness** *n*

**lug** \'ləg\ *vb* **lugged**; **lug·ging**
to find hard to carry or haul

**lug·gage** \'ləg-ij\ *n*
BAGGAGE

**luke·warm** \'lü-'kwȯrm\ *adj*
**1** neither hot nor cold
**2** not very interested or eager ⟨*lukewarm* toward our plan⟩

[1]**lull** \'ləl\ *vb*
to make or become quiet or less watchful

[2]**lull** *n*
a period of calm (as in a storm)

**lul·la·by** \'ləl-ə-ˌbī\ *n, pl* **lul·la·bies**
a song for helping babies to sleep

[1]**lum·ber** \'ləm-bər\ *vb*
to move in an awkward way

[2]**lumber** *n*
timber especially when sawed into boards

[3]**lumber** *vb*
to cut logs **:** saw logs into lumber

**lum·ber·jack** \'ləm-bər-ˌjak\ *n*
a person who works at lumbering

**lum·ber·man** \'ləm-bər-mən\ *n, pl* **lum·ber·men** \-mən\
a person engaged in the lumber business

**lum·ber·yard** \'ləm-bər-ˌyärd\ *n*
a place where a stock of lumber is kept for sale

**lu·mi·nous** \'lü-mə-nəs\ *adj*
shining brightly
**lu·mi·nous·ly** *adv*

[1]**lump** \'ləmp\ *n*
a small uneven mass (as a chunk or a swelling)

[2]**lump** *vb*
**1** to form into a lump
**2** to group together ⟨*lumped* our change to buy some candy⟩

**lu·nar** \'lü-nər\ *adj*
**1** of or relating to the moon
**2** measured by the revolutions of the moon ⟨a *lunar* month⟩

[1]**lu·na·tic** \'lü-nə-ˌtik\ *adj*
INSANE 1, CRAZY

**Word History** In the past many people thought that insanity was affected by the moon. Someone who was insane, they thought, would be at his or her worst when the moon was full. But when there was a new moon he or she might act just like a normal person. We owe the word *lunatic* to the belief that the moon had an effect on madness. *Lunatic* comes from a Latin word that meant "insane." This word was formed from the Latin word for moon.

[2]**lunatic** *n*
an insane person

[1]**lunch** \'lənch\ *n*
**1** a light meal especially when eaten in the middle of the day
**2** food prepared for lunch ⟨a picnic *lunch*⟩

[2]**lunch** *vb*
to eat lunch

**lun·cheon** \'lən-chən\ *n*
**1** [1]LUNCH 1
**2** a formal lunch

**lung** \'ləng\ *n*
either of two organs in the chest that are like bags and are the main breathing structure in animals that breathe air

[1]**lunge** \'lənj\ *n*
a sudden movement forward ⟨the horse started with a *lunge*⟩

[2]**lunge** *vb* **lunged**; **lung·ing**
to push or drive with force ⟨we *lunged* through the crowd⟩ ⟨*lunge* a sword⟩

**lungfish:** an African lungfish

**lung·fish** \'ləng-ˌfish\ *n*
▲ any of several fishes that breathe with structures like lungs as well as with gills

**lu·pine** \'lü-pən\ *n*
▶ a plant related to the clovers that has tall spikes of showy flowers like those of sweet peas

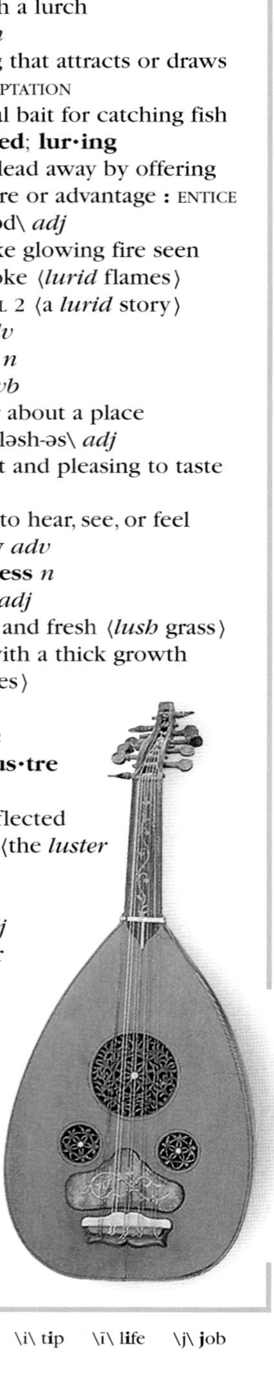

**lupine**

[1]**lurch** \'lərch\ *n*
**1** a sudden roll of a ship to one side
**2** a swaying staggering movement or gait

[2]**lurch** *vb*
to move with a lurch

[1]**lure** \'lu̇r\ *n*
**1** something that attracts or draws one on **:** TEMPTATION
**2** an artificial bait for catching fish

[2]**lure** *vb* **lured**; **lur·ing**
to tempt or lead away by offering some pleasure or advantage **:** ENTICE

**lu·rid** \'lu̇r-əd\ *adj*
**1** looking like glowing fire seen through smoke ⟨*lurid* flames⟩
**2** SENSATIONAL 2 ⟨a *lurid* story⟩
**lu·rid·ly** *adv*
**lu·rid·ness** *n*

**lurk** \'lərk\ *vb*
to hide in or about a place

**lus·cious** \'ləsh-əs\ *adj*
**1** very sweet and pleasing to taste and smell
**2** delightful to hear, see, or feel
**lus·cious·ly** *adv*
**lus·cious·ness** *n*

**lush** \'ləsh\ *adj*
**1** very juicy and fresh ⟨*lush* grass⟩
**2** covered with a thick growth ⟨*lush* pastures⟩
**lush·ly** *adv*
**lush·ness** *n*

**lus·ter** *or* **lus·tre** \'ləs-tər\ *n*
a glow of reflected light **:** SHEEN ⟨the *luster* of a pearl⟩

**lus·trous** \'ləs-trəs\ *adj*
having luster

**lute** \'lüt\ *n*
▶ an old stringed instrument with a body shaped like a pear and usually paired

**lute**

strings played with the fingers

**lux·u·ri·ant** \ˌləg-ˈzhu̇r-ē-ənt, ˌlək-ˈshu̇r-\ *adj*
growing freely and well ⟨a *luxuriant* growth of plants⟩
**lux·u·ri·ant·ly** *adv*

**lux·u·ri·ous** \ˌləg-ˈzhu̇r-ē-əs, ˌlək-ˈshu̇r-\ *adj*
**1** loving pleasure and luxury
**2** very fine and comfortable
**lux·u·ri·ous·ly** *adv*
**lux·u·ri·ous·ness** *n*

**lux·u·ry** \ˈlək-shə-rē, ˈləg-zhə-\ *n, pl* **lux·u·ries**
**1** very rich, pleasant, and comfortable surroundings ⟨live in *luxury*⟩
**2** something desirable but expensive or hard to get ⟨fresh strawberries are a *luxury* in winter⟩
**3** something pleasant but not really needed for one's pleasure or comfort

[1]**-ly** \lē\ *adj suffix*
**1** like : similar to ⟨queen*ly*⟩ ⟨father*ly*⟩
**2** happening in each specified period of time : every ⟨hour*ly*⟩

[2]**-ly** *adv suffix*
**1** in a specified manner ⟨slow*ly*⟩
**2** from a specified point of view

**lynx**

**lye** \ˈlī\ *n*
a dangerous compound containing sodium that dissolves in water and is used in cleaning

**lying** *present participle of* LIE

**lymph** \ˈlimf\ *n*
a clear liquid like blood without the red cells that nourishes the tissues and carries off wastes

**lym·phat·ic** \lim-ˈfat-ik\ *adj*
of or relating to lymph ⟨a *lymphatic* duct⟩

**lym·pho·cyte** \ˈlim-fə-ˌsīt\ *n*
any of the white blood cells of the immune system that play a role in recognizing and destroying foreign cells, particles, or substances that have invaded the body

**lynx** \ˈliŋks\ *n, pl* **lynx** *or* **lynx·es**
◀ any of several wildcats with rather long legs, a short tail, and often ears with small bunches of long hairs at the tip

**lyre** \ˈlīr\ *n*
a stringed instrument like a harp used by the ancient Greeks

[1]**lyr·ic** \ˈlir-ik\ *n*
**1** a lyric poem
**2 lyrics** *pl* the words of a song

[2]**lyric** *adj*
**1** suitable for singing : MUSICAL
**2** expressing personal emotion ⟨*lyric* poetry⟩

**lyr·i·cal** \ˈlir-i-kəl\ *adj*
[2]LYRIC

# Mm

**The sounds of M:** The letter **M** has only one sound in English. It has the same sound in **mat**, **mom**, **demonstrate**, **some**, and **atom**, and also when it is doubled, as in the word **summer**.

**m** \'em\ *n, pl* **m's** *or* **ms** \'emz\ *often cap*
**1** the thirteenth letter of the English alphabet
**2** 1000 in Roman numerals

**ma** \'mä, 'mȯ\ *n, often cap*
[1]MOTHER 1

**ma'am** \'mam\ *n*
MADAM

**mac·ad·am** \mə-'kad-əm\ *n*
a road surface made of small closely packed broken stone

**ma·caque** \mə-'kak, -'käk\ *n*
any of several mostly Asian monkeys with short tails

**mac·a·ro·ni** \,mak-ə-'rō-nē\ *n, pl* **macaronis** *or* **macaronies**
a food that is made of a mixture of flour and water formed into tubes and dried

**mac·a·roon** \,mak-ə-'rün\ *n*
a cookie made of the white of eggs, sugar, and ground almonds or coconut

**ma·caw** \mə-'kȯ\ *n*
► a large parrot of Central and South America with a long tail, a harsh voice, and bright feathers

**macaw:** a scarlet macaw

[1]**mace** \'mās\ *n*
a spice made from the dried outer covering of the nutmeg

[2]**mace** *n*
a fancy club carried before certain officials as a sign of authority

**ma·chete** \mə-'shet-ē\ *n*
a large heavy knife used for cutting sugarcane and underbrush and as a weapon

[1]**ma·chine** \mə-'shēn\ *n*
**1** VEHICLE 2 ⟨a flying *machine*⟩
**2** ▼ a device that combines forces, motion, and energy in a way that does some desired work ⟨a sewing *machine*⟩

[1]**machine 2:** a sewing machine

[2]**machine** *vb* **ma·chined**; **ma·chin·ing**
to shape or finish by tools run by machines

**machine gun** *n*
an automatic gun for continuous firing

**ma·chin·ery** \mə-'shē-nə-rē, -'shēn-rē\ *n*
**1** a group of machines ⟨the *machinery* in a factory⟩
**2** the working parts of a machine
**3** the people and equipment by which something is done ⟨the *machinery* of government⟩

**machine shop** *n*
a workshop in which metal articles are machined and put together

**ma·chin·ist** \mə-'shē-nist\ *n*
a person who makes or works on machines

**mack·er·el** \'mak-ə-rəl, 'mak-rəl\ *n, pl* **mackerel** *or* **mackerels**
► a food fish of the North Atlantic that is green with blue bars above and silvery below

**mackerel**

**mack·i·naw** \'mak-ə-,nȯ\ *n*
a short heavy woolen coat

**ma·cron** \'mā-,krän\ *n*
a mark ˉ placed over a vowel to show that the vowel is long

**mad** \'mad\ *adj* **mad·der**; **mad·dest**
**1** INSANE 1
**2** done or made without thinking ⟨a *mad* promise⟩
**3** ANGRY ⟨he's *mad* at his brother⟩
**4** INFATUATED ⟨*mad* about horses⟩
**5** having rabies ⟨a *mad* dog⟩
**6** marked by intense and often disorganized activity ⟨a *mad* scramble⟩
**mad·ly** *adv*
**mad·ness** *n*

**mad·am** \'mad-əm\ *n, pl* **mes·dames** \mā-'däm, -'dam\
used without a name as a form of polite address to a woman ⟨may I help you, *madam*?⟩

[1]**mad·cap** \'mad-,kap\ *adj*
likely to do something mad or reckless : done for fun without thinking ⟨a *madcap* adventure⟩

[2]**madcap** *n*
a madcap person

**mad·den** \'mad-n\ *vb*
to make mad

**made** *past of* MAKE

**made–up** \'mā-'dəp\ *adj*
showing more imagination than concern with fact ⟨a *made-up* excuse⟩

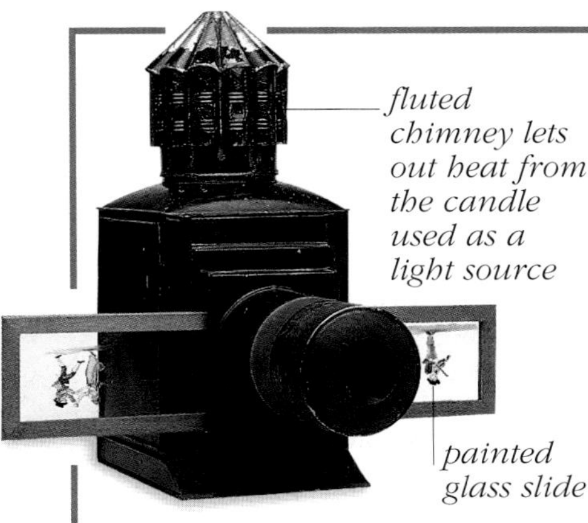
fluted chimney lets out heat from the candle used as a light source
painted glass slide

**magic lantern**

**mad·house** \'mad-ˌhau̇s\ *n*
a place or scene of complete confusion

**mag·a·zine** \'mag-ə-ˌzēn\ *n*
**1** a storehouse or warehouse for military supplies
**2** a place for keeping explosives in a fort or ship
**3** a container in a gun for holding cartridges
**4** a publication issued at regular intervals (as weekly or monthly)

**Word History** The English word *magazine* came from a French word which in turn came from an Arabic word. Both the French and the Arabic words meant "a place where things are stored." At first the English word had the same meaning, and it is still used in this sense. However, a later sense is now more common — that of a collection of written pieces printed at set times. A magazine can be thought of as a storehouse for the written pieces.

**mag·got** \'mag-ət\ *n*
a legless grub that is the larva of a two-winged fly

**[1]mag·ic** \'maj-ik\ *n*
**1** the power to control natural forces possessed by certain persons (as wizards and witches) in folk tales and fiction
**2** a power that seems mysterious ⟨the *magic* of a great name⟩
**3** something that charms ⟨the *magic* of their singing⟩
**4** the art or skill of performing tricks or illusions as if by magic for entertainment

**[2]magic** *adj*
**1** of or relating to magic
**2** having effects that seem to be caused by magic
**3** giving a feeling of enchantment

**mag·i·cal** \'maj-i-kəl\ *adj*
[2]MAGIC 1, 2

**ma·gi·cian** \mə-'jish-ən\ *n*
a person skilled in magic

**magic lantern** *n*
◀ an early kind of slide projector

**mag·is·trate** \'maj-ə-ˌstrāt\ *n*
**1** a chief officer of government
**2** a local official with some judicial power

**mag·ma** \'mag-mə\ *n*
molten rock within the earth

**mag·na·nim·i·ty** \ˌmag-nə-'nim-ət-ē\ *n*
the quality of being magnanimous

**mag·nan·i·mous** \mag-'nan-ə-məs\ *adj*
**1** having a noble and courageous spirit
**2** being generous and forgiving
**mag·nan·i·mous·ly** *adv*

**mag·ne·sium** \mag-'nē-zē-əm, -'nē-zhəm\ *n*
a silvery white metallic chemical element that is lighter than aluminum and is used in lightweight alloys

**mag·net** \'mag-nət\ *n*
▶ a piece of material (as of iron, steel, or alloy) that is able to attract iron

metal paper clip

**magnet**

**mag·net·ic** \mag-'net-ik\ *adj*
**1** acting like a magnet
**2** of or relating to the earth's magnetism
**3** having a great power to attract people

**magnetic field** *n*
the portion of space near a magnetic body within which magnetic forces can be detected

**magnetic needle** *n*
a narrow strip of magnetized steel that is free to swing around to show the direction of the earth's magnetism

**magnetic pole** *n*
**1** either of the poles of a magnet
**2** either of two small regions of the earth which are located near the North and South Poles and toward which a compass needle points

**magnetic tape** *n*
a thin ribbon of plastic coated with a magnetic material on which information (as sound) may be stored

**mag·ne·tism** \'mag-nə-ˌtiz-əm\ *n*
**1** the power to attract that a magnet has
**2** the power to attract others **:** personal charm

**mag·ne·tize** \'mag-nə-ˌtīz\ *vb*
**mag·ne·tized**; **mag·ne·tiz·ing**
to cause to be magnetic

**mag·ne·to** \mag-'nēt-ō\ *n, pl* **mag·ne·tos**
a small generator used especially to produce the spark in some gasoline engines

**mag·nif·i·cent** \mag-'nif-ə-sənt\ *adj*
having impressive beauty **:** very grand ⟨*magnificent* palaces⟩
**mag·nif·i·cent·ly** *adv*

**mag·ni·fy** \'mag-nə-ˌfī\ *vb*
**mag·ni·fied**; **mag·ni·fy·ing**
**1** to enlarge in fact or appearance ⟨a microscope *magnifies* an object seen through it⟩
**2** to cause to seem greater or more important **:** EXAGGERATE ⟨*magnify* a fault⟩

**magnifying glass** *n*
▼ a lens that magnifies something seen through it

feather
magnifying glass
leaf

**magnifying glass**

**mag·ni·tude** \'mag-nə-ˌtüd, -ˌtyüd\ *n*
greatness of size

**mag·no·lia** \mag-'nōl-yə\ *n*
a tree or tall shrub having showy white, pink, yellow, or purple flowers that appear before or sometimes with the leaves

**mag·pie** \'mag-ˌpī\ *n*
a noisy black-and-white bird related to the jays

**ma·hog·a·ny** \mə-'häg-ə-nē\ *n, pl* **ma·hog·a·nies**
a strong reddish brown wood that is used especially for furniture and is obtained from several tropical trees

**maid** \'mād\ *n*
**1** an unmarried girl or woman
**2** a female servant

**[1]maid·en** \'mād-n\ *n*
an unmarried girl or woman

**[2]maiden** *adj*
**1** UNMARRIED
**2** [1]FIRST 2 ⟨a *maiden* voyage⟩

**maid·en·hair fern** \'mād-n-ˌhaər-, -ˌheər-\ *n*
▶ a fern with slender stems and delicate feathery leaves

**maidenhair fern**

**maid·en·hood** \'mād-n-ˌhu̇d\ *n*
the state or time of being a maiden

**maiden name** *n*
a woman's family name before she is married

**maid of honor**
an unmarried woman who stands with the bride at a wedding

**[1]mail** \'māl\ *n*
**1** letters, parcels, and papers sent from one person to another through the post office
**2** the whole system used in the public sending and delivering of mail ⟨do business by *mail*⟩
**3** something that comes in the mail

**[2]mail** *vb*
to send by mail

**[3]mail** *n*
a fabric made of metal rings linked together and used as armor

**mail·box** \'māl-ˌbäks\ *n*
**1** a public box in which to place outgoing mail
**2** a private box (as on a house) for the delivery of incoming mail

**mail carrier** *n*
LETTER CARRIER

**mail·man** \'māl-ˌman\ *n, pl* **mail·men** \-ˌmen\
LETTER CARRIER

**maim** \'mām\ *vb*
to injure badly or cripple by violence

**[1]main** \'mān\ *n*
**1** physical strength : FORCE ⟨with might and *main*⟩
**2** HIGH SEAS ⟨over the bounding *main*⟩
**3** the chief part : essential point ⟨the new workers are in the *main* well trained⟩
**4** a principal line, tube, or pipe of a utility system ⟨water *main*⟩ ⟨gas *main*⟩

**[2]main** *adj*
**1** first in size, rank, or importance : CHIEF ⟨*main* part⟩ ⟨*main* street⟩
**2** PURE 3, SHEER ⟨by *main* force⟩
**main·ly** *adv*

**main·land** \'mān-ˌland\ *n*
a continent or the main part of a continent as distinguished from an offshore island or sometimes from a cape or peninsula

**main·mast** \'mān-ˌmast, -məst\ *n*
the principal mast of a sailing ship

**main·sail** \'mān-ˌsāl, -səl\ *n*
▼ the principal sail on the mainmast

**main·spring** \'mān-ˌspriŋ\ *n*
the principal spring in a mechanical device (as a watch or clock)

**main·stay** \'mān-ˌstā\ *n*
**1** the large strong rope from the maintop of a ship usually to the foot of the foremast
**2** a chief support ⟨the *mainstay* of the family⟩

**main·tain** \mān-'tān\ *vb*
**1** to keep in a particular or desired state ⟨*maintain* one's health⟩
**2** to defend by argument ⟨*maintain* a position⟩
**3** CARRY ON 3, CONTINUE ⟨*maintain* a correspondence⟩
**4** to provide for : SUPPORT ⟨*maintained* my family by working⟩
**5** to insist to be true ⟨*maintained* that we were cheated⟩

**main·te·nance** \'mānt-n-əns\ *n*
**1** the act of maintaining : the state of being maintained ⟨*maintenance* of law and order⟩ ⟨money for the family's *maintenance*⟩
**2** UPKEEP ⟨workers in charge of *maintenance*⟩

**main·top** \'mān-ˌtäp\ *n*
a platform around the head of a mainmast

**maize** \'māz\ *n*
INDIAN CORN

**ma·jes·tic** \mə-'jes-tik\ *adj*
very impressive and dignified : NOBLE
**ma·jes·ti·cal·ly** \-ti-kə-lē\ *adv*

**maj·es·ty** \'maj-ə-stē\ *n, pl* **maj·es·ties**
**1** royal dignity or authority
**2** the quality or state of being majestic
**3** used as a title for a king, queen, emperor, or empress ⟨Your *Majesty*⟩

**[1]ma·jor** \'mā-jər\ *adj*
**1** greater in number, quantity, rank, or importance ⟨the *major* part of the cost⟩ ⟨the *major* leagues⟩
**2** of or relating to a musical scale of eight notes with half steps between the third and fourth and between the seventh and eighth

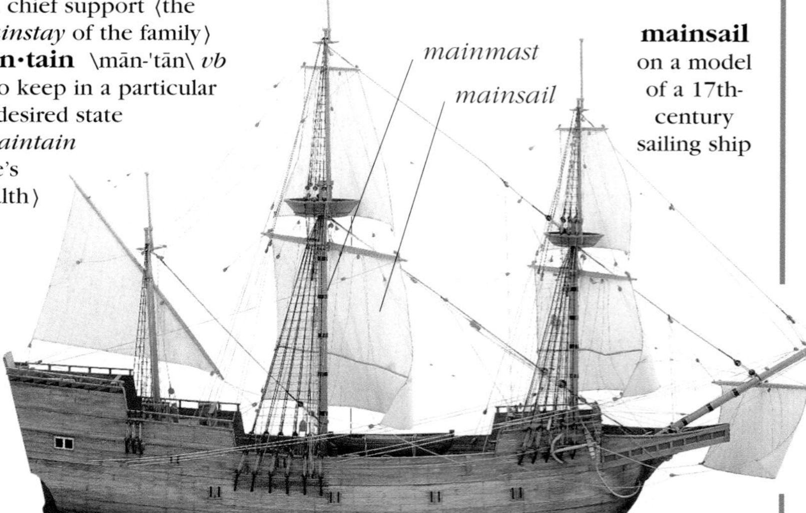


**mainsail** on a model of a 17th-century sailing ship

notes and with whole steps between all the others

**²major** *n*
a commissioned officer in the Army, Air Force, or Marine Corps ranking above a captain

**major general** *n*
a commissioned officer in the Army, Air Force, or Marine Corps ranking above a brigadier general

**ma·jor·i·ty** \mə-'jȯr-ət-ē\ *n, pl* **ma·jor·i·ties**
**1** the age at which one is allowed to vote
**2** a number greater than half of a total
**3** the amount by which a majority is more than a minority ⟨winning by fifty-one to forty-nine, a *majority* of two⟩
**4** a group or party that makes up the greater part of a whole body of persons ⟨the *majority* chose a leader⟩

**¹make** \'māk\ *vb* **made** \'mād\; **mak·ing**
**1** to cause to occur ⟨*make* trouble⟩
**2** to form or put together out of material or parts ⟨*make* a dress⟩ ⟨*make* a chair⟩
**3** to combine to produce ⟨two and two *make* four⟩
**4** to set in order : PREPARE ⟨*make* a bed⟩
**5** to cause to be or become ⟨*made* them happy⟩
**6** ¹DO 1, PERFORM ⟨*make* a speech⟩ ⟨*made* a sweeping motion with his hand⟩
**7** to produce by action ⟨*make* a mess of a job⟩
**8** COMPEL ⟨*make* them go to bed⟩
**9** GET 1, GAIN ⟨*make* money⟩ ⟨*make* friends⟩
**10** to act so as to be ⟨*make* merry⟩ ⟨*make* sure⟩

**Synonyms** MAKE, FORM, and MANUFACTURE mean to cause to come into being. MAKE is a word that can be used of many kinds of creation ⟨*make* a chair⟩ ⟨*made* many friends⟩. FORM suggests that the thing brought into being has a design or structure ⟨the colonies *formed* a new nation⟩. MANUFACTURE suggests making something in a fixed way and usually nowadays by machinery ⟨*manufactures* cars⟩.

**make believe** to act as if something known to be imaginary is real or true

**make good**
**1** FULFILL, COMPLETE ⟨*made* my promise *good*⟩ ⟨*made good* their escape⟩
**2** SUCCEED 3 ⟨*made good* in the job⟩

**²make** *n*
**1** the way in which a thing is made : STRUCTURE
**2** ¹BRAND 4 ⟨a *make* of car⟩

**¹make–be·lieve** \'māk-bə-,lēv\ *n*
a pretending to believe (as in children's play)

**²make–believe** *adj*
not real : IMAGINARY

**make out** *vb*
**1** to write out ⟨*make out* a list⟩ ⟨*make out* a check⟩
**2** UNDERSTAND 1 ⟨I can't *make out* what this letter means⟩
**3** IDENTIFY 3 ⟨couldn't *make out* who it was⟩
**4** ¹FARE ⟨how did you *make out*?⟩

**¹make·shift** \'māk-,shift\ *n*
a thing used as a temporary substitute for another

**²makeshift** *adj*
serving as a temporary substitute ⟨used a folded coat as a *makeshift* pillow⟩

**make·up** \'mā-,kəp\ *n*
**1** the way the parts or elements of something are put together or joined
**2** ▶ materials used in changing one's appearance (as for a play or other entertainment)
**3** any of various cosmetics (as lipstick or powder)

**make up** *vb*
**1** to create from the imagination ⟨*made up* a story⟩
**2** ²FORM 3, COMPOSE ⟨eleven players *make up* the team⟩
**3** ¹RECOMPENSE, ATONE ⟨this will *make up* for your loss⟩
**4** to become friendly again ⟨they quarreled but later *made up*⟩
**5** to put on makeup

**make up one's mind** to reach a decision

**mal-** *prefix*
**1** bad : badly ⟨*mal*treat⟩
**2** abnormal : abnormally ⟨*mal*formation⟩

**mal·ad·just·ed** \,mal-ə-'jəs-təd\ *adj*
not properly adjusted ⟨a *maladjusted* student⟩

**mal·a·dy** \'mal-ə-dē\ *n, pl* **mal·a·dies**
a disease or ailment of body or mind

**ma·lar·ia** \mə-'ler-ē-ə\ *n*
a serious disease with chills and fever that is spread by the bite of one kind of mosquito

**Word History** The English word *malaria* came from two Italian words that together meant "bad air." The sickness that we call *malaria* is spread by mosquitoes. However, people once thought it was caused by bad air. That is why it was called *malaria*.

**¹male** \'māl\ *n*
an individual that produces germ cells (as sperm) that fertilize the eggs of a female

**²male** *adj*
**1** of, relating to, or being the sex that fathers young
**2** bearing stamens but no pistil ⟨a *male* flower⟩
**3** of, relating to, or like that of males
**male·ness** *n*

**makeup 2:**
a girl wearing clown makeup

**[1]mammoth:** reconstruction of a mammoth

**mal·for·ma·tion** \ˌmal-fȯr-ˈmā-shən\ *n*
something that is badly or wrongly formed

**mal·ice** \ˈmal-əs\ *n*
ILL WILL

**ma·li·cious** \mə-ˈlish-əs\ *adj*
**1** doing mean things for pleasure
**2** done just to be mean ⟨*malicious* gossip⟩
**ma·li·cious·ly** *adv*

**[1]ma·lign** \mə-ˈlīn\ *adj*
MALIGNANT 1

**[2]malign** *vb*
to say evil things about **:** SLANDER

**ma·lig·nant** \mə-ˈlig-nənt\ *adj*
**1** evil in influence or result **:** INJURIOUS
**2** MALICIOUS 1
**3** likely to cause death **:** DEADLY
**ma·lig·nant·ly** *adv*

**mall** \ˈmȯl\ *n*
**1** a shaded walk **:** PROMENADE
**2** a usually paved or grassy strip between two roadways
**3** a shopping area in a community with a variety of shops around an often covered space for pedestrians

**mal·lard** \ˈmal-ərd\ *n*
a common wild duck of the northern hemisphere that is the ancestor of the domestic ducks

**mal·lea·ble** \ˈmal-ē-ə-bəl, ˈmal-yə-bəl\ *adj*
capable of being beaten out, extended, or shaped by hammer blows

**mal·let** \ˈmal-ət\ *n*
**1** a hammer with a short handle and a barrel-shaped head of wood or soft material used for driving a tool (as a chisel) or for striking a surface without denting it
**2** a club with a short thick rod for a head and a long thin rod for a handle ⟨croquet *mallet*⟩

**mal·low** \ˈmal-ō\ *n*
► a tall plant related to the hollyhock that has usually lobed leaves and white, rose, or purplish flowers with five petals

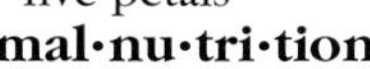

**mallow**

**mal·nu·tri·tion** \ˌmal-nu̇-ˈtrish-ən, -nyu̇-\ *n*
faulty nourishment

**malt** \ˈmȯlt\ *n*
**1** grain and especially barley soaked in water until it has sprouted
**2** MALTED MILK

**malt·ed milk** \ˈmȯl-təd-\ *n*
a beverage made by dissolving a powder made from dried milk and cereals in a liquid (as milk)

**mal·treat** \mal-ˈtrēt\ *vb*
to treat in arough or unkind way **:** ABUSE

**ma·ma** *or* **mam·ma** \ˈmäm-ə\ *n*
[1]MOTHER 1

**mam·mal** \ˈmam-əl\ *n*
► a warm-blooded animal that feeds its young with milk and has a backbone, two pairs of limbs, and a more or less complete covering of hair

**[1]mam·moth** \ˈmam-əth\ *n*
◄ a very large hairy extinct elephant with tusks that curve upward

**[2]mammoth** *adj*
very large **:** HUGE

**mam·my** \ˈmam-ē\ *n, pl* **mammies**
[1]MOTHER 1

**[1]man** \ˈman\ *n, pl* **men** \ˈmen\
**1** a human being **:** PERSON
**2** an adult male human being
**3** the human race **:** MANKIND
**4** a member of the natural family to which human beings belong including both modern humans and extinct related forms
**5** HUSBAND ⟨*man* and wife⟩
**6** an adult male servant or employee
**7** one of the pieces with which various games (as chess or checkers) are played

**[2]man** *vb* **manned**; **man·ning**
**1** to station crew members at ⟨*man* the lifeboats⟩
**2** to do the work of operating ⟨*man* the pumps⟩

**man·age** \ˈman-ij\ *vb* **man·aged**; **man·ag·ing**
**1** to look after and make decisions about **:** be the boss of ⟨*manage* a factory⟩
**2** to achieve what one wants to do ⟨I'll *manage* somehow⟩ ⟨they always *manage* to win⟩
**synonyms** see CONDUCT

**man·age·ment** \ˈman-ij-mənt\ *n*
**1** the managing of something
**2** the people who manage ⟨*management* and labor disagreed⟩

**man·ag·er** \ˈman-ij-ər\ *n*
a person who manages
**man·ag·er·ship** \-ˌship\ *n*

**man·a·tee** \ˈman-ə-ˌtē\ *n*
a mainly tropical water-dwelling mammal that eats plants and has a broad rounded tail

**man·da·rin** \ˈman-də-rən\ *n*
a high public official of the Chinese Empire

**man·date** \ˈman-ˌdāt\ *n*
**1** an order from a higher court to a lower court
**2** a command or instruction from an authority
**3** the instruction given by voters to their elected representatives

## mammal

Mammals live in a wide range of habitats throughout the world, kept warm by a covering of hair, which takes different forms, such as fur, wool, whiskers, and spines. There are three main types of mammals — egg-laying mammals, marsupials, and the largest group, mammals whose young grow inside the female's body, within a placenta, through which they are fed nutrients.

A B C D E F G H I J K L M N O P Q R S T U V W X Y Z

**man·da·tory** \'man-də-ˌtōr-ē\ *adj*
containing or being a command ⟨student attendance is *mandatory*⟩

**man·di·ble** \'man-də-bəl\ *n*
**1** a lower jaw often with its soft parts
**2** either the upper or lower part of the bill of a bird
**3** either of the first pair of mouth parts of some invertebrates (as an insect or crustacean) that often form biting organs

**mandolin**

**man·do·lin** \ˌman-də-'lin, 'man-dl-ən\ *n*
▲ an instrument with four pairs of strings played by plucking

**mane** \'mān\ *n*
long heavy hair growing from the neck or shoulders of an animal
**maned** \'mānd\ *adj*

[1]**ma·neu·ver** \mə-'nü-vər, -'nyü-\ *n*
**1** a planned movement of troops or ships
**2** a training exercise by armed forces
**3** skillful action or management ⟨avoided an accident by a quick *maneuver*⟩

[2]**maneuver** *vb*
**1** to move in a maneuver
**2** to perform a maneuver
**3** to guide skillfully
**ma·neu·ver·able** \-'nü-və-rə-bəl, -'nyü-\ *adj*

**ma·neu·ver·abil·i·ty** \mə-ˌnü-və-rə-'bil-ət-ē, -ˌnyü-\ *n*
the quality or state of being maneuverable

**man·ga·nese** \'mang-gə-ˌnēz\ *n*
a grayish white brittle metallic chemical element that resembles iron

**mange** \'mānj\ *n*
a contagious skin disease usually of domestic animals in which there is itching and loss of hair

**man·ger** \'mān-jər\ *n*
an open box in which food for farm animals is placed

**man·gle** \'mang-gəl\ *vb*
**man·gled**; **man·gling**
**1** to cut or bruise with repeated blows
**2** to spoil while making or performing ⟨*mangle* a speech⟩

**man·go** \'mang-gō\ *n*, *pl* **man·goes** *or* **man·gos**
a juicy, yellowish red mildly tart tropical fruit that is borne by an evergreen tree related to the cashew

**mangy** \'mān-jē\ *adj* **mang·i·er**; **mang·i·est**
**1** having mange or resulting from mange ⟨a *mangy* dog⟩
**2** SHABBY 2 ⟨a *mangy* old rug⟩
**3** SEEDY 2 ⟨a *mangy* restaurant⟩

**man·hole** \'man-ˌhōl\ *n*
a covered hole (as in a street or tank) large enough to let a person pass through

**man·hood** \'man-ˌhu̇d\ *n*
**1** COURAGE
**2** the state of being an adult human male
**3** adult human males ⟨the *manhood* of a nation⟩

**ma·nia** \'mā-nē-ə, -nyə\ *n*
**1** often violent or excited insanity
**2** unreasonable enthusiasm

**ma·ni·ac** \'mā-nē-ˌak\ *n*
a violently insane person

[1]**man·i·cure** \'man-ə-ˌkyu̇r\ *n*
**1** MANICURIST
**2** a treatment for the care of the hands and nails

[2]**manicure** *vb* **man·i·cured**; **man·i·cur·ing**
to give a manicure to

**man·i·cur·ist** \'man-ə-ˌkyu̇r-ist\ *n*
a person who gives manicures

[1]**man·i·fest** \'man-ə-ˌfest\ *adj*
easy to see or recognize : OBVIOUS ⟨their relief was *manifest*⟩

[2]**manifest** *vb*
to show plainly

**man·i·fes·ta·tion** \ˌman-ə-fəs-'tā-shən\ *n*
**1** the act of manifesting
**2** something that makes clear : EVIDENCE ⟨the first *manifestations* of spring⟩

**man·i·fold** \'man-ə-ˌfōld\ *adj*
of many and various kinds ⟨*manifold* activities⟩

**ma·nip·u·late** \mə-'nip-yə-ˌlāt\ *vb* **ma·nip·u·lat·ed**; **ma·nip·u·lat·ing**
**1** to work with the hands or by mechanical means and especially with skill ⟨*manipulate* the levers of a machine⟩
**2** to manage skillfully and especially with intent to deceive ⟨*manipulate* public opinion⟩

**man·kind** *n*
**1** \'man-'kīnd\ human beings
**2** \-ˌkīnd\ men as distinguished from women

**man·ly** \'man-lē\ *adj* **man·li·er**; **man·li·est**
having qualities (as courage) often felt to be proper for a man
**man·li·ness** *n*

**man–made** \'man-'mād\ *adj*
made by people rather than nature

**man·na** \'man-ə\ *n*
food supplied by a miracle to the Israelites in the wilderness

**man·ne·quin** \'man-i-kən\ *n*
a form representing the human figure used especially for displaying clothes

**man·ner** \'man-ər\ *n*
**1** [1]SORT 1
**2** a way of acting ⟨worked in a brisk *manner*⟩
**3** **manners** *pl* behavior toward or in the presence of other people ⟨they have good *manners*⟩

**man·ner·ism** \'man-ə-ˌriz-əm\ *n*
a habit (as of looking or moving in a certain way) that one notices in a person's behavior

**man·ner·ly** \'man-ər-lē\ *adj*
showing good manners : POLITE

**man–of–war** \ˌman-əv-'wȯr\ *n*, *pl* **men–of–war** \men-\
WARSHIP

**man·or** \'man-ər\ *n*
a large estate

**man·sion** \'man-chən\ *n*
a large fine house

**man·slaugh·ter** \'man-ˌslȯt-ər\ *n*
the unintentional but unlawful killing of a person

**man·ta ray** \'mant-ə-\ *n*
any of several very large rays of warm seas that have fins that resemble wings

**man·tel** \'mant-l\ *n*
a shelf above a fireplace

**man·tel·piece** \'mant-l-ˌpēs\ *n*
**1** a shelf above a fireplace along with side pieces
**2** MANTEL

**man·tis** \'mant-əs\ *n*, *pl* **man·tis·es** *or* **man·tes** \'man-ˌtēz\
an insect related to the grasshoppers and roaches that feeds on other

insects which are clasped in the raised front legs

**man·tle** \'mant-l\ *n*
**1** a loose sleeveless outer garment
**2** something that covers or wraps ⟨a *mantle* of snow⟩
**3** a fold of the body wall of a mollusk that produces the shell material
**4** the part of the earth's interior beneath the crust and above the central core

**¹man·u·al** \'man-yə-wəl\ *adj*
**1** of or relating to the hands ⟨*manual* skill⟩
**2** done or operated by the hands ⟨*manual* labor⟩ ⟨a *manual* gearshift⟩
**man·u·al·ly** *adv*

**²manual** *n*
HANDBOOK ⟨a scout *manual*⟩

**manual training** *n*
training in work done with the hands (as woodworking)

**¹man·u·fac·ture** \ˌman-yə-'fak-chər\ *n*
**1** the making of products by hand or machinery
**2** PRODUCTION 2 ⟨the *manufacture* of blood in the body⟩

**²manufacture** *vb*
**man·u·fac·tured**; **man·u·fac·tur·ing**
to make from raw materials by hand or machinery **synonyms** see MAKE
**man·u·fac·tur·er** *n*

**ma·nure** \mə-'nu̇r, -'nyu̇r\ *n*
material (as animal wastes) used to fertilize land

**Word History** Before we had modern machinery all farm work had to be done by hand. Back in those days the French had a verb that meant "to do work by hand" and it came to refer especially to the hard work of making the land grow crops. The English word *manure* came from this Old French verb and at first was used in just the same way. Later, perhaps because keeping the land fertile was such an important part of growing crops, the verb began to be used as a noun meaning "material used to make land fertile."

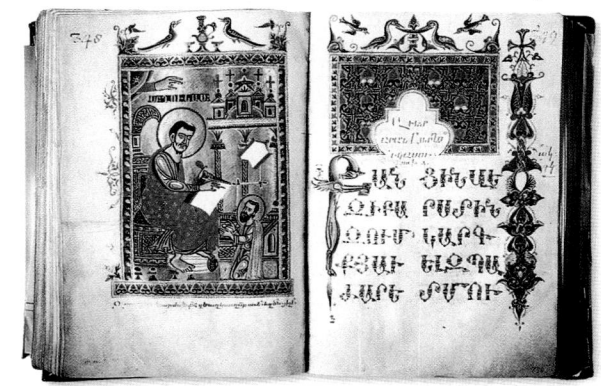

**manuscript 1:** a decorated medieval Armenian manuscript

**man·u·script** \'man-yə-ˌskript\ *n*
**1** ▲ a composition or document written by hand especially before the development of printing ⟨an ancient *manuscript*⟩
**2** a document submitted for publication
**3** HANDWRITING

**¹many** \'men-ē\ *adj* **more** \'mōr\; **most** \'mōst\
**1** amounting to a large number
**2** being one of a large but not fixed number ⟨*many* a day⟩

**²many** *pron*
a large number ⟨*many* of the students left late⟩

**³many** *n*
a large number ⟨a good *many* left early⟩

**¹map** \'map\ *n*
**1** ◄ a picture or chart showing features of an area (as the surface of the earth or the moon)
**2** a picture or chart of the sky showing the position of stars and planets

**Word History** The English word *map* came from a Latin word that in the time of the ancient Romans meant "napkin." Some years later, people began to use the Latin word that meant "napkin" in a new way. They used it for a piece of parchment that had drawn on it a picture or chart of the world or of a part of the world. The shape of the parchment must have reminded these people of the shape of a napkin.

**¹map 1**

There are a number of different types of maps produced to serve a range of functions. For example, city maps show the streets and landmarks of towns and cities, road maps show major and minor roads with their intersections, and satellite maps record the earth's surface. City and road maps are used for finding routes, with city maps giving detailed information on local facilities such as railroad stations.

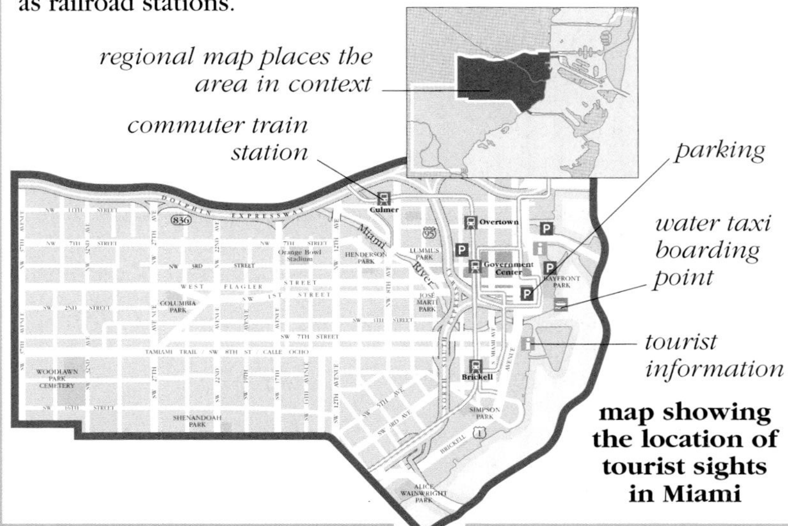


**map showing the location of tourist sights in Miami**

**[2]map** *vb* **mapped**; **map·ping**
**1** to make a map of ⟨*map* the heavens⟩
**2** to plan in detail ⟨*map* out a campaign⟩

**ma·ple** \'mā-pəl\ *n*
▼ any of a group of trees having deeply notched leaves, fruits with two wings, and hard pale wood and including some whose sap is evaporated to a sweet syrup (**maple syrup**) and a brownish sugar (**maple sugar**)

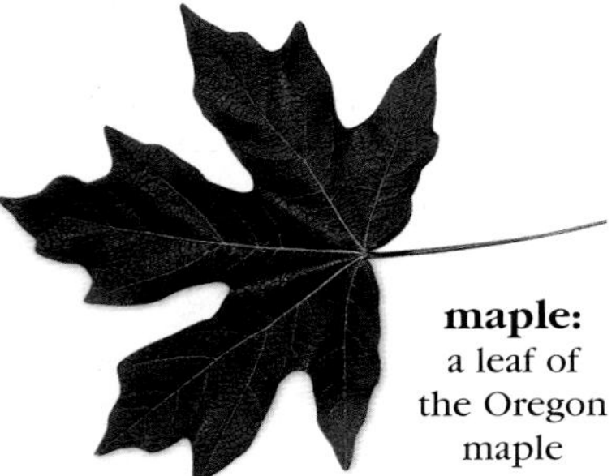

**maple:** a leaf of the Oregon maple

**mar** \'mär\ *vb* **marred**; **mar·ring**
to make a blemish on : SPOIL

**ma·ra·ca** \mə-'räk-ə, -'rak-\ *n*
a musical rhythm instrument made of a dried gourd with seeds or pebbles inside that is usually played in pairs by shaking

**mar·a·thon** \'mar-ə-ˌthän\ *n*
**1** a long-distance running race
**2** a long hard contest

**[1]mar·ble** \'mär-bəl\ *n*
**1** limestone that is capable of taking a high polish and is used in architecture and sculpture
**2** ▼ a little ball (as of glass) used in a children's game (**marbles**)

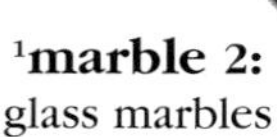

**[1]marble 2:** glass marbles

**[2]marble** *adj*
made of or like marble

**[1]march** \'märch\ *vb*
**1** to move or cause to move along steadily usually with long even steps and in step with others ⟨*march* in a parade⟩
**2** to make steady progress ⟨science *marches* on⟩
**march·er** *n*

**[2]march** *n*
**1** the action of marching
**2** the distance covered in marching ⟨a long day's *march*⟩
**3** a regular step used in marching
**4** a musical piece in a lively rhythm with a strong beat that is suitable to march to

**March** \'märch\ *n*
the third month of the year

**Word History** The English word *March* came from the Latin name for the same month. The Latin name came from *Mars*, the name of the Roman god of war and farming. The planet Mars also got its name from this god.

**mar·chio·ness** \'mär-shə-nəs\ *n*
**1** the wife or widow of a marquess
**2** a woman who holds the rank of a marquess in her own right

**mare** \'maər, 'meər\ *n*
an adult female of the horse or a related animal (as a zebra or donkey)

**mar·ga·rine** \'mär-jə-rən\ *n*
a food product made usually from vegetable oils and skim milk and used as a spread or for cooking

**mar·gin** \'mär-jən\ *n*
**1** the part of a page outside the main body of print or writing
**2** [1]BORDER 1
**3** an extra amount (as of time or money) allowed for use if needed ⟨we have a *margin* of five minutes⟩

**mari·gold** \'mar-ə-ˌgōld\ *n*
any of several plants related to the daisies that are grown for their yellow or brownish red and yellow flower heads

**mar·i·jua·na** \ˌmar-ə-'wä-nə\ *n*
dried leaves and flowers of the hemp plant smoked as a drug

**ma·ri·na** \mə-'rē-nə\ *n*
a dock or basin providing a place to anchor motorboats and yachts

**[1]ma·rine** \mə-'rēn\ *adj*
**1** of or relating to the sea ⟨*marine* paintings⟩ ⟨fish and other *marine* animals⟩
**2** of or relating to the navigation of the sea : NAUTICAL ⟨*marine* charts⟩
**3** of or relating to marines ⟨*marine* barracks⟩

**[2]marine** *n*
**1** the ships of a country ⟨the merchant *marine*⟩
**2** one of a class of soldiers serving on board a ship or in close cooperation with a naval force

**mar·i·ner** \'mar-ə-nər\ *n*
SEAMAN 1, SAILOR

**mar·i·o·nette** \ˌmar-ē-ə-'net, ˌmer-\ *n*
▼ a doll that can be made to move by means of strings : PUPPET

**marionettes** of a horse and a boy

**mar·i·tal** \'mar-ət-l\ *adj*
of or relating to marriage

**mar·i·time** \'mar-ə-ˌtīm\ *adj*
**1** of or relating to ocean navigation or trade ⟨*maritime* law⟩
**2** bordering on or living near the sea ⟨*maritime* nations⟩

**[1]mark** \'märk\ *n*
**1** something designed or serving to record position ⟨high-water *mark*⟩
**2** something aimed at : TARGET
**3** the starting line of a race
**4** INDICATION 2 ⟨a *mark* of friendship⟩

5 a blemish (as a scratch or stain) made on a surface ⟨the blow left a *mark*⟩
6 a written or printed symbol ⟨punctuation *mark*⟩
7 a grade or score showing the quality of work or conduct ⟨good *marks* in school⟩

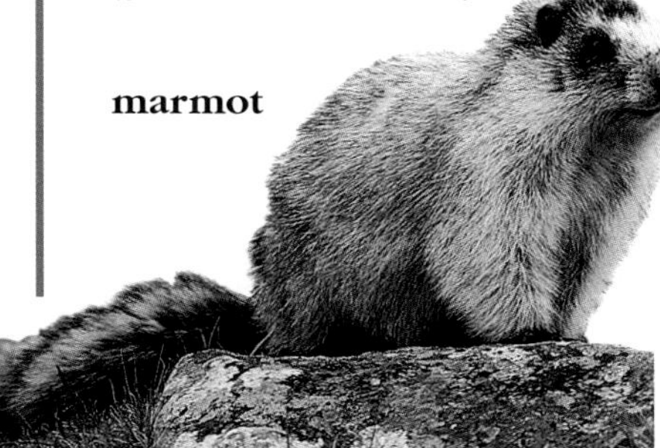
**marmot**

[2]**mark** *vb*
1 to set apart by a line or boundary ⟨*mark* off a tennis court⟩
2 to make a mark on ⟨*mark* the top with a cross⟩
3 to decide and show the value or quality of by marks : GRADE ⟨*mark* the tests⟩
4 to be an important characteristic of ⟨a disease *marked* by fever⟩
5 to take notice of ⟨*mark* my words⟩
**mark·er** *n*

[3]**mark** *n*
a German coin or bill

**marked** \'märkt\ *adj*
1 having a mark or marks
2 NOTICEABLE ⟨speaks with a *marked* accent⟩

[1]**mar·ket** \'mär-kət\ *n*
1 ► a meeting of people at a fixed time and place to buy and sell things
2 a public place where a market is held
3 a store where foods are sold to the public ⟨a meat *market*⟩
4 the region in which something can be sold ⟨*markets* for American cotton⟩

[2]**market** *vb*
to buy or sell in a market

**mar·ket·place** \'mär-kət-ˌplās\ *n*
an open square or place in a town where markets or public sales are held

**mark·ing** \'mär-king\ *n*
a mark made

**marks·man** \'märk-smən\ *n, pl* **marks·men** \-smən\
a person who shoots well
**marks·man·ship** \-ˌship\ *n*

**mar·ma·lade** \'mär-mə-ˌlād\ *n*
a jam containing pieces of fruit and fruit rind ⟨orange *marmalade*⟩

**mar·mo·set** \'mär-mə-ˌset\ *n*
a small monkey of South and Central America with soft fur and a bushy tail

**mar·mot** \'mär-mət\ *n*
◄ a stocky animal with short legs, coarse fur, and bushy tail that is related to the squirrels

[1]**ma·roon** \mə-'rün\ *vb*
to put ashore and abandon on a lonely island or coast

[2]**maroon** *n*
a dark red

**mar·quess** \'mär-kwəs\ *n*
a British nobleman ranking below a duke and above an earl

**mar·quis** \'mär-kwəs\ *n*
MARQUESS

**mar·quise** \mär-'kēz\ *n*
MARCHIONESS

**mar·riage** \'mar-ij\ *n*
1 the legal relationship into which a man and a woman enter with the purpose of making a home and raising a family
2 the act of getting married

**mar·row** \'mar-ō\ *n*
a soft tissue rich in fat and blood vessels that fills the cavities of most bones

[1]**market 1:**
a fruit and vegetable market

**mar·ry** \'mar-ē\ *vb* **mar·ried**; **mar·ry·ing**
1 to join in marriage as husband and wife ⟨they were *married* by a priest⟩
2 to give (as one's child) in marriage
3 to take for husband or wife ⟨*married* a high school sweetheart⟩
4 to enter into a marriage relationship ⟨decide to *marry*⟩

**Mars** \'märz\ *n*
▼ the planet that is fourth in order of distance from the sun, is known for its redness, and has a diameter of about 6800 kilometers

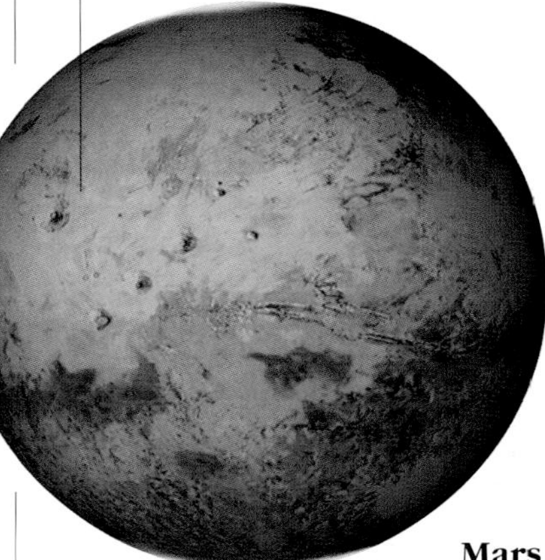

**Mars**

**marsh** \'märsh\ *n*
an area of soft wet land usually overgrown with grasses and related plants

[1]**mar·shal** \'mär-shəl\ *n*
1 a person who arranges and directs ceremonies ⟨*marshal* of the parade⟩
2 an officer of the highest rank in some military forces
3 a federal official having duties similar to those of a sheriff
4 the head of a division of a city government ⟨fire *marshal*⟩

[2]**marshal** *vb* **mar·shaled** *or* **mar·shalled**; **mar·shal·ing** *or* **mar·shal·ling**
to arrange in order ⟨*marshal* troops⟩

**marsh·mal·low** \'märsh-ˌmel-ō, -ˌmal-\ *n*
a soft spongy sweet made from corn syrup, sugar, and gelatin

**marsh marigold** *n*
a swamp plant with shiny leaves and bright yellow flowers like buttercups

**marshy** \'mär-shē\ *adj*
**marsh·i·er**; **marsh·i·est**
like or being a marsh

**mar·su·pi·al** \mär-'sü-pē-əl\ *n*
▶ any of a group of mammals (as kangaroos and opossums) that do not develop a true placenta and that usually have a pouch on the female's abdomen in which the young are carried

**mart** \'märt\ *n*
a trading place : MARKET

**mar·ten** \'märt-n\ *n*
a slender animal larger than the related weasels that eats flesh and is sought for its soft gray or brown fur

**mar·tial** \'mär-shəl\ *adj*
having to do with or suitable for war

**martial art** *n*
an art of combat and self-defense (as karate or judo) that is widely practiced as a sport

**mar·tin** \'märt-n\ *n*
**1** a European swallow with a forked tail
**2** ▲ any of several birds (as the American **purple martin**) resembling or related to the true martin

**martin 2:** a purple martin

**Mar·tin Lu·ther King Day** \'märt-n-'lü-thər-\ *n*
the third Monday in January observed as a legal holiday in some states of the United States

[1]**mar·tyr** \'märt-ər\ *n*
a person who suffers greatly or dies rather than give up his or her religion or principles

[2]**martyr** *vb*
to put to death for refusing to give up a belief

[1]**mar·vel** \'mär-vəl\ *n*
something that causes wonder or astonishment

[2]**marvel** *vb* **mar·veled** *or* **mar·velled**; **mar·vel·ing** *or* **mar·vel·ling**
to be struck with astonishment or wonder ⟨I *marvel* at your skill⟩

**mar·vel·ous** *or* **mar·vel·lous** \'mär-və-ləs\ *adj*
**1** causing wonder or astonishment
**2** of the finest kind or quality
**mar·vel·ous·ly** *adv*

**mas·cot** \'mas-,kät, -kət\ *n*
a person, animal, or object adopted by a group and believed to bring good luck

**mas·cu·line** \'mas-kyə-lən\ *adj*
**1** of the male sex
**2** [2]MALE 3

[1]**mash** \'mash\ *vb*
to make into a soft pulpy mass

[2]**mash** *n*
**1** a mixture of ground feeds used for feeding livestock
**2** a mass of something made soft and pulpy by beating or crushing

[1]**mask** \'mask\ *n*
**1** ▼ a cover for the face or part of the face used for disguise or protection ⟨a Halloween *mask*⟩ ⟨a catcher's *mask*⟩
**2** something that disguises or conceals ⟨a *mask* of friendship⟩
**3** a copy of a face molded in wax or plaster ⟨a death *mask*⟩

[1]**mask 1:** a girl with a bird mask

[2]**mask** *vb*
CONCEAL, DISGUISE ⟨*mask* one's anger⟩

**ma·son** \'mās-n\ *n*
a person who builds or works with stone, brick, or cement

**ma·son·ry** \'mās-n-rē\ *n*, *pl* **ma·son·ries**
**1** the art, trade, or occupation of a mason
**2** the work done by a mason
**3** something built of stone, brick, or concrete

**masque** \'mask\ *n*
**1** [1]MASQUERADE 1
**2** an old form of dramatic entertainment in which the actors wore masks

[1]**mas·quer·ade** \,mas-kə-'rād\ *n*
**1** a party (as a dance) at which people wear masks and costumes
**2** a pretending to be something one is not

[2]**masquerade** *vb*
**mas·quer·ad·ed**; **mas·quer·ad·ing**
**1** to disguise oneself
**2** to pass oneself off as something one is not : POSE ⟨*masquerade* as an expert⟩
**mas·quer·ad·er** *n*

[1]**mass** \'mas\ *n*
**1** an amount of something that holds or clings together ⟨a *mass* of iron ore⟩
**2** BULK 1, SIZE ⟨an elephant's huge *mass*⟩
**3** the principal part : main body ⟨the great *mass* of voters⟩
**4** a large quantity or number ⟨a *mass* of figures⟩
**5 masses** *pl* the body of ordinary or common people

[2]**mass** *vb*
to collect into a mass

**Mass** \'mas\ *n*
a religious service in celebration of the Eucharist

[1]**mas·sa·cre** \'mas-ə-kər\ *n*
the violent and cruel killing of a large number of persons

[2]**massacre** *vb* **mas·sa·cred**; **mas·sa·cring**
to kill in a massacre : SLAUGHTER

[1]**mas·sage** \mə-'säzh\ *n*
treatment of the body by rubbing, kneading, and tapping

[2]**massage** *vb* **mas·saged**; **mas·sag·ing**
to give massage to

**mas·sive** \'mas-iv\ *adj*
very large, heavy, and solid

**mast** \'mast\ *n*
**1** a long pole that rises from the bottom of a ship and supports the sails and rigging
**2** a vertical or nearly vertical tall pole ⟨a *mast* on a derrick⟩
**mast·ed** \'mas-təd\ *adj*

## marsupial

Newborn marsupials wriggle their way to the pouch or nipple, using their large forelimbs to grasp their mother's fur. The young suckle milk and continue to grow until they are ready to fend for themselves. Marsupials are found in Australia, New Guinea, North America, and South America.

koala

bandicoot

*a baby kangaroo is called a joey* \'jō-ē\

features of a female kangaroo

*pouch*

opossum

wombat

**[1]mas·ter** \'mas-tər\ *n*
**1** a male teacher
**2** an artist or performer of great skill
**3** one having authority over another person or thing ⟨the slave's *master*⟩ ⟨*master* of a ship⟩
**4** EMPLOYER
**5** used as a title for a young boy too young to be called *mister* ⟨*Master* Timothy Roe⟩

**[2]master** *vb*
**1** to get control of ⟨*master* your temper⟩
**2** to become skillful at ⟨*master* arithmetic⟩

**master chief petty officer** *n*
a petty officer in the Navy or Coast Guard ranking above a senior chief petty officer

**mas·ter·ful** \'mas-tər-fəl\ *adj*
**1** tending to take control **:** BOSSY
**2** having or showing great skill

**mas·ter·ly** \'mas-tər-lē\ *adj*
showing the knowledge or skill of a master ⟨a *masterly* performance⟩

**mas·ter·piece** \'mas-tər-ˌpēs\ *n*
a work done or made with supreme skill

**master sergeant** *n*
a noncommissioned officer in the Army ranking above a sergeant first class or in the Air Force ranking above a technical sergeant or in the Marine Corps ranking above a gunnery sergeant

**mas·tery** \'mas-tə-rē\ *n*, *pl* **mas·ter·ies**
**1** the position or authority of a master
**2** VICTORY 1 ⟨gained the *mastery* over their opponents⟩
**3** skill that makes one master of something

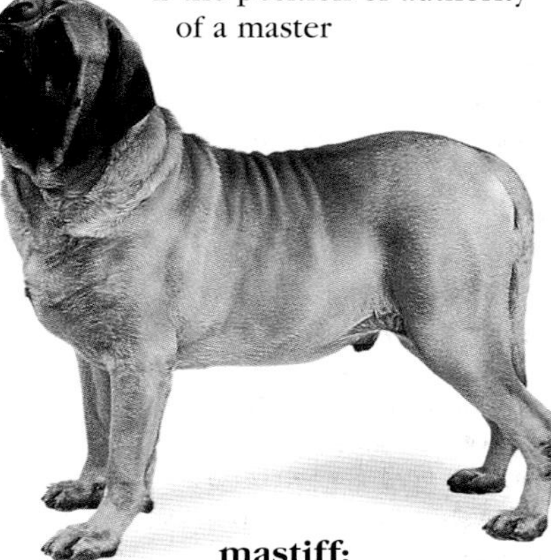

**mastiff:** a bullmastiff \'bu̇l-'mas-təf\

**mast·head** \'mast-ˌhed\ *n*
the top of a mast

**mas·ti·cate** \'mas-tə-ˌkāt\ *vb*
**mas·ti·cat·ed**; **mas·ti·cat·ing**
[1]CHEW

**mas·tiff** \'mas-təf\ *n*
◀ a very large powerful dog with a smooth coat

**[1]mat** \'mat\ *n*
**1** a piece of coarse woven or braided fabric used as a floor or seat covering
**2** a piece of material in front of a door to wipe the shoes on
**3** a piece of material (as cloth or woven straw) used under dishes or vases or as an ornament
**4** a pad or cushion for gymnastics or wrestling
**5** something made up of many tangled strands ⟨a *mat* of weeds⟩

**[2]mat** *vb* **mat·ted**; **mat·ting**
to form into a tangled mass

**mat·a·dor** \'mat-ə-,dȯr\ *n*
▼ a bullfighter who plays the chief human part in a bullfight

*a cape is used to encourage the bull to charge*

**matador:** a Spanish matador in traditional costume

**match·book** \'mach-,bu̇k\ *n*
► a small folder containing rows of paper matches

**match·less** \'mach-ləs\ *adj*
having no equal **:** better than any other of the same kind
**match·less·ly** *adv*

**match·lock** \'mach-,läk\ *n*
a musket with a hole at the rear of the barrel into which a slowly burning cord is lowered to ignite the charge

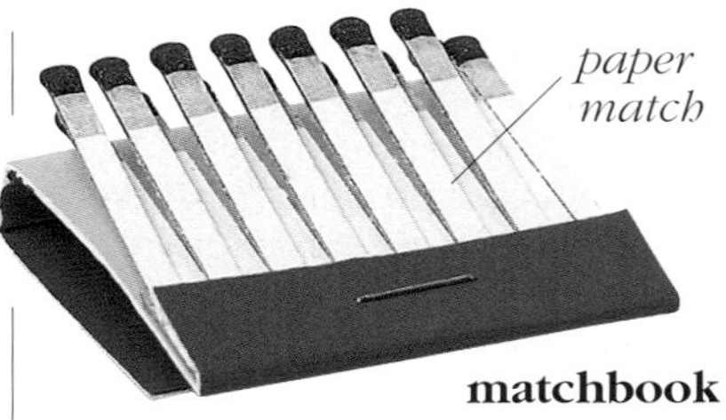


**matchbook**

**[1]match** \'mach\ *n*
**1** a person or thing that is equal to or as good as another ⟨we are a *match* for the enemy⟩
**2** a thing that is exactly like another thing ⟨this cloth is a *match* for that⟩
**3** two people or things that go well together ⟨the curtains and carpet are a good *match*⟩
**4** MARRIAGE 1 ⟨made a good *match*⟩
**5** a contest between two individuals or teams ⟨a tennis *match*⟩ ⟨a boxing *match*⟩ ⟨a soccer *match*⟩

**[2]match** *vb*
**1** to place in competition ⟨*matched* my strength with my rival's⟩
**2** to choose something that is the same as another or goes with it ⟨try to *match* this material⟩
**3** to be the same or suitable to one another ⟨the colors *match*⟩

**[3]match** *n*
**1** a wick or cord that is made to burn evenly and is used for lighting a charge of powder
**2** a short slender piece of material tipped with a mixture that produces fire when scratched

**[1]mate** \'māt\ *n*
**1** COMPANION 1, COMRADE
**2** an officer on a ship used to carry passengers or freight who ranks below the captain
**3** either member of a married couple
**4** either member of a breeding pair of animals
**5** either of two matched objects ⟨lost the *mate* to the glove⟩

**[2]mate** *vb* **mat·ed; mat·ing**
to join as mates **:** MARRY

**[1]ma·te·ri·al** \mə-'tir-ē-əl\ *adj*
**1** of, relating to, or made of matter **:** PHYSICAL ⟨the *material* world⟩
**2** of or relating to a person's bodily needs or wants ⟨*material* comforts⟩
**3** having real importance ⟨facts *material* to the case⟩
**ma·teri·al·ly** *adv*

**[2]material** *n*
**1** the elements, substance, or parts of which something is made or can be made ⟨building *material*⟩
**2 materials** *pl* equipment needed for doing something ⟨writing *materials*⟩

**ma·te·ri·al·ize** \mə-'tir-ē-ə-,līz\ *vb*
**ma·te·ri·al·ized; ma·te·ri·al·iz·ing**
**1** to cause to take on a physical form ⟨the medium claimed to *materialize* the spirits of the dead⟩
**2** to become actual fact ⟨their hopes never *materialized*⟩

**ma·ter·nal** \mə-'tərn-l\ *adj*
**1** of or relating to a mother ⟨*maternal* love⟩
**2** related through one's mother ⟨*maternal* grandparents⟩
**ma·ter·nal·ly** *adv*

**ma·ter·ni·ty** \mə-'tər-nət-ē\ *n*
the state of being a mother

**math** \'math\ *n*
MATHEMATICS

**math·e·mat·i·cal** \,math-ə-'mat-i-kəl\ *adj*
**1** of or relating to mathematics
**2** [2]EXACT ⟨*mathematical* precision⟩
**math·e·mat·i·cal·ly** *adv*

**math·e·ma·ti·cian** \,math-ə-mə-'tish-ən\ *n*
a specialist in mathematics

**math·e·mat·ics** \,math-ə-'mat-iks\ *n*
the science that studies and explains numbers, quantities, measurements, and the relations between them

**mat·i·nee** *or* **mat·i·née** \,mat-n-'ā\ *n*
a musical or dramatic performance in the afternoon

**ma·tri·arch** \'mā-trē-,ärk\ *n*
a woman who is head of a family, group, or state

**mat·ri·mo·ni·al** \,ma-trə-'mō-nē-əl\ *adj*
of or relating to marriage

**mat·ri·mo·ny** \'ma-trə-,mō-nē\ *n*
MARRIAGE 1

**ma·tron** \'mā-trən\ *n*
**1** a married woman
**2** a woman who is in charge of the household affairs of an institution
**3** a woman who looks after women prisoners in a police station or prison

**[1]mat·ter** \'mat-ər\ *n*
**1** something to be dealt with or

considered ⟨a serious *matter*⟩
**2** PROBLEM 2, DIFFICULTY ⟨what's the *matter?*⟩
**3** the substance things are made of **:** something that takes up space and has weight
**4** material substance of a certain kind or function ⟨coloring *matter*⟩ ⟨gray *matter* of the brain⟩
**5** PUS
**6** a more or less definite quantity or amount ⟨a *matter* of ten cents⟩
**7** [1]MAIL 1 ⟨third class *matter*⟩
**no matter** it makes no difference

**[2]matter** *vb*
to be of importance ⟨it does not *matter*⟩

**mat·ter–of–fact** \ˌmat-ər-ə-'fakt\ *adj*
sticking to or concerned with fact ⟨a *matter-of-fact* answer⟩

**mat·ting** \'mat-ing\ *n*
material for mats

**mat·tress** \'ma-trəs\ *n*
**1** a springy pad for use as a resting place usually over springs on a bedstead
**2** a sack that can be filled with air or water and used as a mattress

**[1]ma·ture** \mə-'tu̇r, -'tyu̇r\ *adj*
**1** fully grown or developed **:** ADULT, RIPE
**2** like that of a mature person ⟨a *mature* outlook⟩

**[2]mature** *vb* **ma·tured**; **ma·tur·ing**
to reach maturity

**ma·tu·ri·ty** \mə-'tu̇r-ət-ē, -'tyu̇r-\ *n*
the condition of being mature **:** full development

**[1]maul** \'mȯl\ *n*
a heavy hammer used especially for driving wedges or posts

**[2]maul** *vb*
**1** to beat and bruise severely
**2** to handle roughly

**mauve** \'mōv, 'mȯv\ *n*
a medium purple, violet, or lilac

**maxi-** *prefix*
very long or large

**max·il·la** \mak-'sil-ə\ *n, pl* **max·il·lae** \-'sil-ē\
**1** an upper jaw especially of a mammal
**2** either of the pair of mouth parts next behind the mandibles of an arthropod (as an insect or a crustacean)

**max·im** \'mak-səm\ *n*
a short saying expressing a general truth or rule of conduct

**[1]max·i·mum** \'mak-sə-məm\ *n, pl* **max·i·mums** *or* **max·i·ma** \-sə-mə\
the highest value **:** greatest amount ⟨we had to pay the *maximum*⟩

**[2]maximum** *adj*
as great as possible in amount or degree ⟨*maximum* efficiency⟩

**may** \mā\ *helping verb, past* **might** \mīt\; *present sing & pl* **may**
**1** have permission to ⟨you *may* go now⟩
**2** be in some degree likely to ⟨you *may* be right⟩
**3** used to express a wish ⟨*may* you be happy⟩
**4** used to express purpose ⟨we exercise so that we *may* be strong⟩

**May** \'mā\ *n*
the fifth month of the year

**Word History** The English word *May* came from the Latin name for the same month. The Latin name came from *Maia*, the name of a Roman goddess. Every year on the first of May, the ancient Romans made offerings to this goddess.

**may·be** \'mā-bē\ *adv*
possibly but not certainly

**mayn't** \'mā-ənt, mānt\
may not

**may·on·naise** \'mā-ə-ˌnāz\ *n*
a creamy dressing usually made of egg yolk, oil, and vinegar or lemon juice

**may·or** \'mā-ər\ *n*
an official elected to serve as head of a city or borough

**maze** \'māz\ *n*
► a confusing arrangement of paths or passages

**maze:** aerial view of part of a maze made of rows of hedges

**MB** \'em-'bē\ *n*
MEGABYTE

**me** \mē\ *pron, objective case of* I

**mead·ow** \'med-ō\ *n*
usually moist and low grassland

**mead·ow·lark** \'med-ō-ˌlärk\ *n*
▼ a bird that has brownish upper parts and a yellow breast and is about as large as a robin

**meadowlark**

**mea·ger** *or* **mea·gre** \'mē-gər\ *adj*
**1** having little flesh **:** THIN
**2** INSUFFICIENT ⟨a *meager* income⟩

**[1]meal** \'mēl\ *n*
**1** the food eaten or prepared for eating at one time
**2** the act or time of eating

**[2]meal** *n*
**1** usually coarsely ground seeds of a cereal grass and especially of Indian corn
**2** something like meal in texture ⟨fish *meal*⟩

**mealy** \'mē-lē\ *adj* **meal·i·er**; **meal·i·est**
like meal ⟨a *mealy* powder⟩
**meal·i·ness** *n*

**[1]mean** \'mēn\ *vb* **meant** \'ment\; **mean·ing** \'mē-ning\
**1** to have in mind as a purpose **:** INTEND ⟨I *mean* to go⟩
**2** to intend for a particular use ⟨a book *meant* for children⟩
**3** to have as a meaning **:** SIGNIFY ⟨what does this word *mean*⟩ ⟨those clouds *mean* rain⟩

A B C D E F G H I J K L M N O P Q R S T U V W X Y Z

**[2]mean** *adj*
**1** low in quality, worth, or dignity ⟨*mean* houses⟩ ⟨that was no *mean* achievement⟩
**2** lacking in honor or dignity ⟨your reasons are *mean*⟩
**3** STINGY 1
**4** deliberately unkind ⟨that was a *mean* trick to play⟩
**5** ASHAMED 1 ⟨it made me feel *mean* and unhappy⟩
**mean·ly** *adv*
**mean·ness** *n*

**[3]mean** *adj*
occurring or being in a middle position **:** AVERAGE ⟨*mean* temperature⟩

**[4]mean** *n*
**1** a middle point or something (as a place, time, number, or rate) that falls at or near a middle point **:** MODERATION
**2** ARITHMETIC MEAN
**3 means** *pl* something that helps a person to get what he or she wants ⟨use every *means* you can think of⟩
**4 means** *pl* WEALTH 1 ⟨a person of *means*⟩
**by all means** CERTAINLY 1
**by any means** in any way
**by means of** through the use of
**by no means** certainly not

**me·an·der** \mē-'an-dər\ *vb*
**1** to follow a winding course ⟨a brook *meandering* through the fields⟩
**2** to wander without a goal or purpose ⟨*meander* around town⟩

**mean·ing** \'mē-ning\ *n*
**1** the idea a person intends to express by something said or done ⟨what is the *meaning* of this?⟩
**2** the quality of communicating something or of being important ⟨a look full of *meaning*⟩

**mean·ing·ful** \'mē-ning-fəl\ *adj*
having a meaning or purpose
**mean·ing·ful·ly** \-fə-lē\ *adv*

**mean·ing·less** \'mē-ning-ləs\ *adj*
having no meaning or importance

**[1]mean·time** \'mēn-,tīm\ *n*
the time between two events

**[2]meantime** *adv*
in the meantime

**[1]mean·while** \'mēn-,hwīl, -,wīl\ *n*
[1]MEANTIME

**[2]meanwhile** *adv*
**1** [2]MEANTIME
**2** at the same time

**mea·sles** \'mē-zəlz\ *n sing or pl*
**1** a contagious disease in which there are fever and red spots on the skin
**2** any of several diseases (as **German measles**) resembling true measles

**mea·sly** \'mēz-lē\ *adj* **mea·sli·er**; **mea·sli·est**
so small or unimportant as to be rejected with scorn

**mea·sur·able** \'mezh-ə-rə-bəl\ *adj*
capable of being measured

**[1]mea·sure** \'mezh-ər\ *n*
**1** EXTENT 2, DEGREE, AMOUNT ⟨succeed in large *measure*⟩
**2** the size, capacity, or quantity of something as fixed by measuring ⟨made to *measure*⟩
**3** something (as a yardstick or cup) used in measuring
**4** a unit used in measuring
**5** a system of measuring ⟨liquid *measure*⟩
**6** the notes and rests between bar lines on a musical staff
**7** a way of accomplishing something ⟨take *measures* to stop it⟩ ⟨a safety *measure*⟩
**8** a legislative bill or act

**[2]measure 1:** using a measuring cup to measure bread crumbs

**[2]measure** *vb* **mea·sured**; **mea·sur·ing**
**1** ▲ to find out the size, extent, or amount of ⟨*measure* the cloth with the tape measure⟩
**2** [1]ESTIMATE 1 ⟨*measure* the distance with the eye⟩
**3** to bring into comparison ⟨*measure* your skill against an opponent's⟩
**4** to give a measure of **:** INDICATE ⟨a thermometer *measures* temperature⟩
**5** to have as its measurement ⟨the cloth *measures* ten meters⟩

**mea·sure·ment** \'mezh-ər-mənt\ *n*
**1** the act of measuring
**2** the extent, size, capacity, or amount of something as fixed by measuring
**3** a system of measures

**measure up** *vb*
to satisfy needs or requirements ⟨*measure up* to expectations⟩

**meat** \'mēt\ *n*
**1** solid food ⟨*meat* and drink⟩
**2** the part of something that can be eaten ⟨nut *meats*⟩
**3** animal and especially mammal tissue for use as food
**4** the most important part **:** SUBSTANCE ⟨the *meat* of the story⟩
**meat·less** \-ləs\ *adj*

**meat·ball** \'mēt-,bòl\ *n*
a small ball of chopped or ground meat

**me·chan·ic** \mi-'kan-ik\ *n*
a person who makes or repairs machines

**me·chan·i·cal** \mi-'kan-i-kəl\ *adj*
**1** of or relating to machinery ⟨*mechanical* engineering⟩
**2** made or operated by a machine ⟨a *mechanical* toy⟩
**3** done or produced as if by a machine ⟨sing in a *mechanical* way⟩
**me·chan·i·cal·ly** *adv*

**me·chan·ics** \mi-'kan-iks\ *n sing or pl*
**1** a science dealing with the action of forces on bodies
**2** the way something works or things are done ⟨the *mechanics* of a watch⟩ ⟨the *mechanics* of writing⟩

**mech·a·nism** \'mek-ə-,niz-əm\ *n*
**1** a mechanical device
**2** ▶ the parts by which a machine operates ⟨the *mechanism* of a watch⟩
**3** the parts or steps that make up a process or activity ⟨the *mechanism* of government⟩

**mechanism 2:** visible mechanism of a watch

**mech·a·nize** \'mek-ə-,nīz\ *vb* **mech·a·nized**; **mech·a·niz·ing**
**1** to make mechanical or automatic
**2** to equip with machinery

**med·al** \'med-l\ *n*
▼ a piece of metal often in the form of a coin with design and words in honor of a special event, a person, or an achievement

*ribbon allows medal to be placed around athlete's neck*

**medal:** an athlete's medal

**Word History** The English word *medal* came from a French word meaning "medal." The French word, however, came from an Italian word that was at first the name for a coin worth half as much as another coin. The name for this coin came from a Latin word that meant "middle" or "half." The Italian word came to mean "medal" before finding its way into French and from French into English.

**me·dal·lion** \mə-'dal-yən\ *n*
**1** a large medal
**2** something like a large medal (as in shape) ⟨a doily with a lace *medallion* in the center⟩

**med·dle** \'med-l\ *vb* **med·dled**; **med·dling**
to interest oneself in what is not one's concern

**Synonyms** MEDDLE, INTERFERE, TAMPER mean to concern oneself with something that is not one's own business. MEDDLE stresses intruding in an inconsiderate and annoying fashion ⟨*meddling* in a friend's personal problems⟩. INTERFERE suggests getting in the way of or disturbing someone or something whether intentionally or not ⟨building the dam *interfered* with nature⟩ ⟨a bossy child always *interfering* with the others' play⟩. TAMPER implies intruding or experimenting that is wrong or uncalled-for and likely to be harmful ⟨someone had *tampered* with the lock⟩.

**med·dle·some** \'med-l-səm\ *adj*
given to meddling

**media** *pl of* MEDIUM

**med·i·cal** \'med-i-kəl\ *adj*
of or relating to the science or practice of medicine or to the treatment of disease
**med·i·cal·ly** *adv*

**med·i·cate** \'med-ə-ˌkāt\ *vb* **med·i·cat·ed**; **med·i·cat·ing**
**1** to use medicine on or for ⟨*medicate* a sore throat⟩
**2** to add medicinal material to ⟨*medicated* soap⟩

**med·i·ca·tion** \ˌmed-ə-'kā-shən\ *n*
**1** the act or process of medicating
**2** medicinal material

**me·dic·i·nal** \mə-'dis-n-əl\ *adj*
used or likely to relieve or cure disease
**me·dic·i·nal·ly** *adv*

**med·i·cine** \'med-ə-sən\ *n*
**1** ▼ something used to cure or relieve a disease
**2** a science or art dealing with the prevention, cure, or relief of disease

**medicine dropper** *n*
DROPPER 2

**medicine man** *n*
a member of a primitive tribe believed to have magic powers and called on to cure illnesses and keep away evil spirits

**me·di·eval** *or* **me·di·ae·val** \ˌmēd-ē-'ē-vəl, ˌmed-\ *adj*
of or relating to the Middle Ages

**me·di·o·cre** \ˌmēd-ē-'ō-kər\ *adj*
neither good nor bad **:** ORDINARY

**med·i·tate** \'med-ə-ˌtāt\ *vb* **med·i·tat·ed**; **med·i·tat·ing**
**1** to consider carefully **:** PLAN ⟨*meditate* a trip⟩
**2** to spend time in quiet thinking **:** REFLECT

**med·i·ta·tion** \ˌmed-ə-'tā-shən\ *n*
the act or an instance of meditating

**medicine 1**
Medicines are used to treat a wide variety of ailments, from minor complaints such as a sore throat to life-threatening conditions such as heart disease. A common method for taking medicines is to swallow them in tablet, capsule, or syrup form. Other medicines are given by injection, inhaled through the nose or mouth, introduced in liquid form through a dropper to the eye or ear, or absorbed through the skin as cream or ointment.

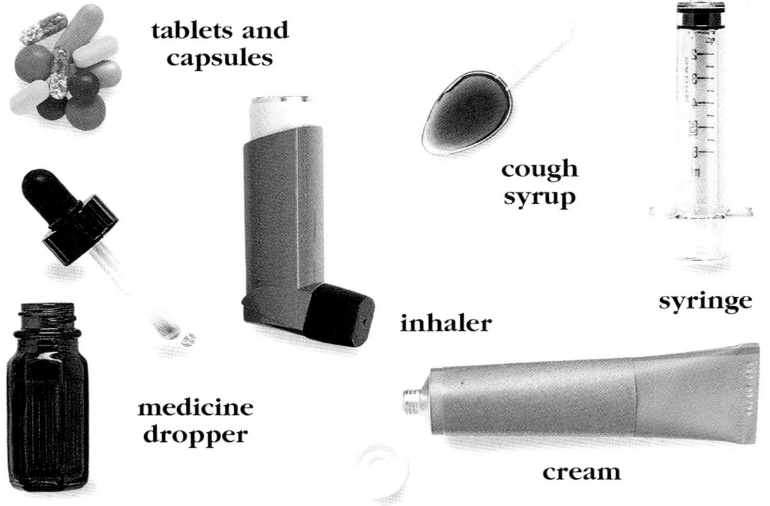

**Med·i·ter·ra·nean** \ˌmed-ə-tə-ˈrā-nē-ən, -ˈrān-yən\ *adj*
of or relating to the Mediterranean sea or to the lands or peoples surrounding it

[1]**me·di·um** \ˈmēd-ē-əm\ *n, pl* **me·di·ums** *or* **me·dia** \-ē-ə\
**1** something that is between or in the middle
**2** the thing by which or through which something is done ⟨money is a *medium* of exchange⟩
**3** the substance in which something lives or acts ⟨the *medium* of air⟩
**4** a person through whom other persons try to communicate with the spirits of the dead

[2]**medium** *adj*
intermediate in amount, quality, position, or degree ⟨*medium* size⟩

**med·ley** \ˈmed-lē\ *n, pl* **medleys**
**1** MIXTURE 2, JUMBLE ⟨a *medley* of tastes⟩
**2** a musical selection made up of a series of different songs or parts of different compositions

**me·dul·la ob·lon·ga·ta** \mə-ˈdəl-ə-ˌäb-ˌlȯng-ˈgät-ə\ *n*
the last part of the brain that joins the spinal cord and is concerned especially with control of involuntary activities (as breathing and beating of the heart)

**meed** \ˈmēd\ *n*
something deserved or earned **:** REWARD ⟨received their *meed* of praise⟩

**meek** \ˈmēk\ *adj*
**1** putting up with injury or abuse with patience
**2** lacking spirit or self-confidence
**meek·ly** *adv*
**meek·ness** *n*

[1]**meet** \ˈmēt\ *vb* **met** \ˈmet\; **meet·ing**
**1** to come upon or across ⟨*met* a friend while shopping⟩
**2** to be at a place to greet or keep an appointment ⟨*meet* me at the airport⟩ ⟨*met* in the park for lunch⟩
**3** to approach from the opposite direction ⟨when you *meet* another car, keep to the right⟩
**4** to come together **:** JOIN, MERGE ⟨where the two rivers *meet*⟩
**5** to be sensed by ⟨sounds that *meet* the ears⟩
**6** to deal with ⟨*meet* problems as they appear⟩
**7** to fulfill the requirements of **:** SATISFY ⟨unable to *meet* your demands⟩
**8** to become acquainted ⟨they *met* at a party⟩
**9** to hold a meeting

[2]**meet** *n*
a meeting for sports competition ⟨track *meet*⟩

**meet·ing** \ˈmēt-ing\ *n*
**1** the act of persons or things that meet
**2** ASSEMBLY 1 ⟨the club holds *meetings* once a month⟩

**meet·ing·house** \ˈmēt-ing-ˌhau̇s\ *n*
a building used for public assembly and especially for Protestant worship

**mega·byte** \ˈmeg-ə-ˌbīt\ *n*
a unit of computer information storage capacity equal to 1,048,576 bytes

**mega·phone** \ˈmeg-ə-ˌfōn\ *n*
▼ a device shaped like a cone that is used to direct the voice and increase its loudness

**megaphone:** a woman speaking through a megaphone

[1]**mel·an·choly** \ˈmel-ən-ˌkäl-ē\ *n*
a sad or gloomy mood

[2]**melancholy** *adj*
SAD 1

[1]**mel·low** \ˈmel-ō\ *adj*
**1** tender and sweet because of ripeness ⟨a *mellow* peach⟩
**2** made mild by age ⟨*mellow* wines⟩ ⟨a *mellow* character⟩
**3** being clear, full, and pure **:** not coarse ⟨a *mellow* sound⟩ ⟨a *mellow* color⟩
**mel·low·ness** *n*

[2]**mellow** *vb*
to make or become mellow

**me·lo·di·ous** \mə-ˈlōd-ē-əs\ *adj*
agreeable to the ear because of its melody
**me·lo·di·ous·ly** *adv*
**me·lo·di·ous·ness** *n*

**mel·o·dy** \ˈmel-əd-ē\ *n, pl* **mel·o·dies**
**1** pleasing arrangement of sounds
**2** a series of musical notes or tones arranged in a definite pattern of pitch and rhythm
**3** the leading part in a musical composition

**mel·on** \ˈmel-ən\ *n*
► a fruit (as a watermelon) having juicy and usually sweet flesh and growing on a vine related to the gourds

**melon:** a watermelon

**melt** \ˈmelt\ *vb*
**1** to change from a solid to a liquid usually through the action of heat ⟨*melt* sugar⟩ ⟨snow *melts*⟩
**2** to grow less **:** DISAPPEAR ⟨clouds *melting* away⟩
**3** to make or become gentle **:** SOFTEN ⟨kindness that *melts* the heart⟩
**4** to lose clear outline ⟨sky *melting* into sea⟩

**melting point** *n*
the temperature at which a solid melts

**mem·ber** \ˈmem-bər\ *n*
**1** a part (as an arm, leg, leaf, or branch) of a person, animal, or plant
**2** one of the individuals (as persons) or units (as species) making up a group
**3** a part of a structure ⟨a horizontal *member* of a bridge⟩

**mem·ber·ship** \ˈmem-bər-ˌship\ *n*
**1** the state or fact of being a member
**2** the whole number of members

**mem·brane** \ˈmem-ˌbrān\ *n*
a thin soft flexible layer especially of animal or plant tissue

**mem·bra·nous** \'mem-brə-nəs\ *adj*
made of or like membrane

**me·men·to** \mi-'ment-ō\ *n, pl* **me·men·tos** *or* **me·men·toes**
▼ something that serves as a reminder ⟨*mementos* of a trip⟩

**memento** of a trip to England

**mem·o·ra·ble** \'mem-ə-rə-bəl, 'mem-rə-bəl\ *adj*
worth remembering : not easily forgotten
**mem·o·ra·bly** \-blē\ *adv*

**mem·o·ran·dum** \,mem-ə-'ran-dəm\ *n, pl* **mem·o·ran·dums** *or* **mem·o·ran·da** \-də\
**1** an informal record or message
**2** a written reminder

**¹me·mo·ri·al** \mə-'mōr-ē-əl\ *adj*
serving to preserve the memory of a person or event ⟨a *memorial* service⟩

**²memorial** *n*
► something by which the memory of a person or an event is kept alive : MONUMENT ⟨the Lincoln *Memorial*⟩

**Memorial Day** *n*
**1** May 30 once observed as a legal holiday in remembrance of war dead
**2** the last Monday in May observed as a legal holiday in most states of the United States

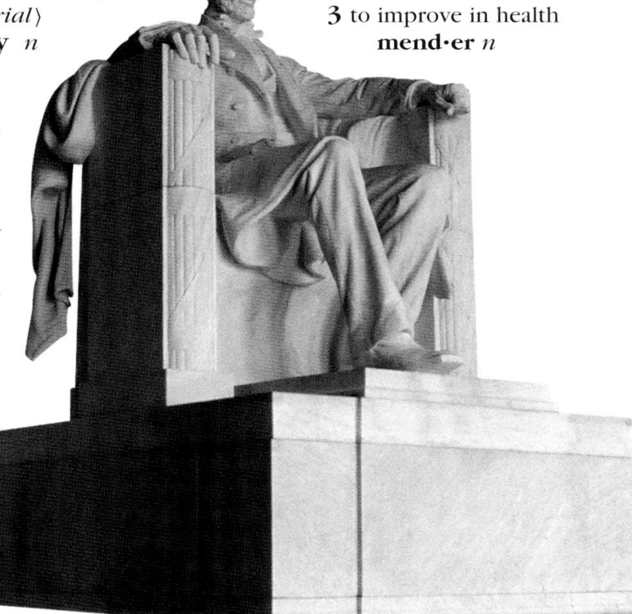

**²memorial:** the Lincoln Memorial in Washington, DC

**mem·o·rize** \'mem-ə-,rīz\ *vb* **mem·o·rized**; **mem·o·riz·ing**
to learn by heart

**mem·o·ry** \'mem-ə-rē, 'mem-rē\ *n, pl* **mem·o·ries**
**1** the power or process of remembering
**2** the store of things learned and kept in the mind ⟨recite from *memory*⟩
**3** the act of remembering and honoring ⟨in *memory* of a great soldier⟩
**4** something remembered ⟨a pleasant *memory*⟩
**5** the time within which past events are remembered ⟨within the *memory* of anyone living today⟩
**6** a device or part in a computer which can receive and store information for use when wanted ⟨a *memory* chip⟩
**7** capacity for storing information ⟨four megabytes of *memory*⟩

**men** *pl of* MAN

**¹men·ace** \'men-əs\ *n*
**1** DANGER 2 ⟨the *menace* of disease⟩
**2** an annoying person

**²menace** *vb* **men·aced**; **men·ac·ing**
THREATEN 1

**me·nag·er·ie** \mə-'naj-ə-rē\ *n*
a collection of confined wild animals

**¹mend** \'mend\ *vb*
**1** IMPROVE, CORRECT ⟨*mend* your ways⟩
**2** to restore to a whole condition
**3** to improve in health
**mend·er** *n*

---

**Synonyms** MEND, PATCH, REPAIR mean to take something that has been damaged and make it usable again. MEND suggests making something that has been broken or damaged once again whole or fit for use ⟨*mend* a piece of china⟩. PATCH refers to mending a hole or tear by using the same or similar material ⟨*patched* my pants with scraps of cloth⟩. PATCH may also suggest a hurried, careless job ⟨just *patch* the roof for now⟩. REPAIR suggests a skillful mending of a complicated thing that has been damaged very much ⟨*repaired* our car⟩.

---

**²mend** *n*
**1** the process of improving ⟨a broken leg on the *mend*⟩
**2** a mended place

**men·folk** \'men-,fōk\ *or* **men·folks** \-,fōks\ *n pl*
the men of a family or community

**men·ha·den** \men-'hād-n\ *n, pl* **menhaden**
a fish of the Atlantic coast of the United States that is related to the herrings and is a source of oil and fertilizer

**¹me·ni·al** \'mē-nē-əl\ *n*
a household servant

**²menial** *adj*
of, relating to, or suitable for servants : not needing skill ⟨*menial* tasks⟩

**men–of–war** *pl of* MAN-OF-WAR

**me·no·rah** \mə-'nōr-ə\ *n*
a holder for candles used in Jewish worship

**men·stru·a·tion** \,men-strə-'wā-shən, men-'strā-shən\ *n*
a periodic discharge of bloody fluid from the uterus

**-ment** \mənt\ *n suffix*
**1** result, goal, or method of a specified action ⟨entangle*ment*⟩ ⟨entertain*ment*⟩
**2** action : process ⟨develop*ment*⟩
**3** place of a specified action ⟨encamp*ment*⟩
**4** state : condition ⟨amaze*ment*⟩

**men·tal** \'ment-l\ *adj*
**1** of or relating to the mind
**2** done in the mind ⟨*mental* arithmetic⟩
**men·tal·ly** *adv*

**men·tal·i·ty** \men-'tal-ət-ē\ *n*
mental power : ability to learn

A B C D E F G H I J K L M N O P Q R S T U V W X Y Z

**men·thol** \'men-,thȯl\ *n*
a white crystalline soothing substance from oils of mint

[1]**men·tion** \'men-chən\ *n*
a brief reference to something

[2]**mention** *vb*
to refer to **:** speak about briefly ⟨barely *mentioned* their contribution⟩

**menu** \'men-yü\ *n*
**1** a list of dishes served at or available for a meal
**2** the dishes or kinds of food served at a meal
**3** ► a list shown on a computer screen from which a user can select an operation for the computer to perform

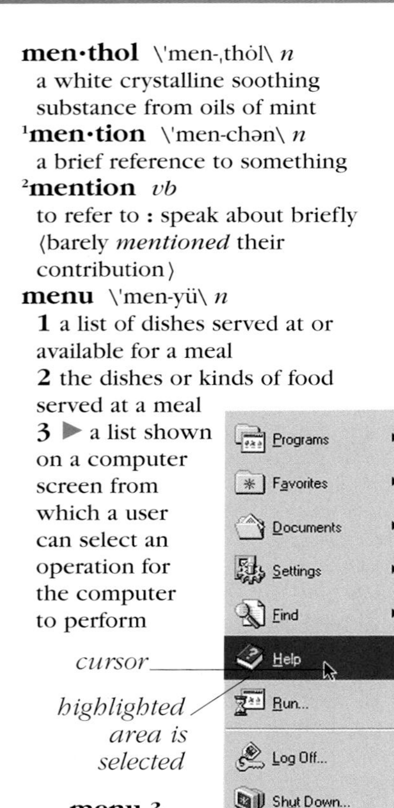


**menu 3**

**Word History** The English word *menu* came from a French word with the same spelling and meaning. The French noun that means "menu" came from an adjective that means "small," "slender," or "detailed." Since a menu is a detailed list, this last meaning must have given English and French the noun *menu*.

[1]**me·ow** \mē-'au̇\ *n*
the cry of a cat

[2]**meow** *vb*
to utter a meow

**mer·can·tile** \'mər-kən-,tēl, -,tīl\ *adj*
of or relating to merchants or trade

[1]**mer·ce·nary** \'mərs-n-,er-ē\ *n, pl* **mer·ce·nar·ies**
a soldier from a foreign country hired to fight in an army

[2]**mercenary** *adj*
**1** doing something only for the pay or reward
**2** greedy for money

**mer·chan·dise** \'mər-chən-,dīz, -,dīs\ *n*
goods bought and sold in trade

**mer·chant** \'mər-chənt\ *n*
**1** a person who carries on trade especially on a large scale or with foreign countries
**2** STOREKEEPER 2

**mer·chant·man** \'mər-chənt-mən\ *n, pl* **mer·chant·men** \-mən\
a ship used in trading

**merchant marine** *n*
**1** the trading ships of a nation
**2** the persons who work in a merchant marine

**mer·ci·ful** \'mər-si-fəl\ *adj*
having or showing mercy or compassion
**mer·ci·ful·ly** \-fə-lē\ *adv*

**mer·ci·less** \'mər-si-ləs\ *adj*
having no mercy **:** PITILESS
**mer·ci·less·ly** *adv*

**mer·cu·ric** \,mər-'kyu̇r-ik\ *adj*
of, relating to, or containing mercury

**mer·cu·ry** \'mər-kyə-rē\ *n*
**1** a heavy silvery white metallic chemical element that is liquid at ordinary temperatures
**2** the column of mercury in a thermometer or barometer
**3** ▼ *cap* the planet that is nearest the sun and has a diameter of about 4700 kilometers

**mercury 3:** the planet Mercury

**mer·cy** \'mər-sē\ *n, pl* **mer·cies**
**1** kind and gentle treatment of a wrongdoer, an opponent, or some unfortunate person
**2** a kind sympathetic disposition **:** willingness to forgive, spare, or help
**3** a blessing as an act of divine love ⟨the *mercies* of God⟩
**4** a fortunate happening ⟨it's a *mercy* that we arrived in time⟩

**mere** \'mir\ *adj, superlative* **mer·est**
nothing more than **:** SIMPLE ⟨*mere* rumors⟩

**mere·ly** \'mir-lē\ *adv*
nothing else than **:** JUST

**merge** \'mərj\ *vb* **merged**; **merg·ing**
to be or cause to be combined or blended into a single unit

**merg·er** \'mər-jər\ *n*
a combination of two or more businesses into one

**me·rid·i·an** \mə-'rid-ē-ən\ *n*
**1** the highest point reached
**2** any imaginary semicircle on the earth reaching from the north to the south pole
**3** a representation of a meridian on a map or globe numbered according to degrees of longitude

**me·ringue** \mə-'rang\ *n*
**1** ▼ a mixture of beaten white of egg and sugar put on pies or cakes and browned
**2** a shell made of baked meringue and filled with fruit or ice cream

meringue

**meringue 1:** a lemon pie with meringue

**me·ri·no** \mə-'rē-nō\ *n, pl* **me·ri·nos**
**1** a sheep of a breed that produces a heavy fleece of white fine wool
**2** a fine soft fabric like cashmere

[1]**mer·it** \'mer-ət\ *n*
**1** the condition or fact of deserving well or ill ⟨students are graded according to *merit*⟩
**2** [2]WORTH 1, VALUE ⟨a suggestion having great *merit*⟩
**3** a quality worthy of praise **:** VIRTUE ⟨the *merit* of honesty⟩

[2]**merit** *vb*
to be worthy of or have a right to ⟨I think I *merit* a higher mark⟩
**synonyms** see DESERVE

**mer·i·to·ri·ous** \,mer-ə-'tōr-ē-əs\ *adj*
deserving reward or honor **:** PRAISEWORTHY
**mer·i·to·ri·ous·ly** *adv*

**mer·maid** \'mər-,mād\ *n*
an imaginary sea creature usually shown with a woman's body and a fish's tail

**mer·man** \'mər-,man\ *n, pl* **mer·men** \-,men\
an imaginary sea creature usually shown with a man's body and a fish's tail

**mer·ri·ment** \'mer-i-mənt\ *n*
GAIETY, MIRTH

**mer·ry** \'mer-ē\ *adj* **mer·ri·er**; **mer·ri·est**
**1** full of good humor and good spirits : JOYOUS
**2** full of gaiety or festivity ⟨a *merry* Christmas⟩
**mer·ri·ly** \'mer-ə-lē\ *adv*

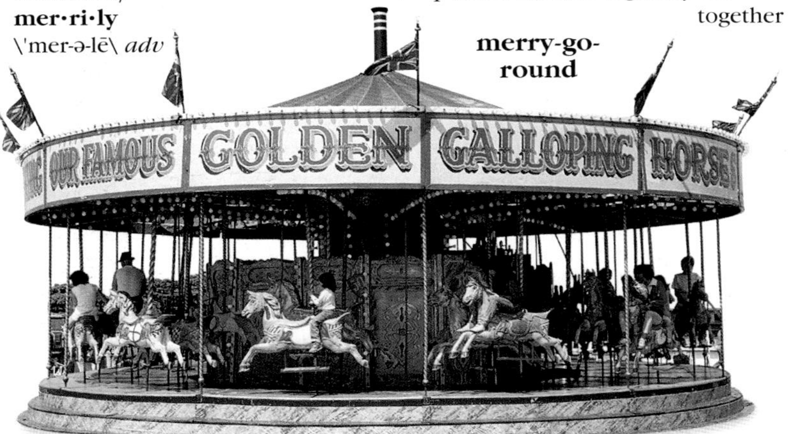

**merry-go-round**

**mer·ry–go–round** \'mer-ē-gō-,raund\ *n*
▲ a circular revolving platform fitted with seats and figures of animals on which people sit for a ride

**mer·ry·mak·er** \'mer-ē-,mā-kər\ *n*
one taking part in merrymaking

**mer·ry·mak·ing** \'mer-ē-,mā-king\ *n*
**1** merry activity
**2** a festive occasion : PARTY

**me·sa** \'mā-sə\ *n*
a hill with a flat top and steep sides

**mesdames** *pl of* MADAM *or of* MRS.

**[1]mesh** \'mesh\ *n*
**1** one of the spaces enclosed by the threads of a net or the wires of a sieve or screen
**2** NETWORK 1, 2
**3** the coming or fitting together of the teeth of two sets of gears

**[2]mesh** *vb*
to fit together : INTERLOCK ⟨gear teeth that *mesh*⟩

**Mes·o·zo·ic** \,mez-ə-'zō-ik, ,mes-\ *n*
an era of geological history which extends from the Paleozoic to the Cenozoic and in which dinosaurs are present and the first birds and mammals and flowering plants appear

**mes·quite** \mə-'skēt\ *n*
a spiny shrub or small tree of the southwestern United States and Mexico that is related to the clovers

**[1]mess** \'mes\ *n*
**1** a group of people (as military personnel) who regularly eat together
**2** the meal eaten by a mess
**3** a state of confusion or disorder ⟨left things in a *mess*⟩

**[2]mess** *vb*
**1** to take meals with a mess
**2** to make dirty or untidy ⟨*messed* the place up⟩
**3** to mix up : BUNGLE ⟨*messed* up the schedule⟩
**4** to work without serious goal : PUTTER
**5** [2]FOOL 2, INTERFERE ⟨you'd better not *mess* with them⟩

**mes·sage** \'mes-ij\ *n*
a communication in writing, in speech, or by signals

**mes·sen·ger** \'mes-n-jər\ *n*
a person who carries a message or does an errand

**Messrs.** *pl of* MR.

**messy** \'mes-ē\ *adj* **mess·i·er**; **mess·i·est**
UNTIDY
**mess·i·ly** \'mes-ə-lē\ *adv*
**mess·i·ness** \'mes-ē-nəs\ *n*

**met** *past of* MEET

**met·a·bol·ic** \,met-ə-'bäl-ik\ *adj*
of or relating to metabolism
**met·a·bol·i·cal·ly** \-i-kə-lē\ *adv*

**me·tab·o·lism** \mə-'tab-ə-,liz-əm\ *n*
the processes by which a living being uses food to obtain energy and build tissue and disposes of waste material

**[1]met·al** \'met-l\ *n*
**1** ▼ a substance (as gold, tin, copper, or bronze) that has a more or less shiny appearance, is a good conductor of electricity and heat, and usually can be made into a wire or hammered into a thin sheet
**2** METTLE ⟨the soldiers showed their *metal*⟩

**[1]metal 1**

Some metals are valued for their beauty and rarity, others for their usefulness. Precious metals such as gold, silver, and platinum are commonly made into jewelry, while weaker, more readily available metals such as aluminum, lead, and tin are used to make a range of practical items. Metals may also be combined to make an alloy — brass, for example, is a combination of copper and zinc.

**gold**

**platinum**

**silver** in its natural form

**lead** pellets

**[2]metal** *adj*
made of metal

**me·tal·lic** \mə-'tal-ik\ *adj*
**1** of, relating to, or being a metal
**2** containing or made of metal

**met·al·lur·gi·cal** \ˌmet-l-'ər-ji-kəl\ *adj*
of or relating to metallurgy

**met·al·lur·gy** \'met-l-ˌər-jē\ *n*
the science of obtaining metals from their ores and preparing them for use

**meta·mor·phic** \ˌmet-ə-'mȯr-fik\ *adj*
formed by the action of pressure, heat, and water that results in a more compact form ⟨a *metamorphic* rock⟩

**meta·mor·pho·sis** \ˌmet-ə-'mȯr-fə-səs\ *n, pl* **meta·mor·pho·ses** \-fə-ˌsēz\
a sudden and very great change especially in appearance or structure

**met·a·phor** \'met-ə-ˌfȯr\ *n*
a figure of speech comparing two unlike things without using *like* or *as* ⟨"their cheeks were roses" is a *metaphor;* "their cheeks were like roses" is a simile⟩

**mete** \'mēt\ *vb* **met·ed**; **met·ing**
ALLOT ⟨*mete* out punishment⟩

**me·te·or** \'mēt-ē-ər\ *n*
▶ one of the small pieces of matter in the solar system that enter the earth's atmosphere where friction causes them to glow and form a streak of light

**me·te·or·ic** \ˌmēt-ē-'ȯr-ik\ *adj*
**1** of or relating to a meteor or group of meteors
**2** like a meteor in speed or in sudden and temporary brilliance ⟨a *meteoric* career⟩

**me·te·or·ite** \'mēt-ē-ə-ˌrīt\ *n*
a meteor that reaches the surface of the earth

**me·te·o·rol·o·gist** \ˌmēt-ē-ə-'räl-ə-jəst\ *n*
a specialist in meteorology

**me·te·o·rol·o·gy** \ˌmēt-ē-ə-'räl-ə-jē\ *n*
a science that deals with the atmosphere, weather, and weather forecasting

**[1]me·ter** \'mēt-ər\ *n*
**1** a planned rhythm in poetry that is usually repeated
**2** the repeated pattern of musical beats in a measure

**[2]meter** *n*
a measure of length on which the metric system is based and which is equal to about 39.37 inches

**[3]meter** *n*
an instrument for measuring and sometimes recording the amount of something ⟨gas *meter*⟩

**-meter** \m-ət-ər\ *n suffix*
instrument for measuring

**meth·od** \'meth-əd\ *n*
**1** a certain way of doing something ⟨a *method* of teaching⟩
**2** careful arrangement : PLAN ⟨work that lacks *method*⟩

**me·thod·i·cal** \mə-'thäd-i-kəl\ *adj*
**1** showing or done or arranged by method ⟨a *methodical* search⟩
**2** following a method out of habit : SYSTEMATIC ⟨*methodical* teachers⟩
**me·thod·i·cal·ly** *adv*

**me·tic·u·lous** \mə-'tik-yə-ləs\ *adj*
extremely or overly careful in dealing with small details

**met·ric** \'me-trik\ *adj*
**1** of or relating to measurement
**2** of or relating to the metric system

**meteor:** an artist's picture of a meteor

**met·ri·cal** \'me-tri-kəl\ *adj*
of or relating to meter (as in poetry or music)

**metric system** *n*
a system of weights and measures in which the meter is the unit of length and the kilogram is the unit of weight

**metric ton** *n*
a unit of weight equal to 1000 kilograms

**met·ro·nome** \'me-trə-ˌnōm\ *n*
▶ a device for marking exact musical tempo by regularly repeated ticks

pendulum

scale of tempos

**metronome**

**me·trop·o·lis** \mə-'träp-ə-ləs\ *n*
**1** the chief or capital city of a country, state, or region
**2** a large or important city

**met·ro·pol·i·tan** \ˌme-trə-'päl-ət-n\ *adj*
of, relating to, or like that of a metropolis ⟨in the *metropolitan* area⟩

**met·tle** \'met-l\ *n*
strength of spirit : COURAGE
**on one's mettle** aroused to do one's best

**[1]mew** \'myü\ *vb*
to make a meow or a similar sound ⟨*mewing* sea gulls⟩

**[2]mew** *n*
MEOW

**[1]Mex·i·can** \'mek-si-kən\ *adj*
of or relating to Mexico or Mexicans

**[2]Mexican** *n*
a person born or living in Mexico

**mi** \'mē\ *n*
the third note of the musical scale

**mi·ca** \'mī-kə\ *n*
a mineral that easily breaks into very thin transparent sheets

**mice** *pl of* MOUSE

**micr-** *or* **micro-** *prefix*
**1** small : tiny ⟨*micro* film⟩
**2** millionth

**mi·crobe** \'mī-ˌkrōb\ *n*
a very tiny and often harmful plant or animal : MICROORGANISM

**mi·cro·com·put·er** \'mī-krō-kəm-ˌpyüt-ər\ *n*
PERSONAL COMPUTER

**mi·cro·film** \'mī-krə-ˌfilm\ *n*
a film on which something (as

printing or a drawing) is recorded in very much smaller size

**mi·crom·e·ter** \mī-ˈkräm-ət-ər\ *n*
**1** an instrument used with a telescope or microscope for measuring very small distances
**2** MICROMETER CALIPER

**micrometer caliper** *n*
an instrument having a rod moved by fine screw threads and used for making exact measurements

**mi·cro·or·gan·ism** \ˌmī-krō-ˈȯr-gə-ˌniz-əm\ *n*
an organism (as a bacterium) of microscopic or less than microscopic size

**mi·cro·phone** \ˈmī-krə-ˌfōn\ *n*
▶ an instrument in which sound is changed into an electrical effect for transmitting or recording (as in radio or television)

*protective covering*

*on/off switch*

**microphone**

**mi·cro·pro·ces·sor** \ˌmī-krō-ˈpräs-ˌes-ər, -ˈprōs-\ *n*
a computer processor

**mi·cro·chip** contained on an integrated-circuit chip

**mi·cro·scope** \ˈmī-krə-ˌskōp\ *n*
an instrument with one or more lenses used to help a person to see something very small by making it appear larger

**mi·cro·scop·ic** \ˌmī-krə-ˈskäp-ik\ *adj*
**1** of, relating to, or conducted with the microscope ⟨a *microscopic* examination⟩
**2** so small as to be visible only through a microscope **:** very tiny
**mi·cro·scop·i·cal·ly** \-i-kə-lē\ *adv*

**¹mi·cro·wave** \ˈmī-krō-ˌwāv\ *n*
**1** a radio wave between one millimeter and one meter in wavelength
**2** MICROWAVE OVEN

**²microwave** *vb*
to cook or heat in a microwave oven

**microwave oven** *n*
an oven in which food is cooked by the heat produced as a result of penetration of the food by microwaves

**¹mid** \ˈmid\ *adj*
being the part in the middle

**²mid** *prep*
AMID

**mid·air** \ˈmid-ˈaər, -ˈeər\ *n*
a region in the air some distance above the ground ⟨planes crashed in *midair*⟩

**mid·day** \ˈmid-ˌdā\ *n*
NOON

**¹mid·dle** \ˈmid-l\ *adj*
**1** equally distant from the ends **:** CENTRAL ⟨the *middle* house in the row⟩
**2** being at neither extreme ⟨of *middle* size⟩

**²middle** *n*
the middle part, point, or position **:** CENTER ⟨in the *middle* of the room⟩

**middle age** *n*
the period of life from about forty to about sixty years of age
**mid·dle–aged** \ˌmid-l-ˈājd\ *adj*

**Middle Ages** *n pl*
▼ the period of European history from about A.D. 500 to about 1500

**middle class** *n*
a social class between that of the wealthy and the poor

**middle school** *n*
a school usually including grades 5 to 8 or 6 to 8

## Middle Ages

The Middle Ages in Europe was the period of history between the Dark Ages following the fall of the Roman Empire, and the Renaissance. In Europe in the Middle Ages, most countries were organized into a feudal system, each ruled by a king who owned most of the land. The king granted land to noblemen — barons and bishops — who, in turn, often divided their lands among lords or knights. At the lowest level of society were the peasants, who worked on land belonging to the local lord. The Catholic Church possessed its own lands and had enormous power.

*royal coat of arms of England*

**stained glass**

*lord overseeing a hunt*

**French painting**

**wooden angel**

*lady*

*knight*

**ornamental wooden shield**

**mid·dy** \'mid-ē\ *n, pl* **middies**
**1** MIDSHIPMAN
**2** a loose blouse with a collar cut wide and square in the back

**midge** \'mij\ *n*
a very small fly or gnat

**midg·et** \'mij-ət\ *n*
one (as a person) that is much smaller than usual or normal

**mid·night** \'mid-ˌnīt\ *n*
twelve o'clock at night

**mid·rib** \'mid-ˌrib\ *n*
the central vein of a leaf

**mid·riff** \'mid-ˌrif\ *n*
**1** the middle part of the surface of the human body
**2** a part of a garment that covers the midriff

**mid·ship·man** \'mid-ˌship-mən\ *n, pl* **mid·ship·men** \-mən\
a student naval officer

[1]**midst** \'midst\ *n*
**1** the inside or central part ⟨in the *midst* of the forest⟩
**2** a position among the members of a group ⟨a stranger in our *midst*⟩
**3** the condition of being surrounded ⟨in the *midst* of dangers⟩

[2]**midst** *prep*
in the midst of

**mid·stream** \'mid-'strēm\ *n*
the part of a stream away from both sides

**mid·sum·mer** \'mid-'səm-ər\ *n*
**1** the middle of summer
**2** the summer solstice

**mid·way** \'mid-ˌwā, -'wā\ *adv or adj*
in the middle of the way or distance : HALFWAY

**mid·win·ter** \'mid-'wint-ər\ *n*
**1** the middle of winter
**2** the winter solstice

**mid·year** \'mid-ˌyir\ *n*
the middle of a year

**mien** \'mēn\ *n*
a person's appearance or way of acting that shows mood or personality

[1]**mildew 1:** leaves infected by mildew

[1]**might** \'mīt\ *past of* MAY
used as a helping verb to show that something is possible but not likely ⟨we *might* arrive before it rains⟩

[2]**might** \'mīt\ *n*
power that can be used (as by a person or group) ⟨our army's *might*⟩

**mightn't** \'mīt-nt\
might not

[1]**mighty** \'mīt-ē\ *adj* **might·i·er**; **might·i·est**
**1** having great power or strength ⟨a *mighty* nation⟩
**2** done by might : showing great power ⟨*mighty* deeds⟩
**3** great in influence, size, or effect ⟨a *mighty* famine⟩
**might·i·ly** \'mīt-l-ē\ *adv*

[2]**mighty** *adv*
[2]VERY 1 ⟨a *mighty* good friend⟩

**mi·grant** \'mī-grənt\ *n*
one that migrates

**mi·grate** \'mī-ˌgrāt\ *vb* **mi·grat·ed**; **mi·grat·ing**
**1** to move from one country or region to another
**2** to pass from one region to another on a regular schedule ⟨birds *migrating* south for the winter⟩

**mi·gra·tion** \mī-'grā-shən\ *n*
**1** the act or an instance of migrating
**2** a group of individuals that are migrating

**mi·gra·to·ry** \'mī-grə-ˌtōr-ē\ *adj*
**1** having a way of life that includes making migrations ⟨*migratory* workers⟩
**2** of or relating to migration

**mike** \'mīk\ *n*
MICROPHONE

**milch** \'milk, 'milch\ *adj*
giving milk : kept for milking ⟨a *milch* cow⟩

**mild** \'mīld\ *adj*
**1** gentle in personality or behavior
**2** not strong or harsh in action or effect ⟨*mild* weather⟩
**mild·ly** *adv*
**mild·ness** *n*

[1]**mil·dew** \'mil-ˌdü, -ˌdyü\ *n*
**1** ◀ a thin whitish growth of fungus on decaying material or on living plants
**2** a fungus that grows as a mildew

[2]**mildew** *vb*
to become affected with mildew

**mile** \'mīl\ *n*
**1** a measure of distance (**statute mile**) equal to 5280 feet (1609 meters)
**2** a measure of distance (**geographical mile** or **nautical mile**) equal to about 6076 feet (1852 meters)

---

**Word History** In English we use the word *mile* for two different lengths. The ancient Roman mile was not the same as either of these. But the English word *mile* comes from the Latin name for the Roman mile. This Latin word came from a phrase that meant "a thousand steps." From the Latin word for "thousand" we also get the words *mill* (a thousandth of a dollar) and *million* (a thousand thousands).

---

**mile·age** \'mī-lij\ *n*
**1** an amount of money given for traveling expenses at a certain rate per mile
**2** distance or distance covered in miles
**3** the number of miles that something (as a car or tire) will travel before wearing out
**4** the average number of miles a car or truck will travel on a gallon of fuel

**mile·stone** \'mīl-ˌstōn\ *n*
**1** ▶ a stone showing the distance in miles to a stated place
**2** an important point in progress or development

**milestone 1:** an old milestone in London, UK

[1]**mil·i·tary** \'mil-ə-ˌter-ē\ *adj*
**1** of or relating to soldiers, the army, or war ⟨*military* drill⟩
**2** carried on by soldiers : supported by armed force ⟨a *military* government⟩

[2]**military** *n, pl* **military**
members of the armed forces

**mi·li·tia** \mə-'lish-ə\ *n*
a body of citizens having some military training but called into service only in emergencies

**[1]milk** \'milk\ *n*
**1** a whitish liquid secreted by the breasts or udder of a female mammal as food for her young
**2** a liquid (as a plant juice) like milk

**[2]milk** *vb*
to draw off the milk of (as by pressing or sucking) ⟨*milk* a cow⟩

**milk·maid** \'milk-,mād\ *n*
DAIRYMAID

**milk·man** \'milk-,man\ *n*, *pl* **milk·men** \-,men\
a person who sells or delivers milk

**milk of mag·ne·sia** \-mag-'nē-shə, -'nē-zhə\
a white liquid containing an oxide of magnesium in water and used as a laxative

**milk shake** *n*
a drink made of milk, a flavoring syrup, and ice cream shaken or mixed thoroughly

**milk tooth** *n*
one of the first and temporary teeth that in humans number twenty

**milk·weed** \'mil-,kwēd\ *n*
any of a group of plants with milky juice and flowers in dense clusters

**milky** \'mil-kē\ *adj* **milk·i·er**; **milk·i·est**
**1** like milk in color or thickness
**2** full of or containing milk
**milk·i·ness** *n*

**Milky Way** *n*
**1** a broad band of light that stretches across the sky and is caused by the light of a very great number of faint stars
**2** MILKY WAY GALAXY

**Milky Way galaxy** *n*
the galaxy of which the sun and the solar system are a part and which contains the stars that make up the Milky Way

**[1]mill** \'mil\ *n*
**1** a building in which grain is ground into flour
**2** a machine used in processing (as by grinding, crushing, stamping, cutting, or finishing) raw material
**3** a factory using machines ⟨a steel *mill*⟩

**[2]mill** *vb*
**1** to grind into flour or powder
**2** to shape or finish by means of a rotating cutter
**3** to give a raised rim to (a coin)
**4** to move about in a circle or in disorder ⟨cattle *milling* about⟩

**[3]mill** *n*
one tenth of a cent

**mil·len·ni·um** \mə-'len-ē-əm\ *n*, *pl* **mil·len·nia** \-ē-ə\ *or* **millenniums**
**1** a period of 1000 years
**2** a 1000th anniversary or its celebration
**mil·len·ni·al** \-ē-əl\ *adj*

**mill·er** \'mil-ər\ *n*
**1** a person who works in or runs a flour mill
**2** a moth whose wings seem to be covered with flour or dust

**mil·let** \'mil-ət\ *n*
an annual grass with clusters of small usually white seeds that is grown as a cereal and for animals to graze

**milli-** *prefix*
thousandth ⟨*milli*meter⟩

**mil·li·gram** \'mil-ə-,gram\ *n*
a unit of weight equal to 1/1000 gram

**mil·li·li·ter** \'mil-ə-,lēt-ər\ *n*
a unit of capacity equal to 1/1000 liter

**mil·li·me·ter** \'mil-ə-,mēt-ər\ *n*
a unit of length equal to 1/1000 meter

**mil·li·ner** \'mil-ə-nər\ *n*
a person who makes, trims, or sells women's hats

**[1]mil·lion** \'mil-yən\ *n*
**1** one thousand thousands **:** 1,000,000
**2** a very large number ⟨*millions* of mosquitoes⟩

**[2]million** *adj*
being 1,000,000

**mil·lion·aire** \,mil-yə-'naər, -'neər\ *n*
a person having a million dollars or more

**[1]mil·lionth** \'mil-yənth\ *adj*
being last in a series of a million

**[2]millionth** *n*
number 1,000,000 in a series

**mil·li·pede** \'mil-ə-,pēd\ *n*
▶ an animal that is an arthropod with a long body somewhat like that of a centipede but with two pairs of legs on most of its many body sections

antenna
segmented body

**millipede**

**mill·stone** \'mil-,stōn\ *n*
either of two circular stones used for grinding grain

**mill wheel** *n*
a waterwheel that drives a mill

**mim·eo·graph** \'mim-ē-ə-,graf\ *n*
a machine for making copies of typewritten, written, or drawn matter by means of stencils

**[1]mim·ic** \'mim-ik\ *n*
one that mimics another

**[2]mimic** *vb* **mim·icked**; **mim·ick·ing**
**1** to imitate very closely
**2** to make fun of by imitating ⟨*mimic* a person's speech⟩
**synonyms** see COPY

**min·a·ret** \,min-ə-'ret\ *n*
▼ a tall slender tower of a mosque with a balcony from which the people are called to prayer

**minarets** on a mosque in Cairo, Egypt

A B C D E F G H I J K L M N O P Q R S T U V W X Y Z

**mince** \'mins\ *vb* **minced**; **minc·ing**
1 to cut or chop very fine ⟨*minced* ham⟩
2 to act or speak in an unnaturally dainty way
3 to keep (what one says) within the bounds of politeness ⟨I'll not *mince* words with you; you know you lied⟩

**mince·meat** \'min-,smēt\ *n*
▼ a mixture of finely chopped and cooked raisins, apples, suet, spices, and sometimes meat that is used chiefly as a filling for pie (**mince pie**)

**mincemeat**

[1]**mind** \'mīnd\ *n*
1 MEMORY 1 ⟨keep my advice in *mind*⟩
2 the part of a person that feels, understands, thinks, wills, and especially reasons ⟨has a fine *mind*⟩
3 INTENTION 1 ⟨I changed my *mind*⟩
4 OPINION 1 ⟨speak your *mind*⟩

[2]**mind** *vb*
1 to pay attention to : HEED ⟨*mind* what you're doing⟩
2 to pay careful attention to and obey ⟨*mind* the teacher⟩
3 to be bothered about ⟨never *mind* that mistake⟩
4 to object to : DISLIKE ⟨I don't *mind* the cold⟩
5 to take charge of ⟨*mind* the children⟩ **synonyms** see OBEY

**mind·ed** \'mīn-dəd\ *adj*
1 having a specified kind of mind ⟨small-*minded*⟩
2 greatly interested in one thing ⟨safety-*minded*⟩

**mind·ful** \'mīnd-fəl\ *adj*
keeping in mind

[1]**mine** \'mīn\ *pron*
that which belongs to me ⟨that glove is *mine*⟩ ⟨those gloves are *mine*⟩

[2]**mine** *n*
1 a pit or tunnel from which minerals (as coal, gold, or diamonds) are taken
2 an explosive buried in the ground and set to explode when disturbed (as by an enemy soldier or vehicle)
3 an explosive placed in a case and sunk in the water to sink enemy ships
4 a rich source of supply ⟨a *mine* of information⟩

[3]**mine** *vb* **mined**; **min·ing**
1 to dig a mine
2 to obtain from a mine ⟨*mine* coal⟩
3 to work in a mine
4 to dig or form mines under a place
5 to lay military mines in or under ⟨*mine* a field⟩ ⟨*mine* a harbor⟩
**min·er** *n*

[1]**min·er·al** \'min-ə-rəl, 'min-rəl\ *n*
1 ▶ a naturally occurring substance (as diamond or quartz) that results from processes other than those of plants and animals
2 a naturally occurring substance (as ore, coal, petroleum, natural gas, or water) obtained for humans to use usually from the ground

[2]**mineral** *adj*
1 of or relating to minerals
2 containing gases or mineral salts ⟨*mineral* water⟩

**mineral kingdom** *n*
a basic group of natural objects that includes objects consisting of matter that does not come from plants and animals

**min·gle** \'ming-gəl\ *vb* **min·gled**; **min·gling**
1 to mix or be mixed so that the original parts can still be recognized
2 to move among others within a group ⟨*mingle* with the crowd⟩

**mini-** *prefix*
very short or small

[1]**min·i·a·ture** \'min-ē-ə-,chu̇r, 'min-i-,chu̇r\ *n*
1 a copy on a much reduced scale
2 a very small portrait especially on ivory or metal

**mink 1**

**Word History** A long time ago books were written by hand. Often titles were done in red to make them stand out against the black ink of the text. The red pigment used for titles was also used for pictures and had a Latin name. The Italians made a word from the Latin name of the red pigment. This Italian word was used for the pictures in books made by hand. The English word *miniature* comes from this Italian word. Since pictures in books done by hand are often quite small, the word *miniature* is used to mean anything that is small.

[2]**miniature** *adj*
very small : represented on a small scale

**min·i·mize** \'min-ə-,mīz\ *vb* **min·i·mized**; **min·i·miz·ing**
to make as small as possible ⟨*minimize* the risks of a dangerous situation⟩

[1]**min·i·mum** \'min-ə-məm\ *n*, *pl* **min·i·ma** \-mə\ *or* **min·i·mums**
the lowest amount

[2]**minimum** *adj*
being the least possible ⟨a *minimum* loss of time⟩

**min·ing** \'mī-ning\ *n*
the process or business of working mines

[1]**min·is·ter** \'min-əs-tər\ *n*
1 a Protestant clergyman
2 a government official at the head of a section of government activities ⟨*minister* of war⟩
3 a person who represents his or her government in a foreign country

[2]**minister** *vb*
to give aid or service ⟨*minister* to the sick⟩

**min·is·try** \'min-əs-trē\ *n*, *pl* **min·is·tries**
1 the act of ministering
2 the office or duties of a minister
3 a body of ministers
4 a section of a government headed by a minister

**mink** \'mingk\ *n*
1 ◀ an animal related to the weasel that has partly webbed feet and lives around water
2 the soft thick usually brown fur of a mink

**min•now** \'min-ō\ *n*
**1** any of various small freshwater fishes (as a shiner) related to the carps
**2** a fish that looks like a true minnow

[1]**mi•nor** \'mī-nər\ *adj*
**1** less in size, importance, or value
**2** of or relating to a musical scale having the third tone lowered a half step

[2]**minor** *n*
a person too young to have full civil rights

**mi•nor•i•ty** \mə-'nȯr-ət-ē\ *n, pl* **mi•nor•i•ties**
**1** the state of being a minor
**2** a number less than half of a total
**3** a part of a population that is in some ways different from others and that is sometimes disliked or given unfair treatment

**min•strel** \'min-strəl\ *n*
**1** an entertainer in the Middle Ages who sang verses and played a harp
**2** one of a group of entertainers with blackened faces who sing, dance, and tell jokes

[1]**mint** \'mint\ *n*
**1** any of a group of fragrant herbs and shrubs (as catnip or peppermint) with square stems
**2** a piece of candy flavored with mint

[2]**mint** *n*
**1** a place where metals are made into coins
**2** a great amount especially of money

[3]**mint** *vb*
**1** [2]COIN 1 ⟨*mint* silver dollars⟩
**2** to make into coin ⟨*mint* silver⟩

**min•u•end** \'min-yə-,wend\ *n*
a number from which another number is to be subtracted

**min•u•et** \,min-yə-'wet\ *n*
a slow stately dance

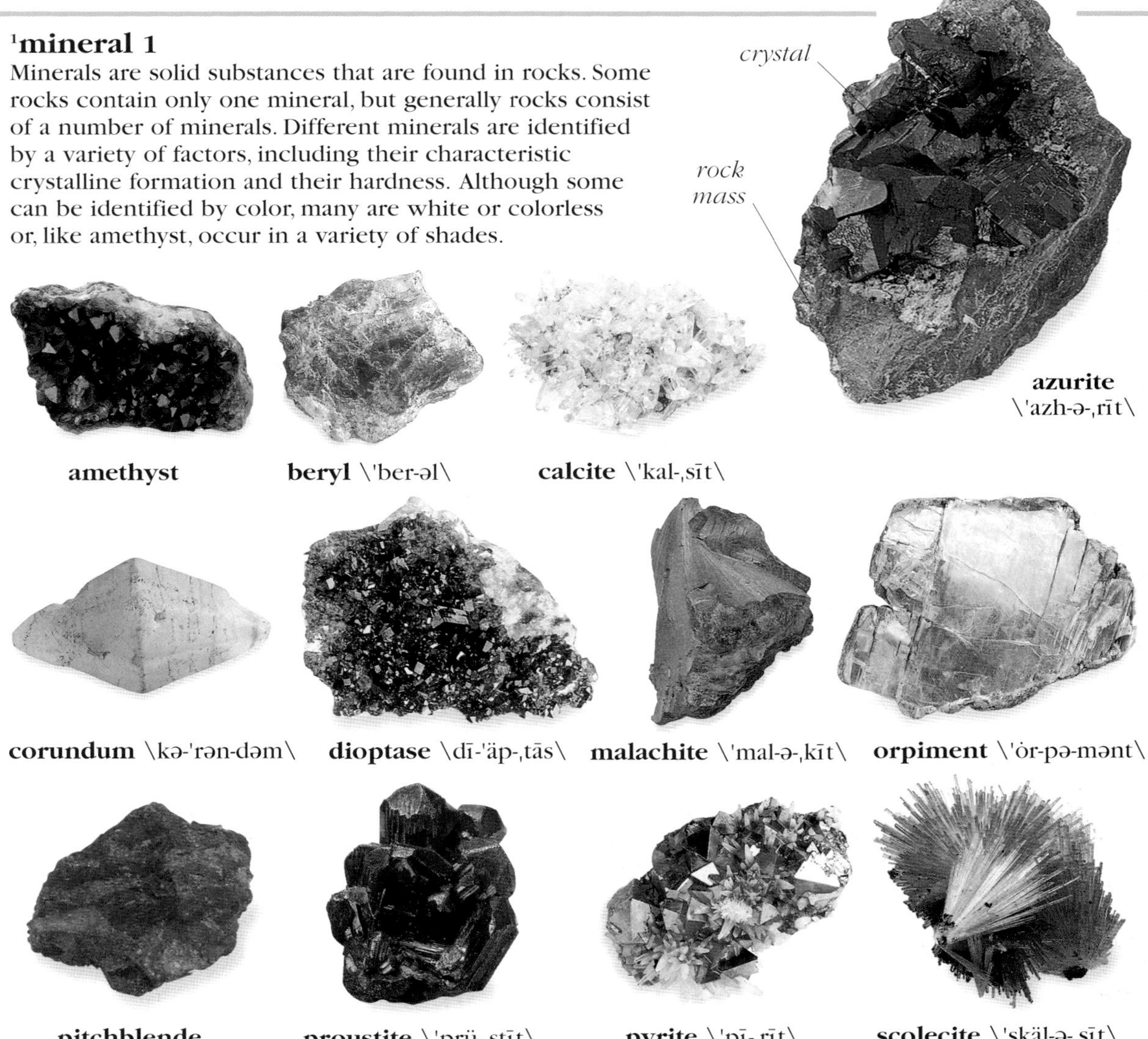


## [1]mineral 1

Minerals are solid substances that are found in rocks. Some rocks contain only one mineral, but generally rocks consist of a number of minerals. Different minerals are identified by a variety of factors, including their characteristic crystalline formation and their hardness. Although some can be identified by color, many are white or colorless or, like amethyst, occur in a variety of shades.

**azurite** \'azh-ə-,rīt\

**amethyst**

**beryl** \'ber-əl\

**calcite** \'kal-,sīt\

**corundum** \kə-'rən-dəm\

**dioptase** \dī-'äp-,tās\

**malachite** \'mal-ə-,kīt\

**orpiment** \'ȯr-pə-mənt\

**pitchblende**

**proustite** \'prü-,stīt\

**pyrite** \'pī-,rīt\

**scolecite** \'skäl-ə-,sīt\

**[1]mi·nus** \'mī-nəs\ *prep*
**1** with the subtraction of **:** LESS ⟨7 *minus* 4 is 3⟩
**2** [1]WITHOUT 2 ⟨went outside *minus* my hat⟩

**[2]minus** *adj*
located in the lower part of a range ⟨a grade of C *minus*⟩

**minus sign** *n*
a sign – used especially in mathematics to indicate subtraction (as in 8 – 6 = 2) or a quantity less than zero (as in –10°)

**[1]min·ute** \'min-ət\ *n*
**1** ▼ the sixtieth part of an hour or of a degree **:** sixty seconds
**2** MOMENT 1 ⟨wait a *minute*⟩
**3 minutes** *pl* a brief record of what happened during a meeting

**[1]minute 1:** a clock with minute markings

**[2]mi·nute** \mī-'nüt, mə-, -'nyüt\ *adj* **mi·nut·er**; **mi·nut·est**
**1** very small **:** TINY
**2** paying attention to small details ⟨a *minute* description⟩
**mi·nute·ly** *adv*

**min·ute·man** \'min-ət-,man\ *n*, *pl* **min·ute·men** \-,men\
a member of a group of armed men ready to fight at a minute's notice immediately before and during the American Revolution

**mir·a·cle** \'mir-i-kəl\ *n*
**1** an extraordinary event taken as a sign of the power of God
**2** something very rare, unusual, or wonderful

**mi·rac·u·lous** \mə-'rak-yə-ləs\ *adj*
being or being like a miracle
**mi·rac·u·lous·ly** *adv*

**mi·rage** \mə-'räzh\ *n*
an illusion sometimes seen at sea, in the desert, or over hot pavement that looks like a pool of water or a mirror in which distant objects are glimpsed

**[1]mire** \'mīr\ *n*
heavy deep mud

**[2]mire** *vb* **mired**; **mir·ing**
to stick or cause to stick fast in mire

**[1]mir·ror** \'mir-ər\ *n*
**1** ▶ a glass coated on the back with a reflecting substance
**2** something that gives a true likeness or description

**[2]mirror** *vb*
to reflect in or as if in a mirror

**mirth** \'mərth\ *n*
the state of being happy or merry as shown by laughter

**mirth·ful** \'mərth-fəl\ *adj*
full of or showing mirth
**mirth·ful·ly** \-fə-lē\ *adv*

**mis-** *prefix*
**1** in a way that is bad or wrong ⟨*mis*judge⟩
**2** bad **:** wrong ⟨*mis*fortune⟩
**3** opposite or lack of ⟨*mis*trust⟩

**mis·ad·ven·ture** \,mis-əd-'ven-chər\ *n*
an unfortunate or unpleasant event

**mis·be·have** \,mis-bi-'hāv\ *vb* **mis·be·haved**; **mis·be·hav·ing**
to behave badly

**mis·car·ry** \mis-'kar-ē\ *vb* **mis·car·ried**; **mis·car·ry·ing**
to go wrong **:** FAIL ⟨the plan *miscarried*⟩

**mis·cel·la·neous** \,mis-ə-'lā-nē-əs, -nyəs\ *adj*
consisting of many things of different sorts

**mis·chance** \mis-'chans\ *n*
**1** bad luck
**2** a piece of bad luck **:** MISHAP

**mis·chief** \'mis-chəf\ *n*
**1** injury or damage caused by a person
**2** conduct that annoys or bothers ⟨keep out of *mischief*⟩

**mis·chie·vous** \'mis-chə-vəs\ *adj*
**1** harming or intended to do harm ⟨*mischievous* gossip⟩
**2** causing or likely to cause minor injury or harm ⟨a *mischievous* puppy⟩
**3** showing a spirit of irresponsible fun or playfulness ⟨*mischievous* behavior⟩
**mis·chie·vous·ly** *adv*
**mis·chie·vous·ness** *n*

**[1]mis·con·duct** \mis-'kän-,dəkt\ *n*
wrong conduct **:** bad behavior

**[1]mirror 1:** a girl looking in a mirror

**[2]mis·con·duct** \,mis-kən-'dəkt\ *vb*
to manage badly

**mis·count** \mis-'kaůnt\ *vb*
to count incorrectly

**mis·cre·ant** \'mis-krē-ənt\ *n*
VILLAIN, RASCAL

**mis·cue** \mis-'kyü\ *n*
[2]MISTAKE 2

**mis·deal** \mis-'dēl\ *vb* **mis·dealt** \-'delt\; **mis·deal·ing** \-'dē-ling\
to deal in an incorrect way ⟨*misdeal* cards⟩

**mis·deed** \mis-'dēd\ *n*
a bad action

**mis·di·rect** \,mis-də-'rekt\ *vb*
to direct incorrectly

**mi·ser** \'mī-zər\ *n*
a stingy person who lives poorly in order to store away money

**mis·er·a·ble** \'miz-ə-rə-bəl, 'miz-ər-bəl\ *adj*
**1** very unsatisfactory ⟨a *miserable* dinner⟩
**2** causing great discomfort ⟨a *miserable* cold⟩
**3** very unhappy or distressed **:** WRETCHED
**mis·er·a·bly** \-blē\ *adv*

**mi·ser·ly** \'mī-zər-lē\ *adj*
of, relating to, or like a miser

**mis·ery** \'miz-ə-rē, 'miz-rē\ *n*, *pl* **mis·er·ies**
suffering or distress due to being poor, in pain, or unhappy

**mis·fit** \mis-'fit, 'mis-,fit\ *n*
**1** something that fits badly

2 a person who cannot adjust to an environment

**mis·for·tune** \mis-'fȯr-chən\ *n*
1 bad luck
2 an unfortunate situation or event

**mis·giv·ing** \mis-'giv-iŋ\ *n*
a feeling of distrust or doubt especially about what is going to happen

**mis·guid·ed** \mis-'gīd-əd\ *adj*
having mistaken ideas or rules of conduct

**mis·hap** \'mis-ˌhap\ *n*
an unfortunate accident

**mis·judge** \mis-'jəj\ *vb* **mis·judged**; **mis·judg·ing**
to judge incorrectly or unjustly

**mis·lay** \mis-'lā\ *vb* **mis·laid** \-'lād\; **mis·lay·ing**
to put in a place later forgotten : LOSE **synonyms** see MISPLACE

**mis·lead** \mis-'lēd\ *vb* **mis·led** \-'led\; **mis·lead·ing**
to lead in a wrong direction or into error

**mis·place** \mis-'plās\ *vb* **mis·placed**; **mis·plac·ing**
1 to put in a wrong place ⟨*misplace* a comma⟩
2 MISLAY

**Synonyms** MISPLACE and MISLAY mean to put in the wrong place. MISPLACE may mean to put something in a place that is not its usual location ⟨someone seems to have *misplaced* the crayons⟩. MISPLACE may also suggest putting something where it should not have been at all ⟨I *misplaced* my confidence in them⟩. MISLAY stresses not only placing something in the wrong location but also forgetting that location ⟨I *mislaid* my keys⟩.

**mis·print** \'mis-ˌprint\ *n*
a mistake in printing

**mis·pro·nounce** \ˌmis-prə-'nau̇ns\ *vb* **mis·pro·nounced**; **mis·pro·nounc·ing**
to pronounce in a way considered incorrect

**mis·pro·nun·ci·a·tion** \ˌmis-prə-ˌnən-sē-'ā-shən\ *n*
incorrect pronunciation

**mis·read** \mis-'rēd\ *vb* **mis·read** \-'red\; **mis·read·ing** \-'rēd-iŋ\
1 to read incorrectly
2 MISUNDERSTAND 2

**mis·rep·re·sent** \ˌmis-ˌrep-ri-'zent\ *vb*
to give a false or misleading idea of

[1]**miss** \'mis\ *vb*
1 to fail to hit, catch, reach, or get ⟨*miss* the target⟩ ⟨*miss* the ball⟩
2 [1]ESCAPE 2 ⟨just *missed* being hit by the falling rock⟩
3 to fail to have or go to ⟨were late and *missed* their lunch⟩ ⟨*miss* the bus⟩
4 to be aware of the absence of : want to be with ⟨*miss* an absent friend⟩

[2]**miss** *n*
failure to hit or catch

[3]**miss** *n*
1 used as a title before the name of an unmarried woman ⟨*Miss* Doe⟩
2 young lady — used without a name as a form of polite address to a girl or young woman ⟨do you need some help, *miss*?⟩

**missile:** launch of a rocket missile

**mis·shap·en** \mis-'shā-pən\ *adj*
badly shaped

**mis·sile** \'mis-əl\ *n*
▶ an object (as a stone, arrow, bullet, or rocket) that is dropped, thrown, shot, or launched usually so as to strike something at a distance

**miss·ing** \'mis-iŋ\ *adj*
1 [1]ABSENT 1 ⟨*missing* persons⟩
2 [2]LOST 4 ⟨a *missing* book⟩

**mis·sion** \'mish-ən\ *n*
1 a group of missionaries
2 a place where the work of missionaries is carried on
3 a group of persons sent by a government to represent it in a foreign country
4 a task that is assigned or begun

[1]**mis·sion·ary** \'mish-ə-ˌner-ē\ *adj*
of or relating to religious missions ⟨a *missionary* society⟩

[2]**missionary** *n, pl* **mis·sion·ar·ies**
a person sent (as to a foreign country) to spread a religious faith

**mis·sive** \'mis-iv\ *n*
[1]LETTER 2

**mis·spell** \mis-'spel\ *vb*
to spell in an incorrect way

**mis·spend** \mis-'spend\ *vb* **mis·spent** \-'spent\; **mis·spend·ing**
[2]WASTE 2

**mis·step** \mis-'step\ *n*
1 a wrong step
2 [2]MISTAKE 2, SLIP

[1]**mist** \'mist\ *n*
1 particles of water floating in the air or falling as fine rain
2 something that keeps one from seeing or understanding clearly ⟨the meaning is lost in the *mist* of time⟩

[2]**mist** *vb*
1 to be or become misty
2 to become or cause to become dim or blurred ⟨eyes *misted* with tears⟩
3 to cover with mist ⟨the windshield was *misted* over⟩

**[1]mis·take** \mə-'stāk\ *vb* **mis·took** \mə-'stu̇k\; **mis·tak·en** \mə-'stā-kən\; **mis·tak·ing**
**1** MISUNDERSTAND 2
**2** to fail to recognize correctly ⟨*mistook* me for someone else⟩

**[2]mistake** *n*
**1** a wrong judgment
**2** a wrong action or statement
**synonyms** see ERROR

**mis·tak·en** \mə-'stā-kən\ *adj*
**1** being in error : judging wrongly ⟨*mistaken* about the time⟩
**2** [2]WRONG 2, INCORRECT ⟨a *mistaken* idea⟩
**mis·tak·en·ly** *adv*

**mis·ter** \'mis-tər\ *n*
**1** *cap* — used sometimes in writing instead of the usual *Mr.*
**2** SIR 2 ⟨do you want a paper, *mister*?⟩

**mis·tle·toe** \'mis-əl-,tō\ *n*
▼ a green plant with waxy white berries that grows on the branches and trunks of trees

berry

**mistletoe:** a sprig of mistletoe

**mis·treat** \mis-'trēt\ *vb*
to treat badly : ABUSE

**mis·tress** \'mis-trəs\ *n*
a woman who has control or authority ⟨the *mistress* of the household⟩

**[1]mis·trust** \mis-'trəst\ *n*
[1]DISTRUST

**[2]mistrust** *vb*
**1** [2]DISTRUST, SUSPECT
**2** to lack confidence in ⟨they *mistrust* your abilities⟩

**misty** \'mis-tē\ *adj* **mist·i·er**; **mist·i·est**
**1** full of mist ⟨a *misty* valley⟩
**2** clouded by or as if by mist ⟨through *misty* eyes⟩
**3** VAGUE 3, INDISTINCT ⟨a *misty* memory⟩
**mist·i·ly** \-tə-lē\ *adv*
**mist·i·ness** \-tē-nəs\ *n*

**mis·un·der·stand** \,mis-,ən-dər-'stand\ *vb* **mis·un·der·stood** \-'stu̇d\; **mis·un·der·stand·ing**
**1** to fail to understand
**2** to take in a wrong meaning or way

**mis·un·der·stand·ing** \,mis-,ən-dər-'stan-ding\ *n*
**1** a failure to understand
**2** DISAGREEMENT 3, QUARREL

**[1]mis·use** \mis-'yüz\ *vb* **mis·used**; **mis·us·ing**
**1** to use in a wrong way
**2** [2]ABUSE 3, MISTREAT

**[2]mis·use** \mis-'yüs\ *n*
incorrect or improper use ⟨*misuse* of public funds⟩

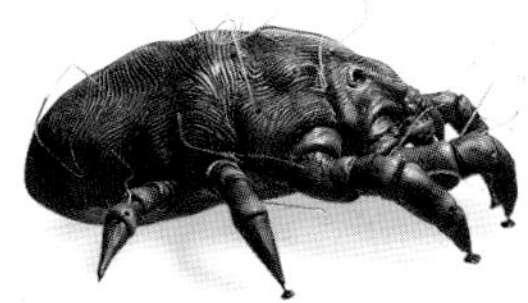

**mite 1:** a model of a mite shown many times its natural size

**mite** \'mīt\ *n*
**1** ▲ any of various tiny spiderlike animals often living on plants, animals, and stored foods
**2** a very small coin or amount of money
**3** a very small object or creature

**mi·to·sis** \mī-'tō-səs\ *n, pl* **mi·to·ses** \-'tō-,sēz\
a process of cell division in which two new nuclei are formed each containing the original number of chromosomes

**mitt** \'mit\ *n*
**1** MITTEN
**2** a baseball catcher's or first baseman's glove

**mit·ten** \'mit-n\ *n*
a covering for the hand and wrist having a separate division for the thumb only

**[1]mix** \'miks\ *vb*
**1** to make into one mass by stirring together : BLEND
**2** to make by combining different things
**3** to become one mass through blending ⟨oil will not *mix* with water⟩
**4** CONFUSE 1
**mixer** *n*

**Synonyms** MIX and BLEND mean to combine into a whole that is more or less the same all over. MIX suggests a fairly complete combining in which the elements may or may not lose their individual identity ⟨*mix* several vegetables for a salad⟩ ⟨*mix* wine and water⟩. BLEND suggests a complete uniting of similar things so that the original parts cannot be separated or recognized ⟨*blend* milk and chocolate syrup⟩.

**[2]mix** *n*
MIXTURE 2

**mixed** \'mikst\ *adj*
**1** made up of two or more kinds ⟨*mixed* candy⟩
**2** made up of persons of both sexes ⟨*mixed* company⟩

**mixed number** *or* **mixed numeral** *n*
a number (as $1\frac{2}{3}$) made up of a whole number and a fraction

**mix·ture** \'miks-chər\ *n*
**1** the act of mixing
**2** something mixed or being mixed
**3** two or more substances mixed together in such a way that each remains unchanged ⟨sand and sugar form a *mixture*⟩

**mix–up** \'mik-,səp\ *n*
an instance of confusion ⟨a *mix-up* about the date⟩

**miz·zen** \'miz-n\ *n*
**1** a fore-and-aft sail set on the mizzenmast
**2** MIZZENMAST

**miz·zen·mast** \'miz-n-,mast, -məst\ *n*
the mast behind or next behind the mainmast

**[1]moan** \'mōn\ *n*
**1** a long low sound showing pain or grief
**2** a mournful sound

**[2]moan** *vb*
**1** COMPLAIN 1
**2** to utter a moan

**moat** \'mōt\ *n*
► a deep wide ditch around the walls of a castle or fort that is usually filled with water

**[1]mob** \'mäb\ *n*
**1** the common masses of people
**2** a rowdy excited crowd

[2]**mob** *vb* **mobbed**; **mob·bing**
to crowd about and attack or annoy

[1]**mo·bile** \'mō-bəl, -,bēl, -,bīl\ *adj*
**1** easily moved : MOVABLE ⟨*mobile* television cameras⟩
**2** changing quickly in expression ⟨a *mobile* face⟩

[2]**mo·bile** \'mō-,bēl\ *n*
an artistic structure whose parts can be moved especially by air currents

**mo·bi·lize** \'mō-bə-,līz\ *vb* **mo·bi·lized**; **mo·bi·liz·ing**
to assemble (as military forces) and make ready for action

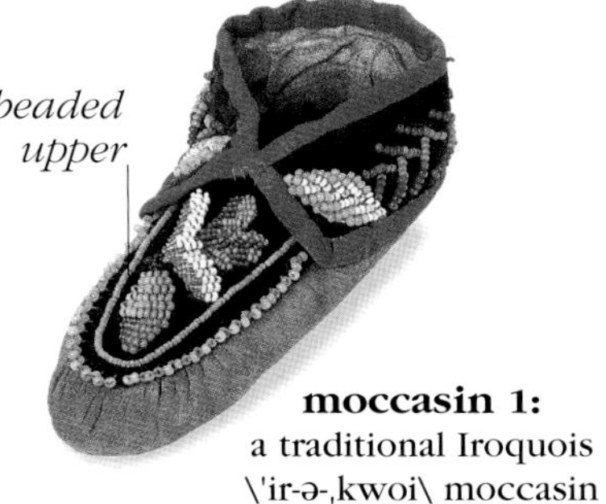

**moccasin 1:** a traditional Iroquois \'ir-ə-,kwoi\ moccasin

**moc·ca·sin** \'mäk-ə-sən\ *n*
**1** ▲ a soft shoe with no heel and the sole and sides made of one piece
**2** a poisonous snake of the southern United States

**moccasin flower** *n*
LADY'S SLIPPER

[1]**mock** \'mäk\ *vb*
**1** to treat with scorn : RIDICULE
**2** [3]MIMIC 2

[2]**mock** *adj*
not real : MAKE-BELIEVE ⟨a *mock* battle⟩

**moat:** a 16th-century French castle with a moat

**mock·ery** \'mäk-ə-rē\ *n, pl* **mock·er·ies**
**1** the act of mocking
**2** a bad imitation : FAKE ⟨a *mockery* of justice⟩

**mock·ing·bird** \'mäk-ing-,bərd\ *n*
▶ a songbird of the southern United States noted for its sweet song and imitations of other birds

**mockingbird**

**mock orange** *n*
SYRINGA

[1]**mode** \'mōd\ *n*
**1** a particular form or variety of something
**2** a form or manner of expressing or acting : WAY ⟨a *mode* of travel⟩

[2]**mode** *n*
a popular fashion or style

[1]**mod·el** \'mäd-l\ *n*
**1** ▶ a small but exact copy of a thing
**2** a pattern or figure of something to be made
**3** a person who sets a good example ⟨a *model* of politeness⟩
**4** a person who poses for an artist or photographer
**5** a person who wears and displays garments that are for sale
**6** a special type of a product ⟨our car is a recent *model*⟩

**Synonyms** MODEL, EXAMPLE, and IDEAL mean something that is set before one for guidance or imitation. MODEL suggests that the thing or person is very worthy of imitation ⟨a saint who can be a *model* for all children⟩. EXAMPLE usually suggests that the person, act, or conduct is likely to be copied, even though this may not always be a good thing ⟨parents are *examples* for their children⟩. IDEAL suggests something, either real or imagined, to be the best of its kind that can exist ⟨the *ideal* of beauty⟩.

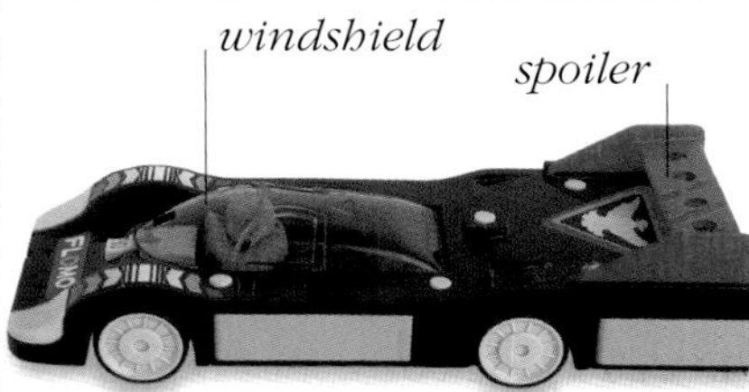

**model:** side view of a model racing car

[2]**model** *vb* **mod·eled** *or* **mod·elled**; **mod·el·ing** *or* **mod·el·ling**
**1** to plan or shape after a pattern ⟨a sports car *modeled* on a racing car⟩
**2** to make a model of ⟨*model* a dog in clay⟩
**3** to act or serve as a model ⟨*model* for an artist⟩

[3]**model** *adj*
**1** worthy of being imitated ⟨a *model* student⟩
**2** being a miniature copy ⟨a *model* airplane⟩

**mo·dem** \'mō-,dem\ *n*
a device that changes electrical signals from one form to another and is used especially to send or receive computer data over a telephone line

A B C D E F G H I J K L M N O P Q R S T U V W X Y Z

**¹mod•er•ate** \'mäd-ə-rət\ *adj*
**1** neither too much nor too little ⟨*moderate* heat⟩
**2** neither very good nor very bad ⟨*moderate* success⟩
**3** not expensive **:** REASONABLE ⟨*moderate* rates⟩
**mod•er•ate•ly** *adv*

**²mod•er•ate** \'mäd-ə-,rāt\ *vb* **mod•er•at•ed**; **mod•er•at•ing**
to make or become less violent or severe

**mod•er•a•tion** \,mäd-ə-'rā-shən\ *n*
**1** the act of moderating
**2** the condition of being moderate

**mod•ern** \'mäd-ərn\ *adj*
**1** of, relating to, or characteristic of the present time or times not long past ⟨*modern* machinery⟩
**2** of the period from about 1500 ⟨*modern* history⟩

**mod•ern•ize** \'mäd-ər-,nīz\ *vb* **mod•ern•ized**; **mod•ern•iz•ing**
to make or become modern

**mod•est** \'mäd-əst\ *adj*
**1** having a limited and not too high opinion of oneself and one's abilities **:** not boastful ⟨a *modest* winner⟩
**2** limited in size or amount ⟨*modest* wealth⟩
**3** clean and proper in thought, conduct, and dress
**mod•est•ly** *adv*

**mod•es•ty** \'mäd-ə-stē\ *n*
the quality of being modest

**mod•i•fi•ca•tion** \,mäd-ə-fə-'kā-shən\ *n*
**1** the act of modifying
**2** the result of modifying **:** a slightly changed form

**mod•i•fi•er** \'mäd-ə-,fī-ər\ *n*
a word (as an adjective or adverb) used with another word to limit its meaning ⟨in the phrase "very big dog" the words "very" and "big" are *modifiers*⟩

**mod•i•fy** \'mäd-ə-,fī\ *vb* **mod•i•fied**; **mod•i•fy•ing**
**1** to make changes in ⟨*modify* a plan⟩
**2** to lower or reduce in amount or scale ⟨*modify* a punishment⟩
**3** to limit in meaning **:** QUALIFY ⟨"green" in the phrase "green gloves" *modifies* the word "gloves"⟩

**mod•u•late** \'mäj-ə-,lāt\ *vb* **mod•u•lat•ed**; **mod•u•lat•ing**
**1** to bring into proper proportion
**2** to tone down **:** SOFTEN ⟨*modulate* your voice⟩

**mod•ule** \'mäj-,ül\ *n*
an independent unit of a spacecraft ⟨a command *module*⟩

**mo•hair** \'mō-,haər, -,heər\ *n*
▼ a fabric or yarn made from the long silky hair of an Asian goat

**mohair** yarn

**Mohammedan, Mohammedanism** *variant of* MUHAMMADAN, MUHAMMADANISM

**moist** \'mȯist\ *adj*
slightly wet **:** DAMP
**moist•ness** *n*

**moist•en** \'mȯis-n\ *vb*
to make moist

**mois•ture** \'mȯis-chər\ *n*
a small amount of liquid that causes moistness

**mo•lar** \'mō-lər\ *n*
a tooth with a broad surface used for grinding **:** a back tooth

---

**Word History** A millstone is a large stone used for grinding grain. We have teeth, called *molars*, that are also used for grinding. The English word *molar* comes from a Latin word that means "mill" or "millstone." The English word *mill* also comes from this Latin word.

---

**mo•las•ses** \mə-'las-əz\ *n*
a thick brown syrup that drains from sugar as it is being made

**¹mold** *or* **mould** \'mōld\ *n*
light rich crumbly earth that contains decaying material

**²mold** *or* **mould** *n*
**1** a hollow form in which something is shaped ⟨a jelly *mold*⟩
**2** ▶ something shaped in a mold ⟨a *mold* of jelly⟩

**³mold** *or* **mould** *vb*
**1** to work and press into shape ⟨*mold* loaves of bread⟩
**2** to form in or as if in a mold

**⁴mold** *n*
**1** an often woolly surface growth of fungus on damp or decaying material
**2** a fungus that forms mold

**⁵mold** *vb*
to become moldy

**mold•er** \'mōl-dər\ *vb*
to crumble to bits by slow decay

**mold•ing** \'mōl-ding\ *n*
**1** the act or work of a person who molds
**2** a strip of material having a shaped surface and used as a decoration (as on a wall or the edge of a table)

**moldy** \'mōl-dē\ *adj* **mold•i•er**; **mold•i•est**
covered with or containing mold

**¹mole** \'mōl\ *n*
a small usually brown spot on the skin

**²mole** *n*
a small burrowing animal with very soft fur and very tiny eyes

**mo•lec•u•lar** \mə-'lek-yə-lər\ *adj*
of or relating to a molecule

**mol•e•cule** \'mäl-i-,kyül\ *n*
**1** the smallest portion of a substance having the properties of the substance ⟨a *molecule* of water⟩
**2** a very small particle

**mole•hill** \'mōl-,hil\ *n*
a little ridge of earth pushed up by moles as they burrow underground

**mo•lest** \mə-'lest\ *vb*
to disturb or injure by interfering

**mol•li•fy** \'mäl-ə-,fī\ *vb* **mol•li•fied**; **mol•li•fy•ing**
to soothe in temper or disposition

**mol•lusk** \'mäl-əsk\ *n*
▶ any of a large group of animals (as clams, snails, and octopuses) most of which live in water and have the body protected by a limy shell

**molt** *or* **moult** \'mōlt\ *vb*
to shed outer material (as hair, shell, or horns) that will be replaced by a new growth

**mol•ten** \'mōlt-n\ *adj*
melted especially by very great heat ⟨*molten* metal⟩

**²mold 2:** a mold of jelly

**mo·lyb·de·num** \mə-'lib-də-nəm\ *n*
a white metallic chemical element used in some steel to give greater strength and hardness

**mom** \'mäm, 'məm\ *n*
[1]MOTHER 1

**mo·ment** \'mō-mənt\ *n*
**1** a very brief time ⟨it disappeared in a *moment*⟩
**2** IMPORTANCE ⟨a subject of great *moment*⟩

**mo·men·tary** \'mō-mən-ˌter-ē\ *adj*
lasting only a moment ⟨a *momentary* fright⟩
**mo·men·tar·i·ly** \ˌmō-mən-'ter-ə-lē\ *adv*

**mo·men·tous** \mō-'ment-əs\ *adj*
very important ⟨a *momentous* decision⟩
**mo·men·tous·ness** *n*

**mo·men·tum** \mō-'ment-əm\ *n*
the force that a moving body has because of its weight and motion

**mom·my** \'mäm-ē, 'məm-ē\ *n*, *pl* **mom·mies**
[1]MOTHER 1

**mon-** *or* **mono-** *prefix*
one : single : alone ⟨*mono*syllable⟩

**mon·arch** \'män-ərk, -ˌärk\ *n*
**1** a person who reigns over a kingdom or empire
**2** a large orange and black American butterfly

**mon·ar·chy** \'män-ər-kē\ *n*, *pl* **mon·ar·chies**
**1** a state or country having a monarch
**2** the system of government by a monarch

**mon·as·tery** \'män-əs-ˌter-ē\ *n*, *pl* **mon·as·ter·ies**
▲ a place where a community of monks live and work

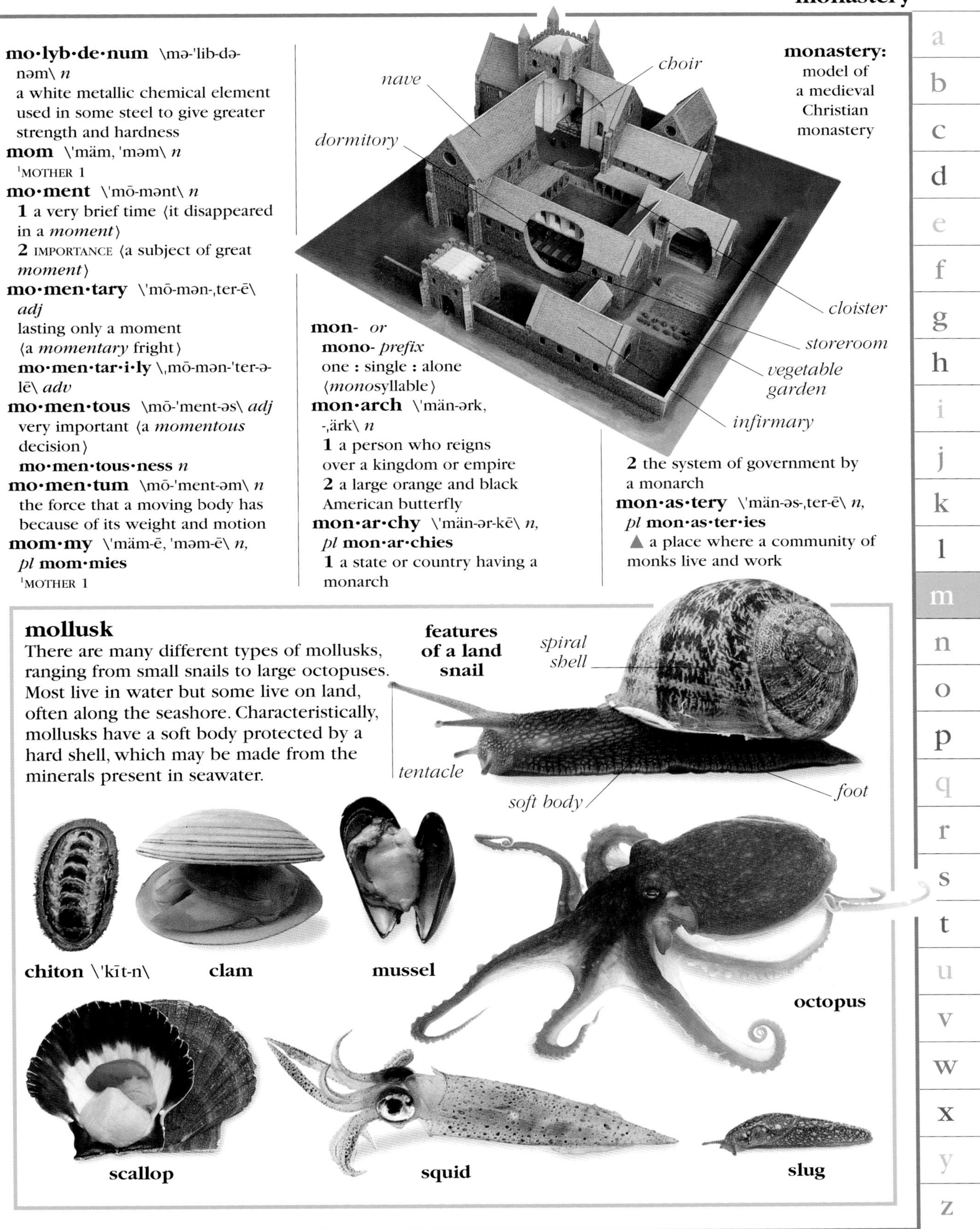


**monastery:** model of a medieval Christian monastery

## mollusk

There are many different types of mollusks, ranging from small snails to large octopuses. Most live in water but some live on land, often along the seashore. Characteristically, mollusks have a soft body protected by a hard shell, which may be made from the minerals present in seawater.

**mo·nas·tic** \mə-'nas-tik\ *adj*
of or relating to monks or monasteries ⟨took *monastic* vows⟩ ⟨*monastic* life⟩

**Mon·day** \'mən-dē\ *n*
the second day of the week

**mon·e·tary** \'män-ə-ˌter-ē\ *adj*
of or relating to money

**mon·ey** \'mən-ē\ *n, pl* **moneys** *or* **mon·ies** \-ēz\
**1** metal (as gold, silver, or copper) coined or stamped and issued for use in buying and selling
**2** a printed or engraved certificate (**paper money**) legal for use in place of metal money
**3** wealth figured in terms of money

**money order** *n*
a piece of paper like a check that can be bought (as at a post office) and that tells another office to pay the sum of money printed on it to the one named

[1]**Mon·go·lian** \män-'gōl-yən\ *adj*
of or relating to Mongolia or the Mongolians

[2]**Mongolian** *n*
a person born or living in Mongolia

**mon·goose** \'män-ˌgüs, 'mäng-ˌgüs\ *n, pl* **mon·goos·es**
▶ a long thin furry animal that eats snakes, eggs, and rodents

[1]**mon·grel** \'məng-grəl, 'mäng-\ *n*
one (as a plant, person, or thing) of mixed or uncertain kind or origin

[2]**mongrel** *adj*
of mixed or uncertain kind or origin

[1]**mon·i·tor** \'män-ət-ər\ *n*
**1** a pupil in a school picked for a special duty (as keeping order)
**2** a person or thing that watches or checks something ⟨a heart *monitor*⟩
**3** a video screen used for display (as of television pictures or computer information)

[2]**monitor** *vb*
to watch or check for a special reason ⟨*monitor* an enemy's radio broadcast⟩

**monk** \'məngk\ *n*
a member of a religious group of men who form a community and promise to stay poor, obey all the laws of their community, and not get married

[1]**mon·key** \'məng-kē\ *n, pl* **monkeys**
**1** any of a group of mostly tropical furry animals that have a long tail and that along with the apes are most closely related to humans in the animal kingdom
**2** a mischievous child

[2]**monkey** *vb* **mon·keyed; mon·key·ing**
**1** to act in a mischievous way ⟨just *monkeying* around⟩
**2** [2]TRIFLE 3, FOOL ⟨don't *monkey* with the lawn mower⟩

**mongoose**
holding an egg

**mon·key·shine** \'məng-kē-ˌshīn\ *n*
PRANK

**monkey wrench** *n*
a wrench with one fixed and one adjustable jaw

**monks·hood** \'məngks-ˌhu̇d\ *n*
▶ a tall poisonous Old World plant related to the buttercups that is grown for its white or purplish flowers that are shaped like hoods or as a source of drugs

**monkshood**

**mono-** see MON-

**mono·gram** \'män-ə-ˌgram\ *n*
a design usually made by combining two or more of a person's initials

**mono·plane** \'män-ə-ˌplān\ *n*
▼ an airplane with only one set of wings

**mo·nop·o·lize** \mə-'näp-ə-ˌlīz\ *vb* **mo·nop·o·lized; mo·nop·o·liz·ing**
to get or have complete control over ⟨*monopolized* the conversation⟩

**mo·nop·o·ly** \mə-'näp-ə-lē\ *n, pl* **mo·nop·o·lies**
**1** complete control of the entire supply of goods or a service in a certain market
**2** complete possession ⟨has no *monopoly* on bad manners⟩
**3** a person or group having a monopoly

## monoplane

The first monoplanes were introduced in the early 20th century. More streamlined in shape than biplanes, they could fly faster and were easier to maneuver. However, their single wings were weak and needed strong wires to brace them to vertical posts called king posts. More powerful, all-metal monoplanes became widespread by the 1930s.

**features of a 1912 monoplane**

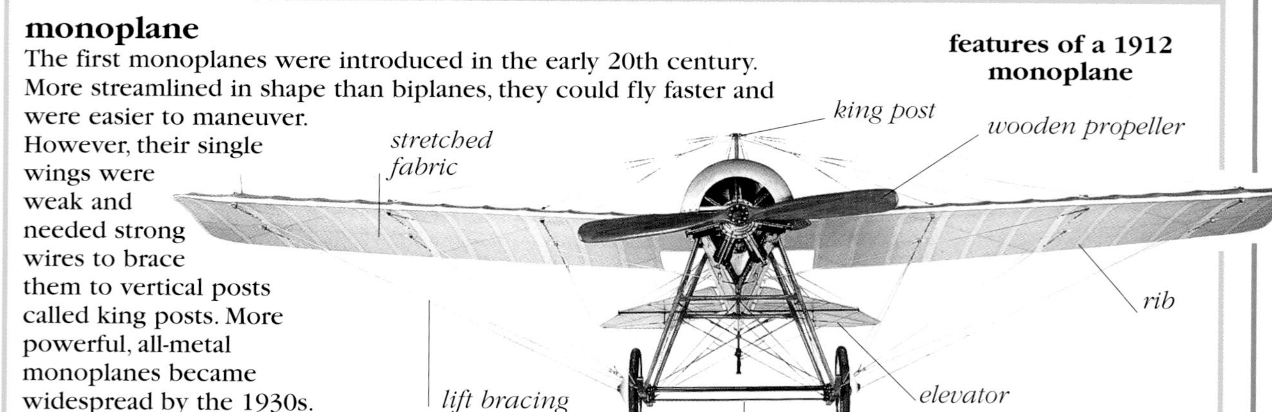

**mono·syl·la·ble** \'män-ə-ˌsil-ə-bəl\ *n*
a word of one syllable

**mo·not·o·nous** \mə-'nät-n-əs\ *adj*
boring from being always the same
**mo·not·o·nous·ly** *adv*

**mo·not·o·ny** \mə-'nät-n-ē\ *n, pl* **mo·not·o·nies**
a boring lack of change

**mon·soon** \män-'sün\ *n*
**1** a wind in the Indian ocean and southern Asia that blows from the southwest from April to October and from the northeast from October to April
**2** the rainy season that comes with the southwest monsoon

**mon·ster** \'män-stər\ *n*
**1** an animal or plant that is very unlike the usual type
**2** a strange or horrible creature
**3** something unusually large
**4** an extremely wicked or cruel person

**mon·strous** \'män-strəs\ *adj*
**1** unusually large **:** ENORMOUS
**2** very bad or wrong ⟨a *monstrous* error⟩
**3** very different from the usual form **:** ABNORMAL
**mon·strous·ly** *adv*

**month** \'mənth\ *n*
one of the twelve parts into which the year is divided

[1]**month·ly** \'mənth-lē\ *adj*
**1** happening, done, or published every month
**2** figured in terms of one month ⟨*monthly* salary⟩
**3** lasting a month

[2]**monthly** *n, pl* **monthlies**
a magazine published every month

**mon·u·ment** \'män-yə-mənt\ *n*
**1** a structure (as a building, stone, or statue) made to keep alive the memory of a person or event
**2** a work, saying, or deed that lasts or is worth keeping or remembering

[1]**moo** \'mü\ *vb* **mooed**; **moo·ing**
to make a moo **:** LOW

[2]**moo** *n, pl* **moos**
the low sound made by a cow

[1]**mood** \'müd\ *n*
a state or frame of mind **:** DISPOSITION ⟨in a good *mood*⟩

[2]**mood** *n*
a set of forms of a verb that show whether the action or state expressed is to be thought of as a fact, a command, or a wish or possibility

**moody** \'müd-ē\ *adj* **mood·i·er**; **mood·i·est**
often feeling gloomy or in a bad mood
**mood·i·ly** \'müd-l-ē\ *adv*
**mood·i·ness** \'müd-ē-nəs\ *n*

[1]**moon** \'mün\ *n*
**1** the natural celestial body that shines by reflecting light from the sun and revolves about the earth in about $29\frac{1}{2}$ days
**2** SATELLITE 1
**3** MONTH

[2]**moon** *vb*
to waste time by daydreaming

**moon·beam** \'mün-ˌbēm\ *n*
a ray of light from the moon

**moon·light** \'mün-ˌlīt\ *n*
the light of the moon

**moon·stone** \'mün-ˌstōn\ *n*
▶ a partly transparent shining stone used as a gem

**moonstone**

[1]**moor** \'mu̇r\ *n*
an area of open land that is too wet or too poor for farming

[2]**moor** *vb*
to fasten in place with cables, lines, or anchors ⟨*moor* a boat⟩

**moor·ing** \'mu̇r-ing\ *n*
**1** a place where or an object to which a boat can be fastened
**2** a chain or line by which an object is moored

**moor·land** \'mu̇r-lənd\ *n*
land consisting of moors

**moose** \'müs\ *n*
▶ a large deerlike animal with broad flattened antlers and humped shoulders that lives in forests of Canada, the northern United States, Europe, and Asia

[1]**mop** \'mäp\ *n*
**1** a tool for cleaning made of a bundle of cloth or yarn or a sponge fastened to a handle
**2** something that looks like a cloth or yarn mop ⟨a *mop* of hair⟩

[2]**mop** *vb* **mopped**; **mop·ping**
to wipe or clean with or as if with a mop

[1]**mope** \'mōp\ *vb* **moped**; **mop·ing**
to be in a dull and sad state of mind

[2]**mope** *n*
a person without any energy or enthusiasm

**mo·raine** \mə-'rān\ *n*
a pile of earth and stones left by a glacier

[1]**mor·al** \'mȯr-əl\ *adj*
**1** concerned with or relating to what is right and wrong in human behavior ⟨*moral* problems⟩ ⟨a *moral* code⟩
**2** able or fit to teach a lesson ⟨a *moral* story⟩
**3** [1]GOOD 7, VIRTUOUS ⟨lead a *moral* life⟩
**4** able to tell right from wrong ⟨humans are *moral* beings⟩
**mor·al·ly** *adv*

[2]**moral** *n*
**1** the lesson to be learned from a story or experience
**2 morals** *pl* moral conduct ⟨people of bad *morals*⟩
**3 morals** *pl* moral teachings or rules of behavior

**mo·rale** \mə-'ral\ *n*
the condition of the mind or feelings (as in relation to enthusiasm, spirit, or hope) of an individual or group

**mo·ral·i·ty** \mə-'ral-ət-ē\ *n, pl* **mo·ral·i·ties**
**1** moral quality **:** VIRTUE ⟨judge the *morality* of an action⟩
**2** moral conduct

**moose:** a young moose

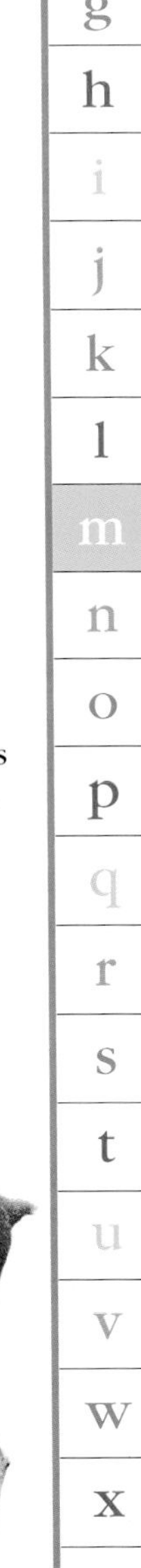

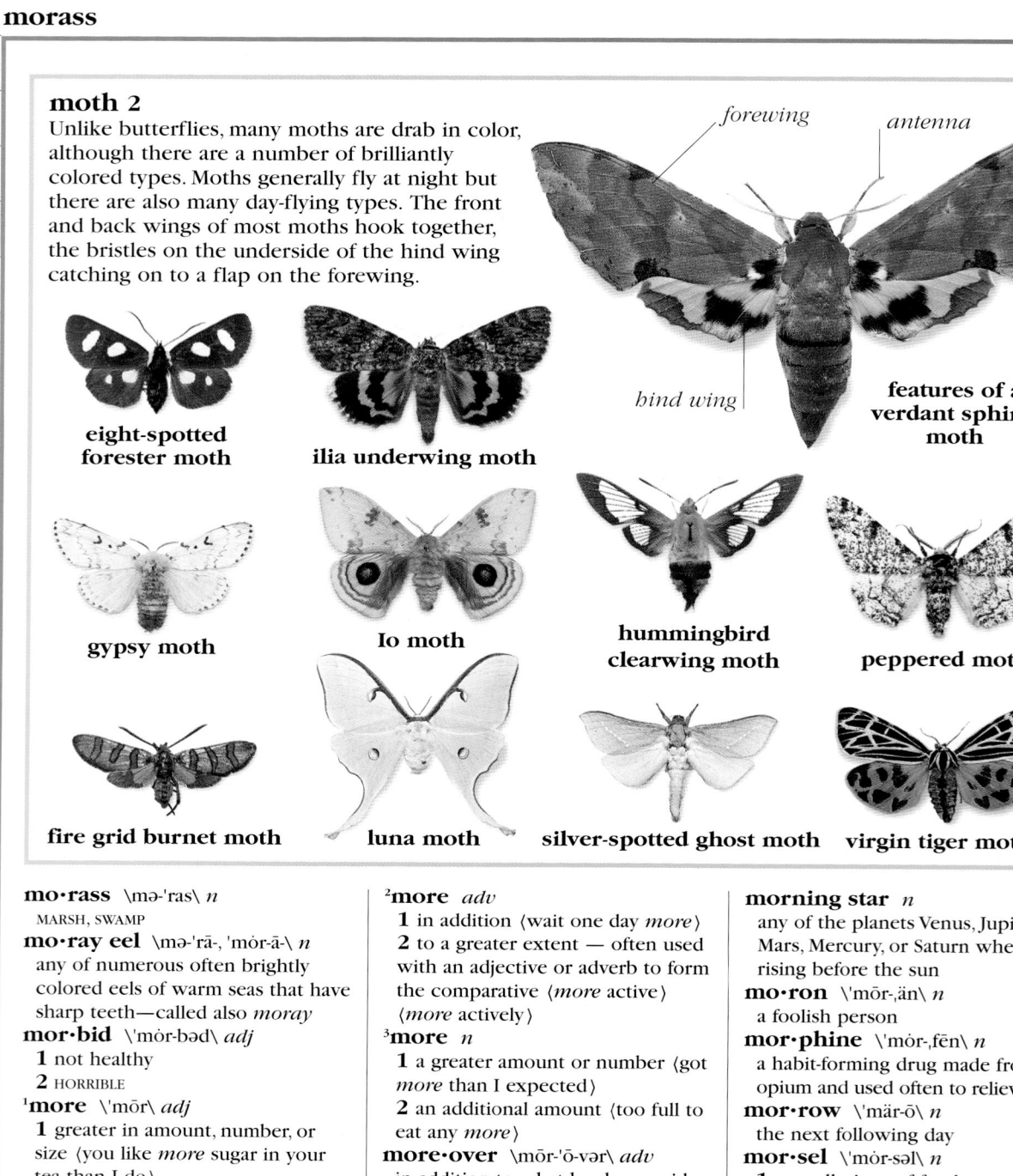

**moth 2**
Unlike butterflies, many moths are drab in color, although there are a number of brilliantly colored types. Moths generally fly at night but there are also many day-flying types. The front and back wings of most moths hook together, the bristles on the underside of the hind wing catching on to a flap on the forewing.

*forewing* *antenna* *hind wing*

**features of a verdant sphinx moth**

**eight-spotted forester moth** **ilia underwing moth**

**gypsy moth** **Io moth** **hummingbird clearwing moth** **peppered moth**

**fire grid burnet moth** **luna moth** **silver-spotted ghost moth** **virgin tiger moth**

**mo·rass** \mə-ˈras\ *n*
MARSH, SWAMP

**mo·ray eel** \mə-ˈrā-, ˈmȯr-ā-\ *n*
any of numerous often brightly colored eels of warm seas that have sharp teeth—called also *moray*

**mor·bid** \ˈmȯr-bəd\ *adj*
**1** not healthy
**2** HORRIBLE

[1]**more** \ˈmōr\ *adj*
**1** greater in amount, number, or size ⟨you like *more* sugar in your tea than I do⟩
**2** [1]EXTRA, ADDITIONAL ⟨take *more* time⟩

**morning glory**

[2]**more** *adv*
**1** in addition ⟨wait one day *more*⟩
**2** to a greater extent — often used with an adjective or adverb to form the comparative ⟨*more* active⟩ ⟨*more* actively⟩

[3]**more** *n*
**1** a greater amount or number ⟨got *more* than I expected⟩
**2** an additional amount ⟨too full to eat any *more*⟩

**more·over** \mōr-ˈō-vər\ *adv*
in addition to what has been said : BESIDES

**morn** \ˈmȯrn\ *n*
MORNING

**morn·ing** \ˈmȯr-ning\ *n*
the early part of the day : the time from sunrise to noon

**morning glory** *n*
◀ a vine that climbs by twisting around something and has large bright flowers that close in the sunshine

**morning star** *n*
any of the planets Venus, Jupiter, Mars, Mercury, or Saturn when rising before the sun

**mo·ron** \ˈmōr-ˌän\ *n*
a foolish person

**mor·phine** \ˈmȯr-ˌfēn\ *n*
a habit-forming drug made from opium and used often to relieve pain

**mor·row** \ˈmär-ō\ *n*
the next following day

**mor·sel** \ˈmȯr-səl\ *n*
**1** a small piece of food : BITE
**2** a small amount : a little piece

[1]**mor·tal** \ˈmȯrt-l\ *adj*
**1** capable of causing death : FATAL ⟨a *mortal* wound⟩
**2** certain to die ⟨we all are *mortal*⟩
**3** very unfriendly ⟨a *mortal* enemy⟩
**4** very great or overpowering ⟨*mortal* fear⟩
**5** [1]HUMAN 1 ⟨*mortal* power⟩
**synonyms** see DEADLY
**mor·tal·ly** *adv*

**[2]mortal** *n*
a human being

**[1]mor·tar** \'mȯrt-ər\ *n*
**1** a strong deep bowl in which substances are pounded or crushed with a pestle
**2** a short light cannon used to shoot shells high into the air

**[2]mortar** *n*
a building material made of lime and cement mixed with sand and water that is spread between bricks or stones so as to hold them together when it hardens

**mor·ti·fy** \'mȯrt-ə-ˌfī\ *vb* **mor·ti·fied**; **mor·ti·fy·ing**
to embarrass greatly **:** SHAME ⟨your bad behavior *mortifies* me⟩

**mo·sa·ic** \mō-'zā-ik\ *n*
► a decoration on a surface made by setting small pieces of glass or stone of different colors into another material so as to make patterns or pictures

**mosaic**

**Moslem** *variant of* MUSLIM

**mosque** \'mäsk\ *n*
a Muslim place of worship

**mos·qui·to** \mə-'skēt-ō\ *n, pl* **mos·qui·toes**
▼ a small two-winged fly the female of which punctures the skin of people and animals to suck their blood

*proboscis*

**mosquito**

**moss** \'mȯs\ *n*
**1** any of a class of plants that have no flowers and grow as small leafy stems in cushion-like patches clinging to rocks, bark, or damp ground
**2** any of various plants (as lichens) resembling moss

**mossy** \'mȯs-ē\ *adj* **moss·i·er**; **moss·i·est**
like or covered with moss

**[1]most** \'mōst\ *adj*
**1** the majority of ⟨*most* people believe this⟩
**2** greatest in amount or extent ⟨the youngest of the group had the *most* courage⟩

**[2]most** *adv*
**1** to the greatest or highest level or extent — often used with an adjective or adverb to form the superlative ⟨*most* active⟩ ⟨*most* actively⟩
**2** to a very great extent ⟨a *most* careful driver⟩

**[3]most** *n*
the greatest amount, number, or part

**most·ly** \'mōst-lē\ *adv*
for the greatest part

**mote** \'mōt\ *n*
a small particle **:** SPECK

**mo·tel** \mō-'tel\ *n*
a building or group of buildings which provide lodgings and in which the rooms are usually reached directly from an outdoor parking area

**moth** \'mȯth\ *n, pl* **moths** \'mȯt͟hz, 'mȯths\
**1** CLOTHES MOTH
**2** ◄ an insect that usually flies at night and has mostly feathery antennae and stouter body, duller coloring, and smaller wings than the related butterflies

**[1]moth·er** \'mət͟h-ər\ *n*
**1** a female parent
**2** a nun in charge of a convent
**3** [1]CAUSE 1, ORIGIN ⟨necessity is the *mother* of invention⟩
**moth·er·hood** \-ˌhu̇d\ *n*
**moth·er·less** \-ləs\ *adj*

**[2]mother** *adj*
**1** of or having to do with a mother ⟨*mother* love⟩
**2** being in the relation of a mother to others ⟨a *mother* church⟩ ⟨our *mother* country⟩
**3** gotten from or as if from one's mother

**[3]mother** *vb*
to be or act as a mother to

**moth·er·board** \'mət͟h-ər-ˌbōrd, -ˌbȯrd\ *n*
▼ the main circuit board especially of a small computer

**moth·er–in–law** \'mət͟h-ər-ən-ˌlȯ\ *n, pl* **mothers–in–law**
the mother of one's husband or wife

**moth·er·ly** \'mət͟h-ər-lē\ *adj*
**1** of, relating to, or characteristic of a mother ⟨*motherly* affection⟩
**2** like a mother **:** MATERNAL

## motherboard

All of a computer's components are attached to the motherboard. The motherboard has a socket that allows a printer or modem to be connected to the computer and another socket for a video card to control the workings of the monitor screen. It also houses the computer's central processing unit (CPU).

**features of a motherboard**

**moth·er–of–pearl** \ˌməth-ər-əv-ˈpərl\ *n*
▶ a hard pearly material that lines the shell of some mollusks (as mussels) and is often used for ornamental objects and buttons

**mother-of-pearl** lining of an abalone shell

[1]**mo·tion** \ˈmō-shən\ *n*
**1** a formal plan or suggestion for action offered according to the rules of a meeting ⟨a *motion* to adjourn⟩
**2** the act or process of changing place or position **:** MOVEMENT
**mo·tion·less** \-ləs\ *adj*
**mo·tion·less·ness** *n*

[2]**motion** *vb*
to direct or signal by a movement or sign ⟨*motioned* them to come forward⟩

**motion picture** *n*
**1** a series of pictures projected on a screen rapidly one after another so as to give the appearance of a continuous picture in which the objects move
**2** MOVIE 1

**mo·ti·vate** \ˈmōt-ə-ˌvāt\ *vb*
**mo·ti·vat·ed**; **mo·ti·vat·ing**
to provide with a reason for doing something ⟨ideas that *motivate* youth⟩

[1]**mo·tive** \ˈmōt-iv\ *n*
a reason for doing something

[2]**motive** *adj*
causing motion ⟨*motive* power⟩

**mot·ley** \ˈmät-lē\ *adj*
**1** having various colors
**2** composed of various often unlike kinds or parts ⟨a *motley* collection of junk⟩

[1]**mo·tor** \ˈmōt-ər\ *n*
**1** a machine that produces motion or power for doing work ⟨an electric *motor*⟩ ⟨a *motor* run by gasoline⟩
**2** [2]AUTOMOBILE
**mo·tored** \ˈmōt-ərd\ *adj*

[2]**motor** *adj*
**1** causing or controlling activity (as motion) ⟨*motor* nerves⟩
**2** equipped with or driven by a motor
**3** of or relating to an automobile
**4** designed for motor vehicles or motorists

[3]**motor** *vb*
[1]DRIVE 3

[1]**mount:** Mount Everest between China and Nepal

**mo·tor·bike** \ˈmōt-ər-ˌbīk\ *n*
a light motorcycle

**mo·tor·boat** \ˈmōt-ər-ˌbōt\ *n*
an often small boat driven by a motor

**mo·tor·cade** \ˈmōt-ər-ˌkād\ *n*
a line of motor vehicles traveling as a group

**mo·tor·car** \ˈmōt-ər-ˌkär\ *n*
[2]AUTOMOBILE

**mo·tor·cy·cle** \ˈmōt-ər-ˌsī-kəl\ *n*
▶ a motorized vehicle for one or two passengers that has two wheels

**mo·tor·ist** \ˈmōt-ə-rist\ *n*
a person who travels by automobile

**mo·tor·ize** \ˈmōt-ə-ˌrīz\ *vb*
**mo·tor·ized**; **mo·tor·iz·ing**
to equip with a motor or with motor-driven vehicles

**motor scooter** *n*
a motorized vehicle having two or three wheels like a child's scooter but having a seat

**motor vehicle** *n*
a motorized vehicle (as an automobile or motorcycle) not operated on rails

**mot·tled** \ˈmät-ld\ *adj*
having spots or blotches of different colors

**mot·to** \ˈmät-ō\ *n, pl* **mottoes**
**1** a phrase or word inscribed on something (as a public building) to suggest its use or nature
**2** a short expression of a guiding rule of conduct

**mould** *variant of* MOLD

**moult** *variant of* MOLT

**mound** \ˈmau̇nd\ *n*
a small hill or heap of dirt

[1]**mount** \ˈmau̇nt\ *n*
▲ a high hill **:** MOUNTAIN — used especially before a proper name ⟨*Mount* Everest⟩

[2]**mount** *vb*
**1** ASCEND, CLIMB ⟨*mount* a ladder⟩
**2** to get up onto something ⟨*mount* a platform⟩ ⟨*mount* a horse⟩
**3** to increase rapidly in amount ⟨*mounting* debts⟩
**4** to prepare for use or display by fastening in position on a support ⟨*mount* a picture on cardboard⟩
**synonyms** see ASCEND

[3]**mount** *n*
that on which a person or thing is or can be mounted ⟨the horse was an excellent *mount*⟩

**moun·tain** \ˈmau̇nt-n\ *n*
**1** an elevation higher than a hill
**2** a great mass or huge number ⟨a *mountain* of mail⟩

**moun·tain·eer** \ˌmau̇nt-n-ˈir\ *n*
**1** a person who lives in the mountains
**2** a mountain climber

**mountain goat** *n*
a goatlike animal of the mountains of western North America with thick white coat and slightly curved black horns

**mountain lion** *n*
COUGAR

## motorcycle

Like bicycles, motorcycles have a streamlined frame, a wheel at the front and back, and controls on the handlebars. Like cars, they also have an engine. The first motorcycle was invented in the mid-19th century. Today, motorcycles are designed for many purposes, including racing and touring, as well as for everyday use. Engine sizes are measured in cubic centimeters, and range from 50cc to more than 1,000cc on the largest and most powerful motorcycles.

**features of a racing motorbike**

*handlebars*

*lightweight frame*

*saddle*

*tire*

**1940s motorcycle for military use**

**1950s motorcycle with a sidecar for a passenger**

**1960s motorcycle for commuting**

**1970s motorcycle for touring**

**1980s motorcycle for commuting**

**1990s 1500cc motorcycle for cruising**

**moun·tain·ous** \'maůnt-n-əs\ *adj*
**1** having many mountains ⟨*mountainous* country⟩
**2** like a mountain in size **:** HUGE

**moun·tain·side** \'maůnt-n-,sīd\ *n*
the side of a mountain

**moun·tain·top** \'maůnt-n-,täp\ *n*
the highest part of a mountain

**mount·ing** \'maůnt-ing\ *n*
something that serves as a mount **:** SUPPORT ⟨a *mounting* for an engine⟩

**mourn** \'mōrn\ *vb*
to feel or show grief or sorrow especially over someone's death
**mourn·er** *n*

**mourn·ful** \'mōrn-fəl\ *adj*
**1** full of sorrow or sadness ⟨a *mournful* face⟩
**2** causing sorrow ⟨*mournful* news⟩
**mourn·ful·ly** \-fə-lē\ *adv*
**mourn·ful·ness** *n*

**mourn·ing** \'mōr-ning\ *n*
**1** the act of sorrowing
**2** an outward sign (as black clothes or an arm band) of grief for a person's death

**mourning dove** *n*
▶ a wild dove of the United States named from its mournful cry

**mourning dove**

**mouse**
\'maůs\ *n, pl* **mice** \'mīs\
**1** a furry gnawing animal like the larger related rats
**2** a person without spirit or courage
**3** a small movable device that is connected to a computer and used to move the cursor and select functions on the screen
**mouse·like** \'maů-,slīk\ *adj*

**mouse pad** *n*
a thin flat pad (as of rubber) on which a computer mouse is used

**mous·er** \'maů-zər\ *n*
a cat good at catching mice

**moustache** *variant of* MUSTACHE

**¹mouth** \'maůth\ *n, pl* **mouths** \'maůthz, 'maůths\
**1** the opening through which food passes into the body **:** the space containing the tongue and teeth
**2** an opening that is like a mouth ⟨the *mouth* of a cave⟩
**3** the place where a stream enters a larger body of water

**²mouth** \'maůth\ *vb*
to repeat without being sincere or without understanding

**mouth·ful** \'maůth-,fůl\ *n*
**1** as much as the mouth will hold
**2** the amount put into the mouth at one time

**mouth organ** *n*
HARMONICA

**mouth·piece**
\'maůth-,pēs\ *n*
▶ the part put to, between, or near the lips ⟨the *mouthpiece* of a trumpet⟩ ⟨the *mouthpiece* of a telephone⟩

*mouthpiece*

**mouthpiece** of a telephone

**mov·able** *or* **move·able** \'mü-və-bəl\ *adj*
**1** possible to move ⟨*movable* desks⟩
**2** changing from one date to another ⟨*movable* holidays⟩

**¹move** \'müv\ *vb* **moved**; **mov·ing**
**1** to go from one place to another ⟨*move* into the shade⟩
**2** to change the place or position of **:** SHIFT
**3** to set in motion ⟨*move* one's feet⟩
**4** to cause to act **:** INFLUENCE ⟨*moved* me to change my mind⟩
**5** to stir the feelings of ⟨the sad story *moved* the children to tears⟩
**6** to change position ⟨*moved* in my chair⟩
**7** to suggest according to the rules in a meeting ⟨*move* to adjourn⟩
**8** to change residence

**²move** *n*
**1** the act of moving a piece in a game
**2** the turn of a player to move ⟨it's your *move*⟩
**3** an action taken to accomplish something **:** MANEUVER ⟨a *move* to end the dispute⟩
**4** the action of moving **:** MOVEMENT

**move·ment** \'müv-mənt\ *n*
**1** the act or process of moving **:** an instance of moving
**2** a program or series of acts working toward a desired end ⟨a *movement* for political action⟩
**3** a mechanical arrangement (as of wheels) for causing a particular motion (as in a clock or watch)
**4** RHYTHM 2, METER
**5** a section of a longer piece of music ⟨a *movement* in a symphony⟩
**6** an emptying of the bowels **:** the material emptied from the bowels

**mov·er** \'mü-vər\ *n*
a person or company that moves the belongings of others (as from one home to another)

**mov·ie** \'mü-vē\ *n*
**1** a story represented in motion pictures
**2** a showing of a movie ⟨let's go to a *movie*⟩

**mov·ing** \'mü-ving\ *adj*
**1** changing place or position ⟨a *moving* target⟩
**2** having the power to stir the feelings or sympathies ⟨a *moving* song⟩
**mov·ing·ly** *adv*

**moving picture** *n*
MOTION PICTURE 1

**¹mow** \'maů\ *n*
the part of a barn where hay or straw is stored

**²mow** \'mō\ *vb* **mowed**; **mowed** *or* **mown** \'mōn\; **mow·ing**
**1** to cut down with a scythe or machine ⟨*mow* grass⟩
**2** to cut the standing plant cover from ⟨*mow* the lawn⟩
**3** to cause to fall in great numbers
**mow·er** \'mō-ər\ *n*

**Mr.** \,mis-tər\ *n, pl* **Messrs.** \,mes-ərz\
used as a title before a man's name ⟨*Mr.* Doe⟩

**Mrs.** \,mis-əz, ,miz-\ *n, pl* **Mes·dames** \mā-'däm, -'dam\
used as a title before a married woman's name ⟨*Mrs.* Doe⟩

**Ms.** \,miz\ *n*
often used instead of *Miss* or *Mrs.* ⟨*Ms.* Jane Doe⟩

**¹much** \'məch\ *adj* **more** \'mōr\; **most** \'mōst\
great in amount or extent ⟨*much* money⟩

**[2]much** *adv* **more**; **most**
**1** to a great or high level or extent ⟨*much* happier⟩
**2** just about : NEARLY ⟨looks *much* as it did years ago⟩

**[3]much** *n*
a great amount or part ⟨*much* that was said is true⟩

**mu·ci·lage** \'myü-sə-lij\ *n*
a water solution of a gum or similar substance used especially to stick things together

**muffin:** a blueberry muffin

**muck** \'mək\ *n*
**1** soft wet soil or barnyard manure
**2** DIRT 1, FILTH

**mu·cous** \'myü-kəs\ *adj*
**1** of, relating to, or like mucus
**2** containing or producing mucus ⟨a *mucous* membrane⟩

**mu·cus** \'myü-kəs\ *n*
a slippery sticky substance produced especially by mucous membranes (as of the nose and throat) which it moistens and protects

**mud** \'məd\ *n*
soft wet earth or dirt

**[1]mud·dle** \'məd-l\ *vb* **mud·dled**; **mud·dling**
**1** to be or cause to be confused or bewildered ⟨*muddled* by too much advice⟩
**2** to mix up in a confused manner ⟨*muddle* the business accounts⟩
**3** to make a mess of : BUNGLE

**[2]muddle** *n*
a state of confusion

**[1]mud·dy** \'məd-ē\ *adj* **mud·di·er**; **mud·di·est**
**1** filled or covered with mud
**2** looking like mud ⟨a *muddy* color⟩
**3** not clear or bright : DULL ⟨a *muddy* skin⟩
**4** being mixed up ⟨*muddy* thinking⟩

**mud·di·ly** \'məd-l-ē\ *adv*

**mud·di·ness** \'məd-ē-nəs\ *n*

**[2]muddy** *vb* **mud·died**; **mud·dy·ing**
**1** to soil or stain with or as if with mud
**2** to make cloudy or dull

**[1]muff** \'məf\ *n*
a soft thick cover into which both hands can be shoved to protect them from cold

**[2]muff** *vb*
to handle awkwardly : BUNGLE

**muf·fin** \'məf-ən\ *n*
◀ a bread made of batter containing eggs and baked in a small cup-shaped container

**muf·fle** \'məf-əl\ *vb* **muf·fled**; **muf·fling**
**1** to wrap up so as to hide or protect
**2** to deaden the sound of

**muf·fler** \'məf-lər\ *n*
**1** a scarf for the neck
**2** a device to deaden the noise of an engine (as of an automobile)

**mug** \'məg\ *n*
a large drinking cup

**mug·gy** \'məg-ē\ *adj* **mug·gi·er**; **mug·gi·est**
being very warm and humid ⟨*muggy* weather⟩
**mug·gi·ness** *n*

**Mu·ham·mad·an** *or* **Mo·ham·med·an** \mō-'ham-əd-ən, mü-, -'häm-\ *n*
MUSLIM

**Mu·ham·mad·an·ism** *or* **Mo·ham·med·an·ism** \mō-'ham-əd-ən-,iz-əm, mü-, -'häm-\ *n*
ISLAM

**mul·ber·ry** \'məl-,ber-ē\ *n*, *pl* **mul·ber·ries**
a tree that bears edible usually purple fruit like berries and has leaves on which silkworms can be fed

**[1]mulch** \'məlch\ *n*
a material (as straw or sawdust) spread over the ground to protect the roots of plants from heat, cold, or drying of the soil or to keep fruit clean

**[2]mulch** *vb*
to cover with mulch

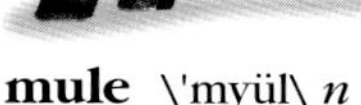

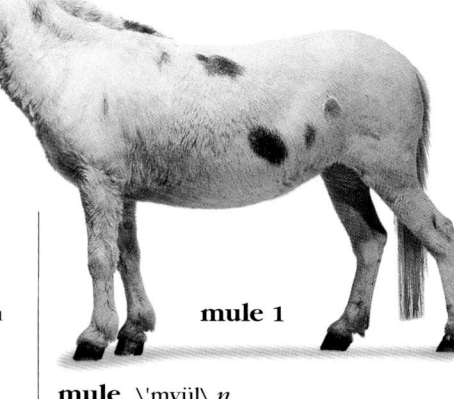

**mule 1**

**mule** \'myül\ *n*
**1** ▲ an animal that is an offspring of a donkey and a horse
**2** a stubborn person

**mule skinner** *n*
a driver of mules

**mu·le·teer** \,myü-lə-'tir\ *n*
a driver of mules

**mul·ish** \'myü-lish\ *adj*
stubborn like a mule
**mul·ish·ly** *adv*
**mul·ish·ness** *n*

**mul·let** \'məl-ət\ *n*
any of various freshwater or saltwater food fishes some mostly gray (**gray mullets**) and others red or golden (**red mullets**)

**multi-** \,məl-ti\ *prefix*
**1** many : much
**2** more than two
**3** many times over

**mul·ti·cul·tur·al** \,məl-,tī-'kəl-chə-rəl\ *adj*
of, relating to, or made up of several different cultures together ⟨a *multicultural* society⟩

**mul·ti·me·dia** \,məl-ti-'mēd-ē-ə\ *adj*
using or composed of more than one form of communication or expression ⟨*multimedia* software that combines sound, video, and text⟩

**[1]mul·ti·ple** \'məl-tə-pəl\ *adj*
being more than one ⟨*multiple* copies of a document⟩

**[2]multiple** *n*
the number found by multiplying one number by another ⟨35 is a *multiple* of 7⟩

**mul·ti·pli·cand** \,məl-tə-plə-'kand\ *n*
a number that is to be multiplied by another number

**mul·ti·pli·ca·tion** \ˌməl-tə-plə-ˈkā-shən\ *n*
a short way of finding out what would be the result of adding a figure the number of times indicated by another figure ⟨the *multiplication* of 7 by 3 gives 21⟩

**mul·ti·pli·er** \ˈməl-tə-ˌplī-ər\ *n*
a number by which another number is multiplied

**mul·ti·ply** \ˈməl-tə-ˌplī\ *vb* **mul·ti·plied**; **mul·ti·ply·ing**
**1** to increase in number **:** make or become more numerous
**2** to find the product of by means of multiplication ⟨*multiply* 7 by 8⟩

**mul·ti·tude** \ˈməl-tə-ˌtüd, -ˌtyüd\ *n*
a great number of persons or things

**mum** \ˈməm\ *adj*
SILENT 1, 4 ⟨keep *mum*⟩

[1]**mum·ble** \ˈməm-bəl\ *vb* **mum·bled**; **mum·bling**
to speak so that words are not clear

[2]**mumble** *n*
speech that is not clear enough to be understood

**mum·my** \ˈməm-ē\ *n, pl* **mummies**
▼ a dead body preserved in the manner of the ancient Egyptians

**mumps** \ˈməmps\ *n sing or pl*
an infectious disease in which there is fever and soreness and swelling of glands and especially of those around the jaw

**munch** \ˈmənch\ *vb*
to chew with a crunching sound

**mu·nic·i·pal** \myu̇-ˈnis-ə-pəl\ *adj*
having to do with the government of a town or city

**muscle 1**
There are three types of muscle: skeletal, smooth, and cardiac. Skeletal muscles are attached to the bones by tendons, usually at one end to a bone that moves, and at the other end to one that does not. Smooth muscles are found in the walls of hollow organs and cardiac muscles are found in the heart.

**diagram of the skeletal muscular system**

**mu·nic·i·pal·i·ty** \myu̇-ˌnis-ə-ˈpal-ət-ē\ *n, pl* **mu·nic·i·pal·i·ties**
a town or city having its own local government

**mu·ni·tions** \myu̇-ˈnish-ənz\ *n*
military equipment and supplies for fighting **:** AMMUNITION

[1]**mu·ral** \ˈmyu̇r-əl\ *adj*
having to do with a wall

[2]**mural** *n*
a painting on a wall

[1]**mur·der** \ˈmərd-ər\ *n*
the intentional and unlawful killing of a human being

[2]**murder** *vb*
**1** to commit murder
**2** to spoil by performing or using badly ⟨*murder* a song⟩ ⟨*murder* the language⟩ **synonyms** see KILL
**mur·der·er** *n*

**mur·der·ous** \ˈmərd-ə-rəs\ *adj*
**1** intending or capable of murder
**2** very hard to bear or withstand ⟨*murderous* heat⟩
**mur·der·ous·ly** *adv*

**murk** \ˈmərk\ *n*
GLOOM 1, DARKNESS

**murky** \ˈmər-kē\ *adj* **murk·i·er**; **murk·i·est**

**mummy:** an ancient Egyptian mummy in its case

1 very dark or gloomy
2 FOGGY 1, MISTY
**murk·i·ness** *n*

**[1]mur·mur** \'mər-mər\ *n*
a low faint sound

**[2]murmur** *vb*
1 to make a murmur
2 to say in a voice too low to be heard clearly

**mus·ca·dine** \'məs-kə-ˌdīn\ *n*
a grape of the southern United States

**mus·cle** \'məs-əl\ *n*
1 ◀ an animal body tissue consisting of long cells that can contract and produce motion
2 a bodily organ that is a mass of muscle tissue attached at either end (as to bones) so that it can make a body part (as an arm) move
3 strength or development of the muscles

**Word History** The English word *muscle* came from a Latin word that meant "small mouse." The movement of the muscles under the skin probably made someone think of a lively mouse.

**mus·cle–bound** \'məs-əl-ˌbau̇nd\ *adj*
having large muscles that do not move and stretch easily

**mus·cu·lar** \'məs-kyə-lər\ *adj*
1 of, relating to, or being muscle
2 done by the muscles
3 STRONG 1

**muse** \'myüz\ *vb* **mused**; **mus·ing**
PONDER

**mu·se·um** \myu̇-'zē-əm\ *n*
a building in which are displayed objects of interest in one or more of the arts or sciences

**[1]mush** \'məsh\ *n*
cornmeal boiled in water

**[2]mush** *vb*
to travel across snow with a sled drawn by dogs

**[1]mush·room** \'məsh-ˌrüm, -ˌru̇m\ *n*
1 ▶ a part of a fungus that bears spores, grows above ground, and suggests an umbrella in shape
2 a fungus that produces mushrooms
3 something shaped like a mushroom

**[2]mushroom** *vb*
to come into being suddenly or grow and develop rapidly

**mushy** \'məsh-ē\ *adj* **mush·i·er**; **mush·i·est**
soft like mush

**mu·sic** \'myü-zik\ *n*
1 the art of producing pleasing or expressive combinations of tones especially with melody, rhythm, and usually harmony
2 compositions made according to the rules of music
3 pleasing sounds
4 a musical composition set down on paper ⟨bring your *music*⟩

**[1]mu·si·cal** \'myü-zi-kəl\ *adj*
1 having to do with music or the writing or performing of music ⟨*musical* instruments⟩
2 pleasing like music ⟨a *musical* voice⟩
3 fond of or talented in music ⟨a *musical* family⟩
4 set to music
**mu·si·cal·ly** *adv*

**[2]musical** *n*
a movie or play that tells a story with both speaking and singing

**music box** *n*
a box that contains a mechanical device which uses gears like those of a clock to play a tune

**mu·si·cian** \myu̇-'zish-ən\ *n*
a person who writes, sings, or plays music with skill and especially as a profession

**[1]mushroom 1**
Mushrooms are fungi that can be found growing wild mainly in damp woodlands and meadows. They are a popular food around the world, and many edible types are cultivated. To reproduce, mushrooms release spores from flaps called gills, or hollows called pores, on the underside of their caps.

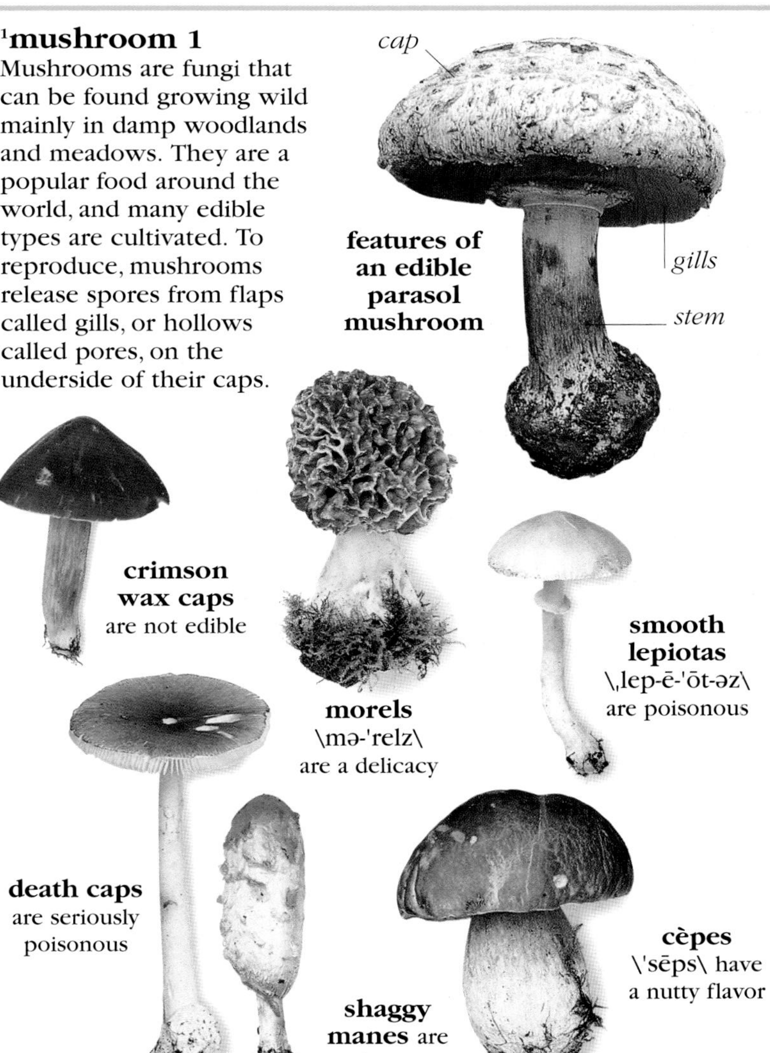


**features of an edible parasol mushroom**

**crimson wax caps** are not edible

**morels** \mə-'relz\ are a delicacy

**smooth lepiotas** \ˌlep-ē-'ōt-əz\ are poisonous

**death caps** are seriously poisonous

**shaggy manes** are poisonous

**cèpes** \'sēps\ have a nutty flavor

a b c d e f g h i j k l m n o p q r s t u v w x y z

**musk** \'məsk\ *n*
**1** a strong-smelling material from a gland of an Asian deer (**musk deer**) used in perfumes
**2** any of several plants with musky odors

**mus·ket** \'məs-kət\ *n*
a firearm that is loaded through the muzzle and that was once used by infantry soldiers

**Word History** The musket was first used in Spain. When the Italians saw the new weapon, they named it after a weapon they already knew — a kind of arrow that sounded a bit like a fly when it whizzed through the air. The arrow got its name from the Italian word that meant "fly." This word in turn came from the Latin word for a fly. The French took their word for the musket from the Italians. The English word *musket* came from this French word.

**mus·ke·teer** \,məs-kə-'tir\ *n*
a soldier armed with a musket

**musk·mel·on** \'məsk-,mel-ən\ *n*
a small round to oval melon with sweet usually green or orange flesh

**musk–ox** \'məs-,käks\ *n*
a shaggy animal like an ox found in Greenland and northern North America

**musk·rat** \'məs-,krat\ *n*
a North American water animal related to the rats that has webbed hind feet and a long scaly tail and is valued for its glossy usually dark brown fur

**musky** \'məs-kē\ *adj* **musk·i·er**; **musk·i·est**
suggesting musk in odor
**musk·i·ness** *n*

**Mus·lim** \'məz-ləm\ *or* **Mos·lem** \'mäz-\ *n*
a person whose religion is Islam

**mus·lin** \'məz-lən\ *n*
a cotton fabric of plain weave

[1]**muss** \'məs\ *n*
[2]DISORDER 1, CONFUSION

[2]**muss** *vb*
to make untidy

**mus·sel** \'məs-əl\ *n*
**1** a sea mollusk that has a long dark shell in two parts and is sometimes used as food
**2** any of various American freshwater clams with shells from which mother-of-pearl is obtained

**must** \məst\ *helping verb, present and past all persons* **must**
**1** to be required to ⟨a person *must* eat to live⟩
**2** to be very likely to ⟨it *must* be time⟩ ⟨*must* have lost it⟩

**mus·tache** *or* **mous·tache** \'məs-,tash, məs-'tash\ *n*
the hair growing on the human upper lip

**mus·tang** \'məs-,tang\ *n*
a small hardy horse of western North America that is half wild

**Word History** Long ago in Spain, stray cattle were rounded up each year and sold. The Spanish word for this roundup of strays came from a Latin phrase that meant "mixed animals." From their word that meant "roundup of strays," the Spanish made another word that meant "a stray animal." In Mexico, this word was used for a kind of wild horse. That is where English *mustang* came from.

**mus·tard** \'məs-tərd\ *n*
▶ yellow powder that is prepared from the seeds of a plant related to the turnips, has a sharp taste, and is used in medicine and as a seasoning for foods

[1]**mus·ter** \'məs-tər\ *n*
**1** a formal military inspection
**2** an assembled group **:** COLLECTION

[2]**muster** *vb*
**1** to call together (as troops) for roll call or inspection
**2** to bring into being or action ⟨*mustering* courage⟩

**mustn't** \'məs-nt\
must not

**musty** \'məs-tē\ *adj* **must·i·er**; **must·i·est**
bad in odor or taste from the effects of dampness or mildew
**must·i·ness** *n*

[1]**mu·tant** \'myüt-nt\ *adj*
of, relating to, or resulting from mutation

[2]**mutant** *n*
a mutant individual

**mu·tate** \'myü-,tāt\ *vb* **mu·tat·ed**; **mu·tat·ing**
**1** to undergo great changes
**2** to undergo mutation

**mu·ta·tion** \myü-'tā-shən\ *n*
a change in a gene or a resulting new trait inherited by an individual

**mustard**

[1]**mute** \'myüt\ *adj* **mut·er**; **mut·est**
**1** unable to speak
**2** not speaking **:** SILENT

[2]**mute** *n*
**1** a person who cannot or does not speak
**2** ▼ a device on a musical instrument that deadens, softens, or muffles its tone

[3]**mute** *vb* **mut·ed**; **mut·ing**
to muffle or reduce the sound of

*mute*

[2]**mute 2:** a mute on a trumpet

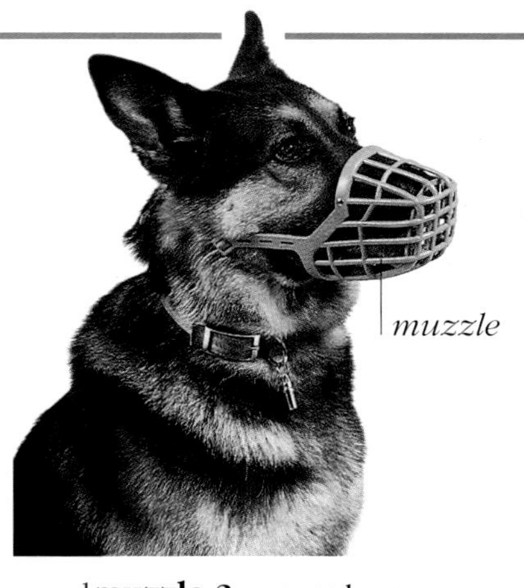


**¹muzzle 2:** a muzzle on a German Shepherd dog

**mu·ti·late** \'myüt-l-,āt\ *vb* **mu·ti·lat·ed**; **mu·ti·lat·ing**
**1** to cut off or destroy a necessary part (as a limb) **:** MAIM
**2** to make imperfect by cutting or changing ⟨*mutilate* a book⟩

**mu·ti·neer** \,myüt-n-'ir\ *n*
a person who is guilty of mutiny

**mu·ti·nous** \'myüt-n-əs\ *adj*
being inclined to or in a state of mutiny
**mu·ti·nous·ly** *adv*

**¹mu·ti·ny** \'myüt-n-ē\ *n, pl* **mu·ti·nies**
**1** refusal to obey authority
**2** a turning of a group (as of sailors) against an officer in authority

**²mutiny** *vb* **mu·ti·nied**; **mu·ti·ny·ing**
to refuse to obey authority

**mutt** \'mət\ *n*
a mongrel dog

**mut·ter** \'mət-ər\ *vb*
**1** to speak in a low voice with lips partly closed
**2** ¹GRUMBLE 1

**mut·ton** \'mət-n\ *n*
the flesh of a mature sheep

**mu·tu·al** \'myü-chə-wəl\ *adj*
**1** given and received in equal amount ⟨*mutual* favors⟩
**2** having the same relation to one another ⟨*mutual* enemies⟩
**3** shared by two or more at the same time ⟨a *mutual* friend⟩
**mu·tu·al·ly** *adv*

**¹muz·zle** \'məz-əl\ *n*
**1** the nose and jaws of an animal
**2** ◀ a fastening or covering for the mouth of an animal to prevent it from biting or eating
**3** the open end of a gun from which the bullet comes out when the gun is fired

**²muzzle** *vb* **muz·zled**; **muz·zling**
**1** to put a muzzle on ⟨*muzzle* your dog⟩
**2** to keep from free expression of ideas or opinions ⟨the dictator *muzzled* the press⟩

**my** \mī, mə\ *adj*
of or relating to me or myself ⟨*my* head⟩ ⟨*my* injuries⟩

**mynah**

**my·nah** *or* **my·na** \'mī-nə\ *n*
▲ an Asian starling that can be trained to pronounce words and is sometimes kept as a cage bird

**¹myr·i·ad** \'mir-ē-əd\ *n*
a large but not specified or counted number ⟨*myriads* of stars visible⟩

**²myriad** *adj*
extremely numerous ⟨the *myriad* grains of sand on the beach⟩

**myrrh** \'mər\ *n*
a brown slightly bitter fragrant material obtained from African and Arabian trees and used especially in perfumes or formerly in incense

**myr·tle** \'mərt-l\ *n*
**1** ▶ an evergreen shrub of southern Europe
**2** ¹PERIWINKLE

**myrtle 1**

**my·self** \mī-'self, mə-\ *pron*
my own self ⟨I hurt *myself*⟩ ⟨I *myself* did it⟩

**mys·te·ri·ous** \mis-'tir-ē-əs\ *adj*
containing a mystery **:** hard to understand **:** SECRET
**mys·te·ri·ous·ly** *adv*
**mys·te·ri·ous·ness** *n*

**mys·tery** \'mis-tə-rē\ *n, pl* **mys·ter·ies**
**1** something that is beyond human power to understand
**2** something that has not been explained
**3** a piece of fiction about a mysterious crime

**mys·ti·fy** \'mis-tə-,fī\ *vb* **mys·ti·fied**; **mys·ti·fy·ing**
CONFUSE 1

**myth** \'mith\ *n*
**1** a legend that tells about a being with more than human powers or an event which cannot be explained or that explains a religious belief or practice
**2** a person or thing existing only in the imagination

**myth·i·cal** \'mith-i-kəl\ *adj*
**1** based on or told of in a myth
**2** IMAGINARY

**my·thol·o·gy** \mi-'thäl-ə-jē\ *n, pl* **my·thol·o·gies**
a collection of myths

# Nn

**The sounds of N:** The consonant **N** has only one sound in English. It sounds the same in **never**, **national**, **intelligent**, **inning**, and **happen**. Double **N** sounds the same as single **N**.

A few words sound as if they begin with **N**, but actually begin with another letter, which is silent. Examples are **gnaw** (with a silent **G**), **knight** (with a silent **K**), and **pneumonia** (with a silent **P**).

Letter **N** is itself silent when it follows **M** at the end of a word, as in **column** and **solemn**.

---

**n** \'en\ *n, pl* **n's** *or* **ns** \'enz\ *often cap*
the fourteenth letter of the English alphabet

**-n** see [1]-EN

**nab** \'nab\ *vb* **nabbed**; **nab•bing**
[1]ARREST 2

**na•cho** \'nä-chō\ *n, pl* **nachos**
a tortilla chip topped with melted cheese and often additional toppings

**[1]nag** \'nag\ *n*
a usually old or worn-out horse

**[2]nag** *vb* **nagged**; **nag•ging**
**1** to find fault continually: COMPLAIN
**2** to annoy continually or again and again ⟨a *nagging* toothache⟩

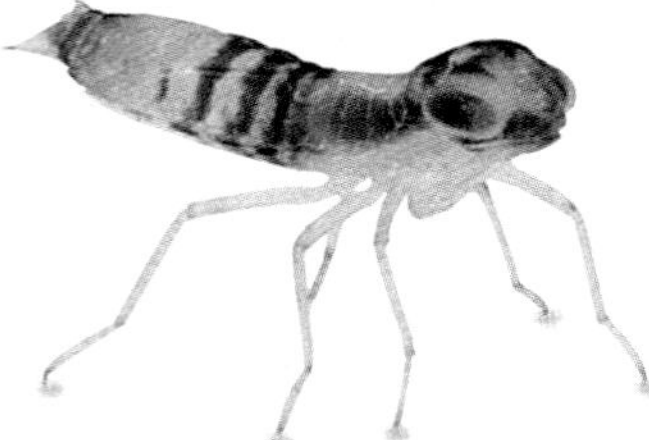

**naiad 2:** a dragonfly naiad

**na•iad** \'nā-əd\ *n, pl* **na•iads** *or* **na•ia•des** \'nā-ə-,dēz\
**1** a nymph believed in ancient times to be living in lakes, rivers, and springs
**2** ▲ the larva of an insect (as a dragonfly) that lives in water

**[1]nail** \'nāl\ *n*
**1** ▶ the horny scale at the end of each finger and toe
**2** a slender pointed piece of metal driven into or through something for fastening

**[2]nail** *vb*
to fasten with or as if with a nail

**nail•brush** \'nāl-,brəsh\ *n*
a brush for cleaning the hands and fingernails

**na•ive** *or* **na•ïve** \nä-'ēv\ *adj*
**1** being simple and sincere
**2** showing lack of experience or knowledge ⟨a child's *naive* belief in fairies⟩
**na•ive•ly** *adv*

**na•ked** \'nā-kəd\ *adj*
**1** having no clothes on : NUDE
**2** lacking a usual or natural covering ⟨*naked* trees⟩
**3** not in its case or covering ⟨a *naked* sword⟩
**4** stripped of anything misleading : PLAIN ⟨the *naked* truth⟩
**5** not aided by an artificial device ⟨seen by the *naked* eye⟩
**na•ked•ly** *adv*
**na•ked•ness** *n*

---

**Synonyms** NAKED and BARE mean being without a natural or usual covering. NAKED suggests that there is neither protective nor ornamental covering ⟨a *naked* baby⟩. BARE stresses that there is no unnecessary covering or that all covering has been removed ⟨*bare* walls⟩.

---

**[1]name** \'nām\ *n*
**1** a word or combination of words by which a person or thing is known
**2** REPUTATION 2 ⟨only you can make a *name* for yourself⟩



**[1]nail 1:** model of a human fingernail in cross section

**[2]name** *vb* **named**; **nam•ing**
**1** to give a name to : CALL ⟨*name* the baby⟩
**2** to refer to by name ⟨can you *name* all the state capitals⟩
**3** to nominate for a job of authority : APPOINT ⟨was *named* to the cabinet⟩
**4** to decide on : CHOOSE ⟨*name* the date for a wedding⟩
**5** [2]MENTION ⟨*name* a price⟩

**[3]name** *adj*
**1** of, relating to, or having a name ⟨wearing a *name* tag⟩
**2** well known because of wide distribution ⟨*name* brands⟩

**name•less** \'nām-ləs\ *adj*
**1** having no name
**2** not marked with a name ⟨a *nameless* grave⟩
**3** [1]UNKNOWN, ANONYMOUS ⟨a *nameless* writer⟩
**4** not to be described ⟨*nameless* fears⟩
**name•less•ness** *n*

**name•ly** \'nām-lē\ *adv*
that is to say ⟨the cat family, *namely*, lions, tigers, and related animals⟩

**name•sake** \'nām-,sāk\ *n*
a person who has the same name as another and especially one named for another

**nan•ny** \'nan-ē\ *n, pl* **nannies**
a child's nurse

**nanny goat** *n*
a female domestic goat

**[1]nap** \'nap\ *vb* **napped**; **nap•ping**
**1** to sleep briefly especially during the day
**2** to be unprepared ⟨was caught *napping*⟩

**[2]nap** *n*
a short sleep especially during the day

[3]**nap** *n*
a hairy or fluffy surface (as on cloth)

**nape** \'nāp\ *n*
the back of the neck

**naph·tha** \'naf-thə, 'nap-thə\ *n*
any of various usually flammable liquids prepared from coal or petroleum and used especially to dissolve substances

**nap·kin** \'nap-kən\ *n*
a small square of cloth or paper used at table to wipe the lips or fingers and protect the clothes

**nar·cis·sus** \när-'sis-əs\ *n, pl* **narcissus** *or* **nar·cis·sus·es** *or* **nar·cis·si** \-'sis-,ī, -ē\
▶ a daffodil with flowers that have short tubes and that grow separately on the stalk

narcissus

[1]**nar·cot·ic** \när-'kät-ik\ *n*
a drug (as opium) that in small doses dulls the senses, relieves pain, and brings on sleep but in larger doses is a dangerous poison

[2]**narcotic** *adj*
**1** acting as or being the source of a narcotic ⟨*narcotic* drugs⟩ ⟨the opium poppy is a *narcotic* plant⟩
**2** of or relating to narcotics or their use or control ⟨*narcotic* laws⟩

**nar·rate** \'nar-,āt, na-'rāt\ *vb* **nar·rat·ed**; **nar·rat·ing**
to tell in full detail ⟨*narrate* the story of one's adventure⟩
**synonyms** see REPORT
**nar·ra·tor** \-ər\ *n*

**nar·ra·tion** \na-'rā-shən\ *n*
**1** the act or process or an instance of narrating
**2** [1]NARRATIVE 1

[1]**nar·ra·tive** \'nar-ət-iv\ *n*
**1** something (as a story) that is narrated
**2** the art or practice of narrating

[2]**narrative** *adj*
of or relating to narration : having the form of a story

[1]**nar·row** \'nar-ō\ *adj*
**1** of slender or less than usual width
**2** limited in size or extent
**3** not broad or open in mind or views
**4** barely successful : CLOSE ⟨a *narrow* escape⟩
**nar·row·ly** *adv*
**nar·row·ness** *n*

[2]**narrow** *vb*
to make or become narrow

[3]**narrow** *n*
a narrow passage connecting two bodies of water — usually used in pl.

**nar·row–mind·ed** \,nar-ō-'mīn-dəd\ *adj*
[1]NARROW 3, INTOLERANT
**nar·row–mind·ed·ly** *adv*
**nar·row–mind·ed·ness** *n*

**nar·whal** \'när-,hwäl, -,wäl\ *n*
▼ an arctic marine animal that is related to the dolphin and in the male has a long twisted ivory tusk

narwhal

[1]**na·sal** \'nā-zəl\ *n*
a nasal sound

[2]**nasal** *adj*
**1** of or relating to the nose
**2** uttered with the nose passage open ⟨the *nasal* consonants \m\, \n\, and \ng\⟩
**na·sal·ly** *adv*

**nas·tur·tium** \nəs-'tər-shəm, nas-\ *n*
an herb with a juicy stem, roundish leaves, red, yellow, or white flowers, and seeds with a sharp taste

**nas·ty** \'nas-tē\ *adj* **nas·ti·er**; **nas·ti·est**
**1** very dirty : FILTHY
**2** INDECENT
**3** [1]MEAN 4 ⟨a *nasty* disposition⟩
**4** HARMFUL, DANGEROUS ⟨a *nasty* fall⟩
**5** very unpleasant ⟨*nasty* weather⟩ ⟨a *nasty* trick⟩
**nas·ti·ly** \'nas-tə-lē\ *adv*
**nas·ti·ness** \'nas-tē-nəs\ *n*

**na·tal** \'nāt-l\ *adj*
of, relating to, or associated with birth ⟨*natal* day⟩

**na·tion** \'nā-shən\ *n*
**1** NATIONALITY 3
**2** a community of people made up of one or more nationalities usually with its own territory and government
**3** COUNTRY

[1]**na·tion·al** \'nash-ən-l\ *adj*
of or relating to a nation ⟨our *national* parks⟩
**na·tion·al·ly** *adv*

[2]**national** *n*
a citizen of a nation

**na·tion·al·ism** \'nash-ən-l-,iz-əm\ *n*
devotion to the interests of a certain country

**na·tion·al·ist** \'nash-ən-l-ist\ *n*
a person who believes in nationalism

**na·tion·al·is·tic** \,nash-ən-l-'is-tik\ *adj*
**1** of, relating to, or favoring nationalism
**2** [1]NATIONAL
**na·tion·al·is·ti·cal·ly** \-ti-kə-lē\ *adv*

**na·tion·al·i·ty** \,nash-ə-'nal-ət-ē\ *n, pl* **na·tion·al·i·ties**
**1** the fact or state of belonging to a nation
**2** the state of being a separate nation
**3** a group of people having a common history, tradition, culture, or language

**na·tion·al·ize** \'nash-ən-l-,īz\ *vb* **na·tion·al·ized**; **na·tion·al·iz·ing**
to place under government control

**na·tion·wide** \,nā-shən-'wīd\ *adj*
extending throughout a nation

[1]**na·tive** \'nāt-iv\ *adj*
**1** NATURAL 1 ⟨*native* ability⟩
**2** born in a certain place or country
**3** belonging to one because of one's place of birth ⟨*native* language⟩
**4** grown, produced, or coming from a certain place ⟨*native* art⟩

[2]**native** *n*
one that is native

**Native American** *n*
a member of any of the first peoples to live in North and South America and especially in the United States

a b c d e f g h i j k l m n o p q r s t u v w x y z

**na·tiv·i·ty** \nə-ˈtiv-ət-ē\ *n, pl* **na·tiv·i·ties**
**1** BIRTH 1
**2** *cap* the birth of Christ : CHRISTMAS

**nat·ty** \ˈnat-ē\ *adj* **nat·ti·er**; **nat·ti·est**
very neat, trim, and stylish
**nat·ti·ly** \ˈnat-l-ē\ *adv*
**nat·ti·ness** \ˈnat-ē-nəs\ *n*

**nat·u·ral** \ˈnach-ə-rəl, ˈnach-rəl\ *adj*
**1** born in or with one ⟨*natural* abilities⟩
**2** being such by nature : BORN ⟨a *natural* musician⟩
**3** found in or produced by nature ⟨*natural* woodland⟩
**4** of or relating to nature ⟨*natural* causes⟩
**5** not made by humans ⟨*natural* rubber⟩
**6** being simple and sincere ⟨*natural* manners⟩
**7** LIFELIKE
**8** being neither sharp nor flat : having neither sharps nor flats
**nat·u·ral·ly** *adv*
**nat·u·ral·ness** *n*

**natural gas** *n*
a flammable gas mixture from below earth's surface that is used especially as a fuel

**nat·u·ral·ist** \ˈnach-ə-rə-list, ˈnach-rə-\ *n*
a person who studies nature and especially plants and animals as they live in nature

**nat·u·ral·i·za·tion** \ˌnach-ə-rə-lə-ˈzā-shən, ˌnach-rə-\ *n*
the act or process of naturalizing : the state of being naturalized

**nat·u·ral·ize** \ˈnach-ə-rə-ˌlīz, ˈnach-rə-\ *vb* **nat·u·ral·ized**; **nat·u·ral·iz·ing**
**1** to become or cause to become established as if native ⟨*naturalize* a plant⟩
**2** to admit to citizenship

**natural number** *n*
the number 1 or any number (as 3, 12, 432) obtained by adding 1 to it one or more times

**natural resource** *n*
▶ something (as a mineral, forest, or kind of animal) that is found in nature and is valuable to humans

**na·ture** \ˈnā-chər\ *n*
**1** the basic character of a person or thing
**2** [1]SORT 1, VARIETY
**3** natural feelings : DISPOSITION, TEMPERAMENT ⟨a generous *nature*⟩
**4** the material universe ⟨the study of *nature*⟩
**5** the working of a living body ⟨leave a cure to *nature*⟩
**6** natural scenery

**[1]naught** *or* **nought** \ˈnȯt\ *pron*
[1]NOTHING 1 ⟨our efforts came to *naught* in the end⟩

**[2]naught** *or* **nought** *n*
ZERO 1, CIPHER

**naugh·ty** \ˈnȯt-ē\ *adj* **naugh·ti·er**; **naugh·ti·est**
behaving in a bad or improper way
**synonyms** see BAD
**naugh·ti·ly** \ˈnȯt-l-ē\ *adv*
**naugh·ti·ness** \ˈnȯt-ē-nəs\ *n*

**nau·sea** \ˈnȯ-zē-ə, ˈnȯ-shə\ *n*
**1** a disturbed condition of the stomach in which one feels like vomiting
**2** deep disgust : LOATHING

**Word History** The English word *nausea* came from a Latin word that meant "seasickness." The Latin word in turn came from a Greek word with the same meaning. This Greek word was formed from another Greek word meaning "sailor" which came from an earlier Greek word that meant "ship." Our word *nausea* has a more general meaning than the Latin or Greek words.

**nau·se·ate** \ˈnȯ-zē-ˌāt, ˈnȯ-shē-\ *vb* **nau·se·at·ed**; **nau·se·at·ing**
to affect or become affected with nausea
**nau·se·at·ing** *adj*
**nau·se·at·ing·ly** *adv*

**nau·seous** \ˈnȯ-shəs, ˈnȯ-zē-əs\ *adj*
**1** suffering from nausea
**2** causing nausea

## natural resource

Natural resources are important for the prosperity and political power of a country. If it has many natural resources, such as fish, minerals, or wood, its people generally enjoy good food, health, and housing. The country can also trade resources with other nations for materials that are lacking locally.

### examples of natural resources

**fish** are used for food

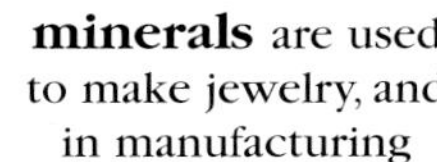

**minerals** are used to make jewelry, and in manufacturing

**wood** is used for fuel, to make furniture, and to build houses

**nau·ti·cal** \'nȯt-i-kəl\ *adj*
of or relating to sailors, navigation, or ships
**nau·ti·cal·ly** *adv*

**na·val** \'nā-vəl\ *adj*
of or relating to a navy or warships ⟨*naval* vessels⟩

**nave** \'nāv\ *n*
▶ the long central main part of a church

**na·vel** \'nā-vəl\ *n*
a hollow in the middle of the abdomen that marks the place where the umbilical cord was attached

**nav·i·ga·bil·i·ty** \,nav-i-gə-'bil-ət-ē\ *n*
the quality or state of being navigable

**nav·i·ga·ble** \'nav-i-gə-bəl\ *adj*
**1** deep enough and wide enough to permit passage of ships
**2** possible to steer ⟨a *navigable* balloon⟩

**nav·i·gate** \'nav-ə-,gāt\ *vb*
**nav·i·gat·ed**; **nav·i·gat·ing**
**1** to travel by water
**2** to sail over, on, or through
**3** to steer a course in a ship or aircraft
**4** to steer or direct the course of (as a boat)

**nav·i·ga·tion** \,nav-ə-'gā-shən\ *n*
**1** the act or practice of navigating
**2** ▼ the science of figuring out the position and course of a ship or aircraft

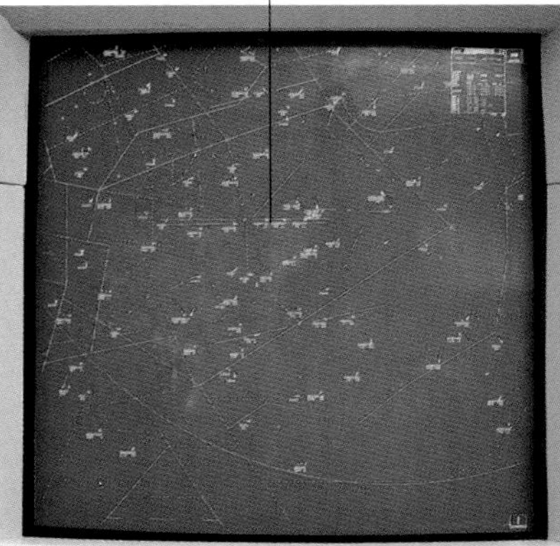


**navigation 2:** a radar screen used by an air traffic controller at an airport to direct aircraft

**nav·i·ga·tor** \'nav-ə-,gāt-ər\ *n*
an officer on a ship or aircraft responsible for its navigation

**nave** of Westminster Abbey, in London, UK

**na·vy** \'nā-vē\ *n, pl* **navies**
**1** a nation's ships of war
**2** the complete naval equipment and organization of a nation
**3** a dark blue

[1]**nay** \'nā\ *adv*
[1]NO 2

[2]**nay** *n*
[3]NO 2

**Na·zi** \'nät-sē\ *n*
a member of a political party controlling Germany from 1933 to 1945

**Ne·an·der·thal man** \nē-,an-dər-,thȯl-\ *n*
a long gone ancient human who made tools of stone and lived by hunting

[1]**near** \'nir\ *adv*
**1** at, within, or to a short distance or time
**2** ALMOST, NEARLY

[2]**near** *prep*
close to ⟨the table *near* the window⟩

[3]**near** *adj*
**1** closely related or associated ⟨a *near* relative⟩
**2** not far away
**3** coming close **:** NARROW ⟨a *near* miss⟩
**4** being the closer of two ⟨the *near* side⟩
**near·ly** *adv*
**near·ness** *n*

[4]**near** *vb*
to come near **:** APPROACH

**near·by** \nir-'bī\ *adv or adj*
close at hand

**near·sight·ed** \'nir-'sīt-əd\ *adj*
able to see near things more clearly than distant ones
**near·sight·ed·ly** *adv*
**near·sight·ed·ness** *n*

**neat** \'nēt\ *adj*
**1** being simple and in good taste ⟨a *neat* suit⟩
**2** SKILLFUL 2 ⟨a *neat* trick⟩
**3** showing care and a concern for order ⟨a *neat* room⟩
**neat·ly** *adv*
**neat·ness** *n*

**Synonyms** NEAT, TIDY, and TRIM mean showing care and a concern for order. NEAT stresses that something is clean in addition to being orderly ⟨your clothes should always be *neat*⟩. TIDY suggests that something is continually kept orderly and neat ⟨I work hard to keep my room *tidy*⟩. TRIM stresses that something is orderly and compact ⟨*trim*, comfortable houses⟩.

**Word History** The English word *neat* can be traced back to a Latin verb that meant "to shine." From this verb, the ancient Romans formed an adjective that meant "shining," "bright," or "clear." The French word that came from this Latin word had the same meanings and came into English as *neat*. English *neat* at first meant "shining," "bright," or "clear." Later it was used to mean "simple and in good taste," "skillful," and "tidy."

**neb·u·la** \'neb-yə-lə\ *n, pl* **neb·u·las** *or* **neb·u·lae** \-,lē\
▼ any of many clouds of gas or dust seen in the sky among the stars

young star

**nebula**

a b c d e f g h i j k l m n o p q r s t u v w x y z

\ng\ sing \ō\ bone \ȯ\ saw \ȯi\ coin \th\ thin \th\ this \ü\ food \u̇\ foot \y\ yet \yü\ few \yu̇\ cure \zh\ vision

A B C D E F G H I J K L M N O P Q R S T U V W X Y Z

**neb·u·lous** \'neb-yə-ləs\ *adj*
not clear : VAGUE
**neb·u·lous·ly** *adv*
**neb·u·lous·ness** *n*

[1]**nec·es·sary** \'nes-ə-,ser-ē\ *adj*
needing to be had or done : ESSENTIAL ⟨food is *necessary* to life⟩ ⟨got the *necessary* work done first⟩
**nec·es·sar·i·ly** \,nes-ə-'ser-ə-lē\ *adv*

[2]**necessary** *n, pl* **nec·es·sar·ies**
something that is needed

**ne·ces·si·tate** \ni-'ses-ə-,tāt\ *vb* **ne·ces·si·tat·ed**; **ne·ces·si·tat·ing**
to make necessary : REQUIRE

**ne·ces·si·ty** \ni-'ses-ət-ē\ *n, pl* **ne·ces·si·ties**
**1** the state of things that forces certain actions ⟨the *necessity* of eating⟩
**2** very great need ⟨call us for help in case of *necessity*⟩
**3** the state of being without or unable to get necessary things : POVERTY ⟨forced by *necessity* to beg⟩
**4** something that is badly needed ⟨bought a few *necessities*⟩

**neck** \'nek\ *n*
**1** the part connecting the head and the main part of the body
**2** the part of a garment covering or nearest to the neck
**3** something like a neck in shape or position ⟨the *neck* of a bottle⟩
**necked** \'nekt\ *adj*
**neck and neck** so nearly equal (as in a race) that one cannot be said to be ahead of the other

**neck·er·chief** \'nek-ər-chif\ *n, pl* **neck·er·chiefs** \-chifs, -,chēvz\
a square of cloth worn folded around the neck like a scarf

**neck·lace** \'nek-ləs\ *n*
an ornament (as a string of beads) worn around the neck

**neck·line** \'nek-,līn\ *n*
the outline of the neck opening of a garment

**neck·tie** \'nek-,tī\ *n*
a narrow length of material worn around the neck and tied in front

**nec·tar** \'nek-tər\ *n*
**1** the drink of the Greek and Roman gods
**2** a sweet liquid given off by plants and used by bees in making honey

**nec·tar·ine** \,nek-tə-'rēn\ *n*
► a peach with a smooth skin

nectarine

**née** *or* **nee** \'nā\ *adj*
BORN 1 — used to identify a woman by her maiden name ⟨Mrs. Jane Doe, *née* Roe⟩

[1]**need** \'nēd\ *n*
**1** something that must be done : OBLIGATION ⟨the *need* to be careful⟩
**2** a lack of something necessary, useful, or desired ⟨in great *need*⟩
**3** something necessary or desired ⟨our daily *needs*⟩

[2]**need** *vb*
**1** to suffer from the lack of something important to life or health ⟨give to those who *need*⟩
**2** to be necessary ⟨something *needs* to be done⟩
**3** to be without : REQUIRE ⟨*need* advice⟩

**need·ful** \'nēd-fəl\ *adj*
[1]NECESSARY
**need·ful·ly** \-fə-lē\ *adv*
**need·ful·ness** *n*

[1]**nee·dle** \'nēd-l\ *n*
**1** ► a slender pointed usually steel device used to make a hole and pull thread through in sewing
**2** a slender pointed piece of metal or plastic (used for knitting)
**3** a leaf (as of a pine) shaped like a needle
**4** a pointer on a dial
**5** a slender hollow instrument by which material is put into or taken from the body through the skin
**nee·dle·like** \'nēd-l-,līk\ *adj*

[2]**needle** *vb* **nee·dled**; **nee·dling**
[1]TEASE, TAUNT

**nee·dle·point** \'nēd-l-,pȯint\ *n*
embroidery done on canvas usually in simple even stitches across counted threads

**need·less** \'nēd-ləs\ *adj*
UNNECESSARY
**need·less·ly** *adv*
**need·less·ness** *n*

**nee·dle·work** \'nēd-l-,wərk\ *n*
work (as sewing or embroidery) done with a needle

**needn't** \'nēd-nt\
need not

**needs** \'nēdz\ *adv*
because of necessity ⟨must *needs* be recognized⟩

**needy** \'nēd-ē\ *adj* **need·i·er**; **need·i·est**
very poor ⟨*needy* people⟩
**need·i·ness** *n*

**ne'er** \neər, naər\ *adv*
NEVER

**ne'er–do–well** \'neər-du̇-,wel, 'naər-\ *n*
a worthless person who will not work

**ne·gate** \ni-'gāt\ *vb* **ne·gat·ed**; **ne·gat·ing**
**1** to deny the existence or truth of
**2** to cause to be ineffective

**ne·ga·tion** \ni-'gā-shən\ *n*
the action of negating : DENIAL

[1]**neg·a·tive** \'neg-ət-iv\ *adj*
**1** making a denial ⟨a *negative* reply⟩
**2** not positive ⟨a *negative* test⟩
**3** not helpful ⟨a *negative* attitude⟩
**4** less than zero and shown by a minus sign ⟨−2 is a *negative* number⟩

canvas
needle

[1]**needle 1:** a needle being used for embroidery

**5** of, being, or relating to electricity of which the electron is the unit and which is produced in a hard rubber rod that has been rubbed with wool ⟨a *negative* charge⟩
**6** having more electrons than protons ⟨a *negative* particle⟩
**7** being the part toward which the electric current flows from the outside circuit ⟨the *negative* pole of a storage battery⟩
**neg·a·tive·ly** *adv*
**neg·a·tiv·i·ty** \,neg-ə-'tiv-ət-ē\ *n*

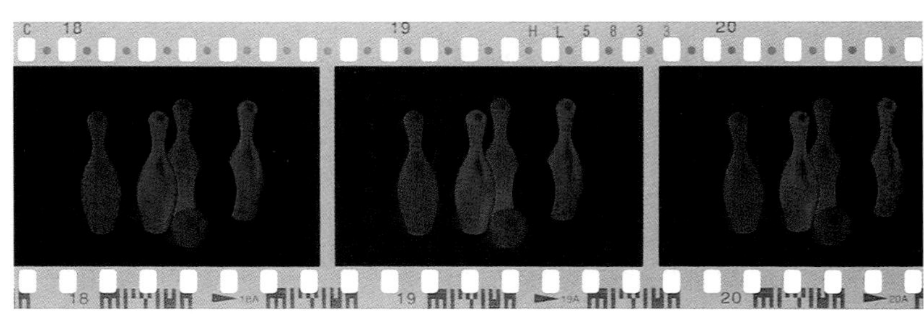
**[2]negative 5:** a strip of photographic color negatives

**[2]neg·a·tive** *n*
**1** something that is the opposite of something else
**2** a negative number
**3** an expression (as the word *no*) that denies or says the opposite
**4** the side that argues or votes against something
**5** ▲ a photographic image on film from which a final picture is made

**[1]ne·glect** \ni-'glekt\ *vb*
**1** to fail to give the right amount of attention to
**2** to fail to do or look after especially because of carelessness

---

**Synonyms** NEGLECT and DISREGARD mean to pass over something without giving it any or enough attention. NEGLECT suggests that one has not given, whether deliberately or not, enough attention to something that deserves or requires attention ⟨you have been *neglecting* your homework⟩. DISREGARD suggests deliberately overlooking something usually because one feels that it is not worth noticing ⟨*disregarded* the "no smoking" sign⟩.

---

**[2]neglect** *n*
**1** an act or instance of neglecting something
**2** the state of being neglected

**ne·glect·ful** \ni-'glekt-fəl\ *adj*
tending to neglect **:** NEGLIGENT
**ne·glect·ful·ly** \-fə-lē\ *adv*
**ne·glect·ful·ness** *n*

**neg·li·gee** \,neg-lə-'zhā\ *n*
a woman's loose robe worn especially while dressing or resting

**neg·li·gence** \'neg-lə-jəns\ *n*
**1** the state of being negligent
**2** an act or instance of being negligent

**neg·li·gent** \'neg-lə-jənt\ *adj*
likely to neglect things **:** CARELESS
**neg·li·gent·ly** *adv*

**neg·li·gi·ble** \'neg-lə-jə-bəl\ *adj*
so small or unimportant as to deserve little or no attention
**neg·li·gi·bly** \-blē\ *adv*

**ne·go·tia·ble** \ni-'gō-shə-bəl\ *adj*
possible to negotiate
**ne·go·tia·bil·i·ty** \ni-,gō-shə-'bil-ət-ē\ *n*

**ne·go·ti·ate** \ni-'gō-shē-,āt\ *vb*
**ne·go·ti·at·ed**; **ne·go·ti·at·ing**
**1** to have a discussion with another in order to settle something ⟨*negotiate* with the enemy for peace⟩
**2** to arrange for by discussing ⟨*negotiate* a loan⟩
**3** to give to someone in exchange for cash or something of equal value ⟨*negotiate* a check⟩
**4** to be successful in getting around, through, or over ⟨*negotiate* a turn⟩
**ne·go·ti·a·tor** \-,āt-ər\ *n*

**ne·go·ti·a·tion** \ni-,gō-shē-'ā-shən\ *n*
the act or process of negotiating or being negotiated

**Ne·gro** \'nē-,grō\ *n, pl* **Ne·groes**
**1** a member of any of the original peoples of Africa south of the Sahara
**2** a person with Negro ancestors
**Negro** *adj*

**[1]neigh** \'nā\ *vb*
to make a neigh

**[2]neigh** *n*
the long loud cry of a horse

**[1]neigh·bor** \'nā-bər\ *n*
**1** a person living or a thing located near another
**2** a fellow human being

**[2]neighbor** *vb*
to be near or next to
**neigh·bor·ing** *adj*

**neigh·bor·hood** \'nā-bər-,hu̇d\ *n*
**1** a place or region near **:** VICINITY
**2** an amount, size, or range that is close to ⟨cost in the *neighborhood* of ten dollars⟩
**3** the people living near one another
**4** a section lived in by neighbors ⟨they are building a new house in our *neighborhood*⟩

**neigh·bor·ly** \'nā-bər-lē\ *adj*
of, relating to, or like neighbors **:** FRIENDLY
**neigh·bor·li·ness** *n*

**[1]nei·ther** \'nē-t͟hər, 'nī-\ *conj*
**1** not either ⟨*neither* good nor bad⟩
**2** also not ⟨our parents did not want to go and *neither* did we⟩

**[2]neither** *pron*
not the one and not the other ⟨*neither* of the bottles is full⟩

**[3]neither** *adj*
not either ⟨*neither* hand⟩

**ne·on** \'nē-,än\ *n*
**1** a colorless gaseous chemical element found in very small amounts in the air and used in electric lamps
**2** a lamp in which the gas contains a large proportion of neon
**3** a sign made up of such lamps

**neo·phyte** \'nē-ə-,fīt\ *n*
**1** a new convert
**2** BEGINNER, NOVICE

**neph·ew** \'nef-yü\ *n*
a son of one's brother or sister

**Nep·tune** \'nep-,tün, -,tyün\ *n*
▼ the planet that is eighth in order of distance from the sun and has a diameter of about 49,000 kilometers

*the four rings of Neptune*

**Neptune**

A B C D E F G H I J K L M N O P Q R S T U V W X Y Z

**nep·tu·ni·um** \nep-'tü-nē-əm, -'tyü-\ *n*
a radioactive chemical element similar to uranium

**nerd** \'nərd\ *n*
**1** a person who is socially awkward, unattractive, or not fashionable
**2** a person who is extremely devoted to study and learning
**nerdy** \'nər-dē\ *adj*

**nerve** \'nərv\ *n*
**1** ▼ one of the bands of nerve fibers that join centers (as the brain) of the nervous system with other parts of the body and carry nerve impulses
**2** FORTITUDE, DARING ⟨a test of *nerve*⟩
**3** IMPUDENCE ⟨you've got a lot of *nerve* asking me that⟩
**4 nerves** *pl* JITTERS
**5** the sensitive soft inner part of a tooth
**nerve·less** \-ləs\ *adj*

**nerve cell** *n*
a cell of the nervous system with fibers that conduct nerve impulses

**nerve fiber** *n*
any of the slender extensions of a nerve cell that carry nerve impulses

**nerve impulse** *n*
a progressive change of a nerve fiber by which information is brought to or orders sent from the central nervous system

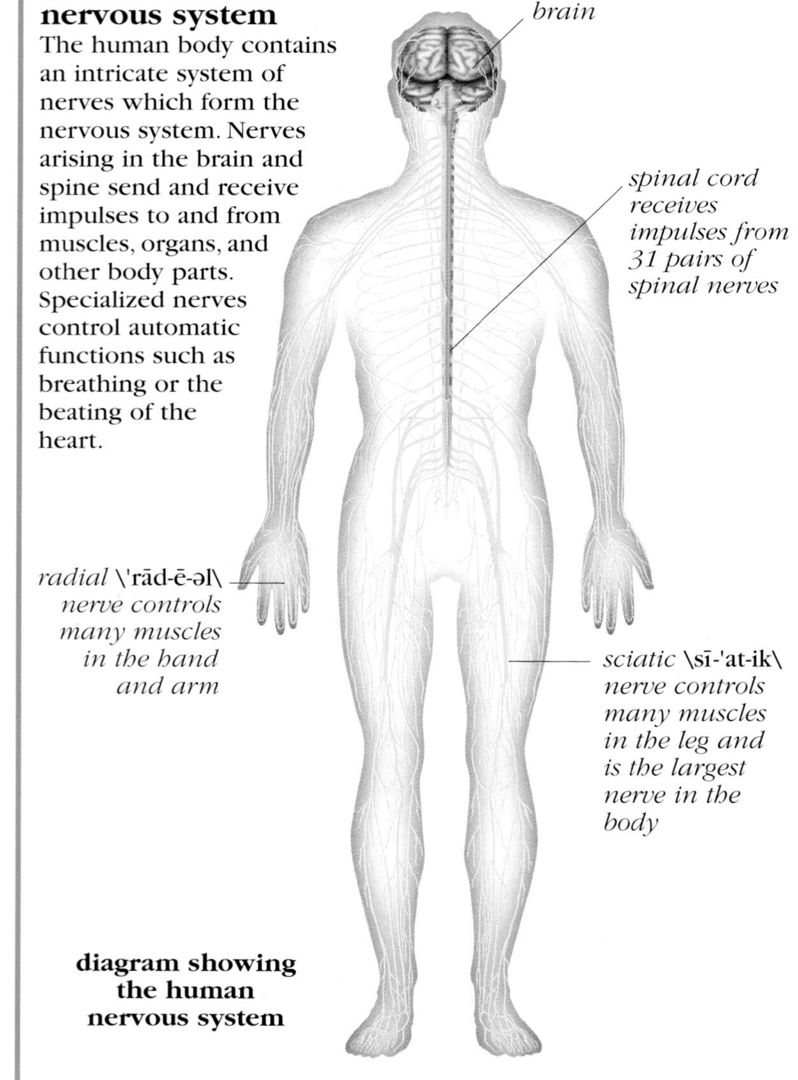
brain
spinal cord receives impulses from 31 pairs of spinal nerves
radial \'rād-ē-əl\ nerve controls many muscles in the hand and arm
sciatic \sī-'at-ik\ nerve controls many muscles in the leg and is the largest nerve in the body

**nervous system**
The human body contains an intricate system of nerves which form the nervous system. Nerves arising in the brain and spine send and receive impulses to and from muscles, organs, and other body parts. Specialized nerves control automatic functions such as breathing or the beating of the heart.

**diagram showing the human nervous system**

**ner·vous** \'nər-vəs\ *adj*
**1** of or relating to nerve cells ⟨*nervous* tissue⟩
**2** of, relating to, or made up of nerves or nervous tissue
**3** easily excited or upset ⟨a *nervous* person⟩
**4** TIMID ⟨*nervous* about answering in class⟩
**ner·vous·ly** *adv*
**ner·vous·ness** *n*

**nervous system** *n*
a system of the body that in vertebrates includes the brain, spinal cord, nerves, and sense organs and receives, interprets, and responds to stimuli from inside and outside the body

**nervy** \'nər-vē\ *adj* **nerv·i·er**; **nerv·i·est**
**1** showing calm courage : BOLD
**2** [1]FORWARD 2
**3** NERVOUS 3
**nerv·i·ness** *n*

**-ness** \nəs\ *n suffix*
state : condition ⟨good*ness*⟩

[1]**nest** \'nest\ *n*
**1** ► a shelter made by a bird for its eggs and young
**2** a place where the eggs of some animals other than birds are laid and hatched ⟨a snake's *nest*⟩
**3** a cozy home : a snug shelter
**4** those living in a nest ⟨a *nest* of robins⟩

[2]**nest** *vb*
to build or live in a nest ⟨*nesting* birds⟩

**nes·tle** \'nes-əl\ *vb* **nes·tled**; **nes·tling** \'nes-ling, -ə-ling\
**1** to lie close and snug : CUDDLE
**2** to settle as if in a nest

**nest·ling** \'nest-ling\ *n*
a young bird not yet able to leave the nest

[1]**net** \'net\ *n*
**1** a fabric made of threads, cords, ropes, or wires that weave in and out with much open space
**2** ► something made of net ⟨a *net* for catching fish⟩
**3** something that traps one as if in a net ⟨a *net* of lies⟩

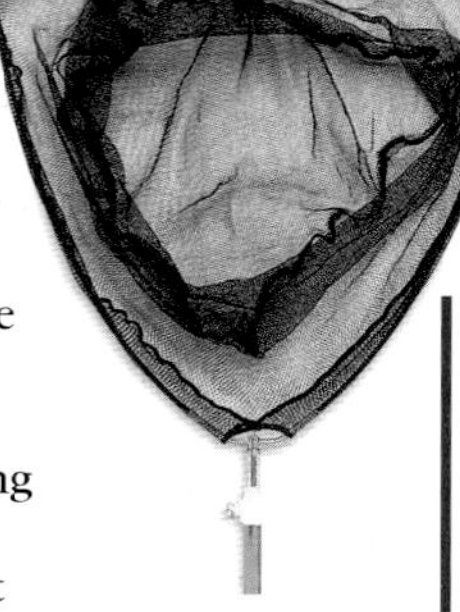

[1]**net 2:** a fishing net

**[1]nest 1**

Birds' nests are built according to the materials available and the predators that threaten the birds' nestlings. Different bird species may raise their young in complex nests woven from grasses, in solid nests constructed from dried mud, or even on tumbled heaps of twigs and feathers.

**features of a European buzzard's nest**

**reed warblers**
live in Europe and build nests slung between reeds

**ovenbirds**
from South America mold their nests from dried mud

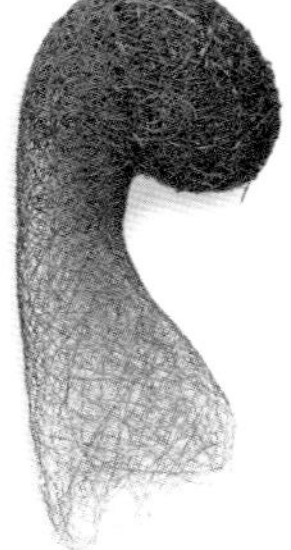
**weaver birds**
found in West Africa weave nests from grass

4 NETWORK 2
5 *often cap* INTERNET

**[2]net** *vb* **net·ted; net·ting**
1 to cover with or as if with a net
2 to catch in or as if in a net

**[3]net** *adj*
remaining after all charges or expenses have been subtracted ⟨*net* profit⟩

**[4]net** *vb* **net·ted; net·ting**
to gain or produce as profit : CLEAR ⟨each sale *nets* ten cents⟩

**net·ting** \'net-iŋ\ *n*
NETWORK 1, 2

**net·tle** \'net-l\ *n*
▶ a tall plant with stinging hairs on the leaves

**net·work** \'net-,wərk\ *n*
1 a net fabric or structure
2 an arrangement of lines or channels crossing as in a net
3 a system of computers connected by communications lines
4 a group of connected radio or television stations

**neu·ron** \'nü-,rän, 'nyü-\ *n*
NERVE CELL

**neu·ter** \'nüt-ər, 'nyüt-\ *adj*
lacking sex organs : having sex organs that are not fully developed

**nettle**

**[1]neu·tral** \'nü-trəl, 'nyü-\ *n*
1 one that does not favor either side in a quarrel, contest, or war
2 a grayish color
3 a position of gears (as in the transmission of a motor vehicle) in which they are not in contact

**[2]neutral** *adj*
1 not favoring either side in a quarrel, contest, or war
2 of or relating to a neutral country
3 being neither one thing nor the other
4 having no color that stands out : GRAYISH
5 neither acid nor basic
6 not electrically charged

**neu·tral·i·ty** \nü-'tral-ət-ē, nyü-\ *n*
the quality or state of being neutral

**neu·tral·ize** \'nü-trə-,līz, 'nyü-\ *vb*
**neu·tral·ized; neu·tral·iz·ing**
1 to make chemically neutral ⟨*neutralize* an acid with lime⟩
2 to make ineffective
**neu·tral·i·za·tion** \,nü-trə-lə-'zā-shən, ,nyü-\ *n*
**neu·tral·iz·er** *n*

**neu·tron** \'nü-,trän, 'nyü-\ *n*
a particle that has a mass nearly equal to that of the proton but no electrical charge and that is present in all atomic nuclei except those of hydrogen

**nev·er** \'nev-ər\ *adv*
1 not ever : at no time
2 not to any extent or in any way ⟨*never* fear⟩

**nev·er·more** \,nev-ər-'mōr\ *adv*
never again

**nev·er·the·less** \,nev-ər-thə-'les\ *adv*
even so : HOWEVER

**[1]new** \'nü, 'nyü\ *adj*
1 not old : RECENT
2 taking the place of one that came before ⟨a *new* teacher⟩
3 recently discovered or learned about ⟨*new* lands⟩
4 not known or experienced before ⟨*new* feelings⟩
5 not accustomed ⟨a person *new* to the job⟩
6 beginning as a repeating of a previous act or thing ⟨a *new* year⟩
7 being in a position, place, or state the first time ⟨*new* member⟩
**new·ness** *n*

a b c d e f g h i j k l m n o p q r s t u v w x y z

**[2]new** *adv*
NEWLY, RECENTLY ⟨*new*-mown hay⟩

**new·born** \'nü-'bȯrn, 'nyü-\ *adj*
**1** ▶ recently born
**2** made new or strong again ⟨*newborn* hopes⟩

**newborn 1:**
a newborn kitten

**new·com·er** \'nü-ˌkəm-ər, 'nyü-\ *n*
**1** one recently arrived
**2** BEGINNER

**new·el** \'nü-əl, 'nyü-\ *n*
a post at the bottom or at a turn of a stairway

**new·fan·gled** \'nü-'fang-gəld, 'nyü-\ *adj*
of the newest style : NOVEL ⟨*newfangled* ideas⟩

**new·ly** \'nü-lē, 'nyü-\ *adv*
not long ago : RECENTLY ⟨a *newly* married couple⟩

**new moon** *n*
**1** the moon's phase when its dark side is toward the earth
**2** the thin curved outline of the moon seen shortly after sunset for a few days after the new moon

**news** \'nüz, 'nyüz\ *n*
**1** a report of recent events ⟨family *news*⟩
**2** material reported in a newspaper or news magazine or on a newscast
**3** an event that is interesting enough to be reported

**news·boy** \'nüz-ˌbȯi, 'nyüz-\ *n*
a person who delivers or sells newspapers

**news·cast** \'nüz-ˌkast, 'nyüz-\ *n*
a radio or television broadcast of news

**news·girl** \'nüz-ˌgərl, 'nyüz-\ *n*
a girl who delivers or sells newspapers

**news·man** \'nüz-mən, 'nyüz-\ *n, pl* **news·men** \-mən\
a person who gathers or reports news

**news·pa·per** \'nüz-ˌpā-pər, 'nyüz-\ *n*
a paper that is printed and sold usually every day or weekly and that contains news, articles of opinion, features, and advertising

**news·pa·per·man** \'nüz-ˌpā-pər-ˌman, 'nyüz-\ *n, pl* **news·pa·per·men** \-ˌmen\
a man who owns or works on a newspaper

**news·pa·per·wom·an** \'nüz-ˌpā-pər-ˌwu̇m-ən, 'nyüz-\ *n, pl* **news·pa·per·wom·en** \-ˌwim-ən\
a woman who owns or works on a newspaper

**news·reel** \'nüz-ˌrēl, 'nyüz-\ *n*
a short motion picture about current events

**news·stand** \'nüz-ˌstand, 'nyüz-\ *n*
a place where newspapers and magazines are sold

**news·wom·an** \'nüz-ˌwu̇m-ən\ *n, pl* **news·wom·en** \-ˌwim-ən\
a woman who gathers or reports news

**New World** *n*
the lands in the western hemisphere and especially North and South America

**newsy** \'nü-zē, 'nyü-\ *adj* **news·i·er**; **news·i·est**
filled with news ⟨a *newsy* letter⟩

**newt** \'nüt, 'nyüt\ *n*
▼ a small salamander that lives mostly in water

**New Year's Day** *n*
January 1 observed as a legal holiday in many countries

**[1]next** \'nekst\ *adj*
coming just before or after ⟨the *next* page⟩ ⟨we were *next* in line⟩

**[2]next** *prep*
NEXT TO

**[3]next** *adv*
**1** in the nearest place, time, or order following ⟨do that *next*⟩
**2** at the first time after this

**next–door** \ˌneks-'dōr\ *adj*
located in the next building, apartment, or room

**[1]next to** *prep*
**1** BESIDE 1 ⟨sat *next to* my friend⟩
**2** following right after ⟨*next* in line⟩

**[2]next to** *adv*
very nearly ⟨it was *next to* impossible⟩

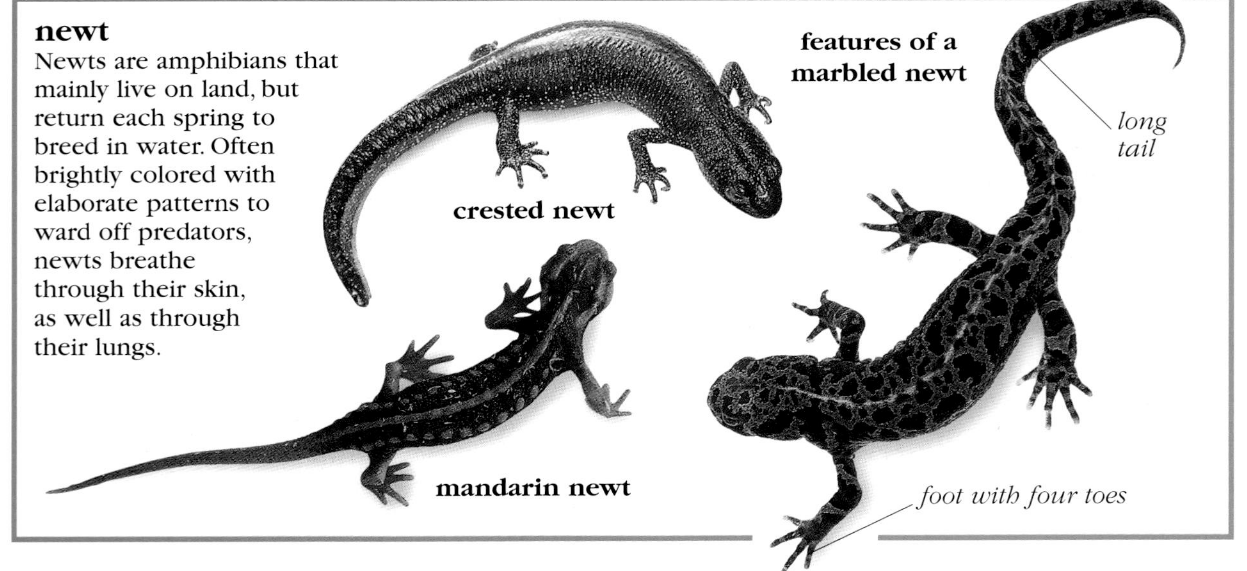
newt
Newts are amphibians that mainly live on land, but return each spring to breed in water. Often brightly colored with elaborate patterns to ward off predators, newts breathe through their skin, as well as through their lungs.
crested newt
mandarin newt
features of a marbled newt
long tail
foot with four toes

**nib** \'nib\ *n*
**1** a pointed object (as the bill of a bird)
**2** the point of a pen

[1]**nib·ble** \'nib-əl\ *vb* **nib·bled**; **nib·bling**
to bite or chew gently or bit by bit
**nib·bler** \'nib-lər\ *n*

[2]**nibble** *n*
**1** an act of nibbling
**2** a very small amount

**nice** \'nīs\ *adj* **nic·er**; **nic·est**
**1** very fussy (as about appearance, manners, or food)
**2** able to recognize small differences between things ⟨has a *nice* ear for music⟩
**3** PLEASING, PLEASANT ⟨a *nice* time⟩
**4** well behaved ⟨*nice* people⟩
**nice·ly** *adv*
**nice·ness** *n*

**Word History** The English word *nice* came from an Old French word that meant "stupid." This Old French word came in turn from a Latin word that meant "ignorant." At first, English *nice* meant "stupid" or "foolish." Later it came to mean "finicky" or "fussy." From these later meanings came the meanings that *nice* has today.

**ni·ce·ty** \'nī-sət-ē\ *n*, *pl* **ni·ce·ties**
**1** something dainty, delicate, or especially nice ⟨the *niceties* of life⟩
**2** a fine detail ⟨*niceties* of workmanship⟩

**niche** \'nich\ *n*
**1** ▶ an open hollow in a wall (as for a statue)
**2** a place, job, or use for which a person or a thing is best fitted ⟨you've found your *niche*⟩

[1]**nick** \'nik\ *n*
**1** a small cut or chip in a surface
**2** the last moment ⟨in the *nick* of time⟩

[2]**nick** *vb*
to make a nick in

[1]**nick·el** \'nik-əl\ *n*
**1** a hard silvery white metallic chemical element that can be highly polished, resists weathering, and is used in alloys
**2** a United States coin worth five cents

**Word History** The coin that is called a *nickel* got its name from the metal called *nickel*. The name of the metal comes from a German word, which is the name of an ore that has nickel in it. This ore has a color like copper, but it has no copper in it. This misleading color must have given the ore its German name, made by putting together two German words. One means "copper" and the other means "goblin."

[2]**nickel** *vb* **nick·eled** *or* **nick·elled**; **nick·el·ing** *or* **nick·el·ling**
to plate with nickel

[1]**nick·er** \'nik-ər\ *vb*
[1]NEIGH, WHINNY

[2]**nicker** *n*
[2]NEIGH

[1]**nick·name** \'nik-,nām\ *n*
**1** a usually descriptive name given in addition to the one belonging to an individual ⟨had the *nickname* "Nosy"⟩
**2** a familiar form of a proper name ⟨"Bill" and "Willie" are *nicknames* for "William"⟩

**niche 1:**
a niche for a statue set into a wall

**Word History** Many years ago there was an English word *ekename* that meant "an extra name." It was made of a word that meant "also" added to the word *name*. It started with a vowel, so *an* was used with this word instead of *a*. When *an ekename* was said fast, it sounded a bit like *a nekename*. As a result, some people thought the word started with *n* and began to spell it *nekename*. They did not know they were taking *n* away from *an*, adding it to *ekename*, and so making a new word. From this new word came the word *nickname* that we use now.

[2]**nickname** *vb* **nick·named**; **nick·nam·ing**
to give a nickname to

**nic·o·tine** \'nik-ə-,tēn\ *n*
a poisonous substance found in small amounts in tobacco and used especially to kill insects

**niece** \'nēs\ *n*
a daughter of one's brother or sister

**nig·gling** \'nig-ling\ *adj*
PETTY 1

[1]**nigh** \'nī\ *adv*
**1** near in time or place
**2** ALMOST, NEARLY

[2]**nigh** *adj*
[3]CLOSE 5, NEAR

**night** \'nīt\ *n*
**1** the time between dusk and dawn when there is no sunlight
**2** NIGHTFALL
**3** the darkness of night

**night·club** \'nīt-,kləb\ *n*
a place of entertainment open at night usually serving food and liquor and having music for dancing

**night crawl·er** \'nīt-,kȯ-lər\ *n*
EARTHWORM

**night·fall** \'nīt-,fȯl\ *n*
the coming of night

**night·gown** \'nīt-,gau̇n\ *n*
a loose garment worn in bed

**night·hawk** \'nīt-,hȯk\ *n*
**1** a bird that is related to the whippoorwill, flies mostly at twilight, and eats insects
**2** a person who stays up late at night

**night·in·gale** \'nīt-n-,gāl\ *n*
▼ a reddish brown Old World thrush noted for the sweet song of the male

nightingale

**[1]night·ly** \'nīt-lē\ *adj*
**1** of or relating to the night or every night
**2** happening or done at night or every night

**[2]nightly** *adv*
**1** every night
**2** at or by night

**night·mare** \'nīt-,maər, -,meər\ *n*
**1** a frightening dream
**2** a horrible experience
**night·mar·ish** \'nīt-,maər-ish, -,meər-\ *adj*

---

**Word History** The *-mare* in *nightmare* comes from an Old English word for a kind of evil spirit. Such spirits were believed to bother people who were sleeping.

---

**night·shirt** \'nīt-,shərt\ *n*
a nightgown like a very long shirt

**night·stick** \'nīt-,stik\ *n*
a police officer's club

**night·time** \'nīt-,tīm\ *n*
NIGHT 1

**nil** \'nil\ *n*
ZERO 4, NOTHING

**nim·ble** \'nim-bəl\ *adj* **nim·bler**; **nim·blest**
**1** quick and light in motion : AGILE ⟨a *nimble* dancer⟩
**2** quick in understanding and learning : CLEVER ⟨a *nimble* mind⟩
**nim·ble·ness** *n*
**nim·bly** \-blē\ *adv*

**nim·bus** \'nim-bəs\ *n, pl* **nim·bi** \-,bī\ *or* **nim·bus·es**
a rain cloud that is evenly gray and that covers the whole sky

**nin·com·poop** \'nin-kəm-,püp, 'ning-\ *n*
[1]FOOL 1

**[1]nine** \'nīn\ *adj*
being one more than eight

**[2]nine** *n*
**1** one more than eight : three times three : 9
**2** the ninth in a set or series

**[1]nine·teen** \nīn-'tēn, nīnt-\ *adj*
being one more than eighteen

**[2]nineteen** *n*
one more than eighteen : 19

**[1]nine·teenth** \nīn-'tēnth, nīnt-\ *adj*
coming right after eighteenth

**[2]nineteenth** *n*
number nineteen in a series

**[1]nine·ti·eth** \'nīnt-ē-əth\ *adj*
coming right after eighty-ninth

**[2]ninetieth** *n*
number ninety in a series

**[1]nine·ty** \'nīnt-ē\ *adj*
being nine times ten

**[2]ninety** *n*
nine times ten : 90

**nin·ja** \'nin-jə\ *n*
a person trained in ancient Japanese arts of fighting and defending oneself and employed especially for espionage and assassinations

**nin·ny** \'nin-ē\ *n, pl* **nin·nies**
[1]FOOL 1

**[1]ninth** \'nīnth\ *adj*
coming right after eighth

**[2]ninth** *n*
**1** number nine in a series
**2** one of nine equal parts

**[1]nip** \'nip\ *vb* **nipped**; **nip·ping**
**1** to catch hold of (as with teeth) and squeeze sharply though not very hard
**2** to cut off by or as if by pinching sharply
**3** to stop the growth or progress of ⟨*nip* plans in the bud⟩
**4** to injure or make numb with cold

**[2]nip** *n*
**1** something that nips
**2** the act of nipping
**3** a small portion : BIT

**[3]nip** *n*
a small amount of liquor

**nip and tuck** \,nip-ən-'tək\ *adj or adv*
so close that the lead shifts rapidly from one contestant to another

**nip·ple** \'nip-əl\ *n*
**1** the part of the breast from which a baby or young animal sucks milk
**2** something (as the mouthpiece of a baby's bottle) like a nipple

**nip·py** \'nip-ē\ *adj* **nip·pi·er**; **nip·pi·est**
CHILLY ⟨a *nippy* day⟩

**nit** \'nit\ *n*
the egg of a louse

**ni·trate** \'nī-,trāt\ *n*
a substance that is made from or has a composition as if made from nitric acid ⟨*nitrates* are used as fertilizers and explosives⟩

**ni·tric acid** \,nī-trik-\ *n*
a strong liquid acid that contains hydrogen, nitrogen, and oxygen and is used in making fertilizers, explosives, and dyes

**ni·tro·gen** \'nī-trə-jən\ *n*
a colorless odorless gaseous chemical element that makes up 78 percent of the atmosphere and forms a part of all living tissues

**nitrogen cycle** *n*
a continuous series of natural processes by which nitrogen passes from air to soil to organisms and back into the air

**nitrogen fix·a·tion** \-fik-'sā-shən\ *n*
the changing of free nitrogen into combined forms especially by bacteria (**nitrogen–fixing bacteria**)

**ni·tro·glyc·er·in** *or* **ni·tro·glyc·er·ine** \,nī-trō-'glis-ə-rən\ *n*
a heavy oily liquid explosive from which dynamite is made

**nit·wit** \'nit-,wit\ *n*
a very silly or stupid person

**[1]no** \nō\ *adv*
**1** not at all : not any ⟨they are *no* better than they should be⟩
**2** not so — used to express disagreement or refusal ⟨*no*, I'm not hungry⟩
**3** used to express surprise, doubt, or disbelief ⟨*no* — you don't say⟩

**[2]no** *adj*
**1** not any ⟨has *no* money⟩
**2** hardly any : very little ⟨finished in *no* time⟩
**3** not a ⟨I'm *no* liar⟩

**[3]no** *n, pl* **noes** *or* **nos**
**1** an act or instance of refusing or denying by the use of the word *no* : DENIAL
**2** a negative vote or decision
**3** *noes or nos, pl* persons voting in the negative

**no·bil·i·ty** \nō-'bil-ət-ē\ *n, pl* **no·bil·i·ties**
1 the quality or state of being noble
2 noble rank
3 the class or a group of nobles

[1]**no·ble** \'nō-bəl\ *adj* **no·bler; no·blest**
1 EMINENT, ILLUSTRIOUS
2 of very high birth or rank
3 having very fine qualities
4 grand in appearance
**no·ble·ness** *n*
**no·bly** \-blē\ *adv*

[2]**noble** *n*
a person of noble birth or rank

**no·ble·man** \'nō-bəl-mən\ *n, pl* **no·ble·men** \-mən\
a man of noble rank

**no·ble·wom·an** \'nō-bəl-,wu̇m-ən\ *n, pl* **no·ble·wom·en** \-,wim-ən\
a woman of noble rank

[1]**no·body** \'nō-,bäd-ē, -bəd-ē\ *pron*
no person : not anybody ⟨*nobody* lives in that house⟩

[2]**nobody** *n, pl* **no·bod·ies**
a person of no importance

**noc·tur·nal** \näk-'tərn-l\ *adj*
1 of, relating to, or happening at night : NIGHTLY
2 ▼ active at night ⟨*nocturnal* insects⟩
**noc·tur·nal·ly** *adv*

**nocturnal 2:** the virgin tiger moth is a nocturnal insect

[1]**nod** \'näd\ *vb* **nod·ded; nod·ding**
1 to bend the head downward or forward (as in bowing, going to sleep, or indicating "yes")
2 to move up and down ⟨daisies *nodded* in the breeze⟩
3 to show by a nod of the head ⟨*nod* agreement⟩

[2]**nod** *n*
the action of bending the head downward and forward

**node** \'nōd\ *n*
► a thickened spot or part (as of a plant stem where a leaf develops)

node

**node** on the stem of a plant

**nod·ule** \'näj-ül\ *n*
a small node (as of a clover root)

**no·el** \nō-'el\ *n*
1 a Christmas carol
2 *cap* the Christmas season

**noes** *pl of* NO

[1]**noise** \'nȯiz\ *n*
1 a loud unpleasant sound
2 [3]SOUND 1 ⟨the *noise* of the wind⟩
**noise·less** \-ləs\ *adj*
**noise·less·ly** *adv*
**noise·less·ness** *n*

**Word History** When we are seasick our stomachs quarrel with us. We are likely to quarrel and complain, too. An Old French word that meant "quarrel" or "loud confused sound" came from a Latin word that meant "seasickness." The English word *noise* came from this Old French word. The word *noise* is related to the word *nausea*.

[2]**noise** *vb* **noised; nois·ing**
to spread by rumor or report ⟨the story was *noised* about⟩

**noise·mak·er** \'nȯiz-,mā-kər\ *n*
a device used to make noise especially at parties

**noisy** \'nȯi-zē\ *adj* **nois·i·er; nois·i·est**
1 making noise
2 full of noise ⟨a *noisy* street⟩
**nois·i·ly** \-zə-lē\ *adv*
**nois·i·ness** \-zē-nəs\ *n*

[1]**no·mad** \'nō-,mad\ *n*
1 ▼ a member of a people having no fixed home but wandering from place to place
2 WANDERER

[2]**nomad** *adj*
NOMADIC 2

**no·mad·ic** \nō-'mad-ik\ *adj*
1 of or relating to nomads
2 roaming about with no special end in mind

**nom·i·nal** \'näm-ən-l\ *adj*
1 being such in name only ⟨the *nominal* president⟩
2 very small : TRIFLING ⟨a *nominal* price⟩
**nom·i·nal·ly** *adv*

**nom·i·nate** \'näm-ə-,nāt\ *vb* **nom·i·nat·ed; nom·i·nat·ing**
to choose as a candidate for election, appointment, or honor ⟨*nominate* a candidate for president⟩
**nom·i·na·tor** \-,nāt-ər\ *n*

**nom·i·na·tion** \,näm-ə-'nā-shən\ *n*
1 the act or an instance of nominating
2 the state of being nominated

**nom·i·na·tive** \'näm-ə-nət-iv\ *adj*
being or belonging to the case of a noun or pronoun that is usually the subject of a verb

**nom·i·nee** \,näm-ə-'nē\ *n*
a person nominated for an office, duty, or position

**non-** *prefix*
not ⟨*non*resident⟩ ⟨*non*stop⟩

**non·al·co·hol·ic** \,nän-,al-kə-'hȯl-ik, -'häl-\ *adj*
containing no alcohol

*a yurt* \'yu̇rt\ *is a light round movable tent of skins or felt*

[1]**nomad 1:** Mongolian nomads

A B C D E F G H I J K L M N O P Q R S T U V W X Y Z

**non·cha·lance** \ˌnän-shə-ˈläns\ *n*
the state of being nonchalant

**non·cha·lant** \ˌnän-shə-ˈlänt\ *adj*
having a confident and easy manner
**non·cha·lant·ly** \-ˈlänt-lē\ *adv*

**non·com·bat·ant** \ˌnän-kəm-ˈbat-nt, ˈnän-ˈkäm-bət-ənt\ *n*
**1** a member (as a chaplain) of the armed forces whose duties do not include fighting
**2** [1]CIVILIAN

**non·com·mis·sioned officer** \ˌnän-kə-ˌmish-ənd-\ *n*
an officer in the Army, Air Force, or Marine Corps appointed from among the enlisted persons

**non·com·mit·tal** \ˌnän-kə-ˈmit-l\ *adj*
not telling or showing what one thinks or has decided ⟨a *noncommittal* answer⟩
**non·com·mit·tal·ly** *adv*

**non·com·mu·ni·ca·ble** \ˌnän-kə-ˈmyü-nə-kə-bəl\ *adj*
not spread from one individual to another ⟨*noncommunicable* diseases⟩

**non·con·duc·tor** \ˌnän-kən-ˈdək-tər\ *n*
a substance that conducts heat, electricity, or sound at a very low rate

**non·con·form·ist** \ˌnän-kən-ˈfȯr-mist\ *n*
a person who does not conform to generally accepted standards or customs

**non·de·script** \ˌnän-di-ˈskript\ *adj*
of no certain class or kind : not easily described

[1]**none** \ˈnən\ *pron*
not any : not one ⟨*none* of the trouble can be blamed on you⟩

[2]**none** *adv*
**1** not at all ⟨arrived *none* too soon⟩
**2** in no way ⟨*none* the worse for wear⟩

**non·en·ti·ty** \nä-ˈnent-ət-ē\ *n, pl* **non·en·ti·ties**
someone or something of no importance

[1]**non·es·sen·tial** \ˌnän-ə-ˈsen-chəl\ *adj*
not essential

[2]**nonessential** *n*
something that is not essential

**none·the·less** \ˌnən-thə-ˈles\ *adv*
NEVERTHELESS

**non·fic·tion** \ˈnän-ˈfik-shən\ *n*
writings that are not fiction

**non·flam·ma·ble** \ˈnän-ˈflam-ə-bəl\ *adj*
not flammable

**non·green** \ˈnän-ˈgrēn\ *adj*
having no chlorophyll ⟨*nongreen* plants⟩

**non·liv·ing** \ˈnän-ˈliv-ing\ *adj*
not living

**non·par·ti·san** \ˈnän-ˈpärt-ə-zən\ *adj*
not partisan : not committed to one party or side

**non·plus** \ˈnän-ˈpləs\ *vb*
**non·plussed**; **non·plus·sing**
to cause to be at a loss as to what to say, think, or do : PERPLEX

**non·poi·son·ous** \ˈnän-ˈpȯiz-n-əs\ *adj*
not poisonous ⟨*nonpoisonous* snakes⟩

**non·prof·it** \ˈnän-ˈpräf-ət\ *adj*
not existing or carried on to make a profit ⟨*nonprofit* organizations⟩

[1]**non·res·i·dent** \ˈnän-ˈrez-ə-dənt\ *adj*
not living in a certain place ⟨a *nonresident* student⟩

[2]**nonresident** *n*
a nonresident person

**non·sched·uled** \ˈnän-ˈskej-üld\ *adj*
licensed to carry passengers or freight by air whenever demand requires ⟨*nonscheduled* airlines⟩

**non·sec·tar·i·an** \ˌnän-sek-ˈter-ē-ən\ *adj*
not limited to a particular religious group

**non·sense** \ˈnän-ˌsens, -səns\ *n*
**1** foolish or meaningless words or actions
**2** things of no importance or value

**non·sen·si·cal** \nän-ˈsen-si-kəl\ *adj*
making no sense : ABSURD
**non·sen·si·cal·ly** *adv*

**non·smok·er** \(ˈ)nän-ˈsmō-kər\ *n*
a person who does not smoke tobacco

**non·smok·ing** \(ˈ)nän-ˈsmō-king\ *adj*
**1** not in the habit of smoking tobacco
**2** reserved for the use of nonsmokers ⟨the *nonsmoking* section of the restaurant⟩

**non·stan·dard** \ˈnän-ˈstan-dərd\ *adj*
not standard

**non·stop** \ˈnän-ˈstäp\ *adv or adj*
without a stop ⟨will fly there *nonstop*⟩ ⟨a *nonstop* flight⟩

**noo·dle** \ˈnüd-l\ *n*
▼ a food like macaroni made with egg and shaped into flat strips — usually used in pl.

**noodle:** a dish of noodles

**nook** \ˈnu̇k\ *n*
**1** an inner corner ⟨a chimney *nook*⟩
**2** a sheltered or hidden place ⟨a shady *nook*⟩

**noon** \ˈnün\ *n*
the middle of the day : twelve o'clock in the daytime

**noon·day** \ˈnün-ˌdā\ *n*
NOON, MIDDAY

**no one** *pron*
[1]NOBODY ⟨*no one* was home⟩

**noon·tide** \ˈnün-ˌtīd\ *n*
NOON

**noon·time** \ˈnün-ˌtīm\ *n*
NOON

**noose** \ˈnüs\ *n*
a loop that passes through a knot at the end of a line so that it gets smaller when the other end of the line is pulled

**nor** \nər, nȯr\ *conj*
and not ⟨neither young *nor* old⟩

**norm** \ˈnȯrm\ *n*
[1]AVERAGE 2

[1]**nor·mal** \ˈnȯr-məl\ *adj*
**1** of the regular or usual kind : REGULAR
**2** of average intelligence
**3** sound in body or mind
**synonyms** see REGULAR
**nor·mal·ly** *adv*

**Word History** People who work with wood use something called a *square* to make and test right angles. The English word *normal* came from the Latin word for this kind of square which also meant "rule" or "pattern." *Normal* at first meant "forming a right angle." Later *normal* came to mean "by a rule or pattern" or "regular."

**[2]normal** *n*
**1** one that is normal
**2** [1]AVERAGE 2

**nor·mal·cy** \'nȯr-məl-sē\ *n*
NORMALITY

**nor·mal·i·ty** \nȯr-'mal-ət-ē\ *n*
the quality or state of being normal

**Nor·man** \'nȯr-mən\ *n*
**1** one of the Scandinavians who conquered Normandy in the tenth century
**2** ▶ one of the people of mixed Norman and French blood who conquered England in 1066

**Norman 2:** section from an 11th-century tapestry depicting Normans

**Norse** \'nȯrs\ *n pl*
**1** people of Scandinavia
**2** people of Norway

**[1]north** \'nȯrth\ *adv*
to or toward the north

**[2]north** *adj*
placed toward, facing, or coming from the north

**[3]north** *n*
**1** the direction to the left of one facing east : the compass point opposite to south
**2** *cap* regions or countries north of a point that is mentioned or understood

**[1]North American** *n*
a person born or living in North America

**[2]North American** *adj*
of or relating to North America or the North Americans

**north·bound** \'nȯrth-,baůnd\ *adj*
going north

**[1]north·east** \nȯr-'thēst\ *adv*
to or toward the direction between north and east

**[2]northeast** *adj*
placed toward, facing, or coming from the northeast

**[3]northeast** *n*
**1** the direction between north and east
**2** *cap* regions or countries northeast of a point that is mentioned or understood

**north·east·er·ly** \nȯr-'thē-stər-lē\ *adv or adj*
**1** from the northeast
**2** toward the northeast

**north·east·ern** \nȯr-'thē-stərn\ *adj*
**1** *often cap* of, relating to, or like that of the Northeast
**2** lying toward or coming from the northeast

**north·er·ly** \'nȯr-thər-lē\ *adj or adv*
**1** toward the north
**2** from the north ⟨a *northerly* wind⟩

**north·ern** \'nȯr-thərn\ *adj*
**1** *often cap* of, relating to, or like that of the North
**2** lying toward or coming from the north

**northern lights** *n pl*
AURORA BOREALIS

**north·land** \'nȯrth-,land\ *n, often cap*
land in the north : the north of a country or region

**north pole** *n*
**1** *often cap N&P* the most northern point of the earth : the northern end of the earth's axis
**2** the end of a magnet that points toward the north when the magnet is free to swing

**North Star** *n*
the star toward which the northern end of the earth's axis very nearly points

**north·ward** \'nȯrth-wərd\ *adv or adj*
toward the north

**[1]north·west** \nȯrth-'west\ *adv*
to or toward the direction between north and west

**[2]northwest** *adj*
placed toward, facing, or coming from the northwest

**[3]northwest** *n*
**1** the direction between north and west
**2** *cap* regions or countries northwest of a point that is mentioned or understood

**north·west·er·ly** \nȯrth-'wes-tər-lē\ *adv or adj*
**1** from the northwest
**2** toward the northwest

**north·west·ern** \nȯrth-'wes-tərn\ *adj*
**1** *often cap* of, relating to, or like that of the Northwest
**2** lying toward or coming from the northwest

**[1]Nor·we·gian** \nȯr-'wē-jən\ *adj*
of or relating to Norway, its people, or the Norwegian language

**[2]Norwegian** *n*
**1** a person who is born or lives in Norway
**2** the language of the Norwegians

**nos** *pl of* NO

**[1]nose** \'nōz\ *n*
**1** ▼ the part of a person's face or an animal's head that contains the nostrils
**2** the sense or organ of smell ⟨a dog with a good *nose*⟩
**3** something (as a point, edge, or the front of an object) that suggests a nose ⟨the *nose* of an airplane⟩
**4** an ability to discover ⟨a *nose* for news⟩

**nosed** \'nōzd\ *adj*

*nose*

**[1]nose 1:** a beagle sniffing a trail

**²nose** *vb* **nosed**; **nos·ing**
**1** to detect by or as if by smell **:** SCENT
**2** to touch or rub with the nose **:** NUZZLE
**3** to search in a nosy way **:** PRY ⟨you're always *nosing* around in someone else's business⟩
**4** to move ahead slowly or carefully ⟨the ship *nosed* into its berth⟩

**nose·bleed** \'nōz-,blēd\ *n*
a bleeding at the nose

**nose cone** *n*
▼ a protective cone forming the forward end of a rocket or missile

**nose cone** on a model rocket

**nose–dive** \'nōz-,dīv\ *vb*
**nose–dived**; **nose–div·ing**
to plunge suddenly or sharply

**nose dive** *n*
**1** a downward plunge (as of an airplane)
**2** a sudden sharp drop (as in prices)

**nos·tal·gia** \nä-'stal-jə\ *n*
a wishing for something past

**nos·tril** \'näs-trəl\ *n*
either of the outer openings of the nose through which one breathes

**nos·trum** \'näs-trəm\ *n*
a medicine of secret formula and doubtful worth **:** a questionable remedy

**nosy** *or* **nos·ey** \'nō-zē\ *adj*
**nos·i·er**; **nos·i·est**
tending to pry into someone else's business

**not** \nät\ *adv*
**1** used to make a word or group of words negative ⟨the books are *not* here⟩
**2** used to stand for the negative of a group of words that comes before ⟨sometimes hard to see and sometimes *not*⟩

**¹no·ta·ble** \'nōt-ə-bəl\ *adj*
**1** deserving special notice **:** REMARKABLE ⟨a *notable* sight⟩
**2** DISTINGUISHED, PROMINENT ⟨a *notable* writer⟩
**no·ta·bly** \-blē\ *adv*

**²notable** *n*
a famous person

**no·ta·rize** \'nōt-ə-,rīz\ *vb*
**no·ta·rized**; **no·ta·riz·ing**
to sign as a notary public to show that a document is authentic

**no·ta·ry public** \,nōt-ə-rē-\ *n, pl* **notaries public** *or* **notary publics**
a public officer who witnesses the making of a document (as a deed) and signs it to show that it is authentic

**no·ta·tion** \nō-'tā-shən\ *n*
**1** the act of noting
**2** ²NOTE 5 ⟨make *notations* on a paper⟩
**3** ▼ a system of signs, marks, or figures used to give specified information ⟨musical *notation*⟩ ⟨scientific *notation*⟩

**¹notch** \'näch\ *n*
**1** a cut in the shape of a V in an edge or surface
**2** a narrow pass between mountains
**3** DEGREE 1, STEP ⟨turn the radio up a *notch*⟩

**²notch** *vb*
to cut or make notches in

**¹note** \'nōt\ *vb* **not·ed**; **not·ing**
**1** to notice or observe with care
**2** to record in writing
**3** to call attention to in speech or writing

**notation 3**

To write down the music they create, composers make signs and symbols, called notation, on a five-line staff divided into parallel bars. The position of each note on, or in the space between, the bars indicates its pitch — how high or low it is to be played. Notation also gives other information, including brief changes in the pitch of the note, the length of a pause, and the speed at which the music is to be played.

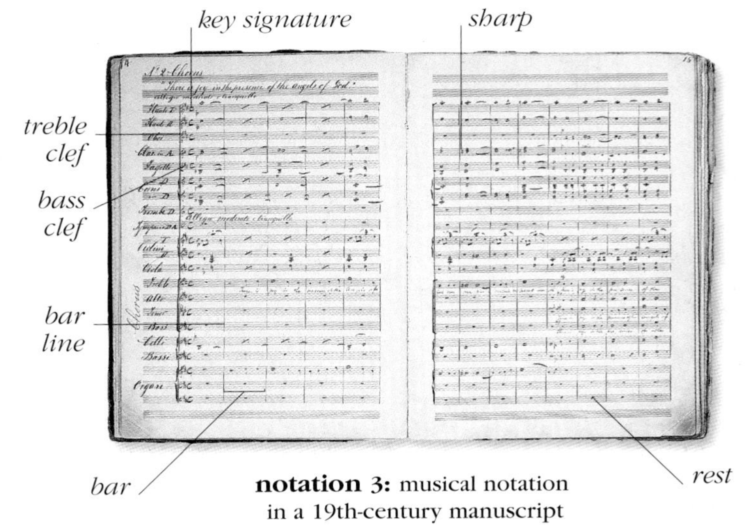


**notation 3:** musical notation in a 19th-century manuscript

[2]**note** *n*
**1** a musical sound : TONE
**2** a symbol in music that by its shape and position on the staff shows the pitch of a tone and the length of time it is to be held
**3** the musical call or song of a bird
**4** a quality that shows a feeling ⟨a *note* of sadness in your voice⟩
**5** something written down often to aid the memory ⟨I'll make a *note* of the appointment⟩
**6** a printed comment in a book that helps explain part of the text
**7** DISTINCTION 3 ⟨artists of *note*⟩
**8** a short written message or letter
**9** careful notice ⟨take *note* of the time⟩
**10** a promise to pay a debt
**11** a piano key
**12** frame of mind : MOOD ⟨began the day on a happy *note*⟩

**note·book** \'nōt-,bu̇k\ *n*
▼ a book of blank pages for writing in

**notebook**

**not·ed** \'nōt-əd\ *adj*
well-known and highly regarded

**note·wor·thy** \'nōt-,wər-t͟hē\ *adj*
worthy of note : REMARKABLE
**note·wor·thi·ness** *n*

[1]**noth·ing** \'nəth-ing\ *pron*
**1** not anything : no thing ⟨there's *nothing* in the box⟩
**2** one of no interest, value, or importance ⟨your opinion is *nothing* to me⟩

[2]**nothing** *adv*
not at all : in no way

[3]**nothing** *n*
**1** something that does not exist
**2** ZERO 1, 4
**3** something of little or no worth or importance
**noth·ing·ness** *n*

[1]**no·tice** \'nōt-əs\ *n*
**1** WARNING ⟨on short *notice*⟩
**2** an indication that an agreement will end at a specified time ⟨gave my employer *notice*⟩
**3** ATTENTION 1, HEED ⟨take no *notice* of them⟩
**4** a written or printed announcement
**5** a brief published criticism (as of a book or play)

[2]**notice** *vb* **no·ticed**; **no·tic·ing**
to take notice of : pay attention to ⟨given to *noticing* details⟩

**no·tice·able** \'nōt-ə-sə-bəl\ *adj*
deserving notice : likely to be noticed
**no·tice·ably** \-blē\ *adv*

**Synonyms** NOTICEABLE and OUTSTANDING mean attracting notice or attention. NOTICEABLE suggests that something is likely to be observed ⟨an essay with many *noticeable* mistakes⟩. OUTSTANDING suggests that something attracts notice because it rises above and is better than others of the same kind ⟨an *outstanding* baseball player⟩.

**no·ti·fi·ca·tion** \,nōt-ə-fə-'kā-shən\ *n*
**1** the act or an instance of notifying
**2** something written or printed that gives notice

**no·ti·fy** \'nōt-ə-,fī\ *vb* **no·ti·fied**; **no·ti·fy·ing**
to give notice to : INFORM ⟨*notify* the police⟩

**no·tion** \'nō-shən\ *n*
**1** IDEA 2 ⟨haven't the faintest *notion* what to do⟩
**2** WHIM ⟨a sudden *notion* to go home⟩
**3** **notions** *pl* small useful articles (as buttons, needles, and thread)

**no·to·ri·e·ty** \,nōt-ə-'rī-ət-ē\ *n*
the state of being notorious

**no·to·ri·ous** \nō-'tōr-ē-əs\ *adj*
widely known for some bad characteristic ⟨a *notorious* thief⟩
**no·to·ri·ous·ly** *adv*

[1]**not·with·stand·ing** \,nät-with-'stan-ding, -wit͟h-\ *prep*
in spite of ⟨we went ahead with our plan *notwithstanding* their objections⟩

[2]**notwithstanding** *adv*
NEVERTHELESS

**nou·gat** \'nü-gət\ *n*
▼ a candy consisting of a sugar paste with nuts or fruit pieces

**nougat**

**nought** *variant of* NAUGHT

**noun** \'nau̇n\ *n*
a word or phrase that is the name of something (as a person, place, or thing) and that is used in a sentence especially as subject or object of a verb or as object of a preposition

**nour·ish** \'nər-ish\ *vb*
to cause to grow or live in a healthy state especially by providing with enough good food
**nour·ish·ing** *adj*

**nour·ish·ment** \'nər-ish-mənt\ *n*
**1** something (as food) that nourishes
**2** the act of nourishing : the state of being nourished

[1]**nov·el** \'näv-əl\ *adj*
**1** new and different from what is already known
**2** original or striking in design or appearance

[2]**novel** *n*
a long made-up story that usually fills a book

**nov·el·ist** \'näv-ə-list\ *n*
a writer of novels

**nov·el·ty** \'näv-əl-tē\ *n*, *pl* **nov·el·ties**
**1** something new or unusual
**2** the quality or state of being novel
**3** a small article of unusual design intended mainly for decoration or adornment

**No·vem·ber** \nō-'vem-bər\ *n*
the eleventh month of the year

**Word History** The first calendar used in ancient Rome began the year with the month of March. November was the ninth month. The Latin name for this month came from the Latin word for nine. The English name *November* comes from the month's Latin name.

a b c d e f g h i j k l m n o p q r s t u v w x y z

A B C D E F G H I J K L M N O P Q R S T U V W X Y Z

**nov•ice** \'näv-əs\ *n*
**1** a new member of a religious community who is preparing to take the vows of religion
**2** a person who has no previous experience with something : BEGINNER

**¹now** \naů\ *adv*
**1** at this time
**2** immediately before the present time ⟨left just *now*⟩
**3** in the time immediately to follow ⟨will leave *now*⟩
**4** used to express command or introduce an important point ⟨*now* this story is interesting⟩
**5** SOMETIMES ⟨*now* one and *now* another⟩
**6** in the present state ⟨*now* what can we do⟩
**7** at the time referred to ⟨*now* the trouble began⟩

**²now** *conj*
in view of the fact that : ²SINCE 2 ⟨*now* you've come, we can begin⟩

**³now** \'naů\ *n*
the present time ⟨up till *now*⟩

**now•a•days** \'naů-ə-ˌdāz\ *adv*
at the present time

**¹no•where** \'nō-ˌhweər, -ˌweər, -ˌhwaər, -ˌwaər\ *adv*
**1** not in or at any place
**2** to no place

**²nowhere** *n*
a place that does not exist

**nox•ious** \'näk-shəs\ *adj*
causing harm ⟨*noxious* fumes⟩

**noz•zle** \'näz-əl\ *n*
▼ a short tube with a taper or constriction often used on a hose or pipe to direct or speed up a flow of fluid

**nozzle** on a garden hose

**-n't** \nt, -nt, ənt\ *adv suffix*
not ⟨is*n't*⟩

**nu•cle•ar** \'nü-klē-ər, 'nyü-\ *adj*
**1** of, relating to, or being a nucleus (as of a cell)
**2** of or relating to the nucleus of the atom ⟨fission is a *nuclear* reaction⟩
**3** produced by a nuclear reaction ⟨*nuclear* energy⟩
**4** of, relating to, or being a weapon whose destructive power comes from an uncontrolled nuclear reaction
**5** relating to or powered by nuclear energy ⟨a *nuclear* submarine⟩

**nu•cle•us** \'nü-klē-əs, 'nyü-\ *n, pl* **nu•clei** \-klē-ˌī\
**1** a central point, group, or mass
**2** a part of cell protoplasm enclosed in a nuclear membrane, containing chromosomes and genes, and concerned especially with the control of vital functions and heredity
**3** the central part of an atom that comprises nearly all of the atomic mass and that consists of protons and neutrons except in hydrogen in which it consists of one proton only

**nude** \'nüd, 'nyüd\ *adj* **nud•er**; **nud•est**
not wearing clothes : NAKED
**nude•ness** *n*

**¹nudge** \'nəj\ *vb* **nudged**; **nudg•ing**
to touch or push gently (as with the elbow) especially in order to attract attention

**²nudge** *n*
a slight push

**nu•di•ty** \'nüd-ət-ē, 'nyüd-\ *n*
the quality or state of being nude

**nug•get** \'nəg-ət\ *n*
► a solid lump especially of precious metal

**nui•sance** \'nüs-ns, 'nyüs-\ *n*
an annoying person or thing

**null** \'nəl\ *adj*
having no legal force : not binding

**null and void** *adj*
NULL

**¹numb** \'nəm\ *adj*
**1** lacking in sensation especially from cold
**2** lacking feelings : INDIFFERENT
**numb•ly** *adv*
**numb•ness** *n*

**²numb** *vb*
to make or become numb

**¹num•ber** \'nəm-bər\ *n*
**1** the total of persons, things, or units taken together : AMOUNT ⟨the *number* of people in a room⟩
**2** a total that is not specified ⟨I got a *number* of presents on my birthday⟩
**3** a quality of a word form that shows whether the word is singular or plural ⟨a verb agrees in *number* with its subject⟩
**4** NUMERAL ⟨the *number* 5⟩
**5** a certain numeral for telling one person or thing from another or from others ⟨a house *number*⟩
**6** one of a series ⟨the March *number* of a magazine⟩

**²number** *vb*
**1** ¹COUNT 1
**2** INCLUDE ⟨was *numbered* among the guests⟩
**3** to limit to a certain number ⟨vacation days are *numbered* now⟩
**4** to give a number to ⟨*number* the pages of a scrapbook⟩
**5** to add up to or have a total of ⟨our group *numbered* ten in all⟩

**num•ber•less** \'nəm-bər-ləs\ *adj*
too many to count ⟨the *numberless* stars in the sky⟩

**number line** *n*
a line in which points are matched to numbers

**nu•mer•al** \'nü-mə-rəl, 'nyü-\ *n*
a symbol or group of symbols representing a number

**nu•mer•a•tion** \ˌnü-mə-'rā-shən, ˌnyü-\ *n*
a system of counting

**nugget** of platinum

**nu•mer•a•tor** \'nü-mə-ˌrāt-ər, 'nyü-\ *n*
the part of a fraction that is above the line ⟨3 is the *numerator* of the fraction $^3/_5$⟩

**nu•mer•i•cal** \nů-'mer-i-kəl, nyů-\ *adj*
of or relating to number : stated in numbers

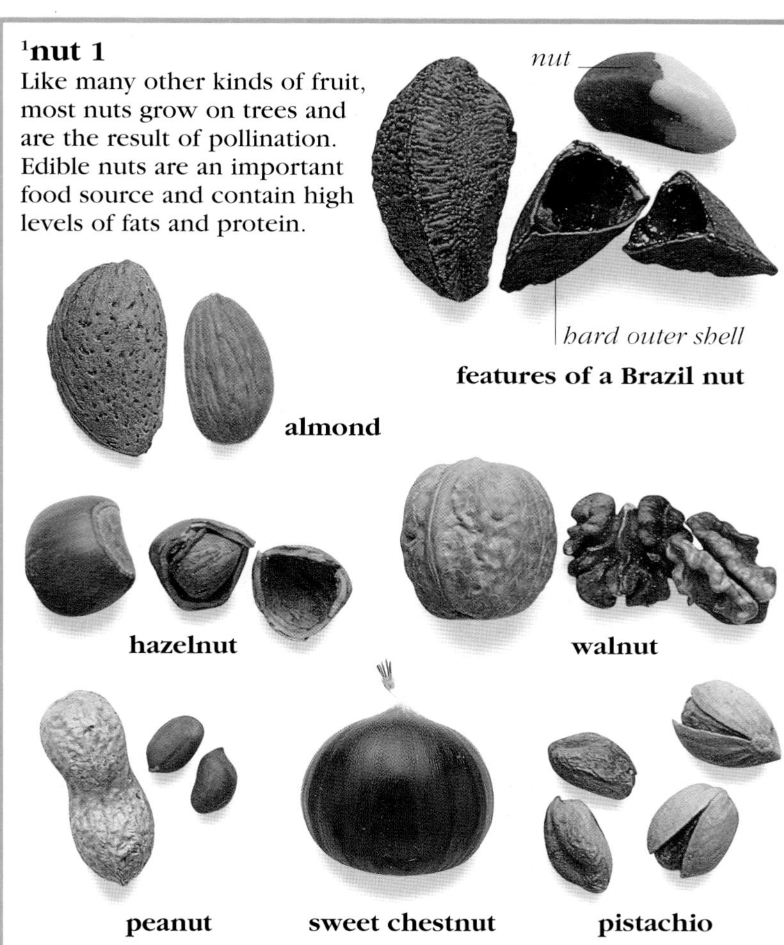


**[1]nut 1**
Like many other kinds of fruit, most nuts grow on trees and are the result of pollination. Edible nuts are an important food source and contain high levels of fats and protein.

**nu·mer·i·cal·ly** *adv*

**nu·mer·ous** \'nü-mə-rəs, 'nyü-\ *adj*
consisting of a large number ⟨*numerous* friends⟩ ⟨a *numerous* family⟩
**nu·mer·ous·ly** *adv*

**num·skull** \'nəm-,skəl\ *n*
a stupid person

**nun** \'nən\ *n*
a woman belonging to a religious community and living by vows

**nun·cio** \'nən-sē-,ō, 'nu̇n-\ *n, pl* **nun·ci·os**
a person who is the pope's representative to a civil government

**nup·tial** \'nəp-shəl\ *adj*
of or relating to marriage or a wedding

**nup·tials** \'nəp-shəlz\ *n pl*
WEDDING

**[1]nurse** \'nərs\ *n*
**1** a woman employed for the care of a young child
**2** a person skilled or trained in the care of the sick

---

**Word History** The English word *nurse* can be traced back to a Latin word that meant "nourishing" or "feeding." In the past some mothers did not feed their babies at their own breasts but hired someone else to do so. The English word *nurse* was first used for such a woman. Later it came to be used for any woman hired to take care of a young child. The word *nurse* is also used now for a person who takes care of sick people.

---

**[2]nurse** *vb* **nursed**; **nurs·ing**
**1** to feed at the breast
**2** to take care of (as a young child or a sick person)
**3** to treat with special care ⟨*nurse* a plant⟩

**nurse·maid** \'nər-,smād\ *n*
[1]NURSE 1

**nurs·ery** \'nər-sə-rē, 'nərs-rē\ *n, pl* **nurs·er·ies**
**1** a place set aside for small children or for the care of small children
**2** a place where young trees, vines, and plants are grown and usually sold

**nurs·ery·man** \'nər-sə-rē-mən, 'nərs-rē-\ *n, pl* **nurs·ery·men** \-mən\
a person whose occupation is the growing of trees, shrubs, and plants

**nursery school** *n*
a school for children usually under five years old

**[1]nur·ture** \'nər-chər\ *n*
**1** UPBRINGING
**2** something (as food) that nourishes

**[2]nurture** *vb* **nur·tured**; **nur·tur·ing**
**1** to supply with food
**2** EDUCATE 2
**3** to provide for growth of

**[1]nut** \'nət\ *n*
**1** ◄ a dry fruit or seed with a firm inner kernel and a hard shell
**2** the often edible kernel of a nut
**3** a piece of metal with a hole in it that is fastened to a bolt by means of a screw thread
**4** a foolish or crazy person
**nut·like** \-,līk\ *adj*

**[2]nut** *vb* **nut·ted**; **nut·ting**
to gather or seek nuts

**nut·crack·er** \'nət-,krak-ər\ *n*
**1** a device used for cracking the shells of nuts
**2** a bird related to the crows that lives mostly on the seeds of pine trees

**nuthatch:** a red-breasted nuthatch

**nut·hatch** \'nət-,hach\ *n*
▲ a small bird that creeps on tree trunks and branches and eats insects

**nut·let** \ˈnət-lət\ *n*
**1** a small nut
**2** a small fruit like a nut

**nut·meg** \ˈnət-ˌmeg\ *n*
▼ a spice that is the ground seeds of a small evergreen tropical tree

*nutmeg seed*
*ground nutmeg*

**nutmeg**

**nu·tri·ent** \ˈnü-trē-ənt, ˈnyü-\ *n*
a substance used in nutrition ⟨green plants make their food from simple *nutrients* such as carbon dioxide and water⟩

**nu·tri·ment** \ˈnü-trə-mənt, ˈnyü-\ *n*
something that nourishes

**nu·tri·tion** \nu̇-ˈtrish-ən, nyu̇-\ *n*
the act or process of nourishing or being nourished **:** the processes by which a living being takes in and uses nutrients

**nu·tri·tion·al** \nu̇-ˈtrish-ən-l, nyu̇-\ *adj*
of or relating to nutrition

**nu·tri·tious** \nu̇-ˈtrish-əs, nyu̇-\ *adj*
providing nutrients **:** NOURISHING

**nu·tri·tive** \ˈnü-trət-iv, ˈnyü-\ *adj*
**1** NUTRITIONAL
**2** NUTRITIOUS

**nut·ty** \ˈnət-ē\ *adj* **nut·ti·er**; **nut·ti·est**
**1** not showing good sense
**2** having a flavor like that of nuts

**nuz·zle** \ˈnəz-əl\ *vb* **nuz·zled**; **nuz·zling**
**1** to push or rub with the nose
**2** to lie close **:** NESTLE

**ny·lon** \ˈnī-ˌlän\ *n*
**1** a synthetic substance used in the making of textiles and plastics
**2** ► a material (as a textile) made from nylon ⟨parachutes are made of *nylon*⟩

**nymph** \ˈnimf\ *n*
**1** one of many goddesses in old legends represented as beautiful young girls living in the mountains, forests, and waters
**2** an immature insect that differs from the adult chiefly in the size and proportions of the body

**nylon 2:**
a jacket made of nylon

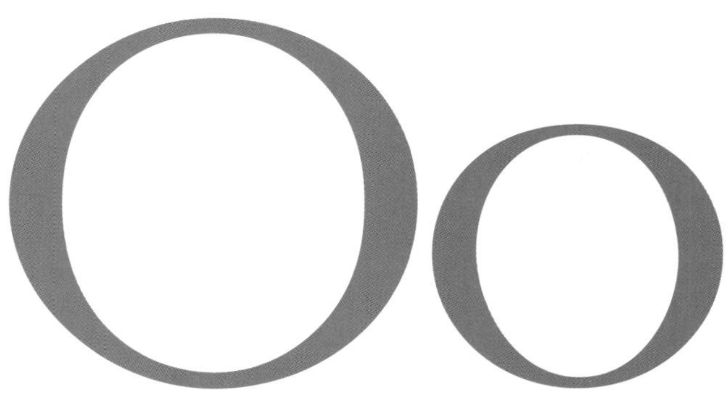

**The sounds of O:** The letter **O** is used for several vowel sounds in English. In many words, it sounds like its own name. This sound is often called "**long O**." Examples are **open**, **hope**, **grocery**, **photo**, and **piano**.

In many others it has the sound called "**short O**." Examples are **opera**, **hop**, **continent**, and **groggy**.

Double **O** does not have the same sound as single **O**. It has several different sounds, for which we also use the letter **U**. The most common sound for double **O** is the "**long U**" sound (as in **boot** and **shoot**). Another sound is the one heard in **foot** and **good**. A third sound of double **O** occurs in the word **flood**.

**o** \'ō\ *n, pl* **o's** *or* **os** \'ōz\ *often cap*
**1** the fifteenth letter of the English alphabet
**2** ZERO 1

**O** *variant of* OH

**oaf** \'ōf\ *n*
a stupid or awkward person
**oaf•ish** \'ō-fish\ *adj*

**oak**

**oak** \'ōk\ *n*
▲ any of various trees and shrubs related to the beech and chestnut whose fruits are acorns and whose tough wood is much used for furniture and flooring

**oak•en** \'ō-kən\ *adj*
made of or like oak

**oar** \'ōr\ *n*
▼ a long pole with a broad blade at one end used for rowing or steering a boat

blade

**oars** for a boat

**oar•lock** \'ōr-,läk\ *n*
a usually U-shaped device for holding an oar in place

**oars•man** \'ōrz-mən\ *n, pl* **oars•men** \-mən\
a person who rows a boat

**oa•sis** \ō-'ā-səs\ *n, pl* **oa•ses** \-,sēz\
a fertile or green spot in a desert

**oat** \'ōt\ *n*
**1** a cereal grass grown for its loose clusters of seeds that are used for human food and animal feed
**2 oats** *pl* a crop or the grain of the oat

**oath** \'ōth\ *n, pl* **oaths** \'ōthz, 'ōths\
**1** a solemn appeal to God or to some deeply respected person or thing to witness to the truth of one's word or the sacredness of a promise ⟨under *oath* to tell the truth⟩
**2** a careless or improper use of a sacred name

**oat•meal** \'ōt-,mēl\ *n*
**1** oats husked and ground into meal or flattened into flakes
**2** a hot cereal made from meal or flakes of oats

**obe•di•ence** \ō-'bēd-ē-əns\ *n*
the act of obeying : willingness to obey

**obe•di•ent** \ō-'bēd-ē-ənt\ *adj*
willing to obey : likely to mind
**obe•di•ent•ly** *adv*

**obe•lisk** \'äb-ə-,lisk, 'ōb-\ *n*
▶ a four-sided pillar that becomes narrower toward the top and ends in a pyramid

**obese** \ō-'bēs\ *adj*
very fat

**obey** \ō-'bā\ *vb* **obeyed**; **obey•ing**
**1** to follow the commands or guidance of
**2** to comply with : carry out ⟨*obey* an order⟩ ⟨*obey* the rules⟩

**Synonyms** OBEY and MIND mean to do what another person says. OBEY suggests that one quickly yields to the authority of another or follows a rule or law ⟨*obey* your parents⟩ ⟨*obey* all traffic laws⟩. MIND is used like *obey* especially when speaking to children but it often stresses paying attention to the wishes or commands of another ⟨*mind* what I said about talking⟩.

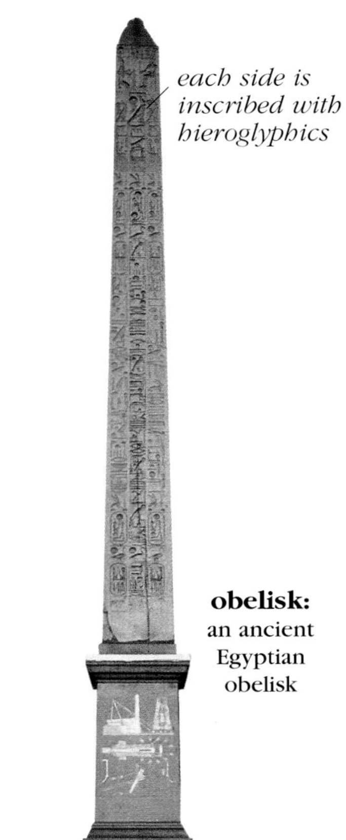


**obelisk:** an ancient Egyptian obelisk

**obit·u·ary** \ō-'bich-ə-,wer-ē\ *n, pl* **obit·u·ar·ies**
a notice of a person's death (as in a newspaper)

[1]**ob·ject** \'äb-jikt\ *n*
**1** something that may be seen or felt ⟨tables and chairs are *objects*⟩
**2** something that arouses feelings in an observer ⟨the *object* of their envy⟩
**3** [1]PURPOSE, AIM ⟨the *object* is to raise money⟩
**4** a noun or a term behaving like a noun that receives the action of a verb or completes the meaning of a preposition

[2]**ob·ject** \əb-'jekt\ *vb*
**1** to offer or mention as an objection ⟨the treasurer *objected* that the funds were too low⟩
**2** to oppose something firmly and usually with words ⟨*object* to a plan⟩

---

**Synonyms** OBJECT and PROTEST mean to oppose something by arguing against it. OBJECT stresses one's great dislike or hatred ⟨I *object* to being called a liar⟩. PROTEST suggests the presenting of objections in speech, writing, or in an organized, public demonstration ⟨groups *protesting* the building of the airport⟩.

---

**ob·jec·tion** \əb-'jek-shən\ *n*
**1** an act of objecting
**2** a reason for or a feeling of disapproval

**ob·jec·tion·able** \əb-'jek-shə-nə-bəl\ *adj*
arousing objection : OFFENSIVE

[1]**ob·jec·tive** \əb-'jek-tiv\ *adj*
**1** being outside of the mind and independent of it
**2** being or belonging to the case of a noun or pronoun that is an object of a transitive verb or a preposition ⟨a noun in the *objective* case⟩
**3** dealing with facts without allowing one's feelings to confuse them ⟨an *objective* report⟩
**ob·jec·tive·ly** *adv*

[2]**objective** *n*
[1]PURPOSE, GOAL

**ob·jec·tiv·i·ty** \,äb-,jek-'tiv-ət-ē\ *n*
the quality or state of being objective

**ob·li·gate** \'äb-lə-,gāt\ *vb* **ob·li·gat·ed**; **ob·li·gat·ing**
**1** to make (someone) do something by law or because it is right
**2** OBLIGE 2

**ob·li·ga·tion** \,äb-lə-'gā-shən\ *n*
**1** an act of making oneself responsible for doing something
**2** something (as the demands of a promise or contract) that requires one to do something
**3** something one must do : DUTY
**4** a feeling of being indebted for an act of kindness

**oblige** \ə-'blīj\ *vb* **obliged**; **oblig·ing**
**1** [2]FORCE 1, COMPEL ⟨the soldiers were *obliged* to retreat⟩
**2** to earn the gratitude of ⟨you will *oblige* me by coming early⟩
**3** to do a favor for or do something as a favor ⟨I'll be glad to *oblige*⟩

**oblig·ing** \ə-'blī-jing\ *adj*
willing to do favors
**oblig·ing·ly** *adv*

**oblique** \ō-'blēk, ə-\ *adj*
neither perpendicular nor parallel
**oblique·ly** *adv*

**oblit·er·ate** \ə-'blit-ə-,rāt\ *vb* **oblit·er·at·ed**; **oblit·er·at·ing**
to remove or destroy completely

**obliv·i·on** \ə-'bliv-ē-ən\ *n*
**1** the state of forgetting or having forgotten or of being unaware or unconscious
**2** the state of being forgotten

**obliv·i·ous** \ə-'bliv-ē-əs\ *adj*
not being conscious or aware ⟨*oblivious* of the crowd⟩ ⟨*oblivious* to the danger⟩
**obliv·i·ous·ly** *adv*
**obliv·i·ous·ness** *n*

[1]**ob·long** \'äb-,lȯng\ *adj*
▼ different from a square, circle, or sphere by being longer in one direction ⟨an *oblong* tablecloth⟩ ⟨an *oblong* melon⟩

[2]**oblong** *n*
an oblong figure or object

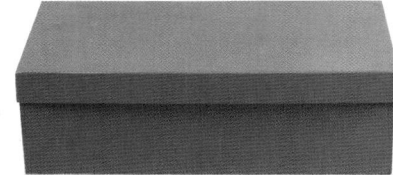

[1]**oblong:** an oblong box

**ob·nox·ious** \äb-'näk-shəs, əb-\ *adj*
very disagreeable : HATEFUL
**ob·nox·ious·ly** *adv*
**ob·nox·ious·ness** *n*

**oboe** \'ō-bō\ *n*
▼ a woodwind instrument with two reeds that has a penetrating tone and a range of nearly three octaves

**oboe:** a musician playing the oboe

---

**Word History** The oboe, the English horn, and the bassoon belong to the same group of woodwind instruments. Of the three the oboe has the highest pitch. The English word *oboe* comes from the Italian name of the instrument. This Italian name comes from the oboe's French name. The French name is made up of two French words. The first means "high" and the second means "wood."

---

**ob·scene** \äb-'sēn, əb-\ *adj*
very shocking to one's sense of what is moral or decent

**ob·scen·i·ty** \äb-'sen-ət-ē, əb-\ *n, pl* **ob·scen·i·ties**
**1** the quality or state of being obscene
**2** something that is obscene

[1]**ob·scure** \äb-'skyu̇r, əb-\ *adj*
**1** [1]DARK 1, GLOOMY
**2** SECLUDED ⟨an *obscure* village in the country⟩
**3** not easily understood or clearly expressed ⟨an *obscure* chapter in a book⟩
**4** not outstanding or famous ⟨an *obscure* poet⟩

[2]**obscure** *vb* **ob·scured**; **ob·scur·ing**
to make obscure

**ob·scu·ri·ty** \äb-'skyu̇r-ət-ē, əb-\ *n, pl* **ob·scu·ri·ties**
**1** the quality or state of being obscure ⟨lived in *obscurity*⟩
**2** something that is obscure ⟨the poems are filled with *obscurities*⟩

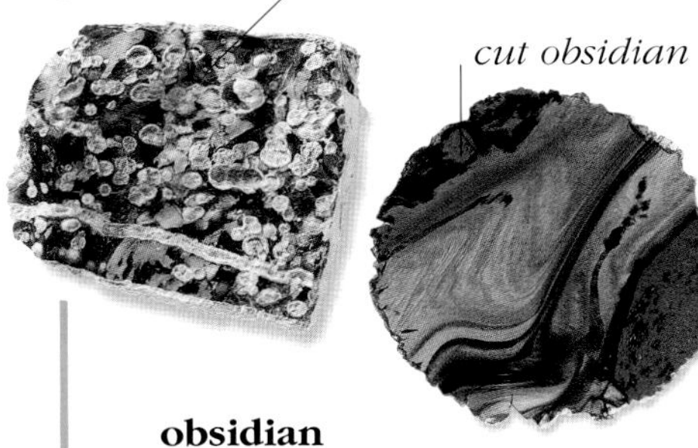


**obsidian**

**ob·serv·able** \əb-'zər-və-bəl\ *adj* NOTICEABLE
**ob·serv·ably** \-blē\ *adv*

**ob·ser·vance** \əb-'zər-vəns\ *n*
**1** an established practice or ceremony ⟨religious *observances*⟩
**2** an act of following a custom, rule, or law ⟨careful *observance* of the speed laws⟩

**ob·ser·vant** \əb-'zər-vənt\ *adj* quick to take notice : WATCHFUL, ALERT
**ob·ser·vant·ly** *adv*

**ob·ser·va·tion** \ˌäb-sər-'vā-shən, -zər-\ *n*
**1** an act or the power of seeing or of fixing the mind upon something
**2** the gathering of information by noting facts or occurrences ⟨weather *observations*⟩
**3** an opinion formed or expressed after observing
**4** the fact of being observed

**ob·ser·va·to·ry** \əb-'zər-və-ˌtōr-ē\ *n, pl* **ob·ser·va·to·ries**
► a place that has instruments for making observations (as of the stars)

**ob·serve** \əb-'zərv\ *vb* **ob·served**; **ob·serv·ing**
**1** to act in agreement with : OBEY ⟨*observe* the law⟩
**2** CELEBRATE 2 ⟨*observe* a religious holiday⟩
**3** [1]WATCH 5 ⟨*observed* their actions carefully⟩
**4** [2]REMARK 2, SAY ⟨*observed* that it was a fine day⟩
**ob·serv·er** *n*

**ob·sess** \əb-'ses\ *vb* to occupy the mind of completely or abnormally ⟨*obsessed* with a new scheme⟩

**ob·ses·sion** \əb-'sesh-ən\ *n* a disturbing and often unreasonable idea or feeling that cannot be put out of the mind

**ob·sid·i·an** \əb-'sid-ē-ən\ *n* ◄ a smooth dark rock formed by the cooling of lava

**ob·so·lete** \ˌäb-sə-'lēt\ *adj* no longer in use : OUT-OF-DATE ⟨*obsolete* words⟩

**ob·sta·cle** \'äb-stə-kəl\ *n* something that stands in the way or opposes : HINDRANCE

**ob·sti·na·cy** \'äb-stə-nə-sē\ *n* the quality or state of being obstinate

**ob·sti·nate** \'äb-stə-nət\ *adj*
**1** sticking stubbornly to an opinion or purpose
**2** not easily overcome or removed ⟨an *obstinate* fever⟩
**ob·sti·nate·ly** *adv*

**ob·struct** \əb-'strəkt\ *vb*
**1** to stop up by an obstacle : BLOCK
**2** to be or come in the way of : HINDER

**ob·struc·tion** \əb-'strək-shən\ *n*
**1** an act of obstructing : the state of being obstructed
**2** something that gets in the way : OBSTACLE

**ob·tain** \əb-'tān\ *vb* to gain or get hold of with effort ⟨*obtain* a ticket⟩ ⟨*obtained* the prisoner's release⟩

**ob·tain·able** \əb-'tā-nə-bəl\ *adj* possible to obtain ⟨tickets were not *obtainable*⟩

**ob·tuse** \äb-'tüs, -'tyüs\ *adj*
**1** not pointed or sharp : BLUNT
**2** ▼ measuring more than a right angle
**3** not quick or keen of understanding or feeling

**obtuse 2:** an obtuse angle

**ob·vi·ous** \'äb-vē-əs\ *adj* easily found, seen, or understood
**ob·vi·ous·ly** *adv*
**ob·vi·ous·ness** *n*

## observatory

Observatories are usually built in remote places, far from bright city lights, where astronomers can observe the movements and other features of stars and planets in the sky. Inside an observatory, huge telescopes view the sky through an opening in the roof and computers collect the data.

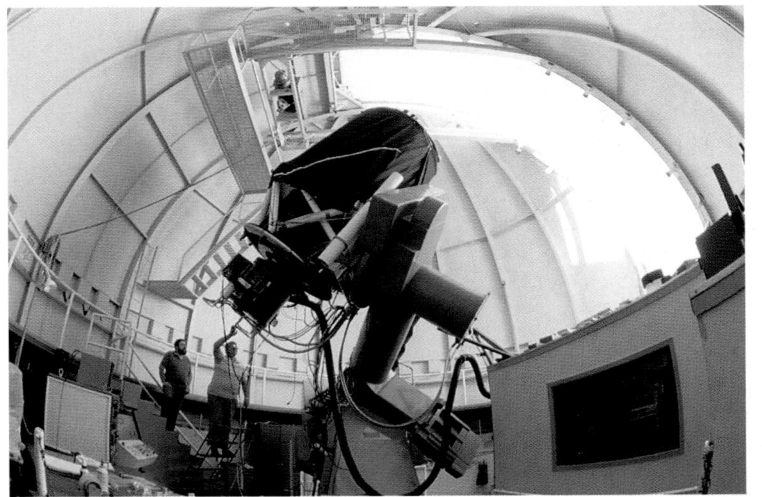

**a telescope inside an observatory**

**oc·ca·sion** \ə-'kā-zhən\ *n*
**1** a suitable opportunity **:** a good chance ⟨take the first *occasion* to write⟩
**2** the time of an event ⟨on the *occasion* of the wedding⟩
**3** a special event ⟨a great *occasion*⟩

**oc·ca·sion·al** \ə-'kā-zhən-l\ *adj*
happening or met with now and then ⟨went to an *occasional* movie⟩
**oc·ca·sion·al·ly** *adv*

**oc·cu·pan·cy** \'äk-yə-pən-sē\ *n, pl* **oc·cu·pan·cies**
the act of occupying or taking possession

**oc·cu·pant** \'äk-yə-pənt\ *n*
a person who occupies or takes possession

**oc·cu·pa·tion** \,äk-yə-'pā-shən\ *n*
**1** one's business or profession ⟨a tailor by *occupation*⟩
**2** the taking possession and control of an area ⟨*occupation* of a conquered country⟩

**ocelot**

**oc·cu·pa·tion·al** \,äk-yə-'pā-shən-l\ *adj*
of or relating to one's occupation
**oc·cu·pa·tion·al·ly** *adv*

**oc·cu·py** \'äk-yə-,pī\ *vb*
**oc·cu·pied**; **oc·cu·py·ing**
**1** to take up the attention or energies of ⟨reading *occupied* me most of the summer⟩
**2** to fill up (an extent of time or space) ⟨sports *occupy* our spare time⟩ ⟨a liter of water *occupies* 1000 cubic centimeters of space⟩
**3** to take or hold possession of ⟨enemy troops *occupied* the town⟩
**4** to live in as an owner or tenant ⟨*occupied* the house three years⟩

**oc·cur** \ə-'kər\ *vb* **oc·curred**; **oc·cur·ring**
**1** to be found or met with **:** APPEAR ⟨a disease that *occurs* among animals⟩
**2** to present itself **:** come by or as if by chance ⟨an accident *occurred* on the way to school⟩ ⟨success doesn't just *occur*, it is earned⟩
**3** to come into the mind ⟨it just *occurred* to me⟩

**oc·cur·rence** \ə-'kər-əns\ *n*
**1** something that occurs
**2** the action or process of occurring **synonyms** see INCIDENT

**ocean** \'ō-shən\ *n*
**1** the whole body of salt water that covers nearly three fourths of the earth
**2** one of the large bodies of water into which the great ocean is divided

**oce·an·ic** \,ō-shē-'an-ik\ *adj*
of or relating to the ocean

**ocean·og·ra·phy** \,ō-shə-'näg-rə-fē\ *n*
a science that deals with the ocean

**oce·lot** \'äs-ə-,lät, 'ō-sə-\ *n*
◄ a medium-sized American wildcat that is tawny or grayish and blotched with black

**o'·clock** \ə-'kläk\ *adv*
according to the clock ⟨the time is one *o'clock*⟩

**octa-** *or* **octo-** *also* **oct-** *prefix*
eight

**oc·ta·gon** \'äk-tə-,gän\ *n*
a flat figure with eight angles and eight sides

**oc·tag·o·nal** \äk-'tag-ən-l\ *adj*
having eight sides

**oc·tave** \'äk-tiv\ *n*
**1** a space of eight steps between musical notes
**2** a tone or note that is eight steps above or below another note or tone

**oc·tet** \äk-'tet\ *n*
a group or set of eight

**Oc·to·ber** \äk-'tō-bər\ *n*
the tenth month of the year

---

**Word History** The calendar first used in ancient Rome started the year with the month of March. October was the eighth month of the year. The Latin name for this month came from the Latin word that meant "eight." The English name *October* comes from the Latin name of the month.

---

**oc·to·pus** \'äk-tə-pəs\ *n, pl* **oc·to·pus·es** *or* **oc·to·pi** \-tə-,pī\
▼ a marine animal with no shell that has a rounded body with eight long flexible arms about its base which have sucking disks able to seize and hold things (as prey)

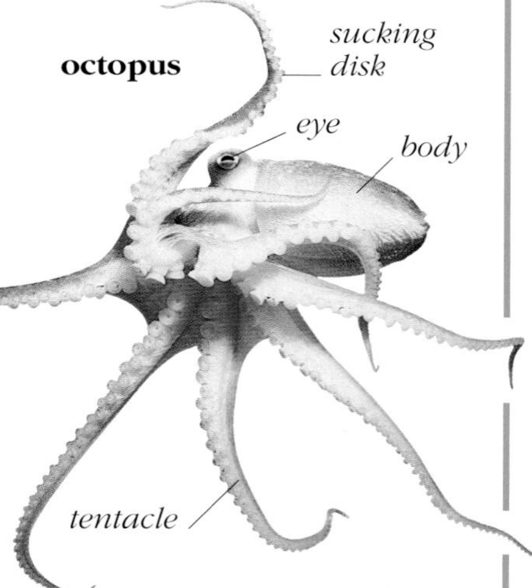


**octopus**

**oc·u·lar** \'äk-yə-lər\ *adj*
of or relating to the eye or eyesight

**odd** \'äd\ *adj*
**1** not one of a pair or a set ⟨an *odd* glove⟩
**2** not capable of being divided by two without leaving a remainder ⟨the *odd* numbers 1, 3, 5, 7, etc.⟩
**3** numbered with an odd number ⟨an *odd* year⟩
**4** some more than the number mentioned ⟨fifty *odd* years ago⟩
**5** not usual, expected, or planned ⟨*odd* jobs⟩ ⟨an *odd* stroke of luck⟩
**6** not usual or traditional ⟨an *odd* thing to do⟩
**odd·ly** *adv*
**odd·ness** *n*

**odd·ball** \'äd-,bȯl\ *n*
a person who behaves strangely

**odd·i·ty** \'äd-ət-ē\ *n, pl* **odd·i·ties**
**1** something odd
**2** the quality or state of being odd

**odds** \'ädz\ *n pl*
**1** a difference in favor of one thing over another ⟨the *odds* are in our favor⟩
**2** DISAGREEMENT 1 ⟨friends who are at *odds*⟩

**odds and ends** *n pl*
things left over **:** miscellaneous things

**ode** \'ōd\ *n*
a lyric poem that expresses a noble feeling with dignity

**odi·ous** \'ōd-ē-əs\ *adj*
causing hatred or strong dislike
: worthy of hatred

**odom·e·ter** \ō-'däm-ət-ər\ *n*
an instrument for measuring the distance traveled (as by a vehicle)

**odor** \'ōd-ər\ *n*
**1** a quality of something that one becomes aware of through the sense of smell
**2** a smell whether pleasant or unpleasant
**odored** \'ōd-ərd\ *adj*
**odor·less** \'ōd-ər-ləs\ *adj*

**odor·ous** \'ōd-ə-rəs\ *adj*
having or giving off an odor

**o'er** \ōr\ *adv or prep*
OVER

**of** \əv, 'əv, 'äv\ *prep*
**1** proceeding from : belonging to ⟨*of* royal blood⟩
**2** CONCERNING ⟨boast *of* success⟩
**3** used to show what has been taken away or what one has been freed from ⟨a tree bare *of* leaves⟩ ⟨cured *of* a cold⟩
**4** on account of ⟨afraid *of* the dark⟩ ⟨died *of* the flu⟩
**5** made from ⟨a house *of* bricks⟩
**6** used to join an amount or a part with the whole which includes it ⟨most *of* the children⟩ ⟨a pound *of* cheese⟩
**7** that is ⟨the city *of* Rome⟩
**8** that has : WITH 8 ⟨a person *of* courage⟩ ⟨a thing *of* no importance⟩

**[1]off** \'ȯf\ *adv*
**1** from a place or position ⟨marched *off*⟩
**2** from a course : ASIDE ⟨turned *off* onto a side street⟩
**3** into sleep ⟨dozed *off* and dropped the book⟩
**4** so as not to be supported, covering or enclosing, or attached ⟨rolled to the edge of the table and *off*⟩ ⟨the lid blew *off*⟩ ⟨the handle fell *off*⟩
**5** so as to be discontinued or finished ⟨turn the radio *off*⟩ ⟨paid *off* their debts⟩
**6** away from work ⟨took the day *off*⟩

**[2]off** \ȯf\ *prep*
**1** away from the surface or top of ⟨*off* the table⟩
**2** at the expense of ⟨lived *off* my parents⟩
**3** released or freed from ⟨*off* duty⟩
**4** below the usual level of ⟨a dollar *off* the price⟩
**5** away from ⟨just *off* the highway⟩

**[3]off** *adj*
**1** more removed or distant ⟨the *off* side⟩
**2** started on the way ⟨*off* on a trip⟩
**3** not taking place ⟨the game is *off*⟩
**4** not operating ⟨the radio is *off*⟩
**5** not correct : WRONG ⟨your guess is way *off*⟩
**6** not entirely sane
**7** small in degree : SLIGHT ⟨an *off* chance⟩
**8** provided for ⟨well *off*⟩

**of·fend** \ə-'fend\ *vb*
**1** to do wrong : SIN ⟨*offend* against the law⟩
**2** to hurt the feelings of : DISTRESS ⟨language that *offends* decent people⟩

**of·fend·er** \ə-'fen-dər\ *n*
a person who offends

**of·fense** *or* **of·fence** \ə-'fens\ *n*
**1** an act of attacking : ASSAULT
**2** an offensive team
**3** the act of offending : the state of being offended
**4** WRONGDOING, SIN

**[1]of·fen·sive** \ə-'fen-siv\ *adj*
**1** relating to or made for or suited to attack ⟨*offensive* weapons⟩
**2** of or relating to the attempt to score in a game or contest ⟨the *offensive* team⟩
**3** causing displeasure or resentment ⟨an *offensive* smell⟩ ⟨an *offensive* question⟩
**of·fen·sive·ly** *adv*
**of·fen·sive·ness** *n*

**[2]offensive** *n*
**1** the state or attitude of one who is making an attack ⟨on the *offensive*⟩
**2** [2]ATTACK 1

**[1]of·fer** \'ȯf-ər\ *vb*
**1** to present as an act of worship : SACRIFICE
**2** to present (something) to be accepted or rejected
**3** to present for consideration : SUGGEST ⟨*offer* a suggestion⟩
**4** to declare one's willingness ⟨*offered* to help⟩
**5** PUT UP 5 ⟨*offered* no resistance to the invaders⟩

**Synonyms** OFFER and PRESENT mean to put before another for acceptance. OFFER suggests that the thing may be accepted or refused ⟨*offered* more coffee to the guests⟩. PRESENT suggests that something is offered with the hope or expectation of its being accepted ⟨peddlers *presented* their goods for our inspection⟩ ⟨the principal *presented* the diplomas⟩.

**[2]offer** *n*
**1** an act of offering
**2** a price suggested by one prepared to buy : BID

**of·fer·ing** \'ȯf-ə-ring, 'ȯf-ring\ *n*
**1** the act of one who offers
**2** something offered
**3** a sacrifice offered as part of worship
**4** a contribution to the support of a church

**off·hand** \'ȯf-'hand\ *adv or adj*
without previous thought or preparation ⟨can't say *offhand* how many there are⟩ ⟨*offhand* remarks⟩

**of·fice** \'ȯf-əs\ *n*
**1** a special duty or post and especially one of authority in government ⟨run for *office*⟩
**2** a place where business is done or a service is supplied ⟨a doctor's *office*⟩

**of·fice·hold·er** \'ȯf-əs-ˌhōl-dər\ *n*
a person who holds public office

**of·fi·cer** \'ȯf-ə-sər\ *n*
**1** ▶ a person given the responsibility of enforcing the law ⟨police *officer*⟩
**2** a person who holds an office ⟨an *officer* of the company⟩
**3** a person who holds a commission in the armed forces ⟨an *officer* of the Navy⟩

**officer 1:** a police officer

**[1]of·fi·cial** \ə-ˈfish-əl\ *n*
OFFICER 2

**[2]official** *adj*
**1** of or relating to an office ⟨*official* duties⟩
**2** having authority to perform a duty ⟨the *official* referee⟩
**3** coming from or meeting the requirements of an authority ⟨an *official* American League baseball⟩
**4** proper for a person in office ⟨an *official* greeting⟩
**of·fi·cial·ly** *adv*

**of·fi·ci·ate** \ə-ˈfish-ē-ˌāt\ *vb* **of·fi·ci·at·ed**; **of·fi·ci·at·ing**
**1** to perform a ceremony or duty ⟨a bishop *officiated* at the wedding⟩
**2** to act as an officer **:** PRESIDE ⟨*officiated* at the annual meeting⟩

**off·ing** \ˈȯf-ing\ *n*
the near future or distance ⟨see trouble in the *offing*⟩

**off–line** \ˈȯf-ˌlīn\ *adj or adv*
not connected to or directly controlled by a computer system ⟨*off-line* data storage⟩ ⟨went *off-line* after sending the e-mail⟩

**[1]off·set** \ˈȯf-ˌset\ *n*
something that serves to make up for something else

**[2]offset** *vb* **offset**; **off·set·ting**
to make up for ⟨gains in one state *offset* losses in another⟩

**off·shoot** \ˈof-ˌshüt\ *n*
a branch of a main stem of a plant

**[1]off·shore** \ˈȯf-ˈshōr\ *adv*
from the shore **:** at a distance from the shore

**[2]off·shore** \ˈȯf-ˌshōr\ *adj*
**1** coming or moving away from the shore ⟨an *offshore* breeze⟩
**2** located off the shore ⟨*offshore* oil⟩

**[1]oil 4:** an oil by contemporary artist Jane Gifford

**offspring:** an adult guinea pig with two offspring

**off·spring** \ˈȯf-ˌspring\ *n, pl* **offspring** *also* **off·springs**
▶ the young of a person, animal, or plant

**off·stage** \ˈȯf-ˈstāj\ *adv or adj*
off or away from the stage

**off–the–rec·ord** \ˌȯf-t͟hə-ˈrek-ərd\ *adj*
given or made in confidence and not for publication ⟨the candidate's *off-the-record* remarks⟩

**oft** \ˈȯft\ *adv*
OFTEN

**of·ten** \ˈȯf-ən, -tən\ *adv*
many times

**of·ten·times** \ˈȯf-ən-ˌtīmz, ˈȯf-tən-\ *adv*
OFTEN

**ogle** \ˈō-gəl\ *vb* **ogled**; **ogling**
to look at (as a person) in a flirting way or with unusual attention or desire

**ogre** \ˈō-gər\ *n*
**1** an ugly giant of fairy tales and folklore who eats people
**2** a dreaded person or object

**oh** *or* **O** \ō, ˈō\ *interj*
**1** used to express an emotion (as surprise or pain)
**2** used in direct address ⟨*Oh*, children, stop that noise⟩

**[1]-oid** \ˌȯid\ *n suffix*
something resembling a specified object or having a specified quality

**[2]-oid** *adj suffix*
resembling **:** having the form or appearance of

**[1]oil** \ˈȯil\ *n*
**1** any of numerous greasy usually liquid substances from plant, animal, or mineral sources that do not dissolve in water and are used especially as lubricants, fuels, and food
**2** PETROLEUM
**3** artists' paints made of pigments and oil
**4** ◀ a painting in oils

**[2]oil** *vb*
to put oil on or in

**oil·cloth** \ˈȯil-ˌklȯth\ *n*
cloth treated with oil or paint so as to be waterproof and used for shelf and table coverings

**oily** \ˈȯi-lē\ *adj* **oil·i·er**; **oil·i·est**
**1** of, relating to, or containing oil
**2** covered or soaked with oil ⟨*oily* rags⟩
**oil·i·ness** *n*

**oint·ment** \ˈȯint-mənt\ *n*
a semisolid usually greasy medicine for use on the skin

**[1]OK** *or* **okay** \ō-ˈkā\ *adv or adj*
all right

**Word History** More than a hundred years ago Boston newspapers were full of abbreviations. Just about anything might be abbreviated. *R.T.B.S.* stood for "remains to be seen." *S.P.* stood for "small potatoes." *N.G.* stood for "no go." *A.R.* stood for "all right." Soon some phrases were spelled wrong on purpose and then abbreviated. *K.G.*, for "know go," was used instead of *N.G. O.W.*, "oll wright," was used instead of *A.R. O.K.*, "oll korrect," was used instead of *A.C.* The fad faded, but the one abbreviation *O.K.* caught on and is still widely used.

**[2]OK** *or* **okay** *n*
APPROVAL

**[3]OK** *or* **okay** *vb* **OK'd** *or* **okayed**; **OK'·ing** *or* **okay·ing**
APPROVE 2, AUTHORIZE

**oka·pi** \ō-ˈkä-pē\ *n*
▼ an animal of the African forests related to the giraffe

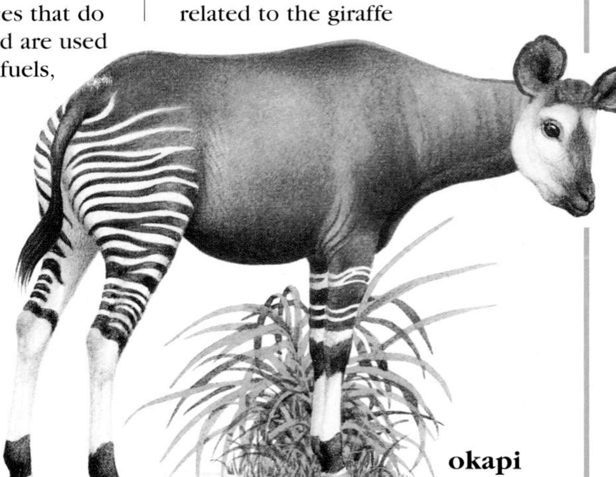

**okapi**

**okra** \'ō-krə\ *n*
▶ a plant related to the hollyhocks and grown for its edible green pods which are used in soups and stews

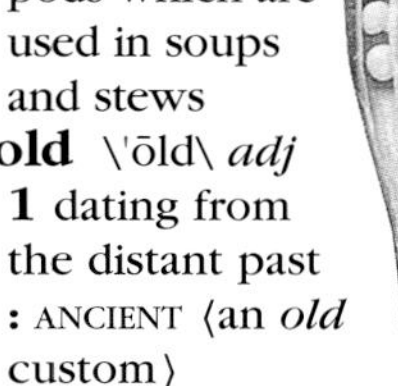

**okra:** okra pods

**¹old** \'ōld\ *adj*
**1** dating from the distant past : ANCIENT ⟨an *old* custom⟩
**2** having lasted or been such for a long time ⟨an *old* friend⟩ ⟨*old* friendships⟩
**3** having existed for a specified length of time ⟨a child three years *old*⟩
**4** having lived a long time ⟨*old* people⟩
**5** FORMER ⟨my *old* students⟩
**6** showing the effects of time or use ⟨wore an *old* coat⟩

**²old** *n*
old or earlier time ⟨in days of *old*⟩

**old·en** \'ōl-dən\ *adj*
of or relating to earlier days

**Old English** *n*
the language of the English people from the earliest documents in the seventh century to about 1100

**old–fash·ioned** \'ōld-'fash-ənd\ *adj*
**1** of, relating to, or like that of an earlier time
**2** holding fast to old ways : CONSERVATIVE

**Old French** *n*
the French language from the ninth to the thirteenth century

**Old Glory** *n*
the flag of the United States

**old maid** *n*
**1** an elderly unmarried woman
**2** a very neat fussy person
**3** a card game in which cards are matched in pairs and the player holding the extra queen at the end loses

**old·ster** \'ōld-stər\ *n*
an old person

**old–time** \,ōld-,tīm\ *adj*
¹OLD 1

**old–tim·er** \'ōld-'tī-mər\ *n*
**1** ¹VETERAN 1
**2** OLDSTER

**old–world** \'ōl-'dwərld\ *adj*
having old-fashioned charm

**Old World** *n*
the lands in the eastern hemisphere and especially Europe but not including Australia

**ol·fac·to·ry** \äl-'fak-tə-rē, ōl-\ *adj*
of or relating to smelling or the sense of smell

**ol·ive** \'äl-iv\ *n*
**1** ▼ an oily fruit that is eaten both ripe and unripe, is the source of an edible oil (**olive oil**), and grows on an evergreen tree with hard smooth shining wood (**olive wood**)
**2** a yellowish green

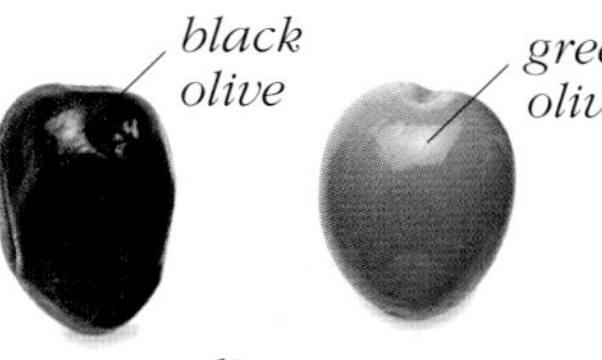


**olive 1**

**Olym·pic** \ə-'lim-pik, ō-\ *adj*
of or relating to the Olympic Games

**Olympic Games** *n pl*
a series of international athletic contests held as separate winter and summer events in a different country every four years

**om·e·lette** *or* **om·e·let** \'äm-ə-lət, 'äm-lət\ *n*
▶ eggs beaten with milk or water, cooked without stirring until firm, and folded in half often over a filling

**Word History** An Old French word that meant "the blade of a sword or knife" came from a Latin word meaning "a thin plate." An omelette, when folded over, looks something like a blade. That is why the French made a word meaning "omelette" from the earlier French word that meant "blade." English *omelette* came from the French word that means "omelette."

**omen** \'ō-mən\ *n*
a happening believed to be a sign or warning of a future event

**om·i·nous** \'äm-ə-nəs\ *adj*
being a sign of evil or trouble to come ⟨*ominous* clouds⟩
**om·i·nous·ly** *adv*
**om·i·nous·ness** *n*

**omis·sion** \ō-'mish-ən\ *n*
**1** something omitted
**2** the act of omitting : the state of being omitted

**omit** \ō-'mit\ *vb* **omit·ted**; **omit·ting**
**1** to leave out : fail to include ⟨*omit* a name from a list⟩
**2** to leave undone : NEGLECT ⟨they *omitted* to tell us how to do it⟩

**om·ni·bus** \'äm-ni-,bəs\ *n*
BUS

**om·nip·o·tent** \äm-'nip-ət-ənt\ *adj*
having power or authority without limit : ALMIGHTY

**¹on** \ȯn, än\ *prep*
**1** over and in contact with ⟨put the books *on* the table⟩
**2** AGAINST 3 ⟨shadows *on* the wall⟩
**3** near or connected with ⟨a town *on* the river⟩
**4** ¹TO 1 ⟨the first house *on* the left⟩
**5** sometime during ⟨*on* Monday⟩
**6** in the state or process of ⟨*on* fire⟩ ⟨*on* sale⟩
**7** ²ABOUT 3 ⟨a book *on* minerals⟩
**8** by means of ⟨talk *on* the phone⟩

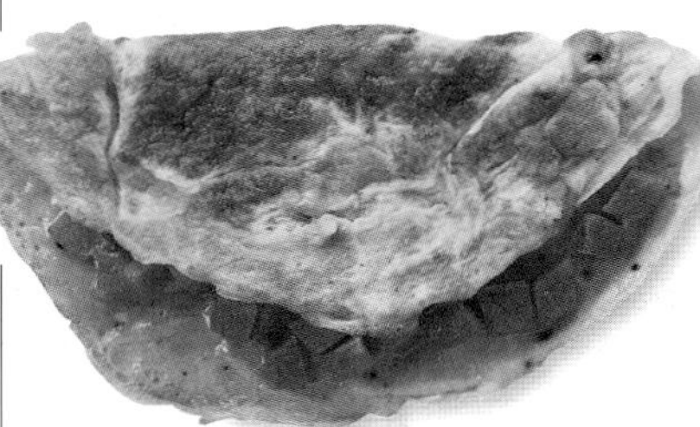

**omelette** with a cheese and ham filling

**²on** \'ȯn, 'än\ *adv*
**1** in or into contact with a surface ⟨put the kettle *on*⟩ ⟨has new shoes *on*⟩
**2** forward in time, space, or action ⟨went *on* home⟩ ⟨the argument went *on* for weeks⟩
**3** from one to another ⟨pass the word *on*⟩ ⟨and so *on*⟩
**4** into operation or a position allowing operation ⟨turn the light *on*⟩

**³on** \'ȯn, 'än\ *adj*
**1** being in operation ⟨the radio is *on*⟩
**2** placed so as to allow operation ⟨the switch is *on*⟩
**3** taking place ⟨the game is *on*⟩
**4** having been planned ⟨has nothing *on* for tonight⟩

**[1]once** \'wəns\ *adv*
**1** one time only ⟨it happened just *once*⟩
**2** at any one time **:** EVER ⟨if we hesitate *once*, all will be lost⟩
**3** at some time in the past **:** FORMERLY ⟨it was *once* done that way⟩

**[2]once** *n*
one single time ⟨just this *once*⟩
**at once**
**1** at the same time ⟨two people talking *at once*⟩
**2** IMMEDIATELY 2 ⟨leave *at once*⟩

**[3]once** *conj*
as soon as **:** WHEN ⟨*once* you've finished your homework, you may watch television⟩

**once–over** \'wən-,sō-vər\ *n*
a quick glance or examination

**on·com·ing** \'on-,kəm-ing, 'än-\ *adj*
coming nearer ⟨an *oncoming* car⟩

**[1]one** \'wən\ *adj*
**1** being a single unit or thing
**2** being a certain unit or thing ⟨early *one* morning⟩
**3** being the same in kind or quality ⟨members of *one* class⟩
**4** not specified ⟨at *one* time or another⟩

**[2]one** *n*
**1** the number denoting a single unit **:** 1
**2** the first in a set or series
**3** a single person or thing

**[3]one** *pron*
**1** a single member or individual ⟨*one* of your friends⟩
**2** any person ⟨*one* never knows⟩

**one another** *pron*
EACH OTHER

**one·self** \,wən-'self\ *pron*
one's own self ⟨one may feel proud of *oneself*⟩

**one–sid·ed** \'wən-'sīd-əd\ *adj*
**1** having or happening on one side only
**2** having one side more developed
**3** favoring one side ⟨a *one-sided* view of the case⟩

**one·time** \'wən-,tīm\ *adj*
FORMER

**one–way** \'wən-'wā\ *adj*
moving or allowing movement in one direction only

**on·go·ing** \'on-,gō-ing, 'än-\ *adj*
being in progress or movement

red onion
white onion
**onion**

**on·ion** \'ən-yən\ *n*
▲ the edible bulb of a plant related to the lilies that has a sharp odor and taste and is used as a vegetable and to season foods

**on–line** \'on-,līn, 'än-\ *adj or adv*
connected to, directly controlled by, or available through a computer system ⟨an *on-line* database⟩ ⟨working *on-line*⟩

**on·look·er** \'on-,lu̇k-ər, 'än-\ *n*
SPECTATOR

**[1]on·ly** \'ōn-lē\ *adj*
**1** best without doubt ⟨the *only* person for me⟩
**2** alone in or of a class or kind **:** SOLE ⟨the *only* survivor⟩

**[2]only** *adv*
**1** as a single fact or instance and nothing more or different ⟨worked *only* in the mornings⟩
**2** no one or nothing other than ⟨*only* you know⟩ ⟨*only* this will do⟩
**3** in the end ⟨it will *only* make you sick⟩
**4** as recently as ⟨*only* last week⟩

**[3]only** *conj*
except that ⟨I'd like to play, *only* I'm too tired⟩

**on·o·mato·poe·ia** \,än-ə-,mat-ə-'pē-ə\ *n*
the forming of a word (as "buzz" or "hiss") in imitation of a natural sound

**on·rush** \'on-,rəsh, 'än-\ *n*
a rushing forward

**on·set** \'on-,set, 'än-\ *n*
**1** [2]ATTACK 1
**2** BEGINNING

**on·slaught** \'än-,slot, 'on-\ *n*
a violent attack

**on·to** \,on-(,)tü, ,än-\ *prep*
to a position on or against ⟨leaped *onto* the horse⟩

**[1]on·ward** \'on-wərd, 'än-\ *adv*
toward or at a point lying ahead in space or time **:** FORWARD

**[2]onward** *adj*
directed or moving onward ⟨the *onward* march of time⟩

**oo·dles** \'üd-lz\ *n pl*
a great quantity

**[1]ooze** \'üz\ *n*
soft mud **:** SLIME

**[2]ooze** *vb* **oozed**; **ooz·ing**
to flow or leak out slowly

**opal** \'ō-pəl\ *n*
▼ a mineral with soft changeable colors that is used as a gem

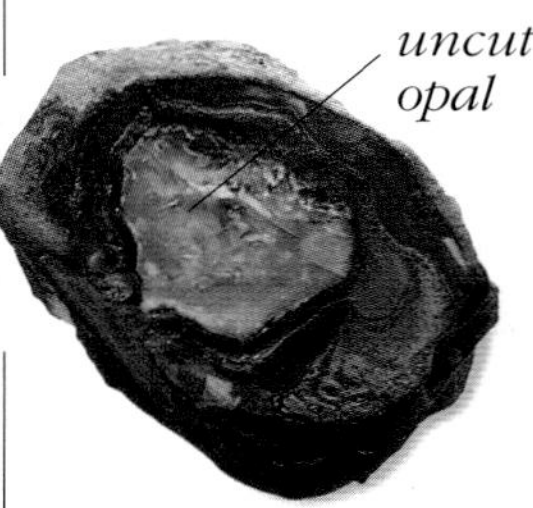


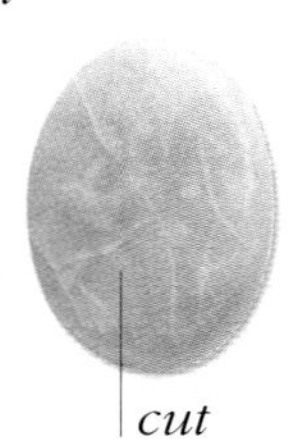


**opal**

**opaque** \ō-'pāk\ *adj*
**1** not letting light through **:** not transparent
**2** not reflecting light **:** DULL ⟨an *opaque* paint⟩

**[1]open** \'ō-pən\ *adj*
**1** not shut or blocked **:** not closed ⟨an *open* window⟩ ⟨*open* books⟩
**2** not enclosed or covered ⟨an *open* boat⟩ ⟨an *open* fire⟩
**3** not secret **:** PUBLIC ⟨an *open* dislike⟩
**4** to be used, entered, or taken part in by all ⟨an *open* golf tournament⟩ ⟨an *open* meeting⟩
**5** easy to enter, get through, or see ⟨*open* country⟩
**6** not drawn together **:** spread out ⟨an *open* flower⟩ ⟨*open* umbrellas⟩
**7** not decided or settled ⟨an *open* question⟩
**8** ready to consider appeals or ideas ⟨an *open* mind⟩
**open·ly** *adv*
**open·ness** *n*

**[2]open** *vb*
**1** to change or move from a shut condition ⟨*open* a book⟩ ⟨the door *opened*⟩
**2** to clear by or as if by removing something in the way ⟨*open* a road blocked with snow⟩
**3** to make or become ready for use ⟨*open* a store⟩ ⟨the office *opens* at eight⟩
**4** to have an opening ⟨the rooms *open* onto a hall⟩

**5** BEGIN 1, START ⟨*open* talks⟩ ⟨*open* fire on an enemy⟩
**open·er** \'ō-pə-nər, 'ōp-nər\ *n*

**[3]open** *n*
open space : OUTDOORS

**open–air** \,ō-pən-'aər, -'eər\ *adj*
OUTDOOR

**open–and–shut** \,ō-pən-ən-'shət\ *adj*
[1]PLAIN 3, OBVIOUS ⟨an *open-and-shut* case⟩

**open·heart·ed** \,ō-pən-'härt-əd\ *adj*
**1** FRANK
**2** GENEROUS 1

**open·ing** \'ōp-ə-ning, 'ōp-ning\ *n*
**1** an act of opening ⟨the *opening* of a new store⟩
**2** an open place : CLEARING
**3** BEGINNING ⟨the *opening* of the speech⟩
**4** OCCASION 1 ⟨waiting for an *opening* to tell the joke⟩
**5** a job opportunity ⟨an *opening* in the legal department⟩

**open letter** *n*
a letter (as one addressed to an official) for the public to see and printed in a newspaper or magazine

**open·work** \'ō-pən-,wərk\ *n*
something made or work done so as to show openings through the fabric or material

**op·era** \'äp-ə-rə, 'äp-rə\ *n*
a play in which the entire text is sung with orchestral accompaniment

**opera glasses** *n*
▼ small binoculars of low power for use in a theater

**opera glasses:**
a pair of 19th-century opera glasses

**op·er·ate** \'äp-ə-,rāt\ *vb*
**op·er·at·ed**; **op·er·at·ing**
**1** to work or cause to work in a proper way ⟨a machine *operating* smoothly⟩ ⟨learn to *operate* a car⟩
**2** to take effect ⟨a drug that *operates* quickly⟩
**3** MANAGE 1 ⟨*operate* a farm⟩ ⟨*operates* a business⟩
**4** to perform surgery : do an operation on (as a person)

**operating system** *n*
a program or series of programs that controls the operation of a computer and directs the processing of the user's programs (as by assigning storage space and controlling input and output functions)

**op·er·a·tion** \,äp-ə-'rā-shən\ *n*
**1** the act, process, method, or result of operating ⟨does the whole *operation* without thinking⟩ ⟨the *operation* of a drug⟩
**2** the quality or state of being able to work ⟨the factory is now in *operation*⟩
**3** ▲ a certain piece or kind of surgery ⟨an *operation* for appendicitis⟩
**4** a process (as addition or multiplication) of getting one mathematical expression from others according to a rule
**5** the process of putting military or naval forces into action ⟨naval *operations*⟩
**6** a single step performed by a computer in carrying out a program

**op·er·a·tion·al** \,äp-ə-'rā-shən-l\ *adj*
**1** of or relating to operation or an operation
**2** ready for operation ⟨the new plant will be *operational* next week⟩

**op·er·a·tor** \'äp-ə-,rāt-ər\ *n*
**1** a person who operates something (as a business)
**2** a person in charge of a telephone switchboard ⟨dial the *operator*⟩

**op·er·et·ta** \,äp-ə-'ret-ə\ *n*
a light play set to music with speaking, singing, and dancing scenes

**operation 3**
Operations are undertaken when a medical team needs to cut into a patient's body in order to treat a disease or an injury. An operation may also be performed to replace organs such as the liver or heart, or to deliver a baby. Operations are generally performed in a hospital operating room by surgeons and nurses. An anesthetist controls the supply of anesthetic to the patient to produce loss of feeling in the area of surgery or to make the patient unconscious throughout the procedure.

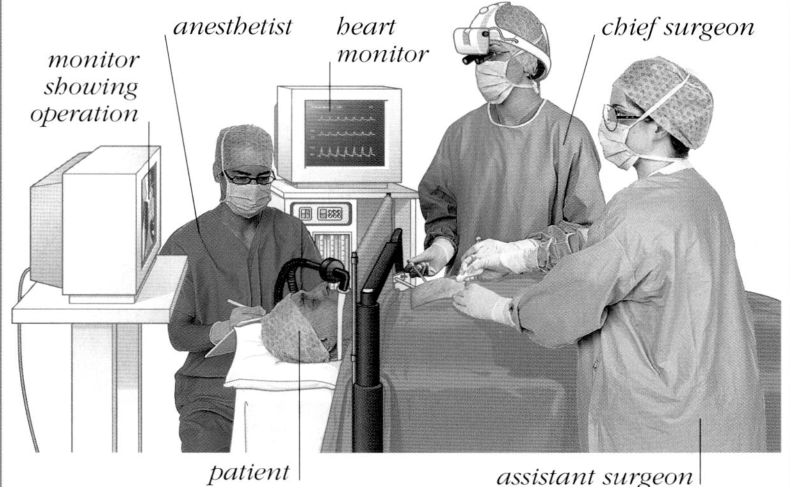


**surgeons performing a heart operation on a patient**

**opin·ion** \ə-ˈpin-yən\ *n*
**1** a belief based on experience and on seeing certain facts but not amounting to sure knowledge ⟨in my *opinion*⟩
**2** a judgment about a person or thing ⟨a high *opinion* of themselves⟩
**3** a statement by an expert after careful study ⟨get an *opinion* from a lawyer⟩

**Synonyms** OPINION and BELIEF mean a judgment that one thinks is true. OPINION suggests that the judgment is not yet final or certain but is founded on some facts ⟨I soon changed my *opinion* of the plan⟩. BELIEF stresses that the judgment is certain and firm in one's own mind but says nothing about the amount or kind of evidence ⟨it's my *belief* that war is sure to come⟩.

**opin·ion·at·ed** \ə-ˈpin-yə-ˌnāt-əd\ *adj*
holding to one's opinions too strongly

**opi·um** \ˈō-pē-əm\ *n*
a bitter brownish narcotic drug that is the dried juice of one kind of poppy

**opos·sum** \ə-ˈpäs-əm\ *n*
▶ a common American animal related to the kangaroos that lives mostly in trees and is active at night

**opossum**

**op·po·nent** \ə-ˈpō-nənt\ *n*
▶ a person or thing that opposes another

**op·por·tu·ni·ty** \ˌäp-ər-ˈtü-nət-ē, -ˈtyü-\ *n, pl* **op·por·tu·ni·ties**
**1** a favorable combination of circumstances, time, and place ⟨write when you have an *opportunity*⟩
**2** a chance to better oneself ⟨felt the new job was a real *opportunity*⟩

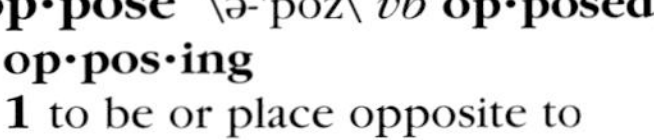

**op·pose** \ə-ˈpōz\ *vb* **op·posed**; **op·pos·ing**
**1** to be or place opposite to something ⟨*oppose* lies with the truth⟩ ⟨good *opposes* evil⟩
**2** to offer resistance to **:** stand against **:** RESIST ⟨*oppose* a plan⟩

[1]**op·po·site** \ˈäp-ə-zət\ *adj*
**1** being at the other end, side, or corner ⟨live on *opposite* sides of the street⟩
**2** being in a position to oppose or cancel out ⟨the *opposite* side of the question⟩
**3** being as different as possible **:** CONTRARY ⟨came to *opposite* conclusions⟩

[2]**opposite** *n*
either of two persons or things that are as different as possible

[3]**opposite** *adv*
on the opposite side

[4]**opposite** *prep*
across from and usually facing or on the same level with ⟨the park *opposite* our house⟩

**op·po·si·tion** \ˌäp-ə-ˈzish-ən\ *n*
**1** the state of being opposite
**2** the action of resisting ⟨offered *opposition* to the plan⟩
**3** a group of persons that oppose someone or something ⟨defeated our *opposition* easily⟩
**4** *often cap* a political party opposed to the party in power

**opponents** practicing combat and self-defense

**op·press** \ə-ˈpres\ *vb*
**1** to cause to feel burdened in spirit ⟨*oppressed* by grief⟩
**2** to control or rule in a harsh or cruel way ⟨a country *oppressed* by a dictator⟩

**op·pres·sion** \ə-ˈpresh-ən\ *n*
**1** cruel or unjust use of power or authority
**2** a feeling of low spirits

**op·pres·sive** \ə-ˈpres-iv\ *adj*
**1** cruel or harsh without just cause ⟨*oppressive* taxes⟩
**2** causing a feeling of oppression ⟨*oppressive* heat⟩
**op·pres·sive·ly** *adv*

**op·tic** \ˈäp-tik\ *adj*
of or relating to seeing or the eye ⟨the *optic* nerve⟩

**op·ti·cal** \ˈäp-ti-kəl\ *adj*
**1** of or relating to the science of optics
**2** of or relating to seeing **:** VISUAL
**3** involving the use of devices that are sensitive to light to get information for a computer ⟨an *optical* scanner⟩

**optical fiber** *n*
a single fiber used in fiber optics

**optical illusion** *n*
ILLUSION 1

**op·ti·cian** \äp-ˈtish-ən\ *n*
a person who prepares eyeglass lenses and sells glasses

**op·tics** \ˈäp-tiks\ *n*
a science that deals with the nature and properties of light and the changes that it undergoes and produces

**op·ti·mism** \ˈäp-tə-ˌmiz-əm\ *n*
a habit of expecting things to turn out for the best

**op·ti·mist** \ˈäp-tə-məst\ *n*
an optimistic person

**op·ti·mis·tic** \ˌäp-tə-ˈmis-tik\ *adj*
showing optimism **:** expecting everything to come out all right **:** HOPEFUL ⟨we are *optimistic* about the progress of the peace talks⟩

**op·ti·mum** \ˈäp-tə-məm\ *adj*
most desirable or satisfactory ⟨under *optimum* conditions⟩

**op·tion** \ˈäp-shən\ *n*
**1** the power or right to choose ⟨have an *option* between milk or juice⟩
**2** a right to buy or sell something at a specified price during a

**orangutan**

specified period ⟨took an *option* on the house⟩

**op·tion·al** \'äp-shən-l\ *adj*
left to one's choice : not required

**op·tom·e·trist** \äp-'täm-ə-trəst\ *n*
a person who prescribes glasses or exercise to improve the eyesight

**op·u·lent** \'äp-yə-lənt\ *adj*
having or showing much wealth ⟨*opulent* homes⟩

**or** \ər, ȯr\ *conj*
used between words or phrases that are choices ⟨juice *or* milk⟩ ⟨pay *or* get out⟩

**¹-or** \ər\ *n suffix*
one that does a specified thing ⟨act*or*⟩ ⟨elevat*or*⟩

**²-or** *n suffix*
condition : activity ⟨demean*or*⟩

**or·a·cle** \'ȯr-ə-kəl\ *n*
**1** a person (as a priestess in ancient Greece) through whom a god is believed to speak
**2** the place where a god speaks through an oracle
**3** an answer given by an oracle

**orac·u·lar** \ȯ-'rak-yə-lər\ *adj*
of, relating to, or serving as an oracle

**oral** \'ōr-əl\ *adj*
**1** ²SPOKEN 1 ⟨an *oral* agreement⟩
**2** of, relating to, given by, or near the mouth ⟨medicine for *oral* use⟩
**oral·ly** *adv*

**or·ange** \'ȯr-inj\ *n*
**1** a sweet juicy fruit with a reddish yellow rind that grows on an evergreen citrus tree with shining leaves and fragrant white flowers
**2** a color between red and yellow

**or·ange·ade** \,ȯr-in-'jād\ *n*
a drink made of orange juice, sugar, and water

**orang·utan** *or* **orang·ou·tan** \ə-'rang-ə-,tang, -,tan\ *n*
◀ a large ape of Borneo and Sumatra that eats plants, lives in trees, and has very long arms and hairless face, feet, and hands

**Word History** Orangutans are found on islands off the southeast coast of Asia. They live among the trees, and — like most apes — they look a bit like people. The people of the islands gave these apes a name that means "man of the forest." The English word *orangutan* comes from the name the apes were given in the language of the islands where they live.

**ora·tion** \ə-'rā-shən\ *n*
an important speech given on a special occasion

**or·a·tor** \'ȯr-ət-ər\ *n*
a public speaker noted for skill and power in speaking

**or·a·tor·i·cal** \,ȯr-ə-'tȯr-i-kəl\ *adj*
of, relating to, or like an orator or oratory
**or·a·tor·i·cal·ly** *adv*

**or·a·to·ry** \'ȯr-ə-,tōr-ē\ *n*
**1** the art of an orator
**2** the style of language used in an oration

**orb** \'ȯrb\ *n*
something in the shape of a ball (as a planet or the eye)

**¹or·bit** \'ȯr-bət\
the path taken by one body circling around another body ⟨the *orbit* of the earth around the sun⟩

**²orbit** *vb*
**1** to move in an orbit around : CIRCLE ⟨the moon *orbits* the earth⟩
**2** to send up so as to move in an orbit ⟨*orbit* a man-made satellite around the earth⟩

**or·chard** \'ȯr-chərd\ *n*
**1** a place where fruit trees are grown
**2** the trees in an orchard

**or·ches·tra** \'ȯr-kə-strə\ *n*
**1** a group of musicians who perform instrumental music using mostly stringed instruments
**2** the front part of the main floor in a theater

**Word History** In ancient Greek plays the chorus danced and sang in a space in front of the stage. The Greek name for this space came from the Greek word that meant "to dance." The English word *orchestra* came from the Greek word for the space in front of a stage. At first the English word was used to refer to such a space but is now used to mean "the front part of the main floor." In today's theaters a group of musicians often sits in the space in front of the stage. Such a group, too, came to be called an *orchestra*.

**or·ches·tral** \ȯr-'kes-trəl\ *adj*
of, relating to, or written for an orchestra

**or·chid** \'ȯr-kəd\ *n*
▼ any of a large group of plants with usually showy flowers with three petals of which the middle petal is enlarged into a lip and differs from the others in shape and color

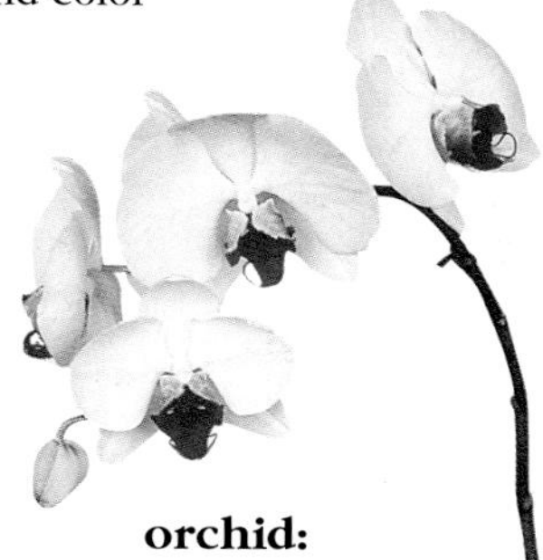

**orchid:**
a moth orchid

**or·dain** \ȯr-'dān\ *vb*
**1** to make a person a Christian minister or priest by a special ceremony
**2** ²DECREE ⟨it was *ordained* by law⟩
**3** DESTINE 1, FATE ⟨we seemed *ordained* to fail⟩

**or·deal** \ȯr-ˈdēl\ *n*
a severe test or experience

**¹or·der** \ˈȯrd-ər\ *vb*
**1** to put into a particular grouping or sequence **:** ARRANGE ⟨dictionary entries are *ordered* alphabetically⟩
**2** to give an order to or for ⟨*order* troops into battle⟩ ⟨*order* a hamburger and a milkshake⟩

**²order** *n*
**1** a group of people united (as by living under the same religious rules or by loyalty to common needs or duties) ⟨an *order* of monks⟩
**2 orders** *pl* the office of a person in the Christian ministry ⟨holy *orders*⟩
**3** a group of related plants or animals that ranks above the family and below the class in scientific classification ⟨bats form an *order* of mammals in the animal kingdom⟩
**4** the arrangement of objects or events in space or time ⟨the *order* of the seasons⟩ ⟨a list of names in alphabetical *order*⟩
**5** the way something should be ⟨kept the room in *order*⟩
**6** the state of things when law or authority is obeyed ⟨restored *order* after the riot⟩
**7** a certain rule or regulation **:** COMMAND ⟨an executive *order*⟩
**8** good working condition ⟨the telephone is out of *order*⟩
**9** a written direction to pay a sum of money
**10** a statement of what one wants to buy ⟨place an *order* for groceries⟩
**11** goods or items bought or sold
**in order to** for the purpose of

**¹or·der·ly** \ˈȯrd-ər-lē\ *adj*
**1** being in good order **:** NEAT, TIDY ⟨an *orderly* room⟩
**2** obeying orders or rules **:** well-behaved ⟨an *orderly* meeting⟩ ⟨*orderly* children⟩
**or·der·li·ness** *n*

**²orderly** *n, pl* **or·der·lies**
**1** a soldier who works for an officer especially to carry messages
**2** a person who does cleaning and general work in a hospital

**or·di·nal** \ˈȯrd-n-əl\ *n*
ORDINAL NUMBER

**ordinal number** *n*
a number that is used to show the place (as first, fifth, twenty-second) taken by an element in a series

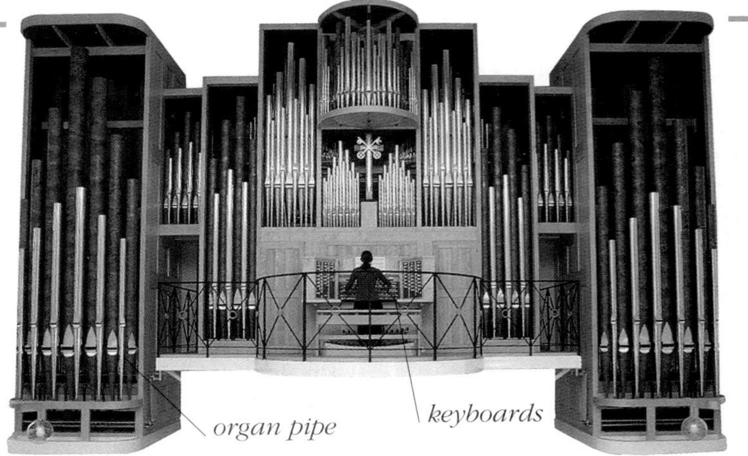

**organ 1:** a large church organ

**or·di·nance** \ˈȯrd-n-əns\ *n*
a law or regulation especially of a city or town

**or·di·nar·i·ly** \ˌȯrd-n-ˈer-ə-lē\ *adv*
in the usual course of events **:** USUALLY ⟨*ordinarily* goes to bed at nine o'clock⟩

**¹or·di·nary** \ˈȯrd-n-ˌer-ē\ *n*
the conditions or events that are usual or normal ⟨nothing out of the *ordinary* about that⟩

**²ordinary** *adj*
**1** to be expected **:** NORMAL, USUAL ⟨an *ordinary* day⟩
**2** neither good nor bad **:** AVERAGE ⟨an *ordinary* student⟩ ⟨just *ordinary* people⟩
**3** not very good **:** MEDIOCRE ⟨a very *ordinary* speech⟩ **synonyms** see COMMON
**or·di·nar·i·ness** *n*

**ord·nance** \ˈȯrd-nəns\ *n*
**1** military supplies (as guns, ammunition, trucks, and tanks)
**2** ARTILLERY 1

**ore** \ˈōr\ *n*
▼ a mineral mined to obtain a substance (as gold) that it contains

**ore:** iron ore

**or·gan** \ˈȯr-gən\ *n*
**1** ▲ a musical instrument played by means of one or more keyboards and having pipes sounded by compressed air
**2** a part of a person, plant, or animal that is specialized to do a particular task ⟨the eye is an *organ* of sight⟩
**3** a way of getting something done ⟨courts are *organs* of government⟩

**or·gan·ic** \ȯr-ˈgan-ik\ *adj*
**1** relating to an organ of the body
**2** having parts that fit or work together ⟨an *organic* whole⟩
**3** relating to or obtained from living things
**4** relating to carbon compounds **:** containing carbon

**or·gan·ism** \ˈȯr-gə-ˌniz-əm\ *n*
**1** something having many related parts and functioning as a whole
**2** a living being made up of organs and able to carry on the activities of life **:** a living person, animal, or plant

**or·gan·ist** \ˈȯr-gə-nist\ *n*
a person who plays an organ

**or·ga·ni·za·tion** \ˌȯr-gə-nə-ˈzā-shən\ *n*
**1** the act or process of organizing ⟨the *organization* of a new club⟩
**2** the state or way of being organized ⟨study the *organization* of city government⟩
**3** a group of persons united for a common purpose ⟨a business *organization*⟩

**or·ga·nize** \ˈȯr-gə-ˌnīz\ *vb*
**or·ga·nized; or·ga·niz·ing**
**1** to make separate parts into one united whole
**2** to put in a certain order ⟨*organized* the documents by date⟩
**3** to arrange by effort and planning ⟨*organized* a field trip⟩
**or·ga·niz·er** *n*

**ori·ent** \'ōr-ē-,ent\ *vb*
**1** to set or arrange in a position especially so as to be lined up with certain points of the compass ⟨*oriented* the house to face east⟩
**2** to acquaint with an existing situation or environment ⟨*orient* new students⟩
**ori·en·ta·tion** \,ōr-ē-ən-'tā-shən\ *n*

**Ori·en·tal** \,ōr-ē-'ent-l\ *adj*
**1** [1]ASIAN
**2** ▼ of or relating to the region that includes the countries of eastern Asia (as China, Japan, Vietnam, and Korea)

**Oriental 2:** a traditional roof tile ornament from eastern Asia

**origami** \,ȯr-ə-'gäm-ē\ *n*
▼ the art of folding paper into three-dimensional figures or designs without cutting the paper or using glue

**or·i·gin** \'ȯr-ə-jən\ *n*
**1** a person's ancestry ⟨people of humble *origin*⟩

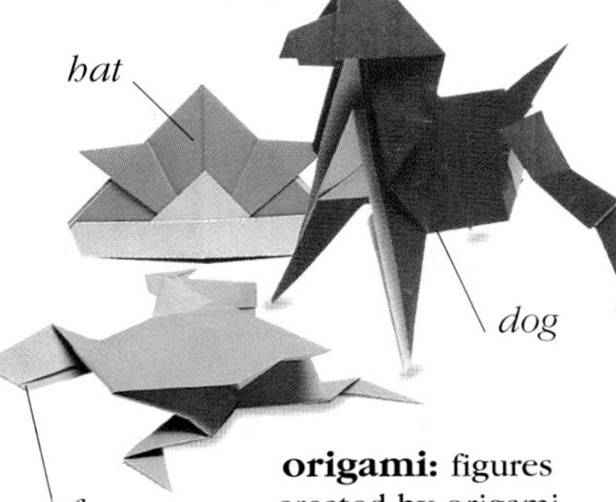


**origami:** figures created by origami

**2** the rise, beginning, or coming from a source ⟨the story has its *origin* in fact⟩
**3** basic source or cause ⟨the *origin* of their quarrel is not known⟩

[1]**orig·i·nal** \ə-'rij-ən-l\ *n*
something from which a copy or translation can be made ⟨the paintings are *originals*⟩ ⟨read the Russian novel in the *original*⟩

[2]**original** *adj*
**1** of or relating to the origin or beginning : FIRST ⟨the *original* part of an old house⟩
**2** not copied from anything else : not translated : NEW ⟨an *original* painting⟩ ⟨an *original* idea⟩
**3** able to think up new things : INVENTIVE ⟨an *original* mind⟩
**orig·i·nal·ly** *adv*

**orig·i·nal·i·ty** \ə-,rij-ə-'nal-ət-ē\ *n*
**1** the quality or state of being original ⟨the *originality* of an idea⟩
**2** the power or ability to think, act, or do something in ways that are new ⟨an artist of great *originality*⟩

**orig·i·nate** \ə-'rij-ə-,nāt\ *vb*
**orig·i·nat·ed**; **orig·i·nat·ing**
**1** to bring into being : cause to be : INVENT, INITIATE ⟨*originate* a new game⟩
**2** to come into being ⟨the custom *originated* in ancient times⟩
**orig·i·na·tor** \-,nāt-ər\ *n*

**ori·ole** \'ōr-ē-,ōl\ *n*
**1** an Old World yellow and black bird related to the crow
**2** ▶ an American songbird related to the blackbird and bobolink that has a bright orange and black male

[1]**or·na·ment** \'ȯr-nə-mənt\ *n*
**1** something that adds beauty : DECORATION ⟨a Christmas-tree *ornament*⟩
**2** the act of beautifying

[2]**or·na·ment** \'ȯr-nə-,ment\ *vb*
DECORATE 1

[1]**or·na·men·tal** \,ȯr-nə-'ment-l\ *adj*
serving to ornament : DECORATIVE

[2]**ornamental** *n*
a plant grown for its beauty

**or·na·men·ta·tion** \,ȯr-nə-mən-'tā-shən\ *n*
**1** the act or process of ornamenting : the state of being ornamented
**2** something that ornaments

**or·nate** \ȯr-'nāt\ *adj*
decorated in a fancy way ⟨wore a traditional costume with an *ornate* headdress⟩
**or·nate·ly** *adv*
**or·nate·ness** *n*

**or·nery** \'ȯr-nə-rē\ *adj* **or·neri·er**; **or·neri·est**
having a bad disposition

[1]**or·phan** \'ȯr-fən\ *n*
a child whose parents are dead

[2]**orphan** *vb*
to cause to become an orphan ⟨*orphaned* as a baby⟩

**or·phan·age** \'ȯr-fə-nij\ *n*
an institution for the care of orphans

**or·tho·don·tist** \,ȯr-thə-'dänt-əst\ *n*
a dentist who adjusts badly placed or irregular teeth

**or·tho·dox** \'ȯr-thə-,däks\ *adj*
**1** holding established beliefs especially in religion ⟨an *orthodox* Christian⟩
**2** approved as measuring up to some standard : CONVENTIONAL ⟨take an *orthodox* approach to a problem⟩

[1]**-ory** \,ōr-ē, ə-rē\ *n suffix, pl* **-ories**
place of or for ⟨observat*ory*⟩

[2]**-ory** *adj suffix*
of, relating to, or associated with ⟨sens*ory*⟩

**oriole 2:** a Bullock's \'bu̇l-əks\ oriole

**os·cil·late** \'äs-ə-,lāt\ *vb*
**os·cil·lat·ed**; **os·cil·lat·ing**
to swing back and forth like a pendulum

**os·mo·sis** \äs-'mō-səs, äz-\ *n*
a passing of material and especially water through a membrane (as of a living cell) that will not allow all kinds of molecules to pass

**os·prey** \'äs-prē\ *n, pl* **ospreys**
▶ a large hawk that feeds chiefly on fish

osprey catching a fish

**os·ten·si·ble** \ä-'sten-sə-bəl\ *adj*
shown in an outward way : APPARENT ⟨the *ostensible* reason⟩
**os·ten·si·bly** \-blē\ *adv*

**os·ten·ta·tious** \,äs-tən-'tā-shəs\ *adj*
having or fond of unnecessary show

**os·tra·cize** \'äs-trə-,sīz\ *vb* **os·tra·cized**; **os·tra·ciz·ing**
to shut out of a group by the agreement of all ⟨was *ostracized* by my friends⟩

**os·trich** \'äs-trich\ *n*
▼ a very large bird of Africa and the Arabian Peninsula that often weighs 300 pounds and runs very swiftly but cannot fly

ostrich

**[1]oth·er** \'ə<u>th</u>-ər\ *adj*
**1** being the one (as of two or more) left ⟨broke my *other* arm⟩
**2** [1]SECOND 1 ⟨every *other* page⟩
**3** [1]EXTRA, ADDITIONAL ⟨some *other* guests are coming⟩

**[2]other** *n*
a remaining or different one ⟨lift one foot and then the *other*⟩ ⟨the *others* will follow us later⟩

**[3]other** *pron*
another thing ⟨there's always something or *other* going on⟩

**oth·er·wise** \'ə<u>th</u>-ər-,wīz\ *adv*
**1** in another way ⟨could not do *otherwise*⟩
**2** in different circumstances ⟨*otherwise* they might have won⟩
**3** in other ways ⟨an *otherwise* busy street⟩

**ot·ter** \'ät-ər\ *n*
▶ a web-footed animal related to the minks that feeds on fish

otter

**ouch** \'aůch\ *interj*
used especially to express sudden pain

**ought** \'ȯt\ *helping verb*
**1** used to show duty ⟨you *ought* to obey your parents⟩
**2** used to show what it would be wise to do ⟨you *ought* to take care of that cough⟩
**3** used to show what is naturally expected ⟨they *ought* to be here by now⟩
**4** used to show what is correct ⟨you *ought* to get nine for the answer⟩

**oughtn't** \'ȯt-nt\
ought not

**ounce** \'aůns\ *n*
**1** a unit of weight equal to $1/16$ pound (about 28 grams)
**2** a unit of liquid capacity equal to $1/16$ pint (about 30 milliliters)

**our** \aůr, är\ *adj*
of or relating to us : done, given, or felt by us ⟨*our* house⟩ ⟨*our* fault⟩

**ours** \aůrz, 'aůrz, ärz\ *pron*
that which belongs to us ⟨this classroom is *ours*⟩ ⟨these desks are *ours*⟩

**our·selves** \aůr-'selvz, är-\ *pron*
our own selves ⟨we amused *ourselves*⟩ ⟨we did it *ourselves*⟩

**-ous** \əs\ *adj suffix*
full of : having : resembling ⟨clamor*ous*⟩ ⟨poison*ous*⟩

**oust** \'aůst\ *vb*
to force or drive out (as from office or from possession of something)

**oust·er** \'aůs-tər\ *n*
the act or an instance of ousting or being ousted

**[1]out** \'aůt\ *adv*
**1** in a direction away from the inside, center, or surface ⟨looked *out* at the snow⟩
**2** away from home, business, or the usual or proper place ⟨went *out* for lunch⟩
**3** beyond control or possession ⟨let a secret *out*⟩
**4** so as to be used up, completed, or discontinued ⟨food supply ran *out*⟩ ⟨filled the form *out*⟩ ⟨blew the candle *out*⟩
**5** in or into the open ⟨the sun came *out*⟩
**6** ALOUD ⟨cried *out* in pain⟩
**7** so as to put out or be put out in baseball ⟨threw the runner *out*⟩

**[2]out** *prep*
**1** outward through ⟨looked *out* the window⟩
**2** outward on or along ⟨drove *out* the road by the river⟩

**[3]out** *adj*
**1** located outside or at a distance
**2** no longer in power or use ⟨the *out* party⟩ ⟨lights are *out*⟩
**3** not confined : not concealed or covered ⟨the secret is *out*⟩ ⟨the sun is *out*⟩
**4** [1]ABSENT 1 ⟨a basket with its bottom *out*⟩ ⟨the barber is *out* today⟩
**5** being no longer at bat and not successful in reaching base
**6** no longer in fashion

**[4]out** *n*
PUTOUT

**out-** *prefix*
in a manner that goes beyond ⟨*out*number⟩ ⟨*out*run⟩

**out–and–out** \ˌau̇t-n-ˌau̇t\ *adj* THOROUGH 1 ⟨an *out-and-out* crook⟩

**out·board motor** \ˌau̇t-ˌbōrd-\ *n* ► a small gasoline engine with an attached propeller that can be fastened to the back end of a small boat

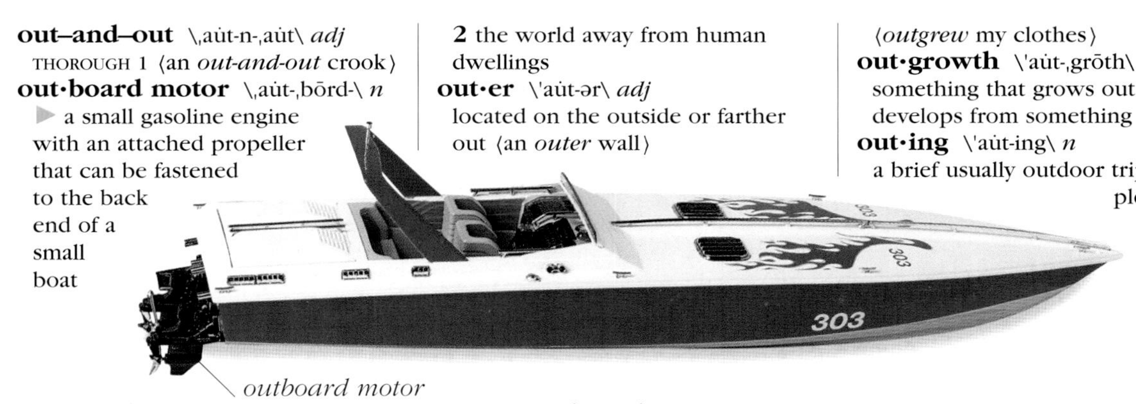

outboard motor

**outboard motor** on a speedboat

**out·break** \ˈau̇t-ˌbrāk\ *n* something (as an epidemic of measles) that breaks out

**out·build·ing** \ˈau̇t-ˌbil-diŋ\ *n* a building (as a shed or stable) separate from a main building

**out·burst** \ˈau̇t-ˌbərst\ *n* **1** a sudden violent expression of strong feeling **2** a sudden increase of activity or growth

[1]**out·cast** \ˈau̇t-ˌkast\ *adj* rejected or cast out

[2]**outcast** *n* a person who is cast out by society

**out·class** \au̇t-ˈklas\ *vb* EXCEL, SURPASS

**out·come** \ˈau̇t-ˌkəm\ *n* [2]RESULT 1

**out·cry** \ˈau̇t-ˌkrī\ *n, pl* **out·cries** **1** a loud and excited cry **2** a strong protest ⟨raised an *outcry* against the new rules⟩

**out·dat·ed** \au̇t-ˈdāt-əd\ *adj* OBSOLETE, OUTMODED ⟨*outdated* methods of farming⟩

**out·dis·tance** \au̇t-ˈdis-təns\ *vb* **out·dis·tanced**; **out·dis·tanc·ing** to go far ahead of (as in a race)

**out·do** \au̇t-ˈdü\ *vb* **out·did** \-ˈdid\; **out·done** \-ˈdən\; **out·do·ing** \-ˈdü-iŋ\; **out·does** \-ˈdəz\ to do better than : SURPASS

**out·door** \ˌau̇t-ˌdōr\ *adj* **1** of or relating to the outdoors ⟨an *outdoor* person⟩ **2** used, being, or done outdoors ⟨*outdoor* sports⟩

[1]**out·doors** \au̇t-ˈdōrz\ *adv* outside a building : in or into the open air ⟨play *outdoors*⟩

[2]**outdoors** *n* **1** the open air **2** the world away from human dwellings

**out·er** \ˈau̇t-ər\ *adj* located on the outside or farther out ⟨an *outer* wall⟩

**out·er·most** \ˈau̇t-ər-ˌmōst\ *adj* farthest out

**outer space** *n* the region beyond earth's atmosphere and especially beyond the solar system

**out·field** \ˈau̇t-ˌfēld\ *n* the part of a baseball field beyond the infield and between the foul lines

**out·field·er** \ˈau̇t-ˌfēl-dər\ *n* a baseball player who plays in the outfield

[1]**out·fit** \ˈau̇t-ˌfit\ *n* **1** the equipment or clothing for a special use ⟨a camping *outfit*⟩ ⟨a sports *outfit*⟩ **2** a group of persons working together or associated in the same activity ⟨soldiers from the same *outfit*⟩

[2]**outfit** *vb* **out·fit·ted**; **out·fit·ting** to supply with an outfit : EQUIP ⟨*outfit* children for school⟩ — **out·fit·ter** *n*

**out·go** \ˈau̇t-ˌgō\ *n, pl* **outgoes** EXPENDITURE 2 ⟨income must be greater than *outgo*⟩

**out·go·ing** \ˈau̇t-ˌgō-iŋ\ *adj* **1** going out ⟨an *outgoing* ship⟩ **2** retiring from a place or position ⟨the *outgoing* president⟩ **3** FRIENDLY 1 ⟨an *outgoing* person⟩

**out·grow** \au̇t-ˈgrō\ *vb* **out·grew** \-ˈgrü\; **out·grown** \-ˈgrōn\; **out·grow·ing** **1** to grow faster than ⟨one plant *outgrew* all the others⟩ **2** ► to grow too large for ⟨*outgrew* my clothes⟩

**out·growth** \ˈau̇t-ˌgrōth\ *n* something that grows out of or develops from something else

**out·ing** \ˈau̇t-iŋ\ *n* a brief usually outdoor trip for pleasure ⟨an *outing* to the beach⟩

**out·land·ish** \au̇t-ˈlan-dish\ *adj* very strange or unusual : BIZARRE ⟨*outlandish* behavior⟩

**out·last** \au̇t-ˈlast\ *vb* to last longer than

[1]**out·law** \ˈau̇t-ˌlȯ\ *n* a lawless person or one who is running away from the law

[2]**outlaw** *vb* to make illegal ⟨dueling was *outlawed*⟩

**out·lay** \ˈau̇t-ˌlā\ *n* EXPENDITURE

**out·let** \ˈau̇t-ˌlet\ *n* **1** a place or opening for letting something out ⟨a lake with several *outlets*⟩ **2** a way of releasing or satisfying a feeling or impulse ⟨needed an *outlet* for my anger⟩ **3** a device (as in a wall) into which the prongs of an electrical plug are inserted for making connection with an electrical circuit

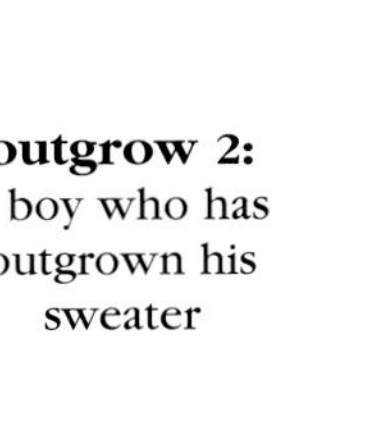

**outgrow 2:** a boy who has outgrown his sweater

A B C D E F G H I J K L M N O P Q R S T U V W X Y Z

**[1]out·line** \'au̇t-ˌlīn\ *n*
**1** a line that traces or forms the outer limits of an object or figure and shows its shape
**2** ▼ a drawing or picture giving only the outlines of a thing **:** this method of drawing
**3** a short treatment of a subject **:** SUMMARY ⟨an *outline* of a composition⟩

**[1]outline 2:** the sketched outline of a man's head

**[2]outline** *vb* **out·lined**; **out·lin·ing**
to make or prepare an outline of

**out·live** \au̇t-'liv\ *vb* **out·lived**; **out·liv·ing**
to live longer than **:** OUTLAST ⟨a rule that has *outlived* its usefulness⟩

**out·look** \'au̇t-ˌlu̇k\ *n*
**1** a view from a certain place ⟨the *outlook* through a window⟩
**2** a way of thinking about or looking at things ⟨a person with a cheerful *outlook*⟩
**3** conditions that seem to lie ahead ⟨the *outlook* for business⟩

**out·ly·ing** \'au̇t-ˌlī-iŋ\ *adj*
being far from a central point **:** REMOTE

**out·mod·ed** \au̇t-'mōd-əd\ *adj*
no longer in style or in use ⟨an *outmoded* dress⟩ ⟨*outmoded* equipment⟩

**out·num·ber** \au̇t-'nəm-bər\ *vb*
to be more than in number

**out of** *prep*
**1** from the inside to the outside of **:** not in ⟨I walked *out of* the room⟩ ⟨they are *out of* town⟩
**2** beyond the limits of ⟨the bird flew *out of* sight⟩ ⟨the patient is *out of* danger⟩
**3** BECAUSE OF ⟨they obeyed *out of* fear⟩
**4** in a group of ⟨I got only one answer right *out of* five⟩
**5** [1]WITHOUT 2 ⟨the store is *out of* bread⟩
**6** FROM 3 ⟨made a table *out of* some boxes and the legs of a chair⟩

**out–of–bounds** \ˌau̇t-əv-'bau̇ndz\ *adv or adj*
outside the limits of the playing field

**out–of–date** \ˌau̇t-əv-'dāt\ *adj*
OUTMODED

**out–of–door** \ˌau̇t-əv-'dōr\ *or* **out–of–doors** \-'dōrz\ *adj*
OUTDOOR 2

**out–of–doors** \ˌau̇t-əv-'dōrz\ *n*
[2]OUTDOORS

**out·pa·tient** \'au̇t-ˌpā-shənt\ *n*
a person who visits a hospital for examination or treatment but who does not stay overnight at the hospital

**out·post** \'au̇t-ˌpōst\ *n*
**1** a guard placed at a distance from a military force or camp
**2** the position taken by an outpost
**3** a settlement on a frontier or in a faraway place

**[1]out·put** \'au̇t-ˌpu̇t\ *n*
**1** something produced ⟨increased steel *output*⟩ ⟨a writer's *output*⟩
**2** the information produced by a computer

**[2]output** *vb* **out·put·ted** *or* **out·put**; **out·put·ting**
to produce as output

**[1]out·rage** \'au̇t-ˌrāj\ *n*
**1** an act of violence or cruelty
**2** an act that hurts someone or shows disrespect for a person's feelings
**3** angry feelings caused by injury or insult

**[2]outrage** *vb* **out·raged**; **out·rag·ing**
**1** to cause to suffer violent injury or great insult
**2** to cause to feel anger or strong resentment ⟨*outraged* by the way we were treated⟩

**out·ra·geous** \au̇t-'rā-jəs\ *adj*
going far beyond what is right, decent, or just

**[1]out·right** \au̇t-'rīt\ *adv*
**1** COMPLETELY ⟨sold the business *outright*⟩
**2** without holding back ⟨laughed *outright* at the story⟩
**3** on the spot **:** INSTANTLY ⟨was killed *outright*⟩

**[2]out·right** \'au̇t-ˌrīt\ *adj*
**1** being exactly what is said ⟨an *outright* lie⟩
**2** given without restriction ⟨an *outright* gift⟩

**out·run** \au̇t-'rən\ *vb* **out·ran** \-'ran\; **out·run**; **out·run·ning**
to run faster than

**out·sell** \au̇t-'sel\ *vb* **out·sold** \-'sōld\; **out·sell·ing**
to sell or be sold more than

**out·set** \'au̇t-ˌset\ *n*
BEGINNING 1, START

**out·shine** \au̇t-'shīn\ *vb* **out·shone** \-'shōn\; **out·shin·ing**
**1** to shine brighter than
**2** OUTDO, SURPASS

**[1]out·side** \au̇t-'sīd\ *n*
**1** a place or region beyond an enclosure or boundary
**2** an outer side or surface ⟨painted white on the *outside*⟩
**3** the greatest amount or limit **:** [3]MOST ⟨will take a week at the *outside*⟩

**[2]outside** *adj*
**1** of, relating to, or being on the outside ⟨the *outside* edge⟩
**2** coming from outside **:** not belonging to a place or group ⟨*outside* influences⟩

**[3]outside** *adv*
on or to the outside **:** OUTDOORS ⟨took the dog *outside*⟩

**[4]outside** *prep*
on or to the outside of **:** beyond the limits of ⟨*outside* the door⟩ ⟨*outside* the law⟩

**out·sid·er** \au̇t-'sīd-ər\ *n*
a person who does not belong to a certain party or group

**out·size** \'au̇t-ˌsīz\ *adj*
unusually large or heavy

**out·skirts** \'au̇t-ˌskərts\ *n pl*
the area that lies away from the center of a place

**out·smart** \au̇t-'smärt\ *vb*
OUTWIT

**out·spo·ken** \au̇t-'spō-kən\ *adj*
direct or open in expression **:** BLUNT ⟨*outspoken* criticism⟩ ⟨an *outspoken* critic⟩
**out·spo·ken·ly** *adv*
**out·spo·ken·ness** *n*

**out·spread** \au̇t-'spred\ *adj*
spread out

**out·stand·ing** \au̇t-ˈstan-diŋ\ *adj*
1 UNPAID ⟨several bills *outstanding*⟩
2 standing out especially because of excellence ⟨a most *outstanding* musician⟩ **synonyms** see NOTICEABLE
**out·stand·ing·ly** *adv*

**out·stay** \au̇t-ˈstā\ *vb*
to stay beyond or longer than ⟨*outstayed* our welcome⟩

**out·stretched** \au̇t-ˈstrecht\ *adj*
stretched out ⟨*outstretched* arms⟩

**out·strip** \au̇t-ˈstrip\ *vb* **out·stripped**; **out·strip·ping**
1 to go faster or farther than ⟨*outstripped* the other runners⟩
2 to do better than : EXCEL

[1]**out·ward** \ˈau̇t-wərd\ *adj*
1 moving or turned toward the outside or away from a center ⟨an *outward* journey⟩
2 showing on the outside ⟨gave no *outward* signs of fear⟩

[2]**outward** *or* **out·wards** \ˈau̇t-wərdz\ *adv*
toward the outside : away from a center ⟨the city stretches *outward* for miles⟩

**out·ward·ly** \ˈau̇t-wərd-lē\ *adv*
on the outside : in outward appearance ⟨*outwardly* calm⟩

**out·weigh** \au̇t-ˈwā\ *vb*
to be greater than in weight or importance

**out·wit** \au̇t-ˈwit\ *vb* **out·wit·ted**; **out·wit·ting**
to get ahead of by cleverness : BEST

**out·worn** \au̇t-ˈwōrn\ *adj*
no longer useful or accepted ⟨*outworn* ideas⟩

[1]**oval** \ˈō-vəl\ *n*
a figure or object having the shape of an egg or ellipse

[2]**oval** *adj*
having the shape of an oval : ELLIPTICAL

**ova·ry** \ˈō-və-rē\ *n*, *pl* **ova·ries**
1 an organ of the body in female animals in which eggs are produced
2 ▶ the larger lower part of the pistil of a flower in which the seeds are formed

seed

ovary

**ovary 2:** cross section showing the ovary of a rose

**ova·tion** \ō-ˈvā-shən\ *n*
a making of a loud noise by many people (as by cheering or clapping) to show great liking or respect

**ov·en** \ˈəv-ən\ *n*
▼ a heated chamber (as in a stove) for baking, heating, or drying

**oven**

[1]**over** \ˈō-vər\ *adv*
1 across a barrier or space ⟨flew *over* to London⟩
2 in a direction down or forward and down ⟨fell *over*⟩
3 across the brim ⟨soup boiled *over*⟩
4 so as to bring the underside up ⟨turned the cards *over*⟩
5 beyond a limit ⟨the show ran a minute *over*⟩
6 more than needed ⟨has two cards left *over*⟩
7 once more : AGAIN ⟨please do it *over*⟩

[2]**over** *prep*
1 above in place : higher than ⟨clouds *over* our heads⟩
2 above in power or value ⟨respected those *over* me⟩
3 on or along the surface of ⟨glide *over* the ice⟩
4 on or to the other side of : ACROSS ⟨jump *over* a puddle⟩
5 down from the top or edge of ⟨fell *over* a cliff⟩

[3]**over** *adj*
1 being more than needed : SURPLUS
2 brought or come to an end ⟨those days are *over*⟩

[1]**over·all** \ˌō-vər-ˈȯl\ *adv*
as a whole : in most ways ⟨did a nice job *overall*⟩

[2]**overall** *adj*
including everything ⟨*overall* expenses⟩

**over·alls** \ˈō-vər-ˌȯlz\ *n pl*
▼ loose pants usually with shoulder straps and a piece in front to cover the chest

**overalls:** a boy wearing overalls

**over·anx·ious** \ˌō-vər-ˈaŋk-shəs\ *adj*
much too anxious

**over·bear·ing** \ˌō-vər-ˈbaər-iŋ, -ˈbeər-\ *adj*
acting in a proud or bossy way toward other people

**over·board** \ˈō-vər-ˌbōrd\ *adv*
1 over the side of a ship into the water ⟨fall *overboard*⟩
2 to extremes of enthusiasm ⟨go *overboard* about a popular singer⟩

**over·bur·den** \ˌō-vər-ˈbərd-n\ *vb*
to burden too heavily

**over·cast** \ˈō-vər-ˌkast\ *adj*
clouded over

**over·charge** \ˌō-vər-ˈchärj\ *vb* **over·charged**; **over·charg·ing**
to charge too much

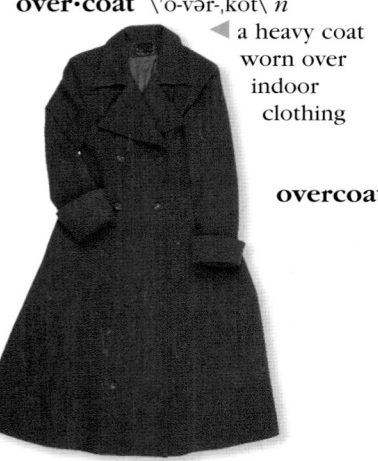

**over·coat** \'ō-vər-,kōt\ *n*
◀ a heavy coat worn over indoor clothing

**overcoat**

**over·come** \,ō-vər-'kəm\ *vb* **over·came** \-'kām\; **overcome**; **over·com·ing**
**1** to win a victory over **:** CONQUER ⟨*overcome* the enemy⟩
**2** to make helpless ⟨*overcome* by gas⟩

**over·con·fi·dent** \,ō-vər-'kän-fə-dənt\ *adj*
too sure of oneself

**over·cooked** \,ō-vər-'kükt\ *adj*
cooked too long

**over·crowd** \,ō-vər-'kraủd\ *vb*
to cause to be too crowded ⟨schools were *overcrowded*⟩

**over·do** \,ō-vər-'dü\ *vb* **over·did** \-'did\; **over·done** \-'dən\; **over·do·ing** \-'dü-iŋ\
**1** to do too much ⟨*overdoes* it getting ready for a party⟩
**2** EXAGGERATE ⟨*overdo* praise⟩
**3** to cook too long

**over·dose** \'ō-vər-,dōs\ *n*
too large a dose (as of a drug)

**over·dress** \,ō-vər-'dres\ *vb*
to dress too well for the occasion

**over·due** \,ō-vər-'dü, -'dyü\ *adj*
**1** not paid when due ⟨*overdue* bills⟩
**2** delayed beyond an expected time ⟨the plane was an hour *overdue*⟩

**over·eat** \,ō-vər-'ēt\ *vb* **over·ate** \-'āt\; **over·eat·en** \-'ēt-n\; **over·eat·ing**
to eat too much

**over·es·ti·mate** \,ō-vər-'es-tə-,māt\ *vb* **over·es·ti·mat·ed**; **over·es·ti·mat·ing**
to estimate too highly ⟨*overestimated* the amount of paper needed⟩

**over·flight** \'ō-vər-,flīt\ *n*
a passage over an area in an airplane

[1]**over·flow** \,ō-vər-'flō\ *vb*
**1** to cover with or as if with water ⟨visitors *overflowed* the town⟩
**2** to flow over the top of ⟨the river *overflowed* its banks⟩
**3** to flow over bounds ⟨the creek *overflows* every spring⟩

[2]**over·flow** \'ō-vər-,flō\ *n*
**1** a flowing over **:** FLOOD
**2** something that flows over **:** SURPLUS

**over·grown** \,ō-vər-'grōn\ *adj*
grown too big ⟨just an *overgrown* puppy⟩

[1]**over·hand** \'ō-vər-,hand\ *adj*
made with a downward movement of the hand or arm

[2]**overhand** *adv*
with an overhand movement ⟨throw the ball *overhand*⟩

**overhand knot** *n*
▼ a simple knot often used to prevent the end of a cord from pulling apart

**overhand knot**

[1]**over·hang** \'ō-vər-,haŋ\ *vb* **over·hung** \-,həŋ\; **over·hang·ing**
to stick out or hang over ⟨an *overhanging* cliff⟩

[2]**overhang** *n*
▼ a part that overhangs ⟨the *overhang* of a roof⟩

[1]**over·haul** \,ō-vər-'hȯl\ *vb*
**1** to make a thorough examination of and make necessary repairs and adjustments on ⟨*overhaul* an automobile engine⟩
**2** to catch up with **:** OVERTAKE ⟨*overhauled* by a police car⟩

[2]**over·haul** \'ō-vər-,hȯl\ *n*
an instance of overhauling

[1]**over·head** \,ō-vər-'hed\ *adv*
**1** above one's head
**2** in the sky ⟨a plane flying *overhead*⟩

[2]**over·head** \'ō-vər-,hed\ *adj*
placed or passing overhead ⟨*overhead* garage doors⟩

[3]**over·head** \'ō-vər-,hed\ *n*
the general expenses (as for rent or heat) of a business

**over·hear** \,ō-vər-'hir\ *vb* **over·heard** \-'hərd\; **over·hear·ing** \-'hir-iŋ\
to hear something said to someone else and not meant for one's own ears

**over·heat** \,ō-vər-'hēt\ *vb*
to heat too much **:** become too hot ⟨the engine *overheated*⟩

**over·joy** \,ō-vər-'jȯi\ *vb*
to make very joyful

[1]**over·land** \'ō-vər-,land\ *adv*
by land rather than by water ⟨travel *overland*⟩

[2]**over·land** *adj*
going overland ⟨an *overland* route⟩

**over·lap** \,ō-vər-'lap\ *vb* **over·lapped**; **over·lap·ping**
to place or be placed so that a part of one covers a part of another ⟨roof shingles are placed so that they *overlap*⟩

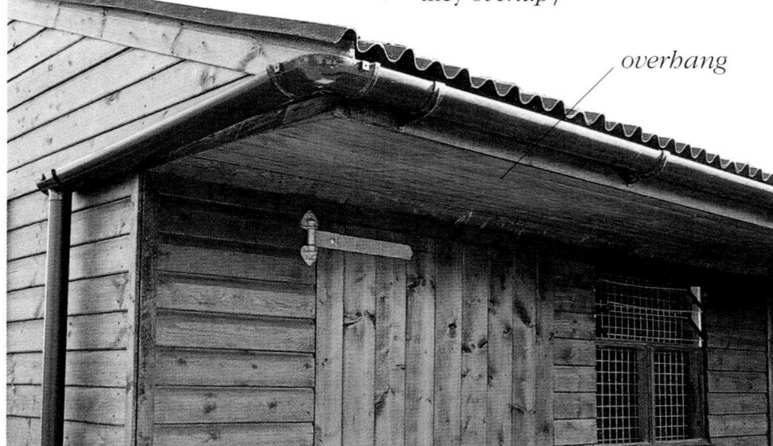


[2]**overhang:** the overhang on a stable roof

[1]**over·lay** \ˌō-vər-ˈlā\ *vb* **over·laid** \-ˈlād\; **over·lay·ing** to lay or spread over or across ⟨a wooden table *overlaid* with ceramic tiles⟩

[2]**over·lay** \ˈō-vər-ˌlā\ *n* something (as a veneer on wood) that is overlaid

**over·load** \ˌō-vər-ˈlōd\ *vb* to put too great a load on ⟨*overload* a truck⟩ ⟨*overload* an electrical circuit⟩

**over·look** \ˌō-vər-ˈlu̇k\ *vb*
**1** to look over : INSPECT
**2** to look down upon from a higher position ⟨a house that *overlooks* a valley⟩
**3** to fail to see : MISS ⟨*overlook* a name on the list⟩
**4** to pass over without notice or blame ⟨*overlook* a mistake⟩

**over·lord** \ˈō-vər-ˌlȯrd\ *n* a lord over other lords

**over·ly** \ˈō-vər-lē\ *adv* by too much ⟨*overly* worried⟩ ⟨an *overly* short skirt⟩

[1]**over·night** \ˌō-vər-ˈnīt\ *adv*
**1** during or through the night ⟨stay *overnight*⟩
**2** [2]FAST 3, QUICKLY ⟨became famous *overnight*⟩

[2]**overnight** *adj*
**1** done or lasting through the night ⟨an *overnight* journey⟩
**2** staying for the night ⟨an *overnight* guest⟩
**3** for use on short trips ⟨an *overnight* bag⟩

**over·pass** \ˈō-vər-ˌpas\ *n* ▶ a crossing (as of two highways or a highway and a railroad) at different levels usually by means of a bridge

**over·pop·u·la·tion** \ˌō-vər-ˌpäp-yə-ˈlā-shən\ *n* the condition of having too many people living in a certain area

**over·pow·er** \ˌō-vər-ˈpau̇-ər\ *vb*
**1** to overcome by greater force
**2** to affect by being too strong ⟨an *overpowering* personality⟩

**over·rate** \ˌō-vər-ˈrāt\ *vb* **over·rat·ed**; **over·rat·ing** to value or praise too highly

**over·ride** \ˌō-vər-ˈrīd\ *vb* **over·rode** \-ˈrōd\; **over·rid·den** \-ˈrid-n\; **over·rid·ing** \-ˈrīd-iŋ\ to push aside as less important ⟨our hunger *overrode* our manners as we grabbed the food⟩

**over·ripe** \ˌō-vər-ˈrīp\ *adj* passed beyond ripeness toward decay ⟨*overripe* fruit⟩

**over·rule** \ˌō-vər-ˈrül\ *vb* **over·ruled**; **over·rul·ing**
**1** to decide against ⟨the chairman *overruled* the suggestion⟩
**2** to set aside a decision or ruling made by someone having less authority ⟨mother *overruled* our plans⟩

**over·run** \ˌō-vər-ˈrən\ *vb* **over·ran** \-ˈran\; **overrun**; **over·run·ning**
**1** to take over and occupy by force ⟨outpost *overrun* by the enemy⟩
**2** to run past ⟨*overran* second base⟩
**3** to spread over so as to cover ⟨a garden *overrun* by weeds⟩

[1]**over·seas** \ˌō-vər-ˈsēz\ *adv* beyond or across the sea ⟨soldiers sent *overseas*⟩

[2]**overseas** *adj* of, relating to, or intended for lands across the sea ⟨*overseas* trade⟩ ⟨*overseas* shipments⟩

**over·see** \ˌō-vər-ˈsē\ *vb* **over·saw** \-ˈsȯ\; **over·seen** \-ˈsēn\; **over·see·ing**
**1** INSPECT 1, EXAMINE
**2** SUPERINTEND

**over·seer** \ˈō-vər-ˌsir\ *n* a person whose business it is to oversee something

**over·shad·ow** \ˌō-vər-ˈshad-ō\ *vb*
**1** to cast a shadow over : DARKEN
**2** to be more important than

**over·shoe** \ˈō-vər-ˌshü\ *n* a shoe (as of rubber) worn over another for protection

**over·shoot** \ˌō-vər-ˈshüt\ *vb* **over·shot** \-ˈshät\; **over·shoot·ing** to miss by going beyond

**over·sight** \ˈō-vər-ˌsīt\ *n*
**1** the act or duty of overseeing : watchful care
**2** an error or a leaving something out through carelessness or haste

**over·sim·pli·fy** \ˌō-vər-ˈsim-plə-ˌfī\ *vb* **over·sim·pli·fied**; **over·sim·pli·fy·ing** to make incorrect or misleading by simplifying too much ⟨*oversimplify* a complicated problem⟩

**over·size** \ˌō-vər-ˈsīz\ *or* **over·sized** \-ˈsīzd\ *adj* larger than the usual or normal size

**over·sleep** \ˌō-vər-ˈslēp\ *vb* **over·slept** \-ˈslept\; **over·sleep·ing** to sleep beyond the usual time or beyond the time set for getting up

**over·spread** \ˌō-vər-ˈspred\ *vb* **overspread**; **over·spread·ing** to spread over or above

*overpass*

**overpass** above a freeway

**over·state** \ˌō-vər-ˈstāt\ *vb* **over·stat·ed**; **over·stat·ing** to put in too strong terms : EXAGGERATE ⟨*overstated* the case⟩

**over·step** \ˌō-vər-ˈstep\ *vb* **over·stepped**; **over·step·ping** to step over or beyond : EXCEED ⟨*overstepped* my authority⟩

**over·stuffed** \ˌō-vər-ˈstəft\ *adj* covered completely and deeply with upholstery ⟨an *overstuffed* chair⟩

**over·sup·ply** \ˌō-vər-sə-ˈplī\ *n, pl* **over·sup·plies** a supply that is too large

**over·take** \ˌō-vər-ˈtāk\ *vb* **over·took** \-ˈtu̇k\; **over·tak·en** \-ˈtā-kən\; **over·tak·ing**
**1** to catch up with and often pass ⟨*overtook* the car ahead⟩
**2** to come upon suddenly or without warning ⟨*overtaken* by rain⟩

¹**over·throw** \ˌō-vər-ˈthrō\ *vb* **over·threw** \-ˈthrü\; **over·thrown** \-ˈthrōn\; **over·throw·ing**
**1** OVERTURN 1
**2** to cause the fall or end of : DEFEAT, DESTROY ⟨a government *overthrown* by rebels⟩

²**over·throw** \ˈō-vər-ˌthrō\ *n* an act of overthrowing : the state of being overthrown : DEFEAT, RUIN

**over·time** \ˈō-vər-ˌtīm\ *n* time spent working that is more than one usually works in a day or a week

**over·ture** \ˈō-vər-ˌchu̇r\ *n*
**1** something first offered or suggested with the hope of reaching an agreement ⟨made *overtures* of peace⟩
**2** a musical composition played by the orchestra at the beginning of an opera or musical play

**over·turn** \ˌō-vər-ˈtərn\ *vb*
**1** to turn over : UPSET
**2** ¹OVERTHROW 2

¹**over·weight** *n*
**1** \ˈō-vər-ˌwāt\ weight that is more than is required or allowed
**2** \ˌō-vər-ˈwāt\ bodily weight that is greater than what is considered normal or healthy

²**over·weight** \ˌō-vər-ˈwāt\ *adj* weighing more than is right, necessary, or allowed

## owl

There are some 130 species of owl, most of which hunt at night. Owls use their large, forward-facing eyes and sharp hearing to locate their prey of small birds, insects, frogs, and rodents — even in total darkness. Special fringed feathers reduce the sound of their flapping wings, allowing owls to swoop down almost silently on their prey.

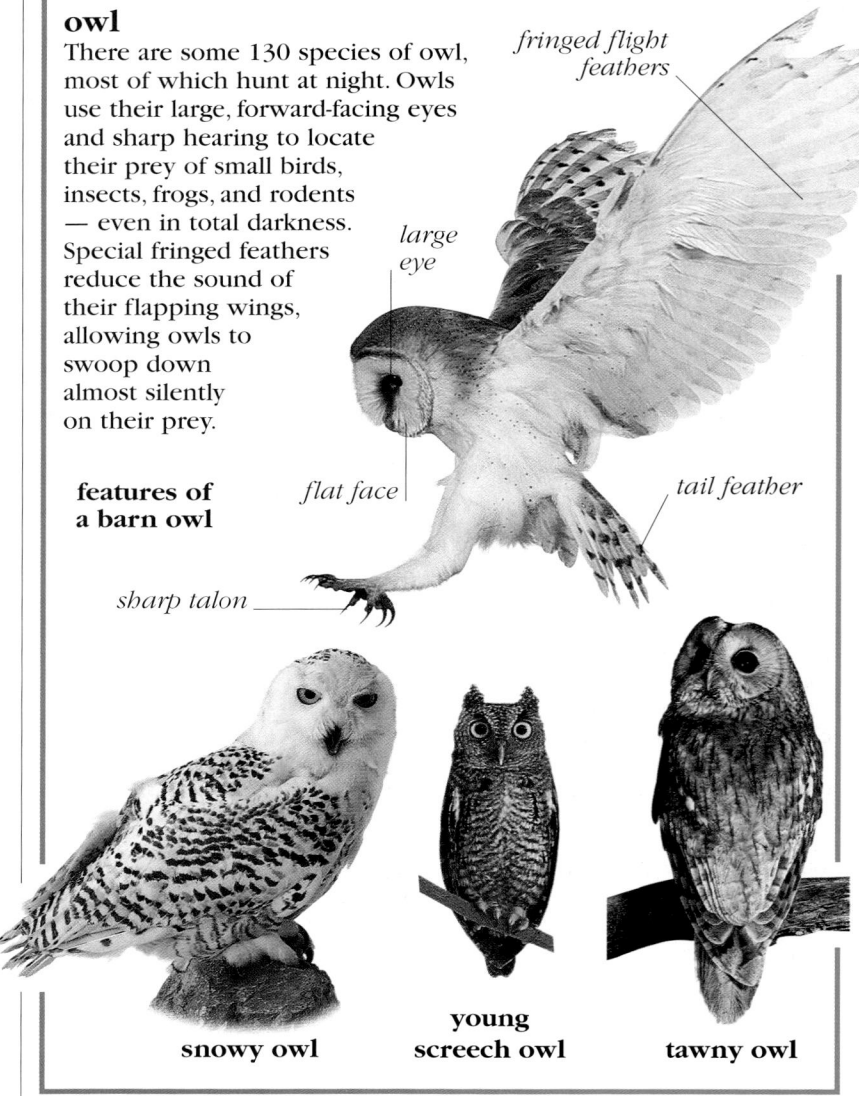

**features of a barn owl**

**snowy owl**

**young screech owl**

**tawny owl**

**over·whelm** \ˌō-vər-ˈhwelm, -ˈwelm\ *vb*
**1** to cover over completely : SUBMERGE ⟨a boat *overwhelmed* by a wave⟩
**2** to overcome completely ⟨were *overwhelmed* by the larger army⟩ ⟨*overwhelmed* with grief⟩

¹**over·work** \ˌō-vər-ˈwərk\ *vb*
**1** to work or cause to work too much or too hard
**2** to make too much use of ⟨*overworked* phrases⟩

²**overwork** *n* too much work

**ovip·a·rous** \ō-ˈvip-ə-rəs\ *adj* reproducing by eggs that hatch outside the parent's body ⟨birds are *oviparous* animals⟩

**ovule** \ˈäv-yül, ˈōv-\ *n* any of the tiny egglike structures in a plant ovary that can develop into seeds

**ovum** \ˈō-vəm\ *n, pl* **ova** \ˈō-və\ EGG CELL

**owe** \ˈō\ *vb* **owed**; **ow·ing**
**1** to be obligated to pay, give, or return ⟨*owe* money⟩
**2** to be in debt to ⟨*owe* the grocer for food⟩
**3** to have as a result ⟨*owe* success to hard work⟩

**owing** \ˈō-ing\ *adj* due to be paid ⟨have bills *owing*⟩

**owing to** *prep*
BECAUSE OF ⟨absent *owing to* illness⟩

**owl** \'au̇l\ *n*
◀ a bird with large head and eyes, hooked bill, and strong claws that is active at night and lives on rats and mice, insects, and small birds
**owl·ish** *adj*

**owl·et** \'au̇-lət\ *n*
a young or small owl

**¹own** \'ōn\ *adj*
belonging to oneself or itself ⟨have one's *own* room⟩

**²own** *vb*
**1** to have or hold as property : POSSESS
**2** ADMIT 3, CONFESS 1 ⟨*own* a mistake⟩

**own·er** \'ō-nər\ *n*
a person who owns something

**own·er·ship** \'ō-nər-ˌship\ *n*
the state or fact of being an owner

**ox** \'äks\ *n, pl* **ox·en** \'äk-sən\ *also* **ox**
**1** one of our common domestic cattle or a closely related animal
**2** an adult castrated male of domestic cattle used especially for meat or for hauling loads : STEER

**ox·bow** \'äks-ˌbō\ *n*
a bend in a river in the shape of a U

**ox·cart** \'äk-ˌskärt\ *n*
a cart pulled by oxen

**ox·ford** \'äks-fərd\ *n*
▶ a low shoe laced and tied over the instep

**oxford**

**ox·i·da·tion** \ˌäk-sə-'dā-shən\ *n*
the process of oxidizing

**ox·ide** \'äk-ˌsīd\ *n*
a compound of oxygen with another element or with a group of elements

**ox·i·dize** \'äk-sə-ˌdīz\ *vb*
**ox·i·dized**; **ox·i·diz·ing**
to combine with oxygen : add oxygen to

**ox·y·gen** \'äk-si-jən\ *n*
a chemical element found in the air as a colorless odorless tasteless gas that is necessary for life

**Word History** People once thought that all acids were formed by adding oxygen to some other substance. This belief turned out not to be true. However, it did give oxygen its name. The first part of the word, *oxy-*, came from a Greek word that meant "acid" or "sharp." The second part, *-gen*, came from a Greek suffix that meant "born."

**oys·ter** \'ȯis-tər\ *n*
▼ a soft gray shellfish that lives on stony bottoms (**oyster beds**) in shallow seawater, has a shell made up of two hinged parts, and is used as food

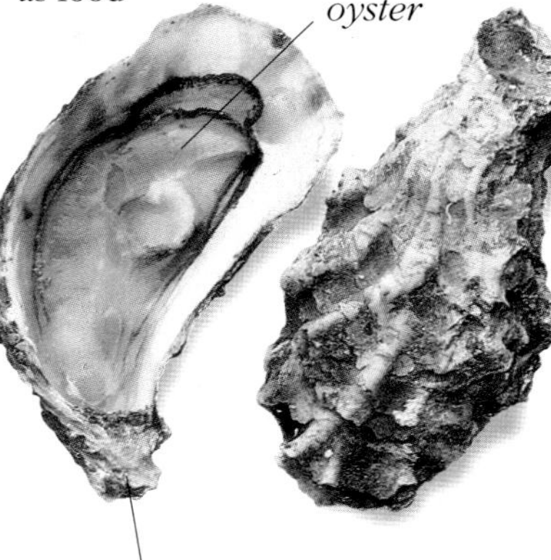


**oyster** in its shell, shown with the shell halves separated

**ozone** \'ō-ˌzōn\ *n*
**1** a faintly blue form of oxygen that is present in the air in small quantities
**2** pure and refreshing air

**ozone layer** *n*
a layer of the upper atmosphere that is characterized by high ozone content which blocks most of the sun's radiation from entering the lower atmosphere

**The sounds of P:** The letter **P** has only one sound in English. It sounds the same in **paper**, **pepper**, **separate**, and **ketchup**. Double **P** sounds the same as single **P**.

The letter **P** combines with **H** to make the sound of **F**, as in **photo**, **gopher**, and **nymph**. Letter **P** is sometimes silent, as in **psalm** and **psychology**. This happens only at the beginning of words.

**p** \'pē\ *n, pl* **p's** *or* **ps** \'pēz\ *often cap*
the sixteenth letter of the English alphabet

**pa** \'pä, 'pò\ *n, often cap*
[1]FATHER 1

[1]**pace** \'pās\ *n*
**1** rate of moving forward or ahead
**2** a manner of walking
**3** a horse's gait in which the legs on the same side move at the same time
**4** a single step or its length

[2]**pace** *vb* **paced**; **pac·ing**
**1** to walk with slow steps
**2** to move at a pace ⟨a *pacing* horse⟩
**3** to measure by steps ⟨*pace* off 300 meters⟩
**4** to walk back and forth across ⟨*pacing* the floor⟩
**5** to set or regulate the pace of

**pa·cif·ic** \pə-'sif-ik\ *adj*
**1** making peace : PEACEABLE
**2** [3]CALM, PEACEFUL
**3** *cap* relating to the Pacific ocean

**pac·i·fy** \'pas-ə-,fī\ *vb* **pac·i·fied**; **pac·i·fy·ing**
to make peaceful or quiet : CALM, SOOTHE ⟨*pacify* a crying baby⟩

**3** to crowd into so as to fill full : CRAM ⟨a *packed* auditorium⟩
**4** to send away ⟨*pack* children off to school⟩
**pack·er** *n*

**Synonyms** PACK, CRAM, and STUFF mean to fill something to its limit or beyond. PACK may suggest a tight filling up in an orderly way ⟨*pack* a trunk⟩ or it may suggest filling up something too much ⟨people were *packed* into the room like sardines⟩. CRAM usually suggests that something has been filled in a forceful, careless, or disorderly way ⟨*crammed* everything into one small box⟩. STUFF suggests filling something as much as it will hold and often to the point of bulging ⟨I *stuffed* my pockets with apples⟩.

**pack·age** \'pak-ij\ *n*
**1** a bundle made up for shipping
**2** a box or case in which goods are shipped or delivered

**pack·et** \'pak-ət\ *n*
a small package

**2** a piece of material that holds ink used in inking rubber stamps
**3** one of the cushioned parts of the underside of the foot of some animals (as a dog)
**4** a floating leaf of a water plant
**5** a tablet of writing or drawing paper

[3]**pad** *vb* **pad·ded**; **pad·ding**
**1** to stuff or cover with soft material
**2** to make longer by adding words ⟨*pad* a speech⟩

**pad·ding** \'pad-ing\ *n*
material used to pad something

[1]**pad·dle** \'pad-l\ *vb* **pad·dled**; **pad·dling**
to move or splash about in the water with the hands or feet : WADE

[2]**paddle** *n*
**1** an instrument like an oar used in moving and steering a small boat (as a canoe)
**2** one of the broad boards at the outer edge of a waterwheel or a paddle wheel
**3** an instrument for beating, mixing, or hitting

[2]**paddle 1:** a double-bladed kayak paddle

[1]**pack** \'pak\ *n*
**1** a bundle arranged for carrying especially on the back of a person or animal
**2** a group of like persons or things : BAND, SET ⟨a Cub Scout *pack*⟩ ⟨a wolf *pack*⟩

[2]**pack** *vb*
**1** to put into a container or bundle ⟨*pack* your clothes⟩
**2** to put things into ⟨*pack* a suitcase⟩

**pack·ing·house** \'pak-ing-,haùs\ *n*
a building for preparing and packing food and especially meat

**pact** \'pakt\ *n*
AGREEMENT 2, TREATY

[1]**pad** \'pad\ *vb* **pad·ded**; **pad·ding**
to walk or run with quiet steps ⟨a lion *padding* about its cage⟩

[2]**pad** *n*
**1** something soft used for protection or comfort : CUSHION

[3]**paddle** *vb* **pad·dled**; **pad·dling**
**1** to move or drive forward with or as if with a paddle
**2** to stir or mix with a paddle
**3** to beat with or as if with a paddle

**paddle wheel** *n*
a wheel with paddles near its outer edge used to drive a boat

**pad·dock** \'pad-ək\ *n*
**1** an enclosed area where animals are put to eat grass or to exercise

2 an enclosed area where racehorses are saddled and paraded

**pad·dy** \'pad-ē\ *n, pl* **paddies**
wet land in which rice is grown

**[1]pad·lock** \'pad-,läk\ *n*
a removable lock that has a curved piece that snaps into a catch

**[2]padlock** *vb*
to fasten with a padlock

**[1]pa·gan** \'pā-gən\ *n*
[2]HEATHEN 1

**[2]pagan** *adj*
of or relating to pagans or their worship : HEATHEN ⟨a *pagan* temple⟩

**[1]page** \'pāj\ *n*
**1** a boy being trained to be a knight in the Middle Ages
**2** a person employed (as by a hotel or the United States congress) to carry messages or run errands

**[1]page 1:** a boy dressed as a 15th-century page

**[2]page** *vb* **paged**; **pag·ing**
to call out the name of (a person) in a public place

**[3]page** *n*
**1** one side of a printed or written sheet of paper
**2** a large section of computer memory
**3** the block of information found at a single World Wide Web address

**pag·eant** \'paj-ənt\ *n*
**1** a grand and fancy public ceremony and display
**2** an entertainment made up of scenes based on history or legend ⟨a Christmas *pageant*⟩

**pa·go·da** \pə-'gōd-ə\ *n*
a tower of several stories built as a temple or memorial in the Far East

**paid** *past of* PAY

**pail** \'pāl\ *n*
**1** a usually round container with a handle : BUCKET

**paddy:** workers in a paddy in Thailand

**2** PAILFUL ⟨poured a *pail* of water down the drain⟩

**pail·ful** \'pāl-,fu̇l\ *n, pl* **pail·fuls** \-,fu̇lz\ *or* **pails·ful** \'pālz-,fu̇l\
the amount a pail holds

**[1]pain** \'pān\ *n*
**1** suffering that accompanies a bodily disorder (as a disease or an injury) ⟨*pain* in the chest⟩
**2** a feeling (as a prick or an ache) that is caused by something harmful and usually makes one try to escape its source
**3** suffering of the mind or emotions : GRIEF
**4 pains** *pl* great care or effort ⟨took *pains* with the garden⟩
**pain·ful** \'pān-fəl\ *adj*
**pain·ful·ly** \-fə-lē\ *adv*
**pain·less** \-ləs\ *adj*

**[2]pain** *vb*
**1** to cause pain in or to
**2** to give or feel pain

**pains·tak·ing** \'pān-,stā-king\ *adj*
taking pains : showing care ⟨a *painstaking* worker⟩
**pains·tak·ing·ly** *adv*

**[1]paint** \'pānt\ *vb*
**1** to cover a surface with or as if with paint ⟨*paint* a wall⟩
**2** to make a picture or design by using paints ⟨*paint* a dog on the sign⟩
**3** to describe clearly
**paint·er** *n*

**[2]paint** *n*
a mixture of coloring matter with a liquid that forms a dry coating when spread on a surface

**paint·brush** \'pānt-,brəsh\ *n*
a brush for applying paint

**paint·ing** *n*
**1** a painted work of art
**2** the art or occupation of painting

**[1]pair** \'paər, 'peər\ *n, pl* **pairs** *also* **pair**
**1** two things that match or are meant to be used together ⟨a *pair* of gloves⟩ ⟨a *pair* of draft horses⟩
**2** a thing having two similar parts that are connected ⟨a *pair* of scissors⟩
**3** a mated couple ⟨a *pair* of robins⟩

**[1]pair 1:** a pair of draft horses

**[2]pair** *vb*
**1** to arrange or join in pairs ⟨the guests *paired* off for dancing⟩
**2** to form a pair : MATCH ⟨this glove doesn't *pair* with that⟩

A B C D E F G H I J K L M N O P Q R S T U V W X Y Z

**pa·ja·mas** \pə-'jäm-əz, -'jam-əz\ *n pl*
loose clothes usually consisting of pants and top that match and that are worn for relaxing or sleeping

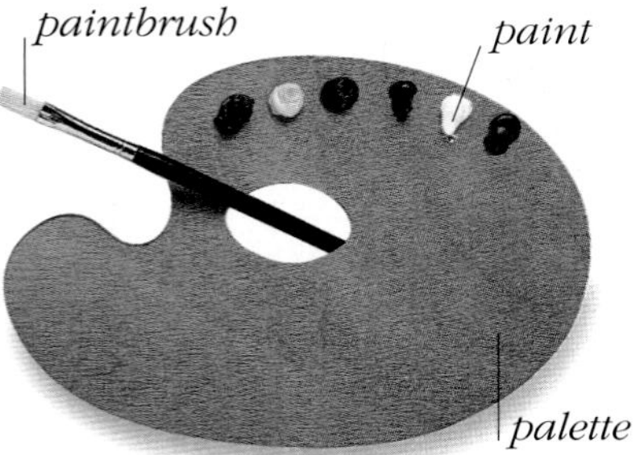

**palette 1**

**Word History** When the English went to India they saw many people wearing light, loose trousers. The English called these trousers *pajamas*. The English word came from a word in a language of India. That word was made up of two words in a language of Iran. The first word meant "leg." The second meant "garment." The English began to use these trousers in place of nightshirts. Later the word *pajamas* came to be used for a two-piece sleeping suit.

**¹Pak·i·stani** \,pak-i-'stan-ē, ,päk-i-'stän-ē\ *n*
a person born or living in Pakistan

**²Pakistani** *adj*
of or relating to Pakistan or the Pakistanis

**pal** \'pal\ *n*
a close friend

**pal·ace** \'pal-əs\ *n*
**1** the home of a ruler
**2** a large or splendid house

**pal·at·able** \'pal-ət-ə-bəl\ *adj*
pleasant to the taste

**pal·ate** \'pal-ət\ *n*
**1** the roof of the mouth made up of a bony front part (**hard palate**) and a soft flexible back part (**soft palate**)
**2** the sense of taste

**¹pale** \'pāl\ *adj* **pal·er**; **pal·est**
**1** not having the warm color of a healthy person
**2** not bright or brilliant ⟨a *pale* star⟩
**3** light in color or shade ⟨*pale* pink⟩
**pale·ness** *n*

**²pale** *vb* **paled**; **pal·ing**
to make or become pale

**Pa·leo·zo·ic** \,pā-lē-ə-'zō-ik\ *n*
an era of geological history ending about 230,000,000 years ago which came before the Mesozoic and in which vertebrates and land plants first appeared

**pal·ette** \'pal-ət\ *n*
**1** ◀ a thin board or tablet on which a painter puts and mixes colors
**2** the set of colors that a painter puts on a palette

**pal·i·sade** \,pal-ə-'sād\ *n*
**1** a fence made of poles to protect against attack
**2** a line of steep cliffs

**¹pall** \'pȯl\ *vb*
to become dull or uninteresting **:** lose the ability to give pleasure

**²pall** *n*
**1** a heavy cloth covering for a coffin, hearse, or tomb
**2** something that makes things dark and gloomy ⟨a *pall* of smoke⟩

**pall·bear·er** \'pȯl-,bar-ər, -,ber-\ *n*
a person who helps to carry or follows a coffin at a funeral

**pal·let** \'pal-ət\ *n*
**1** a mattress of straw
**2** a temporary bed on the floor

**pal·lid** \'pal-əd\ *adj*
¹PALE 1

**pal·lor** \'pal-ər\ *n*
paleness of face

**Word History** *Palm*, the name of a tree, is related to *palm*, the word for the under part of the hand. Both English words come from the same Latin word. This Latin word first meant "palm of the hand." It came to mean "palm tree" as well because the leaves of a palm look something like large outstretched hands.

**²palm** *n*
**1** the under part of the hand between the fingers and the wrist
**2** a measure of length of about seven to ten centimeters

**³palm** *vb*
to hide in the hand ⟨*palm* a coin⟩

**pal·met·to** \pal-'met-ō\ *n, pl* **pal·met·tos** *or* **pal·met·toes**
a low palm with leaves shaped like fans

**palm off** *vb*
to get rid of or pass on in a dishonest way ⟨tried to *palm off* plastic as real leather⟩

**pal·o·mi·no** \,pal-ə-'mē-nō\ *n, pl* **pal·o·mi·nos**
a small strong horse that is light tan or cream in color with a lighter mane and tail

**pal·pi·tate** \'pal-pə-,tāt\ *vb* **pal·pi·tat·ed**; **pal·pi·tat·ing**
¹THROB 1

**pal·sy** \'pȯl-zē\ *n*
**1** PARALYSIS
**2** a trembling of the head or hands that cannot be controlled

**pampas** with grazing sheep in Chile

**¹palm** \'päm, 'pälm\ *n*
any of a group of mostly tropical trees, shrubs, and vines with a simple but often tall stem topped with leaves that are shaped like feathers or fans

**pal·try** \'pȯl-trē\ *adj* **pal·tri·er**; **pal·tri·est**
of little importance **:** PETTY

**pam·pas** \'pam-pəz\ *n pl*
▲ wide treeless plains of South America

**pam·per** \'pam-pər\ *vb* to give someone or someone's desires too much care and attention : INDULGE

**pam·phlet** \'pam-flət\ *n* a short publication without a binding : BOOKLET

**Word History** A long time ago someone whose name we do not know wrote a Latin love poem called *Pamphilus* that became very popular. Many copies of the poem were made. The English formed a word from the name of this poem which they used for any written work too short to be called a book. The modern word *pamphlet* comes from this early English word.

[1]**pan** \'pan\ *n* **1** a shallow open container used for cooking **2** a container somewhat like a cooking pan ⟨the *pans* of a pair of scales⟩

[2]**pan** *vb* **panned**; **pan·ning** to wash earthy material so as to collect bits of metal (as gold)

**pan·cake** \'pan-,kāk\ *n* a flat cake made of thin batter and cooked on both sides on a griddle

**pan·cre·as** \'pang-krē-əs\ *n* a large gland in the abdomen that produces insulin and a fluid (**pancreatic juice**) that aids digestion

**pan·cre·at·ic** \,pang-krē-'at-ik\ *adj* of or relating to the pancreas

**pan·da** \'pan-də\ *n* **1** ▶ a long-tailed mainly plant-eating mammal that is related to and resembles the American raccoon, has long reddish fur, and is found from the Himalayas to China **2** GIANT PANDA

**pan·de·mo·ni·um** \,pan-də-'mō-nē-əm\ *n* wild uproar ⟨*pandemonium* broke loose when the winning run scored⟩

**pane** \'pān\ *n* a sheet of glass (as in a window)

[1]**pan·el** \'pan-l\ *n* **1** a group of persons appointed for some service ⟨a jury *panel*⟩ **2** a group of persons taking part in a discussion or quiz program **3** a part of something (as a door or a wall) often sunk below the level of the frame **4** a piece of material (as plywood) made to form part of a surface (as of a wall) **5** a board into which instruments or controls are set

[2]**panel** *vb* **pan·eled** *or* **pan·elled**; **pan·el·ing** *or* **pan·el·ling** to supply or decorate with panels ⟨*panel* a wall⟩ ⟨a *paneled* ceiling⟩

**pan·el·ing** \'pan-l-ing\ *n* panels joined in a continuous surface

**pang** \'pang\ *n* a sudden sharp attack or feeling (as of hunger or regret)

[1]**pan·ic** \'pan-ik\ *n* a sudden overpowering fear especially without reasonable cause

**Word History** The ancient Greeks had very many gods. One of these, named Pan, was the god of shepherds and hunters. Sometimes he wandered peacefully through the woods, playing a pipe. Sometimes he could also cause sudden fear that seemed to have no reason. People thought that he could make even giants afraid. The Greeks made a word that meant "sudden fright" from the name of this god. The English word *panic* comes from this Greek word.

**panda 1**

[2]**panic** *vb* **pan·icked**; **pan·ick·ing** to affect or be affected by panic

**pan·icky** \'pan-i-kē\ *adj* **1** like or caused by panic ⟨*panicky* fear⟩ **2** feeling or likely to feel panic

**pan·o·rama** \,pan-ə-'ram-ə, -'räm-\ *n* a clear complete view in every direction

**pan out** *vb* to give a good result : SUCCEED

**pan·sy** \'pan-zē\ *n, pl* **pansies** ▼ a garden plant related to the violets that has large velvety flowers with five petals usually in shades of yellow, purple, or brownish red

**pansy**

[1]**pant** \'pant\ *vb* to breathe hard or quickly ⟨*pant* from running⟩

[2]**pant** *n* a panting breath

**pan·ta·loons** \,pant-l-'ünz\ *n pl* PANTS

**pan·ther** \'pan-thər\ *n* **1** LEOPARD **2** COUGAR **3** JAGUAR

**pant·ie** *or* **panty** \'pant-ē\ *n, pl* **pant·ies** a woman's or child's undergarment with short legs or no legs

[1]**pan·to·mime** \'pant-ə-,mīm\ *n* **1** a show in which a story is told by using expressions on the face and movements of the body instead of words **2** a showing or explaining of something through movements of the body and face alone

[2]**pantomime** *vb* **pan·to·mimed**; **pan·to·mim·ing** to tell through pantomime

**pan·try** \'pan-trē\ *n, pl* **pan·tries** a small room where food and dishes are kept

**pants** \'pants\ *n pl* an outer garment reaching from the waist to the ankle or only to the knee and covering each leg separately

**pa·pa** \'pä-pə\ *n*
[1]FATHER 1

**pa·pal** \'pā-pəl\ *adj*
of or relating to the pope

**pa·paw** *n*
**1** \pə-'pȯ\ PAPAYA
**2** \'päp-ȯ, 'pȯp-\ the greenish or yellow edible fruit of a North American tree with shiny leaves and purple flowers

**pa·pa·ya** \pə-'pī-ə\ *n*
▼ a yellow edible fruit that looks like a melon and grows on a tropical American tree

**papaya**

**[1]pa·per** \'pā-pər\ *n*
**1** a material made in thin sheets from fibers (as of wood or cloth)
**2** a sheet or piece of paper
**3** a piece of paper having something written or printed on it **:** DOCUMENT
**4** NEWSPAPER
**5** WALLPAPER
**6** a piece of written schoolwork

**[2]paper** *vb*
to cover or line with paper (as wallpaper) ⟨*paper* a room⟩

**[3]paper** *adj*
**1** made of paper ⟨*paper* carton⟩
**2** like paper in thinness or weakness

**pa·per·back** \'pā-pər-ˌbak\ *n*
a book with a flexible paper binding

**paper clip** *n*
a clip of bent wire used to hold sheets of paper together

**pa·pery** \'pā-pə-rē\ *adj*
like paper

**pa·poose** \pa-'püs\ *n*
a baby of North American Indian parents

**pa·pri·ka** \pə-'prē-kə\ *n*
a mild red spice made from the fruit of some sweet peppers

**pa·py·rus** \pə-'pī-rəs\ *n, pl* **pa·py·rus·es** *or* **pa·py·ri** \-rē, -ˌrī\
**1** a tall African plant related to the grasses that grows especially in Egypt
**2** a material like paper made from papyrus by ancient people and used by them to write on

**par** \'pär\ *n*
**1** a fixed or stated value (as of money or a security)
**2** an equal level ⟨two people with talents on a *par*⟩
**3** the score set for each hole of a golf course

**par·a·ble** \'par-ə-bəl\ *n*
a simple story that teaches a moral truth

**[1]para·chute** \'par-ə-ˌshüt\ *n*
▶ a folding device of light material shaped like an umbrella and used for making a safe jump from an airplane

canopy catches the air to slow the person's descent

**[1]parachute**

**[2]parachute** *vb* **para·chut·ed**; **para·chut·ing**
to transport or come down by parachute

**[1]pa·rade** \pə-'rād\ *n*
**1** great show or display ⟨the exhibition was a *parade* of American history⟩
**2** the formation of troops before an officer for inspection
**3** a public procession ⟨a circus *parade*⟩
**4** a crowd of people walking at an easy pace ⟨the Easter *parade*⟩

**[2]parade** *vb* **pa·rad·ed**; **pa·rad·ing**
**1** to march in an orderly group
**2** SHOW OFF **synonyms** see SHOW

**par·a·dise** \'par-ə-ˌdīs, -ˌdīz\ *n*
**1** the garden of Eden
**2** HEAVEN 2
**3** a place or state of great happiness

**par·a·dox** \'par-ə-ˌdäks\ *n*
a statement that seems to be the opposite of the truth or of common sense and yet is perhaps true

**par·af·fin** \'par-ə-fən\ *n*
a white odorless tasteless substance obtained from wood, coal, or petroleum and used in coating and sealing and in candles

**[1]para·graph** \'par-ə-ˌgraf\ *n*
a part of a piece of writing that is made up of one or more sentences and has to do with one topic or gives the words of one speaker

**[2]paragraph** *vb*
to divide into paragraphs

**par·a·keet** *or* **par·ra·keet** \'par-ə-ˌkēt\ *n*
a small parrot with a long tail

**[1]par·al·lel** \'par-ə-ˌlel\ *adj*
lying or moving in the same direction but always the same distance apart ⟨*parallel* lines⟩ ⟨train tracks are *parallel*⟩

**[2]parallel** *n*
**1** a parallel line or surface
**2** one of the imaginary circles on the earth's surface parallel to the equator that mark latitude
**3** agreement in many or most details ⟨the *parallel* between their lives⟩
**4** COUNTERPART, EQUAL

**[3]parallel** *vb*
**1** to be like or equal to

**2** to move, run, or extend in a direction parallel with ⟨the road *parallels* the river⟩

**par·al·lel·o·gram** \ˌpar-ə-ˈlel-ə-ˌgram\ *n*
▼ a plane figure with four sides whose opposite sides are parallel and equal

**parallelogram**

**pa·ral·y·sis** \pə-ˈral-ə-səs\ *n, pl* **pa·ral·y·ses** \-ˌsēz\
partial or complete loss of one's ability to move or feel

**par·a·lyze** \ˈpar-ə-ˌlīz\ *vb* **par·a·lyzed**; **par·a·lyz·ing**
**1** to affect with paralysis
**2** to destroy or decrease something's energy or ability to act ⟨a city *paralyzed* by snow⟩

**par·a·me·cium** \ˌpar-ə-ˈmē-shē-əm, -shəm\ *n, pl* **par·a·me·cia** \-shē-ə\ *also* **par·a·me·ciums**
a tiny water animal that is a single cell shaped like a slipper

**para·med·ic** \ˌpar-ə-ˈmed-ik\ *n*
a person specially trained to care for a patient before or during the trip to a hospital

**par·a·mount** \ˈpar-ə-ˌmau̇nt\ *adj*
highest in importance or greatness

**par·a·pet** \ˈpar-ə-pət, -ˌpet\ *n*
**1** a wall of earth or stone to protect soldiers
**2** a low wall or fence at the edge of a platform, roof, or bridge

[1]**para·phrase** \ˈpar-ə-ˌfrāz\ *n*
a way of stating something again by giving the meaning in different words

[2]**paraphrase** *vb* **para·phrased**; **para·phras·ing**
to give the meaning of in different words

**par·a·site** \ˈpar-ə-ˌsīt\ *n*
**1** a person who lives at the expense of another
**2** a plant or animal that lives in or on some other living thing and gets food and sometimes shelter from it

**par·a·sit·ic** \ˌpar-ə-ˈsit-ik\ *adj*
of or relating to parasites or their way of life : being a parasite
**par·a·sit·i·cal·ly** \-i-kə-lē\ *adv*

**par·a·sol** \ˈpar-ə-ˌsȯl\ *n*
a light umbrella used as a protection against the sun

**para·troop·er** \ˈpar-ə-ˌtrü-pər\ *n*
a soldier trained and equipped to parachute from an airplane

[1]**par·cel** \ˈpär-səl\ *n*
**1** a plot of land
**2** PACKAGE 1

[2]**parcel** *vb* **par·celed** *or* **par·celled**; **par·cel·ing** *or* **par·cel·ling**
**1** to divide and give out by parts
**2** to wrap up into a package

**parcel post** *n*
a mail service that handles packages

**parch** \ˈpärch\ *vb*
to dry up from heat and lack of moisture

**parch·ment** \ˈpärch-mənt\ *n*
**1** the skin of a sheep or goat prepared so that it can be written on
**2** a paper similar to parchment

[1]**par·don** \ˈpärd-n\ *n*
**1** forgiveness for wrong or rude behavior
**2** a freeing from legal punishment

[2]**pardon** *vb*
**1** to free from penalty for a fault or crime
**2** to allow (a wrong act) to pass without punishment : FORGIVE

**pare** \ˈpaər, ˈpeər\ *vb* **pared**; **par·ing**
**1** to cut or shave off the outside or the ends of
**2** to reduce as if by cutting ⟨*pare* the cost of a trip⟩

**par·ent** \ˈpar-ənt, ˈper-\ *n*
**1** ▶ a father or mother of a child
**2** an animal or plant that produces offspring or seed

**par·ent·age** \ˈpar-ənt-ij, ˈper-\ *n*
a line of ancestors : ANCESTRY

**pa·ren·tal** \pə-ˈrent-l\ *adj*
of or relating to parents

**pa·ren·the·sis** \pə-ˈren-thə-səs\ *n, pl* **pa·ren·the·ses** \-ˌsēz\
**1** a word, phrase, or sentence inserted in a passage to explain or comment on it
**2** one of a pair of marks ( ) used to enclose a word or group of words or to group mathematical terms to be dealt with as a unit
**par·en·thet·ic** \ˌpar-ən-ˈthet-ik\ *or* **par·en·thet·i·cal** \-i-kəl\ *adj*

**par·fait** \pär-ˈfā\ *n*
a dessert made usually of layers of fruit, syrup, ice cream, and whipped cream

**par·ish** \ˈpar-ish\ *n*
**1** a section of a church district under the care of a priest or minister
**2** the persons who live in a parish and attend the parish church
**3** the members of a church
**4** a division in the state of Louisiana that is similar to a county in other states

**parish house** *n*
a building for the educational and social activities of a church

**pa·rish·io·ner** \pə-ˈrish-ə-nər\ *n*
a member or resident of a parish

[1]**park** \ˈpärk\ *n*
**1** an area of land set aside for recreation or for its beauty
**2** an enclosed field for ball games

[2]**park** *vb*
to stop (as an auto or truck) and leave it for a while ⟨never *park* in front of a hydrant⟩

**par·ka** \ˈpär-kə\ *n*
a warm jacket with a hood

**parent 1:**
parents with their child

**park·way** \'pär-,kwā\ *n*
a broad landscaped highway

[1]**par·ley** \'pär-lē\ *n, pl* **parleys**
a discussion with an enemy ⟨a truce *parley*⟩

[2]**parley** *vb* **par·leyed**; **par·ley·ing**
to hold a discussion of terms with an enemy

**par·lia·ment** \'pär-lə-mənt\ *n*
an assembly that is the highest legislative body of a country (as the United Kingdom)

**par·lor** \'pär-lər\ *n*
**1** a room for receiving guests and for conversation
**2** a usually small place of business ⟨beauty *parlor*⟩ ⟨ice cream *parlor*⟩

**pa·ro·chi·al** \pə-'rō-kē-əl\ *adj*
of, relating to, or supported by a religious body (as a church) ⟨a *parochial* school⟩ ⟨*parochial* duties⟩

**pa·role** \pə-'rōl\ *n*
an early release of a prisoner

**parrakeet** *variant of* PARAKEET

**par·rot** \'par-ət\ *n*
▶ a brightly colored tropical bird that has a strong hooked bill and is sometimes trained to imitate human speech

[1]**par·ry** \'par-ē\ *vb* **par·ried**; **par·ry·ing**
**1** to turn aside an opponent's weapon or blow
**2** to avoid by a skillful answer ⟨*parry* an embarrassing question⟩

[2]**parry** *n, pl* **par·ries**
an act or instance of parrying

**pars·ley** \'pär-slē\ *n, pl* **pars·leys**
▼ a garden plant related to the carrot that has finely divided leaves and is used to season or decorate various foods

**parsley**

**pars·nip** \'pär-snəp\ *n*
▶ a vegetable that is the long white root of a plant related to the carrot

**parsnip**

**par·son** \'pärs-n\ *n*
[1]MINISTER 1

**par·son·age** \'pärs-n-ij\ *n*
a house provided by a church for its pastor to live in

[1]**part** \'pärt\ *n*
**1** one of the sections into which something is divided : something less than a whole
**2** a voice or instrument ⟨four-*part* harmony⟩
**3** the music for a voice or instrument ⟨the soprano *part*⟩
**4** a piece of a plant or animal body
**5** a piece of a machine
**6** a person's share or duty ⟨did my *part*⟩
**7** one of the sides in a disagreement ⟨took my *part* in the quarrel⟩
**8** the role of a character in a play
**9** a line along which the hair is divided

---

**Synonyms** PART, PORTION, and SECTION mean something less than the whole to which it belongs. PART suggests only that something is taken away from the whole or thought of as being separate from the rest ⟨a *part* of the room is used for storage⟩. PORTION suggests that a whole has been divided into assigned parts ⟨cut the pie into six *portions*⟩. SECTION suggests that the parts of the whole are recognizable and have been separated by or as if by cutting ⟨this newspaper has four *sections*⟩.

---

[2]**part** *vb*
**1** to leave someone : go away ⟨*part* from a friend⟩
**2** to divide into parts
**3** to hold apart ⟨the fighters were *parted* by friends⟩
**4** to come apart ⟨the rope *parted* under the strain⟩ **synonyms** see SEPARATE

**par·take** \pär-'tāk\ *vb* **par·took** \-'tu̇k\; **par·tak·en** \-'tā-kən\; **par·tak·ing**
to take a share or part ⟨*partake* of a dinner⟩ ⟨*partake* in a ceremony⟩

**part·ed** \'pärt-əd\ *adj*
divided into parts

**par·tial** \'pär-shəl\ *adj*
**1** favoring one side of a question over another ⟨a *partial* judge⟩
**2** fond or too fond of someone or something ⟨*partial* to ice cream sodas⟩
**3** of one part only ⟨a *partial* eclipse⟩
**4** not complete ⟨*partial* deafness⟩ ⟨our show was a *partial* success⟩
**par·tial·ly** \'pär-shə-lē\ *adv*

**par·ti·al·i·ty** \,pär-shē-'al-ət-ē\ *n, pl* **par·ti·al·i·ties**
the quality or state of being partial

**par·tic·i·pant** \pər-'tis-ə-pənt, pär-\ *n*
a person who takes part in something ⟨*participants* in a fight⟩

**par·tic·i·pate** \pər-'tis-ə-,pāt, pär-\ *vb* **par·tic·i·pat·ed**; **par·tic·i·pat·ing**
to join with others in doing something

**par·tic·i·pa·tion** \pär-,tis-ə-'pā-shən\ *n*
the act of participating

**par·ti·ci·ple** \'pärt-ə-,sip-əl\ *n*
a word formed from a verb but often used like an adjective while keeping some verb characteristics (as tense and the ability to take an object) ⟨"crying" in "the crying child ran home" is a *participle*⟩

**par·ti·cle** \'pärt-i-kəl\ *n*
a very small bit of something ⟨not a *particle* of sense⟩ ⟨a *particle* of sand⟩

[1]**par·tic·u·lar** \pər-'tik-yə-lər\ *adj*
**1** relating to one person or thing ⟨each city has its *particular* problems⟩
**2** not usual : SPECIAL ⟨a wind of *particular* force⟩
**3** being one of several ⟨consider each *particular* item⟩
**4** concerned about details ⟨our teacher is very *particular*⟩
**par·tic·u·lar·ly** *adv*

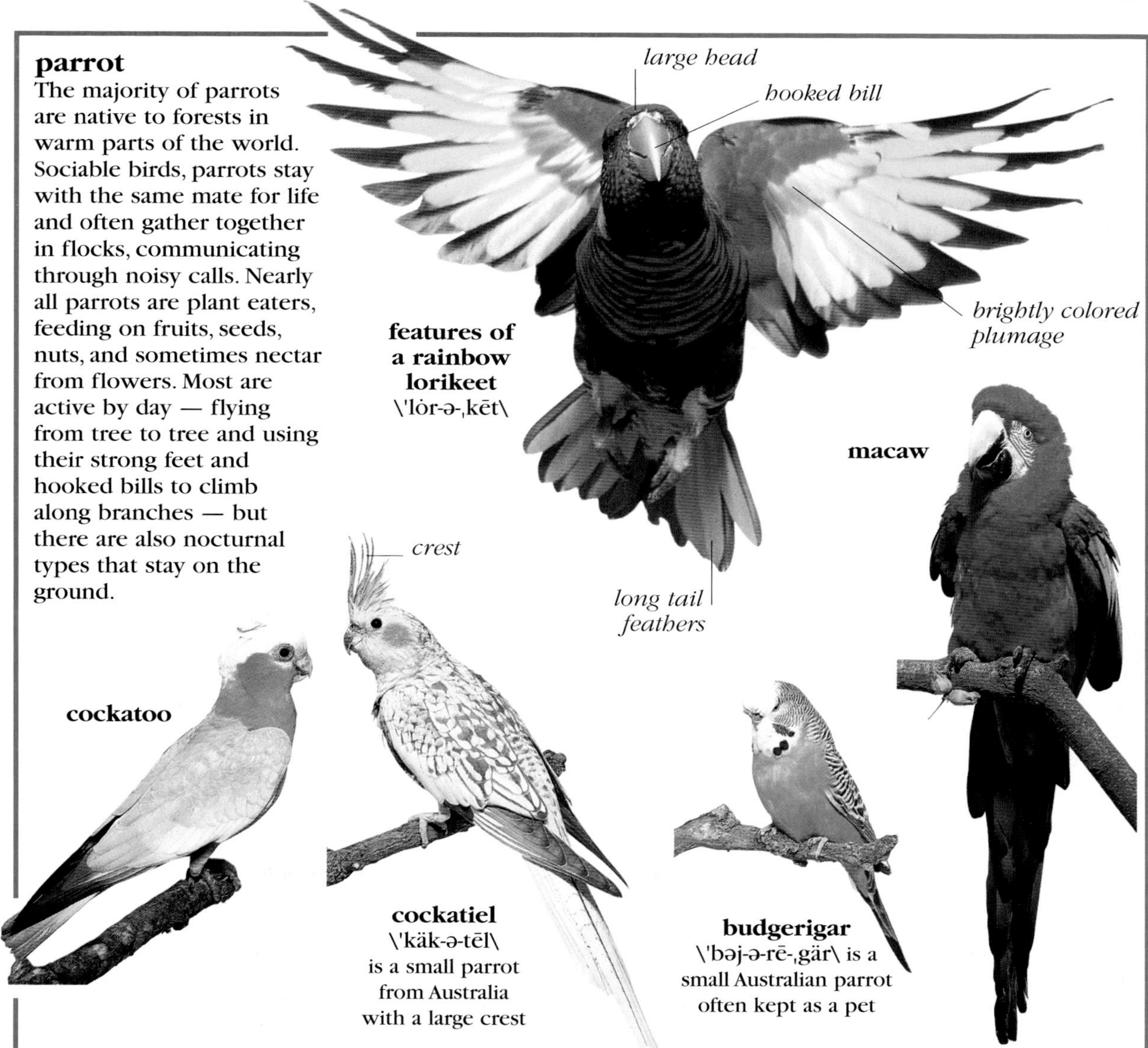


**parrot**
The majority of parrots are native to forests in warm parts of the world. Sociable birds, parrots stay with the same mate for life and often gather together in flocks, communicating through noisy calls. Nearly all parrots are plant eaters, feeding on fruits, seeds, nuts, and sometimes nectar from flowers. Most are active by day — flying from tree to tree and using their strong feet and hooked bills to climb along branches — but there are also nocturnal types that stay on the ground.

**features of a rainbow lorikeet** \'lȯr-ə-ˌkēt\

**macaw**

**cockatoo**

**cockatiel** \'käk-ə-tēl\ is a small parrot from Australia with a large crest

**budgerigar** \'bəj-ə-rē-ˌgär\ is a small Australian parrot often kept as a pet

**[2]particular** *n*
a single fact or detail ⟨the account was correct in every *particular*⟩

**part·ing** \'pärt-ing\ *n*
a place or point where a division or separation occurs

**par·ti·san** \'pärt-ə-zən, -sən\ *n*
**1** a person who aids or approves something (as a party or a point of view) or someone ⟨a *partisan* of the governor⟩
**2** a soldier who lives and fights behind enemy lines
**par·ti·san·ship** \-ˌship\ *n*

**[1]par·ti·tion** \pər-'tish-ən, pär-\ *n*
**1** an act of dividing into parts ⟨the *partition* of a defeated country⟩
**2** something that divides ⟨a *partition* between two rooms⟩

**[2]partition** *vb*
**1** to divide into shares ⟨*partition* an estate⟩
**2** to divide into separate parts or areas ⟨*partitioned* the basement into three rooms⟩

**part·ly** \'pärt-lē\ *adv*
somewhat but not completely ⟨I was *partly* to blame⟩

**part·ner** \'pärt-nər\ *n*
**1** a person who does or shares something with another ⟨my favorite dancing *partner*⟩
**2** either one of a married pair
**3** one who plays with another person on the same side in a game
**4** one of two or more persons who run a business together

**part·ner·ship** \'pärt-nər-ˌship\ *n*
**1** the state of being a partner
**2** a group of people in business together

**part of speech**
a class of words (as adjectives, adverbs, conjunctions, interjections, nouns, prepositions, pronouns, or verbs) identified according to the kinds of ideas they express and the work they do in a sentence

**partook** *past of* PARTAKE

A B C D E F G H I J K L M N O P Q R S T U V W X Y Z

**par·tridge** \'pär-trij\ *n, pl* **partridge** *or* **par·tridg·es**
any of several plump game birds related to the chicken

**partridge:** a European chestnut-bellied partridge

**part–time** \'pärt-'tīm\ *adj*
involving fewer than the usual hours ⟨*part-time* work⟩

**par·ty** \'pärt-ē\ *n, pl* **par·ties**
**1** a group of persons who take one side of a question or share a set of beliefs ⟨a political *party*⟩
**2** a social gathering or the entertainment provided for it
**3** a person or group concerned in some action ⟨a *party* to a lawsuit⟩

[1]**pass** \'pas\ *vb*
**1** [1]MOVE 1, PROCEED
**2** to go away ⟨the pain will soon *pass*⟩
**3** [1]DIE 1 ⟨*pass* on⟩
**4** to go by or move past ⟨*pass* that car⟩
**5** to go or allow to go across, over, or through ⟨they let me *pass*⟩
**6** to move from one place or condition to another ⟨the business has *passed* into other hands⟩
**7** HAPPEN 2
**8** to be or cause to be approved ⟨the senate *passed* the bill⟩
**9** to go successfully through an examination or inspection
**10** to be or cause to be identified or recognized ⟨*pass* for an expert⟩
**11** to transfer or throw to another person ⟨*pass* the salt⟩ ⟨*pass* a football⟩
**pass·er** *n*

[2]**pass** *n*
**1** an opening or way for passing along or through
**2** a gap in a mountain range

[3]**pass** *n*
**1** SITUATION 4 ⟨things have come to a strange *pass*⟩
**2** a written permit to go or come
**3** the act or an instance of passing (as a ball) in a game

**pass·able** \'pas-ə-bəl\ *adj*
**1** fit to be traveled on ⟨*passable* roads⟩
**2** barely good enough ⟨a *passable* imitation⟩
**pass·ably** \-blē\ *adv*

**pas·sage** \'pas-ij\ *n*
**1** the act or process of passing from one place or condition to another ⟨a smooth *passage* over the sea⟩
**2** a means (as a hall) of passing or reaching
**3** the passing of a law
**4** a right or permission to go as a passenger ⟨*passage* at a reduced rate⟩
**5** a brief part of a speech or written work

**pas·sage·way** \'pas-ij-,wā\ *n*
a road or way by which a person or thing may pass

**pas·sen·ger** \'pas-n-jər\ *n*
someone riding on or in a vehicle

**passenger pigeon** *n*
a North American wild pigeon once common but now extinct

**pass·er·by** \,pas-ər-'bī\ *n, pl* **pass·ers·by** \-ərz-'bī\
someone who passes by

[1]**pass·ing** \'pas-ing\ *n*
**1** the act of passing ⟨the *passing* of winter⟩
**2** DEATH 1

[2]**passing** *adj*
**1** going by or past
**2** lasting only for a short time ⟨a *passing* fad⟩
**3** showing haste or lack of attention ⟨a *passing* glance⟩
**4** used for passing ⟨*passing* lanes⟩
**5** showing satisfactory work in a test or course of study ⟨a *passing* mark⟩

**pas·sion** \'pash-ən\ *n*
**1** *cap* the suffering of Christ between the night of the Last Supper and his death
**2** a strong feeling or emotion
**3** strong liking or desire **:** LOVE ⟨a *passion* for music⟩
**4** an object of one's love, liking, or desire

**party 2:** a child's birthday party

**pas·sion·ate** \'pash-ə-nət\ *adj*
**1** easily angered
**2** showing or affected by strong feeling
**pas·sion·ate·ly** *adv*

**pas·sive** \'pas-iv\ *adj*
**1** not acting but acted upon ⟨*passive* spectators⟩
**2** showing that the person or thing represented by the subject is acted

on by the verb ⟨"were met" in "we were met by our friends" is *passive*⟩
**3** offering no resistance ⟨*passive* obedience⟩
**pas•sive•ly** *adv*

**pass out** *vb*
to become unconscious : FAINT

**Pass•over** \'pas-,ō-vər\ *n*
a Jewish holiday celebrated in March or April in honor of the freeing of the Hebrews from slavery in Egypt

**pass•port** \'pas-,pōrt\ *n*
▶ a government document that allows a citizen to leave his or her country

**pass up** *vb*
to let go by : REFUSE

**pass•word** \'pas-,wərd\ *n*
a secret word or phrase that must be spoken by a person before being allowed to pass a guard

**[1]past** \'past\ *adj*
**1** of or relating to a time that has gone by ⟨for the *past* month⟩
**2** expressing a time gone by ⟨the *past* tense of the verb "run" is "ran"⟩
**3** no longer serving ⟨a *past* mayor⟩

**[2]past** *prep*
**1** [2]BEYOND ⟨ten minutes *past* one⟩
**2** going close to and then beyond ⟨walked *past* my house⟩

**[3]past** *n*
**1** a former time
**2** past life or history ⟨the nation's *past*⟩

**[4]past** *adv*
so as to pass by or beyond ⟨a deer ran *past*⟩

**pas•ta** \'päs-tə\ *n*
**1** a dough of flour, eggs, and water made in different shapes and dried or used fresh
**2** a dish of cooked pasta

**[1]paste** \'pāst\ *n*
**1** dough for pies or tarts
**2** a soft smooth mixture
**3** a mixture of flour or starch and water used for sticking things together

**[2]paste** *vb* **past•ed**; **past•ing**
to stick on or together with paste

**paste•board** \'pāst-,bōrd\ *n*
a stiff material made of sheets of paper pasted together or of pulp pressed and dried

**[1]pas•tel** \pas-'tel\ *n*
**1** ▶ a crayon made by mixing ground coloring matter with a watery solution of a gum

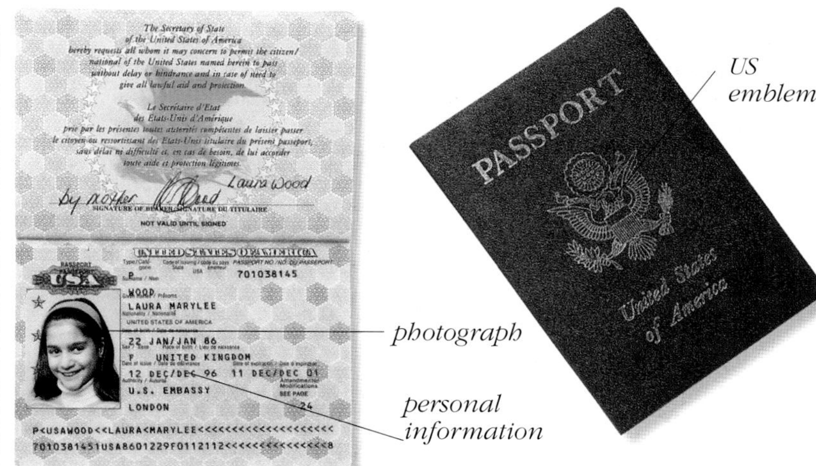

**passport:** a US passport

**2** a drawing made with pastel crayons
**3** a soft pale color

**[2]pastel** *adj*
**1** made with pastels
**2** light and pale in color

**pas•teur•i•za•tion** \,pas-chə-rə-'zā-shən, ,pas-tə-\ *n*
the process or an instance of pasteurizing

**pas•teur•ize** \'pas-chə-,rīz, 'pas-tə-\ *vb* **pas•teur•ized**; **pas•teur•iz•ing**
to keep a liquid (as milk) for a time at a temperature high enough to kill many harmful germs and then cool it rapidly
**pas•teur•iz•er** *n*

**pas•time** \'pas-,tīm\ *n*
something (as a hobby) that helps to make time pass pleasantly

**pas•tor** \'pas-tər\ *n*
a minister or priest in charge of a church

**pas•to•ral** \'pas-tə-rəl\ *adj*
**1** of or relating to shepherds or peaceful rural scenes ⟨*pastoral* poetry⟩
**2** of or relating to the pastor of a church ⟨*pastoral* duties⟩

**[1]pastel 1**

**pas•try** \'pā-strē\ *n, pl* **pas•tries**
**1** sweet baked goods (as pies) made mainly of flour and fat
**2** a piece of pastry

**[1]pas•ture** \'pas-chər\ *n*
**1** plants (as grass) for feeding grazing animals
**2** land on which animals graze

**[2]pasture** *vb* **pas•tured**; **pas•tur•ing**
**1** [1]GRAZE 1
**2** to supply (as cattle) with pasture

**[1]pat** \'pat\ *n*
**1** a light tap with the open hand or a flat instrument
**2** the sound of a pat or tap
**3** a small flat piece (as of butter)

**[2]pat** *adj* **pat•ter**; **pat•test**
**1** exactly suitable ⟨a *pat* answer⟩
**2** learned perfectly ⟨had my lines in the play down *pat*⟩
**3** not changing ⟨stood *pat* against all arguments⟩

**[3]pat** *vb* **pat•ted**; **pat•ting**
to tap or stroke gently with the open hand ⟨*pat* the dog⟩

**[1]patch** \'pach\ *n*
**1** a piece of cloth used to mend or cover a torn or worn place
**2** a small piece or area different from what is around it ⟨a *patch* of snow⟩ ⟨a *patch* of white on a dog's head⟩

**[2]patch** *vb*
to mend or cover with a patch
**synonyms** see MEND

**patch up** *vb*
ADJUST 1 ⟨*patch up* a quarrel⟩

A B C D E F G H I J K L M N O P Q R S T U V W X Y Z

**patch·work** \'pach-ˌwərk\ *n*
pieces of cloth of different colors and shapes sewed together

**[1]pat·ent** *for 1* 'pat-nt, *for 2* 'pat-ər 'pāt-\ *adj*
**1** protected by a patent
**2** OBVIOUS, EVIDENT ⟨a *patent* lie⟩

**[2]pat·ent** \'pat-nt\ *n*
a document that gives the inventor of something the only right to make, use, and sell the invention for a certain number of years

**[3]pat·ent** \'pat-nt\ *vb*
to get a patent for ⟨*patented* their invention⟩

**pa·ter·nal** \pə-'tərn-l\ *adj*
**1** of or relating to a father : FATHERLY
**2** received or inherited from a father
**3** related through the father ⟨my *paternal* grandparents⟩

**path** \'path, 'påth\ *n, pl* **paths** \'pat͟hz, 'påt͟hz\
**1** a track made by traveling on foot ⟨a *path* through the woods⟩
**2** the way or track in which something moves ⟨the *path* of a planet⟩
**3** a way of life or thought
**path·less** \-ləs\ *adj*

**pa·thet·ic** \pə-'thet-ik\ *adj*
making one feel pity, tenderness, or sorrow

**path·way** \'path-ˌwā, 'påth-\ *n*
PATH 1

**pa·tience** \'pā-shəns\ *n*
the ability to be patient or the fact of being patient ⟨need *patience* to do this work⟩

**[1]pa·tient** \'pā-shənt\ *adj*
**1** putting up with pain or troubles without complaint
**2** showing or involving calm self-control ⟨a *patient* teacher⟩ ⟨made a *patient* effort to answer calmly⟩
**pa·tient·ly** *adv*

**[2]patient** *n*
a person under medical care and treatment

**pa·tio** \'pat-ē-ˌō, 'pät-\ *n, pl* **pa·ti·os**
**1** an inner part of a house that is open to the sky
**2** an open area next to a house that is usually paved

**patchwork:**
a section of patchwork

**pa·tri·arch** \'pā-trē-ˌärk\ *n*
**1** the father and ruler of a family or tribe
**2** a respected old man

**pa·tri·ot** \'pā-trē-ət\ *n*
a person who loves his or her country and enthusiastically supports it

**pa·tri·ot·ic** \ˌpā-trē-'ät-ik\ *adj*
having or showing patriotism

**pa·tri·ot·ism** \'pā-trē-ə-ˌtiz-əm\ *n*
love of one's country

**[1]pa·trol** \pə-'trōl\ *n*
**1** the action of going around an area for observation or guard
**2** a person or group doing the act of patrolling
**3** a part of a troop of boy scouts that consists of two or more boys
**4** a part of a troop of girl scouts that usually consists of six or eight girls

**[2]patrol** *vb* **pa·trolled**; **pa·trol·ling**
to go around an area for the purpose of watching or protecting

**pa·trol·man** \pə-'trōl-mən\ *n, pl* **pa·trol·men** \-mən\
a police officer who has a regular beat

**pa·tron** \'pā-trən\ *n*
**1** a person who gives generous support or approval
**2** CUSTOMER
**3** a saint to whom a church or society is dedicated

**pa·tron·age** \'pa-trə-nij, 'pā-trə-\ *n*
**1** the help or encouragement given by a patron
**2** a group of patrons (as of a shop or theater)
**3** the control by officials of giving out jobs, contracts, and favors

**pa·tron·ize** \'pā-trə-ˌnīz, 'pa-trə-\ *vb* **pa·tron·ized**; **pa·tron·iz·ing**
**1** to act as a patron to or of : SUPPORT ⟨*patronize* the arts⟩
**2** to be a customer of ⟨*patronize* a neighborhood store⟩
**3** to treat (a person) as if one were better or more important

**[1]pat·ter** \'pat-ər\ *vb*
**1** to strike again and again with light blows ⟨rain *pattering* on a roof⟩
**2** to run with quick light steps

**[2]patter** *n*
a series of quick light sounds ⟨the *patter* of little feet⟩

**[1]pat·tern** \'pat-ərn\ *n*
**1** something worth copying ⟨a *pattern* of good behavior⟩
**2** a model or guide for making something ⟨a dressmaker's *pattern*⟩
**3** a form or figure used in decoration : DESIGN ⟨a rug with a fancy *pattern*⟩
**pat·terned** \-ərnd\ *adj*

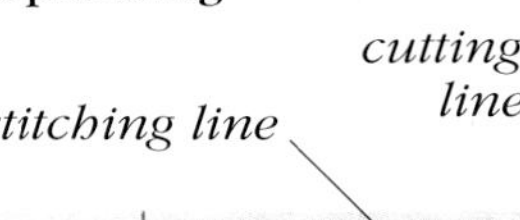

**[1]pattern 2:**
a dressmaker's pattern

**Word History** In early English a person who served as a model to be copied was called a *patron*. Some people began to say *patron* in such a way that the sound of the *r* changed its place. *Patron* soon became *pattern*. After a time *pattern*, the new way of saying the word, was used just for the meaning "a model to be copied." The older *patron* lost that meaning. In this way we got a new word, *pattern*, from the old word, *patron*.

[2]**pattern** *vb*
to make or design by following a pattern

**pat·ty** \'pat-ē\ *n, pl* **pat·ties**
a small flat cake of chopped food ⟨a hamburger *patty*⟩

**pau·per** \'pȯ-pər\ *n*
a very poor person

[1]**pause** \'pȯz\ *n*
**1** a temporary stop
**2** a sign 𝄐 above a musical note or rest to show that the note or rest is to be held longer

[2]**pause** *vb* **paused**; **paus·ing**
to stop for a time : make a pause

**pave** \'pāv\ *vb* **paved**; **pav·ing**
to make a hard surface on (as with concrete or asphalt) ⟨*pave* a street⟩

**pave·ment** \'pāv-mənt\ *n*
**1** a paved surface (as of a street)
**2** material used in paving

**pa·vil·ion** \pə-'vil-yən\ *n*
**1** a very large tent
**2** a building usually with open sides that is used as a place for entertainment or shelter in a park or garden

**pav·ing** \'pā-ving\ *n*
PAVEMENT

[1]**paw** \'pȯ\ *n*
the foot of a four-footed animal (as the lion, dog, or cat) that has claws

[2]**paw** *vb*
**1** to touch in a clumsy or rude way
**2** to touch or scrape with a paw ⟨the dog *pawed* the door⟩
**3** to beat or scrape with a hoof

[1]**pawn** \'pȯn\ *n*
the piece of least value in the game of chess

[2]**pawn** *n*
**1** something of value given as a guarantee (as of payment of a debt)
**2** the condition of being given as a guarantee ⟨have a watch in *pawn*⟩

[3]**pawn** *vb*
to leave as a guarantee for a loan : PLEDGE ⟨*pawn* a watch⟩

**pawn·bro·ker** \'pȯn-ˌbrō-kər\ *n*
a person who makes a business of lending money and keeping personal property as a guarantee

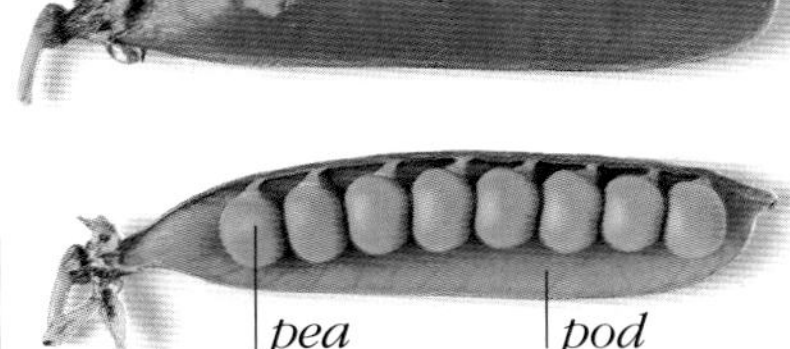


**pea 1:** peas in a pod

**pawn·shop** \'pȯn-ˌshäp\ *n*
a pawnbroker's shop

[1]**pay** \'pā\ *vb* **paid** \'pād\; **pay·ing**
**1** to give (as money) in return for services received or for something bought ⟨*pay* the taxi driver⟩ ⟨*pay* for a ticket⟩
**2** to give what is owed ⟨*pay* a tax⟩
**3** to get revenge on ⟨*pay* them back for the insult⟩
**4** to give or offer freely ⟨*pay* a compliment⟩ ⟨*pay* attention⟩
**5** to get a suitable return for cost or trouble : be worth the effort or pains required ⟨it *pays* to drive carefully⟩
**pay·er** *n*

[2]**pay** *n*
**1** the act of paying : PAYMENT
**2** the state of being paid or employed for money ⟨in the *pay* of the company⟩
**3** SALARY

**pay·able** \'pā-ə-bəl\ *adj*
that may, can, or must be paid

**pay·check** \'pā-ˌchek\ *n*
a check or money received as wages or salary

**pay·ment** \'pā-mənt\ *n*
**1** the act of paying
**2** money given to pay a debt ⟨make *payments* on a car⟩

**pay off** *vb*
**1** to pay in full ⟨*pay off* a debt⟩
**2** to have a good result ⟨hours of practice *paid off* in a successful show⟩

**pay·roll** \'pā-ˌrōl\ *n*
**1** a list of persons who receive pay
**2** the amount of money necessary to pay the employees of a business

**pay up** *vb*
to pay in full especially debts that are overdue

**PC** \ˌpē-'sē\ *n, pl* **PCs** *or* **PC's**
PERSONAL COMPUTER

**pea** \'pē\ *n, pl* **peas** *also* **pease** \'pēz\
**1** ◀ a vegetable that is the round seed found in the pods of a garden plant (**pea vine**) related to the clovers
**2** a plant (as the sweet pea) resembling or related to the garden pea

**peace** \'pēs\ *n*
**1** freedom from public disturbance or war
**2** freedom from upsetting thoughts or feelings
**3** agreement and harmony among persons
**4** an agreement to end a war

**peace·able** \'pē-sə-bəl\ *adj*
PEACEFUL 1, 3

**peace·ful** \'pēs-fəl\ *adj*
**1** liking peace : not easily moved to argue or fight ⟨a *peaceful* people⟩
**2** full of or enjoying peace, quiet, or calm
**3** not involving fighting ⟨settle a dispute by *peaceful* means⟩
**synonyms** see CALM
**peace·ful·ly** \-fə-lē\ *adv*
**peace·ful·ness** *n*

**peace·mak·er** \'pēs-ˌmā-kər\ *n*
a person who settles an argument or stops a fight

**peace pipe** *n*
▼ a decorated pipe of the American Indians used for certain ceremonies

*bowl for tobacco*
*eagle feather decoration*

**peace pipe** of the Menominee \mə-'näm-ə-nē\ tribe of Wisconsin

**peach** \'pēch\ *n*
**1** a fruit that is related to the plum and has a sweet juicy pulp, hairy skin, and a large rough stone
**2** a pale yellowish pink color

**Word History** The ancient Romans used the Latin word that meant "of Iran" as a handy term for anything from the East. They knew, for example, that peaches came from the East and gave the peach a name that meant "apple of Iran." In time, the phrase meaning "apple of Iran" was shortened and the word meaning "of Iran" was used by itself to mean "peach." The English word *peach* comes from the Latin word that meant "of Iran."

**pea•cock** \'pē-,käk\ *n*
the male of a very large Asian pheasant with a very long brightly colored tail that can be spread or raised at will, a small crest, and in most forms brilliant blue or green feathers on the neck and shoulders

**peak** \'pēk\ *n*
**1** the part of a cap that sticks out in front
**2** the pointed top of a hill or mountain ⟨climbed all the way to the *peak*⟩
**3** ▶ a mountain all by itself ⟨a snow-capped *peak* rising from the plain⟩
**4** the highest point of development ⟨at the *peak* of one's career⟩

**[1]peal** \'pēl\ *n*
**1** the sound of bells
**2** a loud sound **:** a series of loud sounds ⟨a *peal* of thunder⟩

**[2]peal** *vb*
to give out peals ⟨bells *pealing* in the distance⟩

**pea•nut** \'pē-,nət\ *n*
a plant related to the peas that has yellow flowers and is grown for its underground pods of oily nutlike edible seeds which yield a valuable oil (**peanut oil**) or are crushed to form a spread (**peanut butter**)

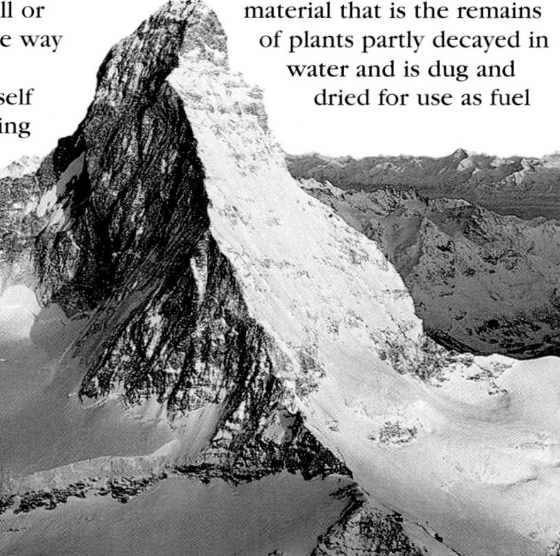

**peak 3**

**pear** \'paər, 'peər\ *n*
the fleshy fruit that grows on a tree related to the apple and is commonly larger at the end opposite the stem

**pearl** \'pərl\ *n*
**1** ▶ a smooth body with a rich luster that is formed within the shell of some mollusks (as the **pearl oyster** of tropical seas) usually around something irritating (as a grain of sand) which has gotten into the shell
**2** MOTHER-OF-PEARL
**3** something like a pearl in shape, color, or value
**4** a pale bluish gray color

**pearly** \'pər-lē\ *adj* **pearl•i•er; pearl•i•est**
like a pearl especially in having a shining surface

**peas•ant** \'pez-nt\ *n*
a farmer owning a small amount of land or a farm worker in European countries

**pease** *pl of* PEA

**peat** \'pēt\ *n*
a blackish or dark brown material that is the remains of plants partly decayed in water and is dug and dried for use as fuel

**peat moss** *n*
a spongy brownish moss of wet areas that is often the chief plant making up peat

**peb•ble** \'peb-əl\ *n*
a small rounded stone

pearl

oyster shell

**pearl 1:** a pearl shown in the oyster shell in which it formed

**pe•can** \pi-'kän, -'kan\ *n*
an oval edible nut that usually has a thin shell and is the fruit of a tall tree of the central and southern United States related to the walnuts

**peccary:** a collared peccary

**pec•ca•ry** \'pek-ə-rē\ *n, pl* **pec•ca•ries**
▲ either of two mostly tropical American animals that gather in herds, are active at night, and look like but are much smaller than the related pigs

**[1]peck** \'pek\ *n*
**1** a unit of capacity equal to one quarter of a bushel
**2** a great deal **:** a large quantity ⟨a *peck* of trouble⟩

**[2]peck** *vb*
**1** to strike or pick up with the bill ⟨birds *pecking* cherries⟩
**2** to strike with a sharp instrument (as a pick)

**[3]peck** *n*
**1** the act of pecking
**2** a mark made by pecking

**pe•cu•liar** \pi-'kyül-yər\ *adj*
**1** one's own **:** of or limited to some one person, thing, or place ⟨a custom *peculiar* to England⟩
**2** different from the usual **:** ODD

**pedestal 1:** a pedestal supporting a statue of an ancient Roman god

**Word History** The word *peculiar* first meant "one's own." You may have some quality that is just your own. No one else has it. That surely makes it unusual. This is how *peculiar* came to mean "unusual" or "odd."

**pe·cu·li·ar·i·ty** \pi-ˌkyü-lē-'ar-ət-ē\ *n, pl* **pe·cu·li·ar·i·ties**
1 the quality or state of being peculiar
2 something peculiar or individual ⟨all of us have some *peculiarities*⟩

**[1]ped·al** \'ped-l\ *n*
a lever worked by the foot or feet

**[2]pedal** *vb* **ped·aled** *or* **ped·alled**; **ped·al·ing** *or* **ped·al·ling**
to use or work the pedals of something ⟨*pedal* a bicycle⟩

**ped·dle** \'ped-l\ *vb* **ped·dled**; **ped·dling**
to go about especially from house to house with goods for sale

**ped·dler** *or* **ped·lar** \'ped-lər\ *n*
someone who peddles

**ped·es·tal** \'ped-əst-l\ *n*
1 ◀ a support or foot of an upright structure (as a column, statue, or lamp)
2 a position of high regard ⟨placed their teacher on a *pedestal*⟩

**pe·des·tri·an** \pə-'des-trē-ən\ *n*
a person who is walking

**pe·di·a·tri·cian** \ˌpēd-ē-ə-'trish-ən\ *n*
a doctor who specializes in the care of babies and children

**ped·i·gree** \'ped-ə-ˌgrē\ *n*
1 a table or list showing the line of ancestors of a person or animal
2 a line of ancestors

**pe·dom·e·ter** \pi-'däm-ət-ər\ *n*
an instrument that measures the distance one covers in walking

**[1]peek** \'pēk\ *vb*
1 to look slyly or cautiously
2 to take a quick glance
**peek·er** *n*

**[2]peek** *n*
a short or sly look

**[1]peel** \'pēl\ *vb*
1 to strip off the skin or bark of
2 to strip or tear off
3 to come off smoothly or in bits

**[2]peel** *n*
▼ an outer covering and especially the skin of a fruit

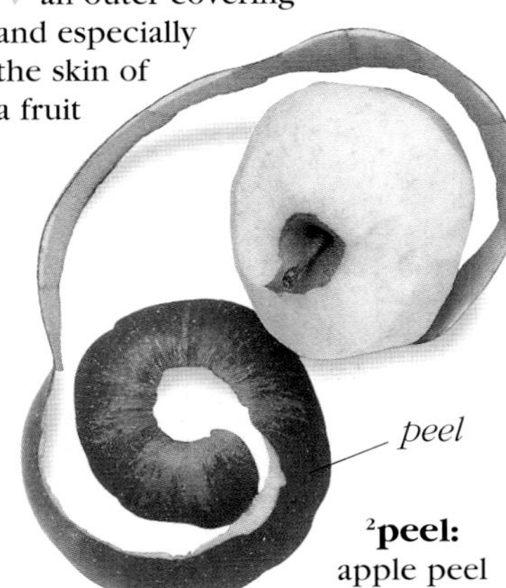


**[2]peel:** apple peel

**[1]peep** \'pēp\ *vb*
to make a weak shrill sound such as a young bird makes
**peep·er** *n*

**[2]peep** *n*
a weak shrill sound

**[3]peep** *vb*
1 to look through or as if through a small hole or a crack : PEEK
2 to show slightly ⟨crocuses *peeping* through the grass⟩

**[4]peep** *n*
1 a brief or sly look
2 the first appearance ⟨the *peep* of dawn⟩

**[1]peer** \'pir\ *n*
1 a person of the same rank or kind : EQUAL
2 a member of one of the five ranks (duke, marquis, earl, viscount, and baron) of the British nobility

**[2]peer** *vb*
1 to look curiously or carefully
2 to come slightly into view : peep out

**peer·less** \'pir-ləs\ *adj*
having no equal

**pee·vish** \'pē-vish\ *adj*
complaining a lot : IRRITABLE
**pee·vish·ly** *adv*
**pee·vish·ness** *n*

**pee·wee** \'pē-ˌwē\ *n*
one that is small

**[1]peg** \'peg\ *n*
1 a slender piece (as of wood or metal) used especially to fasten things together or to hang things on ⟨a clothes *peg*⟩
2 a piece driven into the ground to mark a boundary or to hold something ⟨a *peg* for a tent rope⟩
3 a step or grade in approval or esteem ⟨took them down a *peg*⟩

**[2]peg** *vb* **pegged**; **peg·ging**
1 to mark or fasten with pegs
2 to work hard ⟨I keep *pegging* away at my job⟩

**pel·i·can** \'pel-i-kən\ *n*
a bird with a large bill, webbed feet, and a great pouch on the lower jaw that is used to scoop in fish for food

**pel·la·gra** \pə-'lag-rə, -'lāg-\ *n*
a disease caused by a diet containing too little protein and too little of a necessary vitamin

**pel·let** \'pel-ət\ *n*
1 a little ball (as of food or medicine)
2 a piece of small shot

**pell–mell** \'pel-'mel\ *adv*
1 in crowded confusion
2 in a big hurry

**[1]pelt** \'pelt\ *n*
a skin of an animal especially with its fur or wool

**[2]pelt** *vb*
**1** to strike with repeated blows
**2** HURL, THROW
**3** to beat or pound against something again and again ⟨rain *pelting* on the roof⟩

**pel·vis** \'pel-vəs\ *n*
the bowl-shaped part of the skeleton that supports the lower part of the abdomen and includes the hip bones and the lower bones of the backbone

**[1]pen** \'pen\ *vb* **penned**; **pen·ning**
to shut in a small enclosure

**[2]pen** *n*
a small enclosure especially for animals ⟨a chicken *pen*⟩

**[3]pen** *n*
an instrument for writing with ink

**[4]pen** *vb* **penned**; **pen·ning**
to write with a pen

**pe·nal** \'pē-nl\ *adj*
of or relating to punishment

**pe·nal·ize** \'pē-nl-,īz, 'pen-\ *vb* **pe·nal·ized**; **pe·nal·iz·ing**
to give a penalty to ⟨*penalize* an athlete for a foul⟩

**pen·al·ty** \'pen-l-tē\ *n, pl* **pen·al·ties**
**1** punishment for doing something wrong
**2** a loss or handicap given for breaking a rule in a sport or game

**pence** *pl of* PENNY

**[1]pen·cil** \'pen-səl\ *n*
a device for writing or drawing consisting of a stick of black or colored material enclosed in wood, plastic, or metal

**[2]pencil** *vb* **pen·ciled** *or* **pen·cilled**; **pen·cil·ing** *or* **pen·cil·ling**
to write, mark, or draw with a pencil

**pen·dant** \'pen-dənt\ *n*
▶ an ornament (as on a necklace) allowed to hang free

*chain*
*pendant*
**pendant**

**[1]pend·ing** \'pen-ding\ *prep*
**1** DURING 1
**2** while waiting for ⟨will make no statement *pending* further information⟩

**[2]pending** *adj*
not yet decided ⟨*pending* questions⟩

**pen·du·lum** \'pen-jə-ləm, -dyə-\ *n*
an object hung from a fixed point so as to swing freely back and forth under the action of gravity ⟨the *pendulum* of a clock⟩

**pen·e·trate** \'pen-ə-,trāt\ *vb* **pen·e·trat·ed**; **pen·e·trat·ing**
**1** to pass into or through : PIERCE
**2** to see into or understand

**pen·e·tra·tion** \,pen-ə-'trā-shən\ *n*
**1** the act or process of penetrating
**2** keen understanding

**[2]penitent** *n*
a penitent person

**pen·i·ten·tia·ry** \,pen-ə-'ten-chə-rē\ *n, pl* **pen·i·ten·tia·ries**
a prison for criminals

**pen·knife** \'pen-,nīf\ *n, pl* **pen·knives** \-,nīvz\
a small jackknife

**pen·man** \'pen-mən\ *n, pl* **pen·men** \-mən\
a person who uses a pen : WRITER

**pen·man·ship** \'pen-mən-,ship\ *n*
writing with a pen : style or quality of handwriting

**pen name** *n*
a false name that an author uses on his or her work ⟨a professor who wrote novels under a *pen name*⟩

**penguin:** a penguin diving underwater

**pen·guin** \'pen-gwən, 'peng-\ *n*
▲ a seabird that cannot fly, has very short legs, and is found in the cold regions of the southern hemisphere

**pen·i·cil·lin** \,pen-ə-'sil-ən\ *n*
an antibiotic that is produced by a mold and is used especially against disease-causing round bacteria

**pen·in·su·la** \pə-'nin-sə-lə\ *n*
a piece of land extending out into a body of water

**pe·nis** \'pē-nəs\ *n, pl* **pe·nes** \-,nēz\ *or* **pe·nis·es**
a male organ in mammals used for sexual intercourse and for urinating

**pen·i·tence** \'pen-ə-təns\ *n*
sorrow for one's sins or faults

**[1]pen·i·tent** \'pen-ə-tənt\ *adj*
feeling or showing penitence

**pen·nant** \'pen-ənt\ *n*
**1** a narrow pointed flag used for identification, signaling, or decoration
**2** a flag that serves as the emblem of a championship

**pen·ni·less** \'pen-i-ləs\ *adj*
very poor : having no money

**pen·ny** \'pen-ē\ *n, pl* **pennies** \'pen-ēz\
**1** *or pl* **pence** \'pens\ a coin of the United Kingdom equal to $^1/_{100}$ pound
**2** CENT

**[1]pen·sion** \'pen-chən\ *n*
a sum paid regularly to a person who has retired from work

**[2]pension** *vb*
to grant or give a pension to

**pen•sive** \'pen-siv\ *adj*
lost in sober or sad thought ⟨a *pensive* mood⟩
**pen•sive•ly** *adv*
**pen•sive•ness** *n*

**pent** \'pent\ *adj*
penned up : shut up ⟨*pent*-up feelings⟩

**penta-** *or* **pent-** *prefix*
five

**pen•ta•gon** \'pent-ə-,gän\ *n*
a flat figure having five angles and five sides

**pen•tag•o•nal** \pen-'tag-ən-l\ *adj*
having five sides

**pen•tath•lon** \pen-'tath-lən, -,län\ *n*
an athletic contest made up of five different events in which each person participates

**pent•house** \'pent-,hau̇s\ *n*
an apartment built on the roof of a building

**pe•on** \'pē-,än\ *n*
a member of the landless laboring class in Spanish America

**pe•o•ny** \'pē-ə-nē\ *n, pl* **pe•o•nies**
▼ a plant related to the buttercup that lives for years and is widely grown for its very large usually double white, pink, or red flowers

**peony**

[1]**peo•ple** \'pē-pəl\ *n, pl* **people** *or* **peoples**
**1** a body of persons making up a race, tribe, or nation ⟨the *peoples* of Asia⟩
**2** human beings — often used in compounds instead of *persons* ⟨sales*people*⟩
**3** the persons of a certain group or place ⟨the *people* of this state⟩

[2]**people** *vb* **peo•pled**; **peo•pling**
**1** to supply or fill with people
**2** to dwell on or in

[1]**pep** \'pep\ *n*
brisk energy or liveliness

[2]**pep** *vb* **pepped**; **pep•ping**
to put pep into ⟨cool weather *peps* us up⟩

[1]**pep•per** \'pep-ər\ *n*
**1** a product from the fruit of an East Indian climbing shrub that is sharp in flavor, is used as a seasoning or in medicine, and consists of the whole ground dried berry (**black pepper**) or of the ground seeds alone (**white pepper**)
**2** a plant related to the tomato that is grown for its fruits which may be very sharp in flavor (**hot peppers**) and are used mostly in pickles or dried and ground as a seasoning or may be mild and sweet (**sweet peppers**) and are used mostly as a vegetable

[2]**pepper** *vb*
**1** to season with or as if with pepper
**2** to hit with a shower of blows or objects ⟨hail *peppered* the hikers⟩

**pep•per•mint** \'pep-ər-,mint\ *n*
a mint with stalks of small usually purple flowers that yields an oil (**peppermint oil**) which is sharp in flavor and is used especially to flavor candies

**pep•py** \'pep-ē\ *adj* **pep•pi•er**; **pep•pi•est**
full of pep

**pep•sin** \'pep-sən\ *n*
an enzyme that starts the digestion of proteins in the stomach

**per** \pər\ *prep*
**1** to or for each ⟨ten dollars *per* day⟩
**2** ACCORDING TO 1 ⟨was done *per* instructions⟩

**per an•num** \pər-'an-əm\ *adv*
by the year : in or for each year : ANNUALLY

**per cap•i•ta** \pər-'kap-ət-ə\ *adv or adj*
by or for each person ⟨the *per capita* wealth of a country⟩

**per•ceive** \pər-'sēv\ *vb* **per•ceived**; **per•ceiv•ing**
**1** to become aware of through the senses and especially through sight
**2** UNDERSTAND 1

[1]**per•cent** \pər-'sent\ *adv or adj*
out of every hundred : measured by the number of units as compared with one hundred

[2]**percent** *n, pl* **percent**
a part or fraction of a whole expressed in hundredths ⟨thirty *percent* of the class failed the test⟩

**per•cent•age** \pər-'sent-ij\ *n*
**1** a part of a whole expressed in hundredths
**2** a share of profits

**per•cep•ti•ble** \pər-'sep-tə-bəl\ *adj*
possible to detect ⟨a *perceptible* change⟩

**per•cep•tion** \pər-'sep-shən\ *n*
**1** an act or the result of grasping with one's mind
**2** the ability to grasp (as meanings and ideas) with one's mind
**3** a judgment formed from information grasped

[1]**perch** \'pərch\ *n*
**1** a place where birds roost
**2** a raised seat or position

[2]**perch** *vb*
to sit or rest on or as if on a perch

[3]**perch 1**

[3]**perch** *n, pl* **perch** *or* **perch•es**
**1** ▲ a European freshwater food fish that is mostly olive green and yellow
**2** any of numerous fishes related to or resembling the European perch

**per•chance** \pər-'chans\ *adv*
PERHAPS

**per•co•late** \'pər-kə-,lāt\ *vb* **per•co•lat•ed**; **per•co•lat•ing**
**1** to trickle or cause to trickle through something porous : OOZE ⟨water *percolating* through sand⟩
**2** to prepare (coffee) by passing hot water through ground coffee beans again and again
**per•co•la•tor** \-,lāt-ər\ *n*

**per•co•la•tion** \,pər-kə-'lā-shən\ *n*
the act or process of percolating

**per•cus•sion** \pər-'kəsh-ən\ *n*
**1** a sharp tapping
**2** the striking of an explosive cap to set off the charge in a gun
**3** the musical instruments of a band or orchestra that are played by striking or shaking

## percussion instrument

Percussion instruments may have been the earliest type of musical instrument. Most are used to emphasize rhythm and add impact to music, although some, such as the xylophone, can be tuned to produce separate musical notes.

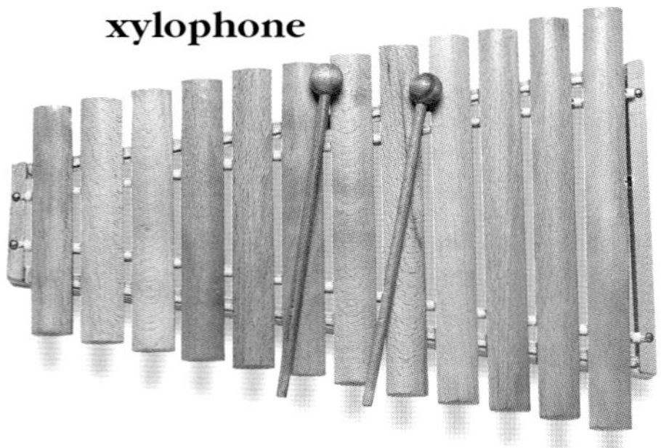

**xylophone**

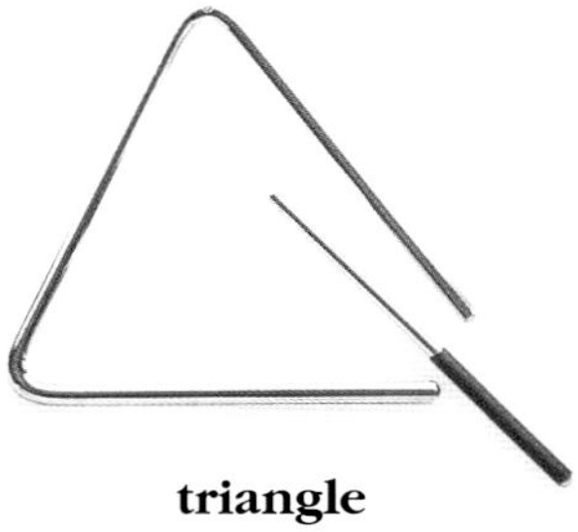

**triangle**

**cymbals**

**tambourine**

**maracas**

**drums**

**percussion instrument** *n*
a musical instrument (as a drum, cymbal, or maraca) sounded by striking or shaking

[1]**pe·ren·ni·al** \pə-'ren-ē-əl\ *adj*
**1** present all through the year ⟨a *perennial* stream⟩
**2** never ending **:** CONTINUOUS ⟨*perennial* joy⟩
**3** living from year to year ⟨a *perennial* plant⟩

[2]**perennial** *n*
a perennial plant

[1]**per·fect** \'pər-fikt\ *adj*
**1** lacking nothing **:** COMPLETE ⟨a *perfect* set of teeth⟩
**2** thoroughly skilled or trained **:** meeting the highest standards ⟨a *perfect* performance⟩
**3** having no mistake, error, or flaw ⟨a *perfect* diamond⟩
**per·fect·ly** *adv*

[2]**per·fect** \pər-'fekt\ *vb*
to make perfect

**per·fec·tion** \pər-'fek-shən\ *n*
**1** completeness in all parts or details
**2** the highest excellence or skill
**3** a quality or thing that cannot be improved

**per·fo·rate** \'pər-fə-ˌrāt\ *vb*
**per·fo·rat·ed; per·fo·rat·ing**
**1** to make a hole through **:** PIERCE
**2** to make many small holes in

**per·form** \pər-'fȯrm\ *vb*
**1** to carry out **:** ACCOMPLISH, DO
**2** to do something needing special skill ⟨*perform* on the piano⟩
**per·form·er** *n*

**per·for·mance** \pər-'fȯr-məns\ *n*
**1** the carrying out of an action ⟨the *performance* of daily chores⟩
**2** a public entertainment

[1]**per·fume** \'pər-ˌfyüm\ *n*
**1** a pleasant smell **:** FRAGRANCE
**2** a liquid used to make things smell nice

[2]**per·fume** \pər-'fyüm\ *vb*
**per·fumed; per·fum·ing**
to make smell nice **:** add a pleasant scent to

**per·haps** \pər-'haps\ *adv*
possibly but not certainly **:** MAYBE

**per·il** \'per-əl\ *n*
**1** the state of being in great danger ⟨in *peril* of death⟩
**2** a cause or source of danger

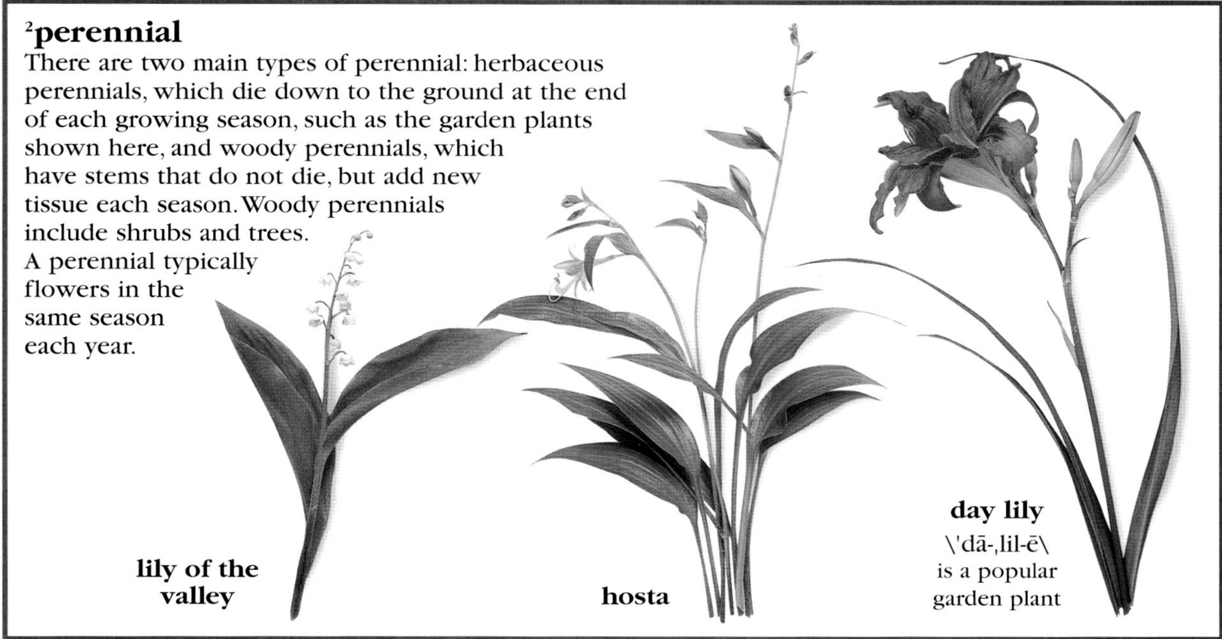


**²perennial**
There are two main types of perennial: herbaceous perennials, which die down to the ground at the end of each growing season, such as the garden plants shown here, and woody perennials, which have stems that do not die, but add new tissue each season. Woody perennials include shrubs and trees. A perennial typically flowers in the same season each year.

**per·il·ous** \'per-ə-ləs\ *adj*
DANGEROUS 1 ⟨sailing along a *perilous* coast⟩
**per·il·ous·ly** *adv*

**pe·rim·e·ter** \pə-'rim-ət-ər\ *n*
**1** the whole outer boundary of a figure or area
**2** the length of the boundary of a figure

**pe·ri·od** \'pir-ē-əd\ *n*
**1** a punctuation mark . used chiefly to mark the end of a declarative sentence or an abbreviation
**2** a portion of time set apart by some quality ⟨a *period* of cool weather⟩
**3** a portion of time that forms a stage in the history of something ⟨the colonial *period*⟩
**4** one of the divisions of a school day

**Synonyms** PERIOD and AGE mean a portion of time. PERIOD can be used of any portion of time, no matter how long or short ⟨a *period* of five minutes⟩ ⟨a new *period* of space exploration⟩. AGE suggests a longer period of time that is associated with an important person ⟨the *age* of Thomas Jefferson⟩ or some outstanding thing ⟨an ice *age*⟩.

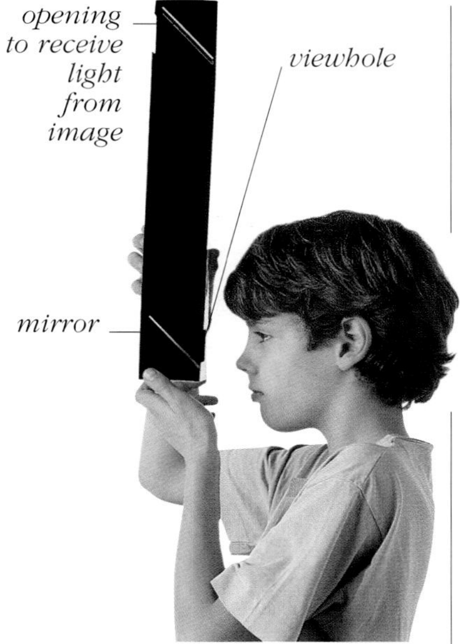


**periscope:** a boy looking through a periscope in cross section

**pe·ri·od·ic** \,pir-ē-'äd-ik\ *adj*
occurring at regular intervals

**¹pe·ri·od·i·cal** \,pir-ē-'äd-i-kəl\ *adj*
**1** PERIODIC
**2** published at regular intervals
**pe·ri·od·i·cal·ly** *adv*

**²periodical** *n*
a periodical publication (as a magazine)

**peri·scope** \'per-ə-,skōp\ *n*
◀ an instrument containing lenses and mirrors by which a person (as on a submarine) can get a view that would otherwise be blocked

**per·ish** \'per-ish\ *vb*
to become destroyed **:** DIE ⟨nations that have *perished* from the earth⟩

**per·ish·able** \'per-ish-ə-bəl\ *adj*
likely to spoil or decay ⟨*perishable* foods such as milk and eggs⟩

**¹per·i·win·kle** \'per-i-,wing-kəl\ *n*
an evergreen plant that spreads along the ground and has shining leaves and blue or white flowers

**²periwinkle** *n*
▶ a small snail that lives along rocky seashores

spiral pattern

**²periwinkle:** a periwinkle's shell

**perk** \'pərk\ *vb*
**1** to lift in a quick, alert, or bold way ⟨a dog *perking* its ears⟩
**2** to make fresher in appearance ⟨*perk* a room up with fresh paint⟩
**3** to become more lively or cheerful ⟨I *perked* up when I heard the good news⟩

A B C D E F G H I J K L M N O P Q R S T U V W X Y Z

**perky** \'pər-kē\ *adj* **perk·i·er**; **perk·i·est**
being lively and cheerful

**per·ma·nence** \'pər-mə-nəns\ *n*
the quality or state of being permanent

**per·ma·nent** \'pər-mə-nənt\ *adj*
lasting or meant to last for a long time : not temporary
**per·ma·nent·ly** *adv*

**per·me·able** \'pər-mē-ə-bəl\ *adj*
having pores or openings that let liquids or gases pass through

**per·me·ate** \'per-mē-,āt\ *vb* **per·me·at·ed**; **per·me·at·ing**
**1** to pass through something that has pores or small openings or is in a loose form ⟨water *permeates* sand⟩
**2** to spread throughout ⟨a room *permeated* with the smell of smoke⟩

**per·mis·sion** \pər-'mish-ən\ *n*
the consent of a person in authority

[1]**per·mit** \pər-'mit\ *vb* **per·mit·ted**; **per·mit·ting**
**1** to give permission : ALLOW
**2** to make possible : give an opportunity ⟨if time *permits*⟩

[2]**per·mit** \'pər-,mit\ *n*
a statement of permission (as a license or pass)

**per·ni·cious** \pər-'nish-əs\ *adj*
causing great damage or harm ⟨a *pernicious* disease⟩ ⟨a *pernicious* habit⟩

**per·ox·ide** \pə-'räk-,sīd\ *n*
an oxide containing much oxygen (as one of hydrogen used as an antiseptic)

[1]**per·pen·dic·u·lar** \,pər-pən-'dik-yə-lər\ *adj*
**1** exactly vertical
**2** being at right angles to a line or surface
**per·pen·dic·u·lar·ly** *adv*

[2]**perpendicular** *n*
a perpendicular line, surface, or position

**per·pe·trate** \'pər-pə-,trāt\ *vb* **per·pe·trat·ed**; **per·pe·trat·ing**
to bring about or carry out : COMMIT ⟨*perpetrate* a crime⟩
**per·pe·tra·tor** \'pər-pə-,trāt-ər\ *n*

**per·pet·u·al** \pər-'pech-ə-wəl\ *adj*
**1** lasting forever : ETERNAL
**2** occurring continually : CONSTANT ⟨*perpetual* arguments⟩
**per·pet·u·al·ly** *adv*

**per·pet·u·ate** \pər-'pech-ə-,wāt\ *vb* **per·pet·u·at·ed**; **per·pet·u·at·ing**
to cause to last a long time

**per·plex** \pər-'pleks\ *vb*
to confuse the mind of : BEWILDER

**per·plex·i·ty** \pər-'plek-sət-ē\ *n, pl* **per·plex·i·ties**
**1** a puzzled or anxious state of mind
**2** something that perplexes

**per·se·cute** \'pər-si-,kyüt\ *vb* **per·se·cut·ed**; **per·se·cut·ing**
to treat continually in a way meant to be cruel and harmful

**per·se·cu·tion** \,pər-si-'kyü-shən\ *n*
**1** the act of persecuting
**2** the state of being persecuted

**per·se·ver·ance** \,pər-sə-'vir-əns\ *n*
the act or power of persevering

**per·se·vere** \,pər-sə-'vir\ *vb* **per·se·vered**; **per·se·ver·ing**
to keep trying to do something in spite of difficulties ⟨*persevered* in learning to speak French⟩

fruit
leaf

**persimmon**

**per·sim·mon** \pər-'sim-ən\ *n*
▲ a fruit of orange color that looks like a plum and grows on a tree related to the ebonies

**per·sist** \pər-'sist\ *vb*
**1** to keep on doing or saying something : continue stubbornly
**2** to last on and on : continue to exist or occur ⟨rain *persisting* for days⟩

**per·sist·ence** \pər-'sis-təns\ *n*
**1** the act or fact of persisting
**2** the quality of being persistent : PERSEVERANCE

**per·sist·ent** \pər-'sis-tənt\ *adj*
continuing to act or exist longer than usual ⟨a *persistent* cold⟩
**per·sist·ent·ly** *adv*

**per·son** \'pərs-n\ *n*
**1** a human being — used in compounds especially by those who prefer to avoid *man* in words that apply to both sexes ⟨chair*person*⟩
**2** the body of a human being ⟨keep your *person* neat⟩
**3** bodily presence ⟨appear in *person*⟩
**4** reference to the speaker, to the one spoken to, or to one spoken of as shown especially by means of certain pronouns

**per·son·age** \'pərs-n-ij\ *n*
an important or famous person

**per·son·al** \'pərs-n-əl\ *adj*
**1** of, relating to, or belonging to a person : not public : not general ⟨*personal* property⟩
**2** made or done in person ⟨*personal* attention⟩
**3** of the person or body ⟨*personal* appearance⟩
**4** relating to a particular person or his or her qualities ⟨make *personal* remarks⟩
**5** intended for one particular person ⟨a *personal* letter⟩
**6** relating to oneself ⟨*personal* pride⟩
**per·son·al·ly** *adv*

**personal computer** *n*
a computer designed for an individual user

**per·son·al·i·ty** \,pərs-n-'al-ət-ē\ *n, pl* **per·son·al·i·ties**
**1** the qualities (as moods or habits) that make one person different from others ⟨your sparkling *personality*⟩
**2** a person's pleasing qualities ⟨is pleasant but doesn't have much *personality*⟩
**3** a person of importance or fame ⟨a dinner attended by movie and television *personalities*⟩

**personal pronoun** *n*
a pronoun (as *I, you, it*, or *they*) used as a substitute for a noun that names a definite person or thing

**per·son·i·fy** \pər-'sän-ə-,fī\ *vb* **per·son·i·fied**; **per·son·i·fy·ing**
to think of or represent as a person

**per·son·nel** \,pərs-n-'el\ *n*
a group of people employed in a business or an organization

**per·spec·tive** \pər-'spek-tiv\ *n*
**1** the art of painting or drawing a scene so that objects in it seem to have their right shape and to be the right distance apart
**2** the power to understand things in their true relationship to each other
**3** the true relationship of objects or events to one another

**per·spi·ra·tion** \,pər-spə-'rā-shən\ *n*
**1** the act or process of perspiring
**2** salty liquid given off from skin glands

**per·spire** \pər-'spīr\ *vb* **per·spired**; **per·spir·ing**
to give off salty liquid through the skin

**per·suade** \pər-'swād\ *vb* **per·suad·ed**; **per·suad·ing**
to win over to a belief or way of acting by argument or earnest request **:** CONVINCE

**per·sua·sion** \pər-'swā-zhən\ *n*
**1** the act of persuading
**2** the power to persuade ⟨you have the gift of *persuasion*⟩
**3** a way of believing **:** BELIEF ⟨two persons of the same *persuasion*⟩

**per·sua·sive** \pər-'swā-siv\ *adj*
able or likely to persuade ⟨a *persuasive* voice⟩
**per·sua·sive·ly** *adv*
**per·sua·sive·ness** *n*

**pert** \'pərt\ *adj*
**1** SAUCY 1
**2** PERKY

**per·tain** \pər-'tān\ *vb*
**1** to belong to as a part, quality, or function ⟨duties *pertaining* to the office of sheriff⟩
**2** to relate to a person or thing ⟨laws *pertaining* to hunting⟩

**per·ti·nent** \'pərt-n-ənt\ *adj*
relating to the subject that is being thought about or discussed **:** RELEVANT ⟨a *pertinent* question⟩

**per·turb** \pər-'tərb\ *vb*
to disturb in mind **:** trouble greatly

**pe·ruse** \pə-'rüz\ *vb* **pe·rused**; **pe·rus·ing**
**1** READ 1
**2** to read through carefully

**per·vade** \pər-'vād\ *vb* **per·vad·ed**; **per·vad·ing**
to spread through all parts of **:** PERMEATE ⟨spicy smells *pervaded* the whole house⟩

**per·verse** \pər-'vərs\ *adj*
stubborn in being against what is right or sensible

**pe·se·ta** \pə-'sāt-ə\ *n*
▶ a Spanish coin or bill

**pe·so** \'pā-sō\ *n, pl* **pesos**
**1** an old silver coin of Spain and Spanish America
**2** a coin of the Philippines or of any of various Latin American countries

**pes·si·mist** \'pes-ə-məst\ *n*
a pessimistic person

**pes·si·mis·tic** \,pes-ə-'mis-tik\ *adj*
**1** having no hope that one's troubles will end or that success or happiness will come **:** GLOOMY
**2** having the belief that evil is more common or powerful than good

**pest** \'pest\ *n*
**1** PESTILENCE
**2** a plant or animal that damages humans or their goods
**3** NUISANCE

**pes·ter** \'pes-tər\ *vb*
to bother again and again
**synonyms** see ANNOY

**pes·ti·cide** \'pes-tə-,sīd\ *n*
a substance used to destroy pests

**pes·ti·lence** \'pes-tə-ləns\ *n*
a contagious often fatal disease that spreads quickly

**pes·tle** \'pes-əl\ *n*
▼ a tool shaped like a small club for crushing substances in a mortar

**[1]pet** \'pet\ *n*
**1** a tame animal kept for pleasure rather than for use

pestle

mortar

**pestle:** a pestle and mortar used to crush pepper

**pesetas**

**2** a person who is treated with special kindness or consideration ⟨teacher's *pet*⟩

**[2]pet** *adj*
**1** kept or treated as a pet
**2** showing fondness ⟨a *pet* name⟩
**3** [2]FAVORITE ⟨my *pet* project⟩

**[3]pet** *vb* **pet·ted**; **pet·ting**
**1** to stroke or pat gently or lovingly
**2** to kiss and caress

**pet·al** \'pet-l\ *n*
one of the often brightly colored modified leaves that make up the corolla of a flower
**pet·aled** *or* **pet·alled** \-ld\ *adj*
**pet·al·less** \-l-ləs\ *adj*

**pet·i·ole** \'pet-ē-,ōl\ *n*
the stalk of a leaf

**pe·tite** \pə-'tēt\ *adj*
having a small trim figure

**[1]pe·ti·tion** \pə-'tish-ən\ *n*
**1** an earnest appeal
**2** a document asking for something

**[2]petition** *vb*
to make a petition to or for
**pe·ti·tion·er** *n*

**pe·trel** \'pe-trəl, 'pē-\ *n*
a small seabird with long wings that flies far from land

**pet·ri·fy** \'pe-trə-,fī\ *vb* **pet·ri·fied**; **pet·ri·fy·ing**
**1** to change plant or animal matter into stone or something like stone ⟨*petrified* trees⟩
**2** to frighten very much

**pe·tro·leum** \pə-'trō-lē-əm, -'trōl-yəm\ *n*
a raw oil that is obtained from wells drilled in the ground and that is the source of gasoline, kerosene, and fuel oils

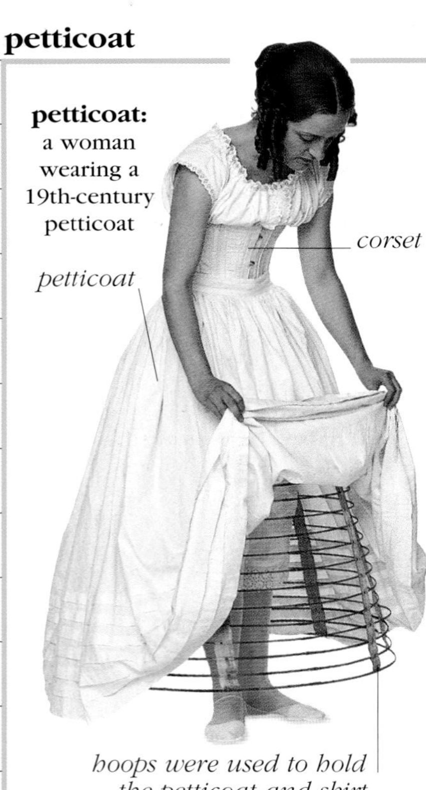


**petticoat:** a woman wearing a 19th-century petticoat

**pet·ti·coat** \'pet-ē-,kōt\ *n*
▲ a skirt worn under a dress or outer skirt

**petting zoo** *n*
a collection of farm animals or gentle exotic animals for children to pet and feed

**pet·ty** \'pet-ē\ *adj* **pet·ti·er**; **pet·ti·est**
**1** small and of no importance ⟨*petty* details⟩
**2** showing or having a mean narrow-minded attitude
**pet·ti·ly** \'pet-l-ē\ *adv*
**pet·ti·ness** \'pet-ē-nəs\ *n*

**petty officer** *n*
an officer in the Navy or Coast Guard appointed from among the enlisted people

**petty officer first class** *n*
a petty officer in the Navy or Coast Guard ranking above a petty officer second class

**petty officer second class** *n*
a petty officer in the Navy or Coast Guard ranking above a petty officer third class

**petty officer third class** *n*
a petty officer in the Navy or Coast Guard ranking above a seaman

**pet·u·lant** \'pech-ə-lənt\ *adj*
easily put in a bad humor : CROSS

**pe·tu·nia** \pə-'tü-nyə, -'tyü-\ *n*
▶ a plant related to the potato grown for its velvety brightly colored flowers that are shaped like funnels

**pew** \'pyü\ *n*
one of the benches with backs and sometimes doors set in rows in a church

**pe·wee** \'pē-,wē\ *n*
a small grayish or greenish brown bird (as a phoebe) that eats flying insects

**pew·ter** \'pyüt-ər\ *n*
**1** a metallic substance made mostly of tin sometimes mixed with copper or antimony that is used in making utensils (as pitchers and bowls)
**2** utensils made of pewter

**phantasy** *variant of* FANTASY

**phan·tom** \'fant-əm\ *n*
an image or figure that can be sensed (as with the eyes or ears) but that is not real

**pha·raoh** \'feər-ō, 'faər-ō\ *n*
▼ a ruler of ancient Egypt

**phar·ma·cist** \'fär-mə-səst\ *n*
a person skilled or engaged in pharmacy

**pharaoh:** a golden mask representing the face of a young pharaoh

**phar·ma·cy** \'fär-mə-sē\ *n, pl* **phar·ma·cies**
**1** the art, practice, or profession of mixing and preparing medicines usually according to a doctor's prescription
**2** the place of business of a pharmacist : DRUGSTORE

**petunia**

**phar·ynx** \'far-ingks\ *n, pl* **pha·ryn·ges** \fə-'rin-,jēz\ *also* **phar·ynx·es**
the space behind the mouth into which the nostrils, gullet, and windpipe open
**pha·ryn·geal** \,far-ən-'jē-əl, fə-'rin-jē-əl\ *adj*

**phase** \'fāz\ *n*
**1** the way that the moon or a planet looks to the eye at any time in its series of changes with respect to how it shines ⟨the new moon and the full moon are two *phases* of the moon⟩
**2** a step or part in a series of events or actions : STAGE
**3** a particular part or feature : ASPECT

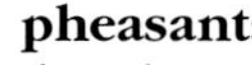

**pheasant:** a domestic breed raised for show

**pheas·ant** \'fez-nt\ *n*
▲ a large brightly colored game bird with a long tail that is related to the chicken

**phe·nom·e·nal** \fi-'näm-ən-l\ *adj*
very remarkable : EXTRAORDINARY ⟨a *phenomenal* memory⟩

**phe·nom·e·non** \fi-'näm-ə-,nän\ *n, pl* **phe·nom·e·na** \-nə\ *or* **phe·nom·e·nons**
**1** *pl phenomena* an observable fact or event
**2** a rare or important fact or event
**3** *pl phenomenons* an extraordinary or exceptional person or thing

[1]**-phil** \ˌfil\ *or* **-phile** \ˌfīl\ *n suffix*
lover : one having a strong attraction to

[2]**-phil** *or* **-phile** *adj suffix*
having a fondness for or strong attraction to

**phil·an·throp·ic** \ˌfil-ən-ˈthräp-ik\ *adj*
of, relating to, or devoted to philanthropy : CHARITABLE
**phil·an·throp·i·cal·ly** \-i-kə-lē\ *adv*

**phi·lan·thro·pist** \fə-ˈlan-thrə-pəst\ *n*
a person who gives generously to help other people

**phi·lan·thro·py** \fə-ˈlan-thrə-pē\ *n, pl* **phi·lan·thro·pies**
**1** active effort to help other people
**2** a philanthropic gift
**3** an organization giving or supported by charitable gifts

**phil·o·den·dron** \ˌfil-ə-ˈden-drən\ *n*
any of several plants that can stand shade and are often grown for their showy leaves

**phi·los·o·pher** \fə-ˈläs-ə-fər\ *n*
**1** a student of philosophy
**2** a person who takes misfortunes with calmness and courage

**phil·o·soph·i·cal** \ˌfil-ə-ˈsäf-i-kəl\ *or* **phil·o·soph·ic** \-ˈsäf-ik\ *adj*
**1** of or relating to philosophy
**2** showing the wisdom and calm of a philosopher
**phil·o·soph·i·cal·ly** *adv*

**phi·los·o·phy** \fə-ˈläs-ə-fē\ *n, pl* **phi·los·o·phies**
**1** the study of the basic ideas about knowledge, right and wrong, reasoning, and the value of things
**2** the philosophical teachings or principles of a person or a group
**3** calmness of temper and judgment

**phlox** \ˈfläks\ *n, pl* **phlox** *or* **phlox·es**
any of a group of plants grown for their showy clusters of usually white, pink, or purplish flowers

**pho·bia** \ˈfō-bē-ə\ *n*
an unreasonable, abnormal, and lasting fear of something

**phoe·be** \ˈfē-bē\ *n*
a common American bird that is grayish brown above and yellowish white below and that eats flying insects

**phon-** *or* **phono-** *prefix*
sound : voice : speech ⟨*phono*graph⟩

[1]**phone** \ˈfōn\ *n*
[1]TELEPHONE

[2]**phone** *vb* **phoned**; **phon·ing**
[2]TELEPHONE

**pho·neme** \ˈfō-ˌnēm\ *n*
one of the smallest units of speech that distinguish one utterance from another

**pho·net·ic** \fə-ˈnet-ik\ *adj*
of or relating to spoken language or speech sounds

**pho·nics** \ˈfän-iks\ *n*
a method of teaching beginners to read and pronounce words by learning the usual sound of letters, letter groups, and syllables

**pho·no·graph** \ˈfō-nə-ˌgraf\ *n*
▶ an instrument that reproduces sounds recorded on a grooved disk

**pho·ny** \ˈfō-nē\ *adj*
not real or genuine ⟨a *phony* dollar bill⟩

**phos·pho·rus** \ˈfäs-fə-rəs\ *n*
a white or yellowish waxlike chemical element that gives a faint glow in moist air and is necessary in some form to life

[1]**pho·to** \ˈfōt-ō\ *n, pl* **photos**
[1]PHOTOGRAPH

[2]**photo** *vb*
[2]PHOTOGRAPH

[1]**pho·to·copy** \ˈfōt-ō-ˌkäp-ē\ *n*
a copy of usually printed material made using a process in which an image is formed by the action of light on an electrically charged surface

[2]**photocopy** *vb*
to make a photocopy of
**pho·to·copi·er** *n*

[1]**pho·to·graph** \ˈfōt-ə-ˌgraf\ *n*
a picture made by photography

[2]**photograph** *vb*
to take a picture of with a camera
**pho·tog·ra·pher** \fə-ˈtäg-rə-fər\ *n*

**pho·to·graph·ic** \ˌfōt-ə-ˈgraf-ik\ *adj*
obtained by or used in photography

**pho·tog·ra·phy** \fə-ˈtäg-rə-fē\ *n*
the making of pictures by means of a camera that directs the image of an object onto a film made sensitive to light

**pho·to·syn·the·sis** \ˌfōt-ə-ˈsin-thə-səs\ *n*
the process by which green plants form carbohydrates from carbon dioxide and water in the presence of light
**pho·to·syn·thet·ic** \-sin-ˈthet-ik\ *adj*

[1]**phrase** \ˈfrāz\ *n*
**1** a brief expression
**2** a group of two or more words that express a single idea but do not form a complete sentence ⟨"out the door" in "they ran out the door" is a *phrase*⟩

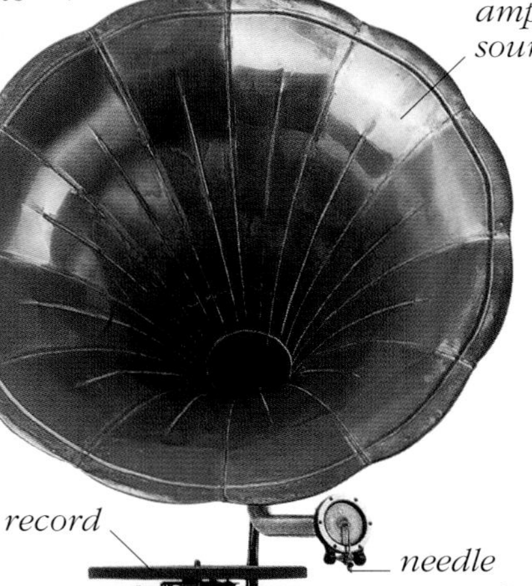


**phonograph:**
an early 20th-century phonograph

[2]**phrase** *vb* **phrased**; **phras·ing**
to express in words ⟨was unable to *phrase* his idea⟩

**phy·lum** \ˈfī-ləm\ *n, pl* **phy·la** \-lə\
a group of animals that ranks above the class in scientific classification and is the highest group of the plant kingdom

**phys ed** \ˈfiz-ˈed\ *n*
PHYSICAL EDUCATION

**phys·i·cal** \ˈfiz-i-kəl\ *adj*
**1** of or relating to nature or the world as we see it : material and not mental, spiritual, or imaginary
**2** of the body : BODILY
**3** of or relating to physics
**phys·i·cal·ly** *adv*

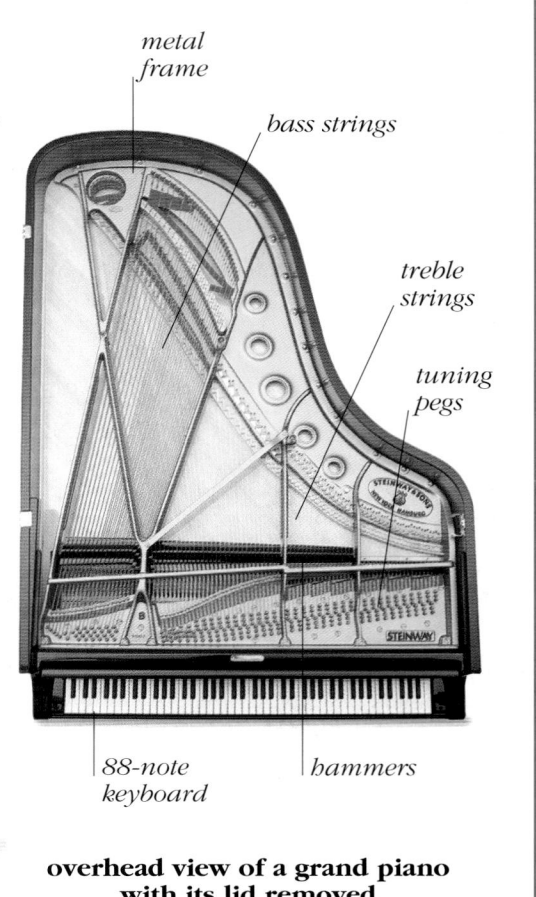

## piano

The piano allows players to produce a wide range of sounds from very high to very low and from very soft to very loud. There are two main types — the upright piano, not shown, which has a vertical frame, and the grand piano, which has a horizontal frame. In both types, metal strings are stretched taut across the frame. When the player presses a key, a felt-tipped hammer strikes the string, which vibrates to produce a note.

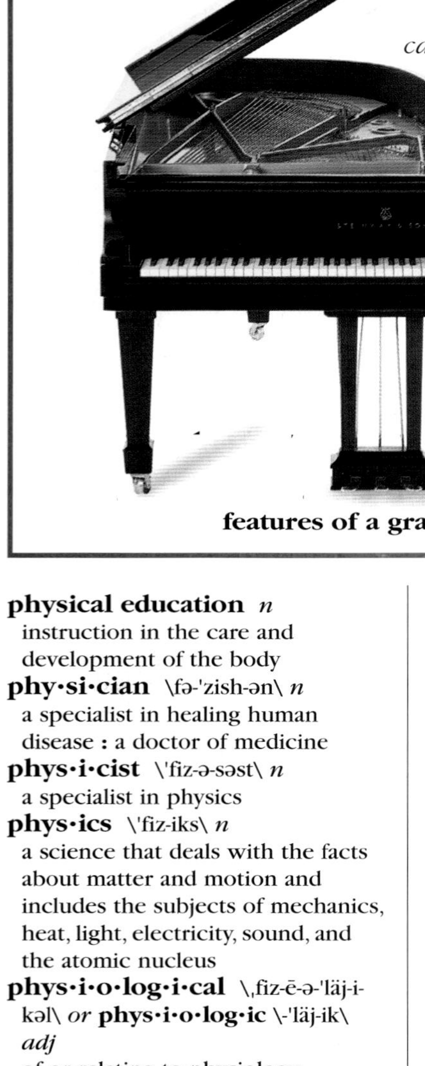


features of a grand piano

overhead view of a grand piano with its lid removed

**physical education** *n* instruction in the care and development of the body

**phy·si·cian** \fə-ˈzish-ən\ *n* a specialist in healing human disease **:** a doctor of medicine

**phys·i·cist** \ˈfiz-ə-səst\ *n* a specialist in physics

**phys·ics** \ˈfiz-iks\ *n* a science that deals with the facts about matter and motion and includes the subjects of mechanics, heat, light, electricity, sound, and the atomic nucleus

**phys·i·o·log·i·cal** \ˌfiz-ē-ə-ˈläj-i-kəl\ *or* **phys·i·o·log·ic** \-ˈläj-ik\ *adj* of or relating to physiology

**phys·i·ol·o·gist** \ˌfiz-ē-ˈäl-ə-jəst\ *n* a specialist in physiology

**phys·i·ol·o·gy** \ˌfiz-ē-ˈäl-ə-jē\ *n* **1** a branch of biology that deals with the working of the living body and its parts (as organs and cells) **2** the processes and activities by which a living being or any of its parts functions

**phy·sique** \fə-ˈzēk\ *n* the build of a person's body

**pi** \ˈpī\ *n, pl* **pis** \ˈpīz\ the symbol π representing the ratio of the circumference of a circle to its diameter or about 3.1416

**pi·a·nist** \pē-ˈan-ist, ˈpē-ə-nist\ *n* a person who plays the piano

**pi·a·no** \pē-ˈan-ō\ *n, pl* **pianos** ▲ a keyboard instrument having steel wire strings that sound when struck by hammers covered with felt

**Word History** The English word *piano* comes from an Italian word spelled like English *piano*. This Italian word comes from another Italian word which comes from a phrase that means "soft and loud." When pianos were first made, people noticed that their softness and loudness could be controlled by the player. That is why the phrase for "soft and loud" was used to refer to this instrument.

**pi·az·za** \pē-ˈat-sə, -ˈaz-ə\ *n* **1** a large open square in an Italian town **2** PORCH, VERANDA

**pic·co·lo** \ˈpik-ə-ˌlō\ *n, pl* **pic·co·los** a small shrill flute

[1]**pick** \ˈpik\ *vb* **1** to strike or work on with a pointed tool **2** to remove bit by bit ⟨*pick* meat from bones⟩ **3** to gather one by one ⟨*pick* cherries⟩ **4** CHOOSE 1, SELECT **5** to eat sparingly or daintily

6 to steal from ⟨*pick* a pocket⟩
7 to start (a fight) with someone else deliberately
8 to unlock without a key
9 to pluck with the fingers or with a pick ⟨*pick* a banjo⟩
**pick·er** *n*
**pick on** [1]TEASE

**[2]pick** *n*
1 PICKAX
2 a slender pointed instrument ⟨ice *pick*⟩
3 a thin piece of metal or plastic used to pluck the strings of a musical instrument
4 the act or opportunity of choosing
5 the best ones ⟨bought only the *pick* of the crop⟩

**pick·ax** \'pik-,aks\ *n*
a heavy tool with a wooden handle and a blade pointed at one or both ends for loosening or breaking up soil or rock

**pick·er·el** \'pik-ə-rəl, 'pik-rəl\ *n*
any of several fairly small fishes that look like the pike

**[1]pick·et** \'pik-ət\ *n*
1 ▶ a pointed stake or slender post (as for making a fence)
2 a soldier or a group of soldiers assigned to stand guard
3 a person stationed before a place of work where there is a strike

**[2]picket** *vb*
1 [2]TETHER ⟨*picket* a horse⟩
2 to walk or stand in front of as a picket ⟨*picket* a factory⟩

**[1]pick·le** \'pik-əl\ *n*
1 a mixture of salt and water or vinegar for keeping foods : BRINE
2 a difficult or very unpleasant condition
3 something (as a cucumber) that has been kept in a pickle of salty water or vinegar

**[2]pickle** *vb* **pick·led**; **pick·ling**
to soak or keep in a pickle

**pick·pock·et** \'pik-,päk-ət\ *n*
a thief who steals from pockets and purses

**pick·up** \'pik-,əp\ *n*
a light truck with an open body and low sides

**pick up** \pik-'əp\ *vb*
1 to take hold of and lift ⟨*picked* the book *up*⟩
2 to stop for and take along ⟨the bus *picked up* passengers⟩
3 to gain by study or experience : LEARN ⟨good readers *pick up* new words from their reading⟩
4 to get by buying : BUY ⟨*pick up* a bargain⟩
5 to come to and follow ⟨*picked up* the outlaw's trail⟩
6 to bring within range of hearing ⟨my radio *picks up* foreign broadcasts⟩
7 to get back speed or strength ⟨business *picked up*⟩

**[1]pic·nic** \'pik-,nik\ *n*
1 an outdoor party with food taken along and eaten in the open
2 a nice experience ⟨a broken leg is no *picnic*⟩

**[2]picnic** *vb* **pic·nicked**; **pic·nick·ing**
to go on a picnic

**[1]picket 1:** a fence made of pickets

**pic·to·graph** \'pik-tə-,graf\ *n*
a diagram showing information by means of pictures

**pic·to·ri·al** \pik-'tōr-ē-əl\ *adj*
1 of or relating to pictures ⟨*pictorial* art⟩
2 using pictures ⟨a *pictorial* magazine⟩

**[1]pic·ture** \'pik-chər\ *n*
1 an image of something formed on a surface (as by drawing, painting, printing, or photography)
2 a very clear description ⟨a word *picture*⟩
3 an exact likeness
4 MOVIE
5 an image on the screen of a television set

**[2]picture** *vb* **pic·tured**; **pic·tur·ing**
1 to draw or paint a picture of
2 to describe very clearly in words
3 to form a mental image of : IMAGINE

**picture graph** *n*
PICTOGRAPH

**pic·tur·esque** \,pik-chə-'resk\ *adj*
like a picture : suggesting a painted scene ⟨a *picturesque* mountain view⟩

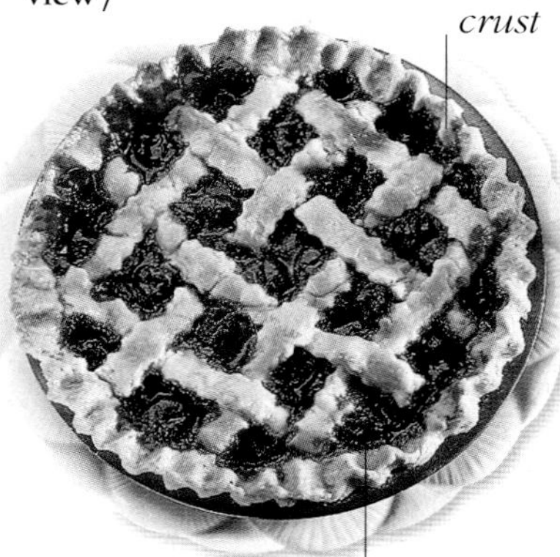


**pie:** a fruit pie

**pie** \'pī\ *n*
▲ a food consisting of a crust and a filling (as of fruit or meat)

**pie·bald** \'pī-,bȯld\ *adj*
spotted or blotched with two colors and especially black and white ⟨a *piebald* horse⟩

**[1]piece** \'pēs\ *n*
1 a part cut, torn, or broken from a thing ⟨a *piece* of string⟩
2 one of a group, set, or mass of things ⟨a *piece* of mail⟩ ⟨a chess *piece*⟩
3 a portion marked off ⟨a *piece* of land⟩
4 a single item or example ⟨a *piece* of news⟩
5 a definite amount or size in which articles are made for sale or use ⟨buy lumber by the *piece*⟩
6 something made or written ⟨a *piece* of music⟩
7 [1]COIN 1 ⟨a fifty-cent *piece*⟩

**[2]piece** *vb* **pieced**; **piec·ing**
**1** to repair or complete by adding a piece or pieces
**2** to make out of pieces ⟨*piece* a puzzle together⟩

**piece·meal** \'pē-,smēl\ *adv*
one piece at a time : little by little

**pied** \'pīd\ *adj*
having blotches of two or more colors

**pier** \'pir\ *n*
**1** a support for a bridge
**2** a structure built out into the water for use as a place to land or walk or to protect or form a harbor

**pigtail:**
a girl wearing her hair in a pigtail

**pierce** \'pirs\ *vb* **pierced**; **pierc·ing**
**1** to run into or through : STAB
**2** to make a hole in or through ⟨have one's ears *pierced*⟩
**3** to force into or through ⟨*pierce* the enemy's line⟩
**4** to penetrate with the eye or mind : see through
**pierc·ing·ly** *adv*

**pi·e·ty** \'pī-ət-ē\ *n, pl* **pieties**
the state or fact of being pious : devotion to one's God

**pig** \'pig\ *n*
**1** a swine especially when not yet mature
**2** a person who lives or acts like a pig
**3** a metal cast (as of iron) poured directly from the smelting furnace into a mold

**pi·geon** \'pij-ən\ *n*
a bird with a stout body, short legs, and smooth feathers

**pi·geon–toed** \,pij-ən-'tōd\ *adj*
having the toes turned in

**pig·gish** \'pig-ish\ *adj*
like a pig especially in greed or dirtiness

**pig·gy·back** \'pig-ē-,bak\ *adv or adj*
on the back or shoulders

**piggy bank** \'pig-ē-\ *n*
a bank for coins often in the shape of a pig

**pig·head·ed** \'pig-'hed-əd\ *adj*
STUBBORN 1, 2

**pig·ment** \'pig-mənt\ *n*
**1** a substance that gives color to other substances
**2** coloring matter in persons, animals, and plants

**pigmy** *variant of* PYGMY

**pig·pen** \'pig-,pen\ *n*
**1** a place where pigs are kept
**2** a dirty place

**pig·sty** \'pig-,stī\ *n*
PIGPEN

**pig·tail** \'pig-,tāl\ *n*
◀ a tight braid of hair

**[1]pike** \'pīk\ *n, pl* **pike** *or* **pikes**
a long slender freshwater fish with a large mouth

**[2]pike** *n*
a long wooden pole with a steel point used long ago as a weapon by soldiers

**[3]pike** *n*
TURNPIKE, ROAD

**[1]pile** \'pīl\ *n*
a large stake or pointed post driven into the ground to support a foundation

**[2]pile** *n*
**1** a mass of things heaped together : HEAP ⟨a *pile* of stones⟩
**2** REACTOR 2

**[3]pile** *vb* **piled**; **pil·ing**
**1** to lay or place in a pile : STACK ⟨*pile* firewood⟩
**2** to heap in large amounts ⟨*pile* a table with food⟩
**3** to move or push forward in a crowd or group ⟨they *piled* into the car⟩

**[4]pile** *n*
a velvety surface of fine short raised fibers ⟨a rug with a thick *pile*⟩

**pil·fer** \'pil-fər\ *vb*
to steal small amounts or articles of small value

**pil·grim** \'pil-grəm\ *n*
**1** a person who travels to a holy place as an act of religious devotion
**2** *cap* one of the English colonists who founded the first permanent settlement in New England at Plymouth in 1620

**pil·grim·age** \'pil-grə-mij\ *n*
a journey made by a pilgrim

**pil·ing** \'pī-ling\ *n*
a structure made of piles

**pill** \'pil\ *n*
▼ medicine or a food supplement in the form of a small rounded mass to be swallowed whole

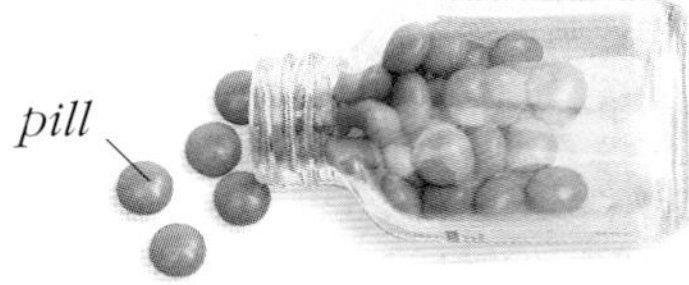


**pill:** a bottle of pills containing Vitamin C

**[1]pil·lage** \'pil-ij\ *n*
the act of robbing by force especially in war

**[2]pillage** *vb* **pil·laged**; **pil·lag·ing**
to take goods and possessions by force

**pil·lar** \'pil-ər\ *n*
**1** a large post that supports something (as a roof)
**2** a column standing alone (as for a monument)
**3** something like a pillar : a main support ⟨a *pillar* of society⟩

**pil·lo·ry** \'pil-ə-rē\ *n, pl* **pil·lo·ries**
a device once used for punishing someone in public consisting of a wooden frame with holes in which the head and hands can be locked

**[1]pil·low** \'pil-ō\ *n*
a bag filled with soft or springy material used as a cushion usually for the head of a person lying down

**[2]pillow** *vb*
**1** to lay on or as if on a pillow
**2** to serve as a pillow for

**pil·low·case** \'pil-ō-,kās\ *n*
a removable covering for a pillow

**[1]pi·lot** \'pī-lət\ *n*
**1** a person who steers a ship
**2** a person especially qualified to guide ships into and out of a port or in dangerous waters
**3** a person who flies or is qualified to fly an aircraft

**²pilot** *vb*
to act as pilot of

**pi·mien·to** \pə-'ment-ō, pəm-'yent-\ *also* **pi·men·to** \pə-'ment-ō\ *n, pl* **pi·mien·tos** *also* **pi·men·tos**
a sweet pepper with a mild thick flesh

**pim·ple** \'pim-pəl\ *n*
a small swelling of the skin often containing pus
**pim·pled** \-pəld\ *adj*
**pim·ply** \-plē\ *adj*

**¹pin** \'pin\ *n*
**1** a slender pointed piece (as of wood or metal) usually having the shape of a cylinder used to fasten articles together or in place
**2** a small pointed piece of wire with a head used for fastening cloth or paper
**3** something (as an ornament or badge) fastened to the clothing by a pin
**4** one of ten pieces set up as the target in bowling

**²pin** *vb* **pinned**; **pin·ning**
**1** to fasten or join with a pin
**2** to hold as if with a pin ⟨*pinned* the snake to the ground with a stick⟩

**pin·a·fore** \'pin-ə-ˌfōr\ *n*
a sleeveless garment with a low neck worn as an apron or a dress

**pin·cer** \'pin-chər, 'pin-sər\ *n*
**1 pincers** *pl* an instrument with two handles and two jaws for gripping something
**2** a claw (as of a lobster) like pincers

**¹pinch** \'pinch\ *vb*
**1** to squeeze between the finger and thumb or between the jaws of an instrument
**2** to squeeze painfully ⟨get a finger *pinched* in a door⟩
**3** to cause to look thin or shrunken ⟨a face *pinched* with cold⟩
**4** to be thrifty or stingy

**²pinch** *n*
**1** a time of emergency ⟨help out in a *pinch*⟩
**2** a painful pressure or stress ⟨felt the *pinch* of hunger⟩
**3** an act of pinching : SQUEEZE
**4** as much as may be picked up between the finger and the thumb ⟨a *pinch* of salt⟩

**pineapple**

**pinch hitter** *n*
**1** a baseball player who is sent in to bat for another
**2** a person who does another's work in an emergency

pin

**pincushion:**
a mouse-shaped pincushion

**pin·cush·ion** \'pin-ˌku̇sh-ən\ *n*
▲ a small cushion in which pins may be stuck when not in use

**¹pine** \'pīn\ *n*
an evergreen tree that has narrow needles for leaves, cones, and a wood that ranges from very soft to hard

**²pine** *vb* **pined**; **pin·ing**
**1** to lose energy, health, or weight through sorrow or worry
**2** to long for very much ⟨*pining* for home⟩ **synonyms** see YEARN

**pine·ap·ple** \'pī-ˌnap-əl\ *n*
◄ the large juicy yellow fruit of a tropical plant that has long stiff leaves with spiny margins

**pin·ey** *also* **piny** \'pī-nē\ *adj*
of, relating to, or like that of pine

**pin·feath·er** \'pin-ˌfe<u>th</u>-ər\ *n*
a new feather just breaking through the skin of a bird

**pin·ion** \'pin-yən\ *n*
**1** the wing or the end part of the wing of a bird
**2** ¹FEATHER 1

**¹pink** \'piŋk\ *n*
**1** any of a group of plants with thick stem joints and narrow leaves that are grown for their showy often fragrant flowers
**2** the highest degree ⟨athletes in the *pink* of condition⟩

**²pink** *n*
a pale red

**³pink** *adj*
of the color pink

**⁴pink** *vb*
to cut cloth, leather, or paper in an ornamental pattern or with an edge with notches

**pink·eye** \'piŋ-ˌkī\ *n*
a very contagious disease of the eyes in which the inner part of the eyelids becomes sore and red

**pink·ish** \'piŋ-kish\ *adj*
somewhat pink

**pin·na·cle** \'pin-ə-kəl\ *n*
**1** a slender tower generally coming to a narrow point at the top
**2** a high pointed peak
**3** the highest point of development or achievement

**pin·point** \'pin-ˌpȯint\ *vb*
to locate or find out exactly

**pint** \'pīnt\ *n*
a unit of capacity equal to one half quart or sixteen ounces (about .47 liter)

**pin·to** \'pin-tō\ *n, pl* **pintos**
▼ a spotted horse or pony

**pinto** horse

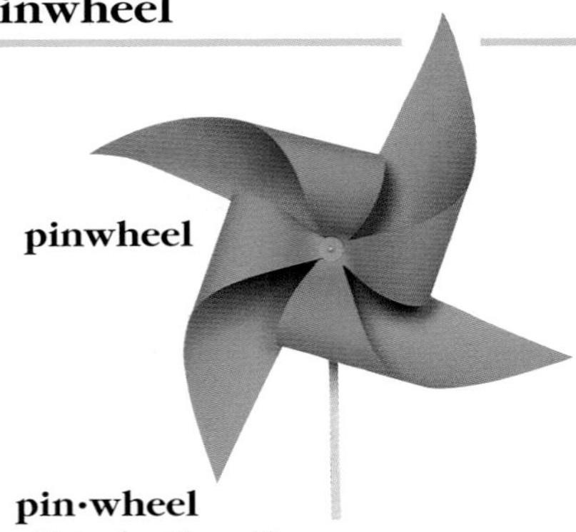
pinwheel

**pin·wheel**
\'pin-,hwēl, -,wēl\ *n*
▲ a toy with fanlike blades at the end of a stick that spin in the wind
**piny** *variant of* PINEY
**[1]pi·o·neer** \,pī-ə-'nir\ *n*
**1** a person who goes before and prepares the way for others to follow
**2** an early settler

---

**Word History** Long ago there were special soldiers who marched ahead of the rest of the French army. They prepared the way for the rest of the army by digging ditches and building bridges. After a time the French word that had been used for any soldier on foot came to be used only for these special soldiers. Later the word was used for anyone who prepared a way for others. The English word *pioneer* came from this French word.

---

**[2]pioneer** *vb*
**1** to explore or open up ways or regions for others to follow
**2** to start up something new or take part in the early development of something
**pi·ous** \'pī-əs\ *adj*
**1** showing respect and honor toward God
**2** making a show of being very good
**pip** \'pip\ *n*
a small fruit seed ⟨orange *pip*⟩
**[1]pipe** \'pīp\ *n*
**1** a musical instrument or part of a musical instrument consisting of a tube (as of wood) played by blowing
**2** one of the tubes in a pipe organ that makes sound when air passes through it
**3** BAGPIPE — usually used in pl.
**4** a long tube or hollow body for transporting a substance (as water, steam, or gas)
**5** a tube with a small bowl at one end for smoking tobacco or for blowing bubbles
**[2]pipe** *vb* **piped**; **pip·ing**
**1** to play on a pipe
**2** to have or utter in a shrill tone
**3** to equip with pipes
**4** to move by means of pipes
**pip·er** *n*
**pipe·line** \'pī-,plīn\ *n*
a line of pipe with pumps and control devices (as for carrying liquids or gases)
**pip·ing** \'pī-ping\ *n*
**1** the music or sound of a person or thing that pipes ⟨the *piping* of frogs⟩
**2** a quantity or system of pipes
**3** a narrow fold of material used to decorate edges or seams
**pi·ra·cy** \'pī-rə-sē\ *n, pl* **pi·ra·cies**
**1** robbery on the high seas
**2** the using of another's work or invention without permission
**pi·ra·nha** \pə-'rän-ə\ *n*
any of various usually small South American freshwater fishes that have very sharp teeth and that may attack human beings and animals in the water
**pi·rate** \'pī-rət\ *n*
▶ a robber on the high seas : a person who commits piracy
**pis** *pl of* PI
**Pi·sces** \'pī-sēz\ *n*
**1** a constellation between Aquarius and Aries imagined as two fish
**2** the twelfth sign of the zodiac or a person born under this sign
**pis·ta·chio** \pə-'stash-ē-,ō\ *n, pl* **pis·ta·chios**
▶ the green edible seed of a small tree related to the sumacs

**pistachios**

**pis·til** \'pist-l\ *n*
the central organ in a flower that contains the ovary and produces the seed
**pis·tol** \'pist-l\ *n*
▶ a short gun made to be aimed and fired with one hand
**pis·ton** \'pis-tən\ *n*
a disk or short cylinder that slides back and forth inside a larger cylinder and is moved by steam in steam engines and by the explosion of fuel in automobiles
**[1]pit** \'pit\ *n*
**1** a cavity or hole in the ground ⟨a gravel *pit*⟩
**2** an area set off from and often sunken below neighboring areas
**3** a hollow area usually of the surface of the body
**4** an indented scar (as from a boil)
**pit·ted** \'pit-əd\ *adj*
**[2]pit** *vb* **pit·ted**; **pit·ting**
**1** to make pits in or scar with pits
**2** to set against another in a fight or contest
**[3]pit** *n*
a hard seed or stone (as of a cherry)
**[4]pit** *vb* **pit·ted**; **pit·ting**
to remove the pits from
**[1]pitch** \'pich\ *n*
**1** a dark sticky substance left over from distilling tar and used in making roofing paper, in waterproofing seams, and in paving
**2** resin from pine trees

**pirate:** a flag of the type formerly flown on pirate ships

**[2]pitch** *vb*
**1** to set up and fix firmly in place ⟨*pitched* a tent⟩
**2** to throw (as hay) usually upward or away from oneself
**3** to throw a baseball to a batter
**4** to plunge or fall forward ⟨*pitch* from a cliff⟩
**5** [1]SLOPE
**6** to fix or set at a certain pitch or level ⟨*pitch* a tune higher⟩
**7** to move in such a way that one end falls while the other end rises ⟨a ship *pitching* in a rough sea⟩

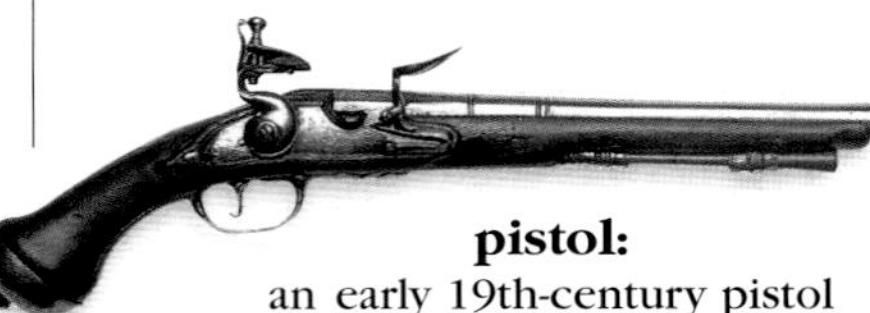
**pistol:** an early 19th-century pistol

[3]**pitch** *n*
**1** the action or manner of pitching
**2** highness or lowness of sound
**3** amount of slope ⟨*pitch* of a roof⟩
**4** the amount or level of something (as a feeling) ⟨excitement reached a high *pitch*⟩
**pitched** \'picht\ *adj*

**pitch·blende** \'pich-,blend\ *n*
a dark mineral that is a source of radium and uranium

[1]**pitch·er** \'pich-ər\ *n*
a container usually with a handle and a lip used for holding and pouring out liquids

[2]**pitcher** *n*
a baseball player who pitches

**pitch·fork** \'pich-,fȯrk\ *n*
a fork with a long handle used in pitching hay or straw

**pizza**

**pit·e·ous** \'pit-ē-əs\ *adj*
seeking or deserving pity ⟨*piteous* cries for help⟩
**pit·e·ous·ly** *adv*

**pit·fall** \'pit-,fȯl\ *n*
**1** a covered or camouflaged pit used to capture animals or people
**2** a danger or difficulty that is hidden or is not easily recognized

**pith** \'pith\ *n*
**1** the loose spongy tissue forming the center of the stem in some plants
**2** the important part ⟨the *pith* of the problem⟩

**piti·able** \'pit-ē-ə-bəl\ *adj*
PITIFUL

**piti·ful** \'pit-i-fəl\ *adj*
**1** causing a feeling of pity or sympathy ⟨a *pitiful* sight⟩
**2** deserving pitying scorn ⟨a *pitiful* excuse⟩

**piti·less** \'pit-i-ləs\ *adj*
having no pity : MERCILESS

**pi·tu·i·tary gland** \pə-'tü-ə-,ter-ē, -'tyü-\ *n*
an endocrine organ at the base of the brain producing several hormones of which one affects growth

[1]**pity** \'pit-ē\ *n*
**1** a sympathetic feeling for the distress of others
**2** a reason or cause of regret

[2]**pity** *vb* **pit·ied**; **pity·ing**
to feel pity for

[1]**piv·ot** \'piv-ət\ *n*
**1** a point or a fixed pin on the end of which something turns
**2** something on which something else turns or depends : a central member, part, or point

[2]**pivot** *vb*
**1** to turn on or as if on a pivot
**2** to provide with, mount on, or attach by a pivot

**pix·el** \'pik-səl\ *n*
any of the small parts that make up an image (as on a computer or television screen)

**pix·ie** *or* **pixy** \'pik-sē\ *n*, *pl* **pix·ies**
a mischievous elf or fairy

**piz·za** \'pēt-sə\ *n*
◀ a dish made usually of flattened bread dough spread with a spiced mixture (as of tomatoes, cheese, and sausage) and baked

**plac·ard** \'plak-ərd, -,ärd\ *n*
a large card for announcing or advertising something : POSTER

**pla·cate** \'plāk-,āt, 'plak-\ *vb* **pla·cat·ed**; **pla·cat·ing**
to calm the anger of : SOOTHE

[1]**place** \'plās\ *n*
**1** a short street
**2** an available space : ROOM ⟨make a *place* for the newcomer⟩
**3** a building or spot set apart for a special purpose ⟨a *place* of worship⟩
**4** a certain region or center of population ⟨a *place* on the map⟩
**5** a piece of land with a house on it ⟨a *place* in the country⟩
**6** position in a scale or series in comparison with another or others ⟨in the first *place*, we have to consider the cost⟩ ⟨finished the race in second *place*⟩
**7** a space (as a seat in a theater) set aside for one's use
**8** usual space or use ⟨paper towels take the *place* of linen⟩
**9** the position of a figure in a numeral
**10** a public square

[2]**place** *vb* **placed**; **plac·ing**
**1** to put or arrange in a certain place or position
**2** to appoint to a job or find a job for
**3** to identify by connecting with a certain time, place, or happening

**place·hold·er** \'plās-,hōl-dər\ *n*
a symbol (as $x$, $\Delta$, $^*$) used in mathematics in the place of a numeral

**place·kick** \'plās-,kik\ *n*
▶ a kick in football made with the ball held in place on the ground

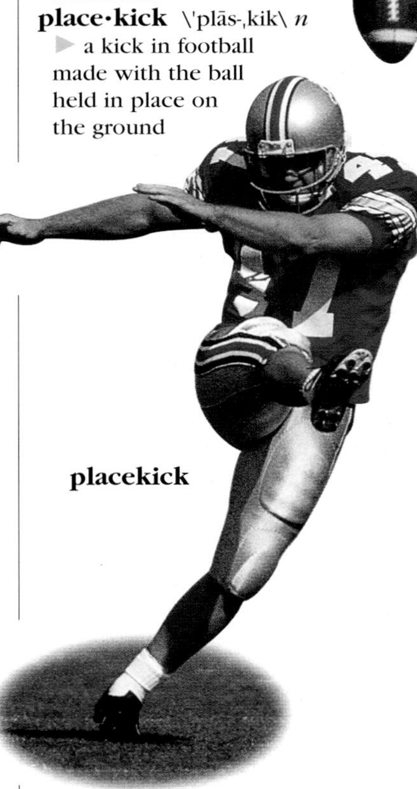

**placekick**

**pla·cen·ta** \plə-'sent-ə\ *n*
an organ that has a large blood supply and joins the fetus of a mammal to its mother's uterus

**pla·gia·rism** \'plā-jə-,riz-əm\ *n*
an act of stealing and passing off as one's own the ideas or words of another

[1]**plague** \'plāg\ *n*
**1** something that causes much distress ⟨a *plague* of locusts⟩
**2** a cause of irritation : NUISANCE
**3** a destructive epidemic disease

A B C D E F G H I J K L M N O P Q R S T U V W X Y Z

**²plague** *vb* **plagued; plagu·ing**
**1** to strike or afflict with disease or distress
**2** ¹TEASE, TORMENT

**plaid** \'plad\ *n*
**1** TARTAN
**2** ▼ a pattern consisting of rectangles formed by crossed lines of various widths

**plaid 2:** cloth with a plaid pattern

**¹plain** \'plān\ *adj*
**1** having no pattern or decoration ⟨a *plain* cloth⟩
**2** open and clear to the sight ⟨in *plain* view⟩
**3** clear to the mind ⟨explained in *plain* words⟩
**4** FRANK ⟨*plain* speaking⟩
**5** of common or average accomplishments or position : ORDINARY ⟨*plain* people⟩
**6** not hard to do : not complicated ⟨*plain* sewing⟩
**7** not handsome or beautiful

**²plain** *n*
a large area of level or rolling treeless land ⟨the *plains* of the West⟩

**³plain** *adv*
in a plain manner

**plain·tive** \'plānt-iv\ *adj*
showing or suggesting sorrow : MOURNFUL, SAD ⟨a *plaintive* sigh⟩

**¹plait** \'plāt, 'plat\ *n*
**1** a flat fold : PLEAT
**2** a flat braid (as of hair)

**²plait** *vb*
**1** ¹PLEAT
**2** ¹BRAID
**3** to make by braiding ⟨*plaiting* a basket⟩

**¹plan** \'plan\ *n*
**1** a drawing or diagram showing the parts or outline of something
**2** a method or scheme of acting, doing, or arranging ⟨vacation *plans*⟩

**Synonyms** PLAN, PLOT, and SCHEME mean a method of making or doing something or achieving an end. PLAN suggests that some thinking was done beforehand and often that there is something written down or pictured ⟨a *plan* for a new school⟩. PLOT suggests a complicated, carefully shaped plan of several parts. PLOT can be used of the plan of a story ⟨a mystery story with a good *plot*⟩ or it can be used of a secret, usually evil plan ⟨a *plot* to take over the government⟩. SCHEME suggests a sly plan often for evil reasons ⟨a *scheme* to cheat the old people⟩.

**²plan** *vb* **planned; plan·ning**
**1** to form a plan of or for : arrange the parts of ahead of time ⟨*plan* a bridge⟩ ⟨*plan* a picnic⟩
**2** to have in mind : INTEND

**¹plane** \'plān\ *vb* **planed; plan·ing**
**1** to smooth or level off with a plane
**2** to remove with or as if with a plane

**²plane** *n*
▼ a tool for smoothing wood

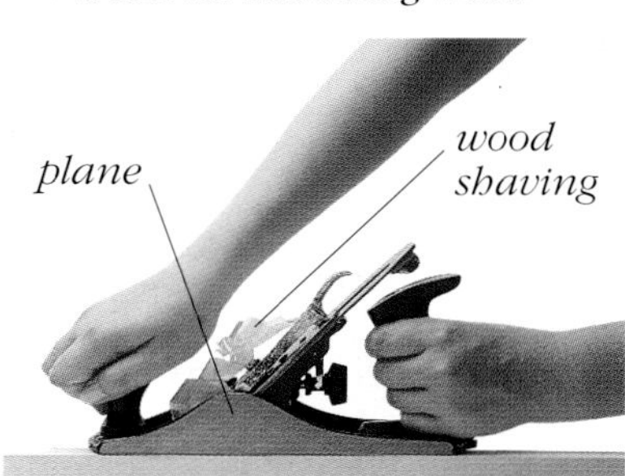


**²plane**

**³plane** *adj*
HORIZONTAL, FLAT ⟨*plane* surface⟩

**⁴plane** *n*
**1** a surface any two points of which can be joined by a straight line lying wholly within it
**2** a level or flat surface
**3** a level of development ⟨exists on a low *plane*⟩
**4** AIRPLANE

**plan·et** \'plan-ət\ *n*
a celestial body other than a comet or meteor that travels in orbit about the sun

**Word History** Most stars seem to have fixed positions when they are compared with other stars. You may look at the sky one night and see three stars in a row. Every night that you can see these three stars at all they will still be in a row. There are certain heavenly bodies that look very much like stars but are not. They seem to wander about among the fixed stars. These heavenly bodies are the planets. The ancient Greeks gave them a name that meant "wanderer." The English word *planet* comes from this Greek name.

**plan·e·tar·i·um** \ˌplan-ə-'ter-ē-əm\ *n*
a building in which there is a device for projecting the images of celestial bodies on a ceiling shaped like a dome

**plan·e·tary** \'plan-ə-ˌter-ē\ *adj*
**1** of or relating to a planet
**2** having a motion like that of a planet

**plank** \'plangk\ *n*
a heavy thick board

**plank·ton** \'plangk-tən\ *n*
▶ the tiny floating plants and animals of a body of water

**plankton** seen under a microscope

**¹plant** \'plant\ *vb*
**1** to place in the ground to grow ⟨*plant* seeds in the spring⟩
**2** to set firmly in or as if in the ground : FIX ⟨*plant* posts for a fence⟩
**3** to introduce as a habit
**4** to cause to become established : SETTLE ⟨*plant* colonies⟩
**5** to stock with something ⟨*plant* a stream with trout⟩

**²plant** *n*
**1** any member of the kingdom of living things (as mosses, ferns, grasses, and trees) with cellulose cell walls, without obvious nervous system or sense organs, and usually without ability to move about

2 the buildings and equipment of an industrial business or an institution ⟨a power *plant*⟩
**plant·like** \'plant-,līk\ *adj*

**[1]plan·tain** \'plant-n\ *n*
any of several common weeds having little or no stem, leaves with parallel veins, and a long stalk of tiny greenish flowers

**[2]plantain** *n*
a banana plant having greenish fruit that is larger, less sweet, and more starchy than the ordinary banana

**plan·ta·tion** \plan-'tā-shən\ *n*
**1** a group of plants and especially trees planted and cared for
**2** a planted area (as an estate) cultivated by laborers
**3** COLONY 1

**plant·er** \'plant-ər\ *n*
**1** one (as a farmer or a machine) that plants crops
**2** a person who owns or runs a plantation
**3** a container in which ornamental plants are grown

**plant kingdom** *n*
a basic group of natural objects that includes all living and extinct plants

**plant louse** *n*
any of various small insects that are related to the true bugs and suck the juices of plants

**plaque** \'plak\ *n*
**1** a flat thin piece (as of metal) used for decoration or having writing cut in it
**2** a thin film containing bacteria and bits of food that forms on the teeth

**plas·ma** \'plaz-mə\ *n*
the watery part of blood, lymph, or milk

**[1]plas·ter** \'plas-tər\ *n*
a paste (as of lime, sand, and water) that hardens when it dries and is used for coating walls and ceilings

**[2]plaster** *vb*
**1** to cover or smear with or as if with plaster
**2** to paste or fasten on especially so as to cover ⟨*plaster* a wall with posters⟩
**plas·ter·er** *n*

**plaster of par·is** \-'par-əs\ *often cap 2d P*
a white powder that mixes with water to form a paste that hardens quickly and is used for casts and molds

**[1]plas·tic** \'plas-tik\ *adj*
**1** capable of being molded or modeled ⟨*plastic* clay⟩
**2** made of plastic ⟨a *plastic* radio cabinet⟩ ⟨a *plastic* raincoat⟩

**[2]plastic** *n*
▼ any of various manufactured materials that can be molded into objects or formed into films or fibers

**[1]plate** \'plāt\ *n*
**1** a thin flat piece of material
**2** metal in sheets ⟨steel *plate*⟩
**3** a piece of metal on which something is engraved or molded ⟨a license *plate*⟩
**4** HOME PLATE
**5** household utensils made of or plated with gold or silver

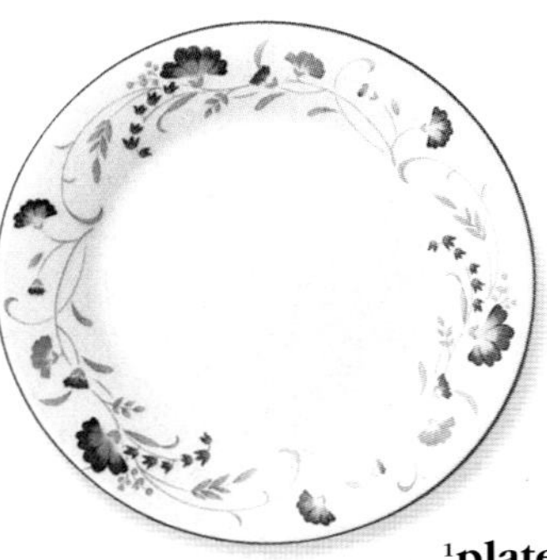

**[1]plate 6**

**6** ▲ a shallow usually round dish
**7** a main course of a meal ⟨a vegetable *plate*⟩ ⟨two dollars a *plate*⟩
**8** a sheet of glass coated with a chemical sensitive to light for use in a camera
**9** an illustration often covering a full page of a book

**[2]plastic**
Since their introduction in the early 20th century, plastics have become some of the most commonly used materials in the world. They are soft or liquid when first made, and can be molded into shape under heat or pressure before they harden. Some plastics, such as those used to make certain plastic bags or bottles, can be reheated and formed into a new shape.

**toy blocks**

**examples of items made from plastic**

**bag**

**toy racket**

**bicycle helmet**

**²plate** *vb* **plat·ed**; **plat·ing**
to cover with a thin layer of metal (as gold or silver)

**pla·teau** \pla-'tō\ *n, pl* **plateaus** *or* **pla·teaux** \-'tōz\
a broad flat area of high land

**plat·form** \'plat-,fȯrm\ *n*
**1** a statement of the beliefs and rules of conduct for which a group stands
**2** a level usually raised surface (as in a railroad station)
**3** a raised floor or stage for performers or speakers
**4** an arrangement of computer components that uses a particular operating system

**plat·i·num** \'plat-n-əm\ *n*
a heavy grayish white metallic chemical element

**pla·toon** \plə-'tün\ *n*
a part of a military company usually made up of two or more squads

**platoon sergeant** *n*
a noncommissioned officer in the Army ranking above a staff sergeant

**plat·ter** \'plat-ər\ *n*
a large plate especially for serving meat

**platy·pus** \'plat-i-pəs\ *n*
▶ a small water-dwelling mammal of Australia that lays eggs and has webbed feet, dense fur, and a bill that resembles that of a duck

**platypus**

**plau·si·ble** \'plȯ-zə-bəl\ *adj*
seeming to be reasonable ⟨a *plausible* excuse⟩
**plau·si·bly** \-blē\ *adv*

**¹play** \'plā\ *n*
**1** exercise or activity for amusement ⟨children at *play*⟩
**2** the action of or a particular action in a game ⟨a great *play* by the shortstop⟩
**3** one's turn to take part in a game ⟨it's your *play*⟩
**4** absence of any bad intention ⟨said it in *play*⟩
**5** quick or light movement ⟨the light *play* of a breeze through the room⟩
**6** freedom of motion ⟨too much *play* in the steering wheel⟩
**7** a story presented on stage

**²play** *vb*
**1** to produce music or sound ⟨*play* the piano⟩ ⟨*play* a CD⟩
**2** to take part in a game of ⟨*play* cards⟩
**3** to take part in sport or recreation : amuse oneself
**4** to handle something idly : TOY ⟨*play* with a watch⟩
**5** to act on or as if on the stage ⟨*play* a part⟩
**6** PRETEND 1 ⟨*play* school⟩
**7** to perform (as a trick) for fun
**8** to play in a game against ⟨*playing* the Dodgers today⟩
**9** ²ACT 2, BEHAVE ⟨*play* fair⟩
**10** to move swiftly or lightly ⟨leaves *playing* in the wind⟩
**11** to put or keep in action ⟨*played* the water hose over the car⟩ **synonyms** see IMPERSONATE
**play hooky** \-'hu̇k-ē\ to stay out of school without permission

**play·act·ing** \'plā-,ak-ting\ *n*
an acting out of make-believe roles

**play·er** \'plā-ər\ *n*
**1** a person who plays a game
**2** a person who plays a musical instrument
**3** a device that reproduces sounds or video images that have been recorded (as on magnetic tape)

**player piano** *n*
a piano containing a mechanical device by which it may be played automatically

**play·ful** \'plā-fəl\ *adj*
**1** full of play : MERRY
**2** HUMOROUS
**play·ful·ly** \-fə-lē\ *adv*
**play·ful·ness** *n*

**play·ground** \'plā-,grau̇nd\ *n*
an area used for games and playing

**play·house** \'plā-,hau̇s\ *n*
**1** THEATER 1
**2** a small house for children to play in

**playing card** *n*
▶ any of a set of cards marked to show rank and suit (**spades**, **hearts**, **diamonds**, or **clubs**) and used in playing various games

**play·mate** \'plā-,māt\ *n*
a companion in play

**play·pen** \'plā-,pen\ *n*
a small enclosure in which a baby is placed to play

**play·thing** \'plā-,thing\ *n*
¹TOY 2

**play·wright** \'plā-,rīt\ *n*
a writer of plays

**pla·za** \'plaz-ə, 'pläz-\ *n*
a public square in a city or town

**plea** \'plē\ *n*
**1** an argument in defense : EXCUSE
**2** an earnest appeal ⟨a *plea* for mercy⟩

**plead** \'plēd\ *vb* **plead·ed** *or* **pled** \'pled\; **plead·ing**
**1** to argue for or against : argue in court ⟨*plead* a case before a jury⟩
**2** to answer to a charge ⟨*plead* guilty⟩
**3** to offer as a defense, an excuse, or an apology ⟨*plead* illness⟩
**4** to make an earnest appeal : BEG

**pleas·ant** \'plez-nt\ *adj*
**1** giving pleasure : AGREEABLE ⟨a *pleasant* day⟩
**2** having pleasing manners, behavior, or appearance
**pleas·ant·ly** *adv*
**pleas·ant·ness** *n*

**¹please** \'plēz\ *vb* **pleased**; **pleas·ing**
**1** to give pleasure or enjoyment to ⟨the gift *pleased* him⟩
**2** to be willing : LIKE, CHOOSE ⟨if you *please*⟩

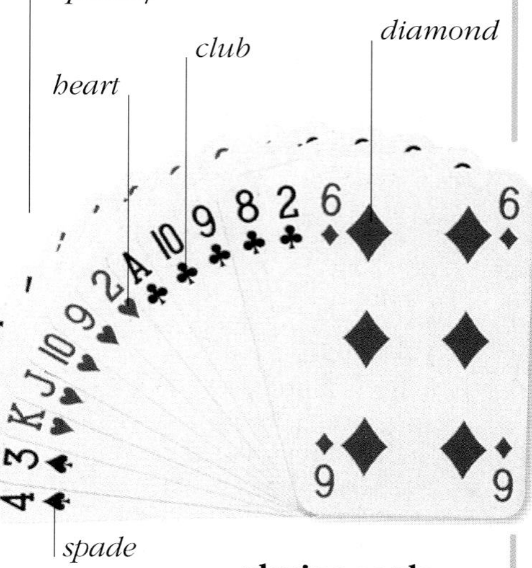


**playing cards**

[2]**please** *adv*
used to show politeness in asking or accepting

**pleas·ing** \'plē-ziŋ\ *adj*
giving pleasure : AGREEABLE
**pleas·ing·ly** *adv*

**plea·sur·able** \'plezh-ə-rə-bəl\ *adj*
PLEASANT 1

**plea·sure** \'plezh-ər\ *n*
**1** a particular desire ⟨what is your *pleasure*⟩
**2** a feeling of enjoyment or satisfaction ⟨took great *pleasure* in gardening⟩ ⟨reading for *pleasure*⟩
**3** something that pleases or delights ⟨the *pleasure* of your company⟩

---

**Synonyms** PLEASURE, JOY and ENJOYMENT mean the agreeable feeling that accompanies getting something good or much wanted. PLEASURE suggests an inner satisfaction rather than an open display of feeling ⟨the *pleasure* felt after helping others⟩. JOY suggests a radiant feeling that is very strong ⟨a life filled with *joy*⟩. ENJOYMENT suggests a conscious reaction to something intended to make one happy ⟨the songs added to our *enjoyment* of the movie⟩.

---

[1]**pleat** \'plēt\ *vb*
to arrange in folds made by doubling material over on itself

[2]**pleat** *n*
a fold (as in cloth) made by doubling material over on itself

**pled** *past of* PLEAD

[1]**pledge** \'plej\ *n*
**1** something handed over to another to ensure that the giver will keep his or her promise or agreement
**2** something that is a symbol of something else ⟨the ring is a *pledge* of love⟩
**3** a promise or agreement that must be kept

[2]**pledge** *vb* **pledged**; **pledg·ing**
**1** to give as a pledge
**2** to hold by a pledge : PROMISE ⟨they *pledged* themselves to secrecy⟩ ⟨I *pledge* allegiance⟩

**plen·te·ous** \'plent-ē-əs\ *adj*
PLENTIFUL 2

**plover:** a European ringed plover

**plen·ti·ful** \'plent-i-fəl\ *adj*
**1** giving or containing plenty : FRUITFUL
**2** present in large numbers or amount : ABUNDANT ⟨*plentiful* rain⟩
**plen·ti·ful·ly** \-fə-lē\ *adv*

**plen·ty** \'plent-ē\ *n*
a full supply : more than enough

**pleu·ri·sy** \'plu̇r-ə-sē\ *n*
a sore swollen state of the membrane that lines the chest often with fever, painful breathing, and coughing

**plex·us** \'plek-səs\ *n, pl* **plex·us·es** *or* **plex·us** \-səs, -ˌsüs\
a network usually of nerves or blood vessels

**pli·able** \'plī-ə-bəl\ *adj*
**1** possible to bend without breaking
**2** easily influenced

**pli·ant** \'plī-ənt\ *adj*
PLIABLE

**pli·ers** \'plī-ərz\ *n pl*
▶ small pincers with long jaws used for bending or cutting wire or handling small things

**pliers**

**plight** \'plīt\ *n*
a usually bad condition or state : PREDICAMENT

**plod** \'pläd\ *vb* **plod·ded**; **plod·ding**
to move or travel slowly but steadily

[1]**plot** \'plät\ *n*
**1** a small area of ground ⟨a cemetery *plot*⟩
**2** the plan or main story of a play or novel
**3** a secret usually evil scheme
**synonyms** see PLAN

[2]**plot** *vb* **plot·ted**; **plot·ting**
**1** to make a map or plan of
**2** to plan or scheme secretly
**plot·ter** *n*

**plo·ver** \'pləv-ər, 'plō-vər\ *n*
◀ any one of several shorebirds having shorter and stouter bills than the related sandpipers

[1]**plow** *or* **plough** \'plau̇\ *n*
**1** a farm machine used to cut, lift, and turn over soil
**2** a device (as a snowplow) used to spread or clear away matter on the ground

[2]**plow** *or* **plough** *vb*
**1** to open, break up, or work with a plow ⟨*plow* a furrow⟩ ⟨*plow* the soil⟩
**2** to move through or cut as a plow does

**plow·share** \'plau̇-ˌsheər, -ˌshaər\ *n*
the part of a plow that cuts the earth

[1]**pluck** \'plək\ *vb*
**1** to pull off : PICK ⟨*pluck* grapes⟩
**2** to remove something (as feathers) from by or as if by plucking ⟨*pluck* a chicken⟩
**3** to seize and remove quickly : SNATCH
**4** to pull at (a string) and let go

[2]**pluck** *n*
**1** a sharp pull : TUG, TWITCH
**2** COURAGE, SPIRIT

**plucky** \'plək-ē\ *adj* **pluck·i·er**; **pluck·i·est**
showing courage : BRAVE

[1]**plug** \'pləg\ *n*
**1** a piece (as of wood or metal) used to stop up or fill a hole
**2** ▶ a device usually on a cord used to make an electrical connection by putting it into another part (as a socket)

[1]**plug 2**

**[2]plug** *vb* **plugged**; **plug·ging**
**1** to stop or make tight with a plug
**2** to keep steadily at work or in action ⟨*plugged* away at my homework⟩
**3** to connect to an electric circuit ⟨*plug* in a lamp⟩

**plum** \'pləm\ *n*
**1** a roundish smooth-skinned edible fruit that has an oblong stone and grows on a tree related to the peaches and cherries
**2** a dark reddish purple
**3** a choice or desirable thing : PRIZE

**plum·age** \'plü-mij\ *n*
the feathers of a bird

**[1]plumb** \'pləm\ *n*
▶ a small weight (as of lead) attached to a line and used to show depth or an exactly straight up-and-down line

*plumb line*

**[1]plumb**

**[2]plumb** *vb*
to measure or test with a plumb ⟨*plumb* the depth of a well⟩ ⟨*plumb* a wall⟩

**plumb·er** \'pləm-ər\ *n*
a person who puts in or repairs plumbing

**Word History** The word *plumber* comes from a Latin word that meant "plumber." The Latin word for a plumber came from a Latin word that meant "lead." In the past water pipes in buildings were often made of lead. The plumbers who put in these pipes and took care of them were workers in lead.

**plumb·ing** \'pləm-ing\ *n*
**1** a plumber's work
**2** a system of pipes for supplying and carrying off water in a building

**plume** \'plüm\ *n*
**1** a large or showy feather of a bird
**2** an ornamental feather or tuft of feathers (as on a hat)
**plumed** \'plümd\ *adj*

**plum·met** \'pləm-ət\ *vb*
to fall straight down ⟨the plane *plummeted* to earth⟩

**[1]plump** \'pləmp\ *vb*
**1** to drop or fall heavily or suddenly ⟨*plumped* down on the couch⟩
**2** to come out in favor of something ⟨*plumping* for my favorite candidate⟩

**[2]plump** *adv*
**1** with a sudden or heavy drop
**2** DIRECTLY 1 ⟨ran *plump* into the wall⟩

**[3]plump** *vb*
to make or become rounded or filled out ⟨*plump* up the pillows⟩

**[4]plump** *adj*
having a pleasingly rounded form : well filled out **synonyms** see FAT
**plump·ness** *n*

**[1]plun·der** \'plən-dər\ *vb*
to rob or steal especially openly and by force (as during war)

**[2]plunder** *n*
something taken by plundering : LOOT

**[1]plunge** \'plənj\ *vb* **plunged**; **plung·ing**
**1** to thrust or force quickly ⟨*plunged* my arm into the pipe⟩
**2** to leap or dive suddenly ⟨*plunged* into the water⟩
**3** to rush, move, or force with reckless haste ⟨*plunged* the family into debt⟩
**4** to dip or move suddenly downward or forward and downward

**[2]plunge** *n*
a sudden dive, rush, or leap

**[1]plu·ral** \'plu̇r-əl\ *adj*
of, relating to, or being a word form used to show more than one ⟨*plural* nouns⟩

**[2]plural** *n*
a form of a word used to show that more than one person or thing is meant

**plu·ral·ize** \'plu̇r-əl-,īz\ *vb* **plu·ral·ized**; **plu·ral·iz·ing**
to make plural or express in the plural form

**[1]plus** \'pləs\ *adj*
falling high in a certain range ⟨a grade of C *plus*⟩

**[2]plus** *prep*
increased by : with the addition of ⟨4 *plus* 5 is 9⟩

**[1]plush** \'pləsh\ *n*
▶ a cloth like a very thick soft velvet

**[2]plush** *adj*
very rich and fine ⟨a *plush* hotel⟩

**plus sign** *n*
a sign + used in mathematics to show addition (as in 8 + 6 = 14) or a quantity greater than zero (as in +10°)

**Plu·to** \'plüt-ō\ *n*
▼ the planet that is farthest away from the sun and has a diameter of about 2300 kilometers

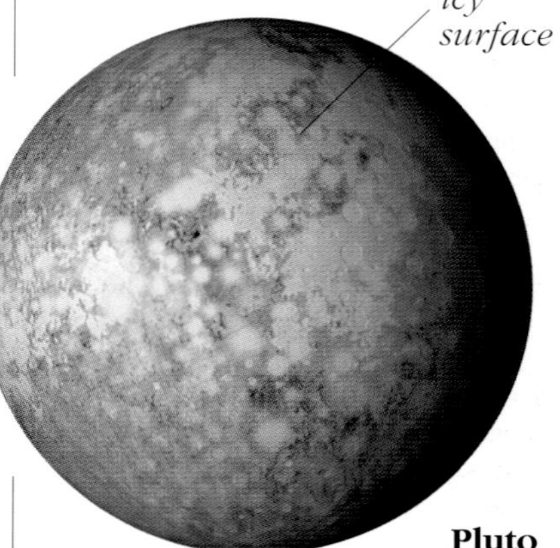

**Pluto**

**plu·to·ni·um** \plü-'tō-nē-əm\ *n*
a radioactive metallic chemical element formed from neptunium and used for releasing atomic energy

**[1]ply** \'plī\ *vb* **plied**; **ply·ing**
**1** to use something steadily or forcefully ⟨*ply* an ax⟩
**2** to keep supplying ⟨*ply* a guest with food⟩
**3** to work hard and steadily at ⟨*ply* a trade⟩

**[2]ply** *n, pl* **plies**
one of the folds, layers, or threads of which something (as yarn or plywood) is made up

**ply·wood** \'plī-,wu̇d\ *n*
a strong board made by gluing together thin sheets of wood under heat and pressure

**[1]plush:** a teddy bear made of plush

**pneu·mat·ic** \nu̇-ˈmat-ik, nyu̇-\ *adj*
**1** of, relating to, or using air, gas, or wind
**2** moved or worked by the pressure of air ⟨a *pneumatic* drill⟩
**3** made to hold or be inflated with compressed air ⟨a *pneumatic* tire⟩

**pneu·mo·nia** \nu̇-ˈmō-nyə, nyu̇-ˈmō-\ *n*
a serious disease in which the lungs are inflamed

[1]**poach** \ˈpōch\ *vb*
to cook slowly in liquid ⟨*poached* eggs⟩

[2]**poach** *vb*
to hunt or fish unlawfully on private property

**pock** \ˈpäk\ *n*
a small swelling like a pimple on the skin (as in smallpox) or the mark it leaves

[1]**pock·et** \ˈpäk-ət\ *n*
**1** a small bag fastened into a garment for carrying small articles
**2** a place or thing like a pocket ⟨a *pocket* of gold in a mine⟩
**3** a condition of the air (as a down current) that causes an airplane to drop suddenly ⟨an air *pocket*⟩

[2]**pocket** *vb*
**1** to put something in a pocket
**2** to take for oneself especially dishonestly ⟨*pocket* the profits⟩

[3]**pocket** *adj*
POCKET-SIZE ⟨a *pocket* dictionary⟩

**pock·et·book** \ˈpäk-ət-ˌbu̇k\ *n*
**1** a case for carrying money or papers in the pocket
**2** HANDBAG
**3** amount of income ⟨a price suited to your *pocketbook*⟩

**pock·et·knife** \ˈpäk-ət-ˌnīf\ *n, pl* **pock·et·knives** \-ˌnīvz\
a knife that has one or more blades that fold into the handle and that can be carried in the pocket

**pock·et–size** \ˈpäk-ət-ˌsīz\ *adj*
small enough to fit in a pocket

**pock·mark** \ˈpäk-ˌmärk\ *n*
the mark left by a pock
**pock·marked** \-ˌmärkt\ *adj*

**pod** \ˈpäd\ *n*
a fruit (as of the pea or bean) that is dry when ripe and then splits open to free its seeds

**po·di·um** \ˈpōd-ē-əm\ *n*
a raised platform especially for the conductor of an orchestra

**po·em** \ˈpō-əm\ *n*
a piece of writing often having rhyme or rhythm which tells a story or describes a feeling

**po·et** \ˈpō-ət\ *n*
a writer of poems

**po·et·ic** \pō-ˈet-ik\ *or* **po·et·i·cal** \-i-kəl\ *adj*
**1** of, relating to, or like that of poets or poetry
**2** written in verse

**po·et·ry** \ˈpō-ə-trē\ *n*
**1** writing usually with a rhythm that repeats **:** VERSE
**2** the writings of a poet

**po·go stick** \ˈpō-gō-\ *n*
a pole with a strong spring at the bottom and two rests for the feet on which a person stands and bounces along

**poin·set·tia** \pȯin-ˈset-ē-ə, -ˈset-ə\ *n*
▼ a tropical plant much used at Christmas with showy usually red leaves that grow like petals around its small greenish flowers

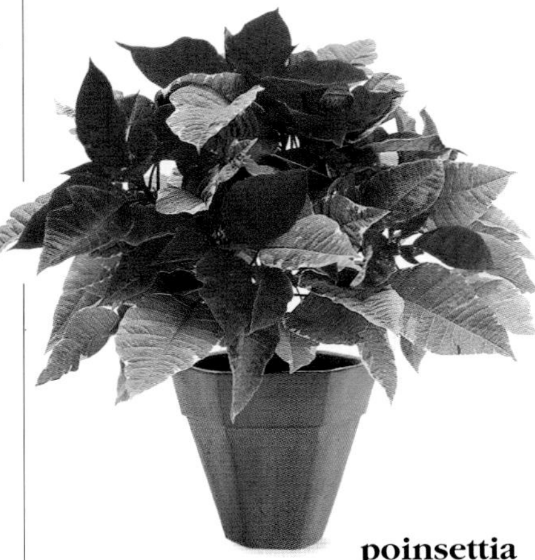
**poinsettia**

[1]**point** \ˈpȯint\ *n*
**1** a separate or particular detail **:** ITEM ⟨explained the main *points* of the plan⟩
**2** an individual quality ⟨has many good *points*⟩
**3** the chief idea or meaning (as of a story or a speech)
**4** [1]PURPOSE, AIM ⟨keep to the *point*⟩ ⟨no *point* in trying any more⟩
**5** a geometric element that has position but no dimensions and is pictured as a small dot
**6** a particular place or position ⟨*points* of interest in the city⟩
**7** a particular stage or moment ⟨the boiling *point*⟩ ⟨at the *point* of death⟩
**8** the sharp end (as of a sword, pin, or pencil)
**9** a piece of land that sticks out
**10** a dot in writing or printing
**11** one of the thirty-two marks indicating direction on a compass
**12** a unit of scoring in a game ⟨scored fifteen *points*⟩
**point·ed** \-əd\ *adj*
**point·less** \-ləs\ *adj*

[2]**point** *vb*
**1** to put a point on ⟨*point* a pencil⟩
**2** to show the position or direction of something by the finger or by standing in a fixed position ⟨*pointed* to the door⟩
**3** to direct someone's attention to ⟨*pointed* out the mistakes⟩
**4** [1]AIM 1, DIRECT ⟨*pointed* the telescope toward Mars⟩ ⟨the arrow *pointed* to the left⟩

[1]**point–blank** \ˈpȯint-ˈblaŋk\ *adj*
**1** aimed at a target from a short distance away ⟨a *point-blank* shot⟩
**2** [1]BLUNT 2 ⟨a *point-blank* refusal⟩

[2]**point–blank** *adv*
in a point-blank manner

**point·er** \ˈpȯint-ər\ *n*
**1** something that points or is used for pointing
**2** a large hunting dog with long ears and short hair that is usually white with colored spots, hunts by scent, and points game
**3** a helpful hint ⟨get a few *pointers* on diving⟩

**point of view**
a way of looking at or thinking about something

[1]**poise** \ˈpȯiz\ *vb* **poised**; **pois·ing**
to hold or make steady by balancing

[2]**poise** *n*
**1** the state of being balanced
**2** a natural self-confident manner ⟨a speaker of great *poise*⟩
**3** BEARING 1

[1]**poi·son** \ˈpȯiz-n\ *n*
a substance that by its chemical action can injure or kill a living thing

[2]**poison** *vb*
**1** to injure or kill with poison
**2** to put poison on or in ⟨gas fumes *poisoned* the air⟩

**poison ivy** *n*
▼ a common woody plant related to the sumacs and having leaves with three leaflets that can cause an itchy rash when touched

**poison ivy**

**poison oak** *n*
a poison ivy that grows as a bush

**poi·son·ous** \'pȯiz-n-əs\ *adj*
containing poison : having or causing an effect of poison

**poison sumac** *n*
a poison oak that grows in wet places

[1]**poke** \'pōk\ *vb* **poked**; **pok·ing**
**1** JAB ⟨*poked* it with a stick⟩
**2** to make by stabbing or piercing ⟨*poked* a hole in the bag⟩
**3** to stick out, or cause to stick out ⟨*poked* my head out of the window⟩
**4** to search over or through usually without purpose : RUMMAGE ⟨*poking* around in the attic⟩
**5** to move slowly or lazily ⟨they were just *poking* along the road⟩

[2]**poke** *n*
a quick thrust : JAB

[1]**pok·er** \'pō-kər\ *n*
a metal rod used for stirring a fire

[2]**po·ker** \'pō-kər\ *n*
a card game in which each player bets on the value of his or her hand

**poky** *or* **pok·ey** \'pō-kē\ *adj* **pok·i·er**; **pok·i·est**
**1** being small and cramped ⟨a *poky* room⟩
**2** so slow as to be annoying

**po·lar** \'pō-lər\ *adj*
**1** of or relating to a pole of the earth or the region around it
**2** coming from or being like a polar region
**3** of or relating to a pole of a magnet

**polar bear** *n*
▶ a large creamy-white bear of arctic regions

**Po·lar·is** \pə-'lar-əs, -'lär-\ *n*
NORTH STAR

[1]**pole** \'pōl\ *n*
a long slender piece (as of wood or metal)

[2]**pole** *vb* **poled**; **pol·ing**
to push or move with a pole ⟨*pole* a boat⟩

[3]**pole** *n*
**1** either end of an axis and especially of the earth's axis
**2** either of the two ends of a magnet
**3** either of the terminals of an electric battery

**Pole** \'pōl\ *n*
a person born or living in Poland

**pole·cat** \'pōl-,kat\ *n*
**1** a small dark European animal that eats flesh and is related to the weasel
**2** SKUNK

**pole·star** \'pōl-,stär\ *n*
NORTH STAR

**pole vault** *n*
a track-and-field contest in which each athlete uses a pole to jump over a high bar

[1]**po·lice** \pə-'lēs\ *vb* **po·liced**; **po·lic·ing**
to keep order in or among ⟨*police* a city⟩

[2]**police** *n, pl* **police**
**1** the department of government that keeps order and enforces law, investigates crimes, and makes arrests
**2** *police pl* members of a police force

**police dog** *n*
a dog trained to help police

**po·lice·man** \pə-'lē-smən\ *n, pl* **po·lice·men** \-smən\
a man who is a police officer

**police officer** *n*
a member of a police force

**po·lice·wom·an** \pə-'lē-,swu̇m-ən\ *n, pl* **po·lice·wom·en** \-,swim-ən\
a woman who is a police officer

[1]**pol·i·cy** \'päl-ə-sē\ *n, pl* **pol·i·cies**
a course of action chosen to guide people in making decisions ⟨a country's foreign *policy*⟩

[2]**policy** *n, pl* **pol·i·cies**
a document that contains the agreement made by an insurance company with a person whose life or property is insured

**po·lio** \'pō-lē-,ō\ *n*
a once common virus disease often affecting children and sometimes causing paralysis

**po·lio·my·eli·tis** \,pō-lē-,ō-,mī-ə-'līt-əs\ *n*
POLIO

[1]**pol·ish** \'päl-ish\ *vb*
**1** to make smooth and glossy usually by rubbing ⟨*polish* silver⟩
**2** to smooth or improve in manners, condition, or style ⟨took a few hours to *polish* the speech⟩
**pol·ish·er** *n*

[2]**polish** *n*
**1** a smooth glossy surface
**2** good manners : REFINEMENT
**3** a substance prepared for use in polishing ⟨shoe *polish*⟩ ⟨metal *polish*⟩

[1]**Pol·ish** \'pō-lish\ *adj*
of or relating to Poland, the Poles, or Polish

[2]**Polish** *n*
the language of the Poles

**polar bear**

**po·lite** \pə-ˈlīt\ *adj* **po·lit·er**; **po·lit·est**
showing courtesy or good manners
**synonyms** see CIVIL
**po·lite·ly** *adv*
**po·lite·ness** *n*

**po·lit·i·cal** \pə-ˈlit-i-kəl\ *adj*
of or relating to politics, government, or the way government is carried on
**po·lit·i·cal·ly** *adv*

**pol·i·ti·cian** \ˌpäl-ə-ˈtish-ən\ *n*
a person who is actively taking part in party politics or in conducting government business

**pol·i·tics** \ˈpäl-ə-ˌtiks\ *n sing or pl*
**1** the science and art of government **:** the management of public affairs
**2** activity in or management of the business of political parties

**pol·ka** \ˈpōl-kə\ *n*
a lively dance for couples or the music for it

**pol·ka dot** \ˈpō-kə-\ *n*
a dot in a pattern of evenly spaced dots

[1]**poll** \ˈpōl\ *n*
**1** the casting or recording of votes or opinions of a number of persons ⟨a *poll* of the persons in the room⟩
**2** the place where votes are cast — usually used in pl. ⟨go to the *polls*⟩

[2]**poll** *vb*
**1** to receive and record the votes of
**2** to receive (votes) in an election
**3** to cast a vote or ballot at a poll

**pol·lack** *or* **pol·lock** \ˈpäl-ək\ *n, pl* **pollack** *or* **pollock**
either of two food fishes of the northern Atlantic and the northern Pacific that are related to the cod

**pol·len** \ˈpäl-ən\ *n*
the fine usually yellow dust in the anthers of a flower that fertilizes the seeds

**pol·li·nate** \ˈpäl-ə-ˌnāt\ *vb* **pol·li·nat·ed**; **pol·li·nat·ing**
to place pollen on the stigma of ⟨bees *pollinating* clover⟩

**pol·li·na·tion** \ˌpäl-ə-ˈnā-shən\ *n*
the act or process of pollinating

**pol·li·wog** *or* **pol·ly·wog** \ˈpäl-ē-ˌwäg\ *n*
TADPOLE

**pol·lut·ant** \pə-ˈlüt-nt\ *n*
something that causes pollution

**pol·lute** \pə-ˈlüt\ *vb* **pol·lut·ed**; **pol·lut·ing**
to make impure ⟨*pollute* a stream⟩
**pol·lut·er** *n*

**pol·lu·tion** \pə-ˈlü-shən\ *n*
the action of polluting or the state of being polluted

**po·lo** \ˈpō-lō\ *n*
a game played by teams of players on horseback who drive a wooden ball with long-handled mallets

**poly-** *prefix*
many **:** much **:** MULTI-

**poly·es·ter** \ˈpäl-ē-ˌes-tər\ *n*
a synthetic fiber used especially in clothing

**poly·gon** \ˈpäl-i-ˌgän\ *n*
a plane figure having three or more straight sides

**poly·mer** \ˈpäl-ə-mər\ *n*
a chemical compound or mixture of compounds that is formed by combination of smaller molecules and consists basically of repeating structural units

**pol·yp** \ˈpäl-əp\ *n*
a small sea animal (as a coral) having a tubelike body closed and attached to something (as a rock) at one end and opening at the other with a mouth surrounded by tentacles

**poncho 1:** a girl wearing a poncho

pomegranate

**pome·gran·ate** \ˈpäm-ˌgran-ət, ˈpäm-ə-\ *n*
▲ a reddish fruit about the size of an orange that has a thick skin and many seeds in a pulp of tart flavor and grows on a tropical Old World tree

[1]**pom·mel** \ˈpəm-əl\ *n*
a rounded knob on the handle of a sword or at the front and top of a saddle

[2]**pommel** *vb* **pom·meled** *or* **pom·melled**; **pom·mel·ing** *or* **pom·mel·ling**
PUMMEL

**pomp** \ˈpämp\ *n*
a show of wealth and splendor

**pom–pom** \ˈpäm-ˌpäm\ *or* **pom·pon** \-ˌpän\ *n*
a fluffy ball used as trimming on clothing

**pomp·ous** \ˈpäm-pəs\ *adj*
**1** making an appearance of importance or dignity
**2** SELF-IMPORTANT
**pomp·ous·ly** *adv*
**pomp·ous·ness** *n*

**pon·cho** \ˈpän-chō\ *n, pl* **ponchos**
**1** ◀ a Spanish-American cloak like a blanket with a slit in the middle for the head
**2** a waterproof garment like a poncho worn as a raincoat

**pond** \ˈpänd\ *n*
a body of water usually smaller than a lake

**pon·der** \ˈpän-dər\ *vb*
to think over carefully

**pon·der·ous** \ˈpän-də-rəs\ *adj*
**1** very heavy
**2** unpleasantly dull ⟨a *ponderous* speech⟩

**pond scum** *n*
a mass of algae in still water or an alga that grows in such masses

**pon·toon** \pän-ˈtün\ *n*
**1** a small boat with a flat bottom

A B C D E F G H I J K L M N O P Q R S T U V W X Y Z

**2** a light watertight float used as one of the supports for a floating bridge **3** a float attached to the bottom of an airplane for landing on water

**po·ny** \'pō-nē\ *n, pl* **ponies**
a small horse

**pony express** *n*
a rapid postal system that operated across the western United States in 1860–61 by changing horses and riders along the way

**po·nytail** \'pō-nē-ˌtāl\ *n*
a hairstyle in which the hair is pulled together and banded usually at the back of the head

**poodle**

**poo·dle** \'püd-l\ *n*
▲ one of an old breed of active intelligent dogs with heavy coats of solid color

**pooh** \'pü, 'pu̇\ *interj*
used to express contempt or disapproval

**¹pool** \'pül\ *n*
**1** a small deep body of usually fresh water ⟨the *pool* below the rock⟩ **2** something like a pool ⟨the lamp cast a *pool* of light⟩ **3** a small body of standing liquid : PUDDLE **4** SWIMMING POOL

**²pool** *n*
**1** ▼ a game of billiards played on a table with six pockets **2** people, money, or things come together or put together for some purpose ⟨a car *pool*⟩

**³pool** *vb*
to contribute to a common fund or effort

**poor** \'pu̇r\ *adj*
**1** not having riches or possessions **2** less than enough ⟨a *poor* crop⟩ **3** worthy of pity ⟨the *poor* dog was killed⟩ **4** low in quality or value ⟨*poor* health⟩
**poor·ly** *adv*
**poor·ness** *n*

**¹pop** \'päp\ *vb* **popped**; **pop·ping**
**1** to burst or cause to burst with a sharp sound ⟨the balloon *popped*⟩ **2** to move suddenly ⟨*pop* into bed⟩ **3** to fire a gun : SHOOT ⟨*popping* at tin cans⟩ **4** to stick out ⟨their eyes *popping* with surprise⟩

**²pop** *n*
**1** a short explosive sound **2** SODA POP

**pop·corn** \'päp-ˌkȯrn\ *n*
**1** corn whose kernels burst open when exposed to high heat to form a white or yellowish mass **2** the kernels after popping ⟨we ate *popcorn* during the movie⟩

**pope** \'pōp\ *n, often cap*
the head of the Roman Catholic Church

**pop·lar** \'päp-lər\ *n*
a tree that has rough bark, catkins for flowers, and a white cottonlike substance around its seeds

**pop·py** \'päp-ē\ *n, pl* **poppies**
► a plant with a hairy stem and showy usually red, yellow, or white flowers

**poppy**

**pop·u·lace** \'päp-yə-ləs\ *n*
**1** the common people **2** POPULATION 1

**²pool 1**
Pool is played on a rectangular table with holes, known as pockets, in the corners and in the center of the longest sides. Players use a long wooden stick called a cue to aim a cue ball toward a colored or striped ball to try to hit it into a pocket. Points are scored by hitting designated balls into pockets, and the player or team that scores an agreed number of points first wins.

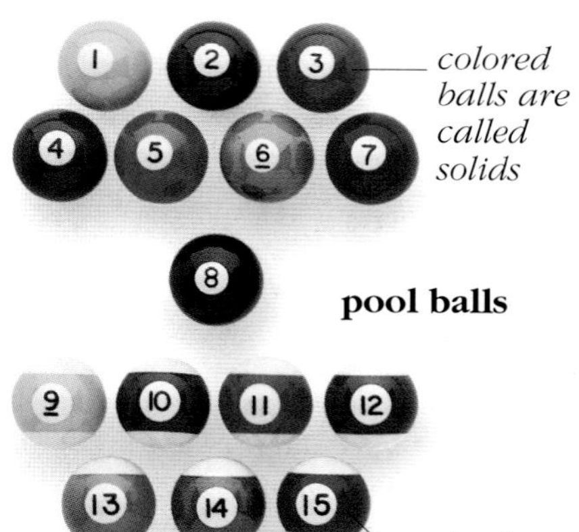

**pool balls**

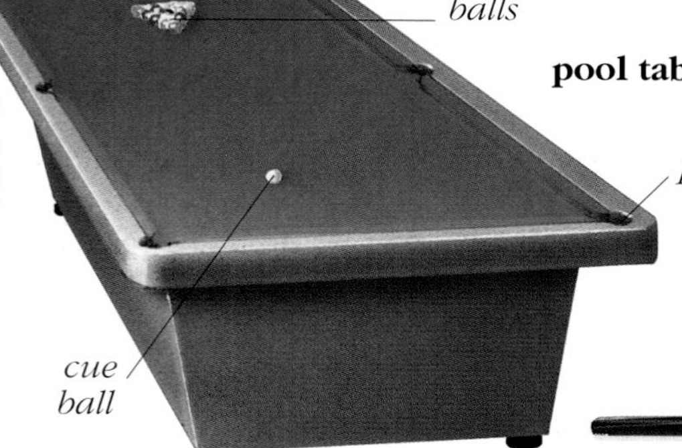

**pool table**

**cue**

**pop·u·lar** \'päp-yə-lər\ *adj*
**1** of, relating to, or coming from the whole body of people ⟨*popular* government⟩
**2** enjoyed or approved by many people ⟨a *popular* game⟩
**pop·u·lar·ly** *adv*

**pop·u·lar·i·ty** \ˌpäp-yə-'lar-ət-ē\ *n*
the quality or state of being popular

**pop·u·late** \'päp-yə-ˌlāt\ *vb* **pop·u·lat·ed**; **pop·u·lat·ing**
to provide with inhabitants

**pop·u·la·tion** \ˌpäp-yə-'lā-shən\ *n*
**1** the whole number of people in a country, city, or area
**2** the people or things living in a certain place

**pop·u·lous** \'päp-yə-ləs\ *adj*
having a large population

**por·ce·lain** \'pōr-sə-lən\ *n*
a hard white ceramic ware used especially for dishes and chemical utensils

**porch** \'pōrch\ *n*
a covered entrance to a building usually with a separate roof

**por·cu·pine** \'pȯr-kyə-ˌpīn\ *n*
▼ a gnawing animal having stiff sharp quills among its hairs

**porcupine**

**Word History** The word *porcupine* is related to the word *pork*. The word *pork* comes from a Latin word that meant "pig." A porcupine looks a little like a spiny pig. The English word *porcupine* comes from two Latin words. The first meant "pig" and the second meant "spine" or "thorn."

**¹pore** \'pōr\ *vb* **pored**; **por·ing**
to read with great attention : STUDY ⟨*pore* over a book⟩

**²pore** *n*
a tiny opening (as in the skin or in the soil)

**por·gy** \'pȯr-gē\ *n, pl* **porgies**
any of several food fishes of the Mediterranean sea and the Atlantic ocean

**pork** \'pōrk\ *n*
the fresh or salted flesh of a pig

**po·rous** \'pōr-əs\ *adj*
**1** full of pores ⟨*porous* wood⟩
**2** capable of absorbing liquids ⟨*porous* blotting paper⟩

**por·poise** \'pȯr-pəs\ *n*
**1** a sea animal somewhat like a small whale with a blunt rounded snout
**2** DOLPHIN 1

**Word History** The word *porpoise* is related to the word *pork*. The word *pork* comes from a Latin word that meant "pig." The snout of the porpoise must have reminded the ancient Romans of a pig's snout. They gave the porpoise a Latin name that meant "pig of the sea." The English word *porpoise* comes from two Latin words. The first meant "pig" and the second meant "fish."

**por·ridge** \'pȯr-ij\ *n*
a food made by boiling meal of a grain or a vegetable (as peas) in water or milk until it thickens

**¹port** \'pōrt\ *n*
**1** a place where ships may ride safe from storms
**2** a harbor where ships load or unload cargo
**3** AIRPORT

**²port** *n*
**1** an opening (as in machinery) for gas, steam, or water to go in or out
**2** PORTHOLE

**³port** *n*
the left side of a ship or airplane looking forward

**por·ta·ble** \'pōrt-ə-bəl\ *adj*
possible to carry or move about

**por·tage** \'pōrt-ij\ *n*
the carrying of boats or goods overland from one body of water to another

**por·tal** \'pōrt-l\ *n*
a grand or fancy door or gate

**port·cul·lis** \pōrt-'kəl-əs\ *n*
a heavy iron gate which can be let down to prevent entrance (as to a castle)

**por·tend** \pȯr-'tend\ *vb*
to give a sign or warning of beforehand

**por·tent** \'pȯr-ˌtent\ *n*
a sign or warning that something is going to happen

**por·ter** \'pōrt-ər\ *n*
**1** a person who carries baggage (as at a terminal)
**2** an attendant on a train

**port·fo·lio** \pōrt-'fō-lē-ˌō\ *n, pl* **port·fo·li·os**
a flat case for carrying papers or drawings

**port·hole** \'pōrt-ˌhōl\ *n*
a small window in the side of a ship or airplane

**por·ti·co** \'pōrt-i-ˌkō\ *n, pl* **por·ti·coes** *or* **por·ti·cos**
▼ a row of columns supporting a roof around or at the entrance of a building

**¹por·tion** \'pōr-shən\ *n*
a part or share of a whole
**synonyms** see PART

**²portion** *vb*
to divide into portions : DISTRIBUTE

**portico** on a theater in Paris, France

**por·trait** \'pōr-trət, -ˌtrāt\ *n*
a picture of a person usually showing the face

**por·tray** \pōr-'trā\ *vb*
**1** to make a portrait of
**2** to picture in words : DESCRIBE
**3** to play the role of ⟨*portray* the villain in a movie⟩

**por·tray·al** \pōr-'trā-əl\ *n*
the act or result of portraying

[1]**Por·tu·guese** \'pōr-chə-ˌgēz\ *adj*
of or relating to Portugal, its people, or the Portuguese language

[2]**Portuguese** *n, pl* **Portuguese**
**1** a person born or living in Portugal
**2** the language of Portugal and Brazil

[1]**pose** \'pōz\ *vb* **posed**; **pos·ing**
**1** to hold or cause to hold a special position of the body ⟨*pose* for a painting⟩
**2** to set forth ⟨*pose* a problem⟩
**3** to pretend to be what one is not ⟨*pose* as a police officer⟩

[2]**pose** *n*
**1** a position of the body held for a special purpose ⟨photographed in different *poses*⟩
**2** a pretended attitude ⟨a *pose* of innocence⟩

**po·si·tion** \pə-'zish-ən\ *n*
**1** the way in which something is placed or arranged
**2** a way of looking at or considering things
**3** the place where a person or thing is ⟨took their *positions* at the head of the line⟩
**4** the rank a person has in an organization or in society
**5** JOB 3

[1]**pos·i·tive** \'päz-ət-iv\ *adj*
**1** definitely and clearly stated ⟨the police had *positive* orders⟩
**2** fully confident : CERTAIN ⟨*positive* that I would win⟩
**3** of, relating to, or having the form of an adjective or adverb that shows no degree of comparison
**4** having a real position or effect ⟨a *positive* change⟩
**5** having the light and shade the same as in the original subject ⟨a *positive* photograph⟩
**6** being greater than zero and often shown by a plus sign ⟨2 or +2 is a *positive* number⟩
**7** of, being, or relating to electricity of a kind that is produced in a glass rod rubbed with silk ⟨a *positive* charge⟩
**8** having a deficiency of electrons ⟨a *positive* particle⟩
**9** being the part from which the electric current flows to the external circuit ⟨the *positive* pole of a storage battery⟩
**10** showing acceptance or approval ⟨a *positive* answer⟩
**11** showing the presence of what is looked for or suspected to be present ⟨the test for tuberculosis was *positive*⟩
**pos·i·tive·ly** *adv*

**portrait:**
a portrait of a woman

[2]**positive** *n*
the positive degree or a positive form of an adjective or adverb

**pos·sess** \pə-'zes\ *vb*
**1** to have and hold as property : OWN
**2** to enter into and control firmly ⟨acted as if *possessed* by a devil⟩
**pos·ses·sor** \-ər\ *n*

**pos·ses·sion** \pə-'zesh-ən\ *n*
**1** the act of possessing or holding as one's own : OWNERSHIP ⟨charged with the *possession* of stolen goods⟩
**2** something that is held as one's own property

[1]**pos·ses·sive** \pə-'zes-iv\ *adj*
**1** being or belonging to the case of a noun or pronoun that shows possession
**2** showing the desire to possess or control

[2]**possessive** *n*
a noun or pronoun in the possessive case

**pos·si·bil·i·ty** \ˌpäs-ə-'bil-ət-ē\ *n, pl* **pos·si·bil·i·ties**
**1** the state or fact of being possible ⟨face the *possibility* of failure⟩
**2** something that may happen

**pos·si·ble** \'päs-ə-bəl\ *adj*
**1** being within the limits of one's ability ⟨a task *possible* to the youngest children⟩
**2** being something that may or may not happen ⟨*possible* dangers⟩
**3** able or fitted to be or to become ⟨a *possible* site for a camp⟩

---

**Synonyms** POSSIBLE and LIKELY mean being such as may become true or actual. POSSIBLE suggests that something is within the limit of what may happen or of what a person or thing may do regardless of the chances for or against it actually happening ⟨it is *possible* that you may get rich⟩. LIKELY suggests that the chances are good that something will actually happen but there is no proof it will ⟨it is *likely* that you will get married⟩.

---

**pos·si·bly** \'päs-ə-blē\ *adv*
**1** by any possibility ⟨that cannot *possibly* be true⟩
**2** PERHAPS ⟨*possibly* it will rain⟩

**pos·sum** \'päs-əm\ *n*
OPOSSUM

[1]**post** \'pōst\ *n*
a piece of solid substance (as metal or timber) placed firmly in an upright position and used especially as a support

[2]**post** *vb*
**1** to fasten on a post, wall, or bulletin board ⟨*post* examination results⟩
**2** to make known publicly as if by posting a notice
**3** to forbid persons from entering or using by putting up warning notices ⟨*post* a trout stream⟩

[3]**post** *vb*
**1** to ride or travel with haste
**2** to send by mail : MAIL
**3** to make familiar with a subject ⟨keep me *posted*⟩

[4]**post** *n*
**1** the place at which a soldier or guard is stationed
**2** a place where a body of troops is stationed
**3** a place or office to which a person is appointed
**4** a trading settlement

[5]**post** *vb*
to station at a post ⟨*post* a guard⟩
**post-** *prefix*
after : later : following : behind
**post·age** \'pō-stij\ *n*
a fee for postal service
**post·al** \'pōst-l\ *adj*
of or relating to the post office or the handling of mail
**postal card** *n*
**1** a blank card with a postage stamp printed on it
**2** POSTCARD 1
**post·card** \'pōst-,kärd\ *n*
**1** ▶ a card on which a message may be sent by mail without an envelope
**2** POSTAL CARD 1
**post·er** \'pō-stər\ *n*
a usually large sheet with writing or pictures on it that is displayed as a notice, advertisement, or for decoration
**pos·ter·i·ty** \pä-'ster-ət-ē\ *n*
**1** the line of individuals descended from one ancestor
**2** all future generations ⟨leave a record for *posterity*⟩
**post·man** \'pōst-mən\ *n, pl* **post·men** \-mən\
LETTER CARRIER
**post·mark** \'pōst-,märk\ *n*
a mark put on a piece of mail especially for canceling the postage stamp
**post·mas·ter** \'pōst-,mas-tər\ *n*
a person in charge of a post office
**post·mis·tress** \'pōst-,mis-trəs\ *n*
a woman in charge of a post office
**post office** *n*
**1** a government agency in charge of the mail
**2** a place where mail is received, handled, and sent out
**post·paid** \'pōst-'pād\ *adv*
with postage paid by the sender

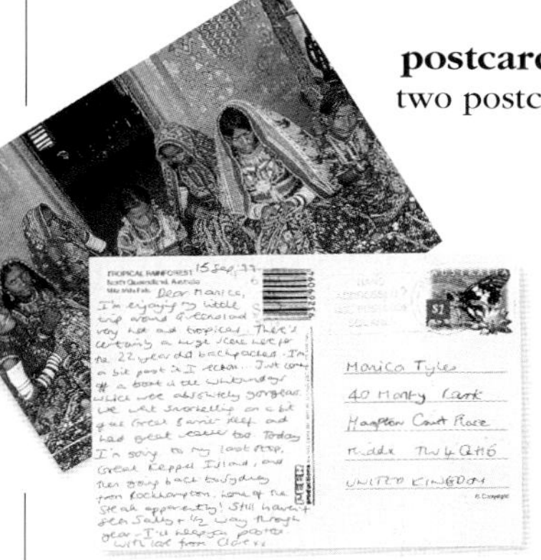
**postcard 1:** two postcards

**post·pone** \pōst-'pōn\ *vb* **post·poned**; **post·pon·ing**
to put off till some later time
**post·pone·ment** \-mənt\ *n*
**post·script** \'pōst-,skript\ *n*
a note added at the end of a finished letter or book
[1]**pos·ture** \'päs-chər\ *n*
the position of one part of the body with relation to other parts : the general way of holding the body
[2]**posture** *vb* **pos·tured**; **pos·tur·ing**
to take on a particular posture : POSE
**po·sy** \'pō-zē\ *n, pl* **posies**
**1** [1]FLOWER 1, 2
**2** BOUQUET
[1]**pot** \'pät\ *n*
**1** a deep rounded container for household purposes
**2** the amount a pot will hold
[2]**pot** *vb* **pot·ted**; **pot·ting**
**1** to put or pack in a pot
**2** to plant (as a flower) in a pot to grow — often used with *up* ⟨*pot* up begonias⟩
**pot·ash** \'pät-,ash\ *n*
potassium or a compound of potassium
**po·tas·si·um** \pə-'tas-ē-əm\ *n*
a silvery soft light metallic chemical element found especially in minerals
**po·ta·to** \pə-'tāt-ō\ *n, pl* **po·ta·toes**
the thick edible underground tuber of a widely grown American plant related to the tomato
**potato chip** *n*
a very thin slice of potato fried crisp
**po·tent** \'pōt-nt\ *adj*
**1** having power or authority ⟨a *potent* ruler⟩
**2** very effective : STRONG ⟨*potent* medicine⟩
**po·ten·tial** \pə-'ten-chəl\ *adj*
existing as a possibility
**po·ten·tial·ly** *adv*
**pot·hole** \'pät-,hōl\ *n*
a deep round hole (as in a stream bed or a road)
**po·tion** \'pō-shən\ *n*
a drink especially of a medicine or of a poison
**pot·luck** \'pät-'lək\ *n*
a meal to which people bring food to share
**pot·shot** \'pät-,shät\ *n*
a shot taken in a casual manner or at an easy target
[1]**pot·ter** \'pät-ər\ *n*
a person who makes pottery
[2]**potter** *vb*
PUTTER
**pot·tery** \'pät-ə-rē\ *n, pl* **pot·ter·ies**
**1** a place where clay articles (as pots, dishes, and vases) are made
**2** ◀ the art of making clay articles
**3** articles made from clay that is shaped while moist and hardened by heat

## pottery 2

Pottery can be made in several ways — for example, from coils or flat slabs of clay, by pressing clay into a mold, or by shaping it on a potter's wheel. This last method involves the potter shaping the wet clay with both hands while the wheel spins, giving the pot an even shape. The pot is then left to dry before it is baked at very high temperatures in an oven called a kiln — this process is known as firing.

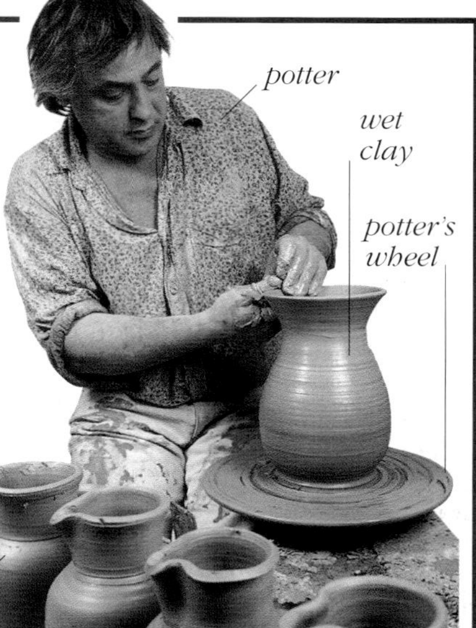


a b c d e f g h i j k l m n o p q r s t u v w x y z

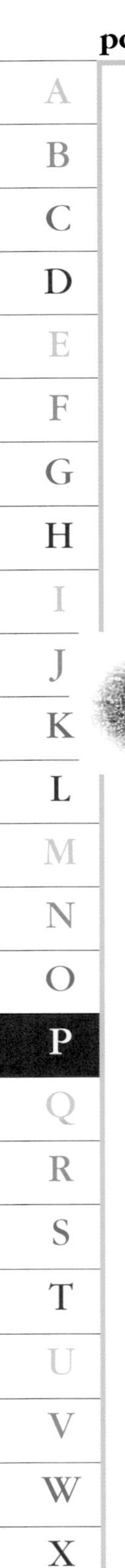


**pouch** \'pau̇ch\ *n*
**1** a small bag with a drawstring
**2** a bag often with a lock for carrying goods or valuables ⟨mail *pouch*⟩
**3** ▶ a bag of folded skin and flesh especially for carrying the young (as on the abdomen of a kangaroo) or for carrying food (as in the cheek of many animals of the rat family)

**poul·tice** \'pōl-təs\ *n*
a soft and heated mass usually containing medicine and spread on the body surface to relieve pain, inflammation, or congestion

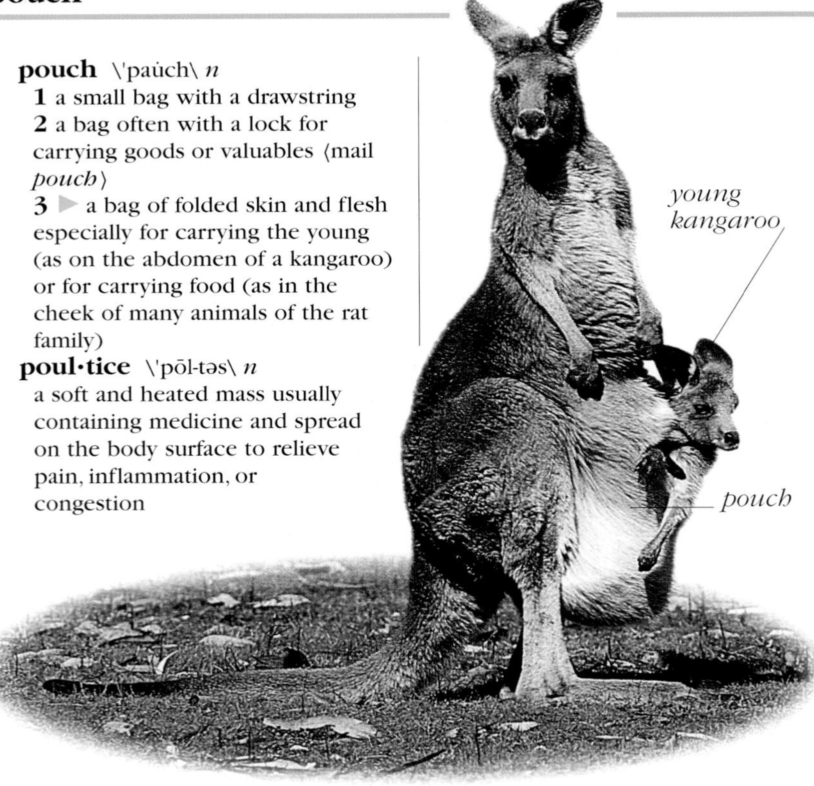


**pouch 3:** a kangaroo with young in its pouch

**poul·try** \'pōl-trē\ *n*
▼ birds (as chickens, turkeys, ducks, and geese) grown to furnish meat or eggs for human food

**[1]pounce** \'pau̇ns\ *vb* **pounced**; **pounc·ing**
**1** to swoop on and seize something with or as if with claws
**2** to leap or attack very quickly

**[2]pounce** *n*
an act of pouncing **:** a sudden swooping or springing on something

**[1]pound** \'pau̇nd\ *n*
**1** a measure of weight equal to sixteen ounces (about .45 kilogram)
**2** a unit of money used in several countries (as the United Kingdom and Egypt)

**[2]pound** *n*
a public enclosure where stray animals are kept ⟨a dog *pound*⟩

**[3]pound** *vb*
**1** to crush to a powder or pulp by beating ⟨*pound* almonds into a paste⟩
**2** to strike heavily again and again ⟨*pound* a piano⟩
**3** to move along heavily ⟨*pounding* through mud⟩

**pour** \'pōr\ *vb*
**1** to flow or cause to flow in a stream
**2** to let loose something without holding back ⟨*poured* out my troubles⟩

## poultry

People have kept poultry for centuries, mainly as a source of meat and eggs, although the feathers of ducks and geese are often used to stuff pillows and quilts. On some modern farms, birds are raised in large numbers in highly controlled conditions to encourage them to grow quickly. Poultry reared in a more natural setting are known as "free range."

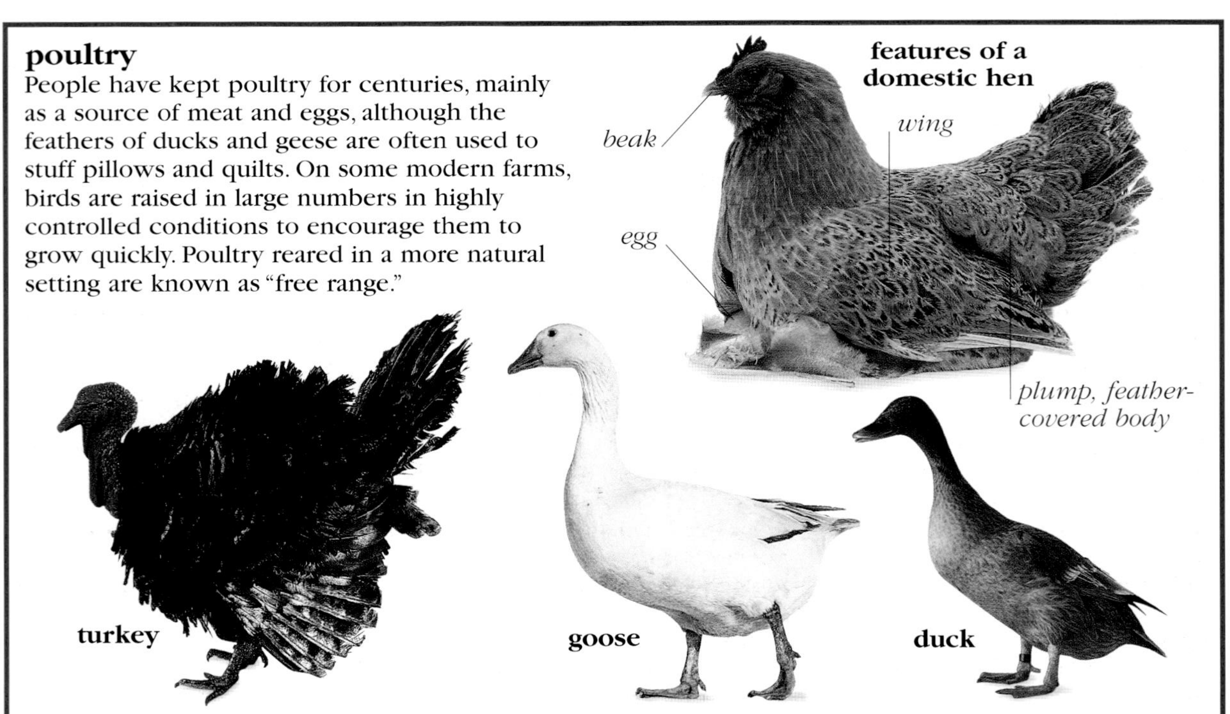

3 to rain hard ⟨it *poured* all day long⟩

**¹pout** \ˈpau̇t\ *vb*
to show displeasure by pushing out one's lips

**²pout** *n*
an act of pouting

**pov·er·ty** \ˈpäv-ərt-ē\ *n*
1 the condition of being poor : lack of money or possessions
2 a lack of something desirable ⟨*poverty* of the soil⟩

**¹pow·der** \ˈpau̇d-ər\ *vb*
1 to sprinkle with or as if with fine particles of something
2 to reduce to powder
3 to use face powder

**²powder** *n*
1 the fine particles made (as by pounding or crushing) from a dry substance
2 something (as a food, medicine, or cosmetic) made in or changed to the form of a powder
3 an explosive used in shooting and in blasting

**powder horn** *n*
a cow or ox horn made into a flask for carrying gunpowder

**pow·dery** \ˈpau̇d-ə-rē\ *adj*
1 made of or like powder
2 easily crumbled
3 sprinkled with powder

**¹pow·er** \ˈpau̇-ər\ *n*
1 possession of control, authority, or influence over others
2 a nation that has influence among other nations
3 the ability to act or to do ⟨lose the *power* to walk⟩
4 physical might : STRENGTH
5 the number of times as shown by an exponent a number is used as a factor to obtain a product ⟨$10^3$ is the third *power* of 10 and means $10 \times 10 \times 10$⟩
6 force or energy used to do work ⟨electric *power*⟩
7 the rate of speed at which work is done
8 the number of times an optical instrument magnifies the apparent size of the object viewed
**pow·er·less** \-ləs\ *adj*

**Synonyms** POWER, ENERGY, and STRENGTH mean the ability to put out effort or force. POWER applies to the ability to act, whether only possible or actually used ⟨the king had the *power* to execute criminals⟩. ENERGY applies to stored-up power that can be used to do work ⟨the sun could be a great source of *energy*⟩. STRENGTH applies to that quality which gives a person or thing the ability to put out force or to oppose another's force or attack ⟨test the *strength* of this rope⟩.

**²power** *vb*
to supply with power

**³power** *adj*
relating to, supplying, or using mechanical or electrical power ⟨*power* sources⟩ ⟨*power* drill⟩

**pow·er·ful** \ˈpau̇-ər-fəl\ *adj*
full of or having power, strength, or influence
**pow·er·ful·ly** \-fə-lē\ *adv*

**pow·er·house** \ˈpau̇-ər-ˌhau̇s\ *n*
1 POWER PLANT
2 a person or thing having unusual strength or energy

**prairie dog:** a black-tailed prairie dog with its young

**power plant** *n*
a building in which electric power is generated

**pow·wow** \ˈpau̇-ˌwau̇\ *n*
1 a North American Indian ceremony or conference
2 a meeting for discussion

**prac·ti·ca·ble** \ˈprak-ti-kə-bəl\ *adj*
possible to do or put into practice

**prac·ti·cal** \ˈprak-ti-kəl\ *adj*
1 engaged in some work ⟨a *practical* farmer⟩
2 of or relating to action and practice rather than ideas or thought
3 capable of being made use of ⟨a *practical* knowledge of carpentry⟩
4 ready to do things rather than just plan or think about them ⟨a *practical* mind⟩

**practical joke** *n*
a joke made up of something done rather than said : a trick played on someone

**prac·ti·cal·ly** \ˈprak-ti-kə-lē\ *adv*
1 ACTUALLY ⟨a clever but *practically* worthless plan⟩
2 ALMOST ⟨*practically* friendless⟩

**¹prac·tice** *or* **prac·tise** \ˈprak-təs\ *vb* **prac·ticed** *or* **prac·tised**; **prac·tic·ing** *or* **prac·tis·ing**
1 to work at often so as to learn well ⟨*practice* music⟩
2 to engage in often or usually ⟨*practice* politeness⟩
3 to follow or work at as a profession ⟨*practice* medicine⟩

**²practice** *also* **practise** *n*
1 actual performance : USE ⟨put into *practice*⟩
2 a usual way of doing ⟨follow the local *practice*⟩
3 repeated action for gaining skill ⟨*practice* makes perfect⟩

**prai·rie** \ˈpreər-ē\ *n*
a large area of level or rolling grassland

**prairie chicken** *n*
a grouse of the Mississippi valley

**prairie dog** *n*
◀ a burrowing animal related to the woodchuck but about the size of a large squirrel that lives in large colonies

**prairie schooner** *n*
a long covered wagon used by pioneers to cross the prairies

**¹praise** \ˈprāz\ *vb* **praised**; **prais·ing**
1 to express approval of
2 to glorify God or a saint especially in song **synonyms** see COMPLIMENT

**²praise** *n*
1 an expression of approval
2 ¹WORSHIP 1

**praise·wor·thy** \ˈprāz-ˌwər-t͟hē\ *adj*
worthy of praise

**prance** \ˈprans\ *vb* **pranced**; **pranc·ing**
1 to rise onto or move on the hind legs
2 to ride on a prancing horse
3 ¹STRUT

**prank** \ˈprangk\ *n*
a mischievous act : PRACTICAL JOKE

A B C D E F G H I J K L M N O P Q R S T U V W X Y Z

**prat·tle** \'prat-l\ *vb* **prat·tled**; **prat·tling**
to talk a great deal without much meaning

**prawn** \'prȯn\ *n*
▼ an edible shellfish that looks like a shrimp

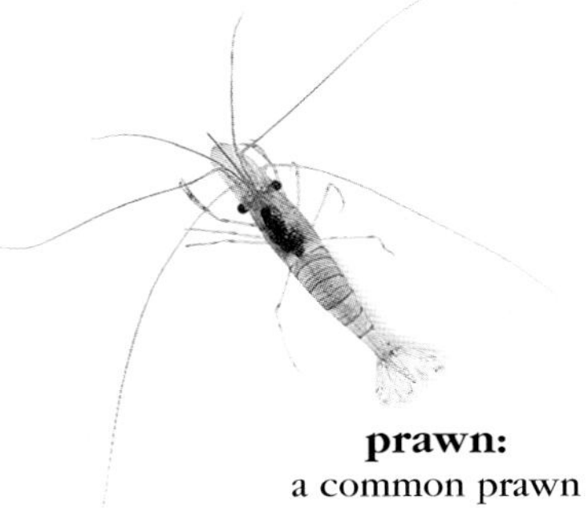
**prawn:** a common prawn

**pray** \'prā\ *vb*
**1** to ask earnestly : BEG
**2** to address God with adoration, pleading, or thanksgiving

**prayer** \'praər, 'preər\ *n*
**1** a request addressed to God ⟨a *prayer* for peace⟩
**2** the act of praying to God ⟨kneel in *prayer*⟩
**3** a set form of words used in praying ⟨the Lord's *prayer*⟩
**4** a religious service that is mostly prayers ⟨evening *prayer*⟩

**praying mantis** \ˌprā-ing-\ *n*
MANTIS

**pre-** *prefix*
**1** earlier than : before ⟨*pre*historic⟩
**2** beforehand ⟨*pre*pay⟩
**3** in front of : front ⟨*pre*molar⟩

**preach** \'prēch\ *vb*
**1** to give a sermon
**2** to urge publicly : ADVOCATE

**preach·er** \'prē-chər\ *n*
**1** a person who preaches
**2** [1]MINISTER 1

**pre·am·ble** \'prē-ˌam-bəl\ *n*
an introduction (as to a law) that often gives the reasons for what follows

**pre·car·i·ous** \pri-'kar-ē-əs, -'ker-\ *adj*
**1** depending on chance or unknown conditions : UNCERTAIN
**2** lacking steadiness or security ⟨*precarious* state of health⟩
**pre·car·i·ous·ly** *adv*
**pre·car·i·ous·ness** *n*

**pre·cau·tion** \pri-'kȯ-shən\ *n*
**1** care taken beforehand
**2** something done beforehand to prevent evil or bring about good results ⟨take all possible *precautions* against fire⟩

**pre·cede** \pri-'sēd\ *vb*
**pre·ced·ed**; **pre·ced·ing**
to be or go before in importance, position, or time

**pre·ce·dent** \'pres-ə-dənt\ *n*
something that can be used as a rule or as a model to be followed in the future

**pre·ced·ing** \pri-'sēd-ing\ *adj*
going before : PREVIOUS

**pre·cinct** \'prē-ˌsingkt\ *n*
**1** an administrative district especially of a town or city ⟨a police *precinct*⟩ ⟨an electoral *precinct*⟩
**2** a surrounding or enclosed area ⟨within school *precincts*⟩

**pre·cious** \'presh-əs\ *adj*
**1** very valuable ⟨diamonds and other *precious* stones⟩
**2** greatly loved : DEAR

**prec·i·pice** \'pres-ə-pəs\ *n*
▼ a very steep and high face of rock or mountain : CLIFF

**pre·cip·i·tate** \pri-'sip-ə-ˌtāt\ *vb*
**pre·cip·i·tat·ed**; **pre·cip·i·tat·ing**
**1** to cause to happen suddenly or unexpectedly ⟨the comment *precipitated* a quarrel⟩
**2** to change from a vapor to a liquid or solid and fall as rain or snow
**3** to separate from a solution ⟨*precipitate* salt from seawater⟩

**pre·cip·i·ta·tion** \pri-ˌsip-ə-'tā-shən\ *n*
**1** unwise haste
**2** water or the amount of water that falls to the earth as hail, mist, rain, sleet, or snow

**pre·cise** \pri-'sīs\ *adj*
**1** exactly stated or explained ⟨follow *precise* rules⟩
**2** very clear ⟨a *precise* voice
**3** very exact : ACCURATE
**pre·cise·ly** *adv*
**pre·cise·ness** *n*

**pre·ci·sion** \pri-'sizh-ən\ *n*
the quality or state of being precise

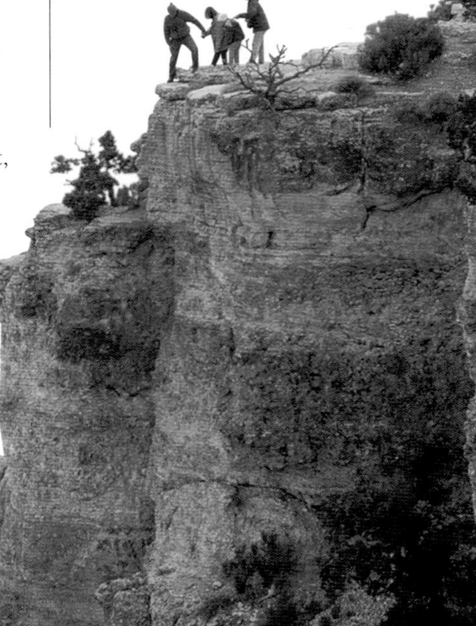
**precipice** at the edge of the Grand Canyon, Arizona

**pre·co·cious** \pri-'kō-shəs\ *adj*
showing qualities or abilities of an adult at an unusually early age
**pre·co·cious·ly** *adv*
**pre·co·cious·ness** *n*

**pre–Co·lum·bi·an** \ˌprē-kə-'ləm-bē-ən\ *adj*
preceding or belonging to the time before the arrival of Columbus in America

**pred·a·tor** \'pred-ət-ər\ *n*
an animal that lives mostly by killing and eating other animals

**pred·a·to·ry** \'pred-ə-ˌtōr-ē\ *adj*
living by preying upon other animals

**pre·de·ces·sor** \'pred-ə-ˌses-ər, 'prēd-\ *n*
a person who has held a position or office before another

**pre·dic·a·ment** \pri-'dik-ə-mənt\ *n*
a bad or difficult situation : FIX

**pred·i·cate** \'pred-i-kət\ *n*
the part of a sentence or clause that tells what is said about the subject ⟨"rang" in "the doorbell rang" is the *predicate*⟩

**predicate adjective** *n*
an adjective that occurs in the predicate after a linking verb and describes the subject ⟨"sweet" in "sugar is sweet" is a *predicate adjective*⟩

**predicate noun** *n*
a noun that occurs in the predicate after a linking verb and refers to the same person or thing as the subject ⟨"parent" in "that person is my parent" is a *predicate noun*⟩

**pre·dict** \pri-'dikt\ *vb*
to figure out and tell beforehand ⟨*predict* the weather⟩ **synonyms** see FORETELL

**pre·dic·tion** \pri-'dik-shən\ *n*
**1** an act of predicting
**2** something that is predicted

**pre·dom·i·nance** \pri-'däm-ə-nəns\ *n*
the quality or state of being predominant

**pre·dom·i·nant** \pri-'däm-ə-nənt\ *adj*
greater than others in number, strength, influence, or authority

**pre·dom·i·nate** \pri-'däm-ə-,nāt\ *vb* **pre·dom·i·nat·ed**; **pre·dom·i·nat·ing**
to be predominant

**preen** \'prēn\ *vb*
**1** to smooth with or as if with the bill ⟨the sparrow *preened* its feathers⟩
**2** to make one's appearance neat and tidy

**pre·fab·ri·cate** \prē-'fab-ri-,kāt\ *vb* **pre·fab·ri·cat·ed**; **pre·fab·ri·cat·ing**
to manufacture the parts of something beforehand so that it can be built by putting the parts together ⟨*prefabricate* houses⟩

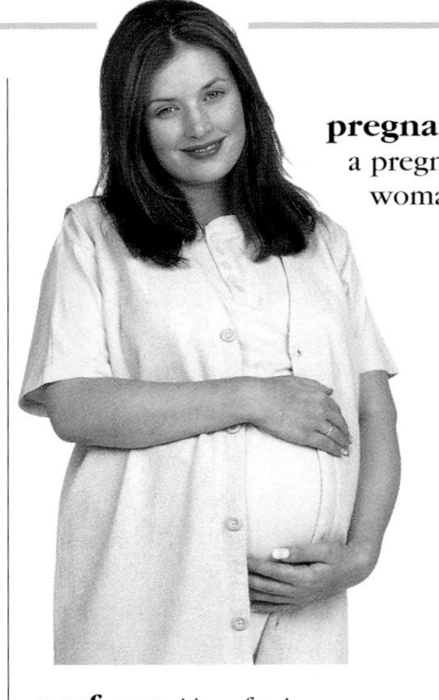

**pregnant 1:** a pregnant woman

**pref·ace** \'pref-əs\ *n*
a section at the beginning that introduces a book or a speech

**pre·fer** \pri-'fər\ *vb* **pre·ferred**; **pre·fer·ring**
to like better ⟨*prefer* chocolate ice cream⟩

**pref·er·a·ble** \'pref-ə-rə-bəl\ *adj*
deserving to be preferred **:** more desirable
**pref·er·a·bly** \-blē\ *adv*

**pref·er·ence** \'pref-ə-rəns, 'pref-rəns\ *n*
**1** a choosing of or special liking for one person or thing rather than another
**2** the power or chance to choose **:** CHOICE
**3** a person or thing that is preferred

**[1]pre·fix** \'prē-,fiks\ *vb*
to put or attach at the beginning of a word **:** add as a prefix

**[2]prefix** *n*
a letter or group of letters that comes at the beginning of a word and has a meaning of its own

**preg·nan·cy** \'preg-nən-sē\ *n, pl* **preg·nan·cies**
the state of being pregnant

**preg·nant** \'preg-nənt\ *adj*
**1** ◀ carrying unborn offspring
**2** full of meaning

**pre·hen·sile** \prē-'hen-səl\ *adj*
adapted for grasping by wrapping around ⟨some monkeys have a *prehensile* tail⟩

**pre·his·tor·ic** \,prē-his-'tȯr-ik\ *adj*
▼ of, relating to, or being in existence in the period before written history began ⟨*prehistoric* animals⟩

**[1]prej·u·dice** \'prej-ə-dəs\ *n*
**1** injury or damage to a case at law or to one's rights
**2** a liking or dislike for one rather than another without good reason

**[2]prejudice** *vb* **prej·u·diced**; **prej·u·dic·ing**
**1** to cause damage to (as a case at law)
**2** to cause prejudice in

**prel·ate** \'prel-ət\ *n*
a clergyman (as a bishop) of high rank

**[1]pre·lim·i·nary** \pri-'lim-ə-,ner-ē\ *n, pl* **pre·lim·i·nar·ies**
something that is preliminary

**prehistoric**

Information about prehistoric life comes from fossils, or from objects made by early humans. By examining these, experts can build up a picture of what life was like before systems of writing were developed to record events. Prehistoric people are known to have found food by hunting animals and gathering fruit, seeds, nuts, and wild vegetables. They made simple clothes from animal skins and later from wool, and lived in caves or in shelters they built.

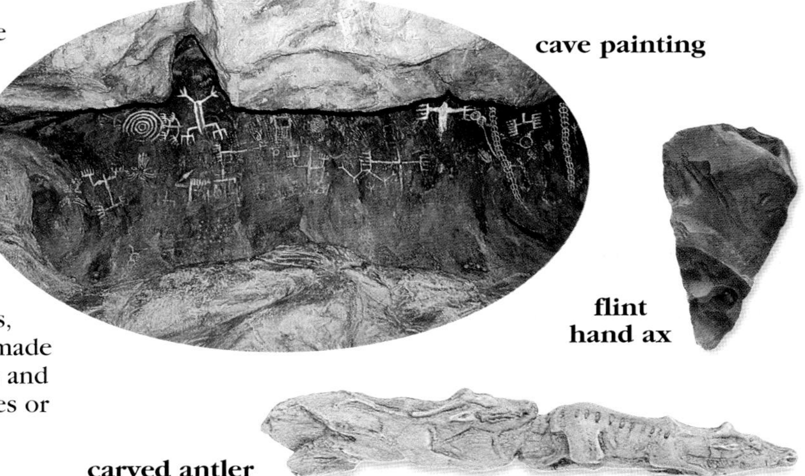

**cave painting**

**flint hand ax**

**carved antler**

A B C D E F G H I J K L M N O P Q R S T U V W X Y Z

**[2]preliminary** *adj*
coming before the main part
: INTRODUCTORY

**pre·lude** \'prel-ˌyüd, 'prā-ˌlüd\ *n*
**1** something that comes before and prepares for the main or more important parts
**2** a short musical introduction (as for an opera)
**3** a piece (as an organ solo) played at the beginning of a church service

**pre·ma·ture** \ˌprē-mə-'tu̇r, -'tyu̇r\ *adj*
happening, coming, or done before the usual or proper time : too early
**pre·ma·ture·ly** *adv*

**pre·med·i·tate** \pri-'med-ə-ˌtāt\ *vb* **pre·med·i·tat·ed**; **pre·med·i·tat·ing**
to think about and plan beforehand

**[1]pre·mier** \pri-'mir, 'prē-mē-ər\ *adj*
first in position or importance : CHIEF

**[2]premier** *n*
PRIME MINISTER

**[1]pre·miere** \pri-'myeər, -'mir\ *adj*
[2]CHIEF 2 ⟨the *premiere* dancer of a group⟩

**[2]premiere** *n*
a first showing or performance ⟨*premiere* of a movie⟩

**prem·ise** \'prem-əs\ *n*
**1** a statement taken to be true and on which an argument or reasoning may be based
**2 premises** *pl* a piece of land with the buildings on it

**pre·mi·um** \'prē-mē-əm\ *n*
**1** a prize to be gained by some special act
**2** a sum over and above the stated value ⟨sell stock at a *premium*⟩
**3** the amount paid for a contract of insurance

**pre·mo·lar** \'prē-'mō-lər\ *n*
any of the teeth that come between the canines and the molars and in humans are normally two in each side of each jaw

**pre·mo·ni·tion** \ˌprē-mə-'nish-ən, 'prem-ə-\ *n*
a feeling that something is going to happen

**pre·oc·cu·pied** \prē-'äk-yə-ˌpīd\ *adj*
lost in thought

**prepaid** *past of* PREPAY

**prep·a·ra·tion** \ˌprep-ə-'rā-shən\ *n*
**1** the act of making ready beforehand for some special reason
**2** something that prepares ⟨finish *preparations* for a trip⟩
**3** something prepared for a particular purpose ⟨a *preparation* for burns⟩

**pre·par·a·to·ry** \pri-'par-ə-ˌtōr-ē\ *adj*
preparing or serving to prepare for something ⟨a *preparatory* school⟩

**pre·pare** \pri-'paər, -'peər\ *vb*
**pre·pared**; **pre·par·ing**
**1** to make ready beforehand for some particular reason ⟨*prepare* for college⟩
**2** to put together the elements of ⟨*prepare* dinner⟩ ⟨*prepare* a vaccine⟩

**pre·pay** \'prē-'pā\ *vb* **pre·paid** \-'pād\; **pre·pay·ing**
to pay or pay for beforehand ⟨*prepay* the shipping charges⟩

**prep·o·si·tion** \ˌprep-ə-'zish-ən\ *n*
a word or group of words that combines with a noun or pronoun to form a phrase that usually acts as an adverb, adjective, or noun

**prep·o·si·tion·al** \ˌprep-ə-'zish-ən-l\ *adj*
of, relating to, or containing a preposition

**pre·pos·ter·ous** \pri-'päs-tə-rəs\ *adj*
making little or no sense : FOOLISH ⟨a *preposterous* excuse⟩

**pre·req·ui·site** \prē-'rek-wə-zət\ *n*
something that is needed beforehand or is necessary to prepare for something else

**[1]pre·school** \'prē-ˌskül\ adj
of or relating to the time in a child's life that ordinarily comes before attendance at school

**[2]preschool** *n*
NURSERY SCHOOL

**pre·school·er** \'prē-'skü-lər\ *n*
a child of preschool age

**pre·scribe** \pri-'skrīb\ *vb*
**pre·scribed**; **pre·scrib·ing**
**1** to lay down as a rule of action : ORDER ⟨*prescribe* longer hours of rest⟩
**2** to order or direct the use of as a remedy ⟨*prescribe* medicine⟩

**pre·scrip·tion** \pri-'skrip -shən\ *n*
**1** a written direction or order for the preparing and use of a medicine
**2** a medicine that is prescribed

**pres·ence** \'prez-ns\ *n*
**1** the fact or condition of being present ⟨no one noticed the stranger's *presence*⟩
**2** position close to a person ⟨in the *presence* of a guest⟩
**3** a person's appearance

**presence of mind**
ability to think clearly and act quickly in an emergency

**[1]pres·ent** \'prez-nt\ *n*
: GIFT 2

**[1]present:**
a present in decorative wrapping

**[2]pre·sent** \pri-'zent\ *vb*
**1** to introduce one person to another
**2** to take (oneself) into another's presence
**3** to bring before the public ⟨*present* a play⟩
**4** to make a gift to
**5** to give as a gift
**6** to offer to view : SHOW, DISPLAY ⟨*presents* a fine appearance⟩
**synonyms** see GIVE, OFFER

**[3]pres·ent** \'prez-nt\ *adj*
**1** not past or future : now going on
**2** being before or near a person or in sight : being at a certain place and not elsewhere
**3** pointing out or relating to time that is not past or future ⟨the *present* tense of a verb⟩

**[4]pres·ent** \'prez-nt\ *n*
the present time : right now

**pre·sent·able** \pri-'zent-ə-bəl\ *adj*
having a satisfactory or pleasing appearance

**pre·sen·ta·tion** \ˌprē-ˌzen-'tā-shən, ˌprez-n-\ *n*
**1** an introduction of one person to another
**2** an act of presenting
**3** something offered or given

**pres·ent·ly** \'prez-nt-lē\ *adv*
**1** before long : SOON
**2** at the present time : NOW

**pres·er·va·tion** \ˌprez-ər-'vā-shən\ *n*
a keeping from injury, loss, or decay

**pre·ser·va·tive** \pri-'zər-vət-iv\ *n*
something (as a substance added to food) that preserves

**¹pre·serve** \pri-'zərv\ *vb* **pre·served**; **pre·serv·ing**
**1** to keep or save from injury or ruin : PROTECT
**2** to prepare (as by canning or pickling) fruits or vegetables for keeping
**3** MAINTAIN 1, CONTINUE ⟨*preserve* silence⟩
**pre·serv·er** *n*

**²preserve** *n*
**1** ▶ fruit cooked in sugar or made into jam or jelly — often used in pl. ⟨strawberry *preserves*⟩
**2** an area where game or fish are protected

**²preserve 1:** a jar of peach preserves

**pre·side** \pri-'zīd\ *vb* **pre·sid·ed**; **pre·sid·ing**
**1** to act as chairperson of a meeting
**2** to be in charge

**pres·i·den·cy** \'prez-ə-dən-sē\ *n, pl* **pres·i·den·cies**
**1** the office of president
**2** the term during which a president holds office

**pres·i·dent** \'prez-əd-ənt\ *n*
**1** a person who presides over a meeting
**2** the chief officer of a company or society
**3** the head of the government and chief executive officer of a modern republic

**pres·i·den·tial** \ˌprez-ə-'den-chəl\ *adj*
of or relating to a president or the presidency

**¹press** \'pres\ *n*
**1** ²CROWD 1, THRONG
**2** a machine that uses pressure to shape, flatten, squeeze,or stamp
**3** a closet for clothing
**4** the act of pressing : PRESSURE
**5** a printing or publishing business
**6** the newspapers and magazines of a country

**²press** *vb*
**1** to bear down upon : push steadily against
**2** to squeeze so as to force out the juice or contents ⟨*press* oranges⟩
**3** to flatten out or smooth by bearing down upon especially by ironing ⟨*press* clothes⟩
**4** to ask or urge strongly ⟨*press* someone to go along⟩
**5** to force or push one's way

**press·ing** \'pres-ing\ *adj*
needing one's immediate attention ⟨*pressing* business⟩

**pres·sure** \'presh-ər\ *n*
**1** the action of pressing or bearing down upon
**2** a force or influence that cannot be avoided ⟨social *pressure*⟩
**3** the force with which one body presses against another
**4** the need to get things done ⟨works well under *pressure*⟩

**pres·tige** \pre-'stēzh\ *n*
importance in the eyes of people : REPUTE

**pres·to** \'pres-tō\ *adv or adj*
suddenly as if by magic

**pre·sume** \pri-'züm\ *vb* **pre·sumed**; **pre·sum·ing**
**1** to undertake without permission or good reason : DARE ⟨*presume* to question a judge's decision⟩
**2** to suppose to be true without proof ⟨*presume* a person innocent until proved guilty⟩

**pre·sump·tion** \pri-'zəmp-shən\ *n*
**1** presumptuous behavior or attitude
**2** a strong reason for believing something to be so
**3** something believed to be so but not proved

**pre·sump·tu·ous** \pri-'zəmp-chə-wəs\ *adj*
going beyond what is proper ⟨punished for *presumptuous* pride⟩
**pre·sump·tu·ous·ly** *adv*
**pre·sump·tu·ous·ness** *n*

**pre·tend** \pri-'tend\ *vb*
**1** to make believe : SHAM
**2** to put forward as true something that is not true ⟨*pretend* friendship⟩
**pre·tend·er** *n*

**pre·tense** *or* **pre·tence** \'prē-ˌtens, pri-'tens\ *n*
**1** a claim usually not supported by facts
**2** an effort to reach a certain condition or quality ⟨makes no *pretense* at completeness⟩

**pre·ten·tious** \pri-'ten-chəs\ *adj*
having or showing pretenses : SHOWY ⟨a *pretentious* house⟩
**pre·ten·tious·ly** *adv*
**pre·ten·tious·ness** *n*

**¹pret·ty** \'prit-ē\ *adj* **pret·ti·er**; **pret·ti·est**
pleasing to the eye or ear especially because of being graceful or delicate ⟨a *pretty* face⟩ ⟨a *pretty* tune⟩ **synonyms** see BEAUTIFUL
**pret·ti·ly** \'prit-l-ē\ *adv*
**pret·ti·ness** \'prit-ē-nəs\ *n*

**²pret·ty** \ˌprit-ē, pərt-ē\ *adv*
in some degree : FAIRLY ⟨*pretty* good⟩

**pret·zel** \'pret-səl\ *n*
▼ a brown cracker that is salted and is usually hard and shaped like a loose knot

**pretzel**

**Word History** The English word *pretzel* comes from a German word. The German word for a pretzel came from a Latin word that meant "having branches like arms." This Latin word was formed from a Latin word that meant "arm." The most common shape for a pretzel is like a knot. This knot shape must have reminded someone of a pair of folded arms.

**pre·vail** \pri-'vāl\ *vb*
**1** to win a victory ⟨*prevailed* over their enemies⟩
**2** to succeed in convincing ⟨we *prevailed* upon them to sing⟩
**3** to be or become usual, common, or widespread ⟨west winds *prevail* in that region⟩

**prev·a·lence** \'prev-ə-ləns\ *n*
the state of being prevalent

**prev·a·lent** \'prev-ə-lənt\ *adj*
accepted, practiced, or happening often or over a wide area

A B C D E F G H I J K L M N O P Q R S T U V W X Y Z

**pre·vent** \pri-ˈvent\ *vb*
**1** to keep from happening ⟨help to *prevent* accidents⟩
**2** to hold or keep back ⟨bad weather *prevented* us from leaving⟩
**pre·vent·able** \-ə-bəl\ *adj*

**pre·ven·tion** \pri-ˈven-chən\ *n*
the act or practice of preventing something ⟨study about the *prevention* of fires⟩

**pre·ven·tive** \prē-ˈvent-iv\ *adj*
used for prevention

**pre·view** \ˈprē-ˌvyü\ *n*
a showing of something (as a movie) before regular showings

**pre·vi·ous** \ˈprē-vē-əs\ *adj*
going before in time or order : PRECEDING
**pre·vi·ous·ly** *adv*

[1]**prey** \ˈprā\ *n*
**1** an animal hunted or killed by another animal for food
**2** a person that is helpless and unable to escape attack : VICTIM
**3** the act or habit of seizing or pouncing upon ⟨birds of *prey*⟩

[2]**prey** *vb*
**1** to seize and eat something as prey ⟨dogs *preying* on small game⟩
**2** to have a harmful effect ⟨fears *preying* on the mind⟩

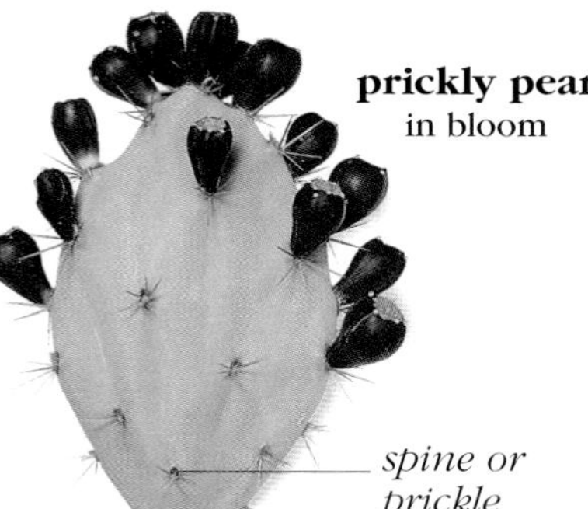

**prickly pear** in bloom

[1]**price** \ˈprīs\ *n*
**1** the quantity of one thing given or asked for something else : the amount of money paid or to be paid
**2** [2]REWARD ⟨a *price* on one's head⟩
**3** the cost at which something is gotten or done ⟨win a victory at the *price* of many lives⟩

**Synonyms** PRICE, CHARGE, and COST mean the amount asked or given in payment for something. PRICE usually refers to what is asked for goods ⟨the *price* of a new car⟩. CHARGE usually refers to the amount asked for services ⟨the doctor's *charge* for an office visit⟩. COST is usually used to state what is paid for something by the buyer rather than what is asked by the seller ⟨the *cost* of our dinner seemed very high⟩.

[2]**price** *vb* **priced**; **pric·ing**
**1** to set a price on
**2** to ask the price of

**price·less** \ˈprī-sləs\ *adj*
too valuable to have a price : not to be bought at any price

[1]**prick** \ˈprik\ *n*
**1** a mark or small wound made by a pointed instrument ⟨the *prick* of a pin⟩
**2** something sharp or pointed
**3** a sensation of being pricked

[2]**prick** *vb*
**1** to pierce slightly with a sharp point
**2** to have or to cause a feeling of or as if of being pricked
**3** to point upward ⟨the horse *pricked* up its ears⟩

**prick·er** \ˈprik-ər\ *n*
[1]PRICKLE 1

[1]**prick·le** \ˈprik-əl\ *n*
**1** a small sharp point (as a thorn)
**2** a slight stinging pain

[2]**prickle** *vb* **prick·led**; **prick·ling**
[2]PRICK 2

**prick·ly** \ˈprik-lē\ *adj* **prick·li·er**; **prick·li·est**
**1** having prickles ⟨a *prickly* cactus⟩
**2** being or having a pricking ⟨a *prickly* sensation⟩ ⟨a *prickly* thumb⟩

**prickly pear** *n*
◀ a usually spiny cactus with flat branching joints and a sweet pulpy fruit shaped like a pear

[1]**pride** \ˈprīd\ *n*
**1** too high an opinion of one's own ability or worth : a feeling of being better than others
**2** a reasonable and justifiable sense of one's own worth : SELF-RESPECT ⟨*pride* in doing good work⟩
**3** a sense of pleasure that comes from some act or possession ⟨take *pride* in their children's high marks⟩
**4** something of which one is proud ⟨that car is my *pride* and joy⟩

[2]**pride** *vb* **prid·ed**; **prid·ing**
to think highly of (oneself) ⟨I *pride* myself on my spelling⟩

**priest** \ˈprēst\ *n*
a person who has the authority to lead or perform religious ceremonies

**priest·ess** \ˈprē-stəs\ *n*
a woman who is a priest

**prim** \ˈprim\ *adj* **prim·mer**; **prim·mest**
very fussy about one's appearance or behavior
**prim·ly** *adv*

**pri·mar·i·ly** \prī-ˈmer-ə-lē\ *adv*
in the first place

[1]**pri·ma·ry** \ˈprī-ˌmer-ē, -mə-rē\ *adj*
**1** first in time or development ⟨the *primary* grades⟩
**2** most important : PRINCIPAL ⟨*primary* duties⟩
**3** not made or coming from something else : BASIC ⟨the *primary* source of trouble⟩
**4** of, relating to, or being the heaviest of three levels of stress in pronunciation

[2]**primary** *n, pl* **pri·ma·ries**
an election in which members of a political party nominate candidates for office

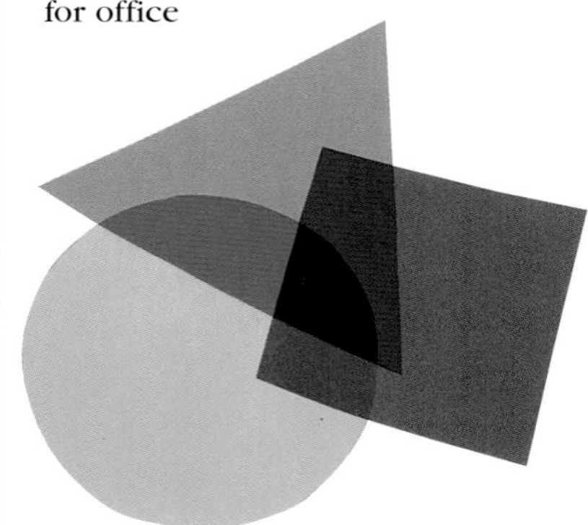
**primary colors** combining to make secondary colors

**primary color** *n*
▲ any of a set of colors from which all other colors may be made with the colors for light being red, green, and blue and for pigments or paint being red, yellow, and blue

**pri·mate** \ˈprī-ˌmāt\ *n*
▶ any of a group of mammals that includes humans together with the apes and monkeys and a few related forms

## primate

Primates usually gather together in social groups. Most live in trees, although some live on the ground. Almost all have forward-facing eyes, long arms, and fingers that are capable of gripping objects. There are two main groups — more highly developed primates called anthropoids, and less developed primates called prosimians \prō-'sim-ē-ənz\. Humans, apes, and monkeys are anthropoids, with a large brain and a high level of intelligence. Prosimians, such as galagos and lemurs, are less intelligent.

**features of an orangutan**

**gibbons** move swiftly through the trees, swinging hand over hand

**squirrel monkeys** live in groups, sometimes of several hundred

**tamarins** inhabit the trees of South American forests

**baboons** are found in the trees and on the ground in open grasslands

**galagos** \gə-'lā-gōz\ have long hind legs that help them leap from branch to branch

**lemurs** spend most of their time in trees

**gorillas** are the largest of the primates, and may weigh up to 330 lb (150 kg)

**[1]prime** \'prīm\ *n*
**1** the first part **:** the earliest stage
**2** the period in life when a person is best in health, looks, or strength
**3** the best individual or part

**[2]prime** *adj*
**1** first in time **:** ORIGINAL ⟨*prime* cost⟩
**2** having no factor except itself and one ⟨3 is a *prime* number⟩
**3** first in importance, rank, or quality

**[3]prime** *vb* **primed**; **prim·ing**
**1** to put a first color or coating on (an unpainted surface)
**2** to put into working order by filling ⟨*prime* a pump⟩
**3** to tell what to say beforehand **:** COACH ⟨*prime* a witness⟩

**prime minister** *n*
the chief officer of the government in some countries

**[1]prim·er** \'prim-ər\ *n*
**1** a small book for teaching children to read
**2** a book of first instructions on a subject

**[2]prim·er** \'prī-mər\ *n*
**1** a device (as a cap) for setting off an explosive
**2** material used to prime a surface

**pri·me·val** \prī-'mē-vəl\ *adj*
belonging to the earliest time **:** PRIMITIVE

**prim·i·tive** \'prim-ət-iv\ *adj*
**1** of or belonging to very early times ⟨*primitive* people⟩
**2** of or belonging to an early stage of development ⟨*primitive* tools⟩

**primp** \'primp\ *vb*
to dress or arrange in a careful or fussy manner

**prim·rose** \'prim-,rōz\ *n*
▶ a low perennial plant with large leaves growing from the base of the stem and showy often yellow or pink flowers

**prince** \'prins\ *n*
**1** MONARCH 1
**2** the son of a monarch
**3** a nobleman of very high or the highest rank

**primrose**

**prin·cess** \'prin-səs, -,ses\ *n*
a daughter or granddaughter of a monarch **:** a female member of a royal family

**[1]prin·ci·pal** \'prin-sə-pəl\ *adj*
highest in rank or importance **:** CHIEF ⟨had the *principal* part in the school play⟩
**prin·ci·pal·ly** *adv*

**[2]principal** *n*
**1** a leading or most important person or thing
**2** the head of a school
**3** a sum of money that is placed to earn interest, is owed as a debt, or is used as a fund

**prin·ci·pal·i·ty** \,prin-sə-'pal-ət-ē\ *n, pl* **prin·ci·pal·i·ties**
a small territory that is ruled by a prince ⟨the *principality* of Monaco⟩

**principal parts** *n pl*
the infinitive, the past tense, and the past and present participles of an English verb

**prin·ci·ple** \'prin-sə-pəl\ *n*
**1** a general or basic truth on which other truths or theories can be based ⟨scientific *principles*⟩
**2** a rule of conduct ⟨a person of high *principles*⟩
**3** a law or fact of nature which makes possible the working of a machine or device ⟨the *principle* of magnetism⟩ ⟨the *principle* of the lever⟩

**[1]print** \'print\ *n*
**1** a mark made by pressure
**2** something which has been stamped with an impression or formed in a mold ⟨a *print* of butter⟩
**3** printed matter
**4** printed letters ⟨clear *print*⟩
**5** a picture, copy, or design taken from an engraving or photographic negative
**6** cloth upon which a design is stamped ⟨a cotton *print*⟩

**[2]print** *vb*
**1** to put or stamp in or on ⟨*print* a seal in wax⟩
**2** to make a copy of by pressing paper against an inked surface (as type or an engraving)
**3** to stamp with a design by pressure ⟨*print* wallpaper⟩
**4** PUBLISH 2 ⟨*print* a newspaper⟩
**5** PRINT OUT
**6** to write in separate letters like those made by a typewriter ⟨*print* your name clearly⟩
**7** to make a picture from a photographic negative

**print·er** \'print-ər\ *n*
**1** a person whose business is printing
**2** a machine that produces printouts

**print·ing** \'print-ing\ *n*
**1** the process of putting something in printed form
**2** the art, practice, or business of a printer

**printing press** *n*
a machine that makes printed copies

**print·out** \'print-,au̇t\ *n*
a printed record produced by a computer

**print out** \(')print-,au̇t\ *vb*
to make a printout of ⟨*print out* a letter⟩

**[1]pri·or** \'prī-ər\ *n*
a monk who is head of a priory

**[2]prior** *adj*
**1** being or happening before something else
**2** being more important than something else

**pri·or·ess** \'prī-ə-rəs\ *n*
a nun who is head of a priory

**pri·or·i·ty** \prī-'ȯr-ət-ē\ *n, pl* **pri·or·i·ties**
the quality or state of coming before another in time or importance

**prior to** *prep*
in advance of **:** BEFORE ⟨must be finished *prior to* July⟩

**pri·o·ry** \'prī-ə-rē\ *n, pl* **pri·o·ries**
a religious house under a prior or prioress

**prism** \'priz-əm\ *n*
▶ a transparent object that usually has three sides and bends light so that it breaks up into rainbow colors

**pris·on** \'priz-n\ *n*
a place where criminals are locked up

*triangular glass prism*

**prism**

**pris•on•er** \'priz-n-ər, 'priz-nər\ *n*
a person who has been captured or locked up

**pri•va•cy** \'prī-və-sē\ *n*
**1** the state of being out of the sight and hearing of other people
**2** SECRECY 2 ⟨talk together in *privacy*⟩

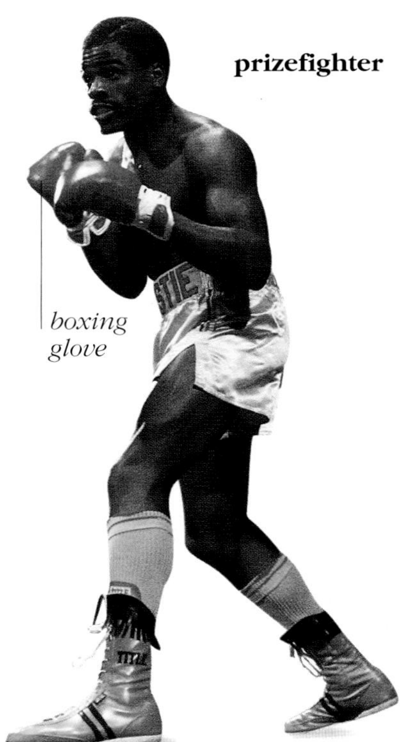

**prizefighter**

**¹pri•vate** \'prī-vət\ *adj*
**1** having to do with or for the use of a single person or group : not public ⟨*private* property⟩
**2** not holding any public office ⟨a *private* citizen⟩
**3** ¹SECRET 1 ⟨*private* meetings⟩
**pri•vate•ly** *adv*
**pri•vate•ness** *n*

**²private** *n*
an enlisted person of the lowest rank in the Marine Corps or of either of the two lowest ranks in the Army

**pri•va•teer** \,prī-və-'tir\ *n*
**1** an armed private ship permitted by its government to make war on ships of an enemy country
**2** a sailor on a privateer

**private first class** *n*
an enlisted person in the Army or Marine Corps ranking above a private

**priv•et** \'priv-ət\ *n*
a shrub with white flowers that is related to the lilac and is often used for hedges

**priv•i•lege** \'priv-ə-lij\ *n*
a right or liberty granted as a favor or benefit especially to some and not others

**priv•i•leged** \'priv-ə-lijd\ *adj*
having more things and a better chance in life than most people ⟨*privileged* classes of society⟩

**¹prize** \'prīz\ *n*
**1** something won or to be won in a contest
**2** something unusually valuable or eagerly sought

**²prize** *adj*
**1** awarded a prize ⟨a *prize* essay⟩
**2** awarded as a prize ⟨*prize* money⟩
**3** outstanding of its kind ⟨a *prize* fool⟩ ⟨a *prize* student⟩

**³prize** *vb* **prized**; **priz•ing**
**1** to estimate the value of
**2** to value highly : TREASURE ⟨*prize* a picture⟩

**⁴prize** *n*
something taken (as in war) by force especially at sea

**prize•fight•er** \'prīz-,fīt-ər\ *n*
◀ a professional boxer

**¹pro** \'prō\ *n, pl* **pros**
an argument or evidence in favor of something ⟨discussed the *pros* and cons⟩

**²pro** *adv*
in favor of something ⟨argue *pro* and con⟩

**³pro** *n or adj*
PROFESSIONAL

**pro-** *prefix*
approving : in favor of

**prob•a•bil•i•ty** \,präb-ə-'bil-ət-ē\ *n, pl* **prob•a•bil•i•ties**
**1** the quality or state of being probable
**2** something probable

**prob•a•ble** \'präb-ə-bəl\ *adj*
reasonably sure but not certain of happening or being true : LIKELY

**prob•a•bly** \'präb-ə-blē\ *adv*
very likely ⟨the clouds are dark and *probably* it will rain⟩

**pro•ba•tion** \prō-'bā-shən\ *n*
a period of trial for finding out or testing a person's fitness (as for a job)

**¹probe** \'prōb\ *n*
**1** a slender instrument for examining a cavity (as a deep wound)
**2** a careful investigation

**²probe** *vb* **probed**; **prob•ing**
**1** to examine with or as if with a probe
**2** to investigate thoroughly

**prob•lem** \'präb-ləm\ *n*
**1** something to be worked out or solved ⟨a *problem* in arithmetic⟩
**2** a person or thing that is hard to understand or deal with

**pro•bos•cis** \prə-'bäs-əs, -kəs\ *n*
▶ a long flexible hollow bodily structure (as the trunk of an elephant or the beak of a mosquito)

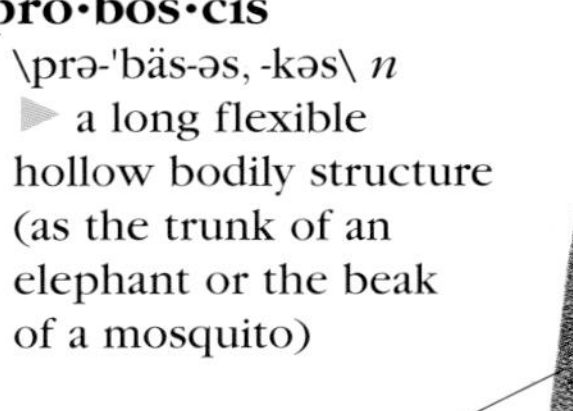
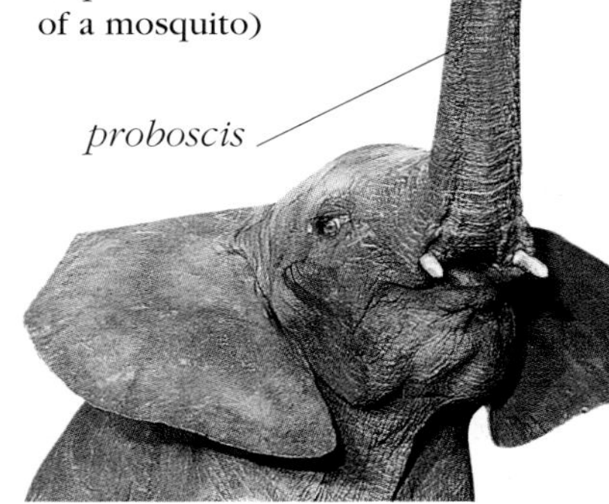

**proboscis** of an elephant

**pro•ce•dure** \prə-'sē-jər\ *n*
**1** the manner or method in which a business or action is carried on
**2** an action or series of actions ⟨the *procedure* of swearing in a club member⟩

**pro•ceed** \prō-'sēd\ *vb*
**1** to come from a source ⟨light *proceeds* from the sun⟩
**2** to go or act by an orderly method ⟨*proceed* according to plan⟩
**3** to go forward or onward : ADVANCE

**pro•ceed•ing** \prō-'sēd-ing\ *n*
**1** PROCEDURE 2
**2** **proceedings** *pl* things that happen

**pro•ceeds** \'prō-,sēdz\ *n pl*
the money or profit that comes from a business deal

**¹pro•cess** \'präs-,es, 'prōs-\ *n*
**1** ²ADVANCE 1 ⟨the *process* of time⟩
**2** a series of actions, motions, or operations leading to some result ⟨a *process* of manufacture⟩
**3** the carrying on of a legal action ⟨due *process*⟩

A B C D E F G H I J K L M N O P Q R S T U V W X Y Z

**²process** *vb*
**1** to change by a special treatment ⟨*process* cheese⟩
**2** to take care of according to a routine ⟨*process* insurance claims⟩
**3** to take in and organize for use in a variety of ways ⟨computers *process* data⟩

**pro·ces·sion** \prə-'sesh-ən\ *n*
**1** continuous forward movement : PROGRESSION
**2** a group of individuals moving along in an orderly often ceremonial way ⟨a funeral *procession*⟩

**pro·ces·sor** \'präs-,es-ər, 'prōs-\ *n*
**1** a person or machine that processes
**2** COMPUTER
**3** the part of a computer that operates on data

**pro·claim** \prō-'klām\ *vb*
to announce publicly : DECLARE ⟨*proclaim* a holiday⟩

**proc·la·ma·tion** \,präk-lə-'mā-shən\ *n*
**1** the act of proclaiming
**2** something proclaimed

**pro·cure** \prə-'kyu̇r\ *vb* **pro·cured**; **pro·cur·ing**
**1** OBTAIN ⟨*procure* a ticket to the game⟩
**2** to bring about or cause to be done ⟨*procured* my friend's release from jail⟩

**¹prod** \'präd\ *vb* **prod·ded**; **prod·ding**
**1** to poke with something
**2** to stir a person or animal to action

**²prod** *n*
**1** something used for prodding ⟨a cattle *prod*⟩
**2** an act of prodding
**3** a sharp urging or reminder

**¹prod·i·gal** \'präd-i-gəl\ *adj*
carelessly wasteful ⟨a *prodigal* spender⟩

**²prodigal** *n*
somebody who wastes money carelessly

**prod·i·gy** \'präd-ə-jē\ *n, pl* **prod·i·gies**
**1** an amazing event or action : WONDER
**2** an unusually talented child

**¹pro·duce** \prə-'düs, -'dyüs\ *vb* **pro·duced**; **pro·duc·ing**
**1** to bring to view : EXHIBIT ⟨*produce* evidence⟩
**2** to bring forth : YIELD ⟨this tree *produces* good fruit⟩
**3** to prepare (as a play) for public presentation
**4** MANUFACTURE ⟨a city that *produces* steel⟩
**pro·duc·er** *n*

**²pro·duce** \'präd-,üs, 'prōd-, -,yüs\ *n*
**1** something produced
**2** fresh fruits and vegetables

**prod·uct** \'präd-əkt\ *n*
**1** the number resulting from the multiplication of two or more numbers ⟨the *product* of 3 and 5 is 15⟩
**2** something produced by manufacture, labor, thought, or growth

**pro·duc·tion** \prə-'dək-shən\ *n*
**1** something produced ⟨a television *production* of a play⟩
**2** the act of producing ⟨*production* of cars⟩
**3** the amount produced ⟨annual *production* of coal⟩

**pro·duc·tive** \prə-'dək-tiv\ *adj*
**1** having the power to produce plentifully ⟨*productive* soil⟩
**2** producing something

**profile** of a famous 19th-century English scientist on a medal

**¹pro·fane** \prō-'fān\ *vb* **pro·faned**; **pro·fan·ing**
to treat with great disrespect
**pro·fan·er** *n*

**²profane** *adj*
showing no respect for God or holy things
**pro·fane·ly** *adv*
**pro·fane·ness** *n*

**pro·fan·i·ty** \prō-'fan-ət-ē\ *n, pl* **pro·fan·i·ties**
profane language

**pro·fess** \prə-'fes\ *vb*
**1** to declare openly ⟨*profess* confidence in a person⟩
**2** PRETEND 2 ⟨*professed* to be my friend⟩

**pro·fes·sion** \prə-'fesh-ən\ *n*
**1** a public declaring or claiming ⟨a *profession* of religious faith⟩
**2** an occupation (as medicine, law, or teaching) that is not mechanical or agricultural and that requires special education
**3** the people working in a profession **synonyms** see TRADE

**¹pro·fes·sion·al** \prə-'fesh-ən-l\ *adj*
**1** of, relating to, or like that of a profession
**2** taking part in an activity (as a sport) that others do for pleasure in order to make money
**pro·fes·sion·al·ly** *adv*

**²professional** *n*
a person whose work is professional

**pro·fes·sor** \prə-'fes-ər\ *n*
a teacher especially of the highest rank at a college or university

**prof·fer** \'präf-ər\ *vb*
¹OFFER 2

**pro·fi·cient** \prə-'fish-ənt\ *adj*
very good at doing something : EXPERT ⟨a *proficient* reader⟩
**pro·fi·cient·ly** *adv*

**pro·file** \'prō-,fīl\ *n*
◀ something (as a head) seen or drawn from the side

**¹prof·it** \'präf-ət\ *n*
**1** the gain or benefit from something ⟨it was to our *profit* to study hard⟩
**2** the gain after all the expenses are subtracted from the total amount received ⟨a business that shows a *profit* of $100 a week⟩
**prof·it·less** \-ləs\ *adj*

**²profit** *vb*
**1** to get some good out of something : GAIN ⟨*profit* by experience⟩
**2** to be of use to (someone) ⟨an agreement that *profited* us all⟩

**prof·it·able** \'präf-ət-ə-bəl\ *adj*
producing profit ⟨a *profitable* business⟩
**prof·it·ably** \-blē\ *adv*

**pro·found** \prə-'fau̇nd\ *adj*
**1** having or showing great knowledge and understanding ⟨a *profound* thinker⟩

2 very deeply felt ⟨*profound* sorrow⟩
**pro·found·ly** *adv*
**pro·found·ness** *n*

**pro·fuse** \prə-'fyüs\ *adj*
very plentiful
**pro·fuse·ly** *adv*
**pro·fuse·ness** *n*

**pro·fu·sion** \prə-'fyü-zhən\ *n*
a plentiful supply : PLENTY

**prog·e·ny** \'präj-ə-nē\ *n*, *pl* **prog·e·nies**
human descendants or animal offspring

[1]**pro·gram** \'prō-,gram, -grəm\ *n*
1 a brief statement or written outline (as of a concert or play)
2 PERFORMANCE 2 ⟨a television *program*⟩
3 a plan of action
4 a set of step-by-step instructions that tell a computer to do something with data

[2]**program** *vb* **pro·grammed** \'prō-,gramd, -grəmd\; **pro·gram·ming**
to provide with a program ⟨*program* a computer⟩

**pro·gram·mer** \'prō-,gra-mər, -grə-\ *n*
a person who creates and tests programs for computers

[1]**prog·ress** \'präg-rəs, -,res\ *n*
1 a moving toward a goal ⟨a ship's *progress*⟩
2 gradual improvement

[2]**pro·gress** \prə-'gres\ *vb*
1 to move forward : ADVANCE ⟨the story *progresses*⟩
2 to move toward a higher, better, or more advanced stage

**pro·gres·sion** \prə-'gresh-ən\ *n*
1 the act of progressing or moving forward
2 a continuous and connected series (as of acts, events, or steps)

**pro·gres·sive** \prə-'gres-iv\ *adj*
1 of, relating to, or showing progress ⟨a *progressive* city⟩
2 taking place gradually or step by step ⟨*progressive* wearing away of the soil⟩
3 favoring or working for gradual political change and social improvement by action of the government
**pro·gres·sive·ly** *adv*
**pro·gres·sive·ness** *n*

**pro·hib·it** \prō-'hib-ət\ *vb*
1 to forbid by authority ⟨parking *prohibited*⟩
2 to make impossible ⟨the high walls *prohibit* escape⟩

**pro·hi·bi·tion** \,prō-ə-'bish-ən\ *n*
1 the act of prohibiting something
2 the forbidding by law of the sale or manufacture of alcoholic liquids for use as beverages

[1]**proj·ect** \'präj-,ekt, -ikt\ *n*
1 a plan or scheme to do something
2 a task or problem in school
3 a group of houses or apartment buildings built according to a single plan

[2]**pro·ject** \prə-'jekt\ *vb*
1 to stick out ⟨a rock that *projects* above the ground⟩
2 to cause to fall on a surface ⟨*project* motion pictures on a screen⟩ ⟨*project* a shadow on the wall⟩

**pro·jec·tile** \prə-'jek-təl\ *n*
something (as a bullet or rocket) that is thrown or driven forward especially from a weapon

**pro·jec·tion** \prə-'jek-shən\ *n*
1 something that sticks out
2 the act or process of projecting on a surface (as by means of motion pictures or slides)

*tray for slides*

**projector** for showing slides

**pro·jec·tor** \prə-'jek-tər\ *n*
▲ a machine for projecting images on a screen

**pro·lif·ic** \prə-'lif-ik\ *adj*
producing young or fruit in large numbers

**pro·long** \prə-'lȯng\ *vb*
to make longer than usual or expected ⟨*prolong* a person's life⟩

**prom** \'präm\ *n*
a usually formal dance given by a high school or college class

**prom·e·nade** \,präm-ə-'nād, -'näd\ *n*
1 a walk or ride for pleasure or to be seen
2 a place for walking

**prom·i·nence** \'präm-ə-nəns\ *n*
1 the quality, condition, or fact of being prominent : DISTINCTION ⟨a person of *prominence*⟩
2 something (as a mountain) that is prominent

**prom·i·nent** \'präm-ə-nənt\ *adj*
1 sticking out beyond the surface
2 attracting attention (as by size or position) : CONSPICUOUS
3 DISTINGUISHED, EMINENT ⟨our town's most *prominent* resident⟩
**prom·i·nent·ly** *adv*

[1]**prom·ise** \'präm-əs\ *n*
1 a statement by a person that he or she will do or not do something ⟨a *promise* to pay within a month⟩
2 a cause or ground for hope ⟨these plans give *promise* of success⟩

[2]**promise** *vb* **prom·ised**; **prom·is·ing**
1 to give a promise about one's own actions ⟨I *promise* to clean my room this afternoon⟩
2 to give reason to expect ⟨the clouds *promise* rain⟩

**prom·is·ing** \'präm-ə-sing\ *adj*
likely to turn out well ⟨a very *promising* pupil⟩

**prom·on·to·ry** \'präm-ən-,tōr-ē\ *n*, *pl* **prom·on·to·ries**
a high point of land sticking out into the sea

**pro·mote** \prə-'mōt\ *vb* **pro·mot·ed**; **pro·mot·ing**
1 to move up in position or rank ⟨was *promoted* to the next grade⟩
2 to help (something) to grow or develop ⟨good soil *promotes* plant growth⟩

**pro·mo·tion** \prə-'mō-shən\ *n*
1 a moving up in position or rank ⟨*promotion* to a higher grade in school⟩
2 the promoting of something (as growth of health)

[1]**prompt** \'prämpt\ *vb*
1 to lead to do something ⟨curiosity *prompted* me to ask the question⟩
2 to remind of something forgotten or poorly learned ⟨*prompt* an actor⟩
3 to be the cause of : INSPIRE ⟨pride *prompted* the act⟩
**prompt·er** *n*

[2]**prompt** *adj*
**1** quick and ready to act ⟨*prompt* to answer⟩
**2** being on time **:** PUNCTUAL ⟨*prompt* in arriving⟩
**3** done at once **:** given without delay ⟨*prompt* assistance⟩
**synonyms** see QUICK
**prompt·ly** *adv*
**prompt·ness** *n*

**prone** \'prōn\ *adj*
**1** likely to be or act a certain way ⟨*prone* to laziness⟩
**2** having the front surface downward ⟨lying *prone* on the floor⟩
**prone·ness** *n*

**prong** \'prȯng\ *n*
**1** one of the sharp points of a fork
**2** a slender part that sticks out (as a point of an antler)

**prong·horn** \'prȯng-,hȯrn\ *n*
▶ an animal like an antelope that lives in the treeless parts of the western United States and Mexico

**pro·noun** \'prō-,nau̇n\ *n*
a word used as a substitute for a noun

**pro·nounce** \prə-'nau̇ns\ *vb* **pro·nounced**; **pro·nounc·ing**
**1** to state in an official or solemn way ⟨the judge *pronounced* sentence⟩
**2** to use the voice to make the sounds of ⟨*pronounce* these words⟩
**3** to say correctly ⟨I can't *pronounce* your name⟩

**pro·nounced** \prə-'nau̇nst\ *adj*
very noticeable ⟨was walking with a *pronounced* limp⟩

**pro·nun·ci·a·tion** \prə-,nən-sē-'ā-shən\ *n*
the act or way of pronouncing a word or words

[1]**proof** \'prüf\ *n*
**1** evidence of truth or correctness ⟨find *proof* of a statement⟩
**2** [1]TEST 1 ⟨put a theory to the *proof*⟩
**3** a printing (as from type) prepared for study and correction
**4** a test print made from a photographic negative

[2]**proof** *adj*
able to keep out something that could be harmful ⟨*proof* against tampering⟩ — usually used in compounds ⟨water*proof*⟩

**proof·read** \'prü-,frēd\ *vb* **proof·read** \-,fred\; **proof·read·ing** \-,frēd-ing\
to read over and fix mistakes in (written or printed matter) ⟨*proofread* your paper before you hand it in⟩
**proof·read·er** *n*

[1]**prop** \'präp\ *n*
something that props or supports

[2]**prop** *vb* **propped**; **prop·ping**
**1** to keep from falling or slipping by providing a support under or against
**2** to give help, encouragement, or support to

**pronghorn**

[3]**prop** *n*
PROPERTY 3

**pro·pa·gan·da** \,präp-ə-'gan-də\ *n*
an organized spreading of certain ideas or the ideas spread in such a way

**prop·a·gate** \'präp-ə-,gāt\ *vb* **prop·a·gat·ed**; **prop·a·gat·ing**
**1** to have or cause to have offspring ⟨*propagate* a fine apple by grafting⟩
**2** to cause (as an idea or belief) to spread out and affect a greater number or wider area ⟨*propagate* a faith⟩

**prop·a·ga·tion** \,präp-ə-'gā-shən\ *n*
an act or process of propagating

**pro·pel** \prə-'pel\ *vb* **pro·pelled**; **pro·pel·ling**
to push or drive usually forward or onward ⟨*propel* a bicycle⟩

**pro·pel·ler** \prə-'pel-ər\ *n*
▶ a device having a hub fitted with blades that is made to turn rapidly by an engine and that drives a ship, power boat, or airplane

**propeller** of a ship

**prop·er** \'präp-ər\ *adj*
**1** referring to one individual only ⟨a *proper* name⟩
**2** belonging naturally to a particular group or individual **:** CHARACTERISTIC ⟨every animal has its *proper* instincts⟩
**3** considered in its true or basic meaning ⟨lived outside the city *proper*⟩
**4** having or showing good manners ⟨*proper* behavior⟩
**5** APPROPRIATE, SUITABLE ⟨the *proper* tool for the job⟩

**proper fraction** *n*
a fraction in which the numerator is smaller than the denominator

**prop·er·ly** \'präp-ər-lē\ *adv*
**1** in a fit or suitable way
**2** according to fact ⟨*properly* speaking, whales are not fish⟩

**proper noun** *n*
a noun that names a particular person, place, or thing ⟨"Tom," "Chicago," and "Friday" are *proper nouns*⟩

**prop·er·ty** \'präp-ərt-ē\ *n, pl* **prop·er·ties**
**1** a special quality of a thing ⟨sweetness is a *property* of sugar⟩
**2** something (as land or money) that is owned ⟨that chair is my aunt's *property*⟩
**3** something other than scenery or costumes that is used in a play or movie

**proph·e·cy** \'präf-ə-sē\ *n, pl* **proph·e·cies**
**1** the sayings of a prophet
**2** something foretold **:** PREDICTION

**proph·e·sy** \'präf-ə-ˌsī\ *vb* **proph·e·sied**; **proph·e·sy·ing**
**1** to speak or write as a prophet
**2** FORETELL, PREDICT

**proph·et** \'präf-ət\ *n*
**1** ▶ one who declares publicly a message that one believes has come from God or a god
**2** a person who predicts the future

**pro·phet·ic** \prə-'fet-ik\ *adj*
of or relating to a prophet or prophecy

**prophet 1:** a 19th-century book illustration showing the prophet Daniel in the lions' den

[1]**pro·por·tion** \prə-'pōr-shən\ *n*
**1** the size, number, or amount of one thing or group of things as compared to that of another thing or group of things ⟨the *proportion* of boys to girls in our class is two to one⟩
**2** a balanced or pleasing arrangement ⟨out of *proportion*⟩
**3** a statement of the equality of two ratios (as $^4/_2 = {}^{10}/_5$)
**4** a fair or just share ⟨did my *proportion* of the work⟩
**5** DIMENSION ⟨a crisis of large *proportions*⟩

[2]**proportion** *vb*
**1** to adjust something to fit with something else
**2** to make the parts of fit well with each other

**pro·por·tion·al** \prə-'pōr-shə-nəl\ *adj*
being in proportion to something else ⟨received allowances *proportional* to their ages⟩
**pro·por·tion·al·ly** *adv*

**pro·pos·al** \prə-'pō-zəl\ *n*
**1** a stating or putting forward of something for consideration
**2** something proposed **:** PLAN
**3** an offer of marriage

**pro·pose** \prə-'pōz\ *vb* **pro·posed**; **pro·pos·ing**
**1** to make a suggestion to be thought over and talked about **:** SUGGEST
**2** to make plans **:** INTEND ⟨*propose* to buy a new house⟩
**3** to suggest for filling a place or office ⟨*propose* someone for membership in the club⟩
**4** to make an offer of marriage

**prop·o·si·tion** \ˌpräp-ə-'zish-ən\ *n*
**1** something proposed
**2** a statement to be proved, explained, or discussed

**pro·pri·e·tor** \prə-'prī-ət-ər\ *n*
a person who owns something **:** OWNER

**pro·pri·ety** \prə-'prī-ət-ē\ *n, pl* **pro·pri·eties**
**1** the quality or state of being proper
**2** correctness in manners or behavior ⟨behave with *propriety*⟩
**3** *proprieties pl* the rules and customs of behavior followed by nice people

**pro·pul·sion** \prə-'pəl-shən\ *n*
**1** the act or process of propelling
**2** something that propels

**pros** *pl of* PRO

**prose** \'prōz\ *n*
**1** the ordinary language that people use in speaking or writing
**2** writing without the repeating rhythm that is used in verse

**pros·e·cute** \'präs-i-ˌkyüt\ *vb* **pros·e·cut·ed**; **pros·e·cut·ing**
**1** to follow up to the end **:** keep at ⟨*prosecute* a war⟩
**2** to carry on a legal action against an accused person to prove his or her guilt

**pros·e·cu·tion** \ˌpräs-i-'kyü-shən\ *n*
**1** the act of prosecuting especially a criminal case in court
**2** the one bringing charges of crime against a person being tried
**3** the state's lawyers in a criminal case ⟨the *prosecution* will try to prove it was murder⟩

**pros·e·cu·tor** \'präs-i-ˌkyüt-ər\ *n*
a person who prosecutes especially a criminal case as lawyer for the state

[1]**pros·pect** \'präs-ˌpekt\ *n*
**1** a wide view ⟨a *prospect* of sea and land⟩
**2** an imagining of something to come ⟨the *prospect* of a good time⟩
**3** something that is waited for or expected **:** POSSIBILITY ⟨not much *prospect* of seeing them again⟩
**4** a possible buyer or customer
**5** a likely candidate ⟨a presidential *prospect*⟩

[2]**prospect** *vb*
to explore especially for mineral deposits

**pro·spec·tive** \prə-'spek-tiv, 'präs-ˌpek-\ *adj*
**1** likely to come about ⟨*prospective* benefits⟩
**2** likely to become ⟨a *prospective* buyer⟩
**pro·spec·tive·ly** *adv*

**pros·pec·tor** \'präs-ˌpek-tər\ *n*
a person who explores a region in search of valuable minerals (as metals or oil)

**pros·per** \'präs-pər\ *vb*
**1** to succeed or make money in something one is doing
**2** [1]FLOURISH 1, THRIVE

**pros·per·i·ty** \präs-'per-ət-ē\ *n*
the state of being prosperous or successful

**pros·per·ous** \'präs-pə-rəs\ *adj*
**1** having or showing success or financial good fortune
**2** strong and healthy in growth ⟨a *prosperous* crop⟩
**pros·per·ous·ly** *adv*

A B C D E F G H I J K L M N O P Q R S T U V W X Y Z

**[1]pros·trate** \'präs-ˌtrāt\ *adj*
**1** stretched out with face on the ground
**2** spread out parallel to the ground ⟨a *prostrate* shrub⟩
**3** lacking strength or energy ⟨*prostrate* with a cold⟩

**[2]prostrate** *vb* **pros·trat·ed**; **pros·trat·ing**
**1** to throw or put into a prostrate position
**2** to bring to a weak and powerless condition ⟨*prostrated* with grief⟩

**pro·tect** \prə-'tekt\ *vb*
to cover or shield from something that would destroy or injure : GUARD
**synonyms** see DEFEND

**pro·tec·tion** \prə-'tek-shən\ *n*
**1** the act of protecting : the state of being protected
**2** a protecting person or thing

**pro·tec·tive** \prə-'tek-tiv\ *adj*
giving or meant to give protection
**pro·tec·tive·ly** *adv*
**pro·tec·tive·ness** *n*

**pro·tec·tor** \prə-'tek-tər\ *n*
a person or thing that protects or is intended to protect

**pro·tein** \'prō-ˌtēn\ *n*
a nutrient containing nitrogen that is found in all living plant or animal cells, is a necessary part of the diet, and is supplied especially by such foods as meat, milk, and eggs

**[1]pro·test** \'prō-ˌtest\ *n*
**1** the act of protesting
**2** a complaint or objection against an idea, an act, or a way of doing things

**[2]pro·test** \prə-'test\ *vb*
**1** to declare positively : ASSERT ⟨*protest* one's innocence⟩
**2** to complain strongly about ⟨the fans *protested* the umpire's decision⟩ **synonyms** see OBJECT

**[1]Prot·es·tant** \'prät-əs-tənt\ *n*
a member of a Christian church other than the Eastern Orthodox Church and the Roman Catholic Church

**[2]Protestant** *adj*
of or relating to Protestants

**pro·ton** \'prō-ˌtän\ *n*
a very small particle that occurs in the nucleus of every atom and has a positive charge of electricity

**pro·to·plasm** \'prōt-ə-ˌplaz-əm\ *n*
the usually colorless and jellylike living part of cells

**pro·to·zo·an** \ˌprōt-ə-'zō-ən\ *n*
any of a large group of mostly microscopic animals whose body is a single cell

**pro·tract** \prō-'trakt\ *vb*
to make longer : draw out in time or space

**pro·trac·tor** \prō-'trak-tər\ *n*
▶ an instrument used for drawing and measuring angles



protractor

**pro·trude** \prō-'trüd\ *vb*
**pro·trud·ed**; **pro·trud·ing**
to stick out or cause to stick out

**proud** \'prȧu̇d\ *adj*
**1** having or showing a feeling that one is better than others : HAUGHTY
**2** having a feeling of pleasure or satisfaction : very pleased ⟨they were *proud* of their clever child⟩
**3** having proper self-respect ⟨too *proud* to beg⟩
**proud·ly** *adv*

**prove** \'prüv\ *vb* **proved**; **proved** *or* **prov·en** \'prü-vən\; **prov·ing**
**1** to test by experiment or by a standard
**2** to convince others of the truth of something by showing the facts
**3** to test the answer to and check the way of solving an arithmetic problem

**prov·erb** \'präv-ˌərb\ *n*
a short well-known saying containing a wise thought : MAXIM, ADAGE ⟨"haste makes waste" is a *proverb*⟩

**pro·ver·bi·al** \prə-'vər-bē-əl\ *adj*
of, relating to, or being a proverb
**pro·ver·bi·al·ly** *adv*

**pro·vide** \prə-'vīd\ *vb*
**pro·vid·ed**; **pro·vid·ing**
**1** to look out for or take care of beforehand ⟨*provide* for a rainy day⟩
**2** to make as a condition ⟨the rules *provide* that all players must do good work in school⟩
**3** to give something that is needed ⟨*provide* books⟩

**pro·vid·ed** \prə-'vīd-əd\ *conj*
IF 1 ⟨we'll start now *provided* you agree⟩

**pro·vid·er** \prə-'vīd-ər\ *n*
one that provides something ⟨a service *provider*⟩

**prov·i·dence** \'präv-ə-dəns\ *n*
**1** *often cap* help or care from God or heaven
**2** *cap* God as the guide and protector of all human beings
**3** PRUDENCE, THRIFT

**prov·ince** \'präv-əns\ *n*
**1** a part of a country having a government of its own (as one of the divisions of the Dominion of Canada)
**2** **provinces** *pl* the part or parts of a country far from the capital or chief city
**3** an area of activity or authority ⟨the *province* of science⟩

**pro·vin·cial** \prə-'vin-chəl\ *adj*
**1** of, relating to, or coming from a province
**2** lacking the social graces and sophistication of the city

**[1]pro·vi·sion** \prə-'vizh-ən\ *n*
**1** the act of providing
**2** something done beforehand
**3** a stock or store of food — usually used in pl. ⟨lay in *provisions* for a holiday⟩
**4** [1]CONDITION 1 ⟨the *provisions* of the contract⟩

**[2]provision** *vb*
to supply with provisions

**prov·o·ca·tion** \ˌpräv-ə-'kā-shən\ *n*
**1** the act of provoking
**2** something that provokes

**pro·voc·a·tive** \prə-'väk-ət-iv\ *adj*
serving or likely to cause a reaction (as interest, curiosity, or anger)
**pro·voc·a·tive·ly** *adv*

**pro·voke** \prə-'vōk\ *vb*
**pro·voked**; **pro·vok·ing**
**1** to cause to become angry ⟨don't *provoke* the dog⟩
**2** to bring about ⟨*provoke* a smile⟩

**pro·vok·ing** \prə-ˈvō-king\ *adj*
causing mild anger
**pro·vok·ing·ly** *adv*

**prow** \ˈpraů\ *n*
▶ the bow of a ship

**prow·ess** \ˈpraů-əs\ *n*
**1** great bravery especially in battle
**2** very great ability

**prowl** \ˈpraůl\ *vb*
to move about quietly and secretly like a wild animal hunting prey
**prowl·er** *n*

**proxy** \ˈpräk-sē\ *n, pl* **prox·ies**
**1** authority to act for another or a paper giving such authority
**2** a person with authority to act for another

**prude** \ˈprüd\ *n*
a person who cares too much about proper speech and conduct
**prud·ish** \-ish\ *adj*

**pru·dence** \ˈprüd-ns\ *n*
skill and good sense in taking care of oneself or of one's doings

**pru·dent** \ˈprüd-nt\ *adj*
**1** clever and careful in action or judgment
**2** careful in trying to avoid mistakes
**pru·dent·ly** *adv*

[1]**prune** \ˈprün\ *n*
a dried plum

[2]**prune** *vb* **pruned**; **prun·ing**
**1** to cut off dead or unwanted parts of a bush or tree
**2** to cut out useless or unwanted parts (as unnecessary words or phrases in a composition)

[1]**pry** \ˈprī\ *vb* **pried**; **pry·ing**
to be nosy about something

[2]**pry** *vb* **pried**; **pry·ing**
**1** to raise or open or try to do so with a lever
**2** to get at with great difficulty ⟨*pry* a secret out of a person⟩

**pry·ing** \ˈprī-ing\ *adj*
rudely nosy ⟨*prying* questions⟩

**psalm** \ˈsäm, ˈsälm\ *n*
**1** a sacred song or poem
**2** *cap* one of the hymns that make up the Old Testament Book of Psalms

**psy·chi·a·trist** \sə-ˈkī-ə-trəst, sī-\ *n*
a specialist in psychiatry

**psy·chi·a·try** \sə-ˈkī-ə-trē, sī-\ *n*
a branch of medicine dealing with problems of the mind, emotions, or behavior

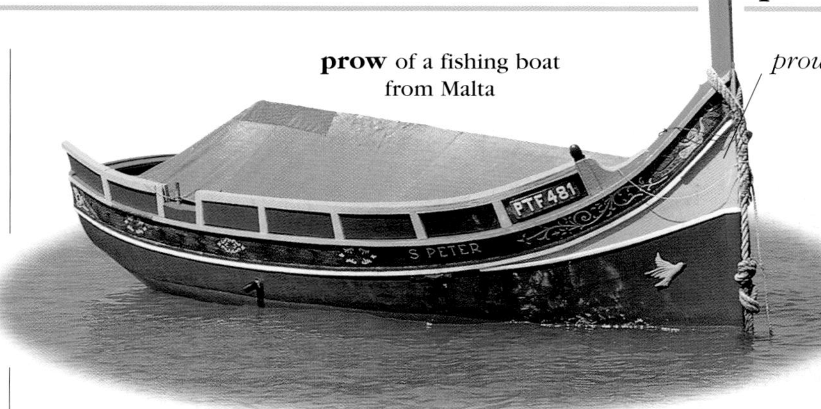


**prow** of a fishing boat from Malta

**psy·cho·log·i·cal** \ˌsī-kə-ˈläj-i-kəl\ *adj*
**1** of or relating to psychology
**2** directed toward or meant to influence the mind ⟨*psychological* warfare⟩

**psy·chol·o·gist** \sī-ˈkäl-ə-jəst\ *n*
a specialist in psychology

**psy·chol·o·gy** \sī-ˈkäl-ə-jē\ *n*
the science that studies facts about the mind and its activities especially in human beings

**pu·ber·ty** \ˈpyü-bərt-ē\ *n*
the age at or period during which a person becomes able to reproduce sexually

[1]**pub·lic** \ˈpəb-lik\ *adj*
**1** of or relating to the people as a whole ⟨*public* opinion⟩
**2** of, relating to, or working for a government or community ⟨*public* prosecutor⟩ ⟨holds *public* office⟩
**3** open to all ⟨a *public* library⟩
**4** known to many people **:** not kept secret ⟨the story became *public*⟩
**5** WELL-KNOWN, PROMINENT ⟨*public* figures⟩
**pub·lic·ly** *adv*

[2]**public** *n*
**1** the people as a whole ⟨open to the *public*⟩
**2** a group of people having common interests ⟨a novelist's *public*⟩

**pub·li·ca·tion** \ˌpəb-lə-ˈkā-shən\ *n*
**1** the act or process of publishing
**2** a printed work (as a book or magazine) made for sale or distribution

**pub·lic·i·ty** \ˌpəb-ˈlis-ət-ē\ *n*
**1** public interest and approval
**2** something (as favorable news) used to attract public interest and approval

**pub·li·cize** \ˈpəb-lə-ˌsīz\ *vb* **pub·li·cized**; **pub·li·ciz·ing**
to give publicity to

**public school** *n*
a free school paid for by taxes and run by a local government

**pub·lish** \ˈpəb-lish\ *vb*
**1** to make widely known
**2** to bring printed works (as books) before the public usually for sale
**pub·lish·er** *n*

**puck** \ˈpək\ *n*
a rubber disk used in hockey

[1]**puck·er** \ˈpək-ər\ *vb*
to draw or cause to draw up into folds or wrinkles ⟨*pucker* one's lips⟩

[2]**pucker** *n*
a fold or wrinkle in a normally even surface

**pudding:**
a Mexican chocolate pudding

**pud·ding** \ˈpůd-ing\ *n*
▲ a soft spongy or creamy dessert

**pud·dle** \ˈpəd-l\ *n*
a very small pool (as of dirty or muddy water)

A B C D E F G H I J K L M N O P Q R S T U V W X Y Z

**pudgy** \'pəj-ē\ *adj* **pudg·i·er**; **pudg·i·est**
being short and plump : CHUBBY

**pueb·lo** \'pweb-lō\ *n, pl* **pueb·los**
▲ an Indian village of Arizona or New Mexico made up of groups of stone or adobe houses with flat roofs

[1]**Puer·to Ri·can** \,pwert-ə-'rē-kən, ,pōrt-\ *adj*
of or relating to Puerto Rico or the Puerto Ricans

[2]**Puerto Rican** *n*
a person born or living in Puerto Rico

[1]**puff** \'pəf\ *vb*
**1** to blow in short gusts
**2** to breathe hard : PANT
**3** to send out small whiffs or clouds (as of smoke)
**4** to swell up or become swollen with or as if with air ⟨the injured eye *puffed* up⟩ ⟨*puffed* out my cheeks⟩

[2]**puff** *n*
**1** a quick short sending or letting out of air, smoke, or steam ⟨*puffs* from a locomotive⟩
**2** a slight swelling
**3** a soft pad for putting powder on the skin

**puf·fin** \'pəf-ən\ *n*
▶ a seabird related to the auks that has a short thick neck and a deep grooved bill marked with several colors

**puffy** \'pəf-ē\ *adj* **puff·i·er**; **puff·i·est**
**1** blowing in puffs ⟨a *puffy* locomotive⟩
**2** BREATHLESS 1 ⟨was still *puffy* after the long run⟩
**3** somewhat swollen ⟨a *puffy* face⟩
**4** like a puff : FLUFFY ⟨a *puffy* marshmallow pie⟩

**pueblo** in New Mexico

**pug** \'pəg\ *n*
**1** a small dog having a thick body, a large round head, a square snout, a curled tail, and usually short hair
**2** a nose turning up at the tip and usually short and thick

[1]**pull** \'pu̇l\ *vb*
**1** to separate from a firm or a natural attachment ⟨*pull* a tooth⟩
**2** to use force on so as to cause or tend to cause movement toward the force ⟨*pulled* the rope⟩
**3** to stretch repeatedly ⟨*pull* taffy⟩
**4** [1]MOVE 1 ⟨a train *pulling* out⟩
**5** to draw apart : TEAR, REND ⟨*pull* a flower to pieces⟩

[2]**pull** *n*
**1** the act or an instance of pulling ⟨two *pulls* on the cord⟩
**2** the effort put forth in moving ⟨a long *pull* up the hill⟩
**3** a device for pulling something
**4** a force that pulls ⟨the *pull* of gravity⟩

**pull–down** \'pu̇l-,dau̇n\ *adj*
appearing on a computer screen below a selected item ⟨a *pull-down* menu⟩

**puffin**

**pul·let** \'pu̇l-ət\ *n*
a young hen

**pul·ley** \'pu̇l-ē\ *n, pl* **pulleys**
▼ a wheel that has a grooved rim in which a belt, rope, or chain runs and that is used to change the direction of a pulling force and in combination to increase the force applied for lifting

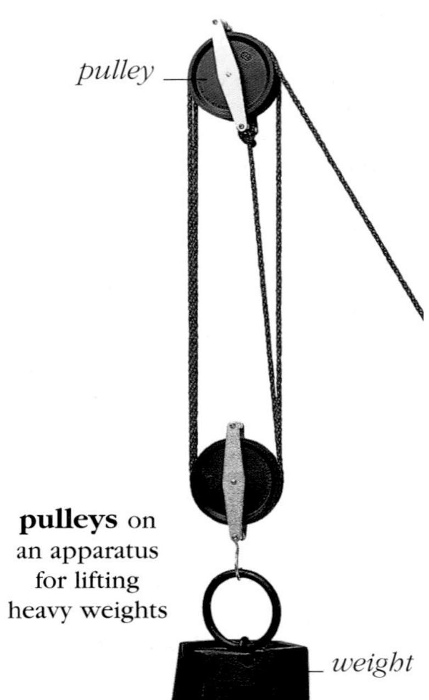


**pulleys** on an apparatus for lifting heavy weights

**pull·over** \'pu̇l-,ō-vər\ *n*
a garment (as a sweater) that is put on by being pulled over the head

**pull through** *vb*
to survive a very difficult or dangerous period ⟨was seriously ill but *pulled through*⟩

**pul·mo·nary** \'pu̇l-mə-,ner-ē, 'pəl-\ *adj*
of or relating to the lungs

**[1]pulp** \ˈpəlp\ *n*
**1** the soft juicy part of a fruit or vegetable ⟨the *pulp* of an orange⟩
**2** a mass of vegetable matter from which the moisture has been squeezed
**3** the soft sensitive tissue inside a tooth
**4** a material prepared usually from wood or rags and used in making paper

**[2]pulp** *vb*
to make into a pulp

**pul·pit** \ˈpu̇l-ˌpit\ *n*
**1** a raised place in which a clergyman stands while preaching or conducting a religious service
**2** preachers in general

**pulp·wood** \ˈpəlp-ˌwu̇d\ *n*
wood (as of aspen or spruce) from which wood pulp is made

**pulpy** \ˈpəl-pē\ *adj* **pulp·i·er**; **pulp·i·est**
like or made of pulp

**pul·sate** \ˈpəl-ˌsāt\ *vb* **pul·sat·ed**; **pul·sat·ing**
to have or show a pulse or beats

**pul·sa·tion** \ˌpəl-ˈsā-shən\ *n*
pulsating movement or action

**pulse** \ˈpəls\ *n*
**1** a regular beating or throbbing (as of the arteries)
**2** one complete beat of a pulse or the number of these in a given period (as a minute) ⟨exercise increases the *pulse*⟩

**pul·ver·ize** \ˈpəl-və-ˌrīz\ *vb* **pul·ver·ized**; **pul·ver·iz·ing**
to beat or grind into a powder or dust

**pu·ma** \ˈpyü-mə, ˈpü-\ *n*
COUGAR

**pum·ice** \ˈpəm-əs\ *n*
▼ a very light porous volcanic glass that is used in powder form for smoothing and polishing

pumice

**pum·mel** \ˈpəm-əl\ *vb* **pum·meled** *or* **pum·melled**; **pum·mel·ing** *or* **pum·mel·ling**
to strike again and again

**[1]pump** \ˈpəmp\ *n*
a device for raising, moving, or compressing fluids

**[2]pump** *vb*
**1** to raise, move, or compress by using a pump ⟨*pump* water⟩
**2** to free (as from water or air) by the use of a pump ⟨*pump* a boat dry⟩
**3** to fill by using a pump ⟨*pump* up tires⟩
**4** to draw, force, or drive onward in the manner of a pump ⟨heart *pumping* blood into the arteries⟩
**5** to question again and again to find out something
**pump·er** *n*

**pum·per·nick·el** \ˈpəm-pər-ˌnik-əl\ *n*
a dark rye bread

**pump·kin** \ˈpəmp-kən\ *n*
▼ a large round orange or yellow fruit of a vine related to the squash vine that is used as a vegetable or as feed for farm animals

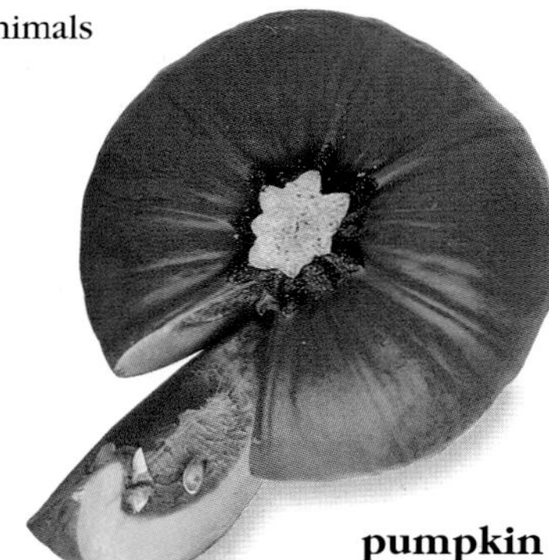
pumpkin

**[1]pun** \ˈpən\ *n*
a form of joking in which a person uses a word in two senses

**[2]pun** *vb* **punned**; **pun·ning**
to make a pun

**[1]punch** \ˈpənch\ *vb*
**1** to care for (range cattle)
**2** to strike with the fist
**3** to press or strike by or as if by punching ⟨*punch* a typewriter⟩
**4** to pierce or stamp with a punch

**[2]punch** *n*
a blow with or as if with the fist

**[3]punch** *n*
a tool for piercing, stamping, or cutting

**[4]punch** *n*
a drink containing several things and often including wine or liquor

**punc·tu·al** \ˈpəngk-chə-wəl\ *adj*
acting at the right time **:** not late

**punc·tu·ate** \ˈpəngk-chə-ˌwāt\ *vb* **punc·tu·at·ed**; **punc·tu·at·ing**
to mark or divide with punctuation marks

**punc·tu·a·tion** \ˌpəngk-chə-ˈwā-shən\ *n*
**1** the act of punctuating
**2** a system of using marks (**punctuation marks**) such as commas and periods to make clear the meaning of written matter

**[1]punc·ture** \ˈpəngk-chər\ *n*
**1** an act of puncturing
**2** a hole or wound made by puncturing

**[2]puncture** *vb* **punc·tured**; **punc·tur·ing**
**1** to pierce with something pointed
**2** to make useless or destroy as if by a puncture ⟨*puncture* an argument⟩

**pun·gent** \ˈpən-jənt\ *adj*
giving a sharp or biting sensation
**pun·gent·ly** *adv*

**pun·ish** \ˈpən-ish\ *vb*
**1** to make suffer for a fault or crime ⟨*punish* a child for lying⟩
**2** to make someone suffer for (as a crime) ⟨*punish* theft with prison⟩

---

**Synonyms** PUNISH and DISCIPLINE mean to put a penalty on someone for doing wrong. PUNISH stresses the giving of some kind of pain or suffering to the wrongdoer rather than trying to reform the person ⟨*punished* the killers by ordering their deaths⟩. DISCIPLINE suggests penalizing the wrongdoer but stresses the effort to bring the person under control ⟨parents must *discipline* their children⟩.

---

**pun·ish·able** \ˈpən-ish-ə-bəl\ *adj*
deserving to be punished ⟨a *punishable* offense⟩

**pun·ish·ment** \ˈpən-ish-mənt\ *n*
**1** the act of punishing **:** the state or fact of being punished
**2** the penalty for a fault or crime

**[1]punk** \ˈpəngk\ *n*
a petty gangster or hoodlum

a b c d e f g h i j k l m n o p q r s t u v w x y z

A B C D E F G H I J K L M N O P Q R S T U V W X Y Z

**[2]punk** *adj*
**1** poor in quality
**2** UNWELL, SICK ⟨feeling *punk* today⟩

**[1]punt** \'pənt\ *vb*
to kick a ball dropped from the hands before it hits the ground
**punt·er** *n*

**puppet 1:** a hand puppet

**[2]punt** *n*
an act or instance of punting a ball

**pu·ny** \'pyü-nē\ *adj* **pu·ni·er**; **pu·ni·est**
small and weak in size or power

**Word History** The English word *puny* first meant "younger" or "lower in rank" and came from an early French word that meant "younger." Someone who is younger than another person was, of course, born later. The French word meaning "younger" was made up of two words. The first of these two French words meant "afterward." The second meant "born."

**pup** \'pəp\ *n*
**1** PUPPY
**2** one of the young of any of several animals (as a seal)

**pu·pa** \'pyü-pə\ *n, pl* **pu·pae** \-,pē\ *or* **pupas**
an insect (as a bee, moth, or beetle) in an intermediate inactive stage of its growth in which it is enclosed in a cocoon or case

**pu·pal** \'pyü-pəl\ *adj*
of, relating to, or being a pupa

**[1]pu·pil** \'pyü-pəl\ *n*
a child in school or under the care of a teacher

**Word History** The Latin word *pupilla* meant "girl." The English word *pupil* that means "a girl or boy in school" comes from that Latin word and a similar word that meant "boy." *Pupilla* is also the ancestor of our word for a pupil of the eye. In Latin this word meant "doll" as well as "girl." If you look in another person's eyes from close up, you can see yourself reflected. You will look like a little doll. That is why a word for a part of the eye was formed from a word meaning "doll" or "girl."

**[2]pupil** *n*
the opening in the iris through which light enters the eye

**pup·pet** \'pəp-ət\ *n*
**1** a doll moved by hand or by strings or wires
**2** one (as a person or government) whose acts are controlled by another

**pup·py** \'pəp-ē\ *n, pl* **puppies**
a young dog

**[1]pur·chase** \'pər-chəs\ *vb* **pur·chased**; **pur·chas·ing**
to get by paying money

**[2]purchase** *n*
**1** an act of purchasing ⟨the *purchase* of supplies⟩
**2** something purchased
**3** a firm hold or grasp or a safe place to stand ⟨could not get a *purchase* on the ledge⟩

**pure** \'pyu̇r\ *adj* **pur·er**; **pur·est**
**1** not mixed with anything else **:** free from everything that might injure or lower the quality ⟨*pure* water⟩ ⟨*pure* French⟩
**2** free from sin **:** INNOCENT, CHASTE
**3** nothing other than **:** ABSOLUTE ⟨*pure* nonsense⟩
**pure·ly** *adv*
**pure·ness** *n*

**pup 2:** a seal pup

**pure·bred** \'pyu̇r-'bred\ *adj*
bred from ancestors of a single breed for many generations

**[1]purge** \'pərj\ *vb* **purged**; **purg·ing**
**1** to make clean
**2** to have or cause frequent bowel movements
**3** to get rid of ⟨the leaders had been *purged*⟩

**[2]purge** *n*
**1** an act or instance of purging
**2** the removal of persons thought to be treacherous or disloyal ⟨a *purge* of party leaders⟩

**pu·ri·fi·ca·tion** \,pyu̇r-ə-fə-'kā-shən\ *n*
an act or instance of purifying or of being purified

**pu·ri·fy** \'pyu̇r-ə-,fī\ *vb* **pu·ri·fied**; **pu·ri·fy·ing**
to make pure **:** free from impurities

**pu·ri·tan** \'pyu̇r-ət-n\ *n*
**1** *cap* a member of a sixteenth and seventeenth century Protestant group in England and New England opposing formal customs of the Church of England
**2** a person who practices or preaches or follows a stricter moral code than most people

**pu·ri·ty** \'pyu̇r-ət-ē\ *n*
**1** freedom from dirt or impurities
**2** freedom from sin or guilt

**pur·ple** \'pər-pəl\ *n*
a color between red and blue

**pur·plish** \'pər-plish\ *adj*
somewhat purple

**[1]pur·pose** \'pər-pəs\ *n*
something set up as a goal to be achieved **:** INTENTION, AIM
**on purpose** PURPOSELY

**[2]purpose** *vb* **pur·posed**; **pur·pos·ing**
to have as one's intention **:** INTEND

**pur·pose·ful** \'pər-pəs-fəl\ *adj*
having a clear purpose or aim
**pur·pose·ful·ly** \-fə-lē\ *adv*
**pur·pose·ful·ness** *n*

**pur·pose·ly** \'pər-pəs-lē\ *adv*
with a clear or known purpose

**purr** \'pər\ *vb*
to make the low murmuring sound of a contented cat or a similar sound

**[1]purse** \'pərs\ *n*
1 a bag or pouch for money
2 HANDBAG
3 the contents of a purse : MONEY 1
4 a sum of money offered as a prize or collected as a present

**[2]purse** *vb* **pursed**; **purs·ing**
to draw into folds ⟨*purse* one's lips⟩

**pur·sue** \pər-'sü\ *vb* **pur·sued**; **pur·su·ing**
1 to follow after in order to catch or destroy : CHASE ⟨*pursued* the retreating enemy⟩
2 to follow with an end in view ⟨*pursue* a wise course⟩
3 to go on with : FOLLOW ⟨*pursue* medical studies⟩ **synonyms** see CHASE
**pur·su·er** *n*

**pur·suit** \pər-'süt\ *n*
1 the act of pursuing
2 ACTIVITY 2, OCCUPATION

**pus** \'pəs\ *n*
thick yellowish matter (as in an abscess or a boil)

**[1]push** \'pu̇sh\ *vb*
1 to press against with force so as to drive or move away ⟨*push* a car to get it started⟩
2 to force forward, downward, or outward ⟨a tree *pushing* its roots deep in the soil⟩
3 to go or make go ahead ⟨*push* a task to completion⟩

**[2]push** *n*
1 a sudden thrust : SHOVE ⟨gave it a *push* and it fell over⟩
2 a steady applying of force in a direction away from the body from which it comes ⟨gave the car a *push* up the hill⟩

**push button** *n*
a small button or knob that when pushed operates something usually by closing an electric circuit

**push·cart** \'pu̇sh-,kärt\ *n*
a cart pushed by hand

**push·over** \'pu̇sh-,ō-vər\ *n*
1 an opponent that is easy to defeat ⟨thought the first team they played would be a *pushover*⟩
2 something easily done ⟨the exam was a *pushover*⟩

**pushy** \'pu̇sh-ē\ *adj* **push·i·er**; **push·i·est**
too aggressive : FORWARD

**puss** \'pu̇s\ *n*
CAT 1

**[1]purse 1**

**pussy** \'pu̇s-ē\ *n, pl* **puss·ies**
CAT 1

**pussy willow** \,pu̇s-ē-\ *n*
a willow with large silky catkins

**put** \'pu̇t\ *vb* **put**; **put·ting**
1 to place in or move into a particular position ⟨*put* the book on the table⟩ ⟨*put* your hand up⟩
2 to bring into a specified state or condition ⟨*puts* the money to good use⟩ ⟨*put* the room in order⟩
3 to cause to stand for or suffer something ⟨was *put* to death⟩ ⟨*puts* them to shame⟩
4 to give expression to ⟨*put* my fear into words⟩ ⟨*puts* the idea clearly⟩
5 to give up to or urge to an activity ⟨if they *put* their minds to it⟩ ⟨*putting* us to work⟩
6 to think something to have : ATTRIBUTE ⟨*puts* a high value on peace⟩
7 to begin a voyage ⟨the ship *put* to sea⟩
**put forward** PROPOSE 1 ⟨*put forward* a new plan⟩

**put away** *vb*
1 to give up : DISCARD ⟨*put away* foolish habits⟩
2 to take in food and drink ⟨*put away* a big dinner⟩

**put by** *vb*
to lay aside : SAVE ⟨*put by* money for fuel⟩

**put down** *vb*
1 to bring to an end by force ⟨*put down* a riot⟩
2 to consider to belong to a particular class or to be due to a particular cause ⟨*put* them *down* as lazy⟩ ⟨we *put* our trouble *down* to carelessness⟩

**put in** *vb*
1 to ask for ⟨*put in* for a job at the school⟩
2 to spend time in a place or activity ⟨*put in* six hours at school⟩

**put off** *vb*
DEFER ⟨*put off* an appointment⟩

**put on** *vb*
1 to dress oneself in ⟨*put* a new jacket *on*⟩
2 PRETEND 2, SHAM ⟨*put on* a show of anger⟩
3 [1]PRODUCE 4 ⟨*put on* the senior play⟩

**put·out** \'pu̇t-,au̇t\ *n*
the causing of a batter or runner to be out in baseball

**put out** \'pu̇t-'au̇t\ *vb*
1 to make use of ⟨*put out* a real effort to succeed⟩
2 EXTINGUISH 1 ⟨be sure to *put out* the light⟩
3 [1]MAKE 2 ⟨the factory *puts out* fine cloth⟩
4 IRRITATE 1, ANNOY ⟨I was very *put out* by the sharp answer⟩
5 to cause to be out (as in baseball) ⟨was *put out* at third base⟩

**pu·trid** \'pyü-trəd\ *adj*
1 ROTTEN 1 ⟨*putrid* meat⟩
2 coming from or suggesting something rotten ⟨a *putrid* smell⟩

**put·ter** \'pət-ər\ *vb*
to act or work without much purpose ⟨*puttering* around the garden⟩

**put through** *vb*
to conclude with success ⟨*put through* a needed reform⟩

**[1]put·ty** \'pət-ē\ *n, pl* **putties**
a soft cement (as for holding glass in a window frame)

**[2]putty** *vb* **put·tied**; **put·ty·ing**
to cement or seal up with putty

**put up** *vb*
1 to make (as food) ready or safe for later use ⟨*put up* a lunch⟩ ⟨*put* vegetables *up* for winter⟩
2 NOMINATE ⟨*put* a candidate *up*⟩
3 to give or get shelter and often food ⟨*put* tourists *up*⟩ ⟨we *put up* at a motel⟩
4 [1]BUILD 1 ⟨*put up* a new school⟩
5 to make by action or effort ⟨*put up* a good fight⟩
**put up to** to urge or cause to do something wrong or unexpected ⟨we were the ones who *put* the others *up to* mischief⟩
**put up with** to stand for : TOLERATE ⟨the coach won't *put up with* any nonsense⟩

a b c d e f g h i j k l m n o p q r s t u v w x y z

\ng\ sing \ō\ bone \ȯ\ saw \ȯi\ coin \th\ thin \th\ this \ü\ food \u̇\ foot \y\ yet \yü\ few \yu̇\ cure \zh\ vision

[1]**pyramid 1:** a pyramid at Giza \'gē-zə\, Egypt

[1]**puz·zle** \'pəz-əl\ *vb* **puz·zled**; **puz·zling**
**1** CONFUSE 1, PERPLEX ⟨*puzzled* by the answer⟩
**2** to solve by thought or by clever guessing ⟨*puzzle* out a mystery⟩

[2]**puzzle** *n*
**1** something that puzzles : MYSTERY
**2** a question, problem, or device intended to test one's skill or cleverness

[1]**pyg·my** *also* **pig·my** \'pig-mē\ *n, pl* **pygmies** *also* **pigmies**
a person or thing very small for its kind : DWARF

[2]**pygmy** *adj*
very small

[1]**pyr·a·mid** \'pir-ə-ˌmid\ *n*
**1** ▲ a large structure built especially in ancient Egypt that usually has a square base and four triangular sides meeting at a point and that contains tombs
**2** something that has the shape of a pyramid
**3** a solid with a polygon for its base and three or more triangles for its sides which meet to form the top

[2]**pyramid** *vb*
to build up in the form of a pyramid

**pyre** \'pīr\ *n*
a heap of wood for burning a dead body

**py·thon** \'pī-ˌthän\ *n*
▼ any of various large nonpoisonous snakes of Africa, Asia, and Australia that squeeze and suffocate their prey

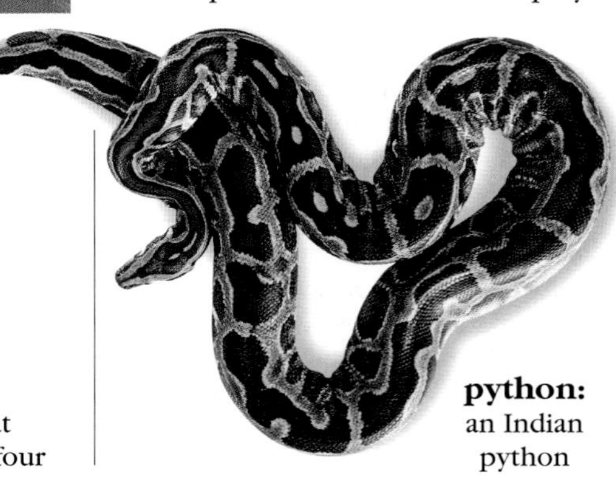

**python:** an Indian python

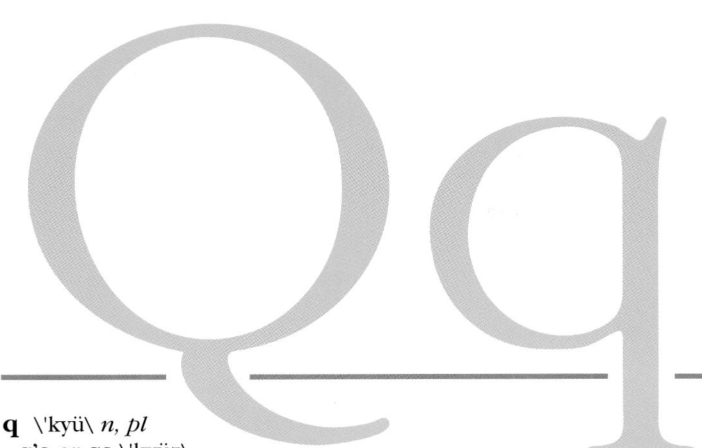

**The sounds of Q:** The letter **Q** in English has the same sound as the letter **K**. **Q** is not used in many words. Most words with this sound are spelled with the letter **K** or **C** or **CK** together, rather than with **Q**. When **Q** is used, it is almost always followed by the letter **U**. In most of these "**-QU-**" words, the two letters together sound like **K** followed by **W**. Examples are **quick**, **square**, **quote**, and **request**. In some words, the **Q** sounds like **K** alone and the **U** is silent, as in **bouquet**, **etiquette**, and **conquer.**

**q** \'kyü\ *n, pl* **q's** *or* **qs** \'kyüz\ *often cap* the seventeenth letter of the English alphabet

[1]**quack** \'kwak\ *vb* to make the cry of a duck

[2]**quack** *n* a cry made by or as if by quacking

[3]**quack** *n* an ignorant person who pretends to have medical knowledge and skill

[4]**quack** *adj*
**1** of, relating to, or like that of a quack
**2** pretending to cure disease ⟨*quack* remedies⟩

**quadri-** \'kwäd-rə\ *or* **quadr-** *or* **quadru-** \'kwäd-rə\ *prefix*
**1** four
**2** fourth

**quad·ri·lat·er·al** \,kwäd-rə-'lat-ə-rəl\ *n* a figure of four sides and four angles

**quad·ru·ped** \'kwäd-rə-,ped\ *n* an animal having four feet

**qua·dru·plet** \kwä-'drüp-lət, -'drəp-\ *n*
**1** one of four offspring born at one birth
**2** a combination of four of a kind

**quag·mire** \'kwag-,mīr\ *n*
**1** soft spongy wet ground that shakes or gives way under the foot
**2** a difficult situation from which it is hard to escape

[1]**quail** \'kwāl\ *n, pl* **quail** *or* **quails** ▼ any of various mostly small plump game birds (as the bobwhite) that are related to the chicken

[1]**quail:** a Japanese quail

[2]**quail** *vb* to lose courage **:** shrink in fear

**quaint** \'kwānt\ *adj*
**1** being or looking unusual or different
**2** pleasingly old-fashioned or unfamiliar
**quaint·ly** *adv*
**quaint·ness** *n*

[1]**quake** \'kwāk\ *vb* **quaked**; **quak·ing**
**1** to shake usually from shock or lack of stability
**2** to tremble or shudder usually from cold or fear

[2]**quake** *n* an instance (as an earthquake) of shaking or trembling

**qual·i·fi·ca·tion** \,kwäl-ə-fə-'kā-shən\ *n*
**1** the act or an instance of qualifying
**2** the state of being qualified
**3** a special skill, knowledge, or ability that fits a person for a particular work or position
**4** LIMITATION 1 ⟨agree without *qualification*⟩

**qual·i·fy** \'kwäl-ə-,fī\ *vb* **qual·i·fied**; **qual·i·fy·ing**
**1** to narrow down or make less general in meaning **:** LIMIT ⟨*qualify* a statement⟩ ⟨adjectives *qualify* nouns⟩
**2** to make less harsh or strict **:** SOFTEN ⟨*qualify* a punishment⟩
**3** to fit by training, skill, or ability for a special purpose
**4** to show the skill or ability needed to be on a team or take part in a contest

**qual·i·ty** \'kwäl-ət-ē\ *n, pl* **qual·i·ties**
**1** basic and individual nature ⟨know the *quality* of one's actions⟩
**2** how good or bad something is ⟨food of excellent *quality*⟩
**3** high social rank ⟨a person of *quality*⟩
**4** what sets a person or thing apart **:** CHARACTERISTIC ⟨the salty *quality* of the water⟩

**qualm** \'kwäm, 'kwälm\ *n*
**1** a sudden attack of illness, faintness, or nausea
**2** a sudden fear
**3** a feeling of doubt or uncertainty that one's behavior is honest or right
**qualm·ish** \-ish\ *adj*

**quan·da·ry** \'kwän-də-rē, -drē\ *n, pl* **quan·da·ries** a state of doubt or puzzled confusion ⟨in a *quandary* about what to do⟩

**quan·ti·ty** \'kwänt-ət-ē\ *n, pl* **quan·ti·ties**
**1** [2]AMOUNT, NUMBER ⟨a *quantity* of information⟩
**2** a large number or amount ⟨a *quantity* of shoes⟩ ⟨*quantities* of money⟩

[1]**quar·an·tine** \'kwȯr-ən-,tēn\ *n*
**1** a halting or forbidding of the moving of people or things out of a certain area to prevent the spread of disease or pests
**2** a period during which a person with a contagious disease is under quarantine
**3** a place (as a hospital) where persons are kept in quarantine

**Word History** Sometimes a ship comes to a port from another place where there is disease or pests.

a b c d e f g h i j k l m n o p q r s t u v w x y z

The ship is often kept apart for a time. No one may go ashore and no goods may be taken off until it is certain that the ship is not carrying the disease or pests. The time for keeping the ship apart was once forty days. This period was called *quarantine*, a word that came from an Italian word. The Italian word came from a French word that meant "a period of forty days."

**²quarantine** *vb* **quar·an·tined**; **quar·an·tin·ing**
to put or hold in quarantine

**¹quar·rel** \'kwȯr-əl\ *n*
**1** a cause of disagreement or complaint
**2** an angry difference of opinion

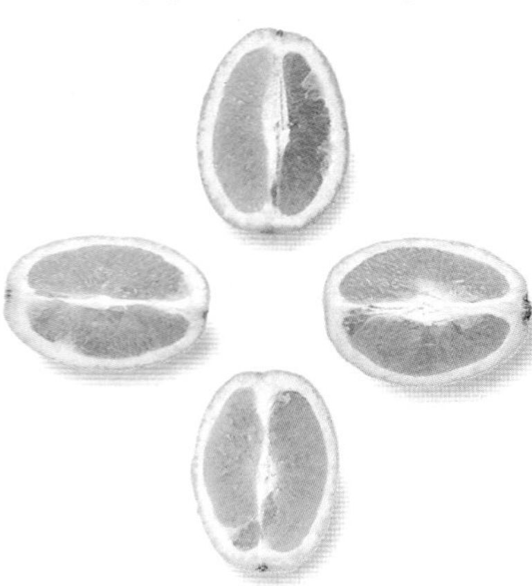

**¹quarter 1:**
an orange divided into quarters

**²quarrel** *vb* **quar·reled** *or* **quar·relled**; **quar·rel·ing** *or* **quar·rel·ling**
**1** to find fault
**2** to argue actively **:** SQUABBLE

**quar·rel·some** \'kwȯr-əl-səm\ *adj*
usually ready to quarrel

**¹quar·ry** \'kwȯr-ē\ *n, pl* **quar·ries**
an animal or bird hunted as game or prey

**Word History** There were hunters long ago, just as there are today. They rewarded their dogs each time they made a kill. The dogs' reward was a part of the slain beast's intestines. The French had a word for this portion fed to the dogs. This French word was taken into English. In time the word for the intestines was used for the hunted beast itself. This early word became our modern English *quarry*.

**²quarry** *n, pl* **quar·ries**
an open pit usually for obtaining building stone, slate, or limestone

**Word History** This word is not related to the word *quarry* that means "game" or "prey." Quarries provide stones for building. Such stones are usually squared. The English word *quarry* comes from a French word meaning "quarry" that came from a word meaning "squared stone." The source of this word was a Latin word that meant "square."

**³quarry** *vb* **quar·ried**; **quar·ry·ing**
**1** to dig or take from or as if from a quarry
**2** to make a quarry in
**quar·ri·er** *n*

**quart** \'kwȯrt\ *n*
a measure of capacity that equals two pints (about .95 liter)

**¹quar·ter** \'kwȯrt-ər\ *n*
**1** ◄ one of four equal parts into which something can be divided
**2** a United States coin worth twenty-five cents
**3** someone or something (as a place, direction, or group) not clearly identified ⟨expects trouble from another *quarter*⟩
**4** a particular division or district of a city
**5 quarters** *pl* a dwelling place ⟨winter *quarters*⟩
**6** MERCY 1 ⟨show no *quarter* to the enemy⟩

**²quarter** *vb*
**1** to divide into four usually equal parts
**2** to provide with lodgings or shelter

**³quarter** *adj*
consisting of or equal to a quarter ⟨give it a *quarter* turn⟩

**quar·ter·deck** \'kwȯrt-ər-,dek\ *n*
the part of the upper deck that is located toward the rear of a ship

**quarter horse** *n*
a stocky muscular saddle horse capable of high speed over short distances

**¹quar·ter·ly** \'kwȯrt-ər-lē\ *adv*
four times a year ⟨interest compounded *quarterly*⟩

**²quarterly** *adj*
coming or happening every three months ⟨a *quarterly* meeting⟩

**³quarterly** *n, pl* **quar·ter·lies**
a magazine published four times a year

**quar·ter·mas·ter** \'kwȯrt-ər-,mas-tər\ *n*
an army officer who provides clothing and supplies for troops

**quar·tet** *also* **quar·tette** \kwȯr-'tet\ *n*
a group or set of four

**quartz** \'kwȯrts\ *n*
▼ a common mineral often found in the form of colorless transparent crystals but sometimes (as in amethysts, agates, and jaspers) brightly colored

**quartz**
While typical quartz rocks are colorless, others may be white, gray, red, purple, pink, yellow, green, brown, or black. Quartz is often used in making jewelry.

**milky quartz**

**smoky quartz**

**rose quartz**

**quay** in Australia

**qua·ver** \'kwā-vər\ *vb*
**1** [1]TREMBLE 1, SHAKE ⟨*quavering* inwardly⟩
**2** to sound in shaky tones ⟨my voice *quavered*⟩

**quay** \'kē, 'kwā\ *n*
▲ a paved bank or a solid artificial landing for loading and unloading ships

**quea·sy** \'kwē-zē\ *adj* **quea·si·er**; **quea·si·est**
**1** somewhat nauseated
**2** full of doubt

**queen** \'kwēn\ *n*
**1** the wife or widow of a king
**2** a woman who rules a kingdom in her own right
**3** a woman of high rank, power, or attractiveness ⟨a society *queen*⟩
**4** ▶ the most powerful piece in the game of chess
**5** a playing card bearing the figure of a queen
**6** a fully developed adult female of social bees, ants, or termites
**queen·ly** *adj*

**queer** \'kwir\ *adj*
oddly unlike the usual or normal ⟨a *queer* smell⟩
**queer·ly** *adv*

**quell** \'kwel\ *vb*
**1** to put down by force ⟨*quell* a riot⟩
**2** [4]QUIET 1, CALM ⟨*quelled* their fears⟩

**quench** \'kwench\ *vb*
**1** to put out (as a fire)
**2** to end by satisfying ⟨*quenched* my thirst⟩

[1]**que·ry** \'kwir-ē, 'kweər-ē\ *n*, *pl* **queries**
**1** [1]QUESTION 1
**2** a question in the mind : DOUBT

[2]**query** *vb* **que·ried**; **que·ry·ing**
**1** to put as a question ⟨*queried* it to their teacher⟩
**2** to ask questions about especially in order to clear up a doubt ⟨*queried* the proceeding⟩
**3** to ask questions of especially to obtain official or expert information ⟨*query* the professor⟩

**queen 4:**
a queen from a modern ornamental chess set

[1]**quest** \'kwest\ *n*
an act or instance of seeking : SEARCH ⟨in *quest* of fame⟩

[2]**quest** *vb*
to search for

[1]**ques·tion** \'kwes-chən\ *n*
**1** something asked ⟨try to make your *questions* short⟩
**2** a topic discussed or argued about ⟨an important *question* of the day⟩
**3** a suggestion to be voted on ⟨put the *question* to the members⟩
**4** an act or instance of asking
**5** OBJECTION 1, DISPUTE ⟨obey without *question*⟩

[2]**question** *vb*
**1** to ask questions of or about
**2** to doubt the correctness of ⟨*question* a decision⟩

**ques·tion·able** \'kwes-chə-nə-bəl\ *adj*
**1** not certain or exact : DOUBTFUL
**2** not believed to be true, sound, or proper ⟨*questionable* motives⟩

**question mark** *n*
a punctuation mark ? used chiefly at the end of a sentence to indicate a direct question

**ques·tion·naire** \,kwes-chə-'naər, -'neər\ *n*
a set of questions to be asked of a number of persons to collect facts about knowledge or opinions

[1]**queue** \'kyü\ *n*
**1** PIGTAIL
**2** a waiting line ⟨a *queue* at a ticket window⟩

**Word History** The English word *queue* comes from a French word that means "tail." A long braid of hair worn at the back of the head looks rather like a tail. A long line of people waiting for something must also have reminded someone of a tail. The French word meaning "tail" came to be used for a pigtail and a waiting line as well. The English word *queue* that comes from this French word does not mean "tail." It does mean "pigtail" or "waiting line."

[2]**queue** *vb* **queued**; **queu·ing** *or* **queue·ing**
to form or line up in a queue ⟨*queuing* up for tickets⟩

**quib·ble** \'kwib-əl\ *vb* **quib·bled**; **quib·bling**
**1** to talk about unimportant things

rather than the main point
**2** to find fault especially over unimportant points
**quib·bler** \'kwib-lər\ *n*

**[1]quick** \'kwik\ *adj*
**1** very swift : SPEEDY ⟨*quick* steps⟩
**2** mentally alert
**3** easily stirred up ⟨*quick* temper⟩
**quick·ly** *adv*
**quick·ness** *n*

**Synonyms** QUICK, PROMPT, and READY mean able to respond right away. QUICK stresses that the response is immediate and often suggests the ability is part of one's nature ⟨always had a *quick* mind⟩. PROMPT suggests that the ability to respond quickly is the product of training and discipline ⟨the store gives *prompt* service⟩. READY suggests ease or smoothness in response ⟨always had a *ready* answer to every question⟩.

**Word History** The word *quick* first meant "alive." Most animals that are alive can move and run, so *quick* came to mean "moving" or "running." From this sense came the sense of *quick* that is most familiar today: "fast." New senses have come from this common sense. *Quick* means "alert," which is "fast in understanding." *Quick* means "sensitive," "reacting fast." *Quick* means "aroused fast or easily."

**[2]quick** *n*
**1** a very tender area of flesh (as under a fingernail)
**2** one's innermost feelings ⟨hurt to the *quick* by the remark⟩

**[3]quick** *adv*
in a quick manner : FAST

**quick·en** \'kwik-ən\ *vb*
**1** REVIVE 1
**2** AROUSE 2 ⟨curiosity *quickened* my interest⟩
**3** to make or become quicker : HASTEN ⟨*quickened* their steps⟩
**4** to begin or show active growth

**quick·sand** \'kwik-,sand\ *n*
a deep mass of loose sand mixed with water into which heavy objects sink

**quick·sil·ver** \'kwik-,sil-vər\ *n*
MERCURY 1

**Word History** The metal mercury has a color like silver. Most metals are solid but this one is not. Mercury moves and flows and acts almost as if it were alive. The word *quick* once meant "alive" or "moving." This is why mercury was given the name *quicksilver*.

**quick–tem·pered** \'kwik-'tem-pərd\ *adj*
easily made angry

**quick–wit·ted** \'kwik-'wit-əd\ *adj*
mentally alert

**[1]qui·et** \'kwī-ət\ *n*
the quality or state of being quiet

**[2]quiet** *adj*
**1** marked by little or no motion or activity : CALM
**2** GENTLE 2, MILD ⟨a *quiet* disposition⟩
**3** not disturbed : PEACEFUL ⟨a *quiet* lunch⟩
**4** free from noise or uproar : STILL ⟨a *quiet* day⟩
**5** not showy (as in color or style)
**6** SECLUDED ⟨a *quiet* nook⟩
**qui·et·ly** *adv*
**qui·et·ness** *n*

**[3]quiet** *adv*
in a quiet manner : QUIETLY

**[4]quiet** *vb*
**1** to cause to be quiet : CALM ⟨*quieted* the crowd⟩
**2** to become quiet ⟨*quieted* down after an exciting day⟩

**qui·etude** \'kwī-ə-,tüd, -,tyüd\ *n*
the state of being quiet : REST

**quill** \'kwil\ *n*
**1** a large stiff feather
**2** the hollow tubelike part of a feather
**3** a spine of a hedgehog or porcupine
**4** ◀ a pen made from a feather



**quill 4**

**[1]quilt:** section from a traditional hand-sewn quilt

**[1]quilt** \'kwilt\ *n*
▲ a bed cover made of two pieces of cloth with a filling of wool, cotton, or down held together by patterned stitching

**[2]quilt** *vb*
to stitch or sew together as in making a quilt

**quince** \'kwins\ *n*
▼ a hard yellow fruit that grows on a shrubby tree related to the apple and is used especially in preserves

**quince**

**qui·nine** \'kwī-,nīn\ *n*
a bitter drug obtained from cinchona bark and used to treat malaria

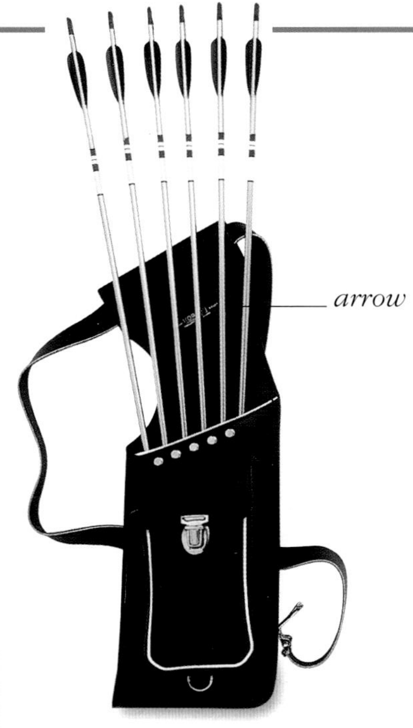


[1]**quiver**

**quin·tet** \kwin-'tet\ *n*
a group or set of five

**quin·tu·plet** \kwin-'təp-lət, -'tüp-\ *n*
**1** a combination of five of a kind
**2** one of five offspring born at one birth

**quirk** \'kwərk\ *n*
a sudden turn, twist, or curve

**quit** \'kwit\ *vb* **quit**; **quit·ting**
to finish doing, using, dealing with, working on, or handling : LEAVE ⟨*quit* a job⟩

**quite** \'kwīt\ *adv*
**1** beyond question or doubt : COMPLETELY ⟨*quite* alone⟩ ⟨*quite* sure⟩
**2** more or less : RATHER ⟨we live *quite* near the school⟩

**quit·ter** \'kwit-ər\ *n*
a person who gives up too easily

[1]**quiv·er** \'kwiv-ər\ *n*
◀ a case for carrying arrows

[2]**quiver** *vb*
to move with a slight trembling motion ⟨leaves *quivering* in the breeze⟩

[3]**quiver** *n*
the act or action of quivering ⟨the *quiver* of a leaf⟩

[1]**quiz** \'kwiz\ *n, pl* **quiz·zes**
a short oral or written test ⟨a *quiz* in history⟩

[2]**quiz** *vb* **quizzed**; **quiz·zing**
to ask a lot of questions of

**quoit** \'kwāt, 'kwȯit\ *n*
a ring (as of rope) tossed at a peg in a game (**quoits**)

**quo·rum** \'kwōr-əm\ *n*
the number of members of a group needed at a meeting in order for business to be legally carried on

**quo·ta** \'kwōt-ə\ *n*
a share assigned to each member of a group ⟨the *quota* of delegates from each state⟩

**quo·ta·tion** \kwō-'tā-shən\ *n*
**1** material (as a passage from a book) that is quoted
**2** the act or process of quoting

**quotation mark** *n*
one of a pair of punctuation marks " " or ' ' used chiefly to indicate the beginning and end of a direct quotation

**quote** \'kwōt\ *vb* **quot·ed**; **quot·ing**
to repeat (someone else's words) exactly ⟨*quote* a favorite poem⟩ ⟨*quote* the president's speech⟩

**Word History** Sometimes passages in books are numbered. The English word *quote* came from a Latin word that meant "to refer to a passage by number." The meaning of the English word is not quite the same. English *quote* means "to repeat the words of a passage exactly." The idea of number has been lost.

**quo·tient** \'kwō-shənt\ *n*
the number obtained by dividing one number by another

# Rr

**The sounds of R:** The letter **R** has only one sound in English. It sounds the same in **rabbit**, **merry**, **February**, **burr**, **bear**, and **radar**. A double **R** sounds the same as a single **R**.

In a few very common words, it has a silent **W** in front of it. Examples are **wrong**, **wrinkle**, and **write**. In a few other words, it is followed by a silent **H**, as in **rhyme**.

**r** \'är\ *n, pl* **r's** *or* **rs** \'ärz\ *often cap*
the eighteenth letter of the English alphabet

**rab·bi** \'rab-ˌī\ *n, pl* **rab·bis**
**1** [1]MASTER 1, TEACHER — used as a term of address for Jewish religious leaders
**2** a professionally trained leader of a Jewish congregation

**rab·bit** \'rab-ət\ *n*
▼ a long-eared short-tailed gnawing mammal that burrows

**rabbit:** a cottontail rabbit

**rab·ble** \'rab-əl\ *n*
**1** a crowd that is noisy and hard to control **:** MOB
**2** a group of people looked down upon as ignorant and hard to handle

**ra·bid** \'rab-əd, 'rā-bəd\ *adj*
**1** very angry **:** FURIOUS
**2** going to extreme lengths (as in interest or opinion)
**3** affected with rabies ⟨a *rabid* dog⟩
**ra·bid·ly** *adv*
**ra·bid·ness** *n*

**ra·bies** \'rā-bēz\ *n*
a deadly disease of the nervous system caused by a virus that is usually passed on through the bite of an infected animal

**rac·coon** \ra-'kün\ *n*
a small North American animal that is mostly gray with a black mask, has a bushy ringed tail, is active mostly at night, and eats small animals, fruits, eggs, and insects

[1]**race** \'rās\ *n*
**1** a strong or rapid current of water
**2** a contest of speed
**3** a contest involving progress toward a goal ⟨the *race* for mayor⟩

[2]**race** *vb* **raced**; **rac·ing**
**1** to take part in a race
**2** to go, move, or drive at top speed
**3** to cause an engine of a motor vehicle in neutral to run fast

[3]**race** *n*
**1** a group of individuals with the same ancestors
**2** a category of humankind that shares distinctive physical traits
**3** a major group of living things ⟨the human *race*⟩

**race·course** \'rā-ˌskōrs\ *n*
a place for racing

**race·horse** \'rās-ˌhȯrs\ *n*
a horse bred or kept for racing

**rac·er** \'rā-sər\ *n*
**1** one that races or is used for racing
**2** any of several long slender active snakes (as a common American blacksnake)

**race·track** \'rā-ˌstrak\ *n*
a usually oval course on which races are run

**ra·cial** \'rā-shəl\ *adj*
of, relating to, or based on race
**ra·cial·ly** *adv*

**rac·ism** \'rā-ˌsiz-əm\ *n*
**1** belief that certain races of people are by birth and nature superior to others
**2** discrimination or hatred based on race

**rac·ist** \'rā-sist\ *adj*
based on or showing racism ⟨a *racist* comment⟩
**racist** *n*

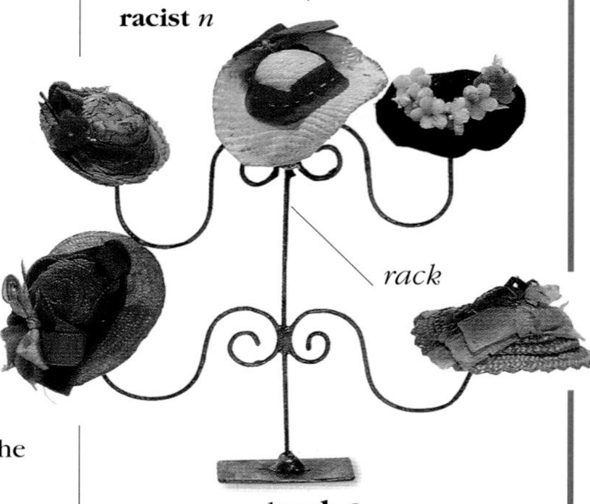


[1]**rack 2:** an early 20th-century hat rack

[1]**rack** \'rak\ *n*
**1** an instrument of torture for stretching the body
**2** ▲ a frame or stand for storing or displaying things ⟨a hat *rack*⟩

[2]**rack** *vb*
**1** to cause to suffer torture, pain, or sorrow
**2** to stretch or strain violently

[1]**rack·et** \'rak-ət\ *n*
a light bat consisting of a handle and a frame with a netting stretched tight across it

[2]**racket** *n*
**1** a loud confused noise
**2** a dishonest scheme for obtaining money (as by cheating or threats)

**radar**
Radio waves transmitted from a radar antenna strike a distant object, such as the airplane shown below, and are reflected back to the source. A computer then calculates the speed and distance of the airplane by the delay in the signal's return.

signal returns to radar antenna

approaching airplane

radio waves sent from radar antenna

radar antenna

**diagram showing how radar tracks an airplane**

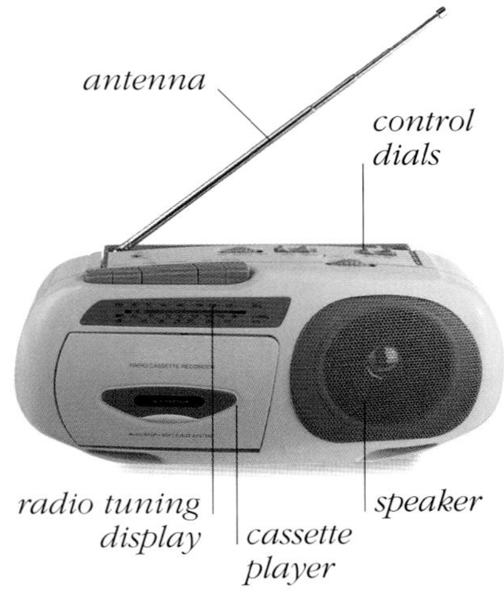


**²radio 2:** a combination radio and cassette player

**rack·e·teer** \,rak-ə-'tir\ *n*
a person who gets money or advantages by using force or threats

**racy** \'rā-sē\ *adj* **rac·i·er**; **rac·i·est**
full of energy or keen enjoyment

**ra·dar** \'rā-,där\ *n*
▲ a radio device for detecting the position of things in the distance and the direction of moving objects (as distant airplanes or ships)

**ra·di·ance** \'rād-ē-əns\ *n*
the quality or state of being radiant

**ra·di·ant** \'rād-ē-ənt\ *adj*
**1** giving out or reflecting rays of light ⟨the *radiant* sun⟩
**2** glowing with love, confidence, or joy ⟨a *radiant* smile⟩
**3** transmitted by radiation
**synonyms** see BRIGHT

**radiant energy** *n*
energy sent out in the form of electromagnetic waves ⟨light and heat are forms of *radiant energy*⟩

**ra·di·ate** \'rād-ē-,āt\ *vb*
**ra·di·at·ed**; **ra·di·at·ing**
**1** to send out rays **:** SHINE
**2** to come forth in the form of rays ⟨light *radiates* from shining bodies⟩
**3** to spread around from or as if from a center ⟨the news *radiated* through the crowd⟩

**ra·di·a·tion** \,rād-ē-'ā-shən\ *n*
**1** the process of radiating and especially of giving off radiant energy in the form of waves or particles
**2** something that is radiated

**ra·di·a·tor** \'rād-ē-,āt-ər\ *n*
a device to heat air (as in a room) or to cool an object (as an automobile engine)

**¹rad·i·cal** \'rad-i-kəl\ *adj*
**1** departing sharply from the usual or ordinary **:** EXTREME
**2** of or relating to radicals in politics
**rad·i·cal·ly** *adv*

**Word History** The English word *radical* which first meant "of a root" comes from a Latin word meaning "root." Since we can speak of the source or origin of something as its root, *radical* came to mean "of the origin." Later, since an extreme change can be said to go to the root of something, *radical* also came to mean "extreme."

**²radical** *n*
a person who favors rapid and sweeping changes especially in laws and methods of government

**radii** *pl of* RADIUS

**¹ra·dio** \'rād-ē-,ō\ *adj*
**1** of or relating to radiant energy
**2** of, relating to, or used in radio

**²radio** *n, pl* **ra·di·os**
**1** the sending or receiving of signals by means of electromagnetic waves without a connecting wire
**2** ▲ a radio receiving set
**3** a radio message
**4** the radio broadcasting industry

**³radio** *vb*
to communicate or send a message to by radio

**ra·dio·ac·tive** \,rād-ē-ō-'ak-tiv\ *adj*
of, caused by, or exhibiting radioactivity

**ra·dio·ac·tiv·i·ty** \,rād-ē-ō-ak-'tiv-ət-ē\ *n*
the giving off of rays of energy or particles by the breaking apart of atoms of certain elements (as uranium)

**radio wave** *n*
an electromagnetic wave used in radio, television, or radar communication

**rad·ish** \'rad-ish\ *n*
▶ the fleshy edible root of a plant related to the mustards

**ra·di·um** \'rād-ē-əm\ *n*
a strongly radioactive element found in very small quantities in various minerals (as pitchblende) and used in the treatment of cancer

**radish**

**ra·di·us** \'rād-ē-əs\ *n, pl* **ra·dii** \-ē-,ī\
**1** the bone on the thumb side of the human forearm or a corresponding bone in lower forms
**2** a straight line extending from the center of a circle to the circumference or from the center of a sphere to the surface
**3** a nearly circular area defined by a radius ⟨within a *radius* of one kilometer from the school⟩

**raf·fle** \'raf-əl\ *n*
the sale of chances for a prize whose winner is the one whose ticket is picked at a drawing

**[1]raft** \'raft\ *n*
a flat structure (as a group of logs fastened together) for support or transportation on water

**[2]raft** *n*
a large amount or number

**raf·ter** \'raf-tər\ *n*
one of the usually sloping timbers that support a roof

**rag** \'rag\ *n*
**1** a waste or worn piece of cloth
**2 rags** *pl* shabby or very worn clothing ⟨dressed in *rags*⟩

**rag·a·muf·fin** \'rag-ə-,məf-ən\ *n*
a poorly clothed and often dirty child

**[1]rage** \'rāj\ *n*
**1** very strong and uncontrolled anger : FURY ⟨flew into a *rage* over the remark⟩
**2** violent action (as of wind or sea)
**3** FAD ⟨the current *rage*⟩
**synonyms** see ANGER

**[3]rail**

**[2]rage** *vb* **raged**; **rag·ing**
**1** to be in a rage
**2** to continue out of control ⟨the fire *raged* for hours⟩

**rag·ged** \'rag-əd\ *adj*
**1** having a rough or uneven edge or outline ⟨*ragged* cliffs⟩
**2** very worn : TATTERED ⟨*ragged* clothes⟩
**3** wearing tattered clothes
**4** done in an uneven way ⟨a *ragged* performance⟩
**rag·ged·ly** *adv*
**rag·ged·ness** *n*

**rag·gedy** \'rag-əd-ē\ *adj*
RAGGED 2, 3

**rag·tag** \'rag-,tag\ *adj*
RAGGED 3

**rag·time** \'rag-,tīm\ *n*
jazz music that has a lively melody and a steady rhythm like a march

**rag·weed** \'rag-,wēd\ *n*
► a common coarse weed with pollen that irritates the eyes and noses of some persons

**ragweed**

**[1]raid** \'rād\ *n*
a sudden attack or invasion

**[2]raid** *vb*
to make a raid on
**raid·er** *n*

**[1]rail** \'rāl\ *n*
**1** a bar extending from one support to another and serving as a guard or barrier
**2** a bar of steel forming a track for wheeled vehicles
**3** RAILROAD ⟨travel by *rail*⟩

**[2]rail** *vb*
to provide with a railing

**[3]rail** *n*
◄ any of a family of wading birds related to the cranes and hunted as game birds

**[4]rail** *vb*
to scold or complain in harsh or bitter language

**rail·ing** \'rā-ling\ *n*
**1** a barrier (as a fence) made up of rails and their supports
**2** material for making rails

**rail·lery** \'rā-lə-rē\ *n, pl* **rail·ler·ies**
an act or instance of making fun of someone in a good-natured way

**[1]rail·road** \'rāl-,rōd\ *n*
**1** a permanent road that has parallel steel rails that make a track for cars
**2** a railroad together with the lands, buildings, locomotives, cars, and other equipment that belong to it

**[2]railroad** *vb*
to work on a railroad

**rail·way** \'rāl-,wā\ *n*
[1]RAILROAD 1

**rai·ment** \'rā-mənt\ *n*
CLOTHING 1

**[1]rain** \'rān\ *n*
**1** water falling in drops from the clouds
**2** a fall of rain
**3** rainy weather
**4** a heavy fall of objects

**[2]rain** *vb*
**1** to fall as water in drops from the clouds
**2** to send down rain
**3** to fall like rain ⟨ashes *rained* from the volcano⟩
**4** to give in large amounts ⟨*rain* advice on a friend⟩
**rain cats and dogs** to rain very hard

**rain·bow** \'rān-,bō\ *n*
▼ an arc of colors that appears in the sky opposite the sun and is caused by the sun shining through rain, mist, or spray

**rainbow:** a double rainbow

**rain·coat** \'rān-ˌkōt\ *n*
a coat of waterproof or water-resistant material

**rain·drop** \'rān-ˌdräp\ *n*
a drop of rain

**rain·fall** \'rān-ˌfȯl\ *n*
**1** [1]RAIN 2
**2** amount of precipitation ⟨annual *rainfall* of eighty centimeters⟩

**rain forest** *n*
▼ a woodland with a high annual rainfall and very tall trees and that is often found in tropical regions

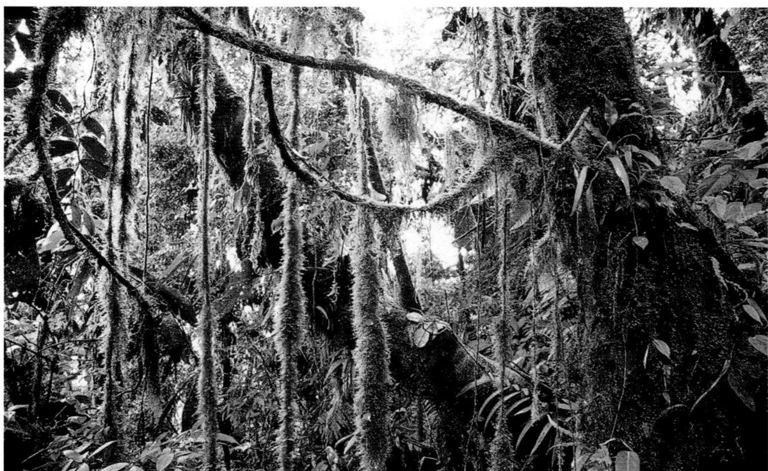

**rain forest:** a section of rain forest in South America

**rain·proof** \'rān-'prüf\ *adj*
not letting in rain

**rain·storm** \'rān-ˌstȯrm\ *n*
a storm of or with rain

**rain·wa·ter** \'rān-ˌwȯt-ər, -ˌwät-\ *n*
water falling or fallen as rain

**rainy** \'rā-nē\ *adj* **rain·i·er**; **rain·i·est**
having much rain ⟨a *rainy* season⟩

[1]**raise** \'rāz\ *vb* **raised**; **rais·ing**
**1** to cause to rise : LIFT ⟨*raise* a window⟩
**2** to give life to : AROUSE ⟨enough noise to *raise* the dead⟩
**3** to set upright by lifting or building ⟨*raise* a monument⟩
**4** PROMOTE 1, ELEVATE ⟨was *raised* to captain⟩
**5** [2]END
**6** COLLECT 2 ⟨*raise* money for a party⟩
**7** to look after the growth and development of : GROW ⟨*raise* hogs for market⟩
**8** to bring up a child : REAR
**9** to give rise to : PROVOKE ⟨*raise* a laugh⟩
**10** to bring to notice ⟨*raise* an objection⟩
**11** [1]INCREASE ⟨*raise* the rent⟩
**12** to make light and airy ⟨*raise* dough⟩
**13** to cause to form on the skin ⟨*raise* a blister⟩ **synonyms** see LIFT
**rais·er** *n*

[2]**raise** *n*
an increase in amount (as of pay)

**rai·sin** \'rāz-n\ *n*
a sweet grape dried for food

**ra·ja** *or* **ra·jah** \'räj-ə\ *n*
an Indian prince

[1]**rake** \'rāk\ *n*
a garden tool with a long handle and a bar with teeth or prongs at the end

[2]**rake** *vb* **raked**; **rak·ing**
**1** to gather, loosen, or smooth with a rake ⟨*rake* leaves⟩
**2** to search through : RANSACK
**3** to sweep the length of with gunfire

[3]**rake** *n*
a person with bad morals and conduct

[1]**ral·ly** \'ral-ē\ *vb* **ral·lied**; **ral·ly·ing**
**1** to bring or come together for a common purpose
**2** to bring back to order
**3** to rouse from low spirits or weakness ⟨the patient *rallied*⟩
**4** [1]REBOUND 2

[2]**rally** *n, pl* **rallies**
**1** the act of rallying
**2** a big meeting held to arouse enthusiasm

[1]**ram** \'ram\ *n*
**1** ▼ a male sheep
**2** BATTERING RAM

*horn*

[1]**ram 1:** a bighorn ram

[2]**ram** *vb* **rammed**; **ram·ming**
**1** to strike or strike against with violence
**2** to force in, down, or together by driving or pressing ⟨*ram* clothes into a suitcase⟩
**3** [2]FORCE 2 ⟨*ram* a bill through congress⟩

**RAM** \'ram\ *n*
RANDOM-ACCESS MEMORY

**Ram·a·dan** \'räm-ə-ˌdän, ˌräm-ə-'dän\ *n*
the ninth month of the Islamic calendar observed as sacred with fasting practiced daily from dawn to sunset

[1]**ram·ble** \'ram-bəl\ *vb* **ram·bled**; **ram·bling**
**1** to go aimlessly from place to place : WANDER ⟨spent a year *rambling* around the country⟩
**2** to talk or write without a clear purpose or point
**3** to grow or extend irregularly ⟨a *rambling* vine⟩ **synonyms** see WANDER

[2]**ramble** *n*
a long stroll with no particular destination

**ram·bler** \'ram-blər\ *n*
a hardy climbing rose with large clusters of small flowers

**ram·bunc·tious** \ram-'bəngk-shəs\ *adj*
UNRULY
**ram·bunc·tious·ly** *adv*
**ram·bunc·tious·ness** *n*

A B C D E F G H I J K L M N O P Q R S T U V W X Y Z

**ram·i·fi·ca·tion** \ˌram-ə-fə-ˈkā-shən\ *n*
**1** a branching out
**2** one thing that comes from another like a branch ⟨study the *ramifications* of a problem⟩

**ram·i·fy** \ˈram-ə-ˌfī\ *vb* **ram·i·fied**; **ram·i·fy·ing**
to spread out or split up into branches or divisions

**ramp** \ˈramp\ *n*
a sloping passage or roadway connecting different levels

**ram·page** \ˈram-ˌpāj\ *n*
a course of violent or reckless action or behavior

**ram·pant** \ˈram-pənt\ *adj*
not checked in growth or spread ⟨fear was *rampant* in the town⟩
**ram·pant·ly** *adv*

**ram·part** \ˈram-ˌpärt\ *n*
a broad bank or wall raised as a protective barrier

**ram·rod** \ˈram-ˌräd\ *n*
a rod for ramming the charge down the barrel in a firearm that is loaded through the muzzle

**ram·shack·le** \ˈram-ˌshak-əl\ *adj*
ready to fall down ⟨a *ramshackle* barn⟩

**ran** *past of* RUN

**¹ranch** \ˈranch\ *n*
**1** a place for the raising of livestock (as cattle) on range
**2** a farm devoted to a special crop ⟨a fruit *ranch*⟩

**²ranch** *vb*
to live or work on a ranch
**ranch·er** *n*

**ran·cid** \ˈran-səd\ *adj*
having the strong disagreeable smell or taste of stale oil or fat ⟨*rancid* butter⟩
**ran·cid·ness** *n*

**ran·cor** \ˈrang-kər\ *n*
deep hatred

**ran·cor·ous** \ˈrang-kə-rəs\ *adj*
showing rancor ⟨a *rancorous* answer⟩
**ran·cor·ous·ly** *adv*

**ran·dom** \ˈran-dəm\ *adj*
lacking a clear plan, purpose, or pattern ⟨a *random* selection of poems⟩
**ran·dom·ly** *adv*
**ran·dom·ness** *n*

**ran·dom–access** \ˌran-dəm-ˈak-ˌses\ *adj*
permitting access to stored data in any order the user desires

**random–access memory** *n*
a computer memory that provides the main storage available to the user for programs and data

**rang** *past of* RING

**¹range** \ˈrānj\ *n*
**1** a series of things in a line ⟨a *range* of mountains⟩
**2** ▼ a cooking stove
**3** open land over which livestock may roam and feed
**4** the distance a gun will shoot
**5** a place where shooting is practiced ⟨a rifle *range*⟩
**6** the distance or amount included or gone over **:** SCOPE ⟨the *range* of one's knowledge⟩
**7** a variety of choices within a scale ⟨new cars with a wide *range* of prices⟩

**¹range 2:** a large range with two ovens

**²range** *vb* **ranged**; **rang·ing**
**1** to set in a row or in proper order
**2** to set in place among others of the same kind
**3** to roam over or through
**4** to come within an upper and a lower limit ⟨prices *range* from three to ten dollars⟩

**rang·er** \ˈrān-jər\ *n*
**1** FOREST RANGER
**2** a member of a body of troops who range over a region
**3** a soldier specially trained in close-range fighting and in raiding tactics

**rangy** \ˈrān-jē\ *adj* **rang·i·er**; **rang·i·est**
tall and slender in body build
**rang·i·ness** *n*

**¹rank** \ˈrangk\ *adj*
**1** strong and active in growth ⟨*rank* weeds⟩
**2** ¹EXTREME 1 ⟨a *rank* beginner⟩
**3** having an unpleasant smell ⟨the room was *rank* with cigarette smoke⟩
**rank·ly** *adv*
**rank·ness** *n*

**²rank** *n*
**1** ³ROW 1, SERIES ⟨*ranks* of houses⟩
**2** a line of soldiers standing side by side
**3 ranks** *pl* the body of enlisted persons in an army ⟨rose from the *ranks*⟩
**4** position within a group ⟨a poet of the first *rank*⟩
**5** high social position
**6** official grade or position ⟨the *rank* of major⟩

**³rank** *vb*
**1** to arrange in lines or in a formation
**2** to arrange in a classification
**3** to take or have a certain position in a group ⟨*ranks* near the top of the class⟩

**ran·kle** \ˈrang-kəl\ *vb* **ran·kled**; **ran·kling**
to cause anger, irritation, or bitterness

**Word History** The words *rankle* and *dragon* are related. *Dragon* came from a Latin word that meant "snake" or "dragon." Certain sores must have looked to people like little snakes. A Latin word that meant "little snake" was used to mean "inflamed sore." This word came from the Latin word that meant "snake" or "dragon." The English word *rankle* came from the Latin word that first meant "little snake" or "inflamed sore." *Rankle* was first used to refer to sores. It meant "to become inflamed." Later it came to be used more often of hurt or bitter feelings.

**ran·sack** \ˈran-ˌsak\ *vb*
**1** to search thoroughly
**2** to search through in order to rob ⟨a burglar *ransacked* the house⟩

**[1]ran·som** \'ran-səm\ *n*
**1** something paid or demanded for the freedom of a captured person
**2** the act of ransoming

**[2]ransom** *vb*
to free from captivity or punishment by paying a price
**ran·som·er** *n*

**rant** \'rant\ *vb*
to talk loudly and wildly
**rant·er** *n*

**[1]rap** \'rap\ *n*
a sharp blow or knock

**[2]rap** *vb* **rapped**; **rap·ping**
to give a quick sharp blow : [1]KNOCK 1

**[3]rap** *vb* **rapped**; **rap·ping**
**1** to talk freely and informally
**2** to perform rap music

**[4]rap** *n*
**1** an informal talk : CHAT
**2** a rhythmic chanting often in unison of rhymed verses to a musical accompaniment

**ra·pa·cious** \rə-'pā-shəs\ *adj*
**1** very greedy
**2** PREDATORY
**ra·pa·cious·ly** *adv*
**ra·pa·cious·ness** *n*

**[1]rape** \'rāp\ *n*
▶ a plant related to the mustards that is grown for animals to graze on and for its seeds used as birdseed and as a source of oil

**[1]rape**

**[2]rape** *vb* **raped**; **rap·ing**
to have sexual intercourse with by force

**[3]rape** *n*
an act of raping

**rap·id** \'rap-əd\ *adj*
very fast **synonyms** see FAST
**rap·id·ly** *adv*

**ra·pid·i·ty** \rə-'pid-ət-ē\ *n*
the quality or state of being rapid

**rap·ids** \'rap-ədz\ *n pl*
▶ a part of a river where the current flows very fast usually over rocks

**ra·pi·er** \'rā-pē-ər\ *n*
a straight sword with a narrow blade having two sharp edges

**rap·port** \ra-'pōr\
friendly relationship : ACCORD

**rapt** \'rapt\ *adj*
showing complete delight or interest ⟨were listening with *rapt* attention⟩

**rap·ture** \'rap-chər\ *n*
a strong feeling of joy, delight, or love

**[1]rare** \'raər, 'reər\ *adj* **rar·er**; **rar·est**
**1** not thick or compact : THIN ⟨the atmosphere is *rare* at high altitudes⟩
**2** very fine : EXCELLENT ⟨a *rare* June day⟩
**3** very uncommon ⟨collect *rare* coins⟩

---

**Synonyms** RARE, SCARCE, and UNCOMMON mean being in short supply. RARE usually applies to an object or quality of which only a few examples are to be found and which is therefore especially appreciated ⟨a *rare* gem⟩ ⟨*rare* beauty⟩. SCARCE applies to something that for a while is in too short supply to meet the demand for it ⟨food was *scarce* that winter⟩. UNCOMMON can be used of anything which is not often found, but usually there is no suggestion that more would be desirable or needed ⟨identical twins are *uncommon*⟩.

---

**[2]rare** *adj* **rar·er**; **rar·est**
cooked so that the inside is still red ⟨*rare* roast beef⟩

**rar·e·fy** \'rar-ə-,fī, 'rer-\ *vb* **rar·e·fied**; **rar·e·fy·ing**
to make or become less dense or solid

**rare·ly** \'raər-lē, 'reər-\ *adv*
not often : SELDOM

**rar·i·ty** \'rar-ət-ē, 'rer-\ *n, pl* **rar·i·ties**
**1** the quality, state, or fact of being rare
**2** something that is uncommon

**ras·cal** \'ras-kəl\ *n*
**1** a mean or dishonest person
**2** a mischievous person

**[1]rash** \'rash\ *adj*
too hasty in decision, action, or speech
**rash·ly** *adv*
**rash·ness** *n*

**[2]rash** *n*
a breaking out of the skin with red spots (as in measles)

**[1]rasp** \'rasp\ *vb*
**1** to rub with or as if with a rough file ⟨*rasp* off the rough edges⟩
**2** IRRITATE 1
**3** to make a harsh sound ⟨a *rasping* voice⟩

**[2]rasp** *n*
**1** a coarse file with cutting points instead of lines
**2** a rasping sound or sensation

**rasp·ber·ry** \'raz-,ber-ē\ *n, pl* **rasp·ber·ries**
a sweet edible red, black, or purple berry

**rapids** on a river

**[1]rat** \'rat\ *n*
**1** ▶ a gnawing animal with brown, black, white, or grayish fur that looks like but is larger than the mouse
**2** a person who betrays friends

[1]rat 1

**[2]rat** *vb* **rat·ted**; **rat·ting**
**1** to betray one's friends
**2** to hunt or catch rats

**[1]rate** \'rāt\ *n*
**1** a price or charge set according to a scale or standard ⟨hotel *rates*⟩
**2** amount of something measured in units of something else ⟨walk at a *rate* of four miles per hour⟩
**at any rate** in any case

**[2]rate** *vb* **rat·ed**; **rat·ing**
**1** CONSIDER 3, REGARD ⟨you are *rated* an expert⟩
**2** to have a rating **:** RANK ⟨our school *rates* high in math⟩
**3** to have a right to **:** DESERVE ⟨*rates* a promotion⟩

**rath·er** \'rath-ər\ *adv*
**1** more willingly ⟨would *rather* stay home⟩
**2** more correctly or truly ⟨ten minutes away, or *rather* nine and a half⟩
**3** INSTEAD ⟨not for better but *rather* for worse⟩
**4** [2]SOMEWHAT ⟨a *rather* cold day⟩

rattle

**[2]rattle 2:** a baby with a rattle

**rat·i·fi·ca·tion** \,rat-ə-fə-'kā-shən\ *n*
the act or process of ratifying

**rat·i·fy** \'rat-ə-fī\ *vb* **rat·i·fied**; **rat·i·fy·ing**
to give legal approval to (as by a vote) ⟨*ratify* the treaty⟩

**rat·ing** \'rāt-ing\ *n*
a position within a grading system ⟨credit *rating*⟩

**ra·tio** \'rā-shō, -shē-,ō\ *n, pl* **ra·tios**
the relationship in number or quantity between two or more things ⟨the *ratio* of births to deaths⟩

**[1]ra·tion** \'rash-ən, 'rā-shən\ *n*
**1** a food allowance for one day
**2 rations** *pl* [1]PROVISION 3
**3** the amount one is allowed by authority ⟨gas *ration*⟩

**[2]ration** *vb*
**1** to control the amount one can use ⟨the government *rationed* gas⟩
**2** to use sparingly ⟨a diet means *rationing* your food⟩

**ra·tio·nal** \'rash-ən-l\ *adj*
**1** having the ability to reason ⟨humans are *rational* creatures⟩
**2** relating to, based on, or showing reason ⟨*rational* thinking⟩
**ra·tio·nal·ly** *adv*

**ra·tio·nale** \,rash-ə-'nal\ *n*
a basic explanation or reason for something

**ra·tio·nal·ize** \'rash-ən-l-,īz\ *vb* **ra·tio·nal·ized**; **ra·tio·nal·iz·ing**
to find believable but untrue reasons for (one's conduct)

**rat·ter** \'rat-ər\ *n*
a dog or cat that catches rats

**[1]rat·tle** \'rat-l\ *vb* **rat·tled**; **rat·tling**
**1** to make or cause to make a rapid series of short sharp sounds
**2** to move with a clatter ⟨the wagon *rattled* down the road⟩
**3** to say or do in a brisk lively way ⟨*rattle* off the answers⟩
**4** to disturb the calmness of **:** UPSET ⟨*rattle* the speaker⟩

**[2]rattle** *n*
**1** a series of short sharp sounds
**2** ◀ a device (as a toy) for making a rattling sound
**3** a rattling organ at the end of a rattlesnake's tail

**rat·tler** \'rat-lər\ *n*
RATTLESNAKE

**rat·tle·snake** \'rat-l-,snāk\ *n*
▶ a poisonous American snake with a rattle at the end of its tail

**rattlesnake**

**rat·tle·trap** \'rat-l-,trap\ *n*
something (as an old car) rickety and full of rattles

**rau·cous** \'rȯ-kəs\ *adj*
**1** being harsh and unpleasant ⟨a *raucous* voice⟩
**2** behaving in a rough and noisy way ⟨a *raucous* crowd⟩
**rau·cous·ly** *adv*
**rau·cous·ness** *n*

**[1]rav·age** \'rav-ij\ *n*
violently destructive action or effect ⟨repair the *ravages* of war⟩

**[2]ravage** *vb* **rav·aged**; **rav·ag·ing**
to attack or act upon with great violence ⟨a forest *ravaged* by fire⟩
**rav·ag·er** *n*

**rave** \'rāv\ *vb* **raved**; **rav·ing**
**1** to talk wildly or as if crazy
**2** to talk with great enthusiasm ⟨*raved* about the new play⟩

**rav·el** \'rav-əl\ *vb* **rav·eled** *or* **rav·elled**; **rav·el·ing** *or* **rav·el·ling**
UNRAVEL 1 ⟨*ravel* out a sweater and use the wool again⟩

**[1]ra·ven** \'rā-vən\ *n*
a large shiny black bird like a crow that is found in northern regions

**[2]raven** *adj*
shiny and black like a raven's feathers

**rav·en·ous** \'rav-ə-nəs\ *adj*
very hungry
**rav·en·ous·ly** *adv*

**ra·vine** \rə-'vēn\ *n*
a small narrow valley with steep sides that is larger than a gully and smaller than a canyon

**rav·ish** \'rav-ish\ *vb*
**1** to seize and take away by force
**2** to overcome with a feeling and especially one of joy or delight

**raw** \'ró\ *adj*
**1** not cooked
**2** being in or nearly in the natural state ⟨*raw* materials⟩
**3** lacking a normal or usual finish ⟨*raw* edge of a seam⟩
**4** having the skin rubbed off
**5** not trained or experienced ⟨*raw* recruits⟩
**6** unpleasantly damp or cold ⟨a *raw* day⟩
**raw·ly** *adv*
**raw·ness** *n*

**raw·hide** \'ró-,hīd\ *n*
**1** a whip of untanned hide
**2** untanned cattle skin

**[1]ray** \'rā\ *n*
▼ a flat broad fish related to the sharks that has its eyes on the top of its head

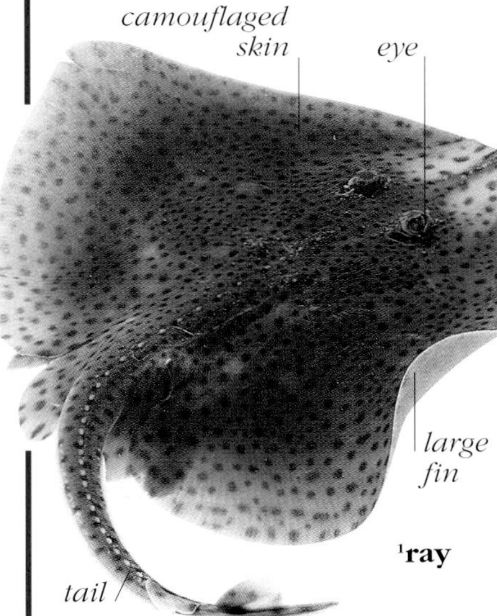


**[1]ray**

**[2]ray** *n*
**1** one of the lines of light that appear to be given off by a bright object ⟨*rays* of sunlight⟩
**2** a thin beam of radiant energy (as light)
**3** light cast in rays
**4** any of a group of lines that spread out from the same center
**5** a straight line extending from a point in one direction only
**6** a plant or animal structure like a ray
**7** a tiny bit : PARTICLE ⟨a *ray* of hope⟩

**ray·on** \'rā-,än\ *n*
a cloth made from fibers produced chemically from cellulose

**raze** \'rāz\ *vb* **razed**; **raz·ing**
to destroy completely by knocking down or breaking to pieces
: DEMOLISH

**ra·zor** \'rā-zər\ *n*
▶ a sharp cutting instrument used to shave off hair



**razor:** a disposable razor

**razz** \'raz\ *vb*
to make fun of : TEASE

**re** \'rā\ *n*
the second note of the musical scale

**re-** *prefix*
**1** again ⟨*re*fill⟩
**2** back : backward ⟨*re*call⟩

**[1]reach** \'rēch\ *vb*
**1** to stretch out
: EXTEND
**2** to touch or move to touch or take by sticking out a part of the body (as the hand) or something held in the hand
**3** to extend or stretch to ⟨their land *reaches* the river⟩
**4** to arrive at : COME ⟨*reached* home late⟩
**5** to communicate with ⟨tried to *reach* them on the phone⟩

**Synonyms** REACH, GAIN, and ACHIEVE mean to arrive at a point or end by work or effort. REACH may apply to anything arrived at by any amount of effort ⟨they *reached* the city after many days⟩ ⟨we have *reached* our goal of a million dollars⟩. GAIN suggests a struggle to arrive at a goal ⟨the slaves *gained* their freedom⟩. ACHIEVE suggests that skill or courage is involved ⟨*achieved* the confidence of the people⟩.

**[2]reach** *n*
**1** an unbroken stretch (as of a river)
**2** the act of reaching especially to take hold of something
**3** ability to stretch (as an arm) so as to touch something ⟨a person with a long *reach*⟩

**re·act** \rē-'akt\ *vb*
**1** to act or behave in response (as to stimulation or an influence) ⟨*reacted* violently to this suggestion⟩
**2** to oppose a force or influence — usually used with *against* ⟨*react* against unfair treatment⟩
**3** to go through a chemical reaction

**re·ac·tion** \rē-'ak-shən\ *n*
**1** an instance of reacting ⟨our *reaction* to the news⟩
**2** a response (as of body or mind) to a stimulus (as a treatment, situation, or stress) ⟨studied the patient's *reaction* to the drug⟩
**3** a chemical change that is brought about by the action of one substance on another and results in a new substance being formed

**re·ac·tion·ary** \rē-'ak-shə-,ner-ē\ *adj*
of, relating to, or favoring old-fashioned political or social ideas

**re·ac·tor** \rē-'ak-tər\ *n*
**1** one that reacts
**2** a device using atomic energy to produce heat

**read** \'rēd\ *vb* **read** \'red\; **read·ing** \'rēd-ing\
**1** to understand language through written symbols for speech sounds
**2** to speak aloud written or printed words ⟨*read* a poem to the class⟩
**3** to learn from what one has seen in writing or printing ⟨*read* about the fire⟩
**4** to discover or figure out the meaning of ⟨*read* palms⟩
**5** to give meaning to ⟨*read* guilt in the child's manner⟩
**6** to show by letters or numbers ⟨the thermometer *reads* zero⟩
**read between the lines** to understand more than is directly stated

**read·able** \'rēd-ə-bəl\ *adj*
able to be read easily

**read·er** \'rēd-ər\ *n*
**1** one that reads
**2** a book for learning or practicing reading

**read·ing** \'rēd-ing\ *n*
**1** something read or for reading
**2** the form in which something is written : VERSION
**3** the number or fact shown on an instrument ⟨take a *reading* from the thermometer⟩

**read–only memory** \'rēd-'ōn-lē-\ *n*
a usually small computer memory that contains special-purpose information (as a program) which cannot be changed

A B C D E F G H I J K L M N O P Q R S T U V W X Y Z

**read•out** \'rēd-au̇t\ *n*
**1** information from an automatic device (as a computer) that is recorded (as on a disk) or presented in a form that can be seen
**2** an electronic device that presents information in a form that can be seen ⟨a calculator's *readout*⟩

**[1]ready** \'red-ē\ *adj* **read•i•er**; **read•i•est**
**1** prepared for use or action ⟨dinner is *ready*⟩
**2** likely to do something ⟨*ready* to cry⟩
**3** WILLING 1 ⟨*ready* to help⟩
**4** showing ease and promptness
**5** available right away **:** HANDY ⟨*ready* money⟩ **synonyms** see QUICK
**read•i•ly** \'red-l-ē\ *adv*
**read•i•ness** \'red-ē-nəs\ *n*

**[2]ready** *vb* **read•ied**; **ready•ing**
to make ready **:** PREPARE

**ready–made** \,red-ē-'mād\ *adj*
made beforehand in large numbers ⟨*ready-made* clothes⟩

**re•al** \'rē-əl, 'rēl\ *adj*
**1** of, relating to, or made up of land and buildings ⟨*real* property⟩
**2** not artificial **:** GENUINE ⟨*real* leather⟩
**3** not imaginary **:** ACTUAL ⟨*real* life⟩
**re•al•ness** *n*

---

**Synonyms** REAL, ACTUAL, and TRUE mean agreeing with known facts. REAL suggests that a thing is what it appears to be ⟨this is a *real* diamond⟩. ACTUAL stresses that someone or something does or did occur or exist ⟨is Santa Claus an *actual* person?⟩. TRUE may apply to something that is real or actual ⟨a *true* story⟩ or to something that agrees with a standard ⟨a whale is not a *true* fish⟩.

---

**real estate** *n*
property consisting of buildings and land

**re•al•ism** \'rē-ə-,liz-əm\ *n*
willingness to face facts or to give in to what is necessary

**re•al•is•tic** \,rē-ə-'lis-tik\ *adj*
**1** true to life or nature ⟨a *realistic* painting⟩
**2** ready to see things as they really are and to deal with them sensibly
**re•al•is•ti•cal•ly** \-ti-kə-lē\ *adv*

**re•al•i•ty** \rē-'al-ət-ē\ *n*, *pl* **re•al•i•ties**
**1** actual existence
**2** someone or something real or actual ⟨the *realities* of life⟩

**re•al•iza•tion** \,rē-ə-lə-'zā-shən\ *n*
the action of realizing **:** the state of being realized

**re•al•ize** \'rē-ə-,līz\ *vb* **re•al•ized**; **re•al•iz•ing**
**1** to bring into being **:** ACCOMPLISH ⟨*realize* a lifelong ambition⟩
**2** to get as a result of effort **:** GAIN ⟨*realize* a large profit⟩
**3** to be aware of **:** UNDERSTAND ⟨*realized* their danger⟩

**re•al•ly** \'rē-ə-lē, 'rē-lē\ *adv*
**1** in fact ⟨didn't *really* mean it⟩
**2** without question ⟨a *really* fine day⟩

**realm** \'relm\ *n*
**1** KINGDOM 1
**2** field of activity or influence ⟨the *realm* of fancy⟩

**real time** *n*
the actual time during which something takes place ⟨a conversation in an on-line chat room happens in *real time*⟩
**real–time** *adj*

**re•al•ty** \'rē-əl-tē\ *n*
REAL ESTATE

**[1]ream** \'rēm\ *n*
**1** a quantity of paper that may equal 480, 500, or 516 sheets
**2 reams** *pl* a great amount ⟨*reams* of notes⟩

**[2]ream** *vb*
**1** to shape or make larger with a reamer
**2** to clean or clear with a reamer

**ream•er** \'rē-mər\ *n*
▶ a tool with cutting edges for shaping or enlarging a hole

**reap** \'rēp\ *vb*
**1** to cut (as grain) or clear (as a field) with a sickle, scythe, or machine
**2** HARVEST ⟨*reap* a crop⟩

**reap•er** \'rē-pər\ *n*
**1** a worker who harvests crops
**2** a machine for reaping grain

*cutting edge*

**reamer**

**re•ap•pear** \,rē-ə-'pir\ *vb*
to appear again

**[1]rear** \'rir\ *vb*
**1** to put up by building **:** CONSTRUCT
**2** to raise or set on end
**3** to take care of the breeding and raising of ⟨*rear* cattle⟩
**4** BRING UP ⟨*rear* children⟩
**5** to rise high
**6** ▼ to rise up on the hind legs ⟨the horse *reared* in fright⟩

**[1]rear 6:** a horse rearing

**[2]rear** *n*
**1** the part (as of an army) or area farthest from the enemy
**2** the space or position at the back

**[3]rear** *adj*
being at the back

**rear admiral** *n*
a commissioned officer in the Navy or Coast Guard ranking above a captain

**re•ar•range** \,rē-ə-'rānj\ *vb* **re•ar•ranged**; **re•ar•rang•ing**
to arrange again usually in a different way

**[1]rea•son** \'rēz-n\ *n*
**1** a statement given to explain a belief or an act ⟨gave a *reason* for my absence⟩
**2** a good basis ⟨have *reasons* for what I did⟩
**3** [1]CAUSE 1 ⟨wanted to know the *reason* for rain⟩

4 the power to think
5 a sound mind

[2]**reason** *vb*
1 to talk with another so as to influence his or her actions or opinions
2 to use the power of reason

**rea·son·able** \'rēz-nə-bəl, -n-ə-bəl\ *adj*
1 not beyond what is usual or expected : MODERATE
2 [1]CHEAP 1, INEXPENSIVE
3 able to reason
**rea·son·able·ness** *n*
**rea·son·ably** \-blē\ *adv*

**re·as·sure** \,rē-ə-'shu̇r\ *vb* **re·as·sured**; **re·as·sur·ing**
1 to assure again
2 to give fresh confidence to : free from fear

[1]**re·bate** \'rē-,bāt\ *vb* **re·bat·ed**; **re·bat·ing**
to make a rebate to or give as a rebate ⟨*rebate* the interest on the bill⟩

[2]**rebate** *n*
a returning of part of a payment or of an amount owed

[1]**reb·el** \'reb-əl\ *adj*
1 being or fighting against one's government or ruler
2 not obeying

[2]**rebel** *n*
a person who refuses to give in to authority

[3]**re·bel** \ri-'bel\ *vb* **re·belled**; **re·bel·ling**
1 to be or fight against authority and especially the authority of one's government
2 to feel or show anger or strong dislike

**re·bel·lion** \ri-'bel-yən\ *n*
1 open opposition to authority ⟨the strict rules caused *rebellion* in the class⟩
2 an open fight against one's government

**re·bel·lious** \ri-'bel-yəs\ *adj*
1 taking part in rebellion ⟨*rebellious* troops⟩
2 tending to fight against or disobey authority
**re·bel·lious·ly** *adv*
**re·bel·lious·ness** *n*

**re·birth** \'rē-'bərth\ *n*
1 a new or second birth
2 a return to importance ⟨a *rebirth* of democratic ideas⟩

**re·born** \'rē-'bȯrn\ *adj*
born again

[1]**re·bound** \'rē-'bau̇nd, ri-\ *vb*
1 to spring back on hitting something
2 to get over a disappointment

[2]**re·bound** \'rē-,bau̇nd\ *n*
1 the action of rebounding : RECOIL
2 an immediate reaction to a disappointment

[1]**re·buff** \ri-'bəf\ *vb*
to refuse or criticize sharply ⟨the suggestion was *rebuffed*⟩

[2]**rebuff** *n*
a refusal to meet an advance or offer

**re·build** \'rē-'bild\ *vb* **re·built** \-'bilt\; **re·build·ing**
1 to make many or important repairs to or changes in ⟨*rebuild* an old house⟩
2 to build again ⟨planned to *rebuild* after the fire⟩

[1]**re·buke** \ri-'byük\ *vb* **re·buked**; **re·buk·ing**
to criticize severely

[2]**rebuke** *n*
an expression of strong disapproval

**re·bus** \'rē-bəs\ *n*
a riddle or puzzle made up of letters, pictures, and symbols whose names sound like the syllables and words of a phrase or sentence ⟨I C U is a *rebus*⟩

**re·but** \ri-'bət\ *vb* **re·but·ted**; **re·but·ting**
to prove to be wrong especially by argument or by proof that the opposite is right

[1]**re·call** \ri-'kȯl\ *vb*
1 to ask or order to come back
2 to bring back to mind ⟨*recall* an address⟩
3 CANCEL 2, REVOKE ⟨*recall* an order⟩

[2]**re·call** \ri-'kȯl, 'rē-,kȯl\ *n*
1 a command to return
2 remembrance of what has been learned or experienced

**re·cap·ture** \'rē-'kap-chər\ *vb* **re·cap·tured**; **re·cap·tur·ing**
1 to capture again
2 to experience again ⟨*recapture* one's youth⟩

**re·cede** \ri-'sēd\ *vb* **re·ced·ed**; **re·ced·ing**
1 to move back or away
2 to slant backward

[1]**re·ceipt** \ri-'sēt\ *n*
1 RECIPE
2 the act of receiving
3 **receipts** *pl* something received ⟨the *receipts* from the sale⟩
4 a written statement saying that money or goods have been received

[2]**receipt** *vb*
1 to give a receipt for
2 to mark as paid

**re·ceive** \ri-'sēv\ *vb* **re·ceived**; **re·ceiv·ing**
1 to take or get something that is given, paid, or sent ⟨*receive* the money⟩ ⟨*receive* a letter⟩
2 to let enter one's household or company : WELCOME ⟨*receive* friends⟩
3 to be at home to visitors
4 [2]EXPERIENCE ⟨*receive* a shock⟩
5 to change incoming radio waves into sounds or pictures

**re·ceiv·er** \ri-'sē-vər\ *n*
1 one that receives
2 a device for changing electricity or radio waves into light or sound ⟨a telephone *receiver*⟩ ⟨a radio *receiver*⟩

**re·cent** \'rēs-nt\ *adj*
1 of or relating to a time not long past ⟨*recent* history⟩
2 having lately appeared to come into being : NEW, FRESH ⟨*recent* events⟩
**re·cent·ly** *adv*
**re·cent·ness** *n*

**re·cep·ta·cle** \ri-'sep-tə-kəl\ *n*
▼ something used to receive and contain smaller objects

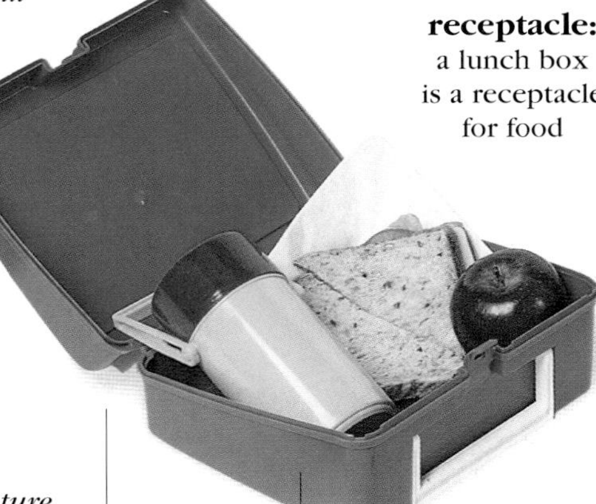

**receptacle:** a lunch box is a receptacle for food

*lunch box*

a b c d e f g h i j k l m n o p q r s t u v w x y z

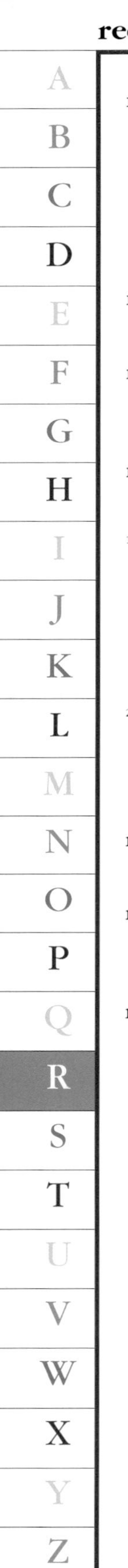


**re·cep·tion** \ri-'sep-shən\ *n*
**1** the act or manner of receiving ⟨a warm *reception*⟩
**2** a social gathering at which someone is often formally introduced or welcomed
**3** the receiving of a radio or television broadcast

**re·cep·tion·ist** \ri-'sep-shə-nist\ *n*
an office employee who greets callers

**re·cep·tive** \ri-'sep-tiv\ *adj*
able or willing to receive ideas
**re·cep·tive·ly** *adv*
**re·cep·tive·ness** *n*

**re·cep·tor** \ri-'sep-tər\ *n*
a cell or group of cells that receives stimuli **:** SENSE ORGAN

**[1]re·cess** \'rē-,ses, ri-'ses\ *n*
**1** a secret or hidden place
**2** a hollow cut or built into a surface ⟨a *recess* lined with books⟩
**3** a brief period for relaxation between work periods ⟨went out to play ball at *recess*⟩

**[2]recess** *vb*
**1** to put into a recess ⟨the light fixture was *recessed* into the ceiling⟩
**2** to interrupt for or take a recess

**re·ces·sion** \ri-'sesh-ən\ *n*
a period of reduced business activity

**re·ces·sive** \ri-'ses-iv\ *adj*
not dominant ⟨*recessive* genes⟩ ⟨a *recessive* trait⟩

**rec·i·pe** \'res-ə-pē\ *n*
▶ a set of instructions for making something (as a food dish) by combining various things

20 MINUTES SERVES 4

HOT DOGS WITH SALSA

You will need
Large saucepan • Colander • Chopping board • Bread knife • Sharp knife Spoon • Bowl • Lemon squeezer

For the hot dogs
4 Frankfurter sausages
4 hot-dog rolls

For the salsa
½ small onion
225 g (8 oz) tomatoes
½ lime
A few drops Tabasco sauce
Salt and pepper

Making the hot dogs
1 Heat a large saucepan of water until it *simmers*, then add the sausages. Cook them for 5 minutes, then drain them.
2 Warm the rolls in the oven for a few minutes, then split each one down the middle. Put a cooked sausage in each roll.

Making the salsa
1 *Chop* the onion finely. Cut the tomatoes in half, then scoop out and discard the seeds. Chop the tomato flesh finely.
2 Put the chopped tomato in a bowl. Add the onion, the juice of half a lime, the Tabasco, and the *seasoning* and mix well.

*Serve the salsa in a small bowl.*
*This hot dog has a squiggle of mustard on top.*
*This one is topped with tomato ketchup.*
*This hot dog is topped with tomato salsa.*

20

*list of ingredients*
*instructions*

**recipe** for making salsa for hot dogs

**re·cip·i·ent** \ri-'sip-ē-ənt\ *n*
one that receives

**re·cip·ro·cal** \ri-'sip-rə-kəl\ *n*
one of a pair of numbers (as 9 and $^1/_9$, $^2/_3$ and $^3/_2$) whose product is one

**re·cit·al** \ri-'sīt-l\ *n*
**1** a reciting of something ⟨the *recital* of their troubles⟩
**2** ▶ a public performance given by one musician ⟨piano *recital*⟩
**3** a public performance by pupils (as dancing pupils)

**recital 2:** a man giving a piano recital

**rec·i·ta·tion** \,res-ə-'tā-shən\ *n*
**1** a complete telling or listing of something
**2** the reciting before an audience of something memorized
**3** a student's oral reply to questions

**re·cite** \ri-'sīt\ *vb* **re·cit·ed**; **re·cit·ing**
**1** to repeat from memory ⟨*recite* a poem⟩
**2** to tell about in detail
**3** to answer questions about a lesson

**reck·less** \'rek-ləs\ *adj*
being or given to wild careless behavior
**reck·less·ly** *adv*
**reck·less·ness** *n*

**reck·on** \'rek-ən\ *vb*
**1** [1]COUNT 1, COMPUTE ⟨*reckon* the days till vacation⟩
**2** to regard or think of as **:** CONSIDER ⟨was *reckoned* among the leaders⟩

**re·claim** \ri-'klām\ *vb*
**1** to make better in behavior or character **:** REFORM
**2** to change to a desirable condition or state ⟨*reclaim* a swamp⟩
**3** to obtain from a waste product or by-product ⟨*reclaimed* rubber⟩

**rec·la·ma·tion** \,rek-lə-'mā-shən\ *n*
the act or process of reclaiming **:** the state of being reclaimed

**re·cline** \ri-'klīn\ *vb* **re·clined**; **re·clin·ing**
**1** to lean backward
**2** to lie down

**rec·og·ni·tion** \,rek-ig-'nish-ən\ *n*
**1** the act of recognizing
**2** special attention or notice ⟨a writer whose work was slow to win *recognition*⟩

**rec·og·nize** \'rek-ig-,nīz\ *vb* **rec·og·nized**; **rec·og·niz·ing**
**1** to know and remember upon seeing ⟨*recognize* an old friend⟩

2 to be willing to acknowledge ⟨*recognized* my own faults⟩
3 to take approving notice of ⟨*recognize* an act of bravery by the award of a medal⟩
4 to show one is acquainted with ⟨*recognize* someone with a nod⟩

**²record 5:** a record on the turntable of a record player

**¹re·coil** \ri-'kȯil\ *vb*
1 to draw back ⟨*recoil* in horror⟩
2 to spring back to a former position ⟨the gun *recoiled* upon firing⟩

**²recoil** *n*
1 the act or action of recoiling
2 a springing back (as of a gun just fired)
3 the distance through which something (as a spring) recoils

**rec·ol·lect** \,rek-ə-'lekt\ *vb*
to call to mind **:** REMEMBER ⟨*recollect* what happened⟩

**rec·ol·lec·tion** \,rek-ə-'lek-shən\ *n*
1 the act or power of recalling to mind **:** MEMORY ⟨a good *recollection*⟩
2 something remembered ⟨my earliest *recollections*⟩

**rec·om·mend** \,rek-ə-'mend\ *vb*
1 to present or support as worthy or fit ⟨*recommended* her for the job⟩ ⟨*recommend* a hotel⟩
2 to make acceptable ⟨the plan has many points to *recommend* it⟩
3 to make a suggestion **:** ADVISE ⟨*recommend* that the matter be dropped⟩

**rec·om·men·da·tion** \,rek-ə-mən-'dā-shən\ *n*
1 the act of recommending
2 a thing or course of action recommended ⟨didn't follow their *recommendation*⟩
3 something that recommends ⟨asked his boss for a *recommendation*⟩

**¹rec·om·pense** \'rek-əm-,pens\ *vb*
**rec·om·pensed**; **rec·om·pens·ing**
to pay for or pay back

**²recompense** *n*
a return for something done, suffered, or given **:** PAYMENT

**rec·on·cile** \'rek-ən-,sīl\ *vb*
**rec·on·ciled**; **rec·on·cil·ing**
1 to make friendly again ⟨*reconcile* friends who have quarreled⟩
2 ¹SETTLE 7, ADJUST ⟨*reconcile* differences of opinion⟩
3 to make agree ⟨a story that cannot be *reconciled* with the facts⟩
4 to cause to give in or accept ⟨*reconcile* oneself to a loss⟩

**re·con·di·tion** \,rē-kən-'dish-ən\ *vb*
to restore to good condition (as by repairing or replacing parts)

**re·con·nais·sance** \ri-'kän-ə-zəns\ *n*
a survey (as of enemy territory) to get information

**re·con·noi·ter** \,rē-kə-'nȯit-ər, ,rek-ə-\ *vb*
to make a reconnaissance (as in preparation for military action)

**re·con·sid·er** \,rē-kən-'sid-ər\ *vb*
to consider again especially with a view to change

**re·con·sid·er·a·tion** \,rē-kən-,sid-ə-'rā-shən\ *n*
the act of reconsidering **:** the state of being reconsidered

**re·con·struct** \,rē-kən-'strəkt\ *vb*
to construct again **:** REBUILD, REMODEL

**¹re·cord** \ri-'kȯrd\ *vb*
1 to set down in writing
2 to register permanently
3 to change sound or visual images into a form (as on magnetic tape) that can be listened to or watched at a later time

**²rec·ord** \'rek-ərd\ *n*
1 the state or fact of being recorded ⟨a matter of *record*⟩
2 something written to preserve an account
3 the known or recorded facts about a person or thing ⟨has a good school *record*⟩
4 a recorded top performance ⟨broke the scoring *record*⟩
5 ◀ something on which sound or visual images have been recorded

**³rec·ord** \'rek-ərd\ *adj*
outstanding among other like things ⟨a *record* crop⟩

**re·cord·er** \ri-'kȯrd-ər\ *n*
1 a person or device that records
2 ▼ a musical instrument like a long hollow whistle with eight finger holes

**recorder 2:** a girl playing a recorder

**re·cord·ing** \ri-'kȯrd-ing\ *n*
²RECORD 5

**¹re·count** \ri-'kau̇nt\ *vb*
to tell all about **:** NARRATE ⟨*recount* an adventure⟩

**²re·count** \'rē-'kau̇nt\ *vb*
to count again

**³re·count** \'rē-,kau̇nt, -'kau̇nt\ *n*
a counting again (as of election votes)

**re·course** \'rē-,kōrs\ *n*
1 a turning for help or protection
2 a source of help or strength

**re·cov·er** \ri-'kəv-ər\ *vb*
1 to get back **:** REGAIN ⟨*recover* a lost wallet⟩
2 to regain normal health, self-confidence, or position
3 to make up for ⟨*recover* lost time⟩
4 RECLAIM 2 ⟨*recover* land from the sea⟩

**re–cov•er** \'rē-'kəv-ər\ *vb*
to cover again

**re•cov•ery** \ri-'kəv-ə-rē, -'kəv-rē\ *n, pl* **re•cov•er•ies**
the act, process, or an instance of recovering

**rec•re•a•tion** \,rek-rē-'ā-shən\ *n*
**1** a refreshing of mind or body after work or worry
**2** ▶ a means of refreshing mind or body ⟨exercise is healthful *recreation*⟩

[1]**re•cruit** \ri-'krüt\ *vb*
**1** to form or strengthen with new members ⟨*recruit* an army⟩
**2** to get the services of ⟨*recruit* engineers⟩
**3** to restore or increase the health or vigor of

[2]**recruit** *n*
a newcomer to a field of activity

**Word History** An early French verb with the meaning "to grow up again" came from a Latin verb meaning "to grow." The French made a noun meaning "fresh growth" from the verb meaning "to grow up again." Someone apparently compared new troops of soldiers to a fresh growth of plants. The noun that meant "fresh growth" came to mean "a new group of soldiers called into service." The English noun *recruit* came from this French noun.

**rectangle**

**rect•an•gle** \'rek-,tang-gəl\ *n*
▲ a four-sided figure with right angles and with opposite sides parallel

**rect•an•gu•lar** \rek-'tang-gyə-lər\ *adj*
shaped like a rectangle

**recreation 2:** a boy and girl playing chess for recreation

**rec•ti•fy** \'rek-tə-,fī\ *vb* **rec•ti•fied**; **rec•ti•fy•ing**
to set or make right

**rec•tor** \'rek-tər\ *n*
PASTOR

**rec•tum** \'rek-təm\ *n, pl* **rec•tums** *or* **rec•ta** \-tə\
the last part of the large intestine

**re•cu•per•ate** \ri-'kü-pə-,rāt, -'kyü-\ *vb* **re•cu•per•at•ed**; **re•cu•per•at•ing**
to regain health or strength

**re•cu•per•a•tion** \ri-,kü-pə-'rā-shən, -,kyü-\ *n*
a getting back to health or strength

**re•cur** \ri-'kər\ *vb* **re•curred**; **re•cur•ring**
to occur or appear again ⟨the fever *recurred*⟩

**re•cur•rence** \ri-'kər-əns\ *n*
the state of occurring again and again

**re•cy•cla•ble** \(,)rē-'sī-kə-lə-bəl\ *adj*
that can be recycled ⟨*recyclable* plastic bottles⟩

**re•cy•cle** \'rē-'sī-kəl\ *vb* **re•cy•cled**; **re•cy•cling**
▶ to process (as paper, glass, or cans) in order to regain materials for human use

**recycle:** articles for recycling

[1]**red** \'red\ *adj* **red•der**; **red•dest**
**1** of the color red
**2** of or relating to Communism or Communists
**red•ness** *n*

[2]**red** *n*
**1** the color of fresh blood or of the ruby
**2** something red in color
**3** a person who seeks or favors revolution
**4** COMMUNIST 2

**red•bird** \'red-,bərd\ *n*
any of several birds (as a cardinal) with mostly red feathers

**red blood cell** *n*
one of the tiny reddish cells of the blood that have no nuclei and carry oxygen from the lungs to the tissues

**redcoat:** model of a redcoat

*musket*

**red•breast** \'red-,brest\ *n*
a bird (as a robin) with a reddish breast

**red•cap** \'red-,kap\ *n*
PORTER 1

**red cell** *n*
RED BLOOD CELL

**red•coat** \'red-,kōt\ *n*
▲ a British soldier especially during the Revolutionary War

**red corpuscle** *n*
RED BLOOD CELL

**red•den** \'red-n\ *vb*
to make or become red

**red·dish** \'red-ish\ *adj*
somewhat red

**re·deem** \ri-'dēm\ *vb*
**1** to buy back ⟨*redeem* a watch from the pawnshop⟩
**2** to ransom, free, or rescue through payment or effort
**3** to free from sin
**4** to make good **:** FULFILL ⟨*redeem* a promise⟩
**5** to make up for ⟨*redeem* a mistake⟩
**re·deem·er** *n*

**re·demp·tion** \ri-'demp-shən\ *n*
the act or process or an instance of redeeming

**red–hand·ed** \'red-'han-dəd\ *adv or adj*
in the act of doing something wrong ⟨was caught *red-handed*⟩

**red·head** \'red-,hed\ *n*
▼ a person having reddish hair

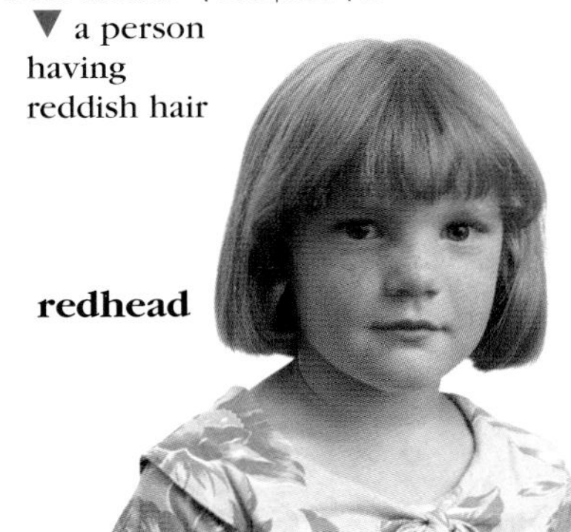

**redhead**

**red–hot** \'red-'hät\ *adj*
**1** glowing red with heat
**2** very active and emotional ⟨*red-hot* anger⟩ ⟨a *red-hot* campaign⟩

**re·di·rect** \,rē-də-'rekt, -dī-\ *vb*
to change the course or direction of

**re·dis·cov·er** \,rē-dis-'kəv-ər\ *vb*
to discover again

**red–let·ter** \'red-'let-ər\ *adj*
of special importance **:** MEMORABLE ⟨a *red-letter* day in my life⟩

**re·do** \'rē-'dü\ *vb* **re·did** \-'did\; **re·done** \-'dən\; **re·do·ing** \-'dü-ing\
to do over or again

**re·dress** \ri-'dres\ *vb*
to set right **:** REMEDY

**red tape** *n*
usually official rules and regulations that waste people's time

*cone*

**redwood**

*the figure shows the huge scale of the tree*

**re·duce** \ri-'düs, -'dyüs\ *vb* **re·duced**; **re·duc·ing**
**1** to make smaller or less ⟨*reduce* expenses⟩
**2** to force to surrender ⟨*reduce* a fort⟩
**3** to lower in grade or rank
**4** to change from one form into another ⟨*reduce* fractions to lowest terms⟩
**5** to lose weight by dieting

**re·duc·tion** \ri-'dək-shən\ *n*
**1** the act of reducing **:** the state of being reduced
**2** something made by reducing ⟨a *reduction* of a picture⟩
**3** the amount by which something is reduced ⟨a ten-cent *reduction* in price⟩

**red·wood** \'red-,wu̇d\ *n*
◀ a tall timber tree of California that bears cones and has a light long-lasting brownish red wood

**reed** \'rēd\ *n*
**1** a tall slender grass of wet areas that has stems with large joints
**2** a stem or a growth or mass of reeds
**3** a thin flexible piece of cane, plastic, or metal fastened to the mouthpiece or over an air opening in a musical instrument (as a clarinet or accordion) and set in vibration by an air current (as the breath)

**reef** \'rēf\ *n*
▼ a chain of rocks or ridge of sand at or near the surface of water

**[1]reek** \'rēk\ *n*
a strong or unpleasant smell

**[2]reek** *vb*
to have a strong or unpleasant smell

**reef:** an overhead view of the Great Barrier Reef, Australia

**[1]reel** \'rēl\ *n*
**1** ▶ a device that can be turned round and round and on which something flexible may be wound
**2** a quantity of something wound on a reel ⟨two *reels* of wire⟩

*reel*

**[1]reel 1:** a reel of film

**[2]reel** *vb*
**1** to wind on a reel
**2** to pull by the use of a reel ⟨*reel* in a fish⟩

**[3]reel** *vb*
**1** to whirl around
**2** to be in a confused state ⟨heads *reeling* with excitement⟩
**3** to fall back (as from a blow)
**4** to walk or move unsteadily **:** STAGGER

**[4]reel** *n*
a reeling motion

**[5]reel** *n*
a lively folk dance

**re·elect** \,rē-ə-'lekt\ *vb*
to elect for another term

**reel off** *vb*
to tell or recite rapidly or easily ⟨*reeled off* the right answers⟩

**re·en·ter** \'rē-'ent-ər\ *vb*
to enter again

**re·es·tab·lish** \,rē-əs-'tab-lish\ *vb*
to establish again

**re·fer** \ri-'fər\ *vb* **re·ferred**; **re·fer·ring**
**1** to send or direct to some person or place for treatment, aid, information, or decision ⟨*refer* a patient to a specialist⟩ ⟨*refer* a student to the dictionary⟩
**2** to call attention ⟨the teacher *referred* to a story in the newspaper⟩
**3** something that refers a reader to another source of information
**4** a person of whom questions can be asked about the honesty or ability of another person
**5** a written statement about someone's honesty or ability
**6** a work (as a dictionary) that contains useful information

**[1]ref·er·ee** \,ref-ə-'rē\ *n*
**1** a person to whom something that is to be investigated or decided is referred
**2** a sports official with final authority for conducting a game or match

**[2]referee** *vb* **ref·er·eed**; **ref·er·ee·ing**
to act or be in charge of as referee

**ref·er·ence** \'ref-ə-rəns, 'ref-rəns\ *n*
**1** the act of referring
**2** a relation to or concern with something ⟨with *reference* to what was said⟩

**ref·er·en·dum** \,ref-ə-'ren-dəm\ *n, pl* **ref·er·en·da** \-də\ *or* **ref·er·en·dums**
the idea or practice of letting the voters approve or disapprove laws

**[1]re·fill** \'rē-'fil\ *vb*
to fill or become filled again

**[2]re·fill** \'rē-,fil\ *n*
a new or fresh supply of something

**re·fine** \ri-'fīn\ *vb* **re·fined**; **re·fin·ing**
**1** to bring to a pure state ⟨*refine* sugar⟩
**2** to make better **:** IMPROVE ⟨*refined* their methods of forecasting the weather⟩

**re·fined** \ri-'fīnd\ *adj*
**1** having or showing good taste or training ⟨*refined* manners⟩
**2** freed from impurities **:** PURE ⟨*refined* gold⟩

**re·fine·ment** \ri-'fīn-mənt\ *n*
**1** the act or process of refining
**2** excellence of manners, feelings, or tastes ⟨a person of *refinement*⟩
**3** something meant to improve something else ⟨*refinements* in a car to increase its efficiency⟩

**re·fin·ery** \ri-'fī-nə-rē\ *n, pl* **re·fin·er·ies**
a building and equipment for refining metals, oil, or sugar

**re·fin·ish** \'rē-'fin-ish\ *vb*
to give (as furniture) a new surface

**re·fit** \'rē-'fit\ *vb* **re·fit·ted**; **re·fit·ting**
to get ready for use again ⟨*refit* a ship⟩

**re·flect** \ri-'flekt\ *vb*
**1** to bend or throw back (waves of light, sound, or heat) ⟨a polished surface *reflects* light⟩
**2** to give back an image or likeness of in the manner of a mirror
**3** to bring as a result ⟨your achievement *reflects* credit on your school⟩
**4** to bring disapproval or blame ⟨our bad conduct *reflects* upon our training⟩
**5** to think seriously ⟨*reflected* on the problem⟩

**re·flec·tion** \ri-'flek-shən\ *n*
**1** the return of light or sound waves from a surface
**2** an image produced by or as if by a mirror
**3** something that brings blame or disgrace ⟨it's a *reflection* on my honesty⟩
**4** an opinion formed or a remark made after careful thought
**5** careful thought ⟨much *reflection* upon the problem⟩

**reflector:** a cyclist wearing a safety reflector over his jacket

**re·flec·tor** \ri-'flek-tər\ *n*
▲ a shiny surface for reflecting light or heat

**re·flex** \'rē-,fleks\ *n*
an action that occurs automatically when a sense organ is stimulated

**reflex act** *n*
REFLEX

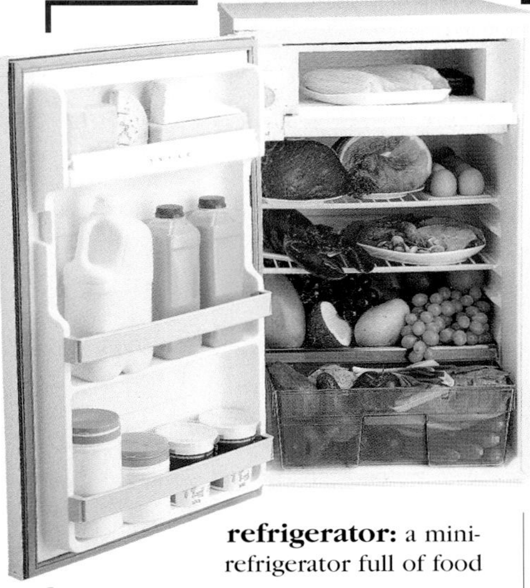

**refrigerator:** a mini-refrigerator full of food

**re•for•est** \'rē-'fȯr-əst\ *vb*
to renew forest growth by planting seeds or young trees

**re•for•es•ta•tion** \,rē-,fȯr-ə-'stā-shən\ *n*
the act of reforesting

[1]**re•form** \ri-'fȯrm\ *vb*
**1** to make better or improve by removal of faults ⟨*reform* a criminal⟩ ⟨wants to *reform* spelling⟩
**2** to correct or improve one's own behavior or habits

[2]**reform** *n*
**1** improvement of what is bad
**2** a removal or correction of a wrong or an error

**ref•or•ma•tion** \,ref-ər-'mā-shən\ *n*
the act of reforming : the state of being reformed

**re•for•ma•to•ry** \ri-'fȯr-mə-,tōr-ē\ *n, pl* **re•for•ma•to•ries**
an institution for reforming usually young or first offenders

**re•form•er** \ri-'fȯr-mər\ *n*
a person who works for reform

**re•fract** \ri-'frakt\ *vb*
to cause to go through refraction

**re•frac•tion** \ri-'frak-shən\ *n*
the bending of a ray when it passes at an angle from one medium into another in which its speed is different (as when light passes from air into water)

**re•frac•to•ry** \ri-'frak-tə-rē\ *adj*
**1** STUBBORN 3
**2** capable of enduring very high temperatures ⟨*refractory* clays⟩

[1]**re•frain** \ri-'frān\ *vb*
to hold oneself back

[2]**refrain** *n*
a phrase or verse repeated regularly in a poem or song

**re•fresh** \ri-'fresh\ *vb*
to make fresh or fresher : REVIVE ⟨sleep *refreshes* the body⟩
**re•fresh•er** *n*

**re•fresh•ment** \ri-'fresh-mənt\ *n*
**1** the act of refreshing : the state of being refreshed
**2** something (as food or drink) that refreshes — often used in pl.

**re•frig•er•ate** \ri-'frij-ə-,rāt\ *vb* **re•frig•er•at•ed**; **re•frig•er•at•ing**
to make or keep cold or cool

**re•frig•er•a•tor** \ri-'frij-ə-,rāt-ər\ *n*
◀ a device or room for keeping articles (as food) cool

**re•fu•el** \'rē-'fyü-əl\ *vb*
to provide with or take on more fuel

**ref•uge** \'ref-yüj\ *n*
**1** shelter or protection from danger or distress
**2** a place that provides shelter or protection ⟨wildlife *refuge*⟩

**ref•u•gee** \,ref-yu̇-'jē\ *n*
a person who flees for safety usually to a foreign country

[1]**re•fund** \ri-'fənd\ *vb*
to give back : REPAY ⟨*refund* the cost⟩

[2]**re•fund** \'rē-,fənd\ *n*
a sum of money refunded

**re•fus•al** \ri-'fyü-zəl\ *n*
the act of refusing

[1]**re•fuse** \ri-'fyüz\ *vb* **re•fused**; **re•fus•ing**
**1** to say one will not accept ⟨*refuse* a job⟩
**2** to say one will not do, give, or allow something ⟨*refused* to help⟩

[2]**ref•use** \'ref-,yüs\ *n*
TRASH 1, RUBBISH

**re•fute** \ri-'fyüt\ *vb* **re•fut•ed**; **re•fut•ing**
to prove wrong by argument or evidence
**re•fut•er** *n*

**re•gain** \ri-'gān\ *vb*
**1** to gain or get again : get back ⟨*regained* my health⟩
**2** to get back to : reach again ⟨*regain* the shore⟩

**re•gal** \'rē-gəl\ *adj*
of, relating to, or suitable for a monarch : ROYAL
**re•gal•ly** *adv*

**re•gale** \ri-'gāl\ *vb* **re•galed**; **re•gal•ing**
**1** to entertain richly
**2** to give pleasure or amusement to

[1]**re•gard** \ri-'gärd\ *n*
**1** [2]LOOK 1 ⟨a tender *regard*⟩
**2** CONSIDERATION 2 ⟨*regard* for others⟩
**3** a feeling of respect ⟨held in high *regard*⟩
**4** **regards** *pl* friendly greetings ⟨give them my *regards*⟩
**5** a point to be considered ⟨be careful in this *regard*⟩

[2]**regard** *vb*
**1** to pay attention to
**2** to show respect or consideration for
**3** to have a high opinion of
**4** to look at
**5** to think of : CONSIDER ⟨*regarded* them as friends⟩

**re•gard•ing** \ri-,gärd-ing\ *prep*
relating to : ABOUT ⟨talked with them *regarding* their behavior⟩

**re•gard•less** \ri-'gärd-ləs\ *adv*
come what may ⟨I will go *regardless*⟩

**regardless of** *prep*
in spite of ⟨*regardless of* race⟩

**re•gat•ta** \ri-'gät-ə, -'gat-\ *n*
▼ a rowing, speedboat, or sailing race or a series of such races

**regatta:** a sailing regatta in Australia

**re•gen•er•ate** \ri-'jen-ə-,rāt\ *vb* **re•gen•er•at•ed**; **re•gen•er•at•ing**
to form (as a lost part) once more ⟨the lizard *regenerated* its lost tail⟩

a b c d e f g h i j k l m n o p q r s t u v w x y z

\ng\ sing \ō\ bone \ȯ\ saw \ȯi\ coin \th\ thin \t͟h\ this \ü\ food \u̇\ foot \y\ yet \yü\ few \yu̇\ cure \zh\ vision

**re·gent** \'rē-jənt\ *n*
**1** a person who governs a kingdom (as during the childhood of the monarch)
**2** a member of a governing board (as of a state university)

**re·gime** \rā-'zhēm, ri-\ *n*
a form or system of government or management

**reg·i·men** \'rej-ə-mən\ *n*
a systematic course of treatment

**reg·i·ment** \'rej-ə-mənt\ *n*
a military unit made up usually of a number of battalions

**re·gion** \'rē-jən\ *n*
**1** an area having no definite boundaries
**2** VICINITY 2 ⟨a pain in the *region* of the heart⟩
**3** a broad geographical area

**re·gion·al** \'rē-jən-l\ *adj*
of, relating to, or characteristic of a certain region

[1]**reg·is·ter** \'rej-əs-tər\ *n*
**1** a written record or list containing regular entries of items or details
**2** a book or system of public records ⟨a *register* of deeds⟩
**3** a device for regulating ventilation or the flow of heated air from a furnace
**4** ▼ a mechanical device (as a **cash register**) that records items

[1]**register 4:** a cash register

[2]**register** *vb*
**1** to enter or enroll in a register (as a list of voters, students, or guests)
**2** to record automatically ⟨the thermometer *registered* zero⟩
**3** to get special protection for by paying extra postage ⟨*register* a letter⟩
**4** to show by expression and bodily movements ⟨*register* surprise⟩

**reg·is·tra·tion** \,rej-ə-'strā-shən\ *n*
**1** the act of registering
**2** an entry in a register
**3** the number of persons registered
**4** a document showing that something is registered ⟨a car *registration*⟩

**reg·is·try** \'rej-ə-strē\ *n, pl* **reg·is·tries**
a place where registration takes place

[1]**re·gret** \ri-'gret\ *vb* **re·gret·ted**; **re·gret·ting**
**1** to mourn the loss or death of
**2** to be sorry for ⟨*regret* one's faults⟩

[2]**regret** *n*
**1** sorrow aroused by events beyond one's control
**2** an expression of sorrow
**3 regrets** *pl* a note politely refusing to accept an invitation ⟨send *regrets*⟩

**re·gret·ful** \ri-'gret-fəl\ *adj*
full of regret
**re·gret·ful·ly** \-fə-lē\ *adv*

**re·gret·ta·ble** \ri-'gret-ə-bəl\ *adj*
deserving regret
**re·gret·ta·bly** \-blē\ *adv*

**re·group** \'rē-'grüp\ *vb*
to form into a new grouping ⟨to subtract 129 from 531 *regroup* 531 into 5 hundreds, 2 tens, and 11 ones⟩

**reg·u·lar** \'reg-yə-lər\ *adj*
**1** formed, built, or arranged according to an established rule, law, principle, or type
**2** even or balanced in form or structure
**3** steady in practice or occurrence ⟨*regular* habits⟩
**4** following established usages or rules
**5** [1]NORMAL 1
**6** of, relating to, or being a permanent army
**reg·u·lar·ly** *adv*

**Synonyms** REGULAR, NORMAL, and TYPICAL mean being of the sort that is considered to be usual, ordinary, or average. REGULAR stresses that something follows a rule, standard, or pattern ⟨a *regular* school holiday⟩. NORMAL stresses that something does not vary from what is the most usual or expected ⟨*normal* behavior for a child of that age⟩. TYPICAL suggests that all the important characteristics of a type, class, or group are shown ⟨a *typical* small American town⟩.

**reg·u·lar·i·ty** \,reg-yə-'lar-ət-ē\ *n*
the quality or state of being regular

**reg·u·late** \'reg-yə-,lāt\ *vb* **reg·u·lat·ed**; **reg·u·lat·ing**
**1** to govern or direct by rule
**2** to bring under the control of authority ⟨*regulate* prices⟩
**3** to bring order or method to ⟨*regulated* my habits⟩
**4** to fix or adjust the time, amount, degree, or rate of
**reg·u·la·tor** \-,lāt-ər\ *n*

**reg·u·la·tion** \,reg-yə-'lā-shən\ *n*
**1** the act of regulating **:** the state of being regulated
**2** a rule or order telling how something is to be done or having the force of law

**re·hears·al** \ri-'hər-səl\ *n*
a private performance or practice session in preparation for a public appearance

**re·hearse** \ri-'hərs\ *vb* **re·hearsed**; **re·hears·ing**
to practice in private in preparation for a public performance ⟨*rehearse* a play⟩

**Word History** A device called a *harrow* is used to break up and smooth soil. Sometimes the first run with the harrow does not break up all the lumps of earth. The farmer then has to take the harrow over the ground more than once. An early French verb meant "to go over again with a harrow." The English verb *rehearse* comes from this early French verb. When we rehearse something we are, so to speak, going over the same ground again and again.

[1]**reign** \'rān\ *n*
**1** the authority or rule of a monarch
**2** the time during which a monarch rules

[2]**reign** *vb*
**1** to rule as a monarch
**2** to be usual or widespread

**re·im·burse** \,rē-əm-'bərs\ *vb* **re·im·bursed**; **re·im·burs·ing**
to pay back **:** REPAY
**re·im·burse·ment** \-mənt\ *n*

**¹rein** \ˈrān\ *n*
**1** ▼ a line or strap attached at either end of the bit of a bridle to control an animal — usually used in pl.
**2** an influence that slows, limits, or holds back ⟨kept the child under a tight *rein*⟩
**3** controlling or guiding power ⟨seized the *reins* of government⟩

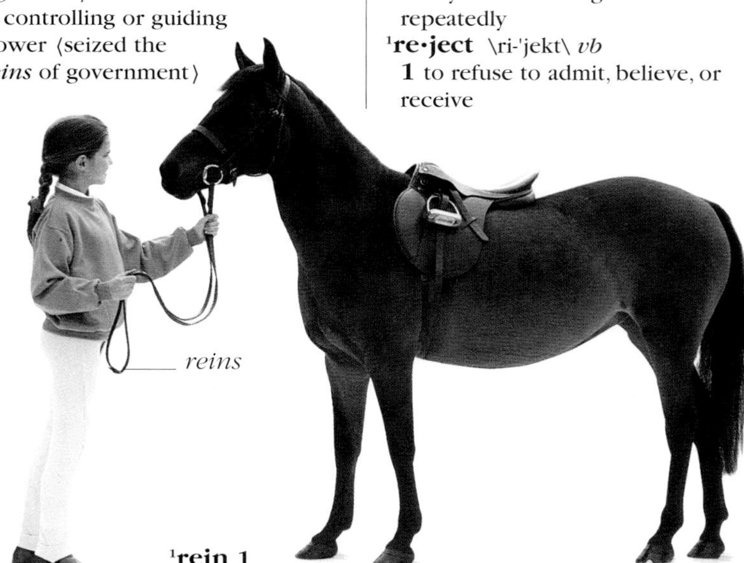


**¹rein 1**

**²rein** *vb*
to check, control, or stop by or as if by reins

**re·in·car·na·tion** \ˌrē-ˌin-ˌkär-ˈnā-shən\ *n*
rebirth of the soul in a new body

**rein·deer** \ˈrān-ˌdir\ *n, pl* **reindeer**
▶ a large deer that has antlers in both the male and the female and is found in northern regions

**re·in·force** \ˌrē-ən-ˈfōrs\ *vb* **re·in·forced**; **re·in·forc·ing**
**1** to strengthen with extra troops or ships
**2** to strengthen with new force, assistance, material, or support ⟨*reinforce* a wall⟩

**re·in·force·ment** \ˌrē-ən-ˈfōr-smənt\ *n*
**1** the act of reinforcing : the state of being reinforced
**2** something that reinforces

**re·in·state** \ˌrē-ən-ˈstāt\ *vb* **re·in·stat·ed**; **re·in·stat·ing**
to place again in a former position or condition
**re·in·state·ment** \-mənt\ *n*

**re·it·er·ate** \rē-ˈit-ə-ˌrāt\ *vb* **re·it·er·at·ed**; **re·it·er·at·ing**
to say or do over again or repeatedly

**¹re·ject** \ri-ˈjekt\ *vb*
**1** to refuse to admit, believe, or receive
**2** to throw away as useless or unsatisfactory
**3** to refuse to consider ⟨*reject* a request⟩

**²re·ject** \ˈrē-ˌjekt\ *n*
a rejected person or thing

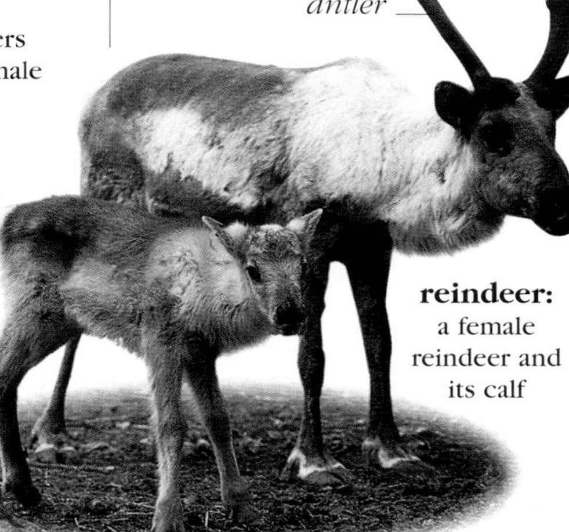


**reindeer:** a female reindeer and its calf

**re·jec·tion** \ri-ˈjek-shən\ *n*
**1** the act of rejecting : the state of being rejected
**2** something rejected

**re·joice** \ri-ˈjȯis\ *vb* **re·joiced**; **re·joic·ing**
**1** to give joy to : GLADDEN ⟨news that *rejoices* the heart⟩
**2** to feel joy ⟨*rejoiced* over their good luck⟩

**re·join** \ri-ˈjȯin\ *vb*
**1** to join again : return to ⟨*rejoined* my family after the trip⟩
**2** to reply sharply

**re·join·der** \ri-ˈjȯin-dər\ *n*
²REPLY

**¹re·lapse** \ri-ˈlaps, ˈrē-ˌlaps\ *n*
a fresh period of an illness after an improvement

**²re·lapse** \ri-ˈlaps\ *vb* **re·lapsed**; **re·laps·ing**
to slip or fall back into a former condition after a change for the better

**re·late** \ri-ˈlāt\ *vb* **re·lat·ed**; **re·lat·ing**
**1** to give an account of : NARRATE ⟨*related* their experiences⟩
**2** to show or have a relationship to or between : CONNECT ⟨the events are *related*⟩ ⟨the lesson *relates* to history⟩

**re·lat·ed** \ri-ˈlāt-əd\ *adj*
connected by common ancestry or by marriage

**re·la·tion** \ri-ˈlā-shən\ *n*
**1** the act of telling or describing
**2** CONNECTION 2 ⟨the *relation* between sleep and death⟩ ⟨the *relation* between teacher and pupils⟩
**3** a related person : RELATIVE
**4** RELATIONSHIP 2
**5** REFERENCE 2, RESPECT ⟨in *relation* to this matter⟩
**6 relations** *pl* business or public affairs ⟨foreign *relations*⟩

**re·la·tion·ship** \ri-ˈlā-shən-ˌship\ *n*
**1** the state of being related or connected
**2** connection by blood or marriage

**¹rel·a·tive** \ˈrel-ət-iv\ *n*
a person connected with another by blood or marriage

**²relative** *adj*
**1** RELEVANT ⟨questions *relative* to world peace⟩
**2** existing in comparison to something else ⟨the *relative* value of two houses⟩
**rel·a·tive·ly** *adv*

**re·lax** \ri-'laks\ *vb*
1 to make or become loose or less tense ⟨*relaxed* my attention⟩
2 to make or become less severe or strict ⟨*relax* discipline⟩
3 to rest or enjoy oneself away from one's usual duties

**re·lax·ation** \,rē-,lak-'sā-shən\ *n*
1 the act or fact of relaxing or of being relaxed
2 a relaxing activity or pastime

**[1]re·lay** \'rē-,lā\ *n*
1 a fresh supply (as of horses or people) arranged to relieve others
2 ► a race between teams in which each team member covers a certain part of the course

**[2]re·lay** \'rē-,lā, ri-'lā\ *vb* **re·layed**; **re·lay·ing**
to pass along by stages ⟨*relay* a message from person to person⟩

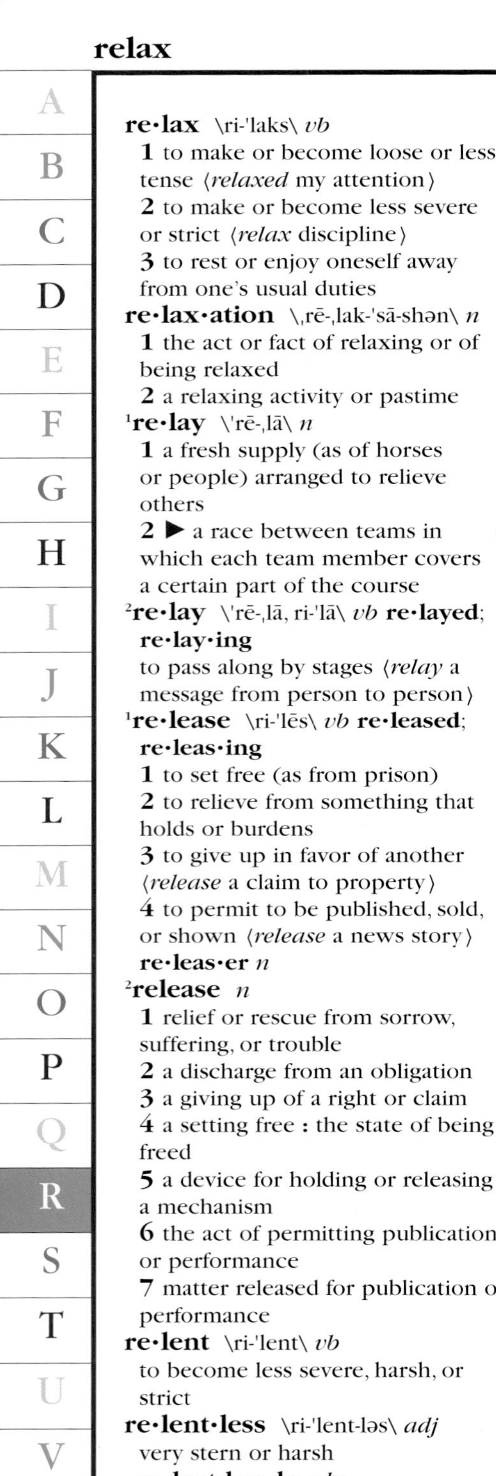

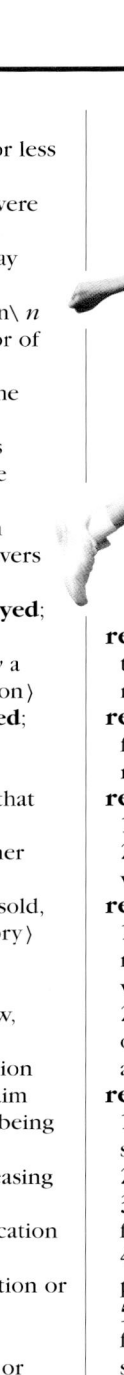

**[1]relay 2:** a runner finishes her part of the relay by passing a stick called a baton to the next runner

**[1]re·lease** \ri-'lēs\ *vb* **re·leased**; **re·leas·ing**
1 to set free (as from prison)
2 to relieve from something that holds or burdens
3 to give up in favor of another ⟨*release* a claim to property⟩
4 to permit to be published, sold, or shown ⟨*release* a news story⟩
**re·leas·er** *n*

**[2]release** *n*
1 relief or rescue from sorrow, suffering, or trouble
2 a discharge from an obligation
3 a giving up of a right or claim
4 a setting free : the state of being freed
5 a device for holding or releasing a mechanism
6 the act of permitting publication or performance
7 matter released for publication or performance

**re·lent** \ri-'lent\ *vb*
to become less severe, harsh, or strict

**re·lent·less** \ri-'lent-ləs\ *adj*
very stern or harsh
**re·lent·less·ly** *adv*
**re·lent·less·ness** *n*

**rel·e·vance** \'rel-ə-vəns\ *n*
relation to the matter at hand

**rel·e·vant** \'rel-ə-vənt\ *adj*
having something to do with the matter at hand ⟨a *relevant* question⟩
**rel·e·vant·ly** *adv*

**re·li·abil·i·ty** \ri-,lī-ə-'bil-ət-ē\ *n*
the quality or state of being reliable

**re·li·able** \ri-'lī-ə-bəl\ *adj*
fit to be trusted : DEPENDABLE
**re·li·ably** \-blē\ *adv*

**re·li·ance** \ri-'lī-əns\ *n*
1 the act of relying
2 the condition or attitude of one who relies

**rel·ic** \'rel-ik\ *n*
1 an object treated with great respect because of its connection with a saint or martyr
2 something left behind after decay or disappearance ⟨*relics* of an ancient civilization⟩

**re·lief** \ri-'lēf\ *n*
1 removal or lightening of something painful or troubling
2 WELFARE 2
3 military assistance in or rescue from a position of difficulty
4 release from a post or from performance of a duty
5 ► elevation of figures or designs from the background (as in sculpture)
6 elevations of a land surface ⟨a map showing *relief*⟩

**re·lieve** \ri-'lēv\ *vb* **re·lieved**; **re·liev·ing**
1 to free partly or wholly from a burden or from distress
2 to release from a post or duty ⟨*relieve* a sentry⟩
3 to break the sameness of ⟨a dark red house *relieved* by white trim⟩
**re·liev·er** *n*

**re·li·gion** \ri-'lij-ən\ *n*
1 the service and worship of God or the supernatural
2 a system of religious beliefs and practices

**re·li·gious** \ri-'lij-əs\ *adj*
1 relating to or showing devotion to God or to the powers or forces believed to govern life ⟨a *religious* person⟩
2 of or relating to religion ⟨*religious* books⟩
3 very devoted and faithful ⟨pay *religious* attention to one's teacher⟩
**re·li·gious·ly** *adv*
**re·li·gious·ness** *n*

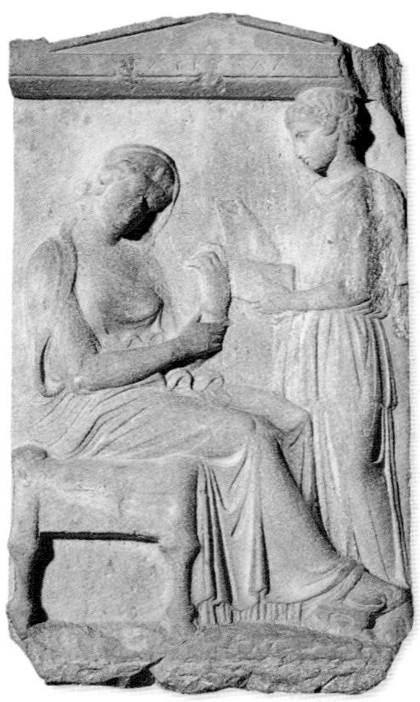

**relief 5:** an ancient Greek relief

**re·lin·quish** \ri-'ling-kwish\ *vb*
GIVE UP 1 **:** let go of

**¹rel·ish** \'rel-ish\ *n*
**1** a pleasing taste
**2** great enjoyment ⟨eats with *relish*⟩
**3** ► a highly seasoned food eaten with other food to add flavor

**²relish** *vb*
**1** to be pleased by **:** ENJOY
**2** to like the taste of

**¹relish 3:** a jar of corn and pepper relish

**re·live** \'rē-'liv\ *vb* **re·lived**; **re·liv·ing**
to experience again (as in the imagination)

**re·luc·tance** \ri-'lək-təns\ *n*
the quality or state of being reluctant

**re·luc·tant** \ri-'lək-tənt\ *adj*
showing doubt or unwillingness ⟨*reluctant* to answer⟩
**re·luc·tant·ly** *adv*

**re·ly** \ri-'lī\ *vb* **re·lied**; **re·ly·ing**
to place faith or confidence **:** DEPEND

**re·main** \ri-'mān\ *vb*
**1** to be left after others have been removed, subtracted, or destroyed ⟨little *remained* after the fire⟩
**2** to be something yet to be done or considered ⟨a fact that *remains* to be proved⟩
**3** to stay after others have gone
**4** to continue unchanged ⟨the weather *remained* cold⟩

**re·main·der** \ri-'mān-dər\ *n*
**1** a remaining group or part
**2** the number left after a subtraction
**3** the number left over from the dividend after division that is less than the divisor

**remains** \ri-'mānz\ *n pl*
**1** whatever is left over or behind ⟨the *remains* of a meal⟩
**2** a dead body

**re·make** \'rē-'māk\ *vb* **re·made** \-'mād\; **re·mak·ing**
to make again or in a different form

**¹re·mark** \ri-'märk\ *n*
**1** a telling of something in speech or writing
**2** a brief comment

**²remark** *vb*
**1** to take note of **:** OBSERVE
**2** to make a comment

**re·mark·able** \ri-'mär-kə-bəl\ *adj*
worth noticing **:** UNUSUAL
**re·mark·able·ness** *n*
**re·mark·ably** \-blē\ *adv*

**re·match** \'rē-'mach\ *n*
a second meeting between the same contestants

**re·me·di·al** \ri-'mēd-ē-əl\ *adj*
intended to make something better ⟨classes in *remedial* reading⟩
**re·me·di·al·ly** *adv*

**¹rem·e·dy** \'rem-ə-dē\ *n, pl* **rem·e·dies**
**1** a medicine or treatment that cures or relieves
**2** something that corrects an evil

**²remedy** *vb* **rem·e·died**; **rem·e·dy·ing**
to provide or serve as a remedy for

**re·mem·ber** \ri-'mem-bər\ *vb*
**1** to bring to mind or think of again
**2** to keep in mind ⟨*remember* your promise⟩
**3** to pass along greetings from ⟨*remember* us to your family⟩

**re·mem·brance** \ri-'mem-brəns\ *n*
**1** the act of remembering
**2** something remembered ⟨a vivid *remembrance*⟩
**3** something (as a souvenir) that brings to mind a past experience

**re·mind** \ri-'mīnd\ *vb*
to cause to remember
**re·mind·er** *n*

**rem·i·nisce** \,rem-ə-'nis\ *vb* **rem·i·nisced**; **rem·i·nisc·ing**
to talk or think about things in the past

**rem·i·nis·cence** \,rem-ə-'nis-ns\ *n*
**1** a recalling or telling of a past experience
**2 reminiscences** *pl* a story of one's memorable experiences

**rem·i·nis·cent** \,rem-ə-'nis-nt\ *adj*
**1** of, relating to, or engaging in reminiscence
**2** reminding one of something else

**re·miss** \ri-'mis\ *adj*
careless in the performance of work or duty
**re·miss·ly** *adv*
**re·miss·ness** *n*

**re·mit** \ri-'mit\ *vb* **re·mit·ted**; **re·mit·ting**
**1** ²PARDON 2
**2** to send money (as in payment)
**re·mit·ter** *n*

**re·mit·tance** \ri-'mit-ns\ *n*
money sent in payment

**rem·nant** \'rem-nənt\ *n*
something that remains or is left over ⟨a *remnant* of cloth⟩

**re·mod·el** \'rē-'mäd-l\ *vb* **re·mod·eled** *or* **re·mod·elled**; **re·mod·el·ing** *or* **re·mod·el·ling**
to change the structure of

**re·mon·strate** \ri-'män-,strāt\ *vb* **re·mon·strat·ed**; **re·mon·strat·ing**
²PROTEST 2

**re·morse** \ri-'mȯrs\ *n*
deep regret for one's sins or for acts that wrong others
**re·morse·ful** \-fəl\ *adj*
**re·morse·less** \-ləs\ *adj*

**¹re·mote** \ri-'mōt\ *adj* **re·mot·er**; **re·mot·est**
**1** far off in place or time ⟨*remote* countries⟩ ⟨*remote* ages⟩
**2** SECLUDED ⟨a *remote* valley⟩
**3** not closely connected or related ⟨a *remote* relative⟩
**4** small in degree ⟨a *remote* possibility⟩
**5** distant in manner **:** ALOOF
**re·mote·ly** *adv*
**re·mote·ness** *n*

**²remote** *n*
REMOTE CONTROL

**remote control** *n*
**1** control (as by a radio signal) of operation from a point some distance away ⟨operated by *remote control*⟩
**2** ► a device for controlling something from a distance ⟨a *remote control* for a VCR⟩

**re·mov·able** \ri-'mü-və-bəl\ *adj*
possible to remove

**remote control 2:** a remote control for a television and VCR

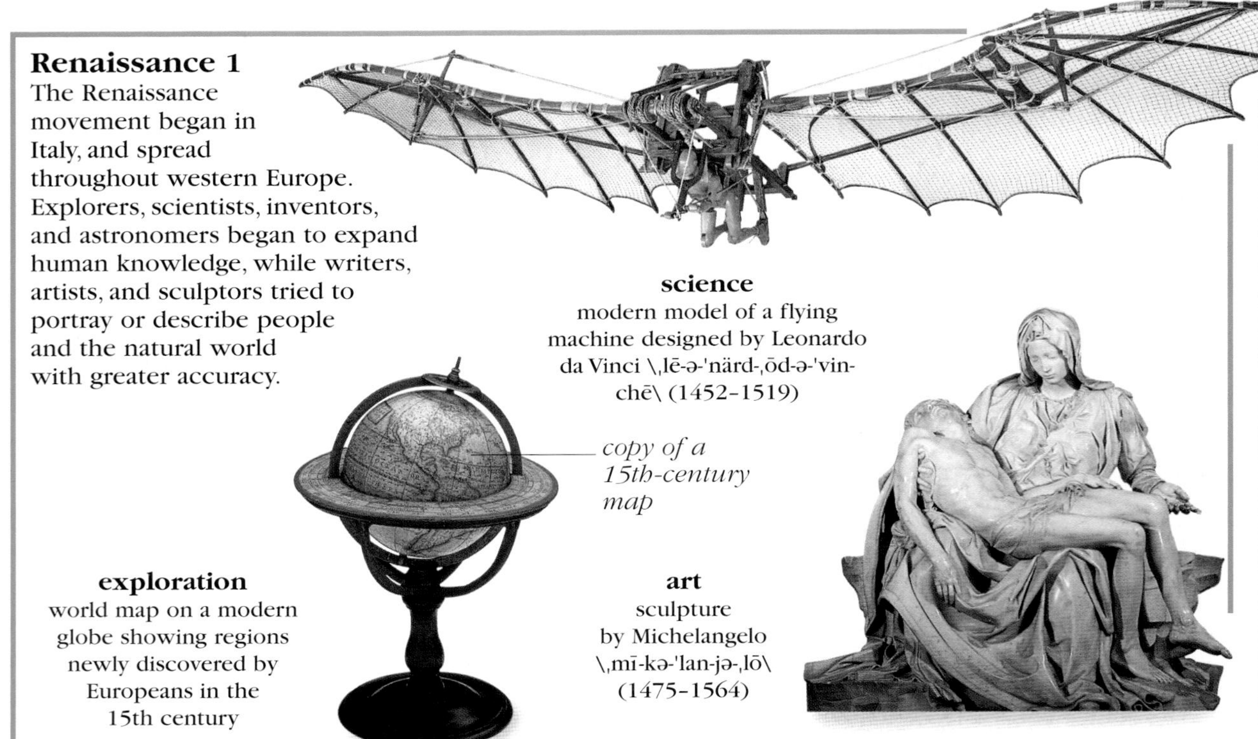

**Renaissance 1**
The Renaissance movement began in Italy, and spread throughout western Europe. Explorers, scientists, inventors, and astronomers began to expand human knowledge, while writers, artists, and sculptors tried to portray or describe people and the natural world with greater accuracy.

**science**
modern model of a flying machine designed by Leonardo da Vinci \ˌlē-ə-ˈnärd-ˌōd-ə-ˈvin-chē\ (1452–1519)

*copy of a 15th-century map*

**exploration**
world map on a modern globe showing regions newly discovered by Europeans in the 15th century

**art**
sculpture by Michelangelo \ˌmī-kə-ˈlan-jə-ˌlō\ (1475–1564)

**re·mov·al** \ri-ˈmü-vəl\ *n*
the act of removing **:** the fact of being removed

**re·move** \ri-ˈmüv\ *vb* **re·moved**; **re·mov·ing**
**1** to move by lifting or taking off or away ⟨please *remove* your hat⟩ ⟨*removed* a book from the shelf⟩
**2** to dismiss from office ⟨the treasurer was *removed* after a year⟩
**3** to get rid of ⟨*remove* the causes of poverty⟩

**re·mov·er** \ri-ˈmü-vər\ *n*
something (as a chemical) used in removing a substance ⟨paint *remover*⟩

**Re·nais·sance** \ˌren-ə-ˈsäns\ *n*
**1** ▲ the period of European history between the fourteenth and seventeenth centuries marked by a fresh interest in ancient art and literature and by the beginnings of modern science
**2** *often not cap* a movement or period of great activity in literature, science, and the arts

**re·name** \rē-ˈnām\ *vb* **re·named**; **re·nam·ing**
to give a new name to ⟨*rename* a street⟩

**rend** \ˈrend\ *vb* **rent** \ˈrent\; **rend·ing**
to tear apart by force

**ren·der** \ˈren-dər\ *vb*
**1** to obtain by heating ⟨*render* lard from fat⟩
**2** to furnish or give to another ⟨*render* a report⟩ ⟨*render* aid⟩
**3** to cause to be or become ⟨*rendered* helpless by the blow⟩
**4** PERFORM 2 ⟨*render* a song⟩

**ren·dez·vous** \ˈrän-di-ˌvü, -dā-\ *n, pl* **ren·dez·vous** \-ˌvüz\
**1** a place agreed on for a meeting
**2** a planned meeting

**ren·di·tion** \ren-ˈdish-ən\ *n*
an act or a result of rendering

**ren·e·gade** \ˈren-i-ˌgād\ *n*
a person who deserts a faith, cause, or party

**re·nege** \ri-ˈnig, -ˈneg\ *vb* **re·neged**; **re·neg·ing**
to go back on a promise or agreement

**re·new** \ri-ˈnü, -ˈnyü\ *vb*
**1** to make or become new, fresh, or strong again
**2** to make, do, or begin again ⟨*renew* a complaint⟩
**3** to put in a fresh supply of ⟨*renew* the water in a tank⟩
**4** to continue in force for a new period ⟨*renew* a lease⟩

**re·new·al** \ri-ˈnü-əl, -ˈnyü-\ *n*
**1** the act of renewing **:** the state of being renewed
**2** something renewed

**re·nounce** \ri-ˈnau̇ns\ *vb* **re·nounced**; **re·nounc·ing**
**1** to give up, abandon, or resign usually by a public declaration ⟨*renounced* the throne⟩
**2** REPUDIATE 1, DISCLAIM ⟨*renounce* one's religion⟩

**ren·o·vate** \ˈren-ə-ˌvāt\ *vb* **ren·o·vat·ed**; **ren·o·vat·ing**
to put in good condition again
**ren·o·va·tor** \-ˌvāt-ər\ *n*

**re·nown** \ri-ˈnau̇n\ *n*
the state of being widely and favorably known

**re·nowned** \ri-ˈnau̇nd\ *adj*
having renown

**[1]rent** \ˈrent\ *n*
money paid for the use of another's property
**for rent** available for use at a price

**[2]rent** *vb*
**1** to take and hold property under an agreement to pay rent

2 to give the possession and use of in return for rent ⟨*rented* a cottage to friends⟩
3 to be for rent ⟨the house *rents* for $700 a month⟩ **synonyms** see HIRE

[3]**rent** *past of* REND

[4]**rent** *n*
an opening (as in cloth) made by tearing

[1]**rent·al** \'rent-l\ *n*
an amount paid or collected as rent

[2]**rental** *adj*
of, relating to, or available for rent

**rent·er** \'rent-ər\ *n*
a person who pays rent for something (as a place to live)

**re·open** \'rē-'ō-pən\ *vb*
to open again

**re·or·ga·nize** \'rē-'ȯr-gə-,nīz\ *vb* **re·or·ga·nized**; **re·or·ga·niz·ing**
to organize again

[1]**re·pair** \ri-'paər, -'peər\ *vb*
1 ▶ to put back in good condition ⟨*repair* a broken toy⟩
2 to make up for⟨*repair* a wrong⟩
**synonyms** see MEND

[2]**repair** *n*
1 the act or process of repairing
2 [1]CONDITION 3 ⟨a house in bad *repair*⟩

**rep·a·ra·tion** \,rep-ə-'rā-shən\ *n*
1 the act of making up for a wrong
2 something paid by a country losing a war to the winner to make up for damages done in the war

**re·past** \ri-'past\ *n*
[1]MEAL

**re·pay** \rē-'pā\ *vb* **re·paid** \-'pād\; **re·pay·ing**
1 to pay back ⟨*repay* a loan⟩
2 to make a return payment to ⟨*repay* a creditor⟩

**re·pay·ment** \rē-'pā-mənt\ *n*
the act or an instance of paying back

**re·peal** \ri-'pēl\ *vb*
to do away with especially by legislative action ⟨*repeal* a law⟩

[1]**re·peat** \ri-'pēt\ *vb*
1 to state or tell again ⟨*repeat* a question⟩ ⟨*repeat* gossip⟩
2 to say from memory : RECITE ⟨*repeat* a poem⟩
3 to make or do again ⟨*repeat* a mistake⟩
**re·peat·er** *n*

[2]**repeat** *n*
1 the act of repeating
2 something repeated

**re·peat·ed** \ri-'pēt-əd\ *adj*
done or happening again and again
**re·peat·ed·ly** *adv*

**re·pel** \ri-'pel\ *vb* **re·pelled**; **re·pel·ling**
1 to drive back ⟨*repel* the enemy⟩
2 to turn away : REJECT ⟨*repel* a suggestion⟩
3 to keep out : RESIST ⟨cloth treated to *repel* water⟩
4 [2]DISGUST ⟨a sight that *repelled* everyone⟩

**re·pel·lent** \ri-'pel-ənt\ *n*
▶ a substance used to keep off pests (as insects)

[1]**repair 1:**
a teddy bear being repaired

**re·pent** \ri-'pent\ *vb*
1 to feel sorrow for one's sin and make up one's mind to do what is right
2 to feel sorry for something done : REGRET ⟨*repent* a rash decision⟩

**re·pen·tance** \ri-'pent-ns\ *n*
the action or process of repenting

**re·pen·tant** \ri-'pent-nt\ *adj*
feeling or showing regret for something one has done
**re·pen·tant·ly** *adv*

**re·per·cus·sion** \,rē-pər-'kəsh-ən\ *n*
1 a return action or effect
2 a widespread, indirect, or unexpected effect of something said or done

**rep·er·toire** \'rep-ər-,twär\ *n*
a list or supply of plays, operas, or pieces that a company or person is prepared to perform

**rep·er·to·ry** \'rep-ər-,tōr-ē\ *n, pl* **rep·er·to·ries**
REPERTOIRE

**rep·e·ti·tion** \,rep-ə-'tish-ən\ *n*
1 the act or an instance of repeating
2 something repeated

**repellent:**
a spray can containing insect repellent

**re·place** \ri-'plās\ *vb* **re·placed**; **re·plac·ing**
1 to put back in a former or proper place ⟨*replace* a card in a file⟩
2 to take the place of ⟨paper money has *replaced* gold coins⟩
3 to put something new in the place of ⟨*replace* a broken dish⟩

**re·place·ment** \ri-'plās-mənt\ *n*
1 the act of replacing : the state of being replaced
2 [1]SUBSTITUTE

**re·plen·ish** \ri-'plen-ish\ *vb*
to make full or complete once more ⟨*replenish* a supply of fuel⟩
**re·plen·ish·er** *n*
**re·plen·ish·ment** \-mənt\ *n*

**re·plete** \ri-'plēt\ *adj*
well supplied ⟨the game was *replete* with thrills⟩
**re·plete·ness** *n*

**rep·li·ca** \'rep-li-kə\ *n*
a very exact copy

[1]**re·ply** \ri-'plī\ *vb* **re·plied**; **re·ply·ing**
to say or do in answer : RESPOND

[2]**reply** *n, pl* **re·plies**
something said, written, or done in answer

[1]**re·port** \ri-'pōrt\ *n*
1 [1]RUMOR
2 REPUTATION 1 ⟨people of evil *report*⟩
3 a usually complete description or statement ⟨a weather *report*⟩
4 an explosive noise ⟨the *report* of a gun⟩

A B C D E F G H I J K L M N O P Q R S T U V W X Y Z

[2]**report** *vb*
**1** to describe or tell something ⟨*reported* what happened⟩ ⟨*reported* that they won⟩
**2** to prepare or present an account of something (as for television or a newspaper)
**3** to present oneself ⟨*report* for duty⟩
**4** to make known to the proper authorities ⟨*report* a fire⟩
**5** to make a charge of misconduct against ⟨will *report* them to the police⟩
**re·port·er** *n*

**Synonyms** REPORT, DESCRIBE, and NARRATE mean to talk or write about something. REPORT suggests the giving of information to others often after one has done some investigation ⟨newspapers *report* important events⟩. DESCRIBE stresses the giving to the hearers or readers a clear mental picture of an event or situation ⟨*describe* a day at school⟩. NARRATE suggests the telling of a story with a beginning and an end ⟨*narrated* a tale about pirates and sailors⟩.

**report card** *n*
a report on a student's grades that is regularly sent by a school to the student's parents or guardian

[1]**re·pose** \ri-'pōz\ *vb* **re·posed**; **re·pos·ing**
**1** to lay at rest
**2** ▼ to lie at rest ⟨*reposing* on the couch⟩

[2]**repose** *n*
**1** a state of resting and especially sleep after effort or strain
**2** freedom from disturbance or excitement : CALM

[1]**repose 2:** a woman reposing on a couch

**rep·re·sent** \,rep-ri-'zent\ *vb*
**1** to present a picture, image, or likeness of : PORTRAY ⟨this picture *represents* a scene at King Arthur's court⟩
**2** to be a sign or symbol of ⟨the flag *represents* our country⟩
**3** to act for or in place of ⟨we elect men and women to *represent* us in Congress⟩

**rep·re·sen·ta·tion** \,rep-ri-,zen-'tā-shən\ *n*
**1** one (as a picture or symbol) that represents something else
**2** the act of representing : the state of being represented (as in a legislative body)

[1]**rep·re·sen·ta·tive** \,rep-ri-'zent-ət-iv\ *adj*
**1** serving to represent ⟨a painting *representative* of a battle⟩
**2** standing or acting for another
**3** carried on by elected representatives ⟨a *representative* government⟩
**4** being a typical example of the thing mentioned ⟨chosen by the class as a *representative* athlete⟩

[2]**representative** *n*
**1** a typical example (as of a group or class)
**2** a person who represents another (as in a legislature)

**re·press** \ri-'pres\ *vb*
to hold in check by or as if by pressure

[1]**re·prieve** \ri-'prēv\ *vb* **re·prieved**; **re·priev·ing**
to delay the punishment of (as a prisoner sentenced to die)

[2]**reprieve** *n*
**1** a postponing of a prison or death sentence
**2** a temporary relief

[1]**rep·ri·mand** \'rep-rə-,mand\ *n*
a severe or formal criticism : CENSURE

[2]**reprimand** *vb*
to criticize (a person) severely or formally

**re·pri·sal** \ri-'prī-zəl\ *n*
an act in return for harm done by another

[1]**re·proach** \ri-'prōch\ *n*
**1** something that calls for blame or disgrace ⟨their dirty yard is a *reproach* to the whole street⟩
**2** an expression of disapproval

[2]**reproach** *vb*
to find fault with : BLAME

**re·pro·duce** \,rē-prə-'düs, -'dyüs\ *vb* **re·pro·duced**; **re·pro·duc·ing**
**1** to produce again ⟨the cooling of steam *reproduces* water⟩
**2** to produce another living thing of the same kind ⟨many plants *reproduce* by means of seeds⟩
**re·pro·duc·er** *n*

**re·pro·duc·tion** \,rē-prə-'dək-shən\ *n*
**1** the act or process of reproducing
**2** [1]COPY 1

**re·pro·duc·tive** \,rē-prə-'dək-tiv\ *adj*
of, relating to, capable of, or concerned with reproduction ⟨*reproductive* cells⟩

**re·proof** \ri-'prüf\ *n*
blame or criticism for a fault

**re·prove** \ri-'prüv\ *vb* **re·proved**; **re·prov·ing**
to express blame or disapproval of : SCOLD ⟨*reprove* a child⟩

**rep·tile** \'rep-təl, -,tīl\ *n*
▶ any of a group of vertebrates (as snakes, lizards, turtles, and alligators) that are cold-blooded, breathe air, and usually have the skin covered with scales or bony plates

**Word History** Most of the animals we call *reptiles* creep or crawl about. Some, like snakes, crawl about on their bellies. Some, like lizards, creep about on little, short legs. The English word *reptile* came from a Latin word that meant "creeping." This Latin word came from a Latin verb meaning "to creep."

## reptile

Related to the dinosaurs, modern reptiles live in habitats throughout the world, avoiding only cold regions and high altitudes. All have dry, scaly skin, which prevents water loss in hot, dry climates, and reproduce by laying eggs, which hatch into fully formed young. Reptiles shed skin as they grow, and many can lose their tail at will to escape a predator; the tail later grows again.

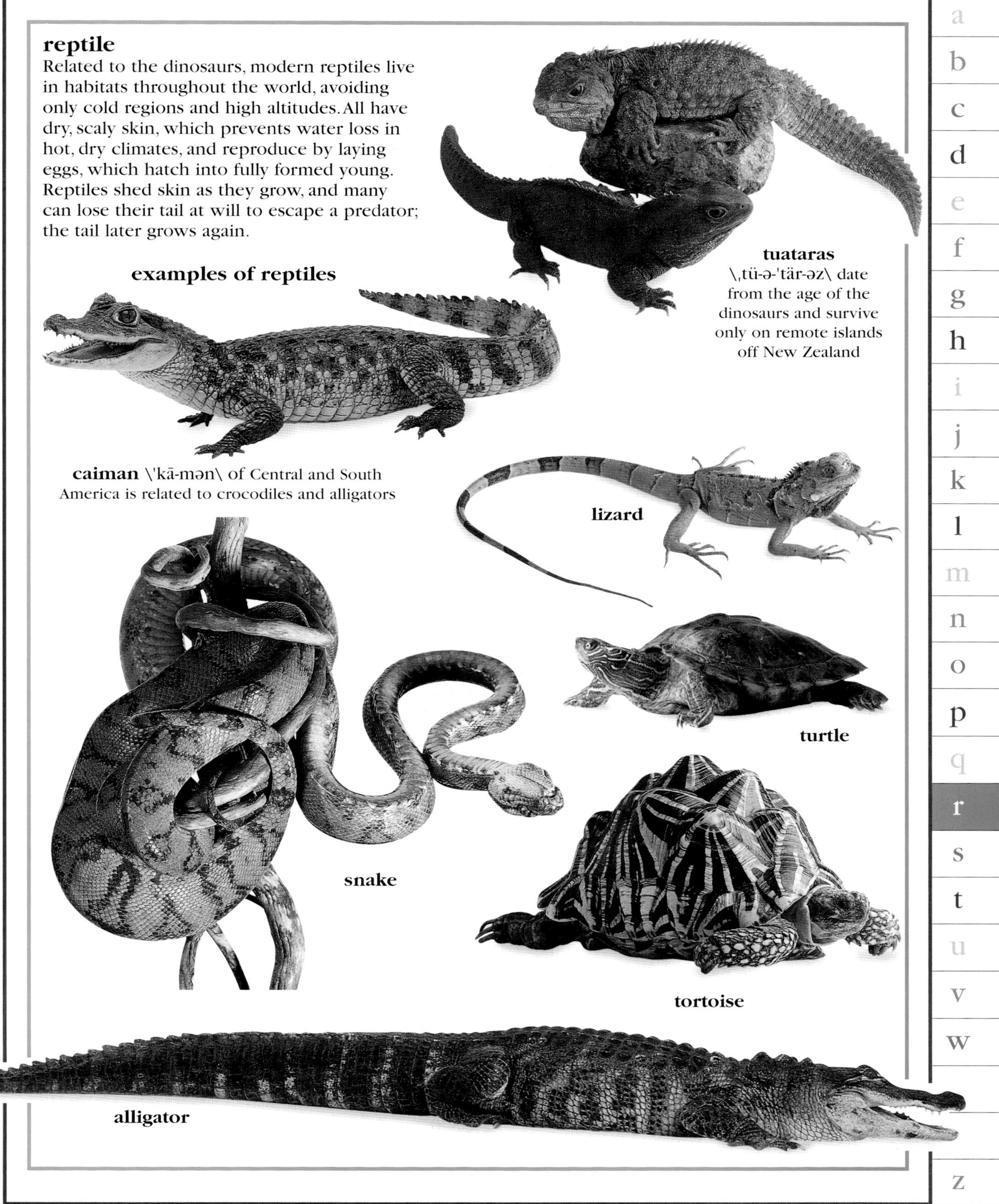


**examples of reptiles**

**tuataras** \,tü-ə-'tär-əz\ date from the age of the dinosaurs and survive only on remote islands off New Zealand

**caiman** \'kā-mən\ of Central and South America is related to crocodiles and alligators

**lizard**

**turtle**

**snake**

**tortoise**

**alligator**

A B C D E F G H I J K L M N O P Q R S T U V W X Y Z

**re·pub·lic** \ri-ˈpəb-lik\ *n*
**1** a government having a chief of state who is not a monarch and who is usually a president
**2** a government in which supreme power lies in the citizens through their right to vote
**3** a state or country having a republican government

[1]**re·pub·li·can** \ri-ˈpəb-li-kən\ *n*
a person who favors a republican form of government

[2]**republican** *adj*
of, relating to, or like a republic ⟨a *republican* form of government⟩

**re·pu·di·ate** \ri-ˈpyüd-ē-ˌāt\ *vb* **re·pu·di·at·ed**; **re·pu·di·at·ing**
**1** to refuse to have anything to do with
**2** to refuse to accept, admit, or pay ⟨*repudiate* a debt⟩

[1]**re·pulse** \ri-ˈpəls\ *vb* **re·pulsed**; **re·puls·ing**
**1** to drive or beat back **:** REPEL
**2** to treat with discourtesy **:** SNUB

[2]**repulse** *n*
**1** [2]REBUFF, SNUB
**2** the action of driving back an attacker

**re·pul·sive** \ri-ˈpəl-siv\ *adj*
causing disgust ⟨a *repulsive* sight⟩
**re·pul·sive·ly** *adv*
**re·pul·sive·ness** *n*

**rep·u·ta·ble** \ˈrep-yət-ə-bəl\ *adj*
having a good reputation ⟨*reputable* citizens⟩
**rep·u·ta·bly** \-blē\ *adv*

**rep·u·ta·tion** \ˌrep-yə-ˈtā-shən\ *n*
**1** overall quality or character as seen or judged by people in general ⟨this car has a good *reputation*⟩
**2** notice by other people of some quality or ability ⟨have the *reputation* of being a good tennis player⟩

[1]**re·pute** \ri-ˈpyüt\ *vb* **re·put·ed**; **re·put·ing**
CONSIDER 3 ⟨a person *reputed* to be a millionaire⟩

[2]**repute** *n*
**1** REPUTATION 1
**2** good reputation **:** HONOR

[1]**re·quest** \ri-ˈkwest\ *n*
**1** an asking for something
**2** something asked for ⟨grant every *request*⟩
**3** the condition of being requested ⟨tickets are available on *request*⟩

[2]**request** *vb*
**1** to make a request to or of ⟨*request* them to sing⟩
**2** to ask for ⟨*request* a loan⟩

**re·qui·em** \ˈrek-wē-əm\ *n*
**1** a mass for a dead person
**2** a musical service or hymn in honor of the dead

**re·quire** \ri-ˈkwīr\ *vb* **re·quired**; **re·quir·ing**
**1** to have a need for ⟨a trick that *requires* skill⟩
**2** [1]ORDER 2, COMMAND ⟨the law *requires* drivers to obey traffic signals⟩

**re·quire·ment** \ri-ˈkwīr-mənt\ *n*
something that is required or necessary ⟨complete all *requirements*⟩ ⟨sleep is a *requirement* for health⟩

[1]**req·ui·site** \ˈrek-wə-zət\ *adj*
needed for reaching a goal or achieving a purpose

[2]**requisite** *n*
REQUIREMENT

**re·read** \ˈrē-ˈrēd\ *vb* **re·read** \-ˈred\; **re·read·ing**
to read again

[1]**res·cue** \ˈres-kyü\ *vb* **res·cued**; **res·cu·ing**
to free from danger or evil **:** SAVE
**res·cu·er** *n*

[2]**rescue** *n*
an act of rescuing

**re·search** \ri-ˈsərch, ˈrē-ˌsərch\ *n*
careful study and investigation for the purpose of discovering and explaining new knowledge
**re·search·er** *n*

**re·sem·blance** \ri-ˈzem-bləns\ *n*
the quality or state of resembling something else

**re·sem·ble** \ri-ˈzem-bəl\ *vb* **re·sem·bled**; **re·sem·bling**
to be like or similar to

**re·sent** \ri-ˈzent\ *vb*
to feel annoyance or anger at ⟨*resent* criticism⟩

**re·sent·ment** \ri-ˈzent-mənt\ *n*
a feeling of angry displeasure at a real or imagined wrong, insult, or injury

**res·er·va·tion** \ˌrez-ər-ˈvā-shən\ *n*
**1** an act of reserving
**2** an arrangement to have something (as a hotel room) held for one's use
**3** something (as land) reserved for a special use ⟨an Indian *reservation*⟩
**4** something that limits ⟨agree without *reservations*⟩

[1]**re·serve** \ri-ˈzərv\ *vb* **re·served**; **re·serv·ing**
**1** to keep in store for future or special use
**2** to hold over to a future time or place ⟨*reserve* judgment⟩
**3** to arrange to have set aside and held for one's use ⟨*reserve* a hotel room⟩

[2]**reserve** *n*
**1** something stored or available for future use ⟨oil *reserves*⟩
**2 reserves** *pl* military forces held back or available for later use
**3** an area of land set apart ⟨wild game *reserve*⟩
**4** an act of reserving
**5** caution in one's words and behavior

**re·served** \ri-ˈzərvd\ *adj*
**1** cautious in words and actions
**2** kept or set apart for future or special use

**res·er·voir** \ˈrez-ərv-ˌwär\ *n*
▼ a place where something (as water) is kept in store for future use

**reservoir** that provides water to a large city

**resin 1**
Resins include amber, balsam, and rosin, as well as frankincense and myrrh. Prized since ancient times, frankincense and myrrh are fragrant resins still used in incense, perfumes, and cosmetics.

pellets of dried frankincense

pellets of dried myrrh

**re•set** \'rē-'set\ *vb* **re•set**; **re•set•ting**
to set again

**re•ship•ment** \'rē-'ship-mənt\ *n*
an act of shipping again

**re•side** \ri-'zīd\ *vb* **re•sid•ed**; **re•sid•ing**
1 to live permanently and continuously : DWELL
2 to have its place : EXIST ⟨the right to decide *resides* in the voters⟩

**res•i•dence** \'rez-ə-dəns\ *n*
1 the act or fact of residing
2 the place where one actually lives
3 a building used for a home
4 the time during which a person lives in a place ⟨a *residence* of ten years⟩

**[1]res•i•dent** \'rez-ə-dənt\ *adj*
1 living in a place for some length of time
2 serving in a full-time position at a certain place ⟨the hospital's *resident* doctors⟩

**[2]resident** *n*
a person who lives in a place

**res•i•den•tial** \,rez-ə-'den-chəl\ *adj*
1 used as a residence or by residents ⟨a *residential* hotel⟩
2 suitable for or containing residences ⟨a *residential* section of the city⟩

**res•i•due** \'rez-ə-,dü, -,dyü\ *n*
whatever remains after a part is taken, set apart, or lost

**re•sign** \ri-'zīn\ *vb*
1 to give up by a formal or official act ⟨*resign* an office⟩
2 to prepare to accept something usually unpleasant ⟨*resigned* myself to the loss⟩

**res•ig•na•tion** \,rez-ig-'nā-shən\ *n*
1 an act of resigning
2 a letter or written statement that gives notice of resignation
3 the feeling of a person who is resigned

**re•signed** \ri-'zīnd\ *adj*
giving in patiently (as to loss or sorrow)
**re•sign•ed•ly** \-'zī-nəd-lē\ *adv*

**res•in** \'rez-n\ *n*
1 ▲ a yellowish or brownish substance obtained from the gum or sap of some trees (as the pine) and used in varnishes and medicine
2 any of various manufactured products that are similar to natural resins in properties and are used especially as plastics

**re•sist** \ri-'zist\ *vb*
1 to withstand the force or effect of ⟨*resist* disease⟩
2 to fight against : OPPOSE ⟨*resist* arrest⟩

**re•sis•tance** \ri-'zis-təns\ *n*
1 an act or instance of resisting
2 the ability to resist ⟨the body's *resistance* to disease⟩
3 an opposing or slowing force ⟨the *resistance* of air to an airplane in motion⟩
4 the opposition offered by a substance to the passage through it of an electric current

**re•sis•tant** \ri-'zis-tənt\ *adj*
giving or capable of resistance

**res•o•lute** \'rez-ə-,lüt\ *adj*
firmly determined
**res•o•lute•ly** *adv*
**res•o•lute•ness** *n*

**res•o•lu•tion** \,rez-ə-'lü-shən\ *n*
1 the act of resolving
2 the act of solving : SOLUTION ⟨the *resolution* of a problem⟩
3 something decided on ⟨New Year *resolutions*⟩
4 firmness of purpose
5 a statement expressing the feelings, wishes, or decisions of a group

**[1]re•solve** \ri-'zälv\ *vb* **re•solved**; **re•solv•ing**
1 to find an answer to : SOLVE ⟨*resolve* a difficulty⟩
2 to reach a firm decision about something ⟨*resolve* to work hard⟩
3 to declare or decide by a formal resolution and vote

**[2]resolve** *n*
1 something resolved
2 firmness of purpose

**res•o•nance** \'rez-n-əns\ *n*
the quality or state of being resonant

**res•o•nant** \'rez-n-ənt\ *adj*
being or making sound with a rich vibrating quality ⟨a *resonant* voice⟩
**res•o•nant•ly** *adv*

**[1]re•sort** \ri-'zȯrt\ *n*
1 one that is looked to for help
2 HANGOUT
3 a place where people go for pleasure, sport, or a change ⟨a ski *resort*⟩ ⟨vacation *resorts*⟩

**[2]resort** *vb*
1 to go often or again and again
2 to seek aid, relief, or advantage ⟨*resorted* to force in order to check the mob⟩

**re•sound** \ri-'zau̇nd\ *vb*
1 to become filled with sound : REVERBERATE ⟨the hall *resounded* with cheers⟩
2 to sound loudly ⟨the organ *resounds* through the hall⟩

**re•source** \'rē-,sōrs\ *n*
1 a new or a reserve source of supply or support
2 **resources** *pl* a usable stock or supply (as of money or products) ⟨America has great natural *resources*⟩
3 the ability to meet and deal with situations

**re•source•ful** \ri-'sōrs-fəl\ *adj*
clever in dealing with problems
**re•source•ful•ly** \-fə-lē\ *adv*
**re•source•ful•ness** *n*

A B C D E F G H I J K L M N O P Q R S T U V W X Y Z

**[1]re·spect** \ri-ˈspekt\ *n*
**1** relation to or concern with something specified ⟨with *respect* to your last letter⟩
**2** high or special regard : ESTEEM
**3 respects** *pl* an expression of regard or courtesy ⟨pay my *respects*⟩
**4** [1]DETAIL 2 ⟨perfect in all *respects*⟩

**[2]respect** *vb*
**1** to consider worthy of high regard : ESTEEM
**2** to pay attention to ⟨*respected* their wishes⟩
**re·spect·er** *n*

**re·spect·able** \ri-ˈspek-tə-bəl\ *adj*
**1** deserving respect ⟨acted in a *respectable* manner⟩
**2** decent or correct in conduct : PROPER ⟨*respectable* people⟩
**3** fair in size or quantity ⟨a *respectable* amount⟩
**4** fit to be seen : PRESENTABLE ⟨*respectable* clothes⟩
**re·spect·ably** \-blē\ *adv*

**re·spect·ful** \ri-ˈspekt-fəl\ *adj* showing respect ⟨a *respectful* manner⟩
**re·spect·ful·ly** \-fə-lē\ *adv*
**re·spect·ful·ness** *n*

**re·spect·ing** \ri-ˌspek-ting\ *prep* CONCERNING ⟨information *respecting* stolen goods⟩

**re·spec·tive** \ri-ˈspek-tiv\ *adj* not the same or shared : SEPARATE ⟨they hurried to their *respective* homes⟩
**re·spec·tive·ly** *adv*

**re·spell** \ˈrē-ˈspel\ *vb* to spell again or in another way ⟨*respelled* pronunciations⟩

**res·pi·ra·tion** \ˌres-pə-ˈrā-shən\ *n*
**1** the act or process of breathing
**2** the physical and chemical processes (as breathing and oxidation) by which a living being gets the oxygen it needs to live

**res·pi·ra·tor** \ˈres-pə-ˌrāt-ər\ *n*
**1** a device covering the mouth or nose especially to prevent the breathing in of something harmful
**2** a device used for aiding one to breathe

**res·pi·ra·to·ry** \ˈres-pə-rə-ˌtōr-ē\ *adj* of, relating to, or concerned with respiration

**respiratory system** *n* a system of the body used in breathing that in human beings consists of the nose, nasal passages, pharynx, larynx, trachea, bronchial tubes, and lungs

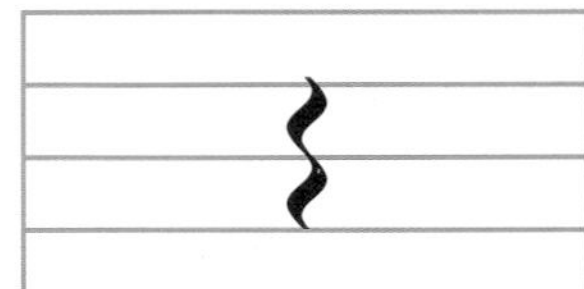

**[1]rest 6:** the musical notation for a single rest beat

**re·spire** \ri-ˈspīr\ *vb* **re·spired**; **re·spir·ing** BREATHE 1

**res·pite** \ˈres-pət\ *n*
**1** a short delay
**2** a period of rest or relief

**re·splen·dent** \ri-ˈsplen-dənt\ *adj* shining brightly : SPLENDID
**re·splen·dent·ly** *adv*

**re·spond** \ri-ˈspänd\ *vb*
**1** to say something in return : REPLY
**2** to act in response : REACT ⟨*respond* to surgery⟩

**re·sponse** \ri-ˈspäns\ *n*
**1** an act or instance of replying : ANSWER ⟨there was no *response* to my question⟩
**2** words said or sung by the people or choir in a religious service
**3** a reaction of a living being (as to a drug)

**re·spon·si·bil·i·ty** \ri-ˌspän-sə-ˈbil-ət-ē\ *n, pl* **re·spon·si·bil·i·ties**
**1** the quality or state of being responsible
**2** the quality of being dependable ⟨show *responsibility* by always doing your homework⟩
**3** something for which one is responsible

**re·spon·si·ble** \ri-ˈspän-sə-bəl\ *adj*
**1** getting the credit or blame for one's acts or decisions ⟨*responsible* for the damage⟩
**2** RELIABLE ⟨*responsible* persons⟩
**3** needing a person to take charge of or be trusted with things of importance ⟨a *responsible* job⟩
**re·spon·si·bly** \-blē\ *adv*

**re·spon·sive** \ri-ˈspän-siv\ *adj*
**1** giving response ⟨a *responsive* glance⟩
**2** quick to respond or react in a sympathetic way
**re·spon·sive·ly** *adv*
**re·spon·sive·ness** *n*

**[1]rest** \ˈrest\ *n*
**1** [1]SLEEP 1
**2** freedom from activity or work
**3** a state of not moving or not doing anything
**4** a place for resting or stopping
**5** a silence in music
**6** ◀ a symbol in music that stands for a certain period of silence in a measure
**7** something used for support ⟨a head *rest*⟩

**[2]rest** *vb*
**1** to get rest by lying down : SLEEP
**2** to give rest to ⟨*rest* your eyes now and then⟩
**3** to lie dead
**4** to not take part in work or activity
**5** to sit or lie fixed or supported ⟨a house *rests* on its foundation⟩
**6** DEPEND 2 ⟨the success of the flight *rests* on the wind⟩
**7** to fix or be fixed in trust or confidence ⟨*rested* their hopes on their children⟩

**[3]rest** *n* something that is left over : REMAINDER

**re·state·ment** \ˈrē-ˈstāt-mənt\ *n* a saying again or in another way

**res·tau·rant** \ˈres-tə-rənt, -ˌränt\ *n* a public eating place

**rest·ful** \ˈrest-fəl\ *adj*
**1** giving rest ⟨a *restful* chair⟩
**2** giving a feeling of rest : QUIET ⟨a *restful* scene⟩
**rest·ful·ly** \-fə-lē\ *adv*
**rest·ful·ness** *n*

**rest·ing** \ˈres-ting\ *adj* DORMANT ⟨a *resting* spore⟩

**res·tive** \ˈres-tiv\ *adj*
**1** resisting control
**2** not being at ease
**res·tive·ly** *adv*
**res·tive·ness** *n*

**rest·less** \ˈrest-ləs\ *adj*
**1** having or giving no rest ⟨a *restless* night⟩
**2** not quiet or calm ⟨the *restless* sea⟩
**rest·less·ly** *adv*
**rest·less·ness** *n*

**res·to·ra·tion** \ˌres-tə-ˈrā-shən\ *n*
**1** ▶ an act of restoring : the condition of being restored
**2** something (as a building) that has been restored

**re·store** \ri-ˈstōr\ *vb* **re·stored**; **re·stor·ing**
**1** to give back : RETURN ⟨*restore* a purse to its owner⟩
**2** to put back into use or service

3 to put or bring back to an earlier or original state

**re·strain** \ri-'strān\ *vb*
1 to keep from doing something ⟨*restrain* a crowd⟩
2 to keep back : CURB ⟨*restrain* anger⟩
**re·strain·er** *n*

**re·straint** \ri-'strānt\ *n*
1 the act of restraining : the state of being restrained
2 a restraining force or influence
3 control over one's thoughts or feelings

**re·strict** \ri-'strikt\ *vb*
to keep within bounds : set limits to

**re·stric·tion** \ri-'strik-shən\ *n*
1 something (as a law or rule) that restricts
2 an act of restricting : the condition of being restricted

**re·stric·tive** \ri-'strik-tiv\ *adj*
serving or likely to restrict
**re·stric·tive·ly** *adv*
**re·stric·tive·ness** *n*

**rest·room** \'rest-,rüm, -,ru̇m\ *n*
a room or set of rooms with sinks and toilets

[1]**re·sult** \ri-'zəlt\ *vb*
1 to come about as an effect ⟨disease *results* from infection⟩
2 to end as an effect ⟨the disease *results* in death⟩

[2]**result** *n*
1 something that comes about as an effect or end ⟨the *results* of war⟩
2 a good effect ⟨this method gets *results*⟩

**re·sume** \ri-'züm\ *vb* **re·sumed**; **re·sum·ing**
1 to take or occupy again ⟨*resume* your seats⟩
2 to begin again ⟨*resume* play⟩

**re·sump·tion** \ri-'zəmp-shən\ *n*
the act of resuming

**res·ur·rect** \,rez-ə-'rekt\ *vb*
1 to raise from the dead : bring back to life
2 to bring to view or into use again ⟨*resurrect* an old song⟩

**res·ur·rec·tion** \,rez-ə-'rek-shən\ *n*
1 *cap* the rising of Christ from the dead
2 *often cap* the rising again to life of all human dead before the final judgment
3 a coming back into use or importance

**re·sus·ci·tate** \ri-'səs-ə-,tāt\ *vb* **re·sus·ci·tat·ed**; **re·sus·ci·tat·ing**
to bring back from apparent death or unconsciousness
**re·sus·ci·ta·tor** \-,tāt-ər\ *n*

**restoration 1**

With the technique of picture restoration shown here, an old painting is first strengthened by soaking with glue. When dry, it is cleaned with a solvent, which is painted onto the surface through a piece of cloth. The area is then covered with plastic film to prevent the liquid from evaporating. Finally, after further cleaning with turpentine, any places where paint has flaked away are carefully repainted.

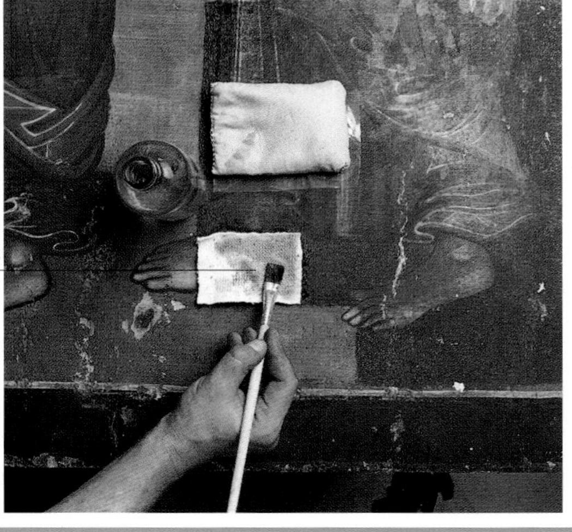

*liquid is applied through fabric*

**restoration of a damaged 15th-century Russian painting**

[1]**re·tail** \'rē-,tāl\ *vb*
to sell in small amounts to people for their own use
**re·tail·er** *n*

[2]**retail** *n*
the sale of products or goods in small amounts to people for their own use

[3]**retail** *adj*
of, relating to, or engaged in selling by retail ⟨*retail* stores⟩ ⟨*retail* prices⟩

**re·tain** \ri-'tān\ *vb*
1 to keep in one's possession or control ⟨*retain* knowledge⟩
2 to hold safe or unchanged ⟨lead *retains* heat⟩

**re·tal·i·ate** \ri-'tal-ē-,āt\ *vb* **re·tal·i·at·ed**; **re·tal·i·at·ing**
to get revenge by returning like for like

**re·tal·i·a·tion** \ri-,tal-ē-'ā-shən\ *n*
the act or an instance of retaliating

**re·tard** \ri-'tärd\ *vb*
to slow up : keep back : DELAY
**re·tard·er** *n*

**retch** \'rech\ *vb*
to vomit or try to vomit

**re·ten·tion** \ri-'ten-chən\ *n*
1 the act of retaining : the state of being retained
2 the power of retaining

**ret·i·na** \'ret-n-ə\ *n, pl* **retinas** *or* **ret·i·nae** \-n-,ē\
the membrane that lines the back part of the eyeball and is the sensitive part for seeing

**re·tire** \ri-'tīr\ *vb* **re·tired**; **re·tir·ing**
1 to get away from action or danger : RETREAT
2 to go away especially to be alone
3 to give up one's job permanently : quit working
4 to go to bed
5 to take out of circulation
**re·tire·ment** \-mənt\ *n*

**re·tired** \ri-'tīrd\ *adj*
not working at active duties or business

**re·tir·ing** \ri-'tīr-ing\ *adj*
[1]SHY 2, RESERVED

[1]**re·tort** \ri-'tȯrt\ *vb*
1 to answer back : reply angrily or sharply
2 to reply with an argument against

[2]**retort** *n*
a quick, clever, or angry reply

A B C D E F G H I J K L M N O P Q R S T U V W X Y Z

**re·trace** \rē-ˈtrās\ *vb* **re·traced**; **re·trac·ing**
to go over once more ⟨*retrace* one's steps⟩

**re·tract** \ri-ˈtrakt\ *vb*
**1** to pull back or in ⟨a cat can *retract* its claws⟩
**2** to take back (as an offer or statement) : WITHDRAW

**¹re·tread** \ˈrē-ˈtred\ *vb* **re·tread·ed**; **re·tread·ing**
to put a new tread on the cord fabric of (a tire)

**²re·tread** \ˈrē-ˌtred\ *n*
a retreaded tire

**¹re·treat** \ri-ˈtrēt\ *n*
**1** an act of going away from something dangerous, difficult, or disagreeable
**2** a military signal for turning away from the enemy
**3** a place of privacy or safety : REFUGE
**4** a period in which a person goes away to pray, think quietly, and study

**²retreat** *vb*
to make a retreat

**re·trieve** \ri-ˈtrēv\ *vb* **re·trieved**; **re·triev·ing**
**1** to find and bring in killed or wounded game ⟨a dog that *retrieves* well⟩
**2** to make good a loss or damage : RECOVER

**re·triev·er** \ri-ˈtrē-vər\ *n*
**1** one that retrieves
**2** a dog that has a water-resistant coat and is skilled in retrieving game

**ret·ro–rock·et** \ˈre-trō-ˌräk-ət\ *n*
► a rocket (as on a space vehicle) used to slow forward motion

**ret·ro·spect** \ˈre-trə-ˌspekt\ *n*
a looking back on things past

**¹re·turn** \ri-ˈtərn\ *vb*
**1** to come or go back
**2** ²ANSWER 1, REPLY
**3** to make an official report of ⟨the jury *returned* a verdict⟩
**4** to bring, carry, send, or put back : RESTORE ⟨*return* a book to the library⟩
**5** ¹YIELD 4, PRODUCE ⟨the loan *returned* good interest⟩
**6** REPAY 1 ⟨*return* borrowed money⟩

**²return** *n*
**1** the act of coming back to or from a place or condition
**2** RECURRENCE ⟨the *return* of spring⟩
**3** a report of the results of voting ⟨election *returns*⟩
**4** a statement of income to be taxed
**5** the profit from labor, investment, or business
**6** the act of returning something (as to an earlier place or condition)
**7** something given (as in payment)

**³return** *adj*
**1** played or given in return ⟨a *return* game⟩
**2** used for returning ⟨*return* ticket⟩

**re·union** \rē-ˈyün-yən\ *n*
**1** the act of reuniting : the state of being reunited
**2** a reuniting of persons after being apart ⟨class *reunion*⟩

**re·unite** \ˌrē-yu̇-ˈnīt\ *vb* **re·unit·ed**; **re·unit·ing**
to come or bring together again after being apart

**rev** \ˈrev\ *vb* **revved**; **rev·ving**
to increase the number of revolutions per minute of (a motor)

**re·veal** \ri-ˈvēl\ *vb*
**1** to make known ⟨*reveal* a secret⟩
**2** to show clearly ⟨the opened door *revealed* a messy room⟩

**rev·eil·le** \ˈrev-ə-lē\ *n*
a signal sounded at about sunrise on a bugle or drum to call soldiers or sailors to duty

**retro-rocket** of a space vehicle used to land astronauts on the moon

*retro-rocket*

**¹rev·el** \ˈrev-əl\ *vb* **rev·eled** *or* **rev·elled**; **rev·el·ing** *or* **rev·el·ling**
**1** to be social in a wild noisy way
**2** to take great pleasure ⟨*reveling* in success⟩

**²revel** *n*
a noisy or merry celebration

**rev·e·la·tion** \ˌrev-ə-ˈlā-shən\ *n*
**1** an act of revealing
**2** something revealed

**rev·el·ry** \ˈrev-əl-rē\ *n, pl* **rev·el·ries**
rough and noisy merrymaking

**¹re·venge** \ri-ˈvenj\ *vb* **re·venged**; **re·veng·ing**
to cause harm or injury in return for ⟨*revenge* a wrong⟩

**²revenge** *n*
**1** an act or instance of revenging
**2** a desire to repay injury for injury
**3** a chance for getting satisfaction

**re·venge·ful** \ri-ˈvenj-fəl\ *adj*
given to or seeking revenge

**rev·e·nue** \ˈrev-ə-ˌnü, -ˌnyü\ *n*
**1** the income from an investment
**2** money collected by a government (as through taxes)

**re·ver·ber·ate** \ri-ˈvər-bə-ˌrāt\ *vb* **re·ver·ber·at·ed**; **re·ver·ber·at·ing**
to continue in or as if in a series of echoes

**re·vere** \ri-ˈvir\ *vb* **re·vered**; **re·ver·ing**
to think of with reverence

**¹rev·er·ence** \ˈrev-ə-rəns, ˈrev-rəns\ *n*
honor and respect mixed with love and awe

**²reverence** *vb* **rev·er·enced**; **rev·er·enc·ing**
to show reverence to or toward

**rev·er·end** \ˈrev-ə-rənd, ˈrev-rənd\ *adj*
**1** worthy of honor and respect
**2** used as a title for a member of the clergy ⟨the *Reverend* John Doe⟩ ⟨the *Reverend* Jane Doe⟩

**rev·er·ent** \ˈrev-ə-rənt, ˈrev-rənt\ *adj*
very respectful
**rev·er·ent·ly** *adv*

**rev·er·ie** *also* **rev·ery** \ˈrev-ə-rē\ *n, pl* **rev·er·ies**
**1** ¹DAYDREAM
**2** the condition of being lost in thought

**re•ver•sal** \ri-'vər-səl\ *n*
an act or the process of reversing

[1]**re•verse** \ri-'vərs\ *adj*
**1** opposite to a previous or normal condition
**2** acting or working in a manner opposite to the usual
**re•verse•ly** *adv*

[2]**reverse** *vb* **re•versed**; **re•vers•ing**
**1** to turn completely around or upside down or inside out
**2** ANNUL ⟨*reverse* a legal decision⟩
**3** to go or cause to go in the opposite direction

[3]**reverse** *n*
**1** something opposite to something else **:** CONTRARY
**2** an act or instance of reversing
**3** the back part of something
**4** a gear that reverses something

**re•vert** \ri-'vərt\ *vb*
to come or go back ⟨*reverted* to savagery⟩

[1]**re•view** \ri-'vyü\ *n*
**1** a military parade put on for high officers
**2** a general survey
**3** a piece of writing about the quality of a book, performance, or show
**4** a fresh study of material studied before

[2]**review** *vb*
**1** to look at a thing again **:** study or examine again ⟨*review* a lesson⟩
**2** to make an inspection of (as troops)
**3** to write a review about (as a book)
**4** to look back on ⟨*review* accomplishments⟩
**re•view•er** *n*

**re•vile** \ri-'vīl\ *vb* **re•viled**; **re•vil•ing**
to speak to in an insulting way
**re•vil•er** *n*

**re•vise** \ri-'vīz\ *vb* **re•vised**; **re•vis•ing**
**1** to look over again to correct or improve ⟨*revise* an essay⟩
**2** to make a new version of ⟨*revise* a dictionary⟩

**re•viv•al** \ri-'vī-vəl\ *n*
**1** a reviving of interest (as in art)
**2** a new presentation of a play or movie
**3** a gaining back of strength or importance ⟨a *revival* of business⟩
**4** a meeting or series of meetings led by a preacher to stir up religious feelings or to make converts

**re•vive** \ri-'vīv\ *vb* **re•vived**; **re•viv•ing**
**1** to bring back or come back to life, consciousness, freshness, or activity
**2** to bring back into use ⟨*revive* an old custom⟩

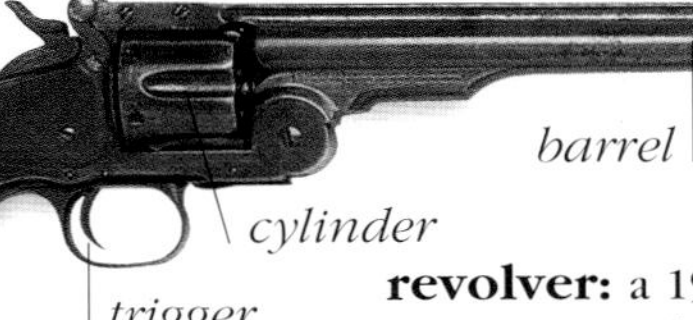

**revolver:** a 19th-century revolver

**re•voke** \ri-'vōk\ *vb* **re•voked**; **re•vok•ing**
to take away or cancel ⟨*revoke* a driver's license⟩

[1]**re•volt** \ri-'vōlt\ *vb*
**1** to rebel against the authority of a ruler or government
**2** to be or cause to be disgusted or shocked

[2]**revolt** *n*
REBELLION, INSURRECTION

**rev•o•lu•tion** \,rev-ə-'lü-shən\ *n*
**1** the action by a celestial body of going round in a fixed course
**2** completion of a course (as of years) **:** CYCLE
**3** a turning round a center or axis **:** ROTATION
**4** a single complete turn (as of a wheel)
**5** a sudden, extreme, or complete change (as in manner of living or working)
**6** the overthrow of one government and the substitution of another by the governed

**rev•o•lu•tion•ary** \,rev-ə-'lü-shə-,ner-ē\ *adj*
**1** of, relating to, or involving revolution ⟨a *revolutionary* war⟩ ⟨*revolutionary* improvements⟩
**2** [1]RADICAL 2 ⟨*revolutionary* ideas⟩

**rev•o•lu•tion•ist** \,rev-ə-'lü-shə-nist\ *n*
a person taking part in or supporting a revolution

**rev•o•lu•tion•ize** \,rev-ə-'lü-shə-,nīz\ *vb* **rev•o•lu•tion•ized**; **rev•o•lu•tion•iz•ing**
to change greatly or completely ⟨*revolutionize* an industry by new methods⟩

**re•volve** \ri-'välv, -'vȯlv\ *vb* **re•volved**; **re•volv•ing**
**1** to think over carefully
**2** to move in an orbit ⟨planets *revolving* around the sun⟩
**3** ROTATE 1

**re•volv•er** \ri-'väl-vər, -'vȯl-\ *n*
◀ a pistol having a revolving cylinder holding several bullets all of which may be shot without loading again

**re•vue** \ri-'vyü\ *n*
a theatrical entertainment consisting usually of short and often funny sketches and songs

[1]**re•ward** \ri-'wȯrd\ *vb*
to give a reward to or for

[2]**reward** *n*
something (as money) given or offered in return for a service (as the return of something lost)

**re•wind** \rē-'wīnd\ *vb* **re•wound** \-'waund\; **re•wind•ing**
to reverse the winding of (as a videotape)

**re•word** \'rē-'wərd\ *vb*
to state in different words

**re•write** \'rē-'rīt\ *vb* **re•wrote** \-'rōt\; **re•writ•ten** \-'rit-n\; **re•writ•ing** \-'rīt-ing\
to write over again especially in a different form

**rhap•so•dy** \'rap-səd-ē\ *n*, *pl* **rhap•so•dies**
a written or spoken expression of extreme praise or delight

**rhea** \'rē-ə\ *n*
▼ a tall flightless South American bird that has three toes on each foot and is like but smaller than the ostrich

**rhea**

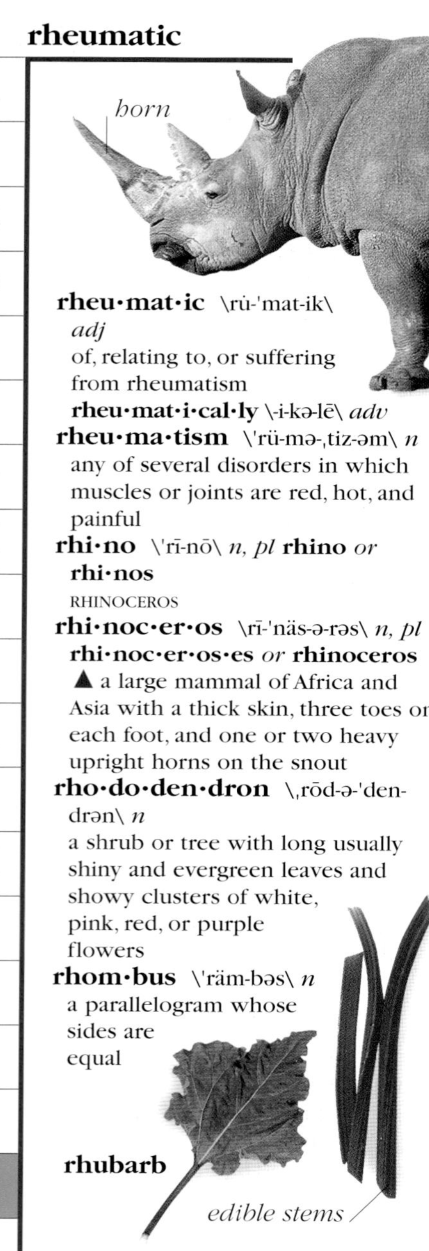


**rheu·mat·ic** \rü-ˈmat-ik\ *adj*
of, relating to, or suffering from rheumatism
**rheu·mat·i·cal·ly** \-i-kə-lē\ *adv*

**rheu·ma·tism** \ˈrü-mə-ˌtiz-əm\ *n*
any of several disorders in which muscles or joints are red, hot, and painful

**rhi·no** \ˈrī-nō\ *n, pl* **rhino** *or* **rhi·nos**
RHINOCEROS

**rhi·noc·er·os** \rī-ˈnäs-ə-rəs\ *n, pl* **rhi·noc·er·os·es** *or* **rhinoceros**
▲ a large mammal of Africa and Asia with a thick skin, three toes on each foot, and one or two heavy upright horns on the snout

**rho·do·den·dron** \ˌrōd-ə-ˈden-drən\ *n*
a shrub or tree with long usually shiny and evergreen leaves and showy clusters of white, pink, red, or purple flowers

**rhom·bus** \ˈräm-bəs\ *n*
a parallelogram whose sides are equal

**rhu·barb** \ˈrü-ˌbärb\ *n*
▲ a plant with broad green leaves and thick juicy pink or red stems that are used for food

[1]**rhyme** *or* **rime** \ˈrīm\ *n*
**1** close similarity in the final sounds of two or more words or lines of verse
**2** a verse composition that rhymes

[2]**rhyme** *or* **rime** *vb* **rhymed** *or* **rimed**; **rhym·ing** *or* **rim·ing**
**1** to make rhymes
**2** to end with the same sound
**3** to cause lines or words to end with a similar sound

**rhythm** \ˈrith-əm\ *n*
**1** a flow of rising and falling sounds produced in poetry by a regular repeating of stressed and unstressed syllables
**2** a flow of sound in music having regular accented beats
**3** a movement or activity in which some action repeats regularly ⟨the *rhythm* of breathing⟩

**rhyth·mic** \ˈrith-mik\ *or* **rhyth·mi·cal** \-mi-kəl\ *adj*
having rhythm
**rhyth·mi·cal·ly** *adv*

[1]**rib** \ˈrib\ *n*
**1** ▼ one of the series of curved bones that are joined in pairs to the backbone of humans and other vertebrates and help to stiffen the body wall
**2** something (as a piece of wire supporting the fabric of an umbrella) that is like a rib in shape or use
**3** one of the parallel ridges in a knitted or woven fabric
**ribbed** \ˈribd\ *adj*

[2]**rib** *vb* **ribbed**; **rib·bing**
**1** to provide or enclose with ribs
**2** to form ribs in (a fabric) in knitting or weaving

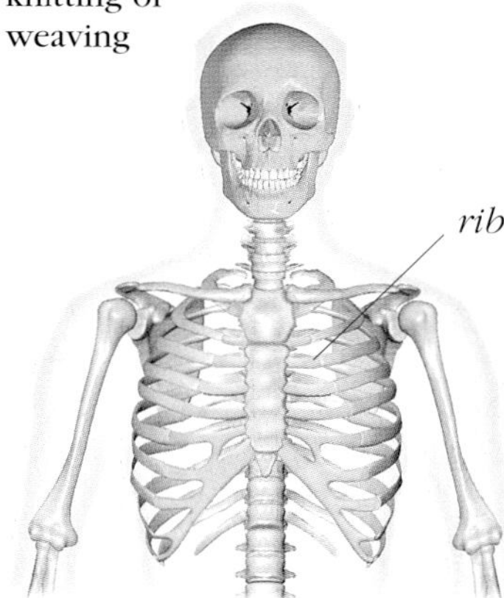


[1]**rib 1:** diagram of the human skeleton showing the ribs

**rib·bon** \ˈrib-ən\ *n*
**1** a narrow strip of fabric (as silk) used for trimming or for tying or decorating packages
**2** a long narrow strip like a ribbon ⟨typewriter *ribbon*⟩
**3** TATTER 1, SHRED ⟨torn to *ribbons*⟩

**rice** \ˈrīs\ *n*
an annual cereal grass widely grown in warm wet regions for its grain that is a chief food in many parts of the world

**rich** \ˈrich\ *adj*
**1** having great wealth ⟨*rich* people⟩
**2** [1]VALUABLE 1, EXPENSIVE ⟨*rich* robes⟩
**3** containing much sugar, fat, or seasoning ⟨*rich* food⟩
**4** high in fuel content ⟨a *rich* mixture⟩
**5** deep and pleasing in color or tone
**6** ABUNDANT ⟨a *rich* harvest⟩
**7** FERTILE 1 ⟨*rich* soil⟩
**rich·ly** *adv*
**rich·ness** *n*

**rich·es** \ˈrich-əz\ *n pl*
things that make one rich : WEALTH

**rick·ets** \ˈrik-əts\ *n*
a disease in which the bones are soft and deformed and which usually attacks the young and is caused by lack of the vitamin that controls the use of calcium and phosphorus

**rick·ety** \ˈrik-ət-ē\ *adj*
SHAKY, UNSOUND ⟨*rickety* stairs⟩

**rick·sha** *or* **rick·shaw** \ˈrik-ˌshȯ\ *n*
▼ a small hooded carriage with two wheels that is pulled by one person and was used originally in Japan

**ricksha:**
a modern bicycle ricksha in Thailand

**[1]ric·o·chet** \'rik-ə-,shā\ *n*
a bouncing off at an angle (as of a bullet off a wall)

**[2]ricochet** *vb* **ric·o·cheted**; **ric·o·chet·ing**
to bounce off at an angle

**rid** \'rid\ *vb* **rid** *also* **rid·ded**; **rid·ding**
to free from something : RELIEVE ⟨*rid* a dog of fleas⟩

**rid·dance** \'rid-ns\ *n*
the act of ridding : the state of being rid of something

**[1]rid·dle** \'rid-l\ *n*
a puzzling question to be solved or answered by guessing

**[2]riddle** *vb* **rid·dled**; **rid·dling**
to pierce with many holes

**[1]ride** \'rīd\ *vb* **rode** \'rōd\; **rid·den** \'rid-n\; **rid·ing** \'rīd-ing\
**1** to go on an animal's back or in a vehicle (as a car)
**2** to sit on and control so as to be carried along ⟨*ride* a bicycle⟩
**3** to float or move on water
**4** to travel over a surface
**5** CARRY 1 ⟨*rode* the child on my shoulders⟩
**rid·er** \'rīd-ər\ *n*

**[2]ride** *n*
**1** a trip on horseback or by vehicle
**2** a mechanical device (as a merry-go-round) that one rides for fun
**3** a means of transportation ⟨wants a *ride* to school⟩

**ridge** \'rij\ *n*
**1** a range of hills or mountains
**2** a raised strip
**3** the line made where two sloping surfaces come together ⟨the *ridge* of a roof⟩
**ridged** \'rijd\ *adj*

**ridge·pole** \'rij-,pōl\ *n*
the highest horizontal timber in a sloping roof to which the upper ends of the rafters are fastened

**[2]rig 2**
Some oil-drilling rigs are built as platforms over the sea, supported by a steel frame attached to the floor of the sea. The platform holds machinery and pipes used to drill wells for oil, which is pumped back to the rig, before being piped ashore or transported by oil tanker. The people who work on the rig also live there, and work in shifts so that the rig is operated day and night. The only way to reach land or to receive supplies is by boat or helicopter.

**model of an oil-drilling rig at sea**

**[1]rid·i·cule** \'rid-ə-,kyül\ *n*
the act of making fun of someone

**[2]ridicule** *vb* **rid·i·culed**; **rid·i·cul·ing**
to make fun of : DERIDE

**ri·dic·u·lous** \rə-'dik-yə-ləs\ *adj*
causing or deserving ridicule : ABSURD
**ri·dic·u·lous·ly** *adv*
**ri·dic·u·lous·ness** *n*

**riff·raff** \'rif-,raf\ *n*
RABBLE 2

**[1]ri·fle** \'rī-fəl\ *vb* **ri·fled**; **ri·fling**
**1** to search through fast and roughly especially in order to steal
**2** [1]STEAL 2

**Word History** There was an early French verb that meant "to scratch or file." This verb was also used to mean "to plunder." The English verb *rifle* came from this early French verb. The English noun *rifle* also came from the early French verb meaning "to scratch or file." The noun *rifle* first meant "a spiral groove cut or filed into the barrel of a gun." Later the word *rifle* came to be used for guns with such spiral grooves in their barrels.

**[2]rifle** *n*
a gun having a long barrel with spiral grooves on its inside

**rift** \'rift\ *n*
**1** an opening made by splitting or separation : CLEFT
**2** a break in friendly relations

**[1]rig** \'rig\ *vb* **rigged**; **rig·ging**
**1** to fit out (as a ship) with rigging
**2** CLOTHE 1, 2, DRESS
**3** EQUIP
**4** to set up usually for temporary use ⟨*rigged* a shelter of branches⟩

**[2]rig** *n*
**1** the shape, number, and arrangement of sails on a ship of one class or type that sets it apart from ships of other classes or types
**2** ◀ apparatus for a certain purpose ⟨oil-drilling *rig*⟩

**rig·ging** \'rig-ing\ *n*
the lines and chains used on a ship especially for moving the sails and supporting the masts and spars

**[1]right** \'rīt\ *adj*
**1** being just or good **:** UPRIGHT
**2** ACCURATE, CORRECT ⟨the *right* answer⟩
**3** SUITABLE, APPROPRIATE ⟨the *right* person for the job⟩

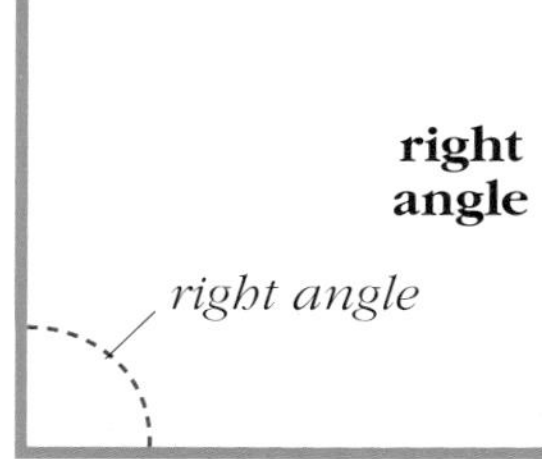


**right angle**

**4** STRAIGHT 1 ⟨a *right* line⟩
**5** of, relating to, located on, or being the side of the body away from the heart ⟨the *right* hand is stronger in most persons⟩
**6** located nearer to the right hand ⟨the *right* arm of my chair⟩
**7** being or meant to be the side on top, in front, or on the outside ⟨landed *right* side up⟩ ⟨turn the socks *right* side out⟩
**8** healthy in mind or body
**right·ly** *adv*
**right·ness** *n*

**[2]right** *n*
**1** the ideal of what is right and good ⟨loyalty, honesty, and faithfulness are elements of the *right*⟩
**2** something to which one has a just claim ⟨the *right* to freedom⟩
**3** the cause of truth or justice
**4** the right side or a part that is on or toward the right side

**[3]right** *adv*
**1** according to what is right ⟨live *right*⟩
**2** in the exact location or position **:** PRECISELY ⟨it's *right* where you left it⟩
**3** in a direct line or course **:** STRAIGHT ⟨went *right* home⟩
**4** according to truth or fact ⟨guessed *right*⟩
**5** in the right way **:** CORRECTLY ⟨you're not doing it *right*⟩
**6** all the way ⟨*right* to the end⟩
**7** without delay **:** IMMEDIATELY ⟨*right* after lunch⟩
**8** on or to the right ⟨turn *right*⟩

**[4]right** *vb*
**1** to make right (something wrong or unjust)
**2** to adjust or restore to a proper state or condition
**3** to bring or bring back to a vertical position
**4** to become vertical

**right angle** *n*
◀ an angle formed by two lines that are perpendicular to each other
**right–an·gled** \'rīt-'ang-gəld\ *adj*

**righ·teous** \'rī-chəs\ *adj*
doing or being what is right ⟨*righteous* people⟩ ⟨a *righteous* action⟩
**righ·teous·ly** *adv*
**righ·teous·ness** *n*

**right·ful** \'rīt-fəl\ *adj*
LAWFUL 2, PROPER ⟨the *rightful* owner⟩
**right·ful·ly** \-fə-lē\ *adv*
**right·ful·ness** *n*

**right–hand** \,rīt-,hand\ *adj*
**1** located on the right
**2** RIGHT-HANDED
**3** relied on most of all

**right–hand·ed** \'rīt-'han-dəd\ *adj*
**1** using the right hand more easily than the left ⟨a *right-handed* pitcher⟩
**2** done or made with or for the right hand
**3** CLOCKWISE

**right–of–way** \,rīt-əv-'wā\ *n, pl* **rights–of–way** \,rīt-səv-\
**1** the right to pass over someone else's land
**2** the right of some traffic to go before other traffic

**right triangle** *n*
a triangle having a right angle

**rig·id** \'rij-əd\ *adj*
**1** not flexible **:** STIFF
**2** STRICT 1, SEVERE ⟨*rigid* discipline⟩
**rig·id·ly** *adv*
**rig·id·ness** *n*

**rig·ma·role** \'rig-mə-,rōl\ *n*
NONSENSE 1

**rig·or** \'rig-ər\ *n*
a harsh severe condition (as of discipline or weather)

**rig·or·ous** \'rig-ə-rəs\ *adj*
**1** very strict
**2** hard to put up with **:** HARSH
**rig·or·ous·ly** *adv*
**rig·or·ous·ness** *n*

**rill** \'ril\ *n*
a very small brook

**rim** \'rim\ *n*
**1** ▶ an outer edge especially of something curved
**2** the outer part of a wheel
**synonyms** see BORDER
**rimmed** \'rimd\ *adj*

**[1]rime** \'rīm\ *n*
[1]FROST 2

**[2]rime** *variant of* RHYME

**rind** \'rīnd\ *n*
a usually hard or tough outer layer ⟨watermelon *rind*⟩

**[1]ring** \'ring\ *n*
**1** ▶ a circular band worn as an ornament or used for holding or fastening
**2** something circular in shape ⟨smoke *ring*⟩
**3** a place for exhibitions (as at a circus) or contests (as in boxing)
**4** a group of persons who work together for selfish or dishonest purposes
**ringed** \'ringd\ *adj*
**ring·like** \'ring-,līk\ *adj*

napkin ring

**[1]ring 1:** a napkin rolled in a napkin ring

**[2]ring** *vb* **ringed**; **ring·ing**
**1** to place or form a ring around
**:** to throw a ring over (a peg or hook) in a game (as quoits)

**[3]ring** *vb* **rang** \'rang\; **rung** \'rəng\; **ring·ing**
**1** to make or cause to make a rich vibrating sound when struck ⟨the bell *rang* clearly⟩ ⟨*ring* the school bell⟩

**rim 1:** a plate with a blue rim

2 to sound a bell ⟨*ring* for the waiter⟩
3 to announce by or as if by striking a bell ⟨*ring* in the New Year⟩
4 to sound loudly ⟨their cheers *rang* out⟩
5 to be filled with talk or report ⟨the whole school *rang* with the news⟩
6 to repeat loudly
7 to seem to be a certain way ⟨their story *rings* true⟩
8 to call on the telephone

**[4]ring** *n*
1 a clear ringing sound made by vibrating metal
2 a tone suggesting that of a bell
3 a loud or continuing noise
4 something that suggests a certain quality ⟨their story had the *ring* of truth⟩
5 a telephone call

**ring·lead·er** \'ring-,lēd-ər\ *n*
a leader especially of a group of persons who cause trouble

**ringlet:** a woman in 19th-century costume with her hair in ringlets

**ring·let** \'ring-lət\ *n*
▲ a long curl

**ring·worm** \'ring-,wərm\ *n*
a contagious skin disease with discolored rings on the skin

**rink** \'ringk\ *n*
a place for skating

**[1]rinse** \'rins\ *vb* **rinsed**; **rins·ing**
1 to wash lightly with water ⟨*rinse* one's mouth⟩
2 to cleanse (as of soap) with clear water ⟨*rinse* the dishes⟩
3 to treat (hair) with a rinse

**[2]rinse** *n*
1 an act of rinsing
2 a liquid used for rinsing
3 a solution that temporarily tints hair

**[1]ri·ot** \'rī-ət\ *n*
1 public violence, disturbance, or disorder
2 a colorful display

**[2]riot** *vb*
to create or take part in a riot

**[1]rip** \'rip\ *vb* **ripped**; **rip·ping**
to cut or tear open
**rip·per** *n*

**[2]rip** *n*
[3]TEAR 2

**ripe** \'rīp\ *adj* **rip·er**; **rip·est**
1 fully grown and developed ⟨*ripe* fruit⟩
2 having mature knowledge, understanding, or judgment
3 [1]READY 1 ⟨*ripe* for action⟩
**ripe·ness** *n*

**rip·en** \'rī-pən\ *vb*
to make or become ripe

**[1]rip·ple** \'rip-əl\ *vb* **rip·pled**; **rip·pling**
1 ▼ to become or cause to become covered with small waves
2 to make a sound like that of water flowing in small waves

**[2]ripple** *n*
1 the disturbing of the surface of water
2 a sound like that of rippling water

**[1]rise** \'rīz\ *vb* **rose** \'rōz\; **ris·en** \'riz-n\; **ris·ing** \'rī-zing\
1 to get up from lying, kneeling, or sitting
2 to get up from sleep or from one's bed
3 to return from death
4 to take up arms
5 to appear above the horizon
6 to go up : ASCEND ⟨smoke *rises*⟩
7 to swell in size or volume ⟨their voices *rose* as they argued⟩
8 to become encouraged ⟨their spirits *rose*⟩
9 to gain a higher rank or position
10 to increase in amount or number ⟨*rising* prices⟩
11 ARISE 3
12 to come into being : ORIGINATE
13 to show oneself equal to a demand or test ⟨*rise* to the occasion⟩
**ris·er** \'rī-zər\ *n*

**[2]rise** *n*
1 an act of rising : a state of being risen
2 BEGINNING 1, ORIGIN
3 an increase in amount, number, or volume
4 an upward slope
5 a spot higher than surrounding ground
6 an angry reaction

**[1]risk** \'risk\ *n*
possibility of loss or injury
**synonyms** see DANGER

**[2]risk** *vb*
1 to expose to danger
2 to take the risk or danger of

**risky** \'ris-kē\ *adj* **risk·i·er**; **risk·i·est**
DANGEROUS 1

**rite** \'rīt\ *n*
1 a set form of conducting a ceremony
2 a ceremonial act or action

**rit·u·al** \'rich-ə-wəl\ *n*
1 an established form for a ceremony
2 a system of rites

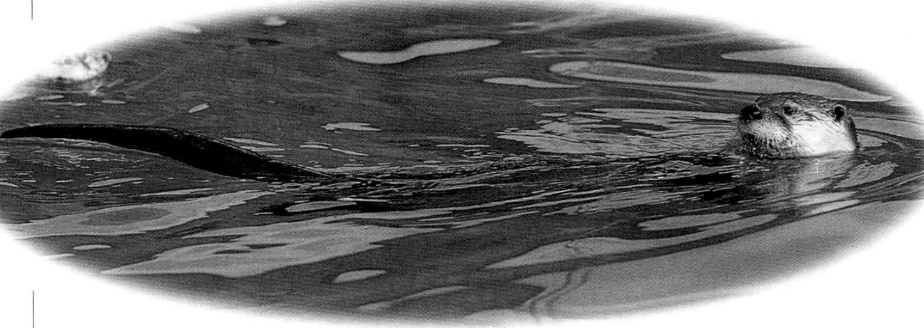

**[1]ripple 1:** an otter rippling the water while swimming

a b c d e f g h i j k l m n o p q r s t u v w x y z

**[1]ri·val** \'rī-vəl\ *n*
one of two or more trying to get what only one can have

**Word History** We can trace the English word *rival* back to a Latin word that meant "stream." Another Latin word was formed from the word that meant "stream." This word meant "one who uses the same stream as another." Those who must share a stream may fight about who has the better right to the water. There will often be disputes like that when two people want the same thing. The Latin word for people who share streams was used for others who are likely to fight, too. It meant "a man in love with the same woman some other man loves." The word *rival* came from this Latin word.

**[2]rival** *adj*
having the same worth ⟨*rival* claims⟩

**[3]rival** *vb* **ri·valed** *or* **ri·valled**; **ri·val·ing** *or* **ri·val·ling**
**1** to be in competition with
**2** [2]EQUAL

**ri·val·ry** \'rī-vəl-rē\ *n, pl* **ri·val·ries**
the act of rivaling **:** the state of being a rival **:** COMPETITION

**riv·er** \'riv-ər\ *n*
**1** a natural stream of water larger than a brook or creek
**2** a large stream ⟨a *river* of oil⟩

**riv·et** \'riv-ət\ *n*
a bolt with a head at one end used for uniting two or more pieces by passing the shank through a hole in each piece and then beating or pressing down the plain end so as to make a second head

**riv·u·let** \'riv-yə-lət\ *n*
a small stream

**roach** \'rōch\ *n*
COCKROACH

**road** \'rōd\ *n*
**1** ▶ an open way for vehicles, persons, and animals
**2** PATH 3, ROUTE ⟨the *road* to prosperity⟩

**road·bed** \'rōd-ˌbed\ *n*
**1** the foundation of a road or railroad
**2** the traveled surface of a road

**road·side** \'rōd-ˌsīd\ *n*
the strip of land along a road **:** the side of a road

**road·way** \'rōd-ˌwā\ *n*
**1** the strip of land over which a road passes
**2** the part of the surface of a road traveled by vehicles

**roam** \'rōm\ *vb*
to go from place to place with no fixed purpose or direction
**synonyms** see WANDER
**roam·er** *n*

**[1]roan** \'rōn\ *adj*
of a dark color (as black or brown) sprinkled with white ⟨a *roan* horse⟩

**[2]roan** *n*
an animal (as a horse) with a roan coat

**[1]roar** \'rōr\ *vb*
**1** to utter a long full loud sound
**2** to laugh loudly
**roar·er** *n*

**[2]roar** *n*
a long shout, bellow, or loud confused noise

**[1]roast** \'rōst\ *vb*
**1** to cook with dry heat (as in an oven)
**2** to be or make very hot
**roast·er** *n*

**[2]roast** *n*
**1** a piece of meat roasted or suitable for roasting
**2** an outing at which food is roasted

**[3]roast** *adj*
cooked by roasting ⟨*roast* beef⟩

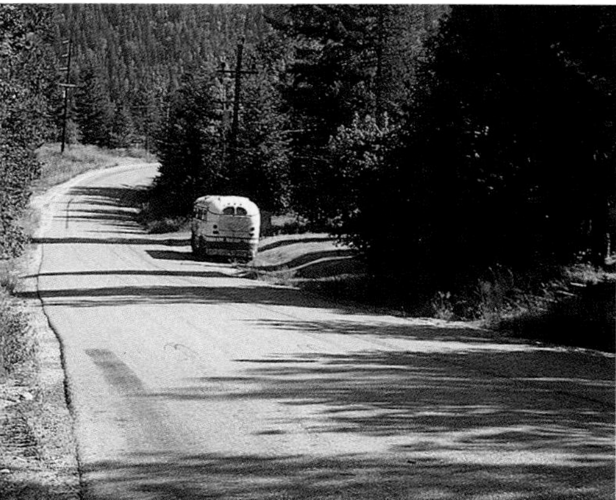

**road 1:** a country road

**rob** \'räb\ *vb* **robbed**; **rob·bing**
**1** to take something away from a person or place in secrecy or by force, threat, or trickery
**2** to keep from getting something due, expected, or desired
**rob·ber** *n*

**rob·bery** \'räb-ə-rē, 'räb-rē\ *n, pl* **rob·ber·ies**
the act or practice of robbing

**[1]robe** \'rōb\ *n*
**1** a long loose or flowing garment ⟨a judge's *robe*⟩
**2** a covering for the lower part of the body ⟨snuggled under the lap *robe*⟩

**[2]robe** *vb* **robed**; **rob·ing**
**1** to put on a robe
**2** [1]DRESS 2 ⟨*robed* in white⟩

**rob·in** \'räb-ən\ *n*
**1** a small European thrush with a yellowish red throat and breast
**2** a large North American thrush with a grayish back and dull reddish breast

**robot 1:** a toy robot

**ro·bot** \'rō-ˌbät\ *n*
**1** ▶ a machine that looks and acts like a human being
**2** a capable but unfeeling person

**Word History** The English word *robot* comes from a play written in 1920. The play was about machines called *robota* that looked like humans and were meant to work like slaves. The word *robota* means "forced labor" in the language of what is now the Czech Republic, where the play was written. The play became very well known outside the country too and the name for the machines was taken into English, with very little change, to be used for machines made to look and act like humans.

**ro·bust** \rō-ˈbəst\ *adj*
strong and vigorously healthy
**ro·bust·ly** *adv*
**ro·bust·ness** *n*

[1]**rock** \ˈräk\ *vb*
**1** to move back and forth as in a cradle
**2** to sway or cause to sway back and forth ⟨an earthquake *rocked* the town⟩

[2]**rock** *n*
**1** a rocking movement
**2** popular music played on instruments that are amplified electronically

[3]**rock** *n*
**1** a large mass of stone
**2** solid mineral deposits
**3** something like a rock in firmness **:** SUPPORT

**rock·er** \ˈräk-ər\ *n*
**1** a curving piece of wood or metal on which an object (as a cradle) rocks
**2** a structure or device that rocks on rockers
**3** a mechanism that works with a rocking motion

[1]**rock·et** \ˈräk-ət\ *n*
**1** a firework that is driven through the air by the gases produced by a burning substance
**2** a jet engine that operates like a firework rocket but carries the oxygen needed for burning its fuel
**3** a bomb, missile, or vehicle that is moved by a rocket

[2]**rocket** *vb*
**1** to rise swiftly
**2** to travel rapidly in or as if in a rocket

**rock·ing chair** \ˈräk-ing-\ *n*
a chair mounted on rockers

**rocking horse** *n*
▶ a toy horse mounted on rockers

**rocking horse**
ornament

**rodent**
There are almost 2,000 species of rodent living in diverse environments around the world. Rodents are generally small, furry, plant-eating creatures with a single pair of sharp incisor teeth, which grow quickly to compensate for constant gnawing. Many rodents are nocturnal, preferring darkness to protect them from predators. Others are camouflaged or run quickly for cover when threatened.

**capybara** \ˌkap-i-ˈbar-ə\ is a South American rodent often found in or near water

**guinea pig**

**rat**

**mouse**

**porcupine**

**squirrel**

**rock ʼnʼ roll** *or* **rock and roll** *n*
[2]ROCK 2

**rock salt** *n*
common salt in large crystals

**rocky** \ˈräk-ē\ *adj* **rock·i·er**; **rock·i·est**
full of or consisting of rocks
**rock·i·ness** *n*

**rod** \ˈräd\ *n*
**1** a straight slender stick or bar
**2** a stick or bundle of twigs used in whipping a person
**3** a measure of length equal to $16\frac{1}{2}$ feet (about 5 meters)
**4** any of the sensory bodies shaped like rods in the retina that respond to faint light
**5** a light flexible pole often with line and a reel attached used in fishing
**rod·like** \-ˌlīk\ *adj*

**rode** *past of* RIDE

**ro·dent** \ˈrōd-nt\ *n*
▲ any of a group of mammals (as squirrels, rats, mice, and beavers) with sharp front teeth used in gnawing

**ro·deo** \ˈrōd-ē-ˌō, rə-ˈdā-ō\ *n, pl* **ro·de·os**
**1** a roundup of cattle
**2** an exhibition that features cowboy skills (as riding and roping)

A B C D E F G H I J K L M N O P Q R S T U V W X Y Z

**roe** *n*
▼ the eggs of a fish especially while still held together in a membrane

**roe deer** *n*
a small deer of Europe and Asia with erect antlers forked at the tip

**roe**

**rogue** \'rōg\ *n*
**1** a dishonest or wicked person
**2** a pleasantly mischievous person

**rogu·ish** \'rō-gish\ *adj*
being or like a rogue
**rogu·ish·ly** *adv*
**rogu·ish·ness** *n*

**role** \'rōl\ *n*
**1** a character assigned or taken on
**2** a part played by an actor or singer
**3** [1]FUNCTION 1 ⟨the *role* of the teacher in education⟩

**role model** *n*
a person whose behavior in a certain role is imitated by others

**[1]roll** \'rōl\ *n*
**1** a writing that may be rolled up : SCROLL
**2** an official list of names
**3** something or a quantity of something that is rolled up or rounded as if rolled
**4** a small piece of baked bread dough

**[2]roll** *vb*
**1** to move by turning over and over on a surface without sliding
**2** to shape or become shaped in rounded form
**3** to make smooth, even, or firm with a roller
**4** to move on rollers or wheels
**5** to sound with a full echoing tone or with a continuous beating sound
**6** to go by : PASS ⟨time *rolled* by⟩
**7** to flow in a continuous stream ⟨the money was *rolling* in⟩
**8** to move with a side-to-side sway ⟨the ship *rolled*⟩

**[3]roll** *n*
**1** a sound produced by rapid strokes on a drum
**2** a heavy echoing sound ⟨the *roll* of thunder⟩
**3** a rolling movement or action

**roll·er** \'rō-lər\ *n*
**1** a turning cylinder over or on which something is moved or which is used to press, shape, or smooth something
**2** a rod on which something (as a map) is rolled up
**3** a small wheel
**4** a long heavy wave on the sea

**roller coaster** *n*
▼ an elevated railway (as in an amusement park) with sharp curves and steep slopes on which cars roll

**roller skate** *n*
a skate that has wheels instead of a runner

**roller coaster:** model of a roller coaster

**roller–skate** *vb*
to ride on roller skates

**rolling pin** *n*
a cylinder (as of wood) used to roll out dough

**ROM** \'räm\ *n*
READ-ONLY MEMORY

**[1]Ro·man** \'rō-mən\ *n*
**1** a person born or living in Rome
**2** a citizen of the Roman Empire
**3** *not cap* roman letters or type

**[2]Roman** *adj*
**1** of or relating to Rome or the Romans
**2** *not cap* of or relating to a type style with upright characters (as in "these definitions")

**[1]ro·mance** \rō-'mans\ *n*
**1** an old tale of knights and noble ladies
**2** an adventure story
**3** a love story
**4** a love affair
**5** an attraction or appeal to one's feelings ⟨the *romance* of the sea⟩

**[2]romance** *vb* **ro·manced**; **ro·manc·ing**
to have romantic thoughts or ideas

**Roman numerals** on a watch face

**Roman numeral** *n*
▲ a numeral in a system of figures based on the ancient Roman system ⟨some *Roman numerals* with corresponding Arabic numerals are I = 1; IV = 4; V = 5; IX = 9; X = 10; XI =11; L = 50; C = 100; D = 500; M = 1000⟩

**ro·man·tic** \rō-'mant-ik\ *adj*
**1** not founded on fact : IMAGINARY
**2** IMPRACTICAL ⟨a *romantic* scheme⟩
**3** stressing or appealing to the emotions or imagination
**4** of, relating to, or associated with love
**ro·man·ti·cal·ly** \-i-kə-lē\ *adv*

**[1]romp** \'rämp\ *n*
rough and noisy play : FROLIC

**[2]romp** *vb*
to play in a rough and noisy way

**romp·er** \'räm-pər\ *n*
a young child's one-piece garment having legs that can be unfastened around the inside — usually used in pl.

**[1]roof** \'rüf, 'ru̇f\ *n, pl* **roofs**
**1** ▼ the upper covering part of a building
**2** something like a roof in form, position, or purpose
**roofed** \'rüft, 'ru̇ft\ *adj*

**[1]roof 1:** a French church with a pitched roof
*gable*

**[2]roof** *vb*
to cover with a roof

**roof·ing** \'rüf-ing, 'ru̇f-\ *n*
material for a roof

**roof·tree** \'rüf-,trē, 'ru̇f-\ *n*
RIDGEPOLE

**[1]rook** \'ru̇k\ *n*
an Old World bird similar to the related crows

**[2]rook** *vb*
[1]CHEAT 1, SWINDLE

**[3]rook** *n*
▶ one of the pieces in the game of chess

**[3]rook**

**rook·ie** \'ru̇k-ē\ *n*
BEGINNER, RECRUIT

**[1]room** \'rüm, 'ru̇m\ *n*
**1** available space ⟨had barely *room* to move⟩
**2** a divided part of the inside of a building
**3** the people in a room
**4 rooms** *pl* LODGING 2
**5** a suitable opportunity ⟨you have *room* to improve your work⟩

**[2]room** *vb*
to provide with or live in lodgings

**room·er** \'rüm-ər, 'ru̇m-\ *n*
LODGER

**rooming house** *n*
a house for renting furnished rooms to lodgers

**room·mate** \'rüm-,māt, 'ru̇m-\ *n*
one of two or more persons sharing a room or dwelling

**roomy** \'rüm-ē, 'ru̇m-\ *adj*
**room·i·er**; **room·i·est**
SPACIOUS
**room·i·ness** *n*

**[1]roost** \'rüst\ *n*
a support on which birds perch

**[2]roost** *vb*
to settle on a roost

**roost·er** \'rüs-tər\ *n*
an adult male chicken

**[1]root** \'rüt, 'ru̇t\ *n*
**1** a leafless underground part of a plant that stores food and holds the plant in place
**2** the part of something by which it is attached
**3** something like a root especially in being a source of support or growth
**4** SOURCE 1 ⟨the *root* of evil⟩
**5** [1]CORE 2 ⟨get to the *root* of the matter⟩
**6** a word or part of a word from which other words are obtained by adding a prefix or suffix ⟨"hold" is the *root* of "holder"⟩
**root·ed** \-əd\ *adj*

**[2]root** *vb*
**1** to form or cause to form roots
**2** to attach by or as if by roots
**3** UPROOT 1 ⟨*root* crime from our cities⟩

**[3]root** *vb*
to turn up or dig with the snout

**[4]root** \'rüt\ *vb*
[2]CHEER 2
**root·er** *n*

**root beer** *n*
a sweet drink flavored with extracts of roots and herbs

**[1]rope** \'rōp\ *n*
**1** ▶ a large stout cord of strands (as of fiber or wire) twisted or braided together
**2** a noose used for hanging
**3** a row or string (as of beads) made by braiding, twining, or threading

**[1]rope 1**

**[2]rope** *vb* **roped**; **rop·ing**
**1** to bind, fasten, or tie with a rope
**2** to set off or divide by a rope ⟨*rope* off a street⟩
**3** [1]LASSO
**rop·er** *n*

**ro·sa·ry** \'rō-zə-rē\ *n, pl* **ro·sa·ries**
▶ a string of beads used in counting prayers

**[1]rose** *past of* RISE

**[2]rose** \'rōz\ *n*
**1** a showy and often fragrant white, yellow, pink, or red flower that grows on a prickly shrub (**rose·bush**) with compound leaves
**2** a moderate purplish red

**rosary:** a Catholic rosary

**rose·mary** \'rōz-ˌmer-ē\ *n* ▶ a fragrant mint that has branching woody stems and is used in cooking and in perfumes

**rosemary**

**ro·sette** \rō-'zet\ *n* a badge or ornament of ribbon gathered in the shape of a rose

**rose·wood** \'rōz-ˌwu̇d\ *n* a reddish or purplish wood streaked with black and that is valued for making furniture

**Rosh Ha·sha·nah** \ˌrōsh-hə-'shō-nə\ *n* the Jewish New Year observed as a religious holiday in September or October

**ros·in** \'räz-n\ *n* a hard brittle yellow to dark red substance obtained especially from pine trees and used in varnishes and on violin bows

**ros·ter** \'räs-tər\ *n* an orderly list usually of people belonging to some group

**ros·trum** \'räs-trəm\ *n, pl* **rostrums** *or* **ros·tra** \-trə\ a stage or platform for public speaking

**rosy** \'rō-zē\ *adj* **ros·i·er**; **ros·i·est**
**1** of the color rose
**2** PROMISING, HOPEFUL ⟨*rosy* prospects⟩

[1]**rot** \'rät\ *vb* **rot·ted**; **rot·ting**
**1** to undergo decay **:** SPOIL
**2** to go to ruin

[2]**rot** *n*
**1** the process of rotting **:** the state of being rotten
**2** a disease of plants or of animals in which tissue decays

**ro·ta·ry** \'rōt-ə-rē\ *adj*
**1** turning on an axis like a wheel
**2** having a rotating part

**ro·tate** \'rō-ˌtāt\ *vb* **ro·tat·ed**; **ro·tat·ing**
**1** to turn about an axis or a center
**2** to do or cause to do something in turn
**3** to pass in a series

**ro·ta·tion** \rō-'tā-shən\ *n*
**1** the act of rotating especially on an axis
**2** the growing of different crops in the same field usually in a regular order

**rote** \'rōt\ *n* repeating from memory of forms or phrases with little or no attention to meaning ⟨learn by *rote*⟩

**ro·tor** \'rōt-ər\ *n*
**1** the part of an electrical machine that turns
**2** ▼ a system of spinning horizontal blades that support a helicopter in the air

rotor

**rotor 2**

**rot·ten** \'rät-n\ *adj*
**1** having rotted
**2** morally bad
**3** very unpleasant or worthless ⟨a *rotten* game⟩
**rot·ten·ly** *adv*
**rot·ten·ness** *n*

**ro·tund** \rō-'tənd\ *adj*
**1** somewhat round
**2** [4]PLUMP
**ro·tund·ly** *adv*
**ro·tund·ness** *n*

**rouge** \'rüzh\ *n* a cosmetic used to give a red color to cheeks or lips

[1]**rough** \'rəf\ *adj*
**1** uneven in surface
**2** not calm ⟨*rough* seas⟩
**3** being harsh or violent ⟨*rough* treatment⟩
**4** coarse or rugged in nature or look
**5** not complete or exact ⟨a *rough* estimate⟩ **synonyms** see HARSH
**rough·ly** *adv*
**rough·ness** *n*

[2]**rough** *n*
**1** uneven ground covered with high grass, brush, and stones
**2** something in a crude or unfinished state

[3]**rough** *vb*
**1** ROUGHEN
**2** to handle roughly **:** BEAT ⟨*roughed* up by hoodlums⟩
**3** to make or shape roughly
**rough it** to live without ordinary comforts

**rough·age** \'rəf-ij\ *n* coarse food (as bran) whose bulk increases the activity of the bowel

**rough·en** \'rəf-ən\ *vb* to make or become rough

**rough·neck** \'rəf-ˌnek\ *n* a rough person **:** ROWDY

[1]**round** \'rau̇nd\ *adj*
**1** having every part of the surface or circumference the same distance from the center
**2** shaped like a cylinder
**3** [4]PLUMP
**4** [1]COMPLETE 1, FULL ⟨a *round* dozen⟩
**5** nearly correct or exact ⟨in *round* numbers⟩
**6** LARGE ⟨a good *round* sum⟩
**7** moving in or forming a circle
**8** having curves rather than angles
**round·ish** \'rau̇n-dish\ *adj*
**round·ly** *adv*
**round·ness** *n*

[2]**round** *adv* [1]AROUND

[3]**round** *n*
**1** something (as a circle or globe) that is round
**2** a song in which three or four singers sing the same melody and words one after another at intervals
**3** a round or curved part (as a rung of a ladder)
**4** an indirect path
**5** a regularly covered route
**6** a series or cycle of repeated actions or events
**7** one shot fired by a soldier or a gun
**8** ammunition for one shot

9 a unit of play in a contest or game
10 a cut of beef especially between the rump and the lower leg

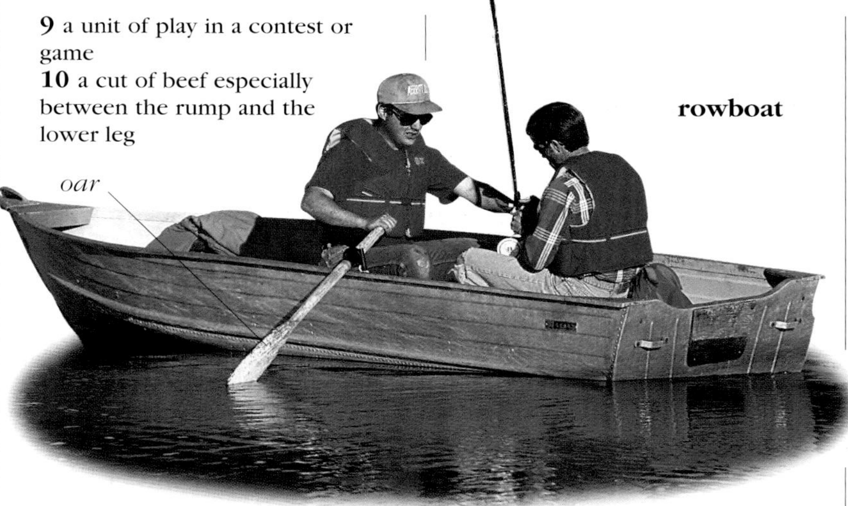

rowboat

⁴**round** *vb*
1 to make or become round
2 to go or pass around
3 to bring to completion ⟨*round* out a career⟩
4 to express as a round number
5 to follow a winding course

⁵**round** *prep*
²AROUND 1, 2, 3 ⟨travel *round* the world⟩

**round·about** \'raün-də-,baüt\ *adj*
not direct ⟨took a *roundabout* route⟩

**round·house** \'raünd-,haüs\ *n, pl* **round·hous·es** \-,haü-zəz\
a circular building where locomotives are kept or repaired

**round trip** *n*
a trip to a place and back usually over the same route

**round–up** \'raün-,dəp\ *n*
1 the gathering together of animals on the range by circling them in vehicles or on horseback and driving them in
2 a gathering together of scattered persons or things
3 ²SUMMARY ⟨a *roundup* of the day's news⟩

**round up** *vb*
1 to collect (as cattle) by circling in vehicles or on horseback and driving
2 to gather in or bring together

**round·worm** \'raün-,dwərm\ *n*
any of a group of worms with long round bodies that are not segmented and that include serious parasites of people and animals

**rouse** \'raüz\ *vb* **roused**; **rous·ing**
1 ¹AWAKE 1
2 to stir up : EXCITE

¹**rout** \'raüt\ *n*
1 a state of wild confusion or disorderly retreat
2 a disastrous defeat ⟨we lost 44–0 — it was a *rout*⟩

²**rout** *vb*
1 to put to flight
2 to defeat completely

¹**route** \'rüt, 'raüt\ *n*
a regular, chosen, or assigned course of travel

²**route** *vb* **rout·ed**; **rout·ing**
1 to send or transport by a selected route
2 to arrange and direct the order of (as a series of factory operations)

¹**rou·tine** \rü-'tēn\ *n*
a standard or usual way of doing

²**routine** *adj*
1 ²COMMONPLACE, ORDINARY
2 done or happening in a standard or usual way
**rou·tine·ly** *adv*

**rove** \'rōv\ *vb* **roved**; **rov·ing**
to wander without definite plan or direction
**rov·er** *n*

¹**row** \'rō\ *vb*
1 to move a boat by means of oars
2 to travel or carry in a rowboat

²**row** *n*
an act or instance of rowing

³**row** *n*
1 a series of persons or things in an orderly sequence
2 ¹WAY 1, STREET

⁴**row** \'raü\ *n*
a noisy disturbance or quarrel

**row·boat** \'rō-,bōt\ *n*
◀ a boat made to be rowed

¹**row·dy** \'raüd-ē\ *adj* **row·di·er**; **row·di·est**
coarse or rough in behavior ⟨don't bring your *rowdy* friends⟩
**row·di·ness** *n*

²**rowdy** *n, pl* **rowdies**
a rowdy person

**roy·al** \'röi-əl\ *adj*
1 of or relating to a sovereign : REGAL
2 fit for a king or queen ⟨gave the team a *royal* welcome⟩
**roy·al·ly** *adv*

**roy·al·ty** \'röi-əl-tē\ *n, pl* **roy·al·ties**
1 royal status or power
2 royal character or conduct
3 members of a royal family
4 a share of a product or profit (as of a mine) claimed by the owner for allowing another to use the property
5 payment made to the owner of a patent or copyright for the use of it

¹**rub** \'rəb\ *vb* **rubbed**; **rub·bing**
1 to move along the surface of a body with pressure
2 to wear away or chafe with friction
3 to cause discontent, irritation, or anger
4 to scour, polish, erase, or smear by pressure and friction
**rub the wrong way** to cause to be angry : IRRITATE

²**rub** *n*
1 something that gets in the way : DIFFICULTY
2 something that is annoying
3 the act of rubbing

**rub·ber** \'rəb-ər\ *n*
1 something used in rubbing
2 ▶ an elastic substance obtained from the milky juice of some tropical plants
3 a synthetic substance like rubber
4 something (as an overshoe) made of rubber

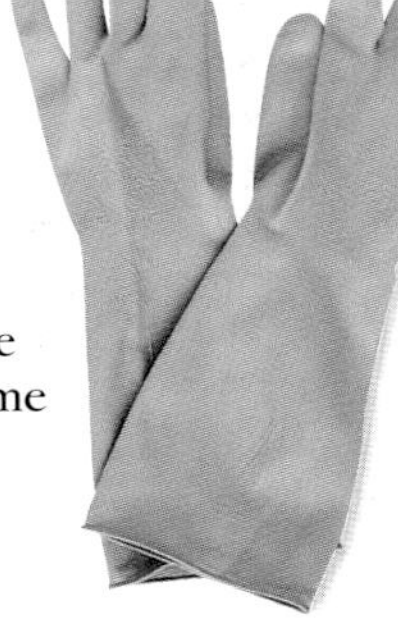
**rubber 2:** a pair of gloves made of rubber

**ruff 1:** a ruff worn by a man in 16th-century dress

**rubber band** *n*
a continuous band made of rubber for holding things together : ELASTIC

**rubber stamp** *n*
a stamp with a printing face of rubber

**rub·bish** \'rəb-ish\ *n*
TRASH

**rub·ble** \'rəb-əl\ *n*
a confused mass of broken or worthless things

**ru·ble** \'rü-bəl\ *n*
a Russian coin or bill

**ru·by** \'rü-bē\ *n, pl* **rubies**
**1** ▼ a precious stone of a deep red color
**2** a deep purplish red

**ruby 1**

**ruck·us** \'rək-əs\ *n*
[4]ROW

**rud·der** \'rəd-ər\ *n*
a movable flat piece attached at the rear of a ship or aircraft for steering

**rud·dy** \'rəd-ē\ *adj* **rud·di·er**; **rud·di·est**
having a healthy reddish color
**rud·di·ness** *n*

**rude** \'rüd\ *adj* **rud·er**; **rud·est**
**1** roughly made
**2** not refined or cultured : UNCOUTH
**3** IMPOLITE
**rude·ly** *adv*
**rude·ness** *n*

**ru·di·ment** \'rüd-ə-mənt\ *n*
a basic principle

**ru·di·men·ta·ry** \,rüd-ə-'ment-ə-rē\ *adj*
**1** ELEMENTARY, SIMPLE
**2** not fully developed

**rue** \'rü\ *vb* **rued**; **ru·ing**
to feel sorrow or regret for

**rue·ful** \'rü-fəl\ *adj*
**1** exciting pity or sympathy
**2** MOURNFUL 1, REGRETFUL

**ruff** \'rəf\ *n*
**1** ◄ a large round collar of pleated muslin or linen worn by men and women in the sixteenth and seventeenth centuries
**2** a fringe of long hair or feathers on the neck of an animal or bird

**ruf·fi·an** \'rəf-ē-ən\ *n*
a brutal cruel person

[1]**ruf·fle** \'rəf-əl\ *vb* **ruf·fled**; **ruf·fling**
**1** to disturb the smoothness of
**2** [1]TROUBLE 1, VEX
**3** to erect (as feathers) in or like a ruff
**4** to make into or provide with a ruffle

[2]**ruffle** *n*
a strip of fabric gathered or pleated on one edge

**rug** \'rəg\ *n*
► a piece of thick heavy fabric usually with a nap or pile used especially as a floor covering

**rug·ged** \'rəg-əd\ *adj*
**1** having a rough uneven surface
**2** involving hardship ⟨*rugged* training⟩
**3** STRONG 9, TOUGH **synonyms** see HARSH
**rug·ged·ly** *adv*
**rug·ged·ness** *n*

[1]**ru·in** \'rü-ən\ *n*
**1** complete collapse or destruction
**2** ▼ **ruins** *pl* the remains of something destroyed
**3** a cause of destruction

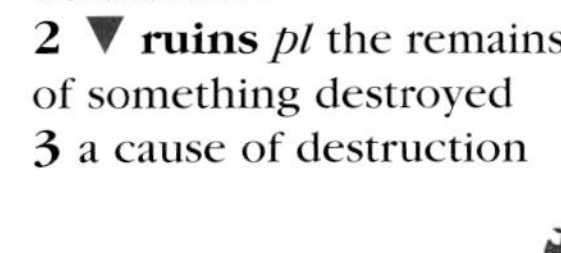

[2]**ruin** *vb*
**1** to reduce to ruins
**2** to damage beyond repair
**3** [3]BANKRUPT

**ru·in·ous** \'rü-ə-nəs\ *adj*
causing or likely to cause ruin : DESTRUCTIVE
**ru·in·ous·ly** *adv*

[1]**rule** \'rül\ *n*
**1** a guide or principle for conduct or action
**2** an accepted method, custom, or habit
**3** the exercise of authority or control : GOVERNMENT
**4** the time of a particular sovereign's reign
**5** RULER 2

**rug** with tassels

[2]**rule** *vb* **ruled**; **rul·ing**
**1** [1]CONTROL 2, DIRECT
**2** to exercise authority over : GOVERN
**3** to be supreme or outstanding in
**4** to give or state as a considered decision

[1]**ruin 2:** the ruins of a 15th-century English abbey

5 to mark with lines drawn along the straight edge of a ruler

**rul·er** \'rü-lər\ *n*
1 [1]SOVEREIGN 1
2 a straight strip (as of wood or metal) with a smooth edge that is marked off in units and used for measuring or as a guide in drawing straight lines

**rum** \'rəm\ *n*
an alcoholic liquor made from sugarcane or molasses

[1]**rum·ble** \'rəm-bəl\ *vb* **rum·bled**; **rum·bling**
to make or move with a low heavy rolling sound

[2]**rumble** *n*
a low heavy rolling sound

[1]**ru·mi·nant** \'rü-mə-nənt\ *n*
an animal (as a cow) that chews the cud

[2]**ruminant** *adj*
1 chewing the cud
2 of or relating to the group of hoofed mammals that chew the cud

**ru·mi·nate** \'rü-mə-,nāt\ *vb* **ru·mi·nat·ed**; **ru·mi·nat·ing**
1 to engage in thought : MEDITATE
2 to bring up and chew again what has been previously swallowed

[1]**rum·mage** \'rəm-ij\ *vb* **rum·maged**; **rum·mag·ing**
to make an active search especially by moving about, turning over, or looking through the contents of a place or container ⟨*rummaging* through the attic for old toys⟩

[2]**rummage** *n*
a confused collection of different articles

**rum·my** \'rəm-ē\ *n*
a card game in which each player tries to lay down cards in groups of three or more

[1]**ru·mor** \'rü-mər\ *n*
1 widely held opinion having no known source : HEARSAY
2 a statement or story that is in circulation but has not been proven to be true

[2]**rumor** *vb*
to tell by rumor : spread a rumor

**rump** \'rəmp\ *n*
1 the back part of an animal's body where the hips and thighs join

[1]**run 1:**
a girl running

2 a cut of beef between the loin and the round

**rum·ple** \'rəm-pəl\ *vb* **rum·pled**; **rum·pling**
[2]WRINKLE, MUSS

**rum·pus** \'rəm-pəs\ *n*
[4]ROW, FRACAS

[1]**run** \'rən\ *vb* **ran** \'ran\; **run**; **run·ning**
1 ▲ to go at a pace faster than a walk
2 to take to flight
3 to move freely about as one wishes
4 to go rapidly or hurriedly
5 to do something by or as if by running ⟨*run* errands⟩
6 to take part in a race
7 to move on or as if on wheels
8 to go back and forth often according to a fixed schedule
9 to migrate or move in schools ⟨the salmon are *running* early this year⟩
10 [2]FUNCTION, OPERATE
11 to continue in force
12 to pass into a specified condition
13 [1]FLOW 1
14 DISSOLVE 1 ⟨dyes guaranteed not to *run*⟩
15 to give off liquid ⟨a *running* sore⟩
16 to tend to develop a specified feature or quality
17 [1]STRETCH 2
18 to be in circulation ⟨the story *runs* that our principal is going to resign⟩
19 [2]TRACE 4
20 to pass over, across, or through
21 to slip through or past ⟨*run* a blockade⟩
22 to cause to penetrate
23 to cause to go ⟨*ran* them out of town⟩ ⟨*ran* my car off the road⟩
24 INCUR
**run into** to meet by chance

[2]**run** *n*
1 an act or the action of running
2 a continuous series especially of similar things ⟨had a long *run* of cloudy days⟩
3 sudden heavy demands from depositors, creditors, or customers ⟨a *run* on a bank⟩
4 the quantity of work turned out in a continuous operation
5 the usual or normal kind ⟨people of the common *run*⟩
6 the distance covered in a period of continuous traveling
7 a regular course or trip
8 freedom of movement ⟨had the *run* of the house⟩
9 a way, track, or path frequented by animals ⟨a deer *run*⟩
10 an enclosure for animals where they may feed and exercise
11 a score made in baseball by a base runner reaching home plate
12 [2]SLOPE 1 ⟨a ski *run*⟩
13 a ravel in a knitted fabric

[1]**run·away** \'rən-ə-,wā\ *n*
1 [2]FUGITIVE
2 a horse that is running out of control

[2]**runaway** *adj*
running away : escaping from control ⟨a *runaway* horse⟩

**run–down** \'rən-'daùn\ *adj*
1 being in poor condition ⟨a *run-down* farm⟩
2 being in poor health

[1]**rung** \'rəng\ *past participle of* RING

a b c d e f g h i j k l m n o p q r s t u v w x y z

\ng\ sing \ō\ bone \ò\ saw \òi\ coin \th\ thin \t͟h\ this \ü\ food \u̇\ foot \y\ yet \yü\ few \yu̇\ cure \zh\ vision

A B C D E F G H I J K L M N O P Q R S T U V W X Y Z

**²rung** *n*
**1** a rounded part placed as a crosspiece between the legs of a chair
**2** ▶ one of the crosspieces of a ladder

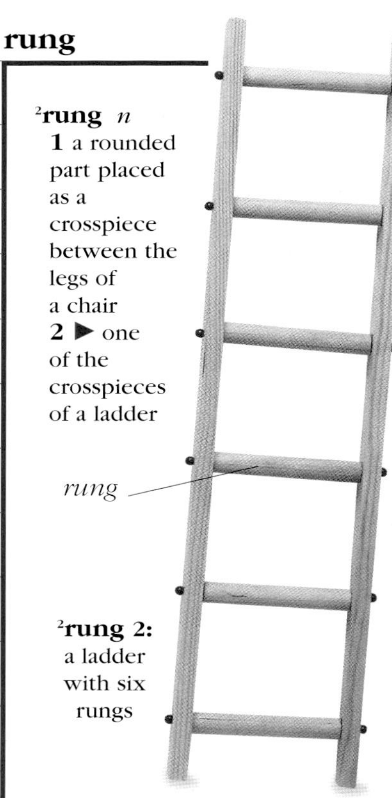


**²rung 2:** a ladder with six rungs

**run–in** \'rən-ˌin\ *n*
an angry dispute : QUARREL

**run·ner** \'rən-ər\ *n*
**1** one that runs
**2** MESSENGER
**3** a thin piece or part on or in which something slides
**4** a slender creeping branch of a plant that roots at the end or at the joints to form new plants
**5** a plant that forms or spreads by runners
**6** a long narrow carpet (as for a hall)

**run·ner–up** \'rən-ə-ˌrəp\ *n, pl* **run·ners–up** \'rən-ər-ˌzəp\
the competitor in a contest who finishes next to the winner

**rupee:** a one-rupee coin from India

**run·ny** \'rən-ē\ *adj*
running or likely to run ⟨a *runny* nose⟩

**run out** *vb*
**1** to come to an end : EXPIRE ⟨time *ran out* before we could tie the game⟩
**2** to become exhausted or used up ⟨our supplies were *running out*⟩
**run out of** to use up the available supply of ⟨better stop before we *run out of* gas⟩

**run over** *vb*
¹OVERFLOW 2

**runt** \'rənt\ *n*
an unusually small person or animal

**²rupture** *vb* **rup·tured**; **rup·tur·ing**
**1** to part by violence : BREAK
**2** to produce a rupture in
**3** to have a rupture

**ru·ral** \'ru̇r-əl\ *adj*
of or relating to the country, country people or life, or agriculture

**rural free delivery** *n*
the free delivery of mail on routes in country districts

**runway 2:** an airplane taking off from a runway

**run·way** \'rən-ˌwā\ *n*
**1** a path beaten by animals in going to and from feeding grounds
**2** ▲ a paved strip of ground on a landing field for the landing and takeoff of aircraft

**ru·pee** \rü-'pē\ *n*
◀ any of various coins (as of India or Pakistan)

**¹rup·ture** \'rəp-chər\ *n*
**1** a break in peaceful or friendly relations
**2** a breaking or tearing apart (as of body tissue)
**3** a condition in which a body part (as a loop of intestine) bulges through the weakened wall of the cavity that contains it

**ruse** \'rüs, 'rüz\ *n*
¹TRICK 4, ARTIFICE

**¹rush** \'rəsh\ *n*
a grasslike marsh plant with hollow stems used in chair seats and mats

**²rush** *vb*
**1** to move forward or act with great haste or eagerness
**2** to perform in a short time or at high speed
**3** ¹ATTACK 1, CHARGE
**rush·er** *n*

**³rush** *n*
**1** a violent forward motion
**2** a burst of activity or speed
**3** an eager migration of people usually to a new place in search of wealth ⟨the gold *rush*⟩

**[4]rush** *adj*
demanding special speed ⟨a *rush* order⟩

**[1]Rus·sian** \'rəsh-ən\ *adj*
of or relating to Russia, its people, or the Russian language

**[2]Russian** *n*
**1** a person born or living in Russia
**2** a language of the Russians

**[1]rust** \'rəst\ *n*
**1** a reddish coating formed on metal (as iron) when it is exposed especially to moist air
**2** ▶ a plant disease caused by fungi that makes spots on plants
**3** a fungus that causes a rust
**rust·like** \-ˌlīk\ *adj*

**[2]rust** *vb*
to make or become rusty

**[1]rus·tic** \'rəs-tik\ *adj*
**1** of, relating to, or suitable for the country
**2** [1]PLAIN 5, SIMPLE

**[2]rustic** *n*
a person living or raised in the country

**[1]rust 2:**
a leaf affected with rust

**[1]rus·tle** \'rəs-əl\ *vb* **rus·tled**; **rus·tling**
**1** to make or cause to make a rustle
**2** to steal (as cattle) from the range
**rus·tler** \'rəs-lər\ *n*

**[2]rustle** *n*
a quick series of small sounds

**rusty** \'rəs-tē\ *adj* **rust·i·er**; **rust·i·est**
**1** affected by rust ⟨a *rusty* nail⟩
**2** less skilled and slow through lack of practice or old age
**rust·i·ness** *n*

**[1]rut** \'rət\ *n*
**1** a track worn by a wheel or by habitual passage
**2** [1]ROUTINE

**[2]rut** *vb* **rut·ted**; **rut·ting**
to make a rut in

**ru·ta·ba·ga** \'rüt-ə-ˌbā-gə\ *n*
a turnip with a large yellow root

**ruth·less** \'rüth-ləs\ *adj*
having no pity **:** CRUEL
**ruth·less·ly** *adv*
**ruth·less·ness** *n*

**-ry** \rē\ *n suffix, pl* **-ries**
-ERY ⟨citizen*ry*⟩

**rye** \'rī\ *n*
a hardy cereal grass grown especially for its edible seeds that are used in flour and animal feeds and in making whiskey

# Ss

**The sounds of S:** The letter **S** has two main sounds in English. These are the "**S**" sound, as in **sad**, and the "**Z**" sound, as in **has**.

The letter **S** has the "**S**" sound in many words, such as **sister**, **scat**, **spend**, **storm**, **mistake**, **miss**, and **hats**.

**S** also has the "**Z**" sound, but only in the middle of a word, as in **easy** and **risen**, or at the end, as in **Mars** and **ponies**.

**S** combines with **H** to form a completely different sound, the sound heard in words like **ship** and **hush**.

In a few words, such as **island** and **aisle**, **S** is silent. A few other words sound as if they begin with **S**, but they actually begin with a silent **P**. An example is **psalm**.

---

**s** \'es\ *n, pl* **s's** *or* **ss** \'es-əz\ *often cap*
**1** the nineteenth letter of the English alphabet
**2** a grade rating a student's work as satisfactory

[1]**-s** \s *after sounds* f, k, p, t, th; əz *after sounds* ch, j, s, sh, z, zh; z *after other sounds*\ *n pl suffix*
used to form the plural of most nouns that do not end in *s, z, sh, ch*, or *y* following a consonant ⟨head*s*⟩ ⟨book*s*⟩ ⟨belief*s*⟩ and with or without an apostrophe to form the plural of abbreviations, numbers, letters, and symbols used as nouns ⟨4*s*⟩ ⟨#*s*⟩ ⟨B'*s*⟩

[2]**-s** *adv suffix*
used to form adverbs showing usual or repeated action or state ⟨always at home Sunday*s*⟩

[3]**-s** *vb suffix*
used to form the third person singular present of most verbs that do not end in *s, z, sh, ch*, or *y* following a consonant ⟨fall*s*⟩ ⟨take*s*⟩ ⟨play*s*⟩

**-'s** *n suffix or pron suffix*
used to form the possessive of singular nouns ⟨elephant*'s*⟩, of plural nouns not ending in *s* ⟨children*'s*⟩, and of some pronouns ⟨anyone*'s*⟩

**Sab·bath** \'sab-əth\ *n*
**1** the seventh day of the week in the Jewish calendar beginning at sundown on Friday and lasting until sundown on Saturday
**2** the first day of the week (as Sunday) kept for rest and worship

**sa·ber** *or* **sa·bre** \'sā-bər\ *n*
► a cavalry sword with a curved blade

hilt    blade

**saber:** a 19th-century English saber

**saber–toothed tiger** \'sā-bər-ˌtütht-\ *n*
a very large prehistoric cat with long sharp curved eyeteeth

**Sa·bin vaccine** \'sā-bən-\ *n*
a material that is taken by mouth to prevent polio

**sa·ble** \'sā-bəl\ *n*
**1** the color black
**2** ▼ a meat-eating animal of northern Europe and Asia that is related to the marten and prized for its soft rich brown fur

**sable 2**

[1]**sab·o·tage** \'sab-ə-ˌtäzh\ *n*
deliberate destruction of or damage to property or machinery (as by enemy agents) to block production or a nation's war effort

[2]**sabotage** *vb* **sab·o·taged**; **sab·o·tag·ing**
to damage or block by sabotage

**sac** \'sak\ *n*
a baglike part of a plant or animal often containing a liquid
**sac·like** \-ˌlīk\ *adj*

**sa·chem** \'sā-chəm\ *n*
a North American Indian chief

[1]**sack** \'sak\ *n*
**1** [1]BAG 1
**2** a sack and its contents ⟨a *sack* of potatoes⟩

[2]**sack** *vb*
to put into a sack

[3]**sack** *vb*
to loot after capture

[4]**sack** *n*
the looting of a city by its conquerors

**sack·ing** \'sak-ing\ *n*
a strong rough cloth (as burlap) from which sacks are made

**sac·ra·ment** \'sak-rə-mənt\ *n*
a religious act or ceremony that is considered especially sacred ⟨baptism is a Christian *sacrament*⟩

**sa·cred** \'sā-krəd\ *adj*
**1** HOLY 1 ⟨the *sacred* name of God⟩
**2** RELIGIOUS 2 ⟨*sacred* songs⟩
**3** deserving to be respected and honored ⟨a *sacred* right⟩
**sa·cred·ness** *n*

[1]**sac·ri·fice** \'sak-rə-ˌfīs\ *n*
**1** the act or ceremony of making an offering to God or a god especially on an altar
**2** something offered as a religious act
**3** an unselfish giving ⟨a *sacrifice* of our time to help others⟩
**4** a loss of profit

[2]**sacrifice** *vb* **sac·ri·ficed**; **sac·ri·fic·ing**
**1** to offer or kill as a sacrifice
**2** to give for the sake of something else ⟨*sacrificed* their lives for their country⟩
**3** to sell at a loss

**sad** \'sad\ *adj* **sad·der**; **sad·dest**
**1** filled with sorrow or unhappiness

2 causing or showing sorrow or gloom
**sad·ly** *adv*
**sad·ness** *n*
**sad·den** \'sad-n\ *vb*
to make or become sad
[1]**sad·dle** \'sad-l\ *n*
1 ▶ a seat (as for a rider on horseback) that is padded and usually covered with leather
2 something like a saddle in shape, position, or use
[2]**saddle** *vb* **sad·dled**; **sad·dling**
1 to put a saddle on ⟨*saddle* a horse⟩
2 to put a load on : BURDEN ⟨*saddled* him with the hardest job⟩
**saddle horse** *n*
a horse suited for or trained for riding
**sa·fa·ri** \sə-'fär-ē\ *n*
a hunting trip especially in Africa
[1]**safe** \'sāf\ *adj* **saf·er**; **saf·est**
1 free or secure from harm or danger
2 successful in reaching base in baseball
3 giving protection or security against danger ⟨a *safe* harbor⟩

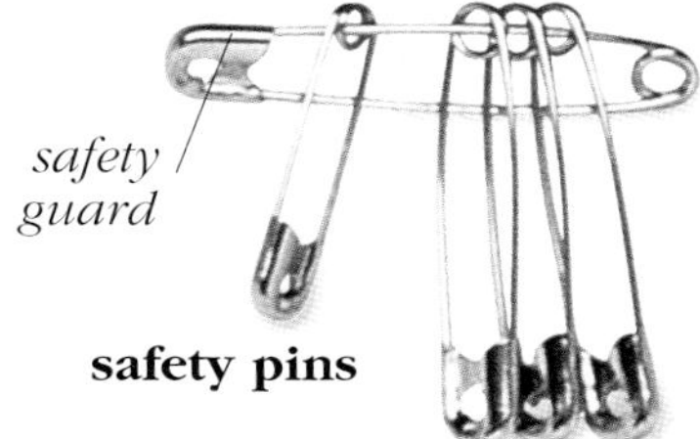

**safety pins**

4 HARMLESS
5 unlikely to be wrong : SOUND ⟨a *safe* answer⟩
6 not likely to take risks : CAREFUL ⟨a *safe* driver⟩
**safe·ly** *adv*
**safe·ness** *n*

**Synonyms** SAFE and SECURE mean free from danger. SAFE suggests freedom from a present danger ⟨felt *safe* as soon as I crossed the street⟩. SECURE suggests freedom from a possible future danger or risk ⟨the locks on the door made us feel *secure*⟩.

[2]**safe** *n*
a metal chest for keeping something (as money) safe

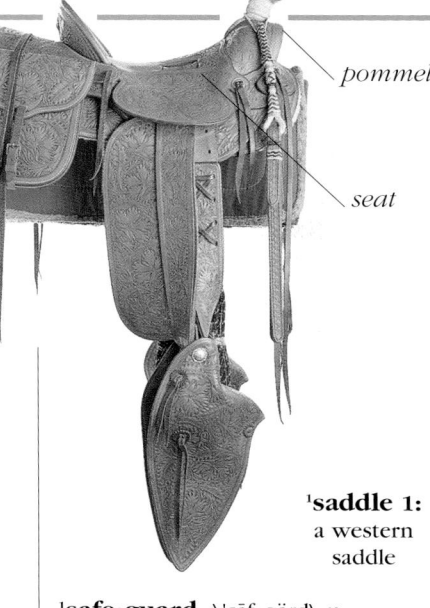

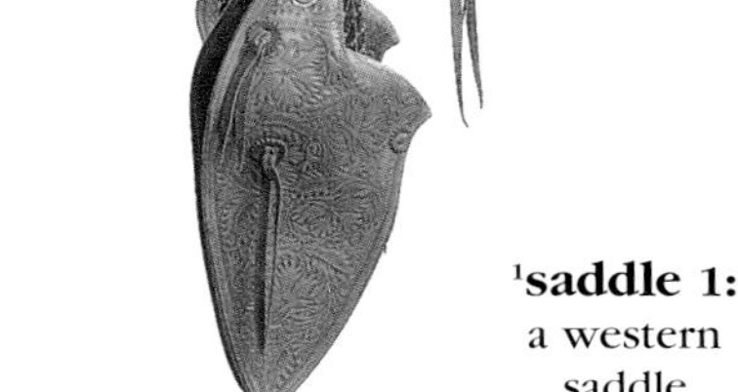

[1]**saddle 1:** a western saddle

[1]**safe·guard** \'sāf-,gärd\ *n*
something that protects and gives safety
[2]**safeguard** *vb*
to keep safe **synonyms** see DEFEND
**safe·keep·ing** \'sāf-'kē-ping\ *n*
the act of keeping safe : protection from danger or loss
**safe·ty** \'sāf-tē\ *n*
freedom from danger : SECURITY
**safety belt** *n*
a belt for holding a person to something (as a car seat)
**safety pin** *n*
◀ a pin that is bent back on itself to form a spring and has a guard that covers the point

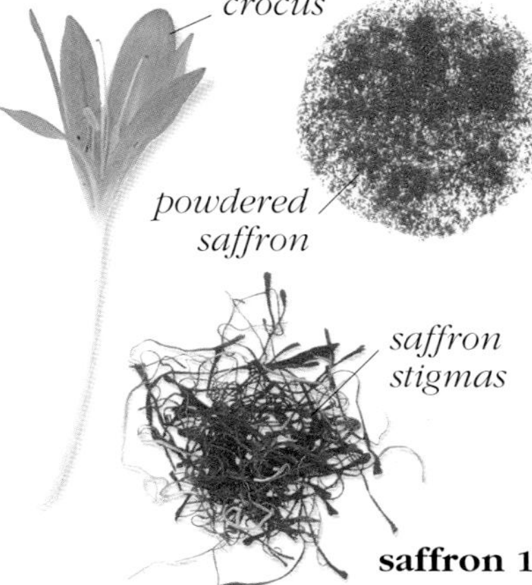

**saffron 1**

**saf·fron** \'saf-rən\ *n*
1 ▲ an orange powder used especially to color or flavor foods that consists of the dried stigmas of a crocus with purple flowers
2 an orange to orange yellow
[1]**sag** \'sag\ *vb* **sagged**; **sag·ging**
1 to sink, settle, or hang below the natural or right level ⟨the roof *sags*⟩
2 to become less firm or strong ⟨our *sagging* spirits⟩
[2]**sag** *n*
a sagging part or area
**sa·ga** \'sä-gə\ *n*
a story of heroic deeds
**sa·ga·cious** \sə-'gā-shəs\ *adj*
quick and wise in understanding and judging
**sa·ga·cious·ly** *adv*
**sa·ga·cious·ness** *n*
[1]**sage** \'sāj\ *adj*
[2]WISE 1
**sage·ly** *adv*
[2]**sage** *n*
a very wise person
[3]**sage** *n*
1 ▶ a mint that grows as a low shrub and has grayish green leaves used to flavor foods
2 a mint grown for its showy usually scarlet flowers
3 SAGEBRUSH

[3]**sage 1**

**sage·brush** \'sāj-,brəsh\ *n*
a western American plant related to the daisies that grows as a low shrub and has a bitter juice and sharp smell
**Sag·it·tar·i·us** \,saj-ə-'ter-ē-əs\ *n*
1 a constellation between Scorpio and Capricorn imagined as a centaur
2 the ninth sign of the zodiac or a person born under this sign
**sa·gua·ro** \sə-'gwä-rō\ *n*, *pl* **sa·gua·ros**
a giant cactus of the southwestern United States
**said** *past of* SAY
[1]**sail** \'sāl\ *n*
1 a sheet of fabric (as canvas) used to catch enough wind to move boats through the water or over ice
2 the sails of a ship considered as a group ⟨lowered *sail* as they approached the bay⟩
3 a trip in a sailing vessel ⟨went for a *sail* on the lake⟩

a b c d e f g h i j k l m n o p q r s t u v w x y z

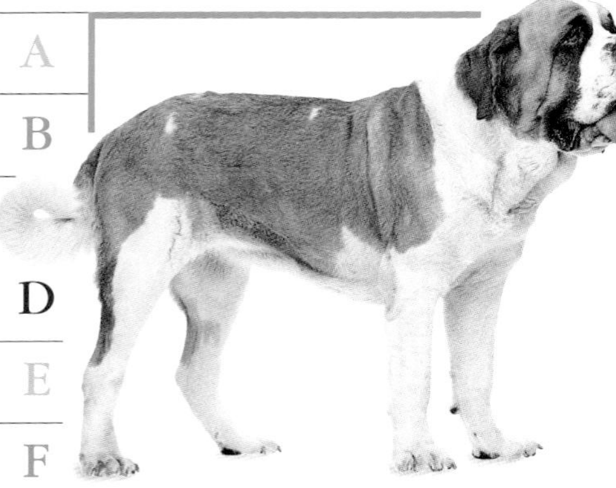
Saint Bernard

²**sail** *vb*
**1** to travel on a boat moved by the wind
**2** to travel by water
**3** to move or pass over by ship
**4** to manage or direct the motion of (a boat or ship moved by the wind)
**5** to move or glide along

**sail·boat** \'sāl-ˌbōt\ *n*
a boat equipped with sails

**sail·fish** \'sāl-ˌfish\ *n*
▶ a fish related to the swordfish but with a large sail-like fin on its back

**sail·or** \'sā-lər\ *n*
a person who sails

**saint** \'sānt\ *n*
**1** a good and holy person and especially one who is declared to be worthy of special honor
**2** a person who is very good especially about helping others

**Saint Ber·nard** \ˌsānt-bər-'närd\ *n*
◀ a very large powerful dog bred originally in the Swiss Alps

**saint·ly** \'sānt-lē\ *adj*
like a saint or like that of a saint ⟨a *saintly* smile⟩
**saint·li·ness** *n*

**sake** \'sāk\ *n*
**1** ¹PURPOSE ⟨for the *sake* of argument⟩
**2** WELFARE 1, BENEFIT ⟨for the *sake* of the country⟩

**sal·able** *or* **sale·able** \'sā-lə-bəl\ *adj*
good enough to sell **:** likely to be bought

**sal·ad** \'sal-əd\ *n*
**1** a dish of raw usually mixed vegetables served with a dressing
**2** a cold dish of meat, shellfish, fruit, or vegetables served with a dressing

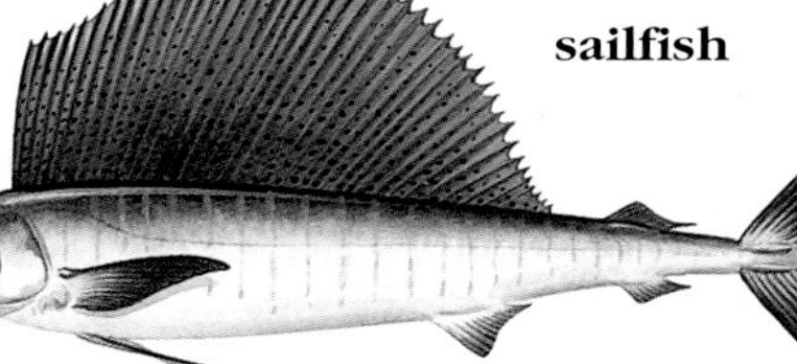
sailfish

**sal·a·man·der** \'sal-ə-ˌman-dər\ *n*
▼ any of a group of animals that are related to the frogs but look like lizards

**sal·a·ry** \'sal-ə-rē, 'sal-rē\ *n*, *pl* **sal·a·ries**
a fixed amount of money paid at regular times for work done

**Word History** In ancient times, salt was used not only to make food taste better but to keep it from spoiling. Because salt was not always easy to get, Roman soldiers were given money to buy salt. The Latin word for salt money came to be used for any money paid to soldiers. Later the same word was used for money paid to public officials. The English word *salary* comes from this Latin word.

**sale** \'sāl\ *n*
**1** an exchange of goods or property for money
**2** the state of being available for purchase ⟨a house offered for *sale*⟩
**3** ¹AUCTION
**4** a selling of goods at lowered prices

**sales·clerk** \'sālz-ˌklərk\ *n*
a person who sells in a store

**sales·man** \'sālz-mən\ *n*, *pl* **sales·men** \-mən\
a person who sells either in a territory or in a store

**sales·per·son** \'sālz-ˌpərs-n\ *n*
one who sells especially in a store

**sales tax** *n*
a tax paid by the buyer on goods bought

**sales·wom·an** \'sālz-ˌwu̇m-ən\ *n*, *pl* **sales·wom·en** \-ˌwim-ən\
a woman who sells either in a territory or in a store

**sa·li·va** \sə-'lī-və\ *n*
a watery fluid that contains

## salamander

There are more than 300 species of salamander that live mainly in cool, temperate areas throughout Europe, North America, and Asia. They have adapted to many habitats, living among trees and shrubs, in crevices, or in water. Some salamanders have lungs, while others breathe through gills or through their skin and the lining of their mouth.

**European fire salamander** prefers damp environments and hunts slow-moving prey at night

**spotted salamander** uses its bright coloration to scare away predators

enzymes which break down starch and is secreted into the mouth from glands in the neck

**sal·i·vary** \'sal-ə-,ver-ē\ *adj*
of, relating to, or producing saliva ⟨*salivary* glands⟩

**Salk vaccine** \'sȯk-\ *n*
a material given by injection to prevent polio

**sal·low** \'sal-ō\ *adj*
of a grayish greenish yellow color ⟨*sallow* skin⟩

**[1]sal·ly** \'sal-ē\ *n, pl* **sallies**
**1** a rushing out to attack especially by besieged soldiers
**2** a funny remark

**[2]sally** *vb* **sal·lied**; **sal·ly·ing**
to rush out

**salm·on** \'sam-ən\ *n*
**1** a large fish (**Atlantic salmon**) of the northern Atlantic Ocean valued for food and sport
**2** any of several fishes (**Pacific salmon**) of the northern Pacific Ocean valued for food and sport

**sa·loon** \sə-'lün\ *n*
**1** a large public hall (as on a passenger ship)
**2** a place where liquors are sold and drunk : BAR

**salsa 1**

**sal·sa** \'sȯl-sə, 'säl-\ *n*
**1** ▲ a spicy sauce of tomatoes, onions, and hot peppers
**2** popular music of Latin American origin with characteristics of jazz and rock

**[1]salt** \'sȯlt\ *n*
**1** a colorless or white substance that consists of sodium and chlorine and is used in seasoning foods, preserving meats and fish, and in making soap and glass
**2** a compound formed by replacement of hydrogen in an acid by a metal or group of elements that act like a metal

**[2]salt** *vb*
to add salt to

**[3]salt** *adj*
containing salt : SALTY

**salt·wa·ter** \'sȯlt-,wȯt-ər, -,wät-\ *adj*
of, relating to, or living in salt water

**salty** \'sȯl-tē\ *adj* **salt·i·er**; **salt·i·est**
of, tasting of, or containing salt

**sal·u·ta·tion** \,sal-yə-'tā-shən\ *n*
**1** an act or action of greeting
**2** a word or phrase used as a greeting at the beginning of a letter

**[1]sa·lute** \sə-'lüt\ *vb* **sa·lut·ed**; **sa·lut·ing**
**1** to address with expressions of kind wishes, courtesy, or honor
**2** to honor by a standard military ceremony
**3** to give a sign of respect to (as a military officer) especially by a smart movement of the right hand to the forehead

**[2]salute** *n*
**1** GREETING 1, SALUTATION
**2** a military show of respect or honor ⟨a twenty-one-gun *salute*⟩
**3** the position taken or the movement made to salute a military officer

**[1]sal·vage** \'sal-vij\ *n*
**1** money paid for saving a wrecked or endangered ship or its cargo or passengers
**2** the act of saving a ship
**3** the saving of possessions in danger of being lost
**4** something that is saved (as from a wreck)

**[2]salvage** *vb* **sal·vaged**; **sal·vag·ing**
to recover (something usable) especially from wreckage

**sal·va·tion** \sal-'vā-shən\ *n*
**1** the saving of a person from the power and the results of sin
**2** something that saves

**[1]salve** \'sav, 'säv\ *n*
a healing or soothing ointment

**[2]salve** *vb* **salved**; **salv·ing**
to quiet or soothe with or as if with a salve

**[1]same** \'sām\ *adj*
**1** not another : IDENTICAL ⟨lived in the *same* house all their lives⟩
**2** UNCHANGED ⟨is always the *same* no matter what happens⟩
**3** very much alike ⟨eat the *same* breakfast every day⟩

**Synonyms** SAME, IDENTICAL, and EQUAL mean not different or not differing from one another. SAME suggests that the things being compared are really one thing and not two or more things ⟨we saw the *same* person⟩. IDENTICAL usually suggests that two or more things are just like each other in every way ⟨the two jewels seemed *identical*⟩. EQUAL suggests that the things being compared are like each other in some particular way ⟨two baseball players of *equal* ability⟩.

**[2]same** *pron*
something identical with or like another ⟨you had an ice cream cone and I had the *same*⟩

**same·ness** \'sām-nəs\ *n*
**1** the quality or state of being the same
**2** MONOTONY

**sam·pan** \'sam-,pan\ *n*
▼ a Chinese boat with a flat bottom that is usually moved with oars

**sampan:** model of a 19th-century sampan

oar
sliding canopy
hold for storing fish

**¹sam·ple** \'sam-pəl\ *n*
a part or piece that shows the quality of the whole

**²sample** *vb* **sam·pled**; **sam·pling**
to judge the quality of by samples
: TEST

**sam·pler** \'sam-plər\ *n*
a piece of cloth with letters or verses embroidered on it

**san·a·to·ri·um** \,san-ə-'tōr-ē-əm\ *n*
a place for the care and treatment usually of people recovering from illness or having a disease likely to last a long time

**sanc·tion** \'sangk-shən\ *n*
**1** approval by someone in charge
**2** an action short of war taken by several nations to make another nation behave

**sanc·tu·ary** \'sangk-chə-,wer-ē\ *n, pl* **sanc·tu·ar·ies**
**1** a holy or sacred place
**2** the most sacred part (as near the altar) of a place of worship
**3** a building for worship
**4** a place of safety ⟨a wildlife *sanctuary*⟩
**5** the state of being protected

**¹sand** \'sand\ *n*
**1** loose material in grains produced by the natural breaking up of rocks
**2** a soil made up mostly of sand

**²sand** *vb*
**1** to sprinkle with sand
**2** to smooth or clean with sand or sandpaper
**sand·er** *n*

**san·dal** \'san-dəl\ *n*
▼ a shoe that is a sole held in place by straps

**sandal:**
a pair of girl's sandals

**san·dal·wood** \'san-dəl-,wu̇d\ *n*
the fragrant yellowish heartwood of an Asian tree

**sand·bag** \'sand-,bag\ *n*
a bag filled with sand and used as a weight (as on a balloon) or as part of a wall or dam

**sand·bar** \'sand-,bär\ *n*
a ridge of sand formed in water by tides or currents

**sand·box** \'sand-,bäks\ *n*
a large box for holding sand especially for children to play in

**sand dollar** *n*
▶ a flat round sea urchin

**sand dollar**

**sand·man** \'sand-,man\ *n, pl* **sand·men** \-,men\
a genie said to make children sleepy by sprinkling sand in their eyes

**¹sand·pa·per** \'sand-,pā-pər\ *n*
paper that has rough material (as sand) glued on one side and is used for smoothing and polishing

**²sandpaper** *vb*
to rub with sandpaper

**sand·pip·er** \'sand-,pī-pər\ *n*
a small shorebird related to the plovers

**sand·stone** \'sand-,stōn\ *n*
rock made of sand held together by a natural cement

**sand·storm** \'sand-,stȯrm\ *n*
a storm of wind (as in a desert) that drives clouds of sand

**¹sand·wich** \'sand-,wich\ *n*
two or more slices of bread or a split roll with a filling (as meat or cheese) between them

**²sandwich** *vb*
to fit in between things

**sandy** \'san-dē\ *adj* **sand·i·er**; **sand·i·est**
**1** full of or covered with sand
**2** of a yellowish gray color

**sane** \'sān\ *adj* **san·er**; **san·est**
**1** having a healthy and sound mind
**2** very sensible
**sane·ness** \-nəs\ *n*

**sang** *past of* SING

**san·i·tar·i·um** \,san-ə-'ter-ē-əm\ *n*
SANATORIUM

**san·i·tary** \'san-ə-,ter-ē\ *adj*
**1** of or relating to health or hygiene
**2** free from filth, infection, or other dangers to health

**san·i·ta·tion** \,san-ə-'tā-shən\ *n*
**1** the act or process of making sanitary
**2** the act of keeping things sanitary

**san·i·ty** \'san-ət-ē\ *n*
the state of being sane

**sank** *past of* SINK

**San·ta Claus** \'sant-ə-,klȯz\ *n*
the spirit of Christmas as represented by a jolly old man in a red suit who gives toys to children

**¹sap** \'sap\ *n*
a watery juice that circulates through a higher plant and carries food and nutrients

**²sap** *vb* **sapped**; **sap·ping**
to weaken or exhaust little by little ⟨it *saps* your strength⟩

**sap·ling** \'sap-ling\ *n*
a young tree

**sap·phire** \'saf-,īr\ *n*
▼ a clear bright blue precious stone

**sapphire**

**Word History** People in ancient India believed that each planet had its own god. They thought of the god of the planet Saturn as a dark man with dark clothes who was very fond of a certain dark gem. It is likely that this gem was the sapphire. The Indians gave this gem a name that meant "dear to Saturn." The English word *sapphire* comes from this old Indian word.

**sap·wood** \'sap-,wu̇d\ *n*
young wood found just beneath the bark of a tree and usually lighter in color than the heartwood

**sar·casm** \'sär-,kaz-əm\ *n*
the use of words that normally mean one thing to mean just the opposite usually to hurt someone's feelings or show scorn

**sar·cas·tic** \sär-'kas-tik\ *adj*
**1** showing or related to sarcasm

2 having the habit of sarcasm
**sar·cas·ti·cal·ly** \-ti-kə-lē\ *adv*

**sar·dine** \sär-'dēn\ *n*
a young or very small fish often preserved in oil and used for food

**sa·ri** \'sä-rē\ *n*
► a piece of clothing worn mainly by women of southern Asia that is a long light cloth wrapped around the body

sari

**sari:**
a girl from India wearing a sari

**sar·sa·pa·ril·la** \,sas-ə-pə-'ril-ə, ,sär-sə-\ *n*
the dried root of a tropical American plant used especially as a flavoring

**[1]sash** \'sash\ *n*
a broad band of cloth worn around the waist or over the shoulder

**[2]sash** *n*
**1** a frame for a pane of glass in a door or window
**2** the movable part of a window

**[1]sass** \'sas\ *n*
a rude fresh reply

**[2]sass** *vb*
to reply to in a rude fresh way

**sas·sa·fras** \'sas-ə-,fras\ *n*
a tall tree of eastern North America whose dried root bark was formerly used in medicine or as a flavoring

**sassy** \'sas-ē\ *adj* **sass·i·er**; **sass·i·est**
given to or made up of sass ⟨*sassy* children⟩ ⟨a *sassy* answer⟩

**sat** *past of* SIT

**Sa·tan** \'sāt-n\ *n*
[1]DEVIL 1

**satch·el** \'sach-əl\ *n*
a small bag for carrying clothes or books

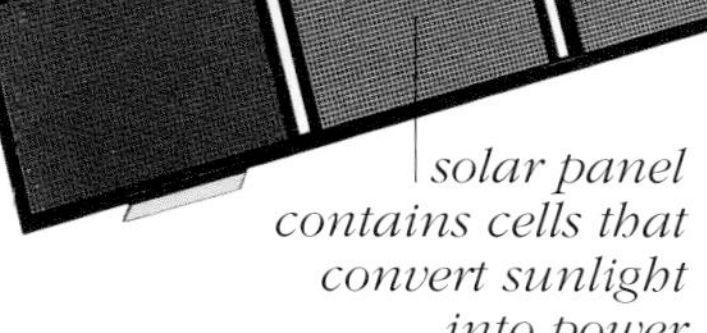


**satellite 2:**
model of a communications satellite

**sat·el·lite** \'sat-l-,īt\ *n*
**1** a smaller body that revolves around a planet
**2** ▲ a vehicle sent out from the earth to revolve around the earth, moon, sun, or a planet
**3** a country controlled by another more powerful country

**satellite dish** *n*
a bowl-shaped antenna for receiving transmissions (as of television programs) from a satellite orbiting the earth

**sat·in** \'sat-n\ *n*
a cloth (as of silk) with a shiny surface

**sat·ire** \'sa-,tīr\ *n*
writing or cartoons meant to make fun of and often show the weaknesses of someone or something ⟨a *satire* on television commercials⟩

**sa·tir·i·cal** \sə-'tir-i-kəl\ *adj*
of, relating to, or showing satire

**sat·is·fac·tion** \,sat-əs-'fak-shən\ *n*
**1** the act of satisfying : the condition of being satisfied
**2** something that satisfies

**sat·is·fac·to·ry** \,sat-əs-'fak-tə-rē\ *adj*
causing satisfaction
**sat·is·fac·to·ri·ly** \-rə-lē\ *adv*
**sat·is·fac·to·ri·ness** \-rē-nəs\ *n*

**sat·is·fy** \'sat-əs-,fī\ *vb* **sat·is·fied**; **sat·is·fy·ing**
**1** to carry out the terms of (as a contract)
**2** to make contented ⟨was *satisfied* with the job⟩
**3** to meet the needs of ⟨it *satisfied* our hunger⟩
**4** CONVINCE ⟨*satisfied* the story is true⟩

**sat·u·rate** \'sach-ə-,rāt\ *vb* **sat·u·rat·ed**; **sat·u·rat·ing**
to soak full or fill to the limit

**Sat·ur·day** \'sat-ər-dē\ *n*
the seventh day of the week

**Saturn**

**Sat·urn** \'sat-ərn\ *n*
▲ the planet that is sixth in distance from the sun and has a diameter of about 115,000 kilometers

**sa·tyr** \'sāt-ər, 'sat-\ *n*
a forest god of the ancient Greeks believed to have the ears and the tail of a horse or goat

**sauce** \'sȯs\ *n*
**1** a tasty liquid poured over food
**2** stewed fruit ⟨cranberry *sauce*⟩

**sauce·pan** \'sȯ-,span\ *n*
a small deep cooking pan with a handle

**sau·cer** \'sȯ-sər\ *n*
a small shallow dish often with a slightly lower center for holding a cup

**sauropod:** *Barosaurus* \\,bar-ə-'sȯr-əs\\ was one of the largest sauropods

**sau·cy** \\'sȯs-ē\\ *adj* **sauc·i·er; sauc·i·est**
**1** being rude and disrespectful
**2** [2]TRIM
**sauc·i·ly** \\-ə-lē\\ *adv*
**sauc·i·ness** \\-ē-nəs\\ *n*

**sau·er·kraut** \\'sau̇-ər-,krau̇t\\ *n*
finely cut cabbage soaked in a salty mixture

**saun·ter** \\'sȯnt-ər\\ *vb*
to walk in a slow relaxed way : STROLL

**sau·ro·pod** \\'sȯr-ə-,päd\\ *n*
▲ any of a group of plant-eating dinosaurs (as a brontosaurus)

**sau·sage** \\'sȯ-sij\\ *n*
**1** spicy ground meat (as pork) usually stuffed in casings
**2** a roll of sausage in a casing

**[1]sav·age** \\'sav-ij\\ *adj*
**1** not tamed : WILD ⟨*savage* beasts⟩
**2** being cruel and brutal : FIERCE ⟨a *savage* attack⟩
**sav·age·ly** *adv*
**sav·age·ness** *n*

---

**Word History** A good place to look for wild animals is in the woods. The English word *savage* at first meant "wild." It comes from a Latin word that meant "woods."

---

**[2]savage** *n*
**1** a person belonging to a group with a low level of civilization
**2** a cruel person

**sav·age·ry** \\'sav-ij-rē\\ *n, pl* **sav·age·ries**
**1** an uncivilized condition ⟨ancient tribes living in *savagery*⟩
**2** savage behavior

**[1]save** \\'sāv\\ *vb* **saved; sav·ing**
**1** to free from danger
**2** to keep from being ruined : PRESERVE ⟨*save* fruits from spoiling⟩
**3** to put aside for later use ⟨*save* a snack for bedtime⟩
**4** to keep from being spent, wasted, or lost ⟨*save* energy⟩
**5** to make unnecessary ⟨*saves* a long detour⟩

**[2]save** *prep*
[1]EXCEPT ⟨took all *save* one⟩

**sav·ing** \\'sā-ving\\ *n*
**1** the act of rescuing
**2** something saved ⟨a *saving* in labor⟩
**3 savings** *pl* money put aside (as in a bank)

**sav·ior** *or* **sav·iour** \\'sāv-yər\\ *n*
**1** a person who saves from ruin or danger
**2** *cap* JESUS

*tooth-edged blade*

**[2]saw 1**

**sa·vo·ry** \\'sā-və-rē\\ *adj*
pleasing to the taste or smell ⟨*savory* sausages⟩

**[1]saw** *past of* SEE

**[2]saw** \\'sȯ\\ *n*
**1** ▲ a tool with a tooth-edged blade for cutting hard material
**2** a machine that operates a toothed blade

**[3]saw** *vb* **sawed; sawed** *or* **sawn** \\'sȯn\\; **saw·ing**
to cut or shape with a saw

**[4]saw** *n*
a common saying : PROVERB

**saw·dust** \\'sȯ-,dəst\\ *n*
tiny bits (as of wood) which fall from something being sawed

**saw·horse** \\'sȯ-,hȯrs\\ *n*
a frame or rack on which wood is rested while being sawed

**saw·mill** \\'sȯ-,mil\\ *n*
a mill or factory having machinery for sawing logs

**saw–toothed** \\'sȯ-'tütht\\ *adj*
having an edge or outline like the teeth of a saw

**sax·o·phone** \\'sak-sə-,fōn\\ *n*
▼ a musical wind instrument with a reed mouthpiece and a bent tubelike metal body with keys

**[1]say** \\'sā\\ *vb* **said** \\'sed\\; **say·ing** \\'sā-ing\\
**1** to express in words
**2** to give as one's opinion or decision : DECLARE ⟨I *say* you are wrong⟩
**3** [1]REPEAT 2, RECITE ⟨*say* one's prayers⟩

**[2]say** *n*
**1** an expression of opinion ⟨everybody had a *say* at the meeting⟩
**2** the power to decide or help decide

**say·ing** \\'sā-ing\\ *n*
PROVERB

**scab** \\'skab\\ *n*
**1** a crust that forms over and protects a sore or wound
**2** a plant disease in which crusted spots form on stems or leaves

**scab·bard** \\'skab-ərd\\ *n*
a protective case or sheath for the blade of a sword or dagger

**scab·by** \\'skab-ē\\ *adj* **scab·bi·er; scab·bi·est**
**1** having scabs
**2** diseased with scab

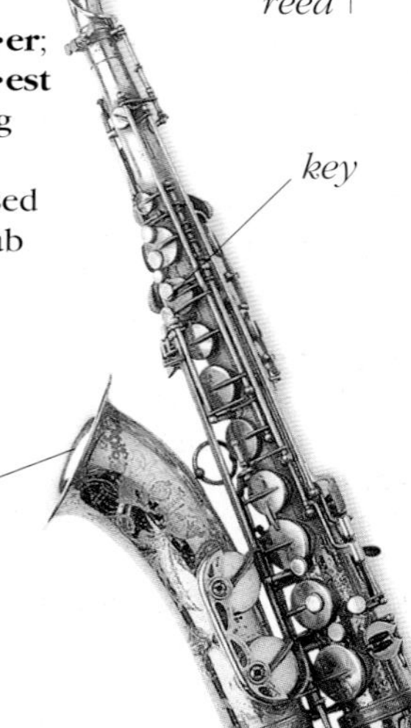


**saxophone:** a tenor saxophone

**sca·bies** \'skā-bēz\ *n, pl* **scabies**
an itch or mange caused by mites living as parasites in the skin

**scaf·fold** \'skaf-əld\ *n*
**1** a raised platform built as a support for workers and their tools and materials
**2** a platform on which a criminal is executed

**[1]scald** \'skȯld\ *vb*
**1** to burn with or as if with hot liquid or steam
**2** to pour very hot water over
**3** to bring to a heat just below the boiling point

**[2]scald** *n*
an injury caused by scalding

**[1]scale** \'skāl\ *n*
**1** either pan of a balance or the balance itself
**2** ▼ an instrument or machine for weighing

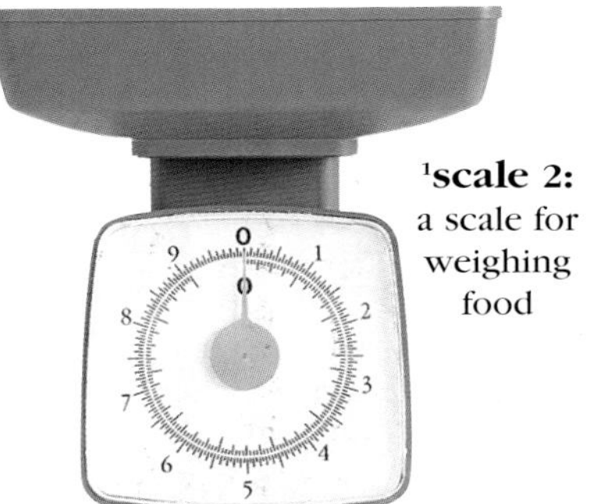

**[1]scale 2:** a scale for weighing food

**[2]scale** *vb* **scaled**; **scal·ing**
**1** to weigh on scales
**2** to have a weight of

**[3]scale** *n*
**1** one of the small stiff plates that cover much of the body of some animals (as fish and snakes)
**2** a thin layer or part (as a special leaf that protects a plant bud) suggesting a fish scale
**scaled** \'skāld\ *adj*
**scale·less** \'skāl-ləs\ *adj*
**scale·like** \-,līk\ *adj*

**[4]scale** *vb* **scaled**; **scal·ing**
**1** to remove the scales of
**2** [2]FLAKE

**[5]scale** *vb* **scaled**; **scal·ing**
**1** to climb by or as if by a ladder
**2** to regulate or set according to a standard — often used with *down* or *up* ⟨had to *scale* down the budget⟩

**[6]scale** *n*
**1** a series of tones going up or down in pitch in fixed steps
**2** a series of spaces marked off by lines and used for measuring distances or amounts
**3** a number of like things arranged in order from the highest to the lowest
**4** the size of a picture, plan, or model of a thing compared to the size of the thing itself
**5** a standard for measuring or judging

**scale insect** *n*
any of a group of insects that are related to the plant lice, suck the juices of plants, and have winged males and wingless females which look like scales attached to the plant

**[1]scallop 1**

**[1]scal·lop** \'skäl-əp, 'skal-\ *n*
**1** ▲ an edible shellfish that is a mollusk with a ribbed shell in two parts
**2** any of a series of rounded half-circles that form a border on an edge (as of lace)

**[2]scallop** *vb*
**1** to bake with crumbs, butter, and milk
**2** to embroider, cut, or edge with scallops

**[1]scalp** \'skalp\ *n*
the part of the skin and flesh of the head usually covered with hair

**[2]scalp** *vb*
to remove the scalp from

**scaly** \'skā-lē\ *adj* **scal·i·er**; **scal·i·est**
covered with or like scales ⟨a *scaly* skin⟩

**scamp** \'skamp\ *n*
RASCAL

**[1]scam·per** \'skam-pər\ *vb*
to run or move lightly

**[2]scamper** *n*
a playful scampering or scurrying

**scan** \'skan\ *vb* **scanned**; **scan·ning**
**1** to read or mark verses so as to show stress and rhythm
**2** to examine or look over ⟨*scanning* the field with binoculars⟩ ⟨*scanned* the headlines⟩
**3** to examine with a sensing device (as a scanner) especially to obtain information

**scan·dal** \'skan-dəl\ *n*
**1** something that causes a general feeling of shame : DISGRACE
**2** talk that injures a person's good name

**scan·dal·ous** \'skan-də-ləs\ *adj*
**1** being or containing scandal
**2** very bad or objectionable ⟨*scandalous* behavior⟩

**Scan·di·na·vian** \,skan-də-'nā-vē-ən, -vyən\ *n*
a person born or living in Scandinavia

**scan·ner** \'skan-ər\ *n*
▼ a device that converts a printed image (as text or a photograph) into a form a computer can use (as for displaying on the screen)

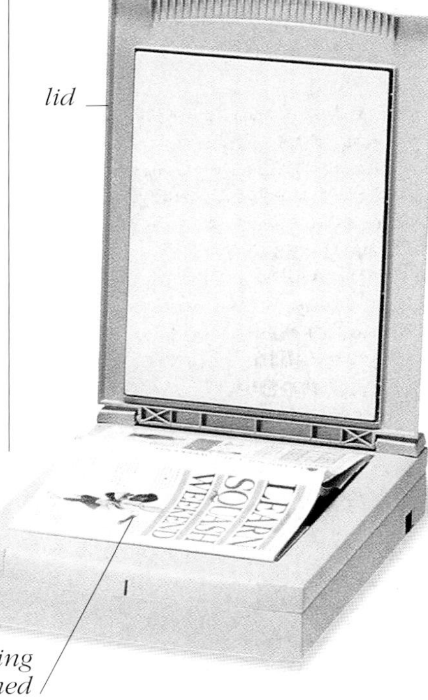


**scanner** with its lid raised

**[1]scant** \'skant\ *adj*
**1** barely enough ⟨a *scant* lunch⟩
**2** not quite full ⟨a *scant* quart of milk⟩
**3** having only a small supply ⟨*scant* of money⟩

scarf

**scarf 1:** a girl wearing a scarf

**²scant** *vb*
to give or use less than needed **:** be stingy with

**scanty** \'skant-ē\ *adj* **scant·i·er; scant·i·est**
barely enough

**¹scar** \'skär\ *n*
**1** a mark left after injured tissue has healed
**2** an ugly mark (as on furniture)
**3** the lasting effect of some unhappy experience

**²scar** *vb* **scarred; scar·ring**
to mark or become marked with a scar

**scar·ab** \'skar-əb\ *n*
▶ a large dark beetle used in ancient Egypt as a symbol of eternal life

**scarab**

**scarce** \'skeərs, 'skaərs\ *adj* **scarc·er; scarc·est**
**1** not plentiful
**2** hard to find **:** RARE **synonyms** see RARE
**scarce·ness** *n*

**scarce·ly** \'skeər-slē, 'skaər-\ *adv*
**1** only just ⟨*scarcely* enough to eat⟩
**2** certainly not

**scar·ci·ty** \'sker-sət-ē, 'skar-\ *n, pl* **scar·ci·ties**
the condition of being scarce

**¹scare** \'skeər, 'skaər\ *vb* **scared; scar·ing**
to be or become frightened suddenly

**²scare** *n*
**1** a sudden fright
**2** a widespread state of alarm

**scare·crow** \'skeər-,krō, 'skaər-\ *n*
a crude human figure set up to scare away birds and animals from crops

**scarf** \'skärf\ *n, pl* **scarves** \'skärvz\ *or* **scarfs**
**1** ◀ a piece of cloth worn loosely around the neck or on the head
**2** a long narrow strip of cloth used as a cover (as on a bureau)

**scar·la·ti·na** \,skär-lə-'tē-nə\ *n*
a mild scarlet fever

**¹scar·let** \'skär-lət\ *n*
a bright red

**²scarlet** *adj*
of the color scarlet

**scarlet fever** *n*
a contagious disease in which there is a sore throat, a high fever, and a rash

**scary** \'skeər-ē, 'skaər-\ *adj* **scar·i·er; scar·i·est**
causing fright ⟨a *scary* movie⟩

**scat** \'skat\ *vb* **scat·ted; scat·ting**
to go away quickly

**scat·ter** \'skat-ər\ *vb*
**1** to toss, sow, or place here and there
**2** to separate and go in different ways ⟨the crowd *scattered*⟩

**scat·ter·brain** \'skat-ər-,brān\ *n*
a flighty thoughtless person
**scat·ter·brained** \-,brānd\ *adj*

**scav·en·ger** \'skav-ən-jər\ *n*
**1** a person who picks over junk or garbage for useful items
**2** an animal that lives on decayed material

**scene** \'sēn\ *n*
**1** a division of an act in a play
**2** a single interesting or important happening in a play or story
**3** the place and time of the action in a play or story
**4** the painted screens and slides used as backgrounds on the stage **:** SCENERY
**5** something that attracts or holds one's gaze **:** VIEW
**6** a display of anger or misconduct

**scen·ery** \'sē-nə-rē, 'sēn-rē\ *n*
**1** the painted scenes used on a stage and the furnishings that go with them
**2** outdoor scenes or views

**sce·nic** \'sē-nik\ *adj*
**1** of or relating to stage scenery
**2** giving views of natural scenery ⟨a *scenic* drive⟩

**¹scent** \'sent\ *n*
**1** an odor left by some animal or person no longer in a place or given off (as by flowers) at a distance
**2** a usual or particular and often agreeable odor
**3** power or sense of smell
**4** a course followed by someone in search or pursuit of something
**5** ¹PERFUME 2

**²scent** *vb*
**1** to become aware of or follow through the sense of smell
**2** to get a hint of
**3** to fill with an odor **:** PERFUME

**scep·ter** *or* **scep·tre** \'sep-tər\ *n*
▼ a rod carried by a ruler as a sign of authority

**scepter:** a 15th-century painting of Isabella I \,iz-ə-'bel-ə\ of Spain holding her scepter

**¹sched·ule** \'skej-ül, -əl\ *n*
**1** a written or printed list
**2** a list of the times set for certain events **:** TIMETABLE
**3** AGENDA, PROGRAM

**²schedule** *vb* **sched·uled; sched·ul·ing**
to form into or add to a schedule

**[1]scheme** \'skēm\ *n*
**1** a plan or program of something to be done : PROJECT
**2** a secret plan : PLOT
**3** an organized design ⟨color *scheme* of a room⟩ **synonyms** see PLAN

**[2]scheme** *vb* **schemed**; **schem·ing**
to form a scheme
**schem·er** *n*

**Schick test** \'shik-\ *n*
a test to find out whether a person might easily catch diphtheria

**schol·ar** \'skäl-ər\ *n*
**1** a student in a school : PUPIL
**2** a person who knows a great deal about one or more subjects

**schol·ar·ly** \'skäl-ər-lē\ *adj*
like that of or suitable to learned persons

**schol·ar·ship** \'skäl-ər-,ship\ *n*
**1** the qualities of a scholar : LEARNING
**2** money given a student to help pay for further education

**scho·las·tic** \skə-'las-tik\ *adj*
of or relating to schools, pupils, or education

**[1]school** \'skül\ *n*
**1** a place for teaching and learning
**2** a session of school
**3** SCHOOLHOUSE
**4** the teachers and pupils of a school
**5** a group of persons who share the same opinions and beliefs

---

**Word History** You may not think of school as a form of leisure. The English word *school*, however, can be traced back to a Greek word meaning "leisure." To the ancient Greeks it seemed only natural to spend leisure time in learning. The Greek word that meant "leisure" came to mean "time spent in learning." Later the word came to mean "a place for learning." English *school* comes from this Greek word.

---

**[2]school** *vb*
TEACH 2, TRAIN

**[3]school** *n*
a large number of one kind of fish or water animals swimming together

**school·bag** \'skül-,bag\ *n*
a bag for carrying schoolbooks

**school·book** \'skül-,bu̇k\ *n*
a book used in schools

**school·boy** \'skül-,bȯi\ *n*
a boy who goes to school

**school·girl** \'skül-,gərl\ *n*
a girl who goes to school

**school·house** \'skül-,hau̇s\ *n*, *pl* **school·hous·es** \-,hau̇-zəz\
a building used as a place for teaching and learning

**school·ing** \'skü-ling\ *n*
EDUCATION 1

**school·mas·ter** \'skül-,mas-tər\ *n*
a man who has charge of a school or teaches in a school

**school·mate** \'skül-,māt\ *n*
a fellow pupil

**school·mis·tress** \'skül-,mis-trəs\ *n*
a woman who has charge of a school or teaches in a school

**school·room** \'skül-,rüm, -,ru̇m\ *n*
CLASSROOM

**school·teach·er** \'skül-,tē-chər\ *n*
a person who teaches in a school

**school·work** \'skül-,wərk\ *n*
lessons done at school or assigned to be done at home

**school·yard** \'skül-,yärd\ *n*
the playground of a school

**schoo·ner** \'skü-nər\ *n*
a ship usually having two masts with the mainmast located toward the center and the shorter mast toward the front

**schwa** \'shwä\ *n*
**1** an unstressed vowel that is the usual sound of the first and last vowels of the English word *America*
**2** the symbol ə commonly used for a schwa and sometimes also for a similarly pronounced stressed vowel (as in *cut* )

**sci·ence** \'sī-əns\ *n*
**1** a branch of knowledge in which what is known is presented in an orderly way
**2** a branch of study that is concerned with collecting facts and forming laws to explain them

**sci·en·tif·ic** \,sī-ən-'tif-ik\ *adj*
**1** of or relating to science or scientists
**2** using or applying the methods of science
**sci·en·tif·i·cal·ly** \-'tif-i-kə-lē\ *adv*

**sci·en·tist** \'sī-ən-təst\ *n*
a person who knows much about science or does scientific work

**scis·sors** \'siz-ərz\ *n sing or pl*
▼ a cutting instrument with two blades fastened together so that the sharp edges slide against each other

**scissors:** a pair of scissors for cutting paper

**scoff** \'skäf, 'sko̊f\ *vb*
to show great disrespect with mocking laughter or behavior

**[1]scold** \'skōld\ *n*
a person given to criticizing and blaming others

**[2]scold** *vb*
to find fault with or criticize in an angry way
**scold·ing** *n*

**[1]scoop** \'sküp\ *n*
**1** a large deep shovel for digging, dipping, or shoveling
**2** a shovellike tool or utensil for digging into a soft substance and lifting out some of it
**3** a motion made with or as if with a scoop
**4** the amount held by a scoop

**[2]scoop** *vb*
**1** to take out or up with or as if with a scoop
**2** to make by scooping

**scoot** \'sküt\ *vb*
to go suddenly and fast

**scoot·er** \'sküt-ər\ *n*
**1** ▼ a vehicle consisting of a narrow base mounted between a front and a back wheel and guided by a handle attached to the front wheel
**2** MOTOR SCOOTER

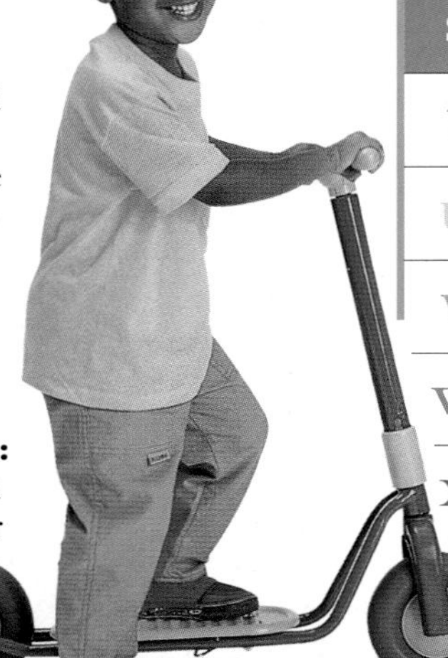

**scooter 1:** a boy with his scooter

**scope** \'skōp\ *n*
**1** space or opportunity for action or thought
**2** the area or amount covered, reached, or viewed

stinger

pincer

**scorpion**

**scorch** \'skȯrch\ *vb*
**1** to burn on the surface
**2** to burn so as to brown or dry out

**[1]score** \'skōr\ *n*
**1** a group of twenty things **:** TWENTY
**2** a line (as a scratch) made with or as if with something sharp
**3** a record of points made or lost (as in a game)
**4** DEBT 2
**5** a duty or an injury kept in mind for later action ⟨have a *score* to settle with you⟩
**6** [1]GROUND 3, REASON ⟨we were tired but wouldn't leave on that *score*⟩
**7** the written or printed form of a musical composition
**score·less** \-ləs\ *adj*

**[2]score** *vb* **scored**; **scor·ing**
**1** to set down in an account **:** RECORD
**2** to keep the score in a game
**3** to cut or mark with a line, scratch, or notch
**4** to make or cause to make a point in a game
**5** ACHIEVE 2, WIN
**6** [2]GRADE 3, MARK

**[1]scorn** \'skȯrn\ *n*
**1** an emotion involving both anger and disgust
**2** a person or thing very much disliked

**[2]scorn** *vb*
to show scorn for **synonyms** see DESPISE

**scorn·ful** \'skȯrn-fəl\ *adj*
feeling or showing scorn
**scorn·ful·ly** \-fə-lē\ *adv*

**Scor·pio** \'skȯr-pē-,ō\ *n*
**1** a constellation between Libra and Sagittarius imagined as a scorpion
**2** the eighth sign of the zodiac or a person born under this sign

**scor·pi·on** \'skȯr-pē-ən\ *n*
◀ an animal related to the spiders that has a long jointed body ending in a slender tail with a poisonous stinger at the end

**Scot** \'skät\ *n*
a person born or living in Scotland

**[1]Scotch** \'skäch\ *adj*
[1]SCOTTISH

**[2]Scotch** *n pl*
[2]SCOTTISH

**scot–free** \'skät-'frē\ *adj*
completely free from duty, harm, or punishment

**[1]Scot·tish** \'skät-ish\ *adj*
of or relating to Scotland or the Scottish

**[2]Scottish** *n pl*
the people of Scotland

**scoun·drel** \'skaùn-drəl\ *n*
a mean or wicked person **:** VILLAIN

**[1]scour** \'skaùr\ *vb*
**1** to rub hard with a rough substance in order to clean
**2** to free or clear from impurities by or as if by rubbing

**[2]scour** *n*
an action or result of scouring

**[3]scour** *vb*
to go or move swiftly about, over, or through in search of something ⟨*scoured* the records for a clue⟩

**[1]scourge** \'skərj\ *n*
**1** [2]WHIP 1
**2** a cause of widespread or great suffering

**[2]scourge** *vb* **scourged**; **scourg·ing**
**1** to whip severely **:** FLOG
**2** to cause severe suffering to **:** AFFLICT

**[1]scout** \'skaùt\ *vb*
**1** to go about in search of information
**2** to make a search

**[2]scout** *n*
**1** a person, group, boat, or plane that scouts
**2** the act of scouting
**3** *often cap* BOY SCOUT
**4** *often cap* GIRL SCOUT

**scout·ing** \'skaùt-ing\ *n*
**1** the act of one that scouts
**2** *often cap* the general activities of Boy Scout and Girl Scout groups

**scout·mas·ter** \'skaùt-,mas-tər\ *n*
the leader of a troop of Boy Scouts

**scow** \'skaù\ *n*
a large boat with a flat bottom and square ends that is used chiefly for loading and unloading ships and for carrying rubbish

**[1]scowl** \'skaùl\ *vb*
[1]FROWN 1

**[2]scowl** *n*
an angry look

**scram** \'skram\ *vb* **scrammed**; **scram·ming**
to go away at once

**[1]scram·ble** \'skram-bəl\ *vb* **scram·bled**; **scram·bling**
**1** to move or climb quickly on hands and knees
**2** to work hard to win or escape something ⟨had to *scramble* to earn a living⟩
**3** to mix together in disorder ⟨don't *scramble* up those papers⟩
**4** to cook the mixed whites and yolks of eggs by stirring them while frying

**[2]scramble** *n*
the act or result of scrambling

**[1]scrap** \'skrap\ *n*
**1** **scraps** *pl* pieces of leftover food
**2** a small bit
**3** waste material (as metal) that can be made fit to use again

**[2]scrap** *vb* **scrapped**; **scrap·ping**
**1** to break up (as a ship) into scrap
**2** to throw away as worthless

**[3]scrap** *n*
[1]QUARREL 2, FIGHT

**scrap·book** \'skrap-,bùk\ *n*
▼ a blank book in which clippings or pictures are kept

**scrapbook** displaying colorful cards

**¹scrape** \'skrāp\ *vb* **scraped**; **scrap·ing**
**1** to remove by repeated strokes of a sharp or rough tool
**2** to clean or smooth by rubbing
**3** to rub or cause to rub so as to make a harsh noise : SCUFF
**4** to hurt or roughen by dragging against a rough surface
**5** to get with difficulty and a little at a time ⟨*scrape* together money for a vacation⟩
**scrap·er** *n*

**²scrape** *n*
**1** the act of scraping
**2** a sound, mark, or injury made by scraping
**3** a disagreeable or trying situation

**¹scratch** \'skrach\ *vb*
**1** to scrape or injure with claws, nails, or an instrument
**2** to make a scraping noise
**3** to erase by scraping

**²scratch** *n*
a mark or injury made by scratching ⟨received a *scratch* while playing with the kitten⟩

**scratchy** \'skrach-ē\ *adj* **scratch·i·er**; **scratch·i·est**
likely to scratch or make sore or raw

**¹scrawl** \'skrȯl\ *vb*
to write quickly and carelessly : SCRIBBLE

**²scrawl** *n*
something written carelessly or without skill

**scraw·ny** \'skrȯ-nē\ *adj* **scraw·ni·er**; **scraw·ni·est**
poorly nourished : SKINNY

**¹scream** \'skrēm\ *vb*
to cry out (as in fright) with a loud and shrill sound

**²scream** *n*
a long cry that is loud and shrill

**¹screech** \'skrēch\ *n*
a shrill harsh cry usually expressing terror or pain

**²screech** *vb*
to cry out usually in terror or pain
**synonyms** see SHOUT

**¹screen** \'skrēn\ *n*
**1** a curtain or wall used to hide or to protect
**2** a network of wire set in a frame for separating finer parts from coarser parts (as of sand)
**3** a frame that holds a usually wire netting and is used to keep out pests (as insects)
**4** the flat surface on which movies are projected
**5** the surface on which the image appears in an electronic display (as on a television set or computer terminal)

**²screen** *vb*
**1** to hide or protect with or as if with a screen
**2** to separate or sift with a screen

**screen saver** *n*
a computer program that usually displays images on the screen of a computer that is on but not in use so as to prevent damage to the screen

**¹screw** \'skrü\ *n*
**1** a nail-shaped or rod-shaped piece of metal with a winding ridge around its length used for fastening and holding pieces together
**2** the act of screwing tight : TWIST
**3** PROPELLER

**²screw** *vb*
**1** to attach or fasten with a screw
**2** to operate, tighten, or adjust with a screw
**3** to turn or twist on a thread on or like that on a screw

**screw·driv·er** \'skrü-ˌdrī-vər\ *n*
▼ a tool for turning screws

**screwdriver**

**¹scrib·ble** \'skrib-əl\ *vb* **scrib·bled**; **scrib·bling**
to write quickly or carelessly
**scrib·bler** \'skrib-lər\ *n*

**²scribble** *n*
something scribbled

**scribe** \'skrīb\ *n*
**1** a teacher of Jewish law
**2** a person who copies writing (as in a book)

**scrim·mage** \'skrim-ij\ *n*
**1** a confused struggle
**2** the action between two football teams when one attempts to move the ball down the field

**script** \'skript\ *n*
**1** the written form of a play or movie or the lines to be said by a radio or television performer
**2** a type used in printing that resembles handwriting
**3** HANDWRITING

**scrip·ture** \'skrip-chər\ *n*
**1** *cap* BIBLE 1
**2** writings sacred to a religious group

**¹scroll 1:** a Hebrew scroll

**¹scroll** \'skrōl\ *n*
**1** ▲ a roll of paper or parchment on which something is written or engraved
**2** an ornament resembling a length of paper usually rolled at both ends

**²scroll** *vb*
to move words or images up or down a display screen as if by unrolling a scroll

**¹scrub** \'skrəb\ *n*
**1** a thick growth of small or stunted shrubs or trees
**2** one of poor size or quality

**²scrub** *vb* **scrubbed**; **scrub·bing**
to rub hard in washing

**³scrub** *n*
the act or an instance or a period of scrubbing

**scrub·by** \'skrəb-ē\ *adj* **scrub·bi·er**; **scrub·bi·est**
**1** of poor size or quality
**2** covered with scrub

**scruff** \'skrəf\ *n*
the loose skin on the back of the neck

**scruffy** \'skrəf-ē\ *adj* **scruff·i·er**; **scruff·i·est**
dirty or shabby in appearance

**scru·ple** \'skrü-pəl\ *n*
**1** a sense of right and wrong that keeps one from doing as one pleases
**2** a feeling of guilt when one does wrong : QUALM

**scru·pu·lous** \'skrü-pyə-ləs\ *adj*
having or showing very careful and strict regard for what is right and proper : CONSCIENTIOUS
**scru·pu·lous·ly** *adv*

**scuba** \'skü-bə\ *n*
equipment used for breathing while swimming underwater

**scuba diver** *n*
a person who swims underwater with scuba gear

**scuff** \'skəf\ *vb*
**1** to scrape the feet while walking
**2** to become rough or scratched through wear

[1]**scuf·fle** \'skəf-əl\ *vb* **scuf·fled**; **scuf·fling**
**1** to struggle in a confused way at close quarters
**2** to shuffle one's feet

[2]**scuffle** *n*
a rough confused struggle

**scull** \'skəl\ *n*
**1** an oar used at the rear of a boat to drive it forward
**2** one of a pair of short oars
**3** a boat driven by one or more pairs of sculls

**sculp·tor** \'skəlp-tər\ *n*
one that sculptures

[1]**sculp·ture** \'skəlp-chər\ *n*
**1** the action or art of making statues by carving or chiseling (as in wood or stone), by modeling (as in clay), or by casting (as in melted metal)
**2** work produced by sculpture ⟨displayed a piece of *sculpture*⟩

[2]**sculpture** *vb* **sculp·tured**; **sculp·tur·ing**
to make sculptures

**scum** \'skəm\ *n*
**1** a film of matter that rises to the top of a boiling or fermenting liquid
**2** a coating on the surface of still water

**scurf** \'skərf\ *n*
thin dry scales or a coating of these (as on a leaf or the skin)

[1]**scur·ry** \'skər-ē\ *vb* **scur·ried**; **scur·ry·ing**
to move in a brisk way

[2]**scurry** *n, pl* **scur·ries**
the act or an instance of scurrying

[1]**scur·vy** \'skər-vē\ *n*
a disease caused by lack of vitamin C in which the teeth loosen, the gums soften, and there is bleeding under the skin

[2]**scurvy** *adj* **scur·vi·er**; **scur·vi·est**
[1]MEAN 4, CONTEMPTIBLE

[1]**scut·tle** \'skət-l\ *n*
a pail or bucket for carrying coal

[2]**scuttle** *n*
a small opening with a lid or cover (as in the deck of a ship)

[3]**scuttle** *vb* **scut·tled**; **scut·tling**
to sink by cutting holes through the bottom or sides

[4]**scuttle** *vb* **scut·tled**; **scut·tling**
to run rapidly from view

**scythe** \'sīth\ *n*
a tool with a curved blade on a long curved handle that is used to mow grass or grain by hand

**sea** \'sē\ *n*
**1** a body of salt water not as large as an ocean and often nearly surrounded by land
**2** OCEAN 1
**3** rough water
**4** something suggesting a sea's great size or depth

**sea anemone** *n*
a hollow sea animal with a flowerlike cluster of tentacles about its mouth

**sea·bird** \'sē-,bərd\ *n*
a bird (as a gull) that lives about the open ocean

**sea·coast** \'sē-,kōst\ *n*
the shore of the sea

**sea cucumber** *n*
▼ a sea animal related to the starfishes and sea urchins that has a long flexible muscular body shaped like a cucumber

**sea cucumber**

**sea dog** *n*
an experienced sailor

**sea·far·er** \'sē-,far-ər, -,fer-\ *n*
a person who travels over the ocean : MARINER

[1]**sea·far·ing** \'sē-,far-ing, -,fer-\ *adj*
of, given to, or employed in seafaring

[2]**seafaring** *n*
a traveling over the sea as work or as recreation

**sea·food** \'sē-,füd\ *n*
▼ edible saltwater fish and shellfish

**seafood:** a plate of seafood

**sea·go·ing** \'sē-,gō-ing\ *adj*
suitable or used for sea travel ⟨a *seagoing* vessel⟩

**sea gull** *n*
a gull that lives near the sea

**sea horse** *n*
a small fish with a head which looks like that of a horse

[1]**seal** \'sēl\ *n*
**1** a sea mammal that swims with flippers, lives mostly in cold regions, mates and bears young on land, eats flesh, and is hunted for fur, hides, or oil
**2** the soft dense fur of a seal

[2]**seal** *n*
**1** something (as a pledge) that makes safe or secure
**2** a device with a cut or raised design or figure that can be stamped or pressed into wax or paper

3 ▼ a piece of wax stamped with a design and used to seal a letter or package
4 a stamp that may be used to close a letter or package ⟨Christmas *seals*⟩
5 something that closes tightly
6 a closing that is tight and perfect

**²seal 3:** a wax seal on an envelope

**³seal** *vb*
1 to mark with a seal
2 to close or make fast with or as if with a seal
**seal·er** *n*

**sea level** *n*
the surface of the sea midway between the average high and low tides

**sea lion** *n*
► a very large seal of the Pacific Ocean

**seal·skin** \'sēl-,skin\ *n*
¹SEAL 2

**¹seam** \'sēm\ *n*
1 the fold, line, or groove made by sewing together or joining two edges or two pieces of material
2 a layer of a mineral or metal ⟨a *seam* of coal⟩

**²seam** *vb*
1 to join with a seam
2 to mark with a line, scar, or wrinkle ⟨a face *seamed* with age⟩

**sea·man** \'sē-mən\ *n, pl* **sea·men** \-mən\
1 a person who helps in the handling of a ship at sea : SAILOR
2 an enlisted person in the Navy or Coast Guard ranking above a seaman apprentice

**seaman apprentice** *n*
an enlisted person in the Navy or Coast Guard ranking above a seaman recruit

**seaman recruit** *n*
an enlisted person of the lowest rank in the Navy or Coast Guard

**seam·stress** \'sēm-strəs\ *n*
a woman who sews especially for a living

**sea·plane** \'sē-,plān\ *n*
an airplane that can rise from and land on water

**sea·port** \'sē-,pōrt\ *n*
a port, harbor, or town within reach of seagoing ships

**sear** \'sir\ *vb*
1 to dry by or as if by heat : PARCH
2 to scorch or make brown on the surface by heat

**¹search** \'sərch\ *vb*
1 to go through carefully and thoroughly in an effort to find something ⟨*search* the house⟩
2 to look in the pockets or the clothing of for something hidden ⟨all of us were *searched*⟩
**synonyms** see SEEK
**search·ing·ly** *adv*

**²search** *n*
an act or instance of searching

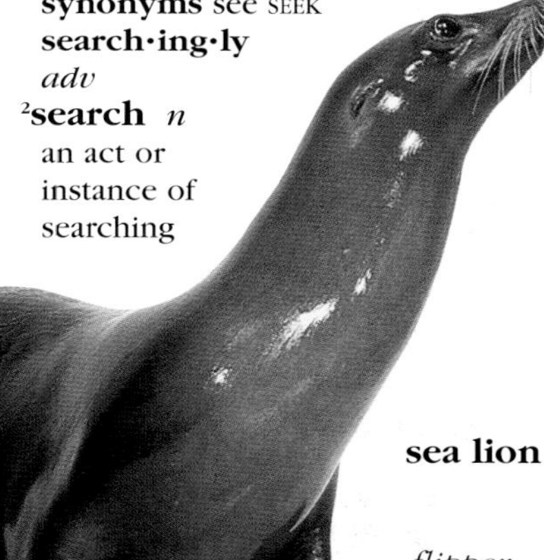


**sea lion**

**search engine** *n*
computer software used to search data (as text or a database) for requested information

**search·light** \'sərch-,līt\ *n*
a lamp for sending a beam of bright light

**sea·shell** \'sē-,shel\ *n*
the shell of a sea creature

**sea·shore** \'sē-,shōr\ *n*
the shore of a sea

**sea·sick** \'sē-,sik\ *adj*
sick at the stomach from the pitching or rolling of a ship
**sea·sick·ness** *n*

**sea·side** \'sē-,sīd\ *n*
SEACOAST

**¹sea·son** \'sēz-n\ *n*
1 one of the four quarters into which a year is commonly divided
2 a period of time associated with something special ⟨the Christmas *season*⟩ ⟨the strawberry *season*⟩

**²season** *vb*
1 to make pleasant to the taste by use of seasoning
2 to make suitable for use (as by aging or drying) ⟨*seasoned* lumber⟩

**sea·son·al** \'sēz-n-əl\ *adj*
of, relating to, or coming only at a certain season ⟨*seasonal* foods⟩

**sea·son·ing** \'sēz-n-ing\ *n*
something added to food to give it more flavor

**¹seat** \'sēt\ *n*
1 something (as a chair) used to sit in or on
2 the part of something on which one rests in sitting ⟨chair *seat*⟩ ⟨*seat* of my pants⟩
3 the place on or at which a person sits ⟨take your *seat*⟩
4 a place that serves as a capital or center ⟨a *seat* of learning⟩
**seat·ed** \'sēt-əd\ *adj*

**²seat** *vb*
1 to place in or on a seat
2 to provide seats for ⟨the hall *seats* 500 persons⟩

**seat belt** *n*
a strap (as in an automobile or airplane) designed to hold a person in a seat

**sea urchin** *n*
▼ a rounded shellfish related to the starfishes that lives on or burrows in the sea bottom and is covered with spines

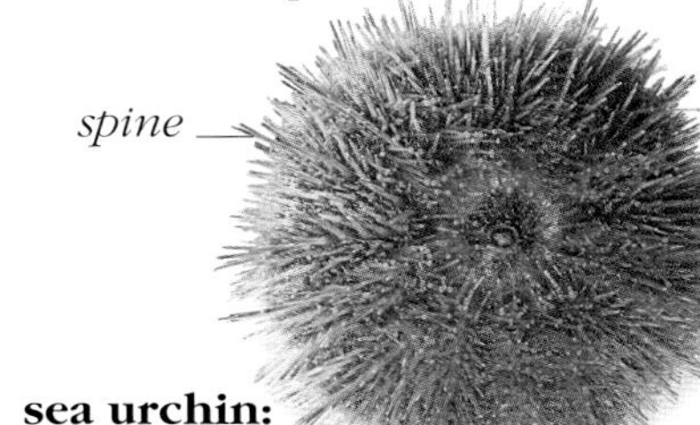


**sea urchin:** overhead view of a sea urchin

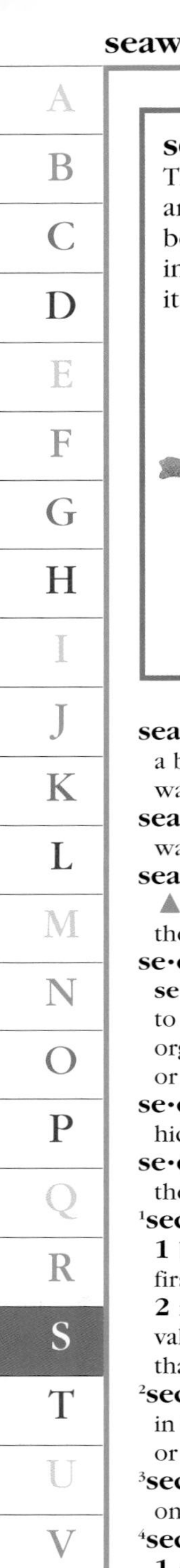


**seaweed**
The three most common types of seaweed are brown, red, or green. Seaweed can be found on the beach, in the sea, and in salty rockpools where it anchors itself onto rocks and solid surfaces.

**brown seaweed** **green seaweed** **red seaweed**

**sea·wall** \'sē-,wȯl\ *n*
a bank or a wall to prevent sea waves from cutting away the shore

**sea·wa·ter** \'sē-,wȯt-ər, -,wät-\ *n*
water in or from the sea

**sea·weed** \'sē-,wēd\ *n*
▲ an alga (as a kelp) that grows in the sea

**se·cede** \si-'sēd\ *vb* **se·ced·ed**; **se·ced·ing**
to end one's association with an organization (as a country, church, or political party)

**se·clud·ed** \si-'klüd-əd\ *adj*
hidden from sight

**se·clu·sion** \si-'klü-zhən\ *n*
the condition of being secluded

[1]**sec·ond** \'sek-ənd\ *adj*
**1** being next after the first ⟨the *second* time⟩
**2** next lower in rank, value, or importance than the first ⟨*second* prize⟩

[2]**second** *adv*
in the second place or rank

[3]**second** *n*
one that is second

[4]**second** *n*
**1** a sixtieth part of a minute of time or of a degree
**2** MOMENT 1, INSTANT

[5]**second** *vb*
to support a motion or nomination so that it may be debated or voted on

**sec·ond·ary** \'sek-ən-,der-ē\ *adj*
**1** second in rank, value, or importance
**2** of, relating to, or being the second of three levels of stress in pronunciation
**3** derived from or coming after something original or primary ⟨*secondary* schools⟩

**sec·ond·hand** \,sek-ənd-'hand\ *adj*
**1** not new **:** having had a previous owner ⟨a *secondhand* automobile⟩
**2** selling used goods

**second lieutenant** *n*
a commissioned officer of the lowest rank in the Army, Air Force, or Marine Corps

**secretary 4:** model of a secretary

**sec·ond·ly** \'sek-ənd-lē\ *adv*
in the second place

**sec·ond–rate** \,sek-ən-'drāt\ *adj*
of ordinary quality or value

**se·cre·cy** \'sē-krə-sē\ *n*, *pl* **se·cre·cies**
**1** the habit of keeping things secret
**2** the quality or state of being secret or hidden

[1]**se·cret** \'sē-krət\ *adj*
**1** hidden from the knowledge of others ⟨keep your plans *secret*⟩
**2** done or working in secrecy ⟨a *secret* agent⟩
**se·cret·ly** *adv*

[2]**secret** *n*
something kept or planned to be kept from others' knowledge

**sec·re·tary** \'sek-rə-,ter-ē\ *n*, *pl* **sec·re·tar·ies**
**1** a person who is employed to take care of records and letters for another person
**2** an officer of a business corporation or society who has charge of the letters and records and who keeps minutes of meetings
**3** a government official in charge of the affairs of a department
**4** ◄ a writing desk with a top section for books

[1]**se·crete** \si-'krēt\ *vb* **se·cret·ed**; **se·cret·ing**
to produce and give off as a secretion ⟨glands that *secrete* mucus⟩

**²se·crete** *vb* **se·cret·ed**; **se·cret·ing**
to put in a hiding place

**se·cre·tion** \si-'krē-shən\ *n*
**1** the act or process of secreting some substance
**2** a substance formed in and given off by a gland that usually performs a useful function in the body ⟨digestive *secretions* contain enzymes⟩
**3** a concealing or hiding of something

**se·cre·tive** \'sē-krət-iv, si-'krēt-\ *adj*
not open or frank

**sect** \'sekt\ *n*
a group within a religion which has a special set of teachings or a special way of doing things

**¹sec·tion** \'sek-shən\ *n*
**1** a part cut off or separated ⟨a *section* of an orange⟩
**2** a part of a written work ⟨the sports *section* of a newspaper⟩

**sedan chair:** porcelain model of a sedan chair made in Russia in the early 20th century

**3** the appearance that a thing has or would have if cut straight through ⟨a drawing of a gun in *section*⟩
**4** a part of a country, group of people, or community ⟨the business *section* of town⟩
**synonyms** see PART

**²section** *vb*
to cut into sections

**sec·tor** \'sek-tər\ *n*
a part of an area or of a sphere of activity

**sec·u·lar** \'sek-yə-lər\ *adj*
**1** not concerned with religion or the church ⟨*secular* affairs⟩ ⟨*secular* music⟩
**2** not bound by a monk's vows **:** not belonging to a religious order ⟨a *secular* priest⟩

**¹se·cure** \si-'kyůr\ *adj* **se·cur·er**; **se·cur·est**
**1** free from danger or risk
**2** strong or firm enough to ensure safety ⟨a *secure* lock⟩
**3** ¹SURE 5, ASSURED ⟨the victory was *secure*⟩ **synonyms** see SAFE

**²secure** *vb* **se·cured**; **se·cur·ing**
**1** to make safe ⟨*secure* troops against attack⟩
**2** to fasten tightly ⟨*secure* a door⟩
**3** to get hold of **:** ACQUIRE ⟨*secure* information⟩ ⟨*secured* a job⟩

**se·cu·ri·ty** \si-'kyůr-ət-ē\ *n, pl* **se·cu·ri·ties**
**1** the state of being secure **:** SAFETY
**2** something given as a pledge of payment ⟨*security* for a loan⟩
**3** something (as a stock certificate) that is evidence of debt or ownership

**se·dan** \si-'dan\ *n*
**1** SEDAN CHAIR
**2** a closed automobile seating four or more persons that has two or four doors and a permanent top

**sedan chair** *n*
◀ a portable and often covered chair made to hold one person and to be carried on two poles by two men

**se·date** \si-'dāt\ *adj*
quiet and steady in manner or conduct
**se·date·ly** *adv*
**se·date·ness** *n*

**¹sed·a·tive** \'sed-ət-iv\ *adj*
tending to calm or to relieve tension

**²sedative** *n*
a sedative medicine

**sedge** \'sej\ *n*
a plant that is like grass but has solid stems and grows in tufts in marshes

**sed·i·ment** \'sed-ə-mənt\ *n*
**1** the material from a liquid that settles to the bottom
**2** material (as stones and sand) carried onto land or into water by water, wind, or a glacier

**sed·i·men·ta·ry** \ˌsed-ə-'ment-ə-rē\ *adj*
of, relating to, or formed from sediment ⟨sandstone is a *sedimentary* rock⟩

**se·duce** \si-'düs, -'dyüs\ *vb* **se·duced**; **se·duc·ing**
to persuade to do wrong ⟨was *seduced* into crime⟩

**¹see** \'sē\ *vb* **saw** \'sȯ\; **seen** \'sēn\; **see·ing**
**1** to have the power of sight **:** view with the eyes
**2** to have experience of **:** UNDERGO ⟨*saw* some action during the war⟩
**3** to understand the meaning or importance of
**4** to make sure ⟨*see* that the job gets done⟩
**5** to attend to ⟨I'll *see* to your order at once⟩
**6** to meet with ⟨the doctor will *see* you now⟩
**7** ACCOMPANY 1, ESCORT ⟨I'll *see* you home⟩

**²see** *n*
**1** the city in which a bishop's church is located
**2** DIOCESE

**¹seed** \'sēd\ *n*
**1** ▼ a tiny resting plant closed in a protective coat and able to develop under suitable conditions into a plant like the one that produced it
**2** a small structure (as a spore or a tiny dry fruit) other than a true seed by which a plant reproduces itself
**3** the descendants of one individual ⟨the *seed* of David⟩
**4** a source of development or growth **:** GERM 2
**seed·ed** \-əd\ *adj*
**seed·less** \-ləs\ *adj*

**¹seed 1:** seeds in a slice of watermelon

**²seed** *vb*
**1** ²SOW 2, PLANT
**2** to produce or shed seeds ⟨a plant that *seeds* early⟩
**3** to take the seeds out of ⟨*seed* raisins⟩

**seed·case** \'sēd-ˌkās\ *n*
a dry hollow fruit (as a pod) that contains seeds

**seed·ling** \'sēd-ling\ *n*
**1** a young plant grown from seed
**2** a young tree before it becomes a sapling

**seed plant** *n*
a plant that reproduces by true seeds

**seed·pod** \'sēd-,päd\ *n*
POD

**seedy** \'sēd-ē\ *adj* **seed·i·er**; **seed·i·est**
**1** having or full of seeds ⟨a *seedy* fruit⟩
**2** poor in condition or quality

**seek** \'sēk\ *vb* **sought** \'sȯt\; **seek·ing**
**1** to try to find ⟨*seek* help⟩
**2** to try to win or get ⟨*seek* fame⟩
**3** to make an attempt ⟨*seek* to end a war⟩

**seen** *past participle of* SEE

**seep** \'sēp\ *vb*
to flow slowly through small openings ⟨water *seeped* into the basement⟩

**seer** \'sir\ *n*
a person who predicts events

**[1]see·saw** \'sē-,sȯ\ *n*
**1** an up-and-down or backward-and-forward motion or movement
**2** ▼ a children's game of riding on the ends of a plank balanced in the middle with one end going up while the other goes down
**3** the plank used in seesaw

**[2]seesaw** *vb*
**1** to ride on a seesaw
**2** to move like a seesaw

**[1]seesaw 2**

**Synonyms** SEEK, SEARCH, and HUNT mean to look for something. SEEK may be used in looking for either material or mental things ⟨*seeking* new friends⟩ ⟨*seek* the truth⟩. SEARCH suggests looking for something in a very careful, thorough way ⟨we *searched* all over the house for the letter⟩. HUNT suggests a long pursuit, as if one were going after game ⟨I *hunted* all day for the right present⟩.

**seem** \'sēm\ *vb*
**1** to give the impression of being : APPEAR ⟨they certainly *seemed* pleased⟩
**2** to suggest to one's own mind ⟨I *seem* to have lost my key⟩

**seem·ing** \'sē-ming\ *adj*
APPARENT 3 ⟨suspicious of our *seeming* enthusiasm⟩
**seem·ing·ly** *adv*

**seethe** \'sēth\ *vb* **seethed**; **seeth·ing**
**1** to move without order as if boiling ⟨flies *seething* around garbage⟩
**2** to be in a state of great excitement ⟨*seethe* with rage⟩

**seg·ment** \'seg-mənt\ *n*
**1** ► any of the parts into which a thing is divided or naturally separates
**2** a part cut off from a figure (as a circle) by means of a line or plane
**3** a part of a straight line included between two points
**seg·ment·ed** \-,ment-əd\ *adj*

**seg·re·gate** \'seg-ri-,gāt\ *vb* **seg·re·gat·ed**; **seg·re·gat·ing**
to set apart from others

**seg·re·ga·tion** \,seg-ri-'gā-shən\ *n*
**1** an act, process, or instance of segregating
**2** enforced separation of a race, class, or group from the rest of society

**seis·mo·graph** \'sīz-mə-,graf, 'sīs-\ *n*
a device that measures and records vibrations of the earth
**seis·mo·graph·ic** \,sīz-mə-'graf-ik, ,sīs-\ *adj*
**seis·mog·ra·phy** \sīz-'mäg-rə-fē, sīs-\ *n*

**seize** \'sēz\ *vb* **seized**; **seiz·ing**
**1** to take possession of by force ⟨*seize* a fortress⟩
**2** to take hold of suddenly or with force **synonyms** see TAKE

**sei·zure** \'sē-zhər\ *n*
an act of seizing : the state of being seized

**sel·dom** \'sel-dəm\ *adv*
not often : RARELY

**[1]se·lect** \sə-'lekt\ *adj*
**1** chosen to include the best or most suitable individuals ⟨*select* committees⟩ ⟨a *select* library⟩
**2** of special value or excellence ⟨a *select* hotel⟩

**[2]select** *vb*
to pick out from a number or group : CHOOSE ⟨*select* a ripe peach⟩ **synonyms** see CHOOSE

**se·lec·tion** \sə-'lek-shən\ *n*
**1** the act or process of selecting
**2** something that is chosen

**se·lec·tive** \sə-'lek-tiv\ *adj*
involving or based on selection

**se·le·ni·um** \sə-'lē-nē-əm\ *n*
a gray powdery chemical element used chiefly in electronic devices

**self** \'self\ *n, pl* **selves** \'selvz\
**1** a person regarded as an individual apart from everyone else
**2** a special side of a person's character ⟨your better *self*⟩

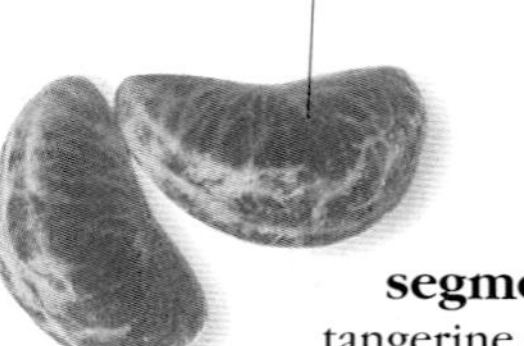


**segment 1:** tangerine segments

**self-** *prefix*
**1** oneself or itself ⟨*self*-governing⟩
**2** of or by oneself or itself

**3** to, with, for, or toward oneself or itself ⟨*self*-respect⟩

**self–ad·dressed** \ˌsel-fə-ˈdrest, ˈsel-ˈfad-ˌrest\ *adj*
addressed for return to the sender

**self–cen·tered** \ˈself-ˈsent-ərd\ *adj*
SELFISH

**self–con·fi·dence** \ˈself-ˈkän-fə-dəns\ *n*
confidence in oneself and one's abilities

**self–con·scious** \ˈself-ˈkän-chəs\ *adj*
too much aware of one's feelings or appearance when in the presence of other people
**self–con·scious·ly** *adv*
**self–con·scious·ness** *n*

**self–con·trol** \ˌself-kən-ˈtrōl\ *n*
control over one's own impulses, emotions, or actions

**self–de·fense** \ˌself-di-ˈfens\ *n*
the act of defending oneself or one's property ⟨acted in *self-defense*⟩

**self–es·teem** \ˌsel-fə-ˈstēm\ *n*
a satisfaction in oneself and one's own abilities

**self–ev·i·dent** \ˈsel-ˈfev-ə-dənt\ *adj*
having no need of proof ⟨*self-evident* truths⟩

**self–gov·ern·ing** \ˈself-ˈgəv-ər-ning\ *adj*
having self-government

**self–gov·ern·ment** \ˈself-ˈgəv-ərn-mənt, -ər-mənt\ *n*
government by action of the people making up a community **:** democratic government

**self–im·por·tant** \ˌsel-fim-ˈpȯrt-nt\ *adj*
believing or acting as if one's importance is greater than it really is

**self·ish** \ˈsel-fish\ *adj*
taking care of oneself without thought for others
**self·ish·ness** *n*

**self·less** \ˈsel-fləs\ *adj*
not selfish
**self·less·ly** *adv*
**self·less·ness** *n*

**self–pro·pelled** \ˌself-prə-ˈpeld\ *adj*
containing within itself the means for its own movement

**self–re·li·ance** \ˌsel-fri-ˈlī-əns\ *n*
trust in one's own efforts and abilities

**self–re·spect** \ˌsel-fri-ˈspekt\ *n*
**1** a proper regard for oneself as a human being
**2** regard for one's standing or position

**self–re·straint** \ˌsel-fri-ˈstrānt\ *n*
proper control over one's actions or emotions

**self–righ·teous** \ˈsel-ˈfrī-chəs\ *adj*
strongly convinced of the rightness of one's actions or beliefs

**self·same** \ˈself-ˌsām\ *adj*
exactly the same

**self–ser·vice** \ˈself-ˈsər-vəs\ *n*
the serving of oneself with things to be paid for to a cashier usually upon leaving

**self–worth** \ˈself-ˈwərth\ *n*
SELF–ESTEEM

**sell** \ˈsel\ *vb* **sold** \ˈsōld\; **sell·ing**
**1** to betray a person or duty ⟨*sell out* their country⟩
**2** to exchange in return for money or something else of value
**3** to be sold or priced ⟨these *sell* for a dollar apiece⟩
**sell·er** *n*

**selves** *pl of* SELF

**sem·a·phore** \ˈsem-ə-ˌfōr\ *n*
**1** a device for sending signals that can be seen by the receiver
**2** ▼ a system of sending signals with two flags held one in each hand

**sem·blance** \ˈsem-bləns\ *n*
outward appearance

**se·mes·ter** \sə-ˈmes-tər\ *n*
either of two terms that make up a school year

---

**Word History** The English word *semester* that means "half a school year" came from a Latin word that meant "every half year." This word in turn came from two Latin words. The first meant "six" and the second meant "month." A half year is, after all, six months.

---

**semi-** *prefix*
**1** half ⟨*semi*circle⟩
**2** partly **:** not completely
**3** partial

**semi·cir·cle** \ˈsem-i-ˌsər-kəl\ *n*
▼ half of a circle

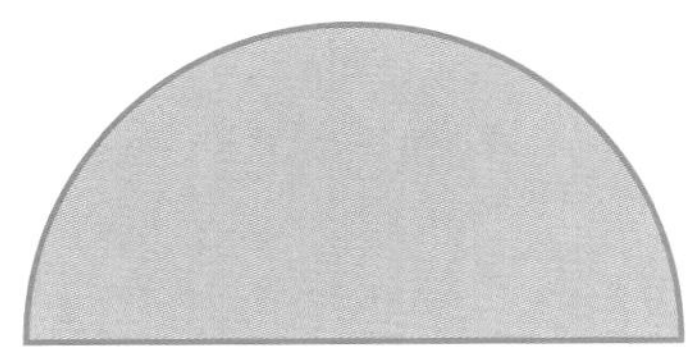

**semicircle**

**semi·cir·cu·lar** \ˌsem-i-ˈsər-kyə-lər\ *adj*
having the form of a semicircle

**semaphore 2:** a series of semaphore signals that spell the word "HELLO"

A B C D E F G H I J K L M N O P Q R S T U V W X Y Z

**semi·co·lon** \'sem-i-ˌkō-lən\ *n*
a punctuation mark ; that can be used to separate parts of a sentence which need clearer separation than would be shown by a comma, to separate main clauses which have no conjunction between, and to separate phrases and clauses containing commas

**semi·con·duc·tor** \ˌsem-i-kən-'dək-tər\ *n*
a solid substance whose ability to conduct electricity is between that of a conductor and that of an insulator

**¹semi·fi·nal** \ˌsem-i-'fīn-l\ *adj*
coming before the final round in a tournament

**²semi·fi·nal** \'sem-i-ˌfīn-l\ *n*
a semifinal match or game

**sem·i·nary** \'sem-ə-ˌner-ē\ *n, pl* **sem·i·nar·ies**
**1** a private school at or above the high school level
**2** a school for the training of priests, ministers, or rabbis

**semi·sol·id** \ˌsem-i-'säl-əd\ *adj*
having the qualities of both a solid and a liquid

**sen·ate** \'sen-ət\ *n*
**1** the upper and smaller branch of a legislature in a country or state
**2** a governing body

**sen·a·tor** \'sen-ət-ər\ *n*
a member of a senate

**send** \'send\ *vb* **sent** \'sent\; **send·ing**
**1** to cause to go ⟨*sent* the pupil home⟩
**2** to set in motion by physical force ⟨*sent* the ball into right field⟩
**3** to cause to happen ⟨whatever fate may *send* us⟩
**4** to cause someone to pass a message on or do an errand ⟨*send* out for coffee⟩
**5** to give an order or request to come or go ⟨*sent* for the child⟩
**6** to bring into a certain condition ⟨*sent* me into a rage⟩
**send·er** *n*

**¹se·nior** \'sēn-yər\ *n*
**1** a person older or higher in rank than someone else
**2** a student in the final year of high school or college

**²senior** *adj*
**1** being older — used to distinguish a father from a son with the same name ⟨John Doe, *Senior*⟩
**2** higher in rank or office ⟨the *senior* partner of the law firm⟩
**3** of or relating to seniors in a high school or college

**senior airman** *n*
an enlisted person in the Air Force who ranks above airman first class but who has not been made sergeant

**senior chief petty officer** *n*
a petty officer in the Navy or Coast Guard ranking above a chief petty officer

**senior master sergeant** *n*
a noncommissioned officer in the Air Force ranking above a master sergeant

**sen·sa·tion** \sen-'sā-shən\ *n*
**1** awareness (as of noise or heat) or a mental process (as seeing or smelling) resulting from stimulation of a sense organ
**2** an indefinite bodily feeling ⟨a *sensation* of flying⟩
**3** a state of excited interest or feeling ⟨the rumor caused a *sensation*⟩
**4** a cause or object of excited interest ⟨the play was a *sensation*⟩

**sen·sa·tion·al** \sen-'sā-shən-l\ *adj*
causing or meant to cause great interest

**¹sense** \'sens\ *n*
**1** a meaning or one of a set of meanings a word, phrase, or story may have
**2** a specialized function or mechanism (as sight, taste, or touch) of the body that involves the action and effect of a stimulus on a sense organ ⟨the pain *sense*⟩
**3** a particular sensation or kind of sensation ⟨a good *sense* of balance⟩
**4** awareness arrived at through or as if through the senses ⟨a vague *sense* of danger⟩
**5** an awareness or understanding of something ⟨a *sense* of humor⟩
**6** the ability to make wise decisions
**7** good reason or excuse ⟨no *sense* in waiting⟩

**²sense** *vb* **sensed**; **sens·ing**
to be or become conscious of ⟨*sense* the approach of a storm⟩

**sense·less** \'sen-sləs\ *adj*
**1** UNCONSCIOUS 2 ⟨knocked *senseless*⟩
**2** STUPID 2
**sense·less·ly** *adv*
**sense·less·ness** *n*

**sense organ** *n*
a bodily structure (as the retina of the eye) that reacts to a stimulus (as light) and activates associated nerves so that they carry impulses to the brain

**sen·si·bil·i·ty** \ˌsen-sə-'bil-ət-ē\ *n, pl* **sen·si·bil·i·ties**
**1** the ability to receive or feel sensations
**2** the emotion or feeling of which a person is capable ⟨a person of keen *sensibility*⟩

**sen·si·ble** \'sen-sə-bəl\ *adj*
**1** possible to take in by the senses or mind ⟨*sensible* impressions⟩
**2** capable of feeling or perceiving ⟨*sensible* to pain⟩
**3** showing or containing good sense or reason ⟨a *sensible* argument⟩
**sen·si·ble·ness** *n*
**sen·si·bly** \-blē\ *adv*

**sen·si·tive** \'sen-sət-iv\ *adj*
**1** capable of responding to stimulation ⟨*sensitive* structures of the ear⟩
**2** easily or strongly affected, impressed, or hurt ⟨a *sensitive* child⟩
**3** readily changed or affected by the action of a certain thing ⟨plants *sensitive* to light⟩
**sen·si·tive·ly** *adv*
**sen·si·tive·ness** *n*

**sen·si·tiv·i·ty** \ˌsen-sə-'tiv-ət-ē\ *n*
the quality or state of being sensitive

**sen·so·ry** \'sen-sə-rē\ *adj*
of or relating to sensation or the senses ⟨*sensory* nerves⟩

**sen·su·al** \'sen-chə-wəl\ *adj*
relating to the pleasing of the senses

**sent** *past of* SEND

**¹sen·tence** \'sent-ns\ *n*
**1** JUDGMENT 1
**2** punishment set by a court ⟨served a *sentence* for robbery⟩
**3** a group of words that makes a statement, asks a question, or expresses a command, wish, or exclamation
**4** a mathematical statement (as an equation) in words or symbols

**²sentence** *vb* **sen·tenced**; **sen·tenc·ing**
to give a sentence to ⟨the judge *sentenced* the prisoner⟩

**sen·ti·ment** \'sent-ə-mənt\ *n*
**1** a thought or attitude influenced by feeling ⟨a strong religious *sentiment*⟩

2 OPINION 1
3 tender feelings of affection or yearning

**sen·ti·men·tal** \ˌsent-ə-ˈment-l\ *adj*
1 influenced strongly by sentiment
2 primarily affecting the emotions ⟨*sentimental* music⟩

**sen·ti·nel** \ˈsent-n-əl\ *n*
SENTRY

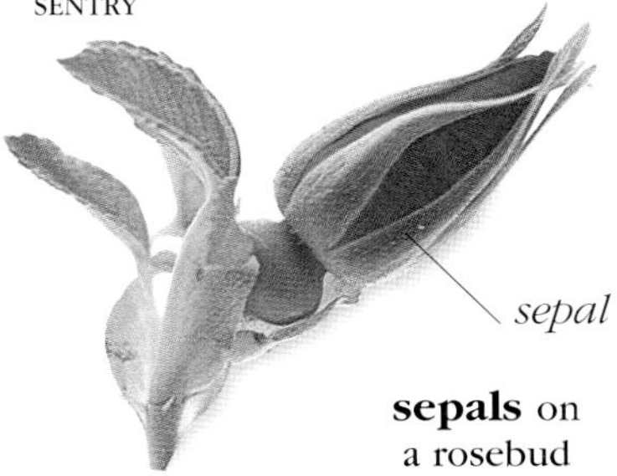

**sepals** on a rosebud

**sen·try** \ˈsen-trē\ *n, pl* **sentries**
a person (as a soldier) on duty as a guard

**se·pal** \ˈsē-pəl, ˈsep-əl\ *n*
▲ one of the specialized leaves that form the calyx of a flower

[1]**sep·a·rate** \ˈsep-ə-ˌrāt\ *vb*
**sep·a·rat·ed**; **sep·a·rat·ing**
1 to set or keep apart ⟨*separate* an egg yolk from the white⟩
2 to make a distinction between ⟨*separate* fact from fiction⟩
3 to cease to be together : PART

**Synonyms** SEPARATE, PART, and DIVIDE mean to break into parts or to keep apart. SEPARATE may suggest that things have been put into groups, or that a thing has been removed from a group, or that something has been inserted between like things ⟨*separate* the good eggs from the bad ones⟩ ⟨a fence *separates* the two yards⟩. PART suggests that the things to be separated are closely joined in some way ⟨only death could *part* the two friends⟩. DIVIDE suggests separating by cutting or breaking into pieces or sections ⟨*divide* the pie into six equal portions⟩.

[2]**sep·a·rate** \ˈsep-ə-rət, ˈsep-rət\ *adj*
1 set or kept apart ⟨the motel contains fifty *separate* units⟩
2 divided from each other ⟨where church and state are *separate*⟩
3 not shared : INDIVIDUAL ⟨we were each busy with our *separate* jobs⟩
4 having independent existence

**sep·a·rate·ly** \ˈsep-ə-rət-lē\ *adv*
apart from others

**sep·a·ra·tion** \ˌsep-ə-ˈrā-shən\ *n*
1 the act of separating : the state of being separated
2 a point or line at which something is divided

**sep·a·ra·tor** \ˈsep-ə-ˌrāt-ər\ *n*
a machine for separating cream from milk

**Sep·tem·ber** \sep-ˈtem-bər\ *n*
the ninth month of the year

**Word History** The first Roman calendar had only ten months. The first month was March. The seventh month was September. The Latin name for this month came from the Latin word that meant "seven." When January and February were later added September kept its name, even though it became the ninth month. English *September* comes from the Latin name of the month.

**sep·tet** \sep-ˈtet\ *n*
a group or set of seven

**sep·ul·cher** *or* **sep·ul·chre** \ˈsep-əl-kər\ *n*
[1]GRAVE, TOMB

**se·quel** \ˈsē-kwəl\ *n*
1 an event that follows or comes afterward : RESULT
2 a book that continues a story begun in another

**se·quence** \ˈsē-kwəns\ *n*
1 the condition or fact of following or coming after something else
2 [2]RESULT 1, SEQUEL
3 the order in which things are or should be connected, related, or dated

**se·quin** \ˈsē-kwən\ *n*
▼ a bit of shiny metal or plastic used as an ornament usually on clothing

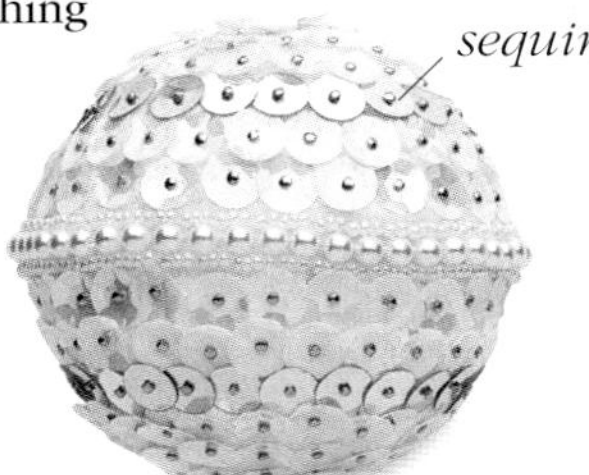

**sequins** covering a Christmas decoration

**se·quoia** \si-ˈkwȯi-ə\ *n*
1 a California tree that grows almost 100 meters tall and has needles as leaves and small egg-shaped cones
2 REDWOOD

**se·ra·pe** \sə-ˈräp-ē, -ˈrap-\ *n*
▼ a colorful woolen shawl or blanket

**serape:**
a folded serape from Mexico

**ser·e·nade** \ˌser-ə-ˈnād\ *n*
music sung or played at night under the window of a lady

**se·rene** \sə-ˈrēn\ *adj*
1 [1]CLEAR 2
2 being calm and quiet ⟨a *serene* manner⟩
**se·rene·ly** *adv*
**se·rene·ness** *n*

**se·ren·i·ty** \sə-ˈren-ət-ē\ *n*
the quality or state of being serene

**serf** \ˈsərf\ *n*
a servant or laborer of olden times who was treated as part of the land worked on and went along with the land if it was sold

**serge** \ˈsərj\ *n*
a woolen cloth that wears well

**ser·geant** \ˈsär-jənt\ *n*
1 a noncommissioned officer in the Army or Marine Corps ranking above a corporal or in the Air Force ranking above an airman first class
2 an officer in a police force

**sergeant first class** *n*
a noncommissioned officer in the Army ranking above a staff sergeant

**sergeant major** *n*
1 the chief noncommissioned officer at a military headquarters
2 a noncommissioned officer in the Marine Corps ranking above a first sergeant
3 a staff sergeant major or command sergeant major in the Army

A B C D E F G H I J K L M N O P Q R S T U V W X Y Z

**[1]se·ri·al** \'sir-ē-əl\ *adj*
arranged in or appearing in parts or numbers that follow a regular order ⟨a *serial* story⟩
**se·ri·al·ly** *adv*

**[2]serial** *n*
a story appearing (as in a magazine or on television) in parts at regular intervals

**se·ries** \'sir-ēz\ *n, pl* **series**
a number of things or events arranged in order and connected by being alike in some way

**se·ri·ous** \'sir-ē-əs\ *adj*
**1** thoughtful or quiet in appearance or manner
**2** requiring much thought or work ⟨a *serious* task⟩
**3** being in earnest **:** not light or casual ⟨give a *serious* answer to a *serious* question⟩
**4** IMPORTANT 1 ⟨*serious* responsibilities⟩
**5** being such as to cause distress or harm ⟨a *serious* accident⟩ ⟨*serious* losses⟩
**se·ri·ous·ly** *adv*
**se·ri·ous·ness** *n*

---

**Synonyms** SERIOUS, SOLEMN, and EARNEST mean not funny or not playful. SERIOUS suggests being concerned or seeming to be concerned about really important things ⟨a *serious* student⟩. SOLEMN stresses dignity along with complete seriousness ⟨the preacher is always very *solemn*⟩. EARNEST stresses that one is sincere and has serious intentions ⟨an *earnest* student working hard for a scholarship⟩.

---

**ser·mon** \'sər-mən\ *n*
**1** a speech usually by a priest, minister, or rabbi for the purpose of giving religious instruction
**2** a serious talk to a person about his or her conduct

**ser·pent** \'sər-pənt\ *n*
a usually large snake

**service station:** a toy service station

**se·rum** \'sir-əm\ *n*
the liquid part that can be separated from coagulated blood, contains antibodies, and is sometimes used to prevent or cure disease

**ser·vant** \'sər-vənt\ *n*
a person hired to perform household or personal services

**[1]serve** \'sərv\ *vb* **served**; **serv·ing**
**1** to be a servant
**2** to give the service and respect due
**3** [2]WORSHIP 1 ⟨*serve* God⟩
**4** to put in **:** SPEND ⟨*served* three years in the army⟩
**5** to be of use **:** answer some purpose ⟨the tree *served* as shelter⟩
**6** to provide helpful services
**7** to be enough for ⟨a pie that will *serve* eight people⟩
**8** to hold an office **:** perform a duty ⟨*serve* on a jury⟩
**9** to help persons to food or set out helpings of food or drink
**10** to furnish with something needed or desired
**11** to make a serve (as in tennis)

**[2]serve** *n*
▶ an act of putting the ball or shuttlecock in play (as in tennis or badminton)

**[1]ser·vice** \'sər-vəs\ *n*
**1** the occupation or function of serving or working as a servant
**2** the work or action of one that serves ⟨gives quick *service*⟩
**3** [2]HELP 1, USE ⟨be of *service* to them⟩
**4** a religious ceremony ⟨the Sunday *service*⟩
**5** a helpful or useful act **:** good turn ⟨did me a *service*⟩
**6** [2]SERVE
**7** a set of dishes or silverware ⟨a silver tea *service*⟩
**8** a branch of public employment or the people working in it
**9** a nation's armed forces ⟨called into the *service*⟩
**10** an organization for supplying some public demand or keeping up and repairing something ⟨bus *service*⟩ ⟨television sales and *service*⟩

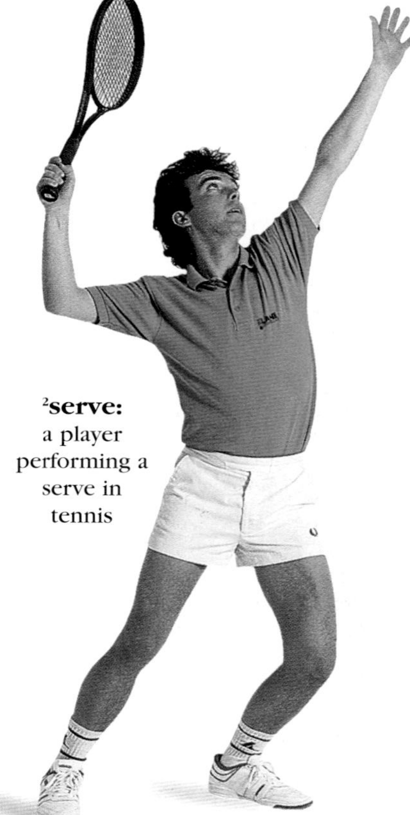
**[2]serve:** a player performing a serve in tennis

**[2]service** *vb* **ser·viced**; **ser·vic·ing**
to work at taking care of or repairing

**ser·vice·able** \'sər-və-sə-bəl\ *adj*
**1** fit for or suited to some use
**2** lasting or wearing well in use ⟨*serviceable* shoes⟩
**ser·vice·able·ness** *n*

**ser·vice·man** \'sər-vəs-ˌman\ *n, pl* **ser·vice·men** \-ˌmen\
a male member of the armed forces

**service station** *n*
◀ a place for servicing motor vehicles especially with gasoline and oil

**ser·vile** \'sər-vəl\ *adj*
**1** of or suitable to a slave ⟨*servile* work⟩
**2** lacking spirit or independence

**serv·ing** \'sər-ving\ *n*
a helping of food

**ser·vi·tude** \'sər-və-ˌtüd, -ˌtyüd\ *n*
the condition of a slave

**ses·sion** \'sesh-ən\ *n*
**1** a single meeting (as of a court, lawmaking body, or school)
**2** a whole series of meetings ⟨congress was in *session* for six months⟩
**3** the time during which a court, congress, or school meets

[1]**set** \'set\ *vb* **set**; **set·ting**
**1** to cause to sit
**2** to cover and warm eggs to hatch them ⟨*setting* hens⟩
**3** to put or fix in a place or condition ⟨*set* the box on the table⟩
**4** to arrange in a desired and especially a normal position ⟨*set* a broken bone⟩
**5** [1]START 5 ⟨*set* a fire⟩
**6** to cause to be, become, or do ⟨*set* the prisoner free⟩
**7** to fix at a certain amount **:** SETTLE ⟨*set* a price⟩
**8** to furnish as a model ⟨*set* an example for others⟩
**9** to put in order for immediate use ⟨*set* the table⟩
**10** to provide (as words or verses) with music
**11** to fix firmly
**12** to become or cause to become firm or solid ⟨wait for the cement to *set*⟩
**13** to form and bring to maturity ⟨the old tree still *sets* a good crop of apples⟩
**14** to pass below the horizon **:** go down ⟨the sun is *setting*⟩
**set about** to begin to do
**set forth** to start out ⟨*set forth* on a journey⟩

[2]**set** *n*
**1** the act or action of setting **:** the condition of being set
**2** a number of persons or things of the same kind that belong or are used together
**3** the form or movement of the body or of its parts ⟨the *set* of the shoulders⟩
**4** an artificial setting for a scene of a play or motion picture
**5** a group of tennis games that make up a match
**6** a collection of mathematical elements
**7** an electronic apparatus ⟨a television *set*⟩

[3]**set** *adj*
**1** fixed by authority ⟨a *set* rule⟩
**2** not very willing to change ⟨*set* in their ways⟩
**3** [1]READY 1 ⟨are you all *set*⟩

**set·back** \'set-ˌbak\ *n*
a slowing of progress **:** a temporary defeat

**set down** *vb*
**1** to place at rest on a surface
**2** to land an aircraft

**set in** *vb*
to make its appearance **:** BEGIN ⟨winter *set in* early⟩

**set off** *vb*
**1** to cause to stand out ⟨dark eyes *set off* by a pale face⟩
**2** to set apart ⟨words *set off* by commas⟩
**3** to cause to start ⟨the story *set* them *off* laughing⟩
**4** EXPLODE 1 ⟨*set* the bomb *off*⟩
**5** to start a journey ⟨*set off* for home⟩

**set on** *vb*
to urge to attack or chase ⟨threatened to *set* the dogs *on* me⟩

**set out** *vb*
**1** UNDERTAKE 1
**2** to begin on a course or journey

**set·tee** \se-'tē\ *n*
a long seat with a back

**set·ter** \'set-ər\ *n*
**1** one that sets
**2** ▼ a large dog that has long hair and is used in hunting birds

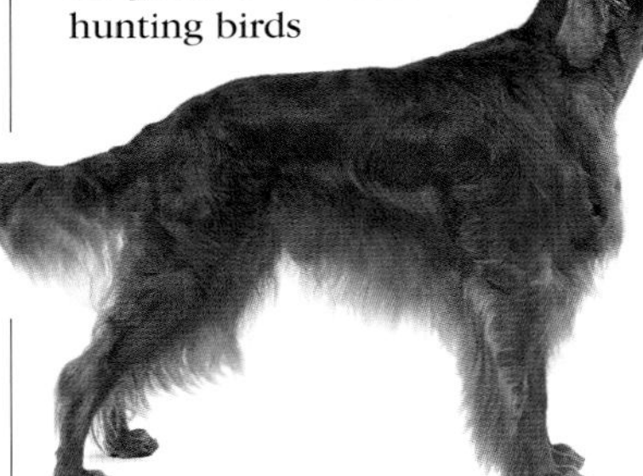

**setter 2:** an Irish setter

**set·ting** \'set-ing\ *n*
**1** the act of one that sets ⟨*setting* of type⟩
**2** that in which something is set or mounted ⟨a gold *setting* for a ruby⟩
**3** the background (as time and place) of the action of a story or play
**4** a batch of eggs for hatching

[1]**set·tle** \'set-l\ *vb* **set·tled**; **set·tling**
**1** to place so as to stay ⟨*settle* oneself in a chair⟩
**2** to come to rest ⟨birds *settling* on a branch⟩ ⟨dust *settled* on the table⟩
**3** to sink gradually to a lower level ⟨the foundations of the house *settled*⟩
**4** to sink in a liquid
**5** to make one's home ⟨*settle* in the country⟩
**6** to apply oneself ⟨*settle* down to work⟩
**7** to fix by agreement
**8** to put in order ⟨*settled* their affairs⟩
**9** to make quiet **:** CALM ⟨*settled* my nerves⟩
**10** DECIDE 1 ⟨*settle* a question⟩
**11** to complete payment on ⟨*settle* a bill⟩
**12** ADJUST 1 ⟨*settle* a quarrel⟩

[2]**settle** *n*
a long wooden bench with arms and a high solid back

**set·tle·ment** \'set-l-mənt\ *n*
**1** the act of settling **:** the condition of being settled
**2** final payment (as of a bill)
**3** the act or fact of establishing colonies ⟨the *settlement* of New England⟩
**4** a place or region newly settled
**5** a small village
**6** an institution that gives help to people in a crowded part of a city

**set·tler** \'set-lər\ *n*
a person who settles in a new region **:** COLONIST

**set up** *vb*
**1** to place or secure in position
**2** to put in operation **:** FOUND, ESTABLISH

[1]**sev·en** \'sev-ən\ *adj*
being one more than six

[2]**seven** *n*
one more than six **:** 7

[1]**sev·en·teen** \ˌsev-ən-'tēn\ *adj*
being one more than sixteen

[2]**seventeen** *n*
one more than sixteen **:** 17

[1]**sev·en·teenth** \ˌsev-ən-'tēnth\ *adj*
coming right after sixteenth

[2]**seventeenth** *n*
number seventeen in a series

[1]**sev·enth** \'sev-ənth\ *adj*
coming right after sixth

**sew 1:** a boy sewing a button onto a shirt

**[2]seventh** *n*
1 number seven in a series
2 one of seven equal parts

**[1]sev·en·ti·eth** \'sev-ən-tē-əth\ *adj*
coming right after sixty-ninth

**[2]seventieth** *n*
number seventy in a series

**[1]sev·en·ty** \'sev-ən-tē, -dē\ *adj*
being seven times ten

**[2]seventy** *n*
seven times ten : 70

**sev·er** \'sev-ər\ *vb*
1 to put or keep apart : DIVIDE
2 to come or break apart

**[1]sev·er·al** \'sev-ə-rəl, 'sev-rəl\ *adj*
1 separate or distinct from others : DIFFERENT ⟨federal union of the *several* states⟩
2 consisting of more than two but not very many ⟨*several* persons⟩

**[2]several** *pron*
a small number : more than two but not many

**se·vere** \sə-'vir\ *adj* **se·ver·er**; **se·ver·est**
1 very strict : HARSH ⟨a *severe* ruler⟩
2 serious in feeling or manner : GRAVE
3 not using unnecessary ornament : PLAIN ⟨a *severe* style⟩
4 hard to bear or deal with ⟨*severe* suffering⟩ ⟨a *severe* test⟩
**se·vere·ly** *adv*
**se·vere·ness** *n*

**se·ver·i·ty** \sə-'ver-ət-ē\ *n*
the quality or state of being severe

**sew** \'sō\ *vb* **sewed**; **sewn** \'sōn\ *or* **sewed**; **sew·ing**
1 ◀ to join or fasten by stitches
2 to work with needle and thread

**sew·age** \'sü-ij\ *n*
waste materials carried off by sewers

**[1]sew·er** \'sō-ər\ *n*
one that sews

**[2]sew·er** \'sü-ər\ *n*
a usually covered drain to carry off water and waste

**sew·er·age** \'sü-ə-rij\ *n*
1 SEWAGE
2 the removal and disposal of sewage by sewers
3 a system of sewers

**sew·ing** \'sō-ing\ *n*
1 the act, method, or occupation of one that sews
2 material being sewed or to be sewed

**sex** \'seks\ *n*
1 either of two divisions of living things and especially humans, one made up of males, the other of females
2 the things that make males and females different from each other
3 sexual activity

**sex·ism** \'sek-,siz-əm\ *n*
distinction and especially unjust distinction based on sex and made against one person or group (as women) in favor of another

**sex·ist** \'sek-sist\ *adj*
based on or showing sexism ⟨a *sexist* remark⟩
**sexist** *n*

**sex·tet** \sek-'stet\ *n*
a group or set of six

**sex·ton** \'sek-stən\ *n*
an official of a church who takes care of church buildings and property

**sex·u·al** \'sek-shə-wəl\ *adj*
1 of or relating to sex or the sexes
2 of, relating to, or being the form of reproduction in which germ cells from two parents combine in fertilization to form a new individual
**sex·u·al·ly** *adv*

**shab·by** \'shab-ē\ *adj* **shab·bi·er**; **shab·bi·est**
1 dressed in worn clothes
2 faded and worn from use or wear
3 not fair or generous ⟨*shabby* treatment⟩
**shab·bi·ly** \'shab-ə-lē\ *adv*
**shab·bi·ness** \'shab-ē-nəs\ *n*

**shack** \'shak\ *n*
HUT, SHANTY

**[1]shack·le** \'shak-əl\ *n*
1 a ring or band that prevents free use of the legs or arms
2 something that prevents free action ⟨the *shackles* of superstition⟩
3 a U-shaped metal device for joining or fastening something

**[2]shackle** *vb* **shack·led**; **shack·ling**
1 to bind or fasten with a shackle
2 HINDER

**shad** \'shad\ *n, pl* **shad**
▼ any of several sea fishes related to the herrings that have deep bodies, swim up rivers to spawn, and are important food fish

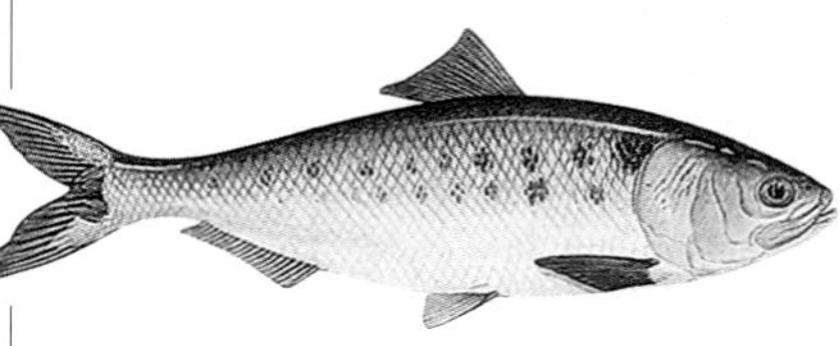

**shad:** an American shad

**[1]shade** \'shād\ *n*
1 partial darkness ⟨the trees cast *shade*⟩
2 space sheltered from light or heat and especially from the sun ⟨sit in the *shade* of a tree⟩
3 **shades** *pl* the shadows that gather as darkness falls ⟨the *shades* of night⟩
4 GHOST, SPIRIT
5 ▼ something that blocks off or cuts down light ⟨a lamp *shade*⟩ ⟨a window *shade*⟩
6 the darkening of some objects in a painting or drawing to suggest that they are in shade
7 the darkness or lightness of a color ⟨four *shades* of brown⟩
8 a very small difference or amount ⟨just a *shade* taller⟩ ⟨*shades* of meaning⟩

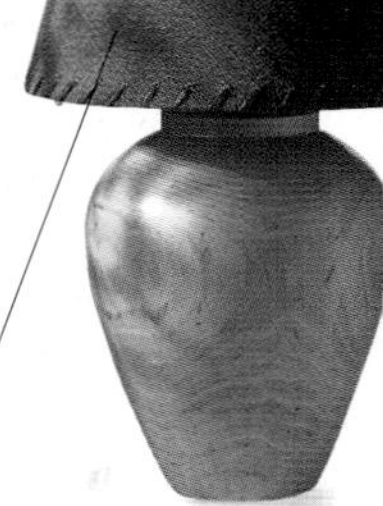

*lamp shade*

**[1]shade 5**

[2]**shade** *vb* **shad·ed**; **shad·ing**
**1** to shelter from light or heat
**2** to mark with shades of light or color ⟨*shade* a drawing⟩
**3** to show or begin to have slight differences of color, value, or meaning

[1]**shad·ow** \'shad-ō\ *n*
**1** [1]SHADE 1 ⟨the valley was in *shadow*⟩
**2** a reflected image
**3** shelter from danger or view
**4** ▶ the dark figure cast on a surface by a body that is between the surface and the light ⟨my *shadow* stays with me⟩
**5** PHANTOM
**6 shadows** *pl* darkness caused by the setting of the sun
**7** a very little bit : TRACE ⟨beyond a *shadow* of doubt⟩

*shadow*

[2]**shadow** *vb*
**1** to cast a shadow upon
**2** to cast gloom over
**3** to follow and watch closely especially in a secret way

**shad·owy** \'shad-ə-wē\ *adj*
**1** not realistic ⟨*shadowy* dreams of glory⟩
**2** full of shadow ⟨a *shadowy* lane⟩

**shady** \'shād-ē\ *adj* **shad·i·er**; **shad·i·est**
**1** sheltered from the sun's rays
**2** not right or honest ⟨*shady* business deals⟩
**shad·i·ness** *n*

**shaft** \'shaft\ *n*
**1** the long handle of a weapon (as a spear)
**2** one of two poles between which a horse is hitched to pull a wagon or carriage
**3** an arrow or its narrow stem
**4** a narrow beam of light
**5** a long narrow part especially when round ⟨the *shaft* of a feather⟩
**6** the handle of a tool or instrument
**7** a bar to support rotating pieces of machinery or to give them motion
**8** a tall monument (as a column)
**9** a mine opening made for finding or mining ore
**10** an opening or passage straight down through the floors of a building ⟨an air *shaft*⟩

**shag·gy** \'shag-ē\ *adj* **shag·gi·er**; **shag·gi·est**
**1** covered with or made up of a long, coarse, and tangled growth (as of hair or vegetation) ⟨a dog with a *shaggy* coat⟩
**2** having a rough or hairy surface ⟨a *shaggy* tweed⟩
**shag·gi·ly** \'shag-ə-lē\ *adv*
**shag·gi·ness** \'shag-ē-nəs\ *n*

[1]**shadow 4:** a boy looking at his shadow

[1]**shake** \'shāk\ *vb* **shook** \'shu̇k\; **shak·en** \'shā-kən\; **shak·ing**
**1** to tremble or make tremble : QUIVER
**2** to make less firm : WEAKEN ⟨had their confidence *shaken*⟩
**3** to move back and forth or to and fro ⟨*shake* your head⟩
**4** to cause to be, become, go, or move by or as if by a shake ⟨*shake* apples from a tree⟩

[2]**shake** *n*
the act or motion of shaking

**shak·er** \'shā-kər\ *n*
one that shakes or is used in shaking ⟨salt *shaker*⟩

**shaky** \'shā-kē\ *adj* **shak·i·er**; **shak·i·est**
easily shaken : UNSOUND ⟨*shaky* arguments⟩
**shak·i·ly** \-kə-lē\ *adv*
**shak·i·ness** \-kē-nəs\ *n*

**shale** \'shāl\ *n*
a rock with a fine grain formed from clay, mud, or silt

**shall** \shəl, 'shal\ *helping verb, past* **should** \shəd, 'shu̇d\; *present sing & pl* **shall**
**1** am or are going to or expecting to : WILL ⟨I *shall* never mention it again⟩
**2** is or are forced to : MUST ⟨they *shall* not pass⟩

[1]**shal·low** \'shal-ō\ *adj*
**1** not deep
**2** showing little knowledge, thought, or feeling
**shal·low·ness** *n*

[2]**shallow** *n*
a shallow place in a body of water — usually used in pl.

[1]**sham** \'sham\ *n*
[3]COUNTERFEIT, IMITATION

[2]**sham** *adj*
not real : FALSE ⟨*sham* battle⟩

[3]**sham** *vb* **shammed**; **sham·ming**
to act in a deceiving way

**sham·ble** \'sham-bəl\ *vb* **sham·bled**; **sham·bling**
to walk in an awkward unsteady way

**sham·bles** \'sham-bəlz\ *n sing or pl*
a place or scene of disorder or destruction

[1]**shame** \'shām\ *n*
**1** a painful emotion caused by having done something wrong or improper
**2** ability to feel shame ⟨have you no *shame*⟩
**3** [1]DISHONOR 1, DISGRACE
**4** something that brings disgrace or causes shame or strong regret

[2]**shame** *vb* **shamed**; **sham·ing**
**1** to make ashamed
**2** [2]DISHONOR
**3** to force by causing to feel shame ⟨they were *shamed* into confessing⟩

**shame·faced** \'shām-'fāst\ *adj*
seeming ashamed
**shame·faced·ly** \-'fā-səd-lē\ *adv*
**shame·faced·ness** \-səd-nəs\ *n*

**shame·ful** \'shām-fəl\ *adj*
bringing shame : DISGRACEFUL ⟨*shameful* behavior⟩
**shame·ful·ly** \-fə-lē\ *adv*
**shame·ful·ness** *n*

**shame·less** \'shām-ləs\ *adj*
having no shame ⟨a *shameless* liar⟩
**shame·less·ly** *adv*
**shame·less·ness** *n*

[1]**sham·poo** \sham-'pü\ *vb*
▼ to wash the hair and scalp

*lather from shampoo*

[1]**shampoo:** a woman shampooing her hair

a b c d e f g h i j k l m n o p q r s t u v w x y z

**[2]shampoo** *n, pl* **sham·poos**
**1** a washing of the hair
**2** a cleaner made for washing the hair

**sham·rock** \'sham-,räk\ *n*
a plant (as some clovers) that has leaves with three leaflets and is used as an emblem by the Irish

**shank** \'shangk\ *n*
**1** the lower part of the human leg **:** the equivalent part of a lower animal
**2** the part of a tool that connects the working part with a part by which it is held or moved ⟨the *shank* of a drill bit⟩

**shan't** \'shant\
shall not

**shan·ty** \'shant-ē\ *n, pl* **shanties**
a small roughly built shelter or dwelling

**[1]shape** \'shāp\ *vb* **shaped**; **shap·ing**
**1** to give a certain form or shape to ⟨*shape* the dough into loaves⟩
**2** DEVISE ⟨*shaped* a secret plan⟩
**3** to make fit especially for some purpose **:** ADAPT ⟨*shaping* the minds of future leaders⟩
**4** to take on a definite form or quality **:** DEVELOP ⟨plans were *shaping* up⟩
**shap·er** *n*

**[2]shape** *n*
**1** outward appearance **:** FORM ⟨the *shape* of a pear⟩
**2** the outline of a body **:** FIGURE ⟨a square *shape*⟩
**3** definite arrangement and form ⟨a plan is taking *shape*⟩
**4** [1]CONDITION 3 ⟨the car is in poor *shape*⟩
**shaped** \,shāpt\ *adj*

**shape·less** \'shā-pləs\ *adj*
**1** having no fixed or regular shape
**2** not shapely
**shape·less·ly** *adv*
**shape·less·ness** *n*

**shape·ly** \'shā-plē\ *adj* **shape·li·er**; **shape·li·est**
having a pleasing shape
**shape·li·ness** *n*

**[1]share** \'sheər, 'shaər\ *n*
**1** a portion belonging to one person
**2** the part given or belonging to one of a number of persons owning something together ⟨sold my *share* of the business⟩
**3** any of the equal portions into which a property or corporation is divided ⟨100 *shares* of stock⟩

**[2]share** *vb* **shared**; **shar·ing**
**1** to divide and distribute in portions ⟨*shared* the lunch⟩
**2** to use, experience, or enjoy with others ⟨*share* a room⟩
**3** to take a part ⟨*share* in planning the program⟩

**share·crop** \'sheər-,kräp, 'shaər-\ *vb* **share·cropped**; **share·crop·ping**
to farm another's land for a share of the crop or profit
**share·crop·per** *n*

**[1]shark** \'shärk\ *n*
▶ any of a group of mostly fierce sea fishes that are typically gray, have a skeleton of cartilage, and include some forms that may attack humans

**[2]shark** *n*
a sly greedy person who takes advantage of others

**[1]shave 1:** a man shaving

**[1]sharp** \'shärp\ *adj*
**1** having a thin edge or fine point ⟨a *sharp* knife⟩
**2** brisk and cold ⟨a *sharp* wind⟩
**3** QUICK-WITTED, SMART ⟨a *sharp* student⟩
**4** ATTENTIVE 1 ⟨keep a *sharp* watch⟩
**5** having very good ability to see or hear ⟨you have *sharp* eyes⟩
**6** ENERGETIC, BRISK ⟨keep up a *sharp* pace⟩
**7** SEVERE 1, ANGRY ⟨a *sharp* reply⟩
**8** very trying to the feelings **:** causing distress ⟨a *sharp* pain⟩ ⟨*sharp* criticism⟩
**9** strongly affecting the senses ⟨a *sharp* taste⟩
**10** ending in a point or edge ⟨a *sharp* peak⟩
**11** involving an abrupt change ⟨a *sharp* drop in the temperature⟩ ⟨a *sharp* turn to the right⟩
**12** DISTINCT 2 ⟨a *sharp* image⟩
**13** raised in pitch by a half step
**14** higher than true pitch
**sharp·ly** *adv*
**sharp·ness** *n*

**[2]sharp** *adv*
**1** in a sharp manner ⟨sang *sharp*⟩
**2** at an exact time ⟨four o'clock *sharp*⟩

**[3]sharp** *n*
**1** a note or tone that is a half step higher than the note named
**2** a sign ♯ that tells that a note is to be made higher by a half step

**sharp·en** \'shär-pən\ *vb*
to make or become sharp or sharper
**sharp·en·er** *n*

**shat·ter** \'shat-ər\ *vb*
**1** to break or fall to pieces
**2** to damage badly **:** RUIN, WRECK ⟨*shattered* hopes⟩

**[1]shave** \'shāv\ *vb* **shaved**; **shaved** *or* **shav·en** \'shā-vən\; **shav·ing**
**1** ◀ to cut or trim off with a sharp blade ⟨*shaved* the hair off my arm⟩
**2** to make bare or smooth by cutting the hair from ⟨the doctor *shaved* my arm⟩
**3** to trim closely ⟨a lawn *shaven* close⟩

**[2]shave** *n*
**1** an operation of shaving
**2** a narrow escape ⟨a close *shave*⟩

**shav·ing** \'shā-ving\ *n*
a thin slice or strip sliced off with a cutting tool ⟨wood *shavings*⟩

**shawl** \'shȯl\ *n*
▼ a square or oblong piece of cloth used especially by women as a loose covering for the head or shoulders

**shawl:** a woman wearing a shawl

## [1]shark

There are about 200 species of shark worldwide. Sharks are cartilaginous fish that range in size from the small lantern shark to the enormous whale shark. They have excellent eyesight and a very good sense of smell, and can accelerate quickly through the water to catch their prey. Not all sharks are a threat to humans; the whale shark, for example, eats only plankton, and most sharks are too shy or live too deep in the ocean to bother people.

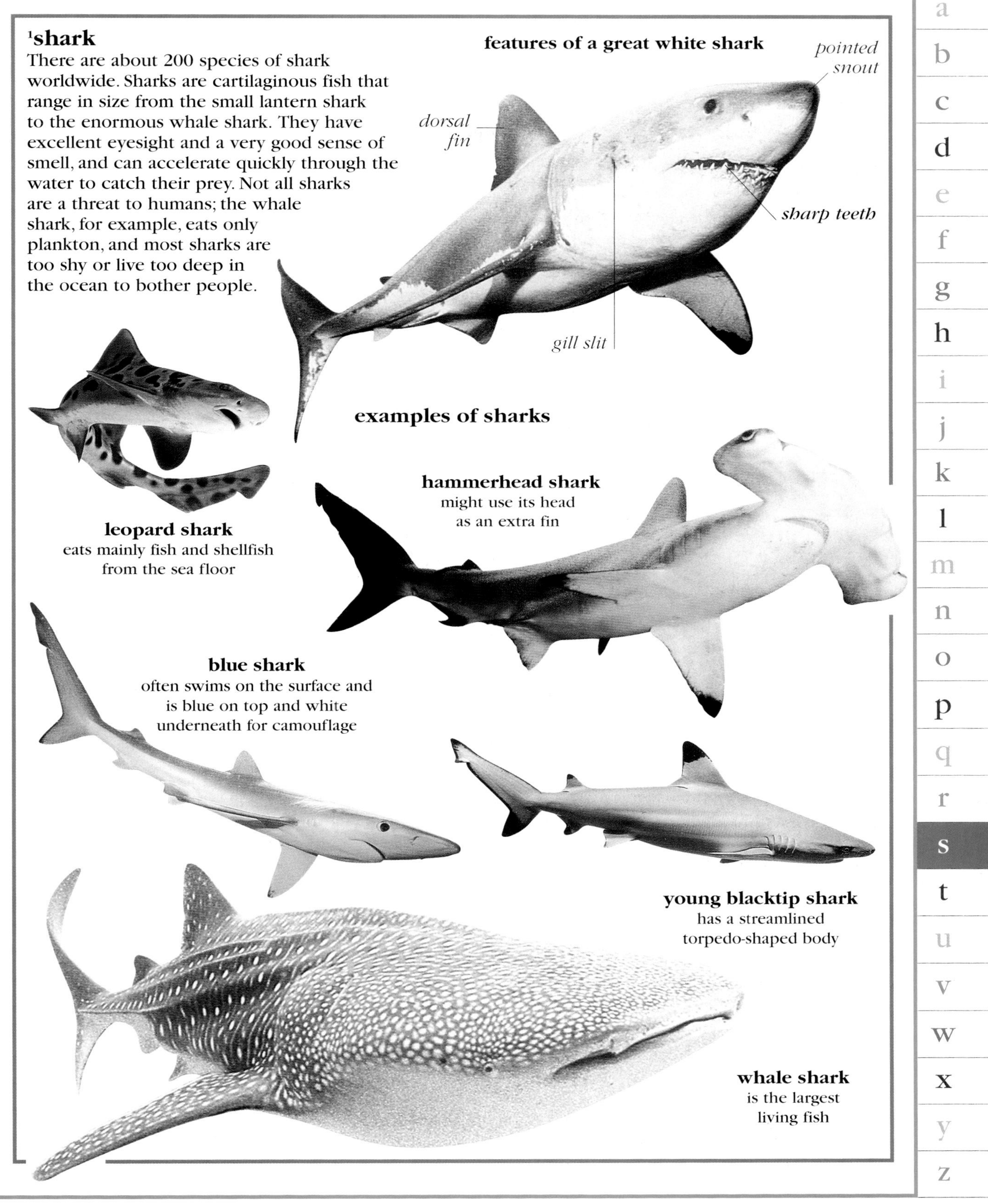


**hammerhead shark** might use its head as an extra fin

**leopard shark** eats mainly fish and shellfish from the sea floor

**blue shark** often swims on the surface and is blue on top and white underneath for camouflage

**young blacktip shark** has a streamlined torpedo-shaped body

**whale shark** is the largest living fish

**she** \ˈshē\ *pron* that female one

**sheaf** \ˈshēf\ *n, pl* **sheaves** \ˈshēvz\
1 ▶ a bundle of stalks and ears of grain
2 a group of things fastened together ⟨a *sheaf* of arrows⟩
**sheaf·like** \ˈshē-ˌflīk\ *adj*

**sheaf 1:** a sheaf of wheat

**shear** \ˈshir\ *vb* **sheared**; **sheared** *or* **shorn** \ˈshōrn\; **shear·ing**
1 to cut the hair or wool from : CLIP ⟨*shear* sheep⟩
2 to strip of as if by cutting ⟨*shorn* of their power⟩
3 to cut or break sharply ⟨a telephone pole *sheared* off by a car⟩
**shear·er** *n*

**shears** \ˈshirz\ *n pl* ▼ a cutting tool like a pair of large scissors

**shears:** a pair of garden shears

**sheath** \ˈshēth\ *n, pl* **sheaths** \ˈshēthz\
1 a case for a blade (as of a knife)
2 a covering (as the outer wings of a beetle) suggesting a sheath in form or use

**sheathe** \ˈshēth\ *vb* **sheathed**; **sheath·ing**
1 to put into a sheath ⟨*sheathe* your sword⟩
2 to cover with something that protects

**sheath·ing** \ˈshē-thing\ *n* the first covering of boards or of waterproof material on the outside wall of a frame house or on a timber roof

**sheaves** *pl of* SHEAF

[1]**shed** \ˈshed\ *vb* **shed**; **shed·ding**
1 to give off in drops ⟨*shed* tears⟩
2 to cause (blood) to flow from a cut or wound
3 to spread abroad ⟨the sun *sheds* light and heat⟩
4 REPEL 3 ⟨raincoats *shed* water⟩
5 to cast (as a natural covering) aside ⟨a snake *sheds* its skin⟩

[2]**shed** *n* a structure built for shelter or storage ⟨a tool *shed*⟩

**she'd** \ˈshēd\ she had : she would

**sheen** \ˈshēn\ *n* a bright or shining condition : LUSTER

**sheep** \ˈshēp\ *n, pl* **sheep**
1 ▶ an animal related to the goat that is raised for meat or for its wool and skin
2 a weak helpless person who is easily led

**sheep·fold** \ˈshēp-ˌfōld\ *n* a pen or shelter for sheep

**sheep·herd·er** \ˈshēp-ˌhərd-ər\ *n* a worker in charge of a flock of sheep

**sheep·ish** \ˈshē-pish\ *adj*
1 like a sheep
2 embarrassed especially over being found out in a fault ⟨a *sheepish* look⟩
**sheep·ish·ly** *adv*
**sheep·ish·ness** *n*

**sheep·skin** \ˈshēp-ˌskin\ *n* the skin of a sheep or leather prepared from it

[1]**sheer** \ˈshir\ *adj*
1 very thin or transparent ⟨*sheer* stockings⟩
2 THOROUGH 1, ABSOLUTE ⟨*sheer* nonsense⟩
3 very steep ⟨a *sheer* cliff⟩
**sheer·ly** *adv*
**sheer·ness** *n*

[2]**sheer** *adv*
1 COMPLETELY
2 straight up or down

[1]**sheet** \ˈshēt\ *n*
1 a broad piece of cloth (as an article of bedding used next to the body)
2 a broad piece of paper (as for writing or printing)
3 a broad surface ⟨a *sheet* of water⟩
4 something that is very thin as compared with its length and width ⟨a *sheet* of iron⟩
**sheet·like** \-ˌlīk\ *adj*

[2]**sheet** *n* a rope or chain used to adjust the angle at which the sail of a boat is set to catch the wind

**sheikh** *or* **sheik** \ˈshēk, ˈshāk\ *n* an Arab chief

**shek·el** \ˈshek-əl\ *n*
1 any of various ancient units of weight (as of the Hebrews)
2 a coin weighing one shekel

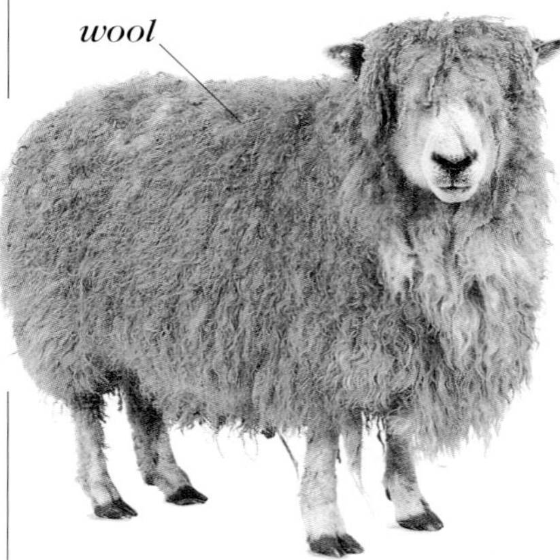


**sheep 1**

**shelf** \ˈshelf\ *n, pl* **shelves** \ˈshelvz\
1 a flat piece (as of board or metal) set above a floor (as on a wall or in a bookcase) to hold things
2 something (as a sandbar or ledge of rock) that suggests a shelf

[1]**shell** \ˈshel\ *n*
1 ▶ a stiff hard covering of an animal (as a turtle, oyster, or beetle)
2 the tough outer covering of an egg
3 the outer covering of a nut, fruit, or seed especially when hard or tough and fibrous
4 something like a shell (as in shape, function, or material) ⟨a pastry *shell*⟩
5 a narrow light racing boat rowed by one or more persons
6 a metal or paper case holding the explosive charge and the shot or object to be fired from a gun or cannon
**shelled** \ˈsheld\ *adj*

[2]**shell** *vb*
1 to take out of the shell or husk ⟨*shell* peas⟩
2 to remove the kernels of grain from (as a cob of Indian corn)
3 to shoot shells at or upon

**she'll** \'shēl\
she shall : she will

**¹shel·lac** \shə-'lak\ *n*
a varnish made from a material given off by an Asian insect dissolved usually in alcohol

**²shellac** *vb* **shel·lacked**; **shel·lack·ing**
to coat with shellac

**shell·fish** \'shel-ˌfish\ *n, pl* **shellfish**
an invertebrate animal that lives in water and has a shell — used mostly of edible forms (as oysters or crabs)

**¹shel·ter** \'shel-tər\ *n*
**1** something that covers or protects
**2** the condition of being protected ⟨find *shelter* with friends⟩

**²shelter** *vb*
**1** to be a shelter for : provide with shelter
**2** to find and use a shelter

**shelve** \'shelv\ *vb* **shelved**; **shelv·ing**
**1** to place or store on shelves
**2** ¹DEFER ⟨*shelve* a plan⟩

**shelves** *pl of* SHELF

**¹shep·herd** \'shep-ərd\ *n*
a person who takes care of sheep

**²shepherd** *vb*
to care for as or as if a shepherd

**shep·herd·ess** \'shep-ərd-əs\ *n*
a woman who takes care of sheep

**sher·bet** \'shər-bət\ *n*
a frozen dessert of fruit juice to which milk, the white of egg, or gelatin is added before freezing

**sher·iff** \'sher-əf\ *n*
the officer of a county who is in charge of enforcing the law

**she's** \'shēz\
she is : she has

**Shet·land pony** \'shet-lənd-\ *n*
▼ any of a breed of small stocky horses with shaggy coats

**Shetland pony**

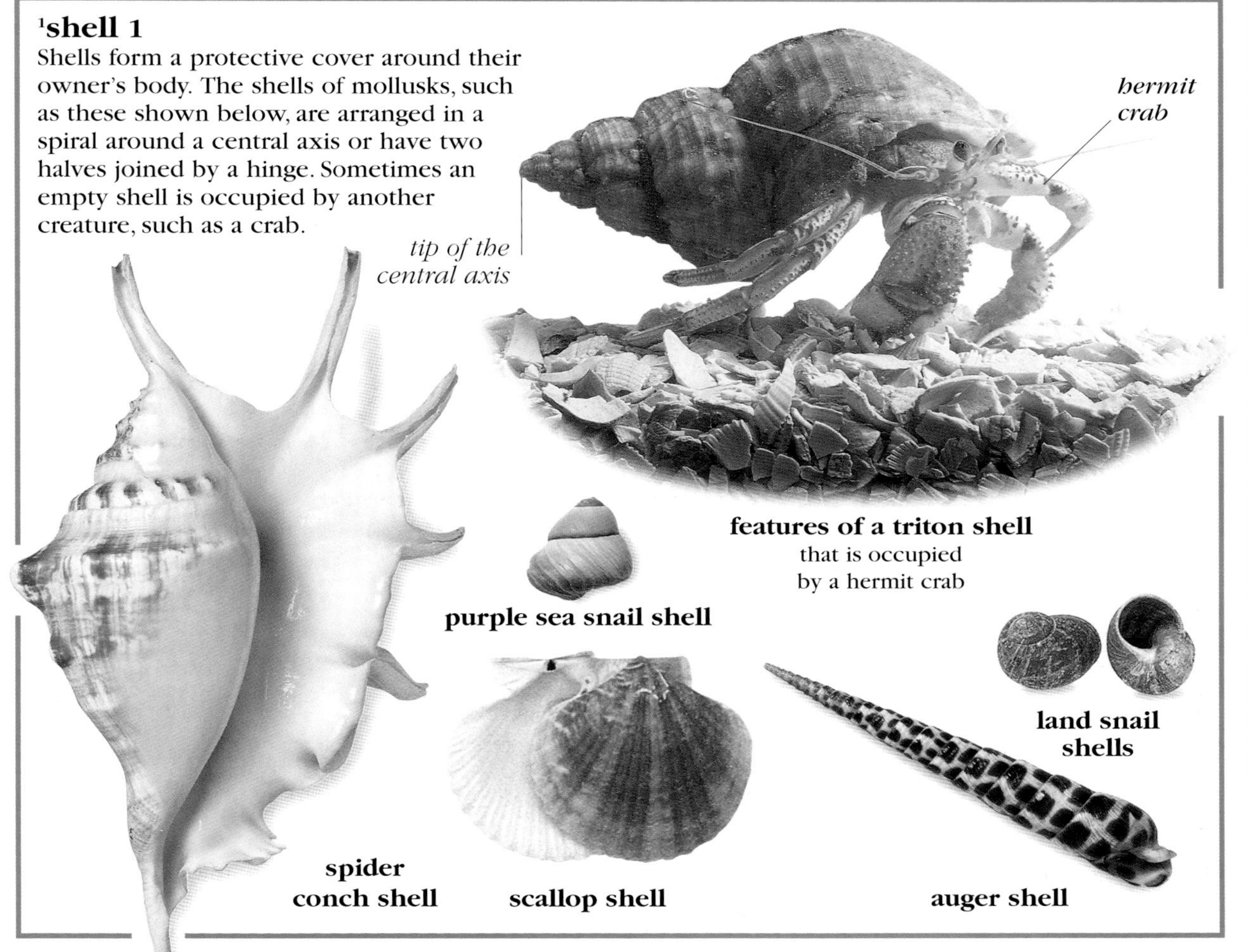


**¹shell 1**
Shells form a protective cover around their owner's body. The shells of mollusks, such as these shown below, are arranged in a spiral around a central axis or have two halves joined by a hinge. Sometimes an empty shell is occupied by another creature, such as a crab.

a b c d e f g h i j k l m n o p q r s t u v w x y z

**[1]shield** \'shēld\ *n*
**1** ▶ a broad piece of armor carried on the arm to protect oneself in battle
**2** something that serves as a defense or protection

**[2]shield** *vb*
to cover or screen with or as if with a shield

**[1]shift** \'shift\ *vb*
**1** to exchange for another of the same kind
**2** to change or remove from one person or place to another ⟨*shift* a bag to the other shoulder⟩
**3** to change the arrangement of gears transmitting power (as in an automobile)
**4** to get along without help **:** FEND ⟨can *shift* for myself⟩

**[2]shift** *n*
**1** the act of shifting **:** TRANSFER
**2** a group of workers who work together during a scheduled period of time
**3** the period during which one group of workers is working
**4** GEARSHIFT

**shift·less** \'shift-ləs\ *adj*
lacking in ambition and energy **:** LAZY
**shift·less·ly** *adv*
**shift·less·ness** *n*

**shifty** \'shif-tē\ *adj* **shift·i·er**; **shift·i·est**
not worthy of trust **:** TRICKY
**shift·i·ly** \-tə-lē\ *adv*
**shift·i·ness** \-tē-nəs\ *n*

**shil·ling** \'shil-ing\ *n*
an old British coin equal to 1/20 pound

**shim·mer** \'shim-ər\ *vb*
to shine with a wavering light **:** GLIMMER ⟨*shimmering* silks⟩

**[1]shin** \'shin\ *n*
▶ the front part of the leg below the knee

**[2]shin** *vb* **shinned**; **shin·ning**
to climb (as a pole) by grasping with arms and legs and moving oneself upward by repeated jerks

**[1]shine** \'shīn\ *vb* **shone** \'shōn\ *or* **shined**; **shin·ing**
**1** to give light ⟨the sun *shone*⟩
**2** to be glossy **:** GLEAM
**3** to be outstanding ⟨*shines* in sports⟩
**4** to make bright by polishing ⟨*shined* my shoes⟩

**[1]shield 1:** a 19th-century warrior's shield from India

**[2]shine** *n*
**1** brightness from light given off or reflected
**2** fair weather **:** SUNSHINE ⟨rain or *shine*⟩
**3** [2]POLISH 1

**shin·er** \'shī-nər\ *n*
**1** a small silvery American freshwater fish related to the carp
**2** an eye discolored by injury **:** a black eye

**[1]shin·gle** \'shing-gəl\ *n*
**1** a small thin piece of building material (as wood or an asbestos composition) for laying in overlapping rows as a covering for the roof or sides of a building
**2** a small sign

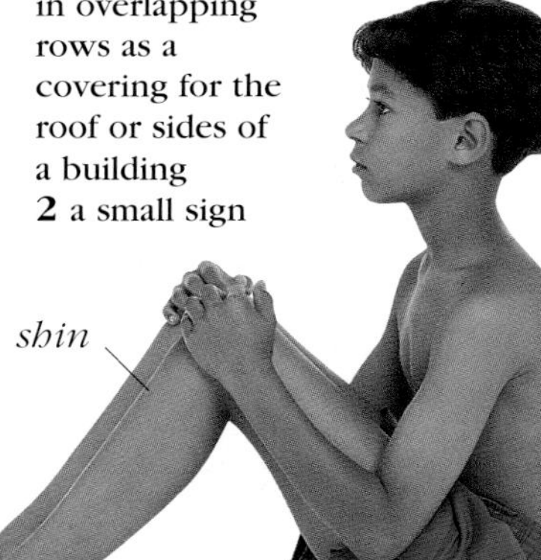


**[1]shin**

**[2]shingle** *vb* **shin·gled**; **shin·gling**
to cover with shingles

**shin·ny** \'shin-ē\ *vb* **shin·nied**; **shin·ny·ing**
[2]SHIN

**shiny** \'shī-nē\ *adj* **shin·i·er**; **shin·i·est**
bright in appearance

**[1]ship** \'ship\ *n*
**1** a large seagoing boat
**2** a ship's crew
**3** AIRSHIP, AIRPLANE
**4** a vehicle for traveling beyond the earth's atmosphere ⟨a rocket *ship*⟩

**[2]ship** *vb* **shipped**; **ship·ping**
**1** to put or receive on board for transportation by water
**2** to cause to be transported ⟨*ship* grain by rail⟩
**3** to take into a ship or boat ⟨*ship* oars⟩
**4** to sign on as a crew member on a ship

**-ship** \,ship\ *n suffix*
**1** state **:** condition **:** quality ⟨friend*ship*⟩
**2** office **:** rank **:** profession ⟨lord*ship*⟩ ⟨author*ship*⟩
**3** skill ⟨horseman*ship*⟩
**4** something showing a quality or state of being ⟨champion*ship*⟩ ⟨town*ship*⟩
**5** one having a specified rank ⟨your Lord*ship*⟩

**ship·board** \'ship-,bōrd\ *n*
**1** a ship's side
**2** [1]SHIP 1 ⟨met on *shipboard*⟩

**ship·ment** \'ship-mənt\ *n*
**1** the act of shipping
**2** the goods shipped

**ship·ping** \'ship-ing\ *n*
**1** the body of ships in one place or belonging to one port or country
**2** the act or business of a person who ships goods

**ship·shape** \'ship-'shāp\ *adj*
being neat and orderly **:** TIDY

**[1]ship·wreck** \'ship-,rek\ *n*
**1** a wrecked ship
**2** the loss or destruction of a ship

**[2]shipwreck** *vb*
**1** to cause to experience shipwreck
**2** to destroy (a ship) by driving ashore or sinking

**ship·yard** \'ship-,yärd\ *n*
a place where ships are built or repaired

**shirk** \'shərk\ *vb*
**1** to get out of doing what one ought to do
**2** AVOID

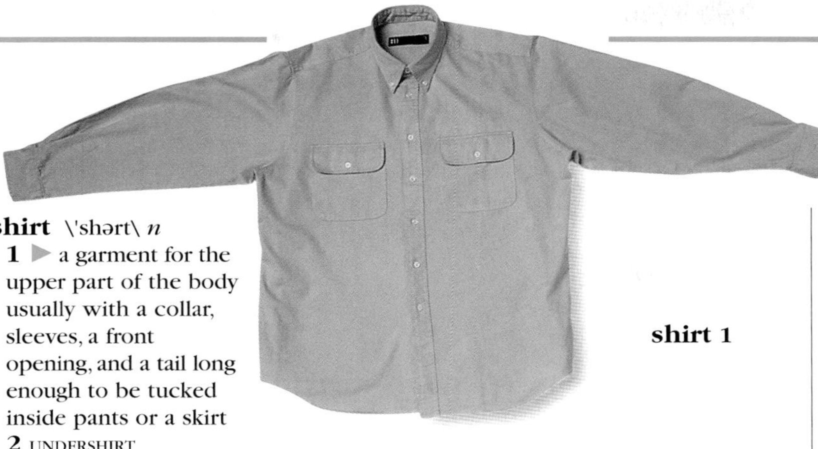
shirt 1

**shirt** \ˈshərt\ *n*
**1** ▶ a garment for the upper part of the body usually with a collar, sleeves, a front opening, and a tail long enough to be tucked inside pants or a skirt
**2** UNDERSHIRT

**[1]shiv·er** \ˈshiv-ər\ *vb*
to be made to shake (as by cold or fear) **:** QUIVER

**[2]shiver** *n*
an instance of shivering

**[1]shoal** \ˈshōl\ *adj*
[1]SHALLOW 1 ⟨*shoal* water⟩

**[2]shoal** *n*
**1** a place where a sea, lake, or river is shallow
**2** a bank or bar of sand just below the surface of the water

**[3]shoal** *n*
[3]SCHOOL ⟨a *shoal* of mackerel⟩

**[1]shock** \ˈshäk\ *n*
a bunch of sheaves of grain or stalks of corn set on end in the field

**[2]shock** *n*
**1** the sudden violent collision of bodies in a fight ⟨the *shock* of battle⟩
**2** a violent shake or jerk ⟨an earthquake *shock*⟩
**3** a sudden and violent disturbance of mind or feelings ⟨a *shock* of surprise⟩
**4** a state of bodily collapse that usually follows severe crushing injuries, burns, or hemorrhage
**5** the effect of a charge of electricity passing through the body of a person or animal

**[3]shock** *vb*
**1** to strike with surprise, horror, or disgust ⟨their behavior *shocked* us⟩
**2** to affect by electrical shock
**3** to drive into or out of by or as if by a shock ⟨*shocked* the public into action⟩

**[4]shock** *n*
a thick bushy mass (as of hair)

**shock·ing** \ˈshäk-ing\ *adj*
causing horror or disgust ⟨a *shocking* crime⟩
**shock·ing·ly** *adv*

**shod·dy** \ˈshäd-ē\ *adj* **shod·di·er; shod·di·est**
poorly done or made ⟨*shoddy* work⟩
**shod·di·ly** \ˈshäd-l-ē\ *adv*
**shod·di·ness** \ˈshäd-ē-nəs\ *n*

**[1]shoe** \ˈshü\ *n*
**1** ▼ an outer covering for the human foot usually having a thick and somewhat stiff sole and heel and a lighter upper part
**2** something (as a horseshoe) like a shoe in appearance or use

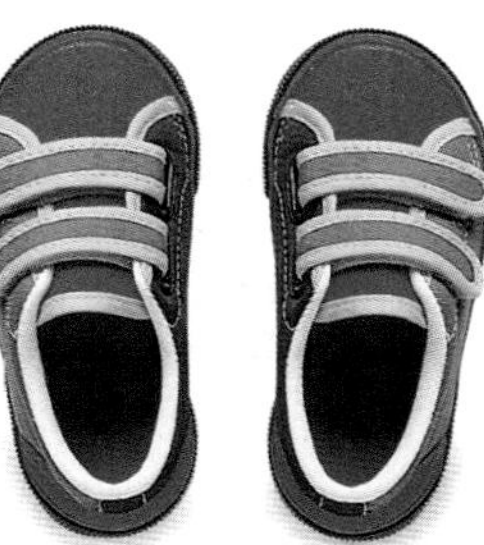
**[1]shoe 1:** a pair of shoes for young children

**[2]shoe** *vb* **shod** \ˈshäd\ *also* **shoed** \ˈshüd\; **shoe·ing**
to put a shoe on **:** furnish with shoes

**shoe·horn** \ˈshü-ˌhórn\ *n*
a curved piece (as of metal) to help in putting on a shoe

**shoe·lace** \ˈshü-ˌlās\ *n*
a lace or string for fastening a shoe

**shoe·mak·er** \ˈshü-ˌmā-kər\ *n*
a person who makes or repairs shoes

**shoe·string** \ˈshü-ˌstring\ *n*
SHOELACE

**shone** *past of* SHINE

**shoo** \ˈshü\ *vb*
to wave, scare, or send away by or as if by crying *shoo*

**shook** *past of* SHAKE

**[1]shoot** \ˈshüt\ *vb* **shot** \ˈshät\; **shoot·ing**
**1** to let fly or cause to be driven forward with force ⟨*shoot* an arrow⟩
**2** to cause a missile to be driven out of ⟨*shoot* a gun⟩
**3** to cause a weapon to discharge a missile ⟨*shoot* at a target⟩
**4** to force (a marble) forward by snapping the thumb
**5** to hit or throw (as a ball or puck) toward a goal
**6** to score by shooting ⟨*shoot* a basket⟩
**7** [2]PLAY 2 ⟨*shot* a round of golf⟩
**8** to strike with a missile from a bow or gun ⟨*shot* a deer⟩
**9** to push or slide into or out of a fastening ⟨*shoot* the door bolt⟩
**10** to thrust forward swiftly ⟨lizards *shooting* out their tongues⟩
**11** to grow rapidly ⟨the corn is *shooting* up⟩
**12** to go, move, or pass rapidly ⟨they *shot* past on skis⟩
**13** to pass swiftly along or through ⟨*shot* the rapids in a canoe⟩
**14** to stream out suddenly **:** SPURT
**shoot·er** *n*

**[2]shoot** *n*
**1** the part of a plant that grows above ground or as much of this as comes from a single bud
**2** a hunting party or trip ⟨a duck *shoot*⟩

**shooting star** *n*
▼ a meteor appearing as a temporary streak of light in the night sky

shooting star

A B C D E F G H I J K L M N O P Q R S T U V W X Y Z

**[1]shop** \'shäp\ *n*
**1** a worker's place of business
**2** a building or room where goods are sold at retail : STORE
**3** a place in which workers are doing a particular kind of work ⟨a repair *shop*⟩

**[2]shop** *vb* **shopped**; **shop·ping**
to visit shops for the purpose of looking over and buying goods
**shop·per** *n*

**shop·keep·er** \'shäp-,kē-pər\ *n*
STOREKEEPER 2

**shop·lift·er** \'shäp-,lif-tər\ *n*
a person who steals merchandise on display in stores

**[1]shore** \'shōr\ *n*
the land along the edge of a body of water (as the sea)

**[2]shore** *vb* **shored**; **shor·ing**
to support with one or more bracing timbers

**shore·bird** \'shōr-,bərd\ *n*
any of various birds (as the plovers) that frequent the seashore

**shore·line** \'shōr-,līn\ *n*
the line where a body of water touches the shore

**shorn** *past participle of* SHEAR

**[1]short** \'shȯrt\ *adj*
**1** not long or tall ⟨a *short* coat⟩
**2** not great in distance ⟨a *short* trip⟩
**3** brief in time ⟨a *short* delay⟩
**4** cut down to a brief length
**5** not coming up to the regular standard ⟨give *short* measure⟩
**6** less in amount than expected or called for ⟨three dollars *short*⟩
**7** less than : not equal to ⟨a little *short* of perfect⟩
**8** not having enough ⟨*short* of money⟩
**9** FLAKY, CRUMBLY ⟨a *short* biscuit⟩
**10** of, relating to, or being one of the vowel sounds \ə,a, e,i, u̇\ and sometimes \ä\ and \ȯ\
**short·ness** *n*

**[2]short** *adv*
**1** with suddenness ⟨stop *short*⟩
**2** so as not to reach as far as expected ⟨fall *short* of the mark⟩

**[3]short** *n*
**1** something shorter than the usual or regular length
**2 shorts** *pl* pants that reach to or almost to the knees
**3 shorts** *pl* short underpants
**4** SHORT CIRCUIT

**short·age** \'shȯrt-ij\ *n*
a lack in the amount needed : DEFICIT ⟨a water *shortage*⟩

**short·cake** \'shȯrt-,kāk\ *n*
▼ a dessert made usually of rich biscuit dough baked and served with sweetened fruit

**shortcake:**
a strawberry shortcake dessert

**short circuit** *n*
an electric connection made between points in an electric circuit between which current does not normally flow

**short·com·ing** \'shȯrt-,kəm-ing\ *n*
FAULT 1

**short·cut** \'shȯrt-,kət\ *n*
a shorter, quicker, or easier way

**short·en** \'shȯrt-n\ *vb*
to make or become short or shorter

**short·en·ing** \'shȯrt-n-ing, 'shȯrt-ning\ *n*
a fatty substance (as lard) used to make pastry flaky

**short·hand** \'shȯrt-,hand\ *n*
a method of rapid writing by using symbols for sounds or words

**short·horn** \'shȯrt-,hȯrn\ *n*
any of a breed of beef cattle developed in England and including good producers of milk from which a separate dairy breed (**milking shorthorn**) has come

**short–lived** \'shȯrt-'līvd, -'livd\ *adj*
living or lasting only a short time

**short·ly** \'shȯrt-lē\ *adv*
**1** in a few words : BRIEFLY
**2** in or within a short time : SOON

**short–sight·ed** \'shȯrt-'sīt-əd\ *adj*
NEARSIGHTED

**short·stop** \'shȯrt-,stäp\ *n*
a baseball infielder whose position is between second and third base

**[1]shot** \'shät\ *n*
**1** the act of shooting
**2** *pl* **shot** a bullet, ball, or pellet for a gun or cannon
**3** something thrown, cast forth, or let fly with force
**4** [2]ATTEMPT, TRY ⟨take another *shot* at the puzzle⟩
**5** the flight of a missile or the distance it travels : RANGE ⟨within rifle *shot*⟩
**6** a person who shoots ⟨that hunter is a good *shot*⟩
**7** a heavy metal ball thrown for distance in a track-and-field contest (**shot put**)
**8** a stroke or throw at a goal ⟨a long *shot* in basketball⟩
**9** an injection of something (as medicine) into the body

**[2]shot** *past of* SHOOT

**shot·gun** \'shät-,gən\ *n*
a gun with a long barrel used to fire shot at short range

**should** \shəd, 'shu̇d\ *past of* SHALL
**1** ought to ⟨you *should* study harder⟩ ⟨they *should* be here soon⟩
**2** happen to ⟨if you *should* see them, say hello for me⟩
**3** used as a politer or less assured form of *shall* ⟨*should* I turn the light out⟩

**[1]shoul·der** \'shōl-dər\ *n*
**1** ▼ the part of the body of a person or animal where the arm or foreleg joins the body
**2** the part of a garment at the wearer's shoulder
**3** a part that resembles a person's shoulder ⟨the *shoulder* of a bottle⟩
**4** the edge of a road

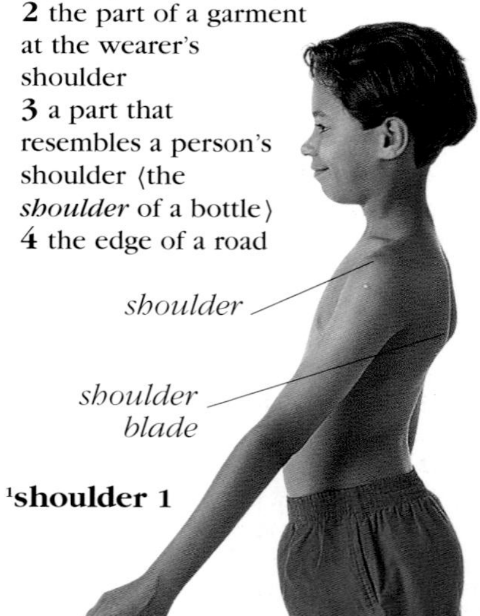


**[1]shoulder 1**

**²shoulder** *vb*
**1** to push with one's shoulder
**2** to accept as one's burden or duty ⟨*shoulder* the blame for a mistake⟩

**shoulder blade** *n*
the flat triangular bone in a person's or animal's shoulder

**shouldn't** \'shu̇d-nt\
should not

**¹shout** \'shau̇t\ *vb*
to make a sudden loud cry (as of joy, pain, or sorrow)

**Synonyms** SHOUT, SHRIEK, and SCREECH mean to utter a loud cry. SHOUT suggests any kind of loud cry that is uttered in order to be heard either far away or above other noise ⟨we *shouted* to them across the river⟩. SHRIEK suggests a high-pitched shrill cry that is a sign of strong feeling (as fear or anger) ⟨the children *shrieked* upon seeing the stranger⟩. SCREECH suggests an extended shriek that is usually without words and very harsh and unpleasant ⟨the cats fought and *screeched*⟩.

**²shout** *n*
a sudden loud cry

**¹shove** \'shəv\ *vb* **shoved**; **shov·ing**
**1** to push with steady force
**2** to push along or away carelessly or rudely ⟨*shove* a person out of the way⟩

**²shove** *n*
the act or an instance of shoving

**¹shov·el** \'shəv-əl\ *n*
**1** ▶ a broad scoop used to lift and throw loose material (as snow)
**2** as much as a shovel will hold

**²shovel** *vb* **shov·eled** *or* **shov·elled**; **shov·el·ing** *or* **shov·el·ling**
**1** to lift or throw with a shovel
**2** to dig or clean out with a shovel ⟨*shovel* a ditch⟩
**3** to throw or carry roughly or in a mass as if with a shovel ⟨*shoveled* food into my mouth⟩

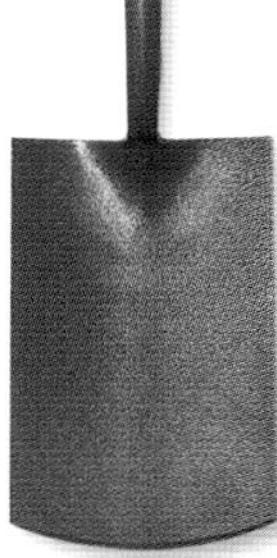
**¹shovel 1**

**¹show** \'shō\ *vb* **showed**; **shown** \'shōn\ *or* **showed**; **show·ing**
**1** to place in sight : DISPLAY
**2** REVEAL 2 ⟨*showed* themselves to be cowards⟩
**3** to give from or as if from a position of authority ⟨*show* them no mercy⟩
**4** TEACH 1, INSTRUCT ⟨*showed* them how to play⟩
**5** PROVE 2 ⟨that *shows* we're right⟩
**6** ¹DIRECT 3, USHER ⟨*showed* them to the door⟩
**7** to be noticeable ⟨the patch hardly *shows*⟩ ⟨determination *showed* in her face⟩

**Synonyms** SHOW, EXHIBIT, and PARADE mean to display something so that it will attract attention. SHOW suggests letting another see or examine ⟨*show* me a picture of your family⟩. EXHIBIT suggests putting something out in public ⟨the children *exhibited* their drawings at the fair⟩. PARADE suggests making a great show of something ⟨look at them *parading* their new bikes⟩.

**²show** *n*
**1** a display made for effect ⟨a *show* of strength⟩ ⟨done for *show*⟩
**2** an appearance meant to deceive : PRETENSE ⟨made a great *show* of friendship⟩
**3** an appearance or display that is basically true or real ⟨answered with some *show* of alarm⟩
**4** an entertainment or exhibition especially by performers (as on TV or the stage)

**show·boat** \'shō-,bōt\ *n*
a river steamboat used as a traveling theater

**show·case** \'shō-,kās\ *n*
a protective glass case in which things are displayed

**¹show·er** \'shau̇-ər\ *n*
**1** a short fall of rain over a small area
**2** something like a shower ⟨a *shower* of sparks⟩
**3** a party where gifts are given especially to a bride or a pregnant woman
**4** a bath in which water is showered on a person or a device for providing such a bath

**²shower** *vb*
**1** to wet with fine spray or drops
**2** to fall in or as if in a shower
**3** to provide in great quantity ⟨*showered* them with gifts⟩
**4** to bathe in a shower

**show·man** \'shō-mən\ *n, pl* **show·men** \-mən\
**1** the producer of a theatrical show
**2** a person having a special skill for presenting something in a dramatic way

**shown** *past participle of* SHOW

**show off** *vb*
to make an obvious display of one's abilities or possessions

**show up** *vb*
**1** to reveal the true nature of : EXPOSE ⟨*shown up* for what they really were⟩
**2** APPEAR 2 ⟨didn't *show up* for work today⟩

**showy** \'shō-ē\ *adj* **show·i·er**; **show·i·est**
**1** attracting attention : STRIKING
**2** given to or being too much outward display : GAUDY
**show·i·ly** \'shō-ə-lē\ *adv*
**show·i·ness** \'shō-ē-nəs\ *n*

**shrank** *past of* SHRINK

**shrap·nel** \'shrap-nl\ *n*
**1** a shell designed to burst and scatter the metal balls with which it is filled along with jagged fragments of the case
**2** metal pieces from an exploded bomb, shell, or mine

**¹shred** \'shred\ *n*
**1** a long narrow piece torn or cut off : STRIP
**2** ²BIT 1, PARTICLE ⟨not a *shred* of evidence⟩

**²shred** *vb* **shred·ded**; **shred·ding**
to cut or tear into shreds

**shrew** \'shrü\ *n*
**1** a small mouselike animal with a long pointed snout and tiny eyes that lives on insects and worms
**2** an unpleasant quarrelsome woman

**shrewd** \'shrüd\ *adj*
showing quick practical cleverness : ASTUTE
**shrewd·ly** *adv*
**shrewd·ness** *n*

A B C D E F G H I J K L M N O P Q R S T U V W X Y Z

[1]**shriek** \'shrēk\ *vb*
to utter a sharp shrill cry
**synonyms** see SHOUT

[2]**shriek** *n*
a sharp shrill cry

**shrike** \'shrīk\ *n*
▼ a grayish or brownish bird with a hooked bill that feeds mostly on insects and often sticks them on thorns before eating them

**shrike**

[1]**shrill** \'shril\ *vb*
to make a high sharp piercing sound : SCREAM

[2]**shrill** *adj*
having a sharp high sound ⟨a *shrill* whistle⟩
**shrill·ness** *n*
**shril·ly** \'shril-lē\ *adv*

**shrimp** \'shrimp\ *n*
**1** a small shellfish related to the crabs and lobsters
**2** a small or unimportant person or thing
**shrimp·like** \'shrim-,plīk\ *adj*

**shrine** \'shrīn\ *n*
**1** a case or box for sacred relics (as the bones of saints)
**2** the tomb of a holy person (as a saint)
**3** ► a place that is considered sacred ⟨the Lincoln Memorial is a *shrine* to all lovers of freedom⟩

**shrink** \'shringk\ *vb* **shrank** \'shrangk\ *also* **shrunk** \'shrəngk\; **shrunk**; **shrink·ing**
**1** to curl up or withdraw in or as if in fear or pain ⟨*shrink* in horror⟩
**2** to make or become smaller ⟨the sweater *shrank* when it got wet⟩

**shrink·age** \'shring-kij\ *n*
the amount by which something shrinks or becomes less

**shriv·el** \'shriv-əl\ *vb* **shriv·eled** *or* **shriv·elled**; **shriv·el·ing** *or* **shriv·el·ling**
to shrink and become dry and wrinkled

[1]**shroud** \'shraủd\ *n*
**1** the cloth placed over or around a dead body
**2** something that covers or shelters like a shroud
**3** one of the ropes that go from the masthead of a boat to the sides to support the mast

[2]**shroud** *vb*
to cover with or as if with a shroud

**shrub** \'shrəb\ *n*
a woody plant having several stems and smaller than most trees

**shrub·bery** \'shrəb-ə-rē\ *n, pl* **shrub·ber·ies**
a group or planting of shrubs

**shrug** \'shrəg\ *vb* **shrugged**; **shrug·ging**
to draw or hunch up the shoulders usually to express doubt, uncertainty, or lack of interest

**shrine 3:** a Catholic shrine to the Virgin Mary in a Spanish church

**shrunk** *past & past participle of* SHRINK

**shrunk·en** \'shrəng-kən\ *adj*
made or grown smaller (as in size or value)

[1]**shuck** \'shək\ *n*
a covering shell or husk

[2]**shuck** *vb*
to free (as an ear of corn) from the shuck

[1]**shud·der** \'shəd-ər\ *vb*
to tremble with fear or horror or from cold

[2]**shudder** *n*
an act of shuddering : SHIVER

[1]**shuf·fle** \'shəf-əl\ *vb* **shuf·fled**; **shuf·fling**
**1** to push out of sight or mix in a disorderly mass ⟨odds and ends *shuffled* in a drawer⟩
**2** to mix cards to change their order in the pack
**3** to move from place to place ⟨*shuffle* chairs⟩
**4** to move in a clumsy dragging way ⟨*shuffled* their feet⟩

[2]**shuffle** *n*
**1** an act of shuffling
**2** [2]JUMBLE
**3** a clumsy dragging walk

**shun** \'shən\ *vb* **shunned**; **shun·ning**
to avoid purposely or by habit

**shunt** \'shənt\ *vb*
**1** to turn off to one side or out of the way : SHIFT ⟨*shunt* cattle into a corral⟩
**2** to switch (as a train) from one track to another

**shut** \'shət\ *vb* **shut**; **shut·ting**
**1** to close or become closed ⟨*shut* the door⟩ ⟨the door *shut* slowly⟩
**2** to close so as to prevent entrance or leaving : BAR ⟨*shut* the cottage for the winter⟩
**3** to keep in a place by enclosing or by blocking the way out : IMPRISON ⟨*shut* them in a jail cell⟩
**4** to close by bringing parts together ⟨*shut* your eyes⟩

**shut–in** \'shət-,in\ *n*
a sick person kept indoors

**shut·out** \'shət-,aủt\ *n*
a game in which one side fails to score

**shut·ter** \'shət-ər\ *n*
1 ▶ a movable cover for a window
2 a device in a camera that opens to let in light when a picture is taken

**¹shut·tle** \'shət-l\ *n*
1 an instrument used in weaving to carry the thread back and forth from side to side through the threads that run lengthwise
2 a vehicle (as a bus or train) that goes back and forth over a short route
3 SPACE SHUTTLE

**²shuttle** *vb* **shut·tled**; **shut·tling**
to move back and forth rapidly or often

**shut·tle·cock**
\'shət-l-,käk\ *n*
▶ a light object (as a piece of cork with feathers stuck in it) used in badminton

**shuttlecock**

**¹shy** \'shī\ *adj*
**shi·er** *or* **shy·er**; **shi·est** *or* **shy·est**
1 easily frightened : TIMID
2 not feeling comfortable around people : not wanting or able to call attention to oneself : BASHFUL
3 having less than a full or an expected amount or number ⟨we were *shy* about ten dollars⟩
**shy·ly** *adv*
**shy·ness** *n*

**Synonyms** SHY and BASHFUL mean feeling awkward with others. SHY suggests not wanting to meet or talk with people either by habit or for special reasons ⟨at the new school I was *shy* at first⟩. BASHFUL suggests being shy and afraid like a very young child ⟨the toddler was *bashful* and would hide when company came⟩.

**²shy** *vb* **shied**; **shy·ing**
1 to draw back in dislike or distaste ⟨*shied* from publicity⟩
2 to move quickly to one side in fright ⟨the horse *shied*⟩

*shutter*

**shutter 1:**
a window with wooden shutters

**sick** \'sik\ *adj*
1 affected with disease or ill health : not well
2 of, relating to, or intended for use in or during illness ⟨*sick* pay⟩
3 affected with or accompanied by nausea ⟨a *sick* headache⟩
4 badly upset by strong emotion (as shame or fear)
5 tired of something from having too much of it ⟨*sick* of flattery⟩
6 filled with disgust ⟨such gossip makes me *sick*⟩

**sick·bed** \'sik-,bed\ *n*
a bed on which a sick person lies

**sick·en** \'sik-ən\ *vb*
to make or become sick

**sick·en·ing** \'sik-ə-ning\ *adj*
causing sickness or disgust ⟨a *sickening* smell⟩
**sick·en·ing·ly** *adv*

**sick·le** \'sik-əl\ *n*
a tool with a sharp curved metal blade and a short handle used to cut grass

**sick·ly** \'sik-lē\ *adj* **sick·li·er**; **sick·li·est**
1 somewhat sick : often ailing ⟨I was *sickly* as a child⟩
2 caused by or associated with ill health ⟨a *sickly* complexion⟩
3 not growing well : SPINDLY ⟨*sickly* plants⟩

**sick·ness** \'sik-nəs\ *n*
1 ill health : ILLNESS
2 a specific disease : MALADY
3 NAUSEA 1

**¹side** \'sīd\ *n*
1 the right or left part of the trunk of the body
2 a place, space, or direction away from or beyond a central point or line ⟨set something to one *side*⟩
3 a surface or line forming a border or face of an object
4 an outer part of a thing considered as facing in a certain direction ⟨the upper *side*⟩
5 a position viewed as opposite to another ⟨can see both *sides* of the question⟩
6 a body of contestants ⟨our *side* won⟩
7 a line of ancestors traced back from either parent ⟨French on my mother's *side*⟩

**²side** *adj*
1 of, relating to, or being on the side ⟨*side* pockets⟩
2 aimed toward or from the side ⟨a *side* thrust⟩
3 related to something in a minor or unimportant way ⟨a *side* remark⟩
4 being in addition to a main portion ⟨a *side* order of French fries⟩

**[3]side** *vb* **sid·ed**; **sid·ing**
to take the same side ⟨*sided* with our friend in the argument⟩

**side·arm** \'sīd-,ärm\ *adv*
with the arm moving out to the side ⟨threw the ball *sidearm*⟩

**side·board** \'sīd-,bōrd\ *n*
a piece of furniture for holding dishes, silverware, and table linen

**side·burns** \'sīd-,bərnz\ *n pl*
hair growing on the side of the face in front of the ears

**sid·ed** \'sīd-əd\ *adj*
having sides often of a stated number or kind ⟨a four-*sided* figure⟩

**side·line** \'sīd-,līn\ *n*
**1** a line marking the side of a playing field or court
**2** a business or a job done in addition to one's regular occupation

**[1]side·long** \'sīd-,lòng\ *adv*
out of the corner of one's eye ⟨glanced *sidelong* at the pie on the table⟩

**[2]sidelong** *adj*
**1** made to one side or out of the corner of one's eye ⟨a *sidelong* look⟩
**2** INDIRECT 2

**side·show** \'sīd-,shō\ *n*
a small show off to the side of a main show or exhibition (as of a circus)

**side·step** \'sīd-,step\ *vb* **side·stepped**; **side·step·ping**
**1** to take a step to the side
**2** to avoid by a step to the side
**3** to avoid answering or dealing with ⟨*sidestep* a question⟩

**side·track** \'sīd-,trak\ *vb*
**1** to transfer from a main railroad line to a side line
**2** to turn aside from a main purpose or direction ⟨*sidetrack* his career⟩

**side·walk** \'sīd-,wȯk\ *n*
a usually paved walk at the side of a street or road

**side·ways** \'sīd-,wāz\ *adv or adj*
**1** from one side ⟨look at it *sideways*⟩
**2** with one side forward ⟨sliding *sideways* down the hill⟩
**3** to one side ⟨moved *sideways* to let them through⟩

**side·wise** \'sīd-,wīz\ *adv or adj*
SIDEWAYS

**sid·ing** \'sīd-iŋ\ *n*
**1** a short railroad track connected with the main track
**2** material (as boards or metal pieces) used to cover the outside walls of frame buildings

**si·dle** \'sīd-l\ *vb* **si·dled**; **si·dling**
to go or move with one side forward ⟨the crab *sidled* away⟩

**siege** \'sēj\ *n*
**1** the moving of an army around a fortified place to capture it
**2** a lasting attack (as of illness)

**si·er·ra** \sē-'er-ə\ *n*
a range of mountains especially with jagged peaks

**si·es·ta** \sē-'es-tə\ *n*
a nap or rest especially at midday

---

**Word History** The ancient Romans counted the hours of the day from sunrise to sunset, an average of about twelve hours. The sixth hour in the Roman day was noon. The Latin name for noon came from the Latin word that meant "sixth." A Spanish word for a nap taken about noon came from the Latin word that meant "noon." English *siesta* comes from the Spanish word.

---

**sieve** \'siv\ *n*
▼ a utensil with meshes or holes to separate finer particles from coarser ones or solids from liquids

*sieve*

**sieve:** sifting flour with a sieve

**sift** \'sift\ *vb*
**1** to pass or cause to pass through a sieve ⟨*sift* flour⟩
**2** to separate or separate out by or as if by passing through a sieve
**3** to test or examine carefully ⟨*sift* evidence⟩
**sift·er** *n*

**[1]sigh** \'sī\ *vb*
**1** to take or let out a long loud breath often as an expression of sadness or weariness
**2** to make a sound like sighing ⟨wind *sighing* in the branches⟩
**3** YEARN ⟨*sighing* for the days of youth⟩

**[2]sigh** *n*
the act or a sound of sighing

**[1]sight** \'sīt\ *n*
**1** something that is seen : SPECTACLE
**2** something that is worth seeing ⟨showed us the *sights* of the city⟩
**3** something that is peculiar, funny, or messy ⟨you're a *sight*⟩
**4** the function, process, or power of seeing : the sense by which one becomes aware of the position, form, and color of objects
**5** the act of seeing
**6** the presence of an object within the field of vision ⟨can't bear the *sight* of it⟩
**7** the distance a person can see ⟨a ship came into *sight*⟩
**8** a device (as a small metal bead on a gun barrel) that aids the eye in aiming or in finding the direction of an object

**[2]sight** *vb*
**1** to get sight of : SEE ⟨*sighted* the ship⟩
**2** to look at through or as if through a sight

**sight·less** \'sīt-ləs\ *adj*
lacking sight : BLIND

**sight·seer** \'sīt-,sē-ər\ *n*
a person who goes about to see places and things of interest

**[1]sign** \'sīn\ *n*
**1** a motion, action, or movement of the hand that means something ⟨made a *sign* for them to be quiet⟩
**2** one of the twelve parts of the zodiac
**3** a symbol (as + or ÷) indicating a mathematical operation
**4** a public notice that advertises something or gives information
**5** something that indicates what is to come ⟨the first *signs* of spring⟩
**6** [1]TRACE 2 ⟨no *sign* of life⟩

**[2]sign** *vb*
**1** to make or place a sign on
**2** to represent or show by a sign or signs
**3** to write one's name on to show that one accepts, agrees with, or will be responsible for ⟨*signed* the order form⟩
**4** to communicate by using sign language

[1]**sig·nal** \'sig-nl\ *n*
**1** a sign, event, or word that serves to start some action ⟨a *signal* to light the fires⟩
**2** a sound, a movement of part of the body, or an object that gives warning or a command ⟨make a *signal* with one's hand⟩ ⟨a traffic *signal*⟩
**3** a radio wave that transmits a message or effect (as in radio or television)

[2]**signal** *vb* **sig·naled** *or* **sig·nalled**; **sig·nal·ing** *or* **sig·nal·ling**
**1** to notify by a signal
**2** to communicate by signals

[3]**signal** *adj*
**1** unusually great ⟨a *signal* honor⟩
**2** used for signaling ⟨a *signal* light⟩

**sig·na·ture** \'sig-nə-ˌchu̇r\ *n*
**1** the name of a person written by that person
**2** a sign or group of signs placed at the beginning of a staff in music to show the key (**key signature**) or the meter (**time signature**)

**sign·board** \'sīn-ˌbōrd\ *n*
a board with a sign or notice on it

**sig·nif·i·cance** \sig-'nif-i-kəns\ *n*
**1** MEANING 1
**2** IMPORTANCE ⟨it's a subject of some *significance*⟩

**sig·nif·i·cant** \sig-'nif-i-kənt\ *adj*
**1** having meaning and especially a special or hidden meaning ⟨gave them a *significant* smile⟩
**2** IMPORTANT 1

**sig·ni·fy** \'sig-nə-ˌfī\ *vb* **sig·ni·fied**; **sig·ni·fy·ing**
**1** [2]MEAN 3, DENOTE
**2** to show especially by a sign **:** make known ⟨*signified* their pleasure⟩
**3** to have importance

**sign language** *n*
▶ a system of hand movements used for communication (as by people who are deaf)

**sign·post** \'sīn-ˌpōst\ *n*
a post with a sign (as for directing travelers)

**si·lage** \'sī-lij\ *n*
fodder fermented (as in a silo) to produce a good juicy feed for livestock

[1]**si·lence** \'sī-ləns\ *n*
**1** the state of keeping or being silent ⟨the teacher motioned for *silence*⟩
**2** the state of there being no sound or noise **:** STILLNESS

[2]**silence** *vb* **si·lenced**; **si·lenc·ing**
**1** to stop the noise or speech of **:** cause to be silent
**2** SUPPRESS 1 ⟨*silence* objections⟩

**si·lent** \'sī-lənt\ *adj*
**1** not speaking **:** not talkative ⟨a *silent* person⟩
**2** free from noise or sound **:** STILL
**3** done or felt without being spoken ⟨*silent* reading⟩ ⟨*silent* prayer⟩
**4** making no mention ⟨they were *silent* about their plan⟩
**5** not active in running a business ⟨a *silent* partner⟩
**6** not pronounced ⟨the *e* in "came" is *silent*⟩

[1]**sil·hou·ette** \ˌsil-ə-'wet\ *n*
**1** ▶ a drawing or picture of the outline of an object filled in with a solid usually black color
**2** a profile portrait done in silhouette
**3** [1]OUTLINE 1

[1]**silhouette 1:** a silhouette of a man

**Word History** A man named *Silhouette* was once in charge of the finances of France. He was a miser who did not like to spend his money or the country's money. According to one story he was too cheap to buy paintings for his walls. He made simple outline drawings to hang in place of paintings. In French and in English *silhouette* still means "an outline drawing."

[2]**silhouette** *vb* **sil·hou·ett·ed**; **sil·hou·ett·ing**
to represent by a silhouette **:** show against a light background ⟨an airplane *silhouetted* against the sky⟩

**sil·i·con** \'sil-i-kən, 'sil-ə-ˌkän\ *n*
a chemical element that is found combined as the most common element next to oxygen in the earth's crust and is used especially in electronic devices

**silk** \'silk\ *n*
**1** a fine fiber that is spun by many insect larvae usually to form their cocoon or by spiders to make their webs and that includes some kinds used for weaving cloth
**2** ▶ thread, yarn, or fabric made from silk
**3** something suggesting silk ⟨the *silk* of an ear of corn⟩

**silk 2:** twists of silk for use in sewing

## sign language

Sign language allows people who are deaf, hard of hearing, or mute, to communicate. There is a sign for each letter of the alphabet to enable the spelling of individual words, as well as signs that represent whole words and names. Sometimes, even a whole sentence can be expressed through one or two signs.

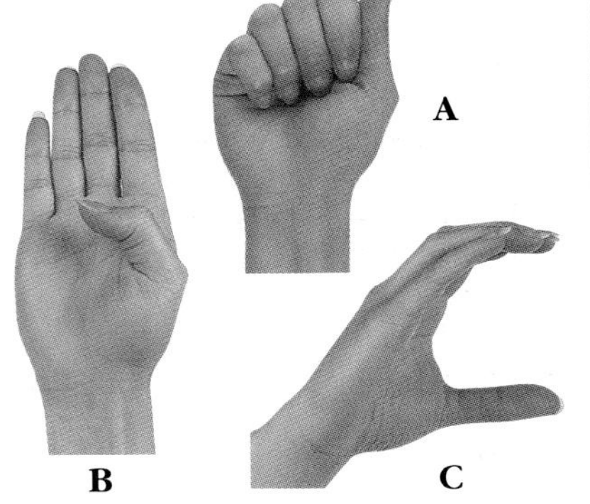

**silk·en** \'sil-kən\ *adj*
1 made of or with silk
2 like silk especially in its soft and smooth feel ⟨*silken* hair⟩

**silk·worm** \'sil-,kwərm\ *n*
▼ a yellowish hairless caterpillar that is the larva of an Asian moth (**silk moth** or **silkworm moth**), is raised in captivity on mulberry leaves, and produces a strong silk that is the silk most used for thread or cloth

**silkworm:** a Chinese silkworm

**silky** \'sil-kē\ *adj* **silk·i·er**; **silk·i·est**
soft and smooth as silk

**sill** \'sil\ *n*
1 a horizontal supporting piece at the base of a structure
2 a heavy horizontal piece (as of wood) that forms the bottom part of a window frame or a doorway

**sil·ly** \'sil-ē\ *adj* **sil·li·er**; **sil·li·est**
1 not very intelligent
2 showing a lack of common sense ⟨a *silly* mistake⟩
3 not serious or important ⟨a *silly* reason⟩ **synonyms** see ABSURD
**sil·li·ness** *n*

**si·lo** \'sī-lō\ *n, pl* **silos**
a covered trench, pit, or especially a tall round building in which silage is made and stored

[1]**silt** \'silt\ *n*
1 particles of small size left as sediment from water
2 a soil made up mostly of silt and containing little clay

[2]**silt** *vb*
to choke, fill, cover, or block with silt

[1]**sil·ver** \'sil-vər\ *n*
1 a soft white metallic chemical element that takes a high polish and is used for money, jewelry and ornaments, and table utensils
2 coin made of silver
3 SILVERWARE ⟨table *silver*⟩
4 a medium gray

[2]**silver** *adj*
1 made of, coated with, or yielding silver
2 having the color of silver

[3]**silver** *vb*
to coat with or as if with silver

**sil·ver·smith** \'sil-vər-,smith\ *n*
a person who makes objects of silver

**sil·ver·ware** \'sil-vər-,waər, -,weər\ *n*
▶ things (as knives, forks, and spoons) made of silver, silver-plated metal, or stainless steel

**sil·very** \'sil-və-rē\ *adj*
having a shine like silver

**sim·i·lar** \'sim-ə-lər\ *adj*
having qualities in common ⟨houses *similar* in design⟩
**sim·i·lar·ly** *adv*

**sim·i·lar·i·ty** \,sim-ə-'lar-ət-ē\ *n, pl* **sim·i·lar·i·ties**
the quality or state of being similar **:** RESEMBLANCE

**sim·i·le** \'sim-ə-,lē\ *n*
a figure of speech comparing two unlike things using *like* or *as* ⟨"their cheeks are like roses" is a *simile*, "their cheeks are roses" is a metaphor⟩

**sim·mer** \'sim-ər\ *vb*
1 to cook gently at or just below the boiling point
2 to be on the point of bursting out with violence or anger

**sim·ple** \'sim-pəl\ *adj* **sim·pler**; **sim·plest**
1 INNOCENT 1, MODEST
2 not rich or important ⟨*simple* folk⟩
3 lacking in education, experience, or intelligence
4 not fancy ⟨neat *simple* clothing⟩
5 having few parts **:** not complicated ⟨a *simple* machine⟩
6 ABSOLUTE 2 ⟨the *simple* truth⟩
7 not hard to understand or solve
8 EASY 1, STRAIGHTFORWARD ⟨a *simple* explanation⟩

**sim·ple·ton** \'sim-pəl-tən\ *n*
a foolish or stupid person

**sim·plic·i·ty** \sim-'plis-ət-ē\ *n, pl* **sim·plic·i·ties**
1 the quality or state of being simple or plain and not complicated or difficult
2 SINCERITY
3 directness or clearness in speaking or writing

**sim·pli·fy** \'sim-plə-,fī\ *vb* **sim·pli·fied**; **sim·pli·fy·ing**
to make simple or simpler **:** make easier

**silverware**

**sim·ply** \'sim-plē\ *adv*
1 in a clear way ⟨explain *simply*⟩
2 in a plain way ⟨dressed *simply*⟩
3 DIRECTLY 1, CANDIDLY ⟨told the story as *simply* as a child would⟩
4 [2]ONLY 1, MERELY ⟨ask a question *simply* out of curiosity⟩
5 in actual fact **:** REALLY, TRULY ⟨*simply* marvelous⟩

**si·mul·ta·neous** \,sī-məl-'tā-nē-əs\ *adj*
existing or taking place at the same time
**si·mul·ta·neous·ly** *adv*

[1]**sin** \'sin\ *n*
1 an action that breaks a religious law
2 an action that is or is felt to be bad

[2]**sin** *vb* **sinned**; **sin·ning**
to be guilty of a sin

[1]**since** \'sins\ *adv*
1 from a definite past time until now ⟨has stayed there ever *since*⟩
2 before the present time **:** AGO ⟨long *since* dead⟩
3 after a time in the past ⟨has *since* become rich⟩

[2]**since** *conj*
1 in the period after ⟨we've played better *since* you joined the team⟩
2 BECAUSE ⟨*since* you have finished your work, you may go⟩

**³since** *prep*
**1** in the period after ⟨haven't seen them *since* last week⟩
**2** continuously from ⟨have lived here *since* 1976⟩

**sin·cere** \sin-'sir\ *adj*
**1** HONEST 2, STRAIGHTFORWARD ⟨a *sincere* person⟩
**2** being what it seems to be : GENUINE ⟨*sincere* good wishes⟩
**sin·cere·ly** *adv*

**sin·cer·i·ty** \sin-'ser-ət-ē\ *n*
freedom from fraud or deception : HONESTY

**sin·ew** \'sin-yü\ *n*
TENDON

**sin·ewy** \'sin-yə-wē\ *adj*
**1** full of tendons : TOUGH, STRINGY ⟨a *sinewy* piece of meat⟩
**2** STRONG 1, POWERFUL ⟨*sinewy* arms⟩

**sin·ful** \'sin-fəl\ *adj*
being or full of sin : WICKED ⟨a *sinful* act⟩ ⟨*sinful* people⟩

**sing** \'sing\ *vb* **sang** \'sang\ *or* **sung** \'səng\; **sung**; **sing·ing**
**1** to produce musical sounds with the voice ⟨*sing* for joy⟩
**2** to express in musical tones ⟨*sing* a song⟩
**3** ¹CHANT 2 ⟨*sing* mass⟩
**4** to make musical sounds ⟨birds *singing* at dawn⟩
**5** to make a small shrill sound ⟨arrows *singing* through the air⟩
**6** to speak with enthusiasm ⟨*sing* their praises⟩
**7** to do something with song ⟨*sing* a baby to sleep⟩
**sing·er** *n*

**¹singe** \'sinj\ *vb* **singed**; **singe·ing**
**1** to burn lightly or on the surface : SCORCH
**2** to remove the hair, down, or fuzz from by passing briefly over a flame ⟨*singe* a plucked chicken⟩

**²singe** *n*
a slight burn

**¹sin·gle** \'sing-gəl\ *adj*
**1** not married
**2** being alone : being the only one
**3** made up of or having only one
**4** having but one row of petals or rays ⟨a *single* rose⟩
**5** being a separate whole : INDIVIDUAL ⟨a *single* thread⟩
**6** of, relating to, or involving only one person

**²single** *vb* **sin·gled**; **sin·gling**
to select or distinguish (as one person or thing) from a number or group ⟨*singled* out for praise⟩

**³single** *n*
**1** a separate individual person or thing
**2** a hit in baseball that enables the batter to reach first base

**sin·gle–hand·ed** \,sing-gəl-'han-dəd\ *adj*
**1** done or managed by one person or with one hand
**2** working alone : lacking help

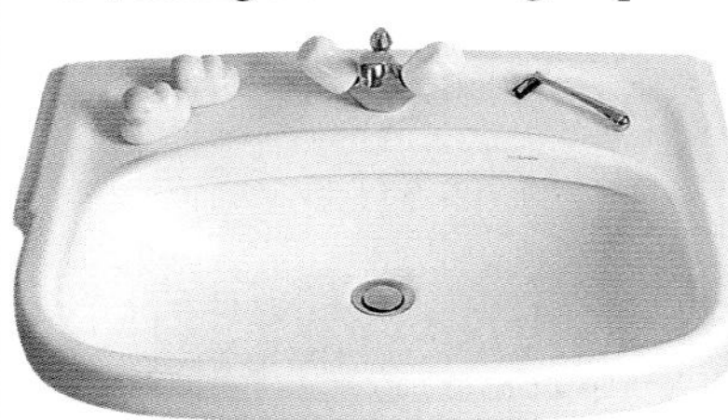

**²sink:** a bathroom sink

**sin·gly** \'sing-gə-lē, 'sing-glē\ *adv*
one by one : INDIVIDUALLY

**¹sin·gu·lar** \'sing-gyə-lər\ *adj*
**1** of, relating to, or being a word form used to show not more than one ⟨a *singular* noun⟩
**2** ¹SUPERIOR 2, EXCEPTIONAL
**3** of unusual quality : UNIQUE
**4** STRANGE 3, ODD ⟨*singular* habits⟩

**²singular** *n*
a form of a word used to show that only one person or thing is meant

**sin·is·ter** \'sin-əs-tər\ *adj*
**1** ¹EVIL 1, CORRUPT
**2** threatening evil, harm, or danger ⟨*sinister* rumors⟩

**¹sink** \'singk\ *vb* **sank** \'sangk\ *or* **sunk** \'səngk\; **sunk**; **sink·ing**
**1** to move or cause to move downward so as to be swallowed up ⟨the ship *sank*⟩
**2** to fall or drop to a lower level ⟨the lake *sank* during the drought⟩
**3** to lessen in amount ⟨the temperature *sank*⟩
**4** to cause to penetrate ⟨*sank* an ax into the tree⟩
**5** to go into or become absorbed ⟨the water *sank* into the ground⟩
**6** to form by digging or boring ⟨*sink* a well⟩
**7** to spend (money) unwisely

**²sink** *n*
◄ a basin usually with water faucets and a drain fixed to a wall or floor

**sin·ner** \'sin-ər\ *n*
a sinful person

**si·nus** \'sī-nəs\ *n*
any of several spaces in the skull mostly connected with the nostrils

**¹sip** \'sip\ *vb* **sipped**; **sip·ping**
to take small drinks of

**²sip** *n*
**1** the act of sipping
**2** a small amount taken by sipping

**¹si·phon** \'sī-fən\ *n*
**1** ▼ a bent pipe or tube through which a liquid can be drawn by air pressure up and over the edge of a container
**2** a tubelike organ in an animal and especially a mollusk or arthropod used to draw in or squirt out a fluid

**¹siphon 1:** a girl using a siphon to fill an aquarium with water

a b c d e f g h i j k l m n o p q r s t u v w x y z

A B C D E F G H I J K L M N O P Q R S T U V W X Y Z

[2]**siphon** *vb*
to draw off by a siphon

**sir** \'sər, sər\ *n*
**1** *cap* — used as a title before the given name of a knight or a baronet ⟨*Sir* Walter Raleigh⟩
**2** used without a name as a form of polite address to a man ⟨may I help you, *sir*?⟩

[1]**sire** \'sīr\ *n*
**1** *often cap* [1]FATHER 1
**2** ANCESTOR
**3** the male parent of an animal

[2]**sire** *vb* **sired**; **sir·ing**
to become the father of

**si·ren** \'sī-rən\ *n*
a device that makes a loud shrill warning sound and is often operated by electricity ⟨an ambulance *siren*⟩

**sir·loin** \'sər-,lȯin\ *n*
a cut of beef taken from the part just in front of the rump

**sirup** *variant of* SYRUP

**si·sal** \'sī-səl, -zəl\ *n*
**1** ▶ a long strong white fiber used to make rope and twine
**2** a Mexican agave whose leaves yield sisal

**sisal 1:** twine made of sisal

**sis·ter** \'sis-tər\ *n*
**1** a female person or animal related to another person or animal by having one or both parents in common
**2** a member of a religious society of women : NUN
**3** a woman related to another by a common tie or interest
**sis·ter·ly** *adj*

**sis·ter·hood** \'sis-tər-,hu̇d\ *n*
**1** the state of being a sister
**2** women joined in a group

**sis·ter–in–law** \'sis-tər-ən-,lȯ\ *n, pl* **sis·ters–in–law**
**1** the sister of one's husband or wife
**2** the wife of one's brother

**sit** \'sit\ *vb* **sat** \'sat\; **sit·ting**
**1** to rest upon the part of the body where the hips and legs join
**2** to cause (as oneself) to be seated ⟨*sat* myself down to write a letter⟩
**3** [2]PERCH
**4** to hold a place as a member of an official group ⟨*sit* in congress⟩
**5** to hold a session ⟨the court *sat* last month⟩
**6** to pose for a portrait or photograph
**7** to be located ⟨the vase *sits* on the table⟩
**8** to remain quiet or still ⟨the car *sits* in the garage⟩

**site** \'sīt\ *n*
**1** the space of ground a building rests upon
**2** the place where something (as a town or event) is found or took place ⟨a famous battle *site*⟩
**3** WEB SITE

**sit·ting** \'sit-ing\ *n*
**1** an act of one that sits : the time taken in such a sitting
**2** SESSION 1 ⟨a *sitting* of the legislature⟩

**sitting room** *n*
LIVING ROOM

**sit·u·at·ed** \'sich-ə-,wāt-əd\ *adj*
**1** having its place ⟨a town *situated* on a hill⟩
**2** being in such financial circumstances ⟨not rich but comfortably *situated*⟩

**sit·u·a·tion** \,sich-ə-'wā-shən\ *n*
**1** LOCATION 2, PLACE
**2** position or place of employment : JOB
**3** position in life : STATUS
**4** the combination of surrounding conditions ⟨a bad *situation*⟩

[1]**six** \'siks\ *adj*
being one more than five

[2]**six** *n*
one more than five : two times three : 6

**six–gun** \'siks-,gən\ *n*
a revolver having six chambers

**six·pence** \'sik-spens\ *n*
**1** the sum of six pence
**2** an old British coin worth six pence

**six–shoot·er** \'siks-,shüt-ər\ *n*
SIX-GUN

[1]**six·teen** \sik-'stēn\ *adj*
being one more than fifteen

[2]**sixteen** *n*
one more than fifteen : four times four : 16

[1]**six·teenth** \sik-'stēnth\ *adj*
coming right after fifteenth

[2]**sixteenth** *n*
number sixteen in a series

[1]**sixth** \'siksth\ *adj*
coming right after fifth

[2]**sixth** *n*
**1** number six in a series
**2** one of six equal parts

[1]**six·ti·eth** \'sik-stē-əth\ *adj*
coming right after fifty-ninth

[2]**sixtieth** *n*
number sixty in a series

[1]**six·ty** \'sik-stē\ *adj*
being six times ten

[2]**sixty** *n*
six times ten : 60

**siz·able** *or* **size·able** \'sī-zə-bəl\ *adj*
fairly large

**size** \'sīz\ *n*
**1** amount of space occupied : BULK
**2** the measurements of a thing ⟨the *size* of a book⟩
**3** one of a series of measures especially of manufactured articles (as clothing) ⟨a *size* 8 shoe⟩
**sized** \'sīzd\ *adj*

**siz·zle** \'siz-əl\ *vb* **siz·zled**; **siz·zling**
to make a hissing or sputtering noise in or as if in frying or burning

[1]**skate** \'skāt\ *n*
a very flat fish related to the sharks that has large and nearly triangular fins

[2]**skate** *n*
**1** a metal runner fitting the sole of the shoe or a shoe with a permanently attached metal runner used for gliding on ice
**2** ROLLER SKATE

[3]**skate** *vb* **skat·ed**; **skat·ing**
**1** to glide along on skates
**2** to slide or move as if on skates
**skat·er** *n*

**skate·board** \'skāt-,bōrd\ *n*
▼ a short board mounted on small wheels that is used for coasting and often for performing athletic stunts
**skate·board·er** \-,bōrd-ər\ *n*
**skate·board·ing** \-ding\ *n*

**skateboard**

**skeleton 1**
At birth the human skeleton has over 300 bones, some of which fuse together during growth, leaving 206 bones in the adult body. About half of these bones can be found in the hands and the feet. The largest bone in the human body is the thigh bone, and the smallest are the group of three tiny bones in each ear.

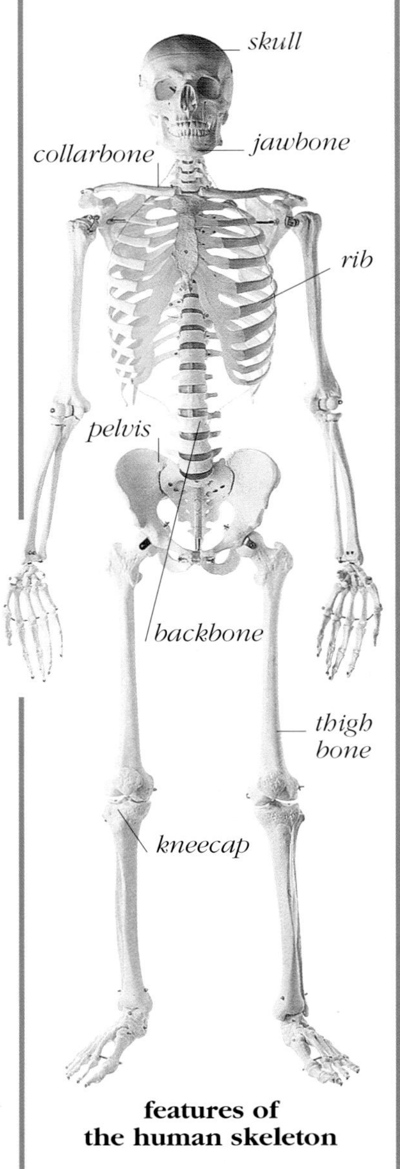


**features of the human skeleton**

**skein** \'skān\ *n*
a quantity of yarn or thread arranged in a loose coil

**skel·e·tal** \'skel-ət-l\ *adj*
of, relating or attached to, forming, or like a skeleton ⟨*skeletal* muscles⟩

**skel·e·ton** \'skel-ət-n\ *n*
**1** ◀ a firm supporting or protecting structure or framework of a living being **:** the usually bony framework of a vertebrate (as a fish, bird, or human)
**2** FRAMEWORK ⟨the steel *skeleton* of a building⟩

**skep·ti·cal** \'skep-ti-kəl\ *adj*
having or showing doubt

**[1]sketch** \'skech\ *n*
**1** a rough outline or drawing showing the main features of something to be written, painted, or built
**2** a short written composition (as a story or essay)

**[2]sketch** *vb*
**1** to make a sketch, rough draft, or outline of
**2** to draw or paint sketches

**sketchy** \'skech-ē\ *adj*
**sketch·i·er**; **sketch·i·est**
**1** like a sketch **:** roughly outlined
**2** lacking completeness or clearness ⟨a *sketchy* description⟩

**[1]ski** \'skē\ *n, pl* **skis**
one of a pair of narrow wooden, metal, or plastic strips bound one on each foot and used in gliding over snow or water

**[2]ski** *vb* **skied**; **ski·ing**
▶ to glide on skis
**ski·er** *n*

**[1]skid** \'skid\ *n*
**1** a support (as a plank) used to raise and hold an object ⟨put a boat on *skids*⟩
**2** one of the logs, planks, or rails along or on which something heavy is rolled or slid
**3** the act of skidding **:** SLIDE

**[2]skid** *vb* **skid·ded**; **skid·ding**
**1** to roll or slide on skids
**2** to slide sideways
**3** [1]SLIDE 1, SLIP ⟨*skid* across the ice⟩

**skiff** \'skif\ *n*
**1** a small light rowboat
**2** a light sailboat that can be rowed

**ski·ing** \'skē-ing\ *n*
the art or sport of gliding and jumping on skis

**skill** \'skil\ *n*
**1** ability that comes from training or practice
**2** a developed or acquired ability

**skilled** \'skild\ *adj*
**1** having skill ⟨a *skilled* mason⟩
**2** requiring skill and training ⟨a *skilled* trade⟩

**skil·let** \'skil-ət\ *n*
a frying pan

**skill·ful** *or* **skil·ful** \'skil-fəl\ *adj*
**1** having or showing skill **:** EXPERT ⟨a *skillful* chef⟩
**2** done or made with skill ⟨a *skillful* repair job⟩
**skill·ful·ly** \-fə-lē\ *adv*

**Synonyms** SKILLFUL and EXPERT mean having the knowledge and experience needed to succeed at what one does. SKILLFUL suggests being very skilled at doing a particular job ⟨a *skillful* truck driver⟩. EXPERT suggests having a thorough knowledge of a subject as well as being very skillful at working in it ⟨an *expert* surgeon⟩.

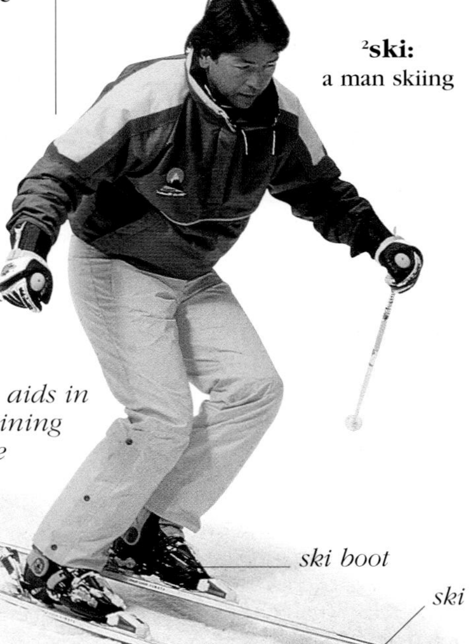


**[2]ski:** a man skiing

A B C D E F G H I J K L M N O P Q R S T U V W X Y Z

**skim** \'skim\ *vb* **skimmed**; **skim·ming**
**1** to clean a liquid of scum or floating substance **:** remove (as cream or film) from the top part of a liquid
**2** to read or examine quickly and not thoroughly
**3** to throw so as to skip along the surface of water
**4** to pass swiftly or lightly over

**skim milk** *n*
milk from which the cream has been taken

**skimp** \'skimp\ *vb*
to give too little or just enough attention or effort to or funds for

**skimpy** \'skim-pē\ *adj* **skimp·i·er**; **skimp·i·est**
not enough especially because of skimping **:** SCANTY

[1]**skin** \'skin\ *n*
**1** the hide especially of a small animal or one that has fur
**2** the outer limiting layer of an animal body that in vertebrate animals (as humans) is made up of two layers of cells forming an inner dermis and an outer epidermis
**3** an outer or surface layer (as of a fruit)
**skin·less** \-ləs\ *adj*
**skinned** \'skind\ *adj*

[2]**skin** *vb* **skinned**; **skin·ning**
**1** to strip, scrape, or rub off the skin of ⟨*skin* one's knee⟩
**2** to remove an outer layer from (as by peeling)

**skin dive** *vb*
to swim below the surface of water with a face mask and sometimes a portable breathing device
**skin diver** *n*

**skin·ny** \'skin-ē\ *adj* **skin·ni·er**; **skin·ni·est**
very thin **synonyms** see LEAN

[1]**skip** \'skip\ *vb* **skipped**; **skip·ping**
**1** to move lightly with leaps and bounds
**2** to bound or cause to bound off one point after another **:** SKIM
**3** to leap over lightly and nimbly
**4** to pass over or omit an item, space, or step ⟨*skip* a page⟩
**5** to fail to attend ⟨*skipped* the meeting⟩

[2]**skip** *n*
**1** a light bounding step
**2** a way of moving by hops and steps

**skip·per** \'skip-ər\ *n*
the master of a ship and especially of a fishing, trading, or pleasure boat

[1]**skir·mish** \'skər-mish\ *n*
**1** a minor fight in war
**2** a minor dispute or contest

[2]**skirmish** *vb*
to take part in a skirmish

[1]**skirt** \'skərt\ *n*
**1** a woman's or girl's garment or part of a garment that hangs from the waist down
**2** either of two flaps on a saddle covering the bars on which the stirrups are hung
**3** a part or attachment serving as a rim, border, or edging

**sky** \'skī\ *n, pl* **skies**
**1** the upper air **:** the vast arch or dome that seems to spread over the earth
**2** WEATHER, CLIMATE ⟨sunny *skies* are predicted⟩

**sky·lark** \'skī-,lärk\ *n*
a European lark noted for its song

**sky·light** \'skī-,līt\ *n*
a window or group of windows in a roof or ceiling

**sky·line** \'skī-,līn\ *n*
**1** the line where earth and sky seem to meet **:** HORIZON

**skyline 2:** the city skyline in Sydney \'sid-nē\, Australia

[2]**skirt** *vb*
**1** [2]BORDER 2
**2** to go or pass around or about the outer edge of

**skit** \'skit\ *n*
a brief sketch in play form

**skit·tish** \'skit-ish\ *adj*
easily frightened ⟨a *skittish* horse⟩

**skulk** \'skəlk\ *vb*
to hide or move in a sly or sneaking way ⟨*skulked* behind a fence⟩

**skull** \'skəl\ *n*
the case of bone or cartilage that forms most of the skeleton of the head and face, encloses the brain, and supports the jaws

**skunk** \'skəngk\ *n*
**1** ▶ a North American animal related to the weasels and minks that has coarse black and white fur and can squirt out a fluid with a very unpleasant smell
**2** a mean person who deserves to be scorned

**skunk 1:** a spotted skunk

**2** ▲ an outline against the sky ⟨buildings forming the *skyline* of a city⟩

**sky·rock·et** \'skī-,räk-ət\ *n*
[1]ROCKET 1

**sky·scrap·er** \'skī-,skrā-pər\ *n*
a very tall building

**sky·writ·ing** \'skī-,rīt-iŋ\ *n*
writing formed in the sky by means of smoke or vapor released from an airplane

**slab** \'slab\ *n*
a flat thick piece or slice (as of stone, wood, or bread)

**¹slack** \'slak\ *adj*
**1** CARELESS 2, NEGLIGENT
**2** not energetic : SLOW ⟨a *slack* pace⟩
**3** not tight or firm ⟨a *slack* rope⟩
**4** not busy or active ⟨business is *slack*⟩

**²slack** *vb*
to make or become looser, slower, or less energetic : LOOSEN, SLACKEN

**³slack** *n*
**1** a stopping of movement or flow
**2** a part (as of a rope or sail) that hangs loose without strain
**3 slacks** *pl* pants especially for informal wear

**slack·en** \'slak-ən\ *vb*
**1** to make slower or less energetic : slow up ⟨*slacken* speed at a crossing⟩
**2** to make less tight or firm : LOOSEN ⟨*slacken* the reins⟩

**slag** \'slag\ *n*
the waste left after the melting of ores and the separation of the metal from them

**slain** *past participle of* SLAY

**slake** \'slāk\ *vb* **slaked**; **slak·ing**
**1** QUENCH 2 ⟨*slaked* my thirst⟩
**2** to cause solid lime to heat and crumble by treating it with water

**¹slam** \'slam\ *n*
**1** a severe blow
**2** a noisy violent closing : BANG

**²slam** *vb* **slammed**; **slam·ming**
**1** to strike or beat hard
**2** to shut with noisy force : BANG ⟨*slam* the door⟩
**3** to put or place with force ⟨*slam* down the money⟩
**4** to criticize harshly

**¹slan·der** \'slan-dər\ *vb*
to make a false and spiteful statement against : DEFAME

**²slander** *n*
a false and spiteful statement that damages another person's reputation

**slang** \'slaŋ\ *n*
an informal nonstandard vocabulary composed mostly of invented words, changed words, and exaggerated or humorous figures of speech

**¹slant** \'slant\ *n*
a direction, line, or surface that is neither level nor straight up and down : SLOPE ⟨the *slant* of a ladder leaning against a wall⟩

**²slant** *vb*
to turn or incline from a straight line or level : SLOPE

**³slant** *adj*
not level or straight up and down

**slant·wise** \'slant-,wīz\ *adv or adj*
so as to slant : at a slant : in a slanting position

**¹slap** \'slap\ *vb* **slapped**; **slap·ping**
**1** to strike with or as if with the open hand
**2** to make a sound like that of slapping
**3** to put, place, or throw with careless haste or force

**²slap** *n*
**1** a quick sharp blow especially with the open hand
**2** a noise like that of a slap

**¹slash** \'slash\ *vb*
**1** to cut by sweeping blows : GASH
**2** to whip or strike with or as if with a cane
**3** to reduce sharply ⟨*slash* prices⟩

**²slash** *n*
**1** an act of slashing
**2** a long cut or slit made by slashing

**slat** \'slat\ *n*
a thin narrow strip of wood, plastic, or metal

**slate** \'slāt\ *n*
**1** ▶ a fine-grained usually bluish gray rock that splits into thin layers or plates and is used mostly for roofing and blackboards
**2** a framed piece of slate used to write on

**¹slaugh·ter** \'slȯt-ər\ *n*
**1** the act of killing
**2** the killing and dressing of animals for food
**3** destruction of many lives especially in battle

**²slaughter** *vb*
**1** ²BUTCHER 1
**2** ¹MASSACRE

**slaugh·ter·house** \'slȯt-ər-,hau̇s\ *n, pl* **slaugh·ter·hous·es** \-,hau̇-zəz\
an establishment where animals are killed and dressed for food

**Slav** \'släv, 'slav\ *n*
a person speaking a Slavic language as a native tongue

**¹slave** \'slāv\ *n*
**1** a person who is owned by another person and can be sold at the owner's will
**2** one who is like a slave in not being his or her own master ⟨a *slave* to alcohol⟩
**3** DRUDGE

---

**Word History** A long time ago the people of western Europe conquered most of the Slavic people of eastern Europe. The Slavs became slaves. The Latin word that meant "Slav" came to be used for all slaves, even if they were not Slavic. The English word *slave* came from the Latin word that meant "Slav." The word *Slav* did, too.

---

**²slave** *vb* **slaved**; **slav·ing**
to work like a slave

**slave·hold·er** \'slāv-,hōl-dər\ *n*
an owner of slaves

**slav·ery** \'slā-və-rē, 'slāv-rē\ *n*
**1** hard tiring labor : DRUDGERY
**2** the state of being a slave : BONDAGE
**3** the custom or practice of owning slaves

**slate 1**

**Slav·ic** \'slav-ik, 'släv-\ *adj*
of, relating to, or characteristic of the Slavs or their languages

**slav·ish** \'slā-vish\ *adj*
**1** of or characteristic of slaves ⟨*slavish* tasks⟩
**2** following or copying something or someone without questioning ⟨*slavish* imitators⟩

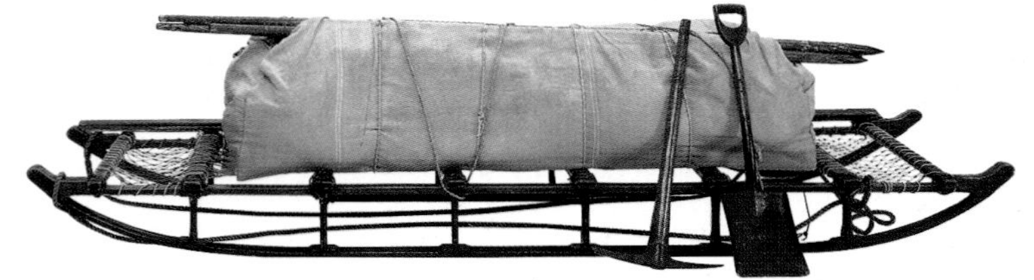

**[1]sled 1:** a sled from the early 1900s loaded with equipment

**slay** \'slā\ *vb* **slew** \'slü\; **slain** \'slān\; **slay·ing**
[1]KILL 1
**slay·er** *n*

**[1]sled** \'sled\ *n*
**1** ▲ a vehicle on runners for carrying loads especially over snow
**2** a small vehicle used mostly by children for sliding on snow and ice

**[2]sled** *vb* **sled·ded**; **sled·ding**
to ride or carry on a sled

**[1]sledge** \'slej\ *n*
SLEDGEHAMMER

**[2]sledge** *n*
a strong heavy sled

**sledge·ham·mer** \'slej-,ham-ər\ *n*
a large heavy hammer usually used with both hands

**[1]sleek** \'slēk\ *vb*
[1]SLICK

**[2]sleek** *adj*
**1** smooth and glossy as if polished ⟨*sleek* dark hair⟩
**2** having a healthy well-groomed look ⟨*sleek* cattle⟩

**[1]sleep** \'slēp\ *n*
**1** a natural periodic loss of consciousness during which the body rests and refreshes itself
**2** an inactive state (as hibernation or trance) like true sleep
**3** DEATH ⟨an animal put to *sleep*⟩
**sleep·less** \-ləs\ *adj*
**sleep·less·ness** *n*

**[2]sleep** *vb* **slept** \'slept\; **sleep·ing**
to take rest in sleep : be or lie asleep

**sleep·er** \'slē-pər\ *n*
**1** one that sleeps
**2** a horizontal beam to support something on or near ground level
**3** a railroad car with berths for sleeping

**sleeping bag** *n*
a large fabric bag that is warmly lined for sleeping outdoors or in a camp or tent

**sleep·over** \'slēp-ō-vər\ *n*
an overnight stay at another's home

**sleep·walk·er** \'slēp-,wȯ-kər\ *n*
a person who walks about while asleep
**sleep·walk·ing** \-,wȯ-king\ *n*

**sleepy** \'slē-pē\ *adj* **sleep·i·er**; **sleep·i·est**
**1** ready to fall asleep : DROWSY
**2** not active, noisy, or busy ⟨a *sleepy* town⟩
**sleep·i·ness** *n*

**[1]sleet** \'slēt\ *n*
frozen or partly frozen rain

**[2]sleet** *vb*
to shower sleet

**sleeve** \'slēv\ *n*
**1** the part of a garment covering the arm
**2** a part that fits over or around something like a sleeve
**sleeved** \'slēvd\ *adj*
**sleeve·less** \'slēv-ləs\ *adj*

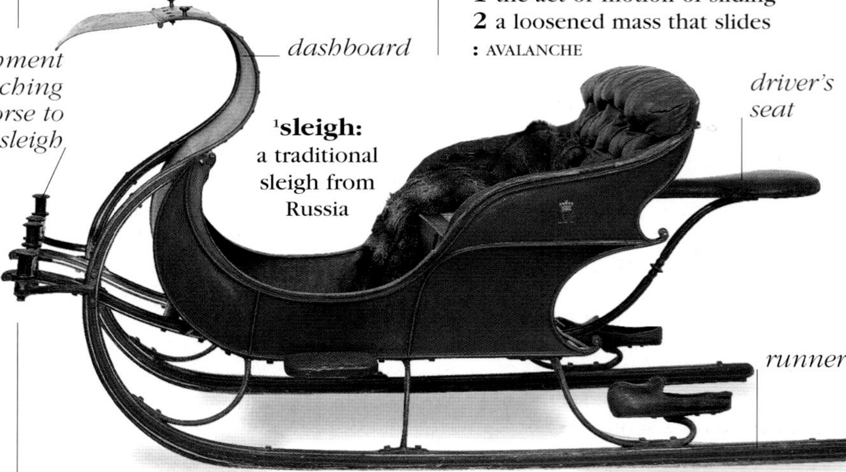


**[1]sleigh:** a traditional sleigh from Russia

**[1]sleigh** \'slā\ *n*
▲ an open usually horse-drawn vehicle with runners for use on snow or ice

**[2]sleigh** *vb*
to drive or ride in a sleigh

**sleight of hand** \,slīt-əv-'hand\
skill and quickness in the use of the hands especially in doing magic tricks

**slen·der** \'slen-dər\ *adj*
**1** gracefully thin
**2** narrow for its height
**3** very little ⟨a *slender* income⟩

**slept** *past of* SLEEP

**slew** *past of* SLAY

**[1]slice** \'slīs\ *vb* **sliced**; **slic·ing**
**1** to cut with or as if with a knife
**2** to cut into thin flat pieces ⟨*sliced* a tomato⟩

**[2]slice** *n*
a thin flat piece cut from something

**[1]slick** \'slik\ *vb*
to make sleek or smooth

**[2]slick** *adj*
**1** having a smooth surface : SLIPPERY
**2** CRAFTY, CLEVER ⟨*slick* sales tricks⟩

**slick·er** \'slik-ər\ *n*
a long loose raincoat

**[1]slide** \'slīd\ *vb* **slid** \'slid\; **slid·ing** \'slīd-ing\
**1** to move or cause to move smoothly over a surface : GLIDE ⟨*slide* over the ice⟩
**2** to move or pass smoothly without much effort ⟨*slid* into the seat⟩

**[2]slide** *n*
**1** the act or motion of sliding
**2** a loosened mass that slides : AVALANCHE
**3** a surface down which a person or thing slides
**4** something that operates or adjusts by sliding
**5** ▼ a transparent picture that can be projected on a screen
**6** a glass plate for holding an object to be examined under a microscope

**[2]slide 5**

**[1]slight** \'slīt\ *adj*
**1** not large or stout ⟨a trim *slight* figure⟩
**2** FLIMSY, FRAIL
**3** not important : TRIVIAL ⟨a *slight* wound⟩
**4** small of its kind or in amount ⟨a *slight* smell of gas⟩
**slight·ly** *adv*

**[2]slight** *vb*
to treat without proper care, respect, or courtesy ⟨felt we had been *slighted* by their actions⟩ ⟨don't *slight* your work⟩

**[3]slight** *n*
**1** an act or an instance of slighting
**2** the state or an instance of being slighted

**slight·ing** \'slīt-iŋ\ *adj*
showing a lack of respect or caring ⟨a *slighting* remark⟩

**[1]slim** \'slim\ *adj* **slim·mer**; **slim·mest**
**1** SLENDER 1
**2** very small ⟨a *slim* chance⟩

**[2]slim** *vb* **slimmed**; **slim·ming**
to make or become slender

**slime** \'slīm\ *n*
**1** soft slippery mud
**2** a soft slippery material (as on the skin of a slug or catfish)

**slimy** \'slī-mē\ *adj* **slim·i·er**; **slim·i·est**
**1** having the feel or look of slime
**2** covered with slime

**[1]sling** \'sliŋ\ *vb* **slung** \'sləŋ\; **sling·ing**
**1** to throw with a sudden sweeping motion : FLING
**2** to hurl with a sling

**[2]sling** *n*
**1** a device (as a short strap with a string attached at each end) for hurling stones
**2** SLINGSHOT
**3** a device (as a rope or chain) by which something is lifted or carried
**4** ► a hanging bandage put around the neck to hold up the arm or hand

**[3]sling** *vb* **slung** \'sləŋ\; **sling·ing**
**1** to put in or move or support with a sling
**2** to hang from two points ⟨*sling* a hammock⟩

**sling·shot** \'sliŋ-ˌshät\ *n*
a forked stick with an elastic band attached for shooting small stones

**slink** \'sliŋk\ *vb* **slunk** \'sləŋk\; **slink·ing**
to move or go by or as if by creeping especially so as not to be noticed (as in fear or shame)

**[1]slip** \'slip\ *vb* **slipped**; **slip·ping**
**1** to move easily and smoothly ⟨*slipped* the knife into the sheath⟩
**2** to move quietly : STEAL ⟨*slipped* from the room⟩
**3** to pass or let pass or escape without being noted, used, or done ⟨time *slipped* by⟩
**4** to get away from ⟨*slipped* the pursuers⟩
**5** to escape the attention of ⟨it just *slipped* my mind⟩
**6** to slide into or out of place or away from a support ⟨*slip* the bolt⟩ ⟨the book *slipped* out of my hand⟩
**7** to slide on a slippery surface so as to lose one's balance ⟨*slipped* on the wet floor⟩
**8** to put on or take off a garment quickly and carelessly ⟨*slipped* out of the coat⟩

**[2]slip** *n*
**1** a ramp where ships can be landed or repaired
**2** a place for a ship between two piers
**3** a secret or quick departure or escape ⟨gave them the *slip*⟩
**4** a small mistake : BLUNDER
**5** the act or an instance of slipping down or out of place ⟨a *slip* on the ice⟩
**6** a sudden mishap
**7** a fall from some level or standard : DECLINE ⟨a *slip* in stock prices⟩

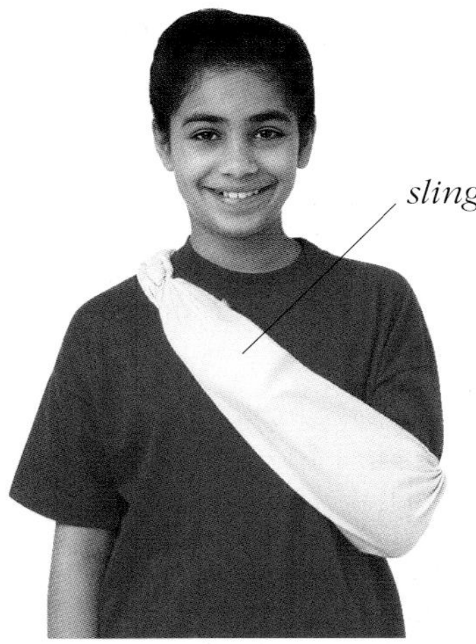

**[2]sling 4:** a girl wearing a sling

**8** an undergarment made in dress length with straps over the shoulders
**9** PILLOWCASE

**[3]slip** *n*
**1** a piece of a plant cut for planting or grafting
**2** a long narrow piece of material
**3** a piece of paper used for some record ⟨a sales *slip*⟩
**4** a young and slender person

**[4]slip** *vb* **slipped**; **slip·ping**
to take slips from (a plant)

**slip·cov·er** \'slip-ˌkəv-ər\ *n*
a cover (as for a sofa or chair) that may be slipped off and on

**slip·knot** \'slip-ˌnät\ *n*
a knot made by tying the end of a line around the line itself to form a loop so that the size of the loop may be changed by slipping the knot

**slip·per** \'slip-ər\ *n*
▼ a light low shoe that is easily slipped on the foot

**slipper:** a pair of slippers

**slip·pery** \'slip-ə-rē\ *adj* **slip·per·i·er**; **slip·per·i·est**
**1** having a surface smooth or wet enough to make something slide or make one lose one's footing or hold ⟨fell on the *slippery* walk⟩
**2** not to be trusted : TRICKY

**slip·shod** \'slip-'shäd\ *adj*
very careless : SLOVENLY ⟨their work was *slipshod*⟩

**slip up** *vb*
to make a mistake

**[1]slit** \'slit\ *n*
a long narrow cut or opening

**[2]slit** *vb* **slit**; **slit·ting**
to make a long narrow cut in : SLASH

**slith·er** \'sli<u>th</u>-ər\ *vb*
[1]GLIDE ⟨a snake *slithering* along⟩

**[1]sliv·er** \'sliv-ər\ *n*
a long slender piece cut or torn off : SPLINTER

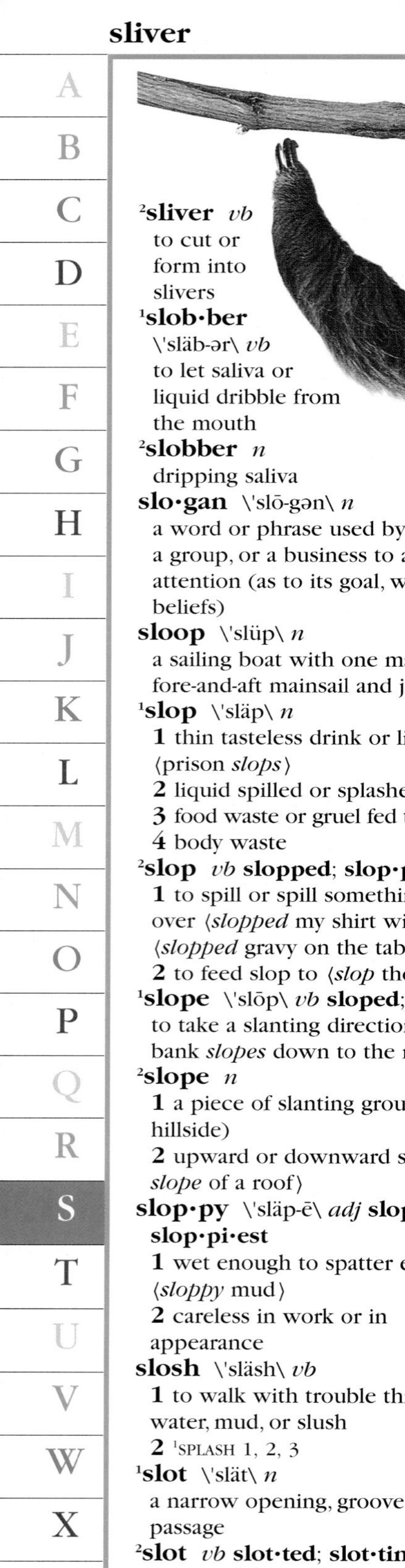

**sloth 2:** a three-toed sloth

[2]**sliver** *vb*
to cut or form into slivers

[1]**slob·ber** \'släb-ər\ *vb*
to let saliva or liquid dribble from the mouth

[2]**slobber** *n*
dripping saliva

**slo·gan** \'slō-gən\ *n*
a word or phrase used by a party, a group, or a business to attract attention (as to its goal, worth, or beliefs)

**sloop** \'slüp\ *n*
a sailing boat with one mast and a fore-and-aft mainsail and jib

[1]**slop** \'släp\ *n*
**1** thin tasteless drink or liquid food ⟨prison *slops*⟩
**2** liquid spilled or splashed
**3** food waste or gruel fed to animals
**4** body waste

[2]**slop** *vb* **slopped**; **slop·ping**
**1** to spill or spill something on or over ⟨*slopped* my shirt with gravy⟩ ⟨*slopped* gravy on the table⟩
**2** to feed slop to ⟨*slop* the pigs⟩

[1]**slope** \'slōp\ *vb* **sloped**; **slop·ing**
to take a slanting direction ⟨the bank *slopes* down to the river⟩

[2]**slope** *n*
**1** a piece of slanting ground (as a hillside)
**2** upward or downward slant ⟨the *slope* of a roof⟩

**slop·py** \'släp-ē\ *adj* **slop·pi·er**; **slop·pi·est**
**1** wet enough to spatter easily ⟨*sloppy* mud⟩
**2** careless in work or in appearance

**slosh** \'släsh\ *vb*
**1** to walk with trouble through water, mud, or slush
**2** [1]SPLASH 1, 2, 3

[1]**slot** \'slät\ *n*
a narrow opening, groove, or passage

[2]**slot** *vb* **slot·ted**; **slot·ting**
to cut a slot in

**sloth** \'slȯth, 'slōth\ *n*
**1** the state of being lazy
**2** ▲ an animal of Central and South America that hangs back downward and moves slowly along the branches of trees on whose leaves, twigs, and fruits it feeds

[1]**slouch** \'slau̇ch\ *n*
**1** a lazy worthless person
**2** a lazy drooping way of standing, sitting, or walking

[2]**slouch** *vb*
to walk, stand, or sit with a slouch

**slough** \'slü, 'slau̇\ *n*
a wet marshy or muddy place

**slov·en·ly** \'sləv-ən-lē\ *adj*
personally untidy

[1]**slow** \'slō\ *adj*
**1** not as smart or as quick to understand as most people
**2** not easily aroused or excited ⟨*slow* to anger⟩
**3** moving, flowing, or going at less than the usual speed ⟨a *slow* stream⟩ ⟨*slow* music⟩
**4** indicating less than is correct ⟨my watch is five minutes *slow*⟩
**5** not lively or active ⟨business was *slow*⟩ ⟨a very *slow* party⟩
**slow·ly** *adv*
**slow·ness** *n*

[2]**slow** *adv*
in a slow way

[3]**slow** *vb*
to make or go slow or slower

**slow·poke** \'slō-,pōk\ *n*
a very slow person

**sludge** \'sləj\ *n*
a soft muddy mass resulting from sewage treatment

[1]**slug**

[1]**slug** \'sləg\ *n*
▶ a long wormlike land mollusk that is related to the snails but has an undeveloped shell or none at all

[2]**slug** *n*
**1** a small piece of shaped metal
**2** BULLET
**3** a metal disk often used in place of a coin

[3]**slug** *n*
a hard blow especially with the fist

[4]**slug** *vb* **slugged**; **slug·ging**
to hit hard with the fist or with a bat

**slug·gard** \'sləg-ərd\ *n*
a lazy person

**slug·ger** \'sləg-ər\ *n*
a boxer or baseball batter who hits hard

**slug·gish** \'sləg-ish\ *adj*
slow in movement or reaction
**slug·gish·ly** *adv*
**slug·gish·ness** *n*

[1]**sluice** \'slüs\ *n*
**1** ▼ an artificial passage for water with a gate for controlling its flow or changing its direction
**2** a device for controlling the flow of water
**3** a sloping trough for washing ore or for floating logs

[2]**sluice** *vb* **sluiced**; **sluic·ing**
**1** to wash in a stream of water running through a sluice
**2** [3]FLUSH 2, DRENCH

[1]**sluice 1:** a sluice in a canal

**slum** \'sləm\ *n*
a very poor crowded dirty section especially of a city

[1]**slum·ber** \'sləm-bər\ *vb*
to be asleep

[2]**slumber** *n*
[1]SLEEP

[1]**slump** \'sləmp\ *vb*
**1** to drop or slide down suddenly **:** COLLAPSE ⟨*slumped* into a chair⟩
**2** [2]SLOUCH ⟨don't *slump* when you walk⟩
**3** to drop sharply ⟨prices *slumped*⟩

[2]**slump** *n*
a big or continued drop especially in prices, business, or performance

**slung** *past of* SLING

**slunk** *past of* SLINK

[1]**slur** \'slər\ *n*
**1** an insulting remark
**2** STIGMA 1, STAIN

[2]**slur** *vb* **slurred**; **slur·ring**
**1** to pass over without proper mention or stress
**2** to run one's speech together so that it is hard to understand

[3]**slur** *n*
a slurred way of talking

**slush** \'sləsh\ *n*
partly melted snow

**sly** \'slī\ *adj* **sli·er** *or* **sly·er**; **sli·est** *or* **sly·est**
**1** both clever and tricky
**2** being sneaky and dishonest
**3** MISCHIEVOUS 3
**sly·ly** *adv*
**sly·ness** *n*

---

**Synonyms** SLY, CUNNING, and TRICKY mean tending to use crooked methods to get what one wants. SLY suggests secrecy and dishonesty as well as skill in hiding one's goals and methods ⟨a *sly* trader of horses⟩. CUNNING suggests using one's intelligence in order to achieve one's ends ⟨the *cunning* lawyer tried every trick⟩. TRICKY, unlike *cunning*, suggests having more plain dishonesty than skill ⟨the *tricky* politicians in this town⟩.

---

**on the sly** so as not to be seen or caught **:** SECRETLY

[1]**smack** \'smak\ *n*
a slight taste, trace, or touch of something

[2]**smack** *vb*
to have a flavor, trace, or suggestion ⟨it *smacks* of garlic⟩

[3]**smack** *vb*
**1** to close and open the lips noisily especially in eating
**2** to kiss usually loudly or hard
**3** to make or give a smack **:** SLAP

[4]**smack** *n*
**1** a quick sharp noise made by the lips (as in enjoyment of some taste)
**2** a loud kiss
**3** a noisy slap or blow

[1]**small** \'smȯl\ *adj*
**1** little in size
**2** few in numbers or members ⟨a *small* crowd⟩
**3** little in amount ⟨a *small* supply⟩
**4** not very much ⟨*small* success⟩
**5** UNIMPORTANT
**6** operating on a limited scale ⟨*small* dealers⟩
**7** lacking in strength ⟨a *small* voice⟩ ⟨*small* beer⟩
**8** not generous **:** MEAN
**9** made up of units of little worth ⟨*small* change⟩
**10** [1]HUMBLE 3, MODEST ⟨a *small* beginning⟩
**11** lowered in pride
**12** being letters that are not capitals
**small·ness** *n*

[2]**small** *n*
a part smaller and usually narrower than the rest ⟨the *small* of the back⟩

**small intestine** *n*
the long narrow upper part of the intestine in which food is mostly digested and from which digested food is absorbed into the body

**small·pox** \'smȯl-ˌpäks\ *n*
an acute disease in which fever and skin eruptions occur and which is believed to be extinct due to vaccination against the virus causing it

[1]**smart** \'smärt\ *adj*
**1** BRISK, SPIRITED ⟨walking at a *smart* pace⟩
**2** quick to learn or do **:** BRIGHT
**3** SAUCY 1
**4** stylish in appearance ⟨a *smart* dresser⟩
**smart·ly** *adv*
**smart·ness** *n*

[2]**smart** *vb*
**1** to cause or feel a sharp stinging pain
**2** to feel distress ⟨*smart* under criticism⟩

[3]**smart** *n*
a stinging pain usually in one spot

**smart al·eck** \'smärt-ˌal-ik\ *n*
a person who likes to show off

[1]**smash** \'smash\ *n*
**1** a violent blow or attack
**2** the action or sound of smashing ⟨broke the plate with a *smash*⟩
**3** a striking success ⟨a box office *smash*⟩

[2]**smash** *vb*
**1** to break in pieces **:** SHATTER
**2** to drive or move violently ⟨the ball *smashed* through the window⟩
**3** to destroy completely **:** WRECK
**4** to go to pieces **:** COLLAPSE

[1]**smear** \'smir\ *n*
a spot or streak made by or as if by an oily or sticky substance **:** SMUDGE

[2]**smear** *vb*
**1** to spread or soil with something oily or sticky **:** DAUB
**2** to spread over a surface
**3** to blacken the good name of

[1]**smell** \'smel\ *vb* **smelled** \'smeld\ *or* **smelt** \'smelt\; **smell·ing**
**1** to become aware of the odor of by means of sense organs located in the nose
**2** to detect by means or use of the sense of smell
**3** to have or give off an odor

[2]**smell** *n*
**1** the sense by which a person or animal becomes aware of an odor
**2** the sensation one gets through the sense of smell **:** ODOR, SCENT

[1]**smelt** \'smelt\ *n, pl* **smelts** *or* **smelt**
▼ a small food fish that looks like the related trouts, lives in coastal sea waters, and swims up rivers to spawn

[1]**smelt**

[2]**smelt** *vb*
to melt (as ore) in order to separate the metal **:** REFINE

**smelt·er** \'smel-tər\ *n*
**1** a person whose work or business is smelting
**2** a place where ores or metals are smelted

**[1]smile** \'smīl\ *vb* **smiled**; **smil·ing**
**1** to have, produce, or show a smile
**2** to look with amusement or scorn
**3** to express by a smile ⟨*smile* approval⟩

**[2]smile** *n*
▼ an expression on the face in which the lips curve upward especially to show amusement or pleasure

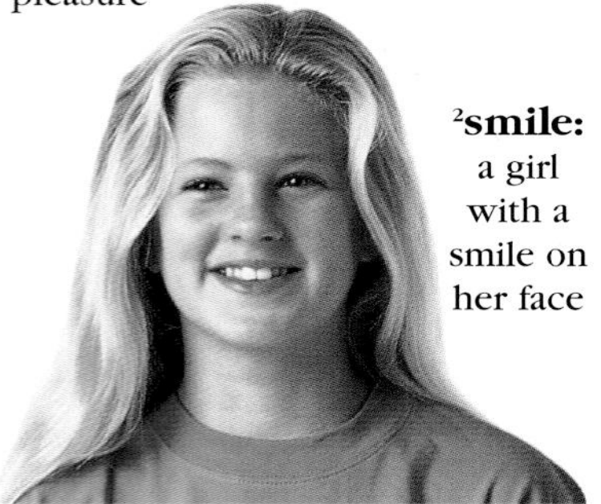

**[2]smile:** a girl with a smile on her face

**smite** \'smīt\ *vb* **smote** \'smōt\; **smit·ten** \'smit-n\; **smit·ing** \'smīt-ing\
to strike hard especially with the hand or a weapon

**smith** \'smith\ *n*
**1** a worker in metals
**2** BLACKSMITH

**smithy** \'smith-ē\ *n, pl* **smith·ies**
the workshop of a smith and especially of a blacksmith

**smock** \'smäk\ *n*
a loose outer garment worn especially for protection of clothing

**smog** \'smäg\ *n*
a fog made heavier and thicker by the action of sunlight on air polluted by smoke and automobile fumes

**[1]smoke** \'smōk\ *n*
**1** the gas of burning materials (as coal, wood, or tobacco) made visible by particles of carbon floating in it
**2** a mass or column of smoke : SMUDGE
**3** the act of smoking tobacco

**[2]smoke** *vb* **smoked**; **smok·ing**
**1** to give out smoke
**2** to draw in and breathe out the fumes of burning tobacco
**3** to drive (as mosquitoes) away by smoke
**4** to expose (as meat) to smoke to give flavor and keep from spoiling
**smok·er** *n*

**smoke de·tec·tor** \-di-'tek-tər\ *n*
a device that sounds an alarm automatically when it detects smoke

**smoke·house** \'smōk-,haủs\ *n, pl* **smoke·hous·es** \-,haủ-zəz\
a building where meat or fish is cured with smoke

**smoke·stack** \'smōk-,stak\ *n*
a large chimney or a pipe for carrying away smoke (as on a factory or ship)

**smoky** \'smō-kē\ *adj* **smok·i·er**; **smok·i·est**
**1** giving off smoke especially in large amounts ⟨*smoky* stoves⟩
**2** like that of smoke ⟨a *smoky* flavor⟩
**3** filled with or darkened by smoke ⟨a *smoky* room⟩

**[1]smol·der** *or* **smoul·der** \'smōl-dər\ *n*
a slow often smoky fire

**[2]smolder** *or* **smoulder** *vb*
**1** to burn slowly usually with smoke and without flame ⟨a fire *smoldering* in the grate⟩
**2** to burn inwardly ⟨anger *smoldered* in my heart⟩

**[1]smooth** \'smüth\ *adj*
**1** not rough or uneven in surface ⟨a *smooth* board⟩
**2** not hairy
**3** free from difficulties or things in the way ⟨a *smooth* path⟩
**4** moving or progressing without breaks, sudden changes, or shifts ⟨a *smooth* stream⟩ ⟨*smooth* speech⟩
**5** able to make things seem right or easy or good : GLIB ⟨a *smooth* excuse⟩
**smooth·ly** *adv*
**smooth·ness** *n*

**[2]smooth** *vb*
**1** to make smooth
**2** [1]POLISH 2, REFINE ⟨*smooth* one's style in writing⟩
**3** to free from trouble or difficulty ⟨*smoothed* the way for us⟩

**smote** *past of* SMITE

**smoth·er** \'sməth-ər\ *vb*
**1** to overcome by depriving of air or exposing to smoke or fumes : SUFFOCATE
**2** to become suffocated
**3** to cover up : SUPPRESS ⟨*smother* a yawn⟩
**4** to cover thickly ⟨steak *smothered* with onions⟩

**[1]smudge** \'sməj\ *vb* **smudged**; **smudg·ing**
to soil or blur by rubbing or smearing

**[2]smudge** *n*
**1** a blurred spot or streak : SMEAR
**2** a smoky fire (as to drive away mosquitoes or protect fruit from frost)

**smug** \'sməg\ *adj* **smug·ger**; **smug·gest**
very satisfied with oneself
**smug·ly** *adv*

**smug·gle** \'sməg-əl\ *vb* **smug·gled**; **smug·gling**
**1** to export or import secretly and unlawfully especially to avoid paying taxes ⟨*smuggle* jewels⟩
**2** to take or bring secretly
**smug·gler** \'sməg-lər\ *n*

**smut** \'smət\ *n*
**1** something (as a particle of soot) that soils or blackens
**2** a destructive disease of plants (as cereal grasses) in which plant parts (as seeds) are replaced by masses of dark spores of the fungus that causes the disease
**3** a fungus that causes smut

**snack** \'snak\ *n*
a light meal : LUNCH

**[1]snag** \'snag\ *n*
**1** a stump or stub of a tree branch especially when hidden under water
**2** a rough or broken part sticking out from something
**3** an unexpected difficulty

**[2]snag** *vb* **snagged**; **snag·ging**
to catch or damage on or as if on a snag ⟨*snag* one's clothes⟩

**snail** \'snāl\ *n*
**1** ▼ a small slow-moving mollusk with a spiral shell into which it can draw itself for safety
**2** a person who moves slowly

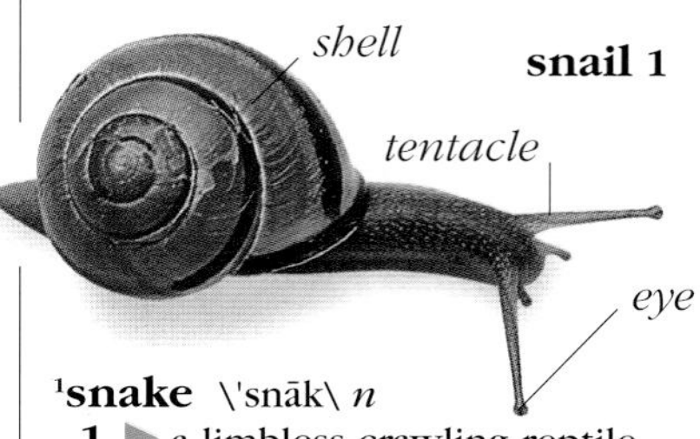


**snail 1**

**[1]snake** \'snāk\ *n*
**1** ► a limbless crawling reptile that has a long body and lives usually on large insects or small animals and birds
**2** a horrid or treacherous person

## [1]snake 1

There are over 2,500 species of snake. Snakes capture their prey by injecting poison into it, suffocating it, or swallowing it alive. They use their forked tongue to smell, taste, and touch. Some snakes can dislocate their jaw to swallow large prey.

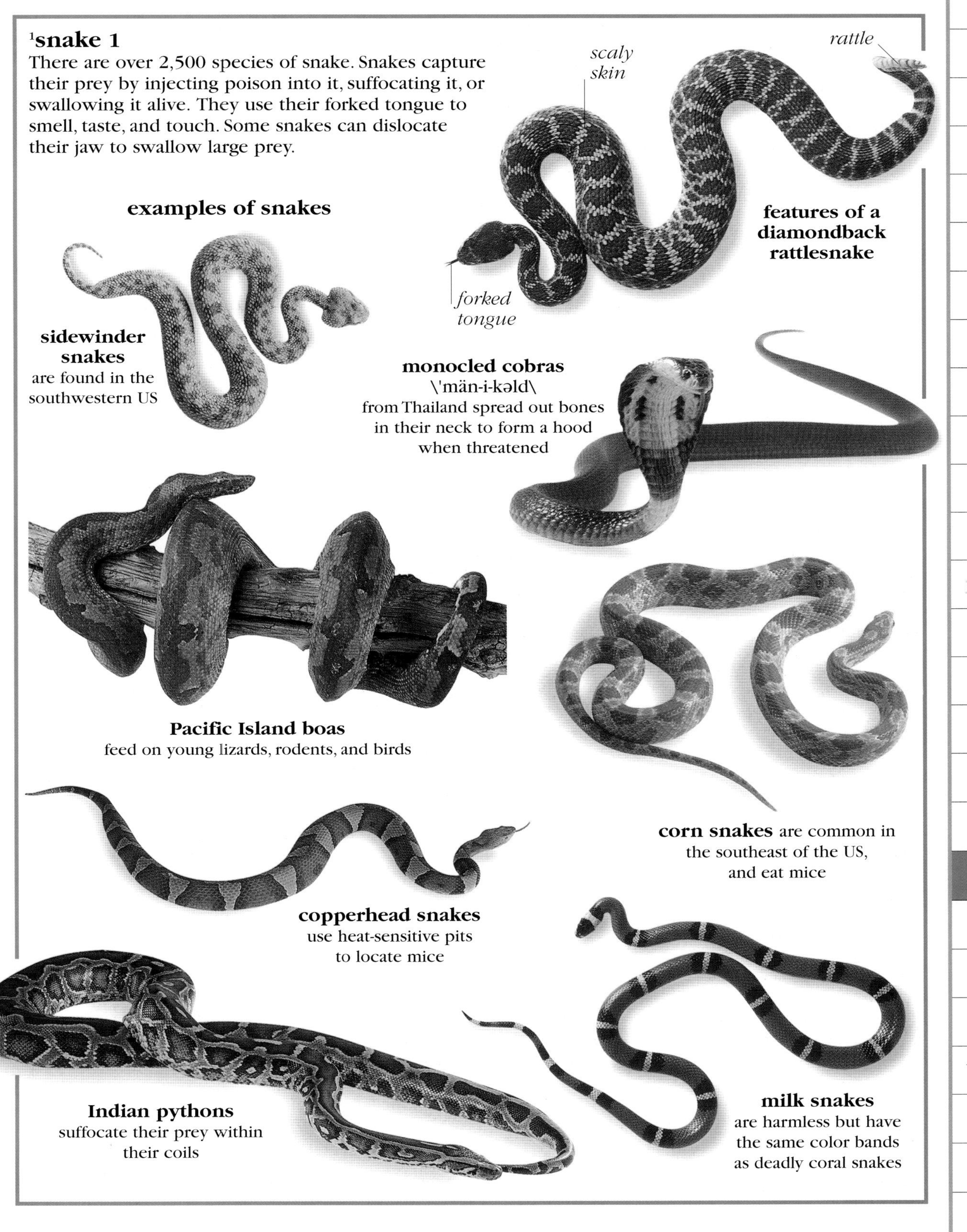


**features of a diamondback rattlesnake**

**examples of snakes**

**sidewinder snakes** are found in the southwestern US

**monocled cobras** \'män-i-kəld\ from Thailand spread out bones in their neck to form a hood when threatened

**Pacific Island boas** feed on young lizards, rodents, and birds

**corn snakes** are common in the southeast of the US, and eat mice

**copperhead snakes** use heat-sensitive pits to locate mice

**Indian pythons** suffocate their prey within their coils

**milk snakes** are harmless but have the same color bands as deadly coral snakes

A B C D E F G H I J K L M N O P Q R S T U V W X Y Z

[2]**snake** *vb* **snaked**; **snak·ing**
to crawl, wind, or move like a snake

**snaky** \'snā-kē\ *adj* **snak·i·er**; **snak·i·est**
**1** of or like a snake
**2** full of snakes

[1]**snap** \'snap\ *vb* **snapped**; **snap·ping**
**1** to grasp or grasp at something suddenly with the mouth or teeth ⟨fish *snapping* at the bait⟩
**2** to grasp at something eagerly ⟨*snapped* at the chance to go⟩
**3** to get, take, or buy at once ⟨*snap* up a bargain⟩
**4** to speak or utter sharply or irritably ⟨*snap* out a command⟩
**5** to break or break apart suddenly and often with a cracking noise ⟨the branch *snapped*⟩
**6** to make or cause to make a sharp or crackling sound ⟨*snap* a whip⟩
**7** to close or fit in place with a quick movement ⟨the lid *snapped* shut⟩
**8** to put into or remove from a position suddenly or with a snapping sound ⟨*snap* off a switch⟩
**9** to close by means of snaps or fasteners
**10** to act or be acted on with snap ⟨*snapped* to attention⟩
**11** to take a snapshot of

[2]**snap** *n*
**1** the act or sound of snapping
**2** something that is easy and presents no problems ⟨that job is a *snap*⟩
**3** a small amount : BIT ⟨doesn't care a *snap*⟩
**4** a sudden spell of harsh weather ⟨a cold *snap*⟩
**5** a catch or fastening that closes or locks with a click ⟨the *snap* on a purse⟩
**6** a thin brittle cookie
**7** SNAPSHOT
**8** smartness of movement or speech : ENERGY

[3]**snap** *adj*
**1** made suddenly or without careful thought ⟨a *snap* judgment⟩
**2** closing with a click or by means of a device that snaps ⟨a *snap* lock⟩
**3** very easy ⟨a *snap* course⟩

**snap·drag·on** \'snap-,drag-ən\ *n*
a garden plant with stalks of mostly white, pink, crimson, or yellow flowers with two lips

**snap·per** \'snap-ər\ *n*
**1** one that snaps
**2** SNAPPING TURTLE
**3** an active sea fish important for sport and food

**snap·ping tur·tle** \,snap-ing-'tərt-l\ *n*
▶ a large American turtle that catches its prey with a snap of the powerful jaws

**snapping turtle:** an alligator snapper

**snap·py** \'snap-ē\ *adj* **snap·pi·er**; **snap·pi·est**
**1** full of life : LIVELY
**2** briskly cold : CHILLY
**3** STYLISH, SMART ⟨a *snappy* suit⟩

**snap·shot** \'snap-,shät\ *n*
a photograph taken usually with an inexpensive hand-held camera

[1]**snare** \'snaər, 'sneər\ *n*
**1** a trap (as a noose) for catching small animals and birds
**2** something by which one is entangled, trapped, or deceived

[2]**snare** *vb* **snared**; **snar·ing**
to catch or entangle by or as if by use of a snare

**snare drum** *n*
▶ a small drum with two heads that has strings stretched across its lower head to produce a rattling sound

[1]**snarl** \'snärl\ *vb*
to get into a tangle

[2]**snarl** *n*
**1** a tangle usually of hairs or thread : KNOT
**2** a tangled situation ⟨a traffic *snarl*⟩

[3]**snarl** *vb*
**1** to growl with a showing of teeth
**2** to speak in an angry way
**3** to utter with a growl

[4]**snarl** *n*
an angry growl

[1]**snatch** \'snach\ *vb*
to take hold of or try to take hold of something quickly or suddenly

[2]**snatch** *n*
**1** an act of snatching
**2** a brief period ⟨slept in *snatches*⟩
**3** something brief, hurried, or in small bits ⟨*snatches* of old songs⟩

[1]**sneak** \'snēk\ *vb* **sneaked** \'snēkt\ *or* **snuck** \'snək\; **sneak·ing**
to move, act, bring, or put in a sly or secret way

[2]**sneak** *n*
**1** a person who acts in a sly or secret way
**2** the act or an instance of sneaking

**sneak·er** \'snē-kər\ *n*
a sports shoe with a rubber sole

**sneaky** \'snē-kē\ *adj* **sneak·i·er**; **sneak·i·est**
behaving in a sly or secret way or showing that kind of behavior ⟨a *sneaky* person⟩ ⟨a *sneaky* trick⟩

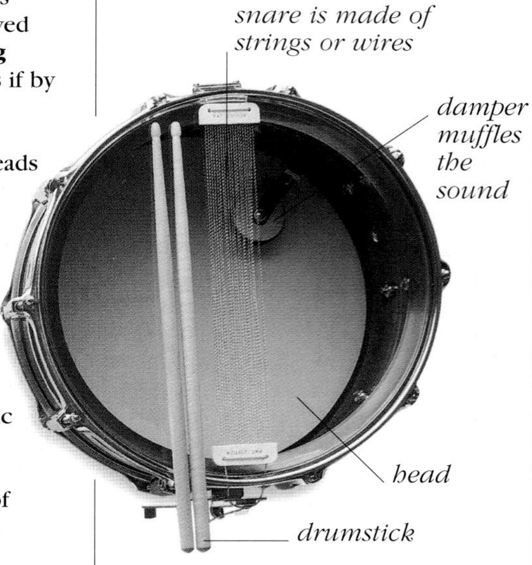

*snare is made of strings or wires*
*damper muffles the sound*
*head*
*drumstick*

**snare drum:** the underside of a snare drum, with the bottom head removed

**[1]sneer** \'snir\ *vb*
**1** to smile or laugh while making a face that shows scorn
**2** to speak or write in a scorning way

**[2]sneer** *n*
a sneering expression or remark

**[1]sneeze** \'snēz\ *vb* **sneezed**; **sneez·ing**
to force out the breath in a sudden loud violent action

**[2]sneeze** *n*
an act or instance of sneezing

**[1]snick·er** \'snik-ər\ *vb*
to give a small and often mean or sly laugh

**[2]snicker** *n*
an act or sound of snickering

**[1]sniff** \'snif\ *vb*
**1** to draw air into the nose in short breaths loud enough to be heard
**2** to show scorn ⟨*sniffed* at simple jobs⟩
**3** to smell by taking short breaths ⟨*sniff* perfume⟩

**[2]sniff** *n*
**1** the act or sound of sniffing
**2** an odor or amount sniffed

**snif·fle** \'snif-əl\ *vb* **snif·fled**; **snif·fling**
**1** to sniff repeatedly
**2** to speak with sniffs ⟨a child *sniffling* about where it hurt⟩

**snif·fles** \'snif-əlz\ *n pl*
a common cold in which the main symptom is a runny nose

**[1]snig·ger** \'snig-ər\ *vb*
[1]SNICKER

**[2]snigger** *n*
[2]SNICKER

**[1]snip** \'snip\ *n*
**1** a small piece that is snipped off ⟨picked up all the *snips* of paper⟩
**2** an act or sound of snipping

**[2]snip** *vb* **snipped**; **snip·ping**
to cut or cut off with or as if with shears or scissors

**[1]snipe** \'snīp\ *n, pl* **snipes** *or* **snipe**
a game bird that lives in marshes and has a long straight bill

**[2]snipe** *vb* **sniped**; **snip·ing**
to shoot from a hiding place (as at individual enemy soldiers)
**snip·er** *n*

**snob** \'snäb\ *n*
a person who imitates, admires, or wants to be friends with people of higher position and looks down on or avoids those felt to be less important

**snout 1**

**snob·bish** \'snäb-ish\ *adj*
of, relating to, or being a snob

**[1]snoop** \'snüp\ *vb*
to look or search especially in a sneaking or nosy way

**[2]snoop** *n*
SNOOPER

**snoop·er** \'snü-pər\ *n*
a person who snoops

**snoot** \'snüt\ *n*
[1]NOSE 1

**[1]snooze** \'snüz\ *vb* **snoozed**; **snooz·ing**
to take a nap

**[2]snooze** *n*
a short sleep **:** NAP

**[1]snore** \'snōr\ *vb* **snored**; **snor·ing**
to breathe with a rough hoarse noise while sleeping

**[2]snore** *n*
an act or sound of snoring ⟨kept awake by his *snores*⟩

**[1]snor·kel** \'snȯr-kəl\ *n*
a tube used by swimmers for breathing with the head underwater

**[2]snorkel** *vb*
to swim underwater using a snorkel

**[1]snort** \'snȯrt\ *vb*
to force air through the nose with a rough harsh sound

**[2]snort** *n*
an act or sound of snorting

**snout** \'snau̇t\ *n*
**1** ▲ a long projecting nose (as of a pig)
**2** the front part of a head (as of a weevil) that sticks out like the snout of a pig
**3** a usually large and ugly human nose

**[1]snow** \'snō\ *n*
**1** small white crystals of ice formed directly from the water vapor of the air
**2** a fall of snowflakes **:** a mass of snowflakes fallen to earth ⟨over a foot of *snow*⟩

**[2]snow** *vb*
**1** to fall or cause to fall in or as snow ⟨it's *snowing*⟩
**2** to cover or shut in with snow

**snow·ball** \'snō-,bȯl\ *n*
a round mass of snow pressed or rolled together

**snow·bird** \'snō-,bərd\ *n*
a small bird (as a junco) seen mostly in winter

**snow–blind** \'snō-,blīnd\ *or* **snow–blind·ed** \-,blīn-dəd\ *adj*
having the eyes red and swollen and unable to see from the effect of glare reflected from snow
**snow blindness** *n*

**snow·blow·er** \'snō-,blō-ər\ *n*
a machine in which rotating parts pick up snow and throw it aside

**snow·board** \'snō-,bōrd\ *n*
a board like a wide ski ridden in a surfing position over snow
**snow·board·er** \'snō-,bōrd-ər\ *n*
**snowboarding** *n*

**snow·bound** \'snō-'bau̇nd\ *adj*
shut in or blocked by snow ⟨*snowbound* mountain passes⟩

**snow·drift** \'snō-,drift\ *n*
a bank of drifted snow

**snow·fall** \'snō-,fȯl\ *n*
**1** a fall of snow
**2** the amount of snow that falls in a single storm or in a certain period

**snow·flake** \'snō-,flāk\ *n*
▼ a snow crystal **:** a small mass of snow crystals

**snowflake:**
magnified view of a snowflake

snowmobile

**snow·man** \'snō-,man\ *n, pl* **snow·men** \-,men\
snow shaped to look like a person

**snow·mo·bile** \'snō-mō-,bēl\ *n*
▲ a motor vehicle designed for travel on snow

**snow·plow** \'snō-,plaù\ *n*
any of various devices used for clearing away snow

[1]**snow·shoe** \'snō-,shü\ *n*
a light frame of wood strung with a net (as of rawhide) and worn under one's shoe to prevent sinking into soft snow

[2]**snowshoe** *vb* **snow·shoed**; **snow·shoe·ing**
to go on snowshoes

**snow·storm** \'snō-,stȯrm\ *n*
a storm of falling snow

**snow thrower** *n*
SNOWBLOWER

**snowy** \'snō-ē\ *adj* **snow·i·er**; **snow·i·est**
**1** having or covered with snow
**2** white like snow

[1]**snub** \'snəb\ *vb* **snubbed**; **snub·bing**
to ignore or treat rudely on purpose

[2]**snub** *n*
an act or an instance of snubbing

**snub–nosed** \'snəb-'nōzd\ *adj*
having a stubby and usually slightly turned-up nose

**snuck** *past of* SNEAK

[1]**snuff** \'snəf\ *vb*
**1** to cut or pinch off the burned end of the wick of a candle
**2** EXTINGUISH 1

[2]**snuff** *vb*
to draw through or into the nose with force

[3]**snuff** *n*
powdered tobacco that is chewed, placed against the gums, or drawn in through the nostrils

[1]**snuf·fle** \'snəf-əl\ *vb* **snuf·fled**; **snuf·fling**
to breathe noisily through a nose that is partly blocked

[2]**snuffle** *n*
the sound made in snuffling

**snug** \'snəg\ *adj* **snug·ger**; **snug·gest**
**1** fitting closely and comfortably ⟨a *snug* coat⟩
**2** COMFORTABLE 1, COZY ⟨a *snug* corner⟩
**3** offering protection or a hiding place ⟨a *snug* harbor⟩
**snug·ly** *adv*

**snug·gle** \'snəg-əl\ *vb* **snug·gled**; **snug·gling**
**1** to curl up comfortably or cozily : CUDDLE
**2** to pull in close to one

[1]**so** \'sō\ *adv*
**1** in the way indicated ⟨said I'd go and did *so*⟩
**2** in the same way : ALSO ⟨they wrote well and *so* did you⟩
**3** [1]THEN 2 ⟨and *so* to bed⟩
**4** to an indicated extent or way ⟨had never felt *so* well⟩
**5** to a great degree : VERY, EXTREMELY ⟨loved them *so*⟩
**6** to a definite but not specified amount ⟨can do only *so* much⟩
**7** most certainly : INDEED ⟨you did *so* say it⟩
**8** THEREFORE ⟨is honest and *so* returned the wallet⟩

[2]**so** *conj*
**1** in order that ⟨be quiet *so* I can sleep⟩
**2** and therefore ⟨we were hungry, *so* we ate⟩

[3]**so** \'sō\ *pron*
**1** the same : THAT ⟨they told me *so*⟩
**2** approximately that ⟨I'd been there a month or *so*⟩

[1]**soak** \'sōk\ *vb*
**1** to lie covered with liquid
**2** to place in a liquid to wet or as if to wet thoroughly
**3** to enter or pass through something by or as if by tiny holes : PERMEATE
**4** to draw out by or as if by soaking in a liquid ⟨*soak* the dirt from clothes⟩
**5** to draw in by or as if by absorption ⟨*soaked* up the sunshine⟩

[2]**soak** *n*
the act or process of soaking : the state of being soaked

[1]**soap** \'sōp\ *n*
a substance that is usually made by the action of alkali on fat, dissolves in water, and is used for washing

[2]**soap** *vb*
to rub soap over or into something

**soap·stone** \'sōp-,stōn\ *n*
► a soft stone having a soapy or greasy feeling

**soapstone:** an owl carved from soapstone in a traditional Eskimo style

**soap·suds** \'sōp-,sədz\ *n pl*
SUDS

**soapy** \'sō-pē\ *adj* **soap·i·er**; **soap·i·est**
**1** smeared with or full of soap
**2** containing or combined with soap
**3** like soap

**soar** \'sōr\ *vb*
to fly or sail through the air often at a great height

[1]**sob** \'säb\ *vb* **sobbed**; **sob·bing**
**1** to cry or express with gasps and catching in the throat ⟨*sobbed* out the story⟩
**2** to make a sobbing sound ⟨the wind *sobs* in the trees⟩

[2]**sob** *n*
**1** an act of sobbing
**2** a sound of or like that of sobbing

[1]**so·ber** \'sō-bər\ *adj*
**1** not drinking too much : TEMPERATE
**2** not drunk
**3** having a serious attitude : SOLEMN ⟨a *sober* child⟩
**4** having a quiet color ⟨*sober* clothes⟩

**5** not fanciful or imagined ⟨a matter of *sober* fact⟩

[2]**sober** *vb*
to make or become sober

**so–called** \'sō-'kȯld\ *adj*
usually but often wrongly so named ⟨my *so-called* friend⟩

**soc·cer** \'säk-ər\ *n*
▼ a game played between two teams of eleven players in which a round inflated ball is moved toward a goal usually by kicking

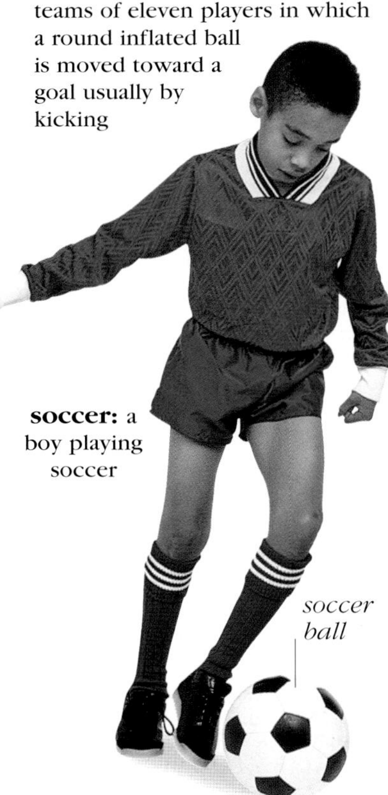

**soccer:** a boy playing soccer

**so·cia·ble** \'sō-shə-bəl\ *adj*
**1** liking to be around other people **:** FRIENDLY
**2** involving pleasant social relations ⟨enjoyed a *sociable* evening⟩

[1]**so·cial** \'sō-shəl\ *adj*
**1** FRIENDLY 1, SOCIABLE ⟨a *social* evening⟩
**2** of or relating to human beings as a group ⟨*social* institutions⟩
**3** living or growing naturally in groups or communities ⟨bees are *social* insects⟩
**4** of, relating to, or based on rank in a particular society ⟨different *social* circles⟩
**5** of or relating to fashionable society ⟨a *social* leader⟩
**so·cial·ly** *adv*

[2]**social** *n*
a friendly gathering usually for a special reason ⟨a church *social*⟩

**so·cial·ism** \'sō-shə-,liz-əm\ *n*
a theory or system of government based on public ownership and control of the means of production and distribution of goods

**so·cial·ist** \'sō-shə-list\ *n*
a person who believes in socialism

**social studies** *n pl*
the studies (as civics, history, and geography) that deal with human relationships and the way society works

**so·ci·ety** \sə-'sī-ət-ē\ *n, pl* **so·ci·et·ies**
**1** friendly association with others
**2** human beings viewed as a system within which the individual lives **:** all of the people ⟨urban *society*⟩
**3** a group of persons with a common interest or purpose ⟨the school French *society*⟩
**4** a part of a community thought of as different in some way ⟨share the interests of musical *society*⟩
**5** the group or set of fashionable persons

[1]**sock** \'säk\ *n, pl* **socks** *or* **sox** \'säks\
► a knitted or woven covering for the foot usually reaching past the ankle and sometimes to the knee

[1]**sock:** a pair of patterned socks

[2]**sock** *vb*
[1]HIT 1, PUNCH

[3]**sock** *n*
[2]PUNCH

**sock·et** \'säk-ət\ *n*
a hollow thing or place that receives or holds something ⟨an electric light *socket*⟩ ⟨eye *socket*⟩

**sock·eye** \'säk-,ī\ *n*
a small Pacific salmon that is the source of most of the salmon with red flesh that we eat

[1]**sod** \'säd\ *n*
the layer of the soil filled with roots (as of grass)

[2]**sod** *vb* **sod·ded**; **sod·ding**
to cover with sod

**so·da** \'sōd-ə\ *n*
**1** a powdery substance like salt used in washing and in making glass or soap
**2** SODIUM BICARBONATE
**3** SODA WATER
**4** SODA POP
**5** a sweet drink made of soda water, flavoring, and ice cream ⟨a chocolate *soda*⟩

**soda fountain** *n*
a counter where soft drinks and ice cream are served

**soda pop** *n*
a flavored beverage containing carbon dioxide

**soda water** *n*
water with carbon dioxide added

**sod·den** \'säd-n\ *adj*
SOGGY

**so·di·um** \'sōd-ē-əm\ *n*
a soft waxy silver-white chemical element occurring in nature in combined form (as in salt)

**sodium bicarbonate** *n*
a white powder used in cooking and medicine

**sodium chlo·ride** \-'klōr-,īd\ *n*
[1]SALT 1

**so·fa** \'sō-fə\ *n*
a long upholstered seat usually with a back and arms

[1]**soft** \'sȯft\ *adj*
**1** having a pleasing or comfortable effect
**2** not bright or glaring ⟨*soft* lights⟩
**3** quiet in pitch or volume ⟨*soft* voices⟩
**4** smooth or delicate in appearance or feel ⟨a *soft* silk⟩
**5** not violent ⟨*soft* breezes⟩
**6** EASY 1 ⟨a *soft* job⟩
**7** sounding as in *ace* and *gem* — used of *c* and *g*
**8** easily affected by emotions ⟨a *soft* heart⟩
**9** lacking in strength ⟨*soft* from good living⟩
**10** not hard, solid, or firm ⟨a *soft* mattress⟩
**11** free from substances that prevent lathering of soap ⟨*soft* water⟩
**12** not containing alcohol ⟨*soft* drinks⟩
**soft·ness** *n*

[2]**soft** *adv*
SOFTLY

## solar system

The sun lies at the center of the solar system, and is orbited by nine planets, most of which are themselves circled by one or more moons. Millions of asteroids, meteors, and comets also orbit the sun.

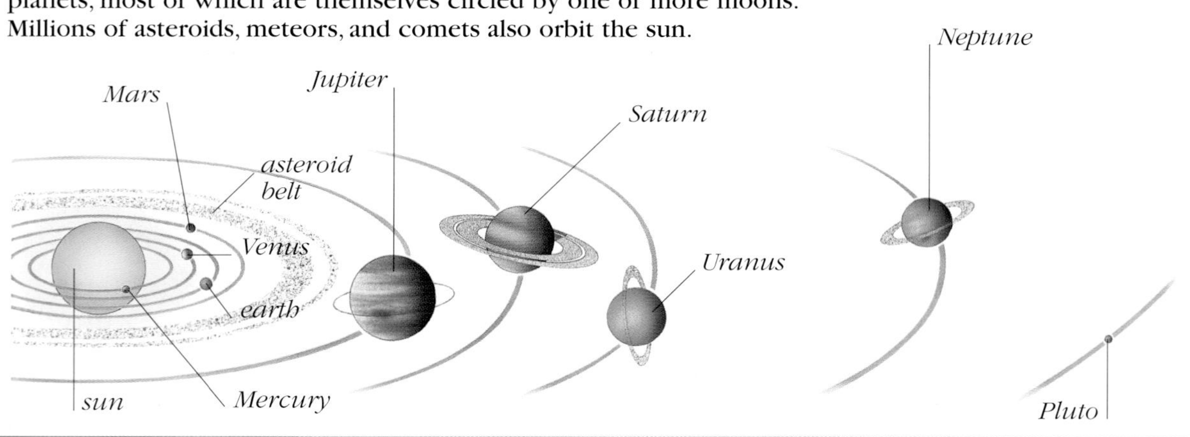


**soft·ball** \ˈsȯft-ˌbȯl\ *n*
**1** a game like baseball played with a larger ball
**2** the ball used in softball

**soft·en** \ˈsȯf-ən\ *vb*
to make or become soft or softer
**soft·en·er** *n*

**soft·ly** \ˈsȯft-lē\ *adv*
in a soft way **:** QUIETLY, GENTLY ⟨speak *softly*⟩ ⟨walked *softly* across the room⟩

**soft·ware** \ˈsȯf-ˌtwa(ə)r, -ˌtwe(ə)r\ *n*
the programs and related information used by a computer

**soft·wood** \ˈsȯf-ˌtwu̇d\ *n*
the wood of a cone-bearing tree (as a pine or spruce)

**sog·gy** \ˈsäg-ē, ˈsȯg-\ *adj* **sog·gi·er**; **sog·gi·est**
heavy with water or moisture ⟨*soggy* ground⟩

**[1]soil** \ˈsȯil\ *vb*
to make or become dirty

**[2]soil** *n*
**1** the loose finely divided surface material of the earth in which plants have their roots
**2** COUNTRY 2, LAND ⟨my native *soil*⟩
**soil·less** \ˈsȯil-ləs\ *adj*

**[1]so·journ** \ˈsō-ˌjərn\ *n*
a temporary stay

**[2]sojourn** *vb*
to stay as a temporary resident

**sol** \ˈsōl\ *n*
the fifth note of the musical scale

**so·lar** \ˈsō-lər\ *adj*
**1** of or relating to the sun
**2** measured by the earth's course around the sun ⟨a *solar* year⟩
**3** produced or made to work by the action of the sun's light or heat ⟨a *solar* furnace⟩

**solar system** *n*
▲ the sun and the planets, asteroids, comets, and meteors that revolve around it

**sold** *past of* SELL

**[1]sol·der** \ˈsäd-ər\ *n*
a metal or a mixture of metals used when melted to join or mend surfaces of metal

**[2]solder** *vb*
to join together or repair with solder

**sol·dier** \ˈsōl-jər\ *n*
a person in military service **:** an enlisted person who is not a commissioned officer

**[1]sole** \ˈsōl\ *n*
▼ a flatfish that has a small mouth and small eyes close together and is a popular food fish

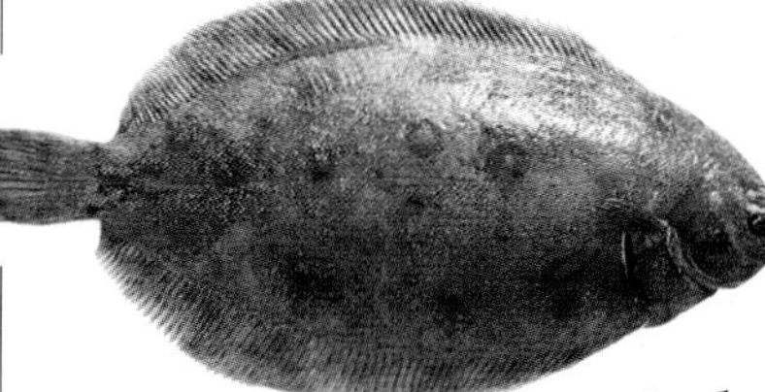

**[1]sole**

**[2]sole** *n*
**1** the bottom of the foot
**2** the bottom of a shoe, slipper, or boot

**[3]sole** *vb* **soled**; **sol·ing**
to furnish with a sole ⟨*sole* shoes⟩

**[4]sole** *adj*
**1** [1]SINGLE 2, ONLY ⟨the *sole* heir⟩
**2** limited or belonging only to the one mentioned ⟨gave me *sole* authority⟩

**sole·ly** \ˈsōl-lē\ *adv*
**1** without another **:** ALONE
**2** [2]ONLY 2 ⟨done *solely* for money⟩

**sol·emn** \ˈsäl-əm\ *adj*
**1** celebrated with religious ceremony **:** SACRED
**2** [1]FORMAL ⟨a *solemn* procession⟩
**3** done or made seriously and thoughtfully ⟨a *solemn* promise⟩
**4** very serious ⟨a *solemn* moment⟩
**5** being dark and gloomy **:** SOMBER ⟨a robe of *solemn* black⟩
**synonyms** see SERIOUS
**sol·emn·ly** *adv*

**so·lem·ni·ty** \sə-ˈlem-nət-ē\ *n, pl* **so·lem·ni·ties**
**1** a solemn ceremony, event, day, or speech
**2** formal dignity

**so·lic·it** \sə-ˈlis-ət\ *vb*
**1** to come to with a request or plea
**2** to try to get ⟨*solicited* the help of their neighbors⟩

**[1]sol·id** \ˈsäl-əd\ *adj*
**1** not hollow
**2** not loose or spongy **:** COMPACT ⟨a *solid* mass of rock⟩
**3** neither liquid nor gaseous
**4** made firmly and well ⟨a *solid* chair⟩

**5** being without a break, interruption, or change ⟨practiced for three *solid* hours⟩
**6** UNANIMOUS ⟨had the *solid* support of her party⟩
**7** RELIABLE, DEPENDABLE ⟨a *solid* citizen⟩
**8** of one material, kind, or color ⟨*solid* gold⟩ **synonyms** see HARD
**sol·id·ly** *adv*
**sol·id·ness** *n*

**²solid** *n*
**1** something that has length, width, and thickness
**2** a solid substance **:** a substance that keeps its size and shape

**so·lid·i·fy** \sə-ˈlid-ə-ˌfī\ *vb* **so·lid·i·fied**; **so·lid·i·fy·ing**
to make or become solid

**so·lid·i·ty** \sə-ˈlid-ət-ē\ *n, pl* **so·lid·i·ties**
the quality or state of being solid

**sol·i·taire** \ˈsäl-ə-ˌtaər, -ˌteər\ *n*
a card game played by one person alone

**sol·i·tary** \ˈsäl-ə-ˌter-ē\ *adj*
**1** all alone ⟨a *solitary* traveler⟩
**2** seldom visited **:** LONELY
**3** growing or living alone **:** not one of a group or cluster ⟨*solitary* insects⟩ **synonyms** see ALONE

**sol·i·tude** \ˈsäl-ə-ˌtüd, -ˌtyüd\ *n*
**1** the quality or state of being alone or away from others **:** SECLUSION
**2** a lonely place

**sombrero:**
a 19th-century straw sombrero

**¹so·lo** \ˈsō-lō\ *n, pl* **solos**
**1** music played or sung by one person either alone or with accompaniment
**2** an action (as in a dance) in which there is only one performer

**²solo** *adv or adj*
²ALONE 2 ⟨fly *solo*⟩ ⟨a *solo* dancer⟩

**³solo** *vb*
to fly solo in an airplane

**so·lo·ist** \ˈsō-lə-wist\ *n*
a person who performs a solo

**sol·stice** \ˈsäl-stəs, ˈsōl-, ˈsȯl-\ *n*
the time of the year when the sun is farthest north (**summer solstice**, about June 22) or south (**winter solstice**, about December 22) of the equator

**sol·u·ble** \ˈsäl-yə-bəl\ *adj*
**1** capable of being dissolved in liquid ⟨sugar is *soluble* in water⟩
**2** capable of being solved or explained ⟨a *soluble* mystery⟩ ⟨a *soluble* problem⟩

**so·lu·tion** \sə-ˈlü-shən\ *n*
**1** the act or process of solving
**2** the result of solving a problem ⟨a correct *solution*⟩
**3** the act or process by which a solid, liquid, or gas is dissolved in a liquid
**4** a liquid in which something has been dissolved

**solve** \ˈsälv, ˈsȯlv\ *vb* **solved**; **solv·ing**
to find the answer to or a solution for

**sol·vent** \ˈsäl-vənt, ˈsȯl-\ *n*
a usually liquid substance in which other substances can be dissolved or dispersed ⟨a *solvent* for removing paint⟩

**som·ber** *or* **som·bre** \ˈsäm-bər\ *adj*
**1** being dark and gloomy **:** DULL ⟨*somber* colors⟩
**2** showing or causing low spirits ⟨a *somber* mood⟩

**som·bre·ro** \səm-ˈbreər-ō\ *n, pl* **som·bre·ros**
◀ a tall hat of felt or straw with a very wide brim worn especially in the Southwest and Mexico

**¹some** \ˈsəm\ *adj*
**1** being one unknown or not specified ⟨*some* person called⟩
**2** being one, a part, or an unspecified number of something ⟨*some* gems are hard⟩
**3** being of an amount or number that is not mentioned ⟨buy *some* flour⟩
**4** being at least one and sometimes all of ⟨*some* years ago⟩

**²some** \ˈsəm\ *pron*
a certain number or amount ⟨*some* of the milk has spilled⟩ ⟨*some* of the puppies are for sale⟩

**¹-some** \ˈsəm\ *adj suffix*
distinguished by a specified thing, quality, state, or action ⟨trouble*some*⟩

**²-some** *n suffix*
group of so many members ⟨four*some*⟩

**¹some·body** \ˈsəm-ˌbäd-ē, -bəd-ē\ *pron*
some person ⟨*somebody* was looking for you⟩

**²somebody** *n, pl* **some·bod·ies**
a person of importance ⟨wanted to be a *somebody*⟩

**some·day** \ˈsəm-ˌdā\ *adv*
at some future time

**some·how** \ˈsəm-ˌhau̇\ *adv*
in one way or another

**some·one** \ˈsəm-wən, -ˌwən\ *pron*
some person ⟨*someone* has to do the job⟩

**¹som·er·sault** \ˈsəm-ər-ˌsȯlt\ *n*
▼ a moving of the body through one complete turn in which the feet move up and over the head

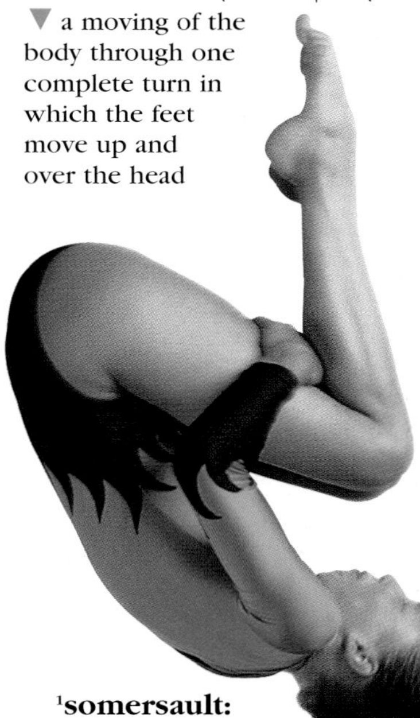

**¹somersault:**
a gymnast performing a somersault in midair

**²somersault** *vb*
to turn a somersault

**some·thing** \ˈsəm-thing\ *pron*
**1** a thing that is not surely known or understood ⟨we'll have to do *something* about it soon⟩
**2** a thing or amount that is clearly known but not named ⟨I have *something* here for you⟩
**3** SOMEWHAT ⟨is *something* of an expert⟩

**some·time** \'səm-,tīm\ *adv*
**1** at a future time ⟨will pay *sometime*⟩
**2** at a time not known or not specified

**some·times** \'səm-,tīmz\ *adv*
now and then : OCCASIONALLY

**some·way** \'səm-,wā\ *adv*
SOMEHOW

[1]**some·what** \'səm-,hwät, -,wät, -,hwət, -,wət\ *pron*
some amount or extent ⟨came as *somewhat* of a surprise⟩

[2]**somewhat** *adv*
to some extent ⟨*somewhat* more comfortable⟩

**some·where** \'səm-,hweər, -,weər, -,hwaər, -,waər\ *adv*
**1** in, at, or to a place not known or named
**2** at some time not specified ⟨*somewhere* around two o'clock⟩

**son** \'sən\ *n*
**1** a male child or offspring
**2** a man or boy closely associated with or thought of as a child of something (as a country, race, or religion) ⟨*sons* of liberty⟩

**so·nar** \'sō-,när\ *n*
a device for detecting objects underwater using sound waves

**so·na·ta** \sə-'nät-ə\ *n*
a musical composition usually for a single instrument consisting of three or four separate sections in different forms and keys

**song** \'sȯng\ *n*
**1** vocal music
**2** poetic composition : POETRY
**3** a short musical composition of words and music
**4** a small amount ⟨can be bought for a *song*⟩

**song·bird** \'sȯng-,bərd\ *n*
a bird that sings

**song·ster** \'sȯng-stər\ *n*
a person or a bird that sings

**son·ic** \'sän-ik\ *adj*
using, produced by, or relating to sound waves

**sonic boom** *n*
a sound like an explosion made by an aircraft traveling at supersonic speed

**son–in–law** \'sən-ən-,lȯ\ *n, pl* **sons–in–law**
the husband of one's daughter

**son·ny** \'sən-ē\ *n, pl* **son·nies**
a young boy — used mostly to address a stranger

**so·no·rous** \sə-'nōr-əs, 'sän-ə-rəs\ *adj*
**1** producing sound (as when struck)
**2** loud, deep, or rich in sound : RESONANT

**soon** \'sün\ *adv*
**1** without delay : before long
**2** in a prompt way : QUICKLY
**3** [1]EARLY 2 ⟨arrived too *soon*⟩
**4** by choice : WILLINGLY ⟨would *sooner* walk than ride⟩

**soot** \'su̇t, 'sət\ *n*
a black powder formed when something is burned : the very fine powder that colors smoke

**soothe** \'sü*th*\ *vb* **soothed**; **sooth·ing**
**1** to please by praise or attention
**2** RELIEVE 1
**3** to calm down : COMFORT

**sooth·say·er** \'süth-,sā-ər\ *n*
a person who claims to foretell events

**sooty** \'su̇t-ē, 'sət-\ *adj* **soot·i·er**; **soot·i·est**
**1** soiled with soot
**2** like soot especially in color

**sop** \'säp\ *vb* **sopped**; **sop·ping**
**1** to soak or dip in or as if in liquid
**2** to mop up (as water)

**soph·o·more** \'säf-,mōr, 'säf-ə-,mōr\ *n*
a student in his or her second year at a high school or college

**so·pra·no** \sə-'pran-ō, -'prän-\ *n, pl* **so·pra·nos**
**1** the highest part in harmony having four parts
**2** the highest singing voice of women or boys
**3** a person having a soprano voice
**4** an instrument having a soprano range or part

**sor·cer·er** \'sȯr-sər-ər\ *n*
a person who practices sorcery or witchcraft : WIZARD

**sor·cer·ess** \'sȯr-sə-rəs\ *n*
a woman who practices sorcery or witchcraft : WITCH

**sor·cery** \'sȯr-sə-rē\ *n, pl* **sor·cer·ies**
the use of magic : WITCHCRAFT

**sor·did** \'sȯrd-əd\ *adj*
**1** very dirty : FOUL ⟨*sordid* surroundings⟩
**2** of low moral quality : VILE ⟨a *sordid* life⟩

[1]**sore** \'sōr\ *adj* **sor·er**; **sor·est**
**1** causing distress ⟨*sore* news⟩
**2** very painful or sensitive : TENDER ⟨muscles *sore* from exercise⟩
**3** hurt or red and swollen so as to be or seem painful
**4** ANGRY
**sore·ly** *adv*
**sore·ness** *n*

[2]**sore** *n*
a sore spot (as an ulcer) on the body usually with the skin broken or bruised and often with infection

**sor·ghum** \'sȯr-gəm\ *n*
**1** a tall grass that looks like Indian corn and is used for forage and grain
**2** syrup from the juice of a sorghum

**so·ror·i·ty** \sə-'rȯr-ət-ē\ *n, pl* **so·ror·i·ties**
a club of girls or women especially at a college

[1]**sor·rel** \'sȯr-əl\ *n*
**1** an animal (as a horse) of a sorrel color
**2** a brownish orange to light brown

[2]**sorrel** *n*
▼ any of several plants with sour juice

[2]**sorrel:** wood sorrel

[1]**sor·row** \'sär-ō\ *n*
**1** sadness or grief caused by loss (as of something loved)
**2** a cause of grief or sadness
**3** a feeling of regret

**Synonyms** SORROW, GRIEF, and WOE mean distress of mind. SORROW suggests a feeling that something has been lost and often feelings of guilt and regret ⟨expressed *sorrow* for having caused the accident⟩. GRIEF stresses feeling great sorrow usually for a particular reason ⟨the *grief* of the parents when their only child died⟩. WOE suggests feeling hopeless and miserable ⟨all my troubles left me in a state of *woe*⟩.

**²sorrow** *vb*
to feel or express sorrow : GRIEVE

**sor·row·ful** \'sär-ō-fəl, -ə-fəl\ *adj*
**1** full of or showing sorrow ⟨a *sorrowful* face⟩
**2** causing sorrow

**sor·ry** \'sär-ē\ *adj* **sor·ri·er**; **sor·ri·est**
**1** feeling sorrow or regret ⟨*sorry* for the mistake⟩
**2** causing sorrow, pity, or scorn : WRETCHED ⟨a *sorry* sight⟩

**¹sort** \'sȯrt\ *n*
**1** a group of persons or things that have something in common : KIND ⟨all *sorts* of people⟩
**2** PERSON 1, INDIVIDUAL ⟨not a bad *sort*⟩
**3** general disposition : NATURE ⟨people of an evil *sort*⟩
**out of sorts**
**1** not feeling well
**2** easily angered : IRRITABLE

**²sort** *vb*
to separate and arrange according to kind or class : CLASSIFY ⟨*sort* mail⟩

**SOS** \,es-ō-'es\ *n*
**1** an international radio code distress signal used especially by ships and airplanes calling for help
**2** a call for help

**¹so–so** \'sō-'sō\ *adv*
fairly well ⟨did *so-so* on the test⟩

**²so–so** *adj*
neither very good nor very bad

**sought** *past of* SEEK

**soul** \'sōl\ *n*
**1** the spiritual part of a person believed to give life to the body
**2** the essential part of something
**3** a person who leads or stirs others to action : LEADER ⟨the *soul* of the campaign⟩
**4** a person's moral and emotional nature
**5** human being : PERSON ⟨a kind *soul*⟩

**¹sound** \'sau̇nd\ *adj*
**1** free from disease or weakness ⟨a *sound* body⟩
**2** free from flaw or decay ⟨*sound* timbers⟩
**3** ¹SOLID 4, FIRM ⟨a building of *sound* construction⟩
**4** free from error ⟨a *sound* argument⟩
**5** based on the truth ⟨*sound* beliefs⟩
**6** THOROUGH 1 ⟨a *sound* beating⟩
**7** ¹DEEP 5, UNDISTURBED ⟨a *sound* sleep⟩
**8** showing good sense : WISE ⟨*sound* advice⟩
**sound·ly** *adv*
**sound·ness** *n*

**²sound** *adv*
to the full extent ⟨*sound* asleep⟩

**³sound** *n*
**1** the sensation experienced through the sense of hearing : an instance or occurrence of this
**2** one of the noises that together make up human speech ⟨the *sound* \s\ in "sit"⟩
**3** the suggestion carried or given by something heard or read ⟨this excuse has a suspicious *sound*⟩
**4** hearing distance : EARSHOT
**sound·less** \'sau̇nd-ləs\ *adj*
**sound·less·ly** *adv*

**⁴sound** *vb*
**1** to make or cause to make a sound or noise ⟨*sound* the trumpet⟩
**2** PRONOUNCE 2 ⟨*sound* each word clearly⟩
**3** to make known : PROCLAIM ⟨*sound* the alarm⟩
**4** to order, signal, or indicate by a sound ⟨the clock *sounded* noon⟩
**5** to make or give an impression : SEEM ⟨the story *sounds* false⟩

**⁵sound** *n*
▼ a long stretch of water that is wider than a strait and often connects two larger bodies of water or forms a channel between the mainland and an island

**⁶sound** *vb*
**1** to measure the depth of (as by a weighted line dropped down from the surface)
**2** to find or try to find the thoughts or feelings of a person ⟨*sounded* them out on the idea⟩

**sound·proof** \'sau̇nd-'prüf\ *adj*
capable of keeping sound from entering or escaping ⟨a *soundproof* room⟩

**sound wave** *n*
a wave that is produced when a sound is made and is responsible for carrying the sound to the ear

**soup** \'süp\ *n*
a liquid food made from the liquid in which vegetables, meat, or fish have been cooked and often containing pieces of solid food

**¹sour** \'sau̇r\ *adj*
**1** having an acid taste
**2** having become acid through spoiling ⟨*sour* milk⟩
**3** suggesting decay ⟨a *sour* smell⟩
**4** not pleasant or friendly ⟨a *sour* look⟩
**5** acid in reaction ⟨*sour* soil⟩
**sour·ish** \-ish\ *adj*
**sour·ly** *adv*
**sour·ness** *n*

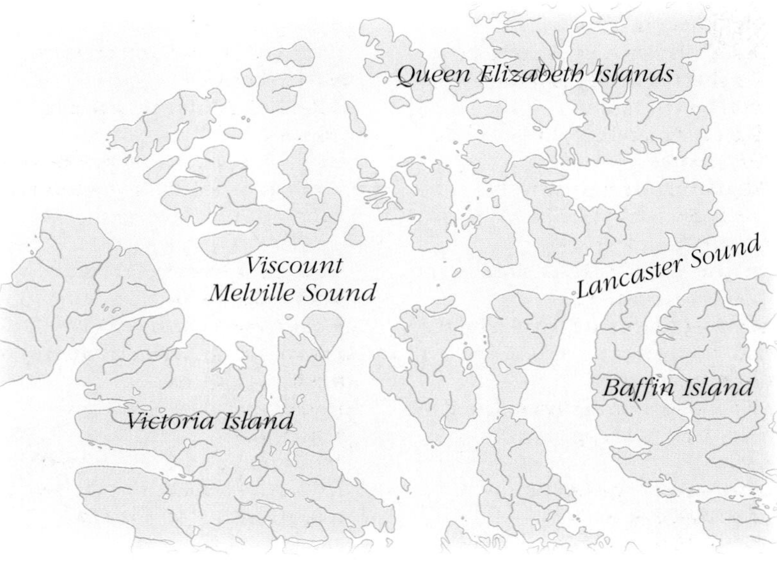


**⁵sound:** map showing the sounds above northern Canada

A B C D E F G H I J K L M N O P Q R S T U V W X Y Z

**²sour** *vb*
to make or become sour

**source** \'sōrs\ *n*
**1** the cause or starting point of something ⟨nobody knows the *source* of the rumor⟩
**2** the beginning of a stream of water
**3** one that supplies information

**sou·sa·phone** \'sü-zə-ˌfōn, -sə-\ *n*
▼ a large circular tuba designed to rest on the player's shoulder and used chiefly in marching bands

**¹south** \'sau̇th\ *adv*
to or toward the south

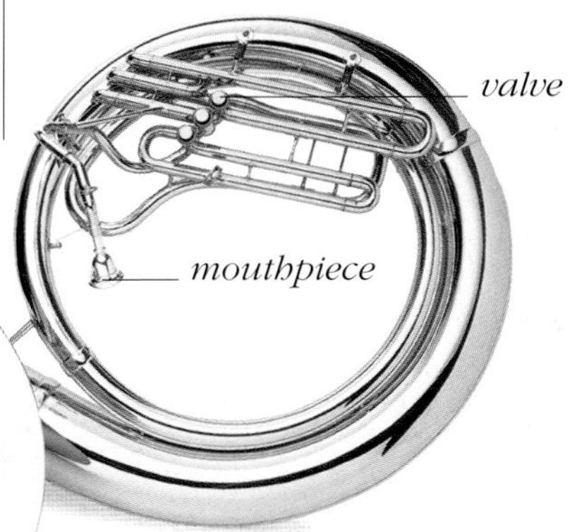

**sousaphone**

**²south** *adj*
placed toward, facing, or coming from the south

**³south** *n*
**1** the direction to the right of one facing east : the compass point opposite to north
**2** *cap* regions or countries south of a point that is mentioned or understood

**¹South American** *adj*
of or relating to South America or the South Americans

**²South American** *n*
a person born or living in South America

**south·bound** \'sau̇th-ˌbau̇nd\ *adj*
going south

**¹south·east** \sau̇-'thēst\ *adv*
to or toward the southeast

**²southeast** *n*
**1** the direction between south and east
**2** *cap* regions or countries southeast of a point that is mentioned or understood

**³southeast** *adj*
placed toward, facing, or coming from the southeast

**south·east·er·ly** \sau̇-'thē-stər-lē\ *adv or adj*
**1** from the southeast
**2** toward the southeast

**south·east·ern** \sau̇-'thē-stərn\ *adj*
**1** *often cap* of, relating to, or like that of the Southeast
**2** lying toward or coming from the southeast

**south·er·ly** \'sə<u>th</u>-ər-lē\ *adj or adv*
**1** toward the south
**2** from the south ⟨a *southerly* wind⟩

**south·ern** \'sə<u>th</u>-ərn\ *adj*
**1** *often cap* of, relating to, or like that of the South
**2** lying toward or coming from the south

**South·ern·er** \'sə<u>th</u>-ər-nər\ *n*
a person who is born or lives in the South

**south·paw** \'sau̇th-ˌpȯ\ *n*
a person (as a baseball pitcher) who is left-handed

**south pole** *n, often cap S&P*
**1** the most southern point of the earth : the southern end of the earth's axis
**2** the end of a magnet that points toward the south when the magnet is free to swing

**south·ward** \'sau̇th-wərd\ *adv or adj*
toward the south

**¹south·west** \sau̇th-'west\ *adv*
to or toward the southwest

**²southwest** *n*
**1** the direction between south and west
**2** *cap* regions or countries southwest of a point that is mentioned or understood

**³southwest** *adj*
placed toward, facing, or coming from the southwest

**south·west·er·ly** \sau̇th-'wes-tər-lē\ *adv or adj*
**1** from the southwest
**2** toward the southwest

**south·west·ern** \sau̇th-'wes-tərn\ *adj*
**1** lying toward or coming from the southwest
**2** *often cap* of, relating to, or like that of the Southwest

**sou·ve·nir** \'sü-və-ˌniər\ *n*
something that serves as a reminder

**sou'·west·er** \sau̇-'wes-tər\ *n*
a waterproof hat with wide slanting brim that is longer in back than in front

**¹sov·er·eign** \'säv-ə-rən, 'säv-rən\ *n*
**1** a person (as a king or queen) or body of persons having the highest power and authority in a state
**2** an old British gold coin

**²sovereign** *adj*
**1** highest in power or authority ⟨a *sovereign* ruler⟩
**2** having independent authority ⟨a *sovereign* state⟩

**sov·er·eign·ty** \'säv-ə-rən-tē, 'säv-rən-\ *n, pl* **sov·er·eign·ties**
**1** supreme power especially over a political unit
**2** freedom from outside control
**3** one (as a country) that is sovereign

**¹sow** \'sau̇\ *n*
▼ an adult female hog

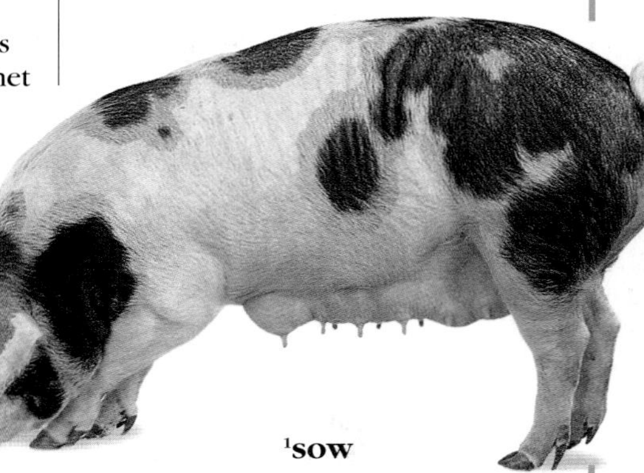
**¹sow**

**²sow** \'sō\ *vb* **sowed**; **sown** \'sōn\ *or* **sowed**; **sow·ing**
**1** to plant or scatter (as seed) for growing
**2** to cover with or as if with scattered seed for growing ⟨*sow* a field to oats⟩
**3** to set in motion **:** cause to exist ⟨*sow* discontent⟩
**sow·er** *n*

**sow bug** \'saù-\ *n*
WOOD LOUSE

**sox** *pl of* SOCK

**soy·bean** \'sȯi-,bēn\ *n*
an annual Asian plant related to the clovers that is widely grown for its edible seeds which yield an oil rich in protein

**soybean oil** *n*
a pale yellow oil that is obtained from soybeans and is used chiefly as a food and in paints and soaps

**soy sauce** \'sȯi-\ *n*
a brown sauce made from soybeans and used especially in Chinese and Japanese cooking

**¹space** \'spās\ *n*
**1** a period of time
**2** a part of a distance, area, or volume that can be measured
**3** a certain place set apart or available ⟨a parking *space*⟩
**4** the area without limits in which all things exist and move
**5** the region beyond the earth's atmosphere
**6** an empty place

**²space** *vb* **spaced**; **spac·ing**
to place with space between

**space·craft** \'spā-,skraft\ *n, pl* **spacecraft**
a vehicle for travel beyond the earth's atmosphere

**space·man** \'spā-,sman, -smən\ *n, pl* **space·men** \'spā-,smen, -smən\
a person who travels outside the earth's atmosphere

**space·ship** \'spās-,ship\ *n*
SPACECRAFT

**space shuttle** *n*
▼ a spacecraft designed to transport people and cargo between earth and space that can be used repeatedly

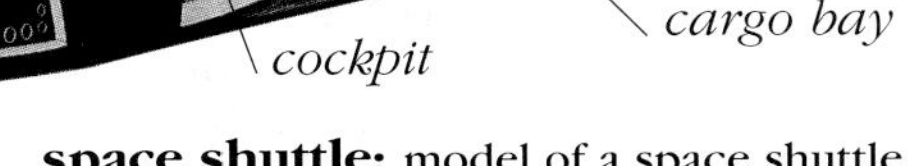

**space shuttle:** model of a space shuttle

**space station** *n*
an artificial satellite designed to stay in orbit permanently and can accomodate humans for long periods

**space suit** *n*
a suit equipped to keep its wearer alive in space

**spa·cious** \'spā-shəs\ *adj*
having ample space

**¹spade** \'spād\ *n*
a digging tool made to be pushed into the ground with the foot

**²spade** *vb* **spad·ed**; **spad·ing**
to dig with a spade

**spa·ghet·ti** \spə-'get-ē\ *n*
pasta made in the form of strings

**¹spam** \'spam\ *n*
e-mail sent to a large number of addresses and usually containing advertising

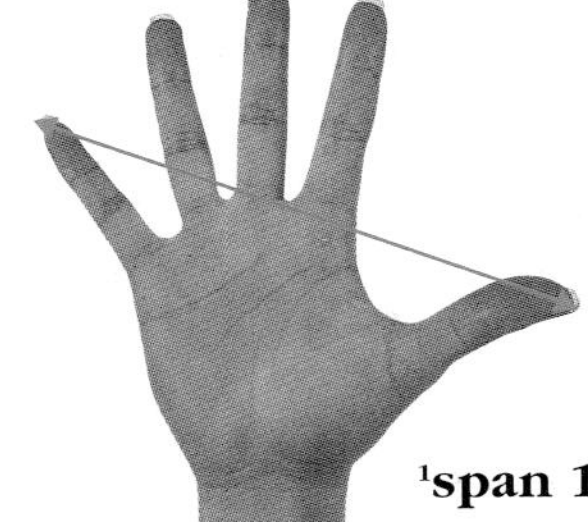
**¹span 1**

**²spam** *vb*
to send spam
**spam·mer** \'spam-ər\ *n*

**¹span** \'span\ *n*
**1** ▲ the distance from the end of the thumb to the end of the little finger when the hand is stretched wide open
**2** a limited portion of time ⟨*span* of life⟩
**3** the spread (as of an arch) from one support to another

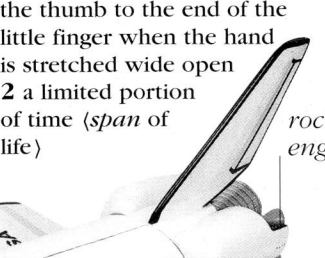

**²span** *vb* **spanned**; **span·ning**
**1** to measure by or as if by the hand stretched wide open
**2** to reach or extend across ⟨a bridge *spans* the river⟩
**3** to place or construct a span over

**³span** *n*
two animals (as mules) worked or driven as a pair

**span·gle** \'spang-gəl\ *n*
SEQUIN

**Span·iard** \'span-yərd\ *n*
a person born or living in Spain

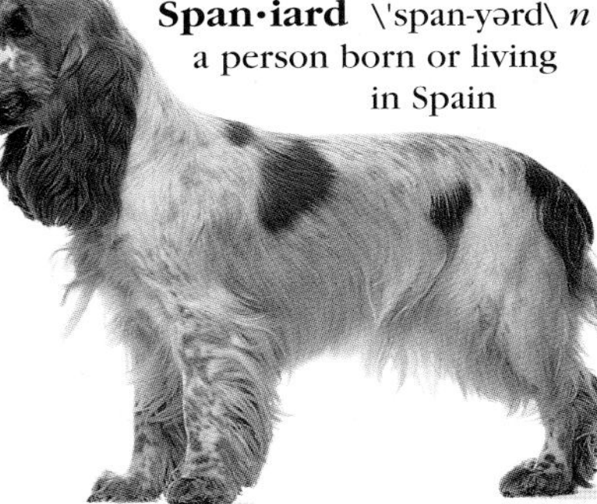
**spaniel:** an English cocker spaniel

**span·iel** \'span-yəl\ *n*
▲ a small or medium-sized dog with a thick wavy coat, long drooping ears, and usually short legs

**Word History** There are many kinds of spaniels today that come from different places in Europe. The ancestors of all spaniels, however, came from Spain. The English word *spaniel* came from an early French word that meant "Spaniard."

**¹Span·ish** \'span-ish\ *adj*
of or relating to Spain, its people, or the Spanish language

**²Spanish** *n*
**1** the language of Spain and the countries colonized by Spaniards
**2 Spanish** *pl* the people of Spain

**spank** \'spangk\ *vb*
to strike on the buttocks with the open hand

**spank·ing** \'spang-king\ *adj*
BRISK 1, LIVELY ⟨a *spanking* breeze⟩

**¹spar** \'spär\ *n*
a long rounded piece of wood or metal (as a mast, yard, or boom) to which a sail is fastened

**²spar** *vb* **sparred**; **spar·ring**
1 to box or make boxing movements with the fists for practice or in fun
2 ²SKIRMISH

**¹spare** \'spaər, 'speər\ *vb* **spared**; **spar·ing**
1 to keep from being punished or harmed **:** show mercy to ⟨will *spare* the prisoners⟩
2 to free of the need to do something ⟨was *spared* the work⟩
3 to keep from using or spending ⟨more pancakes, please, and don't *spare* the syrup⟩
4 to give up especially as not really needed ⟨can you *spare* me a few minutes?⟩ ⟨couldn't *spare* a dime⟩
5 to have left over ⟨got there with time to *spare*⟩

**²spare** *adj* **spar·er**; **spar·est**
1 held in reserve ⟨a *spare* tire⟩
2 being over what is needed ⟨*spare* time⟩
3 somewhat thin
4 SCANTY

**³spare** *n*
1 a spare or duplicate piece or part
2 the knocking down of all ten bowling pins with the first two balls

**spare·ribs** \'spaər-,ribz, 'speər-\ *n pl*
a cut of pork ribs separated from the bacon strips

**spar·ing** \'spaər-ing, 'speər-\ *adj*
careful in the use of money or supplies **synonyms** see ECONOMICAL
**spar·ing·ly** *adv*

**¹spark** \'spärk\ *n*
1 a small bit of burning material
2 a hot glowing bit struck from a mass (as by steel on flint)
3 a short bright flash of electricity between two points
4 ²SPARKLE 1
5 ¹TRACE 2 ⟨showed a *spark* of interest⟩

**²spark** *vb*
1 to give off or cause to give off sparks
2 to set off ⟨*spark* a discussion⟩

**¹spar·kle** \'spär-kəl\ *vb* **spar·kled**; **spar·kling**
1 to throw off sparks
2 to give off small flashes of light ⟨the diamond *sparkled*⟩
3 to be lively or active ⟨the conversation *sparkled*⟩ **synonyms** see GLEAM

**²sparkle** *n*
1 a little flash of light
2 the quality of sparkling ⟨the *sparkle* of a diamond⟩

**spar·kler** \'spär-klər\ *n*
a firework that throws off very bright sparks as it burns

**spark plug** *n*
a device used in an engine to produce a spark that ignites a fuel mixture

**spar·row** \'spar-ō\ *n*
a small brownish bird related to the finches

**sparrow hawk** *n*
▶ a small hawk or falcon

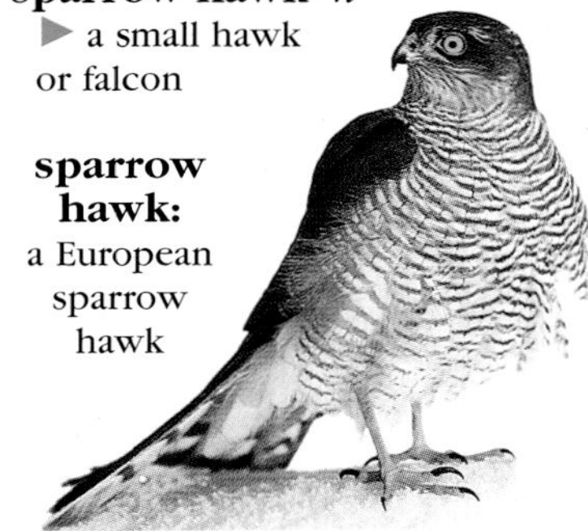

**sparrow hawk:** a European sparrow hawk

**sparse** \'spärs\ *adj* **spars·er**; **spars·est**
not thickly grown or settled
**sparse·ly** *adv*

**spasm** \'spaz-əm\ *n*
1 a sudden involuntary and usually violent contracting of muscles ⟨back *spasms*⟩
2 a sudden, violent, and temporary effort, emotion, or outburst ⟨a *spasm* of coughing⟩

**spas·mod·ic** \spaz-'mäd-ik\ *adj*
relating to or affected by spasm **:** involving spasms ⟨*spasmodic* breathing⟩ ⟨*spasmodic* movements⟩
**spas·mod·i·cal·ly** \-i-kə-lē\ *adv*

**¹spat** \'spat\ *past of* SPIT

**²spat** *n*
a cloth or leather covering for the instep and ankle

**³spat** *n*
a brief unimportant quarrel

**spa·tial** \'spā-shəl\ *adj*
of or relating to space

**¹spat·ter** \'spat-ər\ *vb*
1 to splash with drops or small bits of something wet
2 to scatter by splashing

**²spatter** *n*
1 the act or sound of spattering
2 a drop or splash spattered on something **:** a spot or stain due to spattering

**spat·u·la** \'spach-ə-lə\ *n*
a knifelike instrument with a broad flexible blade that is used mostly for spreading or mixing soft substances or for lifting

**¹spawn** \'spȯn\ *vb*
to produce or deposit eggs or spawn ⟨salmon go up rivers to *spawn*⟩

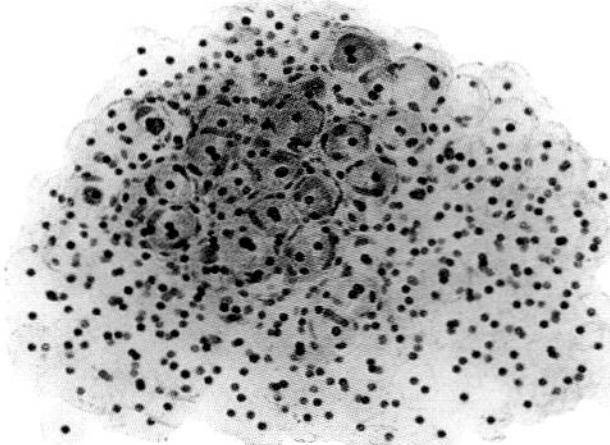

**²spawn:** a mass of spawn produced by frogs

**²spawn** *n*
▲ the eggs of a water animal (as an oyster or fish) that produces many small eggs

**spay** \'spā\ *vb*
to remove the ovaries of (a female animal) ⟨a *spayed* cat⟩

**speak** \'spēk\ *vb* **spoke** \'spōk\; **spo·ken** \'spō-kən\; **speak·ing**
1 to utter words **:** TALK
2 to utter in words ⟨*speak* the truth⟩
3 to mention in speech or writing ⟨*spoke* of being ill⟩
4 to use or be able to use in talking ⟨*speak* French⟩

---

**Synonyms** SPEAK, TALK, and CONVERSE mean to express oneself in words. SPEAK applies to anything said, whether it is understood or not and whether it is heard or not ⟨we didn't know what language they were *speaking*⟩. TALK suggests there is a listener who understands what is said and often that both people do some speaking ⟨we *talked* about school⟩. CONVERSE suggests an exchange of thoughts and opinions ⟨the scientists *conversed* about traveling in space⟩.

---

**speak·er** \'spē-kər\ *n*
1 a person who speaks
2 a person who conducts a meeting
3 LOUDSPEAKER

[1]**spear** \'spir\ *n*
**1** ▲ a weapon with a long straight handle and sharp head or blade used for throwing or jabbing
**2** an instrument with a sharp point and curved hooks used in spearing fish

[2]**spear** *vb*
to strike or pierce with or as if with a spear

[3]**spear** *n*
a usually young blade or sprout (as of grass)

[1]**spear·head** \'spir-,hed\ *n*
**1** the head or point of a spear
**2** the person, thing, or group that is the leading force (as in a development or an attack)

[2]**spearhead** *vb*
to serve as leader of ⟨*spearhead* a campaign for better schools⟩

**spear·mint** \'spir-,mint\ *n*
► a common mint used for flavoring

**spearmint**

**spe·cial** \'spesh-əl\ *adj*
**1** UNUSUAL, EXTRAORDINARY ⟨a *special* occasion⟩
**2** liked very well ⟨a *special* friend⟩
**3** UNIQUE 2 ⟨a *special* case⟩
**4** [1]EXTRA ⟨a *special* edition⟩
**5** meant for a particular purpose or occasion ⟨a *special* diet⟩
**spe·cial·ly** *adv*

**spe·cial·ist** \'spesh-ə-list\ *n*
**1** a person who studies or works at a special occupation or branch of learning ⟨an eye *specialist*⟩
**2** a person working in a special skill in the Army in any of the four ranks equal to the ranks of corporal through sergeant first class

**spe·cial·ize** \'spesh-ə-,līz\ *vb*
**spe·cial·ized**; **spe·cial·iz·ing**
**1** to limit one's attention or energy to one business, subject, or study ⟨*specialize* in jet airplanes⟩

[1]**spear 1:** a medieval European spear used for hunting

**2** to change and develop so as to be suited for some particular use or living conditions ⟨*specialized* sense organs⟩

**spe·cial·ty** \'spesh-əl-tē\ *n, pl* **spe·cial·ties**
**1** a product of a special kind or of special excellence ⟨pancakes were the cook's *specialty*⟩
**2** something a person specializes in

**spe·cies** \'spē-shēz, -sēz\ *n, pl* **species**
**1** a class of things of the same kind and with the same name : KIND, SORT
**2** a category of plants or animals that ranks below a genus in scientific classification and that is made up of individuals able to produce young with one another ⟨the one-humped camel is a different *species* from the two-humped camel⟩

**spe·cif·ic** \spi-'sif-ik\ *adj*
**1** being an actual example of a certain kind of thing ⟨a *specific* case⟩
**2** clearly and exactly presented or stated ⟨*specific* directions⟩
**3** of, relating to, or being a species

**spec·i·fi·ca·tion** \,spes-ə-fə-'kā-shən\ *n*
**1** the act or process of specifying
**2** a single specified item
**3** a description of work to be done or materials to be used — often used in pl. ⟨the architect's *specifications* for a new building⟩

**spec·i·fy** \'spes-ə-,fī\ *vb*
**spec·i·fied**; **spec·i·fy·ing**
**1** to mention or name exactly and clearly ⟨*specify* the cause⟩
**2** to include in a specification ⟨*specify* oak flooring⟩

**spec·i·men** \'spes-ə-mən\ *n*
a part or a single thing that shows what the whole thing or group is like : SAMPLE

**speck** \'spek\ *n*
**1** a small spot or blemish
**2** a very small amount : BIT

[1]**speck·le** \'spek-əl\ *n*
a small mark (as of color)

[2]**speckle** *vb* **speck·led**; **speck·ling**
to mark with speckles

**spec·ta·cle** \'spek-ti-kəl\ *n*
**1** an unusual or impressive public display (as a big parade)
**2** **spectacles** *pl* a pair of glasses held in place by parts passing over the ears

**spec·tac·u·lar** \spek-'tak-yə-lər\ *adj*
STRIKING, SHOWY ⟨a *spectacular* sunset⟩

**spec·ta·tor** \'spek-,tāt-ər\ *n*
a person who looks on (as at a sports event)

**spec·ter** *or* **spec·tre** \'spek-tər\ *n*
GHOST

**spec·trum** \'spek-trəm\ *n, pl* **spec·tra** \-trə\ *or* **spec·trums**
the group of different colors including red, orange, yellow, green, blue, indigo, and violet seen when light passes through a prism and falls on a surface or when sunlight is affected by drops of water (as in a rainbow)

**spec·u·late** \'spek-yə-,lāt\ *vb*
**spec·u·lat·ed**; **spec·u·lat·ing**
**1** MEDITATE 2
**2** to engage in a business deal in which much profit may be made although at a big risk

**spec·u·la·tion** \,spek-yə-'lā-shən\ *n*
**1** [2]GUESS
**2** the taking of a big risk in business in hopes of making a big profit

**speech** \'spēch\ *n*
**1** the communication or expression of thoughts in spoken words
**2** something that is spoken
**3** a public talk
**4** a form of communication (as a language or dialect) used by a particular group
**5** the power of expressing or communicating thoughts by speaking

**speech·less** \'spēch-ləs\ *adj*
**1** unable to speak
**2** not speaking for a time : SILENT ⟨*speechless* with surprise⟩

[1]**speed** \'spēd\ *n*
**1** quickness in movement or action
**2** rate of moving or doing

**[2]speed** *vb* **sped** \'sped\ *or* **speed·ed**; **speed·ing**
**1** to move or cause to move fast : HURRY
**2** to go or drive at too high a speed
**3** to increase the speed of : ACCELERATE

**speed·boat** \'spēd-,bōt\ *n*
▶ a fast motorboat

**speed bump** *n*
a low raised ridge across a roadway (as in a parking lot) to limit vehicle speed

**speed·om·e·ter** \spi-'däm-ət-ər\ *n*
**1** an instrument that measures speed
**2** an instrument that measures speed and records distance traveled

**speedy** \'spēd-ē\ *adj* **speed·i·er**; **speed·i·est**
moving or taking place fast ⟨made a *speedy* recovery⟩
**speed·i·ly** \'spēd-l-ē\ *adv*

**[1]spell** \'spel\ *vb*
**1** to name, write, or print in order the letters of a word
**2** to make up the letters of ⟨"c-a-t" *spells* the word "cat"⟩
**3** to amount to : MEAN ⟨another drought would *spell* famine⟩

**[2]spell** *n*
**1** a spoken word or group of words believed to have magic power : CHARM
**2** a very strong influence

**[3]spell** *n*
**1** one's turn at work or duty
**2** a period spent in a job or occupation
**3** a short period of time
**4** a stretch of a specified kind of weather
**5** a period of bodily or mental distress or disorder

**[4]spell** *vb*
to take the place of for a time : RELIEVE ⟨*spell* a person at shoveling⟩

**spell·bound** \'spel-,baund\ *adj*
held by or as if by a spell

**spell·er** \'spel-ər\ *n*
**1** a person who spells words
**2** a book with exercises for teaching spelling

**spell·ing** \'spel-iŋ\ *n*
**1** the forming of words from letters
**2** the letters composing a word

**speedboat**

**spelling checker** *also* **spell check** *or* **spell checker** *n*
a computer program that shows the user any words that might be incorrectly spelled

**spend** \'spend\ *vb* **spent** \'spent\; **spend·ing**
**1** to use up : pay out
**2** to wear out : EXHAUST
**3** to use wastefully : SQUANDER
**4** to cause or allow (as time) to pass

**spend·thrift** \'spend-,thrift\ *n*
one who spends wastefully

**spent** \'spent\ *adj*
**1** used up
**2** drained of energy

**sperm** \'spərm\ *n*
SPERM CELL

**sperm cell** *n*
a male germ cell

**sperm whale** *n*
▼ a huge whale with a large head having a closed cavity that contains a mixture of wax and oil

**spew** \'spyü\ *vb*
to pour out ⟨a volcano *spewing* lava⟩

**sphere** \'sfir\ *n*
**1** a body (as the moon) shaped like a ball
**2** a figure so shaped that every point on its surface is an equal distance from the center of the figure
**3** a field of influence or activity ⟨a subject outside one's *sphere*⟩

**spher·i·cal** \'sfir-i-kəl, 'sfer-\ *adj*
relating to or having the form of a sphere

**sphinx** \'sfiŋks\ *n*
▼ an Egyptian figure having the body of a lion and the head of a man, a ram, or a hawk

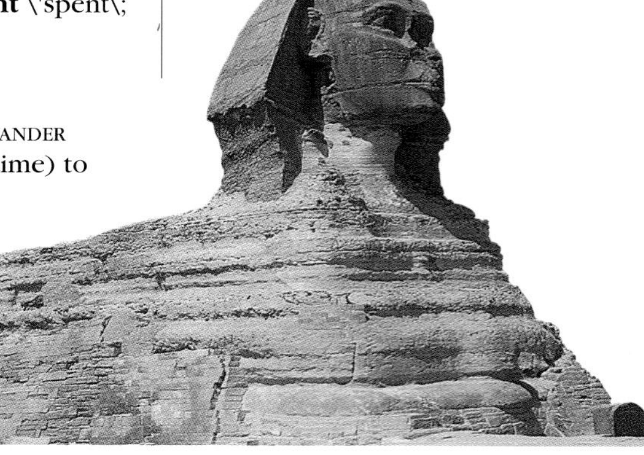

**sphinx:** the Great Sphinx, constructed in the third millennium BC in ancient Egypt

**[1]spice** \'spīs\ *n*
**1** a plant product (as pepper or nutmeg) that has a strong pleasant smell and is used to flavor food
**2** something that adds interest ⟨variety is the *spice* of life⟩

**[2]spice** *vb* **spiced**; **spic·ing**
to season with or as if with spices

**spick–and–span** *or* **spic–and–span** \,spik-ən-'span\ *adj*
**1** quite new and unused
**2** very clean and neat

**spicy** \'spī-sē\ *adj* **spic·i·er**; **spic·i·est**
**1** flavored with or containing spice

**sperm whale:** a pygmy sperm whale

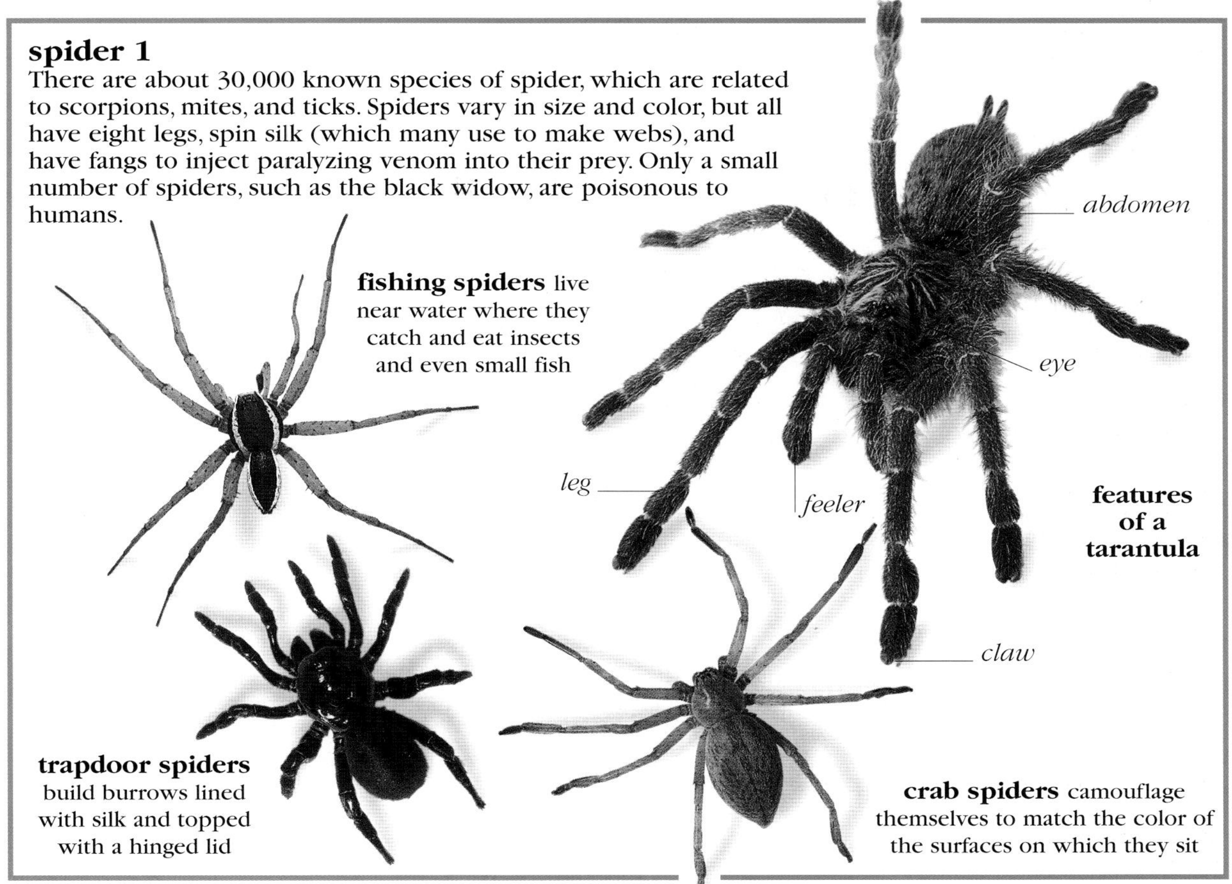


**spider 1**
There are about 30,000 known species of spider, which are related to scorpions, mites, and ticks. Spiders vary in size and color, but all have eight legs, spin silk (which many use to make webs), and have fangs to inject paralyzing venom into their prey. Only a small number of spiders, such as the black widow, are poisonous to humans.

**fishing spiders** live near water where they catch and eat insects and even small fish

**features of a tarantula**

**trapdoor spiders** build burrows lined with silk and topped with a hinged lid

**crab spiders** camouflage themselves to match the color of the surfaces on which they sit

2 somewhat shocking or indecent ⟨a *spicy* story⟩

**spi·der** \'spīd-ər\ *n*
1 ▲ a wingless animal somewhat like an insect but having eight legs instead of six and a body divided into two parts instead of three
2 a cast-iron frying pan

**spi·der·web** \'spīd-ər-ˌweb\ *n*
the silken web spun by most spiders and used as a resting place and a trap for prey

**spig·ot** \'spig-ət, 'spik-\ *n*
1 a plug used to stop the vent in a barrel
2 FAUCET

[1]**spike** \'spīk\ *n*
1 a very large nail
2 one of the metal objects attached to the heel and sole of a shoe (as a baseball shoe) to prevent slipping
3 something pointed like a spike

[2]**spike** *vb* **spiked**; **spik·ing**
1 to fasten with spikes
2 to pierce or cut with or on a spike

[3]**spike** *n*
1 an ear of grain ⟨*spikes* of wheat⟩
2 a long usually rather narrow flower cluster in which the blossoms grow very close to a central stem

[1]**spill** \'spil\ *vb* **spilled** \'spild\ *also* **spilt** \'spilt\; **spill·ing**
1 to cause (blood) to flow by wounding : [1]SHED 2
2 to cause or allow to fall, flow, or run out so as to be wasted or scattered ⟨knocked the glass over and *spilled* the milk⟩
3 to flow or run out, over, or off and become wasted or scattered ⟨filled the jar until it *spilled* over⟩ ⟨the milk *spilled*⟩
4 to make known ⟨*spilled* the secret⟩

[2]**spill** *n*
1 an act of spilling
2 a fall especially from a horse or vehicle
3 something spilled ⟨mop up a *spill* on the floor⟩

[1]**spin** \'spin\ *vb* **spun** \'spən\; **spin·ning**
1 to make yarn or thread from (fibers) ⟨*spin* flax⟩
2 to make (yarn or thread) from fibers ⟨*spin* thread⟩
3 to form threads or a web or cocoon by giving off a sticky fluid that quickly hardens into silk
4 to turn or cause to turn round and round rapidly : TWIRL ⟨*spin* a top⟩
5 to feel as if in a whirl ⟨my head was *spinning*⟩
6 to make up and tell using the imagination ⟨*spin* a yarn⟩
7 to move swiftly on wheels or in a vehicle
8 to make, shape, or produce by or as if by whirling ⟨*spun* sugar⟩

[2]**spin** *n*
1 a rapid whirling motion
2 a short trip in or on a wheeled vehicle ⟨let's take a *spin* on our bikes⟩

A B C D E F G H I J K L M N O P Q R S W X Y Z

**spin·ach** \'spin-ich\ *n*
a leafy plant that is grown for use as food

**spi·nal** \'spī-nᵊl\ *adj*
of, relating to, or located near the backbone or the spinal cord
**spi·nal·ly** *adv*

**spinal column** *n*
BACKBONE 1

**spinal cord** *n*
the thick cord of nervous tissue that extends from the brain down the back, fills the cavity of the backbone, and is concerned especially with reflex action

**spin·dle** \'spin-dᵊl\ *n*
**1** a slender round rod or stick with narrowed ends by which thread is twisted in spinning and on which it is wound
**2** something (as an axle or shaft) which is shaped or turned like a spindle or on which something turns

**spin·dly** \'spin-dlē\ *adj* **spin·dli·er**; **spin·dli·est** being thin and long or tall and usually feeble or weak ⟨a *spindly* plant⟩

**spine** \'spīn\ *n*
**1** BACKBONE 1
**2** a stiff pointed part growing from the surface of a plant or animal

**spine·less** \'spīn-ləs\ *adj*
**1** lacking spines
**2** having no backbone
**3** lacking spirit, courage, or determination

**spin·et** \'spin-ət\ *n*
**1** ▼ an early harpsichord with one keyboard and only one string for each note
**2** a small upright piano

**spinet 2:** an 18th-century spinet from England

**spin·ning jen·ny** \'spin-ing-ˌjen-ē\ *n*, *pl* **spin·ning jen·nies**
an early machine for spinning wool or cotton by means of many spindles

**spinning wheel** *n*
▶ a small machine driven by the hand or foot that is used to spin yarn or thread

**spinning wheel:** an 18th-century spinning wheel

**spin·ster** \'spin-stər\ *n*
an unmarried woman past the usual age for marrying

**spiny** \'spī-nē\ *adj* **spin·i·er**; **spin·i·est**
covered with spines

**spi·ra·cle** \'spir-ə-kəl\ *n*
an opening (as in the head of a whale or the abdomen of an insect) for breathing

**¹spi·ral** \'spī-rəl\ *adj*
**1** winding or circling around a center and gradually getting closer to or farther away from it ⟨the *spiral* curve of a watch spring⟩
**2** ▶ circling around a center like the thread of a screw ⟨a *spiral* staircase⟩
**spi·ral·ly** *adv*

**¹spiral 2:** a spiral staircase in Vatican City

**²spiral** *n*
**1** a single turn or coil in a spiral object
**2** something that has a spiral form

**³spiral** *vb* **spi·raled** *or* **spi·ralled**; **spi·ral·ing** *or* **spi·ral·ling**
to move in a spiral path

**spire** \'spīr\ *n*
**1** a pointed roof especially of a tower
**2** STEEPLE

**spi·rea** *or* **spi·raea** \spī-'rē-ə\ *n*
a shrub related to the roses that bears clusters of small white or pink flowers

**¹spir·it** \'spir-ət\ *n*
**1** a force within a human being thought to give the body life, energy, and power : SOUL
**2** *cap* the active presence of God in human life : the third person of the Trinity
**3** a being (as a ghost) whose existence cannot be explained by the known laws of nature
**4** ¹MOOD ⟨in good *spirits*⟩
**5** a lively or brisk quality
**6** an attitude governing one's actions ⟨said in a *spirit* of fun⟩
**7** PERSON 1 ⟨a bold *spirit*⟩
**8** an alcoholic liquor — usually used in pl.
**9** **spirits** *pl* a solution in alcohol ⟨*spirits* of camphor⟩
**10** real meaning or intention ⟨the *spirit* of the law⟩
**spir·it·less** \-ləs\ *adj*

**²spirit** *vb*
to carry off secretly or mysteriously

**spir·it·ed** \'spir-ət-əd\ *adj*
full of courage or energy

**[1]spir·i·tu·al** \'spir-i-chə-wəl\ *adj*
**1** of, relating to, or consisting of spirit : not bodily or material
**2** of or relating to sacred or religious matters
**spir·i·tu·al·ly** *adv*

**[2]spiritual** *n*
a religious folk song developed especially among Negroes of the southern United States

**[1]spit** \'spit\ *n*
**1** a thin pointed rod for holding meat over a fire
**2** a small point of land that runs out into a body of water

**[2]spit** *vb* **spit** *or* **spat** \'spat\; **spit·ting**
**1** to cause (as saliva) to spurt from the mouth
**2** to express by or as if by spitting ⟨*spitting* an angry answer⟩
**3** to give off usually briskly : EMIT ⟨the fire is *spitting* sparks⟩
**4** to rain lightly or snow in flurries

**[3]spit** *n*
**1** SALIVA
**2** the act of spitting
**3** a foamy material given out by some insects
**4** perfect likeness ⟨the child was the *spit* and image of the parent⟩

**[1]spite** \'spīt\ *n*
dislike or hatred for another person with a wish to torment, anger, or defeat
**in spite of** without being prevented by ⟨failed *in spite of* our efforts⟩

**[2]spite** *vb* **spit·ed**; **spit·ing**
ANNOY, ANGER ⟨did it to *spite* me⟩

**spite·ful** \'spīt-fəl\ *adj*
filled with or showing spite : MALICIOUS
**spite·ful·ly** \-fə-lē\ *adv*

**spit·tle** \'spit-l\ *n*
**1** SALIVA
**2** [3]SPIT 3

**[1]splash** \'splash\ *vb*
**1** to hit (something liquid or sloppy) and cause to move and scatter roughly ⟨*splash* water⟩
**2** to wet or soil by spattering with water or mud ⟨*splashed* by a passing car⟩
**3** to move or strike with a splashing sound ⟨*splash* through a puddle⟩
**4** to spread or scatter like a splashed liquid ⟨the sunset *splashed* the sky with red⟩

**[2]splash** *n*
**1** splashed material
**2** a spot or smear from or as if from splashed liquid
**3** the sound or action of splashing

**[1]splat·ter** \'splat-ər\ *vb*
[1]SPLASH, SPATTER

**[2]splatter** *n*
[2]SPLASH

**spleen** \'splēn\ *n*
an organ near the stomach that destroys worn-out red blood cells and produces some of the white blood cells

**splen·did** \'splen-dəd\ *adj*
**1** having or showing splendor : BRILLIANT
**2** impressive in beauty, excellence, or magnificence ⟨did a *splendid* job⟩ ⟨a *splendid* palace⟩
**3** GRAND 4
**splen·did·ly** *adv*

**Synonyms** SPLENDID, GLORIOUS, and SUPERB mean very impressive. SPLENDID suggests that something is far above the ordinary in excellence or magnificence ⟨what a *splendid* idea⟩ ⟨a *splendid* jewel⟩. GLORIOUS suggests that something is radiant with light or beauty ⟨a *glorious* sunset⟩. SUPERB suggests the highest possible point of magnificence or excellence ⟨a *superb* museum⟩ ⟨the food was *superb*⟩.

**splen·dor** \'splen-dər\ *n*
**1** great brightness ⟨the *splendor* of the sun⟩
**2** POMP, GLORY ⟨the *splendors* of ancient Rome⟩

**[1]splice** \'splīs\ *vb* **spliced**; **splic·ing**
**1** to unite (as two ropes) by weaving together
**2** to unite (as rails or pieces of film) by connecting the ends together

**[2]splice** *n*
a joining or joint made by splicing

**splint** \'splint\ *n*
**1** a thin flexible strip of wood woven together with others in making a chair seat or basket
**2** a device for keeping a broken or displaced bone in place

**[1]splin·ter** \'splint-ər\ *n*
a thin piece split or torn off lengthwise : SLIVER

**[2]splinter** *vb*
to break into splinters

**[1]split** \'split\ *vb* **split**; **split·ting**
**1** to divide lengthwise or by layers ⟨*split* a log⟩
**2** to separate the parts of by putting something between ⟨a river *split* the town⟩
**3** to burst or break apart or in pieces ⟨the melon fell and *split* open⟩
**4** to divide into shares or sections ⟨we *split* the profit⟩

**[2]split 3:** a gymnast performing a split

**[2]split** *n*
**1** a product or result of splitting : CRACK
**2** the act or process of splitting : DIVISION ⟨a *split* in a political party⟩
**3** ▲ the feat of lowering oneself to the floor or leaping into the air with the legs extended in a straight line and in opposite directions

**[3]split** *adj*
divided by or as if by splitting

**[1]spoil** \'spȯil\ *n*
stolen goods : PLUNDER

**[2]spoil** *vb* **spoiled** \'spȯild\ *or* **spoilt** \'spȯilt\; **spoil·ing**
**1** [1]PLUNDER, ROB
**2** to damage badly : RUIN
**3** to damage the quality or effect of ⟨a quarrel *spoiled* the celebration⟩
**4** to decay or lose freshness, value, or usefulness by being kept too long ⟨the milk *spoiled*⟩
**5** to damage the disposition of by letting get away with too much ⟨*spoil* a child⟩

**spoil·age** \'spȯi-lij\ *n*
the action of spoiling or condition of being spoiled ⟨food *spoilage*⟩

**¹spoke** *past of* SPEAK

**²spoke** \'spōk\ *n*
▼ one of the bars or rods extending from the hub of a wheel to the rim

**²spoke:**
spokes on a bicycle wheel

**¹spoken** *past participle of* SPEAK

**²spo·ken** \'spō-kən\ *adj*
**1** expressed in speech : ORAL ⟨a *spoken* message⟩
**2** used in speaking ⟨the *spoken* language⟩
**3** speaking in a specified manner ⟨soft-*spoken*⟩

**spokes·man** \'spōk-smən\ *n, pl* **spokes·men** \'spōk-smən\
SPOKESPERSON

**spokes·per·son** \'spōk-ˌspərs-ⁿn\ *n*
a person who speaks for another or for a group

**spokes·wom·an** \'spōk-ˌswu̇m-ən\ *n, pl* **spokes·wom·en** \-ˌswim-ən\
a woman who is a spokesperson

**¹sponge** \'spənj\ *n*
**1** a springy mass of horny fibers that forms the skeleton of a group of sea animals, is able to absorb water freely, and is used for cleaning
**2** any of a group of water animals that have the form of hollow cell colonies made up of two layers and that include those whose skeletons are sponges
**3** a manufactured product (as of rubber or plastic) having the springy absorbent quality of natural sponge
**4** a pad of folded gauze used in surgery and medicine
**sponge·like** \-ˌlīk\ *adj*

**²sponge** *vb* **sponged**; **spong·ing**
**1** to clean or wipe with a sponge
**2** to absorb with or like a sponge
**3** to get something or live at the expense of another

**spongy** \'spən-jē\ *adj* **spong·i·er**; **spong·i·est**
like a sponge in appearance or in ability to absorb : soft and full of holes or moisture

**¹spon·sor** \'spän-sər\ *n*
**1** a person who takes the responsibility for some other person or thing ⟨agreed to be our *sponsor* at the club⟩
**2** GODPARENT
**3** a person or an organization that pays for or plans and carries out a project or activity
**4** a person or an organization that pays the cost of a radio or television program
**spon·sor·ship** \-ˌship\ *n*

**²sponsor** *vb*
to act as sponsor for

**spon·ta·ne·ous** \spän-'tā-nē-əs\ *adj*
**1** done, said, or produced freely and naturally ⟨*spontaneous* laughter⟩
**2** acting or taking place without any outside force or cause
**spon·ta·ne·ous·ly** *adv*

**spontaneous combustion** *n*
a bursting of material into flame from the heat produced within itself through chemical action

**spook** \'spük\ *n*
GHOST, SPECTER

**spooky** \'spü-kē\ *adj* **spook·i·er**; **spook·i·est**
**1** like a ghost ⟨a *spooky* figure⟩
**2** suggesting the presence of ghosts ⟨a *spooky* place⟩

**¹spool** \'spül\ *n*
► a small cylinder which has a rim or ridge at each end and a hole from end to end for a pin or spindle and on which material (as thread, wire, or tape) is wound

**¹spool:**
a spool of thread

**²spool** *vb*
to wind on a spool

**¹spoon** \'spün\ *n*
a utensil with a shallow bowl and a handle used especially in cooking and eating

**²spoon** *vb*
to take up in or as if in a spoon

**spoon·bill** \'spün-ˌbil\ *n*
▼ a wading bird related to the ibises and having a bill which widens and flattens at the tip

**spoonbill:**
a roseate \'rō-zē-ət\ spoonbill

**spoon·ful** \'spün-ˌfu̇l\ *n, pl* **spoon·fuls** \-ˌfu̇lz\ *or* **spoons·ful** \'spünz-ˌfu̇l\
as much as a spoon can hold

**spore** \'spōr\ *n*
a reproductive body of various plants and some lower animals that consists of a single cell and is able to produce a new individual
**spored** \'spōrd\ *adj*

**¹sport** \'spōrt\ *vb*
**1** to amuse oneself : FROLIC
**2** to speak or act in fun
**3** SHOW OFF ⟨*sport* new shoes⟩

**²sport** *n*
**1** PASTIME, RECREATION
**2** physical activity (as running or an athletic game) engaged in for pleasure ⟨skating is my favorite *sport*⟩
**3** FUN 3 ⟨made *sport* of their embarrassment⟩
**4** a person thought of with respect

to the ideals of sportsmanship ⟨a good *sport*⟩ ⟨a poor *sport*⟩

**sports·man** \'spōrt-smən\ *n, pl* **sports·men** \'spōrt-smən\
a person who engages in or is interested in sports and especially outdoor sports (as hunting and fishing)

**sports·man·ship** \'spōrt-smən-,ship\ *n*
fair play, respect for opponents, and gracious behavior in winning or losing

**sports·wom·an** \'spōrt-,swu̇m-ən\ *n, pl* **sports·wom·en** \-,swim-ən\
a woman who engages in or is interested in sports and especially outdoor sports

**sport–util·i·ty vehicle** \'spōrt-yü-'til-ət-ē-\ *n*
an automobile similar to a station wagon but built on a light truck frame

**[1]spot** \'spät\ *n*
**1** something bad that others know about one : FAULT
**2** a small part that is different (as in color) from the main part
**3** an area soiled or marked (as by dirt)
**4** a particular place ⟨a good *spot* for a picnic⟩
**spot·ted** \'spät-əd\ *adj*
**on the spot**
**1** right away : IMMEDIATELY
**2** at the place of action
**3** in difficulty or danger

**[2]spot** *vb* **spot·ted**; **spot·ting**
**1** to mark or be marked with spots
**2** to single out : IDENTIFY

**spot·less** \'spät-ləs\ *adj*
free from spot or blemish : perfectly clean or pure
**spot·less·ly** *adv*
**spot·less·ness** *n*

**[1]spot·light** \'spät-,līt\ *n*
**1** a spot of light used to show up a particular area, person, or thing (as on a stage)
**2** public notice
**3** ▶ a light to direct a narrow strong beam of light on a small area

**[2]spotlight** *vb* **spot·light·ed** *or* **spot·lit** \'spät-,lit\; **spot·light·ing**
**1** to light up with a spotlight
**2** to bring to public attention

**spotted owl** *n*
a rare brown owl with white spots and dark stripes that is found from British Columbia to southern California and central Mexico

**spot·ty** \'spät-ē\ *adj* **spot·ti·er**; **spot·ti·est**
**1** having spots
**2** not always the same especially in quality ⟨your work has been *spotty*⟩

**spouse** \'spau̇s\ *n*
a married person : HUSBAND, WIFE

**[1]spout** \'spau̇t\ *vb*
**1** to shoot out (liquid) with force ⟨wells *spouting* oil⟩
**2** to speak with a long and quick flow of words so as to sound important
**3** to flow out with force : SPURT

**[2]spout** *n*
**1** a tube, pipe, or hole through which something (as rainwater) spouts
**2** a sudden strong stream of fluid

**[1]sprain** \'sprān\ *n*
**1** a sudden or severe twisting of a joint with stretching or tearing of ligaments
**2** a sprained condition

**[2]sprain** *vb*
to injure by a sudden or severe twist

**sprang** *past of* SPRING

**[1]sprawl** \'sprȯl\ *vb*
**1** to lie or sit with arms and legs spread out
**2** to spread out in an uneven or awkward way ⟨a *sprawling* city⟩

**[1]spotlight 3:** a spotlight used in a film studio

**[2]sprawl** *n*
the act or posture of sprawling

**[1]spray** \'sprā\ *n*
a green or flowering branch or a usually flat arrangement of these

**[2]spray** *n*
**1** liquid flying in fine drops like water blown from a wave
**2** a burst of fine mist (as from an atomizer)
**3** a device (as an atomizer) for scattering a spray of liquid or mist

**[3]spray** *vb*
**1** to scatter or let fall in a spray ⟨*spray* paint⟩
**2** to scatter spray on or into ⟨*spray* an orchard⟩
**spray·er** *n*

**spray gun** *n*
a device for spraying paints, varnishes, or insect poisons

**[1]spread** \'spred\ *vb* **spread**; **spread·ing**
**1** to open over a larger area ⟨*spread* out a map⟩
**2** to stretch out : EXTEND ⟨*spread* my arms wide⟩
**3** SCATTER 1, STREW ⟨*spread* fertilizer⟩
**4** to give out over a period of time or among a group ⟨*spread* work to make it last⟩
**5** to put a layer of on a surface ⟨*spread* butter on bread⟩
**6** to cover something with ⟨*spread* a cloth on the table⟩
**7** to prepare for a meal : SET ⟨*spread* a table⟩
**8** to pass from person to person ⟨the news *spread* rapidly⟩ ⟨flies *spread* disease⟩
**9** to stretch or move apart ⟨*spreading* my fingers⟩

**[2]spread** *n*
**1** the act or process of spreading ⟨the *spread* of education⟩
**2** extent of spreading ⟨the *spread* of a bird's wings⟩
**3** a noticeable display in a magazine or newspaper
**4** a food to be spread on bread or crackers
**5** a very fine meal : FEAST
**6** a cloth cover for a table or bed
**7** distance between two points

**spree** \'sprē\ *n*
an outburst of activity ⟨went on a buying *spree*⟩

**sprig** \'sprig\ *n*
a small shoot or twig

**spright·ly** \'sprīt-lē\ *adj* **spright·li·er**; **spright·li·est**
full of spirit : LIVELY

[1]**spring** \'spring\ *vb* **sprang** \'sprang\ *or* **sprung** \'sprəng\; **sprung**; **spring·ing**
**1** to appear or grow quickly ⟨weeds *sprang* up overnight⟩
**2** to come from by birth or descent ⟨*sprang* from poor parents⟩
**3** to come into being : ARISE ⟨hope *springs* eternal⟩
**4** to move suddenly upward or forward : LEAP
**5** to have (a leak) appear
**6** to move quickly by elastic force ⟨the lid *sprang* shut⟩
**7** [2]WARP 1
**8** to cause to operate suddenly ⟨*spring* a trap⟩

[2]**spring** *n*
**1** a source of supply (as of water coming up from the ground)
**2** the season between winter and summer including in the northern hemisphere usually the months of March, April, and May
**3** a time or season of growth or development
**4** ▶ an elastic body or device that recovers its original shape when it is released after being squeezed or stretched
**5** the act or an instance of leaping up or forward
**6** elastic power or force ⟨a *spring* in your step⟩

[2]**spring 4**

**spring·board** \'spring-,bōrd\ *n*
▼ a flexible board usually fastened at one end and used for jumping high in the air in gymnastics or diving

**springboard:** a springboard used in gymnastics

**spring peep·er** \-'pē-pər\ *n*
▶ a small frog that lives in trees and makes a high peeping sound heard mostly in spring

**spring·time** \'spring-,tīm\ *n*
the season of spring

**springy** \'spring-ē\ *adj* **spring·i·er**; **spring·i·est**
**1** [1]ELASTIC
**2** having or showing a lively and energetic movement ⟨walks with a *springy* step⟩

[1]**sprin·kle** \'spring-kəl\ *vb* **sprin·kled**; **sprin·kling**
**1** to scatter in drops ⟨*sprinkle* water⟩
**2** to scatter over or in or among
**3** to rain lightly
**sprin·kler** \-klər\ *n*

[2]**sprinkle** *n*
**1** a light rain
**2** SPRINKLING

**sprin·kling** \'spring-kling\ *n*
a very small number or amount

[1]**sprint** \'sprint\ *vb*
to run at top speed especially for a short distance
**sprint·er** *n*

[2]**sprint** *n*
**1** a short run at top speed
**2** a race over a short distance

**sprite** \'sprīt\ *n*
ELF, FAIRY

**sprock·et** \'spräk-ət\ *n*
▶ one of many points that stick up on the rim of a wheel (**sprocket wheel**) shaped so as to fit into the links of a chain

*sprocket wheel*
*motorcycle chain*
*sprocket*

**sprockets** on the sprocket wheels of a motorcycle

[1]**sprout** \'sprau̇t\ *vb*
to produce or cause to produce fresh young growth ⟨new twigs *sprouting* from an old tree⟩ ⟨we need rain to *sprout* the seeds⟩

[2]**sprout** *n*
a young stem of a plant especially when coming directly from a seed or root

**spring peeper**

[1]**spruce** \'sprüs\ *vb* **spruced**; **spruc·ing**
to make something or oneself neat or stylish in appearance ⟨*spruce* up a room⟩ ⟨*spruce* up a bit before a meeting⟩

[2]**spruce** *adj* **spruc·er**; **spruc·est**
neat or stylish in appearance

[3]**spruce** *n*
an evergreen tree shaped like a cone with a thick growth of short needles, drooping cones, and light soft wood

**sprung** *past of* SPRING

**spry** \'sprī\ *adj* **spri·er** *or* **spry·er**; **spri·est** *or* **spry·est**
LIVELY 1, ACTIVE ⟨busy *spry* old people⟩

**spun** *past of* SPIN

**spunk** \'spəngk\ *n*
COURAGE, SPIRIT

**Word History** The English word *spunk* comes from a word in a language of Scotland that meant "tinder" or "sponge." This word, in turn, came from a Latin word that meant "sponge." The English word at first meant "tinder," which is a spongy material that catches fire easily. Since the human spirit can also be thought of as catching fire, *spunk* came to mean "spirit" or "pluck."

**[1]spur** \'spər\ *n*
**1** ▼ a pointed device fastened to the back of a rider's boot and used to urge a horse on
**2** something that makes one want to do something **:** INCENTIVE
**3** a stiff sharp point (as a horny spine on the leg of a rooster)
**4** a mass of jagged rock coming out from the side of a mountain
**5** a short section of railway track coming away from the main line
**spurred** \'spərd\ *adj*

*spur*

**[1]spur 1:** spurs on a pair of cowboy boots

**[2]spur** *vb* **spurred**; **spur·ring**
**1** to urge a horse on with spurs
**2** INCITE

**spurn** \'spərn\ *vb*
to reject with scorn ⟨*spurn* an offer⟩

**[1]spurt** \'spərt\ *vb*
**1** to pour out suddenly **:** SPOUT
**2** [1]SQUIRT

**[2]spurt** *n*
a sudden pouring out **:** JET

**[3]spurt** *n*
a brief burst of increased effort

**[4]spurt** *vb*
to make a spurt

**[1]sput·ter** \'spət-ər\ *vb*
**1** to spit or squirt bits of food or saliva noisily from the mouth
**2** to speak in a hasty or explosive way in confusion or excitement ⟨*sputtered* out protests⟩
**3** to make explosive popping sounds ⟨the motor *sputtered* and died⟩

**[2]sputter** *n*
the act or sound of sputtering

**[1]spy** \'spī\ *vb* **spied**; **spy·ing**
**1** to watch secretly
**2** to catch sight of **:** SEE ⟨*spy* land from a ship⟩

**[2]spy** *n, pl* **spies**
**1** a person who watches the movement or actions of others especially in secret
**2** a person who tries secretly to get information especially about an unfriendly country or its plans and actions

**spy·glass** \'spī-ˌglas\ *n*
► a small telescope

**squab** \'skwäb\ *n*
a young pigeon especially when about four weeks old

**[1]squab·ble** \'skwäb-əl\ *n*
a noisy quarrel usually over unimportant things

**[2]squabble** *vb* **squab·bled**; **squab·bling**
to quarrel noisily for little or no reason

**squad** \'skwäd\ *n*
**1** a small group of soldiers
**2** a small group working or playing together ⟨a football *squad*⟩

**squad car** *n*
CRUISER 2

**squad·ron** \'skwäd-rən\ *n*
a group especially of cavalry riders, military airplanes, or naval ships moving and working together

**squal·id** \'skwäl-əd\ *adj*
filthy or degraded from a lack of care or money

**[1]squall** \'skwȯl\ *vb*
to let out a harsh cry or scream

**[2]squall** *n*
a sudden strong gust of wind often with rain or snow

**squal·or** \'skwäl-ər\ *n*
the quality or state of being squalid ⟨live in *squalor*⟩

**squan·der** \'skwän-dər\ *vb*
to spend foolishly **:** WASTE

**[1]square** \'skwaər, 'skweər\ *n*
**1** ▼ an instrument having at least one right angle and two or more straight edges used to mark or test right angles ⟨a carpenter's *square*⟩

**[1]square 1:** a carpenter's square

**2** a flat figure that has four equal sides and four right angles
**3** something formed like a square ⟨the *squares* of a checkerboard⟩
**4** the product of a number or amount multiplied by itself
**5** an open place or area where two or more streets meet
**6** [1]BLOCK 6, 7

*viewing hole*

**spyglass**

**[2]square** *adj* **squar·er**; **squar·est**
**1** having four equal sides and four right angles
**2** forming a right angle
**3** multiplied by itself
**4** having outlines that suggest sharp corners rather than curves
**5** being a unit of area consisting of a square whose sides have a given length ⟨a *square* meter⟩
**6** having a specified length in each of two equal dimensions ⟨ten meters *square*⟩
**7** exactly adjusted
**8** [1]JUST 3, FAIR ⟨a *square* deal⟩
**9** leaving no balance **:** EVEN ⟨make accounts *square*⟩
**10** large enough to satisfy ⟨three *square* meals a day⟩
**square·ly** *adv*

**[3]square** *vb* **squared**; **squar·ing**
**1** to make square **:** form with right angles, straight edges, and flat surfaces
**2** to make straight ⟨*squared* my shoulders⟩
**3** to multiply a number by itself
**4** AGREE 4 ⟨your story does not *square* with the facts⟩
**5** [2]BALANCE 1, SETTLE ⟨*square* an account⟩

**[1]square dance** *n*
a lively dance for sets of four couples who form the sides of a square

**[2]square dance** *vb*
to dance a square dance
**square dancer** *n*
**square dancing** *n*

**square knot** *n*
▼ a knot made of two half-knots tied in opposite directions and typically used to join the ends of two cords

**square knot**

A B C D E F G H I J K L M N O P Q R S T U V W X Y Z

**square–rigged** \'skwaər-'rigd, 'skweər-\ *adj*
having the principal sails extended on yards fastened in a horizontal position to the masts at their center

**square root** *n*
a factor of a number that when multiplied by itself gives the number ⟨the *square root* of 9 is 3⟩

[1]**squash** \'skwäsh\ *vb*
to beat or press into a soft or flat mass : CRUSH

**squid**

[2]**squash** *n*
the fruit of any of several plants related to the gourds that is cooked as a vegetable or used for animal feed

[1]**squat** \'skwät\ *vb* **squat·ted**; **squat·ting**
**1** to crouch by bending the knees fully so as to sit on or close to the heels
**2** to settle without any right on land that one does not own
**3** to settle on government land in order to become the owner of the land

[2]**squat** *adj* **squat·ter**; **squat·test**
**1** bent in a deep crouch
**2** low to the ground
**3** having a short thick body

[3]**squat** *n*
**1** the act of squatting
**2** a squatting posture

[1]**squawk** \'skwȯk\ *vb*
**1** to make a harsh short scream
**2** to complain or protest loudly or with strong feeling

[2]**squawk** *n*
**1** a harsh short scream
**2** a noisy complaint

[1]**squeak** \'skwēk\ *vb*
**1** to make a short shrill cry
**2** to get, win, or pass with trouble : barely succeed ⟨just *squeaked* by⟩

[2]**squeak** *n*
a sharp shrill cry or sound

**squeaky** \'skwē-kē\ *adj* **squeak·i·er**; **squeak·i·est**
likely to squeak ⟨a *squeaky* door⟩

[1]**squeal** \'skwēl\ *vb*
**1** to make a sharp long shrill cry or noise
**2** INFORM 2

[2]**squeal** *n*
a shrill sharp cry or noise

[1]**squeeze** \'skwēz\ *vb* **squeezed**; **squeez·ing**
**1** to press together from the opposite sides or parts of : COMPRESS
**2** to get by squeezing ⟨*squeeze* juice from a lemon⟩
**3** to force or crowd in by compressing ⟨*squeeze* into a box⟩

[2]**squeeze** *n*
an act or instance of squeezing

**squid** \'skwid\ *n*
◀ a sea mollusk that is related to the octopus but has a long body and ten arms

[1]**squint** \'skwint\ *adj*
not able to look in the same direction — used of the two eyes

[2]**squint** *vb*
**1** to have squint eyes
**2** to look or peer with the eyes partly closed

[3]**squint** *n*
**1** the condition of being cross-eyed
**2** the action or an instance of squinting

[1]**squire** \'skwīr\ *n*
**1** a person who carries the shield or armor of a knight
**2** [1]ESCORT 1
**3** an owner of a country estate

[2]**squire** *vb* **squired**; **squir·ing**
to act as a squire or escort for

**squirm** \'skwərm\ *vb*
**1** to twist about like an eel or a worm
**2** to feel very embarrassed

**squir·rel** \'skwər-əl\ *n*
▶ a small gnawing animal (as the common American **red squirrel** and **gray squirrel**) usually with a bushy tail and soft fur and strong hind legs for leaping

**Word History** When a squirrel sits up, its long tail curves up and over its head and sometimes casts a shadow. The English word *squirrel* comes from the Greek word for a squirrel, which was made up of two words. The first meant "shadow." The second meant "tail."

[1]**squirt** \'skwərt\ *vb*
to shoot out liquid in a thin stream : SPURT

[2]**squirt** *n*
**1** an instrument for squirting liquid
**2** a small powerful stream of liquid : JET
**3** the action of squirting

[1]**stab** \'stab\ *n*
**1** a wound produced by or as if by a pointed weapon
**2** [2]THRUST 1
**3** [3]TRY, EFFORT ⟨make a *stab* at it⟩

### squirrel

Squirrels are rodents. Typical squirrels, such as the gray squirrel, red squirrel, and flying squirrel, live in trees. Those that live on the ground, such as chipmunks, are usually called ground squirrels. Both tree-living squirrels and ground squirrels feed on acorns and nuts.

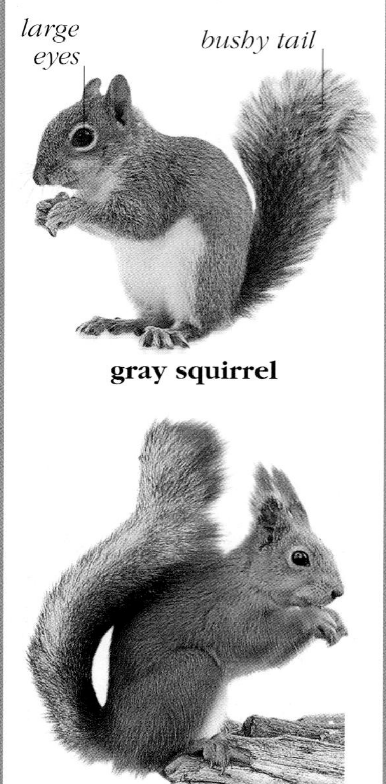


**gray squirrel**

**European red squirrel**

[2]**stab** *vb* **stabbed**; **stab·bing**
**1** to wound or pierce with a stab
**2** [1]DRIVE 2, THRUST ⟨*stab* a fork into meat⟩

**sta·bil·i·ty** \stə-ˈbil-ət-ē\ *n, pl* **sta·bil·i·ties**
the condition of being stable

**sta·bi·lize** \ˈstā-bə-ˌlīz\ *vb* **sta·bi·lized**; **sta·bi·liz·ing**
to make or become stable
**sta·bi·liz·er** *n*

[1]**sta·ble** \ˈstā-bəl\ *n*
a building in which domestic animals are housed and cared for

[2]**stable** *vb* **sta·bled**; **sta·bling**
to put or keep in a stable

[3]**stable** *adj* **sta·bler**; **sta·blest**
**1** not easily changed or affected ⟨a *stable* government⟩
**2** not likely to change suddenly or greatly ⟨a *stable* income⟩
**3** LASTING ⟨a *stable* peace⟩
**4** RELIABLE

**stac·ca·to** \stə-ˈkät-ō\ *adj*
**1** cut short so as not to sound connected ⟨*staccato* notes⟩
**2** played or sung with breaks between notes ⟨a *staccato* passage⟩

[1]**stack** \ˈstak\ *n*
**1** a large pile (as of hay) usually shaped like a cone
**2** a neat pile of objects usually one on top of the other
**3** a large number or amount
**4** CHIMNEY 1, SMOKESTACK
**5** a structure with shelves for storing books

[2]**stack** *vb*
to arrange in or form a stack : PILE

**sta·di·um** \ˈstād-ē-əm\ *n, pl* **sta·di·ums** *or* **sta·dia** \ˈstād-ē-ə\
a large outdoor structure with rows of seats for spectators at sports events

**staff** \ˈstaf\ *n, pl* **staffs** *or* **staves** \ˈstavz\
**1** a pole, stick, rod, or bar used as a support or as a sign of authority ⟨the *staff* of a flag⟩ ⟨a bishop's *staff*⟩
**2** something that is a source of strength ⟨bread is the *staff* of life⟩
**3** the five parallel lines with their four spaces on which music is written
**4** *pl* *staffs* a group of persons serving as assistants to or employees under a chief ⟨a hospital *staff*⟩
**5** *pl* *staffs* a group of military officers who plan and manage for a commanding officer

**staff sergeant** *n*
a noncommissioned officer in the Army, Air Force, or Marine Corps ranking above a sergeant

**staff sergeant major** *n*
a noncommissioned officer in the Army ranking above a master sergeant

[1]**stag** \ˈstag\ *n*
**1** ◀ an adult male deer especially of the larger kind
**2** a man who goes to a social gathering without escorting a woman

[2]**stag** *adj*
intended or thought suitable for men only ⟨a *stag* party⟩

[1]**stage** \ˈstāj\ *n*
**1** a raised floor (as for speaking or giving plays)
**2** a place where something important happens
**3** the theatrical profession or art
**4** a step forward in a journey, a task, a process, or a development : PHASE
**5** STAGECOACH

[2]**stage** *vb* **staged**; **stag·ing**
to produce or show to the public on or as if on the stage ⟨*stages* two plays each year⟩

**stage·coach** \ˈstāj-ˌkōch\ *n*
◀ a coach pulled by horses that runs on a schedule from place to place carrying passengers and mail

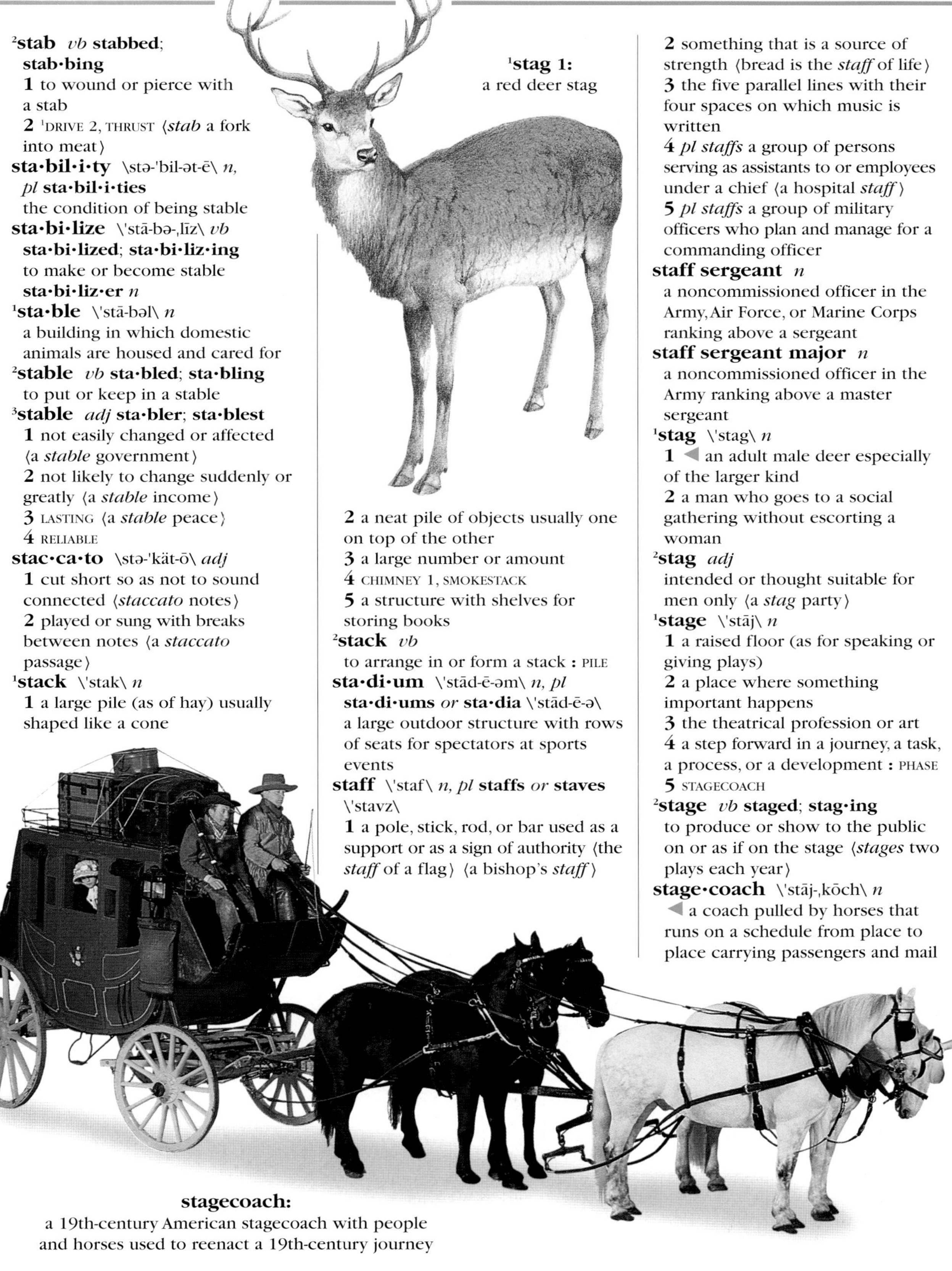

[1]**stag 1:** a red deer stag

**stagecoach:** a 19th-century American stagecoach with people and horses used to reenact a 19th-century journey

A B C D E F G H I J K L M N O P Q R S T U V W X Y Z

**[1]stag·ger** \'stag-ər\ *vb*
**1** to move unsteadily from side to side as if about to fall : REEL
**2** to cause to move unsteadily
**3** to cause great surprise or shock in
**4** to place or arrange in a zigzag but balanced way ⟨*stagger* the nails along either edge of the board⟩

**[2]stagger** *n*
a reeling or unsteady walk

**stag·nant** \'stag-nənt\ *adj*
**1** not flowing ⟨a *stagnant* pool⟩
**2** not active or brisk : DULL ⟨*stagnant* business⟩

**stag·nate** \'stag-,nāt\ *vb* **stag·nat·ed**; **stag·nat·ing**
to be or become stagnant

**[1]stain** \'stān\ *vb*
**1** to soil or discolor especially in spots
**2** [2]COLOR 2, TINGE
**3** [1]CORRUPT 1
**4** [1]DISGRACE

**[2]stain** *n*
**1** [1]SPOT 3, DISCOLORATION
**2** a mark of guilt or disgrace : STIGMA
**3** something (as a dye) used in staining
**stain·less** \-ləs\ *adj*

**stainless steel** *n*
an alloy of steel and chromium that is resistant to stain, rust, and corrosion

**stair** \'staər, 'steər\ *n*
**1** a series of steps or flights of steps for going from one level to another — often used in pl. ⟨ran down the *stairs*⟩
**2** one step of a stairway

**stair·case** \'staər-,kās, 'steər-\ *n*
a flight of stairs with their supporting structure and railings

**stair·way** \'staər-,wā, 'steər-\ *n*
one or more flights of stairs usually with connecting landings

**[1]stake** \'stāk\ *n*
**1** a pointed piece (as of wood) driven or to be driven into the ground as a marker or to support something
**2** a post to which a person is tied to be put to death by burning
**3** something that is put up to be won or lost in gambling ⟨play cards for high *stakes*⟩
**4** the prize in a contest
**5** [1]SHARE 1, INTEREST ⟨a *stake* in the business⟩
**at stake** in a position to be lost if something goes wrong ⟨your job is *at stake*⟩

**[2]stake** *vb* **staked**; **stak·ing**
**1** to mark the limits of by stakes ⟨*stake* out a mining claim⟩
**2** to fasten or support (as plants) with stakes
**3** [2]BET 1
**4** to give money to to help (as with a project)

**sta·lac·tite** \stə-'lak-,tīt\ *n*
a deposit hanging from the roof or side of a cave in the shape of an icicle formed by the partial evaporating of dripping water containing lime

**sta·lag·mite** \stə-'lag-,mīt\ *n*
a deposit like an upside down stalactite formed by the dripping of water containing lime onto the floor of a cave

**[1]stale** \'stāl\ *adj* **stal·er**; **stal·est**
**1** having lost a good taste or quality through age ⟨*stale* bread⟩
**2** used or heard so often as to be dull ⟨*stale* jokes⟩
**3** not so strong, energetic, or effective as before ⟨felt *stale* from lack of exercise⟩
**stale·ly** *adv*
**stale·ness** *n*

**[2]stale** *vb* **staled**; **stal·ing**
to make or become stale

**[1]stalk** \'stȯk\ *n*
**1** a plant stem especially when not woody ⟨*stalks* of asparagus⟩
**2** a slender supporting structure ⟨the *stalk* of a goblet⟩
**stalked** \'stȯkt\ *adj*
**stalk·less** \'stȯk-ləs\ *adj*

**[2]stalk 1:** a cat stalking prey

**[2]stalk** *vb*
**1** ◄ to hunt slowly and quietly ⟨a cat *stalking* a bird⟩
**2** to walk in a stiff or proud manner ⟨*stalked* angrily out of the room⟩
**3** to move through or follow as if stalking prey ⟨famine *stalked* the land⟩
**stalk·er** *n*

**[3]stalk** *n*
**1** the act of stalking
**2** a stalking way of walking

**[1]stall** \'stȯl\ *n*
**1** a compartment for one animal in a stable
**2** a space set off (as for parking an automobile)
**3** a seat in a church choir : a church pew
**4** a booth, stand, or counter where business may be carried on or articles may be displayed for sale

**[2]stall** *vb*
**1** to put or keep in a stall
**2** to stop or cause to stop usually by accident ⟨*stall* an engine⟩

**[3]stall** *n*
a trick to deceive or delay

**[4]stall** *vb*
to distract attention or make excuses to gain time ⟨quit *stalling* and answer the question⟩ ⟨try to *stall* them until I get the place cleaned up⟩

**stal·lion** \'stal-yən\ *n*
a male horse

**stal·wart** \'stȯl-wərt\ *adj*
STURDY, RESOLUTE ⟨a *stalwart* body⟩ ⟨*stalwart* spirits⟩

**sta·men** \'stā-mən\ *n*
▼ any of a row of organs at the center of a flower that bear the anthers which produce the pollen

**stamen:** a pink lily with long stamens

**stam·i·na** \'stam-ə-nə\ *n*
VIGOR 1, ENDURANCE

**¹stam·mer** \'stam-ər\ *vb*
to speak with involuntary stops and much repeating
**stam·mer·er** *n*

**²stammer** *n*
an act or instance of stammering

**¹stamp** \'stamp\ *vb*
**1** to bring the foot down hard and with noise ⟨don't *stamp* around in the house⟩
**2** to put an end to by or as if by hitting with the bottom of the foot ⟨*stamp* out the fire⟩ ⟨*stamp* out crime⟩
**3** to mark or cut out with a tool or device having a design ⟨*stamp* the bill paid⟩ ⟨*stamping* out coins⟩
**4** to attach a postage stamp to
**5** CHARACTERIZE 1 ⟨*stamped* them as cowards⟩

**²stamp** *n*
**1** a device or instrument for stamping
**2** the mark made by stamping
**3** a sign of a special quality ⟨the *stamp* of genius⟩
**4** the act of stamping
**5** ▼ a small piece of paper or a mark attached to something to show that a tax or fee has been paid ⟨a postage *stamp*⟩

**¹stam·pede** \stam-'pēd\ *n*
**1** a wild dash or flight of frightened animals ⟨a cattle *stampede*⟩
**2** a sudden foolish action or movement of a crowd of people ⟨the rumor started a *stampede* of buying⟩

**²stampede** *vb* **stam·ped·ed**; **stam·ped·ing**
**1** to run or cause (as cattle) to run away in panic
**2** to act or cause to act together suddenly and without thought ⟨refused to be *stampeded* by threats⟩

**stance** \'stans\ *n*
way of standing : POSTURE

**stanch** \'stȯnch\ *vb*
to stop or check the flow of (as blood)

**¹stand** \'stand\ *vb* **stood** \'stu̇d\; **stand·ing**
**1** to be in or take a vertical position on one's feet
**2** to take up or stay in a specified position or condition ⟨*stands* first in the class⟩ ⟨*stands* accused⟩ ⟨machines *standing* idle⟩
**3** to have an opinion ⟨how do you *stand* on taxes?⟩
**4** to rest, remain, or set in a usually vertical position ⟨*stand* the box in the corner⟩
**5** to be in a specified place ⟨the house *stands* on the hill⟩
**6** to stay in effect ⟨the order still *stands*⟩
**7** to put up with : ENDURE ⟨can't *stand* pain⟩
**8** UNDERGO ⟨*stand* trial⟩
**9** to perform the duty of ⟨*stand* guard⟩
**stand by** to be or remain loyal or true to ⟨*stand by* a promise⟩
**stand for**
**1** to be a symbol for : REPRESENT
**2** to put up with : PERMIT ⟨won't *stand for* any nonsense⟩

**²stand** *n*
**1** an act of standing
**2** a halt for defense or resistance ⟨made a *stand* against the enemy⟩
**3** a place or post especially where one stands : STATION ⟨took the witness *stand*⟩
**4** a structure containing rows of seats for spectators of a sport or spectacle
**5** a raised area (as for speakers or performers)
**6** a stall or booth often outdoors for a small business
**7** a small structure (as a rack or table) on or in which something may be placed ⟨an umbrella *stand*⟩
**8** POSITION 2 ⟨they took a strong *stand* on the question⟩

**¹stan·dard** \'stan-dərd\ *n*
**1** a figure used as a symbol by an organized body of people
**2** the personal flag of the ruler of a state
**3** something set up as a rule for measuring or as a model ⟨a *standard* of weight⟩ ⟨*standards* of good manners⟩
**4** an upright support ⟨a lamp *standard*⟩

**²standard** *adj*
**1** used as or matching a standard ⟨*standard* weight⟩
**2** regularly and widely used ⟨a *standard* practice in the trade⟩
**3** widely known and accepted to be of good and permanent value ⟨*standard* reference works⟩

### ²stamp 5

Stamps to show payment of postal charges were introduced in the mid-19th century. Most early stamps featured portraits of a country's ruler or its political leaders, but over the years it has become more common for countries to issue stamps showing a wide variety of other subjects as well. Countries occasionally issue stamps that have unusual shapes.

stamp from the Netherlands

stamp from Japan

stamp from the US

1960s stamp from Tonga

stamp from Sri Lanka

**stan·dard·ize** \'stan-dər-ˌdīz\ *vb* **stan·dard·ized; stan·dard·iz·ing** to make standard or alike

**standard time** *n* the time established by law or by common usage over a region or country

**stand by** *vb*
1 to be present ⟨we *stood by* and watched the fight⟩
2 to be or get ready to act ⟨*stand by* to help⟩

**¹stand·ing** \'stan-ding\ *adj*
1 ¹ERECT ⟨*standing* grain⟩
2 not flowing : STAGNANT ⟨a *standing* pool⟩
3 remaining at the same level or amount until canceled ⟨a *standing* offer⟩
4 PERMANENT ⟨a *standing* army⟩

**²standing** *n*
1 the action or position of one that stands
2 length of existence or service ⟨a custom of long *standing*⟩
3 POSITION 4, STATUS ⟨had the highest *standing* in the class⟩

**stand out** *vb* to be easily seen or recognized

**stand·point** \'stand-ˌpȯint\ *n* a way in which things are thought about : POINT OF VIEW

**stand·still** \'stand-ˌstil\ *n* the condition of not being active or busy : STOP ⟨business was at a *standstill*⟩

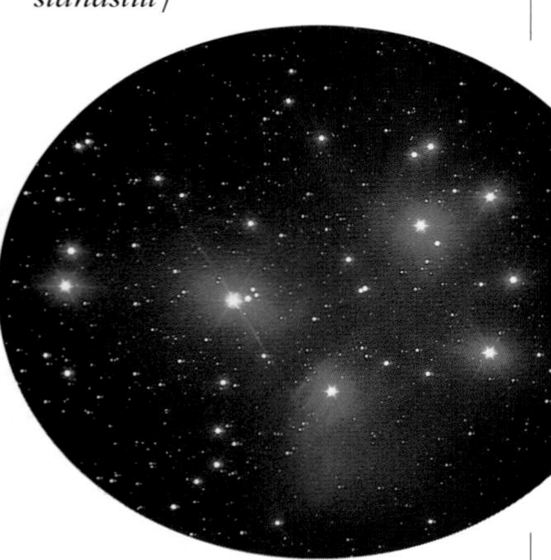

**¹star 1:** stars in the night sky

**stand up** *vb*
1 to stay in good condition ⟨*stands up* well under hard use⟩
2 to fail to keep an appointment with ⟨you *stood* me *up* yesterday⟩

**stand up for** DEFEND 2

**stand up to** to face boldly

**stank** *past of* STINK

**stan·za** \'stan-zə\ *n* a group of lines forming a division of a poem

**¹sta·ple** \'stā-pəl\ *n*
1 a piece of metal shaped like a U with sharp points to be driven into a surface to hold something (as a hook, rope, or wire)
2 a short thin wire with bent ends that is driven through papers and clinched to hold them together or driven through thin material to fasten it to a surface ⟨fasten cardboard to wood with *staples*⟩

**²staple** *vb* **sta·pled; sta·pling** to fasten with staples

**³staple** *n*
1 a chief product of business or farming of a place
2 something that is used widely and often
3 the chief part of something ⟨potatoes are the *staple* of their diet⟩
4 fiber (as cotton or wool) suitable for spinning into yarn

**⁴staple** *adj*
1 much used, needed, or enjoyed usually by many people ⟨a *staple* plot in mystery novels⟩
2 ¹PRINCIPAL, CHIEF ⟨*staple* foods⟩

**sta·pler** \'stā-plər\ *n* a device that staples

**¹star** \'stär\ *n*
1 ◀ any of those celestial bodies except planets which are visible at night and look like fixed points of light
2 a star or especially a planet that is believed in astrology to influence one's life ⟨born under a lucky *star*⟩
3 a figure or thing (as a medal) with five or more points that represents or suggests a star
4 the principal member of a theater or opera company
5 a very talented or popular performer

**²star** *vb* **starred; star·ring**
1 to sprinkle or decorate with or as if with stars
2 to mark with a star as being special or very good
3 to mark with an asterisk
4 to present in the role of a star
5 to play the most important role ⟨*star* in a new play⟩
6 to perform in an outstanding manner

**star·board** \'stär-bərd\ *n* the right side of a ship or airplane looking forward

**¹starch** \'stärch\ *vb* to stiffen with starch

**²starch** *n* a white odorless tasteless substance that is the chief storage form of carbohydrates in plants, is an important food, and has also various household and business uses (as for stiffening clothes)

**starchy** \'stär-chē\ *adj* **starch·i·er; starch·i·est** like or containing starch

**¹stare** \'staər, 'steər\ *vb* **stared; star·ing** to look at hard and long often with wide-open eyes **synonyms** see GAZE

**²stare** *n* the act or an instance of staring

**star·fish** \'stär-ˌfish\ *n* ▶ any of a group of sea animals mostly having five arms that spread out from a central disk and feeding mostly on mollusks

**¹stark** \'stärk\ *adj*
1 ¹BARREN 2, DESOLATE ⟨a *stark* landscape⟩
2 ¹UTTER, ABSOLUTE ⟨*stark* folly⟩

**²stark** *adv* COMPLETELY ⟨*stark* mad⟩

**star·light** \'stär-ˌlīt\ *n* the light given by the stars

**starling**

**star·ling** \'stär-ling\ *n* ▲ a dark brown or in summer greenish black European bird about the size of a robin that is now common and often a pest in the United States

**star·lit** \'stär-ˌlit\ *adj* lighted by the stars

## starfish

Starfish belong to a group of animals with mostly spiny skin and body parts arranged symmetrically around a central axis. Some starfish have smooth skin, but all are protected by a hard outer skeleton made of chalky plates. Starfish move by pumping water through tiny tubes in their feet, which propels them forward.

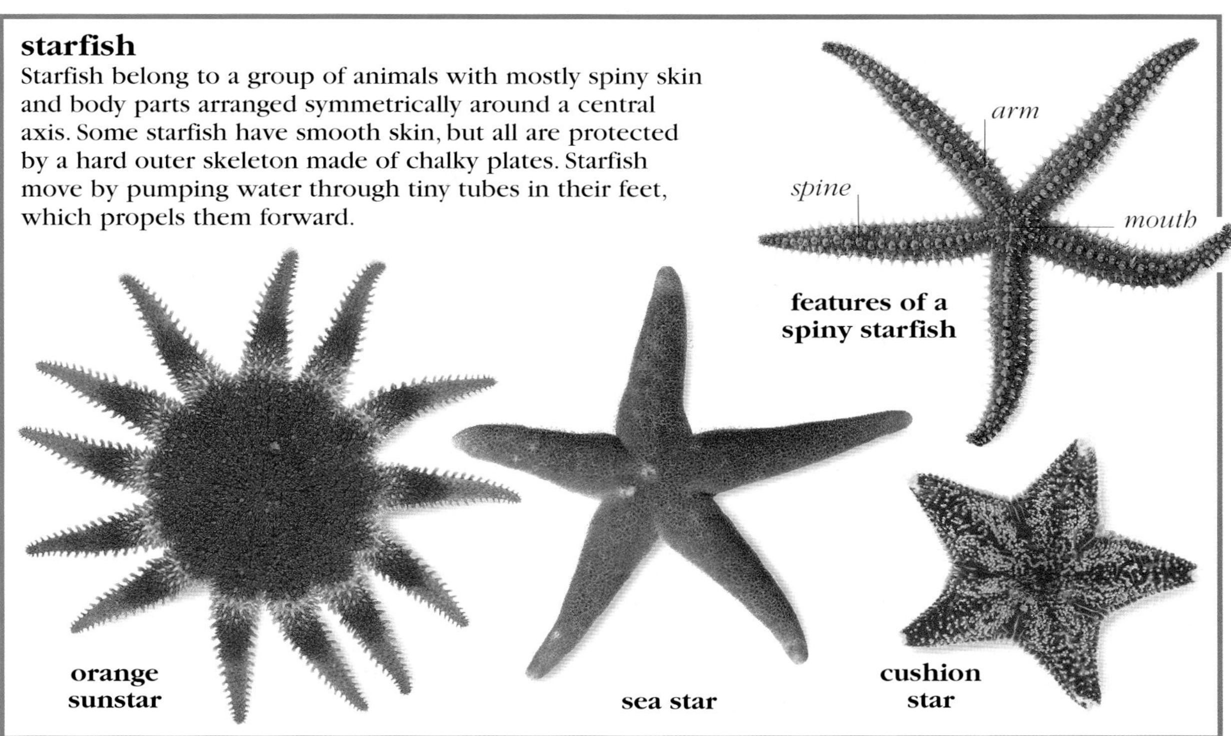


**star•ry** \'stär-ē\ *adj* **star•ri•er**; **star•ri•est**
1 full of stars ⟨*starry* heavens⟩
2 of, relating to, or consisting of stars ⟨*starry* light⟩
3 shining like stars ⟨*starry* eyes⟩

**Stars and Stripes** *n sing or pl*
the flag of the United States

**[1]start** \'stärt\ *vb*
1 to move suddenly and quickly : give a sudden twitch or jerk (as in surprise)
2 to come or bring into being or action ⟨*start* a rumor⟩ ⟨rain is likely to *start* soon⟩
3 to stick out or seem to stick out ⟨their eyes *started* from the sockets⟩
4 SET OUT 2 ⟨*start* for home⟩
5 to set going ⟨*start* the motor⟩

**[2]start** *n*
1 a sudden movement ⟨a *start* of surprise⟩
2 a brief act, movement, or effort ⟨work by fits and *starts*⟩
3 a beginning of movement, action, or development ⟨got an early *start*⟩
4 a place of beginning (as of a race)

**start•er** \'stärt-ər\ *n*
someone or something that starts something or causes something else to start ⟨there were seven *starters* in the race⟩ ⟨the *starter* of a motor⟩

**star•tle** \'stärt-l\ *vb* **star•tled**; **star•tling**
1 to cause to move or jump (as in surprise or fear)
2 to frighten suddenly but slightly

**star•tling** *adj*
causing a moment of fright or surprise

**star•va•tion** \stär-'vā-shən\ *n*
the act or an instance of starving : the condition of being starved

**starve** \'stärv\ *vb* **starved**; **starv•ing**
1 to suffer or die or cause to suffer or die from lack of food
2 to suffer or cause to suffer from a lack of something other than food ⟨a child *starving* for affection⟩

**[1]state** \'stāt\ *n*
1 manner or condition of being ⟨water in the gaseous *state*⟩ ⟨a nervous *state*⟩
2 a body of people living in a certain territory under one government : the government of such a body of people
3 one of the divisions of a nation having a federal government ⟨the United *States* of America⟩

**[2]state** *vb* **stat•ed**; **stat•ing**
1 to set by rule, law, or authority : FIX ⟨at *stated* times⟩
2 to express especially in words ⟨*state* an opinion⟩

**state•house** \'stāt-ˌhaủs\ *n*
the building where the legislature of a state meets

**state•ly** \'stāt-lē\ *adj* **state•li•er**; **state•li•est**
1 having great dignity ⟨*stately* language⟩
2 impressive especially in size : IMPOSING ⟨a *stately* building⟩
**state•li•ness** *n*

**state•ment** \'stāt-mənt\ *n*
1 something that is stated : REPORT, ACCOUNT
2 a brief record of a business account ⟨a monthly bank *statement*⟩

**state•room** \'stāt-ˌrüm, -ˌrủm\ *n*
a private room on a ship or a train

**states•man** \'stāt-smən\ *n*, *pl* **states•men** \'stāt-smən\
a person who is active in government and who gives wise leadership in making policies

A B C D E F G H I J K L M N O P Q R S T U V W X Y Z

[1]**stat·ic** \'stat-ik\ *adj*
**1** showing little change or action ⟨a *static* population⟩
**2** of or relating to charges of electricity (as one produced by friction) that do not flow

[2]**static** *n*
noise produced in a radio or television receiver by atmospheric or electrical disturbances

[1]**sta·tion** \'stā-shən\ *n*
**1** the place or position where a person or thing stands or is assigned to stand or remain
**2** a regular stopping place (as on a bus line) **:** DEPOT
**3** a post or area of duty ⟨military *station*⟩
**4** POSITION 4, RANK ⟨a person of high *station*⟩
**5** a place for specialized observation or for a public service ⟨weather *station*⟩ ⟨police *station*⟩
**6** a collection of radio or television equipment for transmitting or receiving
**7** the place where a radio or television station is

[2]**station** *vb*
to assign to or set in a station or position **:** POST

**sta·tion·ary** \'stā-shə-,ner-ē\ *adj*
**1** having been set in a certain place or post **:** IMMOBILE ⟨a *stationary* laundry tub⟩
**2** not changing **:** STABLE ⟨their weekly income remained *stationary*⟩

**stationery**

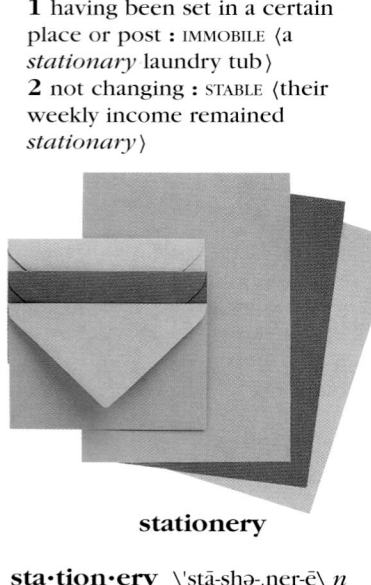

**sta·tion·ery** \'stā-shə-,ner-ē\ *n*
▲ writing paper and envelopes

**station wagon** *n*
an automobile that is longer on the inside than a sedan and has one or more folding or removable seats but no separate luggage compartment

**stat·ue**
\'stach-ü\ *n*
► an image or likeness (as of a person or animal) sculptured, modeled, or cast in a solid substance (as marble or bronze)

**statue:**
a famous statue carved in ancient Greek style in about 150 BC

**stat·ure**
\'stach-ər\ *n*
**1** natural height (as of a person)
**2** quality or fame one has gained (as by growth or development) ⟨artists of *stature*⟩

**sta·tus** \'stāt-əs, 'stat-\ *n*
**1** position or rank of a person or thing ⟨lost my *status* as an amateur⟩
**2** state of affairs **:** SITUATION ⟨the economic *status* of a country⟩

**stat·ute** \'stach-üt\ *n*
LAW 4 ⟨the *statutes* of our state⟩

**staunch** \'stȯnch, 'stänch\ *adj*
**1** strongly built **:** SUBSTANTIAL ⟨*staunch* foundations⟩
**2** LOYAL 2, STEADFAST ⟨they were *staunch* friends for many years⟩
**staunch·ly** *adv*

[1]**stave** \'stāv\ *n*
**1** a wooden stick **:** STAFF
**2** one of a number of narrow strips of wood or iron plates placed edge to edge to form the sides, covering, or lining of something (as a barrel or keg)

[2]**stave** *vb* **staved** *or* **stove** \'stōv\; **stav·ing**
**1** to break in the staves of ⟨*stave* in a boat⟩
**2** to smash a hole in **:** crush or break inward ⟨*staved* in several ribs⟩

**stave off** *vb*
to keep away **:** ward off ⟨*stave off* trouble⟩

**staves** *pl of* STAFF

[1]**stay** \'stā\ *n*
a strong rope or wire used to steady or brace something (as a mast)

[2]**stay** *vb*
to fasten (as a smokestack) with stays

[3]**stay** *vb*
**1** to stop going forward **:** PAUSE
**2** [1]REMAIN 3, 4 ⟨*stayed* after the party to help⟩ ⟨we *stayed* friends for many years⟩
**3** to stand firm
**4** to live for a while ⟨*staying* with friends⟩
**5** [2]CHECK 1, HALT ⟨*stay* an execution⟩

[4]**stay** *n*
**1** the action of bringing to a stop **:** the state of being stopped
**2** a period of living in a place ⟨made a long *stay* in the country⟩

[5]**stay** *n*
**1** [1]PROP, SUPPORT
**2** a thin firm strip (as of steel or plastic) used to stiffen a garment (as a corset) or part of a garment (as a shirt collar)

[6]**stay** *vb*
to hold up ⟨*stay* a person who is about to fall⟩

**stead** \'sted\ *n*
**1** [2]AVAIL — used mostly in the phrase *stand one in good stead*
**2** the place usually taken or duty carried out by the one mentioned ⟨try to get someone to work in your *stead*⟩

**stead·fast** \'sted-,fast\ *adj*
**1** not changing **:** RESOLUTE ⟨a *steadfast* aim⟩
**2** LOYAL 2 ⟨*steadfast* friends⟩
**stead·fast·ly** *adv*
**stead·fast·ness** *n*

[1]**steady** \'sted-ē\ *adj* **steadi·er**; **steadi·est**
**1** firmly fixed in position
**2** direct or sure in action ⟨worked with *steady* hands⟩ ⟨took *steady* aim⟩
**3** showing little change ⟨*steady* prices⟩ ⟨a *steady* flow of water⟩
**4** not easily upset ⟨*steady* nerves⟩
**5** RELIABLE
**stead·i·ly** \'sted-l-ē\ *adv*
**stead·i·ness** \'sted-ē-nəs\ *n*

**²steady** *vb* **stead·ied**; **steady·ing**
to make, keep, or become steady

**steak** \'stāk\ *n*
**1** a slice of meat and especially beef
**2** a slice of a large fish (as salmon)

**¹steal** \'stēl\ *vb* **stole** \'stōl\; **sto·len** \'stō-lən\; **steal·ing**
**1** to come or go quietly or secretly ⟨*stole* out of the room⟩
**2** to take and carry away (something that belongs to another person) without right and with the intention of keeping
**3** to get more than one's share of attention during ⟨*stole* the show⟩
**4** to take or get for oneself secretly or without permission ⟨*stole* a nap⟩

**²steal** *n*
**1** the act or an instance of stealing
**2** ¹BARGAIN 2

**stealth** \'stelth\ *n*
sly or secret action

**stealthy** \'stel-thē\ *adj* **stealth·i·er**; **stealth·i·est**
done in a sly or secret manner
**stealth·i·ly** \-thə-lē\ *adv*

**¹steam** \'stēm\ *n*
**1** the vapor into which water is changed when heated to the boiling point
**2** steam when kept under pressure so that it supplies heat and power ⟨houses heated by *steam*⟩
**3** the mist formed when water vapor cools
**4** driving force : POWER ⟨arrived under their own *steam*⟩

**²steam** *vb*
**1** to rise or pass off as steam
**2** to give off steam or vapor
**3** to move or travel by or as if by the power of steam ⟨the ship *steamed* out of the harbor⟩
**4** to expose to steam (as for cooking)

**steam·boat** \'stēm-,bōt\ *n*
a boat driven by steam

**steam engine** *n*
▶ an engine driven by steam

**steam·er** \'stē-mər\ *n*
**1** a container in which something is steamed
**2** a ship driven by steam
**3** an engine, machine, or vehicle run by steam

**steam·roll·er** \'stēm-'rō-lər\ *n*
a machine formerly driven by steam that has wide heavy rollers for pressing down and smoothing roads

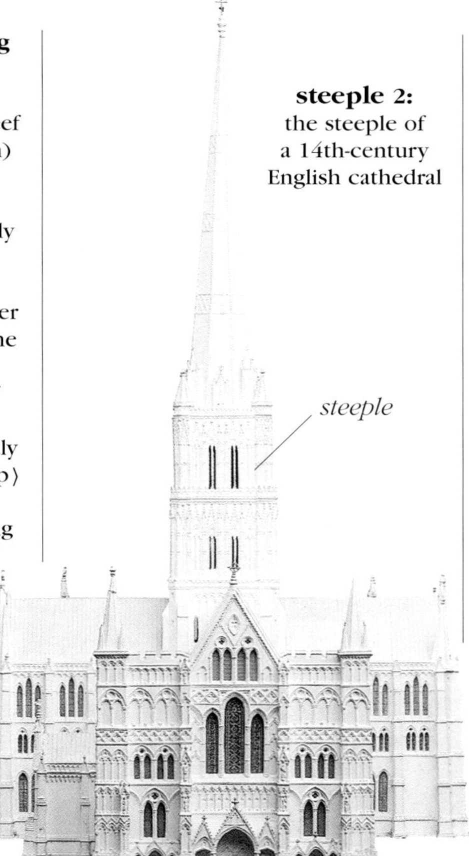


**steeple 2:** the steeple of a 14th-century English cathedral

**steam·ship** \'stēm-,ship\ *n*
STEAMER 2

**steam shovel** *n*
a power machine for digging that was formerly operated by steam

**steam engine:** model of a 19th-century steam engine

**steed** \'stēd\ *n*
a usually lively horse

**¹steel** \'stēl\ *n*
**1** a hard and tough metal made by treating iron with great heat and mixing carbon with it
**2** an article (as a sword) made of steel

**²steel** *vb*
to fill with courage or determination ⟨I *steeled* myself for the struggle⟩

**³steel** *adj*
made of or like steel

**steely** \'stē-lē\ *adj* **steel·i·er**; **steel·i·est**
**1** made of steel
**2** like steel (as in hardness or color)

**¹steep** \'stēp\ *adj*
**1** having a very sharp slope : almost straight up and down
**2** too great or high ⟨*steep* prices⟩
**steep·ly** *adv*
**steep·ness** *n*

**²steep** *vb*
**1** to soak in a liquid ⟨*steep* tea⟩
**2** to fill with or involve deeply ⟨*steeped* in learning⟩ ⟨a story *steeped* with legend⟩

**stee·ple** \'stē-pəl\ *n*
**1** a tall pointed structure usually built on top of a church tower
**2** ◀ a church tower

**stee·ple·chase** \'stē-pəl-,chās\ *n*
**1** a horse race across country
**2** a race on a course that has hedges, walls, and ditches to be crossed

a b c d e f g h i j k l m n o p q r s t u v w x y z

**[1]steer** \'stir\ *n*
a castrated bull usually raised for beef

**[2]steer** *vb*
**1** to control a course or the course of : GUIDE ⟨*steer* by the stars⟩ ⟨*steer* a boat⟩
**2** to follow a course of action
**3** to be guided ⟨this car *steers* well⟩

**steering wheel** *n*
a wheel for steering something by hand

**stego·sau·rus** \ˌsteg-ə-'sȯr-əs\ *n*
a large plant-eating dinosaur having bony plates along its back and tail with spikes at the end of the tail

**[1]stem** \'stem\ *n*
**1** the main stalk of a plant that develops buds and sprouts and usually grows above ground
**2** a plant part (as a leafstalk or flower stalk) that supports some other part
**3** the bow of a ship
**4** a line of ancestors : STOCK
**5** the basic part of a word to which prefixes or suffixes may be added
**6** something like a stalk or shaft ⟨the *stem* of a goblet⟩
**stem·less** \-ləs\ *adj*

**[2]stem** *vb* **stemmed**; **stem·ming**
**1** to make progress against
**2** to check or hold back the progress of

**[3]stem** *vb* **stemmed**; **stem·ming**
**1** to come from a certain source ⟨illness that *stems* from an accident⟩
**2** to remove the stem from ⟨*stem* cherries⟩

**[4]stem** *vb* **stemmed**; **stem·ming**
to stop or check by or as if by damming ⟨*stem* the flow of blood⟩

**stemmed** \'stemd\ *adj*
having a stem

**[1]sten·cil** \'sten-səl\ *n*
**1** ▶ a material (as a sheet of paper, thin wax, or woven fabric) with cut out lettering or a design through which ink, paint, or metallic powder is forced onto a surface to be printed
**2** a pattern, design, or print produced with a stencil

**[1]stencil 1:** a stencil used to decorate a box

**[2]stencil** *vb* **sten·ciled** *or* **sten·cilled**; **sten·cil·ing** *or* **sten·cil·ling**
**1** to mark or paint with a stencil ⟨*stencil* a box with designs⟩
**2** to produce with a stencil ⟨*stencil* a number⟩

**stepping-stone 1:** stepping-stones over a stream

**ste·nog·ra·pher** \stə-'näg-rə-fər\ *n*
one employed chiefly to take and make a copy of dictation

**[1]step** \'step\ *n*
**1** a rest or place for the foot in going up or down : STAIR 2
**2** a movement made by raising one foot and putting it down in another spot
**3** a combination of foot and body movements in a repeated pattern ⟨a waltz *step*⟩
**4** manner of walking
**5** FOOTPRINT
**6** the sound of a footstep
**7** the space passed over in one step
**8** a short distance ⟨the house is only a *step* away⟩
**9** the height of one stair
**10 steps** *pl* [1]COURSE 3 ⟨directed our *steps* toward home⟩
**11** a level, grade, or rank in a scale or series : a stage in a process
**12** [1]MEASURE 7 ⟨took *steps* to correct the condition⟩
**13** a space in music between two notes of a scale or staff that may be a single degree of the scale (**half step**) or two degrees (**whole step**)
**in step** with one's foot or feet moving in time with other feet or in time to music ⟨march *in step*⟩

**[2]step** *vb* **stepped**; **step·ping**
**1** to move by taking a step or steps ⟨*stepped* into the bus⟩
**2** [1]DANCE 1
**3** to go on foot : WALK ⟨*stepped* slowly along the path⟩
**4** to move at a good speed ⟨the car was really *stepping*⟩
**5** to press down with the foot ⟨*step* on the pedal⟩
**6** to come as if at a single step ⟨*step* into a good job⟩
**7** to measure by steps ⟨*step* off ten yards⟩

**step–by–step** \ˌstep-bī-ˈstep\ *adj or adv*
moving or happening by steps one after the other

**step·fa·ther** \ˈstep-ˌfäth-ər, -ˌfäth-\ *n*
the husband of one's mother after the death or divorce of one's real father

**step·lad·der** \ˈstep-ˌlad-ər\ *n*
a light portable set of steps with a hinged frame for steadying

**step·moth·er** \ˈstep-ˌməth-ər\ *n*
the wife of one's father after the death or divorce of one's real mother

**steppe** \ˈstep\ *n*
land that is dry, usually rather level, and covered with grass in regions (as much of southeastern Europe and parts of Asia) of wide temperature range

**step·ping–stone** \ˈstep-ing-ˌstōn\ *n*
**1** ◀ a stone on which to step (as in crossing a stream)
**2** a means of progress or advancement ⟨a *stepping-stone* to success⟩

**step up** *vb*
to increase especially by a series of steps ⟨*step up* production⟩

**-ster** \stər\ *n suffix*
**1** one that does or handles or operates
**2** one that makes or uses ⟨song*ster*⟩
**3** one that is associated with or takes part in ⟨gang*ster*⟩
**4** one that is ⟨young*ster*⟩

**ste·reo** \ˈster-ē-ˌō, ˈstir-\ *n, pl* **ste·re·os**
**1** stereophonic reproduction
**2** a stereophonic sound system

**ste·reo·phon·ic** \ˌster-ē-ə-ˈfän-ik, ˌstir-\ *adj*
of or relating to sound reproduction designed to create the effect of listening to the original

**ste·reo·scope** \ˈster-ē-ə-ˌskōp, ˈstir-\ *n*
an optical instrument that blends two pictures of one subject taken from slightly different points of view into one image that seems to be three-dimensional

[1]**ste·reo·type** \ˈster-ē-ə-ˌtīp, ˈstir-\ *vb*
**1** to make a printing plate by casting melted metal in a mold
**2** to form a fixed mental picture of ⟨*stereotyping* people according to where they live⟩

[2]**stereotype** *n*
**1** a printing plate of a complete page made by casting melted metal in a mold ⟨newspaper pages are often printed from *stereotypes*⟩
**2** a fixed idea that many people have about a thing or a group and that may often be untrue or only partly true

**ste·reo·typed** \ˈster-ē-ə-tīpt, ˈstir-\ *adj*
following a pattern or stereotype **:** lacking individuality

**ste·reo·typ·i·cal** \ˌster-ē-ə-ˈti-pi-kəl\ *also* **ste·reo·typ·ic** \-pik\ *adj*
based on or characteristic of a stereotype ⟨a *stereotypical* reaction⟩
**ste·reo·typ·i·cal·ly** \-pi-kə-lē\ *adv*

**ster·ile** \ˈster-əl\ *adj*
**1** not able to produce fruit, crops, or offspring **:** not fertile ⟨*sterile* soil⟩
**2** free from living germs

**ster·il·ize** \ˈster-ə-ˌlīz\ *vb* **ster·il·ized**; **ster·il·iz·ing**
to make sterile and especially free from harmful germs

[1]**ster·ling** \ˈstər-ling\ *n*
**1** British money
**2** sterling silver **:** articles made from sterling silver

[2]**sterling** *adj*
**1** of or relating to British sterling
**2** being or made of an alloy of 925 parts of silver with 75 parts of copper
**3** EXCELLENT ⟨had a *sterling* voice⟩

[1]**stern** \ˈstərn\ *adj*
**1** hard and severe in nature or manner ⟨a *stern* judge⟩
**2** firm and not changeable ⟨*stern* determination to succeed⟩
**stern·ly** *adv*
**stern·ness** *n*

[2]**stern** *n*
▼ the rear end of a boat

**ster·num** \ˈstər-nəm\ *n, pl* **ster·nums** *or* **ster·na** \-nə\
BREASTBONE

**ste·roid** \ˈstir-ˌȯid, ˈster-\ *n*
any one of a number of chemical compounds (as an anabolic steroid) including many hormones

**stetho·scope** \ˈsteth-ə-ˌskōp\ *n*
▶ an instrument used by doctors for listening to sounds produced in the body and especially in the chest

**stethoscope**

[1]**stew** \ˈstü, ˈstyü\ *n*
**1** food (as meat with vegetables) prepared by slow boiling
**2** a state of excitement, worry, or confusion

[2]**stern:** model of an early 20th-century Norwegian fishing boat

*stern*

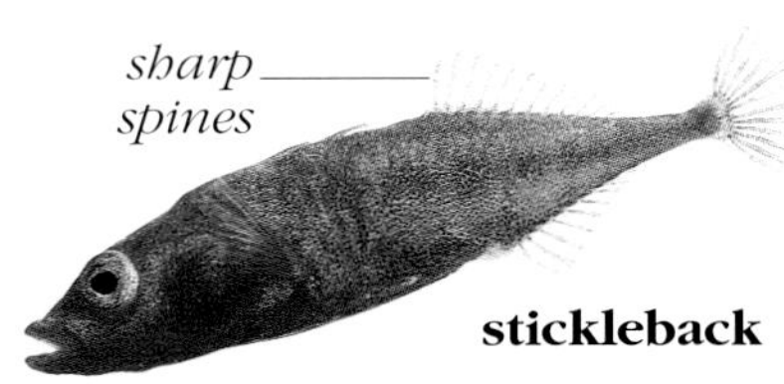


**stickleback**

**[2]stew** *vb*
**1** to boil slowly : SIMMER
**2** to become excited or worried

**stew·ard** \'stü-ərd, 'styü-\ *n*
**1** a manager of a very large home, an estate, or an organization
**2** a person employed to manage the supply and distribution of food (as on a ship)
**3** a worker who serves and looks after the needs of passengers (as on an airplane or ship)

**stew·ard·ess** \'stü-ərd-əs, 'styü-\ *n*
a woman who looks after passengers (as on an airplane or ship)

**[1]stick** \'stik\ *n*
**1** a cut or broken branch or twig
**2** a long thin piece of wood
**3** WALKING STICK 1
**4** something like a stick in shape or use ⟨a *stick* of dynamite⟩

**[2]stick** *vb* **stuck** \'stək\; **stick·ing**
**1** to stab with something pointed
**2** to cause to penetrate ⟨*stuck* a needle in my finger⟩
**3** to put in place by or as if by pushing ⟨*stick* cloves in a ham⟩
**4** to push out, up, into, or under ⟨*stuck* out my hand⟩
**5** to put in a specified place or position ⟨*stuck* a cap on my head⟩
**6** to remain in a place, situation, or environment ⟨decided to *stick* where we were⟩
**7** to halt the movement or action of ⟨the car was *stuck* in the mud⟩
**8** BAFFLE
**9** to burden with something unpleasant ⟨*stuck* with the job of washing the dishes⟩
**10** to cling or cause to cling ⟨the jam *stuck* to the knife⟩ ⟨*stick* a stamp on a letter⟩
**11** to become blocked or jammed ⟨the door is *stuck*⟩

**stick·er** \'stik-ər\ *n*
something (as a slip of paper with gum or glue on its back) that can be stuck to a surface

**stick·le·back** \'stik-əl-,bak\ *n*
◀ a small scaleless fish with sharp spines on its back

**sticky** \'stik-ē\ *adj* **stick·i·er**; **stick·i·est**
**1** ADHESIVE 1
**2** coated with a sticky substance
**3** MUGGY, HUMID ⟨a *sticky* day⟩
**4** tending to stick ⟨*sticky* windows⟩
**stick·i·ness** *n*

**stiff** \'stif\ *adj*
**1** not easily bent ⟨*stiff* leather⟩
**2** not easily moved ⟨*stiff* muscles⟩
**3** FIRM 5
**4** hard fought : STUBBORN ⟨a *stiff* fight⟩
**5** not easy or graceful in manner : FORMAL
**6** POWERFUL, STRONG ⟨a *stiff* wind⟩
**7** not flowing easily : being thick and heavy ⟨*stiff* glue⟩
**8** SEVERE 1 ⟨a *stiff* penalty⟩
**9** DIFFICULT 1 ⟨a *stiff* test⟩
**stiff·ly** *adv*
**stiff·ness** *n*

**stiff·en** \'stif-ən\ *vb*
to make or become stiff or stiffer
**stiff·en·er** *n*

**sti·fle** \'stī-fəl\ *vb* **sti·fled**; **sti·fling**
**1** to kill by depriving of or die from lack of oxygen or air : SMOTHER
**2** to keep in check by deliberate effort ⟨*stifle* one's anger⟩

**stig·ma** \'stig-mə\ *n, pl* **stig·ma·ta** \stig-'mät-ə, 'stig-mət-ə\ *or* **stig·mas**
**1** a mark of disgrace or discredit
**2** the upper part of the pistil of a flower which receives the pollen grains and on which they complete their development

**stile** \'stīl\ *n*
**1** a step or set of steps for crossing a fence or wall
**2** TURNSTILE

**sti·let·to** \stə-'let-ō\ *n, pl* **sti·let·tos** *or* **sti·let·toes**
▼ a slender pointed dagger

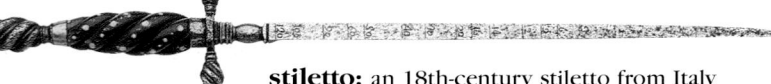

**stiletto:** an 18th-century stiletto from Italy

**[1]still** \'stil\ *adj*
**1** having no motion
**2** making no sound
**3** free from noise and confusion : QUIET
**still·ness** *n*

**[2]still** *vb*
to make or become still : QUIET

**[3]still** *adv*
**1** without motion ⟨sit *still*⟩
**2** up to this or that time ⟨we *still* live there⟩
**3** NEVERTHELESS ⟨they know it's not true, but they *still* believe it⟩
**4** [2]EVEN 4 ⟨ran *still* faster⟩

**[4]still** *n*
[1]QUIET, SILENCE

**[5]still** *n*
**1** a place where alcoholic liquors are made
**2** a device used in distillation

**still·born** \'stil-'bȯrn\ *adj*
born dead

**stilt** \'stilt\ *n*
**1** ▶ one of a pair of tall poles each with a high step or loop for the support of a foot used to lift the person wearing them above the ground in walking
**2** a stake or post used to support a structure above ground or water level

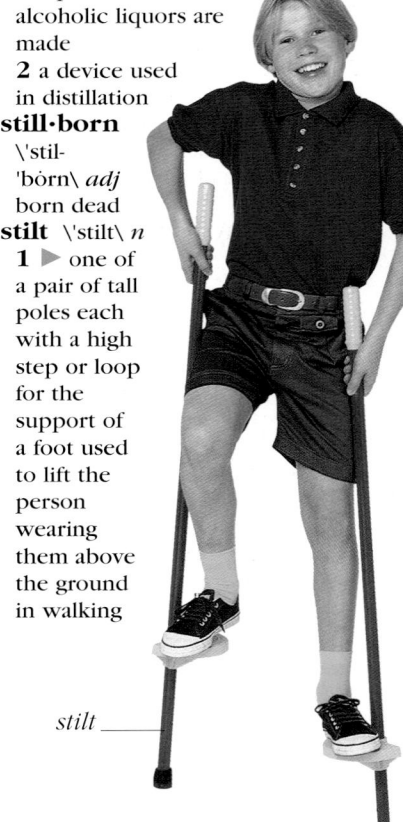

stilt

**stilt 1:** a boy walking on a pair of stilts

**stilt·ed** \'stil-təd\ *adj*
not easy and natural ⟨a *stilted* speech⟩

**[1]stim·u·lant** \'stim-yə-lənt\ *n*
**1** something (as a drug) that makes the body or one of its parts more active for a while ⟨a heart *stimulant*⟩
**2** STIMULUS 1

**[2]stimulant** *adj*
stimulating or tending to stimulate

**stim·u·late** \'stim-yə-,lāt\ *vb* **stim·u·lat·ed**; **stim·u·lat·ing**
**1** to make active or more active **:** ANIMATE, AROUSE
**2** to act toward as a bodily stimulus or stimulant

**stim·u·la·tion** \,stim-yə-'lā-shən\ *n*
an act or result of stimulating

**stim·u·lus** \'stim-yə-ləs\ *n, pl* **stim·u·li** \-,lī, -,lē\
**1** something that stirs or urges to action
**2** an influence that acts usually from outside the body to partly change bodily activity (as by exciting a sense organ) ⟨light, heat, and sound are common *stimuli*⟩

**[1]sting** \'sting\ *vb* **stung** \'stəng\; **sting·ing**
**1** to prick painfully usually with a sharp or poisonous stinger ⟨a bee *stung* my hand⟩
**2** to suffer or affect with sharp quick burning pain ⟨hail *stung* their faces⟩
**3** to cause to suffer severely ⟨*stung* with regret⟩

**[2]sting** *n*
**1** an act of stinging
**2** a wound or pain caused by or as if by stinging
**3** STINGER

**sting·er** \'sting-ər\ *n*
a sharp organ by which an animal (as a wasp or scorpion) wounds and often poisons an enemy

**sting·ray** \'sting-,rā\ *n*
▼ a very flat fish with a stinging spine on its whiplike tail

tail

**stingray**

pectoral fin

**stin·gy** \'stin-jē\ *adj* **stin·gi·er**; **stin·gi·est**
**1** not generous **:** giving or spending as little as possible
**2** very small in amount ⟨a *stingy* portion⟩
**stin·gi·ly** \-jə-lē\ *adv*
**stin·gi·ness** \-jē-nəs\ *n*

**[1]stink** \'stingk\ *vb* **stank** \'stangk\ *or* **stunk** \'stəngk\; **stunk**; **stink·ing**
**1** to give off or cause to have a strong unpleasant smell
**2** to be of very bad quality

**stirrup**

**[2]stink** *n*
a strong unpleasant smell

**stink·bug** \'stingk-,bəg\ *n*
a bug that gives off a bad smell

**stinky** \'sting-kē\ *adj*
having a strong unpleasant smell ⟨*stinky* garbage⟩

**[1]stint** \'stint\ *vb*
to be stingy or saving ⟨don't *stint* when health is concerned⟩

**[2]stint** *n*
an amount of work given to be done

**[1]stir** \'stər\ *vb* **stirred**; **stir·ring**
**1** to make or cause to make a usually slight movement or change of position
**2** to make active (as by pushing, beating, or prodding) ⟨*stir* up the fire⟩
**3** to mix, dissolve, or make by a continued circular movement ⟨*stir* sugar into coffee⟩
**4** AROUSE 2 ⟨*stir* up trouble⟩

**[2]stir** *n*
**1** a state of upset or activity ⟨the whole town is in a *stir*⟩
**2** a slight movement
**3** the act of stirring

**stir·ring** \'stər-ing\ *adj*
LIVELY 3, MOVING ⟨a *stirring* song⟩

**stir·rup** \'stər-əp\ *n*
◀ either of a pair of small light frames often of metal hung by straps from a saddle and used as a support for the foot of a horseback rider

**[1]stitch** \'stich\ *n*
**1** a sudden sharp pain especially in the side
**2** one in-and-out movement of a threaded needle in sewing **:** a portion of thread left in the material after one such movement
**3** a single loop of thread or yarn around a tool (as a knitting needle or crochet hook)
**4** a method of stitching

**[2]stitch** *vb*
**1** to fasten or join with stitches
**2** to make, mend, or decorate with or as if with stitches
**3** SEW 2

**[1]stock** \'stäk\ *n*
**1 stocks** *pl* a wooden frame with holes for the feet or the feet and hands once used to punish a wrongdoer publicly
**2** the wooden part by which a rifle or shotgun is held during firing
**3** an original (as a person, race, or language) from which others descend
**4** the whole supply or amount on hand
**5** farm animals **:** LIVESTOCK, CATTLE
**6** the ownership element in a business which is divided into shares that can be traded independently
**7** liquid in which meat, fish, or vegetables have been simmered
**in stock** on hand **:** in the store and available for purchase

**stock** *vb*
**1** to provide with or get stock or a stock ⟨*stock* a farm⟩ ⟨*stock* up on groceries⟩
**2** to get or keep a stock of ⟨that store *stocks* only the best goods⟩

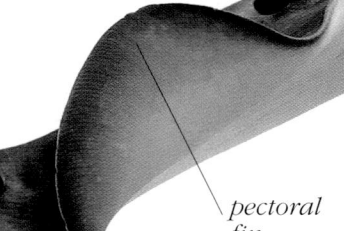

**[3]stock** *adj*
**1** kept regularly in stock ⟨comes in *stock* sizes⟩
**2** commonly used : STANDARD ⟨gave a *stock* answer⟩

**stock·ade** \stä-'kād\ *n*
**1** a line of strong posts set in the ground to form a defense
**2** an enclosure formed by stakes driven into the ground

**stock·bro·ker** \'stäk-,brō-kər\ *n*
a person who handles orders to buy and sell stocks

**stock·hold·er** \'stäk-,hōl-dər\ *n*
an owner of stock

**stock·ing** \'stäk-ing\ *n*
a close-fitting usually knit covering for the foot and leg

**stock market** *n*
a place where shares of stock are bought and sold

**stocky** \'stäk-ē\ *adj* **stock·i·er**; **stock·i·est**
compact, sturdy, and relatively thick in build : THICKSET

**stock·yard** \'stäk-,yärd\ *n*
a yard for stock and especially for keeping livestock about to be slaughtered or shipped

**[1]stole** \'stōl\ *past of* STEAL

**[2]stole** *n*
a long wide scarf worn about the shoulders

**stolen** *past participle of* STEAL

**[1]stom·ach** \'stəm-ək\ *n*
**1** the pouch into which food goes after it leaves the mouth and has passed down the throat
**2** ABDOMEN 1
**3** [2]DESIRE 1, LIKING ⟨had no *stomach* for trouble⟩

**[2]stomach** *vb*
to bear patiently : put up with ⟨I couldn't *stomach* their rude behavior⟩

**stomp** \'stämp, 'stȯmp\ *vb*
to walk heavily or noisily : STAMP ⟨*stomped* angrily out of the room⟩

**[1]stone** \'stōn\ *n*
**1** earth or mineral matter hardened in a mass : ROCK
**2** a piece of rock coarser than gravel ⟨throw *stones*⟩
**3** GEM
**4** a stony mass sometimes present in a diseased organ
**5** the kernel of a fruit in its hard case

## Stone Age

Humans living in the Stone Age began to make tools from stone some two and a half million years ago. Hand-held axes, flint scrapers, and adzes were some of the tools early humans utilized for cutting, grinding, slicing, and preparing animal skins for use. In the later Stone Age, people began to make more sophisticated items, such as flint arrowheads and blades which were used in hunting for food, chopping wood, and carving bone and antler.

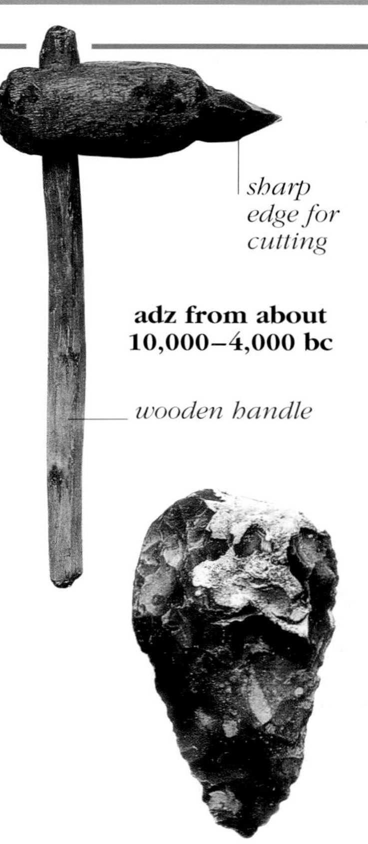


**adz from about 10,000–4,000 bc**

**hand ax from about 300,000–70,000 bc**

**flint scraper from about 1,600,000–200,000 bc**

**6** *pl usually* **stone** an English measure of weight equaling fourteen pounds (about 6.5 kilograms)

**[2]stone** *vb* **stoned**; **ston·ing**
**1** to throw stones at
**2** to remove the stones of ⟨*stone* cherries⟩

**[3]stone** *adj*
of, relating to, or made of stone

**Stone Age** *n*
▲ the oldest period in which human beings are known to have existed : the age during which stone tools were used

**stone–blind** \'stōn-'blīnd\ *adj*
completely blind

**stone–deaf** \'stōn-'def\ *adj*
completely deaf

**stony** \'stō-nē\ *adj* **ston·i·er**; **ston·i·est**
**1** full of stones ⟨*stony* soil⟩
**2** insensitive as stone : UNFEELING ⟨a *stony* stare⟩
**3** hard as stone

**stood** *past of* STAND

**stool** \'stül\ *n*
**1** a seat without back or arms supported by three or four legs or by a central post
**2** FOOTSTOOL
**3** a mass of material discharged from the intestine

**[1]stoop** \'stüp\ *vb*
**1** to bend down or over
**2** to carry the head and shoulders or the upper part of the body bent forward
**3** to do something that is beneath one ⟨*stoop* to lying⟩

**[2]stoop** *n*
a forward bend of the head and shoulders ⟨walks with a *stoop*⟩

**[3]stoop** *n*
a porch, platform, or stairway at the entrance of a house or building

**[1]stop** \'stäp\ *vb* **stopped**; **stop·ping**
**1** to close an opening by filling or blocking it : PLUG ⟨*stopped* my ears with cotton⟩

2 to hold back : RESTRAIN ⟨*stop* a person from going⟩
3 to halt the movement or progress of ⟨*stop* the car⟩
4 to come to an end : CEASE
5 to make a visit : STAY ⟨*stop* with friends⟩

**²stop** *n*
1 ¹END 2, FINISH
2 a set of organ pipes of one tone quality : a control knob for such a set
3 something that delays, blocks, or brings to a halt
4 STOPPER, PLUG
5 the act of stopping : the state of being stopped
6 a halt in a journey : STAY ⟨made a *stop* in the mountains⟩
7 a stopping place ⟨a bus *stop*⟩

**stop·light** \'stäp-ˌlīt\ *n*
1 a light on the rear of a motor vehicle that goes on when the driver presses the brake pedal
2 a signal light used in controlling traffic

**stop·over** \'stäp-ˌō-vər\ *n*
a stop made during a journey

**stop·page** \'stäp-ij\ *n*
the act of stopping : the state of being stopped

**stop·per** \'stäp-ər\ *n*
something (as a cork or plug) used to stop openings

**stop·watch** \'stäp-ˌwäch\ *n*
▼ a watch having a hand that can be started and stopped for exact timing (as of a race)

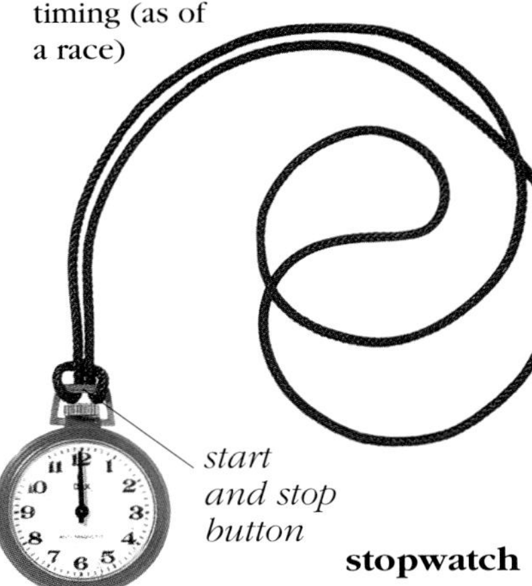

**stopwatch**

**stor·age** \'stōr-ij\ *n*
1 space or a place for storing
2 an amount stored
3 the act of storing : the state of being stored
4 the price charged for storing something

**stork:** a marabou \'mar-ə-ˌbü\ stork

**storage battery** *n*
a battery that can be renewed by passing an electric current through it

**¹store** \'stōr\ *vb* **stored**; **stor·ing**
1 to provide with what is needed : SUPPLY ⟨*store* a ship with goods⟩
2 to place or leave something in a location (as a warehouse, library, or computer memory) to keep for later use or disposal
3 to put somewhere for safekeeping ⟨*store* the jewels in a safe⟩

**²store** *n*
1 **stores** *pl* something collected and kept for future use ⟨a ship's *stores*⟩
2 a large quantity, supply, or number ⟨a *store* of natural resources⟩
3 a place where goods are sold : SHOP ⟨a candy *store*⟩
**in store** ¹READY 1 ⟨we have a big surprise *in store* for you⟩

**store·house** \'stōr-ˌhau̇s\ *n, pl* **store·hous·es** \-ˌhau̇-zəz\
1 a building for storing goods
2 a large supply or source

**store·keep·er** \'stōr-ˌkē-pər\ *n*
1 a person in charge of supplies (as in a factory)
2 an owner or manager of a store or shop

**store·room** \'stōr-ˌrüm, -ˌru̇m\ *n*
a room for storing things not in use

**stork** \'stȯrk\ *n*
◀ a large Old World wading bird that looks like the related herons and includes one European form (the **white stork**) that often nests on roofs and chimneys

**¹storm** \'stȯrm\ *n*
1 a heavy fall of rain, snow, or sleet often with strong wind
2 a violent outburst ⟨a *storm* of protest⟩
3 a violent attack on a defended position ⟨took the fort by *storm*⟩

**²storm** *vb*
1 to blow hard and rain or snow heavily
2 to make a mass attack against
3 to be very angry : RAGE
4 to rush about violently ⟨the mob *stormed* through the streets⟩

**stormy** \'stȯr-mē\ *adj* **storm·i·er**; **storm·i·est**
1 relating to or affected by a storm ⟨a *stormy* sea⟩
2 displaying anger and excitement ⟨a *stormy* meeting⟩
**storm·i·ness** *n*

**¹sto·ry** \'stōr-ē\ *n, pl* **sto·ries**
1 a report about incidents or events : ACCOUNT
2 a short often amusing tale
3 a tale shorter than a novel
4 a widely told rumor
5 ³LIE, FALSEHOOD

**²sto·ry** *or* **sto·rey** \'stōr-ē\ *n, pl* **sto·ries** *or* **sto·reys**
a set of rooms or an area making up one floor level of a building

**stout** \'stau̇t\ *adj*
1 of strong character : BRAVE, FIRM
2 of a strong or lasting sort : STURDY, TOUGH
3 bulky in body : FLESHY
**synonyms** see FAT
**stout·ly** *adv*
**stout·ness** *n*

**¹stove** \'stōv\ *n*
a structure usually of iron or steel that burns fuel or uses electricity to provide heat (as for cooking or heating)

**²stove** *past of* STAVE

**stove·pipe** \'stōv-ˌpīp\ *n*
a metal pipe to carry away smoke from a stove

**stow** \'stō\ *vb*
1 to put away : STORE
2 to arrange in an orderly way : PACK
3 ²LOAD 1

**stow·away** \'stō-ə-,wā\ *n*
a person who hides (as in a ship or airplane) to travel free

**strad·dle** \'strad-l\ *vb* **strad·dled**; **strad·dling**
**1** to stand, sit, or walk with the legs spread wide apart
**2** to stand, sit, or ride with a leg on either side of ⟨*straddle* a horse⟩
**3** to favor or seem to favor two opposite sides of ⟨*straddle* a question⟩

**strag·gle** \'strag-əl\ *vb* **strag·gled**; **strag·gling**
**1** to wander from a straight course or way **:** STRAY
**2** to trail off from others of its kind
**strag·gler** \'strag-lər\ *n*

[1]**straight** \'strāt\ *adj*
**1** following the same direction throughout its length **:** not having curves, bends, or angles ⟨a *straight* line⟩
**2** not straying from the main point or proper course ⟨*straight* thinking⟩
**3** not straying from what is right or honest ⟨a *straight* answer⟩
**4** correctly ordered or arranged ⟨keep accounts *straight*⟩
**straight·ness** *n*

[2]**straight** *adv*
in a straight manner, course, or line

**straight·en** \'strāt-n\ *vb*
**1** to make or become straight
**2** to put in order ⟨*straighten* up a room⟩

**straight·for·ward** \strāt-'fȯr-wərd\ *adj*
being plain and honest **:** FRANK ⟨gave a *straightforward* reply⟩
**straight·for·ward·ly** *adv*
**straight·for·ward·ness** *n*

**straight·way** \'strāt-,wā\ *adv*
IMMEDIATELY 2

[1]**strain** \'strān\ *n*
**1** a line of ancestors to whom a person is related
**2** a group of individuals that cannot be told from related kinds by appearance alone ⟨a new *strain* of wheat⟩
**3** a quality or disposition that runs through a family or race
**4** a small amount **:** TRACE ⟨a *strain* of sadness⟩
**5** MELODY 2, AIR

[2]**strain** *vb*
**1** to stretch or be stretched, pulled, or used to the limit ⟨muscles *straining* under a load⟩
**2** to stretch beyond a proper limit ⟨*strain* the truth⟩
**3** to try one's hardest ⟨*strain* to lift a heavy box⟩
**4** to injure or be injured by too much or too hard use or effort ⟨*strain* one's heart⟩
**5** to press or pass through a strainer **:** FILTER

[3]**strain** *n*
**1** the act of straining
**2** the state of being strained
**3** [2]OVERWORK, WORRY
**4** bodily injury resulting from strain or from a wrench or twist that stretches muscles and ligaments

**strained** \'strānd\ *adj*
**1** not easy or natural ⟨a *strained* smile⟩
**2** brought close to war ⟨*strained* relations between countries⟩

**strain·er** \'strā-nər\ *n*
a device (as a screen, sieve, or filter) to hold back solid pieces while a liquid passes through

**strait** \'strāt\ *n*
**1** a narrow channel connecting two bodies of water
**2** [1]DISTRESS 1, NEED — often used in pl. ⟨in difficult *straits*⟩

[1]**strand** \'strand\ *n*
the land bordering a body of water **:** SHORE, BEACH

[2]**strand** *vb*
**1** to run, drive, or cause to drift onto a strand **:** run aground
**2** to leave in a strange or unfavorable place especially without any chance to get away ⟨*stranded* in a strange city⟩

[3]**strand** *n*
**1** one of the fibers, threads, strings, or wires twisted or braided to make a cord, rope, or cable
**2** something long or twisted like a rope ⟨a *strand* of pearls⟩ ⟨a *strand* of hair⟩

**strange** \'strānj\ *adj* **strang·er**; **strang·est**
**1** of or relating to some other person, place, or thing ⟨the cuckoo lays its eggs in a *strange* nest⟩
**2** UNFAMILIAR 1 ⟨*strange* surroundings⟩
**3** exciting curiosity, surprise, or wonder because of not being usual or ordinary ⟨a *strange* sight⟩
**4** ill at ease **:** SHY ⟨felt *strange* on the first day at school⟩
**strange·ly** *adv*
**strange·ness** *n*

**strang·er** \'strān-jər\ *n*
**1** one who is not in the place where one's home is **:** FOREIGNER
**2** GUEST 1, VISITOR
**3** a person whom one does not know or has not met

**stran·gle** \'strang-gəl\ *vb* **stran·gled**; **stran·gling**
**1** to choke to death by squeezing the throat
**2** to choke in any way
**stran·gler** \-glər\ *n*

[1]**strap** \'strap\ *n*
a narrow strip of flexible material (as leather) used especially for fastening, binding, or wrapping

[2]**strap** *vb* **strapped**; **strap·ping**
**1** to fasten with or attach by means of a strap
**2** BIND 1, 2, CONSTRICT
**3** to whip with a strap

**strap·ping** \'strap-ing\ *adj*
LARGE, STRONG

**strat·a·gem** \'strat-ə-jəm\ *n*
a trick in war to deceive or outwit the enemy

**stra·te·gic** \strə-'tē-jik\ *adj*
**1** of, relating to, or showing the use of strategy ⟨a *strategic* retreat⟩
**2** useful or important in strategy ⟨*strategic* weapons⟩

**strat·e·gy** \'strat-ə-jē\ *n*, *pl* **strat·e·gies**
**1** the skill of using military, naval, and air forces to win a war
**2** a clever plan or method

**strato·sphere** \'strat-ə-,sfir\ *n*
an upper portion of the atmosphere more than eleven kilometers above the earth where temperature changes little and clouds rarely form

**stra·tum** \'strāt-əm, 'strat-\ *n*, *pl* **stra·ta** \-ə\
LAYER 2 ⟨a *stratum* of rock⟩

**stra·tus** \'strāt-əs, 'strat-\ *n*, *pl* **stra·ti** \'strāt-,ī, 'strat-\
a cloud extending over a large area at an altitude of from 600 to 2000 meters

**straw** \'strȯ\ *n*
**1** stalks especially of grain after threshing
**2** a single dry coarse plant stalk **:** a piece of straw

3 a slender tube for sucking up a beverage

**straw·ber·ry** \'strò-,ber-ē\ *n*, *pl* **straw·ber·ries**
▼ the juicy edible usually red fruit of a low plant with white flowers and long slender runners

**strawberries** on the plant

[1]**stray** \'strā\ *n*
a domestic animal that is wandering at large because it is lost or has been abandoned

[2]**stray** *vb*
1 to wander from a group or from the proper place : ROAM ⟨the gate was left open and the cattle *strayed*⟩
2 to go off from a straight or the right course ⟨your story *strays* from the truth⟩

[3]**stray** *adj*
1 having strayed or been lost ⟨a *stray* dog⟩ ⟨found a few *stray* mittens⟩
2 occurring here and there : RANDOM ⟨a few *stray* comments⟩

[1]**streak** \'strēk\ *n*
1 a line or mark of a different color or composition from its background
2 a narrow band of light ⟨a *streak* of lightning⟩
3 a small amount : TRACE, STRAIN ⟨a *streak* of humor⟩
4 a short series of something ⟨a *streak* of luck⟩ ⟨a winning *streak*⟩
**streaked** \'strēkt, 'strē-kəd\ *adj*

[2]**streak** *vb*
1 to make streaks in or on ⟨hair *streaked* with gray⟩
2 to move swiftly : RUSH ⟨a jet *streaking* across the sky⟩

[1]**stream** \'strēm\ *n*
1 a body of water (as a brook or river) flowing on the earth
2 a flow of liquid ⟨a *stream* of tears⟩
3 a steady series (as of words or events) following one another ⟨kept up an endless *stream* of chatter⟩

[2]**stream** *vb*
1 to flow in or as if in a stream ⟨rain *streaming* down the windows⟩
2 to give out a bodily fluid in large amounts ⟨his face *streamed* with sweat⟩
3 to become wet with flowing liquid ⟨windows *streaming* with rain⟩
4 to trail out at full length ⟨hair *streaming* in the wind⟩
5 to pour in large numbers ⟨the people *streamed* into the hall⟩

**stream·er** \'strē-mər\ *n*
1 a flag that streams in the wind : PENNANT
2 a long narrow wavy strip (as of ribbon on a hat) suggesting a banner floating in the wind
3 **streamers** *pl* AURORA BOREALIS

**stream·lined** \'strēm-,līnd\ *adj*
1 designed or constructed to make motion through water or air easier or as if for this purpose ⟨a *streamlined* automobile⟩
2 made shorter, simpler, or more efficient ⟨a *streamlined* course of study⟩

**street** \'strēt\ *n*
1 a public way especially in a city, town, or village
2 the people living along a street ⟨the whole *street* was excited⟩

**street·car** \'strēt-,kär\ *n*
► a passenger vehicle that runs on rails and operates mostly on city streets

**strength** \'strength\ *n*
1 the quality of being strong
2 power to resist force ⟨the *strength* of a rope⟩
3 power to resist attack
4 intensity of light, color, sound, or odor
5 force as measured in numbers ⟨the full *strength* of an army⟩
**synonyms** see POWER

**strength·en** \'streng-thən\ *vb*
to make, grow, or become stronger

**stren·u·ous** \'stren-yə-wəs\ *adj*
1 very active : ENERGETIC ⟨a *strenuous* supporter of the president⟩
2 showing or requiring much energy ⟨*strenuous* exercise⟩
**stren·u·ous·ly** *adv*

**strep·to·my·cin** \,strep-tə-'mīs-n\ *n*
a substance produced by a soil bacterium and used especially in treating tuberculosis

[1]**stress** \'stres\ *n*
1 a force that tends to change the shape of a body
2 something that causes bodily or mental tension : a state of tension resulting from a stress
3 special importance given to something
4 relative prominence of sound : a syllable carrying this stress : ACCENT

[2]**stress** *vb*
1 to expose to stress : STRAIN
2 [1]ACCENT 1 ⟨*stress* the first syllable⟩
3 to give special importance to ⟨*stressed* the need to save energy⟩

**stress mark** *n*
a mark used with a written syllable in the respelling of a word to show that this syllable is to be stressed when spoken

**streetcars** in San Francisco

**[1]stretch** \'strech\ *vb*
**1** to reach out : EXTEND, SPREAD ⟨*stretched* out a hand for the apple⟩
**2** to draw out in length or width or both : EXPAND, ENLARGE
**3** to draw up from a cramped, stooping, or relaxed position ⟨awoke and *stretched* myself⟩
**4** to pull tight ⟨canvas *stretched* over a frame⟩
**5** to cause to reach or continue ⟨*stretch* a wire between two posts⟩
**6** EXAGGERATE
**7** to become extended without breaking ⟨rubber *stretches* easily⟩

**[2]stretch** *n*
**1** the act of extending or drawing out beyond ordinary or normal limits ⟨a *stretch* of the imagination⟩
**2** the extent to which something may be stretched
**3** the act or an instance of stretching the body or one of its parts
**4** a continuous extent in length, area, or time ⟨a fine *stretch* of country⟩

**stretch·er** \'strech-ər\ *n*
**1** one that stretches ⟨a curtain *stretcher*⟩
**2** a light bedlike device for carrying sick or injured persons

**strew** \'strü\ *vb* **strewed**; **strewed** *or* **strewn** \'strün\; **strew·ing**
**1** to spread by scattering ⟨*strew* crumbs for the birds⟩
**2** to cover by or as if by scattering something

**strick·en** \'strik-ən\ *adj*
**1** hit or wounded by or as if by a missile
**2** troubled with disease, misfortune, or sorrow

**strict** \'strikt\ *adj*
**1** permitting no avoidance or escape ⟨*strict* discipline⟩
**2** kept with great care : ABSOLUTE ⟨*strict* secrecy⟩
**3** carefully observing something (as a rule or principle) : EXACT, PRECISE ⟨a *strict* Catholic⟩
**strict·ly** *adv*
**strict·ness** *n*

**[1]stride** \'strīd\ *vb* **strode** \'strōd\; **strid·den** \'strid-n\; **strid·ing** \'strīd-ing\
**1** to walk or run with long even steps
**2** to step over : STRADDLE

**[2]stride** *n*
**1** a long step : the distance covered by such a step
**2** a step forward : ADVANCE ⟨made great *strides* in their studies⟩
**3** a way of striding

**strife** \'strīf\ *n*
**1** bitter and sometimes violent disagreement
**2** [2]STRUGGLE 1, CONTENTION

**[1]strike** \'strīk\ *vb* **struck** \'strək\; **struck** *or* **strick·en** \'strik-ən\; **strik·ing** \'strī-king\
**1** GO 1, PROCEED ⟨*strike* off into the woods⟩
**2** to touch or hit with force ⟨*struck* me with a whip⟩ ⟨lightning never *strikes* twice⟩
**3** to lower (as a flag or sail) usually in salute or surrender
**4** to come into contact or collision with ⟨the ship *struck* a rock⟩
**5** to make a military attack : FIGHT ⟨*strike* for freedom⟩
**6** to remove or cancel with or as if with the stroke of a pen ⟨*strike* a name from the list⟩
**7** to make known by sounding or cause to sound ⟨the clock *struck* one⟩ ⟨*strike* a bell⟩
**8** to affect usually suddenly ⟨*stricken* with a high fever⟩
**9** to produce by stamping with a die or punch ⟨*strike* a medal⟩
**10** to produce by or as if by a blow ⟨*strike* fear into the enemy⟩
**11** to cause to ignite by scratching ⟨*strike* a match⟩
**12** to agree on the arrangements of ⟨*strike* a bargain⟩
**13** to make an impression on ⟨it *struck* me as funny⟩
**14** to come upon : DISCOVER ⟨*strike* oil⟩
**15** to stop work in order to obtain a change in conditions of work

**[2]strike** *n*
**1** an act or instance of striking
**2** a stopping of work by workers to force an employer to agree to demands
**3** a discovery of a valuable mineral deposit
**4** a baseball pitch that is swung at or that passes through a certain area over home plate (**strike zone**) and that counts against the batter
**5** DISADVANTAGE, HANDICAP
**6** the knocking down of all ten bowling pins with the first ball
**7** a military attack

**strike·out** \'strī-ˌkaůt\ *n*
an out in baseball that results from a batter's striking out

**strike out** \strī-'kaůt\ *vb*
to be out in baseball by getting three strikes as a batter

**strik·ing** \'strī-king\ *adj*
attracting attention : REMARKABLE ⟨a *striking* resemblance⟩
**strik·ing·ly** *adv*

**[1]string** \'string\ *n*
**1** a small cord used to bind, fasten, or tie
**2** a thin tough plant structure (as the fiber connecting the halves of a bean pod)
**3** the gut, wire, or plastic cord of a musical instrument that vibrates to produce a tone
**4 strings** *pl* the stringed instruments of an orchestra
**5** a group, series, or line of objects threaded on a string or arranged as if strung together ⟨a *string* of automobiles⟩

**[2]string** *vb* **strung** \'strəng\; **string·ing**
**1** to provide with strings ⟨*string* a violin⟩
**2** to make tense ⟨my nerves were *strung* up⟩
**3** [2]THREAD 4 ⟨*string* beads⟩
**4** to tie, hang, or fasten with string
**5** to remove the strings of ⟨*string* beans⟩
**6** to set or stretch out in a line ⟨*string* wires from tree to tree⟩

**string bass** *n*
DOUBLE BASS

**string bean** *n*
a bean grown primarily for its pods which are eaten before the seeds are full grown

**stringed instrument** \'stringd-\ *n*
▶ a musical instrument (as a violin, guitar, or banjo) sounded by plucking or striking or by drawing a bow across tight strings

**string·er** \'string-ər\ *n*
a long strong piece of wood or metal used for support or strengthening in building (as under a floor)

**stringy** \'string-ē\ *adj* **string·i·er**; **string·i·est**
containing, consisting of, or like string ⟨*stringy* meat⟩ ⟨*stringy* hair⟩

**stringed instrument**
Some stringed instruments can be plucked or strummed, such as the balalaika, sitar, harp, and electric bass. Other instruments, such as the cello, violin, viola, and double bass, are sounded with a bow. The thinner and shorter the string, the higher the note it will produce. Larger instruments, such as the double bass, can produce lower notes.

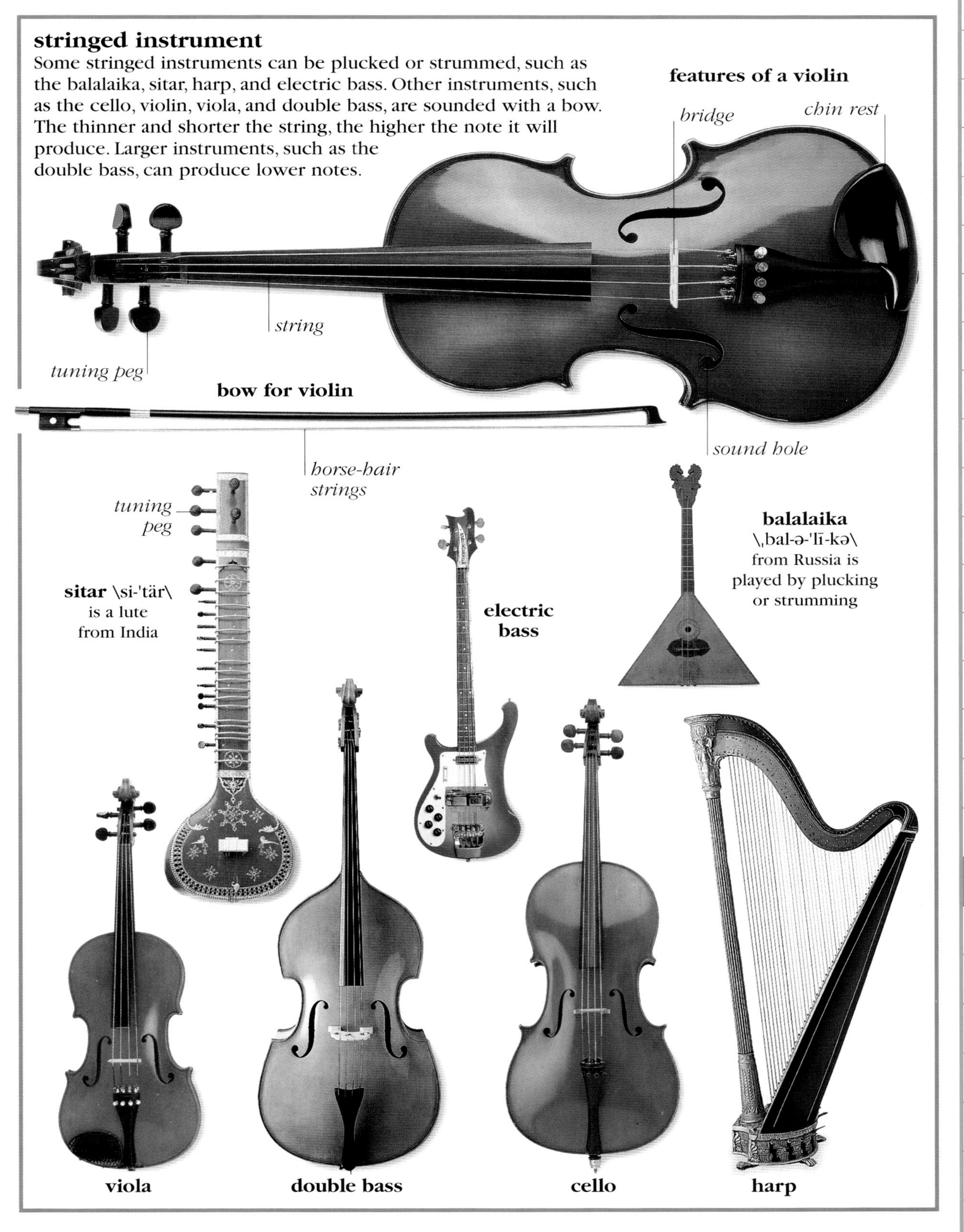

A B C D E F G H I J K L M N O P Q R S T U V W X Y Z

**[1]strip** \'strip\ *vb* **stripped**; **strip·ping**
**1** to remove clothes : UNDRESS
**2** to remove a covering or surface layer from ⟨*strip* furniture for refinishing⟩
**3** to take away all duties, honors, or special rights ⟨they were *stripped* of their rank⟩
**4** to remove furniture, equipment, or accessories from ⟨thieves *stripped* the car⟩
**5** to tear or damage the thread of a screw or bolt

**[2]strip** *n*
a long narrow piece or area

**strip–crop·ping** \'strip-,kräp-iŋ\ *n*
the growing of a food crop (as potatoes) in alternate strips with a crop (as grass) that forms sod and helps keep the soil from being worn away

**[1]stripe** \'strīp\ *vb* **striped**; **strip·ing**
to make stripes on

**[2]stripe** *n*
**1** a line or long narrow division or section of something different in color or appearance from the background
**2** a piece of material often with a special design worn (as on a sleeve) to show military rank or length of service

**striped** \'strīpt, 'strī-pəd\ *adj*
having stripes

**strive** \'strīv\ *vb* **strove** \'strōv\; **striv·en** \'striv-ən\ *or* **strived**; **striv·ing** \'strī-viŋ\
**1** to carry on a conflict or effort : CONTEND ⟨*strive* against fate⟩
**2** to try hard ⟨*strive* to win⟩

**strode** *past of* STRIDE

**[1]stroke** \'strōk\ *vb* **stroked**; **strok·ing**
to rub gently in one direction

**[2]stroke** *n*
**1** the act of striking : BLOW
**2** a single unbroken movement especially in one direction : one of a series of repeated movements (as in swimming or rowing a boat)
**3** the hitting of a ball in a game (as golf or tennis)
**4** a sudden action or process that results in something being struck ⟨a *stroke* of lightning⟩
**5** a sudden or unexpected example ⟨a *stroke* of luck⟩
**6** a sudden weakening or loss of consciousness and powers of voluntary movement that results from the breaking or blocking of an artery in the brain
**7** effort by which something is done or the results of such effort ⟨it was a *stroke* of genius⟩
**8** the sound of striking (as of a clock or bell) ⟨at the *stroke* of midnight⟩
**9** a mark made by a single movement of a brush, pen, or tool

**[1]stroll** \'strōl\ *vb*
to walk in a leisurely manner : RAMBLE

**[2]stroll** *n*
a leisurely walk : RAMBLE

**stroll·er** \'strō-lər\ *n*
▼ a small carriage in which a baby can sit and be pushed around

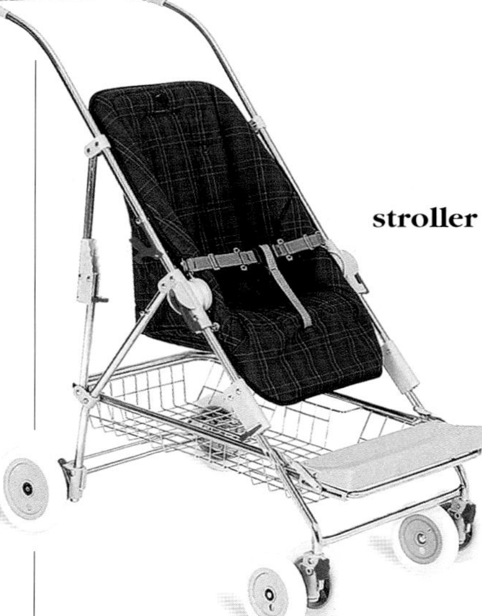

**stroller**

**strong** \'stroŋ\ *adj* **stron·ger** \'stroŋ-gər\; **stron·gest** \'stroŋ-gəst\
**1** having great power in the muscles
**2** HEALTHY 1, 2, ROBUST
**3** having great resources ⟨a *strong* nation⟩
**4** of a specified number ⟨an army 10,000 *strong*⟩
**5** PERSUASIVE ⟨*strong* arguments⟩
**6** having much of some quality ⟨*strong* coffee⟩ ⟨*strong* light⟩
**7** moving with speed and force ⟨a *strong* wind⟩
**8** ENTHUSIASTIC, ZEALOUS
**9** not easily injured or overcome ⟨a *strong* bridge⟩ ⟨a *strong* opponent⟩
**10** well established : FIRM ⟨*strong* beliefs⟩
**strong·ly** \'stroŋ-lē\ *adv*

---

**Synonyms** STRONG, STURDY, and TOUGH mean showing the power to endure opposing force. STRONG suggests great bodily or material power ⟨a *strong* person is needed to lift that⟩ ⟨a *strong* army⟩. STURDY suggests the ability to endure pressure or hard use ⟨a *sturdy* table⟩. TOUGH suggests that something is very firm and elastic ⟨this meat is *tough*⟩ ⟨a *tough* fabric that will last many years⟩.

---

**strong·hold** \'stroŋ-,hōld\ *n*
FORTRESS

**strove** *past of* STRIVE

**struck** *past of* STRIKE

**struc·tur·al** \'strək-chə-rəl\ *adj*
**1** of, relating to, or affecting structure ⟨*structural* weaknesses⟩
**2** used or formed for use in construction ⟨*structural* steel⟩

**struc·ture** \'strək-chər\ *n*
**1** something built (as a house or dam)
**2** the manner in which something is built : CONSTRUCTION
**3** the arrangement or relationship of parts or organs ⟨the *structure* of the body⟩

**[1]strug·gle** \'strəg-əl\ *vb* **strug·gled**; **strug·gling**
**1** to make a great effort to overcome someone or something : STRIVE ⟨*struggled* with the burglar⟩ ⟨*struggling* with money problems⟩
**2** to move with difficulty or with great effort ⟨*struggled* through the snow⟩

**[2]struggle** *n*
**1** a violent effort
**2** [2]FIGHT 1, CONTEST

**strum** \'strəm\ *vb* **strummed**; **strum·ming**
to play on a stringed instrument by brushing the strings with the fingers ⟨*strum* a guitar⟩

**strung** *past of* STRING

[1]**strut** \'strət\ *vb* **strut·ted**; **strut·ting**
to walk in a stiff proud way

[2]**strut** *n*
**1** a bar or brace used to resist lengthwise pressure
**2** a strutting step or walk

[1]**stub** \'stəb\ *n*
**1** a short part remaining after the rest has been removed or used up ⟨a pencil *stub*⟩
**2** a small part of a check kept as a record of what was on the detached check

[2]**stub** *vb* **stubbed**; **stub·bing**
to strike (as the toe) against an object

**stub·ble** \'stəb-əl\ *n*
**1** the stem ends of herbs and especially cereal grasses left in the ground after harvest
**2** a rough growth or surface like stubble in a field **:** a short growth of beard

**stub·born** \'stəb-ərn\ *adj*
**1** refusing to change an opinion or course of action in spite of difficulty or urging ⟨*stubborn* as a mule⟩
**2** PERSISTENT ⟨a *stubborn* cough⟩
**3** difficult to handle, manage, or treat ⟨*stubborn* hair⟩
**stub·born·ly** *adv*
**stub·born·ness** *n*

**stub·by** \'stəb-ē\ *adj* **stub·bi·er**; **stub·bi·est**
short and thick like a stub ⟨*stubby* fingers⟩

**stuc·co** \'stək-ō\ *n, pl* **stuc·cos** *or* **stuc·coes**
a plaster for coating walls

**stuck** *past of* STICK

**stuck–up** \'stək-'əp\ *adj*
VAIN 2, CONCEITED ⟨they're awfully *stuck-up*⟩

[1]**stud** \'stəd\ *n*
**1** one of the smaller vertical braces of the walls of a building to which the wall materials are fastened
**2** a removable device like a button used to fasten something or as an ornament ⟨shirt *studs*⟩
**3** one of the metal cleats used on a snow tire to provide a better grip

[2]**stud** *vb* **stud·ded**; **stud·ding**
**1** to supply or cover with or as if with studs
**2** to set thickly together ⟨water *studded* with islands⟩

**stu·dent** \'stüd-nt, 'styüd-\ *n*
a person who studies especially in school **:** PUPIL

**stu·dio** \'stüd-ē-,ō, 'styüd-\ *n, pl* **stu·di·os**
**1** ▼ the place where an artist, sculptor, or photographer works
**2** a place for the study of an art
**3** a place where movies are made
**4** a place from which radio or television programs are broadcast

**stu·di·ous** \'stüd-ē-əs, 'styüd-\ *adj*
devoted to and fond of study ⟨a *studious* child⟩

[1]**study** \'stəd-ē\ *n, pl* **stud·ies**
**1** use of the mind to get knowledge
**2** a careful investigation or examination of something ⟨the *study* of a disease⟩
**3** a room especially for study, reading, or writing

[2]**study** *vb* **stud·ied**; **study·ing**
**1** to use the mind to learn about something by reading, investigating, or memorizing
**2** to give close attention to ⟨*studied* the request carefully⟩

[1]**stuff** \'stəf\ *n*
**1** materials, supplies, or equipment that people need or use
**2** writing, speech, or ideas of little value ⟨it's just *stuff* and nonsense⟩
**3** something mentioned or understood but not named ⟨wipe that *stuff* off your face⟩
**4** basic part of something **:** SUBSTANCE ⟨shows the *stuff* of greatness⟩

[2]**stuff** *vb*
**1** to fill by packing or crowding things in **:** CRAM ⟨*stuffed* the suitcases⟩
**2** OVEREAT, GORGE ⟨*stuffed* themselves on candy⟩
**3** to fill with a stuffing ⟨*stuff* a turkey⟩
**4** to stop up **:** CONGEST ⟨a *stuffed* nose⟩
**5** to force into something **:** THRUST ⟨*stuffed* the clothes into the drawer⟩ **synonyms** see PACK

### studio 1
Different artists, such as photographers and painters, have specially equipped studios suited to their work. For example, a photographer's studio has a range of lighting devices, camera accessories, and screens. This equipment gives the photographer control over the intensity and color of the lighting, camera angle and focus, and the subject's background.

**a photographer's studio**

**stuff·ing** \'stəf-ing\ *n*
**1** material used in filling up or stuffing something
**2** ▶ a mixture (as of bread crumbs and seasonings) used to stuff meat, vegetables, eggs, or poultry

*stuffing*

**stuffing 2:** vegetable stuffing in a sweet pepper

**stuffy** \'stəf-ē\ *adj* **stuff·i·er**; **stuff·i·est**
**1** needing fresh air ⟨a *stuffy* room⟩
**2** stuffed or choked up ⟨a *stuffy* nose⟩
**3** [1]DULL 8

[1]**stum·ble** \'stəm-bəl\ *vb* **stum·bled**; **stum·bling**
**1** to trip in walking or running
**2** to walk unsteadily
**3** to speak or act in a clumsy manner ⟨*stumbled* through the recitation⟩
**4** to come unexpectedly or accidentally ⟨*stumbled* onto a clue⟩

[2]**stumble** *n*
an act or instance of stumbling

[1]**stump** \'stəmp\ *n*
**1** the part of something (as an arm, a tooth, or a pencil) that remains after the rest has been removed, lost, or worn away : STUB
**2** the part of a tree that remains in the ground after the tree is cut down

[2]**stump** *vb*
**1** PERPLEX, BAFFLE ⟨the question *stumped* the experts⟩
**2** to walk or walk over heavily, stiffly, or clumsily as if with a wooden leg
**3** [2]STUB

**stun** \'stən\ *vb* **stunned**; **stun·ning**
**1** to make dizzy or senseless by or as if by a blow
**2** to affect with shock or confusion : fill with disbelief ⟨*stunned* by the news⟩

**stung** *past of* STING

**stunk** *past of* STINK

**stun·ning** \'stən-ing\ *adj*
**1** able or likely to make a person senseless or confused ⟨a *stunning* blow⟩
**2** unusually lovely or attractive : STRIKING

[1]**stunt** \'stənt\ *vb*
to hold back the normal growth of ⟨*stunt* a tree⟩

[2]**stunt** *n*
an unusual or difficult performance or act ⟨acrobatic *stunts*⟩

**stu·pe·fy** \'stü-pə-,fī, 'styü-\ *vb* **stu·pe·fied**; **stu·pe·fy·ing**
**1** to make stupid, groggy, or numb
**2** ASTONISH, ASTOUND

**stu·pen·dous** \stu̇-'pen-dəs, styu̇-\ *adj*
amazing especially because of great size or height

**stu·pid** \'stü-pəd, 'styü-\ *adj*
**1** slow or dull of mind
**2** showing or resulting from a dull mind or a lack of proper attention ⟨a *stupid* mistake⟩
**3** not interesting or worthwhile ⟨a *stupid* plot⟩
**stu·pid·ly** *adv*

**stu·pid·i·ty** \stu̇-'pid-ət-ē, styu̇-\ *n, pl* **stu·pid·i·ties**
**1** the quality or state of being stupid
**2** a stupid thought, action, or remark

**stu·por** \'stü-pər, 'styü-\ *n*
a condition in which the senses or feelings become dull ⟨in a drunken *stupor*⟩

**stur·dy** \'stərd-ē\ *adj* **stur·di·er**; **stur·di·est**
**1** firmly built or made
**2** strong and healthy in body : ROBUST
**3** RESOLUTE **synonyms** see STRONG
**stur·di·ly** \'stərd-l-ē\ *adv*
**sturd·i·ness** \'stərd-ē-nəs\ *n*

**stur·geon** \'stər-jən\ *n*
a large food fish with tough skin and rows of bony plates

[1]**stut·ter** \'stət-ər\ *vb*
to speak or say in a jerky way with involuntary repeating or interruption of sounds

[2]**stutter** *n*
the act or an instance of stuttering

[1]**sty** \'stī\ *n, pl* **sties**
PIGPEN

[2]**sty** *or* **stye** \'stī\ *n, pl* **sties** *or* **styes**
a painful red swelling on the edge of an eyelid

[1]**style** \'stīl\ *n*
**1** the narrow middle part of the pistil of a flower
**2** a way of speaking or writing
**3** an individual way of doing something ⟨a batter's *style* of holding the bat⟩
**4** a method or manner that is felt to be very respectable, fashionable, or proper : FASHION ⟨dine in *style*⟩ ⟨clothes that are out of *style*⟩ **synonyms** see FASHION

[2]**style** *vb* **styled**; **styl·ing**
**1** to identify by some descriptive term : CALL
**2** to design and make in agreement with an accepted or a new style ⟨well-*styled* hats⟩

**styl·ish** \'stī-lish\ *adj*
having style : FASHIONABLE
**styl·ish·ly** *adv*
**styl·ish·ness** *n*

**sty·lus** \'stī-ləs\ *n, pl* **sty·li** \-,lī\ *or* **sty·lus·es**
▶ a pointed instrument used in ancient times for writing on wax tablets

**stylus:** a bronze stylus from Southeast Asia

[1]**sub** \'səb\ *n*
[1]SUBSTITUTE

[2]**sub** *vb* **subbed**; **sub·bing**
to act as a substitute

[3]**sub** *n*
SUBMARINE

**sub-** *prefix*
**1** under : beneath : below ⟨*sub*marine⟩
**2** lower in importance or rank : lesser
**3** division or part of ⟨*sub*set⟩
**4** so as to form, stress, or deal with lesser parts or relations

**sub·di·vide** \,səb-də-'vīd\ *vb* **sub·di·vid·ed**; **sub·di·vid·ing**
**1** to divide the parts of into more parts
**2** to divide into several parts ⟨*subdivide* a farm into building lots⟩

**sub·di·vi·sion** \,səb-də-'vizh-ən\ *n*
**1** the act of subdividing
**2** one of the parts into which something is subdivided

**sub·due** \səb-ˈdü, -ˈdyü\ *vb* **sub·dued**; **sub·du·ing**
**1** to overcome in battle ⟨*subdued* the enemy⟩
**2** to bring under control ⟨*subduing* one's fears⟩
**3** to reduce the brightness or strength of : SOFTEN ⟨*subdued* light⟩

**sub·head** \ˈsəb-ˌhed\ *or* **sub·head·ing** \-ˌhed-iŋ\ *n* a heading under which one of the divisions of a subject is listed

**[1]sub·ject** \ˈsəb-jikt\ *n*
**1** a person under the authority or control of another
**2** a person who owes loyalty to a monarch or state
**3** a course of study
**4** an individual that is studied or experimented on
**5** the person or thing discussed : TOPIC
**6** the word or group of words about which the predicate makes a statement

**[2]subject** *adj*
**1** owing obedience or loyalty to another
**2** likely to be affected by ⟨*subject* to temptation⟩ ⟨*subject* to colds⟩
**3** depending on ⟨*subject* to your approval⟩

**[3]sub·ject** \səb-ˈjekt\ *vb*
**1** to bring under control or rule
**2** to cause to put up with ⟨unwilling to *subject* us to embarrassment⟩

**sub·lime** \sə-ˈblīm\ *adj*
**1** grand or noble in thought, expression, or manner ⟨*sublime* truths⟩
**2** having beauty enough or being impressive enough to arouse a mixed feeling of admiration and wonder ⟨*sublime* scenery⟩

**submarine** *n*
▼ a naval ship designed to operate underwater

**sub·merge** \səb-ˈmərj\ *vb* **sub·merged**; **sub·merg·ing**
**1** to put under or plunge into water
**2** to cover or become covered with or as if with water ⟨floods *submerged* the town⟩

**sub·mis·sion** \səb-ˈmish-ən\ *n*
**1** the act of submitting something (as for consideration or comment)
**2** the condition of being humble or obedient
**3** the act of submitting to power or authority

**sub·mis·sive** \səb-ˈmis-iv\ *adj* willing to submit to others

**sub·mit** \səb-ˈmit\ *vb* **sub·mit·ted**; **sub·mit·ting**
**1** to leave to the judgment or approval of someone else ⟨*submit* a plan for consideration⟩
**2** to put forward as an opinion, reason, or idea
**3** to yield to the authority, control, or choice of another

**[1]sub·or·di·nate** \sə-ˈbȯrd-n-ət\ *adj*
**1** being in a lower class or rank : INFERIOR
**2** yielding to or controlled by authority

**[2]subordinate** *n* one that is subordinate

**[3]sub·or·di·nate** \sə-ˈbȯrd-n-ˌāt\ *vb* **sub·or·di·nat·ed**; **sub·or·di·nat·ing** to make subordinate

**sub·scribe** \səb-ˈskrīb\ *vb* **sub·scribed**; **sub·scrib·ing**
**1** to make known one's approval by or as if by signing ⟨we *subscribe* to your plan⟩
**2** to agree to give or contribute by signing one's name with the amount promised ⟨*subscribe* fifty dollars to the building fund⟩
**3** to place an order (as for a newspaper) with payment or a promise to pay
— **sub·scrib·er** *n*

**sub·scrip·tion** \səb-ˈskrip-shən\ *n*
**1** an act or instance of subscribing
**2** a thing or amount subscribed ⟨a *subscription* of ten dollars⟩

**sub·se·quent** \ˈsəb-si-kwənt\ *adj* following in time, order, or place ⟨*subsequent* events⟩
— **sub·se·quent·ly** *adv*

**sub·set** \ˈsəb-ˌset\ *n* a mathematical set each of whose members is also a member of a larger set

**sub·side** \səb-ˈsīd\ *vb* **sub·sid·ed**; **sub·sid·ing**
**1** to become lower : SINK ⟨the flood *subsided*⟩
**2** to become quiet or less ⟨the pain *subsided*⟩

**sub·sist** \səb-ˈsist\ *vb* to continue living or being ⟨*subsisting* on bread and water⟩

**sub·sis·tence** \səb-ˈsis-təns\ *n* the smallest amount (as of food and clothing) necessary to support life

**sub·soil** \ˈsəb-ˌsȯil\ *n* a layer of soil lying just under the topsoil

**sub·stance** \ˈsəb-stəns\ *n*
**1** ESSENCE 1
**2** the most important part ⟨the *substance* of a speech⟩
**3** material of a certain kind ⟨an oily *substance*⟩
**4** material belongings : WEALTH ⟨a person of *substance*⟩

**sub·stan·dard** \ˌsəb-ˈstan-dərd\ *adj* being below what is standard

**sub·stan·tial** \səb-ˈstan-chəl\ *adj*
**1** made up of or relating to substance ⟨dreams are not *substantial*⟩
**2** ABUNDANT ⟨a *substantial* meal⟩
**3** PROSPEROUS 1
**4** firmly constructed
**5** large in amount ⟨a *substantial* improvement⟩

**[1]sub·sti·tute** \ˈsəb-stə-ˌtüt, -ˌtyüt\ *n* a person or thing that takes the place of another

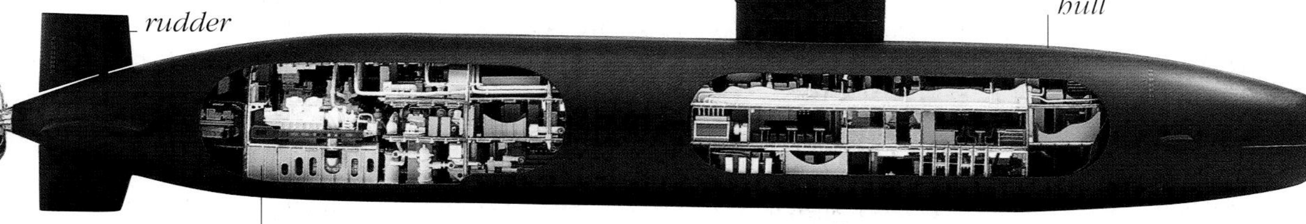


**submarine** with some parts shown in cross section

**²substitute** *vb* **sub·sti·tut·ed**; **sub·sti·tut·ing**
**1** to put in the place of another
**2** to serve as a substitute

**sub·sti·tu·tion** \ˌsəb-stə-ˈtü-shən, -ˈtyü-\ *n*
the act or process of substituting

**sub·tle** \ˈsət-l\ *adj* **sub·tler** \ˈsət-lər\; **sub·tlest** \ˈsət-ləst\
**1** DELICATE 1 ⟨a *subtle* fragrance⟩
**2** SHREWD, KEEN ⟨*subtle* questions⟩
**3** CLEVER 2, SLY
**sub·tly** \ˈsət-lē\ *adv*

**sub·top·ic** \ˈsəb-ˌtäp-ik\ *n*
a topic (as in a composition) that is a division of a main topic

**sub·tract** \səb-ˈtrakt\ *vb*
to take away (as one part or number from another) : DEDUCT

**sub·trac·tion** \səb-ˈtrak-shən\ *n*
the subtracting of one number from another

**sub·tra·hend** \ˈsəb-trə-ˌhend\ *n*
a number that is to be subtracted from another number

**sub·urb** \ˈsəb-ˌərb\ *n*
**1** a part of a city or town near its outer edge
**2** a smaller community close to a city
**3** **suburbs** *pl* the area of homes close to or surrounding a city
**sub·ur·ban** \sə-ˈbər-bən\ *adj or n*

**sub·way** \ˈsəb-ˌwā\ *n*
**1** an underground tunnel
**2** a usually electric underground railway

**suc·ceed** \sək-ˈsēd\ *vb*
**1** to come after : FOLLOW
**2** to take the place of a ruler or leader who has died, resigned, or been removed
**3** to be successful

**suc·cess** \sək-ˈses\ *n*
**1** satisfactory completion of something
**2** the gaining of wealth, respect, or fame
**3** a person or thing that succeeds

**suc·cess·ful** \sək-ˈses-fəl\ *adj*
**1** resulting or ending well or in success
**2** gaining or having gained success
**suc·cess·ful·ly** \-fə-lē\ *adv*

**suc·ces·sion** \sək-ˈsesh-ən\ *n*
**1** the order, act, or right of succeeding to a throne, title, or property
**2** a series of persons or things that follow one after another

**suc·ces·sive** \sək-ˈses-iv\ *adj*
following in order and without interruption
**suc·ces·sive·ly** *adv*

**suc·ces·sor** \sək-ˈses-ər\ *n*
a person who succeeds to a throne, title, property, or office

**suc·cor** \ˈsək-ər\ *n*
²HELP 1, RELIEF

**suc·cu·lent** \ˈsək-yə-lənt\ *adj*
JUICY

**suc·cumb** \sə-ˈkəm\ *vb*
**1** to yield to force or pressure ⟨*succumb* to temptation⟩
**2** ¹DIE 1

**¹such** \ˈsəch, səch\ *adj*
**1** of a kind just specified or to be specified ⟨a bag *such* as a doctor carries⟩
**2** of the same class, type, or sort : SIMILAR ⟨opened three *such* stores⟩
**3** so great : so remarkable ⟨*such* courage⟩

**²such** *pron*
that sort of person, thing, or group ⟨has a plan, if it may be called *such*⟩ ⟨*such* were the Romans⟩ ⟨boards and nails and *such*⟩

**suck** \ˈsək\ *vb*
**1** to draw in liquid and especially mother's milk with the mouth
**2** to draw liquid from by action of the mouth ⟨*suck* an orange⟩
**3** to allow to dissolve gradually in the mouth ⟨*suck* a lollipop⟩
**4** to put (as a thumb) into the mouth and draw on as if sucking
**5** ABSORB 1 ⟨plants *suck* moisture from the soil⟩

**suck·er** \ˈsək-ər\ *n*
**1** one that sucks : SUCKLING
**2** ▼ a freshwater fish related to the carps that has thick soft lips for sucking in food
**3** a new stem from the roots or lower part of a plant
**4** LOLLIPOP
**5** a person easily fooled or cheated

**sucker 2**

**suck·le** \ˈsək-əl\ *vb* **suck·led**; **suck·ling**
▼ to feed from the breast or udder

**suckle:** a cat suckling her kittens

**suck·ling** \ˈsək-ling\ *n*
a young mammal still sucking milk from its mother

**suc·tion** \ˈsək-shən\ *n*
**1** the act or process of sucking
**2** the process of drawing something into a space (as in a pump) by removing air from the space
**3** the force caused by suction

**sud·den** \ˈsəd-n\ *adj*
**1** happening or coming quickly and unexpectedly ⟨a *sudden* shower⟩
**2** met with unexpectedly ⟨a *sudden* turn in the road⟩
**3** ¹STEEP 1
**4** HASTY 2 ⟨a *sudden* decision⟩
**sud·den·ly** *adv*
**sud·den·ness** *n*

**suds** \ˈsədz\ *n pl*
**1** soapy water especially when foamy
**2** the foam on soapy water

**sue** \ˈsü\ *vb* **sued**; **su·ing**
to seek justice or right by bringing legal action

**suede** \ˈswād\ *n*
leather tanned and rubbed so that it is soft and has a nap

**su·et** \ˈsü-ət\ *n*
the hard fat about the kidneys in beef and mutton from which tallow is made

**suf·fer** \ˈsəf-ər\ *vb*
**1** to feel pain
**2** to experience something unpleasant ⟨*suffer* a defeat⟩

3 to bear loss or damage ⟨the business *suffered* during the storm⟩
4 [1]PERMIT
**suf·fer·er** \'səf-ər-ər\ *n*
**suf·fer·ing** \'səf-ə-riŋ, 'səf-riŋ\ *n*
1 the state or experience of one that suffers
2 a cause of distress : HARDSHIP
**suf·fice** \sə-'fīs\ *vb* **suf·ficed**; **suf·fic·ing**
1 to satisfy a need
2 to be enough for
**suf·fi·cient** \sə-'fish-ənt\ *adj*
enough to achieve a goal or fill a need
**suf·fi·cient·ly** *adv*
**suf·fix** \'səf-,iks\ *n*
a letter or group of letters that comes at the end of a word and has a meaning of its own
**suf·fo·cate** \'səf-ə-,kāt\ *vb* **suf·fo·cat·ed**; **suf·fo·cat·ing**
1 to kill by stopping the breath or depriving of oxygen to breathe
2 to be or become choked or smothered
3 to have or cause to have a feeling of smothering
**suf·fo·ca·tion** \,səf-ə-'kā-shən\ *n*
the act of suffocating or state of being suffocated
**suf·frage** \'səf-rij\ *n*
the right to vote
[1]**sug·ar** \'shu̇g-ər\ *n*
1 a sweet substance obtained from sugarcane, sugar beets, or maple syrup
2 any of numerous soluble and usually sweet carbohydrates
[2]**sugar** *vb*
1 to mix, cover, or sprinkle with sugar
2 to make something less hard to take or put up with ⟨*sugar* advice with praise⟩
3 to change to crystals of sugar
**sugar beet** *n*
▶ a large beet with white roots that is grown as a source of sugar

root

**sugar beet**

**sug·ar·cane** \'shu̇g-ər-,kān\ *n*
a tall strong grass with jointed stems widely raised in tropical regions for the sugar it yields
**sugar maple** *n*
▼ an American maple tree with hard strong wood and a sweet sap that yields maple syrup and maple sugar

**sugar maple** leaves in fall

**sug·gest** \səg-'jest, sə-'jest\ *vb*
1 to put (as a thought or desire) into a person's mind
2 to offer as an idea ⟨*suggest* going for a walk⟩
3 to bring into one's mind through close connection or association ⟨smoke *suggests* fire⟩
**sug·ges·tion** \səg-'jes-chən, sə-'jes-\ *n*
1 the act or process of suggesting
2 a thought or plan that is suggested
3 [1]HINT 2 ⟨gray with a *suggestion* of blue⟩
**sug·ges·tive** \səg-'jes-tiv, sə-'jes-\ *adj*
1 giving a suggestion
2 full of suggestions : PROVOCATIVE
3 suggesting something improper or indecent
**sui·cide** \'sü-ə-,sīd\ *n*
1 the act of killing oneself purposely
2 a person who commits suicide
[1]**suit** \'süt\ *n*
1 an action in court for enforcing a right or claim
2 an earnest request
3 COURTSHIP
4 a number of things used together : SET ⟨a *suit* of clothes⟩
5 all the playing cards of one kind (as spades) in a pack
[2]**suit** *vb*
1 to be suitable or satisfactory
2 to make suitable : ADAPT ⟨*suit* the action to the word⟩
3 to be proper for or pleasing with ⟨the scarf does not *suit* the dress⟩
4 to meet the needs or desires of
**suit·abil·i·ty** \,süt-ə-'bil-ət-ē\ *n*
the quality or state of being suitable
**suit·able** \'süt-ə-bəl\ *adj*
being fit or right for a use or group ⟨a movie *suitable* for children⟩
**suit·ably** \-blē\ *adv*
**suit·case** \'süt-,kās\ *n*
a flat rectangular traveling bag
**suite** \'swēt, 'süt\ *n*
1 a number of connected rooms (as in a hotel)
2 a set of matched furniture for a room
**suit·or** \'süt-ər\ *n*
a man who courts a woman
**sul·fur** *or* **sul·phur** \'səl-fər\ *n*
a yellow chemical element that is found widely in nature and is used in making chemicals and paper
**sul·fu·rous** *or* **sul·phu·rous** \'səl-fə-rəs\ *adj*
containing or suggesting sulfur ⟨a *sulfurous* odor⟩
[1]**sulk** \'səlk\ *vb*
to be sullenly silent or irritable
[2]**sulk** *n*
1 the state of one sulking ⟨had a case of the *sulks*⟩
2 a sulky mood or spell ⟨in a *sulk*⟩
[1]**sulky** \'səl-kē\ *adj* **sulk·i·er**; **sulk·i·est**
sulking or given to sulking
[2]**sulky** *n, pl* **sulk·ies**
a light vehicle with two wheels, a seat for the driver only, and usually no body
**sul·len** \'səl-ən\ *adj*
1 not sociable : SULKY
2 GLOOMY 1, DREARY ⟨a *sullen* sky⟩
**sul·len·ly** *adv*
**sul·tan** \'səlt-n\ *n*
a ruler especially of a Muslim state
**sul·ta·na** \,səl-'tan-ə\ *n*
the wife, mother, sister, or daughter of a sultan
**sul·try** \'səl-trē\ *adj* **sul·tri·er**; **sul·tri·est**
very hot and humid ⟨*sultry* summer weather⟩
[1]**sum** \'səm\ *n*
1 a quantity of money
2 the whole amount ⟨the *sum* of your experience⟩
3 the result obtained by adding numbers ⟨the *sum* of 4 and 5 is 9⟩
4 a problem in arithmetic

[2]**sum** *vb* **summed**; **sum·ming**
to find the sum of by adding or counting

**su·mac** *or* **su·mach** \'shü-ˌmak, 'sü-\ *n*
▼ any of a group of trees, shrubs, or woody vines having leaves with many leaflets and loose clusters of red or white berries

flowers

**sumac:** a staghorn \'stag-horn\ sumac

**sum·ma·rize** \'səm-ə-ˌrīz\ *vb* **sum·ma·rized**; **sum·ma·riz·ing**
to tell in or reduce to a summary

[1]**sum·ma·ry** \'səm-ə-rē\ *adj*
**1** expressing or covering the main points briefly : CONCISE ⟨a *summary* account⟩
**2** done without delay ⟨*summary* punishment⟩

[2]**summary** *n, pl* **sum·ma·ries**
a short statement of the main points (as in a book or report)

[1]**sum·mer** \'səm-ər\ *n*
**1** the season between spring and autumn which is in the northern hemisphere usually the months of June, July, and August
**2** YEAR 2 ⟨a youth of sixteen *summers*⟩

[2]**summer** *vb*
to pass the summer

**sum·mer·time** \'səm-ər-ˌtīm\ *n*
the summer season

**sum·mery** \'səm-ə-rē\ *adj*
of, relating to, or typical of summer

**sum·mit** \'səm-ət\ *n*
the highest point (as of a mountain) : TOP

**sum·mon** \'səm-ən\ *vb*
**1** to call or send for : CONVENE
**2** to order to appear before a court of law
**3** to call into being : AROUSE ⟨*summon* up courage⟩
**sum·mon·er** *n*

**sum·mons** \'səm-ənz\ *n, pl* **sum·mons·es**
**1** the act of summoning
**2** a call by authority to appear at a place named or to attend to some duty
**3** a written order to appear in court

**sump·tu·ous** \'səmp-chə-wəs\ *adj*
very expensive or luxurious

**sum up** *vb*
SUMMARIZE

[1]**sun** \'sən\ *n*
**1** ► the celestial body whose light makes our day : the member of the solar system round which the planets revolve
**2** a celestial body like our sun
**3** SUNSHINE 1

[2]**sun** *vb* **sunned**; **sun·ning**
**1** to expose to or as if to the rays of the sun
**2** to sun oneself

**sun·bathe** \'sən-ˌbāth\ *vb* **sun·bathed**; **sun·bath·ing**
[2]SUN 2

**sundial:** an 18th-century brass sundial

**sun·beam** \'sən-ˌbēm\ *n*
a ray of sunlight

**sun·block** \'sən-ˌbläk\ *n*
a strong sunscreen

**sun·bon·net** \'sən-ˌbän-ət\ *n*
a bonnet with a wide curving brim that shades the face and usually a ruffle at the back that protects the neck from the sun

[1]**sun·burn** \'sən-ˌbərn\ *vb* **sun·burned** \-ˌbərnd\ *or* **sun·burnt** \-ˌbərnt\; **sun·burn·ing**
to burn or discolor by the sun

[2]**sunburn** *n*
a sore red state of the skin caused by too much sunlight

**sun·dae** \'sən-dē\ *n*
a serving of ice cream topped with fruit, syrup, or nuts

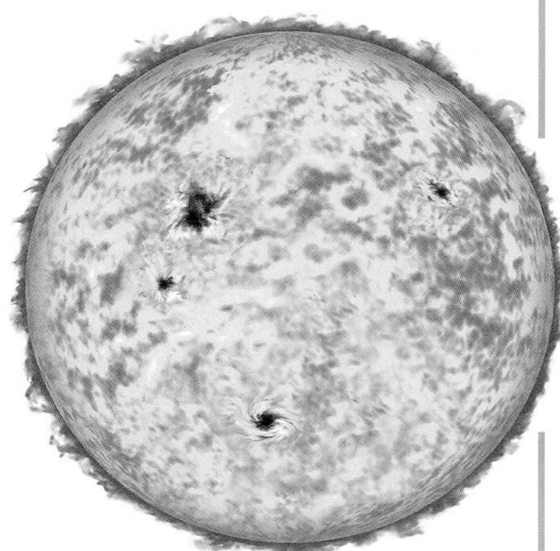

[1]**sun 1**

**Sun·day** \'sən-dē\ *n*
the first day of the week : the Christian Sabbath

**Sunday school** *n*
a school held on Sunday in a church for religious education

**sun·di·al** \'sən-ˌdī-əl\ *n*
◄ a device to show the time of day by the position of the shadow cast onto a marked plate by an object with a straight edge

**sun·down** \'sən-ˌdau̇n\ *n*
SUNSET

**sun·dries** \'sən-drēz\ *n pl*
various small articles or items

**sun·dry** \'sən-drē\ *adj*
more than one or two : VARIOUS ⟨we disagreed for *sundry* reasons⟩

**sun·fish** \'sən-ˌfish\ *n, pl* **sunfish** *or* **sun·fish·es**
any of numerous mostly small and brightly colored American freshwater fishes related to the perches

**sun·flow·er** \'sən-ˌflau̇-ər\ *n*
► a tall plant often grown for its large flower heads with brown center and yellow petals or for its edible oily seeds

**sung** *past of* SING

**sun·glass·es** \'sən-ˌglas-əz\ *n pl*
glasses to protect the eyes from the sun

**sunk** *past of* SINK

**sunflower**

**sunk·en** \'səng-kən\ *adj*
**1** lying at the bottom of a body of water ⟨*sunken* ships⟩
**2** fallen in : HOLLOW ⟨*sunken* cheeks⟩
**3** built or settled below the surrounding or normal level ⟨a *sunken* garden⟩

**sun·less** \'sən-ləs\ *adj*
being without sunlight : DARK

**sun·light** \'sən-,līt\ *n*
SUNSHINE

**sun·lit** \'sən-,lit\ *adj*
lighted by the sun

**sun·ny** \'sən-ē\ *adj* **sun·ni·er**; **sun·ni·est**
**1** bright with sunshine ⟨a *sunny* day⟩
**2** MERRY 1, CHEERFUL ⟨a *sunny* smile⟩

**sun·rise** \'sən-,rīz\ *n*
**1** the apparent rise of the sun above the horizon : the light and color that go with this
**2** the time at which the sun rises

**sun·screen** \'sən-,skrēn\ *n*
a substance used on the skin to help protect it from the sun's ultraviolet radiation

**sun·set** \'sən-,set\ *n*
**1** the apparent passing of the sun below the horizon : the light and color that go with this
**2** the time at which the sun sets

**sun·shade** \'sən-,shād\ *n*
something (as a parasol) used to protect from the sun's rays

**sun·shine** \'sən-,shīn\ *n*
**1** the sun's light or direct rays : the warmth and light given by the sun's rays
**2** something that spreads warmth or happiness

**sun·stroke** \'sən-,strōk\ *n*
a disorder marked by high fever and collapse and caused by too much sun

**sun·tan** \'sən-,tan\ *n*
a browning of skin exposed to the sun

**sun·up** \'sən-,əp\ *n*
SUNRISE

**sun·ward** \'sən-wərd\ *adv or adj*
toward or facing the sun

**su·per** \'sü-pər\ *adj*
**1** very great
**2** very good

**super-** *prefix*
**1** more than ⟨*super*human⟩
**2** extremely : very

**su·perb** \sù-'pərb\ *adj*
outstandingly excellent, impressive, or beautiful **synonyms** see SPLENDID

**su·per·com·put·er** \'sü-pər-kəm-,pyüt-ər\ *n*
a large very fast computer used especially for scientific computations

**su·per·fi·cial** \,sü-pər-'fish-əl\ *adj*
**1** of or relating to the surface or appearance only ⟨a *superficial* cut⟩
**2** not thorough : SHALLOW ⟨a *superficial* piece of work⟩
**su·per·fi·cial·ly** *adv*

**su·per·flu·ous** \sù-'pər-flə-wəs\ *adj*
going beyond what is enough or necessary : EXTRA

**su·per·he·ro** \'sü-pər-,hir-ō, -,hē-rō\ *n*
a fictional hero having extraordinary or superhuman powers

**su·per·high·way** \,sü-pər-'hī-,wā\ *n*
an expressway for high-speed traffic

**su·per·hu·man** \,sü-pər-'hyü-mən, -'yü-mən\ *adj*
going beyond normal human power, size, or ability

**su·per·in·tend** \,sü-pər-in-'tend\ *vb*
to have or exercise the charge of

**su·per·in·ten·dent** \,sü-pər-in-'ten-dənt\ *n*
a person who looks after or manages something (as schools or a building)

[1]**su·pe·ri·or** \sù-'pir-ē-ər\ *adj*
**1** situated higher up : higher in rank, importance, numbers, or quality
**2** excellent of its kind : BETTER
**3** feeling that one is better or more important than others : ARROGANT

[2]**superior** *n*
**1** one that is higher than another in rank, importance, or quality
**2** the head of a religious house or order

**su·pe·ri·or·i·ty** \sù-,pir-ē-'òr-ət-ē\ *n*
the state or fact of being superior

[1]**su·per·la·tive** \sù-'pər-lət-iv\ *adj*
**1** of, relating to, or being the form of an adjective or adverb that shows the highest or lowest degree of comparison
**2** better than all others : SUPREME

[2]**superlative** *n*
the superlative degree or a superlative form in a language

**su·per·mar·ket** \'sü-pər-,mär-kət\ *n*
a self-service market selling foods and household items

**su·per·nat·u·ral** \,sü-pər-'nach-ə-rəl, -'nach-rəl\ *adj*
of or relating to something beyond or outside of nature or the visible universe

**su·per·sede** \,sü-pər-'sēd\ *vb* **su·per·sed·ed**; **su·per·sed·ing**
to take the place or position of

**su·per·son·ic** \,sü-pər-'sän-ik\ *adj*
**1** relating to or being vibrations too rapid to be heard
**2** having a speed from one to five times that of sound ⟨a *supersonic* airplane⟩

**su·per·sti·tion** \,sü-pər-'stish-ən\ *n*
beliefs or practices resulting from ignorance, fear of the unknown, or trust in magic or chance

**su·per·sti·tious** \,sü-pər-'stish-əs\ *adj*
of, relating to, showing, or influenced by superstition

**su·per·vise** \'sü-pər-,vīz\ *vb* **su·per·vised**; **su·per·vis·ing**
SUPERINTEND, OVERSEE

**su·per·vi·sion** \,sü-pər-'vizh-ən\ *n*
the act of supervising : MANAGEMENT

**su·per·vi·sor** \'sü-pər-,vī-zər\ *n*
**1** a person who supervises
**2** an officer in charge of a unit or an operation of a business, government, or school

**sup·per** \'səp-ər\ *n*
**1** the evening meal especially when dinner is eaten at midday
**2** refreshments served late in the evening especially at a social gathering

**sup·plant** \sə-'plant\ *vb*
to take the place of another usually unfairly

**sup·ple** \'səp-əl\ *adj* **sup·pler** \'səp-lər\; **sup·plest** \'səp-ləst\
**1** ADAPTABLE ⟨a *supple* mind⟩
**2** capable of bending or of being bent easily without stiffness, creases, or damage ⟨a *supple* body⟩ ⟨*supple* leather⟩

A B C D E F G H I J K L M N O P Q R S T U V W X Y Z

**[1]sup·ple·ment** \'səp-lə-mənt\ *n*
something that supplies what is needed or adds to something else ⟨a food *supplement*⟩ ⟨the *supplement* at the back of the book⟩

**[2]sup·ple·ment** \'səp-lə-,ment\ *vb*
to add to : COMPLETE ⟨*supplement* their incomes by doing odd jobs⟩

**sup·ple·men·ta·ry** \,səp-lə-'ment-ə-rē\ *adj*
added as a supplement : ADDITIONAL

**sup·pli·cate** \'səp-lə-,kāt\ *vb* **sup·pli·cat·ed**; **sup·pli·cat·ing**
to ask or beg in a humble way : BESEECH

**sup·pli·ca·tion** \,səp-lə-'kā-shən\ *n*
the act of supplicating

**[1]sup·ply** \sə-'plī\ *vb* **sup·plied**; **sup·ply·ing**
**1** to provide for : SATISFY ⟨enough to *supply* the demand⟩
**2** to make available : FURNISH ⟨the trees *supplied* us with shelter⟩ ⟨*supplied* sandwiches for a picnic⟩

**[2]supply** *n, pl* **sup·plies**
**1** the amount of something that is needed or can be gotten ⟨the nation's oil *supply*⟩
**2** [2]STORE 1 ⟨keep a *supply* of pencils in my desk drawer⟩
**3** the act or process of supplying something ⟨engaged in the *supply* of raw materials⟩

**[1]sup·port** \sə-'pōrt\ *vb*
**1** to take sides with : FAVOR ⟨*support* a candidate⟩
**2** to provide evidence for : VERIFY ⟨they cannot *support* this claim⟩
**3** to pay the costs of : MAINTAIN ⟨*supports* a large family⟩
**4** to hold up or in position : serve as a foundation or prop for ⟨posts *support* the porch roof⟩
**5** to keep going : SUSTAIN ⟨not enough air to *support* life⟩
**sup·port·er** *n*

**[2]support** *n*
**1** the act of supporting : the condition of being supported
**2** one that supports

**sup·pose** \sə-'pōz\ *vb* **sup·posed**; **sup·pos·ing**
**1** to think of as true or as a fact for the sake of argument ⟨*suppose* you had to leave⟩
**2** BELIEVE 2, THINK ⟨I *suppose* they are honest⟩
**3** [1]GUESS 1 ⟨who do you *suppose* won⟩

**sup·posed** \sə-'pōzd\ *adj*
**1** believed to be true or real ⟨the *supposed* murderer⟩
**2** forced or required to do something ⟨I am *supposed* to be home early⟩
**sup·pos·ed·ly** \-'pō-zəd-lē\ *adv*

**sup·press** \sə-'pres\ *vb*
**1** to put down (as by authority or force) : SUBDUE ⟨*suppress* a riot⟩
**2** to hold back : REPRESS ⟨could hardly *suppress* a smile⟩

**[2]surf 1:** two people surfing

**sup·pres·sion** \sə-'presh-ən\ *n*
an act or instance of suppressing : the state of being suppressed

**su·prem·a·cy** \sů-'prem-ə-sē\ *n, pl* **su·prem·a·cies**
the highest rank, power, or authority

**su·preme** \sů-'prēm\ *adj*
**1** highest in rank, power, or authority
**2** highest in degree or quality : UTMOST ⟨*supreme* confidence⟩
**3** [1]EXTREME 1, FINAL ⟨the *supreme* sacrifice⟩
**su·preme·ly** *adv*

**Supreme Being** *n*
GOD 1

**Supreme Court** *n*
the highest court of the United States consisting of a chief justice and eight associate justices

**[1]sure** \'shůr\ *adj* **sur·er**; **sur·est**
**1** firmly established : STEADFAST ⟨a *sure* grip⟩ ⟨*sure* foundation⟩
**2** RELIABLE, TRUSTWORTHY ⟨a *sure* remedy⟩
**3** having no doubt : CONFIDENT ⟨I'm *sure* of it⟩
**4** not to be doubted : CERTAIN ⟨speaks from *sure* knowledge⟩
**5** bound to happen ⟨*sure* disaster⟩
**6** bound as if by fate ⟨you are *sure* to win⟩

**[2]sure** *adv*
SURELY 2, 3 ⟨*sure*, we'll be there⟩

**sure·ly** \'shůr-lē\ *adv*
**1** with confidence : CONFIDENTLY ⟨answered their questions *surely*⟩
**2** without doubt ⟨a book you will *surely* enjoy⟩
**3** beyond question : REALLY ⟨I *surely* do miss them⟩

**[1]surf** \'sərf\ *n*
**1** the waves of the sea that splash on the shore
**2** the sound, splash, and foam of breaking waves

**[2]surf** *vb*
**1** ◀ to ride the surf (as on a surfboard)
**2** to scan a wide range of offerings (as on television or the Internet) for something that is interesting or fills a need

**[1]sur·face** \'sər-fəs\ *n*
**1** the outside or any one side of an object
**2** the outside appearance ⟨on the *surface* the plan seems good⟩

**[2]surface** *adj*
**1** of or relating to a surface : acting on a surface
**2** not deep or real ⟨*surface* friendship⟩

**[3]surface** *vb* **sur·faced**; **sur·fac·ing**
**1** to give a surface to : make smooth (as by sanding or paving)
**2** to come to the surface ⟨the submarine *surfaced*⟩

**surf·board** \'sərf-,bōrd\ *n*
a long narrow board that floats and is ridden in surfing

**surf·ing** \'sər-fing\ *n*
the sport of riding waves in to shore usually while standing on a surfboard

**¹surge** \'sərj\ *vb* **surged**; **surg·ing**
**1** to rise and fall with much action
**2** to move in or as if in waves ⟨crowds *surging* through the streets⟩

**²surge** *n*
**1** an onward rush like that of a wave ⟨a *surge* of anger⟩
**2** a large wave ⟨*surges* of water⟩

**sur·geon** \'sər-jən\ *n*
a doctor who specializes in surgery

**sur·gery** \'sər-jə-rē\ *n*, *pl* **sur·ger·ies**
**1** a branch of medicine concerned with the correction of defects, the repair and healing of injuries, and the treatment of diseased conditions by operation
**2** the work done by a surgeon

**sur·gi·cal** \'sər-ji-kəl\ *adj*
of, relating to, or associated with surgery or surgeons ⟨*surgical* dressings⟩

**sur·ly** \'sər-lē\ *adj* **sur·li·er**; **sur·li·est**
having a mean rude disposition : UNFRIENDLY

---

**Word History** The word *surly* comes from the word *sir*. Long ago, some Englishmen who had the title *Sir* became too proud of it. Such men were called *sirly*, a word that meant "overbearing" and "arrogant." Over the years the spelling changed to *surly* and came to be used of anyone who is rude and unfriendly.

---

**¹sur·mise** \sər-'mīz\ *n*
a thought or idea based on very little evidence : ²GUESS

**²surmise** *vb* **sur·mised**; **sur·mis·ing**
to form an idea on very little evidence : ¹GUESS 1

**sur·mount** \sər-'mau̇nt\ *vb*
**1** OVERCOME 1 ⟨*surmount* difficulties⟩
**2** to get to the top of
**3** to be at the top of ⟨a castle *surmounts* the cliff⟩

**sur·name** \'sər-ˌnām\ *n*
a family name : a last name

**sur·pass** \sər-'pas\ *vb*
**1** to be greater, better, or stronger than : EXCEED
**2** to go beyond the reach or powers of ⟨a task that *surpassed* their strength⟩

**¹sur·plus** \'sər-pləs\ *n*
an amount left over : EXCESS

**²surplus** *adj*
left over : EXTRA ⟨*surplus* wheat⟩

**¹sur·prise** \sər-'prīz, sə-'prīz\ *n*
**1** an act or instance of coming upon without warning ⟨they were taken by *surprise*⟩
**2** something that surprises ⟨I have a *surprise* for you⟩
**3** ASTONISHMENT, AMAZEMENT

**²surprise** *vb* **sur·prised**; **sur·pris·ing**
**1** to attack without warning : capture by an unexpected attack
**2** to come upon without warning
**3** to cause to feel wonder or amazement because of being unexpected

---

**Synonyms** SURPRISE, ASTONISH, and AMAZE mean to impress forcibly by being unexpected, startling, or unusual. SURPRISE stresses that something is unexpected even though it by itself is not startling ⟨the sudden storm *surprised* the people at the picnic⟩. ASTONISH means to surprise very much with something that is hard or impossible to believe ⟨the first airplanes *astonished* people⟩. AMAZE stresses that something causes one to wonder and puzzle over it ⟨the magician *amazed* the children by making the rabbit disappear⟩.

---

*instrument for surveying an area of land*

**surveyor**

**sur·pris·ing** \sər-'prī-zing, sə-'prī-zing\ *adj*
causing surprise : UNEXPECTED
**sur·pris·ing·ly** *adv*

**¹sur·ren·der** \sə-'ren-dər\ *vb*
**1** to give oneself or something over to the power, control, or possession of another especially under force : YIELD ⟨*surrender* the fort⟩
**2** RELINQUISH ⟨*surrendered* our place in line⟩

**²surrender** *n*
the act of giving up or yielding oneself or something into the possession or control of someone else

**sur·rey** \'sər-ē\ *n*, *pl* **surreys**
a pleasure carriage that has two wide seats and four wheels and is drawn by horses

**sur·round** \sə-'rau̇nd\ *vb*
to enclose on all sides : ENCIRCLE

**sur·round·ings** \sə-'rau̇n-dingz\ *n pl*
the circumstances, conditions, or things around an individual : ENVIRONMENT

**¹sur·vey** \sər-'vā\ *vb* **sur·veyed**; **sur·vey·ing**
**1** to look over : EXAMINE ⟨the governor *surveyed* the damage caused by the flood⟩
**2** to find out the size, shape, or position of (as an area of land)
**3** to gather information from : make a survey of ⟨*surveyed* the students to find out who was the most popular teacher⟩

**²sur·vey** \'sər-ˌvā\ *n*, *pl* **surveys**
**1** the action or an instance of surveying
**2** something that is surveyed
**3** a careful examination to learn facts ⟨a *survey* of the school system⟩
**4** a history or description that covers a large subject briefly ⟨a *survey* of English literature⟩

**sur·vey·ing** \sər-'vā-ing\ *n*
**1** the act or occupation of a person who makes surveys
**2** a branch of mathematics that teaches how to measure the earth's surface and record these measurements accurately

**sur·vey·or** \sər-'vā-ər\ *n*
◀ a person who surveys or whose occupation is surveying

A B C D E F G H I J K L M N O P Q R S T U V W X Y Z

**sur·viv·al** \sər-ˈvī-vəl\ *n*
**1** a living or continuing longer than another person or thing
**2** one that survives

**sur·vive** \sər-ˈvīv\ *vb* **sur·vived**; **sur·viv·ing**
**1** to remain alive : continue to exist
**2** to live longer than or past the end of ⟨*survived* their children⟩ ⟨at least we *survived* the flood⟩
**sur·vi·vor** \sər-ˈvī-vər\ *n*

**sus·cep·ti·ble** \sə-ˈsep-tə-bəl\ *adj*
**1** of such a nature as to permit ⟨words *susceptible* of being misunderstood⟩
**2** having little resistance ⟨*susceptible* to colds⟩
**3** easily affected or impressed by ⟨*susceptible* to flattery⟩

**¹sus·pect** \ˈsəs-ˌpekt, sə-ˈspekt\ *adj*
thought of with suspicion ⟨a person whose honesty is *suspect*⟩

**²sus·pect** \ˈsəs-ˌpekt\ *n*
a person who is suspected

**³sus·pect** \sə-ˈspekt\ *vb*
**1** to have doubts of : DISTRUST
**2** to imagine to be guilty without proof
**3** to suppose to be true or likely

**sus·pend** \sə-ˈspend\ *vb*
**1** to force to give up some right or office for a time ⟨*suspended* from school⟩
**2** to stop or do away with for a time ⟨*suspend* a rule⟩
**3** to stop operation or action for a time ⟨all business *suspended* during the storm⟩
**4** to hang especially so as to be free except at one point ⟨*suspend* a ball by a thread⟩

**sus·pend·er** \sə-ˈspen-dər\ *n*
► one of a pair of supporting straps that fasten to trousers or a skirt and pass over the shoulders

**sus·pense** \sə-ˈspens\ *n*
uncertainty or worry about the result of something

**sus·pen·sion** \sə-ˈspen-chən\ *n*
**1** the act or an instance of suspending
**2** the state of being suspended
**3** the period during which someone or something is suspended

**sus·pi·cion** \sə-ˈspish-ən\ *n*
**1** an act or instance of suspecting or the state of being suspected ⟨was above *suspicion*⟩
**2** a feeling that something is wrong : DOUBT

**sus·pi·cious** \sə-ˈspish-əs\ *adj*
**1** likely to arouse suspicion ⟨*suspicious* actions⟩
**2** likely to suspect or distrust ⟨*suspicious* of everything new⟩
**3** showing distrust ⟨a *suspicious* glance⟩

**sus·tain** \sə-ˈstān\ *vb*
**1** to give support or relief to : HELP ⟨*sustained* by their faith⟩
**2** to provide with what is needed ⟨machines that *sustain* our economy⟩ ⟨food *sustains* life⟩
**3** to keep up : PROLONG ⟨books that *sustain* our interest⟩
**4** to hold up the weight of : PROP
**5** to keep up the spirits of ⟨hope *sustained* us⟩
**6** to put up with without giving in ⟨*sustaining* the burdens of life⟩
**7** ²EXPERIENCE ⟨the army *sustained* heavy losses⟩
**8** to allow or uphold as true, legal, or fair ⟨the judge *sustained* the plea⟩
**9** CONFIRM 1, PROVE ⟨this report *sustains* our story⟩

**sus·te·nance** \ˈsəs-tə-nəns\ *n*
**1** ²LIVING 3, SUBSISTENCE
**2** the act of sustaining : the state of being sustained
**3** ²SUPPORT 2 ⟨God is our *sustenance* in time of trouble⟩

**suspender:** a boy wearing suspenders

**SUV** \ˌes-ˌyü-ˈvē\ *n*
SPORT-UTILITY VEHICLE

**¹swab** \ˈswäb\ *n*
**1** a yarn mop especially as used on a ship
**2** a wad of absorbent material usually wound around the end of a small stick and used for applying or removing material (as medicine or makeup)

**²swab** *vb* **swabbed**; **swab·bing**
**1** to clean with or as if with a swab
**2** to apply medication to with a swab ⟨*swabbed* the wound with iodine⟩

**¹swag·ger** \ˈswag-ər\ *vb*
to walk with a proud strut

**²swagger** *n*
an act or instance of swaggering

**¹swal·low** \ˈswäl-ō\ *n*
any of a group of small migratory birds with long wings, forked tails, and a graceful flight

**²swallow** *vb*
**1** to take into the stomach through the mouth and throat
**2** to perform the actions used in swallowing something ⟨clear your throat and *swallow* before answering⟩
**3** to take in as if by swallowing : ENGULF ⟨a ship *swallowed* by the waves⟩
**4** to accept or believe without question, protest, or anger ⟨you *swallow* every story you hear⟩ ⟨*swallow* an insult⟩
**5** to keep from expressing or showing : REPRESS ⟨*swallowed* my disgust⟩

**³swallow** *n*
**1** an act of swallowing
**2** an amount that can be swallowed at one time

**swam** *past of* SWIM

**¹swamp** \ˈswämp\ *n*
wet spongy land often partly covered with water

**²swamp** *vb*
**1** to fill or cause to fill with water : sink after filling with water ⟨high waves *swamped* the boat⟩ ⟨the boat *swamped* and we had to swim to shore⟩
**2** OVERWHELM 2 ⟨was *swamped* with work⟩

**swampy** \ˈswäm-pē\ *adj* **swamp·i·er**; **swamp·i·est**
of, relating to, or like a swamp

**swan** \'swän\ *n*
▶ a usually white waterbird with a long neck and a heavy body that is related to but larger than the geese

[1]**swap** \'swäp\ *vb* **swapped**; **swap·ping**
to give in exchange : make an exchange : TRADE

[2]**swap** *n*
[1]EXCHANGE 1, TRADE

[1]**swarm** \'swȯrm\ *n*
**1** a large number of bees that leave a hive together to form a new colony elsewhere
**2** a large moving crowd (as of people or insects)

[2]**swarm** *vb*
**1** to form a swarm and leave the hive ⟨*swarming* bees⟩
**2** to move or gather in a swarm or large crowd ⟨shoppers *swarmed* into the stores⟩
**3** to be filled with a great number : TEEM

**swar·thy** \'swȯr-t͟hē, -thē\ *adj* **swar·thi·er**; **swar·thi·est**
having a dark complexion

[1]**swat** \'swät\ *vb* **swat·ted**; **swat·ting**
to hit with a quick hard blow

[2]**swat** *n*
a hard blow

**swath** \'swäth\ *or* **swathe** \'swät͟h\ *n*
**1** a sweep of a scythe or machine in mowing or the path cut in one course
**2** a row of cut grass (as grain)

[1]**sway** \'swā\ *n*
**1** a slow swinging back and forth or from side to side
**2** a controlling influence or force : RULE ⟨under the *sway* of a tyrant⟩

[2]**sway** *vb*
**1** to swing slowly back and forth or from side to side ⟨tree branches *swaying* in the wind⟩
**2** to change often between one point, position, or opinion and another
**3** [2]INFLUENCE ⟨we were *swayed* by their arguments⟩

**swear** \'swaər, 'sweər\ *vb* **swore** \'swōr\; **sworn** \'swōrn\; **swear·ing**
**1** to make a statement or promise under oath : VOW ⟨*swear* to tell the truth⟩
**2** to give an oath to ⟨*swear* a witness⟩

**swan**

**3** to bind by an oath ⟨*swore* them to secrecy⟩
**4** to take an oath
**5** to use bad or vulgar language : CURSE

[1]**sweat** \'swet\ *vb* **sweat** *or* **sweat·ed**; **sweat·ing**
**1** to give off salty moisture through the pores of the skin : PERSPIRE
**2** to collect moisture on the surface ⟨a pitcher of ice water *sweats* on a hot day⟩
**3** to work hard enough to perspire ⟨*sweat* over a lesson⟩

[2]**sweat** *n*
**1** PERSPIRATION 2
**2** moisture coming from or collecting in drops on a surface
**3** the condition of one sweating

**sweat·er** \'swet-ər\ *n*
a knitted or crocheted jacket or pullover

**sweat gland** *n*
any of numerous small skin glands that give off perspiration

**sweat·shirt** \'swet-,shərt\ *n*
a loose pullover or jacket without a collar and usually with long sleeves

**Swede** \'swēd\ *n*
a person born or living in Sweden

[1]**Swed·ish** \'swēd-ish\ *adj*
of or relating to Sweden, the Swedes, or Swedish

[2]**Swedish** *n*
the language of the Swedes

[1]**sweep** \'swēp\ *vb* **swept** \'swept\; **sweep·ing**
**1** to remove with a broom or brush ⟨*sweep* up the dirt⟩
**2** to clean by removing loose dirt or small trash with a broom or brush ⟨*sweep* the floor⟩
**3** to move over or across swiftly with force or destruction ⟨fire *swept* the village⟩
**4** to move or gather as if with a broom or brush ⟨*swept* the money from the table⟩
**5** to touch a surface as if with a brush ⟨the musician's fingers *swept* the piano keys⟩
**6** to drive along with steady force ⟨was *swept* away by the tide⟩
**7** to move the eyes or an instrument through a wide curve ⟨they *swept* the hill for some sign of the enemy⟩
**sweep·er** *n*

[2]**sweep** *n*
**1** something that sweeps or works with a sweeping motion
**2** an act or instance of sweeping
**3** a complete or easy victory
**4** a curving movement, course, or line ⟨brushed it away with a *sweep* of my hand⟩
**5** [1]RANGE 6, SCOPE ⟨outside the *sweep* of our vision⟩
**6** CHIMNEY SWEEP

[1]**sweep·ing** \'swē-ping\ *n*
**1** the act or action of one that sweeps
**2** **sweepings** *pl* things collected by sweeping

[2]**sweeping** *adj*
**1** moving or extending in a wide curve or over a wide area ⟨gave the audience a *sweeping* glance⟩
**2** EXTENSIVE ⟨*sweeping* changes in teaching methods⟩

**sweep·stakes** *n sing or pl*
a contest in which money or prizes are given to winners picked by chance (as by drawing names from a box)

[1]**sweet** \'swēt\ *adj*
**1** pleasing to the taste
**2** containing or tasting of sugar
**3** pleasing to the mind or feelings : AGREEABLE ⟨*sweet* memories⟩
**4** [1]KINDLY 2, MILD ⟨a *sweet* disposition⟩
**5** FRAGRANT ⟨a *sweet* smell⟩
**6** pleasing to the ear or eye ⟨the *sweet* sounds of a violin⟩
**7** much loved : DEAR
**8** not sour, stale, or spoiled ⟨*sweet* milk⟩
**9** FRESH 1 ⟨*sweet* butter⟩
**sweet·ish** \'swēt-ish\ *adj*
**sweet·ly** *adv*
**sweet·ness** *n*

[2]**sweet** *n*
**1** something (as candy) that is sweet to the taste
**2** [1]DARLING 1, DEAR

**sweet corn** *n*
an Indian corn with kernels rich in sugar that is cooked as a vegetable while young

**sweet·en** \'swēt-n\ *vb*
to make or become sweet or sweeter

**sweet·en·ing** \'swēt-n-ing\ *n*
**1** the act or process of making sweet
**2** something that sweetens

**sweet·heart** \'swēt-ˌhärt\ *n*
a person whom one loves

**sweet·meat** \'swēt-ˌmēt\ *n*
a food (as a piece of candy or candied fruit) rich in sugar

**sweet pea** *n*
a climbing plant related to the peas that is grown for its fragrant flowers of many colors

**sweet potato** *n*
the large sweet edible root of a tropical vine somewhat like a morning glory

**sweet wil·liam** \-'wil-yəm\ *n, often cap W*
a European pink grown for its thick flat clusters of many-colored flowers

[1]**swell** \'swel\ *vb* **swelled**; **swelled** *or* **swol·len** \'swō-lən\; **swell·ing**
**1** to enlarge in an abnormal way usually by pressure from within or by growth ⟨a *swollen* ankle⟩
**2** to grow or make bigger (as in size or value)
**3** to stretch upward or outward **:** BULGE ⟨a breeze *swelled* the sails⟩
**4** to fill or become filled with emotion ⟨a heart *swelling* with gratitude⟩

[2]**swell** *n*
**1** a becoming larger (as in size or value)
**2** a long rolling wave or series of waves in the open sea
**3** a very fashionably dressed person

[3]**swell** *adj*
**1** STYLISH, FASHIONABLE ⟨*swell* clothes⟩
**2** EXCELLENT, FIRST-RATE ⟨we had a *swell* time⟩

**swell·ing** \'swel-ing\ *n*
a swollen lump or part

**swel·ter** \'swel-tər\ *vb*
to suffer, sweat, or be faint from heat

**swept** *past of* SWEEP

[1]**swim 1**

Swimmers combine different movements of the arms, legs, and torso to propel themselves through water in four basic competitive swimming strokes — the crawl, backstroke, breaststroke, and butterfly.

**backstroke**
the swimmer lies face upward in the water, reaching the arms behind the head while the legs kick up and down

**crawl**
the swimmer lies face downward in the water, moving the arms over the head and kicking the legs up and down

**butterfly**
the arms are moved in a circular motion while the legs kick up and down

**breaststroke**
the arms extend in front and the knees draw forward, then the arms sweep back while the legs kick backward

**¹swerve** \'swərv\ *vb* **swerved**; **swerv·ing**
to turn aside suddenly from a straight line or course ⟨*swerved* to avoid an oncoming car⟩

**²swerve** *n*
an act or instance of swerving

**¹swift** \'swift\ *adj*
**1** moving or capable of moving with great speed
**2** occurring suddenly
**3** ¹READY 3, ALERT **synonyms** see FAST
**swift·ly** *adv*
**swift·ness** *n*

**²swift** *adv*
SWIFTLY ⟨a *swift*-flowing stream⟩

**³swift** *n*
a small usually sooty black bird that is related to the hummingbirds but looks like a swallow

**swig** \'swig\ *n*
the amount drunk at one time : GULP

**¹swill** \'swil\ *vb*
to eat or drink greedily

**²swill** *n*
**1** ¹SLOP 3
**2** GARBAGE, REFUSE

**¹swim** \'swim\ *vb* **swam** \'swam\; **swum** \'swəm\; **swim·ming**
**1** ◀ to move through or in water by moving arms, legs, fins, or tail
**2** to glide smoothly and quietly
**3** to float on or in or be covered with or as if with a liquid ⟨meat *swimming* in gravy⟩
**4** to be dizzy : move or seem to move dizzily ⟨my head *swam* in the smoky room⟩
**5** to cross by swimming ⟨*swim* the river⟩
**swim·mer** *n*

**²swim** *n*
**1** an act or period of swimming ⟨enjoyed a good *swim*⟩
**2** the main current of activity ⟨in the social *swim*⟩

**swimming** *adj*
**1** capable of swimming ⟨*swimming* birds⟩
**2** used in or for swimming ⟨a *swimming* cap⟩

**swimming pool** *n*
a tank (as of concrete or plastic) made for swimming

**swim·suit** \'swim-,süt\ *n*
a garment for swimming or bathing

**¹swin·dle** \'swin-dəl\ *vb* **swin·dled**; **swin·dling**
to get money or property from by dishonest means : CHEAT

**²swindle** *n*
an act or instance of swindling

**swin·dler** \'swin-dlər\ *n*
a person who swindles

---

**Word History** A German noun that means "a dizzy person" came to mean "a person who has fantastic schemes." The English word *swindler* came from the German word that means "one who has fantastic schemes." Swindlers often use fantastic schemes to cheat people.

---

**swine** \'swīn\ *n, pl* **swine**
a hoofed domestic animal that comes from the wild boar, has a long snout and bristly skin, and is widely raised for meat

**swine·herd** \'swīn-,hərd\ *n*
a person who tends swine

**¹swing** \'swing\ *vb* **swung** \'swəng\; **swing·ing**
**1** to move rapidly in a sweeping curve ⟨*swing* a bat⟩
**2** to throw or toss in a circle or back and forth ⟨*swing* a lasso⟩
**3** to sway to and fro ⟨sheets *swung* on the clothes line⟩
**4** to hang or be hung so as to move freely back and forth or in a curve ⟨*swing* a hammock between two trees⟩
**5** to turn on a hinge or pivot ⟨the door *swung* open⟩
**6** to manage or handle successfully ⟨able to *swing* the job⟩
**7** to march or walk with free swaying movements

**²swing** *n*
**1** an act of swinging
**2** a swinging movement, blow, or rhythm
**3** the distance through which something swings ⟨measured the *swing* of the pendulum⟩
**4** a swinging seat usually hung by overhead ropes
**5** a style of jazz marked by lively rhythm and played mostly for dancing

**¹swipe** \'swīp\ *n*
a strong sweeping blow

**²swipe** *vb* **swiped**; **swip·ing**
¹STEAL 2

**¹swirl** \'swərl\ *vb*
to move with a whirling or twisting motion

**²swirl** *n*
**1** a whirling mass or motion : EDDY
**2** whirling confusion
**3** a twisting shape or mark ⟨hair worn in a *swirl*⟩

**¹swish** \'swish\ *vb*
to make, move, or strike with a soft rubbing or hissing sound

**²swish** *n*
**1** a hissing sound (as of a whip cutting the air) or a light sweeping or rubbing sound (as of a silk skirt)
**2** a swishing movement

**¹Swiss** \'swis\ *n, pl* **Swiss**
a person born or living in Switzerland

**²Swiss** *adj*
of or relating to Switzerland or the Swiss

**¹switch** \'swich\ *n*
**1** a narrow flexible whip, rod, or twig
**2** an act of switching
**3** a blow with a switch or whip
**4** a change from one thing to another ⟨a *switch* in plans⟩
**5** a device for adjusting the rails of a track so that a train or streetcar may be turned from one track to another
**6** SIDING 1
**7** a device for making, breaking, or changing the connections in an electrical circuit

**²switch** *vb*
**1** to strike or whip with or as if with a switch
**2** to lash from side to side ⟨a cow *switching* its tail⟩
**3** to turn, shift, or change by operating a switch ⟨*switch* off the light⟩
**4** to make a shift or change ⟨*switched* to a new barber⟩

**switch·board** \'swich-,bōrd\ *n*
a panel for controlling the operation of a number of electric circuits used especially to make and break telephone connections

**¹swiv·el** \'swiv-əl\ *n*
a device joining two parts so that one or both can turn freely (as on a bolt or pin)

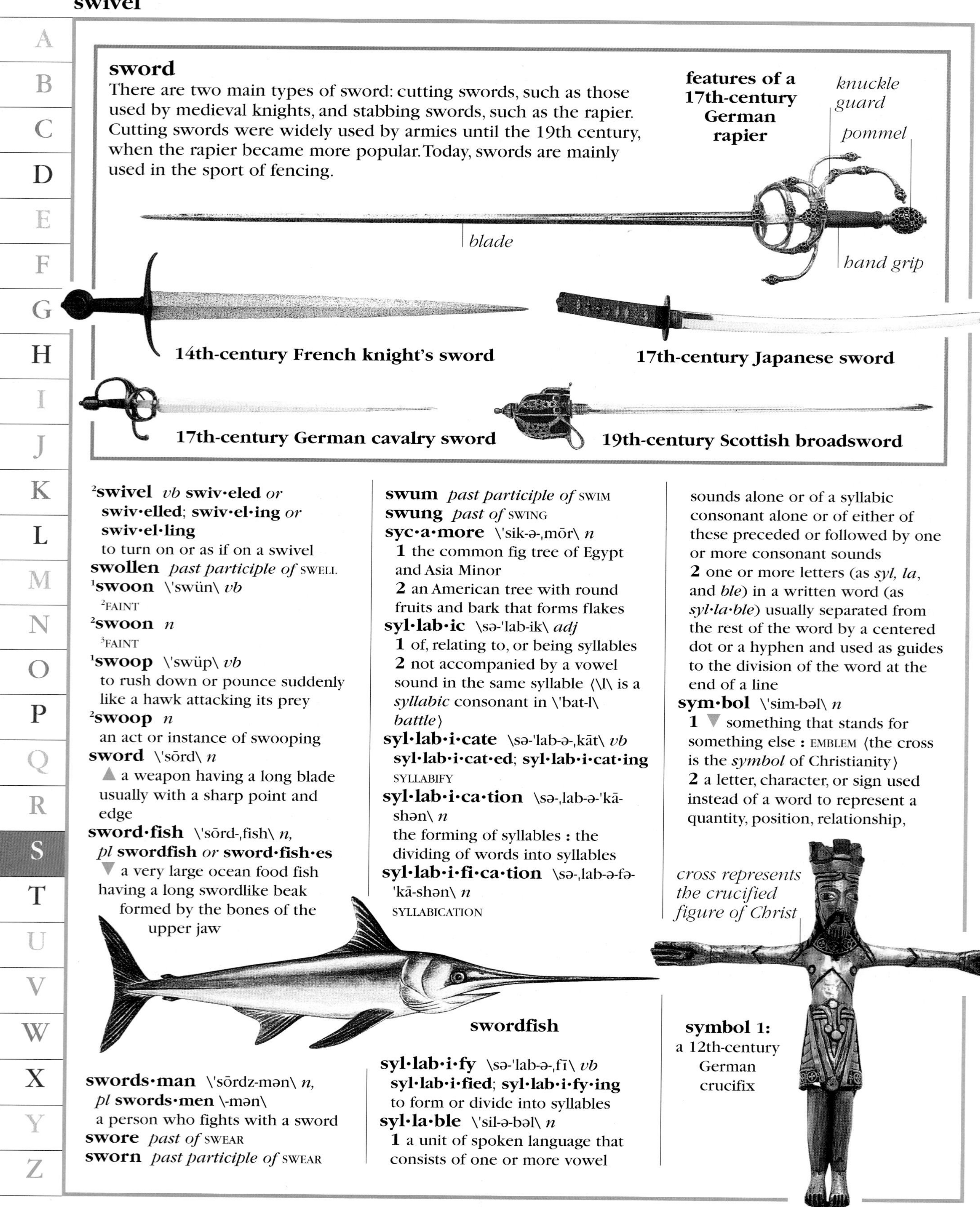


**sword**
There are two main types of sword: cutting swords, such as those used by medieval knights, and stabbing swords, such as the rapier. Cutting swords were widely used by armies until the 19th century, when the rapier became more popular. Today, swords are mainly used in the sport of fencing.

**features of a 17th-century German rapier**

**14th-century French knight's sword**

**17th-century Japanese sword**

**17th-century German cavalry sword**

**19th-century Scottish broadsword**

**²swivel** *vb* **swiv·eled** *or* **swiv·elled**; **swiv·el·ing** *or* **swiv·el·ling**
to turn on or as if on a swivel

**swollen** *past participle of* SWELL

**¹swoon** \'swün\ *vb*
²FAINT

**²swoon** *n*
³FAINT

**¹swoop** \'swüp\ *vb*
to rush down or pounce suddenly like a hawk attacking its prey

**²swoop** *n*
an act or instance of swooping

**sword** \'sōrd\ *n*
▲ a weapon having a long blade usually with a sharp point and edge

**sword·fish** \'sōrd-ˌfish\ *n*, *pl* **swordfish** *or* **sword·fish·es**
▼ a very large ocean food fish having a long swordlike beak formed by the bones of the upper jaw

**swordfish**

**swords·man** \'sōrdz-mən\ *n*, *pl* **swords·men** \-mən\
a person who fights with a sword

**swore** *past of* SWEAR

**sworn** *past participle of* SWEAR

**swum** *past participle of* SWIM

**swung** *past of* SWING

**syc·a·more** \'sik-ə-ˌmōr\ *n*
**1** the common fig tree of Egypt and Asia Minor
**2** an American tree with round fruits and bark that forms flakes

**syl·lab·ic** \sə-'lab-ik\ *adj*
**1** of, relating to, or being syllables
**2** not accompanied by a vowel sound in the same syllable ⟨\l\ is a *syllabic* consonant in \'bat-l\ *battle*⟩

**syl·lab·i·cate** \sə-'lab-ə-ˌkāt\ *vb* **syl·lab·i·cat·ed**; **syl·lab·i·cat·ing**
SYLLABIFY

**syl·lab·i·ca·tion** \sə-ˌlab-ə-'kā-shən\ *n*
the forming of syllables **:** the dividing of words into syllables

**syl·lab·i·fi·ca·tion** \sə-ˌlab-ə-fə-'kā-shən\ *n*
SYLLABICATION

**syl·lab·i·fy** \sə-'lab-ə-ˌfī\ *vb* **syl·lab·i·fied**; **syl·lab·i·fy·ing**
to form or divide into syllables

**syl·la·ble** \'sil-ə-bəl\ *n*
**1** a unit of spoken language that consists of one or more vowel sounds alone or of a syllabic consonant alone or of either of these preceded or followed by one or more consonant sounds
**2** one or more letters (as *syl, la,* and *ble*) in a written word (as *syl·la·ble*) usually separated from the rest of the word by a centered dot or a hyphen and used as guides to the division of the word at the end of a line

**sym·bol** \'sim-bəl\ *n*
**1** ▼ something that stands for something else **:** EMBLEM ⟨the cross is the *symbol* of Christianity⟩
**2** a letter, character, or sign used instead of a word to represent a quantity, position, relationship,

**symbol 1:** a 12th-century German crucifix

direction, or something to be done ⟨the sign + is the *symbol* for addition⟩ **synonyms** see EMBLEM

**sym•bol•ic** \sim-'bäl-ik\ *or* **sym•bol•i•cal** \-i-kəl\ *adj* of, relating to, or using symbols or symbolism ⟨a *symbolic* meaning⟩

**sym•bol•ize** \'sim-bə-ˌlīz\ *vb* **sym•bol•ized**; **sym•bol•iz•ing** to serve as a symbol of ⟨a lion *symbolizes* courage⟩

**sym•met•ri•cal** \sə-'me-tri-kəl\ *or* **sym•met•ric** \-rik\ *adj* having or showing symmetry

**sym•me•try** \'sim-ə-trē\ *n, pl* **sym•me•tries** close agreement in size, shape, and position of parts that are on opposite sides of a dividing line or center : an arrangement involving regular and balanced proportions ⟨the *symmetry* of the human body⟩

**sym•pa•thet•ic** \ˌsim-pə-'thet-ik\ *adj*
**1** fitting one's mood or disposition ⟨a *sympathetic* atmosphere⟩
**2** feeling sympathy ⟨received much help from *sympathetic* friends⟩
**3** feeling favorable ⟨*sympathetic* to their ambitions⟩
**sym•pa•thet•i•cal•ly** \-i-kə-lē\ *adv*

**sym•pa•thize** \'sim-pə-ˌthīz\ *vb* **sym•pa•thized**; **sym•pa•thiz•ing**
**1** to feel or show sympathy ⟨*sympathize* with a family in its sorrow⟩
**2** to be in favor of something ⟨*sympathize* with a friend's ambitions⟩

**sym•pa•thy** \'sim-pə-thē\ *n, pl* **sym•pa•thies**
**1** a relationship between persons or things in which whatever affects one similarly affects the other
**2** readiness to think or feel alike : similarity of likes, interest, or aims that makes a bond of goodwill ⟨*sympathy* between friends⟩
**3** readiness to favor or support ⟨political *sympathies*⟩
**4** the act of or capacity for entering into the feelings or interests of another
**5** sorrow or pity for another
**6** a showing of sorrow for another's loss, grief, or misfortune

**sym•phon•ic** \sim-'fän-ik\ *adj* of or relating to a symphony or symphony orchestra

**sym•pho•ny** \'sim-fə-nē\ *n, pl* **sym•pho•nies**
**1** harmonious arrangement (as of sound or color)
**2** a usually long musical composition for a full orchestra
**3** a large orchestra of wind, string, and percussion instruments

**symp•tom** \'simp-təm\ *n*
**1** a noticeable change in the body or its functions typical of a disease
**2** INDICATION 2, SIGN ⟨*symptoms* of fear⟩

**syn•a•gogue** *or* **syn•a•gog** \'sin-ə-ˌgäg\ *n* a Jewish house of worship

**syn•apse** \'sin-ˌaps\ *n* the point at which a nerve impulse passes from one nerve cell to another

**syn•co•pa•tion** \ˌsing-kə-'pā-shən\ *n* a temporary accenting of a normally weak beat in music to vary the rhythm

**syn•o•nym** \'sin-ə-ˌnim\ *n* a word having the same or almost the same meaning as another word in the same language

**syn•on•y•mous** \sə-'nän-ə-məs\ *adj* alike in meaning

**syn•tax** \'sin-ˌtaks\ *n* the way in which words are put together to form phrases, clauses, or sentences

**syn•the•size** \'sin-thə-ˌsīz\ *vb* **syn•the•sized**; **syn•the•siz•ing** to build up from simpler materials ⟨glands *synthesizing* enzymes⟩

**syn•thet•ic** \sin-'thet-ik\ *adj* produced artificially especially by chemical means : produced by human beings

**sy•rin•ga** \sə-'ring-gə\ *n* a garden shrub with often fragrant flowers of a white or cream color

**sy•ringe** \sə-'rinj\ *n* ▶ a device used to force fluid into or withdraw it from the body or its cavities

syringe

**syr•up** *or* **sir•up** \'sər-əp, 'sir-\ *n*
**1** a thick sticky solution of sugar and water often containing flavoring or a medicine
**2** the juice of a fruit or plant with some of the water removed

**sys•tem** \'sis-təm\ *n*
**1** a group of parts combined to form a whole that works or moves as a unit ⟨a heating *system*⟩
**2** a body that functions as a whole ⟨the disease affected the entire *system*⟩
**3** a group of bodily organs that together carry on some vital function ⟨the nervous *system*⟩
**4** an orderly plan or method of governing or arranging ⟨a democratic *system* of government⟩
**5** regular method or order : ORDERLINESS

**sys•tem•at•ic** \ˌsis-tə-'mat-ik\ *adj*
**1** having, using, or acting on a system
**2** carrying out a plan with thoroughness or regularity ⟨*systematic* efforts⟩
**sys•tem•at•i•cal•ly** \-i-kə-lē\ *adv*

**sys•tem•ic** \sis-'tem-ik\ *adj* of or relating to the body as a whole ⟨*systemic* disease⟩

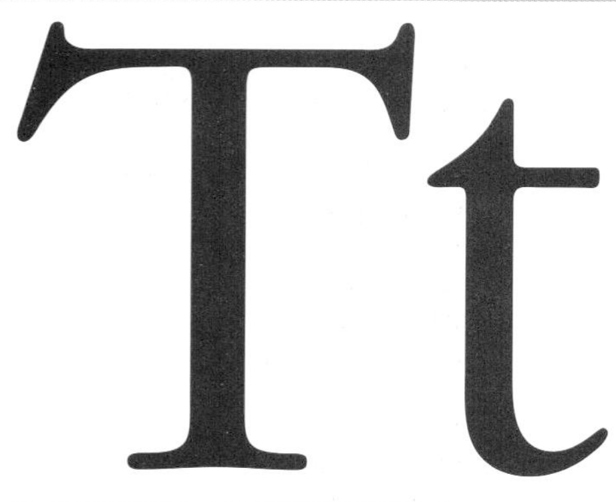

**The sounds of T:** The letter **T** has only one sound in English. It has the same sound in **tell**, **letter**, **lot**, and **mitt**. A double **T** in a word sounds the same as a single **T**.

The letter **T** is sometimes silent, as in **bouquet**, **soften**, and **croquet**.

**T** also combines with the letter **H** to make two different sounds. One is the sound heard in **the**, **weather**, and **bathe**. The other **TH** sound is the one heard in **thick**, **thin**, **thunder**, **ether**, and **bath**. In just a handful of words, the **H** following the **T** is silent, and the **T** has its normal sound, as in **thyme**.

In a few words, **T** has the sound of **CH**, as in **nature**, or **SH**, as in **nation**.

**t** \'tē\ *n, pl* **t's** *or* **ts** \'tēz\ *often cap*
the twentieth letter of the English alphabet
**to a T** just fine **:** EXACTLY

**tab** \'tab\ *n*
**1** a short flap or tag attached to something for filing, pulling, or hanging
**2** a careful watch ⟨keep *tabs* on the weather⟩

**tab•by** \'tab-ē\ *n, pl* **tabbies**
**1** ▼ a domestic cat with a gray or tawny coat striped and spotted with black
**2** a female domestic cat

**Word History** A kind of silk cloth was once made in a district of the city of Baghdad. The Arabic name for this cloth was taken from the name of the district where it was made. The English word *tabby* was first used for this silk cloth and came from the cloth's Arabic name. The cloth called *tabby* had a striped finish and was marked with spots of several colors or shades. That is why striped and mottled cats came to be called *tabbies*.

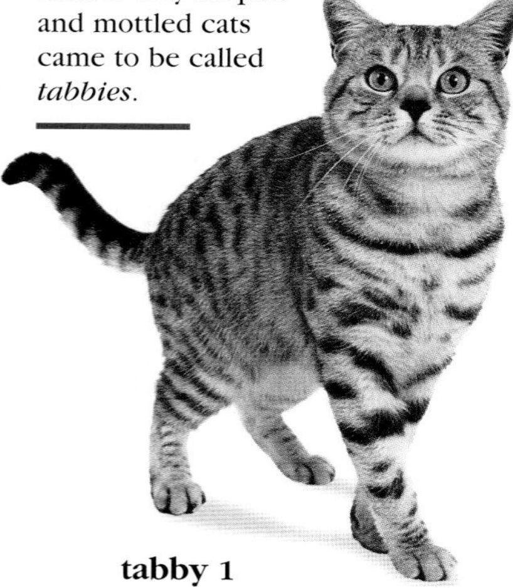

**tabby 1**

**tab•er•na•cle** \'tab-ər-,nak-əl\ *n*
**1** *often cap* a structure of wood hung with curtains used in worship by the Israelites during their wanderings in the wilderness with Moses
**2** a house of worship

**¹ta•ble** \'tā-bəl\ *n*
**1** a piece of furniture having a smooth flat top on legs
**2** food to eat ⟨sets a good *table*⟩
**3** the people around a table
**4** short list ⟨a *table* of contents⟩
**5** an arrangement in rows or columns for reference ⟨multiplication *tables*⟩

**²table** *vb* **ta•bled**; **ta•bling**
**1** TABULATE
**2** to put on a table

**tab•leau** \'tab-,lō\ *n, pl* **tableaus** *or* **tab•leaux** \-,lōz\
a scene or event shown by a group of persons who remain still and silent

**ta•ble•cloth** \'tā-bəl-,klȯth\ *n*
a covering spread over a dining table before the places are set

**ta•ble•land** \'tā-bəl-,land\ *n*
PLATEAU

**ta•ble•spoon** \'tā-bəl-,spün\ *n*
**1** a large spoon used mostly for dishing up food
**2** TABLESPOONFUL

**ta•ble•spoon•ful** \,tā-bəl-'spün-,fu̇l\ *n, pl* **tablespoonfuls** \-,fu̇lz\ *or* **ta•ble•spoons•ful** \-'spünz-,fu̇l\
**1** as much as a tablespoon will hold
**2** a unit of measure used in cooking equal to three teaspoonfuls (about fifteen milliliters)

**tab•let** \'tab-lət\ *n*
**1** a thin flat slab used for writing, painting, or drawing
**2** a number of sheets of writing paper glued together at one edge
**3** a flat and usually round mass of material containing medicine ⟨aspirin *tablets*⟩

**table tennis** *n*
▼ a game played on a table by two or four players who use paddles to hit a small hollow plastic ball back and forth over a net

**table tennis** paddle and ball

**ta•ble•ware** \'tā-bəl-,waər, -,weər\ *n*
utensils (as of china, glass, or silver) for use at the table

**tab•u•late** \'tab-yə-,lāt\ *vb* **tab•u•lat•ed**; **tab•u•lat•ing**
to put in the form of a table

**tac•it** \'tas-ət\ *adj*
understood or made known without being put into words
**tac•it•ly** *adv*

**¹tack** \'tak\ *n*
**1** a small nail with a sharp point and usually a broad flat head for fastening a light object or material to a solid surface
**2** the direction a ship is sailing as shown by the position the sails are set in or the movement of a ship with the sails set in a certain position
**3** a change of course from one tack to another

4 a zigzag movement or course
5 a course of action
6 a temporary stitch used in sewing

[2]**tack** *vb*
1 to fasten with tacks
2 to attach or join loosely
3 to change from one course to another in sailing
4 to follow a zigzag course

[1]**tack·le** \'tak-əl\ *n*
1 a set of special equipment ⟨fishing *tackle*⟩
2 an arrangement of ropes and wheels for hoisting or pulling something heavy
3 an act of tackling

[2]**tackle** *vb* **tack·led**; **tack·ling**
1 to seize and throw (a person) to the ground
2 to begin working on ⟨*tackle* a job⟩

**ta·co** \'täk-ō\ *n, pl* **tacos** \'täk-ōz\
▼ a corn tortilla usually folded and fried and filled with a spicy mixture (as of ground meat and cheese)

**taco:** a plate of tacos

**tact** \'takt\ *n*
a keen understanding of how to get along with other people

**tact·ful** \'takt-fəl\ *adj*
having or showing tact
**tact·ful·ly** \-fə-lē\ *adv*
**tact·ful·ness** *n*

**tac·tic** \'tak-tik\ *n*
a planned action for some purpose

**tac·tics** \'tak-tiks\ *n sing or pl*
1 the science and art of arranging and moving troops or warships for best use
2 a system or method for reaching a goal

**tac·tile** \'tak-təl\ *adj*
of or relating to the sense of touch

**tact·less** \'takt-ləs\ *adj*
having or showing no tact
**tact·less·ly** *adv*
**tact·less·ness** *n*

**tad·pole** \'tad-,pōl\ *n*
▼ the larva of a frog or toad that has a long tail, breathes with gills, and lives in water

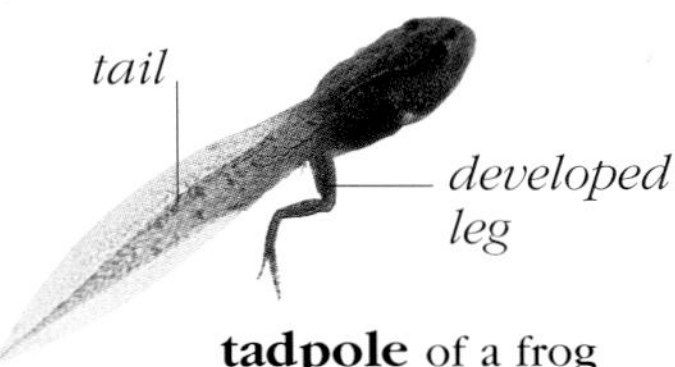


**tadpole** of a frog

**Word History** A young tadpole, which looks like a large head with a tail, will in time become a toad or a frog. The English word *tadpole* comes from an early English word that was made up of two words. The first of these was a word that meant "toad." The second was a word that meant "head."

**taf·fy** \'taf-ē\ *n, pl* **taffies**
a candy made usually of molasses or brown sugar boiled and pulled until soft

[1]**tag** \'tag\ *n*
a small flap or tab fixed or hanging on something ⟨a price *tag*⟩
2 an often quoted saying

[2]**tag** *vb* **tagged**; **tag·ging**
1 to put a tag on
2 to follow closely and continually

[3]**tag** *n*
a game in which one player who is it chases the others and tries to touch one of them to make that person it

[4]**tag** *vb* **tagged**; **tag·ging**
1 to touch in or as if in a game of tag
2 to touch a runner in baseball with the ball and cause the runner to be out

[1]**tail** \'tāl\ *n*
1 ► the rear part of an animal or a usually slender flexible extension of this part
2 something that in shape, appearance, or position is like an animal's tail ⟨the *tail* of a coat⟩
3 the back, last, or lower part of something ⟨the *tail* of an airplane⟩
4 the side or end opposite the head
**tailed** \'tāld\ *adj*
**tail·less** \'tāl-ləs\ *adj*
**tail·like** \'tāl-,līk\ *adj*

[1]**tail 1:** a kangaroo has a muscular tail

[2]**tail** *vb*
to follow closely to keep watch on

**tail·gate** \'tāl-,gāt\ *n*
a panel at the back end of a vehicle that can be let down for loading and unloading

**tail·light** \'tāl-,līt\ *n*
a red warning light at the rear of a vehicle

[1]**tai·lor** \'tā-lər\ *n*
a person whose business is making or making adjustments in men's or women's clothes

[2]**tailor** *vb*
1 to make or make adjustments in (clothes)
2 to change to fit a special need ⟨*tailored* their plans to suit the weather⟩

**tail·pipe** \'tāl-,pīp\ *n*
the pipe carrying off the exhaust gases from the muffler of an engine in a car or truck

**tail·spin** \'tāl-,spin\ *n*
a dive by an airplane turning in a circle

[1]**taint** \'tānt\ *vb*
1 to affect slightly with something bad
2 to rot slightly ⟨*tainted* meat⟩

[2]**taint** *n*
a trace of decay

[1]**take** \'tāk\ *vb* **took** \'tu̇k\; **tak·en** \'tā-kən\; **tak·ing**
**1** to get control of : CAPTURE ⟨*took* the fort⟩
**2** [1]GRASP 1 ⟨*take* it by the handle⟩
**3** to come upon ⟨they were *taken* by suprise⟩
**4** CAPTIVATE ⟨were *taken* with its beauty⟩
**5** to receive into the body ⟨*take* your medicine⟩
**6** to get possession or use of ⟨*took* the book from the table⟩ ⟨will *take* a cottage by the shore for the summer⟩
**7** ASSUME 1 ⟨*take* office⟩
**8** to be formed or used with ⟨prepositions *take* objects⟩
**9** to adopt as one's own or for oneself ⟨*took* my side in the argument⟩ ⟨*took* all the credit⟩
**10** WIN 3 ⟨*took* second prize⟩
**11** CHOOSE 1, SELECT ⟨I'll *take* the red one⟩
**12** to sit in or on ⟨*take* a chair⟩
**13** to use as a way of going from one place to another ⟨*take* the bus⟩ ⟨we'll *take* the highway⟩
**14** REQUIRE ⟨it will *take* a long time⟩ ⟨I *take* a size ten⟩
**15** to find out by special methods ⟨*take* your temperature⟩
**16** to save in some permanent form ⟨*took* down every word of the speech⟩ ⟨*take* a picture⟩
**17** to put up with : ENDURE ⟨I don't have to *take* that from you⟩
**18** BELIEVE 2, 3 ⟨I *took* it to be the truth⟩ ⟨*take* my word for it⟩
**19** to be guided by : FOLLOW ⟨*take* my advice⟩
**20** to become affected suddenly ⟨*took* sick⟩
**21** UNDERSTAND 4, INTERPRET ⟨I *took* it to mean something different⟩
**22** to react in a certain way ⟨*take* pleasure in music⟩ ⟨don't *take* offense⟩
**23** to carry or go with from one place to another ⟨I'll *take* you home⟩ ⟨this bus will *take* us there⟩
**24** REMOVE 3, SUBTRACT ⟨*take* 2 from 4⟩
**25** to do the action of ⟨*take* a walk⟩
**26** to have effect : be successful ⟨the vaccination *took*⟩
**tak·er** *n*

**takeoff 2:**
an aircraft during takeoff

**Synonyms** TAKE, SEIZE, and GRASP mean to get a hold on with or as if with the hand. TAKE can be used of any way of getting something into one's possession or control ⟨*take* this gift⟩ ⟨you *took* more food than you can use⟩. SEIZE suggests the taking of something suddenly and by force ⟨the police officer *seized* the thief in the act of escaping⟩. GRASP stresses taking something in the hand and keeping it there firmly ⟨*grasp* my arm and walk slowly⟩.

**take advantage of**
**1** to make good use of
**2** to treat (someone) unfairly
**take after** RESEMBLE ⟨*take after* their parents⟩
**take care** to be careful
**take care of** to do what is needed : look after
**take effect**
**1** to go into effect ⟨the new rate *takes effect* Monday⟩
**2** to have an intended or expected effect
**take hold** to become attached or established
**take part** to do or join in something together with others ⟨*take part* in the fun⟩
**take place** to come into being and last for a time — used of events or actions ⟨the meeting *took place* yesterday⟩

[2]**take** *n*
**1** the act of taking
**2** something that is taken
**3** a bodily reaction that shows a smallpox vaccination to be successful

**take back** *vb*
to try to cancel (as something said) ⟨*take back* a mean remark⟩

**take in** *vb*
**1** to make smaller ⟨*took* the dress *in*⟩
**2** to receive as a guest ⟨*took in* the travelers for the night⟩
**3** to allow to join ⟨the club is not *taking in* new members⟩
**4** to receive (work) to be done in one's home for pay ⟨*taking in* washing⟩
**5** to have within its limits ⟨the tour *takes in* both museums⟩
**6** to go to ⟨*take in* a movie⟩
**7** to get the meaning of ⟨*took in* the situation at a glance⟩
**8** [1]CHEAT 2 ⟨they were *taken in* by an old trick⟩

**take·off** \'tā-ˌkȯf\ *n*
**1** an imitation especially to mock the original
**2** ▲ an act or instance of taking off from the ground (as by an airplane)
**3** a spot at which one takes off

**take off** \tā-'kȯf\ *vb*
**1** to take away (a covering) : REMOVE ⟨*take* your shoes *off*⟩
**2** DEDUCT ⟨*take off* ten percent⟩
**3** to leave a surface in beginning a flight or leap ⟨the plane is *taking off* now⟩

**take on** *vb*
**1** to begin (a task) or struggle against (an opponent) ⟨*took on* the champion⟩
**2** to gain or show as or as if a part of oneself ⟨the city *took on* a carnival mood⟩
**3** [1]EMPLOY 2 ⟨*take on* more workers⟩
**4** to make an unusual show of one's grief or anger ⟨don't *take on* so⟩

**take over** *vb*
to get control of ⟨military leaders *took over* the government⟩

**take up** *vb*
**1** to get together from many sources ⟨*take up* a collection⟩
**2** to start something for the first time or after a pause ⟨*take up* painting⟩ ⟨*took up* the lesson where we left off⟩
**3** to change by making tighter or shorter ⟨*take up* the dress in the back⟩

**tak·ing** \'tā-king\ *adj*
**1** ATTRACTIVE ⟨*taking* ways⟩
**2** INFECTIOUS 1

**talc** \'talk\ *n*
▼ a soft mineral that has a soapy feel and is used in making talcum powder and for coloring

**talc:**
a rock of talc

**tal·cum powder** \'tal-kəm-\ *n*
a usually perfumed powder for the body made of talc

**tale** \'tāl\ *n*
**1** something told ⟨a *tale* of woe⟩
**2** a story about an imaginary event
**3** [3]LIE
**4** a piece of harmful gossip

**tal·ent** \'tal-ənt\ *n*
**1** unusual natural ability
**2** a special often creative or artistic ability
**3** persons having special ability
**synonyms** see ABILITY

**tal·ent·ed** \'tal-ən-təd\ *adj*

**Word History** *Talent* is the name of a unit of money in ancient Palestine. The Bible has a story about a man who gave three servants talents to keep for him while he was away. One servant received five talents, the second received two, and the third, one. The first two servants invested their money and doubled it. The third hid his one talent in the ground. When the master returned, he praised the first two servants. But he scolded the third, who could give back only what he had been given. The story means that we should make good use of the natural gifts God gives us. From this story came a new meaning of *talent* : "natural gift."

**tal·is·man** \'tal-ə-smən\ *n, pl* **tal·is·mans**
► a ring or stone carved with symbols and believed to have magical powers **:** CHARM

**[1]talk** \'tók\ *vb*
**1** to express in speech **:** SPEAK
**2** to speak about **:** DISCUSS ⟨*talk* business⟩
**3** to cause or influence by talking ⟨*talked* them into agreeing⟩
**4** to use a certain language ⟨*talk* Spanish⟩
**5** to exchange ideas by means of spoken words **:** CONVERSE ⟨let's sit and *talk*⟩
**6** to pass on information other than by speaking ⟨*talk* with one's hands⟩
**7** [2]GOSSIP
**8** to reveal secret information ⟨forced the spy to *talk*⟩
**synonyms** see SPEAK

**talk·er** *n*

**[2]talk** *n*
**1** the act of talking **:** SPEECH
**2** a way of speaking **:** LANGUAGE
**3** CONFERENCE
**4** [1]RUMOR 2, GOSSIP
**5** the topic of comment or gossip ⟨it's the *talk* of the town⟩
**6** an informal address

**talk·a·tive** \'tók-ət-iv\ *adj*
fond of talking

**talk·a·tive·ness** *n*

**talk·ing–to** \'tó-king-,tü\ *n*
an often wordy scolding

**[1]tall** \'tól\ *adj*
**1** having unusually great height
**2** of a stated height ⟨two meters *tall*⟩
**3** made up ⟨a *tall* tale⟩ **synonyms** see HIGH

**tall·ness** *n*

**[2]tall** *adv*
so as to be or look tall ⟨stand *tall*⟩

**tal·low** \'tal-ō\ *n*
a white solid fat obtained by heating fatty tissues of cattle and sheep

**[1]tal·ly** \'tal-ē\ *n, pl* **tallies**
**1** a device for keeping a count
**2** a recorded count
**3** a score or point made (as in a game)

**[2]tally** *vb* **tal·lied**; **tal·ly·ing**
**1** to keep a count of
**2** to make a tally **:** SCORE
**3** CORRESPOND 1

**talisman:** an ancient Egyptian ring serving as a talisman

**tal·on** \'tal-ən\ *n*
▼ the claw of a bird of prey

**tal·oned** \-ənd\ *adj*

**ta·ma·le** \tə-'mä-lē\ *n*
seasoned ground meat rolled in cornmeal, wrapped in corn husks, and steamed

**talon** of an eagle

**tam·bou·rine** \ˌtam-bə-'rēn\ *n*
a small shallow drum with only one head and loose metal disks around the rim that is played by shaking or hitting with the hand

**¹tame** \'tām\ *adj* **tam·er**; **tam·est**
**1** made useful and obedient to humans **:** DOMESTIC 3
**2** not afraid of people
**3** not interesting **:** DULL
**tame·ly** *adv*
**tame·ness** *n*

**²tame** *vb* **tamed**; **tam·ing**
**1** to make or become gentle or obedient
**2** ²HUMBLE
**tam·able** *or* **tame·able** \'tā-mə-bəl\ *adj*
**tam·er** *n*

**tamp** \'tamp\ *vb*
to drive down or in with several light blows

**tam·per** \'tam-pər\ *vb*
to interfere in a secret or incorrect way **synonyms** see MEDDLE

**¹tan** \'tan\ *vb* **tanned**; **tan·ning**
**1** to change hide into leather by soaking in a tannin solution
**2** to make or become brown or tan in color
**3** ¹BEAT 1, THRASH

**²tan** *adj* **tan·ner**; **tan·nest**
of a light yellowish brown color

**³tan** *n*
**1** a brown color given to the skin by the sun or wind
**2** a light yellowish brown color

**tan·a·ger** \'tan-i-jər\ *n*
▼ a very brightly colored bird related to the finches

**tanager:**
a scarlet tanager

**¹tan·dem** \'tan-dəm\ *n*
**1** a carriage pulled by horses hitched one behind the other
**2** TANDEM BICYCLE

**²tandem** *adv*
one behind another

**tandem bicycle** *n*
▼ a bicycle for two people sitting one behind the other

**tang** \'tang\ *n*
a sharp flavor or smell ⟨the *tang* of salt air⟩

**tan·ger·ine** \'tan-jə-ˌrēn\ *n*
a Chinese orange with a loose skin and sweet pulp

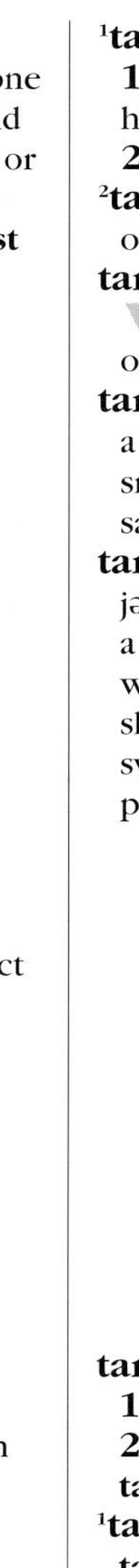

**tandem bicycle:**
a couple riding a tandem bicycle

**tan·gi·ble** \'tan-jə-bəl\ *adj*
**1** possible to touch or handle
**2** actually real **:** MATERIAL
**tan·gi·bly** \-blē\ *adv*

**¹tan·gle** \'tang-gəl\ *vb* **tan·gled**; **tan·gling**
to twist or become twisted together into a mass hard to straighten out again ⟨the dog *tangled* its leash around the bushes⟩

**²tangle** *n*
**1** a tangled twisted mass (as of yarn)
**2** a complicated or confused state

**¹tank** \'tangk\ *n*
**1** an often large container for a liquid ⟨water *tank*⟩ ⟨fish *tank*⟩
**2** an enclosed combat vehicle that has heavy armor and guns and a tread which is an endless belt

**²tank** *vb*
to put, keep, or treat in a tank

**tan·kard** \'tang-kərd\ *n*
a tall cup with one handle and often a lid

**tank·er** \'tang-kər\ *n*
a vehicle or ship with tanks for carrying a liquid ⟨oil *tankers*⟩

**tan·ner** \'tan-ər\ *n*
a person who tans hides into leather

**tan·nery** \'tan-ə-rē\ *n, pl* **tan·ner·ies**
a place where hides are tanned

**tan·nin** \'tan-ən\ *n*
a substance often made from oak bark or sumac and used in tanning, dyeing, and making ink

**tan·ta·lize** \'tant-l-ˌīz\ *vb* **tan·ta·lized**; **tan·ta·liz·ing**
to make miserable by or as if by showing something desirable but keeping it out of reach
**tan·ta·liz·er** *n*

**Word History** There was once, so Greek mythology tells us, a king named Tantalus who was not a good man. He murdered his own son and served his flesh to the gods. For this the king was punished by being made to stand underneath a fruit tree in water up to his chin. If he bent his head to drink, the water got lower and he could not reach it. If he lifted his head to bite into a fruit, the bough went higher and he could not reach it. He was made miserable by food and drink kept just out of reach. The word *tantalize* comes from the name of this mythical king.

**tan·trum** \'tan-trəm\ *n*
an outburst of bad temper

**[1]tap** \'tap\ *n*
FAUCET, SPIGOT
**on tap** on hand : AVAILABLE

**[2]tap** *vb* **tapped; tap·ping**
**1** to let out or cause to flow by making a hole or by pulling out a plug ⟨*tap* wine from a barrel⟩
**2** to make a hole in to draw off a liquid ⟨*tap* maple trees for sap⟩
**3** to draw from or upon ⟨*tapped* my bank to go to the movies⟩
**4** to connect into (a telephone wire) to listen secretly
**tap·per** *n*

**[3]tap** *vb* **tapped; tap·ping**
**1** to hit lightly
**2** to make by striking something lightly again and again ⟨*tap* out a note on the typewriter⟩
**tap·per** *n*

**[4]tap** *n*
a light blow or its sound

**[1]tape** \'tāp\ *n*
**1** a narrow band of cloth
**2** a narrow strip or band of material (as paper, steel, or plastic)
**3** MAGNETIC TAPE
**4** TAPE RECORDING

**[2]tape** *vb* **taped; tap·ing**
**1** to fasten, cover, or hold up with tape
**2** to make a record of on tape

**tape deck** *n*
a device used to play back and often to record on magnetic tapes

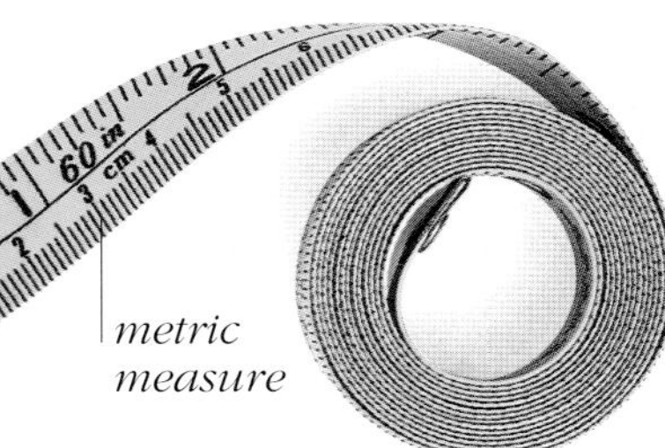


**tape measure**

**tape measure** *n*
▲ a tape marked off for measuring

**[1]ta·per** \'tā-pər\ *n*
**1** a slender candle
**2** a gradual lessening in thickness or width in a long object

**[2]taper** *vb*
**1** to make or become gradually smaller toward one end
**2** to grow gradually less and less

**tape recorder** *n*
a device for recording on and playing back magnetic tapes

**tape recording** *n*
a recording made on magnetic tape

**tap·es·try** \'tap-ə-strē\ *n, pl* **tap·es·tries**
a heavy cloth that has designs or pictures woven into it and is used especially as a wall hanging
**tap·es·tried** \-strēd\ *adj*

**tape·worm** \'tāp-ˌwərm\ *n*
a worm with a long flat body that lives in human or animal intestines

**tap·i·o·ca** \ˌtap-ē-'ō-kə\ *n*
small pieces of starch from roots of a tropical plant used especially in puddings

**ta·pir** \'tā-pər\ *n*
▶ a large hoofed mammal of tropical America, Malaya, and Sumatra that has thick legs, a short tail, and a long flexible snout

**tapir**

**tap·root** \'tap-ˌrüt, -ˌrůt\ *n*
a main root of a plant that grows straight down and gives off smaller side roots

**taps** \'taps\ *n sing or pl*
the last bugle call at night blown as a signal to put out the lights

**[1]tar** \'tär\ *n*
a thick dark sticky liquid made from wood, coal, or peat

**[2]tar** *vb* **tarred; tar·ring**
to cover with or as if with tar

**[3]tar** *n*
SAILOR

**ta·ran·tu·la** \tə-'ran-chə-lə\ *n*
**1** a large European spider whose bite was once believed to cause a wild desire to dance
**2** ▶ any of a group of large hairy spiders of warm regions of North and South America whose bite is sharp but not serious except for some South American species

hairy leg

**tarantula 2:** a red-kneed tarantula

**tar·dy** \'tärd-ē\ *adj* **tar·di·er; tar·di·est**
not on time : LATE
**tar·di·ly** \'tärd-l-ē\ *adv*
**tar·di·ness** \'tärd-ē-nəs\ *n*

**tar·get** \'tär-gət\ *n*
**1** a mark or object to shoot at
**2** a person or thing that is talked about, criticized, or laughed at
**3** a goal to be reached

**tar·iff** \'tar-əf\ *n*
**1** a list of taxes placed by a government on goods coming into a country
**2** the tax or the rate of taxation set up in a tariff list

**[1]tar·nish** \'tär-nish\ *vb*
to make or become dull, dim, or discolored

**[2]tarnish** *n*
a surface coating formed during tarnishing

**tar·pau·lin** \tär-'pò-lən, 'tär-pə-lən\ *n*
a sheet of waterproof canvas

A B C D E F G H I J K L M N O P Q R S T U V W X Y Z

**¹tar·ry** \'tar-ē\ *vb* **tar·ried**; **tar·ry·ing**
**1** to be slow in coming or going
**2** to stay in or at a place

**²tar·ry** \'tär-ē\ *adj*
of, like, or covered with tar

**¹tart** \'tärt\ *adj*
**1** pleasantly sharp to the taste
**2** BITING ⟨a *tart* manner⟩
**tart·ly** *adv*
**tart·ness** *n*

**²tart:**
a cherry tart

**²tart** *n*
▲ a small pie often with no top crust

**tar·tan** \'tärt-n\ *n*
▼ a woolen cloth with a plaid design first made in Scotland

**tartan**

**tar·tar** \'tärt-ər\ *n*
**1** a substance found in the juices of grapes that forms a reddish crust on the inside of wine barrels
**2** a crust that forms on the teeth made up of deposits of saliva, food, and calcium

**task** \'task\ *n*
a piece of assigned work

**Synonyms** TASK, DUTY, and JOB mean a piece of work assigned or to be done. TASK suggests work given by a person in a position of authority ⟨the boss used to give me every difficult *task*⟩. DUTY stresses that one has responsibility to do the work ⟨the *duty* of the police is to protect the people⟩. JOB may suggest that the work is necessary, hard, or important ⟨we all have to do our *job*⟩.

**tas·sel** \'tas-əl\ *n*
**1** a hanging ornament made of a bunch of cords of the same length fastened at one end
**2** something like a tassel ⟨the *tassel* of Indian corn⟩

**¹taste** \'tāst\ *vb* **tast·ed**; **tast·ing**
**1** ²EXPERIENCE
**2** to find out the flavor of something by taking a little into the mouth
**3** to eat or drink usually in small amounts
**4** to recognize by the sense of taste ⟨can *taste* salt in the soup⟩
**5** to have a certain flavor ⟨the milk *tastes* sour⟩
**tast·er** *n*

**²taste** *n*
**1** a small amount tasted
**2** the one of the special senses that recognizes sweet, sour, bitter, or salty flavors and that acts through sense organs (**taste buds**) in the tongue
**3** the quality of something recognized by the sense of taste or by this together with smell and touch : FLAVOR
**4** a personal liking ⟨children with a *taste* for reading⟩ ⟨has very expensive *tastes*⟩
**5** the ability to choose and enjoy what is good or beautiful

**taste·ful** \'tāst-fəl\ *adj*
having or showing good taste
**taste·ful·ly** \-fə-lē\ *adv*
**taste·ful·ness** *n*

**taste·less** \'tāst-ləs\ *adj*
**1** having little flavor
**2** not having or showing good taste
**taste·less·ly** *adv*
**taste·less·ness** *n*

**tasty** \'tās-tē\ *adj* **tast·i·er**; **tast·i·est**
pleasing to the taste ⟨a *tasty* dessert⟩
**tast·i·ness** *n*

**tat·ter** \'tat-ər\ *n*
**1** a part torn and left hanging : SHRED
**2 tatters** *pl* ragged clothing

**tat·tered** \'tat-ərd\ *adj*
**1** torn in or worn to shreds
**2** dressed in ragged clothes

**tat·tle** \'tat-l\ *vb* **tat·tled**; **tat·tling**
**1** PRATTLE
**2** to give away secrets : tell on someone
**tat·tler** \'tat-lər\ *n*

**tat·tle·tale** \'tat-l-,tāl\ *n*
a person who lets secrets out

**¹tat·too** \ta-'tü\ *vb* **tat·tooed**; **tat·too·ing**
to mark the body with a picture or pattern by using a needle to put color under the skin
**tat·too·er** *n*

**²tattoo:**
a New Zealand man with a tribal tattoo

**²tattoo** *n, pl* **tat·toos**
▲ a picture or design made by tattooing

**taught** *past of* TEACH

**¹taunt** \'tȯnt\ *n*
a mean insulting remark

**²taunt** *vb*
to make fun of or say mean insulting things to

**Tau·rus** \'tȯr-əs\ *n*
**1** a constellation between Aries and Gemini imagined as a bull
**2** the second sign of the zodiac or a person born under this sign

**taut** \'tȯt\ *adj*
**1** tightly stretched ⟨a *taut* rope⟩
**2** HIGH-STRUNG, TENSE
**3** kept in good order
**taut·ly** *adv*
**taut·ness** *n*

**tea 2:** a cup of tea

**tav·ern** \'tav-ərn\ *n*
**1** a place where beer and liquor are sold and drunk
**2** INN

**taw·ny** \'tȯ-nē\ *adj* **taw·ni·er**; **taw·ni·est**
of a brownish orange color

**¹tax** \'taks\ *vb*
**1** to require to pay a tax
**2** to accuse of something ⟨*taxed* them with carelessness⟩
**3** to cause a strain on ⟨*taxed* their strength⟩
**tax·er** *n*

**²tax** *n*
**1** money collected by the government from people or businesses for public use
**2** a difficult task

**tax·able** \'tak-sə-bəl\ *adj*
subject to tax ⟨*taxable* property⟩

**tax·a·tion** \tak-'sā-shən\ *n*
**1** the action of taxing
**2** money gotten from taxes

**¹taxi** \'tak-sē\ *n, pl* **tax·is** \-sēz\
TAXICAB

**²taxi** *vb* **tax·ied**; **taxi·ing** *or* **taxy·ing**
**1** to go by taxicab
**2** to run an airplane slowly along the ground under its own power

**taxi·cab** \'tak-sē-,kab\ *n*
an automobile that carries passengers for a fare usually determined by the distance traveled

**taxi·der·my** \'tak-sə-,dər-mē\ *n*
the art of stuffing and mounting the skins of animals

**tax·on·o·my** \tak-'sän-ə-mē\ *n*
**1** the study of classification
**2** a classification (as of animals) using a system that is usually based on relationship

**tax·pay·er** \'tak-,spā-ər\ *n*
a person who pays or is responsible for paying a tax

**TB** \tē-'bē\ *n*
TUBERCULOSIS

**T–ball** \'tē-,bȯl\ *n*
baseball for young children in which the ball is batted from a tee rather than being pitched

**tea** \'tē\ *n*
**1** the dried leaves and leaf buds of a shrub widely grown in eastern and southern Asia
**2** ◀ a drink made by soaking tea in boiling water
**3** a drink or medicine made by soaking plant parts (as dried roots) ⟨ginger *tea*⟩
**4** refreshments often including tea served in late afternoon
**5** a party at which tea is served

**teach** \'tēch\ *vb* **taught** \'tȯt\; **teach·ing**
**1** to show how ⟨*teach* a child⟩
**2** to guide the studies of
**3** to cause to know the unpleasant results of something ⟨that will *teach* you to talk back⟩
**4** to give lessons in ⟨*teach* math⟩

---

**Synonyms** TEACH, INSTRUCT, and TRAIN mean to cause to gain knowledge or skill. TEACH can be used of any method of passing on information or skill so that others may learn ⟨*teach* me how to swim⟩ ⟨*teach* children to read⟩. INSTRUCT stresses that the teaching is done in a formal or orderly manner ⟨teachers will *instruct* all students in the sciences⟩. TRAIN stresses instruction with a particular purpose in mind ⟨*trained* workers to operate the new machines⟩.

---

**teach·er** \'tē-chər\ *n*
a person who teaches

**teaching** *n*
**1** the duties or profession of a teacher
**2** something taught

**tea·cup** \'tē-,kəp\ *n*
a cup used with a saucer for hot drinks

**teak** \'tēk\ *n*
the hard wood of a tall tree which grows in the East Indies and resists decay

**tea·ket·tle** \'tē-,ket-l\ *n*
a covered kettle that is used for boiling water and has a handle and spout

**teal** \'tēl\ *n*
▼ a small wild duck that is very swift in flight

**¹team** \'tēm\ *n*
**1** two or more animals used to pull the same vehicle or piece of machinery
**2** a group of persons who work or play together

**²team** *vb*
**1** to haul with or drive a team
**2** to form a team

**team·mate** \'tēm-,māt\ *n*
a person who belongs to the same team as someone else

**team·ster** \'tēm-stər\ *n*
a worker who drives a team or a truck

**team·work** \'tēm-,wərk\ *n*
the work of a group of persons acting together

**tea·pot** \'tē-,pät\ *n*
a pot for making and serving tea

**¹tear** \'tir\ *n*
a drop of the salty liquid that keeps the eyeballs and inside of the eyelids moist

**²tear** \'taər, 'teər\ *vb* **tore** \'tōr\; **torn** \'tōrn\; **tear·ing**
**1** to pull into two or more pieces by force
**2** LACERATE ⟨fell and *tore* my knee⟩
**3** to remove by force ⟨children *torn* from their parents⟩
**4** to move powerfully or swiftly ⟨*tore* up the street⟩

A B C D E F G H I J K L M N O P Q R S T U V W X Y Z

**³tear** \'taər, 'teər\ *n*
**1** the act of tearing
**2** damage from being torn

**tear·drop** \'tir-,dräp\ *n*
¹TEAR

**tear·ful** \'tir-fəl\ *adj*
flowing with, accompanied by, or causing tears
**tear·ful·ly** \-fə-lē\ *adv*

**¹tease** \'tēz\ *vb* **teased**; **teas·ing**
to annoy again and again
**synonyms** see ANNOY
**teas·er** *n*

**²tease** *n*
**1** the act of teasing : the state of being teased
**2** a person who teases

**teddy bear**

**tea·spoon** \'tē-,spün\ *n*
**1** a small spoon used especially for stirring drinks
**2** TEASPOONFUL

**tea·spoon·ful** \'tē-,spün-,fu̇l\ *n, pl* **teaspoonfuls** \-,fu̇lz\ *or* **tea·spoons·ful** \-,spünz-,fu̇l\
**1** as much as a teaspoon can hold
**2** a unit of measure used especially in cooking and pharmacy equal to about five milliliters

**teat** \'tit, 'tēt\ *n*
NIPPLE 1 — used mostly of domestic animals

**tech·ni·cal** \'tek-ni-kəl\ *adj*
**1** having special knowledge especially of a mechanical or scientific subject
**2** of or relating to a single and especially a practical or scientific subject
**3** according to a strict explanation of the rules
**tech·ni·cal·ly** *adv*

**tech·ni·cal·i·ty** \,tek-nə-'kal-ət-ē\ *n, pl* **tech·ni·cal·i·ties**
something having meaning only to a person with special training

**technical sergeant** *n*
a noncommissioned officer in the Air Force ranking above a staff sergeant

**tech·ni·cian** \tek-'nish-ən\ *n*
a person skilled in the details or techniques of a subject, art, or job ⟨a dental *technician* helps the dentist⟩

**tech·nique** \tek-'nēk\ *n*
**1** the manner in which technical details are used in reaching a goal
**2** technical methods

**tech·no·log·i·cal** \,tek-nə-'läj-i-kəl\ *adj*
of or relating to technology

**tech·nol·o·gist** \tek-'näl-ə-jəst\ *n*
a specialist in technology

**tech·nol·o·gy** \tek-'näl-ə-jē\ *n, pl* **tech·nol·o·gies**
**1** the use of science in solving problems (as in industry or engineering)
**2** a technical method of doing something

**ted·dy bear** \'ted-ē-\ *n*
◀ a stuffed toy bear

**te·dious** \'tēd-ē-əs, 'tē-jəs\ *adj*
tiring because of length or dullness
**te·dious·ly** *adv*
**te·dious·ness** *n*

**tee** \'tē\ *n*
a device (as a post or peg) on which a ball is placed to be hit or kicked in various sports

**teem** \'tēm\ *vb*
to be full of something ⟨the streams *teemed* with fish⟩

**teen·age** \'tēn-,āj\ *or* **teen·aged** \-,ājd\ *adj*
of, being, or relating to teenagers

**teen·ag·er** \'tēn-,ā-jər\ *n*
a person in his or her teens

**teens** \'tēnz\ *n pl*
the years thirteen through nineteen in a person's life

**tee·ny** \'tē-nē\ *adj* **tee·ni·er**; **tee·ni·est**
TINY

**tee shirt** *variant of* T-SHIRT

**tee·ter** \'tēt-ər\ *vb*
**1** to move unsteadily
**2** ²SEESAW

**tee·ter–tot·ter** \'tēt-ər-,tät-ər\ *n*
¹SEESAW

**teeth** *pl of* TOOTH

**teethe** \'tē<u>th</u>\ *vb* **teethed**; **teeth·ing**
to cut one's teeth : grow teeth

**tele-** *or* **tel-** *prefix*
**1** at a distance ⟨*tele*gram⟩
**2** television ⟨*tele*cast⟩

**¹tele·cast** \'tel-i-,kast\ *n*
a program broadcast by television

**²telecast** *vb* **telecast** *also* **tele·cast·ed**; **tele·cast·ing**
to broadcast by television
**tele·cast·er** *n*

**tele·gram** \'tel-ə-,gram\ *n*
a message sent by telegraph

**¹tele·graph** \'tel-ə-,graf\ *n*
an electric device or system for sending messages by a code over connecting wires

**²telegraph** *vb*
**1** to send by telegraph
**2** to send a telegram to

**te·leg·ra·phy** \tə-'leg-rə-fē\ *n*
the use of a telegraph

**tele·mar·ket·ing** \,tel-ə-'mär-kət-iŋ\ *n*
the selling of goods or services by telephone

**¹telephone**

**te·lep·a·thy** \tə-'lep-ə-thē\ *n*
communication which appears to take place from one mind to another without speech or signs

**¹tele·phone** \'tel-ə-,fōn\ *n*
▲ an instrument for transmitting and receiving sounds over long distances by electricity

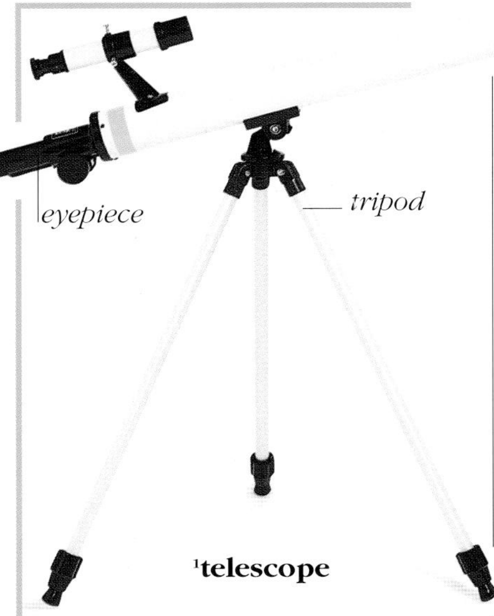

[1]telescope

[2]**telephone** *vb* **tele·phoned**; **tele·phon·ing**
to speak to by telephone

[1]**tele·scope** \'tel-ə-ˌskōp\ *n*
▲ an instrument shaped like a long tube that has lenses for viewing objects at a distance and especially for observing objects in outer space

[2]**telescope** *vb* **tele·scoped**; **tele·scop·ing**
to slide or force one part into another like the sections of a small telescope

**tele·vise** \'tel-ə-ˌvīz\ *vb* **tele·vised**; **tele·vis·ing**
to send (a program) by television

**tele·vi·sion** \'tel-ə-ˌvizh-ən\ *n*
**1** an electronic system of sending images together with sound over a wire or through space by devices that change light and sound into electrical waves and then change these back into light and sound
**2** a television receiving set
**3** television as a way of communicating

**tell** \'tel\ *vb* **told** \'tōld\; **tell·ing**
**1** [1]COUNT 1 ⟨all *told* there were 27 of us⟩
**2** to describe item by item ⟨*tell* a story⟩
**3** [1]SAY 1 ⟨*tell* a lie⟩
**4** to make known ⟨*tell* a secret⟩
**5** to let a person know something : to give information to ⟨I'll *tell* them when they get here⟩
**6** [1]ORDER 2 ⟨*told* us to wait⟩
**7** to find out by observing ⟨learned to *tell* time⟩
**8** to act as a tattletale ⟨don't *tell* on me⟩
**9** to have a noticeable result ⟨the pressure began to *tell* on them⟩
**10** to act as evidence ⟨smiles *telling* of success⟩

**tell·er** \'tel-ər\ *n*
**1** NARRATOR
**2** a person who counts votes
**3** a bank employee who receives and pays out money

[1]**tem·per** \'tem-pər\ *vb*
**1** SOFTEN ⟨the mountains *temper* the wind⟩
**2** to make a substance as thick, firm, or tough as is wanted
**3** to heat and cool a substance (as steel) until it is as hard, tough, or flexible as is wanted

[2]**temper** *n*
**1** the hardness or toughness of a substance (as metal)
**2** characteristic state of feeling
**3** calmness of mind ⟨lost my *temper*⟩
**4** an angry mood ⟨control your *temper*⟩

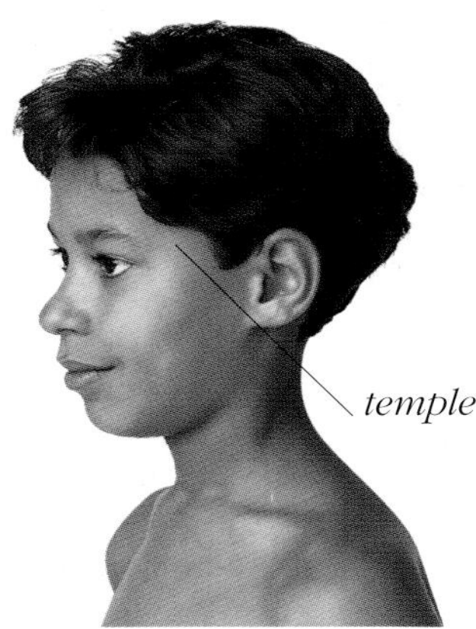

[2]temple

**tem·per·a·ment** \'tem-pə-rə-mənt, -prə-mənt\ *n*
a person's attitude as it affects what he or she says or does ⟨nervous *temperament*⟩

**tem·per·a·men·tal** \ˌtem-pə-rə-'ment-l, -prə-'ment-l\ *adj*
having or showing a nervous sensitive temperament
**tem·per·a·men·tal·ly** *adv*

**tem·per·ance** \'tem-pə-rəns, -prəns\ *n*
**1** control over one's actions, thoughts, or feelings
**2** the use of little or no alcoholic drink

**tem·per·ate** \'tem-pə-rət, -prət\ *adj*
**1** keeping or held within limits : MILD
**2** not drinking much liquor
**3** showing self-control
**4** not too hot or too cold

**tem·per·a·ture** \'tem-pə-rə-ˌchu̇r, -prə-ˌchu̇r, -pə-ˌchu̇r, -chər\ *n*
**1** degree of hotness or coldness as shown by a thermometer
**2** level of heat above what is normal for the human body : FEVER

**tem·pest** \'tem-pəst\ *n*
**1** a strong wind often accompanied by rain, hail, or snow
**2** UPROAR

**tem·pes·tu·ous** \tem-'pes-chə-wəs\ *adj*
very stormy
**tem·pes·tu·ous·ly** *adv*

[1]**tem·ple** \'tem-pəl\ *n*
a building for worship

[2]**temple** *n*
◀ the space between the eye and forehead and the upper part of the ear

**tem·po** \'tem-pō\ *n, pl* **tem·pi** \-ˌpē\ *or* **tempos**
the rate of speed at which a musical composition is played or sung

**tem·po·ral** \'tem-pə-rəl\ *adj*
of, relating to, or limited by time

**tem·po·rary** \'tem-pə-ˌrer-ē\ *adj*
not permanent
**tem·po·rar·i·ly** \ˌtem-pə-'rer-ə-lē\ *adv*

**tempt** \'tempt\ *vb*
**1** to make someone think of doing wrong (as by promise of gain)
**2** to risk the dangers of ⟨*tempt* one's luck⟩
**tempt·er** *n*

**temp·ta·tion** \temp-'tā-shən\ *n*
**1** the act of tempting or the state of being tempted
**2** something that tempts

[1]**ten** \'ten\ *adj*
being one more than nine

[2]**ten** *n*
one more than nine : two times five : 10

**te·na·cious** \tə-'nā-shəs\ *adj*
**1** not easily pulled apart
**2** PERSISTENT

**te·nac·i·ty** \tə-'nas-ət-ē\ *n*
the quality or state of being tenacious

[1]**ten·ant** \'ten-ənt\ *n*
**1** a person who rents property (as a house) from the owner
**2** OCCUPANT, DWELLER

[2]**tenant** *vb*
to hold or live in as a tenant

[1]**tend** \'tend\ *vb*
**1** to pay attention ⟨*tend* strictly to business⟩
**2** to take care of
**3** to manage the operation of ⟨*tend* a machine⟩

[2]**tend** *vb*
**1** to move or turn in a certain direction : LEAD
**2** to be likely

**ten·den·cy** \'ten-dən-sē\ *n, pl* **ten·den·cies**
**1** the direction or course toward something
**2** a leaning toward a particular kind of thought or action

[1]**ten·der** \'ten-dər\ *adj*
**1** not tough ⟨a *tender* steak⟩
**2** DELICATE 4 ⟨*tender* plants⟩
**3** YOUTHFUL 1 ⟨children of *tender* years⟩
**4** feeling or showing love ⟨a *tender* look⟩
**5** very easily hurt ⟨a *tender* scar⟩
**ten·der·ly** *adv*
**ten·der·ness** *n*

[2]**tender** *vb*
**1** to offer in payment
**2** to present for acceptance

[3]**tender** *n*
**1** [2]OFFER
**2** something (as money) that may be offered in payment

[4]**tend·er** \'ten-dər\ *n*
**1** a ship used to attend other ships (as to supply food)
**2** a boat that carries passengers or freight to a larger ship
**3** a car attached to a locomotive for carrying fuel or water

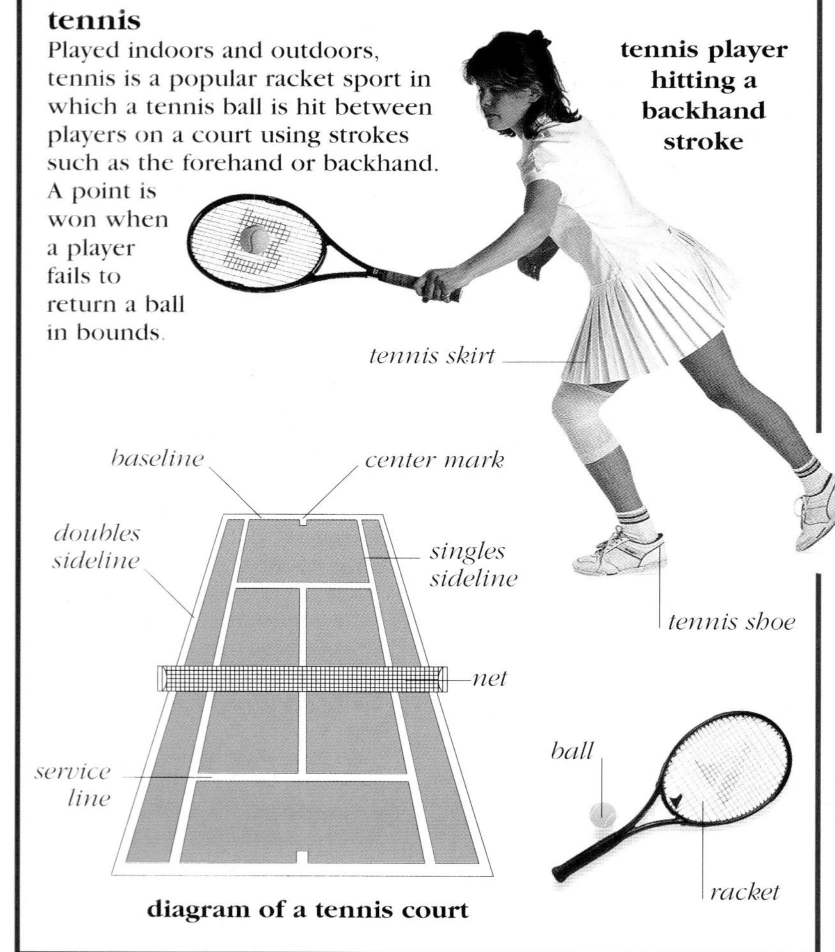
tennis
Played indoors and outdoors, tennis is a popular racket sport in which a tennis ball is hit between players on a court using strokes such as the forehand or backhand. A point is won when a player fails to return a ball in bounds.
tennis player hitting a backhand stroke
tennis skirt
tennis shoe
baseline
center mark
doubles sideline
singles sideline
net
service line
ball
racket
**diagram of a tennis court**

**ten·der·foot** \'ten-dər-,fu̇t\ *n, pl* **ten·der·feet** \-,fēt\ *also* **ten·der·foots**
a person who is not used to a rough outdoor life

**ten·der·heart·ed** \,ten-dər-'härt-əd\ *adj*
easily affected with feelings of love, pity, or sorrow

**ten·don** \'ten-dən\ *n*
a strip or band of tough white fiber connecting a muscle to another part (as a bone)

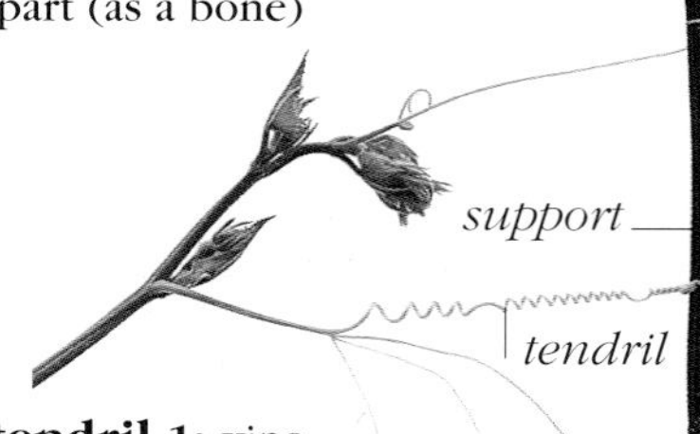
support
tendril
**tendril 1:** vine tendrils clinging to a support

**ten·dril** \'ten-drəl\ *n*
**1** ▲ a slender leafless winding stem by which some climbing plants fasten themselves to a support
**2** something that winds like a plant's tendril ⟨*tendrils* of hair⟩

**ten·e·ment** \'ten-ə-mənt\ *n*
**1** a house used as a dwelling
**2** APARTMENT 1
**3** a building divided into separate apartments for rent

**ten·nis** \'ten-əs\ *n*
◀ a game played on a level court by two or four players who use rackets to hit a ball back and forth across a low net dividing the court

**ten·or** \'ten-ər\ *n*
**1** the next to the lowest part in harmony having four parts
**2** the highest male singing voice
**3** a singer or an instrument having a tenor range or part

**ten·pins** \'ten-,pinz\ *n*
a bowling game played with ten pins

[1]**tense** \'tens\ *n*
a form of a verb used to show the time of the action or state

[2]**tense** *adj* **tens·er**; **tens·est**
**1** stretched tight
**2** feeling or showing nervous tension

3 marked by strain or uncertainty ⟨a *tense* moment⟩
**tense·ly** *adv*
**tense·ness** *n*
**³tense** *vb* **tensed**; **tens·ing**
to make or become tense
**ten·sion** \'ten-chən\ *n*
1 the act of straining or stretching : the condition of being strained or stretched
2 a state of mental unrest
3 a state of unfriendliness
**¹tent** \'tent\ *n*
a portable shelter (as of canvas) stretched and supported by poles
**²tent** *vb*
to live in a tent
**ten·ter** *n*
**ten·ta·cle** \'tent-ə-kəl\ *n*
one of the long thin flexible structures that stick out about the head or the mouth of an animal (as an insect or fish) and are used especially for feeling or grasping
**ten·ta·tive** \'tent-ət-iv\ *adj*
not final ⟨*tentative* plans⟩
**ten·ta·tive·ly** *adv*
**tent caterpillar** *n*
any of several caterpillars that spin tent-like webs in which they live in groups
**¹tenth** \'tenth\ *adj*
coming right after ninth
**²tenth** *n*
1 number ten in a series
2 one of ten equal parts
**te·pee** \'tē-,pē\ *n*
► a tent shaped like a cone and used as a home by some American Indians
**tep·id** \'tep-əd\ *adj*
LUKEWARM 1 ⟨*tepid* water⟩
**¹term** \'tərm\ *n*
1 a period of time fixed especially by law or custom ⟨a school *term*⟩
2 **terms** *pl* conditions that limit the nature and scope of something (as a treaty or a will)
3 a word or expression that has an exact meaning in some uses or is limited to a subject or field ⟨legal *terms*⟩
4 the numerator or denominator of a fraction
5 any one of the numbers in a series
6 **terms** *pl* relationship between people ⟨was on good *terms* with the neighbors⟩
**²term** *vb*
to apply a term to ⟨*termed* them liars⟩
**¹ter·mi·nal** \'tər-mən-l\ *adj*
of, relating to, or forming an end
**²terminal** *n*
1 a part that forms the end : EXTREMITY
2 a device at the end of a wire or on a machine for making an electrical connection
3 either end of a transportation line or a passenger or freight station located at it
4 a device (as in a computer system) used to put in, receive, and display information
**ter·mi·nate** \'tər-mə-,nāt\ *vb* **ter·mi·nat·ed**; **ter·mi·nat·ing**
END, CLOSE
**ter·mi·na·tion** \,tər-mə-'nā-shən\ *n*
1 the end of something
2 the act of ending something
**ter·mi·nus** \'tər-mə-nəs\ *n, pl* **ter·mi·ni** \-,nī, -,nē\ *or* **ter·mi·nus·es**
1 final goal : END
2 either end of a transportation line or travel route

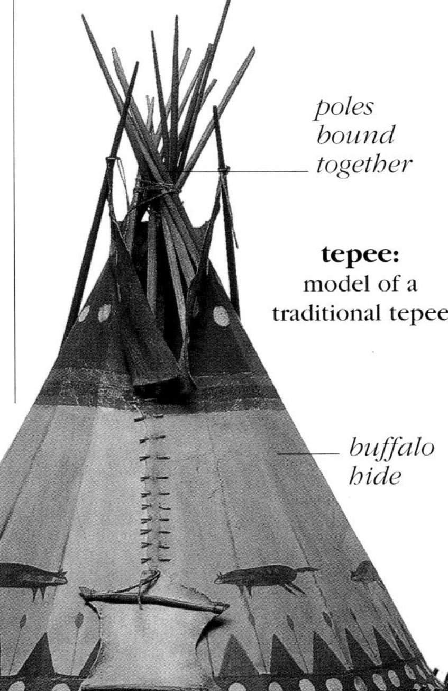

**tepee:** model of a traditional tepee

**ter·mite** \'tər-,mīt\ *n*
▼ a chewing antlike insect of a light color that lives in large colonies and feeds on wood

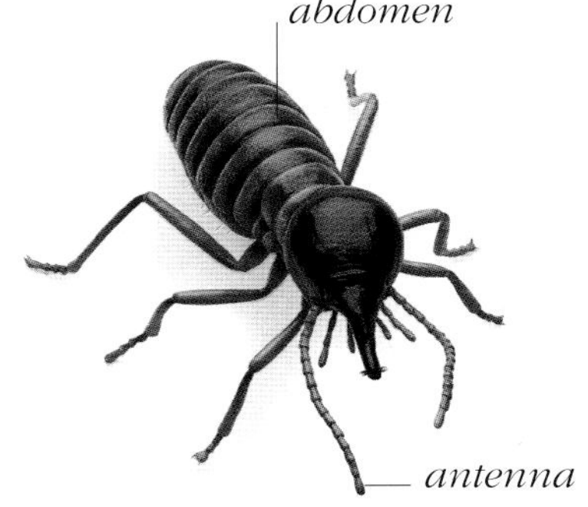

**termite:** model of a termite

**tern** \'tərn\ *n*
any of numerous small slender sea gulls with black cap, white body, and narrow wings
**¹ter·race** \'ter-əs\ *n*
1 a flat roof or open platform
2 a level area next to a building
3 a raised piece of land with the top leveled
4 a row of houses on raised ground or a slope
**²terrace** *vb* **ter·raced**; **ter·rac·ing**
to form into a terrace or supply with terraces
**ter·rain** \tə-'rān\ *n*
the features of the surface of a piece of land
**ter·ra·pin** \'ter-ə-pən\ *n*
a North American turtle that eats flesh and lives in water
**ter·rar·i·um** \tə-'rar-ē-əm, -'rer-\ *n, pl* **ter·rar·ia** \-ē-ə\ *or* **ter·rar·i·ums**
a box usually made of glass that is used for keeping and observing small animals or plants
**ter·res·tri·al** \tə-'res-trē-əl\ *adj*
1 of or relating to the earth or its people
2 living or growing on land
**ter·ri·ble** \'ter-ə-bəl\ *adj*
1 causing great fear ⟨*terrible* weapons⟩
2 very great in degree : INTENSE ⟨a *terrible* fright⟩
3 very bad ⟨*terrible* writing⟩
**ter·ri·bly** \-blē\ *adv*

**ter•ri•er** \'ter-ē-ər\ *n*
any of various usually small dogs originally used by hunters to drive animals from their holes

**Word History** Terriers were first used in hunting small game. Their job was to dig for the animals and drive them from their holes. Terriers got their name because they dug in the earth. The English word *terrier* came from a Latin word that meant "earth."

**ter•rif•ic** \tə-'rif-ik\ *adj*
**1** causing terror : TERRIBLE ⟨*terrific* damage from the storm⟩
**2** very unusual : EXTRAORDINARY ⟨going at *terrific* speed⟩
**3** very good : EXCELLENT
**ter•rif•i•cal•ly** \-i-kə-lē\ *adv*

**ter•ri•fy** \'ter-ə-,fī\ *vb* **ter•ri•fied**; **ter•ri•fy•ing**
to frighten greatly

**ter•ri•to•ri•al** \,ter-ə-'tōr-ē-əl\ *adj*
of or relating to a territory

**ter•ri•to•ry** \'ter-ə-,tōr-ē\ *n*, *pl* **ter•ri•to•ries**
**1** a geographical area belonging to or under the rule of a government
**2** a part of the United States not included within any state but organized with a separate governing body
**3** REGION 1, DISTRICT

**ter•ror** \'ter-ər\ *n*
**1** a state of great fear
**2** a cause of great fear

**ter•ror•ism** \'ter-ər-,iz-əm\ *n*
the use of threat or violence especially as a means of forcing others to do what one wishes

**ter•ror•ize** \'ter-ər-,īz\ *vb* **ter•ror•ized**; **ter•ror•iz•ing**
**1** to fill with terror
**2** to use terrorism against

**terse** \'tərs\ *adj* **ters•er**; **ters•est**
being brief and to the point : CONCISE
**terse•ly** *adv*
**terse•ness** *n*

**[1]test** \'test\ *n*
**1** a means of finding out the nature, quality, or value of something
**2** a set of questions or problems by which a person's knowledge, intelligence, or skills are measured

**Word History** The English word *test* first meant "a small bowl used in analyzing metals." It came from a Latin word that meant "a bowl or pot made of clay." The bowl called a *test* was used to examine things. That is why the word *test* came to mean "examination."

**[2]test** *vb*
to put to a test : EXAMINE

**tes•ta•ment** \'tes-tə-mənt\ *n*
**1** either of two main parts (**Old Testament** and **New Testament**) of the Bible
**2** [2]WILL 3

**tes•ti•fy** \'tes-tə-,fī\ *vb* **tes•ti•fied**; **tes•ti•fy•ing**
to make a formal statement of what one swears is true

**tes•ti•mo•ny** \'tes-tə-,mō-nē\ *n*, *pl* **tes•ti•mo•nies**
a statement made by a witness under oath especially in a court

**tes•tis** \'tes-təs\ *n*, *pl* **tes•tes** \'tes-,tēz\
a male reproductive gland

**test tube** *n*
a plain tube of thin glass closed at one end and used especially in chemistry and biology

sulfur
iron

**test tube**
containing iron and sulfur

**tet•a•nus** \'tet-n-əs, 'tet-nəs\ *n*
a dangerous disease in which spasms of the muscles occur often with locking of the jaws and which is caused by poison from a germ that enters wounds

**[1]teth•er** \'te<u>th</u>-ər\ *n*
a line by which an animal is fastened so as to limit where it can go

**[2]tether** *vb*
to fasten by a tether

**teth•er•ball** \'te<u>th</u>-ər-,bȯl\ *n*
a game played with a ball attached by a string to an upright pole in which the object is to wrap the string around the pole by hitting the ball in a direction opposite to that of the other player

**text** \'tekst\ *n*
**1** the actual words of an author's work
**2** the main body of printed or written matter on a page
**3** a passage from the Bible chosen as the subject of a sermon
**4** TEXTBOOK

**text•book** \'tekst-,bu̇k\ *n*
a book that presents the important information about a subject and is used as a basis of instruction

**tex•tile** \'tek-,stīl, 'teks-təl\ *n*
a woven or knit cloth

**terrier**
There are dozens of breeds of terrier. They are often found exploring and digging tunnels, and make spirited and loyal pets.

**Scottish terrier**

**Jack Russell terrier** \'jak-'rus-əl-\

**Airedale terrier** \'aer-,dāl-\

**tex•ture** \'teks-chər\ *n*
the structure, feel, and appearance of something (as cloth)

**-th** \th\ *or* **-eth** \əth\ *adj suffix*
used to form numbers that show the place of something in a series ⟨hundred*th*⟩ ⟨fortie*th*⟩

**than** \thən, than\ *conj*
when compared to the way in which, the extent to which, or the degree to which ⟨you are older *than* I am⟩

**thank** \'thangk\ *vb*
1 to express gratitude to
2 to hold responsible

**thank•ful** \'thangk-fəl\ *adj*
feeling or showing thanks
: GRATEFUL
**thank•ful•ly** \-fə-lē\ *adv*
**thank•ful•ness** *n*

**thank•less** \'thangk-ləs\ *adj*
1 UNGRATEFUL
2 not appreciated ⟨a necessary but *thankless* job⟩

**thanks** \'thangks\ *n*
1 GRATITUDE
2 an expression of gratitude (as for something received)
**thanks to**
1 with the help of
2 BECAUSE OF

**[2]thatch:**
a cottage with a roof of thatch

**thanks•giv•ing** \thangks-'giv-ing\ *n*
1 the act of giving thanks
2 a prayer expressing gratitude
3 *cap* THANKSGIVING DAY

**Thanksgiving Day** *n*
the fourth Thursday in November observed as a legal holiday for public thanksgiving to God

**[1]that** \that\ *pron, pl* **those** \thōz\
1 the one seen, mentioned, or understood ⟨*that* is my book⟩ ⟨*those* are my shoes⟩
2 the one farther away ⟨this is an elm, *that* is a hickory⟩
3 the one : the kind ⟨the richest ore is *that* found higher up⟩

**[2]that** \thət, that\ *conj*
1 the following, namely ⟨said *that* we'd go⟩
2 which is, namely ⟨a chance *that* it might rain⟩
3 [2]SO 1 ⟨shouted *that* all might hear⟩
4 as to result in the following, namely ⟨so hungry *that* I fainted⟩
5 BECAUSE ⟨glad *that* you came⟩

**[3]that** *adj, pl* **those**
1 being the one mentioned, indicated, or understood ⟨*that* boy⟩
2 being the one farther away ⟨this book or *that* one⟩

**[4]that** \thət, that\ *pron*
1 WHO 3, WHOM, [2]WHICH 2 ⟨the person *that* won the race⟩ ⟨the people *that* you saw⟩ ⟨the food *that* I like⟩
2 in, on, or at which ⟨the year *that* I started school⟩

**[5]that** \'that\ *adv*
to such an extent or degree ⟨need a nail about *that* long⟩

**[1]thatch** \'thach\ *vb*
to cover with thatch

**[2]thatch** *n*
◄ a plant material (as straw) for use as roofing

**[1]thaw** \'thȯ\ *vb*
1 to melt or cause to melt
2 to grow less unfriendly or quiet in manner

**[2]thaw** *n*
1 the action, fact, or process of thawing
2 a period of weather warm enough to thaw ice and snow

**[1]the** *especially before consonant sounds* thə, *before vowel sounds* thē, *4 is often* 'thē\ *definite article*
1 that or those mentioned, seen, or clearly understood ⟨put *the* cat out⟩ ⟨I'll take *the* red one⟩
2 that or those near in space, time, or thought ⟨news of *the* day⟩
3 [1]EACH ⟨forty cookies to *the* box⟩
4 that or those considered best, most typical, or most worth singling out ⟨is *the* person for this job⟩
5 any one typical of or standing for the entire class named ⟨useful tips for *the* beginner⟩
6 all those that are ⟨*the* British⟩

**[2]the** *adv*
1 than before ⟨none *the* wiser⟩
2 to what extent ⟨*the* sooner the better⟩
3 to that extent ⟨the sooner *the* better⟩

**the•ater** *or* **the•atre** \'thē-ət-ər\ *n*
1 ▼ a building in which plays or motion pictures are presented
2 a place like a theater in form or use
3 a place or area where some important action is carried on ⟨a *theater* of war⟩
4 plays or the performance of plays

**the•at•ri•cal** \thē-'at-ri-kəl\ *adj*
of or relating to the theater or the presentation of plays

**theater 1:**
a theater for performing plays

**thee** \thē\ *pron, archaic, objective case of* THOU ⟨"my country, 'tis of *thee* "⟩

**theft** \'theft\ *n*
the act of stealing

**their** \thər, theər, thaər\ *adj*
of or relating to them or themselves especially as owners or as agents or objects of an action ⟨*their* clothes⟩ ⟨*their* deeds⟩ ⟨*their* pain⟩

**theirs** \'theərz, 'thaərz\ *pron*
that which belongs to them ⟨the red house is *theirs*⟩

**them** \thəm, them\ *pron, objective case of* THEY

**theme** \'thēm\ *n*
1 a subject of a work of art, music, or literature
2 a specific quality, characteristic, or concern ⟨a room decorated in a tropical *theme*⟩
3 a written exercise

**theme park** *n*
an amusement park in which the rides and buildings are based on a central theme

**them·selves** \thəm-'selvz\ *pron*
their own selves ⟨they enjoyed *themselves*⟩ ⟨did it *themselves*⟩

[1]**then** \then\ *adv*
**1** at that time
**2** soon after that **:** NEXT
**3** in addition **:** BESIDES
**4** in that case
**5** as an expected result

[2]**then** \'then\ *n*
that time ⟨wait until *then*⟩

[3]**then** \'then\ *adj*
existing or acting at that time ⟨the *then* president⟩

**thence** \'thens\ *adv*
**1** from that place
**2** from that fact

**thence·forth** \'thens-,fōrth\ *adv*
from that time on

**thence·for·ward** \thens-'fȯr-wərd\ *adv*
onward from that place or time

**the·ol·o·gy** \thē-'äl-ə-jē\ *n, pl* **the·ol·o·gies**
the study and explanation of religious faith, practice, and experience

**the·o·ry** \'thē-ə-rē, 'thir-ē\ *n, pl* **the·o·ries**
**1** the general rules followed in a science or an art ⟨music *theory*⟩
**2** a general rule offered to explain experiences or facts ⟨wave *theory* of light⟩
**3** an idea used for discussion or as a starting point for an investigation

**ther·a·peu·tic** \,ther-ə-'pyüt-ik\ *adj*
MEDICINAL

**ther·a·pist** \'ther-ə-pəst\ *n*
a specialist in therapy and especially in methods of treatment other than drugs and surgery

**ther·a·py** \'ther-ə-pē\ *n, pl* **ther·a·pies**
treatment of an abnormal state in the body or mind

[1]**there** \'thaər, 'theər\ *adv*
**1** in or at that place ⟨stand over *there*⟩
**2** to or into that place ⟨take the basket *there* and leave it⟩
**3** in that situation or way ⟨*there* you have a choice⟩

[2]**there** \thaər, theər\ *pron*
used to introduce a sentence in which the subject comes after the verb ⟨*there* is a person outside⟩

[3]**there** \'thaər, 'theər\ *n*
that place ⟨get away from *there*⟩

**there·abouts** \,thar-ə-'bau̇ts, ,ther-\ *or* **there·about** \-'bau̇t\ *adv*
**1** near that place or time
**2** near that number, degree, or amount

**there·af·ter** \tha-'raf-tər, the-\ *adv*
after that

**there·at** \tha-'rat, the-\ *adv*
**1** at that place
**2** because of that

**there·by** \thaər-'bī, theər-\ *adv*
**1** by that
**2** related to that

**there·fore** \'thaər-,fōr, 'theər-\ *adv*
for that reason

**there·in** \tha-'rin, the-\ *adv*
in or into that place, time, or thing ⟨the world and all that is *therein*⟩

**there·of** \tha-'rəv, the-, -'räv\ *adv*
**1** of that or it
**2** from that cause

**there·on** \tha-'rȯn, the-, -'rän\ *adv*
on that

**there·to** \thaər-'tü, theər-\ *adv*
to that

**there·up·on** \'thar-ə-,pȯn, 'ther-, -,pän\ *adv*
**1** on that thing
**2** for that reason
**3** immediately after that **:** at once

**there·with** \thaər-'with, theər-, -'with\ *adv*
with that

**ther·mal** \'thər-məl\ *adj*
of, relating to, caused by, or saving heat

**ther·mom·e·ter** \thər-'mäm-ət-ər, thə-'mäm-\ *n*
▶ an instrument for measuring temperature usually consisting of a sealed glass tube containing a liquid (as colored alcohol) that expands or contracts as the temperature rises or falls

**ther·mos** \'thər-məs\ *n*
a container (as a bottle or jar) that has a vacuum between an inner and an outer wall and is used to keep liquids hot or cold for seveal hours
VACUUM BOTTLE

**ther·mo·stat** \'thər-mə-,stat\ *n*
a device that automatically controls temperature

**the·sau·rus** \thi-'sȯr-əs\ *n, pl* **the·sau·ri** \-'sȯr-,ī, -,ē\ *or* **the·sau·rus·es** \-'sȯr-ə-səz\
a book of words and their synonyms

**these** *pl of* THIS

**the·sis** \'thē-səs\ *n, pl* **the·ses** \-,sēz\
**1** a statement that a person wants to discuss or prove
**2** an essay presenting results of original research

**they** \thā\ *pron*
those individuals **:** those ones

**they'd** \thād\
they had **:** they would

**they'll** \thāl\
they shall **:** they will

**they're** \thər, theər\
they are

**they've** \thāv\
they have

**thi·a·min** \'thī-ə-mən\ *n*
a member of the vitamin B complex whose lack causes beriberi

[1]**thick** \'thik\ *adj*
**1** having great size from one surface to its opposite
**2** heavily built
**3** closely packed together
**4** occurring in large numbers **:** NUMEROUS ⟨mosquitos were *thick* in the shade⟩
**5** not flowing easily ⟨a *thick* milk shake⟩
**6** having haze, fog, or mist
**7** measuring a certain amount in the smallest of three dimensions ⟨two millimeters *thick*⟩
**8** not clearly spoken ⟨*thick* speech⟩
**9** STUPID 1
**synonyms** see DENSE
— **thick·ly** *adv*

glass tube
Celsius scale
Fahrenheit scale

**thermometer**

**²thick** *n*
**1** the most crowded or active part ⟨in the *thick* of the battle⟩
**2** the part of greatest thickness

**thick·en** \'thik-ən\ *vb*
to make or become thick
**thick·en·er** *n*

**thick·et** \'thik-ət\ *n*
a thick usually small patch of bushes or low trees

**thick·ness** \'thik-nəs\ *n*
**1** the quality or state of being thick
**2** the smallest of three dimensions ⟨length, width, and *thickness*⟩

**thick·set** \'thik-'set\ *adj*
**1** closely placed or planted
**2** STOCKY

**thief** \'thēf\ *n, pl* **thieves** \'thēvz\
a person who steals : ROBBER

**thieve** \'thēv\ *vb* **thieved**; **thiev·ing**
¹STEAL 2, ROB

**thiev·ery** \'thē-və-rē\ *n, pl* **thiev·er·ies**
THEFT

**thiev·ish** \'thē-vish\ *adj*
**1** likely to steal
**2** of, relating to, or like a thief

**thigh** \'thī\ *n*
the part of a leg between the knee and the main part of the body

**thim·ble** \'thim-bəl\ *n*
a cap or cover used in sewing to protect the finger that pushes the needle

**¹thin** \'thin\ *adj* **thin·ner**; **thin·nest**
**1** having little size from one surface to its opposite : not thick ⟨*thin* paper⟩
**2** having the parts not close together ⟨*thin* hair⟩
**3** having little body fat
**4** having less than the usual number ⟨attendance was *thin*⟩
**5** not very convincing ⟨a *thin* excuse⟩
**6** somewhat weak or shrill ⟨a *thin* voice⟩ **synonyms** see LEAN
**thin·ly** *adv*
**thin·ness** *n*

**²thin** *vb* **thinned**; **thin·ning**
to make or become thin

**thine** \t͟hīn\ *pron, singular, archaic*
YOURS ⟨"'All the jungle is *thine*,' said Bagheera..."⟩

**thing** \'thing\ *n*
**1** AFFAIR 2, MATTER ⟨have a *thing* or two to take care of⟩
**2 things** *pl* state of affairs ⟨*things* are improving⟩
**3** EVENT 1 ⟨the accident was a terrible *thing*⟩
**4** ¹DEED 1, ACHIEVEMENT ⟨expect great *things* from them⟩
**5** something that exists and can be talked about ⟨all *things* bright and beautiful⟩ ⟨say the first *thing* that pops into your mind⟩ ⟨how do you work this *thing*?⟩
**6 things** *pl* personal possessions ⟨pack your *things*, we're leaving⟩
**7** a piece of clothing ⟨not a *thing* to wear⟩
**8** ¹DETAIL 2 ⟨checks every little *thing*⟩
**9** what is needed or wanted ⟨it's just the *thing* for a cold⟩
**10** an action or interest that one very much enjoys ⟨music is my *thing*⟩

**think** \'thingk\ *vb* **thought** \'thȯt\; **think·ing**
**1** to form or have in the mind ⟨afraid to even *think* what had happened⟩
**2** to have as an opinion or belief ⟨I *think* you can do it⟩
**3** REMEMBER 1 ⟨I didn't *think* to ask⟩
**4** to use the power of reason ⟨you're just not *thinking*⟩
**5** to invent something by thinking ⟨*think* up an excuse⟩
**6** to hold a strong feeling ⟨they *think* highly of you⟩
**7** to care about ⟨I must *think* first of my family⟩
**think·er** *n*

**thin·ner** \'thin-ər\ *n*
a liquid used to thin paint

**¹third** \'thərd\ *adj*
coming right after second

**²third** *n*
**1** number three in a series
**2** one of three equal parts

**¹thirst** \'thərst\ *n*
**1** a feeling of dryness in the mouth and throat that accompanies a need for liquids
**2** the bodily condition that produces thirst ⟨die of *thirst*⟩
**3** a strong desire

**²thirst** *vb*
**1** to feel thirsty
**2** to have a strong desire

**thirsty** \'thər-stē\ *adj* **thirst·i·er**; **thirst·i·est**
**1** feeling thirst
**2** needing moisture ⟨*thirsty* crops⟩
**3** having a strong desire : EAGER
**thirst·i·ly** \'thər-stə-lē\ *adv*

**¹thir·teen** \,thər-'tēn\ *adj*
being one more than twelve

**²thirteen** *n*
one more than twelve : 13

**¹thir·teenth** \,thər-'tēnth\ *adj*
coming right after twelfth

**²thirteenth** *n*
number thirteen in a series

**¹thir·ti·eth** \'thərt-ē-əth\ *adj*
coming right after twenty-ninth

**²thirtieth** *n*
number thirty in a series

**¹thir·ty** \'thərt-ē\ *adj*
being three times ten

**²thirty** *n*
three times ten : 30

**¹this** \t͟his\ *pron, pl* **these** \t͟hēz\
**1** the one close or closest in time or space ⟨*this* is your book⟩ ⟨*these* are my friends⟩
**2** what is in the present or is being seen or talked about ⟨*this* is where it happened⟩

**²this** *adj, pl* **these**
**1** being the one present, near, or just mentioned ⟨*this* morning⟩ ⟨friends all *these* years⟩
**2** being the one nearer or last mentioned ⟨*this* book or that one⟩

**³this** \'t͟his\ *adv*
to the degree suggested by something in the present situation ⟨didn't expect to wait *this* long⟩

**this·tle** \'this-əl\ *n*
▼ a prickly plant related to the daisies that has usually purplish often showy heads of mostly tubular flowers

thistle

**thith·er** \'thit͟h-ər\ *adv*
to that place : THERE

**thong** \'thȯng\ *n*
a strip of leather used especially for fastening something

**tho·rax** \'thōr-,aks\ *n,* *pl* **tho·rax·es** *or* **tho·ra·ces** \'thōr-ə-,sēz\
**1** the part of the body of a mammal that lies between the neck and the abdomen and contains the heart and lungs
**2** the middle of the three main divisions of the body of an insect

**thorn** \'thȯrn\ *n*
**1** a woody plant (as hawthorn) with sharp briers, prickles, or spines
**2** ▼ a short hard sharp-pointed leafless branch on a woody plant

**thorn 2:**
a twig with thorns

**thorny** \'thȯr-nē\ *adj* **thorn·i·er**; **thorn·i·est**
**1** full of or covered with thorns
**2** full of difficulties

**thor·ough** \'thər-ō\ *adj*
**1** being such to the fullest degree **:** COMPLETE ⟨a *thorough* search⟩
**2** careful about little things ⟨a *thorough* worker⟩
**thor·ough·ly** *adv*
**thor·ough·ness** *n*

[1]**thor·ough·bred** \'thər-ō-,bred\ *adj*
**1** bred from the best blood through a long line
**2** *cap* of, relating to, or being a member of the Thoroughbred breed of horses

[2]**thoroughbred** *n*
**1** *cap* any of an English breed of light speedy horses kept mainly for racing
**2** a purebred or pedigreed animal
**3** a very fine person

**thor·ough·fare** \'thər-ō-,faər, -,feər\ *n*
**1** a street or road open at both ends
**2** a main road

**thor·ough·go·ing** \,thər-ə-'gō-iŋ\ *adj*
THOROUGH 1

**those** *pl of* THAT

**thou** \'thau̇\ *pron, singular, archaic*
YOU ⟨"bow, wow, wow, whose dog art *thou* ?"⟩

[1]**though** \'thō\ *conj*
ALTHOUGH ⟨*though* it was raining, we went out⟩

[2]**though** *adv*
HOWEVER 3, NEVERTHELESS ⟨not for long, *though*⟩

[1]**thought** \'thȯt\ *past of* THINK

[2]**thought** *n*
**1** the act or process of thinking and especially of trying to decide about something ⟨give *thought* to the future⟩
**2** power of reasoning and judging
**3** power of imagining
**4** something (as an idea or fancy) formed in the mind

**thought·ful** \'thȯt-fəl\ *adj*
**1** deep in thought
**2** showing careful thinking ⟨a *thoughtful* essay⟩
**3** considerate of others
**thought·ful·ly** \-fə-lē\ *adv*
**thought·ful·ness** *n*

**thought·less** \'thȯt-ləs\ *adj*
**1** not careful and alert
**2** NEGLIGENT ⟨a *thoughtless* mistake⟩
**3** not considerate of others
**thought·less·ly** *adv*
**thought·less·ness** *n*

[1]**thou·sand** \'thau̇z-nd\ *n*
**1** ten times one hundred **:** 1000
**2** a very large number ⟨*thousands* of things to do⟩

[2]**thousand** *adj*
being 1000

[1]**thou·sandth** \'thau̇z-nth\ *adj*
coming right after 999th

[2]**thousandth** *n*
number 1000 in a series

**thrash** \'thrash\ *vb*
**1** THRESH 1
**2** to beat very hard
**3** to move about violently ⟨something was *thrashing* wildly in the brush⟩

[1]**thrash·er** \'thrash-ər\ *n*
one that thrashes

[2]**thrasher** *n*
an American bird (as the common reddish brown **brown thrasher**) related to the thrushes and noted for its song

[1]**thread** \'thred\ *n*
**1** a thin fine cord formed by spinning and twisting short fibers into a continuous strand
**2** something suggesting a thread ⟨a *thread* of light⟩
**3** ▼ the ridge or groove that winds around a screw
**4** a line of reasoning or train of thought that connects the parts of an argument or story
**thread·like** \-,līk\ *adj*

[1]**thread 3:**
a screw showing the thread

[2]**thread** *vb*
**1** to put a thread in working position (as in a needle)
**2** to pass through like a thread ⟨*thread* a pipe with wire⟩
**3** to make one's way through or between
**4** to put together on a thread **:** STRING

**thread·bare** \'thred-,baər, -,beər\ *adj*
**1** worn so much that the thread shows **:** SHABBY
**2** TRITE

**threat** \'thret\ *n*
**1** a showing of an intention to do harm
**2** something that threatens ⟨the *threat* of punishment⟩

**threat·en** \'thret-n\ *vb*
**1** to make threats against
**2** to give warning of by a threat or sign ⟨clouds that *threatened* rain⟩
**threat·en·ing·ly** *adv*

[1]**three** \'thrē\ *adj*
being one more than two

[2]**three** *n*
**1** one more than two **:** 3
**2** the third in a set or series

**3–D** \'thrē-'dē\ *adj*
THREE-DIMENSIONAL 2 ⟨a *3-D* movie⟩

**three–dimensional** *adj*
**1** ▼ of, relating to, or having the three dimensions of length, width, and height ⟨a cube is *three-dimensional*⟩
**2** giving the appearance of depth or varying distances ⟨a *three-dimensional* movie⟩

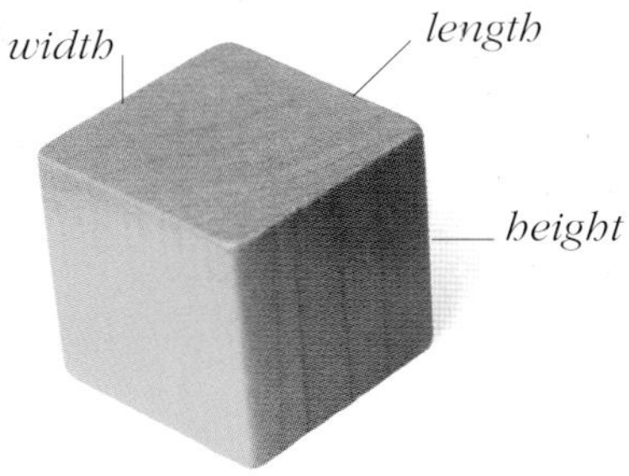


**three-dimensional 1:** a cube is a three-dimensional solid

**three·fold** \'thrē-ˌfōld\ *adj*
being three times as great or as many
**three·score** \'thrē-ˌskōr\ *adj*
SIXTY
**thresh** \'thrash, 'thresh\ *vb*
**1** to separate (as grain from straw) by beating
**2** THRASH 3
**thresh·er** \'thrash-ər, 'thresh-\ *n*
THRESHING MACHINE
**threshing machine** *n*
a machine used in harvesting to separate grain from straw
**thresh·old** \'thresh-ˌōld\ *n*
**1** the sill of a door
**2** a point or place of beginning or entering ⟨at the *threshold* of an adventure⟩
**threw** *past of* THROW
**thrice** \'thrīs\ *adv*
three times
**thrift** \'thrift\ *n*
careful management especially of money
**thrifty** \'thrif-tē\ *adj* **thrift·i·er**; **thrift·i·est**
**1** tending to save money
**2** doing well in health and growth ⟨*thrifty* cattle⟩ **synonyms** see ECONOMICAL
[1]**thrill** \'thril\ *vb*
**1** to have or cause to have a sudden feeling of excitement or pleasure
**2** [1]TREMBLE 2, VIBRATE
**thrill·er** *n*

---

**Word History** The English word *thrill* is related to the English word *through*. Modern English *through* comes from an Old English word that meant "through." An Old English word meaning "hole" was formed from the word meaning "through." An Old English word meaning "to pierce" was formed from the word meaning "hole." The modern word *thrill* comes from the Old English word meaning "to pierce." When you are thrilled you are not really pierced, of course. You do feel, however, as if something has gone through you.

---

[2]**thrill** *n*
**1** a feeling of being thrilled
**2** VIBRATION 3
**thrive** \'thrīv\ *vb* **throve** \'thrōv\ *or* **thrived**; **thriv·en** \'thriv-ən\ *also* **thrived**; **thriv·ing** \'thrī-ving\
**1** to grow very well : FLOURISH
**2** to gain in wealth or possessions
**throat** \'thrōt\ *n*
**1** the part of the neck in front of the backbone
**2** the passage from the mouth to the stomach and lungs ⟨a sore *throat*⟩
**3** something like the throat especially in being an entrance or a narrowed part
[1]**throb** \'thräb\ *vb* **throbbed**; **throb·bing**
**1** to beat hard or fast ⟨our hearts *throbbed* from fright⟩
**2** to beat or rotate in a normal way ⟨the motor *throbbed* quietly⟩
[2]**throb** *n*
[2]BEAT 2, PULSE
**throne** \'thrōn\ *n*
**1** ▶ the chair of state especially of a monarch or bishop
**2** royal power and dignity
[1]**throng** \'thrȯng\ *n*
a large group of assembled persons : CROWD
[2]**throng** *vb*
[1]CROWD 4
[1]**throt·tle** \'thrät-l\ *vb* **throt·tled**; **throt·tling**
**1** STRANGLE 1, CHOKE
**2** to reduce the speed of (an engine) by closing the throttle

[2]**throttle** *n*
**1** a valve for regulating the flow of steam or fuel in an engine
**2** a lever that controls the throttle valve
[1]**through** \thrü\ *prep*
**1** into at one side and out at the other side of ⟨drove a nail *through* the wood⟩
**2** by way of ⟨got in *through* the window⟩
**3** AMONG 1 ⟨a path *through* the trees⟩
**4** by means of ⟨succeeded *through* hard work⟩
**5** over the whole of ⟨the rumor swept *through* school⟩
**6** during the whole of ⟨slept *through* the night⟩
[2]**through** \'thrü\ *adv*
**1** from one end or side to the other ⟨the arm was pierced *through*⟩
**2** from beginning to end ⟨read the book *through* in one evening⟩
**3** to completion ⟨see the job *through*⟩
**4** in or to every part ⟨was wet *through*⟩
**5** into the open ⟨break *through*⟩
[3]**through** \'thrü\ *adj*
**1** allowing free or continuous passage : DIRECT ⟨a *through* road⟩
**2** going from point of origin to destination without changes or transfers ⟨*through* trains⟩
**3** coming from and going to points outside a local zone ⟨*through* traffic⟩
**4** having reached an end ⟨we're *through* with the job⟩

**throne 1:** an ancient Egyptian throne

a b c d e f g h i j k l m n o p q r s t u v w x y z

A B C D E F G H I J K L M N O P Q R S T U V W X Y Z

**[1]through·out** \thrü-'aüt\ *adv*
**1** EVERYWHERE ⟨of one color *throughout*⟩
**2** from beginning to end ⟨remained loyal *throughout*⟩

**[2]throughout** *prep*
**1** in or to every part of ⟨traveling *throughout* the country⟩
**2** during the whole period of ⟨rained *throughout* the day⟩

**throughway** *variant of* THRUWAY

**throve** *past of* THRIVE

**[1]throw** \'thrō\ *vb* **threw** \'thrü\; **thrown** \'thrōn\; **throw·ing**
**1** to send through the air with a quick forward motion of the arm ⟨*throw* a ball⟩
**2** to send through the air in any way
**3** to cause to fall ⟨the horse *threw* the rider⟩
**4** to put suddenly in a certain position or condition ⟨was *thrown* out of work⟩
**5** to put on or take off in a hurry ⟨*throw* on a coat⟩
**6** to move quickly ⟨*throw* in reinforcements⟩
**7** to move (as a switch) to an open or closed position
**8** to give by way of entertainment ⟨*throw* a party⟩
**throw·er** *n*

---

**Synonyms** THROW, TOSS, and HURL mean to drive something swiftly through space often by a movement of the arm. THROW is the broadest word and can be used of almost any motion and driving force ⟨*threw* their caps in the air⟩ ⟨the crash *threw* the driver from the car⟩. TOSS suggests a light or careless throwing ⟨*toss* a coin to see which side comes up⟩ ⟨*tossed* the paper into the wastebasket⟩. HURL suggests a throwing with strong force ⟨the angry mob *hurled* rocks at the police⟩.

---

**[2]throw** *n*
**1** an act of throwing
**2** the distance something is or may be thrown

**throw up** *vb*
[2]VOMIT

**thrum** \'thrəm\ *vb* **thrummed**; **thrum·ming**
to play a stringed instrument idly
**:** STRUM

**thrush** \'thrəsh\ *n*
any of numerous songbirds that eat insects and are usually of a plain color but sometimes spotted below

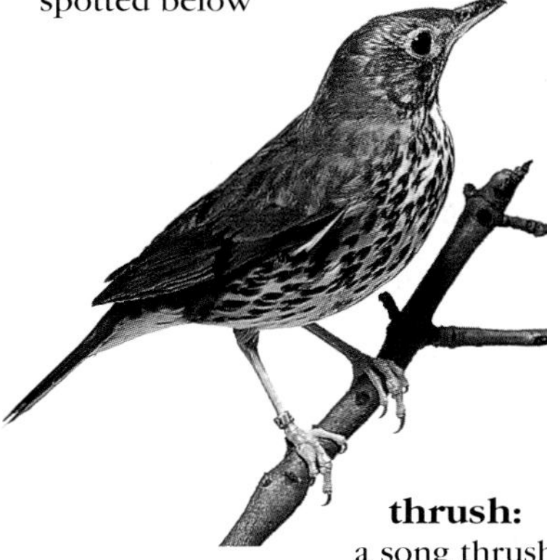

**thrush:** a song thrush

**[1]thrust** \'thrəst\ *vb* **thrust**; **thrust·ing**
**1** to push or drive with force **:** SHOVE
**2** PIERCE 1, STAB
**3** to push forth **:** EXTEND
**4** to press the acceptance of on someone ⟨always *thrusting* new jobs on me⟩

**[2]thrust** *n*
**1** a lunge with a pointed weapon
**2** a military attack
**3** a forward or upward push

**thru·way** *or* **through·way** \'thrü-ˌwā\ *n*
EXPRESSWAY

**[1]thud** \'thəd\ *n*
a dull sound **:** THUMP

**[2]thud** *vb* **thud·ded**; **thud·ding**
to move or strike so as to make a dull sound

**thug** \'thəg\ *n*
RUFFIAN

---

**Word History** In a language of India there is a word that means "thief." This word was used for the members of a certain gang of thieves who strangled the people they robbed. The English word *thug* was taken from the Indian word meaning "thief" and was first used for these vicious Indian thieves.

---

**[1]thumb** \'thəm\ *n*
**1** the short thick finger next to the forefinger
**2** the part of a glove covering the thumb

**[2]thumb** *vb*
**1** to turn the pages of quickly with the thumb
**2** to seek or get (a ride) in a passing automobile by signaling with the thumb

**thumb·tack** \'thəm-ˌtak\ *n*
a tack with a broad flat head for pressing into a board or wall with the thumb

**[1]thump** \'thəmp\ *vb*
**1** to strike or beat with something thick or heavy so as to cause a dull sound
**2** [3]POUND 2, KNOCK

**[2]thump** *n*
**1** a blow with something blunt or heavy
**2** the sound made by a thump

**[1]thun·der** \'thən-dər\ *n*
**1** the loud sound that follows a flash of lightning
**2** a noise like thunder

**[2]thunder** *vb*
**1** to produce thunder
**2** to make a sound like thunder
**3** [1]ROAR 1, SHOUT ⟨*thundered* their approval⟩

**thun·der·bolt** \'thən-dər-ˌbōlt\ *n*
a flash of lightning and the thunder that follows it

**thun·der·cloud** \'thən-dər-ˌklaüd\ *n*
a dark storm cloud that produces lightning and thunder

**thun·der·head** \'thən-dər-ˌhed\ *n*
a rounded mass of dark cloud with white edges often appearing before a thunderstorm

**thun·der·show·er** \'thən-dər-ˌshauər\ *n*
a shower with thunder and lightning

**thun·der·storm** \'thən-dər-ˌstörm\ *n*
a storm with thunder and lightning

**thun·der·struck** \'thən-dər-ˌstrək\ *adj*
stunned as if struck by a thunderbolt

**Thurs·day** \'thərz-dē\ *n*
the fifth day of the week

**thus** \'thəs\ *adv*
**1** in this or that way
**2** to this degree or extent **:** SO ⟨a mild winter *thus* far⟩
**3** because of this or that **:** THEREFORE

**thwart** \'thwȯrt\ *vb*
to oppose successfully

**thy** \t͟hī\ *adj, singular, archaic*
YOUR ⟨"I love *thy* rocks and rills"⟩

**thyme** \'tīm\ *n*
▶ a mint with tiny fragrant leaves used to season foods or formerly in medicine

**thy·roid** \'thī-,rȯid\ *n*
an endocrine gland at the base of the neck that produces a secretion which affects growth, development, and metabolism

**thy·self** \t͟hī-'self\ *pron, archaic*
YOURSELF ⟨"good Romeo, hide *thyself*"⟩

**ti** \'tē\ *n*
the seventh note of the musical scale

**¹tick** \'tik\ *n*
**1** an animal with eight legs that is related to the spiders and attaches itself to humans and animals from which it sucks blood
**2** a wingless fly that sucks blood from sheep

**²tick** *n*
**1** a light rhythmic tap or beat (as of a clock)
**2** a small mark used chiefly to draw attention to something or to check an item on a list

**³tick** *vb*
**1** to make a tick or a series of ticks ⟨a *ticking* clock⟩
**2** to mark, count, or announce by or as if by ticks ⟨a meter *ticking* off the cab fare⟩
**3** OPERATE 1, RUN ⟨tried to understand what makes them *tick*⟩
**4** ²CHECK 4 ⟨*ticked* off each item in the list⟩

**¹tick·et** \'tik-ət\ *n*
**1** a summons or warning issued to a person who breaks a traffic law
**2** a document or token showing that a fare or an admission fee has been paid
**3** a list of candidates for nomination or election
**4** a slip or card recording a sale or giving information

**²ticket** *vb*
**1** to attach a ticket to : LABEL
**2** to give a traffic ticket to

**ticket office** *n*
an office (as of a transportation company or a theater) where tickets are sold and reservations made

**thyme**

**¹tick·le** \'tik-əl\ *vb* **tick·led**; **tick·ling**
**1** to have a tingling or prickling sensation ⟨my foot *tickles*⟩
**2** to excite or stir up agreeably
**3** AMUSE 2
**4** to touch (a body part) lightly so as to excite the surface nerves and cause uneasiness, laughter, or jerky movements

**²tickle** *n*
a tickling sensation

**tick·lish** \'tik-lish\ *adj*
**1** sensitive to tickling
**2** calling for careful handling ⟨a *ticklish* situation⟩

**tid·al** \'tīd-l\ *adj*
of or relating to tides : flowing and ebbing like tides

**tidal wave** *n*
**1** a great wave of the sea that sometimes follows an earthquake
**2** an unusual rise of water along a shore due to strong winds

**tid·bit** \'tid-,bit\ *n*
**1** a small tasty piece of food
**2** a pleasing bit (as of news)

**¹tide** \'tīd\ *n*
**1** the rising and falling of the surface of the ocean caused twice daily by the attraction of the sun and the moon ⟨carried away by the *tide*⟩
**2** something that rises and falls like the tides of the sea

---

**Word History** The English word *tide* at first meant "time" or "a space of time." Later the word was used for the space of time between the rising and falling of the sea's surface. Then *tide* came to mean "the rising and falling of the sea." This is the most common meaning of the word today.

---

**²tide** *vb* **tid·ed**; **tid·ing**
to help to overcome or put up with a difficulty ⟨a loan to *tide* them over⟩

**tide pool** *n*
a pool of salt water left behind when the tide goes out

**tid·ings** \'tīd-ingz\ *n pl*
NEWS 3

**¹ti·dy** \'tīd-ē\ *adj* **ti·di·er**; **ti·di·est**
**1** well ordered and cared for : NEAT
**2** LARGE, SUBSTANTIAL ⟨a *tidy* sum⟩
**synonyms** see NEAT
**ti·di·ness** *n*

---

**Word History** The English word *tidy* comes from the English word *tide*. *Tide* first meant "time," and *tidy* first meant "timely, at the proper time." Soon *tidy* came to mean "in good condition." The current meaning "neat" developed from this sense.

---

**²tidy** *vb* **ti·died**; **ti·dy·ing**
**1** to put in order
**2** to make things tidy ⟨*tidied* up after supper⟩

**¹tie** \'tī\ *n*
**1** a line, ribbon, or cord used for fastening, joining, or closing
**2** a part (as a beam or rod) holding two pieces together
**3** one of the cross supports to which railroad rails are fastened
**4** a connecting link : BOND ⟨family *ties*⟩
**5** an equality in number (as of votes or scores)
**6** a contest that ends with an equal score
**7** NECKTIE

**²tie** *vb* **tied**; **ty·ing** \'tī-ing\ *or* **tie·ing**
**1** to fasten, attach, or close by means of a tie
**2** to form a knot or bow in ⟨*tie* your necktie⟩
**3** to bring together firmly : UNITE
**4** to hold back from freedom of action
**5** to make or have an equal score with in a contest

**tier** \'tir\ *n*
a row, rank, or layer usually arranged in a series one above the other

**ti·ger** \'tī-gər\ *n*
▼ a large Asian flesh-eating animal of the cat family that is light brown with black stripes

tiger

**¹tight** \'tīt\ *adj*
**1** so close in structure as not to allow a liquid or gas to pass through ⟨a *tight* roof⟩
**2** fixed or held very firmly in place ⟨a *tight* jar cover⟩
**3** firmly stretched or drawn : TAUT ⟨a *tight* rope⟩
**4** fitting too closely ⟨*tight* shoes⟩
**5** difficult to get through or out of ⟨in a *tight* spot⟩
**6** firm in control ⟨keeps a *tight* hand on affairs⟩
**7** STINGY 1
**8** very closely packed or compressed ⟨a *tight* bundle⟩
**9** low in supply : SCARCE ⟨money is *tight*⟩
**tight·ly** *adv*
**tight·ness** *n*

**²tight** *adv*
**1** in a firm, secure, or close manner ⟨shut the door *tight*⟩ ⟨hold on *tight*⟩
**2** in a deep and uninterrupted manner : SOUNDLY ⟨sleep *tight*⟩

**tight·en** \'tīt-n\ *vb*
to make or become tight

**tight·rope** \'tīt-,rōp\ *n*
a rope or wire stretched tight on which an acrobat performs

**tights** \'tīts\ *n pl*
a garment closely fitted to the body and covering it usually from the waist down

**tight squeeze** *n*
a difficult situation that one can barely get through

**tight·wad** \'tīt-,wäd\ *n*
a stingy person

**ti·gress** \'tī-grəs\ *n*
a female tiger

**til·de** \'til-də\ *n*
a mark ˜ placed especially over the letter *n* (as in Spanish *señor*) to indicate a sound that is approximately \nyə\

**¹tile** \'tīl\ *n*
**1** a thin piece of material (as plastic, stone, concrete, or rubber) used especially for roofs, walls, floors, or drains
**2** a pipe of earthenware used for a drain

**²tile** *vb* **tiled**; **til·ing**
to cover with tiles

**¹till** \'til\ *prep or conj*
UNTIL ⟨won't finish *till* next week⟩

**²till** *vb*
to work by plowing, sowing, and raising crops on ⟨*till* the fields⟩

**³till** *n*
a drawer for money

**till·age** \'til-ij\ *n*
cultivated land

**til·ler** \'til-ər\ *n*
▶ a lever used to turn the rudder of a boat from side to side

**¹tilt** \'tilt\ *n*
**1** a contest on horseback in which two opponents charging with lances try to unhorse one another : JOUST
**2** ¹SPEED 2 ⟨going at full *tilt*⟩
**3** ¹SLANT

**²tilt** *vb*
**1** to move or shift so as to slant or tip ⟨*tilt* a ladder against a wall⟩
**2** to take part in a contest with lances : JOUST

**tim·ber** \'tim-bər\ *n*
**1** wood suitable for building or for carpentry
**2** a large squared piece of wood ready for use or forming part of a structure

**tim·ber·land** \'tim-bər-,land\ *n*
wooded land especially as a source of timber

**tim·ber·line** \'tim-bər-,līn\ *n*
the upper limit beyond which trees do not grow (as on mountains)

**¹time** \'tīm\ *n*
**1** a period during which an action, process, or condition exists or continues
**2** part of the day when one is free to do as one pleases ⟨found *time* to read⟩
**3** a point or period when something occurs : OCCASION
**4** a set or usual moment or hour for something to occur ⟨arrived on *time*⟩
**5** an historical period : AGE
**6** conditions of a period — usually used in pl. ⟨hard *times*⟩
**7** rate of speed : TEMPO
**8** RHYTHM 2
**9** a moment, hour, day, or year as shown by a clock or calendar
**10** a system of determining time ⟨solar *time*⟩
**11** one of a series of repeated instances or actions ⟨told them many *times*⟩
**12** **times** *pl* multiplied instances ⟨five *times* greater⟩
**13** a person's experience during a certain period ⟨had a good *time*⟩

**tiller** of a sailboat

**at times** SOMETIMES
**for the time being** for the present
**from time to time** once in a while
**in time**
**1** soon enough
**2** as time goes by
**3** at the correct speed in music
**time after time** over and over again
**time and again** over and over again

[2]**time** *vb* **timed**; **tim·ing**
**1** to arrange or set the time or rate at which something happens
**2** to measure or record the time, length of time, or rate of ⟨*time* a performance⟩
**tim·er** *n*

**time capsule** *n*
a container holding records or objects representative of a current culture that is put in a safe place for discovery in the future

**time·keep·er** \'tīm-ˌkē-pər\ *n*
**1** a clerk who keeps records of the time worked by employees
**2** an official who keeps track of the playing time in a sports contest

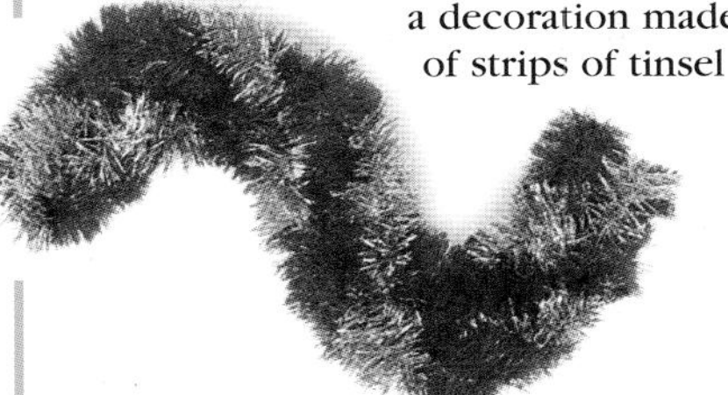
**tinsel 1:** a decoration made of strips of tinsel

**time·less** \'tīm-ləs\ *adj*
not restricted to a certain time or date ⟨a *timeless* theme of friendship⟩

**time·ly** \'tīm-lē\ *adj* **time·li·er**; **time·li·est**
**1** coming early or at the right time
**2** especially suitable to the time

**time·piece** \'tīm-ˌpēs\ *n*
a device (as a clock or watch) to measure the passing of time

**times** \tīmz\ *prep*
multiplied by ⟨2 *times* 4 is 8⟩

**time·ta·ble** \'tīm-ˌtā-bəl\ *n*
a table telling when something (as a bus or train) leaves or arrives

**time zone** *n*
a geographic region within which the same standard time is used

**tim·id** \'tim-əd\ *adj*
feeling or showing a lack of courage or self-confidence : SHY
**tim·id·ly** *adv*
**tim·id·ness** *n*

**tim·o·rous** \'tim-ə-rəs\ *adj*
easily frightened : FEARFUL
**tim·o·rous·ly** *adv*

**tin** \'tin\ *n*
**1** a soft bluish white metallic chemical element used chiefly in combination with other metals or as a coating to protect other metals
**2** something (as a can or sheet) made from tinplate

**tin·der** \'tin-dər\ *n*
material that burns easily and can be used as kindling

**tin·foil** \'tin-ˌfȯil\ *n*
a thin metal sheeting usually of aluminum or an alloy of tin and lead

[1]**tin·gle** \'ting-gəl\ *vb* **tin·gled**; **tin·gling**
to feel or cause a prickling or thrilling sensation

[2]**tingle** *n*
a tingling sensation or condition

**tin·ker** \'ting-kər\ *vb*
to repair or adjust something in an unskilled or experimental manner

[1]**tin·kle** \'ting-kəl\ *vb* **tin·kled**; **tin·kling**
to make or cause to make short high ringing or clinking sounds

[2]**tinkle** *n*
a sound of tinkling

**tin·plate** \'tin-'plāt\ *n*
thin steel sheets covered with tin

**tin·sel** \'tin-səl\ *n*
**1** ◀ a thread, strip, or sheet of metal, paper, or plastic used to produce a glittering effect
**2** something that seems attractive but is of little worth

**tin·smith** \'tin-ˌsmith\ *n*
a worker in tin or sometimes other metals

[1]**tint** \'tint\ *n*
**1** a slight or pale coloring
**2** a shade of a color

[2]**tint** *vb*
to give a tint to : COLOR

**ti·ny** \'tī-nē\ *adj* **ti·ni·er**; **ti·ni·est**
very small

[1]**tip** \'tip\ *vb* **tipped**; **tip·ping**
**1** to turn over
**2** to bend from a straight position : SLANT
**3** to raise and tilt forward

[2]**tip** *vb* **tipped**; **tip·ping**
**1** to attach an end or point to
**2** to cover or decorate the tip of

[3]**tip** *n*
**1** the usually pointed end of something
**2** a small piece or part serving as an end, cap, or point

[4]**tip** *n*
a piece of useful or secret information

[5]**tip** *vb* **tipped**; **tip·ping**
to give a small sum of money for a service ⟨*tipped* the waiter⟩

[6]**tip** *n*
a small sum of money given for a service

[1]**tip·toe** \'tip-ˌtō\ *n*
▼ the position of being balanced on the balls of the feet and toes with the heels raised — usually used with *on* ⟨walking on *tiptoe*⟩

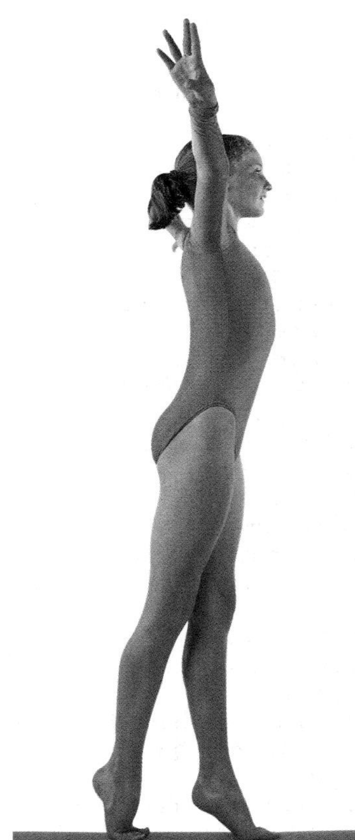
[1]**tiptoe:** a gymnast balancing on tiptoe

[2]**tiptoe** *adv or adj*
on or as if on tiptoe ⟨walked *tiptoe* past the dog⟩

[3]**tiptoe** *vb* **tip·toed**; **tip·toe·ing**
to walk tiptoe

a b c d e f g h i j k l m n o p q r s t u v w x y z

## toad

Toads are carnivorous amphibians that live throughout most of the world, mainly on land, although they do move to streams, ponds, and rivers during the breeding season. Toads have dry warty skin, squat bodies, short stout legs, and less webbing on their feet than frogs.

**cane toad** was introduced to Australia from South America, and has become a pest

**green toad** flattens itself to the ground when threatened

**red-spotted toad** lives at high altitudes in the mountains of Chile

[1]**tip·top** \'tip-'täp\ *n*
the highest point

[2]**tiptop** *adj*
EXCELLENT, FIRST-RATE

[1]**tire** \'tīr\ *vb* **tired**; **tir·ing**
**1** to make or become weary
**2** to wear out the patience or attention of : BORE

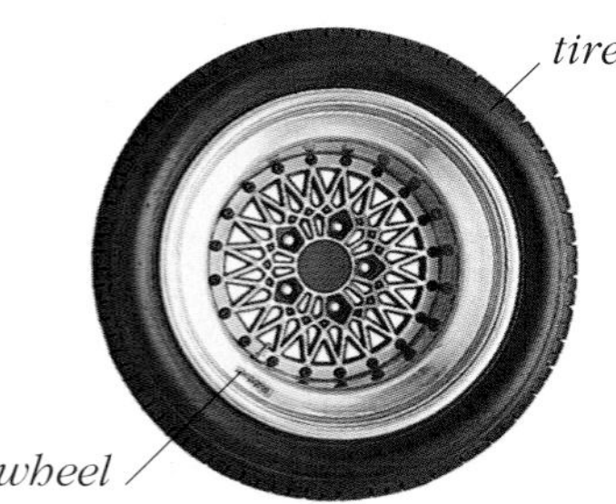


[2]**tire 2:**
an automobile tire

[2]**tire** *n*
**1** a metal band that forms the tread of a wheel
**2** ▲ a rubber cushion that usually contains compressed air and fits around a wheel (as of an automobile)

**tired** \'tīrd\ *adj*
[1]WEARY 1

**tire·less** \'tīr-ləs\ *adj*
able to work a long time without becoming tired
**tire·less·ly** *adv*
**tire·less·ness** *n*

**tire·some** \'tīr-səm\ *adj*
likely to tire one because of length or dullness : BORING
**tire·some·ly** *adv*

**'tis** \'tiz\
it is

**tis·sue** \'tish-ü\ *n*
**1** a fine lightweight fabric
**2** a piece of soft absorbent paper
**3** a mass or layer of cells usually of one kind that together with their supporting structures form a basic structural material of an animal or plant body ⟨muscular *tissue*⟩

**tit** \'tit\ *n*
NIPPLE 1, TEAT

**ti·tan·ic** \tī-'tan-ik\ *adj*
enormous in size, force, or power : GIGANTIC

**ti·tle** \'tīt-l\ *n*
**1** a legal right to the ownership of property
**2** the name given to something (as a book, song, or job) to identify or describe it
**3** a word or group of words attached to a person's name to show an honor, rank, or office ⟨mayor and senator are *titles* of office⟩
**4** CHAMPIONSHIP ⟨won the batting *title*⟩

**tit·mouse** \'tit-,maůs\ *n, pl* **tit·mice** \-,mīs\
► any of several small birds that have long tails and are related to the nuthatches

**TNT** \,tē-,en-'tē\ *n*
an explosive used in artillery shells and bombs and in blasting

[1]**to** \tə, tü\ *prep*
**1** in the direction of ⟨walking *to* school⟩
**2** AGAINST 3, ON ⟨apply salve *to* a burn⟩
**3** as far as ⟨from the top *to* the bottom⟩
**4** so as to become or bring about ⟨broken *to* pieces⟩
**5** [2]BEFORE 3 ⟨it's ten *to* six⟩
**6** [1]UNTIL ⟨from May *to* December⟩
**7** fitting or being a part of ⟨a key *to* the lock⟩
**8** along with ⟨skip *to* the music⟩
**9** in relation to or comparison with ⟨similar *to* that one⟩ ⟨won ten *to* six⟩
**10** in agreement with ⟨made *to* order⟩
**11** within the limits of ⟨*to* my knowledge⟩
**12** contained, occurring, or included in ⟨two pints *to* a quart⟩
**13** TOWARD 3 ⟨our attitude *to* our friends⟩
**14** used to show the one or ones that an action is directed toward ⟨spoke *to* my parents⟩ ⟨gave it *to* them⟩
**15** for no one except ⟨had the room *to* ourselves⟩
**16** into the action of ⟨we got *to* talking⟩
**17** used to mark an infinitive ⟨I like *to* swim⟩

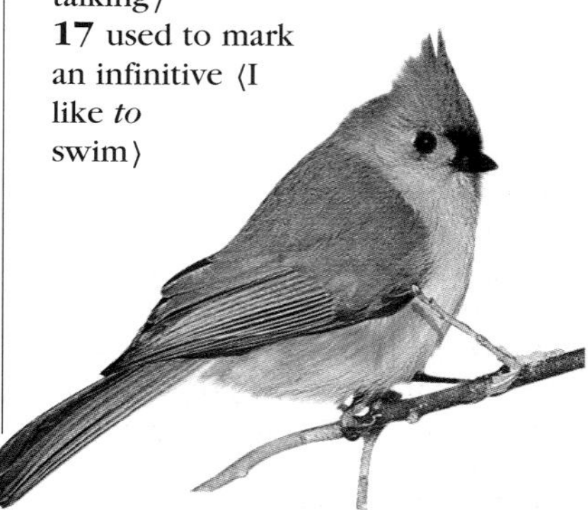

**titmouse**

[2]**to** \'tü\ *adv*
**1** in a direction toward ⟨run *to* and fro⟩
**2** to a conscious state ⟨came *to* an hour after the accident⟩

**toad** \'tōd\ *n*
◄ a tailless leaping amphibian that has rough skin and usually lives on land

**toad·stool** \'tōd-ˌstül\ *n*
a mushroom especially when poisonous or unfit for food

[1]**toast** \'tōst\ *vb*
**1** to make (as bread) crisp, hot, and brown by heat
**2** to warm completely

[2]**toast** *n*
**1** sliced toasted bread
**2** a person in whose honor other people drink
**3** a highly admired person ⟨the *toast* of the town⟩
**4** an act of drinking in honor of a person

[3]**toast** *vb*
to suggest or drink to as a toast

**toast·er** \'tō-stər\ *n*
an electrical appliance for toasting

**tobacco**

**to·bac·co** \tə-'bak-ō\ *n, pl* **to·bac·cos**
▲ a tall plant related to the tomato and potato that has pink or white flowers and broad sticky leaves which are dried and prepared for use in smoking or chewing or as snuff

[1]**to·bog·gan** \tə-'bäg-ən\ *n*
a long light sled made without runners and curved up at the front

[2]**toboggan** *vb*
to slide on a toboggan

[1]**to·day** \tə-'dā\ *adv*
**1** on or for this day
**2** at the present time

[2]**today** *n*
the present day, time, or age

**tod·dler** \'täd-lər\ *n*
a small child

[1]**toe** \'tō\ *n*
**1** one of the separate parts of the front end of a foot
**2** the front end or part of a foot or hoof
**toed** \'tōd\ *adj*

[2]**toe** *vb* **toed**; **toe·ing**
to touch, reach, or kick with the toes

**toe·nail** \'tō-ˌnāl\ *n*
the hard covering at the end of a toe

**to·fu** \'tō-fü\ *n*
a soft food product prepared from soybeans

**to·ga** \'tō-gə\ *n*
► the loose outer garment worn in public by citizens of ancient Rome

**to·geth·er** \tə-'geth-ər\ *adv*
**1** in or into one group, body, or place ⟨gathered *together*⟩
**2** in touch or in partnership with ⟨in business *together*⟩
**3** at one time ⟨they all cheered *together*⟩
**4** one after the other **:** in order ⟨for days *together*⟩
**5** in or by combined effort ⟨worked *together* to win⟩
**6** in or into agreement ⟨get *together* on a plan⟩
**7** considered as a whole ⟨gave more than all the others *together*⟩

[1]**toil** \'tȯil\ *n*
long hard labor

**Word History** To get olive oil you must crush olives. Even in ancient times there were machines for crushing olives. The Latin word for such a machine came from a Latin word that meant "hammer." The Romans made a verb from the word for a machine that crushed olives. This Latin verb meant "to crush." From this Latin verb came an Old French verb that meant "to disturb" or "to argue." The French formed a noun from this verb. This Old French noun meant "confusion" or "battle." An early English noun meaning "battle" or "struggle" came from this Old French noun. Our modern English noun *toil* developed from this early English noun.

**toga:** a man dressed in a toga

[2]**toil** *vb*
**1** to work hard and long
**2** to go on with effort ⟨*toiling* up a steep hill⟩

**toi·let** \'tȯi-lət\ *n*
**1** the act or process of dressing and making oneself neat
**2** BATHROOM
**3** a device for removing body wastes consisting essentially of a bowl that is flushed with water

**to·ken** \'tō-kən\ *n*
**1** an outer sign **:** PROOF ⟨a *token* of friendship⟩
**2** an object used to suggest something that cannot be pictured
**3** SOUVENIR
**4** INDICATION 2
**5** a piece like a coin that has a special use ⟨a bus *token*⟩
**synonyms** see EMBLEM

**told** *past of* TELL

**tol·er·a·ble** \'täl-ə-rə-bəl\ *adj*
**1** capable of being put up with
**2** fairly good ⟨*tolerable* weather⟩
**tol·er·a·bly** \-blē\ *adv*

**tol·er·ance** \'täl-ə-rəns\ *n*
**1** ability to put up with something harmful or bad
**2** sympathy for or acceptance of feelings or habits which are different from one's own

**tol·er·ant** \'täl-ə-rənt\ *adj*
showing tolerance
**tol·er·ant·ly** *adv*

**tol·er·ate** \'täl-ə-,rāt\ *vb* **tol·er·at·ed**; **tol·er·at·ing**
**1** to allow something to be or to be done without making a move to stop it
**2** to stand the action of ⟨*tolerate* a drug⟩

[1]**toll** \'tōl\ *n*
**1** a tax paid for a privilege (as the use of a highway or bridge)
**2** a charge paid for a service
**3** the cost in life or health

[2]**toll** *vb*
**1** to announce or call by the sounding of a bell
**2** to sound with slow strokes

[3]**toll** *n*
the sound of a bell ringing slowly

[1]**tom·a·hawk** \'täm-i-,hȯk\ *n*
▶ a light ax used as a weapon by North American Indians

[2]**tomahawk** *vb*
to cut, strike, or kill with a tomahawk

[1]**tomahawk:** a ceremonial tomahawk

**to·ma·to** \tə-'māt-ō, -'mät-\ *n*, *pl* **to·ma·toes**
a red or yellow juicy fruit that is used as a vegetable or in salads and is produced by a hairy plant related to the potato

**tomb** \'tüm\ *n*
**1** [1]GRAVE
**2** a house or burial chamber for dead people

**tom·boy** \'täm-,bȯi\ *n*
a girl who enjoys things that some people think are more suited to boys

**tomb·stone** \'tüm-,stōn\ *n*
GRAVESTONE

**tom·cat** \'täm-,kat\ *n*
a male cat

[1]**to·mor·row** \tə-'mär-ō\ *adv*
on or for the day after today

[2]**tomorrow** *n*
the day after today

**tom–tom** \'täm-,täm\ *n*
**1** a drum (as a traditional Asian, African or American Indian drum) that is beaten with the hands
**2** a deep drum with a low hollow tone that is usually played with soft mallets or drumsticks and is often part of a drum set in a band

**ton** \'tən\ *n*
a measure of weight equal either to 2000 pounds (about 907 kilograms) (**short ton**) or 2240 pounds (about 1016 kilograms) (**long ton**) with the short ton being more frequently used in the United States and Canada

[1]**tone** \'tōn\ *n*
**1** quality of spoken or musical sound
**2** a sound on one pitch
**3** an individual way of speaking or writing ⟨reply in a friendly *tone*⟩
**4** a shade of color ⟨decorated in soft *tones*⟩
**5** a color that changes another ⟨gray with a blue *tone*⟩
**6** a healthy state of the body or any of its parts
**7** common character or quality

[2]**tone** *vb* **toned**; **ton·ing**
**1** to give tone to : STRENGTHEN ⟨medicine to *tone* up the system⟩
**2** to soften or blend in color, appearance, or sound

**tongs** \'täŋz, 'tȯŋz\ *n pl*
a device for taking hold of something that consists usually of two movable pieces joined at one end

**tongue** \'təŋ\ *n*
**1** ▶ an organ of the mouth used in tasting, in taking and swallowing food, and by human beings in speaking
**2** the power of communication : SPEECH
**3** LANGUAGE 1 ⟨a foreign *tongue*⟩
**4** something like an animal's tongue in being long and fastened at one end

**tongue–tied** \'təŋ-,tīd\ *adj*
unable to speak clearly or freely (as from shyness)

[1]**ton·ic** \'tän-ik\ *adj*
making (as the mind or body) stronger or healthier

[2]**tonic** *n*
**1** a tonic medicine
**2** the first note of a scale

[1]**to·night** \tə-'nīt\ *adv*
on this present night or the night following this present day

[2]**tonight** *n*
the present or the coming night

**ton·nage** \'tən-ij\ *n*
**1** a tax on ships based on tons carried
**2** ships in terms of the total number of tons that are or can be carried
**3** total weight in tons shipped, carried, or mined

**ton·sil** \'tän-səl\ *n*
either of a pair of masses of spongy tissue at the back of the mouth

**ton·sil·li·tis** \,tän-sə-'līt-əs\ *n*
a sore reddened state of the tonsils

**too** \'tü\ *adv*
**1** in addition : ALSO
**2** to a greater than wanted or needed degree ⟨the load was *too* heavy⟩
**3** [2]VERY 1 ⟨the climb was not *too* hard though the hill was steep⟩

**took** *past of* TAKE

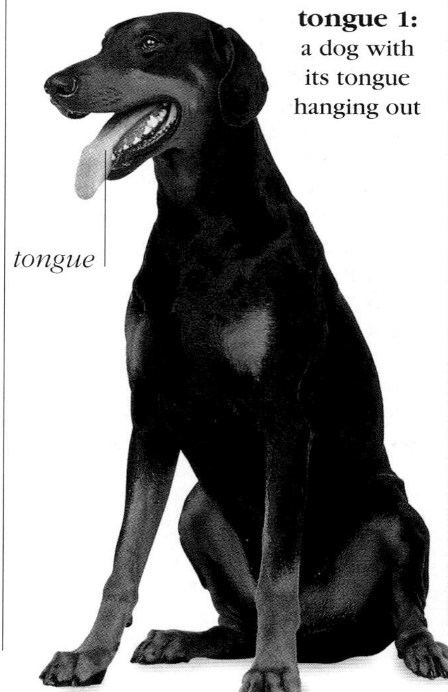


**tongue 1:** a dog with its tongue hanging out

**[1]tool** \'tül\ *n*
**1** ▶ an instrument (as a saw, file, knife, or wrench) used or worked by hand or machine
**2** something that helps to gain an end
**3** a person used by another **:** DUPE
**synonyms** see INSTRUMENT

**[2]tool** *vb*
**1** to shape, form, or finish with a tool
**2** to equip a plant or industry with machines and tools for production

**tool·box** \'tül-,bäks\ *n*
a box for storing or carrying tools

**tool·shed** \'tül-,shed\ *n*
a small building for storing tools

**[1]toot** \'tüt\ *vb*
**1** to sound a short blast
**2** to blow or sound an instrument (as a horn) especially in short blasts

**[2]toot** *n*
a short blast (as on a horn)

**tooth** \'tüth\ *n, pl* **teeth** \'tēth\
**1** one of the hard bony structures set in sockets on the jaws of most vertebrates and used in taking hold of and chewing food and in fighting
**2** something like or suggesting an animal's tooth in shape, arrangement, or action ⟨the *teeth* of a comb⟩
**3** one of the projections around the rim of a wheel that fit between the projections on another part causing the wheel or the other part to move along
**tooth·less** \'tüth-ləs\ *adj*

**tooth·ache** \'tü-,thāk\ *n*
pain in or near a tooth

**tooth·brush** \'tüth-,brəsh\ *n*
▶ a brush for cleaning the teeth
**tooth·brush·ing** \-iŋ\ *n*

**toothed** \'tütht\ *adj*
**1** having teeth or such or so many teeth
**2** JAGGED

**tooth·paste** \'tüth-,pāst\ *n*
a paste for cleaning the teeth

**tooth·pick** \'tüth-,pik\ *n*
a pointed instrument for removing substances caught between the teeth

**toothbrush**

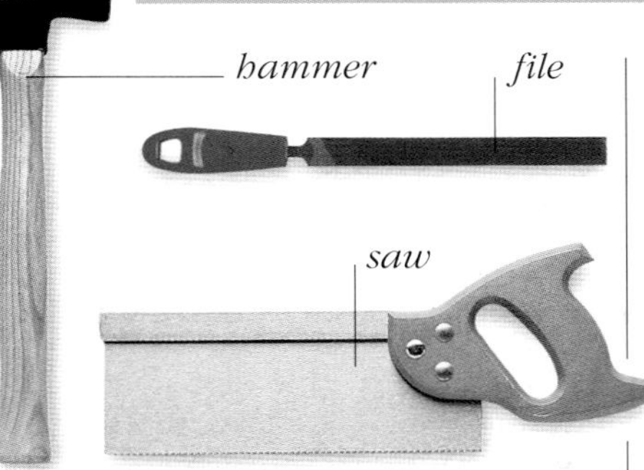


**[1]tool 1:** a selection of carpentry tools

**[1]top** \'täp\ *n*
**1** the highest point, level, or part of something
**2** the upper end, edge, or surface
**3** the stalk and leaves of a plant and especially of one with roots that are used for food ⟨beet *tops*⟩
**4** an upper piece, lid, or covering ⟨put the *top* on the jar⟩
**5** the highest position

**[2]top** *vb* **topped**; **top·ping**
**1** to remove or cut the top of ⟨*top* a tree⟩
**2** to cover with a top or on the top
**3** to be better than
**4** to go over the top of

**[3]top** *adj*
of, relating to, or at the top

**[4]top** *n*
a child's toy with a tapering point on which it can be made to spin

**to·paz** \'tō-,paz\ *n*
a mineral that when occurring as perfect yellow crystals is valued as a gem

**top·coat** \'täp-,kōt\ *n*
a lightweight overcoat

**top·ic** \'täp-ik\ *n*
**1** a heading in an outline of a subject or explanation
**2** the subject or a section of the subject of a speech or writing

**topic sentence** *n*
a sentence that states the main thought of a paragraph

**top·knot** \'täp-,nät\ *n*
a tuft of feathers or hair on the top of the head

**top·mast** \'täp-,mast, -məst\ *n*
the second mast above a ship's deck

**top·most** \'täp-,mōst\ *adj*
highest of all

**top·ple** \'täp-əl\ *vb* **top·pled**; **top·pling**
**1** to fall from being too heavy at the top
**2** to push over

**top·sail** \'täp-,sāl, -səl\ *n*
**1** the sail next above the lowest sail on a mast in a square-rigged ship
**2** the sail above the large sail on a mast in a ship with a fore-and-aft rig

**top·soil** \'täp-,sȯil\ *n*
the rich upper layer of soil in which plants have most of their roots

**top·sy–tur·vy** \,täp-sē-'tər-vē\ *adv or adj*
**1** upside down ⟨the wagon lay *topsy-turvy* at the bottom of the hill⟩
**2** in complete disorder

**torch** \'tȯrch\ *n*
**1** ▼ a flaming light that is made of something which burns brightly and that is usually carried in the hand

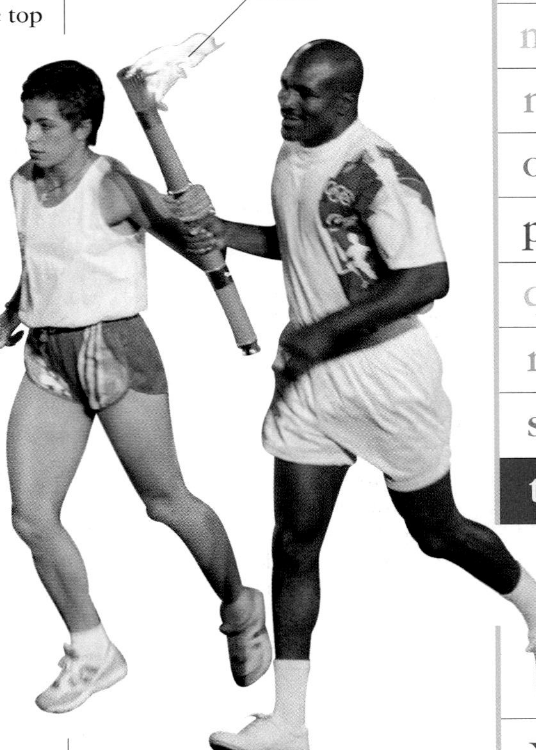


**torch 1:** runners bearing a torch to signal the start of the 1996 Olympic Games in Atlanta

a b c d e f g h i j k l m n o p q r s t x y z

A B C D E F G H I J K L M N O P Q R S T U V W X Y Z

**tortoise 1**
There are about 40 species of tortoise found in warm climates around the world. They can all retract their limbs and heads into their shell for protection from predators. Some species lay as many as 160 eggs at a time.

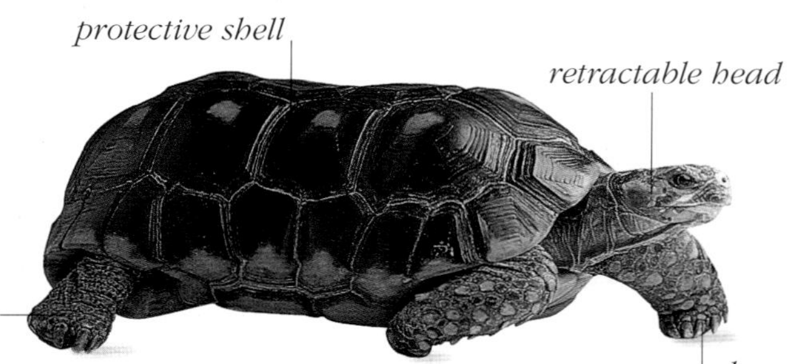


**features of a red-legged tortoise**

hinged section

**hinge-back tortoise** has a hinged rear section that closes for extra protection from predators

**leopard tortoise** is so called because of its spots

**red-eared slider tortoise** is a common pet

2 something that guides or gives light or heat like a torch
3 a portable device for producing a hot flame

**tore** *past of* TEAR

**[1]tor·ment** \'tȯr-ˌment\ *n*
1 extreme pain or distress of body or mind
2 a cause of suffering in mind or body

**[2]tor·ment** \tȯr-'ment\ *vb*
1 to cause severe suffering of body or mind to
2 VEX 1, HARASS

**torn** *past participle of* TEAR

**tor·na·do** \tȯr-'nād-ō\ *n, pl* **tor·na·does** *or* **tor·na·dos**
a violent whirling wind accompanied by a cloud that is shaped like a funnel and moves overland in a narrow path

**[1]tor·pe·do** \tȯr-'pēd-ō\ *n, pl* **tor·pe·does**
a self-propelled underwater weapon shaped like a cigar that is used for blowing up ships

---

**Word History** The English word *torpedo* came from a Latin word that meant "numbness." This Latin word was formed from a Latin word that meant "to be numb." English *torpedo* was first used for a fish that gives an electric shock which can make its victim numb. The explosive device called a *torpedo* was named after the fish. Like a fish, it belongs in water. It can also be said to give a shock to anything it hits.

---

**[2]torpedo** *vb* **tor·pe·doed**; **tor·pe·do·ing**
to hit with or destroy by a torpedo

**tor·pid** \'tȯr-pəd\ *adj*
1 having lost motion or the power of exertion or feeling ⟨a bear *torpid* in winter sleep⟩
2 having too little energy or strength **:** DULL ⟨a *torpid* mind⟩

**tor·rent** \'tȯr-ənt\ *n*
1 a rushing stream of liquid
2 [3]RUSH 1, 2

**tor·rid** \'tȯr-əd\ *adj*
very hot and usually dry

**tor·so** \'tȯr-sō\ *n, pl* **torsos**
the human body except for the head, arms, and legs

**tor·ti·lla** \tȯr-'tē-ə\ *n*
a round flat bread made of corn or wheat flour and usually rolled with a filling and eaten hot

**tor·toise** \'tȯrt-əs\ *n*
1 ▲ any of a family of turtles that live on land
2 TURTLE

**tor·toise·shell** \'tȯrt-əs-ˌshel\ *n*
1 the hornlike covering of the shell of a sea tortoise that is mottled brown and yellow and is used for ornamental objects
2 ▼ any of several brightly colored butterflies

**tortoiseshell 2**

**tor·tu·ous** \'tȯr-chə-wəs\ *adj*
having many twists and turns ⟨a *tortuous* path⟩

**[1]tor·ture** \'tȯr-chər\ *n*
1 the causing of great pain especially to punish or to obtain a confession
2 distress of body or mind

**[2]torture** *vb* **tor·tured**; **tor·tur·ing**
1 to punish or force someone to do or say something by causing great pain

**totem pole** from British Columbia, Canada

**2** to cause great suffering to
**tor·tur·er** *n*

**[1]toss** \'tȯs\ *vb*
**1** to throw or swing to and fro or up and down ⟨waves *tossed* the ship⟩
**2** to throw with a quick light motion
**3** to lift with a sudden motion ⟨the horse *tossed* its head⟩
**4** to be thrown about rapidly ⟨a canoe *tossing* on the waves⟩
**5** to move about restlessly
**6** to stir or mix lightly ⟨*tossed* salad⟩ **synonyms** see THROW

**[2]toss** *n*
an act or instance of tossing

**tot** \'tät\ *n*
a young child

**[1]to·tal** \'tōt-l\ *adj*
**1** of or relating to the whole of something ⟨a *total* eclipse⟩
**2** making up the whole ⟨collected the *total* amount⟩
**3** being such to the fullest degree ⟨*total* ruin⟩
**4** making use of every means to do something ⟨*total* war⟩
**to·tal·ly** *adv*

**[2]total** *n*
**1** a result of addition : SUM
**2** an entire amount

**[3]total** *vb* **to·taled** *or* **to·talled**; **to·tal·ing** *or* **to·tal·ling**
**1** to add up
**2** to amount to : NUMBER

**tote** \'tōt\ *vb* **tot·ed**; **tot·ing**
CARRY 1, HAUL

**to·tem** \'tōt-əm\ *n*
**1** an object (as an animal or plant) serving as the emblem of a family or clan
**2** a carving or picture representing such an object

**totem pole** *n*
◀ a pole or pillar carved and painted with totems and placed before the houses of Indian tribes of the northwest coast of North America

**tot·ter** \'tät-ər\ *vb*
**1** to sway or rock as if about to fall
**2** to move unsteadily : STAGGER

**tou·can** \'tü-ˌkan\ *n*
▶ a brightly colored tropical bird that has a very large beak and feeds on fruit

**[1]touch** \'təch\ *vb*
**1** to feel or handle (as with the fingers) especially so as to be aware of with the sense of touch
**2** to be or cause to be in contact with something
**3** to be or come next to
**4** to hit lightly
**5** [2]HARM ⟨won't dare to *touch* you⟩
**6** to make use of ⟨won't *touch* salt⟩
**7** to refer to in passing
**8** to affect the interest of
**9** to move emotionally ⟨*touched* by your kindness⟩

**[2]touch** *n*
**1** a light stroke or tap
**2** the act or fact of touching or being touched
**3** the special sense by which one is aware of light pressure ⟨soft to the *touch*⟩
**4** an impression gotten through the sense of touch ⟨the soft *touch* of silk⟩
**5** a state of contact or communication ⟨keep in *touch* with friends⟩
**6** a small amount : TRACE

**touch·down** \'təch-ˌdau̇n\ *n*
a score made in football by carrying or catching the ball over the opponent's goal line

**touch·ing** \'təch-ing\ *adj*
causing a feeling of tenderness or pity

**touch pad** *n*
a flat surface on an electronic device (as a microwave oven) divided into several differently marked areas that are touched to make choices in controlling the device

**touch screen** *n*
a display screen (as for a computer) on which the user selects options by touching the screen

**touch–tone** \'təch-'tōn\ *adj*
relating to or being a telephone with push buttons that produce tones corresponding to the numbers

**touch up** *vb*
to improve by or as if by small changes

**touchy** \'təch-ē\ *adj* **touch·i·er**; **touch·i·est**
**1** easily hurt or insulted
**2** calling for tact or careful handling ⟨a *touchy* subject⟩

beak

**toucan**

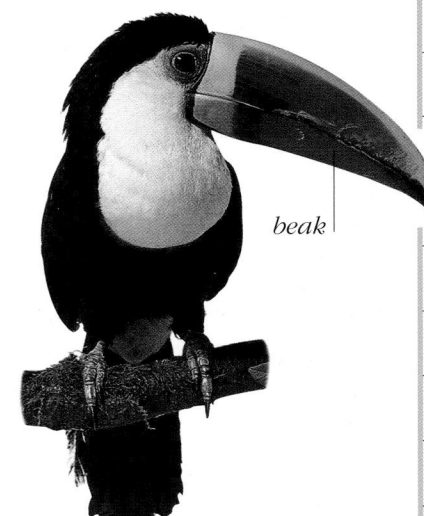

**[1]tough** \'təf\ *adj*
**1** strong or firm but flexible and not brittle ⟨*tough* fibers⟩
**2** not easily chewed ⟨*tough* meat⟩
**3** able to put up with strain or hardship
**4** STUBBORN 1
**5** very difficult ⟨a *tough* problem⟩
**6** LAWLESS 2 ⟨a *tough* neighborhood⟩ **synonyms** see STRONG
**tough·ness** *n*

**[2]tough** *n*
[2]ROWDY, RUFFIAN

A B C D E F G H I J K L M N O P Q R S T U V W X Y Z

**tough·en** \'təf-ən\ *vb*
to make or become tough

**[1]tour** \'tu̇r\ *n*
**1** a fixed period of duty
**2** a trip usually ending at the point where it started ⟨a *tour* of the city⟩
**synonyms** see JOURNEY

**[2]tour** *vb*
to make a tour of **:** travel as a tourist

**tour·ist** \'tu̇r-ist\ *n*
a person who travels for pleasure

**tour·na·ment** \'tu̇r-nə-mənt\ *n*
**1** a contest of skill and courage between knights wearing armor and fighting with blunted lances or swords
**2** a series of contests played for a championship

**tour·ni·quet** \'tu̇r-ni-kət\ *n*
a device (as a bandage twisted tight) for stopping bleeding or blood flow

**tou·sle** \'tau̇-zəl\ *vb* **tou·sled**; **tou·sling**
to put into disorder by rough handling ⟨*tousled* my hair⟩

**[1]tow** \'tō\ *vb*
to draw or pull along behind

**[2]tow** *n*
**1** a rope or chain for towing
**2** an act or instance of towing **:** the fact or state of being towed
**3** something (as a barge) that is towed

**[3]tow** *n*
short broken fiber of flax, hemp, or jute used for yarn, twine, or stuffing

**to·ward** \'tō-ərd, tə-'wȯrd\ *or* **to·wards** \'tō-ərdz, tə-'wȯrdz\ *prep*
**1** in the direction of ⟨heading *toward* town⟩
**2** along a course leading to ⟨efforts *toward* peace⟩
**3** in regard to ⟨attitude *toward* life⟩
**4** so as to face ⟨their backs were *toward* me⟩
**5** [2]NEAR ⟨awoke *toward* morning⟩
**6** as part of the payment for ⟨$1000 *toward* a new car⟩

**tow·el** \'tau̇-əl\ *n*
a cloth or piece of absorbent paper for wiping or drying

**[1]tow·er** \'tau̇-ər\ *n*
**1** ▶ a building or structure that is higher than its length or width, is high with respect to its surroundings, and may stand by itself or be attached to a larger structure
**2** CITADEL 1

**[2]tower** *vb*
to reach or rise to a great height

**tow·er·ing** \'tau̇-ə-ring\ *adj*
**1** rising high **:** TALL
**2** reaching a high point of strength or force ⟨*towering* rage⟩
**3** going beyond proper bounds ⟨*towering* ambition⟩

**tow·head** \'tō-ˌhed\ *n*
a person having soft whitish hair

**town** \'tau̇n\ *n*
**1** a compactly settled area that is usually larger than a village but smaller than a city
**2** CITY 1
**3** the people of a town

**[1]tower 1:** the Eiffel \'ī-fəl\ Tower in Paris, France

**town·ship** \'tau̇n-ˌship\ *n*
**1** a unit of local government in some northeastern and north central states
**2** a division of territory in surveys of United States public lands containing thirty-six square miles (about ninety-three square kilometers)

**tow·path** \'tō-ˌpath, -ˌpȧth\ *n*
a path traveled by people or animals towing boats

**tox·ic** \'täk-sik\ *adj*
of, relating to, or caused by a poison ⟨*toxic* effects⟩

**Word History** Sometimes people put poison on the points of arrows. Even a slight wound from such an arrow can be fatal. The ancient Greeks had a word for the poison used on arrows. A Latin word that meant "poison" came from the Greek word that meant "arrow poison." The English word *toxic* comes from this Latin word.

**tox·in** \'täk-sən\ *n*
a poison produced by an animal, a plant, or germs

**[1]toy** \'tȯi\ *n*
**1** something of little or no value
**2** something for a child to play with
**3** something small of its kind

**[2]toy** *vb*
to amuse oneself as if with a toy

**[1]trace** \'trās\ *n*
**1** a mark left by something that has passed or is past
**2** a very small amount

**[2]trace** *vb* **traced**; **trac·ing**
**1** [2]SKETCH 1
**2** to form (as letters) carefully
**3** to copy (as a drawing) by following the lines or letters as seen through a transparent sheet placed over the thing copied
**4** to follow the footprints, track, or trail of
**5** to study or follow the development and progress of in detail
**trac·er** *n*

**[3]trace** *n*
either of the two straps, chains, or ropes of a harness that fasten a horse to a vehicle

**[1]track 7**
Competition in track usually takes place in a stadium, with a central field area for throwing sports such as shot put, long strips for jumping sports such as long jump, and an oval racetrack for running and hurdling sports.

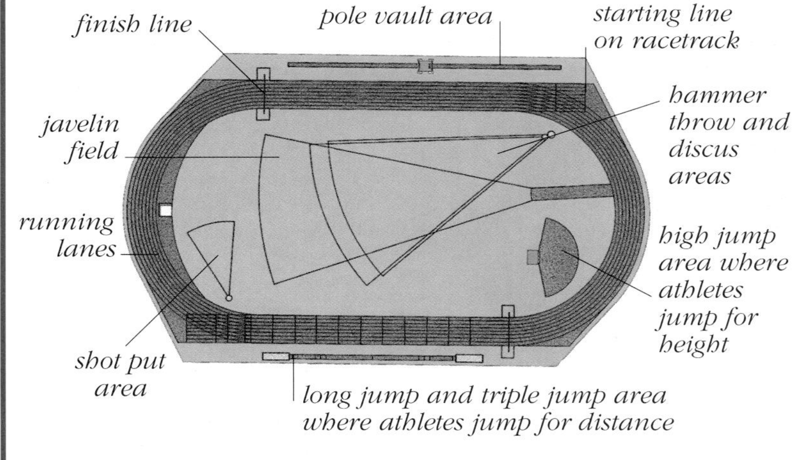


**trace•able** \'trā-sə-bəl\ *adj*
capable of being traced

**tra•chea** \'trā-kē-ə\ *n,* *pl* **tra•che•ae** \-kē-,ē\
**1** WINDPIPE
**2** a breathing tube of an insect

**trac•ing** \'trā-sing\ *n*
**1** the act of a person that traces
**2** something that is traced

**[1]track** \'trak\ *n*
**1** a mark left by something that has gone by ⟨rabbit *tracks*⟩
**2** PATH 1, TRAIL
**3** a course laid out for racing
**4** a way for a vehicle with wheels ⟨railroad *track*⟩
**5** awareness of things or of the order in which things happen or ideas come ⟨lose *track* of time⟩ ⟨keep *track* of expenses⟩
**6** either of two endless metal belts on which a vehicle (as a tank) travels
**7** ▲ track-and-field sports

**[2]track** *vb*
**1** to follow the tracks or traces of
**2** to make tracks on or with

**track–and–field** *adj*
relating to or being sports events (as racing, throwing, and jumping contests) held on an oval running track and on an enclosed field

**[1]tract** \'trakt\ *n*
a pamphlet of political or religious ideas and beliefs

**[2]tract** *n*
**1** an indefinite stretch of land ⟨a large *tract* of forest⟩
**2** a defined area of land ⟨sold off several 40 acre *tracts*⟩
**3** a system of body parts or organs that serve some special purpose ⟨the digestive *tract*⟩

**trac•tor** \'trak-tər\ *n*
**1** ▶ a vehicle that has large rear wheels or moves on endless belts and is used especially for pulling farm implements
**2** a short truck for hauling a trailer

**[1]trade** \'trād\ *n*
**1** the business or work in which a person takes part regularly **:** OCCUPATION
**2** an occupation requiring manual or mechanical skill **:** CRAFT
**3** the persons working in a business or industry
**4** the business of buying and selling items **:** COMMERCE
**5** an act of trading **:** TRANSACTION
**6** a firm's customers

**Synonyms** TRADE, BUSINESS, and PROFESSION mean an occupation requiring skill or training by which one earns a living. TRADE applies chiefly to occupations requiring skilled labor and usually the handling of tools or machines ⟨the *trade* of a carpenter⟩. BUSINESS is used mainly of occupations concerned with the buying or selling of goods and services or of similar occupations such as transportation and finance ⟨the hotel and restaurant *business*⟩. PROFESSION is used of occupations that require a college or university education and much training ⟨the medical *profession*⟩.

**[2]trade** *vb* **trad•ed**; **trad•ing**
**1** to give in exchange for something else
**2** to take part in the exchange, purchase, or sale of goods
**3** to deal regularly as a customer

**trade•mark** \'trād-,märk\ *n*
a device (as a word) that points clearly to the origin or ownership of merchandise to which it is applied and that is legally reserved for use only by the owner

**trad•er** \'trād-ər\ *n*
**1** a person who trades
**2** a ship engaged in trade

**tractor 1**

**trades•man** \'trādz-mən\ *n,* *pl* **trades•men** \-mən\
**1** a person who runs a retail store
**2** CRAFTSMAN 1

**trades•peo•ple** \'trādz-,pē-pəl\ *n pl*
people engaged in trade

**trade wind** *n*
a wind blowing steadily toward the equator from an easterly direction

**trad•ing post** \'trād-ing-\ *n*
a station or store of a trader or trading company set up in a thinly settled region

**tra·di·tion** \trə-'dish-ən\ *n*
**1** the handing down of information, beliefs, or customs from one generation to another
**2** a belief or custom handed down by tradition

**tra·di·tion·al** \trə-'dish-ən-l\ *adj*
**1** handed down from age to age ⟨a *traditional* explanation⟩
**2** based on custom : CONVENTIONAL ⟨the *traditional* Thanksgiving dinner⟩
**tra·di·tion·al·ly** *adv*

[1]**traf·fic** \'traf-ik\ *n*
**1** the business of carrying passengers or goods ⟨the tourist *traffic*⟩
**2** the business of buying and selling : COMMERCE
**3** exchange of information ⟨*traffic* with the enemy⟩
**4** the persons or goods carried by train, boat, or airplane or passing along a road, river, or air route
**5** the movement (as of vehicles) along a route

[2]**traffic** *vb* **traf·ficked**; **traf·fick·ing**
[2]TRADE 2

[1]**train 1:** the train on a dress in early 1900s style

*train*

**traffic light** *n*
a visual signal (as a set of colored lights) for controlling the flow of traffic

**trag·e·dy** \'traj-ə-dē\ *n, pl* **trag·e·dies**
**1** a serious play that has a sorrowful or disastrous ending
**2** a disastrous event

**trag·ic** \'traj-ik\ *adj*
**1** of or relating to tragedy
**2** very unfortunate ⟨a *tragic* end⟩

[1]**trail** \'trāl\ *vb*
**1** to drag or draw along behind ⟨the horse *trailed* its reins⟩
**2** to lag behind
**3** to follow in the tracks of : PURSUE
**4** to hang or let hang so as to touch the ground or float out behind
**5** to become weak, soft, or less ⟨the sound *trailed* off⟩

[2]**trail** *n*
**1** something that trails or is trailed
**2** a trace or mark left by something that has passed or been drawn along
**3** a beaten path
**4** a path marked through a forest or mountainous region

**trail·er** \'trā-lər\ *n*
**1** a vehicle designed to be hauled
**2** a vehicle designed to serve wherever parked as a dwelling or a place of business

[1]**train** \'trān\ *n*
**1** ◀ a part of a gown that trails behind the wearer
**2** the followers of an important person
**3** a moving line of persons, vehicles, or animals ⟨a wagon *train*⟩
**4** a connected series ⟨*train* of thought⟩
**5** a connected series of railway cars usually hauled by a locomotive

[2]**train** *vb*
**1** to direct the growth of (a plant) usually by bending, pruning, and tying
**2** to give or receive instruction, discipline, or drill
**3** to teach in an art, profession, or trade ⟨*train* radio operators⟩
**4** to make ready (as by exercise) for a sport or test of skill
**5** to aim (as a gun) at a target
**synonyms** see TEACH
**train·er** *n*

**train·ing** \'trā-ning\ *n*
**1** the course followed by one who trains or is being trained
**2** the condition of one who has trained for a test or contest ⟨in perfect *training*⟩

**training wheels** *n pl*
a pair of small wheels connected to the rear axle of a bicycle to help a beginning rider keep balance

**trait** \'trāt\ *n*
a quality that sets one person or thing off from another

**trai·tor** \'trāt-ər\ *n*
**1** a person who betrays another's trust or is false to a personal duty
**2** a person who commits treason

**trai·tor·ous** \'trāt-ə-rəs\ *adj*
**1** guilty or capable of treason
**2** amounting to treason ⟨*traitorous* acts⟩ **synonyms** see FAITHLESS
**trai·tor·ous·ly** *adv*

[1]**tramp** \'tramp\ *vb*
**1** to walk heavily
**2** to tread on forcibly and repeatedly
**3** to travel or wander through on foot ⟨*tramp* the woods⟩

[2]**tramp** *n*
**1** a person who wanders from place to place, has no home or job, and often lives by begging or stealing
**2** [2]HIKE
**3** the sounds made by the beat of marching feet

**tram·ple** \'tram-pəl\ *vb* **tram·pled**; **tram·pling**
**1** to tramp or tread heavily so as to bruise, crush, or injure something ⟨*trampled* on the flowers⟩
**2** to crush under the feet ⟨don't *trample* the flowers⟩
**3** to injure or harm by treating harshly and without mercy

**tram·po·line** \,tram-pə-'lēn\ *n*
a canvas sheet or web supported by springs in a metal frame used for springing and landing in acrobatic tumbling

**trance** \'trans\ *n*
**1** STUPOR
**2** a condition like sleep (as deep hypnosis)
**3** a state of being so deeply absorbed in something as not to be aware of one's surroundings

**tran·quil** \'trang-kwəl\ *adj*
very calm and quiet : PEACEFUL ⟨a *tranquil* life⟩ **synonyms** see CALM

**tran·quil·iz·er** \'trang-kwə-,lī-zər\ *n*
a drug used to ease worry and nervous tension

**tran·quil·li·ty** *or* **tran·quil·i·ty** \tran-'kwil-ət-ē\ *n*
the state of being calm : QUIET

**trans-** *prefix*
**1** on or to the other side of : across : beyond ⟨*trans*atlantic⟩
**2** so as to change or transfer

**trans·act** \trans-'akt\ *vb*
to carry on : MANAGE, CONDUCT

**trans·ac·tion** \trans-'ak-shən\ *n*
**1** a business deal
**2 transactions** *pl* the record of the meeting of a club or organization

**trans·at·lan·tic** \ˌtrans-ət-'lant-ik\ *adj*
crossing or being beyond the Atlantic ocean

**tran·scend** \tran-'send\ *vb*
**1** to rise above the limits of
**2** to do better or more than

**trans·con·ti·nen·tal** \ˌtrans-ˌkänt-n-'ent-l\ *adj*
crossing, extending across, or being on the farther side of a continent

**tran·scribe** \tran-'skrīb\ *vb*
**tran·scribed**; **tran·scrib·ing**
to make a copy of

**tran·script** \'tran-ˌskript\ *n*
**1** [1]COPY 1
**2** an official copy of a student's school record

[1]**trans·fer** \trans-'fər\ *vb*
**trans·ferred**; **trans·fer·ring**
**1** to pass or cause to pass from one person, place, or condition to another
**2** to give over the possession or ownership of ⟨*transfer* title to the house to the new owners⟩
**3** to copy (as by printing) from one surface to another by contact
**4** to move to a different place, region, or job
**5** to change from one vehicle or transportation line to another

[2]**trans·fer** \'trans-ˌfər\ *n*
**1** a giving over of right, title, or interest in property by one person to another
**2** an act or process of transferring
**3** someone or something that transfers or is transferred
**4** a ticket allowing a passenger on a bus or train to continue the journey on another route without paying more fare

**trans·fix** \trans-'fiks\ *vb*
to pierce through with or as if with a pointed weapon

**trans·form** \trans-'fȯrm\ *vb*
to change completely ⟨*transform* waterpower into electric power⟩
**trans·form·er** *n*

**trans·for·ma·tion** \ˌtrans-fər-'mā-shən\ *n*
the act or process of transforming : a complete change

**trans·fu·sion** \trans-'fyü-zhən\ *n*
**1** a passing of one thing into another
**2** a transferring (as of blood or salt solution) into a vein of a person or animal

[1]**tran·sient** \'tran-chənt\ *adj*
not lasting or staying long ⟨a *transient* illness⟩

[2]**transient** *n*
a person who is not staying long in a place

**tran·sis·tor** \tran-'zis-tər\ *n*
a small solid electronic device used especially in radios for controlling the flow of electricity

**tran·sit** \'trans-ət, 'tranz-\ *n*
**1** a passing through or across
**2** the act or method of carrying things from one place to another
**3** local transportation of people in public vehicles
**4** a surveyor's instrument for measuring angles

**tran·si·tion** \trans-'ish-ən, tranz-\ *n*
a passing from one state, stage, place, or subject to another : CHANGE

**tran·si·tive** \'trans-ət-iv, 'tranz-\ *adj*
having or containing a direct object ⟨*transitive* verbs⟩

**trans·late** \trans-'lāt\ *vb*
**trans·lat·ed**; **trans·lat·ing**
**1** to change from one state or form to another ⟨*translate* words into action⟩
**2** to turn from one language into another

**trans·la·tion** \trans-'lā-shən\ *n*
the act, process, or result of translating

**trans·lu·cent** \trans-'lüs-nt\ *adj*
not transparent but clear enough to allow rays of light to pass through
**trans·lu·cent·ly** *adv*

**trans·mis·sion** \trans-'mish-ən\ *n*
**1** an act or process of transmitting ⟨the *transmission* of a disease⟩
**2** the gears by which the power is transmitted from the engine to the axle that gives motion to a motor vehicle

**trans·mit** \trans-'mit\ *vb*
**trans·mit·ted**; **trans·mit·ting**
**1** to transfer from one person or place to another
**2** to pass on by or as if by inheritance
**3** to pass or cause to pass through space or through a material ⟨glass *transmits* light⟩
**4** to send out by means of radio waves

**trans·mit·ter** \trans-'mit-ər\ *n*
**1** one that transmits
**2** the instrument in a telegraph system that sends out messages
**3** the part of a telephone that includes the mouthpiece and a device that picks up sound waves and sends them over the wire
**4** the device that sends out radio or television signals

**tran·som** \'tran-səm\ *n*
**1** ▼ a piece that lies crosswise in a structure (as in the frame of a window or of a door that has a window above it)

**transom 1:**
the transom of a doorway

2 a window above a door or another window

**trans·par·en·cy** \trans-ˈpar-ən-sē, -ˈper-\ *n*
the quality or state of being transparent

**trans·par·ent** \trans-ˈpar-ənt, -ˈper-\ *adj*
1 clear enough or thin enough to be seen through
2 easily detected ⟨a *transparent* lie⟩
**trans·par·ent·ly** *adv*

**trans·pi·ra·tion** \ˌtrans-pə-ˈrā-shən\ *n*
an act or instance of transpiring

**trans·pire** \trans-ˈpīr\ *vb*
**trans·pired**; **trans·pir·ing**
1 to give off or pass off in the form of a vapor usually through pores
2 to become known or apparent
3 to come to pass : HAPPEN

**[1]trans·plant** \trans-ˈplant\ *vb*
1 to dig up and plant again in another soil or location ⟨*transplant* seedlings⟩
2 to remove from one place and settle or introduce elsewhere

**[2]trans·plant** \ˈtrans-ˌplant\ *n*
1 something transplanted
2 the process of transplanting

**[1]trans·port** \trans-ˈpōrt\ *vb*
1 to carry from one place to another
2 to fill with delight

**[2]trans·port** \ˈtrans-ˌpōrt\ *n*
1 the act of transporting : TRANSPORTATION
2 a state of great joy or pleasure
3 a ship for carrying soldiers or military equipment
4 a vehicle used to transport persons or goods

**trapezoid**

**trans·por·ta·tion** \ˌtrans-pər-ˈtā-shən\ *n*
1 an act, instance, or means of transporting or being transported
2 public transporting of passengers or goods especially as a business

**trans·pose** \trans-ˈpōz\ *vb*
**trans·posed**; **trans·pos·ing**
1 to change the position or order of ⟨*transpose* the letters in a word⟩
2 to write or perform in a different musical key

**trans·verse** \trans-ˈvərs\ *adj*
lying or being across : placed crosswise
**trans·verse·ly** *adv*

**[1]trap** \ˈtrap\ *n*
1 a device for catching animals
2 something by which one is caught or stopped unawares ⟨set a *trap* for the criminal⟩
3 a light one-horse carriage with springs
4 a device that allows something to pass through but keeps other things out ⟨a *trap* in a drain⟩

**[2]trap** *vb* **trapped**; **trap·ping**
1 to catch in a trap ⟨*trap* game⟩
2 to provide (a place) with traps ⟨*trap* a stream⟩
3 to set traps for animals especially as a business **synonyms** see CATCH
**trap·per** *n*

**trap·door** \ˈtrap-ˈdōr\ *n*
a lifting or sliding door covering an opening in a floor or roof

**tra·peze** \tra-ˈpēz\ *n*
a short horizontal bar hung from two parallel ropes and used by acrobats

**trap·e·zoid** \ˈtrap-ə-ˌzȯid\ *n*
◄ a figure with four sides but with only two sides parallel

**trap·pings** \ˈtrap-ingz\ *n pl*
1 ornamental covering especially for a horse
2 outward decoration or dress

**trash** \ˈtrash\ *n*
1 something of little or no worth
2 low worthless persons

**[1]trav·el** \ˈtrav-əl\ *vb*
**trav·eled** *or* **trav·elled**; **trav·el·ing** *or* **trav·el·ling**
1 to journey from place to place or to a distant place
2 to get around : pass from one place to another ⟨the news *traveled* fast⟩
3 to journey through or over ⟨*travel* the countryside⟩
**trav·el·er** *or* **trav·el·ler** *n*

**Word History** An Old French word that meant "to torture" came from the Latin name of an instrument of torture. In time this Old French word developed milder meanings and came to mean "to trouble" and "to work." Long ago taking a trip was not easy. A journey cost a great deal of work and trouble. The English word *travel* came from the Old French word that meant "to trouble" or "to work."

**[2]travel** *n*
1 the act or a means of traveling ⟨air *travel* is fast⟩
2 [1]JOURNEY, TRIP — often used in pl.
3 the number traveling : TRAFFIC

**traveling bag** *n*
a bag carried by hand and designed to hold a traveler's clothing and personal articles

**tra·verse** \trə-ˈvərs\ *vb*
**tra·versed**; **tra·vers·ing**
to pass through, across, or over

**[1]trawl** \ˈtrȯl\ *vb*
to fish or catch with a trawl

**[2]trawl** *n*
a large net in the shape of a cone dragged along the sea bottom in fishing

**trawl·er** \ˈtrȯ-lər\ *n*
▼ a boat used for trawling

**trawler:**
model of a fishing trawler

**tray** \'trā\ *n*
an open container with a flat bottom and low rim for holding, carrying, or showing articles ⟨a waiter's *tray*⟩

**treach·er·ous** \'trech-ə-rəs\ *adj*
**1** guilty of or likely to commit treachery
**2** not to be trusted ⟨a *treacherous* memory⟩
**3** not safe because of hidden dangers
**treach·er·ous·ly** *adv*

**treach·ery** \'trech-ə-rē\ *n, pl* **treach·er·ies**
**1** a betraying of trust or faith
**2** an act or instance of betraying trust

**¹tread** \'tred\ *vb* **trod** \'träd\; **trod·den** \'träd-n\ *or* **trod**; **tread·ing**
**1** to step or walk on or over
**2** to move on foot : WALK
**3** to beat or press with the feet
**tread water** to keep the body in an up and down position in the water and the head above water by a walking or running motion of the legs helped by moving the hands

**²tread** *n*
**1** a mark made by or as if by treading
**2** the action, manner, or sound of treading
**3** the part of something (as a shoe or tire) that touches a surface
**4** the horizontal part of a step

**trea·dle** \'tred-l\ *n*
a device worked by the foot to drive a machine

**tread·mill** \'tred-,mil\ *n*
**1** ▶ a mill moved by persons treading on steps around the rim of a wheel or by animals walking on an endless belt
**2** a device having an endless belt on which an individual walks or runs in place for exercise
**3** a tiresome routine

**trea·son** \'trēz-n\ *n*
**1** the betraying of a trust
**2** the crime of trying or helping to overthrow the government of one's country or cause its defeat in war

**¹trea·sure** \'trezh-ər\ *n*
**1** wealth (as money or jewels) stored up or held in reserve
**2** something of great value

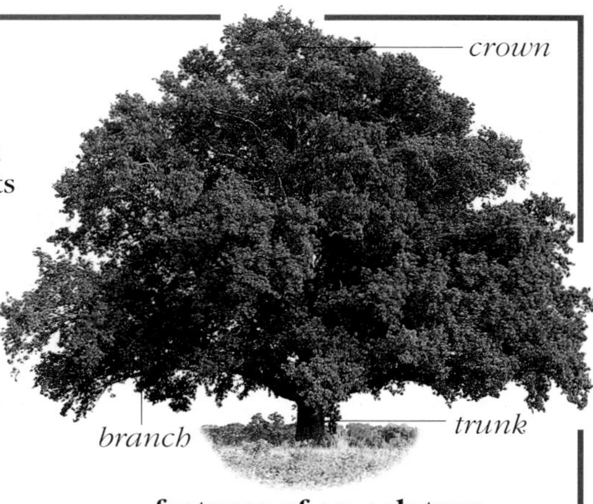


**¹tree 1**
Trees grow in many different environments around the world. Each tree has anchoring roots which pass water and nutrients up the trunk to the branches, to nourish the leaves, flowers, seeds or cones. The tallest trees — sequoias — can grow to a height of more than 360 feet.

**features of an oak tree**

**²treasure** *vb* **trea·sured**; **trea·sur·ing**
to treat as precious : value highly : CHERISH **synonyms** see APPRECIATE

**trea·sur·er** \'trezh-ər-ər\ *n*
a person (as an officer of a club) who has charge of the money

**trea·sury** \'trezh-ə-rē\ *n, pl* **trea·sur·ies**
**1** a place in which stores of wealth are kept
**2** a place where money collected is kept and paid out
**3** *cap* a government department in charge of finances

**treadmill 1:**
a hamster walking in a treadmill

**¹treat** \'trēt\ *vb*
**1** to have as a subject especially in writing
**2** to handle, use, or act toward in a usually stated way ⟨*treat* these flowers gently⟩ ⟨*treat* this as secret⟩
**3** to pay for the food or entertainment of
**4** to give medical or surgical care to : to use a certain medical care on ⟨*treat* a patient for fever⟩ ⟨*treat* cancer with drugs⟩
**5** to expose to some action (as of a chemical) ⟨*treat* soil with lime⟩

**²treat** *n*
**1** an entertainment given without expense to those invited
**2** an often unexpected or unusual source of pleasure or amusement

**treat·ment** \'trēt-mənt\ *n*
**1** the act or manner of treating someone or something
**2** a substance or method used in treating

**trea·ty** \'trēt-ē\ *n, pl* **trea·ties**
an agreement between two or more states or sovereigns

**¹tre·ble** \'treb-əl\ *n*
**1** the highest part in harmony having four parts : SOPRANO 1
**2** an instrument having the highest range or part
**3** a voice or sound that has a high pitch
**4** the upper half of the musical pitch range

**²treble** *adj*
**1** being three times the number or amount
**2** relating to or having the range of a musical treble

**³treble** *vb* **tre·bled**; **tre·bling**
to make or become three times as much

**¹tree** \'trē\ *n*
**1** ▲ a woody plant that lives for years and has a single usually tall main stem with few or no branches on its lower part

**2** a plant of treelike form ⟨a banana *tree*⟩
**3** something suggesting a tree ⟨a clothes *tree*⟩
**tree·less** \-ləs\ *adj*
**tree·like** \-ˌlīk\ *adj*

**²tree** *vb* **treed**; **tree·ing**
to drive to or up a tree

**tree fern** *n*
▼ a tropical fern with a tall woody stalk and a crown of often feathery leaves

**tree fern**

**tree house** *n*
a structure (as a playhouse) built among the branches of a tree

**tre·foil** \'trē-ˌfȯil\ *n*
**1** a clover or related plant having leaves with three leaflets
**2** a fancy design with three leaflike parts

**¹trek** \'trek\ *vb* **trekked**; **trek·king**
to make one's way with difficulty

**²trek** *n*
a slow or difficult journey

**trel·lis** \'trel-əs\ *n*
a frame of lattice used especially as a screen or a support for climbing plants

**¹trem·ble** \'trem-bəl\ *vb* **trem·bled**; **trem·bling**
**1** to shake without control (as from fear or cold) : SHIVER
**2** to move, sound, or happen as if shaken ⟨the building *trembled*⟩ ⟨my voice *trembled*⟩
**3** to have strong fear or doubt

**²tremble** *n*
the act or a period of trembling

**tre·men·dous** \tri-'men-dəs\ *adj*
**1** causing fear or terror : DREADFUL
**2** astonishingly large, strong, or great
**tre·men·dous·ly** *adv*

**trem·or** \'trem-ər\ *n*
**1** a trembling or shaking especially from weakness or disease
**2** a shaking motion of the earth (as during an earthquake)

**trem·u·lous** \'trem-yə-ləs\ *adj*
**1** marked by trembling or shaking ⟨a *tremulous* voice⟩
**2** FEARFUL 2, TIMID

**trench** \'trench\ *n*
a long narrow ditch

**¹trend** \'trend\ *vb*
to have or take a general direction

**²trend** *n*
general direction taken in movement or change ⟨a down *trend* in the stock market⟩ ⟨new *trends* in fashion⟩

**¹tres·pass** \'tres-pəs\ *n*
**1** ¹SIN, OFFENSE
**2** unlawful entry upon someone's land

**²trespass** *vb*
**1** to do wrong : SIN
**2** to enter upon someone's land unlawfully
**tres·pass·er** *n*

**tress** \'tres\ *n*
a long lock of hair

**tres·tle** \'tres-əl\ *n*
**1** a braced frame consisting usually of a horizontal piece with spreading legs at each end that supports something (as the top of a table)
**2** a structure of timbers or steel for supporting a road or railroad over a low place

**T. rex** \tē-'reks\ *n*
TYRANNOSAUR

**tri-** *prefix*
three ⟨*tri*angle⟩

**tri·ad** \'trī-ˌad\ *n*
a chord made up usually of the first, third, and fifth notes of a scale

**tri·al** \'trī-əl\ *n*
**1** the action or process of trying or testing
**2** the hearing and judgment of something in court
**3** a test of faith or of one's ability to continue or stick with something
**4** an experiment to test quality, value, or usefulness
**5** ²ATTEMPT

**tri·an·gle** \'trī-ˌang-gəl\ *n*
**1** a figure that has three sides and three angles
**2** an object that has three sides and three angles ⟨a *triangle* of land⟩
**3** ▼ a musical instrument made of a steel rod bent in the shape of a triangle with one open angle

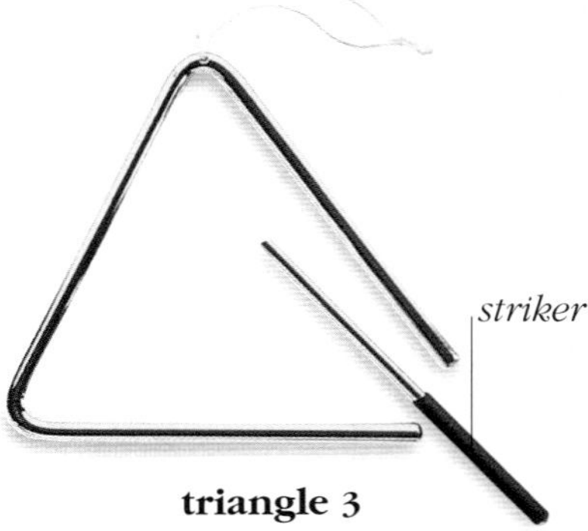


**triangle 3**

**tri·an·gu·lar** \trī-'ang-gyə-lər\ *adj*
**1** of, relating to, or having the form of a triangle
**2** having three angles, sides, or corners ⟨a *triangular* sign⟩
**3** of, relating to, or involving three parts or persons

**trib·al** \'trī-bəl\ *adj*
of, relating to, or like that of a tribe ⟨a *tribal* custom⟩

**tribe** \'trīb\ *n*
**1** a group of people including many families, clans, or generations ⟨an Indian *tribe*⟩
**2** a group of people who are of the same kind or have the same occupation or interest
**3** a group of related plants or animals ⟨the cat *tribe*⟩

**tribes·man** \'trībz-mən\ *n, pl* **tribes·men** \-mən\
a member of a tribe

**trib·u·la·tion** \ˌtrib-yə-'lā-shən\ *n*
**1** distress or suffering resulting from cruel and unjust rule of a leader, persecution, or misfortune
**2** an experience that is hard to bear

**tri·bu·nal** \trī-'byün-l\ *n*
a court of justice

**¹trib·u·tary** \'trib-yə-ˌter-ē\ *adj*
flowing into a larger stream or a lake

**²tributary** *n, pl* **trib·u·tar·ies**
a stream flowing into a larger stream or a lake

**trib·ute** \'trib-yüt\ *n*
**1** a payment made by one ruler or state to another especially to gain peace
**2** a tax put on the people to raise money for tribute
**3** something given to show respect, gratitude, or affection

**tri·cer·a·tops** \trī-'ser-ə-,täps\ *n, pl* **triceratops**
▶ a large plant-eating dinosaur with three horns, a large bony crest around the neck, and hoofed toes

**tri·chi·na** \trə-'kī-nə\ *n, pl* **tri·chi·nae** \-nē\
a small roundworm which enters the body when infected meat is eaten and whose larvae form cysts in the muscles and cause a painful and dangerous disease **(trichinosis)**

**[1]trick** \'trik\ *n*
**1** an action intended to deceive or cheat
**2** a mischievous act : PRANK
**3** an unwise or childish action
**4** an action designed to puzzle or amuse
**5** a quick or clever way of doing something
**6** the cards played in one round of a game

**[2]trick** *vb*
to deceive with tricks : CHEAT

**trick·ery** \'trik-ə-rē\ *n, pl* **trick·er·ies**
the use of tricks to deceive or cheat

**[1]trick·le** \'trik-əl\ *vb* **trick·led**; **trick·ling**
**1** to run or fall in drops
**2** to flow in a thin slow stream

**[2]trickle** *n*
a thin slow stream

**trick or treat** *n*
a children's Halloween practice of asking for treats from door to door and threatening to play tricks on those who refuse

**trick·ster** \'trik-stər\ *n*
a person who uses tricks

**triceratops:** model of a triceratops

**tricky** \'trik-ē\ *adj* **trick·i·er**; **trick·i·est**
**1** likely to use tricks
**2** requiring special care and skill
**synonyms** see SLY

**tri·cy·cle** \'trī-,sik-əl\ *n*
▼ a vehicle with three wheels that is moved usually by pedals

**tricycle:** a boy on his tricycle

**tri·dent** \'trīd-nt\ *n*
a spear with three prongs

**[1]tried** \'trīd\ *past of* TRY

**[2]tried** *adj*
found good or trustworthy through experience or testing ⟨a *tried* and true remedy⟩

**[1]tri·fle** \'trī-fəl\ *n*
**1** something of little importance
**2** a small amount (as of money)

**[2]trifle** *vb* **tri·fled**; **tri·fling**
**1** to talk in a joking way
**2** to act in a playful way
**3** to handle something in an absentminded way : TOY

**tri·fling** \'trī-fling\ *adj*
**1** not serious : FRIVOLOUS
**2** of little value

**trig·ger** \'trig-ər\ *n*
the part of the lock of a gun that is pressed to release the hammer so that it will fire

**[1]trill** \'tril\ *n*
**1** a quick movement back and forth between two musical tones one step apart
**2** [1]WARBLE 1
**3** the rapid vibration of one speech organ against another ⟨pronounce *r*'s with a *trill*⟩

**[2]trill** *vb*
to utter as or with a trill

**tril·lion** \'tril-yən\ *n*
a thousand billions

**tril·li·um** \'tril-ē-əm\ *n*
▼ a plant related to the lilies that has three leaves and a single flower with three petals and that blooms in the spring

**trillium**

**[1]trim** \'trim\ *vb* **trimmed**; **trim·ming**
**1** to put ornaments on : ADORN ⟨*trim* a Christmas tree⟩
**2** to make neat especially by cutting or clipping ⟨*trim* a hedge⟩
**3** to free of unnecessary matter ⟨*trim* a budget⟩ ⟨*trim* a steak⟩
**4** to cause (as a ship) to take the right position in the water by balancing the load carried
**5** to adjust (as an airplane or submarine) for horizontal movement or for motion upward or downward

**6** to adjust (as a sail) to a desired position
**trim·mer** *n*

**[2]trim** *adj* **trim·mer**; **trim·mest**
neat and compact in line or structure **synonyms** see NEAT
**trim·ly** *adv*

**[3]trim** *n*
**1** the state of a ship as being ready for sailing
**2** good condition : FITNESS
**3** material used for ornament or trimming
**4** the woodwork in the finish of a building especially around doors and windows

**trim·ming** \'trim-ing\ *n*
**1** the action of one that trims
**2** something that trims, ornaments, or completes
**3 trimmings** *pl* parts removed by trimming

**trin·ket** \'tring-kət\ *n*
a small ornament (as a jewel)

**trio** \'trē-ō\ *n, pl* **tri·os**
**1** a musical composition for three instruments or voices
**2** a group or set of three

camera

**tripod 2**

**[1]trip** \'trip\ *vb* **tripped**; **trip·ping**
**1** to move (as in dancing) with light quick steps ⟨*tripped* lightly around the room⟩
**2** to catch the foot against something so as to stumble : cause to stumble
**3** to make or cause to make a mistake ⟨their tricky questions *tripped* us up⟩
**4** to release (as a spring) by moving a catch

**[2]trip** *n*
**1** a traveling from one place to another : VOYAGE ⟨a *trip* to Europe⟩
**2** a brief errand having a certain aim or being more or less regular ⟨a *trip* to the dentist⟩
**3** the action of releasing something mechanically
**4** a device for releasing something by tripping a mechanism
**synonyms** see JOURNEY

**tripe** \'trīp\ *n*
a part of the stomach of a cow used for food

**[1]tri·ple** \'trip-əl\ *vb* **tri·pled**; **tri·pling**
to make or become three times as great or as many

**[2]triple** *n*
**1** a sum, amount, or number that is three times as great
**2** a combination, group, or series of three
**3** a hit in baseball that lets the batter reach third base

**[3]triple** *adj*
**1** having three units or parts
**2** being three times as great or as many
**3** repeated three times

**trip·let** \'trip-lət\ *n*
**1** a combination, set, or group of three
**2** one of three offspring born at one birth

**tri·pod** \'trī-,päd\ *n*
**1** something (as a container or stool) resting on three legs
**2** ◄ a stand (as for a camera) having three legs

**trite** \'trīt\ *adj* **trit·er**; **trit·est**
so common that the newness and cleverness have worn off : STALE ⟨*trite* remarks⟩
**trite·ness** *n*

**[1]tri·umph** \'trī-əmf\ *n*
**1** the joy of victory or success
**2** an outstanding victory
**synonyms** see VICTORY

**[2]triumph** *vb*
**1** to celebrate victory or success in high spirits and often with boasting
**2** to gain victory : WIN

**tri·um·phal** \trī-'əm-fəl\ *adj*
of or relating to a triumph

**tri·um·phant** \trī-'əm-fənt\ *adj*
**1** VICTORIOUS, SUCCESSFUL
**2** rejoicing for or celebrating victory
**tri·um·phant·ly** *adv*

**triv·i·al** \'triv-ē-əl\ *adj*
of little worth or importance

**trod** *past of* TREAD

**trodden** *past participle of* TREAD

**[1]troll** \'trōl\ *vb*
**1** to sing the parts of (a song) in succession
**2** to fish with a hook and line drawn through the water

**[2]troll** *n*
a lure or a line with its lure and hook used in trolling

**[3]troll** *n*
a dwarf or giant of folklore living in caves or hills

**trol·ley** \'träl-ē\ *n, pl* **trolleys**
**1** a device (as a grooved wheel on the end of a pole) that carries current from a wire to an electrically driven vehicle
**2** a passenger car that runs on tracks and gets its power through a trolley
**3** a wheeled carriage running on an overhead track

**trom·bone** \träm-'bōn\ *n*
▼ a brass musical instrument made of a long bent tube that has a wide opening at one end and one section that slides in and out to make different tones

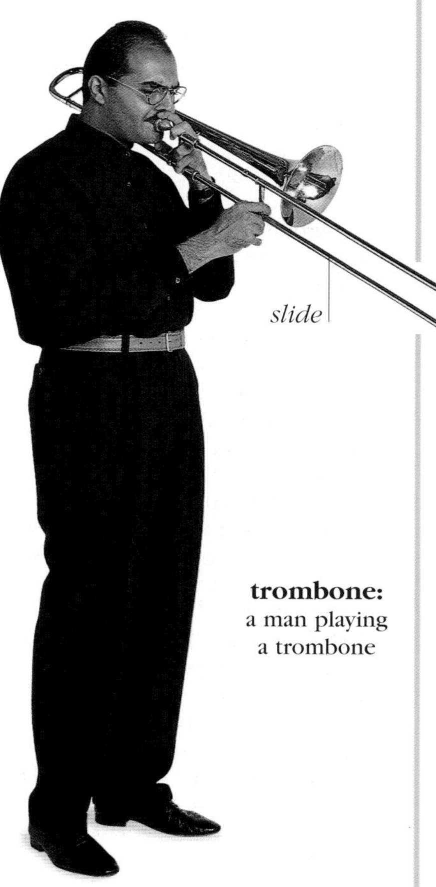


**trombone:** a man playing a trombone

## tropical fish

Tropical fish kept in aquariums are bred from species that live in the warm water of coral reefs and coastal parts of the tropics. As shown below, they exist in a huge variety of shapes, sizes, and colors.

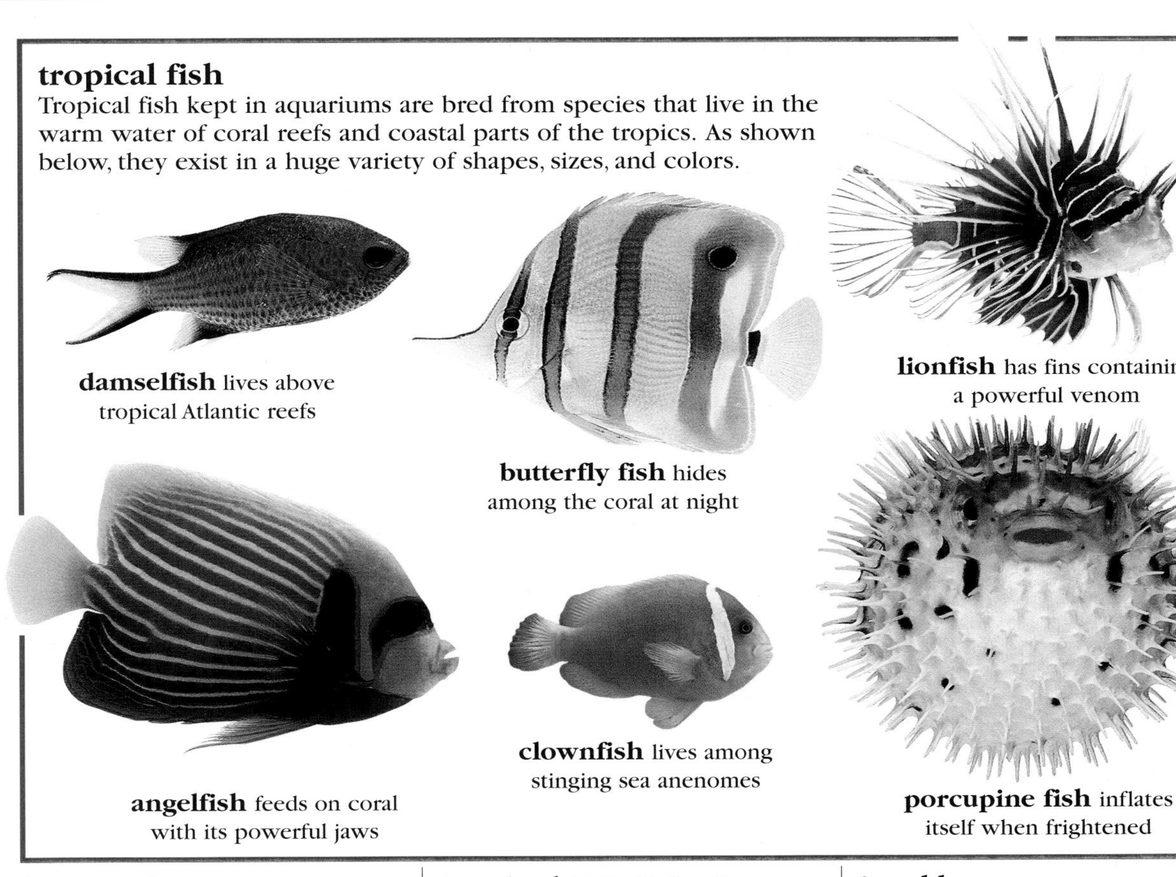

**damselfish** lives above tropical Atlantic reefs

**butterfly fish** hides among the coral at night

**lionfish** has fins containing a powerful venom

**angelfish** feeds on coral with its powerful jaws

**clownfish** lives among stinging sea anemones

**porcupine fish** inflates itself when frightened

[1]**troop** \'trüp\ *n*
**1** a cavalry unit
**2 troops** *pl* armed forces : MILITARY
**3** a group of beings or things
**4** a unit of boy or girl scouts under a leader

[2]**troop** *vb*
to move or gather in groups

**troop·er** \'trü-pər\ *n*
**1** a soldier in a cavalry unit
**2** a mounted police officer
**3** a state police officer

**tro·phy** \'trō-fē\ *n, pl* **trophies**
**1** something taken in battle or conquest especially as a memorial
**2** something given to celebrate a victory or as an award for achievement

**trop·ic** \'träp-ik\ *n*
**1** either of two parallels of the earth's latitude of which one is about $23\frac{1}{2}$ degrees north of the equator and the other about $23\frac{1}{2}$ degrees south of the equator
**2 tropics** *pl, often cap* the region lying between the two tropics

**trop·i·cal** \'träp-i-kəl\ *adj*
of, relating to, or occurring in the tropics

**tropical fish** *n*
▲ any of various small often brightly colored fishes kept in aquariums

[1]**trot** \'trät\ *n*
**1** a moderately fast gait of an animal with four feet in which a front foot and the opposite hind foot move as a pair
**2** a human jogging pace between a walk and a run

[2]**trot** *vb* **trot·ted**; **trot·ting**
**1** to ride, drive, or go at a trot
**2** to cause to go at a trot
**3** to go along quickly : HURRY

[1]**trou·ble** \'trəb-əl\ *vb* **trou·bled**; **trou·bling**
**1** to disturb or become disturbed mentally or spiritually : WORRY
**2** to produce physical disorder in : AFFLICT
**3** to put to inconvenience
**4** to make an effort ⟨do not *trouble* to write⟩

[2]**trouble** *n*
**1** the quality or state of being troubled : MISFORTUNE ⟨people in *trouble*⟩
**2** an instance of distress or disturbance
**3** a cause of disturbance or distress
**4** extra work or effort ⟨took the *trouble* to write⟩
**5** ill health : AILMENT
**6** failure to work normally ⟨had *trouble* with the engine⟩

**trou·ble·some** \'trəb-əl-səm\ *adj*
**1** giving trouble or anxiety ⟨a *troublesome* infection⟩
**2** difficult to deal with
**trou·ble·some·ly** *adv*
**trou·ble·some·ness** *n*

**trough** \'trȯf\ *n*
**1** a long shallow open container especially for water or feed for livestock
**2** a channel for water : GUTTER
**3** a long channel or hollow

**trounce** \'trau̇ns\ *vb* **trounced**; **trounc·ing**
**1** to beat severely : FLOG
**2** to defeat thoroughly

**troupe** \'trüp\ *n*
a group especially of performers on the stage

**trou·sers** \'trau̇-zərz\ *n pl*
PANTS

**trout** \'trau̇t\ *n, pl* **trout**
▼ a freshwater fish related to the salmon and valued for food and sport

**trout:**
a rainbow trout

**trow·el** \'trau̇-əl\ *n*
**1** a small hand tool with a flat blade used for spreading and smoothing mortar or plaster
**2** a small hand tool with a curved blade used by gardeners

**tru·ant** \'trü-ənt\ *n*
**1** a person who neglects his or her duty
**2** a student who stays out of school without permission

**truce** \'trüs\ *n*
**1** ARMISTICE
**2** a short rest especially from something unpleasant

[1]**truck** \'trək\ *n*
**1** [2]BARTER
**2** goods for barter or for small trade
**3** close association ⟨wanted no *truck* with criminals⟩

[2]**truck** *n*
▼ a vehicle (as a strong heavy wagon or motor vehicle) for carrying heavy articles or hauling a trailer

[3]**truck** *vb*
to transport on a truck

**trudge** \'trəj\ *vb* **trudged**; **trudg·ing**
to walk or march steadily and usually with much effort

[1]**true** \'trü\ *adj* **tru·er**; **tru·est**
**1** completely loyal : FAITHFUL
**2** that can be relied on : CERTAIN
**3** agreeing with the facts : ACCURATE ⟨a *true* story⟩
**4** HONEST 1, SINCERE ⟨*true* friendship⟩
**5** properly so called : GENUINE ⟨mosses have no *true* seeds⟩
**6** placed or formed accurately : EXACT ⟨*true* pitch⟩
**7** being or holding by right : LEGITIMATE ⟨the *true* owner⟩ **synonyms** see FAITHFUL, REAL

[2]**true** *adv*
**1** in agreement with fact : TRUTHFULLY
**2** in an accurate manner : ACCURATELY ⟨the bullet flew straight and *true*⟩
**3** without variation from type ⟨breed *true*⟩

[3]**true** *n*
the quality or state of being accurate (as in alignment) ⟨out of *true*⟩

[4]**true** *vb* **trued**; **true·ing** *also* **tru·ing**
to bring to exactly correct condition as to place, position, or shape

**true–blue** \'trü-'blü\ *adj*
very faithful

**truf·fle** \'trəf-əl\ *n*
the edible usually dark and wrinkled fruiting body of a European fungus that grows in the ground

**tru·ly** \'trü-lē\ *adv*
in a true manner

[1]**trum·pet** \'trəm-pət\ *n*
**1** ▼ a brass musical instrument that consists of a tube formed into a long loop with a wide opening at one end and that has valves by which different tones are produced
**2** something that is shaped like a trumpet
**3** a sound like that of a trumpet

[1]**trumpet 1:**
a man playing a trumpet

[2]**trumpet** *vb*
**1** to blow a trumpet
**2** to make a sound like that of a trumpet
**trum·pet·er** *n*

**trumpet creeper** *n*
a North American woody vine having red flowers shaped like trumpets

**trumpet vine** *n*
TRUMPET CREEPER

[1]**trun·dle** \'trən-dəl\ *vb* **trun·dled**; **trun·dling**
to roll along : WHEEL

[2]**trundle** *n*
**1** a small wheel or roller
**2** a cart or truck with low wheels

**trundle bed** *n*
a low bed on small wheels that can be rolled under a higher bed

[2]**truck**

**trunk** \'trəngk\ *n*
**1** the main stem of a tree apart from branches and roots
**2** the body of a person or animal apart from the head, arms, and legs
**3** ▼ a box or chest for holding clothes or other articles especially for traveling
**4** the enclosed space usually in the rear of an automobile for carrying articles
**5** the long round muscular nose of an elephant
**6 trunks** *pl* men's shorts worn chiefly for sports

**trunk 3:** a 19th-century trunk

[1]**truss** \'trəs\ *vb*
**1** to bind or tie firmly
**2** to support, strengthen, or stiffen by a truss

[2]**truss** *n*
**1** a framework of beams or bars used in building and engineering
**2** a device worn to hold a ruptured body part in place

[1]**trust** \'trəst\ *n*
**1** firm belief in the character, strength, or truth of someone or something
**2** a person or thing in which confidence is placed
**3** confident hope
**4** financial credit
**5** a property interest held by one person or organization (as a bank) for the benefit of another
**6** a combination of firms or corporations formed by a legal agreement and often held to reduce competition
**7** something (as a public office) held or managed by someone for the benefit of another
**8** responsibility for safety and well-being

[2]**trust** *vb*
**1** to place confidence **:** DEPEND
**2** to be confident **:** HOPE
**3** to place in one's care or keeping **:** ENTRUST
**4** to rely on or on the truth of **:** BELIEVE
**5** to give financial credit to

**trust·ee** \ˌtrəs-'tē\ *n*
a person who has been given legal responsibility for someone else's property

**trust·ful** \'trəst-fəl\ *adj*
full of trust
**trust·ful·ly** \-fə-lē\ *adv*
**trust·ful·ness** *n*

**trust·ing** \'trəs-ting\ *adj*
having trust, faith, or confidence

**trust·wor·thy** \'trəst-ˌwər-t͟hē\ *adj*
deserving trust and confidence
**trust·wor·thi·ness** *n*

[1]**trusty** \'trəs-tē\ *adj* **trust·i·er**; **trust·i·est**
TRUSTWORTHY, RELIABLE

[2]**trusty** *n, pl* **trust·ies**
a convict considered trustworthy and allowed special privileges

**truth** \'trüth\ *n, pl* **truths** \'trüt͟hz\
**1** the quality or state of being true
**2** the body of real events or facts
**3** a true or accepted statement
**4** agreement with fact or reality

**truth·ful** \'trüth-fəl\ *adj*
telling or being in the habit of telling the truth
**truth·ful·ly** \-fə-lē\ *adv*
**truth·ful·ness** *n*

[1]**try** \'trī\ *vb* **tried** \'trīd\; **try·ing**
**1** to examine or investigate in a court of law
**2** to conduct the trial of
**3** to put to a test
**4** to test to the limit
**5** to melt down (as tallow) and obtain in a pure state
**6** to make an effort to do

[2]**try** *n, pl* **tries**
an effort to do something **:** ATTEMPT

**try·ing** \'trī-ing\ *adj*
hard to bear or put up with

**try on** *vb*
to put on (a garment) to test the fit

**try·out** \'trī-ˌau̇t\ *n*
a test of the ability (as of an athlete or an actor) to fill a part or meet standards

**T–shirt** *also* **tee shirt** \'tē-ˌshərt\ *n*
**1** a cotton undershirt with short sleeves and no collar
**2** a cotton or wool jersey outer shirt designed like a T-shirt

**tsu·na·mi** \su̇-'näm-ē\ *n*
a large sea wave produced especially by an earthquake or volcanic eruption under the sea **:** TIDAL WAVE

[1]**tub** \'təb\ *n*
**1** a wide low container
**2** an old or slow boat
**3** BATHTUB
**4** BATH 1
**5** the amount that a tub will hold

[2]**tub** *vb* **tubbed**; **tub·bing**
to wash or bathe in a tub

**tu·ba** \'tü-bə, 'tyü-\ *n*
a brass musical instrument of lowest pitch with an oval shape and valves for producing different tones

**tube** \'tüb, 'tyüb\ *n*
**1** a long hollow cylinder used especially to carry fluids
**2** a slender channel within a plant or animal body **:** DUCT
**3** a soft container shaped something like a tube whose contents (as toothpaste or glue) can be removed by squeezing
**4** a hollow cylinder of rubber inside a tire to hold air
**5** ELECTRONIC TUBE
**6** TELEVISION — always used with *the*
**tubed** \'tü-bd, 'tyübd\ *adj*
**tube·less** \'tü-bləs, 'tyü-\ *adj*
**tube·like** \'tü-ˌblīk, 'tyü-\ *adj*

**tu·ber** \'tü-bər, 'tyü-\ *n*
► a short fleshy usually underground stem (as of a potato plant) bearing tiny leaves like scales each with a bud at its base

*tuber*

**tubers** on a potato plant

**tu·ber·cu·lo·sis** \tu̇-ˌbər-kyə-'lō-səs, tyu̇-\ *n*
a disease (as of humans or cattle) which is caused by a bacillus and in which fever, wasting, and formation of cheesy nodules especially in the lungs occur

**tu·ber·ous** \'tü-bə-rəs, 'tyü-\ *adj*
of, relating to, or like a tuber

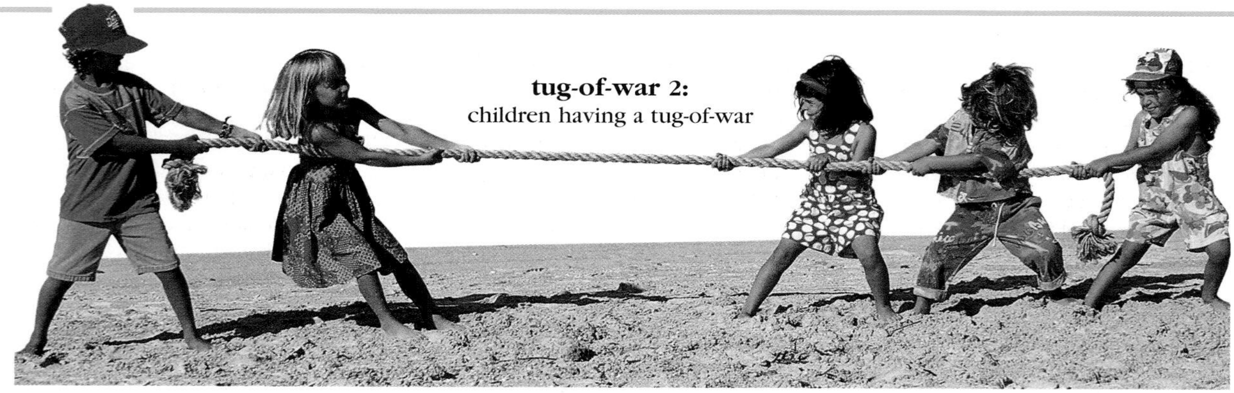

**tug-of-war 2:**
children having a tug-of-war

**tu·bu·lar** \'tü-byə-lər, 'tyü-\ *adj*
**1** having the form of or made up of a tube
**2** made with tubes

**[1]tuck** \'tək\ *vb*
**1** to pull up into a fold
**2** to make stitched folds in
**3** to put or fit into a snug or safe place ⟨*tucked* their money away in the bank⟩
**4** to push in the edges of ⟨*tuck* in your shirt⟩
**5** to cover by tucking in bedclothes ⟨*tucked* the children in for the night⟩

**[2]tuck** *n*
a fold stitched into cloth usually to alter it

**Tues·day** \'tüz-dē, 'tyüz-\ *n*
the third day of the week

**[1]tuft** \'təft\ *n*
**1** a small bunch of long flexible things (as hairs) growing out
**2** a bunch of soft fluffy threads used for ornament
**3** [1]CLUMP 1, CLUSTER

**[2]tuft** *vb*
**1** to provide or decorate with a tuft
**2** to grow in tufts
**3** to make (as upholstery) firm by stitching through the stuffing here and there

**[1]tug** \'təg\ *vb* **tugged; tug·ging**
**1** to pull hard ⟨*tug* at a rope⟩
**2** to move by pulling hard **:** DRAG
**3** to tow with a tugboat

**[2]tug** *n*
**1** an act of tugging **:** PULL
**2** a strong pulling force ⟨the *tug* of gravity⟩
**3** a struggle between two people or forces
**4** TUGBOAT

**tug·boat** \'təg-ˌbōt\ *n*
a small powerful boat used for towing ships

**tug–of–war** \ˌtəg-əv-'wȯr\ *n, pl* **tugs–of–war**
**1** a struggle to win
**2** ▲ a contest in which two teams pull against each other at opposite ends of a rope

**tu·ition** \tu̇-'ish-ən, tyu̇-\ *n*
money paid for instruction (as at a college)

**tu·lip** \'tü-ləp, 'tyü-\ *n*
▼ a plant related to the lilies that grows from a bulb and has a large cup-shaped flower in early spring

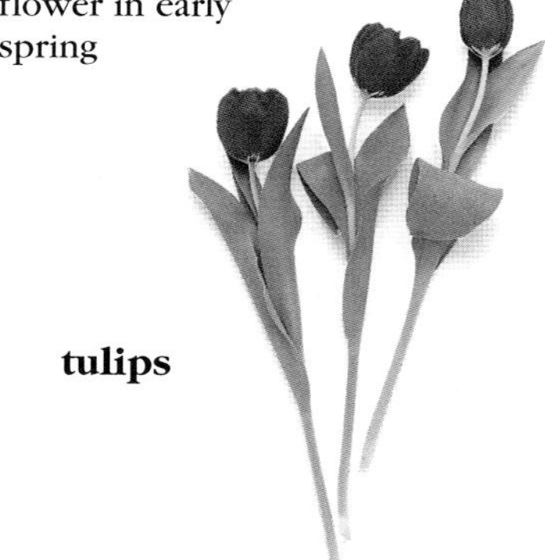

**tulips**

**Word History** We often think of the tulip as a Dutch flower. The Dutch do grow tulips, but they first got the flower from Turkey. The tulip's Latin name came from a Turkish word that meant "turban." A tulip looks just a bit like a turban. The English word *tulip* comes from the Latin name.

**[1]tum·ble** \'təm-bəl\ *vb* **tum·bled; tum·bling**
**1** to perform gymnastic feats of rolling and turning
**2** to fall suddenly and helplessly
**3** to suffer a sudden downward turn or defeat
**4** to move or go in a hurried or confused way
**5** to come to understand
**6** to toss together into a confused mass

**[2]tumble** *n*
**1** a messy state or collection
**2** an act or instance of tumbling and especially of falling down

**tum·ble·down** \'təm-bəl-ˌdau̇n\ *adj*
DILAPIDATED ⟨a *tumbledown* old house⟩

**tum·bler** \'təm-blər\ *n*
**1** a person (as an acrobat) who tumbles
**2** a drinking glass
**3** a movable part of a lock that must be adjusted (as by a key) before the lock will open

**tum·ble·weed** \'təm-bəl-ˌwēd\ *n*
a plant that breaks away from its roots in autumn and is tumbled about by the wind

**tum·my** \'təm-ē\ *n, pl* **tummies**
[1]STOMACH 1, 2

**tu·mor** \'tü-mər, 'tyü-\ *n*
an abnormal growth of body tissue

**tu·mult** \'tü-ˌməlt, 'tyü-\ *n*
**1** UPROAR ⟨the *tumult* raised by the rioters⟩
**2** great confusion of mind

**tu·mul·tu·ous** \tu̇-'məl-chə-wəs, tyu̇-\ *adj*
being or suggesting tumult

**tu·na** \'tü-nə, 'tyü-\ *n, pl* **tuna** *or* **tunas**
▼ a large sea fish valued for food and sport

**tuna**

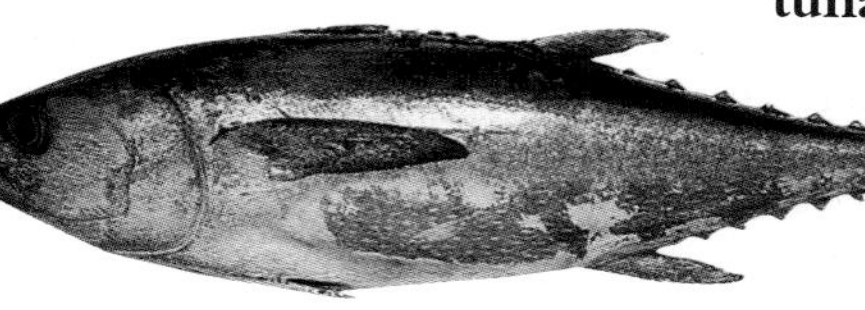

**tun·dra** \'tən-drə\ *n*
a treeless plain of arctic regions

[1]**tune** \'tün, 'tyün\ *n*
**1** a series of pleasing musical tones : MELODY
**2** the main melody of a song
**3** correct musical pitch or key ⟨were singing out of *tune*⟩
**4** AGREEMENT 1, HARMONY ⟨your feelings are in *tune* with mine⟩
**5** general attitude ⟨changed their *tune* when they knew all the facts⟩
**tune·ful** \-fəl\ *adj*

[2]**tune** *vb* **tuned**; **tun·ing**
**1** to adjust in musical pitch ⟨*tuned* my guitar⟩
**2** to come or bring into harmony
**3** to adjust a radio or television set so that it receives clearly — often used with *in*
**4** to put (as an engine) in good working order — often used with *up*
**tun·er** *n*

**tung·sten** \'təng-stən\ *n*
a grayish-white hard metallic chemical element used especially for electrical purposes (as for the fine wire in an electric light bulb) and to make alloys (as steel) harder

**tu·nic** \'tü-nik, 'tyü-\ *n*
**1** a usually knee-length belted garment worn by ancient Greeks and Romans
**2** a shirt or jacket reaching to or just below the hips

**tuning fork** *n*
▶ a metal instrument that gives a fixed tone when struck and is useful for tuning musical instruments

**tuning fork**

[1]**tun·nel** \'tən-l\ *n*
a passage under the ground

[2]**tunnel** *vb* **tun·neled** *or* **tun·nelled**; **tun·nel·ing** *or* **tun·nel·ling**
to make a tunnel

**tun·ny** \'tən-ē\ *n, pl* **tun·nies**
TUNA

**tur·ban** \'tər-bən\ *n*
**1** a head covering worn especially by Muslims and made of a long cloth wrapped around the head or around a cap
**2** a woman's small soft hat with no brim

**tur·bid** \'tər-bəd\ *adj*
dark or discolored with sediment ⟨a *turbid* stream⟩

**tur·bine** \'tər-bən\ *n*
an engine whose central driving shaft is fitted with a series of winglike parts that are whirled around by the pressure of water, steam, or gas

**tur·bot** \'tər-bət\ *n, pl* **turbot**
a large brownish flatfish

**tur·bu·lent** \'tər-byə-lənt\ *adj*
causing or being in a state of unrest, violence, or disturbance

**tu·reen** \tə-'rēn\ *n*
▼ a deep bowl from which food (as soup) is served

**tureen** of soup

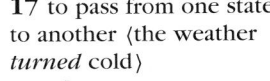

**turf** \'tərf\ *n*
the upper layer of soil bound into a thick mat by roots of grass and other plants

**Turk** \'tərk\ *n*
a person born or living in Turkey

**tur·key** \'tər-kē\ *n, pl* **turkeys**
▶ a large American bird related to the chicken and widely raised for food

---

**Word History** Guinea fowl were once called *turkey-cocks*. They came from Africa, but some people thought they came from Turkey. The birds we call *turkeys* are American. When the English first saw them, some confused them with guinea fowl. That is why the new birds were called *turkey-cocks*, too. The word *turkey* is short for *turkey-cock*.

---

[1]**Turk·ish** \'tər-kish\ *adj*
of or relating to Turkey, the Turks, or Turkish

[2]**Turkish** *n*
the language of the Turks

**tur·moil** \'tər-,mȯil\ *n*
a very confused or disturbed state or condition

[1]**turn** \'tərn\ *vb*
**1** to move or cause to move around a center : ROTATE
**2** to twist so as to bring about a desired end ⟨*turn* the key to unlock the door⟩
**3** [1]WRENCH 2 ⟨*turn* an ankle⟩
**4** to change in position usually by moving through an arc of a circle ⟨they *turned* and walked away⟩ ⟨*turn* the child over in bed⟩ ⟨*turn* pancakes⟩
**5** to think over : PONDER
**6** to become dizzy : REEL
**7** [1]UPSET 3 ⟨*turn* one's stomach⟩
**8** to set in another and especially an opposite direction
**9** to change course or direction ⟨the road *turns* to the left⟩
**10** to go around
**11** to reach or pass beyond
**12** to move or direct toward or away from something ⟨we *turned* toward home⟩
**13** to make an appeal ⟨*turned* to an agency for help⟩
**14** to become or make very unfriendly
**15** to make or become spoiled ⟨the milk *turned*⟩
**16** to cause to be or look a certain way ⟨the weather *turned* the leaves red⟩
**17** to pass from one state to another ⟨the weather *turned* cold⟩

**turkey**

**18** [1]CHANGE 1, TRANSFORM ⟨*turn* lead into gold⟩
**19** TRANSLATE 2
**20** to give a rounded form to (as on a lathe)
**turn a hair** to be or become upset or frightened
**turn tail** to turn so as to run away
**turn the trick** to bring about the desired result
**turn turtle** OVERTURN 1

**[2]turn** *n*
**1** a turning about a center
**2** a change or changing of direction, course, or position
**3** a change or changing of the general state or condition ⟨business took a *turn* for the better⟩
**4** a place at which something turns ⟨a *turn* in the road⟩
**5** a short walk or ride
**6** an act affecting another ⟨do a friend a good *turn*⟩
**7** proper place in a waiting line or time in a schedule ⟨take your *turn*⟩
**8** a period of action or activity **:** SPELL
**9** a special purpose or need ⟨that will serve the *turn*⟩
**10** special quality
**11** the shape or form in which something is molded **:** CAST
**12** a single circle or loop (as of rope passed around an object)
**13** natural or special skill ⟨has a *turn* for writing⟩
**at every turn** all the time **:** CONSTANTLY, CONTINUOUSLY
**to a turn** precisely right

**turn·about** \'tər-nə-ˌbau̇t\ *n*
a change from one direction or one way of thinking or acting to the opposite

**turquoise**

**turn down** *vb*
**1** to fold back or down ⟨*turn down* the bedclothes⟩
**2** to lower by using a control ⟨*turn down* the heat⟩
**3** [1]REFUSE 1, REJECT ⟨*turn down* a job⟩

**tur·nip** \'tər-nəp\ *n*
the thick white or yellow edible root of a plant related to the cabbage

**turn off** *vb*
**1** to turn aside ⟨*turned off* onto another road⟩
**2** to stop by using a control ⟨*turn off* the alarm⟩

**turn on** *vb*
to make work by using a control ⟨*turn on* the light⟩

**turn·out** \'tər-ˌnau̇t\ *n*
a gathering of people for a special reason ⟨a good *turnout* for the meeting⟩

**turn out** *vb*
**1** TURN OFF 2 ⟨who *turned out* the light⟩
**2** to prove to be ⟨it *turned out* to be the cat⟩

**turn·pike** \'tərn-ˌpīk\ *n*
**1** a road that one must pay to use
**2** a main road

**turn·stile** \'tərn-ˌstīl\ *n*
a post having arms that turn around set in an entrance or exit so that persons can pass through only on foot one by one

**turn·ta·ble** \'tərn-ˌtā-bəl\ *n*
a round flat plate that turns a phonograph record

**tur·pen·tine** \'tər-pən-ˌtīn\ *n*
**1** a mixture of oil and resin obtained mostly from pine trees
**2** an oil made from turpentine and used as a solvent and as a paint thinner

**tur·quoise** \'tər-ˌkȯiz, -ˌkwȯiz\ *n*
◀ a blue to greenish gray mineral used in jewelry

**turret 1:** a Spanish castle with turrets

**tur·ret** \'tər-ət\ *n*
**1** ▲ a little tower often at a corner of a building
**2** a low usually rotating structure (as in a tank, warship, or airplane) in which guns are mounted

**tur·tle** \'tərt-l\ *n*
any of a large group of reptiles living on land, in water, or both and having a toothless horny beak and a shell of bony plates which covers the body and into which the head, legs, and tail can usually be drawn

**tur·tle·dove** \'tərt-l-ˌdəv\ *n*
any of several small wild pigeons

**tur·tle·neck** \'tərt-l-ˌnek\ *n*
a high turned-over collar (as of a sweater)

**tusk** \'təsk\ *n*
▼ a very long large tooth (as of an elephant) usually growing in pairs and used in digging and fighting
**tusked** \'təskt\ *adj*

**[1]tus·sle** \'təs-əl\ *n*
**1** a physical contest or struggle
**2** a rough argument or a struggle against difficult odds

**[2]tussle** *vb* **tus·sled; tus·sling**
to struggle roughly **:** SCUFFLE

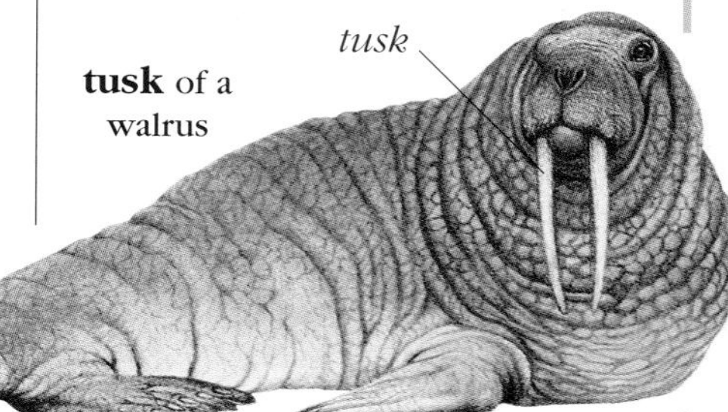

**tusk** of a walrus

**tus·sock** \'təs-ək\ *n*
a compact tuft or clump (as of grass)

**[1]tu·tor** \'tüt-ər, 'tyüt-\ *n*
a person who has the responsibility of instructing and guiding another

**[2]tutor** *vb*
to teach usually individually

**TV** \'tē-'vē\ *n*
TELEVISION

**twad·dle** \'twäd-l\ *n*
silly idle talk

**twain** \'twān\ *n*
[2]TWO 1

**[1]twang** \'twang\ *n*
**1** a harsh quick ringing sound
**2** nasal speech

**[2]twang** *vb*
**1** to sound or cause to sound with a twang
**2** to speak with a nasal twang

**'twas** \twəz, 'twäz\
it was

**[1]tweak** \'twēk\ *vb*
to pinch and pull with a sudden jerk and twist

**[2]tweak** *n*
an act of tweaking

**tweed** \'twēd\ *n*
**1** a rough woolen cloth
**2 tweeds** *pl* tweed clothing (as a suit)

**[1]tweet** \'twēt\ *n*
a chirping sound

**[2]tweet** *vb*
[2]CHIRP

**tweez·ers** \'twē-zərz\ *n pl*
▼ a small instrument that is used like pincers in grasping or pulling something

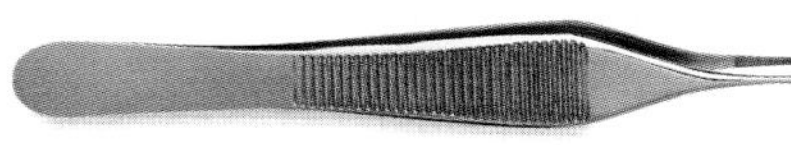

**tweezers**

**[1]twelfth** \'twelfth\ *adj*
coming right after eleventh

**[2]twelfth** *n*
number twelve in a series

**[1]twelve** \'twelv\ *adj*
being one more than eleven

**[2]twelve** *n*
one more than eleven **:** three times four **:** 12

**twelve·month** \'twelv-,mənth\ *n*
YEAR

**[1]twin 1:**
identical twins

**[1]twen·ti·eth** \'twent-ē-əth\ *adj*
coming right after nineteenth

**[2]twentieth** *n*
number twenty in a series

**[1]twen·ty** \'twent-ē\ *adj*
being one more than nineteen

**[2]twenty** *n*
one more than nineteen **:** four times five **:** 20

**twen·ty–first** \,twent-ē-'fərst\ *adj*
coming right after twentieth

**[1]twen·ty–one** \,twent-ē-'wən\ *adj*
being one more than twenty

**[2]twenty–one** *n*
one more than twenty **:** 21

**twice** \'twīs\ *adv*
two times

**twid·dle** \'twid-l\ *vb* **twid·dled**; **twid·dling**
[1]TWIRL ⟨*twiddle* one's thumbs⟩

**twig** \'twig\ *n*
a small shoot or branch

**twi·light** \'twī-,līt\ *n*
the period or the light from the sky between full night and sunrise or between sunset and full night

**twill** \'twil\ *n*
a way of weaving cloth that produces a pattern of diagonal lines

**[1]twin** \'twin\ *n*
**1** ◀ either of two offspring produced at one birth
**2** one of two persons or things closely related to or very like each other

**[2]twin** *adj*
**1** born with one other or as a pair at one birth ⟨*twin* calves⟩
**2** made up of two similar, related, or connected members or parts
**3** being one of a pair

**[1]twine** \'twīn\ *n*
a strong string of two or more strands twisted together

**[2]twine** *vb* **twined**; **twin·ing**
**1** to twist together ⟨*twined* the branches into a wreath⟩
**2** to coil around a support ⟨a vine *twining* around a pole⟩

**[1]twinge** \'twinj\ *vb* **twinged**; **twing·ing** *or* **twinge·ing** to affect with or feel a sudden sharp pain

**[2]twinge** *n*
a sudden sharp stab (as of pain)

**[1]twin·kle** \'twing-kəl\ *vb* **twin·kled**; **twin·kling**
**1** to shine or cause to shine with a flickering or sparkling light ⟨stars *twinkling* in the sky⟩
**2** to appear bright with amusement ⟨eyes *twinkled* at the joke⟩
**3** to move or flutter rapidly

**[2]twinkle** *n*
**1** a very short time
**2** [2]SPARKLE 1, FLICKER

**twin·kling** \'twing-kling\ *n*
[2]TWINKLE 1

**[1]twirl** \'twərl\ *vb*
to turn or cause to turn rapidly ⟨a *twirling* windmill⟩
**twirl·er** *n*

**[2]twirl** *n*
an act of twirling

**[1]twist** \'twist\ *vb*
**1** to unite by winding one thread, strand, or wire around another
**2** [2]TWINE 2
**3** to turn so as to sprain or hurt ⟨*twist* one's ankle⟩
**4** to change the meaning of ⟨you're *twisting* my words; that's not what I meant⟩
**5** to pull off, rotate, or break by a turning force ⟨*twist* a flower from its stem⟩
**6** to follow a winding course ⟨the path *twisted* between the trees⟩

A
B
C
D
E
F
G
H
I
J
K
L
M
N
O
P
Q
R
S
T
U
V
W
X
Y
Z

**²twist** *n*
**1** something that is twisted
**2** ▶ an act of twisting **:** the state of being twisted
**3** a spiral turn or curve
**4** a strong personal tendency **:** BENT
**5** a changing of meaning
**6** something (as a plan of action) that is both surprising and strange
**7** a lively dance in which the hips are twisted

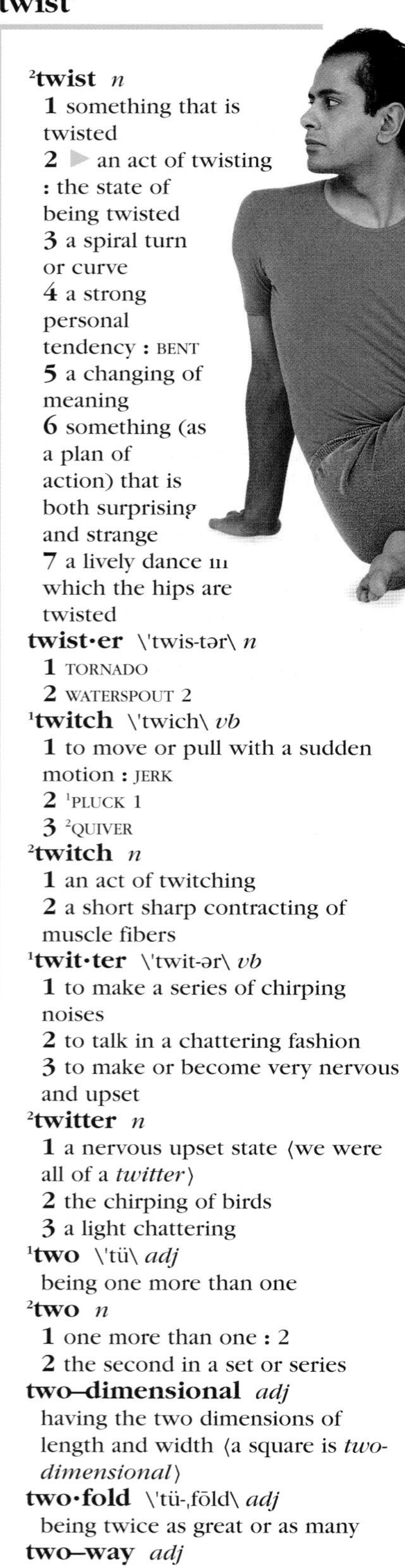

**²twist 2:** a man performing a yoga twist

**twist·er** \'twis-tər\ *n*
**1** TORNADO
**2** WATERSPOUT 2

**¹twitch** \'twich\ *vb*
**1** to move or pull with a sudden motion **:** JERK
**2** ¹PLUCK 1
**3** ²QUIVER

**²twitch** *n*
**1** an act of twitching
**2** a short sharp contracting of muscle fibers

**¹twit·ter** \'twit-ər\ *vb*
**1** to make a series of chirping noises
**2** to talk in a chattering fashion
**3** to make or become very nervous and upset

**²twitter** *n*
**1** a nervous upset state ⟨we were all of a *twitter*⟩
**2** the chirping of birds
**3** a light chattering

**¹two** \'tü\ *adj*
being one more than one

**²two** *n*
**1** one more than one **:** 2
**2** the second in a set or series

**two–dimensional** *adj*
having the two dimensions of length and width ⟨a square is *two-dimensional*⟩

**two·fold** \'tü-,fōld\ *adj*
being twice as great or as many

**two–way** *adj*
**1** moving or acting or allowing movement or action in either direction ⟨*two-way* traffic⟩ ⟨a *two-way* street⟩
**2** involving two persons or groups ⟨communication is a *two-way* process⟩
**3** made to send and receive messages ⟨a *two-way* radio⟩

**two–winged fly** \,tü-,wingd-\ *n*
an insect belonging to the same group as the housefly

**ty·coon** \tī-'kün\ *n*
a very powerful and wealthy business person

**tying** *present participle of* TIE

**¹type** \'tīp\ *n*
**1** a set of letters or figures that are used for printing or the letters or figures printed by them
**2** the special things by which members of a group are set apart from other groups ⟨plants grouped by *type*⟩
**3** VARIETY 3 ⟨a seedless *type* of orange⟩

**²type** *vb* **typed**; **typ·ing**
**1** TYPEWRITE
**2** to identify as belonging to a type

**type·write** \'tī-,prīt\ *vb* **type·wrote** \-,prōt\; **type·writ·ten** \-,prit-n\; **type·writ·ing** \-,prīt-ing\
to write with a typewriter

**type·writ·er** \'tī-,prīt-ər\ *n*
a machine that prints letters or figures when a person pushes its keys down

**type·writ·ing** \'tī-,prīt-ing\ *n*
**1** the use of a typewriter
**2** writing done with a typewriter

**¹ty·phoid** \'tī-,fȯid\ *adj*
**1** of, relating to, or like typhus
**2** of, relating to, or being typhoid

**²typhoid** *n*
a disease in which a person has fever, diarrhea, an inflamed intestine, and great weakness and which is caused by a bacterium (**typhoid bacillus**) that passes from one person to another in dirty food or water

▼ **ty·phoon** \tī-'fün\ *n*
a tropical cyclone in the region of the Philippines or the China Sea

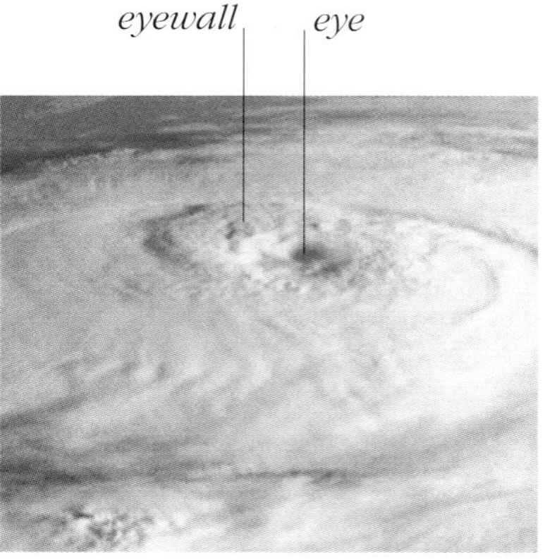


**typhoon:** spiralling winds of over 74 mph cause a typhoon

**ty·phus** \'tī-fəs\ *n*
a disease carried to people especially by body lice and marked by high fever, stupor and delirium, severe headache, and a dark red rash

**typ·i·cal** \'tip-i-kəl\ *adj*
combining or showing the special characteristics of a group or kind ⟨a *typical* Sunday dinner⟩
**synonyms** see REGULAR
**typ·i·cal·ly** *adv*

**typ·i·fy** \'tip-ə-,fī\ *vb* **typ·i·fied**; **typ·i·fy·ing**
**1** REPRESENT 2
**2** to have or include the special or main characteristics of

**typ·ist** \'tī-pist\ *n*
a person who uses a typewriter

**ty·ran·ni·cal** \tə-'ran-i-kəl\ *adj*
of, relating to, or like that of tyranny or a tyrant ⟨*tyrannical* acts⟩

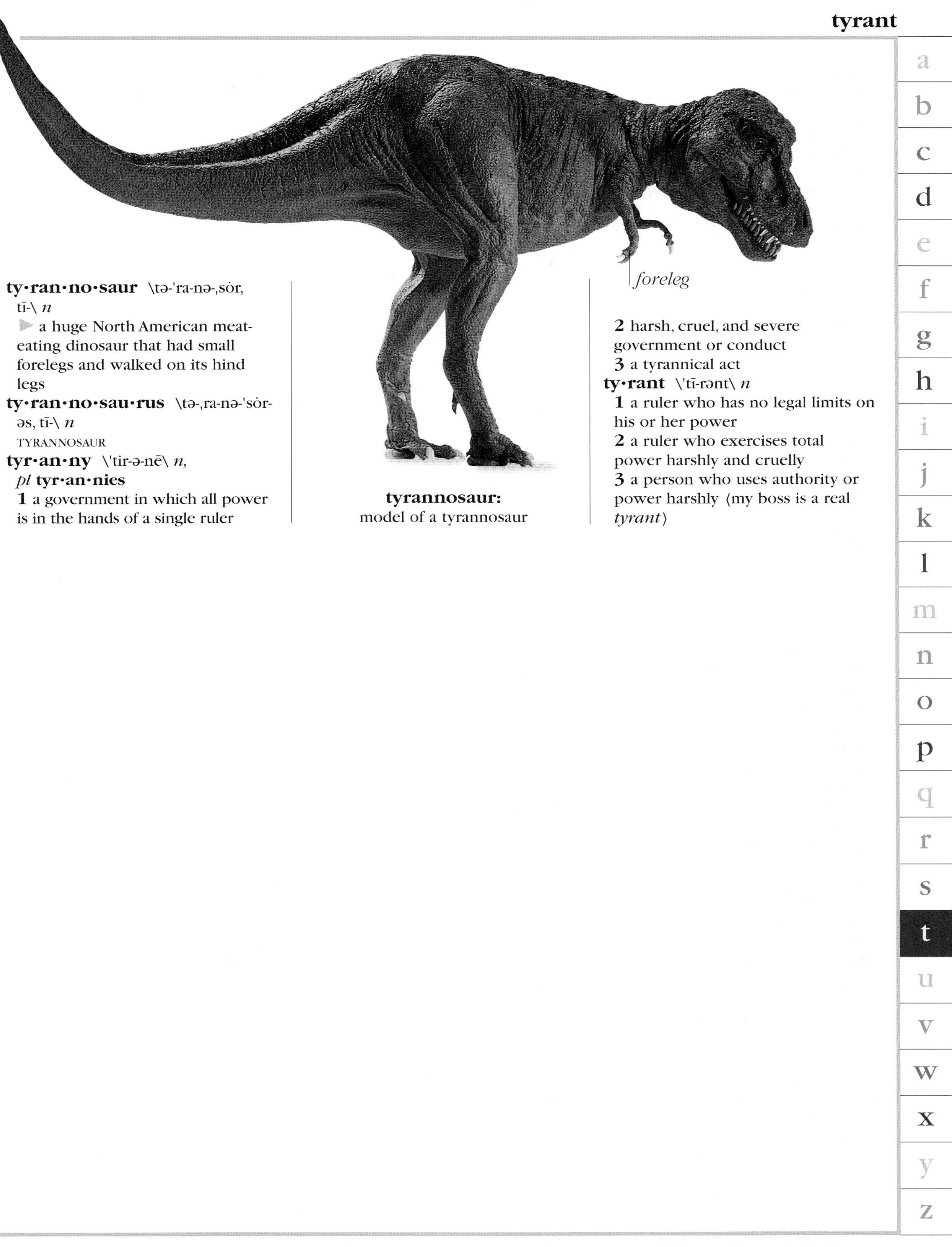


**ty•ran•no•saur** \tə-ˈra-nə-ˌsȯr, tī-\ *n*
▶ a huge North American meat-eating dinosaur that had small forelegs and walked on its hind legs

**ty•ran•no•sau•rus** \tə-ˌra-nə-ˈsȯr-əs, tī-\ *n*
TYRANNOSAUR

**tyr•an•ny** \ˈtir-ə-nē\ *n, pl* **tyr•an•nies**
**1** a government in which all power is in the hands of a single ruler
**2** harsh, cruel, and severe government or conduct
**3** a tyrannical act

**tyrannosaur:** model of a tyrannosaur

**ty•rant** \ˈtī-rənt\ *n*
**1** a ruler who has no legal limits on his or her power
**2** a ruler who exercises total power harshly and cruelly
**3** a person who uses authority or power harshly ⟨my boss is a real *tyrant*⟩

A
B
C
D
E
F
G
H
I
J
K
L
M
N
O
P
Q
R
S
T
U
V
W
X
Y
Z

**The sounds of U**: The letter **U** has three main sounds in English. Its most common sound, often called "**short U**," is the one heard in **but**, **sun**, and **funny**.

**U** has two "long" sounds. Plain "**long U**" is heard in a few common words, such as **rule**. Much more often, "**long U**" is pronounced as if it had a **Y** in front of it. In these words **U** says its own name. Examples are **cute**, **pure**, and **unicorn**.

The third sound of **U** is heard in only a few mostly very common words, such as **full**, **put**, and **sugar**.

The sounds of **U** are often spelled with **O**. See "**The sounds of O**" for examples.

---

**u** \'yü\ *n, pl* **u's** *or* **us** \'yüz\ *often cap*
**1** the twenty-first letter of the English alphabet
**2** a grade rating a student's work as unsatisfactory

**ud·der** \'əd-ər\ *n*
an organ (as of a cow) made up of two or more milk glands enclosed in a common pouch but opening by separate nipples

**ugh** \'əg\ *interj*
used to indicate the sound of a cough or to express disgust or horror

**ug·ly** \'əg-lē\ *adj* **ug·li·er**; **ug·li·est**
**1** unpleasant to look at **:** not attractive ⟨an *ugly* color⟩
**2** [1]OFFENSIVE 3 ⟨*ugly* smells⟩ ⟨*ugly* habits⟩
**3** not pleasant **:** TROUBLESOME ⟨an *ugly* situation⟩ ⟨*ugly* weather⟩
**4** showing a mean or quarrelsome disposition ⟨an *ugly* temper⟩
**ug·li·ness** *n*

**uku·le·le** \,yü-kə-'lā-lē\ *n*
► a musical instrument like a small guitar with four strings

---

**Word History** Years ago a man from Britain lived in Hawaii. He was small and lively and was, it is said, called *ukulele*, which meant "jumping flea" in the language of Hawaii. When a new instrument came to the islands from Portugal the man called "jumping flea" learned to play it well. He made the new instrument popular. It is likely that this small guitar, which we call *ukulele*, got its name from the little man called "jumping flea."

---

**ul·cer** \'əl-sər\ *n*
an open sore in which tissue is eaten away and which may discharge pus

**ul·cer·ate** \'əl-sə-,rāt\ *vb* **ul·cer·at·ed**; **ul·cer·at·ing**
to cause or have an ulcer ⟨an *ulcerated* leg⟩

**ul·cer·ation** \,əl-sə-'rā-shən\ *n*
**1** the process of forming or state of having an ulcer
**2** ULCER

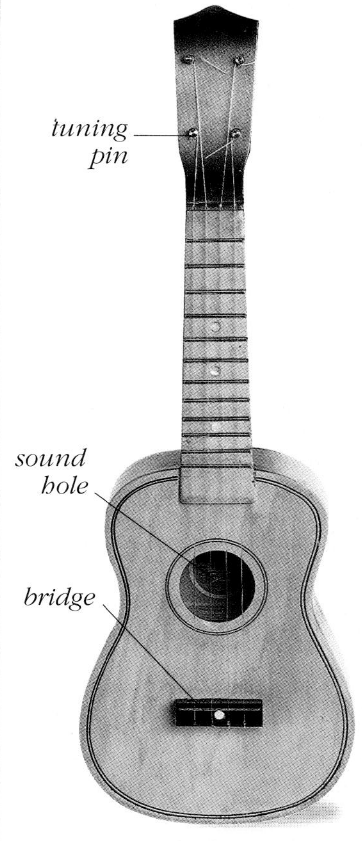


**ukulele**

**ul·cer·ous** \'əl-sə-rəs\ *adj*
being or accompanied by ulceration

**ul·na** \'əl-nə\ *n, pl* **ul·nas** *or* **ul·nae** \-nē\
the bone on the side of the forearm opposite the thumb

**ul·te·ri·or** \,əl-'tir-ē-ər\ *adj*
not seen or made known ⟨*ulterior* motives⟩

**ul·ti·mate** \'əl-tə-mət\ *adj*
**1** last in a series **:** FINAL
**2** [1]EXTREME 1 ⟨the *ultimate* sacrifice⟩
**3** FUNDAMENTAL, ABSOLUTE ⟨*ultimate* reality⟩
**ul·ti·mate·ly** *adv*

**ul·ti·ma·tum** \,əl-tə-'māt-əm\ *n, pl* **ul·ti·ma·tums** *or* **ul·ti·ma·ta** \-'māt-ə\
a final condition or demand that if rejected could end peaceful talks and lead to forceful action

**ul·tra** \'əl-trə\ *adj*
[1]EXTREME 1, EXCESSIVE

**ultra-** *prefix*
**1** beyond in space **:** on the other side ⟨*ultra*violet⟩
**2** beyond the limits of **:** SUPER-
**3** beyond what is ordinary or proper **:** too

**ul·tra·vi·o·let** \,əl-trə-'vī-ə-lət\ *adj*
relating to or producing ultraviolet light

**ultraviolet light** *n*
waves that are like light but cannot be seen, that lie beyond the violet end of the spectrum, and that are found especially along with light from the sun

**um·bil·i·cal cord** \,əm-'bil-i-kəl-\ *n*
a cord joining a fetus to its placenta

**um·brel·la** \ˌəm-ˈbrel-ə\ *n*
► a fabric covering stretched over folding ribs attached to a rod or pole and used as a protection against rain or sun

**Word History** We most often think of an umbrella as something that protects us from the rain. However, its shade can protect us from the hot sun, too. The English word *umbrella* came from an Italian word. This word came from a Latin word for an umbrella used to guard against the sun. This Latin word first meant "small shade." It was formed from a Latin word that meant "shade" or "shadow."

**umbrella**

**umi·ak** \ˈü-mē-ˌak\ *n*
an open Eskimo boat made of a wooden frame covered with hide

**um·pire** \ˈəm-ˌpīr\ *n*
a sports official who rules on plays

[1]**un-** \ˌən, ˈən\ *prefix*
not : IN-, NON- ⟨*un*skilled⟩

[2]**un-** *prefix*
**1** do the opposite of : DE- 1, DIS- 1 ⟨*un*dress⟩ ⟨*un*fold⟩
**2** deprive of, remove a specified thing from, or free or release from ⟨*un*leash⟩ ⟨*un*hand⟩
**3** completely ⟨*un*loose⟩

**un·able** \ˌən-ˈā-bəl\ *adj*
not able

**un·ac·count·able** \ˌən-ə-ˈkau̇nt-ə-bəl\ *adj*
not accountable : not to be explained : STRANGE
**un·ac·count·ably** \-blē\ *adv*

**un·ac·cus·tomed** \ˌən-ə-ˈkəs-təmd\ *adj*
not accustomed : not customary

**un·af·fect·ed** \ˌən-ə-ˈfek-təd\ *adj*
**1** not influenced or changed
**2** free from false behavior intended to impress others : GENUINE
**un·af·fect·ed·ly** *adv*

**un·afraid** \ˌən-ə-ˈfrād\ *adj*
not afraid

**un·aid·ed** \ˌən-ˈād-əd\ *adj*
not aided

**un·al·loyed** \ˌən-l-ˈȯid\ *adj*
PURE 1, 3

**unan·i·mous** \yu̇-ˈnan-ə-məs\ *adj*
**1** having the same opinion ⟨they were *unanimous* in their choice for club president⟩
**2** showing total agreement ⟨a *unanimous* vote⟩

**un·armed** \ˌən-ˈärmd\ *adj*
having no weapons or armor

**un·asked** \ˌən-ˈaskt\ *adj*
not asked or asked for

**un·as·sum·ing** \ˌən-ə-ˈsü-ming\ *adj*
MODEST 1

**un·at·trac·tive** \ˌən-ə-ˈtrak-tiv\ *adj*
not attractive : [1]PLAIN 7

**un·avoid·able** \ˈən-ə-ˈvȯid-ə-bəl\ *adj*
INEVITABLE
**un·avoid·ably** \-blē\ *adv*

[1]**un·aware** \ˌən-ə-ˈwaər, -ˈweər\ *adv*
UNAWARES

[2]**unaware** *adj*
not aware : IGNORANT ⟨*unaware* of danger⟩
**un·aware·ness** *n*

**un·awares** \ˌən-ə-ˈwaərz, -ˈweərz\ *adv*
**1** without knowing : UNINTENTIONALLY
**2** without warning : by surprise ⟨taken *unawares*⟩

**un·bal·anced** \ˌən-ˈbal-ənst\ *adj*
**1** not balanced
**2** not completely sane

**un·bear·able** \ˌən-ˈbar-ə-bəl, -ˈber-\ *adj*
seeming too great or too bad to put up with ⟨*unbearable* pain⟩
**un·bear·ably** \-blē\ *adv*

**un·be·com·ing** \ˌən-bi-ˈkəm-ing\ *adj*
not becoming : not suitable or proper ⟨*unbecoming* clothes⟩ ⟨*unbecoming* behavior⟩
**un·be·com·ing·ly** *adv*

**un·be·lief** \ˌən-bə-ˈlēf\ *n*
lack of belief

**un·be·liev·able** \ˌən-bə-ˈlē-və-bəl\ *adj*
too unlikely to be believed
**un·be·liev·ably** \-blē\ *adv*

**un·be·liev·er** \ˌən-bə-ˈlē-vər\ *n*
**1** a person who doubts what is said
**2** a person who has no religious beliefs

**un·bend** \ˌən-ˈbend\ *vb* **un·bent** \-ˈbent\; **un·bend·ing**
RELAX 3

**un·bend·ing** \ˌən-ˈben-ding\ *adj*
not relaxed and easy in manner

**un·bi·ased** \ˌən-ˈbī-əst\ *adj*
free from bias

**un·bind** \ˌən-ˈbīnd\ *vb* **un·bound** \-ˈbau̇nd\; **un·bind·ing**
**1** to remove a band from : UNTIE
**2** to set free

**un·born** \ˌən-ˈbȯrn\ *adj*
not yet born

**un·bos·om** \ˌən-ˈbu̇z-əm\ *vb*
to tell someone one's own thoughts or feelings

**un·bound·ed** \ˌən-ˈbau̇n-dəd\ *adj*
having no limits ⟨*unbounded* enthusiasm⟩

**un·break·able** \ˌən-ˈbrā-kə-bəl\ *adj*
not easily broken

**un·bro·ken** \ˌən-ˈbrō-kən\ *adj*
**1** not damaged : WHOLE
**2** not tamed for use ⟨an *unbroken* colt⟩
**3** not interrupted

**un·buck·le** \ˌən-ˈbək-əl\ *vb* **un·buck·led**; **un·buck·ling**
to unfasten the buckle of (as a belt)

**un·bur·den** \ˌən-ˈbərd-n\ *vb*
**1** to free from a burden
**2** to free oneself from (as cares)

**un·but·ton** \ˌən-ˈbət-n\ *vb*
to unfasten the buttons of (as a garment)

**un·called–for** \ˌən-ˈkȯld-ˌfȯr\ *adj*
not needed or wanted : not proper ⟨*uncalled-for* remarks⟩

**un·can·ny** \ˌən-ˈkan-ē\ *adj*
**1** MYSTERIOUS, EERIE
**2** suggesting powers or abilities greater than normal for humans ⟨an *uncanny* sense of direction⟩
**un·can·ni·ly** \-ˈkan-l-ē\ *adv*

**un·ceas·ing** \ˌən-ˈsē-sing\ *adj*
never stopping : CONTINUOUS
**un·ceas·ing·ly** *adv*

**un·cer·tain** \ˌən-ˈsərt-n\ *adj*
**1** not exactly known or decided on ⟨an *uncertain* amount⟩
**2** not known for sure

A B C D E F G H I J K L M N O P Q R S T U V W X Y Z

3 not sure
4 likely to change : not dependable ⟨*uncertain* weather⟩
**un·cer·tain·ly** *adv*

**un·cer·tain·ty** \ˌən-ˈsərt-n-tē\ *n, pl* **un·cer·tain·ties**
1 lack of certainty : DOUBT
2 something uncertain

**un·change·able** \ˌən-ˈchān-jə-bəl\ *adj*
not changing or capable of being changed

**un·changed** \ˌən-ˈchānjd\ *adj*
not changed

**un·chang·ing** \ˌən-ˈchān-jing\ *adj*
not changing or able to change

**un·charged** \ˌən-ˈchärjd\ *adj*
having no electric charge

**un·civ·il** \ˌən-ˈsiv-əl\ *adj*
IMPOLITE
**un·civ·il·ly** *adv*

**un·civ·i·lized** \ˌən-ˈsiv-ə-ˌlīzd\ *adj*
1 not civilized : BARBAROUS
2 far away from civilization : WILD

**un·cle** \ˈəng-kəl\ *n*
1 the brother of one's father or mother
2 the husband of one's aunt

**un·clean** \ˌən-ˈklēn\ *adj*
1 not pure and innocent : WICKED
2 not allowed for use by religious law
3 DIRTY 1, FILTHY
**un·clean·ness** *n*

[1]**un·clean·ly** \ˌən-ˈklen-lē\ *adj*
UNCLEAN 1, 3
**un·clean·li·ness** *n*

[2]**un·clean·ly** \ˌən-ˈklēn-lē\ *adv*
in an unclean manner

**un·cleared** \ˌən-ˈklird\ *adj*
not cleared especially of trees or brush

**Un·cle Sam** \ˌəng-kəl-ˈsam\ *n*
▶ the American government, nation, or people pictured or thought of as a person

**un·clothed** \ˌən-ˈklōthd\ *adj*
NAKED 1, 2

**un·com·fort·able** \ˌən-ˈkəm-fərt-ə-bəl, -ˈkəmf-tər-bəl\ *adj*
1 causing discomfort ⟨an *uncomfortable* chair⟩
2 feeling discomfort : UNEASY
**un·com·fort·ably** \-blē\ *adv*

**un·com·mon** \ˌən-ˈkäm-ən\ *adj*
1 not often found or seen : UNUSUAL
2 not ordinary : REMARKABLE
**synonyms** see RARE
**un·com·mon·ly** *adv*
**un·com·mon·ness** *n*

**un·com·pro·mis·ing** \ˌən-ˈkäm-prə-ˌmī-zing\ *adj*
not willing to give in even a little
**un·com·pro·mis·ing·ly** *adv*

**un·con·cern** \ˌən-kən-ˈsərn\ *n*
lack of care or interest : INDIFFERENCE

**un·con·cerned** \ˌən-kən-ˈsərnd\ *adj*
1 not involved or interested ⟨*unconcerned* with winning if the game is fun⟩
2 free of worry ⟨an *unconcerned* smile⟩ ⟨*unconcerned* about the test⟩
**un·con·cern·ed·ly** \-ˈsər-nəd-lē\ *adv*

**un·con·di·tion·al** \ˌən-kən-ˈdish-ən-l\ *adj*
without any special exceptions ⟨*unconditional* surrender⟩
**un·con·di·tion·al·ly** *adv*

**un·con·quer·able** \ˌən-ˈkäng-kə-rə-bəl\ *adj*
not capable of being beaten or overcome

**un·con·scious** \ˌən-ˈkän-chəs\ *adj*
1 not aware ⟨*unconscious* of being watched⟩
2 having lost consciousness ⟨knocked *unconscious* by a fall⟩
3 not intentional or planned ⟨an *unconscious* error⟩
**un·con·scious·ly** *adv*
**un·con·scious·ness** *n*

**Uncle Sam:**
a 19th-century doll representing Uncle Sam

**un·con·sti·tu·tion·al** \ˌən-ˌkän-stə-ˈtü-shən-l, -ˈtyü-\ *adj*
not according to the constitution (as of a government)

**un·con·trol·la·ble** \ˌən-kən-ˈtrō-lə-bəl\ *adj*
hard or impossible to control
**un·con·trol·la·bly** \-blē\ *adv*

**un·con·trolled** \ˌən-kən-ˈtrōld\ *adj*
not being controlled

**un·couth** \ˌən-ˈküth\ *adj*
vulgar in conduct or speech : CRUDE ⟨*uncouth* manners⟩ ⟨*uncouth* people⟩
**un·couth·ly** *adv*

**Word History** The word *uncouth* first meant "unknown" or "strange." It was made up of the prefix *un-* and an Old English word that meant "known." The modern English words *can* and *know* are relatives of this Old English word.

**un·cov·er** \ˌən-ˈkəv-ər\ *vb*
1 to make known ⟨*uncover* a crime⟩
2 to make visible by removing some covering

**un·cul·ti·vat·ed** \ˌən-ˈkəl-tə-ˌvāt-əd\ *adj*
not cultivated ⟨*uncultivated* fields⟩

**un·curl** \ˌən-ˈkərl\ *vb*
to make or become straightened out from a curled position

**un·cut** \ˌən-ˈkət\ *adj*
1 not cut down or cut into ⟨*uncut* forests⟩
2 not shaped by cutting ⟨an *uncut* diamond⟩

**un·daunt·ed** \ˌən-ˈdònt-əd\ *adj*
not discouraged or frightened : FEARLESS

**un·de·cid·ed** \ˌən-di-ˈsīd-əd\ *adj*
1 not settled ⟨the date for the picnic is still *undecided*⟩
2 not having decided ⟨we are still *undecided* about the date⟩

**un·de·clared** \ˌən-di-ˈklaərd, -ˈkleərd\ *adj*
not announced or openly confessed ⟨an *undeclared* war⟩

**un·de·fined** \ˌən-di-ˈfīnd\ *adj*
not defined

**un·de·ni·able** \ˌən-di-ˈnī-ə-bəl\ *adj*
plainly true
**un·de·ni·ably** \-blē\ *adv*

[1]**un·der** \ˈən-dər\ *adv*
**1** in or into a position below or beneath something ⟨the diver went *under* again⟩
**2** below some quantity or level ⟨ten dollars or *under*⟩
**3** so as to be covered or hidden ⟨turned *under* by the plow⟩

[2]**under** *prep*
**1** lower than and topped or sheltered by ⟨*under* a tree⟩
**2** below the surface of ⟨*under* the sea⟩
**3** in or into such a position as to be covered or hidden by ⟨a vest *under* my jacket⟩
**4** commanded or guided by ⟨the soldiers who served *under* George Washington⟩
**5** controlled or limited by ⟨*under* lock and key⟩
**6** affected or influenced by the action or effect of ⟨the disease is *under* treatment⟩
**7** within the division or grouping of ⟨*under* this heading⟩
**8** less or lower than (as in size, amount, or rank) ⟨paid *under* a dollar⟩ ⟨weighs *under* two pounds⟩

[3]**under** *adj*
**1** lying or placed below or beneath
**2** [1]SUBORDINATE 1 ⟨the *under* secretary⟩

**un·der·brush** \ˈən-dər-ˌbrəsh\ *n*
shrubs and small trees growing among large trees

**un·der·clothes** \ˈən-dər-ˌklōz, -ˌklōthz\ *n pl*
UNDERWEAR

**un·der·cloth·ing** \ˈən-dər-ˌklō-thing\ *n*
UNDERWEAR

**un·der·dog** \ˈən-dər-ˌdȯg\ *n*
a person or team thought to have little chance of winning (as an election or a game)

**un·der·foot** \ˌən-dər-ˈfu̇t\ *adv*
**1** under the feet ⟨flowers trampled *underfoot*⟩
**2** close about one's feet **:** in one's way ⟨a puppy always *underfoot*⟩

**un·der·gar·ment** \ˈən-dər-ˌgär-mənt\ *n*
a garment to be worn under another

**un·der·go** \ˌən-dər-ˈgō\ *vb*
**un·der·went** \-ˈwent\; **un·der·gone** \-ˈgȯn\; **un·der·go·ing** \-ˈgō-ing\
to have (something) done or happen to oneself **:** EXPERIENCE ⟨*undergo* an operation⟩

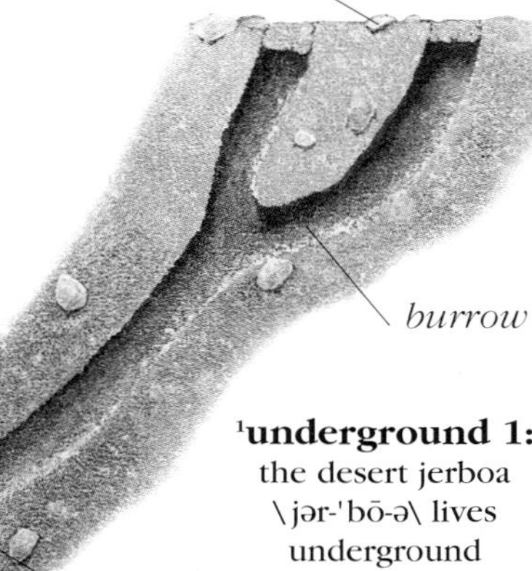

[1]**underground 1:** the desert jerboa \jər-ˈbō-ə\ lives underground

[1]**un·der·ground** \ˌən-dər-ˈgrau̇nd\ *adv*
**1** ▲ beneath the surface of the earth
**2** in or into hiding or secret operation

[2]**un·der·ground** \ˈən-dər-ˌgrau̇nd\ *n*
**1** SUBWAY 2
**2** a secret political movement or group

[3]**un·der·ground** \ˈən-dər-ˌgrau̇nd\ *adj*
**1** being or growing under the surface of the ground
**2** done or happening secretly

**un·der·growth** \ˈən-dər-ˌgrōth\ *n*
UNDERBRUSH

[1]**un·der·hand** \ˈən-dər-ˌhand\ *adv*
in a secret or dishonest manner

[2]**underhand** *adj*
**1** done in secret or so as to deceive
**2** made with an upward movement of the hand or arm ⟨an *underhand* throw⟩

**un·der·hand·ed** \ˌən-dər-ˈhan-dəd\ *adj*
[2]UNDERHAND 1
**un·der·hand·ed·ly** *adv*
**un·der·hand·ed·ness** *n*

**un·der·lie** \ˌən-dər-ˈlī\ *vb*
**un·der·lay** \-ˈlā\; **un·der·lain** \-ˈlān\; **un·der·ly·ing** \-ˈlī-ing\
**1** to be under
**2** to form the foundation of **:** SUPPORT ⟨the ideas that *underlie* democracy⟩

**un·der·line** \ˈən-dər-ˌlīn\ *vb*
**un·der·lined**; **un·der·lin·ing**
**1** to draw a line under
**2** EMPHASIZE

**un·der·lip** \ˌən-dər-ˈlip\ *n*
the lower lip

**un·der·mine** \ˌən-dər-ˈmīn\ *vb*
**un·der·mined**; **un·der·min·ing**
**1** to dig out or wear away the supporting earth beneath ⟨*undermine* a wall⟩
**2** to weaken secretly or little by little ⟨*undermining* their confidence⟩

[1]**un·der·neath** \ˌən-dər-ˈnēth\ *prep*
directly under ⟨wore their bathing suits *underneath* their clothes⟩

[2]**underneath** *adv*
**1** below a surface or object **:** BENEATH ⟨soaked through to the shirt *underneath*⟩
**2** on the lower side ⟨the bread was scorched *underneath*⟩

**un·der·nour·ished** \ˌən-dər-ˈnər-isht\ *adj*
given too little nourishment
**un·der·nour·ish·ment** \-ish-mənt\ *n*

**un·der·pants** \ˈən-dər-ˌpants\ *n pl*
pants worn under an outer garment

**un·der·part** \ˈən-dər-ˌpärt\ *n*
▼ a part lying on the lower side especially of a bird or mammal

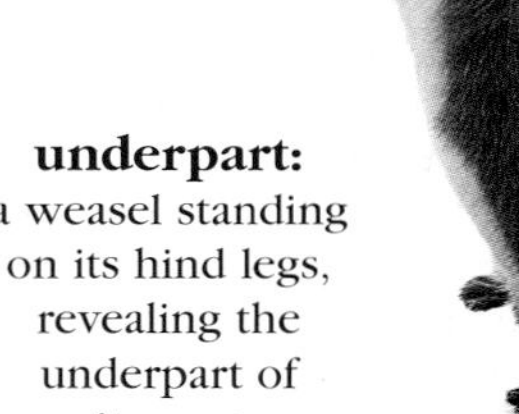

**underpart:** a weasel standing on its hind legs, revealing the underpart of its coat

**un·der·pass** \'ən-dər-ˌpas\ *n*
a passage underneath something (as for a road passing under a railroad or another road)

**un·der·priv·i·leged** \ˌən-dər-'priv-ə-lijd\ *adj*
having fewer advantages than others especially because of being poor

**un·der·rate** \ˌən-dər-'rāt\ *vb*
**un·der·rat·ed**; **un·der·rat·ing**
to rate too low : UNDERVALUE

**un·der·score** \'ən-dər-ˌskōr\ *vb*
**un·der·scored**; **un·der·scor·ing**
UNDERLINE

[1]**un·der·sea** \'ən-dər-'sē\ *adj*
**1** being or done under the sea or under the surface of the sea
**2** used under the surface of the sea ⟨an *undersea* fleet⟩

[2]**un·der·sea** \ˌən-dər-'sē\ *or* **un·der·seas** \-'sēz\ *adv*
under the surface of the sea

**un·der·sell** \ˌən-dər-'sel\ *vb*
**un·der·sold** \-'sōld\; **un·der·sell·ing**
to sell articles cheaper than ⟨*undersell* a competitor⟩

**un·der·shirt** \'ən-dər-ˌshərt\ *n*
a collarless garment with or without sleeves that is worn next to the body

**un·der·side** \'ən-dər-ˌsīd\ *n*
the side or surface lying underneath

**un·der·skirt** \'ən-dər-ˌskərt\ *n*
PETTICOAT

**un·der·stand** \ˌən-dər-'stand\ *vb*
**un·der·stood** \-'stu̇d\; **un·der·stand·ing**
**1** to get the meaning of
**2** to know thoroughly ⟨I *understand* Spanish⟩
**3** to have reason to believe ⟨I *understand* that they will come today⟩
**4** to take as meaning something not openly made known ⟨I *understand* the letter to be a refusal⟩
**5** to have a sympathetic attitude
**6** to accept as settled ⟨it is *understood* that I will pay⟩

**un·der·stand·able** \ˌən-dər-'stan-də-bəl\ *adj*
possible or easy to understand
**un·der·stand·ably** \-blē\ *adv*

[1]**un·der·stand·ing** \ˌən-dər-'stan-ding\ *n*
**1** ability to get the meaning of and judge
**2** AGREEMENT 2 ⟨we've come to an *understanding* about how to decorate the room⟩

[2]**understanding** *adj*
having or showing kind or favorable feelings toward others : SYMPATHETIC

**un·der·study** \'ən-dər-ˌstəd-ē\ *n, pl* **un·der·stud·ies**
an actor who is prepared to take over another actor's part if necessary

**un·der·take** \ˌən-dər-'tāk\ *vb*
**un·der·took** \-'tu̇k\; **un·der·tak·en** \-'tā-kən\; **un·der·tak·ing**
**1** to plan or try to accomplish ⟨*undertook* a trip around the world⟩
**2** to take on as a duty : AGREE ⟨I *undertake* to pay you ten percent interest⟩

**un·der·tak·er** \'ən-dər-ˌtā-kər\ *n*
a person whose business is to prepare the dead for burial and to take charge of funerals

**un·der·tak·ing** \'ən-dər-ˌtā-king\ *n*
**1** the act of a person who undertakes something
**2** the business of an undertaker
**3** something undertaken ⟨learning a language is a serious *undertaking*⟩

**un·der·tone** \'ən-dər-ˌtōn\ *n*
**1** a low or quiet tone ⟨spoke in *undertones*⟩
**2** a partly hidden feeling ⟨an *undertone* of anger in the answer⟩

**un·der·tow** \'ən-dər-ˌtō\ *n*
a current beneath the surface of the water that moves away from or along the shore while the surface water above it moves toward the shore

**un·der·val·ue** \ˌən-dər-'val-yü\ *vb*
**un·der·val·ued**; **un·der·valu·ing**
to value below the real worth

[1]**un·der·wa·ter** \'ən-dər-'wȯt-ər, -'wät-\ *adj*
lying, growing, worn, or operating below the surface of the water

[2]**un·der·wa·ter** \ˌən-dər-'wȯt-ər, -'wät-\ *adv*
under the surface of the water ⟨liked to swim *underwater*⟩

**un·der·wear** \'ən-dər-ˌwaər, -ˌweər\ *n*
clothing worn next to the skin and under other clothing

**un·der·weight** \ˌən-dər-'wāt\ *adj*
weighing less than what is normal, average, or necessary

**underwent** *past of* UNDERGO

**un·der·world** \'ən-dər-ˌwərld\ *n*
the world of organized crime

[1]**un·de·sir·able** \ˌən-di-'zī-rə-bəl\ *adj*
not desirable
**un·de·sir·ably** \-blē\ *adv*

[2]**undesirable** *n*
an undesirable person

**un·de·vel·oped** \ˌən-di-'vel-əpt\ *adj*
not developed

**un·di·gest·ed** \ˌən-dī-'jest-əd, -də-\ *adj*
not digested

**un·dig·ni·fied** \ˌən-'dig-nə-ˌfīd\ *adj*
not dignified

**un·dis·cov·ered** \ˌən-dis-'kəv-ərd\ *adj*
not discovered

**un·dis·put·ed** \ˌən-dis-'pyüt-əd\ *adj*
not disputed : UNQUESTIONABLE ⟨the *undisputed* leader⟩

**un·dis·turbed** \ˌən-dis-'tərbd\ *adj*
not disturbed

**un·do** \ˌən-'dü\ *vb* **un·did** \-'did\; **un·done** \-'dən\; **un·do·ing** \-'dü-ing\; **un·does** \-'dəz\
**1** UNTIE, UNFASTEN ⟨*undo* a knot⟩ ⟨*undo* a boat from its mooring⟩
**2** UNWRAP, OPEN ⟨*undo* a package⟩
**3** to destroy the effect of
**4** to cause the ruin of

**un·do·ing** \ˌən-'dü-ing\ *n*
**1** an act or instance of unfastening
**2** a cause of ruin or destruction ⟨my quick temper was my *undoing*⟩

**un·done** \ˌən-'dən\ *adj*
not done or finished

**un·doubt·ed** \ˌən-'dau̇t-əd\ *adj*
not doubted

**un·doubt·ed·ly** \ˌən-'dau̇t-əd-lē\ *adv*
without doubt : SURELY

**un·dress** \ˌən-'dres\ *vb*
to remove the clothes or covering of

**un·dy·ing** \ˌən-'dī-ing\ *adj*
living or lasting forever : IMMORTAL ⟨*undying* devotion⟩

**un·earth** \ˌən-ˈərth\ *vb*
**1** to drive or draw from the earth : dig up ⟨*unearth* a fox from its den⟩
**2** to bring to light : UNCOVER ⟨*unearthed* a plot to cheat the government⟩

**un·easy** \ˌən-ˈē-zē\ *adj* **un·eas·i·er**; **un·eas·i·est**
**1** not easy in manner : AWKWARD
**2** disturbed by pain or worry : RESTLESS
**un·eas·i·ly** \-zə-lē\ *adv*
**un·eas·i·ness** \-zē-nəs\ *n*

**unfledged:**
a nest of unfledged egret chicks

**un·ed·u·cat·ed** \ˌən-ˈej-ə-ˌkāt-əd\ *adj*
not educated

**un·em·ployed** \ˌən-im-ˈplȯid\ *adj*
not employed : having no job

**un·em·ploy·ment** \ˌən-im-ˈplȯi-mənt\ *n*
the state of being unemployed

**un·end·ing** \ˌən-ˈen-ding\ *adj*
having no ending : ENDLESS
**un·end·ing·ly** *adv*

**un·equal** \ˌən-ˈē-kwəl\ *adj*
**1** not alike (as in size or value)
**2** badly balanced or matched ⟨an *unequal* fight⟩
**3** not having the needed abilities ⟨proved *unequal* to the task⟩
**un·equal·ly** *adv*

**un·equaled** \ˌən-ˈē-kwəld\ *adj*
not equaled

**un·even** \ˌən-ˈē-vən\ *adj*
**1** ODD 2 ⟨*uneven* numbers⟩
**2** not level or smooth ⟨an *uneven* surface⟩
**3** IRREGULAR 3 ⟨*uneven* teeth⟩
**4** varying in quality ⟨an *uneven* performance⟩
**5** UNEQUAL 2
**un·even·ly** *adv*
**un·even·ness** *n*

**un·event·ful** \ˌən-i-ˈvent-fəl\ *adj*
not eventful : including no interesting or important happenings ⟨an *uneventful* vacation⟩
**un·event·ful·ly** \-fə-lē\ *adv*

**un·ex·pect·ed** \ˌən-ik-ˈspek-təd\ *adj*
not expected ⟨an *unexpected* visit⟩
**un·ex·pect·ed·ly** *adv*
**un·ex·pect·ed·ness** *n*

**un·fail·ing** \ˌən-ˈfā-ling\ *adj*
not failing or likely to fail
**un·fail·ing·ly** *adv*

**un·fair** \ˌən-ˈfaər, -ˈfeər\ *adj*
not fair, honest, or just
**un·fair·ly** *adv*
**un·fair·ness** *n*

**un·faith·ful** \ˌən-ˈfāth-fəl\ *adj*
not faithful : DISLOYAL
**un·faith·ful·ly** \-fə-lē\ *adv*
**un·faith·ful·ness** *n*

**un·fa·mil·iar** \ˌən-fə-ˈmil-yər\ *adj*
**1** not well known : STRANGE ⟨look up *unfamiliar* words in your dictionary⟩
**2** not well acquainted ⟨I'm *unfamiliar* with this word⟩

**un·fa·mil·iar·i·ty** \ˌən-fə-ˌmil-ˈyar-ət-ē\ *n*
the quality or state of being unfamiliar

**un·fas·ten** \ˌən-ˈfas-n\ *vb*
to make or become loose : UNDO

**un·fa·vor·able** \ˌən-ˈfā-və-rə-bəl\ *adj*
**1** not approving
**2** likely to make difficult or unpleasant ⟨*unfavorable* weather for a camping trip⟩
**un·fa·vor·ably** \-blē\ *adv*

**un·feel·ing** \ˌən-ˈfē-ling\ *adj*
**1** not able to feel ⟨the *unfeeling* sky⟩
**2** having no kindness or sympathy : CRUEL
**un·feel·ing·ly** *adv*

**un·fin·ished** \ˌən-ˈfin-isht\ *adj*
not finished

**un·fit** \ˌən-ˈfit\ *adj*
**1** not suitable ⟨*unfit* to eat⟩
**2** not qualified
**3** UNSOUND 1, 2 ⟨feeling very *unfit*⟩
**un·fit·ness** *n*

**un·fledged** \ˌən-ˈflejd\ *adj*
◀ not feathered or ready for flight ⟨a nest of *unfledged* robins⟩

**un·fold** \ˌən-ˈfōld\ *vb*
**1** to open the folds of : open up
**2** to lay open to view : REVEAL ⟨*unfold* a plan⟩
**3** to develop gradually

**un·fore·seen** \ˌən-fōr-ˈsēn\ *adj*
not known beforehand

**un·for·get·ta·ble** \ˌən-fər-ˈget-ə-bəl\ *adj*
not likely to be forgotten ⟨an *unforgettable* experience⟩
**un·for·get·ta·bly** \-blē\ *adv*

**un·for·giv·able** \ˌən-fər-ˈgiv-ə-bəl\ *adj*
not to be forgiven or pardoned
**un·for·giv·ably** \-blē\ *adv*

[1]**un·for·tu·nate** \ˌən-ˈfȯr-chə-nət\ *adj*
**1** not fortunate : UNLUCKY
**2** not proper or suitable ⟨an *unfortunate* remark⟩ **synonyms** see UNLUCKY
**un·for·tu·nate·ly** *adv*

[2]**unfortunate** *n*
an unfortunate person

**un·found·ed** \ˌən-ˈfau̇n-dəd\ *adj*
being without a sound basis

**un·friend·ly** \ˌən-ˈfrend-lē\ *adj* **un·friend·li·er**; **un·friend·li·est**
not friendly or favorable : HOSTILE
**un·friend·li·ness** *n*

**un·fruit·ful** \ˌən-ˈfrüt-fəl\ *adj*
**1** not bearing fruit or offspring
**2** not producing a desired result ⟨*unfruitful* efforts⟩

**un·furl** \ˌən-ˈfərl\ *vb*
to open out from a rolled or folded state ⟨*unfurl* a flag⟩

**un·fur·nished** \ˌən-ˈfər-nisht\ *adj*
not supplied with furniture ⟨an *unfurnished* apartment⟩

**un·gain·ly** \ˌən-ˈgān-lē\ *adj* **un·gain·li·er**; **un·gain·li·est**
CLUMSY 1, AWKWARD ⟨an *ungainly* walk⟩
**un·gain·li·ness** *n*

**un·god·ly** \ˌən-ˈgäd-lē\ *adj* **un·god·li·er**; **un·god·li·est**
**1** disobedient to or denying God : IMPIOUS
**2** SINFUL, WICKED

a b c d e f g h i j k l m n o p q r s t u v w x y z

3 not normal or bearable ⟨got up at an *ungodly* hour⟩

**un·gra·cious** \,ən-'grā-shəs\ *adj*
not gracious or polite
**un·gra·cious·ly** *adv*

**un·grate·ful** \,ən-'grāt-fəl\ *adj*
not grateful
**un·grate·ful·ly** \-fə-lē\ *adv*
**un·grate·ful·ness** *n*

**¹un·gu·late** \'əng-gyə-lət\ *adj*
having hooves ⟨horses and cows are *ungulate* animals⟩

**²ungulate** *n*
a hoofed animal

**un·hand** \,ən-'hand\ *vb*
to remove the hand from : let go

**un·hap·py** \,ən-'hap-ē\ *adj*
**un·hap·pi·er**; **un·hap·pi·est**
1 not fortunate : UNLUCKY
2 not cheerful : SAD
3 not suitable
**un·hap·pi·ly** \-'hap-ə-lē\ *adv*
**un·hap·pi·ness** \-'hap-ē-nəs\ *n*

**un·health·ful** \,ən-'helth-fəl\ *adj*
not healthful

**un·healthy** \,ən-'hel-thē\ *adj*
**un·health·i·er**; **un·health·i·est**
1 not good for one's health ⟨an *unhealthy* climate⟩
2 not in good health : SICKLY
3 HARMFUL, BAD ⟨an *unhealthy* situation⟩
**un·health·i·ly** \-thə-lē\ *adv*

**un·heard** \,ən-'hərd\ *adj*
not heard

**un·heard–of** \,ən-'hərd-,əv, -,äv\ *adj*
not known before

**un·hin·dered** \,ən-'hin-dərd\ *adj*
not hindered : not kept back ⟨*unhindered* progress⟩

**un·hitch** \,ən-'hich\ *vb*
to free from being hitched

**un·ho·ly** \,ən-'hō-lē\ *adj*
**un·ho·li·er**; **un·ho·li·est**
1 not holy : WICKED
2 UNGODLY 3 ⟨stop that *unholy* racket⟩
**un·ho·li·ness** *n*

**un·hook** \,ən-'hu̇k\ *vb*
1 to remove from a hook
2 to unfasten the hooks of

**un·horse** \,ən-'hȯrs\ *vb*
**un·horsed**; **un·hors·ing**
to cause to fall from or as if from a horse

**un·hur·ried** \,ən-'hər-ēd\ *adj*
not hurried

**uni-** \'yü-ni\ *prefix*
one : single

## ²uniform

One of the purposes of a uniform is to make a group of people immediately recognizable. Most uniforms are also designed to be comfortable and helpful for the wearers while they work. This is especially important for workers like firefighters and members of the armed forces.

US police officer

British nurse

Australian firefighter

**uni·corn** \'yü-nə-,kȯrn\ *n*
an imaginary animal that looks like a horse with one horn in the middle of the forehead

**un·iden·ti·fied** \,ən-ī-'dent-ə-,fīd\ *adj*
not identified

**uni·fi·ca·tion** \,yü-nə-fə-'kā-shən\ *n*
the act, process, or result of unifying : the state of being unified

**¹uni·form** \'yü-nə-,fȯrm\ *adj*
1 having always the same form, manner, or degree : not changing
2 of the same form with others ⟨hats of *uniform* style⟩
**uni·form·ly** *adv*

**²uniform** *n*
▲ special clothing worn by members of a particular group (as an army)

**uni·formed** \'yü-nə-,fȯrmd\ *adj*
dressed in uniform

**uni·for·mi·ty** \,yü-nə-'fȯr-mət-ē\ *n, pl* **uni·for·mi·ties**
the quality or state or an instance of being uniform

**uniform resource lo·ca·tor** \-'lō-,kāt-ər, -lō-'kā-\ *n*
URL

**uni·fy** \'yü-nə-,fī\ *vb* **uni·fied**; **uni·fy·ing**
to make into or become a unit : UNITE

**un·im·por·tant** \,ən-im-'pȯrt-nt\ *adj*
not important

**un·in·hab·it·ed** \,ən-in-'hab-ət-əd\ *adj*
not lived in or on ⟨an *uninhabited* island⟩

**un·in·tel·li·gi·ble** \,ən-in-'tel-ə-jə-bəl\ *adj*
impossible to understand

**un·in·ten·tion·al** \,ən-in-'ten-chən-l\ *adj*
not intentional
**un·in·ten·tion·al·ly** *adv*

**un·in·ter·est·ed** \,ən-'in-trəs-təd, -'int-ə-rəs-\ *adj*
not interested

**un·in·ter·est·ing** \,ən-'in-trəs-ting, -'int-ə-rəs-\ *adj*
not attracting interest or attention

**un·in·ter·rupt·ed** \,ən-,int-ə-'rəp-təd\ *adj*
not interrupted : CONTINUOUS

**union** \'yün-yən\ *n*
1 an act or instance of uniting two

or more things into one
**2** something (as a nation) formed by a combining of parts or members
**3** a device for connecting parts (as of a machine)
**4** LABOR UNION

**Union** *adj*
of or relating to the side favoring the federal union in the American Civil War

**unique** \yu̇-'nēk\ *adj*
**1** being the only one of its kind
**2** very unusual
**unique·ly** *adv*
**unique·ness** *n*

**uni·son** \'yü-nə-sən\ *n*
**1** sameness of musical pitch
**2** the state of being tuned or sounded at the same pitch or at an octave
**3** exact agreement

**unit** \'yü-nət\ *n*
**1** the least whole number : ONE
**2** a fixed quantity (as of length, time, or value) used as a standard of measurement
**3** a single thing, person, or group forming part of a whole
**4** a part of a school course with a central theme

**unite** \yu̇-'nīt\ *vb* **unit·ed**; **unit·ing**
**1** to put or come together to form a single unit
**2** to bind by legal or moral ties ⟨nations *united* by a treaty⟩
**3** to join in action ⟨the two groups *united* to fight for better schools⟩

**unit·ed** \yu̇-'nīt-əd\ *adj*
**1** made one ⟨*United* States of America⟩
**2** being in agreement

**uni·ty** \'yü-nət-ē\ *n*
**1** the quality or state of being one
**2** the state of those who are in full agreement : HARMONY ⟨live in *unity* with one another⟩

**uni·ver·sal** \,yü-nə-'vər-səl\ *adj*
**1** including, covering, or taking in all or everything
**2** present or happening everywhere
**uni·ver·sal·ly** *adv*

**universal resource lo·ca·tor** \-'lō-,kāt-ər, -lō-'kā-\ *n*
URL

**uni·verse** \'yü-nə-,vərs\ *n*
all created things including the earth and celestial bodies viewed as making up one system

**uni·ver·si·ty** \,yü-nə-'vər-sət-ē\ *n, pl* **uni·ver·si·ties**
an institution of higher learning that gives degrees in special fields (as law and medicine) as well as in the arts and sciences

**un·just** \,ən-'jəst\ *adj*
not just : UNFAIR ⟨an *unjust* decision⟩
**un·just·ly** *adv*

**un·kempt** \,ən-'kempt\ *adj*
**1** not combed ⟨*unkempt* hair⟩
**2** not neat and orderly : UNTIDY

**un·kind** \,ən-'kīnd\ *adj*
not kind or sympathetic ⟨an *unkind* remark⟩
**un·kind·ly** *adv*
**un·kind·ness** *n*

[1]**un·known** \,ən-'nōn\ *adj*
not known ⟨*unknown* lands⟩

[2]**unknown** *n*
one (as a quantity) that is unknown

**un·lace** \,ən-'lās\ *vb* **un·laced**; **un·lac·ing**
to untie the laces of ⟨*unlace* a shoe⟩

**un·latch** \,ən-'lach\ *vb*
to open by lifting a latch

**un·law·ful** \,ən-'lȯ-fəl\ *adj*
not lawful : ILLEGAL
**un·law·ful·ly** \-fə-lē\ *adv*

**un·learned** *adj*
**1** \,ən-'lər-nəd\ : not educated
**2** \-'lərnd\ : not based on experience : INSTINCTIVE

**un·leash** \,ən-'lēsh\ *vb*
to free from or as if from a leash ⟨a storm *unleashed* its fury⟩

**un·less** \ən-,les\ *conj*
except on the condition that ⟨you can't have dessert *unless* you finish your dinner⟩

[1]**un·like** \,ən-'līk\ *adj*
DIFFERENT, UNEQUAL
**un·like·ness** *n*

[2]**unlike** *prep*
**1** different from ⟨you are *unlike* the rest⟩
**2** unusual for ⟨it's *unlike* them to be so late⟩
**3** differently from ⟨I behave *unlike* the others⟩

**un·like·ly** \ən-'lī-klē\ *adj* **un·like·li·er**; **un·like·li·est**
**1** not likely ⟨an *unlikely* story⟩
**2** not promising ⟨an *unlikely* place for fishing⟩
**un·like·li·ness** *n*

**un·lim·it·ed** \,ən-'lim-ət-əd\ *adj*
**1** having no restrictions or controls ⟨*unlimited* freedom⟩
**2** BOUNDLESS, INFINITE

**un·load** \,ən-'lōd\ *vb*
**1** ▼ to take away or off : REMOVE ⟨*unload* cargo⟩
**2** to take a load from ⟨*unload* a ship⟩
**3** to get rid of or be freed from a load or burden ⟨the ship is *unloading*⟩

**un·lock** \,ən-'läk\ *vb*
**1** to unfasten the lock of
**2** to make known ⟨scientists *unlocking* the secrets of nature⟩

**un·looked–for** \,ən-'lu̇kt-,fȯr\ *adj*
not expected ⟨an *unlooked-for* treat⟩

**unload 1:**
cranes being used to unload cargo from a ship

A B C D E F G H I J K L M N O P Q R S T U V W X Y Z

**un·loose** \ˌən-ˈlüs\ *vb* **un·loosed**; **un·loos·ing**
**1** to make looser : RELAX ⟨*unloose* one's grip on a rope⟩
**2** to set free

**un·lucky** \ˌən-ˈlək-ē\ *adj* **un·luck·i·er**; **un·luck·i·est**
**1** not fortunate
**2** likely to bring misfortune
**3** causing distress or regret
**un·luck·i·ly** \-ˈlək-ə-lē\ *adv*
**un·luck·i·ness** \-ˈlək-ē-nəs\ *n*

**Synonyms** UNLUCKY and UNFORTUNATE mean having or experiencing bad luck. UNLUCKY suggests that one continually meets with bad luck no matter how hard one tries or how well one does ⟨an *unlucky* political candidate⟩. UNFORTUNATE suggests not so much simple bad luck as it does an unhappy situation or misery ⟨missionaries helping the *unfortunate* peoples of the world⟩.

**un·man·age·able** \ˌən-ˈman-ij-ə-bəl\ *adj*
hard or impossible to manage

**un·man·ner·ly** \ˌən-ˈman-ər-lē\ *adj*
not having or showing good manners

**un·mar·ried** \ˌən-ˈmar-ēd\ *adj*
not married

**un·mis·tak·able** \ˌən-mə-ˈstā-kə-bəl\ *adj*
impossible to mistake for anything else
**un·mis·tak·ably** \-blē\ *adv*

**un·moved** \ˌən-ˈmüvd\ *adj*
**1** not moved by deep feelings or excitement : CALM
**2** staying in the same place or position

**un·nat·u·ral** \ˌən-ˈnach-ə-rəl, -ˈnach-rəl\ *adj*
**1** not natural or normal
**2** ARTIFICIAL 3
**un·nat·u·ral·ly** *adv*
**un·nat·u·ral·ness** *n*

**un·nec·es·sary** \ˌən-ˈnes-ə-ˌser-ē\ *adj*
not necessary
**un·nec·es·sar·i·ly** \ˈən-ˌnes-ə-ˈser-ə-lē\ *adv*

**un·nerve** \ˌən-ˈnərv\ *vb* **un·nerved**; **un·nerv·ing**
to cause to lose confidence, courage, or self-control

**un·no·tice·able** \ˌən-ˈnōt-ə-sə-bəl\ *adj*
not easily noticed

**un·num·bered** \ˌən-ˈnəm-bərd\ *adj*
**1** not numbered ⟨an *unnumbered* page⟩
**2** INNUMERABLE

**un·ob·served** \ˌən-əb-ˈzərvd\ *adj*
not observed

**un·oc·cu·pied** \ˌən-ˈäk-yə-ˌpīd\ *adj*
**1** not busy
**2**▼ not occupied : EMPTY

**un·pop·u·lar** \ˌən-ˈpäp-yə-lər\ *adj*
not popular

**un·pre·dict·able** \ˌən-pri-ˈdik-tə-bəl\ *adj*
impossible to predict ⟨*unpredictable* hazards of travel⟩

**un·prej·u·diced** \ˌən-ˈprej-ə-dəst\ *adj*
not prejudiced

**un·pre·pared** \ˌən-pri-ˈpaərd, -ˈpeərd\ *adj*
not prepared

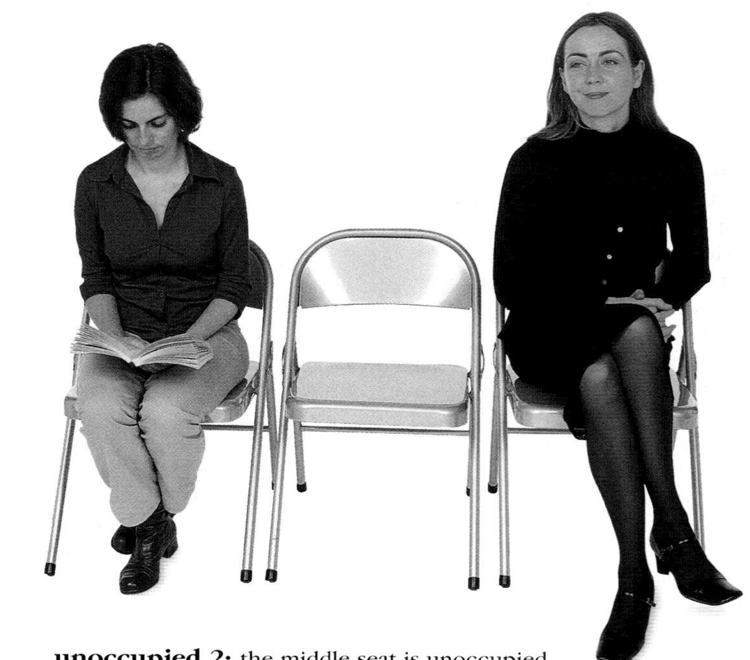

**unoccupied 2:** the middle seat is unoccupied

**un·of·fi·cial** \ˌən-ə-ˈfish-əl\ *adj*
not official
**un·of·fi·cial·ly** *adv*

**un·pack** \ˌən-ˈpak\ *vb*
**1** to separate and remove things that are packed
**2** to open and remove the contents of ⟨*unpack* a suitcase⟩

**un·paid** \ˌən-ˈpād\ *adj*
not paid

**un·paint·ed** \ˌən-ˈpānt-əd\ *adj*
not painted

**un·par·al·leled** \ˌən-ˈpar-ə-ˌleld\ *adj*
having no parallel or equal

**un·pleas·ant** \ˌən-ˈplez-nt\ *adj*
not pleasant
**un·pleas·ant·ly** *adv*
**un·pleas·ant·ness** *n*

**un·prin·ci·pled** \ˌən-ˈprin-sə-pəld\ *adj*
not having or showing high moral principles ⟨*unprincipled* behavior⟩

**un·ques·tion·able** \ˌən-ˈkwes-chə-nə-bəl\ *adj*
being beyond question or doubt
**un·ques·tion·ably** \-blē\ *adv*

**un·rav·el** \ˌən-ˈrav-əl\ *vb* **un·rav·eled** *or* **un·rav·elled**; **un·rav·el·ing** *or* **un·rav·el·ling**
**1** to separate the threads of : UNTANGLE
**2** SOLVE ⟨*unravel* a mystery⟩

**un·re·al** \ˌən-ˈrē-əl\ *adj*
not real

**un·rea·son·able** \ˌən-ˈrēz-n-ə-bəl\ *adj*
not reasonable ⟨*unreasonable*

behavior⟩ ⟨*unreasonable* prices⟩
**un·rea·son·able·ness** *n*
**un·rea·son·ably** \-blē\ *adv*

**un·re·lent·ing** \ˌən-ri-ˈlent-iŋ\ *adj*
**1** not giving in or softening in determination : STERN
**2** not letting up or weakening in energy or pace
**un·re·lent·ing·ly** *adv*

**un·re·li·able** \ˌən-ri-ˈlī-ə-bəl\ *adj*
not reliable

**un·rest** \ˌən-ˈrest\ *n*
a disturbed or uneasy state ⟨political *unrest*⟩

**un·righ·teous** \ˌən-ˈrī-chəs\ *adj*
not righteous
**un·righ·teous·ly** *adv*
**un·righ·teous·ness** *n*

**un·ripe** \ˌən-ˈrīp\ *adj*
▶ not ripe or mature

**un·ri·valed** *or* **un·ri·valled** \ˌən-ˈrī-vəld\ *adj*
having no rival

**un·roll** \ˌən-ˈrōl\ *vb*
**1** to unwind a roll of
**2** to become unrolled

**un·ruf·fled** \ˌən-ˈrəf-əld\ *adj*
**1** not upset or disturbed
**2** ¹SMOOTH 4 ⟨*unruffled* water⟩

**un·ruly** \ˌən-ˈrü-lē\ *adj*
**un·rul·i·er**; **un·rul·i·est**
not yielding easily to rule or restriction
**un·rul·i·ness** *n*

**un·safe** \ˌən-ˈsāf\ *adj*
exposed or exposing to danger ⟨people are *unsafe* on the streets⟩ ⟨the bridge is *unsafe* for heavy trucks⟩

**un·san·i·tary** \ˌən-ˈsan-ə-ˌter-ē\ *adj*
not sanitary

**un·sat·is·fac·to·ry** \ˈən-ˌsat-əs-ˈfak-tə-rē\ *adj*
not satisfactory
**un·sat·is·fac·to·ri·ly** \-rə-lē\ *adv*

**un·sat·is·fied** \ˌən-ˈsat-əs-ˌfīd\ *adj*
not satisfied

**un·say** \ˌən-ˈsā\ *vb* **un·said** \-ˈsed\; **un·say·ing** \-ˈsā-iŋ\
to take back (something said)

**un·schooled** \ˌən-ˈsküld\ *adj*
not trained or taught

**un·sci·en·tif·ic** \ˌən-ˌsī-ən-ˈtif-ik\ *adj*
not scientific
**un·sci·en·tif·i·cal·ly** \-i-kə-lē\ *adv*

**un·scram·ble** \ˌən-ˈskram-bəl\ *vb*
**un·scram·bled**; **un·scram·bling**
to make orderly or clear again ⟨*unscramble* a mix-up about seating⟩ ⟨*unscramble* a radio message⟩

**un·screw** \ˌən-ˈskrü\ *vb*
**1** to remove the screws from
**2** to loosen or withdraw by turning ⟨*unscrew* a light bulb⟩

**un·scru·pu·lous** \ˌən-ˈskrü-pyə-ləs\ *adj*
not scrupulous
**un·scru·pu·lous·ly** *adv*

**un·seal** \ˌən-ˈsēl\ *vb*
to break or remove the seal of : OPEN

**unripe:** a bunch of unripe bananas

**un·sea·son·able** \ˌən-ˈsēz-n-ə-bəl\ *adj*
happening or coming at the wrong time ⟨*unseasonable* weather⟩
**un·sea·son·ably** \-blē\ *adv*

**un·sea·soned** \ˌən-ˈsēz-nd\ *adj*
not made ready or fit for use (as by the passage of time) ⟨*unseasoned* lumber⟩

**un·seat** \ˌən-ˈsēt\ *vb*
**1** to throw from one's seat
**2** to remove from a position of authority

**un·seem·ly** \ˌən-ˈsēm-lē\ *adj*
**un·seem·li·er**; **un·seem·li·est**
not polite or proper

**un·seen** \ˌən-ˈsēn\ *adj*
not seen : INVISIBLE

**un·self·ish** \ˌən-ˈsel-fish\ *adj*
not selfish
**un·self·ish·ly** *adv*
**un·self·ish·ness** *n*

**un·set·tle** \ˌən-ˈset-l\ *vb*
**un·set·tled**; **un·set·tling**
to disturb the quiet or order of : UPSET ⟨heavy food *unsettles* my stomach⟩ ⟨social changes that *unsettle* old beliefs⟩

**un·set·tled** \ˌən-ˈset-ld\ *adj*
**1** not staying the same ⟨*unsettled* weather⟩
**2** not calm ⟨*unsettled* waters⟩
**3** not able to make up one's mind : DOUBTFUL
**4** not paid ⟨an *unsettled* account⟩
**5** not taken over and lived in by settlers

**un·shaped** \ˌən-ˈshāpt\ *adj*
imperfect especially in form ⟨*unshaped* ideas⟩

**un·sheathe** \ˌən-ˈshēth\ *vb*
**un·sheathed**; **un·sheath·ing**
to draw from or as if from a sheath

**un·sight·ly** \ˌən-ˈsīt-lē\ *adj*
not pleasant to look at : UGLY
**un·sight·li·ness** *n*

**un·skilled** \ˌən-ˈskild\ *adj*
**1** not skilled
**2** not needing skill ⟨*unskilled* jobs⟩

**un·skill·ful** \ˌən-ˈskil-fəl\ *adj*
not skillful : not having skill
**un·skill·ful·ly** \-fə-lē\ *adv*

**un·sound** \ˌən-ˈsau̇nd\ *adj*
**1** not healthy or in good condition
**2** being or having a mind that is not normal
**3** not firmly made or placed
**4** not fitting or true ⟨*unsound* argument⟩
**un·sound·ly** *adv*
**un·sound·ness** *n*

**un·speak·able** \ˌən-ˈspē-kə-bəl\ *adj*
**1** impossible to express in words ⟨*unspeakable* beauty⟩
**2** extremely bad ⟨*unspeakable* conduct⟩
**un·speak·ably** \-blē\ *adv*

**un·spec·i·fied** \ˌən-ˈspes-ə-ˌfīd\ *adj*
not specified

**un·spoiled** \ˌən-ˈspȯild\ *adj*
not spoiled

**un·sta·ble** \ˌən-ˈstā-bəl\ *adj*
not stable ⟨an *unstable* boat⟩ ⟨*unstable* prices⟩

**un·steady** \ˌən-ˈsted-ē\ *adj*
**un·stead·i·er**; **un·stead·i·est**
not steady : UNSTABLE
**un·stead·i·ly** \-ˈsted-l-ē\ *adv*

**un·stressed** \ˌən-ˈstrest\ *adj*
not stressed

**un·suc·cess·ful** \ˌən-sək-ˈses-fəl\ *adj*
not successful
**un·suc·cess·ful·ly** \-fə-lē\ *adv*

**un·sup·port·ed** \ˌən-sə-ˈpōrt-əd\ *adj*
**1** not supported or proved ⟨*unsupported* claims⟩
**2** not held up ⟨the roof is *unsupported* in places⟩

**un·sur·passed** \ˌən-sər-ˈpast\ *adj*
not surpassed (as in excellence)

**un·sus·pect·ing** \ˌən-sə-ˈspek-ting\ *adj*
having no suspicion : TRUSTING

**un·tan·gle** \ˌən-ˈtang-gəl\ *vb*
**un·tan·gled**; **un·tan·gling**
**1** to remove a tangle from
**2** to straighten out ⟨*untangle* a problem⟩

**un·tanned** \ˌən-ˈtand\ *adj*
not put through a tanning process

**un·think·able** \ˌən-ˈthing-kə-bəl\ *adj*
not to be thought of or considered as possible

**un·think·ing** \ˌən-ˈthing-king\ *adj*
not taking thought : HEEDLESS ⟨*unthinking* neglect⟩

**un·ti·dy** \ˌən-ˈtī-dē\ *adj*
**un·ti·di·er**; **un·ti·di·est**
not neat
**un·ti·di·ly** \-ˈtīd-l-ē\ *adv*
**un·ti·di·ness** \-ˈtīd-ē-nəs\ *n*

**un·tie** \ˌən-ˈtī\ *vb* **un·tied**; **un·ty·ing** *or* **un·tie·ing**
to free from something that ties, fastens, or holds back ⟨*untie* a package⟩

[1]**un·til** \ən-ˌtil\ *prep*
up to the time of ⟨worked *until* noon⟩

[2]**until** *conj*
up to the time that ⟨wait *until* I call⟩

[1]**un·time·ly** \ˌən-ˈtīm-lē\ *adv*
before a good or proper time

[2]**untimely** *adj*
**1** happening or done before the expected, natural, or proper time ⟨came to an *untimely* end⟩
**2** coming at the wrong time ⟨an *untimely* joke⟩
**un·time·li·ness** *n*

**un·tir·ing** \ˌən-ˈtī-ring\ *adj*
not making or becoming tired : TIRELESS
**un·tir·ing·ly** *adv*

**un·to** \ən-tə, ˈən-tü\ *prep*
[1]TO

**un·told** \ˌən-ˈtōld\ *adj*
**1** not told or made public ⟨*untold* secrets⟩
**2** not counted : VAST ⟨*untold* resources⟩

**un·to·ward** \ˌən-ˈtō-ərd\ *adj*
causing trouble or unhappiness : UNLUCKY ⟨an *untoward* accident⟩

**un·trou·bled** \ˌən-ˈtrəb-əld\ *adj*
not troubled : free from worry

**un·true** \ˌən-ˈtrü\ *adj*
**1** not faithful : DISLOYAL
**2** not correct : FALSE
**un·tru·ly** *adv*

**un·truth** \ˌən-ˈtrüth\ *n*
**1** the state of being false
**2** [3]LIE

**un·truth·ful** \ˌən-ˈtrüth-fəl\ *adj*
not containing or telling the truth : FALSE
**un·truth·ful·ly** \-fə-lē\ *adv*
**un·truth·ful·ness** *n*

**un·used** \ˌən-ˈyüzd, *1 often* -ˈyüst *before "to"*\ *adj*
**1** not accustomed
**2** not having been used before ⟨fresh *unused* linen⟩
**3** not being used ⟨an *unused* chair⟩

**un·usu·al** \ˌən-ˈyü-zhə-wəl\ *adj*
not usual
**un·usu·al·ly** *adv*

**un·ut·ter·able** \ˌən-ˈət-ə-rə-bəl\ *adj*
being beyond one's powers of description ⟨*unutterable* horrors⟩

**un·veil** \ˌən-ˈvāl\ *vb*
to show or make known to the public for the first time ⟨*unveil* a statue⟩ ⟨*unveiled* a new plan for the city⟩

**un·voiced** \ˌən-ˈvȯist\ *adj*
VOICELESS

**un·want·ed** \ˌən-ˈwȯnt-əd\ *adj*
not wanted

**un·wary** \ˌən-ˈwaər-ē, -ˈweər-ē\ *adj*
**un·war·i·er**; **un·war·i·est**
easily fooled or surprised
**un·war·i·ness** *n*

**un·washed** \ˌən-ˈwȯsht, -ˈwäsht\ *adj*
▼ not having been washed : DIRTY

**un·wea·ried** \ˌən-ˈwir-ēd\ *adj*
not tired

**unwashed** carrots

**un·well** \ˌən-ˈwel\ *adj*
being in poor health

**un·whole·some** \ˌən-ˈhōl-səm\ *adj*
not good for bodily, mental, or moral health

**un·wieldy** \ˌən-ˈwēl-dē\ *adj*
hard to handle or control because of size or weight
**un·wield·i·ness** *n*

**un·will·ing** \ˌən-ˈwil-ing\ *adj*
not willing
**un·will·ing·ly** *adv*
**un·will·ing·ness** *n*

**un·wind** \ˌən-ˈwīnd\ *vb* **un·wound** \-ˈwau̇nd\; **un·wind·ing**
**1** UNROLL ⟨*unwind* yarn from a ball⟩ ⟨the fishing line *unwound* from the reel⟩
**2** RELAX 3 ⟨*unwind* after a hard day at the office⟩

**un·wise** \ˌən-ˈwīz\ *adj*
not wise : FOOLISH
**un·wise·ly** *adv*

**un·wor·thy** \ˌən-ˈwər-thē\ *adj*
**un·wor·thi·er**; **un·wor·thi·est**
not worthy
**un·wor·thi·ly** \-thə-lē\ *adv*
**un·wor·thi·ness** \-thē-nəs\ *n*

**un·wrap** \ˌən-ˈrap\ *vb*
**un·wrapped**; **un·wrap·ping**
to remove the wrapping from

**un·writ·ten** \ˌən-ˈrit-n\ *adj*
not in writing : followed by custom ⟨*unwritten* law⟩

**un·yield·ing** \ˌən-ˈyēl-ding\ *adj*
**1** not soft or flexible : HARD
**2** showing or having firmness or determination

[1]**up** \ˈəp\ *adv*
**1** in or to a higher position : away from the center of the earth
**2** from beneath a surface (as ground or water) ⟨come *up* for air⟩
**3** from below the horizon ⟨the sun came *up*⟩
**4** in or into a vertical position ⟨stand *up*⟩
**5** out of bed
**6** with greater force ⟨speak *up*⟩
**7** in or into a better or more advanced state ⟨bring *up* a child⟩
**8** so as to make more active ⟨stir *up* a fire⟩
**9** into being or knowledge ⟨the missing ring turned *up*⟩
**10** for discussion ⟨brought *up* the matter of taxes⟩

**upholstery:** cross section of an armchair showing its layers of upholstery

**11** into the hands of another ⟨gave myself *up*⟩
**12** COMPLETELY ⟨use it *up*⟩
**13** used to show completeness ⟨fill *up* the gas tank⟩
**14** into storage ⟨lay *up* supplies⟩
**15** so as to be closed ⟨seal *up* the package⟩
**16** so as to approach or arrive ⟨walked *up* and said "hello"⟩
**17** in or into pieces ⟨tore it *up*⟩
**18** to a stop ⟨pull *up* at the curb⟩

**²up** *adj*
**1** risen above the horizon or ground ⟨the sun is *up*⟩
**2** being out of bed
**3** unusually high ⟨prices are *up*⟩
**4** having been raised or built ⟨the windows are *up*⟩ ⟨the house is *up*⟩
**5** moving or going upward ⟨an *up* elevator⟩
**6** being on one's feet and busy ⟨likes to be *up* and doing⟩
**7** well prepared ⟨the team was *up* for the game⟩
**8** going on ⟨find out what's *up*⟩
**9** at an end ⟨time is *up*⟩
**10** well informed ⟨*up* on the news⟩

**³up** *prep*
**1** to, toward, or at a higher point of ⟨*up* a ladder⟩
**2** to or toward the beginning of ⟨*up* a river⟩
**3** ¹ALONG 1 ⟨walk *up* the street⟩

**⁴up** *n*
a period or state of doing well ⟨you've had your *ups* and downs⟩

**⁵up** *vb* **upped**; **up·ping**
**1** to act suddenly or surprisingly ⟨*upped* and left home⟩
**2** to make or become higher ⟨*upped* prices by 10 percent⟩

**up·beat** \'əp-ˌbēt\ *n*
a beat in music that is not accented and especially one just before a downbeat

**up·braid** \ˌəp-'brād\ *vb*
to criticize or scold severely

**up·bring·ing** \'əp-ˌbriŋ-iŋ\ *n*
the process of raising and training

**up·com·ing** \ˌəp-ˌkəm-iŋ\ *adj*
coming soon

**up·draft** \'əp-ˌdraft\ *n*
an upward movement of gas (as air)

**up·end** \ˌəp-'end\ *vb*
to set, stand, or rise on end

**up·grade** \'əp-ˌgrād, əp-'grād\ *vb* **up·grad·ed**; **up·grad·ing**
**1** to raise to a higher grade or position
**2** to improve or replace old software or an old device for increased usefulness
**upgrade** *n*

**up·heav·al** \ˌəp-'hē-vəl\ *n*
a period of great change or violent disorder

**¹up·hill** \'əp-'hil\ *adv*
**1** in an upward direction
**2** against difficulties

**²up·hill** \'əp-ˌhil\ *adj*
**1** going up ⟨an *uphill* trail⟩
**2** DIFFICULT 1 ⟨an *uphill* battle⟩

**up·hold** \ˌəp-'hōld\ *vb* **up·held** \-'held\; **up·hold·ing**
**1** to give support to ⟨*upholds* the ideals of the nation⟩
**2** to lift up

**up·hol·ster** \ˌəp-'hōl-stər\ *vb*
to provide with or as if with upholstery
**up·hol·ster·er** *n*

**up·hol·stery** \ˌəp-'hōl-stə-rē\ *n*, *pl* **up·hol·ster·ies**
◀ materials used to make a soft covering for a seat

**Word History** The word *upholstery* comes from the word *uphold*. *Uphold* means "to hold up or support." It once meant "to repair" as well. In early English a new word was formed from the word *uphold*. This word was used for a person who sold or repaired small and used goods. Such people often repaired and re-covered furniture. The word for a person who sold used goods was later used for people who covered chairs, too. The word *upholstery* comes from this early English word.

**up·keep** \'əp-ˌkēp\ *n*
the act or cost of keeping something in good condition

**up·land** \'əp-lənd, -ˌland\ *n*
high land usually far from a coast or sea

**¹up·lift** \ˌəp-'lift\ *vb*
**1** to lift up
**2** to improve the moral, mental, or bodily condition of

**²up·lift** \'əp-ˌlift\ *n*
an act, process, or result of uplifting

**up·on** \ə-'pȯn, ə-'pän\ *prep*
¹ON 1, 2, 3, 4, 8 ⟨the plate *upon* the table⟩

**¹up·per** \'əp-ər\ *adj*
**1** higher in position or rank ⟨the *upper* classes⟩
**2** farther inland ⟨the *upper* Mississippi⟩

**²upper** *n*
▼ something (as the parts of a shoe above the sole) that is upper

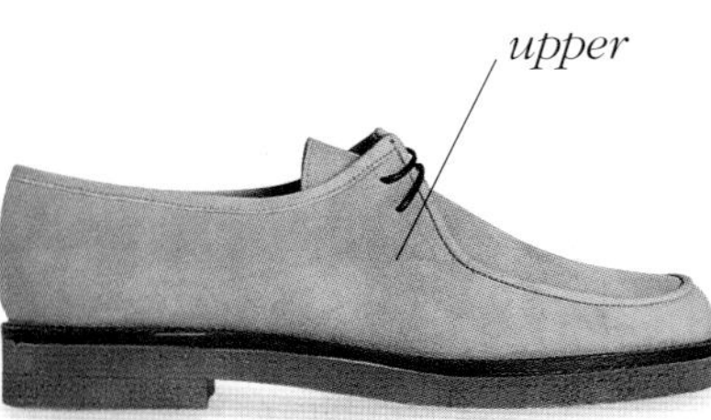


**²upper:** a shoe showing the upper

a b c d e f g h i j k l m n o p q r s t u v w x y z

A B C D E F G H I J K L M N O P Q R S T U V W X Y Z

**upper hand** *n*
ADVANTAGE 1

**up·per·most** \'əp-ər-ˌmōst\ *adj*
**1** farthest up
**2** being in the most important position ⟨the thought is *uppermost* in my mind⟩

**up·raise** \ˌəp-'rāz\ *vb* **up·raised**; **up·rais·ing**
to raise or lift up

[1]**up·right** \'əp-ˌrīt\ *adj*
**1** VERTICAL 2 ⟨an *upright* post⟩
**2** straight in posture
**3** having or showing high moral standards
**up·right·ly** *adv*
**up·right·ness** *n*

**Synonyms** UPRIGHT, HONEST, and JUST mean having or showing a great concern for what is right. UPRIGHT suggests having high moral standards in all areas of life ⟨an *upright* person whose life was an example to the whole community⟩. HONEST suggests dealing with others in a fair and truthful way ⟨an *honest* merchant who wouldn't cheat anyone⟩. JUST stresses that one's fairness comes from both conscious choice and habit ⟨a *just* principal who treats all students alike⟩.

[2]**upright** *n*
**1** the state of being upright
**2** something that is upright

**up·rise** \ˌəp-'rīz\ *vb* **up·rose** \-'rōz\; **up·ris·en** \-'riz-n\; **up·ris·ing** \-'rī-zing\
[1]RISE 1, 2, 7

**up·ris·ing** \'əp-ˌrī-zing\ *n*
REBELLION

**up·roar** \'əp-ˌrōr\ *n*
a state of commotion, excitement, or violent disturbance

**Word History** The word *uproar* appears to be made up of the words *up* and *roar*, but it is not. English *uproar* first meant "revolt." It came from a Dutch word meaning "revolt." This Dutch word was formed from a word meaning "up" and a word meaning "motion." The Dutch word meaning "up" is a relative of English *up*. The Dutch word meaning "motion" is not related to English *roar*.

**up·root** \ˌəp-'rüt, -'ru̇t\ *vb*
**1** to take out by or as if by pulling up by the roots
**2** to take, send, or force away from a country or a traditional home ⟨the war *uprooted* many families⟩

[1]**up·set** \ˌəp-'set\ *vb* **up·set**; **up·set·ting**
**1** to force or be forced out of the usual position : OVERTURN
**2** to worry or make unhappy ⟨the bad news *upset* us all⟩
**3** to make somewhat ill ⟨pizza *upsets* my stomach⟩
**4** to cause confusion in ⟨rain *upset* our plans⟩
**5** to defeat unexpectedly

[2]**up·set** \'əp-ˌset\ *n*
an act or result of upsetting : a state of being upset

**up·shot** \'əp-ˌshät\ *n*
the final result

**up·side** \'əp-ˌsīd\ *n*
the upper side or part

**up·side down** \ˌəp-ˌsīd-'dau̇n\ *adv*
**1** in such a way that the upper part is underneath and the lower part is on top ⟨turned the box *upside down*⟩
**2** in or into great confusion

**upside–down** *adj*
**1** having the upper part underneath and the lower part on top ⟨the letter "u" is an *upside-down* "n"⟩
**2** showing great confusion

[1]**up·stairs** \'əp-'staərz, -'steərz\ *adv*
up the stairs : on or to an upper floor

[2]**up·stairs** \'əp-'staərz, -'steərz\ *adj*
being on or relating to an upper floor ⟨*upstairs* bedrooms⟩

[3]**up·stairs** \'əp-'staərz, -'steərz\ *n*
the part of a building above the ground floor

**up·stand·ing** \ˌəp-'stan-ding\ *adj*
HONEST 2

**up·start** \'əp-ˌstärt\ *n*
a person who gains quick or unexpected success and who makes a great show of pride in that success

**up·stream** \'əp-'strēm\ *adv*
at or toward the beginning of a stream ⟨rowed *upstream*⟩

**up·swing** \'əp-ˌswing\ *n*
a great increase or rise ⟨an *upswing* in business⟩

**urinary**
The urinary system eliminates some waste from the human body through a process that involves the kidneys and the bladder. The kidneys regulate water levels inside the body and filter waste from the blood. This liquid waste travels through a duct from each kidney to the bladder and then passes out of the body in the form of urine.

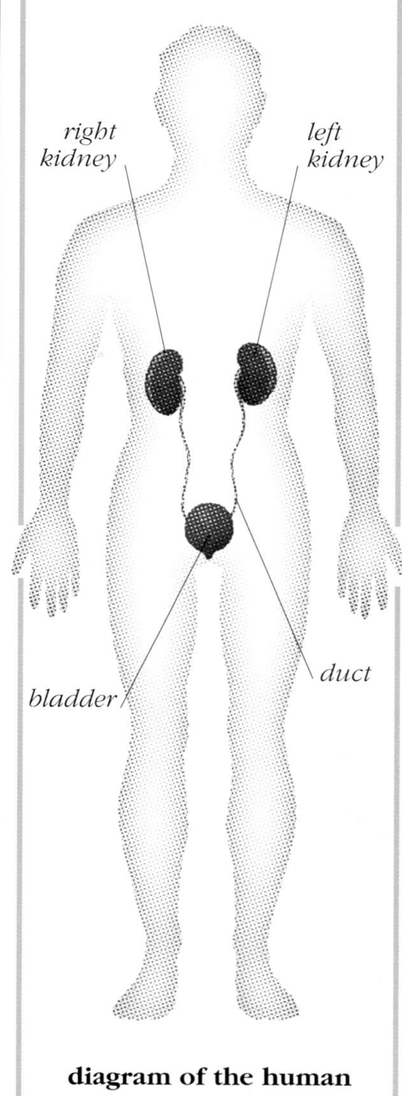


**diagram of the human urinary system**

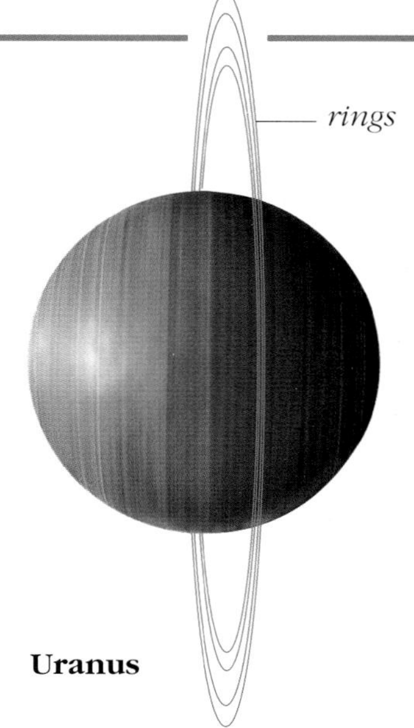

Uranus

**up to** *prep*
**1** as far as ⟨in mud *up to* our ankles⟩
**2** in accordance with ⟨the game was not *up to* our standards⟩
**3** to the limit of ⟨the car holds *up to* six people⟩

**up–to–date** \ˌəp-tə-ˈdāt\ *adj*
**1** lasting up to the present time
**2** knowing, being, or making use of what is new or recent ⟨*up-to-date* information⟩

**up·town** \ˈəp-ˈtau̇n\ *adv*
to, toward, or in what is thought of as the upper part of a town or city

**¹up·turn** \ˈəp-ˌtərn, ˌəp-ˈtərn\ *vb*
to turn upward or up or over

**²up·turn** \ˈəp-ˌtərn\ *n*
an upward turning

**¹up·ward** \ˈəp-wərd\ *or* **up·wards** \-wərdz\ *adv*
**1** in a direction from lower to higher
**2** toward a higher or better state
**3** toward a greater amount or a higher number or rate

**²upward** *adj*
turned toward or being in a higher place or level ⟨an *upward* gaze⟩ ⟨an *upward* movement of prices⟩
**up·ward·ly** *adv*

**up·wind** \ˈəp-ˈwind\ *adv or adj*
in the direction from which the wind is blowing

**ura·ni·um** \yu̇-ˈrā-nē-əm\ *n*
a radioactive metallic chemical element used as a source of atomic energy

**Ura·nus** \ˈyu̇r-ə-nəs, yu̇-ˈrā-nəs\ *n*
◀ the planet that is seventh in order of distance from the sun and has a diameter of about 47,000 kilometers

**ur·ban** \ˈər-bən\ *adj*
of, relating to, or being a city ⟨*urban* life⟩

**ur·chin** \ˈər-chən\ *n*
**1** a mischievous or disrespectful youngster
**2** SEA URCHIN

**Word History** The English word *urchin* first meant "hedgehog." Many years ago some people compared mischievous children to hedgehogs and began calling them *urchins*. The sea urchin got its name because it has spines like a hedgehog.

**-ure** *suffix*
**1** act : process ⟨expos*ure*⟩
**2** office : duty
**3** body performing an office or duty ⟨legislat*ure*⟩

**urea** \yu̇-ˈrē-ə\ *n*
a compound of nitrogen that is the chief solid substance dissolved in the urine of a mammal and is formed by the breaking down of protein

**¹urge** \ˈərj\ *vb* **urged**; **urg·ing**
**1** to try to get (something) accepted : argue in favor of ⟨*urge* a plan⟩
**2** to try to convince ⟨*urge* a guest to stay⟩
**3** ²FORCE 1, DRIVE ⟨the dog *urged* the sheep onward⟩

**²urge** *n*
a strong desire

**ur·gen·cy** \ˈər-jən-sē\ *n*
the quality or state of being urgent

**ur·gent** \ˈər-jənt\ *adj*
**1** calling for immediate action ⟨an *urgent* need⟩
**2** having or showing a sense of urgency ⟨an *urgent* manner⟩
**ur·gent·ly** *adv*

**uri·nal** \ˈyu̇r-ən-l\ *n*
**1** a container for urine
**2** a place for urinating

**uri·nary** \ˈyu̇r-ə-ˌner-ē\ *adj*
◀ of or relating to urine or the organs producing it ⟨the *urinary* bladder⟩

**uri·nate** \ˈyu̇r-ə-ˌnāt\ *vb* **uri·nat·ed**; **uri·nat·ing**
to discharge urine

**uri·na·tion** \ˌyu̇r-ə-ˈnā-shən\ *n*
the act of urinating

**urine** \ˈyu̇r-ən\ *n*
the yellowish liquid produced by the kidneys and given off from the body as waste

**URL** \ˌyü-ˌär-ˈel, ˈərl\ *n*
the address of a computer or a document on the Internet

**urn** \ˈərn\ *n*
**1** ▼ a container usually in the form of a vase resting on a stand
**2** a closed container with a faucet used for serving a hot beverage ⟨coffee *urn*⟩

**us** \əs, ˈəs\ *pron, objective case of* WE

**us·able** \ˈyü-zə-bəl\ *adj*
suitable or fit for use

**us·age** \ˈyü-sij, -zij\ *n*
**1** usual way of doing things
**2** the way in which words and phrases are actually used
**3** the action of using : USE

**¹use** \ˈyüs\ *n*
**1** the act of using something ⟨put knowledge to *use*⟩
**2** the fact or state of being used ⟨a book in daily *use*⟩
**3** way of using ⟨the proper *use* of tools⟩
**4** the ability or power to use something ⟨have the *use* of one's legs⟩

**urn 1:** a ceramic urn

## utensil 1

Cooks use a variety of different utensils in the kitchen. Some utensils, such as knives, bowls, spoons, and pans, have been in use for centuries. Other utensils, such as electric mixers, are newer and were developed to make cooking easier and faster.

5 the quality or state of being useful
6 a reason or need to use ⟨I've no *use* for it⟩
7 LIKING ⟨we have no *use* for such people⟩

[2]**use** \'yüz\ *vb* **used** \'yüzd, *in the phrase "used to" usually* 'yüst\; **us·ing** \'yü-zing\
1 to put into action or service **:** make use of ⟨*use* tools⟩ ⟨*use* good English⟩
2 to take into the body ⟨people who *use* drugs⟩ ⟨I don't *use* sugar in tea⟩
3 to do something by means of ⟨*use* care⟩
4 to behave toward **:** TREAT ⟨*used* the children kindly⟩
5 used with *to* to show a former custom, fact, or state ⟨said winters *used* to be harder⟩
**us·er** *n*

**used** \'yüzd, *2 often* 'yüst *before "to"*\ *adj*
1 SECONDHAND 1 ⟨bought a *used* car⟩
2 having the habit of doing or putting up with something ⟨*used* to flying⟩ ⟨*used* to criticism⟩

**use·ful** \'yüs-fəl\ *adj*
that can be put to use **:** USABLE ⟨*useful* scraps of material⟩
**use·ful·ly** \-fə-lē\ *adv*
**use·ful·ness** *n*

**use·less** \'yü-sləs\ *adj*
being of or having no use
**use·less·ly** *adv*
**use·less·ness** *n*

**us·er–friend·ly** \,yü-zər-'fren(d)-lē\ *adj*
easy to learn, use, understand, or deal with
**user–friendliness** *n*

[1]**ush·er** \'əsh-ər\ *n*
a person who shows people to seats (as in a theater)

[2]**usher** *vb*
1 to show to a place as an usher
2 to come before as if to lead in or announce ⟨a party to *usher* in the new year⟩

**usu·al** \'yü-zhə-wəl\ *adj*
done, found, used or existing most of the time ⟨this is the *usual* state of the house⟩
**usu·al·ly** *adv*

**usurp** \yu̇-'sərp, -'zərp\ *vb*
to take and hold unfairly or by force ⟨*usurp* power from the king⟩
**usurp·er** *n*

**uten·sil** \yu̇-'ten-səl\ *n,*
1 ◀ a tool or container used in a home and especially a kitchen
2 a useful tool
**synonyms** see INSTRUMENT

**uter·us** \'yüt-ə-rəs\ *n, pl* **uteri** \'yüt-ə-,rī\
the organ of a female mammal in which the young develop before birth

**util·i·ty** \yu̇-'til-ət-ē\ *n, pl* **util·i·ties**
1 the quality or state of being useful
2 a business that supplies a public service (as electricity or gas) under special regulation by the government

**uti·li·za·tion** \,yüt-l-ə-'zā-shən\ *n*
the action of utilizing **:** the state of being utilized

**uti·lize** \'yüt-l-,īz\ *vb* **uti·lized**; **uti·liz·ing**
to make use of especially for a certain job

[1]**ut·most** \'ət-,mōst\ *adj*
of the greatest or highest degree or amount ⟨the *utmost* importance⟩

[2]**utmost** *n*
the most possible

[1]**ut·ter** \'ət-ər\ *adj*
in every way **:** TOTAL ⟨*utter* nonsense⟩ ⟨*utter* strangers⟩
**ut·ter·ly** *adv*

[2]**utter** *vb*
1 to send forth as a sound ⟨*uttered* a short cry⟩
2 to express in usually spoken words ⟨*utter* an angry protest⟩

**ut·ter·ance** \'ət-ə-rəns\ *n*
something uttered

a b c d e f g h i j k l m n o p q r s t u v w x y z

**The sounds of V:** The letter **V** has only one sound in English. It sounds the same in **value**, **river**, and **ivory**.

The letter **V** is usually followed by a silent **E** at the end of a word, as in **give**, **five**, and **jive**.

---

**v** \'vē\ *n, pl* **v's** *or* **vs** \'vēz\ *often cap*
**1** the twenty-second letter of the English alphabet
**2** five in Roman numerals

**va·can·cy** \'vā-kən-sē\ *n, pl* **va·can·cies**
**1** something (as an office or hotel room) that is vacant
**2** empty space
**3** the state of being vacant

**va·cant** \'vā-kənt\ *adj*
**1** not filled, used, or lived in ⟨a *vacant* house⟩
**2** free from duties or care
**3** showing a lack of thought **:** FOOLISH **synonyms** see EMPTY

**va·cate** \'vā-ˌkāt\ *vb* **va·cat·ed**; **va·cat·ing**
to leave vacant

[1]**va·ca·tion** \vā-'kā-shən\ *n*
**1** a period during which activity (as of a school) is stopped for a time
**2** a period spent away from home or business in travel or amusement

[2]**vacation** *vb*
to take or spend a vacation
**va·ca·tion·er** *n*

**vac·ci·nate** \'vak-sə-ˌnāt\ *vb* **vac·ci·nat·ed**; **vac·ci·nat·ing**
to inoculate with weak germs in order to protect against a disease

**vac·ci·na·tion** \ˌvak-sə-'nā-shən\ *n*
**1** the act of vaccinating
**2** the scar left by vaccinating

**vac·cine** \vak-'sēn, 'vak-ˌsēn\ *n*
a material (as one containing killed or weakened bacteria or virus) used in vaccinating

---

**Word History** The first vaccine was developed for protection from smallpox. The word *vaccine* comes from the Latin word for "cow." Cows get a disease called cowpox that is something like smallpox but much less serious. People working with cows sometimes used to get cowpox too, and if they did they were protected against smallpox. An English doctor got the idea of making people immune to smallpox by giving them shots of a substance taken from cows that had cowpox. He named the substance *vaccine*, meaning "from cows."

---

**vac·il·late** \'vas-ə-ˌlāt\ *vb* **vac·il·lat·ed**; **vac·il·lat·ing**
to hesitate between courses or opinions **:** be unable to choose

[1]**vac·u·um** \'vak-yə-wəm, -ˌyüm\ *n, pl* **vac·u·ums** *or* **vac·ua** \-yə-wə\
**1** a space completely empty of matter
**2** a space from which most of the air has been removed (as by a pump)
**3** VACUUM CLEANER

[2]**vacuum** *adj*
of, containing, producing, or using a partial vacuum

[3]**vacuum** *vb*
to use a vacuum cleaner on

**vacuum bottle** *n*
THERMOS

**vacuum cleaner** *n*
an electrical appliance for cleaning (as floors or rugs) by suction

**vacuum tube** *n*
an electron tube having a high vacuum

[1]**vag·a·bond** \'vag-ə-ˌbänd\ *adj*
moving from place to place without a fixed home

[2]**vagabond** *n*
a person who leads a vagabond life

**va·gi·na** \və-'jī-nə\ *n*
a canal leading out from the uterus

[1]**va·grant** \'vā-grənt\ *n*
a person who has no steady job and wanders from place to place

[2]**vagrant** *adj*
**1** wandering about from place to place
**2** having no fixed course ⟨*vagrant* breezes⟩

**vague** \'vāg\ *adj* **vagu·er**; **vagu·est**
**1** not clearly expressed ⟨a *vague* answer⟩
**2** not clearly understood ⟨they knew in a *vague* way what they wanted⟩

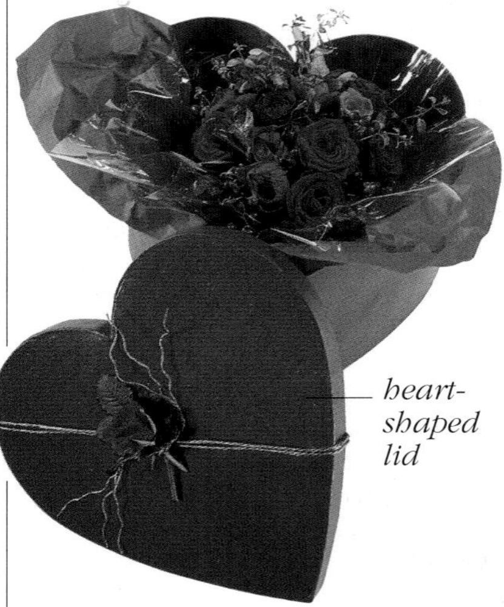


**valentine 2:**
a valentine gift of roses

**3** not clearly outlined **:** SHADOWY
**vague·ly** *adv*
**vague·ness** *n*

**vain** \'vān\ *adj*
**1** having no success ⟨made a *vain* effort to escape⟩
**2** proud of one's looks or abilities

**valley** in Yosemite \yō-ˈsem-ə-tē\ National Park, California

**vain·ly** *adv*
**in vain**
**1** without success
**2** in an unholy way

**vain·glo·ri·ous** \vān-ˈglōr-ē-əs\ *adj*
being vain and boastful
**vain·glo·ri·ous·ly** *adv*
**vain·glo·ri·ous·ness** *n*

**vain·glo·ry** \ˈvān-ˌglōr-ē\ *n*
too much pride especially in what one has done

**vale** \ˈvāl\ *n*
VALLEY

**val·e·dic·to·ri·an** \ˌval-ə-ˌdik-ˈtōr-ē-ən\ *n*
a student usually of the highest standing in a class who gives the farewell speech at the graduation ceremonies

**val·en·tine** \ˈval-ən-ˌtīn\ *n*
**1** a sweetheart given something as a sign of affection on Saint Valentine's Day
**2** ◀ a greeting card or gift sent or given on Saint Valentine's Day

**va·let** \ˈval-ət, ˈval-ā, va-ˈlā\ *n*
a male servant or hotel employee who takes care of a man's clothes and does personal services

**val·iant** \ˈval-yənt\ *adj*
**1** boldly brave
**2** done with courage : HEROIC
**val·iant·ly** *adv*

**val·id** \ˈval-əd\ *adj*
**1** legally binding
**2** based on truth or fact
**val·id·ly** *adv*

**val·i·date** \ˈval-ə-ˌdāt\ *vb*
**val·i·dat·ed**; **val·i·dat·ing**
to make valid

**va·lid·i·ty** \və-ˈlid-ət-ē\ *n*
the quality or state of being valid

**va·lise** \və-ˈlēs\ *n*
TRAVELING BAG

**val·ley** \ˈval-ē\ *n, pl* **valleys**
◀ an area of lowland between ranges of hills or mountains

**val·or** \ˈval-ər\ *n*
COURAGE

**val·or·ous** \ˈval-ə-rəs\ *adj*
having or showing valor
: BRAVE ⟨*valorous* knights⟩
**val·or·ous·ly** *adv*

[1]**valu·able** \ˈval-yə-wə-bəl, ˈval-yə-bəl\ *adj*
**1** worth a large amount of money
**2** of great use or service

[2]**valuable** *n*
a personal possession (as a jewel) of great value

[1]**val·ue** \ˈval-yü\ *n*
**1** a fair return in goods, services, or money for something exchanged
**2** worth in money
**3** worth, usefulness, or importance in comparison with something else ⟨the changing *value* of the dollar⟩
**4** something valuable
**val·ue·less** \-ləs\ *adj*

[2]**value** *vb* **val·ued**; **val·u·ing**
**1** to estimate the worth of ⟨*valued* at two hundred dollars⟩
**2** to think highly of ⟨I *value* your friendship⟩

**valve** \ˈvalv\ *n*
**1** a structure in a tube of the body (as a vein) that closes temporarily to prevent passage of material or allows movement of a fluid in one direction only
**2** a mechanical device by which the flow of liquid, gas, or loose material may be controlled by a movable part
**3** a device on a brass musical instrument that changes the pitch of the tone
**4** one of the separate pieces that make up the shell of some animals (as clams) and are often hinged
**valve·less** \-ləs\ *adj*

**vam·pire** \ˈvam-ˌpīr\ *n*
the body of a dead person believed to come from the grave at night and suck the blood of sleeping persons

**vampire bat** *n*
▼ a bat of tropical America that feeds on the blood of birds and mammals often including domestic animals

**vampire bat**

[1]**van** \ˈvan\ *n*
VANGUARD

[2]**van** *n*
a usually closed wagon or truck for moving goods or animals

**va·na·di·um** \və-ˈnād-ē-əm\ *n*
a metallic chemical element used in making a strong alloy of steel

**van·dal** \ˈvan-dəl\ *n*
a person who destroys or damages property on purpose

**van·dal·ism** \ˈvan-dəl-ˌiz-əm\ *n*
intentional destruction of or damage to property

**van·dal·ize** \ˈvan-dəl-ˌīz\ *vb*
**van·dal·ized**; **van·dal·iz·ing**
to destroy or damage property on purpose

**vane** \ˈvān\ *n*
**1** WEATHER VANE
**2** a flat or curved surface that turns around a center when moved by wind or water

**van·guard** \ˈvan-ˌgärd\ *n*
**1** the troops moving at the front of an army
**2** FOREFRONT

**vanilla beans**

**va·nil·la** \və-ˈnil-ə, -ˈnel-\ *n*
a substance extracted from vanilla beans and used as a flavoring for sweet foods and beverages

**vanilla bean** *n*
▲ the long pod of a tropical American climbing orchid from which vanilla is extracted

**van·ish** \ˈvan-ish\ *vb*
to pass from sight or existence
: DISAPPEAR

**van·i·ty** \'van-ət-ē\ *n, pl* **van·i·ties**
**1** something that is vain
**2** the quality or fact of being vain
**3** a small box for cosmetics

**van·quish** \'vang-kwish\ *vb*
OVERCOME 1

**va·por** \'vā-pər\ *n*
**1** fine bits (as of fog or smoke) floating in the air and clouding it
**2** a substance in the form of a gas ⟨water *vapor*⟩

**va·por·ize** \'vā-pə-,rīz\ *vb* **va·por·ized**; **va·por·iz·ing**
to turn from a liquid or solid into vapor
**va·por·iz·er** \-,rī-zər\ *n*

[1]**var·i·able** \'ver-ē-ə-bəl, 'var-\ *adj*
**1** able to change **:** likely to be changed **:** CHANGEABLE
**2** having differences
**3** not true to type
**var·i·able·ness** *n*
**var·i·ably** \-blē\ *adv*

[2]**variable** *n*
**1** something that is variable
**2** PLACEHOLDER

**var·i·ant** \'ver-ē-ənt, 'var-\ *n*
**1** an individual that shows variation from a type
**2** one of two or more different spellings or pronunciations of a word

**var·i·a·tion** \,ver-ē-'ā-shən, ,var-\ *n*
**1** a change in form, position, or condition
**2** amount of change or difference
**3** departure from what is usual to a group

**var·ied** \'ver-ēd, 'var-\ *adj*
**1** having many forms or types
**2** VARIEGATED 2

**var·ie·gat·ed** \'ver-ē-ə-,gāt-əd, 'ver-i-,gāt-, 'var-\ *adj*
**1** having patches, stripes, or marks of different colors
**2** full of variety

**va·ri·ety** \və-'rī-ət-ē\ *n, pl* **va·ri·et·ies**
**1** the quality or state of having different forms or types
**2** a collection of different things **:** ASSORTMENT
**3** something differing from others of the class to which it belongs
**4** entertainment made up of performances (as dances and songs) that follow one another and are not related

**var·i·ous** \'ver-ē-əs, 'var-\ *adj*
**1** of different kinds

[2]**vault:** an athlete vaulting

**2** different one from another **:** UNLIKE
**3** made up of an indefinite number greater than one ⟨played *various* sports⟩

[1]**var·nish** \'vär-nish\ *n*
a liquid that is spread on a surface and dries into a hard coating

[2]**varnish** *vb*
to cover with or as if with varnish

**var·si·ty** \'vär-sət-ē\ *n, pl* **var·si·ties**
the main team that represents a college, school, or club in contests

**vary** \'ver-ē, 'var-ē\ *vb* **var·ied**; **vary·ing**
**1** to make a partial change in
**2** to make or be of different kinds
**3** DEVIATE
**4** to differ from the usual members of a group. **synonyms** see CHANGE

**vas·cu·lar** \'vas-kyə-lər\ *adj*
of, relating to, containing, or being bodily vessels

**vase** \'vās, 'vāz\ *n*
an often round container of greater depth than width used chiefly for ornament or for flowers

**vas·sal** \'vas-əl\ *n*
a person in the Middle Ages who received protection and land from a lord in return for loyalty and service

**vast** \'vast\ *adj*
very great in size or amount
**vast·ly** *adv*
**vast·ness** *n*

**vat** \'vat\ *n*
a large container (as a tub) especially for holding liquids in manufacturing processes

**vaude·ville** \'vȯd-ə-vəl, 'vȯd-vəl\ *n*
theatrical entertainment made up of songs, dances, and comic acts

[1]**vault** \'vȯlt\ *n*
**1** an arched structure of stone or concrete forming a ceiling or roof
**2** an arch suggesting a vault
**3** a room or compartment for storage or safekeeping
**4** a burial chamber

[2]**vault** *vb*
◀ to leap with the aid of the hands or a pole

[3]**vault** *n*
[2]LEAP

**VCR** \,vē-,sē-'är\ *n*
a device for recording (as television programs) on videocassettes and playing them back

**veal** \'vēl\ *n*
a young calf or its flesh for use as meat

**vec·tor** \'vek-tər\ *n*
a creature (as a fly) that carries disease germs

**vee·jay** \'vē-,jā\ *n*
an announcer of a program (as on television) that features music videos

**veer** \'vir\ *vb*
to change direction or course

**vee·ry** \'vir-ē\ *n, pl* **veeries**
a common brownish woodland thrush of the eastern United States

[1]**veg·e·ta·ble** \'vej-tə-bəl, 'vej-ət-ə-\ *adj*
**1** of, relating to, or made up of plants
**2** gotten from plants ⟨*vegetable* dyes⟩

[2]**vegetable** *n*
**1** [2]PLANT 1
**2** ▶ a plant or plant part grown for use as human food and usually eaten with the main part of a meal

**veg·e·tar·i·an** \,vej-ə-'ter-ē-ən\ *n*
a person who lives on plants and their products

**veg·e·ta·tion** \,vej-ə-'tā-shən\ *n*
plant life or cover (as of an area)

**veg·e·ta·tive** \'vej-ə-,tāt-iv\ *adj*
**1** of, relating to, or functioning in nutrition and growth rather than reproduction
**2** of, relating to, or involving

reproduction by other than sexual means

**ve·he·mence** \'vē-ə-məns\ *n*
the quality or state of being vehement

**ve·he·ment** \'vē-ə-mənt\ *adj*
**1** showing great force or energy
**2** highly emotional
**ve·he·ment·ly** *adv*

**ve·hi·cle** \'vē-ˌik-əl, -ˌhik-\ *n*
**1** a means by which something is expressed, achieved, or shown
**2** something used to transport persons or goods

**[1]veil** \'vāl\ *n*
**1** a piece of cloth or net worn usually by women over the head and shoulders and sometimes over the face
**2** something that covers or hides like a veil ⟨a *veil* of secrecy⟩

**[2]veil** *vb*
to cover or provide with a veil

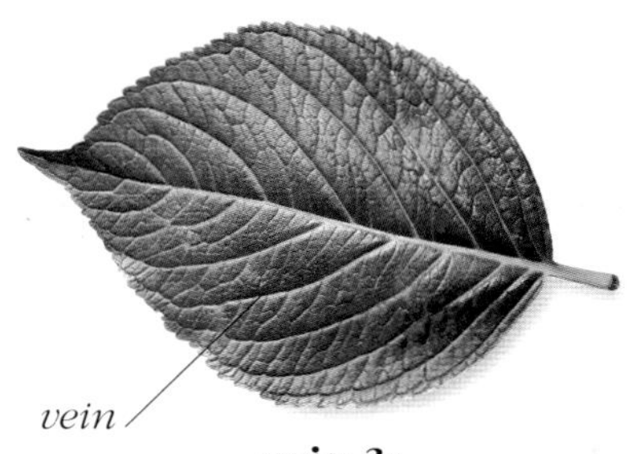


**vein 3:**
the veins of a leaf

**vein** \'vān\ *n*
**1** a long narrow opening in rock filled with mineral matter ⟨a *vein* of gold⟩
**2** one of the blood vessels that carry the blood back to the heart
**3** ▲ one of the bundles of fine tubes that make up the framework of a leaf and carry food, water, and nutrients in the plant
**4** one of the thickened parts that support the wing of an insect
**5** a streak of different color or texture (as in marble)
**6** a style of expression ⟨in a witty *vein*⟩
**veined** \'vānd\ *adj*

**veld** *or* **veldt** \'felt, 'velt\ *n*
an area of grassy land especially in southern Africa

**ve·loc·i·ty** \və-'läs-ət-ē\ *n, pl* **ve·loc·i·ties**
quickness of motion : SPEED

**[1]vel·vet** \'vel-vət\ *n*
a fabric with short soft raised fibers

**[2]velvet** *adj*
**1** made of or covered with velvet
**2** VELVETY

**vel·vety** \'vel-vət-ē\ *adj*
soft and smooth like velvet

**ve·na·tion** \vā-'nā-shən, vē-\ *n*
an arrangement or system of veins

## [2]vegetable 2

Vegetables come in a wide range of types. These include roots, such as lettuce and cabbage; stems, such as asparagus; tubers, such as potatoes; bulbs, such as onions and leeks; flowers, such as broccoli and cauliflower; and fruits, such as tomatoes, corn, peas, peppers, and eggplants. Most vegetables are a good source of vitamins and minerals.

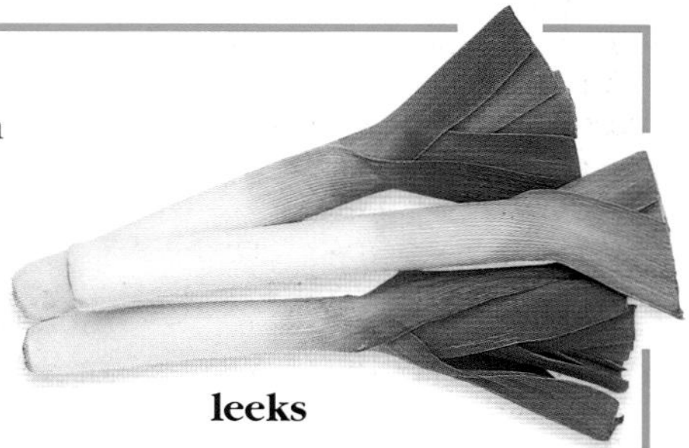

**leeks**

**carrots**

**peas**

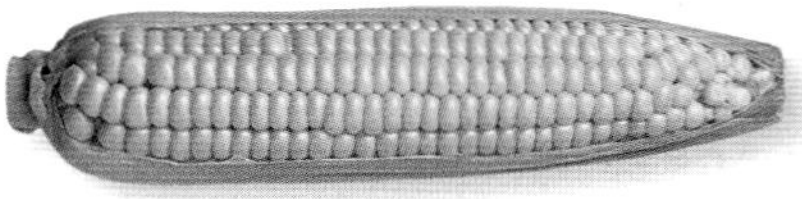

**corn**

**potatoes**

**eggplant**

**lettuce**

**sweet pepper**

**broccoli**

**tomatoes**

**vend** \'vend\ *vb*
to sell or offer for sale
**vend·er** *or* **ven·dor** \'ven-dər\ *n*

**vending machine** *n*
a machine for selling merchandise operated by putting a coin or coins into a slot

**[1]ve·neer** \və-'nir\ *n*
**1** a thin layer of wood bonded to other wood usually to provide a finer surface or a stronger structure
**2** a protective or ornamental facing (as of brick)

**[2]veneer** *vb*
to cover with a veneer

**ven·er·a·ble** \'ven-ə-rə-bəl\ *adj*
**1** deserving to be venerated — often used as a religious title
**2** deserving honor or respect

**ven·er·ate** \'ven-ə-,rāt\ *vb*
**ven·er·at·ed**; **ven·er·at·ing**
to show deep respect for

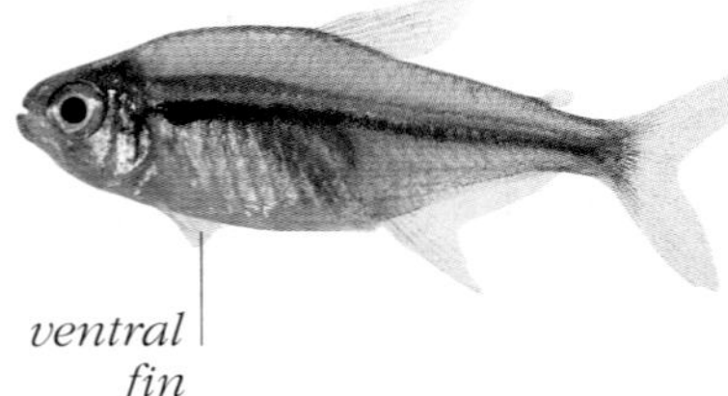


**ventral:** the ventral surface of this fish is silvery-white

**ven·er·a·tion** \,ven-ə-'rā-shən\ *n*
**1** the act of venerating **:** the state of being venerated
**2** a feeling of deep respect

**ve·ne·re·al** \və-'nir-ē-əl\ *adj*
of or relating to sexual intercourse or to diseases that pass from person to person by it

**ve·ne·tian blind** \və-,nē-shən-\ *n*
a blind having thin horizontal slats that can be adjusted to keep out light or to let light come in between them

**ven·geance** \'ven-jəns\ *n*
punishment given in return for an injury or offense

**ven·i·son** \'ven-ə-sən, -ə-zən\ *n*
the flesh of a deer used as food

**ven·om** \'ven-əm\ *n*
poisonous matter produced by an animal (as a snake) and passed to a victim usually by a bite or sting

**ven·om·ous** \'ven-ə-məs\ *adj*
having or producing venom **:** POISONOUS

**ve·nous** \'vē-nəs\ *adj*
of, relating to, or full of veins ⟨*venous* blood⟩

**[1]vent** \'vent\ *vb*
**1** to provide with an outlet
**2** to serve as an outlet for
**3** [3]EXPRESS 1 ⟨*vent* one's anger⟩

**[2]vent** *n*
**1** OUTLET 1, 2
**2** an opening for the escape of a gas or liquid

**ven·ti·late** \'vent-l-,āt\ *vb*
**ven·ti·lat·ed**; **ven·ti·lat·ing**
**1** to discuss freely and openly
**2** to let in air and especially a current of fresh air
**3** to provide with ventilation

**ven·ti·la·tion** \,vent-l-'ā-shən\ *n*
**1** the act or process of ventilating
**2** a system or means of providing fresh air

**ven·ti·la·tor** \'vent-l-,āt-ər\ *n*
a device for letting in fresh air or driving out bad or stale air

**ven·tral** \'ven-trəl\ *adj*
◀ of, relating to, or being on or near the surface of the body that in man is the front but in most animals is the lower surface ⟨a fish's *ventral* fins⟩

**ven·tri·cle** \'ven-tri-kəl\ *n*
the part of the heart from which blood passes into the arteries

**ven·tril·o·quist** \ven-'tril-ə-kwəst\ *n*
a person skilled in speaking in such a way that the voice seems to come from a source other than the speaker

**[1]ven·ture** \'ven-chər\ *vb*
**ven·tured**; **ven·tur·ing**
**1** to expose to risk
**2** to face the risks and dangers of
**3** to offer at the risk of being criticized ⟨*venture* an opinion⟩
**4** to go ahead in spite of danger

**[2]venture** *n*
a task or an act involving chance, risk, or danger

**ven·ture·some** \'ven-chər-səm\ *adj*
**1** tending to take risks
**2** involving risk **synonyms** see ADVENTUROUS
**ven·ture·some·ly** *adv*
**ven·ture·some·ness** *n*

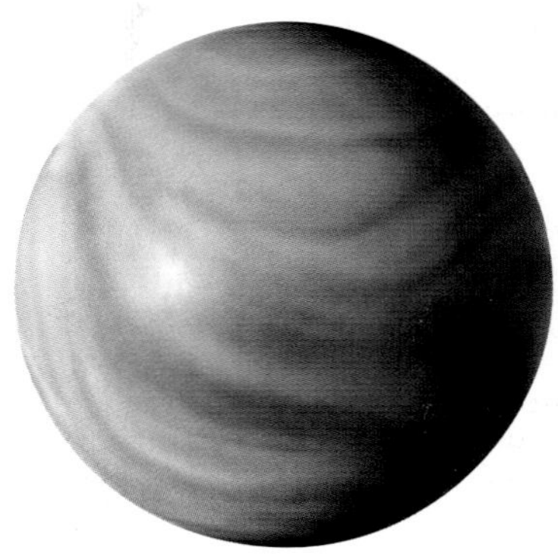

**Venus**

**ven·tur·ous** \'ven-chə-rəs\ *adj*
VENTURESOME
**ven·tur·ous·ly** *adv*
**ven·tur·ous·ness** *n*

**Ve·nus** \'vē-nəs\ *n*
▲ the planet that is second in order of distance from the sun and has a diameter of about 12,200 kilometers

**ve·ran·da** *or* **ve·ran·dah** \və-'ran-də\ *n*
a long porch extending along one or more sides of a building

**verb** \'vərb\ *n*
a word that expresses an act, occurrence, or state of being

**[1]ver·bal** \'vər-bəl\ *adj*
**1** of, relating to, or consisting of words
**2** of, relating to, or formed from a verb ⟨a *verbal* adjective⟩
**3** spoken rather than written
**ver·bal·ly** *adv*

**[2]verbal** *n*
a word that combines characteristics of a verb with those of a noun or adjective

**ver·be·na** \vər-'bē-nə\ *n*
a garden plant with fragrant leaves and heads of white, pink, red, blue, or purple flowers with five petals

**ver·dant** \'vərd-nt\ *adj*
green with growing plants
**ver·dant·ly** *adv*

**ver·dict** \'vər-dikt\ *n*
**1** the decision reached by a jury
**2** JUDGMENT 2, OPINION

**ver·dure** \'vər-jər\ *n*
green vegetation

**[1]verge** \'vərj\ *n*
**1** something that borders, limits, or bounds **:** EDGE

**2** THRESHOLD 2, BRINK ⟨on the *verge* of bankruptcy⟩

[2]**verge** *vb* **verged**; **verg•ing**
to come near to being ⟨this *verges* on madness⟩

**ver•i•fi•ca•tion** \ˌver-ə-fə-ˈkā-shən\ *n*
the act or process of verifying **:** the state of being verified

**ver•i•fy** \ˈver-ə-ˌfī\ *vb* **ver•i•fied**; **ver•i•fy•ing**
**1** to prove to be true or correct **:** CONFIRM
**2** to check or test the accuracy of

**ver•mi•cel•li** \ˌvər-mə-ˈchel-ē\ *n*
a food similar to but thinner than spaghetti

**ver•min** \ˈvər-mən\ *n, pl* **vermin**
small common harmful or objectionable animals (as fleas or mice) that are difficult to get rid of

**Word History** Today we use the term *vermin* for any small common animals that are harmful. Fleas and mice are likely to be called vermin. Even rabbits are called vermin when they invade our gardens. The English word *vermin* came from an early French word that meant much the same thing as today's English word. This French word came from a Latin word that was a bit more specific. The Latin word meant "worm."

**ver•sa•tile** \ˈvər-sət-l\ *adj*
**1** able to do many different kinds of things
**2** having many uses ⟨a *versatile* tool⟩

**ver•sa•til•i•ty** \ˌvər-sə-ˈtil-ət-ē\ *n*
the quality or state of being versatile

**[2]vertebrate**

Vertebrates have an internal skeleton formed of cartilage, bone, or both. The skeleton supports the body and protects the internal organs. Vertebrates include fish, amphibians, reptiles, birds, and mammals.

backbone

**skeleton of a fish**

**bird**
bluebird

**mammal**
wolf

**amphibian**
toad

**reptile**
lizard

**verse** \ˈvərs\ *n*
**1** a line of writing in which words are arranged in a rhythmic pattern
**2** writing in which words are arranged in a rhythmic pattern
**3** STANZA
**4** one of the short parts of a chapter in the Bible

**versed** \ˈvərst\ *adj*
having knowledge or skill as a result of experience, study, or practice

**ver•sion** \ˈvər-zhən\ *n*
**1** a translation especially of the Bible
**2** an account or description from a certain point of view

**ver•sus** \ˈvər-səs\ *prep*
AGAINST 1 ⟨our football team *versus* theirs⟩

**ver•te•bra** \ˈvərt-ə-brə\ *n, pl* **ver•te•brae** \-ˌbrā, -brē\
one of the bony sections making up the backbone

[1]**ver•te•brate** \ˈvərt-ə-brət\ *adj*
**1** having vertebrae or a backbone
**2** of or relating to the vertebrates

[2]**vertebrate** *n*
◀ any of a large group of animals that includes the fishes, amphibians, reptiles, birds, and mammals all of which have a backbone extending down the back of the body

**ver•tex** \ˈvər-ˌteks\ *n, pl* **ver•ti•ces** \ˈvərt-ə-ˌsēz\ *or* **ver•tex•es**
**1** the point opposite to and farthest from the base of a geometrical figure
**2** the common endpoint of the sides of an angle

[1]**ver•ti•cal** \ˈvərt-i-kəl\ *adj*
**1** directly overhead
**2** rising straight up and down from a level surface
**ver•ti•cal•ly** *adv*

[2]**vertical** *n*
something (as a line or plane) that is vertical

**ver•ti•go** \ˈvərt-i-ˌgō\ *n, pl* **ver•ti•goes** *or* **ver•ti•gos**
a dizzy state

[1]**very** \ˈver-ē\ *adj*
**1** [2]EXACT, PRECISE ⟨the *very* heart of the city⟩
**2** exactly suitable or necessary ⟨that's the *very* thing for this job⟩
**3** MERE, BARE ⟨the *very* thought frightened them⟩
**4** exactly the same

**[2]very** *adv*
**1** to a great degree : EXTREMELY
**2** in actual fact : TRULY

**ves·pers** \'ves-pərz\ *n pl, often cap*
a late afternoon or evening church service

**ves·sel** \'ves-əl\ *n*
**1** a hollow utensil (as a cup or bowl) for holding something
**2** a craft larger than a rowboat for navigation of the water
**3** a tube (as an artery) in which a body fluid is contained and carried or circulated

**[1]vest** \'vest\ *vb*
**1** to place or give into the possession or control of some person or authority
**2** to clothe in vestments

**[2]vest** *n*
a sleeveless garment usually worn under a suit coat

**ves·ti·bule** \'ves-tə-,byül\ *n*
a hall or room between the outer door and the inside part of a building

**ves·tige** \'ves-tij\ *n*
a tiny amount or visible sign of something lost or vanished : TRACE

**ves·ti·gial** \ves-'tij-ē-əl, -'ti-jəl\ *adj*
of, relating to, or being a vestige

**vest·ment** \'vest-mənt\ *n*
an outer garment especially for wear during ceremonies or by an official

**[1]vet** \'vet\ *n*
VETERINARIAN

**[2]vet** *n*
[1]VETERAN 2

**[1]vet·er·an** \'vet-ə-rən, 've-trən\ *n*
**1** a person who has had long experience
**2** a former member of the armed forces especially in war

**[2]veteran** *adj*
having gained skill through experience

**vet·er·i·nar·i·an** \,vet-ə-rə-'ner-ē-ən\ *n*
a doctor who treats diseases and injuries of animals

**[1]vet·er·i·nary** \'vet-ə-rə-,ner-ē\ *adj*
of, relating to, or being the medical care of animals and especially domestic animals

**[2]veterinary** *n, pl* **vet·er·i·nar·ies**
VETERINARIAN

**[1]ve·to** \'vēt-ō\ *n, pl* **vetoes**
**1** a forbidding of something by a person in authority
**2** the power of a president, governor, or mayor to prevent something from becoming law

**[2]veto** *vb*
**1** FORBID, PROHIBIT
**2** to prevent from becoming law by use of a veto

**vex** \'veks\ *vb*
**1** to bring trouble, distress, or worry to
**2** to annoy by small irritations

**vex·a·tion** \vek-'sā-shən\ *n*
**1** the quality or state of being vexed
**2** the act of vexing
**3** a cause of trouble or worry

**via** \'vī-ə, 'vē-ə\ *prep*
by way of ⟨went *via* the northern route⟩

**vi·a·ble** \'vī-ə-bəl\ *adj*
**1** capable of living or growing
**2** possible to use or apply ⟨a *viable* plan⟩

**via·duct** \'vī-ə-,dəkt\ *n*
▼ a bridge for carrying a road or railroad over something (as a gorge or highway)

**vi·al** \'vī-əl\ *n*
a small container (as for medicines) that is usually made of glass or plastic

**vi·brant** \'vī-brənt\ *adj*
having or giving the sense of life, vigor, or action ⟨a *vibrant* personality⟩
**vi·brant·ly** *adv*

**vi·brate** \'vī-,brāt\ *vb* **vi·brat·ed**; **vi·brat·ing**
to swing or cause to swing back and forth

**vi·bra·tion** \vī-'brā-shən\ *n*
**1** a rapid motion (as of a stretched cord) back and forth
**2** the action of vibrating : the state of being vibrated
**3** a trembling motion

**vi·bur·num** \vī-'bər-nəm\ *n*
any of a group of shrubs often grown for their broad clusters of usually white flowers

**vic·ar** \'vik-ər\ *n*
**1** a minister in charge of a church who serves under the authority of another minister
**2** a church official who takes the place of or represents a higher official

**vi·car·i·ous** \vī-'ker-ē-əs, -'kar-\ *adj*
experienced or understood as if happening to oneself <got *vicarious* enjoyment from her sister's travels>
**vi·car·i·ous·ly** *adv*
**vi·car·i·ous·ness** *n*

**viaduct** carrying a railroad over a valley

**vice** \'vīs\ *n*
**1** evil conduct or habits
**2** a moral fault or weakness
**vice-** \'vīs\ *prefix*
one that takes the place of ⟨*vice-* president⟩
**vice admiral** *n*
a commissioned officer in the Navy or Coast Guard ranking above a rear admiral
**vice pres·i·dent** \'vīs-'prez-ə-dənt\ *n*
an official (as of a government) whose rank is next below that of the president and who takes the place of the president when necessary
**vice ver·sa** \ˌvī-si-'vər-sə, 'vīs-'vər-\ *adv*
with the order turned around
**vi·cin·i·ty** \və-'sin-ət-ē\ *n, pl* **vi·cin·i·ties**
**1** the state of being close
**2** a surrounding area : NEIGHBORHOOD ⟨there is a school in the *vicinity*⟩
**vi·cious** \'vish-əs\ *adj*
**1** doing evil things : WICKED
**2** very dangerous ⟨a *vicious* dog⟩
**3** filled with or showing unkind feelings ⟨*vicious* gossip⟩
**vi·cious·ly** *adv*
**vi·cious·ness** *n*
**vic·tim** \'vik-təm\ *n*
**1** a living being offered as a religious sacrifice
**2** an individual injured or killed (as by disease)
**3** a person who is cheated, fooled, or hurt by another
**vic·tim·ize** \'vik-tə-ˌmīz\ *vb* **vic·tim·ized**; **vic·tim·iz·ing**
to make a victim of
**vic·tor** \'vik-tər\ *n*
WINNER, CONQUEROR
**vic·to·ri·ous** \vik-'tōr-ē-əs\ *adj*
having won a victory
**vic·to·ri·ous·ly** *adv*
**vic·to·ry** \'vik-tə-rē\ *n, pl* **vic·to·ries**
**1** the defeating of an enemy or opponent
**2** success in a struggle against difficulties

---

**Synonyms** VICTORY, CONQUEST, and TRIUMPH mean a success in a competition or struggle. VICTORY stresses a win over an opponent or difficult problems ⟨a *victory* over disease⟩. CONQUEST stresses the overcoming of someone or something and then bringing the defeated under one's control ⟨Rome's *conquests* in Britain⟩. TRIUMPH suggests an especially great victory that brings honor and glory ⟨a *triumph* for the general⟩.

---

**vict·ual** \'vit-l\ *n*
**1** food fit for humans
**2 victuals** *pl* supplies of food
**vi·cu·ña** *or* **vi·cu·na** \vi-'kün-yə, vī-'kü-nə\ *n*
► a wild animal of the Andes that is related to the llama and produces a fine wool
[1]**vid·eo** \'vid-ē-ˌō\ *n*
**1** TELEVISION
**2** the visual part of television
**3** [1]VIDEOTAPE 1
**4** a videotaped performance of a song ⟨a rock *video*⟩
[2]**video** *adj*
**1** relating to or used in the sending or receiving of television images ⟨a *video* channel⟩
**2** being, relating to, or involving images on a television screen or computer display
**video camera** *n*
a camera (as a camcorder) that records video and usually also audio
**vid·eo·cas·sette** \ˌvid-ē-ō-kə-'set\ *n*
**1** a case containing videotape for use with a VCR
**2** a recording (as of a movie) on a videocassette
**videocassette recorder** *n*
VCR
**video game** *n*
a game played with images on a video screen
[1]**vid·eo·tape** \'vid-ē-ō-ˌtāp\ *n*
**1** a recording of visual images and sound (as of a television production) made on magnetic tape
**2** the magnetic tape used for such a recording
[2]**videotape** *vb*
to make a videotape of
**videotape recorder** *n*
a device for recording on videotape
**vie** \'vī\ *vb* **vied**; **vy·ing**
COMPETE ⟨*vied* for first place⟩
[1]**Viet·nam·ese** \vē-ˌet-nə-'mēz, ˌvē-ət-\ *n*
**1** a person born or living in Vietnam
**2** the language of the Vietnamese
[2]**Vietnamese** *adj*
of or relating to Vietnam, the Vietnamese people, or their language
[1]**view** \'vyü\ *n*
**1** the act of seeing or examining
**2** an opinion or judgment influenced by personal feeling
**3** all that can be seen from a certain place : SCENE ⟨the *view* of the hills⟩
**4** range of vision ⟨no one in *view*⟩
**5** [1]PURPOSE ⟨studied hard with a *view* to getting a scholarship⟩
**6** a picture that represents something that can be seen

**vicuña**

[2]**view** *vb*
**1** to look at carefully ⟨*view* an exhibit⟩
**2** [1]SEE 1
**view·er** *n*
**view·point** \'vyü-ˌpȯint\ *n*
the angle from which something is considered
**vig·il** \'vij-əl\ *n*
**1** the day before a religious feast
**2** keeping watch especially when sleep is usual
**vig·i·lance** \'vij-ə-ləns\ *n*
a staying alert especially to possible danger
**vig·i·lant** \'vij-ə-lənt\ *adj*
alert especially to avoid danger
**vig·i·lant·ly** *adv*
**vig·i·lan·te** \ˌvij-ə-'lant-ē\ *n*
a member of a group of volunteers organized to stop crime and punish criminals especially when the proper officials are not doing so

helmet

**Viking:**
a man dressed as a
10th-century Viking

**vig·or** \'vig-ər\ *n*
**1** strength or energy of body or mind
**2** active strength or force

**vig·or·ous** \'vig-ə-rəs\ *adj*
**1** having vigor
**2** done with vigor
**vig·or·ous·ly** *adv*

**Vi·king** \'vī-king\ *n*
▲ a member of the Scandinavian invaders of the coasts of Europe in the eighth to tenth centuries

**vile** \'vīl\ *adj* **vil·er**; **vil·est**
**1** of little worth
**2** WICKED 1
**3** very objectionable
**vile·ly** \'vīl-lē\ *adv*
**vile·ness** *n*

**vil·i·fy** \'vil-ə-,fī\ *vb* **vil·i·fied**; **vil·i·fy·ing**
to speak of as worthless or wicked

**vil·la** \'vil-ə\ *n*
**1** an estate in the country
**2** a large expensive home especially in the country or suburbs

**vil·lage** \'vil-ij\ *n*
a place where people live that is usually smaller than a town

**vil·lag·er** \'vil-ij-ər\ *n*
a person who lives in a village

**vil·lain** \'vil-ən\ *n*
a wicked person

**vil·lain·ous** \'vil-ə-nəs\ *adj*
WICKED

**vil·lainy** \'vil-ə-nē\ *n, pl* **vil·lain·ies**
conduct or actions of or like those of a villain

**vil·lus** \'vil-əs\ *n, pl* **vil·li** \'vil-,ī, -ē\
one of the tiny extensions that are shaped like fingers, line the small intestine, and are active in absorbing nutrients

**vim** \'vim\ *n*
ENERGY 1, VIGOR

**vin·di·cate** \'vin-də-,kāt\ *vb* **vin·di·cat·ed**; **vin·di·cat·ing**
**1** to free from blame or guilt
**2** to show to be true or correct : JUSTIFY

**vin·dic·tive** \vin-'dik-tiv\ *adj*
likely to seek revenge : meant to be harmful

**vine** \'vīn\ *n*
a plant whose stem requires support and which climbs by tendrils or twining or creeps along the ground
**vine·like** \-,līk\ *adj*

**vin·e·gar** \'vin-i-gər\ *n*
a sour liquid made from cider, wine, or malt and used to flavor or preserve foods

**Word History** The English word *vinegar* came from an Old French word that had the same meaning. Vinegar was thought of as sour wine. The Old French word was made by combining two words. The first meant "wine" and the second meant "sharp" or "sour."

**vin·e·gary** \'vin-i-gə-rē\ *adj*
like vinegar

**vine·yard** \'vin-yərd\ *n*
▼ a field of grapevines

**vin·tage** \'vint-ij\ *n*
**1** the grapes grown or wine made during one season
**2** a usually excellent wine of a certain type, region, and year
**3** the time when something started or was made

**vi·nyl** \'vīn-l\ *n*
a plastic substance or product (as a fiber) made from a synthetic polymer

**¹vi·o·la** \vī-'ō-lə, vē-\ *n*
a hybrid garden flower that looks like but is smaller than a pansy

**²vi·o·la** \vē-'ō-lə\ *n*
an instrument of the violin family slightly larger and having a lower pitch than a violin

**vi·o·late** \'vī-ə-,lāt\ *vb* **vi·o·lat·ed**; **vi·o·lat·ing**
**1** to fail to keep : BREAK
**2** to do harm or damage to
**3** to treat in a disrespectful way
**4** DISTURB 1 ⟨*violate* their privacy⟩
**vi·o·la·tor** \-,lāt-ər\ *n*

**vineyard** in the Napa Valley, California

**vi·o·la·tion** \,vī-ə-'lā-shən\ *n*
an act or instance of violating : the state of being violated

**vi·o·lence** \'vī-ə-ləns\ *n*
**1** the use of force to harm a person or damage property
**2** great force or strength ⟨the *violence* of the storm⟩

**vi·o·lent** \'vī-ə-lənt\ *adj*
**1** showing very strong force ⟨a *violent* storm⟩
**2** ¹EXTREME 1, INTENSE ⟨*violent* pain⟩
**3** caused by force ⟨a *violent* death⟩
**vi·o·lent·ly** *adv*

**vi·o·let** \'vī-ə-lət\ *n*
**1** a wild or garden plant related to the pansies that has small often fragrant white, blue, purple, or yellow flowers
**2** a reddish blue

**violin:**
a girl playing a violin

**vi·o·lin** \,vī-ə-'lin\ *n*
▲ a stringed musical instrument with four strings that is usually held against the shoulder under the chin and played with a bow

**vi·o·lon·cel·lo** \,vī-ə-lən-'chel-ō, ,vē-\ *n, pl* **vi·o·lon·cel·los**
CELLO

**vi·per** \'vī-pər\ *n*
a snake that is or is believed to be poisonous

**vir·eo** \'vir-ē-,ō\ *n, pl* **vir·e·os**
a small songbird that eats insects and is olive-green or grayish in color

**[1]vir·gin** \'vər-jən\ *n*
**1** an unmarried woman devoted to religion
**2** a person who has not had sexual intercourse

**[2]virgin** *adj*
**1** not soiled ⟨*virgin* snow⟩
**2** being a virgin
**3** not changed by human actions ⟨*virgin* forests⟩

**Vir·go** \'vər-gō, 'vir-\ *n*
**1** a constellation between Leo and Libra imagined as a woman
**2** the sixth sign of the zodiac or a person born under this sign

**vir·ile** \'vir-əl, 'vir-,īl\ *adj*
**1** having qualities generally associated with a man
**2** ENERGETIC, VIGOROUS

**vir·tu·al** \'vər-chə-wəl\ *adj*
being almost but not quite complete ⟨the *virtual* ruler of the country⟩ ⟨rain is a *virtual* certainty for the weekend⟩
**vir·tu·al·ly** *adv*

**virtual reality** *n*
an artificial environment which is experienced through sights and sounds provided by a computer and in which one's actions partly decide what happens in the environment

**vir·tue** \'vər-chü\ *n*
**1** moral excellence **:** knowing what is right and acting in a right way
**2** a desirable quality ⟨truth is a *virtue*⟩

**Word History** From the Latin word that meant "man," the Romans formed another word. The second word was used to describe such so-called "manly" qualities as strength and courage. Gradually this word was used for any good qualities in males or females. The English word *virtue* came from this second Latin word.

**vir·tu·o·so** \,vər-chə-'wō-sō, -zō\ *n, pl* **vir·tu·o·sos** *or* **vir·tu·o·si** \-sē, -zē\
a person who is an outstanding performer especially in music

**vir·tu·ous** \'vər-chə-wəs\ *adj*
having or showing virtue
**vir·tu·ous·ly** *adv*

**vir·u·lent** \'vir-ə-lənt\ *adj*
very infectious or poisonous **:** DEADLY

**vi·rus** \'vī-rəs\ *n*
**1** an agent too tiny to be seen by the ordinary microscope that causes disease and that may be a living organism or may be a very special kind of protein molecule
**2** a disease caused by a virus
**3** a usually hidden computer program that causes harm by making copies of itself and inserting them into other programs

**vis·count** \'vī-,kau̇nt\ *n*
a British nobleman ranking below an earl and above a baron

**vis·count·ess** \'vī-,kau̇nt-əs\ *n*
**1** the wife or widow of a viscount
**2** a woman who holds the rank of a viscount in her own right

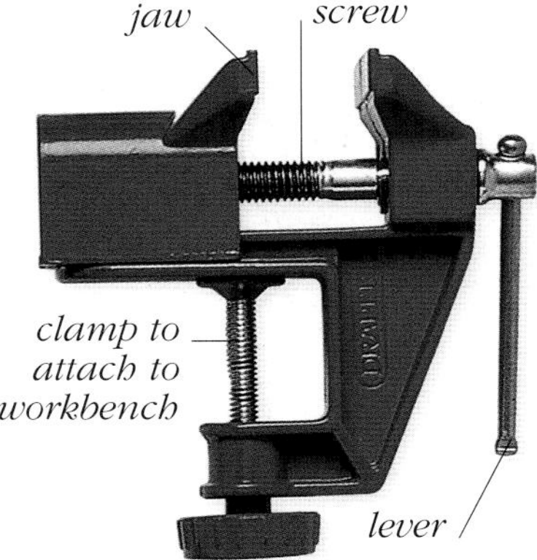


**vise**
for a workshop

**vise** \'vīs\ *n*
▲ a device with two jaws that works by a screw or lever for holding or clamping work

**vis·i·bil·i·ty** \,viz-ə-'bil-ət-ē\ *n*
**1** the quality or state of being visible
**2** the degree of clearness of the atmosphere

**vis·i·ble** \'viz-ə-bəl\ *adj*
**1** capable of being seen
**2** easily seen or understood **:** OBVIOUS
**vis·i·bly** \-blē\ *adv*

**vi·sion** \'vizh-ən\ *n*
**1** something seen in the mind (as in a dream)
**2** a vivid picture created by the imagination
**3** the act or power of imagination
**4** unusual ability to think or plan ahead
**5** the act or power of seeing **:** SIGHT
**6** the special sense by which the qualities of an object (as color) that make up its appearance are perceived

**vi·sion·ary** \'vizh-ə-,ner-ē\ *n, pl* **vi·sion·ar·ies**
a person whose ideas or plans are impractical

**[1]vis·it** \'viz-ət\ *vb*
**1** to go to see in order to comfort or help

A B C D E F G H I J K L M N O P Q R S T U V W X Y Z

**2** to call on as an act of friendship or courtesy or as or for a professional service
**3** to stay with for a time as a guest
**4** to go to for pleasure ⟨*visit* a theater⟩
**5** to come to or upon ⟨we were *visited* by many troubles⟩

**²visit** *n*
**1** a brief stay : CALL
**2** a stay as a guest
**3** a professional call

**vis·i·tor** \'viz-ət-ər\ *n*
a person who visits

---

**Synonyms** VISITOR, GUEST, and CALLER mean someone who visits a person or place. VISITOR is usually used of a person who comes for a reason other than business ⟨I had several surprise *visitors* while at the hospital⟩. GUEST is usually used of an invited visitor who is staying for more than a short time ⟨we had five *guests* over the weekend⟩. CALLER is used of anyone who comes to a home or place of business and may come for personal or business reasons ⟨we had a *caller* from a local charity⟩.

---

**vi·sor** \'vī-zər\ *n*
**1** the movable front upper piece of a helmet
**2** a part that sticks out to protect or shade the eyes

**vis·ta** \'vis-tə\ *n*
a distant view through an opening or along an avenue

**vi·su·al** \'vizh-ə-wəl\ *adj*
**1** of, relating to, or used in vision
**2** obtained by the use of sight ⟨a *visual* impression⟩
**3** appealing to the sense of sight ⟨*visual* aids⟩
**vi·su·al·ly** *adv*

**vi·su·al·ize** \'vizh-ə-wə-,līz\ *vb* **vi·su·al·ized**; **vi·su·al·iz·ing**
to see or form a mental image

**vi·tal** \'vīt-l\ *adj*
**1** of or relating to life
**2** concerned with or necessary to the continuation of life ⟨*vital* organs⟩
**3** full of life and energy
**4** very important
**vi·tal·ly** *adv*

**vi·tal·i·ty** \vī-'tal-ət-ē\ *n, pl* **vi·tal·i·ties**
**1** capacity to live and develop
**2** ENERGY 1

**vi·tals** \'vīt-lz\ *n pl*
the vital organs (as heart, lungs, and liver) of the body

**vi·ta·min** \'vīt-ə-mən\ *n*
any of a group of organic substances that are found in natural foods, are necessary in small quantities to health, and include one (**vitamin A**) found mostly in animal products and needed for good vision, several (**vitamin B complex**) found in many foods and needed especially for growth, one (**vitamin C**) found in fruits and leafy vegetables and used as an enzyme and to prevent scurvy, and another (**vitamin D**) found in fish-liver oils, eggs, and milk and needed for healthy bone development

**vi·va·cious** \və-'vā-shəs, vī-\ *adj*
full of life : LIVELY
**vi·va·cious·ly** *adv*

**vi·vac·i·ty** \və-'vas-ət-ē, vī-\ *n*
the quality or state of being vivacious

**vi·var·i·um** \vī-'var-ē-əm, -'ver-\ *n, pl* **vi·var·ia** \-ē-ə\ *or* **vi·var·i·ums**
an enclosure for keeping or studying plants or animals indoors

**viv·id** \'viv-əd\ *adj*
**1** seeming full of life and freshness ⟨a *vivid* sketch of the children⟩
**2** very strong or bright ⟨*vivid* red⟩
**3** producing strong mental images ⟨a *vivid* description⟩
**4** acting clearly and powerfully ⟨a *vivid* imagination⟩
**viv·id·ly** *adv*
**viv·id·ness** *n*

**vi·vip·a·rous** \vī-'vip-ə-rəs\ *adj*
giving birth to living young rather than laying eggs

**viv·i·sec·tion** \,viv-ə-'sek-shən\ *n*
the operating or experimenting on a living animal usually for scientific study

**vix·en** \'vik-sən\ *n*
a female fox

**vo·cab·u·lary** \vō-'kab-yə-,ler-ē\ *n, pl* **vo·cab·u·lar·ies**
**1** a list or collection of words defined or explained
**2** a stock of words used in a language, by a group or individual, or in relation to a subject

**vo·cal** \'vō-kəl\ *adj*
**1** uttered by the voice : ORAL
**2** composed or arranged for or sung by the human voice
**3** of, relating to, or having the power of producing voice
**vo·cal·ly** *adv*

**vocal cords** *n pl*
membranes at the top of the windpipe that produce vocal sounds when drawn tight and vibrated by the outgoing breath

**vo·cal·ist** \'vō-kə-list\ *n*
SINGER

**vo·ca·tion** \vō-'kā-shən\ *n*
**1** a strong desire for a certain career or course of action
**2** the work in which a person is regularly employed : OCCUPATION

**vo·ca·tion·al** \vō-'kā-shən-l\ *adj*
**1** of, relating to, or concerned with a vocation
**2** concerned with choice of or training in a vocation
**vo·ca·tion·al·ly** *adv*

**vod·ka** \'väd-kə\ *n*
a colorless alcoholic liquor

**vogue** \'vōg\ *n*
**1** the quality or state of being popular at a certain time
**2** a period in which something is in fashion
**3** something that is in fashion at a certain time

**¹voice** \'vȯis\ *n*
**1** sound produced through the mouth by vertebrates and especially by human beings in speaking or shouting
**2** musical sound produced by the vocal cords
**3** SPEECH 5
**4** a sound similar to vocal sound
**5** a means of expression
**6** the right to express a wish, choice, or opinion

**²voice** *vb* **voiced**; **voic·ing**
to express in words ⟨*voice* a complaint⟩

**voice box** *n*
LARYNX

**voiced** \'vȯist\ *adj*
spoken with vibration of the vocal cords ⟨the *voiced* consonants \b\, \d\, and \th\⟩

**voice·less** \'vȯi-sləs\ *adj*
spoken without vibration of the vocal cords ⟨the *voiceless* consonants \p\, \t\, and \th\⟩

## volleyball

Volleyball is played with two teams, usually of six players each. Once the ball is served, it is volleyed back and forth across the net, each team trying to return it to the opponent's side in three or fewer hits. The first team that fails to do this loses the round. If the serving team is the one that loses, the opposing team serves next. Otherwise, the serving team scores and continues serving.

volley ball

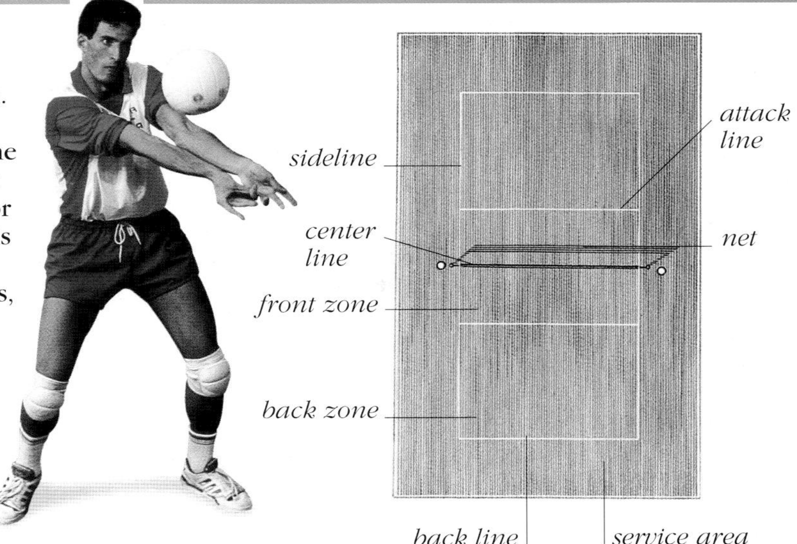


volleyball player striking the ball

volleyball court

**voice mail** *n*
an electronic communication system in which spoken messages are recorded to be played back later

volcano 1

**[1]void** \'vȯid\ *adj*
containing nothing : EMPTY

**[2]void** *n*
empty space

**vol·a·tile** \'väl-ət-l\ *adj*
**1** easily becoming a vapor at a fairly low temperature
**2** likely to change suddenly ⟨a *volatile* disposition⟩ ⟨*volatile* markets⟩

**vol·ca·nic** \väl-'kan-ik, vȯl-\ *adj*
**1** of or relating to a volcano
**2** likely to explode ⟨a *volcanic* temper⟩

**vol·ca·no** \väl-'kā-nō, vȯl-\ *n, pl* **vol·ca·noes** *or* **vol·ca·nos**
**1** ◀ an opening in the earth's crust from which hot or melted rock and steam come
**2** a hill or mountain composed of material thrown out in a volcanic eruption

**Word History** The Romans believed that Vulcanus, the god of fire, had his forge in a fiery mountain on an island off the coast of Italy. The English word *volcano* came (by way of Italian) from the Latin name for the Roman god of fire.

**vole** \'vōl\ *n*
▶ any of various small rodents that look like fat mice or rats with short tails and are sometimes harmful to crops

**vo·li·tion** \vō-'lish-ən\ *n*
the act or power of making one's own choices or decisions : WILL

**[1]vol·ley** \'väl-ē\ *n, pl* **volleys**
**1** a group of missiles (as arrows or bullets) passing through the air
**2** a firing of a number of weapons (as rifles) at the same time
**3** a bursting forth of many things at once
**4** the act of volleying

**[2]volley** *vb* **vol·leyed**; **vol·ley·ing**
**1** to shoot in a volley
**2** to hit an object (as a ball) while it is in the air before it touches the ground

**vol·ley·ball** \'väl-ē-,bȯl\ *n*
▲ a game played by volleying a large ball filled with air across a net

**volt** \'vōlt\ *n*
a unit for measuring the force that moves an electric current

**volt·age** \'vōl-tij\ *n*
electric force measured in volts ⟨the *voltage* of a current⟩

vole

**vol·u·ble** \'väl-yə-bəl\ *adj*
having a smooth and fast flow of words in speaking
**vol·u·bly** \-blē\ *adv*

**vol·ume** \'väl-yəm, -yüm\ *n*
**1** [1]BOOK 1

A B C D E F G H I J K L M N O P Q R S T U V W X Y Z

2 any one of a series of books that together form a complete work or collection
3 space included within limits as measured in cubic units ⟨the *volume* of a cylinder⟩
4 ²AMOUNT
5 the degree of loudness of a sound

**Word History** The earliest books were not like the books we read today. Instead of having pages that could be turned, they were written on rolls of a material something like paper. The Latin word for such a book came from a Latin verb that meant "to roll." The English word *volume* came from this Latin word. At first *volume* meant "scroll" or "book," but later it came to mean "the size of a book" as well. The later meaning led to the more general meaning of "size" or "amount" — as in the volume of a jar or the volume of sales. From this sense came still another meaning: "loudness or intensity of sound."

**vo·lu·mi·nous** \və-'lü-mə-nəs\ *adj*
1 of great volume or bulk
2 filling or capable of filling a large volume or several volumes

**vol·un·tary** \'väl-ən-,ter-ē\ *adj*
1 done, given, or made of one's own free will or choice
2 not accidental : INTENTIONAL
3 of, relating to, or controlled by the will
**vol·un·tar·i·ly** \,väl-ən-'ter-ə-lē\ *adv*

**Synonyms** VOLUNTARY, INTENTIONAL, and DELIBERATE mean done or brought about of one's own will. VOLUNTARY suggests free choice ⟨joining the club is *voluntary*⟩ or control by the will ⟨*voluntary* blinking of the eyes⟩. INTENTIONAL suggests that something is done for a reason and only after some thinking about it ⟨*intentional* neglect of a task⟩. DELIBERATE suggests that one is fully aware of what one is doing and of the likely results of the action ⟨a *deliberate* insult⟩.

**¹vol·un·teer** \,väl-ən-'tir\ *n*
1 a person who volunteers for a service
2 a plant growing without direct human care especially from seeds lost from a previous crop

**²volunteer** *adj*
of, relating to, or done by volunteers ⟨a *volunteer* fire department⟩

**³volunteer** *vb*
1 to offer or give without being asked
2 to offer oneself for a service of one's own free will

**¹vom·it** \'väm-ət\ *n*
material from the stomach gotten rid of through the mouth

**²vomit** *vb*
to rid oneself of the contents of the stomach through the mouth

**vo·ra·cious** \vò-'rā-shəs, və-\ *adj*
1 greedy in eating
2 very eager ⟨a *voracious* reader⟩
**vo·ra·cious·ly** *adv*

**¹vote** \'vōt\ *n*
1 a formal expression of opinion or will (as by ballot)
2 the decision reached by voting
3 the right to vote
4 the act or process of voting
5 a group of voters with some common interest or quality ⟨the farm *vote*⟩

**vulture:** an African vulture

**²vote** *vb* **vot·ed**; **vot·ing**
1 to express one's wish or choice by or as if by a vote
2 to elect, decide, pass, defeat, grant, or make legal by a vote
3 to declare by general agreement

**vot·er** \'vōt-ər\ *n*
a person who votes or who has the legal right to vote

**vouch** \'vaůch\ *vb*
to give a guarantee ⟨the teacher *vouched* for their honesty⟩

**vouch·safe** \vaůch-'sāf\ *vb* **vouch·safed**; **vouch·saf·ing**
to grant as a special favor

**¹vow** \'vaů\ *n*
a solemn promise or statement

**²vow** *vb*
to make a vow : SWEAR

**vow·el** \'vaů-əl\ *n*
1 a speech sound (as \ə\, \ā\, or \ò\) produced without obstruction or audible friction in the mouth
2 a letter (as *a, e, i, o, u*) representing a vowel

**¹voy·age** \'vòi-ij\ *n*
a journey especially by water from one place or country to another

**²voyage** *vb* **voy·aged**; **voy·ag·ing**
to take a trip
**voy·ag·er** *n*

**vul·ca·nize** \'vəl-kə-,nīz\ *vb* **vul·ca·nized**; **vul·ca·niz·ing**
to treat rubber with chemicals in order to give it useful properties (as strength)

**vul·gar** \'vəl-gər\ *adj*
1 of or relating to the common people
2 having poor taste or manners : COARSE
3 offensive in language

**vul·gar·i·ty** \,vəl-'gar-ət-ē\ *n*, *pl* **vul·gar·i·ties**
1 the quality or state of being vulgar
2 a vulgar expression or action

**vul·ner·a·ble** \'vəl-nə-rə-bəl\ *adj*
1 possible to wound or hurt
2 open to attack or damage
**vul·ner·a·bly** \-blē\ *adv*

**vul·ture** \'vəl-chər\ *n*
◀ a large bird related to the hawks and eagles that has a naked head and feeds mostly on animals found dead

**vying** *present participle of* VIE

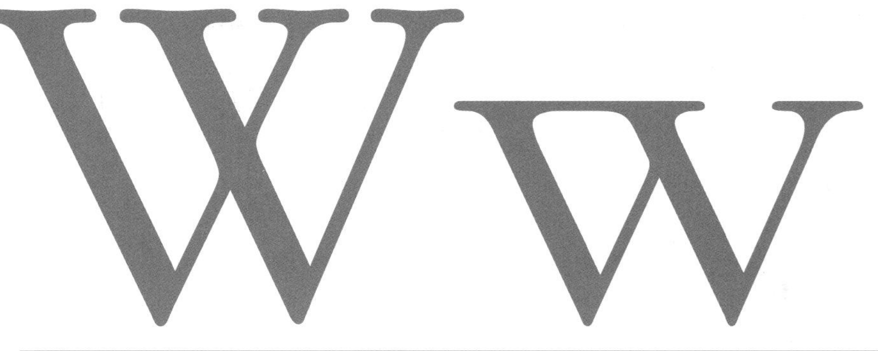

**The sounds of W:** The letter **W** has one sound in English. It sounds the same in **will**, **word**, **twenty**, and **toward**. It is silent in a few words, such as **who** and **two**, and is always silent at the end of a word, as in **yellow**.

The sound of **W** is also made by the letter **U** in most of the words where **U** follows **Q**. Examples are **quick** and **quartz**.

**w** \'dəb-əl-yü\ *n, pl* **w's** *or* **ws** \-yüz\ *often cap*
the twenty-third letter of the English alphabet

**wacky** \'wak-ē\ *or* **whacky** \'hwak-ē, 'wak-\ *adj* **wack·i·er** *or* **whack·i·er**; **wack·i·est** *or* **whack·i·est**
CRAZY 2, INSANE

[1]**wad** \'wäd\ *n*
**1** a small mass or lump
**2** a soft plug or stopper to hold a charge of powder (as in cartridges)
**3** a soft mass of cotton, cloth, or fibers used as a plug or pad

[2]**wad** *vb* **wad·ded**; **wad·ding**
to form into a wad

[1]**wad·dle** \'wäd-l\ *vb* **wad·dled**; **wad·dling**
to walk with short steps swaying like a duck

[2]**waddle** *n*
a waddling walk

**wade** \'wād\ *vb* **wad·ed**; **wad·ing**
**1** to walk through something (as water or snow) that makes it hard to move
**2** to proceed with difficulty ⟨*wading* through homework⟩
**3** to pass or cross by stepping through water ⟨*wade* the stream⟩

**wading bird** *n*
▼ a shorebird or waterbird with long legs that wades in water in search of food

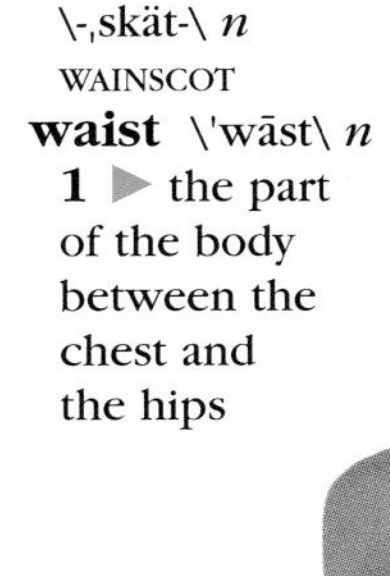

**wading bird:** a grey heron

**wa·fer** \'wā-fər\ *n*
a thin crisp cake or cracker

**waf·fle** \'wäf-əl\ *n*
a crisp cake of batter baked in a waffle iron

**waffle iron** *n*
▼ a cooking utensil with two hinged metal parts that come together for making waffles

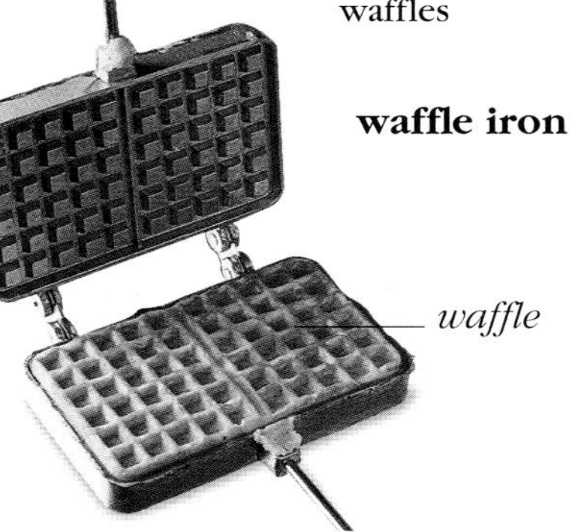


**waffle iron**

**waft** \'wäft, 'waft\ *vb*
to move or be moved lightly by or as if by the action of waves or wind

[1]**wag** \'wag\ *vb* **wagged**; **wag·ging**
to swing to and fro or from side to side ⟨the dog *wagged* its tail⟩

[2]**wag** *n*
**1** a wagging movement
**2** a person full of jokes and humor

[1]**wage** \'wāj\ *n*
**1** payment for work done especially when figured by the hour or day
**2 wages** *sing or pl* something given or received in return **:** REWARD ⟨the *wages* of sin is death⟩

[2]**wage** *vb* **waged**; **wag·ing**
to engage in **:** CARRY ON ⟨*wage* a fight against crime⟩

[1]**wa·ger** \'wā-jər\ *n*
**1** [1]BET 1
**2** the act of betting

[2]**wager** *vb*
to bet on the result of a contest or question
**wa·ger·er** *n*

**wag·gish** \'wag-ish\ *adj*
showing or done in a spirit of harmless mischief

**wag·gle** \'wag-əl\ *vb* **wag·gled**; **wag·gling**
to move backward and forward or from side to side

**wag·on** \'wag-ən\ *n*
a vehicle having four wheels and used for carrying goods

**waif** \'wāf\ *n*
a stray person or animal

[1]**wail** \'wāl\ *vb*
to utter a mournful cry

[2]**wail** *n*
a long cry of grief or pain

**wain·scot** \'wān-skət, -ˌskōt, -ˌskät\ *n*
the bottom part of an inside wall especially when made of material different from the rest

**wain·scot·ing** \'wān-ˌskōt-ing\ *or* **wain·scot·ting** \-ˌskät-\ *n*
WAINSCOT

**waist** \'wāst\ *n*
**1** ► the part of the body between the chest and the hips

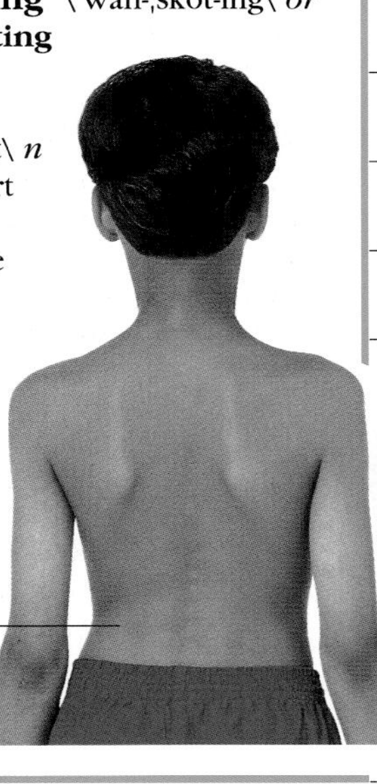


**waist 1**

a b c d e f g h i j k l m n o p q r s t u v w x y

\ng\ sing \ō\ bone \ȯ\ saw \ȯi\ coin \th\ thin \t͟h\ this \ü\ food \u̇\ foot \y\ yet \yü\ few \yu̇\ cure \zh\ vision

**2** the central part of a thing when it is narrower or thinner than the rest
**3** a garment or part of a garment covering the body from the neck to the waist

[1]**wait** \'wāt\ *vb*
**1** to stay in a place looking forward to something that is expected to happen
**2** to serve food as a waiter or waitress
**3** [2]DELAY 1 ⟨*wait* until we're through⟩

[2]**wait** *n*
**1** [2]AMBUSH — used chiefly in the expression *lie in wait*
**2** an act or period of waiting

**wait·er** \'wāt-ər\ *n*
a man who serves food to people at tables (as in a restaurant)

**waiting room** *n*
a room for the use of persons waiting (as for a train)

**wait·ress** \'wā-trəs\ *n*
a girl or woman who serves food to people at tables

**waive** \'wāv\ *vb*
**waived**; **waiv·ing**
to give up claim to

**walking stick 1:** a stick used for hiking

[1]**wake** \'wāk\ *vb*
**waked** *or* **woke** \'wōk\; **waked** *or* **wo·ken** \'wō-kən\; **wak·ing**
**1** to be or stay awake
**2** to stay awake on watch especially over a corpse
**3** [1]AWAKE 1 ⟨*wake* us at six⟩

[2]**wake** *n*
a watch held over the body of a dead person before burial

[3]**wake** *n*
a track or mark left by something moving especially in the water

**wake·ful** \'wāk-fəl\ *adj*
**1** VIGILANT
**2** not sleeping or able to sleep
**wake·ful·ness** *n*

**wak·en** \'wā-kən\ *vb*
[1]AWAKE 1

[1]**walk** \'wȯk\ *vb*
**1** to move or cause to move along on foot at a natural slow pace
**2** to cover or pass over at a walk ⟨*walked* twenty miles⟩
**3** to go or cause to go to first base after four balls in baseball
**walk·er** *n*

[2]**walk** *n*
**1** a going on foot
**2** a place or path for walking
**3** distance to be walked often measured in time required by a walker to cover
**4** position in life or the community
**5** way of walking
**6** an opportunity to go to first base after four balls in baseball

**walk·ie–talk·ie** \ˌwȯ-kē-'tȯ-kē\ *n*
a small portable radio set for receiving and sending messages

**walking stick** *n*
**1** ◀ a stick used in walking
**2** a sticklike insect with a long round body and long thin legs

**walk·out** \'wȯ-ˌkau̇t\ *n*
**1** a labor strike
**2** the leaving of a meeting or organization as a way of showing disapproval

**walk·over** \'wȯ-ˌkō-vər\ *n*
an easy victory

[1]**wall** \'wȯl\ *n*
**1** a solid structure (as of stone) built to enclose or shut off a space
**2** something like a wall that separates one thing from another ⟨a *wall* of mountains⟩
**3** a layer of material enclosing space ⟨the heart *wall*⟩
**walled** \'wȯld\ *adj*

[2]**wall** *vb*
to build a wall in or around

**wall·board** \'wȯl-ˌbōrd\ *n*
a building material (as of wood pulp) made in large stiff sheets and used especially for inside walls and ceilings

**wal·let** \'wäl-ət\ *n*
a small flat case for carrying paper money and personal papers

**wall·eye** \'wȯ-ˌlī\ *n*
a large strong American freshwater sport and food fish that is related to the perches but looks like a pike

[1]**wal·lop** \'wäl-əp\ *vb*
to hit hard

[2]**wallop** *n*
a hard blow

[1]**wal·low** \'wäl-ō\ *vb*
**1** to roll about in or as if in mud
**2** to be too much interested or concerned with ⟨*wallowing* in misery⟩

[2]**wallow** *n*
a muddy or dust-filled hollow where animals wallow

**wall·pa·per** \'wȯl-ˌpā-pər\ *n*
decorative paper for covering the walls of a room

**wal·nut** \'wȯl-ˌnət\ *n*
▼ the edible nut (as the American **black walnut** with a rough shell or the Old World **English walnut** with a smoother shell) that comes from trees related to the hickories and including some valued also for their wood

**Word History** Walnut trees grew in southern Europe for a long time before they were grown in England. As a result the English gave the walnut a name which showed plainly that it was not an English nut. The Old English name for this southern nut meant "a foreign nut." It was formed from two Old English words. The first meant "foreigner." The second meant "nut." The modern English word *walnut* comes from the Old English name.

**walnut:** a branch and the dried nuts from an English walnut tree

**wal·rus** \'wȯl-rəs\ *n*
a large animal of northern seas related to the seals and hunted for its hide, for the ivory tusks of the males, and for oil

[1]**waltz** \'wȯlts\ *n*
a dance in which couples glide to music having three beats to a measure

[2]**waltz** *vb*
to dance a waltz
**waltz·er** *n*

**wam·pum** \'wäm-pəm\ *n*
▼ beads made of shells and once used for money or ornament by North American Indians

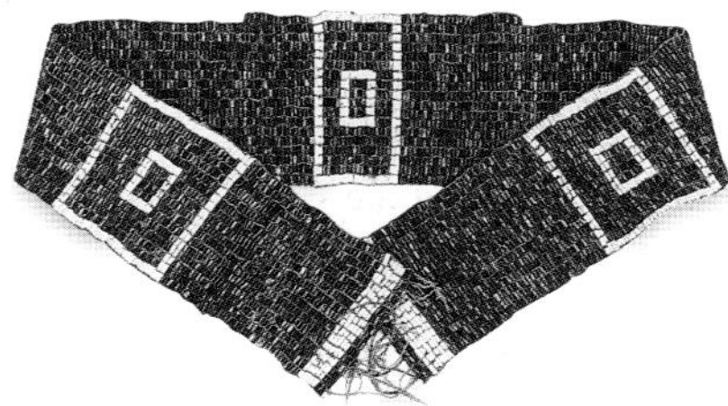

**wampum** woven into an Iroquois \'ir-ə-,kwȯi\ belt

**wan** \'wän\ *adj* **wan·ner**; **wan·nest**
having a pale or sickly color
**wan·ly** *adv*
**wan·ness** *n*

**wand** \'wänd\ *n*
▼ a slender rod (as one carried by a fairy or one used by a magician in doing tricks)

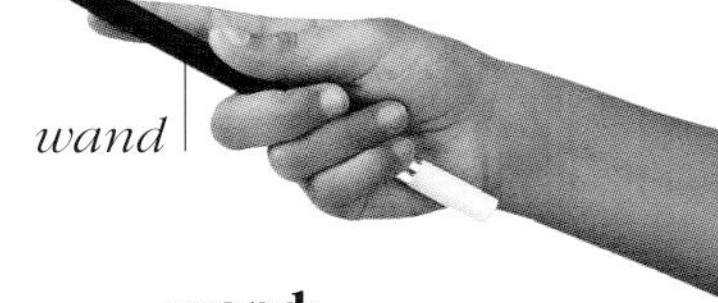


**wand:**
a magician's wand

**wan·der** \'wän-dər\ *vb*
**1** to move about without a goal or purpose : RAMBLE
**2** to follow a winding course
**3** to get off the right path : STRAY
**wan·der·er** *n*

**Synonyms** WANDER, ROAM, and RAMBLE mean to move about from place to place without a reason or plan. WANDER suggests that one does not follow a fixed course while moving about ⟨the tribes *wandered* in the desert for forty years⟩. ROAM suggests a carefree wandering over a wide area often for the sake of enjoyment ⟨I *roamed* over the hills and through the meadows⟩. RAMBLE suggests that one wanders in a careless way and without concern for where one goes ⟨horses *rambling* over the open range⟩.

**wan·der·lust** \'wän-dər-,ləst\ *n*
a strong wish or urge to travel

**wane** \'wān\ *vb* **waned**; **wan·ing**
**1** to grow smaller or less
**2** to lose power or importance : DECLINE

**¹want** \'wȯnt, 'wänt\ *vb*
**1** to be without : LACK
**2** to feel or suffer the need of something
**3** to desire, wish, or long for something

**²want** *n*
**1** ²LACK 2, SHORTAGE ⟨a *want* of common sense⟩
**2** the state of being very poor ⟨they died in *want*⟩
**3** a wish for something : DESIRE

**want·ing** \'wȯnt-ing, 'wänt-\ *adj*
falling below a standard, hope, or need ⟨the plan was found *wanting*⟩

**wan·ton** \'wȯnt-n\ *adj*
**1** PLAYFUL 1 ⟨a *wanton* breeze⟩
**2** not modest or proper : INDECENT
**3** showing no thought or care for the rights, feelings, or safety of others ⟨*wanton* cruelty⟩
**wan·ton·ly** *adv*
**wan·ton·ness** *n*

**¹war** \'wȯr\ *n*
**1** a state or period of fighting between states or nations
**2** the art or science of warfare
**3** a struggle between opposing forces

**²war** *vb* **warred**; **war·ring**
to make war : FIGHT

**¹war·ble** \'wȯr-bəl\ *n*
**1** low pleasing sounds that form a melody (as of a bird)
**2** the action of warbling

**²warble** *vb* **war·bled**; **war·bling**
to sing with a warble

**war·bler** \'wȯr-blər\ *n*
**1** any of a group of Old World birds related to the thrushes and noted for their musical song
**2** any of a group of brightly colored American migratory songbirds that eat insects and have a weak call

**¹ward** \'wȯrd\ *n*
**1** a part of a hospital
**2** one of the parts into which a town or city is divided for management
**3** a person under the protection of a guardian

**²ward** *vb*
**1** to keep watch over : GUARD
**2** to turn aside ⟨*ward* off a blow⟩

**¹-ward** \wərd\ *also* **-wards** \wərdz\ *adj suffix*
**1** that moves, faces, or is pointed toward ⟨wind*ward*⟩
**2** that is found in the direction of

**²-ward** *or* **-wards** *adv suffix*
**1** in a specified direction ⟨up*ward*⟩
**2** toward a specified place

**war·den** \'wȯrd-n\ *n*
**1** a person who sees that certain laws are followed ⟨game *warden*⟩
**2** the chief official of a prison

**ward·robe** \'wȯr-,drōb\ *n*
**1** ▼ a room or closet where clothes are kept
**2** the clothes a person owns

**wardrobe 1:**
a freestanding wardrobe

**ware** \'waər, 'weər\ *n*
**1** manufactured articles or products of art or craft
**2** items (as dishes) of baked clay : POTTERY

**ware·house** \'waər-,hau̇s, 'weər-\ *n, pl* **ware·hous·es** \-,hau̇-zəz\
a building for storing goods and merchandise

**war·fare** \'wȯr-,faər, -,feər\ *n*
**1** military fighting between enemies
**2** strong continued effort : STRUGGLE ⟨our *warfare* against crime⟩

A B C D E F G H I J K L M N O P Q R S T U V W X Y Z

**war·like** \'wȯr-ˌlīk\ *adj*
**1** fond of war
**2** of or relating to war
**3** threatening war

**¹warm** \'wȯrm\ *adj*
**1** somewhat hot ⟨*warm* milk⟩
**2** giving off heat
**3** making a person feel heat or experience no loss of bodily heat ⟨*warm* clothing⟩
**4** having a feeling of warmth
**5** showing strong feeling ⟨a *warm* welcome⟩
**6** newly made : FRESH
**7** near the object sought ⟨keep going, you're getting *warm*⟩
**8** of a color in the range yellow through orange to red
**warm·ly** *adv*

**²warm** *vb*
**1** to make or become warm
**2** to give a feeling of warmth
**3** to become more interested than at first ⟨begin to *warm* to an idea⟩

**warm–blood·ed** \'wȯrm-'bləd-əd\ *adj*
**1** able to keep up a body temperature that is independent of that of the surroundings
**2** warm in feeling
**warm–blood·ed·ness** *n*

**warmth** \'wȯrmth\ *n*
**1** gentle heat
**2** strong feeling

**warm–up** \'wȯr-ˌməp\ *n*
the act or an instance of warming up ⟨a *warm-up* before a game⟩

**warm up** \wȯr-'məp\ *vb*
**1** ▼ to exercise or practice lightly in preparation for more strenuous activity or a performance ⟨*warming up* before an exercise class⟩ ⟨*warm up* for a recital⟩
**2** to run (as a motor) at slow speed before using

**warm up 1:** a woman warming up by stretching

**warn** \'wȯrn\ *vb*
**1** to put on guard : CAUTION
**2** to notify especially in advance

**warn·ing** \'wȯr-ning\ *n*
something that warns ⟨storm *warnings*⟩

**¹warp** \'wȯrp\ *n*
**1** the threads that go lengthwise in a loom and are crossed by the woof
**2** a twist or curve that has developed in something once flat or straight

**²warp** *vb*
**1** to curve or twist out of shape
**2** to cause to judge, choose, or act wrongly ⟨their thinking is *warped* by greed⟩

**war·path** \'wȯr-ˌpath, -ˌpȧth\ *n*
the route taken by a group of American Indians going off to fight
**on the warpath** ready to fight or argue

**war·plane** \'wȯr-ˌplān\ *n*
► a military or naval airplane



**warplane:** front view of a British warplane

**¹war·rant** \'wȯr-ənt\ *n*
**1** a reason or cause for an opinion or action
**2** a document giving legal power

**²warrant** *vb*
**1** to be sure of or that ⟨I'll *warrant* they know the answer⟩
**2** ²GUARANTEE 2 ⟨a toaster *warranted* for ninety days⟩
**3** to call for : JUSTIFY ⟨the report *warrants* careful study⟩

**warrant officer** *n*
**1** an officer in the armed forces in one of the grades between commissioned officers and enlisted persons
**2** a warrant officer of the lowest rank

**war·ren** \'wȯr-ən\ *n*
a place for keeping or raising small game (as rabbits)

**war·rior** \'wȯr-yər, 'wȯr-ē-ər\ *n*
a person who is or has been in warfare

**war·ship** \'wȯr-ˌship\ *n*
a ship armed for combat

**wart** \'wȯrt\ *n*
a small hard lump of thickened skin

**warty** \'wȯr-tē\ *adj* **wart·i·er**; **wart·i·est**
**1** covered with or as if with warts
**2** like a wart

**wary** \'waər-ē, 'weər-ē\ *adj* **war·i·er**; **war·i·est**
very cautious
**war·i·ly** \'war-ə-lē, 'wer-\ *adv*
**war·i·ness** \'war-ē-nəs, 'wer-\ *n*

**was** *past 1st & 3d sing of* BE

**¹wash** \'wȯsh, 'wäsh\ *vb*
**1** to cleanse with water and usually a cleaning agent (as soap)
**2** to wet completely with liquid
**3** to flow along or overflow against ⟨waves *washing* the shore⟩
**4** to remove by the action of water
**5** to stand washing without injury ⟨linen *washes* well⟩

**²wash** *n*
**1** articles (as of clothing) in the laundry
**2** the flow, sound, or action of water
**3** a backward flow of water (as made by the motion of a boat)

4 material carried or set down by water

**wash·able** \'wȯsh-ə-bəl, 'wäsh-\ *adj*
capable of being washed without damage ⟨a *washable* jacket⟩

**wash·board** \'wȯsh-ˌbōrd, 'wäsh-\ *n*
a grooved board to scrub clothes on

**wash·bowl** \'wȯsh-ˌbōl, 'wäsh-\ *n*
a large bowl for water to wash one's hands and face

**wash·er** \'wȯsh-ər, 'wäsh-\ *n*
**1** WASHING MACHINE
**2** a ring (as of metal) used to make something fit tightly or to prevent rubbing

**wash·ing** \'wȯsh-ing, 'wäsh-\ *n*
[2]WASH 1

**washing machine** *n*
a machine used especially for washing clothes and household linen

**wash·out** \'wȯsh-ˌau̇t, 'wäsh-\ *n*
**1** the washing away of earth (as from a road)
**2** a place where earth is washed away
**3** a complete failure

**wash·tub** \'wȯsh-ˌtəb, 'wäsh-\ *n*
a tub for washing clothes or for soaking them before washing

**wasn't** \'wəz-nt, 'wäz-\
was not

**wasp** \'wäsp, 'wȯsp\ *n*
▼ a winged insect related to the bees and ants that has a slender body with the abdomen attached by a narrow stalk and that in females and workers is capable of giving a very painful sting

**wasp·ish** \'wäs-pish, 'wȯs-\ *adj*
[3]CROSS 3, IRRITABLE
**wasp·ish·ly** *adv*
**wasp·ish·ness** *n*

[1]**waste** \'wāst\ *n*
**1** [1]DESERT, WILDERNESS
**2** WASTELAND
**3** the action of wasting : the state of being wasted
**4** material left over or thrown away
**5** material produced in and of no further use to the living body

[2]**waste** *vb* **wast·ed**; **wast·ing**
**1** to bring to ruin
**2** to spend or use carelessly or uselessly
**3** to lose or cause to lose weight, strength, or energy

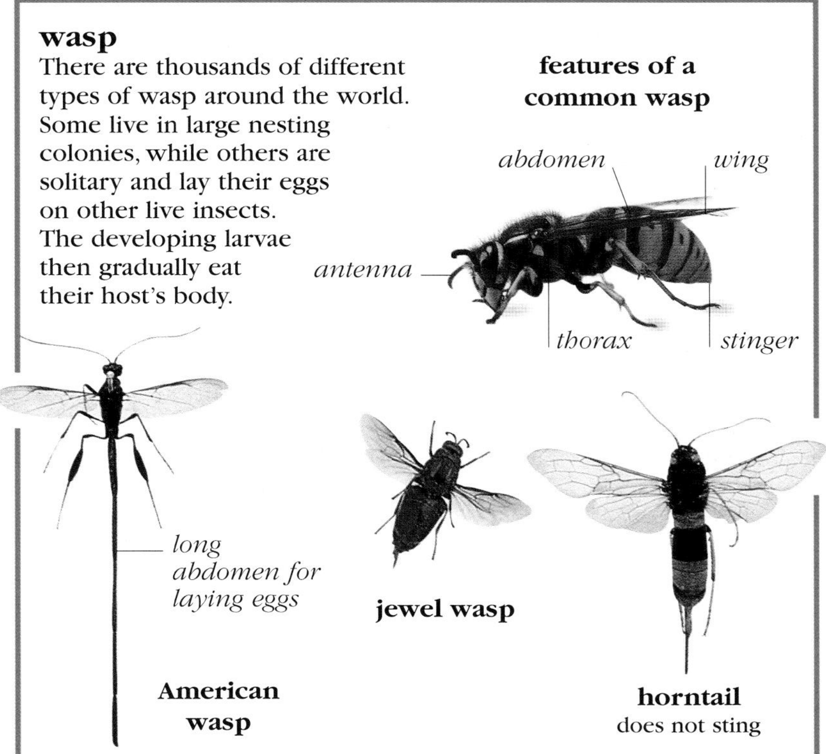

wasp
There are thousands of different types of wasp around the world. Some live in large nesting colonies, while others are solitary and lay their eggs on other live insects. The developing larvae then gradually eat their host's body.
features of a common wasp
abdomen
wing
antenna
thorax
stinger
long abdomen for laying eggs
American wasp
jewel wasp
horntail
does not sting


[3]**waste** *adj*
**1** being wild and not lived in or planted to crops : BARREN
**2** of no further use

**waste·bas·ket** \'wāst-ˌbas-kət\ *n*
an open container for odds and ends to be thrown away

**waste·ful** \'wāst-fəl\ *adj*
**1** wasting or causing waste
**2** spending or using in a careless or foolish way
**waste·ful·ly** \-fə-lē\ *adv*
**waste·ful·ness** *n*

**waste·land** \'wāst-ˌland\ *n*
land that is barren or not fit for crops

[1]**watch** \'wäch\ *vb*
**1** to stay awake
**2** to be on one's guard
**3** to take care of : TEND ⟨*watch* the house until I get back⟩
**4** to be on the lookout ⟨*watching* for a signal⟩
**5** to keep one's eyes on ⟨*watch* a game⟩
**watch·er** *n*

[2]**watch** *n*
**1** an act of keeping awake to guard or protect
**2** close observation
**3** [1]GUARD 2
**4** the time during which one is on duty to watch
**5** ► a small timepiece to be worn or carried

[2]**watch 5:** a watch with a clear face that shows its mechanics

**watch·dog** \'wäch-ˌdȯg\ *n*
a dog kept to watch and guard property

**watch·ful** \'wäch-fəl\ *adj*
ATTENTIVE 1, VIGILANT
**watch·ful·ly** \-fə-lē\ *adv*
**watch·ful·ness** *n*

**watch·man** \'wäch-mən\ *n*, *pl* **watch·men** \-mən\
a person whose job is to watch and guard property at night or when the owners are away

**watch·tow·er** \'wäch-ˌtau̇-ər\ *n*
a tower on which a guard or watchman is placed

**watch·word** \'wäch-,wərd\ *n*
PASSWORD

**[1]wa·ter** \'wȯt-ər, 'wät-\ *n*
**1** the liquid that comes from the clouds as rain and forms streams, lakes, and seas
**2** a liquid that contains or is like water
**3** a body of water or a part of a body of water

**[2]water** *vb*
**1** to wet or supply with water ⟨*water* plants⟩
**2** to add water to
**3** to fill with liquid (as tears)

**wa·ter·bird** \'wȯt-ər-,bərd, 'wät-\ *n*
a swimming or wading bird

**water buffalo** *n*
a buffalo of Asia with large curving horns often used as a work animal

**water clock** *n*
a device or machine for measuring time by the fall or flow of water

**wa·ter·col·or** \'wȯt-ər-,kəl-ər, 'wät-\ *n*
**1** a paint whose liquid part is water
**2** ▼ a picture painted with watercolor
**3** the art of painting with watercolor

**watercolor 2:** a watercolor by contemporary artist Jane Gifford

**wa·ter·course** \'wȯt-ər-,kōrs, 'wät-\ *n*
**1** a channel in which water flows
**2** a stream of water (as a river or brook)

**wa·ter·cress** \'wȯt-ər-,kres, 'wät-\ *n*
▶ a plant related to the mustards that grows in cold flowing waters and is used especially in salads

**wa·ter·fall** \'wȯt-ər-,fȯl, 'wät-\ *n*
▼ a fall of water from a height

**waterfall:** Lower Yosemite \yō-'sem-ət-ē\ Falls, California

**water flea** *n*
a small active often brightly colored freshwater animal related to the crabs and lobsters

**wa·ter·fowl** \'wȯt-ər-,fau̇l, 'wät-\ *n*
**1** a bird that is found in or near water
**2 waterfowl** *pl* swimming birds (as wild ducks and geese) hunted as game

**wa·ter·front** \'wȯt-ər-,frənt, 'wät-\ *n*
land or a section of a town that borders on a body of water

**water hyacinth** *n*
a floating water plant that often blocks streams in the southern United States

**water lily** *n*
any of a group of water plants with rounded floating leaves and showy often fragrant flowers with many petals

**wa·ter·line** \'wȯt-ər-,līn, 'wät-\ *n*
any of several lines marked on the outside of a ship that match the surface of the water when the ship floats evenly

**watercress**

**wa·ter·logged** \'wȯt-ər-,lȯgd, 'wät-, -,lägd\ *adj*
so filled or soaked with water as to be heavy or hard to manage

**wa·ter·mark** \'wȯt-ər-,märk, 'wät-\ *n*
**1** a mark that shows a level to which water has risen
**2** a mark made in paper during manufacture and visible when the paper is held up to the light

**wa·ter·mel·on** \'wȯt-ər-,mel-ən, 'wät-\ *n*
a large edible fruit with a hard outer layer and a sweet red juicy pulp

**water moccasin** *n*
MOCCASIN 2

**water park** *n*
an amusement park with pools and wetted slides

**water polo** *n*
a ball game played in water by teams of swimmers

**wa·ter·pow·er** \'wȯt-ər-,pau̇-ər, 'wät-\ *n*
the power of moving water used to run machinery

**[1]wa·ter·proof** \,wȯt-ər-'prüf, ,wät-\ *adj*
not letting water through ⟨a *waterproof* tent⟩

**[2]waterproof** *vb*
to make waterproof

**wa·ter·shed** \'wȯt-ər-,shed, 'wät-\ *n*
**1** a dividing ridge (as a mountain range) separating one drainage area from others
**2** the whole area that drains into a lake or river

**wa·ter·spout** \'wȯt-ər-,spau̇t, 'wät-\ *n*
**1** a pipe for carrying off water from a roof
**2** a slender cloud that is shaped like a funnel and extends down to a cloud of spray torn up from the surface of a body of water by a whirlwind

**water strid·er** \-'strīd-ər\ *n*
a bug with long legs that skims over the surface of water

**wa·ter·tight** \ˌwȯt-ər-ˈtīt, ˌwät-\ *adj*
so tight as to be waterproof ⟨a *watertight* joint in a pipe⟩

**wa·ter·way** \ˈwȯt-ər-ˌwā, ˈwät-\ *n*
a channel or a body of water by which ships can travel

**wa·ter·wheel** \ˈwȯt-ər-ˌhwēl, ˈwät-, -ˌwēl\ *n*
a wheel turned by a flow of water against it

**wa·ter·works** \ˈwȯt-ər-ˌwərks, ˈwät-\ *n pl*
a system of dams, reservoirs, pumps, and pipes for supplying water (as to a city)

**wa·tery** \ˈwȯt-ə-rē, ˈwät-\ *adj*
**1** of or relating to water
**2** full of or giving out liquid ⟨*watery* eyes⟩
**3** being like water
**4** being soft and soggy

**watt** \ˈwät\ *n*
a unit for measuring electric power

**wat·tle** \ˈwät-l\ *n*
▼ a fleshy flap of skin that hangs from the throat (as of a bird)

**wattle** on a turkey

**¹wave** \ˈwāv\ *vb* **waved**; **wav·ing**
**1** to move like a wave
**2** to move (as one's hand) to and fro as a signal or in greeting
**3** to curve like a wave or series of waves

**²wave** *n*
**1** a moving ridge on the surface of water
**2** a shape like a wave or series of waves ⟨the *wave* in your hair⟩
**3** something that swells and dies away ⟨a *wave* of anger⟩ ⟨a *wave* of buying⟩
**4** a waving motion ⟨a *wave* of the hand⟩
**5** a rolling movement passing along a surface or through the air
**6** a motion that is somewhat like a wave in water and transfers energy from point to point ⟨sound *waves*⟩

**wave·length** \ˈwāv-ˌlength\ *n*
the distance in the line of advance of a wave from any one point to the next similar point

**wave·let** \ˈwāv-lət\ *n*
a little wave

**wa·ver** \ˈwā-vər\ *vb*
**1** to sway one way and the other
**2** to be uncertain in opinion
**3** to move unsteadily

**wavy** \ˈwā-vē\ *adj* **wav·i·er**; **wav·i·est**
like, having, or moving in waves ⟨*wavy* hair⟩
**wav·i·ness** *n*

**¹wax** \ˈwaks\ *n*
**1** a dull yellow sticky substance made by bees and used in building honeycomb **:** BEESWAX
**2** a substance like beeswax

**²wax** *vb*
to treat with wax

**³wax** *vb*
**1** to grow larger or stronger
**2** BECOME 1, GROW ⟨*waxed* angry as the rumor spread⟩

**wax bean** *n*
a string bean with yellow waxy pods

**wax·en** \ˈwak-sən\ *adj*
of or like wax

**wax myrtle** *n*
the bayberry shrub

**wax·wing** \ˈwak-ˌswing\ *n*
► a crested mostly brown bird having smooth feathers (as the American **cedar waxwing** with yellowish belly)

**waxy** \ˈwak-sē\ *adj* **wax·i·er**; **wax·i·est**
**1** being like wax
**2** made of or covered with wax

**¹way** \ˈwā\ *n*
**1** a track for travel **:** PATH, STREET
**2** the course traveled from one place to another **:** ROUTE
**3** a course of action ⟨chose the easy *way*⟩
**4** personal choice as to situation or behavior **:** WISH
**5** the manner in which something is done or happens
**6** a noticeable point
**7** ¹STATE 1
**8** ¹DISTANCE 1 ⟨a short *way*⟩
**9** progress along a course ⟨working my *way* through college⟩
**10** a special or personal manner of behaving
**11** NEIGHBORHOOD 1, DISTRICT
**12** room to advance or pass ⟨make *way*⟩
**13** CATEGORY, KIND ⟨had little in the *way* of help⟩

**²way** *adv*
¹FAR 1 ⟨the sleeves hung *way* down⟩

**way·far·er** \ˈwā-ˌfar-ər, -ˌfer-\ *n*
a traveler especially on foot

**way·lay** \ˈwā-ˌlā\ *vb* **way·laid** \-ˌlād\; **way·lay·ing**
to attack from hiding

**-ways** \ˌwāz\ *adv suffix*
in such a way, direction, or manner ⟨side*ways*⟩

**way·side** \ˈwā-ˌsīd\ *n*
the edge of a road

**way·ward** \ˈwā-wərd\ *adj*
**1** DISOBEDIENT
**2** opposite to what is wished or hoped for

**waxwing:** a Bohemian \bō-ˈhē-mē-ən\ waxwing

**we** \wē\ *pron*
I and at least one other

**weak** \ˈwēk\ *adj*
**1** lacking strength of body, mind, or spirit
**2** not able to stand much strain or force ⟨a *weak* rope⟩
**3** easily overcome ⟨a *weak* argument⟩
**4** not able to function well ⟨*weak* eyes⟩
**5** not rich in some usual or important element ⟨*weak* tea⟩ ⟨*weak* colors⟩

A B C D E F G H I J K L M N O P Q R S T U V W X Y Z

**6** lacking experience or skill
**7** of, relating to, or being the lightest of three levels of stress in pronunciation

---

**Synonyms** WEAK, FEEBLE, and FRAIL mean not strong enough to stand pressure or hard effort. WEAK can be used of either a temporary or permanent loss of strength or power ⟨felt *weak* after the operation⟩ ⟨I have *weak* lungs⟩. FEEBLE stresses very great and pitiful weakness ⟨a *feeble* old beggar wandering in the streets⟩. FRAIL can be used of a person who since birth has had a delicate body ⟨a *frail* child always getting sick⟩ or of any kind of flimsy construction ⟨the *frail* boat was wrecked in the first storm⟩.

---

**weak·en** \'wē-kən\ *vb*
to make or become weak or weaker

**weak·fish** \'wēk-,fish\ *n*
▼ any of several sea fishes related to the perches (as a common sport and market fish of the eastern coast of the United States)

**weakfish**

**weak·ling** \'wē-kling\ *n*
a person or animal that is weak

[1]**weak·ly** \'wē-klē\ *adv*
in a weak manner

[2]**weakly** *adj* **weak·li·er**; **weak·li·est**
not strong or healthy

**weak·ness** \'wēk-nəs\ *n*
**1** lack of strength
**2** a weak point : FLAW

**wealth** \'welth\ *n*
**1** a large amount of money or possessions
**2** a great amount or number ⟨a *wealth* of ideas⟩

**wealthy** \'wel-thē\ *adj* **wealth·i·er**; **wealth·i·est**
having wealth : RICH

**wean** \'wēn\ *vb*
**1** to get a child or young animal used to food other than its mother's milk
**2** to turn one away from desiring a thing one has been fond of

**weap·on** \'wep-ən\ *n*
something (as a gun, knife, or club) to fight with

[1]**wear** \'waər, 'weər\ *vb* **wore** \'wōr\; **worn** \'wōrn\; **wear·ing**
**1** to use as an article of clothing or decoration
**2** to carry on the body ⟨*wearing* a watch⟩
**3** [1]SHOW 1 ⟨*wear* a smile⟩
**4** to damage, waste, or make less by use or by scraping or rubbing
**5** to make tired
**6** to cause or make by rubbing ⟨*wear* a hole in a coat⟩
**7** to last through long use ⟨cloth that *wears* well⟩
**wear·er** *n*

[2]**wear** *n*
**1** the act of wearing : the state of being worn
**2** things worn or meant to be worn ⟨children's *wear*⟩
**3** the result of wearing or use ⟨showing signs of *wear*⟩

**wea·ri·some** \'wir-ē-səm\ *adj*
TEDIOUS, DULL

**wear out** *vb*
**1** to make useless by long or hard use
**2** [1]TIRE 1

[1]**wea·ry** \'wir-ē\ *adj* **wea·ri·er**; **wea·ri·est**
**1** made tired usually from work
**2** having one's patience, pleasure, or interest worn out
**3** causing a loss of strength or interest
**wea·ri·ly** \'wir-ə-lē\ *adv*
**wea·ri·ness** \'wir-ē-nəs\ *n*

[2]**weary** *vb* **wea·ried**; **wea·ry·ing**
to make or become weary

**wea·sel** \'wē-zəl\ *n*
a small slender active animal related to the minks that feeds on small birds and animals (as mice)

[1]**weath·er** \'weth-ər\ *n*
the state of the air and atmosphere in regard to how warm or cold, wet or dry, or clear or stormy it is

[2]**weather** *vb*
**1** to expose to the weather
**2** to change (as in color or structure) by the action of the weather
**3** to be able to last or come safely through ⟨*weather* a storm⟩

[3]**weather** *adj*
[1]WINDWARD

**weath·er·cock** \'weth-ər-,käk\ *n*
▼ a weather vane shaped like a rooster

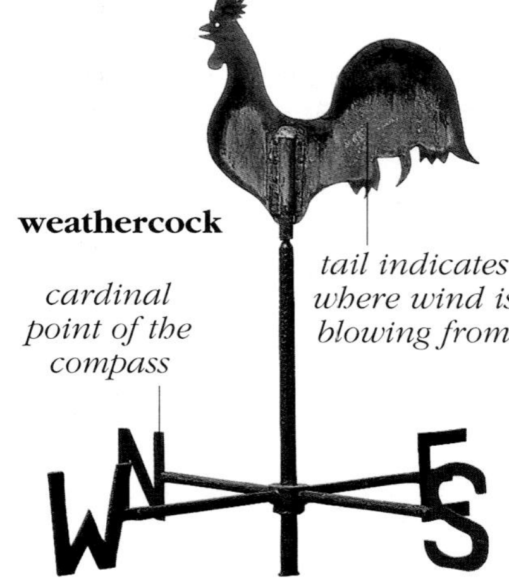


**weathercock**

**weath·er·man** \'weth-ər-,man\ *n*, *pl* **weath·er·men** \-,men\
a person who reports and forecasts the weather

**weath·er·per·son** \'weth-ər-,pərs-n\ *n*
WEATHERMAN

**weather vane** *n*
a movable device attached to something high (as a roof) to show which way the wind is blowing

[1]**weave** \'wēv\ *vb* **wove** \'wōv\; **wo·ven** \'wō-vən\; **weav·ing**
**1** to form (as cloth) by lacing together strands of material
**2** [1]SPIN 3
**3** to make by or as if by lacing parts together ⟨*weave* a tale of adventure⟩
**4** to move back and forth, up and down, or in and out
**weav·er** \'wē-vər\ *n*

[2]**weave** *n*
a method or pattern of weaving

[1]**web** \'web\ *n*
**1** a woven fabric on a loom or coming from a loom
**2** COBWEB 1
**3** something like a cobweb
**4** a membrane especially when joining toes (as of a duck)
**5** *cap* WORLD WIDE WEB

[2]**web** *vb* **webbed**; **web·bing**
to join or surround with a web

**web·foot** \'web-,fu̇t\ *n*, *pl* **web·feet** \-,fēt\
a foot (as of a duck) having the toes joined by webs
**web–foot·ed** \-'fu̇t-əd\ *adj*

**webfoot** of a duck

**Web site** *n*
a group of World Wide Web pages usually containing links to each other and made available on-line by an individual, company, or organization

**wed** \'wed\ *vb* **wed·ded** *also* **wed**; **wed·ding**
**1** MARRY
**2** to attach firmly

**we'd** \wēd\
we had : we should : we would

**wed·ding** \'wed-ing\ *n*
a marriage ceremony

[1]**wedge** \'wej\ *n*
**1** a piece of wood or metal that tapers to a thin edge and is used for splitting (as logs) or for raising something heavy
**2** something (as a piece of cake or a formation of wild geese flying) with a triangular shape

[2]**wedge** *vb* **wedged**; **wedg·ing**
**1** to fasten or tighten with a wedge
**2** to crowd or squeeze in tight

**wed·lock** \'wed-,läk\ *n*
MARRIAGE 1

**Wednes·day** \'wenz-dē\ *n*
the fourth day of the week

**wee** \'wē\ *adj*
very small : TINY

[1]**weed** \'wēd\ *n*
a plant that tends to grow thickly where not wanted and to choke out more desirable plants

[2]**weed** *vb*
**1** to remove weeds from
**2** to get rid of what is not wanted ⟨*weed* out the old computer files⟩

**weedy** \'wēd-ē\ *adj* **weed·i·er**; **weed·i·est**
**1** full of or consisting of weeds
**2** like a weed especially in coarse strong rapid growth
**3** very skinny

**week** \'wēk\ *n*
**1** seven days in a row especially beginning with Sunday and ending with Saturday
**2** the working or school days that come between Sunday and Saturday

**week·day** \'wēk-,dā\ *n*
a day of the week except Sunday or sometimes except Saturday and Sunday

**week·end** \'wē-,kend\ *n*
the period between the close of one work or school week and the beginning of the next

[1]**week·ly** \'wē-klē\ *adj*
**1** happening, done, produced, or published every week
**2** figured by the week ⟨*weekly* pay⟩

[2]**weekly** *n*, *pl* **weeklies**
a newspaper or magazine published every week

**weep** \'wēp\ *vb* **wept** \'wept\; **weep·ing**
to shed tears : CRY

**weep·ing** \'wē-ping\ *adj*
having slender drooping branches ⟨a *weeping* birch⟩

**weeping willow** *n*
a willow originally from Asia that has slender drooping branches

**wee·vil** \'wē-vəl\ *n*
any of various small beetles with a hard shell and a long snout many of which are harmful to fruits, nuts, grain, or trees

**weigh** \'wā\ *vb*
**1** to find the weight of
**2** to think about as if weighing ⟨*weigh* their chances of winning⟩
**3** to measure out on or as if on scales
**4** to lift an anchor before sailing
**5** to have weight or a specified weight ⟨*weigh* one kilogram⟩

**weigh down** *vb*
to cause to bend down

[1]**weight** \'wāt\ *n*
**1** the amount that something weighs
**2** the force with which a body is pulled toward the earth
**3** a unit (as a kilogram) for measuring weight
**4** an object (as a piece of metal) of known weight for balancing a scale in weighing other objects
**5** a heavy object used to hold or press down something
**6** [1]BURDEN 2 ⟨a *weight* on one's mind⟩
**7** strong influence : IMPORTANCE

[1]**weight 4:** weights on a scale

[2]**weight** *vb*
**1** to load or make heavy with a weight
**2** to trouble with a burden

**weighty** \'wāt-ē\ *adj* **weight·i·er**; **weight·i·est**
**1** having much weight : HEAVY
**2** very important

**weird** \'wird\ *adj*
**1** of or relating to witchcraft or magic ⟨the *weird* happenings in the haunted castle⟩
**2** very unusual : STRANGE, FANTASTIC ⟨what a *weird* way to cook an egg!⟩

**Word History** The adjective *weird* came from an earlier noun *weird*, which meant "fate." A long time ago people started to use the noun *weird* as an adjective in a phrase "the Weird Sisters." The Weird Sisters were three goddesses who determined the fates of men and women. At first the adjective *weird* meant "having to do with fate." Later it came to mean "magical," "fantastic," or "strange."

**weirdo** \'wird-ō\ *n*, *pl* **weird·os**
a very strange person

**[1]wel·come** \'wel-kəm\ *vb* **wel·comed**; **wel·com·ing**
**1** to greet with friendship or courtesy
**2** to receive or accept with pleasure

**Word History** When you welcome people to your house you are greeting them as desirable guests. The word *welcome* comes from an Old English word that meant "a desirable guest." It was formed from two words. The first meant "desire" or "wish." The second meant "guest." The word that meant "desire" is related to the modern English word *will*. The word that meant "guest" is related to the modern English word *come*.

**[2]welcome** *adj*
**1** greeted or received gladly ⟨visitors are *welcome*⟩ ⟨a *welcome* rain⟩
**2** giving pleasure : PLEASING ⟨a *welcome* sight⟩
**3** willingly permitted to do, have, or enjoy something ⟨you're *welcome* to come along⟩
**4** used in the phrase "You're welcome" as a reply to an expression of thanks

**[3]welcome** *n*
a friendly greeting

**[1]weld** \'weld\ *vb*
**1** to join two pieces of metal or plastic by heating and allowing the edges to flow together
**2** to join closely
**3** to become or be capable of being welded
**weld·er** *n*

**[2]weld** *n*
a welded joint

**wel·fare** \'wel-ˌfaər, -ˌfeər\ *n*
**1** the state of being or doing well
**2** aid in the form of money or necessities for people who are poor, aged, or disabled

**[1]well** \'wel\ *n*
**1** a source of supply
**2** a hole made in the earth to reach a natural deposit (as of water, oil, or gas)
**3** something suggesting a well

**[2]well** *vb*
to rise to the surface and flow out

**[3]well** *adv* **bet·ter** \'bet-ər\; **best** \'best\
**1** so as to be right : in a satisfactory way ⟨do your work *well*⟩
**2** in a good-hearted or generous way ⟨they always speak *well* of you⟩
**3** in a skillful or expert manner ⟨plays the guitar *well*⟩
**4** by as much as possible : COMPLETELY ⟨we are *well* aware of the problem⟩
**5** with reason or courtesy ⟨I cannot *well* refuse⟩
**6** in such a way as to be pleasing : as one would wish ⟨everything has gone *well* this week⟩
**7** without trouble ⟨we could *well* afford the extra cost⟩
**8** in a thorough manner ⟨shake *well* before using⟩
**9** in a familiar manner ⟨I thought you knew them *well*⟩
**10** by quite a lot ⟨rode *well* ahead⟩ ⟨*well* over a million⟩

**[4]well** *interj*
**1** used to express surprise or doubt
**2** used to begin a conversation or to continue one that was interrupted

**[5]well** *adj*
**1** being in a satisfactory or good state ⟨all is *well*⟩
**2** free or recovered from ill health : HEALTHY
**3** FORTUNATE 1 ⟨it was *well* that we left⟩

**we'll** \wēl\
we shall : we will

**well–be·ing** \'wel-'bē-ing\ *n*
WELFARE 1

**well–bred** \'wel-'bred\ *adj*
having or showing good manners : POLITE

**well–known** \'wel-'nōn\ *adj*
known by many people

**well–nigh** \'wel-'nī\ *adv*
ALMOST

**well–to–do** \ˌwel-tə-'dü\ *adj*
having plenty of money and possessions

**[1]Welsh** \'welsh\ *adj*
of or relating to Wales or the people of Wales

**[2]Welsh** *n*
the people of Wales

**welt** \'welt\ *n*
a ridge raised on the skin by a blow

**[1]wel·ter** \'wel-tər\ *vb*
**1** to twist or roll one's body about
**2** to rise and fall or toss about in or with waves

**[2]welter** *n*
a confused jumble

**wend** \'wend\ *vb*
to go one's way : PROCEED

**went** *past of* GO

**wept** *past of* WEEP

**were** *past 2d sing, past pl, or past subjunctive of* BE

**we're** \wir, wər\
we are

**weren't** \'wərnt\
were not

**were·wolf** \'wir-ˌwu̇lf, 'wər-\ *n, pl* **were·wolves** \-ˌwu̇lvz\
a person in folklore who is changed or is able to change into a wolf

**Word History** The modern English word *werewolf* came from an Old English word that was formed from two other words. The first meant "man" and the second meant "wolf."

**[1]west** \'west\ *adv*
to or toward the west

**[2]west** *adj*
placed toward, facing, or coming from the west

**[3]west** *n*
**1** the direction of sunset : the compass point opposite to east
**2** *cap* regions or countries west of a point that is mentioned or understood

**west·bound** \'west-ˌbau̇nd\ *adj*
going west

**west·er·ly** \'wes-tər-lē\ *adj or adv*
**1** toward the west
**2** from the west ⟨a *westerly* wind⟩

**[1]west·ern** \'wes-tərn\ *adj*
**1** *often cap* of, relating to, or like that of the West
**2** lying toward or coming from the west

**[2]western** *n, often cap*
a story, film, or radio or television show about life in the western United States especially in the last part of the nineteenth century

**west·ward** \'west-wərd\ *adv or adj*
toward the west

**[1]wet** \'wet\ *adj* **wet·ter**; **wet·test**
**1** containing, covered with, or soaked with liquid (as water) ⟨a *wet* cloth⟩
**2** RAINY ⟨*wet* weather⟩
**3** not yet dry ⟨*wet* paint⟩
**wet·ness** *n*

**[2]wet** *n*
**1** [1]WATER
**2** MOISTURE
**3** rainy weather **:** RAIN

**[3]wet** *vb* **wet** *or* **wet·ted**; **wet·ting**
to make wet

**we've** \wēv\
we have

**[1]whack** \'hwak, 'wak\ *vb*
to hit with a hard noisy blow

**[2]whack** *n*
**1** a hard noisy blow
**2** the sound of a whack

**whacky** *variant of* WACKY

**[1]whale** \'hwāl, 'wāl\ *n*
▼ a warm-blooded sea animal that looks like a huge fish but breathes air and feeds its young with its milk

**[2]whale** *vb* **whaled**; **whal·ing**
to hunt whales

**whale·boat** \'hwāl-,bōt, 'wāl-\ *n*
a long rowboat once used by whalers

**whale·bone** \'hwāl-,bōn, 'wāl-\ *n*
a substance like horn from the upper jaw of some whales

**whal·er** \'hwā-lər, 'wā-\ *n*
a person or ship that hunts whales

**wharf** \'hwȯrf, 'wȯrf\ *n, pl* **wharves** \'hwȯrvz, 'wȯrvz\ *or* **wharfs**
a structure built on the shore for loading and unloading ships

**[1]what** \hwät, hwət, wät, wət\ *pron*
**1** which thing or things ⟨*what* happened⟩
**2** which sort of thing or person ⟨*what* is this⟩ ⟨*what* are they, doctors?⟩
**3** that which ⟨do *what* you're told⟩
**what for** [1]WHY
**what if**
**1** what would happen if ⟨*what if* they find out?⟩
**2** what does it matter if ⟨so *what if* they do? I don't care⟩

**[2]what** *adv*
**1** in what way **:** HOW ⟨*what* does it matter⟩
**2** used before one or more phrases that tell a cause ⟨*what* with the cold and the hunger, they nearly died⟩

**[3]what** *adj*
**1** used to ask about the identity of a person, object, or matter ⟨*what* books do you read⟩
**2** how remarkable or surprising ⟨*what* an idea⟩
**3** [2]WHATEVER 1

**[1]what·ev·er** \hwät-'ev-ər, hwət-, wät-, wət-\ *pron*
**1** anything that ⟨take *whatever* you need⟩
**2** no matter what ⟨*whatever* you do, don't cheat⟩
**3** what in the world ⟨*whatever* made you do something as stupid as that⟩

**[2]whatever** *adj*
**1** any and all **:** any … that ⟨take *whatever* money you need⟩
**2** of any kind at all ⟨there's no food *whatever*⟩

**wheat** \'hwēt, 'wēt\ *n*
a cereal grain that grows in tight clusters on the tall stalks of a widely cultivated grass, yields a fine white flour, is the chief source of bread in temperate regions, and is also important in animal feeds

**wheat·en** \'hwēt-n, 'wēt-n\ *adj*
containing or made from wheat ⟨*wheaten* bread⟩

**whee·dle** \'hwēd-l, 'wēd-l\ *vb* **whee·dled**; **whee·dling**
**1** to get (someone) to think or act a certain way by flattering **:** COAX
**2** to gain or get by coaxing or flattering ⟨trying to *wheedle* money out of them⟩

**[1]whale**

There are two main types of whale inhabiting the world's oceans — toothed and baleen \bə-'lēn\ whales. Toothed whales, such as the dolphin, hunt fish and squid. Baleen whales, such as the gray whale, strain fish and plankton from huge gulps of water. Whales have a sleek and powerful body, and a thick layer of blubber keeps them warm and provides a reserve supply of energy. The largest whale is the blue whale, a baleen whale, shown below, which can grow up to 100 ft (32 m) in length, and weigh up to 150 tons (140 metric tons). When born, a blue whale is already the size of an elephant.

**features of a blue whale**

flipper
a blow hole is a nostril in the top of the whale's head
eye
a fluke \'flük\ is one of the lobes of a whale's tail

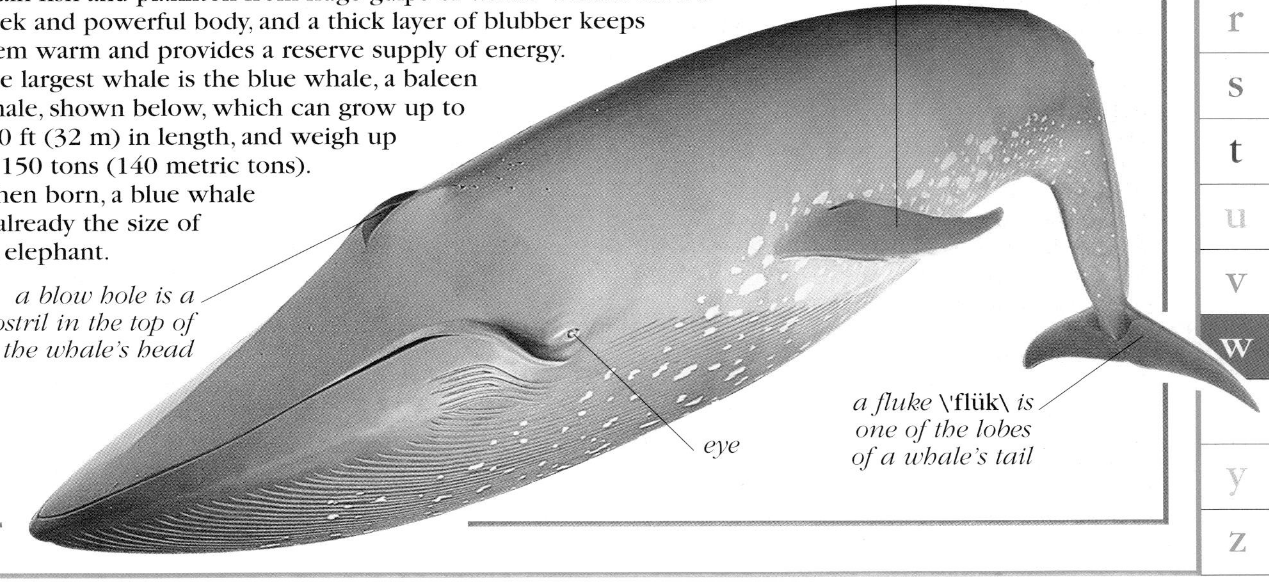

[1]**wheel** \'hwēl, 'wēl\ *n*
**1** a disk or circular frame that can turn on a central point
**2** something like a wheel (as in being round or in turning) ⟨a *wheel* of cheese⟩
**3** something having a wheel as its main part ⟨a spinning *wheel*⟩
**4 wheels** *pl* moving power **:** necessary parts ⟨the *wheels* of government⟩
**wheeled** \'hwēld, wēld\ *adj*

[2]**wheel** *vb*
**1** to carry or move on wheels or in a vehicle with wheels
**2** ROTATE 1
**3** to change direction as if turning on a central point ⟨I *wheeled* and faced them⟩

**wheel·bar·row** \'hwēl-,bar-ō, 'wēl-\ *n*
a small vehicle with two handles and usually one wheel for carrying small loads

**wheel·chair** \'hwēl-,cheər, 'wēl-, -,chaər\ *n*
▼ a chair with wheels in which a disabled or sick person can get about

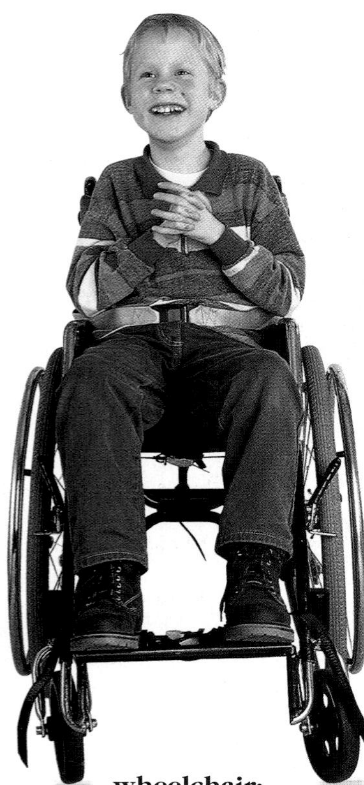

**wheelchair:** a boy sitting in his wheelchair

**wheel·house** \'hwēl-,haủs, 'wēl-\ *n, pl* **wheel·hous·es** \-,haủ-zəz\
a small house containing a ship's steering wheel that is built on or above the top deck

[1]**wheeze** \'hwēz, 'wēz\ *vb* **wheezed**; **wheez·ing**
**1** to breathe with difficulty and usually with a whistling sound
**2** to make a sound like wheezing

[2]**wheeze** *n*
a wheezing sound

**whelk** \'hwelk, 'welk\ *n*
▶ a large sea snail that has a spiral shell and is used in Europe for food

[1]**whelp** \'hwelp, 'welp\ *n*
one of the young of an animal that eats flesh and especially of a dog

[2]**whelp** *vb*
to give birth to whelps

[1]**when** \hwen, wen, hwən, wən\ *adv*
**1** at what time ⟨*when* did you leave⟩
**2** the time at which ⟨not sure of *when* they'd come⟩
**3** at, in, or during which ⟨came at a time *when* things were upset⟩

[2]**when** *conj*
**1** at, during, or just after the time that ⟨leave *when* I do⟩
**2** in the event that **:** IF ⟨*when* you have no family, you're really on your own⟩
**3** ALTHOUGH ⟨why do you tease, *when* you know it's wrong⟩

[3]**when** \,hwen, ,wen\ *pron*
what or which time ⟨since *when* have you been an expert⟩

**whence** \hwens, wens\ *adv*
**1** from what place, source, or cause ⟨*whence* come all these questions⟩
**2** from or out of which ⟨the land *whence* they came⟩

**when·ev·er** \hwen-'ev-ər, wen-, hwən-, wən-\ *conj or adv*
at whatever time ⟨you may leave *whenever* you are ready⟩

[1]**where** \'hweər, 'hwaər, 'weər, 'waər\ *adv*
**1** at, in, or to what place ⟨*where* are they⟩
**2** at or in what way or direction ⟨*where* does this plan lead⟩ ⟨*where* am I wrong⟩

[2]**where** *conj*
**1** at, in, or to the place indicated ⟨sit *where* the light's better⟩
**2** every place that ⟨they go *where* they want to⟩

[3]**where** *n*
what place, source or cause ⟨I don't know *where* that came from⟩

[1]**where·abouts** \'hwer-ə-,baủts, 'hwar-, 'wer-, 'war-\ *adv*
near what place ⟨*whereabouts* did you lose it⟩

**whelk**

[2]**whereabouts** *n sing or pl*
the place where someone or something is

**where·as** \hwer-'az, hwar-, wer-, war-\ *conj*
**1** since it is true that
**2** while just the opposite ⟨water quenches fire, *whereas* gasoline feeds it⟩

**where·by** \hweər-'bī, hwaər-, weər-, waər-\ *adv*
by or through which

**where·fore** \'hweər-,fōr, 'hwaər-, 'weər-, 'waər-\ *adv*
[1]WHY

**where·in** \hwer-'in, hwar-, wer-, war-\ *adv*
**1** in what way
**2** in which

**where·of** \hwer-'əv, hwar-, wer-, war-, -'äv\ *conj*
of what **:** that of which ⟨I know *whereof* I speak⟩

**where·on** \hwer-'ȯn, hwar-, wer-, war-, -'än\ *adv*
on which

**where·up·on** \'hwer-ə-,pȯn, 'hwar-, 'wer-, 'war-, -,pän\ *conj*
and then **:** at which time ⟨the first attempt failed, *whereupon* they tried even harder⟩

[1]**wher·ev·er** \hwer-'ev-ər, hwar-, wer-, war-\ *adv*
where in the world ⟨*wherever* have you been⟩

[2]**wherever** *conj*
**1** at, in, or to whatever place ⟨we can have lunch *wherever* you like⟩
**2** in any situation in which **:** at any time that ⟨*wherever* it is possible, they try to help out⟩

**whet** \'hwet, 'wet\ *vb* **whet·ted**; **whet·ting**
**1** to sharpen the edge of by rubbing on or with a stone
**2** to make (as the appetite) stronger

**wheth·er** \'hwe<u>th</u>-ər, 'we<u>th</u>-\ *conj*
**1** if it is or was true that ⟨see *whether* they've left⟩
**2** if it is or was better ⟨wondered *whether* to stay or go home⟩
**3** used to introduce two or more situations of which only one can occur ⟨the game will be played *whether* it rains or shines⟩

**whet·stone** \'hwet-ˌstōn, 'wet-\ *n*
a stone on which blades are sharpened

**whew** *often read as* 'hwü, 'wü, 'hyü\ *n*
a sound almost like a whistle made as an exclamation chiefly to show amazement, discomfort, or relief

**whey** \'hwā, 'wā\ *n*
the watery part of milk that separates after the milk sours and thickens

**[1]which** \hwich,wich\ *adj*
what certain one or ones ⟨*which* hat should I wear⟩

**[2]which** *pron*
**1** which one or ones ⟨*which* is the right answer⟩
**2** used in place of the name of something other than people at the beginning of a clause ⟨we caught the dog *which* got loose⟩ ⟨the suggestion *which* you made was a good one⟩

**[1]which·ev·er** \hwich-'ev-ər, wich-\ *adj*
being whatever one or ones : no matter which ⟨take *whichever* book you want⟩

**[2]whichever** *pron*
whatever one or ones ⟨buy the sweater or the coat, *whichever* you like better⟩

**[1]whiff** \'hwif, 'wif\ *n*
**1** a small gust
**2** a small amount (as of a scent or a gas) that is breathed in
**3** a very small amount : HINT

**[2]whiff** *vb*
to puff, blow out, or blow away in very small amounts

**[1]while** \'hwīl, 'wīl\ *n*
**1** a period of time ⟨let's rest a *while*⟩
**2** time and effort used in doing something ⟨I'll make it worth your *while* to help out⟩

**[2]while** *conj*
**1** during the time that ⟨someone called *while* you were out⟩
**2** ALTHOUGH ⟨*while* the book is famous, it is seldom read⟩

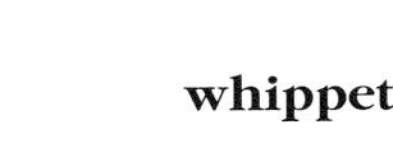

**whippet**

**[3]while** *vb* **whiled**; **whil·ing**
to cause to pass especially in a pleasant way ⟨*while* away time⟩

**whim** \'hwim, 'wim\ *n*
a sudden wish or desire : a sudden change of mind

**[1]whim·per** \'hwim-pər, 'wim-\ *vb*
to cry in low broken sounds : WHINE

**[2]whimper** *n*
a whining cry

**whim·si·cal** \'hwim-zi-kəl, 'wim-\ *adj*
**1** full of whims
**2** DROLL

**[1]whine** \'hwīn, 'wīn\ *vb* **whined**; **whin·ing**
**1** to make a shrill troubled cry or a similar sound ⟨a saw *whining* through knots⟩
**2** to complain by or as if by whining ⟨*whine* about one's troubles⟩

**[2]whine** *n*
a whining cry or sound

**[1]whin·ny** \'hwin-ē, 'win-ē\ *vb* **whin·nied**; **whin·ny·ing**
to neigh usually in a low gentle way

**[2]whinny** *n, pl* **whinnies**
a low gentle neigh

**[1]whip** \'hwip, 'wip\ *vb* **whipped**; **whip·ping**
**1** to move, snatch, or jerk quickly or with force ⟨*whipped* the cloth off the table⟩
**2** to hit with something slender and flexible : LASH
**3** to punish with blows
**4** to beat into foam ⟨*whip* cream⟩
**5** to move back and forth in a lively way ⟨a flag *whipping* in the breeze⟩

**[2]whip** *n*
**1** something used in whipping
**2** a light dessert made with whipped cream or whipped whites of eggs

**whip·pet** \'hwip-ət, 'wip-\ *n*
◀ a small swift dog that is like a greyhound and is often used for racing

**whip·poor·will** \'hwip-ər-ˌwil, 'wip-\ *n*
a bird of eastern North America that flies at night and eats insects and is named from its peculiar call

**[1]whir** \'hwər, 'wər\ *vb* **whirred**; **whir·ring**
to fly, move, or turn rapidly with a buzzing sound

**[2]whir** *n*
a whirring sound

**[1]whirl** \'hwərl, 'wərl\ *vb*
**1** to turn or move in circles rapidly
**2** to feel dizzy ⟨my head *whirls*⟩
**3** to move or carry around or about very rapidly

**[2]whirl** *n*
**1** a whirling movement
**2** something that is or seems to be whirling
**3** a state of busy movement : BUSTLE

**whirl·pool** \'hwərl-ˌpül, 'wərl-\ *n*
a rapid swirl of water with a low place in the center into which floating objects are drawn

**whirl·wind** \'hwərl-ˌwind, 'wərl-\ *n*
a small windstorm in which the air turns rapidly in circles

A B C D E F G H I J K L M N O P Q R S T U V W X Y Z

[1]**whisk** \'hwisk, 'wisk\ *n*
**1** a quick sweeping or brushing motion
**2** ▼ a kitchen utensil of wire used for whipping eggs or cream

[1]**whisk 2**

[2]**whisk** *vb*
**1** to move suddenly and quickly ⟨*whisk* around the corner⟩
**2** to beat into foam
**3** to brush with or as if with a whisk broom ⟨*whisked* dust off the coat⟩

**whisk broom** *n*
a small broom with a short handle used especially as a clothes brush

**whis·ker** \'hwis-kər, 'wis-\ *n*
**1 whiskers** *pl* the part of the beard that grows on the sides of the face and on the chin
**2** one hair of the beard
**3** a long bristle or hair growing near the mouth of an animal

**whis·key** *or* **whis·ky** \'hwis-kē, 'wis-\ *n, pl* **whis·keys** *or* **whis·kies**
a strong drink containing alcohol and usually made from grain

---

**Word History** Most of the people of Ireland and Scotland speak English. Each of these countries has a language of its own as well. The Irish language is a close relative of the Scottish language. The two are only distant relatives of English. The English word *whiskey* has two sources. One is an Irish word. The other is a Scottish word. These words are very much alike. Both mean "water of life."

---

[1]**whis·per** \'hwis-pər, 'wis-\ *vb*
**1** to speak very low
**2** to tell by whispering
**3** to make a low rustling sound ⟨the wind *whispered* in the trees⟩

[2]**whisper** *n*
**1** a low soft way of speaking that can be heard only by persons who are near
**2** the act of whispering
**3** something said in a whisper
**4** [1]HINT 1

[1]**whis·tle** \'hwis-əl, 'wis-\ *n*
**1** a device by which a shrill sound is produced
**2** a shrill sound of or like whistling

[2]**whistle** *vb* **whis·tled**; **whis·tling**
**1** to make a shrill sound by forcing the breath through the teeth or lips
**2** to move, pass, or go with a shrill sound ⟨the arrow *whistled* past⟩
**3** to sound a whistle
**4** to express by whistling ⟨*whistled* my surprise⟩

**whit** \'hwit, 'wit\ *n*
a very small amount ⟨had not a *whit* of sense⟩

[1]**white** \'hwīt, 'wīt\ *adj*
**whit·er**; **whit·est**
**1** of the color white
**2** light or pale in color ⟨*white* wine⟩
**3** pale gray : SILVERY
**4** having a light skin ⟨the *white* races⟩
**5** [1]BLANK 2 ⟨*white* spaces on the page⟩
**6** not intended to cause harm ⟨*white* lies⟩
**7** SNOWY 1 ⟨a *white* Christmas⟩
**white·ness** *n*

[2]**white** *n*
**1** the color of fresh snow : the opposite of black
**2** the white part of something (as an egg)
**3** white clothing
**4** a person belonging to a white race

**white blood cell** *n*
one of the tiny whitish cells of the blood that help fight infection

**white·cap** \'hwīt-,kap, 'wīt-\ *n*
the top of a wave breaking into foam

**white cell** *n*
WHITE BLOOD CELL

**white·fish** \'hwīt-,fish, 'wīt-\ *n*
a freshwater fish related to the trouts that is greenish above and silvery below and is used for food

**white flag** *n*
a flag of plain white raised in asking for a truce or as a sign of surrender

**whit·en** \'hwīt-n, 'wīt-n\ *vb*
to make or become white : BLEACH ⟨*whiten* sheets⟩

**white oak** *n*
a large oak tree known for its hard strong wood that lasts well and is not easily rotted by water

**white–tailed deer** \'hwīt-,tāld-, 'wīt-\ *n*
▼ the common deer of eastern North America with the underside of the tail white

**white-tailed deer**

[1]**white·wash** \'hwīt-,wȯsh, 'wīt-, -,wäsh\ *vb*
**1** to cover with whitewash
**2** to try to hide the wrongdoing of ⟨*whitewash* a politician caught lying⟩

[2]**whitewash** *n*
a mixture (as of lime and water) for making a surface (as a wall) white

**whith·er** \'hwi*th*-ər, 'wi*th*-\ *adv*
**1** to what place
**2** to which place

**whit·ish** \'hwīt-ish, 'wīt-\ *adj*
somewhat white

**whit·tle** \'hwit-l, 'wit-l\ *vb*
**whit·tled**; **whit·tling**
**1** to cut or shave off chips from wood **:** shape by such cutting or shaving
**2** to reduce little by little ⟨*whittle* down their spending⟩

[1]**whiz** *or* **whizz** \'hwiz, 'wiz\ *vb*
**whizzed**; **whiz·zing**
to move, pass, or fly rapidly with a buzzing sound

[2]**whiz** *n*
a buzzing sound ⟨the *whiz* of passing traffic⟩

**who** \hü\ *pron*
**1** what person or people ⟨*who* is that⟩
**2** the person or people that ⟨we know *who* did it⟩
**3** used to stand for a person or people at the beginning of a clause ⟨students *who* need help should ask for it⟩

**whoa** \'wō, 'hō, 'hwō\ *vb*
used as a command to an animal pulling a load to stop

**who·ev·er** \hü-'ev-ər\ *pron*
whatever person ⟨*whoever* wants a snack must tell me now⟩

[1]**whole** \'hōl\ *adj*
**1** completely healthy or sound in condition
**2** not cut up or ground ⟨a *whole* onion⟩
**3** keeping all its necessary elements in being made ready for the market ⟨*whole* milk⟩
**4** made up of all its parts **:** TOTAL ⟨the *whole* family⟩
**5** not scattered or divided ⟨give it my *whole* attention⟩
**6** each one of the ⟨the *whole* ten days⟩
**whole·ness** *n*

[2]**whole** *n*
**1** something that is whole
**2** a sum of all the parts and elements
**on the whole**
**1** all things considered
**2** in most cases

**whole·heart·ed** \'hōl-'härt-əd\ *adj*
not holding back ⟨a *wholehearted* effort⟩

**whole number** *n*
a number that is zero or any of the natural numbers

[1]**whole·sale** \'hōl-,sāl\ *n*
the sale of goods in large quantities to dealers

[2]**wholesale** *adj*
**1** of, relating to, or working at wholesaling
**2** done on a large scale

[3]**wholesale** *vb* **whole·saled**; **whole·sal·ing**
to sell to dealers usually in large lots
**whole·sal·er** *n*

**whole·some** \'hōl-səm\ *adj*
**1** helping to improve or keep the body, mind, or spirit in good condition ⟨*wholesome* food⟩
**2** sound in body, mind, or morals
**whole·some·ness** *n*

**whol·ly** \'hō-lē\ *adv*
to the limit **:** COMPLETELY ⟨a *wholly* honest person⟩

**wick** in a candle

**whom** \hüm\ *pron, objective case of* WHO

**whom·ev·er** \hü-'mev-ər\ *pron, objective case of* WHOEVER

[1]**whoop** \'hüp, 'hu̇p\ *vb*
**1** to shout or cheer loudly and strongly
**2** to make the shrill gasping sound that follows a coughing attack in whooping cough

[2]**whoop** *n*
a whooping sound

**whooping cough** *n*
a bacterial disease especially of children in which severe attacks of coughing are often followed by a shrill gasping intake of breath

**whooping crane** *n*
a large white nearly extinct North American crane that has a loud whooping call

**whop·per** \'hwäp-ər, 'wäp-\
**1** something huge of its kind
**2** a monstrous lie

**whorl** \'hwȯrl, 'wȯrl, 'hwərl, 'wərl\ *n*
**1** a row of parts (as leaves or petals) encircling a stem
**2** something that whirls or winds ⟨a *whorl* of smoke hung over the chimney⟩

[1]**whose** \hüz\ *adj*
of or relating to whom or which ⟨*whose* bag is it⟩ ⟨the book *whose* cover is torn⟩

[2]**whose** *pron*
whose one **:** whose ones

[1]**why** \'hwī, 'wī\ *adv*
for what cause or reason ⟨*why* did you do it⟩

[2]**why** *conj*
**1** the cause or reason for which ⟨we know *why* you did it⟩
**2** for which ⟨here's the reason *why* I did it⟩

[3]**why** *n, pl* **whys**
the cause of or reason for something

[4]**why** \wī, hwī\ *interj*
used to express surprise, uncertainty, approval, disapproval, or impatience ⟨*why*, how did you know that⟩

**wick** \'wik\ *n*
◀ a cord, strip, or ring of loosely woven material through which a liquid (as oil) is drawn to the top in a candle, lamp, or oil stove for burning

**wick·ed** \'wik-əd\ *adj*
**1** bad in behavior, moral state, or effect **:** EVIL
**2** DANGEROUS 2 ⟨a *wicked* storm⟩
**synonyms** see BAD
**wick·ed·ly** *adv*
**wick·ed·ness** *n*

[1]**wick·er** \'wik-ər\ *n*
**1** a flexible twig (as of willow) used in basketry
**2** WICKERWORK

[2]**wicker** *adj*
▼ made of wicker ⟨*wicker* furniture⟩

[2]**wicker:** a wicker basket

A B C D E F G H I J K L M N O P Q R S T U V W X Y Z

**wick·er·work** \'wik-ər-ˌwərk\ *n*
basketry made of wicker

**wick·et** \'wik-ət\ *n*
**1** a small gate or door in or near a larger gate or door
**2** a small window (as in a bank or ticket office) through which business is conducted
**3** ▶ either of the two sets of three rods topped by two crosspieces at which the ball is bowled in cricket
**4** an arch (as of wire) through which the ball is hit in the game of croquet

**[1]wide** \'wīd\ *adj* **wid·er**; **wid·est**
**1** covering a very large area
**2** measured across or at right angles to length ⟨cloth 100 centimeters *wide*⟩
**3** having a large measure across **:** BROAD ⟨a *wide* street⟩
**4** opened as far as possible ⟨eyes *wide* with wonder⟩
**5** not limited ⟨*wide* reading⟩
**6** far from the goal or truth ⟨the shot was *wide*⟩
**wide·ly** *adv*
**wide·ness** *n*

**[2]wide** *adv* **wid·er**; **wid·est**
**1** over a wide area ⟨travel far and *wide*⟩
**2** to the limit **:** COMPLETELY ⟨*wide* open⟩

**wide–awake** \ˌwīd-ə-'wāk\ *adj*
not sleepy, dull, or without energy **:** ALERT

**wid·en** \'wīd-n\ *vb*
to make or become wide or wider

**wig:** a man in 17th-century fashionable dress and wig

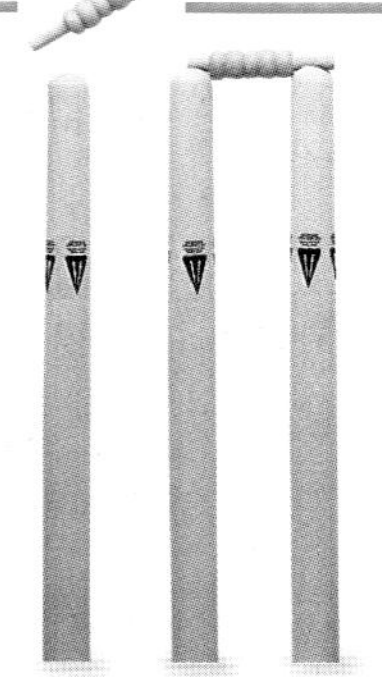

**wicket 3:** a player is sent off the field when the ball knocks a crosspiece off the wicket

**wide·spread** \'wīd-'spred\ *adj*
**1** widely stretched out ⟨*widespread* wings⟩
**2** widely scattered ⟨*widespread* public interest⟩

**[1]wid·ow** \'wid-ō\ *n*
a woman who has lost her husband by death

**[2]widow** *vb*
to make a widow or widower of

**wid·ow·er** \'wid-ə-wər\ *n*
a man who has lost his wife by death

**width** \'width\ *n*
**1** the shortest or shorter side of an object
**2** BREADTH 1

**wield** \'wēld\ *vb*
**1** to use (as a tool) in an effective way ⟨*wield* a broom⟩
**2** [2]EXERCISE 1 ⟨*wield* influence⟩

**wie·ner** \'wē-nər\ *n*
FRANKFURTER

**wife** \'wīf\ *n, pl* **wives** \'wīvz\
a married woman
**wife·ly** *adj*

**wig** \'wig\ *n*
◀ a manufactured covering of natural or artificial hair for the head

**[1]wig·gle** \'wig-əl\ *vb* **wig·gled**; **wig·gling**
**1** to move to and fro in a jerky way
**2** to proceed with twisting and turning movements

**[2]wiggle** *n*
a wiggling motion

**wig·gler** \'wig-lər\ *n*
WRIGGLER

**wig·gly** \'wig-lē\ *adj* **wig·gli·er**; **wig·gli·est**
**1** given to wiggling ⟨a *wiggly* worm⟩
**2** WAVY ⟨*wiggly* lines⟩

**wig·wag** \'wig-ˌwag\ *vb* **wig·wagged**; **wig·wag·ging**
to signal by movement of a flag or light

**wig·wam** \'wig-ˌwäm\ *n*
an Indian hut made of poles spread over with bark, rush mats, or hides

**[1]wild** \'wīld\ *adj*
**1** living in a state of nature and not under human control and care **:** not tame ⟨*wild* game animals⟩
**2** growing or produced in nature **:** not cultivated by people ⟨*wild* honey⟩ ⟨*wild* grapes⟩
**3** not civilized **:** SAVAGE
**4** not kept under control ⟨*wild* rage⟩
**5** wide of the intended goal or course ⟨a *wild* guess⟩ ⟨a *wild* throw⟩
**wild·ly** *adv*
**wild·ness** *n*

**[2]wild** *n*
WILDERNESS

**wild boar**

**wild boar** *n*
▲ an Old World wild hog from which most domestic swine derive

**wild·cat** \'wīld-ˌkat\ *n*
any of various cats (as an ocelot or bobcat) of small or medium size

**wil·der·ness** \'wil-dər-nəs\ *n*
a wild region which is not used for farming and in which few people live

**wild·fire** \'wīld-ˌfīr\ *n*
a fire that destroys a wide area

**wild·flower** \'wīld-ˌflaù-ər\ *n*
the flower of a wild plant or the plant bearing it

**wild·fowl** \'wīld-ˌfaùl\ *n, pl* **wildfowl**
a bird and especially a waterfowl hunted as game

**wild·life** \'wīld-,līf\ *n*
creatures that are neither human nor domesticated : the wild animals of field and forest

**[1]wile** \'wīl\ *n*
a trick meant to trap or deceive

**[2]wile** *vb* **wiled**; **wil·ing**
[2]LURE

**[1]will** \wəl, wil\ *helping verb, past* **would** \wəd, wu̇d\, *present sing & pl* **will**
**1** wish to ⟨they *will* have hamburgers⟩
**2** am, is, or are willing to ⟨I *will* go if you ask me⟩
**3** am, is, or are determined to ⟨we *will* go in spite of the storm⟩
**4** am, is, or are going to ⟨everyone *will* be there⟩
**5** is or are commanded to ⟨you *will* come here at once⟩

**[2]will** \'wil\ *n*
**1** a firm wish or desire ⟨the *will* to win⟩
**2** the power to decide or control what one will do or how one will act
**3** a legal paper in which a person states to whom the things which he or she owns are to be given after death

**[3]will** \'wil\ *vb*
**1** [1]ORDER 2, DECREE ⟨it will happen if God *wills* it⟩
**2** to bring to a certain condition by the power of the will ⟨*will* yourself to sleep⟩
**3** to leave by will ⟨*willed* their property to the children⟩

**will·ful** *or* **wil·ful** \'wil-fəl\ *adj*
**1** STUBBORN 1 ⟨*willful* children⟩
**2** INTENTIONAL ⟨*willful* murder⟩
**will·ful·ly** \-fə-lē\ *adv*
**will·ful·ness** *n*

**will·ing** \'wil-ing\ *adj*
**1** feeling no objection ⟨*willing* to go⟩
**2** not slow or lazy ⟨a *willing* worker⟩
**3** made, done, or given of one's own choice : VOLUNTARY
**will·ing·ly** *adv*
**will·ing·ness** *n*

**wil·low** \'wil-ō\ *n*
**1** ▶ a tree or bush with narrow leaves, catkins for flowers, and tough flexible stems used in making baskets
**2** the wood of the willow tree

**[1]wilt** \'wilt\ *vb*
**1** to lose freshness and become limp ⟨*wilting* roses⟩
**2** to lose strength

**[2]wilt** *n*
a plant disease (as of tomatoes) in which wilting and browning of leaves leads to death of the plant

**wily** \'wī-lē\ *adj* **wil·i·er**; **wil·i·est**
full of tricks : CRAFTY

**win** \'win\ *vb* **won** \'wən\; **win·ning**
**1** to achieve the victory in a contest
**2** to get by effort or skill : GAIN ⟨*win* praise⟩
**3** to obtain by victory ⟨*win* a prize in a contest⟩
**4** to be the victor in ⟨*win* a race⟩
**5** to ask and get the favor of

**wince** \'wins\ *vb* **winced**; **winc·ing**
to draw back (as from pain)

**winch** \'winch\ *n*
a machine that has a roller on which rope is wound for pulling or lifting

**[1]wind** \'wind\ *n*
**1** a movement of the air : BREEZE
**2** power to breathe ⟨the fall knocked the *wind* out of the child⟩
**3** air carrying a scent (as of game)
**4** limited knowledge especially about something secret : HINT ⟨they got *wind* of our plans⟩
**5** **winds** *pl* wind instruments of a band or orchestra

**[2]wind** *vb*
**1** to get a scent of ⟨the dogs *winded* game⟩
**2** to cause to be out of breath

**[3]wind** \'wīnd, 'wind\ *vb* **wound** \'wau̇nd\; **wind·ing**
to sound by blowing ⟨*wind* a horn⟩

**[4]wind** \'wīnd\ *vb* **wound** \'wau̇nd\; **wind·ing**
**1** to twist around ⟨*wind* thread on a spool⟩
**2** to cover with something twisted around : WRAP ⟨*wind* an arm with a bandage⟩
**3** to make the spring of tight ⟨*wound* my watch⟩
**4** to move in a series of twists and turns ⟨the trail *wound* between the trees⟩

**willow 1:** a branch of a white willow

catkin

**[5]wind** \'wīnd\ *n*
[2]BEND

**wind·break** \'wind-,brāk\ *n*
something (as a growth of trees and shrubs) that breaks the force of the wind

**wind·fall** \'wind-,fȯl\ *n*
**1** something (as fruit from a tree) blown down by the wind
**2** an unexpected gift or gain

**wind instrument** *n*
a musical instrument (as a clarinet, harmonica, or trumpet) sounded by the vibration of a stream of air and especially by the player's breath

**wind·lass** \'wind-ləs\ *n*
a winch used especially on ships for pulling and lifting

**wind·mill** \'wind-,mil\ *n*
a mill or a machine (as for pumping water) worked by the wind turning sails or vanes at the top of a tower

**window 3:** a window in use on a computer

**win·dow** \'win-dō\ *n*
**1** an opening in a wall to admit light and air
**2** the glass and frame that fill a window opening
**3** ▲ any of the areas into which a computer display may be divided and on which different types of information may be shown

**Word History** The English word *window* came from a word in an old Scandinavian language. This word was formed from two words. One meant "wind" or "air." The other meant "eye." A window can be thought of as an eye, or hole, through which the wind enters.

**window box** *n*
a box for growing plants in or by a window

**win·dow·pane** \'win-dō-ˌpān\ *n*
a pane in a window

**wind·pipe** \'wind-ˌpīp\ *n*
a tube with a firm wall that connects the pharynx with the lungs and is used in breathing

**wind·proof** \'wind-'prüf\ *adj*
protecting from the wind

**wind·shield** \'wind-ˌshēld\ *n*
a clear screen (as of glass) attached to the body of a vehicle (as a car) in front of the riders to protect them from the wind

**wind·storm** \'wind-ˌstȯrm\ *n*
a storm with strong wind and little or no rain

**wind·up** \'wīn-ˌdəp\ *n*
**1** the last part of something : FINISH
**2** a swing of a baseball pitcher's arm before the pitch is thrown

**wind up** *vb*
**1** to bring to an end : CONCLUDE
**2** to swing the arm before pitching a baseball

**[1]wind·ward** \'win-dwərd\ *adj*
moving or placed toward the direction from which the wind is blowing

**[2]windward** *n*
the side or direction from which the wind is blowing ⟨sail to the *windward*⟩

**windy** \'win-dē\ *adj* **wind·i·er**; **wind·i·est**
having much wind ⟨a *windy* day⟩

**wine** \'wīn\ *n*
**1** ▶ fermented grape juice containing various amounts of alcohol
**2** the usually fermented juice of a plant product (as a fruit) used as a drink

**win·ery** \'wīn-ə-rē\ *n, pl* **win·er·ies**
a place where wine is made

**[1]wing** \'wing\ *n*
**1** ▶ one of the paired limbs or limblike parts with which a bird, bat, or insect flies
**2** something like a wing in appearance, use, or motion ⟨the *wings* of an airplane⟩
**3** a part (as of a building) that sticks out from the main part
**4** a division of an organization
**5 wings** *pl* an area just off the stage of a theater
**wing·like** \-ˌlīk\ *adj*
**on the wing** in flight

**[2]wing** *vb*
to go with wings : FLY

**winged** \'wingd, 'wing-əd\ *adj*
having wings or winglike parts ⟨*winged* insects⟩

**wing·less** \'wing-ləs\ *adj*
having no wings

**wing·spread** \'wing-ˌspred\ *n*
the distance between the tips of the spread wings

**[1]wink** \'wingk\ *vb*
**1** to close and open the eyelids quickly
**2** to close and open one eye quickly as a signal or hint

**[2]wink** *n*
**1** a brief period of sleep
**2** a hint or sign given by winking
**3** an act of winking
**4** a very short time

**win·ner** \'win-ər\ *n*
one that wins

**[1]win·ning** \'win-ing\ *n*
**1** the act of one that wins
**2** something won especially in gambling — often used in pl.

**[2]winning** *adj*
**1** being one that wins ⟨a *winning* team⟩
**2** tending to please or delight ⟨a *winning* smile⟩

**wine 1:** glasses of wine

**[1]wing 1:** the wing of a pigeon

**win·now** \'win-ō\ *vb*
to remove (as waste from grain) by a current of air

**win·some** \'win-səm\ *adj*
[2]WINNING 2

**[1]win·ter** \'wint-ər\ *n*
**1** the season between autumn and spring (as the months of December, January, and February in the northern half of the earth)
**2** YEAR 2 ⟨a person of seventy *winters*⟩

**[2]winter** *vb*
**1** to pass the winter ⟨*wintered* in Florida⟩
**2** to keep, feed, or manage during the winter ⟨*winter* livestock on silage⟩

**win·ter·green** \'wint-ər-ˌgrēn\ *n*
a low evergreen plant with white flowers that look like little bells and are followed by red berries which produce an oil (**oil of wintergreen)** used in medicine and flavoring

**win·ter·time** \'wint-ər-ˌtīm\ *n*
the winter season

**win·try** \'win-trē\ *adj* **win·tri·er**; **win·tri·est**
**1** of, relating to, or characteristic of winter
**2** not friendly : COLD ⟨a *wintry* welcome⟩

**[1]wipe** \'wīp\ *vb* **wiped**; **wip·ing**
**1** to clean or dry by rubbing ⟨*wipe* dishes⟩
**2** to remove by or as if by rubbing ⟨*wipe* away tears⟩
**wip·er** *n*

**[2]wipe** *n*
an act of wiping : RUB

**wipe out** *vb*
to destroy completely

**[1]wire** \'wīr\ *n*
**1** metal in the form of a thread or slender rod
**2** a telephone or telegraph wire or system
**3** TELEGRAM, CABLEGRAM

**[2]wire** *vb* **wired**; **wir·ing**
**1** to provide or equip with wire
**2** to bind, string, or mount with wire
**3** to send or send word to by telegraph

**[1]wire·less** \'wīr-ləs\ *adj*
**1** having no wire
**2** relating to communication by electric waves but without connecting wires : RADIO 2

**[2]wireless** *n*
**1** wireless telegraphy
**2** [2]RADIO

**wiry** \'wīr-ē\ *adj* **wir·i·er**; **wir·i·est**
**1** of or like wire
**2** being slender yet strong and active

**wis·dom** \'wiz-dəm\ *n*
knowledge and the ability to use it to help oneself or others

**wisdom tooth** *n*
the last tooth of the full set on each half of each jaw of an adult

**[1]wise** \'wīz\ *n*
MANNER 2, WAY — used in such phrases as *in any wise, in no wise, in this wise*

**[2]wise** *adj* **wis·er**; **wis·est**
**1** having or showing good sense or good judgment : SENSIBLE
**2** having knowledge or information
**wise·ly** *adv*

**-wise** \,wīz\ *adv suffix*
**1** in the manner of
**2** in the position or direction of ⟨clock*wise*⟩
**3** with regard to

**wise·crack** \'wīz-,krak\ *n*
a clever and often insulting statement usually made in joking

**[1]wish** \'wish\ *vb*
**1** to have a desire for : WANT
**2** to form or express a desire concerning ⟨the teacher *wished* that we would be quiet⟩
**synonyms** see DESIRE

**[2]wish** *n*
**1** an act or instance of wishing
**2** something wished ⟨got my *wish*⟩
**3** a desire for happiness or good fortune ⟨send them my best *wishes*⟩

**wish·bone** \'wish-,bōn\ *n*
a bone in front of a bird's breastbone that is shaped like a V

**wish·ful** \'wish-fəl\ *adj*
having, showing, or based on a wish

**wishy–washy** \'wish-ē-,wȯsh-ē, -,wäsh-\ *adj*
lacking spirit, courage, or determination : WEAK

**wisp** \'wisp\ *n*
**1** a small bunch of hay or straw
**2** a thin piece or strand ⟨*wisps* of hair⟩
**3** a thin streak ⟨*wisps* of smoke⟩

**wispy** \'wis-pē\ *adj* **wisp·i·er**; **wisp·i·est**
being thin and flimsy

**wis·tar·ia** \wis-'tir-ē-ə, -'ter-\ *n*
WISTERIA

**wis·te·ria** \wis-'tir-ē-ə\ *n*
▼ a woody vine related to the beans that is grown for its long clusters of violet, white, or pink flowers

**wisteria** growing up a wall

**wist·ful** \'wist-fəl\ *adj*
feeling or showing a timid longing ⟨a *wistful* expression⟩
**wist·ful·ly** \-fə-lē\ *adv*
**wist·ful·ness** *n*

**wit** \'wit\ *n*
**1** power to think, reason, or decide ⟨a person of little *wit*⟩
**2** normal mental state — usually used in pl. ⟨scared me out of my *wits*⟩
**3** cleverness in making sharp and usually amusing comments
**4** witty comments, expressions, or talk
**5** a witty person

**witch** \'wich\ *n*
**1** a woman believed to have magic powers
**2** an ugly or mean old woman

**witch·craft** \'wich-,kraft\ *n*
the power or doings of a witch

**witch doctor** *n*
a person who uses magic to cure illness and fight off evil spirits

**witch·ery** \'wich-ə-rē\ *n*, *pl* **witch·er·ies**
**1** WITCHCRAFT
**2** power to charm or fascinate

**witch ha·zel** \'wich-,hā-zəl\ *n*
**1** ► a shrub with small yellow flowers in late fall or very early spring
**2** a soothing alcoholic lotion made from witch hazel bark

**witch hazel 1**

**with** \wi<u>th</u>, with\ *prep*
**1** AGAINST 2 ⟨argued *with* the child's parents⟩
**2** in shared relation to ⟨talk *with* friends⟩
**3** having in or as part of it ⟨coffee *with* cream⟩
**4** in regard to ⟨patient *with* children⟩
**5** compared to ⟨identical *with* the rest⟩
**6** in the opinion or judgment of ⟨is the party all right *with* your parents⟩
**7** by the use of ⟨hit me *with* a ruler⟩
**8** so as to show ⟨spoke *with* pride⟩
**9** in the company of ⟨went to the show *with* a friend⟩
**10** in possession of ⟨arrived *with* good news⟩ ⟨animals *with* horns⟩
**11** as well as ⟨hits the ball *with* the best of them⟩

**12** FROM 2 ⟨parting *with* friends⟩
**13** BECAUSE OF ⟨pale *with* anger⟩
**14** DESPITE ⟨*with* all your tricks you failed⟩
**15** if given ⟨*with* your permission, I'll leave⟩
**16** at the time of or shortly after ⟨get up *with* the dawn⟩ ⟨*with* that, I paused⟩
**17** in support of ⟨I'm *with* you all the way⟩
**18** in the direction of ⟨sail *with* the tide⟩

**with·draw** \wi<u>th</u>-'dro̊, with-\ *vb* **with·drew** \-'drü\; **with·drawn** \-'dro̊n\; **with·draw·ing**
**1** to draw back **:** take away ⟨*withdraw* money from the bank⟩
**2** to take back (as something said or suggested)
**3** to go away especially for privacy or safety

**with·draw·al** \wi<u>th</u>-'dro̊-əl, with-\ *n*
an act or instance of withdrawing

**with·er** \'wi<u>th</u>-ər\ *vb*
to shrink up from or as if from loss of natural body moisture **:** WILT

**with·ers** \'wi<u>th</u>-ərz\ *n pl*
the ridge between the shoulder bones of a horse

**with·hold** \with-'hōld, wi<u>th</u>-\ *vb* **with·held** \-'held\; **with·hold·ing**
to refuse to give, grant, or allow ⟨*withhold* permission⟩

[1]**with·in** \wi<u>th</u>-'in, with-\ *adv*
[2]INSIDE ⟨a bomb exploded *within*⟩

[2]**within** *prep*
**1** [4]INSIDE 1 ⟨stay *within* the house⟩
**2** not beyond the limits of ⟨live *within* your income⟩

[1]**with·out** \wi<u>th</u>-'au̇t, with-\ *prep*
**1** [4]OUTSIDE
**2** completely lacking ⟨they're *without* hope⟩
**3** not accompanied by or showing ⟨spoke *without* thinking⟩

[2]**without** *adv*
[3]OUTSIDE

**with·stand** \with-'stand, wi<u>th</u>-\ *vb* **with·stood** \-'stu̇d\; **with·stand·ing**
**1** to hold out against ⟨able to *withstand* the worst weather⟩
**2** to oppose (as an attack) successfully

**wit·less** \'wit-ləs\ *adj*
lacking in wit or intelligence **:** FOOLISH

[1]**wit·ness** \'wit-nəs\ *n*
**1** TESTIMONY ⟨give false *witness*⟩
**2** a person who sees or otherwise has personal knowledge of something ⟨*witnesses* of an accident⟩
**3** a person who gives testimony in court
**4** a person who is present at an action (as the signing of a will) so as to be able to say who did it

[2]**witness** *vb*
**1** to be a witness to
**2** to give testimony to **:** testify as a witness
**3** to be or give proof of ⟨their actions *witness* their guilt⟩

**wit·ted** \'wit-əd\ *adj*
having wit or understanding — used in combination ⟨quick-*witted*⟩ ⟨slow-*witted*⟩

**wit·ty** \'wit-ē\ *adj* **wit·ti·er**; **wit·ti·est**
having or showing wit ⟨a *witty* person⟩

**wives** *pl of* WIFE

**wiz·ard** \'wiz-ərd\ *n*
**1** SORCERER, MAGICIAN
**2** a very clever or skillful person

[1]**wob·ble** \'wäb-əl\ *vb* **wob·bled**; **wob·bling**
to move from side to side in a shaky manner
**wob·bly** \'wäb-lē\ *adj*

[2]**wobble** *n*
a rocking motion from side to side

**woe** \'wō\ *n*
great sorrow, grief, or misfortune **:** TROUBLE ⟨a tale of *woe*⟩
**synonyms** see SORROW

**woe·ful** \'wō-fəl\ *adj*
**1** full of grief or misery ⟨a *woeful* heart⟩
**2** bringing woe or misery ⟨a *woeful* day⟩

**woke** *past of* WAKE

**woken** *past participle of* WAKE

[1]**wolf 1:** a gray wolf

[1]**wolf** \'wu̇lf\ *n, pl* **wolves** \'wu̇lvz\
**1** ▲ a large intelligent doglike wild animal that eats flesh and has ears which stand up and a bushy tail
**2** a person felt to resemble a wolf (as in craftiness or fierceness)
**wolf·ish** \'wu̇l-fish\ *adj*

[2]**wolf** *vb*
to eat greedily

**wolf dog** *n*
**1** WOLFHOUND
**2** the hybrid offspring of a wolf and a domestic dog
**3** a dog that looks like a wolf

**wolf·hound** \'wu̇lf-ˌhau̇nd\ *n*
any of several large dogs used in hunting large animals

**wol·fram** \'wu̇l-frəm\ *n*
TUNGSTEN

**wol·ver·ine** \ˌwu̇l-və-'rēn\ *n*
▼ a blackish wild animal with shaggy fur that is related to the martens and sables, eats flesh, and is found chiefly in the northern parts of North America

**wolverine**

**wolves** *pl of* WOLF

**wom·an** \'wu̇m-ən\ *n, pl* **wom·en** \'wim-ən\
**1** an adult female person
**2** women considered as a group

**wom·an·hood** \'wu̇m-ən-ˌhu̇d\ *n*
1 the state of being a woman
2 womanly characteristics
3 WOMAN 2

**wom·an·kind** \'wu̇m-ən-ˌkīnd\ *n*
WOMAN 2

**wom·an·ly** \'wu̇m-ən-lē\ *adj*
having the characteristics of a woman

**womb** \'wüm\ *n*
UTERUS

**wom·en·folk** \'wim-ən-ˌfōk\ *or* **wom·en·folks** \-ˌfōks\ *n pl*
women especially of one family or group

**won** *past of* WIN

[1]**won·der** \'wən-dər\ *n*
1 something extraordinary : MARVEL
2 a feeling (as of astonishment) caused by something extraordinary

[2]**wonder** *vb*
1 to feel surprise or amazement
2 to be curious or have doubt

**won·der·ful** \'wən-dər-fəl\ *adj*
1 causing wonder : MARVELOUS
2 very good or fine ⟨had a *wonderful* time⟩
**won·der·ful·ly** \-fə-lē\ *adv*

**won·der·ing·ly** \'wən-də-ring-lē\ *adv*
in or as if in wonder ⟨looked at them *wonderingly*⟩

**won·der·land** \'wən-dər-ˌland\ *n*
a place of wonders or surprises

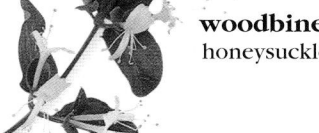

**woodbine:** honeysuckle

**won·der·ment** \'wən-dər-mənt\ *n*
AMAZEMENT

**won·drous** \'wən-drəs\ *adj*
WONDERFUL 1

[1]**wont** \'wȯnt, 'wōnt\ *adj*
being in the habit of doing ⟨slept longer than I was *wont*⟩

[2]**wont** *n*
usual custom : HABIT ⟨slept longer than was my *wont*⟩

**won't** \wōnt\
will not

**woo** \'wü\ *vb* **wooed**; **woo·ing**
1 to try to gain the love of
2 to try to gain ⟨*woo* public favor⟩

**woodpecker:** a great spotted woodpecker

[1]**wood** \'wu̇d\ *n*
1 a thick growth of trees : a small forest — often used in pl.
2 a hard fibrous material that makes up most of the substance of a tree or shrub within the bark and is often used as a building material or fuel

[2]**wood** *adj*
1 WOODEN 1
2 used for or on wood ⟨a *wood* chisel⟩
3 *or* **woods** \'u̇dz\ living or growing in woodland ⟨*woods* herbs⟩

**wood·bine** \'wu̇d-ˌbīn\ *n*
◀ any of several climbing vines of Europe and America (as honeysuckle)

**wood·carv·er** \'wu̇d-ˌkär-vər\ *n*
a person who carves useful or ornamental things from wood

**wood·chuck** \'wu̇d-ˌchək\ *n*
a reddish brown rodent that hibernates : GROUNDHOG

**wood·cock** \'wu̇d-ˌkäk\ *n*
a brown game bird that has a long bill and is related to the snipe

**wood·craft** \'wu̇d-ˌkraft\ *n*
knowledge about the woods and how to take care of oneself in them

**wood·cut·ter** \'wu̇d-ˌkət-ər\ *n*
a person who cuts wood especially as an occupation

**wood·ed** \'wu̇d-əd\ *adj*
covered with trees

**wood·en** \'wu̇d-n\ *adj*
1 made of wood
2 stiff like wood : AWKWARD ⟨a *wooden* posture⟩
3 lacking spirit, ease, or charm ⟨a *wooden* manner⟩

**wood·land** \'wu̇d-lənd, -ˌland\ *n*
land covered with trees and shrubs : FOREST

**wood·lot** \'wu̇d-ˌlät\ *n*
a small wooded section (as of a farm) kept to meet fuel and timber needs

**wood louse** *n*
a small flat gray crustacean that lives usually under stones or bark

**wood·peck·er** \'wu̇d-ˌpek-ər\ *n*
◀ a bird that climbs trees and drills holes in them with its bill in search of insects

**wood·pile** \'wu̇d-ˌpīl\ *n*
a pile of wood especially for use as fuel

**wood·shed** \'wu̇d-ˌshed\ *n*
a shed for storing wood and especially firewood

**woods·man** \'wu̇dz-mən\ *n*, *pl* **woods·men** \-mən\
1 a person who cuts down trees as an occupation
2 a person skilled in woodcraft

**woodsy** \'wu̇d-zē\ *adj*
of, relating to, or suggestive of woodland

**wood thrush** *n*
▼ a large thrush of eastern North America noted for its loud clear song

**wood thrush**

**wood·wind** \'wu̇d-ˌwind\ *n*
one of the group of wind instruments consisting of the flutes, oboes, clarinets, bassoons, and sometimes saxophones

A B C D E F G H I J K L M N O P Q R S T U V W X Y Z

**wood·work** \'wu̇d-ˌwərk\ *n*
work (as the edge around doorways) made of wood

**wood·work·ing** \'wu̇d-ˌwər-king\ *n*
the art or process of shaping or working with wood

**woody** \'wu̇d-ē\ *adj* **wood·i·er**; **wood·i·est**
**1** being mostly woods ⟨*woody* land⟩
**2** of or containing wood or wood fibers ⟨a *woody* stem⟩
**3** very much like wood ⟨*woody* texture⟩

**woof** \'wu̇f, 'wüf\ *n*
**1** the threads that cross the warp in weaving a fabric
**2** a woven fabric or its texture

**wool** \'wu̇l\ *n*
**1** soft heavy wavy or curly hair especially of the sheep
**2** a substance that looks like a mass of wool ⟨glass *wool*⟩
**3** ▼ a material (as yarn) made from wool

**wool 3:**
a skein of wool

**wool·en** *or* **wool·len** \'wu̇l-ən\ *adj*
**1** made of wool
**2** of or relating to wool or cloth made of wool ⟨a *woolen* mill⟩

**wool·ly** \'wu̇l-ē\ *adj* **wool·li·er**; **wool·li·est**
made of or like wool

[1]**word** \'wərd\ *n*
**1** a sound or combination of sounds that has meaning and is spoken by a human being
**2** a written or printed letter or letters standing for a spoken word
**3** a brief remark or conversation
**4** [2]COMMAND 2, ORDER
**5** NEWS ⟨any *word* on how they are⟩
**6** [1]PROMISE 1 ⟨I give you my *word*⟩
**7 words** *pl* remarks said in anger or in a quarrel

[2]**word** *vb*
to express in words : PHRASE

**word·ing** \'wərd-ing\ *n*
the way something is put into words

**word processing** *n*
the production of typewritten documents (as business letters) with automated and usually computerized equipment

**word processor** *n*
**1** a terminal operated by a keyboard for use in word processing usually having a video display and a magnetic storage device
**2** software (as for a computer) to perform word processing

**wordy** \'wərd-ē\ *adj* **word·i·er**; **word·i·est**
using or containing many words or more words than are needed
**word·i·ness** *n*

**wore** *past of* WEAR

[1]**work** \'wərk\ *n*
**1** the use of a person's strength or ability in order to get something done or get some desired result : LABOR ⟨the *work* of a carpenter⟩
**2** OCCUPATION 1, EMPLOYMENT
**3** something that needs to be done : TASK, JOB ⟨have *work* to do⟩
**4** DEED 1, ACHIEVEMENT ⟨honor the club for its good *works*⟩
**5** something produced by effort or hard work ⟨an author's latest *work*⟩
**6 works** *pl* a place where industrial labor is done : PLANT, FACTORY ⟨a locomotive *works*⟩
**7 works** *pl* the working or moving parts of a mechanical device ⟨the *works* of a watch⟩
**8** the way one works : WORKMANSHIP ⟨a job spoiled by careless *work*⟩ **synonyms** see LABOR

[2]**work** *vb* **worked** *or* **wrought** \'rȯt\; **work·ing**
**1** to do work especially for money or because of a need instead of for pleasure : labor or cause to labor
**2** to perform or act or to cause to act as planned : OPERATE ⟨a plan that *worked* well⟩ ⟨*work* a machine⟩
**3** to move or cause to move slowly or with effort ⟨*work* the liquid into a cloth⟩ ⟨the screw *worked* loose⟩
**4** to cause to happen ⟨*work* miracles⟩
**5** [1]MAKE 2, SHAPE ⟨a vase beautifully *wrought*⟩
**6** to carry on one's occupation in, through, or along ⟨two agents *worked* the city⟩
**7** EXCITE 2, PROVOKE ⟨*work* yourself into a rage⟩

**work·able** \'wər-kə-bəl\ *adj*
capable of being worked or done

**work·bench** \'wərk-ˌbench\ *n*
▼ a bench on which work is done (as by mechanics)

**workbench:**
sawing wood on a workbench

**work·book** \'wərk-,bu̇k\ *n*
a book made up of a series of problems or practice examples for a student to use as part of a course of study

**work·er** \'wər-kər\ *n*
**1** a person who works
**2** one of the members of a colony of bees, ants, wasps, or termites that are only partially developed sexually and that do most of the labor and protective work of the colony

**work·ing** \'wər-king\ *adj*
**1** doing work especially for a living ⟨*working* people⟩
**2** relating to work ⟨*working* hours⟩
**3** good enough to allow work or further work to be done ⟨a *working* agreement⟩

**work·ing·man** \'wər-king-,man\ *n, pl* **work·ing·men** \-,men\
a person who works for wages usually at common labor or in industry : a member of the working class

**work·man** \'wərk-mən\ *n, pl* **work·men** \-mən\
**1** WORKINGMAN
**2** a skilled worker (as an electrician or carpenter)

**work·man·ship** \'wərk-mən-,ship\ *n*
**1** the art or skill of a workman
**2** the quality of a piece of work ⟨take pride in good *workmanship*⟩

**work·out** \'wər-,kau̇t\ *n*
an exercise or practice to test or increase ability or performance ⟨the team had a good *workout*⟩

**work out** \,wər-'kau̇t\ *vb*
to invent or solve by effort ⟨*work out* a new kind of machine⟩ ⟨*work* it *out* for yourself⟩

**work·shop** \'wərk-,shäp\ *n*
a shop where work and especially skilled work is carried on

**work·sta·tion** \'wərk-,stā-shən\ *n*
**1** an area with equipment for the performance of a particular task usually by one person
**2** a computer usually connected to a computer network

**world** \'wərld\ *n*
**1** EARTH 3
**2** people in general : HUMANITY
**3** a state of existence ⟨a future *world*⟩
**4** a great number or amount ⟨a *world* of troubles⟩
**5** a part or section of the earth and the people living there

**Word History** The word *world* came from an Old English word that meant "this world" or "lifetime." It was used to refer to the life of human beings on earth as contrasted with life after death. The Old English word that meant "this world" or "lifetime" was formed from two words. The first meant "man." The second meant "old."

**world·ly** \'wərld-lē\ *adj* **world·li·er**; **world·li·est**
of or relating to this world

[1]**world·wide** \'wərl-'dwīd\ *adj*
extending or involving the entire world

[2]**worldwide** *adv*
throughout the world

**World Wide Web** *n*
a part of the Internet designed to allow easier navigation of the network through the use of text and graphics that link to other documents

[1]**worm** \'wərm\ *n*
**1** ► any of various long creeping or crawling animals that usually have soft bodies
**2** a person hated or pitied
**3 worms** *pl* the presence of or disease caused by worms living in the body ⟨a dog with *worms*⟩

[2]**worm** *vb*
**1** to move slowly by creeping or wriggling ⟨*worm* through thick brush⟩
**2** to get hold of or escape from by trickery ⟨*worm* a secret from a friend⟩ ⟨*worm* one's way out of trouble⟩
**3** to free from worms ⟨*worm* a puppy⟩



[1]**worm 1:** an earthworm

**wormy** \'wər-mē\ *adj* **worm·i·er**; **worm·i·est**
containing worms

**worn** *past participle of* WEAR

**worn–out** \'wōr-'nau̇t\ *adj*
**1** useless from long or hard wear
**2** very weary

**wor·ri·some** \'wər-ē-səm\ *adj*
**1** given to worrying
**2** causing worry

[1]**wor·ry** \'wər-ē\ *vb* **wor·ried**; **wor·ry·ing**
**1** to shake or pull at with the teeth
**2** to make anxious or upset ⟨the child's illness *worried* the parents⟩
**3** to feel or express great concern

[2]**worry** *n, pl* **worries**
**1** ANXIETY
**2** a cause of great concern

[1]**worse** \'wərs\ *adj, comparative of* BAD *or of* ILL
**1** more bad or evil : poorer in quality or worth
**2** being in poorer health

[2]**worse** *n*
something worse

[3]**worse** *adv, comparative of* BADLY *or of* ILL
not as well : in a worse way

**wors·en** \'wərs-n\ *vb*
to get worse

[1]**wor·ship** \'wər-shəp\ *n*
**1** deep respect toward God, a god, or a sacred object
**2** too much respect or admiration

[2]**worship** *vb* **wor·shiped** *or* **wor·shipped**; **wor·ship·ing** *or* **wor·ship·ping**
**1** to honor or respect as a divine being
**2** to regard with respect, honor, or devotion
**3** to take part in worship or an act of worship
**wor·ship·er** *or* **wor·ship·per** *n*

[1]**worst** \'wərst\ *adj, superlative of* BAD *or of* ILL
most bad, ill or evil

[2]**worst** *adv, superlative of* ILL *or of* BADLY
in the worst way possible ⟨treated you *worst* of all⟩

[3]**worst** *n*
a person or thing that is worst

[4]**worst** *vb*
to get the better of : DEFEAT

**wor·sted** \'wu̇s-təd, 'wərs-\ *n*
**1** a smooth yarn spun from pure wool

A B C D E F G H I J K L M N O P Q R S T U V W X Y Z

2 a fabric woven from a worsted yarn

**[1]worth** \'wərth\ *n*
1 the quality or qualities of a thing making it valuable or useful
2 value as expressed in money
3 EXCELLENCE 1

**[2]worth** *prep*
1 equal in value to ⟨a painting *worth* thousands⟩
2 having possessions or income equal to ⟨a singer *worth* millions⟩
3 deserving of ⟨well *worth* the effort⟩
4 capable of ⟨ran for all I was *worth*⟩

**worth·less** \'wərth-ləs\ *adj*
1 lacking worth
2 USELESS

**worth·while** \'wərth-'hwīl, -'wīl\ *adj*
being worth the time spent or effort used

**wor·thy** \'wər-thē\ *adj*
**wor·thi·er**; **wor·thi·est**
1 having worth or excellence ⟨a *worthy* goal⟩
2 having enough value or excellence ⟨students *worthy* of promotion⟩
**wor·thi·ness** *n*

**would** \wəd, wu̇d\ *past of* WILL
1 strongly desire : WISH ⟨I *would* that I were gone⟩

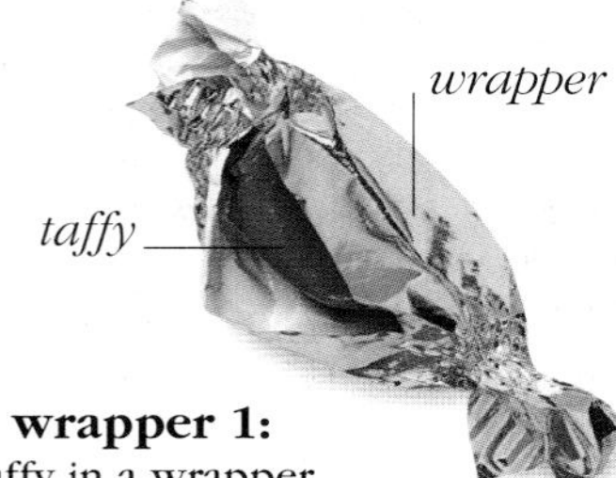


**wrapper 1:**
taffy in a wrapper

2 used as a helping verb to show that something might be likely or meant to happen under certain conditions ⟨I *would* have won except I fell⟩ ⟨they *would* be here by now if they were coming at all⟩ ⟨if I were you, I *would* save my money⟩
3 prefers or prefer to ⟨they *would* die rather than surrender⟩
4 was or were going to ⟨we wish that you *would* go⟩
5 is or are able to : COULD ⟨no stone *would* break that window⟩
6 used as a politer form of *will* ⟨*would* you please turn the radio down⟩

**wouldn't** \'wu̇d-nt\
would not

**[1]wound** \'wünd\ *n*
1 an injury that involves cutting or breaking of bodily tissue (as by violence, accident, or surgery)
2 an injury or hurt to a person's feelings or reputation

**[2]wound** *vb*
1 to hurt by cutting or breaking tissue
2 to hurt the feelings or pride of

**[3]wound** \'wau̇nd\ *past of* WIND

**wove** *past of* WEAVE

**woven** *past participle of* WEAVE

**[1]wran·gle** \'rang-gəl\ *vb*
**wran·gled**; **wran·gling**
1 to have an angry quarrel : BICKER
2 ARGUE 2, DEBATE

**[2]wrangle** *n*
[1]QUARREL 2

**wran·gler** \'rang-glər\ *n*
1 a person who wrangles
2 a worker on a ranch who tends the saddle horses

**[1]wrap** \'rap\ *vb* **wrapped**; **wrap·ping**
1 to cover by winding or folding
2 to enclose in a package
3 to wind or roll together : FOLD
4 to involve completely ⟨*wrapped* in thought⟩

**[2]wrap** *n*
a warm loose outer garment (as a shawl, cape, or coat)

**wrap·per** \'rap-ər\ *n*
1 ◀ what something is wrapped in
2 a person who wraps merchandise
3 a garment that is worn wrapped about the body

**wrap·ping** \'rap-ing\ *n*
something used to wrap something else : WRAPPER

**wrap up** *vb*
1 to bring to an end ⟨that *wraps up* the meeting⟩
2 to put on warm clothing ⟨*wrap up* warm, it's cold outside⟩

**wrath** \'rath\ *n*
violent anger : RAGE

**wrath·ful** \'rath-fəl\ *adj*
1 full of wrath
2 showing wrath

**wreak** \'rēk\ *vb*
to bring down as or as if punishment ⟨*wreak* revenge on an enemy⟩ ⟨the storm *wreaked* destruction⟩

**wreath** \'rēth\ *n, pl* **wreaths** \'rēthz, 'rēths\
▼ something twisted or woven into a circular shape ⟨a *wreath* of flowers⟩

**wreath:**
a decorative wreath

**wreathe** \'rēth\ *vb* **wreathed**; **wreath·ing**
1 to form into wreaths
2 to crown, decorate, or cover with or as if with a wreath ⟨the poet's head was *wreathed* with laurel⟩ ⟨the hill was *wreathed* with mist⟩

**[1]wreck** \'rek\ *n*
1 the remains (as of a ship or vehicle) after heavy damage usually by storm, collision, or fire
2 a person or animal in poor health or without strength
3 the action of breaking up or destroying something

**[2]wreck** *vb*
1 [2]SHIPWRECK 2
2 to damage or destroy by breaking up ⟨*wreck* a car⟩ ⟨*wreck* an old building⟩
3 to bring to ruin or an end ⟨the fire *wrecked* the business⟩ ⟨our picnic was *wrecked* by the storm⟩

**wreck·age** \'rek-ij\ *n*
1 a wrecking or being wrecked
2 the remains of a wreck

**wreck·er** \'rek-ər\ *n*
**1** a person who wrecks something or deals in wreckage
**2** a ship used in salvaging wrecks
**3** a truck for removing wrecked or broken-down cars

**wren** \'ren\ *n*
▼ any of a group of small brown songbirds (as the **house wren**) with short rounded wings and short erect tail

**wren:**
a house wren

**[1]wrench** \'rench\ *vb*
**1** to pull or twist with sudden sharp force ⟨*wrenched* a branch from the tree⟩
**2** to injure or cripple by a sudden sharp twisting or straining ⟨*wrenched* my knee⟩

**[2]wrench** *n*
**1** a violent twist to one side or out of shape
**2** an injury caused by twisting or straining : SPRAIN
**3** ▼ a tool used in turning nuts or bolts

**[2]wrench 3:** a pipe wrench

**wrest** \'rest\ *vb*
**1** to pull away by twisting or wringing
**2** to obtain only by great and steady effort

**[1]wres·tle** \'res-əl\ *vb* **wres·tled**; **wres·tling**
**1** to grasp and attempt to turn, trip, or throw down an opponent or to prevent the opponent from being able to move

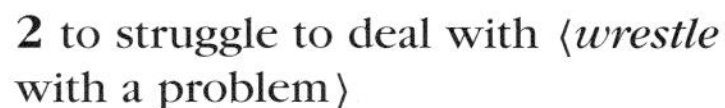

**2** to struggle to deal with ⟨*wrestle* with a problem⟩

**[2]wrestle** *n*
[2]STRUGGLE 1

**wres·tling** \'res-ling\ *n*
a sport in which two opponents wrestle each other

**wretch** \'rech\ *n*
**1** a miserable unhappy person
**2** a very bad person : WRONGDOER

**wretch·ed** \'rech-əd\ *adj*
**1** very unhappy or unfortunate : suffering greatly
**2** causing misery or distress ⟨*wretched* living conditions⟩
**3** of very poor quality : INFERIOR ⟨*wretched* food⟩ ⟨I have a *wretched* memory⟩

**wrig·gle** \'rig-əl\ *vb* **wrig·gled**; **wrig·gling**
**1** to twist or move like a worm : SQUIRM, WIGGLE
**2** to advance by twisting and turning

**wrig·gler** \'rig-lər\ *n*
**1** one that wriggles
**2** a mosquito larva or pupa

**wring** \'ring\ *vb* **wrung** \'rəng\; **wring·ing**
**1** to twist or press so as to squeeze out moisture ⟨*wring* out the clothes⟩
**2** to get by or as if by twisting or pressing ⟨*wring* water from the clothes⟩ ⟨*wrung* a confession from the criminal⟩
**3** to twist so as to strangle ⟨*wrung* its neck⟩
**4** to affect as if by wringing ⟨the bad news *wrung* our hearts⟩

**wring·er** \'ring-ər\ *n*
a machine or device for squeezing liquid out of something (as laundry)

**[1]wrin·kle** \'ring-kəl\ *n*
**1** a crease or small fold (as in the skin or in cloth)
**2** a clever notion or trick ⟨thought up a new *wrinkle*⟩

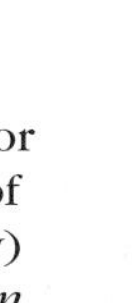

**[2]wrinkle** *vb* **wrin·kled**; **wrin·kling**
to mark or become marked with wrinkles

**wrist** \'rist\ *n*
▼ the joint or the region of the joint between the hand and arm

*wrist*

**wrist**

**wrist·band** \'rist-ˌband\ *n*
**1** the part of a sleeve that goes around the wrist
**2** a band that goes around the wrist (as for support or warmth)

**wrist·watch** \'rist-ˌwäch\ *n*
a watch attached to a bracelet or strap and worn on the wrist

**writ** \'rit\ *n*
an order in writing signed by an officer of a court ordering someone to do or not to do something

**write** \'rīt\ *vb* **wrote** \'rōt\; **writ·ten** \'rit-n\; **writ·ing** \'rīt-ing\
**1** ▼ to form letters or words with pen or pencil
**2** to form the letters or the words of (as on paper)
**3** to put down on paper
**4** to make up and set down for others to read ⟨*write* a novel⟩
**5** to write a letter to

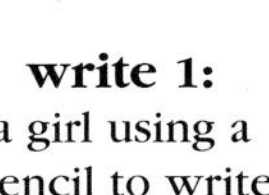

**write 1:**
a girl using a pencil to write

**writ·er** \'rīt-ər\ *n*
a person who writes especially as a business or occupation

**writhe** \'rīth\ *vb* **writhed**; **writh·ing**
**1** to twist and turn this way and that ⟨*writhing* in pain⟩
**2** to suffer from shame or confusion : SQUIRM

**writ·ing** \'rīt-ing\ *n*
**1** the act of a person who writes
**2** HANDWRITING
**3** something (as a letter or book) that is written

[1]**wrong** \'ròng\ *n*
something (as an idea, rule, or action) that is wrong

[2]**wrong** *adj*
**1** not right : SINFUL, EVIL ⟨it is *wrong* to lie⟩
**2** not correct or true : FALSE ⟨your addition is *wrong*⟩
**3** not the one wanted or intended ⟨took the *wrong* train⟩
**4** not suitable ⟨what is *wrong* with this coat⟩
**5** made so as to be placed down or under and not to be seen ⟨the *wrong* side of cloth⟩
**6** not proper ⟨swallowed something the *wrong* way⟩
**wrong·ly** *adv*
**wrong·ness** *n*

[3]**wrong** *adv*
in the wrong direction, manner, or way ⟨answer *wrong*⟩

[4]**wrong** *vb*
to do wrong to

**wrong·do·er** \'ròng-'dü-ər\ *n*
a person who does wrong and especially a moral wrong

**wrong·do·ing** \'ròng-'dü-ing\ *n*
bad behavior or action ⟨guilty of *wrongdoing*⟩

**wrong·ful** \'ròng-fəl\ *adj*
**1** [2]WRONG 1, UNJUST
**2** UNLAWFUL

**wrote** *past of* WRITE

[1]**wrought** \'ròt\ *past of* WORK

[2]**wrought** *adj*
**1** beaten into shape by tools ⟨*wrought* metals⟩
**2** much too excited ⟨don't get all *wrought* up over the test⟩

**wrung** *past of* WRING

**wry** \'rī\ *adj* **wry·er**; **wry·est**
**1** turned abnormally to one side ⟨a *wry* neck⟩
**2** made by twisting the features ⟨a *wry* smile⟩

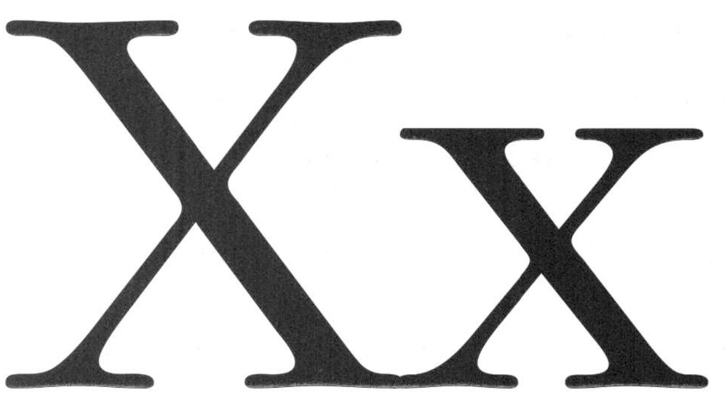

**The sounds of X:** The letter **X** has two main sounds in English. The most common is the sound of **KS**, as in **maximum** and **six**.

Very few words begin with this letter. In those that do, **X** usually has the sound of **Z**, as in **xylophone**. In other words, however, such as the word **X ray**, the **X** is separated from the rest of the word and is pronounced to say its own name.

**x** \'eks\ *n, pl* **x's** *or* **xs** \'ek-səz\ *often cap*
**1** the twenty-fourth letter of the English alphabet
**2** ten in Roman numerals
**3** an unknown quantity

**Xmas** \'kris-məs\ *n*
CHRISTMAS

**Word History** Some people dislike the use of *Xmas* for *Christmas*, saying it is wrong to take *Christ* out of *Christmas*. Really, they are the ones who are wrong, for the *X* in *Xmas* stands for a Greek letter that looks just like our *X* and is the first letter of *Christ* in Greek. For many centuries this letter has been used as an abbreviation and a holy symbol for Christ.

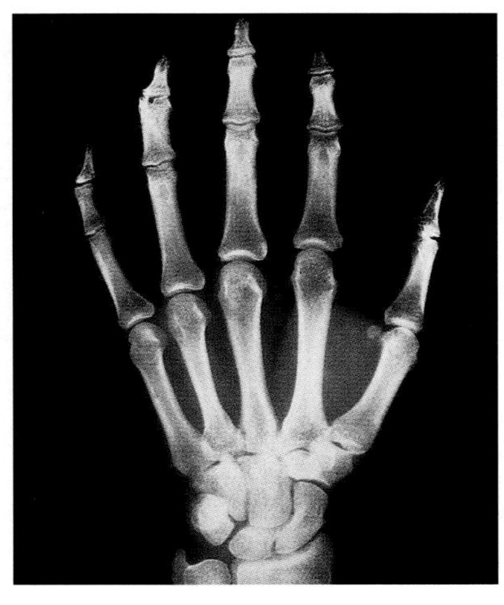

**X ray 2:** an X ray of a human hand

**x–ray** \'eks-ˌrā\ *vb, often cap X*
to examine, treat, or photograph with X rays

**X ray** \'eks-ˌrā\ *n*
**1** a powerful invisible ray made up of very short waves that is somewhat similar to light and that is able to pass through various thicknesses of solids and act on photographic film like light
**2** ◀ a photograph taken by the use of X rays

**Word History** English *X ray* came from the German name of a ray that passes through some solid objects that light cannot pass through. The German scientist who discovered this strange ray did not know why it behaves the way it does. In naming his discovery, he therefore used the letter *x* (the scientific symbol for something unknown) plus the German word for "ray."

**xy·lo·phone** \'zī-lə-ˌfōn\ *n*
▼ a musical instrument consisting of a series of wooden bars of different lengths made to sound the musical scale and played with two wooden hammers

**Word History** The English word *xylophone* came from two Greek words. The first meant "wood." The second meant "sound." The musical sound of a xylophone is made by striking wooden bars.

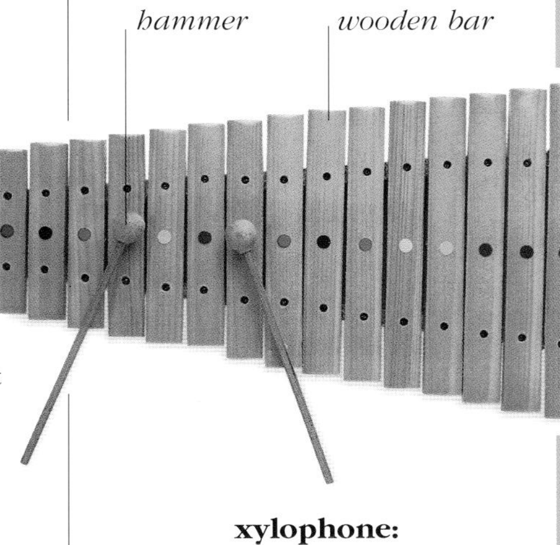


**xylophone:** a toy xylophone

# Y y

**The sounds of Y:** The letter **Y** has one consonant sound in English. That is the sound heard in **yard** and **yellow**.

But this letter also has vowel sounds. One of these is the "long **E**" sound, usually heard at the end of a word, as in **happy**, **pretty**, and **family**. Another is the "long **I**" sound, heard in **type**, **cycle**, and **tyrant**, but also at the end of some words, such as **by** and **cry**. A third vowel sound of **Y** is the "short **Y**" sound, as in **typical** and **mysterious**.

**Y** is sometimes silent, such as when it follows the letter **A** at the end of a word, such as **play** or **stay**.

**[1]yacht:** model of a yacht



**y** \'wī\ *n, pl* **y's** *or* **ys** \'wīz\ *often cap* the twenty-fifth letter of the English alphabet

**[1]-y** *also* **-ey** \ē\ *adj suffix* **-i·er**; **-i·est**
**1** showing, full of, or made of ⟨dirt*y*⟩ ⟨mudd*y*⟩ ⟨ic*y*⟩
**2** like ⟨wintr*y*⟩
**3** devoted to **:** enthusiastic about
**4** tending to ⟨sleep*y*⟩
**5** somewhat **:** rather ⟨chill*y*⟩

**[2]-y** \ē\ *n suffix, pl* **-ies**
**1** state **:** condition **:** quality ⟨jealous*y*⟩
**2** occupation, place of business, or goods dealt with ⟨laundr*y*⟩
**3** whole body or group

**[3]-y** *n suffix, pl* **-ies** occasion or example of a specified action ⟨entreat*y*⟩ ⟨inquir*y*⟩

**[4]-y** see -IE

**[1]yacht** \'yät\ *n* ▲ a small ship used for pleasure cruising or racing

**Word History** Long ago the Dutch built sailing ships designed to chase pirates and smugglers. The Dutch word for such a ship came from a German word that meant "hunting ship." The Dutch gave one of their hunting ships to an English king who used it for pleasure. Other English people made ships like the king's and called them *yachts*, their spelling of the Dutch word. That is how the word *yacht* came into the English language.

**[2]yacht** *vb* to race or cruise in a yacht

**yacht·ing** \'yät-ing\ *n* the action, fact, or recreation of racing or cruising in a yacht

**yachts·man** \'yät-smən\ *n, pl* **yachts·men** \-smən\ a person who owns or sails a yacht

**yak** \'yak\ *n* ▶ a wild or domestic ox of the uplands of Asia that has very long hair

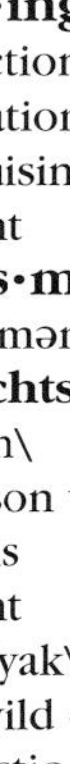

yak

**yam** \'yam\ *n*
**1** ▶ the starchy root of a plant related to the lilies that is an important food in much of the tropics
**2** a sweet potato with a moist and usually orange flesh

**[1]yank** \'yangk\ *n* a strong sudden pull **:** JERK

**[2]yank** *vb* [2]JERK 1 ⟨*yanked* the drawer open⟩

**yam 1:** a cut yam

**Yan·kee** \'yang-kē\ *n*
**1** a person born or living in New England
**2** a person born or living in the northern United States
**3** a person born or living in the United States

**[1]yap** \'yap\ *vb* **yapped**; **yap·ping**
**1** to bark in yaps
**2** [2]SCOLD, CHATTER

**[2]yap** *n*
a quick shrill bark

**[1]yard** \'yärd\ *n*
**1** a small and often fenced area open to the sky and next to a building
**2** the grounds of a building
**3** a fenced area for livestock
**4** an area set aside for a business or activity ⟨a navy *yard*⟩
**5** a system of railroad tracks especially for keeping and repairing cars

**[2]yard** *n*
**1** a measure of length equal to three feet or thirty-six inches (about .91 meter)
**2** a long pole pointed toward the ends that holds up and spreads the top of a sail

**yard·age** \'yärd-ij\ *n*
**1** a total number of yards
**2** the length or size of something measured in yards

**yard·arm** \'yärd-,ärm\ *n*
either end of the yard of a square-rigged ship

**yard·mas·ter** \'yärd-,mas-tər\ *n*
the person in charge of operations in a railroad yard

**yard·stick** \'yärd-,stik\ *n*
**1** a measuring stick a yard long
**2** a rule or standard by which something is measured or judged

**[1]yarn** \'yärn\ *n*
**1** ▶ natural or manufactured fiber (as cotton, wool, or rayon) formed as a continuous thread for use in knitting or weaving
**2** an interesting or exciting story

**[2]yarn** *vb*
to tell a yarn

**yawl** \'yȯl\ *n*
a sailboat having two masts with the shorter one behind the point where the stern enters the water

**[1]yarn 1**

**[1]yawn** \'yȯn\ *vb*
**1** to open wide ⟨a *yawning* cavern⟩
**2** to open the mouth wide usually as a reaction to being tired or bored

**[2]yawn** *n*
a deep drawing in of breath through the wide-open mouth

**ye** \yē\ *pron, archaic*
YOU 1

**[1]yea** \'yā\ *adv*
[1]YES 1 — used in spoken voting

**[2]yea** *n*
**1** a vote in favor of something
**2** a person casting a yea vote

**year** \'yir\ *n*
**1** the period of about 365¼ days required for the earth to make one complete trip around the sun
**2** a period of 365 days or in leap year 366 days beginning January 1
**3** a fixed period of time ⟨the school *year*⟩

**year·book** \'yir-,bu̇k\ *n*
**1** a book published yearly especially as a report
**2** a school publication recording the history and activities of a graduating class

**year·ling** \'yir-ling\ *n*
a person or animal that is or is treated as if a year old

**year·ly** \'yir-lē\ *adj*
[1]ANNUAL 1

**yearn** \'yərn\ *vb*
to feel an eager desire

**Synonyms** YEARN, LONG, and PINE mean to desire something very much. YEARN suggests a very eager desiring along with restless, painful feelings ⟨*yearning* for the day when they would be free⟩. LONG suggests wanting something with one's whole heart and often actually striving to get it ⟨*longing* to become a successful writer⟩. PINE suggests that one grows weak as one continues to desire something that one is not ever going to have ⟨*pining* away for a long lost friend⟩.

**yearn·ing** \'yər-ning\ *n*
an eager desire ⟨a *yearning* for friends⟩

**year–round** \'yir-'rau̇nd\ *adj*
being in operation for the full year

**yeast** \'yēst\ *n*
**1** material that may be found on the surface or at the bottom of sweet liquids, is made up mostly of the cells of a tiny fungus, and causes a reaction in which alcohol is produced
**2** ▼ a commercial product containing living yeast plants and used especially to make bread dough rise
**3** any of the group of tiny fungi that form alcohol or raise bread dough

**yeast 2:**
a cake of dried yeast

**[1]yell** \'yel\ *vb*
to cry or scream loudly

**[2]yell** *n*
**1** [2]SCREAM, SHOUT
**2** a cheer used especially in schools or colleges to encourage athletic teams

**[1]yel·low** \'yel-ō\ *adj*
**1** of the color yellow
**2** COWARDLY

**[2]yellow** *n*
**1** the color in the rainbow between green and orange
**2** something yellow in color

**[3]yellow** *vb*
to turn yellow

**yellow fever** *n*
a disease carried by mosquitoes in hot countries

**yel·low·ish** \'yel-ə-wish\ *adj*
somewhat yellow

**yellow jacket** *n*
a small wasp with yellow markings that usually nests in colonies in the ground

**[1]yelp** \'yelp\ *n*
a quick shrill bark or cry

**[2]yelp** *vb*
to make a quick shrill bark or cry ⟨a dog *yelping* in pain⟩

**yen** \'yen\ *n*
a strong desire **:** LONGING

**yeo·man** \'yō-mən\ *n, pl* **yeo·men** \-mən\
**1** a naval petty officer who works as a clerk
**2** a small farmer who cultivates his or her own land

**-yer** see [2]-ER

**[1]yes** \'yes\ *adv*
**1** used to express agreement ⟨are you ready? *Yes*, I am⟩
**2** used to introduce a phrase with greater emphasis or clearness ⟨we are glad, *yes*, very glad to see you⟩
**3** used to show interest or attention ⟨*yes*, what can I do for you⟩

**[2]yes** *n*
a positive reply

**[1]yes·ter·day** \'yes-tər-dē\ *adv*
on the day next before today

**[2]yesterday** *n*
**1** the day next before this day
**2** time not long past ⟨fashions of *yesterday*⟩

**yes·ter·year** \'yes-tər-ˌyir\ *n*
the recent past

**[1]yet** \'yet\ *adv*
**1** [2]BESIDES ⟨gives *yet* another reason⟩
**2** [2]EVEN 4 ⟨a *yet* higher speed⟩
**3** up to now **:** so far ⟨hasn't done much *yet*⟩
**4** at this or that time ⟨not time to go *yet*⟩
**5** up to the present ⟨is *yet* a new country⟩
**6** at some later time ⟨may *yet* decide to go⟩
**7** NEVERTHELESS

**[2]yet** *conj*
but nevertheless ⟨I was sick *yet* I went to school⟩

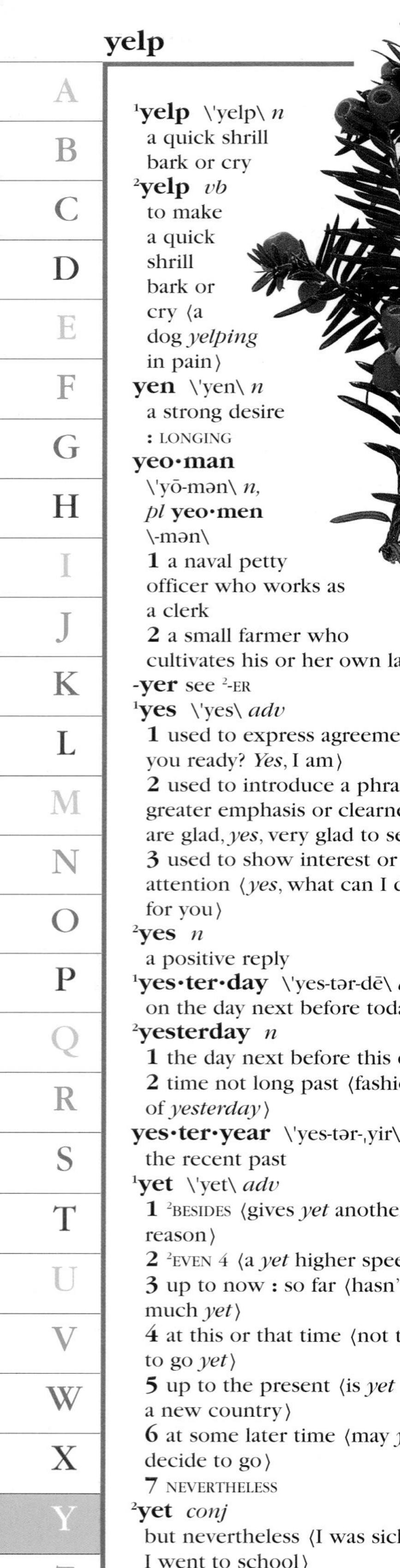

**yew**

**yew** \'yü\ *n*
◀ a tree or shrub with stiff poisonous evergreen leaves, a fleshy fruit, and tough wood used especially for bows and small articles

**Yid·dish** \'yid-ish\ *n*
a language that comes from German and is used by some Jews

**Word History** The language called Yiddish is based on German. The Jews who first spoke this language had a phrase to describe it. This phrase meant "Jewish German." In time this Yiddish phrase was shortened and the first word, which meant "Jewish," was used alone to mean "the language Yiddish." The English word *Yiddish* came from this Yiddish word.

**[1]yield** \'yēld\ *vb*
**1** to give up possession of on claim or demand
**2** to give (oneself) up to a liking, temptation, or habit
**3** to bear as a natural product ⟨the tree *yielded* its first crop last year⟩
**4** to return as income or profit ⟨an investment *yielding* ten percent⟩
**5** to be productive **:** bring good results ⟨the garden *yielded* well⟩
**6** to stop opposing or objecting to something ⟨*yield* to a demand⟩
**7** to give way under physical force so as to bend, stretch, or break ⟨the rope *yielded* under the strain⟩
**8** to admit that someone else is better

**[2]yield** *n*
the amount produced or returned

**[1]yip** \'yip\ *vb* **yipped**; **yip·ping**
[2]YELP — used chiefly of a dog

**[2]yip** *n*
a noise made by or as if by yelping

**[1]yo·del** \'yōd-l\ *vb* **yo·deled** *or* **yo·delled**; **yo·del·ing** *or* **yo·del·ling**
**1** to sing with frequent sudden changes from the natural voice range to a higher range and back
**2** to call or shout in the manner of yodeling
**yo·del·er** *n*

**[2]yodel** *n*
a yodeled shout

**yo·gurt** \'yō-gərt\ *n*
a soft food made of milk that is soured by the addition of bacteria and is often flavored and sweetened

**[1]yoke** \'yōk\ *n*
**1** a wooden bar or frame by which two work animals (as oxen) are harnessed at the heads or necks for drawing a plow or load
**2** a frame fitted to a person's shoulders to carry a load in two equal parts
**3** a clamp that joins two parts to hold or connect them in position
**4** *pl usually* **yoke** two animals yoked together
**5** something that brings to a state of hardship, humiliation, or slavery
**6** SLAVERY 2
**7** [1]TIE 4, BOND
**8** ▼ a fitted or shaped piece at the shoulder of a garment or at the top of a skirt

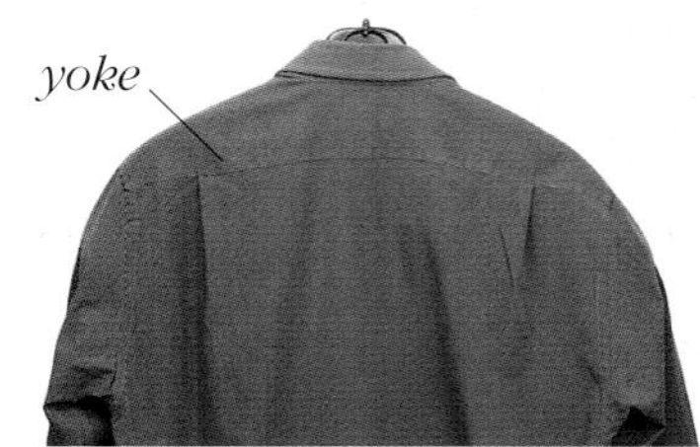


**[1]yoke 8:**
the yoke of a shirt

**[2]yoke** *vb* **yoked**; **yok·ing**
**1** to put a yoke on
**2** to attach a work animal to ⟨*yoke* a plow⟩

**yo·kel** \'yō-kəl\ *n*
a country person with little education or experience

**yolk** \'yōk\ *n*
▼ the yellow inner part of the egg of a bird or reptile containing stored food material for the developing young
**yolked** \'yōkt\ *adj*

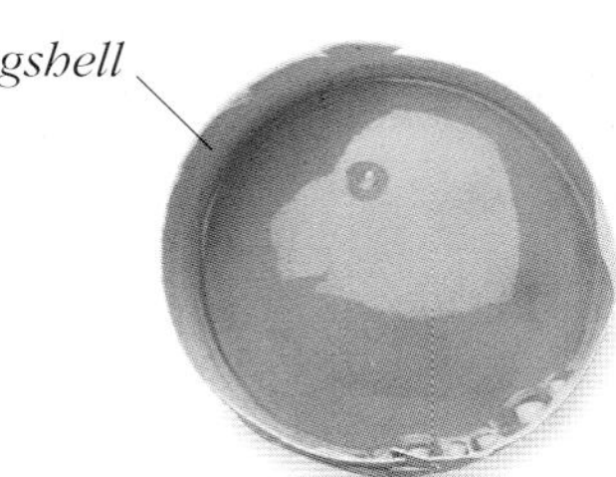


**yolk** of a hen's egg

**Word History** The modern English word *yolk* came from an Old English word that meant "the yellow part of an egg." This Old English word came in turn from an Old English word that meant "yellow." The modern English word *yellow* came from this Old English word, too.

**Yom Kip·pur** \ˌyōm-ki-ˈpu̇r, ˌyȯm-, -ˈkip-ər\ *n*
a Jewish holiday observed in September or October with fasting and prayer

**[1]yon** \ˈyän\ *adj*
[2]YONDER 2

**[2]yon** *adv*
1 [1]YONDER
2 THITHER ⟨ran hither and *yon*⟩

**[1]yon·der** \ˈyän-dər\ *adv*
at or in that place ⟨look *yonder* down the hill⟩

**[2]yonder** *adj*
1 more distant ⟨the *yonder* side of the hill⟩
2 being at a distance within view ⟨*yonder* hills⟩

**yore** \ˈyōr\ *n*
time long past ⟨stories of *yore*⟩

**you** \yü, yə\ *pron*
1 the one or ones these words are spoken or written to
2 [3]ONE 2 ⟨*you* never know what will happen⟩

**you'd** \ˈyüd, ˈyəd\
you had : you would

**you'll** \ˈyül, ˈyəl\
you shall : you will

**[1]young** \ˈyəng\ *adj* **youn·ger** \ˈyəng-gər\; **youn·gest** \ˈyəng-gəst\
1 being in the first or an early stage of life or growth
2 INEXPERIENCED
3 recently come into being : NEW
4 YOUTHFUL 1

**[2]young** *n, pl* **young**
1 **young** *pl* young persons
2 **young** *pl* immature offspring ⟨a cat and her *young*⟩
3 a single recently born or hatched animal

**youn·gest** \ˈyəng-gəst\ *n, pl* **youngest**
one that is the least old especially of a family

**young·ster** \ˈyəng-stər\ *n*
1 a young person : YOUTH
2 CHILD

**your** \yər, ˈyu̇r, ˈyōr\ *adj*
1 of or belonging to you ⟨*your* book⟩
2 by or from you ⟨*your* gifts⟩
3 affecting you ⟨*your* enemies⟩
4 of or relating to one ⟨when you face the north, east is at *your* right⟩
5 used before a title of honor in addressing a person ⟨*your* Majesty⟩ ⟨*your* Holiness⟩

**yo-yo**

**you're** \yər, ˈyu̇r, ˈyōr\
you are

**yours** \ˈyu̇rz, ˈyōrz\ *pron*
that which belongs to you ⟨the bike is *yours*⟩ ⟨the boots are *yours*⟩

**your·self** \yər-ˈself\ *pron, pl* **your·selves** \-ˈselvz\
your own self ⟨you might hurt *yourself* if you're not careful⟩ ⟨you are responsible *yourselves* for the problem⟩

**youth** \ˈyüth\ *n, pl* **youths** \ˈyüt͟hz, ˈyüths\
1 the period of life between being a child and an adult
2 a young man
3 young people ⟨the *youth* of today⟩
4 the quality or state of being young

**youth·ful** \ˈyüth-fəl\ *adj*
1 of or relating to youth
2 being young and not yet fully grown
3 having the freshness of youth
**youth·ful·ly** \-fə-lē\ *adv*
**youth·ful·ness** *n*

**you've** \ˈyüv, yəv\
you have

**[1]yowl** \ˈyau̇l\ *vb*
[1]WAIL

**[2]yowl** *n*
a loud long moaning cry (as of a cat)

**yo–yo** \ˈyō-yō\ *n, pl* **yo–yos** *also* **yo–yoes**
◀ a thick divided disk that is made to fall and rise to the hand by unwinding and winding again on a string

**yuc·ca** \ˈyək-ə\ *n*
▼ a plant related to the lilies that grows in dry regions and has stiff pointed leaves at the base of a tall stiff stalk of usually whitish flowers

**yule** \ˈyül\ *n, often cap*
CHRISTMAS

**yule log** *n, often cap Y*
a large log once put in the fireplace on Christmas Eve as the foundation of the fire

**yule·tide** \ˈyül-ˌtīd\ *n, often cap*
the Christmas season

**yucca**

**The sounds of Z:** The letter **Z** has one main sound in English. It sounds the same in **zero**, **azalea**, **dazzle**, and **buzz**. A double **Z** sounds the same as a single **Z**.

In a very few words the letter **Z** has the sound that **S** has in the word **measure**. An example is **azure**.

**zebu**

**z** \'zē\ *n, pl* **z's** *or* **zs** \'zēz\ *often cap*
the twenty-sixth letter of the English alphabet

[1]**za·ny** \'zā-nē\ *n, pl* **zanies**
**1** [1]CLOWN 2
**2** a silly or foolish person

**Word History** In early Italian plays, there was usually a clown who copied the actions of the chief actor in a comical way. The English word *zany*, which at first meant "clown," came from the Italian name for the stage clown.

[2]**zany** *adj* **za·ni·er**; **za·ni·est**
**1** being or like a zany
**2** FOOLISH, SILLY ⟨a *zany* plan⟩

**zeal** \'zēl\ *n*
eager desire to get something done or see something succeed

**zeal·ous** \'zel-əs\ *adj*
filled with or showing zeal
**zeal·ous·ly** *adv*
**zeal·ous·ness** *n*

**ze·bra** \'zē-brə\ *n*
an African wild animal related to the horses that has a hide striped in black and white or black and buff

**ze·bu** \'zē-byü\ *n*
▲ an Asian domestic ox that differs from the related European cattle in having a large hump over the shoulders and a loose skin with hanging folds

**ze·nith** \'zē-nəth\ *n*
**1** the point in the heavens directly overhead
**2** the highest point

**zeph·yr** \'zef-ər\ *n*
**1** a breeze from the west
**2** a gentle breeze

**zep·pe·lin** \'zep-ə-lən\ *n*
a huge long balloon that has a metal frame and is driven through the air by engines carried on its underside

**ze·ro** \'zē-rō, 'ziər-ō\ *n, pl* **zeros** *or* **zeroes**
**1** the numerical symbol 0 meaning the absence of all size or quantity
**2** the point on a scale (as on a thermometer) from which measurements are made
**3** the temperature shown by the zero mark on a thermometer
**4** a total lack of anything **:** NOTHING
**5** the lowest point

**zest** \'zest\ *n*
**1** an enjoyable or exciting quality
**2** keen enjoyment ⟨eat with *zest*⟩
**zest·ful** \-fəl\ *adj*
**zest·ful·ly** \-fə-lē\ *adv*
**zest·ful·ness** *n*

**Word History** The English word *zest* came from a French word that meant "the peel of an orange or a lemon." Because their flavor made food more tasty and enjoyable, lemon and orange peels were used to season food. In time the word *zest* came to mean any quality that made life more enjoyable.

[1]**zig·zag** \'zig-ˌzag\ *n*
**1** one of a series of short sharp turns or angles in a course
**2** ► a line, path, or pattern that bends sharply this way and that

[2]**zigzag** *adv*
in or by a zigzag path or course ⟨ran *zigzag* across the field⟩

[3]**zigzag** *adj*
having short sharp turns or angles ⟨a *zigzag* road⟩

[4]**zigzag** *vb* **zig·zagged**; **zig·zag·ging**
to form into or move along a zigzag

[1]**zigzag 2:** a zigzag pattern of toy blocks

**zinc** \'zingk\ *n*
a bluish white metal that tarnishes only slightly in moist air and is used mostly to make alloys and to give iron a protective coating

**zing** \'zing\ *n*
**1** a shrill humming sound
**2** a lively or energetic quality

**zin·nia** \'zin-ē-ə, 'zin-yə\ *n*
▼ a tropical American herb related to the daisies that is widely grown for its bright flower heads that last a long time

**zinnia**

**¹zip** \'zip\ *vb* **zipped**; **zip·ping**
**1** to move or act with speed and force
**2** to move or pass with a shrill hissing or humming sound

**²zip** *n*
**1** a sudden shrill hissing sound
**2** ENERGY 1

**³zip** *vb* **zipped**; **zip·ping**
to close or open with a zipper

**zip code** *or* **ZIP Code** *n*
a number consisting of five digits that identifies each postal area in the United States

**zip·per** \'zip-ər\ *n*
a fastener (as for a jacket) consisting of two rows of metal or plastic teeth on strips of tape and a sliding piece that closes an opening by drawing the teeth together
**zip·pered** \-ərd\ *adj*

**zip·py** \'zip-ē\ *adj* **zip·pi·er**; **zip·pi·est**
full of energy **:** LIVELY

**zith·er** \'zith-ər, 'zith-\ *n*
▶ a stringed instrument with thirty to forty tuned strings that are plucked with the fingers or with a pick

**zodiac**

Each constellation of the zodiac is made up of a pattern of stars that are imagined to represent an animal or character from ancient Greek myth. The twelve signs of the zodiac are used in astrology to identify different types of personality and to tell fortunes.

**diagram showing the 12 signs of the zodiac**

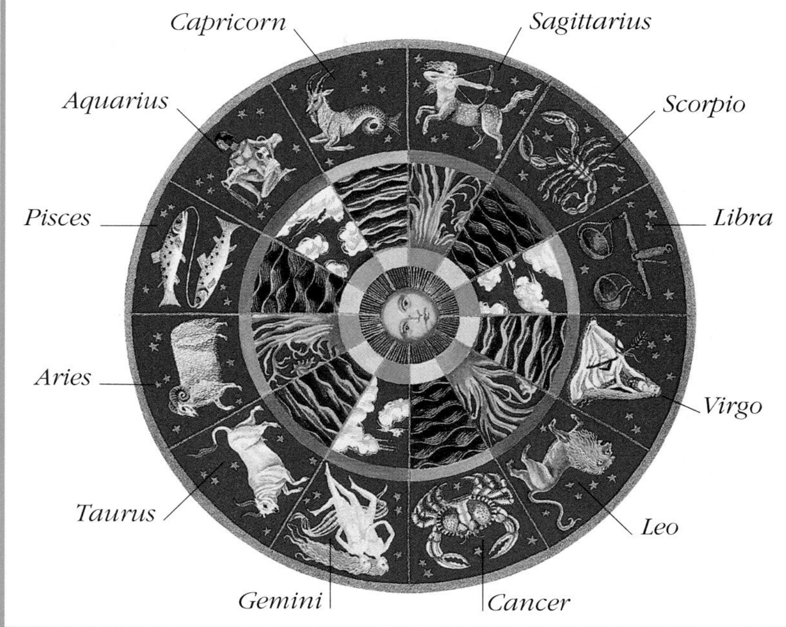


**zo·di·ac** \'zōd-ē-,ak\ *n*
▲ an imaginary belt in the heavens that includes the paths of most of the planets and is divided into twelve constellations or signs

**zom·bie** *or* **zom·bi** \'zäm-bē\ *n*
a person who is believed to have died and been brought back to life

**Word History** The word *zombie* developed from the name of a snake god of western Africa. Africans believed that the snake god could bring the dead back to life. People who were thought to have been brought back from the dead in this way were also called *zombies*. The word *zombie* came into the English language through southern slaves whose roots go back to western Africa.

**¹zone** \'zōn\ *n*
**1** any of the five great parts that

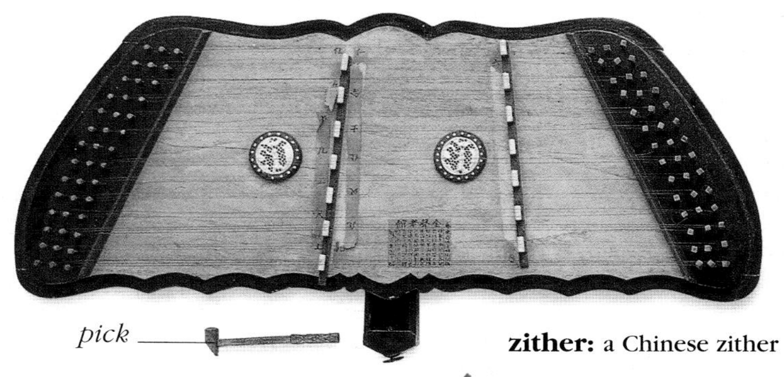


**zither:** a Chinese zither

a b c d e f g h i j k l m n o p q r s t u v w x y z

**zoo:** polar bears in their zoo enclosure

the earth's surface is divided into according to latitude and temperature ⟨one torrid, two frigid, and two temperate *zones*⟩
**2** a band or belt that surrounds ⟨a *zone* of trees⟩
**3** a section set off or marked as different in some way ⟨a war *zone*⟩

**Word History** The ancient Greeks had a word that meant "belt." From that word, the ancient Romans made a Latin word that also meant "belt." The Romans thought of the world as being divided into five regions or five great belts that circled the world. That is why the Latin word that meant "belt" was used to refer to the five divisions. The English word *zone* came from this Latin word.

**[2]zone** *vb* **zoned**; **zon·ing**
to divide into zones for different uses

**zoo** \'zü\ *n, pl* **zoos**
▲ a collection of living animals for display

**zoo·log·i·cal** \ˌzō-ə-'läj-i-kəl\ *adj*
of or relating to zoology

**zoological garden** *n*
a garden or park where wild animals are kept for exhibition

**zo·ol·o·gist** \zō-'äl-ə-jəst\ *n*
a specialist in zoology

**zo·ol·o·gy** \zō-'äl-ə-jē\ *n*
**1** a branch of biology dealing with animals and animal life
**2** animal life (as of a region)

**[1]zoom** \'züm\ *vb*
**1** to speed along with a loud hum or buzz
**2** to move upward quickly at a sharp angle ⟨the airplane *zoomed* into the sky⟩

**[2]zoom** *n*
**1** an act or process of zooming
**2** a zooming sound

**zuc·chi·ni** \zü-'kē-nē\ *n*
a smooth cylinder-shaped green-skinned vegetable that is a type of squash

**zwie·back** \'swē-ˌbak, 'swī-\ *n*
▼ a usually sweetened bread made with eggs that is baked and then sliced and toasted until dry and crisp

**zy·gote** \'zī-ˌgōt\ *n*
the new cell produced when a sperm cell joins with an egg

**zwieback**

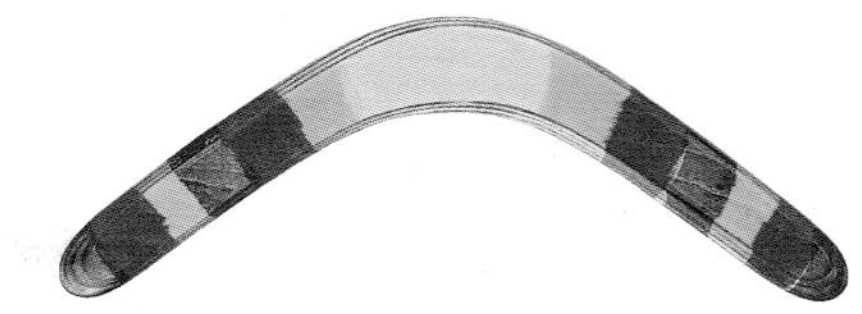

# REFERENCE SECTION

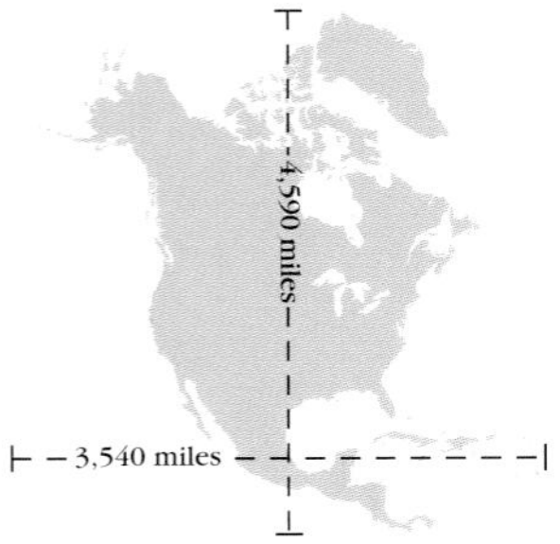

# North America

STRETCHING FROM THE WARM Caribbean islands to icy Greenland, North America is the third-largest continent. Along each side of the mainland are mountain ranges — the Appalachians in the east and the giant Rocky Mountains in the west — that run parallel to one another. Between them lies a vast, flat landscape that includes the Great Plains and the freshwater Great Lakes.

Extent of North American lands

Population: 490,115,017
No. of countries: 22

## Ancient Civilizations

The first European explorers in North America discovered a series of advanced civilizations that had traded and fought with each other. Some of these civilizations, such as the Maya and Aztec, had become dominant in the recent centuries. Others, such as the Adena and Hopewell cultures, had flourished and died hundreds of years before.

## Rocky Mountains

The snow-capped Rocky Mountains run down the length of the west side of North America, stretching from Alaska in the north to beyond Mexico in the south. Moraine \mə-'ran\ Lake, in the Canadian part of the Rockies, is one of many lakes and rivers that run from the mountain range. Rivers flowing east from the Rockies deposit silt on the Great Plains, which helps to develop fertile soil.

## Native Peoples

The Inuit are the original people of Arctic Canada. The children shown here are from a town on the coast of Baffin Island in the Arctic Ocean. It snows here for eight months of the year and children keep warm with modern winter clothes.

## Extreme Climates

| | |
|---|---|
| Hottest place | Death Valley \'deth-,val-ē\, USA |
| Driest place | Bataques \bä-'täk-es\, Mexico |
| Coldest place | Northice \'nȯrth-,īs\, Greenland |
| Wettest place | Henderson Lake \'hen-dərsən\, Canada |

## City Life

More than three quarters of all Americans live in cities or their suburbs, and the population is made up of people from many different ethnic backgrounds. San Francisco, shown here, is one of the oldest cities, renowned for its attractive 19th-century buildings.

## Fact File

| | |
|---|---|
| Largest country | Canada |
| Smallest country | St. Kitts-Nevis |
| Largest city | Mexico City |
| Largest lake | Lake Superior |
| Longest river | Mississippi |

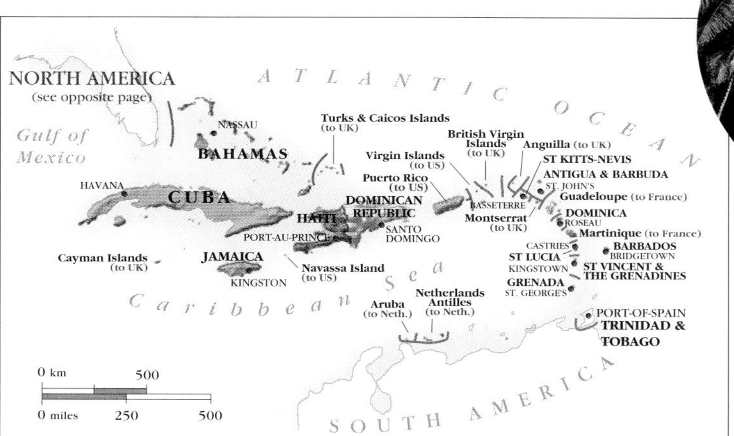

## Caribbean Islands

Characterized by long, sandy beaches, sunny weather, and warm waters, the islands of the Caribbean Sea attract many tourists every year. They are, however, prone to hurricanes, and volcanic eruptions.

# United States of America

THE WORLD'S most powerful industrial nation, the United States has developed over the last three hundred twenty odd years from a wild landscape populated only sparsely by native peoples. Today, the east is remarkable for its busy modern cities, while west of the Mississippi River the dramatic scenery varies from evergreen forests to prairies.

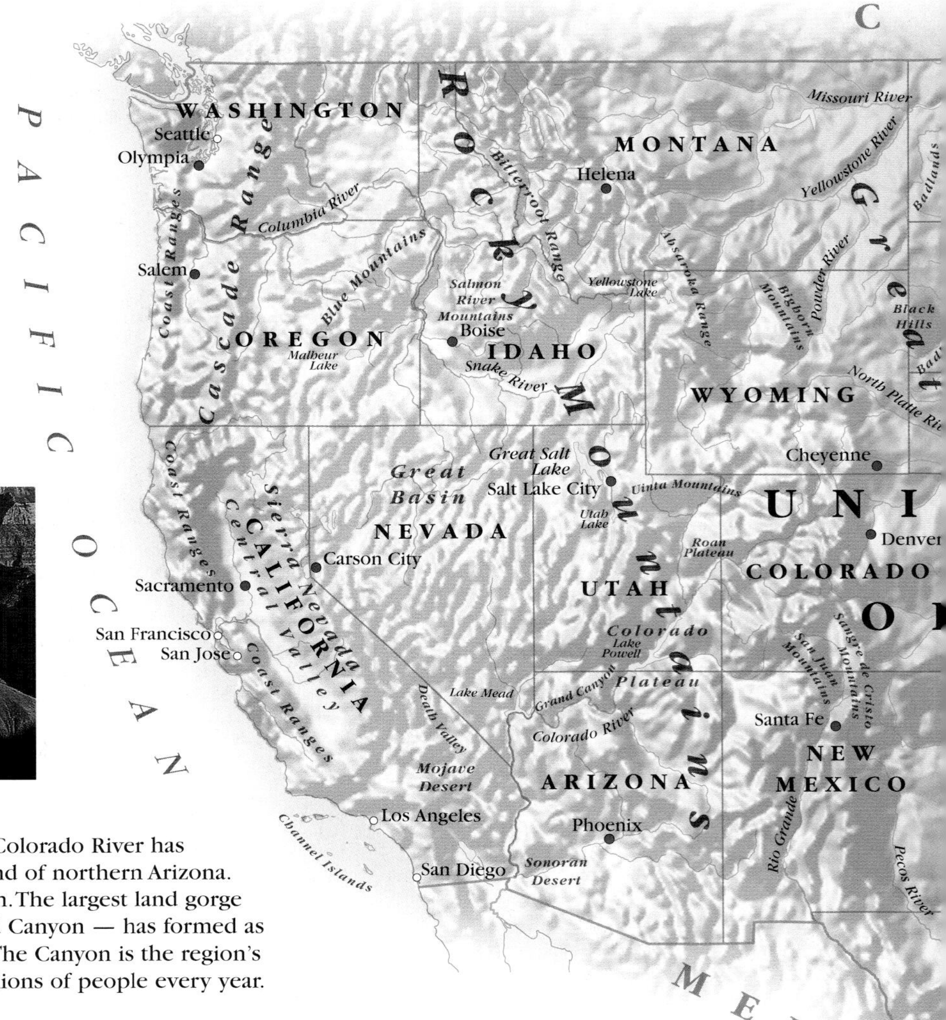

## Grand Canyon

Over the last five million years, the Colorado River has carved its way through the rocky land of northern Arizona. At the same time, plateaus have risen. The largest land gorge in the world — known as the Grand Canyon — has formed as a result of these combined actions. The Canyon is the region's main attraction and is visited by millions of people every year.

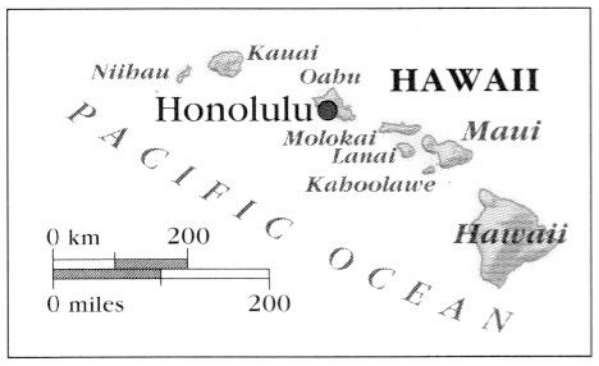

## Hawaiian Islands

Characterized by miles of coastline and a tropical climate, the Hawaiian islands have a thriving tourist industry. Some of the islands are formed by volcanoes that rise out of the sea.

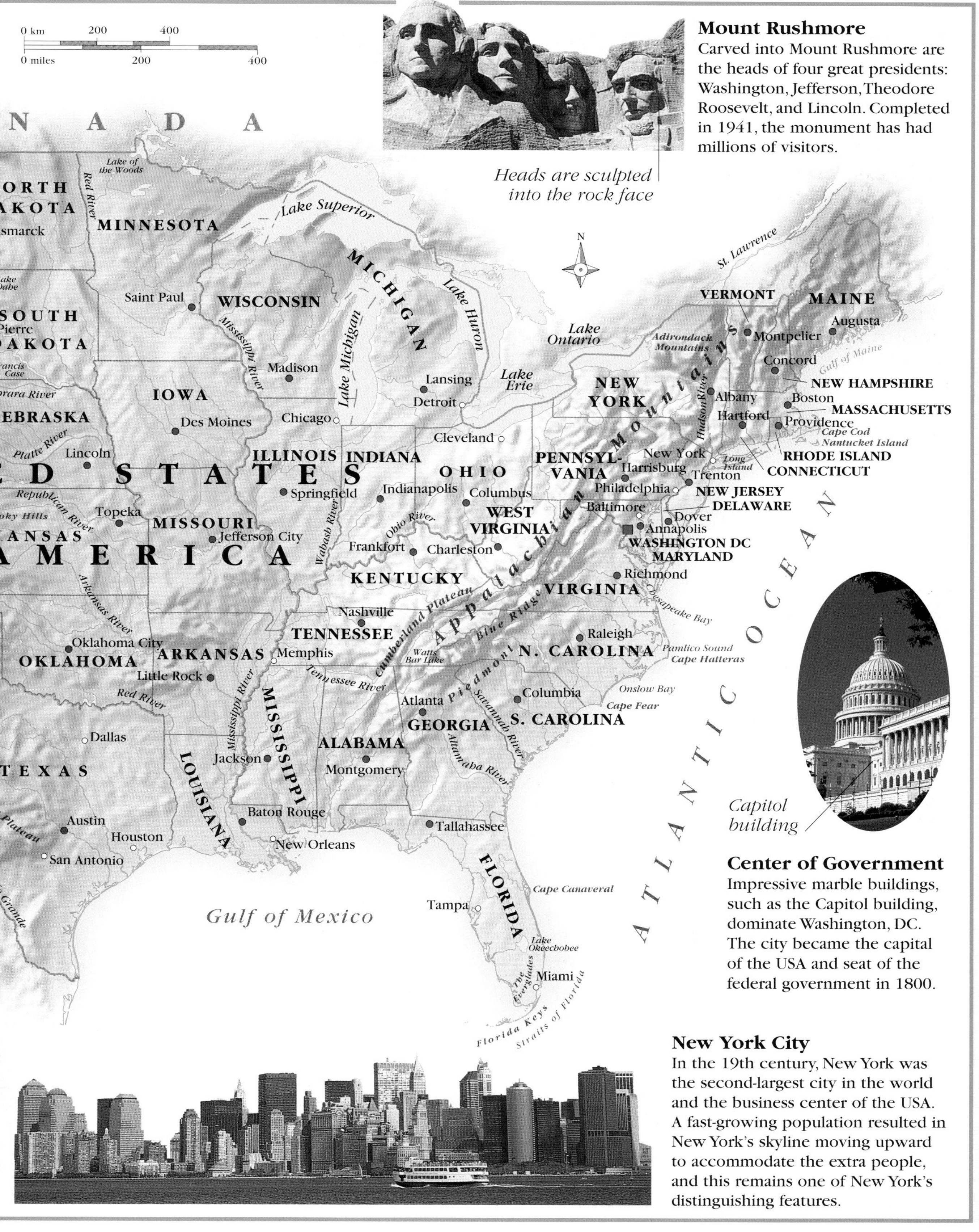


## Mount Rushmore

Carved into Mount Rushmore are the heads of four great presidents: Washington, Jefferson, Theodore Roosevelt, and Lincoln. Completed in 1941, the monument has had millions of visitors.

## Center of Government

Impressive marble buildings, such as the Capitol building, dominate Washington, DC. The city became the capital of the USA and seat of the federal government in 1800.

## New York City

In the 19th century, New York was the second-largest city in the world and the business center of the USA. A fast-growing population resulted in New York's skyline moving upward to accommodate the extra people, and this remains one of New York's distinguishing features.

# South America

ONE OF THE WORLD'S last great wildernesses — the Amazonian rain forest — is found in South America, the fourth-largest continent. Bordering the western coast are the high peaks of the Andes, which are lined with numerous volcanoes. West of the Andes, the climate is dry with arid deserts, while by contrast the Amazon Basin and the Guiana Highlands in the north are humid and tropical.

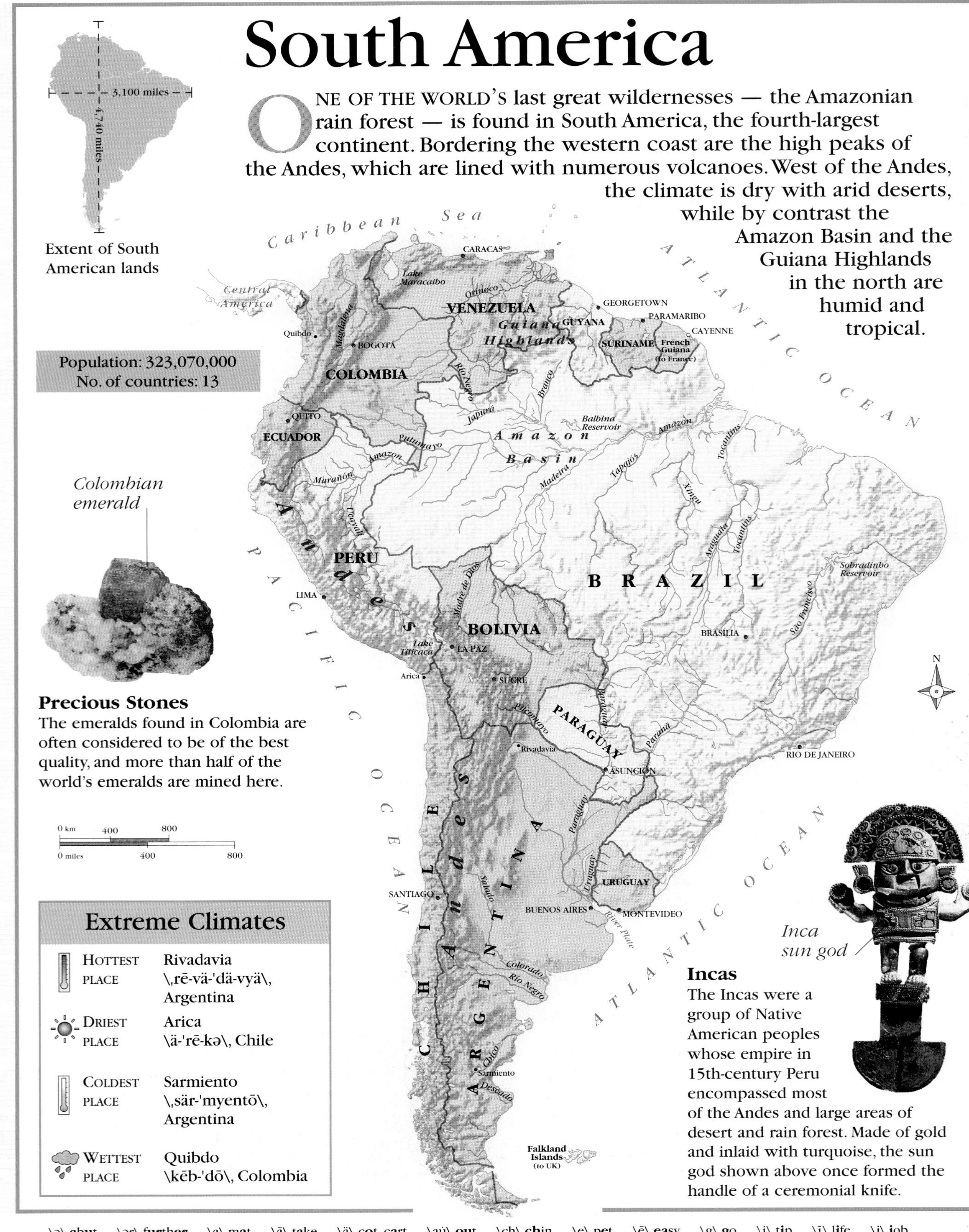


Extent of South American lands

Population: 323,070,000
No. of countries: 13

*Colombian emerald*

**Precious Stones**
The emeralds found in Colombia are often considered to be of the best quality, and more than half of the world's emeralds are mined here.

## Extreme Climates

| | |
|---|---|
| HOTTEST PLACE | Rivadavia \ˌrē-vä-ˈdä-vyä\, Argentina |
| DRIEST PLACE | Arica \ä-ˈrē-kə\, Chile |
| COLDEST PLACE | Sarmiento \ˌsär-ˈmyentō\, Argentina |
| WETTEST PLACE | Quibdo \kēb-ˈdō\, Colombia |

*Inca sun god*

**Incas**
The Incas were a group of Native American peoples whose empire in 15th-century Peru encompassed most of the Andes and large areas of desert and rain forest. Made of gold and inlaid with turquoise, the sun god shown above once formed the handle of a ceremonial knife.

## Volcanic Andes

The Andes run the entire length of South America along a narrow strip of land bordering the Pacific Ocean. Many of the peaks are active or formerly active volcanoes. Despite the intense heat within these lava-filled mountains, the highest are covered in snow all year round.

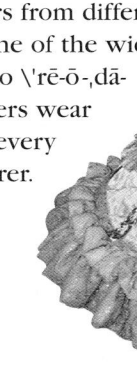

*Flag bearer*

## Carnival Time

One of the world's largest and most spectacular carnivals is held in Brazil, with dancers from different clubs parading along one of the wide avenues of Rio de Janeiro \'rē-ō-ˌdā-zhə-'neər-ō\. The dancers wear elaborate costumes and every club has a flag bearer.

### Fact File

| | |
|---|---|
| LARGEST COUNTRY | Brazil |
| SMALLEST COUNTRY | Suriname |
| LARGEST CITY | São Paulo \ˌsä-ō-'pau̇-lō\ |
| LARGEST LAKE | Lake Titicaca \ˌlāk-ˌtit-i-'käk-ə\ |
| LONGEST RIVER | Amazon |

*Amazon winds through rain forest*

## Amazon

From its source in the Andes Mountains of Peru, the Amazon River flows through a vast depression in the north of the continent and empties into the Atlantic Ocean. The Amazon, with its tributaries, nearby lakes, and swamps forms a network of fresh water that supports a huge area of tropical rain forest. The Amazon floods and deposits fertile silt on surrounding land. For more than half of its length, the Amazon flows through Brazil and is used by large boats to transport cargo inland.

## Buenos Aires

Nearly half of all Argentinians live in or near the capital city of Buenos Aires. One of the major cities in the southern half of the world, it has wide avenues, a subway system, and sophisticated shops. To the west of Buenos Aires, there are vast areas of pampas.

*Plaza in Buenos Aires*

# Europe

ABOUT A QUARTER of the size of Asia and less than half the size of North America, Europe is the second-smallest continent. Irregularly shaped, it has many interlocking areas of land and sea. A vast curve of mountain ranges that include the Pyrenees and the Alps divides the north from the south. Europe's climate is generally temperate, with only a few places affected by extreme weather conditions. Most notable is the area around the Baltic Sea, which freezes over in winter. By contrast, countries along the Mediterranean Sea have milder weather and long, hot summers.

## Fact File

| | |
|---|---|
| LARGEST COUNTRY | (European) Russia |
| SMALLEST COUNTRY | Vatican City |
| LARGEST CITY | Moscow in European Russia |
| LARGEST LAKE | Lake Ladoga |
| LONGEST RIVER | Volga |

Population: 598,424,892
No. of countries: 46

## Swiss Alps

Europe's highest mountains, the Alps form a massive wall that separates northern Europe from the Mediterranean countries. The Swiss Alps are a popular ski resort and attract millions of tourists each year. Clustered in valleys, at the foot of the towering Alps, are picturesque villages and peaceful lakes. On the lower slopes are meadows where dairy cattle graze.

## Folk Art

Made in Eastern Europe for centuries, nesting dolls can represent famous characters, but are mostly painted figures in traditional costumes. This form of folk art reflects the rural lifestyle of much of the population.

*Nesting doll*

## Historic Cities

Italy has some of the world's most beautiful cities. One of the most remarkable is Venice, built on low-lying islands in a lagoon. Many Venetian houses are more than 400 years old and face on to canals, which take the place of roads.

## Dutch Tulips

The largest producer of flowers in Europe is the Netherlands — particularly those grown from bulbs, such as tulips. In spring, the fields of flowers attract many tourists.

## Mediterranean

Near the Mediterranean Sea, the climate is sunny and dry. Fields of lavender are characteristic of the South of France, where crops of fruit and cereal are also widely grown. By contrast, the climate in the north of France is cool and wet.

### Extreme Climates

| | |
|---|---|
| HOTTEST PLACE | Seville \sə'vil\, Spain |
| DRIEST PLACE | Astrakhan \'as-trə-ˌkan\, Russia |
| COLDEST PLACE | Ust' Shchugor \ˌüst-shchü-gȯr\, Russia |
| WETTEST PLACE | Crkvice \'tsər-kə-ˌvēts\, Bosnia |

*Scandinavian ice-hockey players*

## Winter Sports

Scandinavia has deep fjords, lakes, and valleys that were gouged out by glaciers in past ice ages. During the long, cold winters, many of the lakes freeze up and ice hockey can be played outdoors. Long-distance, cross-country skiing is another popular winter sport here, as for many months much of the land becomes covered with deep snowfall.

# Asia

THE LARGEST CONTINENT, Asia has a rich variety of landscapes, climates, and traditions. Two out of every three people in the world live in Asia, and the most populated countries are China and India. In the Himalayas, Mount Everest is the highest place in the world, and the Dead Sea on the border of Israel and Jordan is the lowest. Climates vary from the frozen wastelands of Siberia in the north to the baking hot deserts of the Arabian Peninsula in the south. Toward the center of the continent, the climate is one of extreme contrasts — dry, hot summers and bitterly cold winters.

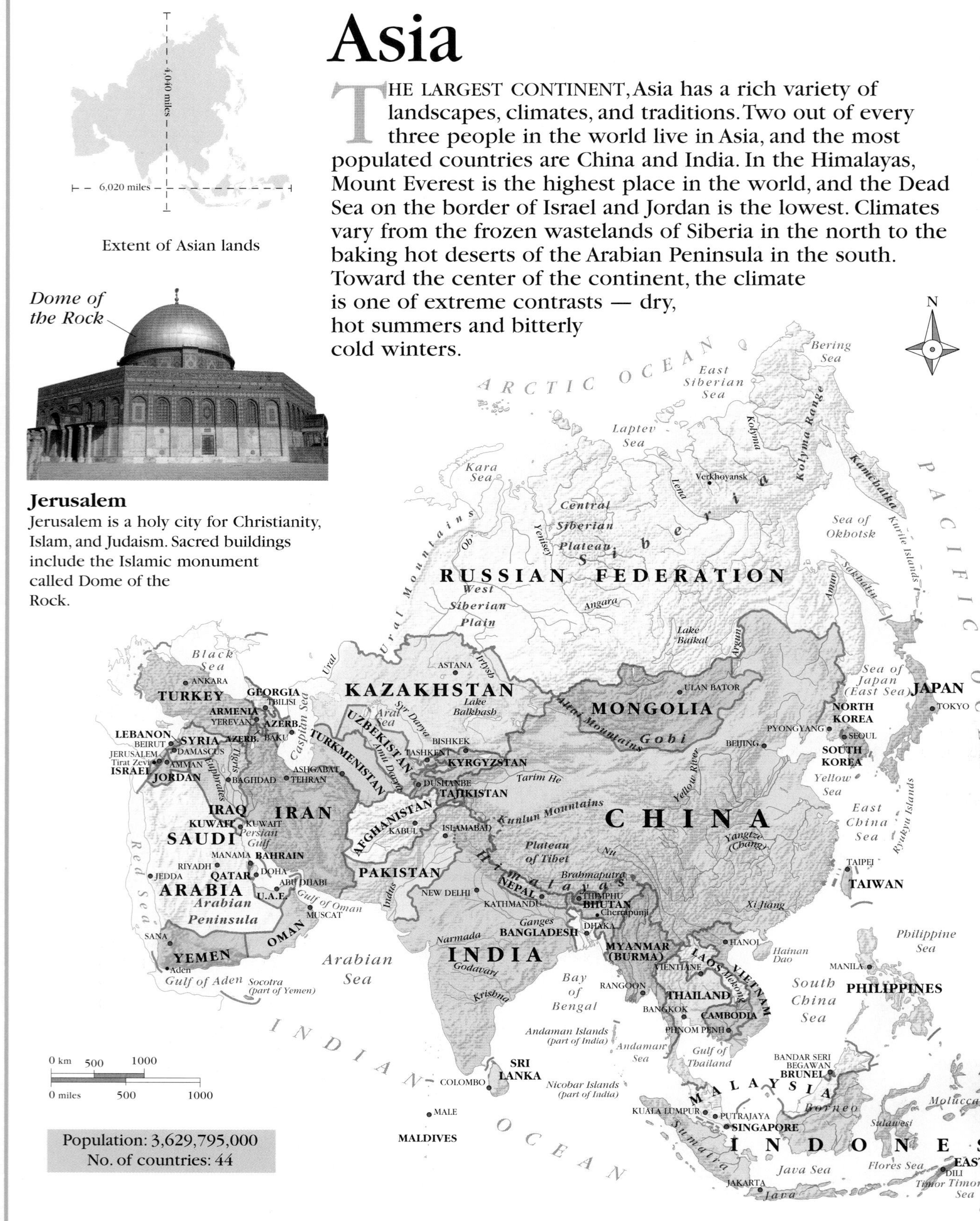


## Jerusalem

Jerusalem is a holy city for Christianity, Islam, and Judaism. Sacred buildings include the Islamic monument called Dome of the Rock.

Population: 3,629,795,000
No. of countries: 44

## Siberia

This vast region — mostly in Asian Russia — is bitterly cold in winter. To the north of Siberia lies the tundra, where part of the soil has been frozen since the end of the Ice Age.

*Mongolian family in traditional dress*

## Mongolia

Mongolia is a remote, sparsely populated country whose rulers once dominated China, central Asia, and eastern Europe. Genghis Khan was a famous Mongol leader.

## Tokyo

Japan has huge economic power, with investments in land and property around the world. Many of its major banks and businesses are found in Tokyo. This busy city is hemmed in by mountains and built around Tokyo Bay.

## Fact File

| | |
|---|---|
| LARGEST COUNTRY | (Asian) Russia |
| SMALLEST COUNTRY | Maldives |
| LARGEST CITY | Tokyo |
| LARGEST LAKE | Caspian Sea |
| LONGEST RIVER | Yangtze (Chang) |

## Extreme Climates

| | |
|---|---|
| HOTTEST PLACE | Tirat Zevi \\,tē-rät-'zevē\\, Israel |
| DRIEST PLACE | Aden \\'äd-ən\\, Yemen |
| COLDEST PLACE | Verkhoyansk \\,vyer-kə-'yänsk\\, Russia |
| WETTEST PLACE | Cherrapunji \\,cher-ə-'pu̇n-jē\\, India |

## Himalayas

Forming a natural border between Tibet and India, the peaks of the Himalayas are permanently snow-capped. Himalaya is thought to mean "home of the snows" in the ancient language called Sanskrit.

*Monument is built in white marble*

## India

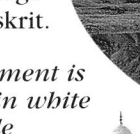

The world's second most populous country, India is a land of contrasts. While many people live in villages and farm small plots of land, India also has huge cities where office blocks stand next to ancient temples and monuments. The most famous monument is the Taj Mahal in northern India, built in the 17th century by an emperor as a tomb for his wife.

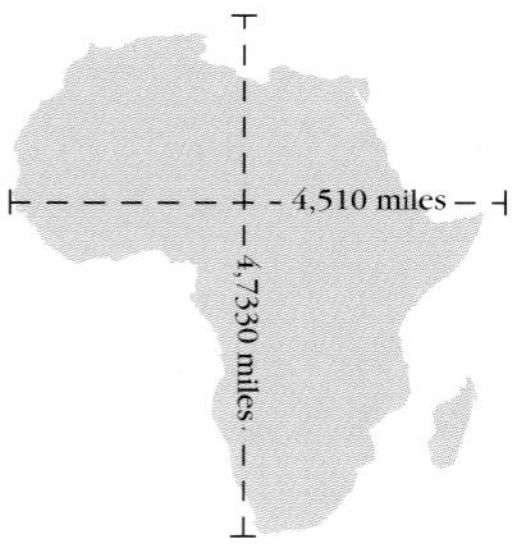


Extent of African lands

# Africa

RAIN FORESTS AND ARID DESERTS dominate much of Africa, which is the world's second-largest continent. The landscapes of northern and southern Africa are hot and dry, with vast deserts stretching over raised platforms of rock. In these deserts — most famously the Sahara — the world's highest-ever temperatures have been recorded. By contrast, large tropical rain forests near to the Equator are home to a wide variety of animal and bird life. In East Africa, the landscape is made distinctive by steep-sided valleys, many of which contain enormous lakes.

Population: 765,722,915
No. of countries: 53

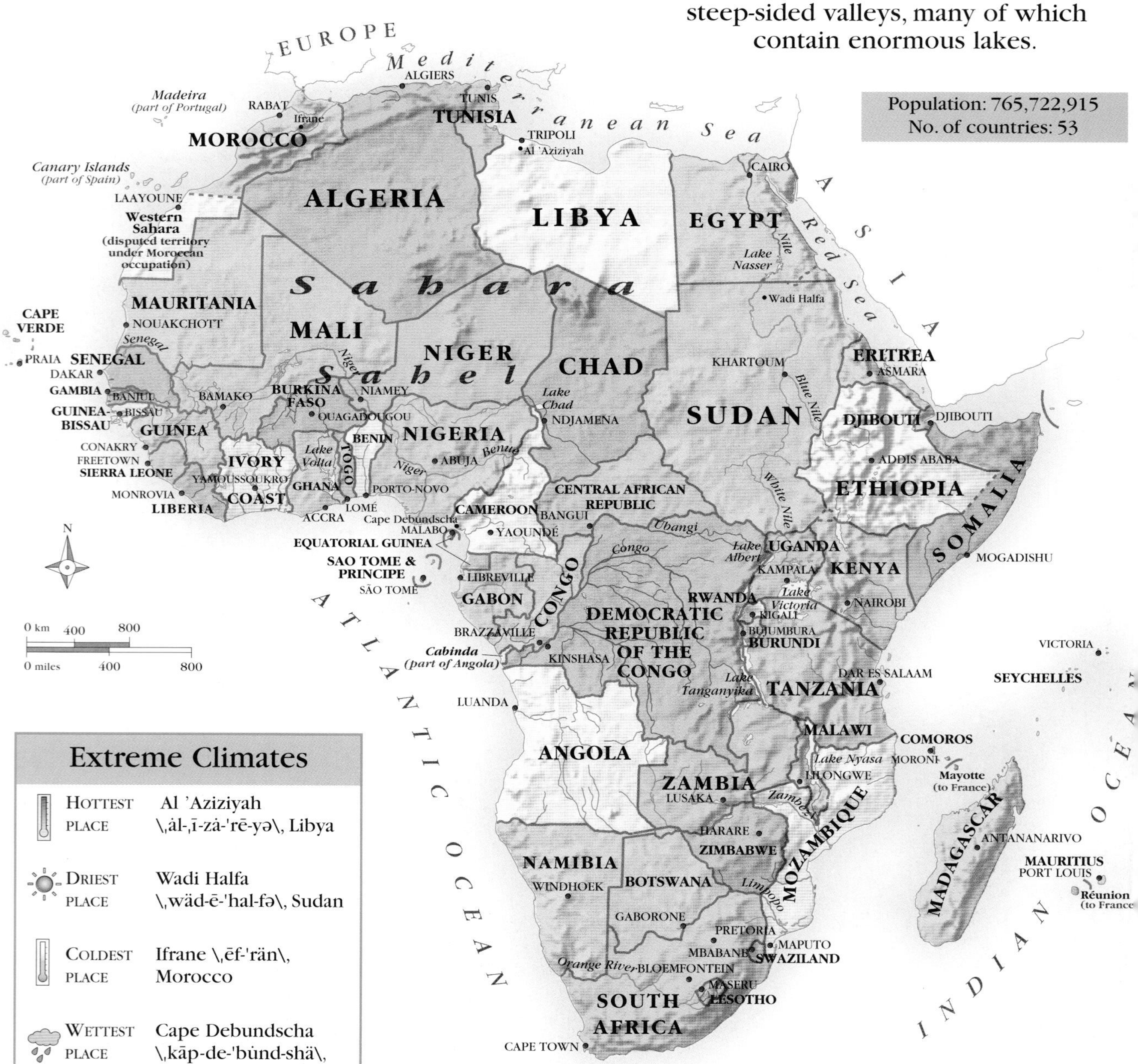


## Extreme Climates

| | | |
|---|---|---|
| HOTTEST PLACE | Al 'Aziziyah \\,al-,ī-zà-'rē-yə\\, Libya | |
| DRIEST PLACE | Wadi Halfa \\,wäd-ē-'hal-fə\\, Sudan | |
| COLDEST PLACE | Ifrane \\,ēf-'rän\\, Morocco | |
| WETTEST PLACE | Cape Debundscha \\,kāp-de-'bu̇nd-shä\\, Cameroon | |

## Mining

The mining industry is one of Africa's most important employers, and is crucial to many of its economies. The continent has large natural reserves of chromium, diamonds, gold, manganese, and platinum.

*Colors vary*

*Diamonds are mined from 125 miles below the earth's surface*

### Fact File

| | |
|---|---|
| Largest country | Sudan |
| Smallest country | Seychelles |
| Largest city | Cairo, Egypt |
| Largest lake | Lake Victoria |
| Longest river | Nile |

*Sphinx is 187 ft (57 m) long and 66 ft (23 m) high*

## Ancient Egypt

Africa is home to one of the world's most ancient civilizations in Egypt. Between 3,000 BC and 30 BC the Egyptians built the first large stone buildings and invented one of the earliest forms of writing. Today, tourists flock to Egypt to see ancient monuments such as the pyramids and the Sphinx.

## Equatorial Rainforest

Near the Equator, where rainfall is plentiful, dense tropical rainforests grow. Differing considerably from the hot desert land of the north, the hot and humid climate here allows large areas of vegetation to flourish.

## Sahara

The largest of Africa's deserts is the Sahara, which covers most of the northern part of the continent. One quarter of this desert land is sandy dunes, while the rest is made up of bare, rocky plains. The northern coast has a hot, dry climate, while further inland the Sahara is swept by strong winds.

*Staff shows elder status*

*Type of bead necklace shows the wearer's age*

## Nomadic Farmers

The quality of Africa's land is dependent on the amount of rainfall a particular area receives, and this has a great impact on the type of farming that takes place there. At the southern edge of the Sahara cultivation and nomadic herding are widely practiced. People from the Masai tribe, shown here, are nomads, moving from place to place in search of fresh grass for their cattle.

# Australasia and Oceania

AUSTRALIA, NEW ZEALAND, and thousands of small islands in the South Pacific Ocean are collectively termed Australasia and Oceania. Australia is the smallest continent, with a mainly flat landscape ranging from desert in the center of the continent to rain forest along the north coast. New Zealand is made up of two large, mountainous islands, while the thousands of tiny islands in the South Pacific are spread across a vast area.

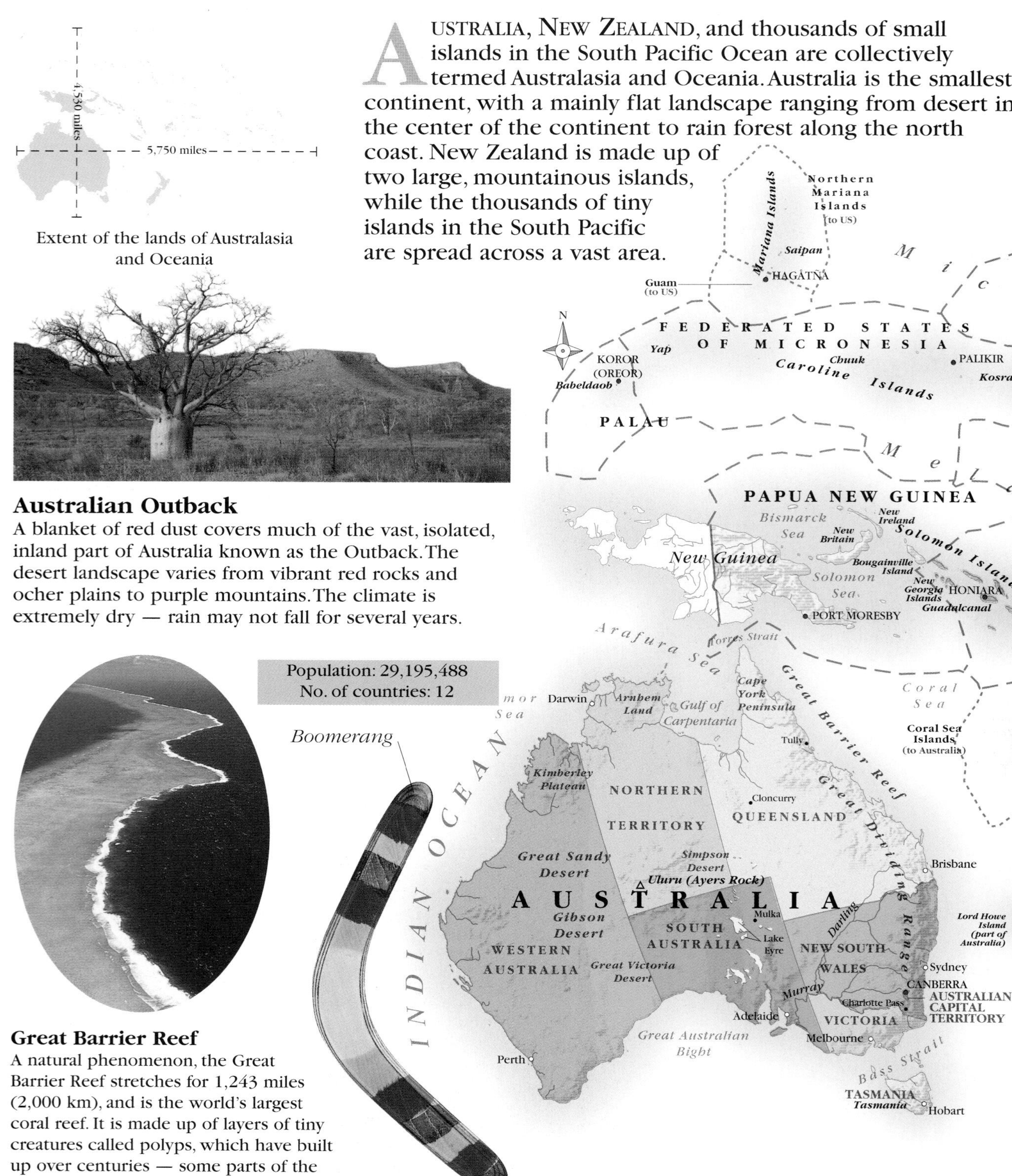


Extent of the lands of Australasia and Oceania

## Australian Outback

A blanket of red dust covers much of the vast, isolated, inland part of Australia known as the Outback. The desert landscape varies from vibrant red rocks and ocher plains to purple mountains. The climate is extremely dry — rain may not fall for several years.

## Great Barrier Reef

A natural phenomenon, the Great Barrier Reef stretches for 1,243 miles (2,000 km), and is the world's largest coral reef. It is made up of layers of tiny creatures called polyps, which have built up over centuries — some parts of the reef date back to 25 million years ago.

## Cook Islands

There are chains of islands along the northern and western edges of the Pacific Ocean. Among these, the Cook Islands are made up of 15 coral and volcanic islands. Citrus fruit and copra production have developed alongside tourism.

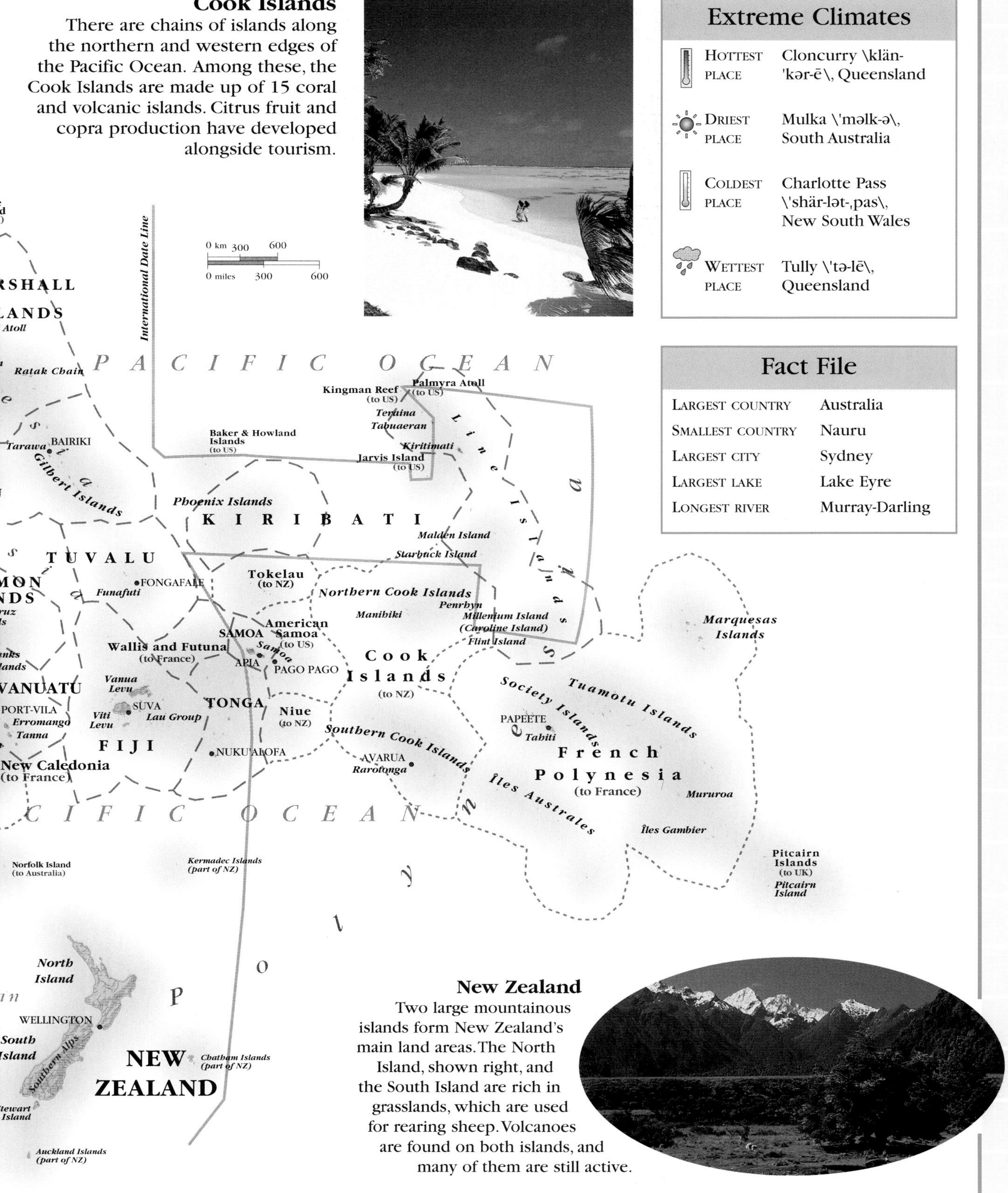


## Extreme Climates

| | |
|---|---|
| HOTTEST PLACE | Cloncurry \klän-'kər-ē\, Queensland |
| DRIEST PLACE | Mulka \'məlk-ə\, South Australia |
| COLDEST PLACE | Charlotte Pass \'shär-lət-,pas\, New South Wales |
| WETTEST PLACE | Tully \'tə-lē\, Queensland |

## Fact File

| | |
|---|---|
| LARGEST COUNTRY | Australia |
| SMALLEST COUNTRY | Nauru |
| LARGEST CITY | Sydney |
| LARGEST LAKE | Lake Eyre |
| LONGEST RIVER | Murray-Darling |

## New Zealand

Two large mountainous islands form New Zealand's main land areas. The North Island, shown right, and the South Island are rich in grasslands, which are used for rearing sheep. Volcanoes are found on both islands, and many of them are still active.

# Flags of the World

THE MAIN COUNTRIES and territories of the world have their own national flags, with a design relevant to that country. For example, a cross symbol indicates a Christian country, and the stars on the American flag represent the number of its member states.

Afghanistan
Asia

Albania
Europe

Algeria
Africa

Andorra
Europe

Angola
Africa

Antigua & Barbuda
North America

Argentina
South America

Armenia
Asia

Australia
Australasia & Oceania

Austria
Europe

Azerbaijan
Asia

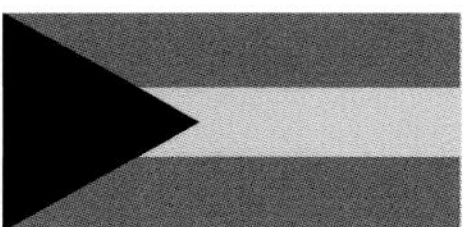
Bahamas
North America

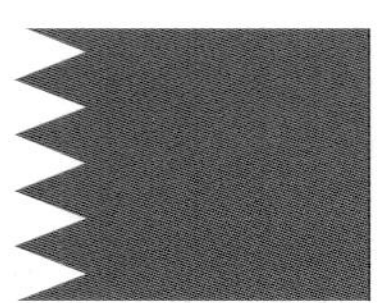
Bahrain
Asia

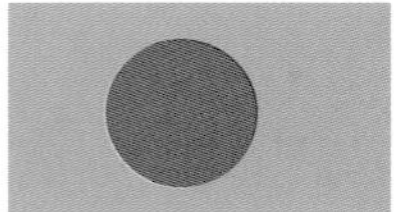
Bangladesh
Asia

Barbados
North America

Belarus
Europe

Belgium
Europe

Belize
North America

Benin
Africa

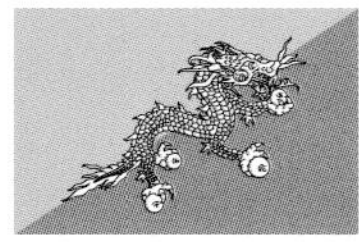
Bhutan
Asia

Bolivia
South America

Bosnia & Herzegovina
Europe

Botswana
Africa

Brazil
South America

Brunei
Asia

Bulgaria
Europe

Burkina Faso
Africa

Burundi
Africa

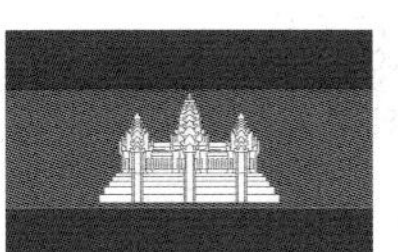

Cambodia
Asia

Cameroon
Africa

Canada
North America

Cape Verde
Africa

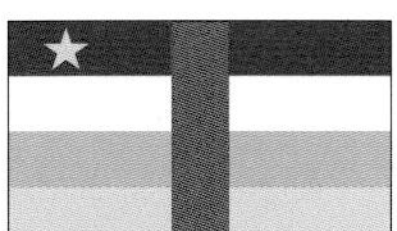

Central African Republic
Africa

Chad
Africa

Chile
South America

China
Asia

Colombia
South America

Comoros
Africa

Congo, Republic of the
Africa

Congo, Democratic Republic of the
Africa

Costa Rica
North America

Croatia
Europe

Cuba
North America

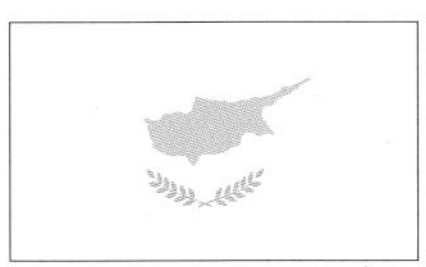

Cyprus
Europe

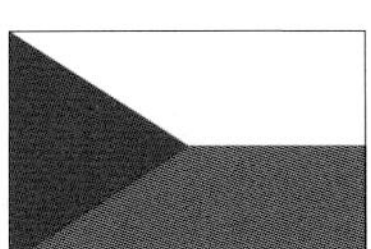

Czech Republic
Europe

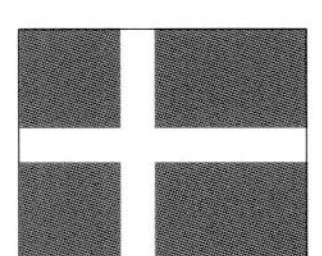

Denmark
Europe

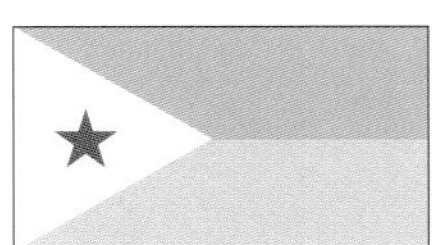

Djibouti
Africa

Dominica
North America

Dominican Republic
North America

East Timor
Asia

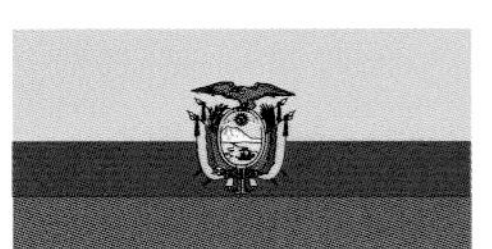

Ecuador
South America

Egypt
Africa

El Salvador
North America

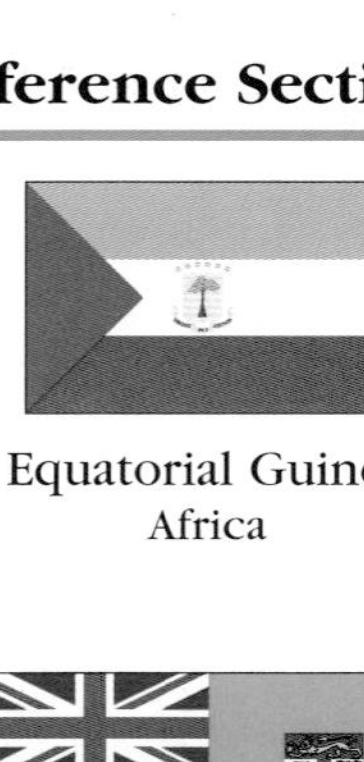

Equatorial Guinea
Africa

Eritrea
Africa

Estonia
Europe

Ethiopia
Africa

Fiji
Australasia & Oceania

Finland
Europe

France
Europe

Gabon
Africa

Gambia
Africa

Georgia
Asia

Germany
Europe

Ghana
Africa

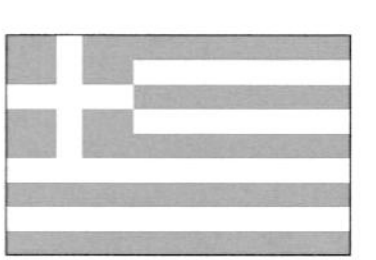

Greece
Europe

Grenada
North America

Guatemala
North America

Guinea
Africa

Guinea-Bissau
Africa

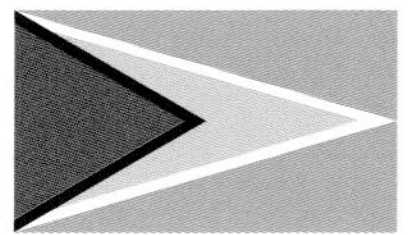

Guyana
South America

Haiti
North America

Honduras
North America

Hungary
Europe

Iceland
Europe

India
Asia

Indonesia
Asia

Iran
Asia

Iraq
Asia

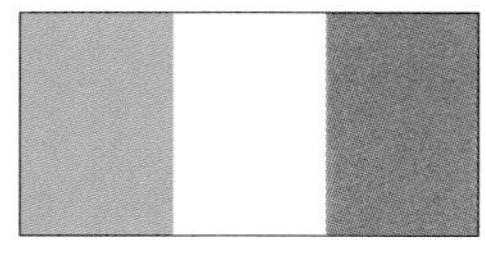

Ireland
Europe

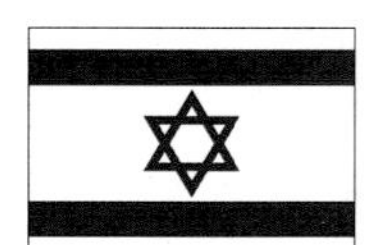

Israel
Asia

Italy
Europe

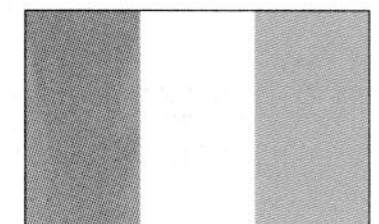
Ivory Coast
Africa

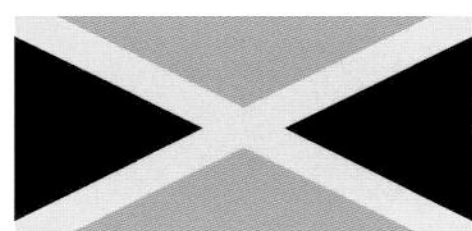
Jamaica
North America

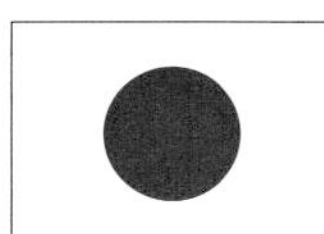
Japan
Asia

Jordan
Asia

Kazakhstan
Asia

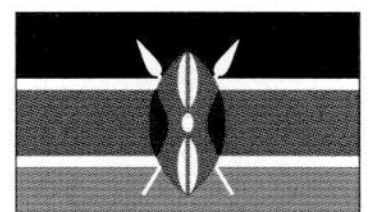
Kenya
Africa

Kiribati
Australasia & Oceania

Kuwait
Asia

Kyrgyzstan
Asia

Laos
Asia

Latvia
Europe

Lebanon
Asia

Lesotho
Africa

Liberia
Africa

Libya
Africa

Liechtenstein
Europe

Lithuania
Europe

Luxembourg
Europe

Macedonia
Europe

Madagascar
Asia

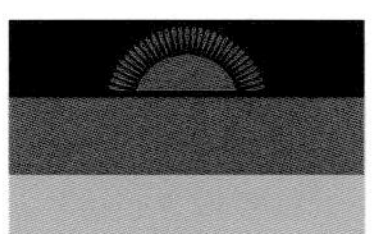
Malawi
Africa

Malaysia
Asia

Maldives
Asia

Mali
Africa

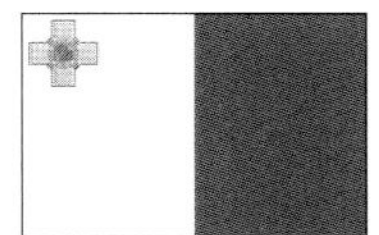
Malta
Europe

Marshall Islands
Australasia & Oceania

Mauritania
Africa

Mauritius
Asia

Mexico
North America

Micronesia
Australasia & Oceania

Moldova
Europe

Monaco
Europe

Mongolia
Asia

Morocco
Africa

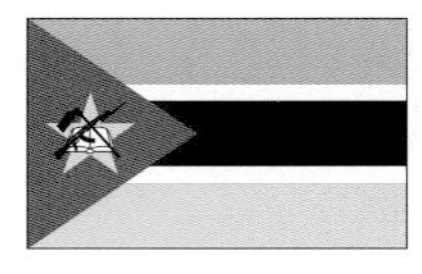

Mozambique
Africa

Myanmar (Burma)
Asia

Namibia
Africa

Nauru
Australasia & Oceania

Nepal
Asia

Netherlands
Europe

New Zealand
Australasia & Oceania

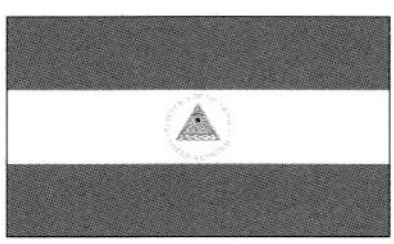

Nicaragua
North America

Niger
Africa

Nigeria
Africa

North Korea
Asia

Norway
Europe

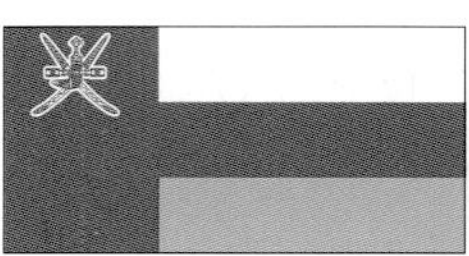

Oman
Asia

Pakistan
Asia

Palau
Australasia & Oceania

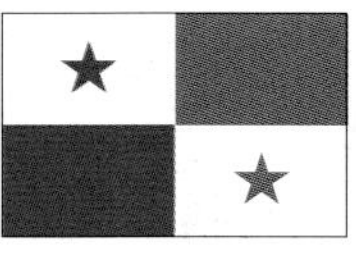

Panama
North America

Papua New Guinea
Australasia & Oceania

Paraguay
South America

Peru
South America

Philippines
Asia

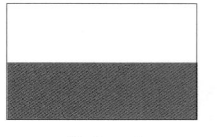

Poland
Europe

Portugal
Europe

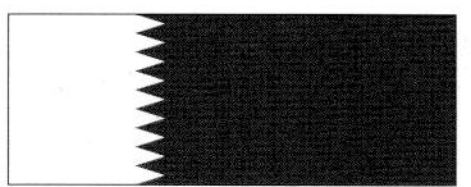
Qatar
Asia

Romania
Europe

Russian Federation
Europe and Asia

Rwanda
Africa

St. Kitts-Nevis
North America

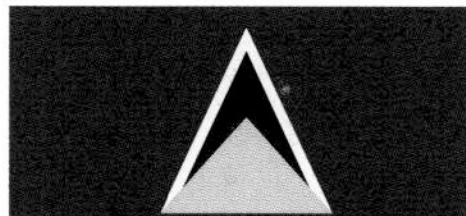
St. Lucia
North America

St. Vincent & the Grenadines
North America

Samoa
Australasia & Oceania

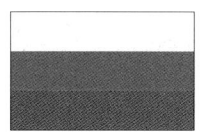
San Marino
Europe

São Tomé & Principe
Africa

Saudi Arabia
Asia

Senegal
Africa

Serbia & Montenegro
Europe

Seychelles
Asia

Sierra Leone
Africa

Singapore
Asia

Slovakia
Europe

Slovenia
Europe

Solomon Islands
Australasia & Oceania

Somalia
Africa

South Africa
Africa

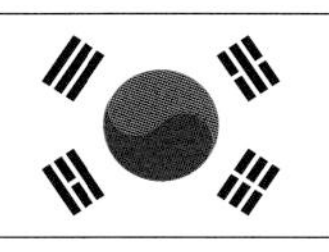
South Korea
Asia

Spain
Europe

Sri Lanka
Asia

Sudan
Africa

Suriname
South America

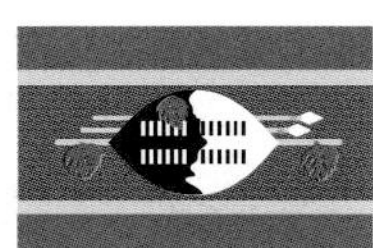
Swaziland
Africa

Sweden
Europe

Switzerland
Europe

Syria
Asia

Tajikistan
Asia

Tanzania
Africa

Thailand
Asia

Togo
Africa

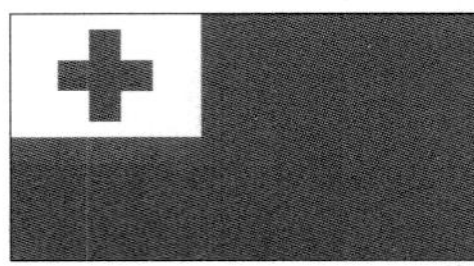
Tonga
Australasia & Oceania

Trinidad & Tobago
North America

Tunisia
Africa

Turkey
Asia and Europe

Turkmenistan
Asia

Tuvalu
Australasia & Oceania

Uganda
Africa

Ukraine
Europe

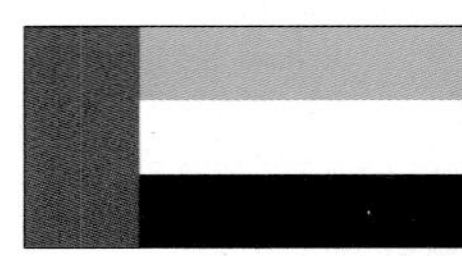
United Arab Emirates
Asia

United Kingdom
Europe

United States of America
North America

Uruguay
South America

Uzbekistan
Asia

Vanuatu
Australasia & Oceania

Vatican City
Europe

Venezuela
South America

Vietnam
Asia

Yemen
Asia

Zambia
Africa

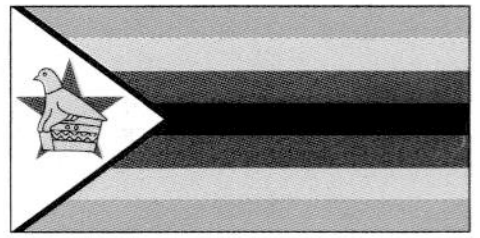
Zimbabwe
Africa

# State Flags

Alabama

Alaska

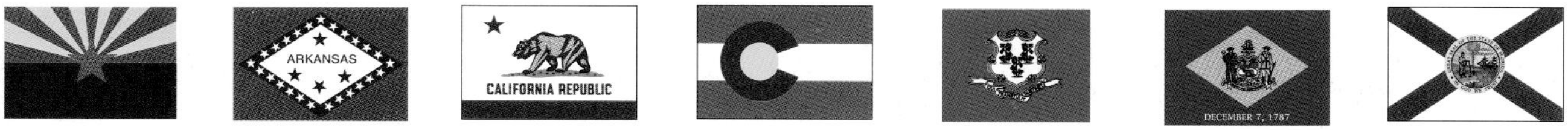

Arizona

Arkansas

California

Colorado

Connecticut

Delaware

Florida

Georgia

Hawaii

Idaho

Illinois

Indiana

Iowa

Kansas

Kentucky

Louisiana

Maine

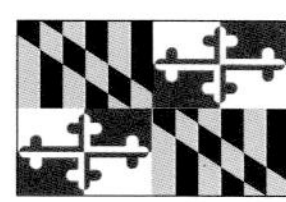
Maryland

Massachusetts

Michigan

Minnesota

Mississippi

Missouri

Montana

Nebraska

Nevada

New Hampshire

New Jersey

New Mexico

New York

North Carolina

North Dakota

Ohio

Oklahoma

Oregon

Pennsylvania

Rhode Island

South Carolina

South Dakota

Tennessee

Texas

Utah

Vermont

Virginia

Washington

West Virginia

Wisconsin

Wyoming

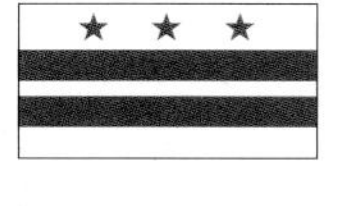
District of Columbia

# States of the USA

THE UNITED STATES OF AMERICA is made up of 50 states, including Alaska in the far north and Hawaii in the Pacific Ocean. The original 13 states on the East Coast were governed by Britain until independence in 1776. Today, each state has its own laws, but is ruled by the national government in Washington, DC.

## States of the USA

| State | Capital | Date of entry into Union |
|---|---|---|
| Alabama \\,al-ə-'bam-ə\\ | Montgomery \\mənt-'gəm-ə-rē, mänt-\\ | 1819 |
| Alaska \\ə-'las-kə\\ | Juneau \\'jü-nō, jü-'nō\\ | 1959 |
| Arizona \\,ar-ə-'zō-nə\\ | Phoenix \\'fē-niks\\ | 1912 |
| Arkansas \\'är-kən-,sȯ\\ | Little Rock \\'lit-l-,räk\\ | 1836 |
| California \\,kal-ə-'fȯr-nyə\\ | Sacramento \\,sak-rə-'ment-ō\\ | 1850 |
| Colorado \\,käl-ə-'rad-ō, -'räd-\\ | Denver \\'den-vər\\ | 1876 |
| Connecticut \\kə-'net-i-kət\\ | Hartford \\'härt-fərd\\ | 1788 |
| Delaware \\'del-ə-,waər, -,weər\\ | Dover \\'dō-vər\\ | 1787 |
| Florida \\'flȯr-əd-ə\\ | Tallahassee \\,tal-ə-'has-ē\\ | 1845 |
| Georgia \\'jȯr-jə\\ | Atlanta \\ət-'lant-ə, at-\\ | 1788 |
| Hawaii \\hə-'wä-ē, -'wȯ-ē\\ | Honolulu \\,hän-l-'ü-,lü, ,hōn-\\ | 1959 |
| Idaho \\'īd-ə-,hō\\ | Boise \\'bȯi-sē, -zē\\ | 1890 |
| Illinois \\,il-ə-'nȯi\\ | Springfield \\'spring-,fēld\\ | 1818 |
| Indiana \\,in-dē-'an-ə\\ | Indianapolis \\,in-dē-ə-'nap-ə-ləs\\ | 1816 |
| Iowa \\'ī-ə-wə\\ | Des Moines \\di-'mȯin\\ | 1846 |
| Kansas \\'kan-zəs\\ | Topeka \\tə-'pē-kə\\ | 1861 |
| Kentucky \\kən-'tək-ē\\ | Frankfort \\'frangk-fərt\\ | 1792 |
| Louisiana \\lu̇-,ē-zē-'an-ə, ,lü-ə-zē-\\ | Baton Rouge \\,bat-n-'rüzh\\ | 1812 |
| Maine \\'mān\\ | Augusta \\ȯ-'gəs-tə, ə-\\ | 1820 |
| Maryland \\'mer-ə-lənd\\ | Annapolis \\ə-'nap-ə-ləs\\ | 1788 |
| Massachusetts \\,mas-ə-'chü-səts, -zəts\\ | Boston \\'bȯ-stən\\ | 1788 |
| Michigan \\'mish-i-gən\\ | Lansing \\'lan-sing\\ | 1837 |
| Minnesota \\,min-ə-'sōt-ə\\ | Saint Paul \\sānt-'pȯl, sənt-\\ | 1858 |
| Mississippi \\,mis-ə-'sip-ē\\ | Jackson \\'jak-sən\\ | 1817 |
| Missouri \\mə-'zu̇r-ē, -'zu̇r-ə\\ | Jefferson City \\,jef-ər-sən-\\ | 1821 |
| Montana \\män-'tan-ə\\ | Helena \\'hel-ə-nə\\ | 1889 |
| Nebraska \\nə-'bras-kə\\ | Lincoln \\'ling-kən\\ | 1867 |
| Nevada \\nə-'vad-ə, -'väd-\\ | Carson City \\,kärs-n-\\ | 1864 |
| New Hampshire \\-'hamp-shər, -,shir\\ | Concord \\'käng-kərd\\ | 1788 |
| New Jersey \\-'jər-zē\\ | Trenton \\'trent-n\\ | 1787 |
| New Mexico \\-'mek-si-,kō\\ | Santa Fe \\,sant-ə-'fā\\ | 1912 |
| New York \\-'yȯrk\\ | Albany \\'ȯl-bə-nē\\ | 1788 |
| North Carolina \\-,kar-ə-'lī-nə\\ | Raleigh \\'rȯ-lē, 'räl-ē\\ | 1789 |
| North Dakota \\-də-'kōt-ə\\ | Bismarck \\'biz-,märk\\ | 1889 |
| Ohio \\ō-'hī-ō\\ | Columbus \\kə-'ləm-bəs\\ | 1803 |
| Oklahoma \\ō-klə-'hō-mə\\ | Oklahoma City | 1907 |
| Oregon \\'ȯr-i-gən, 'är-\\ | Salem \\'sā-ləm\\ | 1859 |

*Glacier in Alaska*

*Arizona desert*

*Volcano in Hawaii*

## States of the USA

| State | Capital | Date of entry into Union |
|---|---|---|
| Pennsylvania \ˌpen-səl-'vān-yə\ | Harrisburg \'har-əs-ˌbərg\ | 1787 |
| Rhode Island \rō-'dī-lənd\ | Providence \'präv-ə-dəns, -ˌdens\ | 1790 |
| South Carolina \-ˌkar-ə-'lī-nə\ | Columbia \kə-'ləm-bē-ə\ | 1788 |
| South Dakota \-də-'kōt-ə\ | Pierre \'piər\ | 1889 |
| Tennessee \ˌten-ə-'sē\ | Nashville \'nash-ˌvil, -vəl\ | 1796 |
| Texas \'tek-səs, -siz\ | Austin \'ȯ-stən\ | 1845 |
| Utah \'yü-ˌtȯ, -ˌtä\ | Salt Lake City | 1896 |
| Vermont \vər-'mänt\ | Montpelier \mänt-'pēl-yər, -'pil-\ | 1791 |
| Virginia \vər-'jin-yə\ | Richmond \'rich-mənd\ | 1788 |
| Washington \'wȯsh-ing-tən, 'wäsh-\ | Olympia \ə-'lim-pē-ə\ | 1889 |
| West Virginia \-vər-'jin-yə\ | Charleston \'chärl-stən\ | 1863 |
| Wisconsin \wis-'kän-sən\ | Madison \'mad-ə-sən\ | 1848 |
| Wyoming \wī-'ō-ming\ | Cheyenne \shī-'an, -'en\ | 1890 |

*Farmland in Pennsylvania*

*Fall in New Hampshire*

*Cattle drive in Texas*

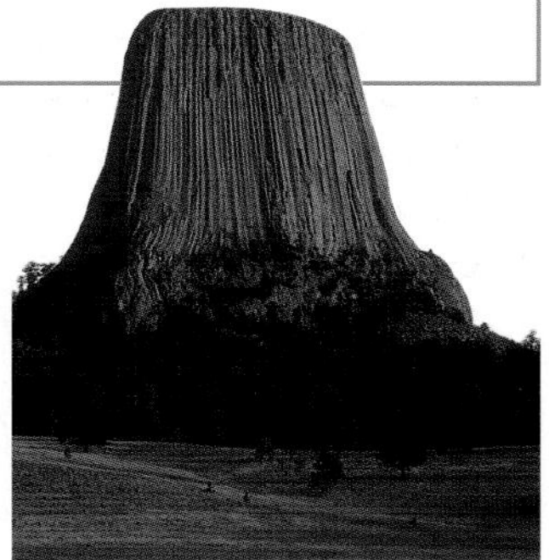
*Devil's Tower, Wyoming*

## Provinces and territories of Canada

Canada is the second-largest country in the world, occupying two-fifths of the North American continent. Divided into 10 provinces and two territories, Canada borders Alaska and the Pacific Ocean to the west, and the Atlantic Ocean to the east. Most of the population lives near the US border, around the Great Lakes.

| Province or Territory | Capital |
|---|---|
| Alberta \al-'bərt-ə\ | Edmonton \'ed-mən-tən\ |
| British Columbia \-kə-'ləm-bē-ə\ | Victoria \vik-'tōr-ē-ə\ |
| Manitoba \ˌman-ə-'tō-bə\ | Winnipeg \'win-ə-ˌpeg\ |
| New Brunswick \-'brenz-wik\ | Fredericton \'fred-rik-tən\ |
| Newfoundland and Labrador \'nü-fənd-lənd-ənd-'lab-rə-ˌdȯr, 'nyü-, -ˌland\ | Saint John's \sānt-'jänz, sənt-\ |
| Northwest Territories | Yellowknife \'yel-ə-ˌnīf\ |
| Nova Scotia \ˌnō-və-'skō-shə\ | Halifax \'hal-ə-ˌfaks\ |
| Nunavut \'nu̇n-ə-vət\ | Iqaluit \i-'kal-ü-it\ |
| Ontario \än-'ter-ē-ō, -'tar-\ | Toronto \tə-'ränt-ō\ |
| Prince Edward Island \-ˌed-wərd-\ | Charlottetown \'shär-lət-ˌtau̇n\ |
| Quebec \kwi-'bek, ki-\ | Quebec |
| Saskatchewan \se-'skach-ə-wən, -ˌwän\ | Regina \ri-'jī-nə\ |
| Yukon Territory \'yü-ˌkän-\ | Whitehorse \'hwīt-ˌhȯrs, 'wīt-\ |

*Harbor in Quebec*

# Presidents of the USA

## Presidents of the USA

| Number | Name and Pronunciation of Surname | Life Dates | Birthplace | Term |
|---|---|---|---|---|
| 1 | George Washington \'wȯsh-ing-tən, 'wäsh-\ | 1732–1799 | Virginia | 1789–1797 |
| 2 | John Adams \'ad-əmz\ | 1735–1826 | Massachusetts | 1797–1801 |
| 3 | Thomas Jefferson \'jef-ər-sən\ | 1743–1826 | Virginia | 1801–1809 |
| 4 | James Madison \'mad-ə-sən\ | 1751–1836 | Virginia | 1809–1817 |
| 5 | James Monroe \mən-'rō\ | 1758–1831 | Virginia | 1817–1825 |
| 6 | John Quincy Adams \'ad-əmz\ | 1767–1848 | Massachusetts | 1825–1829 |
| 7 | Andrew Jackson \'jak-sən\ | 1767–1845 | South Carolina | 1829–1837 |
| 8 | Martin Van Buren \van-'byu̇r-ən\ | 1782–1862 | New York | 1837–1841 |
| 9 | William Henry Harrison \'har-ə-sən\ | 1773–1841 | Virginia | 1841 |
| 10 | John Tyler \'tī-lər\ | 1790–1862 | Virginia | 1841–1845 |
| 11 | James Knox Polk \'pōk\ | 1795–1849 | North Carolina | 1845–1849 |
| 12 | Zachary Taylor \'tā-lər\ | 1784–1850 | Virginia | 1849–1850 |
| 13 | Millard Fillmore \'fil-,mōr\ | 1800–1874 | New York | 1850–1853 |
| 14 | Franklin Pierce \'pirs\ | 1804–1869 | New Hampshire | 1853–1857 |
| 15 | James Buchanan \byü-'kan-ən\ | 1791–1868 | Pennsylvania | 1857–1861 |
| 16 | Abraham Lincoln \'ling-kən\ | 1809–1865 | Kentucky | 1861–1865 |
| 17 | Andrew Johnson \'jän-sən\ | 1808–1875 | North Carolina | 1865–1869 |
| 18 | Ulysses Simpson Grant \'grant\ | 1822–1885 | Ohio | 1869–1877 |
| 19 | Rutherford Birchard Hayes \'hāz\ | 1822–1893 | Ohio | 1877–1881 |
| 20 | James Abram Garfield \'gär-,fēld\ | 1831–1881 | Ohio | 1881 |
| 21 | Chester Alan Arthur \'är-thər\ | 1829–1886 | Vermont | 1881–1885 |
| 22 | Grover Cleveland \'klēv-lənd\ | 1837–1908 | New Jersey | 1885–1889 |
| 23 | Benjamin Harrison \'har-ə-sən\ | 1833–1901 | Ohio | 1889–1893 |
| 24 | Grover Cleveland \'klēv-lənd\ | 1837–1908 | New Jersey | 1893–1897 |
| 25 | William McKinley \mə-'kin-lē\ | 1843–1901 | Ohio | 1897–1901 |
| 26 | Theodore Roosevelt \'rō-zə-,velt\ | 1858–1919 | New York | 1901–1909 |
| 27 | William Howard Taft \'taft\ | 1857–1930 | Ohio | 1909–1913 |
| 28 | Woodrow Wilson \'wil-sən\ | 1856–1924 | Virginia | 1913–1921 |
| 29 | William Gamaliel Harding \'härd-ing\ | 1865–1923 | Ohio | 1921–1923 |
| 30 | Calvin Coolidge \'kü-lij\ | 1872–1933 | Vermont | 1923–1929 |
| 31 | Herbert Clark Hoover \'hü-vər\ | 1874–1964 | Iowa | 1929–1933 |
| 32 | Franklin Delano Roosevelt \'rō-zə-,velt\ | 1882–1945 | New York | 1933–1945 |
| 33 | Harry S. Truman \'trü-mən\ | 1884–1972 | Missouri | 1945–1953 |
| 34 | Dwight David Eisenhower \'īz-n-,hau̇-ər\ | 1890–1969 | Texas | 1953–1961 |
| 35 | John Fitzgerald Kennedy \'ken-ə-dē\ | 1917–1963 | Massachusetts | 1961–1963 |
| 36 | Lyndon Baines Johnson \'jän-sən\ | 1908–1973 | Texas | 1963–1969 |
| 37 | Richard Milhous Nixon \'nik-sən\ | 1913–1994 | California | 1969–1974 |
| 38 | Gerald Rudolph Ford \'fōrd\ | 1913– | Nebraska | 1974–1977 |
| 39 | Jimmy Carter \'kärt-ər\ | 1924– | Georgia | 1977–1981 |
| 40 | Ronald Wilson Reagan \'rā-gən\ | 1911– | Illinois | 1981–1989 |
| 41 | George Herbert Walker Bush \'bu̇sh\ | 1924– | Massachusetts | 1989–1993 |
| 42 | William Jefferson Clinton \'klin-tən\ | 1946– | Arkansas | 1993–2001 |
| 43 | George Walker Bush \'bu̇sh\ | 1946– | Connecticut | 2001– |

*George Washington*

*Theodore Roosevelt*

*Woodrow Wilson*

*William J. Clinton*

## Vice Presidents of the USA

| Number | Name and Pronunciation of Surname | Life Dates | Birthplace | Term |
|---|---|---|---|---|
| 1 | John Adams \'ad-əmz\ | 1735–1826 | Massachusetts | 1789–1797 |
| 2 | Thomas Jefferson \'jef-ər-sən\ | 1743–1826 | Virginia | 1797–1801 |
| 3 | Aaron Burr \'bər\ | 1756–1836 | New Jersey | 1801–1805 |
| 4 | George Clinton \'klint-n\ | 1739–1812 | New York | 1805–1812 |
| 5 | Elbridge Gerry \'ger-ē\ | 1744–1814 | Massachusetts | 1813–1814 |
| 6 | Daniel D. Tompkins \'tämp-kənz\ | 1774–1825 | New York | 1817–1825 |
| 7 | John C. Calhoun \kal-'hün\ | 1782–1850 | South Carolina | 1825–1832 |
| 8 | Martin Van Buren \van-'byu̇r-ən\ | 1782–1862 | New York | 1833–1837 |
| 9 | Richard M. Johnson \'jän-sən\ | 1780–1850 | Kentucky | 1837–1841 |
| 10 | John Tyler \'tī-lər\ | 1790–1862 | Virginia | 1841 |
| 11 | George M. Dallas \'dal-əs\ | 1792–1864 | Pennsylvania | 1845–1849 |
| 12 | Millard Fillmore \'fil-ˌmōr\ | 1800–1874 | New York | 1849–1850 |
| 13 | William R. King \'king\ | 1786–1853 | North Carolina | 1853 |
| 14 | John C. Breckinridge \'brek-ən-rij\ | 1821–1875 | Kentucky | 1857–1861 |
| 15 | Hannibal Hamlin \'ham-lən\ | 1809–1891 | Maine | 1861–1865 |
| 16 | Andrew Johnson \'jän-sən\ | 1808–1875 | North Carolina | 1865 |
| 17 | Schuyler Colfax \'kōl-ˌfaks\ | 1823–1885 | New York | 1869–1873 |
| 18 | Henry Wilson \'wil-sən\ | 1812–1875 | New Hampshire | 1873–1875 |
| 19 | William A. Wheeler \'hwē-lər-, 'wē\ | 1819–1887 | New York | 1877–1881 |
| 20 | Chester A. Arthur \'är-thər\ | 1830–1886 | Vermont | 1881 |
| 21 | Thomas A. Hendricks \'hen-driks\ | 1819–1885 | Ohio | 1885 |
| 22 | Levi P. Morton \'mȯrt-n\ | 1824–1920 | Vermont | 1889–1893 |
| 23 | Adlai E. Stevenson \'stē-vən-sən\ | 1835–1914 | Kentucky | 1893–1897 |
| 24 | Garret A. Hobart \'hō-ˌbärt\ | 1844–1899 | New Jersey | 1897–1899 |
| 25 | Theodore Roosevelt \'rō-zə-ˌvelt\ | 1858–1919 | New York | 1901 |
| 26 | Charles W. Fairbanks \'faər-ˌbangks, 'feər-\ | 1852–1918 | Ohio | 1905–1909 |
| 27 | James S. Sherman \'shər-mən\ | 1855–1912 | New York | 1909–1912 |
| 28 | Thomas R. Marshall \'mär-shəl\ | 1854–1925 | Indiana | 1913–1921 |
| 29 | Calvin Coolidge \'kü-lij\ | 1872–1933 | Vermont | 1921–1923 |
| 30 | Charles G. Dawes \'dȯz\ | 1865–1951 | Ohio | 1925–1929 |
| 31 | Charles Curtis \'kərt-əs\ | 1860–1936 | Kansas | 1929–1933 |
| 32 | John N. Garner \'gär-nər\ | 1868–1967 | Texas | 1933–1941 |
| 33 | Henry A. Wallace \'wäl-əs\ | 1888–1965 | Iowa | 1941–1945 |
| 34 | Harry S. Truman \'trü-mən\ | 1884–1972 | Missouri | 1945 |
| 35 | Alben W. Barkley \'bär-klē\ | 1877–1956 | Kentucky | 1949–1953 |
| 36 | Richard M. Nixon \'nik-sən\ | 1913–1994 | California | 1953–1961 |
| 37 | Lyndon B. Johnson \'jän-sən\ | 1908–1973 | Texas | 1961–1963 |
| 38 | Hubert H. Humphrey \'həm-frē\ | 1911–1978 | South Dakota | 1965–1969 |
| 39 | Spiro T. Agnew \'ag-nü, -nyü\ | 1918–1996 | Maryland | 1969–1973 |
| 40 | Gerald R. Ford \'fōrd\ | 1913– | Nebraska | 1973–1974 |
| 41 | Nelson A. Rockefeller \'räk-i-ˌfel-ər\ | 1908–1979 | Maine | 1974–1977 |
| 42 | Walter F. Mondale \'män-ˌdāl\ | 1928– | Minnesota | 1977–1981 |
| 43 | George H. W. Bush \'bu̇sh\ | 1924– | Massachusetts | 1981–1989 |
| 44 | James Danforth Quayle \'kwāl\ | 1947– | Indiana | 1989–1993 |
| 45 | Albert Gore, Jr. \'gōr\ | 1948– | Washington, DC | 1993–2001 |
| 46 | Richard B. Cheney \'chē-nē\ | 1941– | Nebraska | 2001– |

*John C. Calhoun*

*Hannibal Hamlin*

*Henry A. Wallace*

*James D. Quayle*

# Abbreviations

## Abbreviations

Most of these abbreviations are shown in one form only. Variation in use of periods, in kind of type, and in capitalization is frequent and widespread (as mph, MPH, m.p.h., Mph).

| | |
|---|---|
| **abbr** | abbreviation |
| **AD** | in the year of our Lord |
| **adj** | adjective |
| **adv** | adverb |
| **AK** | Alaska |
| **AL, Ala** | Alabama |
| **alt** | alternate, altitude |
| **a.m., A.M.** | before noon |
| **Am, Amer** | America, American |
| **amt** | amount |
| **anon** | anonymous |
| **ans** | answer |
| **Apr** | April |
| **AR** | Arkansas |
| **Ariz** | Arizona |
| **Ark** | Arkansas |
| **assn** | association |
| **asst** | assistant |
| **atty** | attorney |
| **Aug** | August |
| **ave** | avenue |
| **AZ** | Arizona |
| **Azerb** | Azerbaijan |
| **BC** | before Christ |
| **bet** | between |
| **bldg** | building |
| **blvd** | boulevard |
| **Br, Brit** | Britain, British |
| **bro** | brother |
| **bros** | brothers |
| **bu** | bushel |
| **c** | carat, cent, centimeter, century, chapter, cup |
| **C** | Celsius, centigrade |
| **CA, Cal, Calif** | California |
| **Can, Canad** | Canada, Canadian |
| **cap** | capital, capitalize, capitalized |
| **Capt** | captain |
| **ch** | chapter, church |
| **cm** | centimeter |
| **co** | company, county |
| **CO** | Colorado |
| **COD** | cash on delivery, collect on delivery |
| **col** | column |
| **Col** | colonel, Colorado |
| **Colo** | Colorado |
| **conj** | conjunction |
| **Conn** | Connecticut |
| **cpu** | central processing unit |
| **ct** | cent, court |
| **CT** | Connecticut |
| **cu** | cubic |
| **CZ** | Canal Zone |
| **d** | penny |
| **DC** | District of Columbia |
| **DDS** | doctor of dental surgery |
| **DE** | Delaware |
| **Dec** | December |
| **Del** | Delaware |
| **dept** | department |
| **DMD** | doctor of dental medicine |
| **doz** | dozen |
| **Dr** | doctor |
| **DST** | daylight saving time |
| **E** | east, eastern, excellent |
| **ea** | each |
| **e.g.** | for example |
| **Eng** | England, English |
| **esp** | especially |
| **etc** | et cetera |
| **f** | false, female, forte |
| **F** | Fahrenheit |
| **FBI** | Federal Bureau of Investigation |
| **Feb** | February |
| **fem** | feminine |
| **FL, Fla** | Florida |
| **fr** | father, from |
| **Fri** | Friday |
| **ft** | feet, foot, fort |
| **g** | gram |
| **G** | good |
| **Ga, GA** | Georgia |
| **gal** | gallon |
| **GB** | gigabyte |
| **gen** | general |
| **geog** | geographic, geographical, geography |
| **gm** | gram |
| **gov** | governor |
| **govt** | government |
| **gt** | great |
| **GU** | Guam |
| **HI** | Hawaii |
| **Herz.** | Herzegovina |
| **hr** | hour |
| **HS** | high school |
| **ht** | height |
| **Ia, IA** | Iowa |
| **ID** | Idaho |
| **i.e.** | that is |
| **IL, Ill** | Illinois |
| **in** | inch |
| **IN** | Indiana |
| **inc** | incorporated |
| **Ind** | Indian, Indiana |
| **interj** | interjection |
| **intrans** | intransitive |
| **Jan** | January |
| **jr, jun** | junior |
| **Kan, Kans** | Kansas |
| **KB** | kilobyte |
| **kg** | kilogram |
| **km** | kilometer |
| **KS** | Kansas |
| **Ky, KY** | Kentucky |
| **l** | left, liter |
| **La, LA** | Louisiana |
| **lb** | pound |
| **Lt** | lieutenant |
| **ltd** | limited |
| **m** | male, meter, mile |
| **MA** | Massachusetts |
| **Maj** | major |
| **Mar** | March |
| **masc** | masculine |
| **Mass** | Massachusetts |

**MB** megabyte
**Md** Maryland
**MD** doctor of medicine, Maryland
**Me, ME** Maine
**Mex** Mexican, Mexico
**mg** milligram
**MI, Mich** Michigan
**min** minute
**Minn** Minnesota
**Miss** Mississippi
**ml** milliliter
**mm** millimeter
**MN** Minnesota
**mo** month
**Mo, MO** Missouri
**Mon** Monday
**Mont** Montana
**mpg** miles per gallon
**mph** miles per hour
**MS** Mississippi
**mt** mount, mountain
**MT** Montana

**n** noun
**N** north, northern
**NC** North Carolina
**ND, N Dak** North Dakota
**NE** Nebraska, northeast
**Neb, Nebr** Nebraska
**Nev** Nevada
**NH** New Hampshire
**NJ** New Jersey
**NM, N Mex** New Mexico
**no** north, number
**Nov** November
**NV** Nevada
**NW** northwest
**NY** New York
**NZ** New Zealand

**O** Ohio
**obj** object, objective
**Oct** October
**off** office
**OH** Ohio
**OK, Okla** Oklahoma
**OR, Ore, Oreg** Oregon
**oz** ounce, ounces

**p** page
**Pa, PA** Pennsylvania
**part** participle
**pat** patent
**Penn, Penna** Pennsylvania
**pg** page
**pk** park, peck
**pkg** package
**pl** plural
**p.m., P.M.** afternoon
**PO** post office
**poss** possessive
**pp** pages
**pr** pair
**PR** Puerto Rico
**prep** preposition
**pres** present, president
**prof** professor
**pron** pronoun
**PS** postscript, public school
**pt** pint, point
**PTA** Parent-Teacher Association
**PTO** Parent-Teacher Organization

**qt** quart

**r** right
**rd** road, rod
**recd** received
**reg** region, regular
**res** residence
**Rev** reverend
**RFD** rural free delivery
**RI** Rhode Island
**rpm** revolutions per minute
**RR** railroad
**RSVP** please reply
**rt** right
**rte** route
**Russ Fed** Russian Federation

**S** south, southern
**Sat** Saturday
**SC** South Carolina
**sci** science
**Scot** Scotland, Scottish
**SD, S Dak** South Dakota
**SE** southeast
**sec** second
**Sept** September
**SI** International System of Units
**sing** singular
**so** south
**sq** square
**sr** senior
**Sr** sister
**SS** steamship
**st** state, street
**St** saint
**Sun** Sunday
**SW** southwest

**t** true
**tbs, tbsp** tablespoon
**TD** touchdown
**Tenn** Tennessee
**Tex** Texas
**Thurs, Thu** Thursday
**TN** Tennessee
**trans** transitive
**tsp** teaspoon
**Tues, Tue** Tuesday
**TX** Texas

**UK** United Kingdom
**UN** United Nations
**US** United States
**USA** United States of America
**USSR** Union of Soviet Socialist Republics
**usu** usual, usually
**UT** Utah

**v** verb
**Va, VA** Virginia
**var** variant
**vb** verb
**VG** very good
**vi** verb intransitive
**VI** Virgin Islands
**vol** volume
**VP** vice president
**vs** versus
**vt** verb transitive
**Vt, VT** Vermont

**W** west, western
**WA, Wash** Washington
**Wed** Wednesday
**WI, Wis, Wisc** Wisconsin
**wk** week
**wt** weight
**WV, W Va** West Virginia
**WWW** World Wide Web
**WY, Wyo** Wyoming

**yd** yard
**yr** year

# Pronunciation Guides

## Continents and Nations of the World

| Continent | Ocean |
|---|---|
| Africa \'af-ri-kə\ | Arctic \'ärk-tik, 'ärt-ik\ |
| Antarctica \ant-'ärk-ti-kə, -'är-ti-\ | Atlantic \ət-'lant-ik, at-\ |
| Asia \'ā-zhə, -shə\ | Indian \'in-dē-ən\ |
| Australia \ȯ-'strāl-yə\ | Pacific \pə-'sif-ik\ |
| Europe \'yu̇r-əp\ | |
| North America \-ə-'mer-ə-kə\ | |
| South America | |

## North America

| Nation | Capital |
|---|---|
| Antigua and Barbuda \an-'tē-gə-ənd-bär-'bü-də\ | Saint John's \sānt-'jänz, sənt-\ |
| Bahamas \bə-'häm-əz\ | Nassau \'nas-,ȯ\ |
| Barbados \bär-'bād-əs, -ōz\ | Bridgetown \'brij-,tau̇n\ |
| Belize \bə-'lēz\ | Belmopan \,bel-mō-'pän\ |
| Canada \'kan-ə-də\ | Ottawa \'ät-ə-,wä, -wə\ |
| Costa Rica \,käs-tə-'rē-kə, ,kȯs-\ | San Jose \,san-ə-'zā, -hō-'zā\ |
| Cuba \'kyü-bə\ | Havana \hə-'van-ə\ |
| Dominica \däm-ə-'nē-kə, də-'min-ə-kə\ | Roseau \rō-'zō\ |
| Dominican Republic \də-,min-i-kən-\ | Santo Domingo \,sant-ə-də-'ming-gō\ |
| El Salvador \el-'sal-və-,dor\ | San Salvador \san-'sal-və-,dȯr\ |
| Grenada \grə-'nād-ə\ | Saint George's \sānt-'jȯr-jəz, sənt-\ |
| Greenland \'grēn-lənd\ | Nuuk \'nük\ |
| Guatemala \,gwät-ə-'mäl-ə\ | Guatemala City |
| Haiti \'hāt-ē\ | Port-au-Prince \,pōrt-ō-'prins,-'prans\ |
| Honduras \hän-'du̇r-əs, -'dyu̇r-\ | Tegucigalpa \tə-,gü-sə-'gal-pə\ |
| Jamaica \jə-'mā-kə\ | Kingston \'king-stən\ |
| Mexico \'mek-si-,kō\ | Mexico City |
| Nicaragua \,nik-ə-'räg-wə\ | Managua \mə-'näg-wə\ |
| Panama \'pan-ə-,mä, -,mȯ\ | Panama City |
| Saint Kitts–Nevis \sānt-'kits-'nē-vəs, sənt-\ | Basseterre \bas-'ter, bäs-\ |
| Saint Lucia \sānt-'lü-shə, sənt-\ | Castries \'kas-,trēz, -,trēs\ |
| Saint Vincent and the Grenadines \sānt-'vin-sənt-ənd-th̲ə-,gren-ə-'dēnz, sənt-\ | Kingstown \'kingz-,tau̇n\ |
| Trinidad and Tobago \'trin-ə-,dad-n-tə-'bā-gō\ | Port of Spain \-'spān\ |
| United States of America \-ə-'mer-ə-kə\ | Washington \'wȯsh-ing-tən, 'wäsh-\ |

**Bay**
Hudson Bay \həd-sən-,bā\

**Islands**
Aleutian Islands \ə-'lü-shən-,ī-landz\
Anguilla \ang-'gwil-ə\
Aruba \ə-'rü-bə\
Baffin Island \'baf-ən-,ī-land\
British Virgin Islands \'brit-ish-,vər-jən-,ī-landz\
Cayman Islands \'kā-'man-,ī-landz\
Ellesmere Island \'elz-,mir-'ī-land\
Guadeloupe \'gwäd-l-,üp\
Martinique \,märt-n-'ēk\
Montserrat \,mänt-sə-'rat\
Navassa Island \nə-'va-sə-,ī-land\
Netherlands Antilles \'neth-ər-landz-an-'til-ēz\
Puerto Rico \,pōrt-ə-'rē-kō\
Queen Charlotte Islands \'kwēn-'shär-lət-,ī-landz\
St Pierre and Miquelon \'sānt-'pir-and-'mi-kə-,län\
Turks and Caicos Islands \,tərk-sən-'kā-kəs-,ī-landz\
Vancouver Island \van-'kü-vər-,ī-land\

**Lakes**
Great Bear Lake \'grāt-'baər-,lāk\
Great Slave Lake \'grāt-'slāv-,lāk\
Lake Huron \,lāk-'hyu̇r-ən\
Lake Michigan \,lāk-'mish-i-gən\
Lake Nicaragua \,lāk-,nik-ə-'räg-wə\
Lake Ontario \,lāk-än-'ter-ē-ō\
Lake Superior \,lāk-su̇-'pir-ē-ər\
Lake Winnipeg \'lāk-'win-ə-,peg\

**Rivers**
Mackenzie \mə-'ken-zē\
Rio Grande \,rē-ō-'grand\
St Lawrence \'sānt-'lȯr-ənts\

**Seas**
Beaufort \bō-fərt\
Bering Sea \'bir-ing-,sē\

**Strait**
Davis Strait \'dā-vəs-,strāt\

## South America

| Nation | Capital |
|---|---|
| Argentina \,är-jən-'tē-nə\ | Buenos Aires \,bwā-nə-,saər-ēz, -'seər-, -'sīr-\ |
| Bolivia \bə-'liv-ē-ə\ | La Paz \lə-'paz, -'päz\ |
| | Sucre \'sü-krā\ |
| Brazil \brə-'zil\ | Brasília \brə-'zil-yə\ |
| Chile \'chil-ē\ | Santiago \,sant-ē-'äg-ō, ,sänt-\ |
| Colombia \kə-'ləm-bē-ə\ | Bogotá \,bō-gə-'tȯ, -'tä\ |
| Ecuador \'ek-wə-,dȯr\ | Quito \'kē-tō\ |
| Guyana \gī-'an-ə\ | Georgetown \'jȯrj-,tau̇n\ |
| Paraguay \'par-ə-,gwī, -,gwā\ | Asunción \ə-,sün-sē-'ōn\ |
| Peru \pə-'rü\ | Lima \'lē-mə\ |
| Suriname \'su̇r-ə-,näm-ə\ | Paramaribo \,par-ə-'mar-ə-,bō\ |
| Uruguay \'yu̇r-ə-,gwī, -,gwā\ | Montevideo \,mänt-ə-və-'dā-ō, -'vid-ē-ō\ |
| Venezuela \,ven-ə-zə-'wā-lə\ | Caracas \kə-'rak-əs, -'räk-\ |

## Europe

(* indicates a member of the European Union)

| Nation | Capital |
|---|---|
| Albania \al-'bā-nē-ə\ | Tirane \ti-'rän-ə\ |
| Andorra \an-'dȯr-ə\ | Andorra la Vella \-lä-'vel-ə\ |
| Armenia \är-'mē-nē-ə\ | Yerevan \,yer-ə-'vän\ |
| *Austria \'ȯs-trē-ə\ | Vienna \vē-'en-ə\ |
| Azerbaijan \,az-ər-,bī-'jän\ | Baku \bä-'kü\ |
| Belarus \,bē-lə-'rüs, ,byel-ə-\ | Minsk \'minsk\ |
| *Belgium \'bel-jəm\ | Brussels \'brəs-əlz\ |
| Bosnia and Herzegovina \'bäz-nē-ə-ənd-,hert-sə-gō-'vē-nə, -'gō-vin-ə\ | Sarajevo \,sar-ə-'yā-vō\ |
| Bulgaria \,bəl-'gar-ē-ə, -'ger-\ | Sofia \'sō-fē-ə, 'sȯ-, sō-'-\ |
| Croatia \krō-'ā-shə\ | Zagreb \'zä-,greb\ |
| *Cyprus \'sī-prəs\ | Nicosia \,nik-ə-'sē-ə\ |
| *Czech Republic \'chek-\ | Prague \'präg\ |
| *Denmark \'den-,märk\ | Copenhagen \,kō-pən-'hā-gən, -'hä-\ |
| *Estonia \es-'tō-nē-ə\ | Tallinn \'tal-ən, 'täl-\ |
| *Finland \'fin-lənd\ | Helsinki \'hel-,sing-kē, ,hel-'\ |
| *France \'frans\ | Paris \'par-əs\ |
| Georgia, Republic of \-'jȯr-jə\ | Tbilisi \tə-'blē-sē\ |
| *Germany \'jər-mə-nē\ | Berlin \bər-'lin\ |
| *Greece \'grēs\ | Athens \'ath-ənz\ |
| *Hungary \'həng-gə-rē\ | Budapest \'büd-ə-,pest\ |
| Iceland \'īs-lənd, -,land\ | Reykjavik \'rā-kyə-,vik, -,vēk\ |
| *Ireland \'īr-lənd\ | Dublin \'dəb-lən\ |
| *Italy \'it-l-ē\ | Rome \'rōm\ |
| *Latvia \'lat-vē-ə\ | Riga \'rē-gə\ |
| Liechtenstein \'lik-tən-,stīn\ | Vaduz \vä-'düts\ |
| *Lithuania \,lith-ə-'wā-nē-ə\ | Vilnius \'vil-nē-əs\ |
| *Luxembourg \'lək-səm-,bərg\ | Luxembourg |
| Macedonia, Republic of \-,mas-ə-'dō-nē-ə\ | Skopje \'skȯp-,yā, -yə\ |
| *Malta \'mȯl-tə\ | Valletta \və-'let-ə\ |
| Moldova \mȯl-'dō-və\ | Chisinau \,kē-shē-'nau̇\ |
| Monaco \'män-ə-,kō\ | Monaco |
| *Netherlands \'neth̲-ər-ləndz\ | Amsterdam \'am-stər-,dam\ |
| | The Hague \th̲ə-'hāg\ |
| | Rotterdam \'rät-ər-,dam\ |
| Norway \'nȯr-,wā\ | Oslo \'äz-lō, 'äs-\ |
| *Poland \'pō-lənd\ | Warsaw \'wȯr-,sȯ\ |
| *Portugal \'pȯr-chi-gəl\ | Lisbon \'liz-bən\ |
| Romania \ru̇-'mā-nē-ə, rō-\ | Bucharest \'bü-kə-,rest\ |
| Russia \'rəsh-ə\ | Moscow \'mäs-,kō, -,kau̇\ |
| San Marino \,san-mə-'rē-nō\ | San Marino |
| Serbia and Montenegro \'sər-bē-ə-ənd-,män-tə-'nē-grō\ | Belgrade \'bel-,grād, -,gräd\ |
| *Slovakia \slō-'väk-ē-ə\ | Bratislava \,brät-ə-'släv-ə\ |
| *Slovenia \slō-'vē-nē-ə\ | Ljubljana \lē-,ü-blē-'än-ə\ |
| *Spain \'spān\ | Madrid \mə-'drid\ |
| *Sweden \'swēd-n\ | Stockholm \'stäk-,hōm, -,hōlm\ |

\ə\ abut \ər\ further \a\ mat \ā\ take \ä\ cot, cart \au̇\ out \ch\ chin \e\ pet \ē\ easy \g\ go \i\ tip \ī\ life \j\ job

Switzerland \'swit-sər-lənd\
Ukraine \yü-'krān, 'yü-,\
*United Kingdom
Vatican City \'vat-i-kən-\

**Islands**
Aland \'ō-,län\
Balearic Islands \,ba-lē-'ar-ik-'ī-ləndz\
Channel Islands \'chan-l-,ī-ləndz\
Corsica \'kȯr-si-kə\
Crete \'krēt\
Faeroe Islands \'faər-ō-,ī-ləndz\
Gotland \'gȯt-,länt\
Ibiza \ā-'vis-sä\
Ionian Islands \ī-'ō-ne-ən\
Isle of Man \'īl-əv-'man\
Majorca \mə-'jȯr-kə\
Minorca \mə-'nȯr-kə\
Orkney Islands \'ȯrk-nē-,ī-ləndz\
Outer Hebrides \'aůt-ər-'heb-rə-,dēz\
Sardinia \sär-'din-ē-ə\
Shetland Islands \'shet-lənd-,ī-ləndz\
Sicily \'sis-ə-lē\

**Lakes**
Ladoga \'là-də-gə\
Onega \,ə-'nye-gə\
Vanern \'va-nərn\

Bern \'bərn, 'bern\
Kiev \'kē-,ef, -,ev\
London \'lən-dən\

**Rivers**
Danube \'dan-yüb\
Dnieper \'nē-pər\
Dniester \'nēs-tər\
Elbe \'el-bə\
Ebro \'ā-,brō\
Loire \lə-'wär\
Northern Dvina \'nȯr-thərn-dvē-'nä\
Rhone \'rōn\
Seine \'sān\
Volga \'väl-gə\

**Seas**
Azov \ə-'zȯf\
Baltic \'bȯl-tik\
Barents \'bar-ənts\
Ionian \ī-'ō-ne-ən\
Norwegian \nȯr-'wē-jən\
Tyrrhenian \tə-'rē-nē-ən\

**Other names that appear on the map of Europe:**
Basque Country \'bäsk-,kən-trē\
Bay of Biscay \'bā-əv-'bis-,kā\
Caucasus \'kȯ-kə-səs\
Ceuta \'thā-ü-tä\
Gibraltar \jə-'brȯl-tər\
Gulf of Bothnia \'gəlf-əv-'bäth-nē-ə\
Kaliningrad \kə-'lē-nin-,grát\

Turkey \'tər-kē\
Turkmenistan \tərk-,men-i-'stan, -'stän\
United Arab Emirates \-'em-ər-əts, -,āts\
Uzbekistan \ůz-,bek-i-'stan, -'stän\
Vietnam \vē-'et-'näm, ,vē-ət-, -'nam\
Yemen \'yem-ən\

**Rivers**
Aldan \al-'dün\
Amur \ä-'mür\
Angara \ən-,gə-'rä\
Argun \'är-'gün\
Brahmaputra \,bräm-ə-'pü-trə\
Euphrates \yů-'frāt-ēz\
Ganges \'gan-,jēz\
Godavari \gō-'dä-və-rē\
Indigirka \,in-də-'gir-kə\
Irrawaddy \,ir-ə-'wäd-ē\
Irtysh \ir-'tish\
Kolyma \,kà-lə-'mü\
Krishna \'krish-na\
Lena \'lē-nə\
Mekong \'mā-'kong\
Narmada \nər-'mə-də\
Ob \'äb\
Salween \'sal-,wēn\
Syr Darya \sir-dər-'yä\
Tarim He \'dä-'rēm-,hē\
Tigris \tī-grəs\
Ural \'yůr-əl\
Vitim \və-'tēm\
Yangon \,yän-gōn\
Yangtze \'yang-'sē\
Yenisey \,yi-ni-'sā\

**Mountain ranges**
Himalayas \,him-ə-'lā-əz\
Kunlun Mountains \kün-lün-,maůntnz\

Ankara \'ang-kə-rə\
Ashgabat \'ash-gə-,bät\
Abu Dhabi \,äb-,ü-'däb-ē\
Tashkent \tash-'kent, 'täsh-\
Hanoi \ha-'nȯi, hə-\
Sanaa \san-,ä, san-'ä\

**Desert**
Gobi \'gō-bē\

**Islands**
Andaman Islands \'an-də-mən-'ī- əndz\
Borneo \'bȯr-nē-,ō\
Flores \'flōr-əs\
Hainan Dao \'hī-'nän-,daů\
Luzon \lü-'zän\
Mindanao \,min-də-'nä-ō\
Moluccas \mə-'lək-əz\
Nicobar Islands \'nik-ə-,bür-'ī-landz\
Sakhalin \sak-ə-,lēn\
Socotra \sə-'kō-trə\
Sumatra \sů-'mä-trə\

**Seas**
Aral Sea \'ar-əl-,sē\
Kara Sea \'kär-ə-,sē\
Lapter Sea \'lap-tif-,sē\
Sulawesi \,sü-lə-'wā-sē\

**Other names that appear on the map of Asia:**
Arabian Peninsula \ə-'rā-bē-ən-pə-nin-sə-lə\
Bay of Bengal \,bā-əv-ben-'gȯl\
Gulf of Aden \'gəlf-əv-'äd\
Gulf of Oman \'gəlf-əv-ō-mün\
Kamchatka \kam-'chat-kə\
Plateau of Tibet \pla-'tō-əv-tə-'bet\
West Papua

## Asia

| Nation | Capital |
|---|---|
| Afghanistan \af-'gan-ə-,stan\ | Kabul \'käb-əl, kə-'bül\ |
| Bahrain \bä-'rān\ | Manama \mə-'nam-ə\ |
| Bangladesh \,bän-glə-'desh,,bang-\ | Dhaka \'dak-ə, 'däk-\ |
| Bhutan \bü-'tan, -'tän\ | Thimphu \thim-'pü\ |
| Brunei \brů-'nī, 'brü-,nī\ | Bandar Seri Begawan \,bən-dər-,ser-ē-bə-'gä-wȧn\ |
| Cambodia \kam-'bō-dē-ə\ | Phnom Penh \'nȯm-'pen, pə-'näm-\ |
| China \'chī-nə\ | Beijing |
| East Timor \'tē-,mȯr\ | Dili \'dil-ē\ |
| India \'in-dē-ə\ | New Delhi \-'del-ē\ |
| Indonesia \,in-də-'nē-zhə, -shə\ | Jakarta \jə-'kär-tə\ |
| Iran \i-'ran, i-'rän, ī-'ran\ | Tehran \,tā-ə-'ran, te-'ran, -'rän\ |
| Iraq \i-'räk, i-'rak\ | Baghdad \'bag-,dad\ |
| Israel \'iz-rē-əl\ | Jerusalem \je-'rü-sə-ləm, -zə-\ |
| Japan \jə-'pan, ji-, ja-\ | Tokyo \'tō-kē-ō\ |
| Jordan \'jȯrd-n\ | Amman \a-'män, -'man\ |
| Kazakhstan \,ka-zak-'stan, ,kä-zäk-'stän\ | Astana \ä-'stä-nə\ |
| Korea, North \kə-'rē-ə\ | Pyongyang \pē-'ȯng-'yäng\ |
| Korea, South | Seoul \'sōl\ |
| Kuwait \kə-'wāt\ | Kuwait |
| Kyrgyzstan \,kir-gi-'stan, -'stän\ | Bishkek \bish-'kek\ |
| Laos \'laůs, 'lā-,äs, 'lä-ōs\ | Vientiane \vyen-'tyän\ |
| Lebanon \'leb-ə-nən, -,nän\ | Beirut \bā-'rüt\ |
| Malaysia \mə-'lā-zhə, -shə\ | Kuala Lumpur \,kwäl-ə-'lům-,pủr, -'ləm-\ |
| Maldive Islands \'mȯl-,dēv-, -,dīv-\ | Male \'mäl-ē\ |
| Mongolia \män-'gōl-yə, mäng-\ | Ulaanbaatar \,ü-,län-'bä-,tȯr\ |
| Myanmar \'myän-,mär\ | Yangon \,yän-'gōn\ |
| Nepal \ne-'pȯl, -'päl, -'pal\ | Kathmandu \,kat-,man-'dü\ |
| Oman \ō-'män, -'man\ | Muscat \'məs-,kat, -kət\ |
| Pakistan \,pak-i-'stan, ,päk-i-'stän\ | Islamabad \is-'läm-ə-,bad\ |
| Philippines \,fil-ə-'pēnz\ | Manila \mə-'nil-ə\ |
| Qatar \'kät-ər, 'gät-, 'gət-\ | Doha \'dō-hä\ |
| Saudi Arabia \,saůd-ē-ə-'rā-bē-ə, ,sȯd-, sä-,üd-\ | Riyadh \rē-'äd\ |
| Singapore \,sing-ə-,pōr, -gə-\ | Singapore |
| Sri Lanka \srē-'läng-kə, shrē\ | Colombo \kə-'ləm-bō\ |
| Syria \'sir-ē-ə\ | Damascus \də-'mas-kəs\ |
| Taiwan \,tī-'wän\ | Taipei \'tī-'pā\ |
| Tajikistan \tä-,jē-ki-'stan, -'stän\ | Dushanbe \dü-'sham-bə, -'shäm-\ |
| Thailand \'tī-,land, -lənd\ | Bangkok \'bang-,käk\ |

## Africa

| Nation | Capital |
|---|---|
| Algeria \al-'jir-ē-ə\ | Algiers \al-'jiərz\ |
| Angola \ang-'gō-lə, an-\ | Luanda \lü-'an-də\ |
| Benin \be-'nin, -'nēn\ | Porto-Novo \,pōrt-ə-'nō-vō\ |
| Botswana \bät-'swän-ə\ | Gaborone \,gäb-ə-'rōn\ |
| Burkina Faso \bůr-'kē-nə-'fäs-ō\ | Ouagadougou \,wä-gä-'dü-(,)gü\ |
| Burundi \bů-'rün-dē\ | Bujumbura \,bü-jəm-'bůr-ə\ |
| Cameroon \,kam-ə-'rün\ | Yaoundé \yaů-'dā\ |
| Cape Verde Islands \-,vərd-\ | Praia \'prī-ə\ |
| Central African Republic | Bangui \bäng-'gē\ |
| Chad \'chad\ | Ndjamena \en-'jäm-ə-nə\ |
| Comoros \käm-ə-,rō-\ | Moroni \mȯ-'rō-nē\ |
| Congo, Democratic Republic of \-'kānn-gō\ | Kinshasa \kin-'shä-sə\ |
| Congo, Republic of the | Brazzaville \'braz-ə-,vil\ |
| Djibouti \jə-'büt-ē\ | Djibouti |
| Egypt \'ē-jəpt\ | Cairo \'kī-rō\ |
| Equatorial Guinea \-'gin-ē\ | Malabo \mä-'lä-bō\ |
| Eritrea \,er-i-'trē-ə, -'trā-\ | Asmara \az-'mär-ə, -'mar-\ |
| Ethiopia \,ē-thē-'ō-pē-ə\ | Addis Ababa \,ad-ə-'sab-ə-bə\ |
| Gabon \ga-'bōn\ | Libreville \,lē-brə-,vil, -,vēl\ |
| Gambia \'gam-bē-ə\ | Banjul \'bän-,jül\ |
| Ghana \'gän-ə, 'gan-ə\ | Accra \ə-'krä\ |
| Guinea \'gin-ē\ | Conakry \'kän-ə-krē\ |
| Guinea-Bissau \,gin-ē-bis-'aů\ | Bissau \bis-'aů\ |
| Ivory Coast | Yamoussoukro \,yä-mə-'sü-krō\ |
| Kenya \'ken-yə, 'kēn-\ | Nairobi \nī-'rō-bē\ |
| Lesotho \lə-'sō-tō\ | Maseru \'maz-ə-,rü\ |
| Liberia \lī-'bir-ē-ə\ | Monrovia \mən-'rō-vē-ə\ |
| Libya \'lib-ē-ə\ | Tripoli \'trip-ə-lē\ |
| Madagascar \,mad-ə-'gas-kər\ | Antananarivo \,an-tə-,nan-ə-'rē-vō\ |
| Malawi \mə-'lä-wē\ | Lilongwe \li-'lȯng-wā\ |
| Mali \'mäl-ē, 'mal-\ | Bamako \,bäm-ə-'kō\ |

| | |
|---|---|
| Mauritania \ˌmȯr-ə-ˈtā-nē-ə\ | Nouakchott \nu̇-ˈäk-ˌshät\ |
| Mauritius \mȯ-ˈrish-ē-əs\ | Port Louis \-ˈlü-əs, -ˈlü-ē, -lu̇-ˈē\ |
| Morocco \mə-ˈräk-ō\ | Rabat \rə-ˈbät\ |
| Mozambique \ˌmō-zəm-ˈbēk\ | Maputo \mä-ˈpü-tō\ |
| Namibia \nə-ˈmib-ē-ə\ | Windhoek \ˈvint-ˌhu̇k\ |
| Niger \ˈnī-jər\ | Niamey \ˈnyä-mā\ |
| Nigeria \nī-ˈjir-ē-ə\ | Abuja \ä-ˈbü-jä\ |
| Rwanda \ru̇-ˌän-də\ | Kigali \ki-ˈgäl-ē\ |
| São Tomé and Principe \ˌsau̇t-ə-ˈmā-ən-ˈprin-sə-pə\ | São Tomé |
| Senegal \ˌsen-i-ˈgȯl\ | Dakar \ˈdak-ˌär\ |
| Seychelles \sā-ˈshelz, -ˈshel\ | Victoria \vik-ˈtōr-ē-ə\ |
| Sierra Leone \sē-ˌer-ə-lē-ˈōn\ | Freetown \ˈfrē-ˌtau̇n\ |
| Somalia \sō-ˈmäl-ē-ə\ | Mogadishu \ˌmō-gə-ˈdē-shü, -ˈdi-\ |
| South Africa, Republic of \-ˈaf-ri-kə\ | Pretoria \pri-ˈtōr-ē-ə\<br>Cape Town \ˈkāp-ˌtau̇n\<br>Bloemfontein \ˈblüm-fən-ˌtān, -ˌfān-\ |
| Sudan \sü-ˈdan, -ˈdän\ | Khartoum \kär-ˈtüm\ |
| Swaziland \ˈswäz-ē-ˌland\ | Mbabane \ˌem-bə-ˈbān\ |
| Tanzania \ˌtan-zə-ˈnē-ə\ | Dodoma \dō-ˈdō-mä\ |
| Togo \ˈtō-gō\ | Lomé \lō-mā |
| Tunisia \tü-ˈnē-zhə, tyü-\ | Tunis \ˈtü-nəs, ˈtyü-\ |
| Uganda \yü-ˈgan-də, -ˈgän-\ | Kampala \käm-ˈpäl-ə\ |
| Zambia \ˈzam-bē-ə\ | Lusaka \lü-ˈsäk-ə\ |
| Zimbabwe \zim-ˈbäb-wē\ | Harare \hə-ˈrä-ˌrā\ |

| Lakes | Rivers |
|---|---|
| Albert \ˈal-bərt\ | Benue \ˈbā-nwā\ |
| Chad \ˌchad\ | Limpopo \lim-ˈpō-ˈpō\ |
| Nasser \nä-sər\ | Niger \nī-jər\ |
| Nyasa \nī-ˈa–ə\ | Nile \nīəl\ |
| Tanganyika \ˌtan-gən-ˈyē-kə\ | Senegal \ˌsen-i-gȯ\ |
| Victoria \vik-ˈtōr-ē-ə\ | Ubangi \übang-gē\ |
| Volta \ˈväl-tə\ | Zambezi \zamˈbē-zē\ |

## Australasia and Oceania \ˌō-shē-ˈan-ē-ə, -ˈān-\ (group of islands in the Pacific)

| Nation | Capital |
|---|---|
| Australia \ȯ-ˈstrāl-yə\ | Canberra \ˈkan-bə-rə, -ˌber-ə\ |
| **State** | |
| New South Wales \ˈnü-ˌsau̇th-ˈwāəlz\ | Sydney \ˈsid-nē\ |
| Queensland \ˈkwēnz-land\ | Brisbane \ˈbriz-bən\ |
| South Australia \sau̇th-ȯ-ˈstrāl-yə\ | Adelaide \ˈad-əl-ˌād\ |
| Tasmania \taz-ˈmā-nē-ə\ | Hobart \ˈhō-ˌbärt\ |
| Victoria \vik-ˈtōr-ē-ə\ | Melbourne \ˈmel-bərn\ |
| Western Australia \ˌwes-tərn-ȯ-ˈstrāl-yə\ | Perth \ˈpərth\ |
| **Territory** | |
| Australian Capital Territory | |
| Northern Territory | Darwin \ˈdär-wən\ |
| New Zealand \ˈnü-ˈzē-lənd\ | Wellington \ˈwel-ing-tən\ |

| South Pacific Islands | Capital |
|---|---|
| American Samoa \sə-ˈmōə\ | Pago Pago \ˈpäng-ō-ˈpäng-ō\ |
| Auckland Islands \ˈȯ-klənd-ˌī-ləndz\ | |
| Austral Islands \ˈȯs-trəl-ˌīləndz\ | |
| Babelthuap \ˌbä-bəl-ˈtü-ˌäp\ | |
| Baker and Howland Islands \ˈbā-kər-ənd-ˌhau̇-ī-ləndz\ | |
| Bikini Atoll \bi-ˈkē-nē-ˌa-tȯl\ | |
| Bougainville Island \ˈbü-gən-ˌvil-ˈī-lənd\ | |
| Caroline Islands \ˈkar-ə-ˌlīn-ˌī-ləndz\ | |
| Chatham Islands \ˈchat-əm-ˌī-ləndz\ | |
| Chuuk \ˈchu̇k\ | |
| Cook Islands | |
| Éfaté \ā-ˈfā-tā\ | |
| Erromango \ˌer-ō-ˈmäng-gō\ | Avarua \ˌä-vä-ˈrü-ä\ |
| Fiji \ˈfē-ˌjē\ | Suva \ˈsü-və\ |
| French Polynesia \ˈfrench-ˌpäl-ə-ˈnē-zhə\ | |
| Gambier Islands \ˈgam-ˌbir-ˈī-ləndz\ | |
| Guadalcanal \ˌgwäd-əl-kə-ˈnal\ | |
| Guam \ˈgwäm\ | Agana \ä-ˈgän-yä\ |
| Jarvis Island \ˈjär-vis-ˌī-lənd\ | |
| Kangaroo Island \ˌkang-gə-ˈrü– īlənd\ | |
| Kermadec Islands \kər-ˈma-dək-ˌī-ləndz\ | |
| Kiribati \ˈkir-ə-ˌbas\ | Tarawa \t-ə-ˈrä-wə\ |
| Kiritimati \kə-ˈris-məs\ | |
| Kosrae \ˈkōs-ˌrī\ | |
| Lau Group \ˈlau̇-ˌgrüp\ | |
| Lord Howe Island \ˈlȯrd-ˌhau̇-ˌī-lənd\ | |
| Malden Island \ˈmȯl-dən-ˌī-lənd\ | |
| Malekula \ˌmä-lā-ˈkü-lä\ | |
| Manihiki \ˌmä-nē-ˈhē-kē\ | |
| Mariana Islands \ˌmar-ē-ˈan-ə-ˌī-ləndz\ | |
| Marshall Islands \ˈmär-shəl-\ | Majuro \mə-ˈju̇r-ō\ |
| Melanesia \ˌmel-ə-ˈnē-zhə\ | |
| Micronesia \-ˌmī-krə-ˈnē-zhə\ | Palikir \ˌpä-lē-ˈkir\ |
| Mururoa \ˌmü-rü-ˈrō-ä\ | |
| Nauru \nä-ˈü-rü\ | |
| Norfolk Island \ˈnȯr-fək-ˌī-lənd\ | |
| Northern Mariana Islands \ˈnȯr-thərn-ˌmar-ē-ˈan-ə-ˌī-ləndz\ | |
| Palau \pə-ˈlau̇\ | Koror \ˈkȯr-ˌȯr\ |
| Palmyra Atoll \pal-ˈmī-rə-ˌa-tȯl\ | |
| Papua New Guinea \ˈpap-yə-wə-nü-ˈgin-ē, ˈpäp-ə-wə-, -nyü-\ | Port Moresby \-ˈmōrz-bē\ |
| Penrhyn \ˈpen-ˌrin\ | |
| Pheonix Islands \ˈfē-niks-ˌī-ləndz\ | |
| Pitcairn Island \ˈpit-ˌkarn-ˈī-lənd\ | |
| Pohnpei \ˈpōn-ˌpā\ | |
| Ralik Chain \ˈrä-lik-ˌchān\ | |
| Rarotonga \rar-ə-täng-gə\ | |
| Ratak Chain \ˈrä-ˌtäk-ˌchān\ | |
| Saipan \sī-ˈpan\ | |
| Samoa \sə-ˈmō-ə\ | Apia \ə-ˈpē-ə\ |
| Santa Cruz Islands \ˌsant-ə-ˈkrüz-ˌī-ləndz\ | |
| Solomon Islands \ˈsäl-ə-mən–ˈī-ləndz\ | Honiara \ˌhō-nē-ˈär-ə\ |
| Starbuck Island \ˈstär-ˌbək-ˌī-lənd\ | |
| Stewart Island \ˈstü-ərt-ˌī-lənd\ | |
| Tabuaeran \tə-ˌbü-ə-ˈer-ən | |
| Tahiti \tə-ˈhēt-ē\ | Papeete \ˌpä-pā-ˈā-tā\ |
| Tanna \ˈtä-nä\ | |
| Teraina \ter-ˈī-nə\ | |
| Tokelau \ˈtō-kə-ˌlau̇\ | |
| Tonga \ˈtäng-gə\ | Nuku'alofa \ˌnü-kü-ä-ˈlō-fə\ |
| Tuvalu \tü-ˈväl-ü\ | Funafuti \ˌfü-nə-ˈfüt-ē\ |
| Vanua Levu \ˌvän-ˌwä-lā-ˌvü\ | |
| Vanuatu \ˌvan-ˌwä-ˈtü\ | Port-Vila \pōrt-ˈvē-lə, pȯrt-\ |
| Viti Levu \ˈvē-tē-ˈlā-vü\ | |
| Wallis and Futuna \ˈwä-ləs-ənd-fə-ˈtü-nə\ | |
| Yap \ˈyap\ | |

**Deserts**

Gibson Desert \gib-sən-ˈdez-ərt\
Great Sandy Desert \ˈgrāt-ˌsan-dē-ˈdez-ərt\
Great Victoria Desert \ˈgrāt-vik-ˌtōr-ē-ə-ˈdez-ərt\
Simpson Desert \ˈsimp-sən-ˌdez-ərt\
Tanami Desert \tə-ˈnä-mē-ˌdez-ərt\
Nullarbor Plain \ˌnəl-ə-ˌbȯər-ˈplān\

**Other names that appear on the map of Australasia and Oceania:**

Arnhem Land \ˈär-nəm-ˌland\
Bairiki \ˈbī-ˌrē-kē\
Cape York Peninsula \ˈkāp-yȯrk-pə-ˈnin-sə-lə\
Espiritu Santo \e-ˈspē-rē-ˌtü-ˈsan-tō\
Fongafale \ˌfȯng-gä-ˈfā-lā\
Foveaux Strait \ˈfō-vō-ˌstrāt\
Great Australian Bight \ˈgrāt-ȯ-ˈstrāl-yən-ˌbīt\
Great Barrier Reef \ˈgrāt-ˌbar-ē-ər-ˌrēf\
Gulf of Carpentaria \ˈgəlf-əv-ˌkär-pən-ˈtar-ē-ə\
Hamersley Range \ˈha-mərz-lē-ˌrānj\
Kimberly Plateau \ˈkim-bər-lē-pla-ˌtō\
Murray \ˈmər-ē\
New Caledonia \ˌnü-ˌka-lə-ˈdō-nya\
Nouméa \nü-ˈmā-ə\
Torres Strait \ˈtȯr-əs-ˌstrāt\
Uluru \ü-ˈlü-rü\

\ə\ abut \ər\ further \a\ mat \ā\ take \ä\ cot, cart \au̇\ out \ch\ chin \e\ pet \ē\ easy \g\ go \i\ tip \ī\ life \j\ job

# Signs and Symbols

## Mathematics

| | |
|---|---|
| $+$ | plus; positive ⟨$a+b=c$⟩ |
| $-$ | minus; negative |
| $\pm$ | plus or minus ⟨the square root of $4a^2$ is $\pm 2a$⟩ |
| $\times$ | multiplied by; times ⟨6×4=24⟩ — also indicated by placing a dot between the numbers ⟨6 · 4=24⟩ |
| $\div$ *or* : | divided by ⟨24÷6=4⟩— also indicated by writing the divisor under the dividend with a line between ⟨$\frac{24}{6}$ =4⟩ or by writing the divisor after the dividend with a diagonal between ⟨3/8⟩ |
| $=$ | equals ⟨6+2=8⟩ |
| $\neq$ *or* ≠ | is not equal to |
| $>$ | is greater than ⟨6>5⟩ |
| $<$ | is less than ⟨3<4⟩ |
| $\geqq$ *or* $\geq$ | is greater than or equal to |
| $\leqq$ *or* $\leq$ | is less than or equal to |
| $\not>$ | is not greater than |
| $\not<$ | is not less than is |
| $\approx$ | approximately equal to |
| : | is to; the ratio of |
| $\therefore$ | therefore |
| $\infty$ | infinity |
| $\angle$ | angle; the angle ⟨∠ABC⟩ |
| ∟ | right angle ⟨∟ABC⟩ |
| $\perp$ | the perpendicular; is perpendicular to AB⊥CD⟩ |
| $\parallel$ | parallel; is parallel to ⟨AB‖CD⟩ |
| ⊙ *or* ○ | circle |
| ⌒ | arc of a circle |
| △ | triangle |
| □ | square |
| ▭ | rectangle |
| $\surd$ | square root ⟨as in $\sqrt{4}=2$⟩ |
| ( ) | parentheses — indicate that the quantities enclosed by them are to be taken together |
| [ ] | brackets — indicate that the quantities enclosed by them are to be taken together |
| { } | braces — indicate that the quantities enclosed by them are to be taken together |
| $\pi$ | pi; the number 3.14159265+; the ratio of the circumference of a circle to its diameter |
| ° | degree ⟨60°⟩ |
| ′ | minute(s); foot (feet) ⟨30′⟩ |
| ″ | second(s); inch(es) ⟨30″⟩ |
| $^2$, $^3$, etc. | — used as exponents placed above and at the right of an expression to indicate that it is raised to a power indicated by the figure ⟨$a^2$ is the square of $a$⟩ |
| $\cup$ | union of two sets |
| $\cap$ | intersection of two sets |
| $\subset$ | is included in, is a subset of |
| $\supset$ | contains as a subset |
| $\in$ *or* ∊ | is an element of |
| $\notin$ | is not an element of |
| Λ *or* 0 *or* ∅ *or* { } | empty set |

## Astronomy

| | |
|---|---|
| ☉ | the sun; Sunday |
| ◐, ☾, ☽ | the moon; Monday |
| ● | new moon |
| ☽, ◐, ☽ | first quarter |
| ○, ☺ | full moon |
| ☾, ◑, ☾ | last quarter |
| ☿ | Mercury; Wednesday |
| ♀ | Venus; Friday |
| ⊕, ⊖, ♁ | the earth |
| ♂ | Mars; Tuesday |
| ♃ | Jupiter; Thursday |
| ♄ | Saturn; Saturday |
| ⛢ | Uranus |
| ♆ | Neptune |
| ♇ | Pluto |
| ☄ | comet |
| ✻ | fixed star |

## Miscellaneous

| | |
|---|---|
| & | and |
| &c | et cetera; and so forth |
| / | diagonal *or* slant; used to mean "or" (as in *and/or*), "per" (as in *meters/second*); indicates end of a line of verse; separates the figures of a date (9/29/99) |
| † | died — used especially in genealogies |
| *f/ or f:* | relative aperture of a photographic lens |
| ☠ | poison |
| ℞ | take — used on prescriptions |
| ♀ | female |
| ♂ | male |
| ☮ | peace |
| × | by ⟨3×5 cards⟩ |

## Business

| | |
|---|---|
| @ | at; each ⟨4 apples @ 25¢ = $1.00⟩ |
| c/o | care of |
| # | number if it precedes a numeral ⟨track #3⟩; pound(s) if it follows ⟨a 5# sack of sugar⟩ |
| lb | pound; pounds |
| % | percent |
| ‰ | per thousand |
| $ | dollar(s) |
| ¢ | cent(s) |
| £ | pound(s) |
| © | copyrighted |
| ® | registered trademark |

## Reference Marks

These marks are often placed in written or printed text to direct attention to a footnote:

| | |
|---|---|
| * | asterisk *or* star |
| † | dagger |
| ‡ | double dagger |
| § | section *or* numbered clause |
| ‖ | parallels |
| ¶ | paragraph |

# Picture Index

Page numbers in **bold** refer to entries with additional information

\ng\ si**ng** \ō\ b**o**ne \ȯ\ s**aw** \ȯi\ c**oi**n \th\ **th**in \th̲\ **th**is \ü\ f**oo**d \u̇\ f**oo**t \y\ **y**et \yü\ f**ew** \yu̇\ c**u**re \zh\ vi**s**ion

# Acknowledgments

**Merriam-Webster, Inc., wishes to thank:** Emily B. Arsenault, Daniel B. Brandon, Robert D. Copeland, Kathleen M. Doherty, Adam Groff, G. James Kossuth, Rose Martino, Joan I. Narmontas, Roger W. Pease, Jr., Thomas F. Pitoniak, Donna L. Rickerby, Michael D. Roundy, Maria A. Sansalone, Adrienne M. Scholz, Peter A. Sokolowski, Kory L. Stamper, Mark A. Stevens, and Karen L. Wilkinson for additional editorial and research assistance; Carol A. Fugiel as Senior Clerk

**Dorling Kindersley would like to thank:** Latha Anantharaman, Maggie Crowley, and Jacqueline Jackson for editorial assistance; Pauline Clarke, Darren Holt, Kathryn Thomas, and Olivia Triggs for design assistance; Aoitha Dare, Marie Ducos, Robert Graham, Nicholas Schonberger, and Dipali Singh for additional research; John Plumer for cartography; Umesh Aggarwal, Nicola Erdpresser, Andrew O'Brien, Claudia Shill, and Mabel Wu for additional DTP design; Chuck Wills as US consultant

**Dorling Kindersley would also like to thank the following organizations for their help with research or photography for this dictionary. Unless otherwise stated all are located in the UK:** All Saints Church, York; Angels & Bermans, London; Audifon UK Ltd. Hearing Systems, Horley, Surrey; Blists Hill and Jackfield Tile Museum, Telford, Shropshire; Boosey & Hawkes Music Publishers Ltd, London; British Telecom; Brooking Collection, University of Greenwich, London; Pat Buckler, Canada/Mr Starpasser; Bureau, London; Cambridge Botanic Garden; The Civil War Library and Museum, Philadelphia, Pennsylvania; Danish National Museum, Copenhagen, Denmark; Detmold Open Air Museum, Germany; David Edge; Elvax Door Entry Systems, Rayleigh, Essex; Gables Travel; Glasgow Museums; Alex Gunn; Hamleys Toy Store, London; Mrs Hampton, Briar Stud, Herts./Chatsworth Belle; Harrods Department Store, London; Mrs G. Harwood, Wychwood Stud/Wychwood Dynascha; Highly Sprung, High Wycombe, Bucks.; The History Museum, Moscow, Russia; Horniman Museum, New York; Miss M. Houlden, Amoco Park, Spruce Meadows, Canada; Instituto Incremento Ippico Di Crema/ Weaner; Janet Fitch and Juliet Sheath, London; Eileen Trippier at Kensington Lighting Company Ltd, London; Lady Fischer, Kentucky Horse Park, USA/Roy, Patrick, and Pegasus Of Kilverstone; Sam Tree at Keygrove Marketing Ltd; Bill Leonard; Jim Lockwood/Duke; London Underground; Manchester Museums; David and Jon Maughan; Pat and Joanna Maxwell, Lodge Farm/Altruista; Lyn Moran and John Goddard Fenwick/Neopolitano Dubowina IV; Musée de Saint Malo, France; Musée de l'Empéri, Salon de Provence, France; National Army Museum, London; National Railway Museum, York; Norfolk Rural Life Museum, Gressenhall; Odds Farm Park, High Wycombe, Bucks.; Ministry of Defence, Pattern Room, Nottingham; Pegasus Stables, Newmarket; Anthony Pozner at Hendon Way Motors, London; Purves & Purves, London; Peter Ray; RNLI; Science Museum, London; Shelleys Shoes Ltd., London; Stephen Jones Millinery, London; Texas Instruments; University Marine Biological Station, Millport, Isle of Cumbrae, Scotland; Van Cortlandt Museum, New York; Weald and Downland Open Air Museum, Chichester, West Sussex; West One, London; Whitbread Plc; Cecil Williamson Collection,Witheridge, London; Worthing Art Gallery and Museum; Yorkshire Museum, York; Xerox Corporation, New York

**Illustrators** **While all efforts have been made to acknowledge all illustrators, Dorling Kindersley will be pleased to add any missing credits in future editions:** Joanna Cameron; Luciano Corbello; John Hutchinson; Kenneth Lilly; Chris Orr; Daniel Pyne; Peter Serjeant

**Model-makers** Mark Beesley; Roby Braun; Peter Minister, Model FX; Chris Reynolds and the team at BBC Visual Effects; Thorp Modelmakers; Thurston Watson

**Commissioned photography** **While all efforts have been made to acknowledge all photographers, Dorling Kindersley will be pleased to add any missing credits in future editions:** Max Alexander; Peter Anderson; Dennis Avon; Patrick Baldwin; Geoff Brightling; Paul Bricknell; Jane Burton; Martin Cameron; Peter Chadwick; Tina Chambers; Gordon Clayton; Joe Cornish; Andy Crawford; Geoff Dann; Tom Dobbie; Christine M. Douglas; Philip Dowell; Peter Downs; Mike Dunning; Andreas Einsiedel; David Exton; Neil Fletcher; Jo Foord; Lynton Gardiner; John Garrett; Peter Gathercole; Philip Gatward; Ann George Marsh; John Glover; Paul Goff; Steve Gorton; Christi Graham; Frank Greenaway; Derek Hall; Mark Hamilton; Finbar Hawkins; Peter Hayman; Stephen Haywood; Tim Hayward; John Hepver; Marc Henrie; Norman Hollands; Jacqui Hurst; James Jackson; David Johnson; Colin Keates; Alan Keohane; Gary Kevin; Barnabas and Anabel Kindersley, 'Children Just Like Me'; Dave King; Cyril Laubscher; Richard Leeney; Liz McAulay; Andrew McRobb; Maslowski Photo; Neil Mersh; Graham Miller; Ray Moller; Michael Moran; Tracy Morgan; David Murray; Nick Nicholls; Stephen Oliver; Gary Ombler; Roger Phillips; Susanna Price; Howard Rice; Tim Ridley; Kim Sayer; Philippe Sebert; Tim Shepard; Karl Shone; Steve Shott; Gary Staab; James Stevenson; Clive Streeter; Steve Tanner; Harry Taylor; Kim Taylor; Andreas Von Einsiedel; Colin Walton; David Ward; Matthew Ward; Alan Williams; Alex Wilson; Jerry Young; Michel Zabé

## Agency Photography

**Dorling Kindersley would like to thank the following for their kind permission to reproduce their photographs. Unless otherwise stated all are located in the UK.**

a = above; b = below; c = center; l = left; r = right; t = top

**AKG London Ltd**: 672r, Bibliothèque Nationale, Paris 491tl, Winchester Cathedral Library 409t. **Action Plus**: Chris Barry 839tc, Glyn Kirk 830. **Allsport UK Ltd**: Steven Babineau 379bl, Vincent Laforet 379tr, Tom Pidgeon 581r, Mike Powell 603l, Richard Saker 443r. **American Museum of Natural History, New York**: 777b, 851. **Ardea London Ltd**: M. Iijima 664t. **Barleylands Farm and Animal Centre, Essex**: 847l. **Birmingham Museum and Art Gallery**: 62bl. **Bridgeman Art Library, London**: Ashmolean Museum, Oxford 52bc, Private Collection 679l. **British Library, London**: 752r. **British Museum, London**: 50b, 62bc, 210br, 296r, 375br, 408r, 491cr, 510b, 638b, 769r, 567t. **J. Allan Cash**: 318b, 329r, 625bl, 708b, 883tl, 885cr, b. **Civil Aviation Authority**: 517bl. **Bruce Coleman Collection**: Astrofoto 490b, 693br, Erwin & Peggy Bauer 595, Jonathan Blair 491cc, Nigel Blake 333tl, Fred Bruemmer 612b, Jeff Foott 227br, 376bc, Johnny Johnson 479tl, Michael McKavett 356tl, Luiz Claudio Marigo 344, Dr. Scott Nielsen 102br, Allan G. Potts 483t, Marie Read 427t, Hans Reinhard 210t, John Shaw 481tl. **Corbis**: 497, 900cb, 901cb, Archivo Iconografico, S.A. 444br, Arte & Immagini srl 57b, William A. Bake 564t, Tom Bean 296l, 341, 596b, Morton Beebe, S.F. 457r, Neil Beer 574b, Bettmann 900ct, 901ct, Barnabas Bosshart 614l, Tom Brakefield 339tr, Michael Busselle 697r, S. Carmona 316bl, Roger Chester/Eye Ubiquitous 489c, W. Cody 899t, The Corcoran Gallery of Art 901t, The Corcoran Gallery of Art/Bequest of Mrs. Benjamin Taylor 900t, Philip James Corwin 877c, George B. Diebold 208tl, Macduff Everton 899cc, Kevin Fleming 291b, 415b, 644, D. Robert Franz 620l, Franz-Marc Frei 726c, Lowell Georgia 610t, J.D. Griggs 898b, Darrell Gulin 773r, Dan Guravich 817, George Hall 427b, 768, Historical Picture Archive 607, Horree Zirkzee Produk 738t, Wolfgang Kaehler 378t, 885tr, George Lepp 487b, Massimo Listri 499bl, Bob London 176cra, Wally MacNamee 791br, Lawrence Manning 300b, Gunter Marx 659t, 558r, Buddy Mays 618t, Joe McDonald 499t, 861br, Gail Mooney 38b, Marc Muench 37, Amos Nachoum 689 ctr, Charles O'Rear 54bl, Gianni Dagli Orti 527c, 880br, Christine Osborne 884l, Greg Probst 889b, Progressive Image/Bob Rowan 405b, 444t, Neil Rabinowitz 423c, Roger Ressmeyer 339l, 535b, Lynda Richardson 378b, Bill Ross 899cr, Galen Rowell 506r, 623r, 898c, Ken Schafer 745t, 874t, Phil Schermeister 899cl, Michael T. Sedam 118cl, Vince Streano 322b, Ted Streshinsky 836r, Jim Sugar Photography 240, 264c, 839bl, Adam Woolfitt 879c, Michael S. Yamashita 462, Yogi, Inc. 898t. **Danish National Museum**: 764br. **James Davis Travel Library**: 740t. **Denoyer-Geppert**: 115b, 262t, 437t. **Edinburgh/SUSM**: 764cr. **Philip Dowell** 45cl, bl, 67tl, 68r, 97br, 108t, 111bl, 116tl, tr, b, 135t, 154, 159b, 171l, 254l, 327ctl, ctc, 441bl, br, 453b, 475ctr, 501cbc, 518t, 522bl, 531t, 539c, 540t, 553r, 570tr, cl, bl, 579bl, 589t, 621b, 712b, 831b. **The European Space Centre**: 669tr. **The Eurospace Centre, Transinne, Belgium**: 137t. **Exeter Maritime Museum**: 109tc, 667b. **Flag Fen Excavations**: 62br. **Brooking Collection, University of Greenwich**: 448tl. **Robert Harding Picture Library**: Martyn Chillmaid 818c. **Hibbert/Ralph**: 175c. Hugh McManners 681b. **The Hutchison Library**: J.G. Fuller 772r. **Imperial War Museum**: 352t. **The Jewish Museum, London**: 372. **Frank Lane Picture Agency**: S.C. Brown 622bl, Robin Chittenden 566c, A.R. Hamblin 696t, Eric & David Hosking 459t, 728tr, 732b, Gerard Lecz 481cr, S. Maslowski 494b, Chris Mattison 730t, Mark Newman 556b, Fritz Polking 557b, Leonard Lee Rue 854r, H. Schrempp 722l, Silvestris 633br, G. Stewart 788br, R. Tidman 887cl, Maurice Walker 779l, Larry West 606l, 713b, Martin Withers 610b, E. Woods 376tl. **The London Planetarium**: 433l, 825t. **Melbourne Zoo, Australia**: 475cc. **H. Keith Melton Collection**: 628b. **Mexican Museum Authority**: 876l. **Motorcycle Heritage Museum, Westerville, Ohio**: 507ctr. **Musée d'Orsay, Paris**: 66tl. **Museum of English Rural Life**: 398b. **Museum of London**: 744cl. **Museum of Mankind, London**: 185b, 843l. **The Museum of the Moving Image, London**: 471t, 634t, 729. **Museum of the Order of Saint John**: 149t. **Museum of the Revolution, Moscow, Russia**: 306b. **NASA** 202t, 331. **National Maritime Museum, Greenwich**: 51bl, 119, 166, 206c, 213t, 232, 251t, 302t, 432b, 435b, 456, 472b, 640tl, 706t, 753, 756c. **National Motor Museum, Beaulieu**: 419c. **National Museums of Scotland**: 135c, 424b. **Natural History Museum, London**: 60br, 111l, 321cr, 441tr, 506l, 515r, 660cl, 880cl, 887tl. **Natural History Picture Agency**: A.N.T. 464b, Nigel J. Dennis 475ctl, Pavel German 481ct, Martin Harvey 475t, Derek Karp 475cbl, John Shaw 102tcr, 481cb. **Oxford Scientific Films**: Alan Root/Survival Anglia 173c, DK 127, 382l, Max Gibbs 468bl. **Panos Pictures**: J.C. Callow 361. **Pictor International**: 76, 622br, 793l, 819, 834, 877br, 879t, b, 881tl, cl, 609t. **Pictures**: David Henderson 808t. **Pitt-Rivers Museum, Oxford**: 227bl, 692t. **Planet Earth Pictures**: J. Lythgoe 502c, Doug Perrine 689cbr, 732tl, Marty Snyderman 689t, James D. Watt 689b. **Rex Features**: Peter Brookes 901b, Sipa Press/Trippet 900b.**Royal Artillery Trust**: 67tr. **Royal British Columbia Museum, Victoria**: 474t. **Royal College of Music, Junior Department**: 804tr. **Science Museum, London**: 606r. **Science Photo Library**: David Parker for ESA/CNES/Arianespace 448bc, Petit Format Nestlé 272b, Stammers/Thompson 867l. **Scott Polar Institute**: 367b, 714r. **Seward Ltd, London**: 402c. **South of England Rare Breeds Centre**: 720b, 849l. **The Stock Market**: 551, 779r. **Tony Stone Images**: 662r, 759, James Balog 566b, Paul Chesley 888bl, Florence Douyrou 482l, Chad Ehlers 889t, Robert Frerck 881b, Jason Hawkes 483b, Andy Sacks 291t, Oliver Strewe 888tl. **Carole Stott**: 425l. **Kim Taylor**: 861t. **Telegraph Colour Library**: Bavaria Bildagentur 736l, 806t, 885cl, Colorific/Wayne Sorce/Visions 434br, M. Trigalon 747b. **Trip**: 783b. **Vatican Museums**: 640tr. **The Wallace Collection, London**: 90bl, 195bl, 206bl, 215tr, 764tl, cl. **Warwick Castle**: 335l. **Washington Dolls' House Museum**: 620r. **Barrie Watts**: 252r. **Westminster Cathedral**: 657br. **Elizabeth Whiting Associates**: 701t. **Robin Wigington, Arbour Antiques**: 377. **Chris Wilkinson Architects Ltd, London**: 118tcr. **The Earl of Pembroke & the Trustees of Wilton House**: 706b. **Winchcombe Folk & Police Museum**: Ross Simms 664b. **Jerry Young**: 35, 46b, 57cl, 64tr, 67cr, 89tc, bl, 102tcl, tc, bc, 110t, 139b, 199b, 201b, 205t, 270t, 305 ctc,cbl, 312bc, 322l, 339b, 383bl, 387tr, 392c, 430, 463ctl, br, 527b, 552bl, 643cbr, b, 650t, 655cbl, 708t, 711tl, tr, ctr, 725tl, cl, cr, 733b, 788tr, cr, 792t, 829tr, 832l, 833cr, 860t

**Jacket**: **National Maritime Museum, Greenwich**: back bl

ARCTIC OCEAN
Ellesmere Island
Queen Elizabeth Islands
Greenland
Beaufort Sea
Chukchi Sea
Baffin Bay
Victoria Island
Baffin Island
Brooks Range
Bering Strait
Denmark Strait
Iceland
Great Bear Lake
Great Slave Lake
Hudson Bay
Peninsule d'Ungava
Labrador Sea
Bering Sea
Aleutian Islands
Aleutian Trench
Gulf of Alaska
Rocky Mountains
Canadian Shield
Lake Winnipeg
Laurentian Mountains
Newfoundland
Grand Banks of Newfoundland
Vancouver Island
Great Lakes
St Lawrence
NORTH AMERICA
Bay of Biscay
Iberian Peninsula
Appalachian Mountains
Mendocino Fracture Zone
Great Plains
Azores
Mid-Atlantic Ridge
Mississippi
North American Basin
Madeira
Murray Fracture Zone
Canary Islands
Hawaiian Islands
Tropic of Cancer
Gulf of Mexico
Hawaii
Greater Antilles
Yucatan Peninsula
West Indies
Caribbean Sea
Cape Verde Islands
Lesser Antilles
Middle America Trench
Guiana Basin
PACIFIC OCEAN
Guatemala Basin
Orinoco
Guiana Highlands
ATLANTIC OCEAN
Line Islands
Equator
Galapagos Islands
Amazon
Amazon Basin
Purus
Ascension Island
Marquesas Islands
SOUTH AMERICA
Peru Basin
Peru-Chile Trench
Andes
Brazil Basin
Samoa
Tuamotu Islands
Planalto de Mato Grosso
Brazilian Highlands
Cook Islands
Society Islands
Polynesia
Tropic of Capricorn
Pitcairn Islands
East Pacific Rise
Gran Chaco
Easter Island
Cerro Aconcagua 6959m
Pampas
Southwest Pacific Basin
Argentine Basin
Patagonia
Falkland Islands
Tierra del Fuego
South Georgia
Cape Horn
Drake Passage
Antarctic Circle